EMPLOYMENT, HOURS, AND EARNINGS

STATES AND AREAS

14th Edition
2019

EMPLOYMENT, HOURS, AND EARNINGS

STATES AND AREAS

14th Edition
2019

Edited by Mary Meghan Ryan

Lanham, MD

Published by Bernan Press
An imprint of The Rowman & Littlefield Publishing Group, Inc.
4501 Forbes Boulevard, Suite 200, Lanham, Maryland 20706
www.rowman.com
800-462-6420

6 Tinworth Street, London, SE11 5AL

ISBN-13:   978-1-64143-334-1
e-ISBN-13: 978-1-64143-335-8

♾™ The paper used in this publication meets the minimum requirements of
American National Standard for Information Sciences—Permanence of
Paper for Printed Library Materials, ANSI/NISO Z39.48-1992.

CONTENTS

PART B: METROPOLITAN STATISTICAL AREA (MSA) DATA

APPENDIX

PREFACE

Bernan Press proudly presents the 14th edition of *Employment, Hours, and Earnings: States and Areas, 2019.* A special addition to Bernan Press's *Handbook of U.S. Labor Statistics: Employment, Earnings, Prices, Productivity, and Other Labor Data,* this reference is a consolidated wealth of employment information, providing monthly and annual data on hours worked and earnings made by industry across America for the years 2010 through 2018, including figures and summary information spanning years the same time period. These data, compiled by the Bureau of Labor Statistics, are presented for states and metropolitan statistical areas.

This edition features:

- Nearly 300 tables with data on employment for each state, the District of Columbia, and the nation's 75 largest metropolitan statistical areas (MSAs)

- Detailed, non-seasonally adjusted, industry data organized by month and year

- Hours and earnings data for each state, by industry

- An introduction for each state and the District of Columbia that denotes salient data and noteworthy trends, including changes in population and the civilian labor force, industry increases and declines, employment and unemployment statistics, and a chart detailing employment percentages, by industry

- Ranking of the 75 largest MSAs, including Census population estimates for 2018, unemployment rates for 2010 and 2018, and the percent change in total nonfarm employment from 2010 through 2018

- Concise technical notes that explain pertinent facts about the data, including sources, definitions, and significant changes; and provides references for further guidance

- A comprehensive appendix that details the geographical components of the 75 largest MSAs

The employment, hours, and earnings data in this publication provide a detailed and timely picture of the 50 states, the District of Columbia, and the nation's 75 largest MSAs. These data can be used to analyze key factors affecting state and local economies and to compare national cyclical trends to local-level economic activity.

This reference is an excellent source of information for analysts in both the public and private sectors. Readers who are involved in public policy can use these data to determine the health of the economy, to clearly identify which sectors are growing and which are declining, and to determine the need for federal assistance. State and local jurisdictions can use the data to determine the need for services, including training and unemployment assistance, and for planning and budgetary purposes. In addition, the data can be used to forecast tax revenue. In private industry, the data can be used by business owners to compare their business to the economy as a whole; and to identify suitable areas when making decisions about plant locations, wholesale and retail trade outlets, and for locating a particular sector base.

In this 14th edition, *Employment, Hours, and Earnings: States and Areas* presents monthly and annual average data on employment for each state, the District of Columbia, and the nation's 75 largest metropolitan statistical areas (MSAs). In addition, hours and earnings data are provided, where available, for each state. The industry data are based on the North American Industry Classification System (NAICS), which is discussed in greater detail later in these notes. The employment data are presented on a monthly and annual basis for 2010 through 2018. The hours and earnings data are available from 2014 through 2018.

The Bureau of Labor Statistics (BLS), the statistical agency within the U.S. Department of Labor, conducts the Current Employment Statistics (CES) survey to provide industry data on the employment, hours, and earnings of workers on nonfarm payrolls. The unemployment data and the civilian labor force estimates in this publication were obtained from the Local Area Unemployment Statistics (LAUS) program, which provides monthly employment and unemployment data for approximately 7,000 geographic areas including Census regions and divisions, states, counties, metropolitan areas, and many cities and towns.

The data from both the CES and LAUS are derived from federal and state cooperative collection efforts in which state employment security agencies prepare data using concepts, definitions, and technical procedures prescribed by the BLS. Although the estimation of the two data sets are based on differing methodologies (described in more detail later in this section), their inclusion together in this reference is intended to provide a broad overview of state and local labor market conditions.

THE CURRENT EMPLOYMENT STATISTICS (CES) SURVEY—EMPLOYMENT, HOURS, AND EARNINGS DATA

The CES survey is a monthly survey commonly referred to as the establishment or payroll survey that provides estimates of employment, hours, and earnings data by industry. Its estimates are derived from a sample of about 142,000 private nonfarm businesses and federal, state, and local government entities, which cover approximately 689,000 individual worksites in all 50 states, the District of Columbia, Puerto Rico, the U.S. Virgin Islands, and more than 350 metropolitan areas and divisions. These establishments are classified on the basis of their primary activity by major industry groupings in accordance with NAICS. For an establishment engaging in more than one activity, the entire establishment is included under the industry indicated as the principal activity.

More information on the exact methodology used to obtain data for employment, hours, and earnings was originally detailed in the *BLS Handbook of Methods*. The *Handbook* is updated online and can be found at www.bls.gov/opub/hom. Information on the CES survey can also be found on the BLS website at www.bls.gov/ces/cesprog.htm.

CONCEPTS

Employment is the total number of persons employed either full or part-time in nonfarm business establishments during a specific payroll period. Temporary employees are included as well as civilian government employees. Unpaid family members working in a family-owned business, domestic workers in private homes, farm employees, and self-employed persons are excluded from the CES, as well as military personnel and employees of the Central Intelligence Agency, the National Security Agency, the National Imagery and Mapping Agency, and the Defense Intelligence Agency. In addition, employees on layoff, on leave without pay, on strike for the entire pay period, or who had been hired but did not start work during the pay period are also excluded.

The reference period includes all persons who worked during or received pay for any part of the pay period that includes the 12th of the month, a standard for all federal agencies collecting employment data from business establishments. Workers who are on paid sick leave (when pay is received directly from the employer) or paid holiday or vacation, or who worked during only part of the specified pay period (because of unemployment or strike during the rest of the pay period) are counted as employed. Employees on the payroll of more than one establishment during the pay period are counted in each establishment that reports them, whether the duplication is due to turnover or dual jobholding.

Nonfarm employment includes employment in all goods-producing and service-providing industries. The goods-producing sector includes mining and logging, construction, and manufacturing, the last of which is made up of durable and nondurable goods (these breakdowns are not provided in this publication). The service-providing sector includes both private service-providing and government employment. Private service sector employment includes trade, transportation, and utilities (which is comprised of wholesale trade, retail trade, and transportation and utilities); information; financial activities; professional and business services; educational and health services; leisure and hospitality; and other services. Government employment encompasses federal-, state-, and local-level civilian employees. Subcategories of these industries are available on the BLS website at www.bls.gov/sae.

Unemployment consists of those who were not employed during the reference week but were available for work, except for temporary illness, and had made specific efforts to find employment some time during the 4-week period ending with the reference week. Persons who were waiting to be recalled to a job from which they had been laid off are classified as unemployed even if they have not been looking for another job.

The *unemployment rate* is the number of unemployed persons as a percent of the civilian labor force.

The *civilian labor force* consists of all persons classified as employed or unemployed as described above.

Hours and earnings data for each state are based on reports from industry payrolls and the corresponding hours paid for construction workers, production workers, and nonsupervisory workers. The data include workers who received pay for any part of the pay period that includes the 12th day of the month. Because not all sample respondents report production worker hours and earnings data, insufficient sample sizes preclude hours and earnings data from many sectors in many states. Therefore, the data available, and thus published, vary from state to state.

The payroll for these workers is reported before deductions of any kind, including Social Security, unemployment insurance, group health insurance, withholding taxes, retirement plans, or union dues.

Included in the payroll report of earnings is pay for all hours worked, including overtime, shift premiums, vacations, holiday, and sick-leave pay. Bonuses and commissions are excluded unless they are earned and paid regularly each pay period. Benefits, such as health insurance and contribution to a retirement fund, are also excluded.

Hours include all hours worked (including overtime hours) and hours paid for holidays, vacations, and sick leave during the pay period that includes the 12th day of the month. Average weekly hours differ from the concept of scheduled hours worked because of factors such as unpaid absenteeism, labor turnover, part-time work, and strikes, as well as fluctuations in work schedules. Average weekly hours are typically lower than scheduled hours of work.

Average hourly earnings are derived by dividing gross payrolls by total hours, reflecting the actual earnings of workers (including premium pay). They differ from wage rates, which are the amounts stipulated for a given unit of work or time. Average hourly earnings do not represent total labor costs per hour because they exclude retroactive payments and irregular bonuses, employee benefits, and the employer's share of payroll taxes. Earnings for employees not included in the production worker or nonsupervisory categories are not reflected in the estimates in this publication.

Average weekly earnings are derived by multiplying average weekly hours by average hourly earnings.

Users should note that in the context of historical data, long-term trends in hours and earnings data also reflect structural changes, such as the changing mixes of full-time and part-time employees and highly paid and lower-wage workers within businesses and across industries.

METROPOLITAN STATISTICAL AREAS (MSAs) AND NEW ENGLAND CITY AND TOWN AREAS (NECTAs)

A metropolitan statistical area (MSA) is a core area with a large population nucleus, combined with adjacent communities that have high degrees of economic and social integration with the core area. The standard definition of a MSA is determined by the Office of Management and Budget (OMB), which updates the definition based on the decennial census and updated information provided by the Census Bureau between the censuses. Each MSA must have at least one urbanized area of 50,000 inhabitants or more.

New England city and town areas (NECTAs) are similar to MSAs, but are defined using cities and towns instead of counties in the six New England states. BLS only provides employment data on NECTAs in the New England region. Employment and Unemployment data are provided for the following NECTAs in this publication: Boston–Cambridge–Newton, MA–NH; Hartford–West Hartford–East Hartford, CT; Providence–Warwick, RI–MA; New Haven–Milford, CT; and Worcester, MA. All other areas are MSAs.

The appendix details the geographic components for each MSA and NECTA.

REVISIONS TO THE DATA

North American Industry Classification System (NAICS)

The most far-reaching revision of the CES data occurred when the industrial classification system was changed from the 60-year-old Standard Industrial Classification (SIC) system to the North American Industry Classification System (NAICS) in January 2003. The revision changed the way establishments were classified into industries in order to more accurately reflect the current composition of U.S. businesses. In March 2008, the CES state and area nonfarm payroll series was converted to the 2007 NAICS series. This resulted in relatively minor changes. In February 2012, CES updated the national payroll series to NAICS 2012 from NAICS 2007. This resulted in minor content changes within the Manufacturing and Retail trade sectors as well as minor coding changes within the Utilities and Leisure and hospitality sectors. Several industry titles and descriptions were updated as well.

The CES program updated to the 2017 North American Industry Classification System from the NAICS 2012 System with the February 2, 2018 Employment Situation release. For more information on the NAICS 2012 and 2017 classifications, see www.census.gov/epcd/www/naics.html.

NAICS was adopted as the standard measure of industry classification by statistical agencies in the United States, Canada, and Mexico to enhance the comparability of economic data across the North American Free Trade Association (NAFTA) trade area. Comparison between the NAICS and the old SIC are limited, however, the historical industry series from April 1995 through 2001 are available on both SIC and NAICS bases. The BLS has not updated the SIC data nor (for the most part) linked the historical SIC data with the current NAICS data.

Benchmark Revisions

Employment estimates are adjusted annually to a complete count of jobs—called benchmarks—which are primarily derived from tax reports submitted by employers covered by state unemployment laws (which cover most establishments). In this re-anchoring of sample-based employment estimates to full population counts, the original sample-based estimates are replaced with the benchmark data from the previous year. The benchmark information is used to adjust monthly estimates between the new benchmark and the preceding benchmark, thereby preserving the continuity of the series and establishing the level of employment for the new benchmark month.

Seasonal Adjustment

Over the course of a year, the size of a state's employment level undergoes sharp fluctuations because of changes in the weather, reduced or expanded production, harvests, major holidays, and the like. Because these seasonal events follow a more or less regular pattern each year, adjusting the data on a month-to-month basis may eliminate their influence on data trends. These adjustments make it easier for users to observe the cyclical and other nonseasonal movements in the data series, but it must be noted that the seasonally adjusted series are only an approximation based on past experience. The seasonally adjusted data have a broader margin of error than the unadjusted data because they are subject to both sampling and other errors in the seasonal adjustment process. The data presented in this publication are not seasonally adjusted; therefore, the month-to-month variations in the data contain seasonal variations that may distort month-to-month comparisons. Data for the MSAs are also not seasonally adjusted, as the sample sizes do not allow for reliable estimates for seasonal adjustment factors.

THE LOCAL AREA UNEMPLOYMENT STATISTICS (LAUS) PROGRAM

The Local Area Unemployment Statistics (LAUS) program provides monthly and annual estimates on several labor force concepts, including employment, unemployment, labor force totals, and the employment-population ratio. The unemployment data as well as the civilian labor force estimates presented in this publication are from the LAUS program. The unemployment rate is shown for each state in 2010 and 2018 along with the rank for each state. The rankings are from highest to lowest—a change from earlier editions of *Employment, Hours, and Earnings* but consistent with recent editions. In 2018, unemployment ranged from a low of 2.4 percent in Hawaii to a high of 6.6 percent in Alaska. Therefore, Hawaii is ranked last and Alaska is ranked first. Unemployment data are not available by industry.

The concepts and definitions underlying the LAUS program come from the Current Population Survey (CPS), the household survey conducted by the Census Bureau for the BLS. The LAUS models combine current and historical data from the CPS, Current Employment Statistics (CES), and the State Unemployment Insurance (UI) Systems. Numerous conceptual and technical differences exist between the household and establishment surveys, and estimates of monthly employment changes from these two surveys usually do not match in size or even direction. As a result, the unemployment data and the civilian labor force estimates on each state header page presented in this edition are not directly comparable to the employment data. However, this publication includes this information to provide complementary information on labor market conditions in each state and the District of Columbia. Monthly and annual data are available from the BLS on their website at www.bls.gov/lau. More information on the differences between the surveys, as well as guidance on the complex methods used to obtain the LAUS data, is provided on the BLS website at www.bls.gov/lau/laufaq.htm.

PART A

STATE DATA

ALABAMA
At a Glance

Population:
  2010 census: 4,779,736
  2018 estimate: 4,887,871

Percent change in population:
  2010–2018: 2.3%

Percent change in total nonfarm employment:
  2010–2018: 8.0%

Industry with the largest growth in employment, 2010–2018 (percent):
  Leisure and hospitality, 22.9%

Industry with the largest decline or smallest growth in employment, 2010–2018 (percent):
  Mining and logging, -16.7%

Civilian labor force:
  2010: 2,196,042
  2018: 2,198,837

Unemployment rate and rank among states (highest to lowest):
  2010: 10.5%, 9th
  2018: 3.9%, 22nd

Over-the-year change in unemployment rates:
  2016–2017: -1.4%
  2017–2018: -0.5%

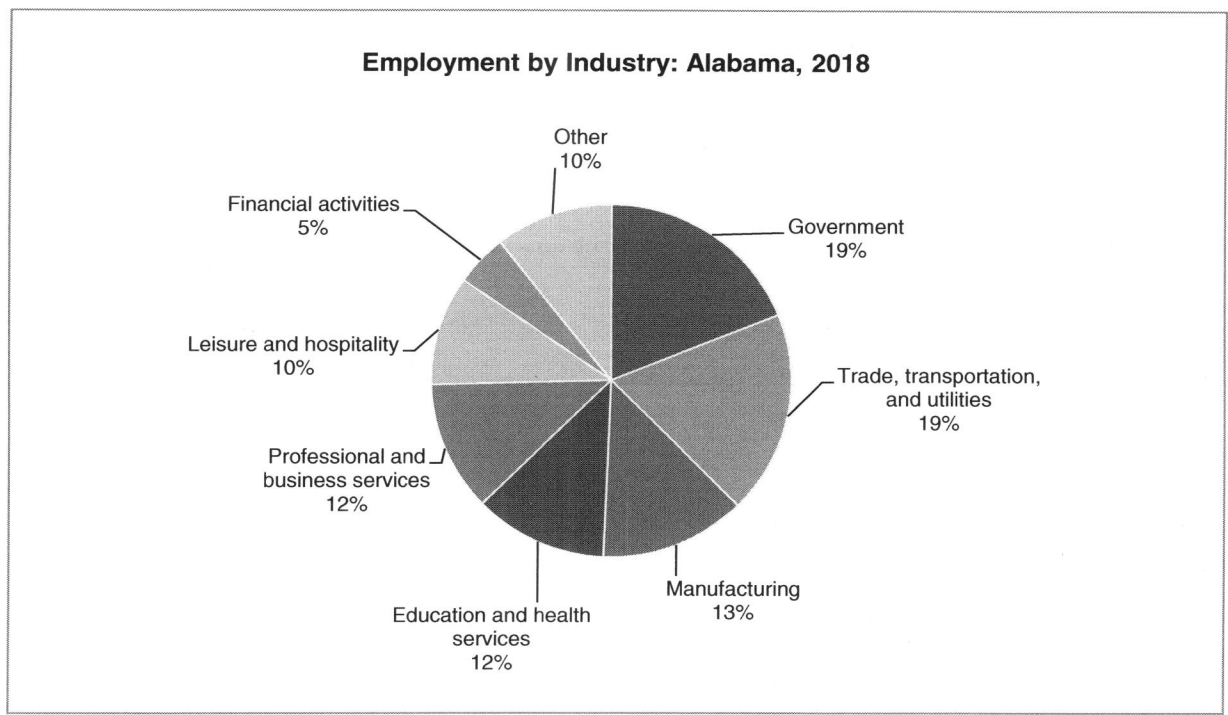

Employment by Industry: Alabama, 2018

Other 10%
Financial activities 5%
Government 19%
Trade, transportation, and utilities 19%
Leisure and hospitality 10%
Manufacturing 13%
Professional and business services 12%
Education and health services 12%

1. Employment by Industry: Alabama, 2010–2018

Industry and year	January	February	March	April	May	June	July	August	September	October	November	December	Annual average
Total Nonfarm													
2010	1,858.3	1,864.4	1,879.8	1,891.4	1,907.1	1,907.8	1,888.2	1,886.9	1,891.7	1,897.7	1,904.3	1,903.6	1,890.1
2011	1,858.7	1,873.6	1,886.2	1,894.6	1,897.3	1,896.9	1,881.7	1,886.9	1,899.9	1,894.4	1,905.3	1,904.7	1,890.0
2012	1,870.4	1,882.8	1,901.5	1,909.6	1,912.5	1,916.7	1,892.7	1,903.4	1,911.2	1,914.0	1,927.5	1,926.2	1,905.7
2013	1,885.5	1,903.4	1,917.8	1,926.4	1,934.2	1,935.2	1,915.2	1,923.2	1,927.4	1,929.6	1,942.6	1,947.2	1,924.0
2014	1,905.7	1,915.4	1,930.0	1,944.1	1,950.5	1,953.2	1,934.1	1,945.0	1,953.0	1,959.0	1,966.3	1,974.0	1,944.2
2015	1,932.5	1,945.0	1,953.7	1,969.1	1,978.2	1,979.7	1,965.9	1,972.4	1,977.6	1,985.9	1,993.7	2,000.1	1,971.2
2016	1,962.9	1,974.7	1,984.8	2,001.5	2,003.7	2,003.9	1,991.6	1,998.0	2,007.0	2,005.7	2,013.5	2,016.2	1,997.0
2017	1,984.4	1,999.0	2,010.7	2,016.5	2,023.0	2,028.1	2,011.3	2,019.5	2,024.5	2,030.6	2,039.2	2,037.0	2,018.7
2018	2,001.9	2,018.5	2,029.9	2,039.9	2,042.9	2,050.9	2,037.1	2,045.3	2,047.2	2,059.9	2,064.4	2,066.6	2,042.0
Total Private													
2010	1,471.3	1,473.8	1,486.4	1,496.9	1,503.7	1,510.6	1,509.4	1,508.0	1,504.2	1,506.3	1,511.7	1,510.4	1,499.4
2011	1,471.5	1,483.0	1,494.6	1,503.6	1,506.8	1,510.2	1,507.6	1,512.9	1,516.1	1,508.3	1,517.6	1,518.8	1,504.3
2012	1,489.3	1,497.6	1,514.1	1,523.8	1,527.5	1,534.9	1,524.6	1,534.4	1,533.2	1,529.9	1,542.1	1,541.1	1,524.4
2013	1,506.3	1,519.4	1,531.4	1,540.9	1,549.4	1,554.7	1,543.6	1,551.4	1,549.4	1,546.6	1,558.0	1,563.5	1,542.9
2014	1,526.8	1,532.6	1,545.9	1,559.4	1,564.6	1,569.9	1,564.2	1,572.6	1,571.9	1,574.1	1,580.3	1,587.3	1,562.5
2015	1,553.7	1,563.0	1,570.7	1,585.3	1,593.0	1,597.0	1,595.3	1,598.8	1,597.8	1,603.3	1,610.1	1,616.0	1,590.3
2016	1,584.4	1,593.0	1,601.8	1,618.0	1,619.1	1,620.3	1,618.9	1,621.6	1,623.5	1,620.4	1,627.0	1,629.0	1,614.8
2017	1,602.8	1,614.2	1,624.4	1,630.0	1,635.3	1,641.3	1,635.9	1,641.4	1,639.4	1,643.3	1,651.0	1,649.3	1,634.0
2018	1,620.2	1,633.2	1,643.0	1,652.0	1,653.9	1,662.5	1,660.8	1,665.6	1,660.5	1,670.8	1,673.7	1,678.0	1,656.2
Goods Producing													
2010	332.3	331.5	334.4	336.7	338.3	339.4	338.6	337.6	336.8	335.5	334.0	331.9	335.6
2011	322.5	326.3	329.0	330.0	331.7	332.5	331.3	332.7	332.7	331.4	332.5	334.0	330.6
2012	328.6	329.9	333.3	335.1	335.5	337.0	336.7	338.2	337.9	339.0	339.1	339.7	335.8
2013	334.7	336.3	340.6	341.1	341.1	342.6	340.8	342.4	341.8	342.1	341.8	343.2	340.7
2014	338.5	339.3	341.7	342.6	344.0	345.7	345.4	346.6	347.6	348.6	348.5	349.5	344.8
2015	345.6	346.8	347.6	348.8	350.0	351.8	351.2	351.6	352.2	353.0	352.9	354.4	350.5
2016	351.4	351.2	352.9	354.8	353.8	354.6	355.2	354.3	356.6	355.0	354.6	356.3	354.2
2017	354.4	356.6	358.0	356.8	357.7	358.5	358.1	358.8	360.0	361.8	361.2	362.4	358.7
2018	358.3	361.8	363.4	363.4	364.1	365.9	366.6	368.3	368.7	371.5	369.2	372.5	366.1
Service-Providing													
2010	1,526.0	1,532.9	1,545.4	1,554.7	1,568.8	1,568.4	1,549.6	1,549.3	1,554.9	1,562.2	1,570.3	1,571.7	1,554.5
2011	1,536.2	1,547.3	1,557.2	1,564.6	1,565.6	1,564.4	1,550.4	1,554.2	1,567.2	1,563.0	1,572.8	1,570.7	1,559.5
2012	1,541.8	1,552.9	1,568.2	1,574.5	1,577.0	1,579.7	1,556.0	1,565.2	1,573.3	1,575.0	1,588.4	1,586.5	1,569.9
2013	1,550.8	1,567.1	1,577.2	1,585.3	1,593.1	1,592.6	1,574.4	1,580.8	1,585.6	1,587.5	1,600.8	1,604.0	1,583.3
2014	1,567.2	1,576.1	1,588.3	1,601.5	1,606.5	1,607.5	1,588.7	1,598.4	1,605.4	1,610.4	1,617.8	1,624.5	1,599.4
2015	1,586.9	1,598.2	1,606.1	1,620.3	1,628.2	1,627.9	1,614.7	1,620.8	1,625.4	1,632.9	1,640.8	1,645.7	1,620.7
2016	1,611.5	1,623.5	1,631.9	1,646.7	1,649.9	1,649.3	1,636.4	1,643.7	1,650.4	1,650.7	1,658.9	1,659.9	1,642.7
2017	1,630.0	1,642.4	1,652.7	1,659.7	1,665.3	1,669.6	1,653.2	1,660.7	1,664.5	1,668.8	1,678.0	1,674.6	1,660.0
2018	1,643.6	1,656.7	1,666.5	1,676.5	1,678.8	1,685.0	1,670.5	1,677.0	1,678.5	1,688.4	1,695.2	1,694.1	1,675.9
Mining and Logging													
2010	11.7	11.7	11.7	11.9	12.0	12.0	12.1	12.2	12.1	12.3	12.2	12.2	12.0
2011	12.1	12.1	12.1	12.3	12.4	12.5	12.3	12.5	12.6	12.5	12.5	12.6	12.4
2012	12.7	12.6	12.5	12.5	12.5	12.6	12.8	12.8	12.7	12.6	12.6	12.6	12.6
2013	12.3	12.3	12.4	12.1	12.2	12.3	11.9	12.0	12.0	11.9	11.9	11.9	12.1
2014	11.8	11.6	11.7	11.7	11.6	11.7	11.8	11.8	11.8	11.7	11.6	11.5	11.7
2015	11.5	11.4	11.3	11.1	11.1	11.1	11.2	11.0	10.9	10.8	10.3	10.2	11.0
2016	9.9	9.5	9.5	9.3	9.2	9.2	9.3	9.2	9.4	9.1	9.3	9.3	9.4
2017	9.6	9.7	9.7	9.7	9.7	9.7	9.8	9.9	10.0	9.9	10.0	10.0	9.8
2018	9.9	9.9	9.9	9.8	9.9	9.9	10.0	10.1	10.1	10.1	10.0	9.9	10.0
Construction													
2010	85.4	85.4	87.4	88.2	89.1	90.2	89.3	88.2	87.8	86.9	85.1	83.5	87.2
2011	77.2	79.2	81.1	80.8	82.0	81.8	81.2	81.1	81.9	81.0	80.7	80.6	80.7
2012	76.7	77.7	79.9	80.3	79.9	80.0	79.7	80.2	80.2	80.7	80.0	79.3	79.6
2013	76.5	76.9	79.9	80.4	79.9	80.1	79.5	80.1	79.5	80.0	78.7	79.3	79.2
2014	76.2	77.4	79.0	79.4	79.9	80.3	80.4	80.9	81.1	82.0	81.2	81.0	79.9
2015	78.5	79.1	79.6	80.9	81.2	82.3	81.9	82.2	82.7	83.4	83.5	84.2	81.6
2016	82.9	82.8	84.6	85.6	84.7	84.4	84.3	83.5	84.9	84.5	83.7	84.7	84.2
2017	83.2	84.1	85.5	84.2	85.1	84.9	84.8	85.2	86.3	87.8	86.6	86.5	85.4
2018	84.2	86.5	88.2	88.5	88.6	89.2	89.3	90.3	90.7	92.0	90.4	91.1	89.1

1. Employment by Industry: Alabama, 2010–2018—*Continued*

Industry and year	January	February	March	April	May	June	July	August	September	October	November	December	Annual average
Manufacturing													
2010	235.2	234.4	235.3	236.6	237.2	237.2	237.2	237.2	236.9	236.3	236.7	236.2	236.4
2011	233.2	235.0	235.8	236.9	237.3	238.2	237.8	239.1	238.2	237.9	239.3	240.8	237.5
2012	239.2	239.6	240.9	242.3	243.1	244.4	244.2	245.2	245.0	245.7	246.5	247.8	243.7
2013	245.9	247.1	248.3	248.6	249.0	250.2	249.4	250.3	250.3	250.2	251.2	252.0	249.4
2014	250.5	250.3	251.0	251.5	252.5	253.7	253.2	253.9	254.7	254.9	255.7	257.0	253.2
2015	255.6	256.3	256.7	256.8	257.7	258.4	258.1	258.4	258.6	258.8	259.1	260.0	257.9
2016	258.6	258.9	258.8	259.9	259.9	261.0	261.6	261.6	262.3	261.4	261.6	262.3	260.7
2017	261.6	262.8	262.8	262.9	262.9	263.9	263.5	263.7	263.7	264.1	264.6	265.9	263.5
2018	264.2	265.4	265.3	265.1	265.6	266.8	267.3	267.9	267.9	269.4	268.8	271.5	267.1
Trade, Transportation, and Utilities													
2010	356.3	355.4	358.3	358.8	360.4	360.9	360.3	360.5	359.5	362.8	368.4	371.7	361.1
2011	358.5	358.6	360.2	361.7	362.0	363.6	363.9	364.5	363.9	364.7	371.2	374.0	363.9
2012	361.6	360.1	363.2	363.4	365.2	366.1	364.0	364.4	364.0	365.9	374.6	376.3	365.7
2013	361.2	361.6	363.8	364.7	366.8	368.8	367.9	368.7	367.6	368.7	376.9	381.2	368.2
2014	366.9	365.5	368.7	369.9	370.6	372.0	372.1	371.9	371.5	372.7	381.6	385.4	372.4
2015	370.8	369.9	372.6	375.0	376.9	377.8	377.8	378.0	376.8	379.2	387.1	390.1	377.7
2016	376.4	375.8	377.3	379.2	379.7	379.8	379.6	378.8	378.7	379.8	386.8	388.7	380.1
2017	376.8	375.3	376.4	377.0	377.6	378.7	377.5	377.7	376.7	378.5	385.3	387.9	378.8
2018	376.4	375.2	377.8	378.4	379.7	379.9	380.1	379.9	378.9	383.3	388.4	390.1	380.7
Wholesale Trade													
2010	71.4	71.3	71.2	71.6	71.9	71.7	71.7	71.7	71.3	71.9	71.7	71.6	71.6
2011	70.7	71.2	71.2	71.6	71.6	71.7	72.1	72.2	72.3	72.6	72.5	72.8	71.9
2012	71.7	71.9	72.3	72.4	72.7	72.8	72.4	72.4	72.4	72.8	72.8	72.8	72.5
2013	71.7	72.1	72.3	72.7	72.9	72.8	72.8	72.9	72.9	73.0	73.2	73.1	72.7
2014	72.0	72.1	72.3	72.6	72.9	73.0	73.0	73.2	73.2	73.4	73.6	73.8	72.9
2015	72.6	72.9	73.1	73.6	73.7	73.6	73.9	73.8	73.7	74.0	73.9	73.8	73.6
2016	72.7	73.0	73.1	73.7	73.7	73.7	73.7	73.5	73.6	73.7	73.5	73.5	73.5
2017	72.6	72.8	72.9	73.3	73.5	73.8	73.6	73.5	73.5	74.0	74.0	74.0	73.5
2018	73.1	73.3	73.6	73.8	74.1	74.3	74.5	74.4	74.4	75.2	74.0	74.0	74.1
Retail Trade													
2010	219.9	219.1	221.8	221.4	222.3	222.8	221.9	222.0	221.1	224.0	229.6	232.2	223.2
2011	221.4	220.6	221.9	223.2	223.1	224.3	224.3	224.4	223.6	224.5	231.0	232.7	224.6
2012	222.4	220.1	222.1	222.1	223.5	223.9	222.5	222.4	221.8	223.4	231.8	232.7	224.1
2013	219.4	219.2	220.9	221.6	223.1	224.8	224.2	224.7	223.5	224.4	232.0	235.2	224.4
2014	223.3	222.1	224.4	225.3	225.7	226.6	226.7	226.2	225.6	226.9	235.1	237.5	227.1
2015	225.1	224.7	226.7	228.5	229.9	230.7	230.4	230.6	229.8	231.8	239.5	241.3	230.8
2016	229.7	229.4	230.8	232.2	232.5	232.5	232.3	231.7	231.3	232.7	239.7	240.1	232.9
2017	230.6	229.1	229.7	230.7	230.8	231.7	231.0	230.6	229.5	230.7	237.2	237.2	231.6
2018	228.6	227.8	229.7	230.1	230.8	230.6	230.2	229.6	228.9	230.7	235.9	236.0	230.7
Transportation and Utilities													
2010	65.0	65.0	65.3	65.8	66.2	66.4	66.7	66.8	67.1	66.9	67.1	67.9	66.4
2011	66.4	66.8	67.1	66.9	67.3	67.6	67.5	67.9	68.0	67.6	67.7	68.5	67.4
2012	67.5	68.1	68.8	68.9	69.0	69.4	69.1	69.6	69.8	69.7	70.0	70.8	69.2
2013	70.1	70.3	70.6	70.4	70.8	71.2	70.9	71.1	71.2	71.3	71.7	72.9	71.0
2014	71.6	71.3	72.0	72.0	72.0	72.4	72.4	72.5	72.7	72.4	72.9	74.1	72.4
2015	73.1	72.3	72.8	72.9	73.3	73.5	73.5	73.6	73.3	73.4	73.7	75.0	73.4
2016	74.0	73.4	73.4	73.3	73.5	73.6	73.6	73.6	73.8	73.4	73.6	75.1	73.7
2017	73.6	73.4	73.8	73.0	73.3	73.2	72.9	73.6	73.7	73.8	74.7	76.7	73.8
2018	74.7	74.1	74.5	74.5	74.8	75.0	75.4	75.9	75.6	77.4	78.5	80.1	75.9
Information													
2010	24.5	24.4	24.3	24.2	24.2	24.3	24.0	23.9	23.8	23.7	23.7	23.6	24.1
2011	23.5	23.4	23.3	23.1	23.3	23.3	23.2	23.1	23.1	22.7	22.8	22.8	23.1
2012	22.9	22.9	23.0	22.8	22.8	22.8	22.7	22.6	22.5	22.2	22.4	22.4	22.7
2013	22.4	22.4	22.3	22.4	22.8	22.9	22.9	22.7	22.5	22.6	22.8	22.9	22.6
2014	22.2	22.1	22.1	22.1	22.1	22.0	22.0	21.9	21.8	21.7	21.9	21.9	22.0
2015	21.6	21.9	21.8	21.6	22.0	21.4	21.5	21.3	21.0	21.0	21.1	21.2	21.5
2016	20.8	20.7	20.6	20.8	21.0	21.0	20.8	20.7	20.5	20.7	20.9	20.9	20.8
2017	20.5	20.7	20.9	20.7	21.1	21.0	21.0	20.7	20.6	20.8	20.9	20.9	20.8
2018	20.7	21.0	21.1	21.6	21.3	21.4	21.0	20.9	20.9	21.0	21.3	21.5	21.1

1. Employment by Industry: Alabama, 2010–2018—*Continued*

Industry and year	January	February	March	April	May	June	July	August	September	October	November	December	Annual average
Financial Activities													
2010	92.1	92.0	92.4	92.3	92.5	92.7	92.2	91.8	91.2	91.7	91.7	91.9	92.0
2011	91.1	91.5	91.6	92.4	93.8	93.0	93.2	92.5	93.3	92.1	92.0	91.8	92.4
2012	90.6	91.1	91.5	91.7	92.2	92.7	93.5	93.4	93.6	93.5	94.0	93.9	92.6
2013	93.2	93.3	93.8	93.7	94.0	94.5	94.7	94.9	94.2	94.6	94.8	95.0	94.2
2014	93.8	93.9	94.2	94.6	95.1	95.5	95.4	95.4	94.4	94.7	94.8	95.2	94.8
2015	94.2	94.3	94.8	95.3	95.8	96.1	96.2	95.9	95.4	95.6	95.6	95.7	95.4
2016	95.1	95.3	95.5	95.9	96.1	96.2	96.4	96.6	96.6	96.6	96.6	96.6	96.1
2017	95.5	95.7	96.0	95.7	96.1	96.3	97.0	97.1	97.5	98.4	97.7	96.5	96.6
2018	95.4	95.5	95.6	95.5	95.8	96.5	96.7	96.8	96.7	97.8	97.4	96.9	96.4
Professional and Business Services													
2010	201.0	202.2	204.1	206.8	207.7	211.7	213.6	212.8	212.9	213.5	214.5	214.6	209.6
2011	208.9	211.9	212.7	213.6	213.0	213.9	213.1	215.3	217.6	216.1	216.0	216.4	214.0
2012	211.0	214.4	216.7	218.1	218.9	220.2	218.1	222.4	221.7	220.3	220.6	219.0	218.5
2013	213.5	217.0	219.0	220.4	220.4	221.8	219.3	221.0	219.7	220.2	220.1	221.6	219.5
2014	216.6	217.4	219.4	222.6	223.4	224.4	224.3	227.5	226.7	228.4	228.2	228.5	224.0
2015	222.5	224.2	225.7	227.8	228.8	228.6	229.5	231.0	230.4	233.3	233.5	234.1	229.1
2016	229.1	230.7	231.9	235.4	234.9	234.3	232.7	234.6	234.1	234.9	235.5	234.9	233.6
2017	231.6	234.3	237.0	237.7	239.0	241.3	238.9	242.1	240.7	242.4	242.6	242.1	239.1
2018	237.5	240.8	242.7	244.4	242.7	245.2	245.0	246.1	245.0	246.4	246.1	245.6	244.0
Education and Health Services													
2010	215.8	217.8	217.3	218.8	219.0	217.7	218.8	220.0	221.3	222.0	223.1	221.5	219.4
2011	218.7	219.6	221.6	221.2	221.0	219.1	218.9	220.1	223.2	222.9	224.7	223.1	221.2
2012	221.5	222.2	223.8	224.9	222.9	222.8	219.7	222.9	225.8	225.0	228.1	228.3	224.0
2013	223.4	228.0	225.8	226.9	229.3	226.4	222.6	225.9	229.5	228.4	231.6	231.8	227.5
2014	225.1	228.6	227.4	229.8	228.9	226.9	224.1	227.3	230.8	232.5	231.3	233.8	228.9
2015	228.6	232.1	229.8	232.6	232.0	231.5	230.8	233.0	235.6	237.3	236.4	238.6	233.2
2016	233.2	236.7	235.6	237.9	237.3	236.4	237.0	239.2	241.6	241.5	240.8	242.4	238.3
2017	237.2	240.8	240.2	241.9	241.0	241.0	239.3	240.9	243.3	243.1	245.1	245.0	241.6
2018	240.8	244.0	243.0	245.1	244.1	244.9	243.3	245.1	246.6	248.3	249.6	249.0	245.3
Leisure and Hospitality													
2010	160.3	161.0	165.9	169.5	171.4	173.0	170.9	171.0	168.8	166.5	166.5	165.5	167.5
2011	159.5	162.3	166.5	171.5	171.8	174.1	173.7	174.7	172.4	168.5	168.0	166.7	169.1
2012	163.1	166.3	170.9	176.1	178.2	180.6	177.7	178.8	176.6	172.7	172.7	171.0	173.7
2013	167.9	170.4	174.8	180.3	183.4	185.4	183.6	184.0	182.5	178.7	179.0	176.8	178.9
2014	173.1	174.8	180.4	185.6	187.9	190.4	188.3	189.6	187.0	183.6	182.3	181.4	183.7
2015	178.8	182.1	186.1	191.1	194.0	196.0	195.1	195.1	193.6	191.3	191.0	189.6	190.3
2016	186.2	190.0	194.6	199.7	202.2	203.2	202.2	202.6	200.5	197.4	197.2	194.4	197.5
2017	192.2	195.7	200.1	204.2	206.5	208.0	207.7	207.9	204.2	202.2	201.4	198.6	202.4
2018	195.8	199.2	203.1	207.1	209.3	211.3	211.5	211.7	206.9	205.6	204.5	204.6	205.9
Other Services													
2010	89.0	89.5	89.7	89.8	90.2	90.9	91.0	90.4	89.9	90.6	89.8	89.7	90.0
2011	88.8	89.4	89.7	90.1	90.2	90.7	90.3	90.0	89.9	89.9	90.4	90.0	90.0
2012	90.0	90.7	91.7	91.7	91.8	92.7	92.2	91.7	91.1	91.3	90.6	90.5	91.3
2013	90.0	90.4	91.3	91.4	91.6	92.3	91.8	91.8	91.6	91.3	91.0	91.0	91.3
2014	90.6	91.0	92.0	92.2	92.6	93.0	92.6	92.4	92.1	91.9	91.7	91.6	92.0
2015	91.6	91.7	92.3	93.1	93.5	93.8	93.2	92.9	92.8	92.6	92.5	92.3	92.7
2016	92.2	92.6	93.4	94.3	94.1	94.8	95.0	94.8	94.9	94.5	94.6	94.8	94.2
2017	94.6	95.1	95.8	96.0	96.3	96.5	96.4	96.2	96.4	96.1	96.2	95.9	96.0
2018	95.3	95.7	96.3	96.5	96.9	97.4	96.6	96.8	96.8	96.9	97.2	97.8	96.7
Government													
2010	387.0	390.6	393.4	394.5	403.4	397.2	378.8	378.9	387.5	391.4	392.6	393.2	390.7
2011	387.2	390.6	391.6	391.0	390.5	386.7	374.1	374.0	383.8	386.1	387.7	385.9	385.8
2012	381.1	385.2	387.4	385.8	385.0	381.8	368.1	369.0	378.0	384.1	385.4	385.1	381.3
2013	379.2	384.0	386.4	385.5	384.8	380.5	371.6	371.8	378.0	383.0	384.6	383.7	381.1
2014	378.9	382.8	384.1	384.7	385.9	383.3	369.9	372.4	381.1	384.9	386.0	386.7	381.7
2015	378.8	382.0	383.0	383.8	385.2	382.7	370.6	373.6	379.8	382.6	383.6	384.1	380.8
2016	378.5	381.7	383.0	383.5	384.6	383.6	372.7	376.4	383.5	385.3	386.5	387.2	382.2
2017	381.6	384.8	386.3	386.5	387.7	386.8	375.4	378.1	385.1	387.3	388.2	387.7	384.6
2018	381.7	385.3	386.9	387.9	389.0	388.4	376.3	379.7	386.7	389.1	390.7	388.6	385.9

2. Average Weekly Hours by Selected Industry: Alabama, 2014–2018

(Not seasonally adjusted)

Industry and year	January	February	March	April	May	June	July	August	September	October	November	December	Annual average
Total Private													
2014	35.0	35.1	36.0	35.6	35.5	35.8	35.4	35.6	35.5	35.2	35.6	35.5	35.5
2015	34.9	35.4	35.4	35.2	35.5	35.5	35.4	35.9	35.4	35.8	35.9	35.6	35.5
2016	35.5	35.6	35.5	35.5	35.8	35.6	35.6	35.4	35.6	36.0	35.3	35.4	35.6
2017	35.3	35.2	35.2	35.2	35.2	35.3	35.4	35.3	34.9	35.6	35.3	35.2	35.3
2018	34.3	35.0	35.3	35.5	35.2	35.4	35.5	35.4	35.8	35.3	35.3	35.9	35.3
Goods-Producing													
2014	41.4	40.2	42.6	41.9	41.9	42.0	41.8	42.5	42.4	41.8	41.7	42.1	41.9
2015	41.2	41.2	41.3	41.2	41.7	41.7	41.6	41.9	40.8	42.2	41.7	42.2	41.6
2016	41.5	41.5	41.4	41.4	42.1	42.2	41.5	41.5	42.1	42.3	41.2	41.3	41.7
2017	40.8	41.0	41.0	40.8	41.8	42.0	41.5	42.3	41.4	42.0	42.4	41.8	41.6
2018	40.0	41.5	42.0	41.7	42.1	41.9	41.0	42.1	42.0	41.6	41.8	42.4	41.7
Construction													
2014	39.5	37.7	40.1	39.8	40.6	40.8	41.3	42.3	42.2	40.3	41.4	40.9	40.6
2015	38.6	39.7	39.6	39.5	41.4	41.5	41.7	41.6	40.1	41.8	41.7	42.4	40.8
2016	41.7	41.3	40.1	41.2	41.6	41.7	41.4	40.5	41.0	41.5	40.3	39.8	41.0
2017	39.6	39.9	39.8	39.8	41.4	40.5	41.2	40.0	39.9	40.7	41.2	40.1	40.4
2018	37.7	39.5	40.5	40.9	42.0	40.3	40.0	40.0	39.7	40.2	40.1	40.3	40.1
Manufacturing													
2014	41.1	40.3	42.1	41.4	41.3	41.4	41.1	41.9	41.7	41.7	41.3	42.1	41.5
2015	41.8	41.6	41.7	41.7	41.4	41.4	41.2	41.8	41.4	42.4	41.8	42.0	41.7
2016	41.5	41.5	41.7	41.4	42.2	42.2	41.3	41.7	42.4	42.5	41.5	41.9	41.8
2017	41.3	41.4	41.5	41.2	42.1	42.8	41.7	43.4	42.2	42.7	43.0	42.7	42.2
2018	41.3	42.5	42.9	42.3	42.3	42.8	41.5	42.1	42.3	41.6	42.1	42.9	42.2
Trade, Transportation, and Utilities													
2014	35.1	35.4	35.8	35.9	35.6	35.6	35.4	35.2	35.1	34.8	34.9	35.2	35.3
2015	34.2	34.6	34.3	34.5	34.6	34.7	34.7	34.9	34.4	34.5	34.5	34.4	34.5
2016	34.1	34.3	33.9	34.0	34.0	34.1	34.3	34.0	33.7	33.8	33.5	33.9	34.0
2017	33.5	33.4	33.4	34.0	33.5	33.6	33.9	33.7	33.2	33.5	33.2	33.5	33.5
2018	32.7	32.8	32.8	33.2	33.0	33.2	33.6	33.3	33.3	33.0	32.9	33.2	33.1
Financial Activities													
2014	35.7	36.7	36.7	36.0	36.2	37.1	36.4	36.5	36.4	36.4	37.9	36.8	36.6
2015	37.0	38.1	38.4	36.8	37.2	37.2	36.9	38.3	37.2	36.9	38.6	37.3	37.5
2016	37.9	37.9	37.2	37.5	38.5	37.9	37.7	37.1	38.3	38.0	37.8	37.3	37.8
2017	39.0	38.4	38.5	38.7	38.2	38.1	38.2	38.0	37.5	38.5	37.9	38.1	38.3
2018	37.6	37.6	37.5	38.1	37.4	37.6	38.4	37.5	38.8	37.7	38.4	39.4	38.0
Professional and Business Services													
2014	35.8	36.3	36.8	36.3	36.5	37.1	36.6	37.2	36.6	36.9	37.6	37.3	36.8
2015	36.3	37.0	36.7	36.5	36.7	36.6	36.7	37.3	36.7	36.7	36.9	36.0	36.7
2016	36.3	36.4	36.5	36.7	37.0	36.5	37.0	37.1	37.1	37.7	37.0	37.0	36.9
2017	37.0	36.6	37.0	36.7	36.8	36.7	37.2	36.9	36.6	37.7	37.0	37.1	36.9
2018	35.8	36.9	37.5	37.4	36.6	37.0	36.9	36.5	37.4	36.7	36.5	37.4	36.9
Education and Health Services													
2014	33.1	33.1	33.3	32.8	32.7	33.2	32.8	33.0	32.6	32.4	33.4	32.4	32.9
2015	32.5	33.4	33.2	33.1	33.3	33.3	33.3	33.8	33.4	33.8	34.6	33.3	33.4
2016	34.0	34.0	33.8	34.0	34.2	33.9	33.9	34.2	34.4	34.8	34.5	34.2	34.2
2017	34.5	34.1	33.8	33.2	32.9	33.1	33.6	33.1	33.5	34.0	33.5	33.5	33.6
2018	32.8	33.4	33.5	34.1	33.2	33.5	33.9	33.5	34.5	33.4	33.5	34.3	33.6
Leisure and Hospitality													
2014	25.4	25.9	26.7	26.5	26.5	26.9	26.5	26.3	26.2	25.7	26.3	26.3	26.3
2015	25.7	26.5	26.6	26.9	26.9	27.3	27.1	26.7	26.0	26.2	25.8	26.1	26.5
2016	25.4	25.5	26.3	26.0	26.1	26.5	26.3	25.8	25.5	26.1	25.8	25.9	25.9
2017	25.3	25.8	26.0	25.9	25.8	26.2	26.2	25.6	25.4	25.9	25.7	25.3	25.8
2018	25.4	26.2	26.5	26.4	26.5	27.2	27.1	26.7	26.9	27.1	26.4	26.6	26.6
Other Services													
2014	31.6	31.9	32.7	32.2	31.1	32.1	30.0	30.2	32.8	32.8	32.6	31.5	31.8
2015	32.0	32.9	33.5	33.1	33.9	33.2	32.1	33.6	32.6	33.8	34.5	34.5	33.3
2016	34.1	34.5	35.2	34.9	34.6	33.9	34.2	33.8	34.1	35.0	33.5	33.5	34.3
2017	32.2	33.1	33.0	33.0	32.6	33.1	33.4	32.4	32.8	33.2	32.9	32.6	32.9
2018	32.3	32.9	33.0	32.8	32.4	32.4	32.9	33.0	33.4	33.6	32.6	32.7	32.8

3. Average Hourly Earnings by Selected Industry: Alabama, 2014–2018

(Dollars, not seasonally adjusted)

Industry and year	January	February	March	April	May	June	July	August	September	October	November	December	Annual average
Total Private													
2014	20.50	20.86	20.72	20.61	20.60	20.85	20.67	20.68	20.73	20.75	20.96	20.78	20.73
2015	21.00	21.40	21.29	20.63	20.62	20.72	20.78	20.99	21.00	21.10	21.31	21.35	21.02
2016	21.64	21.60	21.43	21.83	21.89	21.79	21.97	21.78	21.86	22.25	22.04	22.05	21.85
2017	22.47	22.32	22.24	22.75	22.44	22.20	22.56	22.45	22.87	22.97	22.78	23.05	22.59
2018	23.12	23.03	23.08	23.29	23.07	23.05	23.34	23.18	23.74	23.69	23.84	24.14	23.38
Goods-Producing													
2014	22.29	22.89	22.50	22.46	22.30	22.50	22.39	22.29	22.28	22.51	22.64	22.59	22.47
2015	22.55	22.78	22.60	22.58	22.44	22.46	22.47	22.61	22.90	22.86	23.14	23.12	22.71
2016	23.16	23.32	22.92	23.28	23.27	23.15	23.36	23.22	23.00	23.29	23.23	23.47	23.22
2017	23.60	23.42	23.51	24.06	23.81	23.59	23.83	23.59	24.19	24.30	24.22	24.36	23.88
2018	24.26	24.15	24.46	24.60	24.35	24.25	24.38	24.38	24.95	24.96	25.18	25.12	24.59
Construction													
2014	23.11	23.26	22.37	22.66	22.56	22.41	22.23	22.50	22.31	22.57	22.64	22.93	22.62
2015	23.05	22.82	22.55	22.51	22.06	22.22	22.11	22.32	22.70	22.97	23.08	22.86	22.60
2016	22.75	22.40	22.27	22.58	22.25	22.43	22.21	21.98	21.95	22.10	22.09	22.30	22.28
2017	22.14	22.56	22.30	22.13	22.40	22.27	22.39	22.69	23.05	23.23	23.47	23.54	22.69
2018	23.06	23.07	23.87	23.56	23.31	23.00	23.03	23.48	24.39	24.53	24.65	24.32	23.70
Manufacturing													
2014	22.03	22.38	22.20	22.14	22.00	22.34	22.35	22.12	22.24	22.49	22.67	22.56	22.29
2015	22.36	22.74	22.60	22.53	22.56	22.57	22.62	22.72	23.00	22.85	23.19	23.29	22.75
2016	23.36	23.71	23.18	23.57	23.64	23.44	23.86	23.72	23.41	23.82	23.74	23.97	23.62
2017	24.27	23.81	24.02	24.46	24.08	23.81	24.19	23.70	24.44	24.54	24.30	24.48	24.17
2018	24.52	24.38	24.44	24.77	24.54	24.51	24.72	24.74	25.17	25.13	25.35	25.42	24.81
Trade, Transportation, and Utilities													
2014	18.34	18.69	18.76	18.76	18.71	18.94	18.96	18.85	18.91	18.81	18.74	18.31	18.73
2015	18.92	19.09	18.99	19.13	19.04	18.88	18.99	19.16	19.32	19.17	19.17	18.87	19.06
2016	19.50	19.37	19.46	19.88	19.71	19.75	19.77	19.51	19.64	19.89	19.56	19.23	19.61
2017	19.88	19.67	19.51	19.94	19.58	19.63	19.76	19.81	20.11	20.19	19.87	19.93	19.82
2018	20.05	19.59	19.61	19.79	19.68	19.85	20.09	20.13	20.66	20.86	20.50	20.53	20.12
Financial Activities													
2014	21.01	21.57	22.02	21.74	22.16	22.10	21.89	21.77	21.86	21.89	21.92	21.59	21.80
2015	21.67	22.12	22.14	22.45	22.23	22.89	23.00	22.65	23.08	23.59	23.64	24.14	22.80
2016	24.04	23.63	24.27	25.21	25.62	24.84	25.19	24.93	25.52	26.36	25.87	25.86	25.12
2017	26.52	25.92	25.27	25.80	25.51	25.01	25.40	25.53	25.84	25.93	25.50	25.77	25.67
2018	26.01	26.12	26.55	27.22	27.31	26.89	27.60	27.32	28.16	27.59	27.66	27.77	27.19
Professional and Business Services													
2014	23.72	24.33	24.12	23.94	23.91	24.35	23.95	23.94	24.06	23.89	24.60	24.41	24.11
2015	24.74	26.08	26.09	23.40	23.62	24.17	23.99	24.65	24.70	24.70	25.06	25.38	24.71
2016	25.74	25.28	25.05	25.01	25.60	25.29	25.68	25.45	25.66	25.89	25.71	25.91	25.52
2017	26.40	26.25	26.05	26.60	26.24	26.06	26.82	26.38	26.80	26.73	26.62	27.13	26.51
2018	27.60	27.74	27.42	27.81	27.52	27.81	28.37	27.41	28.30	28.01	28.39	28.73	27.93
Education and Health Services													
2014	21.09	21.57	21.58	21.59	21.51	21.83	21.49	21.52	21.74	21.70	22.11	21.84	21.63
2015	22.16	22.14	21.83	22.04	21.91	22.06	22.17	22.16	22.19	22.49	22.69	22.88	22.23
2016	22.94	22.99	22.72	23.24	22.93	23.16	23.46	22.91	22.88	23.18	23.06	22.96	23.04
2017	23.10	23.25	23.19	24.17	24.01	23.54	23.76	23.70	23.97	24.13	23.93	24.23	23.75
2018	24.31	24.42	24.41	24.44	23.94	24.15	24.10	23.95	24.38	24.48	25.03	24.83	24.37
Leisure and Hospitality													
2014	10.99	11.09	10.94	10.91	10.85	10.86	10.75	11.00	10.79	10.86	10.90	11.03	10.91
2015	10.93	11.16	11.05	11.04	11.00	10.88	10.84	10.97	11.03	10.99	11.08	11.28	11.02
2016	11.23	11.47	11.24	11.18	11.25	11.31	11.30	11.44	11.55	11.72	11.73	11.94	11.45
2017	11.80	11.92	11.83	11.89	11.84	11.76	11.89	11.97	12.08	12.06	12.09	12.25	11.95
2018	12.12	12.27	12.24	12.18	12.30	12.08	12.12	12.20	12.15	12.34	12.21	12.51	12.23
Other Services													
2014	20.55	20.58	20.65	20.11	21.13	21.90	21.76	22.15	21.86	21.49	21.22	21.54	21.24
2015	20.87	21.18	21.52	19.99	20.06	20.23	20.05	20.28	19.72	19.54	19.25	19.12	20.14
2016	19.23	19.17	19.22	19.10	19.04	18.91	19.11	19.15	19.81	19.56	19.55		19.24
2017	20.63	20.86	20.05	20.40	19.99	19.68	19.62	19.60	20.56	21.13	21.52	21.73	20.48
2018	21.02	21.69	21.97	22.47	22.57	22.68	22.75	22.85	23.43	23.10	23.17	22.68	22.54

4. Average Weekly Earnings by Selected Industry: Alabama, 2014–2018

(Dollars, not seasonally adjusted)

Industry and year	January	February	March	April	May	June	July	August	September	October	November	December	Annual average
Total Private													
2014	717.50	732.19	745.92	733.72	731.30	746.43	731.72	736.21	735.92	730.40	746.18	737.69	735.92
2015	732.90	757.56	753.67	726.18	732.01	735.56	735.61	753.54	743.40	755.38	765.03	760.06	746.21
2016	768.22	768.96	760.77	774.97	783.66	775.72	782.13	771.01	778.22	801.00	778.01	780.57	777.86
2017	793.19	785.66	782.85	800.80	789.89	783.66	798.62	792.49	798.16	817.73	804.13	811.36	797.43
2018	793.02	806.05	814.72	826.80	812.06	815.97	828.57	820.57	849.89	836.26	841.55	866.63	825.31
Goods-Producing													
2014	922.81	920.18	958.50	941.07	934.37	945.00	935.90	947.33	944.67	940.92	944.09	951.04	941.49
2015	929.06	938.54	933.38	930.30	935.75	936.58	934.75	947.36	934.32	964.69	964.94	975.66	944.74
2016	961.14	967.78	948.89	963.79	979.67	976.93	969.44	963.63	968.30	985.17	957.08	969.31	968.27
2017	962.88	960.22	963.91	981.65	995.26	990.78	988.95	997.86	1,001.47	1,020.60	1,026.93	1,018.25	993.41
2018	970.40	1,002.23	1,027.32	1,025.82	1,025.14	1,016.08	999.58	1,026.40	1,047.90	1,038.34	1,052.52	1,065.09	1,025.40
Construction													
2014	912.85	876.90	897.04	901.87	915.94	914.33	918.10	951.75	941.48	909.57	937.30	937.84	918.37
2015	889.73	905.95	892.98	889.15	913.28	922.13	921.99	928.51	910.27	960.15	962.44	969.26	922.08
2016	948.68	925.12	893.03	930.30	925.60	935.33	919.49	890.19	899.95	917.15	890.23	887.54	913.48
2017	876.74	900.14	887.54	880.77	927.36	901.94	922.47	907.60	919.70	945.46	966.96	943.95	916.68
2018	869.36	911.27	966.74	963.60	979.02	926.90	921.20	939.20	968.28	986.11	988.47	980.10	950.37
Manufacturing													
2014	905.43	901.91	934.62	916.60	908.60	924.88	918.59	926.83	927.41	937.83	936.27	949.78	925.04
2015	934.65	945.98	942.42	939.50	933.98	934.40	931.94	949.70	952.20	968.84	969.34	978.18	948.68
2016	969.44	983.97	966.61	975.80	997.61	989.17	985.42	989.12	992.58	1,012.35	985.21	1,004.34	987.32
2017	1,002.35	985.73	996.83	1,007.75	1,013.77	1,019.07	1,008.72	1,028.58	1,031.37	1,047.86	1,044.90	1,045.30	1,019.97
2018	1,012.68	1,036.15	1,048.48	1,047.77	1,038.04	1,049.03	1,025.88	1,041.55	1,064.69	1,045.41	1,067.24	1,090.52	1,046.98
Trade, Transportation, and Utilities													
2014	643.73	661.63	671.61	673.48	666.08	674.26	671.18	663.52	663.74	654.59	654.03	644.51	661.17
2015	647.06	660.51	651.36	659.99	658.78	655.14	658.95	668.68	664.61	661.37	661.37	649.13	657.57
2016	664.95	664.39	659.69	675.92	670.14	673.48	678.11	663.34	661.87	672.28	655.26	651.90	666.74
2017	665.98	656.98	651.63	677.96	655.93	659.57	669.86	667.60	667.65	676.37	659.68	667.66	663.97
2018	655.64	642.55	643.21	657.03	649.44	659.02	675.02	670.33	687.98	688.38	674.45	681.60	665.97
Financial Activities													
2014	750.06	791.62	808.13	782.64	802.19	819.91	796.80	794.61	795.70	796.80	830.77	794.51	797.88
2015	801.79	842.77	850.18	826.16	826.96	851.51	848.70	867.50	858.58	870.47	912.50	900.42	855.00
2016	911.12	895.58	902.84	945.38	986.37	941.44	949.66	924.90	977.42	1,001.68	977.89	964.58	949.54
2017	1,034.28	995.33	972.90	998.46	974.48	952.88	970.28	970.14	969.00	998.31	966.45	981.84	983.16
2018	977.98	982.11	995.63	1,037.08	1,021.39	1,011.06	1,059.84	1,024.50	1,092.61	1,040.14	1,062.14	1,094.14	1,033.22
Professional and Business Services													
2014	849.18	883.18	887.62	869.02	872.72	903.39	876.57	890.57	880.60	881.54	924.96	910.49	887.25
2015	898.06	964.96	957.50	854.10	866.85	884.62	880.43	919.45	906.49	906.49	924.71	913.68	906.86
2016	934.36	920.19	914.33	917.87	947.20	923.09	950.16	944.20	951.99	976.05	951.27	958.67	941.69
2017	976.80	960.75	963.85	976.22	965.63	956.40	997.70	973.42	980.88	1,007.72	984.94	1,006.52	978.22
2018	988.08	1,023.61	1,028.25	1,040.09	1,007.23	1,028.97	1,046.85	1,000.47	1,058.42	1,027.97	1,036.24	1,074.50	1,030.62
Education and Health Services													
2014	698.08	713.97	718.61	708.15	703.38	724.76	704.87	710.16	708.72	703.08	738.47	707.62	711.63
2015	720.20	739.48	724.76	729.52	729.60	734.60	738.26	749.01	741.15	760.16	785.07	761.90	742.48
2016	779.96	781.66	767.94	790.16	784.21	785.12	795.29	783.52	787.07	806.66	795.57	785.23	787.97
2017	796.95	792.83	783.82	802.44	789.93	779.17	798.34	784.47	803.00	820.42	801.66	811.71	798.00
2018	797.37	815.63	817.74	833.40	794.81	809.03	816.99	802.33	841.11	817.63	838.51	851.67	818.83
Leisure and Hospitality													
2014	279.15	287.23	292.10	289.12	287.53	292.13	284.88	289.30	282.70	279.10	286.67	290.09	286.93
2015	280.90	295.74	293.93	296.98	295.90	297.02	293.76	292.90	286.78	287.94	285.86	294.41	292.03
2016	285.24	292.49	295.61	290.68	293.63	299.72	297.19	295.15	294.53	305.89	302.63	309.25	296.56
2017	298.54	307.54	307.58	307.95	305.47	308.11	311.52	306.43	306.83	312.35	310.71	309.93	308.31
2018	307.85	321.47	324.36	321.55	325.95	328.58	328.45	325.74	326.84	334.41	322.34	332.77	325.32
Other Services													
2014	649.38	656.50	675.26	647.54	657.14	702.99	652.80	668.93	717.01	704.87	691.77	678.51	675.43
2015	667.84	696.82	720.92	661.67	680.03	671.64	643.61	681.41	642.87	660.45	664.13	659.64	670.66
2016	655.74	661.37	676.54	666.59	657.40	645.46	646.72	645.92	653.02	693.35	655.26	654.93	659.93
2017	664.29	690.47	661.65	673.20	651.67	651.41	655.31	635.04	674.37	701.52	708.01	708.40	673.79
2018	678.95	713.60	725.01	737.02	731.27	734.83	748.48	754.05	782.56	776.16	755.34	741.64	739.31

ALASKA
At a Glance

Population: 2010 census: 710,231 2018 estimate: 737,438	Percent change in population: 2010–2018: 3.8%

Percent change in total nonfarm employment:
2010–2018: 0.7%

Industry with the largest growth in employment, 2010–2018 (percent):
Education and health services, 16.9%

Industry with the largest decline or smallest growth in employment, 2010–2018 (percent):
Mining and logging, -15.3%

Civilian labor force:
2010: 361,913
2018: 356,886

Unemployment rate and rank among states (highest to lowest):
2010: 7.9%, 36th
2018: 6.6%, 1st

Over-the-year change in unemployment rates:
2016–2017: 0.1%
2017–2018: -0.4%

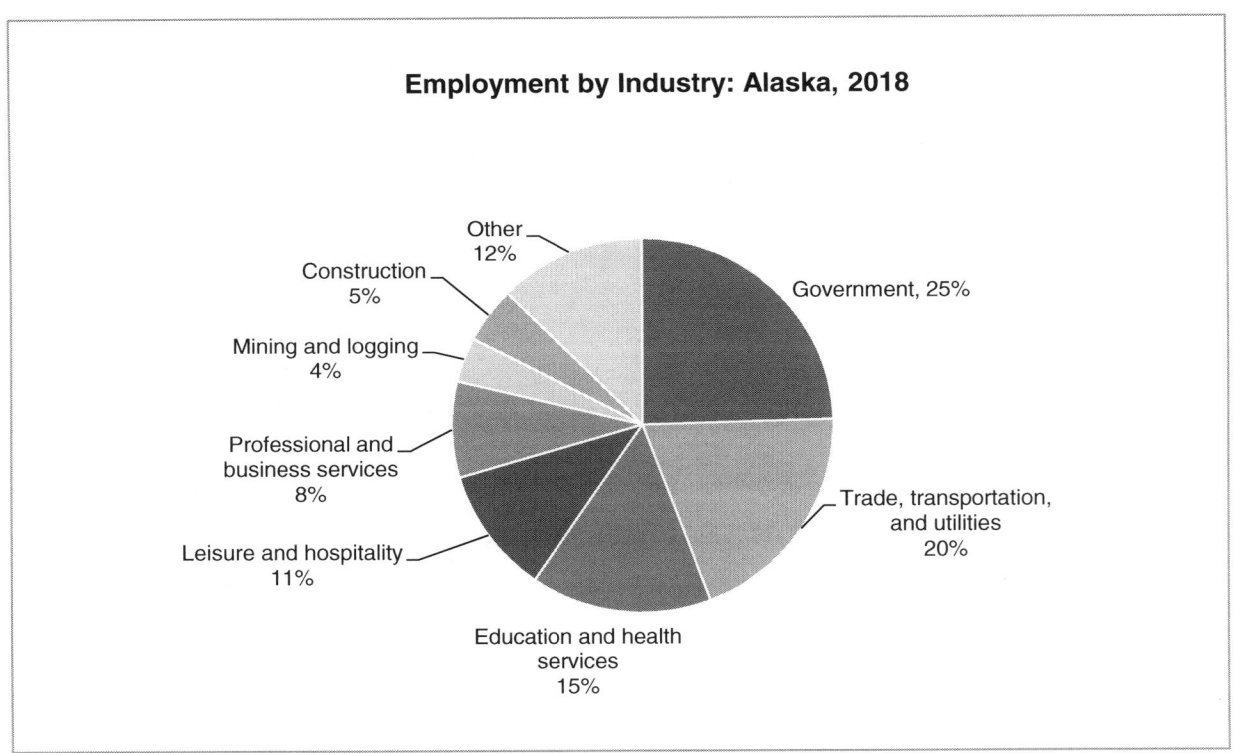

Employment by Industry: Alaska, 2018

- Other 12%
- Construction 5%
- Mining and logging 4%
- Professional and business services 8%
- Leisure and hospitality 11%
- Education and health services 15%
- Government, 25%
- Trade, transportation, and utilities 20%

1. Employment by Industry: Alaska, 2010–2018

(Numbers in thousands, not seasonally adjusted)

Industry and year	January	February	March	April	May	June	July	August	September	October	November	December	Annual average
Total Nonfarm													
2010	303.0	307.0	309.4	315.5	325.7	343.6	349.6	347.8	341.4	324.8	317.5	314.1	325.0
2011	308.6	314.2	316.4	321.2	330.5	348.8	354.0	352.6	347.2	329.4	321.3	318.0	330.2
2012	312.6	320.2	322.9	326.7	337.9	354.5	358.1	357.3	349.0	336.4	325.5	321.8	335.2
2013	314.7	322.3	324.7	329.3	340.1	355.3	360.2	359.8	351.3	333.5	325.1	322.1	336.5
2014	318.6	322.9	325.5	331.2	344.0	356.4	362.4	360.3	350.6	335.1	326.3	324.2	338.1
2015	321.9	326.2	328.4	332.8	345.1	358.0	365.0	360.3	351.1	334.2	324.2	321.4	339.1
2016	317.7	322.1	323.7	330.0	340.2	351.8	358.1	354.0	342.5	328.1	318.0	316.0	333.5
2017	310.5	317.2	318.2	321.9	335.3	349.7	353.6	351.2	340.5	325.2	314.7	312.1	329.2
2018	308.0	314.7	316.3	319.3	332.6	347.0	351.3	349.1	338.7	323.6	313.8	313.7	327.3
Total Private													
2010	219.8	221.8	223.7	228.4	239.9	256.8	268.5	265.8	254.0	237.4	230.7	227.5	239.5
2011	224.4	228.3	230.9	234.7	245.6	263.1	274.0	272.5	261.0	242.7	235.4	232.1	245.4
2012	230.7	234.8	237.0	240.7	253.1	270.2	279.0	276.8	263.4	250.8	240.3	236.8	251.1
2013	233.5	238.2	240.4	244.4	255.9	271.9	282.3	281.0	267.9	250.2	241.7	239.2	253.9
2014	237.2	240.1	242.4	247.2	260.0	273.7	284.5	281.7	267.7	252.2	243.1	241.1	255.9
2015	240.4	243.3	245.3	248.8	261.1	275.5	287.3	282.1	268.3	251.6	241.6	238.9	257.0
2016	236.6	239.9	241.3	246.1	256.5	269.3	281.4	276.3	260.2	245.2	235.2	233.9	251.8
2017	229.6	235.0	235.9	239.2	251.6	267.9	277.9	274.4	259.0	243.5	233.2	230.7	248.2
2018	228.1	233.3	234.8	237.2	249.9	265.9	276.0	272.4	257.8	242.1	232.7	233.0	246.9
Goods Producing													
2010	37.3	38.5	39.5	39.9	42.0	50.0	58.8	56.4	50.1	43.7	39.4	36.3	44.3
2011	37.8	40.0	40.9	41.1	42.8	51.6	60.0	58.3	52.5	45.4	40.5	37.1	45.7
2012	39.7	42.2	43.4	43.6	45.6	54.2	61.3	59.3	52.3	47.4	42.2	38.7	47.5
2013	40.4	43.2	44.4	44.7	45.9	54.1	62.3	60.4	54.6	47.3	42.5	40.3	48.3
2014	43.0	44.8	45.7	47.3	47.7	55.9	63.8	60.8	53.8	47.7	43.7	41.5	49.6
2015	44.2	45.9	46.9	47.3	47.8	55.2	64.4	60.5	52.9	46.5	41.2	39.0	49.3
2016	41.0	43.2	43.7	43.2	43.0	49.7	59.0	54.1	45.5	41.3	36.4	34.4	44.5
2017	34.9	38.6	39.0	38.5	39.1	47.4	55.5	52.5	44.8	39.9	34.6	32.6	41.5
2018	33.8	37.4	37.8	38.0	39.0	46.7	54.9	51.0	44.4	40.3	35.1	34.6	41.1
Service-Providing													
2010	265.7	268.5	269.9	275.6	283.7	293.6	290.8	291.4	291.3	281.1	278.1	277.8	280.6
2011	270.8	274.2	275.5	280.1	287.7	297.2	294.0	294.3	294.7	284.0	280.8	280.9	284.5
2012	272.9	278.0	279.5	283.1	292.3	300.3	296.8	298.0	296.7	289.0	283.3	283.1	287.8
2013	274.3	279.1	280.3	284.6	294.2	301.2	297.9	299.4	296.7	286.2	282.6	281.8	288.2
2014	275.6	278.1	279.8	283.9	296.3	300.5	298.6	299.5	296.8	287.4	282.6	282.7	288.5
2015	277.7	280.3	281.5	285.5	297.3	302.8	300.6	299.8	298.2	287.7	283.0	282.4	289.7
2016	276.7	278.9	280.0	286.8	297.2	302.1	299.1	299.9	297.0	286.8	281.6	281.6	289.0
2017	275.6	278.6	279.2	283.4	296.2	302.3	298.1	298.7	295.7	285.3	280.1	279.5	287.7
2018	274.2	277.3	278.5	281.3	293.6	300.3	296.4	298.1	294.3	283.3	278.7	279.1	286.3
Mining and Logging													
2010	13.8	13.8	14.1	14.4	14.9	15.5	15.9	16.0	15.7	15.3	15.0	15.0	15.0
2011	14.4	14.6	14.8	15.0	15.2	15.8	16.2	16.2	16.1	15.9	15.6	15.8	15.5
2012	15.1	15.3	15.5	16.0	16.4	16.9	17.2	17.4	16.9	16.7	16.4	16.2	16.3
2013	15.8	16.3	16.7	16.6	16.8	17.3	17.3	17.4	17.1	16.5	16.4	16.5	16.7
2014	16.2	16.5	16.7	17.1	17.2	17.6	17.9	17.9	17.7	17.6	17.7	17.8	17.3
2015	17.5	17.5	17.7	17.8	17.6	17.8	17.8	17.8	17.6	17.1	16.4	16.3	17.4
2016	15.7	15.6	15.6	15.1	15.0	14.6	14.3	14.2	13.9	13.7	13.5	13.7	14.6
2017	13.1	13.1	13.1	13.0	13.1	13.4	13.5	13.5	13.2	12.8	12.3	12.4	13.0
2018	12.2	12.3	12.5	12.4	12.7	12.9	12.9	13.0	12.9	12.9	12.5	13.0	12.7
Construction													
2010	13.0	13.1	13.4	14.4	16.7	19.1	20.1	20.4	19.6	18.5	15.8	14.7	16.6
2011	12.8	13.0	13.2	14.5	16.6	18.8	19.5	19.9	19.2	18.2	15.7	14.5	16.3
2012	13.5	13.7	14.1	15.0	17.1	19.6	20.5	21.0	20.0	19.1	16.2	15.1	17.1
2013	13.4	13.9	14.5	15.1	16.9	19.5	20.4	21.4	20.4	18.9	16.6	15.8	17.2
2014	14.5	14.8	15.4	16.1	18.2	20.2	20.9	21.6	20.6	18.7	16.6	15.8	17.8
2015	14.9	15.3	15.9	16.9	18.5	20.2	20.9	20.8	19.5	17.9	15.9	15.0	17.6
2016	13.9	14.2	14.3	15.5	17.3	18.6	19.5	19.2	18.0	16.7	14.6	13.5	16.3
2017	12.2	12.8	13.0	13.9	15.5	17.5	18.0	18.1	17.4	16.3	14.2	13.3	15.2
2018	12.6	13.0	13.5	14.1	16.0	17.9	18.3	18.7	18.1	17.7	15.5	15.4	15.9

1. Employment by Industry: Alaska, 2010–2018—*Continued*

(Numbers in thousands, not seasonally adjusted)

Industry and year	January	February	March	April	May	June	July	August	September	October	November	December	Annual average
Manufacturing													
2010	10.5	11.6	12.0	11.1	10.4	15.4	22.8	20.0	14.8	9.9	8.6	6.6	12.8
2011	10.6	12.4	12.9	11.6	11.0	17.0	24.3	22.2	17.2	11.3	9.2	6.8	13.9
2012	11.1	13.2	13.8	12.6	12.1	17.7	23.6	20.9	15.4	11.6	9.6	7.4	14.1
2013	11.2	13	13.2	13	12.2	17.3	24.6	21.6	17.1	11.9	9.5	8	14.4
2014	12.3	13.5	13.6	14.1	12.3	18.1	25	21.3	15.5	11.4	9.4	7.9	14.5
2015	11.8	13.1	13.3	12.6	11.7	17.2	25.7	21.9	15.8	11.5	8.9	7.7	14.3
2016	11.4	13.4	13.8	12.6	10.7	16.5	25.2	20.7	13.6	10.9	8.3	7.2	13.7
2017	9.6	12.7	12.9	11.6	10.5	16.5	24.0	20.9	14.2	10.8	8.1	6.9	13.2
2018	9.0	12.1	11.8	11.5	10.3	15.9	23.7	19.3	13.4	9.7	7.1	6.2	12.5
Trade, Transportation, and Utilities													
2010	58.9	58.5	58.8	60.5	64.0	66.7	67.5	67.6	65.2	61.6	60.9	61.1	62.6
2011	58.8	58.8	59.6	60.9	64.7	67.1	68.1	68.5	66.4	62.3	61.6	61.5	63.2
2012	59.7	59.5	59.7	61.3	65.2	67.5	68.4	68.5	66.7	64.0	61.9	62.0	63.7
2013	59.9	59.6	59.9	61.4	65.6	67.7	68.4	69.2	67.2	63.1	62.3	62.4	63.9
2014	60.0	60.3	60.3	62.2	67.0	68.4	69.4	69.8	67.5	64.3	62.8	63.0	64.6
2015	61.1	61.2	61.5	63.2	67.5	69.3	70.4	70.6	68.7	65.5	63.9	63.8	65.6
2016	61.6	61.6	61.7	63.9	67.8	69.2	70.0	70.1	67.7	64.9	63.2	63.0	65.4
2017	60.9	60.9	60.9	62.6	66.5	68.5	69.5	69.5	66.9	63.9	62.5	62.2	64.6
2018	60.5	60.3	60.7	62.2	66.5	68.7	69.2	69.5	67.1	63.0	61.9	62.2	64.3
Wholesale Trade													
2010	5.9	5.9	5.9	6.1	6.2	6.4	6.7	6.7	6.4	6.2	6.1	6.1	6.2
2011	6.0	6.0	6.0	6.1	6.2	6.4	6.7	6.7	6.4	6.3	6.1	6.1	6.3
2012	6.0	6.0	6.0	6.1	6.3	6.4	6.6	6.6	6.5	6.4	6.4	6.4	6.3
2013	6.3	6.3	6.4	6.5	6.6	6.7	6.7	6.7	6.6	6.5	6.5	6.5	6.5
2014	6.3	6.3	6.3	6.4	6.5	6.6	6.6	6.6	6.5	6.4	6.3	6.4	6.4
2015	6.3	6.4	6.4	6.5	6.5	6.6	6.7	6.6	6.5	6.5	6.4	6.4	6.5
2016	6.4	6.3	6.3	6.4	6.4	6.5	6.5	6.5	6.4	6.3	6.3	6.2	6.4
2017	6.1	6.2	6.2	6.2	6.4	6.5	6.5	6.5	6.4	6.3	6.3	6.3	6.3
2018	6.3	6.3	6.3	6.4	6.5	6.6	6.6	6.6	6.5	6.4	6.3	6.4	6.4
Retail Trade													
2010	34.0	33.6	33.6	34.6	35.8	37.1	37.3	37.0	36.0	35.1	35.3	35.4	35.4
2011	33.9	33.6	33.8	34.5	35.9	37.1	37.4	37.4	36.6	35.6	35.8	35.8	35.6
2012	34.4	33.9	33.9	34.6	36.1	37.2	37.3	37.2	36.4	35.7	35.6	35.6	35.7
2013	34.2	33.7	33.8	34.5	36.0	37.2	37.5	37.9	37.1	36.0	36.1	36.2	35.9
2014	34.7	34.6	34.6	35.5	37.2	38.2	38.6	38.7	37.6	36.8	36.9	36.9	36.7
2015	35.5	35.2	35.4	36.1	37.7	38.8	39.2	39.2	38.4	37.4	37.5	37.4	37.3
2016	35.8	35.6	35.6	36.5	37.8	38.6	38.8	38.5	37.7	37.0	36.9	36.7	37.1
2017	35.4	35.1	35.0	35.7	36.8	37.9	38.2	37.9	36.9	36.0	36.1	35.8	36.4
2018	34.8	34.3	34.3	34.8	36.2	37.2	37.3	37.2	36.4	35.4	35.4	35.5	35.7
Transportation and Utilities													
2010	19.0	19.0	19.3	19.8	22.0	23.2	23.5	23.9	22.8	20.3	19.5	19.6	21.0
2011	18.9	19.2	19.8	20.3	22.6	23.6	24.0	24.4	23.4	20.4	19.7	19.6	21.3
2012	19.3	19.6	19.8	20.6	22.8	23.9	24.5	24.7	23.8	21.9	19.9	20.0	21.7
2013	19.4	19.6	19.7	20.4	23.0	23.8	24.2	24.6	23.5	20.6	19.7	19.7	21.5
2014	19.0	19.4	19.4	20.3	23.3	23.6	24.2	24.5	23.4	21.1	19.6	19.7	21.5
2015	19.3	19.6	19.7	20.6	23.3	23.9	24.5	24.8	23.8	21.6	20.0	20.0	21.8
2016	19.4	19.7	19.8	21.0	23.6	24.1	24.7	25.1	23.6	21.6	20.0	20.1	21.9
2017	19.4	19.6	19.7	20.7	23.3	24.1	24.8	25.1	23.6	21.6	20.1	20.1	21.8
2018	19.4	19.7	20.1	21.0	23.8	24.9	25.3	25.7	24.2	21.2	20.2	20.3	22.2
Information													
2010	6.3	6.3	6.3	6.3	6.3	6.5	6.6	6.5	6.7	7.0	6.9	6.6	6.5
2011	6.3	6.3	6.4	6.4	6.3	6.4	6.4	6.3	6.2	6.3	6.3	6.3	6.3
2012	6.2	6.2	6.2	6.2	6.3	6.3	6.3	6.2	6.1	6.2	6.1	6.2	6.2
2013	6.0	6.0	6.0	6.1	6.2	6.2	6.2	6.2	6.2	6.2	6.3	6.3	6.2
2014	6.2	6.2	6.2	6.2	6.3	6.2	6.3	6.3	6.2	6.3	6.3	6.3	6.3
2015	6.3	6.3	6.4	6.4	6.3	6.3	6.3	6.3	6.3	6.3	6.3	6.3	6.3
2016	6.2	6.3	6.2	6.4	6.4	6.4	6.4	6.3	6.3	6.1	6.1	6.1	6.3
2017	6.1	6.1	6.1	6.0	6.0	6.0	6.0	5.9	5.9	5.8	5.8	5.8	6.0
2018	5.7	5.7	5.7	5.7	5.7	5.7	5.7	5.6	5.5	5.5	5.5	5.6	5.6

1. Employment by Industry: Alaska, 2010–2018—*Continued*

(Numbers in thousands, not seasonally adjusted)

Industry and year	January	February	March	April	May	June	July	August	September	October	November	December	Annual average
Financial Activities													
2010	11.9	11.8	11.8	12.0	12.2	12.6	12.7	12.7	12.4	12.4	12.2	11.9	12.2
2011	11.9	12.0	12.0	12.0	12.1	12.5	12.7	12.7	12.3	12.1	12.0	11.9	12.2
2012	11.9	11.9	11.8	11.9	12.2	12.5	12.7	12.7	12.2	12.3	12.1	12.1	12.2
2013	11.8	11.9	11.8	12	12.1	12.7	12.9	12.8	12.2	12.2	12	12	12.2
2014	11.9	11.9	11.8	11.9	12.2	12.6	12.7	12.5	12.1	12.0	11.8	11.8	12.1
2015	11.6	11.6	11.6	11.7	12.1	12.8	13.1	12.7	12.3	12.0	12.0	11.7	12.1
2016	11.7	11.6	11.7	11.8	12.0	12.4	12.9	12.8	12.1	11.9	11.9	11.9	12.1
2017	11.5	11.7	11.6	11.8	12.0	12.5	12.6	12.6	11.9	11.8	11.7	11.7	12.0
2018	11.4	11.5	11.5	11.6	11.7	12.4	12.4	12.3	11.7	11.8	11.4	11.3	11.8
Professional and Business Services													
2010	26.4	26.8	26.9	27.0	28.1	29.5	29.6	29.6	29.3	28.3	27.6	27.4	28.0
2011	26.9	27.5	27.5	28.2	29.1	30.3	30.2	29.9	30.0	29.0	28.6	28.6	28.8
2012	28.0	28.6	28.8	29.1	30.3	31.4	31.5	31.5	31.2	30.1	29.4	29.3	29.9
2013	28.6	29.4	29.3	29.8	30.7	31.7	31.8	32.1	31.1	29.9	29.7	29.6	30.3
2014	28.8	28.7	29.3	29.3	30.7	31.2	31.5	31.7	31.1	30.3	29.2	29.5	30.1
2015	29.0	29.3	29.3	29.9	31.0	31.7	31.6	31.5	30.8	29.7	29.1	28.5	30.1
2016	27.6	27.8	27.8	28.8	29.3	30.0	29.8	29.9	29.2	28.0	26.9	27.5	28.6
2017	26.7	27.4	26.9	27.3	28.5	29.4	29.6	29.5	28.7	27.5	27.0	26.6	27.9
2018	26.1	26.7	26.7	26.2	27.4	28.2	28.5	28.7	28.2	27.2	25.7	25.8	27.1
Education and Health Services													
2010	41.7	42.1	42.2	42.8	43.0	43.1	43.3	43.2	43.5	44.0	44.1	44.4	43.1
2011	44.3	44.7	44.8	45.3	45.5	45.5	45.5	45.8	45.8	46.0	46.2	46.6	45.5
2012	46.2	46.9	46.9	47.0	47.3	47.3	46.5	46.6	46.3	47.4	47.6	47.7	47.0
2013	47.3	47.8	47.9	48.2	48.3	48.0	47.9	47.9	47.8	47.9	48.0	48.0	47.9
2014	47.4	47.7	47.8	47.9	47.8	47.6	47.6	47.6	47.4	47.6	47.6	47.6	47.6
2015	47.6	47.9	47.9	47.3	47.3	47.4	47.5	47.2	47.0	47.4	47.5	47.9	47.5
2016	47.8	48.3	48.5	48.8	48.7	48.3	48.8	48.8	48.7	48.8	48.9	49.2	48.6
2017	49.0	49.4	49.7	49.8	50.0	50.1	49.8	49.9	49.6	49.9	50.1	50.2	49.8
2018	50.0	50.4	50.6	50.4	50.4	50.5	50.3	50.3	50.1	50.3	50.9	50.9	50.4
Leisure and Hospitality													
2010	26.4	26.9	27.2	28.6	32.9	36.9	38.4	38.4	35.5	29.2	28.5	28.8	31.5
2011	27.5	28.0	28.6	29.7	33.9	38.3	39.8	39.7	36.5	30.2	29.0	28.9	32.5
2012	27.9	28.4	29.1	30.4	34.7	39.4	40.7	40.5	37.2	32.1	29.7	29.6	33.3
2013	28.4	29.1	29.8	30.8	35.6	39.9	41.2	41.0	37.5	32.4	29.7	29.5	33.7
2014	28.8	29.4	30.3	31.1	36.8	40.3	41.5	41.4	38.1	32.4	30.3	30.3	34.2
2015	29.7	30.2	30.8	31.8	37.7	41.3	42.7	42.3	39.3	33.2	30.6	30.7	35.0
2016	29.9	30.3	30.8	32.1	38.0	42.0	43.2	43.2	39.6	33.2	30.8	31.0	35.3
2017	29.8	30.1	30.9	32.0	38.1	42.4	43.5	43.2	39.9	33.6	30.5	30.7	35.4
2018	29.8	30.5	31.0	32.0	37.9	42.2	43.7	43.8	39.7	33.0	31.5	31.8	35.6
Other Services													
2010	10.9	10.9	11.0	11.3	11.4	11.5	11.6	11.4	11.3	11.2	11.1	11.0	11.2
2011	10.9	11.0	11.1	11.1	11.2	11.4	11.3	11.3	11.3	11.4	11.2	11.2	11.2
2012	11.1	11.1	11.1	11.2	11.5	11.6	11.6	11.5	11.4	11.3	11.3	11.2	11.3
2013	11.1	11.2	11.3	11.4	11.5	11.6	11.6	11.4	11.3	11.2	11.2	11.1	11.3
2014	11.1	11.1	11.0	11.3	11.5	11.5	11.7	11.6	11.5	11.6	11.4	11.1	11.4
2015	10.9	10.9	10.9	11.2	11.4	11.5	11.3	11.0	11.0	11.0	11.0	11.0	11.1
2016	10.8	10.8	10.9	11.1	11.3	11.3	11.3	11.1	11.1	11.0	11.0	10.8	11.0
2017	10.7	10.8	10.8	11.2	11.4	11.6	11.4	11.3	11.3	11.1	11.0	10.9	11.1
2018	10.8	10.8	10.8	11.1	11.3	11.5	11.3	11.2	11.1	11.0	10.7	10.8	11.0
Government													
2010	83.2	85.2	85.7	87.1	85.8	86.8	81.1	82.0	87.4	87.4	86.8	86.6	85.4
2011	84.2	85.9	85.5	86.5	84.9	85.7	80.0	80.1	86.2	86.7	85.9	85.9	84.8
2012	81.9	85.4	85.9	86.0	84.8	84.3	79.1	80.5	85.6	85.6	85.2	85.0	84.1
2013	81.2	84.1	84.3	84.9	84.2	83.4	77.9	78.8	83.4	83.3	83.4	82.9	82.7
2014	81.4	82.8	83.1	84.0	84.0	82.7	77.9	78.6	82.9	82.9	83.2	83.1	82.2
2015	81.5	82.9	83.1	84.0	84.0	82.5	77.7	78.2	82.8	82.6	82.6	82.5	82.0
2016	81.1	82.2	82.4	83.9	83.7	82.5	76.7	77.7	82.3	82.9	82.8	82.1	81.7
2017	80.9	82.2	82.3	82.7	83.7	81.8	75.7	76.8	81.5	81.7	81.5	81.4	81.0
2018	79.9	81.4	81.5	82.1	82.7	81.1	75.3	76.7	80.9	81.5	81.1	80.7	80.4

2. Average Weekly Hours by Selected Industry: Alaska, 2014–2018

(Not seasonally adjusted)

Industry and year	January	February	March	April	May	June	July	August	September	October	November	December	Annual average
Total Private													
2014	33.6	34.5	34.7	34.0	34.1	35.3	35.8	35.3	34.9	34.4	34.3	33.7	34.6
2015	34.1	34.9	35.0	34.0	34.7	35.2	35.8	36.1	34.7	34.2	34.1	33.4	34.7
2016	33.5	34.3	34.2	33.9	34.0	34.5	35.8	35.4	34.5	34.7	34.0	33.6	34.4
2017	34.7	35.1	35.1	34.7	34.6	35.7	36.7	36.3	34.8	34.7	34.2	34.1	35.1
2018	34.0	34.7	34.8	34.4	34.4	35.4	36.6	36.2	35.7	35.0	34.6	34.9	35.1
Goods Producing													
2014	37.9	39.1	40.1	37.1	37.3	37.6	41.8	40.1	39.5	38.9	36.0	37.2	38.7
2015	38.3	39.0	39.7	35.0	37.9	37.8	39.2	39.5	35.6	35.7	34.0	34.5	37.4
2016	35.0	39.1	38.9	35.7	37.3	39.2	43.6	41.3	39.3	37.0	35.3	34.0	38.3
2017	36.6	40.9	40.4	36.2	37.3	38.8	41.2	40.0	35.9	36.0	34.6	34.0	37.9
2018	34.2	37.7	37.3	34.5	35.6	37.6	40.9	40.8	41.0	39.0	37.6	38.4	38.1
Construction													
2014	39.7	39.7	39.2	39.8	37.3	39.1	39.1	40.1	39.3	39.7	35.4	37.1	38.8
2015	36.2	35.5	35.7	38.0	38.4	40.5	40.2	40.4	36.4	38.1	35.5	35.2	37.7
2016	35.3	37.1	36.8	36.9	38.3	40.5	41.7	41.7	39.8	39.3	37.6	35.6	38.6
2017	36.1	36.5	37.7	39.1	40.0	42.7	43.7	44.4	42.7	42.2	39.0	38.4	40.6
2018	37.5	38.1	38.4	38.4	37.1	40.0	40.2	40.7	41.1	39.1	36.7	37.4	38.8
Manufacturing													
2014	31.0	35.8	40.3	37.0	40.2	38.0	47.5	39.1	38.5	35.7	34.7	34.8	38.7
2015	41.0	44.5	45.8	35.0	44.3	37.3	47.1	45.0	38.2	34.0	31.5	31.8	40.8
2016	33.4	40.7	41.1	32.1	33.7	36.6	47.2	40.4	37.8	29.7	26.5	25.6	37.3
2017	34.2	46.7	42.2	29.4	30.8	32.7	37.0	34.0	22.5	21.1	24.0	22.5	32.6
2018	25.0	35.9	33.9	24.0	29.7	30.9	42.0	41.7	39.7	35.8	32.7	32.4	35.0
Trade, Transportation, and Utilities													
2014	33.9	34.1	34.5	33.9	34.3	35.9	35.3	35.2	34.8	34.0	34.4	33.3	34.5
2015	33.0	34.1	34.0	33.7	34.4	34.9	35.3	35.5	35.0	33.3	34.1	33.4	34.3
2016	33.4	33.0	33.0	33.2	34.1	34.6	35.1	35.1	33.7	34.0	33.5	33.9	33.9
2017	34.0	33.5	33.4	34.5	34.1	35.5	35.7	35.1	34.2	33.9	33.8	33.8	34.3
2018	33.9	34.2	34.0	34.4	34.3	35.9	36.5	35.8	34.9	34.3	34.7	34.6	34.8
Professional and Business Services													
2014	34.9	36.0	36.0	35.4	36.3	37.8	37.6	38.2	37.2	36.3	36.2	35.3	36.5
2015	34.8	36.6	36.9	36.9	36.6	37.9	37.8	38.7	37.6	37.6	37.3	35.0	37.0
2016	34.9	36.9	36.8	35.9	35.4	35.0	34.8	35.4	34.8	36.4	34.9	33.7	35.4
2017	35.4	36.2	36.4	36.2	35.1	35.9	36.9	36.7	34.8	35.5	34.4	34.0	35.6
2018	34.2	35.4	35.2	35.2	34.2	36.2	36.6	36.9	36.2	35.1	34.4	35.0	35.5
Leisure and Hospitality													
2014	25.7	27.4	27.6	26.7	26.4	28.7	28.9	28.8	27.7	27.2	27.4	26.5	27.5
2015	26.8	27.3	27.6	27.3	27.4	28.6	29.0	29.7	28.5	26.9	26.6	25.9	27.7
2016	25.4	25.3	25.8	25.8	26.4	27.3	28.1	28.3	25.9	25.6	24.4	24.0	26.2
2017	24.1	24.0	24.6	24.8	26.4	29.0	29.5	29.6	27.6	25.6	25.5	25.5	26.7
2018	24.7	25.1	26.1	25.6	27.6	29.1	30.4	29.3	27.1	25.8	25.4	25.6	27.1

3. Average Hourly Earnings by Selected Industry: Alaska, 2014–2018

(Dollars, not seasonally adjusted)

Industry and year	January	February	March	April	May	June	July	August	September	October	November	December	Annual average
Total Private													
2014	27.10	27.34	26.99	27.19	27.07	26.86	26.66	26.95	27.22	27.76	27.39	27.46	27.15
2015	26.93	27.02	27.41	28.11	27.87	27.75	27.85	28.09	27.90	28.51	28.63	28.60	27.89
2016	27.92	27.73	27.96	28.41	28.48	27.77	27.66	27.89	28.24	28.99	28.81	28.99	28.22
2017	28.13	27.56	27.92	28.47	27.98	27.69	27.57	27.90	28.65	29.43	29.10	29.39	28.28
2018	29.21	29.06	29.06	29.16	28.25	28.12	28.13	28.14	28.77	29.27	29.18	29.41	28.78
Goods Producing													
2014	34.49	34.51	33.39	35.62	36.56	36.07	33.24	34.21	34.48	36.15	35.38	35.66	34.89
2015	30.93	30.60	31.60	36.26	35.57	35.51	34.62	35.39	35.55	36.91	38.16	38.18	34.82
2016	32.70	32.13	32.62	35.98	37.12	33.51	31.61	33.23	34.85	37.81	37.67	38.44	34.44
2017	34.22	31.58	33.10	35.83	36.90	35.05	32.51	33.83	37.28	39.42	38.86	39.87	35.35
2018	37.07	36.23	36.29	36.96	35.73	35.04	33.42	34.03	35.69	37.00	38.37	39.15	35.98
Construction													
2014	36.13	37.06	36.41	37.28	38.17	38.46	38.96	38.44	38.42	38.41	36.25	35.73	37.62
2015	35.94	36.05	37.31	38.72	38.34	39.44	39.05	39.07	38.19	37.49	37.25	37.06	38.00
2016	36.67	37.65	37.51	38.06	38.91	40.09	40.57	40.35	39.51	38.99	38.35	37.93	38.92
2017	37.81	37.30	38.44	38.17	37.86	38.66	38.26	38.89	37.80	37.43	37.10	37.02	37.96
2018	35.97	37.01	37.80	37.93	37.64	38.26	39.01	39.54	38.25	38.04	37.80	37.24	38.00
Manufacturing													
2014	21.34	19.88	18.11	20.34	22.20	19.59	17.19	17.39	18.36	21.09	21.97	23.66	19.41
2015	17.54	16.30	17.24	20.08	20.58	19.21	17.18	19.41	20.32	23.66	25.93	26.96	19.40
2016	20.21	19.17	19.72	23.38	26.47	20.03	17.45	19.12	21.56	24.39	26.64	29.76	20.80
2017	21.15	18.40	19.52	22.61	25.34	21.84	19.83	20.10	24.45	27.80	27.59	30.11	21.73
2018	25.02	22.35	22.70	23.22	25.61	23.58	20.04	21.70	27.16	31.87	36.13	39.13	24.68
Trade, Transportation, and Utilities													
2014	22.15	22.34	22.67	22.52	21.93	21.55	21.76	22.00	22.41	22.85	22.81	22.93	22.31
2015	23.19	22.97	23.27	22.85	22.63	22.26	22.51	22.64	22.60	23.41	23.16	23.42	22.89
2016	23.44	22.90	23.79	23.53	22.98	22.53	22.59	22.56	23.56	23.81	23.74	24.13	23.27
2017	24.06	23.63	23.94	23.99	23.31	23.28	23.52	23.54	24.00	24.36	24.12	24.57	23.84
2018	24.10	23.97	24.50	24.74	24.25	24.10	24.16	24.44	25.37	26.06	25.63	25.75	24.74
Professional and Business Services													
2014	34.64	35.00	34.40	34.64	34.52	33.89	33.80	34.30	34.73	35.47	35.49	33.97	34.56
2015	34.16	33.82	33.95	34.08	34.26	33.57	33.65	34.34	34.34	34.01	34.33	34.26	34.00
2016	33.91	33.28	32.66	33.18	33.48	34.32	34.96	34.46	34.91	35.74	36.26	36.48	34.44
2017	35.25	33.88	34.19	35.07	34.14	33.22	33.58	33.44	35.02	35.31	35.55	35.92	34.50
2018	35.38	35.07	34.81	34.89	33.74	33.50	33.98	33.20	32.98	33.24	33.43	33.69	33.97
Leisure and Hospitality													
2014	16.21	16.96	16.33	16.64	16.52	16.03	16.42	16.48	16.95	16.94	16.98	17.48	16.64
2015	16.96	17.15	17.13	17.19	17.01	16.81	16.79	16.80	16.87	17.58	17.60	18.04	17.11
2016	17.94	17.80	17.56	17.45	17.46	17.29	17.45	17.36	17.31	17.52	17.67	17.79	17.52
2017	17.93	17.61	17.62	17.61	16.77	16.65	16.67	16.76	16.88	17.84	17.65	18.31	17.25
2018	18.25	17.92	18.01	17.96	16.95	16.69	16.65	16.53	16.96	17.33	17.42	17.53	17.24

4. Average Weekly Earnings by Selected Industry: Alaska, 2014–2018

(Dollars, not seasonally adjusted)

Industry and year	January	February	March	April	May	June	July	August	September	October	November	December	Annual average
Total Private													
2014	910.56	943.23	936.55	924.46	923.09	948.16	954.43	951.34	949.98	954.94	939.48	925.40	939.39
2015	918.31	943.00	959.35	955.74	967.09	976.80	997.03	1,014.05	968.13	975.04	976.28	955.24	967.78
2016	935.32	951.14	956.23	963.10	968.32	958.07	990.23	987.31	974.28	1,005.95	979.54	974.06	970.77
2017	976.11	967.36	979.99	987.91	968.11	988.53	1,011.82	1,012.77	997.02	1,021.22	995.22	1,002.20	992.63
2018	993.14	1,008.38	1,011.29	1,003.10	971.80	995.45	1,029.56	1,018.67	1,027.09	1,024.45	1,009.63	1,026.41	1,010.18
Goods Producing													
2014	1,307.17	1,349.34	1,338.94	1,321.50	1,363.69	1,356.23	1,389.43	1,371.82	1,361.96	1,406.24	1,273.68	1,326.55	1,350.24
2015	1,184.62	1,193.40	1,254.52	1,269.10	1,348.10	1,342.28	1,357.10	1,397.91	1,265.58	1,317.69	1,297.44	1,317.21	1,302.27
2016	1,144.50	1,256.28	1,268.92	1,284.49	1,384.58	1,313.59	1,378.20	1,372.40	1,369.61	1,398.97	1,329.75	1,306.96	1,319.05
2017	1,252.45	1,291.62	1,337.24	1,297.05	1,376.37	1,359.94	1,339.41	1,353.20	1,338.35	1,419.12	1,344.56	1,355.58	1,339.77
2018	1,267.79	1,365.87	1,353.62	1,275.12	1,271.99	1,317.50	1,366.88	1,388.42	1,463.29	1,443.00	1,442.71	1,503.36	1,370.84
Construction													
2014	1,434.36	1,471.28	1,427.27	1,483.74	1,423.74	1,503.79	1,523.34	1,541.44	1,509.91	1,524.88	1,283.25	1,325.58	1,459.66
2015	1,301.03	1,279.78	1,331.97	1,471.36	1,472.26	1,597.32	1,569.81	1,578.43	1,390.12	1,428.37	1,322.38	1,304.51	1,432.60
2016	1,294.45	1,396.82	1,380.37	1,404.41	1,490.25	1,623.65	1,691.77	1,682.60	1,572.50	1,532.31	1,441.96	1,350.31	1,502.31
2017	1,364.94	1,361.45	1,449.19	1,492.45	1,514.40	1,650.78	1,671.96	1,726.72	1,614.06	1,579.55	1,446.90	1,421.57	1,541.18
2018	1,348.88	1,410.08	1,451.52	1,456.51	1,396.44	1,530.40	1,568.20	1,609.28	1,572.08	1,487.36	1,387.26	1,392.78	1,474.40
Manufacturing													
2014	661.54	711.70	729.83	752.58	892.44	744.42	816.53	679.95	706.86	752.91	762.36	823.37	751.17
2015	719.14	725.35	789.59	702.80	911.69	716.53	809.18	873.45	776.22	804.44	816.80	857.33	791.52
2016	675.01	780.22	810.49	750.50	892.04	733.10	823.64	772.45	814.97	724.38	705.96	761.86	775.84
2017	723.33	859.28	823.74	664.73	780.47	714.17	733.71	683.40	550.13	586.58	662.16	677.48	708.40
2018	625.50	802.37	769.53	557.28	760.62	728.62	841.68	904.89	1,078.25	1,140.95	1,181.45	1,267.81	863.80
Trade, Transportation, and Utilities													
2014	750.89	761.79	782.12	763.43	752.20	773.65	768.13	774.40	779.87	776.90	784.66	763.57	769.70
2015	765.27	783.28	791.18	770.05	778.47	776.87	794.60	803.72	791.00	779.55	789.76	782.23	785.13
2016	782.90	755.70	785.07	781.20	783.62	779.54	792.91	791.86	793.97	809.54	795.29	818.01	788.85
2017	818.04	791.61	799.60	827.66	794.87	826.44	839.66	826.25	820.80	825.80	815.26	830.47	817.71
2018	816.99	819.77	833.00	851.06	831.78	865.19	881.84	874.95	885.41	893.86	889.36	890.95	860.95
Professional and Business Services													
2014	1,208.94	1,260.00	1,238.40	1,226.26	1,253.08	1,281.04	1,270.88	1,310.26	1,291.96	1,287.56	1,284.74	1,199.14	1,261.44
2015	1,188.77	1,237.81	1,252.76	1,257.55	1,253.92	1,272.30	1,271.97	1,328.96	1,263.36	1,278.78	1,280.51	1,199.10	1,258.00
2016	1,183.46	1,228.03	1,201.89	1,191.16	1,185.19	1,201.20	1,216.61	1,219.88	1,214.87	1,300.94	1,265.47	1,229.38	1,219.18
2017	1,247.85	1,226.46	1,244.52	1,269.53	1,198.31	1,192.60	1,239.10	1,227.25	1,218.70	1,253.51	1,222.92	1,221.28	1,228.20
2018	1,210.00	1,241.48	1,225.31	1,228.13	1,153.91	1,212.70	1,243.67	1,225.08	1,193.88	1,166.72	1,149.99	1,179.15	1,205.94
Leisure and Hospitality													
2014	416.60	464.70	450.71	444.29	436.13	460.06	474.54	474.62	469.52	460.77	465.25	463.22	457.60
2015	454.53	468.20	472.79	469.29	466.07	480.77	486.91	498.96	480.80	472.90	468.16	467.24	473.95
2016	455.68	450.34	453.05	450.21	460.94	472.02	490.35	491.29	448.33	448.51	431.15	426.96	459.02
2017	432.11	422.64	433.45	436.73	442.73	482.85	491.77	496.10	465.89	456.70	450.08	466.91	460.58
2018	450.78	449.79	470.06	459.78	467.82	485.68	506.16	484.33	459.62	447.11	442.47	448.77	467.20

ARIZONA
At a Glance

Population:
2010 census: 6,392,017
2018 estimate: 7,171,646

Percent change in population:
2010–2018: 12.2%

Percent change in total nonfarm employment:
2010–2018: 19.7%

Industry with the largest growth in employment, 2010–2018 (percent):
Construction, 42.4%

Industry with the largest decline or smallest growth in employment, 2010–2018 (percent):
Government, -0.3%

Civilian labor force:
2010: 3,089,705
2018: 3,439,755

Unemployment rate and rank among states (highest to lowest):
2010: 10.4%, 11th
2018: 4.8%, 6th

Over-the-year change in unemployment rates:
2016–2017: -0.5%
2017–2018: -0.1%

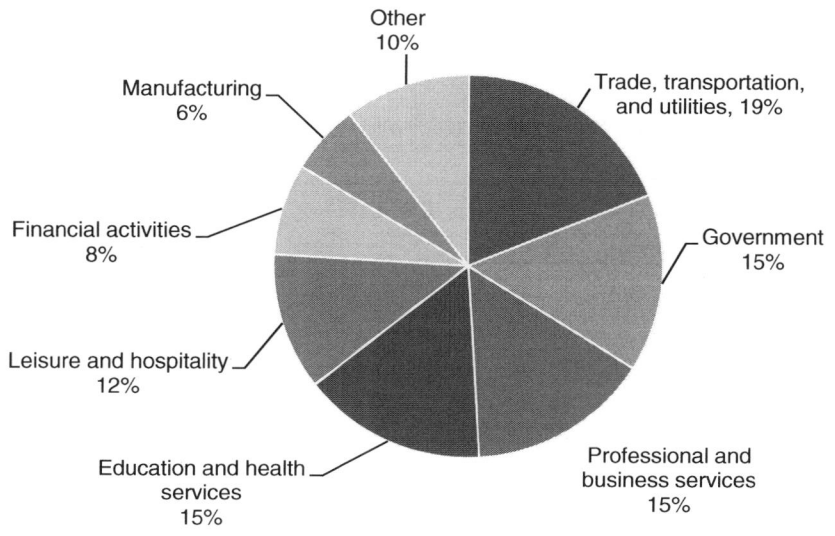

Employment by Industry: Arizona, 2018

Other 10%
Manufacturing 6%
Trade, transportation, and utilities, 19%
Financial activities 8%
Government 15%
Leisure and hospitality 12%
Professional and business services 15%
Education and health services 15%

1. Employment by Industry: Arizona, 2010–2018

(Numbers in thousands, not seasonally adjusted)

Industry and year	January	February	March	April	May	June	July	August	September	October	November	December	Annual average
Total Nonfarm													
2010	2,366.2	2,385.0	2,396.6	2,407.1	2,413.8	2,351.7	2,326.7	2,357.2	2,373.9	2,402.2	2,423.1	2,430.0	2,386.1
2011	2,379.2	2,402.4	2,414.8	2,426.6	2,425.8	2,361.7	2,337.7	2,392.9	2,422.6	2,440.5	2,464.6	2,467.7	2,411.4
2012	2,425.2	2,448.4	2,466.3	2,468.0	2,464.1	2,420.2	2,387.7	2,445.2	2,474.8	2,494.2	2,523.0	2,531.1	2,462.4
2013	2,478.5	2,505.1	2,517.8	2,526.9	2,524.1	2,472.6	2,451.0	2,502.1	2,530.4	2,553.6	2,586.0	2,592.1	2,520.0
2014	2,536.1	2,558.1	2,566.4	2,577.7	2,564.9	2,520.1	2,497.1	2,547.8	2,576.1	2,610.0	2,639.4	2,649.5	2,570.3
2015	2,596.3	2,621.6	2,628.8	2,639.7	2,630.0	2,576.7	2,563.4	2,614.7	2,646.5	2,686.0	2,715.1	2,718.1	2,636.4
2016	2,663.7	2,693.1	2,701.8	2,717.4	2,704.0	2,647.4	2,642.0	2,690.6	2,730.4	2,754.7	2,778.5	2,782.5	2,708.8
2017	2,731.3	2,758.8	2,769.4	2,782.4	2,769.2	2,726.9	2,703.8	2,758.3	2,794.6	2,823.3	2,852.0	2,857.0	2,777.3
2018	2,807.5	2,839.4	2,850.6	2,852.5	2,844.6	2,796.7	2,783.3	2,845.9	2,877.0	2,903.6	2,936.5	2,934.6	2,856.0
Total Private													
2010	1,947.9	1,955.5	1,968.5	1,975.7	1,973.4	1,964.3	1,950.6	1,958.4	1,954.6	1,980.3	1,998.5	2,010.0	1,969.8
2011	1,968.8	1,980.3	1,993.8	2,003.9	2,004.8	1,993.0	1,984.1	1,998.2	2,005.8	2,020.3	2,042.7	2,052.6	2,004.0
2012	2,016.8	2,027.8	2,045.0	2,045.8	2,048.7	2,044.0	2,029.6	2,048.4	2,054.5	2,072.3	2,099.1	2,109.7	2,053.5
2013	2,066.3	2,082.5	2,096.1	2,103.7	2,105.7	2,099.0	2,090.6	2,108.8	2,111.4	2,131.1	2,163.1	2,172.4	2,110.9
2014	2,122.7	2,135.8	2,145.6	2,155.4	2,154.3	2,144.5	2,133.4	2,152.9	2,154.9	2,183.5	2,212.0	2,226.0	2,160.1
2015	2,184.2	2,197.4	2,205.4	2,216.2	2,215.3	2,206.2	2,205.2	2,222.5	2,227.4	2,260.2	2,286.6	2,295.6	2,226.9
2016	2,253.0	2,269.4	2,277.3	2,292.9	2,289.2	2,273.6	2,278.2	2,295.4	2,306.4	2,328.0	2,349.6	2,357.5	2,297.5
2017	2,318.3	2,332.9	2,343.3	2,355.7	2,353.1	2,348.5	2,337.9	2,357.4	2,368.6	2,395.1	2,422.6	2,432.5	2,363.8
2018	2,393.2	2,413.1	2,424.8	2,426.6	2,425.3	2,415.9	2,415.5	2,438.0	2,448.0	2,474.8	2,506.0	2,508.4	2,440.8
Goods Producing													
2010	267.6	267.7	268.5	270.9	271.1	272.6	272.8	272.2	270.4	272.4	271.8	271.2	270.8
2011	266.2	266.1	268.0	269.6	271.6	274.4	275.9	276.4	276.4	276.5	276.0	276.3	272.8
2012	273.5	274.7	278.3	279.3	281.5	285.6	286.8	288.7	288.5	289.0	288.9	288.5	283.6
2013	283.7	285.6	288.0	288.8	291.4	295.3	296.1	296.4	294.6	295.6	295.2	294.5	292.1
2014	292.2	294.2	294.2	295.1	295.4	296.3	295.6	295.7	293.5	295.4	295.0	295.4	294.8
2015	291.2	293.2	293.9	296.3	297.6	300.1	301.5	301.8	300.3	302.8	302.7	303.8	298.8
2016	299.9	303.1	303.9	304.9	305.5	308.8	310.1	310.3	309.3	309.0	309.0	311.1	307.1
2017	309.0	312.0	313.8	315.8	318.5	323.6	324.9	325.9	326.4	329.2	330.7	332.5	321.9
2018	329.1	333.1	335.9	336.0	337.0	341.9	343.9	345.0	345.6	349.1	353.5	354.1	342.0
Service-Providing													
2010	2,098.6	2,117.3	2,128.1	2,136.2	2,142.7	2,079.1	2,053.9	2,085.0	2,103.5	2,129.8	2,151.3	2,158.8	2,115.4
2011	2,113.0	2,136.3	2,146.8	2,157.0	2,154.2	2,087.3	2,061.8	2,116.5	2,146.2	2,164.0	2,188.6	2,191.4	2,138.6
2012	2,151.7	2,173.7	2,188.0	2,188.7	2,182.6	2,134.6	2,100.9	2,156.5	2,186.3	2,205.2	2,234.1	2,242.6	2,178.7
2013	2,194.8	2,219.5	2,229.8	2,238.1	2,232.7	2,177.3	2,154.9	2,205.7	2,235.8	2,258.0	2,290.8	2,297.6	2,227.9
2014	2,243.9	2,263.9	2,272.2	2,282.6	2,269.5	2,223.8	2,201.5	2,252.1	2,282.6	2,314.6	2,344.4	2,354.1	2,275.4
2015	2,305.1	2,328.4	2,334.9	2,343.4	2,332.4	2,276.6	2,261.9	2,312.9	2,346.2	2,383.2	2,412.4	2,414.3	2,337.6
2016	2,363.8	2,390.0	2,397.9	2,412.5	2,398.5	2,338.6	2,331.9	2,380.3	2,421.1	2,445.7	2,469.5	2,471.4	2,401.8
2017	2,422.3	2,446.8	2,455.6	2,466.6	2,450.7	2,403.3	2,378.9	2,432.4	2,468.2	2,494.1	2,521.3	2,524.5	2,455.4
2018	2,478.4	2,506.3	2,514.7	2,516.5	2,507.6	2,454.8	2,439.4	2,500.9	2,531.4	2,554.5	2,583.0	2,580.5	2,514.0
Mining and Logging													
2010	10.8	10.9	10.8	10.9	11.0	11.0	10.8	10.8	10.7	11.0	11.1	11.2	10.9
2011	11.3	11.4	11.5	11.2	11.4	11.6	11.2	11.3	11.4	12.1	12.1	12.2	11.6
2012	12.2	12.3	12.4	12.5	12.6	12.7	12.9	12.9	12.9	12.8	12.9	13.0	12.7
2013	13.0	13.1	13.1	13.3	13.3	13.6	13.6	13.5	13.2	13.2	13.0	13.0	13.2
2014	13.0	13.0	13.0	13.1	13.0	13.3	13.3	13.2	13.1	13.2	13.2	13.2	13.1
2015	12.6	12.7	12.6	12.5	12.6	12.9	12.9	12.7	12.5	12.3	12.2	12.1	12.6
2016	11.8	12.0	11.5	11.5	11.4	11.6	11.6	11.5	11.4	11.4	11.4	11.5	11.6
2017	11.3	11.4	11.4	11.6	11.6	11.9	12.1	12.1	12.0	12.2	12.2	12.3	11.8
2018	12.3	12.5	12.7	13.0	13.1	13.3	13.4	13.5	13.4	13.4	13.5	13.5	13.1
Construction													
2010	109.0	109.0	109.9	111.8	111.6	113.0	113.3	113.0	111.8	113.1	112.0	110.7	111.5
2011	106.6	106.4	107.9	109.4	110.1	112.4	113.7	113.9	113.9	113.1	112.1	111.2	110.9
2012	108.8	109.3	112.0	112.6	114.1	117.0	118.1	119.8	120.1	120.7	120.5	119.5	116.0
2013	116.2	117.6	120.0	120.9	123.1	126.1	126.5	127.4	126.4	127.2	126.9	125.9	123.7
2014	123.7	124.8	124.8	125.9	125.8	125.8	125.4	125.4	124.1	125.9	125.2	124.4	125.1
2015	122.5	123.8	124.7	126.8	127.6	128.5	129.3	129.6	129.0	131.0	130.8	130.9	127.9
2016	128.6	130.9	132.6	133.7	134.2	136.4	138.2	138.5	137.9	138.2	137.5	137.7	135.4
2017	136.8	138.5	140.8	142.5	144.4	147.3	148.0	148.7	149.1	151.4	151.8	152.3	146.0
2018	150.3	152.6	154.5	154.9	156.0	158.5	159.7	160.5	161.0	163.8	166.6	166.8	158.8

1. Employment by Industry: Arizona, 2010–2018—*Continued*

(Numbers in thousands, not seasonally adjusted)

Industry and year	January	February	March	April	May	June	July	August	September	October	November	December	Annual average
Manufacturing													
2010	147.8	147.8	147.8	148.2	148.5	148.6	148.7	148.4	147.9	148.3	148.7	149.3	148.3
2011	148.3	148.3	148.6	149.0	150.1	150.4	151.0	151.2	151.1	151.3	151.8	152.9	150.3
2012	152.5	153.1	153.9	154.2	154.8	155.9	155.8	156.0	155.5	155.5	155.5	156.0	154.9
2013	154.5	154.9	154.9	154.6	155.0	155.6	156.0	155.5	155.0	155.2	155.3	155.6	155.2
2014	155.5	156.4	156.4	156.1	156.6	157.2	156.9	157.1	156.3	156.3	156.6	157.8	156.6
2015	156.1	156.7	156.6	157.0	157.4	158.7	159.3	159.5	158.8	159.5	159.7	160.8	158.3
2016	159.5	160.2	159.8	159.7	159.9	160.8	160.3	160.3	160.0	159.4	160.1	161.9	160.2
2017	160.9	162.1	161.6	161.7	162.5	164.4	164.8	165.1	165.3	165.6	166.7	167.9	164.1
2018	166.5	168.0	168.7	168.1	167.9	170.1	170.8	171.0	171.2	171.9	173.4	173.8	170.1
Trade, Transportation, and Utilities													
2010	466.4	465.1	465.6	466.1	466.4	464.3	461.7	461.6	458.6	464.2	475.0	481.1	466.3
2011	466.4	466.0	467.2	469.2	469.2	468.3	466.8	468.0	466.9	473.3	486.4	489.9	471.5
2012	474.3	471.2	472.8	471.7	472.2	470.8	468.9	469.1	469.8	474.9	489.9	494.2	475.0
2013	473.7	472.1	472.1	473.5	474.5	474.6	474.8	476.9	477.8	483.1	498.1	505.3	479.7
2014	487.2	485.7	486.2	486.6	486.5	486.6	485.6	487.9	487.9	494.4	508.8	516.1	491.6
2015	497.7	496.5	497.4	498.2	498.9	499.6	499.9	502.8	504.5	512.0	526.0	529.1	505.2
2016	509.4	508.7	509.5	511.2	511.2	509.0	510.6	511.9	511.6	520.6	534.9	539.2	515.7
2017	520.6	518.1	517.1	518.0	517.9	518.2	518.3	519.9	520.0	527.1	544.5	546.4	523.8
2018	530.7	527.2	527.6	527.4	529.1	529.0	530.1	531.7	533.8	537.6	554.6	555.1	534.5
Wholesale Trade													
2010	94.6	94.9	95.0	95.0	94.9	94.5	94.0	93.4	92.6	92.9	93.3	93.6	94.1
2011	92.8	93.5	93.5	93.8	93.8	93.7	93.1	92.7	92.5	92.9	93.3	93.4	93.3
2012	92.4	92.9	93.4	93.2	93.2	93.4	93.1	92.9	93.0	93.3	93.7	94.0	93.2
2013	92.6	93.4	93.3	93.5	93.0	93.4	92.8	92.8	92.6	93.5	93.9	94.4	93.3
2014	92.9	93.2	93.5	93.1	93.3	92.9	92.8	92.7	92.6	92.6	92.9	93.6	93.0
2015	92.2	92.4	92.4	92.7	92.9	92.8	92.4	92.5	92.6	93.1	93.6	93.8	92.8
2016	93.4	93.7	93.3	93.5	93.6	93.3	93.5	93.1	93.0	94.3	94.5	94.9	93.7
2017	94.0	94.4	94.4	94.4	94.5	94.5	94.1	94.1	94.2	95.0	95.5	95.8	94.6
2018	95.3	95.7	96.0	96.2	96.6	96.6	97.2	97.4	97.7	98.2	99.4	100.1	97.2
Retail Trade													
2010	291.5	289.9	290.4	290.7	290.8	288.9	287.1	287.0	284.6	288.7	298.2	301.4	290.8
2011	290.1	288.7	289.7	291.1	290.8	289.4	289.1	290.3	289.0	294.1	306.1	307.7	293.0
2012	295.6	291.9	292.6	292.1	292.7	291.0	289.3	289.5	290.2	294.6	308.7	310.8	294.9
2013	293.4	291.0	291.8	293.6	294.2	294.0	295.0	296.8	297.4	300.8	314.2	318.9	298.4
2014	304.2	302.5	302.4	304.0	303.2	303.4	303.1	304.7	304.6	309.7	322.4	326.8	307.6
2015	311.4	309.2	309.7	311.3	311.5	312.2	311.7	313.3	314.2	319.9	331.0	332.3	315.6
2016	316.8	315.8	315.9	316.8	316.7	315.6	316.2	317.5	317.3	323.7	335.5	336.9	320.4
2017	322.8	320.4	320.3	321.0	320.8	320.8	321.6	322.3	321.6	325.7	339.3	338.4	324.6
2018	326.2	323.0	323.1	322.2	323.2	322.7	322.4	323.4	324.3	326.4	340.2	338.5	326.3
Transportation and Utilities													
2010	80.3	80.3	80.2	80.4	80.7	80.9	80.6	81.2	81.4	82.6	83.5	86.1	81.5
2011	83.5	83.8	84.0	84.3	84.6	85.2	84.6	85.0	85.4	86.3	87.0	88.8	85.2
2012	86.3	86.4	86.8	86.4	86.3	86.4	86.5	86.7	86.6	87.0	87.5	89.4	86.9
2013	87.7	87.7	87.0	86.4	87.3	87.2	87.0	87.3	87.8	88.8	90.0	92.0	88.0
2014	90.1	90.0	90.3	89.5	90.0	90.3	89.7	90.5	90.7	92.1	93.5	95.7	91.0
2015	94.1	94.9	95.3	94.2	94.5	94.6	95.8	97.0	97.7	99.0	101.4	103.0	96.8
2016	99.2	99.2	100.3	100.9	100.9	100.1	100.9	101.3	101.3	102.6	104.9	107.4	101.6
2017	103.8	103.3	102.4	102.6	102.6	102.9	102.6	103.5	104.2	106.4	109.7	112.2	104.7
2018	109.2	108.5	108.5	109.0	109.3	109.7	110.5	110.9	111.8	113.0	115.0	116.5	111.0
Information													
2010	37.7	37.9	38.1	38.1	38.0	38.3	37.4	37.3	37.0	36.8	37.4	38.0	37.7
2011	37.7	37.6	37.7	38.0	38.1	38.2	38.6	38.6	38.3	38.7	39.6	39.7	38.4
2012	39.5	40.0	40.2	40.5	41.1	41.0	41.1	41.4	40.8	40.9	42.1	42.2	40.9
2013	42.0	42.6	42.8	42.9	43.9	43.2	43.4	43.6	42.9	43.1	44.0	43.9	43.2
2014	43.7	43.7	44.0	44.4	44.9	45.2	45.6	45.5	44.5	44.9	45.3	45.6	44.8
2015	45.3	46.7	45.6	46.1	46.5	46.1	46.1	45.5	44.8	45.0	45.9	45.8	45.8
2016	46.1	46.9	46.3	46.9	47.3	46.9	46.6	46.0	45.5	46.0	46.1	46.2	46.4
2017	46.0	46.7	46.8	47.4	47.5	47.4	47.0	46.9	46.1	46.6	47.0	47.3	46.9
2018	47.1	48.1	47.2	47.4	47.6	47.3	47.2	47.0	46.4	47.1	47.7	48.2	47.4

1. Employment by Industry: Arizona, 2010–2018—*Continued*

(Numbers in thousands, not seasonally adjusted)

Industry and year	January	February	March	April	May	June	July	August	September	October	November	December	Annual average
Financial Activities													
2010	166.6	167.2	167.6	166.3	166.4	166.5	167.0	167.3	166.6	168.9	169.6	170.9	167.6
2011	168.3	169.2	169.9	170.5	170.4	170.9	171.5	172.1	172.0	172.7	173.4	175.4	171.4
2012	173.5	175.3	175.5	175.2	175.5	175.5	175.6	176.4	176.7	178.9	180.1	181.4	176.6
2013	179.5	182.2	182.2	183.3	184.0	184.6	184.8	185.3	185.4	188.1	189.4	190.0	184.9
2014	187.2	188.1	187.7	189.9	190.0	189.7	189.5	189.8	189.4	191.3	192.5	192.7	189.8
2015	190.7	191.9	192.4	192.4	193.1	193.4	194.5	195.4	195.6	198.0	199.3	200.8	194.8
2016	199.2	200.8	201.2	202.8	202.8	203.1	204.7	205.7	206.7	208.6	210.2	211.2	204.8
2017	210.1	210.8	211.6	212.0	212.2	213.6	214.6	215.5	216.2	218.0	219.0	219.6	214.4
2018	218.1	219.6	219.5	219.8	219.9	220.3	221.6	221.8	221.9	223.0	221.7	222.5	220.8
Professional and Business Services													
2010	333.2	334.6	338.4	340.8	338.6	337.5	335.5	336.2	335.1	342.4	343.8	348.7	338.7
2011	339.3	342.6	344.6	346.1	342.4	341.4	341.4	343.1	344.9	349.2	352.1	356.7	345.3
2012	346.8	348.8	351.8	352.2	351.5	353.8	352.7	356.3	356.4	361.9	368.0	371.4	356.0
2013	365.3	365.5	368.5	370.5	370.1	371.5	369.8	372.0	371.5	377.5	386.9	388.6	373.1
2014	372.3	372.2	374.2	377.2	377.3	377.7	376.6	380.6	381.5	389.7	397.0	400.7	381.4
2015	389.2	388.9	388.4	391.8	390.4	390.2	391.8	394.6	396.4	405.3	412.0	414.9	396.2
2016	403.0	403.7	404.2	409.3	406.3	403.3	409.2	411.5	414.9	418.2	420.4	421.2	410.4
2017	413.4	413.4	413.6	415.5	413.9	413.5	411.2	413.9	417.2	422.9	427.2	430.6	417.2
2018	421.4	424.7	425.7	425.5	424.6	425.4	427.5	432.3	433.2	440.6	446.4	445.5	431.1
Education and Health Services													
2010	341.3	342.7	344.2	344.1	345.1	341.8	339.9	346.6	348.3	354.0	355.5	355.4	346.6
2011	350.9	353.3	354.2	356.0	359.2	351.6	349.3	357.3	361.3	363.5	365.9	367.1	357.5
2012	364.1	367.2	368.0	368.2	368.4	363.6	359.1	367.4	370.5	372.7	374.9	376.4	368.4
2013	369.8	373.2	375.7	376.2	375.0	368.8	366.4	375.0	377.5	378.2	381.3	381.8	374.9
2014	377.0	379.7	380.1	381.6	381.8	376.7	375.1	383.7	386.2	391.2	393.9	396.1	383.6
2015	390.8	394.7	395.6	397.8	397.8	392.3	392.5	400.6	402.3	408.3	410.3	411.2	399.5
2016	407.7	410.5	411.1	413.7	412.7	406.5	406.3	415.2	420.0	422.8	425.7	427.7	415.0
2017	422.4	426.9	427.8	429.6	428.7	423.5	420.4	429.8	434.1	438.1	440.5	442.7	430.4
2018	437.7	442.7	443.9	444.8	443.1	434.1	433.9	445.4	449.6	454.7	458.9	459.4	445.7
Leisure and Hospitality													
2010	247.3	251.7	257.1	261.2	259.1	254.2	248.3	249.8	251.4	253.8	257.1	256.2	253.9
2011	252.1	256.5	263.0	265.3	264.6	259.0	252.7	255.5	259.2	259.8	262.7	261.5	259.3
2012	259.9	265.0	272.2	272.6	271.8	266.5	259.4	263.5	266.0	267.8	268.4	268.8	266.8
2013	266.7	273.6	279.4	280.9	279.2	273.4	268.6	273.3	275.3	278.3	280.7	280.8	275.9
2014	277.0	285.0	291.4	292.6	290.5	284.4	278.3	282.9	284.9	288.6	291.2	291.1	286.5
2015	292.1	297.2	303.6	306.0	303.0	296.7	292.0	295.4	296.9	301.6	302.7	302.6	299.2
2016	300.3	307.3	312.4	315.5	313.9	307.0	302.7	307.2	310.2	314.0	314.2	312.6	309.8
2017	309.5	316.8	324.0	327.7	324.2	318.5	312.4	316.7	319.6	323.2	323.0	322.8	319.9
2018	319.1	326.7	333.5	332.9	330.8	324.5	318.5	322.2	324.3	328.5	328.7	329.9	326.6
Other Services													
2010	87.8	88.6	89.0	88.2	88.7	89.1	88.0	87.4	87.2	87.8	88.3	88.5	88.2
2011	87.9	89.0	89.2	89.2	89.3	89.2	87.9	87.2	86.8	86.6	86.6	86.0	87.9
2012	85.2	85.6	86.2	86.1	86.7	87.2	86.0	85.6	85.8	86.2	86.8	86.8	86.2
2013	85.6	87.7	87.4	87.6	87.6	87.6	86.7	86.3	86.4	87.2	87.5	87.5	87.1
2014	86.1	87.2	87.8	88.0	87.9	87.9	87.1	86.8	87.0	88.0	88.3	88.3	87.5
2015	87.2	88.3	88.5	87.6	88.0	87.8	86.9	86.4	86.6	87.2	87.7	87.4	87.5
2016	87.4	88.4	88.7	88.6	89.5	89.0	88.0	87.6	88.2	88.8	89.1	88.3	88.5
2017	87.3	88.2	88.6	89.7	90.2	90.2	89.1	88.8	89.0	90.0	90.7	90.6	89.4
2018	90.0	91.0	91.5	92.8	93.2	93.4	92.8	92.6	93.2	94.2	94.5	93.7	92.7
Government													
2010	418.3	429.5	428.1	431.4	440.4	387.4	376.1	398.8	419.3	421.9	424.6	420.0	416.3
2011	410.4	422.1	421.0	422.7	421.0	368.7	353.6	394.7	416.8	420.2	421.9	415.1	407.4
2012	408.4	420.6	421.3	422.2	415.4	376.2	358.1	396.8	420.3	421.9	423.9	421.4	408.9
2013	412.2	422.6	421.7	423.2	418.4	373.6	360.4	393.3	419.0	422.5	422.9	419.7	409.1
2014	413.4	422.3	420.8	422.3	410.6	375.6	363.7	394.9	421.2	426.5	427.4	423.5	410.2
2015	412.1	424.2	423.4	423.5	414.7	370.5	358.2	392.2	419.1	425.8	428.5	422.5	409.6
2016	410.7	423.7	424.5	424.5	414.8	373.8	363.8	395.2	424.0	426.7	428.9	425.0	411.3
2017	413.0	425.9	426.1	426.7	416.1	378.4	365.9	400.9	426.0	428.2	429.4	424.5	413.4
2018	414.3	426.3	425.8	425.9	419.3	380.8	367.8	407.9	429.0	428.8	430.5	426.2	415.2

2. Average Weekly Hours by Selected Industry: Arizona, 2014–2018

(Not seasonally adjusted)

Industry and year	January	February	March	April	May	June	July	August	September	October	November	December	Annual average
Total Private													
2014	34.5	35.2	35.2	34.4	34.3	35.0	34.2	34.3	33.9	34.1	34.8	34.6	34.5
2015	34.4	35.1	34.9	34.7	34.6	34.8	34.6	35.1	34.4	34.4	34.6	34.3	34.7
2016	34.1	34.2	34.3	34.3	34.8	34.4	34.3	34.1	34.1	34.7	34.2	34.4	34.3
2017	34.7	34.2	34.4	35.0	34.5	34.8	35.3	34.7	34.7	35.2	34.9	34.8	34.8
2018	34.8	34.7	34.9	35.5	34.8	35.0	35.3	34.8	35.1	34.6	34.6	35.1	34.9
Goods Producing													
2014	39.3	39.1	39.5	39.1	39.0	39.0	38.9	38.4	37.8	37.8	38.4	38.3	38.7
2015	37.8	38.1	38.2	38.6	38.7	39.2	38.6	38.5	37.9	38.2	38.2	38.3	38.4
2016	37.8	37.8	38.3	38.3	39.0	38.8	38.4	38.6	38.3	38.5	37.6	38.3	38.3
2017	37.8	37.5	37.8	38.2	38.1	38.9	38.4	38.7	39.2	39.2	39.3	39.5	38.6
2018	38.9	38.1	38.6	39.5	38.8	39.2	39.3	39.5	39.7	39.8	39.7	40.3	39.3
Construction													
2014	38.6	38.2	38.1	37.7	37.5	37.8	37.5	36.6	35.6	36.1	37.0	36.4	37.3
2015	35.9	36.6	37.0	37.7	38.0	38.2	37.8	37.2	35.9	37.1	36.9	36.8	37.1
2016	36.0	36.4	36.9	37.5	38.1	38.3	37.7	37.6	37.3	37.5	36.2	36.8	37.2
2017	36.0	35.9	36.6	37.3	36.4	38.0	37.4	37.7	38.6	38.6	38.6	38.6	37.5
2018	37.7	36.8	37.4	38.4	37.4	37.6	37.9	38.4	38.6	38.7	38.7	38.8	38.0
Manufacturing													
2014	39.8	39.7	40.5	40.2	40.2	40.0	40.0	40.4	40.2	39.6	39.8	40.2	40.1
2015	39.7	39.3	39.2	39.5	39.4	40.4	39.5	39.7	39.9	39.4	39.4	39.6	39.6
2016	39.7	39.2	39.8	39.3	40.2	39.6	39.6	40.3	40.0	40.1	39.2	40.0	39.8
2017	39.9	39.3	39.2	39.2	39.9	39.8	39.5	39.8	39.8	39.8	40.1	40.6	39.7
2018	40.2	39.5	39.7	40.6	40.4	41.2	41.0	40.8	41.1	41.2	41.1	42.1	40.8
Trade, Transportation, and Utilities													
2014	34.2	35.2	35.2	34.8	34.6	35.0	34.4	34.5	34.6	34.7	35.2	35.1	34.8
2015	34.9	35.4	35.3	35.4	35.3	35.3	35.4	35.5	35.3	35.0	34.7	34.0	35.1
2016	33.8	34.1	34.1	34.5	34.6	34.4	34.5	34.1	34.2	34.8	34.5	34.7	34.4
2017	34.3	33.9	34.4	34.9	34.5	34.8	35.6	34.9	34.9	35.3	34.5	34.6	34.7
2018	34.6	34.2	34.2	34.9	34.6	34.7	35.0	34.4	34.7	34.3	34.1	34.8	34.5
Financial Activities													
2014	38.1	38.7	38.3	38.1	37.8	38.6	38.4	38.8	38.4	38.4	38.8	38.5	38.4
2015	38.7	39.1	39.0	38.9	38.6	38.8	38.8	40.0	39.2	38.9	39.4	39.2	39.1
2016	39.0	38.6	38.7	38.6	39.3	39.1	39.0	39.6	39.3	40.1	39.5	39.2	39.2
2017	40.0	39.0	39.3	39.5	39.3	39.7	40.3	39.6	39.4	39.8	39.4	39.1	39.5
2018	39.6	39.5	39.2	39.9	39.2	39.3	39.9	39.0	39.7	38.9	38.7	39.1	39.3
Professional and Business Services													
2014	35.9	36.8	36.6	35.7	35.5	36.1	35.4	35.5	35.2	35.7	36.3	36.3	35.9
2015	35.7	36.4	36.4	35.9	35.8	36.1	35.9	37.2	36.0	35.9	36.4	36.5	36.2
2016	36.4	36.5	36.8	36.9	37.5	36.9	36.7	36.8	36.6	37.3	36.4	36.5	36.8
2017	36.9	36.6	36.5	37.6	36.6	36.5	37.5	36.6	36.5	37.5	37.0	36.7	36.9
2018	36.4	36.8	37.1	37.8	36.9	37.0	37.9	37.1	36.9	36.1	36.3	36.6	36.9
Education and Health Services													
2014	33.4	34.0	33.9	33.3	33.3	34.2	33.7	33.6	33.5	33.6	34.4	33.7	33.7
2015	33.8	34.4	34.1	33.9	33.8	33.6	33.7	33.9	33.7	33.5	33.8	33.3	33.8
2016	33.4	33.5	33.3	33.0	33.4	32.8	33.0	33.2	33.2	33.5	33.6	33.4	33.3
2017	34.4	33.7	33.5	34.1	33.5	34.0	34.5	34.0	33.8	34.2	34.0	33.8	34.0
2018	33.8	34.0	33.7	34.2	33.7	33.7	34.2	33.7	34.3	33.4	33.3	33.7	33.8
Leisure and Hospitality													
2014	26.3	27.1	27.8	26.3	26.2	26.7	25.4	26.0	25.9	26.3	27.7	26.8	26.5
2015	27.1	28.2	28.2	27.2	27.2	26.9	26.4	26.6	26.0	26.2	26.5	26.2	26.9
2016	26.2	26.5	26.7	26.4	26.7	26.1	26.0	25.4	25.7	26.3	25.9	25.8	26.1
2017	26.0	25.9	26.4	26.8	26.2	25.8	26.4	25.1	25.5	26.0	26.2	26.2	26.0
2018	26.2	26.8	27.3	27.2	26.5	26.3	25.8	25.5	26.1	25.5	25.7	26.0	26.2
Other Services													
2014	31.8	33.4	33.1	32.3	31.2	32.6	31.3	31.7	31.0	31.2	30.7	30.4	31.7
2015	30.9	32.7	31.8	32.5	31.6	32.8	32.1	33.4	31.5	32.2	32.8	32.6	32.2
2016	32.8	32.8	33.2	33.3	33.2	33.1	32.7	33.3	32.7	34.2	33.7	33.7	33.2
2017	34.0	33.9	34.3	34.3	33.6	34.5	34.3	33.6	34.2	35.1	35.0	35.8	34.4
2018	35.1	35.1	35.2	35.7	34.9	35.7	33.9	34.6	35.6	34.8	35.9	34.8	35.1

3. Average Hourly Earnings by Selected Industry: Arizona, 2014–2018

(Not seasonally adjusted)

Industry and year	January	February	March	April	May	June	July	August	September	October	November	December	Annual average
Total Private													
2014	23.25	23.24	23.10	22.98	22.87	22.91	22.86	22.76	22.81	22.74	22.80	22.49	22.90
2015	22.91	23.01	23.00	23.05	22.96	22.95	23.02	23.36	23.25	23.31	23.48	23.26	23.13
2016	23.55	23.70	23.72	23.92	24.17	23.77	23.74	24.24	24.21	24.44	24.32	24.06	23.99
2017	24.71	25.03	24.69	25.26	25.00	24.74	25.44	25.62	25.56	25.84	25.58	25.56	25.26
2018	25.54	25.68	25.45	25.57	25.59	25.46	25.75	25.69	25.75	25.85	25.48	25.76	25.63
Goods Producing													
2014	24.52	24.71	24.67	24.73	24.51	24.59	24.43	24.49	24.35	24.09	24.36	24.23	24.48
2015	24.12	23.94	23.92	24.15	23.61	23.42	23.72	23.73	23.73	23.81	24.28	24.15	23.88
2016	24.25	24.13	24.49	24.43	24.44	24.63	24.74	24.88	24.90	24.78	24.72	24.80	24.60
2017	25.15	25.34	25.04	24.94	24.87	24.89	25.15	24.65	25.15	25.10	24.95	24.92	25.01
2018	25.02	25.06	25.60	25.67	25.89	25.80	26.21	26.24	26.18	26.55	26.23	26.94	25.97
Construction													
2014	24.09	24.23	24.22	24.46	24.33	24.04	24.05	24.18	23.91	23.58	24.04	23.94	24.09
2015	23.67	23.14	23.14	23.49	22.64	22.69	22.94	22.89	23.17	23.01	23.45	23.86	23.17
2016	24.39	24.05	24.51	24.44	24.60	24.73	25.10	25.65	25.55	25.26	25.47	25.72	24.97
2017	25.82	26.27	25.82	25.46	25.27	25.60	25.82	25.48	26.29	25.90	25.48	25.69	25.74
2018	25.76	25.81	26.04	26.09	26.39	25.93	26.38	26.03	26.13	26.34	26.15	26.44	26.13
Manufacturing													
2014	24.85	25.10	25.01	24.85	24.57	24.77	24.45	24.44	24.43	24.43	24.49	24.34	24.64
2015	24.38	24.62	24.60	24.67	24.59	24.13	24.50	24.57	24.28	24.57	25.06	24.38	24.53
2016	24.01	24.12	24.34	24.32	24.17	24.42	24.22	23.87	24.02	24.11	23.73	23.65	24.08
2017	24.30	24.26	24.03	24.24	24.38	24.06	24.38	23.68	23.76	24.12	24.28	24.04	24.13
2018	24.16	24.20	24.94	24.99	25.12	25.46	25.87	26.35	26.05	26.00	26.13	26.99	25.54
Trade, Transportation, and Utilities													
2014	20.61	20.79	20.87	20.49	20.58	20.66	20.66	20.53	20.69	20.68	20.47	20.25	20.60
2015	20.79	20.90	20.41	20.63	20.82	20.54	20.51	20.81	20.69	20.85	21.30	21.57	20.82
2016	22.22	22.33	22.56	22.89	23.17	22.82	22.04	22.77	22.86	23.43	23.09	22.34	22.71
2017	23.54	23.85	23.77	24.78	24.07	23.72	24.81	24.43	24.49	25.20	24.57	24.53	24.32
2018	25.33	25.86	24.55	25.09	24.55	24.60	24.77	24.58	24.73	24.98	24.30	24.08	24.78
Financial Activities													
2014	26.92	26.73	26.92	26.51	26.56	26.33	26.14	25.95	26.12	25.95	26.08	25.91	26.34
2015	25.81	26.17	26.56	26.40	26.37	26.71	26.74	27.35	26.99	27.22	27.28	27.09	26.73
2016	26.76	27.36	27.13	27.01	28.10	27.03	27.35	28.57	28.17	28.84	29.10	27.96	27.80
2017	28.55	28.78	28.25	29.07	28.68	28.37	29.01	29.77	28.85	29.74	29.76	29.49	29.03
2018	28.67	29.73	29.32	29.35	30.34	29.60	30.03	30.90	30.08	30.22	30.52	30.53	29.94
Professional and Business Services													
2014	25.10	25.35	25.19	25.16	24.99	25.28	24.94	25.06	25.18	25.29	25.52	24.04	25.09
2015	25.89	26.30	26.66	26.53	26.30	26.40	26.15	26.67	26.53	26.53	26.23	25.05	26.27
2016	25.07	25.16	25.43	25.99	26.48	25.67	26.01	26.15	26.32	26.51	26.00	25.84	25.89
2017	26.83	26.88	26.87	27.45	27.12	27.08	28.21	28.10	28.12	28.26	27.88	27.90	27.56
2018	27.29	27.16	27.10	27.39	27.49	27.32	27.49	27.26	27.71	27.59	27.80	28.25	27.49
Education and Health Services													
2014	25.08	24.90	24.61	24.88	24.64	24.33	24.65	24.47	24.57	24.48	24.67	24.98	24.69
2015	24.79	24.83	24.80	24.68	24.60	24.72	24.83	25.03	25.14	25.12	25.29	25.22	24.92
2016	25.28	25.16	25.44	25.66	25.35	25.24	25.21	25.23	25.52	25.55	25.49	26.25	25.45
2017	25.73	25.71	26.18	26.25	26.27	26.22	26.67	26.67	26.72	26.74	26.94	26.95	26.43
2018	26.74	26.53	26.74	26.60	26.47	26.47	26.54	26.28	26.58	26.50	26.38	26.63	26.54
Leisure and Hospitality													
2014	13.66	13.70	13.70	13.62	13.57	13.40	13.46	13.41	13.57	13.83	13.77	13.77	13.62
2015	14.01	14.07	13.95	13.97	14.03	13.83	13.94	14.02	14.10	14.15	14.30	14.33	14.06
2016	14.41	14.20	13.92	14.23	14.28	14.13	14.13	14.07	14.09	14.26	14.39	14.36	14.21
2017	14.98	15.09	14.94	15.00	15.13	14.82	14.69	14.82	14.80	15.14	15.20	15.79	15.04
2018	15.98	16.01	16.01	15.72	15.70	15.51	15.57	15.59	15.59	15.87	16.18	16.48	15.85
Other Services													
2014	20.87	21.11	20.20	19.70	19.29	20.14	19.72	20.09	19.23	19.02	19.40	18.92	19.82
2015	19.23	19.58	19.67	19.69	20.29	20.15	20.87	21.36	21.27	21.19	21.21	21.12	20.47
2016	21.25	21.49	21.75	21.83	22.10	21.67	22.01	22.60	22.79	22.57	23.12	22.95	22.18
2017	23.72	23.61	23.27	23.64	23.48	23.60	23.66	23.70	23.99	24.15	23.72	23.67	23.69
2018	22.96	22.91	22.50	22.17	22.46	22.22	23.06	23.05	22.71	22.34	22.00	22.63	22.58

4. Average Weekly Earnings by Selected Industry: Arizona, 2014–2018

(Dollars, not seasonally adjusted)

Industry and year	January	February	March	April	May	June	July	August	September	October	November	December	Annual average
Total Private													
2014	802.13	818.05	813.12	790.51	784.44	801.85	781.81	780.67	773.26	775.43	793.44	778.15	790.05
2015	788.10	807.65	802.70	799.84	794.42	798.66	796.49	819.94	799.80	801.86	812.41	797.82	802.61
2016	803.06	810.54	813.60	820.46	841.12	817.69	814.28	826.58	825.56	848.07	831.74	827.66	822.86
2017	857.44	856.03	849.34	884.10	862.50	860.95	898.03	889.01	886.93	909.57	892.74	889.49	879.05
2018	888.79	891.10	888.21	907.74	890.53	891.10	908.98	894.01	903.83	894.41	881.61	904.18	894.49
Goods Producing													
2014	963.64	966.16	974.47	966.94	955.89	959.01	950.33	940.42	920.43	910.60	935.42	928.01	947.38
2015	911.74	912.11	913.74	932.19	913.71	918.06	915.59	913.61	899.37	909.54	927.50	924.95	916.99
2016	916.65	912.11	937.97	935.67	953.16	955.64	950.02	960.37	953.67	954.03	929.47	949.84	942.18
2017	950.67	950.25	946.51	952.71	947.55	968.22	965.76	953.96	985.88	983.92	980.54	984.34	965.39
2018	973.28	954.79	988.16	1,013.97	1,004.53	1,011.36	1,030.05	1,036.48	1,039.35	1,056.69	1,041.33	1,085.68	1,020.62
Construction													
2014	929.87	925.59	922.78	922.14	912.38	908.71	901.88	884.99	851.20	851.24	889.48	871.42	898.56
2015	849.75	846.92	856.18	885.57	860.32	866.76	867.13	851.51	831.80	853.67	865.31	878.05	859.61
2016	878.04	875.42	904.42	916.50	937.26	947.16	946.27	964.44	953.02	947.25	922.01	946.50	928.88
2017	929.52	943.09	945.01	949.66	919.83	972.80	965.67	960.60	1,014.79	999.74	983.53	991.63	965.25
2018	971.15	949.81	973.90	1,001.86	986.99	974.97	999.80	999.55	1,008.62	1,019.36	1,012.01	1,025.87	992.94
Manufacturing													
2014	989.03	996.47	1,012.91	998.97	987.71	990.80	978.00	987.38	982.09	967.43	974.70	978.47	988.06
2015	967.89	967.57	964.32	974.47	968.85	974.85	967.75	975.43	968.77	968.06	987.36	965.45	971.39
2016	953.20	945.50	968.73	955.78	971.63	967.03	959.11	961.96	966.81	966.81	930.22	946.00	958.38
2017	969.57	953.42	941.98	950.21	972.76	957.59	963.01	942.46	945.65	959.98	973.63	976.02	957.96
2018	971.23	955.90	990.12	1,014.59	1,014.85	1,048.95	1,060.67	1,075.08	1,070.66	1,071.20	1,073.94	1,136.28	1,042.03
Trade, Transportation, and Utilities													
2014	704.86	731.81	734.62	713.05	712.07	723.10	710.70	708.29	715.87	717.60	720.54	710.78	716.88
2015	725.57	739.86	720.47	730.30	734.95	725.06	726.05	738.76	730.36	729.75	739.11	733.38	730.78
2016	751.04	761.45	769.30	789.71	801.68	785.01	760.38	776.46	781.81	815.36	796.61	775.20	781.22
2017	807.42	808.52	817.69	864.82	830.42	825.46	883.24	852.61	854.70	889.56	847.67	848.74	843.90
2018	876.42	884.41	839.61	875.64	849.43	853.62	866.95	845.55	858.13	856.81	828.63	837.98	854.91
Financial Activities													
2014	1,025.65	1,034.45	1,031.04	1,010.03	1,003.97	1,016.34	1,003.78	1,006.86	1,003.01	996.48	1,011.90	997.54	1,011.46
2015	998.85	1,023.25	1,035.84	1,026.96	1,017.88	1,036.35	1,037.51	1,094.00	1,058.01	1,058.86	1,074.83	1,061.93	1,045.14
2016	1,043.64	1,056.10	1,049.93	1,042.59	1,104.33	1,056.87	1,066.65	1,131.37	1,107.08	1,156.48	1,149.45	1,096.03	1,089.76
2017	1,142.00	1,122.42	1,110.23	1,148.27	1,127.12	1,126.29	1,169.10	1,178.89	1,136.69	1,183.65	1,172.54	1,153.06	1,146.69
2018	1,135.33	1,174.34	1,149.34	1,171.07	1,189.33	1,163.28	1,198.20	1,205.10	1,194.18	1,175.56	1,181.12	1,193.72	1,176.64
Professional and Business Services													
2014	901.09	932.88	921.95	898.21	887.15	912.61	882.88	889.63	886.34	902.85	926.38	872.65	900.73
2015	924.27	957.32	970.42	952.43	941.54	953.04	938.79	992.12	955.08	952.43	954.77	914.33	950.97
2016	912.55	918.34	935.82	959.03	993.00	947.22	954.57	962.32	963.31	988.82	946.40	943.16	952.75
2017	990.03	983.81	980.76	1,032.12	992.59	988.42	1,057.88	1,028.46	1,026.38	1,059.75	1,031.56	1,023.93	1,016.96
2018	993.36	999.49	1,005.41	1,035.34	1,014.38	1,010.84	1,041.87	1,011.35	1,022.50	996.00	1,009.14	1,033.95	1,014.38
Education and Health Services													
2014	837.67	846.60	834.28	828.50	820.51	832.09	830.71	822.19	823.10	822.53	848.65	841.83	832.05
2015	837.90	854.15	845.68	836.65	831.48	830.59	836.77	848.52	847.22	841.52	854.80	839.83	842.30
2016	844.35	842.86	847.15	846.78	846.69	827.87	831.93	837.64	847.26	855.93	856.46	876.75	847.49
2017	885.11	866.43	877.03	895.13	880.05	891.48	920.12	906.78	903.14	914.51	915.96	910.91	898.62
2018	903.81	902.02	901.14	909.72	892.04	892.04	907.67	885.64	911.69	885.10	878.45	897.43	897.05
Leisure and Hospitality													
2014	359.26	371.27	380.86	358.21	355.53	357.78	341.88	348.66	351.46	363.73	381.43	369.04	360.93
2015	379.67	396.77	393.39	379.98	381.62	372.03	368.02	372.93	366.60	370.73	378.95	375.45	378.21
2016	377.54	376.30	371.66	375.67	381.28	368.79	367.38	357.38	362.11	375.04	372.70	370.49	370.88
2017	389.48	390.83	394.42	402.00	396.41	382.36	387.82	371.98	377.40	393.64	398.24	413.70	391.04
2018	418.68	429.07	437.07	427.58	416.05	407.91	401.71	397.55	406.90	404.69	415.83	428.48	415.27
Other Services													
2014	663.67	705.07	668.62	636.31	601.85	656.56	617.24	636.85	596.13	593.42	595.58	575.17	628.29
2015	594.21	640.27	625.51	639.93	641.16	660.92	669.93	713.42	670.01	682.32	695.69	688.51	659.13
2016	697.00	704.87	722.10	726.94	733.72	717.28	719.73	752.58	745.23	771.89	779.14	773.42	736.38
2017	806.48	800.38	798.16	810.85	788.93	814.20	811.54	796.32	820.46	847.67	830.20	847.39	814.94
2018	805.90	804.14	792.00	791.47	783.85	793.25	781.73	797.53	808.48	777.43	789.80	787.52	792.56

ARKANSAS
At a Glance

Population:
  2010 census: 2,915,918
  2018 estimate: 3,013,825

Percent change in population:
  2010–2018: 3.4%

Percent change in total nonfarm employment:
  2010–2018: 8.5%

Industry with the largest growth in employment, 2010–2018 (percent):
  Financial activities, 24.0%

Industry with the largest decline or smallest growth in employment, 2010–2018 (percent):
  Mining and logging, -43.9%

Civilian labor force:
  2010: 1,353,338
  2018: 1,351,496

Unemployment rate and rank among states (highest to lowest):
  2010: 8.2%, 31st
  2018: 3.7%, 28th

Over-the-year change in unemployment rates:
  2016–2017: -0.3%
  2017–2018: 0.0%

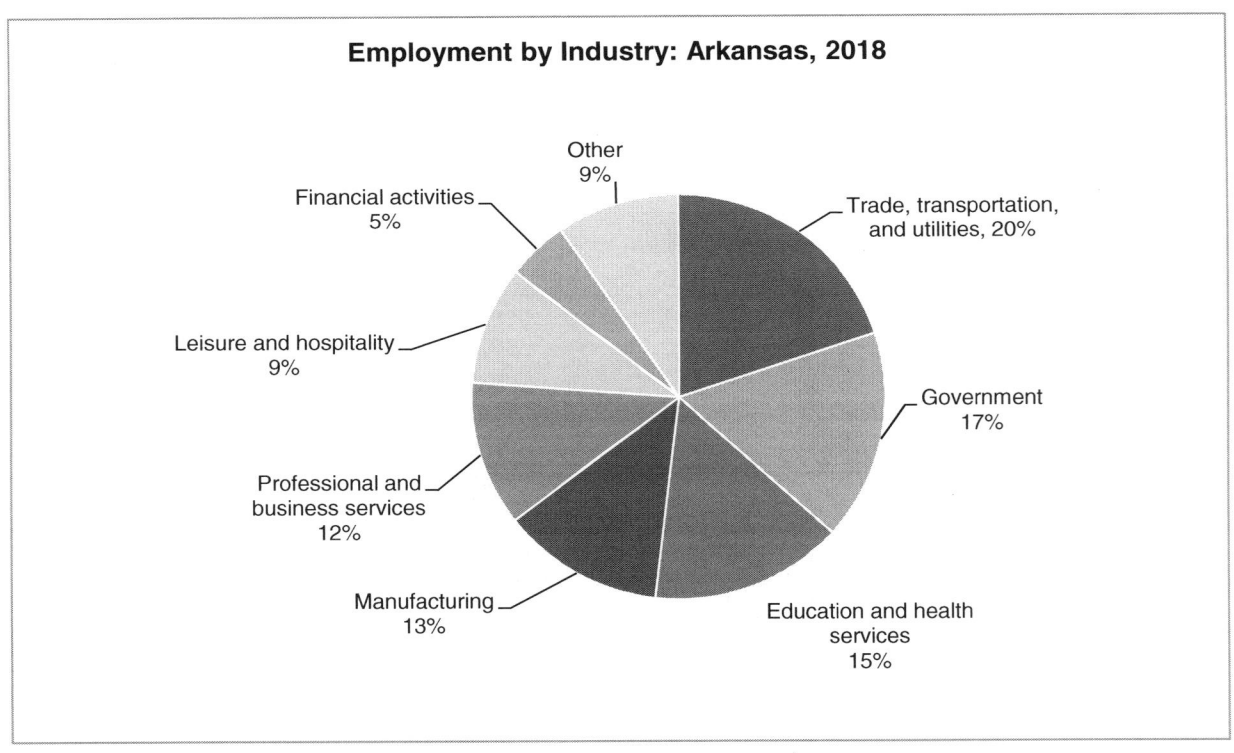

Employment by Industry: Arkansas, 2018

- Other 9%
- Financial activities 5%
- Leisure and hospitality 9%
- Professional and business services 12%
- Manufacturing 13%
- Education and health services 15%
- Education and health services 15%
- Government 17%
- Trade, transportation, and utilities, 20%

1. Employment by Industry: Arkansas, 2010–2018

(Numbers in thousands, not seasonally adjusted)

Industry and year	January	February	March	April	May	June	July	August	September	October	November	December	Annual average
Total Nonfarm													
2010	1,136.0	1,137.6	1,154.0	1,162.9	1,175.2	1,177.6	1,159.0	1,164.3	1,172.2	1,171.2	1,172.3	1,172.8	1,162.9
2011	1,148.3	1,148.2	1,162.0	1,177.9	1,173.9	1,166.3	1,159.7	1,166.4	1,178.3	1,184.0	1,184.6	1,183.8	1,169.5
2012	1,160.4	1,166.2	1,177.7	1,182.9	1,188.1	1,181.8	1,161.9	1,170.9	1,181.0	1,182.8	1,184.9	1,187.1	1,177.1
2013	1,161.7	1,170.6	1,177.3	1,182.9	1,186.5	1,176.7	1,162.2	1,169.2	1,183.6	1,186.4	1,189.8	1,184.8	1,177.6
2014	1,164.4	1,173.0	1,182.0	1,190.5	1,198.3	1,190.1	1,173.7	1,183.9	1,200.1	1,203.1	1,208.5	1,212.1	1,190.0
2015	1,187.0	1,196.6	1,198.1	1,209.6	1,219.1	1,212.2	1,198.9	1,210.0	1,227.3	1,228.8	1,233.9	1,237.1	1,213.2
2016	1,210.5	1,220.2	1,227.9	1,235.9	1,239.0	1,231.8	1,218.2	1,227.0	1,245.3	1,245.3	1,247.7	1,247.5	1,233.0
2017	1,224.5	1,235.6	1,243.1	1,251.2	1,254.5	1,248.7	1,232.0	1,241.3	1,259.3	1,262.0	1,266.6	1,265.8	1,248.7
2018	1,242.8	1,253.1	1,260.2	1,264.7	1,269.1	1,258.7	1,245.9	1,254.9	1,270.3	1,273.2	1,276.7	1,273.3	1,261.9
Total Private													
2010	920.8	920.3	934.1	941.8	947.4	956.2	951.9	954.8	954.5	951.2	950.9	952.6	944.7
2011	931.6	929.5	941.9	957.0	953.1	952.5	960.6	960.3	961.5	963.1	963.0	963.7	953.2
2012	944.4	946.9	957.7	962.6	966.6	967.6	960.5	965.6	964.6	962.6	963.1	966.2	960.7
2013	946.1	951.4	958.0	963.4	967.1	964.6	962.8	965.5	968.1	969.2	972.3	967.8	963.0
2014	952.1	957.2	965.6	974.0	980.8	979.5	975.3	981.3	985.9	987.7	991.0	994.9	977.1
2015	973.8	981.2	982.3	993.8	1,002.3	1,002.1	1,000.7	1,007.4	1,013.6	1,014.2	1,018.2	1,020.9	1,000.9
2016	998.3	1,005.4	1,011.6	1,019.4	1,022.1	1,021.2	1,020.3	1,024.4	1,032.0	1,032.2	1,033.7	1,033.3	1,021.2
2017	1,014.6	1,022.8	1,029.9	1,035.7	1,039.8	1,039.1	1,034.4	1,040.1	1,045.5	1,046.7	1,050.6	1,050.7	1,037.5
2018	1,031.3	1,038.7	1,044.7	1,048.8	1,054.0	1,048.6	1,047.9	1,053.5	1,056.1	1,057.1	1,059.6	1,056.6	1,049.7
Goods Producing													
2010	213.6	212.4	216.8	219.0	220.8	224.8	223.6	223.5	222.2	220.3	219.3	219.3	219.6
2011	214.1	213.9	216.6	218.7	218.1	217.9	220.3	219.1	219.3	217.8	216.7	216.2	217.4
2012	212.7	212.8	214.9	214.7	216.1	216.7	215.0	214.8	213.9	211.3	209.7	210.2	213.6
2013	206.7	206.9	208.0	207.3	208.6	208.9	208.5	208.6	208.4	207.8	207.3	206.2	207.8
2014	205.1	204.4	205.3	207.2	209.2	210.1	210.8	211.3	212.1	212.2	211.4	212.6	209.3
2015	210.8	210.7	209.8	210.5	211.1	212.7	214.0	214.2	215.3	213.8	213.0	213.2	212.4
2016	209.7	209.8	209.9	210.3	210.7	212.7	213.2	212.7	213.4	212.6	211.7	211.8	211.5
2017	210.4	211.6	213.2	213.0	213.8	215.8	215.6	215.8	216.5	215.9	216.4	216.4	214.5
2018	213.2	214.9	215.5	215.2	216.5	218.0	218.3	218.4	219.0	218.3	218.3	219.6	217.1
Service-Providing													
2010	922.4	925.2	937.2	943.9	954.4	952.8	935.4	940.8	950.0	950.9	953.0	953.5	943.3
2011	934.2	934.3	945.4	959.2	955.8	948.4	939.4	947.3	959.0	966.2	967.9	967.6	952.1
2012	947.7	953.4	962.8	968.2	972.0	965.1	946.9	956.1	967.1	971.5	975.2	976.9	963.6
2013	955.0	963.7	969.3	975.6	977.9	967.8	953.7	960.6	975.2	978.6	982.5	978.6	969.9
2014	959.3	968.6	976.7	983.3	989.1	980.0	962.9	972.6	988.0	990.9	997.1	999.5	980.7
2015	976.2	985.9	988.3	999.1	1,008.0	999.5	984.9	995.8	1,012.0	1,015.0	1,020.9	1,023.9	1,000.8
2016	1,000.8	1,010.4	1,018.0	1,025.6	1,028.3	1,019.1	1,005.0	1,014.3	1,031.9	1,032.7	1,036.0	1,035.7	1,021.5
2017	1,014.1	1,024.0	1,029.9	1,038.2	1,040.7	1,032.9	1,016.4	1,025.5	1,042.8	1,046.1	1,050.2	1,049.4	1,034.2
2018	1,029.6	1,038.2	1,044.7	1,049.5	1,052.6	1,040.7	1,027.6	1,036.5	1,051.3	1,054.9	1,058.4	1,053.7	1,044.8
Mining and Logging													
2010	9.9	9.8	10.2	10.6	10.8	11.0	10.9	10.9	11.0	10.9	10.9	11.0	10.7
2011	10.7	10.6	10.8	11.0	10.8	11.0	11.5	11.4	11.5	11.7	11.6	11.6	11.2
2012	11.3	11.3	11.3	11.1	11.1	11.1	10.7	10.5	10.3	10.2	10.1	10.0	10.8
2013	9.6	9.6	9.7	9.5	9.6	9.6	9.7	9.6	9.5	9.3	9.2	9.1	9.5
2014	8.8	8.7	8.7	8.8	9.0	8.9	9.0	9.0	9.1	9.0	9.1	9.1	8.9
2015	8.8	8.7	8.4	8.3	8.1	8.0	8.0	7.9	7.8	7.7	7.6	7.5	8.1
2016	7.1	6.9	6.7	6.3	6.3	6.3	6.2	6.2	6.2	6.0	6.0	6.0	6.4
2017	5.9	5.9	5.9	5.9	6.0	6.1	6.1	6.0	6.0	6.0	6.0	5.9	6.0
2018	5.8	5.9	5.9	5.9	6.0	6.1	5.9	6.0	6.0	6.1	6.0	5.8	6.0
Construction													
2010	46.0	45.0	47.3	48.8	49.7	51.3	51.1	50.8	50.0	48.9	47.8	47.5	48.7
2011	43.6	43.6	45.5	47.3	47.2	48.3	49.3	48.8	49.2	48.7	48.1	47.8	47.3
2012	45.6	46.1	47.5	47.6	48.6	49.4	47.7	48.3	48.5	47.3	46.1	46.0	47.4
2013	43.9	44.4	45.3	45.4	46.4	46.5	46.3	46.3	46.0	45.4	45.2	44.3	45.5
2014	43.9	43.2	43.7	45.0	46.2	46.6	46.8	47.2	47.6	47.6	47.4	47.7	46.1
2015	45.9	46.2	46.0	47.3	48.5	49.5	50.7	51.2	52.2	51.4	50.8	50.4	49.2
2016	48.3	48.6	49.2	50.3	50.5	51.5	51.6	51.1	51.5	51.1	50.1	49.6	50.3
2017	48.7	49.5	50.8	51.1	51.6	52.6	52.0	51.9	52.4	51.4	51.4	50.9	51.2
2018	48.5	49.2	49.5	49.9	50.8	51.6	51.7	51.6	51.9	51.7	51.1	50.2	50.6

1. Employment by Industry: Arkansas, 2010–2018—*Continued*

(Numbers in thousands, not seasonally adjusted)

Industry and year	January	February	March	April	May	June	July	August	September	October	November	December	Annual average
Manufacturing													
2010	157.7	157.6	159.3	159.6	160.3	162.5	161.6	161.8	161.2	160.5	160.6	160.8	160.3
2011	159.8	159.7	160.3	160.4	160.1	158.6	159.5	158.9	158.6	157.4	157.0	156.8	158.9
2012	155.8	155.4	156.1	156.0	156.4	156.2	156.6	156.0	155.1	153.8	153.5	154.2	155.4
2013	153.2	152.9	153.0	152.4	152.6	152.8	152.5	152.7	152.9	153.1	152.9	152.8	152.8
2014	152.4	152.5	152.9	153.4	154.0	154.6	155.0	155.1	155.4	155.6	154.9	155.8	154.3
2015	156.1	155.8	155.4	154.9	154.5	155.2	155.3	155.1	155.3	154.7	154.6	155.3	155.2
2016	154.3	154.3	154.0	153.7	153.9	154.9	155.4	155.4	155.7	155.5	155.6	156.2	154.9
2017	155.8	156.2	156.5	156.0	156.2	157.1	157.5	157.9	158.1	158.5	159.0	159.6	157.4
2018	158.9	159.8	160.1	159.4	159.7	160.3	160.7	160.8	161.1	160.5	161.2	163.6	160.5
Trade, Transportation, and Utilities													
2010	229.5	228.2	231.1	231.5	233.3	235.3	235.3	235.7	234.5	236.3	239.2	241.0	234.2
2011	233.4	231.0	233.5	237.7	236.6	237.5	239.2	238.6	238.3	239.9	242.8	245.0	237.8
2012	237.8	236.6	239.1	240.3	241.3	241.9	241.0	241.3	241.0	240.9	244.6	246.1	241.0
2013	237.8	237.7	239.3	239.6	239.5	239.9	240.8	241.4	240.8	242.1	245.6	246.2	240.9
2014	238.8	238.1	240.2	242.4	243.3	244.3	244.0	245.3	245.4	246.5	250.8	253.0	244.3
2015	244.9	244.6	245.7	248.1	250.3	251.2	250.5	251.7	250.8	252.1	255.7	257.1	250.2
2016	249.1	248.3	249.7	250.1	251.0	251.4	251.6	251.7	251.5	252.1	256.0	256.4	251.6
2017	248.9	247.8	248.0	248.4	249.3	249.9	249.9	250.9	250.1	250.2	254.1	255.4	250.2
2018	249.1	248.4	249.6	249.8	251.2	250.5	250.9	251.6	251.1	252.0	257.1	256.5	251.5
Wholesale Trade													
2010	44.9	44.9	45.5	45.9	46.2	46.6	46.2	45.9	45.6	46.1	45.9	45.9	45.8
2011	45.1	45.0	45.4	46.4	46.1	46.2	46.8	46.5	46.3	46.6	46.4	46.6	46.1
2012	46.0	46.1	46.6	47.3	47.5	47.6	46.9	46.8	46.5	46.3	46.2	46.4	46.7
2013	46.0	46.2	46.6	46.7	46.7	46.6	46.4	46.2	45.9	46.0	45.3	45.1	46.1
2014	45.0	45.3	45.6	45.9	46.1	46.3	46.1	46.2	45.9	46.0	45.9	45.9	45.9
2015	45.3	45.4	45.5	45.5	45.8	45.8	45.8	45.7	45.4	45.6	45.5	45.5	45.6
2016	45.0	45.2	45.4	45.4	45.5	45.5	45.6	45.5	45.4	45.4	45.4	45.6	45.4
2017	45.2	45.5	45.8	45.7	45.9	46.0	46.2	46.3	46.1	46.2	46.4	46.6	46.0
2018	46.7	47.0	47.1	47.1	47.2	47.3	47.5	47.4	47.3	47.8	48.9	48.6	47.5
Retail Trade													
2010	126.8	125.6	127.5	127.8	129.0	130.1	129.9	130.2	129.0	130.5	133.5	134.8	129.6
2011	129.5	127.5	129.1	131.4	130.5	130.9	131.7	131.3	130.4	132.0	135.1	136.2	131.3
2012	131.0	129.9	131.3	132.1	132.6	132.7	132.6	132.5	132.4	132.4	136.1	136.7	132.7
2013	130.7	130.4	131.5	131.9	131.8	131.9	133.4	133.8	133.4	134.6	138.5	139.1	133.4
2014	133.3	132.3	133.6	135.4	135.7	136.4	136.1	136.8	136.4	137.6	141.5	142.6	136.5
2015	136.7	136.5	137.2	139.2	140.8	141.2	140.4	141.6	140.8	142.0	145.8	146.2	140.7
2016	140.3	139.8	140.9	142.1	142.6	142.3	142.5	142.6	141.7	142.6	146.1	145.6	142.4
2017	140.8	139.6	139.5	140.2	140.7	140.5	140.2	140.7	140.0	140.3	143.5	143.5	140.8
2018	138.6	137.6	138.2	138.6	139.4	138.3	138.4	138.8	137.9	138.5	141.6	141.0	138.9
Transportation and Utilities													
2010	57.8	57.7	58.1	57.8	58.1	58.6	59.2	59.6	59.9	59.7	59.8	60.3	58.9
2011	58.8	58.5	59.0	59.9	60.0	60.4	60.7	60.8	61.6	61.3	61.3	62.2	60.4
2012	60.8	60.6	61.2	60.9	61.2	61.6	61.5	62.0	62.1	62.2	62.3	63.0	61.6
2013	61.1	61.1	61.2	61.0	61.0	61.4	61.0	61.4	61.5	61.5	61.8	62.0	61.3
2014	60.5	60.5	61.0	61.1	61.5	61.6	61.8	62.3	63.1	62.9	63.4	64.5	62.0
2015	62.9	62.7	63.0	63.4	63.7	64.2	64.3	64.4	64.6	64.5	64.4	65.4	64.0
2016	63.8	63.3	63.4	62.6	62.9	63.6	63.5	63.6	64.4	64.1	64.5	65.2	63.7
2017	62.9	62.7	62.7	62.5	62.7	63.4	63.5	63.9	64.0	63.7	64.2	65.3	63.5
2018	63.8	63.8	64.3	64.1	64.6	64.9	65.0	65.4	65.9	65.7	66.6	66.9	65.1
Information													
2010	15.3	15.4	15.5	15.4	15.5	15.8	15.3	15.2	15.2	15.1	15.1	15.1	15.3
2011	15.0	15.0	14.9	14.9	14.9	14.9	14.9	14.9	14.7	14.7	14.7	14.7	14.9
2012	14.6	14.6	14.4	14.4	14.5	14.5	14.3	14.3	14.2	14.2	14.2	14.2	14.4
2013	14.0	14.0	13.9	13.8	13.9	13.9	13.9	13.8	13.6	13.6	13.6	13.6	13.8
2014	13.3	13.3	13.2	13.1	13.1	13.0	13.1	12.9	12.7	12.6	12.6	12.6	13.0
2015	12.4	12.4	12.3	12.3	12.5	12.6	13.0	12.7	12.8	12.6	12.7	12.8	12.6
2016	12.5	12.5	12.5	12.5	12.4	12.5	12.4	12.3	12.2	12.3	12.3	12.4	12.4
2017	12.1	12.1	12.0	12.0	11.9	11.8	11.6	11.5	11.3	11.3	11.4	11.1	11.7
2018	11.4	11.3	11.2	11.1	11.2	11.2	11.1	11.1	11.0	11.1	11.4	11.2	11.2

1. Employment by Industry: Arkansas, 2010–2018—*Continued*

(Numbers in thousands, not seasonally adjusted)

Industry and year	January	February	March	April	May	June	July	August	September	October	November	December	Annual average
Financial Activities													
2010	48.7	48.6	48.5	48.8	48.7	49.1	48.9	48.9	48.7	48.8	48.8	49.1	48.8
2011	48.2	48.0	48.2	48.7	48.4	48.6	49.0	48.7	48.3	48.7	48.7	49.0	48.5
2012	48.5	48.6	48.8	49.1	49.5	49.8	49.7	50.1	49.8	50.0	50.2	50.5	49.6
2013	50.1	50.3	50.5	50.8	51.2	51.5	51.5	51.9	51.6	52.0	52.1	52.2	51.3
2014	51.5	51.8	52.0	52.1	52.5	52.7	52.6	52.7	52.2	52.6	52.7	52.9	52.4
2015	52.5	52.6	52.7	53.2	53.7	54.1	54.5	55.0	54.8	55.5	55.7	56.0	54.2
2016	55.7	55.9	56.0	56.5	56.6	57.0	57.3	57.6	57.6	58.1	58.5	58.5	57.1
2017	58.4	58.8	59.2	59.5	59.6	59.8	60.0	60.0	59.4	59.9	59.8	60.0	59.5
2018	59.8	59.8	59.7	60.0	60.4	60.7	61.0	61.2	60.8	60.8	60.6	61.1	60.5
Professional and Business Services													
2010	114.4	115.3	117.6	118.9	118.7	119.6	119.7	120.4	120.7	120.4	119.7	120.3	118.8
2011	118.9	119.8	121.7	123.9	122.5	123.0	125.0	125.5	125.0	125.9	124.8	124.7	123.4
2012	121.8	123.0	124.6	126.2	126.0	125.6	125.8	126.1	126.0	127.1	126.4	127.1	125.5
2013	125.3	127.8	128.8	130.2	130.3	128.0	127.6	127.8	130.8	133.1	133.5	131.4	129.6
2014	128.8	133.2	134.5	134.6	135.2	132.8	131.5	133.1	136.4	138.7	138.9	139.2	134.7
2015	133.1	138.5	137.4	140.1	141.0	138.6	137.8	139.3	142.4	143.7	144.3	144.4	140.1
2016	138.0	142.9	144.0	145.7	144.7	142.4	141.8	143.0	145.9	147.0	146.7	146.3	144.0
2017	141.0	145.4	146.6	147.5	147.7	144.9	143.5	144.5	147.5	148.6	148.3	148.0	146.1
2018	142.8	146.5	147.3	148.4	148.1	144.5	145.0	145.7	147.7	148.0	146.0	144.5	146.2
Education and Health Services													
2010	163.7	164.5	165.2	165.4	165.7	164.6	163.6	165.4	168.2	168.2	168.4	168.5	166.0
2011	165.4	165.2	166.5	168.0	167.0	163.5	164.2	166.2	170.0	171.1	171.7	171.3	167.5
2012	169.5	170.0	170.8	170.3	170.1	167.4	165.6	169.5	172.0	173.5	173.5	173.4	170.5
2013	170.4	171.6	171.5	172.4	172.5	169.2	168.2	170.3	172.8	172.9	173.6	172.9	171.5
2014	170.7	171.3	171.9	172.3	172.9	169.5	168.4	170.4	173.1	173.8	174.1	174.7	171.9
2015	172.8	173.3	173.5	174.6	175.0	172.3	171.7	174.1	177.4	178.3	178.8	179.1	175.1
2016	177.9	178.7	178.8	180.3	180.5	177.8	178.4	180.5	185.7	186.7	186.9	187.2	181.6
2017	185.1	186.4	187.1	188.1	188.4	186.0	184.5	186.6	190.6	191.6	192.0	192.1	188.2
2018	189.7	190.6	191.3	191.6	192.0	188.8	187.5	189.6	192.7	194.3	193.7	192.9	191.2
Leisure and Hospitality													
2010	93.0	93.5	96.6	99.7	101.4	103.0	101.9	102.3	101.6	99.0	97.4	96.5	98.8
2011	93.8	94.0	97.3	101.3	102.1	103.3	103.7	103.7	102.5	101.4	100.1	99.2	100.2
2012	96.6	98.3	101.7	104.0	105.3	107.2	105.4	105.9	104.3	102.2	101.3	101.4	102.8
2013	99.1	100.3	102.9	106.0	107.7	109.4	108.6	108.3	106.7	104.5	103.6	102.3	105.0
2014	101.1	102.2	105.3	108.6	110.7	112.5	110.4	111.1	109.9	107.6	106.9	106.4	107.7
2015	104.4	106.1	107.9	111.6	114.7	115.7	113.8	115.0	114.7	112.7	112.1	111.8	111.7
2016	108.9	110.8	113.8	117.0	119.0	119.3	117.4	118.6	117.5	115.5	113.8	112.7	115.4
2017	110.7	112.5	115.3	118.1	119.4	120.0	118.1	119.4	118.3	117.2	116.2	114.6	116.7
2018	112.6	114.4	117.1	119.4	121.1	121.0	120.2	122.1	119.9	119.2	118.9	117.3	118.6
Other Services													
2010	42.6	42.4	42.8	43.1	43.3	44.0	43.6	43.4	43.4	43.1	43.0	42.8	43.1
2011	42.8	42.6	43.2	43.8	43.5	43.8	44.3	43.6	43.4	43.6	43.5	43.6	43.5
2012	42.9	43.0	43.4	43.6	43.8	44.5	43.7	43.6	43.4	43.4	43.2	43.3	43.5
2013	42.7	42.8	43.1	43.3	43.4	43.8	43.7	43.4	43.4	43.2	43.0	43.0	43.2
2014	42.8	42.9	43.2	43.7	43.9	44.6	44.5	44.5	44.1	43.7	43.6	43.5	43.8
2015	42.9	43.0	43.0	43.4	44.0	44.9	45.4	45.4	45.4	45.5	45.9	46.5	44.6
2016	46.5	46.5	46.9	47.0	47.2	48.1	48.2	48.0	48.2	47.9	47.8	48.0	47.5
2017	48.0	48.2	48.5	49.1	49.7	50.9	51.2	51.4	51.8	52.0	52.4	53.1	50.5
2018	52.7	52.8	53.0	53.3	53.5	53.9	53.9	53.8	53.9	53.4	53.6	53.5	53.4
Government													
2010	215.2	217.3	219.9	221.1	227.8	221.4	207.1	209.5	217.7	220.0	221.4	220.2	218.2
2011	216.7	218.7	220.1	220.9	220.8	213.8	199.1	206.1	216.8	220.9	221.6	220.1	216.3
2012	216.0	219.3	220.0	220.3	221.5	214.2	201.4	205.3	216.4	220.2	221.8	220.9	216.4
2013	215.6	219.2	219.3	219.5	219.4	212.1	199.4	203.7	215.5	217.2	217.5	217.0	214.6
2014	212.3	215.8	216.4	216.5	217.5	210.6	198.4	202.6	214.2	215.4	217.5	217.2	212.9
2015	213.2	215.4	215.8	215.8	216.8	210.1	198.2	202.6	213.7	214.6	215.7	216.2	212.3
2016	212.2	214.8	216.3	216.5	216.9	210.6	197.9	202.6	213.3	213.1	214.0	214.2	211.9
2017	209.9	212.8	213.2	215.5	214.7	209.6	197.6	201.2	213.8	215.3	216.0	215.1	211.2
2018	211.5	214.4	215.5	215.9	215.1	210.1	198.0	201.4	214.2	216.1	217.1	216.7	212.2

2. Average Weekly Hours by Selected Industry: Arkansas, 2014–2018

(Not seasonally adjusted)

Industry and year	January	February	March	April	May	June	July	August	September	October	November	December	Annual average
Total Private													
2014	34.8	35.0	35.3	35.0	34.8	35.3	34.7	34.9	34.8	34.8	34.9	34.8	34.9
2015	34.6	34.7	34.5	34.6	34.3	34.3	34.4	34.9	34.2	34.5	34.8	34.3	34.5
2016	33.7	33.9	33.5	33.9	34.3	34.4	34.6	34.3	34.2	34.7	34.4	34.5	34.2
2017	34.5	34.4	34.5	34.8	34.6	34.9	35.0	34.8	35.0	35.4	34.8	35.1	34.8
2018	34.4	34.6	35.0	35.2	34.7	35.3	35.2	35.1	35.7	35.9	35.6	36.0	35.2
Goods Producing													
2014	40.8	41.1	41.7	41.7	40.9	41.5	39.8	41.3	41.1	41.2	40.8	41.6	41.1
2015	41.0	40.5	39.9	40.5	40.0	40.4	40.1	41.2	39.6	41.1	40.7	40.1	40.4
2016	39.9	39.9	39.0	40.6	40.5	41.6	40.8	41.6	41.0	41.4	41.0	40.9	40.7
2017	40.5	40.2	40.0	39.9	40.4	41.5	40.8	41.3	41.3	42.2	41.6	41.5	40.9
2018	40.3	40.7	41.3	41.5	41.4	41.6	41.1	41.7	42.3	42.4	41.3	41.2	41.4
Construction													
2014	39.9	40.5	42.4	40.5	39.5	40.0	41.1	42.7	39.9	40.1	39.4	40.9	40.6
2015	38.9	36.7	35.6	37.9	37.3	39.3	37.7	38.5	35.4	37.3	37.3	35.7	37.3
2016	35.7	35.8	32.7	36.5	36.9	39.1	38.3	39.6	39.2	37.8	37.4	37.9	37.3
2017	38.6	38.1	38.8	38.0	39.2	41.0	41.0	41.1	40.8	41.3	39.2	39.1	39.7
2018	37.1	37.7	39.3	39.8	41.0	41.3	41.3	40.2	40.2	40.1	38.1	38.7	39.6
Manufacturing													
2014	41.0	41.0	41.3	41.9	41.3	41.7	39.2	40.7	41.4	41.5	40.9	41.8	41.1
2015	41.4	41.4	41.1	40.8	40.6	40.4	40.6	41.6	40.9	41.2	40.8	40.8	41.0
2016	40.7	40.9	41.0	41.2	40.9	41.7	40.9	41.6	40.9	41.9	41.6	41.3	41.2
2017	40.6	40.5	40.0	40.3	40.5	41.5	40.4	41.2	41.3	42.4	42.5	42.3	41.1
2018	41.6	42.0	42.0	42.3	41.5	41.7	40.9	42.3	42.9	43.3	42.7	42.2	42.1
Trade, Transportation, and Utilities													
2014	35.8	35.8	36.8	36.2	36.1	36.5	36.2	36.1	36.1	36.0	35.8	35.9	36.1
2015	35.8	35.9	36.0	35.8	35.3	35.0	34.9	35.6	35.1	34.6	35.0	34.6	35.3
2016	34.1	34.7	34.3	34.2	35.1	35.1	35.0	34.6	34.3	34.7	33.9	34.4	34.5
2017	34.4	34.4	34.3	35.6	35.0	35.4	35.4	35.4	35.8	35.6	35.1	35.5	35.2
2018	35.1	35.2	36.0	36.2	35.6	36.1	36.4	36.0	36.5	35.5	35.3	36.0	35.8
Financial Activities													
2014	35.4	36.4	36.9	36.0	37.5	37.8	36.5	35.5	35.6	35.2	36.8	35.8	36.3
2015	36.7	37.0	37.2	35.7	35.9	35.9	36.0	36.3	35.7	35.7	37.0	36.3	36.3
2016	36.9	36.9	36.6	36.7	37.1	36.1	36.8	36.6	36.6	37.5	36.7	37.2	36.8
2017	38.2	37.3	37.3	38.5	37.7	37.1	38.3	37.5	37.1	38.5	37.3	37.6	37.7
2018	37.8	37.8	37.6	37.7	36.9	37.0	37.8	37.7	37.8	37.6	37.8	38.2	37.6
Professional and Business Services													
2014	36.3	36.2	36.3	36.2	36.1	36.5	35.9	36.4	36.4	36.3	36.7	35.6	36.2
2015	34.9	35.8	35.7	36.2	35.7	35.8	36.1	36.1	36.3	36.1	36.7	35.8	35.9
2016	35.1	35.2	34.6	35.0	35.7	35.2	35.6	34.8	34.2	34.6	34.6	34.7	34.9
2017	34.3	34.3	34.6	35.3	34.6	34.7	35.3	34.7	35.0	35.0	34.6	35.3	34.8
2018	34.1	34.9	35.2	35.7	35.4	35.6	35.6	34.9	35.7	34.7	35.3	35.8	35.3
Education and Health Services													
2014	33.1	33.2	32.8	32.9	32.9	33.3	33.4	33.5	33.5	33.4	33.5	33.5	33.2
2015	33.3	33.6	33.1	33.5	33.4	33.3	33.5	33.7	33.3	33.3	34.2	33.9	33.5
2016	33.8	33.5	33.2	33.1	33.9	33.8	34.4	33.9	34.4	34.6	35.1	35.1	34.1
2017	34.9	34.9	34.3	34.5	34.0	34.0	34.2	33.8	33.6	33.8	33.6	33.3	34.1
2018	32.5	32.6	32.3	32.9	32.4	33.2	32.6	32.4	32.9	32.7	32.4	32.7	32.6
Leisure and Hospitality													
2014	25.1	26.1	26.7	25.9	25.7	26.4	26.3	25.9	25.2	25.6	25.5	25.4	25.8
2015	25.1	25.0	24.9	24.7	25.1	25.3	25.8	25.7	25.0	25.1	25.0	25.1	25.2
2016	24.5	25.2	25.2	25.0	24.9	24.9	25.2	24.8	24.7	25.3	25.0	24.6	24.9
2017	25.1	24.5	25.2	24.6	25.3	25.4	25.5	24.9	24.9	25.7	25.2	25.4	25.1
2018	24.8	25.1	25.6	25.5	25.2	25.9	25.9	25.8	26.5	25.7	25.4	25.9	25.6

3. Average Hourly Earnings by Selected Industry: Arkansas, 2014–2018

(Dollars, not seasonally adjusted)

Industry and year	January	February	March	April	May	June	July	August	September	October	November	December	Annual average
Total Private													
2014	19.55	19.70	19.81	19.47	19.48	19.67	19.53	19.39	19.52	19.40	19.61	19.40	19.54
2015	19.39	19.44	19.61	19.38	19.44	19.29	19.40	19.61	19.51	19.59	19.72	19.69	19.51
2016	20.04	19.88	19.91	19.99	20.04	19.92	20.20	20.07	20.07	20.35	20.18	20.23	20.07
2017	20.38	20.46	20.42	20.67	20.46	20.43	20.66	20.62	20.83	20.75	20.76	20.95	20.62
2018	21.14	21.07	21.01	21.11	20.89	20.76	21.14	21.04	21.37	21.13	21.32	21.75	21.15
Goods Producing													
2014	19.45	19.47	19.62	19.15	19.36	19.50	19.75	19.55	19.62	19.59	19.93	19.66	19.55
2015	19.66	19.82	20.17	20.10	20.15	19.93	20.04	20.28	20.27	20.50	20.32	20.30	20.13
2016	20.22	20.05	20.03	20.04	20.03	19.79	19.97	19.86	20.04	20.27	20.23	20.63	20.10
2017	20.64	21.02	20.84	21.07	20.93	20.88	20.89	20.93	20.91	20.65	21.00	21.38	20.93
2018	21.22	21.35	21.50	21.47	21.49	21.39	21.61	21.53	22.00	21.76	21.68	22.26	21.61
Construction													
2014	20.35	20.35	20.08	20.15	20.61	20.68	20.46	20.14	20.22	20.39	20.66	20.33	20.37
2015	20.33	20.58	21.12	20.94	20.96	20.70	20.76	21.12	21.20	21.88	21.40	21.28	21.03
2016	21.19	21.47	21.56	21.09	20.79	20.65	20.96	21.07	21.13	21.56	21.81	21.87	21.25
2017	21.89	22.15	22.02	21.61	21.79	21.71	21.64	22.17	22.15	21.79	22.04	22.13	21.92
2018	22.29	22.33	22.56	22.20	21.98	21.93	22.14	22.18	22.71	22.75	22.20	23.64	22.40
Manufacturing													
2014	18.97	19.07	19.32	18.70	18.86	18.98	19.34	19.15	19.22	19.09	19.45	19.14	19.11
2015	19.20	19.36	19.76	19.67	19.67	19.45	19.57	19.66	19.56	19.51	19.54	19.66	19.55
2016	19.60	19.24	19.30	19.45	19.54	19.21	19.31	19.07	19.48	19.28	19.92	19.39
2017	19.67	20.19	19.96	20.43	20.17	20.17	20.24	20.18	20.12	19.98	20.41	20.97	20.21
2018	20.76	20.93	20.94	21.09	21.17	21.11	21.27	21.18	21.63	21.27	21.28	21.56	21.19
Trade, Transportation, and Utilities													
2014	19.86	19.69	20.04	19.40	19.50	19.80	19.62	19.45	19.53	19.46	19.50	18.92	19.56
2015	19.09	19.37	19.77	19.24	19.22	19.18	19.31	19.52	19.32	19.42	19.60	19.44	19.37
2016	19.75	19.46	19.64	19.54	19.49	19.30	19.52	19.66	19.60	19.77	19.68	19.42	19.57
2017	19.40	19.50	19.59	19.32	19.43	19.59	19.94	19.74	20.12	20.12	20.14	20.24	19.77
2018	20.98	20.63	20.83	20.94	20.58	20.26	20.78	20.60	21.26	20.98	21.05	22.05	20.91
Financial Activities													
2014	22.86	23.71	23.41	22.66	22.27	23.30	22.86	23.08	22.90	22.78	22.92	23.00	22.98
2015	23.30	23.18	22.82	23.62	23.68	22.60	23.08	23.06	22.95	22.72	23.49	24.02	23.21
2016	23.73	24.34	24.30	24.92	24.71	25.40	25.05	25.29	25.88	26.16	26.37	25.51	25.15
2017	26.24	26.44	25.79	26.13	25.41	26.07	26.79	26.93	27.13	27.52	26.96	26.52	26.50
2018	26.42	27.14	26.39	27.07	26.78	26.90	27.61	27.82	27.16	26.78	27.41	26.98	27.04
Professional and Business Services													
2014	22.32	22.61	22.76	22.24	22.12	22.57	21.93	21.92	21.87	21.88	22.09	22.27	22.21
2015	21.60	21.06	21.30	20.82	20.93	21.15	21.06	21.32	20.83	20.99	21.18	21.02	21.10
2016	21.20	20.93	21.03	21.36	21.78	21.55	21.63	21.36	21.41	21.74	21.12	21.19	21.36
2017	21.45	21.36	21.17	21.45	21.31	21.06	21.16	21.07	21.47	21.49	21.11	21.45	21.30
2018	22.02	21.79	21.46	21.59	21.22	21.05	21.76	21.53	21.48	20.95	21.31	21.51	21.47
Education and Health Services													
2014	20.74	21.28	21.58	21.80	21.72	21.75	21.63	21.37	21.68	21.17	21.51	21.21	21.45
2015	21.09	21.12	21.09	20.66	21.01	20.85	20.91	20.91	20.78	20.81	20.75	20.72	20.89
2016	21.13	21.33	21.40	21.71	21.43	21.59	22.24	22.12	22.03	22.54	22.28	22.65	21.89
2017	22.79	22.23	22.67	23.20	22.93	22.74	23.01	22.96	23.18	22.82	22.66	22.87	22.84
2018	22.71	22.39	22.51	22.42	22.01	22.13	22.29	22.16	22.34	21.84	22.15	22.55	22.29
Leisure and Hospitality													
2014	10.76	10.84	10.50	10.46	10.54	10.58	10.57	10.69	10.75	10.90	10.68	10.91	10.68
2015	10.92	11.02	11.21	11.15	11.05	10.92	10.92	11.26	11.50	11.42	11.60	11.69	11.22
2016	11.76	11.74	11.61	11.44	11.62	11.61	11.62	11.62	11.78	11.76	11.78	11.73	11.67
2017	11.78	12.16	12.18	12.20	12.32	12.11	12.07	12.10	12.19	12.11	12.32	12.25	12.15
2018	12.22	12.33	12.24	12.03	12.07	12.00	12.01	12.05	12.21	12.37	12.61	12.52	12.22

4. Average Weekly Earnings by Selected Industry: Arkansas, 2014–2018

(Dollars, not seasonally adjusted)

Industry and year	January	February	March	April	May	June	July	August	September	October	November	December	Annual average
Total Private													
2014	680.34	689.50	699.29	681.45	677.90	694.35	677.69	676.71	679.30	675.12	684.39	675.12	681.95
2015	670.89	674.57	676.55	670.55	666.79	661.65	667.36	684.39	667.24	675.86	686.26	675.37	673.10
2016	675.35	673.93	666.99	677.66	687.37	685.25	698.92	688.40	686.39	706.15	694.19	697.94	686.39
2017	703.11	703.82	704.49	719.32	707.92	713.01	723.10	717.58	729.05	734.55	722.45	735.35	717.58
2018	727.22	729.02	735.35	743.07	724.88	732.83	744.13	738.50	762.91	758.57	758.99	783.00	744.48
Goods Producing													
2014	793.56	800.22	818.15	798.56	791.82	809.25	786.05	807.42	806.38	807.11	813.14	817.86	803.51
2015	806.06	802.71	804.78	814.05	806.00	805.17	803.60	835.54	802.69	842.55	827.02	814.03	813.25
2016	806.78	800.00	781.17	813.62	811.22	823.26	814.78	826.18	821.64	839.18	829.43	843.77	818.07
2017	835.92	845.00	833.60	840.69	845.57	866.52	852.31	864.41	863.58	871.43	873.60	887.27	856.04
2018	855.17	868.95	887.95	891.01	889.69	889.82	888.17	897.80	930.60	922.62	895.38	917.11	894.65
Construction													
2014	811.97	824.18	851.39	816.08	814.10	827.20	840.91	859.98	806.78	817.64	814.00	831.50	827.02
2015	790.84	755.29	751.87	793.63	781.81	813.51	782.65	813.12	750.48	816.12	798.22	759.70	784.42
2016	756.48	768.63	705.01	769.79	767.15	807.42	802.77	834.37	828.30	814.97	815.69	828.87	792.63
2017	844.95	843.92	854.38	821.18	854.17	890.11	887.24	911.19	903.72	899.93	863.97	865.28	870.22
2018	826.96	841.84	886.61	883.56	901.18	905.71	914.38	891.64	912.94	912.28	845.82	914.87	887.04
Manufacturing													
2014	777.77	781.87	797.92	783.53	778.92	791.47	758.13	779.41	795.71	792.24	795.51	800.05	785.42
2015	794.88	801.50	812.14	802.54	797.38	785.78	794.54	817.86	800.00	803.81	797.23	802.13	801.55
2016	797.72	786.92	791.30	801.34	799.19	801.06	789.78	793.31	790.19	816.21	802.05	822.70	798.87
2017	798.60	817.70	798.40	823.33	816.89	837.06	817.70	831.42	830.96	847.15	867.43	887.03	830.63
2018	863.62	879.06	879.48	892.11	878.56	880.29	869.94	895.91	927.93	920.99	908.66	909.83	892.10
Trade, Transportation, and Utilities													
2014	710.99	704.90	737.47	702.28	703.95	722.70	710.24	702.15	705.03	700.56	698.10	679.23	706.12
2015	683.42	695.38	711.72	688.79	678.47	671.30	673.92	694.91	678.13	671.93	686.00	672.62	683.76
2016	673.48	675.26	673.65	668.27	684.10	677.43	683.20	680.24	672.28	686.02	667.15	668.05	675.17
2017	667.36	670.80	671.94	687.79	680.05	693.49	705.88	698.80	720.30	716.27	706.91	718.52	695.90
2018	736.40	726.18	749.88	758.03	732.65	731.39	756.39	741.60	775.99	744.79	743.07	793.80	748.58
Financial Activities													
2014	809.24	863.04	863.83	815.76	835.13	880.74	834.39	819.34	815.24	801.86	843.46	823.40	834.17
2015	855.11	857.66	848.90	843.23	850.11	811.34	830.88	837.08	819.32	811.10	869.13	871.93	842.52
2016	875.64	898.15	889.38	914.56	916.74	916.94	921.84	925.61	947.21	981.00	967.78	948.97	925.52
2017	1,002.37	986.21	961.97	1,006.01	957.96	967.20	1,026.06	1,009.88	1,006.52	1,059.52	1,005.61	997.15	999.05
2018	998.68	1,025.89	992.26	1,020.54	988.18	995.30	1,043.66	1,048.81	1,026.65	1,006.93	1,036.10	1,030.64	1,016.70
Professional and Business Services													
2014	810.22	818.48	826.19	805.09	798.53	823.81	787.29	797.89	796.07	794.24	810.70	792.81	804.00
2015	753.84	753.95	760.41	753.68	747.20	757.17	760.27	769.65	756.13	757.74	777.31	752.52	757.49
2016	744.12	736.74	727.64	747.60	777.55	758.56	770.03	743.33	732.22	752.20	730.75	735.29	745.46
2017	735.74	732.65	732.48	757.19	737.33	730.78	746.95	731.13	751.45	752.15	730.41	757.19	741.24
2018	750.88	760.47	755.39	770.76	751.19	749.38	774.66	751.40	766.84	726.97	752.24	770.06	757.89
Education and Health Services													
2014	686.49	706.50	707.82	717.22	714.59	724.28	722.44	715.90	726.28	707.08	720.59	710.54	712.14
2015	702.30	709.63	698.08	692.11	701.73	694.31	700.49	704.67	691.97	692.97	709.65	702.41	699.82
2016	714.19	714.56	710.48	718.60	726.48	729.74	765.06	749.87	757.83	779.88	782.03	795.02	746.45
2017	795.37	775.83	777.58	800.40	779.62	773.16	786.94	776.05	778.85	771.32	761.38	761.57	778.84
2018	738.08	729.91	727.07	737.62	713.12	734.72	726.65	717.98	734.99	714.17	717.66	737.39	726.65
Leisure and Hospitality													
2014	270.08	282.92	280.35	270.91	270.88	279.31	277.99	276.87	270.90	279.04	272.34	277.11	275.54
2015	274.09	275.50	279.13	275.41	277.36	276.28	281.74	289.38	287.50	286.64	290.00	293.42	282.74
2016	288.12	295.85	292.57	286.00	289.34	289.09	292.82	288.18	290.97	297.53	294.50	288.56	290.58
2017	295.68	297.92	306.94	300.12	311.70	307.59	307.79	301.29	303.53	311.23	310.46	311.15	304.97
2018	303.06	309.48	313.34	306.77	304.16	310.80	311.06	310.89	323.57	317.91	320.29	324.27	312.83

CALIFORNIA
At a Glance

Population:
   2010 census: 37,253,956
   2018 estimate: 39,557,045

Percent change in population:
   2010–2018: 6.2%

Percent change in total nonfarm employment:
   2010–2018: 20.2%

Industry with the largest growth in employment, 2010–2018 (percent):
   Construction, 53.5%

Industry with the largest decline or smallest growth in employment, 2010–2018 (percent):
   Mining and logging, -6.9%

Civilian labor force:
   2010: 18,336,271
   2018: 19,398,212

Unemployment rate and rank among states (highest to lowest):
   2010: 12.2%, 3rd
   2018: 4.2%, 14th

Over-the-year change in unemployment rates:
   2016–2017: -0.7%
   2017–2018: -0.6%

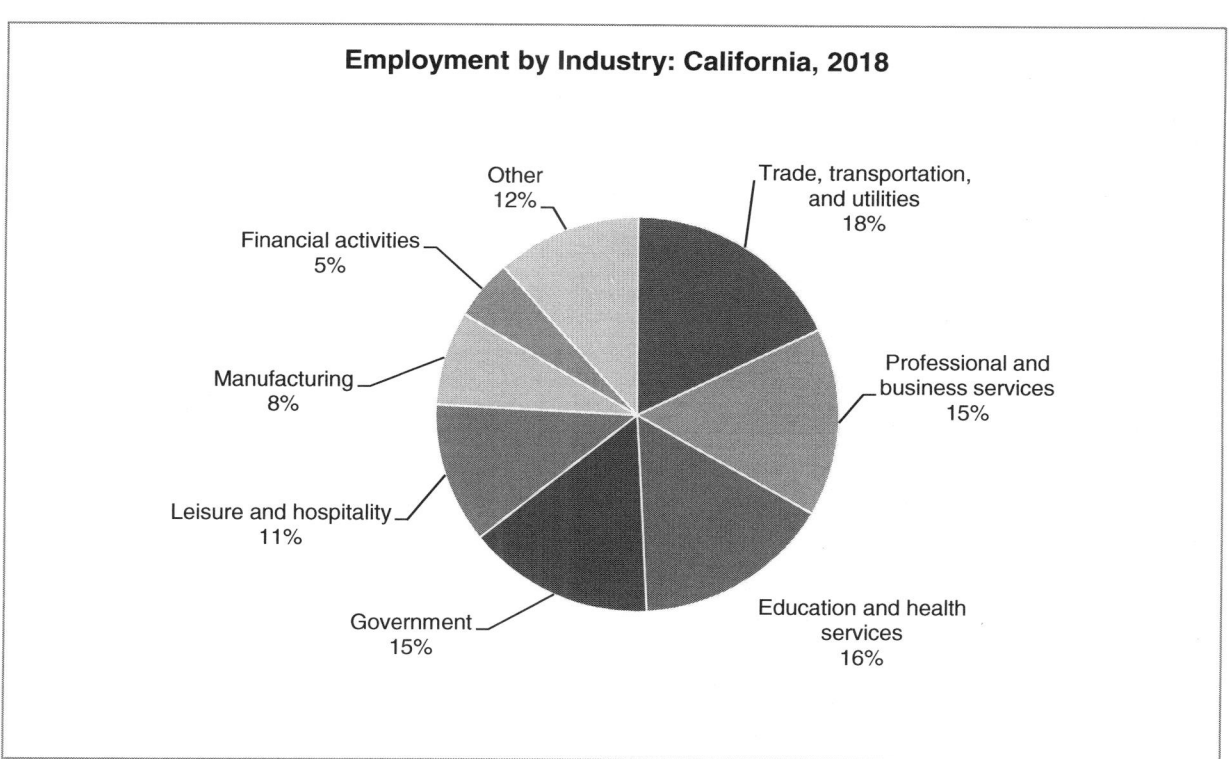

Employment by Industry: California, 2018

- Other 12%
- Trade, transportation, and utilities 18%
- Financial activities 5%
- Professional and business services 15%
- Manufacturing 8%
- Leisure and hospitality 11%
- Education and health services 16%
- Government 15%

1. Employment by Industry: California, 2010–2018

(Numbers in thousands, not seasonally adjusted)

Industry and year	January	February	March	April	May	June	July	August	September	October	November	December	Annual average
Total Nonfarm													
2010	14,048.8	14,089.6	14,158.1	14,290.0	14,382.9	14,395.8	14,187.2	14,209.5	14,266.2	14,413.3	14,464.1	14,494.5	14,283.3
2011	14,197.7	14,280.5	14,339.8	14,405.1	14,452.3	14,471.0	14,324.0	14,370.9	14,467.2	14,574.8	14,655.5	14,677.8	14,434.7
2012	14,435.3	14,532.1	14,626.5	14,664.3	14,763.3	14,830.0	14,658.2	14,737.7	14,803.3	14,945.7	15,061.7	15,084.3	14,761.9
2013	14,796.3	14,922.1	15,000.0	15,065.1	15,148.1	15,178.6	15,032.5	15,146.3	15,200.8	15,344.5	15,482.2	15,498.7	15,151.3
2014	15,230.0	15,327.2	15,411.3	15,477.6	15,564.4	15,595.4	15,435.7	15,573.4	15,645.4	15,800.2	15,914.3	15,938.6	15,576.1
2015	15,662.1	15,757.7	15,846.1	15,919.4	16,000.1	16,038.6	15,980.7	16,077.5	16,142.5	16,330.8	16,424.5	16,448.2	16,052.4
2016	16,150.5	16,261.9	16,284.2	16,431.0	16,481.6	16,468.8	16,394.0	16,469.2	16,552.9	16,694.3	16,787.0	16,793.1	16,480.7
2017	16,462.5	16,582.4	16,671.5	16,744.0	16,838.1	16,883.5	16,730.3	16,816.7	16,902.7	17,054.4	17,164.8	17,189.4	16,836.7
2018	16,880.7	17,008.0	17,059.7	17,119.0	17,179.6	17,226.2	17,050.5	17,151.8	17,191.5	17,344.3	17,440.7	17,449.8	17,175.2
Total Private													
2010	11,604.6	11,629.6	11,677.9	11,763.7	11,810.8	11,864.4	11,857.0	11,898.9	11,895.7	11,965.7	11,998.9	12,051.8	11,834.9
2011	11,773.4	11,834.9	11,870.6	11,935.5	11,982.5	12,013.5	12,045.7	12,098.3	12,130.8	12,166.9	12,229.5	12,276.2	12,029.8
2012	12,052.9	12,123.8	12,198.4	12,238.6	12,329.7	12,404.2	12,406.5	12,480.3	12,485.8	12,559.9	12,655.0	12,692.2	12,385.6
2013	12,433.0	12,530.7	12,587.3	12,652.8	12,725.2	12,765.2	12,793.6	12,874.5	12,865.1	12,945.3	13,058.4	13,092.5	12,777.0
2014	12,837.1	12,912.2	12,971.4	13,026.1	13,101.8	13,143.9	13,156.5	13,264.3	13,264.4	13,349.4	13,440.4	13,478.3	13,162.2
2015	13,215.9	13,291.7	13,360.5	13,423.2	13,497.5	13,541.6	13,650.2	13,716.7	13,706.9	13,828.5	13,903.0	13,937.0	13,589.4
2016	13,659.7	13,748.9	13,743.4	13,883.7	13,921.4	13,924.0	14,012.3	14,056.0	14,059.6	14,137.2	14,209.8	14,223.9	13,965.0
2017	13,919.0	14,017.1	14,085.4	14,138.9	14,220.2	14,279.7	14,309.8	14,369.7	14,365.9	14,451.6	14,541.4	14,575.2	14,272.8
2018	14,293.4	14,401.3	14,432.8	14,488.3	14,538.3	14,593.6	14,620.3	14,688.2	14,650.2	14,726.5	14,799.5	14,821.2	14,587.8
Goods Producing													
2010	1,805.8	1,798.2	1,810.0	1,814.2	1,831.5	1,846.6	1,855.9	1,867.5	1,856.4	1,850.9	1,834.0	1,818.4	1,832.5
2011	1,791.3	1,797.9	1,800.9	1,818.0	1,834.0	1,850.3	1,872.5	1,887.1	1,885.5	1,872.9	1,856.4	1,845.4	1,842.7
2012	1,824.6	1,828.4	1,837.0	1,838.0	1,865.4	1,892.2	1,908.5	1,924.5	1,921.5	1,913.1	1,901.5	1,891.5	1,878.9
2013	1,866.6	1,881.2	1,889.0	1,895.1	1,911.1	1,932.8	1,954.6	1,974.2	1,968.6	1,964.2	1,957.2	1,947.3	1,928.5
2014	1,921.0	1,935.7	1,944.9	1,949.1	1,968.0	1,987.7	2,007.5	2,031.4	2,029.6	2,021.2	2,011.9	1,999.2	1,983.9
2015	1,987.3	1,998.6	2,012.4	2,023.3	2,043.0	2,066.1	2,097.8	2,116.1	2,108.6	2,106.1	2,093.4	2,085.3	2,061.5
2016	2,055.0	2,070.0	2,065.2	2,087.9	2,098.3	2,112.4	2,143.1	2,150.2	2,143.8	2,132.7	2,120.0	2,109.8	2,107.4
2017	2,064.3	2,081.7	2,100.4	2,111.4	2,132.3	2,157.7	2,176.7	2,190.4	2,186.9	2,181.6	2,171.5	2,170.4	2,143.8
2018	2,138.9	2,168.1	2,165.1	2,184.9	2,199.5	2,221.0	2,240.7	2,253.3	2,248.5	2,237.0	2,226.7	2,210.1	2,207.8
Service-Providing													
2010	12,243.0	12,291.4	12,348.1	12,475.8	12,551.4	12,549.2	12,331.3	12,342.0	12,409.8	12,562.4	12,630.1	12,676.1	12,450.9
2011	12,406.4	12,482.6	12,538.9	12,587.1	12,618.3	12,620.7	12,451.5	12,483.8	12,581.7	12,701.9	12,799.1	12,832.4	12,592.0
2012	12,610.7	12,703.7	12,789.5	12,826.3	12,897.9	12,937.8	12,749.7	12,813.2	12,881.8	13,032.6	13,160.2	13,192.8	12,883.0
2013	12,929.7	13,040.9	13,111.0	13,170.0	13,237.0	13,245.8	13,077.9	13,172.1	13,232.2	13,380.3	13,525.0	13,551.4	13,222.8
2014	13,309.0	13,391.5	13,466.4	13,528.5	13,596.4	13,607.7	13,428.2	13,542.0	13,615.8	13,779.0	13,902.4	13,939.4	13,592.2
2015	13,674.8	13,759.1	13,833.7	13,896.1	13,957.1	13,972.5	13,882.9	13,961.4	14,033.9	14,224.7	14,331.1	14,362.9	13,990.9
2016	14,095.5	14,191.9	14,219.0	14,343.1	14,383.3	14,356.4	14,250.9	14,319.0	14,409.1	14,561.6	14,667.0	14,683.3	14,373.3
2017	14,398.2	14,500.7	14,571.1	14,632.6	14,705.8	14,725.8	14,553.6	14,626.3	14,715.8	14,872.8	14,993.3	15,019.0	14,692.9
2018	14,741.8	14,839.9	14,894.6	14,934.1	14,980.1	15,005.2	14,809.8	14,898.5	14,943.0	15,107.3	15,214.0	15,239.7	14,967.3
Mining and Logging													
2010	22.9	22.5	22.9	23.2	24.8	25.2	25.9	25.9	26.0	25.9	25.4	24.8	24.6
2011	24.7	24.9	24.8	25.5	26.2	26.8	27.8	28.1	28.1	28.2	28.0	27.6	26.7
2012	27.3	26.9	26.9	27.0	28.1	28.9	29.6	29.8	29.3	29.2	28.9	28.2	28.3
2013	27.4	27.5	27.3	27.8	28.6	29.0	29.1	29.0	28.8	28.8	28.5	28.0	28.3
2014	27.9	27.9	27.8	28.4	29.2	29.6	30.2	30.3	30.4	30.2	30.0	29.3	29.3
2015	27.8	27.1	26.8	27.0	26.8	26.9	26.9	26.6	26.2	25.7	25.0	24.3	26.4
2016	23.5	22.8	22.2	21.9	22.3	22.7	22.6	22.2	22.0	22.0	21.7	21.3	22.3
2017	20.8	20.6	20.5	21.2	22.0	22.5	22.7	22.8	22.8	22.8	22.6	22.5	22.0
2018	22.0	22.0	21.9	22.1	22.8	23.0	23.5	23.6	23.7	23.5	23.1	23.1	22.9
Construction													
2010	550.9	542.8	549.4	553.9	562.5	568.9	572.6	574.9	566.9	566.6	560.6	549.8	560.0
2011	532.8	535.1	534.4	545.9	554.4	562.9	578.8	584.9	584.2	580.8	575.7	567.5	561.5
2012	556.4	556.3	559.3	561.1	579.1	595.4	605.9	612.3	613.4	617.1	615.7	610.0	590.2
2013	598.0	606.9	613.0	618.1	628.4	640.1	652.8	661.9	658.5	662.3	660.5	652.2	637.7
2014	638.3	645.6	651.8	656.1	667.7	676.3	686.2	697.7	697.2	697.4	696.3	682.7	674.4
2015	681.6	688.0	698.6	707.4	720.1	732.3	749.8	760.2	756.1	767.5	765.7	757.8	732.1
2016	737.7	748.4	744.5	764.2	770.1	777.5	794.4	799.4	797.6	799.6	792.4	782.5	775.7
2017	746.8	761.5	780.7	793.2	806.4	821.1	831.1	837.4	838.1	840.0	836.1	833.0	810.5
2018	815.1	837.1	830.2	846.8	856.0	868.6	878.7	885.9	883.3	878.8	874.8	859.4	859.6

1. Employment by Industry: California, 2010–2018—*Continued*

(Numbers in thousands, not seasonally adjusted)

Industry and year	January	February	March	April	May	June	July	August	September	October	November	December	Annual average
Manufacturing													
2010	1,232.1	1,232.9	1,237.7	1,237.1	1,244.2	1,252.5	1,257.5	1,266.6	1,263.5	1,258.4	1,248.0	1,243.8	1,247.9
2011	1,233.9	1,237.9	1,241.7	1,246.6	1,253.4	1,260.7	1,266.0	1,274.2	1,273.2	1,264.0	1,252.7	1,250.3	1,254.6
2012	1,241.0	1,245.3	1,250.8	1,249.8	1,258.1	1,267.9	1,273.1	1,282.5	1,278.7	1,266.7	1,256.9	1,253.4	1,260.4
2013	1,241.3	1,246.9	1,248.7	1,249.2	1,254.1	1,263.8	1,272.8	1,283.2	1,281.3	1,273.1	1,268.3	1,267.2	1,262.5
2014	1,254.9	1,262.1	1,265.2	1,264.7	1,271.1	1,281.8	1,291.2	1,303.4	1,302.1	1,293.5	1,285.6	1,287.2	1,280.2
2015	1,277.9	1,283.5	1,286.9	1,288.9	1,296.1	1,307.0	1,321.1	1,329.4	1,326.2	1,313.0	1,302.7	1,303.2	1,303.0
2016	1,293.8	1,298.8	1,298.5	1,301.7	1,305.9	1,312.3	1,326.0	1,328.6	1,324.2	1,311.1	1,305.9	1,305.9	1,309.4
2017	1,296.7	1,299.7	1,299.2	1,297.0	1,303.9	1,314.1	1,322.9	1,330.2	1,326.0	1,318.8	1,312.8	1,314.9	1,311.4
2018	1,301.8	1,309.0	1,313.0	1,316.0	1,320.7	1,329.4	1,338.5	1,343.8	1,341.5	1,334.7	1,328.8	1,327.6	1,325.4
Trade, Transportation, and Utilities													
2010	2,584.8	2,565.1	2,563.7	2,575.3	2,589.8	2,598.7	2,601.2	2,612.9	2,612.4	2,634.9	2,690.8	2,727.2	2,613.1
2011	2,626.4	2,610.4	2,609.5	2,625.3	2,637.4	2,643.7	2,652.7	2,665.5	2,666.2	2,684.9	2,749.6	2,777.3	2,662.4
2012	2,686.4	2,655.5	2,658.8	2,665.3	2,683.9	2,696.1	2,702.9	2,713.3	2,715.7	2,734.6	2,818.6	2,838.2	2,714.1
2013	2,731.2	2,715.5	2,713.0	2,717.7	2,736.6	2,748.6	2,758.8	2,771.3	2,764.7	2,789.5	2,875.5	2,906.2	2,769.1
2014	2,797.5	2,778.8	2,778.0	2,785.9	2,800.8	2,812.7	2,819.0	2,838.9	2,837.6	2,860.0	2,940.5	2,975.0	2,835.4
2015	2,867.9	2,846.7	2,851.5	2,855.2	2,872.9	2,878.2	2,904.5	2,920.1	2,918.0	2,943.7	3,013.2	3,035.0	2,908.9
2016	2,929.3	2,913.9	2,911.4	2,928.0	2,935.7	2,929.8	2,957.7	2,971.9	2,965.7	2,996.0	3,070.9	3,094.3	2,967.1
2017	2,995.6	2,961.5	2,963.4	2,973.7	2,984.1	2,989.3	3,001.0	3,016.2	3,012.6	3,040.1	3,124.1	3,146.2	3,017.3
2018	3,036.8	3,010.8	3,008.9	3,010.9	3,022.6	3,026.5	3,040.6	3,050.7	3,045.0	3,060.9	3,139.1	3,166.1	3,051.6
Wholesale Trade													
2010	616.7	617.9	618.8	627.7	631.0	632.9	633.9	634.4	634.0	635.9	636.1	636.8	629.7
2011	631.1	633.8	634.2	640.8	642.5	643.2	645.4	647.3	647.0	646.8	646.6	647.4	642.2
2012	641.9	644.9	647.5	650.4	655.3	657.9	659.5	662.5	661.6	664.5	665.4	665.8	656.4
2013	659.3	662.4	664.3	667.1	670.8	673.3	674.5	675.7	674.4	675.1	678.2	680.5	671.3
2014	675.2	679.4	680.8	680.0	682.5	683.9	683.7	685.8	685.0	685.6	688.3	689.9	683.3
2015	681.2	684.6	684.5	686.8	689.9	690.4	694.8	696.0	694.7	695.5	696.3	697.3	691.0
2016	689.1	691.7	689.5	692.6	693.3	691.7	697.4	697.5	695.1	693.9	693.3	694.7	693.3
2017	688.1	690.4	690.5	694.3	696.9	698.8	699.3	698.8	696.7	698.8	700.0	701.9	696.2
2018	693.8	696.8	696.1	697.0	700.5	700.4	701.9	702.5	698.6	698.4	700.3	700.8	698.9
Retail Trade													
2010	1,507.0	1,486.6	1,485.2	1,487.9	1,495.0	1,499.5	1,501.0	1,509.8	1,507.5	1,526.5	1,581.4	1,610.9	1,516.5
2011	1,530.9	1,512.0	1,509.6	1,514.0	1,520.6	1,525.6	1,532.2	1,539.3	1,539.3	1,556.7	1,620.9	1,643.7	1,545.4
2012	1,569.8	1,537.1	1,535.5	1,535.9	1,545.1	1,548.5	1,552.5	1,557.6	1,557.7	1,573.9	1,655.0	1,667.0	1,569.6
2013	1,579.2	1,558.3	1,554.9	1,556.3	1,567.1	1,574.8	1,579.9	1,587.2	1,581.5	1,603.2	1,680.9	1,703.7	1,593.9
2014	1,614.4	1,590.5	1,590.1	1,594.8	1,599.7	1,607.0	1,612.1	1,623.4	1,618.0	1,636.0	1,708.0	1,731.4	1,627.1
2015	1,647.4	1,626.1	1,625.2	1,626.4	1,636.1	1,637.2	1,650.1	1,657.9	1,655.0	1,674.8	1,735.4	1,749.6	1,660.1
2016	1,669.6	1,652.9	1,648.6	1,654.8	1,657.8	1,653.4	1,666.5	1,674.1	1,667.2	1,689.7	1,750.4	1,761.5	1,678.9
2017	1,693.0	1,664.6	1,660.3	1,666.5	1,667.9	1,667.9	1,673.7	1,680.6	1,675.4	1,692.2	1,757.2	1,766.9	1,688.9
2018	1,695.0	1,670.5	1,665.8	1,664.5	1,669.3	1,667.3	1,676.0	1,680.9	1,674.1	1,685.4	1,748.4	1,766.5	1,688.6
Transportation and Utilities													
2010	461.1	460.6	459.7	459.7	463.8	466.3	466.3	468.7	470.9	472.5	473.3	479.5	466.9
2011	464.4	464.6	465.7	470.5	474.3	474.9	475.1	478.9	479.9	481.4	482.1	486.2	474.8
2012	474.7	473.5	475.8	479.0	483.5	489.7	490.9	493.2	496.4	496.2	498.2	505.4	488.0
2013	492.7	494.8	493.8	494.3	498.7	500.5	504.4	508.4	508.8	511.2	516.4	522.0	503.8
2014	507.9	508.9	507.1	511.1	518.6	521.8	523.2	529.7	534.6	538.4	544.2	553.7	524.9
2015	539.3	536.0	541.8	542.0	546.9	550.6	559.6	566.2	568.3	573.4	581.5	588.1	557.8
2016	570.6	569.3	573.3	580.6	584.6	584.7	593.8	600.3	603.4	612.4	627.2	638.1	594.9
2017	614.5	606.5	612.6	612.9	619.3	622.6	628.0	636.8	640.5	649.1	666.9	677.4	632.3
2018	648.0	643.5	647.0	649.4	652.8	658.8	662.7	667.3	672.3	677.1	690.4	698.8	664.0
Information													
2010	424.8	424.8	428.0	420.0	421.7	427.9	429.0	433.4	433.1	427.6	431.6	438.5	428.4
2011	430.6	430.9	432.3	427.8	427.6	429.8	431.4	433.1	429.5	431.3	429.5	433.3	430.6
2012	426.6	427.6	430.4	433.0	432.1	432.3	437.6	439.8	435.3	440.3	446.6	450.8	436.0
2013	439.9	442.7	444.7	445.3	445.4	449.8	448.0	451.7	451.4	455.1	461.8	461.5	449.8
2014	454.5	454.4	457.5	461.1	458.8	461.0	462.8	468.9	467.8	472.0	471.9	474.1	463.7
2015	467.2	476.4	480.1	480.5	480.9	489.0	489.7	493.3	494.1	501.9	505.2	505.4	488.6
2016	510.7	519.3	518.2	527.9	532.6	528.9	528.4	531.9	528.9	525.4	534.7	533.5	526.7
2017	516.0	538.0	521.2	520.0	520.5	524.8	528.2	531.0	534.5	537.3	539.4	547.4	529.9
2018	536.2	546.7	544.9	531.4	530.1	541.7	537.6	545.7	544.6	558.6	553.1	553.8	543.7

1. Employment by Industry: California, 2010–2018—*Continued*

(Numbers in thousands, not seasonally adjusted)

Industry and year	January	February	March	April	May	June	July	August	September	October	November	December	Annual average
Financial Activities													
2010	755.3	756.5	757.9	757.5	757.3	759.7	759.6	759.4	757.5	761.4	759.7	763.9	758.8
2011	756.9	758.7	759.5	757.3	758.3	761.1	761.4	761.9	760.3	761.8	761.9	766.2	760.4
2012	759.8	763.5	767.4	765.7	768.9	772.8	775.5	776.3	773.6	777.8	778.5	782.5	771.9
2013	773.4	776.8	777.5	779.6	782.3	783.8	786.0	785.7	780.0	783.4	782.7	783.4	781.2
2014	773.7	774.6	774.5	776.1	779.7	782.7	783.7	784.4	780.7	784.6	787.0	789.7	781.0
2015	782.9	786.0	786.6	792.2	796.9	799.7	808.9	809.3	805.0	812.9	813.3	815.3	800.8
2016	808.6	811.3	810.9	818.5	820.4	820.3	828.8	828.6	824.5	827.2	828.4	830.1	821.5
2017	821.7	823.4	823.3	826.5	830.3	831.6	835.9	834.8	830.7	836.5	835.9	839.6	830.9
2018	831.3	834.4	832.8	835.5	837.2	838.8	841.0	840.3	832.6	836.6	837.4	837.1	836.3
Professional and Business Services													
2010	2,016.6	2,038.1	2,048.4	2,069.5	2,069.6	2,088.1	2,091.8	2,104.6	2,099.7	2,134.8	2,132.8	2,134.4	2,085.7
2011	2,078.5	2,102.0	2,108.9	2,117.1	2,119.1	2,128.7	2,148.4	2,161.9	2,173.1	2,188.4	2,195.3	2,201.3	2,143.6
2012	2,166.4	2,198.9	2,214.0	2,219.5	2,228.8	2,250.9	2,252.4	2,272.1	2,274.1	2,304.1	2,315.7	2,317.2	2,251.2
2013	2,268.3	2,299.3	2,311.0	2,324.9	2,329.5	2,336.9	2,355.4	2,378.5	2,376.9	2,394.9	2,407.8	2,406.9	2,349.2
2014	2,360.6	2,380.5	2,393.0	2,401.5	2,410.4	2,416.9	2,421.0	2,445.7	2,444.8	2,479.6	2,493.0	2,497.3	2,428.7
2015	2,427.0	2,441.0	2,454.8	2,458.4	2,458.2	2,468.8	2,500.1	2,515.3	2,507.1	2,549.4	2,563.3	2,569.1	2,492.7
2016	2,498.1	2,514.5	2,499.4	2,520.4	2,512.8	2,518.9	2,540.5	2,550.1	2,555.5	2,564.9	2,568.3	2,563.5	2,533.9
2017	2,509.4	2,533.7	2,550.0	2,548.4	2,561.4	2,579.6	2,599.2	2,611.4	2,608.2	2,627.5	2,642.5	2,641.8	2,584.4
2018	2,594.6	2,619.9	2,629.4	2,641.7	2,643.0	2,657.4	2,669.9	2,689.1	2,683.6	2,711.7	2,714.6	2,709.1	2,663.7
Education and Health Services													
2010	2,103.0	2,120.8	2,127.7	2,148.0	2,145.2	2,128.0	2,099.7	2,101.8	2,129.9	2,152.5	2,159.9	2,169.4	2,132.2
2011	2,135.2	2,160.8	2,168.8	2,174.1	2,171.7	2,151.5	2,119.0	2,124.6	2,159.0	2,183.8	2,196.8	2,210.8	2,163.0
2012	2,181.3	2,218.3	2,236.2	2,233.8	2,238.7	2,223.6	2,191.0	2,207.2	2,232.4	2,265.5	2,276.5	2,290.0	2,232.9
2013	2,265.5	2,297.8	2,310.1	2,319.1	2,320.9	2,291.4	2,264.4	2,280.1	2,304.2	2,339.1	2,354.6	2,360.3	2,309.0
2014	2,333.4	2,363.6	2,375.1	2,374.5	2,377.7	2,355.8	2,334.8	2,356.9	2,384.8	2,418.5	2,429.6	2,433.8	2,378.2
2015	2,410.2	2,440.2	2,450.8	2,459.5	2,463.4	2,441.2	2,434.7	2,446.3	2,472.8	2,511.3	2,521.4	2,527.8	2,465.0
2016	2,494.7	2,526.7	2,532.4	2,553.9	2,557.3	2,535.4	2,515.6	2,524.6	2,557.3	2,605.0	2,615.5	2,621.3	2,553.3
2017	2,592.2	2,628.4	2,645.6	2,648.7	2,655.7	2,636.9	2,609.6	2,627.8	2,659.3	2,693.9	2,704.4	2,706.7	2,650.8
2018	2,680.3	2,711.4	2,722.9	2,726.6	2,728.5	2,715.1	2,690.8	2,713.2	2,729.5	2,762.2	2,763.7	2,774.1	2,726.5
Leisure and Hospitality													
2010	1,440.3	1,449.5	1,462.4	1,496.2	1,509.4	1,526.2	1,533.0	1,535.1	1,522.1	1,514.9	1,503.9	1,516.0	1,500.8
2011	1,475.9	1,490.2	1,505.6	1,523.6	1,540.0	1,553.4	1,564.2	1,568.9	1,560.2	1,545.8	1,543.4	1,545.4	1,534.7
2012	1,518.9	1,536.9	1,556.7	1,582.0	1,605.0	1,625.5	1,632.4	1,641.2	1,626.0	1,615.2	1,610.5	1,615.9	1,597.2
2013	1,588.4	1,610.6	1,632.9	1,657.2	1,682.9	1,702.8	1,709.1	1,714.3	1,700.6	1,697.4	1,695.8	1,705.4	1,674.8
2014	1,676.6	1,698.5	1,719.4	1,742.7	1,767.6	1,786.4	1,791.0	1,799.9	1,780.8	1,774.0	1,768.1	1,772.5	1,756.5
2015	1,743.8	1,767.8	1,787.1	1,811.7	1,836.2	1,851.8	1,865.9	1,869.3	1,854.2	1,853.7	1,845.0	1,852.9	1,828.3
2016	1,823.2	1,846.1	1,858.9	1,893.9	1,909.8	1,923.8	1,940.2	1,941.5	1,925.2	1,923.8	1,914.4	1,916.4	1,901.4
2017	1,873.6	1,897.3	1,923.4	1,945.4	1,967.4	1,988.7	1,990.9	1,989.9	1,964.9	1,965.2	1,956.6	1,957.2	1,951.7
2018	1,916.8	1,944.5	1,962.2	1,984.9	2,001.5	2,015.3	2,022.1	2,019.1	1,992.5	1,984.3	1,990.1	2,000.2	1,986.1
Other Services													
2010	474.0	476.6	479.8	483.0	486.3	489.2	486.8	484.2	484.6	488.7	486.2	484.0	483.6
2011	478.6	484.0	485.1	492.3	494.4	495.0	496.1	495.3	497.0	498.0	496.6	496.5	492.4
2012	488.9	494.7	497.9	501.3	506.9	510.8	506.2	505.9	507.2	509.3	507.1	506.1	503.5
2013	499.7	506.8	509.1	513.9	516.5	519.1	517.3	518.7	518.7	521.7	523.0	521.5	515.5
2014	519.8	526.1	529.0	535.2	538.8	540.7	536.7	538.2	538.3	539.5	538.4	536.7	534.8
2015	529.6	535.0	537.2	542.4	546.0	546.8	548.6	547.0	547.1	549.5	548.2	546.2	543.6
2016	540.1	547.1	547.0	553.2	554.5	554.5	558.0	557.2	558.7	562.2	557.6	555.0	553.8
2017	546.2	553.1	558.1	564.8	568.5	571.1	568.3	568.2	568.8	569.5	567.0	565.9	564.1
2018	558.5	565.5	566.6	572.4	575.9	577.8	577.6	576.8	573.9	575.2	574.8	570.7	572.1
Government													
2010	2,444.2	2,460.0	2,480.2	2,526.3	2,572.1	2,531.4	2,330.2	2,310.6	2,370.5	2,447.6	2,465.2	2,442.7	2,448.4
2011	2,424.3	2,445.6	2,469.2	2,469.6	2,469.8	2,457.5	2,278.3	2,272.6	2,336.4	2,407.9	2,426.0	2,401.6	2,404.9
2012	2,382.4	2,408.3	2,428.1	2,425.7	2,433.6	2,425.8	2,251.7	2,257.4	2,317.5	2,385.8	2,406.7	2,392.1	2,376.3
2013	2,363.3	2,391.4	2,412.7	2,412.3	2,422.9	2,413.4	2,238.9	2,271.8	2,335.7	2,399.2	2,423.8	2,406.2	2,374.3
2014	2,392.9	2,415.0	2,439.9	2,451.5	2,462.6	2,451.5	2,279.2	2,309.1	2,381.0	2,450.8	2,473.9	2,460.3	2,414.0
2015	2,446.2	2,466.0	2,485.6	2,496.2	2,502.6	2,497.0	2,330.5	2,360.8	2,435.6	2,502.3	2,521.5	2,511.2	2,463.0
2016	2,490.8	2,513.0	2,540.8	2,547.3	2,560.2	2,544.8	2,381.7	2,413.2	2,493.3	2,557.1	2,577.2	2,569.2	2,515.7
2017	2,543.5	2,565.3	2,586.1	2,605.1	2,617.9	2,603.8	2,420.5	2,447.0	2,536.8	2,602.8	2,623.4	2,614.2	2,563.9
2018	2,587.3	2,606.7	2,626.9	2,630.7	2,641.3	2,632.6	2,430.2	2,463.6	2,541.3	2,617.8	2,641.2	2,628.6	2,587.4

2. Average Weekly Hours by Selected Industry: California, 2014–2018

(Not seasonally adjusted)

Industry and year	January	February	March	April	May	June	July	August	September	October	November	December	Annual average
Total Private													
2014	33.9	34.9	34.8	34.2	34.2	35.0	34.2	34.5	34.3	34.3	35.0	34.2	34.5
2015	34.1	34.9	35.0	34.4	34.3	34.5	34.5	35.4	34.4	34.5	35.1	34.5	34.6
2016	34.2	34.3	34.1	34.3	34.9	34.3	34.4	34.4	34.3	35.0	34.1	34.2	34.4
2017	34.5	33.9	34.2	34.8	34.3	34.4	35.2	34.6	34.4	35.1	34.5	34.5	34.5
2018	34.0	34.3	34.2	35.1	34.4	34.6	35.0	34.4	35.1	34.3	34.1	35.0	34.5
Goods Producing													
2014	38.2	38.6	38.9	38.6	38.9	38.9	38.3	38.9	38.8	38.8	39.0	38.1	38.7
2015	38.5	38.8	39.1	38.8	38.6	38.9	38.9	39.6	38.2	39.3	39.2	39.3	38.9
2016	38.5	38.5	38.3	38.8	38.8	38.9	38.7	38.9	38.8	39.1	38.4	38.4	38.7
2017	37.5	37.6	38.5	38.4	38.8	39.1	39.0	39.2	39.0	39.2	38.8	39.2	38.7
2018	37.8	38.9	38.4	39.3	39.0	39.0	39.1	39.2	39.4	39.1	38.2	39.2	38.9
Construction													
2014	35.8	36.0	36.5	36.2	36.9	36.7	36.2	36.9	36.5	36.7	36.2	34.9	36.3
2015	36.5	36.6	37.1	36.9	36.5	37.2	37.1	37.7	35.0	37.8	36.9	37.2	36.9
2016	36.2	36.3	35.3	36.7	36.7	37.0	37.0	37.3	36.8	37.4	36.1	36.3	36.6
2017	34.6	35.1	37.0	36.6	37.4	37.6	37.5	37.8	37.5	37.6	37.1	37.7	37.0
2018	34.9	37.1	35.8	37.4	37.4	37.2	37.4	37.5	37.6	37.6	36.1	37.2	36.9
Manufacturing													
2014	39.5	40.1	40.2	40.0	40.2	40.3	39.7	40.2	40.3	40.2	40.8	40.4	40.2
2015	40.0	40.4	40.5	40.2	40.2	40.1	40.2	40.9	40.3	40.3	40.7	40.7	40.4
2016	40.0	39.9	40.2	40.3	40.0	40.3	39.9	40.1	40.2	40.0	39.8	40.1	40.1
2017	39.4	39.3	39.6	39.8	39.8	40.1	40.0	40.0	39.9	40.2	40.0	40.2	39.9
2018	39.7	40.0	40.0	40.4	39.9	40.1	40.2	40.3	40.6	40.2	39.7	40.6	40.1
Trade, Transportation, and Utilities													
2014	34.3	35.3	35.3	35.1	35.2	35.9	35.2	35.6	35.3	34.8	35.2	35.3	35.2
2015	34.4	35.4	35.7	35.2	35.2	35.4	35.5	36.2	35.9	35.3	35.7	35.3	35.4
2016	34.9	35.0	34.8	35.2	35.5	35.2	35.4	35.3	35.2	35.8	34.9	35.3	35.2
2017	35.2	34.9	35.0	35.9	35.5	35.5	36.4	35.7	35.6	35.9	35.7	36.2	35.6
2018	35.3	35.3	35.6	36.3	35.7	35.9	36.4	35.8	36.0	35.1	34.9	35.4	35.6
Information													
2014	37.5	38.9	38.6	37.5	37.0	38.2	36.7	36.8	36.7	36.7	37.8	37.1	37.5
2015	37.2	38.0	37.4	36.7	36.4	36.7	37.3	37.8	36.9	36.9	37.7	36.9	37.2
2016	37.7	37.0	36.9	36.9	37.6	37.1	37.1	37.0	37.3	37.5	37.1	37.0	37.2
2017	38.2	36.8	36.8	37.6	36.7	37.1	38.0	37.0	37.3	38.1	37.3	37.2	37.3
2018	37.5	37.0	37.2	38.0	36.8	37.0	38.1	37.4	38.3	36.9	37.0	38.6	37.5
Financial Activities													
2014	36.3	37.4	37.5	36.4	36.5	37.6	36.5	36.7	36.8	37.0	38.0	37.0	37.0
2015	36.8	37.8	37.8	36.9	36.9	37.0	36.8	38.0	37.0	36.8	37.8	37.0	37.2
2016	36.9	36.9	36.7	36.3	37.2	36.5	36.6	36.6	36.1	37.0	35.7	35.7	36.5
2017	36.6	35.5	35.6	36.8	35.8	36.2	37.3	36.5	36.3	37.3	36.3	36.3	36.4
2018	36.6	36.4	36.4	37.7	36.6	36.7	37.6	36.6	38.0	36.5	36.1	37.0	36.8
Professional and Business Services													
2014	35.4	36.6	36.5	35.7	35.5	36.8	35.8	36.2	35.8	36.0	37.0	35.6	36.1
2015	35.7	36.4	36.9	36.0	35.9	36.2	35.9	37.2	35.8	36.2	37.2	36.2	36.3
2016	35.7	35.9	35.7	36.0	36.8	35.8	35.9	36.0	35.9	37.0	36.0	36.0	36.1
2017	36.7	35.9	36.0	37.0	35.9	35.9	36.9	36.1	36.0	37.1	36.2	36.2	36.3
2018	35.7	36.3	36.0	37.3	36.1	36.2	35.8	35.3	36.5	35.7	35.6	37.0	36.1
Education and Health Services													
2014	33.4	34.1	33.9	33.3	33.1	33.7	33.1	33.0	33.2	33.2	34.0	33.2	33.4
2015	33.3	34.1	33.9	33.1	33.1	33.1	33.1	33.9	33.1	32.8	33.8	32.8	33.3
2016	33.2	33.0	33.2	33.3	33.9	33.1	33.2	33.2	33.3	34.1	33.4	33.3	33.4
2017	34.2	33.5	33.5	34.1	33.5	33.6	34.4	33.6	33.6	34.2	33.7	32.8	33.7
2018	32.9	32.9	32.9	33.9	33.2	33.3	34.1	33.1	34.2	33.5	33.5	34.4	33.5
Leisure and Hospitality													
2014	26.0	27.2	27.3	26.5	26.6	27.6	26.7	27.1	26.5	26.6	27.3	26.3	26.8
2015	26.3	27.4	27.4	26.7	26.7	27.0	27.0	28.0	26.8	26.8	27.3	26.6	27.0
2016	26.4	26.7	26.3	26.4	27.5	26.7	26.9	26.7	25.8	26.7	25.8	25.7	26.5
2017	26.3	25.7	25.9	26.7	26.0	26.1	26.9	26.3	26.0	26.7	25.8	26.0	26.2
2018	25.9	26.2	26.1	26.7	26.2	26.5	27.0	26.5	26.8	26.1	25.9	26.8	26.4
Other Services													
2014	30.9	31.7	31.6	31.0	30.8	31.6	31.2	31.0	31.0	31.2	31.6	30.7	31.2
2015	31.0	32.2	32.4	31.5	31.5	31.6	32.1	33.3	31.6	31.8	32.1	31.6	31.9
2016	31.3	31.6	31.5	31.7	32.6	32.1	32.3	32.5	32.1	33.0	31.8	31.6	32.0
2017	31.9	31.4	32.0	32.4	31.7	32.2	32.8	32.0	31.5	32.1	31.2	31.5	31.9
2018	30.4	31.2	30.6	32.2	31.7	31.7	33.0	32.0	33.0	31.9	31.6	32.6	31.8

3. Average Hourly Earnings by Selected Industry: California, 2014–2018

(Dollars, not seasonally adjusted)

Industry and year	January	February	March	April	May	June	July	August	September	October	November	December	Annual average
Total Private													
2014	27.43	27.60	27.54	27.33	27.24	27.42	27.48	27.31	27.53	27.64	28.01	27.77	27.53
2015	28.03	28.12	28.03	27.95	28.01	27.91	27.95	28.10	27.94	28.16	28.39	28.15	28.06
2016	28.42	28.55	28.48	28.59	28.94	28.60	28.74	28.86	29.11	29.62	29.38	29.39	28.90
2017	29.81	29.73	29.55	29.99	29.75	29.66	30.16	29.89	30.24	30.67	30.26	30.28	30.00
2018	30.48	30.53	30.41	30.71	30.53	30.46	31.04	30.86	31.35	31.30	31.35	31.94	30.92
Goods Producing													
2014	29.54	29.49	29.49	29.46	29.29	29.41	29.69	29.37	29.50	29.53	29.65	29.98	29.53
2015	29.78	29.52	29.53	29.55	29.56	29.52	29.60	29.52	29.57	29.83	29.90	30.01	29.66
2016	30.08	29.87	29.90	30.00	30.38	30.27	30.42	30.52	30.68	31.07	30.94	31.39	30.46
2017	31.65	31.84	31.71	31.92	31.71	31.80	32.33	32.01	32.31	32.60	32.51	32.93	32.12
2018	32.74	32.75	32.76	32.78	32.68	32.78	32.87	32.82	33.17	33.43	33.62	34.31	33.06
Construction													
2014	31.21	31.30	31.37	31.40	31.22	31.17	31.50	31.23	31.42	31.08	31.08	31.65	31.30
2015	31.09	30.81	30.95	31.05	30.73	30.97	31.26	31.31	31.40	31.39	31.59	31.70	31.20
2016	31.67	31.58	31.54	31.43	31.96	32.00	32.41	32.40	32.65	32.74	32.53	33.20	32.19
2017	33.42	33.61	33.55	33.22	33.36	33.42	33.87	33.88	34.19	34.11	34.32	35.09	33.85
2018	34.39	34.46	34.60	34.47	34.51	34.84	35.14	35.34	35.54	35.67	35.61	36.45	35.10
Manufacturing													
2014	28.60	28.45	28.38	28.35	28.18	28.40	28.64	28.23	28.36	28.59	28.76	29.02	28.50
2015	28.94	28.68	28.60	28.60	28.78	28.57	28.50	28.35	28.44	28.77	28.75	28.87	28.65
2016	29.01	28.75	28.86	29.09	29.43	29.25	29.24	29.39	29.47	30.00	29.90	30.19	29.38
2017	30.58	30.71	30.44	31.04	30.55	30.65	31.20	30.69	30.97	31.48	31.18	31.39	30.91
2018	31.58	31.45	31.47	31.48	31.26	31.21	31.13	30.88	31.39	31.74	32.14	32.73	31.54
Trade, Transportation, and Utilities													
2014	21.70	21.80	21.73	21.49	21.38	21.53	21.54	21.52	21.85	21.94	22.18	21.45	21.68
2015	22.54	22.47	22.13	22.26	22.48	22.33	22.36	22.63	22.42	22.67	22.80	22.54	22.47
2016	22.82	23.06	22.77	23.15	23.39	23.07	23.21	23.27	23.45	24.09	23.70	23.63	23.31
2017	24.31	23.83	23.61	24.06	23.67	23.60	23.99	23.59	23.60	23.86	23.36	23.41	23.74
2018	23.58	23.47	23.27	23.68	23.61	23.47	23.79	23.67	23.99	23.90	23.87	24.20	23.71
Information													
2014	40.79	41.06	41.02	40.61	40.31	40.69	40.77	40.66	40.50	41.17	41.44	40.82	40.82
2015	41.02	41.90	41.99	42.24	42.32	41.62	41.34	42.11	41.50	41.36	41.60	41.11	41.67
2016	40.61	40.84	40.50	40.52	41.52	40.50	40.60	40.64	41.03	41.98	41.12	41.06	40.91
2017	41.84	42.02	42.20	43.36	43.15	42.78	43.01	42.72	43.88	44.97	43.63	43.47	43.10
2018	43.95	44.72	44.73	45.88	45.76	45.41	46.09	45.65	47.13	47.08	46.86	48.11	45.97
Financial Activities													
2014	32.27	32.95	33.07	32.83	32.72	33.39	33.69	33.04	33.10	33.45	34.00	33.47	33.17
2015	33.90	34.09	34.28	33.52	33.44	33.28	33.09	33.31	33.17	33.40	34.15	33.68	33.61
2016	33.60	34.39	34.05	34.25	35.44	33.62	33.87	34.83	35.52	36.30	36.23	35.46	34.80
2017	35.43	35.40	34.79	36.06	35.99	35.83	36.84	36.77	37.01	38.31	37.39	37.28	36.44
2018	37.61	38.14	38.07	38.21	38.23	37.01	37.90	38.21	38.58	39.33	39.00	39.32	38.30
Professional and Business Services													
2014	34.59	35.12	35.09	34.59	34.65	35.02	34.88	34.48	34.72	34.53	35.49	35.29	34.88
2015	35.16	35.80	35.85	35.55	35.75	35.62	35.90	36.05	35.56	35.57	36.20	35.29	35.70
2016	36.16	36.42	36.48	36.51	37.30	36.72	37.10	37.02	37.27	38.25	37.78	37.14	37.02
2017	38.19	37.88	37.68	38.39	37.83	37.58	38.37	37.86	38.38	39.14	38.43	38.54	38.20
2018	38.75	38.83	38.61	39.43	39.02	38.97	41.11	40.06	40.88	40.06	40.34	41.31	39.79
Education and Health Services													
2014	28.05	28.07	27.94	27.88	27.90	27.89	27.90	27.94	28.04	28.16	28.39	28.45	28.05
2015	28.40	28.32	28.07	28.11	28.00	28.05	28.16	28.23	28.10	28.41	28.35	28.63	28.24
2016	28.45	28.50	28.52	28.51	28.49	28.69	28.75	28.77	29.00	29.09	29.05	29.68	28.80
2017	29.25	29.37	29.40	29.67	29.68	29.71	30.06	29.81	30.23	30.30	30.31	29.98	29.82
2018	30.34	30.11	30.05	29.89	29.96	30.26	30.46	30.43	30.42	30.53	30.67	31.07	30.35
Leisure and Hospitality													
2014	15.18	15.25	15.20	15.19	15.35	15.29	15.42	15.49	15.64	15.69	15.88	15.95	15.46
2015	15.92	16.05	16.06	16.15	16.20	16.13	16.03	16.10	16.24	16.28	16.33	16.43	16.16
2016	16.73	16.80	16.88	17.06	17.12	17.11	17.12	17.21	17.09	17.10	17.12	17.33	17.06
2017	17.46	17.58	17.51	17.56	17.71	17.58	17.63	17.70	17.87	17.89	17.95	18.11	17.71
2018	18.04	18.07	18.06	18.36	18.19	18.13	18.30	18.50	18.84	18.68	18.75	19.10	18.42
Other Services													
2014	22.35	22.27	22.28	22.41	22.07	22.45	22.51	22.57	22.85	22.97	23.25	23.26	22.60
2015	23.28	23.37	23.52	23.16	23.47	23.33	22.96	23.32	23.66	23.49	23.59	23.30	23.37
2016	23.75	23.62	23.83	23.48	23.37	22.98	22.91	23.12	23.23	23.90	23.91	24.34	23.53
2017	25.19	24.99	24.74	25.37	25.25	24.86	25.70	25.85	26.22	26.50	26.32	26.30	25.61
2018	26.48	26.42	26.66	26.36	25.99	25.95	26.00	26.06	26.63	26.59	26.90	27.65	26.47

4. Average Weekly Earnings by Selected Industry: California, 2014–2018

(Dollars, not seasonally adjusted)

Industry and year	January	February	March	April	May	June	July	August	September	October	November	December	Annual average
Total Private													
2014	929.88	963.24	958.39	934.69	931.61	959.70	939.82	942.20	944.28	948.05	980.35	949.73	949.79
2015	955.82	981.39	981.05	961.48	960.74	962.90	964.28	994.74	961.14	971.52	996.49	971.18	970.88
2016	971.96	979.27	971.17	980.64	1,010.01	980.98	988.66	992.78	998.47	1,036.70	1,001.86	1,005.14	994.16
2017	1,028.45	1,007.85	1,010.61	1,043.65	1,020.43	1,020.30	1,061.63	1,034.19	1,040.26	1,076.52	1,043.97	1,044.66	1,035.00
2018	1,036.32	1,047.18	1,040.02	1,077.92	1,050.23	1,053.92	1,086.40	1,061.58	1,100.39	1,073.59	1,069.04	1,117.90	1,066.74
Goods Producing													
2014	1,128.43	1,138.31	1,147.16	1,137.16	1,139.38	1,144.05	1,137.13	1,142.49	1,144.60	1,145.76	1,156.35	1,142.24	1,142.81
2015	1,146.53	1,145.38	1,154.62	1,146.54	1,141.02	1,148.33	1,151.44	1,168.99	1,129.57	1,172.32	1,172.08	1,179.39	1,153.77
2016	1,158.08	1,150.00	1,145.17	1,164.00	1,178.74	1,177.50	1,177.25	1,187.23	1,190.38	1,214.84	1,188.10	1,205.38	1,178.80
2017	1,186.88	1,197.18	1,220.84	1,225.73	1,230.35	1,243.38	1,260.87	1,254.79	1,260.09	1,277.92	1,261.39	1,290.86	1,243.04
2018	1,237.57	1,273.98	1,257.98	1,288.25	1,274.52	1,278.42	1,285.22	1,286.54	1,306.90	1,307.11	1,284.28	1,344.95	1,286.03
Construction													
2014	1,117.32	1,126.80	1,145.01	1,136.68	1,152.02	1,143.94	1,140.30	1,152.39	1,146.83	1,140.64	1,125.10	1,104.59	1,136.19
2015	1,134.79	1,127.65	1,148.25	1,145.75	1,121.65	1,152.08	1,159.75	1,180.39	1,099.00	1,186.54	1,165.67	1,179.24	1,151.28
2016	1,146.45	1,146.35	1,113.36	1,153.48	1,172.93	1,184.00	1,199.17	1,208.52	1,201.52	1,224.48	1,174.33	1,205.16	1,178.15
2017	1,156.33	1,179.71	1,241.35	1,215.85	1,247.66	1,256.59	1,270.13	1,280.66	1,282.13	1,282.54	1,273.27	1,322.89	1,252.45
2018	1,200.21	1,278.47	1,238.68	1,289.18	1,290.67	1,296.05	1,314.24	1,325.25	1,336.30	1,341.19	1,285.52	1,355.94	1,295.19
Manufacturing													
2014	1,129.70	1,140.85	1,140.88	1,134.00	1,132.84	1,144.52	1,137.01	1,134.85	1,142.91	1,149.32	1,173.41	1,172.41	1,145.70
2015	1,157.60	1,158.67	1,158.30	1,149.72	1,156.96	1,145.66	1,145.70	1,159.52	1,146.13	1,159.43	1,170.13	1,175.01	1,157.46
2016	1,160.40	1,147.13	1,160.17	1,172.33	1,186.03	1,178.78	1,166.68	1,178.54	1,184.69	1,209.00	1,196.00	1,201.56	1,178.14
2017	1,204.85	1,206.90	1,205.42	1,235.39	1,215.89	1,229.07	1,248.00	1,227.60	1,235.70	1,265.50	1,247.20	1,261.88	1,233.31
2018	1,253.73	1,258.00	1,258.80	1,271.79	1,247.27	1,251.52	1,251.43	1,244.46	1,274.43	1,275.95	1,275.96	1,328.84	1,264.75
Trade, Transportation, and Utilities													
2014	744.31	769.54	767.07	754.30	752.58	772.93	758.21	766.11	771.31	763.51	780.74	757.19	763.14
2015	775.38	795.44	790.04	783.55	791.30	790.48	793.78	819.21	804.88	800.25	813.96	795.66	795.44
2016	796.42	807.10	792.40	814.88	830.35	812.06	821.63	821.43	825.44	862.42	827.13	834.14	820.51
2017	855.71	831.67	826.35	863.75	840.29	837.80	873.24	842.16	840.16	856.57	833.95	847.44	845.14
2018	832.37	828.49	828.41	859.58	842.88	842.57	865.96	847.39	863.64	838.89	833.06	856.68	844.08
Information													
2014	1,529.63	1,597.23	1,583.37	1,522.88	1,491.47	1,554.36	1,496.26	1,496.29	1,486.35	1,510.94	1,566.43	1,514.42	1,530.75
2015	1,525.94	1,592.20	1,570.43	1,550.21	1,540.45	1,527.45	1,541.98	1,591.76	1,531.35	1,526.18	1,568.32	1,516.96	1,550.12
2016	1,531.00	1,511.08	1,494.45	1,495.19	1,561.15	1,502.55	1,506.26	1,503.68	1,530.42	1,574.25	1,525.55	1,519.22	1,521.85
2017	1,598.29	1,546.34	1,552.96	1,630.34	1,583.61	1,587.14	1,634.38	1,580.64	1,636.72	1,713.36	1,627.40	1,617.08	1,607.63
2018	1,648.13	1,654.64	1,663.96	1,743.44	1,683.97	1,680.17	1,756.03	1,707.31	1,805.08	1,737.25	1,733.82	1,857.05	1,723.88
Financial Activities													
2014	1,171.40	1,232.33	1,240.13	1,195.01	1,194.28	1,255.46	1,229.69	1,212.57	1,218.08	1,237.65	1,292.00	1,238.39	1,227.29
2015	1,247.52	1,288.60	1,295.78	1,236.89	1,233.94	1,231.36	1,217.71	1,265.78	1,227.29	1,229.12	1,290.87	1,246.16	1,250.29
2016	1,239.84	1,268.99	1,249.64	1,243.28	1,318.37	1,227.13	1,239.64	1,274.78	1,282.27	1,343.10	1,293.41	1,265.92	1,270.20
2017	1,296.74	1,256.70	1,238.52	1,327.01	1,288.44	1,297.05	1,374.13	1,342.11	1,343.46	1,428.96	1,357.26	1,353.26	1,326.42
2018	1,376.53	1,388.30	1,385.75	1,440.52	1,399.22	1,358.27	1,425.04	1,398.49	1,466.04	1,435.55	1,407.90	1,454.84	1,409.44
Professional and Business Services													
2014	1,224.49	1,285.39	1,280.79	1,234.86	1,230.08	1,288.74	1,248.70	1,248.18	1,242.98	1,243.08	1,313.13	1,256.32	1,259.17
2015	1,255.21	1,303.12	1,322.87	1,279.80	1,283.43	1,289.44	1,288.81	1,341.06	1,273.05	1,287.63	1,346.64	1,277.50	1,295.91
2016	1,290.91	1,307.48	1,302.34	1,314.36	1,372.64	1,314.58	1,331.89	1,332.72	1,337.99	1,415.25	1,360.08	1,337.04	1,336.42
2017	1,401.57	1,359.89	1,356.48	1,420.43	1,358.10	1,349.12	1,415.85	1,366.75	1,381.68	1,452.09	1,391.17	1,395.15	1,386.66
2018	1,383.38	1,409.53	1,389.96	1,470.74	1,408.62	1,410.71	1,471.74	1,414.12	1,492.12	1,430.14	1,436.10	1,528.47	1,436.42
Education and Health Services													
2014	936.87	957.19	947.17	928.40	923.49	939.89	923.49	922.02	930.93	934.91	965.26	944.54	936.87
2015	945.72	965.71	951.57	930.44	926.80	928.46	932.10	957.00	930.11	931.85	958.23	939.06	940.39
2016	944.54	940.50	946.86	949.38	965.81	949.64	954.50	955.16	965.70	991.97	970.27	988.34	961.92
2017	1,000.35	983.90	984.90	1,011.75	994.28	998.26	1,034.06	1,001.62	1,015.73	1,036.26	1,021.45	983.34	1,004.93
2018	998.19	990.62	988.65	1,013.27	994.67	1,007.66	1,038.69	1,007.23	1,040.36	1,022.76	1,027.45	1,068.81	1,016.73
Leisure and Hospitality													
2014	394.68	414.80	414.96	402.54	408.31	422.00	411.71	419.78	414.46	417.35	433.52	419.49	414.33
2015	418.70	439.77	440.04	431.21	432.54	435.51	432.81	450.80	435.23	436.30	445.81	437.04	436.32
2016	441.67	448.56	443.94	450.38	470.80	456.84	460.53	459.51	440.92	456.57	441.70	445.38	452.09
2017	459.20	451.81	453.51	468.85	460.46	458.84	474.25	465.51	464.62	477.66	463.11	470.86	464.00
2018	467.24	473.43	471.37	490.21	476.58	480.45	494.10	490.25	504.91	487.55	485.63	511.88	486.29
Other Services													
2014	690.62	705.96	704.05	694.71	679.76	709.42	702.31	699.67	708.35	716.66	734.70	714.08	705.12
2015	721.68	752.51	762.05	729.54	739.31	737.23	737.02	776.56	747.66	746.98	757.24	736.28	745.50
2016	743.38	746.39	750.65	744.32	761.86	737.66	739.99	751.40	745.68	788.70	760.34	769.14	752.96
2017	803.56	784.69	791.68	821.99	800.43	800.49	842.96	827.20	825.93	850.65	821.18	828.45	816.96
2018	804.99	824.30	815.80	848.79	823.88	822.62	858.00	833.92	878.79	848.22	850.04	901.39	841.75

COLORADO
At a Glance

Population:
  2010 census: 5,029,196
  2018 estimate: 5,695,564

Percent change in population:
  2010–2018: 13.2%

Percent change in total nonfarm employment:
  2010–2018: 22.7%

Industry with the largest growth in employment, 2010–2018 (percent):
  Construction, 49.7%

Industry with the largest decline or smallest growth in employment, 2010–2018 (percent):
  Information, 4.0%

Civilian labor force:
  2010: 2,724,417
  2018: 3,096,358

Unemployment rate and rank among states (highest to lowest):
  2010: 8.7%, 24th
  2018: 3.3%, 37th

Over-the-year change in unemployment rates:
  2016–2017: -0.5%
  2017–2018: 0.6%

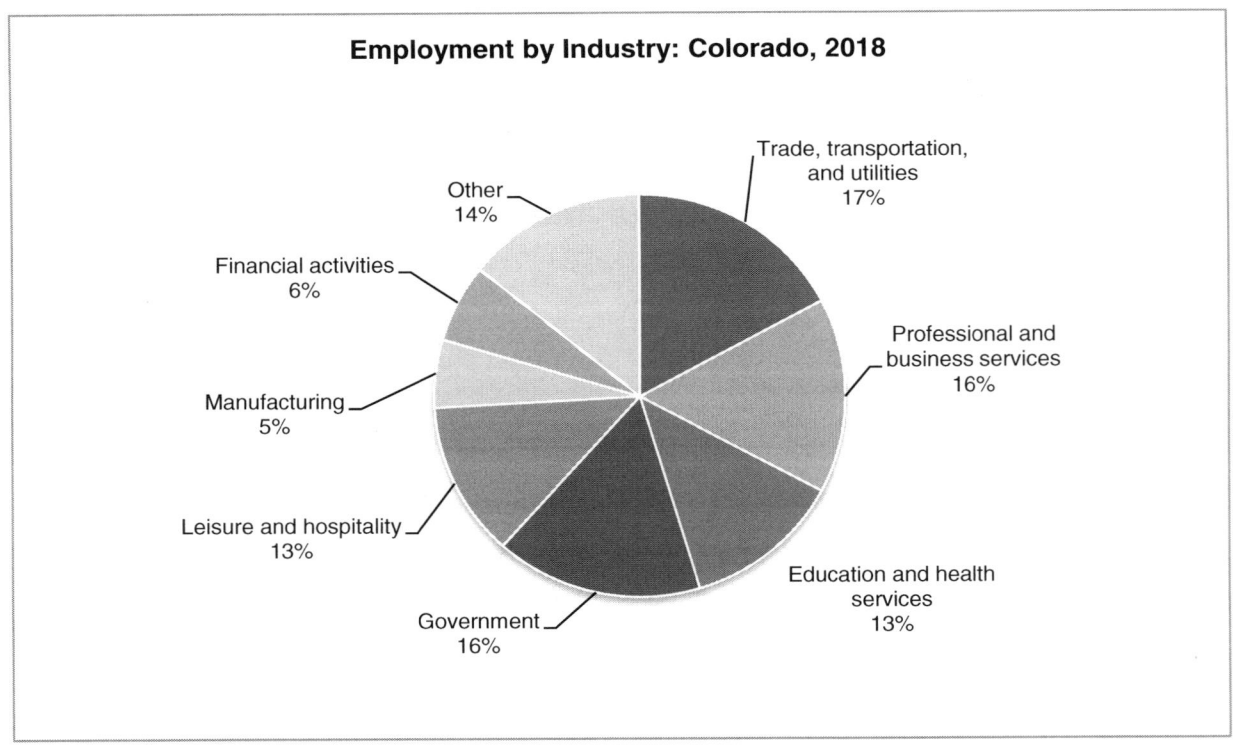

Employment by Industry: Colorado, 2018

Trade, transportation, and utilities 17%
Professional and business services 16%
Education and health services 13%
Government 16%
Leisure and hospitality 13%
Manufacturing 5%
Financial activities 6%
Other 14%

1. Employment by Industry: Colorado, 2010–2018

(Numbers in thousands, not seasonally adjusted)

Industry and year	January	February	March	April	May	June	July	August	September	October	November	December	Annual average
Total Nonfarm													
2010	2,173.6	2,187.2	2,199.9	2,210.6	2,224.4	2,240.0	2,230.2	2,233.2	2,227.6	2,235.1	2,237.4	2,253.6	2,221.1
2011	2,201.8	2,212.1	2,227.7	2,246.8	2,251.4	2,273.4	2,262.1	2,272.9	2,278.8	2,276.4	2,283.4	2,300.5	2,257.3
2012	2,248.4	2,261.9	2,281.2	2,291.4	2,301.8	2,329.3	2,317.9	2,327.7	2,329.0	2,339.9	2,349.7	2,362.3	2,311.7
2013	2,309.9	2,331.0	2,348.4	2,357.3	2,370.1	2,395.3	2,388.3	2,402.2	2,402.0	2,408.0	2,420.1	2,433.6	2,380.5
2014	2,389.7	2,405.1	2,421.9	2,438.6	2,452.6	2,478.0	2,470.5	2,487.1	2,488.0	2,500.2	2,505.2	2,527.1	2,463.7
2015	2,481.4	2,498.3	2,508.7	2,521.7	2,530.6	2,555.3	2,550.3	2,554.8	2,557.1	2,567.0	2,575.5	2,591.6	2,541.0
2016	2,543.2	2,558.4	2,570.0	2,587.0	2,582.2	2,614.4	2,615.5	2,622.0	2,627.5	2,624.6	2,631.1	2,645.2	2,601.8
2017	2,590.8	2,612.5	2,630.8	2,641.6	2,647.2	2,678.4	2,672.2	2,679.5	2,681.0	2,686.4	2,692.7	2,711.7	2,660.4
2018	2,661.1	2,679.8	2,696.4	2,709.3	2,715.4	2,747.9	2,745.8	2,751.7	2,734.8	2,744.8	2,750.4	2,765.8	2,725.3
Total Private													
2010	1,791.6	1,791.8	1,800.5	1,811.0	1,813.2	1,846.0	1,856.3	1,859.7	1,835.2	1,835.3	1,836.5	1,855.5	1,827.7
2011	1,818.9	1,816.7	1,829.8	1,846.9	1,848.6	1,881.6	1,891.0	1,901.1	1,883.9	1,875.7	1,882.1	1,902.3	1,864.9
2012	1,865.1	1,866.0	1,882.1	1,891.1	1,898.0	1,935.9	1,945.3	1,950.6	1,931.3	1,937.0	1,945.0	1,961.1	1,917.4
2013	1,918.7	1,926.1	1,941.0	1,949.3	1,957.6	1,995.2	2,008.1	2,017.2	1,994.4	1,993.7	2,004.4	2,022.7	1,977.4
2014	1,991.2	1,996.2	2,010.2	2,025.8	2,034.9	2,071.8	2,086.4	2,098.6	2,078.0	2,080.9	2,083.6	2,111.1	2,055.7
2015	2,075.4	2,082.0	2,090.1	2,100.6	2,104.2	2,141.2	2,157.2	2,158.6	2,137.8	2,138.9	2,143.8	2,164.6	2,124.5
2016	2,126.2	2,130.4	2,138.6	2,152.5	2,150.7	2,189.9	2,210.1	2,211.2	2,191.1	2,187.9	2,189.3	2,206.2	2,173.7
2017	2,168.4	2,175.7	2,189.2	2,199.9	2,201.4	2,247.3	2,256.4	2,256.4	2,237.2	2,238.7	2,248.2	2,265.6	2,223.7
2018	2,229.9	2,235.5	2,247.8	2,259.5	2,259.8	2,303.6	2,316.9	2,315.6	2,287.2	2,293.9	2,297.2	2,316.3	2,280.3
Goods Producing													
2010	255.0	253.6	254.9	259.3	262.8	268.6	270.8	270.1	268.3	269.2	266.9	265.0	263.7
2011	254.9	253.6	257.5	263.9	266.3	272.6	275.5	277.4	276.0	276.8	275.2	273.1	268.6
2012	265.0	264.5	267.0	271.0	275.9	281.4	283.3	284.3	282.4	284.8	283.3	281.4	277.0
2013	273.6	275.1	278.8	281.8	288.1	295.0	297.6	300.2	298.2	300.8	301.2	299.8	290.9
2014	294.9	295.5	299.2	304.9	311.1	316.9	321.1	322.4	321.5	323.1	322.1	322.0	312.9
2015	314.0	314.2	314.5	317.0	320.0	324.7	326.6	325.5	323.5	323.8	322.0	319.7	320.5
2016	312.2	312.2	314.3	317.4	319.6	324.9	327.8	327.4	326.2	327.2	325.9	324.1	321.6
2017	317.6	319.9	324.1	328.1	331.3	338.9	340.9	341.5	340.0	341.9	341.6	340.6	333.9
2018	335.0	337.2	340.9	344.8	347.6	354.7	355.8	356.1	353.8	353.1	349.3	349.8	348.2
Service-Providing													
2010	1,918.6	1,933.6	1,945.0	1,951.3	1,961.6	1,971.4	1,959.4	1,963.1	1,959.3	1,965.9	1,970.5	1,988.6	1,957.4
2011	1,946.9	1,958.5	1,970.2	1,982.9	1,985.1	2,000.8	1,986.6	1,995.5	2,002.8	1,999.6	2,008.2	2,027.4	1,988.7
2012	1,983.4	1,997.4	2,014.2	2,020.4	2,025.9	2,047.9	2,034.6	2,043.4	2,046.6	2,055.1	2,066.4	2,080.9	2,034.7
2013	2,036.3	2,055.9	2,069.6	2,075.5	2,082.0	2,100.3	2,090.7	2,102.0	2,103.8	2,107.2	2,118.9	2,133.8	2,089.7
2014	2,094.8	2,109.6	2,122.7	2,133.7	2,141.5	2,161.1	2,149.4	2,164.7	2,166.5	2,177.1	2,183.1	2,205.1	2,150.8
2015	2,167.4	2,184.1	2,194.2	2,204.7	2,210.6	2,230.6	2,223.7	2,229.3	2,233.6	2,243.2	2,253.5	2,271.9	2,220.6
2016	2,231.0	2,246.2	2,255.7	2,269.6	2,262.6	2,289.5	2,287.7	2,294.6	2,301.3	2,297.4	2,305.2	2,321.1	2,280.2
2017	2,273.2	2,292.6	2,306.7	2,313.5	2,315.9	2,339.5	2,331.3	2,338.0	2,341.0	2,344.5	2,351.1	2,371.1	2,326.5
2018	2,326.1	2,342.6	2,355.5	2,364.5	2,367.8	2,393.2	2,390.0	2,395.6	2,381.0	2,391.7	2,401.1	2,416.0	2,377.1
Mining and Logging													
2010	22.5	22.8	23.0	23.5	23.9	24.4	25.0	25.2	25.1	25.4	25.5	26.0	24.4
2011	25.7	25.9	26.3	26.8	27.2	27.9	28.5	28.9	28.7	29.5	29.8	30.1	27.9
2012	30.0	30.2	30.3	30.2	30.4	30.7	30.7	30.6	30.1	30.1	29.9	29.9	30.3
2013	29.5	29.6	29.6	29.6	30.0	30.5	30.8	31.2	31.1	31.4	31.6	31.8	30.6
2014	31.8	32.1	32.3	32.7	33.2	33.7	34.5	35.0	35.2	35.8	36.1	36.4	34.1
2015	35.6	34.5	33.1	31.6	31.1	30.7	30.3	29.7	28.9	28.0	27.5	27.1	30.7
2016	26.0	25.4	24.6	23.7	23.3	23.1	22.8	22.9	22.9	22.9	23.0	23.4	23.7
2017	23.5	24.0	24.4	24.9	25.4	26.2	26.6	26.8	26.9	27.1	27.4	27.5	25.9
2018	27.3	27.5	28.0	28.0	28.1	28.5	28.6	28.7	28.5	28.7	28.7	29.0	28.3
Construction													
2010	110.3	108.6	109.6	112.9	115.3	119.3	120.6	119.6	118.2	118.3	115.8	113.1	115.1
2011	104.3	102.7	105.3	110.1	111.6	116.0	117.5	118.6	117.5	117.5	115.7	113.0	112.5
2012	106.5	105.4	107.4	111.0	115.1	119.2	120.5	121.4	120.5	122.4	121.1	119.4	115.8
2013	113.4	114.4	117.5	120.3	125.8	131.1	133.2	135.1	133.7	135.8	135.7	134.0	127.5
2014	130.0	130.0	133.0	137.5	142.2	146.3	148.8	149.3	148.0	148.7	146.8	146.1	142.2
2015	139.8	140.6	141.9	145.6	148.4	151.9	154.0	153.5	152.6	154.0	152.3	150.4	148.8
2016	145.0	145.2	148.0	151.9	154.2	158.8	160.9	160.8	160.3	161.1	159.7	157.1	155.3
2017	151.9	153.6	156.7	159.8	162.2	167.3	168.6	169.2	168.3	169.7	169.0	167.5	163.7
2018	162.9	164.6	166.9	170.0	172.7	177.7	178.3	178.6	177.2	175.9	171.7	170.7	172.3

1. Employment by Industry: Colorado, 2010–2018—*Continued*

(Numbers in thousands, not seasonally adjusted)

Industry and year	January	February	March	April	May	June	July	August	September	October	November	December	Annual average
Manufacturing													
2010	122.2	122.2	122.3	122.9	123.6	124.9	125.2	125.3	125.0	125.5	125.6	125.9	124.2
2011	124.9	125.0	125.9	127.0	127.5	128.7	129.5	129.9	129.8	129.8	129.7	130.0	128.1
2012	128.5	128.9	129.3	129.8	130.4	131.5	132.1	132.3	131.8	132.3	132.3	132.1	130.9
2013	130.7	131.1	131.7	131.9	132.3	133.4	133.6	133.9	133.4	133.6	133.9	134.0	132.8
2014	133.1	133.4	133.9	134.7	135.7	136.9	137.8	138.1	138.3	138.6	139.2	139.5	136.6
2015	138.6	139.1	139.5	139.8	140.5	142.1	142.3	142.3	142.0	141.8	142.2	142.2	141.0
2016	141.2	141.6	141.7	141.8	142.1	143.0	144.1	143.7	143.0	143.2	143.2	143.6	142.7
2017	142.2	142.3	143.0	143.4	143.7	145.4	145.7	145.5	144.8	145.1	145.2	145.6	144.3
2018	144.8	145.1	146.0	146.8	146.8	148.5	148.9	148.8	148.1	148.5	148.9	150.1	147.6
Trade, Transportation, and Utilities													
2010	392.9	391.0	391.5	392.6	394.5	398.5	399.9	400.4	396.4	398.5	404.5	409.4	397.5
2011	395.1	392.5	393.7	397.0	398.9	402.5	403.8	404.6	401.7	403.5	410.7	415.5	401.6
2012	402.5	399.0	401.0	402.5	405.1	409.8	411.1	411.2	409.7	413.3	422.4	426.9	409.5
2013	412.6	410.6	411.7	412.9	415.5	419.9	421.4	423.3	420.6	423.0	432.1	437.8	420.1
2014	424.0	422.3	423.3	425.3	427.8	433.4	434.2	435.5	433.2	436.2	444.5	452.2	432.7
2015	438.2	436.4	437.1	438.7	440.3	445.5	448.3	448.3	445.4	448.9	457.0	463.9	445.7
2016	448.1	445.8	446.1	448.0	449.5	453.1	456.2	456.4	453.7	456.4	463.9	469.9	453.9
2017	456.1	453.3	453.3	454.5	455.2	460.5	462.4	462.8	460.8	463.6	473.7	479.2	461.3
2018	465.7	461.4	462.5	462.7	464.4	469.1	471.7	472.2	469.1	471.2	482.7	484.5	469.8
Wholesale Trade													
2010	90.0	89.8	89.9	90.2	90.4	91.0	91.2	91.2	90.7	91.1	91.1	91.2	90.7
2011	90.4	90.5	90.9	91.4	91.8	92.2	92.5	92.6	92.4	92.2	92.3	92.5	91.8
2012	91.6	91.9	92.5	93.2	93.6	94.4	94.7	94.8	94.6	95.1	95.2	95.6	93.9
2013	94.5	94.9	95.3	95.7	96.1	96.8	96.9	97.0	96.6	97.0	97.3	97.6	96.3
2014	97.0	97.6	97.9	98.6	99.2	99.8	100.3	100.8	100.5	101.0	101.5	102.2	99.7
2015	101.4	101.9	101.9	102.4	102.9	103.3	103.8	103.9	103.5	104.2	104.4	104.7	103.2
2016	103.7	103.9	103.9	104.5	104.6	104.7	105.3	105.0	104.7	105.1	105.2	105.3	104.7
2017	104.8	105.1	105.5	105.8	106.1	106.8	107.0	107.1	106.8	107.0	107.0	107.1	106.3
2018	106.7	107.0	107.2	107.4	107.9	108.8	109.4	109.0	108.6	108.1	108.8	107.3	108.0
Retail Trade													
2010	232.4	230.4	231.0	232.6	234.3	237.4	238.8	238.9	235.7	237.0	242.5	245.3	236.4
2011	234.5	232.4	233.1	235.9	237.3	239.9	240.5	241.3	239.0	240.5	247.0	249.8	239.3
2012	239.5	235.7	237.2	238.1	240.1	243.2	243.9	243.8	242.6	244.4	252.5	255.1	243.0
2013	243.5	241.1	242.1	243.1	245.0	248.4	249.5	250.8	248.6	249.9	257.5	260.9	248.4
2014	249.6	247.4	248.4	249.7	251.0	255.2	255.5	255.8	254.1	256.3	263.2	267.4	254.5
2015	255.7	254.0	255.5	256.8	258.3	262.3	264.2	264.4	262.2	264.7	271.6	275.4	262.1
2016	263.0	261.5	262.6	263.7	265.2	268.1	270.1	270.0	267.7	269.9	276.2	278.6	268.1
2017	267.7	265.0	265.6	266.8	267.5	271.0	272.3	272.2	269.6	271.3	279.0	281.3	270.8
2018	271.3	267.7	268.5	268.6	270.1	272.9	274.8	274.4	270.8	272.3	280.8	280.6	272.7
Transportation and Utilities													
2010	70.5	70.8	70.6	69.8	69.8	70.1	69.9	70.3	70.0	70.4	70.9	72.9	70.5
2011	70.2	69.6	69.7	69.7	69.8	70.4	70.8	70.7	70.3	70.8	71.4	73.2	70.6
2012	71.4	71.4	71.3	71.2	71.4	72.2	72.5	72.6	72.5	73.8	74.7	76.2	72.6
2013	74.6	74.6	74.3	74.1	74.4	74.7	75.0	75.5	75.4	76.1	77.3	79.3	75.4
2014	77.4	77.3	77.0	77.0	77.6	78.4	78.4	78.9	78.6	78.9	79.8	82.6	78.5
2015	81.1	80.5	79.7	79.5	79.1	79.9	80.3	80.0	79.7	80.0	81.0	83.8	80.4
2016	81.4	80.4	79.6	79.8	79.7	80.3	80.8	81.4	81.3	81.4	82.5	86.0	81.2
2017	83.6	83.2	82.2	81.9	81.6	82.7	83.1	83.5	84.4	85.3	87.7	90.8	84.2
2018	87.7	86.7	86.8	86.7	86.4	87.4	87.5	88.8	89.7	90.8	93.1	96.6	89.0
Information													
2010	72.2	71.9	72.0	71.7	71.8	72.3	71.8	72.1	71.5	71.9	72.5	72.5	72.0
2011	72.3	72.2	71.8	71.8	71.6	71.5	71.2	71.1	70.9	70.7	70.8	70.6	71.4
2012	70.2	70.2	70.3	69.7	69.8	70.0	69.6	69.5	69.2	69.4	69.7	69.9	69.8
2013	69.6	69.7	69.7	69.4	69.6	70.2	70.4	70.3	69.7	69.5	70.1	70.1	69.9
2014	70.1	70.2	70.1	69.6	69.8	70.5	71.0	71.2	70.0	70.2	70.5	70.7	70.3
2015	70.3	70.6	70.4	70.0	70.3	70.9	71.3	71.3	70.6	70.6	71.1	71.3	70.7
2016	71.1	71.5	71.5	71.5	71.6	72.0	72.8	72.8	71.8	72.0	72.3	72.1	71.9
2017	71.4	71.7	71.4	71.0	70.8	71.8	71.9	72.0	71.6	72.1	73.3	73.5	71.9
2018	73.8	74.5	74.3	74.7	75.0	75.8	75.8	75.4	74.8	74.7	74.9	74.5	74.9

1. Employment by Industry: Colorado, 2010–2018—*Continued*

(Numbers in thousands, not seasonally adjusted)

Industry and year	January	February	March	April	May	June	July	August	September	October	November	December	Annual average
Financial Activities													
2010	144.9	144.6	144.7	144.3	143.2	144.3	144.7	144.7	143.6	143.8	143.7	145.8	144.4
2011	143.6	143.4	143.5	143.3	142.8	144.0	144.1	144.4	143.7	143.3	144.3	146.3	143.9
2012	144.4	144.7	145.4	145.3	145.2	146.8	147.3	147.7	146.8	147.9	148.3	150.3	146.7
2013	148.6	149.5	150.3	150.1	149.7	151.3	152.1	152.2	151.3	151.5	151.9	153.4	151.0
2014	151.5	152.0	152.2	152.5	152.4	153.7	154.7	155.1	154.1	155.0	155.7	157.8	153.9
2015	156.2	156.9	157.3	157.4	157.4	159.0	160.2	160.5	159.5	160.4	160.7	162.7	159.0
2016	161.4	161.6	161.8	162.2	162.1	163.9	165.3	165.7	164.6	165.2	165.4	167.0	163.9
2017	165.5	166.1	166.6	167.0	166.9	169.0	169.4	169.2	168.3	169.1	169.3	171.1	168.1
2018	169.4	170.0	170.2	170.4	170.0	171.8	173.0	172.3	170.9	169.8	167.9	170.2	170.5
Professional and Business Services													
2010	319.4	321.1	323.8	329.4	331.5	335.7	337.2	337.5	332.8	334.9	333.6	332.6	330.8
2011	328.6	330.0	330.8	338.8	341.4	344.8	346.4	348.9	346.6	346.7	347.2	347.8	341.5
2012	340.3	342.3	345.0	351.8	355.8	360.9	363.0	365.2	362.7	367.5	365.1	363.7	356.9
2013	356.4	359.6	362.9	368.1	371.6	376.7	378.7	381.3	378.2	380.4	379.2	378.5	372.6
2014	370.2	372.2	374.1	381.0	384.5	390.0	391.5	396.8	393.6	397.0	393.4	394.8	386.6
2015	386.8	388.7	390.0	394.9	397.5	401.4	404.3	405.5	402.3	404.9	402.8	402.0	398.4
2016	393.4	395.0	395.8	403.5	403.8	408.9	413.5	413.2	411.2	412.2	410.4	407.7	405.7
2017	398.5	400.6	403.2	409.6	412.3	417.7	419.6	419.8	417.4	419.8	418.6	415.9	412.8
2018	406.9	411.2	413.1	420.4	423.4	428.7	434.3	433.6	428.7	435.7	435.9	435.6	425.6
Education and Health Services													
2010	258.2	260.5	261.3	262.7	263.6	263.2	262.8	264.3	264.7	267.8	268.6	269.6	263.9
2011	267.2	269.2	270.6	271.7	272.3	271.6	271.1	273.4	274.8	276.4	276.9	279.4	272.9
2012	276.6	279.3	280.1	280.4	280.8	280.5	279.9	281.5	282.6	285.2	286.2	288.2	281.8
2013	280.4	282.7	283.4	284.8	285.2	283.7	283.8	286.2	286.8	289.6	291.5	292.7	285.9
2014	290.3	293.1	294.4	296.6	297.5	296.3	295.9	299.0	299.8	303.3	304.6	305.6	298.0
2015	304.7	307.5	308.8	311.4	312.3	312.0	312.5	314.0	314.7	319.2	320.7	321.4	313.3
2016	318.8	321.3	322.4	325.5	325.7	324.9	325.6	326.9	327.8	329.6	330.1	330.4	325.8
2017	327.9	330.7	332.2	333.9	334.4	334.0	332.8	334.2	334.9	337.1	338.0	338.8	334.1
2018	336.2	338.9	339.7	340.7	341.0	339.8	339.1	340.7	340.0	345.2	342.9	343.0	340.6
Leisure and Hospitality													
2010	256.7	257.0	259.9	259.3	253.7	270.1	275.7	277.2	265.6	257.4	255.0	268.6	263.0
2011	265.4	264.1	269.4	267.0	261.6	279.5	284.1	286.0	275.8	264.6	263.4	275.4	271.4
2012	272.0	271.5	278.1	275.0	269.8	289.3	293.7	294.0	281.6	272.5	274.0	284.3	279.7
2013	281.2	282.6	287.4	285.3	280.3	299.6	305.1	304.7	291.7	281.4	280.7	292.4	289.4
2014	291.7	292.4	297.9	296.3	291.8	309.3	315.3	315.4	304.2	294.0	291.0	305.5	300.4
2015	303.0	305.4	309.2	307.9	303.0	322.6	328.1	327.8	317.0	306.5	305.0	318.4	312.8
2016	316.1	317.4	320.8	318.3	312.0	334.0	339.8	339.5	327.3	316.9	313.5	327.6	323.6
2017	324.9	325.9	330.3	327.7	322.1	345.5	349.6	347.2	335.3	326.3	325.3	337.7	333.2
2018	334.8	333.9	338.0	336.4	328.3	351.5	355.1	353.6	339.0	331.7	331.5	345.4	339.9
Other Services													
2010	92.3	92.1	92.4	91.7	92.1	93.3	93.4	93.4	92.3	91.8	91.7	92.0	92.4
2011	91.8	91.7	92.5	93.4	93.7	95.1	94.8	95.3	94.4	93.7	93.6	94.2	93.7
2012	94.1	94.5	95.2	95.4	95.6	97.2	97.4	97.2	96.3	96.4	96.0	96.4	96.0
2013	96.3	96.3	96.8	96.9	97.6	98.8	99.0	99.0	97.9	97.5	97.7	98.0	97.7
2014	98.5	98.5	99.0	99.6	100.0	101.7	102.7	103.2	101.6	102.1	101.8	102.5	100.9
2015	102.2	102.3	102.8	103.3	103.4	105.1	105.9	105.7	104.8	104.6	104.5	105.2	104.2
2016	105.1	105.6	105.9	106.1	106.4	108.2	109.1	109.3	108.5	108.4	107.8	107.4	107.3
2017	106.5	107.5	108.1	108.1	108.4	109.9	109.8	109.7	108.9	108.8	108.4	108.8	108.6
2018	108.1	108.4	109.1	109.4	110.1	112.2	112.1	111.7	110.9	112.5	112.1	113.3	110.8
Government													
2010	382.0	395.4	399.4	399.6	411.2	394.0	373.9	373.5	392.4	399.8	400.9	398.1	393.4
2011	382.9	395.4	397.9	399.9	402.8	391.8	371.1	371.8	394.9	400.7	401.3	398.2	392.4
2012	383.3	395.9	399.1	400.3	403.8	393.4	372.6	377.1	397.7	402.9	404.7	401.2	394.3
2013	391.2	404.9	407.4	408.0	412.5	400.1	380.2	385.0	407.6	414.3	415.7	410.9	403.2
2014	398.5	408.9	411.7	412.8	417.7	406.2	384.1	388.5	410.0	419.3	421.6	416.0	407.9
2015	406.0	416.3	418.6	421.1	426.4	414.1	393.1	396.2	419.3	428.1	431.7	427.0	416.5
2016	417.0	428.0	431.4	434.5	431.5	424.5	405.4	410.8	436.4	436.7	441.8	439.0	428.1
2017	422.4	436.8	441.6	441.7	445.8	431.1	415.8	423.1	443.8	447.7	444.5	446.1	436.7
2018	431.2	444.3	448.6	449.8	455.6	444.3	428.9	436.1	447.6	450.9	453.2	449.5	445.0

2. Average Weekly Hours by Selected Industry: Colorado, 2014–2018

(Not seasonally adjusted)

Industry and year	January	February	March	April	May	June	July	August	September	October	November	December	Annual average
Total Private													
2014	34.2	35.0	34.9	34.1	34.1	35.2	34.5	34.5	34.3	34.4	34.4	34.1	34.5
2015	33.6	34.4	34.4	33.6	33.7	34.0	34.1	34.8	33.9	33.9	34.0	33.2	34.0
2016	33.4	33.2	33.3	33.2	33.9	33.7	33.8	33.8	33.7	34.2	33.3	33.2	33.5
2017	33.1	32.9	32.9	33.7	33.8	33.8	34.4	33.8	33.5	33.9	33.4	33.3	33.5
2018	33.2	33.3	33.5	33.9	33.9	33.9	34.4	33.8	34.2	33.3	33.0	33.6	33.7
Goods Producing													
2014	38.4	39.3	38.9	38.9	38.8	40.0	39.7	40.3	40.0	40.7	38.9	40.5	39.5
2015	39.3	40.1	40.3	39.4	39.0	40.0	40.0	40.8	39.8	40.2	40.1	40.0	39.9
2016	39.5	39.0	39.1	39.3	39.6	39.9	39.7	39.7	39.8	39.9	39.5	38.1	39.4
2017	38.7	39.0	38.8	39.7	39.6	40.7	40.3	39.9	40.2	40.1	39.9	39.4	39.7
2018	39.0	39.2	39.8	40.1	40.5	40.7	40.3	39.7	40.2	40.2	39.3	40.1	39.9
Construction													
2014	37.7	37.9	38.1	38.5	37.5	39.4	39.8	40.4	39.9	40.9	38.4	40.0	39.1
2015	37.8	38.7	39.0	38.7	37.6	39.4	39.8	40.9	39.0	40.3	39.5	39.9	39.2
2016	38.7	37.9	38.5	38.9	39.7	40.0	39.6	40.1	39.8	39.5	38.8	36.6	39.0
2017	36.7	38.0	37.5	38.1	38.1	39.8	39.1	38.7	38.9	38.5	38.4	37.6	38.3
2018	37.1	36.9	38.2	38.2	39.4	39.6	39.2	39.0	39.1	40.1	38.5	39.3	38.7
Manufacturing													
2014	39.5	40.5	39.5	39.2	40.0	40.3	39.2	39.8	39.8	40.1	40.0	39.5	39.8
2015	39.3	40.3	40.4	39.2	39.7	40.1	39.9	40.2	40.1	39.8	40.0	39.6	39.9
2016	39.8	39.5	39.4	39.6	39.3	39.3	39.5	38.9	39.5	40.0	39.7	39.6	39.5
2017	40.4	39.3	39.3	40.2	39.9	40.2	40.2	40.2	39.8	39.9	39.7	39.5	39.9
2018	39.6	39.5	39.6	39.9	39.8	40.1	39.9	39.4	39.8	39.4	39.7	39.8	39.7
Trade, Transportation, and Utilities													
2014	34.7	35.4	35.1	34.3	34.2	35.1	34.4	34.4	34.4	34.5	34.6	34.6	34.6
2015	33.7	34.6	34.5	33.4	34.0	34.2	34.5	34.7	34.5	34.2	34.3	34.0	34.2
2016	33.7	33.7	33.4	33.4	33.6	33.7	33.6	33.7	33.3	33.8	33.0	33.5	33.5
2017	33.3	33.2	32.9	33.5	32.8	33.2	33.9	33.4	33.2	33.7	33.4	33.3	33.3
2018	33.2	33.3	33.0	33.6	33.9	33.8	34.5	33.6	34.2	33.1	33.2	33.6	33.6
Financial Activities													
2014	36.6	37.2	37.5	36.3	36.2	38.3	37.1	37.0	36.9	37.1	38.6	36.9	37.1
2015	36.8	37.7	37.5	36.5	36.4	36.0	36.1	37.4	36.3	36.1	37.6	36.2	36.7
2016	36.8	36.5	36.3	36.8	37.4	37.1	36.9	36.9	37.0	37.9	37.1	36.5	36.9
2017	37.7	36.6	36.5	37.8	36.5	36.6	37.5	36.9	36.8	37.4	36.8	37.1	37.0
2018	36.8	36.8	36.7	37.7	36.3	36.7	37.6	36.4	37.9	36.9	36.4	37.3	37.0
Professional and Business Services													
2014	36.7	37.8	37.5	37.2	36.8	37.8	36.4	36.6	36.7	36.8	36.8	36.2	36.9
2015	36.2	37.0	37.2	36.5	36.6	36.6	36.6	37.2	36.2	36.2	36.2	35.1	36.5
2016	35.4	35.3	35.3	35.6	36.2	35.9	36.0	36.0	36.5	37.0	36.0	35.8	35.9
2017	35.9	35.3	35.4	36.3	35.5	36.3	36.6	35.9	35.4	35.4	35.0	35.3	35.7
2018	35.4	34.8	35.4	36.1	35.7	36.4	37.0	36.8	37.1	35.9	36.1	36.8	36.1
Education and Health Services													
2014	31.4	31.8	32.0	31.2	31.4	32.1	31.6	31.4	31.3	31.4	32.2	31.6	31.6
2015	31.3	32.0	31.9	31.1	31.1	30.9	30.6	31.4	30.7	30.6	31.4	30.5	31.1
2016	31.1	31.0	31.3	31.1	31.7	30.8	31.5	31.3	31.5	31.7	31.3	31.6	31.3
2017	32.2	31.9	31.9	32.9	32.0	32.2	32.9	32.5	31.9	32.4	32.1	31.9	32.2
2018	31.7	31.7	31.8	32.1	31.7	31.4	31.6	31.1	31.4	30.7	30.9	31.7	31.5
Leisure and Hospitality													
2014	26.6	27.3	28.1	26.1	26.5	27.9	27.9	27.9	26.8	26.4	26.0	25.7	26.9
2015	25.9	26.7	26.9	26.0	26.1	26.6	26.8	27.6	26.1	26.2	25.2	25.0	26.3
2016	25.3	25.5	25.9	24.4	26.1	26.2	26.5	26.4	25.7	26.0	24.8	25.0	25.7
2017	24.7	24.7	25.2	24.2	24.6	26.0	26.7	26.1	25.4	25.6	24.5	24.7	25.2
2018	25.5	25.5	25.6	24.8	25.5	26.0	26.5	26.2	25.8	25.0	23.8	24.6	25.4
Other Services													
2014	34.3	34.7	34.0	33.6	33.3	34.4	33.0	34.1	33.7	32.4	32.3	31.0	33.4
2015	29.8	31.0	31.1	30.1	30.4	32.2	32.3	33.6	32.5	32.7	34.2	32.8	31.9
2016	33.5	33.0	33.0	33.1	34.2	33.3	34.1	34.2	33.7	35.6	33.4	33.7	33.7
2017	33.9	33.5	33.6	35.1	33.8	34.4	36.0	35.2	35.1	36.2	35.4	35.2	34.8
2018	34.7	35.0	34.3	35.6	34.6	34.1	34.0	32.9	33.8	33.0	32.6	33.0	34.0

3. Average Hourly Earnings by Selected Industry: Colorado, 2014–2018

(Dollars , not seasonally adjusted)

Industry and year	January	February	March	April	May	June	July	August	September	October	November	December	Annual average
Total Private													
2014	26.04	26.20	26.39	26.35	26.24	26.39	26.10	26.02	26.34	26.34	26.66	26.44	26.29
2015	26.64	26.74	26.81	26.85	26.82	26.41	26.76	27.00	26.81	27.06	27.25	27.02	26.85
2016	27.41	27.47	27.31	27.42	27.31	26.80	26.62	26.60	26.76	27.24	26.97	26.95	27.07
2017	27.42	27.44	27.26	27.74	27.16	27.25	27.65	27.46	27.77	27.95	27.94	28.12	27.60
2018	28.21	28.42	28.39	28.79	28.51	28.66	28.78	28.90	29.38	29.55	29.56	29.88	28.92
Goods Producing													
2014	27.88	27.78	28.25	28.18	28.02	28.29	28.33	28.10	28.60	28.57	28.74	28.79	28.31
2015	29.10	29.28	29.42	29.57	29.54	29.43	29.88	30.08	29.96	29.96	30.19	30.13	29.72
2016	30.93	31.22	31.22	31.17	31.00	30.57	30.49	30.25	30.20	30.48	30.63	30.86	30.74
2017	30.90	31.01	30.58	30.71	30.13	29.71	29.80	29.83	30.12	30.13	30.31	30.87	30.33
2018	30.97	30.71	31.02	30.89	30.84	30.55	30.74	31.07	31.16	31.59	31.88	32.50	31.16
Construction													
2014	26.64	27.04	27.21	26.98	26.90	27.04	27.75	27.53	28.15	28.02	28.43	28.27	27.53
2015	28.06	28.64	28.22	28.44	28.21	27.83	28.04	27.75	27.61	27.78	27.73	27.41	27.96
2016	27.86	28.08	27.81	27.56	27.49	27.25	27.37	27.09	27.00	27.14	26.96	26.85	27.36
2017	26.92	26.76	26.74	27.08	26.86	26.85	26.65	26.93	27.33	27.29	27.84	28.34	27.14
2018	28.31	28.56	28.61	28.49	28.65	28.52	28.71	29.07	29.26	29.90	29.93	30.39	29.05
Manufacturing													
2014	27.42	27.28	27.68	27.42	27.35	27.84	27.20	26.73	27.18	27.27	27.23	27.60	27.35
2015	28.40	28.31	29.19	29.66	29.61	29.76	30.63	30.83	30.50	30.69	31.14	31.49	30.03
2016	32.05	31.89	32.14	32.41	32.22	32.00	31.85	31.93	31.91	32.47	32.89	33.16	32.24
2017	32.67	32.36	31.72	31.48	31.49	31.18	30.45	30.32	30.75	30.89	30.61	31.16	31.25
2018	31.59	30.75	31.09	31.22	31.15	30.66	30.77	31.48	31.37	31.22	31.97	32.21	31.29
Trade, Transportation, and Utilities													
2014	22.96	22.74	23.02	22.94	22.63	23.04	22.50	22.61	22.66	22.92	23.19	22.28	22.79
2015	22.87	22.93	23.08	23.07	22.97	22.65	22.98	23.21	23.02	23.06	22.88	22.65	22.95
2016	23.22	23.23	23.59	23.44	23.26	23.12	22.61	22.67	22.90	22.87	22.37	21.99	22.93
2017	22.31	22.14	22.29	22.31	21.66	21.28	21.81	21.61	22.15	21.88	21.77	21.92	21.93
2018	22.48	23.08	22.80	23.55	23.03	23.34	23.49	23.40	23.67	23.35	23.30	23.94	23.29
Financial Activities													
2014	29.87	31.02	31.20	30.82	31.40	31.81	31.30	31.15	30.87	30.60	30.94	30.37	30.95
2015	30.77	30.85	31.23	31.59	31.57	30.63	31.35	31.94	31.38	31.64	31.63	30.86	31.29
2016	30.82	30.69	30.76	31.12	31.53	30.38	30.43	30.55	31.07	31.84	31.64	31.18	31.00
2017	31.72	31.86	30.97	31.94	31.54	31.12	31.63	31.61	31.66	31.95	31.71	31.85	31.63
2018	32.32	32.67	33.09	34.30	34.06	33.08	34.44	34.51	35.55	35.44	35.42	35.02	34.16
Professional and Business Services													
2014	32.41	32.42	32.62	32.37	32.04	31.94	31.66	31.32	31.48	31.67	32.36	32.03	32.02
2015	32.56	32.48	32.30	32.13	31.86	31.45	32.05	32.43	32.18	32.44	33.32	33.26	32.37
2016	33.65	34.00	33.40	33.00	32.61	31.82	31.91	31.65	31.37	31.92	31.62	31.92	32.38
2017	31.19	31.53	31.32	32.26	31.65	31.54	32.40	31.95	32.10	32.72	33.04	33.60	32.11
2018	34.10	34.53	33.95	34.39	33.93	34.37	34.45	34.81	35.50	35.62	35.92	36.80	34.89
Education and Health Services													
2014	23.76	23.89	24.08	23.97	23.89	24.14	24.45	24.69	25.10	24.63	25.20	25.22	24.43
2015	24.87	25.31	25.30	25.24	25.46	25.81	26.09	25.83	25.99	26.19	26.49	26.43	25.75
2016	26.13	26.03	25.79	25.94	25.62	25.60	25.57	25.49	25.74	26.10	25.62	25.98	25.80
2017	25.77	25.88	25.76	26.05	25.89	25.93	25.89	25.89	25.72	25.91	25.90	26.22	25.90
2018	25.61	25.90	26.25	26.38	25.81	25.95	26.40	26.57	27.36	27.35	28.18	28.08	26.65
Leisure and Hospitality													
2014	15.37	15.35	15.30	15.30	15.13	14.86	14.72	14.79	15.27	15.31	15.30	15.64	15.18
2015	15.82	15.70	16.04	15.89	15.80	15.36	15.43	15.64	15.20	15.65	15.43	15.92	15.65
2016	15.86	16.14	16.18	16.26	16.39	16.18	16.32	16.44	16.63	17.14	16.74	17.03	16.44
2017	17.62	17.71	17.78	17.25	17.32	17.00	17.32	17.19	17.54	18.34	17.86	18.30	17.59
2018	18.17	18.40	18.71	18.66	18.52	18.08	18.05	18.20	18.31	18.61	18.95	19.04	18.46
Other Services													
2014	22.52	23.50	23.88	23.97	23.79	25.26	25.03	24.68	25.06	24.25	23.79	24.19	24.17
2015	23.03	23.24	23.44	23.27	23.32	22.68	23.03	23.63	23.66	24.30	24.23	23.52	23.46
2016	23.42	23.46	23.39	23.87	24.12	23.12	22.76	23.47	24.54	25.05	24.60	25.49	23.95
2017	25.39	26.35	25.94	26.92	26.38	26.61	26.88	26.16	26.48	26.17	26.83	25.90	26.34
2018	25.94	25.77	25.24	25.39	25.30	26.02	26.06	26.37	26.18	27.10	27.31	26.78	26.11

4. Average Weekly Earnings by Selected Industry: Colorado, 2014–2018

(Dollars, not seasonally adjusted)

Industry and year	January	February	March	April	May	June	July	August	September	October	November	December	Annual average
Total Private													
2014	890.57	917.00	921.01	898.54	894.78	928.93	900.45	897.69	903.46	906.10	917.10	901.60	907.01
2015	895.10	919.86	922.26	902.16	903.83	897.94	912.52	939.60	908.86	917.33	926.50	897.06	912.90
2016	915.49	912.00	909.42	910.34	925.81	903.16	899.76	899.08	901.81	931.61	898.10	894.74	906.85
2017	907.60	902.78	896.85	934.84	918.01	921.05	951.16	928.15	930.30	947.51	933.20	936.40	924.60
2018	936.57	946.39	951.07	975.98	966.49	971.57	990.03	976.82	1,004.80	984.02	975.48	1,003.97	974.60
Goods Producing													
2014	1,070.59	1,091.75	1,098.93	1,096.20	1,087.18	1,131.60	1,124.70	1,132.43	1,144.00	1,162.80	1,117.99	1,166.00	1,118.25
2015	1,143.63	1,174.13	1,185.63	1,165.06	1,152.06	1,177.20	1,195.20	1,227.26	1,192.41	1,204.39	1,210.62	1,205.20	1,185.83
2016	1,221.74	1,217.58	1,220.70	1,224.98	1,227.60	1,219.74	1,210.45	1,200.93	1,201.96	1,216.15	1,209.89	1,175.77	1,211.16
2017	1,195.83	1,209.39	1,186.50	1,219.19	1,193.15	1,209.20	1,200.94	1,190.22	1,210.82	1,208.21	1,209.37	1,216.28	1,204.10
2018	1,207.83	1,203.83	1,234.60	1,238.69	1,249.02	1,243.39	1,238.82	1,233.48	1,252.63	1,269.92	1,252.88	1,303.25	1,243.28
Construction													
2014	1,004.33	1,024.82	1,036.70	1,038.73	1,008.75	1,065.38	1,104.45	1,112.21	1,123.19	1,146.02	1,091.71	1,130.80	1,076.42
2015	1,060.67	1,108.37	1,100.58	1,100.63	1,060.70	1,096.50	1,115.99	1,134.98	1,076.79	1,119.53	1,095.34	1,093.66	1,096.03
2016	1,078.18	1,064.23	1,070.69	1,072.08	1,091.35	1,090.00	1,083.85	1,086.31	1,074.60	1,072.03	1,046.05	982.71	1,067.04
2017	987.96	1,016.88	1,002.75	1,031.75	1,023.37	1,068.63	1,042.02	1,042.19	1,063.14	1,050.67	1,069.06	1,065.58	1,039.46
2018	1,050.30	1,053.86	1,092.90	1,088.32	1,128.81	1,129.39	1,125.43	1,133.73	1,144.07	1,198.99	1,152.31	1,194.33	1,124.24
Manufacturing													
2014	1,083.09	1,104.84	1,093.36	1,074.86	1,094.00	1,121.95	1,066.24	1,063.85	1,081.76	1,093.53	1,089.20	1,090.20	1,088.53
2015	1,116.12	1,140.89	1,179.28	1,162.67	1,175.52	1,193.38	1,222.14	1,239.37	1,223.05	1,221.46	1,245.60	1,247.00	1,198.20
2016	1,275.59	1,259.66	1,266.32	1,283.44	1,266.25	1,257.60	1,258.08	1,242.08	1,260.45	1,298.80	1,305.73	1,313.14	1,273.48
2017	1,319.87	1,271.75	1,246.60	1,265.50	1,256.45	1,253.44	1,224.09	1,218.86	1,223.85	1,232.51	1,215.22	1,230.82	1,246.88
2018	1,250.96	1,214.63	1,231.16	1,245.68	1,239.77	1,229.47	1,227.72	1,240.31	1,248.53	1,230.07	1,269.21	1,281.96	1,242.21
Trade, Transportation, and Utilities													
2014	796.71	805.00	808.00	786.84	773.95	808.70	774.00	777.78	779.50	790.74	802.37	770.89	788.53
2015	770.72	793.38	796.26	770.54	780.98	774.63	792.81	805.39	794.19	788.65	784.78	770.10	784.89
2016	782.51	782.85	787.91	782.90	781.54	779.14	759.70	763.98	762.57	773.01	738.21	736.67	768.16
2017	742.92	735.05	733.34	747.39	710.45	706.50	739.36	721.77	735.38	737.36	727.12	729.94	730.27
2018	746.34	768.56	752.40	791.28	780.72	788.89	810.41	786.24	809.51	772.89	773.56	804.38	782.54
Financial Activities													
2014	1,093.24	1,153.94	1,170.00	1,118.77	1,136.68	1,218.32	1,161.23	1,152.55	1,139.10	1,135.26	1,194.28	1,120.65	1,148.25
2015	1,132.34	1,163.05	1,171.13	1,153.04	1,149.15	1,102.68	1,131.74	1,194.56	1,139.09	1,142.20	1,189.29	1,117.13	1,148.34
2016	1,134.18	1,120.19	1,116.59	1,145.22	1,179.22	1,127.10	1,122.87	1,127.30	1,149.59	1,206.74	1,173.84	1,138.07	1,143.90
2017	1,195.84	1,166.08	1,130.41	1,207.33	1,151.21	1,138.99	1,186.13	1,166.41	1,165.09	1,194.93	1,166.93	1,181.64	1,170.31
2018	1,189.38	1,202.26	1,214.40	1,293.11	1,236.38	1,214.04	1,294.94	1,256.16	1,347.35	1,307.74	1,289.29	1,306.25	1,263.92
Professional and Business Services													
2014	1,189.45	1,225.48	1,223.25	1,204.16	1,179.07	1,207.33	1,152.42	1,146.31	1,155.32	1,165.46	1,190.85	1,159.49	1,181.54
2015	1,178.67	1,201.76	1,201.56	1,172.75	1,166.08	1,151.07	1,173.03	1,206.40	1,164.92	1,174.33	1,206.18	1,167.43	1,181.51
2016	1,191.21	1,200.20	1,179.02	1,174.80	1,180.48	1,142.34	1,148.76	1,139.40	1,145.01	1,181.04	1,138.32	1,142.74	1,162.44
2017	1,119.72	1,113.01	1,108.73	1,171.04	1,123.58	1,144.90	1,185.84	1,147.01	1,136.34	1,158.29	1,156.40	1,186.08	1,146.33
2018	1,207.14	1,201.64	1,201.83	1,241.48	1,211.30	1,251.07	1,274.65	1,281.01	1,317.05	1,278.76	1,296.71	1,354.24	1,259.53
Education and Health Services													
2014	746.06	759.70	770.56	747.86	750.15	774.89	772.62	775.27	785.63	773.38	811.44	796.95	771.99
2015	778.43	809.92	807.07	784.96	791.81	797.53	798.35	811.06	797.89	801.41	831.79	806.12	800.83
2016	812.64	806.93	807.23	806.73	812.15	788.48	805.46	797.84	810.81	827.37	801.91	820.97	807.54
2017	829.79	825.57	821.74	857.05	828.48	834.95	851.78	841.43	820.47	839.48	831.39	836.42	833.98
2018	811.84	821.03	834.75	846.80	818.18	814.83	834.24	826.33	859.10	839.65	870.76	890.14	839.48
Leisure and Hospitality													
2014	408.84	419.06	429.93	399.33	400.95	414.59	410.69	412.64	409.24	404.18	397.80	401.95	408.34
2015	409.74	419.19	431.48	413.14	412.38	408.58	413.52	431.66	396.72	410.03	388.84	398.00	411.60
2016	401.26	411.57	419.06	396.74	427.78	423.92	432.48	434.02	427.39	445.64	415.15	425.75	422.51
2017	435.21	437.44	448.06	417.45	426.07	442.00	462.44	448.66	445.52	469.50	437.57	452.01	443.27
2018	463.34	469.20	478.98	462.77	472.26	470.08	478.33	476.84	472.40	465.25	451.01	468.38	468.88
Other Services													
2014	772.44	815.45	811.92	805.39	792.21	868.94	825.99	841.59	844.52	785.70	768.42	749.89	807.28
2015	686.29	720.44	728.98	700.43	708.93	730.30	743.87	793.97	768.95	794.61	828.67	771.46	748.37
2016	784.57	774.18	771.87	790.10	824.90	769.90	776.12	802.67	827.00	891.78	821.64	859.01	807.12
2017	860.72	882.73	871.58	944.89	891.64	915.38	967.68	920.83	929.45	947.35	949.78	911.68	916.63
2018	900.12	901.95	865.73	903.88	875.38	887.28	886.04	867.57	884.88	894.30	890.31	883.74	887.74

CONNECTICUT
At a Glance

Population:
  2010 census: 3,574,097
  2018 estimate: 3,572,665

Percent change in population:
  2010–2018: 0.04%

Percent change in total nonfarm employment:
  2010–2018: 4.8%

Industry with the largest growth in employment, 2010–2018 (percent):
  Transportation and utilities, 20.7%

Industry with the largest decline or smallest growth in employment, 2010–2018 (percent):
  Mining and logging, -16.7%

Civilian labor force:
  2010: 1,911,712
  2018: 1,905,312

Unemployment rate and rank among states (highest to lowest):
  2010: 9.1%, 22nd
  2018: 4.1%, 16th

Over-the-year change in unemployment rates:
  2016–2017: -0.4%
  2017–2018: -0.6%

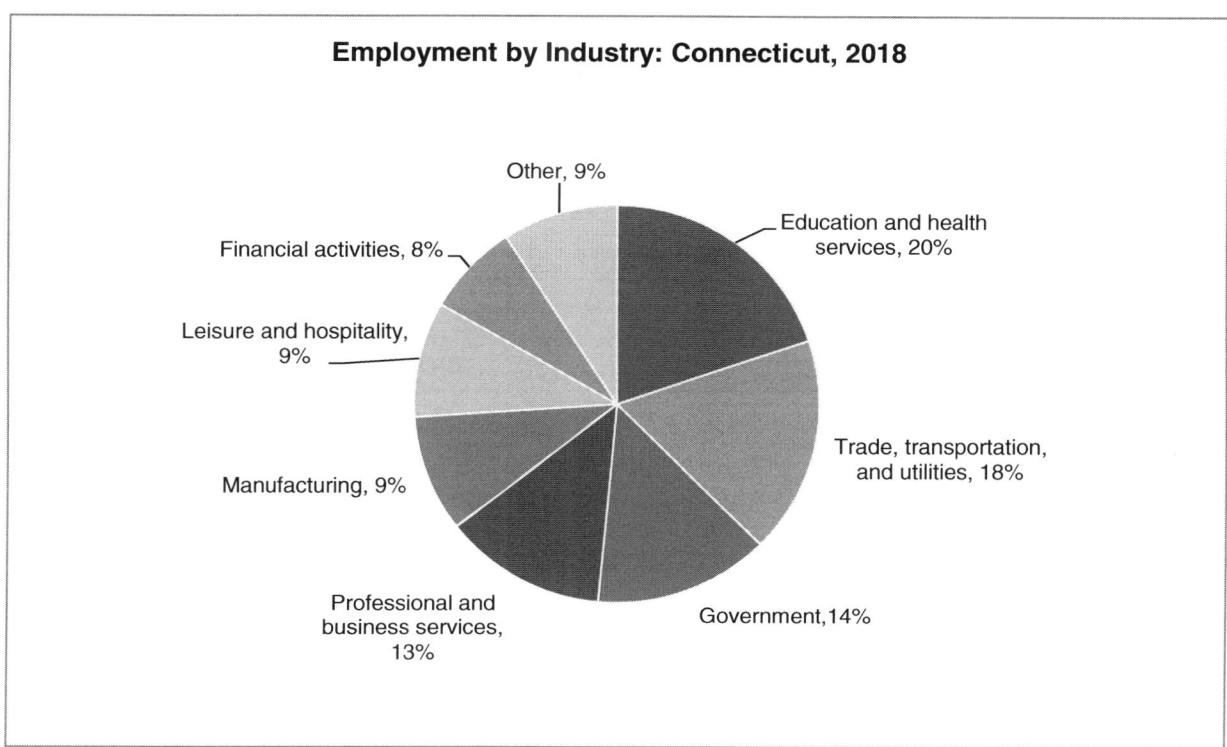

Employment by Industry: Connecticut, 2018

- Other, 9%
- Education and health services, 20%
- Financial activities, 8%
- Trade, transportation, and utilities, 18%
- Leisure and hospitality, 9%
- Manufacturing, 9%
- Government, 14%
- Professional and business services, 13%

1. Employment by Industry: Connecticut, 2010–2018

(Numbers in thousands, not seasonally adjusted)

Industry and year	January	February	March	April	May	June	July	August	September	October	November	December	Annual average
Total Nonfarm													
2010	1,568.7	1,576.8	1,582.6	1,607.8	1,625.9	1,625.9	1,609.0	1,604.7	1,624.5	1,635.9	1,641.2	1,644.6	1,612.3
2011	1,591.7	1,603.0	1,605.6	1,633.4	1,638.3	1,638.5	1,623.8	1,616.0	1,639.2	1,643.4	1,650.9	1,656.2	1,628.3
2012	1,607.1	1,618.5	1,626.1	1,638.0	1,649.2	1,654.2	1,633.7	1,628.2	1,650.8	1,659.4	1,668.3	1,672.8	1,642.2
2013	1,618.3	1,621.6	1,632.5	1,655.3	1,665.8	1,676.3	1,655.9	1,646.7	1,661.4	1,667.8	1,679.0	1,676.4	1,654.8
2014	1,631.0	1,630.6	1,639.9	1,665.6	1,677.9	1,684.1	1,661.2	1,656.4	1,674.0	1,683.5	1,693.0	1,695.4	1,666.1
2015	1,649.7	1,647.6	1,654.8	1,676.2	1,693.3	1,701.4	1,671.2	1,665.1	1,682.8	1,696.7	1,704.5	1,703.9	1,678.9
2016	1,654.9	1,658.0	1,668.5	1,681.6	1,696.3	1,700.8	1,679.7	1,672.3	1,689.5	1,696.4	1,704.3	1,704.3	1,683.9
2017	1,661.5	1,662.1	1,667.5	1,683.2	1,698.3	1,709.0	1,681.9	1,676.4	1,692.5	1,698.5	1,708.8	1,708.7	1,687.4
2018	1,658.7	1,664.6	1,667.4	1,681.1	1,699.0	1,708.5	1,683.6	1,678.4	1,695.0	1,704.3	1,714.2	1,713.3	1,689.0
Total Private													
2010	1,320.7	1,319.7	1,325.0	1,350.8	1,366.1	1,378.8	1,376.9	1,372.9	1,374.1	1,379.7	1,384.0	1,388.9	1,361.5
2011	1,348.1	1,350.3	1,352.3	1,377.4	1,386.9	1,397.9	1,394.6	1,389.6	1,390.3	1,389.8	1,396.4	1,402.0	1,381.3
2012	1,365.9	1,366.3	1,373.7	1,386.0	1,400.9	1,414.3	1,405.9	1,401.8	1,402.9	1,407.8	1,414.4	1,419.0	1,396.6
2013	1,375.2	1,372.2	1,382.0	1,403.8	1,416.1	1,430.2	1,423.1	1,420.0	1,416.8	1,419.6	1,428.1	1,426.8	1,409.5
2014	1,388.1	1,383.2	1,390.8	1,414.6	1,428.4	1,439.9	1,433.4	1,428.7	1,427.9	1,434.0	1,441.0	1,444.9	1,421.2
2015	1,406.1	1,400.3	1,406.3	1,426.5	1,444.8	1,459.2	1,445.2	1,439.5	1,438.0	1,448.0	1,453.5	1,455.4	1,435.2
2016	1,413.5	1,412.2	1,421.3	1,434.4	1,447.9	1,462.6	1,456.9	1,450.6	1,448.8	1,451.9	1,457.1	1,458.9	1,443.0
2017	1,422.0	1,418.2	1,422.9	1,439.4	1,454.9	1,472.3	1,460.4	1,454.6	1,453.6	1,456.5	1,465.3	1,466.4	1,448.9
2018	1,422.7	1,423.3	1,425.0	1,440.4	1,458.5	1,475.6	1,463.2	1,457.9	1,456.2	1,463.0	1,470.5	1,470.9	1,452.3
Goods Producing													
2010	206.4	204.3	205.4	211.3	213.9	217.1	217.6	217.7	217.4	216.9	216.5	215.2	213.3
2011	208.5	208.3	209.3	213.5	216.1	219.3	219.8	220.0	218.7	217.8	217.7	215.8	215.4
2012	209.8	209.1	209.6	212.2	214.1	216.9	217.1	217.1	215.5	215.9	214.9	214.3	213.9
2013	208.9	208.0	209.0	212.9	215.7	218.1	219.0	218.3	216.8	216.0	215.0	213.1	214.2
2014	207.1	206.0	206.6	211.5	214.0	216.5	217.8	217.9	216.4	216.9	215.6	214.2	213.4
2015	208.8	207.2	208.3	213.5	216.9	220.1	219.5	219.8	218.7	218.9	217.8	216.6	215.5
2016	211.0	209.5	211.2	214.8	217.1	220.0	220.9	220.7	218.5	218.2	217.6	215.9	216.3
2017	210.6	209.8	211.1	215.2	218.4	222.4	223.0	222.7	220.5	220.8	219.7	217.9	217.7
2018	211.5	211.8	212.8	216.5	220.1	223.8	224.9	224.4	222.5	222.4	222.1	220.4	219.4
Service-Providing													
2010	1,362.3	1,372.5	1,377.2	1,396.5	1,412.0	1,408.8	1,391.4	1,387.0	1,407.1	1,419.0	1,424.7	1,429.4	1,399.0
2011	1,383.2	1,394.7	1,396.3	1,419.9	1,422.2	1,419.2	1,404.0	1,396.0	1,420.5	1,425.6	1,433.2	1,440.4	1,412.9
2012	1,397.3	1,409.4	1,416.5	1,425.8	1,435.1	1,437.3	1,416.6	1,411.1	1,435.3	1,443.5	1,453.4	1,458.5	1,428.3
2013	1,409.4	1,413.6	1,423.5	1,442.4	1,450.1	1,458.2	1,436.9	1,428.4	1,444.6	1,451.8	1,464.0	1,463.3	1,440.5
2014	1,423.9	1,424.6	1,433.3	1,454.1	1,463.9	1,467.6	1,443.4	1,438.5	1,457.6	1,466.6	1,477.4	1,481.2	1,452.7
2015	1,440.9	1,440.4	1,446.5	1,462.7	1,476.4	1,481.3	1,451.7	1,445.3	1,464.1	1,477.8	1,486.7	1,487.3	1,463.4
2016	1,443.9	1,448.5	1,457.3	1,466.8	1,479.2	1,480.8	1,458.8	1,451.6	1,471.0	1,478.2	1,486.7	1,488.4	1,467.6
2017	1,450.9	1,452.3	1,456.4	1,468.0	1,479.9	1,486.6	1,458.9	1,453.7	1,472.0	1,477.7	1,489.1	1,490.8	1,469.7
2018	1,447.2	1,452.8	1,454.6	1,464.6	1,478.9	1,484.7	1,458.7	1,454.0	1,472.5	1,481.9	1,492.1	1,492.9	1,469.6
Mining and Logging													
2010	0.5	0.5	0.5	0.6	0.6	0.6	0.6	0.6	0.6	0.6	0.6	0.6	0.6
2011	0.5	0.5	0.5	0.5	0.6	0.6	0.6	0.6	0.6	0.6	0.6	0.6	0.6
2012	0.5	0.5	0.5	0.6	0.6	0.6	0.6	0.6	0.6	0.6	0.6	0.5	0.6
2013	0.5	0.5	0.5	0.5	0.6	0.6	0.6	0.6	0.6	0.6	0.6	0.6	0.6
2014	0.5	0.4	0.4	0.5	0.6	0.6	0.6	0.6	0.6	0.6	0.6	0.6	0.6
2015	0.5	0.5	0.5	0.5	0.6	0.6	0.6	0.6	0.6	0.6	0.6	0.6	0.6
2016	0.5	0.5	0.5	0.6	0.6	0.6	0.6	0.6	0.6	0.6	0.6	0.6	0.6
2017	0.5	0.5	0.5	0.5	0.6	0.6	0.6	0.6	0.6	0.6	0.6	0.5	0.6
2018	0.5	0.5	0.5	0.5	0.5	0.5	0.6	0.6	0.6	0.5	0.5	0.5	0.5
Construction													
2010	44.3	42.9	43.6	49.2	50.9	52.3	53.3	53.7	53.1	52.9	52.6	50.9	50.0
2011	45.6	45.3	45.9	50.1	52.1	53.8	54.8	55.0	54.6	54.2	54.2	52.0	51.5
2012	47.1	46.2	47.1	50.0	51.4	52.8	53.9	54.2	53.8	54.3	53.5	52.4	51.4
2013	47.7	46.9	48.0	52.1	54.5	55.7	56.9	57.1	56.7	56.2	55.7	53.5	53.4
2014	48.6	48.0	48.8	53.9	56.6	58.0	59.4	59.7	59.2	59.5	58.4	56.7	55.6
2015	52.1	50.8	51.5	56.5	59.4	60.8	60.9	61.4	60.8	61.7	60.7	59.3	58.0
2016	54.7	53.3	55.0	58.7	60.7	61.9	62.5	62.6	61.5	61.1	60.4	57.8	59.2
2017	53.1	52.4	53.2	57.1	59.7	61.5	61.9	61.9	61.3	61.2	59.8	57.4	58.4
2018	52.1	52.2	53.2	56.7	59.5	61.3	61.9	62.0	61.6	61.6	61.7	59.4	58.6

1. Employment by Industry: Connecticut, 2010–2018—*Continued*

(Numbers in thousands, not seasonally adjusted)

Industry and year	January	February	March	April	May	June	July	August	September	October	November	December	Annual average
Manufacturing													
2010	161.6	160.9	161.3	161.5	162.4	164.2	163.7	163.4	163.7	163.4	163.3	163.7	162.8
2011	162.4	162.5	162.9	162.9	163.4	164.9	164.4	164.4	163.5	163.0	162.9	163.2	163.4
2012	162.2	162.4	162.0	161.6	162.1	163.5	162.6	162.3	161.1	161.0	160.8	161.4	161.9
2013	160.7	160.6	160.5	160.3	160.6	161.8	161.5	160.6	159.5	159.2	158.7	159.0	160.3
2014	158.0	157.6	157.4	157.1	156.8	157.9	157.8	157.6	156.6	156.8	156.6	156.9	157.3
2015	156.2	155.9	156.3	156.5	156.9	158.7	158.0	157.8	157.3	156.6	156.5	156.7	157.0
2016	155.8	155.7	155.7	155.5	155.8	157.5	157.8	157.5	156.4	156.5	156.6	157.5	156.5
2017	157.0	156.9	157.4	157.6	158.1	160.3	160.5	160.2	158.6	159.0	159.3	160.0	158.7
2018	158.9	159.1	159.1	159.3	160.1	162.0	162.4	161.8	160.3	160.3	159.9	160.5	160.3
Trade, Transportation, and Utilities													
2010	282.5	277.6	278.4	278.5	284.8	288.3	283.3	282.6	284.3	287.8	293.9	299.5	285.1
2011	285.8	282.3	282.4	286.4	288.2	290.8	285.2	284.6	286.8	288.4	294.5	300.7	288.0
2012	289.7	284.4	286.3	285.5	290.2	292.9	286.4	285.9	289.2	292.3	300.0	303.5	290.5
2013	290.7	284.9	287.5	289.9	292.8	296.0	289.9	290.0	292.1	295.0	302.3	306.9	293.2
2014	293.6	288.8	290.1	292.1	294.8	297.2	291.2	290.2	293.3	296.5	303.5	308.1	295.0
2015	295.0	289.4	290.6	291.5	296.5	299.6	291.6	290.9	294.8	298.8	306.5	310.8	296.3
2016	297.1	292.6	293.9	293.8	297.6	298.5	293.3	292.0	295.2	298.2	305.3	309.9	297.3
2017	298.3	292.0	291.8	292.4	296.7	298.7	292.0	290.9	295.5	298.3	307.5	311.1	297.1
2018	298.2	292.4	292.2	291.1	296.9	299.5	292.3	291.2	294.4	296.8	304.2	308.2	296.5
Wholesale Trade													
2010	61.1	60.8	61.1	61.4	62.0	62.4	62.3	62.4	62.0	61.9	62.4	62.5	61.9
2011	61.4	61.5	61.6	62.2	62.4	62.8	62.8	62.7	62.4	62.1	62.0	62.3	62.2
2012	61.7	61.7	61.9	62.2	62.3	62.7	62.4	62.2	62.0	62.4	62.3	62.4	62.2
2013	61.4	61.4	61.8	62.0	62.3	62.7	62.5	62.4	62.1	62.1	62.1	62.4	62.1
2014	61.4	61.2	61.4	61.9	62.2	62.4	62.2	61.9	61.8	61.8	61.7	61.9	61.8
2015	61.3	61.2	61.4	61.7	62.0	62.3	61.8	61.6	61.5	61.3	61.1	61.4	61.6
2016	60.8	60.9	61.1	61.5	61.8	62.2	61.9	61.8	61.7	61.5	61.4	61.6	61.5
2017	61.3	61.1	61.2	61.3	61.7	62.2	61.7	61.7	61.6	61.3	61.5	61.9	61.5
2018	61.2	61.1	61.4	61.5	61.9	62.3	61.9	61.8	61.4	61.5	61.3	61.2	61.5
Retail Trade													
2010	176.6	172.1	172.6	173.7	177.1	179.9	178.7	178.4	176.3	179.7	184.9	189.0	178.3
2011	179.2	175.5	175.3	178.1	179.3	181.0	179.1	179.5	177.9	179.8	185.7	190.3	180.1
2012	181.9	176.7	178.1	177.9	181.0	182.9	180.6	180.6	179.2	181.8	189.1	191.4	181.8
2013	181.9	177.2	178.0	179.8	181.9	184.2	182.5	183.2	181.0	183.8	190.5	193.5	183.1
2014	183.9	179.4	180.2	181.7	183.5	185.5	183.7	183.3	181.7	184.4	190.7	193.6	184.3
2015	184.3	179.5	180.2	180.6	184.3	186.7	183.3	183.7	182.2	185.6	191.9	194.5	184.7
2016	185.0	180.7	181.7	181.7	183.9	185.5	184.1	183.8	181.8	184.7	190.7	192.5	184.7
2017	185.5	179.9	179.6	180.9	182.9	184.3	182.9	182.2	180.1	182.8	189.7	191.1	183.5
2018	183.0	177.9	177.4	177.9	180.3	181.8	179.7	179.5	177.4	179.5	185.7	187.7	180.7
Transportation and Utilities													
2010	44.8	44.7	44.7	43.4	45.7	46.0	42.3	41.8	46.0	46.2	46.6	48.0	45.0
2011	45.2	45.3	45.5	46.1	46.5	47.0	43.3	42.4	46.5	46.5	46.8	48.1	45.8
2012	46.1	46.0	46.3	45.4	46.9	47.3	43.4	43.1	48.0	48.1	48.6	49.7	46.6
2013	47.4	46.3	47.7	48.1	48.6	49.1	44.9	44.4	49.0	49.1	49.7	51.0	47.9
2014	48.3	48.2	48.5	48.5	49.1	49.3	45.3	45.0	49.8	50.3	51.1	52.6	. 48.8
2015	49.4	48.7	49.0	49.2	50.2	50.6	46.5	45.6	51.1	51.9	53.5	54.9	50.1
2016	51.3	51.0	51.1	50.6	51.9	50.8	47.3	46.4	51.7	52.0	53.2	55.8	51.1
2017	51.5	51.0	51.0	50.2	52.1	52.2	47.4	47.0	53.8	54.2	56.3	58.1	52.1
2018	54.0	53.4	53.4	51.7	54.7	55.4	50.7	49.9	55.6	55.8	57.2	59.3	54.3
Information													
2010	31.9	31.8	31.7	31.6	31.8	31.7	31.7	32.1	31.9	31.7	31.8	31.9	31.8
2011	31.6	31.6	31.6	31.5	31.3	31.4	31.5	31.5	31.2	31.1	31.4	31.2	31.4
2012	31.3	31.6	31.0	31.0	31.3	31.1	31.2	31.7	31.4	31.5	32.0	31.5	31.4
2013	31.6	32.4	32.1	31.7	32.2	32.3	32.5	32.5	31.9	31.9	32.2	32.2	32.1
2014	31.9	31.9	32.1	32.1	32.1	32.1	32.3	32.5	31.8	31.5	32.6	32.6	32.1
2015	32.2	32.2	32.3	32.4	32.5	32.7	32.6	32.8	32.4	32.4	32.8	32.6	32.5
2016	32.3	32.5	32.2	32.2	32.3	32.4	32.7	33.1	32.3	32.4	32.5	32.1	32.4
2017	31.7	31.9	31.8	31.7	31.7	31.7	31.5	31.7	31.3	31.2	31.7	31.5	31.6
2018	31.6	32.1	31.6	31.7	31.6	31.8	31.7	31.9	31.6	31.9	32.3	32.5	31.9

1. Employment by Industry: Connecticut, 2010–2018—*Continued*

(Numbers in thousands, not seasonally adjusted)

Industry and year	January	February	March	April	May	June	July	August	September	October	November	December	Annual average
Financial Activities													
2010	134.0	134.1	134.5	134.0	134.3	136.2	136.7	137.0	135.2	135.2	135.5	135.8	135.2
2011	135.4	135.2	135.2	134.8	134.9	135.5	136.6	136.3	134.3	133.8	133.9	133.9	135.0
2012	132.9	132.7	132.9	132.5	133.0	134.6	134.8	134.1	132.7	132.4	132.1	132.2	133.1
2013	131.7	131.1	130.8	130.5	130.2	132.1	132.3	131.5	129.5	129.1	129.0	129.2	130.6
2014	128.1	127.7	127.5	127.4	128.3	129.7	130.3	130.0	128.7	128.9	129.0	129.3	128.7
2015	128.9	128.8	129.0	129.4	129.9	131.6	131.9	131.7	129.9	129.9	129.9	130.0	130.1
2016	129.2	128.9	129.4	129.3	129.5	131.1	131.0	130.6	129.0	128.8	128.5	128.4	129.5
2017	127.9	127.4	127.3	127.4	127.7	129.6	129.7	129.1	127.4	127.2	126.7	126.8	127.9
2018	125.5	125.4	125.3	125.0	125.1	127.2	127.2	126.5	125.1	126.4	127.0	127.1	126.1
Professional and Business Services													
2010	184.4	186.6	187.7	195.9	196.1	198.7	198.1	197.9	197.6	198.9	198.3	198.8	194.9
2011	193.1	194.9	194.7	201.6	201.4	203.5	203.0	202.5	203.0	203.9	205.6	205.9	201.1
2012	199.3	199.9	203.4	207.8	207.9	210.0	209.4	209.3	209.2	209.1	209.6	209.0	207.0
2013	201.4	203.5	204.0	209.6	210.5	213.2	212.7	214.1	213.0	213.6	214.2	213.1	210.2
2014	206.6	207.8	208.9	215.5	217.4	218.8	217.7	217.3	216.3	217.6	218.4	218.6	215.1
2015	212.6	214.0	214.6	219.6	221.1	223.4	220.9	220.3	219.4	221.5	221.8	220.7	219.2
2016	213.0	214.0	215.5	220.1	219.8	222.8	221.3	221.1	220.5	220.5	220.0	220.3	219.1
2017	213.2	213.8	215.5	219.9	219.6	222.6	222.0	221.8	220.9	221.5	222.6	221.5	219.6
2018	213.9	215.6	216.5	220.0	221.6	224.2	222.8	223.4	222.1	223.2	222.8	220.2	220.5
Education and Health Services													
2010	301.8	304.9	304.4	308.8	307.3	304.1	302.9	300.6	308.0	312.8	313.9	313.8	306.9
2011	310.1	313.0	312.5	315.8	314.7	310.9	308.8	306.8	314.0	315.8	316.9	317.2	313.0
2012	312.6	317.5	316.6	317.8	317.9	314.9	311.9	310.1	317.9	321.2	322.3	324.1	317.1
2013	315.9	318.8	319.8	323.0	321.1	318.6	315.4	314.4	321.5	324.7	327.1	324.5	320.4
2014	319.7	321.1	321.5	326.2	324.9	322.2	319.5	318.5	325.8	328.9	330.6	330.7	324.1
2015	324.9	326.2	325.3	328.5	327.8	325.8	322.2	320.0	325.5	330.4	331.6	331.5	326.6
2016	325.5	328.7	329.3	330.0	329.2	327.3	326.1	324.2	331.7	334.2	336.2	335.5	329.8
2017	330.3	333.9	333.1	335.6	335.9	332.7	327.3	326.1	334.0	335.7	336.9	338.1	333.3
2018	330.3	335.3	334.0	337.3	336.7	333.3	328.2	326.8	334.7	340.0	340.6	341.0	334.9
Leisure and Hospitality													
2010	120.3	121.3	123.3	130.8	137.4	141.1	144.4	143.1	139.1	135.8	133.6	133.3	133.6
2011	124.3	125.7	127.1	133.6	139.7	144.8	147.9	146.4	142.3	139.5	136.6	137.1	137.1
2012	130.4	131.0	133.8	138.6	145.4	151.6	152.1	150.9	145.3	143.3	141.2	142.3	142.2
2013	134.3	132.7	137.4	144.5	151.4	156.8	157.9	156.2	150.2	147.8	146.6	145.8	146.8
2014	139.8	138.7	142.3	147.4	154.0	159.4	160.1	158.1	152.5	150.4	148.1	148.0	149.9
2015	141.1	140.0	143.1	148.5	156.1	161.3	161.4	158.5	153.3	152.2	149.2	149.1	151.2
2016	142.1	142.6	145.8	150.0	157.7	164.2	165.1	163.1	157.0	155.1	152.7	152.0	154.0
2017	146.1	145.7	148.2	152.7	159.7	167.9	168.2	165.9	158.7	157.1	155.1	154.2	156.6
2018	147.6	146.9	148.2	153.4	160.8	168.6	168.8	166.9	160.2	157.6	156.0	157.1	157.7
Other Services													
2010	59.4	59.1	59.6	59.9	60.5	61.6	62.2	61.9	60.6	60.6	60.5	60.6	60.5
2011	59.3	59.3	59.5	60.2	60.6	61.7	61.8	61.5	60.0	59.5	59.8	60.2	60.3
2012	59.9	60.1	60.1	60.6	61.1	62.3	63.0	62.7	61.7	62.1	62.3	62.1	61.5
2013	60.7	60.8	61.4	61.7	62.2	63.1	63.4	63.0	61.8	61.5	61.7	62.0	61.9
2014	61.3	61.2	61.8	62.4	62.9	64.0	64.5	64.2	63.1	63.3	63.2	63.4	62.9
2015	62.6	62.5	63.1	63.1	64.0	64.7	65.1	65.5	64.0	63.9	63.9	64.1	63.9
2016	63.3	63.4	64.0	64.2	64.7	66.3	66.5	65.8	64.6	64.5	64.3	64.8	64.7
2017	63.9	63.7	64.1	64.5	65.2	66.7	66.7	66.4	65.3	64.7	65.1	65.3	65.1
2018	64.1	63.8	64.4	65.4	65.7	67.2	67.3	66.8	65.6	64.7	65.5	64.4	65.4
Government													
2010	248.0	257.1	257.6	257.0	259.8	247.1	232.1	231.8	250.4	256.2	257.2	255.7	250.8
2011	243.6	252.7	253.3	256.0	251.4	240.6	229.2	226.4	248.9	253.6	254.5	254.2	247.0
2012	241.2	252.2	252.4	252.0	248.3	239.9	227.8	226.4	247.9	251.6	253.9	253.8	245.6
2013	243.1	249.4	250.5	251.5	249.7	246.1	232.8	226.7	244.6	248.2	250.9	249.6	245.3
2014	242.9	247.4	249.1	251.0	249.5	244.2	227.8	227.7	246.1	249.5	252.0	250.5	244.8
2015	243.6	247.3	248.5	249.7	248.5	242.2	226.0	225.6	244.8	248.7	251.0	248.5	243.7
2016	241.4	245.8	247.2	247.2	248.4	238.2	222.8	221.7	240.7	244.5	247.2	245.4	240.9
2017	239.5	243.9	244.6	243.8	243.4	236.7	221.5	221.8	238.9	242.0	243.5	242.3	238.5
2018	236.0	241.3	242.4	240.7	240.5	232.9	220.4	220.5	238.8	241.3	243.7	242.4	236.7

2. Average Weekly Hours by Selected Industry: Connecticut, 2014–2018

(Not seasonally adjusted)

Industry and year	January	February	March	April	May	June	July	August	September	October	November	December	Annual average
Total Private													
2014	33.2	32.8	33.6	33.6	33.5	33.8	33.7	33.8	33.9	33.8	34.2	33.8	33.6
2015	33.5	33.4	33.6	33.4	33.3	33.3	33.4	34.0	33.4	33.7	33.8	33.6	33.5
2016	33.2	33.1	33.2	33.4	34.0	33.6	33.6	33.6	33.9	34.2	33.7	33.7	33.6
2017	33.7	33.0	32.9	33.7	33.6	33.6	33.9	33.8	33.9	34.1	33.9	33.9	33.7
2018	33.6	33.7	33.3	34.1	33.8	33.7	34.2	33.8	34.2	33.9	33.7	34.2	33.9
Goods-Producing													
2014	39.3	37.8	39.7	39.2	39.4	39.8	39.5	39.3	39.6	39.7	40.5	39.8	39.5
2015	39.6	38.9	39.9	39.4	39.2	39.1	39.1	39.9	39.2	39.7	40.2	40.2	39.5
2016	39.8	39.2	39.7	39.7	40.9	40.6	40.3	40.1	40.6	40.3	40.2	39.4	40.1
2017	38.9	38.1	38.3	39.0	39.0	39.1	39.2	39.1	39.2	39.5	39.3	39.9	39.1
2018	39.0	39.1	38.2	40.0	39.0	39.0	40.1	39.5	39.8	39.7	39.2	40.4	39.4
Construction													
2014	36.7	34.5	36.2	36.5	37.4	37.6	38.0	38.1	38.8	38.5	39.1	37.9	37.5
2015	38.2	36.3	38.6	39.0	39.7	38.8	39.6	39.7	38.6	40.2	39.2	39.8	39.0
2016	38.6	37.2	38.4	38.4	40.2	39.5	39.0	38.8	39.9	38.8	38.7	37.0	38.7
2017	36.8	35.8	36.1	37.5	38.5	38.9	37.7	38.3	38.3	37.5	38.3	37.4	37.6
2018	36.8	36.4	35.6	37.6	38.7	38.5	39.6	38.8	37.2	38.9	37.1	39.0	37.9
Manufacturing													
2014	40.3	39.0	40.4	39.7	39.8	40.3	39.8	39.6	39.8	40.1	41.0	40.5	40.0
2015	40.1	40.0	40.6	39.8	39.1	39.3	38.9	40.0	39.6	40.2	41.3	41.0	40.0
2016	40.8	40.5	40.8	40.8	41.5	41.3	41.2	40.9	41.0	41.2	41.1	40.9	41.0
2017	40.1	39.4	39.4	39.9	39.5	39.5	40.2	39.7	39.8	40.6	39.9	40.9	39.9
2018	39.8	40.0	39.2	40.9	40.0	40.0	40.9	40.3	41.5	40.7	40.8	42.2	40.5
Trade, Transportation, and Utilities													
2014	33.1	32.2	33.0	32.9	33.0	33.2	33.5	33.5	33.7	33.1	33.3	33.5	33.2
2015	32.6	32.4	32.7	33.0	32.9	32.8	33.1	33.4	33.6	33.4	32.8	33.1	33.0
2016	32.4	32.6	32.5	32.6	33.1	33.1	32.8	32.8	33.3	33.2	32.7	33.0	32.8
2017	32.4	31.9	31.3	32.2	32.2	32.3	32.7	32.4	32.9	32.5	32.9	32.9	32.4
2018	32.4	32.5	32.2	33.0	33.0	33.1	33.3	33.5	33.9	33.3	33.5	33.5	33.1
Financial Activities													
2014	37.3	38.2	38.3	37.2	37.5	38.2	37.4	37.8	38.0	38.3	38.9	38.3	38.0
2015	38.2	39.1	39.0	38.2	38.1	38.1	37.9	39.0	37.9	38.1	39.4	37.5	38.4
2016	37.2	37.5	37.5	37.4	38.4	37.1	37.1	36.8	37.1	38.6	37.1	36.9	37.4
2017	38.0	36.5	36.5	38.2	36.9	36.7	38.0	37.0	37.0	38.0	37.0	36.9	37.2
2018	37.3	37.1	37.1	37.9	36.9	36.8	38.0	36.8	37.4	36.5	36.3	37.4	37.1
Professional and Business Services													
2014	33.7	34.2	35.0	36.0	35.5	35.9	35.8	35.4	36.0	36.3	36.4	35.5	35.5
2015	34.8	34.9	35.1	34.7	34.7	34.8	34.6	35.2	34.2	34.7	35.2	35.0	34.8
2016	34.3	34.6	34.5	34.9	35.6	35.2	35.1	34.9	34.8	35.6	34.8	34.8	34.9
2017	35.4	34.6	34.6	35.5	35.7	35.8	36.1	35.7	35.5	35.5	34.9	34.6	35.3
2018	34.6	34.5	33.7	34.9	34.7	34.4	34.7	34.0	34.6	34.2	33.7	34.9	34.4
Education and Health Services													
2014	31.3	30.9	31.2	31.2	31.2	31.3	31.4	31.7	31.4	31.4	31.4	31.2	31.3
2015	31.4	31.1	31.2	31.2	31.0	31.2	31.4	31.7	31.3	31.5	31.5	31.1	31.3
2016	31.5	31.1	31.4	31.4	31.6	31.5	31.9	31.9	32.2	32.1	32.3	32.2	31.8
2017	32.2	31.9	31.9	32.2	32.2	32.3	32.5	32.5	32.5	32.4	32.8	32.5	32.3
2018	32.5	32.7	32.3	32.5	32.6	32.4	32.6	32.7	32.8	32.8	32.6	32.7	32.6
Leisure and Hospitality													
2014	24.6	24.1	25.0	25.6	25.6	25.2	25.7	26.2	26.1	26.0	26.2	25.7	25.5
2015	25.3	25.0	25.5	26.1	26.0	25.8	26.0	26.5	25.6	26.0	25.8	25.7	25.8
2016	24.8	25.4	25.6	26.7	26.7	26.3	26.4	26.0	25.7	25.9	25.2	24.9	25.8
2017	24.6	23.8	24.0	25.0	25.4	25.4	26.1	25.7	25.7	25.9	25.9	25.9	25.3
2018	25.3	25.8	25.7	26.3	26.5	26.4	26.9	26.5	26.2	26.1	25.6	25.7	26.1
Other Services													
2014	31.0	30.0	31.0	30.7	30.9	31.2	30.5	30.5	30.2	28.9	30.2	29.9	30.4
2015	29.2	29.2	28.9	29.0	28.8	28.9	29.8	29.5	29.5	30.4	30.6	31.1	29.6
2016	30.5	30.4	30.6	31.4	30.9	30.1	30.7	31.9	32.2	31.9	31.6	31.6	31.2
2017	31.7	30.6	31.7	32.0	32.3	32.3	32.0	32.6	32.1	32.6	32.0	32.3	32.0
2018	31.1	30.7	31.1	32.3	31.6	32.2	32.4	31.7	32.2	33.1	32.9	32.8	32.0

3. Average Hourly Earnings by Selected Industry: Connecticut, 2014–2018

(Dollars, not seasonally adjusted)

Industry and year	January	February	March	April	May	June	July	August	September	October	November	December	Annual average
Total Private													
2014	27.83	28.40	28.15	27.98	27.82	28.13	27.90	27.98	28.26	28.32	28.66	28.47	28.16
2015	28.54	29.13	29.04	28.73	28.68	28.75	28.79	29.35	29.49	29.49	29.89	29.80	29.14
2016	30.28	30.32	30.10	30.52	30.71	30.04	30.18	30.39	30.38	30.95	30.57	30.66	30.43
2017	31.36	31.30	31.39	31.63	31.03	30.78	31.08	30.82	31.00	31.47	30.94	31.18	31.16
2018	31.73	31.58	31.83	32.06	31.40	31.41	31.86	31.78	32.65	32.34	32.39	33.48	32.05
Goods-Producing													
2014	30.27	30.41	30.02	30.05	30.14	30.53	30.38	30.35	30.47	30.47	30.82	30.91	30.41
2015	31.01	30.88	30.84	30.74	30.52	30.27	30.61	31.00	31.25	31.39	31.55	31.67	30.98
2016	31.87	32.22	31.94	31.90	31.89	31.60	31.50	31.20	31.10	30.90	30.55	30.56	31.43
2017	31.04	31.42	31.20	30.47	31.06	31.19	31.04	31.50	31.52	31.90	31.92	31.96	31.36
2018	32.77	32.71	33.53	33.59	33.48	33.48	33.95	34.00	35.03	35.22	34.80	36.02	34.07
Construction													
2014	29.95	30.87	30.20	30.13	30.34	30.25	31.06	31.24	30.67	31.11	30.72	31.30	30.68
2015	31.28	30.72	31.84	31.31	31.05	30.76	31.19	30.78	30.95	31.37	31.07	30.93	31.10
2016	31.29	31.18	31.20	30.86	30.51	30.44	30.57	30.69	30.83	30.85	30.62	31.17	30.83
2017	31.24	31.70	31.98	31.81	30.76	30.99	31.15	31.88	31.13	31.65	31.75	31.23	31.43
2018	32.02	31.25	31.68	30.06	30.01	30.42	31.26	32.06	32.41	33.15	32.15	33.51	31.68
Manfacturing													
2014	30.36	30.27	29.92	30.01	30.04	30.59	30.06	29.95	30.34	30.18	30.88	30.80	30.29
2015	30.93	31.23	30.60	30.67	30.32	30.09	30.38	30.92	31.23	31.28	31.60	31.81	30.93
2016	31.90	32.41	32.05	32.15	32.34	31.98	31.78	31.28	31.04	30.80	30.43	30.27	31.53
2017	30.81	31.17	30.80	30.17	30.96	31.06	30.75	31.13	31.47	31.81	31.81	32.01	31.17
2018	33.04	33.20	33.94	34.65	34.64	34.55	34.70	34.50	35.73	35.79	35.64	37.15	34.81
Trade, Transportation, and Utilities													
2014	23.52	23.89	23.41	24.03	23.70	23.84	23.88	23.64	24.12	24.15	24.21	23.85	23.86
2015	24.45	25.08	24.57	24.30	24.53	24.23	24.18	24.23	24.89	25.01	25.29	25.17	24.67
2016	26.08	26.40	26.42	27.09	26.97	26.21	26.67	26.43	26.68	27.34	26.20	25.77	26.52
2017	26.78	26.82	27.22	27.20	26.76	26.35	26.80	26.24	26.36	26.41	25.99	26.01	26.57
2018	25.97	26.04	25.92	26.07	25.55	25.92	26.04	25.80	26.39	26.06	25.98	26.82	26.05
Financial Activities													
2014	43.82	44.36	44.95	44.20	43.89	45.07	43.84	43.29	43.24	43.00	44.21	42.56	43.87
2015	42.42	43.82	44.04	43.07	43.31	43.61	44.33	46.01	44.45	44.49	44.79	44.95	44.11
2016	44.56	43.39	42.31	45.62	45.89	43.88	44.33	46.15	44.49	47.30	45.57	44.58	44.85
2017	47.54	46.31	47.21	49.68	47.12	46.06	47.10	46.75	46.33	48.17	45.94	46.04	47.03
2018	47.61	46.80	46.93	49.73	47.33	46.76	48.02	48.34	49.93	48.10	48.48	50.28	48.20
Professional and Business Services													
2014	31.42	32.51	32.25	30.98	31.10	31.61	31.20	31.77	32.23	32.33	32.22	32.52	31.84
2015	32.07	32.67	33.10	33.11	32.76	33.84	33.97	34.71	34.50	33.96	34.46	33.95	33.60
2016	35.43	35.27	35.10	34.73	35.35	34.95	34.87	34.89	35.23	35.11	35.00	36.09	35.17
2017	36.36	35.91	36.24	35.99	35.41	35.39	35.78	35.00	35.69	36.09	35.67	35.90	35.78
2018	36.80	36.62	36.80	36.23	35.53	35.41	36.28	36.42	36.71	36.46	36.47	37.24	36.41
Education and Health Services													
2014	24.73	25.07	24.86	25.01	24.84	24.84	25.08	25.31	25.25	25.37	25.59	25.91	25.16
2015	25.72	26.12	25.94	26.05	26.06	26.18	26.05	26.06	26.45	26.39	26.67	27.10	26.23
2016	27.20	27.31	27.41	27.48	27.58	27.57	27.80	28.19	28.33	28.24	28.83	28.81	27.91
2017	28.76	28.81	28.66	28.95	28.56	28.56	28.44	28.55	28.72	28.73	28.43	28.82	28.67
2018	29.04	28.42	28.59	28.88	28.97	29.28	29.28	29.29	29.74	29.64	29.49	29.93	29.22
Leisure and Hospitality													
2014	15.07	15.45	15.34	15.45	15.36	15.37	15.31	15.42	15.62	15.98	16.07	16.10	15.55
2015	16.13	16.49	16.30	16.44	16.37	16.02	15.81	15.89	15.93	16.33	16.60	16.63	16.24
2016	16.75	16.94	16.66	16.63	16.66	16.21	16.23	16.35	16.27	16.60	16.84	17.10	16.59
2017	17.20	17.52	17.49	17.61	17.63	17.06	16.96	16.94	16.99	17.22	17.35	17.80	17.30
2018	17.95	18.04	18.20	18.10	18.14	17.68	17.80	17.57	18.33	18.56	18.40	18.36	18.09
Other Services													
2014	21.97	22.56	23.32	22.72	23.01	22.37	22.17	22.15	22.49	22.14	22.51	22.46	22.49
2015	22.27	22.66	22.19	21.68	22.23	21.98	20.95	21.13	21.58	22.24	22.34	22.08	21.94
2016	22.30	22.42	22.70	22.66	23.28	22.80	22.56	22.74	23.02	23.53	23.95	24.18	23.02
2017	24.82	25.42	24.93	25.04	25.12	24.74	25.46	24.78	25.26	25.21	24.95	25.62	25.11
2018	24.89	25.49	25.82	25.18	25.08	24.70	24.73	24.76	25.03	24.95	25.58	25.18	25.11

4. Average Weekly Earnings by Selected Industry: Connecticut, 2014–2018

(Dollars, not seasonally adjusted)

Industry and year	January	February	March	April	May	June	July	August	September	October	November	December	Annual average
Total Private													
2014	923.96	931.52	945.84	940.13	931.97	950.79	940.23	945.72	958.01	957.22	980.17	962.29	946.18
2015	956.09	972.94	975.74	959.58	955.04	957.38	961.59	997.90	984.97	993.81	1,010.28	1,001.28	976.19
2016	1,005.30	1,003.59	999.32	1,019.37	1,044.14	1,009.34	1,014.05	1,021.10	1,029.88	1,058.49	1,030.21	1,033.24	1,022.45
2017	1,056.83	1,032.90	1,032.73	1,065.93	1,042.61	1,034.21	1,053.61	1,041.72	1,050.90	1,073.13	1,048.87	1,057.00	1,050.09
2018	1,066.13	1,064.25	1,059.94	1,093.25	1,061.32	1,058.52	1,089.61	1,074.16	1,116.63	1,096.33	1,091.54	1,145.02	1,086.50
Goods-Producing													
2014	1,189.61	1,149.50	1,191.79	1,177.96	1,187.52	1,215.09	1,200.01	1,192.76	1,206.61	1,209.66	1,248.21	1,230.22	1,201.20
2015	1,228.00	1,201.23	1,230.52	1,211.16	1,196.38	1,183.56	1,196.85	1,236.90	1,225.00	1,246.18	1,268.31	1,273.13	1,223.71
2016	1,268.43	1,263.02	1,268.02	1,266.43	1,304.30	1,282.96	1,269.45	1,251.12	1,262.66	1,245.27	1,228.11	1,204.06	1,260.34
2017	1,207.46	1,197.10	1,194.96	1,188.33	1,211.34	1,219.53	1,216.77	1,231.65	1,235.58	1,260.05	1,254.46	1,275.20	1,226.18
2018	1,278.03	1,278.96	1,280.85	1,343.60	1,305.72	1,305.72	1,361.40	1,343.00	1,394.19	1,398.23	1,364.16	1,455.21	1,342.36
Construction													
2014	1,099.17	1,065.02	1,093.24	1,099.75	1,134.72	1,137.40	1,180.28	1,190.24	1,190.00	1,197.74	1,201.15	1,186.27	1,150.50
2015	1,194.90	1,115.14	1,229.02	1,221.09	1,232.69	1,193.49	1,235.12	1,221.97	1,194.67	1,261.07	1,217.94	1,231.01	1,212.90
2016	1,207.79	1,159.90	1,198.08	1,185.02	1,226.50	1,202.38	1,192.23	1,190.77	1,230.12	1,196.98	1,184.99	1,153.29	1,193.12
2017	1,149.63	1,134.86	1,154.48	1,192.88	1,184.26	1,205.51	1,174.36	1,221.00	1,192.28	1,186.88	1,216.03	1,168.00	1,181.77
2018	1,178.34	1,137.50	1,127.81	1,130.26	1,161.39	1,171.17	1,237.90	1,243.93	1,205.65	1,289.54	1,192.77	1,306.89	1,200.67
Manfacturing													
2014	1,223.51	1,180.53	1,208.77	1,191.40	1,195.59	1,232.78	1,196.39	1,186.02	1,207.53	1,210.22	1,266.08	1,247.40	1,211.60
2015	1,240.29	1,249.20	1,242.36	1,220.67	1,185.51	1,182.54	1,181.78	1,236.80	1,236.71	1,257.46	1,305.08	1,304.21	1,237.20
2016	1,301.52	1,312.61	1,307.64	1,311.72	1,342.11	1,320.77	1,309.34	1,279.35	1,272.64	1,268.96	1,250.67	1,238.04	1,292.73
2017	1,235.48	1,228.10	1,213.52	1,203.78	1,222.92	1,226.87	1,236.15	1,235.86	1,252.51	1,291.49	1,269.22	1,309.21	1,243.68
2018	1,314.99	1,328.00	1,330.45	1,417.19	1,385.60	1,382.00	1,419.23	1,390.35	1,482.80	1,456.65	1,454.11	1,567.73	1,409.81
Trade, Transportation, and Utilities													
2014	778.51	769.26	772.53	790.59	782.10	791.49	799.98	791.94	812.84	799.37	806.19	798.98	792.15
2015	797.07	812.59	803.44	801.90	807.04	794.74	800.36	809.28	836.30	835.33	829.51	833.13	814.11
2016	844.99	860.64	858.65	883.13	892.71	867.55	874.78	866.90	888.44	907.69	856.74	850.41	869.86
2017	867.67	855.56	851.99	875.84	861.67	851.11	876.36	850.18	867.24	858.33	855.07	855.73	860.87
2018	841.43	846.30	834.62	860.31	843.15	857.95	867.13	864.30	894.62	867.80	870.33	898.47	862.26
Financial Activities													
2014	1,634.49	1,694.55	1,721.59	1,644.24	1,645.88	1,721.67	1,639.62	1,636.36	1,643.12	1,646.90	1,719.77	1,630.05	1,667.06
2015	1,620.44	1,713.36	1,717.56	1,645.27	1,650.11	1,661.54	1,680.11	1,794.39	1,684.66	1,695.07	1,764.73	1,685.63	1,693.82
2016	1,657.63	1,627.13	1,586.63	1,706.19	1,762.18	1,627.95	1,644.64	1,698.32	1,650.58	1,825.78	1,690.65	1,645.00	1,677.39
2017	1,806.52	1,690.32	1,723.17	1,897.78	1,738.73	1,690.40	1,789.80	1,729.75	1,714.21	1,830.46	1,699.78	1,698.88	1,749.52
2018	1,775.85	1,736.28	1,741.10	1,884.77	1,746.48	1,720.77	1,824.76	1,778.91	1,867.38	1,755.65	1,759.82	1,880.47	1,788.22
Professional and Business Services													
2014	1,058.85	1,111.84	1,128.75	1,115.28	1,104.05	1,134.80	1,116.96	1,124.66	1,160.28	1,173.58	1,172.81	1,154.46	1,130.32
2015	1,116.04	1,140.18	1,161.81	1,148.92	1,136.77	1,177.63	1,175.36	1,221.79	1,179.90	1,178.41	1,212.99	1,188.25	1,169.28
2016	1,215.25	1,220.34	1,210.95	1,212.08	1,258.46	1,230.24	1,223.94	1,217.66	1,226.00	1,249.92	1,218.00	1,255.93	1,227.43
2017	1,287.14	1,242.49	1,253.90	1,277.65	1,264.14	1,266.96	1,291.66	1,249.50	1,267.00	1,281.20	1,244.88	1,242.14	1,263.03
2018	1,273.28	1,263.39	1,240.16	1,264.43	1,232.89	1,218.10	1,258.92	1,238.28	1,270.17	1,246.93	1,229.04	1,299.68	1,252.50
Education and Health Services													
2014	774.05	774.66	775.63	780.31	775.01	777.49	787.51	802.33	792.85	796.62	803.53	808.39	787.51
2015	807.61	812.33	809.33	812.76	807.86	816.82	817.97	826.10	827.89	831.29	840.11	842.81	821.00
2016	856.80	849.34	860.67	862.87	871.53	868.46	886.82	899.26	912.23	906.50	931.21	927.68	887.54
2017	926.07	919.04	914.25	932.19	919.63	922.49	924.30	927.88	933.40	930.85	932.50	936.65	926.04
2018	943.80	929.33	923.46	938.60	944.42	948.67	954.53	957.78	975.47	972.19	961.37	978.71	952.57
Leisure and Hospitality													
2014	370.72	372.35	383.50	395.52	393.22	387.32	393.47	404.00	407.68	415.48	421.03	413.77	396.53
2015	408.09	412.25	415.65	429.08	425.62	413.32	411.06	421.09	407.81	424.58	428.28	427.39	418.99
2016	415.40	430.28	426.50	444.02	444.82	426.32	428.47	425.10	418.14	429.94	424.37	425.79	428.02
2017	423.12	416.98	419.76	440.25	447.80	433.32	442.66	435.36	436.64	446.00	449.37	461.02	437.69
2018	454.14	465.43	467.74	476.03	480.71	466.75	478.82	465.61	480.25	484.42	471.04	471.85	472.15
Other Services													
2014	681.07	676.80	722.92	697.50	711.01	697.94	676.19	675.58	679.20	639.85	679.80	671.55	683.70
2015	650.28	661.67	641.29	628.72	640.22	635.22	624.31	623.34	636.61	676.10	683.60	686.69	649.42
2016	680.15	681.57	694.62	711.52	719.35	686.28	692.59	725.41	741.24	750.61	756.82	764.09	718.22
2017	786.79	777.85	790.28	801.28	811.38	799.10	814.72	807.83	810.85	821.85	798.40	827.53	803.52
2018	774.08	782.54	803.00	813.31	792.53	795.34	801.25	784.89	805.97	825.85	841.58	825.90	803.52

DELAWARE
At a Glance

Population:
  2010 census: 897,934
  2018 estimate: 967,171

Percent change in population:
  2010–2018: 7.7%

Percent change in total nonfarm employment:
  2010–2018: 11.5%

Industry with the largest growth in employment, 2010–2018 (percent):
  Transportation and utilities, 36.4%

Industry with the largest decline or smallest growth in employment, 2010–2018 (percent):
  Information, -31.7%

Civilian labor force:
  2010: 434,419
  2018: 482,465

Unemployment rate and rank among states (highest to lowest):
  2010: 8.4%, 29th
  2018: 3.8%, 27th

Over-the-year change in unemployment rates:
  2016–2017: 0.0%
  2017–2018: -0.7%

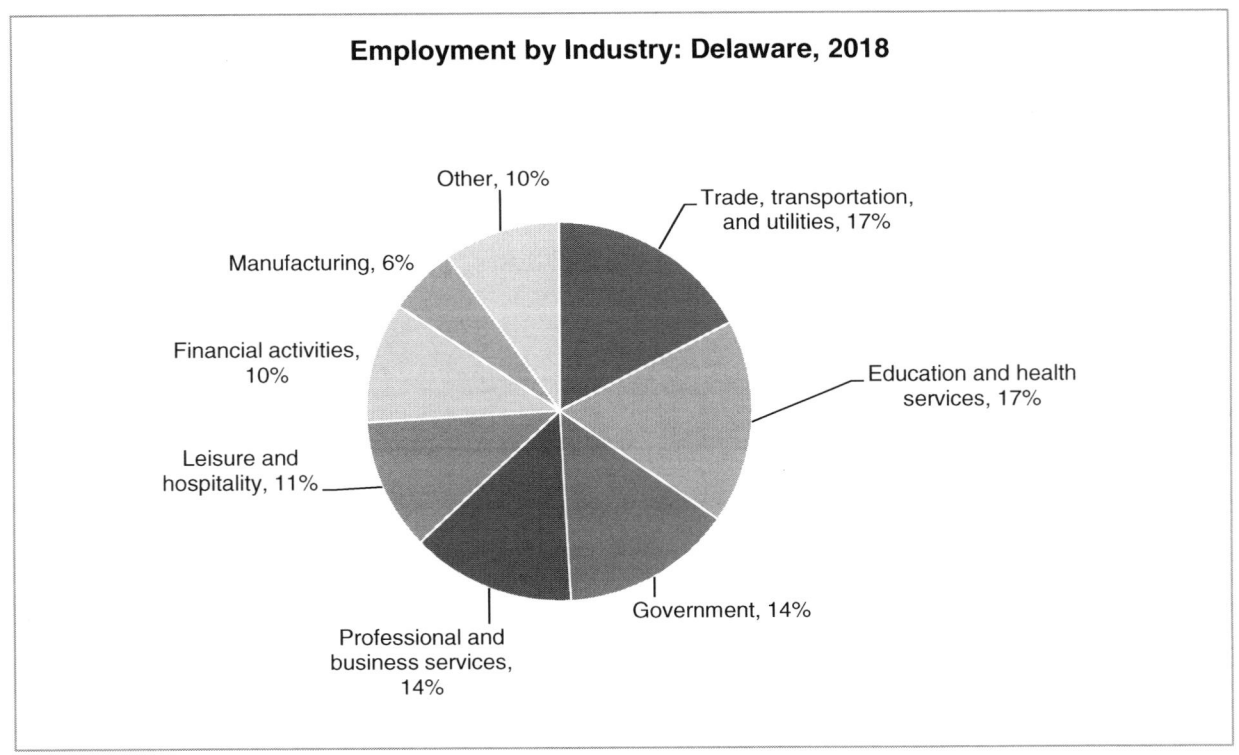

Employment by Industry: Delaware, 2018

Other, 10%
Trade, transportation, and utilities, 17%
Manufacturing, 6%
Financial activities, 10%
Education and health services, 17%
Leisure and hospitality, 11%
Professional and business services, 14%
Government, 14%

1. Employment by Industry: Delaware, 2010–2018

(Numbers in thousands, not seasonally adjusted)

Industry and year	January	February	March	April	May	June	July	August	September	October	November	December	Annual average
Total Nonfarm													
2010	399.9	397.2	404.0	411.6	417.2	420.0	420.2	419.1	419.3	418.1	419.0	420.1	413.8
2011	406.7	407.8	412.0	419.6	420.4	421.6	420.7	418.5	419.9	418.1	420.1	420.9	417.2
2012	406.9	407.9	412.8	416.6	422.4	423.4	423.0	422.2	421.8	423.9	427.2	427.4	419.6
2013	413.2	415.0	419.9	425.0	430.3	432.6	432.4	432.7	432.3	434.6	439.2	436.7	428.7
2014	424.3	423.7	428.3	434.1	440.9	442.9	442.0	441.3	440.9	443.2	448.2	449.0	438.2
2015	433.9	434.0	438.5	443.3	451.2	453.7	454.5	451.4	451.4	452.6	457.4	457.0	448.2
2016	441.1	441.4	445.9	451.0	454.5	457.4	459.0	456.1	455.2	455.5	458.5	458.6	452.9
2017	446.7	446.7	450.0	454.1	457.4	462.4	461.5	458.9	459.3	458.0	462.0	462.0	456.6
2018	448.8	450.8	454.2	459.9	465.5	467.4	466.6	463.4	461.9	464.1	466.6	465.8	461.3
Total Private													
2010	337.9	334.2	339.2	346.3	350.8	356.6	358.7	358.8	355.6	353.3	353.8	354.9	350.0
2011	344.0	344.1	346.9	353.4	355.2	359.3	360.0	358.4	356.4	353.1	354.9	355.9	353.5
2012	344.7	343.9	347.6	351.6	356.9	360.9	362.1	362.4	358.5	359.0	362.0	362.3	356.0
2013	351.8	350.9	354.4	359.4	364.6	369.5	371.2	372.5	368.4	369.1	373.2	371.2	364.7
2014	359.8	358.2	362.0	368.0	374.5	379.5	380.2	380.9	376.2	377.2	382.0	382.9	373.5
2015	369.8	369.2	370.9	376.8	384.0	388.9	391.8	390.2	386.2	386.2	390.9	390.4	382.9
2016	376.5	376.4	379.3	383.8	387.4	393.4	395.7	394.7	389.9	388.4	390.8	391.4	387.3
2017	381.1	380.9	382.2	386.4	389.7	397.4	398.0	397.2	393.0	391.1	394.9	395.0	390.6
2018	384.0	384.8	387.0	392.4	397.8	402.6	402.5	400.9	395.4	395.6	397.8	397.1	394.8
Goods Producing													
2010	44.5	43.0	44.0	45.5	45.6	46.4	46.0	46.2	45.9	46.0	45.7	45.7	45.4
2011	44.1	44.0	44.8	45.9	46.1	46.0	45.8	45.1	45.2	45.3	44.8	44.6	45.1
2012	43.1	42.8	43.1	43.8	44.4	44.6	45.3	45.2	45.0	44.9	45.0	44.8	44.3
2013	44.1	43.6	43.9	44.6	44.9	45.3	45.5	45.8	45.6	46.3	45.8	44.8	45.0
2014	43.7	43.6	44.5	45.1	45.9	46.7	46.8	46.9	46.6	46.7	46.7	46.5	45.8
2015	45.0	45.0	45.0	46.1	46.8	47.1	47.5	47.7	47.9	47.2	46.7	46.7	46.6
2016	45.6	45.8	46.5	46.3	46.6	47.2	47.6	47.9	47.6	47.8	47.8	47.8	47.0
2017	46.9	47.2	47.7	47.8	47.6	48.2	48.3	48.0	48.1	48.0	48.4	48.5	47.9
2018	47.4	47.9	48.3	48.9	49.3	50.0	49.9	50.0	49.8	50.3	50.4	50.6	49.4
Service-Providing													
2010	355.4	354.2	360.0	366.1	371.6	373.6	374.2	372.9	373.4	372.1	373.3	374.4	368.4
2011	362.6	363.8	367.2	373.7	374.3	375.6	374.9	373.4	374.7	372.8	375.3	376.3	372.1
2012	363.8	365.1	369.7	372.8	378.0	378.8	377.7	377.0	376.8	379.0	382.2	382.6	375.3
2013	369.1	371.4	376.0	380.4	385.4	387.3	386.9	386.9	386.7	388.3	393.4	391.9	383.6
2014	380.6	380.1	383.8	389.0	395.0	396.2	395.2	394.4	394.3	396.5	401.5	402.5	392.4
2015	388.9	389.0	393.5	397.2	404.4	406.6	407.0	403.7	403.5	405.4	410.7	410.3	401.7
2016	395.5	395.6	399.4	404.7	407.9	410.2	411.4	408.2	407.6	407.7	410.7	410.8	405.8
2017	399.8	399.5	402.3	406.3	409.8	414.2	413.2	410.9	411.2	410.0	413.6	413.5	408.7
2018	401.4	402.9	405.9	411.0	416.2	417.4	416.7	413.4	412.1	413.8	416.2	415.2	411.9
Mining, Logging, and Construction													
2010	18.0	17.1	18.0	19.3	19.6	20.1	19.9	20.1	19.8	20.1	20.0	19.9	19.3
2011	18.7	18.6	19.3	20.2	20.1	19.9	19.6	19.1	19.2	19.3	18.9	18.8	19.3
2012	17.7	17.3	17.5	18.1	18.5	18.7	19.1	19.2	19.0	19.1	19.3	19.2	18.6
2013	18.6	18.3	18.6	19.3	19.6	19.9	20.2	20.5	20.3	20.8	20.4	19.6	19.7
2014	18.9	18.7	19.4	20.0	20.7	21.2	21.4	21.3	21.0	21.0	21.0	20.8	20.5
2015	19.4	19.4	19.5	20.4	21.1	21.1	21.6	21.7	21.9	21.5	21.0	20.8	20.8
2016	19.8	19.9	20.8	20.5	20.6	21.0	21.4	21.6	21.5	21.7	21.6	21.5	21.0
2017	20.7	20.9	21.6	21.8	21.5	21.9	22.0	21.9	22.0	21.7	21.7	21.6	21.6
2018	20.6	21.0	21.4	22.0	22.4	22.7	22.8	22.8	22.7	23.1	23.1	23.3	22.3
Manufacturing													
2010	26.5	25.9	26.0	26.2	26.0	26.3	26.1	26.1	26.1	25.9	25.7	25.8	26.1
2011	25.4	25.4	25.5	25.7	26.0	26.1	26.2	26.0	26.0	26.0	25.9	25.8	25.8
2012	25.4	25.5	25.6	25.7	25.9	25.9	26.2	26.0	26.0	25.8	25.7	25.6	25.8
2013	25.5	25.3	25.3	25.3	25.3	25.4	25.3	25.3	25.3	25.5	25.4	25.2	25.3
2014	24.8	24.9	25.1	25.1	25.2	25.5	25.4	25.6	25.6	25.7	25.7	25.7	25.4
2015	25.6	25.6	25.5	25.7	25.7	26.0	25.9	26.0	26.0	25.7	25.7	25.9	25.8
2016	25.8	25.9	25.7	25.8	26.0	26.2	26.2	26.3	26.1	26.1	26.2	26.3	26.1
2017	26.2	26.3	26.1	26.0	26.1	26.3	26.3	26.1	26.1	26.3	26.7	26.9	26.3
2018	26.8	26.9	26.9	26.9	26.9	27.3	27.1	27.2	27.1	27.2	27.3	27.3	27.1

1. Employment by Industry: Delaware, 2010–2018—*Continued*

(Numbers in thousands, not seasonally adjusted)

Industry and year	January	February	March	April	May	June	July	August	September	October	November	December	Annual average
Trade, Transportation, and Utilities													
2010	72.4	71.0	72.0	73.1	74.3	75.1	74.8	74.7	74.6	74.9	77.0	77.8	74.3
2011	73.9	73.3	73.6	75.0	75.2	75.9	75.6	75.3	75.4	75.1	77.6	78.4	75.4
2012	74.3	73.4	74.3	74.4	75.7	75.9	75.7	75.6	75.2	76.1	78.9	79.2	75.7
2013	75.0	74.2	75.0	75.8	76.7	77.3	77.3	77.8	77.9	78.9	81.4	82.1	77.5
2014	77.5	76.6	77.1	77.9	78.7	79.5	79.7	80.3	79.7	80.1	82.5	83.8	79.5
2015	79.0	78.5	78.8	79.7	80.4	81.1	81.5	81.7	81.2	82.5	85.2	85.8	81.3
2016	80.8	80.1	80.8	81.3	81.6	81.7	82.1	82.2	82.0	81.8	83.6	84.0	81.8
2017	80.4	79.2	79.1	79.7	80.0	80.7	80.2	81.1	81.1	81.0	83.7	84.2	80.9
2018	79.7	79.1	79.3	80.0	80.8	80.9	80.2	80.1	79.8	79.4	80.8	81.1	80.1
Wholesale Trade													
2010	12.2	12.3	12.3	12.5	12.4	12.4	12.4	12.4	12.4	12.2	12.3	12.2	12.3
2011	12.4	12.4	12.4	12.5	12.4	12.4	12.5	12.4	12.4	12.3	12.3	12.4	12.4
2012	12.3	12.3	12.5	12.4	12.3	12.3	12.3	12.3	12.2	12.1	12.1	12.1	12.3
2013	11.9	11.9	12.0	12.0	12.1	12.1	12.0	12.0	12.0	11.8	11.9	12.0	12.0
2014	11.7	11.6	11.7	11.8	11.9	11.9	11.8	11.8	11.7	11.6	11.7	11.8	11.8
2015	11.5	11.4	11.5	11.5	11.6	11.7	11.5	11.5	11.4	11.4	11.4	11.4	11.5
2016	11.2	11.2	11.2	11.2	11.3	11.2	11.1	11.0	10.9	10.7	10.7	10.7	11.0
2017	10.6	10.5	10.4	10.6	10.6	10.7	10.6	10.6	10.5	10.6	10.6	10.6	10.6
2018	10.5	10.5	10.5	10.7	10.7	10.8	10.8	10.8	10.8	10.8	11.0	11.1	10.8
Retail Trade													
2010	48.0	46.7	47.6	48.5	49.6	50.5	50.9	50.8	49.9	50.3	52.3	53.0	49.8
2011	49.2	48.6	48.9	50.1	50.3	51.1	51.4	51.4	50.5	50.2	52.6	53.1	50.6
2012	49.6	48.7	49.3	49.9	50.7	51.2	51.3	51.1	50.0	50.5	53.0	53.1	50.7
2013	49.5	48.9	49.5	50.2	51.0	51.7	52.1	52.5	51.5	52.2	54.4	54.8	51.5
2014	50.9	50.2	50.6	51.4	52.1	53.2	53.3	53.3	52.2	52.5	54.5	55.2	52.5
2015	51.5	50.9	51.1	51.9	52.5	53.4	53.7	53.6	52.6	53.4	55.8	55.9	53.0
2016	52.3	51.8	52.4	53.0	53.4	54.2	54.7	54.8	53.7	53.7	55.3	55.6	53.7
2017	52.6	52.1	52.1	52.8	53.2	54.0	54.0	54.0	53.0	53.1	55.5	55.7	53.5
2018	52.5	52.1	52.3	52.7	53.4	53.9	53.7	53.4	52.2	52.1	53.3	53.1	52.9
Transportation and Utilities													
2010	12.2	12.0	12.1	12.1	12.3	12.2	11.5	11.5	12.3	12.4	12.4	12.6	12.1
2011	12.3	12.3	12.3	12.4	12.5	12.4	11.7	11.5	12.5	12.6	12.7	12.9	12.3
2012	12.4	12.4	12.5	12.1	12.7	12.4	12.1	12.2	13.0	13.5	13.8	14.0	12.8
2013	13.6	13.4	13.5	13.6	13.6	13.5	13.2	13.3	14.4	14.9	15.1	15.3	14.0
2014	14.9	14.8	14.8	14.7	14.7	14.4	14.6	15.2	15.8	16.0	16.3	16.8	15.3
2015	16.0	16.2	16.2	16.3	16.3	16.0	16.3	16.6	17.2	17.7	18.0	18.5	16.8
2016	17.3	17.1	17.2	17.1	16.9	16.3	16.3	16.4	17.4	17.4	17.6	17.7	17.1
2017	17.2	16.6	16.6	16.3	16.2	16.0	15.6	16.5	17.6	17.3	17.6	17.9	16.8
2018	16.7	16.5	16.5	16.6	16.7	16.2	15.7	15.9	16.8	16.5	16.5	16.9	16.5
Information													
2010	5.9	5.9	6.0	6.1	6.0	6.0	6.0	5.9	6.0	5.9	5.9	5.8	6.0
2011	5.8	5.8	5.8	5.8	5.6	5.8	5.7	5.2	5.7	5.5	5.6	5.7	5.7
2012	5.6	5.6	5.6	5.5	5.5	5.5	5.4	5.5	5.3	5.3	5.3	5.3	5.5
2013	5.3	5.4	5.3	5.3	5.2	5.2	5.2	5.2	5.1	5.0	5.1	5.0	5.2
2014	5.1	4.9	4.9	4.9	5.0	4.9	4.9	5.0	4.8	4.9	4.9	4.8	4.9
2015	4.8	4.7	4.7	4.7	4.8	4.7	4.7	4.6	4.6	4.7	4.7	4.7	4.7
2016	4.6	4.6	4.6	4.6	4.3	4.7	4.7	4.7	4.7	4.6	4.6	4.7	4.6
2017	4.6	4.6	4.6	4.5	4.5	4.6	4.5	4.5	4.4	4.3	4.4	4.3	4.5
2018	4.2	4.3	4.2	4.1	4.1	4.1	4.0	4.0	3.9	3.9	4.0	3.8	4.1

1. Employment by Industry: Delaware, 2010–2018—*Continued*

(Numbers in thousands, not seasonally adjusted)

Industry and year	January	February	March	April	May	June	July	August	September	October	November	December	Annual average
Financial Activities													
2010	42.4	42.5	42.6	42.5	42.4	43.1	43.4	43.4	43.0	42.3	42.3	42.7	42.7
2011	42.3	42.4	42.3	42.4	42.2	42.8	43.1	42.8	42.3	41.4	41.3	41.7	42.3
2012	41.3	41.3	41.5	41.5	42.1	42.7	43.3	43.5	42.7	42.8	42.9	43.3	42.4
2013	42.9	43.2	43.3	43.3	43.5	44.2	44.7	44.7	44.1	44.0	44.3	44.5	43.9
2014	44.1	44.2	44.1	44.3	44.7	45.3	45.5	45.7	45.3	45.4	45.6	46.2	45.0
2015	45.7	46.0	46.1	46.3	46.2	46.6	47.0	47.3	47.2	46.9	47.1	46.9	46.6
2016	46.7	46.8	46.9	46.9	46.8	47.4	47.5	47.5	46.9	47.0	47.3	47.6	47.1
2017	47.3	47.4	47.5	47.5	47.7	48.6	48.6	48.6	48.1	47.9	47.9	48.0	47.9
2018	47.5	47.7	47.6	47.6	47.5	47.9	47.9	47.4	46.9	47.2	47.1	47.1	47.5
Professional and Business Services													
2010	53.2	53.3	53.6	54.3	54.9	55.2	55.8	55.6	55.3	55.8	55.5	56.7	54.9
2011	53.9	54.3	54.3	55.9	55.4	55.7	55.8	55.9	55.8	56.1	57.1	57.6	55.7
2012	54.9	54.6	55.2	56.1	55.9	55.9	56.0	56.2	56.0	57.0	58.5	58.6	56.2
2013	55.9	55.5	56.5	57.5	57.8	58.2	58.7	59.3	58.9	59.4	62.2	60.7	58.4
2014	58.1	57.1	57.8	59.0	59.7	60.0	60.0	59.8	59.6	60.7	64.2	63.6	60.0
2015	59.9	58.9	59.1	59.2	60.6	61.1	61.8	60.7	60.1	61.7	65.1	64.6	61.1
2016	60.5	59.6	59.7	60.6	61.1	62.7	62.8	62.1	61.1	61.7	63.3	64.2	61.6
2017	61.1	60.5	60.2	61.5	61.7	63.1	63.0	62.5	61.8	61.8	63.7	64.7	62.1
2018	61.5	61.3	61.8	63.2	63.6	64.4	64.6	64.1	63.6	64.8	65.9	64.9	63.6
Education and Health Services													
2010	63.7	63.6	64.2	64.8	64.9	64.5	65.1	65.4	65.2	65.3	65.5	65.5	64.8
2011	65.4	65.6	66.2	66.7	66.5	66.2	66.3	66.4	66.8	67.3	67.4	68.0	66.6
2012	67.3	67.4	67.8	68.1	68.4	68.5	68.3	68.4	69.0	69.5	69.7	70.0	68.5
2013	69.3	69.6	69.8	69.8	70.0	69.8	69.9	70.3	70.5	70.9	71.6	71.9	70.3
2014	71.4	71.6	72.1	72.4	72.8	72.4	72.3	72.5	73.0	73.6	74.1	74.3	72.7
2015	74.1	74.4	74.4	75.3	75.6	75.8	75.8	75.3	75.7	76.3	76.5	76.6	75.5
2016	76.1	76.5	76.6	76.8	77.0	76.7	76.9	76.8	77.2	77.6	77.7	77.8	77.0
2017	76.8	77.6	77.6	78.0	78.2	77.8	78.0	77.9	78.5	79.1	79.3	79.3	78.2
2018	79.0	79.1	79.6	79.9	80.2	79.7	79.6	79.3	79.8	81.0	81.5	82.2	80.1
Leisure and Hospitality													
2010	37.8	37.2	38.8	41.8	44.4	47.6	49.1	49.0	47.2	44.8	43.7	42.5	43.7
2011	40.5	40.6	41.8	43.6	46.0	48.5	49.3	49.3	47.0	44.3	43.1	41.9	44.7
2012	40.3	40.8	42.0	44.0	46.6	49.3	49.6	49.4	47.0	45.0	43.3	42.7	45.0
2013	41.1	41.2	42.3	44.6	48.0	50.8	51.2	50.7	47.9	46.2	44.3	43.7	46.0
2014	41.7	41.9	43.1	45.8	49.0	51.9	52.3	51.9	48.7	47.2	45.3	45.0	47.0
2015	43.0	43.3	44.5	46.9	50.8	53.5	54.7	54.1	50.9	48.3	47.0	46.5	48.6
2016	43.9	44.6	45.7	48.5	51.1	54.0	55.2	54.6	51.8	49.3	47.9	46.7	49.4
2017	45.5	45.9	46.9	48.5	51.1	55.2	56.4	55.7	52.6	50.4	48.9	47.5	50.4
2018	46.4	47.1	47.9	50.1	53.6	56.7	57.4	57.2	53.1	50.3	49.3	48.7	51.5
Other Services													
2010	18.0	17.7	18.0	18.2	18.3	18.7	18.5	18.6	18.4	18.3	18.2	18.2	18.3
2011	18.1	18.1	18.1	18.1	18.2	18.4	18.4	18.4	18.2	18.1	18.0	18.0	18.2
2012	17.9	18.0	18.1	18.2	18.3	18.5	18.5	18.6	18.3	18.4	18.4	18.4	18.3
2013	18.2	18.2	18.3	18.5	18.5	18.7	18.7	18.7	18.4	18.4	18.5	18.5	18.5
2014	18.2	18.3	18.4	18.6	18.7	18.8	18.7	18.8	18.5	18.6	18.7	18.7	18.6
2015	18.3	18.4	18.3	18.6	18.8	19.0	18.8	18.8	18.6	18.6	18.6	18.6	18.6
2016	18.3	18.4	18.5	18.8	18.9	19.0	18.9	18.9	18.6	18.6	18.6	18.6	18.7
2017	18.5	18.5	18.6	18.9	18.9	19.2	19.0	18.9	18.4	18.6	18.6	18.5	18.7
2018	18.3	18.3	18.3	18.6	18.7	18.9	18.9	18.8	18.5	18.7	18.8	18.7	18.6
Government													
2010	62.0	63.0	64.8	65.3	66.4	63.4	61.5	60.3	63.7	64.8	65.2	65.2	63.8
2011	62.7	63.7	65.1	66.2	65.2	62.3	60.7	60.1	63.5	65.0	65.2	65.0	63.7
2012	62.2	64.0	65.2	65.0	65.5	62.5	60.9	59.8	63.3	64.9	65.2	65.1	63.6
2013	61.4	64.1	65.5	65.6	65.7	63.1	61.2	60.2	63.9	65.5	66.0	65.5	64.0
2014	64.5	65.5	66.3	66.1	66.4	63.4	61.8	60.4	64.7	66.0	66.2	66.1	64.8
2015	64.1	64.8	67.6	66.5	67.2	64.8	62.7	61.2	65.2	66.4	66.5	66.6	65.3
2016	64.6	65.0	66.6	67.2	67.1	64.0	63.3	61.4	65.3	67.1	67.7	67.2	65.5
2017	65.6	65.8	67.8	67.7	67.7	65.0	63.5	61.7	66.3	66.9	67.1	67.0	66.0
2018	64.8	66.0	67.2	67.5	67.7	64.8	64.1	62.5	66.5	68.5	68.8	68.7	66.4

2. Average Weekly Hours by Selected Industry: Delaware, 2014–2018

(Not seasonally adjusted)

Industry and year	January	February	March	April	May	June	July	August	September	October	November	December	Annual average
Total Private													
2014	31.9	32.0	32.6	32.6	32.7	32.9	33.1	33.5	33.0	32.9	33.5	33.8	32.9
2015	33.1	33.3	33.3	33.2	33.4	33.0	33.4	33.5	33.2	32.5	32.4	33.6	33.2
2016	33.3	33.2	33.3	33.2	33.3	33.4	33.7	33.2	32.9	33.3	32.6	32.8	33.2
2017	32.3	32.1	32.2	33.1	32.3	33.4	34.0	33.5	33.1	32.9	32.8	32.8	32.9
2018	32.9	32.8	32.5	33.2	32.8	33.1	33.7	33.5	33.2	32.5	32.8	33.2	33.0
Goods Producing													
2014	38.6	38.1	38.8	38.8	39.3	39.9	40.4	40.7	40.2	39.4	38.1	38.5	39.3
2015	39.0	38.0	37.9	39.4	39.3	39.0	38.9	39.1	38.7	38.4	36.9	38.6	38.6
2016	39.2	37.7	38.7	38.3	39.0	39.4	39.8	40.0	40.5	40.3	39.1	38.9	39.3
2017	39.6	38.4	38.2	40.1	39.5	40.0	39.8	39.2	39.8	39.6	40.0	39.4	39.5
2018	40.3	39.6	39.1	40.8	40.4	40.3	40.7	40.3	39.7	39.6	40.1	40.1	40.1
Mining, Logging, and Construction													
2014	18.9	18.7	19.4	20.0	20.7	21.2	21.4	21.3	21.0	21.0	21.0	20.8	20.5
2015	19.4	19.4	19.5	20.4	21.1	21.1	21.6	21.7	21.9	21.5	21.0	20.8	20.8
2016	19.8	19.9	20.8	20.5	20.6	21.0	21.4	21.6	21.5	21.7	21.6	21.5	21.0
2017	20.7	20.9	21.6	21.8	21.5	21.9	22.0	21.9	22.0	21.7	21.7	21.6	21.6
2018	20.6	21.0	21.4	22.0	22.4	22.7	22.8	22.8	22.7	23.1	23.1	23.3	22.3
Manufacturing													
2014	39.7	38.9	39.3	39.1	40.0	39.7	40.3	40.2	40.9	39.7	38.8	39.4	39.7
2015	40.6	39.3	38.7	40.2	41.4	40.0	40.9	40.9	40.8	40.4	38.9	39.5	40.1
2016	41.0	39.2	39.1	39.1	40.3	39.9	40.1	40.1	40.6	39.4	39.2	39.9	39.8
2017	41.8	39.4	39.8	41.4	40.8	41.7	41.5	40.7	40.8	40.4	41.4	40.8	40.9
2018	43.2	41.5	40.9	42.5	42.1	42.0	42.1	41.8	41.9	41.9	42.8	41.4	42.0
Trade, Transportation, and Utilities													
2014	31.2	31.4	32.3	32.1	32.3	32.3	32.8	33.6	32.8	32.7	33.7	34.5	32.7
2015	32.4	32.7	32.9	33.2	34.2	34.0	34.1	34.2	34.6	33.1	33.4	35.2	33.7
2016	34.3	34.1	33.5	33.8	33.7	33.9	33.7	33.2	33.4	33.6	33.1	33.8	33.7
2017	33.1	32.6	32.8	33.3	33.1	33.0	33.1	32.8	33.4	33.2	32.4	33.1	33.0
2018	31.8	31.8	31.8	32.4	32.5	33.0	33.2	33.1	33.1	32.1	33.0	32.8	32.6
Financial Activities													
2014	36.1	35.8	36.2	36.1	36.4	36.7	36.3	36.7	36.7	36.9	37.8	37.8	36.6
2015	37.5	38.5	38.3	38.2	38.2	38.4	38.6	38.8	38.4	38.3	38.8	38.5	38.4
2016	38.8	38.4	38.8	38.6	39.3	39.2	38.9	38.9	39.0	39.0	39.0	39.2	38.9
2017	40.1	38.7	38.8	39.5	37.8	38.5	39.4	38.2	38.0	38.1	37.4	37.4	38.5
2018	37.5	37.4	37.9	38.7	36.9	37.4	38.5	37.2	38.5	37.2	37.2	38.3	37.7
Professional and Business Services													
2014	34.4	35.5	35.8	36.4	36.0	35.3	34.7	34.9	34.4	34.7	36.2	36.5	35.4
2015	35.8	36.8	36.9	37.1	36.4	35.2	35.1	35.3	33.7	32.9	32.5	36.0	35.3
2016	35.3	35.9	36.2	36.1	36.5	35.4	35.7	34.9	34.3	36.0	34.1	34.0	35.4
2017	31.0	32.0	31.7	33.3	31.7	32.3	33.8	33.1	31.7	30.4	30.3	30.5	31.8
2018	30.3	30.1	30.7	31.8	32.1	33.5	35.3	35.5	34.2	32.7	33.0	34.0	32.8
Education and Health Services													
2014	31.6	31.1	31.2	31.8	32.2	32.3	32.3	32.8	32.9	32.8	33.0	32.8	32.2
2015	32.6	32.5	32.1	31.7	31.9	32.3	32.3	32.0	32.1	31.7	32.0	32.4	32.1
2016	32.4	32.3	32.4	32.4	32.3	32.6	33.2	32.9	32.5	32.5	32.2	32.0	32.5
2017	32.8	32.6	32.4	32.9	32.4	32.7	32.9	33.0	32.6	33.0	32.8	32.5	32.7
2018	33.1	32.9	32.2	32.7	32.3	32.3	32.2	32.4	32.1	31.9	31.7	31.3	32.3
Leisure and Hospitality													
2014	24.1	24.1	24.7	24.8	24.5	25.2	26.2	26.2	24.9	24.4	24.8	24.9	24.9
2015	24.3	24.4	24.6	24.5	24.9	24.5	26.0	26.3	25.0	24.3	23.8	23.5	24.7
2016	23.0	23.6	23.6	23.7	23.9	25.2	25.7	25.4	24.2	23.9	23.4	23.6	24.2
2017	23.1	23.3	23.9	23.9	23.3	24.6	25.8	25.6	24.3	23.7	24.1	24.0	24.2
2018	23.8	24.1	24.0	24.4	24.3	25.1	26.3	26.1	24.6	24.0	23.3	23.8	24.5

3. Average Hourly Earnings by Selected Industry: Delaware, 2014–2018

(Dollars, not seasonally adjusted)

Industry and year	January	February	March	April	May	June	July	August	September	October	November	December	Annual average
Total Private													
2014	21.95	22.17	21.92	21.61	21.73	21.81	21.37	21.31	21.69	21.74	21.69	21.49	21.70
2015	22.07	22.53	22.56	22.27	22.12	22.08	22.12	22.67	22.87	23.34	23.62	23.27	22.63
2016	24.00	24.13	24.25	24.42	24.38	23.76	23.85	24.09	24.43	25.33	25.16	24.97	24.40
2017	25.79	25.84	25.74	26.00	25.23	26.73	26.63	26.21	26.61	26.82	26.38	26.58	26.22
2018	25.83	26.07	26.33	26.08	25.68	25.49	25.96	25.80	26.54	26.66	26.77	27.21	26.20
Goods Producing													
2014	23.95	24.26	24.48	24.17	24.65	25.07	24.77	25.03	24.93	24.87	25.38	25.00	24.73
2015	24.70	25.16	25.06	24.42	24.44	24.87	25.00	25.50	25.39	25.21	25.34	25.25	25.03
2016	25.10	25.28	25.50	25.34	25.17	25.24	25.68	25.92	25.58	25.97	26.20	25.66	25.56
2017	25.63	25.64	26.04	26.34	25.86	25.39	25.59	25.44	25.92	25.58	25.29	25.41	25.68
2018	24.74	25.06	25.68	25.75	25.74	25.48	26.11	25.77	25.57	26.14	26.12	27.37	25.80
Mining, Logging, and Construction													
2014	26.88	27.03	27.44	27.06	28.11	28.20	27.83	27.40	27.64	27.77	28.19	28.09	27.65
2015	28.19	28.67	28.51	27.70	28.27	28.35	28.60	28.86	28.07	28.05	27.83	28.02	28.26
2016	28.43	29.32	28.89	28.74	28.89	28.45	28.69	29.28	29.07	29.48	29.83	29.00	29.02
2017	28.86	28.64	29.04	29.03	28.78	27.73	27.62	27.19	28.10	27.44	26.58	27.39	28.02
2018	26.79	26.59	27.42	27.60	27.69	26.76	27.32	27.03	26.44	27.97	27.56	28.15	27.29
Manufacturing													
2014	21.85	22.30	22.25	21.92	21.92	22.45	22.18	23.00	22.79	22.55	23.18	22.64	22.42
2015	22.30	22.70	22.56	21.93	21.66	22.21	22.33	22.96	23.37	23.09	23.54	23.14	22.65
2016	22.81	22.43	22.83	22.77	22.42	22.74	23.26	23.17	22.74	22.92	23.22	23.09	22.87
2017	23.38	23.39	23.77	24.26	23.62	23.62	24.04	24.09	24.18	24.11	24.32	23.94	23.89
2018	23.41	23.99	24.44	24.37	24.26	24.51	25.16	24.80	24.92	24.78	25.06	26.75	24.70
Trade, Transportation, and Utilities													
2014	18.69	18.81	18.71	18.21	18.14	18.52	18.15	18.05	18.08	17.95	18.07	18.10	18.28
2015	19.01	18.97	18.95	18.66	18.44	18.67	18.55	18.90	18.76	19.11	19.03	19.02	18.84
2016	19.22	19.13	19.30	19.54	19.95	19.57	19.64	20.15	20.16	20.74	20.59	20.08	19.84
2017	21.00	20.82	20.94	21.60	21.06	21.64	21.47	21.10	21.50	21.89	21.23	21.51	21.32
2018	21.92	21.86	21.92	22.44	21.82	21.54	22.14	22.27	22.23	21.94	22.09	22.01	22.02
Financial Activities													
2014	23.49	23.74	23.29	22.62	23.37	24.71	24.29	24.62	25.15	25.68	27.13	26.12	24.55
2015	25.93	27.28	27.76	26.91	27.21	27.68	28.22	29.60	29.17	29.63	31.14	30.42	28.43
2016	32.14	32.82	33.01	32.24	31.53	30.30	30.67	30.54	30.24	32.35	31.34	31.24	31.53
2017	31.51	32.88	32.24	33.07	30.41	29.68	30.44	30.36	31.00	32.01	31.88	31.13	31.38
2018	31.74	32.25	32.76	32.18	32.49	31.84	32.99	33.02	33.67	33.08	33.56	34.08	32.80
Professional and Business Services													
2014	28.24	28.27	27.45	27.33	27.69	26.73	26.25	26.13	26.46	25.68	23.39	22.89	26.31
2015	24.53	24.74	24.57	24.94	24.90	24.27	24.68	26.25	26.86	26.59	25.71	23.76	25.12
2016	25.60	26.64	26.79	27.38	27.76	27.27	27.73	28.28	29.15	30.22	29.85	29.89	28.05
2017	33.72	34.43	33.95	33.11	32.16	32.12	32.80	32.21	32.71	32.72	32.62	33.17	32.97
2018	30.44	30.59	30.25	30.14	29.33	30.18	31.26	30.52	31.62	31.31	31.79	32.50	30.86
Education and Health Services													
2014	23.10	23.35	23.20	23.21	23.01	23.03	23.24	22.54	22.88	23.35	22.99	23.57	23.12
2015	23.81	23.87	24.11	24.42	24.27	24.12	24.79	24.84	25.37	26.40	25.98	26.16	24.85
2016	26.27	26.22	26.28	27.13	27.30	27.13	27.38	27.58	28.23	29.17	29.18	29.33	27.60
2017	28.44	28.49	28.05	28.27	27.75	27.45	27.13	27.32	27.35	27.77	27.15	27.75	27.74
2018	27.96	28.38	29.35	28.94	28.57	28.58	28.96	29.09	29.22	29.23	28.65	28.43	28.78
Leisure and Hospitality													
2014	13.11	13.37	13.20	13.01	13.05	13.02	12.91	13.09	13.19	13.36	13.16	13.21	13.13
2015	12.94	13.13	13.08	13.08	13.22	13.02	12.93	12.91	13.19	13.35	13.70	13.88	13.19
2016	13.63	13.62	13.74	13.57	13.46	12.95	13.06	13.46	13.89	14.02	14.03	14.19	13.61
2017	14.38	14.76	14.66	14.77	14.86	14.25	14.24	14.41	14.40	14.69	14.41	14.77	14.54
2018	14.52	14.65	14.73	14.51	14.72	14.58	14.77	14.83	15.01	15.30	15.13	15.37	14.84

4. Average Weekly Earnings by Selected Industry: Delaware, 2014–2018

(Dollars, not seasonally adjusted)

Industry and year	January	February	March	April	May	June	July	August	September	October	November	December	Annual average
Total Private													
2014	700.21	709.44	714.59	704.49	710.57	717.55	707.35	713.89	715.77	715.25	726.62	726.36	713.93
2015	730.52	750.25	751.25	739.36	738.81	728.64	738.81	759.45	759.28	758.55	765.29	781.87	751.32
2016	799.20	801.12	807.53	810.74	811.85	793.58	803.75	799.79	803.75	843.49	820.22	819.02	810.08
2017	833.02	829.46	828.83	860.60	814.93	892.78	905.42	878.04	880.79	882.38	865.26	871.82	862.64
2018	849.81	855.10	855.73	865.86	842.30	843.72	874.85	864.30	881.13	866.45	878.06	903.37	864.60
Goods Producing													
2014	924.47	924.31	949.82	937.80	968.75	1,000.29	1,000.71	1,018.72	1,002.19	979.88	966.98	962.50	971.89
2015	963.30	956.08	949.77	962.15	960.49	969.93	972.50	997.05	982.59	968.06	935.05	974.65	966.16
2016	983.92	953.06	986.85	970.52	981.63	994.46	1,022.06	1,036.80	1,035.99	1,046.59	1,024.42	998.17	1,004.51
2017	1,014.95	984.58	994.73	1,056.23	1,021.47	1,015.60	1,018.48	997.25	1,031.62	1,012.97	1,011.60	1,001.15	1,014.36
2018	997.02	992.38	1,004.09	1,050.60	1,039.90	1,026.84	1,062.68	1,038.53	1,015.13	1,035.14	1,047.41	1,097.54	1,034.58
Mining, Logging, and Construction													
2014	1,005.31	997.41	1,050.95	1,039.10	1,079.42	1,130.82	1,127.12	1,134.36	1,086.25	1,083.03	1,045.85	1,047.76	1,070.06
2015	1,040.21	1,040.72	1,049.17	1,063.68	1,037.51	1,065.96	1,041.04	1,067.82	1,021.75	1,012.61	960.14	1,045.15	1,037.14
2016	1,046.22	1,055.52	1,097.82	1,069.13	1,083.38	1,103.86	1,130.39	1,165.34	1,171.52	1,214.58	1,166.35	1,090.40	1,117.27
2017	1,062.05	1,065.41	1,054.15	1,111.85	1,093.64	1,048.19	1,044.04	1,014.19	1,084.66	1,059.18	1,020.67	1,032.60	1,059.16
2018	977.84	986.49	1,006.31	1,065.36	1,066.07	1,030.26	1,065.48	1,037.95	983.57	1,029.30	1,016.96	1,083.78	1,028.83
Manufacturing													
2014	867.45	867.47	874.43	857.07	876.80	891.27	893.85	924.60	932.11	895.24	899.38	892.02	890.07
2015	905.38	892.11	873.07	881.59	896.72	888.40	913.30	939.06	953.50	932.84	915.71	914.03	908.27
2016	935.21	879.26	892.65	890.31	903.53	907.33	932.73	929.12	923.24	903.05	910.22	921.29	910.23
2017	977.28	921.57	946.05	1,004.36	963.70	984.95	997.66	980.46	986.54	974.04	1,006.85	976.75	977.10
2018	1,011.31	995.59	999.60	1,035.73	1,021.35	1,029.42	1,059.24	1,036.64	1,044.15	1,038.28	1,072.57	1,107.45	1,037.40
Trade, Transportation, and Utilities													
2014	583.13	590.63	604.33	584.54	585.92	598.20	595.32	606.48	593.02	586.97	608.96	624.45	597.76
2015	615.92	620.32	623.46	619.51	630.65	634.78	632.56	646.38	649.10	632.54	635.60	669.50	634.91
2016	659.25	652.33	646.55	660.45	672.32	663.42	661.87	668.98	673.34	696.86	681.53	678.70	668.61
2017	695.10	678.73	686.83	719.28	697.09	714.12	710.66	692.08	718.10	726.75	687.85	711.98	703.56
2018	697.06	695.15	697.06	727.06	709.15	710.82	735.05	737.14	735.81	704.27	728.97	721.93	717.85
Financial Activities													
2014	847.99	849.89	843.10	816.58	850.67	906.86	881.73	903.55	923.01	947.59	1,025.51	987.34	898.53
2015	972.38	1,050.28	1,063.21	1,027.96	1,039.42	1,062.91	1,089.29	1,148.48	1,120.13	1,134.83	1,208.23	1,171.17	1,091.71
2016	1,247.03	1,260.29	1,280.79	1,244.46	1,239.13	1,187.76	1,193.06	1,188.01	1,179.36	1,261.65	1,222.26	1,224.61	1,226.52
2017	1,263.55	1,272.46	1,250.91	1,306.27	1,149.50	1,142.68	1,199.34	1,159.75	1,178.00	1,219.58	1,192.31	1,164.26	1,208.13
2018	1,190.25	1,206.15	1,241.60	1,245.37	1,198.88	1,190.82	1,270.12	1,228.34	1,296.30	1,230.58	1,248.43	1,305.26	1,236.56
Professional and Business Services													
2014	971.46	1,003.59	982.71	994.81	996.84	943.57	910.88	911.94	910.22	891.10	846.72	835.49	931.37
2015	878.17	910.43	906.63	925.27	906.36	854.30	866.27	926.63	905.18	874.81	835.58	855.36	886.74
2016	903.68	956.38	969.80	988.42	1,013.24	965.36	989.96	986.97	999.85	1,087.92	1,017.89	1,016.26	992.97
2017	1,045.32	1,101.76	1,076.22	1,102.56	1,019.47	1,037.48	1,108.64	1,066.15	1,036.91	994.69	988.39	1,011.69	1,048.45
2018	922.33	920.76	928.68	958.45	941.49	1,011.03	1,103.48	1,083.46	1,081.40	1,023.84	1,049.07	1,105.00	1,012.21
Education and Health Services													
2014	729.96	726.19	723.84	738.08	740.92	743.87	750.65	739.31	752.75	765.88	758.67	773.10	744.46
2015	776.21	775.78	773.93	774.11	774.21	779.08	800.72	794.88	814.38	836.88	831.36	847.58	797.69
2016	851.15	846.91	851.47	879.01	881.79	884.44	909.02	907.38	917.48	948.03	939.60	938.56	897.00
2017	932.83	928.77	908.82	930.08	899.10	897.62	892.58	901.56	891.61	916.41	890.52	901.88	907.10
2018	925.48	933.70	945.07	946.34	922.81	923.13	932.51	942.52	937.96	932.44	908.21	889.86	929.59
Leisure and Hospitality													
2014	315.95	322.22	326.04	322.65	319.73	328.10	338.24	342.96	328.43	325.98	326.37	328.93	326.94
2015	314.44	320.37	321.77	320.46	329.18	318.99	336.18	339.53	329.75	324.41	326.06	326.18	325.79
2016	313.49	321.43	324.26	321.61	321.69	326.34	335.64	341.88	336.14	335.08	328.30	334.88	329.36
2017	332.18	343.91	350.37	353.00	346.24	350.55	367.39	368.90	349.92	348.15	347.28	354.48	351.87
2018	345.58	353.07	353.52	354.04	357.70	365.96	388.45	387.06	369.25	367.20	352.53	365.81	363.58

DISTRICT OF COLUMBIA
At a Glance

Population:
  2010 census: 601,723
  2018 estimate: 702,455

Percent change in population:
  2010–2018: 16.7%

Percent change in total nonfarm employment:
  2010–2018: 11.2%

Industry with the largest growth in employment, 2010–2018 (percent):
  Mining, logging, and construction, 48.1%

Industry with the largest decline or smallest growth in employment, 2010–2018 (percent):
  Government, -3.6%

Civilian labor force:
  2010: 346,065
  2018: 404,610

Unemployment rate and rank among states (highest to lowest):
  2010: 9.4%, 21st
  2018: 5.6%, 2nd

Over-the-year change in unemployment rates:
  2016–2017: 0.0%
  2017–2018: -0.5%

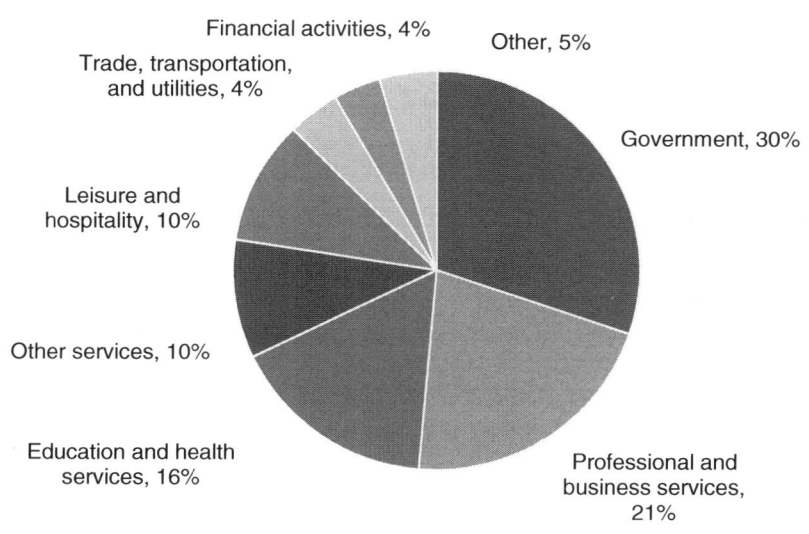

Employment by Industry: District of Columbia, 2018

Financial activities, 4%
Other, 5%
Trade, transportation, and utilities, 4%
Government, 30%
Leisure and hospitality, 10%
Other services, 10%
Education and health services, 16%
Professional and business services, 21%

1. Employment by Industry: District of Columbia, 2010–2018

(Numbers in thousands, not seasonally adjusted)

Industry and year	January	February	March	April	May	June	July	August	September	October	November	December	Annual average
Total Nonfarm													
2010	698.3	695.6	703.5	713.7	715.5	715.5	732.2	707.7	711.1	717.4	718.5	717.5	712.2
2011	713.8	716.9	721.5	727.7	723.8	726.3	740.8	724.7	730.2	729.5	729.2	728.5	726.1
2012	720.6	723.9	728.5	729.1	732.2	730.5	740.7	726.4	733.4	741.1	742.7	741.5	732.6
2013	729.6	734.3	737.5	744.2	744.8	739.0	752.8	738.8	747.4	748.8	752.7	750.6	743.4
2014	732.8	737.5	740.9	746.2	745.4	747.0	759.0	744.4	752.0	757.1	758.6	756.9	748.2
2015	748.1	753.9	755.9	759.1	758.7	760.0	777.0	761.8	765.9	774.5	775.9	776.9	764.0
2016	762.2	770.7	773.2	779.1	774.9	774.9	787.8	773.4	778.7	783.7	784.9	781.9	777.1
2017	771.3	777.9	783.1	783.0	781.9	783.8	794.0	780.3	785.2	791.4	791.8	790.2	784.5
2018	779.9	787.9	791.2	793.3	791.1	793.9	801.5	787.6	791.4	797.6	795.4	795.0	792.2
Total Private													
2010	456.5	454.4	462.1	471.1	470.3	467.6	463.8	461.0	464.6	468.0	469.0	469.1	464.8
2011	466.5	470.0	474.2	481.2	476.8	477.4	479.7	477.7	483.1	485.3	485.5	484.9	478.5
2012	477.9	482.2	486.0	487.9	490.4	486.6	485.5	483.9	491.5	497.9	499.6	499.0	489.0
2013	489.1	494.3	497.1	504.4	505.0	498.7	502.3	500.7	507.7	508.8	512.8	510.5	502.6
2014	499.9	504.1	507.2	513.4	512.1	512.8	512.0	510.7	516.1	520.2	522.3	520.1	512.6
2015	512.3	517.5	519.4	522.6	521.7	522.5	526.0	525.0	528.0	537.1	538.2	537.5	525.7
2016	524.3	532.2	534.5	540.7	535.5	534.5	535.0	534.0	538.0	542.8	543.5	540.0	536.3
2017	530.3	537.6	541.5	544.0	541.9	543.2	542.6	541.8	545.8	553.0	553.8	552.2	544.0
2018	541.8	550.3	553.7	555.9	553.3	555.4	552.8	549.8	554.2	560.3	558.6	557.8	553.7
Goods Producing													
2010	11.3	10.4	11.2	11.8	11.8	11.8	12.2	12.0	11.8	12.1	12.0	12.0	11.7
2011	12.1	12.1	12.3	12.8	13.0	13.2	14.1	14.1	13.8	13.6	13.5	13.6	13.2
2012	13.5	13.8	14.1	14.5	14.7	14.9	15.0	15.0	14.9	15.2	14.9	14.8	14.6
2013	14.5	14.6	14.7	14.5	14.9	15.1	15.7	15.8	15.3	15.1	15.1	15.0	15.0
2014	14.8	14.7	14.9	15.0	15.2	15.5	15.9	15.9	15.6	15.7	15.5	15.3	15.3
2015	14.6	14.5	14.6	14.9	15.2	15.3	16.0	16.2	15.9	16.9	16.9	17.0	15.7
2016	17.0	16.7	17.1	16.9	17.0	17.2	15.9	16.0	15.9	16.5	16.3	16.4	16.6
2017	15.7	16.0	16.1	16.7	16.9	17.2	17.2	17.0	16.9	16.7	16.5	16.5	16.6
2018	16.5	16.8	17.1	17.3	17.2	17.5	17.3	17.1	16.9	16.9	16.7	16.6	17.0
Service-Providing													
2010	687.0	685.2	692.3	701.9	703.7	703.7	720.0	695.7	699.3	705.3	706.5	705.5	700.5
2011	701.7	704.8	709.2	714.9	710.8	713.1	726.7	710.6	716.4	715.9	715.7	714.9	712.9
2012	707.1	710.1	714.4	714.6	717.5	715.6	725.7	711.4	718.5	725.9	727.8	726.7	717.9
2013	715.1	719.7	722.8	729.7	729.9	723.9	737.1	723.0	732.1	733.7	737.6	735.6	728.4
2014	718.0	722.8	726.0	731.2	730.2	731.5	743.1	728.5	736.4	741.4	743.1	741.6	732.8
2015	733.5	739.4	741.3	744.2	743.5	744.7	761.0	745.6	750.0	757.6	759.0	759.9	748.3
2016	745.2	754.0	756.1	762.2	757.9	757.7	771.9	757.4	762.8	767.2	768.6	765.5	760.5
2017	755.6	761.9	767.0	766.3	765.0	766.6	776.8	763.3	768.3	774.7	775.3	773.7	767.9
2018	763.4	771.1	774.1	776.0	773.9	776.4	784.2	770.5	774.5	780.7	778.7	778.4	775.2
Mining, Logging, and Construction													
2010	10.1	9.2	10.1	10.7	10.7	10.7	11.1	11.0	10.7	11.0	11.0	11.0	10.6
2011	11.0	11.1	11.2	11.7	11.9	12.1	13.0	13.1	12.8	12.6	12.5	12.6	12.1
2012	12.5	12.8	13.0	13.5	13.7	13.9	14.0	14.0	13.9	14.2	13.9	13.8	13.6
2013	13.5	13.6	13.7	13.5	13.9	14.1	14.7	14.8	14.3	14.1	14.1	14.0	14.0
2014	13.8	13.7	13.9	14.0	14.2	14.5	14.9	14.9	14.6	14.6	14.4	14.2	14.3
2015	13.6	13.5	13.6	13.9	14.2	14.3	14.9	15.1	14.8	15.8	15.8	15.9	14.6
2016	15.8	15.5	15.9	15.7	15.8	15.9	14.7	14.8	14.7	15.3	15.1	15.2	15.4
2017	14.5	14.8	14.9	15.4	15.6	15.9	15.9	15.7	15.6	15.4	15.2	15.3	15.4
2018	15.2	15.5	15.8	16.0	15.9	16.1	15.9	15.7	15.6	15.6	15.4	15.3	15.7
Manufacturing													
2010	1.2	1.2	1.1	1.1	1.1	1.1	1.1	1.0	1.1	1.1	1.0	1.0	1.1
2011	1.1	1.0	1.1	1.1	1.1	1.1	1.1	1.0	1.0	1.0	1.0	1.0	1.1
2012	1.0	1.0	1.1	1.0	1.0	1.0	1.0	1.0	1.0	1.0	1.0	1.0	1.0
2013	1.0	1.0	1.0	1.0	1.0	1.0	1.0	1.0	1.0	1.0	1.0	1.0	1.0
2014	1.0	1.0	1.0	1.0	1.0	1.0	1.0	1.0	1.0	1.1	1.1	1.1	1.0
2015	1.0	1.0	1.0	1.0	1.0	1.0	1.1	1.1	1.1	1.1	1.1	1.1	1.1
2016	1.2	1.2	1.2	1.2	1.2	1.3	1.2	1.2	1.2	1.2	1.2	1.2	1.2
2017	1.2	1.2	1.2	1.3	1.3	1.3	1.3	1.3	1.3	1.3	1.3	1.2	1.3
2018	1.3	1.3	1.3	1.3	1.3	1.4	1.4	1.4	1.3	1.3	1.3	1.3	1.3

1. Employment by Industry: District of Columbia, 2010–2018—*Continued*

(Numbers in thousands, not seasonally adjusted)

Industry and year	January	February	March	April	May	June	July	August	September	October	November	December	Annual average
Trade, Transportation, and Utilities													
2010	26.9	26.1	26.9	27.4	27.4	27.5	27.4	27.2	27.1	27.6	28.1	28.2	27.3
2011	27.2	27.0	27.1	27.4	27.2	27.2	27.1	27.1	27.3	27.9	28.1	28.3	27.4
2012	27.3	27.4	27.5	27.7	28.0	28.1	28.0	27.9	28.2	28.3	29.1	29.4	28.1
2013	28.4	28.5	28.6	28.6	28.7	28.7	28.7	28.7	29.1	29.4	30.5	30.6	29.0
2014	29.4	29.5	29.8	30.5	30.5	30.7	30.3	30.5	30.7	31.2	32.1	32.1	30.6
2015	31.4	31.3	31.3	31.5	31.6	32.1	32.3	32.1	32.5	32.8	33.4	33.7	32.2
2016	32.1	32.3	32.3	32.6	32.7	33.1	32.7	32.6	32.8	33.1	33.7	33.7	32.8
2017	32.7	32.9	33.1	33.0	33.1	33.4	33.2	33.2	33.5	33.5	34.3	34.4	33.4
2018	33.0	33.0	33.1	33.0	33.1	33.1	33.2	32.9	33.1	33.6	33.5	33.6	33.2
Wholesale Trade													
2010	4.6	4.6	4.6	4.7	4.7	4.7	4.7	4.6	4.5	4.7	4.7	4.7	4.7
2011	4.5	4.5	4.6	4.5	4.5	4.5	4.5	4.7	4.6	4.8	4.8	4.8	4.6
2012	4.7	4.9	4.8	4.9	5.0	5.0	5.0	5.0	5.1	5.0	5.0	5.0	5.0
2013	4.8	4.9	4.9	4.8	4.8	4.8	4.9	4.8	4.9	4.8	4.9	4.8	4.8
2014	4.7	4.8	4.9	4.9	4.9	4.9	4.9	4.9	4.9	5.0	5.0	5.0	4.9
2015	5.0	5.0	5.0	4.7	4.7	4.7	4.8	4.7	4.8	4.8	4.9	4.9	4.8
2016	5.0	5.0	5.0	5.0	5.0	5.0	5.0	5.1	5.0	5.0	4.9	4.9	5.0
2017	5.0	5.0	5.0	4.8	4.8	4.8	4.8	4.9	4.9	4.9	4.9	4.9	4.9
2018	4.8	4.9	4.8	4.8	4.8	4.9	4.9	4.9	4.9	5.1	4.9	4.9	4.9
Retail Trade													
2010	18.3	17.5	18.1	18.4	18.4	18.5	18.4	18.3	18.3	18.6	19.1	19.3	18.4
2011	18.6	18.4	18.3	18.6	18.5	18.4	18.3	18.1	18.5	18.9	19.2	19.5	18.6
2012	18.6	18.5	18.6	18.6	18.8	18.8	18.8	18.7	18.9	19.1	20.0	20.3	19.0
2013	19.5	19.5	19.5	19.6	19.7	19.6	19.6	19.8	20.1	20.5	21.5	21.7	20.1
2014	20.7	20.6	20.7	21.3	21.2	21.3	21.0	21.1	21.4	21.7	22.6	22.7	21.4
2015	22.0	21.8	21.8	22.1	22.1	22.3	22.4	22.4	22.7	23.1	23.7	23.9	22.5
2016	22.6	22.7	22.7	22.8	22.9	23.2	22.7	22.5	22.7	23.0	23.7	23.7	22.9
2017	22.8	23.0	23.1	23.0	23.1	23.2	23.1	23.1	23.3	23.4	24.1	24.3	23.3
2018	23.0	22.9	22.9	22.8	22.8	22.7	22.8	22.6	22.8	23.1	23.2	23.2	22.9
Transportation and Utilities													
2010	4.0	4.0	4.2	4.3	4.3	4.3	4.3	4.3	4.3	4.3	4.3	4.2	4.2
2011	4.1	4.1	4.2	4.3	4.2	4.3	4.3	4.3	4.2	4.2	4.1	4.0	4.2
2012	4.0	4.0	4.1	4.2	4.2	4.3	4.2	4.2	4.2	4.2	4.1	4.1	4.2
2013	4.1	4.1	4.2	4.2	4.2	4.3	4.2	4.1	4.1	4.1	4.1	4.1	4.2
2014	4.0	4.1	4.2	4.3	4.4	4.5	4.4	4.5	4.4	4.5	4.5	4.4	4.4
2015	4.4	4.5	4.5	4.7	4.8	5.1	5.1	5.0	5.0	4.9	4.8	4.9	4.8
2016	4.5	4.6	4.6	4.8	4.8	4.9	5.0	5.0	5.1	5.1	5.1	5.1	4.9
2017	4.9	4.9	5.0	5.2	5.2	5.4	5.3	5.2	5.3	5.2	5.3	5.2	5.2
2018	5.2	5.2	5.4	5.4	5.5	5.5	5.5	5.4	5.4	5.4	5.4	5.5	5.4
Information													
2010	18.5	18.4	18.5	18.7	18.6	18.9	19.0	18.7	18.8	18.7	18.5	18.7	18.7
2011	18.3	18.5	18.6	18.8	18.5	18.7	18.4	17.9	18.2	18.0	18.0	18.2	18.3
2012	17.5	17.7	17.6	17.3	17.4	17.7	17.4	17.7	17.3	17.3	17.6	17.4	17.5
2013	17.1	17.2	17.2	16.9	17.1	17.1	17.3	17.4	16.9	16.6	16.9	16.7	17.0
2014	17.1	17.1	17.1	17.2	17.3	17.4	17.6	17.3	17.2	17.1	17.1	17.1	17.2
2015	16.6	16.7	16.7	17.1	17.2	17.3	17.4	17.3	17.2	17.5	17.5	17.6	17.2
2016	16.9	17.1	17.0	17.0	16.8	17.1	17.2	17.2	17.1	17.3	17.4	17.3	17.1
2017	17.1	17.4	17.5	17.8	17.9	18.0	18.1	18.1	18.1	17.9	18.1	18.4	17.9
2018	18.3	18.7	18.7	18.9	19.0	19.7	19.8	19.4	19.4	19.7	19.8	20.0	19.3
Financial Activities													
2010	26.4	26.3	26.6	26.7	26.7	26.9	26.2	26.1	25.7	26.6	26.8	26.8	26.5
2011	26.7	26.6	26.8	27.1	27.1	27.0	27.3	27.5	27.5	27.5	27.6	27.7	27.2
2012	27.7	27.7	27.7	27.7	27.7	27.9	27.7	27.6	27.6	27.8	27.9	27.8	27.7
2013	27.6	27.8	28.0	28.2	28.1	28.5	28.5	28.6	28.3	28.9	29.0	29.2	28.4
2014	29.1	29.2	29.3	29.1	29.3	29.6	29.8	29.7	29.5	29.5	29.6	29.6	29.4
2015	29.5	29.6	29.7	29.2	29.2	29.3	29.6	29.5	29.2	29.1	29.2	29.0	29.3
2016	29.1	29.1	29.2	29.4	29.3	29.4	29.7	29.7	29.6	29.5	29.4	29.5	29.4
2017	29.3	29.4	29.4	29.3	29.4	29.7	29.9	29.7	29.4	29.5	29.6	29.7	29.5
2018	29.4	29.6	29.6	29.5	29.7	30.1	30.2	30.1	29.8	29.7	29.7	29.5	29.7

1. Employment by Industry: District of Columbia, 2010–2018—*Continued*

(Numbers in thousands, not seasonally adjusted)

Industry and year	January	February	March	April	May	June	July	August	September	October	November	December	Annual average
Professional and Business Services													
2010	145.8	145.8	147.3	148.7	148.6	150.0	149.1	148.2	146.8	147.2	147.2	147.4	147.7
2011	146.7	147.4	148.4	150.4	150.5	151.8	152.7	152.1	150.3	151.8	151.5	151.0	150.4
2012	150.7	151.5	152.7	152.6	152.9	154.4	155.6	154.9	153.7	156.2	156.9	156.5	154.1
2013	153.3	154.6	154.9	155.0	154.9	156.1	157.8	157.5	156.0	156.5	157.7	156.6	155.9
2014	153.7	154.6	155.2	155.9	156.3	158.4	159.1	158.1	158.2	159.1	159.3	159.4	157.3
2015	158.2	159.3	159.5	160.0	160.8	162.8	163.5	163.1	162.0	164.5	164.3	164.2	161.9
2016	162.1	163.3	163.6	165.0	164.7	165.7	166.5	165.2	164.1	165.9	166.3	165.9	164.9
2017	164.7	165.0	165.1	165.7	165.6	167.9	167.6	166.2	165.0	166.7	167.3	167.5	166.2
2018	165.4	166.5	166.7	166.7	167.0	169.6	168.9	167.9	167.4	169.0	167.6	169.1	167.7
Education and Health Services													
2010	107.4	107.2	108.4	111.3	110.4	104.7	103.1	103.5	109.6	109.1	109.9	109.9	107.9
2011	112.7	113.6	114.1	114.3	110.3	108.5	109.4	108.6	115.4	115.1	115.3	115.2	112.7
2012	113.5	114.0	114.0	114.6	114.4	107.8	105.4	106.3	115.4	118.2	119.2	119.5	113.5
2013	116.9	118.5	118.8	123.0	122.2	113.3	114.9	114.5	123.2	124.9	125.7	125.4	120.1
2014	121.4	122.8	122.9	123.9	120.7	118.1	117.3	117.4	122.8	125.4	126.3	125.6	122.1
2015	121.7	125.1	125.1	125.7	122.1	119.5	121.7	121.7	126.3	131.7	132.2	130.9	125.3
2016	125.8	130.2	129.9	130.5	126.1	122.5	124.4	124.9	129.0	131.2	131.8	129.9	128.0
2017	126.5	130.5	130.7	129.3	125.8	123.7	123.7	124.8	129.9	132.9	133.5	131.6	128.6
2018	128.9	132.9	133.0	133.1	129.4	126.2	125.6	126.6	131.3	134.0	135.3	133.4	130.8
Leisure and Hospitality													
2010	56.1	56.1	58.6	61.7	61.4	61.4	60.5	59.6	59.6	60.9	60.4	59.7	59.7
2011	57.2	58.5	60.1	63.9	63.5	63.5	62.6	63.0	63.8	64.3	64.2	63.2	62.3
2012	60.7	62.5	64.4	66.3	67.7	67.4	66.7	66.0	66.3	66.6	65.4	64.7	65.4
2013	63.1	64.6	66.3	69.3	69.9	69.9	69.2	68.6	69.4	68.2	68.5	67.5	67.9
2014	65.4	66.5	68.3	71.6	72.4	71.7	70.5	70.6	71.2	71.4	71.4	70.2	70.1
2015	70.1	70.4	71.8	73.8	74.9	74.6	73.8	74.0	73.9	73.5	73.5	73.7	73.2
2016	70.2	72.1	73.7	77.2	76.6	76.3	74.8	74.9	76.1	75.6	74.6	73.5	74.6
2017	71.3	72.7	75.5	78.1	79.0	78.1	77.3	77.8	78.5	80.3	78.8	78.1	77.1
2018	75.0	76.9	79.4	81.2	81.6	82.0	80.5	79.3	80.3	80.9	79.8	79.5	79.7
Other Services													
2010	64.1	64.1	64.6	64.8	65.4	66.4	66.3	65.7	65.2	65.8	66.1	66.4	65.4
2011	65.6	66.3	66.8	66.5	66.7	67.5	68.1	67.4	66.8	67.1	67.3	67.7	67.0
2012	67.0	67.6	68.0	67.2	67.6	68.4	69.7	68.5	68.1	68.3	68.6	68.9	68.2
2013	68.2	68.5	68.6	68.9	69.2	70.0	70.2	69.6	69.5	69.2	69.4	69.5	69.2
2014	69.0	69.7	69.7	70.2	70.4	71.4	71.5	71.2	70.9	70.8	71.0	70.8	70.6
2015	70.2	70.6	70.7	70.4	70.7	71.6	71.7	71.1	71.0	71.1	71.2	71.4	71.0
2016	71.1	71.4	71.7	72.1	72.3	73.2	73.8	73.5	73.4	73.7	74.0	73.8	72.8
2017	73.0	73.7	74.1	74.1	74.2	75.2	75.6	75.0	74.5	75.5	75.7	76.0	74.7
2018	75.3	75.9	76.1	76.2	76.3	77.2	77.3	76.5	76.0	76.5	76.2	76.1	76.3
Government													
2010	241.8	241.2	241.4	242.6	245.2	247.9	268.4	246.7	246.5	249.4	249.5	248.4	247.4
2011	247.3	246.9	247.3	246.5	247.0	248.9	261.1	247.0	247.1	244.2	243.7	243.6	247.6
2012	242.7	241.7	242.5	241.2	241.8	243.9	255.2	242.5	241.9	243.2	243.1	242.5	243.5
2013	240.5	240.0	240.4	239.8	239.8	240.3	250.5	238.1	239.7	240.0	239.9	240.1	240.8
2014	232.9	233.4	233.7	232.8	233.3	234.2	247.0	233.7	235.9	236.9	236.3	236.8	235.6
2015	235.8	236.4	236.5	236.5	237.0	237.5	251.0	236.8	237.9	237.4	237.7	239.4	238.3
2016	237.9	238.5	238.7	238.4	239.4	240.4	252.8	239.4	240.7	240.9	241.4	241.9	240.9
2017	241.0	240.3	241.6	239.0	240.0	240.6	251.4	238.5	239.4	238.4	238.0	238.0	240.5
2018	238.1	237.6	237.5	237.4	237.8	238.5	248.7	237.8	237.2	237.3	236.8	237.2	238.5

2. Average Weekly Hours by Selected Industry: District of Columbia, 2014–2018

(Not seasonally adjusted)

Industry and year	January	February	March	April	May	June	July	August	September	October	November	December	Annual average
Total Private													
2014	35.8	36.7	36.7	36.0	36.0	36.6	36.0	36.0	35.8	35.8	36.9	35.5	36.2
2015	35.3	36.8	36.4	35.5	35.8	35.6	35.0	35.9	35.0	35.3	36.0	35.2	35.6
2016	35.2	35.3	35.4	35.6	36.4	35.6	35.4	35.3	35.4	36.3	35.4	35.4	35.6
2017	36.1	35.5	35.3	36.4	35.1	35.0	35.9	35.0	35.1	36.0	35.0	35.1	35.5
2018	34.7	34.6	34.7	36.1	34.9	35.0	35.8	34.7	35.8	34.6	35.0	36.1	35.2
Goods-Producing													
2014	39.7	37.6	40.4	39.8	38.9	39.9	41.6	38.6	40.5	38.3	37.8	40.0	39.4
2015	38.3	40.1	40.4	39.0	40.5	40.6	39.0	39.7	38.2	40.6	37.7	40.9	39.6
2016	41.3	39.9	42.3	40.2	38.4	40.9	39.5	40.0	40.7	38.5	37.8	34.4	39.5
2017	36.9	36.9	35.7	37.1	34.7	36.7	35.8	35.3	36.1	35.7	36.6	37.1	36.1
2018	37.9	37.5	38.9	39.7	39.2	39.6	40.8	41.3	39.5	36.3	36.6	37.7	38.8
Trade, Transportation, and Utilities													
2014	35.2	35.6	36.7	36.4	36.8	35.8	35.9	35.5	36.5	35.3	36.5	36.3	36.0
2015	35.4	36.6	35.9	35.7	36.0	35.7	35.3	35.1	37.3	35.9	36.2	36.3	35.9
2016	34.9	34.9	35.0	35.0	34.9	34.3	34.3	33.6	33.8	33.3	33.6	33.0	34.2
2017	33.5	32.5	32.0	33.1	32.9	32.1	32.4	31.4	32.0	31.8	32.0	31.7	32.3
2018	31.0	30.8	31.3	32.1	31.6	32.2	32.3	31.7	32.4	31.7	31.5	31.5	31.7
Professional and Business Services													
2014	37.0	38.3	38.2	37.2	37.3	37.8	36.6	37.1	36.5	36.7	37.9	36.0	37.2
2015	36.0	37.8	37.5	36.2	36.3	36.3	35.4	37.4	35.7	36.1	37.1	36.1	36.5
2016	36.1	36.2	36.1	36.3	37.3	36.3	36.4	36.3	36.4	37.6	36.0	36.6	36.5
2017	37.7	37.0	36.3	38.0	36.4	36.5	37.8	36.6	36.7	38.0	36.3	36.5	37.0
2018	36.2	36.2	35.8	37.8	35.8	35.6	36.8	35.4	36.7	34.9	35.5	37.4	36.2
Leisure and Hospitality													
2014	28.6	29.3	29.7	30.3	30.5	30.7	30.2	29.7	29.6	30.1	30.1	29.7	29.9
2015	28.2	29.1	29.9	30.2	30.7	30.0	29.0	28.7	28.2	28.8	29.0	28.5	29.2
2016	27.3	29.0	29.2	29.7	29.2	28.2	28.3	27.6	27.5	28.2	28.4	28.0	28.4
2017	27.0	27.5	29.8	28.9	28.0	26.8	26.8	27.3	26.7	27.2	27.0	27.5	27.5
2018	25.9	25.6	26.9	27.8	27.5	28.3	27.6	27.3	27.7	27.7	27.5	28.6	27.4
Other Services													
2014	35.1	36.2	36.2	35.2	35.2	36.2	35.7	35.7	35.2	35.7	37.6	35.8	35.8
2015	35.7	37.2	36.1	34.9	35.4	34.8	35.1	36.2	35.5	35.6	36.8	35.2	35.7
2016	35.6	35.2	35.1	35.7	36.6	35.5	35.0	35.2	35.6	37.0	35.7	35.6	35.6
2017	36.8	35.8	35.6	37.2	35.8	36.5	37.7	36.5	36.5	37.6	36.0	35.5	36.5
2018	35.0	35.4	35.1	36.9	35.3	35.6	36.9	35.5	36.9	35.8	36.4	37.5	36.0

3. Average Hourly Earnings by Selected Industry: District of Columbia, 2014–2018

(Dollars, not seasonally adjusted)

Industry and year	January	February	March	April	May	June	July	August	September	October	November	December	Annual average
Total Private													
2014	38.92	39.67	39.21	38.35	38.53	39.14	38.25	38.32	38.86	38.55	39.55	39.26	38.89
2015	39.60	40.48	40.51	38.94	38.18	38.30	37.65	37.97	37.38	36.06	37.36	36.88	38.27
2016	36.57	36.96	36.89	37.44	38.79	37.85	38.38	39.17	39.06	40.10	39.62	39.88	38.40
2017	41.00	39.89	40.00	39.95	39.67	39.57	41.07	40.50	40.88	41.98	41.47	41.75	40.65
2018	42.00	42.66	42.52	42.75	42.13	42.17	43.14	42.80	44.08	43.44	43.73	45.10	43.06
Goods-Producing													
2014	30.77	30.58	29.39	29.12	28.35	28.43	27.34	27.54	27.13	27.33	27.69	28.55	28.49
2015	27.87	27.93	28.78	28.09	28.01	28.19	27.61	28.60	30.33	29.24	30.66	30.33	28.84
2016	30.97	30.27	29.74	29.39	30.41	29.89	29.64	30.33	29.85	29.41	29.36	30.99	30.02
2017	30.28	30.95	31.35	30.85	31.35	31.71	31.82	32.92	32.32	32.57	33.26	33.32	31.90
2018	33.50	33.46	32.60	33.29	32.34	32.96	32.59	31.83	32.10	32.92	32.91	33.49	32.82
Trade, Transportation, and Utilities													
2014	25.72	24.76	24.06	24.19	23.57	23.42	23.15	23.10	23.11	23.58	23.75	23.53	23.81
2015	24.18	24.74	24.88	24.46	24.54	24.63	25.01	26.11	25.43	25.82	26.63	25.68	25.19
2016	26.90	26.65	27.40	27.37	27.78	27.55	27.80	28.03	27.92	26.87	26.41	26.26	27.24
2017	27.29	26.29	25.57	26.27	26.31	25.65	26.74	26.62	26.25	26.69	26.30	25.78	26.31
2018	27.35	26.93	26.64	26.84	26.67	26.27	26.60	26.56	26.41	26.10	26.33	26.25	26.58
Professional and Business Services													
2014	47.85	49.44	49.01	48.06	48.45	49.35	47.62	47.84	48.22	47.66	49.21	48.63	48.45
2015	48.54	49.33	48.95	47.45	47.73	47.54	46.49	47.38	46.84	46.49	47.75	47.30	47.65
2016	47.29	47.09	46.53	46.48	48.16	47.13	47.16	47.52	47.16	48.54	47.57	47.54	47.35
2017	48.53	46.62	46.51	45.13	44.61	44.91	47.13	46.09	46.94	48.07	48.27	49.11	46.83
2018	47.87	48.49	49.18	49.29	48.90	49.65	50.74	50.66	52.42	51.55	51.94	54.18	50.42
Leisure and Hospitality													
2014	17.83	17.44	17.38	17.15	16.69	16.98	17.06	17.35	17.74	18.09	17.80	18.26	17.47
2015	18.08	17.97	18.49	18.07	17.94	17.71	17.64	17.67	17.79	17.85	17.86	17.70	17.90
2016	16.88	16.81	17.44	17.42	17.64	17.74	17.95	17.66	18.22	18.24	18.89	19.49	17.87
2017	19.20	19.22	20.38	19.59	19.61	18.97	19.73	18.89	19.45	20.60	18.82	19.00	19.47
2018	19.72	21.14	19.75	20.05	19.78	19.78	19.67	20.10	20.13	20.47	21.18	21.65	20.28
Other Services													
2014	41.87	42.71	41.75	41.97	42.79	42.96	43.15	43.07	44.61	44.24	44.92	45.05	43.27
2015	45.35	46.56	46.83	45.39	45.09	45.26	44.73	46.26	45.50	44.42	45.68	45.38	45.54
2016	46.12	46.80	47.07	47.43	48.33	46.96	47.59	48.02	47.48	48.22	47.60	48.23	47.50
2017	49.88	48.76	49.16	50.09	49.72	49.04	50.05	49.48	50.03	50.96	49.49	49.81	49.72
2018	51.31	52.49	52.76	53.44	53.68	53.29	53.48	53.80	55.75	55.59	54.81	56.00	53.89

4. Average Weekly Earnings by Selected Industry: District of Columbia, 2014–2018

(Dollars, not seasonally adjusted)

Industry and year	January	February	March	April	May	June	July	August	September	October	November	December	Annual average
Total Private													
2014	1,393.34	1,455.89	1,439.01	1,380.60	1,387.08	1,432.52	1,377.00	1,379.52	1,391.19	1,380.09	1,459.40	1,393.73	1,407.82
2015	1,397.88	1,489.66	1,474.56	1,382.37	1,366.84	1,363.48	1,317.75	1,363.12	1,308.30	1,272.92	1,344.96	1,298.18	1,362.41
2016	1,287.26	1,304.69	1,305.91	1,332.86	1,411.96	1,347.46	1,358.65	1,382.70	1,382.72	1,455.63	1,402.55	1,411.75	1,367.04
2017	1,480.10	1,416.10	1,412.00	1,454.18	1,392.42	1,384.95	1,474.41	1,417.50	1,434.89	1,511.28	1,451.45	1,465.43	1,443.08
2018	1,457.40	1,476.04	1,475.44	1,543.28	1,470.34	1,475.95	1,544.41	1,485.16	1,578.06	1,503.02	1,530.55	1,628.11	1,515.71
Goods-Producing													
2014	1,221.57	1,149.81	1,187.36	1,158.98	1,102.82	1,134.36	1,137.34	1,063.04	1,098.77	1,046.74	1,046.68	1,142.00	1,122.51
2015	1,067.42	1,119.99	1,162.71	1,095.51	1,134.41	1,144.51	1,076.79	1,135.42	1,158.61	1,187.14	1,155.88	1,240.50	1,142.06
2016	1,279.06	1,207.77	1,258.00	1,181.48	1,167.74	1,222.50	1,170.78	1,213.20	1,214.90	1,132.29	1,109.81	1,066.06	1,185.79
2017	1,117.33	1,142.06	1,119.20	1,144.54	1,087.85	1,163.76	1,139.16	1,162.08	1,166.75	1,162.75	1,217.32	1,236.17	1,151.59
2018	1,269.65	1,254.75	1,268.14	1,321.61	1,267.73	1,305.22	1,329.67	1,314.58	1,267.95	1,195.00	1,204.51	1,262.57	1,273.42
Trade, Transportation, and Utilities													
2014	905.34	881.46	883.00	880.52	867.38	838.44	831.09	820.05	843.52	832.37	866.88	854.14	857.16
2015	855.97	905.48	893.19	873.22	883.44	879.29	882.85	916.46	948.54	926.94	964.01	932.18	904.32
2016	938.81	930.09	959.00	957.95	969.52	944.97	953.54	941.81	943.70	894.77	887.38	866.58	931.61
2017	914.22	854.43	818.24	869.54	865.60	823.37	866.38	835.87	840.00	848.74	841.60	817.23	849.81
2018	847.85	829.44	833.83	861.56	842.77	845.89	859.18	841.95	855.68	827.37	829.40	826.88	842.59
Professional and Business Services													
2014	1,770.45	1,893.55	1,872.18	1,787.83	1,807.19	1,865.43	1,742.89	1,774.86	1,760.03	1,749.12	1,865.06	1,750.68	1,802.34
2015	1,747.44	1,864.67	1,835.63	1,717.69	1,732.60	1,725.70	1,645.75	1,772.01	1,672.19	1,678.29	1,771.53	1,707.53	1,739.23
2016	1,707.17	1,704.66	1,679.73	1,687.22	1,796.37	1,710.82	1,716.62	1,724.98	1,716.62	1,825.10	1,712.52	1,739.96	1,728.28
2017	1,829.58	1,724.94	1,688.31	1,714.94	1,623.80	1,639.22	1,781.51	1,686.89	1,722.70	1,826.66	1,752.20	1,792.52	1,732.71
2018	1,732.89	1,755.34	1,760.64	1,863.16	1,750.62	1,767.54	1,867.23	1,793.36	1,923.81	1,799.10	1,843.87	2,026.33	1,825.20
Leisure and Hospitality													
2014	509.94	510.99	516.19	519.65	509.05	521.29	515.21	515.30	525.10	544.51	535.78	542.32	522.35
2015	509.86	522.93	552.85	545.71	550.76	531.30	511.56	507.13	501.68	514.08	517.94	504.45	522.68
2016	460.82	487.49	509.25	517.37	515.09	500.27	507.99	487.42	501.05	514.37	536.48	545.72	507.51
2017	518.40	528.55	607.32	566.15	549.08	508.40	528.76	515.70	519.32	560.32	508.14	522.50	535.43
2018	510.75	541.18	531.28	557.39	543.95	559.77	542.89	548.73	557.60	567.02	582.45	619.19	555.67
Other Services													
2014	1,469.64	1,546.10	1,511.35	1,477.34	1,506.21	1,555.15	1,540.46	1,537.60	1,570.27	1,579.37	1,688.99	1,612.79	1,549.07
2015	1,619.00	1,732.03	1,690.56	1,584.11	1,596.19	1,575.05	1,570.02	1,674.61	1,615.25	1,581.35	1,681.02	1,597.38	1,625.78
2016	1,641.87	1,647.36	1,652.16	1,693.25	1,768.88	1,667.08	1,665.65	1,690.30	1,690.29	1,784.14	1,699.32	1,716.99	1,691.00
2017	1,835.58	1,745.61	1,750.10	1,863.35	1,779.98	1,789.96	1,886.89	1,806.02	1,826.10	1,916.10	1,781.64	1,768.26	1,814.78
2018	1,795.85	1,858.15	1,851.88	1,971.94	1,894.90	1,897.12	1,973.41	1,909.90	2,057.18	1,990.12	1,995.08	2,100.00	1,940.04

FLORIDA
At a Glance

Population:
  2010 census: 18,801,310
  2018 estimate: 21,299,325

Percent change in population:
  2010–2018: 13.3%

Percent change in total nonfarm employment:
  2010–2018: 22.4%

Industry with the largest growth in employment, 2010–2018 (percent):
  Construction, 54.1%

Industry with the largest decline or smallest growth in employment, 2010–2018 (percent):
  Government, -0.2%

Civilian labor force:
  2010: 9,212,066
  2018: 10,234,770

Unemployment rate and rank among states (highest to lowest):
  2010: 11.1%, 6th
  2018: 3.6%, 30th

Over-the-year change in unemployment rates:
  2016–2017: -0.6%
  2017–2018: -0.6%

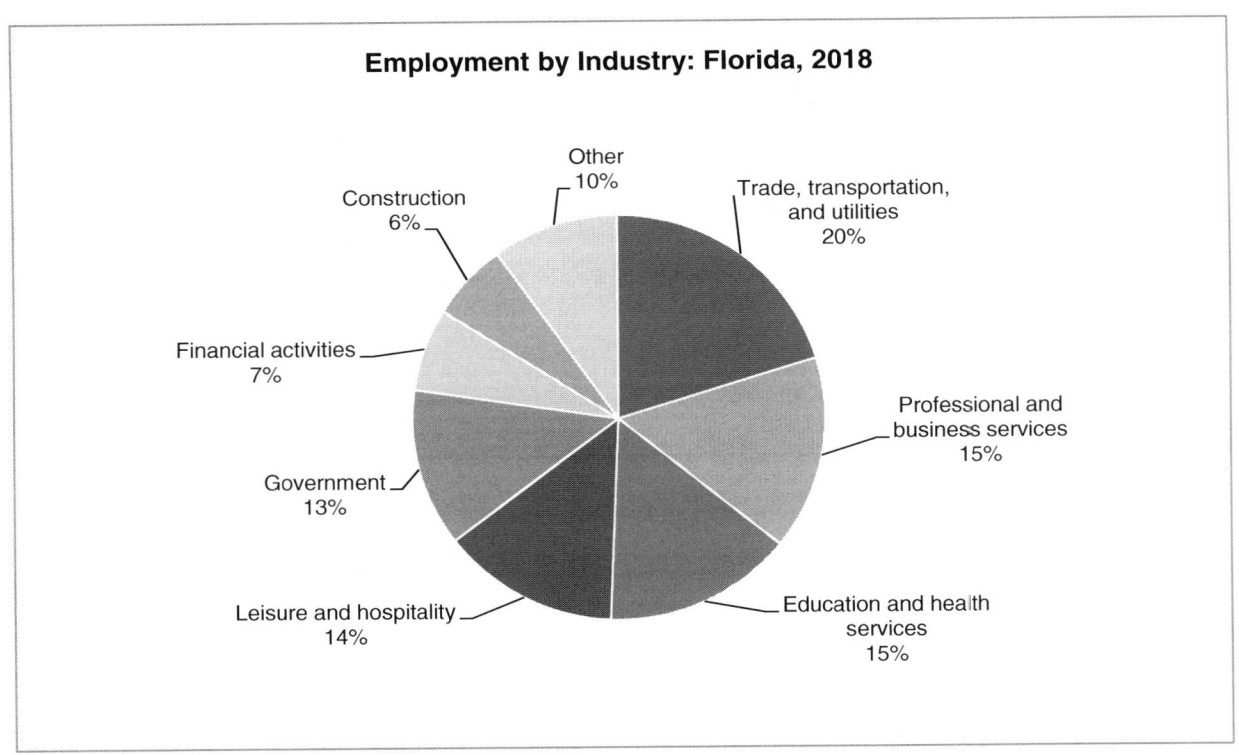

Employment by Industry: Florida, 2018

- Other 10%
- Trade, transportation, and utilities 20%
- Construction 6%
- Professional and business services 15%
- Financial activities 7%
- Education and health services 15%
- Government 13%
- Leisure and hospitality 14%

1. Employment by Industry: Florida, 2010–2018

(Numbers in thousands, not seasonally adjusted)

Industry and year	January	February	March	April	May	June	July	August	September	October	November	December	Annual average
Total Nonfarm													
2010	7,096.4	7,148.2	7,195.5	7,215.2	7,239.1	7,117.5	7,060.4	7,145.2	7,135.9	7,199.5	7,260.2	7,289.2	7,175.2
2011	7,175.7	7,227.1	7,274.0	7,311.1	7,280.9	7,166.9	7,129.1	7,214.6	7,242.2	7,283.8	7,359.7	7,392.9	7,254.8
2012	7,285.4	7,348.2	7,408.3	7,427.4	7,417.5	7,323.2	7,268.9	7,366.7	7,383.1	7,455.5	7,544.2	7,569.1	7,399.8
2013	7,446.3	7,523.4	7,577.1	7,587.2	7,589.1	7,497.9	7,461.9	7,569.7	7,582.8	7,650.9	7,754.9	7,785.1	7,585.5
2014	7,665.3	7,738.4	7,794.6	7,824.0	7,830.9	7,731.5	7,702.4	7,814.6	7,833.3	7,921.5	8,017.5	8,060.8	7,827.9
2015	7,943.1	8,016.5	8,068.0	8,094.8	8,100.9	8,008.2	7,987.1	8,092.5	8,109.3	8,224.5	8,321.4	8,362.8	8,110.8
2016	8,238.8	8,315.1	8,360.9	8,397.5	8,386.6	8,274.0	8,275.1	8,371.3	8,408.6	8,467.8	8,567.4	8,596.0	8,388.3
2017	8,488.1	8,550.5	8,590.8	8,593.6	8,594.4	8,492.8	8,455.3	8,549.7	8,390.3	8,638.6	8,747.4	8,778.0	8,572.5
2018	8,655.1	8,735.2	8,776.2	8,779.3	8,773.6	8,676.3	8,645.4	8,767.4	8,774.5	8,855.3	8,954.8	8,989.9	8,781.9
Total Private													
2010	5,973.0	6,017.7	6,064.5	6,078.8	6,074.8	6,067.5	6,024.7	6,031.2	6,018.0	6,074.8	6,132.4	6,169.9	6,060.6
2011	6,059.0	6,099.8	6,148.2	6,185.0	6,167.0	6,145.7	6,114.4	6,128.8	6,147.3	6,173.4	6,249.1	6,287.9	6,158.8
2012	6,188.6	6,238.6	6,299.4	6,324.2	6,324.8	6,315.5	6,266.9	6,289.5	6,295.0	6,354.8	6,440.4	6,471.3	6,317.4
2013	6,353.8	6,420.2	6,472.4	6,484.9	6,496.7	6,492.3	6,465.5	6,496.1	6,497.8	6,554.2	6,652.9	6,689.5	6,506.4
2014	6,577.9	6,641.0	6,693.1	6,725.9	6,740.3	6,729.7	6,703.4	6,742.1	6,749.9	6,823.9	6,916.5	6,962.4	6,750.5
2015	6,853.9	6,914.9	6,963.1	6,989.6	7,003.0	6,999.6	6,980.4	7,010.5	7,016.8	7,115.0	7,210.7	7,257.4	7,026.2
2016	7,138.7	7,203.7	7,246.2	7,280.8	7,276.2	7,249.8	7,253.6	7,276.3	7,295.5	7,349.2	7,443.7	7,475.0	7,290.7
2017	7,373.6	7,422.6	7,460.1	7,468.5	7,474.4	7,462.8	7,428.8	7,452.0	7,279.1	7,512.8	7,617.3	7,650.2	7,466.9
2018	7,532.5	7,602.9	7,640.9	7,647.1	7,648.5	7,637.6	7,615.2	7,657.5	7,650.2	7,724.2	7,818.9	7,857.1	7,669.4
Goods Producing													
2010	660.7	662.5	664.9	668.7	669.4	672.7	673.6	670.9	666.3	661.6	658.6	657.2	665.6
2011	643.3	645.8	648.8	651.6	653.2	655.7	656.3	657.6	660.0	657.1	658.5	658.9	653.9
2012	649.1	652.3	658.2	657.6	662.3	667.4	665.7	670.8	672.4	674.2	677.7	677.4	665.4
2013	666.4	672.6	679.0	683.2	690.3	695.6	697.4	704.3	706.5	708.5	713.4	715.5	694.4
2014	706.3	713.6	717.3	722.9	731.3	736.6	739.4	744.8	747.4	752.9	754.4	756.1	735.3
2015	748.3	755.2	761.4	766.5	774.1	782.4	785.5	789.7	793.4	805.0	808.8	811.6	781.8
2016	804.5	813.5	819.4	826.6	831.5	837.7	842.6	845.2	850.6	853.0	858.6	860.7	837.0
2017	852.9	861.9	868.4	868.2	873.9	881.5	879.6	883.3	850.2	887.0	891.6	895.2	874.5
2018	888.3	902.2	909.4	911.3	914.3	923.2	921.9	926.8	927.3	932.5	931.2	935.3	918.6
Service-Providing													
2010	6,435.7	6,485.7	6,530.6	6,546.5	6,569.7	6,444.8	6,386.8	6,474.3	6,469.6	6,537.9	6,601.6	6,632.0	6,509.6
2011	6,532.4	6,581.3	6,625.2	6,659.5	6,627.7	6,511.2	6,472.8	6,557.0	6,582.2	6,626.7	6,701.2	6,734.0	6,600.9
2012	6,636.3	6,695.9	6,750.1	6,769.8	6,755.2	6,655.8	6,603.2	6,695.9	6,710.7	6,781.3	6,866.5	6,891.7	6,734.4
2013	6,779.9	6,850.8	6,898.1	6,904.0	6,898.8	6,802.3	6,764.5	6,865.4	6,876.3	6,942.4	7,041.5	7,069.6	6,891.1
2014	6,959.0	7,024.8	7,077.3	7,101.1	7,099.6	6,994.9	6,963.0	7,069.8	7,085.9	7,168.6	7,263.1	7,304.7	7,092.7
2015	7,194.8	7,261.3	7,306.6	7,328.3	7,326.8	7,225.8	7,201.6	7,302.8	7,315.9	7,419.5	7,512.6	7,551.2	7,328.9
2016	7,434.3	7,501.6	7,541.5	7,570.9	7,555.1	7,436.3	7,432.5	7,526.1	7,558.0	7,614.8	7,708.8	7,735.3	7,551.3
2017	7,635.2	7,688.6	7,722.4	7,725.4	7,720.5	7,611.3	7,575.7	7,666.4	7,540.1	7,751.6	7,855.8	7,882.8	7,698.0
2018	7,766.8	7,833.0	7,866.8	7,868.0	7,859.3	7,753.1	7,723.5	7,840.6	7,847.2	7,922.8	8,023.6	8,054.6	7,863.3
Mining and Logging													
2010	5.3	5.3	5.2	5.3	5.3	5.4	5.4	5.5	5.5	5.6	5.6	5.7	5.4
2011	5.7	5.7	5.7	5.6	5.6	5.6	5.6	5.6	5.6	5.6	5.6	5.6	5.6
2012	5.6	5.6	5.6	5.6	5.6	5.6	5.6	5.6	5.6	5.5	5.6	5.7	5.6
2013	5.7	5.7	5.7	5.6	5.6	5.5	5.6	5.6	5.6	5.6	5.6	5.7	5.6
2014	5.6	5.6	5.6	5.7	5.7	5.7	5.7	5.7	5.6	5.7	5.6	5.7	5.7
2015	5.7	5.7	5.7	5.8	5.8	5.8	5.8	5.8	5.8	5.8	5.7	5.7	5.8
2016	5.8	5.7	5.8	5.8	5.8	5.8	5.8	5.6	5.6	5.5	5.6	5.5	5.7
2017	5.7	5.7	5.7	5.6	5.6	5.6	5.5	5.6	5.5	5.6	5.6	5.7	5.6
2018	5.7	5.7	5.7	5.7	5.7	5.8	5.8	5.8	5.8	5.8	5.8	5.9	5.8
Construction													
2010	347.5	349.3	351.7	355.1	354.0	356.2	358.1	355.8	351.6	347.4	343.5	340.5	350.9
2011	328.6	330.3	332.8	334.4	335.0	336.4	337.5	338.1	340.7	337.6	338.3	337.9	335.6
2012	328.8	331.1	335.3	335.1	338.7	343.2	342.7	347.0	349.3	350.6	352.9	352.1	342.2
2013	344.4	348.6	353.7	356.8	362.2	366.1	369.2	375.1	376.7	378.2	380.9	381.6	366.1
2014	373.7	379.5	383.2	387.7	394.0	398.7	401.7	405.9	408.0	411.5	412.3	412.8	397.4
2015	407.2	412.5	416.8	421.0	426.6	432.4	435.3	438.6	441.6	450.6	453.4	454.9	432.6
2016	449.5	456.7	460.9	467.4	471.2	475.9	479.8	482.3	487.3	489.6	493.1	494.2	475.7
2017	488.3	494.7	499.6	499.9	504.4	509.9	509.5	512.7	487.3	517.4	520.0	521.8	505.5
2018	517.8	529.3	534.7	536.5	538.1	544.6	543.3	547.1	548.0	551.7	548.9	550.8	540.9

1. Employment by Industry: Florida, 2010–2018—*Continued*

(Numbers in thousands, not seasonally adjusted)

Industry and year	January	February	March	April	May	June	July	August	September	October	November	December	Annual average
Manufacturing													
2010	307.9	307.9	308.0	308.3	310.1	311.1	310.1	309.6	309.2	308.6	309.5	311.0	309.3
2011	309.0	309.8	310.3	311.6	312.6	313.7	313.2	313.9	313.7	313.9	314.6	315.4	312.6
2012	314.7	315.6	317.3	316.9	318.0	318.6	317.4	318.2	317.5	318.1	319.2	319.6	317.6
2013	316.3	318.3	319.6	320.8	322.5	324.0	322.6	323.6	324.2	324.7	326.9	328.2	322.6
2014	327.0	328.5	328.5	329.5	331.6	332.2	332.0	333.2	333.8	335.7	336.5	337.6	332.2
2015	335.4	337.0	338.9	339.7	341.7	344.2	344.4	345.3	346.0	348.6	349.7	351.0	343.5
2016	349.2	351.1	352.7	353.4	354.5	356.0	357.0	357.3	357.7	357.9	359.9	361.0	355.6
2017	358.9	361.5	363.1	362.7	363.9	366.0	364.6	365.0	357.4	364.0	366.0	367.7	363.4
2018	364.8	367.2	369.0	369.1	370.5	372.8	372.8	373.9	373.5	375.0	376.5	378.6	372.0
Trade, Transportation, and Utilities													
2010	1,459.7	1,458.3	1,462.7	1,463.5	1,465.1	1,463.6	1,452.6	1,456.0	1,451.3	1,468.8	1,502.9	1,525.5	1,469.2
2011	1,479.1	1,477.2	1,481.9	1,490.3	1,488.9	1,486.2	1,484.4	1,488.8	1,490.1	1,501.7	1,541.4	1,560.6	1,497.6
2012	1,517.1	1,514.3	1,520.6	1,520.7	1,524.9	1,521.6	1,513.5	1,516.2	1,518.1	1,531.3	1,575.9	1,592.3	1,530.5
2013	1,544.3	1,544.4	1,548.2	1,549.4	1,553.5	1,555.3	1,551.1	1,556.0	1,556.0	1,573.6	1,622.9	1,645.7	1,566.7
2014	1,590.8	1,593.4	1,598.1	1,602.5	1,604.6	1,603.8	1,599.2	1,607.7	1,609.1	1,630.1	1,682.0	1,708.9	1,619.2
2015	1,654.8	1,654.4	1,658.4	1,659.9	1,662.1	1,665.6	1,659.3	1,667.0	1,662.9	1,683.7	1,732.1	1,756.9	1,676.4
2016	1,693.1	1,693.3	1,696.1	1,699.9	1,701.3	1,696.6	1,698.4	1,702.2	1,702.0	1,715.7	1,766.5	1,787.3	1,712.7
2017	1,735.8	1,727.4	1,727.2	1,728.4	1,728.6	1,725.5	1,721.4	1,725.4	1,690.8	1,740.5	1,804.8	1,824.8	1,740.1
2018	1,771.3	1,767.0	1,767.0	1,765.4	1,767.3	1,765.1	1,762.7	1,766.4	1,767.7	1,783.3	1,834.7	1,852.3	1,780.9
Wholesale Trade													
2010	306.9	308.0	308.2	307.9	309.3	308.3	305.8	306.2	305.7	307.7	308.7	311.0	307.8
2011	304.4	305.7	306.5	307.7	307.2	306.4	305.5	305.5	306.0	307.0	308.2	311.1	306.8
2012	306.7	308.5	309.9	310.9	311.8	311.0	309.9	310.3	310.8	312.9	315.0	316.1	311.2
2013	311.6	313.5	314.3	314.0	314.9	313.8	312.0	312.5	312.9	314.5	317.0	318.6	314.1
2014	315.5	317.8	318.1	318.9	320.5	319.5	318.8	320.5	320.7	323.4	326.3	328.2	320.7
2015	325.1	326.2	327.0	326.7	327.6	327.4	326.7	327.3	327.6	330.0	331.7	333.5	328.1
2016	329.5	331.0	331.3	332.4	332.8	331.0	330.8	331.5	331.7	332.5	335.0	337.1	332.2
2017	333.9	335.2	336.1	336.7	338.2	337.5	337.0	336.9	333.9	337.7	340.0	342.4	337.1
2018	341.2	343.6	344.3	344.8	345.3	345.2	345.1	345.8	346.0	347.5	348.4	352.6	345.8
Retail Trade													
2010	926.8	923.4	927.0	928.6	929.3	929.4	921.9	924.9	921.3	934.7	965.0	979.2	934.3
2011	943.9	939.8	942.3	947.9	947.2	945.3	944.1	948.5	948.8	958.6	994.1	1,004.8	955.4
2012	972.6	966.8	971.0	970.6	973.6	970.6	964.5	966.9	968.1	977.6	1,016.8	1,026.2	978.8
2013	989.4	986.4	988.3	989.2	992.2	995.0	994.3	997.8	996.8	1,011.4	1,054.7	1,069.7	1,005.4
2014	1,025.7	1,024.7	1,027.6	1,031.0	1,031.0	1,031.3	1,027.8	1,033.3	1,034.0	1,050.3	1,094.7	1,111.0	1,043.5
2015	1,068.1	1,067.5	1,069.4	1,070.6	1,071.4	1,074.1	1,068.2	1,074.0	1,068.8	1,083.9	1,124.4	1,139.1	1,081.6
2016	1,088.6	1,087.8	1,089.1	1,091.3	1,092.0	1,089.2	1,091.1	1,094.7	1,092.8	1,103.7	1,146.2	1,156.8	1,101.9
2017	1,117.3	1,108.7	1,106.2	1,107.1	1,105.3	1,102.5	1,100.0	1,103.5	1,076.0	1,115.1	1,168.7	1,176.8	1,115.6
2018	1,132.8	1,127.3	1,125.4	1,123.8	1,123.2	1,119.9	1,117.4	1,118.7	1,118.0	1,129.0	1,170.1	1,173.1	1,131.6
Transportation and Utilities													
2010	226.0	226.9	227.5	227.0	226.5	225.9	224.9	224.9	224.3	226.4	229.2	235.3	227.1
2011	230.8	231.7	233.1	234.7	234.5	234.5	234.8	234.8	235.3	236.1	239.1	244.7	235.3
2012	237.8	239.0	239.7	239.2	239.5	240.0	239.1	239.0	239.2	240.8	244.1	250.0	240.6
2013	243.3	244.5	245.6	246.2	246.4	246.5	244.8	245.7	246.3	247.7	251.2	257.4	247.1
2014	249.6	250.9	252.4	252.6	253.1	253.0	252.6	253.9	254.4	256.4	261.0	269.7	255.0
2015	261.6	260.7	262.0	262.6	263.1	264.1	264.4	265.7	266.5	269.8	276.0	284.3	266.7
2016	275.0	274.5	275.7	276.2	276.5	276.4	276.5	276.0	277.5	279.5	285.3	293.4	278.5
2017	284.6	283.5	284.9	284.6	285.1	285.5	284.4	285.0	280.9	287.7	296.1	305.6	287.3
2018	297.3	296.1	297.3	296.8	298.8	300.0	300.2	301.9	303.7	306.8	316.2	326.6	303.5
Information													
2010	137.8	137.5	138.2	137.3	137.1	137.2	136.9	136.9	136.1	136.7	137.2	136.8	137.1
2011	136.3	136.4	136.3	135.9	136.0	135.9	135.8	135.5	135.3	135.1	135.6	135.4	135.8
2012	134.2	134.1	133.9	133.9	133.6	133.5	133.5	133.1	132.0	134.0	134.0	134.1	133.7
2013	132.9	133.2	133.7	133.6	133.6	134.4	134.6	134.6	134.0	134.7	135.4	135.9	134.2
2014	135.6	136.2	136.1	136.2	136.2	137.2	136.8	135.9	135.1	135.7	136.9	136.8	136.2
2015	135.7	135.9	135.8	135.6	136.5	136.3	136.8	136.9	136.1	137.1	138.2	139.0	136.7
2016	136.4	137.3	136.8	136.9	137.6	137.4	138.1	138.4	136.5	136.9	138.7	138.5	137.5
2017	137.8	139.6	139.4	138.3	139.4	138.9	137.9	138.4	135.2	136.9	139.1	139.7	138.4
2018	138.0	140.6	139.5	138.5	139.3	139.4	138.4	139.7	137.7	140.2	142.4	142.3	139.7

1. Employment by Industry: Florida, 2010–2018—*Continued*

(Numbers in thousands, not seasonally adjusted)

Industry and year	January	February	March	April	May	June	July	August	September	October	November	December	Annual average
Financial Activities													
2010	473.3	474.6	476.4	475.9	477.2	479.1	478.8	479.0	476.2	480.7	482.7	485.9	478.3
2011	479.2	481.1	483.6	484.8	484.7	485.4	487.3	488.7	489.8	490.8	491.8	495.4	486.9
2012	489.2	492.2	494.8	496.9	498.3	500.5	500.6	501.6	500.8	505.3	507.6	510.1	499.8
2013	503.7	506.4	509.1	510.5	511.6	514.3	514.7	515.7	514.6	517.4	519.7	521.9	513.3
2014	513.5	515.5	518.1	519.6	521.6	522.7	523.9	524.6	523.4	527.4	529.3	531.6	522.6
2015	526.8	528.7	531.0	532.4	533.8	535.1	536.9	537.7	535.8	541.1	543.7	545.1	535.7
2016	540.1	542.3	543.4	546.0	546.8	547.6	548.8	549.7	550.2	553.9	556.0	560.2	548.8
2017	554.9	557.5	559.5	560.0	561.2	563.8	564.2	564.4	561.3	569.1	570.2	570.9	563.1
2018	565.8	569.2	571.0	572.3	573.3	575.4	576.2	577.0	575.8	582.1	588.2	593.8	576.7
Professional and Business Services													
2010	981.9	994.0	1,002.3	1,005.0	1,005.3	1,009.9	1,006.2	1,011.9	1,012.3	1,027.2	1,031.8	1,038.6	1,010.5
2011	1,019.5	1,033.1	1,040.4	1,048.0	1,040.9	1,039.0	1,031.8	1,034.4	1,038.0	1,044.0	1,054.1	1,061.4	1,040.4
2012	1,039.7	1,055.7	1,066.9	1,080.4	1,078.8	1,078.5	1,070.9	1,077.4	1,078.3	1,099.4	1,111.5	1,114.4	1,079.3
2013	1,087.5	1,105.6	1,114.1	1,115.4	1,120.1	1,119.3	1,116.3	1,124.0	1,124.6	1,139.3	1,152.0	1,154.1	1,122.7
2014	1,132.8	1,145.6	1,151.5	1,160.0	1,166.9	1,163.3	1,161.5	1,173.0	1,174.4	1,192.5	1,204.5	1,210.0	1,169.7
2015	1,189.1	1,201.9	1,206.6	1,217.7	1,222.8	1,220.2	1,223.2	1,227.5	1,228.6	1,253.0	1,265.7	1,270.5	1,227.2
2016	1,254.7	1,267.2	1,275.3	1,283.9	1,280.8	1,277.5	1,285.2	1,291.3	1,293.2	1,311.7	1,321.0	1,317.8	1,288.3
2017	1,305.2	1,312.3	1,315.9	1,320.2	1,321.5	1,324.9	1,324.9	1,327.7	1,297.2	1,350.1	1,360.6	1,359.8	1,326.7
2018	1,335.4	1,344.6	1,349.5	1,355.2	1,357.6	1,361.5	1,363.0	1,372.1	1,368.0	1,389.4	1,401.8	1,403.3	1,366.8
Education and Health Services													
2010	1,059.3	1,066.7	1,071.5	1,072.8	1,074.2	1,066.5	1,057.2	1,061.3	1,066.9	1,081.0	1,086.6	1,086.2	1,070.9
2011	1,077.4	1,085.1	1,087.5	1,096.2	1,094.8	1,083.9	1,075.1	1,082.4	1,094.2	1,100.2	1,107.1	1,108.5	1,091.0
2012	1,093.8	1,101.9	1,106.3	1,112.0	1,113.0	1,104.3	1,091.8	1,103.6	1,113.0	1,119.9	1,125.1	1,126.7	1,109.3
2013	1,115.0	1,125.9	1,129.6	1,131.7	1,131.3	1,120.3	1,108.0	1,121.1	1,128.3	1,137.7	1,145.1	1,145.6	1,128.3
2014	1,134.4	1,145.3	1,148.8	1,158.4	1,159.8	1,149.6	1,140.9	1,157.2	1,166.4	1,177.9	1,184.6	1,188.1	1,159.3
2015	1,176.4	1,186.8	1,191.2	1,196.0	1,199.9	1,190.4	1,180.9	1,193.8	1,205.6	1,221.7	1,229.0	1,230.5	1,200.2
2016	1,219.8	1,229.6	1,232.3	1,243.1	1,243.4	1,229.3	1,227.7	1,239.9	1,252.9	1,263.1	1,268.9	1,274.0	1,243.7
2017	1,261.0	1,272.8	1,274.5	1,279.0	1,280.3	1,267.7	1,256.4	1,272.1	1,261.3	1,289.5	1,294.9	1,297.6	1,275.6
2018	1,284.9	1,297.8	1,300.8	1,303.1	1,301.4	1,290.3	1,281.1	1,301.6	1,309.6	1,325.5	1,330.2	1,337.7	1,305.3
Leisure and Hospitality													
2010	904.3	926.1	948.8	955.1	946.9	939.3	923.1	920.2	915.0	922.3	935.5	942.7	931.6
2011	931.6	946.6	973.1	979.7	970.6	963.2	948.9	947.2	945.5	949.1	964.1	970.6	957.5
2012	968.0	988.7	1,017.0	1,019.1	1,010.8	1,006.3	990.7	987.0	980.1	988.5	1,005.1	1,011.7	997.8
2013	1,001.8	1,027.3	1,052.2	1,052.4	1,047.3	1,043.8	1,035.6	1,031.6	1,024.1	1,030.9	1,049.2	1,054.3	1,037.5
2014	1,047.5	1,070.9	1,100.0	1,102.7	1,096.3	1,093.6	1,080.4	1,076.5	1,071.3	1,081.9	1,097.6	1,102.8	1,085.1
2015	1,096.7	1,123.3	1,147.9	1,149.0	1,140.9	1,135.9	1,125.4	1,124.5	1,120.1	1,135.9	1,152.1	1,160.7	1,134.4
2016	1,147.8	1,174.8	1,194.6	1,195.4	1,186.3	1,175.6	1,166.2	1,163.1	1,162.2	1,166.4	1,183.0	1,186.6	1,175.2
2017	1,179.9	1,202.9	1,225.7	1,225.3	1,220.0	1,211.3	1,197.0	1,193.7	1,144.3	1,191.6	1,205.7	1,209.7	1,200.6
2018	1,199.6	1,229.0	1,249.2	1,246.6	1,240.5	1,227.7	1,218.4	1,220.6	1,210.9	1,215.4	1,232.1	1,234.7	1,227.1
Other Services													
2010	296.0	298.0	299.7	300.5	299.6	299.2	296.3	295.0	293.9	296.5	297.1	297.0	297.4
2011	292.6	294.5	296.6	298.5	297.9	296.4	294.8	294.2	294.4	295.4	296.5	297.1	295.7
2012	297.5	299.4	301.7	303.6	303.1	303.4	300.2	299.8	300.3	302.2	303.5	304.6	301.6
2013	302.2	304.8	306.5	308.7	309.0	309.3	307.8	308.8	309.7	312.1	315.2	316.5	309.2
2014	317.0	320.5	323.2	323.6	323.6	322.9	321.3	322.4	322.8	325.5	327.2	328.1	323.2
2015	326.1	328.7	330.8	332.5	332.9	333.7	332.4	333.4	334.3	337.5	341.1	343.1	333.9
2016	342.3	345.7	348.3	349.0	348.5	348.1	346.6	346.5	347.9	348.5	351.0	349.9	347.7
2017	346.1	348.2	349.5	349.1	349.5	349.2	347.4	347.0	338.8	348.1	350.4	352.5	348.0
2018	349.2	352.5	354.5	354.7	354.8	355.0	353.5	353.3	353.2	355.8	358.3	357.7	354.4
Government													
2010	1,123.4	1,130.5	1,131.0	1,136.4	1,164.3	1,050.0	1,035.7	1,114.0	1,117.9	1,124.7	1,127.8	1,119.3	1,114.6
2011	1,116.7	1,127.3	1,125.8	1,126.1	1,113.9	1,021.2	1,014.7	1,085.8	1,094.9	1,110.4	1,110.6	1,105.0	1,096.0
2012	1,096.8	1,109.6	1,108.9	1,103.2	1,092.7	1,007.7	1,002.0	1,077.2	1,088.1	1,100.7	1,103.8	1,097.8	1,082.4
2013	1,092.5	1,103.2	1,104.7	1,102.3	1,092.4	1,005.6	996.4	1,073.6	1,085.0	1,096.7	1,102.0	1,095.6	1,079.2
2014	1,087.4	1,097.4	1,101.5	1,098.1	1,090.6	1,001.8	999.0	1,072.5	1,083.4	1,097.6	1,101.0	1,098.4	1,077.4
2015	1,089.2	1,101.6	1,104.9	1,105.2	1,097.9	1,008.6	1,006.7	1,082.0	1,092.5	1,109.5	1,110.7	1,105.4	1,084.5
2016	1,100.1	1,111.4	1,114.7	1,116.7	1,110.4	1,024.2	1,021.5	1,095.0	1,113.1	1,118.6	1,123.7	1,121.0	1,097.5
2017	1,114.5	1,127.9	1,130.7	1,125.1	1,120.0	1,030.0	1,026.5	1,097.7	1,111.2	1,125.8	1,130.1	1,127.8	1,105.6
2018	1,122.6	1,132.3	1,135.3	1,132.2	1,125.1	1,038.7	1,030.2	1,109.9	1,124.3	1,131.1	1,135.9	1,132.8	1,112.5

2. Average Weekly Hours by Selected Industry: Florida, 2014–2018

(Not seasonally adjusted)

Industry and year	January	February	March	April	May	June	July	August	September	October	November	December	Annual average
Total Private													
2014	34.2	34.6	34.6	34.4	34.2	34.5	34.3	34.4	34.3	34.2	34.6	34.4	34.4
2015	34.1	34.7	34.7	34.3	34.2	34.1	34.2	34.5	33.9	34.1	34.5	34.3	34.3
2016	34.2	34.2	34.2	34.2	34.3	33.9	34.1	33.8	33.7	33.9	34.0	34.2	34.0
2017	34.4	34.3	34.3	34.6	34.1	34.1	34.5	34.2	32.7	35.1	34.9	35.0	34.3
2018	34.7	35.0	35.0	35.1	34.6	34.8	34.9	34.7	34.8	34.4	34.6	34.7	34.8
Goods-Producing													
2014	39.2	39.6	40.0	39.9	40.0	40.2	39.9	40.2	40.3	40.0	40.6	40.5	40.0
2015	39.4	39.6	40.2	39.8	39.9	40.1	39.9	40.1	38.7	40.1	40.5	40.4	39.9
2016	39.4	39.3	39.3	39.5	39.3	38.5	39.0	39.1	39.4	39.3	40.0	40.2	39.4
2017	40.2	40.2	40.1	39.6	40.0	39.8	40.2	40.5	35.3	41.1	40.9	41.2	39.9
2018	40.5	40.7	40.5	40.6	40.3	40.8	40.6	40.9	40.7	40.5	40.9	40.7	40.6
Construction													
2014	38.0	38.4	38.9	38.5	39.2	39.2	38.9	39.4	39.5	39.5	39.4	39.7	39.1
2015	38.1	38.6	39.4	38.8	39.2	39.4	39.2	39.6	38.0	40.1	40.2	40.2	39.3
2016	38.6	38.9	38.7	38.8	38.9	38.2	38.7	39.0	39.5	39.1	40.0	39.9	39.0
2017	39.8	39.8	39.8	39.0	39.5	39.0	39.8	40.0	33.9	40.0	40.1	40.1	39.3
2018	39.6	39.5	39.5	39.6	39.6	40.1	40.1	40.5	40.0	40.1	40.4	40.1	39.9
Manufacturing													
2014	40.5	40.9	41.0	41.2	40.6	41.0	40.7	40.8	41.0	40.2	41.8	41.1	40.9
2015	40.7	40.5	40.9	40.7	40.4	40.7	40.5	40.6	39.6	40.2	40.9	40.8	40.5
2016	40.5	40.0	41.1	40.3	39.9	39.5	39.9	39.8	39.8	40.1	40.5	41.0	40.1
2017	40.8	40.9	40.8	40.6	40.7	40.8	40.7	41.2	37.3	42.6	42.0	43.2	41.0
2018	42.1	42.6	42.1	42.1	41.4	41.7	41.3	41.5	41.7	41.1	41.4	41.3	41.7
Trade, Transportation, and Utilities													
2014	32.6	32.9	33.0	33.2	32.8	32.9	33.0	33.2	33.1	33.3	33.6	33.8	33.1
2015	33.2	33.8	33.6	33.5	33.5	33.2	33.2	33.3	33.4	33.3	33.4	33.5	33.4
2016	33.3	33.4	33.1	33.0	33.0	32.6	32.5	32.2	32.1	32.2	32.4	33.4	32.8
2017	33.0	33.0	33.1	33.4	32.9	32.7	33.0	32.7	32.1	34.3	34.1	34.4	33.2
2018	33.8	33.8	34.1	34.0	33.8	33.9	33.7	33.4	33.5	32.9	33.2	33.0	33.6
Financial Activities													
2014	37.4	37.5	37.6	37.0	37.2	37.9	37.2	37.1	37.6	37.4	38.4	37.7	37.5
2015	37.7	38.7	38.6	37.9	37.7	37.7	37.9	38.6	37.9	37.9	38.6	38.1	38.1
2016	37.9	38.0	37.9	37.7	38.0	37.6	37.9	37.7	37.7	38.0	38.4	37.9	37.9
2017	38.5	37.9	37.6	38.1	37.6	37.7	38.3	37.8	37.2	38.5	38.1	38.1	38.0
2018	38.1	38.1	38.0	38.7	37.4	37.7	38.5	38.0	38.2	37.5	37.3	37.7	37.9
Professional and Business Services													
2014	35.9	36.5	36.4	35.5	35.6	36.3	35.8	36.0	35.7	35.8	36.2	35.6	35.9
2015	35.0	36.0	35.8	35.6	35.7	35.7	35.6	36.3	35.4	35.6	36.0	35.6	35.7
2016	35.5	35.4	35.5	35.9	36.2	35.7	35.8	35.7	36.0	36.5	36.0	35.8	35.8
2017	36.5	36.2	36.0	36.8	36.0	36.1	36.7	36.1	34.7	36.9	36.6	36.4	36.3
2018	36.3	36.6	36.6	36.9	36.4	36.6	36.7	36.4	37.3	36.5	36.3	36.7	36.6
Education and Health Services													
2014	34.9	35.2	35.0	35.0	34.9	34.9	34.9	35.0	35.0	34.9	35.3	34.8	35.0
2015	35.1	35.1	35.2	34.8	34.8	34.7	34.8	34.9	34.6	34.5	34.9	34.5	34.8
2016	35.2	35.0	34.9	35.0	35.0	34.7	34.7	34.4	34.2	34.1	34.0	34.1	34.6
2017	34.3	34.2	33.7	34.1	34.0	33.8	34.3	34.0	34.0	34.3	34.3	34.5	34.1
2018	34.2	34.5	34.3	34.6	34.2	34.2	34.2	34.2	34.5	34.3	34.5	34.4	34.3
Leisure and Hospitality													
2014	28.1	28.9	29.3	28.7	28.2	28.4	28.4	28.2	27.5	27.6	28.2	28.1	28.3
2015	28.4	29.1	29.2	28.4	27.8	27.7	27.8	28.0	27.0	27.1	27.7	27.5	28.0
2016	27.6	28.3	28.3	28.0	27.6	27.7	27.9	27.4	26.9	26.9	27.8	27.5	27.7
2017	27.9	28.2	29.0	28.9	27.9	28.0	28.1	27.9	25.0	28.1	28.1	28.3	28.0
2018	28.4	29.4	29.6	29.0	28.2	28.3	28.5	28.0	27.3	27.5	28.2	28.3	28.4
Other Services													
2014	32.7	33.2	33.1	32.5	32.7	32.5	31.9	33.0	32.2	32.4	32.6	33.2	32.7
2015	32.7	32.7	33.1	32.4	31.9	32.5	32.4	33.0	32.7	33.2	33.3	33.4	32.8
2016	33.2	33.4	33.4	33.4	34.0	33.9	33.8	33.7	33.4	33.3	33.4	33.2	33.5
2017	33.4	33.3	33.0	33.0	32.8	33.1	33.2	33.3	30.0	32.5	32.0	33.1	32.7
2018	32.8	33.7	33.6	33.9	33.3	33.7	34.1	33.6	33.4	33.0	33.7	34.3	33.6

3. Average Hourly Earnings by Selected Industry: Florida, 2014–2018

(Dollars, not seasonally adjusted)

Industry and year	January	February	March	April	May	June	July	August	September	October	November	December	Annual average
Total Private													
2014	22.14	22.18	22.09	22.26	22.12	22.22	22.22	22.27	22.22	22.17	22.28	22.13	22.19
2015	22.32	22.53	22.45	22.42	22.51	22.41	22.55	22.80	22.80	22.81	22.98	22.88	22.63
2016	22.73	22.88	23.12	23.06	23.33	23.23	23.11	23.36	23.48	23.93	23.69	23.74	23.31
2017	23.90	23.84	23.78	24.12	23.92	23.67	24.05	23.96	24.80	24.11	24.06	24.29	24.04
2018	24.38	24.42	24.40	24.79	24.80	24.72	24.87	24.72	25.20	25.11	25.00	25.32	24.81
Goods-Producing													
2014	22.96	22.96	22.76	22.52	22.34	22.45	22.69	22.71	22.61	22.59	22.52	22.62	22.64
2015	23.01	22.92	22.95	22.93	23.03	22.90	23.12	23.43	23.36	23.23	23.41	23.18	23.13
2016	23.30	23.31	23.45	23.80	23.91	24.14	24.46	24.48	24.68	24.97	24.86	25.08	24.22
2017	25.06	24.95	24.99	25.36	25.40	25.20	25.46	25.18	26.10	24.72	24.83	25.07	25.18
2018	25.19	25.29	25.36	25.72	25.99	25.91	25.77	25.83	26.16	26.31	26.13	26.35	25.84
Construction													
2014	22.24	22.22	22.16	22.08	21.88	21.97	22.35	22.28	22.21	22.31	22.39	22.13	22.19
2015	22.44	22.41	22.48	22.68	22.66	22.64	22.75	23.07	22.93	22.89	23.31	23.33	22.81
2016	23.12	23.18	22.94	23.28	23.28	23.20	23.65	23.46	23.85	24.27	24.22	24.45	23.59
2017	24.53	24.47	24.63	24.90	25.08	24.94	25.01	24.88	25.82	24.22	24.43	24.73	24.79
2018	24.99	24.74	24.84	25.25	25.54	25.43	25.11	25.30	25.66	25.84	25.37	25.49	25.30
Manufacturing													
2014	23.78	23.81	23.44	23.03	22.92	23.06	23.17	23.29	23.15	23.02	22.69	23.30	23.22
2015	23.74	23.57	23.58	23.29	23.56	23.27	23.62	23.93	23.97	23.72	23.57	24.06	23.66
2016	24.39	24.24	24.70	24.96	25.13	25.62	25.76	26.07	26.00	26.11	25.91	26.06	25.42
2017	25.93	25.72	25.58	25.97	25.85	25.54	26.12	25.64	26.49	25.49	25.45	25.59	25.77
2018	25.51	26.08	26.11	26.37	26.62	26.61	26.80	26.64	26.92	27.02	27.26	27.63	26.63
Trade, Transportation, and Utilities													
2014	19.37	19.57	19.49	19.38	18.97	19.07	19.29	19.36	19.21	19.10	19.23	19.03	19.25
2015	19.58	19.82	19.55	19.68	20.12	20.02	20.28	20.44	20.58	20.05	20.08	20.45	20.06
2016	20.35	20.49	21.10	20.68	20.78	21.41	20.82	20.86	20.65	20.72	20.46	20.13	20.70
2017	20.60	20.55	20.66	21.10	20.89	20.87	21.24	20.75	21.84	21.10	21.30	21.34	21.02
2018	21.52	21.68	21.81	22.45	22.25	22.20	22.37	21.81	22.32	22.35	22.24	22.58	22.13
Financial Activities													
2014	26.40	26.32	26.60	26.27	26.03	26.54	26.32	26.41	26.06	26.21	26.43	26.26	26.32
2015	26.34	27.22	28.07	27.22	27.14	27.09	27.04	27.87	27.30	27.17	28.03	27.74	27.36
2016	27.17	27.72	27.78	26.86	28.09	26.83	26.87	28.48	27.75	28.76	28.82	28.37	27.80
2017	28.87	28.73	28.17	29.12	28.68	27.65	28.66	29.06	28.87	28.97	29.17	29.12	28.76
2018	29.31	29.67	29.50	30.45	30.96	30.68	31.21	31.17	31.86	31.28	32.18	32.25	30.88
Professional and Business Services													
2014	25.41	25.45	25.38	25.65	25.80	25.94	25.79	25.75	25.92	25.76	26.03	25.75	25.72
2015	25.90	26.05	26.03	25.94	25.74	25.63	25.84	26.12	26.22	26.30	26.69	26.39	26.08
2016	26.42	26.67	26.61	26.85	27.10	27.04	27.03	26.69	27.05	27.74	27.56	27.97	27.07
2017	28.04	28.03	28.14	28.50	28.06	27.95	28.46	28.40	29.59	28.79	28.27	28.62	28.40
2018	29.00	28.90	28.66	28.81	28.82	28.92	29.30	29.28	29.94	29.66	29.29	29.75	29.20
Education and Health Services													
2014	24.69	24.60	24.44	24.38	24.19	24.08	24.00	23.97	24.08	24.11	24.06	24.32	24.24
2015	24.01	24.27	24.31	24.38	24.19	24.11	24.18	24.23	24.44	24.70	24.61	24.38	24.32
2016	24.13	24.37	24.48	24.49	24.39	24.32	24.42	24.57	24.93	25.49	25.27	25.52	24.70
2017	25.40	25.42	25.40	25.59	25.53	25.24	25.41	25.49	26.01	25.72	25.72	26.18	25.59
2018	26.26	26.11	26.19	26.15	26.16	26.16	26.09	26.31	26.35	26.33	26.23	26.48	26.24
Leisure and Hospitality													
2014	13.60	13.75	13.75	13.69	13.69	13.67	13.65	13.85	13.84	14.03	14.19	14.15	13.82
2015	14.48	14.53	14.33	14.27	14.36	14.06	14.20	14.14	14.22	14.55	14.65	14.68	14.37
2016	14.72	14.82	14.89	14.95	14.95	14.80	14.85	14.91	15.15	15.49	15.47	15.61	15.05
2017	15.63	15.80	15.81	15.66	15.54	15.17	15.26	15.25	15.46	15.50	15.59	15.64	15.53
2018	15.55	15.84	15.94	15.99	15.77	15.28	15.40	15.38	15.54	15.73	15.93	16.16	15.71
Other Services													
2014	19.11	19.06	19.09	19.25	19.37	19.55	19.37	19.75	19.60	19.26	19.62	19.49	19.38
2015	19.54	19.76	19.74	19.69	19.97	20.22	20.46	20.55	20.26	20.35	20.79	20.57	20.17
2016	20.55	20.74	20.84	21.11	21.14	21.22	21.59	21.48	21.95	21.82	21.37	21.19	21.25
2017	20.81	20.76	20.73	20.67	20.37	19.93	19.98	19.95	20.69	19.96	20.15	20.60	20.38
2018	19.96	20.38	20.41	20.77	20.62	20.44	20.63	20.14	20.45	20.57	20.12	20.65	20.43

4. Average Weekly Earnings by Selected Industry: Florida, 2014–2018

(Dollars, not seasonally adjusted)

Industry and year	January	February	March	April	May	June	July	August	September	October	November	December	Annual average
Total Private													
2014	757.19	767.43	764.31	765.74	756.50	766.59	762.15	766.09	762.15	758.21	770.89	761.27	763.34
2015	761.11	781.79	779.02	769.01	769.84	764.18	771.21	786.60	772.92	777.82	792.81	784.78	776.21
2016	777.37	782.50	790.70	788.65	800.22	787.50	788.05	789.57	791.28	811.23	805.46	811.91	792.54
2017	822.16	817.71	815.65	834.55	815.67	807.15	829.73	819.43	810.96	846.26	839.69	850.15	824.57
2018	845.99	854.70	854.00	870.13	858.08	860.26	867.96	857.78	876.96	863.78	865.00	878.60	863.39
Goods-Producing													
2014	900.03	909.22	910.40	898.55	893.60	902.49	905.33	912.94	911.18	903.60	914.31	916.11	905.60
2015	906.59	907.63	922.59	912.61	918.90	918.29	922.49	939.54	904.03	931.52	948.11	936.47	922.89
2016	918.02	916.08	921.59	940.10	939.66	929.39	953.94	957.17	972.39	981.32	994.40	1,008.22	954.27
2017	1,007.41	1,002.99	1,002.10	1,004.26	1,016.00	1,002.96	1,023.49	1,019.79	921.33	1,015.99	1,015.55	1,032.88	1,004.68
2018	1,020.20	1,029.30	1,027.08	1,044.23	1,047.40	1,057.13	1,046.26	1,056.45	1,064.71	1,065.56	1,068.72	1,072.45	1,049.10
Construction													
2014	845.12	853.25	862.02	850.08	857.70	861.22	869.42	877.83	877.30	881.25	882.17	878.56	867.63
2015	854.96	865.03	885.71	879.98	888.27	892.02	891.80	913.57	871.34	917.89	937.06	937.87	896.43
2016	892.43	901.70	887.78	903.26	905.59	886.24	915.26	914.94	942.08	948.96	968.80	975.56	920.01
2017	976.29	973.91	980.27	971.10	990.66	972.66	995.40	995.20	875.30	968.80	979.64	991.67	974.25
2018	989.60	977.23	981.18	999.90	1,011.38	1,019.74	1,006.91	1,024.65	1,026.40	1,036.18	1,024.95	1,022.15	1,009.47
Manufacturing													
2014	963.09	973.83	961.04	948.84	930.55	945.46	943.02	950.23	949.15	925.40	948.44	957.63	949.70
2015	966.22	954.59	964.42	947.90	951.82	947.09	956.61	971.56	949.21	953.54	964.01	981.65	958.23
2016	987.80	969.60	990.47	1,005.89	1,002.69	1,011.99	1,027.82	1,037.59	1,034.80	1,047.01	1,049.36	1,068.46	1,019.34
2017	1,057.94	1,051.95	1,043.66	1,054.38	1,052.10	1,042.03	1,063.08	1,056.37	988.08	1,085.87	1,068.90	1,105.49	1,056.57
2018	1,073.97	1,111.01	1,099.23	1,110.18	1,102.07	1,109.64	1,106.84	1,105.56	1,122.56	1,110.52	1,128.56	1,141.12	1,110.47
Trade, Transportation, and Utilities													
2014	631.46	643.85	643.17	643.42	622.22	627.40	636.57	642.75	635.85	636.03	646.13	643.21	637.18
2015	650.06	669.92	656.88	659.28	674.02	664.66	673.30	680.65	687.37	667.67	670.67	685.08	670.00
2016	677.66	684.37	698.41	682.44	685.74	697.97	676.65	671.69	662.87	667.18	662.90	672.34	678.96
2017	679.80	678.15	683.85	704.74	687.28	682.45	700.92	678.53	701.06	723.73	726.33	734.10	697.86
2018	727.38	732.78	743.72	763.30	752.05	752.58	753.87	728.45	747.72	735.32	738.37	745.14	743.57
Financial Activities													
2014	987.36	987.00	1,000.16	971.99	968.32	1,005.87	979.10	979.81	979.86	980.25	1,014.91	990.00	987.00
2015	993.02	1,053.41	1,083.50	1,031.64	1,023.18	1,021.29	1,024.82	1,075.78	1,034.67	1,029.74	1,081.96	1,056.89	1,042.42
2016	1,029.74	1,053.36	1,052.86	1,012.62	1,067.42	1,008.81	1,018.37	1,073.70	1,054.50	1,104.38	1,092.28	1,086.57	1,053.62
2017	1,111.50	1,088.87	1,059.19	1,109.47	1,078.37	1,042.41	1,097.68	1,098.47	1,073.96	1,115.35	1,111.38	1,109.47	1,092.88
2018	1,116.71	1,130.43	1,121.00	1,178.42	1,157.90	1,156.64	1,201.59	1,184.46	1,217.05	1,173.00	1,200.31	1,215.83	1,170.35
Professional and Business Services													
2014	912.22	928.93	923.83	910.58	918.48	941.62	923.28	927.00	925.34	922.21	942.29	916.70	923.35
2015	906.50	937.80	931.87	923.46	918.92	914.99	919.90	948.16	928.19	936.28	960.84	939.48	931.06
2016	937.91	944.12	944.66	963.92	981.02	965.33	967.67	952.83	973.80	1,012.51	992.16	1,001.33	969.11
2017	1,023.46	1,014.69	1,013.04	1,048.80	1,010.16	1,009.00	1,044.48	1,025.24	1,026.77	1,062.35	1,034.68	1,041.77	1,030.92
2018	1,052.70	1,057.74	1,048.96	1,063.09	1,049.05	1,058.47	1,075.31	1,065.79	1,116.76	1,082.59	1,063.23	1,091.83	1,068.72
Education and Health Services													
2014	861.68	865.92	855.40	853.30	844.23	840.39	837.60	838.95	842.80	841.44	849.32	846.34	848.40
2015	842.75	851.88	855.71	848.42	841.81	836.62	841.46	845.63	845.62	852.15	858.89	841.11	846.34
2016	849.38	852.95	854.35	857.15	853.65	843.90	847.37	845.21	852.61	869.21	859.18	870.23	854.62
2017	871.22	869.36	855.98	872.62	868.02	853.11	871.56	866.66	884.34	882.20	882.20	903.21	872.62
2018	898.09	900.80	898.32	904.79	894.67	894.67	892.28	899.80	909.08	903.12	904.94	910.91	900.03
Leisure and Hospitality													
2014	382.16	397.38	402.88	392.90	386.06	388.23	387.66	390.57	380.60	387.23	400.16	397.62	391.11
2015	411.23	422.82	418.44	405.27	399.21	389.46	394.76	395.92	383.94	394.31	405.81	403.70	402.36
2016	406.27	419.41	421.39	418.60	412.62	409.96	414.32	408.53	407.54	416.68	430.07	429.28	416.89
2017	436.08	445.56	458.49	452.57	433.57	424.76	428.81	425.48	386.50	435.55	438.08	442.61	434.84
2018	441.62	465.70	471.82	463.71	444.71	432.42	438.90	430.64	424.24	432.58	449.23	457.33	446.16
Other Services													
2014	624.90	632.79	631.88	625.63	633.40	635.38	617.90	651.75	631.12	624.02	639.61	647.07	633.73
2015	638.96	646.15	653.39	637.96	637.04	657.15	662.90	678.15	662.50	675.62	692.31	687.04	661.58
2016	682.26	692.72	696.06	705.07	718.76	719.36	729.74	723.88	733.13	726.61	713.76	703.51	711.88
2017	695.05	691.31	684.09	682.11	668.14	659.68	663.34	664.34	620.70	648.70	644.80	681.86	666.43
2018	654.69	686.81	685.78	704.10	686.65	688.83	703.48	676.70	683.03	678.81	678.04	708.30	686.45

GEORGIA
At a Glance

Population:
2010 census: 9,687,653
2018 estimate: 10,519,475

Percent change in population:
2010–2018: 8.6%

Percent change in total nonfarm employment:
2010–2018: 17.6%

Industry with the largest growth in employment, 2010–2018 (percent):
Professional and business services, 31.3%

Industry with the largest decline or smallest growth in employment, 2010–2018 (percent):
Government, -0.8%

Civilian labor force:
2010: 4,696,676
2018: 5,107,656

Unemployment rate and rank among states (highest to lowest):
2010: 10.5%, 9th
2018: 3.9%, 22nd

Over-the-year change in unemployment rates:
2016–2017: -0.7%
2017–2018: -0.8%

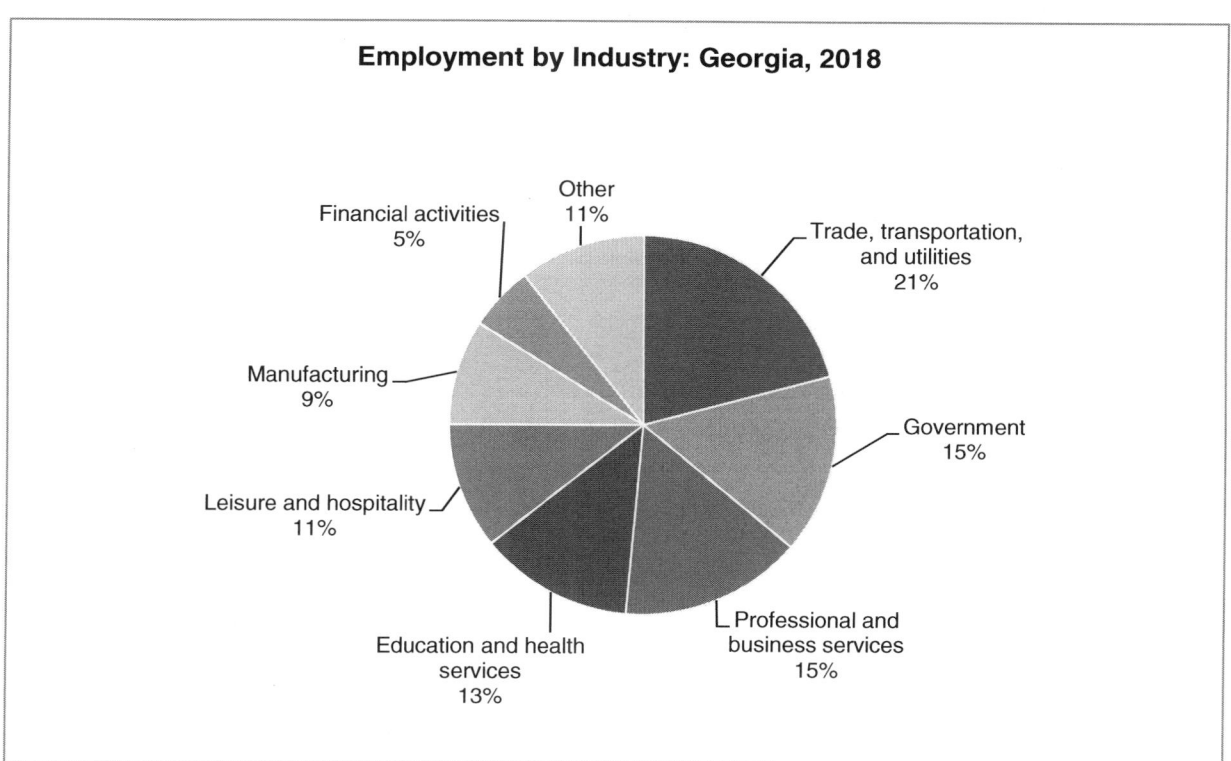

Employment by Industry: Georgia, 2018

- Other 11%
- Financial activities 5%
- Trade, transportation, and utilities 21%
- Manufacturing 9%
- Government 15%
- Leisure and hospitality 11%
- Professional and business services 15%
- Education and health services 13%

1. Employment by Industry: Georgia, 2010–2018

(Numbers in thousands, not seasonally adjusted)

Industry and year	January	February	March	April	May	June	July	August	September	October	November	December	Annual average
Total Nonfarm													
2010	3,794.6	3,807.2	3,827.3	3,859.2	3,891.0	3,866.8	3,852.5	3,868.5	3,859.0	3,892.6	3,905.6	3,896.7	3,860.1
2011	3,804.5	3,855.6	3,876.9	3,916.7	3,926.4	3,904.2	3,885.6	3,910.1	3,909.5	3,929.2	3,948.7	3,935.1	3,900.2
2012	3,876.2	3,897.7	3,921.2	3,954.8	3,971.8	3,957.0	3,926.0	3,961.0	3,954.7	3,991.7	4,022.6	4,009.4	3,953.7
2013	3,949.6	3,977.6	3,992.6	4,026.5	4,039.5	4,023.1	4,005.2	4,043.6	4,043.2	4,078.5	4,107.1	4,101.4	4,032.3
2014	4,036.1	4,045.6	4,087.3	4,129.1	4,152.7	4,138.8	4,129.6	4,173.9	4,171.9	4,199.3	4,232.9	4,242.2	4,145.0
2015	4,161.2	4,187.9	4,208.1	4,236.1	4,261.9	4,262.3	4,243.1	4,277.9	4,282.1	4,321.7	4,344.8	4,356.9	4,262.0
2016	4,278.1	4,302.6	4,315.7	4,361.3	4,373.8	4,369.9	4,353.0	4,386.7	4,398.8	4,418.6	4,453.2	4,456.4	4,372.3
2017	4,368.1	4,393.8	4,420.4	4,437.4	4,451.1	4,458.3	4,429.8	4,469.7	4,457.0	4,501.4	4,531.4	4,528.7	4,453.9
2018	4,444.2	4,476.8	4,504.2	4,521.0	4,539.4	4,542.7	4,518.2	4,560.2	4,557.2	4,588.2	4,611.1	4,616.2	4,540.0
Total Private													
2010	3,093.0	3,101.1	3,118.6	3,150.5	3,168.9	3,163.5	3,174.1	3,182.3	3,169.2	3,197.6	3,208.1	3,202.4	3,160.8
2011	3,116.0	3,160.5	3,179.7	3,223.4	3,231.3	3,221.6	3,223.3	3,235.4	3,224.0	3,238.7	3,255.2	3,244.6	3,212.8
2012	3,192.6	3,209.1	3,227.4	3,260.9	3,280.1	3,274.1	3,269.3	3,286.8	3,270.1	3,300.8	3,325.7	3,318.1	3,267.9
2013	3,264.5	3,287.0	3,300.8	3,334.5	3,352.5	3,350.7	3,353.7	3,375.6	3,363.8	3,392.8	3,418.0	3,415.3	3,350.8
2014	3,362.4	3,367.3	3,405.8	3,445.4	3,467.9	3,467.7	3,478.6	3,501.1	3,491.0	3,514.0	3,542.8	3,557.0	3,466.8
2015	3,484.1	3,505.1	3,524.5	3,552.2	3,580.5	3,590.7	3,590.7	3,604.8	3,601.6	3,634.2	3,654.5	3,669.7	3,582.7
2016	3,598.9	3,617.3	3,634.2	3,674.4	3,687.8	3,691.3	3,699.8	3,709.5	3,711.7	3,727.6	3,756.1	3,764.9	3,689.5
2017	3,686.5	3,705.7	3,730.1	3,745.4	3,761.3	3,774.9	3,769.3	3,786.3	3,765.4	3,806.0	3,832.9	3,833.7	3,766.5
2018	3,754.5	3,782.2	3,808.3	3,825.5	3,840.9	3,855.4	3,850.8	3,869.0	3,860.5	3,887.0	3,905.5	3,914.6	3,846.2
Goods Producing													
2010	502.2	501.4	502.4	504.1	507.7	507.5	510.2	510.6	509.2	508.9	508.2	505.0	506.5
2011	494.1	503.1	506.6	510.7	512.1	512.6	513.6	513.6	511.1	509.8	508.8	506.3	508.5
2012	501.5	503.1	504.7	506.5	508.1	508.5	509.5	510.8	510.1	511.5	512.7	510.1	508.1
2013	505.7	508.1	511.0	510.9	513.9	515.4	517.6	520.0	519.6	521.7	524.2	523.6	516.0
2014	521.0	523.6	528.3	531.4	535.3	538.5	542.2	545.7	546.3	548.5	549.0	550.8	538.4
2015	547.2	551.2	551.9	555.2	558.9	562.0	562.6	563.8	565.0	567.6	567.8	571.1	560.4
2016	566.7	570.4	572.9	576.4	577.7	581.4	584.7	585.9	586.9	587.0	589.8	591.7	581.0
2017	587.1	590.8	592.9	591.7	594.3	599.1	598.3	599.1	598.1	600.4	601.3	604.5	596.5
2018	599.6	606.6	609.4	609.2	612.3	617.3	615.6	617.5	618.6	618.7	617.6	621.8	613.7
Service-Providing													
2010	3,292.4	3,305.8	3,324.9	3,355.1	3,383.3	3,359.3	3,342.3	3,357.9	3,349.8	3,383.7	3,397.4	3,391.7	3,353.6
2011	3,310.4	3,352.5	3,370.3	3,406.0	3,414.3	3,391.6	3,372.0	3,396.5	3,398.4	3,419.4	3,439.9	3,428.8	3,391.7
2012	3,374.7	3,394.6	3,416.5	3,448.3	3,463.7	3,448.5	3,416.5	3,450.2	3,444.6	3,480.2	3,509.9	3,499.3	3,445.6
2013	3,443.9	3,469.5	3,481.6	3,515.6	3,525.6	3,507.7	3,487.6	3,523.6	3,523.6	3,556.8	3,582.9	3,577.8	3,516.4
2014	3,515.1	3,522.0	3,559.0	3,597.7	3,617.4	3,600.3	3,587.4	3,628.2	3,625.6	3,650.8	3,683.9	3,691.4	3,606.6
2015	3,614.0	3,636.7	3,656.2	3,680.9	3,703.0	3,700.3	3,680.5	3,714.1	3,717.1	3,754.1	3,777.0	3,785.8	3,701.6
2016	3,711.4	3,732.2	3,742.8	3,784.9	3,796.1	3,788.5	3,768.3	3,800.8	3,811.9	3,831.6	3,863.4	3,864.7	3,791.4
2017	3,781.0	3,803.0	3,827.5	3,845.7	3,856.8	3,859.2	3,831.5	3,870.6	3,858.9	3,901.0	3,930.1	3,924.2	3,857.5
2018	3,844.6	3,870.2	3,894.8	3,911.8	3,927.1	3,925.4	3,902.6	3,942.7	3,938.6	3,969.5	3,993.5	3,994.4	3,926.3
Mining and Logging													
2010	9.4	9.3	9.3	9.3	9.3	9.3	9.4	9.4	9.4	9.4	9.4	9.2	9.3
2011	9.1	9.2	9.1	9.1	9.1	9.1	9.2	9.2	9.1	9.0	9.0	8.8	9.1
2012	8.7	8.8	8.6	8.7	8.7	8.7	8.8	8.8	8.6	8.8	8.8	8.7	8.7
2013	8.8	8.8	8.8	9.0	9.0	8.9	9.0	9.0	9.0	9.1	9.2	9.1	9.0
2014	9.1	9.0	9.1	8.9	9.0	8.9	9.1	9.1	9.1	9.1	9.2	9.2	9.1
2015	9.1	9.1	9.1	9.1	9.1	9.1	9.1	9.2	9.2	9.2	9.1	9.2	9.1
2016	9.4	9.4	9.5	9.5	9.4	9.5	9.5	9.6	9.6	9.5	9.6	9.6	9.5
2017	9.5	9.5	9.5	9.5	9.5	9.5	9.5	9.5	9.4	9.5	9.4	9.4	9.5
2018	9.6	9.6	9.6	9.5	9.5	9.6	9.5	9.5	9.5	9.4	9.4	9.3	9.5
Construction													
2010	148.2	148.6	149.1	150.2	151.2	150.9	152.4	152.1	151.1	150.7	149.9	146.1	150.0
2011	138.5	144.1	146.9	148.8	148.5	148.8	149.3	148.9	148.2	147.4	145.7	143.4	146.5
2012	139.2	140.3	141.1	141.9	141.9	142.1	143.6	144.5	143.7	144.5	144.6	142.2	142.5
2013	139.4	140.9	143.1	143.4	146.2	147.2	148.8	150.3	150.4	151.4	152.7	151.1	147.1
2014	149.2	150.8	153.1	155.3	157.6	159.3	161.7	163.1	163.6	165.6	164.8	165.2	159.1
2015	162.3	164.5	164.4	168.0	169.1	171.1	171.6	172.0	172.2	174.2	173.5	174.7	169.8
2016	170.3	172.8	174.5	176.8	178.1	180.3	183.0	183.0	184.2	184.3	185.3	185.3	179.8
2017	181.8	183.7	185.0	184.1	186.3	188.6	187.5	187.7	188.0	189.0	188.9	190.1	186.7
2018	185.9	190.2	192.5	193.5	195.4	198.0	198.0	198.5	198.8	201.4	200.5	201.5	196.2

1. Employment by Industry: Georgia, 2010–2018—*Continued*

(Numbers in thousands, not seasonally adjusted)

Industry and year	January	February	March	April	May	June	July	August	September	October	November	December	Annual average
Manufacturing													
2010	344.6	343.5	344.0	344.6	347.2	347.3	348.4	349.1	348.7	348.8	348.9	349.7	347.1
2011	346.5	349.8	350.6	352.8	354.5	354.7	355.1	355.5	353.8	353.4	354.1	354.1	352.9
2012	353.6	354.0	355.0	355.9	357.5	357.7	357.1	357.5	357.8	358.2	359.3	359.2	356.9
2013	357.5	358.4	359.1	358.5	358.7	359.3	359.8	360.7	360.2	361.2	362.3	363.4	359.9
2014	362.7	363.8	366.1	367.2	368.7	370.3	371.4	373.5	373.6	373.8	375.0	376.4	370.2
2015	375.8	377.6	378.4	378.1	380.7	381.8	381.9	382.6	383.6	384.2	385.2	387.2	381.4
2016	387.0	388.2	388.9	390.1	390.2	391.6	392.2	393.3	393.1	393.2	394.9	396.8	391.6
2017	395.8	397.6	398.4	398.1	398.5	401.0	401.3	401.9	400.7	401.9	403.0	405.0	400.3
2018	404.1	406.8	407.3	406.2	407.4	409.7	408.1	409.5	410.3	407.9	407.7	411.0	408.0
Trade, Transportation, and Utilities													
2010	796.4	793.8	795.2	799.0	803.5	802.9	805.5	806.7	802.3	815.1	826.4	831.0	806.5
2011	800.7	805.2	807.8	814.7	817.7	816.2	816.7	818.1	814.6	824.2	838.1	840.6	817.9
2012	819.2	816.2	818.3	823.8	828.9	825.8	826.1	827.1	823.7	834.2	852.9	853.9	829.2
2013	827.6	825.6	825.7	830.4	834.7	835.0	839.1	843.0	839.4	849.5	866.5	873.4	840.8
2014	848.9	843.9	849.2	857.7	861.7	861.6	864.8	867.2	865.4	878.4	898.7	908.7	867.2
2015	876.6	873.5	877.6	883.3	888.3	891.2	891.4	893.6	893.2	906.1	925.1	932.5	894.4
2016	902.4	899.4	902.1	905.3	908.4	908.2	910.2	909.3	909.7	917.5	939.3	949.0	913.4
2017	916.3	913.9	917.0	917.1	919.1	921.1	922.5	924.0	921.5	932.0	955.8	960.5	926.7
2018	929.1	928.3	931.7	935.9	939.5	940.5	941.3	941.5	942.8	947.2	966.8	970.9	943.0
Wholesale Trade													
2010	187.6	187.8	187.5	188.9	189.3	188.8	189.4	189.4	187.9	189.8	189.6	188.4	188.7
2011	187.0	188.0	187.9	190.0	190.8	190.1	191.2	191.7	190.8	192.4	192.4	191.5	190.3
2012	190.6	191.7	191.6	193.1	194.3	193.5	194.7	195.2	194.0	196.4	196.8	196.2	194.0
2013	194.2	195.1	194.5	195.8	196.1	195.8	196.2	196.4	195.3	197.8	198.4	198.0	196.1
2014	197.2	197.8	197.9	199.0	199.8	200.0	200.8	201.3	200.9	202.7	204.1	204.3	200.5
2015	202.2	203.3	203.9	204.5	205.7	206.0	206.9	207.2	206.8	209.1	209.2	208.9	206.1
2016	206.6	206.4	206.9	207.8	208.0	208.2	208.1	207.7	207.7	207.7	207.8	208.5	207.6
2017	206.2	207.2	207.6	207.6	207.9	209.0	209.6	209.4	209.7	210.2	210.7	211.5	208.9
2018	210.4	211.9	212.7	213.2	214.1	215.9	216.2	216.1	216.4	217.0	217.6	218.2	215.0
Retail Trade													
2010	432.8	429.9	431.3	434.0	436.7	436.1	437.3	438.0	434.4	443.2	454.3	457.6	438.8
2011	435.6	437.0	438.6	443.2	444.5	442.9	443.0	443.1	440.2	447.5	460.2	461.4	444.8
2012	444.8	440.8	442.5	445.4	448.4	446.2	446.2	446.4	444.2	451.6	468.7	468.0	449.4
2013	447.1	445.8	446.7	450.0	452.9	453.7	457.1	460.0	458.1	464.6	479.3	483.9	458.3
2014	462.5	458.3	461.6	465.6	467.8	467.5	469.1	469.8	468.4	475.3	492.8	497.8	471.4
2015	471.5	469.9	473.2	478.3	480.4	482.4	480.6	482.0	481.8	487.9	504.0	507.0	483.3
2016	483.8	482.3	485.0	487.5	489.0	487.7	489.3	488.9	488.4	493.9	510.6	513.4	491.7
2017	492.4	490.5	491.8	492.7	493.0	492.6	492.7	492.9	488.7	495.3	513.2	513.8	495.8
2018	493.0	490.4	492.4	493.7	495.4	493.2	493.6	492.3	491.5	493.9	509.4	508.8	495.6
Transportation and Utilities													
2010	176.0	176.1	176.4	176.1	177.5	178.0	178.8	179.3	180.0	182.1	182.5	185.0	179.0
2011	178.1	180.2	181.3	181.5	182.4	183.2	182.5	183.3	183.6	184.3	185.5	187.7	182.8
2012	183.8	183.7	184.2	185.3	186.2	186.1	185.2	185.5	185.5	186.2	187.4	189.7	185.7
2013	186.3	184.7	184.5	184.6	185.7	185.5	185.8	186.6	186.0	187.1	188.8	191.5	186.4
2014	189.2	187.8	189.7	193.1	194.1	194.1	194.9	196.1	196.1	200.4	201.8	206.6	195.3
2015	202.9	200.3	200.5	200.5	202.2	202.8	203.9	204.4	204.6	209.1	211.9	216.6	205.0
2016	212.0	210.7	210.2	210.0	211.4	212.3	212.8	212.7	213.6	215.9	220.9	227.1	214.1
2017	217.7	216.2	217.6	216.8	218.2	219.5	220.2	221.7	223.1	226.5	231.9	235.2	222.1
2018	225.7	226.0	226.6	229.0	230.0	231.4	231.5	233.1	234.9	236.3	239.8	243.9	232.4
Information													
2010	99.5	99.5	99.8	100.0	100.3	99.8	98.6	98.5	98.1	96.6	97.4	97.8	98.8
2011	97.0	97.8	97.7	98.4	98.3	97.7	98.5	98.7	98.3	98.7	100.2	98.4	98.3
2012	98.3	99.5	99.4	99.1	100.3	100.1	100.8	101.1	100.8	102.1	102.6	102.6	100.6
2013	100.4	101.5	101.7	102.7	103.5	102.7	103.4	103.7	103.7	105.6	105.5	105.7	103.3
2014	105.5	106.4	107.0	108.0	108.7	110.1	110.1	109.4	109.0	111.0	111.7	111.8	109.1
2015	108.6	109.5	109.6	110.7	113.0	113.1	115.3	113.3	111.3	115.8	116.7	116.9	112.8
2016	110.5	112.4	110.7	113.6	113.2	113.4	114.9	112.7	113.9	115.0	115.9	114.5	113.4
2017	114.6	116.3	116.3	117.3	118.1	118.0	117.4	120.0	117.4	123.6	123.2	120.2	118.5
2018	114.0	115.0	115.4	113.6	113.5	113.6	113.0	114.6	115.0	116.8	116.6	113.7	114.6

1. Employment by Industry: Georgia, 2010–2018—*Continued*

(Numbers in thousands, not seasonally adjusted)

Industry and year	January	February	March	April	May	June	July	August	September	October	November	December	Annual average
Financial Activities													
2010	216.6	216.4	216.3	216.7	218.0	218.3	218.4	219.2	218.5	220.7	221.4	222.0	218.5
2011	219.3	219.9	220.0	222.8	223.4	223.7	224.2	225.1	225.0	226.2	226.5	226.6	223.6
2012	225.4	225.9	226.2	226.1	226.3	226.4	227.3	227.6	226.3	228.2	229.3	229.0	227.0
2013	226.8	227.7	228.0	228.9	229.3	229.3	229.8	230.4	228.8	230.7	231.9	231.2	229.4
2014	229.6	229.9	230.2	230.9	231.8	231.8	232.3	232.9	231.3	233.2	233.4	233.5	231.7
2015	231.7	232.2	232.6	233.8	234.6	235.2	235.4	235.0	234.1	235.9	236.2	236.8	234.5
2016	235.2	235.4	235.6	236.8	238.1	238.8	240.3	240.1	239.8	241.0	241.3	241.6	238.7
2017	238.6	239.7	240.7	240.8	242.3	244.1	244.6	244.6	244.4	246.2	246.2	247.3	243.3
2018	243.7	245.5	246.2	246.5	247.3	248.7	249.1	249.3	249.1	251.2	250.5	251.5	248.2
Professional and Business Services													
2010	505.8	510.4	515.7	524.3	525.8	527.4	530.5	532.0	531.8	540.9	541.0	540.3	527.2
2011	519.3	532.6	536.5	547.0	545.2	545.6	545.5	549.8	550.5	551.7	553.9	552.5	544.2
2012	538.7	545.9	550.5	558.0	561.3	565.3	561.4	566.7	563.5	569.8	574.1	573.1	560.7
2013	563.2	573.4	576.8	582.5	584.6	587.5	586.5	591.7	591.8	598.5	602.2	599.2	586.5
2014	589.6	592.0	605.1	608.6	613.9	615.6	619.3	625.0	624.9	626.9	631.9	631.6	615.4
2015	615.9	623.4	627.7	627.4	635.1	638.3	638.9	642.6	643.4	648.8	647.7	650.5	636.6
2016	636.7	642.5	645.5	652.4	653.6	654.5	661.5	666.6	668.8	672.1	673.6	674.8	658.6
2017	657.6	662.2	667.2	668.7	670.0	674.7	676.0	681.6	676.8	686.0	690.5	689.0	675.0
2018	673.0	679.7	685.5	686.6	685.6	689.8	688.9	697.0	693.8	706.5	710.0	712.1	692.4
Education and Health Services													
2010	466.4	470.0	470.9	473.5	475.8	469.5	471.9	477.9	477.7	484.9	485.0	483.0	475.5
2011	476.1	482.9	482.7	487.2	486.5	478.4	478.6	484.9	486.2	492.0	492.3	489.9	484.8
2012	486.2	490.9	491.2	495.6	496.3	488.9	487.7	497.2	497.9	503.7	505.3	503.4	495.4
2013	501.2	506.0	506.0	510.8	511.8	504.3	501.6	510.5	512.0	517.3	520.6	518.4	510.0
2014	513.4	515.4	518.4	521.8	523.4	516.7	516.6	527.2	528.6	530.1	532.4	534.4	523.2
2015	529.5	533.4	534.5	535.6	537.8	533.4	532.8	541.4	544.7	551.8	553.8	554.2	540.2
2016	551.5	556.7	557.5	560.4	560.9	554.7	553.1	561.0	563.8	568.6	569.8	569.2	560.6
2017	562.0	566.3	568.8	568.7	569.9	564.5	562.5	569.9	570.9	576.0	577.6	577.2	569.5
2018	572.6	578.0	578.9	581.8	583.6	578.7	578.6	587.9	589.0	594.4	595.8	595.2	584.5
Leisure and Hospitality													
2010	355.1	358.0	366.3	379.0	382.7	383.4	382.9	382.6	377.7	375.8	374.0	370.6	374.0
2011	358.5	365.8	375.1	387.8	392.5	391.3	390.5	390.8	385.0	382.8	382.4	378.8	381.8
2012	372.6	376.0	385.5	398.5	404.9	404.2	401.3	402.2	395.1	397.1	394.9	393.7	393.8
2013	387.9	392.1	399.3	414.6	420.3	421.6	420.8	422.2	415.5	416.3	414.1	412.0	411.4
2014	403.6	404.8	416.1	433.1	438.4	437.7	437.3	438.5	431.6	432.1	431.6	432.3	428.1
2015	422.0	428.1	436.5	450.9	456.5	459.8	456.0	458.1	453.8	452.5	451.8	451.7	448.1
2016	441.2	445.2	454.1	472.1	477.7	480.4	475.7	475.7	471.7	469.0	469.2	467.1	466.6
2017	454.5	459.9	469.8	482.4	487.4	491.8	487.0	487.6	478.4	484.4	481.4	478.4	478.6
2018	467.2	472.5	483.5	493.3	498.6	504.4	502.0	500.1	491.8	491.6	490.4	491.6	490.6
Other Services													
2010	151.0	151.6	152.0	153.9	155.1	154.7	156.1	154.8	153.9	154.7	154.7	152.7	153.8
2011	151.0	153.2	153.3	154.8	155.6	156.1	155.7	154.4	153.3	153.3	153.0	151.5	153.8
2012	150.7	151.6	151.6	153.3	154.0	154.9	155.2	154.1	152.7	154.2	153.9	152.3	153.2
2013	151.7	152.6	152.3	153.7	154.4	154.9	154.9	154.1	153.0	153.2	153.0	151.8	153.3
2014	150.8	151.3	151.5	153.9	154.7	155.7	156.0	155.2	153.9	153.8	154.1	153.9	153.7
2015	152.6	153.8	154.1	155.3	156.3	157.7	158.3	157.0	156.1	155.7	155.4	156.0	155.7
2016	154.7	155.3	155.8	157.4	158.2	159.9	159.4	158.2	157.1	157.4	157.2	157.0	157.3
2017	155.8	156.6	157.4	158.7	160.2	161.6	161.0	159.5	157.9	157.4	156.9	156.6	158.3
2018	155.3	156.6	157.7	158.6	160.5	162.4	162.3	161.1	160.4	160.6	157.8	157.8	159.3
Government													
2010	701.6	706.1	708.7	708.7	722.1	703.3	678.4	686.2	689.8	695.0	697.5	694.3	699.3
2011	688.5	695.1	697.2	693.3	695.1	682.6	662.3	674.7	685.5	690.5	693.5	690.5	687.4
2012	683.6	688.6	693.8	693.9	691.7	682.9	656.7	674.2	684.6	690.9	696.9	691.3	685.8
2013	685.1	690.6	691.8	692.0	687.0	672.4	651.5	668.0	679.4	685.7	689.1	686.1	681.6
2014	673.7	678.3	681.5	683.7	684.8	671.1	651.0	672.8	680.9	685.3	690.1	685.2	678.2
2015	677.1	682.8	683.6	683.9	681.4	671.6	652.4	673.1	680.5	687.5	690.3	687.2	679.3
2016	679.2	685.3	681.5	686.9	686.0	678.6	653.2	677.2	687.1	691.0	697.1	691.5	682.9
2017	681.6	688.1	690.3	692.0	689.8	683.4	660.5	683.4	691.6	695.4	698.5	695.0	687.5
2018	689.7	694.6	695.9	695.5	698.5	687.3	667.4	691.2	696.7	701.2	705.6	701.6	693.8

2. Average Weekly Hours by Selected Industry: Georgia, 2014–2018

(Not seasonally adjusted)

Industry and year	January	February	March	April	May	June	July	August	September	October	November	December	Annual average
Total Private													
2014	34.6	34.0	35.8	35.2	35.2	35.8	35.2	35.4	35.3	35.1	35.6	35.2	35.2
2015	34.8	35.3	35.3	34.8	35.2	35.2	35.1	35.6	34.8	34.9	35.1	34.8	35.1
2016	34.4	34.7	34.7	34.8	35.2	34.9	34.8	34.6	34.6	35.2	34.8	34.9	34.8
2017	34.8	34.4	34.4	34.8	34.5	34.9	35.0	34.6	34.0	35.2	34.8	34.7	34.7
2018	34.2	34.6	34.8	35.2	34.8	35.0	35.2	34.8	35.2	34.6	34.7	35.3	34.9
Goods-Producing													
2014	40.2	37.4	42.1	41.3	41.3	42.0	41.8	41.9	42.0	41.4	41.9	42.2	41.3
2015	40.7	40.4	40.6	40.5	41.4	41.4	41.7	42.3	40.8	41.6	41.0	41.9	41.2
2016	40.3	40.4	41.0	40.7	41.4	41.5	40.6	40.7	41.0	41.3	41.4	41.0	40.9
2017	39.8	39.9	40.0	40.3	40.6	41.2	41.3	41.0	39.5	41.5	41.5	41.2	40.7
2018	39.9	41.1	41.4	41.9	41.5	41.5	41.8	42.0	41.9	41.2	41.4	42.9	41.5
Construction													
2014	38.6	34.9	41.6	41.6	41.8	41.9	43.0	42.7	42.6	40.9	42.2	42.4	41.2
2015	40.0	39.5	39.8	39.7	42.2	42.0	42.3	42.3	40.4	42.5	41.2	42.4	41.2
2016	40.4	40.3	41.4	40.8	41.6	41.2	41.6	40.9	41.4	40.9	41.0	39.5	40.9
2017	39.2	39.4	39.0	39.8	40.5	40.5	40.8	40.1	38.6	41.1	40.4	40.1	40.0
2018	37.7	39.9	41.0	42.2	41.5	41.0	41.1	41.3	41.1	40.7	40.1	41.8	40.8
Manufacturing													
2014	41.1	38.8	42.4	41.1	41.0	42.0	41.0	41.3	41.5	41.7	41.7	42.1	41.3
2015	41.3	41.0	41.1	41.0	40.8	40.9	41.2	42.2	40.9	40.9	40.7	41.4	41.1
2016	40.0	40.1	40.4	40.3	40.9	41.3	39.6	40.2	40.4	41.3	41.4	41.7	40.6
2017	40.1	40.0	40.3	40.4	40.6	41.6	41.4	41.5	40.1	41.7	42.2	41.8	41.0
2018	41.3	41.8	41.7	41.8	41.5	41.8	42.3	42.4	42.5	41.5	42.6	43.9	42.1
Trade, Transportation, and Utilities													
2014	34.3	33.8	35.4	35.1	35.0	35.4	35.0	35.4	35.3	34.9	35.5	35.2	35.0
2015	34.7	35.4	35.3	35.0	35.2	34.9	34.8	35.1	34.3	34.5	34.7	34.6	34.9
2016	34.2	34.6	34.1	34.3	34.6	34.3	34.3	34.2	34.1	34.5	34.2	34.4	34.3
2017	33.9	33.8	33.9	34.5	34.0	34.3	34.9	34.4	33.9	34.6	34.6	34.8	34.3
2018	34.2	34.3	34.4	34.5	34.5	35.2	35.3	34.8	35.1	34.4	34.5	34.7	34.7
Financial Activities													
2014	36.7	37.7	38.0	37.0	37.3	38.1	36.4	36.5	36.2	36.4	38.0	36.7	37.1
2015	36.6	38.1	38.1	36.9	36.9	37.3	37.1	38.6	37.4	37.1	38.9	37.6	37.5
2016	37.4	37.3	37.3	37.2	38.4	37.3	37.2	37.0	37.3	37.9	36.8	36.8	37.3
2017	38.5	37.3	36.9	38.2	36.6	36.7	38.2	36.6	36.8	38.7	37.1	36.8	37.4
2018	36.8	37.1	36.7	38.0	36.7	37.0	38.0	37.1	38.4	36.8	37.5	38.3	37.4
Professional and Business Services													
2014	35.8	36.2	37.8	36.8	36.4	37.4	36.1	36.6	36.3	36.3	37.1	36.0	36.6
2015	35.9	36.5	36.4	35.4	35.6	35.9	35.4	36.0	35.1	34.3	34.8	34.2	35.5
2016	33.6	33.9	34.3	34.8	35.3	34.8	34.8	34.9	34.6	35.8	34.6	34.8	34.7
2017	35.0	34.4	33.9	34.5	34.2	34.9	33.8	33.9	33.3	35.1	34.2	34.5	34.3
2018	33.9	34.5	34.8	35.7	35.4	35.4	35.4	35.1	35.8	35.1	35.0	35.9	35.2
Education and Health Services													
2014	34.9	34.5	35.3	34.7	34.8	35.4	34.9	35.1	35.2	35.2	35.6	34.9	35.0
2015	34.9	35.2	35.3	34.7	34.8	34.7	34.9	35.3	34.9	35.1	35.6	35.1	35.0
2016	35.3	35.2	35.3	35.1	35.3	34.9	35.2	34.6	34.7	35.6	35.5	35.7	35.2
2017	35.8	35.3	35.3	35.4	35.3	35.3	35.4	35.4	34.8	35.4	34.9	34.8	35.3
2018	34.6	34.6	34.4	34.6	34.4	34.4	34.4	34.1	34.4	33.9	34.2	34.6	34.4
Leisure and Hospitality													
2014	25.9	25.5	27.5	27.0	27.3	27.4	27.0	26.8	26.5	26.5	26.7	26.6	26.7
2015	26.2	26.8	26.7	26.8	26.8	26.7	26.5	27.0	26.4	26.7	26.6	26.4	26.6
2016	25.9	26.8	26.8	27.1	27.2	27.1	26.9	26.4	26.1	26.6	26.5	26.6	26.7
2017	26.0	26.5	26.6	26.7	26.6	26.6	26.5	26.0	25.5	26.7	26.5	26.2	26.4
2018	25.8	26.6	27.1	27.1	26.8	27.1	27.1	26.5	26.4	26.5	26.5	26.8	26.7
Other Services													
2014	31.7	31.7	32.9	32.6	32.9	34.4	34.2	33.9	33.7	32.9	33.8	33.6	33.2
2015	33.1	33.7	34.6	33.9	34.2	34.1	34.6	35.1	34.7	34.3	34.4	33.9	34.2
2016	33.3	34.6	34.0	34.5	34.2	33.8	33.7	32.9	33.0	33.2	32.9	32.6	33.6
2017	32.8	32.4	31.9	32.7	32.6	32.1	32.6	31.8	30.0	31.6	31.8	31.3	32.0
2018	30.5	31.5	31.7	31.9	30.4	30.9	30.8	30.0	30.6	31.2	30.0	30.5	30.8

3. Average Hourly Earnings by Selected Industry: Georgia, 2014–2018

(Dollars, not seasonally adjusted)

Industry and year	January	February	March	April	May	June	July	August	September	October	November	December	Annual average
Total Private													
2014	23.07	23.64	23.10	22.95	22.90	23.32	23.19	23.46	23.39	23.48	23.90	23.62	23.34
2015	23.86	24.06	23.92	23.65	23.50	23.39	23.55	23.84	23.71	24.11	24.28	24.13	23.84
2016	24.40	24.27	24.23	24.21	24.58	24.18	24.36	24.50	24.52	25.07	24.63	24.71	24.48
2017	25.53	25.20	25.10	25.58	25.15	25.85	26.37	26.31	26.64	26.68	26.15	26.33	25.91
2018	26.53	26.62	26.38	26.80	26.34	26.26	26.60	26.49	27.11	26.95	26.45	26.75	26.61
Goods-Producing													
2014	22.94	23.55	22.84	22.73	22.99	23.22	23.17	23.16	22.98	23.06	23.34	23.28	23.10
2015	23.30	23.47	23.19	23.20	23.12	23.26	23.48	23.89	23.99	24.09	24.34	24.73	23.68
2016	24.95	24.91	25.04	24.87	25.05	24.76	24.91	24.89	24.84	24.82	24.49	24.62	24.84
2017	24.75	24.59	24.42	24.42	24.28	24.31	24.50	24.22	24.60	24.37	24.48	24.47	24.45
2018	24.27	24.37	24.48	24.84	24.57	24.43	24.74	24.57	25.35	25.42	25.47	25.22	24.82
Construction													
2014	23.00	23.58	22.67	22.30	22.52	22.76	22.73	22.67	22.36	22.56	22.75	22.55	22.68
2015	22.88	23.19	23.09	23.26	23.18	22.87	23.10	23.30	23.36	23.51	24.14	23.85	23.32
2016	24.35	24.10	24.36	24.36	24.42	24.58	24.38	24.46	24.51	25.04	24.62	25.00	24.52
2017	24.57	24.84	24.84	24.73	24.35	24.95	24.99	24.87	25.40	25.07	25.58	25.39	24.97
2018	25.09	25.40	25.28	25.68	25.24	25.28	25.61	25.52	26.30	26.67	26.61	26.59	25.79
Manufacturing													
2014	22.86	23.46	22.87	22.91	23.21	23.45	23.41	23.44	23.37	23.35	23.70	23.77	23.32
2015	23.60	23.66	23.27	23.30	23.16	23.55	23.77	24.30	24.42	24.51	24.51	25.33	23.95
2016	25.33	25.39	25.36	25.19	25.44	24.88	25.27	25.22	25.10	24.67	24.42	24.42	25.05
2017	24.83	24.41	24.15	24.40	24.39	24.11	24.43	24.03	24.31	24.06	23.92	24.04	24.25
2018	23.91	23.88	24.13	24.45	24.27	24.00	24.32	24.03	24.47	24.37	24.67	24.71	24.27
Trade, Transportation, and Utilities													
2014	21.00	21.59	21.21	21.22	21.23	21.51	21.42	21.75	21.75	21.79	22.02	21.72	21.52
2015	22.44	22.26	22.25	21.94	21.68	21.43	21.56	21.48	21.49	21.58	21.33	21.30	21.72
2016	21.67	21.22	21.70	21.72	21.68	21.60	21.77	21.62	21.82	22.40	21.90	22.23	21.78
2017	23.29	22.65	22.52	22.85	22.52	22.91	23.08	23.13	23.29	22.90	22.89	22.92	22.91
2018	23.37	23.32	23.22	23.89	23.60	23.59	23.94	23.71	24.03	23.71	23.22	23.76	23.62
Financial Activities													
2014	30.71	31.89	30.69	30.78	30.56	31.07	30.90	30.46	30.17	30.14	30.54	29.72	30.64
2015	29.47	29.98	30.16	29.33	29.46	29.03	29.06	29.32	29.13	29.09	28.95	28.45	29.28
2016	28.52	29.42	28.79	28.60	30.46	29.06	29.84	31.68	30.85	32.65	32.11	32.36	30.37
2017	32.69	32.45	32.49	33.40	32.94	32.04	33.17	32.84	33.62	34.14	33.57	33.13	33.05
2018	33.95	33.90	34.12	33.91	33.12	32.84	34.19	34.21	34.85	34.58	34.69	35.82	34.19
Professional and Business Services													
2014	26.86	27.28	26.73	26.31	26.41	27.06	26.85	27.17	27.20	27.30	28.12	27.80	27.10
2015	28.29	28.97	28.63	28.06	28.02	27.76	28.16	29.01	28.56	29.18	30.09	29.60	28.69
2016	30.24	30.00	29.55	29.79	30.44	29.63	29.87	29.90	29.98	30.54	30.04	29.85	29.99
2017	31.67	30.82	30.57	31.40	30.37	32.44	34.43	33.86	34.19	33.86	32.92	33.61	32.52
2018	33.13	33.69	32.93	33.35	32.70	32.83	32.97	32.51	33.36	33.12	33.07	33.13	33.06
Education and Health Services													
2014	24.21	24.38	24.08	24.17	23.92	24.61	24.32	25.18	24.90	25.08	25.34	25.29	24.63
2015	24.94	25.05	24.90	25.14	24.83	24.98	24.91	25.02	25.06	25.86	25.52	25.50	25.15
2016	25.39	25.55	25.13	25.38	25.22	25.46	25.60	25.75	25.77	26.38	26.32	26.32	25.69
2017	26.59	26.88	27.20	27.80	27.58	27.62	27.90	28.69	29.05	29.44	27.90	28.31	27.91
2018	28.85	29.08	28.86	29.20	28.74	28.62	29.00	29.73	29.57	30.15	29.95	30.06	29.32
Leisure and Hospitality													
2014	12.02	12.11	12.08	11.94	11.95	11.73	11.74	11.91	11.96	12.05	12.42	12.37	12.02
2015	12.47	12.48	12.57	12.47	12.58	12.38	12.47	12.58	12.58	12.59	12.70	12.74	12.55
2016	12.75	12.70	12.74	12.77	12.71	12.45	12.54	12.54	12.73	12.83	12.65	12.78	12.68
2017	12.87	12.92	12.92	13.03	13.14	13.07	13.03	13.06	13.08	13.13	13.06	13.39	13.06
2018	13.22	13.22	13.21	13.38	13.45	13.29	13.31	13.28	13.38	13.51	13.51	13.70	13.37
Other Services													
2014	19.26	19.72	19.91	20.57	19.66	19.91	20.45	20.40	20.45	20.55	20.35	20.81	20.18
2015	20.76	20.86	20.58	21.14	20.99	21.03	20.91	22.00	21.56	21.61	21.60	21.59	21.22
2016	21.54	21.22	21.31	20.80	20.98	20.29	20.84	21.01	20.68	20.85	20.85	20.53	20.91
2017	20.54	21.16	20.99	20.83	20.66	20.98	20.83	21.40	21.46	21.36	21.47	21.95	21.13
2018	21.99	22.50	23.02	23.89	23.48	23.38	23.01	23.91	24.59	24.66	24.84	24.41	23.64

4. Average Weekly Earnings by Selected Industry: Georgia, 2014–2018

(Dollars, not seasonally adjusted)

Industry and year	January	February	March	April	May	June	July	August	September	October	November	December	Annual average
Total Private													
2014	798.22	803.76	826.98	807.84	806.08	834.86	816.29	830.48	825.67	824.15	850.84	831.42	934.42
2015	830.33	849.32	844.38	823.02	827.20	823.33	826.61	848.70	825.11	841.44	852.23	839.72	960.78
2016	839.36	842.17	840.78	842.51	865.22	843.88	847.73	847.70	848.39	882.46	857.12	862.38	1,002.87
2017	888.44	866.88	863.44	890.18	867.68	902.17	922.95	910.33	905.76	939.14	910.02	913.65	998.80
2018	907.33	921.05	918.02	943.36	916.63	919.10	936.32	921.85	954.27	932.47	917.82	944.28	1,052.23
Goods-Producing													
2014	922.19	880.77	961.56	938.75	949.49	975.24	968.51	970.40	965.16	954.68	977.95	982.42	954.03
2015	948.31	948.19	941.51	939.60	957.17	962.96	979.12	1,010.55	978.79	1,002.14	997.94	1,036.19	975.62
2016	1,005.49	1,006.36	1,026.64	1,012.21	1,037.07	1,027.54	1,011.35	1,013.02	1,018.44	1,025.07	1,013.89	1,009.42	1,015.96
2017	985.05	981.14	976.80	984.13	985.77	1,001.57	1,011.85	993.02	971.70	1,011.36	1,015.92	1,008.16	995.12
2018	968.37	1,001.61	1,013.47	1,040.80	1,019.66	1,013.85	1,034.13	1,031.94	1,062.17	1,047.30	1,054.46	1,081.94	1,030.03
Construction													
2014	887.80	822.94	943.07	927.68	941.34	953.64	977.39	968.01	952.54	922.70	960.05	956.12	934.42
2015	915.20	916.01	918.98	923.42	978.20	960.54	977.13	985.59	943.74	999.18	994.57	1,011.24	960.78
2016	983.74	971.23	1,008.50	993.89	1,015.87	1,012.70	1,014.21	1,000.41	1,014.71	1,024.14	1,009.42	987.50	1,002.87
2017	963.14	978.70	968.76	984.25	986.18	1,010.48	1,019.59	997.29	980.44	1,030.38	1,033.43	1,018.14	998.80
2018	945.89	1,013.46	1,036.48	1,083.70	1,047.46	1,036.48	1,052.57	1,053.98	1,080.93	1,085.47	1,067.06	1,111.46	1,052.23
Manufacturing													
2014	939.55	910.25	969.69	941.60	951.61	984.90	959.81	968.07	969.86	973.70	988.29	1,000.72	963.12
2015	974.68	970.06	956.40	955.30	944.93	963.20	979.32	1,025.46	998.78	1,002.46	997.56	1,048.66	984.35
2016	1,013.20	1,018.14	1,024.54	1,015.16	1,040.50	1,027.54	1,000.69	1,013.84	1,014.04	1,018.87	1,010.99	1,018.31	1,017.03
2017	995.68	976.40	973.25	985.76	990.23	1,002.98	1,011.40	997.25	974.83	1,003.30	1,009.42	1,004.87	994.25
2018	987.48	998.18	1,006.22	1,022.01	1,007.21	1,003.20	1,028.74	1,018.87	1,039.98	1,011.36	1,050.94	1,084.77	1,021.77
Trade, Transportation, and Utilities													
2014	720.30	729.74	750.83	744.82	743.05	761.45	749.70	769.95	767.78	760.47	781.71	764.54	753.20
2015	778.67	788.00	785.43	767.90	763.14	747.91	750.29	753.95	737.11	744.51	740.15	736.98	758.03
2016	741.11	734.21	739.97	745.00	750.13	740.88	746.71	739.40	744.06	772.80	748.98	764.71	747.05
2017	789.53	765.57	763.43	788.33	765.68	785.81	805.49	795.67	789.53	792.34	791.99	797.62	785.81
2018	799.25	799.88	798.77	824.21	814.20	830.37	845.08	825.11	843.45	815.62	801.09	824.47	819.61
Financial Activities													
2014	1,127.06	1,202.25	1,166.22	1,138.86	1,139.89	1,183.77	1,124.76	1,111.79	1,092.15	1,097.10	1,160.52	1,090.72	1,136.74
2015	1,078.60	1,142.24	1,149.10	1,082.28	1,087.07	1,082.82	1,078.13	1,131.75	1,089.46	1,079.24	1,126.16	1,069.72	1,098.00
2016	1,066.65	1,097.37	1,073.87	1,063.92	1,169.66	1,083.94	1,110.05	1,172.16	1,150.71	1,237.44	1,181.65	1,190.85	1,132.80
2017	1,258.57	1,210.39	1,198.88	1,275.88	1,205.60	1,175.87	1,267.09	1,201.94	1,237.22	1,321.22	1,245.45	1,219.18	1,236.07
2018	1,249.36	1,257.69	1,252.20	1,288.58	1,215.50	1,215.08	1,299.22	1,269.19	1,338.24	1,272.54	1,300.88	1,371.91	1,278.71
Professional and Business Services													
2014	961.59	987.54	1,010.39	968.21	961.32	1,012.04	969.29	994.42	987.36	990.99	1,043.25	1,000.80	991.86
2015	1,015.61	1,057.41	1,042.13	993.32	997.51	996.58	996.86	1,044.36	1,002.46	1,000.87	1,047.13	1,012.32	1,018.50
2016	1,016.06	1,017.00	1,013.57	1,036.69	1,074.53	1,031.12	1,039.48	1,043.51	1,037.31	1,093.33	1,039.38	1,038.78	1,040.65
2017	1,108.45	1,060.21	1,036.32	1,083.30	1,038.65	1,132.16	1,163.73	1,147.85	1,138.53	1,188.49	1,125.86	1,159.55	1,115.44
2018	1,123.11	1,162.31	1,145.96	1,190.60	1,157.58	1,162.18	1,167.14	1,141.10	1,194.29	1,162.51	1,157.45	1,189.37	1,163.71
Education and Health Services													
2014	844.93	841.11	850.02	838.70	832.42	871.19	848.77	883.82	876.48	882.82	902.10	882.62	862.05
2015	870.41	881.76	878.97	872.36	864.08	866.81	869.36	883.21	874.59	907.69	908.51	895.05	880.25
2016	896.27	899.36	887.09	890.84	890.27	888.55	901.12	890.95	894.22	939.13	934.36	939.62	904.29
2017	951.92	948.86	960.16	984.12	973.57	974.99	987.66	1,015.63	1,010.94	1,042.18	973.71	985.19	985.22
2018	998.21	1,006.17	992.78	1,010.32	988.66	984.53	997.60	1,013.79	1,017.21	1,022.09	1,024.29	1,040.08	1,008.61
Leisure and Hospitality													
2014	311.32	308.81	332.20	322.38	326.24	321.40	316.98	319.19	316.94	319.33	331.61	329.04	320.93
2015	326.71	334.46	335.62	334.20	337.14	330.55	330.46	339.66	332.11	336.15	337.82	336.34	333.83
2016	330.23	340.36	341.43	346.07	345.71	337.40	337.33	331.06	332.25	341.28	335.23	339.95	338.56
2017	334.62	342.38	343.67	347.90	349.52	347.66	345.30	339.56	333.54	350.57	346.09	350.82	344.78
2018	341.08	351.65	357.99	362.60	360.46	360.16	360.70	351.92	353.23	358.02	358.02	367.16	356.98
Other Services													
2014	610.54	625.12	655.04	670.58	646.81	684.90	699.39	691.56	689.17	676.10	687.83	699.22	669.98
2015	687.16	702.98	712.07	716.65	717.86	717.12	723.49	772.20	748.13	741.22	743.04	731.90	725.72
2016	717.28	734.21	724.54	717.60	717.52	685.80	702.31	691.23	682.44	692.22	685.97	669.28	702.58
2017	673.71	685.58	669.58	681.14	673.52	673.46	679.06	680.52	643.80	674.98	682.75	687.04	676.16
2018	670.70	708.75	729.73	762.09	713.79	722.44	708.71	717.30	752.45	769.39	745.20	744.51	728.11

HAWAII
At a Glance

Population:
  2010 census: 1,360,301
  2018 estimate: 1,420,491

Percent change in population:
  2010–2018: 4.4%

Percent change in total nonfarm employment:
  2010–2018: 11.9%

Industry with the largest growth in employment, 2010–2018 (percent):
  Transportation and utilities, 27.1%

Industry with the largest decline or smallest growth in employment, 2010–2018 (percent):
  Wholesale trade, 2.3%

Civilian labor force:
  2010: 647,249
  2018: 678,734

Unemployment rate and rank among states (highest to lowest):
  2010: 6.9%, 43rd
  2018: 2.4%, 51st

Over-the-year change in unemployment rates:
  2016–2017: -0.6%
  2017–2018: 0.0%

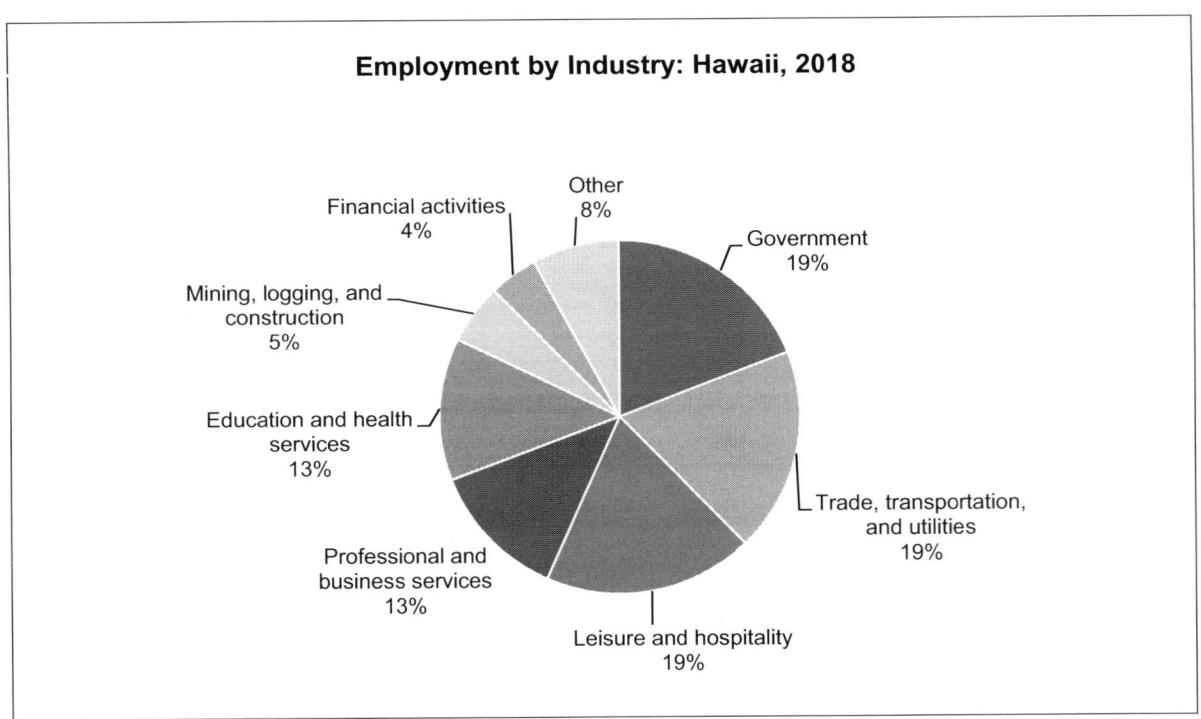

Employment by Industry: Hawaii, 2018

- Financial activities 4%
- Other 8%
- Government 19%
- Mining, logging, and construction 5%
- Education and health services 13%
- Professional and business services 13%
- Trade, transportation, and utilities 19%
- Leisure and hospitality 19%

1. Employment by Industry: Hawaii, 2010–2018

(Numbers in thousands, not seasonally adjusted)

Industry and year	January	February	March	April	May	June	July	August	September	October	November	December	Annual average
Total Nonfarm													
2010	578.9	583.9	587.4	586.6	589.9	586.2	581.2	577.7	584.8	589.6	597.2	599.2	586.9
2011	580.7	592.2	595.7	592.6	593.5	591.3	587.6	584.8	593.8	597.1	603.1	608.4	593.4
2012	584.8	600.3	602.9	604.2	607.5	606.1	599.1	605.7	607.5	611.7	623.0	622.8	606.3
2013	600.3	615.8	618.7	615.7	620.5	617.6	613.7	611.7	619.7	624.2	631.1	634.4	618.6
2014	618.7	623.4	627.0	625.4	628.8	624.9	619.0	622.0	627.4	630.4	639.0	637.8	627.0
2015	627.4	632.8	636.4	635.4	637.6	635.8	630.1	633.8	636.4	642.4	648.2	654.3	637.6
2016	635.7	643.3	645.8	644.3	646.6	643.8	639.8	642.9	648.4	649.0	657.4	656.2	646.1
2017	645.6	651.8	655.6	653.8	655.9	653.6	645.4	644.5	653.7	654.9	659.9	665.3	653.3
2018	649.0	656.4	659.4	656.1	657.7	656.8	647.1	651.0	654.0	658.7	664.8	667.7	656.6
Total Private													
2010	456.6	458.5	459.9	459.0	460.1	460.1	460.2	461.2	462.5	464.3	466.5	471.6	461.7
2011	460.5	465.3	468.0	465.5	465.3	465.8	468.0	469.3	471.3	471.2	475.7	480.3	468.9
2012	469.7	472.8	474.6	475.7	478.5	480.2	480.4	483.1	483.8	485.2	491.0	493.9	480.7
2013	484.6	487.8	490.3	490.3	491.3	492.6	494.9	495.7	495.9	497.2	503.1	505.7	494.1
2014	494.0	495.1	498.4	497.5	499.3	498.7	499.7	501.2	502.6	503.3	507.5	511.6	500.7
2015	502.6	504.5	507.7	506.7	508.2	509.6	511.4	512.2	511.7	514.8	519.8	524.5	511.1
2016	512.8	515.4	516.8	517.7	517.5	517.6	521.0	523.2	523.0	521.3	525.5	529.1	520.1
2017	520.9	522.6	526.2	524.8	526.4	527.6	528.3	529.9	529.4	528.6	532.3	536.7	527.8
2018	526.7	528.6	531.6	529.2	528.9	531.5	529.5	531.8	530.1	532.3	533.5	537.8	531.0
Goods Producing													
2010	42.2	41.9	42.0	41.7	41.7	41.5	41.7	41.6	41.7	42.1	42.2	42.4	41.9
2011	40.6	41.2	41.3	41.6	41.6	42.2	42.7	42.7	43.1	42.6	42.6	42.8	42.1
2012	41.7	41.8	41.8	41.7	41.9	42.6	42.7	43.1	43.6	43.8	44.1	44.1	42.7
2013	43.2	43.5	44.0	44.0	44.6	44.5	45.0	45.1	45.2	45.0	45.5	45.5	44.6
2014	44.1	44.4	44.8	44.7	45.4	45.8	46.5	46.9	47.1	47.3	47.3	47.3	46.0
2015	46.0	46.4	47.0	47.5	48.0	48.8	49.7	50.0	50.1	51.3	51.7	52.2	49.1
2016	51.2	51.8	52.1	52.1	52.3	52.5	53.1	53.1	52.4	51.8	51.8	51.6	52.2
2017	49.9	50.2	50.6	50.3	50.5	51.0	50.8	51.0	50.8	50.1	50.5	50.6	50.5
2018	49.4	49.7	50.0	50.0	49.9	50.4	50.5	50.5	50.3	51.2	50.0	51.0	50.2
Service-Providing													
2010	536.7	542.0	545.4	544.9	548.2	544.7	539.5	536.1	543.1	547.5	555.0	556.8	545.0
2011	540.1	551.0	554.4	551.0	551.9	549.1	544.9	542.1	550.7	554.5	560.5	565.6	551.3
2012	543.1	558.5	561.1	562.5	565.6	563.5	556.4	562.6	563.9	567.9	578.9	578.7	563.6
2013	557.1	572.3	574.7	571.7	575.9	573.1	568.7	566.6	574.5	579.2	585.6	588.9	574.0
2014	574.6	579.0	582.2	580.7	583.4	579.1	572.5	575.1	580.3	583.1	591.7	590.5	581.0
2015	581.4	586.4	589.4	587.9	589.6	587.0	580.4	583.8	586.3	591.1	596.5	602.1	588.5
2016	584.5	591.5	593.7	592.2	594.3	591.3	586.7	589.8	596.0	597.2	605.6	604.6	594.0
2017	595.7	601.6	605.0	603.5	605.4	602.6	594.6	593.5	602.9	604.8	609.4	614.7	602.8
2018	599.6	606.7	609.4	606.1	607.8	606.4	596.6	600.5	603.7	607.5	614.8	616.7	606.3
Mining, Logging, and Construction													
2010	29.0	28.8	28.9	28.8	28.8	28.7	28.9	28.7	28.8	29.1	29.1	29.2	28.9
2011	27.6	28.0	28.1	28.4	28.4	29.0	29.5	29.4	29.6	29.2	29.1	29.3	28.8
2012	28.4	28.4	28.5	28.5	28.8	29.4	29.5	29.8	30.2	30.4	30.5	30.5	29.4
2013	29.8	30.1	30.5	30.7	31.2	31.0	31.4	31.5	31.5	31.3	31.6	31.7	31.0
2014	30.6	30.9	31.1	31.1	31.8	32.0	32.5	32.7	33.1	33.3	33.2	33.1	32.1
2015	32.0	32.3	33.0	33.5	34.0	34.7	35.6	35.8	36.0	37.1	37.5	37.9	35.0
2016	37.2	37.7	38.0	38.0	38.2	38.3	38.8	38.7	38.2	37.6	37.6	37.2	38.0
2017	35.9	36.1	36.4	36.0	36.2	36.6	36.4	36.5	36.3	35.6	35.9	35.9	36.2
2018	34.9	35.2	35.6	35.6	35.8	36.3	36.5	36.5	36.4	37.1	36.1	36.8	36.1

1. Employment by Industry: Hawaii, 2010–2018—*Continued*

(Numbers in thousands, not seasonally adjusted)

Industry and year	January	February	March	April	May	June	July	August	September	October	November	December	Annual average
Manufacturing													
2010	13.2	13.1	13.1	12.9	12.9	12.8	12.8	12.9	12.9	13.0	13.1	13.2	13.0
2011	13.0	13.2	13.2	13.2	13.2	13.2	13.2	13.3	13.5	13.4	13.5	13.5	13.3
2012	13.3	13.4	13.3	13.2	13.1	13.2	13.2	13.3	13.4	13.4	13.6	13.6	13.3
2013	13.4	13.4	13.5	13.3	13.4	13.5	13.6	13.6	13.7	13.7	13.9	13.8	13.6
2014	13.5	13.5	13.7	13.6	13.6	13.8	14.0	14.2	14.0	14.0	14.1	14.2	13.9
2015	14.0	14.1	14.0	14.0	14.0	14.1	14.1	14.2	14.1	14.2	14.2	14.3	14.1
2016	14.0	14.1	14.1	14.1	14.1	14.2	14.3	14.4	14.2	14.2	14.2	14.4	14.2
2017	14.0	14.1	14.2	14.3	14.3	14.4	14.4	14.5	14.5	14.5	14.6	14.7	14.4
2018	14.5	14.5	14.4	14.4	14.1	14.1	14.0	14.0	13.9	14.1	13.9	14.2	14.2
Trade, Transportation, and Utilities													
2010	109.7	109.1	108.9	109.1	108.8	109.3	109.7	110.1	109.7	110.3	112.0	113.9	110.1
2011	110.7	110.3	110.4	110.0	110.0	110.3	111.0	111.2	111.1	112.2	114.4	116.0	111.5
2012	113.4	112.6	113.2	112.9	113.5	114.1	114.4	114.7	114.8	115.2	118.6	119.7	114.8
2013	115.9	115.5	115.9	115.5	115.7	116.2	116.4	116.7	116.8	116.9	119.5	121.0	116.8
2014	117.0	116.1	116.4	116.2	116.5	116.8	117.3	117.0	117.1	117.9	120.4	122.6	117.6
2015	119.2	118.5	118.9	118.5	118.6	118.9	119.1	119.3	118.9	119.5	121.9	123.4	119.6
2016	119.7	119.0	118.9	118.5	118.6	118.5	119.7	120.1	120.5	120.8	123.1	125.3	120.2
2017	121.6	120.4	120.5	120.3	120.5	121.0	121.4	122.0	121.8	122.3	124.7	126.2	121.9
2018	123.1	122.0	122.1	121.9	122.1	122.3	122.8	122.8	122.2	122.1	123.5	124.1	122.6
Wholesale Trade													
2010	17.5	17.5	17.5	17.5	17.5	17.6	17.7	17.6	17.5	17.6	17.6	17.7	17.6
2011	17.3	17.3	17.2	17.3	17.4	17.4	17.4	17.5	17.4	17.5	17.6	17.7	17.4
2012	17.5	17.4	17.5	17.4	17.5	17.6	17.6	17.7	17.7	17.7	17.8	17.9	17.6
2013	17.7	17.6	17.7	17.6	17.6	17.6	17.6	17.6	17.6	17.6	17.6	17.6	17.6
2014	17.5	17.5	17.6	17.5	17.6	17.6	17.6	17.6	17.6	17.8	17.8	18.1	17.7
2015	17.8	17.8	17.9	17.8	17.9	17.9	17.9	18.0	17.9	17.8	17.8	17.9	17.9
2016	17.7	17.6	17.6	17.7	17.7	17.8	17.9	17.9	17.9	17.9	17.9	18.1	17.8
2017	17.8	17.8	17.8	17.8	17.8	17.9	17.9	17.9	17.9	17.9	18.0	18.1	17.9
2018	17.8	17.8	17.8	17.7	17.8	17.8	17.8	17.7	17.7	18.1	18.2	18.0	17.9
Retail Trade													
2010	66.0	65.4	65.3	65.3	65.0	65.5	65.7	65.8	65.5	65.8	67.5	68.9	66.0
2011	66.6	66.0	66.2	65.9	65.8	66.1	66.6	66.6	66.7	67.3	69.3	70.5	67.0
2012	68.3	67.7	67.8	67.6	68.0	68.3	68.4	68.4	68.4	68.8	71.7	72.6	68.8
2013	69.4	68.8	69.1	68.7	68.8	69.1	69.3	69.4	69.4	69.4	72.0	73.1	69.7
2014	69.6	68.7	68.8	68.7	68.8	69.4	69.7	69.4	69.6	69.9	72.1	73.6	69.9
2015	70.7	70.0	70.3	70.0	69.9	70.1	70.3	70.4	70.3	70.8	73.1	74.0	70.8
2016	70.9	70.3	70.2	69.6	69.4	69.2	70.0	70.1	70.6	70.9	72.8	74.1	70.7
2017	71.5	70.3	70.3	70.2	70.4	70.6	70.9	71.1	70.7	71.2	73.6	74.5	71.3
2018	72.2	71.1	71.1	71.0	71.1	71.2	71.6	71.6	71.1	70.8	71.9	72.2	71.4
Transportation and Utilities													
2010	26.2	26.2	26.1	26.3	26.3	26.2	26.3	26.7	26.7	26.9	26.9	27.3	26.5
2011	26.8	27.0	27.0	26.8	26.8	26.8	27.0	27.1	27.0	27.4	27.5	27.8	27.1
2012	27.6	27.5	27.9	27.9	28.0	28.2	28.4	28.6	28.7	28.7	29.1	29.2	28.3
2013	28.8	29.1	29.1	29.2	29.3	29.5	29.5	29.7	29.8	29.9	29.9	30.3	29.5
2014	29.9	29.9	30.0	30.0	30.1	29.8	30.0	30.0	29.9	30.2	30.5	30.9	30.1
2015	30.7	30.7	30.7	30.7	30.8	30.9	30.9	30.9	30.7	30.9	31.0	31.5	30.9
2016	31.1	31.1	31.1	31.2	31.5	31.5	31.8	32.1	32.0	32.0	32.4	33.1	31.7
2017	32.3	32.3	32.4	32.3	32.3	32.5	32.6	33.0	33.2	33.2	33.1	33.6	32.7
2018	33.1	33.1	33.2	33.2	33.2	33.3	33.4	33.5	33.4	33.2	33.4	33.9	33.3
Information													
2010	8.9	9.7	9.9	9.5	10.7	10.0	8.8	9.4	11.1	9.8	9.4	10.3	9.8
2011	8.5	9.4	10.2	8.1	8.0	7.8	8.3	8.3	8.2	8.3	8.6	8.7	8.5
2012	8.3	8.4	8.5	8.4	8.4	7.8	8.1	8.3	8.4	8.6	9.2	8.9	8.4
2013	8.3	8.4	8.5	8.4	8.0	7.9	9.6	8.4	8.8	9.4	9.6	9.9	8.8
2014	8.3	8.4	8.5	8.3	8.8	8.1	8.2	8.7	8.8	8.5	8.7	8.7	8.5
2015	8.5	8.6	8.6	8.4	8.3	8.2	8.7	8.6	8.5	8.7	9.6	9.7	8.7
2016	8.2	8.6	8.4	8.5	9.0	8.4	8.7	9.7	9.1	8.7	9.6	8.7	8.8
2017	8.9	9.1	9.2	9.1	9.8	8.9	9.0	10.0	9.2	8.2	8.3	8.5	9.0
2018	8.4	8.9	9.0	8.9	8.9	9.4	8.1	9.8	9.3	9.3	9.7	9.7	9.1

1. Employment by Industry: Hawaii, 2010–2018—*Continued*

(Numbers in thousands, not seasonally adjusted)

Industry and year	January	February	March	April	May	June	July	August	September	October	November	December	Annual average
Financial Activities													
2010	27.1	27.0	27.1	26.9	26.9	26.8	27.0	26.9	26.8	26.9	26.9	26.9	26.9
2011	26.5	26.5	26.6	26.6	26.5	26.5	26.7	26.7	26.6	26.5	26.8	26.8	26.6
2012	26.3	26.5	26.6	26.5	26.6	26.8	26.8	26.8	26.8	26.9	27.0	27.0	26.7
2013	26.7	26.8	27.0	27.1	27.2	27.2	27.3	27.2	27.3	27.2	27.3	27.5	27.2
2014	27.1	27.2	27.4	27.4	27.5	27.7	27.8	27.8	27.7	27.7	27.8	28.1	27.6
2015	27.7	27.9	28.1	28.1	28.2	28.3	28.3	28.2	28.0	28.0	27.9	28.3	28.1
2016	28.1	28.2	28.3	28.3	28.3	28.5	28.8	28.8	28.6	28.6	28.6	28.8	28.5
2017	28.5	28.5	28.7	28.5	28.6	28.7	28.6	28.6	28.6	28.7	28.7	29.0	28.6
2018	28.7	28.6	28.8	28.8	28.7	28.7	28.7	28.6	28.6	28.7	29.3	29.3	28.8
Professional and Business Services													
2010	70.2	70.6	70.9	70.9	70.9	71.2	72.0	71.9	72.0	72.6	72.8	73.6	71.6
2011	73.3	74.4	75.0	75.3	74.8	75.0	74.8	75.5	75.8	75.9	76.5	77.7	75.3
2012	75.1	75.8	76.1	76.8	77.2	77.4	76.9	77.9	77.3	78.0	78.7	79.2	77.2
2013	78.1	79.0	79.5	79.5	79.1	79.3	79.8	80.4	80.1	81.3	82.1	82.2	80.0
2014	81.3	81.5	82.1	82.3	82.0	82.0	81.6	82.2	82.2	82.1	82.8	83.3	82.1
2015	82.1	82.3	82.7	82.5	82.4	82.5	82.7	82.3	82.1	82.8	83.0	83.1	82.5
2016	81.3	82.0	81.9	82.3	81.4	81.4	81.9	82.1	82.0	81.8	82.2	82.6	81.9
2017	81.3	81.6	82.2	81.8	81.9	82.8	82.6	82.5	82.0	82.3	82.9	83.1	82.3
2018	81.6	81.9	82.7	82.1	81.9	82.5	82.4	82.9	82.4	82.8	83.3	83.2	82.5
Education and Health Services													
2010	74.5	75.2	75.6	75.2	75.6	75.3	74.9	74.6	74.6	75.9	75.9	76.3	75.3
2011	73.9	75.8	75.9	75.7	76.0	75.2	75.6	75.1	76.2	76.3	77.0	77.5	75.9
2012	75.0	76.4	76.1	76.7	77.4	76.8	76.7	77.2	77.9	78.1	78.3	79.1	77.1
2013	77.5	78.7	79.0	79.0	79.0	79.2	78.3	78.7	79.2	78.7	80.0	79.6	78.9
2014	77.8	78.4	79.0	79.0	79.0	78.3	78.3	78.4	79.4	79.7	80.2	80.9	79.0
2015	79.9	81.0	81.7	81.7	81.7	81.3	81.0	81.0	82.1	82.5	82.8	83.7	81.7
2016	81.6	81.9	82.9	83.2	82.7	82.3	82.5	82.2	83.5	82.9	83.1	83.7	82.7
2017	82.9	83.3	84.2	84.3	84.1	83.2	84.3	83.6	85.6	85.4	85.3	86.4	84.4
2018	84.7	85.7	86.4	86.1	85.7	85.6	84.7	84.9	85.9	86.4	87.0	87.0	85.8
Leisure and Hospitality													
2010	98.8	99.4	99.8	99.7	99.4	100.0	100.2	100.8	100.7	100.7	101.4	102.3	100.3
2011	101.5	101.9	102.9	102.4	102.5	102.9	103.0	103.8	104.1	103.2	103.7	104.7	103.1
2012	104.3	105.4	106.3	106.5	107.1	108.3	108.6	108.7	108.4	108.1	108.5	109.5	107.5
2013	108.6	109.5	110.0	110.3	111.1	111.8	111.9	112.5	111.7	111.9	112.4	113.2	111.2
2014	112.0	112.6	113.5	113.2	113.6	113.4	113.5	113.6	113.6	113.4	113.5	113.7	113.3
2015	112.8	113.2	113.8	113.3	114.1	114.5	115.1	116.0	115.1	115.1	115.8	117.1	114.7
2016	115.8	116.9	117.2	117.5	117.9	118.6	118.9	119.9	119.4	119.3	119.6	120.9	118.5
2017	120.4	121.8	123.0	122.6	123.0	123.9	123.7	124.2	123.4	123.7	123.8	124.7	123.2
2018	123.1	123.8	124.5	123.5	123.9	124.5	124.2	124.4	123.3	123.7	122.5	125.3	123.9
Other Services													
2010	25.2	25.6	25.7	26.0	26.1	26.0	25.9	25.9	25.9	26.0	25.9	25.9	25.8
2011	25.5	25.8	25.7	25.8	25.9	25.9	25.9	26.0	26.2	26.2	26.1	26.1	25.9
2012	25.6	25.9	26.0	26.2	26.4	26.4	26.2	26.4	26.6	26.5	26.6	26.4	26.3
2013	26.3	26.4	26.4	26.5	26.6	26.5	26.6	26.7	26.8	26.8	26.7	26.8	26.6
2014	26.4	26.5	26.7	26.4	26.5	26.6	26.5	26.6	26.7	26.7	26.8	27.0	26.6
2015	26.4	26.6	26.9	26.7	26.9	27.1	26.8	26.8	26.9	26.9	27.1	27.0	26.8
2016	26.9	27.0	27.1	27.3	27.3	27.4	27.4	27.3	27.5	27.4	27.5	27.5	27.3
2017	27.4	27.7	27.8	27.9	28.0	28.1	27.9	28.0	28.0	27.9	28.1	28.2	27.9
2018	27.7	28.0	28.1	27.9	27.8	28.1	28.1	27.9	28.1	28.1	28.2	28.2	28.0
Government													
2010	122.3	125.4	127.5	127.6	129.8	126.1	121.0	116.5	122.3	125.3	130.7	127.6	125.2
2011	120.2	126.9	127.7	127.1	128.2	125.5	119.6	115.5	122.5	125.9	127.4	128.1	124.6
2012	115.1	127.5	128.3	128.5	129.0	125.9	118.7	122.6	123.7	126.5	132.0	128.9	125.6
2013	115.7	128.0	128.4	125.4	129.2	125.0	118.8	116.0	123.8	127.0	128.0	128.7	124.5
2014	124.7	128.3	128.6	127.9	129.5	126.2	119.3	120.8	124.8	127.1	131.5	126.2	126.2
2015	124.8	128.3	128.7	128.7	129.4	126.2	118.7	121.6	124.7	127.6	128.4	129.8	126.4
2016	122.9	127.9	129.0	126.6	129.1	126.2	118.8	119.7	125.4	127.7	131.9	127.1	126.0
2017	124.7	129.2	129.4	129.0	129.5	126.0	117.1	114.6	124.3	126.3	127.6	128.6	125.5
2018	122.3	127.8	127.8	126.9	128.8	125.3	117.6	119.2	123.9	126.4	131.3	129.9	125.6

2. Average Weekly Hours by Selected Industry: Hawaii, 2014–2018

(Not seasonally adjusted)

Industry and year	January	February	March	April	May	June	July	August	September	October	November	December	Annual average
Total Private													
2014	33.2	34.2	34.2	33.4	33.1	34.3	33.6	33.6	33.5	33.1	33.9	33.5	33.6
2015	33.2	34.1	34.1	33.0	33.0	32.9	33.3	34.0	32.6	32.6	33.5	33.0	33.3
2016	32.8	32.6	32.6	32.7	33.6	32.4	32.9	32.7	32.3	33.6	32.1	32.4	32.7
2017	33.7	32.6	32.3	33.8	32.6	32.8	34.1	32.8	32.8	33.6	33.0	32.9	33.1
2018	33.0	32.5	32.5	33.4	32.3	32.5	33.8	32.4	33.4	32.4	32.5	33.4	32.8
Goods-Producing													
2014	36.5	36.6	36.7	37.0	37.1	35.9	37.5	36.3	37.0	35.4	36.2	37.3	36.6
2015	36.6	36.5	36.9	37.3	37.8	35.0	36.9	36.5	34.3	36.6	35.9	38.5	36.6
2016	38.5	37.6	37.7	37.1	37.5	36.4	37.1	37.3	36.2	37.7	35.3	36.6	37.1
2017	36.5	36.7	37.1	36.4	37.2	35.2	37.9	37.1	36.4	37.3	37.4	36.9	36.8
2018	37.1	35.3	36.8	37.2	36.2	34.2	37.2	36.1	36.3	37.3	36.3	38.4	36.5
Mining, Logging, and Construction													
2014	37.0	36.8	37.1	37.5	38.3	35.8	37.9	36.5	37.1	34.2	35.0	36.8	36.7
2015	36.2	36.3	37.1	37.6	37.6	34.3	36.1	35.7	33.4	35.9	35.3	38.2	36.1
2016	38.3	37.6	37.2	37.0	37.2	36.2	36.8	37.2	35.7	37.4	34.4	36.4	36.8
2017	36.7	36.4	36.9	35.5	36.9	34.7	38.1	37.2	36.3	37.3	38.7	37.7	36.9
2018	38.3	35.7	37.7	38.0	36.4	34.4	37.8	36.8	36.8	37.8	36.8	39.7	37.2
Manufacturing													
2014	35.1	35.9	35.9	35.7	34.4	36.0	36.4	35.8	36.8	37.9	39.2	38.2	36.5
2015	37.6	37.2	36.6	36.8	38.3	36.6	38.5	38.7	36.6	38.5	37.5	39.2	37.7
2016	39.1	37.5	38.8	37.2	38.1	37.0	38.0	37.4	37.4	38.5	37.6	37.5	37.9
2017	36.2	37.7	37.7	38.7	37.9	36.4	37.6	37.1	36.7	37.2	34.4	35.1	36.8
2018	34.1	34.4	34.6	35.1	35.6	33.9	35.8	34.4	34.8	35.9	34.9	34.9	34.9
Trade, Transportation, and Utilities													
2014	33.3	34.4	34.3	33.5	33.2	34.4	33.7	33.8	33.3	33.4	34.3	34.2	33.8
2015	33.7	34.7	34.7	33.5	33.4	34.2	34.0	34.6	34.3	33.8	34.4	33.8	34.1
2016	33.8	33.6	33.5	33.6	34.0	33.5	34.1	33.6	33.5	34.8	33.4	33.7	33.7
2017	34.7	33.6	33.0	34.8	33.1	33.8	34.8	33.0	33.4	34.5	33.8	34.1	33.9
2018	34.0	33.4	33.0	34.5	33.3	34.3	35.7	33.8	35.5	33.8	34.0	35.1	34.2
Professional and Business Services													
2014	34.8	35.9	35.7	34.5	34.2	35.0	34.5	35.3	34.9	33.6	33.8	34.6	34.7
2015	34.2	34.6	34.8	34.3	33.8	33.3	33.7	34.1	33.0	33.4	35.0	34.6	34.1
2016	33.2	33.2	33.4	34.1	35.0	33.3	34.2	34.9	35.1	36.0	35.1	36.0	34.4
2017	36.5	35.0	35.3	35.8	34.9	34.3	35.7	34.7	34.7	35.0	34.6	34.5	35.1
2018	34.5	34.0	34.8	35.0	33.9	34.3	34.7	33.8	34.6	33.6	33.5	34.6	34.3
Education and Health Services													
2014	32.6	33.1	33.2	32.3	32.5	33.9	32.6	32.3	32.6	32.6	33.5	32.9	32.8
2015	31.9	32.7	31.7	31.5	31.2	31.6	31.7	32.9	31.6	31.2	32.1	31.6	31.8
2016	31.7	31.9	31.6	31.7	32.9	31.7	32.1	31.4	31.1	31.6	30.7	30.7	31.6
2017	32.5	31.7	31.5	32.7	31.8	32.0	33.0	32.1	32.5	32.8	32.1	32.4	32.3
2018	32.8	32.4	32.0	33.2	32.3	32.4	33.4	32.4	33.5	32.5	32.6	32.4	32.7
Leisure and Hospitality													
2014	30.4	31.7	31.6	30.3	29.7	31.6	30.5	30.3	29.9	29.6	31.2	29.1	30.5
2015	29.6	31.1	31.0	29.2	29.6	29.6	30.0	31.0	28.8	28.7	30.3	28.5	29.8
2016	28.8	28.8	28.3	28.8	30.5	28.9	28.9	28.8	28.3	29.9	28.4	28.4	28.9
2017	30.4	28.8	28.3	29.9	28.7	29.4	30.7	29.3	29.2	29.8	29.4	28.6	29.4
2018	29.0	28.8	28.5	28.9	27.5	27.5	29.1	27.4	27.9	27.2	27.7	28.1	28.1

3. Average Hourly Earnings by Selected Industry: Hawaii, 2014–2018

(Dollars, not seasonally adjusted)

Industry and year	January	February	March	April	May	June	July	August	September	October	November	December	Annual average
Total Private													
2014	23.98	24.02	24.13	24.08	24.29	24.34	24.43	24.51	24.62	24.57	24.60	24.40	24.33
2015	24.51	24.61	24.62	24.60	24.62	24.45	24.45	24.52	24.47	24.73	24.85	25.08	24.63
2016	25.14	25.29	25.18	25.32	25.37	25.48	25.46	25.41	25.67	25.63	25.48	25.59	25.42
2017	25.78	25.67	25.68	25.90	25.93	25.86	26.21	26.36	26.45	26.68	26.56	26.91	26.17
2018	27.37	27.18	27.33	27.85	27.47	27.66	27.81	27.85	28.08	27.82	27.98	28.42	27.74
Goods-Producing													
2014	31.58	31.68	31.82	32.24	32.78	32.09	32.76	33.49	34.26	33.13	33.13	33.25	32.70
2015	33.54	32.75	33.15	33.54	33.27	32.60	32.28	32.42	32.77	33.15	32.50	33.14	32.92
2016	32.79	32.52	32.41	33.13	32.44	33.06	32.84	33.33	33.29	33.70	33.52	33.88	33.07
2017	34.50	33.49	33.62	34.12	34.34	33.98	35.06	34.25	34.53	34.37	34.34	34.46	34.26
2018	35.32	35.35	35.47	35.77	35.63	34.79	35.47	36.52	36.97	36.02	36.72	37.45	35.97
Mining, Logging, and Construction													
2014	36.31	36.67	36.86	37.30	37.77	37.54	38.36	39.54	40.47	39.86	39.92	39.85	38.39
2015	40.19	38.91	38.97	39.11	38.98	38.11	37.23	37.43	38.14	38.41	37.28	37.98	38.37
2016	37.75	37.17	37.18	37.75	37.07	37.77	37.60	38.00	38.29	38.81	38.94	39.25	37.95
2017	39.56	38.58	38.51	39.37	39.39	38.73	39.82	39.01	39.34	39.09	38.52	38.66	39.05
2018	39.36	39.81	39.83	40.43	40.32	39.09	39.74	41.01	41.82	40.63	41.50	42.06	40.49
Manufacturing													
2014	20.30	20.00	20.00	20.10	19.83	19.55	19.26	19.23	19.47	18.77	18.89	18.47	19.46
2015	18.89	18.92	19.24	19.86	19.69	19.90	20.62	20.74	20.29	20.35	20.66	20.63	19.99
2016	19.90	20.02	20.11	20.81	20.20	20.60	20.32	20.79	20.46	20.61	20.39	20.36	20.38
2017	21.29	20.90	21.36	21.91	21.89	22.53	22.84	22.22	22.59	22.74	22.77	23.41	22.20
2018	24.42	24.10	23.72	23.25	23.49	23.52	23.73	24.04	23.57	23.22	23.65	23.89	23.72
Trade, Transportation, and Utilities													
2014	23.03	23.21	23.14	23.18	23.52	23.43	23.40	23.52	23.29	23.67	24.25	23.39	23.42
2015	23.91	24.45	24.33	24.43	24.10	23.70	23.63	24.02	23.70	23.77	24.15	24.12	24.03
2016	24.26	24.40	24.24	24.46	24.67	24.84	24.76	24.95	25.23	25.04	24.62	24.51	24.67
2017	25.22	24.87	25.20	25.63	25.55	25.60	25.41	25.63	25.81	25.96	25.39	25.68	25.50
2018	26.01	26.09	26.24	27.06	26.77	26.66	26.84	26.86	27.23	26.95	26.88	27.83	26.79
Professional and Business Services													
2014	23.75	24.00	24.52	24.32	24.35	24.74	24.47	24.70	24.76	24.25	24.01	23.44	24.28
2015	23.34	23.46	23.40	23.14	23.46	23.49	23.35	23.30	23.20	23.85	24.23	23.65	23.49
2016	23.21	24.08	23.94	24.27	25.07	25.18	25.45	25.55	26.04	25.97	25.89	26.09	25.09
2017	25.52	26.04	25.77	25.98	25.68	25.67	26.09	25.55	25.40	26.00	25.53	25.45	25.72
2018	25.96	25.60	25.88	25.94	25.76	26.08	26.36	26.28	26.25	25.66	26.27	26.54	26.05
Education and Health Services													
2014	26.11	26.04	26.11	25.64	26.01	26.27	26.54	26.54	26.67	27.01	26.98	26.95	26.41
2015	26.98	27.18	26.52	25.97	26.32	26.69	26.84	26.64	26.87	27.52	27.26	27.72	26.88
2016	27.83	27.95	27.82	27.55	26.95	26.56	26.59	26.21	26.38	26.24	26.08	26.10	26.86
2017	26.61	27.08	27.08	27.14	27.57	28.04	28.57	29.16	29.51	29.69	30.08	30.29	28.42
2018	30.71	30.81	31.15	31.93	30.96	31.72	31.59	31.75	32.32	32.72	33.21	32.15	31.76
Leisure and Hospitality													
2014	18.78	18.68	18.59	18.44	18.34	18.78	18.86	18.64	18.92	18.96	18.60	18.78	18.70
2015	19.25	19.15	19.17	18.93	19.20	19.44	19.73	19.45	19.38	19.13	19.63	19.51	19.33
2016	20.29	19.96	19.81	19.64	19.94	20.30	20.48	20.08	20.21	20.18	20.17	20.36	20.12
2017	21.17	20.95	20.75	20.94	20.78	21.06	21.21	21.21	20.92	20.90	20.92	21.39	21.02
2018	21.50	21.74	21.48	21.47	20.84	21.33	20.96	21.11	20.53	20.38	20.50	20.57	21.04

4. Average Weekly Earnings by Selected Industry: Hawaii 2014–2018

(Dollars, not seasonally adjusted)

Industry and year	January	February	March	April	May	June	July	August	September	October	November	December	Annual average
Total Private													
2014	796.14	821.48	825.25	804.27	804.00	834.86	820.85	823.54	824.77	813.27	833.94	817.40	817.49
2015	813.73	839.20	839.54	811.80	812.46	804.41	814.19	833.68	797.72	806.20	832.48	827.64	820.18
2016	824.59	824.45	820.87	827.96	852.43	825.55	837.63	830.91	829.14	861.17	817.91	829.12	831.23
2017	868.79	836.84	829.46	875.42	845.32	848.21	893.76	864.61	867.56	896.45	876.48	885.34	866.23
2018	903.21	883.35	888.23	930.19	887.28	898.95	939.98	902.34	937.87	901.37	909.35	949.23	909.87
Goods-Producing													
2014	1,152.67	1,159.49	1,167.79	1,192.88	1,216.14	1,152.03	1,228.50	1,215.69	1,267.62	1,172.80	1,199.31	1,240.23	1,196.82
2015	1,227.56	1,195.38	1,223.24	1,251.04	1,257.61	1,141.00	1,191.13	1,183.33	1,124.01	1,213.29	1,166.75	1,275.89	1,204.87
2016	1,262.42	1,222.75	1,221.86	1,229.12	1,216.50	1,203.38	1,218.36	1,243.21	1,205.10	1,270.49	1,183.26	1,240.01	1,226.90
2017	1,259.25	1,229.08	1,247.30	1,241.97	1,277.45	1,196.10	1,328.77	1,270.68	1,256.89	1,282.00	1,284.32	1,271.57	1,260.77
2018	1,310.37	1,247.86	1,305.30	1,330.64	1,289.81	1,189.82	1,319.48	1,318.37	1,342.01	1,343.55	1,332.94	1,438.08	1,312.91
Mining, Logging, and Construction													
2014	1,343.47	1,349.46	1,367.51	1,398.75	1,446.59	1,343.93	1,453.84	1,443.21	1,501.44	1,363.21	1,397.20	1,466.48	1,408.91
2015	1,454.88	1,412.43	1,445.79	1,470.54	1,465.65	1,307.17	1,344.00	1,336.25	1,273.88	1,378.92	1,315.98	1,450.84	1,385.16
2016	1,445.83	1,397.59	1,383.10	1,396.75	1,379.00	1,367.27	1,383.68	1,413.60	1,366.95	1,451.49	1,339.54	1,428.70	1,396.56
2017	1,451.85	1,404.31	1,421.02	1,397.64	1,453.49	1,343.93	1,517.14	1,451.17	1,428.04	1,458.06	1,490.72	1,457.48	1,440.95
2018	1,507.49	1,421.22	1,501.59	1,536.34	1,467.65	1,344.70	1,502.17	1,509.17	1,538.98	1,535.81	1,527.20	1,669.78	1,506.23
Manufacturing													
2014	712.53	718.00	718.00	717.57	682.15	703.80	701.06	688.43	716.50	711.38	740.49	705.55	710.29
2015	710.26	703.82	704.18	730.85	754.13	728.34	793.87	802.64	742.61	783.48	774.75	808.70	753.62
2016	778.09	750.75	780.27	774.13	769.62	762.20	772.16	777.55	765.20	793.49	766.66	763.50	772.40
2017	770.70	787.93	805.27	847.92	829.63	820.09	858.78	824.36	829.05	845.93	783.29	821.69	816.96
2018	832.72	829.04	820.71	816.08	836.24	797.33	849.53	826.98	820.24	833.60	825.39	833.76	827.83
Trade, Transportation, and Utilities													
2014	766.90	798.42	793.70	776.53	780.86	805.99	788.58	794.98	775.56	790.58	831.78	799.94	791.60
2015	805.77	848.42	844.25	818.41	804.94	810.54	803.42	831.09	812.91	803.43	830.76	815.26	819.42
2016	819.99	819.84	812.04	821.86	838.78	832.14	844.32	838.32	845.21	871.39	822.31	825.99	831.38
2017	875.13	835.63	831.60	891.92	845.71	865.28	884.27	845.79	862.05	895.62	858.18	875.69	864.45
2018	884.34	871.41	865.92	933.57	891.44	914.44	958.19	907.87	966.67	910.91	913.92	976.83	916.22
Professional and Business Services													
2014	826.50	861.60	875.36	839.04	832.77	865.90	844.22	871.91	864.12	814.80	811.54	811.02	842.52
2015	798.23	811.72	814.32	793.70	792.95	782.22	786.90	794.53	765.60	796.59	848.05	818.29	801.01
2016	770.57	799.46	799.60	827.61	877.45	838.49	870.39	891.70	914.00	934.92	908.74	939.24	863.10
2017	931.48	911.40	909.68	930.08	896.23	880.48	931.41	886.59	881.38	910.00	883.34	878.03	902.77
2018	895.62	870.40	900.62	907.90	873.26	894.54	914.69	888.26	908.25	862.18	880.05	918.28	893.52
Education and Health Services													
2014	851.19	861.92	866.85	828.17	845.33	890.55	865.20	857.24	869.44	880.53	903.83	886.66	866.25
2015	860.66	888.79	840.68	818.06	821.18	843.40	850.83	876.46	849.09	858.62	875.05	875.95	854.78
2016	882.21	891.61	879.11	873.34	886.66	841.95	853.54	822.99	820.42	829.18	800.66	801.27	848.78
2017	864.83	858.44	853.02	887.48	876.73	897.28	942.81	936.04	959.08	973.83	965.57	981.40	917.97
2018	1,007.29	998.24	996.80	1,060.08	1,000.01	1,027.73	1,055.11	1,028.70	1,082.72	1,063.40	1,082.65	1,041.66	1,038.55
Leisure and Hospitality													
2014	570.91	592.16	587.44	558.73	544.70	593.45	575.23	564.79	565.71	561.22	580.32	546.50	570.35
2015	569.80	595.57	594.27	552.76	568.32	575.42	591.90	602.95	558.14	549.03	594.79	556.04	576.03
2016	584.35	574.85	560.62	565.63	608.17	586.67	591.87	578.30	571.94	603.38	572.83	578.22	581.47
2017	643.57	603.36	587.23	626.11	596.39	619.16	651.15	621.45	610.86	622.82	615.05	611.75	617.99
2018	623.50	626.11	612.18	620.48	573.10	586.58	609.94	578.41	572.79	554.34	567.85	578.02	591.22

IDAHO
At a Glance

Population:
    2010 census: 1,567,582
    2018 estimate: 1,754,208

Percent change in population:
    2010–2018: 11.9%

Percent change in total nonfarm employment:
    2010–2018: 22.2%

Industry with the largest growth in employment, 2010–2018 (percent):
    Construction, 56.9%

Industry with the largest decline or smallest growth in employment, 2010–2018 (percent):
    Information, -7.3%

Civilian labor force:
    2010: 761,056
    2018: 857,049

Unemployment rate and rank among states (highest to lowest):
    2010: 9.0%, 23rd
    2018: 2.8%, 45th

Over-the-year change in unemployment rates:
    2016–2017: -0.6%
    2017–2018: -0.4%

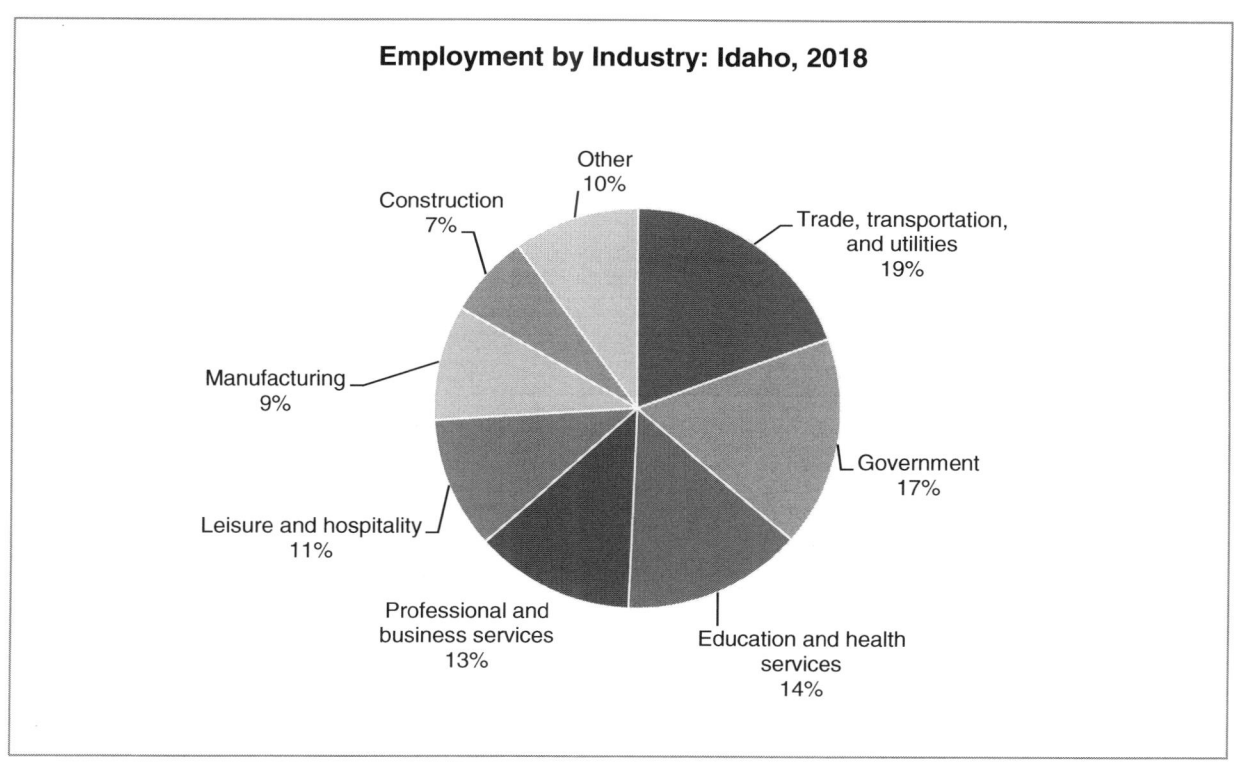

Employment by Industry: Idaho, 2018

Other 10%

Construction 7%

Trade, transportation, and utilities 19%

Manufacturing 9%

Government 17%

Leisure and hospitality 11%

Professional and business services 13%

Education and health services 14%

1. Employment by Industry: Idaho, 2010–2018

(Numbers in thousands, not seasonally adjusted)

Industry and year	January	February	March	April	May	June	July	August	September	October	November	December	Annual average
Total Nonfarm													
2010	581.3	587.0	591.7	600.6	609.6	610.1	608.5	609.8	612.1	613.1	609.6	605.5	603.2
2011	585.7	592.0	594.9	605.3	612.1	615.7	616.4	617.9	623.5	621.6	620.8	618.5	610.4
2012	596.3	602.5	607.6	613.3	623.9	628.0	626.3	628.2	634.1	634.9	634.3	630.9	621.7
2013	611.8	619.5	625.6	630.7	641.0	644.5	641.7	642.6	646.0	650.6	648.7	645.6	637.4
2014	630.8	637.6	642.9	649.4	657.0	661.7	659.4	659.2	661.6	664.1	662.0	660.6	653.9
2015	646.0	652.1	659.4	664.4	674.0	678.6	679.1	676.4	682.5	683.9	682.6	681.1	671.7
2016	666.7	675.4	682.6	687.8	694.6	700.8	702.8	701.1	706.6	705.9	705.2	701.6	694.3
2017	688.8	695.5	703.7	707.3	716.8	725.1	721.2	720.5	725.6	726.0	725.6	723.5	715.0
2018	710.7	720.0	725.1	731.2	740.5	748.2	746.9	745.5	746.5	748.5	745.0	740.0	737.3
Total Private													
2010	466.3	467.4	470.9	478.4	484.1	489.8	496.1	497.3	493.9	493.3	490.8	487.0	484.6
2011	472.5	473.3	475.6	485.2	491.0	498.4	505.2	506.6	505.9	502.3	502.0	499.7	493.1
2012	483.0	484.7	489.4	494.2	503.1	511.0	516.0	517.4	515.7	514.0	514.0	511.1	504.5
2013	496.3	499.8	505.5	511.1	519.9	527.0	531.8	533.0	528.4	530.3	529.2	527.1	520.0
2014	515.6	518.2	522.4	529.0	535.9	543.6	547.7	547.7	543.0	542.6	541.1	541.0	535.7
2015	530.0	532.2	538.6	543.3	551.1	559.4	566.3	564.9	562.2	561.2	560.5	559.9	552.5
2016	549.3	553.7	559.8	565.5	571.0	579.5	587.4	586.6	583.8	581.1	581.1	578.8	573.1
2017	568.6	572.3	579.5	582.6	590.4	601.0	604.5	604.4	601.3	599.1	599.4	597.9	591.8
2018	589.2	594.2	598.6	604.6	612.8	623.2	628.6	627.9	620.7	619.7	617.5	612.9	612.5
Goods Producing													
2010	83.5	82.8	83.6	85.7	87.8	90.1	91.5	92.4	91.8	91.7	89.9	86.4	88.1
2011	82.5	82.7	83.5	86.1	88.5	91.1	92.6	93.3	93.0	93.7	92.9	90.4	89.2
2012	86.6	86.4	87.1	88.8	91.9	94.8	96.2	96.8	96.0	96.6	95.6	94.1	92.6
2013	90.8	91.7	93.2	94.6	97.7	99.9	100.9	101.6	100.7	101.0	99.6	97.7	97.5
2014	95.1	94.9	95.6	97.4	99.7	102.3	103.6	104.0	103.5	103.6	102.2	101.0	100.2
2015	98.1	98.6	100.4	102.1	104.4	106.7	107.5	108.0	107.1	107.8	106.9	105.3	104.4
2016	103.1	104.0	105.9	108.0	109.8	111.9	113.9	114.2	113.3	111.7	111.2	109.7	109.7
2017	107.1	108.0	110.3	111.7	114.3	117.5	118.6	119.0	118.3	118.5	118.0	116.6	114.8
2018	113.8	115.2	116.4	117.8	121.0	124.1	125.2	125.4	124.3	124.1	122.9	119.7	120.8
Service-Providing													
2010	497.8	504.2	508.1	514.9	521.8	520.0	517.0	517.4	520.3	521.4	519.7	519.1	515.1
2011	503.2	509.3	511.4	519.2	523.6	524.6	523.8	524.6	530.5	527.9	527.9	528.1	521.2
2012	509.7	516.1	520.5	524.5	532.0	533.2	530.1	531.4	538.1	538.3	538.7	536.8	529.1
2013	521.0	527.8	532.4	536.1	543.3	544.6	540.8	541.0	545.3	549.6	549.1	547.9	539.9
2014	535.7	542.7	547.3	552.0	557.3	559.4	555.8	555.2	558.1	560.5	559.8	559.6	553.6
2015	547.9	553.5	559.0	562.3	569.6	571.9	571.6	568.4	575.4	576.1	575.7	575.8	567.3
2016	563.6	571.4	576.7	579.8	584.8	588.9	588.9	586.9	593.3	594.2	594.0	591.9	584.5
2017	581.7	587.5	593.4	595.6	602.5	607.6	602.6	601.5	607.3	607.5	607.6	606.9	600.1
2018	596.9	604.8	608.7	613.4	619.5	624.1	621.7	620.1	622.2	624.4	622.1	620.3	616.5
Mining and Logging													
2010	3.0	2.9	2.8	2.9	3.2	3.7	3.9	4.1	4.1	4.1	3.8	3.5	3.5
2011	3.4	3.4	3.3	3.1	3.3	3.9	4.3	4.4	4.4	4.4	4.3	4.1	3.9
2012	3.9	3.8	3.4	3.2	3.7	4.3	4.5	4.5	4.4	4.2	4.0	4.0	4.0
2013	3.8	3.7	3.6	3.5	3.9	4.2	4.3	4.3	4.2	4.2	4.1	3.9	4.0
2014	3.8	3.8	3.3	3.2	3.6	4.0	4.2	4.2	4.1	4.1	3.9	3.8	3.8
2015	3.6	3.5	3.4	3.5	3.8	4.1	4.2	4.1	4.1	3.9	3.8	3.8	3.8
2016	3.6	3.5	3.3	3.4	3.8	4.0	4.1	4.2	4.1	4.0	3.8	3.8	3.8
2017	3.6	3.5	3.1	2.7	3.3	3.7	3.9	3.8	3.8	3.8	3.5	3.4	3.5
2018	3.3	3.3	3.0	2.8	3.5	3.7	3.9	3.9	3.8	3.9	3.6	3.5	3.5
Construction													
2010	28.1	27.6	28.6	30.2	31.8	32.9	33.9	34.2	33.7	32.9	31.8	29.4	31.3
2011	25.7	25.6	26.2	28.5	30.3	32.1	33	33.5	32.9	32.9	32.7	30.8	30.4
2012	27.5	27.3	28.0	29.4	31.3	32.8	33.9	34.2	33.8	33.8	32.9	31.8	31.4
2013	28.8	29.4	30.6	31.8	33.8	35.2	36.1	36.6	36.3	36.1	35.2	33.6	33.6
2014	31.7	31.4	32.5	34.1	35.8	37.4	38.2	38.9	38.5	38.0	37.3	36.3	35.8
2015	34.0	34.5	36.1	37.2	38.7	39.9	40.5	40.8	39.7	40.0	39.1	38.2	38.2
2016	36.3	37.1	38.7	40.6	41.9	43.3	44.5	44.7	44.4	43.5	43.1	41.5	41.6
2017	39.0	39.7	41.9	43.6	45.2	47.1	47.8	48.0	47.4	47.2	46.7	45.7	44.9
2018	43.4	44.5	45.7	47.3	49.4	51.7	52.3	52.6	51.8	51.6	50.5	48.2	49.1

1. Employment by Industry: Idaho, 2010–2018—*Continued*

(Numbers in thousands, not seasonally adjusted)

Industry and year	January	February	March	April	May	June	July	August	September	October	November	December	Annual average
Manufacturing													
2010	52.4	52.3	52.2	52.6	52.8	53.5	53.7	54.1	54.0	54.7	54.3	53.5	53.3
2011	53.4	53.7	54.0	54.5	54.9	55.1	55.1	55.4	55.7	56.4	55.9	55.5	55.0
2012	55.2	55.3	55.7	56.2	56.9	57.7	57.8	58.1	57.8	58.6	58.7	58.3	57.2
2013	58.2	58.6	59.0	59.3	60.0	60.5	60.5	60.7	60.2	60.7	60.3	60.2	59.9
2014	59.6	59.7	59.8	60.1	60.3	60.9	61.2	60.9	60.9	61.5	61.0	60.9	60.6
2015	60.5	60.6	60.9	61.4	61.9	62.7	62.8	63.1	63.3	63.9	64.0	63.3	62.4
2016	63.2	63.4	63.9	64.0	64.1	64.6	65.3	65.3	64.8	64.2	64.3	64.4	64.3
2017	64.5	64.8	65.3	65.4	65.8	66.7	66.9	67.2	67.1	67.5	67.8	67.5	66.4
2018	67.1	67.4	67.7	67.7	68.1	68.7	69.0	68.9	68.7	68.6	68.8	68.0	68.2
Trade, Transportation, and Utilities													
2010	117.6	116.5	117.0	118.5	119.7	120.1	120.8	121.8	120.6	121.3	122.5	122.7	119.9
2011	117.6	117.0	117.5	119.4	120.4	120.8	122.5	123.3	123.5	123.6	125.5	125.7	121.4
2012	121.4	120.5	121.5	122.0	123.8	124.7	125.9	126.2	126.2	126.7	128.7	128.5	124.7
2013	123.5	123.3	124.0	125.2	126.6	127.2	128.5	128.8	128.6	129.0	130.4	130.8	127.2
2014	126.9	126.1	127.0	128.6	129.8	130.7	131.6	131.8	131.4	132.1	134.0	134.6	130.4
2015	130.5	130.3	131.6	132.5	133.8	134.6	136.1	136.1	135.9	136.7	138.7	139.1	134.7
2016	133.9	134.0	134.7	135.7	136.0	136.7	138.0	138.7	138.7	139.2	140.9	140.9	137.3
2017	136.4	135.9	136.6	137.2	138.1	139.2	140.0	140.6	140.2	140.7	142.7	143.2	139.2
2018	139.5	139.0	139.5	140.6	141.9	142.7	143.7	144.8	143.9	144.0	145.5	144.8	142.5
Wholesale Trade													
2010	23.7	23.6	23.8	24.3	24.5	24.5	24.8	24.8	24.5	24.7	24.4	24.4	24.3
2011	23.9	24.0	24.2	24.7	24.9	24.9	25.4	25.4	25.4	25.5	25.3	25.3	24.9
2012	24.9	25.0	25.4	25.7	26.0	26.0	26.7	26.2	26.3	26.4	26.2	26.2	25.9
2013	26.0	26.3	26.4	26.7	26.8	26.9	27.6	26.9	27.1	27.1	26.8	26.8	26.8
2014	26.7	26.7	27.1	27.3	27.4	27.5	28.0	27.3	27.2	27.2	27.2	27.3	27.2
2015	26.8	27.1	27.2	27.1	27.3	27.4	28.0	27.7	27.6	27.6	27.7	27.7	27.4
2016	27.4	27.7	27.9	27.9	27.9	28.0	28.4	28.4	28.2	28.1	28.2	28.1	28.0
2017	27.6	27.9	28.1	28.2	28.4	28.5	28.7	28.7	28.6	28.6	28.6	28.8	28.4
2018	28.8	29.1	29.2	29.3	29.5	29.6	30.1	30.2	29.9	30.0	30.1	29.9	29.6
Retail Trade													
2010	73.4	72.5	73.2	74.1	75.0	75.2	75.5	76.0	75.0	75.4	76.8	76.7	74.9
2011	72.9	72.2	72.5	73.8	74.8	75.2	76.1	76.4	76.3	76.5	78.6	78.4	75.3
2012	75.1	74.3	74.9	75.4	76.8	77.6	78.1	78.2	77.8	78.2	80.5	80.1	77.3
2013	76.0	75.5	76.1	77.5	78.7	79.3	80.0	80.4	79.8	79.9	81.6	81.6	78.9
2014	78.1	77.4	78.1	79.4	80.6	81.5	81.7	81.8	81.1	81.7	83.6	83.6	80.7
2015	80.4	80.2	81.2	82.3	83.4	84.3	85.1	85.1	84.5	85.1	87.1	87.0	83.8
2016	83.0	82.8	83.3	84.4	84.8	85.7	86.6	86.7	86.4	87.0	88.5	88.1	85.6
2017	85.1	84.4	84.8	85.3	85.8	86.9	87.6	87.7	87.1	87.3	89.1	88.8	86.7
2018	85.8	84.9	85.3	86.2	87.4	88.2	88.7	88.8	88.0	88.1	89.3	89.0	87.5
Transportation and Utilities													
2010	20.5	20.4	20.0	20.1	20.2	20.4	20.5	21.0	21.1	21.2	21.3	21.6	20.7
2011	20.8	20.8	20.8	20.9	20.7	20.7	21.0	21.5	21.8	21.6	21.6	22.0	21.2
2012	21.4	21.2	21.2	20.9	21.0	21.1	21.1	21.8	22.1	22.1	22.0	22.2	21.5
2013	21.5	21.5	21.5	21.0	21.1	21.0	20.9	21.5	21.7	22.0	22.0	22.4	21.5
2014	22.1	22.0	21.8	21.9	21.8	21.7	21.9	22.7	23.1	23.2	23.2	23.7	22.4
2015	23.3	23.0	23.2	23.1	23.1	22.9	23.0	23.3	23.8	24.0	23.9	24.4	23.4
2016	23.5	23.5	23.5	23.4	23.3	23.0	23.0	23.6	24.1	24.1	24.2	24.7	23.7
2017	23.7	23.6	23.7	23.7	23.9	23.8	23.7	24.2	24.5	24.8	25.0	25.6	24.2
2018	24.9	25.0	25.0	25.1	25.0	24.9	24.9	25.8	26.0	25.9	26.1	25.9	25.4
Information													
2010	9.8	9.7	9.7	9.6	9.7	9.7	9.7	9.7	9.5	9.4	9.5	9.5	9.6
2011	9.4	9.3	9.3	9.5	9.6	9.6	9.6	9.6	9.4	9.4	9.4	9.5	9.5
2012	9.4	9.4	9.4	9.3	9.4	9.4	9.5	9.5	9.2	9.3	9.3	9.3	9.4
2013	9.1	9.1	9.3	9.4	9.4	9.4	9.4	9.4	9.1	9.2	9.4	9.3	9.3
2014	9.1	9.2	9.2	9.3	9.4	9.4	9.4	9.5	9.1	9.3	9.5	9.5	9.3
2015	9.1	9.2	9.2	9.2	9.3	9.3	9.3	9.2	9.1	9.3	9.4	9.5	9.3
2016	8.8	8.9	8.9	9.0	9.0	9.0	9.1	9.2	9.0	9.2	9.2	9.3	9.1
2017	9.0	9.0	9.0	8.9	9.0	9.0	9.0	9.0	8.9	8.9	9.0	8.9	9.0
2018	8.9	8.9	8.9	8.9	9.0	9.0	9.0	8.9	8.8	8.8	8.6	8.6	8.9

1. Employment by Industry: Idaho, 2010–2018—*Continued*

(Numbers in thousands, not seasonally adjusted)

Industry and year	January	February	March	April	May	June	July	August	September	October	November	December	Annual average
Financial Activities													
2010	28.7	28.6	28.7	28.9	29.1	29.2	29.7	29.5	29.2	29.4	29.4	29.6	29.2
2011	29.2	29.2	29.2	29.5	29.7	29.9	30.4	30.3	30.3	30.2	30.2	30.3	29.9
2012	29.5	29.5	29.6	30.1	30.3	30.5	30.8	30.8	30.5	30.7	30.7	30.9	30.3
2013	30.4	30.6	30.7	30.8	31.1	31.3	31.4	31.6	31.3	31.5	31.5	31.9	31.2
2014	31.8	32.2	32.4	32.5	32.7	32.8	33.4	33.1	32.9	32.7	32.8	32.8	32.7
2015	32.7	32.7	32.9	33.1	33.2	33.5	34.0	33.7	33.4	33.6	33.4	33.4	33.3
2016	33.1	33.1	33.4	33.4	33.6	34.0	34.6	34.4	34.2	34.4	34.5	34.8	34.0
2017	34.4	34.5	34.7	34.7	35.0	35.2	35.7	35.7	35.3	35.5	35.6	35.8	35.2
2018	35.4	35.6	35.8	36.1	36.5	36.7	37.4	37.1	36.7	36.7	36.6	36.7	36.4
Professional and Business Services													
2010	71.5	72.1	73.1	75.0	75.7	76.0	77.4	78.0	77.1	77.8	77.5	76.7	75.7
2011	74.0	74.0	74.4	75.9	76.7	77.6	78.7	79.6	79.3	78.4	78.0	77.0	77.0
2012	73.1	73.8	75.2	76.1	77.1	78.6	78.9	80.0	79.4	79.2	79.7	77.9	77.4
2013	74.5	75.3	76.9	77.4	79.0	80.7	80.8	81.9	81.1	82.1	82.2	81.6	79.5
2014	78.2	79.5	80.4	81.6	81.8	82.7	82.2	82.9	82.6	82.4	82.2	81.8	81.5
2015	79.7	79.8	80.8	81.8	82.5	83.5	84.9	85.5	84.9	83.6	83.6	82.8	82.8
2016	82.4	83.2	84.9	87.2	87.7	88.7	89.8	89.9	89.2	89.4	89.5	88.4	87.5
2017	87.1	87.8	89.3	90.2	91.6	92.8	92.9	93.3	92.7	91.9	92.1	91.4	91.1
2018	88.8	90.7	91.7	93.6	94.1	95.9	96.5	96.7	95.1	96.2	96.5	95.1	94.2
Education and Health Services													
2010	80.2	82.4	82.9	83.2	83.3	82.9	82.9	81.2	83.5	85.0	85.1	84.9	83.1
2011	84.7	85.3	85.5	85.8	86.1	86.1	85.1	83.6	85.9	86.8	86.9	87.3	85.8
2012	85.9	86.8	87.2	87.2	87.7	87.5	86.6	85.3	87.9	88.8	88.9	89.0	87.4
2013	88.0	89.3	89.6	90.2	90.2	89.4	89.6	88.3	89.0	91.7	92.0	92.0	89.9
2014	91.8	92.6	92.6	93.2	93.3	93.3	92.6	92.6	91.2	92.4	94.3	94.3	94.7	93.0
2015	93.9	95.0	95.6	96.2	96.1	96.1	96.3	94.2	96.5	97.9	98.3	98.5	96.2
2016	97.5	98.7	99.1	98.5	98.9	98.7	98.7	96.9	99.8	100.3	100.9	100.3	99.0
2017	100.9	102.1	103.2	102.1	102.3	102.2	101.7	99.7	102.5	103.5	103.7	103.2	102.3
2018	104.4	105.6	105.9	105.7	106.1	105.6	105.8	104.1	104.5	106.3	106.5	106.5	105.6
Leisure and Hospitality													
2010	54.2	54.3	54.9	56.6	57.8	60.6	62.3	63.2	61.2	57.8	56.1	56.5	58.0
2011	54.6	55.2	55.7	58.0	58.8	61.9	64.3	65.2	63.1	59.0	57.8	58.1	59.3
2012	56.1	57.2	58.2	59.4	61.4	63.7	65.8	66.7	64.8	61.0	59.7	60.0	61.2
2013	58.8	59.1	60.3	61.9	64.0	66.8	68.5	68.5	66.1	63.9	62.1	61.9	63.5
2014	61.0	61.8	63.0	64.0	66.6	70.1	71.4	71.7	68.0	65.5	63.5	64.1	65.9
2015	63.3	63.8	65.1	65.3	68.3	71.8	74.1	74.3	71.7	68.7	66.7	67.7	68.4
2016	67.2	68.3	69.2	69.8	71.8	76.0	78.0	78.3	75.1	72.5	70.6	71.3	72.3
2017	69.8	70.9	72.1	73.3	75.3	79.7	81.1	81.6	78.4	75.3	73.5	74.1	75.4
2018	73.7	74.4	75.5	76.9	78.8	83.1	84.8	84.6	81.8	77.7	75.3	75.5	78.5
Other Services													
2010	20.8	21.0	21.0	20.9	21.0	21.2	21.8	21.5	21.0	20.9	20.8	20.7	21.1
2011	20.5	20.6	20.5	21.0	21.2	21.4	22.0	21.7	21.4	21.2	21.3	21.4	21.2
2012	21.0	21.1	21.2	21.3	21.5	21.8	22.3	22.1	21.7	21.7	21.4	21.4	21.5
2013	21.2	21.4	21.5	21.6	21.9	22.3	22.7	22.9	22.5	21.9	22.0	21.9	22.0
2014	21.7	21.9	22.2	22.4	22.6	23.0	23.5	23.5	23.1	22.7	22.6	22.5	22.6
2015	22.7	22.8	23.0	23.1	23.5	23.9	24.1	23.9	23.6	23.6	23.5	23.6	23.4
2016	23.3	23.5	23.7	23.9	24.2	24.5	25.3	25.0	24.5	24.4	24.3	24.1	24.2
2017	23.9	24.1	24.3	24.5	24.8	25.4	25.5	25.5	25.0	24.8	24.8	24.7	24.8
2018	24.7	24.8	24.9	25.0	25.4	26.1	26.2	26.3	25.6	25.9	25.6	26.0	25.5
Government													
2010	115.0	119.6	120.8	122.2	125.5	120.3	112.4	112.5	118.2	119.8	118.8	118.5	118.6
2011	113.2	118.7	119.3	120.1	121.1	117.3	111.2	111.3	117.6	119.3	118.8	118.8	117.2
2012	113.3	117.8	118.2	119.1	120.8	117.0	110.3	110.8	118.4	120.9	120.3	119.8	117.2
2013	115.5	119.7	120.1	119.6	121.1	117.5	109.9	109.6	117.6	120.3	119.5	118.5	117.4
2014	115.2	119.4	120.5	120.4	121.1	118.1	111.7	111.5	118.6	121.5	120.9	119.6	118.2
2015	116.0	119.9	120.8	121.1	122.9	119.2	112.8	111.5	120.3	122.7	122.1	121.2	119.2
2016	117.4	121.7	122.8	122.3	123.6	121.3	115.4	114.5	122.8	124.8	124.1	122.8	121.1
2017	120.2	123.2	124.2	124.7	126.4	124.1	116.7	116.1	124.3	126.9	126.2	125.6	123.2
2018	121.5	125.8	126.5	126.6	127.7	125.0	118.3	117.6	125.8	128.8	127.5	127.1	124.9

2. Average Weekly Hours by Selected Industry: Idaho, 2014–2018

(Not seasonally adjusted)

Industry and year	January	February	March	April	May	June	July	August	September	October	November	December	Annual average
Total Private													
2014	32.5	33.5	33.5	33.0	32.9	34.1	33.3	33.9	33.5	33.3	34.0	33.3	33.4
2015	32.6	33.7	33.7	33.3	33.4	33.6	33.9	34.5	33.2	33.2	33.5	32.7	33.4
2016	32.5	32.4	32.4	32.8	33.6	33.1	33.3	33.2	32.9	33.7	32.8	32.3	32.9
2017	32.3	32.5	32.8	33.9	33.5	33.7	34.4	34.0	33.9	34.5	33.7	33.6	33.6
2018	33.1	33.4	33.3	34.3	33.9	34.2	34.8	34.2	34.7	33.7	33.7	34.0	33.9
Goods-Producing													
2014	37.6	38.9	38.7	39.3	37.9	39.0	39.0	40.0	40.1	39.4	39.2	38.8	39.0
2015	38.5	39.2	39.4	39.4	39.4	39.5	39.5	39.8	37.7	38.5	38.2	37.4	38.9
2016	37.8	37.1	37.4	38.1	38.7	38.9	38.9	39.0	38.8	39.5	38.9	37.2	38.4
2017	37.2	38.0	38.5	39.5	40.2	40.0	39.9	40.2	40.0	40.4	39.7	38.8	39.4
2018	37.7	39.1	38.0	38.8	39.5	39.8	39.5	39.8	40.6	39.1	39.2	38.9	39.2
Construction													
2014	31.7	31.2	33.0	35.3	36.0	37.0	37.5	38.4	37.8	38.2	36.8	36.1	35.9
2015	35.3	36.3	36.6	37.8	38.6	38.8	37.7	38.3	35.7	36.4	35.8	34.8	36.9
2016	35.8	35.0	35.4	36.5	37.4	38.1	37.9	38.1	38.0	37.7	37.4	35.6	37.0
2017	33.9	35.4	36.6	38.4	39.7	39.0	38.7	39.7	38.8	39.5	37.4	36.6	37.9
2018	34.5	36.4	36.3	37.1	38.8	39.4	38.9	39.6	40.5	38.6	38.9	37.6	38.1
Manufacturing													
2014	40.1	41.6	40.9	41.0	39.0	40.4	40.2	41.2	41.5	40.3	40.4	40.0	40.5
2015	39.9	40.2	40.4	39.8	39.5	39.4	40.0	40.3	38.8	39.7	39.6	39.0	39.7
2016	39.1	38.4	38.9	39.3	39.6	39.6	39.3	39.4	39.3	39.8	39.3	37.5	39.1
2017	39.0	39.2	39.5	39.7	40.1	40.4	40.3	40.3	40.7	40.9	41.2	40.2	40.1
2018	39.9	41.1	39.8	40.8	40.4	40.4	40.1	39.9	40.7	39.5	39.4	40.2	40.2
Trade, Transportation, and Utilities													
2014	32.0	32.5	32.7	32.9	33.3	34.1	33.8	34.5	34.1	34.0	34.5	33.8	33.5
2015	33.0	33.7	33.9	33.4	33.9	34.0	34.3	34.6	33.8	33.2	33.4	33.5	33.7
2016	32.3	32.4	32.5	32.8	33.6	33.2	33.2	33.0	32.8	33.3	32.4	32.6	32.8
2017	32.1	32.5	32.7	34.0	33.6	34.0	34.5	34.0	33.8	34.8	33.6	33.8	33.6
2018	33.2	33.6	33.9	34.6	34.3	34.6	35.5	34.7	34.9	34.2	33.9	34.5	34.3
Financial Activities													
2014	36.0	38.1	37.1	34.9	35.6	37.5	35.3	36.3	36.3	36.1	38.6	36.9	36.5
2015	37.2	39.6	38.4	38.6	38.1	37.9	37.8	38.8	37.1	37.6	38.8	36.9	38.0
2016	37.8	37.5	37.1	37.2	38.7	37.0	36.7	36.4	36.9	37.8	37.6	37.0	37.3
2017	38.5	37.3	37.8	39.3	38.0	37.6	39.6	38.2	38.5	39.6	38.4	38.6	38.5
2018	38.1	38.2	38.6	39.8	38.1	38.2	39.6	38.6	38.9	38.4	38.5	39.1	38.7
Professional and Business Services													
2014	34.3	35.7	35.7	35.1	35.6	36.9	35.7	36.5	36.0	36.1	37.3	36.3	35.9
2015	35.8	37.0	36.9	36.4	36.0	36.3	36.0	37.3	36.1	36.0	36.5	35.5	36.3
2016	35.3	35.5	35.6	35.6	36.1	35.6	36.3	36.0	36.3	36.6	35.7	35.1	35.8
2017	35.6	35.4	35.7	36.6	35.5	35.3	36.0	35.4	35.8	36.1	35.0	35.0	35.6
2018	34.7	34.9	35.2	36.2	35.6	35.4	36.1	35.3	36.3	34.5	34.7	34.9	35.3
Education and Health Services													
2014	30.5	31.0	31.0	30.3	30.1	31.1	29.9	30.0	29.7	29.5	30.7	30.2	30.3
2015	29.2	30.1	30.0	29.7	29.4	29.7	29.8	30.5	29.6	29.3	30.2	29.2	29.7
2016	28.9	28.6	28.8	28.9	29.6	29.4	29.7	29.7	29.5	30.4	29.6	29.5	29.4
2017	30.1	30.0	29.9	30.4	29.6	30.3	30.8	30.4	31.2	30.9	30.8	30.3	30.4
2018	30.7	30.2	30.3	31.2	30.6	30.8	31.0	30.6	31.0	30.7	30.7	31.2	30.8
Leisure and Hospitality													
2014	24.3	25.7	25.8	25.0	24.8	26.3	25.5	26.0	24.4	24.5	24.6	23.8	25.1
2015	23.1	24.6	24.7	23.4	24.0	24.7	26.2	26.6	24.7	24.6	24.8	23.9	24.7
2016	23.5	24.3	23.9	24.1	25.5	24.6	25.2	24.7	23.3	24.2	23.1	22.8	24.1
2017	21.3	21.8	22.4	23.0	23.0	23.5	24.8	24.3	22.9	23.6	22.4	22.3	23.0
2018	22.2	22.3	22.5	23.8	23.3	23.9	25.2	24.6	24.3	22.5	22.4	23.0	23.4

3. Average Hourly Earnings by Selected Industry: Idaho, 2014–2018

(Dollars, not seasonally adjusted)

Industry and year	January	February	March	April	May	June	July	August	September	October	November	December	Annual average
Total Private													
2014	21.10	21.32	21.24	21.21	21.24	21.09	21.19	21.31	21.53	21.68	21.78	21.71	21.37
2015	22.01	22.11	21.85	22.04	22.01	21.90	21.83	22.20	22.06	22.25	22.34	22.39	22.08
2016	22.60	22.52	22.45	22.71	22.49	22.08	22.09	22.16	22.32	22.49	22.41	22.44	22.39
2017	22.85	22.62	22.40	22.57	22.43	22.23	22.50	22.30	22.40	22.62	22.49	22.61	22.50
2018	22.62	22.75	22.72	22.95	22.79	22.70	22.89	22.71	23.08	23.02	22.87	23.09	22.85
Goods-Producing													
2014	22.84	22.88	22.44	22.41	22.63	22.38	23.04	22.47	22.80	22.92	23.05	23.04	22.74
2015	23.32	23.58	23.59	23.94	23.86	24.03	23.81	23.82	23.58	23.34	23.01	23.87	23.65
2016	23.47	22.92	22.72	23.02	22.63	22.46	22.17	22.08	22.24	22.30	22.45	22.53	22.57
2017	22.69	22.32	22.50	22.47	22.55	22.64	23.05	22.47	22.77	23.10	23.05	23.43	22.76
2018	23.08	23.14	23.48	23.58	23.66	23.58	23.97	23.88	23.76	23.56	23.83	24.08	23.64
Construction													
2014	20.60	21.07	20.28	19.83	20.00	20.05	19.88	19.92	20.26	20.81	21.30	21.54	20.45
2015	21.12	21.25	21.40	21.10	21.16	21.10	20.42	20.77	20.96	21.00	21.20	21.75	21.09
2016	21.42	20.53	20.92	21.32	20.79	20.86	20.69	20.69	21.37	21.41	21.82	22.12	21.16
2017	22.78	22.64	22.88	22.42	22.72	22.93	23.02	22.46	22.72	23.19	22.76	23.54	22.84
2018	23.44	24.11	24.12	24.23	24.47	24.23	24.94	24.68	24.48	24.36	24.78	24.83	24.42
Manufacturing													
2014	23.45	23.40	23.00	23.04	23.22	22.86	23.69	23.00	23.31	23.33	23.31	23.27	23.24
2015	23.72	24.06	24.11	25.00	24.93	25.31	25.41	25.30	24.90	24.49	24.17	25.07	24.71
2016	24.71	24.40	23.80	24.06	23.74	23.38	22.94	22.72	22.42	22.51	22.41	22.25	23.27
2017	22.15	21.80	21.99	22.41	22.18	22.03	22.07	21.49	21.95	22.29	22.57	22.88	22.15
2018	22.39	22.05	22.45	22.55	22.48	22.60	22.66	22.70	22.68	22.36	22.54	23.00	22.54
Trade, Transportation, and Utilities													
2014	18.16	18.49	18.88	18.35	18.81	18.65	18.46	18.57	19.05	19.48	19.23	19.32	18.80
2015	19.84	19.47	19.24	18.95	19.16	19.07	19.36	19.89	19.69	19.87	20.05	19.64	19.52
2016	19.93	19.86	19.89	19.80	19.57	19.18	19.20	19.17	19.30	19.52	18.96	18.80	19.43
2017	19.56	19.11	19.04	19.19	19.15	18.91	19.49	19.51	19.50	19.43	19.24	19.30	19.29
2018	19.31	19.62	19.63	20.24	20.17	20.01	20.28	19.99	21.00	20.90	20.40	20.61	20.19
Financial Activities													
2014	20.59	20.82	21.16	21.87	21.73	22.30	22.37	23.93	22.82	23.70	24.71	24.25	22.54
2015	25.11	26.15	25.86	26.14	26.77	25.62	25.85	27.61	25.63	25.67	26.65	25.80	26.08
2016	26.61	26.51	25.46	25.74	25.53	24.56	24.55	25.38	25.01	25.73	25.50	25.07	25.47
2017	25.86	26.37	25.30	25.06	25.31	25.46	24.87	25.44	25.54	25.58	25.22	24.83	25.40
2018	25.23	25.65	25.16	25.23	24.70	24.84	25.22	25.22	24.88	24.83	24.56	25.15	25.05
Professional and Business Services													
2014	27.24	27.90	28.13	28.96	28.64	28.50	28.47	28.70	28.71	28.52	28.47	28.44	28.40
2015	28.72	29.17	28.60	29.03	28.97	28.85	28.84	29.15	29.74	30.09	29.91	29.68	29.23
2016	30.53	31.02	30.93	31.37	30.95	30.52	30.68	31.14	30.67	30.54	30.41	30.20	30.75
2017	30.23	29.81	29.79	29.81	29.28	28.81	29.11	28.40	28.16	28.74	28.27	28.35	29.05
2018	29.01	28.99	28.53	29.02	28.40	28.56	28.68	28.07	28.58	28.55	28.94	29.51	28.73
Education and Health Services													
2014	21.42	21.82	21.30	21.22	21.18	21.40	21.99	22.06	22.17	22.03	22.17	22.65	21.78
2015	22.39	22.11	21.92	21.92	21.52	21.50	21.44	21.46	21.49	21.50	21.53	21.79	21.70
2016	21.75	21.92	22.18	22.61	22.56	22.37	22.57	22.13	22.72	22.42	22.61	23.13	22.42
2017	23.47	23.59	22.69	23.09	23.00	22.78	23.18	22.39	22.14	22.41	22.82	23.30	22.90
2018	23.12	23.32	23.53	23.26	23.20	23.25	23.59	23.23	22.82	22.34	22.22	22.19	23.00
Leisure and Hospitality													
2014	12.19	12.15	12.12	11.96	12.00	11.82	11.87	11.89	11.86	11.80	11.91	12.01	11.96
2015	12.08	12.15	12.13	12.17	11.97	11.86	11.83	11.96	11.97	11.85	11.83	12.15	11.99
2016	12.05	12.14	12.11	12.29	12.20	12.11	12.26	12.26	12.37	12.48	12.33	12.68	12.27
2017	13.19	13.04	12.97	13.00	12.93	12.70	12.99	12.94	13.06	13.20	13.00	13.24	13.02
2018	12.82	12.90	12.85	12.70	12.72	12.73	12.93	13.23	13.49	13.66	13.37	13.92	13.11

4. Average Weekly Earnings by Selected Industry: 2014–2018

(Dollars, not seasonally adjusted)

Industry and year	January	February	March	April	May	June	July	August	September	October	November	December	Annual average
Total Private													
2014	685.75	714.22	711.54	699.93	698.80	719.17	705.63	722.41	721.26	721.94	740.52	722.94	713.76
2015	717.53	745.11	736.35	733.93	735.13	735.84	740.04	765.90	732.39	738.70	748.39	732.15	737.47
2016	734.50	729.65	727.38	744.89	755.66	730.85	735.60	735.71	734.33	757.91	735.05	724.81	736.63
2017	738.06	735.15	734.72	765.12	751.41	749.15	774.00	758.20	759.36	780.39	757.91	759.70	756.00
2018	748.72	759.85	756.58	787.19	772.58	776.34	796.57	776.68	800.88	775.77	770.72	785.06	774.62
Goods-Producing													
2014	858.78	890.03	868.43	880.71	857.68	872.82	898.56	898.80	914.28	903.05	903.56	893.95	886.86
2015	897.82	924.34	929.45	943.24	940.08	949.19	940.50	948.04	888.97	898.59	878.98	892.74	919.99
2016	887.17	850.33	849.73	877.06	875.78	873.69	862.41	861.12	862.91	880.85	873.31	838.12	866.69
2017	844.07	848.16	866.25	887.57	906.51	905.60	919.70	903.29	910.80	933.24	915.09	909.08	896.74
2018	870.12	904.77	892.24	914.90	934.57	938.48	946.82	950.42	964.66	921.20	934.14	936.71	926.69
Construction													
2014	653.02	657.38	669.24	700.00	720.00	741.85	745.50	764.93	765.83	794.94	783.84	777.59	734.16
2015	745.54	771.38	783.24	797.58	816.78	818.68	769.83	795.49	748.27	764.40	758.96	756.90	778.22
2016	766.84	718.55	740.57	778.18	777.55	794.77	784.15	788.29	812.06	807.16	816.07	787.47	782.92
2017	772.24	801.46	837.41	860.93	901.98	894.27	890.87	891.66	881.54	916.01	851.22	861.56	865.64
2018	808.68	877.60	875.56	898.93	949.44	954.66	970.17	977.33	991.44	940.30	963.94	933.61	930.40
Manufacturing													
2014	940.35	973.44	940.70	944.64	905.58	923.54	952.34	947.60	967.37	940.20	941.72	930.80	941.22
2015	946.43	967.21	974.04	995.00	984.74	997.21	1,016.40	1,019.59	966.12	972.25	957.13	977.73	980.99
2016	966.16	936.96	925.82	945.56	940.10	925.85	901.54	895.17	881.11	895.90	880.71	834.38	909.86
2017	863.85	854.56	868.61	889.68	889.42	890.01	889.42	866.05	893.37	911.66	929.88	919.78	888.22
2018	893.36	906.26	893.51	920.04	908.19	913.04	908.67	905.73	923.08	883.22	888.08	924.60	906.11
Trade, Transportation, and Utilities													
2014	581.12	600.93	617.38	603.72	626.37	635.97	623.95	640.67	649.61	662.32	663.44	653.02	629.80
2015	654.72	656.14	652.24	632.93	649.52	648.38	664.05	688.19	665.52	659.68	669.67	657.94	657.82
2016	643.74	643.46	646.43	649.44	657.55	636.78	637.44	632.61	633.04	650.02	614.30	612.88	637.30
2017	627.88	621.08	622.61	652.46	643.44	642.94	672.41	663.34	659.10	676.16	646.46	652.34	648.14
2018	641.09	659.23	665.46	700.30	691.83	692.35	719.94	693.65	732.90	714.78	691.56	711.05	692.52
Financial Activities													
2014	741.24	793.24	785.04	763.26	773.59	836.25	789.66	868.66	828.37	855.57	953.81	894.83	822.71
2015	934.09	1,035.54	993.02	1,009.00	1,019.94	971.00	977.13	1,071.27	950.87	965.19	1,034.02	952.02	991.04
2016	1,005.86	994.13	944.57	957.53	988.01	908.72	900.99	923.83	922.87	972.59	958.80	927.59	950.03
2017	995.61	983.60	956.34	984.86	961.78	957.30	984.85	971.81	983.29	1,012.97	968.45	958.44	977.90
2018	961.26	979.83	971.18	1,004.15	941.07	948.89	998.71	973.49	967.83	953.47	945.56	983.37	969.44
Professional and Business Services													
2014	934.33	996.03	1,004.24	1,016.50	1,019.58	1,051.65	1,016.38	1,047.55	1,033.56	1,029.57	1,061.93	1,032.37	1,019.56
2015	1,028.18	1,079.29	1,055.34	1,056.69	1,042.92	1,047.26	1,038.24	1,087.30	1,073.61	1,083.24	1,091.72	1,053.64	1,061.05
2016	1,077.71	1,101.21	1,101.11	1,116.77	1,117.30	1,086.51	1,113.68	1,121.04	1,113.32	1,117.76	1,085.64	1,060.02	1,100.85
2017	1,076.19	1,055.27	1,063.50	1,091.05	1,039.44	1,016.99	1,047.96	1,005.36	1,008.13	1,037.51	989.45	992.25	1,034.18
2018	1,006.65	1,011.75	1,004.26	1,050.52	1,011.04	1,011.02	1,035.35	990.87	1,037.45	984.98	1,004.22	1,029.90	1,014.17
Education and Health Services													
2014	653.31	676.42	660.30	642.97	637.52	665.54	657.50	661.80	658.45	649.89	680.62	684.03	659.93
2015	653.79	665.51	651.90	651.02	632.69	638.55	638.91	654.53	636.10	629.95	650.21	636.27	644.49
2016	628.58	626.91	638.78	653.43	667.78	657.68	670.33	657.26	670.24	681.57	669.26	682.34	659.15
2017	706.45	707.70	678.43	701.94	680.80	690.23	713.94	680.66	690.77	692.47	702.86	705.99	696.16
2018	709.78	704.26	712.96	725.71	709.92	716.10	731.29	710.84	707.42	685.84	682.15	692.33	708.40
Leisure and Hospitality													
2014	296.22	312.26	312.70	299.00	297.60	310.87	302.69	309.14	289.38	289.10	292.99	285.84	300.20
2015	279.05	298.89	299.61	284.78	287.28	292.94	309.95	318.14	295.66	291.51	293.38	290.39	296.15
2016	283.18	295.00	289.43	296.19	311.10	297.91	308.95	302.82	288.22	302.02	284.82	289.10	295.71
2017	280.95	284.27	290.53	299.00	297.39	298.45	322.15	314.44	299.07	311.52	291.20	295.25	299.46
2018	284.60	287.67	289.13	302.26	296.38	304.25	325.84	325.46	327.81	307.35	299.49	320.16	306.77

ILLINOIS
At a Glance

Population:
  2010 census: 12,830,632
  2018 estimate: 12,741,080

Percent change in population:
  2010–2018: -0.7%

Percent change in total nonfarm employment:
  2010–2018: 9.1%

Industry with the largest growth in employment, 2010–2018 (percent):
  Transportation and utilities, 25.8%

Industry with the largest decline or smallest growth in employment, 2010–2018 (percent):
  Mining and logging, -14.3%

Civilian labor force:
  2010: 6,625,321
  2018: 6,469,668

Unemployment rate and rank among states (highest to lowest):
  2010: 10.4%, 11th
  2018: 4.3%, 11th

Over-the-year change in unemployment rates:
  2016–2017: -0.9%
  2017–2018: -0.6%

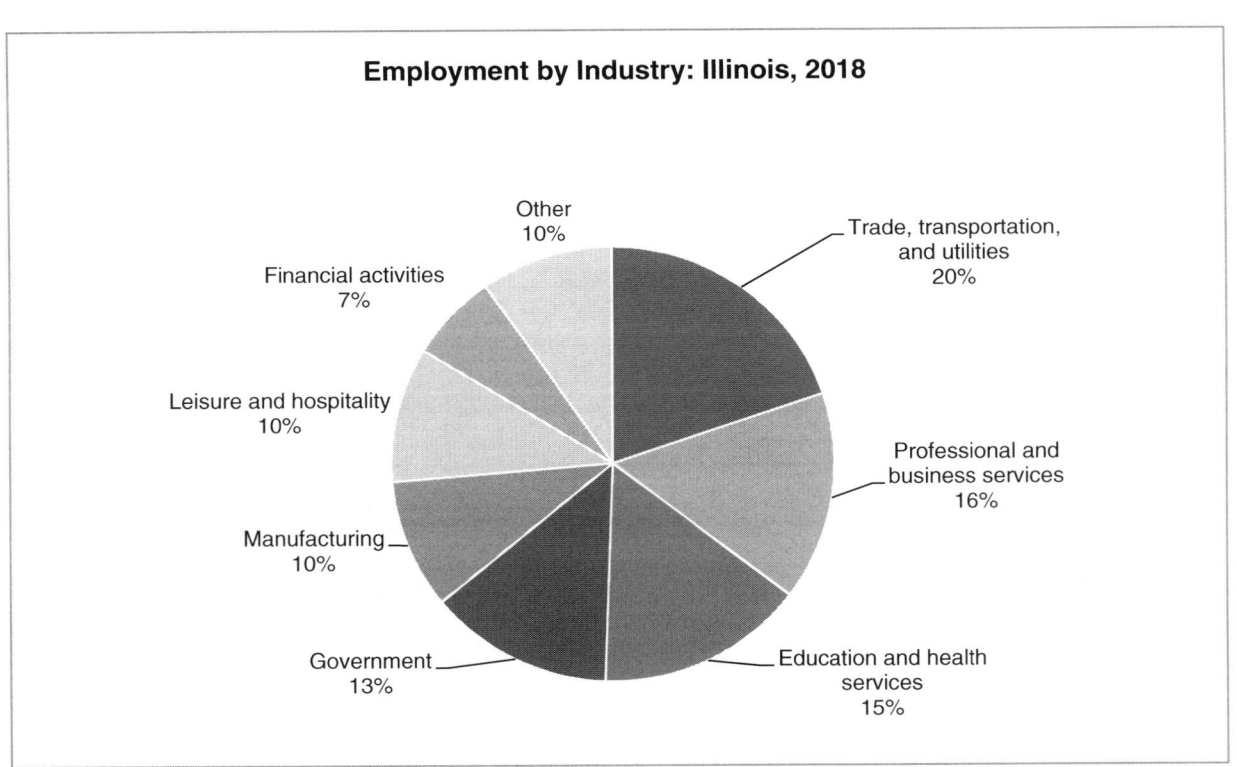

Employment by Industry: Illinois, 2018

- Other 10%
- Trade, transportation, and utilities 20%
- Financial activities 7%
- Professional and business services 16%
- Leisure and hospitality 10%
- Manufacturing 10%
- Education and health services 15%
- Government 13%

1. Employment by Industry: Illinois, 2010–2018

(Numbers in thousands, not seasonally adjusted)

Industry and year	January	February	March	April	May	June	July	August	September	October	November	December	Annual average
Total Nonfarm													
2010	5,461.9	5,484.2	5,517.2	5,595.8	5,654.9	5,661.5	5,595.1	5,622.2	5,651.0	5,686.5	5,697.8	5,687.2	5,609.6
2011	5,526.1	5,546.3	5,590.7	5,667.6	5,702.6	5,721.7	5,680.5	5,695.3	5,728.1	5,741.5	5,751.9	5,746.7	5,674.9
2012	5,596.1	5,620.3	5,673.3	5,731.4	5,775.9	5,799.1	5,747.3	5,768.1	5,807.7	5,815.7	5,836.1	5,824.2	5,749.6
2013	5,658.1	5,689.3	5,723.1	5,771.7	5,832.8	5,851.9	5,803.4	5,825.3	5,855.3	5,867.3	5,884.1	5,880.9	5,803.6
2014	5,712.0	5,734.6	5,778.1	5,855.0	5,915.9	5,935.5	5,883.3	5,900.2	5,928.6	5,961.7	5,971.8	5,969.9	5,878.9
2015	5,790.1	5,820.1	5,853.1	5,945.9	6,011.4	6,030.9	5,988.6	5,991.7	6,019.8	6,056.9	6,057.0	6,051.8	5,968.1
2016	5,880.1	5,901.9	5,933.5	6,010.1	6,040.8	6,062.0	6,027.1	6,031.9	6,063.6	6,090.1	6,102.7	6,084.4	6,019.0
2017	5,912.3	5,938.7	5,982.1	6,035.0	6,086.8	6,125.3	6,072.3	6,088.3	6,109.8	6,126.8	6,146.3	6,137.5	6,063.4
2018	5,962.6	5,994.6	6,046.8	6,078.5	6,134.5	6,171.1	6,132.1	6,142.2	6,158.9	6,197.8	6,205.9	6,183.8	6,117.4
Total Private													
2010	4,617.8	4,617.8	4,651.1	4,724.0	4,768.9	4,805.6	4,789.0	4,813.4	4,801.4	4,827.9	4,838.0	4,834.4	4,757.4
2011	4,696.8	4,696.2	4,739.6	4,811.3	4,848.2	4,886.9	4,882.4	4,902.6	4,892.5	4,897.3	4,904.6	4,904.5	4,838.6
2012	4,776.7	4,780.2	4,830.3	4,884.7	4,929.3	4,971.3	4,960.6	4,982.0	4,970.7	4,969.9	4,987.9	4,981.0	4,918.7
2013	4,837.8	4,847.7	4,881.2	4,927.7	4,985.7	5,025.0	5,016.9	5,041.4	5,020.6	5,030.8	5,044.6	5,043.9	4,975.3
2014	4,901.4	4,905.9	4,946.9	5,014.8	5,073.2	5,110.6	5,096.7	5,116.3	5,092.9	5,119.2	5,129.6	5,128.4	5,053.0
2015	4,976.4	4,984.9	5,016.7	5,104.0	5,168.3	5,203.6	5,198.3	5,205.1	5,184.0	5,212.8	5,215.5	5,209.3	5,139.9
2016	5,064.8	5,068.5	5,095.8	5,170.8	5,202.8	5,231.2	5,234.7	5,243.9	5,222.9	5,251.0	5,262.4	5,237.7	5,190.5
2017	5,098.0	5,105.2	5,145.6	5,197.2	5,249.4	5,294.9	5,280.2	5,296.0	5,269.5	5,288.9	5,306.7	5,297.8	5,235.8
2018	5,151.4	5,164.7	5,211.2	5,244.5	5,298.7	5,342.6	5,342.5	5,351.3	5,319.1	5,359.4	5,364.8	5,342.8	5,291.1
Goods Producing													
2010	731.4	729.9	740.1	761.2	771.2	783.0	779.0	790.3	788.3	791.9	786.4	771.7	768.7
2011	744.0	743.0	755.4	773.5	784.6	797.1	799.8	802.6	796.6	793.7	788.3	777.1	779.6
2012	750.0	749.4	761.8	775.9	784.5	796.9	801.2	802.1	799.6	797.9	791.1	781.8	782.7
2013	753.2	753.7	759.7	768.5	783.4	794.7	797.1	799.0	795.2	794.1	791.6	778.9	780.8
2014	753.1	753.1	765.1	780.3	794.4	806.6	809.8	812.5	809.6	812.5	808.0	800.4	792.1
2015	771.5	771.7	780.8	798.3	811.7	822.2	823.6	823.8	821.0	819.5	813.2	803.2	805.0
2016	775.6	775.8	785.4	799.2	806.8	817.4	818.2	817.3	812.8	811.5	807.8	792.5	801.7
2017	766.7	768.4	778.7	793.0	806.8	821.2	822.5	823.8	820.7	820.8	817.5	808.8	804.1
2018	783.6	787.5	801.7	812.6	827.4	840.2	841.4	841.0	837.5	842.4	830.9	815.7	821.8
Service-Providing													
2010	4,730.5	4,754.3	4,777.1	4,834.6	4,883.7	4,878.5	4,816.1	4,831.9	4,862.7	4,894.6	4,911.4	4,915.5	4,840.9
2011	4,782.1	4,803.3	4,835.3	4,894.1	4,918.0	4,924.6	4,880.7	4,892.7	4,931.5	4,947.8	4,963.6	4,969.6	4,895.3
2012	4,846.1	4,870.9	4,911.5	4,955.5	4,991.4	5,002.2	4,946.1	4,966.0	5,008.1	5,017.8	5,045.0	5,042.4	4,966.9
2013	4,904.9	4,935.6	4,963.4	5,003.2	5,049.4	5,057.2	5,006.3	5,026.3	5,060.1	5,073.2	5,092.5	5,102.0	5,022.8
2014	4,958.9	4,981.5	5,013.0	5,074.7	5,121.5	5,128.9	5,073.5	5,087.7	5,119.0	5,149.2	5,163.8	5,169.5	5,086.8
2015	5,018.6	5,048.4	5,072.3	5,147.6	5,199.7	5,208.7	5,165.0	5,167.9	5,198.8	5,237.4	5,243.8	5,248.6	5,163.1
2016	5,104.5	5,126.1	5,148.1	5,210.9	5,234.0	5,244.6	5,208.9	5,214.6	5,250.8	5,278.6	5,294.9	5,291.9	5,217.3
2017	5,145.6	5,170.3	5,203.4	5,242.0	5,280.0	5,304.1	5,249.8	5,264.5	5,289.1	5,306.0	5,328.8	5,328.7	5,259.4
2018	5,179.0	5,207.1	5,245.1	5,265.9	5,307.1	5,330.9	5,290.7	5,301.2	5,321.4	5,355.4	5,375.0	5,368.1	5,295.6
Mining and Logging													
2010	8.4	8.4	8.5	9.0	9.1	9.3	9.5	9.4	9.6	9.6	9.5	9.4	9.1
2011	9.0	8.8	9.0	9.3	9.5	9.7	10.0	10.1	10.1	10.1	10.1	9.8	9.6
2012	9.6	9.6	9.9	10.3	10.3	10.4	10.6	10.6	10.4	10.2	10.2	10.0	10.2
2013	9.6	9.5	9.3	9.4	9.7	9.9	10.0	9.9	9.8	9.8	9.8	9.6	9.7
2014	9.4	9.2	9.5	9.7	10.1	10.2	10.1	10.2	10.3	10.2	10.2	10.2	9.9
2015	9.6	9.4	9.4	9.5	9.7	9.7	9.6	9.6	9.2	9.0	8.8	8.6	9.3
2016	8.2	8.0	7.9	8.0	8.1	8.2	8.0	8.2	8.1	8.1	8.2	7.8	8.1
2017	7.6	7.6	7.8	8.0	7.9	8.0	8.0	7.9	7.8	7.8	7.8	7.7	7.8
2018	7.4	7.3	7.5	7.7	7.9	8.0	8.1	8.1	8.0	8.1	8.0	7.7	7.8
Construction													
2010	172.5	169.9	178.9	196.6	203.5	210.9	206.6	215.1	213.4	214.0	207.1	190.6	198.3
2011	168.9	167.7	177.2	192.3	201.7	209.5	212.4	214.0	210.2	206.3	200.1	188.7	195.8
2012	166.1	163.9	173.0	185.0	191.8	199.2	202.5	203.1	201.7	202.1	194.8	186.2	189.1
2013	164.4	164.6	170.1	180.6	194.1	201.3	207.1	208.2	207.4	206.8	202.0	189.8	191.4
2014	168.8	168.4	177.3	192.8	204.2	212.4	217.6	219.4	218.8	220.4	215.0	205.6	201.7
2015	182.3	181.8	190.0	208.8	219.1	225.4	228.5	230.1	229.4	229.8	224.1	214.0	213.6
2016	192.4	192.2	202.1	215.8	222.5	230.8	233.0	233.3	231.7	231.9	226.7	211.7	218.7
2017	191.4	194.7	202.5	214.7	225.3	232.5	234.2	235.2	233.7	233.7	228.4	217.4	220.3
2018	197.3	198.3	210.6	219.3	231.6	240.5	241.2	241.0	239.9	241.6	231.4	216.4	225.8

1. Employment by Industry: Illinois, 2010–2018—*Continued*

(Numbers in thousands, not seasonally adjusted)

Industry and year	January	February	March	April	May	June	July	August	September	October	November	December	Annual average
Manufacturing													
2010	550.5	551.6	552.7	555.6	558.6	562.8	562.9	565.8	565.3	568.3	569.8	571.7	561.3
2011	566.1	566.5	569.2	571.9	573.4	577.9	577.4	578.5	576.3	577.3	578.1	578.6	574.3
2012	574.3	575.9	578.9	580.6	582.4	587.3	588.1	588.4	587.5	585.6	586.1	585.6	583.4
2013	579.2	579.6	580.3	578.5	579.6	583.5	580.0	580.9	578.0	577.5	579.8	579.5	579.7
2014	574.9	575.5	578.3	577.8	580.1	584.0	582.1	582.9	580.5	581.9	582.8	584.6	580.5
2015	579.6	580.5	581.4	580.0	582.9	587.1	585.5	584.1	582.4	580.7	580.3	580.6	582.1
2016	575.0	575.6	575.4	575.4	576.2	578.4	577.2	575.8	573.0	571.5	572.9	573.0	575.0
2017	567.7	566.1	568.4	570.3	573.6	580.7	580.3	580.7	579.2	579.3	581.3	583.7	575.9
2018	578.9	581.9	583.6	585.6	587.9	591.7	592.1	591.9	589.6	592.7	591.5	591.6	588.3
Trade, Transportation, and Utilities													
2010	1,107.7	1,098.0	1,102.3	1,112.1	1,121.4	1,126.5	1,122.1	1,125.9	1,122.6	1,131.6	1,149.8	1,163.2	1,123.6
2011	1,123.7	1,114.5	1,120.0	1,131.0	1,137.9	1,143.3	1,139.6	1,143.7	1,143.3	1,150.0	1,169.1	1,183.0	1,141.6
2012	1,139.2	1,128.2	1,136.4	1,141.0	1,149.9	1,153.5	1,151.4	1,154.5	1,153.2	1,160.8	1,186.3	1,192.5	1,153.9
2013	1,145.6	1,136.5	1,140.6	1,147.1	1,157.4	1,164.1	1,161.1	1,165.9	1,162.8	1,168.8	1,190.4	1,203.4	1,162.0
2014	1,156.3	1,145.2	1,152.1	1,161.3	1,173.7	1,181.0	1,176.7	1,181.6	1,179.4	1,188.0	1,210.3	1,222.8	1,177.4
2015	1,175.1	1,167.0	1,172.6	1,184.4	1,197.0	1,204.8	1,200.1	1,203.7	1,201.7	1,210.7	1,230.0	1,238.8	1,198.8
2016	1,190.8	1,183.8	1,187.3	1,200.0	1,204.4	1,207.0	1,206.4	1,208.5	1,203.8	1,219.4	1,238.9	1,252.0	1,208.5
2017	1,202.4	1,191.6	1,194.0	1,197.2	1,202.6	1,209.6	1,206.0	1,208.9	1,206.7	1,214.5	1,241.2	1,251.5	1,210.5
2018	1,206.8	1,194.4	1,199.9	1,202.2	1,210.9	1,216.6	1,215.0	1,213.1	1,206.0	1,222.1	1,247.0	1,258.9	1,216.1
Wholesale Trade													
2010	279.8	279.0	280.6	283.0	284.3	285.8	285.4	285.4	284.2	284.9	284.6	284.8	283.5
2011	281.8	281.8	283.5	286.2	287.3	289.6	289.9	289.4	288.5	289.0	288.6	289.6	287.1
2012	286.6	286.9	289.8	291.1	292.6	295.0	293.8	293.4	292.7	293.3	293.6	293.8	291.9
2013	290.6	290.6	292.3	293.9	295.7	298.3	297.2	296.1	295.3	295.8	296.3	296.6	294.9
2014	292.9	292.9	294.1	294.8	296.9	298.5	297.4	296.8	295.2	297.1	297.8	297.4	296.0
2015	293.6	292.9	294.5	296.8	299.1	301.0	299.7	298.4	296.8	296.6	295.9	296.0	296.8
2016	291.0	290.9	291.6	294.4	294.6	296.6	296.2	295.3	295.1	295.0	295.0	295.2	294.2
2017	290.6	291.1	292.1	293.9	295.3	297.9	297.3	295.8	294.4	295.5	295.4	296.4	294.6
2018	291.9	292.8	294.5	295.2	296.2	298.3	298.1	296.7	295.6	297.7	298.7	300.2	296.3
Retail Trade													
2010	581.1	572.2	574.7	579.4	585.8	591.3	590.2	590.4	583.7	590.4	607.4	617.3	588.7
2011	587.2	577.7	580.4	587.0	591.4	596.0	594.8	597.3	592.5	598.3	616.5	626.0	595.4
2012	593.2	582.1	585.6	587.2	592.5	596.9	596.4	595.9	591.7	598.6	622.3	625.0	597.3
2013	592.9	583.8	585.5	587.8	594.7	602.0	600.8	601.8	597.5	602.9	621.5	630.6	600.2
2014	595.6	585.1	588.6	595.8	602.7	609.7	608.2	608.5	604.5	610.8	629.5	637.1	606.3
2015	603.5	596.3	599.7	605.8	613.0	619.7	618.5	619.8	616.6	623.0	639.9	644.1	616.7
2016	613.0	606.6	607.8	615.4	618.4	621.9	621.9	621.7	613.1	621.1	637.5	643.5	620.2
2017	615.2	605.4	605.5	607.9	609.5	615.1	612.5	610.7	602.9	608.5	628.4	633.3	612.9
2018	603.0	591.8	594.7	596.5	602.0	605.4	604.1	600.8	592.1	602.3	620.8	625.6	603.3
Transportation and Utilities													
2010	246.8	246.8	247.0	249.7	251.3	249.4	246.5	250.1	254.7	256.3	257.8	261.1	251.5
2011	254.7	255.0	256.1	257.8	259.2	257.7	254.9	257.0	262.3	262.7	264.0	267.4	259.1
2012	259.4	259.2	261.0	262.7	264.8	261.6	261.2	265.2	268.8	268.9	270.4	273.7	264.7
2013	262.1	262.1	262.8	265.4	267.0	263.8	263.1	268.0	270.0	270.1	272.6	276.2	266.9
2014	267.8	267.2	269.4	270.7	274.1	272.8	271.1	276.3	279.7	280.1	283.0	288.3	275.0
2015	278.0	277.8	278.4	281.8	284.9	284.1	281.9	285.5	288.3	291.1	294.2	298.7	285.4
2016	286.8	286.3	287.9	290.2	291.4	288.5	288.3	291.5	295.6	303.3	306.4	313.3	294.1
2017	296.6	295.1	296.4	295.4	297.8	296.6	296.2	302.4	309.4	310.5	317.4	321.8	303.0
2018	311.9	309.8	310.7	310.5	312.7	312.9	312.8	315.6	318.3	322.1	327.5	333.1	316.5
Information													
2010	103.2	102.2	102.2	102.3	102.8	103.0	101.5	101.6	100.6	100.9	101.1	101.6	101.9
2011	100.5	99.9	100.1	100.4	100.7	101.1	101.4	101.3	99.8	99.9	100.4	100.4	100.5
2012	100.1	99.7	100.2	100.4	101.2	100.2	100.3	100.3	99.0	99.8	100.1	100.5	100.2
2013	99.2	98.8	98.8	100.0	99.9	99.9	98.8	98.3	97.3	98.0	98.5	98.9	98.9
2014	97.7	97.8	98.8	99.4	98.8	99.3	99.1	99.8	98.1	99.3	99.4	100.3	99.0
2015	99.6	99.6	99.6	101.0	101.6	101.3	100.2	100.5	99.1	100.4	100.8	101.1	100.4
2016	97.6	97.2	97.5	98.2	97.7	97.0	97.0	98.9	97.3	100.8	101.5	100.8	98.5
2017	99.4	99.8	100.0	98.4	98.6	98.3	97.0	97.8	95.5	94.9	94.9	94.8	97.5
2018	94.6	94.4	94.7	94.5	93.8	94.0	95.3	96.0	93.7	94.5	93.3	93.6	94.4

1. Employment by Industry: Illinois, 2010–2018—*Continued*

(Numbers in thousands, not seasonally adjusted)

Industry and year	January	February	March	April	May	June	July	August	September	October	November	December	Annual average
Financial Activities													
2010	370.4	369.8	370.0	371.3	372.2	375.0	374.7	375.0	371.7	373.6	373.5	374.9	372.7
2011	369.9	369.7	369.5	370.2	370.9	373.5	375.3	375.3	372.4	374.3	373.1	373.9	372.3
2012	369.9	370.5	371.3	373.0	374.7	378.3	379.3	379.9	377.5	377.1	376.8	378.6	375.6
2013	375.2	375.5	375.7	378.1	378.7	382.6	382.4	381.9	379.4	379.7	378.9	379.6	379.0
2014	375.4	374.9	375.1	375.4	377.2	380.2	381.3	382.4	378.1	379.3	378.4	379.8	378.1
2015	376.7	376.6	376.6	380.4	382.5	386.5	387.5	387.6	383.0	384.3	383.6	384.6	382.5
2016	380.6	381.0	381.3	384.1	384.9	388.3	391.1	391.4	387.8	389.6	389.2	390.1	386.6
2017	387.8	388.1	388.9	390.8	392.1	397.6	400.7	400.7	396.9	397.7	397.7	399.8	394.9
2018	394.7	395.4	396.9	398.2	399.1	404.3	407.0	407.5	403.4	405.0	404.8	404.7	401.8
Professional and Business Services													
2010	754.3	758.4	761.3	787.9	791.6	801.3	805.6	811.1	807.9	818.0	817.7	815.7	794.2
2011	787.7	791.2	797.1	818.5	818.8	829.8	835.4	840.7	840.8	845.0	844.3	840.0	824.1
2012	817.5	820.3	829.7	848.8	855.4	868.4	867.7	875.3	875.4	874.9	878.6	872.6	857.1
2013	839.0	846.9	853.2	868.5	879.7	891.1	893.4	902.5	898.9	908.4	909.5	906.9	883.2
2014	871.3	877.3	882.3	901.8	911.4	920.8	919.5	926.1	922.3	928.9	929.5	921.5	909.4
2015	885.5	890.2	892.1	914.4	922.6	930.7	937.3	937.8	932.7	945.2	941.2	933.3	921.9
2016	905.8	908.0	909.4	924.5	924.6	933.6	940.6	944.5	944.7	950.7	950.6	939.3	931.4
2017	906.2	909.4	917.2	931.1	939.6	952.8	952.1	956.8	952.7	960.6	964.2	956.4	941.6
2018	917.7	927.2	930.2	935.1	941.9	955.1	964.0	970.0	968.6	973.4	975.4	957.9	951.4
Education and Health Services													
2010	817.5	825.2	829.6	830.6	833.4	828.1	820.8	821.7	832.8	843.2	848.1	848.3	831.6
2011	837.3	844.8	850.0	848.7	849.5	844.2	835.6	837.4	850.8	857.1	860.4	863.7	848.3
2012	852.4	861.7	865.7	864.2	863.9	861.1	850.8	854.3	866.4	869.8	873.3	874.3	863.2
2013	866.4	876.2	881.1	876.1	876.5	869.0	859.0	866.1	876.2	882.4	886.5	887.8	875.3
2014	875.8	884.6	888.6	890.1	890.0	881.2	872.0	875.5	884.1	893.8	897.6	899.6	886.1
2015	885.8	892.3	896.4	902.4	905.7	897.0	891.5	892.0	901.0	911.1	914.2	914.6	900.3
2016	904.1	911.5	913.3	919.2	921.0	911.8	905.8	906.8	915.7	923.3	925.8	924.1	915.2
2017	914.3	923.5	927.7	927.2	928.9	918.6	910.0	912.1	922.8	931.0	934.6	934.1	923.7
2018	922.2	933.0	938.1	937.2	938.1	929.0	918.2	920.2	930.4	944.5	950.5	946.9	934.0
Leisure and Hospitality													
2010	482.2	483.3	492.7	511.6	528.1	538.8	536.7	539.2	530.4	520.3	513.2	510.0	515.5
2011	488.5	487.6	500.1	519.6	534.4	544.1	542.6	549.5	538.5	527.7	520.6	516.1	522.4
2012	501.1	503.1	516.0	532.8	548.8	558.8	557.7	564.4	549.9	540.8	532.8	531.4	536.5
2013	513.4	513.5	524.1	541.1	560.0	571.2	571.8	574.0	559.7	549.7	540.0	538.1	546.4
2014	524.3	524.5	534.3	554.8	573.5	584.2	581.9	584.3	570.1	565.2	555.0	552.2	558.7
2015	533.9	538.0	547.3	571.5	594.1	605.4	603.6	606.1	594.2	589.8	580.8	581.5	578.9
2016	561.5	561.8	571.3	594.5	611.2	622.5	622.0	623.1	610.3	604.3	597.8	587.5	597.3
2017	572.6	575.8	588.4	606.8	627.0	640.0	636.1	640.6	622.1	616.2	604.1	598.4	610.7
2018	581.5	581.7	596.7	611.7	632.8	646.0	644.0	646.9	626.3	622.2	608.4	608.9	617.3
Other Services													
2010	251.1	251.0	252.9	247.0	248.2	249.9	248.6	248.6	247.1	248.4	248.2	249.0	249.2
2011	245.2	245.5	247.4	249.4	251.4	253.8	252.7	252.1	250.3	249.6	248.4	250.3	249.7
2012	246.5	247.3	249.2	248.6	250.9	254.1	252.2	251.2	249.7	248.8	248.9	249.3	249.7
2013	245.8	246.6	248.0	248.3	250.1	252.4	253.3	253.7	251.1	249.7	249.2	250.3	249.9
2014	247.5	248.5	250.6	251.7	254.2	257.3	256.4	254.1	251.2	252.2	251.4	251.8	252.2
2015	248.3	249.5	251.3	251.6	253.1	255.7	254.5	253.6	251.3	251.8	251.7	252.2	252.1
2016	248.8	249.4	250.3	251.1	252.2	253.6	253.6	253.4	250.5	251.4	250.8	251.4	251.4
2017	248.6	248.6	250.7	252.7	253.8	256.8	255.8	255.3	252.1	253.2	252.5	254.0	252.8
2018	250.3	251.1	253.0	253.0	254.7	257.4	257.6	256.6	253.2	255.3	254.5	256.2	254.4
Government													
2010	844.1	866.4	866.1	871.8	886.0	855.9	806.1	808.8	849.6	858.6	859.8	852.8	852.2
2011	829.3	850.1	851.1	856.3	854.4	834.8	798.1	792.7	835.6	844.2	847.3	842.2	836.3
2012	819.4	840.1	843.0	846.7	846.6	827.8	786.7	786.1	837.0	845.8	848.2	843.2	830.9
2013	820.3	841.6	841.9	844.0	847.1	826.9	786.5	783.9	834.7	836.5	839.5	837.0	828.3
2014	810.6	828.7	831.2	840.2	842.7	824.9	786.6	783.9	835.7	842.5	842.2	841.5	825.9
2015	813.7	835.2	836.4	841.9	843.1	827.3	790.3	786.6	835.8	844.1	841.5	842.5	828.2
2016	815.3	833.4	837.7	839.3	838.0	830.8	792.4	788.0	840.7	839.1	840.3	846.7	828.5
2017	814.3	833.5	836.5	837.8	837.4	830.4	792.1	792.3	840.3	837.9	839.6	839.7	827.7
2018	811.2	829.9	835.6	834.0	835.8	828.5	789.6	790.9	839.8	838.4	841.1	841.0	826.3

2. Average Weekly Hours by Selected Industry: Illinois, 2014–2018

(Not seasonally adjusted)

Industry and year	January	February	March	April	May	June	July	August	September	October	November	December	Annual average
Total Private													
2014	34.0	34.6	34.6	34.3	34.3	34.8	34.2	34.4	34.3	34.3	34.9	34.3	34.4
2015	33.9	34.5	34.4	34.1	34.2	34.3	34.2	34.8	34.2	34.4	34.7	34.3	34.3
2016	33.9	33.8	33.9	33.9	34.3	34.2	34.1	34.0	34.2	34.6	34.1	34.0	34.1
2017	33.9	33.7	33.7	34.1	33.9	34.2	34.5	34.3	34.3	34.6	34.4	34.3	34.2
2018	33.7	33.8	34.0	34.5	34.1	34.3	34.8	34.1	34.9	34.1	34.1	34.4	34.2
Goods-Producing													
2014	39.4	39.5	39.2	39.5	39.5	39.9	39.8	40.0	39.6	39.8	40.2	40.2	39.7
2015	39.5	39.6	39.7	39.7	39.9	39.8	39.5	40.1	39.0	39.4	39.5	39.8	39.6
2016	39.3	39.0	39.3	39.4	39.7	39.9	39.6	39.5	39.6	40.0	39.9	39.1	39.5
2017	38.7	38.9	38.8	38.8	39.6	39.9	39.5	40.2	40.0	39.7	40.1	40.0	39.5
2018	39.3	39.2	40.0	40.0	39.6	40.0	40.4	40.0	40.4	39.9	39.7	40.4	39.9
Construction													
2014	35.5	36.9	36.6	37.6	37.1	38.2	38.8	38.6	37.1	37.6	38.0	37.7	37.5
2015	36.7	36.3	36.7	37.1	37.2	37.8	37.6	38.6	35.7	36.5	35.4	35.7	36.8
2016	33.8	34.3	35.0	36.2	36.3	37.0	36.9	37.2	37.2	38.1	37.7	36.3	36.4
2017	35.6	36.2	36.0	36.5	37.6	38.2	36.8	38.2	38.0	37.0	37.2	36.9	37.1
2018	35.6	35.7	37.5	37.0	37.2	38.0	38.7	38.3	39.0	38.5	37.4	38.0	37.6
Manufacturing													
2014	40.9	41.3	41.0	41.0	41.1	41.1	40.6	40.9	40.9	40.9	41.3	41.3	41.0
2015	40.6	40.8	40.9	40.8	41.1	40.8	40.4	40.8	40.6	39.5	40.2	40.6	40.6
2016	40.7	40.2	40.5	40.2	40.6	40.9	40.6	40.3	40.5	40.7	40.8	40.2	40.5
2017	39.8	39.8	39.8	39.6	40.4	40.5	40.6	41.0	40.9	41.0	41.4	41.4	40.5
2018	40.9	40.7	41.1	41.4	40.8	41.0	41.2	40.9	41.1	40.6	40.9	41.5	41.0
Trade, Transportation, and Utilities													
2014	34.4	35.0	35.1	35.0	34.9	35.4	35.0	35.0	35.1	34.9	35.3	35.1	35.0
2015	34.3	34.8	34.5	34.2	34.4	34.4	34.5	34.8	34.7	34.8	35.0	34.7	34.6
2016	34.0	34.0	34.1	34.1	34.4	34.4	34.3	34.3	34.6	34.8	34.1	34.3	34.3
2017	33.6	33.8	33.9	34.7	34.3	34.7	35.1	34.6	34.9	35.2	35.0	35.2	34.6
2018	34.1	34.3	34.6	35.0	35.0	35.0	35.4	34.8	35.4	34.5	34.7	34.7	34.8
Information													
2014	36.9	37.6	37.7	36.6	36.3	36.9	36.4	36.0	36.5	36.2	36.9	36.0	36.7
2015	36.2	36.7	36.6	36.1	35.8	36.4	36.4	36.6	35.9	35.6	36.3	35.5	36.2
2016	35.7	35.2	35.3	35.2	35.5	35.0	35.2	35.1	35.3	35.6	35.2	35.3	35.3
2017	35.8	34.5	34.9	36.1	35.2	35.2	36.1	35.6	36.3	37.4	36.7	36.3	35.8
2018	36.7	36.3	36.9	37.5	37.4	36.4	38.1	37.2	38.1	37.2	37.2	37.8	37.2
Financial Activities													
2014	36.3	37.4	37.2	36.1	36.2	37.1	35.1	35.5	35.5	35.7	36.0	34.6	36.1
2015	35.1	36.4	36.3	35.4	35.6	35.8	35.7	36.9	36.0	35.9	36.3	35.4	35.9
2016	35.4	35.5	35.4	35.6	36.6	35.9	36.1	35.8	36.1	37.3	36.2	36.3	36.0
2017	37.1	36.1	36.0	37.0	35.7	36.1	38.2	37.1	36.7	37.6	36.7	36.4	36.7
2018	36.6	36.6	36.5	37.8	36.4	36.6	37.8	36.6	38.0	36.5	36.3	37.8	37.0
Professional and Business Services													
2014	35.6	36.6	36.4	36.0	35.9	36.6	35.8	36.0	35.7	36.0	36.7	35.5	36.1
2015	35.3	36.4	35.9	35.7	35.7	36.1	35.9	36.9	35.6	36.8	37.3	36.4	36.2
2016	35.8	35.6	35.9	36.1	36.6	36.2	36.2	36.0	36.1	37.0	36.0	35.7	36.1
2017	36.3	36.0	35.6	36.0	35.9	36.2	36.2	36.1	35.9	36.5	36.0	35.8	36.0
2018	35.1	35.6	35.4	36.2	35.6	35.9	36.2	35.5	36.3	35.9	35.7	35.7	35.8
Education and Health Services													
2014	32.5	32.8	32.7	32.3	32.4	32.8	32.6	32.5	32.4	32.4	33.1	32.5	32.6
2015	32.4	32.4	32.5	32.3	32.3	32.3	32.3	32.6	32.4	32.2	32.6	32.3	32.4
2016	32.2	32.2	32.1	32.0	32.2	32.1	32.1	31.9	32.1	32.2	32.1	32.1	32.1
2017	32.4	31.8	31.7	32.0	31.6	31.7	32.2	31.9	31.8	31.9	32.1	31.9	31.9
2018	32.0	31.8	31.8	32.3	31.8	32.0	32.6	32.0	32.8	31.9	32.3	32.5	32.1
Leisure and Hospitality													
2014	24.5	25.5	25.9	25.7	26.0	25.8	25.5	25.7	25.7	25.6	25.9	25.7	25.6
2015	24.6	25.6	25.9	25.6	26.0	26.1	26.1	26.4	26.2	26.1	25.8	25.8	25.9
2016	24.9	25.3	25.4	25.5	25.9	25.7	25.7	25.7	25.5	25.8	25.7	25.1	25.5
2017	24.8	25.0	25.3	25.6	25.6	25.9	25.8	25.8	25.8	26.1	25.6	25.8	25.6
2018	24.2	24.5	25.2	25.1	25.4	25.6	25.8	25.3	25.6	25.4	24.9	25.2	25.2
Other Services													
2014	30.8	31.3	31.4	31.0	31.4	31.9	31.0	31.4	31.6	31.9	32.5	31.7	31.5
2015	32.1	32.8	33.3	32.5	32.3	32.2	32.4	33.3	32.7	32.7	33.7	32.5	32.7
2016	32.6	31.8	32.1	32.0	32.4	32.3	32.7	32.3	32.6	33.5	32.9	33.1	32.5
2017	33.1	32.8	32.4	32.8	32.4	32.5	32.9	32.4	32.1	31.9	31.6	31.7	32.4
2018	31.5	31.7	31.9	32.2	31.1	31.9	32.5	31.5	32.5	31.2	31.1	31.5	31.7

3. Average Hourly Earnings by Selected Industry: Illinois, 2014–2018

(Dollars, not seasonally adjusted)

Industry and year	January	February	March	April	May	June	July	August	September	October	November	December	Annual average
Total Private													
2014	25.05	25.33	25.41	25.24	25.25	25.33	25.25	25.42	25.47	25.52	25.89	25.64	25.40
2015	25.75	26.12	25.99	25.78	25.71	25.62	25.76	26.02	25.95	26.24	26.55	26.31	25.98
2016	26.56	26.46	26.48	26.53	26.69	26.28	26.42	26.54	26.63	26.98	26.69	26.65	26.58
2017	26.95	26.66	26.62	26.92	26.53	26.48	26.89	26.59	26.94	27.15	27.00	27.12	26.82
2018	27.29	27.34	27.23	27.70	27.28	27.23	27.82	27.69	28.31	28.24	28.25	28.67	27.76
Goods-Producing													
2014	26.44	26.48	26.53	26.72	27.05	27.34	27.62	27.86	27.91	28.11	28.08	27.99	27.36
2015	27.79	27.96	27.95	27.86	28.08	28.25	28.72	28.88	28.59	29.74	29.83	29.72	28.62
2016	28.98	28.83	28.91	29.20	29.29	29.02	29.21	29.29	29.16	29.26	28.80	28.78	29.06
2017	28.38	28.39	28.50	28.40	28.52	28.85	29.10	29.02	29.48	29.08	29.23	29.20	28.86
2018	28.87	28.76	29.12	29.39	29.66	29.63	30.16	30.44	31.04	31.20	30.97	31.19	30.06
Construction													
2014	33.66	34.27	33.98	33.87	34.03	34.32	34.50	34.80	35.56	35.54	35.57	35.90	34.72
2015	35.05	36.03	36.21	35.96	36.15	36.19	36.69	36.90	36.33	36.30	37.06	37.47	36.39
2016	36.16	36.09	36.44	36.35	36.66	36.46	36.83	36.88	37.03	37.06	36.96	37.25	36.71
2017	36.73	36.55	36.90	35.58	35.92	35.90	36.40	36.55	37.64	36.54	37.39	37.59	36.64
2018	37.11	36.79	37.12	37.10	37.17	37.08	37.84	37.90	38.92	39.10	38.81	39.26	37.89
Manufacturing													
2014	24.56	24.40	24.49	24.53	24.83	24.90	25.04	25.25	25.16	25.38	25.35	25.28	24.93
2015	25.52	25.50	25.31	25.06	25.15	25.23	25.59	25.59	25.60	26.52	26.55	26.38	25.66
2016	26.29	26.11	25.93	26.10	26.06	25.56	25.64	25.65	25.41	25.55	25.08	25.32	25.72
2017	25.19	25.14	25.08	25.29	25.10	25.45	25.71	25.37	25.56	25.68	25.58	25.75	25.41
2018	25.85	25.73	25.73	26.09	26.14	25.97	26.25	26.63	26.95	27.06	27.14	27.43	26.42
Trade, Transportation, and Utilities													
2014	22.75	23.00	23.22	23.08	23.13	23.04	22.84	22.88	22.97	22.95	23.22	22.87	23.00
2015	23.23	23.35	23.27	23.38	23.30	23.18	23.29	23.60	23.56	23.19	23.46	23.10	23.33
2016	23.55	23.24	23.29	23.53	23.72	23.41	23.50	23.43	23.60	23.86	23.64	23.37	23.51
2017	23.87	23.36	23.39	23.71	23.53	23.45	23.87	23.61	23.86	24.06	24.03	23.80	23.72
2018	24.31	24.13	23.86	24.62	24.27	24.40	24.90	24.75	25.20	25.05	24.71	25.10	24.61
Information													
2014	29.77	31.32	31.81	31.59	31.42	31.69	31.63	31.61	31.60	31.63	32.15	31.42	31.47
2015	31.23	31.92	32.24	31.57	31.80	31.38	31.63	32.46	31.68	31.93	32.31	31.93	31.84
2016	31.80	32.08	32.06	31.88	32.18	31.40	31.72	31.98	32.03	32.74	32.11	31.84	31.99
2017	33.14	32.76	32.69	33.75	32.68	33.41	34.81	32.96	33.24	34.62	33.89	34.91	33.57
2018	35.21	34.91	34.14	35.04	34.59	35.86	35.75	35.99	37.07	36.75	36.83	37.58	35.81
Financial Activities													
2014	31.73	32.63	32.47	32.38	32.42	31.84	32.02	33.09	33.29	33.14	34.67	34.16	32.81
2015	34.01	35.34	35.67	34.95	34.25	33.61	33.71	34.32	34.56	34.81	35.54	34.88	34.64
2016	36.06	36.27	36.20	36.47	37.20	35.78	36.58	37.48	37.61	38.30	37.78	37.44	36.94
2017	38.62	37.54	38.40	39.57	38.44	37.74	37.50	36.91	37.42	38.09	37.65	37.73	37.96
2018	37.77	37.82	37.82	39.28	38.12	37.59	38.69	38.15	39.32	38.76	39.56	39.65	38.55
Professional and Business Services													
2014	28.66	29.21	29.39	28.57	28.63	28.86	28.48	28.31	28.51	28.34	29.22	28.68	28.74
2015	28.98	29.91	29.49	28.91	28.79	28.60	28.70	28.89	28.91	28.59	29.27	28.94	28.99
2016	29.82	29.59	29.70	29.69	29.83	29.33	29.32	29.47	29.60	30.15	30.00	30.11	29.72
2017	30.58	30.32	30.10	30.65	29.58	29.57	30.51	29.62	30.20	30.68	30.09	30.54	30.20
2018	31.25	31.34	31.55	31.95	31.02	30.91	31.73	31.00	31.86	31.56	31.81	32.79	31.57
Education and Health Services													
2014	24.97	24.78	24.97	25.16	24.89	24.84	24.83	25.03	24.63	24.68	24.61	24.88	24.85
2015	24.61	24.63	24.64	24.52	24.61	24.61	24.54	24.57	24.76	25.64	25.65	25.56	24.87
2016	25.43	25.58	25.54	25.01	25.04	24.91	25.06	25.12	25.09	25.21	25.11	25.08	25.18
2017	25.16	25.32	24.89	25.06	25.08	24.94	25.18	25.26	25.27	25.40	25.43	25.81	25.23
2018	24.96	25.45	24.97	24.85	24.84	24.89	25.17	25.34	25.64	25.74	25.85	25.93	25.31
Leisure and Hospitality													
2014	12.58	12.82	12.77	12.88	13.02	13.18	13.27	13.38	13.54	13.73	13.94	14.09	13.28
2015	13.93	14.03	13.85	13.94	13.99	13.97	14.11	14.13	14.18	14.24	14.35	14.51	14.11
2016	14.43	14.47	14.57	14.61	14.71	14.70	14.64	14.69	14.84	15.02	15.02	15.64	14.78
2017	15.03	15.10	15.13	15.21	15.47	15.22	15.09	15.21	15.46	15.45	15.49	15.71	15.30
2018	15.84	15.79	15.74	15.81	15.87	15.73	15.94	15.97	16.12	16.52	16.52	16.98	16.07
Other Services													
2014	24.15	24.57	24.48	24.42	24.39	24.61	24.38	24.81	25.10	25.20	25.50	25.39	24.75
2015	25.35	25.64	25.15	25.06	25.22	25.09	25.04	25.64	25.40	25.85	25.97	26.48	25.49
2016	26.43	26.55	26.26	26.94	27.26	26.48	26.17	26.37	26.69	27.06	26.39	26.23	26.57
2017	26.44	25.98	26.10	26.03	25.31	25.09	25.18	25.51	26.23	26.56	26.28	26.51	25.93
2018	26.96	27.12	27.20	27.54	26.81	26.10	26.76	26.89	27.50	27.42	27.55	28.20	27.17

4. Average Weekly Earnings by Selected Industry: Illinois, 2014–2018

(Dollars, not seasonally adjusted)

Industry and year	January	February	March	April	May	June	July	August	September	October	November	December	Annual average
Total Private													
2014	851.70	876.42	879.19	865.73	866.08	881.48	863.55	874.45	873.62	875.34	903.56	879.45	873.76
2015	872.93	901.14	894.06	879.10	879.28	878.77	880.99	905.50	887.49	902.66	921.29	902.43	891.11
2016	900.38	894.35	897.67	899.37	915.47	898.78	900.92	902.36	910.75	933.51	910.13	906.10	906.38
2017	913.61	898.44	897.09	917.97	899.37	905.62	927.71	912.04	924.04	939.39	928.80	930.22	917.24
2018	919.67	924.09	925.82	955.65	930.25	933.99	968.14	944.23	988.02	962.98	963.33	986.25	949.39
Goods-Producing													
2014	1,041.74	1,045.96	1,039.98	1,055.44	1,068.48	1,090.87	1,099.28	1,114.40	1,105.24	1,118.78	1,128.82	1,125.20	1,086.19
2015	1,097.71	1,107.22	1,109.62	1,106.04	1,120.39	1,124.35	1,134.44	1,158.09	1,115.01	1,171.76	1,178.29	1,182.86	1,133.35
2016	1,138.91	1,124.37	1,136.16	1,150.48	1,162.81	1,157.90	1,156.72	1,156.96	1,154.74	1,170.40	1,149.12	1,125.30	1,147.87
2017	1,098.31	1,104.37	1,105.80	1,101.92	1,129.39	1,151.12	1,149.45	1,166.60	1,179.20	1,154.48	1,172.12	1,168.00	1,139.97
2018	1,134.59	1,127.39	1,164.80	1,175.60	1,174.54	1,185.20	1,218.46	1,217.60	1,254.02	1,244.88	1,229.51	1,260.08	1,199.39
Construction													
2014	1,194.93	1,264.56	1,243.67	1,273.51	1,262.51	1,311.02	1,338.60	1,343.28	1,319.28	1,336.30	1,351.66	1,353.43	1,302.00
2015	1,286.34	1,307.89	1,328.91	1,334.12	1,344.78	1,367.98	1,379.54	1,424.34	1,296.98	1,324.95	1,311.92	1,337.68	1,339.15
2016	1,222.21	1,237.89	1,275.40	1,315.87	1,330.76	1,349.02	1,359.03	1,371.94	1,377.52	1,411.99	1,393.39	1,352.18	1,336.24
2017	1,307.59	1,323.11	1,328.40	1,298.67	1,350.59	1,371.38	1,339.52	1,396.21	1,430.32	1,351.98	1,390.91	1,387.07	1,359.34
2018	1,321.12	1,313.40	1,392.00	1,372.70	1,382.72	1,409.04	1,464.41	1,451.57	1,517.88	1,505.35	1,451.49	1,491.88	1,424.66
Manufacturing													
2014	1,004.50	1,007.72	1,004.09	1,005.73	1,020.51	1,023.39	1,016.62	1,032.73	1,029.04	1,038.04	1,046.96	1,044.06	1,022.13
2015	1,036.11	1,040.40	1,035.18	1,022.45	1,033.67	1,029.38	1,033.84	1,044.07	1,039.36	1,047.54	1,067.31	1,071.03	1,041.80
2016	1,070.00	1,049.62	1,050.17	1,049.22	1,058.04	1,045.40	1,040.98	1,033.70	1,029.11	1,039.89	1,023.26	1,017.86	1,041.66
2017	1,002.56	1,000.57	998.18	1,001.48	1,014.04	1,030.73	1,043.83	1,040.17	1,045.40	1,052.88	1,059.01	1,066.05	1,029.11
2018	1,057.27	1,047.21	1,057.50	1,080.13	1,066.51	1,064.77	1,081.50	1,089.17	1,107.65	1,098.64	1,110.03	1,138.35	1,083.22
Trade, Transportation, and Utilities													
2014	782.60	805.00	815.02	807.80	807.24	815.62	799.40	800.80	806.25	800.96	819.67	802.74	805.00
2015	796.79	812.58	802.82	799.60	801.52	797.39	803.51	821.28	817.53	807.01	821.10	801.57	807.22
2016	800.70	790.16	794.19	802.37	815.97	805.30	806.05	803.65	816.56	830.33	806.12	801.59	806.39
2017	802.03	789.57	792.92	822.74	807.08	813.72	837.84	816.91	832.71	846.91	841.05	837.76	820.71
2018	828.97	827.66	825.56	861.70	849.45	854.00	881.46	861.30	892.08	864.23	857.44	870.97	856.43
Information													
2014	1,098.51	1,177.63	1,199.24	1,156.19	1,140.55	1,169.36	1,151.33	1,137.96	1,153.40	1,145.01	1,186.34	1,131.12	1,154.95
2015	1,130.53	1,171.46	1,179.98	1,139.68	1,138.44	1,142.23	1,151.33	1,188.04	1,137.31	1,136.71	1,172.85	1,133.52	1,152.61
2016	1,135.26	1,129.22	1,131.72	1,122.18	1,142.39	1,099.00	1,116.54	1,122.50	1,130.66	1,165.54	1,130.27	1,123.95	1,129.25
2017	1,186.41	1,130.22	1,140.88	1,218.38	1,150.34	1,176.03	1,256.64	1,173.38	1,206.61	1,294.79	1,243.76	1,267.23	1,201.81
2018	1,292.21	1,267.23	1,259.77	1,314.00	1,293.67	1,305.30	1,362.08	1,338.83	1,412.37	1,367.10	1,370.08	1,420.52	1,332.13
Financial Activities													
2014	1,151.80	1,220.36	1,207.88	1,168.92	1,173.60	1,181.26	1,123.90	1,174.70	1,181.80	1,183.10	1,248.12	1,181.94	1,184.44
2015	1,193.75	1,286.38	1,294.82	1,237.23	1,219.30	1,203.24	1,203.45	1,266.41	1,244.16	1,249.68	1,290.10	1,234.75	1,243.58
2016	1,276.52	1,287.59	1,281.48	1,298.33	1,361.52	1,284.50	1,320.54	1,341.78	1,357.72	1,428.59	1,367.64	1,359.07	1,329.84
2017	1,432.80	1,355.19	1,382.40	1,464.09	1,372.31	1,362.41	1,432.50	1,369.36	1,373.31	1,432.18	1,381.76	1,373.37	1,393.13
2018	1,382.38	1,384.21	1,380.43	1,484.78	1,387.57	1,375.79	1,462.48	1,396.29	1,494.16	1,414.74	1,436.03	1,498.77	1,426.35
Professional and Business Services													
2014	1,020.30	1,069.09	1,069.80	1,028.52	1,027.82	1,056.28	1,019.58	1,019.16	1,017.81	1,020.24	1,072.37	1,018.14	1,037.51
2015	1,022.99	1,088.72	1,058.69	1,032.09	1,027.80	1,032.46	1,030.33	1,066.04	1,029.20	1,052.11	1,091.77	1,053.42	1,049.44
2016	1,067.56	1,053.40	1,066.23	1,071.81	1,091.78	1,061.75	1,061.38	1,060.92	1,068.56	1,115.55	1,080.00	1,074.93	1,072.89
2017	1,110.05	1,091.52	1,071.56	1,103.40	1,061.92	1,070.43	1,104.46	1,069.28	1,084.18	1,119.82	1,083.24	1,093.33	1,087.20
2018	1,096.88	1,115.70	1,116.87	1,156.59	1,104.31	1,109.67	1,148.63	1,100.50	1,156.52	1,133.00	1,135.62	1,170.60	1,130.21
Education and Health Services													
2014	811.53	812.78	816.52	812.67	806.44	814.75	809.46	813.48	798.01	799.63	814.59	808.60	810.11
2015	797.36	798.01	800.80	792.00	794.90	794.90	792.64	800.98	802.22	825.61	836.19	825.59	805.79
2016	818.85	823.68	819.83	800.32	806.29	799.61	804.43	801.33	805.39	811.76	806.03	805.07	808.28
2017	815.18	805.18	789.01	801.92	792.53	790.60	810.80	805.79	803.59	810.26	816.30	823.34	804.84
2018	798.72	809.31	794.05	802.66	789.91	796.48	820.54	810.88	840.99	821.11	834.96	842.73	812.45
Leisure and Hospitality													
2014	308.21	326.91	330.74	331.02	338.52	340.04	338.39	343.87	347.98	351.49	361.05	362.11	339.97
2015	342.68	359.17	358.72	356.86	363.74	364.62	368.27	373.03	371.52	371.66	370.23	374.36	365.45
2016	359.31	366.09	370.08	372.56	380.99	377.79	376.25	377.53	378.42	387.52	386.01	392.56	376.89
2017	372.74	377.50	382.79	389.38	396.03	394.20	389.32	392.42	398.87	403.25	396.54	405.32	391.68
2018	383.33	386.86	396.65	396.83	403.10	402.69	411.25	404.04	412.67	419.61	411.35	427.90	404.96
Other Services													
2014	743.82	769.04	768.67	757.02	765.85	785.06	755.78	779.03	793.16	803.88	828.75	804.86	779.63
2015	813.74	840.99	837.50	814.45	814.61	807.90	811.30	853.81	830.58	845.30	875.19	860.60	833.52
2016	861.62	844.29	842.95	862.08	883.22	855.30	855.76	851.75	870.09	906.51	868.23	868.21	863.53
2017	875.16	852.14	845.64	853.78	820.04	815.43	828.42	826.52	841.98	847.26	830.45	840.37	840.13
2018	849.24	859.70	867.68	886.79	833.79	832.59	869.70	847.04	893.75	855.50	856.81	888.30	861.29

INDIANA
At a Glance

Population:
  2010 census: 6,483,802
  2018 estimate: 6,691,878

Percent change in population:
  2010–2018: 3.2%

Percent change in total nonfarm employment:
  2010–2018: 12.3%

Industry with the largest growth in employment, 2010–2018 (percent):
  Transportation and utilities, 24.2%

Industry with the largest decline or smallest growth in employment, 2010–2018 (percent):
  Information, -17.6%

Civilian labor force:
  2010: 3,175,192
  2018: 3,381,713

Unemployment rate and rank among states (highest to lowest):
  2010: 10.4%, 11th
  2018: 3.4%, 32nd

Over-the-year change in unemployment rates:
  2016–2017: -0.8%
  2017–2018: -0.2%

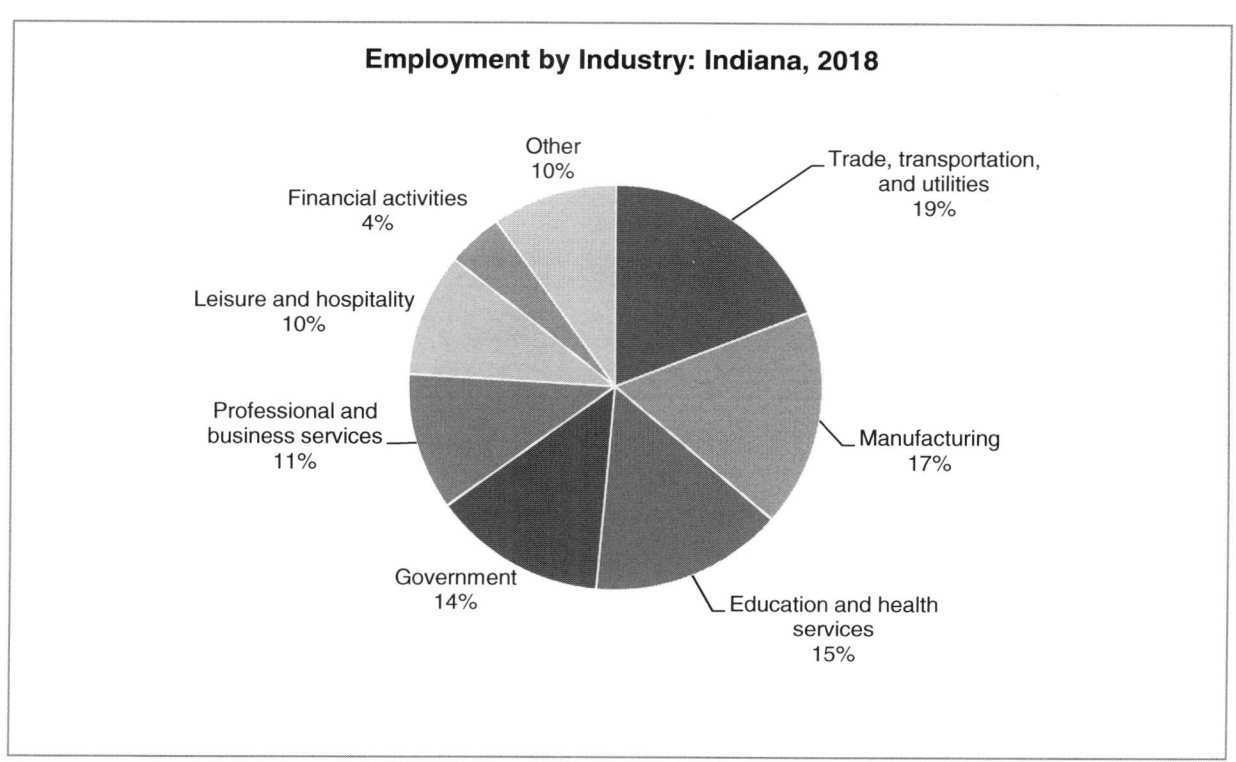

Employment by Industry: Indiana, 2018

- Other 10%
- Financial activities 4%
- Leisure and hospitality 10%
- Professional and business services 11%
- Government 14%
- Trade, transportation, and utilities 19%
- Manufacturing 17%
- Education and health services 15%

1. Employment by Industry: Indiana, 2010–2018

(Numbers in thousands, not seasonally adjusted)

Industry and year	January	February	March	April	May	June	July	August	September	October	November	December	Annual average
Total Nonfarm													
2010	2,722.0	2,729.8	2,761.6	2,805.3	2,833.1	2,803.7	2,775.1	2,806.5	2,829.1	2,841.8	2,840.9	2,833.5	2,798.5
2011	2,765.2	2,776.4	2,808.5	2,849.7	2,873.5	2,838.1	2,808.3	2,844.5	2,889.6	2,892.3	2,893.6	2,895.8	2,844.6
2012	2,826.3	2,846.4	2,874.7	2,901.2	2,924.5	2,902.9	2,849.7	2,910.6	2,943.1	2,944.4	2,949.9	2,945.4	2,901.6
2013	2,859.7	2,887.5	2,907.2	2,934.7	2,947.4	2,932.1	2,880.5	2,950.6	2,970.7	2,978.7	3,002.4	2,997.6	2,937.4
2014	2,885.2	2,913.2	2,941.6	2,978.2	3,006.6	2,988.9	2,932.9	2,986.9	3,008.3	3,022.3	3,039.3	3,043.1	2,978.9
2015	2,954.3	2,970.8	2,993.8	3,030.1	3,057.0	3,044.3	2,992.0	3,040.0	3,067.5	3,078.6	3,092.8	3,096.4	3,034.8
2016	3,007.9	3,031.0	3,052.1	3,078.8	3,093.3	3,071.6	3,038.8	3,081.0	3,115.9	3,112.8	3,126.3	3,118.6	3,077.3
2017	3,045.7	3,063.1	3,084.8	3,110.7	3,133.9	3,125.1	3,070.2	3,113.4	3,142.7	3,146.4	3,159.2	3,160.2	3,113.0
2018	3,078.9	3,098.4	3,120.7	3,137.8	3,167.4	3,152.4	3,105.2	3,149.9	3,169.0	3,177.3	3,188.6	3,182.2	3,144.0
Total Private													
2010	2,281.9	2,280.6	2,312.4	2,351.7	2,372.7	2,379.2	2,382.4	2,395.0	2,389.3	2,398.0	2,397.9	2,395.4	2,361.4
2011	2,335.8	2,339.3	2,369.5	2,407.3	2,427.1	2,427.2	2,425.3	2,442.2	2,449.7	2,450.5	2,450.2	2,452.3	2,414.7
2012	2,392.8	2,406.6	2,432.6	2,461.6	2,487.7	2,495.3	2,483.0	2,497.2	2,504.4	2,503.0	2,508.8	2,509.3	2,473.5
2013	2,435.0	2,449.6	2,468.7	2,495.7	2,522.2	2,530.7	2,518.4	2,537.2	2,538.3	2,540.8	2,560.5	2,557.2	2,512.9
2014	2,468.4	2,477.6	2,503.8	2,541.1	2,573.6	2,579.5	2,561.4	2,576.5	2,576.0	2,584.7	2,600.1	2,602.5	2,553.8
2015	2,526.1	2,535.7	2,558.4	2,593.8	2,623.8	2,630.9	2,620.0	2,630.2	2,627.2	2,640.4	2,652.7	2,654.8	2,607.8
2016	2,579.2	2,593.5	2,612.1	2,643.0	2,661.5	2,665.2	2,666.1	2,670.9	2,675.5	2,676.4	2,687.5	2,681.2	2,651.0
2017	2,616.4	2,629.3	2,647.7	2,674.4	2,697.1	2,712.9	2,696.2	2,700.7	2,701.6	2,706.9	2,717.7	2,717.1	2,684.8
2018	2,648.6	2,663.1	2,683.6	2,700.7	2,725.4	2,737.7	2,728.3	2,732.0	2,728.9	2,737.4	2,745.6	2,740.4	2,714.3
Goods Producing													
2010	539.7	537.7	547.8	563.7	571.1	578.1	584.0	585.3	581.3	582.3	576.9	573.7	568.5
2011	561.5	561.5	571.6	583.1	590.0	598.3	598.7	603.7	603.7	605.2	598.9	598.1	589.5
2012	587.3	588.8	597.5	606.9	614.9	625.1	625.3	626.4	622.8	622.0	617.5	616.0	612.5
2013	600.0	604.3	608.9	616.2	622.4	631.0	627.2	631.4	627.7	628.9	628.7	625.1	621.0
2014	609.0	611.1	620.2	629.2	637.4	648.1	645.1	649.4	645.9	647.3	647.4	646.3	636.4
2015	631.3	631.3	637.8	645.3	653.6	661.6	661.2	663.2	659.6	659.4	659.1	657.1	651.7
2016	641.6	642.4	647.7	656.5	661.3	669.5	670.8	670.6	668.5	668.5	668.6	666.1	661.0
2017	655.2	657.3	663.2	670.0	676.8	685.8	685.0	683.6	683.1	682.6	683.3	682.7	675.7
2018	669.6	672.3	678.4	683.4	689.4	699.6	698.1	697.9	695.2	697.1	697.9	695.6	689.5
Service-Providing													
2010	2,182.3	2,192.1	2,213.8	2,241.6	2,262.0	2,225.6	2,191.1	2,221.2	2,247.8	2,259.5	2,264.0	2,259.8	2,230.1
2011	2,203.7	2,214.9	2,236.9	2,266.6	2,283.5	2,239.8	2,209.6	2,240.8	2,285.9	2,287.1	2,294.7	2,297.7	2,255.1
2012	2,239.0	2,257.6	2,277.2	2,294.3	2,309.6	2,277.8	2,224.4	2,284.2	2,320.3	2,322.4	2,332.4	2,329.4	2,289.1
2013	2,259.7	2,283.2	2,298.3	2,318.5	2,325.0	2,301.1	2,253.3	2,319.2	2,343.0	2,349.8	2,373.7	2,372.5	2,316.4
2014	2,276.2	2,302.1	2,321.4	2,349.0	2,369.2	2,340.8	2,287.8	2,337.5	2,362.4	2,375.0	2,391.9	2,396.8	2,342.5
2015	2,323.0	2,339.5	2,356.0	2,384.8	2,403.4	2,382.7	2,330.8	2,376.8	2,407.9	2,419.2	2,433.7	2,439.3	2,383.1
2016	2,366.3	2,388.6	2,404.4	2,422.3	2,432.0	2,402.1	2,368.0	2,410.4	2,447.4	2,444.3	2,457.7	2,452.5	2,416.3
2017	2,390.5	2,405.8	2,421.6	2,440.7	2,457.1	2,439.3	2,385.2	2,429.8	2,459.6	2,463.8	2,475.9	2,477.5	2,437.2
2018	2,409.3	2,426.1	2,442.3	2,454.4	2,478.0	2,452.8	2,407.1	2,452.0	2,473.8	2,480.2	2,490.7	2,486.6	2,454.4
Mining and Logging													
2010	6.2	6.2	6.4	6.6	6.6	6.6	6.7	6.7	6.8	6.7	6.7	6.6	6.6
2011	6.3	6.4	6.6	6.7	6.8	6.9	6.9	7.0	6.9	7.0	7.0	6.9	6.8
2012	6.8	6.8	6.9	7.0	7.1	7.1	7.1	7.1	7.0	7.0	6.9	6.8	7.0
2013	6.7	6.7	6.7	6.9	7.0	7.1	7.1	7.1	7.2	7.1	7.1	7.1	7.0
2014	6.7	6.6	6.9	7.2	7.3	7.5	7.4	7.4	7.3	7.1	7.2	7.2	7.2
2015	6.9	6.7	6.8	6.9	7.0	7.0	6.9	6.9	6.7	6.7	6.7	6.5	6.8
2016	6.2	6.3	6.2	6.3	6.3	6.3	6.3	6.3	6.3	6.1	5.9	5.9	6.2
2017	5.7	5.7	5.8	6.0	6.0	6.1	6.1	6.1	6.2	6.2	6.4	6.1	6.0
2018	5.9	6.0	6.0	6.2	6.2	6.3	6.4	6.3	6.4	6.4	6.3	6.2	6.2
Construction													
2010	100.3	98.3	104.6	115.0	118.3	121.1	126.1	124.8	121.9	123.1	120.9	114.0	115.7
2011	104.3	102.3	108.0	115.9	121.3	124.5	128.5	129.2	129.2	129.3	127.5	122.1	120.2
2012	112.5	111.2	116.9	123.8	127.4	130.9	131.9	132.0	131.6	130.8	127.5	123.7	125.0
2013	111.2	112.2	116.0	122.0	126.0	129.6	130.6	129.2	127.4	128.4	126.8	121.0	123.4
2014	108.3	107.5	113.4	120.3	124.8	129.8	131.7	130.4	128.9	129.6	128.2	124.1	123.1
2015	112.9	112.4	116.6	124.5	129.8	132.5	133.4	134.4	133.1	134.0	132.9	129.8	127.2
2016	117.2	116.6	121.1	129.9	133.4	136.9	138.4	138.5	139.2	139.9	138.5	132.8	131.9
2017	124.3	124.7	129.7	136.6	141.3	144.3	145.3	144.5	144.6	143.5	141.8	138.1	138.2
2018	126.8	127.5	132.8	138.1	142.2	147.0	147.5	147.1	146.3	148.5	147.1	145.0	141.3

1. Employment by Industry: Indiana, 2010–2018—*Continued*

(Numbers in thousands, not seasonally adjusted)

Industry and year	January	February	March	April	May	June	July	August	September	October	November	December	Annual average
Manufacturing													
2010	433.2	433.2	436.8	442.1	446.2	450.4	451.2	453.8	452.6	452.5	449.3	453.1	446.2
2011	450.9	452.8	457.0	460.5	461.9	466.9	463.3	467.5	467.6	468.9	464.4	469.1	462.6
2012	468.0	470.8	473.7	476.1	480.4	487.1	486.3	487.3	484.2	484.2	483.1	485.5	480.6
2013	482.1	485.4	486.2	487.3	489.4	494.3	489.5	495.1	493.1	493.4	494.8	497.0	490.6
2014	494.0	497.0	499.9	501.7	505.3	510.8	506.0	511.6	509.7	510.6	512.0	515.0	506.1
2015	511.5	512.2	514.4	513.9	516.8	522.1	520.9	521.9	519.8	518.7	519.5	520.8	517.7
2016	518.2	519.5	520.4	520.3	521.6	526.3	526.1	525.8	523.0	522.5	524.2	527.4	522.9
2017	525.2	526.9	527.7	527.4	529.5	535.4	533.6	533.0	532.3	532.9	535.1	538.5	531.5
2018	536.9	538.8	539.6	539.1	541.0	546.3	544.2	544.5	542.5	542.2	544.5	544.4	542.0
Trade, Transportation, and Utilities													
2010	532.0	526.8	531.9	537.2	542.1	544.5	545.1	544.9	541.7	547.6	555.6	558.0	542.3
2011	538.6	535.5	538.9	545.6	551.0	553.0	552.8	553.7	551.5	556.1	565.2	568.5	550.9
2012	549.1	545.4	549.6	553.8	560.2	563.3	561.3	560.7	560.3	563.9	576.6	578.2	560.2
2013	553.0	551.4	553.8	559.3	567.2	571.2	568.0	570.0	568.8	572.1	584.8	588.2	567.3
2014	561.8	559.0	562.6	567.1	573.7	576.2	574.5	575.3	573.2	576.2	587.6	592.5	573.3
2015	568.9	566.1	569.4	573.9	581.6	585.3	584.2	586.1	583.7	589.5	599.8	605.0	582.8
2016	585.2	583.9	586.3	589.5	593.4	594.3	595.7	595.1	594.6	596.2	606.7	609.9	594.2
2017	589.3	586.6	587.8	591.7	595.0	598.4	595.2	595.4	594.2	597.0	609.2	611.7	596.0
2018	589.2	586.7	589.1	590.0	596.7	600.0	599.0	597.9	597.5	602.5	611.9	609.2	597.5
Wholesale Trade													
2010	111.0	110.8	111.7	112.7	113.1	113.4	114.1	113.2	112.6	112.9	112.3	112.0	112.5
2011	111.6	111.8	112.6	113.7	114.6	115.2	115.7	115.0	114.4	114.5	114.6	114.5	114.0
2012	113.4	113.6	114.4	115.1	116.0	116.9	117.0	116.0	115.6	115.5	115.3	115.3	115.3
2013	113.5	114.0	114.7	115.6	116.5	117.3	117.3	116.5	115.9	116.0	116.1	116.2	115.8
2014	114.3	114.5	115.3	116.1	117.4	118.1	118.1	117.7	116.9	116.9	117.2	117.6	116.7
2015	116.3	116.6	117.3	118.0	119.0	119.3	118.7	118.3	117.4	117.5	117.4	117.4	117.8
2016	116.3	116.3	116.8	117.4	117.9	118.4	118.3	117.5	117.0	117.1	117.1	117.2	117.3
2017	116.5	116.9	117.3	117.9	118.7	120.0	119.7	119.5	118.8	118.9	119.0	119.3	118.5
2018	118.2	118.7	119.3	119.6	120.7	121.5	121.8	121.3	120.8	120.4	120.5	120.9	120.3
Retail Trade													
2010	299.7	294.9	297.8	300.9	304.4	305.9	305.6	305.3	302.0	306.8	314.5	316.9	304.6
2011	301.2	297.1	299.3	303.5	306.7	307.2	306.1	306.8	304.7	308.4	316.5	318.9	306.4
2012	304.5	299.8	302.1	305.0	309.2	310.4	309.1	308.3	307.8	310.5	321.3	321.3	309.1
2013	303.1	300.7	302.0	306.0	311.4	313.9	311.7	313.1	311.4	314.4	324.2	326.5	311.5
2014	306.5	303.8	305.9	309.5	313.0	314.5	313.1	313.7	311.9	314.8	324.2	326.7	313.1
2015	309.6	307.1	308.9	312.5	317.1	319.1	318.0	318.7	317.0	321.1	329.5	331.4	317.5
2016	315.6	315.0	316.3	319.8	322.4	323.3	322.6	322.0	321.7	324.1	332.6	333.5	322.4
2017	321.3	318.6	318.9	322.1	324.4	325.1	322.4	321.8	320.5	323.0	332.6	332.8	323.6
2018	318.3	315.7	317.6	317.6	321.9	323.5	322.5	321.0	320.5	324.0	330.9	326.2	321.6
Transportation and Utilities													
2010	121.3	121.1	122.4	123.6	124.6	125.2	125.4	126.4	127.1	127.9	128.8	129.1	125.2
2011	125.8	126.6	127.0	128.4	129.7	130.6	131.0	131.9	132.4	133.2	134.1	135.1	130.5
2012	131.2	132.0	133.1	133.7	135.0	136.0	135.2	136.4	136.9	137.9	140.0	141.6	135.8
2013	136.4	136.7	137.1	137.7	139.3	140.0	139.0	140.4	141.5	141.7	144.5	145.5	140.0
2014	141.0	140.7	141.4	141.5	143.3	143.6	143.3	143.9	144.4	144.5	146.2	148.2	143.5
2015	143.0	142.4	143.2	143.4	145.5	146.9	147.5	149.1	149.3	150.9	152.9	156.2	147.5
2016	153.3	152.6	153.2	152.3	153.1	152.6	154.8	155.6	155.9	155.0	157.0	159.2	154.6
2017	151.5	151.1	151.6	151.7	151.9	153.3	153.1	154.1	154.9	155.1	157.6	159.6	153.8
2018	152.7	152.3	152.2	152.8	154.1	155.0	154.7	155.6	156.2	158.1	160.5	162.1	155.5
Information													
2010	36.0	35.8	35.8	35.8	36.2	36.5	35.9	35.7	35.1	35.0	35.1	35.0	35.7
2011	34.5	34.3	34.5	34.5	35.0	35.2	35.2	35.3	35.2	35.2	35.5	35.6	35.0
2012	35.7	35.7	35.9	35.7	36.0	36.2	36.0	35.9	35.6	35.9	36.0	36.0	35.9
2013	35.9	35.8	36.0	36.0	36.0	36.3	36.5	36.1	35.7	35.7	35.8	36.0	36.0
2014	35.5	35.4	35.6	35.5	35.7	36.0	35.9	35.6	34.9	34.6	34.6	34.5	35.3
2015	34.2	34.0	33.9	33.8	34.0	34.3	34.1	33.7	33.2	33.0	33.2	33.3	33.7
2016	32.9	33.0	32.9	32.9	33.1	33.2	32.9	32.7	32.4	32.7	32.4	32.5	32.8
2017	32.5	32.3	32.6	32.0	32.2	32.1	31.6	31.2	30.6	30.5	30.8	30.9	31.6
2018	30.0	29.8	29.8	29.7	29.9	29.9	29.4	29.1	28.8	28.8	28.9	28.8	29.4

1. Employment by Industry: Indiana, 2010–2018—*Continued*

(Numbers in thousands, not seasonally adjusted)

Industry and year	January	February	March	April	May	June	July	August	September	October	November	December	Annual average
Financial Activities													
2010	129.9	129.4	129.7	129.7	130.4	131.7	132.3	132.2	130.9	131.6	131.3	131.7	130.9
2011	130.9	130.9	131.3	131.0	131.9	132.5	132.6	132.0	130.9	130.7	130.3	130.5	131.3
2012	129.0	128.9	129.2	129.5	130.2	131.0	130.8	130.3	129.4	129.2	129.0	129.4	129.7
2013	127.6	127.3	127.3	127.8	128.9	129.8	130.0	129.6	128.6	128.4	128.3	128.8	128.5
2014	126.2	126.2	126.4	126.7	127.8	129.0	129.2	129.3	128.8	129.0	129.4	129.5	128.1
2015	128.3	128.6	129.0	129.2	130.5	132.0	132.1	132.5	131.7	132.5	132.4	133.2	131.0
2016	131.6	131.8	132.0	132.6	133.5	134.8	135.7	135.7	134.8	135.0	134.8	135.4	134.0
2017	133.5	134.0	134.3	135.0	135.9	137.7	137.8	138.1	137.3	137.5	137.6	138.2	136.4
2018	136.5	137.1	137.5	138.0	138.9	141.0	141.0	140.6	139.2	138.4	138.3	138.1	138.7
Professional and Business Services													
2010	258.2	259.6	264.2	274.0	275.7	278.5	279.7	284.3	283.1	285.7	286.3	287.1	276.4
2011	276.9	277.9	283.8	290.5	288.9	288.7	289.1	294.0	297.1	297.6	297.5	296.6	289.9
2012	284.2	290.1	294.7	298.9	301.1	304.8	302.2	306.2	307.1	307.0	306.5	304.8	300.6
2013	292.3	293.7	298.7	304.6	305.7	309.0	310.6	316.0	317.0	317.9	326.4	324.2	309.7
2014	306.5	307.4	312.4	321.9	325.7	324.7	321.2	327.3	328.0	332.3	337.6	335.9	323.4
2015	319.2	318.4	322.3	332.4	334.1	335.3	334.0	335.0	333.1	337.0	341.4	340.2	331.9
2016	322.3	322.1	325.3	333.7	333.2	335.0	337.6	339.6	340.3	340.0	343.1	339.8	334.3
2017	324.7	325.4	329.8	334.7	336.5	340.5	338.3	341.6	342.1	343.2	345.9	344.6	337.3
2018	333.4	334.6	338.7	342.1	342.5	345.4	343.8	347.1	345.0	345.2	348.4	346.2	342.7
Education and Health Services													
2010	417.2	421.1	425.6	423.3	421.4	408.9	406.0	411.1	422.2	425.6	427.0	425.7	419.6
2011	419.6	423.6	424.6	428.9	427.3	412.2	411.8	416.3	430.4	430.4	431.1	432.3	424.0
2012	425.6	431.9	431.3	434.5	433.1	417.9	413.7	421.6	439.8	439.9	442.0	443.0	431.2
2013	434.7	442.9	442.7	441.5	439.8	426.5	422.5	429.0	441.3	442.8	445.5	443.9	437.8
2014	433.3	439.4	440.0	442.6	443.1	430.7	423.9	427.8	440.3	443.7	445.8	446.9	438.1
2015	437.9	448.3	449.5	452.8	452.3	439.9	435.4	439.6	451.8	458.2	459.8	459.2	448.7
2016	450.3	460.5	460.6	460.8	460.1	447.7	444.8	448.5	461.5	467.1	468.5	466.9	458.1
2017	459.9	468.8	468.6	470.6	471.1	464.9	458.3	460.8	471.7	475.6	475.4	474.5	468.4
2018	466.7	475.0	475.7	476.2	476.1	465.9	462.4	465.4	477.5	484.5	487.4	489.5	475.2
Leisure and Hospitality													
2010	256.3	257.7	263.5	273.4	280.9	284.8	283.1	285.9	279.8	274.8	270.5	269.1	273.3
2011	259.7	261.1	268.7	277.3	286.2	289.3	287.5	289.7	284.1	278.9	275.5	274.3	277.7
2012	266.2	269.6	277.1	284.7	293.6	297.5	294.8	297.3	291.2	286.1	282.5	282.5	285.3
2013	272.8	274.6	280.5	289.0	299.7	302.6	299.7	301.2	296.4	291.8	287.6	286.8	290.2
2014	273.8	275.7	281.9	292.9	303.8	307.2	304.5	305.7	299.7	296.6	292.7	291.7	293.9
2015	282.0	284.4	290.7	299.7	310.1	313.5	310.2	312.0	306.6	302.9	298.6	298.2	300.7
2016	288.1	291.7	298.3	307.5	316.5	319.2	317.1	317.9	312.8	306.9	303.5	300.6	306.7
2017	292.5	295.8	301.1	309.8	317.7	320.3	317.6	318.8	312.3	309.5	304.7	303.5	308.6
2018	294.1	297.8	303.4	309.6	319.4	321.6	321.0	321.3	314.0	308.1	301.6	301.5	309.5
Other Services													
2010	112.6	112.5	113.9	114.6	114.9	116.2	116.3	115.6	115.2	115.4	115.2	115.1	114.8
2011	114.1	114.5	116.1	116.4	116.8	118.0	117.6	117.5	116.8	116.4	116.2	116.4	116.4
2012	115.7	116.2	117.3	117.6	118.6	119.5	118.9	118.8	118.2	119.0	118.7	119.4	118.2
2013	118.7	119.6	120.8	121.3	122.5	124.3	123.9	123.9	122.8	123.2	123.4	124.2	122.4
2014	122.3	123.4	124.7	125.2	126.4	127.6	127.1	126.1	125.2	125.0	125.0	125.2	125.3
2015	124.3	124.6	125.8	126.7	127.6	129.0	128.8	128.1	127.5	127.9	128.4	128.6	127.3
2016	127.2	128.1	129.0	129.5	130.4	131.5	131.5	130.8	130.6	130.0	129.9	130.0	129.9
2017	128.8	129.1	130.3	130.6	131.9	133.2	132.4	131.2	130.3	131.0	130.8	131.0	130.9
2018	129.1	129.8	131.0	131.7	132.5	134.3	133.6	132.7	131.7	132.8	131.2	131.5	131.8
Government													
2010	440.1	449.2	449.2	453.6	460.4	424.5	392.7	411.5	439.8	443.8	443.0	438.1	437.2
2011	429.4	437.1	439.0	442.4	446.4	410.9	383.0	402.3	439.9	441.8	443.4	443.5	429.9
2012	433.5	439.8	442.1	439.6	436.8	407.6	366.7	413.4	438.7	441.4	441.1	436.1	428.1
2013	424.7	437.9	438.5	439.0	425.2	401.4	362.1	413.4	432.4	437.9	441.9	440.4	424.6
2014	416.8	435.6	437.8	437.1	433.0	409.4	371.5	410.4	432.3	437.6	439.2	440.6	425.1
2015	428.2	435.1	435.4	436.3	433.2	413.4	372.0	409.8	440.3	438.2	440.1	441.6	427.0
2016	428.7	437.5	440.0	435.8	431.8	406.4	372.7	410.1	440.4	436.4	438.8	437.4	426.3
2017	429.3	433.8	437.1	436.3	436.8	412.2	374.0	412.7	441.1	439.5	441.5	443.1	428.1
2018	430.3	435.3	437.1	437.1	442.0	414.7	376.9	417.9	440.1	439.9	443.0	441.8	429.7

2. Average Weekly Hours by Selected Industry: Indiana, 2014–2018

(Not seasonally adjusted)

Industry and year	January	February	March	April	May	June	July	August	September	October	November	December	Annual average
Total Private													
2014	33.7	34.6	34.9	34.6	34.8	35.3	34.8	35.1	35.0	35.0	35.4	35.4	34.9
2015	34.7	35.0	35.0	34.8	35.0	34.9	34.8	35.3	34.5	34.9	35.0	35.1	34.9
2016	34.5	34.3	34.3	34.5	34.8	34.7	34.7	34.9	34.9	35.2	35.1	34.7	34.7
2017	34.7	34.5	34.6	34.7	34.8	35.4	35.4	35.5	35.2	35.4	35.6	35.7	35.1
2018	34.8	35.1	35.2	35.1	34.9	35.1	35.4	35.1	35.3	35.1	35.0	35.5	35.1
Goods Producing													
2014	39.4	40.5	40.5	40.5	41.0	41.4	40.2	40.9	40.6	40.5	41.5	41.1	40.7
2015	40.5	40.6	40.6	40.1	40.6	40.3	39.7	40.9	39.5	40.9	41.2	41.0	40.5
2016	40.0	39.5	39.4	39.7	40.2	39.5	39.3	40.0	40.2	41.0	40.3	40.1	39.9
2017	39.9	40.1	39.8	39.9	40.8	41.5	40.9	41.7	41.1	41.5	41.4	41.3	40.8
2018	39.7	40.0	40.7	39.7	39.6	39.8	40.0	40.0	40.4	40.7	40.2	41.3	40.2
Construction													
2014	34.8	34.5	35.9	37.7	36.0	37.9	38.1	39.0	37.9	37.3	38.1	38.0	37.2
2015	36.9	36.8	36.4	37.8	38.9	39.4	38.2	39.3	35.9	38.2	37.5	37.4	37.8
2016	35.3	34.7	35.3	36.5	37.2	38.1	37.9	37.8	38.2	39.2	38.5	36.1	37.2
2017	35.8	37.2	36.7	38.1	39.6	41.1	39.9	41.1	40.2	40.4	40.2	40.6	39.3
2018	38.2	38.7	39.0	39.4	40.3	39.8	41.1	40.2	39.7	41.1	40.3	40.4	39.9
Manufacturing													
2014	40.1	41.6	41.4	40.9	42.0	41.9	40.3	40.9	40.9	40.9	42.1	41.6	41.2
2015	41.1	41.3	41.5	40.6	40.9	40.4	40.0	41.3	40.6	41.2	41.9	41.7	41.0
2016	41.0	40.6	40.4	40.5	41.0	39.9	39.7	40.8	41.0	41.7	41.0	41.5	40.8
2017	41.3	41.0	40.8	40.5	41.3	41.7	41.4	42.0	41.5	42.0	42.0	41.6	41.4
2018	40.2	40.4	41.3	41.9	41.1	41.4	41.1	41.4	42.0	41.8	41.3	42.7	41.4
Trade, Transportation, and Utilities													
2014	33.4	33.8	34.3	33.8	34.3	34.6	34.5	34.6	34.4	34.5	34.7	34.9	34.3
2015	33.7	34.5	34.7	34.5	34.9	34.5	34.9	34.8	34.7	34.4	34.4	35.0	34.6
2016	34.3	34.2	34.0	34.0	34.4	34.4	34.3	34.4	34.4	34.4	34.8	34.2	34.3
2017	34.0	33.3	33.7	34.5	34.1	34.6	34.9	34.5	34.4	34.6	35.0	35.5	34.4
2018	34.5	34.3	34.5	35.0	34.7	34.8	34.7	34.9	34.7	33.9	34.5	34.7	34.6
Financial Activities													
2014	36.5	36.7	37.0	36.5	36.9	37.3	36.4	36.6	36.4	36.4	37.2	36.6	36.7
2015	36.8	37.2	37.3	36.3	36.6	36.4	36.1	37.4	36.3	35.9	36.2	35.2	36.5
2016	36.8	35.8	35.6	36.0	36.2	35.5	36.7	36.4	36.8	37.3	36.8	37.0	36.4
2017	38.6	37.4	37.5	38.0	37.7	37.6	38.7	38.0	38.0	38.5	38.2	37.8	38.0
2018	38.1	37.9	37.9	38.0	36.8	36.3	37.2	35.9	36.6	35.9	36.3	36.8	37.0
Professional and Business Services													
2014	34.1	35.9	36.3	36.1	36.5	37.1	36.0	36.9	36.8	36.9	36.9	37.1	36.4
2015	36.2	36.3	36.2	36.0	36.2	36.0	35.7	36.4	34.7	35.4	35.3	35.5	35.8
2016	34.4	34.6	35.0	35.4	35.7	35.6	35.5	35.4	34.9	36.3	35.7	35.3	35.3
2017	35.7	35.4	35.0	35.6	35.2	35.7	35.5	35.8	35.5	35.7	35.9	36.1	35.6
2018	34.7	35.9	35.2	35.7	36.0	35.7	36.4	35.4	35.8	35.5	34.8	35.8	35.6
Education and Health Services													
2014	32.9	33.3	33.3	33.3	33.3	33.5	33.6	33.3	33.4	33.5	33.8	33.8	33.4
2015	33.5	33.7	33.7	34.0	33.9	34.0	33.9	34.1	33.9	33.7	33.9	34.0	33.9
2016	33.8	33.6	33.7	33.9	34.0	34.2	34.2	34.7	34.9	34.6	34.8	34.0	34.2
2017	33.8	33.6	34.3	33.5	33.6	34.4	34.1	34.1	33.8	33.7	34.2	34.5	34.0
2018	34.3	34.9	34.7	34.6	34.8	35.1	35.2	35.0	35.3	35.2	34.6	34.7	34.9
Leisure and Hospitality													
2014	23.3	25.0	25.2	25.2	25.2	25.8	26.0	25.9	25.5	25.4	25.4	26.1	25.4
2015	24.7	25.3	25.3	25.1	25.3	25.5	25.7	25.5	24.8	25.0	24.7	25.2	25.2
2016	24.2	24.6	24.7	24.7	24.3	24.8	25.1	24.9	24.8	24.5	24.3	23.8	24.6
2017	23.9	24.4	24.9	24.7	24.8	25.7	25.8	25.9	25.4	25.4	25.3	25.0	25.1
2018	24.3	25.1	25.3	25.1	25.3	26.1	26.5	25.9	25.3	25.4	25.0	24.8	25.4
Other Services													
2014	27.9	29.1	29.7	29.0	28.4	29.2	28.9	28.2	29.2	29.1	29.1	29.0	28.9
2015	29.2	29.1	29.8	29.6	29.5	30.5	29.8	29.7	29.5	28.6	28.9	29.6	29.5
2016	28.8	28.7	28.8	29.5	30.3	30.9	30.8	29.1	29.1	28.9	29.1	28.5	29.4
2017	29.1	28.9	29.0	29.3	28.4	29.4	29.9	29.1	29.0	29.3	29.0	28.6	29.1
2018	28.7	28.9	29.2	29.1	25.7	26.8	27.9	27.3	26.8	27.2	27.8	28.4	27.8

3. Average Hourly Earnings by Selected Industry: Indiana, 2014–2018

(Dollars, not seasonally adjusted)

Industry and year	January	February	March	April	May	June	July	August	September	October	November	December	Annual average
Total Private													
2014	22.57	22.62	22.62	22.72	22.49	22.60	22.52	22.53	22.44	22.54	22.90	22.70	22.61
2015	23.00	22.86	22.78	22.71	22.65	22.65	22.75	22.97	22.93	22.89	23.07	23.00	22.85
2016	23.32	23.24	23.15	23.45	23.41	23.20	23.40	23.36	23.60	24.09	23.85	24.15	23.52
2017	24.39	24.37	24.09	24.55	24.40	24.04	24.52	24.30	24.70	24.77	24.47	24.84	24.45
2018	25.02	24.98	25.12	25.28	24.73	24.36	24.63	24.78	24.93	24.94	24.92	25.26	24.91
Goods Producing													
2014	24.90	25.25	25.27	25.47	25.16	25.34	25.32	25.21	25.03	25.16	25.46	25.30	25.24
2015	25.30	25.29	25.36	25.13	25.03	25.17	25.23	25.50	25.42	25.26	25.65	25.40	25.31
2016	25.48	25.58	25.55	25.85	25.84	25.46	25.57	25.76	25.80	26.43	26.23	26.23	25.82
2017	26.77	26.49	26.46	27.11	26.91	26.89	27.23	26.70	26.93	27.07	26.72	27.19	26.88
2018	27.14	27.27	26.78	27.64	27.10	27.15	27.44	27.22	27.84	27.93	27.84	27.95	27.45
Construction													
2014	25.95	27.24	26.90	26.89	26.77	27.81	27.75	26.93	26.52	27.05	27.01	26.76	26.99
2015	26.94	26.83	27.31	27.13	26.33	26.58	26.70	27.19	27.05	27.33	27.07	26.88	26.94
2016	27.20	27.15	27.31	27.73	27.71	27.17	26.95	27.29	27.82	27.92	27.86	27.83	27.51
2017	27.65	27.32	27.89	28.83	29.20	29.78	29.64	29.30	29.55	29.27	29.01	28.74	28.92
2018	28.57	28.32	28.61	28.53	28.60	28.24	28.77	28.43	29.23	29.85	29.24	29.77	28.87
Manufacturing													
2014	24.50	24.70	24.80	25.04	24.70	24.58	24.40	24.55	24.44	24.46	24.88	24.77	24.65
2015	24.79	24.84	24.82	24.52	24.64	24.74	24.79	24.99	24.99	24.65	25.26	25.01	24.84
2016	25.10	25.25	25.14	25.38	25.36	24.99	25.22	25.36	25.22	26.02	25.77	25.83	25.39
2017	26.57	26.29	26.01	26.52	26.06	25.69	26.25	25.61	25.82	26.16	25.76	26.54	26.10
2018	26.56	26.79	26.52	27.21	26.38	26.60	27.05	26.88	27.43	27.24	27.37	27.35	26.95
Trade, Transportation, and Utilities													
2014	20.68	20.62	20.76	20.79	20.57	20.70	20.52	20.58	20.29	20.36	20.80	20.47	20.59
2015	20.94	20.64	20.78	20.74	20.56	20.46	20.44	20.37	20.41	20.02	20.13	20.14	20.46
2016	20.29	20.04	20.01	20.45	20.48	20.52	20.94	20.64	21.27	21.54	21.12	21.35	20.73
2017	20.80	20.76	20.47	20.40	20.16	20.63	21.13	20.91	21.47	21.58	21.10	21.53	20.92
2018	22.21	21.94	21.83	21.51	21.24	21.63	21.70	21.54	22.00	22.00	21.72	22.38	21.81
Financial Activities													
2014	25.06	24.93	24.85	25.10	24.67	24.30	24.06	24.10	23.75	23.75	23.72	23.53	24.31
2015	23.31	23.08	23.03	23.13	23.22	22.85	23.49	23.88	24.24	24.31	24.39	24.96	23.66
2016	25.33	25.59	26.00	26.30	26.23	25.82	25.64	25.37	25.91	26.66	26.50	27.36	26.06
2017	26.24	26.42	26.48	28.02	27.05	27.36	27.14	27.17	27.87	27.74	27.97	28.62	27.35
2018	27.37	28.50	28.40	28.89	28.44	28.56	28.71	28.84	29.48	29.09	28.90	29.79	28.74
Professional and Business Services													
2014	23.51	23.80	23.94	23.68	23.74	24.14	24.28	23.84	23.93	24.13	24.63	24.66	24.04
2015	25.33	25.73	25.42	24.87	24.72	24.99	25.08	25.33	25.53	25.12	25.17	25.00	25.19
2016	26.07	25.68	25.66	25.92	25.92	25.45	26.22	25.60	25.99	26.14	25.51	26.04	25.85
2017	26.96	26.48	26.23	26.58	26.28	25.97	26.64	26.25	26.17	26.11	25.69	25.89	26.26
2018	26.55	26.26	26.38	26.23	26.05	25.57	25.86	25.23	25.73	25.36	25.36	25.78	25.86
Education and Health Services													
2014	23.99	23.63	23.75	24.03	23.86	23.89	23.89	24.04	24.21	24.17	24.54	24.28	24.03
2015	24.53	24.51	24.33	24.77	24.90	24.68	25.08	25.20	24.88	25.29	25.15	25.13	24.87
2016	25.49	25.48	25.07	25.66	25.48	25.48	25.43	25.28	25.22	25.71	25.56	26.04	25.49
2017	26.88	27.19	26.36	27.16	27.54	26.23	27.34	27.11	27.51	27.32	27.03	27.48	27.10
2018	27.42	27.13	28.03	27.95	26.65	25.10	25.87	27.10	25.77	26.09	26.58	26.76	26.70
Leisure and Hospitality													
2014	12.28	12.66	12.34	12.17	12.11	12.20	12.22	12.17	12.36	12.50	12.67	12.85	12.37
2015	12.78	12.91	12.81	12.75	12.62	12.51	12.44	12.57	12.77	13.02	13.30	13.55	12.83
2016	13.34	13.50	13.27	13.25	13.29	12.94	13.01	13.28	13.51	13.63	13.79	13.88	13.38
2017	13.74	13.54	13.45	13.52	13.57	13.28	13.55	13.67	14.07	14.35	14.36	14.25	13.78
2018	14.38	14.27	14.38	14.67	14.29	13.91	13.94	14.01	13.94	13.83	14.04	14.22	14.15
Other Services													
2014	17.85	17.57	17.18	17.61	17.66	17.47	17.47	17.99	17.77	17.66	17.84	18.09	17.68
2015	17.71	17.65	17.66	17.50	17.68	17.58	17.17	17.91	17.91	18.12	18.56	18.81	17.87
2016	19.16	19.42	19.79	19.89	19.82	19.90	19.60	20.32	19.54	20.13	20.06	20.81	19.87
2017	20.93	20.92	20.92	21.30	21.10	20.39	20.60	21.72	22.06	22.54	22.31	22.62	21.45
2018	23.01	24.19	24.19	23.88	24.82	23.79	23.46	24.90	23.97	23.41	23.16	23.01	23.81

4. Average Weekly Earnings by Selected Industry: Indiana, 2014–2018

(Dollars, not seasonally adjusted)

Industry and year	January	February	March	April	May	June	July	August	September	October	November	December	Annual average
Total Private													
2014	760.61	782.65	789.44	786.11	782.65	797.78	783.70	790.80	785.40	788.90	810.66	803.58	789.09
2015	798.10	800.10	797.30	790.31	792.75	790.49	791.70	810.84	791.09	798.86	807.45	807.30	797.47
2016	804.54	797.13	794.05	809.03	814.67	805.04	811.98	815.26	823.64	847.97	837.14	838.01	816.14
2017	846.33	840.77	833.51	851.89	849.12	851.02	868.01	862.65	869.44	876.86	871.13	886.79	858.20
2018	870.70	876.80	884.22	887.33	863.08	855.04	871.90	869.78	880.03	875.39	872.20	896.73	874.34
Goods Producing													
2014	981.06	1,022.63	1,023.44	1,031.54	1,031.56	1,049.08	1,017.86	1,031.09	1,016.22	1,018.98	1,056.59	1,039.83	1,027.27
2015	1,024.65	1,026.77	1,029.62	1,007.71	1,016.22	1,014.35	1,001.63	1,042.95	1,004.09	1,033.13	1,056.78	1,041.40	1,025.06
2016	1,019.20	1,010.41	1,006.67	1,026.25	1,038.77	1,005.67	1,004.90	1,030.40	1,037.16	1,083.63	1,057.07	1,051.82	1,030.22
2017	1,068.12	1,062.25	1,053.11	1,081.69	1,097.93	1,115.94	1,113.71	1,113.39	1,106.82	1,123.41	1,106.21	1,122.95	1,096.70
2018	1,077.46	1,090.80	1,089.95	1,097.31	1,073.16	1,080.57	1,097.60	1,088.80	1,124.74	1,136.75	1,119.17	1,154.34	1,103.49
Construction													
2014	903.06	939.78	965.71	1,013.75	963.72	1,054.00	1,057.28	1,050.27	1,005.11	1,008.97	1,029.08	1,016.88	1,004.03
2015	994.09	987.34	994.08	1,025.51	1,024.24	1,047.25	1,019.94	1,068.57	971.10	1,044.01	1,015.13	1,005.31	1,018.33
2016	960.16	942.11	964.04	1,012.15	1,030.81	1,035.18	1,021.41	1,031.56	1,062.72	1,094.46	1,072.61	1,004.66	1,023.37
2017	989.87	1,016.30	1,023.56	1,098.42	1,156.32	1,223.96	1,182.64	1,204.23	1,187.91	1,182.51	1,166.20	1,166.84	1,136.56
2018	1,091.37	1,095.98	1,115.79	1,124.08	1,152.58	1,123.95	1,182.45	1,142.89	1,160.43	1,226.84	1,178.37	1,202.71	1,151.91
Manufacturing													
2014	982.45	1,027.52	1,026.72	1,024.14	1,037.40	1,029.90	983.32	1,004.10	999.60	1,000.41	1,047.45	1,030.43	1,015.58
2015	1,018.87	1,025.89	1,030.03	995.51	1,007.78	999.50	991.60	1,032.09	1,014.59	1,015.58	1,058.39	1,042.92	1,018.44
2016	1,029.10	1,025.15	1,015.66	1,027.89	1,039.76	997.10	1,001.23	1,034.69	1,034.02	1,085.03	1,056.57	1,071.95	1,035.91
2017	1,097.34	1,077.89	1,061.21	1,074.06	1,076.28	1,071.27	1,086.75	1,075.62	1,071.53	1,098.72	1,081.92	1,104.06	1,080.54
2018	1,067.71	1,082.32	1,095.28	1,140.10	1,084.22	1,101.24	1,111.76	1,112.83	1,152.06	1,138.63	1,130.38	1,167.85	1,115.73
Trade, Transportation, and Utilities													
2014	690.71	696.96	712.07	702.70	705.55	716.22	707.94	712.07	697.98	702.42	721.76	714.40	706.24
2015	705.68	712.08	721.07	715.53	717.54	705.87	713.36	708.88	708.23	688.69	692.47	704.90	707.92
2016	695.95	685.37	680.34	695.30	704.51	705.89	718.24	710.02	731.69	740.98	734.98	730.17	711.04
2017	707.20	691.31	689.84	703.80	687.46	713.80	737.44	721.40	738.57	746.67	738.50	764.32	719.65
2018	766.25	752.54	753.14	752.85	737.03	752.72	752.99	751.75	763.40	745.80	749.34	776.59	754.63
Financial Activities													
2014	914.69	914.93	919.45	916.15	910.32	906.39	875.78	882.06	864.50	864.50	882.38	861.20	892.18
2015	857.81	858.58	859.02	839.62	849.85	831.74	847.99	893.11	879.91	872.73	882.92	878.59	863.59
2016	932.14	916.12	925.60	946.80	949.53	916.61	940.99	923.47	953.49	994.42	975.20	1,012.32	948.58
2017	1,012.86	988.11	993.00	1,064.76	1,019.79	1,028.74	1,050.32	1,032.46	1,059.06	1,067.99	1,068.45	1,081.84	1,039.30
2018	1,042.80	1,080.15	1,076.36	1,097.82	1,046.59	1,036.73	1,068.01	1,035.36	1,078.97	1,044.33	1,049.07	1,096.27	1,063.38
Professional and Business Services													
2014	801.69	854.42	869.02	854.85	866.51	895.59	874.08	879.70	880.62	890.40	908.85	914.89	875.06
2015	916.95	934.00	920.20	895.32	894.86	899.64	895.36	922.01	885.89	889.25	888.50	887.50	901.80
2016	896.81	888.53	898.10	917.57	925.34	906.02	930.81	906.24	907.05	948.88	910.71	919.21	912.51
2017	962.47	937.39	918.05	946.25	925.06	927.13	945.72	939.75	929.04	932.13	922.27	934.63	934.86
2018	921.29	942.73	928.58	936.41	937.80	912.85	941.30	893.14	921.13	900.28	882.53	922.92	920.62
Education and Health Services													
2014	789.27	786.88	790.88	800.20	794.54	800.32	802.70	800.53	808.61	809.70	829.45	820.66	802.60
2015	821.76	825.99	819.92	842.18	844.11	839.12	850.21	859.32	843.43	852.27	852.59	854.42	843.09
2016	861.56	856.13	844.86	869.87	866.32	871.42	869.71	877.22	880.18	889.57	889.49	885.36	871.76
2017	908.54	913.58	904.15	909.86	925.34	902.31	932.29	924.45	929.84	920.68	924.43	948.06	921.40
2018	940.51	946.84	972.64	967.07	927.42	881.01	910.62	948.50	909.68	918.37	919.67	928.57	931.83
Leisure and Hospitality													
2014	286.12	316.50	310.97	306.68	305.17	314.76	317.72	315.20	315.18	317.50	321.82	335.39	314.20
2015	315.67	326.62	324.09	320.03	319.29	319.01	319.71	320.54	316.70	325.50	328.51	341.46	323.32
2016	322.83	332.10	327.77	327.28	322.95	320.91	326.55	330.67	335.05	333.94	335.10	330.34	329.15
2017	328.39	330.38	334.91	333.94	336.54	341.30	349.59	354.05	357.38	364.49	363.31	356.25	345.88
2018	349.43	358.18	363.81	368.22	361.54	363.05	369.41	362.86	352.68	351.28	351.00	352.66	359.41
Other Services													
2014	498.02	511.29	510.25	510.69	501.54	510.12	504.88	507.32	518.88	513.91	519.14	524.61	510.95
2015	517.13	513.62	526.27	518.00	521.56	536.19	511.67	531.93	534.54	518.23	536.38	556.78	527.17
2016	551.81	557.35	569.95	586.76	600.55	614.91	603.68	591.31	568.61	581.76	583.75	593.09	584.18
2017	609.06	604.59	606.68	624.09	599.24	599.47	615.94	632.05	639.74	660.42	646.99	646.93	624.20
2018	660.39	699.09	706.35	694.91	637.87	637.57	654.53	679.77	642.40	636.75	643.85	653.48	661.92

IOWA
At a Glance

Population:
  2010 census: 3,046,355
  2018 estimate: 3,156,145

Percent change in population:
  2010–2018: 3.6%

Percent change in total nonfarm employment:
  2010–2018: 7.8%

Industry with the largest growth in employment, 2010–2018 (percent):
  Construction, 25.8%

Industry with the largest decline or smallest growth in employment, 2010–2018 (percent):
  Information, -23.3%

Civilian labor force:
  2010: 1,678,281
  2018: 1,686,840

Unemployment rate and rank among states (highest to lowest):
  2010: 6.0%, 47th
  2018: 2.5%, 49th

Over-the-year change in unemployment rates:
  2016–2017: -0.5%
  2017–2018: -0.6%

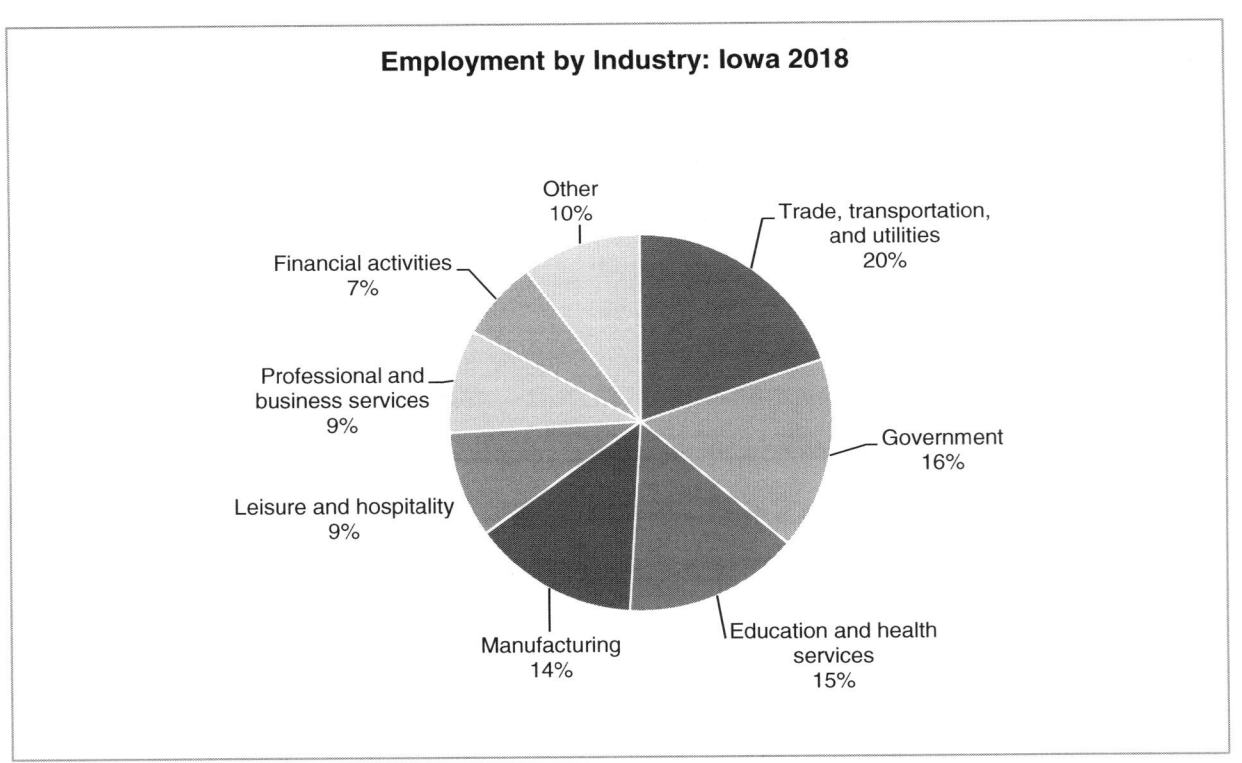

Employment by Industry: Iowa 2018

- Other 10%
- Trade, transportation, and utilities 20%
- Financial activities 7%
- Professional and business services 9%
- Government 16%
- Leisure and hospitality 9%
- Manufacturing 14%
- Education and health services 15%

1. Employment by Industry: Iowa, 2010–2018

(Numbers in thousands, not seasonally adjusted)

Industry and year	January	February	March	April	May	June	July	August	September	October	November	December	Annual average
Total Nonfarm													
2010	1,432.3	1,437.3	1,449.8	1,477.1	1,488.8	1,486.3	1,457.5	1,455.7	1,474.3	1,490.6	1,493.8	1,487.8	1,469.3
2011	1,443.8	1,449.9	1,460.9	1,489.1	1,500.4	1,499.8	1,477.8	1,479.9	1,501.5	1,509.5	1,513.7	1,507.7	1,486.2
2012	1,467.3	1,474.5	1,488.8	1,510.8	1,524.1	1,524.1	1,500.5	1,505.4	1,519.8	1,528.8	1,533.7	1,527.4	1,508.8
2013	1,484.0	1,493.2	1,501.7	1,520.7	1,542.0	1,543.6	1,527.6	1,532.6	1,545.2	1,547.9	1,554.4	1,547.5	1,528.4
2014	1,504.0	1,512.5	1,522.6	1,548.0	1,564.4	1,564.0	1,540.5	1,545.4	1,561.8	1,566.1	1,569.9	1,565.1	1,547.0
2015	1,525.8	1,532.9	1,543.1	1,564.8	1,577.2	1,578.9	1,556.7	1,555.2	1,567.6	1,578.3	1,580.8	1,575.5	1,561.4
2016	1,535.1	1,543.6	1,554.9	1,578.9	1,585.0	1,582.4	1,565.9	1,567.7	1,581.7	1,588.0	1,588.3	1,578.6	1,570.8
2017	1,536.4	1,547.5	1,554.9	1,578.1	1,585.8	1,589.5	1,565.8	1,568.0	1,580.1	1,588.5	1,591.9	1,586.5	1,572.8
2018	1,547.8	1,558.1	1,563.8	1,583.3	1,599.9	1,602.8	1,578.7	1,579.2	1,588.4	1,603.5	1,606.7	1,597.8	1,584.2
Total Private													
2010	1,182.0	1,181.5	1,191.5	1,218.7	1,225.5	1,228.7	1,224.7	1,223.6	1,223.0	1,232.6	1,233.5	1,229.0	1,216.2
2011	1,194.3	1,194.4	1,204.4	1,231.2	1,241.2	1,244.5	1,241.9	1,243.5	1,247.5	1,251.7	1,254.9	1,249.5	1,233.3
2012	1,215.7	1,218.4	1,232.0	1,252.5	1,264.2	1,269.7	1,265.9	1,266.0	1,265.4	1,270.5	1,273.9	1,268.2	1,255.2
2013	1,233.9	1,236.7	1,244.7	1,263.3	1,281.2	1,287.3	1,288.8	1,290.8	1,288.3	1,288.4	1,293.5	1,287.2	1,273.7
2014	1,251.4	1,254.9	1,264.4	1,289.2	1,303.8	1,309.7	1,304.5	1,306.4	1,303.3	1,304.9	1,307.3	1,303.8	1,292.0
2015	1,271.1	1,273.4	1,283.7	1,305.0	1,316.0	1,323.2	1,320.3	1,318.2	1,312.3	1,317.0	1,317.9	1,312.9	1,305.9
2016	1,279.3	1,282.7	1,294.0	1,316.9	1,322.0	1,323.5	1,328.5	1,326.7	1,322.9	1,324.6	1,323.2	1,314.3	1,313.2
2017	1,276.8	1,284.4	1,291.4	1,313.7	1,321.4	1,328.0	1,323.9	1,322.1	1,319.2	1,323.5	1,325.8	1,321.6	1,312.7
2018	1,287.3	1,294.2	1,300.1	1,318.3	1,334.4	1,340.2	1,336.4	1,333.6	1,328.1	1,337.6	1,339.5	1,331.4	1,323.4
Goods Producing													
2010	250.3	248.7	252.2	263.8	266.5	270.7	272.4	272.2	270.9	270.8	269.7	263.9	264.3
2011	254.2	253.5	257.6	267.0	272.2	277.4	279.8	279.8	278.7	277.4	276.3	271.1	270.4
2012	261.7	261.0	266.4	275.1	280.5	285.3	286.5	286.2	283.7	283.7	281.7	278.3	277.5
2013	268.8	268.6	270.9	278.1	286.0	291.4	293.5	294.3	292.0	292.4	291.6	286.5	284.5
2014	276.4	276.4	280.3	290.9	297.3	302.4	303.3	303.5	300.6	299.6	298.6	294.0	293.6
2015	284.9	284.1	287.4	296.1	299.4	304.0	305.0	303.5	300.8	301.1	299.4	295.0	296.7
2016	284.3	282.9	289.4	297.0	299.2	304.0	306.1	306.1	303.4	301.8	298.5	292.8	297.1
2017	281.0	280.9	284.6	292.4	296.3	301.0	301.4	300.4	299.6	300.0	299.4	296.3	294.4
2018	285.2	285.9	290.2	297.8	304.4	310.5	311.9	310.9	309.3	312.6	312.6	303.8	302.9
Service-Providing													
2010	1,182.0	1,188.6	1,197.6	1,213.3	1,222.3	1,215.6	1,185.1	1,183.5	1,203.4	1,219.8	1,224.1	1,223.9	1,204.9
2011	1,189.6	1,196.4	1,203.3	1,222.1	1,228.2	1,222.4	1,198.0	1,200.1	1,222.8	1,232.1	1,237.4	1,236.6	1,215.8
2012	1,205.6	1,213.5	1,222.4	1,235.7	1,243.6	1,238.8	1,214.0	1,219.2	1,236.1	1,245.1	1,252.0	1,249.1	1,231.3
2013	1,215.2	1,224.6	1,230.8	1,242.6	1,256.0	1,252.2	1,234.1	1,238.3	1,253.2	1,255.5	1,262.8	1,261.0	1,243.9
2014	1,227.6	1,236.1	1,242.3	1,257.1	1,267.1	1,261.6	1,237.2	1,241.9	1,261.2	1,266.5	1,271.3	1,271.1	1,253.4
2015	1,240.9	1,248.8	1,255.7	1,268.7	1,277.8	1,274.9	1,251.7	1,251.7	1,266.8	1,277.2	1,281.4	1,280.5	1,264.7
2016	1,250.8	1,260.7	1,265.5	1,281.9	1,285.8	1,278.4	1,259.8	1,261.6	1,278.3	1,286.2	1,289.8	1,285.8	1,273.7
2017	1,255.4	1,266.6	1,270.3	1,285.7	1,289.5	1,288.5	1,264.4	1,267.6	1,280.5	1,288.5	1,292.5	1,290.2	1,278.3
2018	1,262.6	1,272.2	1,273.6	1,285.5	1,295.5	1,292.3	1,266.8	1,268.3	1,279.1	1,290.9	1,294.1	1,294.0	1,281.2
Mining and Logging													
2010	1.6	1.7	1.8	2.3	2.3	2.3	2.3	2.3	2.3	2.4	2.3	2.1	2.1
2011	1.7	1.8	1.8	2.2	2.3	2.4	2.4	2.4	2.4	2.4	2.3	2.2	2.2
2012	1.8	1.9	2.1	2.2	2.4	2.4	2.4	2.4	2.4	2.3	2.3	2.2	2.2
2013	1.8	1.8	2.0	2.1	2.4	2.5	2.5	2.5	2.5	2.4	2.4	2.3	2.3
2014	1.8	1.8	1.9	2.2	2.4	2.5	2.4	2.4	2.4	2.3	2.3	2.2	2.2
2015	1.8	1.9	2.1	2.3	2.4	2.5	2.5	2.5	2.4	2.3	2.2	2.1	2.3
2016	1.7	1.7	1.9	2.4	2.4	2.5	2.5	2.5	2.5	2.3	2.2	2.1	2.2
2017	1.9	2.0	2.2	2.4	2.5	2.5	2.5	2.5	2.5	2.5	2.5	2.4	2.4
2018	1.9	2.2	2.4	2.5	2.6	2.7	2.7	2.7	2.7	2.6	2.6	2.5	2.5
Construction													
2010	51.6	50.3	52.3	62.2	64.7	67.2	68.1	67.2	66.1	66.0	64.5	58.8	61.6
2011	50.6	49.6	52.1	60.8	64.5	67.4	69.0	69.3	68.6	68.3	66.8	61.4	62.4
2012	54.1	52.9	56.5	63.8	67.4	69.9	70.5	70.6	69.2	69.2	67.0	63.9	64.6
2013	56.1	55.3	56.5	63.0	69.5	72.8	74.9	75.6	74.1	74.4	73.3	67.9	67.8
2014	59.9	59.5	62.4	72.0	77.0	80.3	81.3	82.2	81.2	81.1	79.7	74.9	74.3
2015	67.2	66.8	69.3	77.8	80.2	82.8	84.2	83.9	82.7	83.6	82.4	78.0	78.2
2016	68.6	67.9	73.4	81.1	82.8	85.6	88.0	88.4	87.3	86.7	83.8	77.3	80.9
2017	66.9	66.9	69.5	75.7	78.7	81.2	81.1	80.9	79.9	79.6	78.3	74.1	76.1
2018	65.0	65.0	68.7	74.8	80.0	83.4	84.2	84.3	82.9	84.9	82.8	73.4	77.5

1. Employment by Industry: Iowa, 2010–2018—*Continued*

(Numbers in thousands, not seasonally adjusted)

Industry and year	January	February	March	April	May	June	July	August	September	October	November	December	Annual average
Manufacturing													
2010	197.1	196.7	198.1	199.3	199.5	201.2	202.0	202.7	202.5	202.4	202.9	203.0	200.6
2011	201.9	202.1	203.7	204.0	205.4	207.6	208.4	208.1	207.7	206.7	207.2	207.5	205.9
2012	205.8	206.2	207.8	209.1	210.7	213.0	213.6	213.2	212.1	212.2	212.4	212.2	210.7
2013	210.9	211.5	212.4	213.0	214.1	216.1	216.1	216.2	215.4	215.6	215.9	216.3	214.5
2014	214.7	215.1	216.0	216.7	217.9	219.6	219.6	218.9	217.0	216.2	216.6	216.9	217.1
2015	215.9	215.4	216.0	216.0	216.8	218.7	218.3	217.1	215.7	215.2	214.8	214.9	216.2
2016	214.0	213.3	214.1	213.5	214.0	215.9	215.6	215.2	213.6	212.8	212.5	213.4	214.0
2017	212.2	212.0	212.9	214.3	215.1	217.3	217.8	217.0	217.2	217.9	218.6	219.8	216.0
2018	218.3	218.7	219.1	220.5	221.8	224.4	225.0	223.9	223.7	225.1	227.2	227.9	223.0
Trade, Transportation, and Utilities													
2010	294.2	291.4	293.3	298.0	300.0	301.6	300.6	300.1	297.4	300.8	304.5	306.3	299.0
2011	295.4	293.8	295.8	300.4	303.6	304.9	304.0	303.7	302.3	304.9	309.8	311.9	302.5
2012	300.9	298.8	300.2	303.7	306.8	308.5	308.1	307.7	306.8	308.6	314.6	315.6	306.7
2013	304.1	302.5	304.3	307.3	310.9	312.7	312.3	311.5	309.9	311.8	317.6	318.4	310.3
2014	306.8	305.0	306.1	310.1	312.1	314.1	312.4	311.9	310.2	312.8	318.3	320.9	311.7
2015	310.4	308.7	310.2	312.6	314.7	317.2	316.1	314.6	312.4	315.3	319.8	321.0	314.4
2016	311.1	309.8	310.6	314.0	315.1	315.6	317.4	316.5	313.7	315.3	319.7	322.1	315.1
2017	311.1	309.7	310.1	313.6	314.9	316.3	315.2	314.2	311.8	314.0	318.9	320.8	314.2
2018	309.9	307.6	307.7	310.9	313.7	315.2	314.1	312.6	310.0	311.7	318.8	319.3	312.6
Wholesale Trade													
2010	64.2	63.9	64.4	66.6	66.3	66.3	66.2	65.5	65.3	66.3	66.2	65.5	65.6
2011	64.5	64.4	65.0	66.5	67.0	67.2	67.2	66.6	66.8	67.9	68.2	67.7	66.6
2012	66.3	66.4	67.5	68.6	68.9	69.1	68.9	68.3	68.3	68.6	68.8	68.0	68.1
2013	66.8	66.9	67.3	68.6	69.8	69.7	69.2	68.7	67.8	68.8	69.4	68.5	68.5
2014	67.1	67.0	67.3	69.0	69.5	69.6	69.0	68.4	67.7	68.8	69.1	68.3	68.4
2015	66.7	66.4	66.8	68.1	68.0	68.2	67.7	67.1	66.5	67.4	67.4	66.5	67.2
2016	65.4	65.3	66.0	67.1	67.0	66.9	66.9	66.2	66.1	66.6	66.7	66.0	66.4
2017	64.9	65.0	65.5	66.6	66.9	67.0	66.6	66.1	65.8	66.4	66.5	66.3	66.1
2018	65.0	64.9	65.5	66.3	66.9	67.0	66.6	66.0	65.8	65.9	66.5	66.5	66.1
Retail Trade													
2010	171.4	169.1	170.0	171.6	173.6	174.6	173.7	173.3	170.7	172.6	176.0	177.5	172.8
2011	170.8	169.1	170.1	172.6	174.7	175.5	175.1	175.0	173.3	174.8	179.0	180.9	174.2
2012	173.5	171.3	171.2	173.1	175.3	176.1	176.1	176.0	174.8	176.3	181.8	182.6	175.7
2013	174.6	172.8	173.8	175.6	177.3	178.7	178.9	178.6	177.8	178.8	183.3	183.9	177.8
2014	176.6	175.0	175.3	176.8	178.0	179.1	178.2	177.9	176.4	177.8	182.2	183.7	178.1
2015	177.1	175.9	176.8	178.9	180.9	182.3	181.6	180.9	179.1	181.3	185.1	186.0	180.5
2016	180.0	179.4	179.3	181.8	183.1	182.9	183.7	183.7	181.2	182.6	186.1	187.0	182.6
2017	180.6	179.4	178.9	181.3	182.1	182.7	182.1	181.6	179.7	180.9	184.9	185.3	181.6
2018	178.7	177.0	176.1	178.1	179.7	180.2	179.7	178.7	176.4	177.6	181.5	181.0	178.7
Transportation and Utilities													
2010	58.6	58.4	58.9	59.8	60.1	60.7	60.7	61.3	61.4	61.9	62.3	63.3	60.6
2011	60.1	60.3	60.7	61.3	61.9	62.2	61.7	62.1	62.2	62.2	62.6	63.3	61.7
2012	61.1	61.1	61.5	62.0	62.6	63.3	63.1	63.4	63.7	63.7	64.0	65.0	62.9
2013	62.7	62.8	63.2	63.1	63.8	64.3	64.2	64.2	64.3	64.2	64.9	66.0	64.0
2014	63.1	63.0	63.5	64.3	64.6	65.4	65.2	65.6	66.1	66.2	67.0	68.9	65.2
2015	66.6	66.4	66.6	65.6	65.8	66.7	66.8	66.6	66.8	66.6	67.3	68.5	66.7
2016	65.7	65.1	65.3	65.1	65.0	65.8	66.8	66.6	66.4	66.1	66.9	69.1	66.2
2017	65.6	65.3	65.7	65.7	65.9	66.6	66.5	66.5	66.3	66.7	67.5	69.2	66.5
2018	66.2	65.7	66.1	66.5	67.1	68.0	67.8	67.9	67.8	68.2	70.8	71.8	67.8
Information													
2010	29.0	29.2	29.1	29.2	29.2	28.8	28.6	28.3	27.7	28.3	28.4	28.7	28.7
2011	28.3	28.4	28.4	28.4	28.5	28.1	28.0	27.8	27.6	27.5	27.7	27.6	28.0
2012	27.3	27.5	27.6	27.3	27.2	27.2	26.9	26.6	26.3	26.6	26.8	26.6	27.0
2013	26.1	26.5	26.6	26.5	26.6	26.4	26.2	26.1	25.8	25.6	25.7	25.8	26.2
2014	25.9	25.9	26.0	26.2	26.2	26.0	25.7	25.5	25.4	25.6	25.3	25.5	25.8
2015	25.1	25.3	25.2	25.1	25.2	25.0	24.2	23.9	23.4	23.6	23.6	23.3	24.4
2016	23.1	23.1	22.8	22.8	22.8	22.8	22.9	22.7	22.4	22.3	22.2	22.2	22.7
2017	22.1	22.0	22.0	22.0	22.1	22.3	22.4	22.3	22.1	22.0	22.1	22.1	22.1
2018	22.0	22.1	22.1	22.1	22.2	22.3	22.2	22.1	21.9	22.0	21.6	21.6	22.0

1. Employment by Industry: Iowa, 2010–2018—*Continued*

(Numbers in thousands, not seasonally adjusted)

Industry and year	January	February	March	April	May	June	July	August	September	October	November	December	Annual average
Financial Activities													
2010	101.2	100.9	101.2	100.8	101.2	101.9	101.7	101.6	100.8	101.1	101.1	101.7	101.3
2011	100.7	100.4	100.3	100.4	100.7	101.0	101.3	101.4	100.5	100.3	100.6	101.1	100.7
2012	100.2	100.1	100.5	101.2	101.6	102.5	102.5	102.3	101.8	102.1	102.3	103.0	101.7
2013	102.5	102.4	102.6	103.2	103.6	104.3	104.4	104.3	103.6	104.0	104.3	104.5	103.6
2014	103.5	103.3	103.5	103.6	103.7	104.8	104.5	104.8	104.0	104.2	104.2	104.7	104.1
2015	104.0	104.0	104.5	104.9	105.3	106.5	106.6	106.6	106.0	106.1	106.4	107.4	105.7
2016	107.1	107.0	107.2	107.3	107.6	108.5	109.1	108.6	108.1	108.1	108.1	108.9	108.0
2017	108.0	107.9	108.0	108.4	108.8	109.8	110.1	109.8	108.9	108.9	108.9	109.5	108.9
2018	108.7	108.4	108.2	108.3	109.0	109.8	110.2	109.9	108.9	109.1	109.4	109.6	109.1
Professional and Business Services													
2010	115.9	117.0	117.9	122.0	121.4	122.3	124.0	124.4	123.4	125.6	125.4	124.9	122.0
2011	121.8	122.0	121.9	125.3	124.5	125.1	127.4	127.9	128.4	129.5	129.3	127.7	125.9
2012	125.1	126.1	127.7	130.1	129.7	131.6	132.8	132.6	132.4	132.6	131.7	130.0	130.2
2013	127.3	128.0	128.8	131.5	131.7	133.7	134.3	135.3	134.5	135.5	135.9	135.1	132.6
2014	131.5	132.5	132.1	136.3	137.2	138.4	139.0	140.0	138.5	139.9	139.1	137.8	136.9
2015	134.9	135.4	135.9	139.3	139.9	141.3	140.9	141.6	139.1	140.1	139.7	137.9	138.8
2016	134.7	135.5	135.4	139.8	138.8	139.5	141.6	141.3	140.4	141.4	140.7	138.7	139.0
2017	134.1	135.6	135.8	140.7	139.9	141.6	141.7	141.7	140.5	140.4	140.5	139.1	139.3
2018	136.8	138.3	137.7	140.5	141.3	142.2	143.3	142.7	141.6	142.7	142.5	142.4	141.0
Education and Health Services													
2010	214.2	216.3	217.8	217.6	215.0	208.4	203.0	202.7	212.4	219.7	220.6	221.0	214.1
2011	215.6	218.0	219.1	221.5	218.6	211.3	205.6	206.0	216.6	224.0	225.0	225.2	217.2
2012	219.6	222.8	224.2	223.8	221.6	214.2	208.4	209.6	218.5	225.5	226.8	226.1	220.1
2013	221.5	223.6	224.2	223.8	223.5	215.7	214.3	215.0	223.8	225.0	225.8	226.1	221.9
2014	220.3	223.5	225.7	226.5	225.1	218.2	214.8	215.3	223.7	226.6	227.1	227.5	222.9
2015	222.4	225.1	226.8	228.6	226.8	220.5	219.3	219.8	227.5	230.7	231.0	231.5	225.8
2016	227.3	231.3	232.7	234.7	232.5	223.2	221.8	222.2	230.9	234.8	235.3	234.1	230.1
2017	229.0	235.1	235.7	236.6	234.9	227.7	224.6	225.7	233.2	237.8	238.2	237.7	233.0
2018	233.3	238.4	238.7	238.6	237.3	229.9	225.2	227.1	234.0	237.9	237.8	238.2	234.7
Leisure and Hospitality													
2010	120.9	121.7	123.2	130.0	134.8	137.3	137.1	137.4	133.9	129.3	127.1	125.8	129.9
2011	122.1	122.2	124.9	131.7	136.4	139.6	138.7	139.8	136.5	131.1	129.4	127.9	131.7
2012	124.0	125.4	128.3	133.7	138.8	141.9	142.5	142.6	138.2	133.3	131.8	130.8	134.3
2013	126.4	127.9	130.0	135.3	140.7	144.5	144.9	145.2	140.4	135.5	134.1	132.2	136.4
2014	128.8	130.1	132.1	136.8	142.7	145.8	145.0	145.7	141.8	137.1	135.5	134.5	138.0
2015	130.8	132.3	134.8	139.4	145.4	148.8	148.6	148.8	144.1	140.8	138.9	137.5	140.9
2016	133.1	134.6	137.3	142.7	147.1	150.4	150.0	150.2	145.3	142.6	140.7	137.9	142.7
2017	134.5	136.1	138.0	142.7	146.8	150.8	150.3	150.3	145.9	143.3	140.7	138.7	143.2
2018	134.8	136.8	138.4	142.9	148.8	151.6	151.2	150.6	145.2	144.1	139.5	138.9	143.6
Other Services													
2010	56.3	56.3	56.8	57.3	57.4	57.7	57.3	56.9	56.5	57.0	56.7	56.7	56.9
2011	56.2	56.1	56.4	56.5	56.7	57.1	57.1	57.1	56.9	57.0	56.8	57.0	56.7
2012	56.9	56.7	57.1	57.6	58.0	58.5	58.2	58.4	57.7	58.1	58.2	57.8	57.8
2013	57.2	57.2	57.3	57.6	58.2	58.6	58.9	59.1	58.3	58.6	58.5	58.6	58.2
2014	58.2	58.2	58.6	58.8	59.5	60.0	59.8	59.7	59.1	59.1	59.2	58.9	59.1
2015	58.6	58.5	58.9	59.0	59.3	59.9	59.6	59.4	59.0	59.3	59.1	59.3	59.2
2016	58.6	58.5	58.6	58.6	58.9	59.5	59.6	59.1	58.7	58.3	58.0	57.6	58.7
2017	57.0	57.1	57.2	57.3	57.7	58.5	58.2	57.7	57.2	57.1	57.1	57.4	57.5
2018	56.6	56.7	57.1	57.2	57.7	58.7	58.3	57.7	57.2	57.5	57.3	57.6	57.5
Government													
2010	250.3	255.8	258.3	258.4	263.3	257.6	232.8	232.1	251.3	258.0	260.3	258.8	253.1
2011	249.5	255.5	256.5	257.9	259.2	255.3	235.9	236.4	254.0	257.8	258.8	258.2	252.9
2012	251.6	256.1	256.8	258.3	259.9	254.4	234.6	239.4	254.4	258.3	259.8	259.2	253.6
2013	250.1	256.5	257.0	257.4	260.8	256.3	238.8	241.8	256.9	259.5	260.9	260.3	254.7
2014	252.6	257.6	258.2	258.8	260.6	254.3	236.0	239.0	258.5	261.2	262.6	261.3	255.1
2015	254.7	259.5	259.4	259.8	261.2	255.7	236.4	237.0	255.3	261.3	262.9	262.6	255.5
2016	255.8	260.9	260.9	262.0	263.0	258.9	237.4	241.0	258.8	263.4	265.1	264.3	257.6
2017	259.6	263.1	263.5	264.4	264.4	261.5	241.9	245.9	260.9	265.0	266.1	264.9	260.1
2018	260.5	263.9	263.7	265.0	265.5	262.6	242.3	245.6	260.3	265.9	267.2	266.4	260.7

2. Average Weekly Hours by Selected Industry: Iowa, 2014–2018

(Not seasonally adjusted)

Industry and year	January	February	March	April	May	June	July	August	September	October	November	December	Annual average
Total Private													
2014	34.2	35.1	35.0	35.0	34.9	35.7	35.2	35.3	35.1	35.2	35.4	34.8	35.1
2015	34.2	34.8	34.7	34.7	34.6	34.8	34.9	35.3	34.5	34.8	34.7	34.3	34.7
2016	33.8	33.8	34.0	34.4	34.6	35.1	34.8	34.8	34.7	35.1	34.7	34.2	34.5
2017	34.1	34.0	33.8	34.6	34.2	34.6	34.5	34.4	34.4	34.6	34.7	34.3	34.4
2018	33.6	33.7	33.9	34.2	34.4	34.7	34.9	34.5	34.8	34.8	34.6	34.7	34.4
Goods Producing													
2014	40.0	40.6	40.7	41.2	41.5	42.5	42.0	42.0	41.4	42.0	41.8	41.3	41.4
2015	40.3	40.5	40.6	41.1	40.9	41.1	41.1	41.8	40.0	41.7	41.3	41.3	41.0
2016	39.3	39.9	40.6	41.5	41.2	42.9	41.8	41.8	41.8	42.2	42.7	40.6	41.4
2017	39.6	40.0	40.0	40.4	40.4	40.9	40.5	40.6	40.7	40.8	41.0	40.4	40.5
2018	38.9	39.2	39.4	39.8	40.3	40.7	40.9	40.3	41.2	40.2	40.0	40.3	40.1
Construction													
2014	38.7	38.4	39.8	42.6	42.0	43.6	43.3	43.3	41.3	43.8	41.9	40.4	41.8
2015	38.6	38.5	38.9	40.4	40.6	41.2	41.9	42.9	38.9	42.0	41.7	41.7	40.7
2016	38.1	39.3	41.8	43.8	43.2	47.3	45.1	45.2	45.2	45.5	45.3	41.4	43.6
2017	39.2	39.3	39.2	40.5	40.4	41.5	41.4	41.7	41.4	39.5	40.3	38.6	40.3
2018	35.4	36.0	37.4	38.3	40.4	41.2	41.8	41.0	42.4	38.6	39.4	39.5	39.5
Manufacturing													
2014	40.5	41.4	41.0	40.7	41.3	42.0	41.5	41.5	41.6	41.3	41.9	41.9	41.4
2015	41.1	41.4	41.4	41.6	41.2	41.2	40.9	41.4	40.7	41.7	41.2	41.2	41.2
2016	40.1	40.4	40.3	40.3	40.1	40.3	40.1	40.0	39.9	40.3	41.3	40.4	40.3
2017	39.5	40.0	40.1	40.1	40.2	40.4	39.8	39.8	40.2	41.2	40.8	40.6	40.2
2018	39.6	39.8	39.7	39.8	39.7	39.9	39.9	39.4	39.8	40.5	39.8	39.9	39.8
Trade, Transportation, and Utilities													
2014	32.8	33.2	32.8	33.1	33.2	33.7	33.2	33.1	33.1	32.7	32.8	32.0	33.0
2015	31.7	32.2	31.8	31.9	32.1	32.5	32.5	32.8	33.0	32.5	32.1	31.8	32.2
2016	31.8	31.8	31.7	32.0	32.2	32.5	32.3	32.2	32.3	32.4	31.9	32.1	32.1
2017	32.4	32.1	32.3	33.0	32.7	33.0	32.9	32.8	32.7	32.6	32.9	32.5	32.7
2018	31.9	32.1	33.0	32.9	33.7	33.8	33.8	33.4	33.2	32.8	32.6	32.5	33.0
Financial Activities													
2014	38.4	39.1	38.8	38.3	38.2	39.2	38.5	38.7	38.7	38.7	39.6	38.8	38.7
2015	38.2	39.2	39.0	38.7	38.2	38.3	38.2	38.7	38.1	38.1	39.0	37.7	38.4
2016	37.9	38.0	37.7	38.0	38.8	37.9	38.0	37.8	37.8	39.0	37.7	37.5	38.0
2017	38.2	37.1	36.8	37.6	37.2	37.6	38.0	37.6	37.5	38.4	37.8	38.0	37.6
2018	38.2	38.1	37.8	38.6	37.9	38.1	38.5	38.0	38.7	38.1	38.1	38.6	38.2
Professional and Business Services													
2014	34.5	36.9	37.3	36.5	34.7	35.9	35.2	35.5	35.3	36.2	36.7	36.0	35.9
2015	35.0	36.2	36.3	36.0	35.9	35.9	36.4	36.8	35.2	35.7	35.9	35.6	35.9
2016	34.9	34.7	34.9	35.7	35.7	35.7	35.5	35.6	35.3	36.0	34.9	34.7	35.3
2017	34.5	34.5	34.4	35.1	34.8	35.0	35.2	35.0	35.2	35.0	35.2	34.6	34.9
2018	33.9	34.3	34.3	34.9	35.3	36.1	36.3	35.9	36.6	35.5	35.4	34.3	35.2
Education and Health Services													
2014	31.3	31.4	31.5	31.6	31.5	32.4	31.9	32.0	32.1	32.0	32.2	31.8	31.8
2015	31.8	31.9	31.7	31.6	31.6	31.9	32.3	32.5	32.1	31.9	32.3	31.7	31.9
2016	32.0	31.4	31.3	31.8	32.0	32.2	32.0	32.0	32.2	32.3	32.5	32.3	32.0
2017	32.5	31.9	31.2	32.1	31.3	31.5	31.9	31.3	31.6	31.6	31.6	31.2	31.6
2018	31.1	30.6	30.6	31.5	30.8	31.1	31.8	31.2	31.3	30.9	30.9	31.2	31.1
Leisure and Hospitality													
2014	23.7	24.8	24.9	24.6	25.1	25.7	25.6	25.4	24.8	25.0	24.7	24.7	24.9
2015	23.5	24.7	24.8	24.2	24.4	24.8	25.2	25.7	24.5	24.3	24.1	23.8	24.5
2016	23.4	23.7	24.0	23.7	24.1	24.7	24.7	24.7	24.2	24.4	23.9	23.8	24.1
2017	23.7	23.9	23.7	24.3	23.8	24.5	24.5	24.1	23.7	24.2	23.9	24.0	24.0
2018	23.2	23.4	23.8	23.8	24.2	24.6	24.8	24.0	23.7	23.5	23.4	23.9	23.9
Other Services													
2014	28.2	28.5	28.7	28.6	28.6	29.9	29.4	29.4	29.6	29.4	30.0	29.9	29.2
2015	30.0	30.5	29.4	28.7	28.7	29.2	29.6	29.4	28.5	28.3	26.9	26.9	28.8
2016	26.8	25.9	26.5	25.8	27.1	28.5	28.2	28.7	28.7	28.6	29.3	29.4	27.8
2017	29.1	29.2	28.1	28.1	28.6	30.2	30.1	30.1	29.9	30.6	30.3	30.7	29.6
2018	30.1	30.6	30.6	30.7	30.8	31.8	31.0	31.7	31.5	31.2	31.6	31.8	31.1

3. Average Hourly Earnings by Selected Industry: Iowa, 2014–2018

(Dollars, not seasonally adjusted)

Industry and year	January	February	March	April	May	June	July	August	September	October	November	December	Annual average
Total Private													
2014	21.92	21.86	21.87	21.68	21.71	21.81	21.75	21.79	21.92	22.02	22.09	22.11	21.88
2015	22.10	22.28	22.35	22.48	22.57	22.31	22.37	23.01	22.99	22.94	22.51	22.67	22.55
2016	22.75	22.79	23.06	23.37	23.37	23.39	23.27	23.08	23.23	23.57	23.42	23.34	23.23
2017	23.33	23.26	23.44	23.47	23.11	23.03	23.39	23.23	23.49	23.55	23.70	24.00	23.42
2018	23.98	23.72	23.86	23.95	23.90	23.92	24.11	24.15	24.68	24.45	24.44	24.67	24.16
Goods Producing													
2014	22.88	22.96	23.00	23.02	22.78	23.03	22.92	23.29	23.35	23.52	23.73	24.15	23.22
2015	23.87	24.18	24.11	24.14	24.16	24.01	24.27	24.57	24.44	23.48	22.90	23.20	23.94
2016	23.21	23.69	24.14	24.96	25.32	26.07	25.49	25.24	25.49	25.93	25.85	25.70	25.13
2017	25.42	24.98	25.21	25.18	24.60	24.78	25.19	24.77	25.02	25.07	25.30	26.12	25.13
2018	25.54	25.23	25.49	25.81	25.96	26.17	26.65	26.40	26.76	26.37	26.56	27.04	26.19
Construction													
2014	25.03	24.97	24.76	24.86	24.43	24.42	24.35	24.59	24.91	25.27	25.54	26.05	24.92
2015	25.89	25.80	26.00	25.29	25.19	25.54	25.35	25.84	26.17	26.90	27.54	28.53	26.19
2016	28.61	29.59	29.35	29.87	29.76	31.96	31.14	30.57	30.66	30.37	30.98	30.22	30.36
2017	29.14	28.49	28.20	26.99	26.54	26.02	26.22	25.95	26.08	26.08	26.53	25.97	26.77
2018	25.48	25.77	25.36	26.05	26.59	27.32	27.82	27.69	27.90	27.85	28.10	28.34	27.14
Manufacturing													
2014	22.09	22.22	22.34	22.27	22.08	22.42	22.27	22.71	22.69	22.71	22.93	23.39	22.51
2015	23.17	23.61	23.47	23.64	23.70	23.33	23.79	23.98	23.69	24.90	24.15	23.72	23.76
2016	23.52	23.48	23.73	24.09	24.48	24.28	24.15	23.85	24.00	24.74	24.11	25.15	24.13
2017	25.12	24.66	25.01	25.50	24.61	25.04	25.33	24.74	24.98	25.01	25.10	26.53	25.14
2018	25.91	25.37	25.77	25.69	25.63	25.55	25.85	25.55	26.00	25.46	25.62	26.29	25.72
Trade, Transportation, and Utilities													
2014	18.81	18.76	18.88	18.81	18.79	18.79	18.94	19.23	19.36	19.15	19.45	19.15	19.01
2015	19.22	19.55	19.56	20.11	20.23	19.53	19.80	20.68	20.62	21.14	20.57	20.95	20.17
2016	21.28	21.00	21.19	21.48	21.03	20.80	20.89	20.78	21.19	21.33	21.13	20.93	21.08
2017	21.32	21.38	21.35	21.84	21.10	20.88	21.23	21.04	21.36	21.05	21.13	21.00	21.22
2018	21.63	21.42	21.52	21.48	21.50	21.49	21.43	21.51	22.39	22.10	21.90	22.26	21.72
Financial Activities													
2014	28.52	28.72	28.82	28.56	28.45	28.22	28.08	27.65	27.72	28.16	27.51	27.40	28.15
2015	27.61	27.28	27.79	28.13	28.19	27.87	27.77	28.15	28.16	28.42	28.73	28.73	28.07
2016	28.84	28.89	29.64	29.70	29.96	29.43	29.47	29.23	29.57	30.16	30.24	30.00	29.60
2017	30.12	30.15	30.80	30.72	30.54	30.13	30.62	30.52	30.73	30.85	31.13	31.47	30.65
2018	31.32	31.14	31.58	31.81	31.60	31.86	32.06	31.93	32.35	31.97	32.02	32.15	31.82
Professional and Business Services													
2014	23.45	22.86	23.02	22.37	23.59	24.29	23.84	23.79	23.94	23.66	24.14	23.99	23.58
2015	23.88	24.33	24.14	23.61	24.18	24.07	24.27	24.63	24.71	24.82	23.19	23.16	24.09
2016	23.48	23.61	23.76	23.98	24.29	24.49	24.75	24.40	24.51	25.07	25.09	25.84	24.45
2017	25.16	25.13	25.44	25.60	25.73	25.61	25.76	25.49	25.57	25.99	25.95	26.92	25.70
2018	26.53	26.20	26.28	26.10	25.92	25.76	25.99	26.17	26.00	26.08	25.83	26.32	26.09
Education and Health Services													
2014	21.13	20.80	20.77	20.53	20.62	20.54	20.61	20.19	20.33	20.16	20.14	20.21	20.50
2015	20.20	20.40	20.68	20.69	20.74	20.92	20.55	20.68	20.88	21.09	20.97	21.19	20.75
2016	21.01	21.06	21.23	21.10	21.00	20.98	21.13	21.00	21.20	21.39	21.13	21.14	21.12
2017	21.32	21.19	21.28	21.17	21.10	21.28	21.41	21.59	21.59	21.60	21.83	21.61	21.41
2018	21.63	21.31	21.25	21.19	21.23	21.03	20.91	21.13	21.25	21.06	21.25	21.06	21.19
Leisure and Hospitality													
2014	12.53	12.65	12.45	12.50	12.37	12.25	12.09	12.13	12.37	12.37	12.38	12.71	12.39
2015	12.72	12.61	12.30	12.43	12.47	12.19	12.22	12.49	12.46	12.60	12.79	12.95	12.51
2016	12.82	12.84	12.74	12.94	12.80	12.49	12.63	12.51	12.84	12.87	12.85	13.06	12.78
2017	12.79	13.02	12.89	12.81	12.88	12.50	12.78	12.81	13.03	13.05	13.15	13.28	12.91
2018	13.52	13.48	13.46	13.51	13.50	13.27	13.33	13.46	13.77	13.88	13.92	14.08	13.59
Other Services													
2014	19.36	19.52	19.54	19.70	19.49	19.13	19.56	19.69	19.24	20.07	20.21	20.06	19.63
2015	20.57	21.11	21.09	21.14	21.37	20.48	20.50	20.61	20.56	20.61	20.07	19.97	20.68
2016	19.82	19.38	19.45	20.05	19.82	19.27	19.40	19.49	20.26	19.80	18.91	18.62	19.52
2017	18.60	19.27	19.11	19.22	18.96	18.34	18.20	18.03	18.14	18.48	18.40	18.38	18.58
2018	18.41	18.58	18.67	18.81	18.97	19.08	19.39	19.71	19.65	19.52	20.33	20.60	19.32

4. Average Weekly Earnings by Selected Industry: Iowa, 2014–2018

(Dollars, not seasonally adjusted)

Industry and year	January	February	March	April	May	June	July	August	September	October	November	December	Annual average
Total Private													
2014	749.66	767.29	765.45	758.80	757.68	778.62	765.60	769.19	769.39	775.10	781.99	769.43	767.99
2015	755.82	775.34	775.55	780.06	780.92	776.39	780.71	812.25	793.16	798.31	781.10	777.58	782.49
2016	768.95	770.30	784.04	803.93	808.60	820.99	809.80	803.18	806.08	827.31	812.67	798.23	801.44
2017	795.55	790.84	792.27	812.06	790.36	796.84	806.96	799.11	808.06	814.83	822.39	823.20	805.65
2018	805.73	799.36	808.85	819.09	822.16	830.02	841.44	833.18	858.86	850.86	845.62	856.05	831.10
Goods Producing													
2014	915.20	932.18	936.10	948.42	945.37	978.78	962.64	978.18	966.69	987.84	991.91	997.40	961.31
2015	961.96	979.29	978.87	992.15	988.14	986.81	997.50	1,027.03	977.60	979.12	945.77	958.16	981.54
2016	912.15	945.23	980.08	1,035.84	1,043.18	1,118.40	1,065.48	1,055.03	1,065.48	1,094.25	1,103.80	1,043.42	1,040.38
2017	1,006.63	999.20	1,008.40	1,017.27	993.84	1,013.50	1,020.20	1,005.66	1,018.31	1,022.86	1,037.30	1,055.25	1,017.77
2018	993.51	989.02	1,004.31	1,027.24	1,046.19	1,065.12	1,089.99	1,063.92	1,102.51	1,060.07	1,062.40	1,089.71	1,050.22
Construction													
2014	968.66	958.85	985.45	1,059.04	1,026.06	1,064.71	1,054.36	1,064.75	1,028.78	1,106.83	1,070.13	1,052.42	1,041.66
2015	999.35	993.30	1,011.40	1,021.72	1,022.71	1,052.25	1,062.17	1,108.54	1,018.01	1,129.80	1,148.42	1,189.70	1,065.93
2016	1,090.04	1,162.89	1,226.83	1,308.31	1,285.63	1,511.71	1,404.41	1,381.76	1,385.83	1,381.84	1,403.39	1,251.11	1,323.70
2017	1,142.29	1,119.66	1,105.44	1,093.10	1,072.22	1,079.83	1,085.51	1,082.12	1,079.71	1,030.16	1,069.16	1,002.44	1,078.83
2018	901.99	927.72	948.46	997.72	1,074.24	1,125.58	1,162.88	1,135.29	1,182.96	1,075.01	1,107.14	1,119.43	1,072.03
Manufacturing													
2014	894.65	919.91	915.94	906.39	911.90	941.64	924.21	942.47	943.90	937.92	960.77	980.04	931.91
2015	952.29	977.45	971.66	983.42	976.44	961.20	973.01	992.77	964.18	1,038.33	994.98	977.26	978.91
2016	943.15	948.59	956.32	970.83	981.65	978.48	968.42	954.00	957.60	997.02	995.74	1,016.06	972.44
2017	992.24	986.40	1,002.90	1,022.55	989.32	1,011.62	1,008.13	984.65	1,004.20	1,030.41	1,024.08	1,077.12	1,010.63
2018	1,026.04	1,009.73	1,023.07	1,022.46	1,017.51	1,019.45	1,031.42	1,006.67	1,034.80	1,031.13	1,019.68	1,048.97	1,023.66
Trade, Transportation, and Utilities													
2014	616.97	622.83	619.26	622.61	623.83	633.22	628.81	636.51	640.82	626.21	637.96	612.80	627.33
2015	609.27	629.51	622.01	641.51	649.38	634.73	643.50	678.30	680.46	687.05	660.30	666.21	649.47
2016	676.70	667.80	671.72	687.36	677.17	676.00	674.75	669.12	684.44	691.09	674.05	671.85	676.67
2017	690.77	686.30	689.61	720.72	689.97	689.04	698.47	690.11	698.47	686.23	695.18	682.50	693.89
2018	690.00	687.58	710.16	706.69	724.55	726.36	724.33	718.43	743.35	724.88	713.94	723.45	716.76
Financial Activities													
2014	1,095.17	1,122.95	1,118.22	1,093.85	1,086.79	1,106.22	1,081.08	1,070.06	1,072.76	1,089.79	1,089.40	1,063.12	1,089.41
2015	1,054.70	1,069.38	1,083.81	1,088.63	1,076.86	1,067.42	1,060.81	1,089.41	1,072.90	1,082.80	1,120.47	1,083.12	1,077.89
2016	1,093.04	1,097.82	1,117.43	1,128.60	1,162.45	1,115.40	1,119.86	1,104.89	1,117.75	1,176.24	1,140.05	1,125.00	1,124.80
2017	1,150.58	1,118.57	1,133.44	1,155.07	1,136.09	1,132.89	1,163.56	1,147.55	1,152.38	1,184.64	1,176.71	1,195.86	1,152.44
2018	1,196.42	1,186.43	1,193.72	1,227.87	1,197.64	1,213.87	1,234.31	1,213.34	1,251.95	1,218.06	1,219.96	1,240.99	1,215.52
Professional and Business Services													
2014	809.03	843.53	858.65	816.51	818.57	872.01	839.17	844.55	845.08	856.49	885.94	863.64	846.52
2015	835.80	880.75	876.28	849.96	868.06	864.11	883.43	906.38	869.79	886.07	832.52	824.50	864.83
2016	819.45	819.27	829.22	856.09	867.15	874.29	878.63	868.64	865.20	902.52	875.64	896.65	863.09
2017	868.02	866.99	875.14	898.56	895.40	896.35	906.75	892.15	900.06	909.65	913.44	931.43	896.93
2018	899.37	898.66	901.40	910.89	914.98	929.94	943.44	939.50	951.60	925.84	914.38	902.78	918.37
Education and Health Services													
2014	661.37	653.12	654.26	648.75	649.53	665.50	657.46	646.08	652.59	645.12	648.51	642.68	651.90
2015	642.36	650.76	655.56	653.80	655.38	667.35	663.77	672.10	670.25	672.77	677.33	671.72	661.93
2016	672.32	661.28	664.50	670.98	672.00	675.56	676.16	672.00	682.64	690.73	686.73	682.82	675.84
2017	692.90	675.96	663.94	679.56	660.43	670.32	682.98	675.77	682.24	682.56	689.83	674.23	676.56
2018	672.69	652.09	650.25	667.49	653.88	654.03	664.94	659.26	665.13	650.75	656.63	657.07	659.01
Leisure and Hospitality													
2014	296.96	313.72	310.01	307.50	310.49	314.83	309.50	308.10	306.78	309.25	305.79	313.94	308.51
2015	298.92	311.47	305.04	300.81	304.27	302.31	307.94	320.99	305.27	306.18	308.24	308.21	306.50
2016	299.99	304.31	305.76	306.68	308.48	308.50	311.96	309.00	310.73	314.03	307.12	310.83	308.00
2017	303.12	311.18	305.49	311.28	306.54	306.25	313.11	308.72	308.81	315.81	314.29	318.72	309.84
2018	313.66	315.43	320.35	321.54	326.70	326.44	330.58	323.04	326.35	326.18	325.73	336.51	324.80
Other Services													
2014	545.95	556.32	560.80	563.42	557.41	571.99	575.06	578.89	569.50	590.06	606.30	599.79	573.20
2015	617.10	643.86	620.05	606.72	613.32	598.02	606.80	605.93	585.96	583.26	539.88	537.19	595.58
2016	531.18	501.94	515.43	517.29	537.12	549.20	547.08	559.36	581.46	566.28	554.06	547.43	542.66
2017	541.26	562.68	536.99	540.08	542.26	553.87	547.82	542.70	542.39	565.49	557.52	564.27	549.97
2018	554.14	568.55	571.30	577.47	584.28	606.74	601.09	624.81	618.98	609.02	642.43	655.08	600.85

KANSAS
At a Glance

Population:
  2010 census: 2,853,118
  2018 estimate: 2,911,505

Percent change in population:
  2010–2018: 2.0%

Percent change in total nonfarm employment:
  2010–2018: 6.5%

Industry with the largest growth in employment, 2010–2018 (percent):
  Transportation and utilities, 20.0%

Industry with the largest decline or smallest growth in employment, 2010–2018 (percent):
  Information, -30.2%

Civilian labor force:
  2010: 1,500,764
  2018: 1,482,220

Unemployment rate and rank among states (highest to lowest):
  2010: 7.1%, 41st
  2018: 3.4%, 32nd

Over-the-year change in unemployment rates:
  2016–2017: -0.3%
  2017–2018: -0.3%

Employment by Industry: Kansas, 2018

- Other, 10%
- Financial activities, 5%
- Leisure and hospitality, 9%
- Manufacturing, 12%
- Professional and business services, 13%
- Education and health services, 14%
- Government, 18%
- Trade, transportation, and utilities, 19%

1. Employment by Industry: Kansas, 2010–2018

(Numbers in thousands, not seasonally adjusted)

Industry and year	January	February	March	April	May	June	July	August	September	October	November	December	Annual average
Total Nonfarm													
2010	1,301.9	1,305.3	1,316.1	1,334.8	1,347.0	1,342.8	1,318.5	1,319.1	1,332.9	1,348.0	1,345.8	1,345.6	1,329.8
2011	1,315.5	1,317.0	1,326.7	1,347.6	1,353.9	1,340.9	1,325.2	1,328.4	1,348.2	1,357.6	1,359.5	1,355.0	1,339.6
2012	1,331.8	1,339.6	1,351.3	1,360.0	1,370.8	1,366.1	1,337.3	1,344.2	1,361.0	1,374.8	1,377.6	1,375.2	1,357.5
2013	1,341.7	1,352.8	1,359.0	1,375.2	1,380.8	1,374.5	1,354.1	1,359.8	1,382.7	1,391.8	1,397.4	1,395.4	1,372.1
2014	1,359.1	1,370.3	1,381.4	1,394.9	1,403.5	1,396.4	1,375.1	1,379.5	1,397.3	1,408.9	1,412.3	1,412.0	1,390.9
2015	1,374.6	1,387.3	1,392.7	1,402.5	1,410.5	1,405.6	1,384.7	1,387.1	1,404.8	1,417.0	1,418.9	1,418.1	1,400.3
2016	1,381.9	1,392.4	1,397.9	1,413.5	1,413.4	1,403.4	1,387.0	1,388.6	1,410.8	1,420.0	1,422.0	1,417.8	1,404.1
2017	1,379.8	1,395.2	1,400.8	1,403.1	1,407.2	1,400.8	1,385.3	1,388.8	1,410.3	1,420.1	1,426.7	1,425.1	1,403.6
2018	1,388.1	1,403.0	1,405.4	1,416.2	1,421.0	1,414.6	1,398.8	1,409.2	1,423.4	1,434.1	1,440.3	1,435.5	1,415.8
Total Private													
2010	1,042.0	1,041.9	1,048.5	1,065.8	1,070.9	1,076.0	1,076.6	1,075.7	1,070.0	1,081.3	1,081.4	1,080.7	1,067.6
2011	1,053.9	1,053.6	1,061.5	1,079.5	1,084.9	1,084.6	1,087.0	1,088.4	1,085.8	1,091.8	1,093.7	1,092.2	1,079.7
2012	1,074.1	1,076.7	1,086.8	1,095.5	1,103.1	1,110.9	1,102.8	1,104.3	1,101.9	1,108.9	1,111.3	1,111.1	1,099.0
2013	1,085.7	1,089.5	1,095.4	1,109.3	1,116.8	1,123.6	1,121.9	1,124.0	1,122.1	1,127.2	1,132.0	1,131.8	1,114.9
2014	1,104.7	1,108.1	1,117.9	1,131.3	1,139.9	1,144.2	1,141.0	1,143.1	1,137.8	1,144.2	1,147.3	1,148.7	1,134.0
2015	1,119.9	1,124.7	1,128.9	1,138.2	1,146.3	1,152.6	1,151.5	1,151.6	1,146.3	1,153.9	1,155.6	1,156.1	1,143.8
2016	1,129.2	1,131.5	1,135.2	1,149.6	1,151.1	1,151.6	1,154.8	1,153.7	1,151.5	1,156.0	1,158.1	1,154.3	1,148.1
2017	1,127.1	1,133.3	1,138.2	1,140.4	1,144.9	1,150.1	1,152.6	1,152.9	1,151.2	1,155.9	1,161.6	1,161.1	1,147.4
2018	1,134.3	1,140.0	1,141.7	1,151.8	1,157.1	1,163.1	1,164.3	1,164.1	1,160.8	1,168.4	1,174.1	1,170.1	1,157.5
Goods Producing													
2010	212.1	211.6	213.7	219.3	220.7	223.7	225.6	225.5	224.2	224.7	222.7	220.6	220.4
2011	212.2	211.6	215.5	219.6	221.1	223.2	225.0	225.1	224.3	225.8	224.5	223.4	220.9
2012	219.9	219.6	223.7	223.8	226.4	228.5	229.1	228.7	228.3	228.1	226.8	224.5	225.6
2013	219.9	220.7	222.8	226.5	228.3	230.5	230.9	231.2	231.0	231.6	232.0	230.8	228.0
2014	225.5	227.6	230.0	232.4	234.1	236.9	235.5	235.8	234.0	234.4	233.2	232.4	232.7
2015	224.5	227.7	229.3	229.0	232.3	234.1	233.7	232.5	232.4	232.4	231.7	230.8	230.9
2016	225.2	225.0	227.0	228.5	228.8	230.5	230.6	230.6	230.1	230.1	229.6	227.6	228.6
2017	223.9	225.6	227.1	226.0	227.4	230.7	230.9	229.5	230.1	230.2	229.8	230.2	228.5
2018	224.1	227.1	228.6	230.4	232.1	235.8	236.6	236.8	236.4	235.6	236.1	235.4	232.9
Service-Providing													
2010	1,089.8	1,093.7	1,102.4	1,115.5	1,126.3	1,119.1	1,092.9	1,093.6	1,108.7	1,123.3	1,123.1	1,125.0	1,109.5
2011	1,103.3	1,105.4	1,111.2	1,128.0	1,132.8	1,117.7	1,100.2	1,103.3	1,123.9	1,131.8	1,135.0	1,131.6	1,118.7
2012	1,111.9	1,120.0	1,127.6	1,136.2	1,144.4	1,137.6	1,108.2	1,115.5	1,132.7	1,146.7	1,150.8	1,150.7	1,131.9
2013	1,121.8	1,132.1	1,136.2	1,148.7	1,152.5	1,144.0	1,123.2	1,128.6	1,151.7	1,160.2	1,165.4	1,164.6	1,144.1
2014	1,133.6	1,142.7	1,151.4	1,162.5	1,169.4	1,159.5	1,139.6	1,143.7	1,163.3	1,174.5	1,179.1	1,179.6	1,158.2
2015	1,150.1	1,159.6	1,163.4	1,173.5	1,178.2	1,171.5	1,151.0	1,154.6	1,172.4	1,184.6	1,187.2	1,187.3	1,169.5
2016	1,156.7	1,167.4	1,170.9	1,185.0	1,184.6	1,172.9	1,156.4	1,158.0	1,180.7	1,189.9	1,192.4	1,190.2	1,175.4
2017	1,155.9	1,169.6	1,173.7	1,177.1	1,179.8	1,170.1	1,154.4	1,159.3	1,180.2	1,189.9	1,196.9	1,194.9	1,175.2
2018	1,164.0	1,175.9	1,176.8	1,185.8	1,188.9	1,178.8	1,162.2	1,172.4	1,187.0	1,198.5	1,204.2	1,200.1	1,182.9
Mining and Logging													
2010	7.8	7.9	8.0	8.3	8.3	8.4	8.5	8.5	8.5	8.8	8.6	8.6	8.4
2011	8.4	8.3	8.5	8.8	8.8	9.0	9.5	9.5	9.4	9.5	9.5	9.6	9.1
2012	9.5	9.5	9.6	9.6	9.8	10.0	10.3	10.3	10.1	10.5	10.5	10.5	10.0
2013	10.1	10.1	10.1	10.4	10.5	10.5	10.7	10.6	10.5	10.6	10.7	10.8	10.5
2014	10.4	10.3	10.4	10.6	10.7	10.6	10.6	10.6	10.5	10.5	10.4	10.3	10.5
2015	9.9	9.3	8.9	8.6	8.6	8.6	8.5	8.4	8.1	7.8	7.7	7.7	8.5
2016	7.2	6.9	6.8	6.7	6.8	6.8	6.9	6.9	6.8	6.7	6.8	6.7	6.8
2017	6.6	6.6	6.7	6.7	6.7	6.8	6.8	6.8	6.8	6.8	6.7	6.7	6.7
2018	6.6	6.6	6.7	6.8	6.7	6.8	6.8	6.9	6.9	6.9	6.8	6.8	6.8
Construction													
2010	47.2	46.7	49.2	53.8	54.7	56.9	58.6	58.4	57.4	57.6	55.5	53.2	54.1
2011	47.1	46.8	49.9	52.6	53.9	55.2	56.0	55.8	55.6	56.3	54.7	53.1	53.1
2012	50.5	50.5	53.9	54.8	56.2	57.8	57.6	57.2	56.7	56.2	54.9	53.5	55.0
2013	50.0	50.9	52.1	55.4	56.7	59.0	59.7	60.2	59.9	60.1	59.6	57.9	56.8
2014	55.3	54.6	57.4	59.8	61.6	62.6	63.2	62.3	61.1	61.4	59.7	58.7	59.8
2015	55.1	56.1	58.3	61.5	61.8	62.7	63.8	63.4	62.7	63.3	62.5	61.2	61.0
2016	57.3	57.2	59.8	61.2	61.6	63.5	64.0	63.4	63.1	63.2	62.3	60.3	61.4
2017	57.5	58.4	59.9	59.3	60.1	61.8	62.4	61.8	60.8	61.0	60.2	59.8	60.3
2018	56.4	56.8	58.7	59.9	61.2	63.3	63.8	63.8	63.5	62.6	62.0	60.7	61.1

1. Employment by Industry: Kansas, 2010–2018—*Continued*

(Numbers in thousands, not seasonally adjusted)

Industry and year	January	February	March	April	May	June	July	August	September	October	November	December	Annual average
Manufacturing													
2010	157.1	157.0	156.5	157.2	157.7	158.4	158.5	158.6	158.3	158.3	158.6	158.8	157.9
2011	156.7	156.5	157.1	158.2	158.4	159.0	159.5	159.8	159.3	160.0	160.3	160.7	158.8
2012	159.9	159.6	160.2	159.4	160.4	160.7	161.2	161.2	161.5	161.4	161.4	160.5	160.6
2013	159.8	159.7	160.6	160.7	161.1	161.0	160.5	160.4	160.6	160.9	161.7	162.1	160.8
2014	159.8	162.7	162.2	162.0	161.8	163.7	161.7	162.9	162.4	162.5	163.1	163.4	162.4
2015	159.5	162.3	162.1	158.9	161.9	162.8	161.4	160.7	161.6	161.3	161.5	161.9	161.3
2016	160.7	160.9	160.4	160.6	160.6	160.2	159.7	160.3	160.2	160.2	160.5	160.6	160.4
2017	159.8	160.6	160.5	160.0	160.6	162.1	161.7	160.9	162.5	162.4	162.9	163.7	161.5
2018	161.1	163.7	163.2	163.7	164.2	165.7	166.0	166.1	166.0	166.1	167.3	167.9	165.1
Trade, Transportation, and Utilities													
2010	246.7	245.2	246.3	249.1	250.7	251.9	251.4	251.0	249.6	253.0	256.2	257.6	250.7
2011	249.5	248.3	247.6	252.4	253.9	253.4	253.2	253.3	252.3	254.6	258.5	259.6	253.1
2012	252.3	250.5	251.6	253.2	254.9	256.8	253.7	253.9	253.5	256.1	260.0	261.0	254.8
2013	252.9	251.8	252.3	253.6	255.3	256.7	256.3	257.3	256.5	258.9	263.4	265.1	256.7
2014	256.2	254.2	257.0	258.8	260.5	261.3	261.2	261.9	260.4	263.2	267.4	269.7	261.0
2015	261.0	258.8	259.5	261.2	263.6	265.3	264.7	265.1	263.9	266.8	270.5	271.8	264.4
2016	263.1	262.6	262.6	265.5	266.5	266.1	267.2	266.9	265.7	268.2	272.8	274.6	266.8
2017	264.9	264.0	263.6	263.0	264.4	264.3	265.5	267.9	267.8	269.6	275.7	276.6	267.3
2018	267.6	265.7	265.2	266.3	268.0	267.9	268.0	268.2	267.6	271.2	275.4	273.6	268.7
Wholesale Trade													
2010	55.3	55.3	55.5	56.9	56.9	57.7	57.6	56.8	56.2	56.6	56.1	56.0	56.4
2011	55.7	55.7	56.0	56.6	56.9	57.5	57.6	57.1	56.6	56.8	56.6	56.8	56.7
2012	56.1	56.1	56.4	56.3	56.7	58.0	57.0	56.7	56.1	56.4	56.2	56.3	56.5
2013	55.9	55.8	55.8	56.1	56.4	57.2	58.5	57.9	57.4	57.9	57.8	57.9	57.1
2014	57.1	56.7	57.9	57.9	58.4	59.1	59.5	58.9	58.5	58.9	58.7	58.7	58.4
2015	58.5	58.4	58.5	58.4	58.9	59.8	59.8	59.2	58.6	59.2	58.9	58.7	58.9
2016	58.0	58.0	57.7	58.5	58.8	59.4	59.6	59.0	58.5	58.8	58.5	58.3	58.6
2017	57.6	57.7	57.8	57.8	58.2	59.1	59.4	58.9	58.5	58.9	58.8	58.7	58.5
2018	58.5	58.4	58.6	58.8	59.0	59.8	59.9	59.4	59.0	59.4	59.1	58.6	59.0
Retail Trade													
2010	139.6	138.1	138.8	140.0	141.3	141.4	140.8	140.5	139.4	141.4	144.6	145.6	141.0
2011	139.3	138.2	139.2	141.3	142.2	142.0	141.8	141.6	140.8	142.4	146.2	146.7	141.8
2012	141.5	139.8	140.7	141.7	142.7	143.1	142.6	142.2	142.1	143.6	147.5	148.1	143.0
2013	141.4	140.5	141.2	142.2	143.1	144.0	143.9	144.5	144.2	145.5	149.4	150.7	144.2
2014	144.0	142.7	143.8	145.4	146.2	146.7	146.6	146.7	145.5	147.3	151.2	152.5	146.6
2015	145.9	144.6	145.3	147.1	148.8	150.1	149.6	149.4	148.4	150.7	153.9	154.2	149.0
2016	148.6	148.2	148.5	150.1	150.3	149.9	150.7	150.0	148.5	150.1	153.4	153.8	150.2
2017	148.2	147.2	146.9	146.6	147.2	146.6	147.4	147.5	145.8	147.1	150.9	151.0	147.7
2018	145.6	144.4	144.3	144.9	145.9	145.5	145.6	145.2	144.0	145.6	148.8	147.4	145.6
Transportation and Utilities													
2010	51.8	51.8	52.0	52.2	52.5	52.8	53.0	53.7	54.0	55.0	55.5	56.0	53.4
2011	54.5	54.4	52.4	54.5	54.8	53.9	53.8	54.6	54.9	55.4	55.7	56.1	54.6
2012	54.7	54.6	54.5	55.2	55.5	55.7	54.1	55.0	55.3	56.1	56.3	56.6	55.3
2013	55.6	55.5	55.3	55.3	55.8	55.5	53.9	54.9	54.9	55.5	56.2	56.5	55.4
2014	55.1	54.8	55.3	55.5	55.9	55.5	55.1	56.3	56.4	57.0	57.5	58.5	56.1
2015	56.6	55.8	55.7	55.7	55.9	55.4	55.3	56.5	56.9	56.9	57.7	58.9	56.4
2016	56.5	56.4	56.4	56.9	57.4	56.8	56.9	57.9	58.7	59.3	60.9	62.5	58.1
2017	59.1	59.1	58.9	58.6	59.0	58.6	58.7	61.5	63.5	63.6	66.0	66.9	61.1
2018	63.5	62.9	62.3	62.6	63.1	62.6	62.5	63.6	64.6	66.2	67.5	67.6	64.1
Information													
2010	28.2	27.9	27.7	27.7	27.4	27.1	26.7	26.3	25.8	25.6	25.5	25.5	26.8
2011	25.2	25.1	25.0	24.6	23.9	23.8	23.6	23.3	22.9	22.9	22.9	22.9	23.8
2012	23.3	23.0	23.1	23.0	23.0	23.0	22.8	22.6	22.4	22.5	22.5	22.5	22.8
2013	22.1	22.1	22.0	22.1	22.1	22.2	22.5	22.5	22.2	22.2	22.3	22.5	22.2
2014	22.4	22.2	22.1	22.1	22.1	22.1	22.1	21.9	21.5	21.6	21.6	21.6	21.9
2015	21.2	21.2	21.2	21.1	21.1	21.2	21.2	21.1	20.7	20.8	20.9	21.0	21.1
2016	21.0	21.0	20.8	20.8	20.7	20.7	20.7	20.5	20.1	19.8	19.9	19.9	20.5
2017	20.0	19.8	19.7	19.6	19.6	19.4	19.3	19.1	18.8	18.9	18.9	18.9	19.3
2018	18.9	18.9	18.8	18.9	18.8	18.7	18.7	18.5	18.4	18.4	18.6	18.7	18.7

1. Employment by Industry: Kansas, 2010–2018—*Continued*

(Numbers in thousands, not seasonally adjusted)

Industry and year	January	February	March	April	May	June	July	August	September	October	November	December	Annual average
Financial Activities													
2010	71.7	71.6	71.4	71.9	72.3	72.4	72.5	72.4	71.7	72.7	72.7	73.1	72.2
2011	71.9	71.8	72.0	72.7	73.8	74.0	74.5	74.6	74.2	74.7	74.8	75.2	73.7
2012	74.7	75.3	75.7	76.1	76.2	76.9	77.0	76.9	76.2	76.6	77.0	77.3	76.3
2013	76.5	76.7	76.5	77.3	77.9	78.9	79.0	78.8	78.2	78.3	78.5	78.6	77.9
2014	77.4	77.3	77.5	77.6	77.9	78.4	78.4	78.6	78.1	78.5	78.6	78.9	78.1
2015	78.1	78.2	78.4	78.5	78.6	79.1	79.5	79.3	78.3	78.7	78.8	78.9	78.7
2016	79.1	78.9	78.6	79.7	79.7	79.7	80.1	80.0	79.1	79.0	78.9	78.8	79.3
2017	78.1	78.1	77.9	77.7	77.6	78.2	78.5	78.2	77.4	77.8	77.8	77.9	77.9
2018	76.7	76.7	76.5	76.9	77.1	77.8	77.8	77.6	76.8	77.2	77.4	77.2	77.1
Professional and Business Services													
2010	145.6	145.7	147.3	153.0	152.2	152.9	155.0	155.0	153.0	156.3	155.9	156.3	152.4
2011	152.6	153.3	154.9	158.4	157.3	156.4	158.0	158.8	159.2	160.4	160.6	159.2	157.4
2012	157.5	158.7	160.3	163.1	163.3	165.3	163.8	164.5	164.7	167.8	167.4	167.9	163.7
2013	164.5	166.0	167.7	171.4	171.1	173.2	174.2	175.1	175.4	175.9	176.6	177.2	172.4
2014	172.6	174.0	175.7	178.6	178.6	180.2	179.7	180.5	179.9	181.8	182.2	182.8	178.9
2015	176.0	176.8	177.4	179.7	179.5	180.5	181.2	181.8	180.7	182.6	182.1	182.4	180.1
2016	175.5	175.3	175.7	178.9	177.7	177.7	179.7	179.5	180.5	181.3	181.0	180.0	178.6
2017	173.3	173.8	175.1	178.2	178.0	178.9	181.0	180.3	180.0	180.3	180.7	180.4	178.3
2018	175.1	176.4	176.8	179.8	178.9	180.3	181.5	181.6	180.9	182.2	183.5	183.0	180.0
Education and Health Services													
2010	179.1	180.1	180.1	179.5	180.1	179.3	178.2	178.5	179.8	182.5	183.2	183.5	180.3
2011	183.8	184.2	184.3	185.9	186.3	184.4	183.2	183.8	185.3	186.5	187.0	186.9	185.1
2012	184.5	185.2	185.5	186.2	186.9	186.2	184.3	185.2	186.7	188.2	188.9	189.5	186.4
2013	186.9	187.0	187.3	188.3	188.7	187.9	185.8	186.2	187.3	188.8	189.4	189.0	187.7
2014	187.1	187.6	187.8	189.9	191.0	190.0	188.7	189.1	190.9	192.2	193.2	193.0	190.0
2015	192.0	193.2	192.9	195.1	195.2	194.0	193.5	193.4	194.1	195.9	196.4	196.4	194.3
2016	194.7	195.9	195.5	197.0	196.6	194.9	195.3	194.7	196.8	198.1	198.1	197.6	196.3
2017	195.1	196.8	196.8	197.1	196.7	196.0	195.4	195.6	196.9	198.8	199.3	198.9	197.0
2018	197.2	198.6	198.0	199.0	199.0	199.0	197.7	197.8	199.6	202.7	202.7	202.5	199.5
Leisure and Hospitality													
2010	107.1	108.2	110.3	113.4	115.8	117.4	116.3	116.2	114.9	114.2	113.4	112.5	113.3
2011	108.3	108.5	111.4	115.1	117.9	119.2	118.9	119.1	117.0	115.9	114.8	114.4	115.0
2012	112.3	114.3	116.9	120.2	122.5	124.5	122.8	123.3	120.4	119.7	119.1	118.9	119.6
2013	114.9	116.4	118.2	121.1	124.6	125.6	124.7	124.4	122.7	122.4	120.5	119.6	121.3
2014	115.6	116.7	119.0	122.7	126.8	126.8	127.0	126.9	124.6	123.6	122.4	122.1	122.9
2015	119.5	120.9	122.7	125.6	127.9	129.9	129.4	129.7	127.1	126.8	125.6	125.1	125.9
2016	121.1	122.8	124.7	128.2	130.4	131.6	130.8	131.1	128.4	128.4	126.7	125.1	127.4
2017	121.8	124.4	127.2	128.1	130.7	132.5	131.9	132.0	129.7	128.8	128.0	127.0	128.5
2018	124.1	125.6	126.9	129.3	132.1	132.9	132.9	132.5	130.2	130.7	129.4	129.2	129.7
Other Services													
2010	51.5	51.6	51.7	51.9	51.7	51.3	50.9	50.8	51.0	52.3	51.8	51.6	51.5
2011	50.4	50.8	50.8	50.8	50.7	50.2	50.6	50.4	50.6	51.0	50.6	50.6	50.6
2012	49.6	50.1	50.0	49.9	49.9	49.7	49.3	49.2	49.7	49.9	49.6	49.5	49.7
2013	48.0	48.8	48.6	49.0	48.8	48.6	48.5	48.5	48.8	49.1	49.3	49.0	48.8
2014	47.9	48.5	48.8	49.2	48.9	48.5	48.4	48.4	48.4	48.9	48.7	48.2	48.6
2015	47.6	47.9	47.5	48.0	48.1	48.5	48.3	48.7	49.1	49.9	49.6	49.7	48.6
2016	49.5	50.0	50.3	51.0	50.7	50.4	50.4	50.4	50.8	51.1	51.1	50.7	50.5
2017	50.0	50.8	50.8	50.7	50.5	50.1	50.1	50.3	50.5	51.5	51.4	51.2	50.7
2018	50.6	51.0	50.9	51.2	51.1	50.7	51.1	51.1	50.9	50.4	51.0	50.5	50.9
Government													
2010	259.9	263.4	267.6	269.0	276.1	266.8	241.9	243.4	262.9	266.7	264.4	264.9	262.3
2011	261.6	263.4	265.2	268.1	269.0	256.3	238.2	240.0	262.4	265.8	265.8	262.8	259.9
2012	257.7	262.9	264.5	264.5	267.7	255.2	234.5	239.9	259.1	265.9	266.3	264.1	258.5
2013	256.0	263.3	263.6	265.9	264.0	250.9	232.2	235.8	260.6	264.6	265.4	263.6	257.2
2014	254.4	262.2	263.5	263.6	263.6	252.2	234.1	236.4	259.5	264.7	265.0	263.3	256.9
2015	254.7	262.6	263.8	264.3	264.2	253.0	233.2	235.5	258.5	263.1	263.3	262.0	256.5
2016	252.7	260.9	262.7	263.9	262.3	251.8	232.2	234.9	259.3	264.0	263.9	263.5	256.0
2017	252.7	261.9	262.6	262.7	262.3	250.7	232.7	235.9	259.1	264.2	265.1	264.0	256.2
2018	253.8	263.0	263.7	264.4	263.9	251.5	234.5	245.1	262.6	265.7	266.2	265.4	258.3

2. Average Weekly Hours by Selected Industry: Kansas, 2014–2018

(Not seasonally adjusted)

Industry and year	January	February	March	April	May	June	July	August	September	October	November	December	Annual average
Total Private													
2014	34.0	34.4	34.8	34.4	34.4	35.0	34.6	34.7	34.6	34.5	35.2	34.5	34.6
2015	34.2	34.5	34.6	34.0	34.1	34.6	34.4	34.9	34.0	34.2	34.4	33.8	34.3
2016	33.6	33.5	33.5	33.4	33.7	34.0	33.8	33.8	33.8	34.5	33.9	33.8	33.8
2017	33.7	33.8	33.7	34.1	33.6	34.3	34.6	34.2	34.1	34.5	34.2	34.3	34.1
2018	33.6	33.8	33.9	34.5	34.0	34.6	34.9	34.4	34.8	34.2	34.2	34.7	34.3
Goods Producing													
2014	41.0	40.6	40.8	41.0	41.1	41.1	41.3	41.9	41.7	41.4	41.9	41.8	41.3
2015	40.8	40.1	40.8	40.0	39.8	40.3	40.2	40.7	39.7	40.8	40.7	40.4	40.4
2016	39.5	39.6	40.0	39.6	39.5	40.6	39.5	40.1	39.9	40.7	40.4	40.3	40.0
2017	38.4	39.6	39.7	39.8	39.9	40.4	40.4	40.8	40.7	40.7	41.3	41.8	40.3
2018	39.7	40.6	40.8	40.8	41.0	41.4	41.2	40.9	41.1	40.6	40.8	41.0	40.8
Construction													
2014	38.6	36.3	39.4	39.6	40.2	38.2	39.5	40.0	38.6	37.7	37.9	39.1	38.8
2015	38.1	37.7	39.0	36.9	36.1	37.6	37.5	40.0	36.4	38.7	38.1	36.7	37.7
2016	35.9	36.0	37.4	37.5	37.3	39.3	37.6	38.7	37.6	39.6	38.9	37.6	37.8
2017	35.5	36.4	36.8	37.1	37.0	38.6	38.6	38.7	38.3	38.4	38.4	38.1	37.7
2018	34.8	37.0	36.8	37.9	38.7	39.3	39.3	38.4	39.1	38.0	38.7	39.3	38.2
Manufacturing													
2014	41.9	42.2	42.0	42.0	42.0	43.0	42.4	43.1	43.6	43.5	44.2	43.3	42.8
2015	42.4	42.2	42.7	42.4	42.5	42.4	42.1	41.7	42.4	42.6	42.8	43.3	42.5
2016	42.1	42.2	42.1	41.5	41.3	41.7	41.1	41.2	41.6	41.5	41.5	42.1	41.7
2017	40.3	40.8	40.9	40.7	41.1	40.9	41.0	41.7	41.7	41.8	42.3	43.6	41.4
2018	42.4	42.3	42.6	42.1	41.9	42.3	42.0	42.1	42.1	42.0	41.8	41.8	42.1
Trade, Transportation, and Utilities													
2014	33.5	33.9	34.4	34.1	34.0	34.4	33.7	33.8	34.0	34.1	34.6	34.3	34.1
2015	33.4	34.5	34.5	33.9	33.8	34.2	34.4	34.8	34.2	33.8	33.9	33.4	34.1
2016	32.9	32.9	32.6	32.9	32.7	33.1	33.6	33.0	32.8	33.9	33.0	33.4	33.1
2017	33.4	33.1	33.4	33.9	33.4	34.1	34.4	33.6	33.6	33.6	33.5	33.6	33.6
2018	33.1	33.2	33.8	34.1	34.0	34.8	34.6	33.6	34.1	33.2	33.2	33.1	33.7
Financial Activities													
2014	35.5	37.0	36.9	35.9	36.2	36.4	35.8	35.5	35.3	35.0	36.7	35.3	36.0
2015	35.5	36.6	36.4	35.9	36.1	36.1	36.3	37.4	36.2	36.2	37.4	36.6	36.4
2016	36.4	36.5	36.8	37.1	37.6	36.9	37.3	37.0	36.5	37.8	36.6	36.5	36.9
2017	37.9	37.1	36.3	37.3	36.2	36.4	37.3	36.3	36.8	37.8	36.9	36.8	36.9
2018	36.9	37.0	36.1	37.5	35.9	36.3	37.5	36.7	37.7	36.7	36.5	37.7	36.9
Professional and Business Services													
2014	35.0	35.7	37.2	36.7	36.8	37.2	36.7	37.0	36.8	36.5	37.5	36.1	36.6
2015	35.9	36.4	36.8	36.3	36.5	37.0	36.3	37.0	35.8	36.2	36.1	35.6	36.3
2016	35.4	35.1	34.9	34.8	35.2	35.1	34.6	34.4	34.7	35.6	34.8	33.8	34.9
2017	34.5	34.6	34.5	34.9	34.6	35.8	35.8	35.5	35.5	36.3	36.1	36.0	35.4
2018	35.4	35.7	35.6	36.5	35.7	36.1	36.6	36.1	36.7	36.4	36.0	37.0	36.2
Education and Health Services													
2014	31.4	32.1	32.2	31.5	31.4	32.7	32.0	31.9	32.2	31.7	33.0	31.9	32.0
2015	32.4	32.7	32.5	31.9	32.1	32.4	32.4	33.1	32.4	32.2	33.0	31.7	32.4
2016	32.5	32.2	32.2	32.0	32.6	32.5	32.2	32.3	32.6	32.8	32.3	32.4	32.4
2017	32.8	32.2	31.9	32.8	31.7	31.9	32.6	31.8	31.9	32.3	31.6	31.7	32.1
2018	31.8	31.7	31.6	32.5	31.6	32.2	32.8	32.4	32.7	32.0	32.3	32.7	32.2
Leisure and Hospitality													
2014	23.0	23.3	23.6	23.3	23.6	24.5	24.1	23.6	23.3	23.4	23.2	23.2	23.5
2015	22.8	23.3	23.3	23.0	23.6	24.2	23.7	24.1	23.0	23.5	23.4	22.6	23.4
2016	22.2	22.5	23.0	22.9	22.9	23.7	23.6	23.8	23.7	23.7	23.8	23.4	23.3
2017	23.0	23.9	24.0	24.2	24.0	24.7	25.1	24.6	23.9	24.4	24.0	23.7	24.1
2018	23.1	23.7	24.2	24.3	24.0	24.8	24.9	24.6	24.5	24.2	23.8	24.1	24.2
Other Services													
2014	30.7	29.1	30.0	29.0	30.4	31.4	30.6	30.8	29.8	29.4	29.4	29.2	30.0
2015	29.6	29.2	28.2	29.3	30.2	30.6	30.5	31.3	29.2	29.7	29.5	29.3	29.7
2016	30.0	30.1	29.2	29.8	30.5	31.5	30.6	30.8	29.7	30.2	29.2	29.8	30.1
2017	29.7	30.9	30.1	29.8	30.0	31.6	32.1	31.0	30.0	30.8	30.5	29.7	30.5
2018	29.2	29.8	29.7	30.5	30.2	31.3	31.8	31.1	31.4	30.4	29.8	31.1	30.5

3. Average Hourly Earnings by Selected Industry: Kansas, 2014–2018

(Dollars, not seasonally adjusted)

Industry and year	January	February	March	April	May	June	July	August	September	October	November	December	Annual average
Total Private													
2014	21.78	22.07	22.03	21.97	21.85	21.89	21.96	22.09	22.21	22.19	22.52	22.45	22.09
2015	22.51	22.66	22.48	22.26	22.32	22.17	22.36	22.56	22.61	22.78	22.97	23.18	22.57
2016	22.98	22.90	22.71	22.99	22.80	22.46	22.69	22.80	22.92	23.17	23.03	23.05	22.88
2017	23.38	23.29	23.18	23.31	23.05	22.83	23.16	23.12	23.38	23.51	23.33	23.50	23.25
2018	23.59	23.87	23.69	24.02	23.84	23.89	24.15	23.98	24.34	24.45	24.43	24.85	24.10
Goods Producing													
2014	22.93	23.09	23.67	23.53	23.59	23.59	23.68	23.65	24.12	24.26	24.35	24.46	23.75
2015	24.31	23.94	24.09	23.41	23.84	24.01	24.14	24.38	24.33	25.11	25.17	26.02	24.40
2016	25.46	25.45	25.22	25.35	24.95	24.78	24.86	25.13	25.09	25.37	25.24	25.20	25.17
2017	25.34	25.18	24.92	24.69	24.35	24.39	24.45	24.05	24.35	24.37	24.21	24.60	24.57
2018	24.69	24.60	24.34	24.68	24.51	24.58	24.85	24.39	24.57	24.59	24.13	24.68	24.55
Construction													
2014	23.90	24.24	24.25	24.21	24.26	23.41	23.36	23.77	23.57	24.26	24.19	24.25	23.96
2015	25.03	24.40	24.25	23.34	23.56	23.79	24.03	24.56	24.76	24.42	24.35	24.33	24.23
2016	25.06	25.02	24.76	24.96	24.79	24.85	24.87	25.36	25.52	25.65	25.45	25.81	25.18
2017	26.24	26.08	25.87	25.95	25.46	25.26	25.33	25.08	25.39	25.54	25.45	25.68	25.60
2018	26.31	25.89	25.68	25.70	25.96	25.97	26.05	25.58	26.44	25.96	26.43	27.13	26.10
Manufacturing													
2014	22.26	22.36	23.14	23.17	23.20	23.61	23.86	23.51	24.37	24.16	24.37	24.50	23.56
2015	23.88	23.61	23.92	23.26	23.80	23.97	24.07	24.08	23.92	24.19	24.44	25.97	24.10
2016	24.79	24.88	24.70	24.79	24.40	24.13	24.28	24.55	24.44	24.82	24.75	24.51	24.59
2017	24.52	24.32	24.02	23.61	23.34	23.54	23.57	23.05	23.36	23.32	23.21	23.78	23.63
2018	23.66	23.75	23.46	23.87	23.45	23.53	23.93	23.45	23.23	23.60	22.64	23.11	23.47
Trade, Transportation, and Utilities													
2014	20.28	20.46	20.30	20.67	20.51	20.22	20.16	20.48	20.74	20.66	21.12	20.75	20.53
2015	21.62	21.82	21.78	22.14	21.92	21.66	21.47	21.64	21.49	21.73	21.78	21.70	21.73
2016	21.75	21.75	21.60	21.76	21.85	21.33	21.58	21.87	22.40	22.36	22.34	22.18	21.90
2017	22.84	22.49	21.81	22.22	22.16	21.78	22.21	22.09	22.31	22.38	21.89	21.47	22.13
2018	21.88	21.96	22.10	22.27	22.18	22.19	22.35	22.21	22.80	22.35	22.63	22.55	22.29
Financial Activities													
2014	26.31	26.54	26.16	26.46	26.39	28.10	28.49	28.24	27.86	27.61	28.81	27.60	27.38
2015	28.01	28.52	26.00	25.78	26.12	25.43	26.67	27.44	27.18	27.11	27.02	26.90	26.85
2016	27.01	26.75	26.63	27.64	27.52	27.13	27.64	27.47	27.74	28.41	28.26	27.98	27.52
2017	27.78	28.20	28.71	28.46	28.09	27.24	28.14	28.99	28.20	28.66	28.86	28.82	28.34
2018	28.55	30.07	30.00	31.48	30.92	31.88	31.88	31.21	31.19	31.00	31.39	31.54	30.93
Professional and Business Services													
2014	23.80	24.23	24.11	23.65	23.29	23.30	23.25	23.27	23.34	23.69	23.83	24.15	23.65
2015	23.99	24.87	24.98	24.49	24.57	24.32	24.82	25.24	25.52	25.13	25.61	25.36	24.91
2016	25.23	25.22	24.99	25.54	25.16	24.72	25.17	25.46	25.36	25.76	25.41	26.02	25.34
2017	26.62	26.74	26.96	27.30	26.57	26.17	26.67	26.50	26.67	27.09	26.84	27.71	26.82
2018	28.28	28.44	27.95	28.31	28.36	28.43	28.94	28.85	29.39	29.98	29.87	30.65	28.97
Education and Health Services													
2014	21.64	22.00	21.82	21.78	21.72	21.68	21.78	21.99	22.19	21.96	22.09	22.26	21.91
2015	21.79	21.59	21.40	21.16	21.03	20.89	20.76	20.86	21.11	21.05	21.25	21.69	21.21
2016	21.43	21.20	20.97	21.30	20.94	20.79	20.99	20.78	20.74	21.10	20.88	20.72	20.99
2017	20.81	21.11	21.00	21.39	21.47	21.45	21.59	21.55	22.16	22.12	22.12	22.28	21.59
2018	22.00	22.27	22.01	22.05	21.89	21.87	22.04	22.14	22.28	22.30	22.28	22.58	22.14
Leisure and Hospitality													
2014	11.44	11.55	11.74	11.59	11.72	11.50	11.57	11.59	11.69	11.65	11.79	12.16	11.67
2015	11.85	11.97	11.88	11.82	11.79	11.72	11.82	11.88	12.08	11.94	12.02	12.26	11.92
2016	12.13	12.07	11.96	11.92	11.95	11.74	11.91	11.85	11.99	12.10	12.31	12.40	12.02
2017	12.46	12.35	12.32	12.33	12.39	12.27	12.21	12.30	12.44	12.46	12.57	12.67	12.39
2018	12.68	13.12	13.12	13.09	12.99	12.82	12.82	13.01	12.93	13.14	13.04	13.24	13.00
Other Services													
2014	21.38	21.98	21.53	21.51	21.35	21.95	21.72	21.78	21.97	21.57	21.72	21.48	21.66
2015	21.39	21.27	21.34	20.84	20.84	21.02	20.90	20.67	20.68	21.51	21.85	21.55	21.15
2016	21.76	21.83	21.90	21.81	22.00	22.07	22.17	21.99	22.11	21.55	21.42	21.42	21.84
2017	21.44	20.72	21.27	20.93	20.99	21.45	21.04	21.16	20.96	21.19	20.80	20.86	21.07
2018	21.99	21.18	21.43	21.81	21.36	21.19	21.87	21.60	21.79	22.56	22.83	22.70	21.86

4. Average Weekly Earnings by Selected Industry: Kansas, 2014–2018

(Dollars, not seasonally adjusted)

Industry and year	January	February	March	April	May	June	July	August	September	October	November	December	Annual average
Total Private													
2014	740.52	759.21	766.64	755.77	751.64	766.15	759.82	766.52	768.47	765.56	792.70	774.53	764.31
2015	769.84	781.77	777.81	756.84	761.11	767.08	769.18	787.34	768.74	779.08	790.17	783.48	774.15
2016	772.13	767.15	760.79	767.87	768.36	763.64	766.92	770.64	774.70	799.37	780.72	779.09	773.34
2017	787.91	787.20	781.17	794.87	774.48	783.07	801.34	790.70	797.26	811.10	797.89	806.05	792.83
2018	792.62	806.81	803.09	828.69	810.56	826.59	842.84	824.91	847.03	836.19	835.51	862.30	826.63
Goods Producing													
2014	940.13	937.45	965.74	964.73	969.55	969.55	977.98	990.94	1,005.80	1,004.36	1,020.27	1,022.43	980.88
2015	991.85	959.99	982.87	936.40	948.83	967.60	970.43	992.27	965.90	1,024.49	1,024.42	1,051.21	985.76
2016	1,005.67	1,007.82	1,008.80	1,003.86	985.53	1,006.07	981.97	1,007.71	1,001.09	1,032.56	1,019.70	1,015.56	1,006.80
2017	973.06	997.13	989.32	982.66	971.57	985.36	987.78	981.24	991.05	991.86	999.87	1,028.28	990.17
2018	980.19	998.76	993.07	1,006.94	1,004.91	1,017.61	1,023.82	997.55	1,009.83	998.35	984.50	1,011.88	1,001.64
Construction													
2014	922.54	879.91	955.45	958.72	975.25	894.26	922.72	950.80	909.80	914.60	916.80	948.18	929.65
2015	953.64	919.88	945.75	861.25	850.52	894.50	901.13	982.40	901.26	945.05	927.74	892.91	913.47
2016	899.65	900.72	926.02	936.00	924.67	976.61	935.11	981.43	959.55	1,015.74	990.01	970.46	951.80
2017	931.52	949.31	952.02	962.75	942.02	975.04	977.74	970.60	972.44	980.74	977.28	978.41	965.12
2018	915.59	957.93	945.02	974.03	1,004.65	1,020.62	1,023.77	982.27	1,033.80	986.48	1,022.84	1,066.21	997.02
Manufacturing													
2014	932.69	943.59	971.88	973.14	974.40	1,015.23	1,011.66	1,013.28	1,062.53	1,050.96	1,077.15	1,060.85	1,008.37
2015	1,012.51	996.34	1,021.38	986.22	1,011.50	1,016.33	1,013.35	1,004.14	1,014.21	1,030.49	1,046.03	1,124.50	1,024.25
2016	1,043.66	1,049.94	1,039.87	1,028.79	1,007.72	1,006.22	997.91	1,011.46	1,016.70	1,030.03	1,027.13	1,031.87	1,025.40
2017	988.16	992.26	982.42	960.93	959.27	962.79	966.37	961.19	974.11	974.78	981.78	1,036.81	978.28
2018	1,003.18	1,004.63	999.40	1,004.93	982.56	995.32	1,005.06	987.25	977.98	991.20	946.35	966.00	988.09
Trade, Transportation, and Utilities													
2014	679.38	693.59	698.32	704.85	697.34	695.57	679.39	692.22	705.16	704.51	730.75	711.73	700.07
2015	722.11	752.79	751.41	750.55	740.90	740.77	738.57	753.07	734.96	734.47	738.34	724.78	740.99
2016	715.58	715.58	704.16	715.90	714.50	706.02	725.09	721.71	734.72	758.00	737.22	740.81	724.89
2017	762.86	744.42	728.45	753.26	740.14	742.70	764.02	742.22	749.62	751.97	733.32	721.39	743.57
2018	724.23	729.07	746.98	759.41	754.12	772.21	773.31	746.26	777.48	742.02	751.32	746.41	751.17
Financial Activities													
2014	934.01	981.98	965.30	949.91	955.32	1,022.84	1,019.94	1,002.52	983.46	966.35	1,057.33	974.28	985.68
2015	994.36	1,043.83	946.40	925.50	942.93	918.02	968.12	1,026.26	983.92	981.38	1,010.55	984.54	977.34
2016	983.16	976.38	979.98	1,025.44	1,034.75	1,001.10	1,030.97	1,016.39	1,012.51	1,073.90	1,034.32	1,021.27	1,015.49
2017	1,052.86	1,046.22	1,042.17	1,061.56	1,016.86	991.54	1,049.62	1,052.34	1,037.76	1,083.35	1,064.93	1,060.58	1,045.75
2018	1,053.50	1,112.59	1,083.00	1,180.50	1,110.03	1,157.24	1,195.50	1,145.41	1,175.86	1,137.70	1,145.74	1,189.06	1,141.32
Professional and Business Services													
2014	833.00	865.01	896.89	867.96	857.07	866.76	853.28	860.99	858.91	864.69	893.63	871.82	865.59
2015	861.24	905.27	919.26	888.99	896.81	899.84	900.97	933.88	913.62	909.71	924.52	902.82	904.23
2016	893.14	885.22	872.15	888.79	885.63	867.67	870.88	875.82	879.99	917.06	884.27	879.48	884.37
2017	918.39	925.20	930.12	952.77	919.32	936.89	954.79	940.75	946.79	983.37	968.92	997.56	949.43
2018	1,001.11	1,015.31	995.02	1,033.32	1,012.45	1,026.32	1,059.20	1,041.49	1,078.61	1,091.27	1,075.32	1,134.05	1,048.71
Education and Health Services													
2014	679.50	706.20	702.60	686.07	682.01	708.94	696.96	701.48	714.52	696.13	728.97	710.09	701.12
2015	706.00	705.99	695.50	675.00	675.06	676.84	672.62	690.47	683.96	677.81	701.25	687.57	687.20
2016	696.48	682.64	675.23	681.60	682.64	675.68	675.88	671.19	676.12	692.08	674.42	671.33	680.08
2017	682.57	679.74	669.90	701.59	680.60	684.26	703.83	685.29	706.90	714.48	698.99	706.28	693.04
2018	699.60	705.96	695.52	716.63	691.72	704.21	722.91	717.34	728.56	713.60	719.64	738.37	712.91
Leisure and Hospitality													
2014	263.12	269.12	277.06	270.05	276.59	281.75	278.84	273.52	272.38	272.61	273.53	282.11	274.25
2015	270.18	278.90	276.80	271.86	278.24	283.62	280.13	286.31	277.84	280.59	281.27	277.08	278.93
2016	269.29	271.58	275.08	272.97	273.66	278.24	281.08	282.03	284.16	286.77	292.98	290.16	280.07
2017	286.58	295.17	295.68	298.39	297.36	303.07	306.47	302.58	297.32	304.02	301.68	300.28	298.60
2018	292.91	310.94	317.50	318.09	311.76	317.94	319.22	320.05	316.79	317.99	310.35	319.08	314.60
Other Services													
2014	656.37	639.62	645.90	623.79	649.04	689.23	664.63	670.82	654.71	634.16	638.57	627.22	649.80
2015	633.14	621.08	601.79	610.61	629.37	643.21	637.45	646.97	603.86	638.85	644.58	631.42	628.16
2016	652.80	657.08	639.48	649.94	671.00	695.21	678.40	677.29	656.67	650.81	625.46	638.32	657.38
2017	636.77	640.25	640.23	623.71	629.70	677.82	675.38	655.96	628.80	652.65	634.40	619.54	642.64
2018	642.11	631.16	636.47	665.21	645.07	663.25	695.47	671.76	684.21	685.82	680.33	705.97	666.73

KENTUCKY
At a Glance

Population:
  2010 census: 4,339,367
  2018 estimate: 4,468,402

Percent change in population:
  2010–2018: 3.0%

Percent change in total nonfarm employment:
  2010–2018: 9.7%

Industry with the largest growth in employment, 2010–2018 (percent):
  Transportation and utilities, 27.7%

Industry with the largest decline or smallest growth in employment, 2010–2018 (percent):
  Mining and logging, -54.8%

Civilian labor force:
  2010: 2,054,375
  2018: 2,061,622

Unemployment rate and rank among states (highest to lowest):
  2010: 10.2%, 16th
  2018: 4.3%, 11th

Over-the-year change in unemployment rates:
  2016–2017: -0.2%
  2017–2018: -0.6%

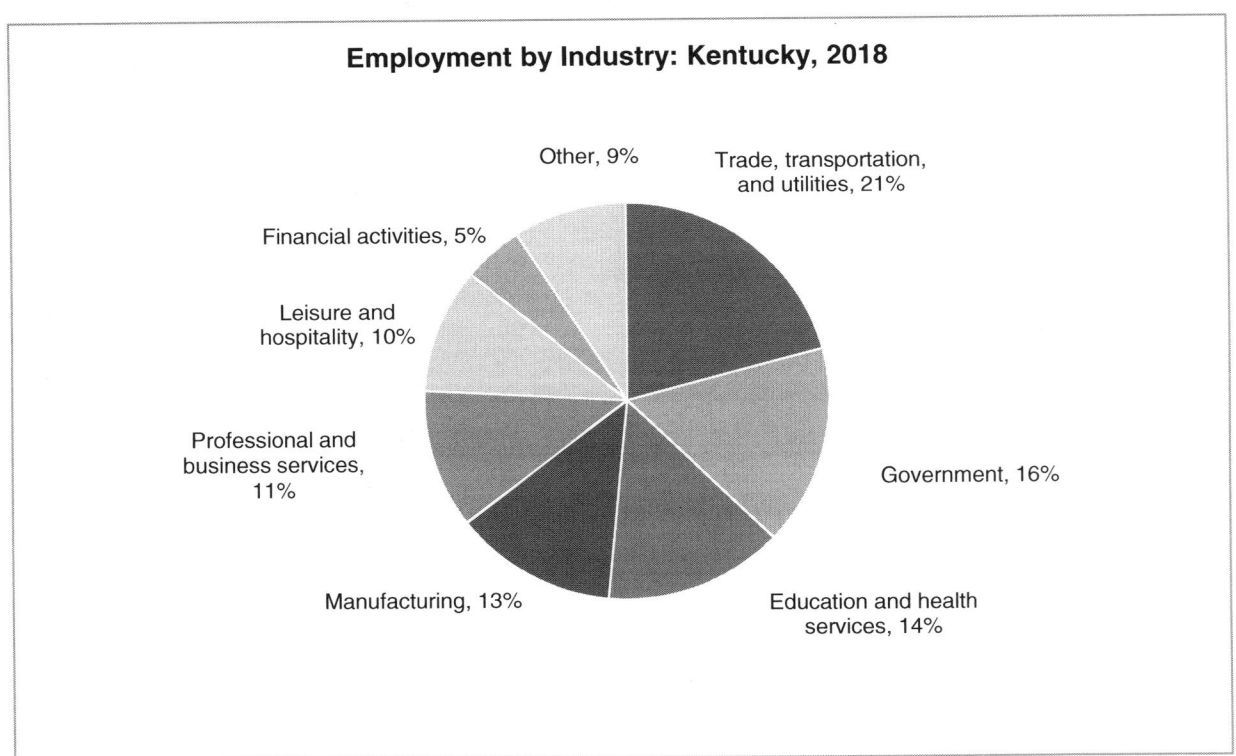

Employment by Industry: Kentucky, 2018

Other, 9%
Trade, transportation, and utilities, 21%
Financial activities, 5%
Leisure and hospitality, 10%
Professional and business services, 11%
Government, 16%
Manufacturing, 13%
Education and health services, 14%

1. Employment by Industry: Kentucky, 2010–2018

(Numbers in thousands, not seasonally adjusted)

Industry and year	January	February	March	April	May	June	July	August	September	October	November	December	Annual average
Total Nonfarm													
2010	1,715.7	1,709.1	1,733.2	1,760.2	1,775.5	1,776.3	1,755.5	1,761.0	1,772.0	1,781.1	1,787.8	1,792.4	1,760.0
2011	1,739.1	1,744.3	1,762.2	1,783.4	1,786.9	1,792.3	1,773.8	1,792.0	1,800.8	1,800.9	1,814.1	1,814.7	1,783.7
2012	1,772.1	1,776.6	1,794.5	1,809.5	1,822.1	1,825.5	1,801.7	1,813.3	1,819.4	1,823.5	1,837.6	1,838.9	1,811.2
2013	1,791.2	1,794.8	1,809.6	1,825.6	1,837.7	1,835.2	1,817.3	1,837.4	1,842.6	1,846.4	1,863.9	1,865.2	1,830.6
2014	1,812.4	1,810.5	1,829.2	1,854.1	1,866.0	1,863.7	1,849.1	1,867.0	1,871.0	1,878.8	1,892.5	1,899.2	1,857.8
2015	1,847.8	1,844.8	1,854.3	1,876.0	1,893.3	1,893.6	1,873.5	1,888.9	1,896.7	1,906.5	1,924.1	1,928.4	1,885.7
2016	1,873.6	1,876.7	1,888.0	1,907.2	1,917.8	1,913.2	1,903.9	1,914.1	1,921.3	1,923.0	1,934.5	1,937.0	1,909.2
2017	1,886.6	1,893.6	1,905.5	1,918.7	1,927.4	1,931.2	1,907.0	1,914.8	1,929.8	1,935.8	1,953.4	1,949.2	1,921.1
2018	1,892.2	1,903.6	1,914.5	1,931.4	1,941.2	1,945.7	1,919.6	1,931.2	1,939.9	1,940.5	1,959.1	1,960.2	1,931.6
Total Private													
2010	1,404.3	1,394.5	1,415.6	1,439.3	1,447.2	1,454.4	1,449.9	1,454.8	1,454.4	1,460.5	1,466.1	1,471.9	1,442.7
2011	1,423.4	1,423.7	1,439.4	1,458.9	1,462.4	1,471.7	1,465.7	1,477.8	1,478.1	1,476.3	1,487.8	1,488.1	1,462.8
2012	1,450.0	1,450.0	1,465.8	1,479.0	1,492.6	1,501.9	1,493.0	1,499.5	1,496.5	1,498.1	1,511.0	1,512.6	1,487.5
2013	1,470.6	1,469.2	1,482.5	1,496.5	1,508.4	1,511.6	1,506.4	1,520.4	1,516.4	1,522.2	1,537.8	1,539.0	1,506.8
2014	1,491.8	1,488.3	1,505.1	1,526.7	1,538.6	1,541.6	1,537.7	1,547.8	1,546.2	1,554.1	1,567.2	1,575.2	1,535.0
2015	1,529.1	1,524.9	1,533.8	1,552.2	1,570.0	1,575.9	1,570.6	1,578.6	1,578.4	1,585.6	1,602.1	1,606.6	1,567.3
2016	1,557.8	1,559.5	1,568.3	1,586.9	1,597.0	1,598.8	1,600.6	1,602.7	1,603.3	1,606.0	1,616.1	1,618.9	1,593.0
2017	1,572.6	1,576.5	1,587.0	1,598.4	1,606.3	1,615.5	1,606.5	1,609.2	1,611.5	1,617.3	1,633.2	1,629.4	1,605.3
2018	1,581.5	1,587.9	1,596.8	1,613.4	1,622.0	1,631.7	1,623.0	1,628.2	1,623.8	1,623.8	1,640.8	1,642.4	1,617.9
Goods Producing													
2010	292.2	286.2	293.3	298.1	299.4	300.9	299.9	303.7	304.7	305.1	303.5	301.9	299.1
2011	292.6	293.2	296.8	301.8	303.0	307.3	302.9	308.8	309.2	308.1	309.2	307.4	303.4
2012	302.4	300.8	305.5	308.2	311.2	315.3	314.9	316.1	315.8	315.4	315.4	314.0	311.3
2013	306.7	306.2	308.8	310.8	314.3	317.2	314.3	318.4	319.4	319.7	320.1	319.4	314.6
2014	311.4	311.8	316.6	320.5	324.7	327.2	327.8	330.4	330.3	330.9	332.0	330.5	324.5
2015	323.2	322.4	323.5	325.8	331.8	333.8	332.1	336.2	336.6	336.3	336.0	335.7	331.1
2016	327.7	327.3	330.5	334.2	336.2	338.9	339.7	339.1	339.3	337.8	338.8	338.1	335.6
2017	331.2	332.3	335.5	336.9	338.5	340.9	340.5	340.4	340.5	340.1	340.5	339.4	338.1
2018	331.8	332.9	335.6	338.1	340.6	342.9	341.8	343.4	341.9	344.0	344.4	345.2	340.2
Service-Providing													
2010	1,423.5	1,422.9	1,439.9	1,462.1	1,476.1	1,475.4	1,455.6	1,457.3	1,467.3	1,476.0	1,484.3	1,490.5	1,460.9
2011	1,446.5	1,451.1	1,465.4	1,481.6	1,483.9	1,485.0	1,470.9	1,483.2	1,491.6	1,492.8	1,504.9	1,507.3	1,480.4
2012	1,469.7	1,475.8	1,489.0	1,501.3	1,510.9	1,510.2	1,486.8	1,497.2	1,503.6	1,508.1	1,522.2	1,524.9	1,500.0
2013	1,484.5	1,488.6	1,500.8	1,514.8	1,523.4	1,518.0	1,503.0	1,519.0	1,523.2	1,526.7	1,543.8	1,545.8	1,516.0
2014	1,501.0	1,498.7	1,512.6	1,533.6	1,541.3	1,536.5	1,521.3	1,536.6	1,540.7	1,547.9	1,560.5	1,568.7	1,533.3
2015	1,524.6	1,522.4	1,530.8	1,550.2	1,561.5	1,559.8	1,541.4	1,552.7	1,560.1	1,570.2	1,588.1	1,592.7	1,554.5
2016	1,545.9	1,549.4	1,557.5	1,573.0	1,581.6	1,574.3	1,564.2	1,575.0	1,582.0	1,585.2	1,595.7	1,598.9	1,573.6
2017	1,555.4	1,561.3	1,570.0	1,581.8	1,588.9	1,590.3	1,566.5	1,574.4	1,589.3	1,595.7	1,612.9	1,609.8	1,583.0
2018	1,560.4	1,570.7	1,578.9	1,593.3	1,600.6	1,602.8	1,577.8	1,587.8	1,598.0	1,596.5	1,614.7	1,615.0	1,591.4
Mining and Logging													
2010	21.3	21.3	21.5	21.8	21.9	22.3	22.2	22.4	22.5	22.4	22.5	22.7	22.1
2011	22.0	22.1	22.3	22.7	22.9	23.2	23.4	23.5	23.4	23.2	23.2	23.3	22.9
2012	23.0	22.5	22.1	21.6	21.1	21.0	20.4	19.9	19.5	18.7	18.6	18.1	20.5
2013	17.6	17.2	17.6	17.5	17.6	17.8	17.7	17.6	17.5	17.2	17.1	16.9	17.4
2014	16.2	16.1	16.3	16.4	16.7	16.8	16.7	16.8	16.7	16.7	16.6	16.5	16.5
2015	15.3	15.1	14.6	14.4	14.4	14.3	14.0	13.7	13.5	13.3	12.8	12.4	14.0
2016	11.6	11.1	11.0	10.5	10.4	10.4	10.2	10.1	10.1	10.2	10.3	10.3	10.5
2017	10.1	10.2	10.4	10.4	10.4	10.4	10.3	10.3	10.2	10.2	10.0	9.8	10.2
2018	9.3	9.3	9.5	10.0	10.1	10.2	10.3	10.3	10.3	10.4	10.3	10.3	10.0
Construction													
2010	63.6	61.5	64.7	68.2	68.7	69.2	71.1	70.6	70.1	70.6	69.3	66.7	67.9
2011	60.4	60.7	63.7	67.5	69.0	71.3	70.9	71.3	70.6	69.5	69.4	67.3	67.6
2012	62.2	62.3	64.3	66.9	68.4	69.9	70.1	70.0	69.7	69.0	68.5	66.5	67.3
2013	61.4	61.5	63.5	65.7	68.3	70.0	71.1	71.4	71.9	71.7	71.3	69.4	68.1
2014	64.1	64.1	68.4	71.3	73.8	75.3	75.9	76.1	76.7	77.2	76.8	74.4	72.8
2015	69.1	68.8	70.0	74.5	76.5	77.7	80.0	79.0	79.0	79.3	78.3	77.1	75.8
2016	71.3	70.7	73.2	76.8	78.0	79.4	79.8	78.9	79.2	78.4	78.2	76.7	76.7
2017	71.5	72.0	74.9	76.1	77.8	79.6	80.0	79.9	80.4	80.2	79.0	77.2	77.4
2018	71.7	72.4	74.8	77.1	79.3	80.7	80.9	80.8	80.9	80.6	79.1	78.8	78.1

1. Employment by Industry: Kentucky, 2010–2018—*Continued*

(Numbers in thousands, not seasonally adjusted)

Industry and year	January	February	March	April	May	June	July	August	September	October	November	December	Annual average
Manufacturing													
2010	207.3	203.4	207.1	208.1	208.8	209.4	206.6	210.7	212.1	212.1	211.7	212.5	209.2
2011	210.2	210.4	210.8	211.6	211.1	212.8	208.6	214.0	215.2	215.4	216.6	216.8	212.8
2012	217.2	216.0	219.1	219.7	221.7	224.4	224.4	226.2	226.6	227.7	228.3	229.4	223.4
2013	227.7	227.5	227.7	227.6	228.4	229.4	225.5	229.4	230.0	230.8	231.7	233.1	229.1
2014	231.1	231.6	231.9	232.8	234.2	235.1	235.2	237.5	236.9	237.0	238.6	239.6	235.1
2015	238.8	238.5	238.9	236.9	240.9	241.8	238.1	243.5	244.1	243.7	244.9	246.2	241.4
2016	244.8	245.5	246.3	246.9	247.8	249.1	249.7	250.1	250.0	249.2	250.3	251.1	248.4
2017	249.6	250.1	250.2	250.4	250.3	250.9	250.2	250.2	249.9	249.7	251.5	252.4	250.5
2018	250.8	251.2	251.3	251.0	251.2	252.0	250.6	252.3	250.7	253.0	255.0	256.1	252.1
Trade, Transportation, and Utilities													
2010	354.4	351.8	354.8	357.2	359.7	360.9	360.2	361.0	359.5	363.6	370.0	375.0	360.7
2011	358.7	356.7	359.8	362.0	363.0	365.1	364.6	366.1	365.1	366.9	376.1	379.4	365.3
2012	363.5	361.7	364.6	366.0	368.8	370.3	368.2	368.9	368.8	368.6	376.4	379.1	368.7
2013	364.0	362.2	364.5	365.5	368.2	369.6	368.5	370.6	369.7	371.2	380.1	385.1	369.9
2014	368.6	366.4	369.2	371.3	374.6	376.4	375.0	377.8	377.2	379.8	388.0	395.3	376.6
2015	379.4	376.9	378.8	381.0	384.5	386.1	384.9	387.1	386.2	388.7	396.5	400.9	385.9
2016	388.6	387.5	389.7	391.9	394.1	393.5	396.0	396.7	395.5	396.6	405.1	410.8	395.5
2017	393.6	391.7	393.2	394.0	396.7	398.0	396.7	398.1	399.3	401.1	413.2	416.8	399.4
2018	400.3	397.9	399.2	400.2	402.8	405.3	404.4	403.9	402.0	402.1	412.2	415.6	403.8
Wholesale Trade													
2010	70.3	70.1	70.4	70.2	70.6	70.8	70.9	70.8	70.6	70.9	71.1	71.2	70.7
2011	70.1	70.4	70.7	70.5	70.5	70.9	71.3	71.5	71.4	71.2	71.3	71.7	71.0
2012	70.6	70.8	71.0	71.1	71.4	71.7	71.5	71.9	72.0	71.9	72.0	72.2	71.5
2013	71.9	72.1	72.3	72.3	72.5	72.9	72.6	72.9	72.7	72.3	72.5	73.2	72.5
2014	72.2	72.3	72.6	72.6	72.9	73.0	72.6	73.0	72.7	72.4	72.5	73.2	72.7
2015	72.1	72.1	72.0	72.1	72.7	73.0	73.0	73.2	73.0	73.0	73.2	73.7	72.8
2016	73.1	72.9	73.2	73.3	73.7	73.6	73.7	73.3	73.1	72.7	73.1	73.7	73.3
2017	72.9	73.2	73.4	74.1	74.5	74.8	74.4	74.2	74.1	73.9	74.2	75.0	74.1
2018	74.3	74.6	74.6	74.8	74.8	75.3	75.4	75.1	74.6	75.7	76.3	75.9	75.1
Retail Trade													
2010	197.0	195.2	197.6	199.5	201.1	200.7	200.6	200.7	198.8	201.7	205.9	207.6	200.5
2011	198.3	196.2	198.3	200.7	201.3	201.5	200.6	201.2	199.3	201.2	207.0	208.7	201.2
2012	199.8	197.3	199.7	201.3	203.5	204.2	202.8	202.4	201.8	202.8	209.0	209.6	202.9
2013	199.7	198.1	199.6	200.9	202.8	203.5	203.0	203.6	202.4	203.9	210.1	212.4	203.3
2014	200.9	199.4	200.9	203.3	204.9	205.8	204.7	205.7	204.2	205.8	212.0	215.3	205.2
2015	205.4	204.2	206.0	208.0	210.2	211.2	209.7	210.3	209.1	210.3	216.2	218.5	209.9
2016	210.1	210.1	211.7	214.2	215.3	214.5	215.4	215.6	214.1	216.0	221.7	222.9	215.1
2017	214.1	211.9	212.6	213.6	215.0	214.9	213.9	214.1	214.1	215.0	222.3	222.2	215.3
2018	213.0	211.9	212.8	213.6	215.8	215.6	215.0	214.2	212.7	211.2	218.6	219.0	214.5
Transportation and Utilities													
2010	87.1	86.5	86.8	87.5	88.0	89.4	88.7	89.5	90.1	91.0	93.0	96.2	89.5
2011	90.3	90.1	90.8	90.8	91.2	92.7	92.7	93.4	94.4	94.5	97.8	99.0	93.1
2012	93.1	93.6	93.9	93.6	93.9	94.4	93.9	94.6	95.0	93.9	95.4	97.3	94.4
2013	92.4	92.0	92.6	92.3	92.9	93.2	92.9	94.1	94.6	95.0	97.5	99.8	94.1
2014	95.5	94.7	95.7	95.4	96.8	97.6	97.7	99.1	100.3	101.6	103.5	106.8	98.7
2015	101.9	100.6	100.8	100.9	101.6	101.9	102.2	103.6	104.1	105.4	107.1	108.7	103.2
2016	105.4	104.5	104.8	104.4	105.1	105.4	106.9	107.8	108.3	107.9	110.3	114.2	107.1
2017	106.6	106.6	107.2	106.3	107.2	108.3	108.4	109.8	111.1	112.2	116.7	119.6	110.0
2018	113.0	111.4	111.8	111.8	112.2	114.4	114.0	114.6	114.7	115.2	117.3	120.7	114.3
Information													
2010	24.6	24.5	24.6	24.6	24.8	24.9	24.4	24.5	24.5	24.6	25.0	25.8	24.7
2011	25.4	25.2	25.1	25.0	25.0	25.0	25.0	25.0	24.6	24.8	25.2	25.3	25.1
2012	25.0	24.8	24.6	24.5	24.7	24.5	24.5	24.5	24.1	24.2	24.5	24.5	24.5
2013	24.3	24.4	24.4	24.1	24.3	24.3	24.1	24.2	23.9	24.0	24.0	24.0	24.2
2014	24.2	24.0	24.0	23.8	23.9	23.9	23.7	23.8	23.6	23.8	23.6	23.5	23.8
2015	23.3	23.1	23.0	22.7	22.9	22.8	22.8	22.8	22.5	22.6	22.8	22.7	22.8
2016	22.7	22.8	22.8	22.7	22.9	23.0	23.2	23.3	23.2	23.1	23.1	23.3	23.0
2017	22.6	22.7	22.8	22.7	22.8	22.7	22.7	22.4	22.2	22.2	21.9	22.1	22.5
2018	22.0	22.1	22.0	22.1	22.2	22.3	21.8	22.0	22.0	21.6	21.9	21.8	22.0

1. Employment by Industry: Kentucky, 2010–2018—*Continued*

(Numbers in thousands, not seasonally adjusted)

Industry and year	January	February	March	April	May	June	July	August	September	October	November	December	Annual average
Financial Activities													
2010	86.4	86.0	86.0	86.2	86.2	86.4	86.3	85.7	85.1	85.0	85.0	85.5	85.8
2011	84.4	84.6	84.7	84.2	84.3	85.0	85.2	85.5	85.6	85.4	85.4	86.0	85.0
2012	85.5	85.4	85.8	85.7	86.1	87.0	87.4	87.5	87.7	87.5	87.9	88.3	86.8
2013	87.8	87.7	88.1	88.1	88.5	89.0	89.5	89.9	89.5	89.1	89.3	89.7	88.9
2014	88.9	88.6	88.7	89.1	89.8	90.2	90.8	90.9	90.8	91.1	91.6	92.3	90.2
2015	91.2	91.2	91.3	91.1	91.8	92.5	92.8	92.9	92.7	92.6	93.1	93.4	92.2
2016	92.7	92.9	92.8	92.9	93.5	93.9	94.2	94.0	93.9	94.2	94.1	95.1	93.7
2017	93.5	93.5	93.7	93.7	94.0	94.7	94.1	94.1	93.9	93.8	93.7	93.7	93.9
2018	92.3	92.1	92.1	92.5	92.9	93.6	93.5	93.8	93.5	94.1	93.0	93.0	93.0
Professional and Business Services													
2010	174.9	172.8	175.3	180.8	181.0	183.7	183.4	183.8	184.6	185.5	187.2	192.0	182.1
2011	182.1	181.4	183.6	187.2	185.8	187.7	188.7	192.2	192.8	193.5	195.2	198.1	189.0
2012	188.9	188.1	189.6	192.3	193.3	195.7	194.2	197.1	196.6	199.4	203.7	206.7	195.5
2013	196.1	194.4	196.4	199.8	201.1	201.9	201.0	207.0	205.7	210.2	217.8	218.9	204.2
2014	207.5	203.3	207.0	211.1	213.0	212.0	211.6	214.8	213.9	218.4	225.7	228.2	213.9
2015	214.9	210.7	212.3	215.2	217.7	219.6	218.4	220.0	219.8	222.6	230.0	233.4	219.6
2016	218.0	215.1	213.0	216.2	217.0	216.1	214.9	215.9	217.8	220.5	224.3	223.9	217.7
2017	214.7	212.0	211.5	212.7	212.6	215.3	214.1	215.6	217.6	219.9	224.0	223.1	216.1
2018	212.9	213.3	213.7	216.7	215.8	218.1	216.3	218.2	218.7	217.1	222.8	224.7	217.4
Education and Health Services													
2010	249.7	250.6	252.5	253.7	254.3	253.3	253.1	253.8	255.9	257.6	258.2	258.0	254.2
2011	255.0	255.7	256.4	257.5	257.2	255.9	255.4	256.7	259.5	259.8	259.9	258.7	257.3
2012	257.0	258.7	259.6	259.5	259.8	259.6	257.9	259.3	260.5	261.7	262.4	262.4	259.9
2013	259.1	260.5	261.5	261.8	261.0	258.5	259.0	260.6	261.6	263.2	263.0	261.9	261.0
2014	258.6	260.1	259.9	260.9	259.3	257.9	256.3	258.2	261.5	263.5	261.1	262.9	260.0
2015	259.5	261.6	262.1	263.6	263.1	261.7	260.8	261.8	265.3	269.1	268.9	269.7	263.9
2016	264.1	267.5	267.2	266.6	266.5	266.0	265.9	267.5	270.7	272.7	271.7	272.8	268.3
2017	267.9	271.7	271.5	273.3	271.7	272.6	269.7	270.8	273.6	276.2	277.5	276.6	272.8
2018	272.3	276.1	275.9	278.6	277.1	277.8	274.8	276.6	279.6	281.9	283.7	285.7	278.3
Leisure and Hospitality													
2010	154.2	155.2	160.5	169.7	172.7	175.0	173.4	173.4	171.6	170.0	168.4	165.0	167.4
2011	157.5	159.1	164.6	173.4	176.2	177.6	175.8	175.8	173.9	170.6	170.0	166.4	170.1
2012	161.3	164.2	169.2	176.1	182.3	182.9	179.8	180.5	177.8	176.3	175.8	172.7	174.9
2013	168.4	169.3	173.8	181.2	185.8	185.8	185.3	185.0	182.2	180.9	179.6	176.1	179.5
2014	169.8	171.0	176.0	185.9	188.9	189.8	188.6	188.0	185.1	183.5	181.3	179.3	182.3
2015	175.0	176.3	179.4	189.4	194.1	194.7	194.7	193.4	191.3	189.9	190.0	186.5	187.9
2016	180.1	182.0	187.3	196.7	200.7	201.4	201.0	200.5	197.5	194.8	193.7	189.5	193.8
2017	184.4	187.3	192.8	199.2	203.7	204.8	203.0	202.0	198.8	198.4	197.2	192.5	197.0
2018	185.6	188.6	192.8	199.2	204.4	205.3	204.8	204.5	200.8	197.6	197.2	190.6	197.6
Other Services													
2010	67.9	67.4	68.6	69.0	69.1	69.3	69.2	68.9	68.5	69.1	68.8	68.7	68.7
2011	67.7	67.8	68.4	67.8	67.9	68.1	68.1	67.7	67.4	67.2	66.8	66.8	67.6
2012	66.4	66.3	66.9	66.7	66.4	66.6	66.1	65.6	65.2	65.0	64.9	64.9	65.9
2013	64.2	64.5	65.0	65.2	65.2	65.3	64.7	64.7	64.4	63.9	63.9	63.9	64.6
2014	62.8	63.1	63.7	64.1	64.4	64.2	63.9	63.9	63.8	63.1	63.9	63.2	63.7
2015	62.6	62.7	63.4	63.4	64.1	64.7	64.1	64.4	64.0	63.8	64.8	64.3	63.9
2016	63.9	64.4	65.0	65.7	66.1	66.0	65.7	65.7	65.4	66.3	65.3	65.4	65.4
2017	64.7	65.3	66.0	65.9	66.3	66.5	65.7	65.8	65.6	65.6	65.2	65.2	65.7
2018	64.3	64.9	65.5	66.0	66.2	66.4	65.6	65.8	65.3	65.4	65.6	65.8	65.6
Government													
2010	311.4	314.6	317.6	320.9	328.3	321.9	305.6	306.2	317.6	320.6	321.7	320.5	317.2
2011	315.7	320.6	322.8	324.5	324.5	320.6	308.1	314.2	322.7	324.6	326.3	326.6	320.9
2012	322.1	326.6	328.7	330.5	329.5	323.6	308.7	313.8	322.9	325.4	326.6	326.3	323.7
2013	320.6	325.6	327.1	329.1	329.3	323.6	310.9	317.0	326.2	324.2	326.1	326.2	323.8
2014	320.6	322.2	324.1	327.4	327.4	322.1	311.4	319.2	324.8	324.7	325.3	324.0	322.8
2015	318.7	319.9	320.5	323.8	323.3	317.7	302.9	310.3	318.3	320.9	322.0	321.8	318.3
2016	315.8	317.2	319.7	320.3	320.8	314.4	303.3	311.4	318.0	317.0	318.4	318.1	316.2
2017	314.0	317.1	318.5	320.3	321.1	315.7	300.5	305.6	318.3	318.5	320.2	319.8	315.8
2018	310.7	315.7	317.7	318.0	319.2	314.0	296.6	303.0	316.1	316.7	318.3	317.8	313.7

2. Average Weekly Hours by Selected Industry: Kentucky, 2014–2018

(Not seasonally adjusted)

Industry and year	January	February	March	April	May	June	July	August	September	October	November	December	Annual average
Total Private													
2014	33.7	34.6	34.6	34.6	34.8	35.2	34.8	34.9	35.0	35.0	35.5	35.6	34.9
2015	34.9	34.4	35.0	35.1	35.2	35.5	35.4	35.7	35.3	35.5	35.7	35.8	35.3
2016	34.8	34.8	35.1	35.1	35.0	35.5	35.2	35.0	35.1	35.4	35.3	35.4	35.1
2017	35.3	34.9	34.8	34.9	34.6	35.1	35.3	35.3	35.1	35.3	35.0	35.2	35.1
2018	33.8	34.7	34.8	35.0	34.8	35.2	35.3	35.1	35.6	35.5	35.2	35.5	35.0
Goods Producing													
2014	38.6	39.4	39.7	39.7	40.0	40.6	40.4	40.8	40.6	40.7	41.5	41.9	40.3
2015	41.1	39.8	40.5	40.9	41.4	41.6	41.0	41.8	40.8	41.2	41.2	42.0	41.1
2016	40.1	39.6	39.9	40.2	40.0	41.2	40.1	40.6	40.9	40.7	41.2	40.9	40.5
2017	40.6	40.3	40.1	40.1	40.2	40.8	41.1	41.4	40.8	41.4	40.8	41.4	40.8
2018	39.1	40.4	40.3	41.1	40.8	40.6	40.8	42.0	42.1	42.0	41.3	41.9	41.0
Construction													
2014	34.9	34.6	35.9	36.3	36.9	37.5	38.0	38.8	37.9	36.1	38.2	38.6	37.1
2015	38.1	36.7	36.9	37.8	39.6	39.8	39.8	40.4	38.1	41.1	39.7	40.5	39.1
2016	38.4	36.5	38.4	39.5	38.1	39.8	38.5	38.7	38.9	38.8	38.8	38.4	38.6
2017	38.4	38.5	38.4	38.6	38.3	40.0	41.3	40.7	39.4	40.5	39.1	39.3	39.4
2018	36.0	37.2	37.1	38.6	39.1	38.7	40.0	39.0	39.3	39.4	37.9	38.6	38.4
Manufacturing													
2014	39.8	41.1	41.0	40.8	40.9	41.6	41.1	41.3	41.3	41.8	42.3	42.6	41.3
2015	41.2	39.9	40.8	41.2	41.4	41.8	40.9	41.7	41.2	41.2	41.7	42.5	41.3
2016	40.7	41.2	41.0	40.9	41.1	41.9	40.7	41.3	41.6	41.5	42.2	41.8	41.3
2017	41.2	40.8	40.6	40.6	40.9	41.0	40.9	41.5	41.2	41.4	41.1	41.9	41.1
2018	39.7	41.1	41.1	41.8	41.1	41.0	40.9	42.3	42.5	42.2	41.9	42.4	41.5
Trade, Transportation, and Utilities													
2014	33.8	34.7	34.7	34.7	35.5	35.4	35.0	34.9	35.4	35.2	35.9	36.2	35.1
2015	34.7	34.7	35.3	35.7	35.9	36.0	35.8	36.2	36.0	35.9	36.2	36.3	35.7
2016	34.6	35.2	35.0	34.8	34.7	35.2	35.4	34.5	34.2	34.6	34.0	34.5	34.7
2017	33.6	33.5	33.7	33.9	33.7	33.7	33.9	33.8	33.7	33.5	33.5	33.8	33.7
2018	31.9	32.5	33.1	33.3	33.3	33.9	33.9	33.8	34.2	34.1	34.1	34.2	33.5
Financial Activities													
2014	36.0	37.0	36.6	36.1	36.5	37.6	36.4	36.2	36.5	36.6	37.2	36.1	36.6
2015	35.9	36.0	36.9	36.0	36.3	36.7	36.7	37.1	36.6	37.2	37.6	37.0	36.7
2016	36.6	35.8	35.9	36.3	36.9	36.7	36.3	36.3	36.0	36.6	35.8	35.3	36.2
2017	36.3	35.6	35.8	36.9	35.8	36.4	37.1	36.7	37.1	38.2	37.4	37.6	36.7
2018	37.7	38.0	37.8	38.4	37.6	37.6	37.7	36.9	38.2	37.1	37.6	38.1	37.7
Professional and Business Services													
2014	34.8	36.7	36.4	36.9	36.3	36.7	35.4	35.9	35.8	35.7	35.9	36.2	36.1
2015	35.7	35.6	35.8	36.1	36.0	36.1	36.4	36.5	35.8	36.3	36.5	36.4	36.1
2016	36.1	36.2	36.8	36.5	36.6	37.4	36.9	37.2	37.1	37.7	37.3	37.6	37.0
2017	37.5	37.1	36.8	36.7	36.0	36.7	37.0	36.4	36.6	36.8	36.5	36.1	36.7
2018	35.1	36.0	35.7	36.1	35.7	36.6	36.0	35.4	35.7	35.7	35.3	35.2	35.7
Education and Health Services													
2014	33.7	34.2	34.0	34.2	34.0	34.4	34.3	34.4	34.5	34.6	35.0	34.8	34.3
2015	34.7	34.2	34.6	34.5	34.5	34.7	35.0	35.2	35.0	34.9	35.3	34.8	34.8
2016	34.5	34.6	34.8	35.0	35.0	34.6	34.4	34.1	34.4	34.7	34.7	34.6	34.6
2017	35.4	34.6	34.6	34.8	34.4	34.9	35.0	34.2	34.1	34.1	34.4	34.3	34.6
2018	33.5	34.4	34.3	34.3	34.1	34.3	34.6	34.3	34.9	35.0	34.6	34.9	34.4
Leisure and Hospitality													
2014	24.4	25.3	25.6	25.7	25.4	26.0	25.6	25.3	25.2	25.2	25.1	25.2	25.3
2015	24.2	23.8	24.7	24.8	24.3	24.9	24.9	24.9	24.6	25.1	24.9	25.4	24.7
2016	24.1	24.3	25.0	25.2	25.0	25.5	25.7	25.5	25.6	25.8	25.8	25.9	25.3
2017	25.6	25.3	25.5	25.6	25.5	26.4	26.8	26.6	26.2	26.4	26.0	26.3	26.0
2018	24.8	26.0	26.4	26.5	26.7	26.9	27.2	26.4	26.2	26.8	26.1	26.4	26.4

3. Average Hourly Earnings by Selected Industry: Kentucky, 2014–2018

(Dollars, not seasonally adjusted)

Industry and year	January	February	March	April	May	June	July	August	September	October	November	December	Annual average
Total Private													
2014	20.36	20.60	20.63	20.40	20.23	20.32	20.46	20.50	20.35	20.51	20.87	21.13	20.53
2015	21.21	21.26	21.17	21.13	21.08	20.97	21.16	21.14	21.08	20.90	20.94	20.98	21.08
2016	21.25	21.06	21.13	21.27	21.16	21.10	21.24	21.14	21.24	21.55	21.34	21.58	21.26
2017	21.92	21.74	21.76	22.01	21.87	21.67	21.94	21.74	21.86	21.82	21.73	21.80	21.82
2018	22.18	21.86	21.82	22.21	22.04	21.78	22.13	21.88	22.18	22.09	22.43	22.73	22.11
Goods Producing													
2014	21.33	21.35	21.33	21.55	21.29	21.36	21.51	21.72	21.88	22.10	22.34	23.43	21.78
2015	22.71	22.71	22.75	22.94	22.78	22.68	23.10	22.72	22.62	22.73	22.93	22.97	22.80
2016	22.77	22.75	22.80	22.97	23.13	23.02	23.16	22.85	22.76	23.04	22.86	23.32	22.95
2017	23.42	23.24	23.14	23.37	23.41	23.47	23.36	23.25	23.20	23.18	22.99	23.03	23.25
2018	22.98	22.64	22.77	23.08	23.07	22.65	23.11	22.86	23.14	22.78	23.06	23.13	22.94
Construction													
2014	21.33	21.08	20.74	21.08	20.85	20.70	21.55	21.99	22.12	22.63	22.77	23.31	21.72
2015	23.11	23.46	23.61	23.73	23.50	23.72	24.63	23.99	23.45	23.42	23.90	23.92	23.72
2016	24.03	24.71	24.05	24.29	24.97	24.94	24.15	24.12	23.63	24.36	23.87	23.91	24.25
2017	23.67	24.23	24.54	24.88	24.88	25.27	25.03	25.15	25.43	25.40	25.44	25.97	25.02
2018	25.37	25.43	25.63	25.75	25.86	24.97	24.84	24.42	25.09	24.85	25.23	25.28	25.21
Manufacturing													
2014	21.27	21.56	21.62	21.75	21.43	21.54	21.42	21.46	21.54	21.74	21.91	23.27	21.72
2015	22.24	22.15	22.17	22.38	22.19	21.89	22.13	21.80	21.94	21.96	22.04	22.03	22.07
2016	21.66	21.50	21.74	21.93	21.96	21.74	22.32	21.91	22.04	22.14	22.11	22.78	21.99
2017	23.00	22.50	22.20	22.40	22.40	22.32	22.33	21.99	22.12	22.04	21.81	21.77	22.24
2018	21.93	21.46	21.57	21.90	21.77	21.49	22.17	22.00	22.09	21.63	21.91	21.98	21.83
Trade, Transportation, and Utilities													
2014	19.55	19.54	19.77	19.50	19.58	19.75	19.76	19.63	19.61	19.71	19.70	19.59	19.64
2015	20.04	20.00	19.89	20.10	20.01	20.18	20.09	20.25	20.17	20.08	20.03	19.89	20.06
2016	20.70	20.30	20.44	20.48	19.95	20.05	20.39	20.40	20.50	20.79	20.29	20.46	20.40
2017	20.95	20.68	20.77	21.16	21.05	21.04	21.17	21.01	21.24	20.91	20.85	20.74	20.96
2018	21.20	20.93	20.83	21.36	21.01	20.99	21.48	21.19	21.22	21.54	21.70	21.90	21.29
Financial Activities													
2014	22.25	22.63	22.65	21.93	22.10	22.47	22.36	22.37	22.08	22.12	22.46	22.17	22.30
2015	22.31	22.68	22.44	22.92	22.25	22.34	22.69	23.16	22.86	23.11	23.07	23.14	22.75
2016	23.44	24.08	23.95	23.71	23.58	23.25	23.64	23.34	23.86	24.66	24.39	25.02	23.91
2017	26.03	26.09	26.19	26.78	26.04	26.28	27.22	26.47	26.64	26.90	27.19	27.34	26.61
2018	28.31	27.79	27.14	27.73	27.84	27.35	27.81	26.88	26.86	26.30	26.37	26.83	27.27
Professional and Business Services													
2014	20.65	20.64	21.26	20.90	20.76	20.90	20.87	20.46	20.81	20.64	20.66	20.34	20.74
2015	20.84	21.33	21.54	21.09	21.24	21.28	21.88	22.29	22.16	22.19	22.33	22.21	21.71
2016	22.82	22.57	22.66	22.65	23.07	22.71	22.48	22.02	21.95	22.25	22.20	22.13	22.45
2017	22.89	23.16	23.19	23.65	23.51	23.02	23.51	23.50	23.32	23.28	23.15	23.52	23.31
2018	24.10	23.77	23.79	23.78	23.56	23.19	23.31	23.17	23.67	23.30	23.37	23.38	23.53
Education and Health Services													
2014	23.20	23.50	23.28	23.36	22.93	22.85	23.31	23.13	23.34	23.32	23.77	24.10	23.34
2015	24.34	24.18	24.02	23.65	23.87	23.48	23.47	23.12	23.26	23.29	22.89	23.22	23.56
2016	23.08	22.71	22.75	22.41	22.10	22.27	22.56	22.66	22.70	22.96	22.88	22.99	22.67
2017	22.84	22.70	22.75	22.62	22.66	22.39	22.89	22.51	22.55	22.68	22.52	22.54	22.64
2018	23.30	23.00	23.00	23.64	23.17	23.07	23.57	23.43	23.64	23.77	24.18	24.40	23.52
Leisure and Hospitality													
2014	10.62	10.80	10.79	10.75	10.77	10.75	10.72	11.01	11.08	11.20	11.26	11.39	10.93
2015	11.37	11.55	11.36	11.41	11.33	11.19	11.31	11.44	11.34	11.47	11.51	11.58	11.40
2016	11.46	11.55	11.59	11.53	11.69	11.55	11.48	11.59	11.70	11.82	11.76	12.01	11.65
2017	11.95	12.12	12.20	12.10	12.18	11.90	12.04	12.11	12.29	12.44	12.40	12.69	12.20
2018	12.57	12.69	12.61	12.55	12.57	12.50	12.52	12.54	12.83	12.80	12.82	13.04	12.67

4. Average Weekly Earnings by Selected Industry: Kentucky, 2014–2018

(Dollars, not seasonally adjusted)

Industry and year	January	February	March	April	May	June	July	August	September	October	November	December	Annual average
Total Private													
2014	686.13	712.76	713.80	705.84	704.00	715.26	712.01	715.45	712.25	717.85	740.89	752.23	716.50
2015	740.23	731.34	740.95	741.66	742.02	744.44	749.06	754.70	744.12	741.95	747.56	751.08	744.12
2016	739.50	732.89	741.66	746.58	740.60	749.05	747.65	739.90	745.52	762.87	753.30	763.93	746.23
2017	773.78	758.73	757.25	768.15	756.70	760.62	774.48	767.42	767.29	770.25	760.55	767.36	765.88
2018	749.68	758.54	759.34	777.35	766.99	766.66	781.19	767.99	789.61	784.20	789.54	806.92	773.85
Goods Producing													
2014	823.34	841.19	846.80	855.54	851.60	867.22	869.00	886.18	888.33	899.47	927.11	981.72	877.73
2015	933.38	903.86	921.38	938.25	943.09	943.49	947.10	949.70	922.90	936.48	944.72	964.74	937.08
2016	913.08	900.90	909.72	923.39	925.20	948.42	928.72	927.71	930.88	937.73	941.83	953.79	929.48
2017	950.85	936.57	927.91	937.14	941.08	957.58	960.10	962.55	946.56	959.65	937.99	953.44	948.60
2018	898.52	914.66	917.63	948.59	941.26	919.59	942.89	960.12	974.19	956.76	952.38	969.15	940.54
Construction													
2014	744.42	729.37	744.57	765.20	769.37	776.25	818.90	853.21	838.35	816.94	869.81	899.77	805.81
2015	880.49	860.98	871.21	896.99	930.60	944.06	980.27	969.20	893.45	962.56	948.83	968.76	927.45
2016	922.75	901.92	923.52	959.46	951.36	992.61	929.78	933.44	919.21	945.17	926.16	918.14	936.05
2017	908.93	932.86	942.34	960.37	952.90	1010.80	1033.74	1023.61	1001.94	1028.70	994.70	1020.62	985.79
2018	913.32	946.00	950.87	993.95	1011.13	966.34	993.60	952.38	986.04	979.09	956.22	975.81	968.06
Manufacturing													
2014	846.55	886.12	886.42	887.40	876.49	896.06	880.36	886.30	889.60	908.73	926.79	991.30	897.04
2015	916.29	883.79	904.54	922.06	918.67	915.00	905.12	909.06	903.93	904.75	919.07	936.28	911.49
2016	881.56	885.80	891.34	896.94	902.56	910.91	908.42	904.88	916.86	918.81	933.04	952.20	908.19
2017	947.60	918.00	901.32	909.44	916.16	915.12	913.30	912.59	911.34	912.46	896.39	912.16	914.06
2018	870.62	882.01	886.53	915.42	894.75	881.09	906.75	930.60	938.83	912.79	918.03	931.95	905.95
Trade, Transportation, and Utilities													
2014	660.79	678.04	686.02	676.65	695.09	699.15	691.60	685.09	694.19	693.79	707.23	709.16	689.36
2015	695.39	694.00	702.12	717.57	718.36	726.48	719.22	733.05	726.12	720.87	725.09	722.01	716.14
2016	716.22	714.56	715.40	712.70	692.27	705.76	721.81	703.80	701.10	719.33	689.86	705.87	707.88
2017	703.92	692.78	699.95	717.32	709.39	709.05	717.66	710.14	715.79	700.49	698.48	701.01	706.35
2018	676.28	680.23	689.47	711.29	699.63	711.56	728.17	716.22	725.72	734.51	739.97	748.98	713.22
Financial Activities													
2014	801.00	837.31	828.99	791.67	806.65	844.87	813.90	809.79	805.92	809.59	835.51	800.34	816.18
2015	800.93	816.48	828.04	825.12	807.68	819.88	832.72	859.24	836.68	859.69	867.43	856.18	834.93
2016	857.90	862.06	859.81	860.67	870.10	853.28	858.13	847.24	858.96	902.56	873.16	883.21	865.54
2017	944.89	928.80	937.60	988.18	932.23	956.59	1009.86	971.45	988.34	1027.58	1016.91	1027.98	976.59
2018	1067.29	1056.02	1025.89	1064.83	1046.78	1028.36	1048.44	991.87	1026.05	975.73	991.51	1022.22	1028.08
Professional and Business Services													
2014	718.62	757.49	773.86	771.21	753.59	767.03	738.80	734.51	745.00	736.85	741.69	736.31	748.71
2015	743.99	759.35	771.13	761.35	764.64	768.21	796.43	813.59	793.33	805.50	815.05	808.44	783.73
2016	823.80	817.03	833.89	826.73	844.36	849.35	829.51	819.14	814.35	838.83	828.06	832.09	830.65
2017	858.38	859.24	853.39	867.96	846.36	844.83	869.87	855.40	853.51	856.70	844.98	849.07	855.48
2018	845.91	855.72	849.30	858.46	841.09	848.75	839.16	820.22	845.02	831.81	824.96	822.98	840.02
Education and Health Services													
2014	781.84	803.70	791.52	798.91	779.62	786.04	799.53	795.67	805.23	806.87	831.95	838.68	800.56
2015	844.60	826.96	831.09	815.93	823.52	814.76	821.45	813.82	814.10	812.82	808.02	808.06	819.89
2016	796.26	785.77	791.70	784.35	773.50	770.54	776.06	772.71	780.88	796.71	793.94	795.45	784.38
2017	808.54	785.42	787.15	787.18	779.50	781.41	801.15	769.84	768.96	773.39	774.69	773.12	783.34
2018	780.55	791.20	788.90	810.85	790.10	791.30	815.52	803.65	825.04	831.95	836.63	851.56	809.09
Leisure and Hospitality													
2014	259.13	273.24	276.22	276.28	273.56	279.50	274.43	278.55	279.22	282.24	282.63	287.03	276.53
2015	275.15	274.89	280.59	282.97	275.32	278.63	281.62	284.86	278.96	287.90	286.60	294.13	281.58
2016	276.19	280.67	289.75	290.56	292.25	294.53	295.04	295.55	299.52	304.96	303.41	311.06	294.75
2017	305.92	306.64	311.10	309.76	310.59	314.16	322.67	322.13	322.00	328.42	322.40	333.75	317.20
2018	311.74	329.94	332.90	332.58	335.62	336.25	340.54	331.06	336.15	343.04	334.60	344.26	334.49

LOUISIANA
At a Glance

Population:
    2010 census: 4,533,372
    2018 estimate: 4,659,978

Percent change in population:
    2010–2018: 2.8%

Percent change in total nonfarm employment:
    2010–2018: 4.9%

Industry with the largest growth in employment, 2010–2018 (percent):
    Construction, 24.4%

Industry with the largest decline or smallest growth in employment, 2010–2018 (percent):
    Mining and logging, -31.7%

Civilian labor force:
    2010: 2,086,076
    2018: 2,103,495

Unemployment rate and rank among states (highest to lowest):
    2010: 8.0%, 35th
    2018: 4.9%, 4th

Over-the-year change in unemployment rates:
    2016–2017: -1.0%
    2017–2018: -0.2%

Employment by Industry: Louisiana, 2018

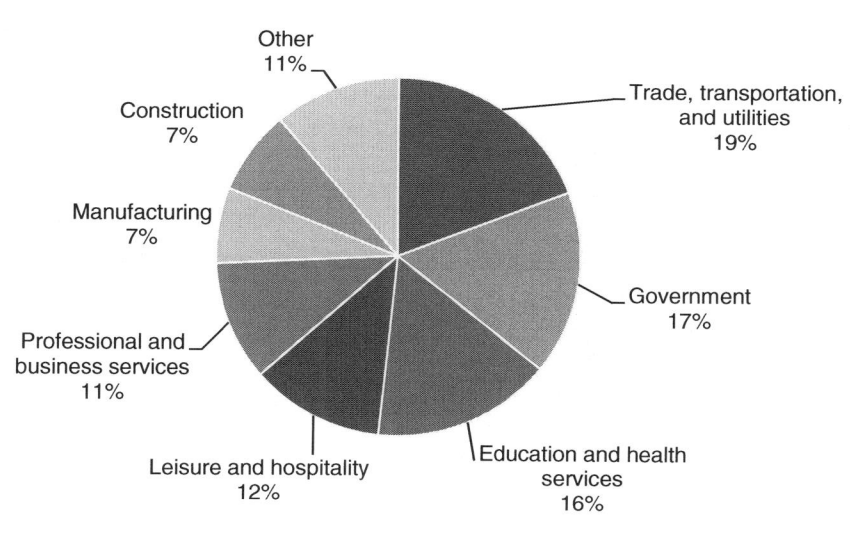

- Other 11%
- Construction 7%
- Manufacturing 7%
- Professional and business services 11%
- Leisure and hospitality 12%
- Education and health services 16%
- Government 17%
- Trade, transportation, and utilities 19%

1. Employment by Industry: Louisiana, 2010–2018

(Numbers in thousands, not seasonally adjusted)

Industry and year	January	February	March	April	May	June	July	August	September	October	November	December	Annual average
Total Nonfarm													
2010	1,858.6	1,867.1	1,884.3	1,893.3	1,901.3	1,899.1	1,876.5	1,879.7	1,889.3	1,899.1	1,904.1	1,905.9	1,888.2
2011	1,875.3	1,889.6	1,901.2	1,910.3	1,911.7	1,899.8	1,891.0	1,898.4	1,913.0	1,920.9	1,927.8	1,927.5	1,905.5
2012	1,897.5	1,911.7	1,923.3	1,937.6	1,944.0	1,934.2	1,910.7	1,920.3	1,924.3	1,942.3	1,954.8	1,954.1	1,929.6
2013	1,920.9	1,939.9	1,948.8	1,956.5	1,959.7	1,956.1	1,938.7	1,953.4	1,959.8	1,977.2	1,988.2	1,979.7	1,956.6
2014	1,950.5	1,961.5	1,973.5	1,980.1	1,989.2	1,984.4	1,972.4	1,986.8	1,994.2	2,012.9	2,021.0	2,021.6	1,987.3
2015	1,985.6	1,991.2	1,992.7	1,998.8	2,003.2	1,995.8	1,984.4	1,988.6	1,990.9	2,009.9	2,010.3	2,005.1	1,996.4
2016	1,968.0	1,971.6	1,976.3	1,984.0	1,985.7	1,975.1	1,961.6	1,956.3	1,974.1	1,981.7	1,985.7	1,978.0	1,974.8
2017	1,952.4	1,969.8	1,972.5	1,975.7	1,983.4	1,975.3	1,954.3	1,962.2	1,968.9	1,981.7	1,989.2	1,984.8	1,972.5
2018	1,953.0	1,965.5	1,982.8	1,984.7	1,990.7	1,984.6	1,966.8	1,978.7	1,980.2	1,998.2	2,001.7	1,991.0	1,981.5
Total Private													
2010	1,489.7	1,493.5	1,508.4	1,517.5	1,520.6	1,526.2	1,521.3	1,523.8	1,525.6	1,531.4	1,535.0	1,538.6	1,519.3
2011	1,514.9	1,525.0	1,536.7	1,546.0	1,549.0	1,543.4	1,545.1	1,550.8	1,553.7	1,557.3	1,563.7	1,566.4	1,546.0
2012	1,544.8	1,554.8	1,567.2	1,580.5	1,588.0	1,584.5	1,572.3	1,580.7	1,575.6	1,588.4	1,600.2	1,600.3	1,578.1
2013	1,577.5	1,591.8	1,600.9	1,609.0	1,613.1	1,615.5	1,609.1	1,624.8	1,620.1	1,636.2	1,644.9	1,639.0	1,615.2
2014	1,617.8	1,624.4	1,637.7	1,645.1	1,654.6	1,654.1	1,654.3	1,665.6	1,661.1	1,677.0	1,683.2	1,686.9	1,655.2
2015	1,657.1	1,658.2	1,661.0	1,665.9	1,670.9	1,667.6	1,667.3	1,668.8	1,659.8	1,676.9	1,675.2	1,673.5	1,666.9
2016	1,640.8	1,640.4	1,646.1	1,652.8	1,652.8	1,647.1	1,645.9	1,638.9	1,643.0	1,647.2	1,649.1	1,644.2	1,645.7
2017	1,624.1	1,636.8	1,640.6	1,643.0	1,650.5	1,648.7	1,639.8	1,645.9	1,641.6	1,649.8	1,656.7	1,654.0	1,644.3
2018	1,628.9	1,636.8	1,653.4	1,653.3	1,659.3	1,658.1	1,651.7	1,659.9	1,652.1	1,666.1	1,667.7	1,659.5	1,653.9
Goods Producing													
2010	306.4	306.0	309.6	310.5	311.6	315.0	315.1	315.1	314.3	315.4	312.7	312.5	312.0
2011	307.7	310.6	313.8	316.7	316.4	316.3	319.4	319.2	320.6	320.4	317.7	316.4	316.3
2012	315.7	319.6	322.5	323.1	326.0	327.7	323.3	325.6	326.4	328.2	327.8	325.0	324.2
2013	320.4	325.0	328.4	328.6	330.3	333.2	332.4	334.1	334.4	338.5	336.1	331.5	331.1
2014	331.3	333.5	337.6	336.4	341.5	341.5	345.1	347.2	347.8	351.4	345.8	343.3	341.9
2015	337.8	335.7	334.3	330.8	330.1	331.1	332.9	332.4	330.9	334.7	328.5	324.3	332.0
2016	316.9	315.9	316.3	313.3	312.8	315.2	316.2	311.2	313.8	315.4	311.9	309.8	314.1
2017	309.6	313.6	315.0	315.5	318.1	319.8	319.6	319.9	317.2	320.2	317.3	316.9	316.9
2018	312.1	316.3	323.1	321.5	324.1	327.4	326.1	326.2	323.8	326.0	320.0	315.2	321.8
Service-Providing													
2010	1,552.2	1,561.1	1,574.7	1,582.8	1,589.7	1,584.1	1,561.4	1,564.6	1,575.0	1,583.7	1,591.4	1,593.4	1,576.2
2011	1,567.6	1,579.0	1,587.4	1,593.6	1,595.3	1,583.5	1,571.6	1,579.2	1,592.4	1,600.5	1,610.1	1,611.1	1,589.3
2012	1,581.8	1,592.1	1,600.8	1,614.5	1,618.0	1,606.5	1,587.4	1,594.7	1,597.9	1,614.1	1,627.0	1,629.1	1,605.3
2013	1,600.5	1,614.9	1,620.4	1,627.9	1,629.4	1,622.9	1,606.3	1,619.3	1,625.4	1,638.7	1,652.1	1,648.2	1,625.5
2014	1,619.2	1,628.0	1,635.9	1,643.7	1,647.7	1,642.9	1,627.3	1,639.6	1,646.4	1,661.5	1,675.2	1,678.3	1,645.5
2015	1,647.8	1,655.5	1,658.4	1,668.0	1,673.1	1,664.7	1,651.5	1,656.2	1,660.0	1,675.2	1,681.8	1,680.8	1,664.4
2016	1,651.1	1,655.7	1,660.0	1,670.7	1,672.9	1,659.9	1,645.4	1,645.1	1,660.3	1,666.3	1,673.8	1,668.2	1,660.8
2017	1,642.8	1,656.2	1,657.5	1,660.2	1,665.3	1,655.5	1,634.7	1,642.3	1,651.7	1,661.5	1,671.9	1,667.9	1,655.6
2018	1,640.9	1,649.2	1,659.7	1,663.2	1,666.6	1,657.2	1,640.7	1,652.5	1,656.4	1,672.2	1,681.7	1,675.8	1,659.7
Mining and Logging													
2010	50.3	51.4	51.9	52.5	53.1	53.6	53.1	53.3	52.9	53.2	52.9	53.0	52.6
2011	52.4	52.9	53.1	54.1	53.9	54.6	55.6	55.8	55.8	55.7	55.7	55.9	54.6
2012	56.9	57.7	57.4	56.1	56.6	56.5	54.8	55.1	54.5	54.7	54.7	54.2	55.8
2013	54.0	54.4	54.6	55.0	55.3	55.8	56.0	56.3	55.9	55.9	55.7	55.3	55.4
2014	55.2	55.0	55.1	54.6	55.3	55.3	55.8	55.8	55.6	55.7	55.4	55.2	55.3
2015	54.1	51.9	50.5	48.4	48.0	46.9	46.7	46.3	45.3	44.3	42.9	42.5	47.3
2016	41.6	40.4	39.4	38.2	37.4	37.2	37.3	36.6	36.3	36.1	35.5	35.6	37.6
2017	34.6	34.6	34.7	34.8	35.1	35.5	35.7	35.5	35.3	35.4	35.4	35.4	35.2
2018	35.2	35.3	35.5	35.7	35.9	36.0	36.3	36.5	36.4	36.7	35.7	35.4	35.9
Construction													
2010	119.5	118.7	120.6	119.5	119.7	122.5	123.9	123.6	123.4	123.5	121.8	121.1	121.5
2011	118.4	120.3	122.8	124.4	123.5	122.5	123.4	122.5	123.1	122.3	120.3	118.8	121.9
2012	119.2	122.1	124.4	125.2	126.5	127.6	125.2	127.0	128.8	130.6	130.1	127.8	126.2
2013	124.5	128.4	131.1	130.6	131.1	132.3	131.4	132.2	132.8	135.6	133.6	129.7	131.1
2014	129.7	132.8	136.6	135.4	138.8	138.2	141.2	142.9	144.2	146.8	141.8	139.6	139.0
2015	136.6	137.5	138.9	138.0	137.9	139.8	141.8	142.1	142.6	147.6	143.8	140.7	140.6
2016	136.8	137.6	139.8	138.3	138.7	141.6	143.1	139.7	142.5	144.6	142.1	139.9	140.4
2017	141.4	144.8	146.1	146.2	148.3	148.8	149.1	149.4	147.5	149.8	146.8	146.2	147.0
2018	143.0	147.1	153.0	151.4	153.3	155.5	154.4	153.9	152.0	153.8	150.0	145.2	151.1

1. Employment by Industry: Louisiana, 2010–2018—*Continued*

(Numbers in thousands, not seasonally adjusted)

Industry and year	January	February	March	April	May	June	July	August	September	October	November	December	Annual average
Manufacturing													
2010	136.6	135.9	137.1	138.5	138.8	138.9	138.1	138.2	138.0	138.7	138.0	138.4	137.9
2011	136.9	137.4	137.9	138.2	139.0	139.2	140.4	140.9	141.7	142.4	141.7	141.7	139.8
2012	139.6	139.8	140.7	141.8	142.9	143.6	143.3	143.5	143.1	142.9	143.0	143.0	142.3
2013	141.9	142.2	142.7	143.0	143.9	145.1	145.0	145.6	145.7	147.0	146.8	146.5	144.6
2014	146.4	145.7	145.9	146.4	147.4	148.0	148.1	148.5	148.0	148.9	148.6	148.5	147.5
2015	147.1	146.3	144.9	144.4	144.2	144.4	144.4	144.0	143.0	142.8	141.8	141.1	144.0
2016	138.5	137.9	137.1	136.8	136.7	136.4	135.8	134.9	135.0	134.7	134.3	134.3	136.0
2017	133.6	134.2	134.2	134.5	134.7	135.5	134.8	135.0	134.4	135.0	135.1	135.3	134.7
2018	133.9	133.9	134.6	134.4	134.9	135.9	135.4	135.8	135.4	135.5	134.3	134.6	134.9
Trade, Transportation, and Utilities													
2010	359.5	358.5	361.6	364.1	365.5	366.3	365.9	366.5	366.0	370.4	376.3	379.8	366.7
2011	369.7	368.8	370.6	373.0	373.9	373.0	373.8	373.8	373.1	374.5	381.2	384.1	374.1
2012	373.5	372.0	374.7	376.2	377.5	377.2	375.5	375.8	374.7	378.8	387.5	389.5	377.7
2013	377.9	376.5	379.7	380.1	380.3	381.4	380.8	382.4	383.1	384.7	391.0	395.5	382.8
2014	383.1	381.6	384.2	385.5	387.2	388.5	387.9	389.6	389.4	391.8	399.4	405.2	389.5
2015	392.3	389.4	391.1	391.7	392.6	393.0	392.0	392.6	390.3	393.5	398.9	401.4	393.2
2016	388.9	386.7	387.8	387.9	387.6	386.5	386.3	385.5	384.5	386.3	392.6	394.9	388.0
2017	383.3	380.9	381.9	381.8	382.2	381.6	379.5	380.5	378.6	379.5	387.2	388.7	382.1
2018	379.3	377.4	379.5	378.6	379.9	378.4	378.3	379.6	377.4	377.4	383.8	384.0	379.5
Wholesale Trade													
2010	69.1	69.3	69.8	70.1	70.4	70.5	70.5	70.7	70.5	71.2	71.1	71.1	70.4
2011	71.5	71.7	72.0	71.4	71.9	71.9	72.4	72.4	72.4	72.5	72.6	72.7	72.1
2012	71.8	72.0	72.3	72.6	72.6	72.7	72.4	72.4	72.0	72.3	72.5	72.5	72.3
2013	72.6	72.7	73.1	73.0	73.1	73.2	73.1	73.4	73.3	73.4	73.5	73.4	73.2
2014	72.3	72.5	72.8	72.9	73.3	73.3	73.2	73.4	73.6	73.6	73.6	73.8	73.2
2015	73.0	72.7	72.9	72.5	72.5	72.4	72.2	72.2	71.7	72.0	71.6	71.7	72.3
2016	71.1	71.0	70.7	70.9	70.7	70.4	70.6	70.5	70.4	70.2	69.8	70.0	70.5
2017	68.9	69.4	69.6	69.6	69.7	69.8	69.8	69.9	69.8	69.3	69.2	69.3	69.5
2018	68.9	69.3	69.6	69.4	69.6	69.7	70.1	70.1	69.5	68.8	68.5	68.8	69.4
Retail Trade													
2010	215.1	214.1	216.2	216.7	217.2	217.2	216.2	216.0	215.6	218.4	224.5	226.8	217.8
2011	218.7	217.7	219.2	221.2	221.4	220.6	220.1	219.5	218.6	219.9	226.4	228.1	221.0
2012	220.4	218.8	220.4	221.2	222.0	221.7	220.9	220.3	219.5	222.9	230.6	231.8	222.5
2013	221.3	219.3	221.4	221.7	221.9	223.0	222.8	223.6	224.2	225.0	231.0	233.8	224.1
2014	223.6	222.4	223.8	224.9	225.8	227.4	226.8	227.2	226.6	228.6	235.8	239.6	227.7
2015	229.3	228.5	230.4	231.1	231.9	233.0	232.4	232.8	231.3	234.5	240.6	241.9	233.1
2016	233.0	232.1	233.6	234.4	234.2	234.4	234.1	233.3	232.3	234.8	241.4	242.7	235.0
2017	233.8	231.3	231.8	231.7	231.8	231.3	229.2	229.8	228.1	229.4	236.1	236.0	231.7
2018	228.3	225.8	227.3	226.4	227.1	226.3	225.4	225.4	224.1	224.2	229.0	228.4	226.5
Transportation and Utilities													
2010	75.3	75.1	75.6	77.3	77.9	78.6	79.2	79.8	79.9	80.8	80.7	81.9	78.5
2011	79.5	79.4	79.4	80.4	80.6	80.5	81.3	81.9	82.1	82.1	82.2	83.3	81.1
2012	81.3	81.2	82.0	82.4	82.9	82.8	82.2	83.1	83.2	83.6	84.4	85.2	82.9
2013	84.0	84.5	85.2	85.4	85.3	85.2	84.9	85.4	85.6	86.3	86.5	88.3	85.6
2014	87.2	86.7	87.6	87.7	88.1	87.8	87.9	89.0	89.2	89.6	90.0	91.8	88.6
2015	90.0	88.2	87.8	88.1	88.2	87.6	87.4	87.6	87.3	87.0	86.7	87.8	87.8
2016	84.8	83.6	83.5	82.6	82.7	81.7	81.6	81.7	81.8	81.3	81.4	82.2	82.4
2017	80.6	80.2	80.5	80.5	80.7	80.5	80.5	80.8	80.7	80.8	81.9	83.4	80.9
2018	82.1	82.3	82.6	82.8	83.2	82.4	82.8	84.1	83.8	84.4	86.3	86.8	83.6
Information													
2010	24.4	24.8	24.5	25.3	25.8	26.4	23.4	23.5	25.6	23.6	24.0	24.7	24.7
2011	23.4	23.5	25.1	23.7	24.6	24.0	22.9	22.9	23.0	23.6	23.5	24.2	23.7
2012	23.2	23.9	23.9	27.1	28.0	25.4	24.8	24.7	24.3	23.9	25.0	25.7	25.0
2013	25.4	26.9	26.3	27.0	27.7	28.0	25.5	25.5	24.4	26.3	27.6	25.7	26.4
2014	23.6	25.0	26.0	26.3	27.8	27.0	26.6	25.3	24.3	25.4	27.4	26.8	26.0
2015	24.8	26.6	25.5	27.5	29.0	28.1	27.5	26.2	24.9	25.1	25.8	26.2	26.4
2016	24.8	24.6	24.5	24.1	23.9	23.4	23.9	23.9	22.3	22.6	24.1	22.5	23.7
2017	21.9	24.2	23.8	24.1	25.0	22.8	22.3	22.5	22.1	22.6	22.9	22.5	23.1
2018	22.5	23.7	24.4	24.0	24.0	22.8	21.7	21.6	21.4	22.7	23.3	23.2	22.9

1. Employment by Industry: Louisiana, 2010–2018—*Continued*

(Numbers in thousands, not seasonally adjusted)

Industry and year	January	February	March	April	May	June	July	August	September	October	November	December	Annual average
Financial Activities													
2010	90.0	90.2	90.8	90.8	91.0	91.7	92.2	92.2	91.8	92.2	92.0	92.4	91.4
2011	91.9	92.3	92.3	91.8	91.9	91.6	91.6	91.3	91.7	91.9	91.7	91.7	91.8
2012	90.8	91.2	91.6	91.4	91.5	91.6	91.4	91.4	91.1	91.7	92.4	92.7	91.6
2013	91.4	91.4	91.6	91.9	92.4	92.9	92.9	93.3	93.5	93.8	93.6	93.2	92.7
2014	92.2	92.1	92.0	92.3	92.8	93.1	93.6	94.2	94.0	94.4	94.6	94.6	93.3
2015	93.6	93.5	93.6	93.2	93.3	93.6	93.3	93.4	92.7	93.3	93.3	93.4	93.4
2016	92.4	92.4	92.3	92.7	93.0	92.4	93.3	92.9	93.2	93.4	93.0	92.8	92.8
2017	91.7	91.9	91.8	91.8	91.9	91.8	92.1	91.8	91.5	91.6	91.7	91.7	91.8
2018	90.5	90.7	90.7	90.8	90.9	91.1	91.4	91.3	90.8	91.5	91.9	92.1	91.1
Professional and Business Services													
2010	186.7	188.3	190.1	192.0	192.7	194.6	195.7	194.9	193.6	194.4	193.7	193.5	192.5
2011	191.3	193.9	193.8	195.4	195.4	194.9	194.6	196.4	196.6	197.7	197.7	198.0	195.5
2012	195.9	198.2	199.9	204.0	204.5	203.2	202.1	202.4	201.7	204.4	204.7	203.4	202.0
2013	200.8	206.9	205.9	205.9	205.7	205.7	205.6	207.7	205.8	210.1	211.0	210.2	206.8
2014	207.9	208.9	210.6	212.3	210.2	210.7	210.5	211.0	210.6	214.2	215.4	216.9	211.6
2015	212.1	212.9	213.7	215.4	215.0	213.5	214.6	214.9	212.4	215.9	214.5	213.0	214.0
2016	209.5	210.6	210.6	214.8	213.1	209.9	209.9	208.3	211.7	211.9	210.5	208.2	210.8
2017	206.3	209.9	209.4	208.5	209.1	208.5	209.0	209.2	209.5	212.9	214.5	212.1	209.9
2018	209.8	210.8	212.8	213.6	212.6	212.9	212.5	213.2	212.3	216.0	215.4	214.4	213.0
Education and Health Services													
2010	267.8	268.8	270.4	272.2	270.2	267.7	268.4	270.3	272.8	274.7	275.1	275.1	271.1
2011	272.5	274.7	275.7	277.1	276.6	273.1	273.5	276.1	279.0	281.2	282.7	282.2	277.0
2012	277.8	280.1	281.6	282.5	283.1	281.4	279.3	283.1	283.4	286.5	287.0	286.9	282.7
2013	286.7	288.5	288.8	289.1	288.7	284.9	284.4	292.1	293.1	297.5	297.8	296.7	290.7
2014	295.3	295.9	296.1	297.2	297.5	294.3	294.1	299.7	300.9	303.2	303.0	302.4	298.3
2015	301.4	301.8	301.8	304.0	304.3	301.1	300.6	304.7	305.7	309.0	309.1	309.4	304.4
2016	306.2	306.9	307.2	309.7	310.0	307.8	307.9	310.9	312.4	313.1	313.1	313.9	309.9
2017	311.6	313.3	313.2	314.0	314.2	312.9	308.9	313.3	314.9	315.4	316.2	315.7	313.6
2018	311.7	313.5	313.2	314.2	314.8	311.6	311.2	316.3	316.3	320.8	322.1	320.8	315.5
Leisure and Hospitality													
2010	187.9	189.6	193.6	195.9	197.1	197.7	194.8	195.3	195.7	194.5	195.3	194.7	194.3
2011	192.6	195.0	198.9	201.6	203.7	203.6	202.2	203.9	202.5	201.1	202.4	203.1	200.9
2012	201.6	203.1	205.9	208.6	209.5	209.6	208.0	209.7	206.1	206.6	207.4	208.6	207.1
2013	206.6	207.6	210.7	214.8	216.1	217.1	215.4	217.6	213.7	213.3	215.7	214.3	213.6
2014	212.4	215.0	218.5	221.9	224.0	225.2	222.8	224.7	220.5	222.5	223.7	223.6	221.2
2015	221.3	224.1	226.5	228.3	231.0	231.6	230.6	229.2	227.8	230.0	230.1	230.7	228.4
2016	227.1	228.4	232.1	234.8	237.1	236.5	233.3	231.5	230.6	230.4	229.9	228.6	231.7
2017	226.2	229.4	231.7	233.6	236.0	236.8	234.5	234.8	234.2	234.0	233.6	233.3	233.2
2018	230.1	231.2	236.2	236.9	238.7	239.5	236.6	237.9	236.3	237.3	236.8	235.6	236.1
Other Services													
2010	67.0	67.3	67.8	66.7	66.7	66.8	65.8	66.0	65.8	66.2	65.9	65.9	66.5
2011	65.8	66.2	66.5	66.7	66.5	66.9	67.1	67.2	67.2	66.9	66.8	66.7	66.7
2012	66.3	66.7	67.1	67.6	67.9	68.4	67.9	68.0	67.9	68.3	68.4	68.5	67.8
2013	68.3	69.0	69.5	71.6	71.9	72.3	72.1	72.1	72.1	72.0	72.1	71.9	71.2
2014	72.0	72.4	72.7	73.2	73.6	73.8	73.7	73.9	73.6	74.1	73.9	74.1	73.4
2015	73.8	74.2	74.5	75.0	75.6	75.6	75.8	75.4	75.1	75.4	75.0	75.1	75.0
2016	75.0	74.9	75.3	75.5	75.3	75.4	75.1	74.7	74.5	74.1	74.0	73.5	74.8
2017	73.5	73.6	73.8	73.7	74.0	74.5	73.9	73.9	73.6	73.6	73.3	73.1	73.7
2018	72.9	73.2	73.5	73.7	74.3	74.4	73.9	73.8	73.8	74.4	74.4	74.2	73.9
Government													
2010	368.9	373.6	375.9	375.8	380.7	372.9	355.2	355.9	363.7	367.7	369.1	367.3	368.9
2011	360.4	364.6	364.5	364.3	362.7	356.4	345.9	347.6	359.3	363.6	364.1	361.1	359.5
2012	352.7	356.9	356.1	357.1	356.0	349.7	338.4	339.6	348.7	353.9	354.6	353.8	351.5
2013	343.4	348.1	347.9	347.5	346.6	340.6	329.6	328.6	339.7	341.0	343.3	340.7	341.4
2014	332.7	337.1	335.8	335.0	334.6	330.3	318.1	321.2	333.1	335.9	337.8	334.7	332.2
2015	328.5	333.0	331.7	332.9	332.3	328.2	317.1	319.8	331.1	333.0	335.1	331.6	329.5
2016	327.2	331.2	330.2	331.2	332.9	328.0	315.7	317.4	331.1	334.5	336.6	333.8	329.2
2017	328.3	333.0	331.9	332.7	332.9	326.6	314.5	316.3	327.3	331.9	332.5	330.8	328.2
2018	324.1	328.7	329.4	331.4	331.4	326.5	315.1	318.8	328.1	332.1	334.0	331.5	327.6

2. Average Weekly Hours by Selected Industry: Louisiana, 2014–2018

(Not seasonally adjusted)

Industry and year	January	February	March	April	May	June	July	August	September	October	November	December	Annual average
Total Private													
2014	35.5	36.2	36.5	36.0	36.1	36.4	36.1	36.4	36.2	36.4	36.8	36.6	36.3
2015	35.9	36.4	35.9	35.7	35.8	35.9	35.9	36.3	35.4	35.9	35.9	35.8	35.9
2016	35.3	35.1	34.6	35.0	35.5	35.2	35.1	34.2	34.9	35.6	35.1	35.2	35.1
2017	35.4	35.4	35.4	35.4	35.4	35.3	35.8	35.3	35.5	35.9	35.5	35.4	35.5
2018	34.9	35.5	36.3	36.4	36.2	36.4	36.4	36.0	36.4	36.0	36.0	36.6	36.1
Goods Producing													
2014	43.1	42.8	43.1	42.8	43.1	43.0	42.8	43.6	43.0	43.4	43.6	44.0	43.2
2015	42.2	42.1	40.6	41.0	41.5	41.3	41.3	41.8	40.3	42.5	42.3	42.4	41.6
2016	41.8	40.6	39.3	40.8	41.9	41.3	41.2	39.8	41.1	42.6	41.3	41.7	41.1
2017	41.7	42.4	42.4	40.7	42.5	42.0	42.6	41.7	42.8	42.3	42.0	42.1	42.1
2018	41.4	42.8	44.4	43.9	44.7	44.6	43.6	43.1	43.0	43.4	43.4	44.1	43.5
Construction													
2014	41.8	41.9	42.5	42.9	43.2	41.8	42.8	43.4	42.8	42.3	41.6	42.2	42.4
2015	40.3	40.6	38.6	40.0	40.9	41.5	41.4	41.5	38.6	41.8	41.5	42.3	40.8
2016	40.7	40.6	37.8	40.2	42.2	41.5	40.9	38.7	41.1	42.6	40.6	40.3	40.6
2017	41.4	42.1	41.5	38.5	41.9	41.2	41.4	40.6	41.4	41.4	40.5	40.9	41.1
2018	39.7	41.0	42.9	42.0	43.4	43.1	42.7	41.9	42.0	43.8	41.7	42.9	42.3
Manufacturing													
2014	43.3	42.3	42.6	42.2	42.8	43.1	42.3	42.6	42.5	44.6	45.4	45.7	43.3
2015	43.9	43.2	42.5	42.2	41.9	40.9	41.1	41.2	40.7	42.3	42.3	42.1	42.0
2016	42.0	39.9	40.1	40.9	40.6	40.4	40.2	39.4	40.2	41.3	41.0	42.1	40.7
2017	41.3	42.2	42.1	41.6	42.1	41.9	42.6	42.3	43.9	43.2	43.2	43.0	42.4
2018	42.3	43.8	44.8	45.2	45.0	44.8	43.9	43.8	43.3	42.2	44.3	44.7	44.0
Trade, Transportation, and Utilities													
2014	34.9	35.7	35.8	35.5	35.8	35.7	35.7	36.1	36.2	36.1	36.2	36.2	35.8
2015	35.6	35.9	36.1	36.2	36.4	36.1	36.3	36.6	35.9	35.4	35.9	36.1	36.0
2016	35.2	35.4	35.1	35.4	35.9	35.7	35.6	34.5	35.4	35.5	35.0	35.5	35.3
2017	35.1	35.0	35.2	35.3	35.1	34.9	35.2	35.1	35.1	35.1	35.1	35.0	35.1
2018	34.7	35.0	35.5	36.0	35.3	35.6	35.6	35.4	35.8	35.2	35.4	35.8	35.4
Financial Activities													
2014	38.4	39.2	39.3	38.3	38.1	38.6	37.3	37.6	37.5	37.3	39.2	37.9	38.2
2015	37.6	38.7	38.5	37.5	37.9	38.0	37.9	38.9	37.4	37.4	38.6	37.3	38.0
2016	37.5	37.5	37.6	36.7	37.3	37.3	36.7	36.0	36.4	37.6	36.2	36.3	36.9
2017	36.5	35.8	35.8	36.3	35.2	35.8	37.2	35.7	36.6	37.4	36.8	36.7	36.3
2018	37.1	37.4	37.5	38.4	37.6	38.5	38.7	39.2	39.6	37.8	38.2	39.4	38.3
Professional and Business Services													
2014	35.9	37.3	37.1	37.2	36.9	37.8	36.7	37.5	37.6	37.9	38.6	37.9	37.4
2015	37.6	38.2	37.6	37.2	36.9	36.9	37.0	37.8	36.6	37.2	37.7	37.6	37.4
2016	36.5	36.2	36.1	36.3	37.2	37.0	36.8	36.7	37.2	38.2	37.1	37.4	36.9
2017	37.8	37.3	36.6	37.7	37.0	37.4	38.0	37.4	37.1	38.3	37.5	37.1	37.4
2018	36.7	36.6	37.2	38.0	37.4	37.6	38.6	37.7	38.4	37.6	37.7	38.6	37.7
Education and Health Services													
2014	32.8	33.4	33.5	33.0	33.0	33.8	33.8	33.7	33.5	33.6	34.3	33.9	33.5
2015	33.9	33.9	33.7	33.5	33.3	33.7	34.1	34.1	33.9	34.0	34.2	34.0	33.9
2016	34.1	33.7	33.4	33.6	33.9	33.8	33.9	33.5	33.4	33.9	33.5	33.5	33.7
2017	34.1	33.5	33.4	33.7	33.2	33.4	34.0	33.5	33.8	34.0	33.8	34.0	33.7
2018	33.5	33.9	34.1	34.1	33.6	33.8	33.9	33.8	34.7	33.4	33.5	34.1	33.9
Leisure and Hospitality													
2014	26.8	27.5	28.5	27.7	27.6	27.6	27.3	27.1	26.9	27.7	28.0	27.9	27.5
2015	27.2	28.5	28.2	28.0	28.2	28.4	28.1	27.9	27.4	27.6	27.7	27.3	27.9
2016	26.5	27.5	27.5	27.5	27.3	26.8	26.5	25.4	26.1	26.6	27.3	26.7	26.8
2017	26.8	27.2	27.5	27.4	27.0	26.6	26.9	26.5	26.4	27.0	27.0	27.1	26.9
2018	26.0	27.1	27.6	27.5	27.1	27.3	27.4	26.7	26.6	26.7	26.3	27.0	26.9

3. Average Hourly Earnings Selected Industry: Louisiana, 2014–2018

(Dollars, not seasonally adjusted)

Industry and year	January	February	March	April	May	June	July	August	September	October	November	December	Annual average
Total Private													
2014	22.09	22.11	22.21	22.11	22.10	22.21	22.23	22.18	22.11	22.04	22.05	21.94	22.11
2015	22.12	22.15	22.31	22.26	21.98	21.94	21.93	22.24	22.15	22.31	22.55	22.38	22.19
2016	22.51	22.39	22.41	22.53	22.63	22.47	22.49	22.65	22.87	23.11	22.87	22.83	22.65
2017	23.09	23.03	23.00	22.85	22.81	22.76	23.07	22.89	23.02	23.14	23.09	23.08	22.99
2018	23.31	23.34	23.21	23.37	23.31	23.19	23.49	23.39	23.75	23.88	23.77	23.81	23.49
Goods Producing													
2014	26.21	26.71	26.72	26.73	26.65	26.64	26.60	26.55	26.20	26.01	25.86	26.18	26.42
2015	26.39	26.30	26.74	26.41	26.12	25.93	26.18	26.38	26.39	26.27	26.51	26.58	26.35
2016	26.76	26.84	27.06	26.89	26.75	26.59	26.74	26.89	27.20	27.26	26.94	26.83	26.90
2017	26.80	27.06	27.14	26.74	26.58	26.36	26.92	26.74	26.62	26.96	26.80	27.16	26.82
2018	27.10	26.97	26.66	26.78	26.56	26.52	26.84	26.53	26.95	27.13	26.89	27.46	26.86
Construction													
2014	24.14	25.03	25.05	24.65	24.92	24.80	24.39	24.61	24.25	24.54	24.41	24.78	24.63
2015	25.28	25.29	25.47	25.14	24.63	24.29	24.68	24.52	24.56	25.17	25.08	25.29	24.95
2016	25.30	25.31	25.62	25.93	25.70	25.55	25.68	25.76	26.63	26.81	26.39	26.67	25.96
2017	26.66	27.18	26.74	26.06	26.21	26.03	26.36	25.95	26.28	26.36	26.33	26.58	26.40
2018	26.31	26.70	26.43	26.62	26.37	26.21	26.39	25.68	26.32	26.44	26.67	27.98	26.50
Manufacturing													
2014	26.53	26.45	26.29	26.08	25.73	26.00	26.69	26.52	26.23	25.41	25.29	25.58	26.06
2015	25.76	25.54	26.44	26.02	25.83	25.83	25.88	26.33	26.26	25.46	25.93	25.95	25.93
2016	26.28	26.51	26.52	26.07	25.90	25.74	26.09	26.24	25.95	26.10	25.89	25.60	26.07
2017	25.45	25.71	26.04	26.16	25.84	25.54	26.27	25.84	25.86	26.29	25.93	26.33	25.94
2018	26.17	25.77	25.50	25.68	25.41	25.64	26.05	25.46	25.73	25.81	25.35	25.74	25.69
Trade, Transportation, and Utilities													
2014	20.50	20.60	20.83	20.53	20.70	21.05	21.34	21.00	21.19	20.98	20.86	20.49	20.84
2015	20.62	20.61	20.86	20.86	20.62	20.89	20.50	20.94	20.76	20.78	20.50	20.79	20.73
2016	20.72	20.37	20.13	20.37	20.40	20.30	20.04	20.30	20.39	20.24	20.02	19.82	20.26
2017	20.07	20.03	19.93	20.28	20.16	20.20	20.50	20.42	20.78	20.79	21.05	20.64	20.40
2018	20.92	20.95	21.04	21.38	21.56	21.42	21.92	21.88	22.22	22.23	22.33	21.90	21.65
Financial Activities													
2014	21.88	22.03	22.16	21.99	21.92	22.41	22.17	22.70	22.92	23.35	23.50	23.07	22.51
2015	23.63	23.89	23.97	24.67	23.98	24.12	24.53	24.92	24.85	24.96	26.12	25.40	24.59
2016	25.54	25.55	25.53	26.12	25.99	24.70	25.12	26.01	26.04	26.89	26.47	26.30	25.85
2017	27.74	26.94	28.09	27.43	26.63	25.79	26.22	26.38	26.41	26.53	26.66	26.74	26.80
2018	27.32	27.72	27.32	27.05	26.90	26.16	26.44	26.04	26.78	25.74	25.76	26.40	26.63
Professional and Business Services													
2014	25.59	25.59	25.95	25.62	25.67	25.93	25.81	25.59	25.36	25.02	25.36	25.27	25.56
2015	25.70	26.16	26.21	25.90	25.52	25.59	25.56	26.00	25.60	25.75	26.26	25.50	25.81
2016	25.55	25.48	25.72	25.24	25.59	25.43	25.48	25.14	25.40	25.93	25.68	25.98	25.55
2017	26.22	25.85	25.93	25.82	25.91	26.35	26.86	26.26	26.17	26.19	25.94	26.19	26.14
2018	26.55	26.68	26.09	26.29	25.77	25.81	26.34	26.04	26.46	26.52	27.29	26.97	26.40
Education and Health Services													
2014	19.10	19.20	19.04	18.97	18.77	18.62	18.46	18.42	18.43	18.40	18.36	18.28	18.67
2015	18.33	18.40	18.65	19.04	18.91	18.58	18.50	18.78	19.00	19.49	19.98	19.98	18.98
2016	20.04	20.29	20.66	21.33	21.67	21.77	21.83	21.92	22.30	22.59	22.83	22.77	21.67
2017	23.09	22.95	22.84	22.96	22.80	22.74	22.81	22.77	22.89	23.02	22.93	22.73	22.88
2018	22.86	22.79	22.72	23.03	22.91	22.91	23.11	23.02	23.12	23.30	23.38	23.71	23.07
Leisure and Hospitality													
2014	12.53	12.70	12.79	12.62	12.65	12.37	12.65	12.69	12.87	13.13	13.13	13.28	12.79
2015	13.29	13.12	13.07	13.06	12.96	12.87	12.87	12.88	12.98	13.16	13.16	13.31	13.06
2016	13.32	13.35	13.60	13.53	13.35	13.21	13.16	13.34	13.35	13.53	13.48	13.51	13.39
2017	13.47	13.51	13.57	13.56	13.41	13.24	13.14	13.11	13.27	13.35	13.49	13.56	13.39
2018	13.36	13.65	13.62	13.58	13.51	13.52	13.43	13.51	13.44	13.63	13.74	13.80	13.57

4. Average Weekly Earnings Selected Industry: Louisiana, 2014–2018

(Dollars, not seasonally adjusted)

Industry and year	January	February	March	April	May	June	July	August	September	October	November	December	Annual average
Total Private													
2014	784.20	800.38	810.67	795.96	797.81	808.44	802.50	807.35	800.38	802.26	811.44	803.00	802.59
2015	794.11	806.26	800.93	794.68	786.88	787.65	787.29	807.31	784.11	800.93	809.55	801.20	796.62
2016	794.60	785.89	775.39	788.55	803.37	790.94	789.40	774.63	798.16	822.72	802.74	803.62	795.02
2017	817.39	815.26	814.20	808.89	807.47	803.43	825.91	808.02	817.21	830.73	819.70	817.03	816.15
2018	813.52	828.57	842.52	850.67	843.82	844.12	855.04	842.04	864.50	859.68	855.72	871.45	847.99
Goods Producing													
2014	1,129.65	1,143.19	1,151.63	1,144.04	1,148.62	1,145.52	1,138.48	1,157.58	1,126.60	1,128.83	1,127.50	1,151.92	1,141.34
2015	1,113.66	1,107.23	1,085.64	1,082.81	1,083.98	1,070.91	1,081.23	1,102.68	1,063.52	1,116.48	1,121.37	1,126.99	1,096.16
2016	1,118.57	1,089.70	1,063.46	1,097.11	1,120.83	1,098.17	1,101.69	1,070.22	1,117.92	1,161.28	1,112.62	1,118.81	1,105.59
2017	1,117.56	1,147.34	1,150.74	1,088.32	1,129.65	1,107.12	1,146.79	1,115.06	1,139.34	1,140.41	1,125.60	1,143.44	1,129.12
2018	1,121.94	1,154.32	1,183.70	1,175.64	1,187.23	1,182.79	1,170.22	1,143.44	1,158.85	1,177.44	1,167.03	1,210.99	1,168.41
Construction													
2014	1,009.05	1,048.76	1,064.63	1,057.49	1,076.54	1,036.64	1,043.89	1,068.07	1,037.90	1,038.04	1,015.46	1,045.72	1,044.31
2015	1,018.78	1,026.77	983.14	1,005.60	1,007.37	1,008.04	1,021.75	1,017.58	948.02	1,052.11	1,040.82	1,069.77	1,017.96
2016	1,029.71	1,027.59	968.44	1,042.39	1,084.54	1,060.33	1,050.31	996.91	1,094.49	1,142.11	1,071.43	1,074.80	1,053.98
2017	1,103.72	1,144.28	1,109.71	1,003.31	1,098.20	1,072.44	1,091.30	1,053.57	1,087.99	1,091.30	1,066.37	1,087.12	1,085.04
2018	1,044.51	1,094.70	1,133.85	1,118.04	1,144.46	1,129.65	1,126.85	1,075.99	1,105.44	1,158.07	1,112.14	1,200.34	1,120.95
Manufacturing													
2014	1,148.75	1,118.84	1,119.95	1,100.58	1,101.24	1,120.60	1,128.99	1,129.75	1,114.78	1,133.29	1,148.17	1,169.01	1,128.40
2015	1,130.86	1,103.33	1,123.70	1,098.04	1,082.28	1,056.45	1,063.67	1,084.80	1,068.78	1,076.96	1,096.84	1,092.50	1,089.06
2016	1,103.76	1,057.75	1,063.45	1,066.26	1,051.54	1,039.90	1,048.82	1,033.86	1,043.19	1,077.93	1,061.49	1,077.76	1,061.05
2017	1,051.09	1,084.96	1,096.28	1,088.26	1,087.86	1,070.13	1,119.10	1,093.03	1,135.25	1,135.73	1,120.18	1,132.19	1,099.86
2018	1,106.99	1,128.73	1,142.40	1,160.74	1,143.45	1,148.67	1,143.60	1,115.15	1,114.11	1,089.18	1,123.01	1,150.58	1,130.36
Trade, Transportation, and Utilities													
2014	715.45	735.42	745.71	728.82	741.06	751.49	761.84	758.10	767.08	757.38	755.13	741.74	746.07
2015	734.07	739.90	753.05	755.13	750.57	754.13	744.15	766.40	745.28	735.61	735.95	750.52	746.28
2016	729.34	721.10	706.56	721.10	732.36	724.71	713.42	700.35	721.81	718.52	700.70	703.61	715.18
2017	704.46	701.05	701.54	715.88	707.62	704.98	721.60	716.74	729.38	729.73	738.86	722.40	716.04
2018	725.92	733.25	746.92	769.68	761.07	762.55	780.35	774.55	795.48	782.50	790.48	784.02	766.41
Financial Activities													
2014	840.19	863.58	870.89	842.22	835.15	865.03	826.94	853.52	859.50	870.96	921.20	874.35	859.88
2015	888.49	924.54	922.85	925.13	908.84	916.56	929.69	969.39	929.39	933.50	1,008.23	947.42	934.42
2016	957.75	958.13	959.93	958.60	969.43	921.31	921.90	936.36	947.86	1,011.06	958.21	954.69	953.87
2017	1,012.51	964.45	1,005.62	995.71	937.38	923.28	975.38	941.77	966.61	992.22	981.09	981.36	972.84
2018	1,013.57	1,036.73	1,024.50	1,038.72	1,011.44	1,007.16	1,023.23	1,020.77	1,060.49	972.97	984.03	1,040.16	1,019.93
Professional and Business Services													
2014	918.68	954.51	962.75	953.06	947.22	980.15	947.23	959.63	953.54	948.26	978.90	957.73	955.94
2015	966.32	999.31	985.50	963.48	941.69	944.27	945.72	982.80	936.96	957.90	990.00	958.80	965.29
2016	932.58	922.38	928.49	916.21	951.95	940.91	937.66	922.64	944.88	990.53	952.73	971.65	942.80
2017	991.12	964.21	949.04	973.41	958.67	985.49	1,020.68	982.12	970.91	1,003.08	972.75	971.65	977.64
2018	974.39	976.49	970.55	999.02	963.80	970.46	1,016.72	981.71	1,016.06	997.15	1,028.83	1,041.04	995.28
Education and Health Services													
2014	626.48	641.28	637.84	626.01	619.41	629.36	623.95	620.75	617.41	618.24	629.75	619.69	625.45
2015	621.39	623.76	628.51	637.84	629.70	626.15	630.85	640.40	644.10	662.66	683.32	679.32	643.42
2016	683.36	683.77	690.04	716.69	734.61	735.83	740.04	734.32	744.82	765.80	764.81	762.80	730.28
2017	787.37	768.83	762.86	773.75	756.96	759.52	775.54	762.80	773.68	782.68	775.03	772.82	771.06
2018	765.81	772.58	774.75	785.32	769.78	774.36	783.43	778.08	802.26	778.22	783.23	808.51	782.07
Leisure and Hospitality													
2014	335.80	349.25	364.52	349.57	349.14	341.41	345.35	343.90	346.20	363.70	367.64	370.51	351.73
2015	361.49	373.92	368.57	365.68	365.47	365.51	361.65	359.35	355.65	363.22	364.53	363.36	364.37
2016	352.98	367.13	374.00	372.08	364.46	354.03	348.74	338.84	348.44	359.90	368.00	360.72	358.85
2017	361.00	367.47	373.18	371.54	362.07	352.18	353.47	347.42	350.33	360.45	364.23	367.48	360.19
2018	347.36	369.92	375.91	373.45	366.12	369.10	367.98	360.72	357.50	363.92	361.36	372.60	365.03

MAINE
At a Glance

Population:
 2010 census: 1,328,361
 2018 estimate: 1,338,404

Percent change in population:
 2010–2018: 0.8%

Percent change in total nonfarm employment:
 2010–2018: 6.0%

Industry with the largest growth in employment, 2010–2018 (percent):
 Professional and business services, 20.1%

Industry with the largest decline or smallest growth in employment, 2010–2018 (percent):
 Information, -16.1%

Civilian labor force:
 2010: 695,182
 2018: 698,745

Unemployment rate and rank among states (highest to lowest):
 2010: 8.1%, 32nd
 2018: 3.4%, 32nd

Over-the-year change in unemployment rates:
 2016–2017: -0.4%
 2017–2018: 0.0%

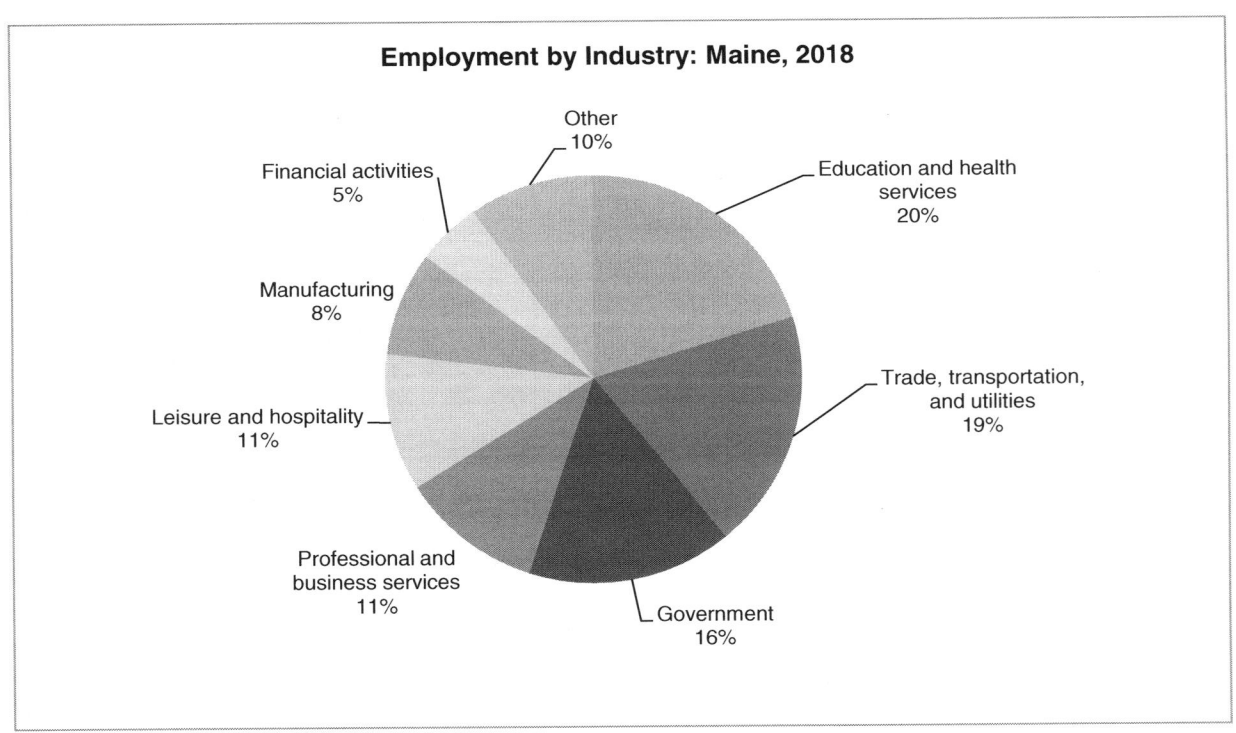

Employment by Industry: Maine, 2018

Other 10%
Financial activities 5%
Education and health services 20%
Manufacturing 8%
Trade, transportation, and utilities 19%
Leisure and hospitality 11%
Professional and business services 11%
Government 16%

1. Employment by Industry: Maine, 2010–2018

(Numbers in thousands, not seasonally adjusted)

Industry and year	January	February	March	April	May	June	July	August	September	October	November	December	Annual average
Total Nonfarm													
2010	572.0	572.9	574.8	583.8	599.1	604.4	604.8	604.4	604.4	603.9	598.8	596.3	593.3
2011	572.3	574.2	575.4	582.9	594.5	605.9	610.6	610.2	608.9	606.4	601.3	597.6	595.0
2012	575.1	577.3	578.8	587.6	602.3	613.4	613.7	613.5	610.9	608.9	601.7	598.7	598.5
2013	577.9	578.3	579.9	588.8	604.5	616.4	619.9	618.8	616.4	615.0	605.3	603.2	602.0
2014	580.2	581.7	583.6	591.7	607.5	621.2	623.0	622.8	619.0	617.1	609.4	608.5	605.5
2015	586.5	585.4	588.2	598.0	613.6	626.5	630.4	629.5	624.5	621.2	614.0	613.0	610.9
2016	593.5	595.2	597.6	606.7	619.7	634.0	638.2	636.7	631.0	627.7	622.1	619.5	618.5
2017	601.6	600.8	604.7	611.3	624.1	641.2	642.4	640.9	636.8	632.2	626.4	626.6	624.1
2018	607.0	609.0	610.3	618.5	631.1	647.4	647.3	644.9	640.5	634.7	628.7	624.4	628.7
Total Private													
2010	468.3	466.6	467.0	476.2	489.0	499.7	512.9	513.5	501.4	497.0	491.4	489.1	489.3
2011	469.2	468.9	469.8	477.9	489.9	504.2	518.4	518.9	506.6	501.9	496.0	493.3	492.9
2012	474.1	473.5	474.6	483.8	497.4	512.4	521.8	521.5	509.3	504.4	497.3	494.4	497.0
2013	476.3	475.3	476.3	485.4	500.8	516.6	529.2	528.7	516.1	511.6	502.3	500.1	501.6
2014	480.7	480.3	481.3	489.5	505.3	520.4	532.6	532.8	518.5	514.0	506.1	505.1	505.6
2015	487.0	484.3	486.2	496.2	512.2	526.9	539.2	538.5	524.4	519.1	511.5	510.8	511.4
2016	494.9	494.0	495.5	504.5	517.7	533.4	546.6	545.0	530.0	524.9	518.3	516.9	518.5
2017	502.4	499.5	502.4	509.0	522.2	540.8	550.6	549.4	535.4	529.3	523.0	523.5	524.0
2018	507.7	507.3	508.3	515.9	528.9	546.3	555.6	553.7	539.3	531.7	525.2	521.2	528.4
Goods Producing													
2010	73.9	72.9	73.2	74.8	78.0	79.4	80.0	80.9	80.3	80.3	80.0	78.1	77.7
2011	74.7	73.8	74.1	75.3	77.9	80.5	81.5	82.0	81.3	81.0	80.8	79.4	78.5
2012	75.1	74.5	74.6	76.7	79.4	81.5	82.1	82.1	81.3	80.8	79.8	77.9	78.8
2013	74.1	73.5	73.6	75.2	78.3	80.7	81.9	82.2	81.3	81.2	80.4	78.4	78.4
2014	73.9	73.7	73.7	75.1	78.7	81.2	82.0	82.3	81.3	81.1	81.3	79.7	78.7
2015	75.3	74.3	74.5	76.5	79.4	81.9	83.0	83.3	82.4	82.1	82.1	80.8	79.6
2016	76.9	76.3	76.5	78.0	80.5	83.0	83.6	83.6	82.3	82.1	82.2	80.9	80.5
2017	77.7	76.9	77.5	78.7	80.8	83.9	84.3	84.8	84.0	84.1	84.0	82.9	81.6
2018	79.3	79.2	79.9	81.3	83.5	85.7	85.8	86.3	85.0	84.7	84.4	81.8	83.1
Service-Providing													
2010	498.1	500.0	501.6	509.0	521.1	525.0	524.8	523.5	524.1	523.6	518.8	518.2	515.7
2011	497.6	500.4	501.3	507.6	516.6	525.4	529.1	528.2	527.6	525.4	520.5	518.2	516.5
2012	500.0	502.8	504.2	510.9	522.9	531.9	531.6	531.4	529.6	528.1	521.9	520.8	519.7
2013	503.8	504.8	506.3	513.6	526.2	535.7	538.0	536.6	535.1	533.8	524.9	524.8	523.6
2014	506.3	508.0	509.9	516.6	528.8	540.0	541.0	540.5	537.7	536.0	528.1	528.8	526.8
2015	511.2	511.1	513.7	521.5	534.2	544.6	547.4	546.2	542.1	539.1	531.9	532.2	531.3
2016	516.6	518.9	521.1	528.7	539.2	551.0	554.6	553.1	548.7	545.6	539.9	538.6	538.0
2017	523.9	523.9	527.2	532.6	543.3	557.3	558.1	556.1	552.8	548.1	542.4	543.7	542.5
2018	527.7	529.8	530.4	537.2	547.6	561.7	561.5	558.6	555.5	550.0	544.3	542.6	545.6
Mining and Logging													
2010	2.7	2.7	2.6	1.9	2.1	2.5	2.7	2.7	2.7	2.7	2.6	2.6	2.5
2011	2.6	2.6	2.6	1.9	1.8	2.4	2.7	2.7	2.7	2.7	2.7	2.7	2.5
2012	2.6	2.6	2.5	1.8	1.9	2.4	2.6	2.7	2.7	2.7	2.6	2.6	2.5
2013	2.6	2.6	2.4	1.8	1.9	2.3	2.5	2.6	2.6	2.6	2.6	2.6	2.4
2014	2.6	2.6	2.6	2.1	1.7	2.3	2.6	2.6	2.6	2.6	2.6	2.6	2.5
2015	2.5	2.5	2.6	2.0	1.8	2.3	2.6	2.6	2.6	2.5	2.5	2.5	2.4
2016	2.4	2.5	2.3	1.7	1.7	2.3	2.4	2.4	2.4	2.4	2.4	2.4	2.3
2017	2.3	2.3	2.3	1.7	1.6	2.1	2.3	2.3	2.4	2.4	2.3	2.3	2.2
2018	2.3	2.3	2.3	1.9	1.7	2.2	2.3	2.3	2.4	2.3	2.3	2.3	2.2
Construction													
2010	21.3	20.6	20.6	22.8	25.0	25.7	26.2	26.5	26.6	26.6	25.9	24.4	24.4
2011	22.0	21.3	21.4	23.2	25.3	27.0	27.7	27.7	27.6	27.6	26.9	25.6	25.3
2012	22.9	22.2	22.3	24.5	26.6	27.4	27.7	27.8	27.4	27.1	26.1	24.7	25.6
2013	22.3	21.9	21.9	23.9	26.1	27.2	27.8	28.0	27.8	27.8	26.8	25.3	25.6
2014	22.7	22.5	22.5	23.9	26.7	27.7	28.3	28.4	28.0	27.9	27.2	25.8	26.0
2015	23.3	22.7	22.7	24.5	27.2	28.4	29.0	29.0	28.4	28.5	27.9	26.9	26.5
2016	24.8	24.3	24.5	26.3	28.1	29.2	29.7	29.4	28.8	28.8	28.3	27.3	27.5
2017	25.5	24.9	25.2	26.7	28.4	29.9	30.2	30.3	30.0	30.2	29.7	28.8	28.3
2018	26.6	26.4	26.8	28.1	30.1	30.7	31.0	30.9	30.3	30.2	28.8	26.3	28.9

1. Employment by Industry: Maine, 2010–2018—*Continued*

(Numbers in thousands, not seasonally adjusted)

Industry and year	January	February	March	April	May	June	July	August	September	October	November	December	Annual average
Manufacturing													
2010	49.9	49.6	50.0	50.1	50.9	51.2	51.1	51.7	51.0	51.0	51.5	51.1	50.8
2011	50.1	49.9	50.1	50.2	50.8	51.1	51.1	51.6	51.0	50.7	51.2	51.1	50.7
2012	49.6	49.7	49.8	50.4	50.9	51.7	51.8	51.6	51.2	51.0	51.1	50.6	50.8
2013	49.2	49.0	49.3	49.5	50.3	51.2	51.6	51.6	50.9	50.8	51.0	50.5	50.4
2014	48.6	48.6	48.6	49.1	50.3	51.2	51.1	51.3	50.7	50.6	51.5	51.3	50.2
2015	49.5	49.1	49.2	50.0	50.4	51.2	51.4	51.7	51.4	51.1	51.7	51.4	50.7
2016	49.7	49.5	49.7	50.0	50.7	51.5	51.5	51.8	51.1	50.9	51.5	51.2	50.8
2017	49.9	49.7	50.0	50.3	50.8	51.9	51.8	51.8	52.2	51.6	51.5	52.0	51.8	51.1
2018	50.4	50.5	50.8	51.3	51.7	52.8	52.5	53.1	52.3	52.2	53.3	53.2	52.0
Trade, Transportation, and Utilities													
2010	114.0	111.5	111.0	112.0	114.4	117.3	118.8	119.3	116.4	117.9	119.5	120.8	116.1
2011	113.8	111.6	110.8	112.2	114.1	117.3	118.8	119.4	117.3	118.6	120.4	121.2	116.3
2012	114.5	112.2	111.7	112.4	115.2	118.5	119.2	119.7	117.3	118.6	121.0	121.1	116.8
2013	113.8	111.4	110.9	112.1	115.1	119.0	121.1	121.5	121.9	119.2	119.9	121.7	122.6	117.4
2014	115.1	113.7	113.0	114.2	116.8	119.8	121.3	121.9	119.6	120.4	122.1	123.2	118.4
2015	115.8	113.9	113.4	115.0	117.8	121.0	122.6	122.7	120.2	120.7	121.9	123.1	119.0
2016	116.6	115.0	114.9	116.1	118.5	121.7	123.2	123.2	120.8	120.5	122.0	122.9	119.6
2017	117.3	114.8	114.8	115.8	118.1	121.6	123.2	123.0	120.3	120.4	121.7	122.9	119.5
2018	117.4	115.5	115.2	116.2	118.4	121.4	122.1	121.5	119.6	119.6	121.1	121.7	119.1
Wholesale Trade													
2010	18.3	18.2	18.3	18.5	18.7	19.0	19.2	19.3	19.0	19.0	18.9	18.9	18.8
2011	18.5	18.4	18.3	18.6	18.7	19.2	19.5	19.5	19.3	19.2	19.1	19.2	19.0
2012	18.7	18.6	18.6	18.9	19.3	19.8	19.9	19.9	19.6	19.5	19.4	19.3	19.3
2013	18.7	18.7	18.7	18.8	19.3	19.9	20.1	20.1	19.8	19.7	19.5	19.5	19.4
2014	18.9	18.8	18.9	19.1	19.6	20.0	20.2	20.2	20.0	20.0	19.8	19.7	19.6
2015	19.3	19.2	19.2	19.4	19.8	20.2	20.5	20.5	20.2	20.1	19.8	19.8	19.8
2016	19.2	19.1	19.2	19.4	19.8	20.1	20.4	20.3	20.0	19.8	19.5	19.4	19.7
2017	19.0	18.8	18.9	19.1	19.5	19.9	20.0	19.9	19.7	19.6	19.4	19.4	19.4
2018	19.0	19.0	19.0	19.2	19.5	19.9	20.1	20.0	19.6	19.5	19.4	19.4	19.5
Retail Trade													
2010	79.7	77.6	77.1	77.9	79.8	82.0	83.2	83.7	81.1	82.3	83.8	84.5	81.1
2011	79.4	77.6	77.0	78.0	79.7	81.9	83.1	83.6	81.4	82.6	84.2	84.6	81.1
2012	79.7	77.7	77.4	78.0	80.0	82.3	83.1	83.5	81.1	82.3	84.4	84.2	81.1
2013	79.0	76.8	76.4	77.4	79.6	82.3	84.2	84.5	82.2	82.8	84.3	84.7	81.2
2014	79.6	78.4	77.8	78.7	80.4	82.5	83.9	84.3	82.0	82.5	83.9	84.6	81.6
2015	79.3	77.9	77.6	78.7	80.7	83.1	84.3	84.4	82.0	82.6	83.8	84.7	81.6
2016	80.1	78.8	78.7	79.4	81.0	83.3	84.7	84.7	82.3	82.3	83.8	84.2	81.9
2017	80.2	78.2	78.2	79.0	80.3	82.7	84.2	84.1	81.4	81.4	82.7	83.3	81.3
2018	80.0	78.3	78.2	79.0	80.5	82.7	83.6	83.1	81.3	81.3	82.6	82.7	81.1
Transportation and Utilities													
2010	16.0	15.7	15.6	15.6	15.9	16.3	16.4	16.3	16.3	16.6	16.8	17.4	16.2
2011	15.9	15.6	15.5	15.6	15.7	16.2	16.2	16.3	16.6	16.8	17.1	17.4	16.2
2012	16.1	15.9	15.7	15.5	15.9	16.4	16.2	16.3	16.6	16.8	17.2	17.6	16.4
2013	16.1	15.9	15.8	15.9	16.2	16.8	16.8	16.9	17.2	17.4	17.9	18.4	16.8
2014	16.6	16.5	16.3	16.4	16.8	17.3	17.2	17.4	17.6	17.9	18.4	18.9	17.3
2015	17.2	16.8	16.6	16.9	17.3	17.7	17.8	17.8	18.0	18.0	18.3	18.6	17.6
2016	17.3	17.1	17.0	17.3	17.7	18.3	18.1	18.2	18.5	18.4	18.7	19.3	18.0
2017	18.1	17.8	17.7	17.7	18.3	19.0	19.0	19.0	19.2	19.4	19.6	20.2	18.8
2018	18.4	18.2	18.0	18.0	18.4	18.8	18.4	18.4	18.7	18.8	19.1	19.6	18.6
Information													
2010	8.8	8.8	8.7	8.7	8.8	8.8	8.8	8.7	8.7	8.6	8.6	8.5	8.7
2011	8.4	8.3	8.3	8.3	8.3	8.3	8.4	8.3	8.2	8.1	8.1	8.1	8.3
2012	8.0	8.0	8.0	7.9	7.9	7.9	7.9	7.9	7.8	7.8	7.8	7.8	7.9
2013	7.8	7.7	7.7	7.7	7.7	7.7	7.7	7.7	7.6	7.5	7.5	7.5	7.7
2014	7.5	7.4	7.4	7.4	7.4	7.6	7.6	7.6	7.6	7.6	7.2	7.2	7.5
2015	7.3	7.3	7.5	7.6	7.7	7.9	7.9	7.8	7.6	7.7	7.8	7.7	7.7
2016	7.7	7.7	7.7	7.7	7.8	7.8	7.9	7.8	7.7	7.7	7.7	7.7	7.7
2017	7.6	7.5	7.5	7.4	7.4	7.4	7.4	7.4	7.3	7.3	7.2	7.4	7.4
2018	7.5	7.4	7.4	7.4	7.4	7.5	7.5	7.5	7.3	7.1	6.9	6.9	7.3

1. Employment by Industry: Maine, 2010–2018—*Continued*

(Numbers in thousands, not seasonally adjusted)

Industry and year	January	February	March	April	May	June	July	August	September	October	November	December	Annual average
Financial Activities													
2010	30.2	30.3	30.4	30.5	30.6	31.0	31.1	31.1	30.7	30.5	30.3	30.4	30.6
2011	30.0	30.1	30.2	30.0	30.3	30.7	31.0	31.0	30.4	30.4	30.2	30.4	30.4
2012	29.9	29.8	29.8	29.9	30.2	30.6	30.9	30.8	30.2	30.0	29.8	29.9	30.2
2013	29.8	29.7	29.9	30.0	30.4	30.8	31.2	31.1	30.6	30.4	30.4	30.4	30.4
2014	29.9	29.8	29.9	30.0	30.4	30.8	31.0	31.2	30.5	30.4	30.3	30.4	30.4
2015	30.1	30.0	30.0	30.2	30.6	31.0	31.3	31.4	30.8	30.7	30.6	30.8	30.6
2016	30.5	30.5	30.6	30.8	31.2	31.6	31.9	31.9	31.3	31.1	30.8	31.0	31.1
2017	30.8	30.7	30.9	30.9	31.3	31.9	32.2	32.2	31.8	31.6	31.6	31.7	31.5
2018	31.2	31.3	31.3	31.5	32.0	32.5	32.6	32.6	32.3	31.8	31.9	31.9	31.9
Professional and Business Services													
2010	55.7	55.5	55.6	57.1	57.9	58.4	59.0	59.0	58.4	58.6	58.7	58.2	57.7
2011	56.6	57.0	57.1	58.7	59.4	60.5	61.0	61.2	60.8	60.5	60.4	59.3	59.4
2012	58.0	57.9	57.9	59.6	60.2	61.5	61.5	61.7	61.3	61.4	60.9	60.4	60.2
2013	58.9	59.7	59.3	61.0	62.3	63.7	64.2	64.3	63.8	63.6	62.8	62.6	62.2
2014	60.6	61.4	61.7	63.1	64.8	66.0	66.2	66.2	65.5	65.5	64.7	64.2	64.2
2015	62.6	63.3	63.3	64.4	66.6	67.2	67.4	67.2	66.3	66.4	65.7	65.3	65.5
2016	63.9	64.1	63.8	65.9	67.0	68.3	68.8	68.5	67.6	67.4	66.8	66.7	66.6
2017	64.8	65.4	65.4	66.3	67.8	69.1	69.1	69.0	68.0	68.2	68.0	67.8	67.4
2018	67.0	67.2	67.3	68.2	69.6	71.0	71.1	70.9	70.0	70.1	70.4	69.3	69.3
Education and Health Services													
2010	117.5	119.3	119.3	119.8	119.6	117.5	117.2	117.0	119.3	120.3	120.3	120.2	118.9
2011	117.1	119.3	119.6	120.1	119.9	118.1	118.0	118.2	120.2	122.0	122.1	122.0	119.7
2012	119.5	121.6	121.6	121.9	122.2	119.9	119.6	119.0	121.5	123.1	122.9	122.7	121.3
2013	120.6	122.4	122.4	122.9	122.2	120.2	119.9	119.7	122.5	123.6	123.4	122.7	121.9
2014	121.6	122.3	122.5	122.9	121.9	120.6	119.9	119.9	122.4	123.4	123.5	122.8	122.0
2015	122.3	122.7	123.3	123.9	123.2	122.1	121.9	121.7	124.0	124.2	124.4	124.3	123.2
2016	124.3	125.0	125.7	125.5	124.9	123.1	123.3	123.0	125.7	126.7	127.0	126.9	125.1
2017	126.7	127.2	128.0	128.0	127.2	126.0	125.2	124.7	127.5	127.5	127.9	128.1	127.0
2018	126.9	127.7	127.6	127.9	127.0	125.6	125.3	125.1	127.7	128.6	128.8	128.3	127.2
Leisure and Hospitality													
2010	48.9	49.0	49.5	53.8	60.0	67.4	77.6	77.4	67.7	61.1	54.3	53.4	60.0
2011	49.3	49.5	50.3	53.6	59.9	68.5	79.1	78.4	68.4	61.3	54.2	53.1	60.5
2012	49.6	50.0	51.3	55.5	62.3	72.2	79.9	79.8	69.8	62.6	55.1	54.6	61.9
2013	51.3	50.9	52.3	56.0	63.9	73.3	81.8	81.0	70.3	64.7	55.5	55.3	63.0
2014	51.7	51.7	52.7	56.2	64.3	73.0	82.8	82.0	70.4	64.3	56.0	56.6	63.5
2015	52.9	52.3	53.5	57.5	65.5	73.9	82.9	82.4	71.7	65.8	57.6	57.2	64.4
2016	53.9	54.2	55.0	59.1	66.1	75.8	85.2	84.6	72.8	67.6	60.1	59.2	66.1
2017	56.1	55.9	57.1	60.4	67.8	78.6	86.6	85.9	74.7	68.4	60.9	60.8	67.8
2018	56.9	57.3	58.0	61.6	68.8	79.9	88.1	87.0	75.2	67.5	59.5	59.3	68.3
Other Services													
2010	19.3	19.3	19.3	19.5	19.7	19.9	20.4	20.1	19.9	19.7	19.7	19.5	19.7
2011	19.3	19.3	19.4	19.7	20.1	20.3	20.6	20.4	20.0	20.0	19.8	19.8	19.9
2012	19.5	19.5	19.7	19.9	20.0	20.3	20.7	20.5	20.1	20.1	20.0	20.0	20.0
2013	20.0	20.0	20.2	20.5	20.9	21.2	21.4	21.2	20.8	20.7	20.6	20.6	20.7
2014	20.4	20.3	20.4	20.6	21.0	21.4	21.8	21.7	21.2	21.3	21.0	21.0	21.0
2015	20.7	20.5	20.7	21.1	21.4	21.9	22.2	22.0	21.4	21.5	21.4	21.6	21.4
2016	21.1	21.2	21.3	21.4	21.7	22.1	22.7	22.4	21.8	21.8	21.7	21.6	21.7
2017	21.4	21.1	21.2	21.5	21.8	22.3	22.6	22.4	21.8	21.8	21.7	21.9	21.8
2018	21.5	21.7	21.6	21.8	22.2	22.7	23.1	22.8	22.2	22.3	22.2	22.0	22.2
Government													
2010	103.7	106.3	107.8	107.6	110.1	104.7	91.9	90.9	103.0	106.9	107.4	107.2	104.0
2011	103.1	105.3	105.6	105.0	104.6	101.7	92.2	91.3	102.3	104.5	105.3	104.3	102.1
2012	101.0	103.8	104.2	103.8	104.9	101.0	91.9	92.0	101.6	104.5	104.4	104.3	101.5
2013	101.6	103.0	103.6	103.4	103.7	99.8	90.7	90.1	100.3	103.4	103.0	103.1	100.5
2014	99.5	101.4	102.3	102.2	102.2	100.8	90.4	90.0	100.5	103.1	103.3	103.4	99.9
2015	99.5	101.1	102.0	101.8	101.4	99.6	91.2	91.0	100.1	102.1	102.5	102.2	99.5
2016	98.6	101.2	102.1	102.2	102.0	100.6	91.6	91.7	101.0	102.8	103.8	102.6	100.0
2017	99.2	101.3	102.3	102.3	101.9	100.4	91.8	91.5	101.4	102.9	103.4	103.1	100.1
2018	99.3	101.7	102.0	102.6	102.2	101.1	91.7	91.2	101.2	103.0	103.5	103.2	100.2

2. Average Weekly Hours by Selected Industry: Maine, 2014–2018

(Not seasonally adjusted)

Industry and year	January	February	March	April	May	June	July	August	September	October	November	December	Annual average
Total Private													
2014	33.6	33.8	33.7	33.8	33.9	33.9	34.3	34.3	34.2	34.1	34.1	33.9	34.0
2015	33.9	34.0	34.1	33.9	34.3	34.3	34.6	34.7	34.5	34.3	34.3	34.1	34.3
2016	33.5	33.6	33.8	33.8	34.0	33.9	34.1	34.2	34.0	34.4	34.0	33.7	33.9
2017	33.6	33.0	33.6	34.0	34.1	34.1	34.5	34.5	34.3	34.2	34.1	33.9	34.0
2018	33.7	33.9	33.2	34.3	34.3	34.4	34.8	34.5	34.3	34.2	33.9	34.5	34.2
Goods Producing													
2014	40.8	39.9	40.0	40.0	40.0	40.1	40.6	40.1	40.6	40.4	39.7	39.7	40.2
2015	40.2	39.7	40.1	40.2	41.4	41.5	41.8	41.8	40.9	41.8	41.2	41.4	41.0
2016	40.5	39.9	40.7	40.6	41.3	41.4	41.6	41.6	41.2	41.6	40.9	39.9	40.9
2017	40.5	38.7	40.0	40.6	40.9	41.3	41.2	41.6	41.4	41.2	40.7	40.3	40.7
2018	40.3	39.9	38.0	40.1	40.3	40.1	40.3	40.4	40.1	39.6	38.8	40.3	39.9
Construction													
2014	38.7	38.5	37.3	37.2	39.0	38.3	40.1	38.3	39.7	39.4	38.9	37.1	38.6
2015	37.3	37.2	37.1	38.5	40.7	41.0	41.6	40.7	39.5	40.9	40.4	40.1	39.7
2016	39.1	37.7	39.2	39.3	41.1	41.6	42.1	41.4	41.1	41.3	40.4	39.1	40.3
2017	39.6	36.7	37.9	39.4	40.2	40.8	40.3	41.6	41.6	40.8	40.4	39.4	40.0
2018	39.4	39.1	36.8	39.7	40.8	40.1	40.6	39.8	39.1	38.6	37.1	38.8	39.2
Manufacturing													
2014	40.2	39.0	39.7	40.1	39.8	40.0	39.6	40.0	39.9	39.8	38.9	39.7	39.7
2015	40.3	39.6	40.5	40.1	40.9	40.9	40.8	41.4	40.8	41.6	41.1	41.6	40.8
2016	40.5	40.3	40.9	40.8	41.1	40.9	41.2	41.5	41.1	41.6	40.7	40.0	40.9
2017	40.7	38.9	40.4	40.7	40.7	41.0	41.2	41.1	41.0	41.1	40.6	40.5	40.6
2018	40.4	39.8	38.4	39.6	39.2	39.5	39.3	40.3	40.5	40.0	39.7	40.9	39.8
Trade, Transportation, and Utilities													
2014	32.1	32.5	32.1	32.4	32.9	33.2	33.6	33.7	33.8	33.2	33.4	33.9	33.1
2015	33.1	33.8	33.4	33.1	33.7	33.4	34.3	34.2	34.8	33.7	33.5	34.1	33.8
2016	33.3	33.5	33.4	33.9	33.7	33.9	34.6	34.8	34.3	34.6	34.2	34.6	34.1
2017	33.6	32.9	33.8	33.9	34.4	34.5	35.1	34.9	34.3	34.0	34.1	34.5	34.2
2018	33.6	33.6	33.0	34.0	34.3	34.1	34.7	34.7	34.3	33.9	34.0	34.1	34.0
Professional and Business Services													
2014	32.4	33.9	33.2	33.4	33.6	33.8	33.3	33.4	33.2	33.3	33.8	33.6	33.4
2015	33.7	34.1	34.6	33.9	34.1	34.4	34.3	34.8	34.3	34.7	35.1	34.4	34.4
2016	33.2	33.6	33.9	34.4	35.0	34.3	34.2	33.7	33.5	34.8	34.2	33.9	34.1
2017	35.1	34.0	34.5	35.2	34.7	34.7	35.4	34.8	35.1	35.3	34.2	34.5	34.8
2018	34.2	34.5	33.7	35.1	35.1	35.3	35.8	35.4	35.4	35.3	35.2	35.9	35.1
Education and Health Services													
2014	34.3	33.5	33.6	33.7	33.8	33.9	34.2	34.0	34.0	33.9	34.0	33.8	33.9
2015	34.4	34.3	34.1	34.1	34.1	34.0	34.0	33.7	33.9	33.5	33.7	33.4	33.9
2016	33.1	33.3	33.1	33.0	33.0	33.1	33.1	33.5	33.6	33.3	33.3	33.1	33.2
2017	32.8	32.0	32.3	32.4	32.5	32.4	32.6	32.5	32.7	32.4	32.6	32.4	32.5
2018	32.2	32.4	32.3	32.9	32.7	33.0	33.1	32.7	33.1	32.9	32.7	33.2	32.8
Leisure and Hospitality													
2014	23.9	24.8	25.1	25.3	25.4	25.4	27.7	28.0	26.2	27.0	25.4	24.7	25.9
2015	24.5	24.3	25.1	25.2	25.6	26.2	27.3	27.9	26.4	25.8	25.3	24.4	25.8
2016	24.3	25.0	24.9	24.7	25.1	25.5	27.0	27.4	26.0	26.0	24.9	23.3	25.5
2017	24.0	23.5	25.0	25.6	25.6	26.5	27.6	28.1	26.7	26.5	25.8	24.7	26.0
2018	24.8	25.5	24.3	25.6	26.1	26.8	28.6	28.1	27.1	27.4	25.2	25.8	26.5

3. Average Hourly Earnings by Selected Industry: Maine, 2014–2018

(Dollars, not seasonally adjusted)

Industry and year	January	February	March	April	May	June	July	August	September	October	November	December	Annual average
Total Private													
2014	21.23	21.41	21.65	21.39	21.23	21.07	20.90	20.85	21.41	21.35	21.74	21.75	21.33
2015	21.93	22.00	22.11	21.94	21.67	21.46	21.42	21.54	21.82	22.01	22.20	22.24	21.85
2016	22.36	22.29	22.22	22.28	22.20	21.88	21.77	21.87	22.38	22.55	22.66	22.66	22.25
2017	23.05	23.43	23.44	23.24	23.28	22.79	22.74	22.84	23.32	23.39	23.56	23.66	23.22
2018	23.85	23.77	23.92	23.90	23.63	23.46	23.32	23.49	24.00	24.11	24.35	24.58	23.86
Goods Producing													
2014	23.43	23.58	23.37	23.23	23.40	23.26	22.81	23.13	23.23	23.26	23.63	23.63	23.33
2015	23.64	23.35	23.13	23.18	22.89	22.80	22.93	23.37	22.85	23.22	23.26	23.68	23.19
2016	23.38	23.43	23.65	23.62	23.79	23.44	23.40	23.25	23.51	24.11	24.01	23.62	23.62
2017	23.64	24.00	24.06	23.67	24.04	23.53	23.78	23.79	24.27	24.15	24.13	24.43	23.96
2018	24.39	24.23	24.54	24.54	24.09	24.15	23.89	23.87	24.05	24.20	24.21	24.86	24.24
Construction													
2014	22.65	23.02	22.75	22.61	22.36	22.14	21.44	21.93	22.03	22.43	22.46	23.16	22.38
2015	23.30	23.27	22.67	22.81	22.44	21.98	22.24	22.71	22.31	22.44	22.74	23.07	22.63
2016	23.27	23.98	23.31	23.31	23.11	23.30	23.19	22.87	23.49	23.90	23.55	23.98	23.43
2017	24.01	24.24	24.55	24.16	23.82	23.54	23.64	23.58	23.97	23.68	23.92	24.47	23.94
2018	24.55	24.65	24.89	24.94	24.44	24.11	23.61	23.91	23.92	23.89	24.35	25.06	24.33
Manufacturing													
2014	24.47	24.53	24.36	24.11	24.32	24.16	23.93	24.17	24.32	24.16	24.75	24.31	24.30
2015	24.29	23.86	23.79	23.70	23.41	23.57	23.71	24.16	23.52	24.00	23.71	24.21	23.83
2016	23.69	23.46	23.96	23.80	24.17	23.71	23.74	23.68	23.78	24.02	24.80	24.30	23.93
2017	23.69	24.17	23.96	23.73	24.51	23.92	24.25	24.21	24.76	24.76	24.57	24.73	24.28
2018	24.61	24.24	24.57	24.46	24.25	24.53	24.50	24.20	24.49	24.69	24.43	24.97	24.50
Trade, Transportation, and Utilities													
2014	18.95	19.20	19.51	19.53	19.10	19.11	19.17	18.81	19.42	19.08	19.34	19.29	19.21
2015	19.88	19.83	19.91	19.97	20.09	20.00	20.10	20.03	20.26	20.28	20.45	20.22	20.09
2016	20.87	20.59	20.49	20.38	20.29	19.98	19.86	19.84	20.13	20.08	20.12	20.02	20.21
2017	20.68	21.04	21.08	20.53	20.90	20.42	20.11	20.25	20.40	20.23	20.25	20.31	20.51
2018	20.33	20.27	20.17	20.08	20.10	20.01	20.05	20.29	20.47	20.72	21.07	20.86	20.37
Professional and Business Services													
2014	23.60	23.83	24.27	23.80	23.41	23.40	23.66	23.53	24.15	23.99	24.15	24.26	23.84
2015	24.47	24.31	24.51	24.21	23.73	23.95	24.26	24.19	24.50	24.11	24.47	24.31	24.25
2016	24.73	24.89	24.49	24.66	24.40	24.07	24.60	24.74	25.19	25.18	25.06	25.15	24.76
2017	25.72	26.34	26.61	26.11	25.71	25.75	26.06	25.85	26.26	26.09	26.48	26.84	26.15
2018	26.73	26.77	27.40	27.27	26.66	26.55	26.85	27.07	27.65	27.61	27.71	28.15	27.20
Education and Health Services													
2014	21.32	21.43	21.90	21.28	21.34	21.22	21.55	21.43	21.86	22.12	22.23	22.36	21.67
2015	22.15	22.51	23.04	22.50	22.14	21.88	21.86	22.21	22.66	23.18	23.20	23.24	22.55
2016	22.83	22.72	22.82	23.03	23.10	23.07	23.09	23.18	23.51	23.73	23.72	23.89	23.23
2017	24.49	24.82	24.89	25.16	25.20	24.83	25.18	25.37	25.58	25.77	25.86	25.94	25.26
2018	26.60	26.10	26.02	26.18	26.13	26.28	26.47	26.20	26.49	26.45	26.30	26.38	26.30
Leisure and Hospitality													
2014	13.34	13.35	13.30	13.22	13.22	13.07	13.00	13.34	13.50	13.33	13.64	13.82	13.32
2015	13.41	13.60	13.51	13.76	13.57	13.48	13.37	13.54	13.86	14.18	14.25	14.62	13.74
2016	14.36	14.15	14.12	14.36	14.26	14.05	14.03	14.27	14.72	15.06	14.85	15.22	14.43
2017	15.15	15.40	15.35	15.42	15.39	15.09	14.90	15.20	15.54	15.82	15.76	15.86	15.38
2018	15.95	16.07	16.34	16.20	16.28	16.11	15.80	16.06	16.56	16.93	17.09	17.13	16.34

4. Average Weekly Earnings by Selected Industry: Maine, 2014–2018

(Dollars, not seasonally adjusted)

Industry and year	January	February	March	April	May	June	July	August	September	October	November	December	Annual average
Total Private													
2014	713.33	723.66	729.61	722.98	719.70	714.27	716.87	715.16	732.22	728.04	741.33	737.33	725.22
2015	743.43	748.00	753.95	743.77	743.28	736.08	741.13	747.44	752.79	754.94	761.46	758.38	749.46
2016	749.06	748.94	751.04	753.06	754.80	741.73	742.36	747.95	760.92	775.72	770.44	763.64	754.28
2017	774.48	773.19	787.58	790.16	793.85	777.14	784.53	787.98	799.88	799.94	803.40	802.07	789.48
2018	803.75	805.80	794.14	819.77	810.51	807.02	811.54	810.41	823.20	824.56	825.47	848.01	816.01
Goods Producing													
2014	955.94	940.84	934.80	929.20	936.00	932.73	926.09	927.51	943.14	939.70	938.11	938.11	937.87
2015	950.33	927.00	927.51	931.84	947.65	946.20	958.47	976.87	934.57	970.60	958.31	980.35	950.79
2016	946.89	934.86	962.56	958.97	982.53	970.42	973.44	967.20	968.61	990.50	986.10	958.00	966.06
2017	957.42	928.80	962.40	961.00	983.24	971.79	979.74	989.66	1004.78	994.98	982.09	984.53	975.17
2018	982.92	966.78	932.52	984.05	970.83	968.42	962.77	964.35	964.41	958.32	939.35	1001.86	967.18
Construction													
2014	876.56	886.27	848.58	841.09	872.04	847.96	859.74	839.92	874.59	883.74	873.69	859.24	863.87
2015	869.09	865.64	841.06	878.19	913.31	901.18	925.18	924.30	881.25	917.80	918.70	925.11	898.41
2016	909.86	904.05	913.75	916.08	949.82	969.28	976.30	946.82	965.44	987.07	951.42	937.62	944.23
2017	950.80	889.61	930.45	951.90	957.56	960.43	952.69	980.93	997.15	966.14	966.37	964.12	957.60
2018	967.27	963.82	915.95	990.12	997.15	966.81	958.57	951.62	935.27	922.15	903.39	972.33	953.74
Manufacturing													
2014	983.69	956.67	967.09	966.81	967.94	966.40	947.63	966.80	970.37	961.57	962.78	965.11	964.71
2015	978.89	944.86	963.50	950.37	957.47	964.01	967.37	1,000.22	959.62	998.40	974.48	1,007.14	972.26
2016	959.45	945.44	979.96	971.04	993.39	969.74	978.09	982.72	977.36	999.23	1,009.36	972.00	978.74
2017	964.18	940.21	967.98	965.81	997.56	980.72	999.10	995.03	1,015.16	1,017.64	997.54	1,001.57	985.77
2018	994.24	964.75	943.49	968.62	950.60	968.94	962.85	975.26	991.85	987.60	969.87	1,021.27	975.10
Trade, Transportation, and Utilities													
2014	608.30	624.00	626.27	632.77	628.39	634.45	644.11	633.90	656.40	633.46	645.96	653.93	635.85
2015	658.03	670.25	664.99	661.01	677.03	668.00	689.43	685.03	705.05	683.44	685.08	689.50	679.04
2016	694.97	689.77	684.37	690.88	683.77	677.32	687.16	690.43	690.46	694.77	688.10	692.69	689.16
2017	694.85	692.22	712.50	695.97	718.96	704.49	705.86	706.73	699.72	687.82	690.53	700.70	701.44
2018	683.09	681.07	665.61	682.72	689.43	682.34	695.74	704.06	702.12	702.41	716.38	711.33	692.58
Professional and Business Services													
2014	764.64	807.84	805.76	794.92	786.58	790.92	787.88	785.90	801.78	798.87	816.27	815.14	796.26
2015	824.64	828.97	848.05	820.72	809.19	823.88	832.12	841.81	840.35	836.62	858.90	836.26	834.20
2016	821.04	836.30	830.21	848.30	854.00	825.60	841.32	833.74	843.87	876.26	857.05	852.59	844.32
2017	902.77	895.56	918.05	919.07	892.14	893.53	922.52	899.58	921.73	920.98	905.62	925.98	910.02
2018	914.17	923.57	923.38	957.18	935.77	937.22	961.23	958.28	978.81	974.63	975.39	1010.59	954.72
Education and Health Services													
2014	731.28	717.91	735.84	717.14	721.29	719.36	737.01	728.62	743.24	749.87	755.82	755.77	734.61
2015	761.96	772.09	785.66	767.25	754.97	743.92	743.24	748.48	768.17	776.53	781.84	776.22	764.45
2016	755.67	756.58	755.34	759.99	762.30	763.62	764.28	776.53	789.94	790.21	789.88	790.76	771.24
2017	803.27	794.24	803.95	815.18	819.00	804.49	820.87	824.53	836.47	834.95	843.04	840.46	820.95
2018	856.52	845.64	840.45	861.32	854.45	867.24	876.16	856.74	876.82	870.21	860.01	875.82	862.64
Leisure and Hospitality													
2014	318.83	331.08	333.83	334.47	335.79	331.98	360.10	373.52	353.70	359.91	346.46	341.35	344.99
2015	328.55	330.48	339.10	346.75	347.39	353.18	365.00	377.77	365.90	365.84	360.53	356.73	354.49
2016	348.95	353.75	351.59	354.69	357.93	358.28	378.81	391.00	382.72	391.56	369.77	354.63	367.97
2017	363.60	361.90	383.75	394.75	393.98	399.89	411.24	427.12	414.92	419.23	406.61	391.74	399.88
2018	395.56	409.79	397.06	414.72	424.91	431.75	451.88	451.29	448.78	463.88	430.67	441.95	433.01

MARYLAND
At a Glance

Population:
  2010 census: 5,773,552
  2018 estimate: 6,042,718

Percent change in population:
  2010–2018: 4.7%

Percent change in total nonfarm employment:
  2010–2018: 8.8%

Industry with the largest growth in employment, 2010–2018 (percent):
  Transportation and utilities, 28.5%

Industry with the largest decline or smallest growth in employment, 2010–2018 (percent):
  Information, -17.0%

Civilian labor force:
  2010: 3,073,826
  2018: 3,197,137

Unemployment rate and rank among states (highest to lowest):
  2010: 7.7%, 38th
  2018: 3.9%, 22nd

Over-the-year change in unemployment rates:
  2016–2017: -0.2%
  2017–2018: -0.4%

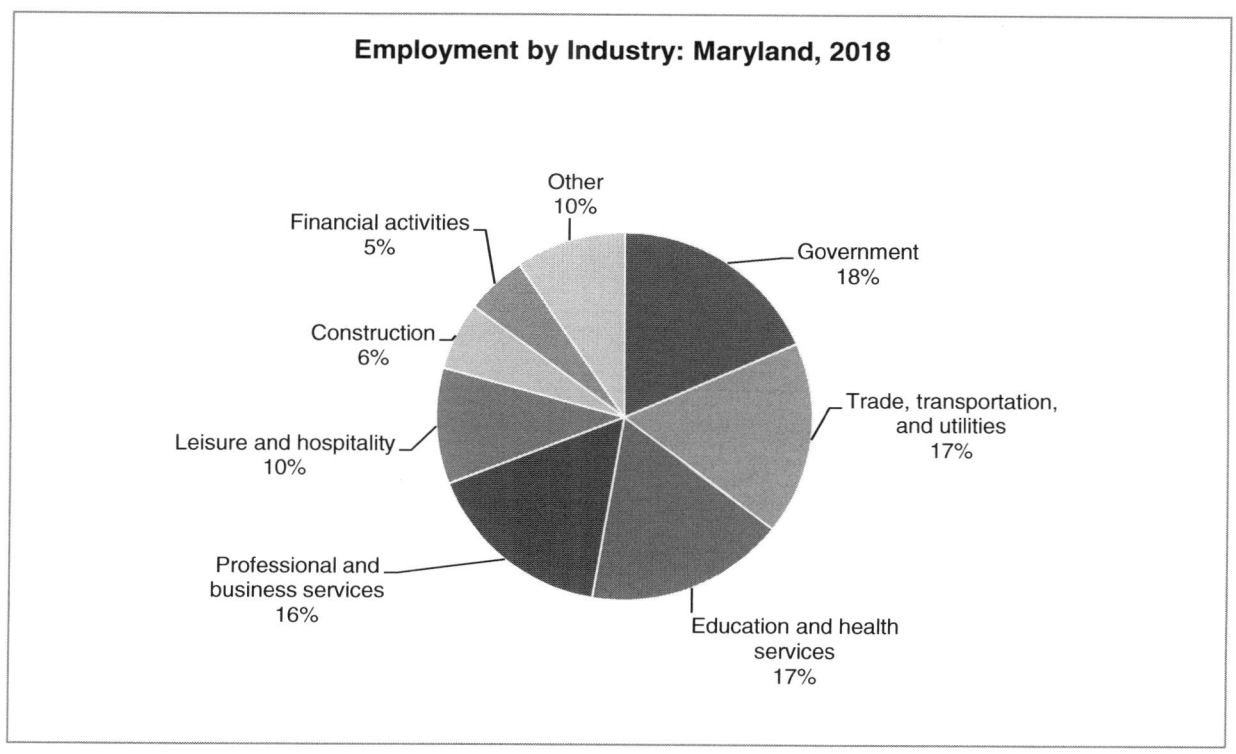

Employment by Industry: Maryland, 2018

- Other 10%
- Financial activities 5%
- Construction 6%
- Leisure and hospitality 10%
- Professional and business services 16%
- Education and health services 17%
- Government 18%
- Trade, transportation, and utilities 17%

1. Employment by Industry: Maryland, 2010–2018

(Numbers in thousands, not seasonally adjusted)

Industry and year	January	February	March	April	May	June	July	August	September	October	November	December	Annual average
Total Nonfarm													
2010	2,450.8	2,429.2	2,487.2	2,524.5	2,548.5	2,555.8	2,536.3	2,532.1	2,535.5	2,549.4	2,553.1	2,557.5	2,521.7
2011	2,478.2	2,495.1	2,522.9	2,547.4	2,561.9	2,569.0	2,560.8	2,550.1	2,560.2	2,571.4	2,575.7	2,580.9	2,547.8
2012	2,510.7	2,527.1	2,556.4	2,571.3	2,590.3	2,601.3	2,582.4	2,582.2	2,593.3	2,602.2	2,608.2	2,614.1	2,578.3
2013	2,539.3	2,555.8	2,579.1	2,598.4	2,619.6	2,630.1	2,610.8	2,608.8	2,613.6	2,618.2	2,632.3	2,627.3	2,602.8
2014	2,549.4	2,561.3	2,584.6	2,615.6	2,642.7	2,654.2	2,628.4	2,635.7	2,642.5	2,654.2	2,664.5	2,665.9	2,624.9
2015	2,583.1	2,600.1	2,617.8	2,655.0	2,684.3	2,693.8	2,675.7	2,673.8	2,678.1	2,698.1	2,706.2	2,709.2	2,664.6
2016	2,624.5	2,635.9	2,661.4	2,695.5	2,708.7	2,715.2	2,702.5	2,703.6	2,714.7	2,722.3	2,737.8	2,739.2	2,696.8
2017	2,659.7	2,679.2	2,696.0	2,717.4	2,739.9	2,753.6	2,732.5	2,729.8	2,733.8	2,746.8	2,760.7	2,752.6	2,725.2
2018	2,679.6	2,703.5	2,721.7	2,741.6	2,764.8	2,775.7	2,751.6	2,747.8	2,744.5	2,758.7	2,771.2	2,771.0	2,744.3
Total Private													
2010	1,962.3	1,929.0	1,977.9	2,014.5	2,031.2	2,054.7	2,052.1	2,049.3	2,038.4	2,040.3	2,039.6	2,046.4	2,019.6
2011	1,985.2	1,985.9	2,006.9	2,033.8	2,049.0	2,069.0	2,074.7	2,069.4	2,059.3	2,056.2	2,063.5	2,068.3	2,043.4
2012	2,018.7	2,017.4	2,041.2	2,057.3	2,077.8	2,105.2	2,104.0	2,104.6	2,093.4	2,089.3	2,094.3	2,100.9	2,075.3
2013	2,046.0	2,046.7	2,065.6	2,084.4	2,106.4	2,129.1	2,130.0	2,129.1	2,113.4	2,108.0	2,118.5	2,117.2	2,099.5
2014	2,059.0	2,054.6	2,074.8	2,105.2	2,133.5	2,154.0	2,153.5	2,156.3	2,140.0	2,142.8	2,149.9	2,154.8	2,123.2
2015	2,092.5	2,093.0	2,107.1	2,142.2	2,171.0	2,190.0	2,197.1	2,194.2	2,174.1	2,187.3	2,192.5	2,195.2	2,161.4
2016	2,132.4	2,130.0	2,149.3	2,182.9	2,197.4	2,216.6	2,226.0	2,223.7	2,210.8	2,210.9	2,223.2	2,224.4	2,194.0
2017	2,164.6	2,168.1	2,181.1	2,203.3	2,224.4	2,249.8	2,255.5	2,251.9	2,233.9	2,235.1	2,245.1	2,240.7	2,221.1
2018	2,186.2	2,191.7	2,206.3	2,227.3	2,249.4	2,270.9	2,274.8	2,269.4	2,244.1	2,244.8	2,254.9	2,256.2	2,239.7
Goods Producing													
2010	256.7	246.6	255.1	262.2	264.2	267.1	268.1	267.5	265.5	263.5	262.7	260.6	261.7
2011	253.6	252.3	254.8	259.5	261.2	264.4	265.8	264.9	262.1	261.2	260.4	259.7	260.0
2012	252.2	250.2	252.5	255.0	255.8	260.4	261.6	261.4	258.7	257.9	257.5	256.8	256.7
2013	249.6	248.6	250.6	254.8	256.9	259.7	260.8	261.2	259.2	257.5	258.1	254.8	256.0
2014	247.7	246.0	248.9	254.8	257.8	261.2	261.6	262.6	260.9	260.9	261.3	259.7	257.0
2015	250.8	250.5	252.2	257.8	261.0	264.8	267.3	268.6	267.1	268.9	268.6	268.2	262.2
2016	260.3	258.0	262.0	266.7	268.6	271.5	272.9	273.0	271.8	271.6	271.4	271.4	268.3
2017	262.9	264.2	265.0	268.5	270.3	274.5	274.9	275.3	273.4	273.0	273.3	272.3	270.6
2018	264.2	265.5	267.7	270.3	272.3	275.6	278.1	278.3	275.9	276.8	274.0	274.1	272.7
Service-Providing													
2010	2,194.1	2,182.6	2,232.1	2,262.3	2,284.3	2,288.7	2,268.2	2,264.6	2,270.0	2,285.9	2,290.4	2,296.9	2,260.0
2011	2,224.6	2,242.8	2,268.1	2,287.9	2,300.7	2,304.6	2,295.0	2,285.2	2,298.1	2,310.2	2,315.3	2,321.2	2,287.8
2012	2,258.5	2,276.9	2,303.9	2,316.3	2,334.5	2,340.9	2,320.8	2,320.8	2,334.6	2,344.3	2,350.7	2,357.3	2,321.6
2013	2,289.7	2,307.2	2,328.5	2,343.6	2,362.7	2,370.4	2,350.0	2,347.6	2,354.4	2,360.7	2,374.2	2,372.5	2,346.8
2014	2,301.7	2,315.3	2,335.7	2,360.8	2,384.9	2,393.0	2,366.8	2,373.1	2,381.6	2,393.3	2,403.2	2,406.2	2,368.0
2015	2,332.3	2,349.6	2,365.6	2,397.2	2,423.3	2,429.0	2,408.4	2,405.2	2,411.0	2,429.2	2,437.6	2,441.0	2,402.5
2016	2,364.2	2,377.9	2,399.4	2,428.8	2,440.1	2,443.7	2,429.6	2,430.6	2,442.9	2,450.7	2,466.4	2,467.8	2,428.5
2017	2,396.8	2,415.0	2,431.0	2,448.9	2,469.6	2,479.1	2,457.6	2,454.5	2,460.4	2,473.8	2,487.4	2,480.3	2,454.5
2018	2,415.4	2,438.0	2,454.0	2,471.3	2,492.5	2,500.1	2,473.5	2,469.5	2,468.6	2,481.9	2,497.2	2,496.9	2,471.6
Mining and Logging													
2010	1.3	1.2	1.3	1.4	1.4	1.4	1.4	1.4	1.4	1.4	1.4	1.4	1.4
2011	1.3	1.3	1.4	1.4	1.4	1.4	1.5	1.5	1.5	1.5	1.5	1.5	1.4
2012	1.4	1.4	1.4	1.5	1.5	1.5	1.5	1.5	1.5	1.5	1.5	1.5	1.5
2013	1.3	1.3	1.4	1.4	1.4	1.4	1.4	1.5	1.5	1.4	1.4	1.4	1.4
2014	1.5	1.5	1.6	1.7	1.7	1.7	1.7	1.7	1.7	1.7	1.7	1.6	1.7
2015	1.5	1.6	1.6	1.6	1.6	1.6	1.7	1.7	1.7	1.5	1.5	1.5	1.6
2016	1.4	1.4	1.4	1.5	1.5	1.5	1.4	1.4	1.4	1.4	1.4	1.4	1.4
2017	1.3	1.3	1.3	1.3	1.3	1.3	1.3	1.3	1.3	1.3	1.3	1.3	1.3
2018	1.3	1.2	1.3	1.3	1.3	1.3	1.3	1.3	1.3	1.3	1.3	1.3	1.3
Construction													
2010	137.2	129.6	136.9	143.1	145.0	147.4	148.6	148.7	147.7	146.5	146.2	144.1	143.4
2011	136.7	136.0	138.1	142.4	143.9	146.6	148.2	147.6	146.0	145.6	145.1	144.3	143.4
2012	138.1	137.3	139.3	141.5	142.4	145.9	147.1	147.5	146.9	146.7	146.1	145.2	143.7
2013	139.4	138.7	140.5	144.8	146.8	149.1	150.3	150.8	149.9	148.6	149.0	146.0	146.2
2014	141.0	139.5	142.3	147.6	150.5	153.1	153.8	154.7	153.7	153.3	153.0	151.8	149.5
2015	144.2	143.8	145.5	150.9	153.9	156.5	158.3	159.6	158.9	160.9	160.3	159.6	154.4
2016	153.9	152.0	155.8	159.8	161.1	163.5	165.1	165.0	164.4	164.3	163.5	163.3	161.0
2017	156.3	157.2	157.7	160.7	162.2	165.7	166.1	166.3	165.0	164.2	164.1	163.1	162.4
2018	156.3	157.7	159.5	161.4	163.0	165.3	167.3	167.4	165.8	166.5	164.2	163.3	163.1

1. Employment by Industry: Maryland, 2010–2018—*Continued*

(Numbers in thousands, not seasonally adjusted)

Industry and year	January	February	March	April	May	June	July	August	September	October	November	December	Annual average
Manufacturing													
2010	118.2	115.8	116.9	117.7	117.8	118.3	118.1	117.4	116.4	115.6	115.1	115.1	116.9
2011	115.6	115.0	115.3	115.7	115.9	116.4	116.1	115.8	114.6	114.1	113.8	113.9	115.2
2012	112.7	111.5	111.8	112.0	111.9	113.0	113.0	112.4	110.3	109.7	109.9	110.1	111.5
2013	108.9	108.6	108.7	108.6	108.7	109.2	109.1	108.9	107.8	107.5	107.7	107.4	108.4
2014	105.2	105.0	105.0	105.5	105.6	106.4	106.1	106.2	105.5	105.9	106.6	106.3	105.8
2015	105.1	105.1	105.1	105.3	105.5	106.7	107.3	107.3	106.5	106.5	106.8	107.1	106.2
2016	105.0	104.6	104.8	105.4	106.0	106.5	106.4	106.6	106.0	105.9	106.5	106.7	105.9
2017	105.3	105.7	106.0	106.5	106.8	107.5	107.5	107.7	107.1	107.5	107.9	107.9	107.0
2018	106.6	106.6	106.9	107.6	108.0	109.0	109.5	109.6	108.8	109.0	108.5	109.5	108.3
Trade, Transportation, and Utilities													
2010	428.6	417.9	426.9	433.5	437.0	440.6	437.9	438.2	436.3	441.6	449.8	456.6	437.1
2011	435.9	431.3	434.0	438.4	441.4	444.0	442.7	443.7	442.9	446.2	455.9	463.1	443.3
2012	443.5	438.6	443.2	444.5	448.1	450.6	447.5	447.5	448.3	450.5	461.7	467.8	449.3
2013	445.5	440.0	442.3	443.9	448.3	451.3	449.8	450.3	448.9	451.6	463.0	469.9	450.4
2014	448.1	441.1	444.4	448.0	451.7	455.9	454.2	455.3	453.5	457.5	468.8	477.0	454.6
2015	453.7	447.9	449.6	455.3	460.0	464.7	462.9	462.5	461.4	467.2	476.9	483.3	462.1
2016	460.1	455.3	457.8	462.0	465.2	467.0	465.9	467.1	466.3	469.8	481.5	486.5	467.0
2017	464.2	457.1	457.8	462.1	465.5	469.0	467.4	468.0	466.7	470.5	485.7	487.7	468.5
2018	466.3	461.0	461.2	463.1	466.4	469.7	467.1	466.6	465.3	464.5	476.5	481.5	467.4
Wholesale Trade													
2010	83.3	82.8	83.7	84.6	85.2	85.4	85.1	85.1	84.2	84.9	84.9	85.1	84.5
2011	83.9	84.0	84.4	84.9	85.5	85.6	85.9	85.8	85.3	85.2	85.0	85.1	85.1
2012	83.9	84.1	84.9	85.2	85.9	86.3	86.0	85.9	85.4	85.4	85.3	85.3	85.3
2013	84.1	84.1	84.4	84.7	84.9	85.1	84.5	84.3	83.8	83.7	83.8	83.9	84.3
2014	82.6	82.5	82.6	83.0	83.6	83.9	83.8	83.8	83.3	83.4	83.4	84.1	83.3
2015	82.9	82.9	83.1	84.1	84.5	85.0	85.2	84.9	84.5	84.8	84.7	84.6	84.3
2016	83.9	83.7	83.7	84.4	84.7	84.8	84.9	85.0	84.5	84.7	84.7	84.6	84.5
2017	83.8	83.6	84.0	84.5	84.9	85.5	85.4	85.3	84.8	84.8	84.8	84.8	84.7
2018	84.0	84.2	84.1	84.5	85.0	85.8	85.9	86.0	85.7	86.4	85.8	85.7	85.3
Retail Trade													
2010	271.7	262.7	269.3	272.7	275.7	278.4	278.0	278.4	275.6	279.6	287.2	291.8	276.8
2011	276.4	272.2	274.1	276.8	278.6	280.8	280.1	281.1	279.2	282.6	291.2	296.5	280.8
2012	281.6	276.8	280.1	280.5	282.9	284.6	283.5	283.5	282.7	285.1	295.0	298.4	284.6
2013	281.9	277.7	279.2	280.6	283.6	285.9	286.6	287.2	284.2	286.8	296.2	300.2	285.8
2014	284.6	279.4	281.5	283.9	286.0	289.4	289.9	290.4	287.0	290.3	298.5	303.1	288.7
2015	286.6	282.0	283.4	286.8	290.0	293.4	292.1	291.9	288.9	292.8	300.5	303.6	291.0
2016	288.7	284.4	286.9	288.0	290.4	291.9	292.0	292.5	289.3	292.2	300.0	302.8	291.6
2017	288.2	282.8	283.4	285.7	287.5	289.7	289.0	289.2	286.0	288.7	299.3	299.7	289.1
2018	285.2	280.8	281.2	282.7	285.1	286.3	286.4	285.9	282.3	280.5	290.3	291.1	284.8
Transportation and Utilities													
2010	73.6	72.4	73.9	76.2	76.1	76.8	74.8	74.7	76.5	77.1	77.7	79.7	75.8
2011	75.6	75.1	75.5	76.7	77.3	77.6	76.7	76.8	78.4	78.4	79.7	81.5	77.4
2012	78.0	77.7	78.2	78.8	79.3	79.7	78.0	78.1	80.2	80.0	81.4	84.1	79.5
2013	79.5	78.2	78.7	78.6	79.8	80.3	78.7	78.8	80.9	81.1	83.0	85.8	80.3
2014	80.9	79.2	80.3	81.1	82.1	82.6	80.5	81.1	83.2	83.8	86.9	89.8	82.6
2015	84.2	83.0	83.1	84.4	85.5	86.3	85.6	85.7	88.0	89.6	91.7	95.1	86.9
2016	87.5	87.2	87.2	89.6	90.1	90.3	89.0	89.6	92.5	92.9	96.8	99.1	91.0
2017	92.2	90.7	90.4	91.9	93.1	93.8	93.0	93.5	95.9	97.0	101.6	103.2	94.7
2018	97.1	96.0	95.9	95.9	96.3	97.6	94.8	94.7	97.3	97.6	100.4	104.7	97.4
Information													
2010	43.2	43.6	45.0	44.8	44.7	45.5	44.1	43.1	43.9	43.4	42.3	44.2	44.0
2011	41.3	41.9	42.1	41.4	41.2	41.1	41.2	38.1	40.2	40.2	40.9	40.7	40.9
2012	39.8	39.9	39.9	38.8	39.1	40.5	40.4	40.5	40.1	39.5	39.8	40.7	39.9
2013	39.7	39.8	40.0	39.5	39.6	39.7	39.8	39.8	39.2	39.2	39.8	39.6	39.6
2014	40.2	38.8	38.8	38.6	39.6	38.7	38.9	39.9	38.3	39.3	38.9	39.0	39.1
2015	38.8	38.3	38.4	39.0	39.2	38.3	38.8	38.4	37.8	38.9	38.7	38.6	38.6
2016	37.6	37.9	37.7	38.9	36.0	39.0	38.9	38.3	38.1	37.8	38.0	38.5	38.1
2017	37.5	38.2	38.0	37.6	37.6	38.0	37.5	37.3	37.1	37.1	37.2	37.3	37.5
2018	36.2	36.7	36.5	36.6	36.7	37.0	36.4	36.4	35.5	36.1	36.9	36.4	36.5

1. Employment by Industry: Maryland, 2010–2018—*Continued*

(Numbers in thousands, not seasonally adjusted)

Industry and year	January	February	March	April	May	June	July	August	September	October	November	December	Annual average
Financial Activities													
2010	141.9	141.3	142.1	142.4	142.9	144.5	144.6	144.4	143.5	143.9	144.2	145.2	143.4
2011	142.3	142.6	143.0	143.3	143.3	144.1	144.2	143.5	142.6	142.7	142.3	142.7	143.1
2012	141.7	141.7	141.8	141.6	142.4	143.7	144.3	144.3	143.7	143.8	144.2	144.7	143.2
2013	143.5	143.5	143.9	144.4	145.0	146.4	147.0	146.5	145.6	145.2	145.3	145.5	145.2
2014	143.4	143.3	143.1	143.8	144.5	145.7	146.1	146.1	144.9	145.4	145.5	146.0	144.8
2015	144.4	144.7	144.8	145.4	145.7	147.0	147.0	146.6	144.6	144.9	144.6	144.5	145.4
2017	143.9	144.4	144.6	145.0	145.7	147.5	149.1	149.0	147.5	147.4	145.8	145.6	146.3
2018	144.3	144.5	144.7	145.1	145.2	145.8	145.7	145.1	143.7	143.5	143.0	142.0	144.4
Professional and Business Services													
2010	374.0	370.8	380.0	388.5	389.1	394.9	394.7	395.0	393.1	397.2	394.7	395.9	389.0
2011	385.9	387.0	391.5	398.4	398.9	404.2	407.4	408.3	407.1	407.4	408.5	408.1	401.1
2012	398.4	399.1	405.2	408.2	411.0	415.7	416.1	419.3	417.6	417.9	419.0	417.5	412.1
2013	408.3	410.9	416.2	416.9	418.6	422.7	423.0	425.9	423.5	422.5	424.2	421.2	419.5
2014	411.2	413.8	417.6	424.6	428.2	431.0	431.8	432.8	429.6	431.3	431.2	429.9	426.1
2015	417.9	419.5	422.8	431.6	434.7	437.4	441.1	442.2	436.5	442.4	442.4	439.6	434.0
2016	429.2	429.7	433.2	441.2	441.7	445.4	448.3	450.1	445.9	446.2	446.4	443.3	441.7
2017	434.7	435.0	438.4	441.9	444.3	449.4	450.6	451.4	448.1	448.1	448.3	446.0	444.7
2018	438.4	440.7	444.8	449.2	451.5	455.1	458.0	458.7	453.4	452.6	454.7	454.3	451.0
Education and Health Services													
2010	396.2	392.6	400.1	402.2	402.1	399.8	399.3	397.3	401.4	405.0	406.6	406.8	400.8
2011	402.2	406.4	408.0	408.8	408.4	405.3	405.9	404.7	409.1	412.8	414.2	414.1	408.3
2012	411.5	415.5	417.5	418.2	418.1	416.7	416.3	414.6	418.7	422.4	422.6	424.5	418.1
2013	418.4	422.4	424.1	425.1	424.9	422.8	421.8	420.4	424.1	427.6	428.7	428.7	424.1
2014	422.0	424.9	427.6	428.4	429.1	428.1	427.0	426.9	430.7	433.5	435.6	436.5	429.2
2015	430.7	434.7	436.4	439.9	440.7	438.2	438.0	436.0	439.4	445.3	447.5	447.1	439.5
2016	440.5	443.4	445.6	448.7	448.3	443.6	447.8	444.5	449.3	454.3	456.0	456.3	448.2
2017	449.0	453.9	455.8	456.9	457.1	455.2	460.5	458.1	462.0	467.1	468.2	468.3	459.3
2018	463.5	468.1	469.3	471.0	471.6	469.8	469.5	466.9	469.2	476.7	480.9	481.0	471.5
Leisure and Hospitality													
2010	209.2	205.0	214.9	226.9	236.6	246.8	248.1	248.9	240.8	231.9	225.6	223.5	229.9
2011	211.8	212.1	220.4	229.9	240.5	250.7	252.7	252.2	242.7	233.6	229.2	227.7	233.6
2012	220.8	221.7	229.8	239.0	251.1	264.4	264.7	264.7	254.8	246.6	239.4	238.4	244.6
2013	232.3	232.7	239.4	249.0	261.9	274.5	275.5	273.5	261.6	254.1	248.9	247.2	254.2
2014	237.1	237.5	244.3	255.7	270.5	279.9	280.3	279.8	269.0	262.5	256.1	254.0	260.6
2015	244.9	245.9	250.8	262.6	278.1	287.1	288.8	287.1	275.4	267.9	261.9	261.9	267.7
2016	251.1	251.9	258.9	269.4	280.7	291.6	291.7	290.7	280.7	272.7	271.6	269.7	273.4
2017	260.2	262.8	268.4	277.7	289.7	300.6	299.8	298.2	285.5	278.2	272.9	269.7	280.3
2018	260.7	262.4	268.6	278.0	291.1	302.3	304.0	302.1	287.2	278.2	272.4	271.4	281.5
Other Services													
2010	112.5	111.2	113.8	114.0	114.6	115.5	115.3	114.9	113.9	113.8	113.7	113.6	113.9
2011	112.2	112.3	113.1	114.1	114.1	115.2	114.8	114.0	112.6	112.1	112.1	112.2	113.2
2012	110.8	110.7	111.3	112.0	112.2	113.2	113.1	112.3	111.5	110.7	110.1	110.5	111.5
2013	108.7	108.8	109.1	110.8	111.2	112.0	112.3	111.5	111.3	110.3	110.5	110.3	110.6
2014	109.3	109.2	110.1	111.3	112.1	113.5	113.6	112.9	113.1	112.4	112.5	112.7	111.9
2015	111.3	111.5	112.1	110.6	111.6	112.5	113.2	112.8	111.9	111.8	111.9	112.0	111.9
2016	111.3	111.5	112.2	112.9	113.3	113.9	114.9	114.3	113.7	113.4	113.4	113.2	113.2
2017	112.2	112.5	113.1	113.6	114.2	115.6	115.7	114.6	113.6	113.7	113.7	113.8	113.9
2018	112.6	112.8	113.5	114.0	114.6	115.6	116.0	115.3	113.9	116.4	116.5	115.5	114.7
Government													
2010	488.5	500.2	509.3	510.0	517.3	501.1	484.2	482.8	497.1	509.1	513.5	511.1	502.0
2011	493.0	509.2	516.0	513.6	512.9	500.0	486.1	480.7	500.9	515.2	512.2	512.6	504.4
2012	492.0	509.7	515.2	514.0	512.5	496.1	478.4	477.6	499.9	512.9	513.9	513.2	503.0
2013	493.3	509.1	513.5	514.0	513.2	501.0	480.8	479.7	500.2	510.2	513.8	510.1	503.2
2014	490.4	506.7	509.8	510.4	509.2	500.2	474.9	479.4	502.5	511.4	514.6	511.1	501.7
2015	490.6	507.1	510.7	512.8	513.3	503.8	478.6	479.6	504.0	510.8	513.7	514.0	503.3
2016	492.1	505.9	512.1	512.6	511.3	498.6	476.5	479.9	503.9	511.4	514.6	514.8	502.8
2017	495.1	511.1	514.9	514.1	515.5	503.8	477.0	477.9	499.9	511.7	515.6	511.9	504.0
2018	493.4	511.8	515.4	514.3	515.4	504.8	476.8	478.4	500.4	513.9	516.3	514.8	504.6

2. Average Weekly Hours by Selected Industry: Maryland, 2014–2018

(Not seasonally adjusted)

Industry and year	January	February	March	April	May	June	July	August	September	October	November	December	Annual average
Total Private													
2014	33.8	33.6	34.4	34.1	34.2	34.6	34.3	34.3	34.2	33.9	34.5	33.7	34.1
2015	33.3	33.9	34.1	34.1	34.3	34.3	34.5	34.7	34.5	34.6	34.6	34.3	34.3
2016	33.6	33.7	34.1	34.2	34.2	34.4	34.3	34.4	34.7	35.0	34.5	34.4	34.3
2017	34.4	34.3	34.0	34.8	34.2	34.4	34.5	34.0	34.3	34.7	34.5	34.4	34.4
2018	33.9	34.2	34.2	34.9	34.1	34.3	34.8	34.3	34.2	33.7	33.6	34.1	34.2
Goods Producing													
2014	38.5	36.3	39.2	39.6	39.6	40.4	40.4	40.1	40.0	39.1	40.0	38.8	39.4
2015	37.5	37.8	38.6	38.9	39.6	40.0	39.9	39.8	39.4	40.6	39.1	40.3	39.3
2016	38.9	38.1	39.3	39.5	38.4	39.5	39.1	39.3	39.4	39.3	38.2	37.7	38.9
2017	38.0	38.3	37.3	38.3	38.4	39.1	38.9	38.7	39.2	39.4	39.5	39.8	38.7
2018	38.2	38.5	39.2	39.6	39.3	38.6	39.0	39.3	38.5	38.9	38.1	39.8	38.9
Mining, Logging, and Construction													
2014	37.9	34.4	38.6	38.9	39.2	40.0	40.7	39.7	39.8	38.6	39.6	37.9	38.8
2015	35.9	36.7	36.9	37.8	39.2	39.5	39.4	39.0	37.6	39.9	37.7	39.9	38.3
2016	38.5	36.6	39.1	39.0	37.8	39.7	39.3	39.4	39.4	39.5	37.6	37.3	38.6
2017	37.7	37.8	36.3	38.0	37.6	38.4	38.2	37.6	37.6	37.7	38.2	38.6	37.8
2018	36.7	37.1	38.2	39.1	38.4	37.9	38.2	39.1	37.7	38.9	37.6	39.6	38.2
Manufacturing													
2014	39.3	38.9	40.0	40.6	40.3	40.9	40.1	40.6	40.3	39.8	40.5	40.0	40.1
2015	39.7	39.3	41.1	40.4	40.2	40.7	40.7	41.0	42.0	41.7	41.2	41.0	40.7
2016	39.4	40.3	39.7	40.4	39.3	39.3	38.8	39.3	39.3	39.0	39.0	38.3	39.3
2017	38.5	39.0	38.7	38.8	39.7	40.3	39.9	40.3	41.7	42.0	41.4	41.6	40.2
2018	40.4	40.5	40.8	40.4	40.7	39.8	40.2	39.5	39.8	38.9	39.0	40.2	40.0
Trade, Transportation, and Utilities													
2014	32.2	32.1	33.5	33.2	33.4	33.6	33.7	33.6	33.5	33.2	33.6	33.2	33.2
2015	32.4	32.9	33.2	33.1	33.5	33.4	34.1	33.9	34.5	33.4	33.6	33.6	33.5
2016	32.3	32.6	32.9	33.0	33.3	33.7	33.6	33.4	34.0	34.2	34.0	34.7	33.5
2017	34.2	33.8	33.5	34.2	33.8	33.9	34.3	33.7	34.2	34.7	34.6	34.0	34.1
2018	33.7	33.7	33.8	34.1	33.9	34.1	34.1	33.9	34.3	33.7	33.9	34.1	33.9
Financial Activities													
2014	37.3	37.2	37.3	36.8	36.9	37.6	37.1	37.3	37.0	37.1	37.9	37.3	37.2
2015	37.6	38.2	38.3	37.5	37.9	37.7	37.6	38.5	38.0	38.1	38.0	37.6	37.9
2016	37.7	38.1	38.3	37.8	38.6	38.5	38.6	38.3	38.0	38.6	38.0	38.3	38.2
2017	38.3	37.8	37.8	38.3	37.3	37.6	38.1	37.3	37.3	37.3	37.6	37.1	37.6
2018	37.3	37.3	37.5	38.2	36.9	37.2	38.2	37.2	38.2	37.4	38.1	38.3	37.7
Professional and Business Services													
2014	36.1	36.5	36.5	36.1	36.0	36.7	35.7	35.7	35.5	35.2	36.0	34.8	35.9
2015	34.7	35.8	35.8	35.8	35.7	35.7	35.4	36.1	35.5	36.2	36.5	35.7	35.7
2016	35.3	35.3	36.0	36.4	36.4	36.6	36.0	36.1	36.1	37.4	36.6	36.2	36.2
2017	36.4	36.3	36.2	37.8	36.6	37.4	37.1	36.9	37.0	37.8	37.1	37.1	37.0
2018	36.4	37.0	36.8	37.9	36.1	36.4	37.4	36.3	35.0	34.9	34.5	35.2	36.2
Education and Health Services													
2014	33.1	33.0	33.0	32.9	32.8	32.8	32.9	33.1	33.0	32.6	32.9	32.7	32.9
2015	32.6	33.0	32.8	32.6	32.7	32.8	33.0	32.9	32.9	33.2	33.5	32.8	32.9
2016	33.3	33.0	33.2	33.2	33.1	33.1	33.6	33.4	33.4	33.5	33.6	33.3	33.3
2017	33.2	33.0	33.0	33.3	33.1	33.0	33.4	33.2	33.1	32.8	32.7	33.1	33.1
2018	33.3	33.3	33.0	33.5	33.2	33.5	33.4	33.2	33.9	33.2	33.4	33.2	33.3
Leisure and Hospitality													
2014	24.9	24.7	25.4	25.0	25.3	25.8	26.1	26.2	25.9	25.5	25.4	25.4	25.5
2015	25.2	25.3	25.8	26.1	26.8	27.3	27.6	28.0	26.9	26.7	26.7	26.5	26.6
2016	24.9	26.0	26.0	26.1	26.1	26.1	26.4	26.3	26.2	25.8	25.6	25.3	25.9
2017	25.1	25.4	25.3	26.2	26.2	25.6	26.1	25.5	25.4	25.7	25.4	25.2	25.6
2018	24.3	25.1	24.8	25.7	25.8	26.7	27.5	26.8	26.2	26.3	26.1	26.0	26.0
Other Services													
2014	32.6	32.9	34.0	32.9	33.1	33.4	32.8	32.6	32.6	32.9	33.7	33.8	33.1
2015	32.1	33.3	33.5	33.6	34.0	33.6	33.7	32.9	32.6	32.3	32.5	32.3	33.0
2016	31.3	31.5	31.8	32.0	31.9	32.6	32.3	32.2	31.6	31.4	30.7	30.6	31.7
2017	31.1	31.6	30.5	31.5	31.4	31.7	32.5	32.1	32.6	32.2	31.6	31.8	31.7
2018	31.8	32.0	32.5	33.4	33.9	33.1	33.3	33.6	34.3	34.0	33.7	34.6	33.4

3. Average Hourly Earnings by Selected Industry: Maryland, 2014–2018

(Dollars, not seasonally adjusted)

Industry and year	January	February	March	April	May	June	July	August	September	October	November	December	Annual average
Total Private													
2014	27.42	27.82	27.41	27.28	27.09	27.29	27.15	27.19	27.46	27.18	27.50	27.45	27.35
2015	27.64	27.71	27.77	27.28	27.08	26.81	26.75	27.28	27.20	27.20	27.69	27.38	27.31
2016	27.38	27.20	27.11	27.17	27.47	26.94	27.06	27.22	27.19	27.51	27.58	27.39	27.27
2017	28.23	27.79	27.86	27.88	27.47	27.56	28.15	27.96	29.07	29.49	29.38	29.23	28.34
2018	29.39	29.74	29.66	30.15	29.68	29.18	29.40	29.09	29.94	29.26	29.42	29.93	29.57
Goods Producing													
2014	27.02	27.15	26.33	26.34	26.18	26.42	26.13	26.20	26.12	26.42	26.73	26.59	26.46
2015	26.73	26.59	26.56	26.26	26.23	26.36	26.19	26.21	26.30	26.05	26.37	26.44	26.35
2016	26.03	26.20	26.25	26.43	26.84	26.50	26.86	27.03	27.53	27.62	28.29	28.48	27.01
2017	28.80	28.84	28.95	28.88	28.74	29.03	29.59	29.03	29.63	29.51	29.77	30.03	29.24
2018	30.18	30.13	30.06	30.10	30.15	30.38	30.25	29.96	30.01	29.86	29.64	30.05	30.06
Mining, Logging, and Construction													
2014	27.30	27.78	26.86	26.86	26.71	27.07	26.68	26.83	26.92	27.53	27.17	27.30	27.07
2015	27.62	27.31	27.17	27.07	26.87	26.91	26.85	26.51	26.49	26.34	26.26	26.66	26.82
2016	26.52	26.47	26.40	26.77	26.89	26.49	27.00	27.49	27.80	27.87	28.54	28.97	27.28
2017	29.53	29.62	29.93	29.43	29.62	30.16	30.84	30.22	30.58	30.56	30.81	31.11	30.21
2018	31.56	31.67	31.63	31.52	31.58	31.97	32.20	31.55	31.54	31.13	30.99	31.55	31.57
Manufacturing													
2014	26.66	26.40	25.62	25.63	25.44	25.50	25.32	25.28	24.95	24.84	26.11	25.61	25.61
2015	25.61	25.66	25.80	25.17	25.31	25.58	25.23	25.78	26.04	25.62	26.53	26.12	25.71
2016	25.33	25.84	26.02	25.94	26.76	26.52	26.64	26.31	27.10	27.22	27.92	27.75	26.61
2017	27.72	27.71	27.58	28.05	27.47	27.35	27.72	27.31	28.30	28.05	28.31	28.50	27.85
2018	28.33	28.02	27.86	28.02	28.09	28.06	27.39	27.53	27.79	27.91	27.65	27.84	27.87
Trade, Transportation, and Utilities													
2014	20.06	20.87	20.31	20.62	20.46	20.29	20.88	20.65	21.63	21.27	21.50	22.35	20.92
2015	22.65	22.69	22.27	22.40	22.04	21.99	22.02	22.30	22.11	22.68	22.66	22.29	22.34
2016	22.96	22.86	23.08	23.45	23.31	23.14	23.59	23.70	23.86	24.08	23.98	23.49	23.47
2017	24.16	23.93	23.94	24.99	24.19	24.20	24.95	24.45	24.31	24.40	24.10	24.42	24.34
2018	24.60	24.73	24.54	24.35	24.39	24.22	23.90	23.95	24.19	24.15	23.79	24.21	24.25
Financial Activities													
2014	32.48	32.96	32.72	32.69	32.68	32.50	32.78	33.25	33.08	33.02	33.71	34.06	33.00
2015	33.76	34.57	34.96	35.50	35.58	35.11	35.45	36.52	36.66	36.36	37.73	36.82	35.75
2016	36.33	37.14	37.52	37.84	37.86	37.37	37.37	39.41	39.66	39.94	39.75	39.28	38.28
2017	40.57	40.20	39.20	39.70	38.83	38.01	37.58	38.47	36.81	37.97	37.60	37.59	38.54
2018	38.65	39.13	37.98	38.24	38.45	37.36	37.77	38.22	37.58	37.77	38.84	38.39	38.20
Professional and Business Services													
2014	34.16	34.87	34.79	33.75	33.88	34.48	34.02	34.30	34.22	33.93	34.74	34.51	34.30
2015	34.51	34.53	34.57	33.49	33.35	33.16	33.08	34.07	33.64	33.31	34.42	34.18	33.85
2016	33.31	32.58	31.83	31.87	32.68	31.67	31.99	32.31	32.64	33.25	33.51	33.88	32.63
2017	34.71	33.66	33.67	33.67	33.15	33.34	34.71	34.22	34.87	36.25	35.92	35.20	34.46
2018	34.87	34.84	35.00	36.45	35.38	33.91	34.94	34.23	36.60	36.76	36.99	37.83	35.63
Education and Health Services													
2014	27.58	27.21	27.16	26.92	26.57	26.61	26.72	26.53	26.46	26.76	26.44	26.30	26.77
2015	26.34	26.08	26.11	25.96	25.66	25.58	25.68	25.52	26.01	25.45	25.38	25.38	25.76
2016	25.28	25.20	25.22	25.42	25.52	25.36	25.54	25.30	25.47	25.33	25.11	24.95	25.31
2017	25.25	25.22	25.29	25.55	25.79	25.84	25.80	25.23	25.33	25.39	25.35	25.44	25.46
2018	25.74	26.16	26.47	26.87	26.73	26.75	27.24	27.27	27.77	27.85	28.12	28.09	27.10
Leisure and Hospitality													
2014	14.88	14.77	14.64	15.28	14.96	14.85	14.71	14.65	15.19	14.81	15.06	14.88	14.89
2015	15.08	15.10	15.23	15.48	15.95	15.18	14.82	15.04	15.06	15.32	15.09	15.16	15.21
2016	15.34	15.26	15.35	15.19	15.33	15.16	15.04	15.25	15.46	14.79	14.58	14.79	15.13
2017	15.10	15.43	15.33	15.07	15.36	15.19	14.93	15.17	15.71	14.69	14.72	15.05	15.15
2018	15.28	15.62	15.19	15.10	15.10	14.70	14.81	14.42	15.58	15.34	15.69	16.44	15.25
Other Services													
2014	24.40	23.91	23.83	24.16	24.45	24.62	24.56	25.07	25.72	25.48	25.45	25.11	24.73
2015	26.11	26.02	26.29	25.40	25.36	25.82	26.05	27.68	27.09	27.66	27.60	27.10	26.51
2016	28.24	28.31	28.86	27.82	28.49	28.00	28.10	28.42	28.98	29.92	29.22	29.24	28.63
2017	29.97	29.01	29.60	29.43	28.67	28.84	29.17	30.10	30.34	30.27	30.10	30.33	29.65
2018	30.66	30.64	30.47	30.49	29.98	31.10	30.79	30.02	30.55	30.68	30.73	31.45	30.63

4. Average Weekly Earnings by Selected Industry: Maryland, 2014–2018

(Dollars, not seasonally adjusted)

Industry and year	January	February	March	April	May	June	July	August	September	October	November	December	Annual average
Total Private													
2014	926.80	934.75	942.90	930.25	926.48	944.23	931.25	932.62	939.13	921.40	948.75	925.07	932.64
2015	920.41	939.37	946.96	930.25	928.84	919.58	922.88	946.62	938.40	941.12	958.07	939.13	936.73
2016	919.97	916.64	924.45	929.21	939.47	926.74	928.16	936.37	943.49	962.85	951.51	942.22	935.36
2017	971.11	953.20	947.24	970.22	939.47	948.06	971.18	950.64	997.10	1,023.30	1,013.61	1,005.51	974.90
2018	996.32	1,017.11	1,014.37	1,052.24	1,012.09	1,000.87	1,023.12	997.79	1,023.95	986.06	988.51	1,020.61	1,011.29
Goods Producing													
2014	1,040.27	985.55	1,032.14	1,043.06	1,036.73	1,067.37	1,055.65	1,050.62	1,044.80	1,033.02	1,069.20	1,031.69	1,042.52
2015	1,002.38	1,005.10	1,025.22	1,021.51	1,038.71	1,054.40	1,044.98	1,043.16	1,036.22	1,057.63	1,031.07	1,065.53	1,035.56
2016	1,012.57	998.22	1,031.63	1,043.99	1,030.66	1,046.75	1,050.23	1,062.28	1,084.68	1,085.47	1,080.68	1,073.70	1,050.69
2017	1,094.40	1,104.57	1,079.84	1,106.10	1,103.62	1,135.07	1,151.05	1,123.46	1,161.50	1,162.69	1,175.92	1,195.19	1,131.59
2018	1,152.88	1,160.01	1,178.35	1,191.96	1,184.90	1,172.67	1,179.75	1,177.43	1,155.39	1,161.55	1,129.28	1,195.99	1,169.33
Mining, Logging, and Construction													
2014	1,034.67	955.63	1,036.80	1,044.85	1,047.03	1,082.80	1,085.88	1,065.15	1,071.42	1,062.66	1,075.93	1,034.67	1,050.32
2015	991.56	1,002.28	1,002.57	1,023.25	1,053.30	1,062.95	1,057.89	1,033.89	996.02	1,050.97	990.00	1,063.73	1,027.21
2016	1,021.02	968.80	1,032.24	1,044.03	1,016.44	1,051.65	1,061.10	1,083.11	1,095.32	1,100.87	1,073.10	1,080.58	1,053.01
2017	1,113.28	1,119.64	1,086.46	1,118.34	1,113.71	1,158.14	1,178.09	1,136.27	1,149.81	1,152.11	1,176.94	1,200.85	1,141.94
2018	1,158.25	1,174.96	1,208.27	1,232.43	1,212.67	1,211.66	1,230.04	1,233.61	1,189.06	1,210.96	1,165.22	1,249.38	1,205.97
Manufacturing													
2014	1,047.74	1,026.96	1,024.80	1,040.58	1,025.23	1,042.95	1,015.33	1,026.37	1,005.49	988.63	1,057.46	1,024.40	1,026.96
2015	1,016.72	1,008.44	1,060.38	1,016.87	1,017.46	1,041.11	1,026.86	1,056.98	1,093.68	1,068.35	1,093.04	1,070.92	1,046.40
2016	998.00	1,041.35	1,032.99	1,047.98	1,051.67	1,042.24	1,033.63	1,033.98	1,065.03	1,061.58	1,088.88	1,062.83	1,045.77
2017	1,067.22	1,080.69	1,067.35	1,088.34	1,090.56	1,102.21	1,106.03	1,100.59	1,180.11	1,178.10	1,172.03	1,185.60	1,119.57
2018	1,144.53	1,134.81	1,136.69	1,132.01	1,143.26	1,116.79	1,101.08	1,087.44	1,106.04	1,085.70	1,078.35	1,119.17	1,114.80
Trade, Transportation, and Utilities													
2014	645.93	669.93	680.39	684.58	683.36	681.74	703.66	693.84	724.61	706.16	722.40	742.02	694.54
2015	733.86	746.50	739.36	741.44	738.34	734.47	750.88	755.97	762.80	757.51	761.38	748.94	748.39
2016	741.61	745.24	759.33	773.85	776.22	779.82	792.62	791.58	811.24	823.54	815.32	815.10	786.25
2017	826.27	808.83	801.99	854.66	817.62	820.38	855.79	823.97	831.40	846.68	833.86	830.28	829.99
2018	829.02	833.40	829.45	830.34	826.82	825.90	814.99	811.91	829.72	813.86	806.48	825.56	822.08
Financial Activities													
2014	1,211.50	1,226.11	1,220.46	1,202.99	1,205.89	1,222.00	1,216.14	1,240.23	1,223.96	1,225.04	1,277.61	1,270.44	1,227.60
2015	1,269.38	1,320.57	1,338.97	1,331.25	1,348.48	1,323.65	1,332.92	1,406.02	1,393.08	1,385.32	1,433.74	1,384.43	1,354.93
2016	1,369.64	1,415.03	1,437.02	1,430.35	1,461.40	1,438.75	1,435.15	1,509.40	1,507.08	1,541.68	1,510.50	1,504.42	1,462.30
2017	1,553.83	1,519.56	1,481.76	1,520.51	1,448.36	1,429.18	1,431.80	1,434.93	1,373.01	1,416.28	1,413.76	1,394.59	1,449.10
2018	1,441.65	1,459.55	1,424.25	1,460.77	1,418.81	1,389.79	1,442.81	1,421.78	1,435.56	1,412.60	1,479.80	1,470.34	1,440.14
Professional and Business Services													
2014	1,233.18	1,272.76	1,269.84	1,218.38	1,219.68	1,265.42	1,214.51	1,224.51	1,214.81	1,194.34	1,250.64	1,200.95	1,231.37
2015	1,197.50	1,236.17	1,237.61	1,198.94	1,190.60	1,183.81	1,171.03	1,229.93	1,194.22	1,205.82	1,256.33	1,220.23	1,208.45
2016	1,175.84	1,150.07	1,145.88	1,160.07	1,189.55	1,159.12	1,151.64	1,166.39	1,178.30	1,243.55	1,226.47	1,226.46	1,181.21
2017	1,263.44	1,221.86	1,218.85	1,272.73	1,213.29	1,246.92	1,287.74	1,262.72	1,290.19	1,370.25	1,332.63	1,305.92	1,275.02
2018	1,269.27	1,289.08	1,288.00	1,381.46	1,277.22	1,234.32	1,306.76	1,242.55	1,281.00	1,282.92	1,276.16	1,331.62	1,289.81
Education and Health Services													
2014	912.90	897.93	896.28	885.67	871.50	872.81	879.09	878.14	873.18	872.38	869.88	860.01	880.73
2015	858.68	860.64	856.41	846.30	839.08	839.02	847.44	839.61	855.73	844.94	850.23	832.46	847.50
2016	841.82	831.60	837.30	843.94	844.71	839.42	858.14	845.02	850.70	848.56	843.70	830.84	842.82
2017	838.30	832.26	834.57	850.82	853.65	852.72	861.72	837.64	838.42	832.79	828.95	842.06	842.73
2018	857.14	871.13	873.51	900.15	887.44	896.13	909.82	905.36	941.40	924.62	939.21	932.59	902.43
Leisure and Hospitality													
2014	370.51	364.82	371.86	382.00	378.49	383.13	383.93	383.83	393.42	377.66	382.52	377.95	379.70
2015	380.02	382.03	392.93	404.03	427.46	414.41	409.03	421.12	405.11	409.04	402.90	401.74	404.59
2016	381.97	396.76	399.10	396.46	400.11	395.68	397.06	401.08	405.05	381.58	373.25	374.19	391.87
2017	379.01	391.92	387.85	394.83	402.43	388.86	389.67	386.84	399.03	377.53	373.89	379.26	387.84
2018	371.30	392.06	376.71	388.07	389.58	392.49	407.28	386.46	408.20	403.44	409.51	427.44	396.50
Other Services													
2014	795.44	786.64	810.22	794.86	809.30	822.31	805.57	817.28	838.47	838.29	857.67	848.72	818.56
2015	838.13	866.47	880.72	853.44	862.24	867.55	877.89	910.67	883.13	893.42	897.00	875.33	874.83
2016	883.91	891.77	917.75	890.24	908.83	912.80	907.63	915.12	915.77	939.49	897.05	894.74	907.57
2017	932.07	916.72	902.80	927.05	900.24	914.23	948.03	966.21	989.08	974.69	951.16	964.49	939.91
2018	974.99	980.48	990.28	1,018.37	1,016.32	1,029.41	1,025.31	1,008.67	1,047.87	1,043.12	1,035.60	1,088.17	1,023.04

MASSACHUSETTS
At a Glance

Population:
  2010 census: 6,547,629
  2018 estimate: 6,902,149

Percent change in population
2010–2018: 5.4%

Percent change in total nonfarm employment:
  2010–2018: 13.0%

Industry with the largest growth in employment, 2010–2018 (percent):
  Construction, 46.6%

Industry with the largest decline or smallest growth in employment, 2010–2018 (percent):
  Manufacturing, -3.2 %

Civilian labor force:
  2010: 3,480,083
  2018: 3,805,450

Unemployment rate and rank among states (highest to lowest):
  2010: 8.3%, 30th
  2018: 3.3%, 37th

Over-the-year change in unemployment rates:
  2016–2017: -0.1%
  2017–2018: -0.5%

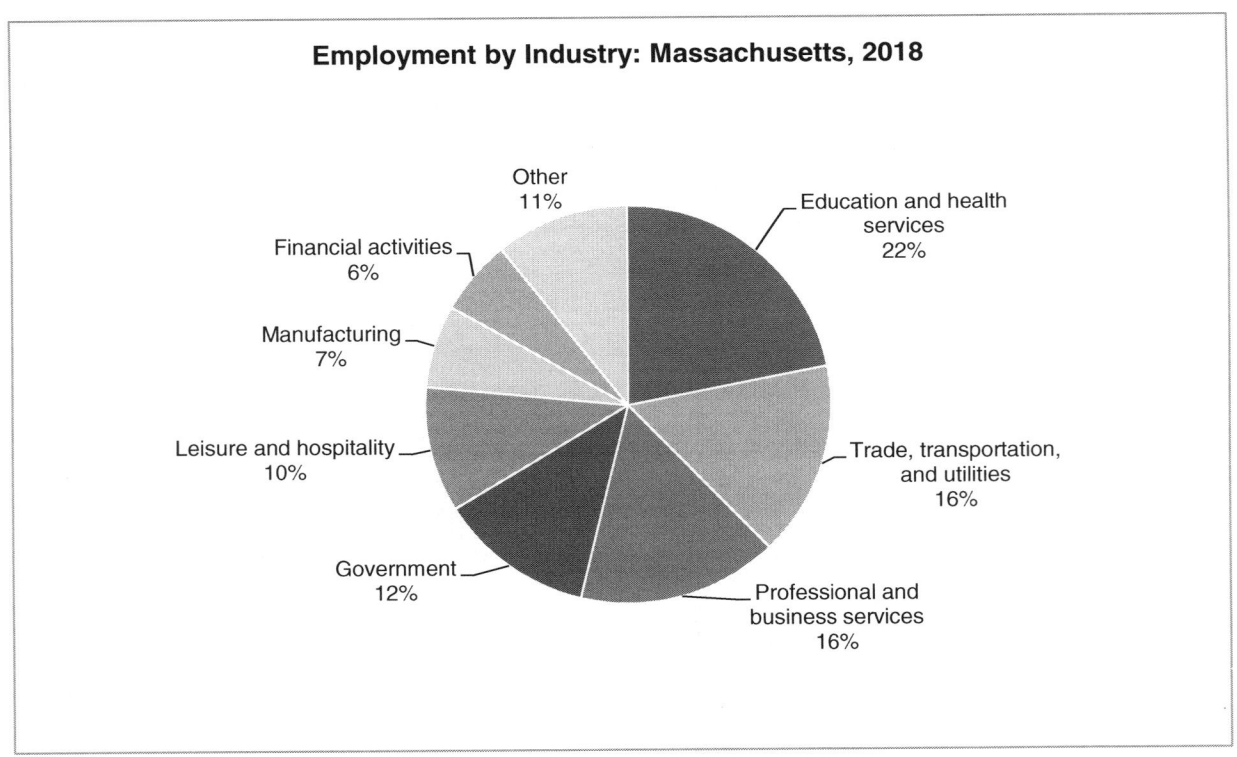

Employment by Industry: Massachusetts, 2018

Other
11%

Education and health services
22%

Financial activities
6%

Manufacturing
7%

Leisure and hospitality
10%

Trade, transportation, and utilities
16%

Government
12%

Professional and business services
16%

1. Employment by Industry: Massachusetts, 2010–2018

(Numbers in thousands, not seasonally adjusted)

Industry and year	January	February	March	April	May	June	July	August	September	October	November	December	Annual average
Total Nonfarm													
2010	3,145.9	3,148.6	3,161.0	3,214.4	3,250.1	3,253.4	3,237.7	3,222.6	3,240.2	3,267.2	3,264.4	3,264.3	3,222.5
2011	3,166.6	3,179.3	3,194.0	3,250.8	3,271.4	3,288.8	3,283.2	3,266.7	3,294.5	3,307.5	3,304.8	3,305.0	3,259.4
2012	3,216.4	3,226.8	3,254.1	3,291.6	3,320.7	3,359.4	3,328.5	3,320.0	3,339.5	3,354.8	3,359.4	3,353.2	3,310.4
2013	3,258.8	3,273.2	3,298.5	3,353.5	3,387.6	3,417.0	3,383.8	3,378.5	3,390.1	3,413.0	3,416.1	3,414.6	3,365.4
2014	3,313.2	3,331.9	3,353.3	3,413.6	3,449.7	3,476.9	3,457.2	3,436.9	3,462.7	3,491.9	3,499.1	3,499.8	3,432.2
2015	3,384.5	3,387.8	3,417.6	3,478.6	3,523.7	3,553.0	3,537.3	3,519.4	3,518.4	3,553.3	3,557.5	3,556.8	3,499.0
2016	3,450.0	3,468.7	3,494.6	3,551.7	3,579.4	3,607.6	3,608.1	3,592.7	3,598.1	3,607.0	3,613.5	3,610.0	3,565.1
2017	3,506.8	3,520.4	3,540.3	3,595.1	3,627.0	3,672.8	3,647.9	3,634.0	3,635.5	3,651.0	3,655.5	3,653.5	3,611.7
2018	3,545.7	3,573.3	3,586.0	3,628.9	3,662.2	3,708.2	3,673.6	3,655.9	3,659.0	3,679.6	3,678.0	3,664.8	3,642.9
Total Private													
2010	2,707.4	2,702.4	2,713.7	2,763.1	2,789.9	2,811.4	2,831.9	2,825.1	2,803.7	2,820.4	2,813.9	2,815.1	2,783.2
2011	2,733.8	2,734.1	2,748.4	2,805.4	2,823.9	2,852.8	2,881.3	2,873.3	2,858.2	2,864.4	2,861.0	2,859.3	2,824.7
2012	2,784.7	2,782.9	2,807.1	2,844.9	2,872.4	2,920.4	2,924.8	2,922.3	2,899.2	2,907.9	2,907.8	2,903.6	2,873.2
2013	2,825.0	2,822.2	2,846.1	2,896.9	2,931.5	2,972.6	2,975.1	2,976.5	2,948.4	2,959.1	2,958.0	2,956.1	2,922.3
2014	2,869.2	2,873.8	2,894.6	2,949.0	2,986.5	3,025.9	3,040.1	3,027.7	3,008.7	3,029.1	3,029.4	3,032.4	2,980.5
2015	2,940.2	2,928.6	2,954.4	3,013.1	3,062.4	3,098.6	3,118.0	3,111.2	3,069.7	3,092.9	3,093.8	3,091.7	3,047.9
2016	3,005.2	3,009.4	3,028.6	3,087.9	3,115.3	3,153.5	3,185.8	3,178.8	3,140.4	3,143.9	3,143.0	3,143.7	3,111.3
2017	3,057.8	3,059.7	3,079.2	3,131.7	3,163.6	3,215.8	3,228.4	3,222.2	3,183.0	3,189.0	3,189.9	3,188.5	3,159.1
2018	3,099.1	3,111.7	3,125.9	3,166.3	3,198.5	3,248.4	3,253.3	3,244.3	3,201.2	3,212.3	3,206.6	3,193.4	3,188.4
Goods Producing													
2010	348.1	343.1	345.5	355.1	361.5	367.5	371.1	370.2	367.5	367.8	365.9	361.6	360.4
2011	347.3	343.7	346.1	357.9	364.2	371.3	375.4	376.0	372.5	371.1	369.0	365.5	363.3
2012	354.2	350.9	355.0	362.5	367.1	375.4	376.5	376.9	373.9	374.4	372.9	369.8	367.5
2013	357.7	355.0	357.6	366.2	374.5	381.3	383.3	384.3	381.1	380.0	378.0	374.5	372.8
2014	363.7	360.4	362.4	371.7	379.9	386.4	388.7	389.1	385.6	386.8	386.6	383.7	378.8
2015	372.0	367.1	370.0	382.7	391.8	398.1	400.2	400.3	395.4	396.8	395.7	393.4	388.6
2016	381.3	375.8	379.8	388.9	395.1	401.4	402.8	402.3	398.5	398.3	396.6	394.1	392.9
2017	381.4	378.0	380.4	390.7	397.4	405.2	408.6	409.2	405.5	406.1	404.5	400.4	397.3
2018	387.6	387.3	390.1	398.4	405.9	413.5	413.3	411.6	408.2	407.3	406.3	399.5	402.4
Service-Providing													
2010	2,797.8	2,805.5	2,815.5	2,859.3	2,888.6	2,885.9	2,866.6	2,852.4	2,872.7	2,899.4	2,898.5	2,902.7	2,862.1
2011	2,819.3	2,835.6	2,847.9	2,892.9	2,907.2	2,917.5	2,907.8	2,890.7	2,922.0	2,936.4	2,935.8	2,939.5	2,896.1
2012	2,862.2	2,875.9	2,899.1	2,929.1	2,953.6	2,984.0	2,952.0	2,943.1	2,965.6	2,980.4	2,986.5	2,983.4	2,942.9
2013	2,901.1	2,918.2	2,940.9	2,987.3	3,013.1	3,035.7	3,000.5	2,994.2	3,009.0	3,033.0	3,038.1	3,040.1	2,992.6
2014	2,949.5	2,971.5	2,990.9	3,041.9	3,069.8	3,090.5	3,068.5	3,047.8	3,077.1	3,105.1	3,112.5	3,116.1	3,053.4
2015	3,012.5	3,020.7	3,047.6	3,095.9	3,131.9	3,154.9	3,137.1	3,119.1	3,123.0	3,156.5	3,161.8	3,163.4	3,110.4
2016	3,068.7	3,092.9	3,114.8	3,162.8	3,184.3	3,206.2	3,205.3	3,190.4	3,199.6	3,208.7	3,216.9	3,215.9	3,172.2
2017	3,125.4	3,142.4	3,159.9	3,204.4	3,229.6	3,267.6	3,239.3	3,224.8	3,230.0	3,244.9	3,251.0	3,253.1	3,214.4
2018	3,158.1	3,186.0	3,195.9	3,230.5	3,256.3	3,294.7	3,260.3	3,244.3	3,250.8	3,272.3	3,271.7	3,265.3	3,240.5
Mining and Logging													
2010	1.0	1.0	1.0	1.2	1.3	1.3	1.2	1.2	1.2	1.1	1.1	1.1	1.1
2011	0.9	0.9	0.9	1.1	1.2	1.2	1.2	1.2	1.2	1.1	1.1	1.1	1.1
2012	0.9	0.8	0.9	0.9	1.0	1.0	1.0	1.0	1.0	1.0	1.0	1.0	1.0
2013	0.8	0.8	0.9	1.0	1.0	1.0	1.0	1.1	1.1	1.1	1.0	1.0	1.0
2014	0.9	0.9	0.9	1.0	1.1	1.1	1.1	1.1	1.1	1.1	1.1	1.0	1.0
2015	0.9	0.9	0.9	1.1	1.1	1.1	1.2	1.1	1.2	1.1	1.1	1.1	1.1
2016	1.0	1.0	1.0	1.1	1.2	1.2	1.2	1.2	1.2	1.2	1.1	1.1	1.1
2017	1.0	1.0	1.0	1.1	1.1	1.2	1.2	1.2	1.2	1.2	1.2	1.1	1.1
2018	1.0	1.0	1.0	1.1	1.1	1.1	1.1	1.1	1.1	1.1	1.1	1.0	1.1
Construction													
2010	96.2	92.4	94.5	103.4	108.7	112.8	116.3	115.6	114.0	113.3	111.5	107.3	107.2
2011	96.8	94.2	95.8	105.9	111.7	116.7	120.7	121.1	119.4	118.0	116.4	112.6	110.8
2012	103.4	100.4	103.9	111.5	115.6	120.5	123.5	123.9	122.1	122.5	121.3	118.0	115.6
2013	108.9	106.8	108.7	116.9	124.3	128.5	131.9	132.3	130.2	129.6	127.6	123.3	122.4
2014	114.9	112.4	113.9	122.9	130.5	135.1	138.1	138.2	136.5	137.2	136.5	133.1	129.1
2015	123.8	119.0	121.4	133.3	141.8	145.9	148.9	149.4	146.6	148.2	146.9	144.4	139.1
2016	135.0	130.6	134.1	143.2	148.7	152.3	155.0	154.4	152.5	152.7	151.4	148.1	146.5
2017	137.6	134.8	137.2	147.0	153.3	158.3	161.5	161.9	160.2	160.4	158.8	153.6	152.1
2018	143.4	143.7	146.0	154.3	160.9	165.6	166.0	165.2	163.3	162.6	161.6	154.2	157.2

1. Employment by Industry: Massachusetts, 2010–2018—*Continued*

(Numbers in thousands, not seasonally adjusted)

Industry and year	January	February	March	April	May	June	July	August	September	October	November	December	Annual average
Manufacturing													
2010	250.9	249.7	250.0	250.5	251.5	253.4	253.6	253.4	252.3	253.4	253.3	253.2	252.1
2011	249.6	248.6	249.4	250.9	251.3	253.4	253.5	253.7	251.9	251.9	251.5	251.8	251.5
2012	249.9	249.7	250.2	250.1	250.5	253.9	252.0	252.0	250.8	250.9	250.6	250.8	251.0
2013	248.0	247.4	248.0	248.3	249.2	251.8	250.4	250.9	249.8	249.3	249.4	250.2	249.4
2014	247.9	247.1	247.6	247.8	248.3	250.2	249.5	249.8	248.0	248.5	249.0	249.6	248.6
2015	247.3	247.2	247.7	248.3	248.9	251.1	250.1	249.8	247.6	247.5	247.7	247.9	248.4
2016	245.3	244.2	244.7	244.6	245.2	247.9	246.6	246.7	244.8	244.4	244.1	244.9	245.3
2017	242.8	242.2	242.2	242.6	243.0	245.7	245.9	246.1	244.1	244.5	244.5	245.7	244.1
2018	243.2	242.6	243.1	243.0	243.9	246.8	246.2	245.3	243.8	243.6	243.6	244.3	244.1
Trade, Transportation, and Utilities													
2010	536.8	527.8	528.2	534.7	541.2	548.1	544.9	544.6	541.2	547.9	554.9	564.4	542.9
2011	541.1	533.9	533.9	540.3	544.3	551.1	548.9	548.7	547.7	551.8	559.5	567.0	547.4
2012	545.2	535.0	537.1	539.8	547.7	557.6	552.1	551.8	549.9	554.7	565.0	570.4	550.5
2013	547.8	539.0	540.7	546.2	553.8	563.2	557.3	557.9	555.7	558.3	567.4	575.4	555.2
2014	555.2	547.3	548.3	553.7	560.1	568.6	562.7	552.3	562.2	567.7	577.7	586.7	561.9
2015	563.0	550.5	552.7	559.2	567.0	576.3	572.3	571.9	568.0	572.7	581.4	588.3	568.6
2016	567.4	559.4	560.6	566.4	572.3	580.9	579.1	578.5	573.4	576.7	585.6	594.3	574.6
2017	574.0	564.0	564.1	570.4	576.4	587.5	584.1	583.5	579.0	582.2	592.0	598.9	579.7
2018	579.5	570.2	568.1	571.1	578.0	587.9	581.8	580.0	574.8	578.0	589.1	594.6	579.4
Wholesale Trade													
2010	120.7	120.1	120.3	120.7	121.7	122.5	122.9	122.7	121.4	122.2	122.0	122.0	121.6
2011	120.4	120.2	119.9	121.3	121.3	121.6	122.5	121.8	120.4	120.4	120.0	120.1	120.8
2012	119.1	118.8	119.2	120.3	120.9	122.1	122.2	122.3	121.0	121.7	121.7	121.6	120.9
2013	120.4	120.2	120.6	121.5	121.9	123.0	123.5	123.4	122.4	122.8	122.7	122.7	122.1
2014	121.4	121.1	121.3	122.4	122.8	123.8	124.0	123.7	122.6	122.8	122.9	123.0	122.7
2015	121.4	120.6	120.7	122.3	122.8	123.9	124.5	124.3	123.2	123.5	123.4	123.5	122.8
2016	122.3	122.0	122.1	123.5	123.8	124.8	126.0	125.9	124.6	124.8	124.4	124.5	124.1
2017	123.2	123.1	123.3	124.5	125.0	126.3	126.5	126.2	124.6	124.7	124.6	124.7	124.7
2018	123.5	123.5	123.7	123.7	124.1	125.6	125.1	124.7	123.3	122.9	123.3	123.5	123.9
Retail Trade													
2010	334.6	326.7	327.1	331.8	335.9	340.9	341.8	342.8	336.2	341.8	349.2	356.2	338.8
2011	338.8	332.0	331.9	336.1	339.0	344.0	345.0	346.5	341.7	346.2	354.4	360.4	343.0
2012	343.3	333.8	335.1	336.4	342.3	349.3	348.1	348.6	343.1	347.0	357.6	360.8	345.5
2013	343.6	334.9	336.1	339.8	345.4	351.8	349.9	351.6	345.3	347.6	356.6	362.7	347.1
2014	347.2	339.6	339.9	343.2	347.1	352.7	351.3	342.1	347.5	352.8	361.8	367.3	349.4
2015	351.3	340.4	342.2	345.7	351.3	357.7	357.1	357.5	349.8	354.3	362.9	368.0	353.2
2016	352.5	345.3	346.3	349.3	353.3	359.3	360.1	360.7	351.7	353.9	362.2	367.6	355.2
2017	353.5	344.3	344.2	348.5	352.0	359.3	359.9	360.3	351.9	355.0	364.2	368.0	355.1
2018	354.8	346.5	344.1	346.3	351.3	357.9	357.9	357.0	348.5	351.8	360.3	363.2	353.3
Transportation and Utilities													
2010	81.5	81.0	80.8	82.2	83.6	84.7	80.2	79.1	83.6	83.9	83.7	86.2	82.5
2011	81.9	81.7	82.1	82.9	84.0	85.5	81.4	80.4	85.6	85.2	85.1	86.5	83.5
2012	82.8	82.4	82.8	83.1	84.5	86.2	81.8	80.9	85.8	86.0	85.7	88.0	84.2
2013	83.8	83.9	84.0	84.9	86.5	88.4	83.9	82.9	88.0	87.9	88.1	90.0	86.0
2014	86.6	86.6	87.1	88.1	90.2	92.1	87.4	86.5	92.1	92.1	93.0	96.4	89.9
2015	90.3	89.5	89.8	91.2	92.9	94.7	90.7	90.1	95.0	94.9	95.1	96.8	92.6
2016	92.6	92.1	92.2	93.6	95.2	96.8	93.0	91.9	97.1	98.0	99.0	102.2	95.3
2017	97.3	96.6	96.6	97.4	99.4	101.9	97.7	97.0	102.5	102.5	103.2	106.2	99.9
2018	101.2	100.2	100.3	101.1	102.6	104.4	98.8	98.3	103.0	103.3	105.5	107.9	102.2
Information													
2010	85.0	85.1	85.2	85.4	86.0	87.0	86.1	85.6	85.0	83.8	84.1	84.5	85.2
2011	83.6	83.7	84.1	84.1	84.6	85.8	87.1	83.5	85.7	85.8	85.6	86.0	85.0
2012	85.7	85.4	85.7	86.0	86.6	88.5	89.6	88.9	86.4	86.5	86.0	85.9	86.8
2013	85.0	85.1	85.1	85.6	86.0	87.7	88.1	87.9	86.7	86.3	88.0	86.6	86.5
2014	85.0	85.2	85.3	86.0	86.9	88.2	88.6	88.2	87.1	87.2	87.4	87.8	86.9
2015	87.5	87.2	87.5	87.9	88.1	89.4	89.9	89.6	88.3	88.9	89.1	89.2	88.6
2016	88.9	89.0	88.4	89.4	86.3	90.2	91.1	91.7	90.6	90.6	90.6	90.6	89.8
2017	89.8	91.0	90.7	91.2	92.6	92.4	93.0	93.7	92.0	91.7	92.0	92.1	91.9
2018	90.7	91.4	90.4	90.3	90.0	91.7	92.2	93.1	91.3	92.1	92.7	92.1	91.5

1. Employment by Industry: Massachusetts, 2010–2018—*Continued*

(Numbers in thousands, not seasonally adjusted)

Industry and year	January	February	March	April	May	June	July	August	September	October	November	December	Annual average
Financial Activities													
2010	214.6	213.9	213.6	213.7	214.8	216.5	217.8	217.6	214.8	214.4	213.9	215.0	215.1
2011	212.4	212.1	212.1	213.0	213.3	215.5	217.4	217.4	214.7	213.9	213.1	213.5	214.0
2012	211.4	211.5	211.5	211.8	212.8	215.9	216.5	216.7	213.4	213.0	212.7	213.3	213.4
2013	211.1	211.2	211.6	211.9	213.2	216.1	216.8	217.4	213.8	213.5	213.4	214.1	213.7
2014	211.6	211.4	211.6	212.6	214.3	217.1	218.1	218.0	214.7	215.0	215.1	215.8	214.6
2015	213.5	213.0	213.1	214.1	215.6	218.7	222.0	222.2	218.0	218.6	218.9	219.1	217.2
2016	217.6	217.7	217.2	218.7	219.8	222.6	225.6	225.6	221.4	220.6	220.3	221.4	220.7
2017	218.8	219.0	218.8	219.4	220.7	225.0	225.8	225.8	222.0	221.6	221.0	222.0	221.7
2018	219.5	219.8	220.0	220.4	221.2	224.8	225.7	225.3	221.5	220.8	219.3	219.9	221.5
Professional and Business Services													
2010	452.9	453.0	455.1	467.9	469.9	474.7	479.3	478.4	472.9	478.0	476.8	475.5	469.5
2011	466.1	467.0	467.0	483.6	483.9	490.4	495.7	494.1	491.3	494.5	494.3	492.0	485.0
2012	478.2	478.5	484.7	496.0	498.3	507.8	508.7	508.7	504.6	507.0	507.8	503.3	498.6
2013	490.8	494.0	496.6	510.3	514.2	521.7	523.2	523.9	517.7	520.5	521.6	518.2	512.7
2014	504.0	505.0	506.8	521.5	525.8	533.9	537.1	538.2	533.2	537.0	536.3	533.4	526.0
2015	519.0	519.1	522.3	537.8	544.7	552.7	556.8	556.6	548.3	554.5	554.8	550.5	543.1
2016	534.5	536.7	539.0	556.1	558.4	567.2	574.5	574.1	566.5	569.4	569.4	565.5	559.3
2017	551.3	553.6	556.8	569.8	572.3	582.5	586.4	584.5	577.1	579.9	580.7	575.1	572.5
2018	562.0	564.3	568.1	579.9	583.7	594.9	598.2	598.2	589.0	591.3	591.2	585.5	583.9
Education and Health Services													
2010	675.0	686.1	689.3	688.9	683.0	666.5	669.8	667.8	681.7	694.2	697.8	697.4	683.1
2011	682.9	694.2	698.1	700.0	693.4	677.9	682.9	680.7	695.2	704.6	709.3	709.3	694.0
2012	696.5	708.2	712.4	711.7	706.9	694.5	694.6	693.2	706.4	717.3	721.8	722.0	707.1
2013	708.1	715.8	721.4	725.8	720.7	708.9	707.0	703.6	714.3	726.6	729.5	731.3	717.8
2014	711.5	726.5	731.9	740.3	735.4	724.0	727.9	725.3	734.4	749.9	755.2	755.8	734.8
2015	734.9	748.3	754.9	760.6	760.3	747.0	749.0	745.3	754.0	770.1	775.4	774.3	756.2
2016	756.3	772.0	775.8	781.1	778.7	761.4	770.9	766.6	778.5	787.1	791.4	791.6	776.0
2017	773.2	787.2	792.4	796.0	792.9	781.4	782.4	779.3	790.4	796.4	800.7	803.7	789.7
2018	780.2	797.7	801.5	805.0	800.1	787.4	790.1	784.5	796.7	809.2	812.7	809.4	797.9
Leisure and Hospitality													
2010	279.4	278.1	280.6	299.6	314.2	328.3	337.4	336.5	322.0	316.5	302.9	299.0	307.9
2011	284.9	283.6	289.5	307.0	319.9	337.2	347.4	347.1	330.9	322.9	310.4	306.0	315.6
2012	296.1	295.9	301.5	316.3	330.8	353.8	358.2	358.6	341.2	331.8	318.3	315.4	326.5
2013	303.1	300.7	309.3	325.0	341.7	361.5	365.1	367.5	350.1	345.2	331.1	326.3	335.6
2014	311.0	310.3	318.1	331.2	350.3	369.1	376.4	376.8	357.8	352.1	337.9	335.8	343.9
2015	319.8	314.6	322.6	337.7	360.2	377.0	385.8	384.3	363.2	356.9	344.5	342.7	350.8
2016	327.8	327.4	334.4	351.8	368.0	388.6	398.0	397.1	375.8	365.4	353.8	350.7	361.6
2017	336.3	334.3	341.4	358.5	374.3	399.5	404.3	403.1	380.5	374.9	362.8	360.0	369.2
2018	345.1	346.4	351.9	363.5	380.5	403.5	406.9	407.2	382.5	375.5	358.2	354.4	373.0
Other Services													
2010	115.6	115.3	116.2	117.8	119.3	122.8	125.5	124.4	118.6	117.8	117.6	117.7	119.1
2011	115.5	115.9	117.6	119.5	120.3	123.6	126.5	125.8	120.2	119.8	119.8	120.0	120.4
2012	117.4	117.5	119.2	120.8	122.2	126.9	128.6	127.5	123.4	123.2	123.3	123.5	122.8
2013	121.4	121.4	123.8	125.9	127.4	132.2	134.3	134.0	129.0	128.7	129.0	129.7	128.1
2014	127.2	127.7	130.2	132.0	133.8	138.6	140.6	139.8	133.7	133.4	133.2	133.4	133.6
2015	130.5	128.8	131.3	133.1	134.7	139.4	142.0	141.0	134.5	134.4	134.0	134.2	134.8
2016	131.4	131.4	133.4	135.5	136.7	141.2	143.8	142.9	135.7	135.8	135.3	135.5	136.6
2017	133.0	132.6	134.6	135.7	137.0	142.3	143.8	143.1	136.5	136.2	136.2	136.3	137.3
2018	134.5	134.6	135.8	137.7	139.1	144.7	145.1	144.4	137.2	138.1	137.1	138.0	138.9
Government													
2010	438.5	446.2	447.3	451.3	460.2	442.0	405.8	397.5	436.5	446.8	450.5	449.2	439.3
2011	432.8	445.2	445.6	445.4	447.5	436.0	401.9	393.4	436.3	443.1	443.8	445.7	434.7
2012	431.7	443.9	447.0	446.7	448.3	439.0	403.7	397.7	440.3	446.9	451.6	449.6	437.2
2013	433.8	451.0	452.4	456.6	456.1	444.4	408.7	402.0	441.7	453.9	458.1	458.5	443.1
2014	444.0	458.1	458.7	464.6	463.2	451.0	417.1	409.2	454.0	462.8	469.7	467.4	451.7
2015	444.3	459.2	463.2	465.5	461.3	454.4	419.3	408.2	448.7	460.4	463.7	465.1	451.1
2016	444.8	459.3	466.0	463.8	464.1	454.1	422.3	413.9	457.7	463.1	470.5	466.3	453.8
2017	449.0	460.7	461.1	463.4	463.4	457.0	419.5	411.8	452.5	462.0	465.6	465.0	452.6
2018	446.6	461.6	460.1	462.6	463.7	459.8	420.3	411.6	457.8	467.3	471.4	471.4	454.5

2. Average Weekly Hours by Selected Industry: Massachusetts, 2014–2018

(Not seasonally adjusted)

Industry and year	January	February	March	April	May	June	July	August	September	October	November	December	Annual average
Total Private													
2014	33.0	33.1	33.3	33.2	33.2	33.5	33.2	33.4	33.4	33.3	33.7	33.4	33.3
2015	33.1	33.0	33.4	33.3	33.5	33.5	33.6	33.9	33.5	33.5	33.8	33.7	33.5
2016	33.2	33.0	33.2	33.3	33.7	33.5	33.6	33.5	33.5	33.8	33.4	33.5	33.5
2017	33.6	33.0	33.0	33.6	33.4	33.4	33.7	33.5	33.6	33.7	33.5	33.5	33.5
2018	33.1	33.2	32.5	33.5	33.4	33.4	33.7	33.5	33.6	33.2	33.3	33.8	33.4
Goods Producing													
2014	39.2	38.8	39.6	39.7	39.6	39.5	39.1	39.4	40.0	39.3	39.9	39.5	39.5
2015	39.3	38.0	39.5	39.2	39.6	39.9	39.5	39.9	38.8	39.4	39.5	40.3	39.4
2016	39.6	38.9	39.6	39.4	40.0	40.1	39.9	39.8	39.9	39.6	39.5	39.6	39.7
2017	39.7	38.2	38.4	38.9	39.1	39.3	39.1	39.4	39.6	39.2	39.7	39.4	39.2
2018	38.9	39.0	37.3	39.2	39.5	39.8	39.2	39.3	38.9	38.6	38.9	40.2	39.1
Construction													
2014	37.6	36.8	37.5	38.3	38.5	37.8	37.8	37.8	38.9	37.3	37.7	37.3	37.8
2015	37.4	35.1	37.8	37.7	38.9	39.3	38.9	39.2	37.5	38.0	37.7	39.2	38.1
2016	38.1	36.5	38.1	37.9	39.0	39.6	39.2	38.9	39.5	38.4	38.0	37.9	38.5
2017	37.8	36.5	36.3	38.0	38.1	38.5	38.0	38.6	38.7	37.9	38.7	38.5	38.0
2018	37.3	37.5	34.8	38.2	39.1	39.7	39.0	39.2	38.6	38.3	38.5	40.4	38.4
Manufacturing													
2014	39.8	39.6	40.4	40.2	40.0	40.3	39.6	40.2	40.4	40.3	41.1	40.9	40.2
2015	40.5	39.7	40.5	40.1	40.1	40.3	40.0	40.5	39.8	40.1	40.5	40.7	40.2
2016	40.2	40.0	40.3	40.1	40.4	40.3	40.3	40.4	40.2	40.4	40.5	40.6	40.3
2017	40.7	39.6	39.9	40.3	40.4	40.4	40.4	40.4	40.4	40.7	40.4	40.6	40.4
2018	40.2	40.1	39.1	39.9	39.7	39.7	39.2	39.3	39.2	38.9	39.2	40.1	39.5
Trade, Transportation, and Utilities													
2014	32.5	32.2	32.5	32.7	32.9	33.1	33.1	33.3	33.2	33.0	33.1	33.5	32.9
2015	32.4	32.1	32.7	32.9	33.1	33.3	33.5	33.1	33.1	32.9	33.3	33.6	33.0
2016	32.6	32.4	32.7	33.0	33.3	33.5	33.6	33.4	33.8	33.8	33.7	34.5	33.4
2017	33.3	32.8	32.9	33.5	33.4	33.3	33.6	33.3	33.4	33.3	33.4	33.9	33.3
2018	32.6	32.4	31.7	33.0	33.3	33.0	33.0	33.0	33.1	32.6	33.0	33.0	32.8
Information													
2014	36.4	37.1	37.5	36.2	36.3	37.7	36.5	36.7	36.7	36.7	38.1	36.4	36.9
2015	37.1	38.5	38.5	37.2	37.9	37.3	37.7	39.1	37.6	37.5	38.7	37.4	37.9
2016	38.2	38.1	38.1	38.1	39.1	37.7	37.8	38.2	38.0	39.6	38.4	37.8	38.3
2017	39.6	38.2	37.9	39.5	38.2	38.0	39.6	37.7	38.0	39.1	37.5	37.8	38.4
2018	37.9	37.7	37.6	39.4	37.8	37.9	39.6	38.1	39.8	38.3	38.5	39.9	38.5
Financial Activities													
2014	36.2	37.1	37.1	36.6	36.5	37.0	36.2	36.3	36.5	36.5	37.0	36.4	36.6
2015	36.5	37.1	37.1	36.7	36.6	36.5	36.7	37.4	36.7	36.7	37.3	36.6	36.8
2016	36.2	36.3	36.5	36.2	37.1	36.7	36.8	36.8	36.8	37.7	37.0	37.3	36.8
2017	37.9	37.5	37.2	38.0	37.3	37.1	38.0	37.1	37.5	38.1	37.8	37.8	37.6
2018	37.7	37.7	37.5	38.1	37.2	37.6	38.1	37.5	38.3	37.6	37.8	38.3	37.8
Professional and Business Services													
2014	35.8	36.3	36.3	36.0	36.1	36.6	35.9	35.8	35.8	35.8	36.8	35.6	36.1
2015	35.4	36.0	36.1	35.9	36.2	36.1	35.8	36.8	36.0	36.3	37.1	36.7	36.2
2016	36.3	35.7	36.1	36.2	37.0	36.4	36.1	36.0	35.9	36.7	35.9	35.8	36.2
2017	36.1	35.4	35.2	36.4	35.7	35.9	36.2	35.7	36.0	36.4	36.0	36.1	35.9
2018	35.7	36.1	35.5	36.9	36.3	36.4	36.8	36.3	36.8	35.9	35.8	37.2	36.3
Education and Health Services													
2014	31.8	31.8	31.6	31.6	31.5	31.8	31.6	31.6	31.8	32.0	32.0	31.9	31.8
2015	31.8	31.7	31.7	31.5	31.5	31.7	31.8	31.9	32.1	32.1	31.9	31.7	31.8
2016	31.5	31.5	31.5	31.6	31.6	31.4	31.8	31.7	31.7	31.8	31.5	31.6	31.6
2017	32.0	31.7	31.6	31.7	31.7	31.6	31.8	31.9	31.9	32.0	31.7	31.5	31.8
2018	31.6	31.5	31.0	31.5	31.3	31.4	31.7	31.6	31.5	31.6	31.7	31.5	31.5
Leisure and Hospitality													
2014	23.9	24.0	24.8	25.1	25.5	25.3	25.8	26.0	25.5	25.2	25.0	25.0	25.1
2015	24.6	24.1	25.3	25.4	26.1	25.6	26.2	26.2	25.7	25.4	25.2	25.1	25.4
2016	24.2	24.8	24.6	25.1	25.4	25.3	25.8	25.4	25.2	25.0	25.0	24.2	25.0
2017	24.0	23.9	24.5	25.3	25.4	25.5	26.0	26.2	25.7	25.4	24.8	24.5	25.1
2018	23.7	24.2	23.7	24.6	24.7	24.9	25.7	25.7	25.0	24.8	24.2	24.6	24.7
Other Services													
2014	27.4	27.9	28.3	28.3	28.2	28.0	29.3	29.7	28.9	28.9	29.1	29.0	28.6
2015	29.1	28.9	29.1	29.1	28.7	28.6	29.9	30.4	29.7	29.0	29.8	29.6	29.3
2016	29.5	28.8	28.8	28.7	28.8	28.8	30.2	30.4	29.2	29.0	28.5	28.4	29.1
2017	28.6	28.2	28.7	29.1	29.1	29.0	30.5	30.1	29.6	29.3	29.5	29.9	29.3
2018	29.8	29.9	29.2	29.7	30.1	29.6	30.8	31.2	31.0	30.6	30.8	30.7	30.3

3. Average Hourly Earnings by Selected Industry: Massachusetts, 2014–2018

(Dollars, not seasonally adjusted)

Industry and year	January	February	March	April	May	June	July	August	September	October	November	December	Annual average
Total Private													
2014	29.50	29.87	29.67	29.35	29.22	29.16	29.04	29.27	29.56	29.77	30.22	29.82	29.54
2015	30.50	30.59	30.39	30.25	30.20	29.95	29.91	30.23	30.41	30.82	31.22	30.98	30.46
2016	31.39	31.27	31.07	31.09	31.10	30.76	30.85	30.76	31.35	31.85	31.73	31.82	31.25
2017	32.29	32.30	32.18	32.32	31.73	31.64	31.91	31.54	32.10	32.48	32.64	32.60	32.14
2018	32.69	33.09	33.23	33.32	32.98	32.90	33.01	32.80	33.55	33.42	33.46	33.82	33.19
Goods Producing													
2014	30.66	30.54	30.27	30.37	30.23	30.40	31.08	30.84	30.80	30.96	30.89	31.51	30.72
2015	31.74	31.70	31.55	31.67	31.67	31.44	31.68	32.08	31.81	32.33	32.45	32.34	31.88
2016	31.90	31.95	32.16	31.95	31.95	31.95	32.16	32.16	32.27	32.34	32.01	32.29	32.09
2017	32.64	33.04	33.39	33.69	33.55	33.71	33.59	33.75	34.25	34.26	34.47	34.81	33.78
2018	34.52	34.55	35.05	34.79	34.89	35.01	35.07	34.72	35.22	35.58	35.98	34.94	35.03
Construction													
2014	35.22	34.89	34.59	34.51	33.89	34.08	34.23	34.54	34.46	34.48	35.03	35.70	34.62
2015	36.38	36.43	36.57	36.70	36.11	35.59	35.98	36.19	35.82	36.68	36.64	37.17	36.34
2016	36.52	36.39	36.69	36.53	36.74	36.59	36.61	36.64	36.56	36.44	36.41	37.14	36.61
2017	37.50	37.23	37.41	37.31	36.91	37.26	36.92	36.63	36.86	36.31	36.56	37.09	36.98
2018	36.62	36.75	37.43	36.65	37.13	37.15	37.67	37.19	37.69	38.36	39.41	36.65	37.41
Manufacturing													
2014	28.60	28.61	28.35	28.47	28.45	28.41	29.36	28.77	28.71	29.00	28.60	29.26	28.72
2015	29.41	29.51	29.16	29.12	29.18	29.03	29.11	29.57	29.44	29.60	29.80	29.31	29.35
2016	29.16	29.46	29.49	29.19	29.00	28.89	29.24	29.26	29.50	29.78	29.35	29.49	29.32
2017	29.96	30.40	30.89	31.35	31.37	31.40	31.39	31.42	32.14	32.73	32.92	33.14	31.60
2018	33.02	32.99	33.43	33.39	33.10	33.25	32.92	32.81	33.27	33.41	33.34	33.73	33.22
Trade, Transportation, and Utilities													
2014	24.89	25.05	24.99	25.11	24.81	24.68	24.83	24.36	24.57	24.84	24.94	24.36	24.78
2015	25.20	24.72	24.82	25.08	24.78	24.47	25.02	24.61	24.73	25.45	25.32	25.18	24.95
2016	26.08	25.60	25.56	25.31	25.71	25.87	25.92	26.00	26.34	26.91	26.74	26.22	26.03
2017	26.78	26.55	26.52	26.52	26.07	26.01	26.42	25.81	26.28	26.79	26.71	26.21	26.39
2018	26.63	27.01	27.24	27.08	27.03	26.89	27.42	27.14	27.81	27.91	27.56	27.12	27.24
Information													
2014	43.62	42.96	42.16	41.30	42.66	41.93	41.55	43.13	42.23	43.36	43.73	43.29	42.66
2015	45.49	45.80	45.35	45.78	45.23	45.88	44.95	43.97	45.14	45.64	46.01	46.36	45.46
2016	47.50	46.54	45.99	45.52	44.89	45.19	44.46	43.43	44.81	45.73	45.28	45.45	45.39
2017	47.10	45.62	45.55	46.24	44.67	45.10	46.53	45.59	45.00	45.89	45.54	46.69	45.80
2018	46.21	46.96	47.54	47.36	46.98	47.93	47.57	47.68	48.28	48.77	48.04	48.68	47.68
Financial Activities													
2014	34.37	35.49	35.52	36.14	36.23	34.76	35.13	35.61	36.86	36.65	37.18	36.48	35.87
2015	37.54	37.25	37.81	37.86	37.42	37.61	37.68	38.54	38.06	38.79	39.10	38.95	38.06
2016	40.10	39.78	38.90	40.22	39.90	38.42	40.26	39.47	40.03	41.05	40.92	40.25	39.95
2017	41.01	41.22	41.90	42.22	41.08	41.22	41.68	41.73	42.30	42.57	42.73	42.31	41.83
2018	41.91	42.59	42.39	43.05	43.25	42.92	42.81	42.43	42.63	42.49	43.22	44.16	42.82
Professional and Business Services													
2014	37.16	37.71	37.94	36.60	36.63	36.81	36.49	37.28	37.44	37.66	38.32	38.08	37.34
2015	38.89	39.18	39.15	38.28	38.32	37.77	37.93	38.70	38.70	38.71	39.33	38.65	38.63
2016	39.52	39.98	39.75	39.67	39.76	38.97	39.03	38.92	39.88	40.25	39.92	40.34	39.66
2017	41.61	41.20	41.20	41.25	40.43	40.05	40.57	40.10	40.23	40.72	40.67	40.04	40.66
2018	40.96	41.51	41.66	41.89	41.21	40.74	41.15	41.11	41.94	41.35	41.63	42.70	41.49
Education and Health Services													
2014	28.46	28.91	28.55	28.35	28.16	28.40	28.11	28.54	28.62	28.76	29.34	28.66	28.58
2015	28.90	28.84	28.40	28.41	28.88	28.73	28.32	28.58	29.13	29.23	29.96	29.89	28.95
2016	29.46	29.22	28.85	29.20	29.15	29.07	29.21	28.92	29.28	29.56	29.88	30.19	29.34
2017	29.42	29.74	29.20	29.38	29.00	29.22	29.44	28.97	29.65	29.98	30.48	31.07	29.63
2018	30.23	30.69	30.49	30.87	30.52	30.96	30.94	30.63	31.00	30.59	30.23	30.91	30.67
Leisure and Hospitality													
2014	15.53	15.66	15.56	15.46	15.48	15.31	15.21	15.35	15.53	15.59	15.72	15.71	15.50
2015	15.66	15.82	15.70	15.63	15.75	15.62	15.72	15.67	15.77	15.91	15.78	15.72	15.73
2016	15.77	15.88	16.06	16.01	15.89	15.88	15.87	16.22	16.65	16.82	16.96	17.30	16.27
2017	17.22	17.42	17.42	17.30	17.50	17.20	17.15	17.21	17.58	17.66	17.81	17.83	17.44
2018	17.78	18.03	18.13	17.94	18.05	17.50	17.44	17.66	18.27	18.57	18.67	19.10	18.08
Other Services													
2014	22.38	22.78	22.62	22.61	22.66	22.71	21.92	22.08	23.33	23.38	23.52	23.71	22.80
2015	23.97	24.66	24.44	24.54	24.67	24.49	23.45	23.81	25.31	25.59	25.75	26.12	24.72
2016	26.00	26.55	26.21	26.08	26.69	26.14	25.05	25.03	26.86	27.18	27.02	27.19	26.31
2017	27.62	28.04	27.85	27.95	27.86	27.16	26.41	26.32	27.74	27.31	27.53	27.51	27.42
2018	27.94	27.94	28.45	28.33	28.01	27.64	26.84	27.14	29.04	29.35	28.91	29.25	28.23

4. Average Weekly Earnings by Selected Industry: Massachusetts, 2014–2018

(Dollars, not seasonally adjusted)

Industry and year	January	February	March	April	May	June	July	August	September	October	November	December	Annual average
Total Private													
2014	973.50	988.70	988.01	974.42	970.10	976.86	964.13	977.62	987.30	991.34	1,018.41	995.99	983.68
2015	1,009.55	1,009.47	1,015.03	1,007.33	1,011.70	1,003.33	1,004.98	1,024.80	1,018.74	1,032.47	1,055.24	1,044.03	1,020.41
2016	1,042.15	1,031.91	1,031.52	1,035.30	1,048.07	1,030.46	1,036.56	1,030.46	1,050.23	1,076.53	1,059.78	1,065.97	1,046.88
2017	1,084.94	1,065.90	1,061.94	1,085.95	1,059.78	1,056.78	1,075.37	1,056.59	1,078.56	1,094.58	1,093.44	1,092.10	1,076.69
2018	1,082.04	1,098.59	1,079.98	1,116.22	1,101.53	1,098.86	1,112.44	1,098.80	1,127.28	1,109.54	1,114.22	1,143.12	1,108.55
Goods Producing													
2014	1,201.87	1,184.95	1,198.69	1,205.69	1,197.11	1,200.80	1,215.23	1,215.10	1,232.00	1,216.73	1,232.51	1,244.65	1,213.44
2015	1,247.38	1,204.60	1,246.23	1,241.46	1,254.13	1,254.46	1,251.36	1,279.99	1,234.23	1,273.80	1,281.78	1,303.30	1,256.07
2016	1,263.24	1,242.86	1,273.54	1,258.83	1,278.00	1,281.20	1,283.18	1,279.97	1,287.57	1,280.66	1,264.40	1,278.68	1,273.97
2017	1,295.81	1,262.13	1,282.18	1,310.54	1,311.81	1,324.80	1,313.37	1,329.75	1,356.30	1,342.99	1,368.46	1,371.51	1,324.18
2018	1,342.83	1,347.45	1,307.37	1,363.77	1,378.16	1,393.40	1,374.74	1,364.50	1,370.06	1,373.39	1,399.62	1,404.59	1,369.67
Construction													
2014	1,324.27	1,283.95	1,297.13	1,321.73	1,304.77	1,288.22	1,293.89	1,305.61	1,340.49	1,286.10	1,320.63	1,331.61	1,308.64
2015	1,360.61	1,278.69	1,382.35	1,383.59	1,404.68	1,398.69	1,399.62	1,418.65	1,343.25	1,393.84	1,381.33	1,457.06	1,384.55
2016	1,391.41	1,328.24	1,397.89	1,384.49	1,432.86	1,448.96	1,435.11	1,425.30	1,444.12	1,399.30	1,383.58	1,407.61	1,409.49
2017	1,417.50	1,358.90	1,357.98	1,417.78	1,406.27	1,434.51	1,402.96	1,413.92	1,426.48	1,376.15	1,414.87	1,427.97	1,405.24
2018	1,365.93	1,378.13	1,302.56	1,400.03	1,451.78	1,474.86	1,469.13	1,457.85	1,454.83	1,469.19	1,517.29	1,480.66	1,436.54
Manufacturing													
2014	1,138.28	1,132.96	1,145.34	1,144.49	1,138.00	1,144.92	1,162.66	1,156.55	1,159.88	1,168.70	1,175.46	1,196.73	1,154.54
2015	1,191.11	1,171.55	1,180.98	1,167.71	1,170.12	1,169.91	1,164.40	1,197.59	1,171.71	1,186.96	1,206.90	1,192.92	1,179.87
2016	1,172.23	1,178.40	1,188.45	1,170.52	1,171.60	1,164.27	1,178.37	1,182.10	1,185.90	1,203.11	1,188.68	1,197.29	1,181.60
2017	1,219.67	1,204.14	1,233.13	1,262.46	1,267.66	1,271.70	1,268.78	1,269.68	1,307.78	1,322.29	1,336.55	1,335.54	1,276.64
2018	1,327.40	1,322.90	1,307.11	1,332.26	1,314.07	1,320.03	1,290.46	1,289.43	1,304.18	1,299.65	1,306.93	1,352.57	1,312.19
Trade, Transportation, and Utilities													
2014	808.93	806.61	812.18	821.10	816.25	816.91	821.87	811.19	815.72	819.72	825.51	816.06	815.26
2015	816.48	793.51	811.61	825.13	820.22	814.85	838.17	814.59	818.56	837.31	843.16	846.05	823.35
2016	850.21	829.44	835.81	835.23	856.14	866.65	870.91	868.40	890.29	909.56	901.14	904.59	869.40
2017	891.77	870.84	872.51	888.42	870.74	866.13	887.71	859.47	877.75	892.11	892.11	888.52	893.47
2018	868.14	875.12	863.51	893.64	900.10	887.37	904.86	895.62	920.51	909.87	909.48	894.96	893.47
Information													
2014	1,587.77	1,593.82	1,581.00	1,495.06	1,548.56	1,580.76	1,516.58	1,582.87	1,549.84	1,591.31	1,666.11	1,575.76	1,574.15
2015	1,687.68	1,763.30	1,745.98	1,703.02	1,714.22	1,711.32	1,694.62	1,719.23	1,697.26	1,711.50	1,780.59	1,733.86	1,722.93
2016	1,814.50	1,773.17	1,752.22	1,734.31	1,755.20	1,703.66	1,680.59	1,659.03	1,702.78	1,810.91	1,738.75	1,718.01	1,738.44
2017	1,865.16	1,742.68	1,726.35	1,826.48	1,706.39	1,713.80	1,842.59	1,718.74	1,710.00	1,794.30	1,707.75	1,764.88	1,758.72
2018	1,751.36	1,770.39	1,787.50	1,865.98	1,775.84	1,816.55	1,883.77	1,816.61	1,921.54	1,867.89	1,849.54	1,942.33	1,835.68
Financial Activities													
2014	1,244.19	1,316.68	1,317.79	1,322.72	1,322.40	1,286.12	1,271.71	1,292.64	1,345.39	1,337.73	1,375.66	1,327.87	1,312.84
2015	1,370.21	1,381.98	1,402.75	1,389.46	1,369.57	1,372.77	1,382.86	1,441.40	1,396.80	1,423.59	1,458.43	1,425.57	1,400.61
2016	1,451.62	1,444.01	1,419.85	1,455.96	1,480.29	1,410.01	1,481.57	1,452.50	1,473.10	1,547.59	1,514.04	1,501.33	1,470.16
2017	1,554.28	1,545.75	1,558.68	1,604.36	1,532.28	1,529.26	1,583.84	1,548.18	1,586.25	1,621.92	1,615.19	1,599.32	1,572.81
2018	1,580.01	1,605.64	1,589.63	1,640.21	1,608.90	1,613.79	1,631.06	1,591.13	1,632.73	1,597.62	1,633.72	1,691.33	1,618.60
Professional and Business Services													
2014	1,330.33	1,368.87	1,377.22	1,317.60	1,322.34	1,347.25	1,309.99	1,334.62	1,340.35	1,348.23	1,410.18	1,355.65	1,347.97
2015	1,376.71	1,410.48	1,413.32	1,374.25	1,387.18	1,363.50	1,357.89	1,424.16	1,393.20	1,405.17	1,459.14	1,418.46	1,398.41
2016	1,434.58	1,427.29	1,434.98	1,436.05	1,471.12	1,418.51	1,408.98	1,401.12	1,431.69	1,477.18	1,433.13	1,444.17	1,435.69
2017	1,502.12	1,458.48	1,450.24	1,501.50	1,443.35	1,437.80	1,468.63	1,431.57	1,448.28	1,482.21	1,464.12	1,445.44	1,459.69
2018	1,462.27	1,498.51	1,478.93	1,545.74	1,495.92	1,482.94	1,514.32	1,492.29	1,543.39	1,484.47	1,490.35	1,588.44	1,506.09
Education and Health Services													
2014	905.03	919.34	902.18	895.86	887.04	903.12	888.28	901.86	910.12	920.32	938.88	914.25	908.84
2015	919.02	914.23	900.28	894.92	909.72	910.74	900.58	911.70	935.07	938.28	955.72	947.51	920.61
2016	927.99	920.43	908.78	922.72	921.14	912.80	928.88	916.76	928.18	940.01	941.22	954.00	927.14
2017	941.44	942.76	922.72	931.35	919.30	923.35	936.19	924.14	945.84	959.36	966.22	978.71	942.23
2018	955.27	966.74	945.19	972.41	955.28	972.14	980.80	967.91	976.50	966.64	958.29	973.67	966.11
Leisure and Hospitality													
2014	371.17	375.84	385.89	388.05	394.74	387.34	392.42	399.10	396.02	392.87	393.00	392.75	389.05
2015	385.24	381.26	397.21	397.00	411.08	399.87	411.86	410.55	405.29	404.11	397.66	394.57	399.54
2016	381.63	393.82	395.08	401.85	403.61	401.76	409.45	411.99	419.58	420.50	424.00	418.66	406.75
2017	413.28	416.34	426.79	437.69	444.50	438.60	445.90	450.90	451.81	448.56	441.69	436.84	437.74
2018	421.39	436.33	429.68	441.32	445.84	435.75	448.21	453.86	456.75	460.54	451.81	469.86	446.58
Other Services													
2014	613.21	635.56	640.15	639.86	639.01	635.88	642.26	655.78	674.24	675.68	684.43	687.59	652.08
2015	697.53	712.67	711.20	714.11	708.03	700.41	701.16	723.82	751.71	742.11	767.35	773.15	724.30
2016	767.00	764.64	754.85	748.50	768.67	752.83	756.51	760.91	784.31	788.22	770.07	772.20	765.62
2017	789.93	790.73	799.30	813.35	810.73	787.64	805.51	792.23	821.10	800.18	812.14	822.55	803.41
2018	832.61	835.41	830.74	841.40	843.10	818.14	826.67	846.77	900.24	898.11	890.43	897.98	855.37

MICHIGAN
At a Glance

Population:
  2010 census: 9,883,640
  2018 estimate: 9,995,915

Percent change in population:
  2010–2018: 1.1%

Percent change in total nonfarm employment:
  2010–2018: 14.4%

Industry with the largest growth in employment, 2010–2018 (percent):
  Construction, 39.1%

Industry with the largest decline or smallest growth in employment, 2010–2018 (percent):
  Government, -4.6%

Civilian labor force:
  2010: 4,798,954
  2018: 4,902,069

Unemployment rate and rank among states (highest to lowest):
  2010: 12.6%, 2nd
  2018: 4.1%, 16th

Over-the-year change in unemployment rates:
  2016–2017: -0.4%
  2017–2018: -0.5%

Employment by Industry: Michigan, 2018

- Other 9%
- Financial activities 5%
- Leisure and hospitality 10%
- Manufacturing 14%
- Government 14%
- Trade, transportation, and utilities 18%
- Education and health services 15%
- Professional and business services 15%

1. Employment by Industry: Michigan, 2010–2018

(Numbers in thousands, not seasonally adjusted)

Industry and year	January	February	March	April	May	June	July	August	September	October	November	December	Annual average
Total Nonfarm													
2010	3,752.2	3,768.7	3,781.2	3,839.0	3,896.1	3,908.1	3,846.1	3,851.5	3,913.8	3,941.7	3,942.5	3,922.7	3,863.6
2011	3,832.0	3,847.0	3,874.4	3,926.4	3,972.9	3,986.0	3,931.6	3,952.6	4,012.7	4,033.8	4,038.6	4,017.4	3,952.1
2012	3,929.6	3,948.5	3,976.6	4,015.6	4,061.2	4,068.9	4,007.2	4,026.5	4,076.6	4,095.2	4,102.9	4,093.2	4,033.5
2013	4,004.4	4,029.4	4,051.5	4,068.6	4,138.5	4,149.9	4,072.6	4,105.9	4,156.7	4,181.3	4,185.7	4,169.6	4,109.5
2014	4,065.1	4,098.7	4,114.9	4,136.4	4,212.1	4,242.6	4,163.2	4,180.3	4,215.7	4,245.6	4,253.9	4,251.7	4,181.7
2015	4,141.4	4,157.7	4,173.8	4,205.8	4,274.4	4,289.9	4,225.2	4,237.3	4,275.8	4,313.0	4,316.1	4,307.5	4,243.2
2016	4,214.6	4,232.9	4,249.9	4,300.2	4,341.7	4,364.5	4,308.8	4,315.3	4,364.4	4,379.7	4,394.4	4,370.0	4,319.7
2017	4,281.8	4,297.2	4,317.4	4,345.8	4,400.2	4,427.5	4,341.6	4,363.9	4,400.6	4,417.9	4,427.0	4,407.9	4,369.1
2018	4,319.2	4,348.6	4,375.2	4,391.9	4,448.2	4,484.8	4,401.1	4,423.3	4,445.4	4,470.2	4,468.3	4,447.3	4,418.6
Total Private													
2010	3,110.5	3,113.3	3,125.3	3,180.5	3,239.0	3,274.5	3,261.4	3,275.5	3,283.7	3,295.6	3,294.3	3,282.6	3,228.0
2011	3,207.0	3,210.8	3,236.0	3,288.8	3,349.4	3,376.6	3,366.5	3,390.9	3,393.0	3,401.8	3,403.9	3,391.5	3,334.7
2012	3,313.8	3,320.6	3,348.3	3,388.0	3,445.3	3,472.8	3,451.7	3,470.8	3,464.3	3,472.3	3,476.6	3,475.7	3,425.0
2013	3,401.3	3,413.4	3,436.5	3,453.2	3,534.3	3,564.1	3,525.6	3,560.9	3,552.0	3,564.0	3,567.4	3,558.9	3,511.0
2014	3,468.0	3,487.9	3,503.7	3,525.1	3,612.8	3,657.8	3,617.1	3,634.9	3,616.4	3,630.3	3,636.2	3,640.9	3,585.9
2015	3,546.7	3,549.4	3,564.2	3,596.3	3,674.2	3,709.4	3,679.8	3,693.1	3,681.1	3,697.6	3,700.0	3,696.3	3,649.0
2016	3,619.2	3,622.7	3,635.9	3,686.3	3,743.4	3,777.7	3,756.7	3,763.1	3,755.2	3,760.6	3,769.9	3,752.8	3,720.3
2017	3,680.8	3,683.5	3,701.3	3,729.9	3,795.0	3,834.1	3,784.8	3,808.4	3,785.4	3,793.5	3,800.6	3,787.0	3,765.4
2018	3,716.7	3,728.6	3,752.9	3,772.1	3,841.4	3,889.9	3,842.1	3,859.7	3,829.7	3,845.2	3,840.8	3,827.0	3,812.2
Goods Producing													
2010	559.6	556.8	559.7	577.7	593.3	605.8	608.8	609.4	619.4	622.5	618.0	608.2	594.9
2011	593.3	593.7	599.0	615.3	633.3	647.6	647.7	658.6	657.9	658.5	658.1	651.9	634.6
2012	636.5	635.0	642.0	652.0	666.9	678.6	680.3	685.0	683.8	683.0	679.0	675.8	666.5
2013	659.0	659.8	664.9	668.5	690.2	702.4	696.0	710.5	710.0	712.2	710.3	698.9	690.2
2014	682.4	691.3	693.7	701.5	725.7	746.9	741.5	749.1	741.1	742.1	743.0	739.2	724.8
2015	718.0	717.7	719.8	730.7	749.9	764.3	760.8	766.5	764.7	762.5	762.1	754.7	747.6
2016	742.7	739.5	741.9	759.4	770.2	784.0	779.7	781.3	781.2	780.4	783.6	771.7	768.0
2017	761.5	760.8	763.5	774.5	790.6	803.5	789.8	803.7	796.1	796.8	795.9	788.1	785.4
2018	772.7	778.6	785.0	793.6	810.3	823.9	817.5	824.3	819.6	820.9	816.2	812.0	806.2
Service-Providing													
2010	3,192.6	3,211.9	3,221.5	3,261.3	3,302.8	3,302.3	3,237.3	3,242.1	3,294.4	3,319.2	3,324.5	3,314.5	3,268.7
2011	3,238.7	3,253.3	3,275.4	3,311.1	3,339.6	3,338.4	3,283.9	3,294.0	3,354.8	3,375.3	3,380.5	3,365.5	3,317.5
2012	3,293.1	3,313.5	3,334.6	3,363.6	3,394.3	3,390.3	3,326.9	3,341.5	3,392.8	3,412.2	3,423.9	3,417.4	3,367.0
2013	3,345.4	3,369.6	3,386.6	3,400.1	3,448.3	3,447.5	3,376.6	3,395.4	3,446.7	3,469.1	3,475.4	3,470.7	3,419.3
2014	3,382.7	3,407.4	3,421.2	3,434.9	3,486.4	3,495.7	3,421.7	3,431.2	3,474.6	3,503.5	3,510.9	3,512.5	3,456.9
2015	3,423.4	3,440.0	3,454.0	3,475.1	3,524.5	3,525.6	3,464.4	3,470.8	3,511.1	3,550.5	3,554.0	3,552.8	3,495.5
2016	3,471.9	3,493.4	3,508.0	3,540.8	3,571.5	3,580.5	3,529.1	3,534.0	3,583.2	3,599.3	3,610.8	3,598.3	3,551.7
2017	3,520.3	3,536.4	3,553.9	3,571.3	3,609.6	3,624.0	3,551.8	3,560.2	3,604.5	3,621.1	3,631.1	3,619.8	3,583.7
2018	3,546.5	3,570.0	3,590.2	3,598.3	3,637.9	3,660.9	3,583.6	3,599.0	3,625.8	3,649.3	3,652.1	3,635.3	3,612.4
Mining and Logging													
2010	6.6	6.5	6.2	6.8	7.2	7.5	7.6	7.6	7.5	7.5	7.3	7.0	7.1
2011	6.7	6.7	6.7	7.0	7.5	7.8	7.9	7.9	7.8	7.9	7.8	7.6	7.4
2012	7.4	7.5	7.3	7.7	8.0	8.0	8.0	8.1	8.2	8.1	7.9	7.7	7.8
2013	7.5	7.5	7.5	7.5	8.1	8.3	8.4	8.5	8.4	8.4	8.3	8.0	8.0
2014	7.8	7.9	7.9	7.9	8.3	8.6	8.6	8.6	8.5	8.5	8.3	8.1	8.3
2015	7.7	7.6	7.5	7.5	7.8	8.0	7.7	7.7	7.7	7.7	7.7	7.4	7.7
2016	7.1	7.0	7.0	7.1	7.2	7.4	7.4	7.4	7.2	7.4	7.0	6.9	7.2
2017	6.6	6.5	6.6	7.0	7.3	7.5	7.5	7.5	7.4	7.4	7.3	7.1	7.1
2018	6.6	6.8	6.9	7.0	7.3	7.6	7.5	7.5	7.5	7.4	7.2	6.9	7.2
Construction													
2010	102.8	100.0	103.4	114.5	123.7	129.1	133.6	134.5	133.8	134.5	129.4	120.4	121.6
2011	108.0	104.9	107.4	114.5	126.1	133.9	138.9	139.6	137.6	135.7	132.3	124.6	125.3
2012	113.2	110.1	114.0	122.1	129.9	135.4	137.9	138.7	138.5	137.6	133.1	127.9	128.2
2013	118.3	115.4	117.2	121.1	135.7	140.4	144.5	145.7	144.7	145.2	140.7	133.0	133.5
2014	122.8	122.2	122.8	128.9	144.0	151.5	153.6	155.5	154.9	153.7	149.4	142.4	141.8
2015	130.6	128.6	131.4	140.5	152.0	158.4	159.1	159.6	158.4	158.8	154.5	147.3	148.3
2016	137.2	135.4	138.9	149.4	159.6	163.5	165.4	165.9	165.4	165.8	162.6	151.9	155.1
2017	143.5	142.0	145.6	154.9	166.7	172.8	174.4	175.2	173.1	172.1	167.3	158.6	162.2
2018	149.3	149.1	153.4	160.6	174.0	180.8	181.8	182.2	178.4	179.2	173.5	168.5	169.2

1. Employment by Industry: Michigan, 2010–2018—*Continued*

(Numbers in thousands, not seasonally adjusted)

Industry and year	January	February	March	April	May	June	July	August	September	October	November	December	Annual average
Manufacturing													
2010	450.2	450.3	450.1	456.4	462.4	469.2	467.6	467.3	478.1	480.5	481.3	480.8	466.2
2011	478.6	482.1	484.9	493.8	499.7	505.9	500.9	511.1	512.5	514.9	518.0	519.7	501.8
2012	515.9	517.4	520.7	522.2	529.0	535.2	534.4	538.2	537.1	537.3	538.0	540.2	530.5
2013	533.2	536.9	540.2	539.9	546.4	553.7	543.1	556.3	556.9	558.6	561.3	557.9	548.7
2014	551.8	561.2	563.0	564.7	573.4	586.8	579.3	585.0	577.7	579.9	585.3	588.7	574.7
2015	579.7	581.5	580.9	582.7	590.1	597.9	594.0	599.2	598.6	596.0	599.9	600.0	591.7
2016	598.4	597.1	596.0	602.9	603.4	613.1	606.9	608.0	608.6	607.2	614.0	612.9	605.7
2017	611.4	612.3	611.3	612.6	616.6	623.2	607.9	621.0	615.6	617.3	621.3	622.4	616.1
2018	616.8	622.7	624.7	626.0	629.0	635.5	628.2	634.6	633.7	634.3	635.5	636.6	629.8
Trade, Transportation, and Utilities													
2010	694.6	687.4	690.3	698.9	709.8	716.3	716.6	716.2	711.0	718.4	729.0	733.1	710.1
2011	704.1	698.3	699.9	709.1	720.4	726.4	728.3	728.4	724.5	728.7	741.5	745.6	721.3
2012	714.9	707.9	712.5	717.5	729.2	734.8	734.7	734.3	730.1	734.6	751.3	753.7	729.6
2013	725.7	721.1	724.4	727.9	741.5	749.7	750.4	751.4	745.3	750.5	764.1	770.7	743.6
2014	739.4	735.6	737.1	743.3	757.5	765.1	761.7	763.1	758.9	764.8	779.8	787.0	757.8
2015	755.8	749.9	752.0	758.9	771.6	778.2	772.8	773.6	769.8	775.0	789.4	795.5	770.2
2016	765.1	760.3	762.1	770.3	781.2	786.6	784.2	785.8	780.8	786.1	799.4	802.9	780.4
2017	774.6	767.9	771.1	778.2	786.9	793.1	787.9	790.2	785.0	790.5	804.4	807.0	786.4
2018	778.1	772.7	775.1	778.5	791.7	798.6	795.3	797.9	791.8	796.0	810.3	810.9	791.4
Wholesale Trade													
2010	146.3	146.6	147.4	149.3	150.9	151.6	151.5	151.9	150.8	151.6	151.9	151.7	150.1
2011	150.2	150.6	151.4	153.1	154.9	155.9	156.1	156.5	155.7	155.8	156.2	156.2	154.4
2012	154.2	154.8	155.8	157.3	159.2	160.4	160.6	160.5	159.7	160.0	159.9	160.4	158.6
2013	159.2	159.7	160.8	161.4	163.3	164.3	164.1	164.0	163.1	163.1	163.2	164.0	162.5
2014	162.5	163.1	163.4	164.7	167.2	168.4	167.4	167.6	166.1	165.8	166.2	167.0	165.8
2015	164.8	165.0	165.6	166.7	168.5	169.7	168.6	168.5	166.9	166.9	167.0	167.5	167.1
2016	165.5	165.8	166.0	167.9	169.8	170.8	170.5	170.2	168.8	168.9	169.1	169.2	168.5
2017	167.4	167.8	168.8	170.6	172.2	173.4	172.5	172.4	170.9	170.4	170.4	170.8	170.6
2018	169.4	170.2	170.6	171.5	173.3	174.8	173.8	173.5	172.2	171.8	172.0	172.1	172.1
Retail Trade													
2010	437.8	431.1	432.3	438.6	446.5	450.6	451.6	450.2	445.4	450.6	460.4	463.5	446.6
2011	439.4	433.7	434.1	440.6	447.8	451.0	452.8	451.8	448.2	452.3	464.3	467.0	448.6
2012	441.8	434.3	437.5	440.9	448.6	451.7	452.2	451.2	447.5	451.2	467.4	467.6	449.3
2013	444.4	439.1	441.1	443.6	453.0	458.6	460.8	460.5	455.6	459.8	472.1	476.0	455.4
2014	449.2	445.2	446.2	451.5	460.4	465.3	463.6	464.2	460.7	467.0	480.5	482.9	461.4
2015	457.2	453.1	454.6	458.8	467.8	472.0	468.8	470.2	466.7	471.5	483.7	486.4	467.6
2016	463.0	459.4	460.5	466.5	473.7	476.9	475.9	477.2	471.9	476.2	487.6	489.2	473.2
2017	467.5	462.2	463.6	468.2	473.4	477.0	474.7	475.2	470.5	475.1	486.3	485.6	473.3
2018	465.2	459.2	460.5	462.8	471.9	475.6	474.4	474.5	467.5	470.5	482.2	480.5	470.4
Transportation and Utilities													
2010	110.5	109.7	110.6	111.0	112.4	114.1	113.5	114.1	114.8	116.2	116.7	117.9	113.5
2011	114.5	114.0	114.4	115.4	117.7	119.5	119.4	120.1	120.6	120.6	121.0	122.4	118.3
2012	118.9	118.8	119.2	119.3	121.4	122.7	121.9	122.6	122.9	123.4	124.0	125.7	121.7
2013	122.1	122.3	122.5	122.9	125.2	126.8	125.5	126.9	126.6	127.6	128.8	130.7	125.7
2014	127.7	127.3	127.5	127.1	129.9	131.4	130.7	131.3	132.1	132.0	133.1	137.1	130.6
2015	133.8	131.8	131.8	133.4	135.3	136.5	135.4	134.9	136.2	136.6	138.7	141.6	135.5
2016	136.6	135.1	135.6	135.9	137.7	138.9	137.8	138.4	140.1	141.0	142.7	144.5	138.7
2017	139.7	137.9	138.7	139.4	141.3	142.7	140.7	142.6	143.6	145.0	147.7	150.6	142.5
2018	143.5	143.3	144.0	144.2	146.5	148.2	147.1	149.9	152.1	153.7	156.1	158.3	148.9
Information													
2010	54.3	54.2	53.9	54.2	54.8	55.3	54.8	57.0	56.5	54.0	54.0	54.2	54.8
2011	53.8	53.5	53.4	52.1	52.7	52.8	53.1	53.2	52.7	53.6	53.8	53.8	53.2
2012	53.4	53.2	53.1	52.9	53.2	53.2	53.6	54.2	52.9	53.2	53.5	53.6	53.3
2013	54.0	54.2	54.4	55.0	55.4	55.9	56.0	56.1	55.3	55.3	56.0	56.1	55.3
2014	56.3	56.0	56.3	57.1	57.4	58.2	59.0	58.6	57.1	57.9	58.0	57.6	57.5
2015	56.5	56.3	56.3	55.9	56.6	57.2	57.7	56.8	56.4	56.0	56.4	56.5	56.6
2016	56.7	56.5	56.7	56.9	57.5	58.1	58.5	57.9	57.4	56.8	57.4	57.1	57.3
2017	56.5	56.3	56.8	56.2	56.7	56.9	56.7	56.4	56.1	56.0	56.3	56.7	56.5
2018	55.9	55.5	55.4	55.2	55.9	56.3	56.6	56.5	55.6	55.6	55.9	55.5	55.8

1. Employment by Industry: Michigan, 2010–2018—*Continued*

(Numbers in thousands, not seasonally adjusted)

Industry and year	January	February	March	April	May	June	July	August	September	October	November	December	Annual average
Financial Activities													
2010	186.2	185.8	185.0	184.7	186.7	188.9	190.0	190.7	189.2	189.3	189.6	190.7	188.1
2011	190.4	190.9	191.5	191.0	192.2	194.1	195.7	196.5	194.1	193.4	193.6	194.4	193.2
2012	192.2	192.6	193.3	194.5	196.2	198.4	199.9	200.0	197.3	197.3	197.5	198.3	196.5
2013	198.5	199.1	199.5	201.0	203.3	206.4	207.1	207.3	203.4	202.8	202.8	202.8	202.8
2014	202.2	202.0	201.8	202.1	204.9	207.2	207.4	207.4	204.3	203.2	203.4	204.2	204.2
2015	202.7	202.3	202.5	204.0	207.3	210.1	210.7	210.9	208.2	208.5	208.6	209.2	207.1
2016	208.5	208.3	208.5	210.0	212.6	215.2	216.6	216.8	214.1	213.8	213.9	215.1	212.8
2017	215.4	215.3	215.1	216.1	217.9	221.4	221.2	220.7	217.4	216.4	216.3	216.4	217.5
2018	215.8	216.0	216.3	217.0	219.0	222.6	222.5	222.2	218.9	217.9	219.6	220.1	219.0
Professional and Business Services													
2010	498.5	504.5	504.8	516.5	524.2	527.8	517.5	525.1	536.9	547.1	548.3	541.9	524.4
2011	537.1	542.3	548.9	560.9	569.5	564.2	552.3	561.5	575.1	585.2	584.6	574.7	563.0
2012	568.6	574.2	578.6	590.5	599.1	591.8	576.4	585.7	595.3	603.9	603.2	599.4	588.9
2013	593.3	600.1	606.1	606.8	623.0	617.7	591.4	606.8	618.4	626.4	627.2	623.3	611.7
2014	606.5	613.3	616.3	617.5	633.4	633.8	612.4	619.0	627.7	639.2	638.9	637.7	624.6
2015	622.8	626.2	627.3	635.9	646.5	644.6	627.1	630.8	638.6	651.2	648.8	643.8	637.0
2016	631.4	634.0	635.5	646.0	652.4	652.3	638.6	641.1	651.1	658.5	659.0	651.9	646.0
2017	640.3	642.0	646.9	648.6	659.9	660.9	638.8	643.1	650.0	656.4	659.5	652.2	649.9
2018	646.4	651.8	657.4	659.6	668.6	675.6	648.7	655.0	659.1	671.5	670.4	662.9	660.6
Education and Health Services													
2010	603.6	609.4	610.9	611.9	613.8	609.6	605.3	605.6	610.3	618.9	621.8	620.8	611.8
2011	610.8	615.1	618.0	622.0	622.1	618.6	616.0	617.1	623.8	630.4	633.1	633.2	621.7
2012	623.3	630.6	632.6	632.3	632.6	630.5	624.0	625.9	631.3	638.5	641.2	642.4	632.1
2013	630.1	636.5	638.6	639.6	639.8	637.8	631.8	633.4	638.6	644.1	647.7	646.2	638.7
2014	635.1	642.0	643.8	641.7	643.9	641.4	632.1	633.6	638.8	644.6	647.3	648.8	641.1
2015	639.8	645.3	648.3	645.9	649.4	647.6	641.6	645.2	647.7	658.9	661.3	663.2	649.5
2016	652.5	658.6	659.8	662.5	665.4	662.0	658.0	658.6	664.3	669.2	671.6	672.4	662.9
2017	661.7	667.5	669.0	670.3	673.7	671.4	666.3	668.0	673.1	678.4	681.2	682.0	671.9
2018	674.1	679.8	682.3	682.0	682.9	680.8	672.3	672.6	675.4	682.0	682.6	681.6	679.0
Leisure and Hospitality													
2010	349.9	350.7	355.4	371.2	389.7	402.0	400.0	403.3	393.9	379.2	367.8	367.6	377.6
2011	353.6	352.7	359.8	372.0	391.3	403.2	404.1	406.0	397.0	384.2	372.2	370.2	380.5
2012	360.0	361.5	369.2	380.0	398.2	413.2	411.3	413.7	402.7	391.8	381.3	382.7	388.8
2013	372.3	373.7	378.3	385.0	410.4	422.0	420.4	422.8	410.5	402.5	389.5	390.9	398.2
2014	377.8	378.8	385.3	393.4	419.7	433.4	431.6	433.5	419.2	409.1	397.5	398.2	406.5
2015	386.4	386.9	392.5	399.5	425.4	438.1	439.4	439.9	427.9	417.5	405.8	405.2	413.7
2016	396.6	399.2	404.7	414.7	435.7	449.3	451.4	452.1	438.1	428.2	417.7	415.0	425.2
2017	406.2	408.5	413.2	422.2	443.3	458.6	457.2	459.4	442.6	433.7	421.9	419.7	432.2
2018	410.6	410.3	416.7	420.8	445.3	461.7	460.5	462.1	442.8	434.5	420.2	417.3	433.6
Other Services													
2010	163.8	164.5	165.3	165.4	166.7	168.8	168.4	168.2	166.5	166.2	165.8	166.1	166.3
2011	163.9	164.3	165.5	166.4	167.9	169.7	169.3	169.6	167.9	167.8	167.0	167.7	167.3
2012	164.9	165.6	167.0	168.3	169.9	172.3	171.5	172.0	170.9	170.0	169.6	169.8	169.3
2013	168.4	168.9	170.3	169.4	170.7	172.2	172.2	172.5	170.5	170.2	169.8	170.0	170.5
2014	168.3	168.9	169.4	168.5	170.3	171.8	171.4	170.6	169.3	169.4	168.3	168.2	169.5
2015	164.7	164.8	165.5	165.5	167.5	169.3	169.7	169.4	167.8	168.0	167.6	168.2	167.3
2016	165.7	166.3	166.7	166.5	168.4	170.2	169.7	169.5	168.2	167.6	167.3	166.7	167.7
2017	164.6	165.2	165.7	163.8	166.0	168.3	166.9	166.9	165.1	165.3	165.1	164.9	165.7
2018	163.1	163.9	164.7	165.4	167.7	170.4	168.7	169.1	166.5	166.8	165.6	166.7	166.6
Government													
2010	641.7	655.4	655.9	658.5	657.1	633.6	584.7	576.0	630.1	646.1	648.2	640.1	635.6
2011	625.0	636.2	638.4	637.6	623.5	609.4	565.1	561.7	619.7	632.0	634.7	625.9	617.4
2012	615.8	627.9	628.3	627.6	615.9	596.1	555.5	555.7	612.3	622.9	626.3	617.5	608.5
2013	603.1	616.0	615.0	615.4	604.2	585.8	547.0	545.0	604.7	617.3	618.3	610.7	598.5
2014	597.1	610.8	611.2	611.3	599.3	584.8	546.1	545.4	599.3	615.3	617.7	610.8	595.8
2015	594.7	608.3	609.6	609.5	600.2	580.5	545.4	544.2	594.7	615.4	616.1	611.2	594.2
2016	595.4	610.2	614.0	613.9	598.3	586.8	552.1	552.2	609.2	619.1	624.5	617.2	599.4
2017	601.0	613.7	616.1	615.9	605.2	593.4	556.8	555.5	615.2	624.4	626.4	620.9	603.7
2018	602.5	620.0	622.3	619.8	606.8	594.9	559.0	563.6	615.7	625.0	627.5	620.3	606.5

2. Average Weekly Hours by Selected Industry: Michigan, 2014–2018

(Not seasonally adjusted)

Industry and year	January	February	March	April	May	June	July	August	September	October	November	December	Annual average
Total Private													
2014	33.8	34.4	34.2	34.1	34.2	34.7	34.3	34.5	34.5	34.4	34.7	34.7	34.4
2015	34.1	34.3	34.5	34.3	34.6	34.7	34.3	34.9	34.1	34.3	34.5	34.3	34.4
2016	33.8	33.8	33.9	34.2	34.3	34.4	34.4	34.5	34.7	34.9	34.4	34.5	34.3
2017	34.4	34.4	34.4	34.6	34.8	34.9	34.9	34.9	34.9	35.0	34.6	34.7	34.7
2018	34.3	34.4	34.5	34.7	34.8	35.0	35.0	34.9	35.2	34.7	34.6	34.7	34.7
Goods Producing													
2014	40.8	41.7	41.4	41.1	41.5	41.8	40.9	41.1	41.5	41.0	41.1	42.1	41.3
2015	40.6	40.9	41.5	41.1	41.8	42.0	40.7	41.9	39.7	41.3	40.8	41.1	41.1
2016	39.9	39.7	40.1	40.7	40.4	40.9	40.3	40.6	41.1	41.5	40.7	40.8	40.6
2017	40.6	40.7	40.9	40.5	41.6	41.7	41.1	41.8	41.9	41.9	41.0	41.5	41.3
2018	41.0	41.0	41.2	41.3	41.4	41.8	41.2	41.4	41.8	41.3	40.9	41.3	41.3
Construction													
2014	36.8	37.1	36.5	37.3	37.5	39.6	38.8	38.7	39.6	38.9	37.8	38.7	38.2
2015	37.7	37.2	38.1	38.3	39.5	39.6	39.2	39.9	37.4	40.3	37.7	38.3	38.7
2016	36.6	36.5	36.8	37.8	38.4	39.3	39.8	39.4	39.4	39.9	39.1	37.8	38.5
2017	37.7	37.9	37.3	38.7	40.5	40.7	39.9	41.4	41.1	39.4	38.3	37.8	39.3
2018	37.6	37.7	37.8	38.4	39.6	41.2	40.9	40.2	39.8	40.4	38.5	38.8	39.3
Manufacturing													
2014	41.5	42.5	42.3	41.9	42.5	42.3	41.4	41.7	41.9	41.6	42.0	43.0	42.1
2015	41.3	41.8	42.3	41.8	42.4	42.7	41.1	42.5	40.4	41.7	41.8	41.9	41.8
2016	40.9	40.6	40.9	41.4	40.9	41.3	40.4	40.9	41.5	41.9	41.1	41.6	41.1
2017	41.3	41.4	41.8	40.9	41.9	42.0	41.5	41.9	42.1	42.8	42.0	42.8	41.9
2018	42.1	42.1	42.4	42.4	42.1	42.1	41.4	41.9	42.5	41.6	41.8	42.1	42.0
Trade, Transportation, and Utilities													
2014	32.9	33.2	33.2	33.2	33.3	33.8	33.8	33.9	33.7	33.5	33.8	33.8	33.5
2015	33.1	33.1	33.2	33.2	33.4	33.2	33.4	33.7	33.7	33.1	33.4	33.5	33.3
2016	32.8	32.7	32.8	33.0	33.2	33.4	33.6	33.5	34.0	34.1	33.8	34.0	33.4
2017	33.4	33.4	33.3	34.1	34.0	34.1	34.2	33.8	33.9	33.8	33.9	34.0	33.8
2018	33.2	33.0	33.1	33.2	33.7	33.7	34.0	33.5	33.7	32.9	33.4	33.2	33.4
Information													
2014	36.4	37.5	37.1	36.4	36.1	37.3	37.2	37.1	37.9	36.3	36.9	36.3	36.9
2015	36.7	36.9	37.0	36.8	36.7	37.9	37.8	37.7	37.0	35.8	36.8	36.4	37.0
2016	37.0	36.2	35.8	34.9	35.3	35.7	36.6	35.6	35.9	35.8	35.7	35.8	35.9
2017	36.9	35.8	36.3	36.1	35.6	36.2	36.7	36.3	36.0	36.5	35.8	36.2	36.2
2018	35.5	35.9	36.2	35.7	36.9	35.8	36.7	37.2	37.1	36.6	35.7	35.6	36.2
Financial Activities													
2014	35.7	36.1	36.0	35.3	35.5	36.3	35.6	35.9	35.7	36.0	36.7	35.9	35.9
2015	36.4	37.0	37.3	36.9	37.1	37.0	36.9	36.9	36.5	36.4	36.9	36.7	36.8
2016	37.0	36.8	36.8	36.7	37.3	37.0	36.8	36.8	36.6	37.1	36.7	36.9	36.9
2017	37.0	36.6	36.7	37.2	36.8	36.4	37.0	36.5	36.5	37.2	36.6	36.7	36.8
2018	36.5	36.6	36.6	37.0	36.2	36.6	36.9	36.6	37.0	36.3	36.1	37.0	36.6
Professional and Business Services													
2014	36.0	36.3	36.1	35.9	36.0	36.7	35.9	36.1	36.2	36.2	36.5	36.5	36.2
2015	35.8	36.2	36.3	35.9	36.1	36.2	35.3	36.0	35.0	35.8	36.0	35.3	35.8
2016	35.1	35.3	35.4	35.9	36.2	36.1	35.7	36.2	36.2	36.6	35.7	35.9	35.9
2017	36.1	36.0	36.1	36.4	36.2	36.2	36.2	36.0	35.9	36.6	35.9	35.9	36.1
2018	35.3	35.8	36.0	36.4	36.3	36.5	36.5	36.3	37.0	36.5	36.3	36.5	36.3
Education and Health Services													
2014	32.2	32.6	32.5	32.2	32.3	32.4	32.2	32.5	32.5	32.5	33.0	32.7	32.5
2015	32.5	32.6	32.8	32.6	32.7	32.6	32.6	32.9	32.7	32.5	33.0	32.7	32.7
2016	32.8	32.7	32.6	32.8	32.9	32.7	33.1	32.9	33.2	33.0	32.9	32.8	32.9
2017	33.0	32.9	33.0	33.1	32.8	32.9	33.0	33.1	33.3	33.2	33.2	33.1	33.1
2018	33.1	33.1	33.1	33.2	33.3	33.4	33.3	33.4	33.9	33.6	33.5	33.3	33.4
Leisure and Hospitality													
2014	22.6	23.5	23.6	23.8	23.9	24.6	24.7	24.9	24.2	23.9	23.6	23.6	23.9
2015	23.2	23.6	23.6	23.5	24.1	24.4	25.1	25.4	24.6	24.1	23.9	23.9	24.1
2016	22.9	23.4	23.5	23.9	24.4	24.7	25.3	25.6	24.9	24.6	24.3	24.0	24.3
2017	24.1	24.1	24.3	24.2	25.4	25.5	26.1	26.0	25.3	25.1	24.6	24.5	25.0
2018	24.1	24.5	24.6	24.4	25.1	25.8	26.2	25.8	25.1	24.4	23.7	24.1	24.8
Other Services													
2014	29.9	30.5	30.2	31.0	30.6	31.1	30.9	31.6	31.9	31.8	32.5	32.5	31.2
2015	32.4	32.1	32.4	31.9	32.2	32.7	32.4	33.2	32.8	32.5	32.4	31.8	32.4
2016	31.1	31.2	31.3	31.7	32.1	31.1	31.6	31.7	31.3	31.6	31.1	31.3	31.4
2017	30.6	31.3	31.1	31.5	31.4	31.8	31.2	31.5	31.3	31.3	31.3	31.4	31.3
2018	30.8	31.6	31.2	31.2	31.1	31.2	31.2	31.4	31.3	31.3	31.4	31.2	31.2

3. Average Hourly Earnings by Selected Industry: Michigan, 2014–2018

(Dollars, not seasonally adjusted)

Industry and year	January	February	March	April	May	June	July	August	September	October	November	December	Annual average
Total Private													
2014	23.52	23.70	23.84	23.70	23.46	23.50	23.30	23.29	23.58	23.61	23.86	23.64	23.58
2015	23.88	23.97	23.95	23.86	23.70	23.61	23.92	24.28	24.26	24.40	24.45	24.33	24.05
2016	24.32	24.23	24.22	24.04	24.02	23.74	23.88	23.80	23.91	24.37	24.25	24.34	24.09
2017	24.74	24.57	24.49	24.82	24.36	24.17	24.52	24.25	24.64	25.05	24.93	25.27	24.65
2018	25.45	25.27	25.26	25.59	25.37	25.37	25.56	25.43	25.94	25.95	26.20	26.43	25.65
Goods Producing													
2014	24.73	24.77	25.05	25.05	24.87	24.78	24.70	24.71	25.04	24.84	24.95	25.00	24.87
2015	25.08	25.09	25.16	25.12	24.93	24.84	24.97	25.57	25.61	25.36	25.41	25.57	25.23
2016	25.20	25.15	25.25	24.62	24.70	24.58	24.89	24.80	24.99	25.41	25.40	25.77	25.06
2017	26.05	25.80	26.00	26.43	26.05	26.13	26.41	26.06	26.23	26.33	26.01	26.55	26.17
2018	26.59	26.49	26.41	26.50	26.57	26.69	26.98	27.01	27.28	27.28	27.28	27.21	26.86
Construction													
2014	25.81	25.70	26.29	26.62	25.92	25.45	25.57	25.94	26.11	25.44	25.06	25.94	25.80
2015	25.76	25.90	26.31	26.40	26.07	25.59	25.90	26.16	26.14	26.51	26.67	27.29	26.23
2016	26.54	26.81	26.91	27.13	26.93	26.87	27.12	26.96	27.10	27.07	27.19	27.52	27.02
2017	27.49	27.34	27.84	27.38	27.43	27.28	27.54	27.77	27.84	27.51	27.27	28.06	27.56
2018	27.94	27.94	28.27	27.70	27.95	28.01	28.32	28.39	28.83	29.00	28.73	29.44	28.39
Manufacturing													
2014	24.61	24.69	24.89	24.77	24.67	24.62	24.45	24.35	24.72	24.67	24.93	24.81	24.68
2015	24.99	25.00	24.99	24.86	24.64	24.65	24.74	25.43	25.51	25.07	24.97	25.05	24.99
2016	24.85	24.76	24.85	24.03	24.14	23.98	24.28	24.21	24.42	24.96	24.91	25.33	24.56
2017	25.67	25.40	25.52	26.11	25.60	25.73	25.78	25.21	25.46	25.78	25.45	25.98	25.64
2018	26.10	25.99	25.76	26.06	25.93	26.06	26.32	26.35	26.63	26.54	26.69	26.43	26.24
Trade, Transportation, and Utilities													
2014	20.82	20.92	21.04	20.77	20.75	20.68	20.51	20.43	20.63	20.57	20.73	20.41	20.68
2015	20.62	20.64	20.46	20.46	20.43	20.47	20.71	20.96	20.96	20.81	20.91	20.53	20.66
2016	20.94	20.70	20.57	20.62	20.40	20.26	20.28	20.45	19.98	20.26	20.19	19.95	20.38
2017	20.57	20.63	20.51	20.87	20.56	20.65	21.07	21.06	21.37	21.73	21.94	22.08	21.09
2018	22.34	22.30	21.61	22.11	21.98	21.95	22.05	21.93	22.46	22.50	22.43	22.60	22.19
Information													
2014	29.81	29.81	30.74	31.05	30.97	31.06	30.51	30.56	30.89	31.27	31.12	31.42	30.77
2015	30.71	30.66	31.47	31.39	31.27	31.43	31.08	31.64	31.40	31.12	31.61	31.54	31.28
2016	32.32	32.33	31.23	31.78	32.27	30.90	30.34	31.00	30.82	31.74	32.44	31.87	31.58
2017	31.10	32.87	32.59	32.62	33.16	31.52	32.01	32.18	32.59	33.12	33.38	33.40	32.54
2018	32.85	34.08	34.09	34.62	33.76	34.13	33.91	33.41	34.16	35.37	35.05	35.48	34.24
Financial Activities													
2014	23.62	24.13	24.64	24.18	24.47	25.05	25.15	25.18	26.02	25.81	26.51	26.61	25.12
2015	26.84	27.49	27.70	27.79	27.67	27.16	27.25	27.68	27.80	27.83	28.74	28.01	27.67
2016	27.62	27.79	27.63	27.98	28.48	27.82	27.90	28.46	29.12	29.28	29.52	29.57	28.44
2017	29.81	29.40	29.04	30.03	29.21	28.63	29.08	28.46	29.50	30.03	30.00	30.56	29.48
2018	30.35	30.79	30.50	31.32	30.74	30.59	31.31	31.22	31.23	31.19	31.40	31.85	31.04
Professional and Business Services													
2014	29.99	30.72	30.90	30.65	29.84	30.21	29.67	29.47	29.30	29.52	29.95	29.17	29.94
2015	29.79	29.88	29.95	29.14	29.07	29.06	30.31	30.78	30.28	30.19	30.22	30.49	29.93
2016	30.21	30.16	30.20	29.89	29.88	29.47	29.68	29.04	29.40	30.31	29.37	29.71	29.77
2017	30.39	29.76	29.38	29.76	29.07	28.65	29.30	28.75	29.12	30.09	29.62	30.42	29.52
2018	30.20	29.36	30.09	30.64	30.20	30.36	30.78	30.25	30.96	30.21	31.06	31.45	30.47
Education and Health Services													
2014	23.08	23.01	22.98	23.02	22.95	23.10	23.23	23.35	23.61	23.48	23.64	23.47	23.24
2015	23.69	23.73	23.58	23.98	23.80	23.77	24.39	24.44	24.51	25.59	25.03	24.87	24.29
2016	24.81	24.72	24.85	24.86	24.77	24.79	25.21	24.83	24.79	25.04	25.08	25.04	24.90
2017	25.12	25.16	24.93	25.13	24.77	24.52	24.86	24.41	24.74	24.84	24.84	24.87	24.85
2018	25.59	25.31	25.48	25.60	25.64	25.84	26.13	25.92	26.30	26.57	27.07	27.56	26.09
Leisure and Hospitality													
2014	12.33	12.23	12.12	12.08	12.13	11.98	11.98	12.00	12.32	12.57	12.65	12.81	12.26
2015	12.58	12.55	12.59	12.63	12.50	12.28	12.26	12.43	12.49	12.57	12.57	12.66	12.50
2016	12.65	12.60	12.63	12.65	12.80	12.60	12.79	13.08	13.13	13.29	13.59	13.66	12.96
2017	13.61	13.67	13.87	14.04	13.92	13.68	13.99	14.11	14.32	14.50	14.50	14.43	14.06
2018	14.52	14.60	14.66	14.74	14.63	14.30	14.23	14.21	14.34	14.69	14.57	14.71	14.51
Other Services													
2014	19.87	20.14	20.10	20.52	20.05	19.81	19.89	20.13	20.08	20.38	20.51	20.39	20.16
2015	20.89	21.15	20.90	20.99	21.34	21.37	21.33	21.51	21.89	21.01	21.40	20.83	21.22
2016	20.83	20.72	20.94	20.75	21.25	20.47	20.63	21.01	20.81	20.81	21.11	21.01	20.86
2017	21.53	21.22	21.64	21.58	21.55	21.59	21.87	22.02	22.22	22.64	22.64	22.84	21.94
2018	22.94	22.65	22.60	22.96	22.75	22.42	22.40	22.40	23.08	23.18	23.15	23.57	22.84

4. Average Weekly Earnings by Selected Industry: Michigan, 2014–2018

(Dollars, not seasonally adjusted)

Industry and year	January	February	March	April	May	June	July	August	September	October	November	December	Annual average
Total Private													
2014	794.98	815.28	815.33	808.17	802.33	815.45	799.19	803.51	813.51	812.18	827.94	820.31	811.15
2015	814.31	822.17	826.28	818.40	820.02	819.27	820.46	847.37	827.27	836.92	843.53	834.52	827.32
2016	822.02	818.97	821.06	822.17	823.89	816.66	821.47	821.10	829.68	850.51	834.20	839.73	826.29
2017	851.06	845.21	842.46	858.77	847.73	843.53	855.75	846.33	859.94	876.75	862.58	876.87	855.36
2018	872.94	869.29	871.47	887.97	882.88	887.95	894.60	887.51	913.09	900.47	906.52	917.12	890.06
Goods Producing													
2014	1,008.98	1,032.91	1,037.07	1,029.56	1,032.11	1,035.80	1,010.23	1,015.58	1,039.16	1,018.44	1,025.45	1,052.50	1,027.13
2015	1,018.25	1,026.18	1,044.14	1,032.43	1,042.07	1,043.28	1,016.28	1,071.38	1,016.72	1,047.37	1,036.73	1,050.93	1,036.95
2016	1,005.48	998.46	1,012.53	1,002.03	997.88	1,005.32	1,003.07	1,006.88	1,027.09	1,054.52	1,033.78	1,051.42	1,017.44
2017	1,057.63	1,050.06	1,063.40	1,070.42	1,083.68	1,089.62	1,085.45	1,089.31	1,099.04	1,103.23	1,066.41	1,101.83	1,080.82
2018	1,090.19	1,086.09	1,088.09	1,094.45	1,100.00	1,115.64	1,111.58	1,118.21	1,140.30	1,126.66	1,115.75	1,123.77	1,109.32
Construction													
2014	949.81	953.47	959.59	992.93	972.00	1,007.82	992.12	1,003.88	1,033.96	989.62	947.27	1,003.88	985.56
2015	971.15	963.48	1,002.41	1,011.12	1,029.77	1,013.36	1,015.28	1,043.78	977.64	1,068.35	1,005.46	1,045.21	1,015.10
2016	971.36	978.57	990.29	1,025.51	1,034.11	1,055.99	1,079.38	1,062.22	1,067.74	1,080.09	1,063.13	1,040.26	1,040.27
2017	1,036.37	1,036.19	1,038.43	1,059.61	1,110.92	1,110.30	1,098.85	1,149.68	1,144.22	1,083.89	1,044.44	1,060.67	1,083.11
2018	1,050.54	1,053.34	1,068.61	1,063.68	1,106.82	1,154.01	1,158.29	1,141.28	1,147.43	1,171.60	1,106.11	1,142.27	1,115.73
Manufacturing													
2014	1,021.32	1,049.33	1,052.85	1,037.86	1,048.48	1,041.43	1,012.23	1,015.40	1,035.77	1,026.27	1,047.06	1,066.83	1,039.03
2015	1,032.09	1,045.00	1,057.08	1,039.15	1,044.74	1,052.56	1,016.81	1,080.78	1,030.60	1,045.42	1,043.75	1,049.60	1,044.58
2016	1,016.37	1,005.26	1,016.37	994.84	987.33	990.37	980.91	990.19	1,013.43	1,045.82	1,023.80	1,053.73	1,009.42
2017	1,060.17	1,051.56	1,066.74	1,067.90	1,072.64	1,080.66	1,069.87	1,056.30	1,071.87	1,103.38	1,068.90	1,111.94	1,074.32
2018	1,098.81	1,094.18	1,092.22	1,104.94	1,091.65	1,097.13	1,089.65	1,104.07	1,131.78	1,104.06	1,115.64	1,112.70	1,102.08
Trade, Transportation, and Utilities													
2014	684.98	694.54	698.53	689.56	690.98	698.98	693.24	692.58	695.23	689.10	700.67	689.86	692.78
2015	682.52	683.18	679.27	679.27	682.36	679.60	691.71	706.35	706.35	688.81	698.39	687.76	687.98
2016	686.83	676.89	674.70	680.46	677.28	676.68	681.41	685.08	679.32	690.87	682.42	678.30	680.69
2017	687.04	689.04	682.98	711.67	699.04	704.17	720.59	711.83	724.44	734.47	743.77	750.72	712.84
2018	741.69	735.90	715.29	734.05	740.73	739.72	749.70	734.66	756.90	740.25	749.16	750.32	741.15
Information													
2014	1,085.08	1,117.88	1,140.45	1,130.22	1,118.02	1,158.54	1,134.97	1,133.78	1,170.73	1,135.10	1,148.33	1,140.55	1,135.41
2015	1,127.06	1,131.35	1,164.39	1,155.15	1,147.61	1,191.20	1,174.82	1,192.83	1,161.80	1,114.10	1,163.25	1,148.06	1,157.36
2016	1,195.84	1,170.35	1,118.03	1,109.12	1,139.13	1,103.13	1,110.44	1,103.60	1,106.44	1,136.29	1,158.11	1,140.95	1,133.72
2017	1,147.59	1,176.75	1,183.02	1,177.58	1,180.50	1,141.02	1,174.77	1,168.13	1,173.24	1,208.88	1,195.00	1,209.08	1,177.95
2018	1,166.18	1,223.47	1,234.06	1,235.93	1,245.74	1,221.85	1,244.50	1,242.85	1,267.34	1,294.54	1,251.29	1,263.09	1,239.49
Financial Activities													
2014	843.23	871.09	887.04	853.55	868.69	909.32	895.34	903.96	928.91	929.16	972.92	955.30	901.81
2015	976.98	1,017.13	1,033.21	1,025.45	1,026.56	1,004.92	1,005.53	1,021.39	1,014.70	1,013.01	1,060.51	1,027.97	1,018.26
2016	1,021.94	1,022.67	1,016.78	1,026.87	1,062.30	1,029.34	1,026.72	1,047.33	1,065.79	1,086.29	1,083.38	1,091.13	1,049.44
2017	1,102.97	1,076.04	1,065.77	1,117.12	1,074.93	1,042.13	1,075.96	1,038.79	1,076.75	1,117.12	1,098.00	1,121.55	1,084.86
2018	1,107.78	1,126.91	1,116.30	1,158.84	1,112.79	1,119.59	1,155.34	1,142.65	1,155.51	1,132.20	1,133.54	1,178.45	1,136.06
Professional and Business Services													
2014	1,079.64	1,115.14	1,115.49	1,100.34	1,074.24	1,108.71	1,065.15	1,063.87	1,060.66	1,068.62	1,093.18	1,064.71	1,083.83
2015	1,066.48	1,081.66	1,087.19	1,046.13	1,049.43	1,051.97	1,069.94	1,108.08	1,059.80	1,080.80	1,087.92	1,076.30	1,071.49
2016	1,060.37	1,064.65	1,069.08	1,073.05	1,081.66	1,063.87	1,059.58	1,051.25	1,064.28	1,109.35	1,048.51	1,066.59	1,068.74
2017	1,097.08	1,071.36	1,060.62	1,083.26	1,052.33	1,037.13	1,060.66	1,035.00	1,045.41	1,101.29	1,063.36	1,092.08	1,065.67
2018	1,066.06	1,051.09	1,083.24	1,115.30	1,096.26	1,108.14	1,123.47	1,098.08	1,145.52	1,102.67	1,127.48	1,147.93	1,106.06
Education and Health Services													
2014	743.18	750.13	746.85	741.24	741.29	748.44	748.01	758.88	767.33	763.10	780.12	767.47	755.30
2015	769.93	773.60	773.42	781.75	778.26	774.90	795.11	804.08	801.48	831.68	825.99	813.25	794.28
2016	813.77	808.34	810.11	815.41	814.93	810.63	834.45	816.91	823.03	826.32	825.13	821.31	819.21
2017	828.96	827.76	822.69	831.80	812.46	806.71	820.38	807.97	823.84	824.69	824.69	823.20	822.54
2018	847.03	837.76	843.39	849.92	853.81	863.06	870.13	865.73	891.57	892.75	906.85	917.75	871.41
Leisure and Hospitality													
2014	278.66	287.41	286.03	287.50	289.91	294.71	295.91	298.80	298.14	300.42	298.54	302.32	293.01
2015	291.86	296.18	297.12	296.81	301.25	299.63	307.73	315.72	307.25	302.94	300.42	302.57	301.25
2016	289.69	294.84	296.81	302.34	312.32	311.22	323.59	334.85	326.94	326.93	330.24	327.84	314.93
2017	328.00	329.45	337.04	339.77	353.57	348.84	365.14	366.86	362.30	363.95	356.70	353.54	351.50
2018	349.93	357.70	360.64	359.66	367.21	368.94	372.83	366.62	359.93	358.44	345.31	354.51	359.85
Other Services													
2014	594.11	614.27	607.02	636.12	613.53	616.09	614.60	636.11	640.55	648.08	666.58	662.68	628.99
2015	676.84	678.92	677.16	669.58	687.15	698.80	691.09	714.13	717.99	682.83	693.36	662.39	687.53
2016	647.81	646.46	655.42	657.78	682.13	636.62	651.91	666.02	651.35	658.23	656.52	657.61	655.00
2017	658.82	664.19	673.00	679.77	676.67	686.56	682.34	693.63	695.49	708.63	708.63	717.18	686.72
2018	706.55	715.74	705.12	716.35	707.53	699.50	698.88	703.36	722.40	725.53	726.91	735.38	712.61

MINNESOTA
At a Glance

Population:
   2010 census: 5,303,925
   2018 estimate: 5,611,179

Percent change in population:
   2010–2018: 5.8%

Percent change in total nonfarm employment:
   2010–2018: 12.0%

Industry with the largest growth in employment, 2010–2018 (percent):
   Construction, 39.8%

Industry with the largest decline or smallest growth in employment, 2010–2018 (percent):
   Information, -8.9%

Civilian labor force:
   2010: 2,938,795
   2018: 3,070,224

Unemployment rate and rank among states (highest to lowest):
   2010: 7.4%, 39th
   2018: 2.9%, 44th

Over-the-year change in unemployment rates:
   2016–2017: -0.5%
   2017–2018: -0.5%

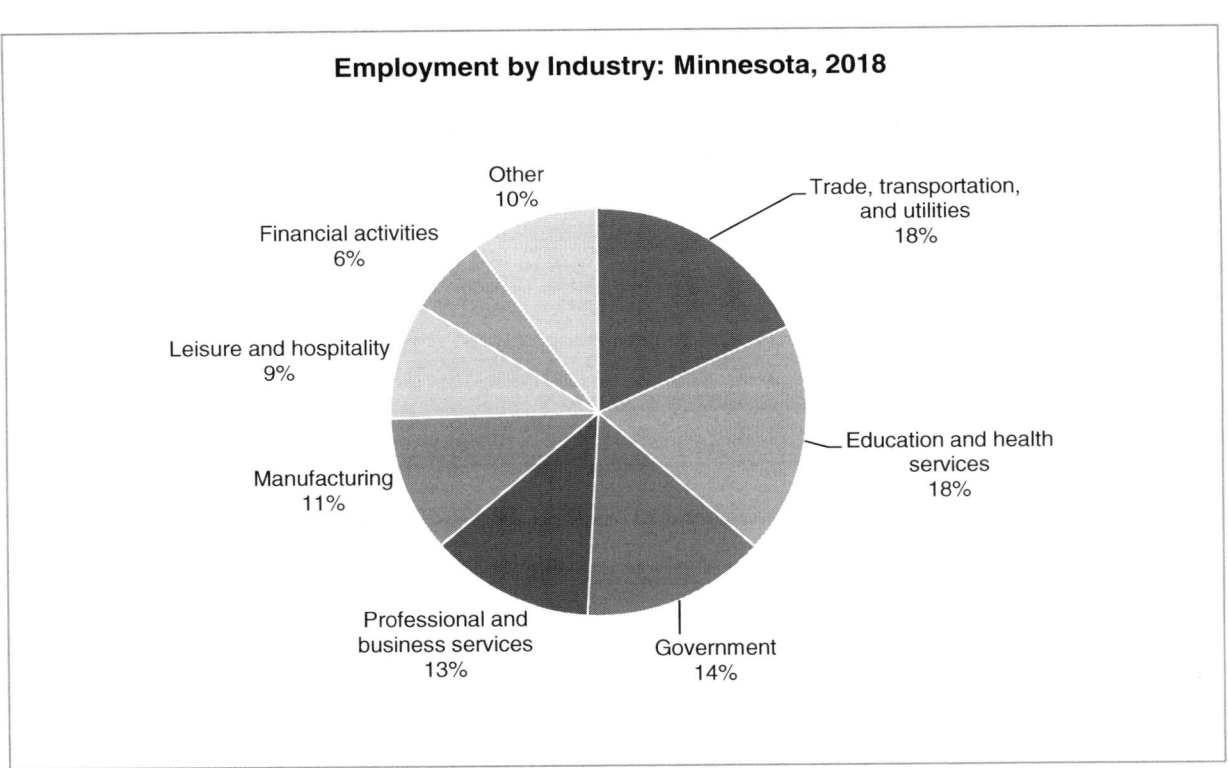

Employment by Industry: Minnesota, 2018

- Other 10%
- Trade, transportation, and utilities 18%
- Financial activities 6%
- Leisure and hospitality 9%
- Education and health services 18%
- Manufacturing 11%
- Professional and business services 13%
- Government 14%

1. Employment by Industry: Minnesota, 2010–2018

(Numbers in thousands, not seasonally adjusted)

Industry and year	January	February	March	April	May	June	July	August	September	October	November	December	Annual average
Total Nonfarm													
2010	2,567.0	2,568.7	2,578.2	2,626.4	2,660.5	2,679.8	2,645.9	2,650.6	2,653.0	2,682.0	2,678.2	2,664.5	2,637.9
2011	2,603.7	2,609.9	2,619.2	2,667.9	2,705.1	2,723.7	2,670.9	2,702.1	2,722.8	2,728.5	2,723.7	2,714.8	2,682.7
2012	2,646.6	2,653.3	2,668.5	2,709.6	2,740.2	2,762.1	2,722.3	2,739.7	2,756.4	2,771.3	2,771.4	2,759.6	2,725.1
2013	2,699.3	2,711.6	2,719.4	2,742.6	2,790.7	2,812.2	2,767.5	2,787.7	2,804.2	2,820.5	2,815.6	2,804.1	2,773.0
2014	2,731.5	2,740.2	2,743.0	2,784.5	2,830.8	2,855.9	2,826.8	2,837.4	2,836.7	2,853.1	2,850.3	2,841.1	2,810.9
2015	2,772.4	2,783.1	2,789.7	2,839.2	2,877.5	2,898.2	2,874.7	2,878.9	2,875.3	2,898.0	2,894.5	2,882.8	2,855.4
2016	2,818.8	2,828.1	2,832.2	2,880.3	2,909.3	2,921.4	2,915.1	2,924.1	2,923.4	2,933.8	2,928.1	2,912.6	2,893.9
2017	2,868.4	2,874.6	2,882.4	2,914.3	2,944.7	2,976.3	2,951.3	2,953.3	2,952.7	2,964.4	2,960.0	2,946.7	2,932.4
2018	2,899.0	2,905.1	2,900.6	2,924.7	2,972.4	2,996.9	2,980.5	2,980.9	2,972.8	2,987.0	2,975.9	2,956.7	2,954.4
Total Private													
2010	2,150.3	2,145.2	2,152.8	2,200.1	2,229.9	2,254.0	2,256.6	2,267.4	2,248.2	2,259.7	2,252.4	2,239.7	2,221.4
2011	2,190.1	2,188.6	2,198.2	2,245.9	2,283.6	2,305.9	2,309.9	2,324.6	2,317.4	2,309.4	2,302.5	2,293.7	2,272.5
2012	2,236.6	2,235.3	2,250.2	2,288.9	2,319.9	2,345.6	2,346.6	2,360.5	2,348.6	2,349.2	2,344.5	2,335.3	2,313.4
2013	2,285.9	2,289.1	2,298.7	2,321.2	2,367.6	2,395.7	2,394.5	2,410.1	2,393.7	2,395.3	2,386.4	2,377.8	2,359.7
2014	2,315.5	2,315.0	2,318.3	2,357.1	2,403.1	2,432.9	2,434.4	2,447.5	2,424.1	2,425.1	2,419.4	2,413.1	2,392.1
2015	2,354.4	2,357.9	2,366.5	2,411.9	2,449.8	2,476.3	2,481.0	2,488.2	2,463.2	2,470.6	2,464.2	2,453.6	2,436.5
2016	2,397.8	2,401.0	2,404.6	2,455.9	2,484.0	2,501.7	2,520.6	2,529.4	2,508.2	2,506.6	2,498.8	2,487.5	2,474.7
2017	2,443.8	2,445.6	2,454.4	2,487.3	2,519.3	2,549.9	2,551.1	2,555.0	2,530.9	2,530.5	2,523.7	2,515.4	2,508.9
2018	2,471.2	2,472.1	2,469.3	2,493.7	2,542.1	2,567.9	2,576.9	2,581.1	2,552.3	2,554.2	2,539.8	2,526.3	2,528.9
Goods Producing													
2010	363.0	358.3	359.8	375.4	386.4	397.6	404.4	405.9	402.5	402.1	395.2	385.1	386.3
2011	373.0	371.3	373.7	386.1	399.5	411.3	417.2	420.5	416.2	414.6	407.2	398.0	399.1
2012	383.1	381.1	386.5	398.8	409.4	421.7	424.9	427.4	422.5	420.1	412.4	404.1	407.7
2013	390.0	388.9	392.6	399.1	416.0	428.6	431.6	435.8	431.4	429.3	423.3	413.0	415.0
2014	399.7	398.7	400.8	410.9	428.3	442.1	446.7	449.8	443.8	442.4	435.0	427.9	427.2
2015	413.8	413.3	416.8	431.2	443.0	455.3	460.0	460.4	453.3	451.0	443.8	434.5	439.7
2016	417.1	415.8	418.8	433.4	444.0	453.9	458.7	459.5	453.4	451.3	444.3	432.5	440.2
2017	420.8	421.0	425.1	435.0	447.7	460.1	463.0	463.1	456.3	456.7	448.2	439.5	444.7
2018	425.5	424.4	426.7	433.5	451.7	466.4	470.6	471.9	465.6	465.1	456.4	448.8	450.6
Service-Providing													
2010	2,204.0	2,210.4	2,218.4	2,251.0	2,274.1	2,282.2	2,241.5	2,244.7	2,250.5	2,279.9	2,283.0	2,279.4	2,251.6
2011	2,230.7	2,238.6	2,245.5	2,281.8	2,305.6	2,312.4	2,253.7	2,281.6	2,306.6	2,313.9	2,316.5	2,316.8	2,283.6
2012	2,263.5	2,272.2	2,282.0	2,310.8	2,330.8	2,340.4	2,297.4	2,312.3	2,333.9	2,351.2	2,359.0	2,355.5	2,317.4
2013	2,309.3	2,322.7	2,326.8	2,343.5	2,374.7	2,383.6	2,335.9	2,351.9	2,372.8	2,391.2	2,392.3	2,391.1	2,358.0
2014	2,331.8	2,341.5	2,342.2	2,373.6	2,402.5	2,413.8	2,380.1	2,387.6	2,392.9	2,410.7	2,415.3	2,413.2	2,383.8
2015	2,358.6	2,369.8	2,372.9	2,408.0	2,434.5	2,442.9	2,414.7	2,418.5	2,422.0	2,447.0	2,450.7	2,448.3	2,415.7
2016	2,401.7	2,412.3	2,413.4	2,446.9	2,465.3	2,467.5	2,456.4	2,464.6	2,470.0	2,482.5	2,483.8	2,480.1	2,453.7
2017	2,447.6	2,453.6	2,457.3	2,479.3	2,497.0	2,516.2	2,488.3	2,490.2	2,496.4	2,507.7	2,511.8	2,507.2	2,487.7
2018	2,473.5	2,480.7	2,473.9	2,491.2	2,520.7	2,530.5	2,509.9	2,509.0	2,507.2	2,521.9	2,519.5	2,507.9	2,503.8
Mining and Logging													
2010	5.3	5.4	5.4	5.7	6.0	5.6	6.5	6.5	6.4	6.5	6.3	6.0	6.0
2011	6.0	6.2	6.1	6.1	6.5	6.8	7.0	7.1	6.9	7.0	6.9	6.6	6.6
2012	6.6	6.6	6.6	6.8	7.0	7.3	7.4	7.5	7.2	7.2	7.1	6.8	7.0
2013	6.6	6.6	6.7	6.6	6.9	7.2	7.2	7.4	7.2	7.2	7.1	6.9	7.0
2014	6.6	6.7	6.7	6.8	7.1	7.3	7.6	7.6	7.4	7.5	7.4	7.1	7.2
2015	6.8	6.9	7.0	7.1	7.3	7.4	7.6	7.2	6.9	6.8	6.7	6.4	7.0
2016	5.5	5.4	5.7	5.7	6.4	6.4	6.6	6.7	6.7	6.8	6.5	6.2	6.2
2017	6.1	6.2	6.3	6.3	6.6	6.8	6.8	6.8	6.8	6.8	6.8	6.6	6.6
2018	6.3	6.4	6.5	6.2	6.7	6.9	7.0	7.1	7.0	6.8	6.6	6.4	6.7
Construction													
2010	73.3	69.5	70.2	81.9	89.4	95.6	99.2	99.8	98.0	97.9	92.8	83.4	87.6
2011	74.2	72.7	74.5	83.3	93.6	101.1	103.8	105.6	103.8	102.5	97.3	88.8	91.8
2012	77.4	75.9	79.7	90.0	98.0	104.4	106.9	108.2	105.2	104.0	98.2	91.4	94.9
2013	80.5	80.0	82.4	88.9	102.7	110.3	113.4	116.2	114.2	112.8	107.7	98.1	100.6
2014	87.9	86.7	88.9	96.5	110.6	119.3	122.1	123.4	120.4	119.0	112.3	105.2	107.7
2015	94.4	93.9	96.3	109.3	119.2	127.0	130.2	130.6	126.6	125.1	118.6	110.8	115.2
2016	97.3	96.4	98.6	112.2	121.1	127.1	129.8	129.6	126.8	125.3	120.1	110.0	116.2
2017	100.7	100.8	104.2	113.6	124.1	131.4	133.2	133.3	130.0	129.2	121.9	114.8	119.8
2018	103.2	102.1	103.6	109.1	124.7	134.2	136.8	137.1	133.8	134.9	128.6	121.6	122.5

1. Employment by Industry: Minnesota, 2010–2018—*Continued*

(Numbers in thousands, not seasonally adjusted)

Industry and year	January	February	March	April	May	June	July	August	September	October	November	December	Annual average
Manufacturing													
2010	284.4	283.4	284.2	287.8	291.0	296.4	298.7	299.6	298.1	297.7	296.1	295.7	292.8
2011	292.8	292.4	293.1	296.7	299.4	303.4	306.4	307.8	305.5	305.1	303.0	302.6	300.7
2012	299.1	298.6	300.2	302.0	304.4	310.0	310.6	311.7	310.1	308.9	307.1	305.9	305.7
2013	302.9	302.3	303.5	303.6	306.4	311.1	311.0	312.2	310.0	309.3	308.5	308.0	307.4
2014	305.2	305.3	305.2	307.6	310.6	315.5	317.0	318.8	316.0	315.9	315.3	315.6	312.3
2015	312.6	312.5	313.5	314.8	316.5	320.9	322.2	322.6	319.8	319.1	318.5	317.3	317.5
2016	314.3	314.0	314.5	315.5	316.5	320.4	322.3	323.2	319.9	319.2	317.7	316.3	317.8
2017	314.0	314.0	314.6	315.1	317.0	321.9	323.0	323.0	319.5	320.7	319.5	318.1	318.4
2018	316.0	315.9	316.6	318.2	320.3	325.3	326.8	327.7	324.8	323.4	321.2	320.8	321.4
Trade, Transportation, and Utilities													
2010	480.4	474.9	475.6	484.4	489.5	494.1	489.3	489.2	487.5	491.8	498.6	500.8	488.0
2011	482.5	478.6	480.2	489.9	496.7	498.8	497.2	498.1	498.4	500.0	507.2	510.6	494.9
2012	493.1	486.4	489.2	496.1	502.4	504.5	501.1	502.7	501.1	505.5	514.7	515.0	501.0
2013	499.7	494.7	495.8	499.0	508.5	512.9	508.8	512.4	510.3	513.8	521.3	524.7	508.5
2014	504.4	499.6	500.4	508.2	515.5	519.4	516.7	518.2	513.4	518.4	525.4	530.9	514.2
2015	511.5	507.0	508.3	517.1	523.5	528.0	525.0	526.2	521.6	527.0	533.9	537.0	522.2
2016	519.1	516.0	516.6	525.6	530.8	531.8	532.7	534.1	529.2	533.4	539.2	543.6	529.3
2017	529.4	525.0	524.7	531.0	536.3	539.8	537.2	537.2	532.8	536.6	544.6	548.7	535.3
2018	533.1	528.7	528.1	531.0	539.4	540.3	539.8	539.3	534.2	537.7	545.0	547.7	537.0
Wholesale Trade													
2010	118.9	118.6	118.9	120.9	121.5	122.9	122.8	122.5	120.8	121.9	121.9	121.3	121.1
2011	119.9	120.0	120.5	123.0	124.7	125.0	125.7	125.6	124.2	124.4	124.2	123.9	123.4
2012	122.9	122.9	124.0	126.1	127.0	128.3	128.7	128.0	126.5	126.9	127.0	126.9	126.3
2013	125.3	125.4	125.8	126.9	129.1	129.9	129.8	129.6	127.9	128.4	128.9	128.1	127.9
2014	126.4	126.3	126.7	128.1	130.3	131.2	131.1	130.9	129.1	129.8	130.0	129.8	129.1
2015	127.8	127.5	127.9	130.1	130.5	131.7	131.9	131.5	129.4	129.9	129.9	129.3	129.8
2016	127.3	127.2	127.5	129.8	130.5	130.3	131.0	130.7	128.7	128.7	128.5	128.1	129.0
2017	127.9	127.6	127.9	129.4	130.6	131.4	131.7	131.4	129.6	130.0	130.2	130.1	129.8
2018	128.7	128.8	129.1	130.0	131.8	132.8	132.4	132.2	130.3	130.0	130.7	131.0	130.7
Retail Trade													
2010	272.8	267.9	268.2	273.7	277.8	281.2	279.3	280.5	276.3	278.0	284.0	286.1	277.2
2011	272.6	268.4	269.1	275.6	280.0	283.0	282.5	284.2	281.6	282.2	289.5	292.2	280.1
2012	279.3	272.8	274.4	277.8	282.3	284.9	283.1	284.7	281.7	284.7	293.4	293.5	282.7
2013	282.0	276.5	277.5	279.6	285.5	290.4	288.8	291.2	287.5	288.5	295.1	298.6	286.8
2014	283.2	278.9	279.4	284.0	288.4	292.4	292.2	293.1	287.1	289.9	296.4	300.4	288.8
2015	286.6	282.4	283.3	287.9	293.5	298.0	296.7	298.1	292.5	295.7	302.0	304.1	293.4
2016	291.9	288.9	289.4	294.7	298.4	300.7	302.9	303.3	296.3	299.2	304.2	306.3	298.0
2017	295.9	292.0	292.0	296.1	299.2	302.4	302.1	302.2	295.5	297.9	304.6	307.0	298.9
2018	296.5	292.2	291.6	293.0	299.2	301.8	302.3	301.9	295.3	298.7	304.9	306.2	298.6
Transportation and Utilities													
2010	88.7	88.4	88.5	89.8	90.2	90.0	87.2	86.2	90.4	91.9	92.7	93.4	89.8
2011	90.0	90.2	90.6	91.3	92.0	90.8	89.0	88.3	92.6	93.4	93.5	94.5	91.4
2012	90.9	90.7	90.8	92.2	93.1	91.3	89.3	90.0	92.9	93.9	94.3	94.6	92.0
2013	92.4	92.8	92.5	92.5	93.9	92.6	90.2	91.6	94.9	96.9	97.3	98.0	93.8
2014	94.8	94.4	94.3	96.1	96.8	95.8	93.4	94.2	97.2	98.7	99.0	100.7	96.3
2015	97.1	97.1	97.1	99.1	99.5	98.3	96.4	96.6	99.7	101.4	102.0	103.6	99.0
2016	99.9	99.9	99.7	101.1	101.9	100.8	98.8	100.1	104.2	105.5	106.5	109.2	102.3
2017	105.6	105.4	104.8	105.5	106.5	106.0	103.4	103.6	107.7	108.7	109.8	111.6	106.6
2018	107.9	107.7	107.4	108.0	108.4	105.7	105.1	105.2	108.6	109.0	109.4	110.5	107.7
Information													
2010	54.4	54.4	54.3	54.1	54.0	54.2	54.4	54.4	53.7	53.8	53.9	53.7	54.1
2011	53.7	53.3	53.1	53.8	53.8	54.1	54.3	54.6	54.0	53.8	53.8	53.8	53.8
2012	52.9	53.0	53.0	53.5	53.9	54.0	54.0	54.0	53.6	53.7	53.6	53.8	53.6
2013	53.1	53.2	53.1	53.1	53.3	53.3	53.8	53.6	52.8	52.7	53.0	53.1	53.2
2014	52.6	52.5	52.2	52.2	52.4	52.8	53.1	53.1	52.1	52.2	52.0	52.4	52.5
2015	51.4	51.2	51.1	51.1	51.4	51.7	52.0	52.0	51.0	50.9	51.1	50.9	51.3
2016	50.2	50.2	50.2	50.4	50.6	50.6	51.0	51.4	51.3	50.8	50.7	50.8	50.7
2017	50.4	50.3	50.3	50.4	50.4	50.6	50.5	50.9	49.9	49.7	49.9	50.0	50.3
2018	49.6	49.7	49.2	49.1	49.2	49.5	49.7	49.8	48.7	48.7	49.1	49.5	49.3

1. Employment by Industry: Minnesota, 2010–2018—*Continued*

(Numbers in thousands, not seasonally adjusted)

Industry and year	January	February	March	April	May	June	July	August	September	October	November	December	Annual average
Financial Activities													
2010	160.5	160.3	160.2	160.5	161.1	162.8	163.3	163.6	162.3	163.7	163.5	164.6	162.2
2011	162.4	162.4	162.3	162.4	163.1	163.7	164.5	164.8	163.1	162.9	162.7	163.0	163.1
2012	162.5	163.1	163.2	164.1	165.5	167.6	168.5	168.9	168.0	168.9	169.2	170.1	166.6
2013	169.4	170.0	170.2	170.1	170.9	172.6	173.4	173.1	171.3	171.4	171.3	171.7	171.3
2014	169.8	169.4	169.5	170.1	171.1	173.0	173.4	173.1	170.9	171.1	171.0	171.7	171.2
2015	171.7	171.6	171.6	172.9	174.2	176.1	177.8	177.8	175.3	175.9	176.0	176.5	174.8
2016	175.1	175.5	175.6	177.0	177.7	179.0	181.5	181.4	179.6	180.1	180.0	180.6	178.6
2017	180.3	180.4	180.7	180.9	181.8	184.2	185.3	185.0	182.7	182.8	182.5	183.2	182.5
2018	182.0	182.1	182.1	183.1	183.5	185.7	186.8	186.8	184.5	184.6	184.5	183.8	184.1
Professional and Business Services													
2010	308.8	309.8	309.7	318.8	321.2	325.2	328.9	333.1	327.8	332.4	332.9	331.2	323.3
2011	324.1	325.0	326.8	335.5	337.5	340.8	345.4	349.5	348.1	349.5	348.2	346.4	339.7
2012	335.1	335.3	337.0	344.1	345.7	349.4	352.2	355.8	352.5	355.4	353.9	353.5	347.5
2013	344.3	347.5	348.6	352.3	355.1	360.5	361.6	365.5	361.7	366.6	363.8	363.5	357.6
2014	351.4	352.2	352.1	357.2	361.2	366.1	369.1	372.3	366.9	371.4	372.6	367.8	363.4
2015	357.2	358.4	358.0	367.2	370.5	372.1	374.7	375.8	369.3	377.0	376.6	372.5	369.1
2016	363.1	365.1	362.2	372.6	373.5	375.6	381.0	381.2	379.4	383.2	380.1	377.9	374.6
2017	368.4	367.6	368.5	373.9	375.5	378.5	380.5	381.0	376.9	380.4	380.6	376.6	375.7
2018	371.9	372.4	368.3	374.7	378.4	380.0	383.7	384.2	379.3	384.2	382.0	377.5	378.1
Education and Health Services													
2010	451.3	456.4	458.3	461.1	461.3	456.2	450.9	453.0	456.2	463.4	465.5	464.0	458.1
2011	460.9	464.6	464.7	469.7	470.3	464.7	459.7	461.9	468.7	472.2	473.6	474.1	467.1
2012	468.0	473.7	474.0	476.2	476.2	469.9	467.4	470.8	478.6	483.5	485.6	484.9	475.7
2013	481.1	486.6	486.4	490.3	490.5	483.6	480.7	483.5	489.6	495.0	497.0	495.5	488.3
2014	489.8	495.1	495.0	498.4	498.4	491.9	488.9	491.7	498.9	502.3	504.4	503.8	496.6
2015	496.7	503.4	504.2	505.4	506.3	500.3	498.9	501.1	509.1	513.1	515.2	514.3	505.7
2016	511.8	516.5	516.3	522.1	520.9	513.3	514.7	518.1	522.9	524.1	529.8	529.9	520.0
2017	525.4	531.4	531.5	535.3	534.7	531.1	528.2	529.9	537.0	539.7	541.9	541.9	534.0
2018	537.4	543.0	543.2	545.8	546.4	541.2	538.4	539.6	544.5	549.1	548.5	543.6	543.4
Leisure and Hospitality													
2010	219.5	218.5	221.3	232.1	242.3	248.5	250.2	252.6	244.5	237.7	228.8	226.4	235.2
2011	220.8	220.4	223.8	233.7	247.5	255.9	255.1	258.3	252.7	241.1	234.6	232.3	239.7
2012	227.7	228.4	232.5	240.6	251.0	260.6	261.4	263.7	256.6	246.2	239.3	238.0	245.5
2013	233.3	232.9	235.9	241.3	256.4	266.4	267.8	269.1	261.1	252.1	243.2	243.0	250.2
2014	236.7	236.9	237.5	247.7	262.6	272.6	271.7	274.5	264.7	253.7	245.9	245.6	254.2
2015	240.3	240.8	243.6	252.8	266.4	277.0	277.1	279.3	269.9	260.9	253.1	253.0	259.5
2016	248.1	248.1	250.4	259.3	270.7	280.7	283.6	286.0	275.6	267.1	258.5	256.2	265.4
2017	254.0	255.0	257.9	264.8	276.4	287.9	289.4	291.0	279.9	269.5	261.6	261.0	270.7
2018	259.0	259.1	259.1	263.5	279.8	289.3	291.7	293.8	282.0	271.5	261.7	263.2	272.8
Other Services													
2010	112.4	112.6	113.6	113.7	114.1	115.4	115.2	115.6	113.7	114.8	114.0	113.9	114.1
2011	112.7	113.0	113.6	114.8	115.2	116.6	116.5	116.9	116.2	115.3	115.2	115.5	115.1
2012	114.2	114.3	114.8	115.5	115.8	117.9	117.1	117.2	115.7	115.9	115.8	115.9	115.8
2013	115.0	115.3	116.1	116.0	116.9	117.8	116.8	117.1	115.5	114.4	113.5	113.3	115.6
2014	111.1	110.6	110.8	112.4	113.6	115.0	114.8	114.8	113.4	113.6	113.1	113.0	113.0
2015	111.8	112.2	112.9	114.2	114.5	115.8	115.5	115.6	113.7	114.8	114.5	114.9	114.2
2016	113.3	113.8	114.5	115.5	115.8	116.8	117.4	117.7	116.8	116.6	116.2	116.0	115.9
2017	115.1	114.9	115.7	116.0	116.5	117.7	117.0	116.9	115.4	115.1	114.4	114.5	115.8
2018	112.7	112.7	112.6	113.0	113.7	115.5	116.2	115.7	113.5	113.3	112.6	112.2	113.6
Government													
2010	416.7	423.5	425.4	426.3	430.6	425.8	389.3	383.2	404.8	422.3	425.8	424.8	416.5
2011	413.6	421.3	421.0	422.0	421.5	417.8	361.0	377.5	405.4	419.1	421.2	421.1	410.2
2012	410.0	418.0	418.3	420.7	420.3	416.5	375.7	379.2	407.8	422.1	426.9	424.3	411.7
2013	413.4	422.5	420.7	421.4	423.1	416.5	373.0	377.6	410.5	425.2	429.2	426.3	413.3
2014	416.0	425.2	424.7	427.4	427.7	423.0	392.4	389.9	412.6	428.0	430.9	428.0	418.8
2015	418.0	425.2	423.2	427.3	427.7	421.9	393.7	390.7	412.1	427.4	430.3	429.2	418.9
2016	421.0	427.1	427.6	424.4	425.3	419.7	394.5	394.7	415.2	427.2	429.3	425.1	419.3
2017	424.6	429.0	428.0	427.0	425.4	426.4	400.2	398.3	421.8	433.9	436.3	431.3	423.5
2018	427.8	433.0	431.3	431.0	430.3	429.0	403.6	399.8	420.5	432.8	436.1	430.4	425.5

2. Average Weekly Hours by Selected Industry: Minnesota, 2014–2018

(Not seasonally adjusted)

Industry and year	January	February	March	April	May	June	July	August	September	October	November	December	Annual average
Total Private													
2014	33.2	33.9	34.0	33.7	34.0	34.5	34.2	34.3	34.1	34.1	34.2	33.9	34.0
2015	33.5	33.9	33.9	33.6	33.8	34.1	34.2	34.8	33.9	34.0	34.2	33.7	34.0
2016	33.5	33.4	33.5	33.7	34.3	34.3	34.1	34.1	34.1	34.5	34.2	33.9	34.0
2017	34.0	33.8	33.8	34.2	33.9	34.1	34.4	34.2	34.1	34.4	34.1	33.9	34.1
2018	33.5	33.7	33.7	34.0	34.0	34.1	34.3	34.3	34.4	33.6	33.8	34.1	34.0
Goods Producing													
2014	39.7	40.2	40.6	40.4	41.1	41.4	41.2	41.8	41.4	41.3	40.4	40.3	40.8
2015	39.2	39.3	39.2	39.1	39.7	40.1	39.6	40.4	38.9	39.5	39.3	39.1	39.5
2016	38.8	38.8	38.8	39.1	39.2	39.7	39.2	39.5	39.9	39.5	39.6	38.7	39.2
2017	38.6	39.1	39.5	39.0	39.6	39.8	39.9	40.3	40.4	39.9	39.5	39.6	39.6
2018	38.9	39.1	39.4	39.1	39.8	40.1	39.9	40.4	40.6	39.7	39.5	39.8	39.7
Construction													
2014	37.7	37.0	38.2	38.3	40.6	40.9	41.6	42.0	41.2	40.8	37.6	37.5	39.6
2015	36.3	37.0	37.0	38.2	40.2	41.6	41.2	42.1	38.6	40.3	38.8	38.1	39.3
2016	37.5	37.6	37.9	38.4	38.9	40.9	41.0	40.4	40.8	41.0	40.0	37.8	39.5
2017	37.5	38.4	38.6	38.7	40.1	40.5	40.4	41.0	40.4	40.2	38.9	38.4	39.5
2018	37.2	37.4	37.9	37.2	39.2	40.8	40.4	40.6	40.3	38.5	38.9	39.3	39.1
Manufacturing													
2014	40.2	41.0	41.1	40.7	41.0	41.3	40.6	41.4	41.3	41.3	41.3	41.0	41.0
2015	39.8	39.8	39.8	39.3	39.6	39.6	39.0	39.9	39.4	39.6	40.0	39.8	39.6
2016	39.4	39.3	39.5	39.6	39.6	39.5	38.6	39.3	39.6	38.8	39.4	39.0	39.3
2017	39.0	39.3	39.9	39.3	39.4	39.5	39.7	39.9	40.3	39.6	39.6	39.9	39.6
2018	39.5	39.7	39.9	39.9	40.1	39.7	39.5	40.1	40.5	39.8	39.4	39.6	39.8
Trade, Transportation, and Utilities													
2014	32.4	32.9	33.1	33.2	33.8	33.6	33.7	33.4	33.7	33.4	33.5	33.3	33.3
2015	32.7	33.2	32.8	32.6	32.7	33.0	33.3	33.8	33.3	32.9	33.0	32.9	33.0
2016	32.0	32.2	32.3	32.3	33.2	33.0	33.1	32.7	32.9	33.2	32.7	32.9	32.7
2017	32.3	31.7	31.8	32.4	31.9	32.2	32.8	32.4	32.2	32.0	32.6	32.8	32.3
2018	31.7	31.9	31.7	32.1	32.5	32.4	32.8	32.6	32.8	31.7	32.3	32.2	32.2
Financial Activities													
2014	37.1	37.7	37.7	36.5	36.8	37.9	36.6	37.1	36.7	36.9	37.7	36.8	37.1
2015	37.0	37.4	37.3	36.9	36.6	36.8	36.5	37.5	36.5	36.7	37.6	36.7	37.0
2016	37.3	37.2	37.0	36.9	38.0	37.4	37.2	36.8	37.2	38.1	37.2	37.3	37.3
2017	38.6	37.7	37.5	38.6	37.5	37.8	38.8	37.5	37.6	38.5	37.6	37.4	37.9
2018	38.1	37.8	37.5	38.6	37.7	38.0	37.9	37.7	38.1	38.0	37.7	38.2	37.9
Professional and Business Services													
2014	34.4	36.1	36.1	35.3	35.7	36.8	35.8	36.0	35.4	35.8	36.4	35.5	35.8
2015	35.4	36.4	36.6	35.8	36.2	36.4	36.3	37.5	35.6	36.7	37.3	35.8	36.3
2016	35.5	35.1	35.4	35.2	36.4	37.6	37.1	37.2	37.0	37.9	37.8	37.1	36.6
2017	38.0	37.6	36.8	37.7	37.2	37.5	37.4	37.1	36.8	37.7	37.1	36.2	37.3
2018	35.8	36.6	36.5	37.0	36.6	36.6	36.8	36.7	37.0	36.0	36.2	37.1	36.6
Education and Health Services													
2014	31.1	31.1	31.0	31.3	31.1	31.3	31.2	31.4	31.6	31.7	32.0	32.2	31.4
2015	32.2	32.4	32.6	32.5	32.6	32.9	33.2	33.2	33.3	33.1	33.2	33.2	32.9
2016	33.1	32.9	33.0	33.2	33.5	32.9	33.1	33.1	32.9	33.3	33.5	33.5	33.2
2017	33.9	33.6	33.6	34.1	33.7	33.7	34.0	33.9	34.1	34.6	34.2	34.2	34.0
2018	34.3	34.4	34.2	34.3	34.1	34.2	34.3	34.3	34.0	33.3	33.2	33.5	34.0
Leisure and Hospitality													
2014	22.2	23.4	23.5	23.1	23.5	24.3	24.0	24.1	23.4	23.2	23.3	22.6	23.4
2015	22.4	23.1	23.4	22.7	23.0	24.0	24.1	24.7	23.6	23.5	23.4	22.6	23.4
2016	22.8	22.7	22.8	23.0	23.5	24.0	23.6	23.7	22.6	23.3	22.4	22.0	23.1
2017	22.0	22.1	22.2	22.1	22.1	23.1	23.3	22.8	22.2	22.5	21.5	21.2	22.3
2018	21.1	21.4	21.5	21.4	21.6	22.2	22.9	22.5	22.3	21.4	20.8	21.5	21.7
Other Services													
2014	31.1	31.6	31.4	30.9	30.7	31.4	30.9	30.6	30.6	30.5	30.9	29.9	30.9
2015	30.4	31.3	30.5	30.1	30.6	30.1	31.0	31.2	29.8	29.6	30.2	29.0	30.3
2016	29.7	29.8	29.1	29.3	30.0	29.6	28.4	29.3	29.1	29.6	28.8	28.5	29.3
2017	28.0	28.1	28.2	28.8	28.8	28.8	29.0	28.3	27.9	28.8	28.0	28.7	28.5
2018	28.4	28.8	29.0	29.1	28.8	29.1	29.1	29.0	29.0	28.7	29.1	29.8	29.0

3. Average Hourly Earnings by Selected Industry: Minnesota, 2014–2018

(Dollars, not seasonally adjusted)

Industry and year	January	February	March	April	May	June	July	August	September	October	November	December	Annual average
Total Private													
2014	26.00	25.95	25.83	25.86	25.81	25.73	25.60	25.58	25.75	25.68	25.88	25.82	25.79
2015	26.08	26.08	26.32	25.98	25.79	25.71	25.80	25.98	26.00	26.39	26.32	26.36	26.06
2016	26.71	26.54	27.05	26.90	26.99	26.64	26.95	26.88	27.32	27.63	27.78	27.85	27.11
2017	28.20	28.26	28.28	28.88	28.25	27.94	28.42	28.20	28.58	28.77	28.54	28.67	28.42
2018	28.71	28.57	28.88	29.03	28.88	28.77	29.08	28.88	29.38	29.35	29.32	29.82	29.06
Goods Producing													
2014	26.72	26.44	26.58	26.68	27.07	26.83	26.85	26.68	26.91	26.64	26.28	26.47	26.68
2015	26.72	26.42	26.38	26.57	26.44	26.35	26.58	26.58	26.37	26.74	26.29	26.26	26.48
2016	26.61	26.62	26.53	27.11	27.21	27.37	28.11	27.80	28.31	28.55	28.26	28.43	27.60
2017	28.32	28.35	28.06	28.67	28.62	28.37	28.67	28.44	28.61	28.76	28.43	28.57	28.49
2018	28.52	28.26	28.23	28.42	28.45	28.47	28.62	28.47	28.87	28.99	28.71	29.00	28.59
Construction													
2014	28.70	28.78	28.58	28.63	29.75	28.73	28.92	29.18	29.89	29.74	30.02	30.21	29.30
2015	30.49	30.73	30.78	30.36	30.73	30.31	30.27	30.60	30.68	30.84	30.19	30.48	30.53
2016	30.63	30.31	30.61	30.95	31.29	31.53	31.80	31.59	32.26	32.46	32.33	32.53	31.59
2017	32.06	32.03	32.20	31.70	32.18	32.30	32.34	32.53	32.37	33.03	32.15	32.27	32.29
2018	32.43	31.98	32.27	32.71	32.50	32.21	32.50	32.71	33.16	33.42	33.26	33.29	32.73
Manufacturing													
2014	25.93	25.57	25.76	25.83	25.87	25.90	25.80	25.38	25.39	25.08	24.69	25.06	25.52
2015	25.42	24.98	24.91	25.12	24.71	24.58	24.90	24.75	24.55	24.97	24.73	24.70	24.86
2016	25.19	25.30	25.07	25.63	25.58	25.59	26.30	25.94	26.44	26.66	26.41	26.83	25.91
2017	26.91	26.90	26.44	27.31	26.92	26.44	26.86	26.44	26.82	26.78	26.77	27.04	26.80
2018	27.00	26.82	26.70	26.76	26.69	26.72	26.82	26.47	26.88	27.07	26.73	27.20	26.82
Trade, Transportation, and Utilities													
2014	22.85	22.52	22.54	23.12	22.98	22.87	22.45	22.53	22.57	22.46	22.77	22.25	22.66
2015	22.92	22.72	22.68	22.63	22.52	22.10	22.24	22.20	22.21	22.27	22.01	22.03	22.37
2016	21.96	21.79	21.69	21.93	22.01	21.76	21.56	21.46	21.74	21.77	21.62	21.18	21.70
2017	21.93	21.68	21.39	22.30	21.84	21.77	22.25	22.05	22.59	22.57	22.47	22.16	22.09
2018	22.68	22.82	22.44	23.35	23.30	23.37	23.73	23.30	24.12	23.68	23.71	24.13	23.39
Financial Activities													
2014	33.08	33.46	33.08	32.96	32.55	32.29	31.66	31.19	31.14	31.15	31.88	31.46	32.16
2015	30.88	31.59	31.64	31.79	32.24	32.39	32.43	32.27	32.20	32.59	32.98	33.45	32.21
2016	32.21	33.33	33.61	33.96	34.45	34.01	34.92	34.92	35.19	35.82	36.13	36.33	34.59
2017	35.89	37.11	35.91	36.59	36.82	36.71	37.78	36.97	37.62	38.78	37.97	38.57	37.23
2018	38.13	38.29	39.01	39.38	39.07	38.95	40.17	39.91	40.50	40.31	40.62	41.24	39.64
Professional and Business Services													
2014	28.60	28.55	28.38	28.06	27.95	28.39	28.54	28.83	29.29	28.93	29.96	30.52	28.84
2015	30.97	30.86	31.58	30.79	31.20	31.19	31.25	31.71	32.13	32.15	32.91	32.99	31.66
2016	33.72	33.25	34.54	33.06	33.41	32.70	33.47	33.18	33.40	33.79	33.79	34.47	33.56
2017	34.83	34.43	35.11	35.39	34.26	33.79	34.84	34.46	34.51	34.58	34.49	35.25	34.66
2018	34.21	34.01	34.66	34.93	34.32	34.83	35.15	35.63	35.78	35.80	35.70	36.05	35.10
Education and Health Services													
2014	26.52	26.61	26.37	26.33	26.28	25.96	26.14	26.06	26.18	26.32	26.26	26.18	26.27
2015	26.37	26.65	27.10	26.58	26.01	26.16	26.33	26.56	26.55	27.14	26.71	26.87	26.59
2016	27.04	27.23	27.57	27.79	27.74	27.18	27.31	27.14	27.39	27.66	27.47	27.77	27.44
2017	28.07	28.45	28.95	29.60	28.60	28.76	29.13	29.06	29.37	29.46	29.38	29.68	29.05
2018	30.02	29.81	30.18	30.01	29.97	29.57	29.72	29.55	29.61	29.45	29.35	29.63	29.74
Leisure and Hospitality													
2014	13.89	13.89	13.88	13.81	13.73	13.55	13.51	13.85	14.28	14.41	14.64	14.78	14.01
2015	14.66	14.87	14.89	14.88	14.51	14.55	14.62	15.12	15.23	15.37	15.48	15.50	14.97
2016	15.37	15.56	15.90	15.61	15.59	15.14	15.30	15.54	16.10	16.35	16.60	16.68	15.80
2017	16.75	16.82	16.95	16.88	16.56	16.04	16.05	16.22	16.64	16.82	17.28	17.30	16.67
2018	17.20	17.18	17.20	17.37	17.10	16.54	16.34	16.41	16.76	16.99	17.34	17.41	16.96
Other Services													
2014	23.49	22.77	22.34	22.75	23.05	23.35	23.21	23.26	23.22	23.01	22.50	23.06	23.00
2015	22.53	22.21	22.06	22.29	22.14	21.83	21.68	22.44	22.74	23.10	22.75	22.86	22.38
2016	22.55	22.36	22.77	22.48	22.57	22.35	22.57	21.98	22.39	22.51	23.03	23.34	22.57
2017	23.03	22.52	22.61	23.55	23.62	22.77	23.05	22.90	23.22	22.76	23.03	23.29	23.03
2018	22.80	22.61	22.11	21.92	22.01	21.84	21.79	21.87	22.43	22.36	22.89	23.58	22.35

4. Average Weekly Earnings by Selected Industry: Minnesota, 2014–2018

(Dollars, not seasonally adjusted)

Industry and year	January	February	March	April	May	June	July	August	September	October	November	December	Annual average
Total Private													
2014	863.20	879.71	878.22	871.48	877.54	887.69	875.52	877.39	878.08	875.69	885.10	875.30	876.86
2015	873.68	884.11	892.25	872.93	871.70	876.71	882.36	904.10	881.40	897.26	900.14	888.33	886.04
2016	894.79	886.44	906.18	906.53	925.76	913.75	919.00	916.61	931.61	953.24	950.08	944.12	921.74
2017	958.80	955.19	955.86	987.70	957.68	952.75	977.65	964.44	974.58	989.69	973.21	971.91	969.12
2018	961.79	962.81	973.26	987.02	981.92	981.06	997.44	990.58	1010.67	986.16	991.02	1016.86	988.04
Goods Producing													
2014	1060.78	1062.89	1079.15	1077.87	1112.58	1110.76	1106.22	1115.22	1114.07	1100.23	1061.71	1066.74	1088.54
2015	1047.42	1038.31	1034.10	1038.89	1049.67	1056.64	1052.57	1073.83	1025.79	1056.23	1033.20	1026.77	1045.96
2016	1032.47	1032.86	1029.36	1060.00	1066.63	1086.59	1101.91	1098.10	1129.57	1127.73	1119.10	1100.24	1081.92
2017	1093.15	1108.49	1108.37	1118.13	1133.35	1129.13	1143.93	1146.13	1155.84	1147.52	1122.99	1131.37	1128.20
2018	1109.43	1104.97	1112.26	1111.22	1132.31	1141.65	1141.94	1150.19	1172.12	1150.90	1134.05	1154.20	1135.02
Construction													
2014	1081.99	1064.86	1091.76	1096.53	1207.85	1175.06	1203.07	1225.56	1231.47	1213.39	1128.75	1132.88	1160.28
2015	1106.79	1137.01	1138.86	1159.75	1235.35	1260.90	1247.12	1288.26	1184.25	1242.85	1171.37	1161.29	1199.83
2016	1148.63	1139.66	1160.12	1188.48	1217.18	1289.58	1303.80	1276.24	1316.21	1330.86	1293.20	1229.63	1247.81
2017	1202.25	1229.95	1242.92	1226.79	1290.42	1308.15	1306.54	1333.73	1307.75	1327.81	1250.64	1239.17	1275.46
2018	1206.40	1196.05	1223.03	1216.81	1274.00	1314.17	1313.00	1328.03	1336.35	1286.67	1293.81	1308.30	1279.74
Manufacturing													
2014	1042.39	1048.37	1058.74	1051.28	1060.67	1069.67	1047.48	1050.73	1048.61	1035.80	1019.70	1027.46	1046.32
2015	1011.72	994.20	991.42	987.22	978.52	973.37	971.10	987.53	967.27	988.81	989.20	983.06	984.46
2016	992.49	994.29	990.27	1014.95	1012.97	1010.81	1015.18	1019.44	1047.02	1034.41	1040.55	1046.37	1018.26
2017	1049.49	1057.17	1054.96	1073.28	1060.65	1044.38	1066.34	1054.96	1080.85	1060.49	1060.09	1078.90	1061.28
2018	1066.50	1064.75	1065.33	1067.72	1070.27	1060.78	1059.39	1061.45	1088.64	1077.39	1053.16	1077.12	1067.44
Trade, Transportation, and Utilities													
2014	740.34	740.91	746.07	767.58	776.72	768.43	756.57	752.50	760.61	750.16	762.80	740.93	754.58
2015	749.48	754.30	743.90	737.74	736.40	729.30	740.59	750.36	739.59	732.68	726.33	724.79	738.21
2016	702.72	701.64	700.59	708.34	730.73	718.08	713.64	701.74	715.25	722.76	706.97	696.82	709.59
2017	708.34	687.26	680.20	722.52	.696.70	700.99	729.80	714.42	727.40	722.24	732.52	726.85	713.51
2018	718.96	727.96	711.35	749.54	757.25	757.19	778.34	759.58	791.14	750.66	765.83	776.99	753.16
Financial Activities													
2014	1227.27	1261.44	1247.12	1203.04	1197.84	1223.79	1158.76	1157.15	1142.84	1149.44	1201.88	1157.73	1193.14
2015	1142.56	1181.47	1180.17	1173.05	1179.98	1191.95	1183.70	1210.13	1175.30	1196.05	1240.05	1227.62	1191.77
2016	1201.43	1239.88	1243.57	1253.12	1309.10	1271.97	1299.02	1285.06	1309.07	1364.74	1344.04	1355.11	1290.21
2017	1385.35	1399.05	1346.63	1412.37	1380.75	1387.64	1465.86	1386.38	1414.51	1493.03	1427.67	1442.52	1411.02
2018	1452.75	1447.36	1462.88	1520.07	1472.94	1480.10	1522.44	1504.61	1543.05	1531.78	1531.37	1575.37	1502.36
Professional and Business Services													
2014	983.84	1030.66	1024.52	990.52	997.82	1044.75	1021.73	1037.88	1036.87	1035.69	1090.54	1083.46	1032.47
2015	1096.34	1123.30	1155.83	1102.28	1129.44	1135.32	1134.38	1189.13	1143.83	1179.91	1227.54	1181.04	1149.26
2016	1197.06	1167.08	1222.72	1163.71	1216.12	1229.52	1241.74	1234.30	1235.80	1280.64	1277.26	1278.84	1228.30
2017	1323.54	1294.57	1292.05	1334.20	1274.47	1267.13	1303.02	1278.47	1269.97	1303.67	1279.58	1276.05	1292.82
2018	1224.72	1244.77	1265.09	1292.41	1256.11	1274.78	1293.52	1307.62	1323.86	1288.80	1292.34	1337.46	1284.66
Education and Health Services													
2014	824.77	827.57	817.47	824.13	817.31	812.55	815.57	818.28	827.29	834.34	840.32	843.00	824.88
2015	849.11	863.46	883.46	863.85	847.93	860.66	874.16	881.79	884.12	898.33	886.77	892.08	874.81
2016	895.02	895.87	909.81	922.63	929.29	894.22	903.96	898.33	901.13	921.08	920.25	930.30	911.01
2017	951.57	955.92	972.72	1009.36	963.82	969.21	990.42	985.13	1001.52	1019.32	1004.80	1015.06	987.70
2018	1029.69	1025.46	1032.16	1029.34	1021.98	1011.29	1019.40	1013.57	1006.74	980.69	974.42	992.61	1011.16
Leisure and Hospitality													
2014	308.36	325.03	326.18	319.01	322.66	329.27	324.24	333.79	334.15	334.31	341.11	334.03	327.83
2015	328.38	343.50	348.43	337.78	333.73	349.20	352.34	373.46	359.43	361.20	362.23	350.30	350.30
2016	350.44	353.21	362.52	359.03	366.37	363.36	361.08	368.30	363.86	380.96	371.84	366.96	364.98
2017	368.50	371.72	376.29	373.05	365.98	370.52	373.97	369.82	369.41	378.45	371.52	366.76	371.74
2018	362.92	367.65	369.80	371.72	369.36	367.19	374.19	369.23	373.75	363.59	360.67	374.32	368.03
Other Services													
2014	730.54	719.53	701.48	702.98	707.64	733.19	717.19	711.76	710.53	701.81	695.25	689.49	710.70
2015	684.91	695.17	672.83	670.93	677.48	657.08	672.08	700.13	677.65	683.76	687.05	662.94	678.11
2016	669.74	666.33	662.61	658.66	677.10	661.56	640.99	644.01	651.55	666.30	663.26	665.19	661.30
2017	644.84	632.81	637.60	678.24	680.26	655.78	668.45	648.07	647.84	655.49	644.84	668.42	656.36
2018	647.52	651.17	641.19	637.87	633.89	635.54	634.09	634.23	650.47	641.73	666.10	702.68	648.15

MISSISSIPPI

At a Glance

Population:
2010 census: 2,967,297
2018 estimate: 2,986,530

Percent change in population:
2010–2018: 0.6%

Percent change in total nonfarm employment:
2010–2018: 5.7%

Industry with the largest growth in employment, 2010–2018 (percent):
Transportation and utilities, 24.9%

Industry with the largest decline or smallest growth in employment, 2010–2018 (percent):
Mining or logging, -20.7%

Civilian labor force:
2010: 1,306,608
2018: 1,275,721

Unemployment rate and rank among states (highest to lowest):
2010: 10.4%, 11th
2018: 4.8%, 6th

Over-the-year change in unemployment rates:
2016–2017: -0.7%
2017–2018: -0.3%

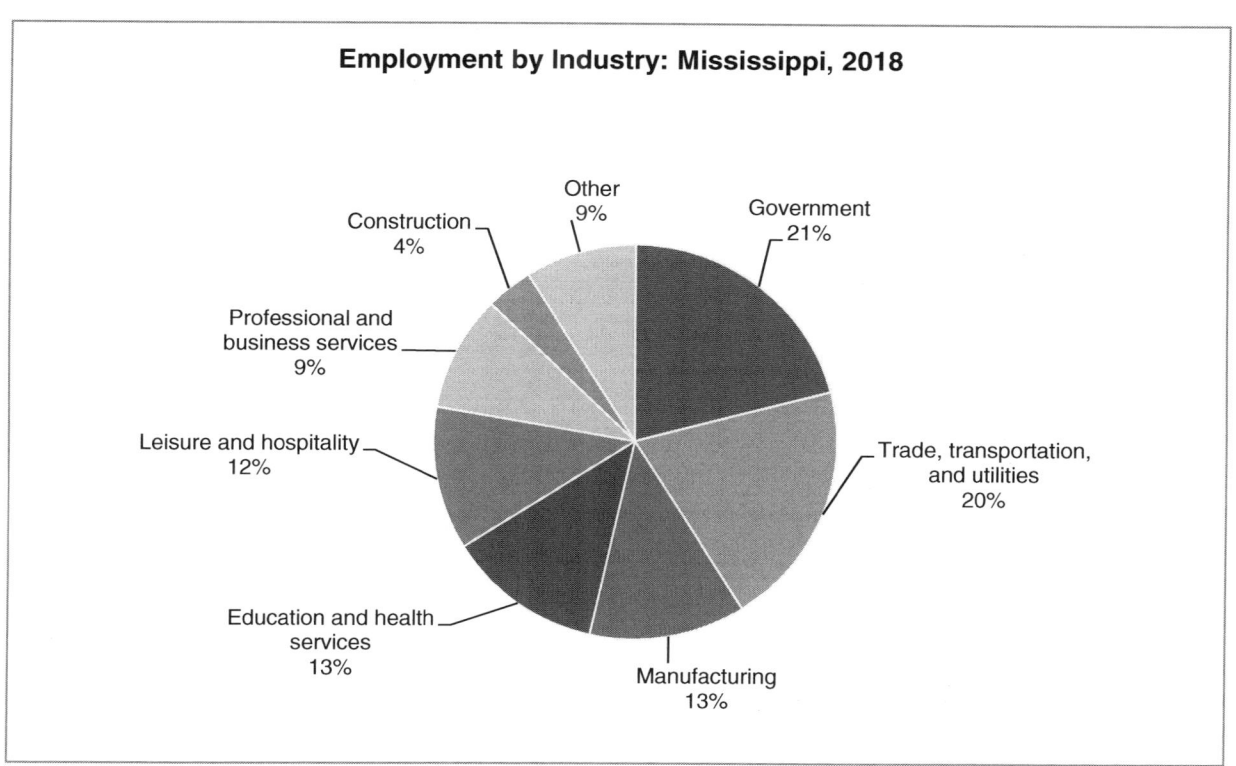

Employment by Industry: Mississippi, 2018

Other 9%
Construction 4%
Government 21%
Professional and business services 9%
Trade, transportation, and utilities 20%
Leisure and hospitality 12%
Education and health services 13%
Manufacturing 13%

1. Employment by Industry: Mississippi, 2010–2018

(Numbers in thousands, not seasonally adjusted)

Industry and year	January	February	March	April	May	June	July	August	September	October	November	December	Annual average
Total Nonfarm													
2010	1,072.3	1,077.9	1,087.8	1,098.0	1,104.7	1,100.7	1,083.5	1,089.5	1,098.4	1,100.0	1,099.5	1,098.1	1,092.5
2011	1,078.2	1,084.1	1,094.3	1,100.0	1,100.1	1,093.7	1,078.4	1,088.9	1,099.0	1,098.8	1,101.6	1,097.7	1,092.9
2012	1,085.3	1,095.4	1,103.7	1,107.4	1,108.2	1,100.5	1,086.5	1,102.0	1,107.7	1,107.4	1,112.7	1,110.7	1,102.3
2013	1,092.6	1,104.6	1,110.2	1,114.7	1,115.2	1,110.0	1,094.1	1,108.8	1,118.5	1,118.1	1,125.2	1,123.1	1,111.3
2014	1,107.4	1,110.7	1,116.8	1,124.3	1,124.3	1,118.1	1,104.8	1,118.3	1,125.8	1,128.9	1,135.0	1,135.0	1,120.8
2015	1,113.9	1,123.0	1,124.7	1,134.3	1,139.2	1,129.7	1,120.7	1,131.0	1,140.0	1,145.9	1,150.1	1,152.1	1,133.7
2016	1,133.5	1,143.3	1,146.0	1,150.7	1,149.4	1,138.3	1,133.5	1,143.3	1,152.5	1,153.2	1,158.1	1,153.6	1,146.3
2017	1,137.6	1,147.1	1,150.6	1,154.9	1,153.9	1,147.7	1,136.9	1,148.3	1,156.1	1,157.9	1,166.0	1,161.7	1,151.6
2018	1,138.4	1,146.3	1,151.8	1,157.0	1,157.4	1,149.9	1,137.6	1,152.1	1,158.3	1,165.8	1,173.6	1,169.0	1,154.8
Total Private													
2010	823.9	826.2	834.3	845.7	849.3	849.9	844.9	847.7	850.6	849.6	850.2	849.8	843.5
2011	833.0	836.6	846.0	851.2	852.0	849.5	841.8	847.1	851.5	849.8	853.1	852.7	847.0
2012	839.9	847.0	854.4	858.6	859.6	856.6	851.2	860.3	860.7	858.5	863.7	865.0	856.3
2013	847.9	856.3	861.5	865.8	867.0	866.6	859.7	868.1	871.2	870.4	877.6	879.4	866.0
2014	864.2	864.2	869.6	876.6	877.5	875.9	870.4	878.2	879.2	881.1	888.2	891.7	876.4
2015	871.6	877.5	878.4	888.7	893.1	888.7	886.5	891.6	894.6	899.2	904.0	909.4	890.3
2016	890.9	896.6	898.8	902.9	902.7	896.7	899.0	903.8	906.1	906.4	911.6	911.1	902.2
2017	896.1	901.8	904.1	909.8	910.1	908.4	903.5	909.6	910.8	912.3	920.7	920.0	908.9
2018	898.5	903.2	907.5	914.0	915.4	911.4	905.9	914.4	914.6	920.7	928.5	927.7	913.5
Goods Producing													
2010	190.1	189.5	192.0	196.5	197.0	196.7	195.8	195.5	194.8	194.6	193.8	193.4	194.1
2011	190.0	190.3	193.4	193.7	195.3	195.4	193.4	193.1	193.9	193.4	192.6	192.5	193.1
2012	191.1	193.0	194.5	195.9	195.9	195.6	194.4	195.3	195.2	195.0	194.5	194.8	194.6
2013	191.5	194.0	194.6	195.8	197.9	198.7	197.4	198.1	199.0	199.7	199.3	198.7	197.1
2014	196.9	196.7	198.7	199.3	200.1	200.4	198.0	197.7	197.1	197.4	196.5	197.0	198.0
2015	193.7	195.1	194.5	195.9	197.1	197.2	196.9	196.0	196.7	196.3	195.0	196.0	195.9
2016	194.5	195.4	196.0	194.5	193.9	193.6	194.3	194.1	194.8	194.1	194.1	194.4	194.5
2017	193.0	194.1	194.2	194.0	194.1	195.4	194.1	194.9	195.1	195.3	195.8	195.5	194.6
2018	192.4	193.6	195.0	196.5	196.8	196.5	195.1	194.7	195.4	195.5	196.5	197.2	195.4
Service-Providing													
2010	882.2	888.4	895.8	901.5	907.7	904.0	887.7	894.0	903.6	905.4	905.7	904.7	898.4
2011	888.2	893.8	900.9	906.3	904.8	898.3	885.0	895.8	905.1	905.4	909.0	905.2	899.8
2012	894.2	902.4	909.2	911.5	912.3	904.9	892.1	906.7	912.5	912.4	918.2	915.9	907.7
2013	901.1	910.6	915.6	918.9	917.3	911.3	896.7	910.7	919.5	918.4	925.9	924.4	914.2
2014	910.5	914.0	918.1	925.0	924.2	917.7	906.8	920.6	928.7	931.5	938.5	938.0	922.8
2015	920.2	927.9	930.2	938.4	942.1	932.5	923.8	935.0	943.3	949.6	955.1	956.1	937.9
2016	939.0	947.9	950.0	956.2	955.5	944.7	939.2	949.2	957.7	959.1	964.0	959.2	951.8
2017	944.6	953.0	956.4	960.9	959.8	952.3	942.8	953.4	961.0	962.6	970.2	966.2	956.9
2018	946.0	952.7	956.8	960.5	960.6	953.4	942.5	957.4	962.9	970.3	977.1	971.8	959.3
Mining and Logging													
2010	8.1	8.1	8.4	8.8	8.9	8.9	8.9	9.0	9.0	9.0	8.9	8.8	8.7
2011	8.8	8.8	9.0	9.0	9.1	9.1	9.3	9.3	9.2	9.1	9.1	9.0	9.1
2012	9.0	9.1	9.2	9.3	9.3	9.3	9.4	9.4	9.4	9.2	9.3	9.2	9.3
2013	8.9	9.0	9.0	9.1	9.2	9.2	9.3	9.3	9.2	9.1	9.1	9.1	9.1
2014	9.1	8.9	9.0	9.0	9.1	9.3	9.3	9.4	9.4	9.4	9.4	9.3	9.2
2015	8.9	8.7	8.3	8.2	8.2	8.1	7.9	7.9	7.8	7.5	7.4	7.3	8.0
2016	7.2	7.1	6.9	6.7	6.8	6.8	6.8	6.9	7.0	7.0	7.0	7.0	6.9
2017	7.0	6.9	7.0	6.9	6.9	7.0	6.9	7.0	7.0	6.9	6.9	6.9	6.9
2018	6.7	6.8	6.9	6.9	6.9	6.9	6.8	6.9	6.9	6.9	6.9	6.8	6.9
Construction													
2010	45.6	45.7	47.6	50.6	50.8	50.7	50.5	50.7	50.8	50.6	50.3	49.5	49.5
2011	46.9	47.2	49.1	49.3	50.3	50.5	49.3	48.8	49.5	49.1	48.2	47.2	48.8
2012	46.0	47.6	48.8	50.0	49.8	48.9	47.9	48.4	48.7	48.4	47.9	47.6	48.3
2013	46.2	48.6	49.3	50.3	52.2	52.9	52.6	52.5	53.0	53.2	52.0	50.5	51.1
2014	48.8	48.6	50.3	50.9	51.5	51.2	50.1	49.0	48.3	47.7	46.9	46.8	49.2
2015	44.5	45.8	45.8	46.5	46.8	46.4	47.1	46.2	46.5	46.2	45.2	45.5	46.0
2016	43.8	44.8	45.7	44.7	44.3	44.1	44.7	44.1	44.5	44.2	44.0	43.3	44.4
2017	42.4	43.0	43.4	43.5	43.2	43.6	43.6	43.7	44.2	44.4	44.2	43.1	43.5
2018	41.4	42.3	43.7	45.4	45.5	44.6	44.1	43.8	44.1	43.4	43.3	43.1	43.7

1. Employment by Industry: Mississippi, 2010–2018—*Continued*

(Numbers in thousands, not seasonally adjusted)

Industry and year	January	February	March	April	May	June	July	August	September	October	November	December	Annual average
Manufacturing													
2010	136.4	135.7	136.0	137.1	137.3	137.1	136.4	135.8	135.0	135.0	134.6	135.1	136.0
2011	134.3	134.3	135.3	135.4	135.9	135.8	134.8	135.0	135.2	135.2	135.3	136.3	135.2
2012	136.1	136.3	136.5	136.6	136.8	137.4	137.1	137.5	137.1	137.4	137.3	138.0	137.0
2013	136.4	136.4	136.3	136.4	136.5	136.6	135.5	136.3	136.8	137.4	138.2	139.1	136.8
2014	139.0	139.2	139.4	139.4	139.5	139.9	138.6	139.3	139.4	140.3	140.2	140.9	139.6
2015	140.3	140.6	140.4	141.2	142.1	142.7	141.9	141.9	142.4	142.6	142.4	143.2	141.8
2016	143.5	143.5	143.4	143.1	142.8	142.7	142.8	143.1	143.3	142.9	143.1	144.1	143.2
2017	143.6	144.2	143.8	143.6	144.0	144.8	143.6	144.2	143.9	144.0	144.7	145.5	144.2
2018	144.3	144.5	144.4	144.2	144.4	145.0	144.2	144.0	144.4	145.2	146.3	147.3	144.9
Trade, Transportation, and Utilities													
2010	210.0	209.3	210.9	212.5	213.4	213.1	212.3	212.9	212.4	213.8	216.9	219.4	213.1
2011	212.1	211.8	213.8	214.7	214.9	214.2	213.4	214.2	213.8	214.0	218.1	220.3	214.6
2012	213.5	212.9	213.8	214.4	215.4	215.0	214.7	215.1	214.7	214.3	218.8	220.5	215.3
2013	212.8	212.2	212.9	213.7	214.6	215.6	215.6	216.7	216.6	216.7	222.4	225.0	216.2
2014	216.9	216.3	217.1	217.8	218.3	219.2	219.1	220.2	219.5	221.3	226.7	229.4	220.2
2015	221.1	220.7	220.9	223.5	224.3	224.5	223.4	224.3	224.3	226.3	231.6	234.3	224.9
2016	226.5	226.0	226.1	228.3	228.7	228.1	228.9	229.2	229.5	231.2	236.5	238.1	229.8
2017	230.5	229.1	228.8	229.5	229.5	230.0	230.1	231.0	230.5	231.7	237.4	238.5	231.4
2018	229.9	228.9	229.4	229.6	230.7	230.4	229.9	230.0	229.4	230.9	237.0	237.4	231.1
Wholesale Trade													
2010	33.7	33.7	33.5	33.8	33.8	33.9	33.8	34.2	33.8	33.8	33.7	34.2	33.8
2011	33.8	33.9	33.8	33.8	33.9	33.7	33.8	34.2	34.1	33.8	33.8	34.3	33.9
2012	34.1	34.2	33.9	33.7	33.8	33.8	33.8	34.1	33.9	33.5	33.6	33.8	33.9
2013	33.9	33.9	33.6	33.5	33.7	33.7	33.5	33.9	33.8	33.4	33.4	33.9	33.7
2014	33.7	33.8	33.4	33.5	33.5	33.6	33.6	34.0	33.7	33.6	33.6	34.2	33.7
2015	34.1	34.1	33.6	33.8	33.9	33.9	33.7	34.0	33.9	33.9	33.8	34.1	33.9
2016	34.0	33.9	33.5	33.5	33.7	33.7	33.8	34.2	34.2	34.1	34.0	34.4	33.9
2017	34.5	34.6	34.3	34.1	34.1	34.2	34.1	34.5	34.2	34.2	34.0	34.5	34.3
2018	34.2	34.3	33.9	33.9	34.1	34.1	34.0	34.5	34.2	34.6	34.6	34.5	34.2
Retail Trade													
2010	130.3	129.7	131.3	132.1	133.0	132.6	131.9	131.7	131.2	132.2	135.4	137.0	132.4
2011	131.2	130.8	132.4	133.4	133.5	133.1	132.4	132.3	131.7	132.4	136.3	137.7	133.1
2012	132.4	131.7	132.6	133.3	133.8	133.5	133.2	132.7	132.1	132.6	136.8	137.7	133.5
2013	130.8	130.2	131.1	131.8	132.3	133.3	133.6	133.7	133.6	133.7	138.8	140.4	133.6
2014	133.7	133.3	134.4	134.8	134.9	135.6	135.3	135.4	134.9	135.8	140.4	142.0	135.9
2015	135.5	135.3	135.8	137.6	138.1	138.3	137.5	137.6	137.3	138.5	143.0	144.4	138.2
2016	138.5	138.7	139.0	140.7	140.5	139.8	140.3	139.8	139.9	141.1	145.2	145.5	140.8
2017	140.3	139.3	139.5	140.2	140.1	140.0	139.8	139.8	139.4	139.8	143.9	143.8	140.5
2018	138.3	137.5	138.1	138.4	138.8	138.1	137.8	137.2	136.7	137.2	141.0	140.6	138.3
Transportation and Utilities													
2010	46.0	45.9	46.1	46.6	46.6	46.6	46.6	47.0	47.4	47.8	47.8	48.2	46.9
2011	47.1	47.1	47.6	47.5	47.5	47.4	47.2	47.7	48.0	47.8	48.0	48.3	47.6
2012	47.0	47.0	47.3	47.4	47.8	47.7	47.7	48.3	48.7	48.2	48.4	49.0	47.9
2013	48.1	48.1	48.2	48.4	48.6	48.6	48.5	49.1	49.2	49.6	50.2	50.7	48.9
2014	49.5	49.2	49.3	49.5	49.9	50.0	50.2	50.8	50.9	51.9	52.7	53.2	50.6
2015	51.5	51.3	51.5	52.1	52.3	52.3	52.2	52.7	53.1	53.9	54.8	55.8	52.8
2016	54.0	53.4	53.6	54.1	54.5	54.6	54.8	55.2	55.4	56.0	57.3	58.2	55.1
2017	55.7	55.2	55.0	55.2	55.3	55.8	56.2	56.7	56.9	57.7	59.5	60.2	56.6
2018	57.4	57.1	57.4	57.3	57.8	58.2	58.1	58.3	58.5	59.1	61.4	62.3	58.6
Information													
2010	12.2	12.2	12.3	12.1	12.2	12.3	12.3	12.3	12.6	12.7	12.3	12.2	12.3
2011	12.0	12.0	12.0	11.9	12.0	12.1	12.1	12.1	12.1	12.1	12.2	12.4	12.1
2012	12.5	12.5	12.5	12.5	12.5	12.5	12.6	12.4	12.4	12.4	12.7	12.7	12.5
2013	12.8	12.8	12.7	12.7	12.6	12.8	12.7	12.7	12.8	12.8	12.9	13.2	12.8
2014	13.8	13.0	13.0	12.8	12.7	12.8	12.8	13.0	13.0	13.1	13.4	13.3	13.1
2015	12.8	12.8	12.7	12.5	12.8	12.7	12.7	12.5	12.6	12.7	12.7	12.8	12.7
2016	12.4	12.3	12.1	12.0	12.2	12.2	12.3	12.2	12.0	12.1	12.2	12.1	12.2
2017	11.7	11.8	11.8	11.7	11.8	11.7	11.6	11.5	11.3	11.4	11.4	11.3	11.6
2018	11.1	11.1	11.0	11.0	11.0	11.1	11.0	11.0	10.8	10.9	11.0	10.9	11.0

1. Employment by Industry: Mississippi, 2010–2018—*Continued*

(Numbers in thousands, not seasonally adjusted)

Industry and year	January	February	March	April	May	June	July	August	September	October	November	December	Annual average
Financial Activities													
2010	44.5	44.4	44.5	44.5	44.7	44.8	44.7	44.5	44.4	44.2	44.2	44.4	44.5
2011	43.9	44.0	44.0	44.3	44.1	44.4	44.2	44.3	44.2	44.1	44.2	44.2	44.2
2012	43.9	43.9	44.0	44.1	44.3	44.3	44.3	44.4	44.2	43.9	44.0	44.0	44.1
2013	43.6	43.8	43.9	43.9	43.8	43.9	43.7	43.8	43.6	43.8	43.9	43.9	43.8
2014	43.2	43.3	43.2	43.1	43.5	43.5	43.4	43.6	43.4	43.4	43.7	43.7	43.4
2015	43.3	43.3	43.3	43.4	43.7	43.7	43.8	43.8	43.6	43.9	44.1	44.4	43.7
2016	43.8	43.9	43.8	44.1	44.1	44.1	44.3	44.3	44.1	44.2	44.2	44.2	44.1
2017	43.8	43.8	43.9	43.9	44.0	44.4	44.2	44.2	44.2	44.4	44.3	44.4	44.1
2018	44.2	44.2	44.3	44.3	44.6	44.6	44.6	44.6	44.5	44.6	44.3	44.2	44.4
Professional and Business Services													
2010	86.0	87.6	88.2	90.6	92.8	96.2	95.7	94.1	95.5	94.6	94.1	94.1	92.5
2011	92.2	93.3	94.5	95.4	94.7	94.2	92.2	93.4	94.4	94.5	94.9	94.0	94.0
2012	92.3	94.7	96.7	96.8	97.0	96.3	94.3	97.6	98.1	98.4	99.4	99.5	96.8
2013	97.3	100.3	101.1	100.5	99.7	98.8	96.0	99.4	98.6	98.6	99.9	101.5	99.3
2014	99.9	99.7	99.7	101.7	100.6	99.9	99.0	102.2	102.9	103.4	105.2	106.6	101.7
2015	102.6	103.8	103.6	105.2	105.2	103.8	104.0	106.9	107.0	109.1	110.3	112.5	106.2
2016	108.0	109.8	109.5	108.6	107.3	106.0	106.4	107.5	108.0	108.8	109.0	109.3	108.2
2017	106.3	108.3	108.4	108.8	107.8	106.9	105.0	106.5	107.1	108.5	110.9	111.7	108.0
2018	107.1	107.6	108.3	109.3	108.0	107.4	106.4	109.5	111.2	114.0	114.1	114.4	109.8
Education and Health Services													
2010	129.6	130.3	130.7	131.1	130.0	126.8	125.9	129.1	132.7	133.6	133.6	132.4	130.5
2011	131.7	132.5	132.7	133.0	131.3	128.9	127.6	130.2	134.5	134.9	134.6	133.6	132.1
2012	132.7	134.1	134.4	134.2	132.2	129.7	129.0	132.0	134.5	135.4	135.3	134.5	133.2
2013	133.4	134.7	135.0	135.7	133.6	130.4	129.3	131.6	135.7	136.1	136.2	135.1	133.9
2014	133.7	134.5	134.6	135.5	134.2	131.3	131.7	135.0	137.3	137.7	138.3	137.6	135.1
2015	136.7	137.9	138.0	138.6	138.7	134.8	134.4	136.4	139.4	140.7	140.8	139.9	138.0
2016	138.9	140.1	140.2	141.1	141.0	137.0	136.9	139.9	141.9	142.5	142.4	141.9	140.3
2017	141.8	143.6	143.8	145.1	144.4	141.2	140.7	143.4	146.1	146.1	146.3	145.2	144.0
2018	143.6	145.4	144.5	145.6	145.1	141.8	141.3	145.1	146.2	146.9	147.4	146.5	145.0
Leisure and Hospitality													
2010	113.4	114.8	117.3	119.6	120.4	121.3	119.7	120.9	119.7	117.8	117.4	116.2	118.2
2011	113.8	115.4	118.1	120.6	121.8	122.2	121.1	122.2	121.0	119.1	118.9	118.2	119.4
2012	116.4	118.4	120.7	122.7	124.1	124.7	123.4	124.9	123.0	120.8	120.6	120.5	121.7
2013	118.2	119.9	122.5	124.7	125.9	127.0	126.0	126.9	126.0	123.9	124.2	123.3	124.0
2014	121.3	122.1	124.5	127.6	129.1	129.3	127.2	127.2	126.9	125.8	125.1	124.7	125.9
2015	122.2	124.4	125.8	129.7	131.3	131.8	131.2	131.9	131.2	130.4	129.6	129.6	129.1
2016	126.9	129.0	130.9	134.1	135.3	135.3	135.4	136.4	135.6	133.3	133.0	130.9	133.0
2017	129.1	130.9	132.8	136.3	137.9	137.9	137.1	137.5	135.7	134.2	133.8	132.6	134.7
2018	129.4	131.4	133.8	136.4	137.8	137.9	136.2	138.3	135.9	136.1	136.7	136.2	135.5
Other Services													
2010	38.1	38.1	38.4	38.8	38.8	38.7	38.5	38.4	38.5	38.3	37.9	37.7	38.4
2011	37.3	37.3	37.5	37.6	37.9	38.1	37.8	37.6	37.6	37.7	37.6	37.5	37.6
2012	37.5	37.5	37.8	38.0	38.2	38.5	38.5	38.6	38.6	38.3	38.4	38.5	38.2
2013	38.3	38.6	38.8	38.8	38.9	39.4	39.0	38.9	38.9	38.8	38.8	38.7	38.8
2014	38.5	38.6	38.8	38.8	39.0	39.5	39.2	39.3	39.1	39.0	39.3	39.4	39.0
2015	39.2	39.5	39.6	39.9	40.0	40.2	40.1	39.8	39.8	39.8	39.9	39.9	39.8
2016	39.9	40.1	40.2	40.2	40.2	40.4	40.5	40.2	40.2	40.2	40.2	40.2	40.2
2017	39.9	40.2	40.4	40.5	40.6	40.9	40.7	40.6	40.8	40.7	40.8	40.8	40.6
2018	40.8	41.0	41.2	41.3	41.4	41.7	41.4	41.2	41.2	41.8	41.5	40.9	41.3
Government													
2010	248.4	251.7	253.5	252.3	255.4	250.8	238.6	241.8	247.8	250.4	249.3	248.3	249.0
2011	245.2	247.5	248.3	248.8	248.1	244.2	236.6	241.8	247.5	249.0	248.5	245.0	245.9
2012	245.4	248.4	249.3	248.8	248.6	243.9	235.3	241.7	247.0	248.9	249.0	245.7	246.0
2013	244.7	248.3	248.7	248.9	248.2	243.4	234.4	240.7	247.3	247.7	247.6	243.7	245.3
2014	243.2	246.5	247.2	247.7	246.8	242.2	234.4	240.1	246.6	247.8	246.8	243.3	244.4
2015	242.3	245.5	246.3	245.6	246.1	241.0	234.2	239.4	245.4	246.7	246.1	242.7	243.4
2016	242.6	246.7	247.2	247.8	246.7	241.6	234.5	239.5	246.4	246.8	246.5	242.5	244.1
2017	241.5	245.3	246.5	245.1	243.8	239.3	233.4	238.7	245.3	245.6	245.3	241.7	242.6
2018	239.9	243.1	244.3	243.0	242.0	238.5	231.7	237.7	243.7	245.1	245.1	241.3	241.3

2. Average Weekly Hours by Selected Industry: Mississippi, 2014–2018

(Not seasonally adjusted)

Industry and year	January	February	March	April	May	June	July	August	September	October	November	December	Annual average
Total Private													
2014	35.5	35.6	36.0	35.5	35.5	36.1	35.7	35.9	36.0	35.7	36.0	35.6	35.8
2015	35.0	35.3	35.3	34.4	34.6	34.8	34.7	35.1	34.2	34.7	35.0	34.7	34.8
2016	34.6	34.5	34.2	34.3	34.8	34.5	34.9	34.5	34.9	35.3	34.9	34.9	34.7
2017	34.9	34.7	34.6	34.7	34.8	34.9	35.2	34.7	34.8	35.0	34.7	34.8	34.8
2018	34.4	34.7	34.7	34.9	34.6	34.8	35.0	34.5	34.8	34.4	34.4	35.3	34.7
Goods Producing													
2014	42.5	41.3	42.0	41.8	41.3	42.1	41.7	42.4	43.1	42.7	42.5	42.3	42.1
2015	41.1	40.9	41.0	39.6	40.4	40.5	40.1	41.1	39.7	41.1	41.7	41.8	40.7
2016	41.5	41.4	41.1	41.3	42.1	41.3	42.0	41.3	41.6	42.3	41.7	42.0	41.6
2017	41.2	41.4	41.0	40.0	40.9	41.5	41.7	41.0	41.5	41.4	41.6	42.0	41.3
2018	39.7	41.6	41.5	41.5	41.0	41.6	41.0	41.2	40.8	40.6	40.1	41.7	41.0
Construction													
2014	40.2	38.9	42.2	41.0	42.2	42.2	43.5	44.0	44.3	43.8	44.3	43.7	42.5
2015	40.8	40.7	40.6	36.1	38.5	37.6	38.2	38.6	36.5	40.0	40.1	40.5	39.0
2016	40.6	40.5	39.3	38.8	42.3	41.7	41.7	40.4	41.5	41.6	40.5	39.8	40.7
2017	40.4	40.5	39.5	40.3	40.5	41.4	41.1	40.0	41.2	40.9	41.2	42.0	40.7
2018	36.9	38.9	40.6	41.6	42.2	40.6	40.5	39.8	39.3	40.0	37.1	39.0	39.7
Manufacturing													
2014	42.8	41.9	42.7	42.9	41.7	42.5	41.4	42.1	42.9	42.5	42.0	42.1	42.3
2015	41.6	41.3	41.7	41.7	41.8	42.3	41.5	42.7	41.4	42.2	42.9	42.9	42.0
2016	42.3	42.3	42.3	42.7	42.5	41.6	42.6	42.2	42.0	42.9	42.5	43.2	42.4
2017	41.8	42.0	41.7	40.2	41.2	41.7	42.0	41.4	41.6	41.5	41.6	41.9	41.6
2018	40.3	41.6	41.1	40.9	40.0	41.5	40.7	41.2	41.0	40.5	40.9	42.3	41.0
Trade, Transportation, and Utilities													
2014	35.3	35.9	36.2	35.6	35.8	36.2	36.1	35.7	35.8	35.1	35.3	35.0	35.7
2015	34.3	35.1	35.2	34.5	34.9	34.7	34.6	34.7	34.2	33.9	34.1	33.7	34.5
2016	33.4	33.1	32.7	32.8	33.3	33.4	33.8	33.4	33.3	34.1	33.9	33.9	33.4
2017	33.8	33.6	34.5	34.9	34.6	34.5	34.6	34.9	34.8	35.2	34.7	35.1	34.6
2018	34.3	34.4	34.7	34.6	34.6	34.5	35.1	34.3	34.6	34.2	34.3	35.0	34.5
Financial Activities													
2014	37.8	39.2	39.2	38.3	38.1	40.0	38.5	38.6	38.2	37.3	39.2	37.4	38.5
2015	37.6	38.9	39.2	36.3	36.4	36.6	36.7	39.1	36.7	37.4	39.1	36.7	37.6
2016	37.3	36.9	36.8	37.3	38.5	36.8	37.0	36.4	36.4	37.5	36.1	35.8	36.9
2017	36.9	36.2	35.5	36.3	36.1	36.4	37.2	35.6	36.6	36.1	34.9	34.9	36.1
2018	34.5	35.4	35.6	36.7	34.8	35.6	37.0	35.9	37.6	36.3	36.6	38.8	36.2
Professional and Business Services													
2014	34.6	34.9	35.3	34.5	35.0	35.6	34.8	35.7	35.7	35.5	36.0	35.6	35.3
2015	35.1	36.3	36.2	35.3	35.4	35.6	35.6	36.7	35.1	36.1	36.1	35.8	35.8
2016	35.3	35.0	34.8	34.4	35.1	35.3	34.9	35.0	35.3	34.5	33.8	34.2	34.8
2017	34.3	34.1	33.6	33.4	34.0	33.9	34.2	33.9	33.7	34.8	34.1	34.0	34.0
2018	32.7	33.6	33.5	34.5	33.9	34.6	34.4	34.2	34.4	34.3	34.4	35.2	34.1
Education and Health Services													
2014	33.5	33.4	33.3	33.1	33.2	33.7	33.5	33.8	33.7	33.6	34.3	33.8	33.6
2015	33.7	33.9	33.5	33.6	33.3	33.1	33.4	34.1	33.6	33.7	34.0	33.5	33.6
2016	34.2	33.9	33.8	33.9	34.2	34.2	34.4	34.2	34.7	35.1	35.0	34.8	34.4
2017	34.9	34.5	34.0	34.5	34.0	34.2	34.7	34.3	34.1	34.0	34.1	33.7	34.2
2018	33.7	33.9	33.5	34.1	33.5	33.5	33.8	33.2	33.7	33.0	33.8	33.7	33.6
Leisure and Hospitality													
2014	27.0	27.5	28.3	27.5	27.6	27.6	27.5	27.4	26.9	27.3	27.1	27.3	27.4
2015	26.7	28.0	28.2	26.7	26.8	27.3	27.7	26.2	25.8	26.1	26.3	26.1	26.8
2016	26.0	26.8	26.5	26.7	27.2	26.5	27.0	26.2	26.5	26.8	26.6	26.6	26.6
2017	26.7	26.9	27.2	27.7	27.6	27.7	27.6	26.9	26.9	26.9	26.9	26.8	27.2
2018	25.9	27.2	27.4	27.3	27.7	27.4	27.7	27.0	27.1	27.4	26.6	27.0	27.1

3. Average Hourly Earnings by Selected Industry: Mississippi, 2014–2018

(Dollars, not seasonally adjusted)

Industry and year	January	February	March	April	May	June	July	August	September	October	November	December	Annual average
Total Private													
2014	19.65	19.75	19.57	19.44	19.13	19.37	19.36	19.36	19.31	19.27	19.29	19.22	19.39
2015	19.31	19.76	19.90	19.79	19.57	19.55	19.64	19.79	19.77	19.69	19.89	19.86	19.71
2016	19.87	19.69	19.66	19.95	20.05	19.94	20.08	19.96	20.03	20.28	20.05	20.09	19.97
2017	20.40	20.33	20.23	20.32	20.10	20.16	20.50	20.53	20.77	20.64	20.63	20.34	20.41
2018	20.01	20.00	20.08	20.18	20.19	20.16	20.45	20.20	20.60	20.64	20.53	20.96	20.34
Goods Producing													
2014	20.48	20.77	20.37	20.11	19.95	20.26	20.56	20.73	20.81	20.54	20.18	20.22	20.42
2015	20.14	20.41	20.84	20.87	20.65	20.68	20.83	20.77	20.75	20.79	21.08	21.41	20.77
2016	21.29	21.37	21.35	21.90	22.46	22.82	22.82	22.62	22.93	23.03	23.12	23.31	22.42
2017	23.04	22.73	22.77	22.70	22.56	22.59	22.87	22.88	22.97	22.90	22.81	22.73	22.80
2018	22.82	22.53	22.45	22.44	22.53	22.42	22.60	22.37	22.90	22.73	22.87	23.15	22.65
Construction													
2014	21.09	21.74	21.30	20.95	20.75	20.88	21.46	21.61	21.63	21.69	21.60	21.93	21.38
2015	21.63	21.42	22.27	22.19	21.72	22.45	22.12	22.08	21.95	21.89	22.13	22.47	22.02
2016	22.17	22.28	22.61	22.40	22.86	22.75	22.24	22.04	22.24	22.22	22.45	22.94	22.43
2017	22.48	22.76	22.74	22.51	22.40	22.56	22.37	22.68	22.56	22.51	22.72	23.04	22.61
2018	22.91	22.85	22.45	22.37	22.77	22.80	22.97	22.49	23.04	22.58	22.50	22.66	22.70
Manufacturing													
2014	20.06	20.23	19.91	19.63	19.54	19.87	20.04	20.30	20.40	19.97	19.53	19.48	19.91
2015	19.48	19.91	20.14	20.23	20.16	19.90	20.23	20.17	20.22	20.34	20.70	21.04	20.21
2016	20.98	21.07	20.96	21.68	22.32	22.75	22.98	22.77	23.16	23.31	23.34	23.43	22.40
2017	23.25	22.77	22.85	22.82	22.65	22.67	23.14	23.06	23.20	23.12	22.91	22.74	22.93
2018	22.86	22.51	22.47	22.48	22.51	22.29	22.52	22.35	22.84	22.82	22.64	23.00	22.61
Trade, Transportation, and Utilities													
2014	18.86	18.60	18.52	18.68	18.35	18.77	18.61	18.67	18.43	18.55	18.47	18.27	18.56
2015	18.20	18.38	18.38	18.38	17.80	18.00	18.22	18.42	18.39	18.47	18.33	18.03	18.25
2016	18.26	18.11	18.26	18.70	18.89	18.39	18.76	18.61	19.18	19.35	18.94	18.66	18.68
2017	19.41	20.01	19.62	19.86	20.06	20.05	20.20	20.69	21.05	20.79	20.58	19.77	20.18
2018	19.47	19.53	19.55	20.13	20.16	19.75	20.13	19.98	19.90	20.24	19.99	20.52	19.95
Financial Activities													
2014	24.18	24.99	25.07	24.20	23.97	23.68	23.34	23.22	22.95	23.24	24.14	23.43	23.87
2015	23.51	25.13	25.02	24.54	24.43	24.83	24.83	25.03	25.31	25.21	26.29	26.40	25.05
2016	25.13	26.34	25.77	25.53	25.35	24.71	24.61	24.57	23.98	24.29	23.97	23.61	24.83
2017	24.13	24.26	23.96	23.50	22.28	22.03	22.27	22.16	22.48	22.51	22.13	22.37	22.84
2018	22.84	22.19	22.59	23.42	23.47	22.94	24.37	23.80	24.71	23.70	23.77	24.22	23.52
Professional and Business Services													
2014	21.81	22.09	22.12	21.99	21.79	21.92	21.84	21.60	21.30	21.35	21.86	21.70	21.78
2015	21.78	22.61	22.73	22.30	22.12	21.56	21.55	21.82	21.74	21.39	21.60	20.84	21.83
2016	20.89	20.95	20.64	20.76	20.85	20.41	20.48	20.09	20.05	21.05	21.02	21.39	20.71
2017	21.35	21.30	21.19	21.52	20.85	21.16	21.27	20.97	21.33	21.03	21.07	20.49	21.12
2018	20.17	19.99	20.36	19.82	19.92	19.98	20.53	20.25	20.69	20.91	20.44	22.16	20.45
Education and Health Services													
2014	19.82	19.75	19.72	19.77	19.44	19.50	19.52	19.49	19.58	19.57	19.37	19.57	19.59
2015	19.95	20.13	20.24	20.41	20.38	20.45	20.75	20.80	20.86	20.78	20.74	21.02	20.54
2016	21.03	21.12	21.18	21.20	21.07	21.15	21.38	21.29	20.99	20.93	20.28	20.27	20.99
2017	20.38	20.55	20.59	20.90	20.74	20.95	21.26	20.83	20.93	20.99	21.22	21.34	20.89
2018	21.40	21.51	21.56	21.67	21.64	21.76	21.89	21.31	21.23	21.42	21.00	21.40	21.48
Leisure and Hospitality													
2014	12.17	12.24	11.98	11.81	11.76	11.78	11.80	11.86	11.73	11.85	11.80	11.80	11.88
2015	11.99	11.98	12.05	11.76	11.79	11.71	11.79	11.75	11.80	11.58	11.70	11.67	11.80
2016	11.89	11.91	11.91	12.05	12.00	11.63	11.73	11.74	11.87	11.93	11.80	11.80	11.85
2017	11.65	11.85	11.90	12.12	12.15	12.14	12.12	12.11	12.12	12.26	12.17	12.09	12.06
2018	12.18	12.25	12.20	12.19	12.15	12.18	12.24	12.25	12.34	12.40	12.54	12.66	12.30

4. Average Weekly Earnings by Selected Industry: Mississippi, 2014–2018

(Dollars, not seasonally adjusted)

Industry and year	January	February	March	April	May	June	July	August	September	October	November	December	Annual average
Total Private													
2014	697.58	703.10	704.52	690.12	679.12	699.26	691.15	695.02	695.16	687.94	694.44	684.23	694.16
2015	675.85	697.53	702.47	680.78	677.12	680.34	681.51	694.63	676.13	683.24	696.15	689.14	685.91
2016	687.50	679.31	672.37	684.29	697.74	687.93	700.79	688.62	699.05	715.88	699.75	701.14	692.96
2017	711.96	705.45	699.96	705.10	699.48	703.58	721.60	712.39	722.80	722.40	715.86	707.83	710.27
2018	688.34	694.00	696.78	704.28	698.57	701.57	715.75	696.90	716.88	710.02	706.23	739.89	705.80
Goods Producing													
2014	870.40	857.80	855.54	840.60	823.94	852.95	857.35	878.95	896.91	877.06	857.65	855.31	859.68
2015	827.75	834.77	854.44	826.45	834.26	837.54	835.28	853.65	823.78	854.47	879.04	894.94	845.34
2016	883.54	884.72	877.49	904.47	945.57	942.47	958.44	934.21	953.89	974.17	964.10	979.02	932.67
2017	949.25	941.02	933.57	908.00	922.70	937.49	953.68	938.08	953.26	948.06	948.90	954.66	941.64
2018	905.95	937.25	931.68	931.26	923.73	932.67	926.60	921.64	934.32	922.84	917.09	965.36	928.65
Construction													
2014	847.82	845.69	898.86	858.95	875.65	881.14	933.51	950.84	958.21	950.02	956.88	958.34	908.65
2015	882.50	871.79	904.16	801.06	836.22	844.12	844.98	852.29	801.18	875.60	887.41	910.04	858.78
2016	900.10	902.34	888.57	869.12	966.98	948.68	927.41	890.42	922.96	924.35	909.23	913.01	912.90
2017	908.19	921.78	898.23	907.15	907.20	933.98	919.41	907.20	929.47	920.66	936.06	967.68	920.23
2018	845.38	888.87	911.47	930.59	960.89	925.68	930.29	895.10	905.47	903.20	834.75	883.74	901.19
Manufacturing													
2014	858.57	847.64	850.16	842.13	814.82	844.48	829.66	854.63	875.16	848.73	820.26	820.11	842.19
2015	810.37	822.28	839.84	843.59	842.69	841.77	839.55	861.26	837.11	858.35	888.03	902.62	848.82
2016	887.45	891.26	886.61	925.74	948.60	946.40	978.95	960.89	972.72	1000.00	991.95	1012.18	949.76
2017	971.85	956.34	952.85	917.36	933.18	945.34	971.88	954.68	965.12	959.48	953.06	952.81	953.89
2018	921.26	936.42	923.52	919.43	900.40	925.04	916.56	920.82	936.44	924.21	925.98	972.90	927.01
Trade, Transportation, and Utilities													
2014	665.76	667.74	670.42	665.01	656.93	679.47	671.82	666.52	659.79	651.11	651.99	639.45	662.59
2015	624.26	645.14	646.98	634.11	621.22	624.60	630.41	639.17	628.94	626.13	625.05	607.61	629.63
2016	609.88	599.44	597.10	613.36	629.04	614.23	634.09	621.57	638.69	659.84	642.07	632.57	623.91
2017	656.06	672.34	676.89	693.11	694.08	691.73	698.92	722.08	732.54	731.81	714.13	693.93	698.23
2018	667.82	671.83	678.39	696.50	697.54	681.38	706.56	685.31	688.54	692.21	685.66	718.20	688.28
Financial Activities													
2014	914.00	979.61	982.74	926.86	913.26	947.20	898.59	896.29	876.69	866.85	946.29	876.28	919.00
2015	883.98	977.56	980.78	890.80	889.25	908.78	911.26	978.67	928.88	942.85	1027.94	968.88	941.88
2016	937.35	971.95	948.34	952.27	975.98	909.33	910.57	894.35	872.87	910.88	865.32	845.24	916.23
2017	890.40	878.21	850.58	853.05	804.31	801.89	828.44	788.90	822.77	812.61	772.34	780.71	824.52
2018	787.98	785.53	804.20	859.51	816.76	816.66	901.69	854.42	929.10	860.31	869.98	939.74	851.42
Professional and Business Services													
2014	754.63	770.94	780.84	758.66	762.65	780.35	760.03	771.12	760.41	757.93	786.96	772.52	768.83
2015	764.48	820.74	822.83	787.19	783.05	767.54	767.18	800.79	763.07	772.18	779.76	746.07	781.51
2016	737.42	733.25	718.27	714.14	731.84	720.47	714.75	703.15	707.77	726.23	710.48	731.54	720.71
2017	732.31	726.33	711.98	718.77	708.90	717.32	727.43	710.88	718.82	731.84	718.49	696.66	718.08
2018	659.56	671.66	682.06	683.79	675.29	691.31	706.23	692.55	711.74	717.21	703.14	780.03	697.35
Education and Health Services													
2014	663.97	659.65	656.68	654.39	645.41	657.15	653.92	658.76	659.85	657.55	664.39	661.47	658.22
2015	672.32	682.41	678.04	685.78	678.65	676.90	693.05	709.28	700.90	700.29	705.16	704.17	690.14
2016	719.23	715.97	715.88	718.68	720.59	723.33	735.47	728.12	728.35	734.64	709.80	705.40	722.06
2017	711.26	708.98	700.06	721.05	705.16	716.49	737.72	714.47	713.71	713.66	723.60	719.16	714.44
2018	721.18	729.19	722.26	738.95	724.94	728.96	739.88	707.49	715.45	706.86	709.80	721.18	721.73
Leisure and Hospitality													
2014	328.59	336.60	339.03	324.78	324.58	325.13	324.50	324.96	315.54	323.51	319.78	322.14	325.51
2015	320.13	335.44	339.81	313.99	315.97	319.68	326.58	307.85	304.44	302.24	307.71	304.59	316.24
2016	309.14	319.19	315.62	321.74	326.40	308.20	316.71	307.59	314.56	319.72	313.88	313.88	315.21
2017	311.06	318.77	323.68	335.72	335.34	336.28	334.51	325.76	326.03	329.79	327.37	324.01	328.03
2018	315.46	333.20	334.28	332.79	336.56	333.73	339.05	330.75	334.41	339.76	333.56	341.82	333.33

MISSOURI
At a Glance

Population:
  2010 census: 5,988,927
  2018 estimate: 6,126,452

Percent change in population:
  2010–2018: 2.3%

Percent change in total nonfarm employment:
  2010–2018: 8.3%

Industry with the largest growth in employment, 2010–2018 (percent):
  Professional and business services, 21.2%

Industry with the largest decline or smallest growth in employment, 2010–2018 (percent):
  Information, -16.1%

Civilian labor force:
  2010: 3,056,484
  2018: 3,052,386

Unemployment rate and rank among states (highest to lowest):
  2010: 9.6%, 19th
  2018: 3.2%, 39th

Over-the-year change in unemployment rates:
  2016–2017: -0.8%
  2017–2018: -0.6%

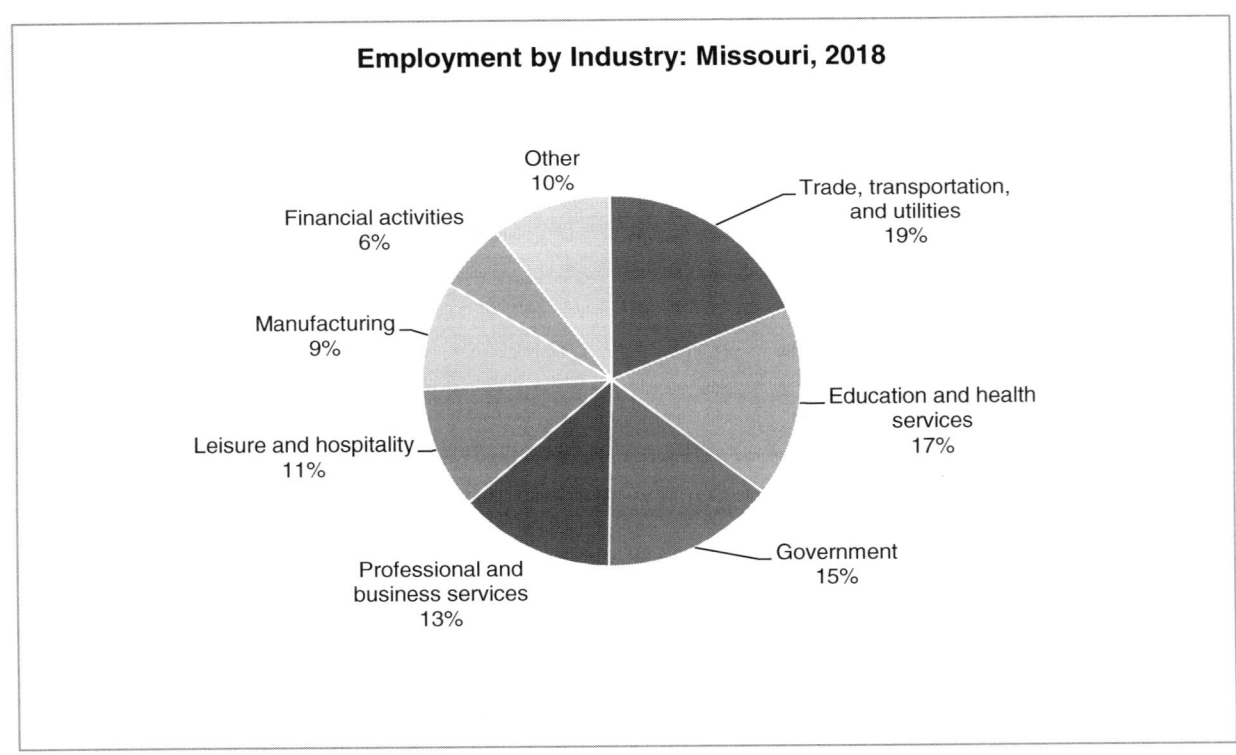

Employment by Industry: Missouri, 2018

Other 10%
Financial activities 6%
Manufacturing 9%
Leisure and hospitality 11%
Professional and business services 13%
Government 15%
Education and health services 17%
Trade, transportation, and utilities 19%

1. Employment by Industry: Missouri, 2010–2018

(Numbers in thousands, not seasonally adjusted)

Industry and year	January	February	March	April	May	June	July	August	September	October	November	December	Annual average
Total Nonfarm													
2010	2,604.2	2,616.3	2,646.5	2,680.2	2,698.4	2,688.9	2,638.5	2,666.1	2,683.3	2,691.4	2,690.0	2,685.0	2,665.7
2011	2,614.6	2,620.1	2,654.5	2,694.7	2,706.2	2,697.1	2,654.1	2,662.1	2,693.0	2,697.9	2,700.9	2,699.4	2,674.6
2012	2,633.5	2,644.9	2,675.7	2,701.3	2,719.2	2,715.4	2,666.8	2,683.5	2,707.3	2,721.5	2,727.3	2,725.2	2,693.5
2013	2,655.0	2,673.3	2,693.9	2,729.0	2,748.6	2,742.1	2,693.6	2,712.2	2,736.4	2,751.4	2,753.4	2,747.2	2,719.7
2014	2,669.8	2,690.0	2,712.6	2,761.7	2,780.1	2,769.7	2,725.3	2,744.9	2,762.9	2,785.7	2,788.4	2,787.7	2,748.2
2015	2,726.5	2,744.6	2,763.3	2,812.9	2,835.2	2,831.4	2,793.8	2,801.6	2,823.8	2,844.4	2,849.7	2,848.6	2,806.3
2016	2,777.7	2,793.9	2,817.7	2,862.5	2,870.2	2,873.0	2,831.0	2,844.8	2,870.2	2,882.4	2,881.3	2,873.8	2,848.2
2017	2,812.6	2,836.1	2,852.9	2,884.9	2,896.2	2,903.6	2,853.5	2,863.5	2,888.2	2,896.1	2,902.0	2,899.2	2,874.1
2018	2,826.8	2,845.7	2,866.4	2,897.3	2,908.9	2,914.1	2,874.5	2,883.3	2,901.0	2,912.9	2,911.5	2,906.2	2,887.4
Total Private													
2010	2,154.3	2,157.0	2,184.0	2,217.2	2,227.5	2,242.2	2,240.3	2,246.0	2,235.3	2,240.1	2,237.6	2,235.0	2,218.0
2011	2,172.0	2,172.4	2,204.4	2,240.7	2,251.2	2,261.0	2,260.1	2,260.8	2,252.3	2,250.7	2,251.5	2,250.5	2,235.6
2012	2,196.5	2,197.8	2,226.3	2,249.7	2,267.0	2,280.4	2,274.6	2,279.0	2,266.1	2,273.0	2,277.9	2,276.9	2,255.4
2013	2,218.3	2,226.8	2,245.1	2,278.3	2,297.8	2,308.8	2,305.0	2,312.6	2,300.3	2,307.6	2,308.4	2,303.5	2,284.4
2014	2,239.0	2,249.2	2,270.3	2,315.5	2,332.7	2,339.2	2,338.0	2,346.6	2,328.0	2,343.5	2,345.7	2,346.6	2,316.2
2015	2,294.0	2,300.0	2,316.5	2,366.6	2,387.3	2,395.7	2,401.8	2,401.4	2,388.2	2,403.9	2,407.4	2,406.3	2,372.4
2016	2,346.7	2,355.7	2,376.1	2,420.3	2,425.8	2,436.8	2,437.3	2,441.6	2,430.0	2,437.0	2,435.6	2,428.4	2,414.3
2017	2,378.6	2,394.8	2,410.5	2,440.8	2,450.4	2,464.6	2,457.8	2,460.7	2,449.6	2,452.4	2,457.4	2,455.3	2,439.4
2018	2,392.7	2,405.3	2,423.9	2,453.3	2,464.1	2,477.7	2,481.2	2,481.7	2,463.4	2,470.0	2,467.4	2,463.9	2,453.7
Goods Producing													
2010	344.4	342.3	349.5	355.7	356.8	362.8	362.1	364.0	362.1	363.1	360.3	357.4	356.7
2011	342.5	341.3	349.3	356.2	359.6	364.6	366.6	363.8	364.4	361.9	359.3	357.7	357.3
2012	350.3	349.5	356.0	359.5	362.1	367.1	367.3	367.7	364.6	363.6	361.4	359.8	360.7
2013	351.0	352.8	355.4	361.1	366.5	371.9	370.9	372.7	371.2	370.3	368.2	364.4	364.7
2014	353.3	356.3	362.9	368.4	372.8	376.8	377.7	379.0	377.2	377.7	376.5	375.9	371.2
2015	367.2	367.8	372.1	378.0	381.9	385.9	387.1	386.4	385.3	385.5	384.1	384.7	380.5
2016	375.8	376.2	381.1	387.8	388.4	394.5	394.3	394.6	393.3	394.1	393.0	391.6	388.7
2017	382.8	385.7	387.3	391.0	393.8	400.2	399.9	399.8	398.5	395.2	396.6	397.0	394.0
2018	385.1	388.5	393.5	396.4	397.7	405.9	407.1	406.7	405.2	405.6	402.3	401.7	399.6
Service-Providing													
2010	2,259.8	2,274.0	2,297.0	2,324.5	2,341.6	2,326.1	2,276.4	2,302.1	2,321.2	2,328.3	2,329.7	2,327.6	2,309.0
2011	2,272.1	2,278.8	2,305.2	2,338.5	2,346.6	2,332.5	2,287.5	2,298.3	2,328.6	2,336.0	2,341.6	2,341.7	2,317.3
2012	2,283.2	2,295.4	2,319.7	2,341.8	2,357.1	2,348.3	2,299.5	2,315.8	2,342.7	2,357.9	2,365.9	2,365.4	2,332.7
2013	2,304.0	2,320.5	2,338.5	2,367.9	2,382.1	2,370.2	2,322.7	2,339.5	2,365.2	2,381.1	2,385.2	2,382.8	2,355.0
2014	2,316.5	2,333.7	2,349.7	2,393.3	2,407.3	2,392.9	2,347.6	2,365.9	2,385.7	2,408.0	2,411.9	2,411.8	2,377.0
2015	2,359.3	2,376.8	2,391.2	2,434.9	2,453.3	2,445.5	2,406.7	2,415.2	2,438.5	2,458.9	2,465.6	2,463.9	2,425.8
2016	2,401.9	2,417.7	2,436.6	2,474.7	2,481.8	2,478.5	2,436.7	2,450.2	2,476.9	2,488.3	2,488.3	2,482.2	2,459.5
2017	2,429.8	2,450.4	2,465.6	2,493.9	2,502.4	2,503.4	2,453.6	2,463.7	2,489.7	2,500.9	2,505.4	2,502.2	2,480.1
2018	2,441.7	2,457.2	2,472.9	2,500.9	2,511.2	2,508.2	2,467.4	2,476.6	2,495.8	2,507.3	2,509.2	2,504.5	2,487.7
Mining and Logging													
2010	3.8	3.9	4.1	4.3	4.3	4.4	4.4	4.4	4.3	4.3	4.3	4.2	4.2
2011	3.9	3.8	4.2	4.3	4.3	4.4	4.4	4.4	4.4	4.3	4.3	4.1	4.2
2012	3.9	3.9	4.1	4.2	4.2	4.3	4.2	4.2	4.2	4.2	4.1	4.1	4.1
2013	3.8	3.9	3.9	4.1	4.2	4.2	4.3	4.3	4.2	4.1	4.1	3.9	4.1
2014	3.6	3.7	3.9	4.1	4.1	4.2	4.2	4.2	4.3	4.2	4.2	4.1	4.1
2015	4.0	4.0	4.1	4.2	4.2	4.1	4.1	4.2	4.2	4.1	4.1	4.0	4.1
2016	4.0	3.9	4.0	4.1	4.1	4.2	4.2	4.1	4.1	4.1	4.1	4.1	4.1
2017	4.0	4.1	4.1	4.2	4.2	4.2	4.3	4.3	4.3	4.3	4.3	4.3	4.2
2018	4.1	4.2	4.3	4.3	4.4	4.5	4.5	4.5	4.4	4.5	4.4	4.3	4.4
Construction													
2010	97.7	95.6	101.0	106.7	106.8	110.8	112.1	111.4	110.2	110.0	107.6	104.1	106.2
2011	91.7	90.5	96.9	102.8	105.3	108.4	110.4	109.7	108.7	107.3	104.9	102.8	103.3
2012	96.1	94.9	99.7	102.6	105.7	108.4	109.2	109.6	108.2	107.3	105.8	104.7	104.4
2013	96.8	97.5	99.5	104.1	108.6	112.5	114.6	113.8	113.2	113.0	111.0	107.2	107.7
2014	100.7	99.1	105.4	108.9	111.6	114.0	115.9	115.8	114.6	114.3	112.6	111.5	110.4
2015	104.1	104.2	107.6	112.8	115.2	117.3	119.0	119.4	118.5	119.5	118.3	117.9	114.5
2016	111.1	110.2	114.5	120.5	121.1	124.8	125.3	125.4	124.8	124.9	123.7	122.0	120.7
2017	115.5	116.7	118.6	121.3	123.5	127.1	127.4	127.2	126.1	125.9	124.3	123.0	123.1
2018	113.1	114.9	119.1	121.7	124.6	127.9	127.9	127.3	126.5	126.2	121.2	119.9	122.5

1. Employment by Industry: Missouri, 2010–2018—*Continued*

(Numbers in thousands, not seasonally adjusted)

Industry and year	January	February	March	April	May	June	July	August	September	October	November	December	Annual average
Manufacturing													
2010	242.9	242.8	244.4	244.7	245.7	247.6	245.6	248.2	247.6	248.8	248.4	249.1	246.3
2011	246.9	247.0	248.2	249.1	250.0	251.8	251.8	249.7	251.3	250.3	250.1	250.8	249.8
2012	250.3	250.7	252.2	252.7	252.2	254.4	253.9	253.9	252.2	252.1	251.5	251.0	252.3
2013	250.4	251.4	252.0	252.9	253.7	255.2	252.0	254.6	253.8	253.2	253.1	253.3	253.0
2014	249.0	253.5	253.6	255.4	257.1	258.6	257.6	259.0	258.3	259.2	259.7	260.3	256.8
2015	259.1	259.6	260.4	261.0	262.5	264.5	264.0	262.8	262.6	261.9	261.7	262.8	261.9
2016	260.7	262.1	262.6	263.2	263.2	265.5	264.8	265.1	264.4	265.1	265.2	265.5	264.0
2017	263.3	264.9	264.6	265.5	266.1	268.9	268.2	268.3	268.1	265.0	268.0	269.7	266.7
2018	267.9	269.4	270.1	270.4	268.7	273.5	274.7	274.9	274.3	274.9	276.7	277.5	272.8
Trade, Transportation, and Utilities													
2010	505.4	501.1	505.6	509.5	513.3	514.0	511.5	513.2	510.9	513.0	520.3	523.8	511.8
2011	505.8	502.5	507.0	514.2	515.8	515.5	512.3	513.1	512.1	513.0	521.7	525.0	513.2
2012	506.4	501.5	505.1	507.8	512.1	512.5	509.8	511.1	510.7	513.6	524.0	526.2	511.7
2013	505.8	501.7	503.9	510.2	514.1	515.6	514.1	516.4	514.9	525.2	528.9	533.2	514.8
2014	512.2	508.7	512.1	517.6	521.5	523.8	521.0	523.1	521.5	525.2	535.2	539.9	521.8
2015	521.0	517.4	520.0	533.1	537.9	539.5	538.7	539.0	537.3	542.0	550.9	554.8	536.0
2016	535.4	533.5	536.1	541.4	543.7	542.9	543.4	543.6	541.2	544.6	553.4	556.8	543.0
2017	539.5	537.1	539.0	542.0	543.3	544.0	541.4	541.7	539.9	543.4	553.6	556.5	543.5
2018	538.6	535.6	537.4	541.5	544.7	544.5	544.5	545.4	542.7	543.7	552.7	552.6	543.7
Wholesale Trade													
2010	114.0	113.7	114.6	115.1	115.4	115.6	115.4	114.7	114.1	114.6	114.3	114.8	114.7
2011	112.9	113.1	113.8	115.1	115.1	115.8	115.7	115.2	114.9	114.9	114.9	115.6	114.8
2012	114.6	114.7	115.6	115.9	116.4	117.2	116.7	116.6	116.1	116.1	116.1	116.4	116.0
2013	114.3	114.6	115.1	116.8	117.4	117.8	117.6	117.5	117.2	117.7	117.9	118.6	116.9
2014	116.9	117.3	117.7	118.3	119.0	119.6	119.4	119.2	118.3	118.3	118.3	118.6	118.4
2015	117.0	116.8	117.0	117.8	118.4	118.8	119.4	118.4	117.4	117.7	117.6	118.0	117.9
2016	116.8	116.8	117.1	118.2	118.2	118.8	119.6	118.3	117.4	117.5	117.6	118.1	117.9
2017	117.3	117.7	118.1	118.8	119.1	120.2	119.9	119.3	119.3	119.4	120.0	120.8	119.2
2018	119.0	119.5	119.9	120.5	121.0	121.7	122.3	121.7	121.5	121.6	121.5	121.3	121.0
Retail Trade													
2010	295.1	291.7	294.7	296.3	299.3	301.2	300.1	300.4	297.9	299.6	307.0	309.4	299.4
2011	296.1	292.5	295.7	300.3	302.2	303.0	301.5	301.8	300.4	300.1	310.5	312.5	301.5
2012	298.4	294.4	297.1	299.1	301.9	302.5	301.5	300.6	300.1	302.5	312.6	313.3	302.0
2013	297.6	293.5	294.8	298.4	301.2	303.4	302.3	302.9	301.1	304.3	313.3	316.0	302.4
2014	299.7	296.3	298.9	302.9	305.4	308.0	306.4	306.5	305.1	308.2	317.5	320.4	306.3
2015	304.7	302.0	304.3	308.6	311.8	314.1	312.7	312.8	311.0	315.3	323.2	325.2	312.1
2016	310.1	308.7	310.5	314.5	316.2	316.3	316.9	316.6	314.3	316.8	324.8	326.0	316.0
2017	312.0	309.4	310.6	312.5	313.3	314.3	313.8	312.9	310.4	313.2	322.0	322.8	313.9
2018	309.2	305.8	307.3	309.5	311.5	311.9	312.0	310.9	308.4	310.0	317.3	317.4	310.9
Transportation and Utilities													
2010	96.3	95.7	96.3	98.1	98.6	97.2	96.0	98.1	98.9	98.8	99.0	99.6	97.7
2011	96.8	96.9	97.5	98.8	98.5	96.7	95.1	96.1	96.8	96.3	96.3	96.9	96.9
2012	93.4	92.4	92.4	92.8	93.8	92.8	91.6	93.9	94.5	95.0	95.3	96.5	93.7
2013	93.9	93.6	94.0	95.0	95.5	94.4	94.2	96.0	96.6	96.8	97.7	98.6	95.5
2014	95.6	95.1	95.5	96.4	97.1	96.2	95.2	97.4	98.1	98.7	99.4	100.9	97.1
2015	99.3	98.6	98.7	106.7	107.7	106.6	106.6	107.8	108.9	109.0	110.1	111.6	106.0
2016	108.5	108.0	108.5	108.7	109.3	107.8	106.9	108.7	109.5	110.3	111.0	112.7	109.2
2017	110.2	110.0	110.3	110.7	110.9	109.5	107.7	109.5	110.2	110.8	111.6	112.9	110.4
2018	110.4	110.3	110.2	111.5	112.2	110.9	110.2	112.8	112.8	112.1	113.9	113.9	111.8
Information													
2010	58.9	58.7	58.8	61.4	61.1	61.5	60.6	60.5	60.3	60.3	60.1	60.1	60.2
2011	58.6	58.4	58.3	59.3	59.6	59.8	60.0	59.9	59.9	59.4	59.4	59.5	59.3
2012	58.8	58.5	58.4	58.5	58.8	58.8	59.1	58.8	58.5	58.2	58.1	58.1	58.6
2013	57.6	57.9	58.0	57.5	57.8	58.0	57.7	57.5	57.1	57.3	57.3	57.5	57.6
2014	56.6	56.6	56.8	56.7	56.7	56.9	56.7	56.1	55.5	55.1	55.0	54.9	56.1
2015	54.6	54.4	54.3	54.4	54.7	54.8	55.0	54.4	53.6	53.5	53.6	53.9	54.3
2016	53.1	53.1	53.1	52.3	52.5	52.6	52.3	52.2	51.9	51.9	51.7	51.8	52.4
2017	51.3	51.2	51.3	51.1	51.3	51.5	51.5	51.3	51.0	50.7	50.7	50.8	51.1
2018	50.6	50.6	50.6	50.7	50.8	51.1	50.7	50.1	49.8	50.0	50.4	50.5	50.5

1. Employment by Industry: Missouri, 2010–2018—*Continued*

(Numbers in thousands, not seasonally adjusted)

Industry and year	January	February	March	April	May	June	July	August	September	October	November	December	Annual average
Financial Activities													
2010	162.0	161.9	162.2	163.1	163.6	164.6	164.8	164.0	162.9	163.6	163.5	163.4	163.3
2011	160.9	161.2	161.5	161.9	162.2	162.6	163.4	163.7	162.8	163.8	164.1	164.2	162.7
2012	162.6	163.2	164.0	163.7	164.5	165.2	165.7	165.9	164.7	165.8	166.1	165.7	164.8
2013	163.1	163.5	163.6	165.2	165.6	166.3	167.3	166.9	165.7	165.8	165.9	165.4	165.4
2014	163.4	163.7	163.5	165.3	166.2	166.8	167.5	167.5	165.9	166.4	166.4	166.7	165.8
2015	165.2	165.4	165.6	167.0	168.3	169.4	170.3	170.0	168.3	169.0	169.3	169.5	168.1
2016	167.9	168.3	168.6	169.7	170.4	171.5	172.2	172.1	171.3	171.3	171.7	172.2	170.6
2017	171.6	172.2	172.9	173.4	174.6	176.2	175.9	175.6	174.3	174.2	173.8	174.1	174.1
2018	172.3	172.5	172.3	173.0	173.7	174.8	175.3	175.0	173.3	172.9	172.5	172.5	173.3
Professional and Business Services													
2010	307.2	310.1	313.0	319.6	317.6	320.0	322.2	323.7	321.6	324.0	323.3	324.3	318.9
2011	318.7	320.4	325.1	331.2	329.5	331.2	329.8	330.1	330.0	331.1	331.7	332.7	328.5
2012	325.9	327.1	331.9	336.1	336.2	339.1	337.5	338.2	337.3	340.3	342.1	342.3	336.2
2013	332.9	336.8	341.7	345.9	346.6	349.0	348.9	351.3	349.2	352.5	352.9	353.1	346.7
2014	341.6	344.7	347.8	356.1	356.1	357.5	356.7	360.1	358.4	362.9	363.7	364.9	355.9
2015	354.8	358.1	361.9	368.8	369.4	369.5	372.4	373.6	372.7	378.1	379.2	379.1	369.8
2016	367.1	371.2	374.1	382.5	380.3	381.2	381.4	383.8	382.9	384.0	382.9	379.9	379.3
2017	370.8	375.2	379.0	385.4	382.9	385.0	383.2	384.6	385.1	386.4	387.6	384.7	382.5
2018	374.5	379.2	382.7	388.3	387.1	387.4	389.7	390.9	388.8	390.6	389.1	389.2	386.5
Education and Health Services													
2010	413.1	417.3	418.6	421.1	421.3	419.1	418.8	419.6	424.2	429.0	430.5	430.7	421.9
2011	425.9	429.5	430.9	432.2	430.4	426.5	426.4	427.0	430.9	433.0	434.4	433.8	430.1
2012	429.1	432.8	432.9	433.3	433.0	430.0	430.5	432.5	435.5	439.0	439.7	440.6	434.1
2013	434.9	440.2	438.5	443.9	441.7	436.0	436.7	437.5	439.3	444.9	445.3	442.7	440.1
2014	437.2	443.1	439.9	447.9	445.6	439.5	442.0	442.8	443.9	451.5	452.5	449.7	444.6
2015	449.4	452.8	449.9	458.0	456.5	451.8	455.4	454.9	455.4	462.9	463.6	459.5	455.8
2016	456.2	460.2	459.2	466.2	463.6	458.5	462.9	463.5	466.1	472.5	472.6	469.7	464.3
2017	466.7	473.2	470.7	476.9	475.7	469.8	472.1	472.7	475.0	480.5	480.8	479.2	474.4
2018	472.7	478.6	476.0	482.1	479.5	474.0	477.3	476.5	477.1	485.0	484.4	482.6	478.8
Leisure and Hospitality													
2010	248.2	250.3	260.5	274.5	281.3	286.9	286.9	287.9	281.2	274.5	267.3	263.2	271.9
2011	248.8	248.2	260.1	271.2	279.3	285.4	286.0	288.0	277.8	274.1	266.7	263.5	270.8
2012	251.0	252.5	264.2	276.0	284.7	291.4	288.6	289.2	280.1	277.6	271.6	269.4	274.7
2013	258.7	259.0	268.7	281.3	291.8	297.3	295.1	296.0	289.7	285.1	277.3	274.8	281.2
2014	263.5	264.4	274.5	289.5	298.9	302.4	301.1	303.1	291.7	290.9	283.0	280.9	287.0
2015	269.1	270.9	278.7	292.5	303.2	308.2	306.7	307.4	300.8	297.5	291.5	289.4	293.0
2016	276.8	278.5	288.5	303.5	309.7	317.1	312.6	314.2	306.6	301.8	293.8	290.5	299.5
2017	280.8	285.1	294.7	304.7	312.1	319.9	316.5	318.2	309.9	306.1	298.9	297.4	303.7
2018	284.7	286.0	296.3	305.5	314.5	322.4	319.5	320.7	311.1	307.1	301.7	300.8	305.9
Other Services													
2010	115.1	115.3	115.8	112.3	112.5	113.3	113.4	113.1	112.1	112.6	112.3	112.1	113.3
2011	110.8	110.9	112.2	114.5	114.8	115.4	115.6	115.2	114.4	114.4	114.2	114.1	113.9
2012	112.4	112.7	113.8	114.8	115.6	116.3	116.1	115.6	114.7	114.9	114.9	114.8	114.7
2013	114.3	114.9	115.3	113.2	113.7	114.7	114.3	114.3	113.2	112.9	112.6	112.4	113.8
2014	111.2	111.7	112.8	114.0	114.9	115.5	115.3	114.9	113.9	113.8	113.4	113.7	113.8
2015	112.7	113.2	114.0	114.8	115.4	116.6	116.2	115.7	114.8	115.4	115.2	115.4	115.0
2016	114.4	114.7	115.4	116.9	117.2	118.5	118.2	117.6	116.7	116.8	116.5	115.9	116.6
2017	115.1	115.1	115.6	116.3	116.7	118.0	117.3	116.8	115.9	115.9	115.4	115.6	116.1
2018	114.2	114.3	115.1	115.8	116.1	117.6	117.1	116.4	115.4	115.1	114.3	114.0	115.5
Government													
2010	449.9	459.3	462.5	463.0	470.9	446.7	398.2	420.1	448.0	451.3	452.4	450.0	447.7
2011	442.6	447.7	450.1	454.0	455.0	436.1	394.0	401.3	440.7	447.2	449.4	448.9	438.9
2012	437.0	447.1	449.4	451.6	452.2	435.0	392.2	404.5	441.2	448.5	449.4	448.3	438.0
2013	436.7	446.5	448.8	450.7	450.8	433.3	388.6	399.6	436.1	443.8	445.0	443.7	435.3
2014	430.8	440.8	442.3	446.2	447.4	430.5	387.3	398.3	434.9	442.2	442.7	441.1	432.0
2015	432.5	444.6	446.8	446.3	447.9	435.7	392.0	400.2	435.6	440.5	442.3	442.3	433.9
2016	431.0	438.2	441.6	442.2	444.4	436.2	393.7	403.2	440.2	445.4	445.7	445.4	433.9
2017	434.0	441.3	442.4	444.1	445.8	439.0	395.7	402.8	438.6	443.7	444.6	443.9	434.7
2018	434.1	440.4	442.5	444.0	444.8	436.4	393.3	401.6	437.6	442.9	444.1	442.3	433.7

2. Average Weekly Hours by Selected Industry: Missouri, 2014–2018

(Not seasonally adjusted)

Industry and year	January	February	March	April	May	June	July	August	September	October	November	December	Annual average
Total Private													
2014	33.6	34.3	34.5	34.1	34.1	34.6	34.3	34.2	34.0	33.8	34.5	34.2	34.2
2015	33.7	34.2	34.2	34.0	33.5	33.7	33.7	34.4	33.6	33.8	34.0	33.7	33.9
2016	33.4	33.3	33.3	33.7	33.7	33.3	33.3	33.2	33.3	33.8	33.1	33.0	33.4
2017	33.1	33.1	33.3	34.0	33.6	33.7	34.1	33.7	33.6	33.8	33.2	33.1	33.5
2018	32.6	32.9	33.2	33.8	33.6	34.0	34.5	33.9	34.4	33.9	33.5	33.8	33.7
Goods Producing													
2014	37.9	38.1	38.5	38.9	39.2	39.4	39.5	39.6	38.4	38.5	39.2	40.0	38.9
2015	38.8	39.1	38.6	39.0	39.0	39.7	39.2	40.0	38.2	39.6	38.7	39.5	39.1
2016	38.7	39.1	39.3	39.6	39.4	39.8	39.7	39.7	39.9	40.3	39.0	39.2	39.5
2017	38.4	39.5	39.4	39.2	39.7	40.0	40.3	40.5	40.5	40.4	39.6	40.0	39.8
2018	38.8	39.2	39.2	40.3	40.2	40.5	41.3	40.6	41.1	40.2	39.4	40.2	40.1
Construction													
2014	34.0	33.1	35.0	35.2	35.5	36.0	37.5	37.3	36.5	35.0	35.9	37.4	35.8
2015	36.4	35.6	36.1	36.3	35.9	37.6	36.7	38.0	34.9	38.2	35.5	38.2	36.6
2016	36.0	36.5	36.5	36.4	35.8	37.9	37.0	36.9	37.4	38.3	35.6	36.9	36.8
2017	34.4	36.4	35.9	36.1	36.4	36.9	37.3	36.6	37.2	37.2	35.7	35.4	36.3
2018	33.4	34.7	35.6	36.6	36.9	37.0	37.6	36.4	37.0	35.6	34.2	35.9	36.0
Manufacturing													
2014	39.9	40.6	40.3	40.8	41.1	41.1	40.4	40.7	39.3	40.3	40.9	41.3	40.6
2015	39.9	40.7	39.7	40.2	40.4	40.8	40.5	41.0	39.9	40.6	40.7	40.3	40.4
2016	40.2	40.5	40.8	41.3	41.3	40.8	41.1	41.1	41.2	41.4	40.8	40.5	40.9
2017	40.6	41.2	41.1	40.7	41.3	41.5	41.8	42.7	42.3	42.1	41.6	42.2	41.6
2018	41.3	41.4	40.9	42.0	41.7	42.1	43.0	42.5	43.0	41.7	41.1	41.6	41.9
Trade, Transportation, and Utilities													
2014	33.3	34.0	34.5	34.2	33.8	34.1	33.8	33.6	33.9	33.6	33.8	34.2	33.9
2015	33.1	33.6	33.5	33.6	33.4	33.9	33.8	34.2	34.1	34.1	34.2	34.2	33.8
2016	33.4	33.4	33.2	33.7	33.7	34.1	33.7	33.7	33.9	34.4	33.6	33.2	33.7
2017	32.8	33.0	33.6	34.3	33.6	33.6	33.6	33.3	33.3	33.2	32.8	32.5	33.3
2018	31.7	31.9	32.5	32.8	33.0	33.5	33.8	33.3	33.7	33.3	33.2	33.0	33.0
Financial Activities													
2014	36.8	38.0	37.8	36.8	36.7	37.1	36.0	36.1	36.0	35.9	37.6	36.5	36.8
2015	36.5	37.6	37.6	36.9	36.8	36.8	37.1	37.8	36.5	36.2	37.2	36.2	36.9
2016	36.0	35.3	35.7	36.3	37.0	34.4	34.8	34.7	34.4	35.3	34.6	34.7	35.3
2017	36.3	35.3	34.8	36.7	35.8	35.5	36.6	35.7	35.6	36.8	35.5	35.6	35.8
2018	35.7	35.7	35.7	37.4	36.2	36.3	37.7	36.6	37.6	37.1	36.4	37.4	36.6
Professional and Business Services													
2014	35.8	36.8	36.6	36.8	36.6	37.5	36.7	36.8	36.4	36.1	37.1	35.8	36.6
2015	35.8	36.7	36.5	36.1	35.5	35.6	35.4	37.0	35.7	36.2	36.3	35.4	36.0
2016	35.2	34.9	35.0	35.7	35.9	35.6	35.9	35.5	35.4	36.4	35.7	35.5	35.6
2017	36.2	35.3	35.2	36.6	35.2	36.0	36.0	36.0	35.0	34.9	34.3	34.0	35.4
2018	33.8	34.0	34.1	34.5	34.5	35.7	35.4	35.4	35.0	34.4	33.8	34.2	34.6
Education and Health Services													
2014	32.3	32.5	32.8	32.1	32.2	33.2	32.8	32.6	32.6	32.5	33.6	32.7	32.7
2015	32.8	33.1	33.1	32.8	33.0	32.3	33.0	33.5	33.2	32.3	33.9	33.0	33.0
2016	33.5	32.6	32.6	32.6	33.1	32.6	32.7	32.6	32.9	33.2	32.7	32.7	32.8
2017	33.8	33.2	32.8	33.6	32.6	32.7	33.4	32.5	32.7	33.3	32.7	32.5	33.0
2018	32.3	31.9	32.3	33.3	32.2	32.3	33.7	32.5	33.5	32.7	32.5	32.9	32.7
Leisure and Hospitality													
2014	24.0	25.0	25.4	24.9	25.1	25.8	26.1	25.9	25.5	25.5	25.6	25.5	25.4
2015	24.8	25.8	26.4	25.9	25.1	25.8	25.7	25.7	25.3	25.4	25.1	24.7	25.5
2016	24.6	24.9	25.2	25.3	24.9	24.6	25.0	24.8	24.0	24.2	24.0	23.2	24.6
2017	22.5	23.4	23.9	24.0	24.6	25.2	25.6	24.9	24.7	24.9	24.5	24.5	24.4
2018	23.3	24.2	24.5	24.7	24.6	25.2	25.3	24.9	24.9	24.5	24.5	24.9	24.6

3. Average Hourly Earnings by Selected Industry: Missouri, 2014–2018

(Dollars, not seasonally adjusted)

Industry and year	January	February	March	April	May	June	July	August	September	October	November	December	Annual average
Total Private													
2014	22.12	22.28	22.22	22.11	21.93	21.97	21.74	21.78	21.83	21.91	22.17	21.90	21.99
2015	22.07	22.20	22.15	21.99	22.18	22.00	22.00	22.07	22.08	22.04	22.21	22.12	22.09
2016	22.25	22.17	22.23	22.16	22.32	22.19	22.42	22.32	22.85	23.11	23.24	23.25	22.54
2017	23.94	23.49	23.59	23.90	23.57	23.52	24.02	23.78	24.20	24.32	24.35	24.26	23.91
2018	24.59	24.63	24.49	24.85	24.60	24.27	24.75	24.63	25.04	24.88	24.81	25.17	24.73
Goods Producing													
2014	25.92	25.88	25.95	25.62	25.74	25.50	25.86	25.87	25.97	26.28	26.41	26.33	25.95
2015	26.24	25.53	25.78	25.28	25.30	25.21	25.46	25.83	26.33	25.91	26.00	26.39	25.77
2016	25.93	25.85	26.62	26.18	26.51	26.36	26.65	26.68	27.00	27.37	27.55	27.21	26.67
2017	26.99	27.25	27.44	27.81	27.54	27.66	28.15	28.07	28.30	28.18	28.01	27.96	27.79
2018	28.56	28.15	28.20	28.69	28.26	28.16	28.74	28.42	28.49	28.11	28.51	28.27	28.38
Construction													
2014	26.51	26.36	26.36	26.44	26.95	26.51	27.16	26.92	27.18	27.44	27.95	27.88	27.00
2015	27.61	27.66	28.07	27.73	28.07	27.77	28.15	28.17	28.41	28.42	28.20	28.48	28.07
2016	27.38	26.97	27.40	27.53	28.17	27.64	28.04	28.53	29.14	29.30	28.81	29.03	28.19
2017	28.20	28.82	29.02	29.10	28.85	28.97	29.29	29.58	29.35	29.59	29.27	29.31	29.13
2018	30.06	29.79	29.70	30.33	30.17	30.33	30.17	30.08	30.05	30.48	30.39	30.43	30.17
Manufacturing													
2014	25.03	25.13	25.23	24.78	24.80	24.67	24.91	25.05	25.10	25.53	25.51	25.46	25.10
2015	25.50	24.51	24.69	24.10	24.00	23.98	24.19	24.72	24.95	24.65	24.96	25.01	24.60
2016	25.07	25.13	26.07	25.36	25.62	25.61	25.88	25.64	25.79	26.28	26.82	26.19	25.79
2017	26.31	26.42	26.68	27.18	26.96	27.09	27.66	27.48	27.93	27.67	27.58	27.51	27.21
2018	28.06	27.54	27.63	28.03	27.56	27.34	28.21	27.81	27.92	27.46	28.07	27.63	27.77
Trade, Transportation, and Utilities													
2014	20.47	20.62	20.70	20.91	20.51	20.53	20.18	19.99	19.90	19.81	19.95	19.19	20.22
2015	19.72	19.88	19.85	19.83	19.87	19.46	19.56	19.60	19.61	19.61	19.58	19.29	19.65
2016	19.71	19.41	19.50	19.63	19.59	19.98	19.62	20.12	20.20	20.64	20.38	20.75	19.97
2017	22.44	21.11	21.21	21.55	21.18	21.27	21.63	21.33	21.71	21.93	21.79	21.83	21.58
2018	22.04	21.64	21.42	22.05	21.91	21.92	22.07	22.16	22.89	22.89	22.43	23.11	22.22
Financial Activities													
2014	26.64	27.25	26.76	26.61	26.43	26.38	26.11	26.33	26.10	26.04	26.69	26.32	26.48
2015	26.55	27.08	26.90	26.61	26.61	26.17	25.87	26.15	26.14	26.01	26.51	26.24	26.40
2016	27.20	27.07	26.81	27.16	27.20	26.93	28.04	27.38	28.34	28.24	29.85	29.12	27.77
2017	30.12	28.33	28.99	29.10	28.77	29.02	30.43	29.65	30.36	30.48	30.84	31.20	29.78
2018	31.37	31.18	31.24	31.61	31.05	30.11	30.90	30.18	30.46	30.44	30.26	30.58	30.78
Professional and Business Services													
2014	25.17	25.41	25.22	24.78	24.84	25.21	24.82	24.82	25.10	25.34	25.71	25.42	25.15
2015	25.80	26.52	26.55	26.28	26.35	26.24	26.34	26.86	26.95	26.80	27.33	26.96	26.59
2016	27.55	27.61	27.05	26.91	27.10	26.68	26.99	26.87	27.17	27.51	27.49	27.76	27.22
2017	28.99	29.10	29.05	29.34	28.88	28.58	29.48	28.97	29.55	29.69	28.87	29.11	29.13
2018	29.41	29.91	29.65	29.50	29.41	28.99	29.88	29.89	30.31	29.62	29.88	30.27	29.73
Education and Health Services													
2014	19.18	19.27	19.17	19.09	18.77	18.38	18.33	18.51	18.49	18.51	18.49	18.56	18.73
2015	18.52	18.72	18.75	18.82	18.64	18.98	18.99	18.36	18.09	18.12	18.18	18.32	18.54
2016	18.09	18.34	18.70	18.83	19.17	19.13	19.31	19.29	19.67	19.53	19.96	19.87	19.16
2017	19.73	19.90	20.03	20.16	20.00	19.98	19.83	19.57	19.67	19.62	19.41	19.41	19.78
2018	19.34	19.80	19.42	19.50	19.74	19.50	19.66	20.10	19.99	20.14	20.34	20.71	19.86
Leisure and Hospitality													
2014	12.74	12.66	12.82	12.66	12.48	12.44	12.35	12.42	12.68	12.66	12.83	13.09	12.65
2015	12.95	13.04	12.96	12.96	13.28	13.09	13.07	13.09	13.11	13.34	13.23	13.42	13.13
2016	13.33	13.51	13.35	13.51	13.46	13.27	13.40	13.36	13.75	13.72	13.57	13.90	13.51
2017	13.99	13.93	14.10	13.93	13.75	13.75	13.79	13.91	14.27	14.21	14.39	14.60	14.05
2018	14.82	14.80	14.71	14.85	14.73	14.42	14.38	14.53	14.77	14.71	14.68	15.06	14.70

4. Average Weekly Earnings by Selected Industry: Missouri, 2014–2018

(Dollars, not seasonally adjusted)

Industry and year	January	February	March	April	May	June	July	August	September	October	November	December	Annual average
Total Private													
2014	743.23	764.20	766.59	753.95	747.81	760.16	745.68	744.88	742.22	740.56	764.87	748.98	752.06
2015	743.76	759.24	757.53	747.66	743.03	741.40	741.40	759.21	741.89	744.95	755.14	745.44	748.85
2016	743.15	738.26	740.26	746.79	752.18	738.93	746.59	741.02	760.91	781.12	769.24	767.25	752.84
2017	792.41	777.52	785.55	812.60	791.95	792.62	819.08	801.39	813.12	822.02	808.42	803.01	800.99
2018	801.63	810.33	813.07	839.93	826.56	825.18	853.88	834.96	861.38	843.43	831.14	850.75	833.40
Goods Producing													
2014	982.37	986.03	999.08	996.62	1,009.01	1,004.70	1,021.47	1,024.45	997.25	1,011.78	1,035.27	1,053.20	1,009.46
2015	1,018.11	998.22	995.11	985.92	986.70	1,000.84	998.03	1,033.20	1,005.81	1,026.04	1,006.20	1,042.41	1,007.61
2016	1,003.49	1,010.74	1,046.17	1,036.73	1,044.49	1,049.13	1,058.01	1,059.20	1,077.30	1,103.01	1,074.45	1,066.63	1,053.47
2017	1,036.42	1,076.38	1,081.14	1,090.15	1,093.34	1,106.40	1,134.45	1,136.84	1,146.15	1,138.47	1,109.20	1,118.40	1,106.04
2018	1,108.13	1,103.48	1,105.44	1,156.21	1,136.05	1,140.48	1,186.96	1,153.85	1,170.94	1,130.02	1,123.29	1,136.45	1,138.04
Construction													
2014	901.34	872.52	922.60	930.69	956.73	954.36	1,018.50	1,004.12	992.07	960.40	1,003.41	1,042.71	966.60
2015	1,005.00	984.70	1,013.33	1,006.60	1,007.71	1,044.15	1,033.11	1,070.46	991.51	1,085.64	1,001.10	1,087.94	1,027.36
2016	985.68	984.41	1,000.10	1,002.09	1,008.49	1,047.56	1,037.48	1,052.76	1,089.84	1,122.19	1,025.64	1,071.21	1,037.39
2017	970.08	1,049.05	1,041.82	1,050.51	1,050.14	1,068.99	1,092.52	1,082.63	1,091.82	1,100.75	1,044.94	1,037.57	1,057.42
2018	1,004.00	1,033.71	1,057.32	1,110.08	1,113.27	1,122.21	1,134.39	1,094.91	1,111.85	1,085.09	1,039.34	1,092.44	1,086.12
Manufacturing													
2014	998.70	1,020.28	1,016.77	1,011.02	1,019.28	1,013.94	1,006.36	1,019.54	986.43	1,028.86	1,043.36	1,051.50	1,019.06
2015	1,017.45	997.56	980.19	968.82	969.60	978.38	979.70	1,013.52	995.51	1,000.79	1,015.87	1,007.90	993.84
2016	1,007.81	1,017.77	1,063.66	1,047.37	1,058.11	1,044.89	1,063.67	1,053.80	1,062.55	1,087.99	1,094.26	1,060.70	1,054.81
2017	1,068.19	1,088.50	1,096.55	1,106.23	1,113.45	1,124.24	1,156.19	1,173.40	1,181.44	1,164.91	1,147.33	1,160.92	1,131.94
2018	1,158.88	1,140.16	1,130.07	1,177.26	1,149.25	1,151.01	1,213.03	1,181.93	1,200.56	1,145.08	1,153.68	1,149.41	1,163.56
Trade, Transportation, and Utilities													
2014	681.65	701.08	714.15	715.12	693.24	700.07	682.08	671.66	674.61	665.62	674.31	656.30	685.46
2015	652.73	667.97	664.98	666.29	663.66	659.69	661.13	670.32	668.70	668.70	669.64	659.72	664.17
2016	658.31	648.29	647.40	661.53	660.18	681.32	661.19	678.04	684.78	710.02	684.77	688.90	672.99
2017	736.03	696.63	712.66	739.17	711.65	714.67	726.77	710.29	722.94	728.08	714.71	709.48	718.61
2018	698.67	690.32	696.15	723.24	723.03	734.32	745.97	737.93	771.39	762.24	744.68	762.63	733.26
Financial Activities													
2014	980.35	1,035.50	1,011.53	979.25	969.98	978.70	939.96	950.51	939.60	934.84	1,003.54	960.68	974.46
2015	969.08	1,018.21	1,011.44	981.91	979.25	963.06	959.78	988.47	954.11	941.56	986.17	949.89	974.16
2016	979.20	955.57	957.12	985.91	1,006.40	926.39	975.79	950.09	974.90	996.87	1,032.81	1,010.46	980.28
2017	1,093.36	1,000.05	1,008.85	1,067.97	1,029.97	1,030.21	1,113.74	1,058.51	1,080.82	1,121.66	1,094.82	1,110.72	1,066.12
2018	1,119.91	1,113.13	1,115.27	1,182.21	1,124.01	1,092.99	1,164.93	1,104.59	1,145.30	1,129.32	1,101.46	1,143.69	1,126.55
Professional and Business Services													
2014	901.09	935.09	923.05	911.90	909.14	945.38	910.89	913.38	913.64	914.77	953.84	910.04	920.49
2015	923.64	973.28	969.08	948.71	935.43	934.14	932.44	993.82	962.12	970.16	992.08	954.38	957.24
2016	969.76	963.59	946.75	960.69	972.89	949.81	968.94	953.89	961.82	1,001.36	981.39	985.48	969.03
2017	1,049.44	1,027.23	1,022.56	1,073.84	1,016.58	1,028.88	1,061.28	1,042.92	1,034.25	1,036.18	990.24	989.74	1,031.20
2018	994.06	1,016.94	1,011.07	1,017.75	1,014.65	1,034.94	1,057.75	1,058.11	1,060.85	1,018.93	1,009.94	1,035.23	1,028.66
Education and Health Services													
2014	619.51	626.28	628.78	612.79	604.39	610.22	601.22	603.43	602.77	601.58	621.26	606.91	612.47
2015	607.46	619.63	620.63	617.30	615.12	613.05	626.67	615.06	600.59	585.28	616.30	604.56	611.82
2016	606.02	597.88	609.62	613.86	634.53	623.64	631.44	628.85	647.14	648.40	652.69	649.75	628.45
2017	666.87	660.68	656.98	677.38	652.00	653.35	662.32	636.03	643.21	653.35	634.71	630.83	652.74
2018	624.68	631.62	627.27	649.35	635.63	629.85	662.54	653.25	669.67	658.58	661.05	681.36	649.42
Leisure and Hospitality													
2014	305.76	316.50	325.63	315.23	313.25	320.95	322.34	321.68	323.34	322.83	328.45	333.80	321.31
2015	321.16	336.43	342.14	335.66	333.33	337.72	335.90	336.41	331.68	338.84	332.07	331.47	334.82
2016	327.92	336.40	336.42	341.80	335.15	326.44	335.00	331.33	330.00	332.02	325.68	322.48	332.35
2017	314.78	325.96	336.99	334.32	338.25	346.50	353.02	346.36	352.47	353.83	352.56	357.70	342.82
2018	345.31	358.16	360.40	366.80	362.36	363.38	363.81	361.80	367.77	360.40	359.66	374.99	361.62

MONTANA
At a Glance

Population:
2010 census: 989,415
2018 estimate: 1,062,305

Percent change in population:
2010–2018: 7.4%

Percent change in total nonfarm employment:
2010–2018: 11.6%

Industry with the largest growth in employment, 2010–2018 (percent):
Construction, 26.5%

Industry with the largest decline or smallest growth in employment, 2010–2018 (percent):
Information, -13.7%

Civilian labor force:
2010: 500,525
2018: 528,244

Unemployment rate and rank among states (highest to lowest):
2010: 7.3%, 40th
2018: 3.7%, 28th

Over-the-year change in unemployment rates:
2016–2017: -0.2%
2017–2018: -0.2%

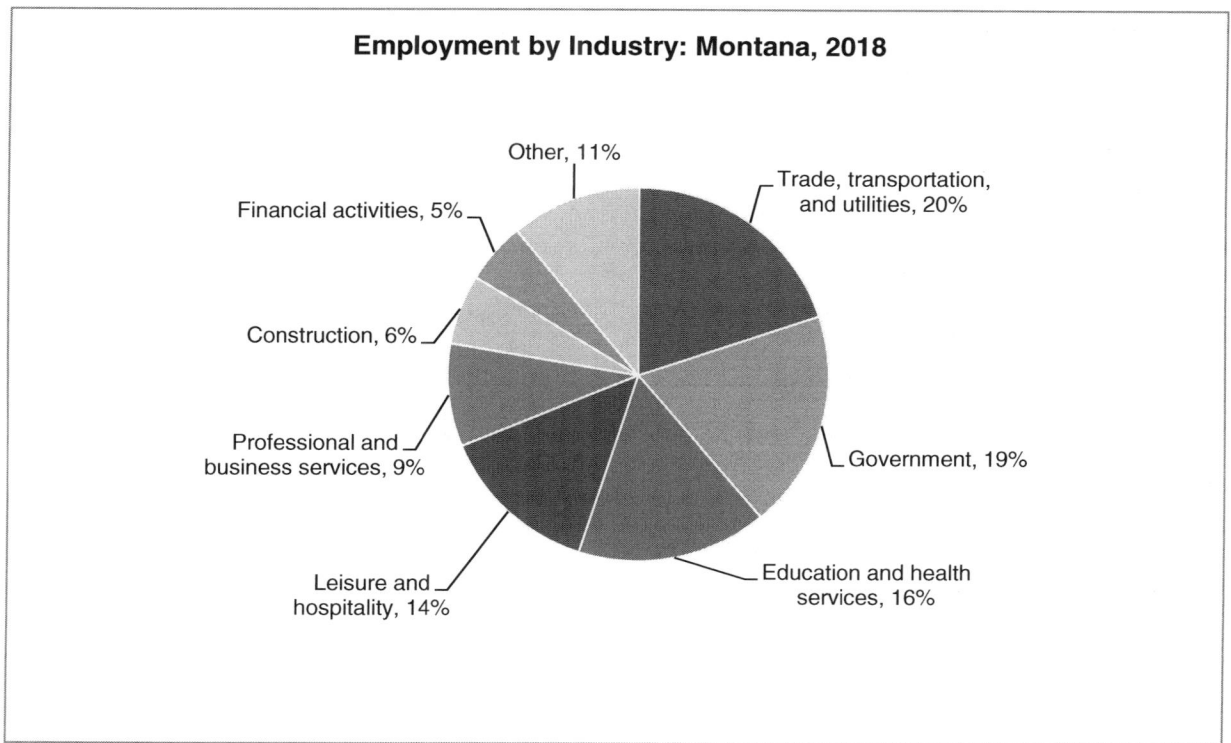

Employment by Industry: Montana, 2018

- Other, 11%
- Financial activities, 5%
- Construction, 6%
- Professional and business services, 9%
- Leisure and hospitality, 14%
- Trade, transportation, and utilities, 20%
- Government, 19%
- Education and health services, 16%

1. Employment by Industry: Montana, 2010–2018

(Numbers in thousands, not seasonally adjusted)

Industry and year	January	February	March	April	May	June	July	August	September	October	November	December	Annual average
Total Nonfarm													
2010	413.3	413.9	418.5	423.7	432.4	437.3	436.8	437.3	435.6	433.1	428.3	427.4	428.1
2011	413.7	415.8	419.8	425.7	433.4	438.5	437.3	440.4	441.2	438.2	434.6	434.6	431.1
2012	422.8	423.9	427.8	434.5	443.6	448.4	448.3	450.1	449.9	447.0	443.0	443.6	440.2
2013	432.3	435.5	438.7	444.5	452.5	456.6	454.2	457.0	455.6	454.7	450.9	450.8	448.6
2014	437.8	441.1	442.7	449.1	456.2	462.0	461.4	462.5	460.3	457.4	452.7	454.7	453.2
2015	444.9	448.9	452.8	458.6	464.5	469.2	468.7	469.5	468.1	468.4	464.7	465.8	462.0
2016	452.5	455.7	459.2	465.1	471.2	476.4	474.0	475.2	474.6	471.6	469.2	468.6	467.8
2017	457.5	459.6	463.4	469.5	476.4	482.3	479.1	480.0	478.1	476.3	472.4	473.5	472.3
2018	463.1	464.5	467.7	472.7	481.4	487.8	485.0	486.1	483.6	481.9	478.7	478.3	477.6
Total Private													
2010	323.1	322.6	325.4	331.1	336.3	344.3	348.1	348.7	344.0	339.9	335.4	334.8	336.1
2011	324.3	324.8	327.8	333.9	340.2	347.7	352.9	354.6	350.4	347.0	343.8	344.0	341.0
2012	334.1	334.3	337.4	344.2	351.2	359.3	362.1	364.5	359.6	356.0	352.0	353.1	350.7
2013	342.0	344.0	346.8	353.1	360.4	367.4	370.4	372.2	366.2	363.0	359.7	361.0	358.9
2014	349.7	349.7	351.0	357.8	364.1	372.3	375.8	377.0	370.0	365.7	360.9	363.8	363.2
2015	356.4	357.9	360.9	366.3	371.6	379.6	383.5	383.9	377.5	375.4	372.4	373.8	371.6
2016	363.7	364.8	367.1	372.7	377.4	384.7	388.3	388.7	383.1	378.6	376.2	376.2	376.8
2017	367.3	368.4	371.6	377.2	383.4	391.3	392.6	393.1	386.0	382.9	380.2	382.1	381.3
2018	373.4	374.1	376.8	381.4	389.0	397.5	399.1	399.9	392.8	389.2	386.5	386.8	387.2
Goods Producing													
2010	42.2	41.6	42.4	44.9	46.7	48.3	49.5	50.0	49.5	49.8	47.9	45.1	46.5
2011	41.6	41.6	42.5	45.4	47.3	49.3	50.9	51.7	51.4	51.5	49.9	48.1	47.6
2012	44.8	44.5	45.4	48.5	50.5	52.0	52.8	53.5	53.3	53.5	51.7	50.6	50.1
2013	46.3	46.8	47.7	50.4	53.7	54.3	54.5	55.1	54.3	54.6	53.5	51.7	51.9
2014	48.1	47.7	48.5	51.1	53.6	56.0	56.7	56.6	55.3	56.0	53.5	53.0	53.0
2015	49.8	50.0	50.7	52.3	54.3	56.2	57.1	56.8	55.4	56.0	54.3	53.0	53.8
2016	49.4	49.5	50.2	52.5	54.2	55.8	56.2	56.4	55.3	55.3	54.8	52.8	53.5
2017	49.6	50.3	51.3	53.5	56.0	57.2	57.3	57.4	56.2	56.5	55.0	54.3	54.6
2018	51.0	51.1	52.3	54.8	58.0	59.1	59.5	59.9	59.2	59.0	57.2	55.1	56.4
Service-Providing													
2010	371.1	372.3	376.1	378.8	385.7	389.0	387.3	387.3	386.1	383.3	380.4	382.3	381.6
2011	372.1	374.2	377.3	380.3	386.1	389.2	386.4	388.7	389.8	386.7	384.7	386.5	383.5
2012	378.0	379.4	382.4	386.0	393.1	396.4	395.5	396.6	396.6	393.5	391.3	393.0	390.2
2013	386.0	388.7	391.0	394.1	398.8	402.3	399.7	401.9	401.3	400.1	397.4	399.1	396.7
2014	389.7	393.4	394.2	398.0	402.6	406.0	404.7	405.9	405.0	401.4	399.2	401.7	400.2
2015	395.1	398.9	402.1	406.3	410.2	413.0	411.6	412.7	412.7	412.4	410.4	412.8	408.2
2016	403.1	406.2	409.0	412.6	417.0	420.6	417.8	418.8	419.3	416.3	414.4	415.8	414.2
2017	407.9	409.3	412.1	416.0	420.4	425.1	421.8	422.6	421.9	419.8	417.4	419.2	417.8
2018	412.1	413.4	415.4	417.9	423.4	428.7	425.5	426.2	424.4	422.9	421.5	423.2	421.2
Mining and Logging													
2010	6.9	6.9	7.0	7.1	7.3	7.5	7.7	7.9	7.8	7.8	7.7	7.5	7.4
2011	7.4	7.5	7.6	7.6	7.8	8.0	8.5	8.8	8.6	8.7	8.8	8.7	8.2
2012	8.7	8.8	8.7	8.8	9.0	9.4	9.7	9.9	9.7	9.8	9.7	9.8	9.3
2013	9.1	9.3	9.3	9.2	9.5	9.7	9.6	9.7	9.6	9.4	9.5	9.4	9.4
2014	8.9	8.8	8.7	8.7	9.0	9.2	9.4	9.5	9.4	9.5	9.3	9.2	9.1
2015	8.8	8.6	8.4	8.1	8.2	8.4	8.4	8.3	8.0	7.9	7.7	7.5	8.2
2016	7.1	7.0	6.8	6.9	7.0	7.1	7.0	7.0	6.9	6.9	6.9	6.8	7.0
2017	6.7	6.7	6.6	6.5	6.7	6.9	7.1	7.2	7.0	7.1	6.9	6.9	6.9
2018	6.8	6.9	6.9	6.8	7.1	7.4	7.5	7.5	7.4	7.5	7.4	7.3	7.2
Construction													
2010	18.9	18.4	19.3	21.7	23.1	24.3	25.2	25.4	25.1	25.2	23.3	20.8	22.6
2011	17.9	17.8	18.5	21.3	22.9	24.5	25.5	25.9	25.9	25.6	24.0	22.1	22.7
2012	19.3	19.0	20.0	22.5	24.0	24.9	25.2	25.6	25.7	25.4	23.7	22.4	23.1
2013	19.6	19.8	20.7	23.2	26.0	26.1	26.2	26.7	26.1	26.2	24.9	23.2	24.1
2014	20.8	20.5	21.5	23.8	25.8	27.7	28.1	27.9	26.9	27.2	25.2	24.6	25.0
2015	22.4	22.7	23.7	25.4	27.2	28.6	29.3	29.1	28.1	28.5	27.1	25.9	26.5
2016	23.1	23.3	24.3	26.4	27.9	29.2	29.5	29.6	28.7	28.5	27.9	26.1	27.0
2017	23.5	24.1	25.1	27.5	29.6	30.3	30.1	30.1	29.1	29.1	27.8	27.1	27.8
2018	24.3	24.2	25.3	28.0	30.5	30.9	31.3	31.5	30.9	30.6	29.0	27.2	28.6

1. Employment by Industry: Montana, 2010–2018—Continued

(Numbers in thousands, not seasonally adjusted)

Industry and year	January	February	March	April	May	June	July	August	September	October	November	December	Annual average
Manufacturing													
2010	16.4	16.3	16.1	16.1	16.3	16.5	16.6	16.7	16.6	16.8	16.9	16.8	16.5
2011	16.3	16.3	16.4	16.5	16.6	16.8	16.9	17.0	16.9	17.2	17.1	17.3	16.8
2012	16.8	16.7	16.7	17.2	17.5	17.7	17.9	18.0	17.9	18.3	18.3	18.4	17.6
2013	17.6	17.7	17.7	18.0	18.2	18.5	18.7	18.7	18.6	19.0	19.1	19.1	18.4
2014	18.4	18.4	18.3	18.6	18.8	19.1	19.2	19.2	19.0	19.3	19.0	19.2	18.9
2015	18.6	18.7	18.6	18.8	18.9	19.2	19.4	19.4	19.3	19.6	19.5	19.6	19.1
2016	19.2	19.2	19.1	19.2	19.3	19.5	19.7	19.8	19.7	19.9	20.0	19.9	19.5
2017	19.4	19.5	19.6	19.5	19.7	20.0	20.1	20.1	20.1	20.3	20.3	20.3	19.9
2018	19.9	20.0	20.1	20.0	20.4	20.8	20.7	20.9	20.9	20.9	20.8	20.6	20.5
Trade, Transportation, and Utilities													
2010	84.2	83.5	83.9	84.8	85.9	86.8	86.6	86.6	85.9	85.8	86.4	87.0	85.6
2011	83.9	83.5	83.6	84.8	86.0	87.0	87.3	87.7	86.9	87.1	88.1	88.7	86.2
2012	85.7	85.3	85.7	86.8	88.4	89.7	89.7	90.0	89.6	90.0	91.1	91.7	88.6
2013	88.3	88.1	88.4	89.8	91.4	92.1	92.1	92.6	91.6	92.2	93.2	94.1	91.2
2014	90.7	90.1	90.1	91.1	92.6	93.5	93.4	93.7	93.0	93.0	94.2	95.1	92.5
2015	92.1	91.7	92.3	93.3	94.3	95.1	95.1	95.3	94.6	95.2	96.4	97.0	94.4
2016	93.7	93.1	93.5	94.2	95.4	95.8	95.4	95.7	95.0	94.5	95.0	95.4	94.7
2017	92.9	92.3	92.6	93.6	94.6	95.4	95.2	95.3	94.6	94.5	95.6	95.9	94.4
2018	93.4	92.9	93.1	93.4	94.8	95.7	95.8	95.9	94.9	95.2	95.9	96.7	94.8
Wholesale Trade													
2010	15.2	15.2	15.3	15.5	15.6	15.7	15.7	15.6	15.5	15.4	15.4	15.3	15.5
2011	15.0	15.1	15.2	15.4	15.6	15.7	15.8	15.9	15.7	15.7	15.7	15.8	15.6
2012	15.6	15.6	15.9	16.1	16.2	16.4	16.5	16.5	16.4	16.4	16.4	16.4	16.2
2013	16.4	16.5	16.7	16.9	17.1	17.1	17.1	17.1	16.8	16.8	16.8	16.8	16.8
2014	16.5	16.4	16.6	16.7	16.9	17.0	17.0	17.0	16.8	16.8	16.9	16.9	16.8
2015	16.9	16.9	17.1	17.3	17.4	17.5	17.5	17.5	17.2	17.3	17.4	17.4	17.3
2016	17.1	17.1	17.2	17.2	17.3	17.4	17.3	17.3	17.0	17.0	17.0	16.9	17.2
2017	16.8	16.8	16.9	17.0	17.2	17.3	17.3	17.3	17.0	17.1	17.2	17.0	17.1
2018	17.0	17.0	17.1	17.2	17.4	17.5	17.4	17.3	17.1	17.4	17.4	17.4	17.3
Retail Trade													
2010	53.7	53.0	53.2	53.9	54.7	55.6	55.5	55.6	54.6	54.7	55.3	55.6	54.6
2011	53.2	52.7	52.8	53.7	54.5	55.3	55.7	55.8	55.1	55.2	56.1	56.3	54.7
2012	53.9	53.3	53.4	54.1	55.3	56.2	56.3	56.2	55.6	56.0	57.1	57.2	55.4
2013	54.1	53.6	53.7	55.0	56.0	56.8	57.2	57.3	56.4	57.0	57.9	58.3	56.1
2014	55.6	55.2	55.1	56.2	57.3	58.1	58.4	58.5	57.6	57.8	58.8	59.1	57.3
2015	56.8	56.5	56.9	57.9	58.8	59.5	59.7	59.8	59.0	59.4	60.4	60.5	58.8
2016	58.3	57.8	58.1	59.0	59.8	60.4	60.3	60.4	59.7	59.3	59.9	59.9	59.4
2017	58.1	57.5	57.7	58.4	59.1	59.7	59.8	59.8	59.0	59.0	60.0	59.9	59.0
2018	58.0	57.6	57.7	57.9	59.0	59.8	60.1	60.1	59.0	59.3	59.7	59.9	59.0
Transportation and Utilities													
2010	15.3	15.3	15.4	15.4	15.6	15.5	15.4	15.4	15.8	15.7	15.7	16.1	15.6
2011	15.7	15.7	15.6	15.7	15.9	16.0	15.8	16.0	16.1	16.2	16.3	16.6	16.0
2012	16.2	16.4	16.4	16.6	16.9	17.1	16.9	17.3	17.6	17.6	17.6	18.1	17.1
2013	17.8	18.0	18.0	17.9	18.3	18.2	17.8	18.2	18.4	18.4	18.5	19.0	18.2
2014	18.6	18.5	18.4	18.2	18.4	18.4	18.0	18.2	18.6	18.4	18.5	19.1	18.4
2015	18.4	18.3	18.3	18.1	18.1	18.1	17.9	18.0	18.4	18.5	18.6	19.1	18.3
2016	18.3	18.2	18.2	18.0	18.3	18.0	17.8	18.0	18.3	18.2	18.1	18.6	18.2
2017	18.0	18.0	18.0	18.2	18.3	18.4	18.1	18.2	18.6	18.4	18.4	19.0	18.3
2018	18.4	18.3	18.3	18.3	18.4	18.4	18.3	18.5	18.8	18.5	18.8	19.4	18.5
Information													
2010	7.3	7.4	7.4	7.3	7.3	7.5	7.4	7.3	7.2	7.2	7.2	7.2	7.3
2011	7.1	7.2	7.2	7.2	7.2	7.3	7.3	7.3	7.2	7.2	7.2	7.1	7.2
2012	6.9	7.0	6.9	6.8	6.9	6.9	6.9	7.0	6.9	6.9	7.0	7.0	6.9
2013	6.8	7.0	6.9	6.8	6.9	6.8	6.8	6.8	6.7	6.7	6.7	6.7	6.8
2014	6.5	6.5	6.4	6.4	6.4	6.4	6.4	6.4	6.4	6.3	6.3	6.3	6.4
2015	6.3	6.4	6.3	6.3	6.4	6.4	6.4	6.4	6.4	6.4	6.5	6.4	6.4
2016	6.3	6.4	6.3	6.3	6.3	6.3	6.3	6.3	6.3	6.4	6.5	6.4	6.3
2017	6.4	6.3	6.3	6.3	6.3	6.3	6.5	6.6	6.5	6.5	6.5	6.5	6.4
2018	6.4	6.5	6.5	6.3	6.4	6.4	6.3	6.3	6.3	6.3	6.1	6.2	6.3

1. Employment by Industry: Montana, 2010–2018—*Continued*

(Numbers in thousands, not seasonally adjusted)

Industry and year	January	February	March	April	May	June	July	August	September	October	November	December	Annual average
Financial Activities													
2010	21.0	21.0	21.1	21.0	21.1	21.4	21.5	21.4	21.1	21.2	20.9	21.2	21.2
2011	20.7	20.7	20.8	20.7	20.8	21.2	21.4	21.3	21.2	21.6	21.6	21.9	21.2
2012	20.9	20.9	20.9	21.0	21.3	21.7	21.9	22.0	21.9	21.9	21.8	22.2	21.5
2013	21.6	21.7	21.8	22.2	22.3	22.6	23.0	23.2	22.9	23.2	23.1	23.4	22.6
2014	22.9	23.1	23.1	23.3	23.4	23.7	24.0	24.0	23.6	23.6	23.5	23.8	23.5
2015	23.4	23.4	23.5	23.4	23.6	23.9	24.1	24.2	23.9	24.0	23.9	24.3	23.8
2016	23.8	23.8	23.8	23.8	23.9	24.3	24.5	24.5	24.2	24.3	24.2	24.4	24.1
2017	24.0	23.9	24.1	24.3	24.5	24.7	24.9	24.8	24.5	24.6	24.6	24.9	24.5
2018	24.4	24.4	24.4	24.5	24.7	25.1	25.3	25.2	24.9	25.2	25.3	25.8	24.9
Professional and Business Services													
2010	37.2	37.5	37.9	39.1	39.4	40.1	40.8	40.7	40.0	40.7	39.9	39.8	39.4
2011	38.8	39.0	39.4	40.6	41.0	41.5	42.0	42.1	41.1	40.6	40.2	39.5	40.5
2012	38.9	39.0	39.5	40.9	41.2	41.7	42.0	41.9	40.8	40.7	39.9	39.5	40.5
2013	38.1	38.3	38.6	39.6	40.1	40.8	41.5	40.9	40.0	39.9	39.3	39.0	39.7
2014	37.6	38.1	38.3	39.3	39.9	40.6	41.1	41.4	40.4	39.7	38.7	38.6	39.5
2015	38.7	39.1	39.5	40.6	40.6	41.5	42.2	42.1	41.1	40.8	40.1	39.9	40.5
2016	39.0	39.4	39.9	40.7	41.0	41.4	42.2	42.0	41.0	40.8	40.4	40.2	40.7
2017	39.3	39.7	40.1	40.9	41.7	42.3	42.5	42.5	41.4	41.7	41.1	41.1	41.2
2018	40.4	40.7	40.9	42.0	43.0	43.8	43.9	44.1	43.3	43.5	43.5	43.3	42.7
Education and Health Services													
2010	63.1	63.3	63.5	63.9	63.9	63.8	63.1	63.2	64.0	64.3	64.5	64.6	63.8
2011	63.9	64.2	64.3	64.2	64.7	64.5	63.9	64.5	65.6	66.4	66.5	67.1	65.0
2012	66.8	67.2	67.3	67.5	67.9	67.3	66.6	67.2	67.7	68.1	68.4	68.8	67.6
2013	68.3	68.6	68.8	68.9	69.1	68.8	68.0	68.6	69.5	69.9	70.1	70.3	69.1
2014	69.7	69.9	70.1	70.9	70.7	70.1	69.1	69.4	70.0	70.5	70.8	71.2	70.2
2015	70.7	71.1	71.4	72.2	72.2	71.8	71.0	71.4	72.3	73.1	73.5	73.6	72.0
2016	73.7	74.2	74.4	74.4	74.3	74.1	73.9	74.2	75.3	75.5	75.8	76.0	74.7
2017	76.2	76.5	76.8	76.7	76.9	76.5	75.8	76.0	76.7	77.2	77.5	77.7	76.7
2018	77.5	77.8	77.9	77.7	77.5	76.9	76.0	76.4	76.7	77.0	77.1	77.5	77.2
Leisure and Hospitality													
2010	51.5	51.7	52.4	53.4	55.2	59.4	62.4	62.8	59.6	54.2	52.0	53.3	55.7
2011	51.9	52.1	53.3	54.2	56.2	59.8	62.9	63.0	60.0	55.6	53.4	54.5	56.4
2012	53.4	53.5	54.7	55.4	57.5	62.3	64.6	65.2	61.7	57.1	54.6	55.9	58.0
2013	55.4	56.1	57.1	57.8	59.1	64.1	66.7	67.1	63.5	58.6	55.9	57.9	59.9
2014	56.8	56.8	57.1	58.0	59.6	64.3	67.1	67.6	63.7	58.6	56.1	58.4	60.3
2015	57.7	58.4	59.3	60.2	62.1	66.5	69.4	69.6	65.8	61.7	59.5	61.4	62.6
2016	59.9	60.5	61.0	62.6	64.0	68.5	71.3	71.1	67.4	63.1	60.9	62.5	64.4
2017	60.8	61.1	62.0	63.4	64.7	70.1	71.8	71.8	67.5	63.3	61.3	63.0	65.1
2018	61.9	62.3	63.0	63.9	65.7	71.3	73.2	73.0	68.6	63.8	62.2	63.4	66.0
Other Services													
2010	16.6	16.6	16.8	16.7	16.8	17.0	16.8	16.7	16.7	16.7	16.6	16.6	16.7
2011	16.4	16.5	16.7	16.8	17.0	17.1	17.2	17.0	17.0	17.0	16.9	17.1	16.9
2012	16.7	16.9	17.0	17.3	17.5	17.7	17.6	17.7	17.7	17.8	17.5	17.4	17.4
2013	17.2	17.4	17.5	17.6	17.8	17.9	17.8	17.9	17.7	17.9	17.9	17.9	17.7
2014	17.4	17.5	17.4	17.7	17.9	17.7	18.0	17.9	17.6	18.0	17.8	17.4	17.7
2015	17.7	17.8	17.9	18.0	18.1	18.2	18.2	18.1	18.0	18.2	18.2	18.2	18.1
2016	17.9	17.9	18.0	18.2	18.3	18.5	18.5	18.5	18.6	18.7	18.6	18.5	18.4
2017	18.1	18.3	18.4	18.5	18.7	18.8	18.6	18.7	18.6	18.6	18.6	18.7	18.6
2018	18.4	18.4	18.7	18.8	18.9	19.2	19.1	19.1	18.9	19.2	19.2	18.8	18.9
Government													
2010	90.2	91.3	93.1	92.6	96.1	93.0	88.7	88.6	91.6	93.2	92.9	92.6	92.0
2011	89.4	91.0	92.0	91.8	93.2	90.8	84.4	85.8	90.8	91.2	90.8	90.6	90.2
2012	88.7	89.6	90.4	90.3	92.4	89.1	86.2	85.6	90.3	91.0	91.0	90.5	89.6
2013	90.3	91.5	91.9	91.4	92.1	89.2	83.8	84.8	89.4	91.7	91.2	89.8	89.8
2014	88.1	91.4	91.7	91.3	92.1	89.7	85.6	85.5	90.3	91.7	91.8	90.9	90.0
2015	88.5	91.0	91.9	92.3	92.9	89.6	85.2	85.6	90.6	93.0	92.3	92.0	90.4
2016	88.8	90.9	92.1	92.4	93.8	91.7	85.7	86.5	91.5	93.0	93.0	92.4	91.0
2017	90.2	91.2	91.8	92.3	93.0	91.0	86.5	86.9	92.1	93.4	92.2	91.4	91.0
2018	89.7	90.4	90.9	91.3	92.4	90.3	85.9	86.2	90.8	92.7	92.2	91.5	90.4

2. Average Weekly Hours by Selected Industry: Montana, 2014–2018

(Not seasonally adjusted)

Industry and year	January	February	March	April	May	June	July	August	September	October	November	December	Annual average
Total Private													
2014	32.2	33.0	32.8	32.4	32.7	33.7	33.0	33.1	32.8	32.7	33.0	32.3	32.8
2015	32.1	32.7	32.5	32.0	32.5	32.7	32.9	33.5	32.7	32.5	33.0	32.3	32.6
2016	32.1	32.3	32.3	32.4	33.0	33.1	33.2	33.4	32.8	33.3	32.6	32.4	32.7
2017	32.6	32.1	32.2	33.0	32.7	33.3	33.7	33.4	32.8	33.3	32.5	32.5	32.9
2018	32.3	32.5	32.6	33.2	33.3	33.7	34.2	33.8	34.3	33.4	33.1	33.7	33.4
Goods Producing													
2014	36.3	37.0	37.2	37.6	38.4	39.4	38.2	37.5	38.2	38.6	37.2	37.4	37.8
2015	36.1	36.8	36.8	37.1	38.2	38.5	38.0	38.2	36.8	37.3	37.7	37.7	37.4
2016	36.2	37.2	37.3	37.8	38.0	38.7	38.5	38.5	38.4	38.1	37.5	35.8	37.7
2017	35.4	35.6	35.1	36.6	37.0	38.0	37.3	37.5	36.6	37.5	35.8	36.3	36.6
2018	35.6	35.5	36.5	37.2	38.0	38.6	38.9	39.1	40.0	39.1	38.0	39.1	38.1
Construction													
2014	34.5	35.6	35.4	36.4	38.4	39.0	37.8	37.0	38.1	38.8	37.0	37.3	37.2
2015	35.5	36.0	36.5	37.4	39.1	38.8	38.1	38.4	36.8	37.4	37.3	37.8	37.5
2016	35.9	36.5	36.6	37.6	37.6	39.1	38.1	38.5	37.9	37.2	37.5	35.5	37.4
2017	34.5	35.8	35.9	36.9	37.9	39.7	38.3	38.2	36.7	38.5	35.7	36.1	37.1
2018	34.6	34.1	35.9	37.1	39.1	39.9	40.7	40.5	40.8	39.7	38.0	39.3	38.5
Trade, Transportation, and Utilities													
2014	32.3	33.1	33.0	32.5	32.9	33.6	33.5	33.4	33.2	32.9	33.2	33.0	33.0
2015	32.8	33.1	32.8	32.3	32.7	33.2	33.4	34.4	33.5	33.1	33.4	32.9	33.1
2016	32.6	32.8	32.5	32.4	32.9	32.8	32.9	33.1	32.7	33.1	32.4	32.9	32.8
2017	32.4	31.7	32.0	33.1	32.6	33.3	33.8	33.7	32.9	33.4	32.9	32.9	32.9
2018	32.2	32.0	32.0	32.6	32.8	33.6	34.4	33.8	33.9	32.9	32.9	33.2	33.0
Financial Activities													
2014	37.3	38.2	38.0	36.5	36.8	37.7	35.7	36.1	35.8	35.7	37.2	35.0	36.6
2015	35.3	36.1	36.0	34.9	35.3	35.0	35.4	36.3	35.6	35.5	36.8	35.1	35.6
2016	35.9	35.4	35.3	35.6	35.6	35.5	35.5	35.5	35.5	35.8	35.5	35.4	35.5
2017	36.0	36.1	36.0	37.1	36.2	36.2	36.2	35.9	36.4	35.9	36.2	36.3	36.2
2018	36.0	36.8	36.5	37.0	36.8	37.0	37.2	37.5	38.0	37.3	37.2	37.4	37.0
Professional and Business Services													
2014	32.7	33.8	33.6	33.5	33.6	34.9	33.1	34.4	34.6	34.1	35.0	34.3	34.0
2015	34.2	34.8	34.2	33.6	34.5	34.4	34.1	34.9	34.6	33.7	34.8	33.9	34.3
2016	34.4	34.6	35.4	35.0	35.9	35.6	35.7	36.2	34.2	34.6	34.2	34.2	35.1
2017	34.8	33.7	32.7	34.2	33.4	33.4	34.6	34.1	34.2	34.5	33.1	33.2	33.8
2018	33.7	34.4	34.2	35.2	35.2	35.8	35.4	35.0	35.9	35.1	34.5	35.1	35.0
Education and Health Services													
2014	33.7	33.8	33.6	33.2	33.3	34.0	33.6	33.6	33.3	33.3	34.0	33.5	33.6
2015	33.6	34.1	34.0	33.7	33.6	33.6	33.8	34.0	33.9	33.8	34.1	33.7	33.8
2016	33.5	33.5	33.5	33.8	33.9	33.9	33.7	34.2	34.3	34.8	34.6	34.5	34.0
2017	35.1	34.7	34.9	35.3	34.6	35.0	35.4	34.8	34.8	35.2	35.1	34.5	35.0
2018	34.6	34.9	34.8	35.0	34.7	34.2	34.5	34.2	34.7	34.3	34.1	34.9	34.6
Leisure and Hospitality													
2014	22.2	23.5	23.7	22.7	23.4	25.2	25.4	25.5	24.1	23.5	24.0	22.6	23.9
2015	22.5	23.8	23.4	22.4	23.3	24.1	25.4	25.9	24.0	23.4	23.5	22.4	23.7
2016	22.8	22.6	22.7	22.7	24.6	25.1	25.9	25.6	24.3	24.6	22.9	22.8	24.0
2017	23.7	23.3	23.7	23.2	23.2	24.6	26.0	25.6	24.1	24.4	23.0	23.3	24.0
2018	23.4	23.4	23.9	23.9	23.8	25.2	26.4	25.7	25.3	23.5	23.1	24.2	24.4

3. Average Hourly Earnings by Selected Industry: Montana, 2014–2018

(Dollars, not seasonally adjusted)

Industry and year	January	February	March	April	May	June	July	August	September	October	November	December	Annual average
Total Private													
2014	21.23	21.53	21.26	21.35	21.33	21.30	21.25	21.13	21.46	21.82	21.68	21.74	21.42
2015	21.81	22.10	21.73	21.78	21.90	21.81	21.78	22.29	22.13	22.25	22.65	22.37	22.05
2016	22.17	22.38	21.98	22.37	22.44	22.13	22.27	22.11	22.58	22.79	22.67	22.72	22.38
2017	23.05	22.72	22.72	23.06	22.96	22.75	23.03	22.90	23.34	23.54	23.49	23.63	23.10
2018	23.61	23.68	23.75	23.89	23.81	23.62	23.70	23.73	24.11	23.92	23.97	24.09	23.83
Goods Producing													
2014	23.11	23.22	23.28	23.47	23.60	24.10	23.31	23.36	23.25	23.34	23.85	24.13	23.51
2015	23.79	23.75	23.83	24.51	24.70	24.58	24.20	24.95	25.38	25.05	24.97	24.30	24.52
2016	24.02	23.86	23.67	24.13	24.43	24.70	24.18	23.63	24.18	24.11	24.18	24.22	24.12
2017	24.33	23.87	24.27	24.10	24.17	24.57	24.72	25.10	25.30	25.66	25.82	25.99	24.84
2018	25.94	26.22	26.46	26.72	26.94	27.02	26.70	26.66	27.28	27.35	27.49	27.95	26.92
Construction													
2014	24.18	24.56	24.56	24.88	25.06	25.84	24.25	24.43	23.98	24.13	24.74	25.20	24.66
2015	24.30	24.32	24.22	24.59	25.27	24.99	24.19	25.09	25.46	25.43	25.28	25.28	24.90
2016	25.32	25.15	24.69	25.14	25.47	25.80	24.60	24.64	24.81	24.81	24.39	24.73	24.96
2017	24.61	25.06	24.68	24.51	24.88	25.62	24.96	25.54	25.60	26.32	26.03	26.12	25.35
2018	25.85	26.22	26.61	26.77	27.32	27.60	26.87	26.77	27.23	27.36	27.56	28.39	27.10
Trade, Transportation, and Utilities													
2014	19.89	19.69	20.01	19.84	20.04	19.73	19.66	19.72	19.98	19.95	20.16	19.97	19.89
2015	20.13	20.02	19.93	19.98	19.76	19.95	20.12	20.05	20.20	19.97	19.99	19.78	19.99
2016	20.76	20.64	20.48	20.91	21.02	20.80	21.05	20.57	20.95	20.59	20.14	19.85	20.65
2017	20.40	20.48	20.27	20.71	20.70	20.52	20.92	20.63	21.04	21.11	20.81	20.75	20.70
2018	21.05	21.20	21.05	21.27	21.20	21.18	21.07	21.21	21.34	20.85	20.61	20.40	21.03
Financial Activities													
2014	22.46	22.80	22.54	22.30	21.98	23.02	23.26	22.92	23.52	23.35	23.74	23.56	22.95
2015	23.20	23.38	24.10	24.08	24.23	24.29	24.27	25.07	24.98	24.98	25.34	25.12	24.43
2016	25.00	25.33	26.19	26.13	26.26	25.52	26.01	25.78	26.23	26.64	26.41	26.18	25.97
2017	26.71	25.12	25.12	25.58	25.14	25.02	25.19	25.15	25.52	25.33	25.19	25.35	25.37
2018	25.76	25.90	26.01	25.79	25.61	25.00	25.25	25.40	25.60	25.35	25.33	25.72	25.56
Professional and Business Services													
2014	23.80	23.72	23.80	23.33	23.22	23.20	23.17	22.87	23.43	23.33	23.80	23.57	23.43
2015	23.62	23.96	23.78	23.29	23.06	22.85	23.08	22.86	23.36	24.11	24.24	24.56	23.55
2016	24.32	24.01	24.16	24.46	24.83	23.91	23.46	23.51	25.19	25.66	25.55	25.99	24.57
2017	26.10	25.59	25.80	25.90	25.75	25.71	25.85	25.49	26.23	26.21	26.93	27.00	26.04
2018	26.54	26.76	26.65	26.65	26.19	25.72	25.99	25.81	26.76	25.90	26.41	26.86	26.34
Education and Health Services													
2014	22.86	24.26	22.94	23.34	23.16	23.27	24.01	23.52	23.89	23.83	23.24	23.63	23.49
2015	24.19	25.26	23.74	23.59	24.22	24.20	24.38	25.83	24.06	24.13	25.48	24.96	24.51
2016	24.38	25.89	24.13	24.42	24.47	24.40	25.21	25.47	25.30	25.66	25.74	26.08	25.11
2017	26.35	25.88	25.76	26.43	26.17	26.02	26.97	26.45	26.69	26.81	26.50	27.13	26.43
2018	26.75	26.35	26.43	26.46	26.14	26.24	27.19	26.87	26.64	26.48	26.59	26.64	26.56
Leisure and Hospitality													
2014	12.32	12.41	12.36	12.45	12.27	12.02	12.12	12.29	12.45	12.42	12.36	12.63	12.33
2015	12.79	13.00	12.97	13.03	13.14	13.02	13.01	13.13	13.22	13.41	13.43	13.44	13.13
2016	13.53	13.85	13.67	13.87	13.80	13.68	13.91	13.79	13.87	13.99	13.87	14.04	13.82
2017	14.14	14.11	14.05	14.30	14.00	13.76	13.96	13.92	14.09	14.41	14.18	14.23	14.09
2018	14.22	14.33	14.47	14.68	14.60	14.43	14.47	14.54	14.90	15.05	14.95	15.08	14.64

4. Average Weekly Earnings by Selected Industry: Montana, 2014–2018

(Dollars, not seasonally adjusted)

Industry and year	January	February	March	April	May	June	July	August	September	October	November	December	Annual average
Total Private													
2014	683.61	710.49	697.33	691.74	697.49	717.81	701.25	699.40	703.89	713.51	715.44	702.20	702.58
2015	700.10	722.67	706.23	696.96	711.75	713.19	716.56	746.72	723.65	723.13	747.45	722.55	718.83
2016	711.66	722.87	709.95	724.79	740.52	732.50	739.36	738.47	740.62	758.91	739.04	736.13	731.83
2017	751.43	729.31	731.58	760.98	750.79	757.58	776.11	764.86	765.55	783.88	763.43	767.98	759.99
2018	762.60	769.60	774.25	793.15	792.87	795.99	810.54	802.07	826.97	798.93	793.41	811.83	795.92
Goods Producing													
2014	838.89	859.14	866.02	882.47	906.24	949.54	890.44	876.00	888.15	900.92	887.22	902.46	888.68
2015	858.82	874.00	876.94	909.32	943.54	946.33	919.60	953.09	933.98	934.37	941.37	916.11	917.05
2016	869.52	887.59	882.89	912.11	928.34	955.89	930.93	909.76	928.51	918.59	906.75	867.08	909.32
2017	861.28	849.77	851.88	882.06	894.29	933.66	922.06	941.25	925.98	962.25	924.36	943.44	909.14
2018	923.46	930.81	965.79	993.98	1,023.72	1,042.97	1,038.63	1,042.41	1,091.20	1,069.39	1,044.62	1,092.85	1,025.65
Construction													
2014	834.21	874.34	869.42	905.63	962.30	1,007.76	916.65	903.91	913.64	936.24	915.38	939.96	917.35
2015	862.65	875.52	884.03	919.67	988.06	969.61	921.64	963.46	936.93	951.08	942.94	955.58	933.75
2016	908.99	917.98	903.65	945.26	957.67	1,008.78	937.26	948.64	940.30	922.93	914.63	877.92	933.50
2017	849.05	897.15	886.01	904.42	942.95	1,017.11	955.97	975.63	939.52	1,013.32	929.27	942.93	940.49
2018	894.41	894.10	955.30	993.17	1,068.21	1,101.24	1,093.61	1,084.19	1,110.98	1,086.19	1,047.28	1,115.73	1,043.35
Trade, Transportation, and Utilities													
2014	642.45	651.74	660.33	644.80	659.32	662.93	658.61	658.65	663.34	656.36	669.31	659.01	656.37
2015	660.26	662.66	653.70	645.35	646.15	662.34	672.01	689.72	676.70	661.01	667.67	550.76	661.67
2016	676.78	676.99	665.60	677.48	691.56	682.24	692.55	680.87	685.07	681.53	652.54	653.07	677.32
2017	660.96	649.22	648.64	685.50	674.82	683.32	707.10	695.23	692.22	705.07	684.65	682.68	681.03
2018	677.81	678.40	673.60	693.40	695.36	711.65	724.81	716.90	723.43	685.97	678.07	677.28	693.99
Financial Activities													
2014	837.76	870.96	856.52	813.95	808.86	867.85	830.38	827.41	842.02	833.60	883.13	824.60	839.97
2015	818.96	844.02	867.60	840.39	855.32	850.15	859.16	910.04	889.29	886.79	932.51	881.71	869.71
2016	897.50	896.68	924.51	930.23	934.86	905.96	923.36	915.19	931.17	953.71	937.56	926.77	921.94
2017	961.56	906.83	904.32	949.02	910.07	905.72	911.88	902.89	928.93	909.35	911.88	920.21	918.39
2018	927.36	953.12	949.37	954.23	942.45	925.00	939.30	952.50	972.80	945.56	942.28	961.93	945.72
Professional and Business Services													
2014	778.26	801.74	799.68	781.56	780.19	809.68	766.93	786.73	810.68	795.55	833.00	808.45	796.62
2015	807.80	833.81	813.28	782.54	795.57	786.04	787.03	797.81	808.26	812.51	843.55	832.58	807.77
2016	836.61	830.75	855.26	856.10	891.40	851.20	837.52	851.06	861.50	908.36	884.03	888.86	862.41
2017	908.28	862.38	843.66	885.78	860.05	858.71	894.41	869.21	897.07	904.25	891.38	896.40	880.15
2018	894.40	920.54	911.43	938.08	921.89	920.78	920.05	903.35	960.68	909.09	911.15	942.79	921.90
Education and Health Services													
2014	770.38	819.99	770.78	774.89	771.23	791.18	806.74	790.27	795.54	793.54	790.16	791.61	789.26
2015	812.78	861.37	807.16	794.98	813.79	813.12	824.04	878.22	815.63	815.59	868.87	841.15	828.44
2016	816.73	867.32	808.36	825.40	829.53	827.16	849.58	871.07	867.79	892.97	890.60	899.76	853.74
2017	924.89	898.04	899.02	932.98	905.48	910.70	954.74	920.46	928.81	943.71	930.15	935.99	925.05
2018	925.55	919.62	919.76	926.10	907.06	897.41	938.06	918.95	924.41	908.26	906.72	929.74	918.98
Leisure and Hospitality													
2014	273.50	291.64	292.93	282.62	287.12	302.90	307.85	313.40	300.05	291.87	296.64	285.44	294.69
2015	287.78	309.40	303.50	291.87	306.16	313.78	330.45	340.07	317.28	313.79	315.61	301.06	311.18
2016	308.48	313.01	310.31	314.85	339.48	343.37	360.27	353.02	337.04	344.15	317.62	320.11	331.68
2017	335.12	328.76	332.99	331.76	324.80	338.50	362.96	356.35	339.57	351.60	326.14	331.56	338.16
2018	332.75	335.32	345.83	350.85	347.48	363.64	382.01	373.68	376.97	353.68	345.35	364.94	357.22

NEBRASKA
At a Glance

Population:
  2010 census: 1,826,341
  2018 estimate: 1,929,268

Percent change in population:
  2010–2018: 5.6%

Percent change in total nonfarm employment:
  2010–2018: 8.3%

Industry with the largest growth in employment, 2010–2018 (percent):
  Construction, 25.4%

Industry with the largest decline or smallest growth in employment, 2010–2018 (percent):
  Wholesale trade, -0.5%

Civilian labor force:
  2010: 993,398
  2018: 1,020,197

Unemployment rate and rank among states (highest to lowest):
  2010: 4.6%, 50th
  2018: 2.8%, 45th

Over-the-year change in unemployment rates:
  2016–2017: -0.2%
  2017–2018: -0.1%

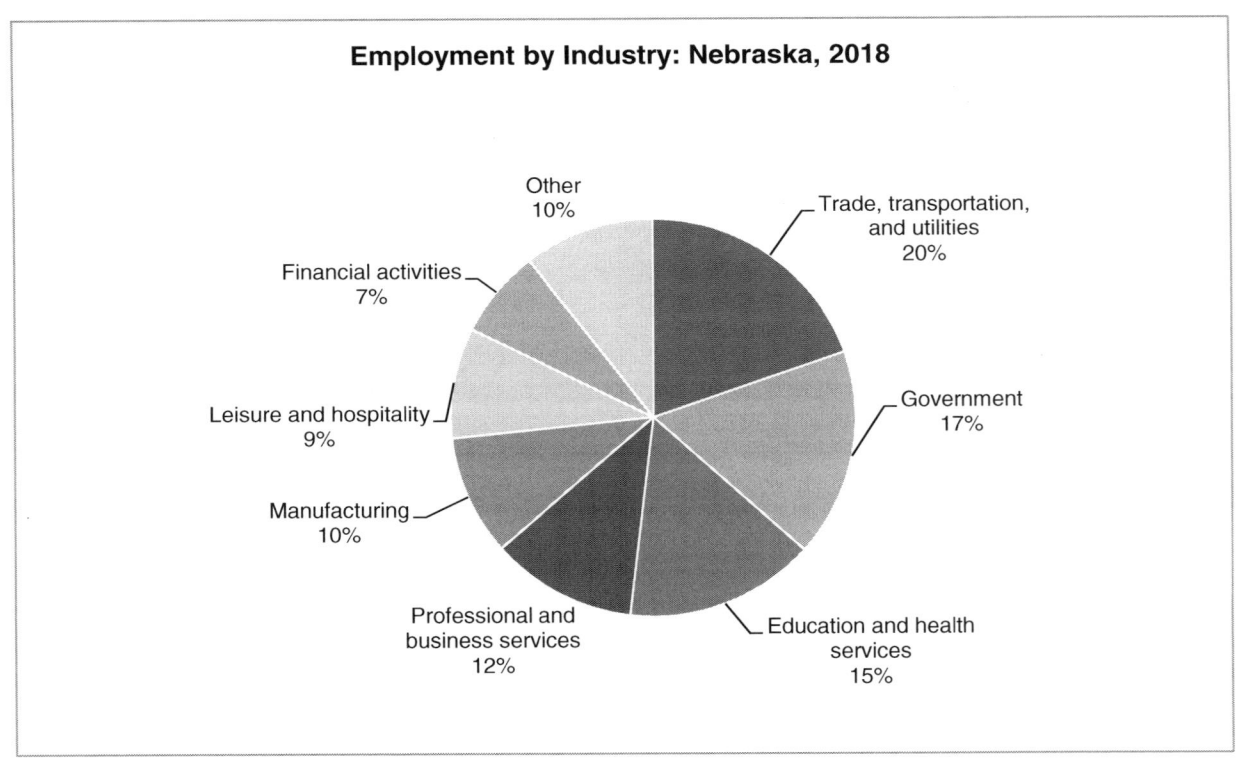

Employment by Industry: Nebraska, 2018

- Other 10%
- Trade, transportation, and utilities 20%
- Financial activities 7%
- Government 17%
- Leisure and hospitality 9%
- Manufacturing 10%
- Professional and business services 12%
- Education and health services 15%

1. Employment by Industry: Nebraska, 2010–2018

(Numbers in thousands, not seasonally adjusted)

Industry and year	January	February	March	April	May	June	July	August	September	October	November	December	Annual average
Total Nonfarm													
2010	921.5	924.9	930.9	944.5	954.5	956.7	946.9	947.9	948.3	955.5	954.8	953.7	945.0
2011	928.5	931.8	939.1	953.6	960.7	959.9	950.4	952.9	957.5	964.5	966.9	965.7	952.6
2012	945.0	947.7	957.6	967.4	977.9	976.8	967.0	969.3	973.5	979.2	981.4	981.5	968.7
2013	955.6	959.6	965.7	975.8	989.2	987.5	978.2	982.6	986.4	993.1	995.6	994.7	980.3
2014	970.8	975.7	981.4	991.9	1,002.7	1,000.2	989.8	992.6	996.6	1,002.8	1,002.9	1,005.7	992.8
2015	980.6	985.9	992.9	1,005.3	1,013.9	1,014.2	1,006.3	1,009.2	1,011.9	1,018.7	1,018.9	1,020.4	1,006.5
2016	992.5	996.1	1,006.0	1,015.8	1,024.4	1,023.0	1,015.7	1,016.0	1,022.5	1,024.9	1,023.8	1,020.3	1,015.1
2017	998.2	1,004.2	1,010.7	1,019.3	1,026.4	1,027.9	1,016.3	1,018.6	1,020.5	1,026.4	1,028.4	1,028.6	1,018.8
2018	1,002.5	1,007.1	1,013.8	1,022.0	1,033.8	1,034.6	1,024.9	1,025.2	1,027.3	1,028.3	1,031.0	1,027.2	1,023.1
Total Private													
2010	754.6	755.4	759.6	772.5	779.3	784.5	784.5	785.3	780.5	783.6	782.8	782.5	775.4
2011	761.3	762.3	769.3	782.2	788.5	791.8	791.3	792.1	790.9	793.2	795.5	795.1	784.5
2012	777.8	778.0	787.7	796.5	804.4	809.8	807.2	807.9	805.3	808.1	809.9	810.8	800.3
2013	788.5	790.2	796.1	805.1	815.1	818.8	817.7	821.0	818.0	820.7	823.1	823.3	811.5
2014	802.8	804.8	810.5	820.7	828.3	831.6	829.5	830.8	826.3	829.5	829.6	833.2	823.1
2015	812.5	814.8	821.2	831.5	838.8	843.7	843.6	844.9	841.2	843.5	844.0	846.1	835.5
2016	822.3	823.5	832.0	840.7	846.9	849.3	850.7	851.7	848.1	848.3	847.1	844.8	842.1
2017	826.5	830.5	836.3	844.2	849.6	853.0	851.2	852.3	847.5	850.7	852.8	853.7	845.7
2018	830.9	833.8	839.4	847.0	856.0	859.8	858.6	858.7	853.2	852.3	854.5	851.3	849.6
Goods Producing													
2010	128.9	128.9	129.4	133.8	135.7	138.1	138.0	137.5	136.7	136.2	135.4	133.3	134.3
2011	128.7	128.4	130.7	134.1	136.0	137.8	138.1	137.4	137.0	137.1	137.3	135.9	134.9
2012	132.5	131.6	134.1	136.5	139.1	141.4	141.3	141.4	140.8	140.9	140.5	139.7	138.3
2013	134.8	135.5	136.7	139.9	143.2	145.2	145.4	145.7	145.0	144.4	143.9	141.6	141.8
2014	138.1	138.1	139.6	144.3	146.1	148.2	148.6	148.6	147.3	147.6	146.1	145.7	144.9
2015	141.0	141.7	143.8	147.2	148.8	150.2	150.6	150.6	149.6	149.6	148.7	147.5	147.4
2016	143.0	142.8	145.7	148.0	149.7	151.5	151.8	151.7	150.7	150.5	149.4	147.4	148.5
2017	143.8	145.0	147.0	149.6	151.3	153.1	153.1	153.1	152.0	152.6	152.4	151.9	150.4
2018	146.5	146.8	149.0	152.2	154.2	156.2	157.3	157.2	155.6	155.1	154.5	152.5	153.1
Service-Providing													
2010	792.6	796.0	801.5	810.7	818.8	818.6	808.9	810.4	811.6	819.3	819.4	820.4	810.7
2011	799.8	803.4	808.4	819.5	824.7	822.1	812.3	815.5	820.5	827.4	829.6	829.8	817.8
2012	812.5	816.1	823.5	830.9	838.8	835.4	825.7	827.9	832.7	838.3	840.9	841.8	830.4
2013	820.8	824.1	829.0	835.9	846.0	842.3	832.8	836.9	841.4	848.7	851.7	853.1	838.6
2014	832.7	837.6	841.8	847.6	856.6	852.0	841.2	844.0	849.3	855.2	856.8	860.0	847.9
2015	839.6	844.2	849.1	858.1	865.1	864.0	855.7	858.6	862.3	869.1	870.2	872.9	859.1
2016	849.5	853.3	860.3	867.8	874.7	871.5	863.9	864.3	871.8	874.4	874.4	872.9	866.6
2017	854.4	859.2	863.7	869.7	875.1	874.8	863.2	865.5	868.5	873.8	876.0	876.7	868.4
2018	856.0	860.3	864.8	869.8	879.6	878.4	867.6	868.0	871.7	873.2	876.5	874.7	870.1
Mining and Logging													
2010	0.8	0.8	0.8	0.9	1.0	1.0	1.0	1.0	1.0	1.0	1.0	0.9	0.9
2011	0.9	0.9	0.9	1.0	1.1	1.1	1.1	1.1	1.1	1.1	1.1	1.0	1.0
2012	1.0	1.0	1.1	1.1	1.2	1.2	1.2	1.4	1.2	1.2	1.1	1.1	1.2
2013	0.9	1.0	1.0	1.1	1.1	1.1	1.1	1.1	1.1	1.1	1.1	1.0	1.1
2014	1.1	1.0	1.1	1.2	1.2	1.2	1.2	1.2	1.1	1.2	1.2	1.1	1.2
2015	1.0	1.0	1.1	1.2	1.1	1.1	1.1	1.1	1.1	1.1	1.0	1.0	1.1
2016	0.9	0.9	1.0	1.0	1.0	1.0	1.0	1.0	1.0	1.0	1.0	1.0	1.0
2017	0.9	0.9	1.0	1.1	1.1	1.1	1.1	1.1	1.1	1.1	1.1	1.1	1.1
2018	1.0	1.0	1.0	1.1	1.1	1.2	1.2	1.2	1.1	1.1	1.1	1.1	1.1
Construction													
2010	37.6	37.3	37.7	41.5	42.9	44.9	44.8	44.5	43.6	43.2	42.0	39.8	41.7
2011	36.0	35.6	37.4	40.2	41.6	42.9	43.1	42.8	42.3	42.2	41.5	39.9	40.5
2012	37.7	36.9	38.9	41.3	43.2	44.6	44.4	44.6	44.1	44.5	43.6	42.5	42.2
2013	38.8	38.9	39.9	42.8	45.6	47.1	47.7	47.7	47.0	46.3	45.4	43.3	44.2
2014	40.4	40.1	41.7	45.8	47.6	49.2	49.7	49.3	48.5	48.9	47.2	46.6	46.3
2015	42.9	43.3	45.1	48.6	50.3	51.6	52.2	51.9	51.2	51.2	50.3	49.0	49.0
2016	45.4	45.3	47.7	50.4	51.9	53.6	53.7	53.5	52.8	52.5	51.3	49.0	50.6
2017	46.1	46.8	48.5	50.9	52.2	53.7	53.7	53.5	52.7	52.7	52.0	51.0	51.2
2018	47.1	46.8	48.7	51.8	53.6	55.2	55.6	55.4	54.2	54.1	53.7	51.8	52.3

1. Employment by Industry: Nebraska, 2010–2018—*Continued*

(Numbers in thousands, not seasonally adjusted)

Industry and year	January	February	March	April	May	June	July	August	September	October	November	December	Annual average
Manufacturing													
2010	90.5	90.8	90.9	91.4	91.8	92.2	92.2	92.0	92.1	92.0	92.4	92.6	91.7
2011	91.8	91.9	92.4	92.9	93.3	93.8	93.9	93.5	93.6	93.8	94.7	95.0	93.4
2012	93.8	93.7	94.1	94.1	94.7	95.6	95.7	95.4	95.5	95.2	95.8	96.1	95.0
2013	95.1	95.6	95.8	96.0	96.5	97.0	96.6	96.9	96.9	97.0	97.4	97.3	96.5
2014	96.6	97.0	96.8	97.3	97.3	97.8	97.7	98.1	97.7	97.5	97.7	98.0	97.5
2015	97.1	97.4	97.6	97.4	97.4	97.5	97.3	97.6	97.3	97.3	97.4	97.5	97.4
2016	96.7	96.6	97.0	96.6	96.8	96.9	97.1	97.2	96.9	97.0	97.1	97.4	96.9
2017	96.8	97.3	97.5	97.6	98.0	98.3	98.3	98.5	98.2	98.8	99.3	99.8	98.2
2018	98.4	99.0	99.3	99.3	99.5	99.8	100.5	100.6	100.3	99.9	99.7	99.6	99.7
Trade, Transportation, and Utilities													
2010	192.5	191.2	192.2	194.4	196.1	196.1	195.5	195.4	194.4	197.2	200.0	202.4	195.6
2011	193.6	192.5	193.6	196.2	197.3	197.6	197.4	198.2	197.9	199.1	203.0	204.6	197.6
2012	197.0	195.0	196.2	198.2	199.8	199.9	199.1	198.6	198.6	200.4	204.5	206.5	199.5
2013	197.8	196.1	197.1	198.4	200.8	201.4	200.8	201.3	200.5	202.1	206.4	209.3	201.0
2014	200.9	199.4	200.1	202.0	204.0	204.4	203.5	204.1	203.0	204.9	208.7	212.2	203.9
2015	202.9	202.2	202.8	204.9	206.6	207.8	206.5	207.0	205.4	207.2	210.5	212.7	206.4
2016	202.7	201.6	202.1	203.5	204.6	204.5	204.3	203.8	202.6	203.7	206.4	207.5	203.9
2017	200.3	199.7	200.1	201.6	203.0	202.6	201.9	202.0	200.9	202.0	206.8	208.1	202.4
2018	199.9	199.2	199.8	200.3	202.1	202.4	201.7	201.5	199.1	199.9	204.1	205.0	201.3
Wholesale Trade													
2010	39.6	39.6	39.8	40.7	41.0	41.2	41.0	40.5	40.2	40.4	40.2	40.2	40.4
2011	39.6	39.6	39.9	40.5	40.8	41.1	41.1	40.8	40.7	40.9	41.0	41.1	40.6
2012	40.3	40.3	40.7	41.3	41.6	41.8	41.6	41.1	40.8	41.0	41.0	41.3	41.1
2013	40.6	40.6	41.0	41.5	42.2	42.5	42.3	41.8	41.5	41.8	41.9	42.3	41.7
2014	41.9	41.6	42.1	42.6	43.1	43.5	43.4	42.8	42.3	42.3	42.2	42.5	42.5
2015	41.5	41.4	41.7	42.3	42.6	42.9	42.6	42.3	41.7	41.8	41.8	41.8	42.0
2016	41.3	41.0	41.3	41.7	42.0	42.2	42.2	41.6	41.1	41.0	40.8	40.7	41.4
2017	40.1	40.1	40.3	40.9	41.2	41.4	41.2	40.7	40.2	40.4	40.5	40.8	40.7
2018	39.8	39.8	40.0	40.5	40.9	41.2	40.8	40.5	39.7	39.3	39.8	39.9	40.2
Retail Trade													
2010	102.4	101.2	101.9	102.8	104.1	104.2	103.7	103.6	102.6	104.7	107.2	108.6	103.9
2011	102.8	101.9	102.4	103.9	104.6	104.6	104.3	104.8	104.2	105.2	108.7	109.7	104.8
2012	104.2	102.4	103.1	104.2	105.2	105.3	104.9	104.7	104.6	106.3	109.8	110.5	105.4
2013	104.3	103.3	103.9	104.6	105.7	106.1	106.0	106.3	105.8	107.1	110.8	112.2	106.3
2014	106.3	105.2	105.3	106.8	108.0	108.2	108.0	108.4	107.6	109.0	111.8	113.4	108.2
2015	107.9	107.3	107.6	108.6	109.5	110.3	109.7	109.9	108.7	110.2	113.1	114.2	109.8
2016	108.8	108.4	108.5	109.9	110.6	110.5	110.6	110.4	109.4	110.5	113.0	113.4	110.3
2017	108.5	107.8	108.0	108.9	109.5	109.1	108.8	108.9	108.0	108.8	112.6	112.7	109.3
2018	107.5	106.8	106.8	107.1	108.2	108.3	108.2	107.7	105.9	106.5	109.9	109.6	107.7
Transportation and Utilities													
2010	50.5	50.4	50.5	50.9	51.0	50.7	50.8	51.3	51.6	52.1	52.6	53.6	51.3
2011	51.2	51.0	51.3	51.8	51.9	51.9	52.0	52.6	53.0	53.0	53.3	53.8	52.2
2012	52.5	52.3	52.4	52.7	53.0	52.8	52.6	52.8	53.2	53.1	53.7	54.7	53.0
2013	52.9	52.2	52.2	52.3	52.9	52.8	52.5	53.2	53.2	53.2	53.7	54.8	53.0
2014	52.7	52.6	52.7	52.6	52.9	52.7	52.1	52.9	53.1	53.6	54.7	56.3	53.2
2015	53.5	53.5	53.5	54.0	54.5	54.6	54.2	54.8	55.0	55.2	55.6	56.7	54.6
2016	52.6	52.2	52.3	51.9	52.0	51.8	51.5	51.8	52.1	52.2	52.6	53.4	52.2
2017	51.7	51.8	51.8	51.8	52.3	52.1	51.9	52.4	52.7	52.8	53.7	54.6	52.5
2018	52.6	52.6	53.0	52.7	53.0	52.9	52.7	53.3	53.5	54.1	54.4	55.5	53.4
Information													
2010	17.7	17.6	17.5	17.4	17.5	17.6	17.5	17.5	17.4	17.4	17.5	17.6	17.5
2011	17.4	17.5	17.4	17.3	17.3	17.5	17.8	17.7	17.7	17.7	17.8	17.8	17.6
2012	17.7	17.8	17.8	17.8	17.7	17.8	17.7	17.8	17.7	17.7	17.8	17.8	17.8
2013	17.7	17.8	17.8	17.7	17.7	17.7	17.7	17.7	17.7	17.8	17.8	17.8	17.7
2014	17.8	17.7	17.6	17.6	17.6	17.7	17.7	17.8	17.8	17.8	18.0	18.0	17.8
2015	17.9	18.0	18.0	18.1	18.2	18.3	18.4	18.5	18.3	18.5	18.5	18.6	18.3
2016	18.5	18.5	18.4	18.5	18.3	18.3	18.4	18.4	18.5	18.5	18.5	18.6	18.5
2017	18.4	18.4	18.3	18.3	18.2	18.2	18.2	18.1	17.9	18.0	17.9	18.0	18.2
2018	17.8	17.9	17.7	17.7	17.7	17.8	17.7	17.6	17.5	17.5	17.5	17.5	17.7

1. Employment by Industry: Nebraska, 2010–2018—*Continued*

(Numbers in thousands, not seasonally adjusted)

Industry and year	January	February	March	April	May	June	July	August	September	October	November	December	Annual average
Financial Activities													
2010	67.8	67.9	68.1	68.2	68.4	69.1	69.2	69.3	68.9	69.1	69.0	69.2	68.7
2011	68.9	68.9	69.0	69.6	69.7	70.0	70.0	70.0	69.9	69.9	70.1	70.5	69.7
2012	69.8	69.7	69.9	70.1	70.4	70.8	70.8	70.7	70.4	70.6	70.7	71.1	70.4
2013	70.3	70.4	70.5	70.5	70.9	71.2	71.3	71.2	70.8	71.0	71.1	71.2	70.9
2014	71.0	71.0	71.1	70.8	70.9	71.3	71.4	71.0	70.6	70.7	70.7	70.7	70.9
2015	70.0	69.8	69.8	70.1	70.4	71.0	71.2	71.1	70.8	71.3	71.4	71.8	70.7
2016	71.2	71.3	71.4	71.6	71.8	72.1	72.6	72.5	71.9	71.9	71.9	72.1	71.9
2017	71.7	71.8	71.9	72.2	72.3	73.0	73.2	73.2	72.9	73.2	73.0	73.4	72.7
2018	72.7	73.2	73.2	73.7	74.1	74.4	74.6	74.4	74.0	74.0	73.8	74.7	73.9
Professional and Business Services													
2010	97.4	97.5	97.8	100.5	100.6	101.8	102.8	102.6	102.6	103.1	102.4	102.7	101.0
2011	99.5	100.1	100.8	102.8	102.9	103.7	104.9	104.9	105.7	105.8	105.3	105.2	103.5
2012	103.9	104.8	105.4	106.7	107.1	109.3	109.3	108.9	108.8	109.0	108.7	108.4	107.5
2013	106.4	106.9	107.5	109.1	109.8	111.1	111.6	111.7	111.8	113.5	113.2	113.7	110.5
2014	110.4	111.8	112.4	113.8	114.1	115.0	115.0	114.7	114.5	114.9	114.8	115.1	113.9
2015	113.5	114.4	115.1	117.4	117.6	119.1	119.4	118.8	118.8	118.5	118.2	118.2	117.4
2016	115.7	116.4	117.5	120.0	120.2	120.9	120.7	120.9	120.4	119.9	119.3	119.5	119.3
2017	116.5	116.9	117.9	119.3	118.9	119.9	120.2	119.5	119.5	120.0	119.6	119.7	119.0
2018	116.0	116.9	117.5	118.8	119.3	120.3	120.4	119.6	120.2	121.0	120.6	119.4	119.2
Education and Health Services													
2010	138.7	140.1	140.4	140.5	140.9	140.3	140.2	140.9	140.8	141.8	141.9	142.0	140.7
2011	141.1	141.9	142.2	143.1	143.5	142.2	141.3	142.0	143.0	144.7	145.1	145.2	142.9
2012	143.2	144.5	146.1	145.9	146.0	144.8	144.2	145.5	146.6	147.8	148.0	148.2	145.9
2013	145.5	146.6	147.3	147.8	147.8	146.0	145.5	146.5	147.0	148.0	148.2	148.3	147.0
2014	145.7	147.3	148.5	148.5	148.6	146.7	146.1	147.2	148.0	149.4	149.3	149.8	147.9
2015	147.7	148.4	149.0	149.1	149.3	147.6	148.5	149.5	150.7	152.2	152.4	152.8	149.8
2016	150.0	151.2	152.6	151.9	152.8	151.2	152.3	153.2	154.5	155.3	155.3	154.7	152.9
2017	153.2	154.7	155.2	154.4	155.2	153.2	152.8	153.6	154.5	156.1	156.1	155.9	154.6
2018	154.3	155.4	155.9	155.9	156.3	154.7	154.0	155.0	155.7	156.6	157.0	155.9	155.6
Leisure and Hospitality													
2010	75.3	75.8	77.3	80.7	83.0	84.3	84.1	85.1	83.1	82.2	80.1	78.7	80.8
2011	76.1	76.8	79.0	82.4	85.0	86.1	85.1	85.5	83.4	82.6	80.7	79.6	81.9
2012	77.7	78.5	81.7	84.7	87.4	88.6	87.8	88.1	85.6	85.0	83.0	82.4	84.2
2013	79.8	80.5	82.2	84.7	87.8	88.9	88.4	89.9	88.4	87.4	86.1	84.9	85.8
2014	82.7	83.2	84.8	86.8	89.9	90.8	90.1	90.6	88.4	87.3	85.1	84.8	87.0
2015	82.9	83.5	85.8	87.6	90.6	92.3	91.7	92.4	90.9	89.3	87.5	87.5	88.5
2016	84.8	85.3	87.8	90.4	92.7	93.8	93.7	94.5	92.8	91.6	89.4	88.3	90.4
2017	86.3	87.6	89.3	91.8	93.9	96.0	95.1	96.2	93.2	92.3	90.4	89.9	91.8
2018	87.4	88.0	89.7	91.6	95.2	96.6	95.6	96.4	94.0	91.7	90.6	89.7	92.2
Other Services													
2010	36.3	36.4	36.9	37.0	37.1	37.2	37.2	37.0	36.6	36.6	36.5	36.6	36.8
2011	36.0	36.2	36.6	36.7	36.8	36.9	36.7	36.4	36.3	36.3	36.2	36.3	36.5
2012	36.0	36.1	36.5	36.6	36.9	37.2	37.0	36.9	36.8	36.7	36.7	36.7	36.7
2013	36.2	36.4	37.0	37.0	37.1	37.3	37.0	37.0	36.8	36.5	36.4	36.5	36.8
2014	36.2	36.3	36.4	36.9	37.1	37.5	37.1	36.8	36.7	36.9	36.9	36.9	36.8
2015	36.6	36.8	36.9	37.1	37.3	37.4	37.3	37.0	36.7	36.9	36.8	37.0	37.0
2016	36.4	36.4	36.5	36.8	36.8	37.0	36.9	36.7	36.7	36.9	36.9	36.7	36.7
2017	36.3	36.4	36.6	37.0	36.8	37.0	36.7	36.6	36.6	36.5	36.6	36.8	36.7
2018	36.3	36.4	36.6	36.8	37.1	37.4	37.3	37.0	37.1	36.5	36.4	36.6	36.8
Government													
2010	166.9	169.5	171.3	172.0	175.2	172.2	162.4	162.6	167.8	171.9	172.0	171.2	169.6
2011	167.2	169.5	169.8	171.4	172.2	168.1	159.1	160.8	166.6	171.3	171.4	170.6	168.2
2012	167.2	169.7	169.9	170.9	173.5	167.0	159.8	161.4	168.2	171.1	171.5	170.7	168.4
2013	167.1	169.4	169.6	170.7	174.1	168.7	160.5	161.6	168.4	172.4	172.5	171.4	168.9
2014	168.0	170.9	170.9	171.2	174.4	168.6	160.3	161.8	170.3	173.3	173.3	172.5	169.6
2015	168.1	171.1	171.7	173.8	175.1	170.5	162.7	164.3	170.7	175.2	174.9	174.3	171.0
2016	170.2	172.6	174.0	175.1	177.5	173.7	165.0	164.3	174.4	176.6	176.7	175.5	173.0
2017	171.7	173.7	174.4	175.1	176.8	174.9	165.1	166.3	173.0	175.7	175.6	174.9	173.1
2018	171.6	173.3	174.4	175.0	177.8	174.8	166.3	166.5	174.1	176.0	176.5	175.9	173.5

2. Average Weekly Hours by Selected Industry: Nebraska, 2014–2018

(Not seasonally adjusted)

Industry and year	January	February	March	April	May	June	July	August	September	October	November	December	Annual average
Total Private													
2014	33.4	33.8	34.1	33.8	34.1	35.0	34.4	34.4	34.1	34.1	34.3	33.9	34.1
2015	33.6	34.3	34.2	33.8	33.9	34.4	34.3	34.9	33.9	34.3	34.2	33.8	34.1
2016	33.4	33.3	33.4	34.0	34.1	34.2	34.0	34.1	33.8	34.5	33.6	33.6	33.8
2017	33.9	33.6	33.8	34.3	33.8	34.3	34.6	34.2	34.3	34.6	34.2	34.2	34.2
2018	33.4	33.6	33.6	34.2	33.8	34.0	34.3	33.6	34.1	33.5	33.4	33.8	33.8
Goods-Producing													
2014	40.0	39.5	40.3	40.5	41.3	41.6	41.1	41.3	40.7	40.8	40.1	40.7	40.7
2015	40.0	41.0	40.4	40.5	40.9	41.2	41.3	42.3	40.4	41.8	40.3	40.4	40.9
2016	40.2	39.4	40.0	42.1	40.6	41.8	41.8	42.4	40.5	41.2	39.9	39.5	40.8
2017	39.8	40.3	41.0	41.1	40.5	40.8	41.0	41.3	41.7	40.8	40.8	41.1	40.9
2018	39.3	40.0	39.5	40.4	40.6	40.9	40.2	40.3	40.7	39.3	39.6	40.0	40.1
Mining, Logging, and Construction													
2014	37.4	36.2	39.1	40.0	41.3	42.0	41.5	41.5	40.1	41.4	38.6	39.5	40.0
2015	37.6	39.7	40.2	39.3	39.2	41.1	42.0	43.0	41.6	42.5	40.6	40.4	40.7
2016	38.3	38.5	39.6	42.9	40.5	42.0	42.6	42.7	38.2	39.7	38.5	36.4	40.1
2017	35.8	36.6	37.3	39.4	38.8	40.1	40.1	41.3	41.1	39.8	40.8	40.3	39.4
2018	37.3	38.5	39.2	41.1	42.2	43.6	41.7	41.5	41.7	38.3	39.3	40.2	40.5
Manufacturing													
2014	41.2	40.9	40.8	40.8	41.3	41.4	41.0	41.2	41.0	40.6	40.8	41.3	41.0
2015	41.1	41.6	40.5	41.1	41.8	41.2	40.9	41.9	39.7	41.4	40.1	40.4	41.0
2016	41.1	39.8	40.2	41.7	40.7	41.8	41.4	42.3	41.8	42.1	40.6	41.1	41.2
2017	41.7	42.1	42.8	42.0	41.4	41.1	41.5	41.3	42.0	41.4	40.9	41.6	41.6
2018	40.4	40.6	39.7	40.1	39.7	39.4	39.3	39.6	40.1	39.8	39.7	39.9	39.9
Trade, Transportation, and Utilities													
2014	33.4	33.7	34.1	34.2	34.5	35.1	34.8	34.3	33.8	34.1	33.8	33.9	34.1
2015	33.1	33.7	33.8	33.7	33.5	34.3	34.0	34.2	33.4	33.9	33.5	33.6	33.7
2016	32.5	32.7	32.8	33.1	33.6	33.4	33.6	33.2	33.1	33.5	32.6	32.7	33.1
2017	32.3	32.0	32.1	32.8	32.4	32.9	32.5	32.3	32.7	32.8	32.8	32.6	32.5
2018	31.3	31.9	32.1	32.9	32.9	33.0	32.4	32.0	32.0	31.8	32.1	32.1	32.2
Financial Activities													
2014	37.3	38.5	38.6	37.7	37.7	39.4	38.0	38.0	37.9	38.0	39.5	37.8	38.2
2015	38.1	39.2	38.9	38.0	37.9	38.1	38.0	39.7	38.0	38.2	39.0	38.1	38.4
2016	37.9	39.2	38.1	38.0	38.4	39.2	38.5	37.9	38.4	38.0	39.0	38.0	38.4	38.3
2017	39.7	38.4	38.1	39.0	37.7	38.3	39.0	37.9	38.3	38.7	38.0	38.4	38.5
2018	38.4	38.2	38.3	39.0	38.2	38.7	39.2	37.0	38.4	38.3	37.0	38.1	38.2
Professional and Business Services													
2014	34.0	35.1	35.1	34.5	34.9	36.4	35.5	36.1	35.6	36.2	36.5	36.3	35.5
2015	35.7	36.4	36.2	35.7	35.5	36.0	35.4	36.3	35.5	35.9	36.4	35.1	35.8
2016	35.1	34.9	35.0	35.3	35.4	35.1	34.9	35.1	35.2	36.0	34.6	34.5	35.1
2017	34.8	34.2	34.5	35.5	35.1	35.5	36.0	35.4	35.0	36.1	36.1	35.3	35.3
2018	34.9	34.3	34.0	34.5	34.2	34.2	34.9	33.9	34.8	34.4	34.5	35.4	34.5
Education and Health Services													
2014	31.6	32.0	32.0	31.8	31.8	32.9	32.5	32.4	32.3	31.9	32.6	31.7	32.1
2015	31.2	31.8	31.9	31.4	31.6	32.3	32.4	32.3	32.2	31.8	32.3	31.1	31.9
2016	30.9	30.7	30.9	31.0	31.4	31.1	31.0	30.9	30.9	31.6	30.7	30.7	31.0
2017	31.1	30.8	31.2	31.9	31.3	31.6	32.1	31.7	31.7	32.3	31.6	31.7	31.6
2018	31.5	31.5	31.7	32.4	31.8	31.8	32.5	32.2	32.5	31.7	31.8	31.8	31.9
Leisure and Hospitality													
2014	21.0	22.0	22.4	21.9	22.1	23.6	22.6	23.1	22.7	22.7	22.6	22.0	22.4
2015	22.2	22.8	23.0	22.0	22.8	23.9	23.2	23.4	22.5	22.8	22.8	22.9	22.9
2016	22.3	22.3	22.5	22.5	22.9	23.5	22.9	22.5	22.9	23.0	22.7	22.0	22.7
2017	22.3	22.4	22.3	22.1	22.1	23.6	23.6	23.2	22.7	23.2	22.8	22.7	22.8
2018	21.9	22.6	22.7	22.3	22.5	23.3	23.7	22.8	23.2	22.7	22.1	22.9	22.7

3. Average Hourly Earnings by Selected Industry: Nebraska, 2014–2018

(Dollars, not seasonally adjusted)

Industry and year	January	February	March	April	May	June	July	August	September	October	November	December	Annual average
Total Private													
2014	21.18	21.23	21.35	21.26	21.16	21.21	21.24	21.33	21.38	21.51	21.66	21.74	21.36
2015	21.98	22.03	22.08	21.85	21.91	21.72	21.93	22.50	22.60	22.34	22.65	22.51	22.18
2016	22.76	22.88	22.84	22.94	23.04	22.78	23.02	22.97	23.19	23.37	23.04	22.94	22.98
2017	23.83	23.57	23.80	24.20	24.05	23.78	24.13	23.95	24.20	24.54	24.62	24.63	24.11
2018	24.82	24.49	24.58	25.01	24.54	24.52	24.78	24.54	25.28	24.76	24.68	25.37	24.78
Goods-Producing													
2014	20.34	19.91	20.10	20.36	20.33	20.33	20.55	20.59	20.46	20.61	20.75	21.02	20.45
2015	21.10	21.13	21.03	21.05	21.30	21.22	21.44	21.86	22.44	21.67	21.75	21.33	21.45
2016	21.36	21.83	22.10	22.13	21.74	21.66	22.00	21.84	21.88	21.98	21.80	22.27	21.88
2017	22.43	22.36	22.50	22.67	22.66	22.81	23.03	23.14	23.36	23.49	23.79	24.10	23.04
2018	24.27	23.98	23.97	24.44	23.77	24.17	24.39	24.31	24.19	24.14	23.87	24.81	24.19
Mining, Logging, and Construction													
2014	21.74	22.13	22.12	22.16	21.78	21.74	21.32	21.60	21.41	21.35	21.31	21.90	21.69
2015	22.15	21.99	21.62	21.80	21.79	21.71	22.24	22.89	23.84	22.81	22.40	21.81	22.28
2016	22.16	23.33	23.32	23.77	22.81	22.48	23.00	22.77	22.70	22.74	22.55	23.25	22.91
2017	22.98	23.27	23.30	22.52	22.76	22.77	22.78	23.42	23.66	23.76	23.95	24.69	23.33
2018	25.09	24.89	24.91	25.07	24.46	25.07	25.70	26.00	25.61	25.78	25.34	26.97	25.42
Manufacturing													
2014	19.79	19.08	19.25	19.51	19.61	19.60	20.14	20.06	19.99	20.22	20.48	20.61	19.86
2015	20.67	20.75	20.75	20.69	21.06	20.96	20.99	21.29	21.65	21.04	21.41	21.09	21.03
2016	21.00	21.14	21.50	21.23	21.16	21.19	21.42	21.31	21.46	21.58	21.42	21.82	21.35
2017	22.20	21.97	22.15	22.74	22.61	22.83	23.17	22.98	23.20	23.35	23.70	23.80	22.89
2018	23.90	23.56	23.50	24.09	23.36	23.61	23.61	23.31	23.37	23.27	23.07	23.65	23.53
Trade, Transportation, and Utilities													
2014	19.13	19.17	19.51	19.37	19.37	19.24	19.36	19.81	19.65	19.82	19.91	19.50	19.49
2015	19.69	19.64	19.51	19.42	19.41	19.20	19.34	20.00	19.70	19.59	19.68	19.50	19.56
2016	20.09	20.36	20.14	20.13	20.61	20.36	20.61	20.55	20.69	20.71	20.38	19.96	20.38
2017	21.21	20.90	21.03	21.48	21.52	21.31	21.69	21.41	21.66	21.87	21.99	21.91	21.50
2018	21.86	21.28	21.54	21.70	21.46	21.49	21.37	21.03	21.95	21.39	20.98	21.34	21.45
Financial Activities													
2014	26.45	27.14	27.12	26.58	26.53	26.97	26.17	26.34	26.09	26.10	26.84	26.81	26.60
2015	26.78	27.58	27.75	27.93	27.73	27.32	27.24	28.34	28.05	28.11	29.02	28.39	27.86
2016	28.88	28.34	28.86	29.64	29.83	29.08	29.26	29.50	29.63	30.17	29.80	29.91	29.41
2017	30.51	29.78	30.43	31.54	30.41	29.72	30.41	29.79	29.89	30.37	30.03	30.06	30.25
2018	30.04	30.00	30.17	31.34	30.26	30.06	30.27	30.31	30.80	29.19	30.09	31.05	30.30
Professional and Business Services													
2014	25.04	25.21	25.46	25.45	25.45	25.61	25.62	25.62	25.70	25.72	25.98	25.99	25.58
2015	26.65	26.25	26.69	26.42	26.63	26.53	26.69	26.69	26.84	26.46	26.94	27.01	26.65
2016	26.85	26.95	26.78	27.00	27.16	27.02	27.30	27.01	27.13	27.48	26.78	26.03	26.96
2017	27.49	27.07	27.79	28.34	28.29	27.82	28.26	27.95	28.26	28.77	29.09	28.80	28.17
2018	29.55	29.60	29.96	29.83	29.36	29.01	29.38	29.17	30.07	29.64	29.88	30.42	29.66
Education and Health Services													
2014	22.36	22.01	21.89	21.93	21.70	21.58	21.79	21.64	22.07	22.07	21.68	22.08	21.90
2015	22.22	22.28	22.33	22.27	22.30	22.13	22.43	22.73	22.87	22.56	22.46	22.52	22.43
2016	22.68	22.45	22.24	22.15	22.10	22.32	22.25	22.14	22.70	22.24	22.26	22.14	22.30
2017	22.91	22.86	23.07	23.34	23.43	23.41	23.69	23.74	24.31	24.58	24.96	24.92	23.78
2018	24.89	24.64	24.60	24.63	24.63	24.61	24.87	24.57	25.28	25.01	24.84	25.81	24.87
Leisure and Hospitality													
2014	11.72	11.80	11.94	11.91	11.96	11.85	11.84	11.78	11.86	12.11	12.13	12.27	11.93
2015	12.33	12.27	12.28	12.30	12.37	12.23	12.41	12.67	12.84	12.88	13.07	13.28	12.58
2016	13.34	13.68	13.33	13.53	13.42	13.13	13.25	13.28	13.33	13.31	13.35	13.59	13.37
2017	13.78	13.73	13.53	13.53	13.48	13.35	13.36	13.41	13.40	13.45	13.51	13.54	13.50
2018	13.81	13.79	13.64	13.84	13.73	13.57	13.82	13.74	13.80	13.91	14.06	14.25	13.83

4. Average Weekly Earnings by Selected Industry: Nebraska, 2014–2018

(Dollars, not seasonally adjusted)

Industry and year	January	February	March	April	May	June	July	August	September	October	November	December	Annual average
Total Private													
2014	707.41	717.57	728.04	718.59	721.56	742.35	730.66	733.75	729.06	733.49	742.94	736.99	728.38
2015	738.53	755.63	755.14	738.53	742.75	747.17	752.20	785.25	766.14	766.26	774.63	760.84	756.34
2016	760.18	761.90	762.86	779.96	785.66	779.08	782.68	783.28	783.82	806.27	774.14	770.78	776.72
2017	807.84	791.95	804.44	830.06	812.89	815.65	834.90	819.09	830.06	849.08	842.00	842.35	824.56
2018	828.99	822.86	825.89	855.34	829.45	833.68	849.95	824.54	862.05	829.46	824.31	857.51	837.56
Goods-Producing													
2014	813.60	786.45	810.03	824.58	839.63	845.73	844.61	850.37	832.72	840.89	832.08	855.51	832.32
2015	844.00	866.33	849.61	852.53	871.17	874.26	885.47	924.68	906.58	905.81	876.53	861.73	877.31
2016	858.67	860.10	884.00	931.67	882.64	905.39	919.60	926.02	886.14	905.58	869.82	879.67	892.70
2017	892.71	901.11	922.50	931.74	917.73	930.65	944.23	955.68	974.11	958.39	970.63	990.51	942.34
2018	953.81	959.20	946.82	987.38	965.06	988.55	980.48	979.69	984.53	948.70	945.25	992.40	970.02
Mining, Logging, and Construction													
2014	813.08	801.11	864.89	886.40	899.51	913.08	884.78	896.40	858.54	883.89	822.57	865.05	867.60
2015	832.84	873.00	869.12	856.74	854.17	892.28	934.08	984.27	991.74	969.43	909.44	881.12	906.80
2016	848.73	898.21	923.47	1,019.73	923.81	944.16	979.80	972.28	867.14	902.78	868.18	846.30	918.69
2017	822.68	851.68	869.09	887.29	883.09	913.08	913.48	967.25	972.43	945.65	977.16	995.01	919.20
2018	935.86	958.27	976.47	1,030.38	1,032.21	1,093.05	1,071.69	1,079.00	1,067.94	987.37	995.86	1,084.19	1,029.51
Manufacturing													
2014	815.35	780.37	785.40	796.01	809.89	811.44	825.74	826.47	819.59	820.93	835.58	851.19	814.26
2015	849.54	863.20	840.38	850.36	880.31	863.55	858.49	892.05	859.51	871.06	858.54	852.04	862.23
2016	863.10	841.37	864.30	885.29	861.21	885.74	886.79	901.41	897.03	908.52	869.65	896.80	879.62
2017	925.74	924.94	948.02	955.08	936.05	938.31	961.56	949.07	974.40	966.69	969.33	990.08	952.22
2018	965.56	956.54	932.95	966.01	927.39	930.23	927.87	923.08	937.14	926.15	915.88	943.64	938.85
Trade, Transportation, and Utilities													
2014	638.94	646.03	665.29	662.45	668.27	675.32	673.73	679.48	664.17	675.86	672.96	661.05	664.61
2015	651.74	661.87	659.44	654.45	650.24	658.56	657.56	684.00	657.98	664.10	659.28	655.20	659.17
2016	652.93	665.77	660.59	666.30	692.50	680.02	692.50	682.26	684.84	693.79	664.39	652.69	674.58
2017	685.08	668.80	675.06	704.54	697.25	701.10	704.93	691.54	708.28	717.34	721.27	714.27	698.75
2018	684.22	678.83	691.43	713.93	706.03	709.17	692.39	672.96	702.40	680.20	673.46	685.01	690.69
Financial Activities													
2014	986.59	1,044.89	1,046.83	1,002.07	1,000.18	1,062.62	994.46	1,000.92	988.81	991.80	1,060.18	1,013.42	1,016.12
2015	1,020.32	1,081.14	1,079.48	1,061.34	1,050.97	1,040.89	1,035.12	1,125.10	1,065.90	1,073.80	1,131.78	1,081.66	1,069.82
2016	1,094.55	1,079.75	1,096.68	1,138.18	1,169.34	1,119.58	1,108.95	1,132.80	1,125.94	1,176.63	1,132.40	1,148.54	1,126.40
2017	1,211.25	1,143.55	1,159.38	1,230.06	1,146.46	1,138.28	1,185.99	1,129.04	1,144.79	1,175.32	1,141.14	1,154.30	1,164.63
2018	1,153.54	1,146.00	1,155.51	1,222.26	1,155.93	1,163.32	1,186.58	1,121.47	1,182.72	1,117.98	1,113.33	1,183.01	1,157.46
Professional and Business Services													
2014	851.36	884.87	893.65	878.03	888.21	932.20	909.51	924.88	914.92	931.06	948.27	943.44	908.09
2015	951.41	955.50	966.18	943.19	945.37	955.08	944.83	968.85	952.82	949.91	980.62	948.05	954.07
2016	942.44	940.56	937.30	953.10	961.46	948.40	952.77	948.05	954.98	989.28	926.59	898.04	946.30
2017	956.65	925.79	958.76	1,006.07	992.98	987.61	1,017.36	989.43	989.10	1,038.60	1,050.15	1,016.64	994.40
2018	1,031.30	1,015.28	1,018.64	1,029.14	1,004.11	992.14	1,025.36	988.86	1,046.44	1,019.62	1,030.86	1,076.87	1,023.27
Education and Health Services													
2014	706.58	704.32	700.48	697.37	690.06	709.98	708.18	701.14	712.86	704.03	706.77	699.94	702.99
2015	693.26	708.50	712.33	699.28	704.68	714.80	726.73	734.18	736.41	717.41	725.46	700.37	715.52
2016	700.81	689.22	687.22	686.65	693.94	694.15	689.75	684.13	701.43	702.78	683.38	679.70	691.30
2017	712.50	704.09	719.78	744.55	733.36	739.76	760.45	752.56	770.63	793.93	788.74	789.96	751.45
2018	784.04	776.16	779.82	798.01	783.23	782.60	808.28	791.15	821.60	792.82	789.91	820.76	793.35
Leisure and Hospitality													
2014	246.12	259.60	267.46	260.83	264.32	279.66	267.58	272.12	269.22	274.90	274.14	269.94	267.23
2015	273.73	279.76	282.44	270.60	282.04	292.30	287.91	296.48	288.90	293.66	298.00	304.11	288.08
2016	297.48	305.06	299.93	304.43	307.32	308.56	303.43	298.80	305.26	306.13	303.05	298.98	303.50
2017	307.29	307.55	301.72	299.01	297.91	315.06	315.30	311.11	304.18	312.04	308.03	307.36	307.80
2018	302.44	311.65	309.63	308.63	308.93	316.18	327.53	313.27	320.16	315.76	310.73	326.33	313.94

NEVADA
At a Glance

Population:
   2010 census: 2,700,551
   2018 estimate: 3,034,392

Percent change in population:
   2010–2018: 12.4%

Percent change in total nonfarm employment:
   2010–2018: 24.0%

Industry with the largest growth in employment, 2010–2018 (percent):
   Construction, 51.3%

Industry with the largest decline or smallest growth in employment, 2010–2018 (percent):
   Government, 4.7%

Civilian labor force:
   2010: 1,358,578
   2018: 1,500,377

Unemployment rate and rank among states (highest to lowest):
   2010: 13.5%, 1st
   2018: 4.6%, 8th

Over-the-year change in unemployment rates:
   2016–2017: -0.6%
   2017–2018: -0.5%

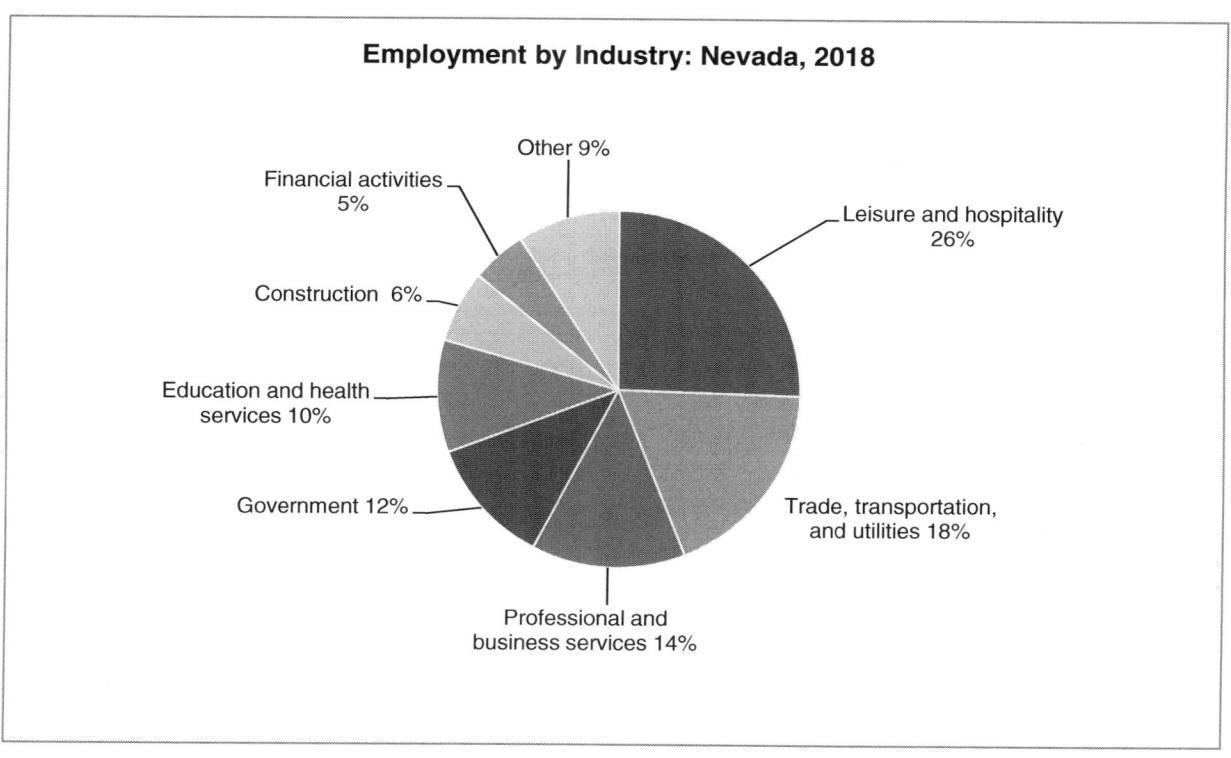

Employment by Industry: Nevada, 2018

Other 9%
Financial activities 5%
Construction 6%
Education and health services 10%
Government 12%
Professional and business services 14%
Leisure and hospitality 26%
Trade, transportation, and utilities 18%

1. Employment by Industry: Nevada, 2010–2018

(Numbers in thousands, not seasonally adjusted)

Industry and year	January	February	March	April	May	June	July	August	September	October	November	December	Annual average
Total Nonfarm													
2010	1,104.4	1,105.8	1,108.8	1,120.9	1,128.3	1,124.3	1,116.7	1,114.0	1,116.0	1,124.1	1,126.0	1,124.6	1,117.8
2011	1,106.8	1,109.6	1,114.8	1,126.6	1,130.6	1,128.7	1,122.7	1,122.2	1,132.4	1,137.9	1,139.2	1,136.9	1,125.7
2012	1,120.2	1,123.5	1,130.9	1,139.5	1,148.1	1,150.0	1,139.2	1,145.6	1,153.8	1,160.6	1,165.5	1,160.6	1,144.8
2013	1,145.0	1,148.8	1,158.4	1,168.3	1,176.1	1,178.9	1,171.0	1,178.5	1,182.9	1,189.6	1,198.0	1,195.3	1,174.2
2014	1,179.9	1,186.7	1,198.1	1,208.4	1,218.9	1,216.2	1,209.0	1,220.2	1,229.6	1,239.7	1,243.3	1,244.1	1,216.2
2015	1,227.8	1,232.9	1,241.5	1,252.8	1,259.3	1,256.5	1,249.9	1,259.3	1,268.8	1,281.4	1,287.5	1,288.8	1,258.9
2016	1,263.9	1,271.2	1,279.9	1,292.5	1,296.3	1,295.6	1,299.2	1,303.2	1,316.3	1,319.8	1,325.7	1,323.6	1,298.9
2017	1,306.9	1,314.8	1,329.5	1,328.9	1,341.0	1,340.2	1,337.3	1,342.3	1,354.7	1,362.5	1,368.4	1,369.1	1,341.3
2018	1,345.9	1,359.1	1,368.7	1,374.2	1,384.1	1,382.8	1,381.0	1,391.8	1,400.2	1,413.5	1,416.8	1,419.5	1,386.5
Total Private													
2010	952.1	948.8	951.0	963.0	967.1	970.6	969.1	969.2	964.1	970.6	972.1	970.8	964.0
2011	955.8	955.0	960.4	971.9	976.2	981.1	980.5	979.8	983.8	987.4	988.4	985.1	975.5
2012	973.2	973.4	979.1	987.7	995.9	1,002.6	996.9	1,003.4	1,003.9	1,008.9	1,013.0	1,007.2	995.4
2013	995.4	996.9	1,005.3	1,015.2	1,022.6	1,029.5	1,028.5	1,033.1	1,031.7	1,036.6	1,043.7	1,039.9	1,023.2
2014	1,029.0	1,032.9	1,042.9	1,053.5	1,063.3	1,067.3	1,064.9	1,075.0	1,075.9	1,084.5	1,087.6	1,087.5	1,063.7
2015	1,075.2	1,077.4	1,084.5	1,096.1	1,102.2	1,104.1	1,103.3	1,111.7	1,112.4	1,124.8	1,129.2	1,129.0	1,104.2
2016	1,109.1	1,113.0	1,119.8	1,133.5	1,136.7	1,143.7	1,148.0	1,151.5	1,156.5	1,159.8	1,164.2	1,160.9	1,141.4
2017	1,150.2	1,153.0	1,166.5	1,168.0	1,178.9	1,183.6	1,183.3	1,186.0	1,190.0	1,200.0	1,204.6	1,204.2	1,180.7
2018	1,188.5	1,195.8	1,204.6	1,212.4	1,221.4	1,224.6	1,228.9	1,237.6	1,236.5	1,248.7	1,252.4	1,254.3	1,225.5
Goods Producing													
2010	108.6	107.1	107.1	109.7	110.7	111.5	111.4	111.3	109.6	110.2	109.1	107.1	109.5
2011	102.8	102.8	101.3	102.7	103.8	105.4	106.4	106.8	106.4	106.5	105.2	104.0	104.5
2012	100.8	100.6	101.8	103.4	105.5	107.7	108.6	110.5	110.3	110.5	110.2	109.5	106.6
2013	106.6	107.5	108.8	110.7	111.3	113.4	114.2	116.0	115.6	116.2	116.1	114.5	112.6
2014	113.7	113.9	114.9	116.3	118.2	119.5	121.2	122.5	122.4	123.1	122.7	122.2	119.2
2015	121.0	121.6	121.8	123.3	125.3	126.4	127.1	129.2	129.2	131.5	131.2	131.5	126.6
2016	128.5	128.8	129.2	130.5	131.2	133.2	135.0	135.6	136.0	136.9	136.8	137.1	133.2
2017	135.6	137.7	141.0	142.2	144.5	147.0	147.8	148.1	149.6	150.5	149.9	150.0	145.3
2018	148.5	150.7	152.2	155.7	157.6	160.5	161.9	163.7	164.3	166.1	166.1	169.4	159.7
Service-Providing													
2010	995.8	998.7	1,001.7	1,011.2	1,017.6	1,012.8	1,005.3	1,002.7	1,006.4	1,013.9	1,016.9	1,017.5	1,008.4
2011	1,004.0	1,006.8	1,013.5	1,023.9	1,026.8	1,023.3	1,016.3	1,015.4	1,026.0	1,031.4	1,034.0	1,032.9	1,021.2
2012	1,019.4	1,022.9	1,029.1	1,036.1	1,042.6	1,042.3	1,030.6	1,035.1	1,043.5	1,050.1	1,055.3	1,051.1	1,038.2
2013	1,038.4	1,041.3	1,049.6	1,057.6	1,064.8	1,065.5	1,056.8	1,062.5	1,067.3	1,073.4	1,081.9	1,080.8	1,061.7
2014	1,066.2	1,072.8	1,083.2	1,092.1	1,100.7	1,096.7	1,087.8	1,097.7	1,107.2	1,116.6	1,120.6	1,121.9	1,097.0
2015	1,106.8	1,111.3	1,119.7	1,129.5	1,134.0	1,130.1	1,122.8	1,130.1	1,139.6	1,149.9	1,156.3	1,157.3	1,132.3
2016	1,135.4	1,142.4	1,150.7	1,162.0	1,165.1	1,162.4	1,164.2	1,167.6	1,180.3	1,182.9	1,188.9	1,186.5	1,165.7
2017	1,171.3	1,177.1	1,188.5	1,186.7	1,196.5	1,193.2	1,189.5	1,194.2	1,205.1	1,212.0	1,218.5	1,219.1	1,196.0
2018	1,197.4	1,208.4	1,216.5	1,218.5	1,226.5	1,222.3	1,219.1	1,228.1	1,235.9	1,247.4	1,250.7	1,250.1	1,226.7
Mining and Logging													
2010	11.5	11.5	11.7	11.7	12.0	12.4	12.7	12.7	12.4	12.4	12.7	12.8	12.2
2011	12.8	13.0	13.2	13.4	13.7	14.3	14.6	14.6	14.5	14.5	14.6	14.7	14.0
2012	14.4	14.6	15.0	15.2	15.4	15.8	16.1	16.1	15.9	15.7	15.6	15.6	15.5
2013	15.4	15.5	15.4	15.3	15.3	15.4	15.7	15.6	15.0	14.8	14.8	14.7	15.2
2014	14.4	14.1	14.2	14.2	14.3	14.5	14.6	14.6	14.4	14.6	14.7	14.7	14.4
2015	14.3	14.3	14.3	14.4	14.4	14.5	14.6	14.5	14.0	13.9	13.7	13.6	14.2
2016	13.4	13.3	13.3	13.6	13.7	13.8	14.0	14.0	13.8	13.9	14.0	14.0	13.7
2017	13.9	13.9	13.9	13.9	13.9	14.2	14.5	14.5	14.4	14.4	14.4	14.4	14.2
2018	14.2	14.3	14.2	14.3	14.4	14.8	14.9	14.9	14.7	14.6	14.6	14.6	14.5
Construction													
2010	59.3	57.9	57.7	60.0	60.7	60.9	60.5	60.6	59.2	59.9	58.5	56.4	59.3
2011	52.4	52.1	50.2	51.3	51.9	52.6	53.3	53.5	53.1	53.1	51.9	50.6	52.2
2012	48.0	47.6	48.1	49.3	51.0	52.4	52.9	54.6	54.8	55.2	55.1	54.4	52.0
2013	51.9	52.4	53.6	55.3	55.6	57.2	57.8	59.5	59.6	60.3	60.1	58.6	56.8
2014	58.1	58.6	59.5	61.0	62.5	63.4	64.9	66.3	66.4	66.9	66.3	65.8	63.3
2015	65.2	65.7	65.8	67.2	69.0	69.7	70.4	72.5	72.9	75.0	74.6	74.9	70.2
2016	72.4	72.5	72.9	73.9	74.3	75.9	77.1	77.6	78.2	78.6	78.3	78.1	75.8
2017	77.1	78.8	81.5	82.0	83.9	85.4	84.6	84.4	85.3	85.9	85.0	84.6	83.2
2018	83.1	84.5	85.3	87.7	88.8	90.2	90.8	92.1	92.1	92.9	93.0	96.1	89.7

1. Employment by Industry: Nevada, 2010–2018—*Continued*

(Numbers in thousands, not seasonally adjusted)

Industry and year	January	February	March	April	May	June	July	August	September	October	November	December	Annual average
Manufacturing													
2010	37.8	37.7	37.7	38.0	38.0	38.2	38.2	38.0	38.0	37.9	37.9	37.9	37.9
2011	37.6	37.7	37.9	38.0	38.2	38.5	38.5	38.7	38.8	38.9	38.7	38.7	38.4
2012	38.4	38.4	38.7	38.9	39.1	39.5	39.6	39.8	39.6	39.6	39.5	39.5	39.2
2013	39.3	39.6	39.8	40.1	40.4	40.8	40.7	40.9	41.0	41.1	41.2	41.2	40.5
2014	41.2	41.2	41.2	41.1	41.4	41.6	41.7	41.6	41.6	41.6	41.7	41.7	41.5
2015	41.5	41.6	41.7	41.7	41.9	42.2	42.1	42.2	42.3	42.6	42.9	43.0	42.1
2016	42.7	43.0	43.0	43.0	43.2	43.5	43.9	44.0	44.0	44.4	44.5	45.0	43.7
2017	44.6	45.0	45.6	46.3	46.7	47.4	48.7	49.2	49.9	50.2	50.5	51.0	47.9
2018	51.2	51.9	52.7	53.7	54.4	55.5	56.2	56.7	57.5	58.6	58.5	58.7	55.5
Trade, Transportation, and Utilities													
2010	208.3	206.0	206.1	206.8	207.7	208.8	209.4	209.8	209.4	211.4	215.6	217.0	209.7
2011	208.6	207.1	207.7	209.1	210.1	210.8	211.7	212.4	212.8	215.0	220.7	221.7	212.3
2012	214.6	212.4	213.5	214.5	215.7	216.8	216.7	217.2	218.0	219.5	226.4	226.3	217.6
2013	217.8	215.8	215.3	216.3	219.0	220.3	221.3	221.9	222.6	224.9	231.4	233.0	221.6
2014	224.4	223.2	224.6	225.8	227.2	228.1	228.4	229.8	230.7	234.0	240.1	242.2	229.9
2015	234.1	232.4	233.3	234.5	235.9	236.5	236.5	237.6	238.4	241.0	246.7	248.0	237.9
2016	236.9	236.3	236.8	238.4	239.2	239.5	240.5	242.0	242.6	244.7	251.9	252.2	241.8
2017	244.8	243.0	243.0	243.6	244.9	245.9	246.5	247.7	249.0	252.1	260.4	262.4	248.6
2018	252.1	250.4	250.2	250.6	252.1	253.1	254.2	255.6	255.8	258.7	264.6	268.0	255.5
Wholesale Trade													
2010	32.4	32.3	32.4	32.6	32.7	32.8	32.7	32.7	32.6	32.8	32.6	32.6	32.6
2011	32.2	32.3	32.4	32.4	32.5	32.6	32.6	32.5	32.4	32.4	32.3	32.4	32.4
2012	32.0	32.0	32.2	32.2	32.3	32.4	32.5	32.4	32.3	32.4	32.4	32.5	32.3
2013	32.0	32.1	32.2	32.4	32.5	32.7	32.9	32.9	33.0	33.0	33.2	33.2	32.7
2014	32.9	33.1	33.3	33.4	33.4	33.5	33.7	33.8	33.9	33.9	33.9	34.1	33.6
2015	33.7	33.8	33.9	34.0	34.0	34.1	34.1	34.1	34.2	34.3	34.3	34.4	34.1
2016	33.7	33.8	33.6	33.9	34.0	34.0	34.2	34.4	34.4	34.5	34.7	34.8	34.2
2017	34.8	34.9	35.1	35.3	35.5	35.7	35.7	35.7	35.7	35.8	35.8	36.0	35.5
2018	36.1	36.3	36.3	36.5	36.7	37.1	37.5	37.6	37.5	37.1	36.9	37.6	36.9
Retail Trade													
2010	125.5	123.5	123.7	124.2	124.8	125.4	126.0	126.4	126.1	127.7	131.9	132.8	126.5
2011	126.1	124.4	124.8	125.5	126.3	126.6	127.0	127.6	127.7	129.4	134.8	135.2	128.0
2012	129.8	127.8	128.6	129.2	129.9	130.6	130.3	130.7	131.2	132.4	139.0	138.5	131.5
2013	131.7	129.9	130.0	130.7	132.3	133.1	133.7	134.3	134.4	136.1	141.7	143.0	134.2
2014	135.6	134.0	134.6	135.3	136.3	136.9	137.0	138.0	138.5	141.5	146.9	148.1	138.6
2015	141.0	139.5	140.5	141.3	142.1	142.4	142.3	143.1	142.8	145.0	149.7	150.0	143.3
2016	141.6	140.9	141.3	142.0	142.4	142.6	142.8	143.8	143.8	145.7	151.5	150.9	144.1
2017	144.7	143.1	142.7	143.2	144.2	144.3	144.3	144.7	145.0	147.2	153.7	154.0	145.9
2018	146.3	144.9	144.5	144.6	145.8	146.3	146.9	148.0	148.1	149.9	153.8	155.0	147.8
Transportation and Utilities													
2010	50.4	50.2	50.0	50.0	50.2	50.6	50.7	50.7	50.7	50.9	51.1	51.6	50.6
2011	50.3	50.4	50.5	51.2	51.3	51.6	52.1	52.3	52.7	53.2	53.6	54.1	51.9
2012	52.8	52.6	52.7	53.1	53.5	53.8	53.9	54.1	54.5	54.7	55.0	55.3	53.8
2013	54.1	53.8	53.1	53.2	54.2	54.5	54.7	54.7	55.2	55.8	56.5	56.8	54.7
2014	55.9	56.1	56.7	57.1	57.5	57.7	57.7	58.0	58.3	58.6	59.3	60.0	57.7
2015	59.4	59.1	58.9	59.2	59.8	60.0	60.1	60.4	61.4	61.7	62.7	63.6	60.5
2016	61.6	61.6	61.9	62.5	62.8	62.9	63.5	63.8	64.4	64.5	65.7	66.5	63.5
2017	65.3	65.0	65.2	65.1	65.2	65.9	66.5	67.3	68.3	69.1	70.9	72.4	67.2
2018	69.7	69.2	69.4	69.5	69.6	69.7	69.8	70.0	70.2	71.7	73.9	75.4	70.7
Information													
2010	12.5	12.6	12.5	12.8	12.8	12.8	13.0	12.7	12.6	12.6	12.9	12.8	12.7
2011	12.6	12.5	12.6	12.9	13.0	13.0	12.8	12.7	12.9	13.3	12.6	13.0	12.8
2012	12.5	12.6	12.7	12.6	12.9	12.9	12.6	13.0	12.9	13.5	14.7	13.2	13.0
2013	12.3	12.6	12.8	13.0	13.3	14.2	13.4	13.2	13.2	13.3	13.6	13.4	13.2
2014	13.0	13.3	13.1	14.3	15.1	15.8	13.8	13.7	13.9	13.9	14.4	14.1	14.0
2015	13.7	14.1	13.9	14.1	14.2	14.5	14.0	14.2	13.8	14.3	15.1	14.5	14.2
2016	14.5	14.7	14.1	15.2	15.0	15.2	15.1	14.4	14.5	14.6	14.4	14.3	14.7
2017	14.7	14.5	14.5	15.3	15.6	16.1	15.0	15.3	14.9	15.4	15.7	15.4	15.2
2018	15.0	15.2	15.2	16.3	16.8	16.3	15.3	15.4	15.0	15.3	15.5	15.3	15.6

1. Employment by Industry: Nevada, 2010–2018—*Continued*

(Numbers in thousands, not seasonally adjusted)

Industry and year	January	February	March	April	May	June	July	August	September	October	November	December	Annual average
Financial Activities													
2010	52.9	52.5	52.5	53.3	53.0	52.9	53.0	52.7	52.5	53.1	52.8	53.0	52.9
2011	52.4	52.1	52.1	52.5	52.4	52.6	52.7	52.3	52.7	52.9	52.7	53.0	52.5
2012	52.6	52.7	53.0	53.9	54.2	54.6	54.5	54.8	54.9	55.7	55.7	55.8	54.4
2013	55.4	56.1	56.7	56.6	57.0	57.0	56.5	56.5	56.4	56.8	57.1	57.3	56.6
2014	56.1	56.2	56.3	56.3	57.0	56.9	56.7	57.2	57.4	58.1	58.3	58.5	57.1
2015	57.9	58.4	58.5	59.4	60.0	59.9	60.3	60.4	60.5	61.7	61.7	62.4	60.1
2016	61.5	61.7	62.0	62.4	62.9	62.7	63.0	63.2	63.3	63.6	63.7	63.9	62.8
2017	63.5	64.2	64.1	64.7	65.5	65.4	66.0	66.1	66.1	66.7	66.6	66.7	65.5
2018	66.4	67.3	67.6	67.7	68.3	68.1	68.5	68.5	68.2	68.5	69.4	69.4	68.2
Professional and Business Services													
2010	135.0	133.3	133.5	135.4	135.9	136.5	135.0	137.1	135.0	137.7	138.2	138.0	135.9
2011	138.7	137.2	137.6	139.0	138.8	139.6	138.9	139.3	141.5	143.0	142.8	141.9	139.9
2012	144.6	143.7	142.4	143.5	144.2	145.5	141.8	145.7	146.4	148.0	147.5	145.3	144.9
2013	148.9	147.2	148.9	150.4	151.3	150.3	147.8	150.8	148.9	151.6	152.8	151.7	150.1
2014	153.0	153.0	154.1	155.1	155.8	155.8	153.3	157.1	157.2	162.2	161.7	161.1	156.6
2015	163.5	161.6	162.8	166.1	165.9	164.7	163.9	167.9	167.9	172.6	173.4	173.3	167.0
2016	172.1	170.5	172.4	175.4	174.3	176.5	176.0	177.1	179.9	181.9	180.9	178.1	176.3
2017	180.7	178.0	182.2	178.7	180.7	180.7	180.8	181.2	182.4	186.9	185.9	184.9	181.9
2018	185.8	185.7	186.6	186.7	187.7	186.6	189.9	193.6	192.6	198.8	198.1	195.2	190.6
Education and Health Services													
2010	99.7	100.1	100.6	101.5	101.7	101.4	101.1	101.1	101.4	103.0	103.3	103.6	101.5
2011	103.1	104.0	104.7	105.3	105.3	105.5	104.9	105.4	105.9	106.5	107.1	107.5	105.4
2012	106.9	107.8	108.1	108.6	109.1	108.6	107.4	108.7	108.5	109.1	109.2	109.6	108.5
2013	108.7	110.1	110.6	111.0	111.4	111.4	111.0	111.8	112.3	113.1	113.5	113.4	111.5
2014	112.6	113.8	114.4	114.8	115.2	115.5	115.2	116.0	116.4	117.8	118.0	118.3	115.7
2015	117.0	118.1	118.8	119.6	119.8	120.3	120.5	121.5	122.3	124.2	124.2	124.7	120.9
2016	123.5	124.8	125.1	126.0	126.5	126.6	127.1	128.1	128.8	130.1	130.7	131.4	127.4
2017	129.7	131.0	131.8	132.4	133.1	133.2	131.8	133.9	134.8	136.1	136.9	137.2	133.5
2018	136.6	138.2	139.1	139.4	140.1	140.1	139.4	141.4	142.0	143.8	143.1	143.6	140.6
Leisure and Hospitality													
2010	302.5	304.5	305.7	310.5	312.1	313.6	312.8	311.2	310.6	309.6	307.9	307.3	309.0
2011	306.0	307.5	312.4	317.9	320.1	321.3	320.1	318.0	319.0	317.9	315.1	311.7	315.6
2012	309.1	311.4	315.0	318.2	320.8	322.6	321.5	319.6	319.0	318.4	316.2	314.7	317.2
2013	313.3	315.0	319.3	323.7	325.4	328.7	330.0	328.6	328.6	326.6	325.0	322.5	323.9
2014	322.1	325.2	330.8	335.4	338.8	339.6	340.1	342.6	341.9	339.0	336.6	335.6	335.6
2015	332.8	335.8	339.7	342.9	344.5	344.6	343.9	343.7	343.3	342.4	339.8	337.3	340.9
2016	334.7	338.0	341.2	346.1	347.8	350.0	350.6	350.3	350.1	346.1	344.9	343.9	345.3
2017	341.5	344.8	349.7	350.4	353.5	353.9	353.7	352.2	351.8	351.0	348.0	346.6	349.8
2018	343.4	347.5	352.5	354.3	356.6	357.0	357.1	356.5	355.5	355.2	353.5	352.0	353.4
Other Services													
2010	32.6	32.7	33.0	33.0	33.2	33.1	33.4	33.3	33.0	33.0	32.3	32.0	32.9
2011	31.6	31.8	32.0	32.5	32.7	32.9	33.0	32.9	32.6	32.3	32.2	32.3	32.4
2012	32.1	32.2	32.6	33.0	33.5	33.9	33.8	33.9	33.9	34.2	33.1	32.8	33.3
2013	32.4	32.6	32.9	33.5	33.9	34.2	34.3	34.3	34.1	34.1	34.2	34.1	33.7
2014	34.1	34.3	34.7	35.5	36.0	36.1	36.2	36.1	36.0	36.4	35.8	35.5	35.6
2015	35.2	35.4	35.7	36.2	36.6	37.2	37.1	37.2	37.0	37.1	37.1	37.3	36.6
2016	37.4	38.2	39.0	39.5	39.8	40.0	40.7	40.8	41.3	41.9	40.9	40.0	40.0
2017	39.7	39.8	40.2	40.7	41.1	41.4	41.7	41.5	41.4	41.3	41.2	41.0	40.9
2018	40.7	40.8	41.2	41.7	42.2	42.9	42.6	42.9	43.1	42.3	42.1	41.4	42.0
2019													
Government													
2010	152.3	157.0	157.8	157.9	161.2	153.7	147.6	144.8	151.9	153.5	153.9	153.8	153.8
2011	151.0	154.6	154.4	154.7	154.4	147.6	142.2	142.4	148.6	150.5	150.8	151.8	150.3
2012	147.0	150.1	151.8	151.8	152.2	147.4	142.3	142.2	149.9	151.7	152.5	153.4	149.4
2013	149.6	151.9	153.1	153.1	153.5	149.4	142.5	145.4	151.2	153.0	154.3	155.4	151.0
2014	150.9	153.8	155.2	154.9	155.6	148.9	144.1	145.2	153.7	155.2	155.7	156.6	152.5
2015	152.6	155.5	157.0	156.7	157.1	152.4	146.6	147.6	156.4	156.6	158.3	159.8	154.7
2016	154.8	158.2	160.1	159.0	159.6	151.9	151.2	151.7	159.8	160.0	161.5	162.7	157.5
2017	156.7	161.8	163.0	160.9	162.1	156.6	154.0	156.3	164.7	162.5	163.8	164.9	160.6
2018	157.4	163.3	164.1	161.8	162.7	158.2	152.1	154.2	163.7	164.8	164.4	165.2	161.0

2. Average Weekly Hours by Selected Industry: Nevada, 2014–2018

(Not seasonally adjusted)

Industry and year	January	February	March	April	May	June	July	August	September	October	November	December	Annual average
Total Private													
2014	33.1	33.3	33.5	33.3	33.2	33.7	33.5	33.8	33.6	33.4	33.6	33.2	33.4
2015	33.2	33.5	33.6	33.4	33.5	33.6	33.7	34.1	33.7	33.6	33.9	33.4	33.6
2016	33.3	33.3	33.3	33.6	34.1	34.0	34.2	34.4	34.1	34.5	33.8	34.1	33.9
2017	34.1	33.5	33.9	34.3	34.1	34.2	34.6	34.3	34.1	34.5	34.0	33.9	34.1
2018	33.6	33.6	33.9	34.0	33.8	34.1	34.5	34.4	34.6	34.0	34.3	34.5	34.1
Goods-Producing													
2014	39.0	38.2	38.0	37.7	37.8	38.4	38.1	38.6	38.1	38.6	37.6	38.4	38.2
2015	37.7	37.7	38.7	38.7	38.4	38.8	38.1	38.3	38.0	38.5	38.1	38.2	38.3
2016	38.2	37.9	38.2	38.5	39.4	38.9	38.4	39.0	38.9	38.9	37.5	38.2	38.5
2017	37.2	37.5	37.9	37.5	38.4	38.7	39.2	39.2	38.7	39.1	38.4	39.1	38.4
2018	38.0	38.7	38.9	39.1	39.6	39.5	38.9	39.8	39.6	39.1	40.0	40.4	39.3
Construction													
2014	36.7	36.4	36.4	35.6	35.4	36.0	36.1	36.9	36.7	37.3	36.0	36.8	36.4
2015	36.0	36.5	37.6	37.5	37.1	37.8	37.0	37.2	37.2	38.1	36.5	36.0	37.0
2016	36.3	36.6	36.7	36.9	37.6	36.5	35.7	36.5	36.4	36.6	35.0	36.1	36.4
2017	34.5	34.4	35.3	35.0	36.0	35.8	36.2	36.4	36.1	36.9	36.5	37.0	35.9
2018	35.9	37.1	37.5	37.2	37.9	37.8	37.5	38.3	37.6	38.0	38.5	39.4	37.8
Trade, Transportation, and Utilities													
2014	32.5	33.1	33.7	33.6	33.4	34.0	34.1	34.5	34.2	34.2	34.4	34.4	33.9
2015	33.9	34.5	35.5	34.6	35.2	35.4	35.6	35.9	36.3	35.7	36.6	36.0	35.4
2016	35.2	35.0	35.2	35.4	35.9	36.3	35.8	35.5	35.7	35.8	34.9	35.7	35.5
2017	35.4	35.0	35.3	36.1	35.6	35.8	36.2	35.5	35.4	35.3	35.1	35.0	35.5
2018	34.9	34.6	34.7	34.9	34.6	34.7	35.3	34.4	34.9	33.8	34.1	34.2	34.6
Financial Activities													
2014	38.4	38.5	38.7	38.1	38.1	38.6	37.9	37.5	37.0	37.3	38.6	36.9	38.0
2015	37.1	37.6	37.7	37.7	37.9	37.0	37.4	37.8	38.3	37.3	37.5	36.7	37.5
2016	37.0	37.1	36.5	37.6	38.1	37.7	38.3	37.6	37.3	36.6	36.7	37.5	37.3
2017	38.2	36.9	37.2	38.3	38.1	38.4	38.7	38.1	37.6	38.0	37.8	37.2	37.9
2018	37.5	37.2	37.5	38.7	37.9	37.9	38.5	38.0	38.5	37.7	35.9	37.8	37.8
Professional and Business Services													
2014	34.7	35.0	34.5	34.4	34.3	35.4	34.8	35.2	34.8	34.8	35.6	35.0	34.9
2015	34.9	35.2	33.9	34.3	34.1	34.3	34.6	35.8	34.0	34.1	34.2	33.9	34.4
2016	33.3	33.9	33.4	34.1	34.5	34.3	34.3	35.2	34.4	35.9	34.7	34.9	34.4
2017	35.4	34.7	34.8	35.5	35.0	35.5	35.4	35.3	34.9	35.8	34.9	34.8	35.2
2018	34.0	34.3	34.8	35.0	34.4	34.8	35.3	35.9	36.2	35.3	35.2	35.9	35.1
Leisure and Hospitality													
2014	29.9	30.2	30.6	30.2	30.0	30.5	30.3	30.6	30.4	30.1	30.1	29.3	30.2
2015	29.8	30.1	30.2	29.9	30.1	30.2	30.5	30.4	30.0	29.7	29.9	29.4	30.0
2016	29.3	29.3	29.6	29.3	29.3	29.5	30.0	30.4	30.1	30.5	29.9	29.4	29.7
2017	29.9	29.5	30.0	30.1	30.1	29.8	30.0	29.9	29.7	29.7	29.3	28.6	29.7
2018	29.3	29.0	29.5	29.4	28.8	29.2	29.6	29.7	29.7	29.6	29.6	29.0	29.4

3. Average Hourly Earnings by Selected Industry: Nevada, 2014–2018

(Dollars, not seasonally adjusted)

Industry and year	January	February	March	April	May	June	July	August	September	October	November	December	Annual average
Total Private													
2014	20.85	20.89	20.79	20.86	20.75	20.87	20.72	20.83	20.91	21.03	21.45	21.41	20.95
2015	21.61	21.88	21.95	21.85	21.78	21.73	21.87	22.12	22.11	22.16	22.24	22.08	21.95
2016	22.28	22.27	22.20	22.22	22.25	22.07	21.88	22.05	22.02	22.20	22.16	22.20	22.15
2017	22.70	22.51	22.47	22.48	22.33	22.33	22.42	22.50	22.51	22.67	22.64	22.70	22.52
2018	22.83	22.85	22.88	23.24	23.40	23.24	23.26	23.46	23.45	23.40	23.87	24.07	23.34
Goods-Producing													
2014	25.43	25.81	25.51	25.72	25.06	25.75	25.76	25.53	25.63	25.62	25.67	26.03	25.63
2015	26.10	26.41	26.43	26.52	26.11	26.14	26.78	26.76	27.13	27.16	26.97	27.11	26.64
2016	27.24	27.31	27.14	27.55	27.34	27.41	27.42	27.11	27.49	27.08	27.37	27.15	27.30
2017	27.94	27.65	27.44	27.23	27.42	27.55	27.73	27.91	28.18	28.45	27.95	28.27	27.82
2018	28.58	28.79	28.61	28.46	28.66	28.52	29.06	28.85	29.01	29.36	30.40	31.13	29.15
Construction													
2014	26.43	27.60	26.78	27.39	26.82	27.84	27.40	27.24	26.68	26.46	26.69	27.01	27.02
2015	26.21	26.40	26.64	26.71	27.16	27.06	28.25	28.26	28.40	28.36	28.00	28.08	27.50
2016	28.11	28.47	27.95	28.14	27.77	27.79	27.79	27.84	27.42	27.25	27.51	27.26	27.77
2017	28.52	28.26	27.81	27.43	27.77	27.65	27.84	28.11	28.24	28.70	28.13	28.67	28.10
2018	28.77	29.13	29.02	28.30	28.80	28.76	29.36	29.33	29.43	29.91	31.08	31.77	29.52
Trade, Transportation, and Utilities													
2014	19.54	19.61	19.27	19.78	19.41	19.26	19.21	19.19	19.41	19.37	19.62	19.41	19.42
2015	19.82	19.93	19.89	19.92	19.79	19.55	19.53	19.45	19.67	19.57	19.65	19.34	19.67
2016	20.01	19.85	20.13	20.22	20.05	19.84	20.00	20.05	20.06	20.46	20.20	20.18	20.09
2017	20.64	20.76	20.46	20.50	19.97	20.06	20.06	19.90	19.70	19.80	19.41	19.67	20.07
2018	19.40	19.68	19.53	19.60	19.77	19.52	19.88	19.70	19.67	19.69	19.44	19.82	19.64
Financial Activities													
2014	21.18	21.31	21.38	21.04	21.28	22.11	21.85	22.01	21.26	21.85	22.17	21.75	21.60
2015	22.19	22.69	22.96	23.49	23.85	23.89	26.20	26.57	26.11	26.33	25.98	26.49	24.76
2016	26.28	25.48	25.20	24.69	26.01	25.34	24.82	25.32	24.94	25.58	24.94	25.56	25.34
2017	24.89	25.53	25.84	25.94	25.60	25.89	26.01	26.24	26.40	26.33	26.34	26.18	25.94
2018	26.65	26.84	26.90	27.05	26.96	26.76	25.82	26.13	26.57	26.05	27.26	27.33	26.69
Professional and Business Services													
2014	24.78	24.37	24.32	24.38	24.28	24.22	23.82	23.94	23.72	23.32	23.61	23.39	24.00
2015	23.63	24.54	24.77	24.12	24.24	24.14	24.30	24.55	24.03	24.31	24.48	23.90	24.25
2016	24.46	24.90	24.59	24.09	24.05	23.73	23.93	23.81	23.60	24.27	24.09	24.18	24.13
2017	24.74	24.40	24.44	24.52	24.76	24.05	24.55	24.74	24.53	24.65	24.84	25.24	24.62
2018	25.79	25.83	25.92	26.34	26.65	26.34	26.68	27.06	26.92	26.57	26.54	26.34	26.43
Leisure and Hospitality													
2014	15.52	15.48	15.53	15.51	15.55	15.45	15.45	15.50	15.86	15.93	16.16	16.26	15.68
2015	16.58	16.28	16.13	15.97	16.20	15.94	15.91	16.06	16.29	16.35	16.64	16.49	16.23
2016	16.64	16.75	16.88	16.77	16.89	17.10	16.72	16.91	17.12	16.95	17.09	16.86	16.89
2017	17.45	17.31	17.35	17.42	17.17	17.30	17.09	17.17	17.42	17.20	17.28	17.14	17.27
2018	17.51	17.12	17.34	17.45	17.75	17.63	17.53	17.71	17.60	17.78	17.75	17.51	17.56

4. Average Weekly Earnings by Selected Industry: Nevada, 2014–2018

(Dollars, not seasonally adjusted)

Industry and year	January	February	March	April	May	June	July	August	September	October	November	December	Annual average
Total Private													
2014	690.14	695.64	696.47	694.64	688.90	703.32	694.12	704.05	702.58	702.40	720.72	710.81	699.73
2015	717.45	732.98	737.52	729.79	729.63	730.13	737.02	754.29	745.11	744.58	753.94	737.47	737.52
2016	741.92	741.59	739.26	746.59	758.73	750.38	748.30	758.52	750.88	765.90	749.01	757.02	750.89
2017	774.07	754.09	761.73	771.06	761.45	763.69	775.73	771.75	767.59	782.12	769.76	769.53	767.93
2018	767.09	767.76	775.63	790.16	790.92	792.48	802.47	807.02	811.37	795.60	818.74	830.42	795.89
Goods-Producing													
2014	991.77	985.94	969.38	969.64	947.27	988.80	981.46	985.46	976.50	988.93	965.19	999.55	979.07
2015	983.97	995.66	1,022.84	1,026.32	1,002.62	1,014.23	1,020.32	1,024.91	1,030.94	1,045.66	1,027.56	1,035.60	1,020.31
2016	1,040.57	1,035.05	1,036.75	1,060.68	1,077.20	1,066.25	1,052.93	1,057.29	1,069.36	1,053.41	1,026.38	1,037.13	1,051.05
2017	1,039.37	1,036.88	1,039.98	1,021.13	1,052.93	1,066.19	1,087.02	1,094.07	1,090.57	1,112.40	1,073.28	1,105.36	1,068.29
2018	1,086.04	1,114.17	1,112.93	1,112.79	1,134.94	1,126.54	1,130.43	1,148.23	1,148.80	1,147.98	1,216.00	1,257.65	1,145.60
Construction													
2014	969.98	1,004.64	974.79	975.08	949.43	1,002.24	989.14	1,005.16	979.16	986.96	960.84	993.97	983.53
2015	943.56	963.60	1,001.66	1,001.63	1,007.64	1,022.87	1,045.25	1,051.27	1,056.48	1,080.52	1,022.00	1,010.88	1,017.50
2016	1,020.39	1,042.00	1,025.77	1,038.37	1,044.15	1,014.34	992.10	1,016.16	998.09	997.35	962.85	984.09	1,010.83
2017	983.94	972.14	981.69	960.05	999.72	989.87	1,007.81	1,023.20	1,019.46	1,059.03	1,026.75	1,060.79	1,008.79
2018	1,032.84	1,080.72	1,088.25	1,052.76	1,091.52	1,087.13	1,101.00	1,123.34	1,106.57	1,136.58	1,196.58	1,251.74	1,115.86
Trade, Transportation, and Utilities													
2014	635.05	649.09	649.40	664.61	648.29	654.84	655.06	662.06	663.82	662.45	674.93	667.70	658.34
2015	671.90	687.59	706.10	689.23	696.61	692.07	695.27	698.26	714.02	698.65	719.19	696.24	696.32
2016	704.35	694.75	708.58	715.79	719.80	720.19	716.00	711.78	716.14	732.47	704.98	720.43	713.20
2017	730.66	726.60	722.24	740.05	710.93	718.15	726.17	706.45	697.38	698.94	681.29	688.45	712.49
2018	677.06	680.93	677.69	684.04	684.04	677.34	701.76	677.68	686.48	665.52	662.90	677.84	679.54
Financial Activities													
2014	813.31	820.44	827.41	801.62	810.77	853.45	828.12	825.38	786.62	815.01	855.76	802.58	820.80
2015	823.25	853.14	865.59	885.57	903.92	883.93	979.88	1,004.35	1,000.01	982.11	974.25	972.18	928.50
2016	972.36	945.31	919.80	928.34	990.98	955.32	950.61	952.03	930.26	936.23	915.30	958.50	945.18
2017	950.80	942.06	961.25	993.50	975.36	994.18	1,006.59	999.74	992.64	1,000.54	995.65	973.90	983.13
2018	999.38	998.45	1,008.75	1,046.84	1,021.78	1,014.20	994.07	992.94	1,022.95	982.09	978.63	1,033.07	1,008.88
Professional and Business Services													
2014	859.87	852.95	839.04	838.67	832.80	857.39	828.94	842.69	825.46	811.54	840.52	818.65	837.60
2015	824.69	863.81	839.70	827.32	826.58	828.00	840.78	878.89	817.02	828.97	837.22	810.21	834.20
2016	814.52	844.11	821.31	821.47	829.73	813.94	820.80	838.11	811.84	871.29	835.92	843.88	830.07
2017	875.80	846.68	850.51	870.46	866.60	853.78	869.07	873.32	856.10	882.47	866.92	878.35	866.62
2018	876.86	885.97	902.02	921.90	916.76	916.63	941.80	971.45	974.50	937.92	934.21	945.61	927.69
Leisure and Hospitality													
2014	464.05	467.50	475.22	468.40	466.50	471.23	468.14	474.30	482.14	479.49	486.42	476.42	473.54
2015	494.08	490.03	487.13	477.50	487.62	481.39	485.26	488.22	488.70	485.60	497.54	484.81	486.90
2016	487.55	490.78	499.65	491.36	494.88	504.45	501.60	514.06	515.31	516.98	510.99	495.68	501.63
2017	521.76	510.65	520.50	524.34	516.82	515.54	512.70	513.38	517.37	510.84	506.30	490.20	512.92
2018	513.04	496.48	511.53	513.03	511.20	514.80	518.89	525.99	522.72	526.29	525.40	507.79	516.26

NEW HAMPSHIRE
At a Glance

Population:
  2010 census: 1,316,470
  2018 estimate: 1,356,458

Percent change in population:
  2010–2018: 3.0%

Percent change in total nonfarm employment:
  2010–2018: 9.2%

Industry with the largest growth in employment, 2010–2018 (percent):
  Construction, 25.7%

Industry with the largest decline or smallest growth in employment, 2010–2018 (percent):
  Financial activities, -1.4%

Civilian labor force:
  2010: 738,257
  2018: 761,752

Unemployment rate and rank among states (highest to lowest):
  2010: 5.8%, 48th
  2018: 2.5%, 49th

Over-the-year change in unemployment rates:
  2016–2017: -0.2%
  2017–2018: -0.2%

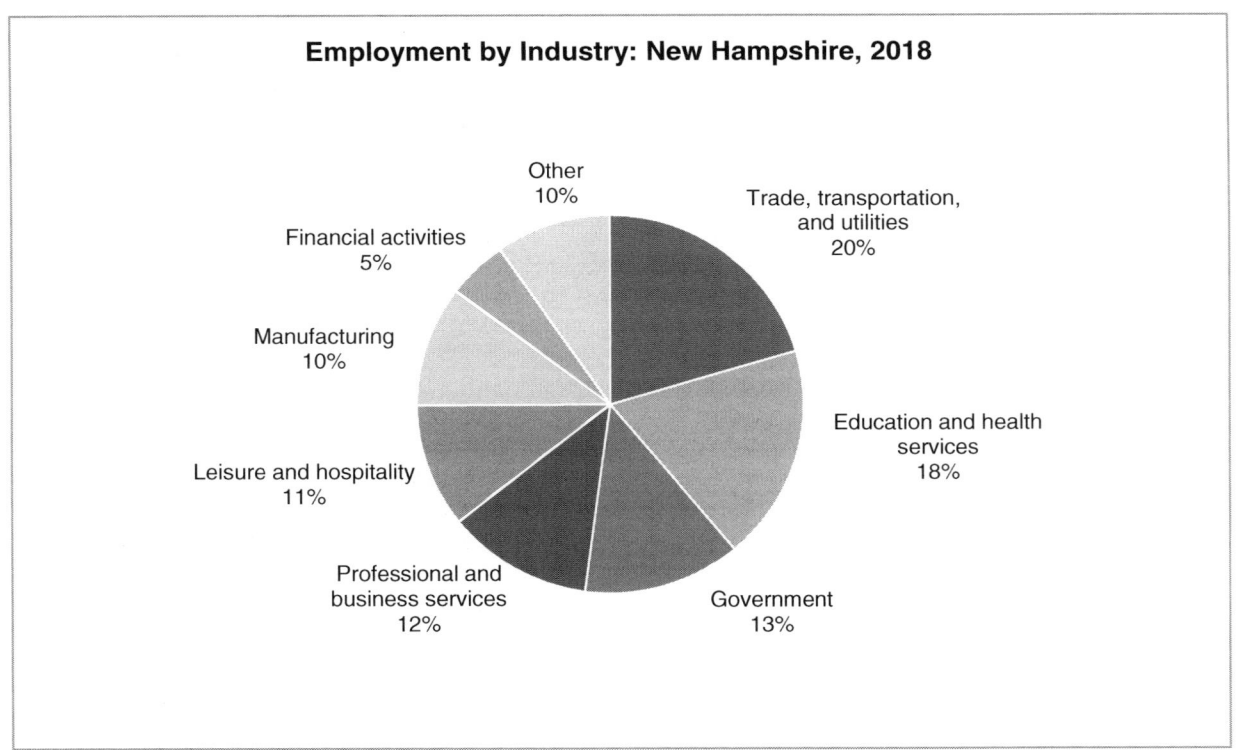

Employment by Industry: New Hampshire, 2018

- Other 10%
- Trade, transportation, and utilities 20%
- Financial activities 5%
- Manufacturing 10%
- Education and health services 18%
- Leisure and hospitality 11%
- Professional and business services 12%
- Government 13%

1. Employment by Industry: New Hampshire, 2010–2018

(Numbers in thousands, not seasonally adjusted)

Industry and year	January	February	March	April	May	June	July	August	September	October	November	December	Annual average
Total Nonfarm													
2010	608.6	611.4	614.5	618.6	628.7	632.0	624.2	624.1	629.5	630.7	629.2	633.3	623.7
2011	612.8	615.8	617.8	623.6	629.9	633.5	627.4	626.4	633.6	633.9	634.3	636.9	627.2
2012	619.0	619.6	623.1	626.7	634.3	641.4	635.7	637.3	641.0	641.0	640.2	642.3	633.5
2013	624.0	626.8	627.3	632.1	642.0	646.5	639.5	642.0	641.9	646.3	646.1	649.6	638.7
2014	630.5	633.6	634.2	639.6	647.0	654.7	649.1	643.3	651.3	654.6	653.2	656.9	645.7
2015	639.2	640.2	643.3	648.2	659.1	664.5	660.0	658.7	660.9	665.3	665.5	668.9	656.2
2016	652.4	656.7	656.5	662.6	669.2	674.8	672.1	672.2	675.6	675.4	675.4	678.2	668.4
2017	661.5	662.8	664.6	669.7	677.2	685.5	680.6	680.4	680.2	681.3	680.0	684.2	675.7
2018	667.5	671.1	671.1	673.7	682.4	691.0	685.0	684.8	682.9	687.5	686.7	687.9	681.0
Total Private													
2010	513.4	511.1	513.0	518.4	527.1	537.3	541.3	541.7	533.6	532.5	530.1	534.4	527.8
2011	520.8	519.0	520.7	527.7	533.4	543.5	549.0	549.4	541.4	538.7	538.1	540.5	535.2
2012	527.7	525.1	527.7	531.9	539.7	553.5	555.7	557.7	547.6	545.9	544.4	545.7	541.9
2013	533.8	532.3	533.4	538.2	547.9	558.5	562.4	563.5	551.9	551.8	551.5	554.2	548.3
2014	540.9	539.9	540.1	545.5	555.0	566.0	570.1	564.3	559.2	559.8	557.6	561.2	555.0
2015	549.3	546.9	548.8	554.1	565.4	576.3	581.4	581.1	570.2	571.5	570.7	574.0	565.8
2016	563.2	562.0	562.2	568.3	576.2	587.2	593.8	593.1	583.2	581.5	580.4	583.3	577.9
2017	573.2	569.8	570.4	576.0	583.8	598.2	602.3	600.6	588.8	587.1	586.2	589.7	585.5
2018	578.5	578.3	577.2	580.2	589.1	603.4	606.1	604.8	591.5	594.8	593.7	594.2	591.0
Goods Producing													
2010	84.5	83.7	84.3	86.6	88.4	89.4	90.1	90.7	90.0	90.4	89.7	89.1	88.1
2011	86.2	85.7	86.6	88.9	89.9	91.0	91.6	91.9	91.2	90.9	90.6	89.7	89.5
2012	86.7	86.0	86.7	88.6	89.4	90.6	90.8	91.0	90.6	90.5	89.5	88.7	89.1
2013	86.5	86.0	86.4	88.1	89.8	91.2	91.2	91.5	90.7	91.0	91.1	90.4	89.5
2014	87.9	87.5	87.8	89.8	91.1	92.3	92.4	92.7	91.6	91.6	91.6	91.3	90.6
2015	89.2	88.3	88.6	90.7	92.5	94.1	94.7	94.8	94.3	94.7	94.1	93.9	92.5
2016	92.1	91.4	91.6	93.6	94.8	96.2	96.8	96.6	95.7	95.8	95.8	95.5	94.7
2017	94.0	93.5	94.1	95.2	96.3	97.9	98.4	98.1	97.6	97.6	97.2	96.9	96.4
2018	95.0	95.0	95.4	96.9	98.3	100.1	100.8	100.8	99.6	99.9	99.5	98.6	98.3
Service-Providing													
2010	524.1	527.7	530.2	532.0	540.3	542.6	534.1	533.4	539.5	540.3	539.5	544.2	535.7
2011	526.6	530.1	531.2	534.7	540.0	542.5	535.8	534.5	542.4	543.0	543.7	547.2	537.6
2012	532.3	533.6	536.4	538.1	544.9	550.8	544.9	546.3	550.4	550.5	550.7	553.6	544.4
2013	537.5	540.8	540.9	544.0	552.2	555.3	548.3	550.5	551.2	555.3	555.0	559.2	549.2
2014	542.6	546.1	546.4	549.8	555.9	562.4	556.7	550.6	559.7	563.0	561.6	565.6	555.0
2015	550.0	551.9	554.7	557.5	566.6	570.4	565.3	563.9	566.6	570.6	571.4	575.0	563.7
2016	560.3	565.3	564.9	569.0	574.4	578.6	575.3	575.6	579.9	579.6	579.6	582.7	573.8
2017	567.5	569.3	570.5	574.5	580.9	587.6	582.2	582.3	582.6	583.7	582.8	587.3	579.3
2018	572.5	576.1	575.7	576.8	584.1	590.9	584.2	584.0	583.3	587.6	587.2	589.3	582.6
Mining and Logging													
2010	0.8	0.8	0.8	0.9	0.9	1.0	1.0	1.0	1.0	0.9	0.9	0.9	0.9
2011	0.8	0.8	0.8	0.8	0.9	0.9	1.0	1.0	1.0	1.0	1.0	0.9	0.9
2012	0.8	0.8	0.8	0.9	0.9	1.0	1.0	1.0	1.0	1.0	0.9	0.9	0.9
2013	0.8	0.8	0.8	0.9	0.9	1.0	1.0	1.0	1.0	1.0	1.0	1.0	0.9
2014	0.9	0.9	0.9	0.9	1.0	1.0	1.0	1.1	1.1	1.1	1.0	1.0	1.0
2015	0.9	0.9	0.9	0.9	0.9	1.0	1.0	1.0	1.0	1.0	1.0	1.0	1.0
2016	0.9	0.9	0.9	0.9	1.0	1.0	1.1	1.1	1.0	1.0	1.0	1.0	1.0
2017	0.9	0.9	0.9	0.9	0.9	1.0	1.0	1.0	1.0	1.0	1.0	0.9	1.0
2018	0.9	0.9	0.9	0.9	1.0	1.0	1.0	1.1	1.0	1.1	1.0	1.0	1.0
Construction													
2010	18.9	18.2	18.6	20.4	21.7	22.2	23.0	23.2	22.9	23.1	22.6	21.7	21.4
2011	19.6	19.1	19.7	21.7	22.5	23.1	23.6	23.6	23.5	23.5	23.2	22.4	22.1
2012	20.0	19.5	20.1	21.8	22.6	23.2	23.5	23.7	23.7	23.6	22.8	21.9	22.2
2013	20.3	19.8	20.2	21.7	23.2	23.8	23.8	23.9	23.7	23.6	23.5	22.7	22.5
2014	20.8	20.6	20.9	22.7	23.7	24.2	24.7	24.7	24.2	24.3	24.2	23.5	23.2
2015	21.8	21.1	21.2	22.9	24.5	25.2	25.7	25.8	25.9	26.2	25.5	25.1	24.2
2016	23.6	23.0	23.3	25.0	25.8	26.4	27.0	26.8	26.6	26.6	26.3	25.6	25.5
2017	24.5	24.2	24.6	25.8	26.7	27.4	27.8	27.8	27.6	27.6	27.1	26.5	26.5
2018	25.0	24.8	24.9	26.2	27.2	28.0	28.4	28.3	27.8	28.0	27.5	26.6	26.9

1. Employment by Industry: New Hampshire, 2010–2018—Continued

(Numbers in thousands, not seasonally adjusted)

Industry and year	January	February	March	April	May	June	July	August	September	October	November	December	Annual average
Manufacturing													
2010	64.8	64.7	64.9	65.3	65.8	66.2	66.1	66.5	66.1	66.4	66.2	66.5	65.8
2011	65.8	65.8	66.1	66.4	66.5	67.0	67.0	67.3	66.7	66.4	66.4	66.4	66.5
2012	65.9	65.7	65.8	65.9	65.9	66.4	66.3	66.3	65.9	65.9	65.8	65.9	66.0
2013	65.4	65.4	65.4	65.5	65.7	66.4	66.4	66.6	66.0	66.4	66.6	66.7	66.0
2014	66.2	66.0	66.0	66.2	66.4	67.1	66.7	66.9	66.3	66.2	66.4	66.8	66.4
2015	66.5	66.3	66.5	66.9	67.1	67.9	68.0	68.0	67.4	67.5	67.6	67.8	67.3
2016	67.6	67.5	67.4	67.7	68.0	68.8	68.7	68.7	68.1	68.2	68.5	68.9	68.2
2017	68.6	68.4	68.6	68.5	68.7	69.5	69.6	69.3	69.0	69.0	69.1	69.5	69.0
2018	69.1	69.3	69.6	69.8	70.1	71.1	71.4	71.4	70.8	70.8	71.0	71.0	70.5
Trade, Transportation, and Utilities													
2010	131.3	128.9	129.1	129.9	132.1	134.1	133.4	133.2	131.6	133.3	135.9	138.6	132.6
2011	132.5	130.0	130.2	131.5	132.8	134.9	134.1	134.1	133.4	134.4	137.0	139.7	133.7
2012	134.1	131.5	132.1	132.5	134.2	137.6	136.8	137.1	135.2	135.7	139.3	140.5	135.6
2013	134.6	132.2	132.6	134.0	136.0	137.9	137.3	137.3	135.5	136.0	139.1	141.4	136.2
2014	135.4	133.3	133.4	134.0	135.9	137.9	137.3	131.2	136.8	137.7	140.5	142.6	136.3
2015	136.5	133.8	133.9	134.8	137.0	138.9	138.1	138.4	136.9	138.0	141.0	143.3	137.6
2016	138.0	136.3	136.3	137.3	139.2	140.7	140.4	140.5	139.3	140.0	142.8	145.1	139.7
2017	139.7	136.9	136.6	137.7	138.8	141.2	140.8	140.7	139.1	139.5	142.3	144.2	139.8
2018	138.8	137.0	136.6	137.2	138.8	140.8	139.6	139.7	138.1	139.5	142.9	143.1	139.3
Wholesale Trade													
2010	25.4	25.3	25.4	25.5	25.7	25.8	25.9	25.8	25.6	25.8	25.8	25.8	25.7
2011	25.6	25.6	25.7	25.9	26.0	26.1	26.1	26.0	25.9	26.0	25.9	26.1	25.9
2012	26.0	25.9	26.0	26.3	26.4	26.6	26.7	26.7	26.5	26.4	26.4	26.4	26.4
2013	26.2	26.1	26.2	26.3	26.5	26.7	26.7	26.7	26.5	26.4	26.5	26.6	26.5
2014	26.4	26.4	26.5	26.6	26.8	27.0	27.1	27.2	27.0	27.0	27.1	27.1	26.9
2015	26.8	26.8	26.8	27.0	27.3	27.4	27.4	27.4	27.2	27.3	27.3	27.4	27.2
2016	27.2	27.1	27.1	27.3	27.5	27.6	27.6	27.6	27.5	27.4	27.5	27.6	27.4
2017	27.4	27.3	27.3	27.6	27.7	28.1	28.0	28.0	27.7	27.7	27.8	27.9	27.7
2018	27.7	27.8	27.8	27.9	28.0	28.3	28.3	28.2	28.0	28.6	28.9	28.6	28.2
Retail Trade													
2010	91.7	89.4	89.5	90.2	91.8	93.4	93.6	93.6	91.2	92.5	95.1	97.2	92.4
2011	92.3	90.0	90.0	90.9	91.8	93.6	93.7	93.9	92.4	93.4	96.2	98.2	93.0
2012	93.6	91.2	91.5	91.6	92.9	95.8	95.8	95.8	93.5	94.2	97.9	98.5	94.4
2013	93.7	91.5	91.7	92.9	94.4	95.9	96.1	96.0	93.7	94.5	97.4	99.1	94.7
2014	94.3	92.2	92.1	92.7	94.0	95.5	95.7	89.4	94.3	95.2	97.8	99.4	94.4
2015	94.6	92.1	92.2	92.9	94.3	95.8	95.7	95.9	93.8	94.8	97.8	99.5	95.0
2016	95.0	93.5	93.5	94.0	95.3	96.6	97.1	97.3	95.2	96.0	98.5	99.8	96.0
2017	96.1	93.4	93.2	93.8	94.7	96.4	96.6	96.6	94.5	95.1	97.8	98.8	95.6
2018	94.7	92.9	92.5	93.0	94.2	95.5	95.2	95.2	93.0	93.8	96.9	96.8	94.5
Transportation and Utilities													
2010	14.2	14.2	14.2	14.2	14.6	14.9	13.9	13.8	14.8	15.0	15.0	15.6	14.5
2011	14.6	14.4	14.5	14.7	15.0	15.2	14.3	14.2	15.1	15.0	14.9	15.4	14.8
2012	14.5	14.4	14.6	14.6	14.9	15.2	14.3	14.6	15.2	15.1	15.0	15.6	14.8
2013	14.7	14.6	14.7	14.8	15.1	15.3	14.5	14.6	15.3	15.1	15.2	15.7	15.0
2014	14.7	14.7	14.8	14.7	15.1	15.4	14.5	14.6	15.5	15.5	15.6	16.1	15.1
2015	15.1	14.9	14.9	14.9	15.4	15.7	15.0	15.1	15.9	15.9	15.9	16.4	15.4
2016	15.8	15.7	15.7	16.0	16.4	16.5	15.7	15.6	16.6	16.6	16.8	17.7	16.3
2017	16.2	16.2	16.1	16.3	16.4	16.7	16.2	16.1	16.9	16.7	16.7	17.5	16.5
2018	16.4	16.3	16.3	16.3	16.6	17.0	16.1	16.3	17.1	17.1	17.1	17.7	16.7
Information													
2010	11.8	11.7	11.7	11.5	11.4	11.5	11.5	11.4	11.2	11.1	11.0	11.0	11.4
2011	11.0	11.0	11.0	11.1	11.3	11.4	11.6	11.6	11.6	11.6	11.8	11.8	11.4
2012	11.8	11.9	12.0	12.0	12.1	12.2	12.3	12.3	12.0	12.0	12.0	12.1	12.1
2013	12.0	11.9	11.9	11.9	11.9	12.0	12.0	12.0	11.8	11.8	11.9	11.9	11.9
2014	12.0	12.0	12.1	12.1	12.2	12.2	12.3	12.3	12.2	12.4	12.0	11.9	12.1
2015	12.1	12.1	12.5	12.6	12.7	12.8	12.8	12.7	12.5	12.5	12.6	12.6	12.5
2016	12.6	12.6	12.5	12.5	12.5	12.6	12.8	12.7	12.4	12.5	12.5	12.7	12.6
2017	12.6	12.5	12.4	12.5	12.8	13.0	12.9	12.8	12.5	12.5	12.4	12.5	12.6
2018	12.4	12.4	12.3	12.3	12.3	12.7	12.7	12.6	12.3	12.3	12.3	12.3	12.4

1. Employment by Industry: New Hampshire, 2010–2018—*Continued*

(Numbers in thousands, not seasonally adjusted)

Industry and year	January	February	March	April	May	June	July	August	September	October	November	December	Annual average
Financial Activities													
2010	35.5	35.0	35.1	35.0	34.9	35.2	35.3	35.0	34.5	34.4	34.2	34.3	34.9
2011	33.9	33.6	33.6	33.7	33.5	33.8	33.9	33.8	33.6	33.4	33.4	33.3	33.6
2012	33.1	33.1	33.2	33.3	33.6	34.3	34.3	34.5	34.0	34.1	33.9	33.9	33.8
2013	33.6	33.6	33.6	33.7	34.0	34.4	34.6	34.7	34.0	34.0	33.9	34.0	34.0
2014	33.5	33.4	33.5	33.5	33.7	34.1	34.3	34.3	33.6	33.5	33.3	33.4	33.7
2015	33.1	33.1	33.1	33.2	33.5	33.9	34.5	34.7	34.2	34.2	34.2	34.2	33.8
2016	34.2	34.2	34.2	34.5	34.5	35.2	35.5	35.5	34.9	34.8	34.6	34.6	34.7
2017	34.8	34.7	34.6	34.4	34.7	35.3	35.4	35.4	34.9	34.7	34.7	34.8	34.9
2018	34.4	34.4	34.3	34.4	34.3	35.0	34.8	34.8	34.1	34.0	34.0	34.4	34.4
Professional and Business Services													
2010	61.6	61.6	62.0	64.5	64.9	65.4	65.6	65.9	65.1	66.2	66.6	66.1	64.6
2011	64.8	64.7	64.6	67.2	67.2	68.2	68.5	68.5	68.3	68.6	69.5	68.7	67.4
2012	67.0	66.5	67.1	69.0	69.5	70.3	70.1	70.9	70.5	70.9	71.2	70.5	69.5
2013	68.8	69.6	69.2	70.6	71.9	72.7	73.3	73.5	72.7	73.5	74.3	74.1	72.0
2014	72.9	72.9	72.5	74.7	75.7	76.7	77.2	77.7	76.4	77.2	77.4	77.3	75.7
2015	75.4	76.4	76.1	77.8	78.8	79.9	80.2	80.6	80.0	80.6	80.8	80.4	78.9
2016	78.3	78.2	78.0	80.2	80.6	81.4	81.8	81.9	81.3	81.7	81.5	81.2	80.5
2017	79.4	79.7	79.8	81.7	82.3	83.9	84.0	83.9	82.9	83.1	83.2	82.5	82.2
2018	81.1	81.1	81.6	82.0	82.9	84.7	84.6	84.6	83.4	84.8	83.5	83.7	83.2
Education and Health Services													
2010	111.0	112.2	112.8	112.5	112.6	112.0	111.1	110.8	112.7	113.1	113.5	113.9	112.4
2011	112.5	113.9	114.5	114.2	114.1	113.0	112.3	112.0	113.7	114.6	114.4	114.7	113.7
2012	113.9	114.9	115.0	114.7	114.6	114.2	113.0	113.2	114.7	115.3	115.7	116.3	114.6
2013	115.3	116.2	116.4	115.4	115.4	114.6	113.6	113.9	115.0	115.8	116.3	116.4	115.4
2014	114.6	115.9	116.0	116.1	115.7	115.5	114.6	114.4	115.7	116.9	117.3	117.5	115.9
2015	117.0	117.5	118.1	118.1	118.3	117.6	117.0	116.3	117.4	119.2	120.2	120.6	118.1
2016	119.7	120.6	121.3	121.7	121.8	120.9	120.8	120.4	122.1	123.1	123.6	124.0	121.7
2017	123.3	123.6	123.5	124.3	124.3	124.1	123.3	122.8	124.0	124.9	125.5	125.9	124.1
2018	125.0	126.2	125.0	125.7	125.8	125.4	124.4	124.3	125.5	127.5	127.8	127.3	125.8
Leisure and Hospitality													
2010	56.9	57.2	57.1	57.4	61.5	67.9	72.2	72.6	66.8	62.2	57.4	59.5	62.4
2011	58.0	58.1	58.0	58.9	62.1	68.2	73.7	74.1	66.8	62.6	58.8	60.0	63.3
2012	58.7	58.9	59.2	59.3	63.5	71.0	75.0	75.2	67.7	64.4	60.0	61.0	64.5
2013	60.4	60.3	60.6	61.6	65.8	72.2	76.7	76.8	68.9	66.5	61.8	62.8	66.2
2014	61.5	61.8	61.7	61.9	67.0	73.2	77.7	77.5	69.2	67.0	62.1	64.0	67.1
2015	62.8	62.5	63.1	63.3	68.6	74.8	79.6	79.2	70.9	68.4	63.8	64.9	68.5
2016	64.4	64.8	64.5	64.6	68.7	75.7	80.6	80.5	73.1	69.1	65.3	66.2	69.8
2017	65.6	65.1	65.5	65.7	69.9	77.4	82.0	81.6	73.1	70.1	66.3	68.2	70.9
2018	67.2	67.5	67.1	66.8	71.5	78.6	83.2	82.1	73.3	71.4	67.8	68.9	72.1
Other Services													
2010	20.8	20.8	20.9	21.0	21.3	21.8	22.1	22.1	21.7	21.8	21.8	21.9	21.5
2011	21.9	22.0	22.2	22.2	22.5	23.0	23.3	23.4	22.8	22.6	22.6	22.6	22.6
2012	22.4	22.3	22.4	22.5	22.8	23.3	23.4	23.5	22.9	23.0	22.8	22.7	22.8
2013	22.6	22.5	22.7	22.9	23.1	23.5	23.7	23.8	23.3	23.2	23.1	23.2	23.1
2014	23.1	23.1	23.1	23.4	23.7	24.1	24.3	24.2	23.7	23.5	23.4	23.2	23.6
2015	23.2	23.2	23.4	23.6	24.0	24.3	24.5	24.4	24.0	23.9	24.0	24.1	23.9
2016	23.9	23.9	23.8	23.9	24.1	24.5	25.1	25.0	24.4	24.5	24.3	24.0	24.3
2017	23.8	23.8	23.9	24.5	24.7	25.4	25.5	25.3	24.7	24.7	24.6	24.7	24.6
2018	24.6	24.7	24.9	24.9	25.2	26.1	26.0	25.9	25.2	25.4	25.9	25.9	25.4
Government													
2010	95.2	100.3	101.5	100.2	101.6	94.7	82.9	82.4	95.9	98.2	99.1	98.9	95.9
2011	92.0	96.8	97.1	95.9	96.5	90.0	78.4	77.0	92.2	95.2	96.2	96.4	92.0
2012	91.3	94.5	95.4	94.8	94.6	87.9	80.0	79.6	93.4	95.1	95.8	96.6	91.6
2013	90.2	94.5	93.9	93.9	94.1	88.0	77.1	78.5	90.0	94.5	94.6	95.4	90.4
2014	89.6	93.7	94.1	94.1	92.0	88.7	79.0	79.0	92.1	94.8	95.6	95.7	90.7
2015	89.9	93.3	94.5	94.1	93.7	88.2	78.6	77.6	90.7	93.8	94.8	94.9	90.3
2016	89.2	94.7	94.3	94.3	93.0	87.6	78.3	79.1	92.4	93.9	95.0	94.9	90.6
2017	88.3	93.0	94.2	93.7	93.4	87.3	78.3	79.8	91.4	94.2	93.8	94.5	90.2
2018	89.0	92.8	93.9	93.5	93.3	87.6	78.9	80.0	91.4	92.7	93.0	93.7	90.0

2. Average Weekly Hours by Selected Industry: New Hampshire, 2014–2018

(Not seasonally adjusted)

Industry and year	January	February	March	April	May	June	July	August	September	October	November	December	Annual average
Total Private													
2014	33.2	32.9	33.1	33.3	33.4	33.4	33.4	33.5	33.5	33.5	33.7	33.3	33.4
2015	32.9	32.9	33.5	33.6	33.7	33.5	33.9	34.2	33.7	33.8	33.9	33.8	33.6
2016	33.3	33.2	33.1	33.6	34.0	33.7	34.0	34.0	34.2	34.5	34.1	34.0	33.8
2017	33.9	33.4	33.5	34.4	34.3	34.1	34.2	34.3	34.0	33.8	33.8	33.6	33.9
2018	33.0	33.1	32.4	33.5	33.6	33.4	33.6	33.6	33.8	33.4	33.4	33.5	33.4
Goods-Producing													
2014	39.6	39.0	39.1	39.2	40.1	40.2	39.7	39.5	39.9	39.4	39.7	39.5	39.6
2015	38.9	38.7	39.4	39.1	39.2	39.2	39.5	39.5	38.5	38.9	39.5	39.6	39.2
2016	39.5	38.8	38.8	39.2	40.0	39.8	39.7	39.7	40.0	40.0	39.4	38.4	39.4
2017	38.8	37.3	37.7	38.6	39.1	39.0	38.5	39.4	39.8	39.7	40.2	39.8	39.0
2018	39.6	39.5	38.1	39.8	40.7	40.5	39.9	40.4	40.5	40.1	39.9	40.6	40.0
Manufacturing													
2014	41.1	40.7	40.8	40.5	40.9	41.3	40.5	40.2	40.9	40.4	41.0	40.9	40.8
2015	40.7	40.4	40.6	40.2	40.0	40.3	40.2	40.1	39.4	39.4	40.2	40.4	40.2
2016	40.3	39.5	39.6	39.8	40.6	40.4	40.1	39.9	40.4	40.2	40.1	39.7	40.0
2017	40.2	38.6	38.8	39.2	40.0	40.3	39.7	40.8	41.2	41.3	41.3	41.4	40.2
2018	41.3	41.4	40.3	41.4	41.7	41.5	41.4	41.6	42.1	41.0	41.3	41.6	41.4
Trade, Transportation, and Utilities													
2014	32.4	32.0	32.4	32.4	32.9	32.8	32.8	33.0	33.0	32.6	32.7	32.5	32.6
2015	31.8	32.1	32.9	33.0	33.5	33.4	33.9	34.2	34.4	33.9	33.9	34.0	33.4
2016	33.0	33.0	32.8	33.3	33.7	33.5	33.8	33.6	33.7	33.8	33.6	34.5	33.5
2017	33.4	33.0	32.8	34.3	34.1	33.6	34.0	33.9	33.5	33.4	33.4	33.7	33.6
2018	32.4	32.0	32.0	33.4	33.3	33.1	33.4	33.2	33.6	33.6	33.9	33.4	33.1
Professional and Business Services													
2014	36.4	35.6	35.9	36.5	36.2	36.1	35.9	35.8	36.0	36.2	36.4	35.8	36.1
2015	35.0	35.2	35.6	35.4	36.3	36.1	35.7	36.0	35.4	35.7	36.3	35.8	35.7
2016	34.4	34.9	35.2	35.9	36.8	35.7	35.5	35.6	36.7	37.7	37.3	37.4	36.1
2017	37.6	36.7	36.8	38.8	38.4	37.8	37.8	37.7	37.6	36.3	36.0	35.7	37.3
2018	35.3	35.6	35.2	36.0	36.3	36.2	35.8	35.9	36.7	35.9	36.3	37.0	36.0
Education and Health Services													
2014	33.0	32.6	32.6	32.5	32.8	32.9	32.6	32.8	33.0	33.0	33.0	32.5	32.8
2015	32.6	32.3	32.7	32.8	32.4	32.7	32.7	32.7	32.0	32.2	32.0	31.7	32.4
2016	31.9	31.6	31.4	31.6	31.6	31.5	31.9	32.2	32.9	31.9	32.0	31.9	31.9
2017	31.8	31.4	31.6	31.7	31.5	31.3	31.4	31.4	31.7	31.3	31.3	31.3	31.5
2018	30.9	31.5	31.0	31.5	31.3	31.2	31.6	31.5	31.5	31.3	31.5	31.6	31.4
Leisure and Hospitality													
2014	21.8	22.3	22.6	23.1	22.5	23.1	25.2	25.8	23.6	24.1	24.1	23.5	23.5
2015	22.9	22.9	23.7	24.3	24.3	23.9	25.8	26.2	25.4	25.2	24.7	24.3	24.5
2016	23.7	24.1	24.1	24.9	24.8	25.3	26.2	26.7	25.4	25.7	24.8	24.3	25.1
2017	24.4	23.5	24.1	24.5	25.2	26.0	26.9	27.0	25.0	24.8	24.7	23.8	25.1
2018	24.0	24.1	22.7	23.8	24.6	25.3	26.3	26.6	25.5	25.0	23.4	23.6	24.7

3. Average Hourly Earnings by Selected Industry: New Hampshire, 2014–2018

(Dollars, not seasonally adjusted)

Industry and year	January	February	March	April	May	June	July	August	September	October	November	December	Annual average
Total Private													
2014................	24.36	24.60	24.60	24.57	24.33	24.18	23.91	23.83	24.39	24.33	24.44	24.41	24.33
2015................	24.61	24.92	24.82	25.09	24.93	24.63	24.52	24.52	24.86	25.21	25.45	25.27	24.90
2016................	25.88	25.85	25.66	25.62	25.38	25.11	25.07	25.43	25.85	26.35	26.16	26.23	25.72
2017................	26.70	26.75	26.68	26.65	25.98	25.83	25.55	25.65	26.37	26.49	26.36	26.67	26.30
2018................	26.69	26.89	26.84	26.79	26.35	26.17	26.19	25.93	26.82	26.86	26.66	26.91	26.59
Goods-Producing													
2014................	26.26	26.52	26.53	26.59	26.39	26.41	26.45	26.44	26.62	26.69	26.35	26.16	26.45
2015................	26.19	26.60	26.51	26.66	26.64	26.26	26.39	26.28	26.86	27.12	26.61	26.98	26.59
2016................	27.52	26.95	26.57	26.58	26.36	26.49	26.62	27.06	27.02	27.21	27.07	27.65	26.92
2017................	26.95	27.01	27.27	27.19	26.50	26.56	26.15	26.18	26.25	26.42	26.34	26.46	26.59
2018................	26.10	26.19	26.71	26.74	26.35	26.39	26.49	26.19	26.50	26.45	26.42	26.83	26.45
Manufacturing													
2014................	25.74	25.95	26.07	25.95	25.52	25.73	25.77	25.93	25.91	26.20	25.99	25.58	25.86
2015................	25.75	26.18	26.02	26.40	26.33	25.98	26.01	25.74	26.58	26.65	26.24	26.77	26.22
2016................	27.28	26.70	26.54	26.71	26.46	26.84	27.07	27.42	26.86	27.36	27.02	27.48	26.98
2017................	26.80	26.90	26.41	26.41	25.47	25.92	25.70	25.70	25.72	25.80	25.50	25.71	25.99
2018................	25.14	25.09	25.54	25.42	25.34	25.17	25.47	25.25	25.24	25.34	25.41	25.81	25.35
Trade, Transportation, and Utilities													
2014................	20.86	21.26	21.62	21.29	21.09	21.22	21.00	21.16	20.98	21.14	21.39	21.52	21.21
2015................	21.72	22.14	21.53	21.81	22.02	21.65	21.80	22.16	22.46	22.79	23.01	22.24	22.12
2016................	22.58	22.07	22.09	21.95	22.04	21.53	21.67	21.85	22.02	22.57	22.27	22.04	22.06
2017................	22.70	22.49	22.43	22.80	22.19	22.00	22.05	22.19	22.63	22.68	22.25	22.38	22.40
2018................	22.86	23.09	23.29	23.45	23.23	23.09	23.28	23.07	23.76	23.80	23.33	23.75	23.34
Professional and Business Services													
2014................	28.42	28.93	28.86	28.27	28.96	28.61	28.24	28.16	28.38	28.27	27.98	28.55	28.46
2015................	28.99	28.54	28.55	28.40	27.91	28.08	28.31	27.29	27.61	28.30	28.47	28.28	28.22
2016................	29.88	30.65	30.55	29.66	28.54	28.39	29.18	29.30	29.63	30.57	30.43	30.42	29.76
2017................	31.75	31.89	31.69	30.43	30.21	30.94	30.39	30.04	30.72	31.13	31.00	31.48	30.95
2018................	31.71	32.02	30.60	30.40	29.43	29.57	29.81	29.57	30.69	31.05	30.66	31.38	30.56
Education and Health Services													
2014................	26.82	26.76	26.39	26.28	26.00	25.90	25.99	25.68	26.36	26.06	25.78	26.00	26.17
2015................	25.91	26.34	26.51	27.49	27.64	27.22	27.31	27.16	27.73	27.77	27.74	28.19	27.25
2016................	28.41	28.48	28.40	28.45	28.07	27.90	28.20	28.27	28.28	28.57	28.66	28.83	28.38
2017................	28.89	29.44	29.29	29.54	29.06	29.34	29.62	29.66	29.47	29.61	29.78	30.08	29.48
2018................	29.57	29.25	29.11	28.93	28.81	28.69	28.65	28.13	28.76	28.67	28.21	28.40	28.76
Leisure and Hospitality													
2014................	13.74	13.92	13.74	13.94	13.83	13.40	13.07	12.83	13.78	13.86	13.69	13.96	13.61
2015................	13.75	14.06	13.92	14.09	13.78	13.44	13.26	13.55	14.06	14.30	14.51	14.54	13.91
2016................	14.45	14.66	14.47	14.64	14.60	14.25	13.96	14.24	14.86	14.97	14.89	14.95	14.56
2017................	14.70	14.91	14.93	15.05	14.94	14.51	14.17	14.27	14.75	15.02	15.11	15.05	14.75
2018................	14.60	15.03	15.29	15.43	15.34	14.81	14.60	14.82	15.10	15.49	15.71	15.89	15.15

4. Average Weekly Earnings by Selected Industry: New Hampshire, 2014–2018

(Dollars, not seasonally adjusted)

Industry and year	January	February	March	April	May	June	July	August	September	October	November	December	Annual average
Total Private													
2014	808.75	809.34	814.26	818.18	812.62	807.61	798.59	798.31	817.07	815.06	823.63	812.85	812.62
2015	809.67	819.87	831.47	843.02	840.14	825.11	831.23	838.58	837.78	852.10	862.76	854.13	836.64
2016	861.80	858.22	849.35	860.83	862.92	846.21	852.38	864.62	884.07	909.08	892.06	891.82	869.34
2017	905.13	893.45	893.78	916.76	891.11	880.80	873.81	879.80	896.58	895.36	890.97	896.11	891.57
2018	880.77	890.06	869.62	897.47	885.36	874.08	879.98	871.25	906.52	897.12	890.44	901.49	888.11
Goods-Producing													
2014	1,039.90	1,034.28	1,037.32	1,042.33	1,058.24	1,061.68	1,050.07	1,044.38	1,062.14	1,051.59	1,046.10	1,033.32	1,047.42
2015	1,018.79	1,029.42	1,044.49	1,042.41	1,044.29	1,029.39	1,042.41	1,038.06	1,034.11	1,054.97	1,051.10	1,068.41	1,042.33
2016	1,087.04	1,045.66	1,030.92	1,041.94	1,054.40	1,054.30	1,056.81	1,074.28	1,080.80	1,088.40	1,066.56	1,061.76	1,060.65
2017	1,045.66	1,007.47	1,028.08	1,049.53	1,036.15	1,035.84	1,006.78	1,031.49	1,044.75	1,048.87	1,058.87	1,053.11	1,037.01
2018	1,033.56	1,034.51	1,017.65	1,064.25	1,072.45	1,068.80	1,056.95	1,058.08	1,073.25	1,060.65	1,054.16	1,089.30	1,058.00
Manufacturing													
2014	1,057.91	1,056.17	1,063.66	1,050.98	1,043.77	1,062.65	1,043.69	1,042.39	1,059.72	1,058.48	1,065.59	1,046.22	1,055.09
2015	1,048.03	1,057.67	1,056.41	1,061.28	1,053.20	1,046.99	1,045.60	1,032.17	1,047.25	1,050.01	1,054.85	1,081.51	1,054.04
2016	1,099.38	1,054.65	1,050.98	1,063.06	1,074.28	1,084.34	1,085.51	1,094.06	1,085.14	1,099.87	1,083.50	1,090.96	1,079.20
2017	1,077.36	1,038.34	1,024.71	1,035.27	1,018.80	1,044.58	1,020.29	1,048.56	1,059.66	1,065.54	1,053.15	1,064.39	1,044.80
2018	1,038.28	1,038.73	1,029.26	1,052.39	1,056.68	1,044.56	1,054.46	1,050.40	1,062.60	1,038.94	1,049.43	1,073.70	1,049.49
Trade, Transportation, and Utilities													
2014	675.86	680.32	700.49	689.80	693.86	696.02	688.80	698.28	692.34	689.16	699.45	699.40	691.45
2015	690.70	710.69	708.34	719.73	737.67	723.11	739.02	757.87	772.62	772.58	780.04	756.16	738.81
2016	745.14	728.31	724.55	730.94	742.75	721.26	732.45	734.16	742.07	762.87	748.27	760.38	739.01
2017	758.18	742.17	735.70	782.04	756.68	739.20	749.70	752.24	758.11	757.51	743.15	754.21	752.64
2018	740.66	738.88	745.28	783.23	773.56	764.28	777.55	765.92	798.34	799.68	790.89	793.25	772.55
Professional and Business Services													
2014	1,034.49	1,029.91	1,036.07	1,031.86	1,048.35	1,032.82	1,013.82	1,008.13	1,021.68	1,023.37	1,018.47	1,022.09	1,027.41
2015	1,014.65	1,004.61	1,016.38	1,005.36	1,013.13	1,013.69	1,010.67	982.44	977.39	1,010.31	1,033.46	1,012.42	1,007.45
2016	1,027.87	1,069.69	1,075.36	1,064.79	1,050.27	1,013.52	1,035.89	1,043.08	1,087.42	1,152.49	1,135.04	1,137.71	1,074.34
2017	1,193.80	1,170.36	1,166.19	1,180.68	1,160.06	1,169.53	1,148.74	1,132.51	1,155.07	1,130.02	1,116.00	1,123.84	1,154.44
2018	1,119.36	1,139.91	1,077.12	1,094.40	1,068.31	1,070.43	1,067.20	1,061.56	1,126.32	1,114.70	1,112.96	1,161.06	1,100.16
Education and Health Services													
2014	885.06	872.38	860.31	854.10	852.80	852.11	847.27	842.30	869.88	859.98	850.74	845.00	858.38
2015	844.67	850.78	866.88	901.67	895.54	890.09	893.04	888.13	887.36	894.19	887.68	893.62	882.90
2016	906.28	899.97	891.76	899.02	887.01	878.85	899.58	910.29	930.41	911.38	917.12	919.68	905.32
2017	918.70	924.42	925.56	936.42	915.39	918.34	930.07	931.32	934.20	926.79	932.11	941.50	928.62
2018	913.71	921.38	902.41	911.30	901.75	895.13	905.34	886.10	905.94	897.37	888.62	897.44	903.06
Leisure and Hospitality													
2014	299.53	310.42	310.52	322.01	311.18	309.54	329.36	331.01	325.21	334.03	329.93	328.06	319.84
2015	314.88	321.97	329.90	342.39	334.85	321.22	342.11	355.01	357.12	360.36	358.40	353.32	340.80
2016	342.47	353.31	348.73	364.54	362.08	360.53	365.75	380.21	377.44	384.73	369.27	363.29	365.46
2017	358.68	350.39	359.81	368.73	376.49	377.26	381.17	385.29	368.75	372.50	373.22	358.19	370.23
2018	350.40	362.22	347.08	367.23	377.36	374.69	383.98	394.21	385.05	387.25	367.61	375.00	374.21

NEW JERSEY
At a Glance

Population:
2010 census: 8,791,894
2018 estimate: 8,908,520

Percent change in population:
2010–2018: 1.3%

Percent change in total nonfarm employment:
2010–2018: 8.2%

Industry with the largest growth in employment, 2010–2018 (percent):
Transportation and utilities, 31.5%

Industry with the largest decline or smallest growth in employment, 2010–2018 (percent):
Information, -10.4%

Civilian labor force:
2010: 4,555,330
2018: 4,422,942

Unemployment rate and rank among states (highest to lowest):
2010: 9.5%, 20th
2018: 4.1%, 16th

Over-the-year change in unemployment rates:
2016–2017: -0.4%
2017–2018: -0.5%

Employment by Industry: New Jersey, 2018

Other 10%

Trade, transportation, and utilities 21%

Manufacturing 6%

Financial activities 6%

Leisure and hospitality 9%

Education and health services 17%

Government 14%

Professional and business services 16%

1. Employment by Industry: New Jersey, 2010–2018

(Numbers in thousands, not seasonally adjusted)

Industry and year	January	February	March	April	May	June	July	August	September	October	November	December	Annual average
Total Nonfarm													
2010	3,765.0	3,757.3	3,787.6	3,838.5	3,883.5	3,926.8	3,855.5	3,830.7	3,832.0	3,851.3	3,863.9	3,869.9	3,838.5
2011	3,743.7	3,753.8	3,783.1	3,826.4	3,856.0	3,906.0	3,851.6	3,828.4	3,852.3	3,865.6	3,884.7	3,892.3	3,837.0
2012	3,783.2	3,800.7	3,837.9	3,851.5	3,899.0	3,960.5	3,885.0	3,875.6	3,897.7	3,911.2	3,913.6	3,938.1	3,879.5
2013	3,825.9	3,842.6	3,875.9	3,895.7	3,936.8	3,996.4	3,934.1	3,927.5	3,941.4	3,953.9	3,977.7	3,977.6	3,923.8
2014	3,848.9	3,850.4	3,882.4	3,938.2	3,985.3	4,032.8	3,972.9	3,957.5	3,974.1	3,991.1	4,013.0	4,024.1	3,955.9
2015	3,887.0	3,894.6	3,927.0	3,968.3	4,021.2	4,069.6	4,016.2	4,003.4	4,017.5	4,048.2	4,071.0	4,077.0	4,000.1
2016	3,941.8	3,955.5	3,992.5	4,035.1	4,071.1	4,130.1	4,082.2	4,065.8	4,087.5	4,102.4	4,125.6	4,135.6	4,060.4
2017	4,007.3	4,021.9	4,044.5	4,079.6	4,136.6	4,205.7	4,131.6	4,118.0	4,133.9	4,156.7	4,180.4	4,190.3	4,117.2
2018	4,047.7	4,070.7	4,087.5	4,126.0	4,175.1	4,244.2	4,170.0	4,154.5	4,162.9	4,192.3	4,212.6	4,213.9	4,154.8
Total Private													
2010	3,124.7	3,110.1	3,137.4	3,186.8	3,221.6	3,270.6	3,245.8	3,242.6	3,227.3	3,227.5	3,233.7	3,243.6	3,206.0
2011	3,134.1	3,132.5	3,159.7	3,200.3	3,234.3	3,285.4	3,270.5	3,262.1	3,256.7	3,245.7	3,259.6	3,270.0	3,225.9
2012	3,178.0	3,182.2	3,215.0	3,232.3	3,283.2	3,340.7	3,308.4	3,310.3	3,303.7	3,293.0	3,294.3	3,318.8	3,271.7
2013	3,217.3	3,219.7	3,252.6	3,283.0	3,327.4	3,383.0	3,360.8	3,361.4	3,348.9	3,335.7	3,356.0	3,358.1	3,317.0
2014	3,245.0	3,233.9	3,264.9	3,312.6	3,366.0	3,414.1	3,395.1	3,390.1	3,379.5	3,376.1	3,392.3	3,405.8	3,348.0
2015	3,288.4	3,282.6	3,313.3	3,351.7	3,408.6	3,457.3	3,444.9	3,439.0	3,429.0	3,438.8	3,455.2	3,464.7	3,397.8
2016	3,345.8	3,346.0	3,378.1	3,421.7	3,459.1	3,519.8	3,511.4	3,504.2	3,496.8	3,493.4	3,511.9	3,525.0	3,459.4
2017	3,410.2	3,411.2	3,431.7	3,468.2	3,526.2	3,591.0	3,557.4	3,552.1	3,544.5	3,547.9	3,568.0	3,578.4	3,515.6
2018	3,453.7	3,462.8	3,479.9	3,516.6	3,567.6	3,631.9	3,597.6	3,590.0	3,573.4	3,581.6	3,597.1	3,598.7	3,554.2
Goods Producing													
2010	372.3	368.4	372.5	382.0	386.5	390.0	389.6	389.0	387.8	387.8	387.4	382.7	383.0
2011	364.4	362.1	368.4	376.3	380.2	384.8	385.4	386.6	384.3	383.2	382.5	379.0	378.1
2012	365.1	363.2	366.2	369.9	372.9	376.8	375.5	376.8	376.0	376.3	376.2	376.9	372.7
2013	364.0	362.5	367.3	374.5	378.5	382.8	382.8	385.3	384.5	385.3	385.1	379.3	377.7
2014	365.6	362.1	367.6	378.7	384.8	388.1	389.6	390.6	390.5	389.7	388.6	385.8	381.8
2015	372.1	368.7	372.8	383.3	389.9	395.0	397.1	397.4	395.3	398.0	397.1	396.0	388.6
2016	383.7	381.3	387.4	393.6	398.0	402.8	404.4	404.5	401.7	403.2	402.6	400.3	397.0
2017	386.3	387.3	389.7	397.5	403.9	409.4	409.3	409.8	407.9	408.3	408.3	406.6	402.0
2018	390.5	394.0	396.8	402.8	407.8	413.7	412.0	411.9	409.1	413.8	414.8	412.9	406.7
Service-Providing													
2010	3,392.7	3,388.9	3,415.1	3,456.5	3,497.0	3,536.8	3,465.9	3,441.7	3,444.2	3,463.5	3,476.5	3,487.2	3,455.5
2011	3,379.3	3,391.7	3,414.7	3,450.1	3,475.8	3,521.2	3,466.2	3,441.8	3,468.0	3,482.4	3,502.2	3,513.3	3,458.9
2012	3,418.1	3,437.5	3,471.7	3,481.6	3,526.1	3,583.7	3,509.5	3,498.8	3,521.7	3,534.9	3,537.4	3,561.2	3,506.9
2013	3,461.9	3,480.1	3,508.6	3,521.2	3,558.3	3,613.6	3,551.3	3,542.2	3,556.9	3,568.6	3,592.6	3,598.3	3,546.1
2014	3,483.3	3,488.3	3,514.8	3,559.5	3,600.5	3,644.7	3,583.3	3,566.9	3,583.6	3,601.4	3,624.4	3,638.3	3,574.1
2015	3,514.9	3,525.9	3,554.2	3,585.0	3,631.3	3,674.6	3,619.1	3,606.0	3,622.2	3,650.2	3,673.9	3,681.0	3,611.5
2016	3,558.1	3,574.2	3,605.1	3,641.5	3,673.1	3,727.3	3,677.8	3,661.3	3,685.8	3,699.2	3,723.0	3,735.3	3,663.5
2017	3,621.0	3,634.6	3,654.8	3,682.1	3,732.7	3,796.3	3,722.3	3,708.2	3,726.0	3,748.4	3,772.1	3,783.7	3,715.2
2018	3,657.2	3,676.7	3,690.7	3,723.2	3,767.3	3,830.5	3,758.0	3,742.6	3,753.8	3,778.5	3,797.8	3,801.0	3,748.1
Mining and Logging													
2010	1.2	1.3	1.3	1.4	1.4	1.4	1.4	1.4	1.4	1.4	1.4	1.4	1.4
2011	1.2	1.2	1.2	1.3	1.3	1.4	1.3	1.3	1.3	1.3	1.3	1.3	1.3
2012	1.2	1.2	1.2	1.3	1.3	1.3	1.3	1.3	1.3	1.3	1.3	1.3	1.3
2013	1.2	1.1	1.2	1.3	1.3	1.4	1.4	1.4	1.4	1.4	1.4	1.4	1.3
2014	1.3	1.3	1.4	1.4	1.5	1.5	1.5	1.5	1.4	1.4	1.5	1.5	1.4
2015	1.4	1.4	1.3	1.4	1.4	1.4	1.4	1.4	1.4	1.5	1.4	1.4	1.4
2016	1.3	1.3	1.3	1.3	1.4	1.4	1.4	1.3	1.3	1.3	1.3	1.3	1.3
2017	1.2	1.2	1.3	1.3	1.3	1.3	1.3	1.3	1.3	1.4	1.4	1.4	1.3
2018	1.3	1.3	1.3	1.4	1.4	1.4	1.4	1.4	1.4	1.4	1.4	1.4	1.4
Construction													
2010	119.8	116.7	120.8	129.2	132.4	134.2	135.2	134.8	133.7	134.2	133.9	128.8	129.5
2011	114.2	112.4	118.3	126.9	130.9	134.3	137.2	138.3	137.4	137.5	137.2	134.2	129.9
2012	123.6	122.1	123.3	127.9	129.8	132.5	133.3	134.4	133.7	134.3	134.7	135.3	130.4
2013	125.8	124.6	128.0	135.8	139.2	141.6	142.6	144.4	143.6	144.1	143.5	137.6	137.6
2014	127.6	124.4	129.2	138.1	143.3	145.3	148.1	149.2	149.8	149.6	148.7	145.7	141.6
2015	134.7	132.0	135.4	145.7	150.5	153.1	155.3	155.7	153.6	156.2	155.2	152.8	148.4
2016	143.0	140.3	145.3	152.0	155.3	157.8	159.7	159.8	157.8	158.7	157.7	154.8	153.5
2017	143.8	144.6	146.6	153.8	158.2	161.1	161.6	162.4	161.3	161.2	160.7	158.2	156.1
2018	145.1	148.2	150.3	155.5	159.4	162.3	162.3	162.1	160.9	163.3	164.2	161.6	157.9

1. Employment by Industry: New Jersey, 2010–2018—*Continued*

(Numbers in thousands, not seasonally adjusted)

Industry and year	January	February	March	April	May	June	July	August	September	October	November	December	Annual average
Manufacturing													
2010	251.3	250.4	250.4	251.4	252.7	254.4	253.0	252.8	252.7	252.2	252.1	252.5	252.2
2011	249.0	248.5	248.9	248.1	248.0	249.1	246.9	247.0	245.6	244.4	244.0	243.5	246.9
2012	240.3	239.9	241.7	240.7	241.8	243.0	240.9	241.1	241.0	240.7	240.2	240.3	241.0
2013	237.0	236.8	238.1	237.4	238.0	239.8	238.8	239.5	239.5	239.8	240.2	240.3	238.8
2014	236.7	236.4	237.0	239.2	240.0	241.3	240.0	239.9	239.3	238.7	238.4	238.6	238.8
2015	236.0	235.3	236.1	236.2	238.0	240.5	240.4	240.3	240.3	240.3	240.5	241.8	238.8
2016	239.4	239.7	240.8	240.3	241.3	243.6	243.3	243.4	242.6	243.2	243.6	244.2	242.1
2017	241.3	241.5	241.8	242.4	244.4	247.0	246.4	246.1	245.3	245.7	246.2	247.0	244.6
2018	244.1	244.5	245.2	245.9	247.0	250.0	248.3	248.4	246.8	249.1	249.2	249.9	247.4
Trade, Transportation, and Utilities													
2010	800.0	788.4	791.0	798.6	806.1	816.4	807.5	806.9	806.8	813.3	826.1	840.3	808.5
2011	804.8	797.8	800.5	804.8	810.5	820.8	813.1	812.8	814.3	818.1	834.8	847.6	815.0
2012	816.1	806.7	811.2	808.1	821.3	831.9	819.7	817.4	820.5	823.5	838.9	850.8	822.2
2013	815.3	806.4	810.4	813.6	822.4	834.1	826.8	826.0	827.3	831.8	851.2	860.8	827.2
2014	824.4	814.3	819.5	824.4	835.0	845.2	837.9	837.8	838.7	843.7	863.1	876.3	838.4
2015	838.6	829.5	833.5	838.9	850.7	862.7	854.8	854.5	855.2	861.4	879.0	886.5	853.8
2016	851.0	844.0	847.5	852.6	861.0	868.8	865.2	864.2	866.2	874.0	894.9	906.2	866.3
2017	870.5	860.5	861.0	865.1	874.6	887.6	880.8	880.7	883.0	886.5	911.1	920.9	881.9
2018	883.6	873.8	873.2	874.4	884.3	892.5	885.7	881.7	882.0	892.6	913.2	920.7	888.1
Wholesale Trade													
2010	208.0	206.7	206.7	207.6	207.9	209.3	208.8	208.3	207.6	207.7	208.0	208.3	207.9
2011	205.5	207.0	208.1	209.3	210.3	211.9	212.3	212.5	211.2	211.2	211.5	213.2	210.3
2012	210.8	211.3	212.3	212.0	213.1	215.0	214.1	213.8	213.6	212.9	213.4	213.8	213.0
2013	210.4	210.2	211.2	211.6	212.6	214.3	214.2	214.1	213.5	213.3	213.7	213.8	212.7
2014	210.5	211.1	212.2	212.8	214.5	215.9	215.6	215.3	215.2	214.9	215.7	216.5	214.2
2015	213.1	212.9	213.9	214.5	215.7	217.2	217.0	216.9	215.6	215.6	215.6	216.2	215.4
2016	212.8	213.0	213.8	214.3	215.2	216.3	216.7	216.7	215.7	215.6	216.1	216.8	215.3
2017	213.4	213.4	213.9	214.6	215.5	217.4	216.7	216.5	215.7	214.7	215.5	216.3	215.3
2018	213.7	213.8	214.0	214.7	216.0	217.7	218.2	216.8	216.8	216.6	215.0	215.7	215.8
Retail Trade													
2010	430.8	421.2	423.8	427.6	434.2	442.0	440.7	441.4	434.7	440.5	451.7	462.0	437.6
2011	435.9	427.9	428.8	432.0	435.8	443.4	442.3	442.7	437.6	440.9	455.2	464.2	440.6
2012	441.4	431.0	433.9	433.4	441.1	448.4	444.8	444.3	439.7	443.1	457.4	465.4	443.7
2013	439.9	431.5	433.7	436.0	442.8	452.2	451.6	452.2	446.8	450.6	466.6	473.6	448.1
2014	446.8	438.2	441.4	444.9	451.4	459.1	459.2	459.2	452.9	456.5	471.1	480.2	455.1
2015	452.7	444.5	446.8	450.1	458.3	466.8	464.5	465.4	460.0	463.2	477.2	481.0	460.9
2016	455.5	448.1	450.2	453.3	458.8	464.9	464.9	465.5	459.2	461.9	475.8	482.9	461.8
2017	459.0	450.6	450.8	452.9	458.1	466.4	465.3	465.1	458.4	460.5	476.5	479.7	461.9
2018	457.3	449.8	449.4	450.2	456.9	462.5	460.4	458.9	452.6	456.8	470.7	472.1	458.1
Transportation and Utilities													
2010	161.2	160.5	160.5	163.4	164.0	165.1	158.0	157.2	164.5	165.1	166.4	170.0	163.0
2011	163.4	162.9	163.6	163.5	164.4	165.5	158.5	157.6	165.5	166.0	168.1	170.2	164.1
2012	163.9	164.4	165.0	162.7	167.1	168.5	160.8	159.3	167.2	167.5	168.1	171.6	165.5
2013	165.0	164.7	165.5	166.0	167.0	167.6	161.0	159.7	167.0	167.9	170.9	173.4	166.3
2014	167.1	165.0	165.9	166.7	169.1	170.2	163.1	163.3	170.6	172.3	176.3	179.6	169.1
2015	172.8	172.1	172.8	174.3	176.7	178.7	173.3	172.2	179.6	182.6	186.2	189.3	177.6
2016	182.7	182.9	183.5	185.0	187.0	187.6	183.6	182.0	191.3	196.5	203.0	206.5	189.3
2017	198.1	196.5	196.3	197.6	201.0	203.8	198.8	199.1	208.9	211.3	219.1	224.9	204.6
2018	212.6	210.2	209.8	209.5	211.4	212.3	207.1	206.0	212.6	219.2	227.5	232.9	214.3
Information													
2010	79.1	78.9	79.1	78.1	78.0	78.9	77.4	77.5	77.3	77.0	75.2	77.6	77.8
2011	74.1	73.9	74.0	74.9	75.1	76.2	77.5	71.5	77.2	74.9	75.1	75.1	75.0
2012	75.3	75.7	76.2	75.1	75.2	75.7	76.3	76.1	75.5	74.6	74.6	74.7	75.4
2013	73.4	73.7	73.3	73.4	73.6	74.3	74.4	74.7	73.2	73.3	73.9	73.6	73.7
2014	72.8	72.7	73.0	73.8	74.1	74.4	74.3	74.3	73.6	73.0	72.4	72.9	73.4
2015	72.5	72.2	72.1	72.0	72.9	73.8	73.4	73.0	72.3	72.4	72.8	72.9	72.7
2016	71.3	71.4	71.1	71.8	67.6	72.2	73.2	72.4	71.8	71.1	71.4	72.4	71.5
2017	70.9	72.0	71.4	70.7	71.0	72.2	70.6	70.7	70.4	70.1	70.5	70.8	70.9
2018	69.1	71.2	70.0	69.6	70.1	71.4	69.9	70.7	69.2	68.5	68.9	67.6	69.7

1. Employment by Industry: New Jersey, 2010–2018—Continued

(Numbers in thousands, not seasonally adjusted)

Industry and year	January	February	March	April	May	June	July	August	September	October	November	December	Annual average
Financial Activities													
2010	247.4	247.0	247.4	247.7	248.0	251.1	250.7	250.7	248.7	247.6	247.6	248.3	248.5
2011	245.5	245.4	245.8	245.8	246.6	249.4	248.9	249.0	246.7	244.1	244.2	244.6	246.3
2012	243.0	243.0	244.1	245.2	246.9	250.2	249.5	249.6	247.4	246.7	246.7	248.5	246.7
2013	249.6	250.0	250.5	249.8	250.4	252.9	252.6	252.0	249.2	247.4	246.3	246.5	249.8
2014	241.9	241.0	241.3	241.6	242.9	245.4	245.7	245.2	242.9	242.0	242.7	243.4	243.0
2015	240.1	240.3	241.4	241.8	243.2	245.8	246.5	246.2	243.9	243.3	243.2	244.1	243.3
2016	240.7	240.3	240.3	241.6	242.9	246.2	248.3	248.4	246.2	246.1	245.8	246.9	244.5
2017	244.9	245.5	246.9	247.2	249.1	252.7	253.1	252.7	250.4	250.3	250.7	251.9	249.6
2018	248.1	248.1	249.2	250.0	251.1	254.6	254.4	254.1	251.8	248.4	247.3	249.2	250.5
Professional and Business Services													
2010	566.2	568.6	575.8	589.0	592.6	602.7	599.2	601.7	600.3	602.1	603.3	602.4	592.0
2011	585.4	586.5	592.4	603.1	606.1	615.1	614.3	616.7	616.8	618.6	620.2	617.4	607.7
2012	596.4	600.1	608.2	615.6	621.8	631.7	626.0	632.8	634.5	632.7	637.8	638.9	623.0
2013	612.1	615.4	624.3	628.1	635.5	644.9	641.8	646.3	644.6	640.9	643.8	643.2	635.1
2014	617.6	618.8	620.8	632.7	638.8	645.7	643.1	645.1	646.2	650.4	654.5	655.2	639.1
2015	626.1	628.1	635.5	643.7	649.4	654.7	654.7	657.1	658.8	667.0	669.4	668.1	651.1
2016	636.8	639.0	646.4	660.0	663.7	674.0	671.6	673.1	676.1	674.0	678.4	681.0	664.5
2017	648.6	650.3	655.3	661.8	672.0	683.0	673.3	673.9	678.4	681.1	682.9	683.3	670.3
2018	649.8	653.0	658.0	668.3	676.2	686.5	675.6	677.2	679.3	681.2	685.0	677.3	672.3
Education and Health Services													
2010	599.1	600.4	604.3	604.2	605.2	603.5	592.2	589.2	596.7	606.2	607.9	607.5	601.4
2011	598.4	603.6	607.6	607.8	609.6	609.1	597.9	595.0	606.4	611.9	614.9	619.1	606.8
2012	611.0	619.4	624.3	620.9	626.3	625.3	611.3	609.4	621.3	628.8	626.8	632.6	621.5
2013	623.6	630.1	635.6	637.3	640.6	637.0	624.0	622.1	633.8	640.7	646.3	646.3	634.8
2014	633.5	636.6	644.1	647.6	652.5	650.6	639.6	635.9	648.8	656.2	660.4	664.3	647.5
2015	649.9	655.0	660.8	660.5	664.3	662.8	649.7	645.6	658.5	667.6	671.6	673.7	660.0
2016	663.0	668.5	673.7	674.6	676.2	675.7	664.5	660.9	678.7	687.0	688.5	689.8	675.1
2017	682.3	687.6	692.2	695.4	700.2	697.9	680.9	677.3	696.6	706.0	708.2	710.3	694.6
2018	698.3	707.0	709.1	711.0	713.8	711.7	693.1	688.6	705.5	717.1	720.4	722.8	708.2
Leisure and Hospitality													
2010	303.4	302.0	309.6	326.7	343.4	362.7	365.7	364.5	349.7	333.1	325.9	323.5	334.2
2011	303.7	305.2	311.7	326.9	344.2	364.1	368.7	367.1	350.5	334.2	327.4	325.8	335.8
2012	311.1	314.0	323.2	334.6	353.8	379.9	382.2	381.2	363.8	346.3	329.9	331.6	346.0
2013	317.8	319.6	328.2	341.5	360.3	386.4	388.7	386.2	370.5	350.9	343.8	342.3	353.0
2014	325.7	325.0	333.4	346.9	368.8	391.9	393.2	390.7	370.8	353.6	343.1	339.8	356.9
2015	324.0	324.1	331.0	345.0	369.3	389.8	397.3	395.0	377.5	360.9	353.3	354.2	360.1
2016	332.6	334.6	343.6	357.2	378.0	404.5	409.9	407.2	385.9	367.3	359.5	357.2	369.8
2017	338.9	340.8	347.6	361.5	384.6	413.2	416.6	415.1	389.0	376.4	367.1	365.1	376.3
2018	347.5	348.8	356.2	370.6	392.0	424.8	431.7	431.6	405.3	387.8	375.6	374.6	387.2
Other Services													
2010	157.2	156.4	157.7	160.5	161.8	165.3	163.5	163.1	160.0	160.4	160.3	161.3	160.6
2011	157.8	158.0	159.3	160.7	162.0	165.9	164.7	163.4	160.5	160.7	160.5	161.4	161.2
2012	160.0	160.1	161.6	162.9	165.0	169.2	167.9	167.0	164.7	164.1	163.4	164.8	164.2
2013	161.5	162.0	163.0	164.8	166.1	170.6	169.7	168.8	165.8	165.4	165.6	166.1	165.8
2014	163.5	163.4	165.2	166.9	169.1	172.8	171.7	170.5	168.0	167.5	167.5	168.1	167.9
2015	165.1	164.7	166.2	166.5	168.9	172.7	171.4	170.2	167.5	168.2	168.8	169.2	168.3
2016	166.7	166.9	168.1	170.3	171.7	175.6	174.3	173.5	170.2	170.7	170.8	171.2	170.8
2017	167.8	167.2	167.6	169.0	170.8	175.0	172.8	171.9	168.8	169.2	169.2	169.5	169.9
2018	166.8	166.9	167.4	169.9	172.3	176.7	175.2	174.2	171.2	172.2	171.9	173.6	171.5
Government													
2010	640.3	647.2	650.2	651.7	661.9	656.2	609.7	588.1	604.7	623.8	630.2	626.3	632.5
2011	609.6	621.3	623.4	626.1	621.7	620.6	581.1	566.3	595.6	619.9	625.1	622.3	611.1
2012	605.2	618.5	622.9	619.2	615.8	619.8	576.6	565.3	594.0	618.2	619.3	619.3	607.8
2013	608.6	622.9	623.3	612.7	609.4	613.4	573.3	566.1	592.5	618.2	621.7	619.5	606.8
2014	603.9	616.5	617.5	625.6	619.3	618.7	577.8	567.4	594.6	615.0	620.7	618.3	607.9
2015	598.6	612.0	613.7	616.6	612.6	612.3	571.3	564.4	588.5	609.4	615.8	612.3	602.3
2016	596.0	609.5	614.4	613.4	612.0	610.3	570.8	561.6	590.7	609.0	613.7	610.6	601.0
2017	597.1	610.7	612.8	611.4	610.4	614.7	574.2	565.9	589.4	608.8	612.4	611.9	601.6
2018	594.0	607.9	607.6	609.4	607.5	612.3	572.4	564.5	589.5	610.7	615.5	615.2	600.5

2. Average Weekly Hours by Selected Industry: New Jersey, 2014–2018

(Not seasonally adjusted)

Industry and year	January	February	March	April	May	June	July	August	September	October	November	December	Annual average
Total Private													
2014	33.4	33.0	33.8	33.6	33.6	33.9	33.8	33.8	33.8	33.6	33.9	33.8	33.7
2015	33.2	33.5	33.7	33.7	33.7	33.7	33.9	34.2	33.9	33.9	34.0	34.0	33.8
2016	33.6	33.6	33.5	33.8	34.0	33.9	34.1	33.9	34.8	35.1	34.5	34.7	34.1
2017	34.4	33.8	33.7	34.5	34.0	33.8	34.1	33.8	33.9	34.1	34.1	34.0	34.0
2018	33.6	33.8	33.6	34.1	34.0	33.9	34.2	34.1	34.5	34.2	34.1	34.8	34.1
Goods-Producing													
2014	38.5	37.1	39.1	38.8	38.9	39.1	38.8	38.5	39.0	38.6	38.5	39.3	38.7
2015	38.3	37.9	38.8	38.6	38.7	38.9	38.6	38.6	38.1	39.0	38.6	39.1	38.6
2016	38.4	38.2	38.5	38.8	38.5	39.1	39.2	38.9	38.9	39.3	38.7	39.1	38.8
2017	37.9	37.4	37.3	38.5	38.7	38.8	38.5	38.9	39.0	39.0	39.1	39.1	38.5
2018	38.6	38.2	38.4	39.1	39.8	39.8	39.7	39.7	39.5	39.4	39.2	40.5	39.3
Construction													
2014	36.3	34.4	38.1	37.9	38.1	37.7	37.9	37.6	38.5	37.7	36.9	38.1	37.5
2015	37.1	36.6	38.1	37.8	38.5	38.3	37.9	37.6	37.1	39.1	37.2	38.1	37.8
2016	37.2	37.1	38.0	38.5	38.5	39.1	39.3	38.8	38.0	38.9	37.8	38.2	38.3
2017	37.6	37.1	36.7	37.8	36.5	37.0	37.3	37.4	37.1	36.9	36.7	37.3	37.1
2018	36.8	36.2	36.4	37.5	39.2	38.9	39.4	38.7	38.0	38.7	37.4	38.4	38.0
Manufacturing													
2014	39.6	38.5	39.7	39.3	39.3	39.9	39.3	39.0	39.3	39.3	39.4	40.0	39.4
2015	38.9	38.5	39.1	39.0	38.7	39.2	39.0	39.1	38.6	38.9	39.4	39.7	39.0
2016	39.1	38.8	38.8	38.9	38.4	39.0	39.0	38.9	39.4	39.4	39.3	39.6	39.1
2017	37.9	37.4	37.6	38.8	40.1	40.0	39.4	40.0	40.3	40.5	40.8	40.5	39.4
2018	40.0	39.8	39.9	40.3	40.3	40.5	39.9	40.3	40.4	39.8	40.4	41.9	40.3
Trade, Transportation, and Utilities													
2014	33.8	33.2	34.1	34.2	34.0	33.9	34.2	34.2	34.3	33.9	34.0	34.4	34.0
2015	33.4	33.6	33.8	34.0	34.2	34.0	34.3	34.5	34.7	34.0	34.3	34.2	34.1
2016	33.4	33.6	33.7	33.9	34.4	34.3	34.6	34.4	34.6	34.7	34.5	35.3	34.3
2017	34.3	33.9	33.8	34.8	34.7	34.8	35.0	34.7	35.1	34.9	35.1	35.2	34.7
2018	34.2	34.0	34.1	34.5	34.4	34.4	34.8	34.6	35.1	34.5	34.7	34.8	34.5
Financial Activities													
2014	35.6	37.1	36.4	36.1	36.0	37.0	35.7	36.2	36.2	36.5	37.0	36.3	36.3
2015	36.3	37.0	37.3	36.6	36.5	36.6	37.0	37.4	36.5	36.8	37.4	36.9	36.9
2016	37.1	37.2	37.2	37.0	38.0	37.0	36.8	37.2	37.1	38.0	36.8	36.7	37.2
2017	38.1	36.7	36.7	38.0	36.8	36.7	37.4	36.4	36.8	38.1	37.1	37.2	37.2
2018	37.1	37.2	37.0	38.0	36.8	37.0	37.5	36.5	38.1	37.1	37.0	38.4	37.3
Professional and Business Services													
2014	35.6	34.9	35.8	35.6	35.9	36.7	35.9	36.0	35.7	35.5	36.1	35.4	35.8
2015	35.2	36.0	35.8	35.5	35.5	35.4	35.4	35.8	35.1	35.7	35.5	35.9	35.6
2016	35.7	35.6	35.6	36.1	36.1	35.7	35.7	35.6	35.9	36.4	35.7	35.5	35.8
2017	35.7	34.7	34.8	35.8	34.9	35.1	35.3	34.9	34.9	35.7	35.3	35.1	35.2
2018	34.8	35.3	35.0	35.9	35.4	35.5	35.9	35.5	36.1	35.6	34.8	36.0	35.5
Education and Health Services													
2014	30.7	30.5	30.9	30.9	30.7	30.8	31.0	31.0	31.1	31.0	31.2	31.3	30.9
2015	31.2	31.4	31.5	31.4	31.6	31.6	31.7	31.9	31.7	31.7	31.9	31.6	31.6
2016	32.0	31.7	31.7	31.8	32.0	32.0	31.9	31.8	31.9	32.1	31.9	31.9	31.9
2017	32.2	31.9	31.7	32.1	31.9	32.2	32.3	32.0	32.1	32.3	32.3	32.6	32.1
2018	32.6	32.6	32.4	32.8	32.7	32.7	32.2	32.8	33.1	33.1	33.3	33.7	32.8
Leisure and Hospitality													
2014	26.4	26.0	27.0	26.9	27.3	27.4	28.1	28.2	27.3	27.1	26.9	26.4	27.1
2015	26.0	26.1	26.2	26.9	26.7	26.6	27.4	27.7	27.1	26.8	26.8	26.5	26.8
2016	26.1	26.8	26.6	26.8	26.8	26.6	27.6	27.6	28.1	27.9	27.6	27.0	27.1
2017	26.8	26.5	26.6	27.5	27.0	26.4	27.2	26.9	26.4	26.4	26.1	25.8	26.6
2018	25.2	26.1	25.4	26.0	26.0	25.9	27.2	27.1	26.9	26.9	26.1	26.5	26.3
Other Services													
2014	29.1	29.3	29.5	28.8	29.4	29.7	30.0	29.9	29.8	29.3	29.9	29.5	29.5
2015	29.1	29.1	29.2	28.8	29.2	29.3	30.0	30.9	29.8	30.1	30.3	30.1	29.7
2016	29.7	29.5	28.9	29.8	30.1	30.2	31.1	30.6	30.6	30.5	30.4	30.7	30.2
2017	31.0	30.3	29.7	30.3	29.5	29.2	30.4	29.5	29.3	29.8	30.1	30.3	29.9
2018	30.5	30.1	29.9	30.7	29.8	30.0	32.0	31.3	30.4	29.8	30.1	30.7	30.4

3. Average Hourly Earnings by Selected Industry: New Jersey, 2014–2018

(Dollars, not seasonally adjusted)

Industry and year	January	February	March	April	May	June	July	August	September	October	November	December	Annual average
Total Private													
2014	26.66	27.10	27.09	26.80	26.63	26.74	26.62	26.64	27.02	27.04	27.42	27.15	26.91
2015	27.68	28.13	28.13	27.55	27.61	27.59	27.46	27.72	27.79	27.82	28.12	27.73	27.78
2016	27.82	27.99	27.99	28.08	28.27	27.77	27.75	27.93	28.19	28.72	28.37	28.43	28.11
2017	29.18	28.51	28.23	28.63	29.64	29.38	29.36	29.20	29.44	29.87	29.44	29.16	29.18
2018	29.55	29.61	29.80	29.99	29.52	29.26	29.66	29.35	29.99	29.91	30.12	30.20	29.75
Goods-Producing													
2014	27.60	27.62	28.21	28.49	28.49	28.86	29.32	29.29	29.65	29.49	29.86	30.05	28.93
2015	29.58	29.95	30.01	29.99	30.21	29.98	30.08	29.95	29.98	30.05	30.25	30.12	30.02
2016	30.04	29.95	30.01	30.47	30.98	30.69	30.63	30.66	30.67	31.05	30.75	31.24	30.60
2017	31.53	31.22	31.54	31.60	31.01	31.18	31.47	31.04	31.09	31.05	30.73	31.69	31.26
2018	31.61	31.40	31.14	32.21	31.55	31.89	32.14	32.01	32.28	32.45	32.72	32.54	32.01
Construction													
2014	32.65	32.95	33.61	33.98	34.02	34.46	35.15	35.30	36.19	35.86	36.12	36.08	34.78
2015	35.07	35.75	35.60	35.46	35.54	35.68	35.49	34.91	34.78	34.60	34.67	34.08	35.12
2016	34.29	34.67	34.78	34.41	34.72	34.05	34.37	34.31	34.91	35.30	34.91	35.44	34.68
2017	35.40	35.74	36.61	36.35	35.45	35.88	35.74	35.30	35.45	35.44	34.68	35.82	35.65
2018	36.31	36.32	36.36	37.52	36.73	37.09	37.21	36.78	37.17	37.07	38.12	37.60	37.04
Manufacturing													
2014	26.24	26.15	26.42	26.41	26.22	26.52	26.61	26.51	26.50	26.38	26.50	26.84	26.44
2015	26.74	27.12	27.19	27.01	27.18	26.86	27.10	27.18	27.28	27.39	27.77	27.87	27.23
2016	27.69	27.37	27.23	28.13	28.67	28.60	28.22	28.24	27.93	28.42	28.15	28.58	28.11
2017	29.12	28.48	28.52	28.69	28.23	28.08	28.55	28.27	28.22	28.20	28.22	28.94	28.45
2018	28.55	28.13	27.71	28.21	27.62	27.98	28.38	28.54	28.91	29.23	29.14	29.26	28.48
Trade, Transportation, and Utilities													
2014	23.53	23.75	23.55	23.52	23.38	23.15	23.39	23.53	23.72	23.72	23.94	23.42	23.55
2015	24.25	24.62	24.50	23.99	24.24	24.38	24.52	24.89	25.01	24.92	24.84	23.67	24.49
2016	23.91	24.09	24.18	24.18	24.26	24.34	24.61	24.67	25.00	25.11	24.97	24.71	24.51
2017	26.21	26.42	25.02	24.88	25.40	24.79	25.46	25.64	25.82	26.00	25.65	25.43	25.56
2018	26.03	26.42	26.26	26.12	26.04	25.78	26.39	26.43	26.48	26.41	26.22	26.11	26.22
Financial Activities													
2014	33.07	33.54	34.08	32.45	33.12	33.67	33.61	33.52	34.17	34.07	35.05	34.18	33.72
2015	34.93	36.13	36.41	35.37	35.72	35.67	35.42	36.17	35.94	35.64	36.71	35.91	35.84
2016	36.20	36.52	36.67	36.72	38.45	36.55	37.54	38.90	38.79	40.29	39.64	38.58	37.92
2017	38.60	38.21	37.79	39.34	38.38	38.55	38.60	39.06	38.77	40.17	39.90	39.95	38.95
2018	41.25	41.26	40.85	41.86	42.27	40.64	41.98	41.70	42.03	41.43	42.57	42.42	41.69
Professional and Business Services													
2014	32.92	34.33	33.96	33.24	32.63	32.94	32.32	32.14	32.45	32.52	33.15	32.78	32.94
2015	31.70	32.59	32.70	31.66	31.63	31.78	31.88	32.47	32.61	32.29	32.60	31.62	32.13
2016	32.71	32.87	33.05	33.15	33.21	32.48	32.27	32.40	32.22	33.00	32.45	32.78	32.71
2017	33.70	31.08	31.44	32.75	33.64	33.26	34.27	33.76	33.98	34.97	34.06	34.58	33.48
2018	35.16	35.11	35.38	35.73	34.64	34.34	34.90	34.47	35.55	35.20	35.59	36.07	35.18
Education and Health Services													
2014	25.37	25.44	25.32	25.46	25.67	25.83	25.89	26.08	26.24	26.03	26.23	26.31	25.83
2015	26.95	27.08	27.12	27.10	27.41	27.66	27.66	27.65	27.46	27.69	27.92	28.10	27.49
2016	27.33	27.59	27.34	27.50	27.26	27.14	27.10	27.01	27.36	27.34	27.10	27.38	27.29
2017	27.28	27.28	27.11	27.15	27.05	26.87	27.01	26.93	27.01	27.09	27.10	27.22	27.09
2018	27.13	27.23	27.53	27.20	26.86	27.05	27.75	27.06	27.76	28.01	28.07	28.05	27.48
Leisure and Hospitality													
2014	14.54	14.49	14.53	14.67	14.67	14.55	14.39	14.33	14.69	14.76	14.83	15.06	14.62
2015	15.01	15.10	14.93	14.91	15.05	14.89	14.71	14.65	14.86	14.89	14.90	14.98	14.90
2016	14.96	14.87	14.87	14.88	14.95	14.89	14.77	14.74	15.17	15.48	15.37	15.52	15.04
2017	15.71	15.64	15.62	15.96	15.89	16.78	16.44	16.47	16.78	16.76	16.71	16.93	16.32
2018	16.58	16.33	16.71	16.73	16.88	16.55	16.28	16.33	16.84	16.73	17.07	16.95	16.66
Other Services													
2014	23.32	23.17	23.27	23.02	22.72	22.65	22.60	22.32	23.24	23.04	22.88	22.76	22.91
2015	22.61	22.34	22.47	22.48	21.72	21.71	21.12	20.99	21.77	22.02	22.61	22.56	22.02
2016	22.34	23.65	23.54	23.74	23.63	23.23	22.55	22.38	23.48	24.17	23.74	24.08	23.37
2017	25.91	26.00	25.74	25.85	25.72	25.55	23.94	23.75	25.45	25.16	25.19	25.55	25.31
2018	25.25	25.60	25.38	25.32	25.06	25.26	24.24	24.03	24.50	23.98	23.92	24.37	24.73

4. Average Weekly Earnings by Selected Industry: New Jersey, 2014–2018

(Dollars, not seasonally adjusted)

Industry and year	January	February	March	April	May	June	July	August	September	October	November	December	Annual average
Total Private													
2014	890.44	894.30	915.64	900.48	894.77	906.49	899.76	900.43	913.28	908.54	929.54	917.67	906.87
2015	918.98	942.36	947.98	928.44	930.46	929.78	930.89	948.02	942.08	943.10	956.08	942.82	938.96
2016	934.75	940.46	937.67	949.10	961.18	941.40	946.28	946.83	981.01	1,008.07	978.77	986.52	958.55
2017	1,003.79	963.64	951.35	987.74	1,007.76	993.04	1,001.18	986.96	998.02	1,018.57	1,003.90	991.44	992.12
2018	992.88	1,000.82	1,001.28	1,022.66	1,003.68	991.91	1,014.37	1,000.84	1,034.66	1,022.92	1,027.09	1,050.96	1,014.48
Goods-Producing													
2014	1,062.60	1,024.70	1,103.01	1,105.41	1,108.26	1,128.43	1,137.62	1,127.67	1,156.35	1,138.31	1,149.61	1,180.97	1,119.59
2015	1,132.91	1,135.11	1,164.39	1,157.61	1,169.13	1,166.22	1,161.09	1,156.07	1,142.24	1,171.95	1,167.65	1,177.69	1,158.77
2016	1,153.54	1,144.09	1,155.39	1,182.24	1,192.73	1,199.98	1,200.70	1,192.67	1,193.06	1,220.27	1,190.03	1,221.48	1,187.28
2017	1,194.99	1,167.63	1,176.44	1,216.60	1,200.09	1,209.78	1,211.60	1,207.46	1,212.51	1,210.95	1,201.54	1,239.08	1,203.51
2018	1,220.15	1,199.48	1,195.78	1,259.41	1,255.69	1,269.22	1,275.96	1,270.80	1,275.06	1,278.53	1,282.62	1,317.87	1,257.99
Construction													
2014	1,185.20	1,133.48	1,280.54	1,287.84	1,296.16	1,299.14	1,332.19	1,327.28	1,393.32	1,351.92	1,332.83	1,374.65	1,304.25
2015	1,301.10	1,308.45	1,356.36	1,340.39	1,368.29	1,366.54	1,345.07	1,312.62	1,290.34	1,352.86	1,289.72	1,298.45	1,327.54
2016	1,275.59	1,286.26	1,321.64	1,324.79	1,336.72	1,331.36	1,350.74	1,331.23	1,326.58	1,373.17	1,319.60	1,353.81	1,328.24
2017	1,331.04	1,325.95	1,343.59	1,374.03	1,293.93	1,327.56	1,333.10	1,320.22	1,315.20	1,307.74	1,272.76	1,336.09	1,322.62
2018	1,336.21	1,314.78	1,323.50	1,407.00	1,439.82	1,442.80	1,466.07	1,423.39	1,412.46	1,434.61	1,425.69	1,443.84	1,407.52
Manufacturing													
2014	1,039.10	1,006.78	1,048.87	1,037.91	1,030.45	1,058.15	1,045.77	1,033.89	1,041.45	1,036.73	1,044.10	1,073.60	1,041.74
2015	1,040.19	1,044.12	1,063.13	1,053.39	1,051.87	1,052.91	1,056.90	1,062.74	1,053.01	1,065.47	1,094.14	1,106.44	1,061.97
2016	1,082.68	1,061.96	1,056.52	1,094.26	1,100.93	1,115.40	1,100.58	1,098.54	1,100.44	1,119.75	1,106.30	1,131.77	1,099.10
2017	1,103.65	1,065.15	1,072.35	1,113.17	1,132.02	1,123.20	1,124.87	1,130.80	1,137.27	1,142.10	1,151.38	1,172.07	1,120.93
2018	1,142.00	1,119.57	1,105.63	1,136.86	1,113.09	1,133.19	1,132.36	1,150.16	1,167.96	1,163.35	1,177.26	1,225.99	1,147.74
Trade, Transportation, and Utilities													
2014	795.31	788.50	803.06	804.38	794.92	784.79	799.94	804.73	813.60	804.11	813.96	805.65	800.70
2015	809.95	827.23	828.10	815.66	829.01	828.92	841.04	858.71	867.85	847.28	852.01	809.51	835.11
2016	798.59	809.42	814.87	819.70	834.54	834.86	851.51	848.65	865.00	871.32	861.47	872.26	840.69
2017	899.00	895.64	845.68	865.82	881.38	862.69	891.10	889.71	906.28	907.40	900.32	895.14	886.93
2018	890.23	898.28	895.47	901.14	895.78	886.83	918.37	914.48	929.45	911.15	909.83	908.63	904.59
Financial Activities													
2014	1,177.29	1,244.33	1,240.51	1,171.45	1,192.32	1,245.79	1,199.88	1,213.42	1,236.95	1,243.56	1,296.85	1,240.73	1,224.04
2015	1,267.96	1,336.81	1,358.09	1,294.54	1,303.78	1,305.52	1,310.54	1,352.76	1,311.81	1,311.55	1,375.20	1,325.08	1,322.50
2016	1,343.02	1,358.54	1,364.12	1,358.64	1,461.10	1,352.35	1,381.47	1,447.08	1,439.11	1,531.02	1,458.75	1,415.89	1,410.62
2017	1,470.66	1,402.31	1,386.89	1,494.92	1,412.38	1,414.79	1,443.64	1,421.78	1,426.74	1,530.48	1,480.29	1,486.14	1,448.94
2018	1,530.38	1,534.87	1,511.45	1,590.68	1,555.54	1,503.68	1,574.25	1,522.05	1,601.34	1,537.05	1,575.09	1,628.93	1,555.04
Professional and Business Services													
2014	1,171.95	1,198.12	1,215.77	1,183.34	1,171.42	1,208.90	1,160.29	1,157.04	1,158.47	1,154.46	1,196.72	1,160.41	1,179.25
2015	1,115.84	1,173.24	1,170.66	1,123.93	1,122.87	1,125.01	1,128.55	1,162.43	1,144.61	1,152.75	1,157.30	1,135.16	1,143.83
2016	1,167.75	1,170.17	1,176.58	1,196.72	1,198.88	1,159.54	1,152.04	1,153.44	1,156.70	1,201.20	1,158.47	1,163.69	1,171.02
2017	1,203.09	1,078.48	1,094.11	1,172.45	1,174.04	1,167.43	1,209.73	1,178.22	1,185.90	1,248.43	1,202.32	1,213.76	1,178.50
2018	1,223.57	1,239.38	1,238.30	1,282.71	1,226.26	1,219.07	1,252.91	1,223.69	1,283.36	1,253.12	1,238.53	1,298.52	1,248.89
Education and Health Services													
2014	778.86	775.92	782.39	786.71	788.07	795.56	802.59	808.48	816.06	806.93	818.38	823.50	798.15
2015	840.84	850.31	854.28	850.94	866.16	874.06	876.82	882.04	870.48	877.77	890.65	887.96	868.68
2016	874.56	874.60	866.68	874.50	872.32	868.48	864.49	858.92	872.78	877.61	864.49	873.42	870.55
2017	878.42	870.23	859.39	871.52	862.90	865.21	872.42	861.76	867.02	875.01	875.33	887.37	869.59
2018	884.44	887.70	891.97	892.16	878.32	884.54	893.55	887.57	918.86	927.13	934.73	945.29	901.34
Leisure and Hospitality													
2014	383.86	376.74	392.31	394.62	400.49	398.67	404.36	404.11	401.04	400.00	398.93	397.58	396.20
2015	390.26	394.11	391.17	401.08	401.84	396.07	403.05	405.81	402.71	399.05	399.32	396.97	399.32
2016	390.46	398.52	395.54	398.78	400.66	396.07	407.65	406.82	426.28	431.89	424.21	419.04	407.58
2017	421.03	414.46	415.49	438.90	429.03	442.99	447.17	443.04	442.99	442.46	436.13	436.79	434.11
2018	417.82	426.21	424.43	434.98	438.88	428.65	442.82	442.54	453.00	450.04	445.53	449.18	438.16
Other Services													
2014	678.61	678.88	686.47	662.98	667.97	672.71	678.00	667.37	692.55	675.07	684.11	671.42	675.85
2015	657.95	650.09	656.12	647.42	634.22	636.10	633.60	648.59	648.75	662.80	685.08	679.06	653.99
2016	663.50	697.68	680.31	707.45	711.26	701.55	701.31	684.83	718.49	737.19	721.70	739.26	705.77
2017	803.21	787.80	764.48	783.26	758.74	746.06	727.78	700.63	745.69	749.77	758.22	774.17	756.77
2018	770.13	770.56	758.86	777.32	746.79	757.80	775.68	752.14	744.80	714.60	719.99	748.16	751.79

NEW MEXICO
At a Glance

Population:
  2010 census: 2,059,179
  2018 estimate: 2,095,428

Percent change in population:
  2010–2018: 1.8%

Percent change in total nonfarm employment:
  2010–2018: 4.8%

Industry with the largest growth in employment, 2010–2018 (percent):
  Mining and logging, 32.4%

Industry with the largest decline or smallest growth in employment, 2010–2018 (percent):
  Information, -17.4%

Civilian labor force:
  2010: 936,088
  2018: 940,359

Unemployment rate and rank among states (highest to lowest):
  2010: 8.1%, 32nd
  2018: 4.9%, 4th

Over-the-year change in unemployment rates:
  2016–2017: -0.7%
  2017–2018: -1.0%

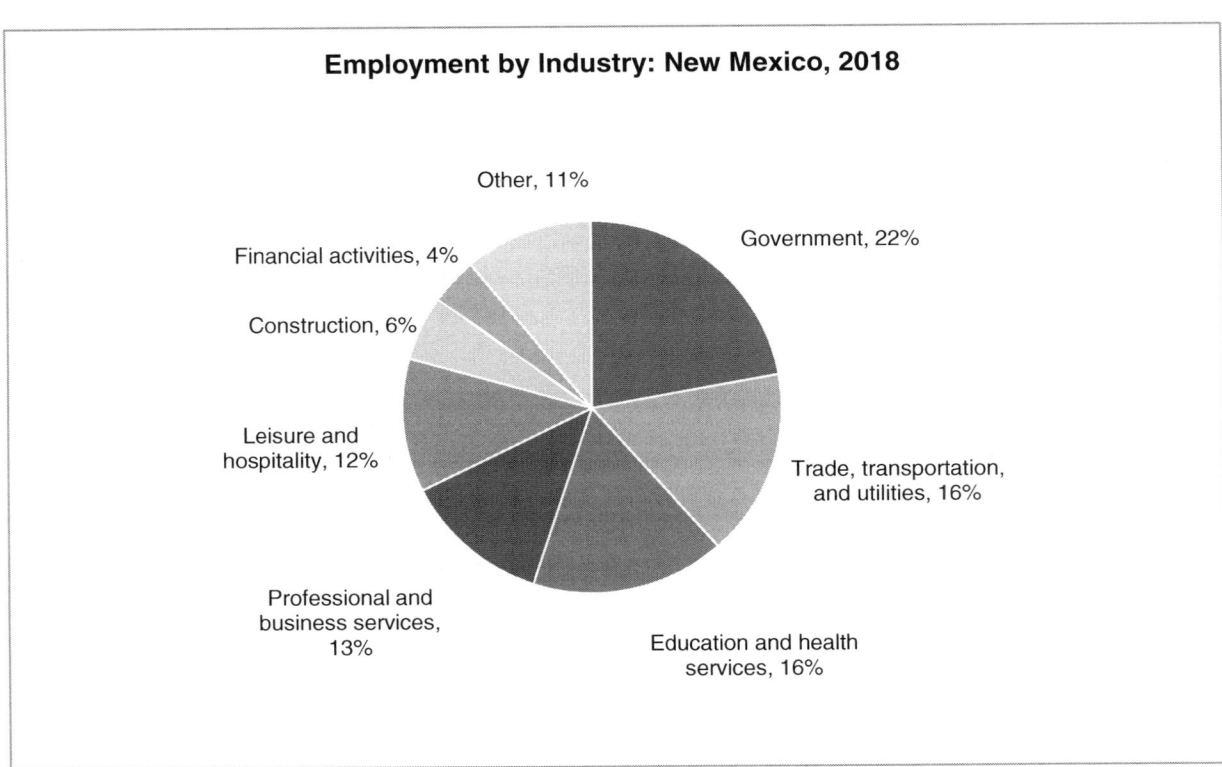

Employment by Industry: New Mexico, 2018

Other, 11%
Government, 22%
Financial activities, 4%
Construction, 6%
Trade, transportation, and utilities, 16%
Leisure and hospitality, 12%
Professional and business services, 13%
Education and health services, 16%

1. Employment by Industry: New Mexico, 2010–2018

(Numbers in thousands, not seasonally adjusted)

Industry and year	January	February	March	April	May	June	July	August	September	October	November	December	Annual average
Total Nonfarm													
2010	789.3	795.9	801.0	807.0	810.6	808.2	801.1	802.6	803.8	807.8	806.4	807.3	803.4
2011	788.0	795.9	800.1	806.5	806.9	804.3	797.9	801.2	807.6	806.5	805.7	805.9	802.2
2012	786.7	796.0	801.4	804.1	806.5	803.8	795.6	801.2	807.5	819.2	818.7	816.0	804.7
2013	799.6	806.0	807.8	815.6	819.2	805.6	801.6	810.7	813.7	820.0	820.3	820.0	811.7
2014	806.0	809.9	811.6	819.2	825.6	812.2	812.1	821.4	824.2	833.3	833.2	833.3	820.2
2015	817.9	822.9	824.7	829.6	830.6	820.4	816.3	825.7	827.9	834.7	835.2	831.5	826.5
2016	818.4	826.4	825.5	832.4	832.9	821.1	817.3	826.7	832.2	832.4	832.9	833.6	827.7
2017	818.4	824.6	827.8	834.4	834.4	829.9	822.8	831.6	836.3	838.2	840.3	840.7	831.6
2018	828.6	836.1	838.0	842.8	843.5	841.0	833.5	843.8	845.3	850.6	851.6	851.5	842.2
Total Private													
2010	595.0	595.3	597.7	601.9	603.8	607.9	608.0	610.0	606.5	606.5	605.5	607.2	603.8
2011	595.5	597.4	600.6	607.1	608.7	611.9	613.2	614.9	613.1	610.0	609.5	608.6	607.5
2012	598.5	601.1	605.4	608.7	610.6	614.9	613.1	616.1	614.0	622.8	622.1	620.0	612.3
2013	609.7	610.9	611.6	619.2	622.1	620.9	623.0	626.6	621.6	625.7	626.4	626.2	620.3
2014	616.9	616.1	617.4	624.5	629.8	628.1	632.1	636.0	631.5	638.6	638.1	638.5	629.0
2015	628.8	629.0	629.7	636.6	638.8	637.5	640.9	642.7	637.4	642.7	641.9	639.6	637.1
2016	631.3	633.6	631.7	638.4	639.9	637.8	642.6	643.9	641.5	641.3	640.6	642.4	638.8
2017	633.9	634.3	636.7	642.5	644.5	647.1	647.5	649.2	647.1	648.3	649.8	650.2	644.3
2018	643.6	646.2	647.5	652.4	655.8	657.7	658.3	661.7	657.5	660.8	660.9	662.2	655.4
Goods Producing													
2010	88.7	88.3	88.4	89.9	90.7	91.7	92.6	93.3	93.1	93.8	92.6	91.9	91.3
2011	89.5	89.3	91.1	92.4	93.1	94.2	95.1	96.0	95.7	95.3	94.4	93.3	93.3
2012	91.4	91.8	92.7	93.3	94.2	95.7	95.6	96.5	96.1	98.9	97.2	96.1	95.0
2013	94.1	94.7	95.0	96.3	96.8	97.6	98.2	99.6	98.9	100.3	99.2	97.5	97.4
2014	96.5	95.6	95.9	96.9	98.0	98.6	100.0	100.4	99.8	102.3	100.9	100.5	98.8
2015	98.9	97.6	96.7	97.2	96.8	97.0	97.7	97.5	96.5	97.3	95.5	94.3	96.9
2016	91.9	91.4	90.3	90.4	89.7	89.7	89.6	89.5	89.6	90.1	89.1	89.1	90.0
2017	88.5	89.2	90.1	91.5	92.5	93.7	94.3	94.6	94.9	95.9	95.6	95.6	93.0
2018	95.3	96.8	97.3	98.4	98.8	99.8	99.3	99.7	99.4	100.1	99.8	99.9	98.7
Service-Providing													
2010	700.6	707.6	712.6	717.1	719.9	716.5	708.5	709.3	710.7	714.0	713.8	715.4	712.2
2011	698.5	706.6	709.0	714.1	713.8	710.1	702.8	705.2	711.9	711.2	711.3	712.6	708.9
2012	695.3	704.2	708.7	710.8	712.3	708.1	700.0	704.7	711.4	720.3	721.5	719.9	709.8
2013	705.5	711.3	712.8	719.3	722.4	708.0	703.4	711.1	714.8	719.7	721.1	722.5	714.3
2014	709.5	714.3	715.7	722.3	727.6	713.6	712.1	721.0	724.4	731.0	732.3	732.8	721.4
2015	719.0	725.3	728.0	732.4	733.8	723.4	718.6	728.2	731.4	737.4	739.7	737.2	729.5
2016	726.5	735.0	735.2	742.0	743.2	731.4	727.7	737.2	742.6	742.3	743.8	744.5	737.6
2017	729.9	735.4	737.7	742.9	741.9	736.2	728.5	737.0	741.4	742.3	744.7	745.1	738.6
2018	733.3	739.3	740.7	744.4	744.7	741.2	734.2	744.1	745.9	750.5	751.8	751.6	743.5
Mining and Logging													
2010	17.4	17.6	17.6	17.9	18.3	18.7	18.9	18.9	18.8	19.2	19.3	19.6	18.5
2011	19.7	20.0	20.2	20.6	21.0	21.4	21.7	22.1	22.3	22.6	22.9	23.2	21.5
2012	23.2	23.4	23.3	23.5	23.8	24.2	24.4	24.5	24.6	25.1	24.9	24.9	24.2
2013	25.2	25.4	25.5	25.8	26.0	26.2	26.4	26.5	26.2	26.4	26.7	26.6	26.1
2014	26.8	26.9	27.2	27.6	27.7	28.0	28.2	28.1	28.2	28.9	29.0	29.0	28.0
2015	28.9	28.1	27.0	26.3	25.7	25.4	25.4	25.3	24.7	24.1	23.4	22.9	25.6
2016	22.1	21.2	20.5	20.0	19.6	19.5	19.2	19.0	19.0	19.1	19.2	19.3	19.8
2017	19.6	20.0	20.2	20.5	20.7	21.0	21.3	21.2	21.5	22.0	22.2	22.4	21.1
2018	23.0	23.8	23.8	24.1	24.3	24.9	24.9	24.9	24.7	25.1	25.1	25.7	24.5
Construction													
2010	42.7	42.2	42.3	43.4	43.5	43.9	44.6	44.6	44.3	44.4	43.9	43.0	43.6
2011	40.9	40.5	41.9	42.7	43.0	43.4	43.8	43.4	42.7	42.2	41.6	40.5	42.2
2012	38.9	39.2	40.2	40.5	40.9	41.8	41.5	41.6	41.1	43.2	42.5	41.8	41.1
2013	40.1	40.5	40.9	41.6	41.8	42.2	42.6	43.2	43.0	44.2	43.8	42.4	42.2
2014	41.7	40.9	40.9	41.4	42.4	42.8	43.6	43.6	43.1	45.1	44.1	43.7	42.8
2015	42.3	42.1	42.2	43.5	43.5	43.7	44.3	43.9	43.7	44.8	44.4	43.7	43.5
2016	42.9	43.3	43.1	43.5	43.1	43.2	43.5	43.4	43.4	43.9	43.5	43.4	43.4
2017	42.8	43.3	44.1	45.2	45.8	46.4	46.3	46.4	46.6	46.7	46.6	45.3	45.5
2018	45.8	46.5	47.0	47.6	47.6	47.8	47.2	47.1	47.0	47.5	47.6	47.3	47.2

1. Employment by Industry: New Mexico, 2010–2018—*Continued*

(Numbers in thousands, not seasonally adjusted)

Industry and year	January	February	March	April	May	June	July	August	September	October	November	December	Annual average
Manufacturing													
2010	28.6	28.5	28.5	28.6	28.9	29.1	29.1	29.8	30.0	30.2	29.4	29.3	29.2
2011	28.9	28.8	29.0	29.1	29.1	29.4	29.6	30.5	30.7	30.5	29.9	29.6	29.6
2012	29.3	29.2	29.2	29.3	29.5	29.7	29.7	30.4	30.4	30.6	29.8	29.4	29.7
2013	28.8	28.8	28.6	28.9	29.0	29.2	29.2	29.9	29.7	29.7	28.7	28.5	29.1
2014	28.0	27.8	27.8	27.9	27.9	27.8	28.2	28.7	28.5	28.3	27.8	27.8	28.0
2015	27.7	27.4	27.5	27.4	27.6	27.9	28.0	28.3	28.1	28.4	27.7	27.7	27.8
2016	26.9	26.9	26.7	26.9	27.0	27.0	26.9	27.1	27.2	27.1	26.4	26.4	26.9
2017	26.1	25.9	25.8	25.8	26.0	26.3	26.7	27.0	26.8	27.2	26.8	26.9	26.4
2018	26.5	26.5	26.5	26.7	26.9	27.1	27.2	27.7	27.7	27.5	27.1	26.9	27.0
Trade, Transportation, and Utilities													
2010	132.0	131.0	131.7	131.9	132.6	132.7	133.0	133.7	132.5	133.5	135.2	136.2	133.0
2011	131.9	131.0	131.3	132.7	133.4	133.4	133.0	133.6	133.6	134.8	136.9	137.6	133.6
2012	134.0	133.3	133.9	134.2	134.9	135.0	135.0	135.2	135.3	137.4	139.4	139.8	135.6
2013	135.2	134.5	134.1	135.3	136.0	136.1	137.0	137.6	136.4	138.0	140.1	141.1	136.8
2014	136.5	135.9	135.9	137.1	137.6	137.3	138.3	138.6	138.3	139.8	141.4	142.5	138.3
2015	138.4	138.0	138.2	139.0	139.7	138.8	139.5	139.8	139.0	140.3	142.0	142.4	139.6
2016	138.3	137.3	137.2	138.4	138.5	137.6	138.7	139.0	138.2	139.0	140.9	140.9	138.7
2017	136.8	135.5	135.3	135.7	136.0	136.0	136.2	136.6	135.8	137.0	139.5	140.0	136.7
2018	137.0	136.3	136.3	136.7	137.5	137.1	137.5	138.4	137.3	137.8	139.9	139.4	137.6
Wholesale Trade													
2010	21.5	21.5	21.5	21.6	21.7	21.9	21.8	21.6	21.2	21.1	21.0	21.0	21.5
2011	20.7	20.6	20.7	20.8	21.0	21.3	21.3	21.3	21.2	21.1	20.9	21.0	21.0
2012	20.8	21.0	21.2	21.2	21.4	21.7	21.8	21.6	21.5	21.7	21.6	21.6	21.4
2013	21.2	21.4	21.3	21.5	21.6	21.7	21.7	21.8	21.4	21.5	21.5	21.5	21.5
2014	21.3	21.4	21.4	21.5	21.7	21.7	21.8	21.8	21.7	21.8	21.6	21.7	21.6
2015	21.3	21.3	21.4	21.5	21.6	21.6	21.7	21.6	21.4	21.6	21.5	21.5	21.5
2016	21.5	21.5	21.4	21.5	21.4	21.3	21.4	21.4	21.1	21.1	21.1	21.1	21.3
2017	20.8	20.8	20.9	20.9	21.1	21.1	21.3	21.1	20.9	20.9	20.9	21.0	21.0
2018	20.9	20.9	20.8	20.9	21.0	21.1	21.2	21.2	21.0	20.9	20.8	20.8	21.0
Retail Trade													
2010	88.9	88.0	88.7	88.7	89.2	89.6	89.8	90.3	89.2	90.1	91.9	92.6	89.8
2011	89.0	88.1	88.5	89.6	90.0	89.9	89.6	89.9	89.8	90.8	93.1	93.4	90.1
2012	90.2	89.2	89.5	89.9	90.2	90.3	90.3	90.3	90.4	91.9	94.0	94.2	90.9
2013	90.4	89.6	89.5	90.5	90.9	91.3	92.1	92.3	91.4	92.7	94.9	95.5	91.8
2014	91.5	90.8	91.0	91.8	91.8	92.0	92.7	92.7	92.2	93.3	95.1	95.6	92.5
2015	92.5	92.0	92.1	92.8	93.4	92.9	93.4	93.6	93.1	94.0	95.8	95.9	93.5
2016	92.3	91.5	91.7	92.8	92.9	92.6	93.3	93.2	92.6	93.5	95.3	94.8	93.0
2017	91.8	90.5	90.2	90.7	90.7	91.0	90.9	91.1	90.2	91.2	93.6	93.5	91.3
2018	91.1	90.4	90.5	90.6	91.2	91.0	91.2	91.5	90.5	91.2	92.6	92.2	91.2
Transportation and Utilities													
2010	21.6	21.5	21.5	21.6	21.7	21.2	21.4	21.8	22.1	22.3	22.3	22.6	21.8
2011	22.2	22.3	22.1	22.3	22.4	22.2	22.1	22.4	22.6	22.9	22.9	23.2	22.5
2012	23.0	23.1	23.2	23.1	23.3	23.0	22.9	23.3	23.4	23.8	23.8	24.0	23.3
2013	23.6	23.5	23.3	23.3	23.5	23.1	23.2	23.5	23.6	23.8	23.7	24.1	23.5
2014	23.7	23.7	23.5	23.8	24.1	23.6	23.8	24.1	24.4	24.7	24.7	25.2	24.1
2015	24.6	24.7	24.7	24.7	24.7	24.3	24.4	24.6	24.5	24.7	24.7	25.0	24.6
2016	24.5	24.3	24.1	24.1	24.2	23.7	24.0	24.4	24.5	24.4	24.5	25.0	24.3
2017	24.2	24.2	24.2	24.1	24.2	23.9	24.0	24.4	24.7	24.9	25.0	25.5	24.4
2018	25.0	25.0	25.0	25.2	25.3	25.0	25.1	25.7	25.8	25.7	26.5	26.4	25.5
Information													
2010	14.2	14.6	14.7	15.3	14.7	15.0	13.8	14.1	14.1	13.7	14.0	14.3	14.4
2011	13.8	13.4	13.6	14.4	14.6	14.3	13.6	13.1	12.4	12.6	13.0	12.6	13.5
2012	13.2	13.7	14.3	13.9	13.6	13.1	13.3	14.0	13.2	13.0	14.0	13.1	13.5
2013	13.1	13.6	12.9	13.6	14.2	13.6	13.2	12.8	12.3	12.4	12.6	12.3	13.1
2014	11.6	12.0	12.2	12.3	12.8	12.7	12.4	12.8	11.9	12.5	13.2	13.0	12.5
2015	11.7	12.2	12.6	13.0	13.5	13.0	13.0	13.7	12.6	12.5	12.7	11.9	12.7
2016	11.5	12.8	12.3	13.4	12.9	12.7	13.3	13.2	13.2	13.3	13.8	13.6	13.0
2017	12.9	11.9	12.3	13.2	12.4	12.9	12.4	12.2	12.0	12.4	11.9	11.7	12.4
2018	11.4	12.0	11.9	11.7	11.8	12.3	11.8	12.2	11.8	12.0	12.0	11.9	11.9

1. Employment by Industry: New Mexico, 2010–2018—*Continued*

(Numbers in thousands, not seasonally adjusted)

Industry and year	January	February	March	April	May	June	July	August	September	October	November	December	Annual average
Financial Activities													
2010	33.3	33.1	33.3	32.9	33.7	33.0	33.0	32.9	32.6	32.7	32.7	33.0	33.0
2011	32.5	32.4	32.4	32.6	32.5	32.5	32.7	32.6	32.5	32.5	32.5	32.7	32.5
2012	32.3	32.5	32.7	32.6	32.6	32.8	32.9	32.8	32.6	33.3	33.3	33.3	32.8
2013	33.0	32.9	32.9	33.0	33.0	33.0	33.2	33.2	33.1	33.3	33.6	33.8	33.2
2014	33.1	33.1	33.2	33.2	33.2	33.2	33.4	33.3	33.0	33.3	33.3	33.4	33.2
2015	33.2	33.2	33.2	33.2	33.3	33.2	33.4	33.4	33.0	33.4	33.5	33.7	33.3
2016	33.5	33.6	33.5	33.6	33.6	33.5	33.5	33.5	33.4	33.6	33.6	33.7	33.6
2017	33.6	33.6	33.6	33.9	33.9	33.9	34.1	34.1	33.9	34.2	34.2	34.3	33.9
2018	34.1	34.1	34.1	34.1	34.1	34.1	34.4	34.4	34.1	33.9	34.3	34.6	34.2
Professional and Business Services													
2010	99.3	99.6	99.1	100.3	99.6	100.6	101.1	101.4	101.1	101.1	100.6	100.7	100.4
2011	98.9	101.0	99.6	100.3	100.0	100.4	101.4	101.2	101.6	99.7	99.0	98.7	100.2
2012	96.6	96.7	97.2	98.5	97.8	99.1	97.9	98.2	98.2	99.3	99.2	98.3	98.1
2013	98.0	98.3	98.1	99.6	99.4	98.9	99.8	99.9	98.8	99.3	98.8	99.0	99.0
2014	98.1	98.0	97.5	99.5	99.3	98.9	100.0	100.6	98.9	99.6	99.3	99.7	99.1
2015	98.4	98.5	98.4	99.4	99.2	99.5	100.8	100.9	99.8	100.7	100.4	100.4	99.7
2016	99.2	99.5	99.3	100.7	100.6	101.2	103.1	103.0	102.8	102.2	101.9	102.3	101.3
2017	102.1	102.8	102.8	104.2	103.8	104.7	105.5	105.8	105.5	104.9	105.7	105.8	104.5
2018	104.5	104.8	104.7	105.9	105.9	106.5	107.2	107.9	107.8	108.2	106.6	107.0	106.4
Education and Health Services													
2010	119.3	119.9	120.4	120.1	120.1	117.8	117.1	117.0	120.2	120.8	121.4	121.6	119.6
2011	120.5	121.0	121.6	122.2	122.2	119.4	119.3	119.9	122.9	123.0	123.1	122.6	121.5
2012	121.8	122.9	122.8	122.9	122.9	120.5	120.1	120.2	123.3	124.5	124.8	125.0	122.6
2013	123.9	124.2	124.7	125.6	125.6	121.6	120.0	121.6	125.0	125.9	126.7	126.4	124.3
2014	126.1	126.7	126.7	127.5	128.1	124.0	123.4	125.5	129.4	131.1	131.4	131.3	127.6
2015	131.0	131.8	132.0	133.4	134.0	130.7	129.6	131.2	134.9	137.1	137.7	136.4	133.3
2016	137.3	138.4	138.0	139.4	139.4	135.2	134.5	136.6	139.3	140.0	139.4	140.4	138.2
2017	139.3	140.1	139.9	140.2	140.1	136.5	135.1	136.6	139.4	139.8	139.9	139.5	138.9
2018	139.3	139.5	139.3	140.3	140.4	137.3	136.1	137.8	140.3	141.4	142.2	142.1	139.7
Leisure and Hospitality													
2010	80.7	81.1	82.4	83.8	84.6	86.2	86.1	86.3	84.9	83.3	81.8	82.4	83.6
2011	81.4	82.0	83.5	84.9	85.2	86.4	86.5	87.3	86.2	84.7	83.3	83.8	84.6
2012	82.0	82.6	84.0	85.4	86.6	88.4	88.3	89.4	87.3	87.9	86.1	86.4	86.2
2013	84.9	85.1	86.2	88.1	89.1	90.0	91.4	91.9	89.3	88.8	87.8	88.6	88.4
2014	87.7	87.3	88.4	90.2	92.5	92.9	93.9	94.4	91.9	91.6	90.5	90.2	91.0
2015	89.7	89.9	90.9	93.6	94.3	94.9	96.2	95.8	93.5	93.5	92.4	93.0	93.1
2016	92.3	93.0	93.5	94.6	97.0	97.5	99.1	98.8	96.8	95.1	94.0	94.8	95.5
2017	93.4	93.6	95.0	95.8	97.4	98.7	99.1	99.1	97.4	96.0	95.1	95.4	96.3
2018	94.3	94.7	95.8	97.2	98.8	99.7	101.0	101.0	98.1	98.6	97.5	99.2	98.0
Other Services													
2010	27.5	27.7	27.7	27.7	27.8	30.9	31.3	31.3	28.0	27.6	27.2	27.1	28.5
2011	27.0	27.3	27.5	27.6	27.7	31.3	31.6	31.2	28.2	27.4	27.3	27.3	28.5
2012	27.2	27.6	27.8	27.9	28.0	30.3	30.0	29.8	28.0	28.5	28.1	28.0	28.4
2013	27.5	27.6	27.7	27.7	28.0	30.1	30.2	30.0	27.8	27.7	27.6	27.5	28.3
2014	27.3	27.5	27.6	27.8	28.3	30.5	30.7	30.4	28.3	28.4	28.1	27.9	28.6
2015	27.5	27.8	27.7	27.8	28.0	30.4	30.7	30.4	28.1	27.9	27.7	27.5	28.5
2016	27.3	27.6	27.6	27.9	28.2	30.4	30.8	30.3	28.2	28.0	27.9	27.6	28.5
2017	27.3	27.6	27.7	28.0	28.4	30.7	30.8	30.2	28.2	28.1	27.9	27.9	28.6
2018	27.7	28.0	28.1	28.1	28.5	30.9	31.0	30.3	28.7	28.8	28.6	28.1	28.9
Government													
2010	194.3	200.6	203.3	205.1	206.8	200.3	193.1	192.6	197.3	201.3	200.9	2C0.1	199.6
2011	192.5	198.5	199.5	199.4	198.2	192.4	184.7	186.3	194.5	196.5	196.2	197.3	194.7
2012	188.2	194.9	196.0	195.4	195.9	188.9	182.5	185.1	193.5	196.4	196.6	196.0	192.5
2013	189.9	195.1	196.2	196.4	197.1	184.7	178.6	184.1	192.1	194.3	193.9	193.8	191.4
2014	189.1	193.8	194.2	194.7	195.8	184.1	180.0	185.4	192.7	194.7	195.1	194.8	191.2
2015	189.1	193.9	195.0	193.0	191.8	182.9	175.4	183.0	190.5	192.0	193.3	191.9	189.3
2016	187.1	192.8	193.8	194.0	193.0	183.3	174.7	182.8	190.7	191.1	192.3	191.2	188.9
2017	184.5	190.3	191.1	191.9	189.9	182.8	175.3	182.4	189.2	189.9	190.5	190.5	187.4
2018	185.0	189.9	190.5	190.4	187.7	183.3	175.2	182.1	187.8	189.8	190.7	189.3	186.8

2. Average Weekly Hours by Selected Industry: New Mexico, 2014–2018

(Not seasonally adjusted)

Industry and year	January	February	March	April	May	June	July	August	September	October	November	December	Annual average
Total Private													
2014	34.4	34.7	35.1	34.7	34.8	35.2	34.7	34.7	34.5	34.5	34.9	34.6	34.7
2015	33.9	34.3	34.3	33.9	33.8	34.1	34.3	34.9	34.2	34.2	34.3	34.0	34.2
2016	33.4	33.5	33.3	33.5	33.7	33.4	33.5	33.6	33.4	33.9	33.4	33.2	33.5
2017	33.5	33.2	33.2	33.9	33.7	34.0	34.0	33.6	33.4	34.1	33.7	33.7	33.7
2018	33.2	33.6	33.7	34.1	33.9	34.0	34.4	33.9	34.1	33.7	33.8	34.0	33.9
Goods-Producing													
2014	42.2	42.1	42.9	42.9	42.1	42.2	40.9	41.2	40.2	40.6	40.5	40.2	41.5
2015	38.9	39.5	39.2	39.9	39.7	39.7	39.7	40.9	39.5	40.8	41.3	41.1	40.0
2016	39.9	39.9	39.6	40.2	39.8	40.0	40.0	40.6	40.2	40.7	40.1	40.3	40.1
2017	40.0	39.1	39.3	38.9	39.8	40.2	39.3	39.6	39.5	39.8	40.1	40.4	39.7
2018	39.0	39.3	39.7	39.9	40.6	40.5	40.3	40.4	40.0	39.9	40.8	40.9	40.1
Construction													
2014	39.0	38.4	39.4	40.0	39.9	40.7	39.1	39.6	38.1	38.5	38.5	38.1	39.1
2015	35.6	37.0	36.1	37.3	37.2	37.3	38.1	39.2	36.3	38.2	38.8	38.1	37.4
2016	37.7	38.2	38.1	38.7	37.7	38.5	38.5	39.2	38.8	39.9	39.1	39.2	38.6
2017	39.3	37.9	38.2	37.7	39.2	39.5	38.6	39.1	38.3	38.8	39.3	39.4	38.8
2018	38.0	38.4	39.1	39.2	40.3	40.1	39.8	40.5	38.9	39.4	40.6	40.4	39.6
Trade, Transportation, and Utilities													
2014	34.1	34.7	35.2	34.6	34.9	35.3	34.9	34.7	34.6	35.0	35.0	35.0	34.8
2015	34.1	34.3	34.7	34.1	34.4	34.6	34.6	35.0	34.8	34.3	33.8	34.3	34.4
2016	33.2	33.3	32.4	33.0	33.6	33.0	33.7	33.8	33.9	33.9	33.5	33.3	33.4
2017	32.5	32.9	32.9	33.2	33.1	33.8	34.1	33.6	33.8	34.3	33.5	33.8	33.5
2018	33.1	34.0	33.8	34.5	34.2	34.2	34.5	34.2	34.4	33.7	33.8	34.2	34.0
Professional and Business Services													
2014	36.2	36.6	36.5	36.3	36.5	36.6	35.5	36.2	35.9	35.6	36.7	35.7	36.2
2015	35.4	35.5	35.6	35.0	34.7	35.0	34.9	35.7	35.2	35.8	36.2	35.1	35.3
2016	35.3	35.4	35.1	35.1	35.2	34.6	35.0	35.4	34.7	35.6	34.6	34.2	35.0
2017	34.9	34.8	34.7	36.4	35.9	35.8	36.0	35.4	35.4	36.1	35.6	35.7	35.6
2018	35.8	36.1	35.7	36.6	35.7	35.5	35.9	35.3	35.8	35.7	35.6	35.1	35.7
Education and Health Services													
2014	32.9	32.7	32.9	32.4	32.9	33.2	33.7	33.3	33.5	33.4	34.0	34.6	33.3
2015	33.9	34.1	33.9	33.6	33.6	34.0	33.3	33.7	33.6	33.2	33.5	33.5	33.7
2016	32.8	32.5	32.6	32.3	32.7	32.5	32.2	32.0	31.8	32.2	32.3	32.2	32.3
2017	33.0	32.1	31.8	32.6	32.5	32.5	32.7	32.3	32.4	32.6	32.2	32.2	32.4
2018	32.1	32.2	32.4	32.7	32.5	32.5	33.4	32.8	33.4	32.9	32.9	33.5	32.8
Leisure and Hospitality													
2014	25.9	26.7	27.5	26.0	26.7	27.3	27.4	27.2	26.6	26.0	26.2	25.7	26.6
2015	25.1	26.0	26.0	25.0	25.4	26.0	26.5	26.9	26.0	26.1	25.8	25.7	25.9
2016	25.4	25.8	26.4	26.0	26.7	26.8	26.5	26.8	26.5	26.9	26.0	25.7	26.3
2017	26.1	26.0	27.0	27.1	26.9	26.8	27.1	26.5	25.6	26.7	25.6	25.6	26.4
2018	25.3	25.6	26.3	26.5	26.5	27.2	27.0	26.5	26.3	26.0	25.4	25.8	26.2

3. Average Hourly Earnings by Selected Industry: New Mexico, 2014–2018

(Dollars, not seasonally adjusted)

Industry and year	January	February	March	April	May	June	July	August	September	October	November	December	Annual average
Total Private													
2014	20.34	20.44	20.45	20.52	20.57	20.70	20.50	20.40	20.44	20.54	20.47	20.48	20.49
2015	20.62	20.65	20.67	20.48	20.52	20.21	20.23	20.32	20.48	20.45	20.57	20.41	20.47
2016	20.59	20.65	20.48	20.46	20.38	20.32	20.44	20.48	20.71	20.94	20.83	20.93	20.60
2017	20.99	20.95	20.91	21.26	21.08	20.86	21.37	21.27	21.37	21.39	21.52	21.57	21.21
2018	21.65	21.56	21.56	21.82	21.73	21.55	21.85	21.96	22.19	22.17	22.23	22.20	21.88
Goods-Producing													
2014	23.84	23.95	23.54	23.55	23.78	23.53	23.52	23.59	23.83	23.64	23.74	23.81	23.69
2015	24.03	23.89	23.89	23.42	23.93	23.50	23.89	23.88	24.11	23.63	23.82	23.62	23.80
2016	23.73	23.47	23.21	22.71	22.17	22.47	22.46	22.39	22.61	22.54	22.96	22.54	22.77
2017	22.56	22.95	22.80	22.65	22.68	22.74	23.16	23.27	23.19	23.15	23.44	23.06	22.98
2018	22.83	23.00	22.99	23.36	23.18	23.56	23.87	24.22	24.33	24.74	25.11	24.52	23.82
Construction													
2014	21.38	21.24	21.08	21.42	21.54	21.23	21.44	21.44	21.53	20.96	21.06	20.73	21.25
2015	21.14	21.14	21.29	20.94	21.38	20.68	20.60	20.94	20.98	20.67	20.74	20.86	20.94
2016	21.11	20.99	21.24	20.62	20.61	20.94	20.93	21.16	21.54	21.52	22.02	21.60	21.19
2017	21.61	22.08	21.89	21.66	21.98	22.18	22.47	22.74	22.61	22.59	22.96	22.86	22.31
2018	22.77	22.91	22.56	22.64	22.72	22.93	22.67	23.27	23.44	23.89	24.28	24.84	23.25
Trade, Transportation, and Utilities													
2014	18.77	18.66	18.57	18.35	18.32	18.23	18.24	17.89	17.73	17.58	17.46	16.94	18.05
2015	17.50	17.41	17.35	17.45	17.15	16.62	16.58	17.26	16.81	16.53	16.91	16.40	16.99
2016	16.58	16.53	16.74	16.45	16.65	16.66	16.73	17.13	17.39	17.61	17.58	17.57	16.97
2017	17.78	17.75	17.71	18.46	18.21	18.25	18.83	18.58	18.76	19.09	18.89	19.13	18.46
2018	19.22	19.04	19.28	19.89	20.04	19.67	20.05	19.82	20.19	19.70	19.31	19.68	19.66
Professional and Business Services													
2014	25.80	26.05	26.26	26.08	25.72	25.99	25.80	26.03	26.21	26.14	26.00	26.16	26.02
2015	26.26	26.47	26.38	26.29	26.58	26.31	26.18	26.30	26.27	26.46	26.32	26.59	26.37
2016	27.15	27.09	26.49	26.75	27.03	27.16	27.26	27.37	27.45	27.91	27.68	27.77	27.26
2017	28.29	28.38	28.37	29.12	28.65	27.80	28.69	28.46	28.04	28.02	28.12	27.99	28.33
2018	28.22	27.86	27.65	27.64	27.13	27.35	27.96	27.68	28.38	28.44	28.75	28.46	27.96
Education and Health Services													
2014	20.38	20.63	20.75	21.37	21.28	21.61	21.52	21.18	21.23	21.51	20.99	21.19	21.14
2015	20.79	20.88	21.01	20.44	20.33	20.13	20.45	20.53	20.74	20.67	20.65	20.59	20.60
2016	20.31	20.74	20.55	20.79	20.60	20.24	20.28	20.39	20.47	20.86	20.40	21.14	20.57
2017	20.55	20.48	20.48	20.35	20.34	20.31	20.56	20.52	20.50	20.43	20.65	21.05	20.52
2018	21.40	21.02	21.04	21.05	21.13	21.01	21.10	21.26	20.99	21.10	21.22	22.02	21.20
Leisure and Hospitality													
2014	12.13	12.06	12.11	11.97	12.04	12.38	12.63	12.52	12.14	12.38	12.43	12.59	12.29
2015	12.41	12.73	12.72	12.49	12.79	12.70	13.06	12.84	13.05	13.08	13.03	13.17	12.84
2016	13.29	13.40	13.31	13.18	13.11	13.58	13.99	13.70	13.52	13.51	13.22	13.30	13.43
2017	13.09	13.03	13.08	12.84	12.82	13.18	13.31	13.39	13.23	13.14	13.32	13.42	13.15
2018	13.43	13.61	13.40	13.34	13.61	13.71	13.88	13.97	13.55	13.79	13.71	13.75	13.65

4. Average Weekly Earnings by Selected Industry: New Mexico, 2014–2018

(Dollars, not seasonally adjusted)

Industry and year	January	February	March	April	May	June	July	August	September	October	November	December	Annual average
Total Private													
2014	699.70	709.27	717.80	712.04	715.84	728.64	711.35	707.88	705.18	708.63	714.40	708.61	711.00
2015	699.02	708.30	708.98	694.27	693.58	689.16	693.89	709.17	700.42	699.39	705.55	693.94	700.07
2016	687.71	691.78	681.98	685.41	686.81	678.69	684.74	688.13	691.71	709.87	695.72	694.88	690.10
2017	703.17	695.54	694.21	720.71	710.40	709.24	726.58	714.67	713.76	729.40	725.22	726.91	714.78
2018	718.78	724.42	726.57	744.06	736.65	732.70	751.64	744.44	756.68	747.13	751.37	754.80	741.73
Goods-Producing													
2014	1,006.05	1,008.30	1,009.87	1,010.30	1,001.14	992.97	961.97	971.91	957.97	959.78	961.47	957.16	983.14
2015	934.77	943.66	936.49	934.46	950.02	932.95	948.43	976.69	952.35	964.10	983.77	970.78	952.00
2016	946.83	936.45	919.12	912.94	882.37	898.80	898.40	909.03	908.92	917.38	920.70	908.36	913.08
2017	902.40	897.35	896.04	881.09	902.66	914.15	910.19	921.49	916.01	921.37	939.94	931.62	912.31
2018	890.37	903.90	912.70	932.06	941.11	954.18	961.96	978.49	973.20	987.13	1,024.49	1,002.87	955.18
Construction													
2014	833.82	815.62	830.55	856.80	859.45	864.06	838.30	849.02	820.29	806.96	810.81	789.81	830.88
2015	752.58	782.18	768.57	781.06	795.34	771.36	784.86	820.85	761.57	789.59	804.71	794.77	783.16
2016	795.85	801.82	809.24	797.99	777.00	806.19	805.81	829.47	835.75	858.65	860.98	846.72	817.93
2017	849.27	836.83	836.20	816.58	861.62	876.11	867.34	889.13	865.96	876.49	902.33	900.68	865.63
2018	865.26	879.74	882.10	887.49	915.62	919.49	902.27	942.44	911.82	941.27	985.77	1,003.54	920.70
Trade, Transportation, and Utilities													
2014	640.06	647.50	653.66	634.91	639.37	643.52	636.58	620.78	613.46	615.30	611.10	592.90	628.14
2015	596.75	597.16	602.05	595.05	589.96	575.05	573.67	604.10	584.99	566.98	571.56	562.52	584.46
2016	550.46	550.45	542.38	542.85	559.44	549.78	563.80	578.99	589.52	596.98	588.93	585.08	566.80
2017	577.85	583.98	582.66	612.87	602.75	616.85	642.10	624.29	634.09	654.79	632.82	646.59	618.41
2018	636.18	647.36	651.66	686.21	685.37	672.71	691.73	677.84	694.54	663.89	652.68	673.06	668.44
Professional and Business Services													
2014	933.96	953.43	958.49	946.70	938.78	951.23	915.90	942.29	940.94	930.58	954.20	933.91	941.92
2015	929.60	939.69	939.13	920.15	922.33	920.85	913.68	938.91	924.70	947.27	952.78	933.31	930.86
2016	958.40	958.99	929.80	938.93	951.46	939.74	954.10	968.90	952.52	993.60	957.73	949.73	954.10
2017	987.32	987.62	984.44	1,059.97	1,028.54	995.24	1,032.84	1,007.48	992.62	1,011.52	1,001.07	999.24	1,008.55
2018	1,010.28	1,005.75	987.11	1,011.62	968.54	970.93	1,003.76	977.10	1,016.00	1,015.31	1,023.50	998.95	998.17
Education and Health Services													
2014	670.50	674.60	682.68	692.39	700.11	717.45	725.22	705.29	711.21	718.43	713.66	733.17	703.96
2015	704.78	712.01	712.24	686.78	683.09	684.42	680.99	691.86	696.86	686.24	691.78	689.77	694.22
2016	666.17	674.05	669.93	671.52	673.62	657.80	653.02	652.48	650.95	671.69	658.92	680.71	664.41
2017	678.15	657.41	651.26	663.41	661.05	660.08	672.31	662.80	664.20	666.02	664.93	677.81	664.85
2018	686.94	676.84	681.70	688.34	686.73	682.83	704.74	697.33	701.07	694.19	698.14	737.67	695.36
Leisure and Hospitality													
2014	314.17	322.00	333.03	311.22	321.47	337.97	346.06	340.54	322.92	321.88	325.67	323.56	326.91
2015	311.49	330.98	330.72	312.25	324.87	330.20	346.09	345.40	339.30	341.39	336.17	338.47	332.56
2016	337.57	345.72	351.38	342.68	350.04	363.94	370.74	367.16	358.28	363.42	343.72	341.81	353.21
2017	341.65	338.78	353.16	347.96	344.86	353.22	360.70	354.84	338.69	350.84	340.99	343.55	347.16
2018	339.78	348.42	352.42	353.51	360.67	372.91	374.76	370.21	356.37	358.54	348.23	354.75	357.63

NEW YORK
At a Glance

Population:
  2010 census: 19,378,102
  2018 estimate: 19,542,209

Percent change in population:
  2010–2018: 0.8%

Percent change in total nonfarm employment:
  2010–2018: 13.2%

Industry with the largest growth in employment, 2010–2018 (percent):
  Construction, 29.9%

Industry with the largest decline or smallest growth in employment, 2010–2018 (percent):
  Manufacturing, -3.1%

Civilian labor force:
  2010: 9,595,362
  2018: 9,574,706

Unemployment rate and rank among states (highest to lowest):
  2010: 8.6%, 27th
  2018: 4.1%, 16th

Over-the-year change in unemployment rates:
  2016–2017: -0.2%
  2017–2018: -0.6%

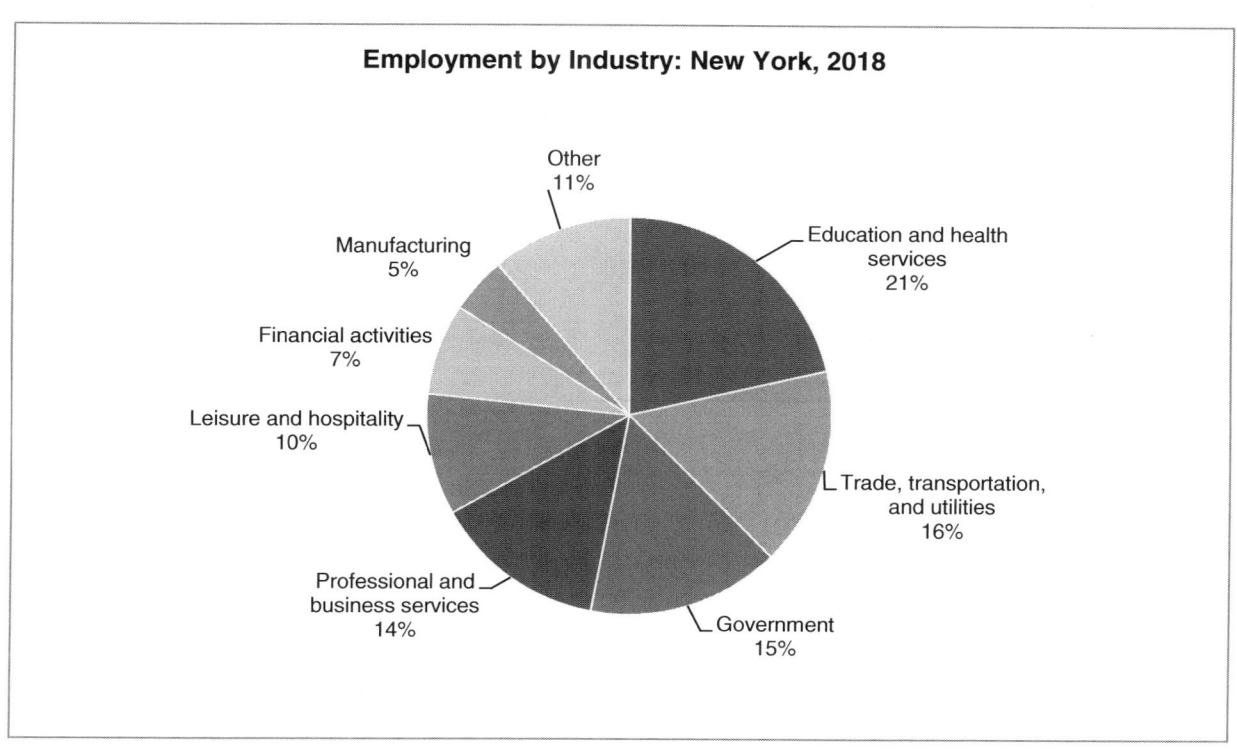

Employment by Industry: New York, 2018

- Other 11%
- Manufacturing 5%
- Financial activities 7%
- Leisure and hospitality 10%
- Professional and business services 14%
- Education and health services 21%
- Trade, transportation, and utilities 16%
- Government 15%

1. Employment by Industry: New York, 2010–2018

(Numbers in thousands, not seasonally adjusted)

Industry and year	January	February	March	April	May	June	July	August	September	October	November	December	Annual average
Total Nonfarm													
2010	8,324.0	8,372.6	8,428.2	8,542.1	8,625.7	8,628.0	8,526.0	8,487.5	8,533.1	8,662.0	8,696.9	8,707.2	8,544.4
2011	8,462.2	8,525.3	8,570.3	8,686.3	8,717.8	8,741.2	8,692.6	8,660.2	8,713.5	8,811.3	8,850.1	8,868.1	8,691.6
2012	8,590.6	8,671.9	8,727.5	8,785.8	8,866.3	8,882.5	8,791.2	8,780.4	8,828.0	8,953.5	8,953.9	9,005.6	8,819.8
2013	8,693.7	8,770.2	8,828.9	8,922.7	8,977.9	9,001.8	8,948.6	8,925.2	8,981.3	9,108.2	9,154.9	9,164.5	8,956.5
2014	8,831.0	8,919.9	8,973.1	9,069.4	9,153.1	9,188.3	9,136.1	9,121.0	9,146.2	9,274.5	9,319.3	9,337.9	9,122.5
2015	9,018.3	9,089.2	9,135.7	9,230.3	9,324.6	9,357.0	9,318.2	9,287.7	9,301.5	9,445.6	9,488.5	9,498.2	9,291.2
2016	9,176.5	9,256.7	9,317.1	9,421.1	9,446.7	9,493.2	9,458.7	9,429.2	9,451.5	9,557.9	9,599.8	9,611.6	9,435.0
2017	9,306.0	9,395.3	9,431.8	9,499.1	9,583.1	9,639.0	9,573.3	9,551.1	9,570.7	9,688.1	9,736.6	9,746.8	9,560.1
2018	9,409.0	9,520.9	9,567.0	9,634.6	9,710.1	9,774.0	9,698.5	9,666.0	9,668.0	9,780.5	9,810.1	9,799.9	9,669.9
Total Private													
2010	6,823.1	6,848.1	6,898.6	7,006.0	7,048.1	7,073.5	7,053.1	7,046.3	7,070.0	7,155.4	7,181.1	7,195.3	7,033.2
2011	6,964.7	7,005.7	7,047.8	7,157.2	7,193.6	7,228.3	7,216.0	7,194.7	7,240.7	7,300.4	7,334.2	7,353.9	7,186.4
2012	7,122.4	7,170.5	7,223.1	7,281.5	7,358.0	7,386.3	7,340.3	7,347.1	7,376.2	7,461.9	7,461.5	7,507.3	7,336.3
2013	7,242.1	7,287.3	7,343.1	7,437.3	7,486.5	7,521.1	7,506.3	7,498.6	7,544.2	7,627.8	7,667.6	7,678.3	7,486.7
2014	7,396.5	7,450.0	7,498.4	7,589.8	7,672.3	7,714.5	7,698.4	7,696.5	7,707.2	7,796.9	7,833.1	7,852.6	7,658.9
2015	7,580.0	7,619.8	7,660.9	7,753.7	7,840.0	7,878.5	7,874.3	7,856.3	7,852.7	7,963.3	7,995.3	8,004.2	7,823.3
2016	7,725.7	7,777.2	7,830.2	7,930.3	7,956.6	8,007.8	8,006.7	7,988.2	7,991.3	8,067.0	8,101.9	8,109.2	7,957.7
2017	7,843.8	7,905.0	7,937.2	8,003.1	8,086.5	8,147.6	8,114.9	8,104.9	8,106.2	8,191.7	8,234.1	8,243.1	8,076.5
2018	7,948.7	8,030.3	8,072.4	8,137.2	8,206.8	8,269.0	8,234.2	8,214.3	8,197.0	8,276.5	8,297.1	8,288.3	8,181.0
Goods Producing													
2010	737.5	730.0	739.6	762.4	773.3	783.9	789.4	794.1	789.5	786.4	780.3	764.6	769.3
2011	729.3	726.9	736.8	757.8	774.3	788.1	796.7	802.1	796.6	793.5	788.1	776.4	772.2
2012	746.6	743.2	752.9	767.5	780.3	794.5	798.3	801.4	796.7	796.2	787.3	783.9	779.1
2013	755.2	749.7	757.8	776.3	792.2	801.4	806.9	811.9	806.3	808.9	803.3	790.0	788.3
2014	757.7	751.4	762.6	784.4	804.6	818.8	826.4	830.2	825.1	827.9	823.0	812.2	802.0
2015	777.1	770.5	782.3	806.8	826.9	839.6	847.0	849.1	841.8	847.2	842.4	832.1	821.9
2016	800.1	795.2	807.3	825.3	837.9	848.5	854.9	856.7	849.9	850.5	844.4	830.3	833.4
2017	802.2	801.5	807.5	825.9	841.7	854.3	858.5	860.5	855.4	856.8	852.6	840.5	838.1
2018	806.8	812.3	819.3	834.8	852.7	865.8	869.9	869.9	863.8	865.2	857.2	844.8	846.9
Service-Providing													
2010	7,586.5	7,642.6	7,688.6	7,779.7	7,852.4	7,844.1	7,736.6	7,693.4	7,743.6	7,875.6	7,916.6	7,942.6	7,775.2
2011	7,732.9	7,798.4	7,833.5	7,928.5	7,943.5	7,953.1	7,895.9	7,858.1	7,916.9	8,017.8	8,062.0	8,091.7	7,919.4
2012	7,844.0	7,928.7	7,974.6	8,018.3	8,086.0	8,088.0	7,992.9	7,979.0	8,031.3	8,157.3	8,166.6	8,221.7	8,040.7
2013	7,938.5	8,020.5	8,071.1	8,146.4	8,185.7	8,200.4	8,141.7	8,113.3	8,175.0	8,299.3	8,351.6	8,374.5	8,168.2
2014	8,073.3	8,168.5	8,210.5	8,285.0	8,348.5	8,369.5	8,309.7	8,290.8	8,321.1	8,446.6	8,496.3	8,525.7	8,320.5
2015	8,241.2	8,318.7	8,353.4	8,423.5	8,497.7	8,517.4	8,471.2	8,438.6	8,459.7	8,598.4	8,646.1	8,666.1	8,469.3
2016	8,376.4	8,461.5	8,509.8	8,595.8	8,608.8	8,644.7	8,603.8	8,572.5	8,601.6	8,707.4	8,755.4	8,781.3	8,601.6
2017	8,503.8	8,593.8	8,624.3	8,673.2	8,741.4	8,784.7	8,714.8	8,690.6	8,715.3	8,831.3	8,884.0	8,906.3	8,722.0
2018	8,602.2	8,708.6	8,747.7	8,799.8	8,857.4	8,908.2	8,828.6	8,796.1	8,804.2	8,915.3	8,952.9	8,955.1	8,823.0
Mining and Logging													
2010	4.4	4.5	4.7	5.3	5.6	5.7	5.7	5.8	5.8	5.6	5.5	5.1	5.3
2011	4.3	4.4	4.5	5.1	5.4	5.6	5.7	5.8	5.8	5.8	5.6	5.4	5.3
2012	4.5	4.6	4.9	5.3	5.5	5.6	5.7	5.6	5.6	5.6	5.3	5.0	5.3
2013	4.3	4.3	4.5	5.0	5.4	5.3	5.3	5.3	5.4	5.5	5.3	5.0	5.1
2014	4.4	4.5	4.6	5.0	5.4	5.6	5.7	5.7	5.6	5.7	5.5	5.2	5.2
2015	4.6	4.6	4.7	5.1	5.5	5.7	5.8	5.7	5.7	5.6	5.5	5.3	5.3
2016	4.4	4.5	4.7	5.0	5.3	5.5	5.5	5.5	5.4	5.2	5.2	4.8	5.1
2017	4.2	4.4	4.5	4.8	5.1	5.2	5.4	5.4	5.3	5.4	5.3	5.1	5.0
2018	4.6	4.7	4.8	5.2	5.5	5.7	5.8	5.8	5.8	5.8	5.6	5.2	5.4
Construction													
2010	280.3	273.2	281.3	302.6	310.8	317.6	325.6	329.6	324.3	320.3	315.3	300.4	306.8
2011	273.6	270.8	279.1	296.1	310.1	319.6	329.8	333.6	328.8	325.9	321.4	310.2	308.3
2012	288.1	284.0	291.7	305.5	315.0	325.0	330.6	333.3	328.8	328.9	323.4	320.0	314.5
2013	299.1	294.4	300.7	316.5	330.1	336.3	344.1	347.4	342.8	345.5	340.4	327.5	327.1
2014	304.1	298.3	308.5	328.7	346.2	355.8	365.2	367.6	364.0	366.4	361.8	351.2	343.2
2015	323.7	316.7	326.2	349.3	366.9	375.2	382.2	384.7	378.9	383.6	379.7	370.2	361.4
2016	345.7	340.3	351.1	370.0	381.7	388.7	395.6	398.2	393.4	393.3	388.9	375.8	376.9
2017	355.5	353.8	358.4	377.5	391.5	400.2	405.9	408.3	404.9	405.4	401.8	390.5	387.8
2018	364.2	368.3	374.3	388.7	404.6	413.7	417.3	417.4	413.6	414.2	408.5	395.6	398.4

1. Employment by Industry: New York, 2010–2018—*Continued*

(Numbers in thousands, not seasonally adjusted)

Industry and year	January	February	March	April	May	June	July	August	September	October	November	December	Annual average
Manufacturing													
2010	452.8	452.3	453.6	454.5	456.9	460.6	458.1	458.7	459.4	460.5	459.5	459.1	457.2
2011	451.4	451.7	453.2	456.6	458.8	462.9	461.2	462.7	462.0	461.8	461.1	460.8	458.7
2012	454.0	454.6	456.3	456.7	459.8	463.9	462.0	462.5	462.3	461.7	458.6	458.9	459.3
2013	451.8	451.0	452.6	454.8	456.7	459.8	457.5	459.2	458.1	457.9	457.6	457.5	456.2
2014	449.2	448.6	449.5	450.7	453.0	457.4	455.5	456.9	455.5	455.8	455.7	455.8	453.6
2015	448.8	449.2	451.4	452.4	454.5	458.7	459.0	458.7	457.2	458.0	457.2	456.6	455.1
2016	450.0	450.4	451.5	450.3	450.9	454.3	453.8	453.0	451.1	452.0	450.3	449.7	451.4
2017	442.5	443.3	444.6	443.6	445.1	448.9	447.2	446.8	445.2	446.0	445.5	444.9	445.3
2018	438.0	439.3	440.2	440.9	442.6	446.4	446.8	446.7	444.4	445.2	443.1	444.0	443.1
Trade, Transportation, and Utilities													
2010	1,435.9	1,416.9	1,423.8	1,440.3	1,453.7	1,472.9	1,454.6	1,455.6	1,463.5	1,480.9	1,505.9	1,525.6	1,460.8
2011	1,464.5	1,447.3	1,449.5	1,461.7	1,474.2	1,493.9	1,474.5	1,478.4	1,488.3	1,500.9	1,531.5	1,554.5	1,484.9
2012	1,494.5	1,474.2	1,478.9	1,481.3	1,503.0	1,520.2	1,492.1	1,497.2	1,508.5	1,523.3	1,553.1	1,574.4	1,508.4
2013	1,501.9	1,478.8	1,489.2	1,500.6	1,516.4	1,536.9	1,522.6	1,520.0	1,532.8	1,547.6	1,585.0	1,604.1	1,528.0
2014	1,531.6	1,513.4	1,517.9	1,529.6	1,545.3	1,563.6	1,547.3	1,547.5	1,556.3	1,574.0	1,607.2	1,627.5	1,555.1
2015	1,555.8	1,535.7	1,537.0	1,544.4	1,564.3	1,581.3	1,562.1	1,560.6	1,567.6	1,580.6	1,612.5	1,627.7	1,569.1
2016	1,557.5	1,540.8	1,543.2	1,553.7	1,561.2	1,576.3	1,558.1	1,554.8	1,563.7	1,579.1	1,609.5	1,627.3	1,568.8
2017	1,562.3	1,540.0	1,540.5	1,544.5	1,562.7	1,577.2	1,558.1	1,554.7	1,563.3	1,576.6	1,612.1	1,628.9	1,568.4
2018	1,559.8	1,540.9	1,539.5	1,543.4	1,558.4	1,572.0	1,551.1	1,545.5	1,552.0	1,570.0	1,608.1	1,615.2	1,563.0
Wholesale Trade													
2010	316.7	316.3	318.0	320.1	322.1	324.6	325.2	325.2	324.7	326.4	327.3	328.5	322.9
2011	322.1	321.6	323.0	325.6	327.4	330.1	330.2	330.6	329.2	330.0	330.0	331.6	327.6
2012	326.7	327.4	328.6	329.6	331.1	333.6	332.7	332.3	330.4	332.5	332.1	333.8	330.9
2013	328.1	328.2	328.9	330.7	332.1	335.3	335.5	334.9	333.5	333.6	334.6	335.9	332.6
2014	330.7	330.2	330.5	332.9	334.9	337.2	337.3	337.2	335.5	336.8	338.2	339.3	335.1
2015	334.1	333.6	334.4	334.9	337.0	339.5	339.9	339.3	337.2	338.2	338.5	339.8	337.2
2016	333.4	333.5	333.1	333.5	334.1	336.1	336.1	335.4	333.2	333.9	334.2	335.2	334.3
2017	329.3	329.7	330.2	332.4	334.2	336.8	336.0	335.3	334.2	333.9	334.7	335.5	333.5
2018	328.6	328.7	329.4	329.0	330.4	332.8	332.5	331.2	329.4	328.3	327.6	326.5	329.5
Retail Trade													
2010	859.8	843.5	847.7	856.7	866.2	881.3	877.5	879.4	872.5	886.9	908.7	923.5	875.3
2011	877.8	863.1	863.2	873.4	881.5	895.7	892.8	897.0	892.3	904.5	932.1	949.1	893.5
2012	905.6	885.4	887.6	891.1	905.0	916.7	912.0	912.7	908.9	921.3	949.8	962.0	913.2
2013	908.9	892.7	896.3	903.4	915.2	930.1	929.4	930.6	926.1	938.2	971.3	984.6	927.2
2014	927.7	912.4	914.5	921.4	931.0	945.5	942.9	945.5	939.1	953.1	980.8	993.9	942.3
2015	939.9	922.9	923.1	928.1	941.1	953.0	948.1	948.1	941.6	952.0	979.4	986.4	947.0
2016	937.0	922.0	923.1	931.0	936.8	947.6	945.4	944.9	938.3	951.2	977.0	986.1	945.0
2017	940.5	919.9	918.5	924.5	934.5	943.7	940.2	938.4	930.3	942.5	970.9	979.4	940.3
2018	933.6	918.1	915.6	918.8	929.0	937.3	932.2	929.9	920.4	934.9	968.8	972.5	934.3
Transportation and Utilities													
2010	259.4	257.1	258.1	263.5	265.4	267.0	251.9	251.0	266.3	267.6	269.9	273.6	262.6
2011	264.6	262.6	263.3	262.7	265.3	268.1	251.5	250.8	266.8	266.4	269.4	273.8	263.8
2012	262.2	261.4	262.7	260.6	266.9	269.9	247.4	252.2	269.2	269.5	271.2	278.6	264.3
2013	264.9	257.9	264.0	266.5	269.1	271.5	257.7	254.5	273.2	275.8	279.1	283.6	268.2
2014	273.2	270.8	272.9	275.3	279.4	280.9	267.1	264.8	281.7	284.1	288.2	294.3	277.7
2015	281.8	279.2	279.5	281.4	286.2	288.8	274.1	273.2	288.8	290.4	294.6	301.5	285.0
2016	287.1	285.3	287.0	289.2	290.3	292.6	276.6	274.5	292.2	294.0	298.3	306.0	289.4
2017	292.5	290.4	291.8	287.6	294.0	296.7	281.9	281.0	298.8	300.2	306.5	314.0	294.6
2018	297.6	294.1	294.5	295.6	299.0	301.9	286.4	284.4	302.2	306.8	311.7	316.2	299.2
Information													
2010	249.8	250.0	251.5	250.8	252.2	253.9	255.2	255.5	254.4	256.4	257.2	259.2	253.8
2011	252.0	252.8	254.1	256.5	256.8	258.3	259.3	244.1	258.8	257.9	258.9	260.1	255.8
2012	255.2	256.1	256.8	258.8	261.0	262.6	260.4	260.1	258.9	260.5	261.4	261.7	259.5
2013	253.8	255.3	256.8	258.8	260.6	263.1	262.8	264.2	263.5	265.6	267.3	268.0	261.7
2014	260.1	263.3	264.2	262.6	263.2	267.2	265.2	266.3	264.1	267.1	267.2	263.3	265.0
2015	261.8	263.2	263.5	262.9	263.8	265.9	268.5	267.0	266.0	270.4	271.4	272.5	266.4
2016	262.3	263.4	265.0	266.9	255.4	269.0	273.9	272.9	271.0	272.7	273.6	275.0	268.4
2017	264.5	268.0	269.0	266.4	268.1	272.3	274.1	276.5	276.1	277.0	279.4	280.4	272.7
2018	265.3	272.9	275.5	270.8	273.0	278.9	278.2	279.4	277.0	278.1	278.6	275.0	275.2

1. Employment by Industry: New York, 2010–2018—*Continued*

(Numbers in thousands, not seasonally adjusted)

Industry and year	January	February	March	April	May	June	July	August	September	October	November	December	Annual average
Financial Activities													
2010	655.9	656.7	658.4	662.9	664.8	674.3	677.3	677.5	670.2	671.3	672.9	677.4	668.3
2011	671.2	672.0	673.4	675.3	676.7	687.5	692.1	693.3	683.7	682.7	682.7	685.9	681.4
2012	676.3	678.0	677.5	676.8	678.1	688.0	690.7	689.6	679.6	682.3	681.9	686.8	682.1
2013	671.0	672.9	672.6	674.5	675.3	685.5	690.5	689.3	680.2	682.4	684.8	689.5	680.7
2014	679.0	680.9	682.6	682.4	686.4	699.0	703.8	703.6	693.8	695.4	696.8	702.1	692.2
2015	691.9	692.9	694.0	695.0	698.3	710.2	715.9	715.3	704.7	708.5	709.3	712.4	704.0
2016	704.8	705.3	705.6	705.3	708.0	718.4	722.9	722.9	709.4	710.3	711.7	716.1	711.7
2017	704.7	706.4	707.3	704.8	708.1	721.9	725.6	725.9	714.3	715.7	717.4	721.3	714.5
2018	709.5	712.5	711.9	712.2	715.2	729.5	733.3	732.0	720.0	719.6	716.9	716.6	719.1
Professional and Business Services													
2010	1,059.7	1,065.4	1,073.0	1,096.6	1,097.0	1,111.5	1,115.7	1,115.2	1,105.4	1,117.5	1,119.4	1,120.7	1,099.8
2011	1,093.1	1,098.8	1,107.3	1,130.9	1,131.4	1,149.6	1,155.5	1,154.3	1,149.6	1,150.7	1,157.3	1,157.6	1,136.3
2012	1,127.4	1,133.4	1,144.7	1,160.5	1,166.5	1,184.2	1,184.6	1,187.4	1,180.1	1,193.9	1,196.8	1,199.6	1,171.6
2013	1,162.6	1,168.9	1,177.8	1,194.6	1,198.7	1,214.9	1,220.7	1,219.6	1,209.9	1,221.8	1,224.8	1,225.0	1,203.3
2014	1,184.6	1,193.2	1,198.4	1,220.6	1,229.5	1,243.2	1,250.7	1,251.5	1,240.7	1,251.9	1,258.4	1,259.4	1,231.8
2015	1,223.6	1,230.4	1,234.4	1,256.8	1,266.5	1,284.5	1,291.2	1,288.6	1,275.2	1,290.4	1,293.2	1,290.5	1,268.8
2016	1,253.3	1,259.1	1,268.0	1,287.6	1,289.9	1,307.2	1,316.2	1,314.0	1,306.1	1,313.5	1,318.1	1,314.2	1,295.6
2017	1,275.9	1,285.2	1,290.0	1,305.1	1,314.4	1,335.5	1,338.5	1,334.5	1,326.6	1,331.5	1,338.5	1,338.3	1,317.8
2018	1,297.3	1,307.3	1,315.5	1,329.4	1,339.5	1,363.3	1,364.7	1,363.5	1,347.6	1,355.9	1,355.9	1,348.4	1,340.7
Education and Health Services													
2010	1,656.1	1,693.3	1,704.3	1,710.8	1,694.3	1,641.0	1,607.5	1,595.7	1,659.4	1,722.7	1,737.2	1,740.7	1,680.3
2011	1,689.0	1,731.9	1,738.8	1,752.9	1,726.7	1,668.4	1,644.1	1,633.5	1,695.8	1,755.8	1,766.0	1,771.1	1,714.5
2012	1,718.4	1,764.6	1,775.9	1,778.5	1,768.5	1,704.7	1,675.8	1,672.7	1,740.8	1,799.6	1,800.5	1,812.8	1,751.1
2013	1,758.4	1,808.7	1,820.1	1,832.0	1,802.2	1,745.6	1,718.8	1,715.9	1,799.6	1,849.2	1,862.3	1,863.7	1,798.0
2014	1,797.4	1,848.0	1,860.5	1,868.6	1,853.8	1,807.8	1,781.7	1,781.2	1,837.2	1,892.4	1,906.6	1,908.5	1,845.3
2015	1,847.4	1,894.7	1,905.0	1,913.8	1,897.9	1,850.9	1,828.5	1,821.8	1,869.2	1,943.4	1,959.4	1,962.9	1,891.2
2016	1,898.2	1,950.9	1,962.5	1,977.4	1,959.3	1,913.5	1,889.6	1,884.3	1,937.2	1,997.6	2,012.9	2,018.0	1,950.1
2017	1,954.0	2,011.0	2,019.7	2,023.5	2,012.0	1,971.1	1,937.1	1,932.9	1,986.6	2,054.9	2,070.1	2,073.0	2,003.8
2018	2,008.0	2,070.7	2,081.6	2,091.9	2,076.3	2,030.7	2,006.6	2,001.8	2,050.4	2,106.5	2,120.4	2,130.6	2,064.6
Leisure and Hospitality													
2010	673.2	680.2	690.4	721.3	749.2	771.3	787.4	787.8	765.2	753.6	741.6	739.5	738.4
2011	704.0	712.6	722.7	751.6	780.0	807.7	820.6	818.0	795.5	785.5	775.8	773.0	770.6
2012	734.7	750.2	762.6	782.5	820.9	849.3	858.7	861.0	833.0	824.1	800.3	805.8	806.9
2013	764.1	776.0	790.1	818.2	855.8	886.2	897.1	891.2	867.3	863.3	850.2	847.4	842.2
2014	802.8	814.2	824.8	850.2	893.9	918.6	927.4	921.6	896.7	890.5	875.1	874.1	874.2
2015	829.9	838.8	849.5	876.4	920.5	941.6	957.8	951.4	927.9	917.2	901.0	898.9	900.9
2016	850.6	860.9	875.6	906.1	934.2	963.5	980.1	973.5	945.7	932.0	920.1	917.4	921.6
2017	876.2	888.6	897.7	923.6	966.3	999.3	1,009.2	1,008.6	973.5	964.8	949.5	945.8	950.3
2018	896.3	905.7	918.8	941.4	975.3	1,009.9	1,014.6	1,008.4	975.1	965.3	943.1	940.2	957.8
Other Services													
2010	355.0	355.6	357.6	360.9	363.6	364.7	366.0	364.9	362.4	366.6	366.6	367.6	362.6
2011	361.6	363.4	365.2	370.5	373.5	374.8	373.2	371.0	372.4	373.4	373.9	375.3	370.7
2012	369.3	370.8	373.8	375.6	379.7	382.8	379.7	377.7	378.6	382.0	380.2	382.3	377.7
2013	375.1	377.0	378.7	382.3	385.3	387.5	386.9	386.5	384.6	389.0	389.9	390.6	384.5
2014	383.3	385.6	387.4	391.4	395.6	396.3	395.9	394.6	393.3	397.7	398.8	399.5	393.3
2015	392.5	393.6	395.2	397.6	401.8	404.5	403.3	402.5	400.3	405.6	406.1	407.2	400.9
2016	398.9	401.6	403.0	408.0	410.7	411.4	411.0	409.1	408.3	411.3	411.6	410.9	408.0
2017	404.0	404.3	405.5	409.3	413.2	416.0	413.8	411.3	410.4	414.4	414.5	414.9	411.0
2018	405.7	408.0	410.3	413.3	416.4	418.9	415.8	413.8	411.1	415.9	416.9	417.5	413.6
Government													
2010	1,500.9	1,524.5	1,529.6	1,536.1	1,577.6	1,554.5	1,472.9	1,441.2	1,463.1	1,506.6	1,515.8	1,511.9	1,511.2
2011	1,497.5	1,519.6	1,522.5	1,529.1	1,524.2	1,512.9	1,476.6	1,465.5	1,472.8	1,510.9	1,515.9	1,514.2	1,505.1
2012	1,468.2	1,501.4	1,504.4	1,504.3	1,508.3	1,496.2	1,450.9	1,433.3	1,451.8	1,491.6	1,492.4	1,498.3	1,483.4
2013	1,451.6	1,482.9	1,485.8	1,485.4	1,491.4	1,480.7	1,442.3	1,426.6	1,437.1	1,480.4	1,487.3	1,486.2	1,469.8
2014	1,434.5	1,469.9	1,474.7	1,479.6	1,480.8	1,473.8	1,437.7	1,424.5	1,439.0	1,477.6	1,486.2	1,485.3	1,463.6
2015	1,438.3	1,469.4	1,474.8	1,476.6	1,484.6	1,478.5	1,443.9	1,431.4	1,448.8	1,482.3	1,493.2	1,494.0	1,468.0
2016	1,450.8	1,479.5	1,486.9	1,490.8	1,490.1	1,485.4	1,452.0	1,441.0	1,460.2	1,490.9	1,497.9	1,502.4	1,477.3
2017	1,462.2	1,490.3	1,494.6	1,496.0	1,496.6	1,491.4	1,458.4	1,446.2	1,464.5	1,496.4	1,502.5	1,503.7	1,483.6
2018	1,460.3	1,490.6	1,494.6	1,497.4	1,503.3	1,505.0	1,464.3	1,451.7	1,471.0	1,504.0	1,513.0	1,511.6	1,488.9

2. Average Weekly Hours by Selected Industry: New York, 2014–2018

(Not seasonally adjusted)

Industry and year	January	February	March	April	May	June	July	August	September	October	November	December	Annual average
Total Private													
2014	33.4	33.6	33.8	33.6	33.6	34.0	33.8	33.9	33.8	33.6	34.0	33.7	33.7
2015	33.5	33.7	33.8	33.5	33.7	33.7	33.8	34.2	33.7	33.7	34.0	33.7	33.7
2016	33.4	33.2	33.2	33.3	33.6	33.5	33.7	33.8	33.6	33.7	33.4	33.5	33.5
2017	33.5	33.1	32.8	33.5	33.3	33.5	33.8	33.5	33.4	33.7	33.4	33.4	33.4
2018	32.9	33.0	32.9	33.4	33.2	33.3	33.6	33.4	33.6	33.2	33.0	33.6	33.3
Goods-Producing													
2014	38.1	37.4	37.9	38.3	38.7	38.6	38.7	38.9	39.1	38.7	38.8	38.9	38.5
2015	38.7	38.0	38.8	38.9	39.3	39.1	39.1	39.0	38.2	38.9	38.8	39.0	38.8
2016	38.5	37.7	38.7	38.5	38.7	38.8	38.7	38.4	38.5	38.2	37.8	37.8	38.4
2017	37.4	36.9	36.4	37.8	38.2	38.4	38.0	38.3	38.7	38.6	38.5	38.4	38.0
2018	37.7	37.9	37.7	38.4	38.6	38.8	38.7	38.5	38.2	38.6	37.9	38.9	38.3
Construction													
2014	36.0	34.7	35.4	36.2	36.6	36.3	37.0	37.3	37.5	36.6	36.7	36.5	36.4
2015	36.6	35.6	37.1	37.5	38.6	38.2	38.6	38.5	37.3	38.1	37.8	38.3	37.7
2016	37.5	35.9	38.0	37.6	37.9	38.1	37.9	37.7	37.9	37.0	36.4	36.7	37.4
2017	36.0	35.2	34.7	36.5	37.1	37.3	37.0	37.5	37.7	37.4	37.1	37.3	36.8
2018	36.3	36.9	36.3	37.2	37.8	38.1	38.0	37.7	37.4	38.2	36.9	38.4	37.5
Manufacturing													
2014	39.1	39.0	39.3	39.5	40.0	40.1	39.8	40.0	40.2	40.3	40.3	40.6	39.9
2015	40.1	39.6	39.9	39.7	39.7	39.7	39.3	39.2	38.7	39.3	39.4	39.4	39.5
2016	39.2	38.9	39.1	39.1	39.3	39.3	39.3	38.9	38.9	39.2	39.0	38.8	39.1
2017	38.6	38.3	37.9	38.4	38.7	38.8	38.3	38.5	39.1	39.3	39.4	39.2	38.7
2018	38.8	38.6	38.9	39.4	39.2	39.3	39.2	39.1	38.8	38.8	39.1	39.5	39.1
Trade, Transportation, and Utilities													
2014	33.7	33.8	34.2	34.2	34.2	34.4	34.5	34.5	34.6	34.2	34.5	34.6	34.3
2015	34.0	34.2	34.2	34.0	34.1	33.9	34.1	34.4	34.6	34.1	34.5	34.0	34.2
2016	33.3	33.3	33.1	33.3	33.6	33.5	33.8	34.0	34.1	33.9	33.7	34.3	33.7
2017	33.3	32.9	32.9	33.4	33.2	33.3	33.6	33.5	33.7	33.5	33.7	33.9	33.4
2018	32.8	32.8	32.8	33.3	33.2	33.5	33.7	33.4	33.6	33.1	33.2	33.7	33.3
Information													
2014	34.6	34.6	34.7	34.3	34.5	34.7	33.9	34.3	34.2	34.1	34.7	33.9	
2015	34.6	35.0	34.8	34.3	34.4	34.3	34.8	35.4	34.9	35.1	35.5	34.8	
2016	35.1	34.5	34.4	34.3	34.8	34.2	34.4	34.6	34.6	34.7	34.8	34.5	
2017	35.3	35.3	35.0	35.2	35.8	35.7	36.0	35.2	35.5	36.3	35.6	35.9	
2018	35.4	35.8	35.5	36.0	35.3	35.3	36.2	35.7	36.6	35.3	34.9	36.0	
Financial Activities													
2014	36.8	37.9	38.0	36.9	37.0	37.8	37.0	37.0	36.7	36.8	37.9	36.8	37.2
2015	36.6	37.9	37.9	37.0	37.3	37.4	37.4	38.6	37.5	37.6	37.7	37.4	37.5
2016	37.3	37.0	36.8	36.4	37.1	36.4	36.7	36.7	35.8	37.1	36.8	36.6	36.7
2017	37.2	36.8	36.6	37.8	37.2	37.8	38.6	37.9	37.5	38.6	37.7	37.4	37.6
2018	37.3	37.3	37.2	38.2	37.4	37.5	37.9	37.4	37.9	37.4	37.2	38.0	37.6
Professional and Business Services													
2014	34.6	35.2	35.1	34.6	34.6	35.5	35.0	35.2	35.0	34.8	35.7	34.8	35.0
2015	34.7	35.5	35.4	34.5	34.7	34.8	34.4	35.3	34.4	34.8	35.6	34.8	34.9
2016	34.6	34.5	34.6	34.7	35.3	35.1	35.3	35.5	35.2	35.7	34.9	34.9	35.0
2017	35.4	34.8	34.4	35.3	34.6	34.7	35.3	34.6	34.3	35.0	34.3	34.2	34.7
2018	33.9	34.3	34.2	35.3	34.4	34.5	35.2	34.7	35.6	34.7	34.4	35.3	34.7
Education and Health Services													
2014	32.3	32.2	32.3	32.1	32.0	32.3	32.0	32.1	32.1	31.9	32.1	31.7	32.1
2015	31.8	31.8	31.8	31.8	31.9	32.0	32.2	32.3	32.1	31.9	32.0	31.9	32.0
2016	32.1	31.9	31.7	31.7	31.8	31.8	32.0	32.1	32.2	32.1	32.0	32.1	32.0
2017	32.3	32.1	31.7	31.8	31.9	31.9	32.0	32.0	31.8	31.9	31.8	31.8	31.9
2018	31.6	31.4	31.4	31.4	31.3	31.3	31.4	31.6	31.5	31.2	31.3	31.5	31.4
Leisure and Hospitality													
2014	27.0	27.4	27.6	27.9	28.2	28.1	28.4	28.5	27.8	28.0	28.1	28.1	27.9
2015	27.7	27.9	27.8	28.3	28.6	28.3	28.7	29.0	28.1	28.3	28.2	28.2	28.3
2016	27.2	27.7	27.8	28.1	28.3	28.4	28.7	28.9	28.5	28.4	28.2	28.1	28.2
2017	27.5	27.2	27.4	28.1	28.2	28.3	28.6	28.4	28.1	28.2	27.9	28.0	28.0
2018	27.1	27.6	27.4	27.4	28.1	28.1	28.4	28.2	28.0	28.0	27.6	28.1	27.8
Other Services													
2014	30.9	31.9	32.0	31.7	31.6	32.2	31.9	32.1	32.0	31.9	32.2	31.3	31.8
2015	31.2	31.7	31.4	31.2	31.5	30.8	31.4	32.0	31.2	31.1	31.3	30.9	31.3
2016	30.9	30.8	30.8	30.8	31.3	31.1	31.4	31.5	31.1	31.0	30.8	30.9	31.0
2017	31.0	30.3	30.1	31.0	30.5	30.9	31.4	31.0	30.8	31.3	30.8	31.2	30.9
2018	30.9	30.8	30.8	31.1	30.7	30.7	31.7	31.5	31.6	31.1	30.9	31.5	31.1

3. Average Hourly Earnings by Selected Industry: New York, 2014–2018

(Dollars, not seasonally adjusted)

Industry and year	January	February	March	April	May	June	July	August	September	October	November	December	Annual average
Total Private													
2014	28.02	28.29	28.26	28.09	27.93	28.28	27.87	27.83	28.08	28.23	28.62	28.34	28.15
2015	28.70	29.03	28.98	28.85	28.55	28.45	28.44	28.75	28.62	28.76	29.23	29.02	28.78
2016	29.26	29.49	29.25	29.11	29.20	28.71	28.99	29.37	29.19	29.64	29.34	29.28	29.24
2017	30.15	29.97	29.99	30.29	29.75	29.63	30.12	29.72	30.07	30.49	30.22	30.47	30.08
2018	30.81	30.95	30.88	31.18	30.75	30.65	31.26	30.90	31.45	31.35	31.57	31.97	31.15
Goods-Producing													
2014	29.10	28.71	28.81	29.15	29.11	28.98	29.25	29.46	29.61	29.65	29.72	29.83	29.29
2015	29.65	29.38	29.89	29.63	29.63	29.71	29.89	29.84	30.03	30.36	30.58	30.84	29.96
2016	30.34	30.17	30.65	30.71	30.66	30.37	30.65	30.84	30.80	30.81	30.69	30.75	30.62
2017	30.85	30.63	31.04	30.93	30.95	31.01	31.46	31.55	31.58	31.57	31.82	32.20	31.31
2018	32.24	32.63	32.49	32.69	32.63	32.80	33.07	33.24	33.37	33.76	33.52	34.01	33.05
Construction													
2014	35.54	35.06	35.40	35.69	35.46	34.84	34.85	35.26	35.57	35.83	35.89	35.64	35.42
2015	35.76	35.19	36.15	35.58	35.12	35.79	36.04	35.92	36.09	36.73	37.16	37.89	36.14
2016	37.27	37.25	37.77	37.39	36.60	36.31	37.10	37.14	37.11	37.22	37.01	37.10	37.10
2017	37.23	37.12	37.51	36.93	36.92	36.81	37.21	37.41	37.29	37.26	37.75	38.14	37.30
2018	38.16	38.59	38.65	38.62	38.28	38.01	38.27	38.66	38.58	39.22	38.85	39.38	38.61
Manufacturing													
2014	25.83	25.86	25.64	25.67	25.63	25.81	26.04	26.00	25.88	25.78	25.87	26.39	25.87
2015	26.13	26.19	26.20	25.89	25.76	25.42	25.35	25.19	25.46	25.37	25.40	25.67	25.67
2016	25.63	25.62	25.63	25.76	26.18	25.76	25.55	25.80	25.57	25.65	25.66	25.83	25.72
2017	25.94	25.74	26.13	26.08	25.95	26.07	26.35	26.17	26.42	26.46	26.41	26.83	26.21
2018	27.14	27.40	27.24	27.41	27.27	27.75	27.77	27.72	28.06	27.96	28.06	28.53	27.70
Trade, Transportation, and Utilities													
2014	23.06	23.32	23.41	23.50	23.27	23.34	23.18	23.07	22.96	22.89	22.53	22.40	23.07
2015	22.83	23.18	23.19	23.41	22.92	22.89	22.87	22.94	22.97	23.27	23.46	23.89	23.15
2016	23.91	24.05	23.98	23.95	23.73	23.43	23.72	24.48	23.63	23.85	23.75	23.44	23.82
2017	24.37	24.40	24.30	24.56	24.47	24.37	24.61	24.33	24.58	24.68	24.45	24.42	24.46
2018	25.15	25.21	25.68	25.66	25.61	25.15	25.39	25.53	25.80	25.80	25.73	25.90	25.55
Information													
2014	41.21	41.03	41.18	40.55	40.14	42.05	41.04	41.01	41.25	41.10	41.85	40.76	41.10
2015	39.93	40.86	41.20	41.51	40.66	40.61	40.91	41.85	41.07	40.85	41.35	40.40	40.94
2016	40.80	42.79	40.64	40.37	41.76	40.58	40.76	42.25	40.71	41.87	41.40	41.85	41.32
2017	42.87	42.47	42.14	43.84	43.80	44.19	45.13	44.01	44.82	45.36	45.94	47.36	44.36
2018	47.12	47.80	46.47	47.02	46.13	44.67	46.46	46.91	46.92	46.89	47.44	48.00	46.82
Financial Activities													
2014	40.59	41.01	41.25	41.23	41.23	42.85	41.14	40.53	41.19	41.85	43.92	42.58	41.62
2015	43.44	44.02	43.73	43.39	43.12	42.62	42.23	43.28	42.62	42.95	43.98	42.40	43.15
2016	41.99	43.81	43.18	42.29	43.65	41.74	42.00	43.74	43.17	44.62	43.38	43.61	43.10
2017	44.43	44.26	43.80	44.90	43.26	42.51	43.73	42.55	43.19	44.92	43.35	44.23	43.76
2018	44.52	44.10	43.71	44.36	43.91	43.69	44.96	43.49	45.06	44.00	44.64	45.35	44.32
Professional and Business Services													
2014	34.14	34.81	34.94	34.39	34.25	35.00	34.18	34.16	34.51	34.89	35.46	35.17	34.66
2015	35.89	36.45	36.19	35.79	35.64	35.31	35.31	35.89	35.38	35.48	36.30	35.73	35.78
2016	36.52	36.57	35.96	35.90	35.71	35.05	35.63	35.64	36.00	36.72	36.09	36.25	36.00
2017	38.13	37.27	37.50	37.95	36.75	36.66	37.45	36.55	37.29	38.34	37.76	38.00	37.47
2018	37.62	37.84	37.84	38.47	37.84	37.92	39.14	38.15	39.20	39.08	39.55	40.11	38.58
Education and Health Services													
2014	24.79	25.00	24.64	24.60	24.50	24.39	24.54	24.59	24.73	24.76	24.83	24.80	24.68
2015	25.02	25.02	24.83	25.04	24.80	24.74	24.94	24.82	24.88	24.65	24.99	24.95	24.89
2016	25.27	25.27	25.12	25.13	25.08	25.09	25.33	25.14	25.32	25.30	25.21	25.18	25.20
2017	25.48	25.53	25.78	25.75	25.55	25.59	25.80	25.73	25.98	25.75	25.84	26.00	25.73
2018	26.50	26.53	26.38	26.48	26.25	26.33	26.78	26.38	26.57	26.59	26.85	27.03	26.56
Leisure and Hospitality													
2014	17.77	17.93	17.85	17.84	17.84	17.15	16.74	16.66	17.41	17.99	18.22	18.50	17.64
2015	18.16	18.28	18.18	18.24	17.84	17.38	17.25	17.32	17.89	18.17	18.64	18.60	17.98
2016	18.77	18.83	18.92	19.23	19.25	18.80	18.63	18.98	19.49	19.70	19.76	19.67	19.17
2017	19.75	19.70	19.71	19.80	19.61	19.01	18.97	19.03	19.48	19.92	19.99	20.32	19.59
2018	20.40	20.82	20.63	20.77	20.30	20.01	19.79	19.92	20.23	20.64	21.06	21.62	20.50
Other Services													
2014	23.77	24.27	24.51	24.16	24.02	24.31	23.78	23.81	24.79	24.36	25.31	25.35	24.37
2015	25.42	26.15	26.44	26.21	26.36	26.71	26.25	26.56	27.29	26.98	27.23	27.20	26.57
2016	27.08	27.44	27.20	26.87	27.09	26.75	26.81	26.49	26.77	27.27	27.88	27.58	27.10
2017	27.94	28.37	28.04	28.08	27.65	27.05	26.96	26.98	27.12	27.14	27.20	27.15	27.47
2018	27.40	27.47	27.58	27.91	27.21	27.24	27.14	26.94	27.79	27.70	28.38	28.85	27.64

4. Average Weekly Earnings by Selected Industry: New York, 2014–2018

(Dollars, not seasonally adjusted)

Industry and year	January	February	March	April	May	June	July	August	September	October	November	December	Annual average
Total Private													
2014	935.87	950.54	955.19	943.82	938.45	961.52	942.01	943.44	949.10	948.53	973.08	955.06	948.66
2015	961.45	978.31	979.52	966.48	962.14	958.77	961.27	983.25	964.49	969.21	993.82	977.97	969.89
2016	977.28	979.07	971.10	969.36	981.12	961.79	976.96	992.71	980.78	998.87	979.96	980.88	979.54
2017	1,010.03	992.01	983.67	1,014.72	990.68	992.61	1,018.06	995.62	1,004.34	1,027.51	1,009.35	1,017.70	1,004.67
2018	1,013.65	1,021.35	1,015.95	1,041.41	1,020.90	1,020.65	1,050.34	1,032.06	1,056.72	1,040.82	1,041.81	1,074.19	1,037.30
Goods-Producing													
2014	1,108.71	1,073.75	1,091.90	1,116.45	1,126.56	1,118.63	1,131.98	1,145.99	1,157.75	1,147.46	1,153.14	1,160.39	1,127.67
2015	1,147.46	1,116.44	1,159.73	1,152.61	1,164.46	1,161.66	1,168.70	1,163.76	1,147.15	1,181.00	1,186.50	1,202.76	1,162.45
2016	1,168.09	1,137.41	1,186.16	1,182.34	1,186.54	1,178.36	1,186.16	1,184.26	1,185.80	1,176.94	1,160.08	1,162.35	1,175.81
2017	1,153.79	1,130.25	1,129.86	1,169.15	1,182.29	1,190.78	1,195.48	1,208.37	1,222.15	1,218.60	1,225.07	1,236.48	1,189.78
2018	1,215.45	1,236.68	1,224.87	1,255.30	1,259.52	1,272.64	1,279.81	1,279.74	1,274.73	1,303.14	1,270.41	1,322.99	1,265.82
Construction													
2014	1,279.44	1,216.58	1,253.16	1,291.98	1,297.84	1,264.69	1,289.45	1,315.20	1,333.88	1,311.38	1,317.16	1,300.86	1,289.29
2015	1,308.82	1,252.76	1,341.17	1,334.25	1,355.63	1,367.18	1,391.14	1,382.92	1,346.16	1,399.41	1,404.65	1,451.19	1,362.48
2016	1,397.63	1,337.28	1,435.26	1,405.86	1,387.14	1,383.41	1,406.09	1,400.18	1,406.47	1,377.14	1,347.16	1,361.57	1,387.54
2017	1,340.28	1,306.62	1,301.60	1,347.95	1,369.73	1,373.01	1,376.77	1,402.88	1,405.83	1,393.52	1,400.53	1,422.62	1,372.64
2018	1,385.21	1,423.97	1,403.00	1,436.66	1,446.98	1,448.18	1,454.26	1,457.48	1,442.89	1,498.20	1,433.57	1,512.19	1,447.88
Manufacturing													
2014	1,009.95	1,008.54	1,007.65	1,013.97	1,025.20	1,034.98	1,036.39	1,040.00	1,040.38	1,038.93	1,042.56	1,071.43	1,032.21
2015	1,047.81	1,037.12	1,045.38	1,027.83	1,022.67	1,009.17	996.26	987.45	985.30	997.04	1,000.76	1,011.40	1,013.97
2016	1,004.70	996.62	1,002.13	1,007.22	1,028.87	1,012.37	1,004.12	1,003.62	994.67	1,005.48	1,000.74	1,002.20	1,005.65
2017	1,001.28	985.84	990.33	1,001.47	1,004.27	1,011.52	1,009.21	1,007.55	1,033.02	1,039.88	1,040.55	1,051.74	1,014.33
2018	1,053.03	1,057.64	1,059.64	1,079.95	1,068.98	1,090.58	1,088.58	1,083.85	1,088.73	1,084.85	1,097.15	1,126.94	1,083.07
Trade, Transportation, and Utilities													
2014	777.12	788.22	800.62	803.70	795.83	802.90	799.71	795.92	794.42	782.84	777.29	775.04	791.30
2015	776.22	792.76	793.10	795.94	781.57	775.97	779.87	789.14	794.76	793.51	809.37	812.26	791.73
2016	796.20	800.87	793.74	797.54	797.33	784.91	801.74	832.32	805.78	808.52	800.38	803.99	802.73
2017	811.52	802.76	799.47	820.30	812.40	811.52	826.90	815.06	828.35	826.78	823.97	827.84	816.96
2018	824.92	826.89	842.30	854.48	850.25	842.53	855.64	852.70	866.88	853.98	854.24	872.83	850.82
Information													
2014	1,425.87	1,419.64	1,428.95	1,390.87	1,384.83	1,459.14	1,391.26	1,406.64	1,410.75	1,401.51	1,452.20	1,381.76	1,413.84
2015	1,381.58	1,430.10	1,433.76	1,423.79	1,398.70	1,392.92	1,423.67	1,481.49	1,433.34	1,433.84	1,467.93	1,405.92	1,424.71
2016	1,432.08	1,476.26	1,398.02	1,384.69	1,453.25	1,387.84	1,402.14	1,461.85	1,408.57	1,452.89	1,440.72	1,443.83	1,429.67
2017	1,513.31	1,499.19	1,474.90	1,543.17	1,568.04	1,577.58	1,624.68	1,549.15	1,591.11	1,646.57	1,635.46	1,700.22	1,579.22
2018	1,668.05	1,711.24	1,649.69	1,692.72	1,628.39	1,576.85	1,681.85	1,674.69	1,717.27	1,655.22	1,655.66	1,728.00	1,671.47
Financial Activities													
2014	1,493.71	1,554.28	1,567.50	1,521.39	1,525.51	1,619.73	1,522.18	1,499.61	1,511.67	1,540.08	1,664.57	1,566.94	1,548.26
2015	1,589.90	1,668.36	1,657.37	1,605.43	1,608.38	1,593.99	1,579.40	1,670.61	1,598.25	1,614.92	1,658.05	1,585.76	1,618.13
2016	1,566.23	1,620.97	1,589.02	1,539.36	1,619.42	1,519.34	1,541.40	1,605.26	1,545.49	1,655.40	1,596.38	1,596.13	1,581.77
2017	1,652.80	1,628.77	1,603.08	1,697.22	1,609.27	1,606.88	1,687.98	1,612.65	1,619.63	1,733.91	1,634.30	1,654.20	1,645.38
2018	1,660.60	1,644.93	1,626.01	1,694.55	1,642.23	1,638.38	1,703.98	1,626.53	1,707.77	1,645.60	1,660.61	1,723.30	1,666.43
Professional and Business Services													
2014	1,181.24	1,225.31	1,226.39	1,189.89	1,185.05	1,242.50	1,196.30	1,202.43	1,207.85	1,214.17	1,265.92	1,223.92	1,213.10
2015	1,245.38	1,293.98	1,281.13	1,234.76	1,236.71	1,228.79	1,214.66	1,266.92	1,217.07	1,234.70	1,292.28	1,243.40	1,248.72
2016	1,263.59	1,261.67	1,244.22	1,245.73	1,260.56	1,230.26	1,257.74	1,265.22	1,267.20	1,310.90	1,259.54	1,265.13	1,260.00
2017	1,349.80	1,297.00	1,290.00	1,339.64	1,271.55	1,272.10	1,321.99	1,264.63	1,279.05	1,341.90	1,295.17	1,299.60	1,300.21
2018	1,275.32	1,297.91	1,294.13	1,357.99	1,301.70	1,308.24	1,377.73	1,323.81	1,395.52	1,356.08	1,360.52	1,415.88	1,338.73
Education and Health Services													
2014	800.72	805.00	795.87	789.66	784.00	787.80	785.28	789.34	793.83	789.84	797.04	786.16	792.23
2015	795.64	795.64	789.59	796.27	791.12	791.68	803.07	801.69	798.65	786.34	799.68	795.91	796.48
2016	811.17	806.11	796.30	796.62	797.54	797.86	810.56	806.99	815.30	812.13	806.72	808.28	806.40
2017	823.00	819.51	817.23	818.85	815.05	816.32	825.60	823.36	826.16	821.43	821.71	826.80	820.79
2018	837.40	833.04	828.33	831.47	821.63	824.13	840.89	833.61	836.96	829.61	840.41	851.45	833.98
Leisure and Hospitality													
2014	479.79	491.28	492.66	497.74	503.09	481.92	475.42	474.81	484.00	503.72	511.98	519.85	492.16
2015	503.03	510.01	505.40	516.19	510.22	491.85	495.08	502.28	502.71	514.21	525.65	524.52	508.83
2016	510.54	521.59	525.98	540.36	544.78	533.92	534.68	548.52	555.47	559.48	557.23	552.73	540.59
2017	543.13	535.84	540.05	556.38	553.00	537.98	542.54	540.45	547.39	561.74	557.72	568.96	548.52
2018	552.84	574.63	565.26	569.10	570.43	562.28	562.04	561.74	566.44	577.92	581.26	607.52	569.90
Other Services													
2014	734.49	774.21	784.32	765.87	759.03	782.78	758.58	764.30	793.28	777.08	814.98	793.46	774.97
2015	793.10	828.96	830.22	817.75	830.34	822.67	824.25	849.92	851.45	839.08	852.30	840.48	831.64
2016	836.77	845.15	837.76	827.60	847.92	833.79	839.95	834.44	832.55	845.37	858.70	852.22	840.10
2017	866.14	859.61	844.00	870.48	843.33	835.85	846.54	836.38	835.30	849.48	837.76	847.08	848.82
2018	846.66	846.08	849.46	868.00	835.35	836.27	860.34	848.61	878.16	861.47	876.94	908.78	859.60

NORTH CAROLINA
At a Glance

Population:
  2010 census: 9,535,483
  2018 estimate: 10,383,620

Percent change in population:
  2010–2018: 8.9%

Percent change in total nonfarm employment:
  2010–2018: 16.0%

Industry with the largest growth in employment, 2010–2018 (percent):
  Transportation and utilities, 31.0%

Industry with the largest decline or smallest growth in employment, 2010–2018 (percent):
  Government, 1.7%

Civilian labor force:
  2010: 4,616,691
  2018: 4,981,834

Unemployment rate and rank among states (highest to lowest):
  2010: 10.9%, 7th
  2018: 3.9%, 22nd

Over-the-year change in unemployment rates:
  2016–2017: -0.6%
  2017–2018: -0.6%

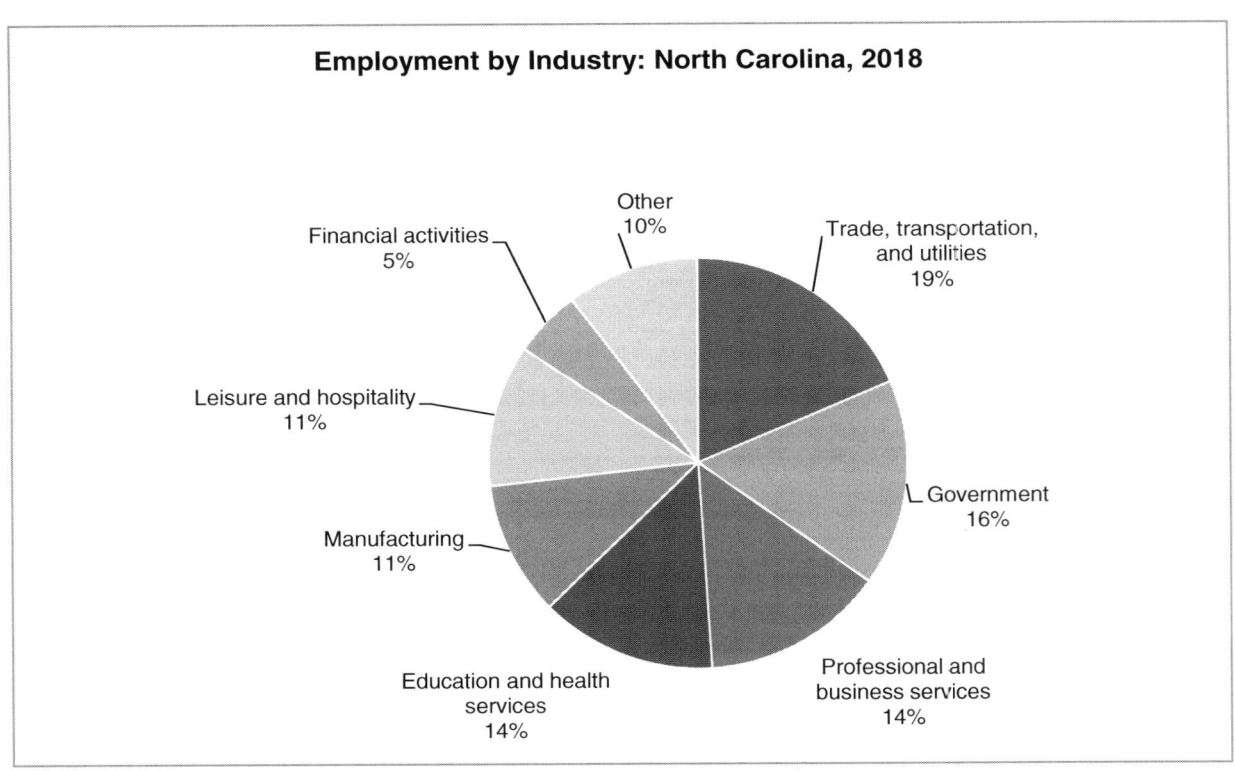

Employment by Industry: North Carolina, 2018

- Other 10%
- Financial activities 5%
- Trade, transportation, and utilities 19%
- Leisure and hospitality 11%
- Government 16%
- Manufacturing 11%
- Education and health services 14%
- Professional and business services 14%

1. Employment by Industry: North Carolina, 2010–2018

(Numbers in thousands, not seasonally adjusted)

Industry and year	January	February	March	April	May	June	July	August	September	October	November	December	Annual average
Total Nonfarm													
2010	3,790.1	3,795.4	3,831.0	3,864.7	3,905.4	3,884.7	3,808.3	3,875.2	3,890.9	3,919.4	3,929.2	3,918.9	3,867.8
2011	3,824.6	3,859.7	3,889.5	3,921.1	3,940.9	3,926.5	3,851.1	3,924.1	3,944.4	3,958.5	3,973.5	3,968.0	3,915.2
2012	3,897.9	3,922.3	3,955.9	3,981.4	4,013.3	3,987.3	3,909.7	3,993.0	4,016.4	4,037.7	4,056.7	4,052.5	3,985.3
2013	3,964.2	3,993.6	4,022.7	4,050.1	4,077.0	4,056.2	3,983.0	4,064.3	4,090.7	4,114.9	4,131.4	4,130.4	4,056.5
2014	4,039.7	4,040.3	4,088.0	4,131.4	4,166.9	4,151.9	4,076.1	4,152.0	4,172.1	4,207.2	4,223.5	4,226.8	4,139.7
2015	4,141.4	4,164.5	4,183.8	4,221.2	4,260.6	4,251.4	4,178.6	4,246.5	4,271.8	4,309.4	4,325.0	4,330.2	4,240.4
2016	4,239.9	4,265.1	4,297.4	4,338.5	4,362.0	4,353.2	4,284.5	4,346.7	4,372.3	4,389.7	4,416.4	4,409.4	4,339.6
2017	4,320.0	4,355.7	4,376.7	4,395.4	4,427.1	4,426.8	4,358.2	4,422.9	4,433.4	4,464.5	4,481.9	4,474.6	4,411.4
2018	4,395.0	4,433.0	4,459.1	4,489.8	4,528.4	4,521.1	4,441.9	4,508.2	4,483.3	4,527.9	4,540.4	4,530.1	4,488.2
Total Private													
2010	3,066.9	3,066.5	3,095.8	3,123.9	3,146.4	3,166.9	3,178.6	3,185.7	3,170.3	3,186.4	3,191.3	3,184.6	3,146.9
2011	3,101.5	3,130.1	3,155.5	3,185.7	3,205.7	3,226.7	3,230.8	3,241.7	3,231.6	3,232.3	3,241.1	3,241.3	3,202.0
2012	3,178.8	3,195.2	3,225.5	3,250.0	3,278.8	3,298.3	3,298.8	3,309.0	3,298.3	3,303.4	3,316.3	3,318.2	3,272.6
2013	3,239.4	3,259.8	3,285.5	3,313.2	3,340.3	3,364.8	3,367.3	3,380.8	3,370.5	3,378.1	3,392.3	3,394.8	3,340.6
2014	3,316.9	3,312.4	3,356.9	3,395.2	3,429.1	3,452.3	3,457.2	3,469.4	3,455.3	3,473.5	3,483.7	3,493.9	3,424.7
2015	3,413.2	3,430.6	3,447.6	3,483.5	3,522.3	3,546.1	3,553.4	3,560.0	3,549.5	3,570.9	3,582.0	3,588.7	3,520.7
2016	3,513.7	3,528.6	3,553.6	3,597.5	3,620.5	3,638.3	3,646.9	3,653.0	3,640.0	3,643.6	3,664.1	3,663.2	3,613.6
2017	3,586.4	3,612.8	3,630.4	3,649.1	3,681.6	3,711.4	3,716.1	3,722.2	3,694.9	3,716.8	3,730.0	3,726.7	3,681.5
2018	3,658.1	3,687.4	3,709.1	3,739.6	3,773.8	3,800.5	3,793.8	3,804.1	3,745.6	3,780.6	3,787.3	3,782.3	3,755.2
Goods Producing													
2010	606.8	603.4	608.4	612.4	615.0	618.9	621.3	620.8	620.7	618.7	616.5	614.1	614.8
2011	597.9	603.6	608.4	610.9	615.0	618.2	619.0	620.2	619.4	615.7	614.6	613.7	613.1
2012	606.0	608.8	614.1	615.1	618.9	621.6	622.0	622.2	622.7	621.4	621.8	622.0	618.1
2013	610.3	612.9	616.1	618.1	621.8	626.4	626.6	626.7	627.5	627.5	627.5	627.9	622.4
2014	617.3	617.9	624.5	626.1	631.5	636.7	638.6	640.2	641.9	645.7	646.4	648.1	634.6
2015	639.9	643.0	646.5	650.2	655.9	660.5	662.1	663.5	663.6	666.1	665.4	667.5	657.0
2016	659.9	662.1	664.9	668.6	670.2	674.4	677.1	676.5	676.3	674.2	677.2	677.8	671.6
2017	668.0	674.3	675.9	677.4	680.6	687.0	688.2	688.3	687.5	687.9	689.0	691.1	682.9
2018	683.6	688.7	692.8	695.8	700.4	707.4	707.2	707.8	704.7	703.3	701.7	700.3	699.5
Service-Providing													
2010	3,183.3	3,192.0	3,222.6	3,252.3	3,290.4	3,265.8	3,187.0	3,254.4	3,270.2	3,300.7	3,312.7	3,304.8	3,253.0
2011	3,226.7	3,256.1	3,281.1	3,310.2	3,325.9	3,308.3	3,232.1	3,303.9	3,325.0	3,342.8	3,358.9	3,354.3	3,302.1
2012	3,291.9	3,313.5	3,341.8	3,366.3	3,394.4	3,365.7	3,287.7	3,370.8	3,393.7	3,416.3	3,434.9	3,430.5	3,367.3
2013	3,353.9	3,380.7	3,406.6	3,432.0	3,455.2	3,429.8	3,356.4	3,437.6	3,463.2	3,487.4	3,503.9	3,502.5	3,434.1
2014	3,422.4	3,422.4	3,463.5	3,505.3	3,535.4	3,515.2	3,437.5	3,511.8	3,530.2	3,561.5	3,577.1	3,578.7	3,505.1
2015	3,501.5	3,521.5	3,537.3	3,571.0	3,604.7	3,590.9	3,516.5	3,583.0	3,608.2	3,643.3	3,659.6	3,662.7	3,583.4
2016	3,580.0	3,603.0	3,632.5	3,669.9	3,691.8	3,678.8	3,607.4	3,670.2	3,696.0	3,715.5	3,739.2	3,731.6	3,668.0
2017	3,652.0	3,681.4	3,700.8	3,718.0	3,746.5	3,739.8	3,670.0	3,734.6	3,745.9	3,776.6	3,792.9	3,783.5	3,728.5
2018	3,711.4	3,744.3	3,766.3	3,794.0	3,828.0	3,813.7	3,734.7	3,800.4	3,778.6	3,824.6	3,838.7	3,829.8	3,788.7
Mining and Logging													
2010	5.6	5.5	5.6	5.6	5.6	5.6	5.8	5.7	5.7	5.7	5.6	5.6	5.6
2011	5.5	5.6	5.6	5.5	5.5	5.6	5.7	5.7	5.7	5.6	5.6	5.6	5.6
2012	5.5	5.5	5.6	5.5	5.5	5.6	5.6	5.6	5.6	5.6	5.6	5.5	5.6
2013	5.4	5.4	5.4	5.5	5.5	5.5	5.5	5.6	5.6	5.6	5.6	5.6	5.5
2014	5.4	5.4	5.5	5.5	5.5	5.6	5.6	5.6	5.6	5.5	5.5	5.5	5.5
2015	5.5	5.5	5.5	5.5	5.5	5.6	5.6	5.6	5.6	5.6	5.5	5.5	5.5
2016	5.6	5.5	5.6	5.6	5.6	5.7	5.7	5.7	5.7	5.6	5.6	5.6	5.6
2017	5.6	5.6	5.7	5.5	5.6	5.6	5.8	5.8	5.8	5.8	5.9	5.9	5.7
2018	5.8	5.8	5.9	5.8	5.8	5.9	5.9	5.9	5.7	5.7	5.7	5.5	5.8
Construction													
2010	171.8	169.7	173.8	177.3	178.5	179.9	180.7	180.2	178.5	177.7	176.2	173.5	176.5
2011	162.5	167.2	170.7	172.9	175.2	176.8	177.7	177.7	177.1	174.8	173.7	172.8	173.3
2012	166.5	167.6	171.2	172.1	173.4	173.5	174.0	174.3	173.6	172.9	172.4	172.1	172.0
2013	165.6	166.6	169.5	172.2	174.3	175.7	176.3	176.8	176.8	176.6	176.8	175.5	173.6
2014	169.7	169.3	173.9	175.6	178.7	180.9	182.7	183.5	183.4	185.2	184.5	184.3	179.3
2015	178.4	180.1	182.3	186.1	189.8	191.7	193.4	193.9	193.7	194.8	193.7	194.2	189.3
2016	190.6	191.6	195.0	199.0	200.2	202.5	204.2	204.0	204.5	204.2	205.1	204.9	200.5
2017	198.8	202.5	204.3	206.1	207.9	211.0	212.1	211.9	211.8	212.4	212.7	213.4	208.7
2018	209.3	211.8	215.1	218.0	221.0	224.6	223.9	224.5	222.9	223.1	220.7	219.1	219.5

1. Employment by Industry: North Carolina, 2010–2018—*Continued*

(Numbers in thousands, not seasonally adjusted)

Industry and year	January	February	March	April	May	June	July	August	September	October	November	December	Annual average
Manufacturing													
2010	429.4	428.2	429.0	429.5	430.9	433.4	434.8	434.9	436.5	435.3	434.7	435.0	432.6
2011	429.9	430.8	432.1	432.5	434.3	435.8	435.6	436.8	436.6	435.3	435.3	435.3	434.2
2012	434.0	435.7	437.3	437.5	440.0	442.5	442.4	442.3	443.5	442.9	443.8	444.4	440.5
2013	439.3	440.9	441.2	440.4	442.0	445.2	444.8	444.3	445.1	445.3	445.1	446.8	443.4
2014	442.2	443.2	445.1	445.0	447.3	450.2	450.3	451.1	452.9	455.0	456.4	458.3	449.8
2015	456.0	457.4	458.7	458.6	460.6	463.2	463.1	464.0	464.3	465.7	466.2	467.8	462.1
2016	463.7	465.0	464.3	464.0	464.4	466.2	467.2	466.8	466.1	464.4	466.5	467.3	465.5
2017	463.6	466.2	465.9	465.8	467.1	470.4	470.3	470.6	469.9	469.7	470.4	471.8	468.5
2018	468.5	471.1	471.8	472.0	473.6	476.9	477.4	477.4	476.1	474.5	475.3	475.7	474.2
Trade, Transportation, and Utilities													
2010	698.0	694.6	700.9	704.5	710.0	712.8	713.6	714.9	709.7	715.3	727.8	733.6	711.3
2011	707.1	707.4	712.6	717.7	721.2	723.9	727.8	729.0	725.8	730.5	743.6	750.0	724.7
2012	726.6	722.6	728.9	732.5	738.7	742.1	743.1	741.9	740.8	744.4	761.0	765.4	740.7
2013	736.4	734.7	739.6	742.7	748.6	753.2	755.3	757.0	754.5	761.0	777.3	785.7	753.8
2014	755.8	749.4	757.1	762.5	767.9	772.8	771.8	774.2	771.5	779.2	795.6	805.5	771.9
2015	773.0	771.5	776.5	782.7	788.7	794.2	795.0	796.3	793.4	801.1	816.4	824.5	792.8
2016	794.3	792.2	796.5	803.7	808.1	810.4	812.0	813.5	810.2	814.2	831.8	841.1	810.7
2017	810.6	807.7	809.7	811.4	815.9	821.3	823.2	824.7	819.5	826.1	843.4	849.8	821.9
2018	820.6	821.0	823.5	825.3	831.3	835.5	834.0	834.9	824.7	832.5	854.3	861.6	833.3
Wholesale Trade													
2010	158.9	159.4	160.4	161.2	161.5	161.4	162.0	162.2	161.3	162.2	162.6	162.8	161.3
2011	161.0	162.0	162.8	163.7	163.9	164.4	165.3	165.3	165.2	165.0	165.5	165.7	164.2
2012	164.0	164.8	166.4	167.3	168.1	168.6	169.0	169.1	168.7	169.0	169.2	169.0	167.8
2013	166.6	167.7	168.7	168.4	169.0	169.6	169.7	170.1	169.9	170.2	170.8	171.0	169.3
2014	169.3	169.7	170.7	170.7	171.3	171.9	172.0	172.6	172.0	172.7	172.8	173.2	171.6
2015	170.8	171.5	172.5	172.6	173.4	174.1	174.4	174.6	173.8	174.6	175.1	175.5	173.6
2016	173.8	174.4	175.1	176.7	177.0	177.2	177.6	177.5	176.9	177.1	177.4	177.9	176.6
2017	176.0	177.0	177.2	177.5	178.4	179.7	179.9	180.2	179.5	180.3	180.3	181.1	178.9
2018	179.4	180.5	181.3	181.1	181.7	183.1	183.1	183.8	182.4	182.5	183.6	182.2	182.1
Retail Trade													
2010	427.1	423.4	427.8	429.7	433.8	436.1	435.8	436.8	432.3	436.4	447.8	452.6	435.0
2011	430.4	429.2	432.6	435.9	439.1	440.5	443.1	443.8	440.0	444.7	456.8	461.2	441.4
2012	443.2	438.6	442.1	445.2	450.2	452.5	453.2	451.8	450.3	453.4	469.1	471.3	451.7
2013	447.9	446.4	449.4	452.5	457.0	460.2	462.2	462.4	459.8	465.4	479.6	485.2	460.7
2014	460.6	455.7	460.9	465.8	469.4	472.5	471.8	472.8	469.7	475.9	490.4	496.0	471.8
2015	471.3	469.6	472.8	477.5	482.0	486.0	486.5	487.0	484.6	490.5	503.4	507.0	484.9
2016	483.9	482.8	485.7	491.4	495.1	496.2	497.5	498.4	495.1	498.7	512.4	515.7	496.1
2017	493.2	490.8	492.3	493.2	495.6	498.4	499.5	499.3	494.5	499.6	514.5	515.6	498.9
2018	495.0	494.0	495.2	496.9	501.4	502.9	501.5	500.5	490.8	498.4	512.5	517.5	500.6
Transportation and Utilities													
2010	112.0	111.8	112.7	113.6	114.7	115.3	115.8	115.9	116.1	116.7	117.4	118.2	115.0
2011	115.7	116.2	117.2	118.1	118.2	119.0	119.4	119.9	120.6	120.8	121.3	123.1	119.1
2012	119.4	119.2	120.4	120.0	120.4	121.0	120.9	121.0	121.8	122.0	122.7	125.1	121.2
2013	121.9	120.6	121.5	121.8	122.6	123.4	123.4	124.5	124.8	125.4	126.9	129.5	123.9
2014	125.9	124.0	125.5	126.0	127.2	128.4	128.0	128.8	129.8	130.6	132.4	136.3	128.6
2015	130.9	130.4	131.2	132.6	133.3	134.1	134.1	134.7	135.0	136.0	137.9	142.0	134.4
2016	136.6	135.0	135.7	135.6	136.0	137.0	136.9	137.6	138.2	138.4	142.0	147.5	138.0
2017	141.4	139.9	140.2	140.7	141.9	143.2	143.8	145.2	145.5	146.2	148.6	153.1	144.1
2018	146.2	146.5	147.0	147.3	148.2	149.5	149.4	150.6	151.5	151.6	158.2	161.9	150.7
Information													
2010	67.7	67.7	67.9	67.8	68.3	68.6	68.7	68.6	68.4	68.3	68.7	68.8	68.3
2011	67.9	68.0	67.9	68.4	68.4	68.9	69.3	69.5	69.2	69.3	69.6	69.5	68.8
2012	69.1	69.2	69.0	69.1	69.0	69.5	69.6	69.3	68.6	68.8	69.1	69.3	69.1
2013	69.2	69.5	69.4	69.3	69.9	70.1	70.6	70.6	70.0	70.7	71.5	71.9	70.2
2014	71.0	71.3	71.4	71.3	72.0	72.9	73.4	73.6	73.2	73.9	74.3	75.0	72.8
2015	74.2	74.7	74.8	74.9	76.4	76.8	77.0	76.9	76.3	76.8	77.5	77.9	76.2
2016	77.3	78.5	77.7	78.5	79.2	79.0	79.5	78.8	77.8	78.8	79.1	79.2	78.6
2017	78.2	78.6	78.6	78.7	78.6	79.0	79.0	79.0	78.0	78.3	79.2	79.2	78.7
2018	79.0	79.6	79.5	79.6	81.3	81.0	80.3	79.7	79.3	79.5	80.5	80.5	80.0

1. Employment by Industry: North Carolina, 2010–2018—*Continued*

(Numbers in thousands, not seasonally adjusted)

Industry and year	January	February	March	April	May	June	July	August	September	October	November	December	Annual average
Financial Activities													
2010	197.1	197.4	198.1	198.3	199.0	200.7	201.5	201.8	200.5	200.5	200.4	200.5	199.7
2011	198.4	198.9	199.1	199.7	201.2	203.1	203.7	204.0	201.6	201.4	201.0	201.2	201.1
2012	198.5	199.3	200.7	201.4	202.3	204.4	204.5	204.9	203.4	204.3	204.0	204.2	202.7
2013	201.8	202.4	203.0	205.2	206.4	208.7	209.0	209.5	208.0	208.0	207.7	208.0	206.5
2014	207.2	207.2	208.2	209.1	211.0	213.6	215.1	216.0	214.7	214.3	214.3	215.1	212.2
2015	212.6	213.7	214.0	215.4	217.4	220.1	222.0	222.0	221.3	222.2	222.0	223.0	218.8
2016	220.9	221.9	222.3	223.7	225.2	227.7	229.7	230.3	228.7	229.5	229.1	230.0	226.6
2017	226.9	227.7	228.6	230.1	231.6	234.8	236.9	236.7	235.1	236.0	235.3	236.1	233.0
2018	234.0	235.4	236.3	237.8	239.4	242.5	242.7	242.8	240.4	241.9	241.1	240.7	239.6
Professional and Business Services													
2010	462.2	465.1	470.1	477.9	478.0	482.9	489.5	493.7	494.9	506.2	504.7	503.8	485.8
2011	491.3	501.0	504.4	510.4	509.7	514.1	517.2	521.6	525.2	527.2	527.2	526.5	514.7
2012	515.7	523.2	527.4	531.7	533.3	536.8	534.4	540.8	540.2	543.3	543.2	543.0	534.4
2013	527.2	536.3	540.0	544.9	546.4	549.7	549.7	557.9	558.7	563.1	563.0	559.8	549.7
2014	547.8	549.0	558.0	569.2	571.0	575.1	577.7	581.1	580.4	586.1	583.8	584.4	572.0
2015	570.8	576.7	577.1	585.8	589.2	592.3	595.2	600.6	601.6	607.9	608.2	605.4	592.6
2016	590.4	594.8	599.5	607.8	607.3	610.6	613.0	614.9	616.4	618.1	619.2	613.9	608.8
2017	602.0	609.6	612.8	614.1	616.6	623.8	623.7	625.1	622.2	628.2	630.6	626.1	619.6
2018	614.1	621.2	623.8	632.5	632.9	638.4	639.0	645.5	638.3	650.1	642.8	635.2	634.5
Education and Health Services													
2010	533.8	535.8	537.4	538.1	538.4	533.9	532.6	534.5	533.0	541.1	542.6	540.3	536.8
2011	532.4	538.6	538.8	541.4	540.9	536.7	533.2	536.2	540.7	544.9	546.7	546.1	539.7
2012	541.4	546.2	546.5	547.0	549.1	545.8	543.2	546.4	551.1	556.0	557.4	558.2	549.0
2013	550.7	556.2	557.5	558.0	559.0	555.4	554.2	557.9	562.3	564.4	565.9	565.3	558.9
2014	557.8	560.3	565.5	568.0	569.7	564.7	565.1	569.4	571.0	576.3	577.7	576.6	568.5
2015	566.6	571.8	571.0	572.2	574.3	569.5	567.8	569.3	574.3	582.1	583.6	582.8	573.8
2016	575.0	579.7	581.8	585.9	587.0	581.3	582.0	586.6	590.2	594.7	596.5	595.5	586.4
2017	590.3	597.2	596.1	598.1	600.3	594.6	594.3	598.5	600.0	608.8	608.4	606.4	599.4
2018	602.5	610.3	610.2	613.5	615.6	609.6	607.0	611.8	608.7	615.4	617.1	617.0	611.6
Leisure and Hospitality													
2010	365.6	366.7	376.2	388.8	400.4	410.2	412.3	413.1	406.1	398.5	393.2	386.9	393.2
2011	371.1	376.4	387.3	400.3	411.7	421.4	420.2	421.7	411.9	404.9	400.4	396.2	402.0
2012	384.5	388.4	400.4	413.5	425.9	434.4	437.5	439.2	427.4	421.3	415.6	412.1	416.7
2013	400.4	403.0	413.4	428.1	440.3	451.6	453.2	453.1	442.5	437.1	432.2	430.4	432.1
2014	415.7	413.3	426.2	442.1	457.8	466.2	465.2	465.2	454.7	449.9	443.9	441.7	445.2
2015	430.3	432.9	440.7	454.2	470.5	481.7	482.1	480.4	470.0	466.2	460.5	459.3	460.7
2016	448.8	452.1	462.8	479.8	492.8	502.4	500.8	499.9	488.6	483.0	479.9	475.5	480.5
2017	461.5	468.1	478.4	488.5	505.9	516.2	516.6	516.6	500.6	498.4	491.4	485.3	494.0
2018	472.7	478.8	489.8	501.4	517.6	528.9	526.7	525.3	496.4	502.4	496.9	493.8	502.6
Other Services													
2010	135.7	135.8	136.8	136.1	137.3	138.9	139.1	138.3	137.0	137.8	137.4	136.6	137.2
2011	135.4	136.2	137.0	136.9	137.6	140.4	140.4	139.5	137.8	138.4	138.0	138.1	138.0
2012	137.0	137.5	138.5	139.7	141.6	143.7	144.5	144.3	144.1	143.9	144.2	144.0	141.9
2013	143.4	144.8	146.5	146.9	147.9	149.7	148.7	148.1	147.0	146.3	147.2	145.8	146.9
2014	144.3	144.0	146.0	146.9	148.2	150.3	150.3	149.7	147.9	148.1	147.7	147.5	147.6
2015	145.8	146.3	147.0	148.1	149.9	151.0	152.2	151.0	149.0	148.5	148.4	148.3	148.8
2016	147.1	147.3	148.1	149.5	150.7	152.5	152.8	152.5	151.8	151.1	151.3	150.2	150.4
2017	148.9	149.6	150.3	150.8	152.1	154.7	154.2	153.3	152.0	153.1	152.7	152.7	152.0
2018	151.6	152.4	153.2	153.7	155.3	157.2	156.9	156.3	153.1	155.5	152.9	153.2	154.3
Government													
2010	723.2	728.9	735.2	740.8	759.0	717.8	629.7	689.5	720.6	733.0	737.9	734.3	720.8
2011	723.1	729.6	734.0	735.4	735.2	699.8	620.3	682.4	712.8	726.2	732.4	726.7	713.2
2012	719.1	727.1	730.4	731.4	734.5	689.0	610.9	684.0	718.1	734.3	740.4	734.3	712.8
2013	724.8	733.8	737.2	736.9	736.7	691.4	615.7	683.5	720.2	736.8	739.1	735.6	716.0
2014	722.8	727.9	731.1	736.2	737.8	699.6	618.9	682.6	716.8	733.7	739.8	732.9	715.0
2015	728.2	733.9	736.2	737.7	738.3	705.3	625.2	686.5	722.3	738.5	743.0	741.5	719.7
2016	726.2	736.5	743.8	741.0	741.5	714.9	637.6	693.7	732.3	746.1	752.3	746.2	726.0
2017	733.6	742.9	746.3	746.3	745.5	715.4	642.1	700.7	738.5	747.7	751.9	747.9	729.9
2018	736.9	745.6	750.0	750.2	754.6	720.6	648.1	704.1	737.7	747.3	753.1	747.8	733.0

2. Average Weekly Hours by Selected Industry: North Carolina, 2014–2018

(Not seasonally adjusted)

Industry and year	January	February	March	April	May	June	July	August	September	October	November	December	Annual average
Total Private													
2014	34.0	33.3	35.2	34.8	34.7	35.2	34.7	34.9	34.7	34.6	35.1	34.7	34.7
2015	34.2	34.5	34.9	34.4	34.6	34.5	34.5	35.0	34.3	34.6	34.6	34.4	34.5
2016	33.8	33.8	34.1	34.3	34.5	34.4	34.5	34.4	34.4	34.6	34.5	34.3	34.3
2017	34.0	34.4	34.3	34.7	34.4	34.7	34.9	34.4	34.5	34.9	34.5	34.4	34.5
2018	33.9	34.7	34.5	35.2	34.7	35.0	35.1	34.8	34.0	34.4	34.2	33.8	34.5
Goods-Producing													
2014	40.0	38.8	42.8	42.3	42.0	42.7	41.7	42.1	41.9	41.6	42.2	41.9	41.7
2015	40.2	40.5	41.3	40.6	41.1	40.9	40.9	41.3	40.3	41.0	40.5	41.2	40.8
2016	39.8	39.7	40.8	40.8	40.8	41.0	40.7	40.6	40.9	40.6	41.4	40.5	40.6
2017	39.0	40.4	40.3	40.1	40.8	41.1	40.6	40.3	40.3	40.8	40.8	40.6	40.4
2018	39.2	40.3	40.0	40.8	40.8	41.5	40.8	40.9	38.3	40.4	39.9	38.3	40.1
Construction													
2014	38.5	35.4	41.2	40.0	40.7	41.3	40.8	40.9	40.0	40.2	40.7	40.6	40.1
2015	37.2	39.0	40.3	39.3	40.9	41.1	41.1	41.4	39.6	40.6	39.4	41.2	40.1
2016	38.8	38.1	40.9	40.3	40.3	41.3	40.8	40.0	40.6	40.4	41.1	39.0	40.1
2017	36.8	39.4	39.5	39.7	40.6	41.0	40.6	39.7	39.4	39.9	40.0	40.1	39.7
2018	38.1	39.3	38.5	40.5	40.7	41.0	40.0	40.1	36.3	38.8	37.7	36.3	38.9
Manufacturing													
2014	40.8	40.3	43.5	43.4	42.7	43.4	42.2	42.8	42.9	42.4	43.0	42.6	42.5
2015	41.7	41.3	41.8	41.3	41.3	40.9	40.8	41.3	40.7	41.1	40.9	41.0	41.2
2016	40.1	40.3	40.5	41.0	41.0	40.7	40.4	40.7	40.9	40.5	41.4	41.1	40.7
2017	40.5	41.1	40.9	40.3	41.0	41.3	40.7	40.8	40.9	41.3	41.2	40.8	40.9
2018	39.8	40.8	40.8	40.8	40.7	41.6	41.1	41.2	39.4	41.2	41.1	39.8	40.7
Trade, Transportation, and Utilities													
2014	33.9	33.1	34.8	34.5	34.4	34.7	34.4	34.3	34.2	34.1	34.2	34.3	34.2
2015	33.8	34.2	34.4	34.3	34.5	34.4	34.6	35.1	34.7	34.6	34.4	34.3	34.4
2016	33.6	34.0	34.1	34.3	34.7	34.6	34.5	34.8	34.7	34.7	34.6	34.7	34.4
2017	34.4	34.6	34.5	35.1	34.8	34.8	35.0	34.5	34.6	34.8	34.3	34.6	34.7
2018	35.0	35.4	35.3	35.8	35.3	35.3	35.3	35.0	34.5	34.6	34.2	33.7	34.9
Information													
2014	36.2	37.0	37.5	36.7	36.4	37.3	35.1	36.5	35.5	35.6	36.9	35.6	36.4
2015	35.4	36.4	36.3	35.7	35.7	36.3	36.1	36.9	36.2	35.9	36.9	35.1	36.1
2016	36.2	36.1	35.8	36.1	36.3	35.5	36.8	35.8	36.0	36.7	36.0	35.5	36.1
2017	36.6	37.0	37.5	38.0	36.4	37.7	39.4	38.2	38.1	37.6	36.4	36.6	37.5
2018	36.0	36.6	36.8	38.6	37.1	37.7	38.1	36.9	38.3	36.9	36.5	37.7	37.3
Financial Activities													
2014	36.4	36.8	36.9	36.2	36.2	37.1	36.2	36.2	36.3	36.8	37.8	36.7	36.6
2015	37.1	38.3	38.5	37.5	37.6	37.6	37.6	38.3	37.5	37.8	38.9	38.1	37.9
2016	38.2	38.2	38.4	38.5	39.2	38.6	38.7	38.3	38.3	38.9	38.0	37.9	38.4
2017	39.0	38.3	37.8	39.0	37.6	38.0	38.8	37.7	38.0	39.2	38.4	38.5	38.4
2018	37.9	38.4	37.8	38.8	37.7	37.5	38.3	37.4	38.5	37.9	37.7	38.0	38.0
Professional and Business Services													
2014	35.4	35.2	36.8	36.4	36.4	37.1	36.4	36.7	36.2	36.4	37.1	36.1	36.4
2015	35.7	36.3	36.7	36.0	36.0	36.2	35.8	36.7	35.4	36.2	36.6	35.7	36.1
2016	35.0	35.0	35.0	35.2	35.7	35.6	35.7	35.7	35.6	36.3	35.5	35.6	35.5
2017	35.5	35.5	35.6	36.1	35.8	36.2	36.5	36.0	36.2	36.7	36.1	35.5	36.0
2018	34.7	35.6	35.5	36.6	35.4	35.9	36.4	35.8	36.0	35.3	35.2	35.7	35.7
Education and Health Services													
2014	32.5	31.9	32.8	32.6	32.6	32.9	32.6	32.8	32.9	32.5	33.0	32.5	32.6
2015	32.5	32.3	32.6	32.2	32.3	32.3	32.1	32.5	32.1	32.2	32.4	32.2	32.3
2016	31.9	31.5	31.4	31.8	32.2	31.8	32.1	31.7	31.8	32.1	31.9	32.0	31.9
2017	32.2	32.1	32.0	32.5	32.3	32.3	32.7	32.3	32.6	32.9	32.5	32.5	32.4
2018	32.1	32.9	32.5	33.1	32.8	32.9	33.0	32.8	32.3	32.3	32.6	32.7	32.7
Leisure and Hospitality													
2014	25.0	24.2	26.0	25.9	25.7	26.2	26.2	26.6	26.0	26.0	26.0	26.0	25.8
2015	25.4	25.8	26.1	26.0	25.9	26.1	26.2	26.5	25.6	25.6	25.7	25.6	25.9
2016	24.7	25.4	25.9	25.8	25.9	26.0	26.3	26.2	25.9	26.0	26.2	25.7	25.8
2017	24.7	25.7	25.8	26.0	25.8	26.2	26.5	26.3	25.8	26.3	26.2	25.7	25.9
2018	24.9	25.9	26.2	26.5	26.6	26.9	26.8	26.7	25.2	26.7	26.4	25.7	26.2
Other Services													
2014	30.2	28.8	30.9	30.9	31.1	31.1	31.3	31.3	30.7	30.9	32.0	31.3	30.9
2015	31.1	31.3	31.9	30.7	31.2	30.8	31.2	31.4	30.8	30.6	30.6	29.9	31.0
2016	29.9	29.5	30.2	30.8	30.7	30.6	30.8	30.8	30.3	30.3	29.8	30.2	30.3
2017	29.4	30.4	29.8	30.9	29.3	29.7	30.4	29.8	29.0	29.6	28.9	28.9	29.7
2018	28.6	29.3	29.4	30.5	30.2	30.5	31.4	31.0	29.2	29.9	29.0	28.7	29.8

3. Average Hourly Earnings by Selected Industry: North Carolina, 2014–2018

(Dollars, not seasonally adjusted)

Industry and year	January	February	March	April	May	June	July	August	September	October	November	December	Annual average
Total Private													
2014	21.81	22.47	22.16	21.69	21.62	21.72	21.60	21.63	21.84	21.78	22.10	21.82	21.85
2015	22.05	22.36	22.03	22.04	22.11	22.04	22.14	22.54	22.35	22.49	22.85	22.66	22.31
2016	22.98	23.19	23.20	23.25	23.46	23.31	23.28	23.45	23.53	23.85	23.70	23.63	23.41
2017	24.06	23.99	24.01	24.33	23.99	23.77	24.17	23.97	24.19	24.46	24.19	24.27	24.12
2018	24.78	24.85	24.78	25.02	24.72	24.57	24.83	24.73	25.53	25.05	25.19	25.66	24.97
Goods-Producing													
2014	20.86	21.34	20.82	20.62	20.72	20.83	21.07	20.95	21.21	21.17	21.24	21.22	21.00
2015	21.56	21.55	21.36	21.50	21.49	21.38	21.26	21.43	21.42	21.46	21.70	21.84	21.50
2016	21.70	21.91	21.88	21.98	22.08	22.14	22.02	22.06	21.85	22.32	21.97	22.31	22.02
2017	22.61	22.50	22.71	22.75	22.81	22.87	23.22	22.99	23.31	23.34	23.21	23.44	22.98
2018	23.74	23.79	23.71	23.86	23.46	23.51	23.57	23.45	23.68	23.57	23.74	24.10	23.68
Construction													
2014	20.66	21.65	20.94	20.81	20.68	20.84	21.13	20.96	21.29	21.38	21.24	21.47	21.09
2015	22.33	21.80	21.71	22.02	21.73	21.90	21.69	21.92	22.23	22.48	22.74	22.77	22.11
2016	22.38	22.49	22.25	22.28	22.53	22.22	21.76	22.08	22.18	22.51	22.10	22.63	22.28
2017	23.00	22.95	23.03	22.93	22.88	23.12	23.54	23.27	23.81	23.70	23.68	23.80	23.32
2018	24.11	24.21	24.07	24.04	24.30	24.32	24.36	24.36	24.72	24.58	24.96	25.07	24.42
Manufacturing													
2014	20.90	21.24	20.81	20.57	20.77	20.85	21.07	20.95	21.22	21.09	21.28	21.13	20.99
2015	21.25	21.44	21.19	21.27	21.35	21.09	21.01	21.15	20.97	20.89	21.14	21.31	21.17
2016	21.33	21.59	21.64	21.83	21.84	22.12	22.20	22.06	21.67	22.20	21.97	22.21	21.89
2017	22.51	22.29	22.53	22.68	22.75	22.71	23.05	22.81	23.02	23.15	22.96	23.26	22.81
2018	23.55	23.55	23.49	23.73	23.32	23.35	23.43	23.19	23.36	23.22	23.27	23.74	23.43
Trade, Transportation, and Utilities													
2014	21.29	21.57	21.96	21.01	20.95	21.07	20.73	20.78	21.13	20.46	20.72	20.43	21.00
2015	20.66	21.08	20.45	20.56	20.36	20.64	20.64	21.03	21.15	21.47	21.28	20.98	20.86
2016	21.50	21.40	21.72	21.72	21.77	21.93	22.13	21.87	21.99	22.05	22.04	21.79	21.83
2017	22.15	21.79	22.38	22.72	22.34	22.17	22.52	22.13	22.52	22.64	22.28	22.13	22.31
2018	23.37	22.93	22.83	23.27	22.86	22.90	23.05	22.85	23.52	23.20	23.04	23.30	23.09
Information													
2014	31.85	33.95	32.05	31.18	31.82	32.15	32.40	32.36	33.26	33.28	34.96	33.91	32.77
2015	34.11	36.40	35.36	35.71	35.55	35.07	34.93	35.93	35.65	36.13	37.15	36.77	35.74
2016	37.31	39.39	37.23	38.48	38.62	37.86	37.85	37.70	38.66	39.52	38.41	39.28	38.36
2017	39.63	39.08	36.97	38.50	36.60	37.22	38.33	36.74	38.06	39.01	38.08	38.87	38.09
2018	38.25	40.51	39.13	37.93	37.21	36.78	36.53	37.34	38.35	37.56	37.92	38.35	37.98
Financial Activities													
2014	27.41	27.99	27.33	26.26	26.56	27.25	26.76	27.34	27.77	28.30	27.68	27.03	27.31
2015	27.14	27.56	28.88	28.23	28.88	28.66	29.24	30.33	29.66	29.93	30.87	30.11	29.15
2016	31.06	32.68	32.02	31.68	32.46	32.03	32.32	33.70	33.22	33.46	32.96	32.66	32.53
2017	33.51	34.50	33.81	34.49	33.87	33.30	34.07	34.28	34.24	34.36	33.30	32.24	33.83
2018	32.71	33.85	34.56	34.48	34.57	33.97	34.56	34.67	36.00	35.92	36.48	37.13	34.92
Professional and Business Services													
2014	25.78	27.25	27.15	26.53	26.01	26.27	26.00	25.78	26.08	26.10	26.74	26.44	26.34
2015	26.54	27.08	26.45	26.43	26.49	26.17	26.72	27.13	26.87	26.58	27.47	27.26	26.77
2016	27.71	28.00	28.57	28.56	28.69	28.39	28.32	28.29	28.64	28.88	28.58	28.48	28.43
2017	29.09	28.86	29.03	29.31	28.40	28.09	28.70	27.78	28.19	28.98	28.44	28.87	28.64
2018	29.26	29.45	29.40	29.86	29.46	29.46	29.99	29.85	31.14	29.89	30.54	31.24	29.97
Education and Health Services													
2014	22.10	22.42	22.12	22.33	22.31	22.02	22.17	22.32	21.66	21.81	22.45	22.22	22.16
2015	22.27	22.50	22.08	22.33	22.77	22.75	22.88	23.25	22.27	22.50	22.74	22.58	22.58
2016	22.70	22.65	22.68	22.87	23.45	23.10	22.69	23.55	23.54	23.85	24.44	23.78	23.28
2017	23.64	24.33	23.71	24.18	24.48	23.83	23.98	24.80	23.93	24.21	24.29	24.35	24.15
2018	24.70	24.74	24.73	24.94	25.17	24.69	24.92	24.80	24.17	24.53	24.44	24.76	24.72
Leisure and Hospitality													
2014	12.56	12.63	12.50	12.40	12.34	12.27	12.18	12.30	12.58	12.55	12.62	12.65	12.46
2015	12.63	12.43	12.33	12.38	12.43	12.34	12.23	12.38	12.44	12.63	12.64	12.88	12.47
2016	12.77	12.76	12.70	12.77	12.77	12.72	12.71	12.85	12.86	12.98	12.98	13.11	12.83
2017	13.09	12.90	12.97	13.11	13.17	13.19	13.23	13.25	13.39	13.45	13.68	13.81	13.27
2018	13.83	13.94	13.85	13.86	13.94	13.76	13.80	14.01	14.21	14.09	14.05	14.31	13.97
Other Services													
2014	17.90	18.49	17.89	17.57	17.76	17.85	17.65	17.75	18.26	18.45	18.56	17.93	18.00
2015	18.52	18.71	18.76	18.52	18.89	18.79	18.75	19.10	19.08	18.88	19.50	19.40	18.91
2016	19.68	19.72	19.65	19.83	20.19	20.08	19.93	19.97	20.40	20.54	20.83	20.67	20.13
2017	21.49	21.32	22.03	22.34	22.08	21.82	22.03	22.48	23.13	23.21	23.52	23.96	22.44
2018	23.42	23.54	23.84	24.15	24.01	23.82	24.24	23.65	27.90	26.26	26.13	26.11	24.74

4. Average Weekly Earnings by Selected Industry: North Carolina, 2014–2018

(Dollars, not seasonally adjusted)

Industry and year	January	February	March	April	May	June	July	August	September	October	November	December	Annual average
Total Private													
2014	741.54	748.25	780.03	754.81	750.21	764.54	749.52	754.89	757.85	753.59	775.71	757.15	758.20
2015	754.11	771.42	768.85	758.18	765.01	760.38	763.83	788.90	766.61	778.15	790.61	779.50	769.70
2016	776.72	783.82	791.12	797.48	809.37	801.86	803.16	806.68	809.43	825.21	817.65	810.51	802.96
2017	818.04	825.26	823.54	844.25	825.26	824.82	843.53	824.57	834.56	853.65	834.56	834.89	832.14
2018	840.04	862.30	854.91	880.70	857.78	859.95	871.53	860.60	868.02	861.72	861.50	867.31	861.47
Goods-Producing													
2014	834.40	827.99	891.10	872.23	870.24	889.44	878.62	882.00	888.70	880.67	896.33	889.12	875.70
2015	866.71	872.78	882.17	872.90	883.24	874.44	869.53	885.06	863.23	879.86	878.85	899.81	877.20
2016	863.66	869.83	892.70	896.78	900.86	907.74	896.21	895.64	893.67	906.19	909.56	903.56	894.01
2017	881.79	909.00	915.21	912.28	930.65	939.96	942.73	926.50	939.39	952.27	946.97	951.66	928.39
2018	930.61	958.74	948.40	973.49	957.17	975.67	961.66	959.11	906.94	952.23	947.23	923.03	949.57
Construction													
2014	795.41	766.41	862.73	832.40	841.68	860.69	862.10	857.26	851.60	859.48	864.47	871.68	845.71
2015	830.68	850.20	874.91	865.39	888.76	900.09	891.46	907.49	880.31	912.69	895.96	938.12	886.61
2016	868.34	856.87	910.03	897.88	907.96	917.69	887.81	883.20	900.51	909.40	908.31	882.57	893.43
2017	846.40	904.23	909.69	910.32	928.93	947.92	955.72	923.82	938.11	945.63	947.20	954.38	925.80
2018	918.59	951.45	926.70	973.62	989.01	997.12	974.40	976.84	897.34	953.70	940.99	910.04	949.94
Manufacturing													
2014	852.72	855.97	905.24	892.74	886.88	904.89	889.15	896.66	910.34	894.22	915.04	900.14	892.08
2015	886.13	885.47	885.74	878.45	881.76	862.58	857.21	873.50	853.48	858.58	864.63	873.71	872.20
2016	855.33	870.08	876.42	895.03	895.44	900.28	896.88	897.84	886.30	899.10	909.56	912.83	890.92
2017	911.66	916.12	921.48	914.00	932.75	937.92	938.14	930.65	941.52	956.10	945.95	949.01	932.93
2018	937.29	960.84	958.39	968.18	949.12	971.36	962.97	955.43	920.38	956.66	956.40	944.85	953.60
Trade, Transportation, and Utilities													
2014	721.73	713.97	764.21	724.85	720.68	731.13	713.11	712.75	722.65	697.69	708.62	700.75	718.20
2015	698.31	720.94	703.48	705.21	702.42	710.02	714.14	738.15	733.91	742.86	732.03	719.61	717.58
2016	722.40	727.60	740.65	745.00	755.42	758.78	763.49	761.08	763.05	765.14	762.58	756.11	750.95
2017	761.96	753.93	772.11	797.47	777.43	771.52	788.20	763.49	779.19	787.87	764.20	765.70	774.16
2018	817.95	811.72	805.90	833.07	806.96	808.37	813.67	799.75	811.44	802.72	787.97	785.21	805.84
Information													
2014	1,152.97	1,256.15	1,201.88	1,144.31	1,158.25	1,199.20	1,137.24	1,181.14	1,180.73	1,184.77	1,290.02	1,207.20	1,192.83
2015	1,207.49	1,324.96	1,283.57	1,274.85	1,269.14	1,273.04	1,260.97	1,325.82	1,290.53	1,297.07	1,370.84	1,290.63	1,290.21
2016	1,350.62	1,421.98	1,332.83	1,389.13	1,401.91	1,344.03	1,392.88	1,349.66	1,391.76	1,450.38	1,382.76	1,394.44	1,384.80
2017	1,450.46	1,445.96	1,386.38	1,463.00	1,332.24	1,403.19	1,510.20	1,403.47	1,450.09	1,466.78	1,386.11	1,422.64	1,428.38
2018	1,377.00	1,482.67	1,439.98	1,464.10	1,380.49	1,386.61	1,391.79	1,377.85	1,468.81	1,385.96	1,384.08	1,445.80	1,416.65
Financial Activities													
2014	997.72	1,030.03	1,008.48	950.61	961.47	1,010.98	968.71	989.71	1,008.05	1,041.44	1,046.30	992.00	999.55
2015	1,006.89	1,055.55	1,111.88	1,058.63	1,085.89	1,077.62	1,099.42	1,161.64	1,112.25	1,131.35	1,200.84	1,147.19	1,104.79
2016	1,186.49	1,248.38	1,229.57	1,219.68	1,272.43	1,236.36	1,250.78	1,290.71	1,272.33	1,301.59	1,252.48	1,237.81	1,249.15
2017	1,306.89	1,321.35	1,278.02	1,345.11	1,273.51	1,265.40	1,321.92	1,292.36	1,301.12	1,346.91	1,278.72	1,241.24	1,299.07
2018	1,239.71	1,299.84	1,306.37	1,337.82	1,303.29	1,273.88	1,323.65	1,296.66	1,386.00	1,361.37	1,375.30	1,410.94	1,326.96
Professional and Business Services													
2014	912.61	959.20	999.12	965.69	946.76	974.62	946.40	946.13	944.10	950.04	992.05	954.48	958.78
2015	947.48	983.00	970.72	951.48	953.64	947.35	956.58	995.67	951.20	962.20	1,005.40	973.18	966.40
2016	969.85	980.00	999.95	1,005.31	1,024.23	1,010.68	1,011.02	1,009.95	1,019.58	1,048.34	1,014.59	1,013.89	1,009.27
2017	1,032.70	1,024.53	1,033.47	1,058.09	1,016.72	1,016.86	1,047.55	1,000.08	1,020.48	1,063.57	1,026.68	1,024.89	1,031.04
2018	1,015.32	1,048.42	1,043.70	1,092.88	1,042.88	1,057.61	1,091.64	1,068.63	1,121.04	1,055.12	1,075.01	1,115.27	1,069.93
Education and Health Services													
2014	718.25	715.20	725.54	727.96	727.31	724.46	722.74	732.10	712.61	708.83	740.85	722.15	722.42
2015	723.78	726.75	719.81	719.03	735.47	734.83	734.45	755.63	714.87	724.50	736.78	727.08	729.33
2016	724.13	713.48	712.15	727.27	755.09	734.58	728.35	746.54	748.57	765.59	779.64	760.96	742.63
2017	761.21	780.99	758.72	785.85	790.70	769.71	784.15	801.04	780.12	796.51	789.43	791.38	782.46
2018	792.87	813.95	803.73	825.51	825.58	812.30	822.36	813.44	780.69	792.32	796.74	809.65	808.34
Leisure and Hospitality													
2014	314.00	305.65	325.00	321.16	317.14	321.47	319.12	327.18	327.08	326.30	328.12	328.90	321.47
2015	320.80	320.69	321.81	321.88	321.94	322.07	320.43	328.07	318.46	323.33	324.85	329.73	322.97
2016	315.42	324.10	328.93	329.47	330.74	330.72	334.27	336.67	333.07	337.48	340.08	336.93	331.01
2017	323.32	331.53	334.63	340.86	339.79	345.58	350.60	348.48	345.46	353.74	358.42	354.92	343.69
2018	344.37	361.05	362.87	367.29	370.80	370.14	369.84	374.07	358.09	376.20	370.92	367.77	366.01
Other Services													
2014	540.58	532.51	552.80	542.91	552.34	555.14	552.45	555.58	560.58	570.11	593.92	561.21	556.20
2015	575.97	585.62	598.44	568.56	589.37	578.73	585.00	599.74	587.66	577.73	596.70	580.06	586.21
2016	588.43	581.74	593.43	610.76	619.83	614.45	613.84	615.08	618.12	622.36	620.73	624.23	609.94
2017	631.81	648.13	656.49	690.31	646.94	648.05	669.71	669.90	670.77	687.02	679.73	692.44	666.47
2018	669.81	689.72	700.90	736.58	725.10	726.51	761.14	733.15	814.68	785.17	757.77	749.36	737.25

NORTH DAKOTA
At a Glance

Population:
 2010 census: 672,591
 2018 estimate: 760,077

Percent change in population:
 2010–2018: 13.0%

Percent change in total nonfarm employment:
 2010–2018: 15.3%

Industry with the largest growth in employment, 2010–2018 (percent):
 Mining and logging, 93.5%

Industry with the largest decline or smallest growth in employment, 2010–2018 (percent):
 Information, -15.1%

Civilian labor force:
 2010: 378,342
 2018: 404,299

Unemployment rate and rank among states (highest to lowest):
 2010: 3.8%, 51st
 2018: 2.6%, 48th

Over-the-year change in unemployment rates:
 2016–2017: -0.4%
 2017–2018: -0.1%

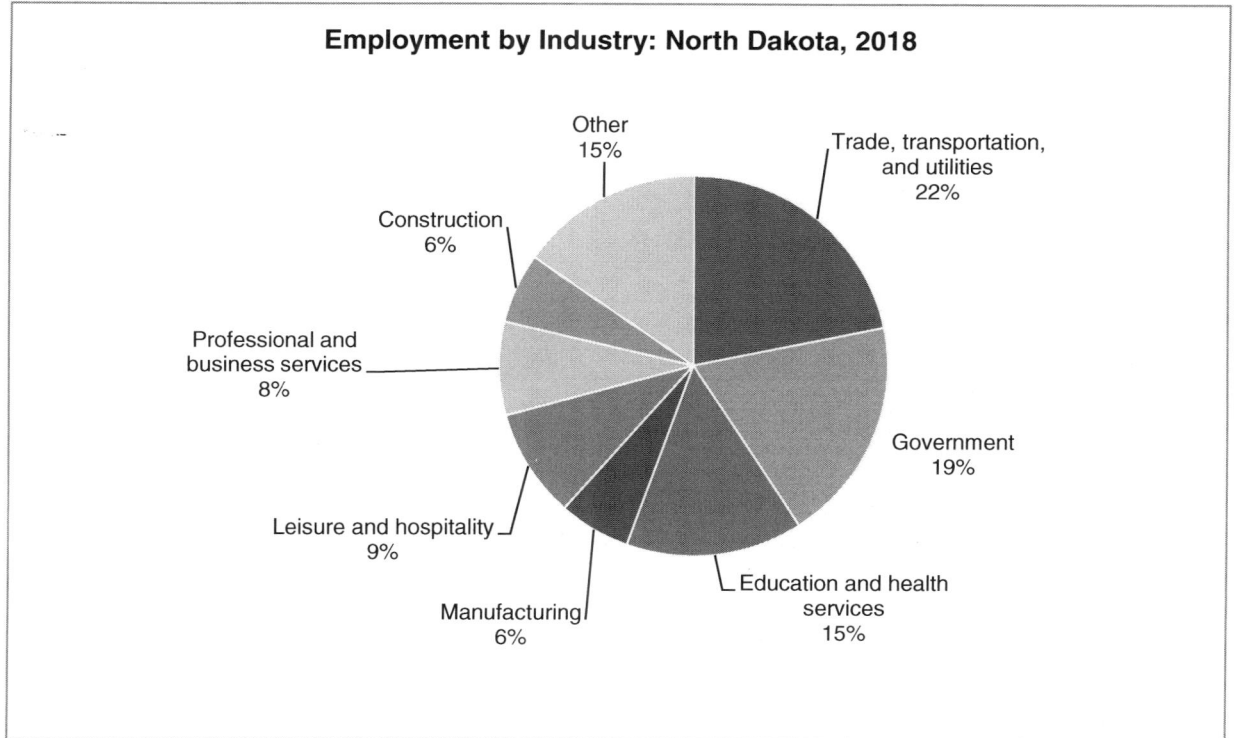

Employment by Industry: North Dakota, 2018

Other 15%
Trade, transportation, and utilities 22%
Construction 6%
Professional and business services 8%
Government 19%
Leisure and hospitality 9%
Manufacturing 6%
Education and health services 15%

1. Employment by Industry: North Dakota, 2010–2018

(Numbers in thousands, not seasonally adjusted)

Industry and year	January	February	March	April	May	June	July	August	September	October	November	December	Annual average
Total Nonfarm													
2010	360.1	362.5	365.9	374.0	379.1	379.9	371.2	372.9	382.9	388.3	387.6	387.5	376.0
2011	377.5	379.2	382.7	389.0	396.1	397.9	391.9	395.5	408.3	412.2	413.6	415.0	396.6
2012	408.3	411.6	416.1	424.2	432.0	436.1	429.0	430.8	439.3	442.0	439.0	439.1	429.0
2013	428.1	431.3	433.9	436.2	446.9	450.0	442.0	444.1	454.0	456.8	457.2	453.1	444.5
2014	441.3	445.1	447.6	453.8	463.3	466.8	462.2	463.5	470.5	475.1	474.1	471.8	461.3
2015	455.6	455.1	453.9	455.5	460.1	458.7	450.7	448.6	453.3	454.0	450.6	445.7	453.5
2016	428.2	428.4	427.6	433.2	438.3	437.6	434.6	434.1	439.9	439.9	437.4	432.1	434.3
2017	421.4	423.0	424.1	430.1	435.6	436.0	430.2	429.6	435.3	436.7	434.7	432.9	430.8
2018	422.3	423.9	425.4	428.4	438.0	439.4	434.6	433.9	439.7	441.8	438.1	435.2	433.4
Total Private													
2010	280.7	281.5	284.0	292.0	296.2	299.9	301.0	302.4	302.4	306.1	305.3	305.1	296.4
2011	297.3	297.8	301.3	307.5	314.3	318.4	322.6	325.8	328.3	330.5	332.3	333.2	317.4
2012	328.6	330.5	334.9	342.7	350.5	356.6	358.7	360.8	358.7	359.5	356.6	356.6	349.6
2013	347.6	349.6	352.0	354.6	364.5	369.5	371.0	373.5	373.2	374.5	374.8	370.5	364.6
2014	361.2	363.3	365.7	372.2	380.9	386.7	388.5	390.1	389.7	393.1	392.2	389.3	381.1
2015	375.7	373.6	371.5	372.8	376.6	377.8	376.0	374.3	371.6	369.6	365.9	361.0	372.2
2016	345.6	343.8	342.7	348.3	352.2	354.2	357.6	357.4	356.2	354.8	352.2	346.9	351.0
2017	338.0	338.3	339.7	345.5	350.4	353.5	354.5	353.7	352.6	352.4	350.6	348.0	348.1
2018	339.8	340.1	341.4	344.8	353.0	357.1	358.4	357.4	356.8	357.6	353.9	350.2	350.9
Goods Producing													
2010	46.6	47.1	48.1	52.0	54.7	56.3	58.0	59.0	59.4	60.2	59.2	58.0	54.9
2011	54.9	55.0	56.5	59.9	63.4	66.0	68.7	70.4	71.6	72.8	72.8	71.4	65.3
2012	69.4	70.5	72.6	76.7	80.4	83.6	85.3	86.0	85.0	84.5	81.3	79.6	79.6
2013	76.2	76.6	77.5	79.2	84.7	87.9	88.9	90.3	89.6	89.6	88.7	84.7	84.5
2014	80.5	81.1	82.1	86.1	90.7	94.5	96.0	97.3	97.1	98.2	96.9	93.6	91.2
2015	88.1	85.3	83.2	83.4	85.1	85.8	85.3	85.2	83.4	82.1	79.1	74.9	83.4
2016	67.7	66.4	65.9	69.3	71.8	74.5	76.4	76.6	75.9	74.5	71.9	67.0	71.5
2017	63.1	63.3	64.1	67.3	70.5	72.7	73.7	73.4	73.3	72.9	71.0	68.7	69.5
2018	65.3	65.3	66.1	68.2	72.9	76.3	77.1	77.4	77.3	77.4	75.2	72.2	72.6
Service-Providing													
2010	313.5	315.4	317.8	322.0	324.4	323.6	313.2	313.9	323.5	328.1	328.4	329.5	321.1
2011	322.6	324.2	326.2	329.1	332.7	331.9	323.2	325.1	336.7	339.4	340.8	343.6	331.3
2012	338.9	341.1	343.5	347.5	351.6	352.5	343.7	344.8	354.3	357.5	357.7	359.5	349.4
2013	351.9	354.7	356.4	357.0	362.2	362.1	353.1	353.8	364.4	367.2	368.5	368.4	360.0
2014	360.8	364.0	365.5	367.7	372.6	372.3	366.2	366.2	373.4	376.9	377.2	378.2	370.1
2015	367.5	369.8	370.7	372.1	375.0	372.9	365.4	363.4	369.9	371.9	371.5	370.8	370.1
2016	360.5	362.0	361.7	363.9	366.5	363.1	358.2	357.5	364.0	365.4	365.5	365.1	362.8
2017	358.3	359.7	360.0	362.8	365.1	363.3	356.5	356.2	362.0	363.8	363.7	364.2	361.3
2018	357.0	358.6	359.3	360.2	365.1	363.1	357.5	356.5	362.4	364.4	362.9	363.0	360.8
Mining and Logging													
2010	7.6	8.3	8.8	9.4	10.0	10.6	11.2	11.7	12.1	12.5	12.7	13.2	10.7
2011	13.5	14.0	14.5	15.2	15.9	16.3	17.1	17.7	18.3	19.0	20.2	21.0	16.9
2012	21.3	22.2	23.2	23.9	24.6	25.4	26.1	26.1	25.6	25.2	24.9	24.8	24.4
2013	24.6	25.1	25.5	25.5	26.0	26.4	26.3	26.6	26.6	26.9	27.6	27.4	26.2
2014	27.5	28.0	28.3	28.9	29.4	30.0	30.3	30.9	31.2	31.8	32.0	32.0	30.0
2015	30.5	28.6	26.8	24.8	23.6	23.0	22.1	21.7	20.8	19.6	19.1	18.6	23.3
2016	17.2	16.6	15.5	15.0	14.6	14.5	14.6	14.7	14.9	15.1	15.4	15.5	15.3
2017	15.4	15.9	16.3	17.0	17.6	18.3	19.1	18.9	18.9	19.1	19.2	19.2	17.9
2018	19.0	19.1	19.4	20.1	20.8	21.2	21.5	21.6	21.6	21.7	21.3	21.6	20.7
Construction													
2010	17.2	16.9	17.4	20.4	22.4	23.1	24.1	24.6	24.2	24.4	23.2	21.5	21.6
2011	18.5	18.1	18.9	21.1	23.8	25.7	27.6	28.8	29.2	29.4	28.1	25.8	24.6
2012	23.7	23.7	24.5	27.9	30.6	32.6	33.6	34.1	33.7	33.6	31.1	29.8	29.9
2013	27.1	26.9	27.3	28.8	33.1	35.6	36.7	37.8	37.2	36.6	35.3	31.7	32.8
2014	27.7	27.8	28.4	31.5	35.4	38.2	39.3	40.0	39.6	40.1	38.6	35.6	35.2
2015	32.2	31.4	31.1	33.1	35.8	37.1	37.7	37.8	37.0	36.9	34.5	31.3	34.7
2016	26.0	25.4	25.9	29.7	32.7	35.3	36.9	37.1	36.3	34.7	32.0	27.5	31.6
2017	23.8	23.5	23.8	26.0	28.2	29.4	29.6	29.5	29.3	28.5	26.6	24.3	26.9
2018	21.2	21.0	21.4	22.6	26.4	29.0	29.4	29.6	29.5	29.0	27.6	24.6	25.9

1. Employment by Industry: North Dakota, 2010–2018—*Continued*

(Numbers in thousands, not seasonally adjusted)

Industry and year	January	February	March	April	May	June	July	August	September	October	November	December	Annual average
Manufacturing													
2010	21.8	21.9	21.9	22.2	22.3	22.6	22.7	22.7	23.1	23.3	23.3	23.3	22.6
2011	22.9	22.9	23.1	23.6	23.7	24.0	24.0	23.9	24.1	24.4	24.5	24.6	23.8
2012	24.4	24.6	24.9	24.9	25.2	25.6	25.6	25.8	25.7	25.7	25.3	25.0	25.2
2013	24.5	24.6	24.7	24.9	25.6	25.9	25.9	25.9	25.8	26.1	25.8	25.6	25.4
2014	25.3	25.3	25.4	25.7	25.9	26.3	26.4	26.4	26.3	26.3	26.3	26.0	26.0
2015	25.4	25.3	25.3	25.5	25.7	25.7	25.5	25.7	25.6	25.6	25.5	25.0	25.5
2016	24.5	24.4	24.5	24.6	24.5	24.7	24.9	24.8	24.7	24.7	24.5	24.0	24.6
2017	23.9	23.9	24.0	24.3	24.7	25.0	25.0	25.0	25.1	25.3	25.2	25.2	24.7
2018	25.1	25.2	25.3	25.5	25.7	26.1	26.2	26.2	26.2	26.7	26.3	26.0	25.9
Trade, Transportation, and Utilities													
2010	77.4	77.3	77.6	79.4	80.4	80.7	80.6	80.8	80.6	82.1	83.1	83.8	80.3
2011	81.8	81.9	82.2	83.8	85.3	85.8	86.5	87.2	87.5	89.1	90.9	92.5	86.2
2012	91.1	91.5	92.4	94.4	96.2	97.1	97.4	97.7	97.3	98.5	99.5	100.0	96.1
2013	97.7	97.9	98.3	98.9	101.1	101.4	101.7	102.3	102.3	102.9	104.3	104.8	101.1
2014	102.2	102.7	103.0	104.3	105.8	105.9	106.1	106.2	105.9	107.2	108.3	109.0	105.6
2015	105.4	105.1	104.7	104.9	105.0	104.5	103.8	102.4	102.0	101.9	102.1	102.0	103.7
2016	98.2	97.1	96.1	96.8	96.9	95.8	96.1	95.8	95.4	95.8	96.4	96.4	96.4
2017	94.0	93.8	93.5	94.3	95.0	94.6	94.6	94.2	94.1	94.6	95.6	95.9	94.5
2018	93.4	93.2	93.1	93.6	95.1	94.5	94.4	94.2	93.9	94.5	94.8	95.2	94.2
Wholesale Trade													
2010	20.0	20.1	20.3	21.0	21.3	21.4	21.3	21.3	21.2	21.5	21.5	21.7	21.1
2011	21.4	21.5	21.7	22.2	22.8	23.1	22.9	22.8	22.7	23.0	23.2	23.6	22.6
2012	23.5	23.7	24.1	24.9	25.4	25.6	25.6	25.6	25.4	25.5	25.6	25.7	25.1
2013	25.4	25.5	25.7	26.0	26.9	27.0	26.8	26.7	26.4	26.5	26.6	26.7	26.4
2014	26.4	26.4	26.6	27.0	27.4	27.6	27.4	27.5	27.2	27.4	27.6	27.6	27.2
2015	27.2	27.0	27.0	27.3	27.3	27.1	26.7	26.5	26.1	25.9	25.6	25.5	26.6
2016	24.9	24.6	24.5	24.9	24.9	24.5	24.5	24.3	23.9	23.9	23.8	23.7	24.4
2017	23.5	23.6	23.7	24.1	24.4	24.3	24.1	23.9	23.6	23.7	23.8	23.7	23.9
2018	23.4	23.4	23.5	23.8	24.4	24.3	24.1	24.1	23.8	23.9	23.9	24.1	23.9
Retail Trade													
2010	42.5	42.2	42.2	42.7	43.2	43.3	43.3	43.2	42.9	43.7	44.6	44.9	43.2
2011	43.2	43.0	42.9	43.5	44.0	43.8	44.2	44.3	44.3	44.9	46.2	46.6	44.2
2012	45.0	44.9	44.9	45.6	46.2	46.6	46.7	46.7	46.6	47.4	48.6	49.0	46.5
2013	47.4	47.3	47.3	47.3	48.1	48.2	48.5	48.9	49.0	49.4	50.5	50.9	48.6
2014	49.0	49.3	49.3	49.6	50.2	50.2	50.3	49.9	49.8	50.6	51.7	52.4	50.2
2015	50.0	50.0	50.0	50.1	50.5	50.5	50.5	49.9	50.0	50.4	51.2	51.4	50.4
2016	49.3	48.8	48.5	48.8	49.0	48.7	49.0	48.8	48.6	49.0	49.8	49.7	49.0
2017	48.0	47.6	47.2	47.3	47.5	47.4	47.5	47.3	47.1	47.4	48.4	48.5	47.6
2018	47.0	46.9	46.7	46.6	47.3	46.8	46.8	46.4	46.1	46.8	47.5	47.4	46.9
Transportation and Utilities													
2010	14.9	15.0	15.1	15.7	15.9	16.0	16.0	16.3	16.5	16.9	17.0	17.2	16.0
2011	17.2	17.4	17.6	18.1	18.5	18.9	19.4	20.1	20.5	21.2	21.5	22.3	19.4
2012	22.6	22.9	23.4	23.9	24.6	24.9	25.1	25.4	25.3	25.6	25.3	25.3	24.5
2013	24.9	25.1	25.3	25.6	26.1	26.2	26.4	26.7	26.9	27.0	27.2	27.2	26.2
2014	26.8	27.0	27.1	27.7	28.2	28.1	28.4	28.8	28.9	29.2	29.0	29.0	28.2
2015	28.2	28.1	27.7	27.5	27.2	26.9	26.6	26.0	25.9	25.6	25.3	25.1	26.7
2016	24.0	23.7	23.1	23.1	23.0	22.6	22.6	22.7	22.9	22.9	22.8	23.0	23.0
2017	22.5	22.6	22.6	22.9	23.1	22.9	23.0	23.0	23.4	23.5	23.4	23.7	23.1
2018	23.0	22.9	22.9	23.2	23.4	23.4	23.5	23.7	24.0	23.8	23.4	23.7	23.4
Information													
2010	7.3	7.3	7.3	7.3	7.3	7.4	7.3	7.3	7.2	7.2	7.2	7.2	7.3
2011	7.1	7.1	7.1	7.1	7.1	7.2	7.2	7.2	7.1	7.0	7.1	7.1	7.1
2012	7.0	6.9	6.9	6.9	6.9	7.0	7.0	7.0	6.9	6.9	6.9	6.9	6.9
2013	6.9	6.8	6.7	6.7	6.8	6.9	6.9	6.9	6.8	6.8	6.8	6.8	6.8
2014	6.8	6.8	6.8	6.8	6.9	6.8	6.8	6.9	6.8	6.8	6.7	6.7	6.8
2015	6.6	6.6	6.6	6.6	6.6	6.6	6.6	6.6	6.6	6.6	6.7	6.7	6.6
2016	6.6	6.7	6.7	6.6	6.6	6.7	6.7	6.7	6.6	6.6	6.6	6.7	6.7
2017	6.6	6.6	6.5	6.5	6.5	6.5	6.5	6.5	6.5	6.5	6.4	6.5	6.5
2018	6.5	6.3	6.3	6.2	6.2	6.2	6.2	6.2	6.2	6.1	6.1	6.0	6.2

1. Employment by Industry: North Dakota, 2010–2018—*Continued*

(Numbers in thousands, not seasonally adjusted)

Industry and year	January	February	March	April	May	June	July	August	September	October	November	December	Annual average
Financial Activities													
2010	20.1	20.1	20.1	20.4	20.5	20.7	20.7	20.8	20.7	20.8	20.8	21.2	20.6
2011	20.8	20.8	20.8	21.0	21.2	21.2	21.3	21.3	21.3	21.3	21.4	21.5	21.2
2012	21.2	21.3	21.4	21.6	21.8	22.0	22.1	22.1	22.0	22.2	22.2	22.5	21.9
2013	22.2	22.3	22.5	22.6	22.8	23.0	23.1	23.2	23.1	23.4	23.5	23.6	22.9
2014	23.5	23.6	23.6	23.8	23.9	24.1	24.2	24.4	24.2	24.6	24.6	24.8	24.1
2015	24.4	24.3	24.4	24.4	24.5	24.5	24.5	24.5	24.3	24.3	24.3	24.2	24.4
2016	24.0	24.0	23.9	23.7	23.8	23.8	24.1	24.1	24.0	24.2	24.4	24.4	24.0
2017	24.1	24.1	24.2	24.2	24.2	24.3	24.4	24.4	24.4	24.4	24.4	24.5	24.3
2018	24.2	24.2	24.2	24.4	24.4	24.4	24.5	24.3	24.2	24.2	24.5	24.2	24.3
Professional and Business Services													
2010	27.8	28.0	28.1	28.6	28.4	29.1	28.7	28.8	28.9	29.5	29.3	29.1	28.7
2011	28.4	28.5	29.1	29.5	29.7	30.3	31.3	31.7	31.7	31.6	31.3	31.2	30.4
2012	31.1	31.0	31.5	32.3	33.0	33.8	34.1	34.6	34.4	34.5	34.2	34.1	33.2
2013	33.3	33.9	33.9	34.2	34.7	35.2	35.6	35.6	35.7	35.7	35.4	34.9	34.8
2014	34.5	34.6	35.2	35.9	36.5	37.8	38.3	38.0	38.2	38.3	37.8	37.2	36.9
2015	35.9	36.1	35.9	36.3	36.9	37.9	37.9	37.8	37.4	37.1	35.9	35.8	36.7
2016	34.1	34.1	33.8	34.8	35.1	35.6	36.0	35.9	35.2	34.9	34.4	34.2	34.8
2017	33.6	33.6	33.7	34.5	34.8	35.7	35.7	35.7	35.0	34.6	34.1	33.8	34.6
2018	33.3	33.5	33.6	33.9	34.6	35.4	35.7	35.6	35.3	35.2	34.8	34.3	34.6
Education and Health Services													
2010	54.1	54.1	54.5	54.8	54.6	55.1	55.2	55.1	55.1	55.7	55.5	55.7	55.0
2011	55.6	55.6	55.8	56.0	56.1	56.1	56.1	56.1	56.6	56.6	56.8	57.1	56.2
2012	56.8	57.1	57.2	57.3	57.6	57.9	57.6	57.9	58.0	58.1	58.1	58.6	57.7
2013	58.1	58.4	58.6	58.7	58.8	58.5	58.4	58.4	58.9	59.5	59.5	59.6	58.8
2014	59.1	59.3	59.1	59.0	59.1	58.9	58.7	58.9	59.3	59.7	60.1	60.0	59.3
2015	59.5	60.0	60.1	60.1	60.3	60.1	60.0	60.1	60.5	60.6	61.2	61.2	60.3
2016	60.8	61.4	61.5	61.9	61.9	61.4	62.1	62.2	62.6	62.9	63.1	63.2	62.1
2017	62.6	62.8	63.0	63.4	63.6	63.1	62.7	62.8	63.3	63.6	63.6	63.6	63.2
2018	63.4	63.6	63.7	63.8	63.7	63.2	63.2	63.0	63.6	63.8	64.2	64.7	63.7
Leisure and Hospitality													
2010	32.3	32.4	33.0	34.1	34.9	35.2	35.1	35.3	35.1	35.0	34.6	34.6	34.3
2011	33.4	33.5	34.2	34.5	35.8	36.3	36.0	36.4	36.8	36.3	36.3	36.7	35.5
2012	36.1	36.3	36.9	37.4	38.5	39.1	39.0	39.4	39.1	38.7	38.2	38.7	38.1
2013	37.3	37.6	38.2	38.0	39.1	40.1	40.1	40.4	40.3	40.1	40.0	39.6	39.2
2014	38.2	38.8	39.3	39.5	41.2	41.9	41.6	41.7	41.5	41.5	41.0	41.1	40.6
2015	39.3	39.6	39.9	40.6	41.6	41.9	41.6	41.6	41.4	41.0	40.7	40.3	40.8
2016	38.7	38.5	39.2	39.6	40.4	40.8	40.7	40.7	41.1	40.4	40.0	39.5	40.0
2017	38.6	38.8	39.2	39.6	40.1	41.2	41.4	41.4	40.9	40.7	40.2	39.8	40.2
2018	38.6	38.9	39.2	39.5	40.8	41.7	41.9	41.4	40.9	41.0	39.2	38.8	40.2
Other Services													
2010	15.1	15.2	15.3	15.4	15.4	15.4	15.4	15.3	15.4	15.6	15.6	15.5	15.4
2011	15.3	15.4	15.6	15.7	15.7	15.5	15.5	15.5	15.7	15.8	15.7	15.7	15.6
2012	15.9	15.9	16.0	16.1	16.1	16.1	16.2	16.1	16.0	16.1	16.2	16.2	16.1
2013	15.9	16.1	16.3	16.3	16.5	16.5	16.3	16.4	16.5	16.5	16.6	16.5	16.4
2014	16.4	16.4	16.6	16.8	16.8	16.8	16.8	16.7	16.7	16.8	16.8	16.9	16.7
2015	16.5	16.6	16.7	16.5	16.6	16.5	16.3	16.1	16.0	16.0	15.9	15.9	16.3
2016	15.5	15.6	15.6	15.6	15.7	15.6	15.5	15.4	15.4	15.5	15.4	15.5	15.5
2017	15.4	15.3	15.5	15.7	15.7	15.4	15.5	15.3	15.1	15.1	15.3	15.2	15.4
2018	15.1	15.1	15.2	15.2	15.3	15.4	15.4	15.3	15.4	15.4	15.1	14.8	15.2
Government													
2010	79.4	81.0	81.9	82.0	82.9	80.0	70.2	70.5	80.5	82.2	82.3	82.4	79.6
2011	80.2	81.4	81.4	81.5	81.8	79.5	69.3	69.7	80.0	81.7	81.3	81.8	79.1
2012	79.7	81.1	81.2	81.5	81.5	79.5	70.3	70.0	80.6	82.5	82.4	82.5	79.4
2013	80.5	81.7	81.9	81.6	82.4	80.5	71.0	70.6	80.8	82.3	82.4	82.6	79.9
2014	80.1	81.8	81.9	81.6	82.4	80.1	73.7	73.4	80.8	82.0	81.9	82.5	80.2
2015	79.9	81.5	82.4	82.7	83.5	80.9	74.7	74.3	81.7	84.4	84.7	84.7	81.3
2016	82.6	84.6	84.9	84.9	86.1	83.4	77.0	76.7	83.7	85.1	85.2	85.2	83.3
2017	83.4	84.7	84.4	84.6	85.2	82.5	75.7	75.9	82.7	84.3	84.1	84.9	82.7
2018	82.5	83.8	84.0	83.6	85.0	82.3	76.2	76.5	82.9	84.2	84.2	85.0	82.5

2. Average Weekly Hours by Selected Industry: North Dakota, 2014–2018

(Not seasonally adjusted)

Industry and year	January	February	March	April	May	June	July	August	September	October	November	December	Annual average
Total Private													
2014	34.2	35.5	35.2	35.0	35.4	36.7	36.3	36.5	36.2	36.2	36.3	35.4	35.8
2015	34.5	35.0	34.9	34.6	34.7	35.3	35.3	36.0	35.2	35.4	35.3	34.8	35.1
2016	34.1	34.1	33.7	34.2	34.9	34.7	34.7	34.9	34.6	35.1	34.2	33.8	34.4
2017	34.2	33.9	33.8	35.0	35.1	35.4	35.7	35.5	35.0	35.3	34.6	34.5	34.8
2018	33.6	34.3	34.5	35.2	35.5	35.9	36.3	36.0	36.2	35.1	34.8	35.5	35.2
Goods-Producing													
2014	40.3	41.7	42.4	41.8	43.3	44.1	45.0	44.5	45.0	44.8	43.7	43.1	43.4
2015	41.5	40.6	41.8	40.8	40.6	42.3	42.3	43.3	42.2	42.5	42.0	42.2	41.8
2016	40.0	40.4	40.5	40.6	41.4	41.5	41.2	42.6	41.9	42.8	40.6	39.1	41.1
2017	39.5	39.4	39.5	40.9	42.6	42.5	43.2	43.7	42.9	44.0	41.9	41.4	41.9
2018	39.7	40.9	41.7	42.1	42.8	43.2	44.6	44.5	44.3	42.9	41.8	43.1	42.7
Construction													
2014	39.9	39.9	40.8	41.3	45.2	46.2	47.7	46.0	46.8	46.6	42.8	43.2	44.2
2015	41.6	39.0	41.4	41.9	40.9	44.6	44.4	45.3	43.5	44.5	42.1	41.9	42.7
2016	38.6	39.9	41.0	41.9	44.1	44.2	42.9	44.1	43.9	45.0	41.5	38.6	42.4
2017	38.5	38.7	38.8	40.4	43.7	43.6	43.6	45.0	42.9	45.1	40.4	39.1	41.9
2018	35.6	37.5	38.7	38.3	41.9	42.7	44.2	44.4	44.3	42.0	40.8	41.6	41.4
Manufacturing													
2014	38.2	39.4	38.9	38.6	39.3	39.3	39.6	40.7	40.9	39.8	40.5	40.1	39.6
2015	38.2	39.1	39.4	38.6	38.6	38.9	38.9	41.0	40.6	40.5	40.2	41.1	39.6
2016	39.4	39.2	39.2	39.0	39.1	39.6	39.4	40.4	39.7	40.8	39.5	39.0	39.6
2017	38.5	38.2	38.8	39.4	40.2	39.3	40.1	39.6	39.8	39.1	38.8	38.6	39.2
2018	38.2	39.2	38.4	39.2	38.5	38.3	39.2	39.2	38.9	38.6	38.6	39.2	38.8
Trade, Transportation, and Utilities													
2014	35.1	36.5	36.2	35.8	35.7	37.5	36.5	37.1	36.3	36.6	37.0	36.3	36.4
2015	35.5	36.1	35.3	35.4	35.5	35.6	35.9	36.0	35.7	35.8	35.3	34.9	35.6
2016	34.2	34.0	33.8	34.7	35.4	35.4	35.4	34.9	34.9	34.9	34.5	34.3	34.7
2017	34.3	33.8	33.7	35.3	35.1	35.5	35.9	35.4	35.0	35.2	34.9	34.8	34.9
2018	34.0	34.1	34.1	34.7	36.2	35.9	36.0	35.7	36.3	35.3	35.1	35.3	35.2
Financial Activities													
2014	36.9	38.3	37.5	36.9	36.7	38.0	36.4	36.3	36.5	36.1	38.7	36.9	37.1
2015	36.9	37.5	36.5	35.0	34.2	34.3	34.8	36.3	34.9	35.0	37.6	35.0	35.7
2016	35.2	34.9	34.8	35.7	37.2	35.6	36.6	35.9	37.0	38.3	36.1	36.9	36.2
2017	38.3	36.6	36.9	37.3	35.2	35.9	37.1	35.8	36.2	37.1	36.5	36.6	36.7
2018	36.2	36.8	36.7	37.8	37.0	37.2	37.5	37.2	38.1	37.7	37.6	38.0	37.3
Professional and Business Services													
2014	36.0	38.9	37.5	37.6	39.2	39.9	39.0	38.9	39.1	39.3	39.0	38.0	38.5
2015	36.8	38.4	38.1	38.4	38.9	39.1	38.4	39.1	38.1	38.9	37.8	36.8	38.3
2016	36.0	36.8	35.9	36.0	37.7	37.0	36.3	36.9	37.3	38.3	37.2	37.5	36.9
2017	37.7	37.0	38.1	39.0	38.4	37.8	38.6	37.3	35.9	36.4	34.8	34.8	37.2
2018	33.5	34.6	35.6	37.0	36.8	36.8	37.0	36.1	37.2	35.6	35.0	35.2	35.9
Education and Health Services													
2014	32.2	32.3	32.0	32.2	31.6	32.7	31.5	32.1	31.9	31.6	31.8	31.6	32.0
2015	31.7	32.3	32.3	32.7	32.5	32.9	32.6	32.6	32.2	32.3	32.6	32.1	32.4
2016	32.1	32.3	31.7	31.7	31.8	31.8	32.0	31.6	31.4	31.5	31.9	31.8	31.8
2017	32.0	32.1	31.6	32.3	32.1	32.5	32.6	32.9	32.6	32.3	32.7	32.6	32.4
2018	32.8	33.1	32.7	33.6	33.0	34.0	34.2	33.9	34.1	33.2	33.6	34.4	33.5
Leisure and Hospitality													
2014	22.1	23.3	23.7	23.4	23.6	24.7	23.8	24.7	23.8	23.6	24.3	23.4	23.7
2015	22.3	23.9	23.5	22.7	23.9	24.4	24.1	25.2	23.6	23.8	24.3	24.0	23.8
2016	23.9	23.5	23.1	23.4	24.1	23.5	23.4	23.7	22.0	22.8	22.6	22.1	23.2
2017	23.3	22.8	22.9	24.0	24.8	24.8	24.5	24.4	23.2	23.3	22.5	23.0	23.7
2018	22.3	22.9	23.0	23.8	23.5	24.6	24.7	24.5	24.3	22.9	23.3	23.9	23.7
Other Services													
2014	26.4	28.7	26.8	24.4	25.0	27.4	28.7	29.3	25.4	24.7	26.3	25.2	26.5
2015	24.4	25.2	25.8	25.2	26.4	26.6	26.2	27.8	26.8	26.4	27.9	27.5	26.3
2016	28.2	27.5	27.1	29.2	29.3	27.6	28.9	28.7	29.2	29.7	28.9	28.9	28.6
2017	28.8	29.7	29.3	31.7	31.0	31.4	32.9	31.5	31.7	32.5	31.9	31.2	31.1
2018	30.0	32.4	31.7	32.4	31.1	31.2	31.1	31.1	30.5	30.4	31.2	32.2	31.3

3. Average Hourly Earnings by Selected Industry: North Dakota, 2014–2018

(Dollars, not seasonally adjusted)

Industry and year	January	February	March	April	May	June	July	August	September	October	November	December	Annual average
Total Private													
2014	24.89	25.07	24.91	24.95	24.78	24.69	24.76	24.59	24.98	24.94	24.92	24.97	24.87
2015	25.07	24.95	25.13	25.38	25.22	24.85	25.26	25.54	25.44	25.63	25.55	25.40	25.29
2016	26.25	25.68	25.66	25.89	25.94	25.40	25.62	25.70	25.78	26.01	25.64	25.72	25.77
2017	25.69	25.55	25.60	26.04	25.96	26.02	26.23	26.14	26.31	26.41	26.43	26.27	26.06
2018	26.31	26.32	26.20	26.29	26.19	26.51	26.66	26.65	27.18	26.86	26.91	27.08	26.60
Goods-Producing													
2014	27.87	27.98	28.27	27.66	27.38	27.23	27.12	27.04	27.43	27.49	27.43	27.78	27.53
2015	27.45	27.37	27.80	27.60	27.37	27.07	27.41	27.73	27.38	27.85	27.53	27.29	27.49
2016	27.74	27.47	27.87	28.07	27.89	27.28	27.40	27.74	27.75	28.18	27.58	27.98	27.74
2017	28.31	27.90	27.99	28.60	28.56	28.43	28.63	28.73	28.65	28.81	28.36	28.51	28.48
2018	28.13	27.85	28.31	28.25	28.23	28.71	28.88	28.87	29.18	29.26	29.58	30.29	28.83
Construction													
2014	28.80	28.81	29.39	28.91	27.89	27.62	27.86	27.64	28.18	27.98	28.17	29.23	28.28
2015	29.75	28.66	29.18	28.44	28.38	28.14	28.11	28.76	27.87	28.70	27.96	28.31	28.50
2016	28.26	28.12	28.54	28.41	27.86	27.31	27.47	28.37	28.13	28.71	27.70	28.32	28.08
2017	28.61	28.50	28.74	28.91	28.91	29.11	29.64	29.39	29.27	29.34	28.55	28.84	29.03
2018	28.76	28.63	28.71	28.88	29.19	29.40	29.00	28.94	29.24	29.66	29.51	30.17	29.21
Manufacturing													
2014	23.33	23.39	23.57	23.06	23.07	22.90	22.74	22.96	23.04	23.25	22.80	22.55	23.05
2015	21.33	21.46	21.73	22.04	22.11	21.41	22.04	22.13	22.42	22.86	22.95	22.43	22.08
2016	23.27	23.23	23.54	23.56	23.68	23.57	23.48	23.55	23.86	24.31	24.21	24.55	23.73
2017	24.61	24.02	24.15	25.35	25.15	24.19	24.28	24.29	24.56	24.67	24.94	24.63	24.57
2018	24.63	24.18	24.59	24.38	23.87	24.06	24.24	24.18	24.64	24.54	24.99	25.47	24.48
Trade, Transportation, and Utilities													
2014	24.37	25.39	24.88	24.73	24.90	24.86	24.67	24.44	24.95	24.61	24.97	24.58	24.78
2015	25.36	25.01	24.99	25.47	25.09	24.98	25.16	25.34	25.42	25.32	25.07	25.01	25.19
2016	25.54	25.13	24.98	25.37	25.32	24.91	25.11	24.58	24.88	25.26	25.02	25.03	25.10
2017	25.34	25.70	25.80	26.60	26.13	26.19	26.47	25.87	25.95	25.97	25.95	25.71	25.98
2018	26.06	26.14	26.42	26.53	26.46	27.28	27.70	27.33	28.00	27.37	26.95	26.64	26.92
Financial Activities													
2014	24.58	24.65	23.54	24.21	24.00	23.98	24.44	23.95	23.43	23.65	23.22	23.47	23.92
2015	24.06	24.42	25.35	25.91	26.45	26.08	27.55	27.42	25.65	26.99	27.24	26.80	26.15
2016	26.68	26.37	26.13	26.74	27.07	26.43	27.01	28.03	27.61	28.54	27.70	28.30	27.24
2017	29.90	28.50	28.47	29.35	29.99	29.70	30.87	31.10	31.43	31.26	30.79	30.88	30.19
2018	32.26	32.12	31.14	31.55	31.48	32.17	31.97	32.40	32.11	31.17	31.95	32.15	31.87
Professional and Business Services													
2014	29.59	28.94	28.88	28.81	28.37	27.84	27.53	27.94	28.36	28.30	28.26	28.55	28.42
2015	28.00	28.06	28.12	28.68	28.83	28.00	28.82	29.30	29.43	29.17	29.50	29.24	28.76
2016	28.63	27.54	28.08	28.86	29.29	27.96	28.59	28.86	29.33	29.95	29.09	29.50	28.82
2017	26.97	27.35	27.30	27.01	27.07	27.87	27.14	27.95	28.24	28.64	28.98	29.73	27.82
2018	29.02	29.18	28.16	28.33	27.82	27.51	27.92	28.10	29.22	29.59	29.45	29.51	28.63
Education and Health Services													
2014	23.49	23.44	23.50	24.08	23.56	23.58	23.96	23.86	24.29	24.03	24.18	24.41	23.86
2015	24.27	24.41	24.17	24.44	24.46	24.21	24.45	24.90	25.42	25.43	25.59	25.70	24.79
2016	25.90	25.39	25.21	25.11	25.22	24.88	24.86	25.21	25.16	25.05	25.20	24.77	25.16
2017	24.71	24.69	24.87	24.62	24.71	24.94	25.01	24.93	25.22	25.37	25.59	25.43	25.01
2018	25.60	25.92	25.48	25.30	25.20	25.11	24.93	25.15	25.65	25.69	25.87	25.90	25.48
Leisure and Hospitality													
2014	13.10	13.06	13.15	13.36	13.22	13.15	13.34	13.22	13.57	13.77	13.77	13.92	13.39
2015	14.16	14.06	14.15	14.28	14.14	13.99	14.06	14.13	14.35	14.40	14.43	14.50	14.22
2016	14.20	14.40	14.41	14.51	14.51	14.49	14.58	14.53	14.76	14.83	14.86	15.02	14.59
2017	15.61	15.01	15.03	15.51	15.46	15.08	15.03	15.08	15.20	15.20	15.30	15.37	15.24
2018	14.92	15.10	14.89	15.12	15.03	14.80	14.83	14.86	15.03	15.11	14.87	15.43	15.00
Other Services													
2014	23.31	22.06	22.44	23.47	22.57	22.79	22.76	22.23	23.26	23.72	22.81	22.41	22.80
2015	22.88	23.10	23.43	23.04	22.85	22.91	23.37	23.22	22.78	23.03	23.54	23.48	23.14
2016	22.30	22.99	22.92	22.42	23.22	22.50	23.67	23.71	23.78	22.65	22.77	23.00	22.99
2017	21.68	21.36	21.34	22.20	22.37	22.42	22.91	22.92	23.20	23.27	22.80	22.27	22.41
2018	22.52	22.31	21.77	21.96	21.34	21.57	21.30	21.38	22.15	22.31	22.82	23.16	22.05

4. Average Weekly Earnings by Selected Industry: North Dakota, 2014–2018

(Dollars, not seasonally adjusted)

Industry and year	January	February	March	April	May	June	July	August	September	October	November	December	Annual average
Total Private													
2014	851.24	889.99	876.83	873.25	877.21	906.12	898.79	897.54	904.28	902.83	904.60	883.94	890.35
2015	864.92	873.25	877.04	878.15	875.13	877.21	891.68	919.44	895.49	907.30	901.92	883.92	887.68
2016	895.13	875.69	864.74	885.44	905.31	881.38	889.01	896.93	891.99	912.95	876.89	869.34	886.49
2017	878.60	866.15	865.28	911.40	911.20	921.11	936.41	927.97	920.85	932.27	914.48	906.32	906.89
2018	884.02	902.78	903.90	925.41	929.75	951.71	967.76	959.40	983.92	942.79	936.47	961.34	936.32
Goods-Producing													
2014	1,123.16	1,166.77	1,198.65	1,156.19	1,185.55	1,200.84	1,220.40	1,203.28	1,234.35	1,231.55	1,198.69	1,197.32	1,194.80
2015	1,139.18	1,111.22	1,162.04	1,126.08	1,111.22	1,145.06	1,159.44	1,200.71	1,155.44	1,183.63	1,156.26	1,151.64	1,149.08
2016	1,109.60	1,109.79	1,128.74	1,139.64	1,154.65	1,132.12	1,128.88	1,181.72	1,162.73	1,206.10	1,119.75	1,094.02	1,140.11
2017	1,118.25	1,099.26	1,105.61	1,169.74	1,216.66	1,208.28	1,236.82	1,255.50	1,229.09	1,267.64	1,188.28	1,180.31	1,193.31
2018	1,116.76	1,139.07	1,180.53	1,189.33	1,208.24	1,240.27	1,288.05	1,284.72	1,292.67	1,255.25	1,236.44	1,305.50	1,231.04
Construction													
2014	1,149.12	1,149.52	1,199.11	1,193.98	1,260.63	1,276.04	1,328.92	1,271.44	1,318.82	1,303.87	1,205.68	1,262.74	1,249.98
2015	1,237.60	1,117.74	1,208.05	1,191.64	1,160.74	1,255.04	1,248.08	1,302.83	1,212.35	1,277.15	1,177.12	1,186.19	1,216.95
2016	1,090.84	1,121.99	1,170.14	1,190.38	1,228.63	1,207.10	1,178.46	1,251.12	1,234.91	1,291.95	1,149.55	1,093.15	1,190.59
2017	1,101.49	1,102.95	1,115.11	1,167.96	1,263.37	1,269.20	1,292.30	1,322.55	1,255.68	1,323.23	1,153.42	1,127.64	1,216.36
2018	1,023.86	1,073.63	1,111.08	1,106.10	1,223.06	1,255.38	1,281.80	1,284.94	1,295.33	1,245.72	1,204.01	1,255.07	1,209.29
Manufacturing													
2014	891.21	921.57	916.87	890.12	906.65	899.97	900.50	934.47	942.34	925.35	923.40	904.26	912.78
2015	814.81	839.09	856.16	850.74	853.45	832.85	857.36	907.33	910.25	925.83	922.59	921.87	874.37
2016	916.84	910.62	922.77	918.84	925.89	933.37	925.11	951.42	947.24	991.85	956.30	957.45	939.71
2017	947.49	917.56	937.02	998.79	1,011.03	950.67	973.63	961.88	977.49	964.60	967.67	950.72	963.14
2018	940.87	947.86	944.26	955.70	919.00	921.50	950.21	947.86	958.50	947.24	964.61	998.42	949.82
Trade, Transportation, and Utilities													
2014	855.39	926.74	900.66	885.33	888.93	932.25	900.46	906.72	905.69	900.73	923.89	892.25	901.99
2015	900.28	902.86	882.15	901.64	890.70	889.29	903.24	912.24	907.49	906.46	884.97	872.85	896.76
2016	873.47	854.42	844.32	880.34	896.33	881.81	888.89	857.84	868.31	881.57	863.19	858.53	870.97
2017	869.16	868.66	869.46	938.98	917.16	929.75	950.27	915.80	908.25	914.14	905.66	894.71	906.70
2018	886.04	891.37	900.92	920.59	957.85	979.35	997.20	975.68	1,016.40	966.16	945.95	940.39	947.58
Financial Activities													
2014	907.00	944.10	882.75	893.35	880.80	911.24	889.62	869.39	855.20	853.77	898.61	866.04	887.43
2015	887.81	915.75	925.28	906.85	904.59	894.54	958.74	995.35	895.19	944.65	1,024.22	938.00	933.56
2016	939.14	920.31	909.32	954.62	1,007.00	940.91	988.57	1,006.28	1,021.57	1,093.08	999.97	1,044.27	986.09
2017	1,145.17	1,043.10	1,050.54	1,094.76	1,055.65	1,066.23	1,145.28	1,113.38	1,137.77	1,159.75	1,123.84	1,130.21	1,107.97
2018	1,167.81	1,182.02	1,142.84	1,192.59	1,164.76	1,196.72	1,198.88	1,205.28	1,223.39	1,175.11	1,201.32	1,221.70	1,188.75
Professional and Business Services													
2014	1,065.24	1,125.77	1,083.00	1,083.26	1,112.10	1,110.82	1,073.67	1,086.87	1,108.88	1,112.19	1,102.14	1,084.90	1,094.17
2015	1,030.40	1,077.50	1,071.37	1,101.31	1,121.49	1,094.80	1,106.69	1,145.63	1,121.28	1,134.71	1,115.10	1,076.03	1,101.51
2016	1,030.68	1,013.47	1,008.07	1,038.96	1,104.23	1,034.52	1,037.82	1,064.93	1,094.01	1,147.09	1,082.15	1,106.25	1,063.46
2017	1,016.77	1,011.95	1,040.13	1,053.39	1,039.49	1,053.49	1,047.60	1,042.54	1,013.82	1,042.50	1,008.50	1,034.60	1,034.90
2018	972.17	1,009.63	1,002.50	1,048.21	1,023.78	1,012.37	1,033.04	1,014.41	1,086.98	1,053.40	1,030.75	1,038.75	1,027.82
Education and Health Services													
2014	756.38	757.11	752.00	775.38	744.50	771.07	754.74	765.91	774.85	759.35	768.92	771.36	763.52
2015	769.36	788.44	780.69	799.19	794.95	796.51	797.07	811.74	818.52	821.39	834.23	824.97	803.20
2016	831.39	820.10	799.16	795.99	802.00	791.18	795.52	796.64	790.02	789.08	803.88	787.69	800.09
2017	790.72	792.55	785.89	795.23	793.19	810.55	815.33	820.20	822.17	819.45	836.79	829.02	810.32
2018	839.68	857.95	833.20	850.08	831.60	853.74	852.61	852.59	874.67	852.91	869.23	890.96	853.58
Leisure and Hospitality													
2014	289.51	304.30	311.66	312.62	311.99	324.81	317.49	326.53	322.97	324.97	334.61	325.73	317.34
2015	315.77	336.03	332.53	324.16	337.95	341.36	338.85	356.08	338.66	342.72	350.65	348.00	338.44
2016	339.38	338.40	332.87	339.53	349.69	340.52	341.17	344.36	324.72	338.12	335.84	331.94	338.49
2017	363.71	342.23	344.19	372.24	383.41	373.98	368.24	367.95	352.64	354.16	344.25	353.51	361.19
2018	332.72	345.79	342.47	359.86	353.21	364.08	366.30	364.07	365.23	346.02	346.47	368.78	355.50
Other Services													
2014	615.38	633.12	601.39	572.67	564.25	624.45	653.21	651.34	590.80	585.88	599.90	564.73	604.20
2015	558.27	582.12	604.49	580.61	603.24	609.41	612.29	645.52	610.50	607.99	656.77	645.70	608.58
2016	628.86	632.23	621.13	654.66	680.35	621.00	684.06	680.48	694.38	672.71	658.05	664.70	657.51
2017	624.38	634.39	625.26	703.74	693.47	703.99	753.74	721.98	735.44	756.28	727.32	694.82	696.95
2018	675.60	722.84	690.11	711.50	663.67	672.98	662.43	664.92	675.58	678.22	711.98	745.75	690.17

OHIO
At a Glance

Population:
  2010 census: 11,536,504
  2018 estimate: 11,689,442

Percent change in population:
  2010–2018: 1.3%

Percent change in total nonfarm employment:
  2010–2018: 10.4%

Industry with the largest growth in employment, 2010–2018 (percent):
  Construction, 29.9%

Industry with the largest decline or smallest growth in employment, 2010–2018 (percent):
  Information, -8.9%

Civilian labor force:
  2010: 5,846,886
  2018: 5,754,931

Unemployment rate and rank among states (highest to lowest):
  2010: 10.3%, 15th
  2018: 4.6%, 8th

Over-the-year change in unemployment rates:
  2016–2017: 0.0%
  2017–2018: -0.4%

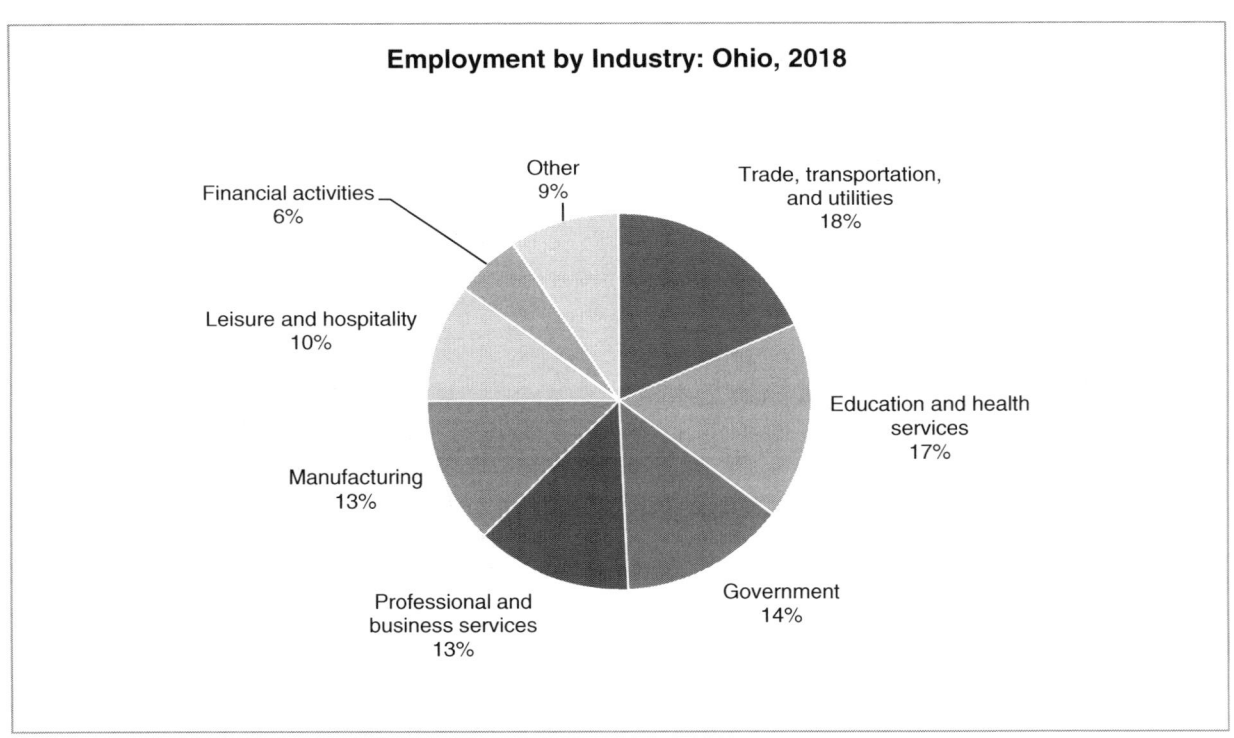

Employment by Industry: Ohio, 2018

- Other 9%
- Trade, transportation, and utilities 18%
- Financial activities 6%
- Leisure and hospitality 10%
- Education and health services 17%
- Manufacturing 13%
- Professional and business services 13%
- Government 14%

1. Employment by Industry: Ohio, 2010–2018

(Numbers in thousands, not seasonally adjusted)

Industry and year	January	February	March	April	May	June	July	August	September	October	November	December	Annual average
Total Nonfarm													
2010	4,904.9	4,910.5	4,944.9	5,022.8	5,080.6	5,076.9	5,043.7	5,047.3	5,069.2	5,106.7	5,116.3	5,106.9	5,035.9
2011	4,959.5	4,981.1	5,015.1	5,092.4	5,132.9	5,131.8	5,128.2	5,145.0	5,159.0	5,172.9	5,192.4	5,184.5	5,107.9
2012	5,050.8	5,082.4	5,129.8	5,188.9	5,247.0	5,248.8	5,210.2	5,223.7	5,232.7	5,265.6	5,275.9	5,263.8	5,201.6
2013	5,113.5	5,142.8	5,171.7	5,248.9	5,317.3	5,303.5	5,276.0	5,297.1	5,303.6	5,330.8	5,355.3	5,341.2	5,266.8
2014	5,180.3	5,203.9	5,238.6	5,319.4	5,391.3	5,379.1	5,348.3	5,378.5	5,384.8	5,423.6	5,442.4	5,437.9	5,344.0
2015	5,273.5	5,295.6	5,322.2	5,403.2	5,473.8	5,460.6	5,445.8	5,456.6	5,453.5	5,494.0	5,505.3	5,498.7	5,423.6
2016	5,346.9	5,369.1	5,401.5	5,479.3	5,522.2	5,504.1	5,496.5	5,501.9	5,514.4	5,541.2	5,560.3	5,534.9	5,481.0
2017	5,404.7	5,427.1	5,455.4	5,515.1	5,562.9	5,564.7	5,532.4	5,546.2	5,543.8	5,582.7	5,596.9	5,577.5	5,525.8
2018	5,434.3	5,469.4	5,494.6	5,543.4	5,593.4	5,600.9	5,577.1	5,591.6	5,583.0	5,614.8	5,617.1	5,599.6	5,559.9
Total Private													
2010	4,121.6	4,114.9	4,146.9	4,220.4	4,260.6	4,288.6	4,300.8	4,310.0	4,298.0	4,311.4	4,317.5	4,312.1	4,250.2
2011	4,188.1	4,195.1	4,226.6	4,303.8	4,345.1	4,366.0	4,382.6	4,400.6	4,386.1	4,388.1	4,405.4	4,404.3	4,332.7
2012	4,290.1	4,301.4	4,344.8	4,400.9	4,452.2	4,486.1	4,468.2	4,482.7	4,462.2	4,480.3	4,489.2	4,483.0	4,428.4
2013	4,353.7	4,366.4	4,395.5	4,467.4	4,531.8	4,557.2	4,546.7	4,566.3	4,538.7	4,553.5	4,572.2	4,567.3	4,501.4
2014	4,430.5	4,434.2	4,467.6	4,539.9	4,605.3	4,628.5	4,622.3	4,645.5	4,610.7	4,638.7	4,655.2	4,655.9	4,577.9
2015	4,518.4	4,519.1	4,545.8	4,618.7	4,687.6	4,705.8	4,706.8	4,715.1	4,681.7	4,705.8	4,715.5	4,714.4	4,652.9
2016	4,588.7	4,591.2	4,623.0	4,686.2	4,733.6	4,748.8	4,756.9	4,759.3	4,733.3	4,744.8	4,759.8	4,746.3	4,706.0
2017	4,626.7	4,635.1	4,662.4	4,720.7	4,772.7	4,806.4	4,790.8	4,800.5	4,763.8	4,785.6	4,796.4	4,785.8	4,745.6
2018	4,661.3	4,676.6	4,700.9	4,748.0	4,803.2	4,838.8	4,835.5	4,842.0	4,801.8	4,825.2	4,824.5	4,811.5	4,780.8
Goods Producing													
2010	766.0	761.6	769.2	788.7	802.1	813.6	819.2	822.7	820.4	822.8	820.1	811.0	801.5
2011	786.1	784.9	794.6	811.7	822.3	834.3	844.1	852.3	849.3	849.7	849.8	843.3	826.9
2012	818.8	819.3	829.1	841.8	853.4	865.6	863.4	867.9	863.7	860.8	859.3	852.4	849.6
2013	829.4	829.2	835.5	848.4	864.6	876.7	874.7	882.6	879.0	879.4	879.0	869.0	862.3
2014	845.8	845.1	855.2	871.5	889.0	901.8	901.4	909.6	905.0	907.3	906.3	898.3	886.4
2015	872.5	870.7	876.5	893.4	909.5	918.1	917.2	920.9	914.9	915.2	912.4	906.1	902.3
2016	881.0	879.6	887.2	899.2	908.6	917.9	917.9	917.2	911.8	911.1	909.7	901.0	903.5
2017	881.8	882.0	891.6	906.7	921.2	935.3	930.7	935.2	926.0	928.9	927.1	920.7	915.6
2018	894.5	901.8	909.6	919.7	933.7	947.5	947.9	949.5	943.4	944.5	939.2	933.7	930.4
Service-Providing													
2010	4,138.9	4,148.9	4,175.7	4,234.1	4,278.5	4,263.3	4,224.5	4,224.6	4,248.8	4,283.9	4,296.2	4,295.9	4,234.4
2011	4,173.4	4,196.2	4,220.5	4,280.7	4,310.6	4,297.5	4,284.1	4,292.7	4,309.7	4,323.2	4,342.6	4,341.2	4,281.0
2012	4,232.0	4,263.1	4,300.7	4,347.1	4,393.6	4,383.2	4,346.8	4,355.8	4,369.0	4,404.8	4,416.6	4,411.4	4,352.0
2013	4,284.1	4,313.6	4,336.2	4,400.5	4,452.7	4,426.8	4,401.3	4,414.5	4,424.6	4,451.4	4,476.3	4,472.2	4,404.5
2014	4,334.5	4,358.8	4,383.4	4,447.9	4,502.3	4,477.3	4,446.9	4,468.9	4,479.8	4,516.3	4,536.1	4,539.6	4,457.7
2015	4,401.0	4,424.9	4,445.7	4,509.8	4,564.3	4,542.5	4,528.6	4,535.7	4,538.6	4,578.8	4,592.9	4,592.6	4,521.3
2016	4,465.9	4,489.5	4,514.3	4,580.1	4,613.6	4,586.2	4,578.6	4,584.7	4,602.6	4,630.1	4,650.6	4,633.9	4,577.5
2017	4,522.9	4,545.1	4,563.8	4,608.4	4,641.7	4,629.4	4,601.7	4,611.0	4,617.8	4,653.8	4,669.8	4,656.8	4,610.2
2018	4,539.8	4,567.6	4,585.0	4,623.7	4,659.7	4,653.4	4,629.2	4,642.1	4,639.6	4,670.3	4,677.9	4,665.9	4,629.5
Mining and Logging													
2010	10.5	10.5	10.5	11.2	11.4	11.5	11.7	11.6	11.7	11.6	11.5	11.3	11.3
2011	10.7	10.7	10.9	11.2	11.3	11.4	11.6	11.7	11.7	11.7	11.6	11.4	11.3
2012	11.0	10.8	11.0	11.4	11.6	11.7	11.8	11.7	11.6	11.5	11.6	11.4	11.4
2013	11.3	11.3	11.8	12.2	12.5	12.5	12.7	12.9	12.9	13.5	13.5	13.3	12.5
2014	13.1	13.3	13.7	14.2	14.6	14.9	15.4	15.8	15.7	15.8	15.9	15.8	14.9
2015	15.2	14.8	14.7	14.5	14.6	14.3	14.1	14.0	13.8	13.3	13.0	12.6	14.1
2016	11.6	11.2	11.3	11.3	11.2	11.2	11.1	11.2	11.0	11.4	11.4	11.2	11.3
2017	10.4	10.6	11.0	11.2	11.3	11.4	11.7	11.9	11.9	12.0	11.9	11.7	11.4
2018	11.5	11.8	12.2	12.0	12.2	12.4	12.4	12.6	12.4	12.6	12.5	12.2	12.2
Construction													
2010	147.4	142.8	149.6	162.8	170.2	176.8	183.1	183.4	181.0	182.5	178.6	167.9	168.8
2011	150.2	147.9	154.2	167.0	175.1	183.0	190.7	193.6	192.6	190.8	187.7	180.8	176.1
2012	162.9	160.3	165.8	176.1	184.0	189.6	191.9	192.4	191.1	191.5	187.3	179.9	181.1
2013	163.0	161.7	166.0	176.2	188.6	195.5	198.8	201.0	199.7	200.2	196.6	185.1	186.0
2014	169.1	166.6	174.9	188.0	199.9	207.3	211.0	211.9	209.5	209.4	205.1	195.6	195.7
2015	175.9	173.9	179.2	193.5	205.4	210.8	213.7	214.8	212.6	213.5	209.9	202.5	200.5
2016	185.6	184.5	192.0	203.6	211.6	217.9	218.2	217.0	214.8	214.6	212.0	201.9	206.1
2017	187.6	189.6	197.3	213.4	226.2	233.3	233.0	233.0	229.8	227.3	222.1	212.9	217.1
2018	193.1	195.1	202.6	212.6	224.2	231.2	234.0	234.3	231.6	232.1	224.7	216.4	219.3

1. Employment by Industry: Ohio, 2010–2018—*Continued*

(Numbers in thousands, not seasonally adjusted)

Industry and year	January	February	March	April	May	June	July	August	September	October	November	December	Annual average
Manufacturing													
2010	608.1	608.3	609.1	614.7	620.5	625.3	624.4	627.7	627.7	628.7	630.0	631.8	621.4
2011	625.2	626.3	629.5	633.5	635.9	639.9	641.8	647.0	645.0	647.2	650.5	651.1	639.4
2012	644.9	648.2	652.3	654.3	657.8	664.3	659.7	663.8	661.0	657.8	660.4	661.1	657.1
2013	655.1	656.2	657.7	660.0	663.5	668.7	663.2	668.7	666.4	665.7	668.9	670.6	663.7
2014	663.6	665.2	666.6	669.3	674.5	679.6	675.0	681.9	679.8	682.1	685.3	686.9	675.8
2015	681.4	682.0	682.6	685.4	689.5	693.0	689.4	692.1	688.5	688.4	689.5	691.0	687.7
2016	683.8	683.9	683.9	684.3	685.8	688.8	688.6	689.0	686.0	685.1	686.3	687.9	686.1
2017	683.8	681.8	683.3	682.1	683.7	690.6	686.0	690.3	684.3	689.6	693.1	696.1	687.1
2018	689.9	694.9	694.8	695.1	697.3	703.9	701.5	702.6	699.4	699.8	702.0	705.1	698.9
Trade, Transportation, and Utilities													
2010	932.1	922.3	927.2	934.9	943.2	947.4	946.4	947.3	941.1	951.7	967.8	978.0	945.0
2011	934.0	928.4	931.6	944.5	950.5	954.9	956.7	959.6	954.8	964.0	984.6	994.9	954.9
2012	953.7	946.7	953.9	958.8	969.0	972.5	968.2	969.1	965.8	976.2	998.5	1,004.5	969.7
2013	961.1	953.4	957.3	965.2	976.9	981.4	979.4	981.1	975.2	985.4	1,009.7	1,019.0	978.8
2014	971.6	964.7	967.9	978.2	989.2	993.4	990.8	994.9	989.1	1,002.9	1,026.0	1,037.8	992.2
2015	992.8	985.5	989.2	997.3	1,008.1	1,010.6	1,008.9	1,010.7	1,004.1	1,015.4	1,037.6	1,047.9	1,009.0
2016	1,005.7	998.4	1,001.2	1,006.7	1,014.9	1,015.5	1,015.5	1,018.0	1,012.0	1,022.5	1,046.3	1,057.4	1,017.8
2017	1,012.8	1,003.6	1,005.0	1,010.8	1,017.9	1,020.6	1,019.8	1,020.7	1,013.5	1,025.8	1,051.0	1,056.0	1,021.5
2018	1,016.4	1,007.0	1,008.4	1,012.6	1,023.0	1,025.0	1,025.0	1,024.5	1,017.6	1,029.8	1,049.6	1,053.1	1,024.3
Wholesale Trade													
2010	210.9	210.7	210.9	212.1	212.7	213.6	214.3	213.9	212.1	212.5	212.1	211.8	212.3
2011	209.8	210.1	210.8	213.2	214.6	215.8	217.3	217.7	216.8	217.6	217.7	218.4	215.0
2012	216.8	217.6	218.6	219.3	220.9	222.5	222.3	222.2	220.8	221.8	221.8	222.2	220.6
2013	219.3	219.6	220.3	221.9	223.5	224.3	224.5	224.5	223.1	224.4	225.3	225.9	223.1
2014	223.0	224.1	225.2	226.1	228.8	229.8	230.4	230.4	229.0	229.8	230.5	231.5	228.2
2015	228.0	228.7	229.8	229.9	231.5	232.1	232.1	231.6	229.3	230.1	230.5	230.6	230.4
2016	228.5	228.5	228.9	228.8	230.0	230.7	230.8	230.6	228.8	229.1	229.2	229.8	229.5
2017	227.5	228.0	228.5	229.5	230.9	232.6	232.4	232.2	230.5	231.6	232.2	233.1	230.8
2018	230.4	231.1	231.9	233.3	234.9	236.5	237.4	236.7	235.2	236.0	237.8	239.2	235.0
Retail Trade													
2010	543.0	534.9	539.1	544.4	550.4	552.7	552.0	552.5	547.4	556.0	571.2	579.1	551.9
2011	544.0	538.5	540.6	549.3	552.7	555.3	555.2	556.2	550.8	558.5	576.9	583.9	555.2
2012	551.1	543.5	549.1	552.8	559.2	560.1	556.6	556.5	554.0	561.8	581.6	584.2	559.2
2013	552.9	545.8	548.8	554.6	562.6	565.2	563.5	564.1	559.4	566.9	586.2	592.1	563.5
2014	555.3	549.2	550.8	559.1	564.3	566.8	563.8	566.0	560.7	571.4	589.7	594.9	566.0
2015	561.0	555.4	557.8	563.8	570.5	571.8	570.1	571.0	566.1	573.8	591.7	597.4	570.9
2016	568.1	563.0	564.8	569.4	574.6	574.6	573.8	575.1	568.8	575.4	592.1	596.4	574.7
2017	567.3	560.2	560.9	565.1	568.8	569.1	568.6	568.1	561.8	570.1	589.2	590.5	570.0
2018	564.7	556.5	556.7	558.5	565.8	564.0	564.2	562.9	556.3	560.8	575.0	573.3	563.2
Transportation and Utilities													
2010	178.2	176.7	177.2	178.4	180.1	181.1	180.1	180.9	181.6	183.2	184.5	187.1	180.8
2011	180.2	179.8	180.2	182.0	183.2	183.8	184.2	185.7	187.2	187.9	190.0	192.6	184.7
2012	185.8	185.6	186.2	186.7	188.9	189.9	189.3	190.4	191.0	192.6	195.1	198.1	190.0
2013	188.9	188.0	188.2	188.7	190.8	191.9	191.4	192.5	192.7	194.1	198.2	201.0	192.2
2014	193.3	191.4	191.9	193.0	196.1	196.8	196.6	198.5	199.4	201.7	205.8	211.4	198.0
2015	203.8	201.4	201.6	203.6	206.1	206.7	206.7	208.1	208.7	211.5	215.4	219.9	207.8
2016	209.1	206.9	207.5	208.5	210.3	210.2	210.9	212.3	214.4	218.0	225.0	231.2	213.7
2017	218.0	215.4	215.6	216.2	218.2	218.9	218.8	220.4	221.2	224.1	229.6	232.4	220.7
2018	221.3	219.4	219.8	220.8	222.3	224.5	223.4	224.9	226.1	233.0	236.8	240.6	226.1
Information													
2010	78.6	78.2	78.0	77.5	77.7	77.6	78.0	78.0	77.1	76.9	77.2	77.3	77.7
2011	76.2	75.9	75.5	76.0	76.4	76.5	76.9	76.8	76.3	76.0	76.2	76.1	76.2
2012	75.2	75.0	74.8	74.8	75.1	75.6	75.6	75.1	74.6	74.9	75.3	75.6	75.1
2013	75.0	75.5	75.6	75.6	75.6	76.0	76.1	75.8	74.9	74.6	74.5	74.9	75.3
2014	73.2	73.1	73.1	73.4	73.3	72.9	73.0	72.8	71.5	71.1	71.7	72.3	72.6
2015	70.9	71.3	71.2	71.8	71.9	72.3	72.2	72.2	71.4	71.8	72.3	72.7	71.8
2016	71.6	71.7	71.8	71.7	72.1	72.5	72.8	72.7	72.2	72.0	72.5	72.4	72.2
2017	71.7	71.8	71.4	71.9	72.3	72.3	72.5	72.5	71.9	71.1	71.7	71.8	71.9
2018	71.1	71.4	70.8	70.9	71.2	71.8	71.2	71.0	70.1	70.3	70.0	69.5	70.8

1. Employment by Industry: Ohio, 2010–2018—*Continued*

(Numbers in thousands, not seasonally adjusted)

Industry and year	January	February	March	April	May	June	July	August	September	October	November	December	Annual average
Financial Activities													
2010	274.5	274.0	273.6	274.9	276.0	277.3	279.0	278.9	277.1	278.3	278.6	279.3	276.8
2011	277.5	277.5	277.4	277.9	278.6	278.8	278.9	278.7	277.9	277.5	277.5	277.7	278.0
2012	275.7	275.7	276.4	277.9	279.6	281.5	282.5	282.4	280.4	281.8	282.7	282.8	280.0
2013	279.6	280.1	280.3	282.8	284.7	286.8	287.2	287.4	285.2	285.5	286.3	286.3	284.4
2014	283.7	284.5	284.9	285.4	288.2	290.0	290.4	291.2	288.5	289.4	290.7	290.9	288.2
2015	288.6	289.0	289.0	290.7	293.4	295.6	296.4	296.9	294.1	296.0	296.2	296.2	293.5
2016	294.6	295.7	296.1	298.4	299.9	301.5	303.7	303.9	302.1	303.4	303.8	304.7	300.7
2017	302.5	302.8	303.0	304.5	306.1	308.6	308.6	308.7	306.9	307.4	306.9	307.0	306.1
2018	305.7	306.7	305.8	306.8	308.7	311.0	312.2	311.4	307.9	306.7	305.5	306.2	307.9
Professional and Business Services													
2010	599.0	600.8	606.0	624.7	625.6	633.3	637.6	642.6	639.9	645.7	646.7	645.1	628.9
2011	627.9	631.5	637.8	653.2	652.2	655.9	662.4	667.0	666.0	668.4	670.6	670.2	655.3
2012	652.2	656.1	662.3	674.4	676.7	681.5	681.9	687.4	684.4	692.7	691.9	687.5	677.4
2013	660.9	666.1	670.9	689.2	694.9	698.9	697.6	705.2	703.2	708.9	712.0	710.8	693.2
2014	687.9	690.1	694.2	709.8	713.7	716.2	718.9	725.6	719.3	726.9	730.0	726.8	713.3
2015	700.6	698.5	701.4	715.4	722.1	725.0	729.2	731.5	723.1	735.2	733.5	728.5	720.3
2016	706.8	706.8	711.3	728.3	729.5	732.1	737.5	737.5	735.0	738.1	738.5	730.3	727.6
2017	709.4	710.7	712.0	723.9	728.0	733.8	731.7	734.4	729.1	737.1	739.8	731.7	726.8
2018	711.7	715.1	717.6	728.5	730.8	737.3	739.3	741.4	735.1	742.8	741.9	732.6	731.2
Education and Health Services													
2010	832.0	837.7	840.8	841.7	837.5	825.7	825.0	826.4	843.5	852.2	854.4	852.1	839.1
2011	839.8	847.9	848.8	854.3	856.1	841.8	838.3	839.5	853.2	860.7	862.8	863.2	850.5
2012	854.2	862.4	864.0	867.3	867.2	858.9	849.4	853.3	864.5	874.5	876.3	874.6	863.9
2013	863.4	874.1	873.5	879.7	880.3	870.4	867.6	872.1	877.9	888.2	893.4	891.6	877.7
2014	876.5	883.8	885.8	890.9	891.6	880.2	877.0	881.5	888.7	900.2	903.8	903.5	888.6
2015	889.2	896.9	898.3	904.4	907.2	896.7	895.4	898.4	906.0	914.8	918.6	919.1	903.8
2016	905.7	913.7	916.4	920.3	921.4	909.2	908.7	912.5	921.9	928.3	930.1	927.6	918.0
2017	916.8	925.5	927.9	930.5	931.6	923.5	917.5	920.9	929.3	936.9	938.5	936.9	928.0
2018	925.0	933.0	933.1	935.8	936.4	928.4	924.2	930.1	936.5	947.8	953.5	949.6	936.1
Leisure and Hospitality													
2010	436.7	437.3	448.5	472.0	492.3	505.5	506.7	506.1	492.6	476.8	466.2	462.4	475.3
2011	442.6	444.6	455.6	479.5	500.9	514.4	515.0	517.1	500.8	484.0	476.1	471.2	483.5
2012	454.0	459.2	474.2	495.0	518.5	535.0	532.0	533.3	516.4	505.9	492.7	492.7	500.7
2013	474.1	477.3	490.4	513.0	540.2	551.6	550.1	548.8	532.4	521.8	508.3	507.0	517.9
2014	485.9	486.9	499.5	522.1	549.1	560.8	558.3	557.8	539.0	529.6	516.3	515.1	526.7
2015	495.6	498.2	509.8	533.0	561.0	571.5	571.4	569.8	556.2	544.2	532.7	531.5	539.6
2016	513.1	514.7	527.0	547.9	571.8	583.6	584.1	581.5	564.1	554.0	543.8	539.1	552.1
2017	519.3	525.4	537.0	556.9	578.6	593.1	592.0	591.3	573.6	564.4	548.6	548.5	560.7
2018	526.7	530.8	543.6	560.4	584.5	600.4	598.8	598.2	577.7	569.5	552.0	553.6	566.4
Other Services													
2010	202.7	203.0	203.6	206.0	206.2	208.2	208.9	208.0	206.3	207.0	206.5	206.9	206.1
2011	204.0	204.4	205.3	206.7	208.1	209.4	210.3	209.6	207.8	207.8	207.8	207.7	207.4
2012	206.3	207.0	210.1	210.9	212.7	215.5	215.2	214.2	212.4	213.5	212.5	212.9	211.9
2013	210.2	210.7	212.0	213.5	214.6	215.4	214.0	213.3	210.9	209.7	209.0	208.7	211.8
2014	205.9	206.0	207.0	208.6	211.2	213.2	212.5	212.1	209.6	211.3	210.4	211.2	209.9
2015	208.2	209.0	210.4	212.7	214.4	216.0	216.1	214.7	211.9	213.2	212.2	212.4	212.6
2016	210.2	210.6	212.0	213.7	215.4	216.5	216.7	216.0	214.2	215.4	215.1	213.8	214.1
2017	212.4	213.3	214.5	215.5	217.0	219.2	218.0	216.8	213.5	214.0	212.8	213.2	215.0
2018	210.2	210.8	212.0	213.3	214.9	217.4	216.9	215.9	213.5	213.8	212.8	213.2	213.7
Government													
2010	783.3	795.6	798.0	802.4	820.0	788.3	742.9	737.3	771.2	795.3	798.8	794.8	785.7
2011	771.4	786.0	788.5	788.6	787.8	765.8	745.6	744.4	772.9	784.8	787.0	780.2	775.3
2012	760.7	781.0	785.0	788.0	794.8	762.7	742.0	741.0	770.5	785.3	786.7	780.8	773.2
2013	759.8	776.4	776.2	781.5	785.5	746.3	729.3	730.8	764.9	777.3	783.1	773.9	765.4
2014	749.8	769.7	771.0	779.5	786.0	750.6	726.0	733.0	774.1	784.9	787.2	782.0	766.2
2015	755.1	776.5	776.4	784.5	786.2	754.8	739.0	741.5	771.8	788.2	789.8	784.3	770.7
2016	758.2	777.9	778.5	793.1	788.6	755.3	739.6	742.6	781.1	796.4	800.5	788.6	775.0
2017	778.0	792.0	793.0	794.4	790.2	758.3	741.6	745.7	780.0	797.1	800.5	791.7	780.2
2018	773.0	792.8	793.7	795.4	790.2	762.1	741.6	749.6	781.2	789.6	792.6	788.1	779.2

2. Average Weekly Hours by Selected Industry: Ohio, 2014–2018

(Not seasonally adjusted)

Industry and year	January	February	March	April	May	June	July	August	September	October	November	December	Annual average
Total Private													
2014	33.3	34.1	34.1	34.0	34.6	34.4	34.1	34.3	34.3	34.3	34.6	34.5	34.2
2015	33.8	34.1	34.3	34.0	34.2	34.3	34.1	34.6	34.1	34.4	34.6	34.4	34.2
2016	34.0	34.0	34.1	34.2	34.4	34.3	34.3	34.3	34.4	34.7	34.4	34.4	34.3
2017	34.3	34.1	34.1	34.3	34.3	34.4	34.4	34.3	34.4	34.7	34.4	34.4	34.4
2018	33.7	34.2	34.3	34.6	34.3	34.4	34.5	34.3	34.5	34.3	34.3	34.7	34.4
Goods-Producing													
2014	39.8	40.8	40.8	41.0	40.9	41.3	40.6	41.1	41.3	41.3	41.3	41.4	41.0
2015	40.3	40.3	40.6	40.4	40.6	40.8	40.0	40.7	39.8	41.0	40.5	40.5	40.5
2016	39.8	39.8	40.1	40.3	40.3	40.5	40.4	40.5	40.9	41.0	40.9	40.5	40.4
2017	39.9	40.0	39.8	40.0	40.6	41.0	40.4	41.1	40.8	41.1	40.9	40.8	40.5
2018	39.5	40.6	40.6	40.9	40.4	40.7	40.4	40.8	40.8	40.8	40.5	41.0	40.6
Construction													
2014	37.3	38.4	38.0	39.0	38.5	39.7	39.4	39.4	40.1	39.1	38.3	38.1	38.8
2015	36.9	37.5	37.7	38.4	39.2	39.0	39.2	40.0	37.9	40.3	38.0	38.7	38.6
2016	36.8	37.2	37.8	38.7	37.9	39.6	39.6	39.2	39.6	39.7	39.4	37.9	38.7
2017	36.6	37.5	36.8	38.3	39.4	40.6	38.9	40.4	40.0	39.1	38.9	37.8	38.8
2018	36.2	37.5	38.5	39.3	39.4	39.5	40.1	39.9	39.3	39.1	38.3	38.9	38.9
Manufacturing													
2014	40.5	41.3	41.4	41.4	41.4	41.5	40.7	41.4	41.5	41.8	42.0	42.1	41.4
2015	41.1	40.9	41.2	40.8	40.8	41.1	40.1	40.7	40.5	41.1	41.2	41.0	40.9
2016	40.6	40.5	40.7	40.7	41.0	40.8	40.7	41.0	41.4	41.6	41.7	41.6	41.0
2017	41.3	41.0	41.0	40.7	41.2	41.3	41.2	41.4	41.1	41.8	41.7	41.9	41.3
2018	40.6	41.5	41.2	41.2	40.4	40.8	40.0	40.8	41.3	41.4	41.5	41.9	41.1
Trade, Transportation, and Utilities													
2014	33.9	34.4	34.3	34.1	34.5	34.6	34.7	34.7	34.8	34.6	34.8	34.8	34.5
2015	33.8	34.3	34.4	34.5	34.8	34.7	34.8	35.2	35.1	34.8	35.1	35.2	34.7
2016	34.2	34.4	34.2	34.7	34.9	35.0	34.9	34.8	34.8	34.8	34.6	35.3	34.7
2017	34.6	34.2	34.5	34.9	34.7	34.7	34.9	34.8	34.9	35.0	34.7	35.1	34.8
2018	33.9	34.1	34.4	34.5	34.5	34.5	34.6	34.3	34.4	34.0	34.5	34.5	34.4
Financial Activities													
2014	36.5	37.7	37.3	36.8	36.9	37.4	36.6	37.0	36.8	36.7	38.1	36.4	37.0
2015	36.7	37.8	38.6	37.3	37.3	36.7	36.6	37.4	36.3	36.6	37.2	36.2	37.1
2016	36.3	35.7	35.3	35.8	36.8	35.8	36.4	35.8	35.8	37.0	36.0	35.9	36.1
2017	37.2	36.1	36.3	37.0	36.2	36.5	36.6	35.8	36.2	36.9	36.2	36.1	36.4
2018	36.1	36.6	36.4	37.1	36.2	36.6	36.8	36.5	37.4	36.4	36.5	36.9	36.6
Professional and Business Services													
2014	35.2	36.3	36.4	36.1	35.7	36.5	35.5	35.5	35.8	35.6	35.9	35.7	35.8
2015	34.8	35.7	35.9	35.4	35.3	35.4	35.2	35.8	35.1	35.8	36.3	35.9	35.6
2016	35.4	35.4	35.6	35.6	36.0	35.2	34.7	35.1	35.4	36.0	35.3	35.3	35.4
2017	35.7	35.5	35.4	35.9	35.8	35.7	36.0	35.8	36.0	36.6	35.8	35.8	35.8
2018	35.4	35.8	35.9	36.5	35.9	36.0	36.3	35.8	36.6	36.4	36.3	37.0	36.2
Education and Health Services													
2014	31.1	31.3	31.3	31.2	31.0	30.4	30.6	30.7	30.9	31.1	31.8	31.7	31.1
2015	31.7	31.6	31.8	31.8	32.0	32.2	32.2	32.5	32.5	32.4	32.8	32.5	32.2
2016	32.7	32.2	32.4	32.4	32.5	32.4	32.4	32.5	32.5	32.7	32.8	32.5	32.5
2017	32.5	32.4	32.4	32.6	32.5	32.3	32.3	32.4	32.6	32.8	33.0	32.9	32.6
2018	32.5	32.7	32.6	32.8	32.6	32.6	32.8	32.6	32.7	32.6	32.6	32.7	32.7
Leisure and Hospitality													
2014	22.1	23.3	23.5	23.5	23.9	24.5	24.3	24.6	24.0	24.0	24.0	24.1	23.8
2015	23.1	23.8	24.0	23.7	24.2	24.5	24.8	24.9	24.1	24.4	24.4	24.6	24.2
2016	23.7	24.2	24.1	23.8	24.1	24.7	24.8	24.6	23.9	24.3	24.1	23.6	24.2
2017	23.5	23.8	24.1	23.7	24.0	24.5	24.5	24.3	23.7	24.0	23.8	23.8	24.0
2018	22.9	23.8	24.1	24.4	24.4	24.7	25.0	24.7	24.3	24.3	24.1	24.3	24.3
Other Services													
2014	29.4	30.6	30.7	29.9	30.1	29.9	29.5	29.6	29.8	30.1	30.4	30.1	30.0
2015	30.1	30.3	31.1	30.6	30.5	31.0	30.8	31.8	30.3	30.2	30.8	31.0	30.7
2016	30.8	30.9	31.9	32.3	32.1	31.7	32.2	32.4	32.7	32.7	32.2	32.6	32.0
2017	32.0	32.4	32.1	33.1	32.3	32.3	32.3	32.2	32.3	33.0	32.4	31.8	32.4
2018	31.1	31.4	31.5	32.0	31.2	31.2	31.1	30.5	30.6	30.3	29.8	30.6	30.9

3. Average Hourly Earnings by Selected Industry: Ohio, 2014–2018

(Dollars, not seasonally adjusted)

Industry and year	January	February	March	April	May	June	July	August	September	October	November	December	Annual average
Total Private													
2014	22.41	22.53	22.46	22.35	21.69	21.84	21.80	21.92	22.20	22.14	22.36	22.29	22.16
2015	22.51	22.63	22.67	22.57	22.48	22.38	22.51	22.80	22.90	22.76	22.98	22.93	22.68
2016	23.12	23.10	23.09	23.39	23.42	23.15	23.33	23.23	23.55	23.86	23.70	23.86	23.40
2017	24.08	23.88	23.91	24.01	23.75	23.70	24.19	23.94	24.17	24.30	24.23	24.35	24.04
2018	24.68	24.58	24.58	24.76	24.46	24.38	24.81	24.77	25.25	25.12	25.09	25.40	24.82
Goods-Producing													
2014	24.59	24.68	24.70	24.68	24.41	24.57	24.69	24.70	24.89	24.82	24.74	24.72	24.68
2015	24.56	24.51	24.65	24.67	24.66	24.61	24.90	24.99	25.00	24.75	24.78	25.10	24.77
2016	24.96	25.04	25.30	25.60	25.71	25.67	25.90	25.78	25.88	26.11	26.19	26.28	25.71
2017	26.11	26.09	26.21	26.41	26.39	26.49	26.74	26.55	26.98	27.00	27.03	27.06	26.60
2018	27.07	27.07	27.21	27.27	27.24	27.03	27.39	27.45	27.69	27.86	27.86	28.33	27.46
Construction													
2014	25.50	26.10	26.23	26.12	25.87	26.03	26.31	26.16	26.85	26.43	25.94	26.03	26.15
2015	25.75	25.55	25.97	26.03	26.56	26.33	26.87	26.91	27.05	26.77	26.68	26.94	26.49
2016	26.82	26.86	26.93	27.42	27.48	27.24	26.93	26.90	26.92	27.19	27.11	26.83	27.06
2017	26.81	26.84	27.32	26.88	27.76	27.75	27.71	27.95	28.35	28.47	27.89	27.40	27.64
2018	27.47	27.77	27.93	27.93	28.09	27.72	28.29	28.70	28.83	29.32	29.48	29.76	28.47
Manufacturing													
2014	24.36	24.36	24.36	24.33	24.06	24.21	24.25	24.33	24.34	24.38	24.46	24.43	24.32
2015	24.34	24.30	24.38	24.37	24.18	24.19	24.34	24.44	24.49	24.17	24.31	24.62	24.34
2016	24.56	24.66	24.98	25.15	25.25	25.26	25.66	25.49	25.70	25.89	26.01	26.26	25.41
2017	26.01	25.95	25.92	26.32	25.87	25.98	26.36	25.91	26.36	26.36	26.67	26.93	26.22
2018	26.87	26.78	26.92	26.97	26.82	26.70	26.96	26.82	27.15	27.22	27.20	27.75	27.02
Trade, Transportation, and Utilities													
2014	20.32	20.74	20.91	20.97	20.53	20.60	20.29	20.53	20.79	20.62	20.75	20.64	20.64
2015	21.00	21.19	21.35	21.34	21.16	21.16	21.32	21.56	21.67	21.69	21.76	21.35	21.38
2016	21.88	21.77	21.95	22.33	22.07	21.95	22.14	22.04	22.34	22.69	22.31	22.14	22.14
2017	22.79	22.51	22.73	23.07	22.73	22.73	22.93	22.59	22.55	22.63	22.43	22.40	22.67
2018	22.82	22.44	22.65	22.89	22.54	22.63	22.94	23.02	23.45	23.04	22.65	22.85	22.83
Financial Activities													
2014	27.90	27.41	27.19	27.08	26.75	26.75	27.08	26.92	27.23	27.31	27.47	27.26	27.19
2015	27.39	27.93	27.47	27.15	26.78	26.46	26.55	27.58	27.39	26.87	26.76	26.87	27.10
2016	26.89	27.21	27.78	27.92	28.23	28.36	28.09	28.52	29.35	30.34	30.20	30.63	28.64
2017	30.80	30.81	30.84	30.78	30.18	29.92	29.90	29.76	30.15	30.06	29.56	29.87	30.22
2018	29.92	30.36	29.97	30.01	29.74	29.47	30.05	29.76	29.74	29.82	30.28	30.83	30.00
Professional and Business Services													
2014	25.57	25.80	25.49	25.03	24.81	24.99	24.78	24.76	24.62	24.38	25.14	25.00	25.03
2015	25.39	25.71	25.71	25.44	25.40	25.21	25.40	25.98	25.93	25.81	26.49	26.23	25.73
2016	27.03	27.07	26.71	26.93	27.06	26.66	26.93	26.87	26.82	27.07	26.86	27.11	26.93
2017	27.34	27.11	27.31	27.22	26.60	26.83	27.48	26.89	27.17	27.69	27.75	27.94	27.28
2018	28.61	28.58	28.45	28.88	28.12	27.86	28.68	28.23	28.89	28.69	28.56	28.89	28.54
Education and Health Services													
2014	21.56	21.61	21.57	21.60	21.59	21.69	21.84	22.13	22.54	22.42	22.61	22.69	21.99
2015	23.02	22.88	22.78	22.61	22.57	22.41	22.30	22.43	22.67	22.36	22.46	22.70	22.60
2016	22.48	22.25	22.20	22.51	22.83	22.26	22.22	21.94	22.41	22.55	22.31	22.61	22.38
2017	22.84	22.61	22.53	22.60	22.50	22.14	22.66	22.49	22.63	22.65	22.65	22.85	22.60
2018	23.25	22.95	22.98	23.04	22.94	23.03	23.18	23.21	23.73	23.60	23.62	23.63	23.27
Leisure and Hospitality													
2014	12.80	12.75	12.65	12.63	12.53	12.29	12.29	12.21	12.36	12.39	12.42	12.56	12.48
2015	12.69	12.64	12.61	12.68	12.46	12.41	12.34	12.40	12.51	12.50	12.58	12.79	12.54
2016	12.73	12.75	12.81	13.01	13.00	12.67	12.78	12.86	13.07	13.30	13.34	13.53	12.98
2017	13.51	13.57	13.53	13.47	13.54	13.20	13.25	13.41	13.51	13.50	13.52	13.69	13.47
2018	13.71	13.73	13.71	13.70	13.75	13.61	13.70	13.84	14.08	14.20	14.31	14.60	13.91
Other Services													
2014	19.22	19.43	19.33	18.92	19.15	19.35	19.46	19.52	19.84	20.30	20.28	20.36	19.60
2015	20.25	20.77	20.79	20.71	21.00	20.81	21.15	21.34	21.76	21.03	21.49	21.29	21.04
2016	21.08	20.81	20.44	20.75	20.82	20.85	21.24	21.04	21.17	21.20	21.41	21.51	21.03
2017	21.85	21.69	21.52	21.56	21.69	21.49	21.82	21.76	21.64	21.61	21.54	21.46	21.64
2018	21.79	22.28	22.22	22.26	22.08	22.13	22.59	22.51	22.84	22.65	23.02	23.42	22.48

4. Average Weekly Earnings by Selected Industry: Ohio, 2014–2018

(Dollars, not seasonally adjusted)

Industry and year	January	February	March	April	May	June	July	August	September	October	November	December	Annual average
Total Private													
2014	746.25	768.27	765.89	759.90	750.47	751.30	743.38	751.86	761.46	759.40	773.66	769.01	757.87
2015	760.84	771.68	777.58	767.38	768.82	767.63	767.59	788.88	780.89	782.94	795.11	788.79	775.66
2016	786.08	785.40	787.37	799.94	805.65	794.05	800.22	796.79	810.12	827.94	815.28	820.78	802.62
2017	825.94	814.31	815.33	823.54	814.63	815.28	832.14	821.14	831.45	843.21	833.51	837.64	826.98
2018	831.72	840.64	843.09	856.70	838.98	838.67	855.95	849.61	871.13	861.62	860.59	881.38	853.81
Goods-Producing													
2014	978.68	1,006.94	1,007.76	1,011.88	998.37	1,014.74	1,002.41	1,015.17	1,027.96	1,025.07	1,021.76	1,023.41	1,011.88
2015	989.77	987.75	1,000.79	996.67	1,001.20	1,004.09	996.00	1,017.09	995.00	1,014.75	1,003.59	1,016.55	1,003.19
2016	993.41	996.59	1,014.53	1,031.68	1,036.11	1,039.64	1,046.36	1,044.09	1,058.49	1,070.51	1,071.17	1,064.34	1,038.68
2017	1,041.79	1,043.60	1,043.16	1,056.40	1,071.43	1,086.09	1,080.30	1,091.21	1,100.78	1,109.70	1,105.53	1,104.05	1,077.30
2018	1,069.27	1,099.04	1,104.73	1,115.34	1,100.50	1,100.12	1,106.56	1,119.96	1,129.75	1,136.69	1,128.33	1,161.53	1,114.88
Construction													
2014	951.15	1,002.24	996.74	1,018.68	996.00	1,033.39	1,036.61	1,030.70	1,076.69	1,033.41	993.50	991.74	1,014.62
2015	950.18	958.13	979.07	999.55	1,041.15	1,026.87	1,053.30	1,076.40	1,025.20	1,078.83	1,013.84	1,042.58	1,022.51
2016	986.98	999.19	1,017.95	1,061.15	1,041.49	1,078.70	1,066.43	1,054.48	1,066.03	1,079.44	1,068.13	1,016.86	1,047.22
2017	981.25	1,006.50	1,005.38	1,029.50	1,093.74	1,126.65	1,077.92	1,129.18	1,134.00	1,113.18	1,084.92	1,035.72	1,072.43
2018	994.41	1,041.38	1,075.31	1,097.65	1,106.75	1,094.94	1,134.43	1,145.13	1,133.02	1,146.41	1,129.08	1,157.66	1,107.48
Manufacturing													
2014	986.58	1,006.07	1,008.50	1,007.26	996.08	1,004.72	986.98	1,007.26	1,010.11	1,019.08	1,027.32	1,028.50	1,006.85
2015	1,000.37	993.87	1,004.46	994.30	986.54	994.21	976.03	994.71	991.85	993.39	1,001.57	1,009.42	995.51
2016	997.14	998.73	1,016.69	1,023.61	1,035.25	1,030.61	1,044.36	1,045.09	1,063.98	1,077.02	1,084.62	1,092.42	1,041.81
2017	1,074.21	1,063.95	1,062.72	1,071.22	1,065.84	1,072.97	1,086.03	1,072.67	1,083.40	1,101.85	1,112.14	1,128.37	1,082.89
2018	1,090.92	1,111.37	1,109.10	1,111.16	1,083.53	1,089.36	1,078.40	1,094.26	1,121.30	1,126.91	1,128.80	1,162.73	1,110.52
Trade, Transportation, and Utilities													
2014	688.85	713.46	717.21	715.08	708.29	712.76	704.06	712.39	723.49	713.45	722.10	718.27	712.08
2015	709.80	726.82	734.44	736.23	736.37	734.25	741.94	758.91	760.62	754.81	763.78	751.52	741.89
2016	748.30	748.89	750.69	774.85	770.24	768.25	772.69	766.99	777.43	789.61	771.93	781.54	768.26
2017	788.53	769.84	784.19	805.14	788.73	788.73	800.26	786.13	787.00	792.05	778.32	786.24	788.92
2018	773.60	765.20	779.16	789.71	777.63	780.74	793.72	789.59	806.68	783.36	781.43	788.33	785.35
Financial Activities													
2014	1,018.35	1,033.36	1,014.19	996.54	987.08	1,000.45	991.13	996.04	1,002.06	1,002.28	1,046.61	992.26	1,006.03
2015	1,005.21	1,055.75	1,060.34	1,012.70	998.89	971.08	971.73	1,031.49	994.26	983.44	995.47	972.69	1,005.41
2016	976.11	971.40	980.63	999.54	1,038.86	1,015.29	1,022.48	1,021.02	1,050.73	1,122.58	1,087.20	1,099.62	1,033.90
2017	1,145.76	1,112.24	1,119.49	1,138.86	1,092.52	1,092.08	1,094.34	1,065.41	1,091.43	1,109.21	1,070.07	1,078.31	1,100.01
2018	1,080.11	1,111.18	1,090.91	1,113.37	1,076.59	1,078.60	1,105.84	1,086.24	1,112.28	1,085.45	1,105.22	1,137.63	1,098.00
Professional and Business Services													
2014	900.06	936.54	927.84	903.58	885.72	912.14	879.69	878.98	881.40	867.93	902.53	892.50	896.07
2015	883.57	917.85	922.99	900.58	896.62	892.43	894.08	930.08	910.14	924.00	961.59	941.66	915.99
2016	956.86	958.28	950.88	958.71	974.16	938.43	934.47	943.14	949.43	974.52	948.16	956.98	953.32
2017	976.04	962.41	966.77	977.20	952.28	957.83	989.28	962.66	978.12	1,013.45	993.45	1,000.25	976.62
2018	1,012.79	1,023.16	1,021.36	1,054.12	1,009.51	1,002.96	1,041.08	1,010.63	1,057.37	1,044.32	1,036.73	1,068.93	1,033.15
Education and Health Services													
2014	670.52	676.39	675.14	673.92	669.29	659.38	668.30	679.39	696.49	697.26	719.00	719.27	683.89
2015	729.73	723.01	724.40	719.00	722.24	721.60	718.06	728.98	736.78	724.46	736.69	737.75	727.72
2016	735.10	716.45	719.28	729.32	741.98	721.22	719.93	713.05	728.33	737.39	731.77	734.83	727.35
2017	742.30	732.56	729.97	736.76	731.25	715.12	731.92	728.68	737.74	742.92	747.45	751.77	736.76
2018	755.63	750.47	749.15	755.71	747.84	750.78	760.30	756.65	775.97	769.36	770.01	772.70	760.93
Leisure and Hospitality													
2014	282.88	297.08	297.28	296.81	299.47	301.11	298.65	300.37	296.64	297.36	298.08	302.70	297.02
2015	293.14	300.83	302.64	300.52	301.53	304.05	306.03	308.76	301.49	305.00	306.95	314.63	303.47
2016	301.70	308.55	308.72	309.64	313.30	312.95	316.94	316.36	312.37	323.19	321.49	319.31	314.12
2017	317.49	322.97	326.07	319.24	324.96	323.40	324.63	325.86	320.19	324.00	321.78	325.82	323.28
2018	313.96	326.77	330.41	334.28	335.50	336.17	342.50	341.85	342.14	345.06	344.87	354.78	338.01
Other Services													
2014	565.07	594.56	593.43	565.71	576.42	578.57	574.07	577.79	591.23	611.03	616.51	612.84	588.00
2015	609.53	629.33	646.57	633.73	640.50	645.11	651.42	678.61	659.33	635.11	661.89	659.99	645.93
2016	649.26	643.03	652.04	670.23	668.32	660.95	683.93	681.70	692.26	693.24	689.40	701.23	672.96
2017	699.20	702.76	690.79	713.64	700.59	694.13	704.79	700.67	698.97	713.13	697.90	682.43	701.14
2018	677.67	699.59	699.93	712.32	688.90	690.46	702.55	686.56	698.90	686.30	686.00	716.65	694.63

OKLAHOMA
At a Glance

Population:
2010 census: 3,751,351
2018 estimate: 3,943,079

Percent change in population:
2010–2018: 5.1%

Percent change in total nonfarm employment:
2010–2018: 8.5%

Industry with the largest growth in employment, 2010–2018 (percent):
Transportation and utilities, 32.4%

Industry with the largest decline or smallest growth in employment, 2010–2018 (percent):
Information, -18.1%

Civilian labor force:
2010: 1,768,284
2018: 1,841,872

Unemployment rate and rank among states (highest to lowest):
2010: 6.8%, 44th
2018: 3.4%, 32nd

Over-the-year change in unemployment rates:
2016–2017: -0.6%
2017–2018: -0.8%

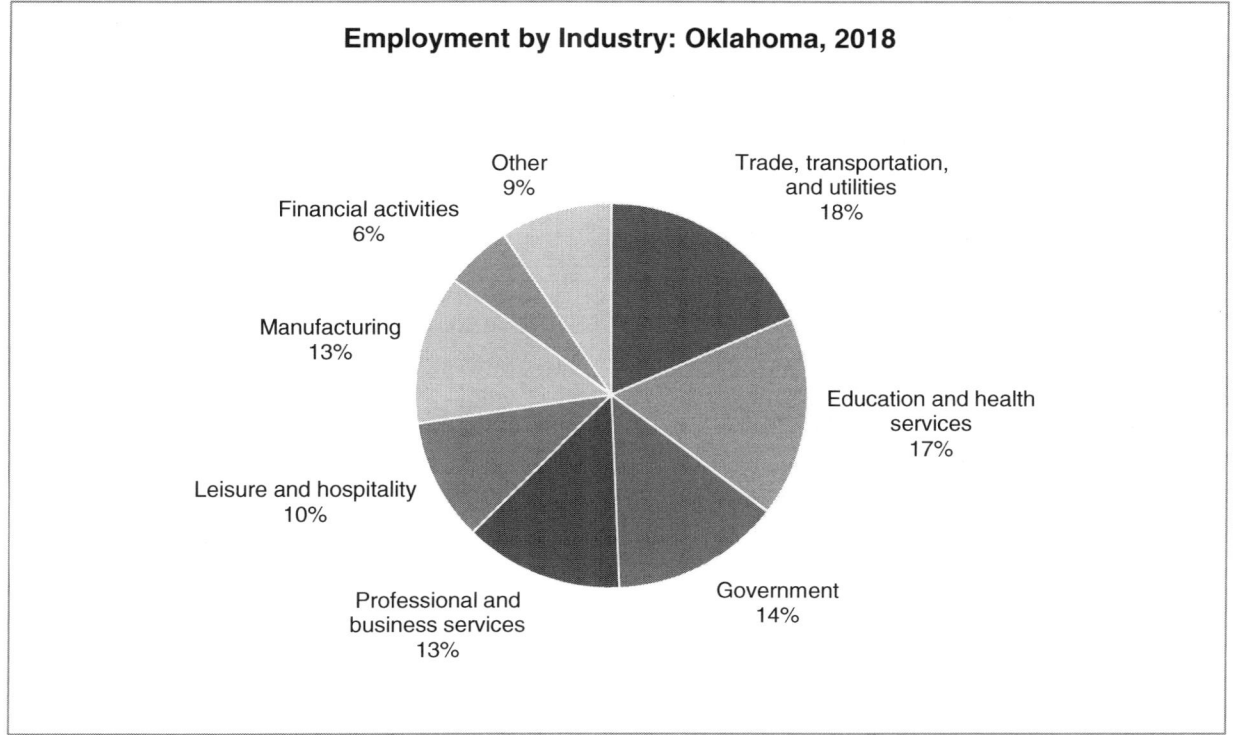

Employment by Industry: Oklahoma, 2018

Other
9%

Trade, transportation,
and utilities
18%

Financial activities
6%

Manufacturing
13%

Education and health
services
17%

Leisure and hospitality
10%

Professional and
business services
13%

Government
14%

1. Employment by Industry: Oklahoma, 2010–2018

(Numbers in thousands, not seasonally adjusted)

Industry and year	January	February	March	April	May	June	July	August	September	October	November	December	Annual average
Total Nonfarm													
2010	1,521.4	1,528.4	1,544.0	1,556.9	1,569.4	1,564.2	1,549.9	1,550.7	1,558.1	1,571.9	1,575.9	1,580.3	1,555.9
2011	1,541.6	1,541.7	1,564.9	1,580.7	1,584.6	1,578.3	1,564.9	1,573.3	1,594.6	1,597.8	1,602.4	1,607.5	1,577.7
2012	1,575.0	1,589.9	1,602.7	1,614.9	1,622.7	1,617.3	1,595.8	1,608.3	1,621.0	1,634.4	1,642.2	1,644.4	1,614.1
2013	1,600.9	1,614.7	1,626.3	1,634.2	1,645.8	1,636.5	1,620.9	1,633.3	1,645.7	1,650.6	1,660.0	1,654.4	1,635.3
2014	1,623.1	1,633.4	1,643.7	1,653.0	1,662.5	1,654.3	1,641.9	1,654.2	1,664.7	1,675.5	1,683.1	1,687.6	1,656.4
2015	1,655.0	1,662.9	1,664.6	1,671.8	1,675.3	1,666.7	1,654.6	1,659.3	1,669.2	1,676.4	1,680.3	1,678.8	1,667.9
2016	1,642.4	1,652.2	1,654.1	1,660.7	1,658.9	1,646.9	1,635.2	1,644.6	1,657.5	1,658.8	1,664.9	1,665.2	1,653.5
2017	1,624.6	1,639.0	1,650.7	1,660.5	1,666.2	1,666.2	1,651.4	1,660.7	1,676.9	1,679.4	1,685.6	1,688.6	1,662.5
2018	1,656.1	1,668.2	1,681.1	1,681.2	1,690.3	1,687.7	1,675.1	1,685.5	1,698.6	1,705.0	1,711.8	1,708.6	1,687.4
Total Private													
2010	1,175.2	1,176.5	1,189.1	1,202.0	1,208.6	1,215.6	1,213.5	1,217.1	1,215.3	1,221.7	1,225.5	1,229.3	1,207.5
2011	1,200.3	1,195.5	1,216.8	1,230.9	1,234.6	1,240.2	1,241.1	1,245.9	1,248.2	1,247.3	1,251.0	1,254.0	1,233.8
2012	1,232.0	1,239.4	1,250.6	1,262.6	1,269.8	1,277.5	1,268.4	1,274.3	1,272.7	1,280.1	1,286.2	1,289.0	1,266.9
2013	1,255.4	1,261.3	1,271.6	1,279.1	1,289.2	1,294.5	1,291.8	1,298.8	1,297.7	1,296.5	1,304.1	1,300.5	1,286.7
2014	1,278.4	1,281.4	1,290.7	1,299.8	1,307.2	1,312.6	1,312.9	1,319.0	1,316.4	1,319.6	1,326.5	1,332.1	1,308.1
2015	1,308.3	1,308.6	1,310.0	1,315.6	1,317.5	1,322.6	1,323.0	1,322.0	1,317.3	1,317.2	1,319.8	1,318.9	1,316.7
2016	1,291.5	1,293.9	1,294.4	1,301.1	1,299.9	1,301.0	1,302.0	1,305.5	1,304.3	1,303.7	1,308.5	1,308.6	1,301.2
2017	1,278.1	1,285.2	1,295.1	1,305.5	1,310.7	1,322.0	1,319.3	1,323.4	1,326.6	1,326.4	1,331.8	1,335.0	1,313.3
2018	1,310.1	1,316.1	1,328.1	1,329.6	1,336.7	1,345.1	1,344.1	1,349.3	1,349.7	1,353.0	1,358.6	1,355.4	1,339.7
Goods Producing													
2010	230.8	230.6	233.4	237.0	239.2	242.4	243.6	244.5	244.4	247.7	247.5	249.4	240.9
2011	244.6	244.1	249.1	253.4	254.7	258.4	260.4	261.2	262.4	263.7	264.0	265.2	256.8
2012	262.2	263.7	266.5	268.4	270.6	273.9	273.3	273.8	273.2	276.5	277.2	277.5	271.4
2013	270.9	272.1	274.0	274.3	276.7	280.0	278.8	280.4	279.8	280.4	280.2	279.7	277.3
2014	275.0	275.9	277.5	277.6	279.9	282.1	284.1	286.7	286.1	287.6	288.0	289.0	282.5
2015	285.4	284.0	280.6	276.2	274.0	274.9	275.1	273.4	271.5	269.4	266.7	265.0	274.7
2016	260.9	260.5	257.6	256.0	254.8	255.4	255.5	255.2	255.5	254.3	253.6	254.4	256.1
2017	250.2	252.3	253.7	254.4	256.7	261.4	262.3	263.6	264.9	264.1	263.9	265.6	259.4
2018	261.9	264.4	267.0	267.1	269.1	272.5	272.6	274.4	275.2	274.1	276.6	278.6	271.1
Service-Providing													
2010	1,290.6	1,297.8	1,310.6	1,319.9	1,330.2	1,321.8	1,306.3	1,306.2	1,313.7	1,324.2	1,328.4	1,330.9	1,315.1
2011	1,297.0	1,297.6	1,315.8	1,327.3	1,329.9	1,319.9	1,304.5	1,312.1	1,332.2	1,334.1	1,338.4	1,342.3	1,320.9
2012	1,312.8	1,326.2	1,336.2	1,346.5	1,352.1	1,343.4	1,322.5	1,334.5	1,347.8	1,357.9	1,365.0	1,366.9	1,342.7
2013	1,330.0	1,342.6	1,352.3	1,359.9	1,369.1	1,356.5	1,342.1	1,352.9	1,365.9	1,370.2	1,379.8	1,374.7	1,358.0
2014	1,348.1	1,357.5	1,366.2	1,375.4	1,382.6	1,372.2	1,357.8	1,367.5	1,378.6	1,387.9	1,395.1	1,398.6	1,374.0
2015	1,369.6	1,378.9	1,384.0	1,395.6	1,401.3	1,391.8	1,379.5	1,385.9	1,397.7	1,407.0	1,413.6	1,413.8	1,393.2
2016	1,381.5	1,391.7	1,396.5	1,404.7	1,404.1	1,391.5	1,379.7	1,389.4	1,402.0	1,404.5	1,411.3	1,410.8	1,397.3
2017	1,374.4	1,386.7	1,397.0	1,406.1	1,409.5	1,404.8	1,389.1	1,397.1	1,412.0	1,415.3	1,421.7	1,423.0	1,403.1
2018	1,394.2	1,403.8	1,414.1	1,414.1	1,421.2	1,415.2	1,402.5	1,411.1	1,423.4	1,430.9	1,435.2	1,430.0	1,416.3
Mining, Logging, and Construction													
2010	103.4	103.2	105.6	108.2	109.8	112.2	113.0	113.8	113.8	116.2	115.3	116.4	110.9
2011	112.6	111.9	115.6	118.1	119.0	121.6	122.4	123.1	123.7	124.5	124.3	124.9	120.1
2012	122.4	123.2	125.3	126.6	128.4	130.7	130.6	130.9	130.3	132.7	133.8	133.6	129.0
2013	128.7	129.8	131.5	132.1	134.4	137.0	136.0	137.8	137.6	138.2	137.8	137.1	134.8
2014	133.3	133.3	134.6	134.2	135.6	136.8	138.4	141.0	140.4	141.4	141.3	141.5	137.7
2015	138.7	137.2	134.8	131.8	130.2	131.6	132.6	132.0	130.8	129.6	127.6	126.0	131.9
2016	123.3	122.6	121.2	120.8	120.2	121.3	122.0	122.0	122.5	122.2	121.0	121.3	121.7
2017	119.2	120.1	121.6	121.9	123.7	127.0	127.8	128.8	130.1	129.3	128.8	129.4	125.6
2018	126.4	128.1	130.1	130.1	131.5	133.8	134.6	136.5	137.0	136.4	137.3	139.5	133.4
Manufacturing													
2010	127.4	127.4	127.8	128.8	129.4	130.2	130.6	130.7	130.6	131.5	132.2	133.0	130.0
2011	132.0	132.2	133.5	135.3	135.7	136.8	138.0	138.1	138.7	139.2	139.7	140.3	136.6
2012	139.8	140.5	141.2	141.8	142.2	143.2	142.7	142.9	142.9	143.8	143.4	143.9	142.4
2013	142.2	142.3	142.5	142.2	142.3	143.0	142.8	142.6	142.2	142.2	142.4	142.6	142.4
2014	141.7	142.6	142.9	143.4	144.3	145.3	145.7	145.7	145.7	146.2	146.7	147.5	144.8
2015	146.7	146.8	145.8	144.4	143.8	143.3	142.5	141.4	140.7	139.8	139.1	139.0	142.8
2016	137.6	137.9	136.4	135.2	134.6	134.1	133.5	133.2	133.0	132.1	132.6	133.1	134.4
2017	131.0	132.2	132.1	132.5	133.0	134.4	134.5	134.8	134.8	134.8	135.1	136.2	133.8
2018	135.5	136.3	136.9	137.0	137.6	138.7	138.0	137.9	138.2	137.7	139.3	139.1	137.7

1. Employment by Industry: Oklahoma, 2010–2018—*Continued*

(Numbers in thousands, not seasonally adjusted)

Industry and year	January	February	March	April	May	June	July	August	September	October	November	December	Annual average
Trade, Transportation, and Utilities													
2010	265.5	264.1	266.7	268.0	269.9	271.1	270.7	270.5	268.5	270.8	275.6	277.9	269.9
2011	268.4	266.8	271.0	273.8	274.4	275.0	274.8	276.4	275.9	277.0	282.0	284.2	275.0
2012	276.5	275.3	278.2	280.0	282.0	283.3	281.9	282.0	282.1	285.2	290.9	293.3	282.6
2013	280.5	280.7	282.7	284.7	287.0	288.3	288.5	289.7	289.6	290.8	297.1	299.4	288.3
2014	290.3	289.5	291.2	291.8	293.5	295.4	294.6	295.4	295.3	297.4	303.0	307.1	295.4
2015	295.7	295.3	296.5	298.2	299.5	301.2	300.5	300.3	299.6	302.2	308.0	310.7	300.6
2016	297.3	296.4	297.4	299.1	299.2	298.8	297.9	298.8	297.5	299.3	306.6	306.1	299.5
2017	294.3	292.4	292.9	294.0	294.7	295.3	295.2	295.6	295.8	298.6	305.8	306.5	296.8
2018	296.2	293.9	295.5	295.8	297.1	297.5	298.3	299.2	299.7	302.6	307.9	307.1	299.2
Wholesale Trade													
2010	51.9	52.0	52.3	52.7	53.1	53.5	53.3	53.2	53.2	53.8	54.0	54.0	53.1
2011	53.4	53.6	54.5	54.6	54.7	54.9	55.1	55.1	55.0	55.2	55.2	55.3	54.7
2012	55.0	55.5	56.1	56.4	56.9	57.3	56.8	56.7	56.7	57.3	57.5	57.8	56.7
2013	57.0	57.2	57.4	57.5	57.9	58.3	58.0	58.0	58.0	58.1	58.4	58.4	57.9
2014	58.5	58.6	58.9	59.0	59.3	59.8	59.4	59.6	59.6	60.1	60.3	60.5	59.5
2015	59.1	59.2	59.0	58.8	58.6	59.0	58.7	58.2	57.9	58.0	57.7	57.9	58.5
2016	56.8	57.0	56.8	57.0	56.9	56.8	56.6	56.4	56.1	55.9	56.1	56.1	56.5
2017	55.6	55.7	56.0	56.3	56.7	57.3	56.8	56.8	56.9	57.5	57.7	58.0	56.8
2018	56.8	56.9	57.0	56.9	57.1	57.7	57.7	57.5	57.7	57.9	57.6	57.6	57.4
Retail Trade													
2010	166.0	164.5	166.7	167.4	168.7	169.4	169.0	169.0	166.9	168.7	173.0	174.4	168.6
2011	167.2	165.3	168.2	170.2	170.4	170.2	169.6	170.9	170.5	171.1	175.9	177.1	170.6
2012	170.3	168.6	170.6	171.8	172.8	173.1	172.2	172.1	172.1	174.2	179.4	180.9	173.2
2013	170.0	169.4	170.9	172.4	174.0	174.5	174.7	175.8	175.8	176.9	182.4	184.3	175.1
2014	175.6	174.9	175.5	176.5	177.5	178.5	178.3	178.8	178.7	179.8	184.5	187.4	178.8
2015	178.9	179.0	180.1	181.6	182.8	183.7	183.0	183.4	183.0	184.2	188.6	190.3	183.2
2016	181.4	181.3	182.7	183.9	184.1	183.9	183.0	183.7	182.4	183.2	188.3	187.6	183.8
2017	179.4	177.7	177.6	178.7	178.6	178.5	178.3	178.4	177.4	178.3	183.4	183.9	179.2
2018	177.3	175.6	176.7	177.2	177.6	176.9	177.1	177.8	177.5	178.9	182.4	181.6	178.1
Transportation and Utilities													
2010	47.6	47.6	47.7	47.9	48.1	48.2	48.4	48.3	48.4	48.3	48.6	49.5	48.2
2011	47.8	47.9	48.3	49.0	49.3	49.9	50.1	50.4	50.4	50.7	50.9	51.8	49.7
2012	51.2	51.2	51.5	51.8	52.3	52.9	52.9	53.2	53.3	53.7	54.0	54.6	52.7
2013	53.5	54.1	54.4	54.8	55.1	55.5	55.8	55.9	55.8	55.8	56.3	56.7	55.3
2014	56.2	56.0	56.8	56.3	56.7	57.1	56.9	57.0	57.0	57.5	58.2	59.2	57.1
2015	57.7	57.1	57.4	57.8	58.1	58.5	58.8	58.7	58.7	60.0	61.7	62.5	58.9
2016	59.1	58.1	57.9	58.2	58.2	58.1	58.3	58.7	59.0	60.2	62.2	62.4	59.2
2017	59.3	59.0	59.3	59.0	59.4	59.5	60.1	60.4	61.5	62.8	64.7	64.6	60.8
2018	62.1	61.4	61.8	61.7	62.4	62.9	63.5	63.9	64.5	65.8	67.9	67.9	63.8
Information													
2010	25.1	24.8	24.5	24.7	24.6	24.3	24.4	24.0	23.8	23.6	23.7	23.7	24.3
2011	23.3	23.1	22.9	23.0	23.1	23.1	23.2	23.1	22.8	22.9	23.0	23.0	23.0
2012	22.8	22.7	22.7	22.6	22.6	22.5	22.6	22.3	22.1	22.2	22.2	22.3	22.5
2013	21.8	21.7	21.6	21.9	22.0	22.1	22.0	21.8	21.5	21.7	21.8	21.7	21.8
2014	21.4	21.3	21.3	21.3	21.3	21.3	21.5	21.2	21.1	20.8	20.9	21.2	21.2
2015	20.8	20.9	21.0	20.9	21.3	21.3	21.2	21.1	21.1	21.4	21.7	21.8	21.2
2016	21.2	21.4	21.3	21.2	21.3	21.4	21.3	21.1	20.9	20.9	21.0	21.3	21.2
2017	20.9	20.9	20.9	20.8	20.8	20.7	20.5	20.3	20.1	19.9	20.0	20.2	20.5
2018	19.9	19.9	19.9	19.9	20.0	20.0	20.1	19.9	19.7	19.9	19.6	19.8	19.9
Financial Activities													
2010	78.1	78.1	78.2	78.1	78.4	78.6	78.3	78.2	77.7	77.9	78.0	78.4	78.2
2011	77.0	76.8	77.3	77.6	77.5	77.9	77.9	78.1	77.7	77.8	77.8	78.2	77.6
2012	77.2	77.6	77.7	77.8	78.2	78.6	78.5	78.5	78.0	78.3	78.4	79.1	78.2
2013	78.2	78.4	78.5	78.3	78.9	79.1	79.3	79.2	79.0	79.1	79.5	79.6	78.9
2014	78.7	78.8	79.0	79.2	79.4	79.8	80.0	80.1	79.4	79.5	80.0	80.5	79.5
2015	79.5	79.4	79.3	79.4	79.8	79.8	80.0	79.6	79.3	79.3	79.2	79.5	79.5
2016	78.6	78.6	78.4	78.5	78.6	78.8	79.1	79.0	78.7	78.9	78.9	79.5	78.8
2017	77.9	78.1	78.4	78.7	78.9	79.4	79.0	79.1	78.9	79.0	79.1	79.7	78.9
2018	78.4	78.4	78.8	78.8	79.1	79.7	79.6	79.6	79.3	79.5	79.9	79.2	79.2

1. Employment by Industry: Oklahoma, 2010–2018—*Continued*

(Numbers in thousands, not seasonally adjusted)

Industry and year	January	February	March	April	May	June	July	August	September	October	November	December	Annual average
Professional and Business Services													
2010	165.4	166.5	168.6	171.1	171.6	173.7	174.9	175.9	175.7	177.3	176.7	176.3	172.8
2011	171.7	171.0	174.1	176.9	176.6	176.7	177.7	178.5	178.8	179.0	177.6	177.6	176.4
2012	173.4	176.8	177.5	179.1	179.5	181.9	180.5	182.7	181.6	183.3	183.1	181.2	180.1
2013	176.7	178.1	180.6	180.6	181.7	182.6	182.7	184.0	183.4	184.0	184.7	182.4	181.8
2014	179.7	180.7	182.7	184.8	185.5	186.2	186.3	187.0	185.5	187.1	187.8	186.8	185.0
2015	184.9	183.9	184.3	185.4	185.0	185.2	186.1	185.8	183.7	185.0	184.1	183.7	184.8
2016	180.1	180.4	179.9	182.2	181.6	182.4	182.6	183.5	183.7	184.2	183.2	182.9	182.2
2017	179.0	181.3	183.5	185.0	185.2	188.0	188.0	188.8	189.1	189.3	188.6	188.2	186.2
2018	185.2	187.6	189.3	188.6	188.6	192.6	192.6	193.3	193.3	193.3	191.9	188.7	190.4
Education and Health Services													
2010	219.0	219.7	220.5	221.8	221.7	221.1	219.9	221.1	222.5	224.1	224.4	224.7	221.7
2011	220.5	219.6	221.6	222.5	222.9	222.7	222.0	223.3	225.2	225.3	225.8	226.1	223.1
2012	223.3	224.4	225.1	226.4	226.6	225.8	223.4	225.8	227.4	228.2	228.8	229.6	226.2
2013	226.3	227.2	227.8	227.9	228.1	226.9	225.5	227.1	228.6	229.0	229.5	228.4	227.7
2014	226.2	226.8	227.3	228.5	228.3	227.5	226.4	227.6	228.7	229.4	229.9	230.4	228.1
2015	228.5	229.1	229.4	230.9	231.0	230.6	230.8	231.9	233.9	234.2	234.6	234.1	231.6
2016	232.7	233.5	233.6	234.0	233.3	231.8	232.4	233.4	235.0	235.2	235.2	235.3	233.8
2017	231.3	232.7	233.2	235.5	235.9	235.4	234.5	235.3	237.4	237.6	237.4	237.7	235.3
2018	235.0	236.1	236.8	235.9	236.1	234.8	234.5	235.7	236.9	237.5	238.5	238.1	236.3
Leisure and Hospitality													
2010	131.5	132.8	136.8	140.6	142.2	142.9	141.1	142.1	142.0	139.7	139.1	138.5	139.1
2011	135.3	134.7	140.7	144.6	146.3	147.0	146.2	147.0	147.0	143.7	142.9	142.0	143.1
2012	139.4	141.4	145.3	148.8	150.6	151.5	148.8	150.1	149.7	147.9	147.5	148.0	147.4
2013	143.7	145.6	148.7	151.9	155.0	155.1	154.7	156.5	156.1	152.4	152.2	150.4	151.9
2014	148.7	149.9	152.9	157.2	159.0	159.4	158.8	160.3	159.6	156.9	156.1	156.1	156.2
2015	152.8	154.9	157.0	162.3	164.4	166.5	165.5	166.9	165.4	163.2	163.0	161.7	162.0
2016	158.3	160.4	163.5	166.9	167.4	167.8	168.2	169.5	167.8	165.7	164.5	163.3	165.3
2017	158.8	160.9	165.2	169.3	170.0	172.2	170.2	171.2	170.6	168.0	167.1	166.8	167.5
2018	163.6	165.4	169.6	172.3	175.2	175.7	174.4	175.4	173.7	173.9	172.3	171.8	171.9
Other Services													
2010	59.8	59.9	60.4	60.7	61.0	61.5	60.6	60.8	60.7	60.6	60.5	60.4	60.6
2011	59.5	59.4	60.1	59.1	59.1	59.4	58.9	58.3	58.4	57.9	57.9	57.7	58.8
2012	57.2	57.5	57.6	59.5	59.7	60.0	59.4	59.1	58.6	58.5	58.1	58.0	58.6
2013	57.3	57.5	57.7	59.5	59.8	60.4	60.3	60.1	59.7	59.1	59.1	58.9	59.1
2014	58.4	58.5	58.8	59.4	60.3	60.9	61.2	60.7	60.7	60.9	60.8	61.0	60.1
2015	60.7	61.1	61.9	62.3	62.5	63.1	63.8	63.0	62.8	62.5	62.5	62.4	62.4
2016	62.4	62.7	62.7	63.2	63.7	64.6	65.0	65.0	65.2	65.2	65.5	65.8	64.3
2017	65.7	66.6	67.3	67.8	68.5	69.6	69.6	69.5	69.8	69.9	69.9	70.3	68.7
2018	69.9	70.4	71.2	71.2	71.5	72.3	72.0	71.8	71.9	72.2	71.9	72.1	71.5
Government													
2010	346.2	351.9	354.9	354.9	360.8	348.6	336.4	333.6	342.8	350.2	350.4	351.0	348.5
2011	341.3	346.2	348.1	349.8	350.0	338.1	323.8	327.4	346.4	350.5	351.4	353.5	343.9
2012	343.0	350.5	352.1	352.3	352.9	339.8	327.4	334.0	348.3	354.3	356.0	355.4	347.2
2013	345.5	353.4	354.7	355.1	356.6	342.0	329.1	334.5	348.0	354.1	355.9	353.9	348.6
2014	344.7	352.0	353.0	353.2	355.3	341.7	329.0	335.2	348.3	355.9	356.6	355.5	348.4
2015	346.7	354.3	354.6	356.2	357.8	344.1	331.6	337.3	351.9	359.2	360.5	359.9	351.2
2016	350.9	358.3	359.7	359.6	359.0	345.9	333.2	339.1	353.2	355.1	356.4	356.6	352.3
2017	346.5	353.8	355.6	355.0	355.5	344.2	332.1	337.3	350.3	353.0	353.8	353.6	349.2
2018	346.0	352.1	353.0	351.6	353.6	342.6	331.0	336.2	348.9	352.0	353.2	353.2	347.8

2. Average Weekly Hours by Selected Industry: Oklahoma, 2014–2018

(Not seasonally adjusted)

Industry and year	January	February	March	April	May	June	July	August	September	October	November	December	Annual average
Total Private													
2014	35.1	35.4	35.6	35.3	35.0	35.7	35.0	35.3	35.1	34.8	35.4	35.2	35.2
2015	34.7	35.1	35.1	34.4	34.2	34.8	34.5	35.3	34.3	34.7	35.1	35.1	34.8
2016	35.0	34.8	34.5	34.7	35.2	35.0	35.3	35.0	35.1	35.7	35.0	35.1	35.0
2017	35.3	35.4	35.3	35.9	35.3	35.6	36.1	35.5	35.5	36.0	35.4	35.4	35.5
2018	35.0	34.9	35.3	35.6	35.3	35.6	35.8	35.5	35.9	35.7	35.7	36.3	35.6
Goods-Producing													
2014	40.5	40.3	41.3	41.0	41.1	41.0	40.7	41.9	41.2	40.5	41.1	41.6	41.0
2015	40.7	40.4	40.2	39.9	39.3	40.7	40.0	40.9	39.5	40.9	41.3	41.2	40.4
2016	40.7	40.3	39.9	40.6	41.1	41.2	41.3	41.2	41.3	41.9	40.8	40.8	40.9
2017	40.3	40.9	41.1	41.5	41.4	41.1	41.6	41.1	41.0	41.9	41.3	41.8	41.3
2018	40.9	41.4	41.9	41.3	41.6	41.7	41.3	41.3	42.2	41.3	42.0	42.7	41.6
Construction													
2014	40.4	40.6	42.8	43.0	42.7	42.1	41.8	44.3	42.3	40.1	40.4	40.2	41.7
2015	40.3	40.7	40.6	41.0	39.5	41.3	41.1	41.7	39.8	41.9	42.7	42.2	41.1
2016	42.3	42.3	41.2	42.8	43.1	43.3	43.5	42.4	42.5	43.1	41.1	42.0	42.5
2017	41.2	42.4	42.0	42.3	42.3	42.8	43.7	42.7	41.0	43.3	42.0	42.4	42.3
2018	40.9	41.9	42.7	41.5	41.8	41.2	41.1	41.0	41.9	39.5	40.1	41.2	41.2
Manufacturing													
2014	40.5	40.1	40.8	40.5	40.8	40.8	40.5	40.8	40.4	40.8	41.7	41.9	40.8
2015	40.6	39.8	39.5	38.8	38.8	39.9	38.7	40.0	38.9	40.3	40.4	40.6	39.7
2016	39.8	39.0	39.3	39.3	39.8	39.9	40.1	40.9	40.5	40.8	40.1	39.4	39.9
2017	39.0	39.1	39.8	39.6	39.9	39.2	39.2	39.3	40.4	40.2	40.5	41.0	39.8
2018	40.2	40.5	40.7	40.5	41.0	41.1	40.5	40.7	41.3	41.9	43.0	43.6	41.3
Trade, Transportation, and Utilities													
2014	34.6	35.2	35.1	35.2	35.2	35.6	34.9	35.1	35.3	34.6	35.2	35.2	35.1
2015	34.7	35.3	35.5	34.9	35.1	35.2	35.3	36.1	35.1	34.7	34.8	35.2	35.2
2016	34.7	35.0	34.8	34.9	35.1	35.3	35.0	34.8	35.1	35.4	34.4	34.9	35.0
2017	35.3	35.3	35.7	36.5	35.8	36.4	36.5	35.9	35.6	35.8	35.0	34.9	35.7
2018	34.6	34.3	34.5	35.0	34.8	35.3	35.6	35.4	35.7	35.0	34.7	35.4	35.0
Financial Activities													
2014	36.6	37.4	37.4	36.0	36.0	37.4	36.1	35.7	35.7	35.2	36.6	35.8	36.3
2015	35.7	36.6	37.0	36.1	35.7	36.0	35.5	37.2	36.4	35.9	37.1	36.2	36.3
2016	35.6	35.5	35.8	36.0	37.1	35.4	35.8	35.5	36.6	36.9	35.6	35.6	35.9
2017	37.3	37.9	37.0	38.1	36.1	37.1	37.9	36.2	35.9	38.0	36.0	35.9	36.9
2018	36.7	36.7	36.8	39.1	37.9	38.3	39.2	37.7	39.0	37.5	38.0	38.1	37.9
Professional and Business Services													
2014	36.2	37.0	36.8	36.4	35.8	37.1	35.8	35.7	35.7	35.2	36.2	35.4	36.1
2015	35.0	35.8	35.7	35.3	34.6	35.2	34.4	35.0	33.5	34.8	35.4	35.1	35.0
2016	35.7	35.2	35.4	35.6	36.1	35.7	36.4	35.6	36.0	36.7	36.3	36.3	35.9
2017	37.0	36.4	36.5	36.8	36.3	36.5	37.1	36.6	37.0	37.4	36.6	36.4	36.7
2018	35.9	35.7	36.0	36.6	36.1	36.0	35.9	35.5	35.7	35.0	35.1	35.3	35.7
Education and Health Services													
2014	34.0	34.0	33.6	33.5	33.5	33.9	33.7	33.6	33.3	33.5	33.8	33.3	33.6
2015	33.2	33.4	33.3	32.7	33.2	33.4	33.9	34.4	33.6	33.8	34.4	33.7	33.6
2016	34.0	33.3	32.9	33.1	33.6	33.7	34.3	34.2	34.3	34.8	34.4	34.4	33.9
2017	35.1	34.5	34.3	35.1	34.2	34.3	35.5	34.5	34.7	35.0	34.8	34.7	34.7
2018	35.0	34.4	34.4	35.0	34.5	34.8	35.9	35.3	35.9	34.8	35.0	35.5	35.0
Leisure and Hospitality													
2014	25.7	26.0	26.4	26.0	25.3	26.5	25.6	26.0	25.6	25.9	26.2	26.0	25.9
2015	25.2	26.0	26.3	25.8	25.6	26.5	25.9	26.5	26.4	26.0	26.2	26.3	26.1
2016	25.3	26.5	26.2	26.0	26.8	26.5	26.7	26.8	26.0	26.7	26.5	26.2	26.4
2017	25.0	26.0	26.3	26.7	26.4	26.6	26.7	26.2	26.2	26.3	26.1	26.1	26.2
2018	24.9	25.7	26.3	26.6	26.1	26.6	25.8	25.6	25.3	24.9	24.7	25.3	25.7

3. Average Hourly Earnings by Selected Industry: Oklahoma, 2014–2018

(Dollars, not seasonally adjusted)

Industry and year	January	February	March	April	May	June	July	August	September	October	November	December	Annual average
Total Private													
2014	21.15	21.52	21.37	21.46	21.44	21.52	21.39	21.53	21.64	21.73	22.06	21.66	21.54
2015	21.85	21.95	21.91	21.79	21.80	21.63	21.67	21.83	21.84	21.82	21.99	21.68	21.82
2016	21.68	21.84	21.88	21.91	21.99	21.80	22.09	21.94	22.23	22.37	22.31	22.35	22.03
2017	22.61	22.62	22.64	22.93	22.75	22.66	23.05	22.94	23.08	23.15	22.96	23.04	22.87
2018	23.05	23.32	23.05	23.31	23.18	23.42	23.83	23.92	24.18	24.24	24.26	24.39	23.69
Goods-Producing													
2014	21.96	22.57	22.71	23.14	23.25	23.54	23.23	23.26	23.67	23.57	23.99	23.44	23.20
2015	23.78	23.94	24.16	23.82	24.01	23.80	23.88	24.01	24.24	24.10	24.32	24.16	24.02
2016	23.63	24.04	24.02	23.76	24.26	24.14	24.20	24.33	24.36	24.58	24.59	24.66	24.21
2017	24.50	24.51	24.77	25.12	25.20	25.09	25.42	25.52	25.62	25.92	25.33	25.60	25.23
2018	25.79	26.00	26.09	26.62	26.15	26.49	26.79	26.98	27.16	26.65	26.82	27.07	26.56
Construction													
2014	20.91	21.40	20.99	21.15	21.47	21.35	21.36	20.93	21.32	21.37	21.61	21.30	21.26
2015	21.56	21.61	21.51	21.35	21.77	21.35	21.23	21.36	21.81	21.81	21.79	22.08	21.60
2016	21.15	21.26	21.81	21.33	21.86	21.68	22.18	21.98	22.26	22.06	22.27	22.10	21.83
2017	21.82	22.05	22.02	22.12	22.79	22.64	22.55	22.92	23.08	23.38	22.79	23.00	22.61
2018	23.13	23.53	23.30	23.56	23.37	23.77	23.86	23.82	24.26	24.05	24.38	24.50	23.80
Manufacturing													
2014	21.11	21.39	21.45	21.63	21.53	21.76	21.48	21.85	22.19	22.15	22.49	22.22	21.78
2015	22.51	22.69	23.00	22.89	23.08	23.16	23.53	23.74	23.95	23.76	24.15	23.82	23.35
2016	23.56	24.00	23.61	23.71	24.07	24.11	23.67	23.82	23.70	24.12	23.55	23.74	23.81
2017	23.35	23.58	23.53	23.99	23.88	23.64	24.24	24.29	24.33	24.59	24.13	24.24	23.99
2018	24.52	24.75	25.03	25.32	24.79	24.71	24.96	25.52	25.27	24.97	25.21	25.49	25.05
Trade, Transportation, and Utilities													
2014	19.84	19.68	19.70	19.54	19.25	19.27	19.43	19.72	19.81	19.90	20.17	19.68	19.67
2015	19.90	19.77	19.58	19.60	20.01	19.61	19.82	19.91	19.76	19.96	20.17	19.53	19.80
2016	19.70	19.85	20.25	20.30	20.50	20.61	21.18	20.72	20.82	20.84	21.08	20.90	20.57
2017	21.23	20.78	20.98	21.36	21.40	21.19	21.90	21.65	21.96	22.05	21.72	21.83	21.51
2018	22.19	22.69	22.25	23.17	22.98	23.50	23.87	24.31	24.24	23.49	23.69	23.59	23.34
Financial Activities													
2014	24.13	24.41	24.18	24.20	24.04	24.17	23.82	24.00	23.81	23.92	24.02	23.87	24.05
2015	24.18	24.62	24.34	24.74	24.73	25.02	24.91	25.62	25.14	25.70	25.84	25.86	25.06
2016	25.34	25.80	25.37	25.67	25.98	25.70	25.78	26.06	27.04	27.05	26.97	26.63	26.12
2017	27.10	27.28	26.99	27.07	26.94	26.27	27.14	26.25	25.72	25.52	25.71	25.34	26.45
2018	24.80	24.65	24.36	24.18	24.51	24.14	25.03	25.36	26.01	26.04	26.00	26.57	25.14
Professional and Business Services													
2014	22.89	23.44	23.23	23.09	23.18	23.60	23.37	23.82	23.99	24.32	24.61	24.23	23.65
2015	24.56	24.76	24.66	24.11	23.99	23.89	23.89	24.03	24.15	23.80	24.10	23.80	24.15
2016	23.89	23.69	23.36	23.27	23.14	22.75	22.63	22.58	22.69	23.02	22.90	23.18	23.09
2017	23.40	23.22	23.14	23.01	22.36	22.26	22.43	22.40	22.61	22.99	23.15	23.44	22.86
2018	23.36	23.63	22.97	23.06	23.26	23.26	23.67	23.57	24.08	24.37	24.18	24.38	23.65
Education and Health Services													
2014	22.50	23.10	22.57	22.96	22.86	22.86	23.01	22.85	22.95	23.26	23.67	23.23	22.99
2015	23.05	23.37	23.30	23.67	23.26	23.10	23.14	23.12	23.11	22.85	22.85	22.46	23.10
2016	22.59	23.13	23.44	23.72	23.23	22.99	23.61	23.11	23.73	23.69	23.33	23.33	23.33
2017	23.33	23.37	23.61	24.26	24.09	24.31	24.45	24.45	24.54	24.33	24.28	24.13	24.10
2018	23.95	24.26	24.03	23.99	23.83	24.19	24.73	24.41	24.65	25.42	24.59	24.60	24.39
Leisure and Hospitality													
2014	10.70	11.11	10.99	11.02	11.24	10.94	10.97	11.12	11.18	11.21	11.53	11.54	11.13
2015	11.57	11.65	11.68	11.64	11.69	11.64	11.67	11.78	12.02	12.06	12.18	12.23	11.82
2016	12.46	12.46	12.50	12.53	12.61	12.30	12.52	12.48	12.51	12.74	12.67	12.75	12.54
2017	13.07	12.91	12.83	12.82	12.84	12.72	12.58	12.63	12.74	12.64	12.66	12.72	12.76
2018	12.70	12.68	12.64	12.63	12.63	12.45	12.46	12.66	12.87	13.05	13.20	13.35	12.77

4. Average Weekly Earnings by Selected Industry: Oklahoma, 2014–2018

(Dollars, not seasonally adjusted)

Industry and year	January	February	March	April	May	June	July	August	September	October	November	December	Annual average
Total Private													
2014	742.37	761.81	760.77	757.54	750.40	768.26	748.65	760.01	759.56	756.20	780.92	762.43	758.21
2015	758.20	770.45	769.04	749.58	745.56	752.72	747.62	770.60	749.11	757.15	771.85	760.97	759.34
2016	758.80	760.03	754.86	760.28	774.05	763.00	779.78	767.90	780.27	798.61	780.85	784.49	771.05
2017	798.13	800.75	799.19	823.19	803.08	806.70	832.11	814.37	819.34	833.40	812.78	815.62	811.89
2018	806.75	813.87	813.67	829.84	818.25	833.75	853.11	849.16	868.06	865.37	866.08	885.36	843.36
Goods-Producing													
2014	889.38	909.57	937.92	948.74	955.58	965.14	945.46	974.59	975.20	954.59	985.99	975.10	951.20
2015	967.85	967.18	971.23	950.42	943.59	968.66	955.20	982.01	957.48	985.69	1004.42	995.39	970.41
2016	961.74	968.81	958.40	964.66	997.09	994.57	999.46	1002.40	1006.07	1029.90	1003.27	1006.13	990.19
2017	987.35	1002.46	1018.05	1042.48	1043.28	1031.20	1057.47	1048.87	1050.42	1086.05	1046.13	1070.08	1042.00
2018	1054.81	1076.40	1093.17	1099.41	1087.84	1104.63	1106.43	1114.27	1146.15	1100.65	1126.44	1155.89	1104.90
Construction													
2014	844.76	868.84	898.37	909.45	916.77	898.84	892.85	927.20	901.84	856.94	873.04	856.26	886.54
2015	868.87	879.53	873.31	875.35	859.92	881.76	872.55	890.71	868.04	913.84	930.43	931.78	887.76
2016	894.65	899.30	898.57	912.92	942.17	938.74	964.83	931.95	946.05	950.79	915.30	928.20	927.78
2017	898.98	934.92	924.84	935.68	964.02	968.99	985.44	978.68	946.28	1012.35	957.18	975.20	956.40
2018	946.02	985.91	994.91	977.74	976.87	979.32	980.65	976.62	1016.49	949.98	977.64	1009.40	980.56
Manufacturing													
2014	854.96	857.74	875.16	876.02	878.42	887.81	869.94	891.48	896.48	903.72	937.83	931.02	888.62
2015	913.91	903.06	908.50	888.13	895.50	924.08	910.61	949.60	931.66	957.53	975.66	967.09	927.00
2016	937.69	936.00	927.87	931.80	957.99	961.99	949.17	974.24	959.85	984.10	944.36	935.36	950.02
2017	910.65	921.98	936.49	950.00	952.81	926.69	950.21	954.60	982.93	988.52	977.27	993.84	954.80
2018	985.70	1002.38	1018.72	1025.46	1016.39	1015.58	1010.88	1038.66	1043.65	1046.24	1084.03	1111.36	1034.57
Trade, Transportation, and Utilities													
2014	686.46	692.74	691.47	687.81	677.60	686.01	678.11	692.17	699.29	688.54	709.98	692.74	690.42
2015	690.53	697.88	695.09	684.04	702.35	690.27	699.65	718.75	693.58	692.61	701.92	687.46	696.96
2016	683.59	694.75	704.70	708.47	719.55	727.53	741.30	721.06	730.78	737.74	725.15	729.41	719.95
2017	749.42	733.53	748.99	779.64	766.12	771.32	799.35	777.24	781.78	789.39	760.20	761.87	767.91
2018	767.77	778.27	767.63	810.95	799.70	829.55	849.77	860.57	865.37	822.15	822.04	835.09	816.90
Financial Activities													
2014	883.16	912.93	904.33	871.20	865.44	903.96	859.90	856.80	850.02	841.98	879.13	854.55	873.02
2015	863.23	901.09	900.58	893.11	882.86	900.72	884.31	953.06	915.10	922.63	958.66	936.13	909.68
2016	902.10	915.90	908.25	924.12	963.86	909.78	922.92	925.13	989.66	998.15	960.13	948.03	937.71
2017	1010.83	1033.91	998.63	1031.37	972.53	974.62	1028.61	950.25	923.35	969.76	925.56	909.71	976.01
2018	910.16	904.66	896.45	945.44	928.93	924.56	981.18	956.07	1014.39	976.50	988.00	1012.32	952.81
Professional and Business Services													
2014	828.62	867.28	854.86	840.48	829.84	875.56	836.65	850.37	856.44	856.06	890.88	857.74	853.77
2015	859.60	886.41	880.36	851.08	830.05	840.93	821.82	841.05	809.03	828.24	853.14	835.38	845.25
2016	852.87	833.89	826.94	828.41	835.35	812.18	823.73	803.85	816.84	844.83	831.27	841.43	828.93
2017	865.80	845.21	844.61	846.77	811.67	812.49	832.15	819.84	836.57	859.83	847.29	853.22	838.96
2018	838.62	843.59	826.92	844.00	839.69	837.36	849.75	836.74	859.66	852.95	848.72	860.61	844.31
Education and Health Services													
2014	765.00	785.40	758.35	769.16	765.81	774.95	775.44	767.76	764.24	779.21	800.05	773.56	772.46
2015	765.26	780.56	775.89	774.01	772.23	771.54	784.45	795.33	776.50	772.33	786.04	756.90	776.16
2016	768.06	770.23	771.18	785.13	780.53	774.76	809.82	790.36	813.94	824.41	802.55	802.55	790.89
2017	818.88	806.27	809.82	851.53	823.88	833.83	867.98	843.53	851.54	851.55	844.94	837.31	836.27
2018	838.25	834.54	826.63	839.65	822.14	841.81	887.81	861.67	884.94	884.62	860.65	873.30	853.65
Leisure and Hospitality													
2014	274.99	288.86	290.14	286.52	284.37	289.91	280.83	289.12	286.21	290.34	302.09	300.04	288.27
2015	291.56	302.90	307.18	300.31	299.26	308.46	302.25	312.17	317.33	313.56	319.12	321.65	308.50
2016	315.24	330.19	327.50	325.78	337.95	325.95	334.28	334.46	325.26	340.16	335.76	334.05	331.06
2017	326.75	335.66	337.43	342.29	338.98	338.35	335.89	330.91	333.79	332.43	330.43	331.99	334.31
2018	316.23	325.88	332.43	335.96	329.64	331.17	321.47	324.10	325.61	324.95	326.04	337.76	328.19

OREGON
At a Glance

Population:
  2010 census: 3,831,074
  2018 estimate: 4,190,713

Percent change in population:
  2010–2018: 9.4%

Percent change in total nonfarm employment:
  2010–2018: 19.2%

Industry with the largest growth in employment, 2010–2018 (percent):
  Construction, 55.0%

Industry with the largest decline or smallest growth in employment, 2010–2018 (percent):
  Government, -1.6%

Civilian labor force:
  2010: 1,984,039
  2018: 2,104,516

Unemployment rate and rank among states (highest to lowest):
  2010: 10.6%, 8th
  2018: 4.2%, 14th

Over-the-year change in unemployment rates:
  2016–2017: -0.7%
  2017–2018: 0.1%

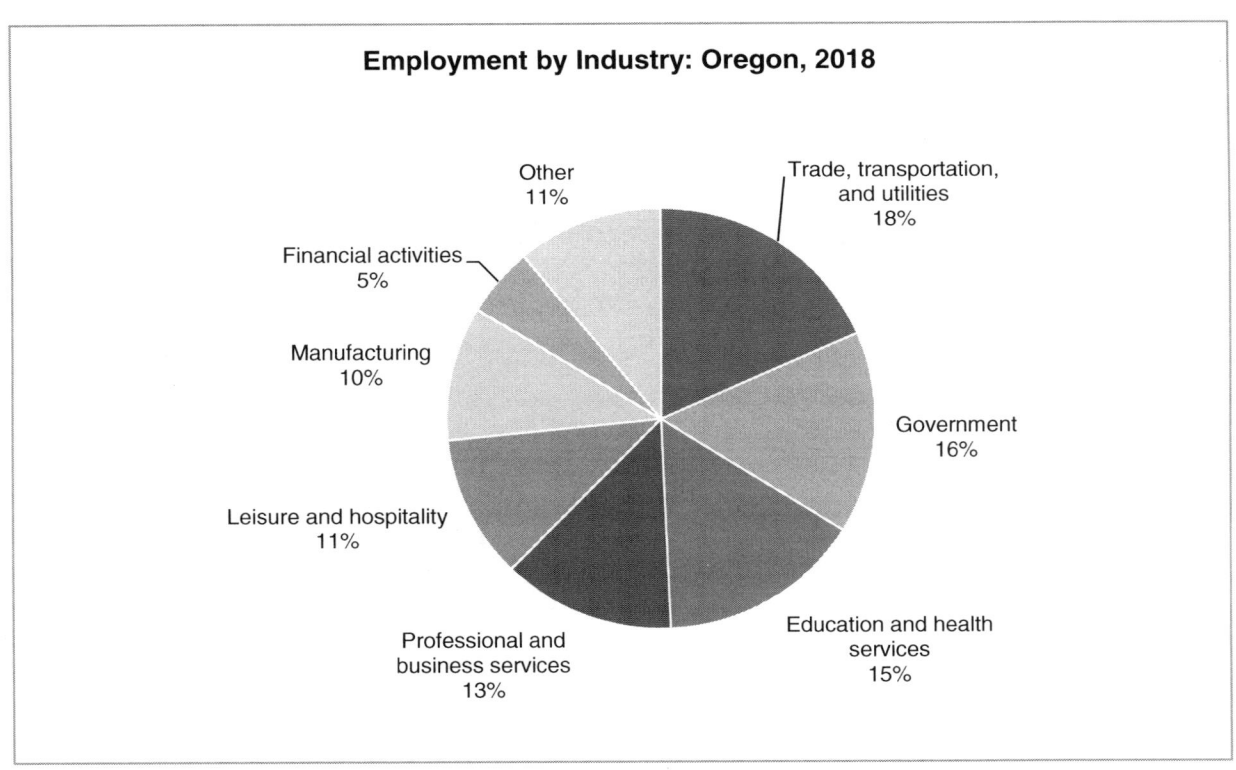

Employment by Industry: Oregon, 2018

- Other 11%
- Trade, transportation, and utilities 18%
- Financial activities 5%
- Manufacturing 10%
- Government 16%
- Leisure and hospitality 11%
- Education and health services 15%
- Professional and business services 13%

1. Employment by Industry: Oregon, 2010–2018

(Numbers in thousands, not seasonally adjusted)

Industry and year	January	February	March	April	May	June	July	August	September	October	November	December	Annual average
Total Nonfarm													
2010	1,562.6	1,570.6	1,578.9	1,596.7	1,611.4	1,621.1	1,597.5	1,598.2	1,607.0	1,628.8	1,626.6	1,620.8	1,601.7
2011	1,583.4	1,596.2	1,603.1	1,617.8	1,624.7	1,634.9	1,611.1	1,614.8	1,628.4	1,640.9	1,642.3	1,638.9	1,619.7
2012	1,599.7	1,612.8	1,620.1	1,632.1	1,646.0	1,654.5	1,632.1	1,639.4	1,649.1	1,665.7	1,666.1	1,661.3	1,639.9
2013	1,622.2	1,639.2	1,647.9	1,664.7	1,679.7	1,686.6	1,666.4	1,674.6	1,689.5	1,704.3	1,709.4	1,705.5	1,674.2
2014	1,673.1	1,681.3	1,693.8	1,710.5	1,724.8	1,734.3	1,714.0	1,722.9	1,738.1	1,753.7	1,758.3	1,759.1	1,722.0
2015	1,725.5	1,740.7	1,750.2	1,772.0	1,786.2	1,797.6	1,776.4	1,781.6	1,794.3	1,813.4	1,817.0	1,817.3	1,781.0
2016	1,782.5	1,801.7	1,811.5	1,827.9	1,837.9	1,846.9	1,825.3	1,833.0	1,847.0	1,861.4	1,867.9	1,860.5	1,833.6
2017	1,815.0	1,842.6	1,853.8	1,871.6	1,882.5	1,896.9	1,871.6	1,876.2	1,886.8	1,899.6	1,905.3	1,902.1	1,875.3
2018	1,871.3	1,886.2	1,895.1	1,903.8	1,916.6	1,925.6	1,899.7	1,906.7	1,919.2	1,931.6	1,931.2	1,926.6	1,909.5
Total Private													
2010	1,263.9	1,267.2	1,274.0	1,289.2	1,296.5	1,306.6	1,316.1	1,320.5	1,323.4	1,325.9	1,320.4	1,319.3	1,301.9
2011	1,283.9	1,292.7	1,299.3	1,313.3	1,317.8	1,327.7	1,339.2	1,345.3	1,349.4	1,343.7	1,342.4	1,341.9	1,324.7
2012	1,307.2	1,315.1	1,321.7	1,334.3	1,344.5	1,353.3	1,363.5	1,372.1	1,371.0	1,370.2	1,367.9	1,366.4	1,348.9
2013	1,332.4	1,343.7	1,352.3	1,369.2	1,380.9	1,388.7	1,401.9	1,410.7	1,412.5	1,410.0	1,411.6	1,409.3	1,385.3
2014	1,380.5	1,384.4	1,396.1	1,411.2	1,422.2	1,431.2	1,442.6	1,451.8	1,454.8	1,452.2	1,453.7	1,455.9	1,428.1
2015	1,425.8	1,436.3	1,444.4	1,462.1	1,473.2	1,484.0	1,499.0	1,505.4	1,506.3	1,506.5	1,506.8	1,507.8	1,479.8
2016	1,477.0	1,491.0	1,499.1	1,514.9	1,522.1	1,530.1	1,541.2	1,550.7	1,551.0	1,547.9	1,550.9	1,546.6	1,526.9
2017	1,508.1	1,527.6	1,536.4	1,554.6	1,562.9	1,576.2	1,583.0	1,588.6	1,588.0	1,585.0	1,588.4	1,587.2	1,565.5
2018	1,577.4	1,586.6	1,594.4	1,602.9	1,613.0	1,620.9	1,629.1	1,636.2	1,632.2	1,630.1	1,626.9	1,623.8	1,614.5
Goods Producing													
2010	228.8	227.9	229.2	232.1	235.0	239.4	246.1	247.4	246.9	245.8	240.0	236.0	237.9
2011	230.7	232.6	234.3	238.3	240.6	244.9	251.2	254.6	253.3	250.3	246.5	244.1	243.5
2012	238.0	239.0	239.6	242.2	246.8	251.0	257.4	260.6	257.0	255.7	249.6	246.3	248.6
2013	241.7	243.8	245.7	249.8	254.0	258.2	264.5	267.0	265.6	265.1	261.5	258.9	256.3
2014	256.3	256.0	258.5	261.7	265.5	269.0	274.4	276.7	275.2	272.5	269.4	268.1	266.9
2015	264.9	266.2	268.1	270.9	274.4	279.1	285.3	286.3	284.9	283.3	279.8	278.2	276.8
2016	274.6	277.6	279.2	281.7	284.6	287.7	291.8	294.7	292.1	291.1	288.2	285.6	285.7
2017	278.2	282.5	285.0	289.5	293.3	298.5	303.0	304.9	302.4	302.4	299.8	299.1	294.9
2018	295.4	298.1	299.7	301.7	305.4	309.4	315.6	316.4	313.6	312.9	307.7	306.6	306.9
Service-Providing													
2010	1,333.8	1,342.7	1,349.7	1,364.6	1,376.4	1,381.7	1,351.4	1,350.8	1,360.1	1,383.0	1,386.6	1,384.8	1,363.8
2011	1,352.7	1,363.6	1,368.8	1,379.5	1,384.1	1,390.0	1,359.9	1,360.2	1,375.1	1,390.6	1,395.8	1,394.8	1,376.3
2012	1,361.7	1,373.8	1,380.5	1,389.9	1,399.2	1,403.5	1,374.7	1,378.8	1,392.1	1,410.0	1,416.5	1,415.0	1,391.3
2013	1,380.5	1,395.4	1,402.2	1,414.9	1,425.7	1,428.4	1,401.9	1,407.6	1,423.9	1,439.2	1,447.9	1,446.6	1,417.9
2014	1,416.8	1,425.3	1,435.3	1,448.8	1,459.3	1,465.3	1,439.6	1,446.2	1,462.9	1,481.2	1,488.9	1,491.0	1,455.1
2015	1,460.6	1,474.5	1,482.1	1,501.1	1,511.8	1,518.5	1,491.1	1,495.3	1,509.4	1,530.1	1,537.2	1,539.1	1,504.2
2016	1,507.9	1,524.1	1,532.3	1,546.2	1,553.3	1,559.2	1,533.5	1,538.3	1,554.9	1,570.3	1,579.7	1,574.9	1,547.9
2017	1,536.8	1,560.1	1,568.8	1,582.1	1,589.2	1,598.4	1,568.6	1,571.3	1,584.4	1,597.2	1,605.5	1,603.0	1,580.5
2018	1,575.9	1,588.1	1,595.4	1,602.1	1,611.2	1,616.2	1,584.1	1,590.3	1,605.6	1,618.7	1,623.5	1,620.0	1,602.6
Mining and Logging													
2010	5.8	5.8	5.9	6.1	6.2	6.6	6.9	6.9	6.8	6.6	6.3	6.1	6.3
2011	5.9	6.1	6.1	6.2	6.4	6.6	7.0	7.1	7.2	7.1	7.0	6.9	6.6
2012	6.3	6.4	6.3	6.4	6.7	7.0	7.1	7.3	7.1	7.2	7.0	6.9	6.8
2013	6.5	6.6	6.6	6.8	7.1	7.3	7.5	7.6	7.5	7.4	7.3	7.1	7.1
2014	7.0	7.0	6.9	7.0	7.1	7.3	7.5	7.6	7.4	7.3	7.3	7.1	7.2
2015	7.0	7.0	7.0	7.0	7.3	7.4	7.5	7.3	7.3	7.4	7.2	7.1	7.2
2016	7.0	7.0	6.9	6.9	7.2	7.2	7.3	7.4	7.3	7.2	7.1	7.0	7.1
2017	6.6	6.7	6.6	6.8	6.9	7.1	7.3	7.3	7.1	7.2	7.2	7.2	7.0
2018	7.0	7.1	7.1	7.1	7.2	7.3	7.4	7.4	7.3	7.5	7.4	7.2	7.3
Construction													
2010	63.4	62.7	63.4	65.0	66.6	68.4	71.8	72.6	72.1	71.5	68.1	66.1	67.6
2011	62.1	62.9	63.6	66.4	67.8	70.0	72.4	73.5	73.6	72.2	70.2	68.6	68.6
2012	65.0	65.4	65.4	67.1	69.6	70.9	73.9	75.7	74.0	73.1	70.0	67.9	69.8
2013	64.9	66.2	67.9	70.6	73.6	75.2	78.4	79.8	79.2	79.6	78.2	76.3	74.2
2014	74.9	74.5	76.3	78.2	80.5	81.6	83.9	84.8	84.2	82.2	80.4	79.2	80.1
2015	77.3	77.7	78.7	80.0	81.7	83.8	86.6	87.8	87.2	87.8	85.9	84.6	83.3
2016	82.1	84.5	85.5	88.0	89.7	91.2	93.8	95.4	95.0	94.8	93.4	91.6	90.4
2017	87.2	90.2	92.1	94.9	97.2	99.7	102.2	103.6	103.1	102.8	101.1	100.5	97.9
2018	98.2	99.7	100.9	102.3	104.6	106.2	108.9	110.3	108.9	108.2	105.3	103.5	104.8

1. Employment by Industry: Oregon, 2010–2018—*Continued*

(Numbers in thousands, not seasonally adjusted)

Industry and year	January	February	March	April	May	June	July	August	September	October	November	December	Annual average
Manufacturing													
2010	159.6	159.4	159.9	161.0	162.2	164.4	167.4	167.9	168.0	167.7	165.6	163.8	163.9
2011	162.7	163.6	164.6	165.7	166.4	168.3	171.8	174.0	172.5	171.0	169.3	168.6	168.2
2012	166.7	167.2	167.9	168.7	170.5	173.1	176.4	177.6	175.9	175.4	172.6	171.5	172.0
2013	170.3	171.0	171.2	172.4	173.3	175.7	178.6	179.6	178.9	178.1	176.0	175.5	175.1
2014	174.4	174.5	175.3	176.5	177.9	180.1	183.0	184.3	183.6	183.0	181.7	181.8	179.7
2015	180.6	181.5	182.4	183.9	185.4	187.9	191.2	191.2	190.4	188.1	186.7	186.5	186.3
2016	185.5	186.1	186.8	186.8	187.7	189.3	190.7	191.9	189.8	189.1	187.7	187.0	188.2
2017	184.4	185.6	186.3	187.8	189.2	191.7	193.5	194.0	192.2	192.4	191.5	191.4	190.0
2018	190.2	191.3	191.7	192.3	193.6	195.9	199.3	198.7	197.4	197.2	195.0	195.9	194.9
Trade, Transportation, and Utilities													
2010	297.6	295.2	295.4	298.1	299.4	301.3	303.3	304.7	305.6	307.4	311.8	314.9	302.9
2011	301.4	299.3	299.7	302.0	303.7	305.5	307.1	307.8	309.0	309.8	315.4	317.4	306.5
2012	305.0	302.5	303.3	305.2	308.2	310.7	310.6	312.3	313.1	314.5	320.8	322.9	310.8
2013	310.7	309.9	310.3	313.1	316.0	317.4	319.5	322.0	323.0	323.3	329.5	331.4	318.8
2014	319.7	317.1	317.5	319.9	322.9	324.6	326.6	329.2	329.9	331.6	337.7	341.4	326.5
2015	328.6	326.9	327.9	330.5	333.2	335.6	337.3	339.3	339.7	340.8	345.7	348.7	336.2
2016	335.2	334.1	334.8	336.7	338.4	340.4	342.5	345.3	344.8	345.5	352.8	354.3	342.1
2017	343.8	342.4	342.7	344.3	345.9	348.0	349.2	350.7	350.9	351.4	358.6	360.2	349.0
2018	348.5	345.1	345.4	346.7	349.4	350.8	351.6	354.0	354.9	357.2	361.5	361.2	352.2
Wholesale Trade													
2010	65.2	65.3	65.0	65.8	66.1	66.0	66.7	66.5	66.7	66.9	66.6	66.4	66.1
2011	65.4	65.8	66.0	66.5	66.9	66.9	67.3	67.4	67.2	67.4	67.1	66.9	66.7
2012	66.0	66.5	66.7	67.5	68.1	67.9	68.4	68.7	68.6	68.7	68.5	68.4	67.8
2013	68.9	69.5	69.3	70.0	70.3	70.2	71.1	71.3	71.3	71.1	71.3	71.2	70.5
2014	70.6	70.8	70.7	70.9	70.9	71.2	71.7	71.9	72.0	72.1	72.0	72.1	71.4
2015	71.4	71.8	71.6	72.0	72.3	72.4	73.2	73.6	73.6	73.5	73.8	73.9	72.8
2016	72.7	73.2	73.2	73.7	73.6	73.8	74.3	74.8	74.4	74.3	74.5	74.5	73.9
2017	74.0	74.6	74.5	74.9	75.2	75.3	75.3	75.2	75.2	75.1	75.2	75.3	75.0
2018	74.4	74.8	74.7	75.0	75.4	75.5	75.8	76.1	75.9	76.4	75.9	75.6	75.5
Retail Trade													
2010	180.6	178.4	178.8	180.1	181.1	182.7	184.7	185.9	185.5	187.0	192.0	194.3	184.3
2011	183.2	180.8	180.9	182.4	183.4	184.9	186.6	187.0	187.1	187.8	193.4	194.7	186.0
2012	185.2	182.1	182.5	183.8	185.9	188.1	188.9	189.7	189.3	190.8	196.9	198.1	188.4
2013	187.7	185.9	186.2	188.1	190.6	191.8	194.1	195.7	195.6	196.0	201.7	202.7	193.0
2014	192.6	189.8	190.6	192.5	195.1	196.3	198.7	200.2	200.1	201.2	206.9	208.7	197.7
2015	198.2	196.4	197.4	199.9	202.0	203.3	205.7	206.9	206.4	207.1	211.0	212.2	203.9
2016	202.3	201.3	201.8	202.8	204.3	205.9	208.2	209.8	208.8	209.7	214.6	214.5	207.0
2017	207.2	205.8	206.1	207.6	208.5	210.0	211.8	212.6	212.2	212.5	218.1	217.9	210.9
2018	209.8	207.0	207.2	208.0	209.9	210.7	212.3	213.5	212.8	214.1	217.5	215.9	211.6
Transportation and Utilities													
2010	51.8	51.5	51.6	52.2	52.2	52.6	51.9	52.3	53.4	53.5	53.2	54.2	52.5
2011	52.8	52.7	52.8	53.1	53.4	53.7	53.2	53.4	54.7	54.6	54.9	55.8	53.8
2012	53.8	53.9	54.1	53.9	54.2	54.7	53.3	53.9	55.2	55.0	55.4	56.4	54.5
2013	54.1	54.5	54.8	55.0	55.1	55.4	54.3	55.0	56.1	56.2	56.5	57.5	55.4
2014	56.5	56.5	56.2	56.5	56.9	57.1	56.2	57.1	57.8	58.3	58.8	60.6	57.4
2015	59.0	58.7	58.9	58.6	58.9	59.9	58.4	58.8	59.7	60.2	60.9	62.6	59.6
2016	60.2	59.6	59.8	60.2	60.5	60.7	60.0	60.7	61.6	61.5	63.7	65.3	61.2
2017	62.6	62.0	62.1	61.8	62.2	62.7	62.1	62.9	63.5	63.8	65.3	67.0	63.2
2018	64.3	63.3	63.5	63.7	64.1	64.6	63.5	64.4	66.2	66.7	68.1	69.7	65.2
Information													
2010	31.3	31.5	31.6	31.5	31.9	32.3	31.6	32.0	31.8	31.5	31.9	31.9	31.7
2011	31.5	31.6	32.0	31.8	31.6	31.6	31.8	31.9	31.7	31.5	31.7	31.6	31.7
2012	31.2	31.4	31.9	32.3	32.1	32.5	32.7	32.5	32.1	32.4	32.5	32.3	32.2
2013	32.0	32.1	32.2	32.2	32.0	31.9	32.0	32.3	32.5	32.6	32.7	32.7	32.3
2014	31.7	31.9	32.2	32.3	31.6	31.8	32.2	32.4	32.5	32.5	32.7	32.7	32.2
2015	32.1	32.4	32.5	32.7	32.5	32.7	33.5	33.9	33.4	32.9	33.2	33.4	32.9
2016	32.7	33.2	33.3	33.2	33.6	33.5	33.3	33.7	34.6	34.1	34.1	33.8	33.6
2017	33.6	34.1	33.8	35.0	34.5	34.5	34.2	34.5	34.6	34.1	34.2	33.7	34.2
2018	33.7	34.1	34.4	34.2	33.9	33.9	34.4	34.3	34.0	34.1	34.4	34.4	34.2

1. Employment by Industry: Oregon, 2010–2018—*Continued*

(Numbers in thousands, not seasonally adjusted)

Industry and year	January	February	March	April	May	June	July	August	September	October	November	December	Annual average
Financial Activities													
2010	92.7	92.3	92.4	93.4	93.5	94.0	94.5	94.3	93.7	93.6	93.1	93.7	93.4
2011	91.5	91.9	91.6	91.9	92.0	92.6	92.8	92.6	91.8	91.6	91.0	91.5	91.9
2012	89.7	89.8	89.5	90.1	90.1	90.5	91.8	91.9	91.2	91.4	91.1	91.3	90.7
2013	89.9	90.1	90.2	91.3	91.6	91.8	93.3	93.1	92.7	92.7	92.4	92.5	91.8
2014	90.7	90.6	90.5	91.6	92.3	93.0	93.8	94.2	93.8	93.8	93.6	94.2	92.7
2015	93.0	93.0	92.9	94.2	94.8	95.1	96.3	96.7	95.8	96.5	95.9	96.5	95.1
2016	94.7	94.6	94.6	95.9	96.5	97.2	98.5	99.1	98.5	98.4	98.6	99.0	97.1
2017	97.5	97.7	98.2	98.8	99.6	100.3	101.7	101.6	100.9	101.4	101.4	101.4	100.0
2018	100.4	100.7	100.9	101.5	102.2	102.4	103.7	103.7	102.7	101.7	102.0	102.0	102.0
Professional and Business Services													
2010	180.3	182.3	183.9	188.1	188.1	189.5	192.2	193.3	192.7	193.9	192.8	192.6	189.1
2011	187.0	189.3	190.7	194.0	193.5	195.2	199.5	200.2	200.5	199.8	199.3	199.5	195.7
2012	195.4	197.4	198.4	200.9	201.1	203.0	205.5	206.9	205.4	205.8	205.8	206.3	202.7
2013	199.5	201.6	204.0	207.3	208.2	210.5	214.4	215.9	214.9	214.7	214.4	215.0	210.0
2014	210.2	212.1	214.6	217.7	218.6	221.1	223.9	226.3	226.0	225.3	224.7	224.7	220.4
2015	219.5	221.5	223.2	227.4	228.4	230.1	233.5	234.8	234.3	235.7	235.1	235.4	229.9
2016	231.2	233.7	235.4	239.0	238.8	240.3	242.9	244.1	242.4	242.4	241.7	240.5	239.4
2017	235.1	239.2	240.7	244.3	244.2	247.5	248.0	248.6	247.8	247.5	246.6	246.0	244.6
2018	243.5	246.1	247.5	248.3	248.4	249.2	251.0	252.5	251.1	250.9	251.6	248.2	249.0
Education and Health Services													
2010	224.0	227.5	228.6	229.3	228.5	225.1	221.2	221.3	227.9	233.2	234.3	234.0	227.9
2011	229.8	233.4	234.6	235.1	233.8	230.1	225.8	226.4	233.4	237.5	238.7	238.1	233.1
2012	232.6	237.7	238.8	239.6	237.8	232.8	228.9	230.0	236.9	240.7	242.0	241.8	236.6
2013	236.9	242.3	242.8	244.2	243.0	237.8	233.4	234.7	241.6	246.2	247.3	246.5	241.4
2014	242.6	246.4	248.3	249.0	247.3	243.5	239.7	240.2	248.2	252.6	254.2	254.3	247.2
2015	249.9	255.6	256.0	258.1	256.5	253.0	249.7	250.6	258.0	262.3	264.3	263.5	256.5
2016	259.6	265.1	265.7	266.8	264.5	260.1	257.5	259.8	267.4	271.4	272.9	272.0	265.2
2017	265.7	273.3	274.4	275.2	273.9	269.2	265.3	266.9	274.3	277.5	279.3	278.7	272.8
2018	292.5	297.1	297.8	297.4	295.8	291.9	286.9	289.0	295.6	298.1	299.1	299.4	295.1
Leisure and Hospitality													
2010	153.3	154.4	156.5	160.3	163.1	167.4	170.2	170.9	167.9	163.6	160.2	160.0	162.3
2011	156.2	158.3	159.9	163.4	165.6	170.6	173.8	174.6	172.3	166.2	163.0	162.9	165.6
2012	159.1	160.7	163.4	166.7	170.4	174.9	178.7	180.1	177.7	171.9	168.9	168.5	170.1
2013	164.9	166.6	169.5	173.5	177.6	182.7	186.2	187.0	183.8	177.4	175.6	174.5	176.6
2014	171.6	172.5	176.2	180.3	184.5	188.3	192.2	193.1	189.4	184.1	181.7	181.1	182.9
2015	178.9	181.2	184.1	187.9	192.5	197.4	201.7	202.1	198.8	193.2	190.8	190.0	191.6
2016	187.4	190.2	193.2	197.7	201.4	206.3	210.4	209.4	206.5	200.2	198.0	197.6	199.9
2017	193.0	196.0	198.9	204.1	207.6	214.0	217.2	217.0	213.1	206.8	204.8	204.3	206.4
2018	200.3	201.8	204.8	208.8	212.9	218.1	220.8	221.4	216.0	209.7	206.6	207.4	210.7
Other Services													
2010	55.9	56.1	56.4	56.4	57.0	57.6	57.0	56.6	56.9	56.9	56.3	56.2	56.6
2011	55.8	56.3	56.5	56.8	57.0	57.2	57.2	57.2	57.4	57.0	56.8	56.8	56.8
2012	56.2	56.6	56.8	57.3	58.0	57.9	57.9	57.8	57.6	57.8	57.2	57.0	57.3
2013	56.8	57.3	57.6	57.8	58.5	58.4	58.6	58.7	58.4	58.0	58.2	57.8	58.0
2014	57.7	57.8	58.3	58.7	59.5	59.9	59.8	59.7	59.8	59.8	59.7	59.4	59.2
2015	58.9	59.5	59.7	60.4	60.9	61.0	61.7	61.7	61.4	61.8	62.0	62.1	60.9
2016	61.6	62.5	62.9	63.9	64.3	64.6	64.3	64.6	64.7	64.8	64.6	63.8	63.9
2017	61.2	62.4	62.7	63.4	63.9	64.2	64.4	64.4	64.0	63.9	63.7	63.8	63.5
2018	63.1	63.6	63.9	64.3	65.0	65.2	65.1	64.9	64.3	65.5	64.0	64.6	64.5
Government													
2010	298.7	303.4	304.9	307.5	314.9	314.5	281.4	277.7	283.6	302.9	306.2	301.5	299.8
2011	299.5	303.5	303.8	304.5	306.9	307.2	271.9	269.5	279.0	297.2	299.9	297.0	295.0
2012	292.5	297.7	298.4	297.8	301.5	301.2	268.6	267.3	278.1	295.5	298.2	294.9	291.0
2013	289.8	295.5	295.6	295.5	298.8	297.9	264.5	263.9	277.0	294.3	297.8	296.2	288.9
2014	292.6	296.9	297.7	299.3	302.6	303.1	271.4	271.1	283.3	301.5	304.6	303.2	293.9
2015	299.7	304.4	305.8	309.9	313.0	313.6	277.4	276.2	288.0	306.9	310.2	309.5	301.2
2016	305.5	310.7	312.4	313.0	315.8	316.8	284.1	282.3	296.0	313.5	317.0	313.9	306.8
2017	306.9	315.0	317.4	317.0	319.6	320.7	288.6	287.6	298.8	314.6	316.9	314.9	309.8
2018	293.9	299.6	300.7	300.9	303.6	304.7	270.6	270.5	287.0	301.5	304.3	302.8	295.0

2. Average Weekly Hours by Selected Industry: Oregon, 2014–2018

(Not seasonally adjusted)

Industry and year	January	February	March	April	May	June	July	August	September	October	November	December	Annual average
Total Private													
2014	32.9	33.8	34.3	33.7	33.6	34.7	33.7	34.1	33.9	33.7	34.4	33.5	33.9
2015	33.3	34.6	34.4	33.6	33.7	34.0	34.0	35.0	33.8	33.7	34.5	33.5	34.0
2016	33.4	33.7	33.5	33.9	34.7	34.2	34.4	34.4	34.3	35.1	34.0	33.3	34.1
2017	33.5	33.9	33.7	34.9	33.7	34.0	34.7	34.2	34.2	34.9	33.8	33.8	34.1
2018	33.3	33.9	33.6	34.7	33.9	34.0	34.7	34.2	35.0	33.9	33.8	34.4	34.1
Goods-Producing													
2014	38.2	38.2	39.3	38.8	38.9	39.5	38.7	39.3	39.7	39.5	39.6	39.0	39.1
2015	38.9	39.7	39.4	38.8	38.6	39.2	39.2	39.6	38.1	38.7	38.9	38.5	39.0
2016	38.0	38.0	38.1	38.4	39.2	38.9	38.7	38.9	39.3	39.4	38.6	37.3	38.6
2017	36.8	38.6	38.6	39.3	38.7	39.3	39.5	39.4	39.5	39.9	38.8	38.5	38.9
2018	37.6	38.1	38.1	38.8	38.6	38.6	38.7	39.0	39.4	38.7	38.3	38.9	38.6
Construction													
2014	35.7	34.7	36.2	36.0	36.5	37.1	36.7	38.1	38.0	37.2	36.6	36.2	36.6
2015	36.4	36.9	36.3	36.3	35.7	37.2	37.2	37.5	35.2	36.4	35.7	35.4	36.3
2016	35.6	35.6	35.6	36.9	36.8	37.5	37.2	37.6	37.6	37.2	36.3	35.0	36.6
2017	33.8	37.0	37.4	37.9	37.5	38.8	39.1	38.9	38.9	39.0	37.1	37.3	37.8
2018	36.1	36.2	36.5	37.5	38.0	38.0	38.1	39.0	38.5	38.0	36.7	37.5	37.5
Manufacturing													
2014	38.9	39.4	40.4	39.8	39.8	40.4	39.4	39.6	40.4	40.3	40.8	40.3	40.0
2015	40.0	40.5	40.4	39.5	39.5	39.8	39.7	40.3	39.2	39.3	40.1	39.8	39.8
2016	39.0	38.9	39.1	39.0	40.2	39.4	39.2	39.3	39.9	40.4	39.7	39.2	39.4
2017	39.1	39.8	39.7	40.4	39.7	39.8	40.1	39.9	40.1	40.5	39.8	39.3	39.9
2018	38.7	39.4	39.4	39.8	39.2	39.4	39.5	39.4	40.3	39.4	39.5	40.0	39.5
Trade, Transportation, and Utilities													
2014	33.7	34.6	35.0	34.6	34.8	35.5	35.1	35.2	34.8	34.1	34.7	34.2	34.7
2015	33.5	35.1	35.1	34.4	34.9	34.9	35.0	35.8	35.4	34.7	35.5	34.5	34.9
2016	34.2	34.5	34.7	35.4	35.9	35.3	35.6	35.5	35.4	36.1	34.9	34.8	35.2
2017	34.3	34.6	34.5	36.0	34.9	34.9	35.7	35.1	35.1	35.9	34.5	34.7	35.0
2018	34.2	35.3	34.8	35.6	35.3	35.2	35.7	35.1	35.6	34.8	34.7	35.4	35.1
Financial Activities													
2014	35.7	37.1	36.9	35.1	35.1	37.6	35.6	36.0	36.0	35.5	37.6	35.8	36.2
2015	35.7	37.1	36.5	35.6	35.3	35.4	35.4	36.9	36.2	36.2	37.0	36.4	36.1
2016	37.0	36.6	36.7	36.6	38.2	37.0	37.5	37.2	38.5	39.8	38.3	37.9	37.6
2017	38.4	37.7	38.7	38.0	37.1	37.4	38.1	37.4	38.3	37.7	36.7	36.8	37.7
2018	36.4	37.6	37.3	39.2	37.4	37.5	37.5	37.0	38.3	36.8	37.0	37.6	37.5
Professional and Business Services													
2014	34.2	35.6	35.8	35.0	34.5	36.2	35.2	35.2	35.1	35.1	35.5	34.5	35.2
2015	34.2	35.5	35.3	34.6	34.4	35.2	35.0	36.0	34.4	34.7	35.8	34.4	35.0
2016	34.5	35.0	34.5	35.0	35.9	35.0	35.0	35.0	34.7	36.3	35.2	34.1	35.0
2017	35.0	35.5	35.2	36.9	35.5	35.9	36.7	35.7	35.9	37.1	36.2	36.2	36.0
2018	35.6	36.1	35.9	37.2	35.7	35.9	36.3	35.3	37.0	35.6	35.5	36.3	36.0
Education and Health Services													
2014	31.3	32.5	32.3	31.6	31.4	32.6	31.0	31.7	31.9	31.7	33.0	32.2	31.9
2015	32.1	33.5	33.1	32.4	32.6	32.6	32.4	33.7	32.9	32.9	34.0	33.2	33.0
2016	33.3	33.2	32.8	33.2	33.8	34.1	34.2	34.1	33.1	34.2	33.3	32.7	33.5
2017	33.4	33.3	32.7	33.9	32.5	32.5	33.3	33.0	32.7	33.3	32.5	32.9	33.0
2018	32.6	32.8	32.4	33.5	32.7	32.9	33.7	33.2	34.1	32.5	32.9	33.6	33.1
Leisure and Hospitality													
2014	23.4	24.5	25.8	24.9	24.8	26.4	25.1	26.3	25.2	24.9	25.7	24.2	25.1
2015	24.1	25.8	25.8	24.8	25.1	25.6	26.1	27.4	25.5	25.0	25.5	24.3	25.4
2016	24.0	25.0	24.3	24.8	25.7	25.1	25.9	26.6	25.8	26.3	24.7	24.2	25.2
2017	24.5	24.8	24.7	26.1	24.9	25.4	26.6	26.0	25.3	25.9	24.6	24.6	25.3
2018	24.5	24.7	24.9	25.8	24.9	25.1	26.5	25.8	25.9	24.8	24.3	24.4	25.1
Other Services													
2014	29.1	29.2	30.2	29.8	30.0	30.7	29.6	29.9	29.3	28.7	29.8	27.7	29.5
2015	28.4	30.1	28.9	28.5	28.6	29.1	29.0	29.8	28.2	28.3	28.8	26.7	28.7
2016	27.0	27.7	27.4	27.8	29.4	28.0	28.8	28.7	28.1	29.8	28.4	27.7	28.2
2017	28.4	29.0	28.3	30.0	28.9	29.0	30.5	28.9	29.3	30.1	28.7	28.8	29.2
2018	28.2	29.3	29.0	30.7	29.7	30.0	31.1	29.9	31.2	29.0	29.6	30.5	29.9

3. Average Hourly Earnings by Selected Industry: Oregon, 2014–2018

(Dollars, not seasonally adjusted)

Industry and year	January	February	March	April	May	June	July	August	September	October	November	December	Annual average
Total Private													
2014	23.09	23.05	22.86	22.80	22.84	22.83	22.77	22.61	22.88	22.92	23.10	23.14	22.91
2015	23.36	23.34	23.38	23.32	23.36	23.28	23.32	23.43	23.57	23.78	24.01	24.12	23.53
2016	24.29	24.35	24.23	24.62	24.66	24.39	24.56	24.53	25.00	25.24	25.20	25.54	24.72
2017	26.01	25.56	25.50	25.64	25.21	25.30	25.55	25.49	25.79	25.93	25.83	26.06	25.66
2018	25.95	25.83	25.83	26.04	25.90	26.01	26.27	26.21	26.53	26.50	26.56	26.97	26.22
Goods-Producing													
2014	24.44	24.31	24.14	24.28	24.13	24.28	24.27	24.02	24.18	24.11	24.28	24.27	24.22
2015	24.32	24.17	24.25	24.36	24.21	24.39	24.49	24.49	24.41	24.71	24.78	25.12	24.48
2016	25.20	25.16	25.13	25.36	25.45	25.29	25.43	25.45	25.74	25.76	25.82	26.19	25.50
2017	26.19	25.94	25.93	26.06	26.36	26.23	26.29	26.03	26.45	26.56	26.28	26.61	26.25
2018	26.62	26.31	26.68	26.92	26.84	26.80	27.22	27.29	27.42	27.69	27.65	28.39	27.16
Construction													
2014	28.65	28.67	28.51	28.48	28.35	28.19	28.26	27.91	28.30	28.00	27.95	28.23	28.28
2015	28.29	28.00	28.29	28.23	28.15	28.33	28.67	28.75	28.61	28.78	28.80	29.84	28.57
2016	29.57	29.23	29.35	29.51	29.68	29.39	29.61	29.88	29.85	29.91	30.19	30.08	29.70
2017	30.65	30.21	29.98	30.21	30.58	30.05	30.40	30.22	30.71	30.51	30.38	30.81	30.39
2018	30.51	30.35	30.32	30.29	29.85	29.83	30.82	30.68	30.27	30.78	30.45	31.34	30.46
Manufacturing													
2014	22.86	22.76	22.68	22.73	22.55	22.84	22.84	22.54	22.59	22.69	22.98	22.83	22.74
2015	22.86	22.81	22.78	22.97	22.77	22.81	22.75	22.65	22.68	22.94	23.07	23.10	22.85
2016	23.29	23.38	23.28	23.42	23.54	23.34	23.46	23.26	23.77	23.78	23.69	24.40	23.55
2017	24.19	23.88	23.92	24.03	24.25	24.27	24.16	23.86	24.16	24.51	24.25	24.41	24.16
2018	24.76	24.32	24.57	24.96	25.02	24.94	25.05	25.16	25.70	25.85	26.07	26.73	25.27
Trade, Transportation, and Utilities													
2014	20.28	20.19	19.85	19.82	19.76	19.84	19.80	19.37	19.48	19.64	19.70	19.44	19.76
2015	19.93	19.73	19.82	19.67	19.74	19.71	19.91	19.73	19.69	19.82	19.88	19.78	19.78
2016	20.31	20.29	20.36	21.25	21.65	21.23	21.84	21.74	21.98	22.32	22.21	22.21	21.47
2017	23.05	22.34	22.51	22.52	22.17	22.72	22.85	22.49	22.43	22.90	22.22	22.32	22.54
2018	21.94	22.17	22.09	22.39	22.30	22.34	22.61	22.32	22.72	22.53	22.27	22.44	22.35
Financial Activities													
2014	24.46	24.29	24.21	24.11	24.70	25.40	25.72	26.19	26.00	26.34	26.37	27.44	25.45
2015	27.39	27.90	27.92	27.74	27.87	27.95	27.48	27.98	27.59	27.81	28.00	28.45	27.84
2016	27.41	28.20	28.29	29.73	28.25	27.64	28.00	27.92	28.63	29.02	28.66	28.45	28.36
2017	29.35	28.64	28.52	30.17	28.70	29.81	30.58	31.71	31.24	31.35	31.43	31.70	30.27
2018	31.73	31.55	31.49	33.03	33.40	33.02	33.18	32.60	32.62	31.94	32.46	32.95	32.51
Professional and Business Services													
2014	26.44	26.85	27.03	26.55	26.44	26.78	26.25	26.25	26.36	26.06	26.17	25.96	26.43
2015	26.22	26.18	26.38	26.41	26.64	26.16	26.26	26.37	26.72	26.91	27.56	27.41	26.61
2016	27.57	27.85	27.73	27.80	27.97	27.71	27.33	27.49	28.20	28.54	28.12	29.03	27.95
2017	29.62	29.18	29.01	29.26	28.66	28.57	29.31	29.06	30.03	30.24	30.35	30.48	29.49
2018	30.87	30.35	30.31	30.64	30.43	30.74	31.05	31.16	31.64	31.40	31.77	32.26	31.05
Education and Health Services													
2014	24.84	24.72	24.67	24.86	24.90	24.87	25.30	25.30	25.46	25.65	25.82	25.98	25.20
2015	26.26	26.22	26.19	26.49	26.70	26.76	27.30	27.45	27.66	27.60	27.81	27.76	27.03
2016	27.92	27.99	27.97	28.20	28.04	28.09	28.60	28.41	29.11	29.15	29.05	29.44	28.50
2017	29.58	29.27	29.10	29.14	29.05	29.16	29.21	29.54	29.36	29.31	29.26	29.69	29.31
2018	29.28	29.08	28.99	28.87	28.81	28.85	29.07	28.96	28.87	28.98	28.99	29.28	29.00
Leisure and Hospitality													
2014	14.14	14.10	14.03	13.87	13.98	13.83	13.66	13.68	13.86	13.72	13.79	14.12	13.89
2015	14.03	14.10	14.01	14.27	14.20	13.97	13.93	14.02	14.40	14.58	14.63	14.70	14.23
2016	14.62	14.69	14.76	14.76	14.89	14.91	15.06	15.03	15.10	15.23	15.19	15.38	14.97
2017	15.36	15.31	15.44	15.54	15.53	15.38	15.70	15.62	15.79	15.91	16.08	16.23	15.66
2018	16.25	16.26	16.18	16.20	16.16	16.31	16.54	16.51	16.85	16.77	16.73	17.13	16.49
Other Services													
2014	20.86	20.82	20.34	20.35	20.25	20.14	20.31	20.19	20.53	20.58	21.20	21.80	20.60
2015	21.44	21.27	21.49	21.67	21.61	21.81	21.51	21.98	22.04	22.10	22.20	22.40	21.79
2016	22.47	21.96	22.13	22.23	21.98	22.27	22.15	22.34	22.75	22.53	22.35	22.73	22.32
2017	22.83	22.53	22.24	22.10	21.81	22.11	21.91	21.69	21.90	21.98	22.14	22.82	22.16
2018	22.74	22.78	22.83	22.68	21.83	22.64	23.04	23.11	23.10	23.38	23.38	23.08	22.88

4. Average Weekly Earnings by Selected Industry: Oregon, 2014–2018

(Dollars, not seasonally adjusted)

Industry and year	January	February	March	April	May	June	July	August	September	October	November	December	Annual average
Total Private													
2014	759.66	779.09	784.10	768.36	767.42	792.20	767.35	771.00	775.63	772.40	794.64	775.19	776.65
2015	777.89	807.56	804.27	783.55	787.23	791.52	792.88	820.05	796.67	801.39	828.35	808.02	800.02
2016	811.29	820.60	811.71	834.62	855.70	834.14	844.86	843.83	857.50	885.92	856.80	850.48	842.95
2017	871.34	866.48	859.35	894.84	849.58	860.20	886.59	871.76	882.02	904.96	873.05	880.83	875.01
2018	864.14	875.64	867.89	903.59	878.01	884.34	911.57	896.38	928.55	898.35	897.73	927.77	894.10
Goods-Producing													
2014	933.61	928.64	948.70	942.06	938.66	959.06	939.25	943.99	959.95	952.35	961.49	946.53	947.00
2015	946.05	959.55	955.45	945.17	934.51	956.09	960.01	969.80	930.02	956.28	963.94	967.12	954.72
2016	957.60	956.08	957.45	973.82	997.64	983.78	984.14	990.01	1,011.58	1,014.94	996.65	976.89	984.30
2017	963.79	1,001.28	1,000.90	1,024.16	1,020.13	1,030.84	1,038.46	1,025.58	1,044.78	1,059.74	1,019.66	1,024.49	1,021.13
2018	1,000.91	1,002.41	1,016.51	1,044.50	1,036.02	1,034.48	1,053.41	1,064.31	1,080.35	1,071.60	1,059.00	1,104.37	1,048.38
Construction													
2014	1,022.81	994.85	1,032.06	1,025.28	1,034.78	1,045.85	1,037.14	1,063.37	1,075.40	1,041.60	1,022.97	1,021.93	1,035.05
2015	1,029.76	1,033.20	1,026.93	1,024.75	1,004.96	1,053.88	1,066.52	1,078.13	1,007.07	1,047.59	1,028.16	1,056.34	1,037.09
2016	1,052.69	1,040.59	1,044.86	1,088.92	1,092.22	1,102.13	1,101.49	1,123.49	1,122.36	1,112.65	1,095.90	1,052.80	1,087.02
2017	1,035.97	1,117.77	1,121.25	1,144.96	1,146.75	1,165.94	1,188.64	1,175.56	1,194.62	1,189.89	1,127.10	1,149.21	1,148.74
2018	1,101.41	1,098.67	1,106.68	1,135.88	1,134.30	1,133.54	1,174.24	1,196.52	1,165.40	1,169.64	1,117.52	1,175.25	1,142.25
Manufacturing													
2014	889.25	896.74	916.27	904.65	897.49	922.74	899.90	892.58	912.64	914.41	937.58	920.05	909.60
2015	914.40	923.81	920.31	907.32	899.42	907.84	903.18	912.80	889.06	901.54	925.11	919.38	909.43
2016	908.31	909.48	910.25	913.38	946.31	919.60	919.63	914.12	948.42	960.71	940.49	956.48	927.87
2017	945.83	950.42	949.62	970.81	962.73	965.95	968.82	952.01	968.82	992.66	965.15	959.31	963.98
2018	958.21	958.21	968.06	993.41	980.78	982.64	989.48	991.30	1,035.71	1,018.49	1,029.77	1,069.20	998.17
Trade, Transportation, and Utilities													
2014	683.44	698.57	694.75	685.77	687.65	704.32	694.98	681.82	677.90	669.72	683.59	664.85	685.67
2015	667.66	692.52	695.68	676.65	688.93	687.88	696.85	706.33	697.03	687.75	705.74	682.41	690.32
2016	694.60	700.01	706.49	752.25	777.24	749.42	777.50	771.77	778.09	805.75	775.13	772.91	755.74
2017	790.62	772.96	776.60	810.72	773.73	792.93	815.75	789.40	787.29	822.11	766.59	774.50	788.90
2018	750.35	782.60	768.73	797.08	787.19	786.37	807.18	783.43	808.83	784.04	772.77	794.38	784.49
Financial Activities													
2014	873.22	901.16	893.35	846.26	866.97	955.04	915.63	942.84	936.00	935.07	991.51	982.35	921.29
2015	977.82	1,035.09	1,019.08	987.54	983.81	989.43	972.79	1,032.46	998.76	1,006.72	1,036.00	1,035.58	1,005.02
2016	1,014.17	1,032.12	1,038.24	1,088.12	1,079.15	1,022.68	1,050.00	1,038.62	1,102.26	1,155.00	1,097.68	1,078.26	1,066.34
2017	1,127.04	1,079.73	1,103.72	1,146.46	1,064.77	1,114.89	1,165.10	1,185.95	1,196.49	1,181.90	1,153.48	1,166.56	1,141.18
2018	1,154.97	1,186.28	1,174.58	1,294.78	1,249.16	1,238.25	1,244.25	1,206.20	1,249.35	1,175.39	1,201.02	1,238.92	1,219.13
Professional and Business Services													
2014	904.25	955.86	967.67	929.25	912.18	969.44	924.00	924.00	925.24	914.71	929.04	895.62	930.34
2015	896.72	929.39	931.21	913.79	916.42	920.83	919.10	949.32	919.17	933.78	986.65	942.90	931.35
2016	951.17	974.75	956.69	973.00	1,004.12	969.85	956.55	962.15	978.54	1,036.00	989.82	989.92	978.25
2017	1,036.70	1,035.89	1,021.15	1,079.69	1,017.43	1,025.66	1,075.68	1,037.44	1,078.08	1,121.90	1,098.67	1,103.38	1,061.64
2018	1,098.97	1,095.64	1,088.13	1,139.81	1,086.35	1,103.57	1,127.12	1,099.95	1,170.68	1,117.84	1,127.84	1,171.04	1,117.80
Education and Health Services													
2014	777.49	803.40	796.84	785.58	781.86	810.76	784.30	802.01	812.17	813.11	852.06	836.56	803.88
2015	842.95	878.37	866.89	858.28	870.42	872.38	884.52	925.07	910.01	908.04	945.54	921.63	891.99
2016	929.74	929.27	917.42	936.24	947.75	957.87	978.12	968.78	963.54	996.93	967.37	962.69	954.75
2017	987.97	974.69	951.57	987.85	944.13	947.70	972.69	974.82	960.07	976.02	950.95	976.80	967.23
2018	954.53	953.82	939.28	967.15	942.09	949.17	979.66	961.47	984.47	941.85	953.77	983.81	959.90
Leisure and Hospitality													
2014	330.88	345.45	361.97	345.36	346.70	365.11	342.87	359.78	349.27	341.63	354.40	341.70	348.64
2015	338.12	363.78	361.46	353.90	356.42	357.63	363.57	384.15	367.20	364.50	373.07	357.21	361.44
2016	350.88	367.25	358.67	366.05	382.67	374.24	390.05	399.80	389.58	400.55	375.19	372.20	377.24
2017	376.32	379.69	381.37	405.59	386.70	390.65	417.62	406.12	399.49	412.07	395.57	399.26	396.20
2018	398.13	401.62	402.88	417.96	402.38	409.38	438.31	425.96	436.42	415.90	406.54	417.97	413.90
Other Services													
2014	607.03	607.94	614.27	606.43	607.50	618.30	601.18	603.68	601.53	590.65	631.76	603.86	607.70
2015	608.90	640.23	621.06	617.60	618.05	634.67	623.79	655.00	621.53	625.43	639.36	598.08	625.37
2016	606.69	608.29	606.36	617.99	646.21	623.56	637.92	641.16	639.28	671.39	634.74	629.62	629.42
2017	648.37	653.37	629.39	663.00	630.31	641.19	668.26	626.84	641.67	661.60	635.42	657.22	647.07
2018	641.27	667.45	662.07	696.28	648.35	679.20	716.54	690.99	720.72	678.02	692.05	703.94	684.11

PENNSYLVANIA
At a Glance

Population:
  2010 census: 12,702,379
  2018 estimate: 12,807,060

Percent change in population:
  2010–2018: 0.8%

Percent change in total nonfarm employment:
  2010–2018: 6.8%

Industry with the largest growth in employment, 2010–2018 (percent):
  Transportation and utilities, 24.6%

Industry with the largest decline or smallest growth in employment, 2010–2018 (percent):
  Government, -8.8%

Civilian labor force:
  2010: 6,380,949
  2018: 6,424,421

Unemployment rate and rank among states (highest to lowest):
  2010: 8.5%, 28th
  2018: 4.3%, 11th

Over-the-year change in unemployment rates:
  2016–2017: -0.5%
  2017–2018: -0.6%

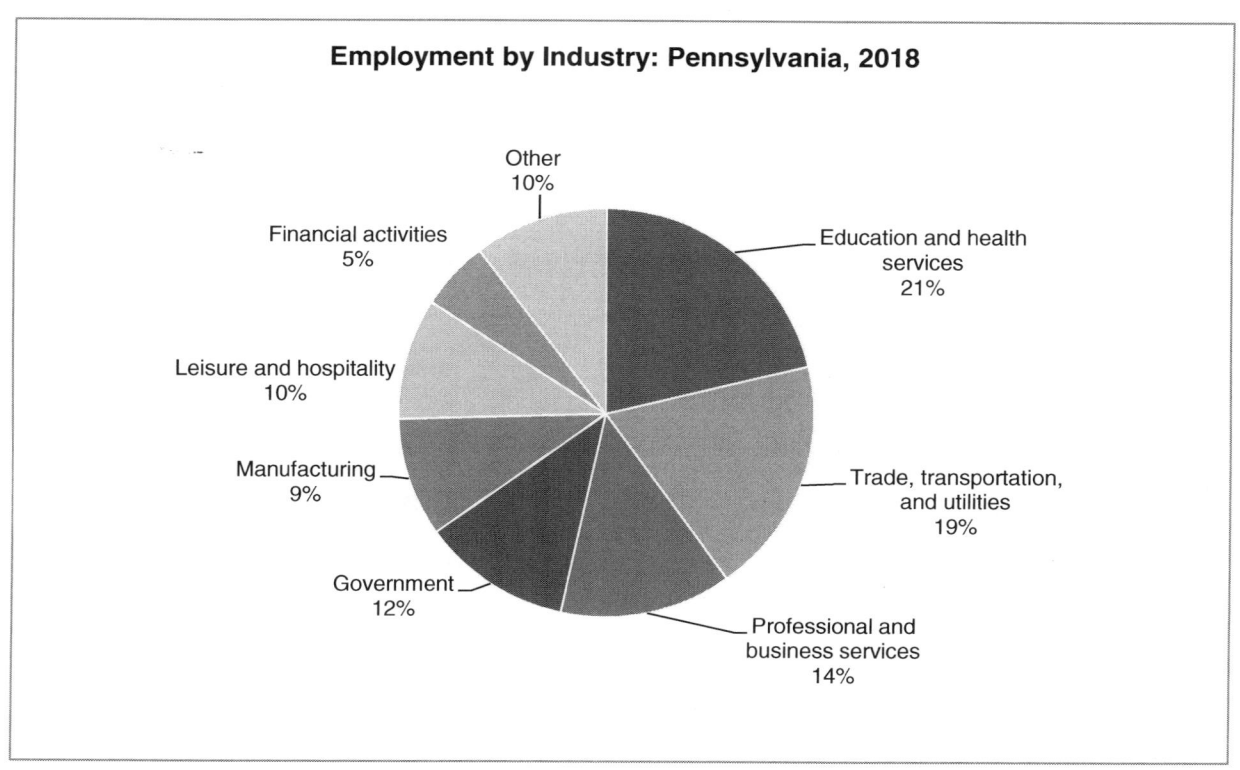

Employment by Industry: Pennsylvania, 2018

- Other 10%
- Financial activities 5%
- Leisure and hospitality 10%
- Manufacturing 9%
- Government 12%
- Education and health services 21%
- Trade, transportation, and utilities 19%
- Professional and business services 14%

1. Employment by Industry: Pennsylvania, 2010–2018

(Numbers in thousands, not seasonally adjusted)

Industry and year	January	February	March	April	May	June	July	August	September	October	November	December	Annual average
Total Nonfarm													
2010	5,473.1	5,483.8	5,541.4	5,622.7	5,677.9	5,673.5	5,605.7	5,601.3	5,650.9	5,703.7	5,722.3	5,712.1	5,622.4
2011	5,555.3	5,587.4	5,631.2	5,700.4	5,730.7	5,729.7	5,654.8	5,648.0	5,713.1	5,748.4	5,772.6	5,759.4	5,685.9
2012	5,600.9	5,647.6	5,702.1	5,742.0	5,774.9	5,760.3	5,687.4	5,688.4	5,748.9	5,780.8	5,797.9	5,781.8	5,726.1
2013	5,620.0	5,664.1	5,702.7	5,745.5	5,784.7	5,771.1	5,705.7	5,710.5	5,766.2	5,797.3	5,818.9	5,800.9	5,740.6
2014	5,648.6	5,669.3	5,717.2	5,787.9	5,830.4	5,825.4	5,757.8	5,765.7	5,824.0	5,869.5	5,888.3	5,879.2	5,788.6
2015	5,708.7	5,736.3	5,760.6	5,835.4	5,878.0	5,869.6	5,811.1	5,811.4	5,865.8	5,908.9	5,924.9	5,913.8	5,835.4
2016	5,754.5	5,785.4	5,828.1	5,894.2	5,913.0	5,892.1	5,861.0	5,854.5	5,927.5	5,955.8	5,972.2	5,956.3	5,882.9
2017	5,810.4	5,849.0	5,871.1	5,938.4	5,975.8	5,957.9	5,913.9	5,914.8	5,985.4	6,014.5	6,037.7	6,026.2	5,941.3
2018	5,873.3	5,918.3	5,946.2	6,008.8	6,040.1	6,027.5	5,982.3	5,984.8	6,041.8	6,087.0	6,085.9	6,075.6	6,006.0
Total Private													
2010	4,712.6	4,702.1	4,753.6	4,829.3	4,876.0	4,894.2	4,891.0	4,892.6	4,886.9	4,920.2	4,932.8	4,929.8	4,851.8
2011	4,793.1	4,808.1	4,850.2	4,919.1	4,960.1	4,977.6	4,966.1	4,964.2	4,972.8	4,992.6	5,009.8	5,001.0	4,934.6
2012	4,870.5	4,893.5	4,946.6	4,986.9	5,022.4	5,036.7	5,014.4	5,014.0	5,018.9	5,036.2	5,049.0	5,036.9	4,993.8
2013	4,897.7	4,922.6	4,961.3	5,003.1	5,041.1	5,060.9	5,044.6	5,045.2	5,048.5	5,065.9	5,080.8	5,067.3	5,019.9
2014	4,935.9	4,941.1	4,988.6	5,056.8	5,105.7	5,118.7	5,101.6	5,107.6	5,112.2	5,144.1	5,159.0	5,155.0	5,077.2
2015	5,008.5	5,016.6	5,040.3	5,110.1	5,159.3	5,170.9	5,157.9	5,154.8	5,158.3	5,191.9	5,202.4	5,197.1	5,130.7
2016	5,057.9	5,069.8	5,109.6	5,175.2	5,200.7	5,199.1	5,205.8	5,199.3	5,216.4	5,236.7	5,248.2	5,236.9	5,179.6
2017	5,113.8	5,132.3	5,152.9	5,218.9	5,258.6	5,265.3	5,258.5	5,258.0	5,275.0	5,297.4	5,315.9	5,309.6	5,238.0
2018	5,176.6	5,203.3	5,229.2	5,291.1	5,326.7	5,334.4	5,326.4	5,324.7	5,330.5	5,369.8	5,365.0	5,359.7	5,303.1
Goods Producing													
2010	766.9	759.0	773.6	796.8	807.6	818.7	823.2	823.1	818.9	818.6	815.9	804.4	802.2
2011	781.1	778.6	793.4	811.4	823.6	835.5	842.0	843.7	840.0	840.6	837.4	827.8	821.3
2012	805.9	805.4	816.1	826.3	833.4	845.4	845.9	845.2	842.0	838.8	830.1	820.0	829.5
2013	798.2	797.0	806.6	819.1	830.2	840.6	842.4	843.5	840.5	838.2	831.5	817.1	825.4
2014	799.2	795.7	808.0	827.1	840.7	851.4	855.6	856.2	851.2	852.4	848.0	837.7	835.3
2015	814.9	809.7	815.8	834.6	846.9	856.2	858.3	857.1	850.7	847.1	839.4	828.6	838.3
2016	805.2	797.5	808.4	821.6	829.1	838.3	841.3	839.5	833.8	833.7	829.2	820.1	824.8
2017	802.7	803.3	810.8	829.8	843.7	856.0	858.7	858.0	853.4	853.2	849.7	843.0	838.5
2018	820.7	822.4	832.3	846.1	857.0	869.7	873.0	871.7	866.7	867.9	862.0	855.3	853.7
Service-Providing													
2010	4,706.2	4,724.8	4,767.8	4,825.9	4,870.3	4,854.8	4,782.5	4,778.2	4,832.0	4,885.1	4,906.4	4,907.7	4,820.1
2011	4,774.2	4,808.8	4,837.8	4,889.0	4,907.1	4,894.2	4,812.8	4,804.3	4,873.1	4,907.8	4,935.2	4,931.6	4,864.7
2012	4,795.0	4,842.2	4,886.0	4,915.7	4,941.5	4,914.9	4,841.5	4,843.2	4,906.9	4,942.0	4,967.8	4,961.8	4,896.5
2013	4,821.8	4,867.1	4,896.1	4,926.4	4,954.5	4,930.5	4,863.3	4,867.0	4,925.7	4,959.1	4,987.4	4,983.8	4,915.2
2014	4,849.4	4,873.6	4,909.2	4,960.8	4,989.7	4,974.0	4,902.2	4,909.5	4,972.8	5,017.1	5,040.3	5,041.5	4,953.3
2015	4,893.8	4,926.6	4,944.8	5,000.8	5,031.1	5,013.4	4,952.8	4,954.3	5,015.1	5,061.8	5,085.5	5,085.2	4,997.1
2016	4,949.3	4,987.9	5,019.7	5,072.6	5,083.9	5,053.8	5,019.7	5,015.0	5,093.7	5,122.1	5,143.0	5,136.2	5,058.1
2017	5,007.7	5,045.7	5,060.3	5,108.6	5,132.1	5,101.9	5,055.2	5,056.8	5,132.0	5,161.3	5,188.0	5,183.2	5,102.7
2018	5,052.6	5,095.9	5,113.9	5,162.7	5,183.1	5,157.8	5,109.3	5,113.1	5,175.1	5,219.1	5,223.9	5,220.3	5,152.2
Mining and Logging													
2010	22.5	22.9	23.7	25.4	26.1	26.9	27.6	28.0	28.7	29.0	29.6	29.4	26.7
2011	29.5	30.2	30.9	32.0	33.0	34.1	34.7	35.1	35.6	36.3	37.1	37.4	33.8
2012	37.0	37.7	38.0	37.8	37.8	38.0	37.5	37.1	36.7	36.3	36.0	35.4	37.1
2013	34.7	34.9	35.5	35.9	36.4	36.7	36.7	36.4	36.3	36.5	36.3	36.1	36.0
2014	35.4	35.6	36.0	37.0	37.6	38.0	38.6	38.9	38.9	39.0	39.1	39.0	37.8
2015	38.3	36.9	36.4	35.5	35.2	35.1	34.3	33.2	32.1	31.1	30.2	29.5	34.0
2016	27.4	26.3	25.9	25.1	24.9	24.6	24.3	24.2	24.2	24.3	24.4	24.4	25.0
2017	24.2	24.8	25.2	25.8	26.6	27.2	27.5	27.6	27.8	27.9	28.1	27.9	26.7
2018	27.3	27.3	27.6	28.2	28.5	28.9	29.2	29.2	29.1	29.1	29.3	29.2	28.6
Construction													
2010	190.7	184.7	195.6	214.2	221.4	226.4	230.4	230.2	227.0	225.8	222.3	211.1	215.0
2011	193.6	191.3	202.4	216.4	224.8	231.5	236.2	237.2	235.5	236.1	232.3	221.4	221.6
2012	204.8	204.3	212.5	221.7	226.7	233.6	235.1	235.6	236.2	235.2	227.8	218.5	224.3
2013	202.0	201.2	209.2	220.3	228.8	233.9	236.8	238.9	237.8	235.3	228.4	213.8	223.9
2014	201.5	198.3	207.6	225.0	234.9	240.5	244.2	244.5	243.2	243.8	237.9	226.2	229.0
2015	209.3	205.9	211.5	230.1	240.4	246.7	249.5	251.5	250.0	250.4	244.8	234.8	235.4
2016	218.3	213.3	223.4	237.4	243.4	248.5	252.4	252.0	250.4	249.9	245.3	234.6	239.1
2017	221.2	221.1	226.0	243.0	254.7	261.6	264.4	264.4	262.6	262.4	257.7	248.9	249.0
2018	230.9	232.0	239.5	251.8	259.8	266.9	269.2	268.7	266.8	266.3	263.4	254.0	255.8

1. Employment by Industry: Pennsylvania, 2010–2018—*Continued*

(Numbers in thousands, not seasonally adjusted)

Industry and year	January	February	March	April	May	June	July	August	September	October	November	December	Annual average
Manufacturing													
2010	553.7	551.4	554.3	557.2	560.1	565.4	565.2	564.9	563.2	563.8	564.0	563.9	560.6
2011	558.0	557.1	560.1	563.0	565.8	569.9	571.1	571.4	568.9	568.2	568.0	569.0	565.9
2012	564.1	563.4	565.6	566.8	568.9	573.8	573.3	572.5	569.1	567.3	566.3	566.1	568.1
2013	561.5	560.9	561.9	562.9	565.0	570.0	568.9	568.2	566.4	566.4	566.8	567.2	565.5
2014	562.3	561.8	564.4	565.1	568.2	572.9	572.8	572.8	569.1	569.6	571.0	572.5	568.5
2015	567.3	566.9	567.9	569.0	571.3	574.4	574.5	572.4	568.6	565.6	564.4	564.3	568.9
2016	559.5	557.9	559.1	559.1	560.8	565.2	564.6	563.3	559.2	559.5	559.5	561.1	560.7
2017	557.3	557.4	559.6	561.0	562.4	567.2	566.8	566.0	563.0	562.9	563.9	566.2	562.8
2018	562.5	563.1	565.2	566.1	568.7	573.9	574.6	573.8	570.8	572.5	569.3	572.1	569.4
Trade, Transportation, and Utilities													
2010	1,062.2	1,043.8	1,053.9	1,060.8	1,073.0	1,077.6	1,064.7	1,065.9	1,070.9	1,084.0	1,103.1	1,118.5	1,073.2
2011	1,076.5	1,065.5	1,068.9	1,077.8	1,085.4	1,085.2	1,074.2	1,074.7	1,081.4	1,090.8	1,112.9	1,125.8	1,084.9
2012	1,083.6	1,072.3	1,080.9	1,083.8	1,093.5	1,093.0	1,082.4	1,083.4	1,089.1	1,098.8	1,125.1	1,133.8	1,093.3
2013	1,088.2	1,077.6	1,082.2	1,084.9	1,093.8	1,095.7	1,082.6	1,085.9	1,090.2	1,099.5	1,122.9	1,135.1	1,094.9
2014	1,091.0	1,077.7	1,085.2	1,092.0	1,103.6	1,108.3	1,093.6	1,097.3	1,103.7	1,115.4	1,138.5	1,153.3	1,105.0
2015	1,107.1	1,093.3	1,097.4	1,104.2	1,116.8	1,120.9	1,108.0	1,108.9	1,113.5	1,123.1	1,145.5	1,160.1	1,116.6
2016	1,114.1	1,102.6	1,106.9	1,112.1	1,120.9	1,119.1	1,111.5	1,111.2	1,117.2	1,125.9	1,148.8	1,163.8	1,121.2
2017	1,120.0	1,105.7	1,103.6	1,110.7	1,116.9	1,116.0	1,107.5	1,109.0	1,117.6	1,125.6	1,152.1	1,162.6	1,120.6
2018	1,121.2	1,110.3	1,112.5	1,117.1	1,126.3	1,126.8	1,117.2	1,116.5	1,122.5	1,133.8	1,155.5	1,162.2	1,126.8
Wholesale Trade													
2010	215.5	214.2	215.6	216.8	218.3	219.3	219.5	219.7	218.1	219.0	218.7	219.0	217.8
2011	216.9	216.7	217.7	219.0	219.8	220.3	220.2	219.8	218.5	218.8	218.6	218.7	218.8
2012	215.9	216.1	217.3	217.9	218.8	220.3	219.5	219.1	217.8	217.6	217.3	218.0	218.0
2013	215.0	215.1	216.3	216.7	217.7	218.7	218.2	218.0	217.4	216.7	216.8	217.4	217.0
2014	214.8	214.5	215.3	216.0	217.7	219.4	219.9	220.0	218.6	219.3	219.8	220.2	218.0
2015	217.4	217.1	217.5	218.0	219.2	219.6	219.8	219.2	217.0	216.9	216.3	216.0	217.8
2016	213.2	212.5	212.5	213.3	214.0	214.3	214.7	214.0	212.5	212.4	212.2	212.4	213.2
2017	210.6	210.5	210.6	211.5	212.8	214.5	215.2	215.1	214.2	214.5	214.9	215.6	213.3
2018	213.8	214.2	215.0	216.1	217.1	218.6	219.3	219.2	217.6	217.6	216.2	216.3	216.8
Retail Trade													
2010	616.3	600.2	607.4	611.7	620.0	623.8	621.6	622.1	614.6	625.1	642.9	653.2	621.6
2011	621.4	610.4	611.8	618.0	623.4	625.0	623.7	625.4	618.7	626.9	646.8	655.9	625.6
2012	625.6	613.4	619.0	621.1	628.3	630.8	629.4	630.8	623.8	632.2	656.8	660.8	631.0
2013	626.7	616.3	618.5	620.7	627.1	631.5	629.4	630.8	623.1	631.6	651.8	660.2	630.6
2014	626.2	614.1	618.7	623.3	630.6	635.3	631.7	633.5	626.1	634.1	653.5	662.4	632.5
2015	628.6	616.6	619.0	623.3	632.2	637.3	634.6	634.6	626.5	634.0	653.0	660.0	633.3
2016	628.8	619.5	622.4	626.5	632.6	635.2	635.6	635.4	625.7	632.1	649.5	656.5	633.3
2017	628.8	616.8	615.1	620.1	622.3	625.3	624.2	623.6	616.2	622.6	642.2	646.4	625.3
2018	619.6	610.2	611.5	613.7	619.2	621.9	620.7	618.1	610.1	615.0	632.8	633.9	618.9
Transportation and Utilities													
2010	230.4	229.4	230.9	232.3	234.7	234.5	223.6	224.1	238.2	239.9	241.5	246.3	233.8
2011	238.2	238.4	239.4	240.8	242.2	239.9	230.3	229.5	244.2	245.1	247.5	251.2	240.6
2012	242.1	242.8	244.6	244.8	246.4	241.9	233.5	233.5	247.5	249.0	251.0	255.0	244.3
2013	246.5	246.2	247.4	247.5	249.0	245.5	235.0	237.1	249.7	251.2	254.3	257.5	247.2
2014	250.0	249.1	251.2	252.7	255.3	253.6	242.0	243.8	259.0	262.0	265.2	270.7	254.6
2015	261.1	259.6	260.9	262.9	265.4	264.0	253.6	255.1	270.0	272.2	276.2	284.1	265.4
2016	272.1	270.6	272.0	272.3	274.3	269.6	261.2	261.8	279.0	281.4	287.1	294.9	274.7
2017	280.6	278.4	277.9	279.1	281.8	276.2	268.1	270.3	287.2	288.5	295.0	300.6	282.0
2018	287.8	285.9	286.0	287.3	290.0	286.3	277.2	279.2	294.8	301.2	306.5	312.0	291.2
Information													
2010	94.2	93.5	93.5	93.5	93.8	94.9	94.9	93.8	93.5	91.7	92.0	92.2	93.5
2011	90.8	90.8	90.9	91.6	92.2	92.7	92.4	87.8	91.4	91.9	92.8	90.8	91.3
2012	90.1	89.6	90.7	90.1	91.4	91.1	91.0	91.5	90.5	90.0	90.9	90.1	90.6
2013	89.0	88.6	88.5	88.1	88.2	88.2	88.3	87.9	86.8	87.9	87.2	87.3	88.0
2014	85.2	85.0	85.2	86.2	85.8	86.2	86.5	86.0	85.3	85.1	85.3	85.8	85.6
2015	83.8	84.1	84.6	84.6	85.2	86.1	86.1	86.5	85.4	85.1	84.9	85.4	85.2
2016	83.8	83.8	84.0	84.8	81.4	86.3	86.5	86.3	84.8	85.0	84.7	84.3	84.6
2017	83.3	83.8	83.1	83.8	84.7	86.0	85.3	85.7	84.0	84.3	84.6	84.8	84.5
2018	84.0	85.2	85.3	86.4	86.2	86.7	86.1	85.9	85.6	86.3	86.3	85.0	85.8

1. Employment by Industry: Pennsylvania, 2010–2018—*Continued*

(Numbers in thousands, not seasonally adjusted)

Industry and year	January	February	March	April	May	June	July	August	September	October	November	December	Annual average
Financial Activities													
2010	311.6	310.2	310.9	310.6	311.9	313.3	313.2	312.6	308.9	309.5	309.5	310.1	311.0
2011	308.2	307.1	307.2	307.5	308.4	310.6	311.1	311.2	308.3	308.1	308.2	308.9	308.7
2012	306.8	306.8	307.4	307.3	309.0	312.2	312.6	312.4	309.6	309.5	310.1	310.6	309.5
2013	308.9	309.5	310.0	311.2	312.5	315.9	316.6	317.0	313.7	314.0	314.6	315.1	313.3
2014	312.6	313.0	313.3	313.4	315.3	318.2	318.9	318.8	315.0	314.9	315.1	316.2	315.4
2015	312.8	313.5	313.6	314.0	316.1	319.3	320.2	320.1	316.2	316.2	316.4	316.8	316.3
2016	314.5	314.3	314.4	315.0	316.4	319.4	320.5	320.6	317.8	317.5	318.0	318.9	317.3
2017	316.6	317.7	318.4	318.3	320.3	324.0	325.1	324.8	322.0	321.6	321.9	322.6	321.1
2018	320.5	321.4	321.5	322.5	324.3	327.8	329.1	329.0	325.9	326.7	328.2	328.7	325.5
Professional and Business Services													
2010	664.1	665.6	672.0	689.6	691.7	697.5	698.7	701.4	699.1	708.0	711.8	711.7	692.6
2011	693.5	695.3	701.8	717.1	720.2	725.4	724.6	727.6	728.4	733.0	735.4	732.2	719.5
2012	712.5	715.3	724.3	734.8	737.8	742.7	740.5	742.0	741.4	747.5	749.1	745.5	736.1
2013	726.1	732.3	739.4	749.3	752.4	758.5	758.8	760.7	755.0	760.1	763.2	756.7	751.0
2014	737.5	739.8	746.0	761.4	766.8	770.2	768.9	772.5	769.8	777.3	784.1	780.7	764.6
2015	758.4	760.2	762.3	777.3	782.4	785.4	786.2	786.4	785.3	800.1	804.7	802.2	782.6
2016	776.1	776.6	782.0	797.8	797.9	798.0	801.0	799.0	803.9	809.9	811.0	806.4	796.6
2017	786.3	784.7	787.9	801.0	805.0	805.5	804.3	804.3	807.8	812.5	814.3	808.1	801.8
2018	787.5	789.2	791.9	805.9	809.2	810.3	809.4	809.0	809.2	817.4	811.9	803.5	804.5
Education and Health Services													
2010	1,108.0	1,128.9	1,132.2	1,136.1	1,129.8	1,108.7	1,106.3	1,102.5	1,127.1	1,151.6	1,154.2	1,149.7	1,127.9
2011	1,123.4	1,150.7	1,153.0	1,154.1	1,146.1	1,125.9	1,118.9	1,115.8	1,145.5	1,163.4	1,168.7	1,163.7	1,144.1
2012	1,138.3	1,167.4	1,173.0	1,172.2	1,160.2	1,134.2	1,126.1	1,121.0	1,157.0	1,175.7	1,179.2	1,172.3	1,156.4
2013	1,146.0	1,175.4	1,177.4	1,176.0	1,160.7	1,138.8	1,131.9	1,127.1	1,166.1	1,183.2	1,191.4	1,182.3	1,163.0
2014	1,159.8	1,182.1	1,187.4	1,195.9	1,181.7	1,157.1	1,151.6	1,146.8	1,186.4	1,205.4	1,211.1	1,201.7	1,180.6
2015	1,175.2	1,198.9	1,198.6	1,206.9	1,192.4	1,166.3	1,162.5	1,156.7	1,194.8	1,216.8	1,221.4	1,214.3	1,192.1
2016	1,194.1	1,221.3	1,224.0	1,233.8	1,219.9	1,187.5	1,188.8	1,185.5	1,229.8	1,245.5	1,250.6	1,242.6	1,218.6
2017	1,220.8	1,250.8	1,252.2	1,256.8	1,244.9	1,213.8	1,213.0	1,210.0	1,256.0	1,273.0	1,279.4	1,275.1	1,245.5
2018	1,247.9	1,280.5	1,280.9	1,287.3	1,273.3	1,243.4	1,239.2	1,241.6	1,281.8	1,307.1	1,306.6	1,307.4	1,274.8
Leisure and Hospitality													
2010	459.4	456.1	469.6	492.9	516.8	529.2	535.1	538.7	517.5	505.2	494.8	492.0	500.6
2011	471.4	471.2	484.4	506.7	529.9	544.4	544.8	546.4	524.5	511.6	501.4	498.3	511.3
2012	482.6	485.4	500.5	518.1	541.3	558.7	557.3	561.3	535.9	523.1	512.8	512.9	524.2
2013	492.7	493.6	507.3	523.5	549.8	565.9	568.3	567.8	544.1	531.7	518.8	522.6	532.2
2014	501.8	499.2	511.9	529.6	557.7	569.7	568.9	573.0	547.9	540.7	524.3	526.7	537.6
2015	506.2	506.3	515.5	535.9	564.3	577.9	578.0	581.4	558.9	549.4	535.9	534.4	545.3
2016	516.9	519.6	533.3	552.1	575.3	587.5	592.4	594.2	569.8	558.6	546.4	542.7	557.4
2017	527.9	530.2	539.4	560.8	582.7	600.2	600.9	603.3	576.2	568.6	555.4	554.6	566.7
2018	538.8	537.9	547.0	565.7	588.8	604.2	606.4	606.4	578.4	572.1	555.4	558.3	571.6
Other Services													
2010	246.2	245.0	247.9	249.0	251.4	254.3	254.9	254.6	251.0	251.6	251.5	251.2	250.7
2011	248.2	248.9	250.6	252.9	254.3	257.9	258.1	257.0	253.3	253.2	253.0	253.5	253.4
2012	250.7	251.3	253.7	254.3	255.8	259.4	258.6	257.2	253.4	252.8	251.7	251.7	254.2
2013	248.6	248.6	249.9	251.0	253.5	257.3	255.7	255.3	252.1	251.3	251.2	251.1	252.1
2014	248.8	248.6	251.6	251.2	254.1	257.6	257.6	257.0	252.9	252.9	252.6	252.9	253.2
2015	250.1	250.6	252.5	252.6	255.2	258.8	258.6	257.7	253.5	254.1	254.2	255.3	254.4
2016	253.2	254.1	256.6	258.0	259.8	263.0	263.8	263.0	259.3	260.6	259.5	258.1	259.1
2017	256.2	256.1	257.5	257.7	260.4	263.8	263.7	262.9	258.0	258.6	258.5	258.8	259.4
2018	256.0	256.4	257.8	260.1	261.6	265.5	266.0	264.6	260.4	258.5	259.1	259.3	260.4
Government													
2010	760.5	781.7	787.8	793.4	801.9	779.3	714.7	708.7	764.0	783.5	789.5	782.3	770.6
2011	762.2	779.3	781.0	781.3	770.6	752.1	688.7	683.8	740.3	755.8	762.8	758.4	751.4
2012	730.4	754.1	755.5	755.1	752.5	723.6	673.0	674.4	730.0	744.6	748.9	744.9	732.3
2013	722.3	741.5	741.4	742.4	743.6	710.2	661.1	665.3	717.7	731.4	738.1	733.6	720.7
2014	712.7	728.2	728.6	731.1	724.7	706.7	656.2	658.1	711.8	725.4	729.3	724.2	711.4
2015	700.2	719.7	720.3	725.3	718.7	698.7	653.2	656.6	707.5	717.0	722.5	716.7	704.7
2016	696.6	715.6	718.5	719.0	712.3	693.0	655.2	655.2	711.1	719.1	724.0	719.4	703.3
2017	696.6	716.7	718.2	719.5	717.2	692.6	655.4	656.8	710.4	717.1	721.8	716.6	703.2
2018	696.7	715.0	717.0	717.7	713.4	693.1	655.9	660.1	711.3	717.2	720.9	715.9	702.9

2. Average Weekly Hours by Selected Industry: Pennsylvania, 2014–2018

(Not seasonally adjusted)

Industry and year	January	February	March	April	May	June	July	August	September	October	November	December	Annual average
Total Private													
2014	33.1	33.1	33.8	33.7	33.8	34.0	33.9	33.8	33.8	33.8	34.2	33.8	33.7
2015	33.5	33.7	33.8	33.8	34.0	34.1	34.0	34.3	33.8	34.1	34.3	34.2	34.0
2016	33.7	33.6	33.6	33.7	33.9	33.8	33.8	33.8	33.8	34.1	33.8	33.8	33.8
2017	33.7	33.5	33.1	33.9	33.8	33.9	34.0	33.9	34.1	34.1	34.1	33.9	33.8
2018	33.4	33.8	33.7	34.3	34.1	34.2	34.5	34.4	34.6	34.3	34.1	34.7	34.2
Goods-Producing													
2014	39.0	38.0	39.6	39.6	39.7	40.1	39.7	39.5	39.8	39.9	40.0	39.3	39.5
2015	38.8	39.3	39.6	39.9	40.2	40.7	40.3	40.3	39.6	40.5	40.1	40.3	40.0
2016	39.6	39.0	39.5	39.7	39.9	40.1	39.8	40.2	40.0	40.3	40.3	40.0	39.9
2017	40.1	39.5	38.5	39.6	40.3	40.4	40.0	39.9	40.4	40.1	40.6	40.1	40.0
2018	39.8	40.0	40.0	40.7	40.6	40.7	40.4	40.4	40.0	40.3	39.5	40.9	40.3
Construction													
2014	37.8	37.7	38.8	39.4	39.7	40.2	39.7	38.5	39.6	39.3	39.8	38.0	39.1
2015	37.3	38.3	39.4	40.6	41.7	42.5	42.2	42.0	39.6	41.0	39.4	39.5	40.4
2016	38.5	37.5	39.4	39.5	40.0	40.2	40.2	39.9	40.1	40.7	40.0	38.7	39.6
2017	38.4	37.5	36.5	38.5	39.3	40.1	39.3	39.0	39.4	38.4	38.9	37.9	38.6
2018	37.4	38.0	38.0	39.3	39.9	40.0	40.4	39.7	38.2	39.3	37.3	38.3	38.9
Manufacturing													
2014	39.6	38.3	40.0	39.8	39.8	40.1	39.8	40.1	40.0	40.3	40.3	40.2	39.9
2015	39.7	39.9	39.9	39.8	39.7	40.0	39.6	39.7	39.7	40.0	40.2	40.4	39.9
2016	39.8	39.4	39.5	39.8	39.9	40.0	39.5	40.3	40.0	40.2	40.6	40.8	40.0
2017	41.0	40.7	39.6	40.3	40.9	40.7	40.3	40.4	41.0	40.9	41.3	41.1	40.7
2018	40.9	40.9	40.9	41.3	40.8	40.9	40.3	40.7	41.0	40.9	40.5	41.6	40.9
Trade, Transportation, and Utilities													
2014	33.3	32.8	33.8	33.8	34.0	34.0	34.2	34.1	34.3	34.0	34.3	34.3	33.9
2015	33.5	33.7	33.8	33.8	34.3	34.3	34.2	34.5	34.4	34.2	34.5	34.8	34.2
2016	33.9	34.0	33.9	33.9	34.1	34.1	34.1	34.2	34.5	34.4	34.1	34.7	34.2
2017	34.0	33.7	33.4	34.5	34.4	34.5	34.9	34.8	35.0	34.7	35.0	35.0	34.5
2018	33.9	34.0	34.2	34.5	34.7	34.5	35.0	34.9	35.2	34.7	35.0	35.2	34.7
Information													
2014	30.7	32.9	31.7	30.3	31.3	33.3	32.2	32.3	32.2	32.0	33.5	32.5	32.1
2015	32.4	34.4	34.0	33.5	33.5	33.1	33.5	34.0	33.0	33.6	33.5	32.6	33.4
2016	32.9	32.7	32.2	32.6	32.5	32.2	32.5	32.1	32.2	32.1	32.1	31.5	32.3
2017	30.9	31.7	31.3	32.0	30.7	30.6	31.5	30.9	30.6	30.9	30.6	30.7	31.0
2018	30.3	30.9	31.0	32.0	31.4	32.1	32.3	31.6	32.3	32.0	32.9	32.4	31.8
Financial Activities													
2014	36.2	36.8	36.9	36.8	36.8	37.1	36.6	36.6	36.8	36.9	37.4	36.8	36.8
2015	37.1	37.5	37.7	37.3	37.3	37.2	36.8	37.5	36.9	36.9	37.6	36.9	37.2
2016	37.0	37.0	37.0	37.2	37.4	36.9	37.3	37.3	37.2	37.5	37.5	37.3	37.2
2017	37.9	37.5	37.2	38.0	37.6	37.2	37.6	37.1	37.0	37.7	37.1	36.9	37.4
2018	37.0	37.0	36.9	37.6	36.9	37.0	37.1	36.8	37.3	36.7	36.6	37.3	37.0
Professional and Business Services													
2014	35.5	36.1	36.5	36.3	36.3	36.5	35.7	35.6	35.4	35.6	36.4	35.7	36.0
2015	34.9	35.5	35.7	35.5	35.8	35.8	35.8	36.4	35.2	35.9	36.5	36.0	35.8
2016	35.7	35.4	35.6	35.6	36.3	35.8	35.8	35.7	35.5	36.6	35.8	35.6	35.8
2017	35.4	35.3	34.8	36.0	35.6	35.5	36.0	35.6	35.8	36.1	35.5	35.4	35.6
2018	34.7	35.2	35.3	36.3	35.8	35.8	36.3	35.8	36.4	35.9	35.4	36.5	35.8
Education and Health Services													
2014	31.9	31.8	32.3	32.2	32.2	32.5	32.5	32.4	32.3	32.4	32.8	32.5	32.3
2015	32.7	32.5	32.6	32.5	32.6	32.5	32.7	32.7	32.6	32.6	33.0	32.9	32.7
2016	32.9	32.6	32.6	32.6	32.7	32.7	32.7	32.5	32.7	32.6	32.4	32.5	32.6
2017	32.5	32.2	32.1	32.4	32.5	32.5	32.4	32.4	32.6	32.5	32.4	32.4	32.4
2018	32.4	32.7	32.5	32.9	32.8	33.1	33.6	33.4	33.7	33.5	33.6	33.6	33.2
Leisure and Hospitality													
2014	24.0	24.4	24.9	25.0	25.3	25.3	25.5	25.4	24.8	25.0	24.9	24.6	24.9
2015	24.2	24.6	24.6	24.9	25.1	25.1	25.0	25.6	24.7	25.1	24.8	24.6	24.9
2016	23.3	24.3	24.2	24.3	24.6	24.6	24.7	24.7	24.4	24.6	24.3	23.9	24.3
2017	24.1	24.3	24.0	24.8	24.6	24.9	24.9	24.9	24.7	25.1	25.0	25.0	24.7
2018	23.9	25.0	24.8	25.4	25.3	25.3	25.4	25.4	25.3	25.3	24.3	25.0	25.0
Other Services													
2014	27.9	28.2	29.0	28.8	28.6	28.8	29.4	29.6	29.2	29.1	29.7	29.1	29.0
2015	29.4	29.3	29.4	29.1	29.2	29.1	29.9	30.3	30.0	30.0	30.1	29.6	29.6
2016	29.4	29.3	29.1	28.7	29.4	29.1	28.8	29.4	28.7	28.8	28.5	28.3	29.0
2017	28.6	28.4	28.1	29.4	28.5	28.7	29.6	29.0	29.0	28.8	29.0	28.9	28.8
2018	29.0	29.2	28.5	28.9	29.2	29.0	29.9	30.5	31.0	29.8	29.7	30.3	29.6

3. Average Hourly Earnings by Selected Industry: Pennsylvania, 2014–2018

(Dollars, not seasonally adjusted)

Industry and year	January	February	March	April	May	June	July	August	September	October	November	December	Annual average
Total Private													
2014	23.80	24.11	23.88	23.76	23.58	23.73	23.55	23.55	23.68	23.59	23.81	23.76	23.73
2015	23.95	24.10	24.23	24.11	24.05	24.08	24.13	24.27	24.36	24.35	24.59	24.42	24.22
2016	24.68	24.58	24.49	24.51	24.51	24.41	24.61	24.54	24.78	25.04	24.95	25.02	24.68
2017	25.20	25.03	25.07	25.21	24.86	24.86	24.98	24.90	25.16	25.35	25.15	25.45	25.10
2018	25.57	25.54	25.53	25.70	25.58	25.52	25.71	25.48	25.96	25.88	26.05	26.38	25.74
Goods-Producing													
2014	25.23	25.70	25.40	25.40	25.04	25.17	25.12	25.21	25.20	25.13	25.31	25.33	25.27
2015	25.26	25.21	25.41	25.38	25.67	25.72	25.89	25.99	25.92	25.95	25.86	25.56	25.66
2016	25.60	25.60	25.61	25.64	25.79	26.07	26.57	26.39	26.52	26.71	26.47	26.67	26.14
2017	26.70	26.61	26.78	27.09	26.70	26.93	26.92	26.95	27.08	27.00	26.78	27.22	26.90
2018	26.96	27.05	26.92	27.18	27.09	26.99	27.38	27.20	27.48	27.45	27.45	27.55	27.23
Construction													
2014	27.81	28.48	28.10	27.86	27.24	27.54	27.84	28.28	28.14	27.99	28.30	28.87	28.03
2015	28.83	29.09	29.14	28.76	29.32	28.91	29.20	29.31	29.33	29.52	29.52	29.72	29.23
2016	29.73	30.11	29.80	29.56	29.79	29.99	30.68	30.27	29.88	30.20	29.48	30.03	29.97
2017	29.99	30.18	30.44	30.01	30.04	30.72	30.01	29.89	30.07	29.89	29.60	30.15	30.08
2018	29.93	30.35	30.14	30.40	30.30	30.27	30.43	30.44	30.68	30.86	30.76	31.09	30.48
Manufacturing													
2014	24.15	24.57	24.29	24.31	24.01	24.05	23.81	23.83	23.88	23.88	23.98	23.92	24.05
2015	23.92	23.76	23.91	23.89	23.96	24.03	24.12	24.19	24.23	24.13	24.12	24.03	24.02
2016	24.21	24.09	24.03	24.08	24.14	24.38	24.65	24.47	24.86	24.98	25.02	25.17	24.51
2017	25.27	25.14	25.25	25.72	25.25	25.24	25.57	25.63	25.76	25.76	25.60	26.01	25.52
2018	25.83	25.76	25.62	25.71	25.55	25.34	25.84	25.59	26.00	25.80	25.93	25.90	25.74
Trade, Transportation, and Utilities													
2014	20.54	20.78	20.36	20.33	20.14	20.47	20.40	20.45	20.47	20.38	20.47	20.36	20.43
2015	20.88	20.78	21.36	21.41	21.21	21.09	21.04	21.13	21.11	21.05	21.04	20.75	21.07
2016	21.43	21.43	21.07	21.08	20.99	20.97	21.09	20.94	21.09	21.33	21.20	20.81	21.12
2017	21.31	21.25	21.35	21.49	21.09	21.40	21.35	21.21	21.45	21.62	21.41	21.74	21.39
2018	22.08	22.00	22.23	22.63	22.86	22.67	22.84	22.70	23.09	22.88	22.72	23.01	22.65
Information													
2014	27.33	27.71	28.60	28.28	27.81	28.58	28.06	27.40	28.35	28.21	29.29	28.95	28.22
2015	28.60	29.72	29.85	29.47	29.65	29.69	29.58	29.47	29.29	29.81	30.21	29.89	29.61
2016	29.75	29.68	29.59	30.36	30.12	30.54	30.53	30.46	30.74	31.10	31.21	31.99	30.50
2017	31.70	31.27	31.10	32.27	31.66	30.80	31.20	31.56	32.15	32.14	32.48	32.77	31.76
2018	33.13	34.22	33.76	33.86	33.22	32.48	32.66	31.94	32.47	32.51	31.80	31.87	32.81
Financial Activities													
2014	31.17	31.27	31.14	30.96	30.79	30.93	30.79	30.73	30.99	30.90	31.50	31.33	31.04
2015	31.38	31.86	31.62	31.74	31.50	31.44	31.35	32.25	31.99	32.06	32.79	33.51	31.96
2016	33.04	33.13	33.53	33.42	34.03	33.43	33.68	34.40	34.84	35.31	34.91	35.19	34.08
2017	34.95	34.54	34.42	34.16	33.36	33.00	33.43	33.03	33.25	33.86	33.41	34.23	33.80
2018	34.22	34.20	34.51	34.90	35.11	34.62	35.23	35.42	36.19	35.84	36.25	37.88	35.37
Professional and Business Services													
2014	29.79	30.64	30.66	30.18	30.13	30.44	29.99	30.06	29.99	29.45	29.96	30.26	30.13
2015	30.72	31.16	31.11	30.50	30.53	30.81	30.92	31.13	31.31	31.25	31.92	31.49	31.08
2016	32.11	31.98	31.91	31.84	31.88	31.73	31.79	31.76	31.94	32.30	32.17	32.65	32.01
2017	33.00	32.45	32.56	32.47	31.91	31.79	32.14	31.93	32.25	32.46	32.18	32.54	32.30
2018	32.49	32.62	32.37	32.51	31.83	31.89	32.32	31.83	32.48	32.19	32.74	33.58	32.40
Education and Health Services													
2014	22.58	22.46	22.25	22.37	22.46	22.38	22.44	22.35	22.50	22.54	22.51	22.41	22.44
2015	22.40	22.58	22.48	22.48	22.46	22.57	22.73	22.81	23.15	22.84	23.10	23.10	22.73
2016	23.03	22.90	22.77	22.93	22.83	22.69	22.88	22.74	22.98	23.02	23.10	23.14	22.92
2017	23.11	23.13	23.00	23.28	23.16	23.19	23.45	23.39	23.61	23.78	23.72	23.84	23.39
2018	23.87	23.72	23.62	23.50	23.42	23.74	23.60	23.35	23.84	23.88	24.16	24.13	23.74
Leisure and Hospitality													
2014	14.64	14.71	14.59	14.47	14.34	14.19	14.03	13.98	14.16	14.19	14.16	14.07	14.28
2015	13.92	13.92	13.82	13.91	13.75	13.66	13.47	13.44	13.71	13.79	13.87	13.91	13.76
2016	13.81	13.82	13.84	13.83	13.85	13.72	13.71	13.81	14.08	14.24	14.34	14.60	13.97
2017	14.51	14.62	14.69	14.74	14.92	14.56	14.41	14.51	14.87	15.07	15.08	15.21	14.76
2018	15.45	15.30	15.42	15.22	15.40	15.02	14.95	14.88	15.13	15.13	15.35	15.41	15.21
Other Services													
2014	20.88	21.07	21.06	20.53	20.26	20.26	19.74	19.73	20.26	20.53	20.56	20.67	20.45
2015	20.82	20.73	21.19	21.00	20.80	20.56	20.34	20.28	20.65	20.83	20.74	21.11	20.75
2016	21.00	20.93	20.87	20.58	20.40	19.81	19.82	19.56	20.19	20.17	20.40	20.79	20.37
2017	20.73	20.46	20.88	21.00	21.05	20.81	20.45	20.95	21.06	21.54	21.41	21.81	21.01
2018	22.18	22.25	22.26	22.79	22.85	22.76	22.81	22.71	22.94	23.77	23.84	24.02	22.94

4. Average Weekly Earnings by Selected Industry: Pennsylvania, 2014–2018

(Dollars, not seasonally adjusted)

Industry and year	January	February	March	April	May	June	July	August	September	October	November	December	Annual average
Total Private													
2014	787.78	798.04	807.14	800.71	797.00	806.82	798.35	795.99	800.38	797.34	814.30	803.09	799.70
2015	802.33	812.17	818.97	814.92	817.70	821.13	820.42	832.46	823.37	830.34	843.44	835.16	823.48
2016	831.72	825.89	822.86	825.99	830.89	825.06	831.82	829.45	837.56	853.86	843.31	845.68	834.18
2017	849.24	838.51	829.82	854.62	840.27	842.75	849.32	844.11	857.96	864.44	857.62	862.76	848.38
2018	854.04	863.25	860.36	881.51	872.28	872.78	887.00	876.51	898.22	887.68	888.31	915.39	880.31
Goods-Producing													
2014	983.97	976.60	1,005.84	1,005.84	994.09	1,009.32	997.26	995.80	1,002.96	1,002.69	1,012.40	995.47	998.17
2015	980.09	990.75	1,006.24	1,012.66	1,031.93	1,046.80	1,043.37	1,047.40	1,026.43	1,050.98	1,036.99	1,030.07	1,026.40
2016	1,013.76	998.40	1,011.60	1,017.91	1,029.02	1,045.41	1,057.49	1,060.88	1,060.80	1,076.41	1,066.74	1,066.80	1,042.99
2017	1,070.67	1,051.10	1,031.03	1,072.76	1,076.01	1,087.97	1,076.80	1,075.31	1,094.03	1,082.70	1,087.27	1,091.52	1,076.00
2018	1,073.01	1,082.00	1,076.80	1,106.23	1,099.85	1,098.49	1,106.15	1,098.88	1,099.20	1,106.24	1,084.28	1,126.80	1,097.37
Construction													
2014	1,051.22	1,073.70	1,090.28	1,097.68	1,081.43	1,107.11	1,105.25	1,088.78	1,114.34	1,100.01	1,126.34	1,097.06	1,095.97
2015	1,075.36	1,114.15	1,148.12	1,167.66	1,222.64	1,228.68	1,232.24	1,231.02	1,161.47	1,210.32	1,163.09	1,173.94	1,180.89
2016	1,144.61	1,129.13	1,174.12	1,167.62	1,191.60	1,205.60	1,233.34	1,207.77	1,198.19	1,229.14	1,179.20	1,162.16	1,186.81
2017	1,151.62	1,131.75	1,111.06	1,155.39	1,180.57	1,231.87	1,179.39	1,165.71	1,184.76	1,147.78	1,151.44	1,142.69	1,161.09
2018	1,119.38	1,153.30	1,145.32	1,194.72	1,208.97	1,210.80	1,229.37	1,208.47	1,171.98	1,212.80	1,147.35	1,190.75	1,185.67
Manufacturing													
2014	956.34	941.03	971.60	967.54	955.60	964.41	947.64	955.58	955.20	962.36	966.39	961.58	959.60
2015	949.62	948.02	954.01	950.82	951.21	961.20	955.15	960.34	961.93	965.20	969.62	970.81	958.40
2016	963.56	949.15	949.19	958.38	963.19	975.20	973.68	986.14	994.40	1,004.20	1,015.81	1,026.94	980.40
2017	1,036.07	1,023.20	999.90	1,036.52	1,032.73	1,027.27	1,030.47	1,035.45	1,056.16	1,053.58	1,057.28	1,069.01	1,038.66
2018	1,056.45	1,053.58	1,047.86	1,061.82	1,042.44	1,036.41	1,041.35	1,041.51	1,066.00	1,055.22	1,050.17	1,077.44	1,052.77
Trade, Transportation, and Utilities													
2014	683.98	681.58	688.17	687.15	684.76	695.98	697.68	697.35	702.12	692.92	702.12	698.35	692.58
2015	699.48	700.29	721.97	723.66	727.50	723.39	719.57	728.99	726.18	719.91	725.88	722.10	720.59
2016	726.48	728.62	714.27	714.61	715.76	715.08	719.17	716.15	727.61	733.75	722.92	722.11	722.30
2017	724.54	716.13	713.09	741.41	725.50	738.30	745.12	738.11	750.75	750.21	749.35	760.90	737.96
2018	748.51	748.00	760.27	780.74	793.24	782.12	799.40	792.23	812.77	793.94	795.20	809.95	785.96
Information													
2014	839.03	911.66	906.62	856.88	870.45	951.71	903.53	885.02	912.87	902.72	981.22	940.88	905.86
2015	926.64	1,022.37	1,014.90	987.25	993.28	982.74	990.93	1,001.98	966.57	1,001.62	1,012.04	974.41	988.97
2016	978.78	970.54	952.80	989.74	978.90	983.39	992.23	977.77	989.83	998.31	1,001.84	1,007.69	985.15
2017	979.53	991.26	973.43	1,032.64	971.96	942.48	982.80	975.20	983.79	993.13	993.89	1,006.04	984.56
2018	1,003.84	1,057.40	1,046.56	1,083.52	1,043.11	1,042.61	1,054.92	1,009.30	1,048.78	1,040.32	1,046.22	1,032.59	1,043.36
Financial Activities													
2014	1,128.35	1,150.74	1,149.07	1,139.33	1,133.07	1,147.50	1,126.91	1,124.72	1,140.43	1,140.21	1,178.10	1,152.94	1,142.27
2015	1,164.20	1,194.75	1,192.07	1,183.90	1,174.95	1,169.57	1,153.68	1,209.38	1,180.43	1,183.01	1,232.90	1,236.52	1,188.91
2016	1,222.48	1,225.81	1,240.61	1,243.22	1,272.72	1,233.57	1,256.26	1,283.12	1,296.05	1,324.13	1,309.13	1,312.59	1,267.78
2017	1,324.61	1,295.25	1,280.42	1,298.08	1,254.34	1,227.60	1,256.97	1,225.41	1,230.25	1,276.52	1,239.51	1,263.09	1,264.12
2018	1,266.14	1,265.40	1,273.42	1,312.24	1,295.56	1,280.94	1,307.03	1,303.46	1,349.89	1,315.33	1,326.75	1,412.92	1,308.69
Professional and Business Services													
2014	1,057.55	1,106.10	1,119.09	1,095.53	1,093.72	1,111.06	1,070.64	1,070.14	1,061.65	1,048.42	1,090.54	1,080.28	1,084.68
2015	1,072.13	1,106.18	1,110.63	1,082.75	1,092.97	1,103.00	1,106.94	1,133.13	1,102.11	1,121.88	1,165.08	1,133.64	1,112.66
2016	1,146.33	1,132.09	1,136.00	1,133.50	1,157.24	1,135.93	1,138.08	1,133.83	1,133.87	1,182.18	1,151.69	1,162.34	1,145.96
2017	1,168.20	1,145.49	1,133.09	1,168.92	1,136.00	1,128.55	1,157.04	1,136.71	1,154.55	1,171.81	1,142.39	1,151.92	1,149.88
2018	1,127.40	1,148.22	1,142.66	1,180.11	1,139.51	1,141.66	1,173.22	1,139.51	1,182.27	1,155.62	1,159.00	1,225.67	1,159.92
Education and Health Services													
2014	720.30	714.23	718.68	720.31	723.21	727.35	729.30	724.14	726.75	730.30	738.33	728.33	724.81
2015	732.48	733.85	732.85	730.60	732.20	733.53	743.27	745.89	754.69	744.58	762.30	759.99	743.27
2016	757.69	746.54	742.30	747.52	746.54	741.96	748.18	739.05	751.45	750.45	748.44	752.05	747.19
2017	751.08	744.79	738.30	754.27	752.70	753.68	759.78	757.84	769.69	772.85	768.53	772.42	757.84
2018	773.39	775.64	767.65	773.15	768.18	785.79	792.96	779.89	803.41	799.98	811.78	810.77	788.17
Leisure and Hospitality													
2014	351.36	358.92	363.29	361.75	362.80	359.01	357.77	355.09	351.17	354.75	352.58	346.12	355.57
2015	336.86	342.43	339.97	346.36	345.13	342.87	336.75	344.06	338.64	346.13	343.98	342.19	342.62
2016	321.77	335.83	334.93	336.07	340.71	337.51	338.64	341.11	343.55	350.30	348.46	348.94	339.47
2017	349.69	355.27	352.56	365.55	367.03	362.54	358.81	361.30	367.29	378.26	377.00	380.25	364.57
2018	369.26	382.50	382.42	386.59	389.62	380.01	379.73	377.95	382.79	382.79	373.01	385.25	380.25
Other Services													
2014	582.55	594.17	610.74	591.26	579.44	583.49	580.36	584.01	591.59	597.42	610.63	601.50	593.05
2015	612.11	607.39	622.99	611.10	607.36	598.30	608.17	614.48	619.50	624.90	624.27	624.86	614.20
2016	617.40	613.25	607.32	590.65	599.76	576.47	570.82	575.06	579.45	580.90	581.40	588.36	590.73
2017	592.88	581.06	586.73	617.40	599.93	597.25	605.32	607.55	610.74	620.35	620.89	630.31	605.09
2018	643.22	649.70	634.41	658.63	667.22	660.04	682.02	692.66	711.14	708.35	708.05	727.81	679.02

RHODE ISLAND
At a Glance

Population:
  2010 census: 1,052,567
  2018 estimate: 1,057,315

Percent change in population:
  2010–2018: 0.5%

Percent change in total nonfarm employment:
  2010–2018: 8.3%

Industry with the largest growth in employment, 2010–2018 (percent):
  Professional and business services, 28.0%

Industry with the largest decline or smallest growth in employment, 2010–2018 (percent):
  Information, -30.6%

Civilian labor force:
  2010: 566,704
  2018: 555,807

Unemployment rate and rank among states (highest to lowest):
  2010: 11.2%, 4th
  2018: 4.1%, 16th

Over-the-year change in unemployment rates:
  2016–2017: -0.8%
  2017–2018: -0.3%

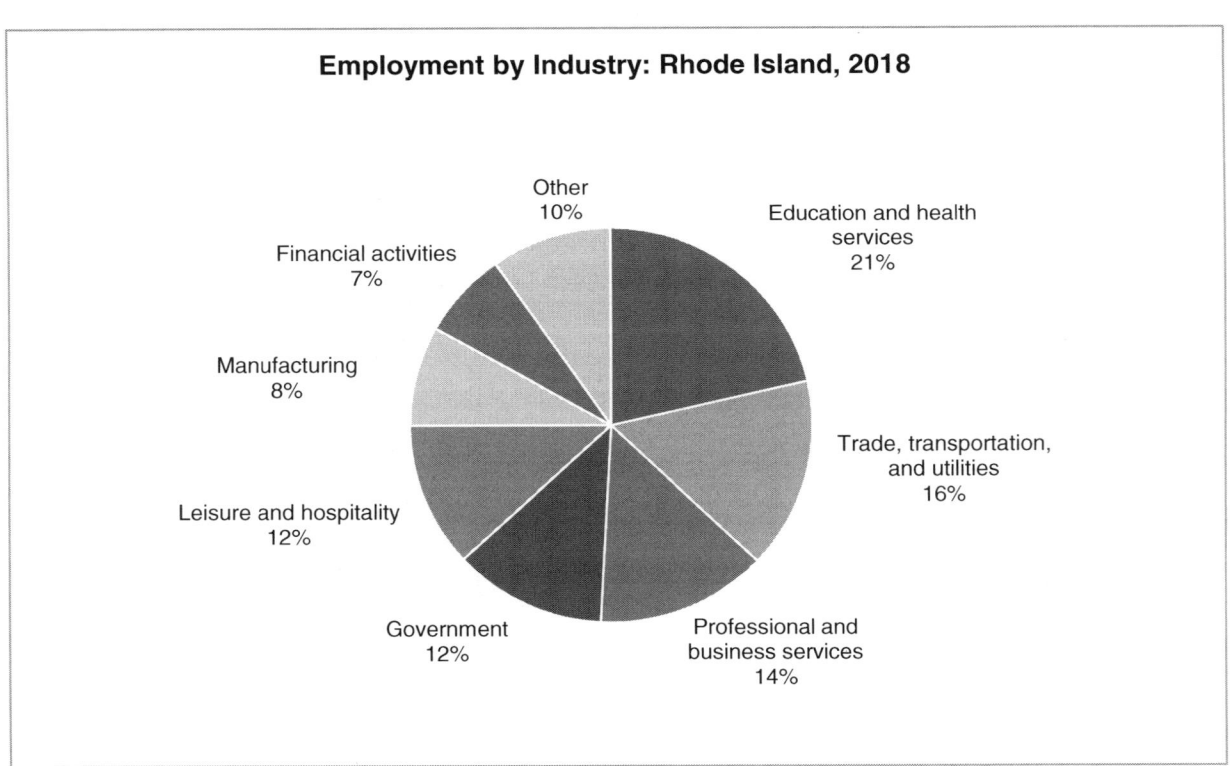

Employment by Industry: Rhode Island, 2018

- Other 10%
- Education and health services 21%
- Financial activities 7%
- Trade, transportation, and utilities 16%
- Manufacturing 8%
- Professional and business services 14%
- Leisure and hospitality 12%
- Government 12%

1. Employment by Industry: Rhode Island, 2010–2018

(Numbers in thousands, not seasonally adjusted)

Industry and year	January	February	March	April	May	June	July	August	September	October	November	December	Annual average
Total Nonfarm													
2010	443.6	445.7	449.0	455.9	463.4	463.6	459.3	460.1	464.0	463.9	464.6	462.3	458.0
2011	444.5	447.9	451.0	460.1	465.8	467.8	461.7	461.0	466.0	467.4	467.3	465.3	460.5
2012	449.1	454.0	457.1	463.2	470.3	472.2	464.3	466.5	472.8	472.1	471.2	472.1	465.4
2013	455.1	457.4	461.3	467.8	475.1	479.0	472.6	473.4	478.3	480.6	479.2	477.1	471.4
2014	460.9	464.3	466.4	476.5	484.1	485.4	480.2	480.2	486.0	486.9	486.8	486.7	478.7
2015	469.8	468.4	472.4	483.2	491.5	492.3	488.0	486.2	491.5	493.7	493.9	493.1	485.3
2016	475.0	478.0	481.8	488.9	493.8	496.4	492.1	490.9	494.4	496.2	495.5	493.5	489.7
2017	477.4	481.2	482.9	491.5	497.9	501.3	495.9	496.4	498.0	499.2	499.7	498.8	493.4
2018	478.9	485.1	486.9	494.2	501.7	504.4	499.0	498.2	501.3	503.0	500.7	499.3	496.1
Total Private													
2010	381.3	383.4	386.3	393.2	398.6	400.5	400.8	401.9	403.5	402.3	402.5	400.5	396.2
2011	383.1	386.5	389.1	398.3	403.8	406.2	405.0	404.3	406.2	406.4	406.0	404.0	399.9
2012	388.5	393.1	396.1	402.1	408.4	411.6	408.1	409.9	413.2	411.4	410.1	410.9	405.3
2013	394.5	396.9	400.3	407.0	413.4	418.1	415.5	416.6	418.5	419.5	418.1	415.7	411.2
2014	400.2	403.7	405.5	415.4	422.1	424.2	423.0	423.5	425.7	425.8	425.3	425.5	418.3
2015	408.9	407.5	411.5	422.2	429.8	431.5	431.1	429.9	432.0	432.9	432.9	431.9	425.2
2016	414.3	417.1	420.6	428.0	432.4	435.6	434.6	433.9	434.4	435.0	434.1	432.1	429.3
2017	416.6	420.1	421.7	430.4	436.1	439.7	438.1	439.0	437.6	437.5	438.2	436.9	432.7
2018	417.7	423.8	425.5	432.8	439.0	442.5	441.3	441.1	440.6	441.1	438.7	437.0	435.1
Goods Producing													
2010	54.2	53.8	54.0	55.5	56.8	57.7	57.1	58.2	58.0	57.9	57.8	56.9	56.5
2011	54.0	53.4	53.9	55.6	56.5	57.4	56.9	57.4	57.0	56.9	56.8	56.2	56.0
2012	53.5	53.2	54.0	55.3	55.9	57.1	56.2	57.2	56.9	57.1	56.9	56.6	55.8
2013	53.9	53.2	54.2	55.5	56.6	57.4	56.5	57.8	57.8	57.8	57.9	57.2	56.3
2014	54.8	54.5	54.8	56.9	58.3	59.0	58.5	59.0	58.8	58.9	58.8	58.4	57.6
2015	56.1	55.0	55.5	57.5	58.7	59.4	59.3	59.7	59.5	59.7	59.9	59.5	58.3
2016	56.7	56.2	56.9	58.3	59.2	59.9	59.6	60.0	59.5	59.8	59.5	59.0	58.7
2017	56.7	56.5	56.7	58.5	59.3	60.2	59.7	60.3	59.9	60.0	60.1	59.9	59.0
2018	57.1	58.0	58.5	59.5	60.4	61.0	60.2	60.8	60.7	60.5	59.9	59.8	59.7
Service-Providing													
2010	389.4	391.9	395.0	400.4	406.6	405.9	402.2	401.9	406.0	406.0	406.8	405.4	401.5
2011	390.5	394.5	397.1	404.5	409.3	410.4	404.8	403.6	409.0	410.5	410.5	409.1	404.5
2012	395.6	400.8	403.1	407.9	414.4	415.1	408.1	409.3	415.9	415.0	414.3	415.5	409.6
2013	401.2	404.2	407.1	412.3	418.5	421.6	416.1	415.6	420.5	422.8	421.3	419.9	415.1
2014	406.1	409.8	411.6	419.6	425.8	426.4	421.7	421.2	427.2	428.0	428.0	428.3	421.1
2015	413.7	413.4	416.9	425.7	432.8	432.9	428.7	426.5	432.0	434.0	434.0	433.6	427.0
2016	418.3	421.8	424.9	430.6	434.6	436.5	432.5	430.9	434.9	436.4	436.0	434.5	431.0
2017	420.7	424.7	426.2	433.0	438.6	441.1	436.2	436.1	438.1	439.2	439.6	438.9	434.4
2018	421.8	427.1	428.4	434.7	441.3	443.4	438.8	437.4	440.6	442.5	440.8	439.5	436.4
Mining and Logging													
2010	0.1	0.1	0.1	0.2	0.2	0.2	0.2	0.2	0.2	0.2	0.2	0.2	0.2
2011	0.1	0.1	0.1	0.2	0.2	0.2	0.2	0.2	0.2	0.2	0.2	0.2	0.2
2012	0.1	0.1	0.2	0.2	0.2	0.2	0.2	0.2	0.2	0.2	0.2	0.2	0.2
2013	0.2	0.1	0.2	0.2	0.2	0.2	0.2	0.2	0.2	0.2	0.2	0.2	0.2
2014	0.1	0.1	0.2	0.2	0.2	0.2	0.3	0.2	0.2	0.2	0.2	0.2	0.2
2015	0.2	0.2	0.2	0.2	0.2	0.2	0.2	0.2	0.2	0.2	0.2	0.2	0.2
2016	0.2	0.2	0.2	0.2	0.2	0.2	0.2	0.2	0.2	0.2	0.2	0.2	0.2
2017	0.2	0.2	0.2	0.2	0.2	0.2	0.2	0.2	0.2	0.2	0.2	0.2	0.2
2018	0.1	0.1	0.2	0.2	0.2	0.2	0.2	0.2	0.2	0.2	0.2	0.2	0.2
Construction													
2010	13.9	13.5	13.9	15.5	16.4	16.9	17.3	17.5	17.0	16.9	16.7	15.8	15.9
2011	13.6	13.0	13.4	15.0	15.9	16.6	17.2	17.1	16.8	16.8	16.8	16.2	15.7
2012	14.3	13.8	14.5	15.7	16.1	16.9	17.2	17.1	16.8	16.8	16.7	16.3	16.0
2013	14.1	13.7	14.3	15.5	16.5	16.9	17.3	17.4	17.3	17.2	17.0	16.2	16.1
2014	14.4	14.0	14.3	16.0	17.1	17.5	17.8	17.7	17.5	17.5	17.3	16.8	16.5
2015	14.8	14.0	14.4	16.2	17.3	17.8	18.3	18.3	18.2	18.3	18.3	17.9	17.0
2016	16.0	15.5	16.1	17.6	18.5	18.9	19.3	19.4	19.2	19.3	18.9	18.2	18.1
2017	16.4	16.2	16.3	17.9	18.7	19.3	19.5	19.6	19.3	19.3	19.2	18.7	18.4
2018	16.5	17.2	17.4	18.7	19.6	20.1	20.3	20.3	20.3	20.4	19.9	19.7	19.2

1. Employment by Industry: Rhode Island, 2010–2018—*Continued*

(Numbers in thousands, not seasonally adjusted)

Industry and year	January	February	March	April	May	June	July	August	September	October	November	December	Annual average
Manufacturing													
2010	40.2	40.2	40.0	39.8	40.2	40.6	39.6	40.5	40.8	40.8	40.9	40.9	40.4
2011	40.3	40.3	40.4	40.4	40.4	40.6	39.5	40.1	40.0	39.9	39.8	39.8	40.1
2012	39.1	39.3	39.3	39.4	39.6	40.0	38.8	39.9	39.9	40.1	40.0	40.1	39.6
2013	39.6	39.4	39.7	39.8	39.9	40.3	39.0	40.2	40.3	40.4	40.7	40.8	40.0
2014	40.3	40.4	40.3	40.7	41.0	41.3	40.4	41.1	41.1	41.2	41.3	41.4	40.9
2015	41.1	40.8	40.9	41.1	41.2	41.4	40.8	41.2	41.1	41.2	41.4	41.4	41.1
2016	40.5	40.5	40.6	40.5	40.5	40.8	40.1	40.4	40.1	40.3	40.4	40.6	40.4
2017	40.1	40.1	40.2	40.4	40.4	40.7	40.0	40.5	40.4	40.5	40.7	41.0	40.4
2018	40.5	40.7	40.9	40.6	40.6	40.7	39.7	40.3	40.2	39.9	39.8	39.9	40.3
Trade, Transportation, and Utilities													
2010	71.9	71.5	71.8	71.4	71.7	72.8	72.3	72.3	72.9	73.4	74.5	75.1	72.6
2011	72.1	71.7	71.9	72.7	73.7	74.3	73.5	73.6	74.4	74.9	76.1	77.1	73.8
2012	73.8	73.0	73.2	73.6	74.6	75.5	74.1	74.1	74.9	75.2	76.4	76.8	74.6
2013	72.6	72.2	72.0	72.6	73.7	74.6	73.9	74.0	74.4	75.1	76.2	77.1	74.0
2014	73.5	73.1	73.0	73.8	74.7	75.6	74.6	75.1	75.5	76.1	77.4	78.8	75.1
2015	75.0	74.1	74.1	75.2	76.1	77.1	76.2	76.2	76.9	77.0	78.5	79.6	76.3
2016	75.6	75.0	75.0	75.4	76.2	76.8	75.9	76.0	76.5	76.8	78.3	79.0	76.4
2017	75.5	75.0	74.7	75.8	76.7	77.3	76.4	76.3	77.0	77.6	79.1	80.0	76.8
2018	76.2	76.0	75.7	76.1	77.2	77.9	77.1	77.0	77.3	77.9	79.6	80.4	77.4
Wholesale Trade													
2010	15.5	15.6	15.6	15.6	15.8	15.9	15.9	15.9	15.9	15.9	16.0	16.0	15.8
2011	15.7	15.8	15.9	16.0	16.3	16.4	16.5	16.5	16.6	16.7	16.7	16.9	16.3
2012	16.7	16.7	16.8	16.8	17.0	17.0	17.0	16.9	16.9	16.9	16.9	16.8	16.9
2013	16.4	16.4	16.5	16.4	16.6	16.7	16.7	16.8	16.7	16.8	16.8	16.8	16.6
2014	16.6	16.7	16.7	16.6	16.8	16.8	16.8	17.0	16.9	17.0	17.0	17.1	16.8
2015	16.8	16.8	16.8	16.9	17.0	17.0	17.0	17.0	16.9	16.7	16.9	16.9	16.9
2016	16.5	16.5	16.4	16.7	16.7	16.7	16.6	16.6	16.6	16.5	16.6	16.6	16.6
2017	16.4	16.4	16.4	16.4	16.5	16.5	16.5	16.4	16.3	16.5	16.6	16.6	16.5
2018	16.4	16.5	16.5	16.5	16.5	16.6	16.5	16.5	16.4	16.5	16.6	16.4	16.5
Retail Trade													
2010	46.5	46.0	46.3	45.6	45.6	46.3	46.5	46.6	46.2	46.7	47.7	48.0	46.5
2011	46.0	45.5	45.6	46.1	46.6	46.9	46.8	47.1	46.7	47.2	48.4	48.8	46.8
2012	46.4	45.7	45.8	46.1	46.7	47.3	46.9	46.9	46.8	47.2	48.3	48.5	46.9
2013	45.8	45.3	45.0	45.5	46.2	46.8	46.9	46.8	46.5	47.1	48.1	48.6	46.6
2014	46.2	45.8	45.6	46.4	47.0	47.5	47.4	47.5	47.2	47.7	48.8	49.6	47.2
2015	47.0	46.4	46.4	47.1	47.6	48.5	48.4	48.4	48.2	48.5	49.7	50.3	48.0
2016	47.8	47.3	47.4	47.4	47.9	48.3	48.4	48.5	48.1	48.5	49.7	49.9	48.3
2017	47.7	47.2	47.0	48.0	48.6	48.9	48.8	48.9	48.6	48.8	50.1	50.3	48.6
2018	47.8	47.7	47.2	47.7	48.5	48.9	49.0	49.1	48.5	49.2	50.4	50.6	48.7
Transportation and Utilities													
2010	9.9	9.9	9.9	10.2	10.3	10.6	9.9	9.8	10.8	10.8	10.8	11.1	10.3
2011	10.4	10.4	10.4	10.6	10.8	11.0	10.2	10.0	11.1	11.0	11.0	11.4	10.7
2012	10.7	10.6	10.6	10.7	10.9	11.2	10.2	10.3	11.2	11.1	11.2	11.5	10.9
2013	10.4	10.5	10.5	10.7	10.9	11.1	10.3	10.4	11.2	11.2	11.3	11.7	10.9
2014	10.7	10.6	10.7	10.8	10.9	11.3	10.4	10.6	11.4	11.4	11.6	12.1	11.0
2015	11.2	10.9	10.9	11.2	11.5	11.6	10.8	10.8	11.8	11.8	11.9	12.4	11.4
2016	11.3	11.2	11.2	11.3	11.6	11.8	10.9	10.9	11.8	11.8	12.0	12.5	11.5
2017	11.4	11.4	11.3	11.4	11.6	11.9	11.1	11.0	12.1	12.3	12.4	13.1	11.8
2018	12.0	11.8	12.0	11.9	12.2	12.4	11.6	11.4	12.4	12.2	12.6	13.4	12.2
Information													
2010	8.4	8.4	8.6	8.4	8.3	8.3	8.4	8.7	8.8	8.6	8.7	8.6	8.5
2011	8.2	8.2	8.3	8.8	8.9	8.8	8.6	7.8	8.4	8.2	8.3	8.5	8.4
2012	8.1	8.2	8.2	8.0	7.8	8.0	7.7	7.8	7.6	7.6	7.5	7.6	7.8
2013	7.5	7.6	7.4	7.2	7.4	7.4	7.2	7.3	7.1	7.1	7.2	7.2	7.3
2014	7.3	7.1	7.0	7.1	7.2	7.1	7.1	7.3	7.1	7.0	7.0	7.1	7.1
2015	6.8	6.7	6.8	6.9	6.9	6.7	6.8	6.7	6.8	6.9	6.2	6.1	6.7
2016	6.0	6.1	6.0	6.2	5.4	6.2	6.3	6.1	6.2	6.1	6.1	6.2	6.1
2017	6.2	6.3	6.2	6.2	6.2	6.3	6.1	6.1	6.2	6.0	6.1	6.0	6.2
2018	5.8	6.0	5.9	5.8	5.7	5.8	5.7	6.0	6.0	6.0	6.1	5.9	5.9

1. Employment by Industry: Rhode Island, 2010–2018—*Continued*

(Numbers in thousands, not seasonally adjusted)

Industry and year	January	February	March	April	May	June	July	August	September	October	November	December	Annual average
Financial Activities													
2010	31.7	31.7	31.9	31.8	32.0	32.2	32.3	32.2	32.3	32.5	32.6	32.7	32.2
2011	32.1	32.2	32.3	32.4	32.4	32.9	32.5	32.6	32.6	32.6	32.9	32.8	32.5
2012	32.6	32.8	33.0	33.0	33.4	33.6	33.5	33.5	33.6	33.6	33.6	33.7	33.3
2013	33.4	33.6	33.9	33.9	34.0	34.2	34.3	34.1	34.0	34.0	33.9	34.2	34.0
2014	33.8	33.8	33.8	34.1	34.2	34.4	34.5	34.3	34.3	34.2	34.2	34.3	34.2
2015	34.0	34.1	34.4	34.6	34.9	35.1	34.9	34.8	35.1	35.7	36.1	36.2	35.0
2016	35.3	35.5	35.6	35.5	35.5	35.8	35.8	35.7	35.6	35.7	35.8	35.8	35.6
2017	35.5	35.6	35.6	35.6	35.8	36.1	36.0	36.1	36.0	35.7	35.9	35.8	35.8
2018	35.3	35.4	35.3	35.4	35.3	35.6	35.5	35.3	35.2	35.5	35.4	35.2	35.4
Professional and Business Services													
2010	50.2	50.2	51.1	54.0	54.2	54.9	54.4	54.6	54.7	54.8	54.6	53.7	53.5
2011	51.5	51.9	52.3	54.2	54.6	55.2	54.9	55.3	55.8	55.9	55.7	54.6	54.3
2012	52.8	53.1	54.1	56.1	56.6	57.5	56.9	57.3	57.2	57.1	57.2	57.2	56.1
2013	55.0	55.6	56.1	58.4	59.0	60.3	59.6	60.2	60.3	60.7	60.4	59.7	58.8
2014	57.0	57.7	58.0	60.5	61.2	61.8	61.7	62.3	62.4	63.0	63.0	62.9	61.0
2015	60.0	60.0	60.7	63.7	64.7	65.0	65.0	64.9	64.7	65.1	65.5	65.2	63.7
2016	62.9	63.1	63.7	65.6	66.0	66.6	66.6	66.9	67.0	67.3	67.1	66.6	65.8
2017	64.2	64.8	64.9	67.1	67.4	68.4	68.8	69.0	68.6	68.7	68.8	68.4	67.4
2018	65.3	65.7	66.3	68.3	68.9	69.6	69.7	70.0	69.7	69.5	69.6	69.1	68.5
Education and Health Services													
2010	99.8	102.2	102.9	102.8	102.8	98.1	97.8	97.8	101.6	103.1	103.8	104.1	101.4
2011	99.7	102.8	103.7	104.4	104.3	99.7	98.8	98.3	101.7	104.7	104.9	104.2	102.3
2012	100.7	104.7	104.9	104.1	104.6	100.0	98.7	99.0	104.7	105.8	105.6	106.4	103.3
2013	103.3	105.5	106.3	105.7	105.5	102.2	100.9	100.5	105.0	107.2	107.5	105.8	104.6
2014	103.4	105.9	106.5	107.2	106.7	102.4	101.7	101.1	106.0	107.6	108.1	107.9	105.4
2015	104.4	105.8	106.9	107.7	106.9	103.3	102.6	101.7	106.1	108.2	108.5	107.9	105.8
2016	104.2	107.1	108.0	108.4	108.2	103.1	102.3	101.8	105.7	108.0	108.1	107.5	106.0
2017	104.2	106.8	108.2	108.8	108.4	103.5	102.7	102.7	105.8	107.6	108.3	107.8	106.2
2018	103.3	106.8	107.4	108.2	108.1	103.8	102.9	102.2	106.4	109.2	109.7	109.4	106.5
Leisure and Hospitality													
2010	43.6	44.0	44.4	47.6	50.8	54.3	55.5	55.2	53.1	50.0	48.3	47.3	49.5
2011	44.0	44.6	45.0	48.1	51.1	55.0	56.1	55.8	53.8	50.9	48.9	48.2	50.1
2012	45.2	46.2	46.8	49.8	53.1	56.9	57.6	57.6	55.4	52.5	50.4	49.9	51.8
2013	46.8	47.2	48.2	51.3	54.6	58.9	59.6	59.5	57.3	55.1	52.5	51.9	53.6
2014	48.4	49.4	50.1	53.3	56.9	60.4	61.0	60.6	58.6	56.3	54.0	53.2	55.2
2015	50.2	49.6	50.6	54.0	58.5	61.4	62.2	62.0	59.9	57.4	55.2	54.5	56.3
2016	51.1	51.6	52.7	55.7	58.8	63.4	63.9	63.4	60.9	58.4	56.2	55.0	57.6
2017	51.9	52.6	53.0	55.6	59.3	64.2	64.5	64.7	61.2	59.0	56.8	56.0	58.2
2018	52.5	53.5	53.9	56.8	60.5	65.1	66.1	65.8	62.2	58.9	55.4	54.0	58.7
Other Services													
2010	21.5	21.6	21.6	21.7	22.0	22.2	23.0	22.9	22.1	22.0	22.2	22.1	22.1
2011	21.5	21.7	21.7	22.1	22.3	22.9	23.7	23.5	22.5	22.3	22.4	22.4	22.4
2012	21.8	21.9	21.9	22.2	22.4	23.0	23.4	23.4	22.9	22.5	22.5	22.7	22.6
2013	22.0	22.0	22.2	22.4	22.6	23.1	23.5	23.2	22.6	22.5	22.5	22.6	22.6
2014	22.0	22.2	22.3	22.5	22.9	23.5	23.9	23.8	23.0	22.7	22.8	22.9	22.9
2015	22.4	22.2	22.5	22.6	23.1	23.5	24.1	23.9	23.0	22.9	23.0	22.9	23.0
2016	22.5	22.5	22.7	22.9	23.1	23.8	24.2	24.0	23.0	22.9	23.0	23.0	23.1
2017	22.4	22.5	22.4	22.8	23.0	23.7	23.9	23.8	22.9	22.9	23.1	23.0	23.0
2018	22.2	22.4	22.5	22.7	22.9	23.7	24.1	24.0	23.1	23.6	23.0	23.2	23.1
Government													
2010	62.3	62.3	62.7	62.7	64.8	63.1	58.5	58.2	60.5	61.6	62.1	61.8	61.7
2011	61.4	61.4	61.9	61.8	62.0	61.6	56.7	56.7	59.8	61.0	61.3	61.3	60.6
2012	60.6	60.9	61.0	61.1	61.9	60.6	56.2	56.6	59.6	60.7	61.1	61.2	60.1
2013	60.6	60.5	61.0	60.8	61.7	60.9	57.1	56.8	59.8	61.1	61.1	61.4	60.2
2014	60.7	60.6	60.9	61.1	62.0	61.2	57.2	56.7	60.3	61.1	61.5	61.2	60.4
2015	60.9	60.9	60.9	61.0	61.7	60.8	56.9	56.3	59.5	60.8	61.0	61.2	60.2
2016	60.7	60.9	61.2	60.9	61.4	60.8	57.5	57.0	60.0	61.2	61.4	61.4	60.4
2017	60.8	61.1	61.2	61.1	61.8	61.6	57.8	57.4	60.4	61.7	61.5	61.9	60.7
2018	61.2	61.3	61.4	61.4	62.7	61.9	57.7	57.1	60.7	61.9	62.0	62.3	61.0

2. Average Weekly Hours by Selected Industry: Rhode Island, 2014–2018

(Not seasonally adjusted)

Industry and year	January	February	March	April	May	June	July	August	September	October	November	December	Annual average
Total Private													
2014	32.7	32.6	32.8	33.0	33.0	33.3	33.3	33.0	33.0	33.0	33.1	33.1	33.0
2015	32.8	32.5	32.9	32.9	33.1	33.6	33.6	33.5	33.3	32.9	33.1	32.9	33.1
2016	32.5	32.4	32.5	32.5	32.9	33.0	33.0	33.0	32.8	32.4	32.3	32.7	32.7
2017	32.6	31.7	32.0	33.0	32.9	32.9	33.2	33.2	33.1	33.2	33.3	33.4	32.9
2018	33.0	33.4	32.5	33.6	33.7	33.4	33.5	33.4	33.3	33.1	33.2	33.6	33.3
Goods-Producing													
2014	38.7	38.3	38.9	39.4	38.9	39.3	38.2	38.0	38.3	38.6	38.3	39.1	38.7
2015	38.2	37.7	38.7	38.1	37.4	38.0	37.7	37.1	37.7	37.0	37.4	38.9	37.8
2016	37.9	37.6	38.4	38.0	38.4	38.8	38.4	38.2	38.2	38.1	38.2	38.8	38.3
2017	38.1	37.3	37.1	38.0	37.6	37.4	37.2	37.9	37.7	37.2	37.6	38.3	37.6
2018	36.6	37.8	35.8	38.5	38.2	37.8	37.7	37.6	37.2	37.0	37.3	38.2	37.5
Construction													
2014	38.4	36.7	38.0	38.9	38.8	38.8	37.4	36.2	36.5	36.4	36.1	36.6	37.4
2015	36.7	35.6	37.5	36.6	35.5	36.0	35.6	34.6	34.6	33.7	35.4	36.4	35.6
2016	35.8	33.8	36.2	35.1	36.5	37.1	36.7	36.1	35.6	35.9	35.9	35.6	35.9
2017	35.5	34.9	33.8	36.1	35.9	35.1	33.8	34.0	33.4	31.8	32.4	32.3	34.1
2018	29.5	31.3	28.9	32.6	32.9	32.1	32.5	32.8	32.4	32.7	32.6	34.2	32.1
Manufacturing													
2014	39.3	39.3	39.6	39.8	39.1	39.8	38.8	39.0	39.3	39.6	39.3	40.2	39.4
2015	38.9	38.5	39.2	38.8	38.3	38.9	38.6	38.1	39.0	38.4	38.2	39.9	38.7
2016	38.7	39.1	39.3	39.2	39.1	39.4	39.0	39.1	39.4	39.1	39.2	40.2	39.2
2017	39.2	38.3	38.4	38.7	38.3	38.4	38.9	39.2	39.4	39.7	40.0	41.2	39.1
2018	40.1	40.8	39.1	41.3	40.9	40.6	40.4	40.2	39.8	39.3	39.9	40.2	40.2
Trade, Transportation, and Utilities													
2014	33.3	33.1	33.4	34.4	34.3	34.2	34.4	34.4	34.4	33.8	33.7	33.9	33.9
2015	32.4	31.8	32.6	32.4	32.6	32.8	32.9	32.9	33.1	32.7	32.6	32.3	32.6
2016	31.2	31.2	31.0	31.5	31.8	32.1	32.6	32.3	32.3	32.3	32.2	32.7	31.9
2017	32.2	31.4	32.3	33.5	33.4	33.4	34.0	33.6	33.7	33.5	33.8	34.1	33.3
2018	33.2	33.5	32.2	32.9	33.5	33.6	33.5	32.7	33.3	33.0	33.1	33.1	33.1
Professional and Business Services													
2014	33.7	33.7	34.0	34.4	34.1	34.5	34.5	33.8	34.4	34.2	34.6	34.7	34.2
2015	34.8	34.7	35.3	35.3	36.4	36.1	36.1	35.8	35.1	35.3	35.7	34.8	35.5
2016	35.4	34.8	35.3	35.7	35.9	36.1	35.3	35.8	35.5	34.8	34.6	35.1	35.3
2017	35.1	34.6	34.6	35.2	35.8	35.8	35.2	35.5	35.8	35.3	35.5	35.2	35.3
2018	34.9	35.5	34.3	35.6	36.0	35.9	36.1	35.8	36.3	35.7	36.2	36.2	35.7
Education and Health Services													
2014	31.2	31.0	31.2	31.2	31.4	31.7	32.1	31.9	31.9	32.4	32.3	32.1	31.7
2015	32.2	32.0	32.2	32.1	32.1	32.0	32.0	32.5	32.2	31.8	32.1	31.3	32.0
2016	31.5	31.1	31.2	30.9	31.5	31.1	31.5	31.7	31.9	32.1	31.9	32.0	31.5
2017	32.5	32.2	32.2	32.8	32.8	33.0	32.7	32.1	32.6	33.0	33.1	33.2	32.7
2018	33.3	33.4	33.2	33.8	33.7	34.0	33.8	34.1	33.8	34.0	33.7	34.0	33.7
Leisure and Hospitality													
2014	25.2	24.9	25.6	25.4	25.4	25.5	26.7	26.5	25.1	24.3	23.9	23.7	25.2
2015	23.9	23.3	24.0	25.0	25.6	27.1	28.0	27.7	26.7	25.4	25.2	24.6	25.6
2016	23.4	24.0	23.8	23.8	24.6	25.0	25.3	25.4	24.3	23.9	24.0	23.7	24.3
2017	23.2	21.9	22.8	24.3	24.1	24.1	25.0	25.3	24.2	24.2	24.1	24.1	24.0
2018	23.5	24.5	23.5	24.9	25.2	25.4	26.4	26.4	25.1	25.1	24.6	24.9	25.0

3. Average Hourly Earnings by Selected Industry: Rhode Island, 2014–2018

(Dollars, not seasonally adjusted)

Industry and year	January	February	March	April	May	June	July	August	September	October	November	December	Annual average
Total Private													
2014	25.79	25.68	25.53	25.28	24.99	25.00	24.58	24.62	24.74	24.92	25.13	24.98	25.10
2015	25.24	25.59	25.49	25.15	25.02	24.13	24.26	24.31	24.68	25.14	25.36	25.09	24.94
2016	25.91	26.05	25.66	26.14	25.99	25.70	25.54	25.88	25.90	26.34	26.51	26.24	25.99
2017	26.88	27.01	26.81	26.91	26.72	26.48	26.63	26.67	27.08	27.32	27.43	27.65	26.97
2018	27.86	27.93	28.04	27.89	27.65	27.31	27.45	27.35	27.48	27.40	27.83	27.99	27.68
Goods-Producing													
2014	27.51	27.33	27.36	27.13	27.03	27.26	27.42	26.88	26.96	27.20	27.41	27.53	27.25
2015	27.27	27.32	26.89	26.39	26.12	25.33	25.58	25.38	25.33	25.44	25.90	25.39	26.01
2016	25.30	24.83	24.99	25.05	25.04	25.11	25.01	25.12	25.15	25.17	25.19	24.98	25.08
2017	25.30	25.10	25.25	25.08	25.19	25.37	25.44	25.08	25.46	25.05	25.28	25.68	25.27
2018	25.70	25.66	26.25	25.76	25.94	26.18	26.51	26.07	26.18	26.32	26.71	26.90	26.18
Construction													
2014	29.32	29.94	29.38	29.22	29.13	29.75	28.51	28.84	28.78	28.62	28.81	29.48	29.13
2015	29.25	29.70	29.25	28.52	29.11	27.78	27.57	27.72	28.82	28.60	28.89	28.83	28.63
2016	28.20	28.38	28.81	29.17	29.33	28.92	28.96	29.31	29.41	28.90	28.54	28.63	28.90
2017	29.19	28.68	28.91	28.19	28.90	28.66	28.67	28.72	29.86	29.82	30.31	31.26	29.25
2018	31.27	32.03	33.43	31.71	31.77	32.04	31.56	31.01	31.55	31.88	32.03	31.78	31.81
Manufacturing													
2014	26.65	26.24	26.44	26.05	25.94	25.97	26.72	25.81	25.65	26.05	26.33	26.23	26.17
2015	25.94	26.01	25.43	25.20	24.77	24.20	24.59	24.32	23.86	24.12	24.57	23.97	24.74
2016	24.13	23.61	23.58	23.54	23.40	23.65	23.42	23.39	23.41	23.62	23.78	23.52	23.59
2017	23.74	23.74	23.85	23.60	23.43	23.78	23.91	23.14	23.50	23.36	23.37	23.32	23.56
2018	23.64	23.38	24.10	23.84	23.63	23.80	24.46	24.07	23.87	23.65	24.24	24.45	23.92
Trade, Transportation, and Utilities													
2014	21.37	21.32	21.17	20.95	20.40	20.69	20.45	20.68	20.47	20.48	20.67	20.23	20.73
2015	20.48	20.31	20.09	19.66	20.01	19.88	20.02	20.01	20.23	20.66	20.55	19.70	20.13
2016	20.46	20.71	20.56	20.78	20.76	21.00	20.73	21.35	21.26	21.89	22.52	21.68	21.16
2017	22.21	22.49	23.36	23.24	23.43	23.67	23.60	23.84	24.29	24.65	24.81	24.70	23.72
2018	25.49	25.55	26.40	25.88	25.79	26.27	26.74	26.59	26.94	26.88	27.21	26.88	26.39
Professional and Business Services													
2014	30.17	30.23	29.92	29.41	28.86	28.82	27.96	28.65	28.17	28.71	29.47	29.74	29.16
2015	30.40	31.09	30.94	29.84	29.73	29.29	29.50	29.88	29.78	29.91	29.83	29.22	29.93
2016	30.03	30.15	29.79	30.14	30.11	30.05	30.12	30.32	30.95	31.26	31.47	31.33	30.48
2017	32.01	31.85	31.77	31.88	31.25	31.15	31.69	31.55	31.76	31.92	31.64	32.33	31.73
2018	32.85	33.08	33.17	32.99	32.08	31.88	32.03	32.16	32.28	32.63	32.39	32.34	32.48
Education and Health Services													
2014	22.75	22.99	23.13	23.21	23.35	23.38	23.61	23.66	23.67	23.66	23.42	23.22	23.34
2015	23.06	23.65	23.91	24.25	24.65	24.75	25.23	25.03	25.75	26.38	26.86	27.16	25.06
2016	27.53	27.86	27.35	27.55	27.65	27.78	27.98	27.66	27.75	28.39	28.22	28.22	27.83
2017	29.12	28.95	28.86	29.46	30.03	29.95	30.36	30.71	31.07	31.34	31.02	31.75	30.22
2018	30.77	30.41	30.42	30.61	30.24	29.97	29.96	29.38	28.42	27.94	27.98	29.34	29.61
Leisure and Hospitality													
2014	13.83	13.68	13.62	13.67	13.71	13.55	13.65	13.81	13.80	14.10	14.07	14.04	13.79
2015	14.40	14.58	14.66	14.49	14.39	13.99	14.27	14.50	14.84	15.25	15.02	15.42	14.63
2016	15.60	15.83	15.75	15.83	15.82	15.50	15.57	15.66	15.82	15.89	15.90	16.13	15.77
2017	16.16	16.53	16.34	16.23	16.02	16.12	16.17	15.95	16.22	16.20	16.18	16.28	16.19
2018	16.40	16.50	16.58	16.51	16.67	16.51	16.65	16.58	16.81	16.64	16.87	16.96	16.64

4. Average Weekly Earnings by Selected Industry: Rhode Island, 2014–2018

(Dollars, not seasonally adjusted)

Industry and year	January	February	March	April	May	June	July	August	September	October	November	December	Annual average
Total Private													
2014	843.33	837.17	837.38	834.24	824.67	832.50	818.51	812.46	816.42	822.36	831.80	826.84	828.30
2015	827.87	831.68	838.62	827.44	828.16	810.77	815.14	814.39	821.84	827.11	839.42	825.46	825.51
2016	842.08	844.02	833.95	849.55	855.07	848.10	842.82	854.04	849.52	853.42	856.27	858.05	849.87
2017	876.29	856.22	857.92	888.03	879.09	871.19	884.12	885.44	896.35	907.02	913.42	923.51	887.31
2018	919.38	932.86	911.30	937.10	931.81	912.15	919.58	913.49	915.08	906.94	923.96	940.46	921.74
Goods-Producing													
2014	1,064.64	1,046.74	1,064.30	1,068.92	1,051.47	1,071.32	1,047.44	1,021.44	1,032.57	1,049.92	1,049.80	1,076.42	1,054.58
2015	1,041.71	1,029.96	1,040.64	1,005.46	976.89	962.54	964.37	941.60	954.94	941.28	968.66	987.67	983.18
2016	958.87	933.61	959.62	951.90	961.54	974.27	960.38	959.58	960.73	958.98	962.26	969.22	960.56
2017	963.93	936.23	936.78	953.04	947.14	948.84	946.37	950.53	959.84	931.86	950.53	983.54	950.15
2018	940.62	969.95	939.75	991.76	990.91	989.60	999.43	980.23	973.90	973.84	996.28	1,027.58	981.75
Construction													
2014	1,125.89	1,098.80	1,116.44	1,136.66	1,130.24	1,154.30	1,066.27	1,044.01	1,050.47	1,041.77	1,040.04	1,078.97	1,089.46
2015	1,073.48	1,057.32	1,096.88	1,043.83	1,033.41	1,000.08	981.49	959.11	997.17	963.82	1,022.71	1,049.41	1,019.23
2016	1,009.56	959.24	1,042.92	1,023.87	1,070.55	1,072.93	1,062.83	1,058.09	1,047.00	1,037.51	1,024.59	1,019.23	1,037.51
2017	1,036.25	1,000.93	977.16	1,017.66	1,037.51	1,005.97	969.05	976.48	997.32	948.28	982.04	1,009.70	997.43
2018	922.47	1,002.54	966.13	1,033.75	1,045.23	1,028.48	1,025.70	1,017.13	1,022.22	1,042.48	1,044.18	1,086.88	1,021.10
Manufacturing													
2014	1,047.35	1,031.23	1,047.02	1,036.79	1,014.25	1,033.61	1,036.74	1,006.59	1,008.05	1,031.58	1,034.77	1,054.45	1,031.10
2015	1,009.07	1,001.39	996.86	977.76	948.69	941.38	949.17	926.59	930.54	926.21	938.57	956.40	957.44
2016	933.83	923.15	926.69	922.77	914.94	931.81	913.38	914.55	922.35	923.54	932.18	945.50	924.73
2017	930.61	909.24	915.84	913.32	897.37	913.15	930.10	907.09	925.90	927.39	934.80	960.78	921.20
2018	947.96	953.90	942.31	984.59	966.47	966.28	988.18	967.61	950.03	929.45	967.18	982.89	961.58
Trade, Transportation, and Utilities													
2014	711.62	705.69	707.08	720.68	699.72	707.60	703.48	711.39	704.17	692.22	696.58	685.80	702.75
2015	663.55	645.86	654.93	636.98	652.33	652.06	658.66	658.33	669.61	675.58	669.93	636.31	656.24
2016	638.35	646.15	637.36	654.57	660.17	674.10	675.80	689.61	686.70	707.05	725.14	708.94	675.00
2017	715.16	706.19	754.53	778.54	782.56	790.58	802.40	801.02	818.57	825.78	838.58	842.27	789.88
2018	846.27	855.93	850.08	851.45	863.97	882.67	895.79	869.49	897.10	887.04	900.65	889.73	873.51
Professional and Business Services													
2014	1,016.73	1,018.75	1,017.28	1,011.70	984.13	994.29	964.62	968.37	969.05	981.88	1,019.66	1,031.98	997.27
2015	1,057.92	1,078.82	1,092.18	1,053.35	1,082.17	1,057.37	1,064.95	1,069.70	1,045.28	1,055.82	1,064.93	1,016.86	1,062.52
2016	1,063.06	1,049.22	1,051.59	1,076.00	1,080.95	1,084.81	1,063.24	1,085.46	1,098.73	1,087.85	1,088.86	1,099.68	1,075.94
2017	1,123.55	1,102.01	1,099.24	1,122.18	1,118.75	1,115.17	1,115.49	1,120.03	1,137.01	1,126.78	1,123.22	1,138.02	1,120.07
2018	1,146.47	1,174.34	1,137.73	1,174.44	1,154.88	1,144.49	1,156.28	1,151.33	1,171.76	1,164.89	1,172.52	1,170.71	1,159.54
Education and Health Services													
2014	709.80	712.69	721.66	724.15	733.19	741.15	757.88	754.75	755.07	766.58	756.47	745.36	739.88
2015	742.53	756.80	769.90	778.43	791.27	792.00	807.36	813.48	829.15	838.88	862.21	850.11	801.92
2016	867.20	866.45	853.32	851.30	870.98	863.96	881.37	876.82	885.23	911.32	900.22	903.04	876.65
2017	946.40	932.19	929.29	966.29	984.98	988.35	992.77	985.79	1,012.88	1,034.22	1,026.76	1,054.10	988.19
2018	1,024.64	1,015.69	1,009.94	1,034.62	1,019.09	1,018.98	1,012.65	1,001.86	960.60	949.96	942.93	997.56	997.86
Leisure and Hospitality													
2014	348.52	340.63	348.67	347.22	348.23	345.53	364.46	365.97	346.38	342.63	336.27	332.75	347.51
2015	344.16	339.71	351.84	362.25	368.38	379.13	399.56	401.65	396.23	387.35	378.50	379.33	374.53
2016	365.04	379.92	374.85	376.75	389.17	387.50	393.92	397.76	384.43	379.77	381.60	382.28	383.21
2017	374.91	362.01	372.55	394.39	386.08	388.49	404.25	403.54	392.52	392.04	389.94	392.35	388.56
2018	385.40	404.25	389.63	411.10	420.08	419.35	439.56	437.71	421.93	417.66	415.00	422.30	416.00

SOUTH CAROLINA
At a Glance

Population:
  2010 census: 4,625,364
  2018 estimate: 5,084,127

Percent change in population:
  2010–2018: 9.9%

Percent change in total nonfarm employment:
  2010–2018: 18.4%

Industry with the largest growth in employment, 2010–2018 (percent):
  Transportation and utilities, 39.4%

Industry with the largest decline or smallest growth in employment, 2010–2018 (percent):
  Government, 3.9%

Civilian labor force:
  2010: 2,155,668
  2018: 2,323,209

Unemployment rate and rank among states (highest to lowest):
  2010: 11.2%, 4th
  2018: 3.4%, 32nd

Over-the-year change in unemployment rates:
  2016–2017: -0.7%
  2017–2018: -0.9%

Employment by Industry: South Carolina, 2018

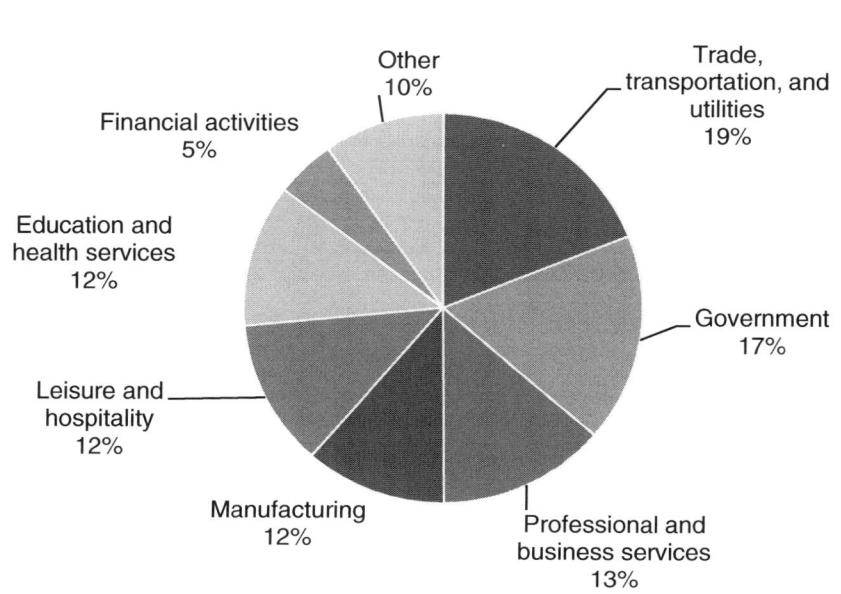

Other 10%

Financial activities 5%

Education and health services 12%

Leisure and hospitality 12%

Manufacturing 12%

Professional and business services 13%

Government 17%

Trade, transportation, and utilities 19%

1. Employment by Industry: South Carolina, 2010–2018

(Numbers in thousands, not seasonally adjusted)

Industry and year	January	February	March	April	May	June	July	August	September	October	November	December	Annual average
Total Nonfarm													
2010	1,760.0	1,771.1	1,789.5	1,816.5	1,837.4	1,832.4	1,816.6	1,821.1	1,817.8	1,822.0	1,826.1	1,825.2	1,811.3
2011	1,779.2	1,798.9	1,819.5	1,842.5	1,851.3	1,850.8	1,833.8	1,839.5	1,841.0	1,840.4	1,847.4	1,846.1	1,832.5
2012	1,813.6	1,830.0	1,851.6	1,866.0	1,877.6	1,881.9	1,859.9	1,866.9	1,870.4	1,874.8	1,891.0	1,887.4	1,864.3
2013	1,844.4	1,860.5	1,878.2	1,897.0	1,911.5	1,917.2	1,899.7	1,906.2	1,912.8	1,919.0	1,932.7	1,933.0	1,901.0
2014	1,891.7	1,898.9	1,928.9	1,951.2	1,966.5	1,968.0	1,945.9	1,953.3	1,960.9	1,972.6	1,987.9	1,990.0	1,951.3
2015	1,944.8	1,960.1	1,979.2	1,998.3	2,016.7	2,021.1	2,008.6	2,014.7	2,016.7	2,031.0	2,042.7	2,046.4	2,006.7
2016	1,997.4	2,015.0	2,033.4	2,057.0	2,068.2	2,068.8	2,058.8	2,063.3	2,068.3	2,063.0	2,084.5	2,085.5	2,055.3
2017	2,046.4	2,063.9	2,080.3	2,093.3	2,106.7	2,113.2	2,097.4	2,096.8	2,091.1	2,105.3	2,122.2	2,121.2	2,094.8
2018	2,101.8	2,119.8	2,131.3	2,142.2	2,156.2	2,163.8	2,148.1	2,148.9	2,131.9	2,158.5	2,168.0	2,173.1	2,145.3
Total Private													
2010	1,405.5	1,413.0	1,429.4	1,455.8	1,466.8	1,474.1	1,474.9	1,476.2	1,466.7	1,468.0	1,471.3	1,471.1	1,456.1
2011	1,430.1	1,446.6	1,465.9	1,488.7	1,498.7	1,503.5	1,501.3	1,503.8	1,492.8	1,489.1	1,494.9	1,494.2	1,484.1
2012	1,466.0	1,477.0	1,497.3	1,511.8	1,523.1	1,531.0	1,523.7	1,529.0	1,518.2	1,517.9	1,530.0	1,528.7	1,512.8
2013	1,492.4	1,504.0	1,520.1	1,538.1	1,553.5	1,565.1	1,562.2	1,567.2	1,560.0	1,561.6	1,573.7	1,575.0	1,547.7
2014	1,538.5	1,541.7	1,570.2	1,591.5	1,606.5	1,613.9	1,606.5	1,610.3	1,603.4	1,610.5	1,624.9	1,626.8	1,595.4
2015	1,587.3	1,598.0	1,616.2	1,634.2	1,652.6	1,663.1	1,664.2	1,666.6	1,655.0	1,665.7	1,676.0	1,678.7	1,646.5
2016	1,636.4	1,650.1	1,666.6	1,689.5	1,701.4	1,707.0	1,709.0	1,710.8	1,703.6	1,696.3	1,716.3	1,716.0	1,691.9
2017	1,683.1	1,697.0	1,711.3	1,724.3	1,737.9	1,749.0	1,744.2	1,741.1	1,723.8	1,735.0	1,749.6	1,749.1	1,728.8
2018	1,733.9	1,749.6	1,760.1	1,770.3	1,784.7	1,797.1	1,792.1	1,790.2	1,762.0	1,785.8	1,791.9	1,798.1	1,776.3
Goods Producing													
2010	286.2	286.0	287.4	290.1	291.4	292.5	292.2	291.8	291.5	291.2	291.6	293.1	290.4
2011	287.3	291.0	294.2	295.9	297.0	298.5	298.1	298.5	298.2	298.0	298.8	299.8	296.3
2012	296.6	298.7	301.0	300.6	302.2	302.8	301.2	302.4	302.1	302.7	303.5	304.3	301.5
2013	302.0	303.5	306.1	306.4	308.1	309.2	308.2	309.3	310.0	310.2	311.5	312.5	308.1
2014	309.9	310.2	313.1	314.6	317.0	318.6	317.6	317.3	318.1	319.9	321.2	322.9	316.7
2015	320.5	322.3	323.6	324.2	326.3	329.0	327.8	328.1	329.2	329.5	331.1	332.0	327.0
2016	330.8	332.3	333.9	334.7	336.3	338.3	339.6	339.4	340.8	339.1	342.0	343.8	337.6
2017	341.9	343.9	345.1	344.9	347.4	350.4	350.1	345.8	345.3	345.2	347.0	348.8	346.3
2018	350.2	353.5	354.3	354.5	355.9	355.9	357.9	354.4	353.6	354.8	355.8	356.3	354.8
Service-Providing													
2010	1,473.8	1,485.1	1,502.1	1,526.4	1,546.0	1,539.9	1,524.4	1,529.3	1,526.3	1,530.8	1,534.5	1,532.1	1,520.9
2011	1,491.9	1,507.9	1,525.3	1,546.6	1,554.3	1,552.3	1,535.7	1,541.0	1,542.8	1,542.4	1,548.6	1,546.3	1,536.3
2012	1,517.0	1,531.3	1,550.6	1,565.4	1,575.4	1,579.1	1,558.7	1,564.5	1,568.3	1,572.1	1,587.5	1,583.1	1,562.8
2013	1,542.4	1,557.0	1,572.1	1,590.6	1,603.4	1,608.0	1,591.5	1,596.9	1,602.8	1,608.8	1,621.2	1,620.5	1,592.9
2014	1,581.8	1,588.7	1,615.8	1,636.6	1,649.5	1,649.4	1,628.3	1,636.0	1,642.8	1,652.7	1,666.7	1,667.1	1,634.6
2015	1,624.3	1,637.8	1,655.6	1,674.1	1,690.4	1,692.1	1,680.8	1,686.6	1,687.5	1,701.5	1,711.6	1,714.4	1,679.7
2016	1,666.6	1,682.7	1,699.5	1,722.3	1,731.9	1,730.5	1,719.2	1,723.9	1,727.5	1,723.9	1,742.5	1,741.7	1,717.7
2017	1,704.5	1,720.0	1,735.2	1,748.4	1,759.3	1,762.8	1,747.3	1,751.0	1,745.8	1,760.1	1,775.2	1,772.4	1,748.5
2018	1,751.6	1,766.3	1,777.0	1,787.7	1,800.3	1,807.9	1,790.2	1,794.5	1,778.3	1,803.7	1,812.2	1,816.8	1,790.5
Mining and Logging													
2010	4.0	4.0	4.0	4.0	4.0	4.0	4.0	4.0	4.0	4.0	3.9	3.9	4.0
2011	3.9	3.9	4.0	4.0	4.0	4.0	3.9	3.9	3.9	3.9	3.9	3.9	3.9
2012	3.9	3.9	3.9	3.9	3.9	3.9	3.8	3.8	3.8	3.8	3.8	3.8	3.9
2013	3.8	3.8	3.8	3.8	3.8	3.8	3.8	3.8	3.8	3.8	3.8	3.9	3.8
2014	3.8	3.7	3.8	3.8	3.9	3.9	3.9	3.9	3.9	3.9	3.9	3.9	3.9
2015	3.9	3.9	3.9	3.9	3.9	4.0	4.0	4.1	4.1	4.0	4.0	4.0	4.0
2016	4.0	4.1	4.1	4.1	4.2	4.2	4.2	4.2	4.3	4.2	4.2	4.3	4.2
2017	4.2	4.2	4.3	4.2	4.3	4.3	4.3	4.3	4.2	4.2	4.2	4.2	4.2
2018	4.4	4.4	4.4	4.4	4.5	4.5	4.5	4.6	4.4	4.4	4.4	4.4	4.4
Construction													
2010	77.8	77.3	78.5	80.4	81.0	81.5	81.6	80.7	80.2	79.9	79.6	79.0	79.8
2011	74.5	76.1	77.3	77.9	78.6	78.8	78.5	78.3	78.0	78.0	78.0	77.6	77.6
2012	75.8	77.0	78.3	77.5	78.6	79.3	79.0	79.5	79.3	79.2	79.1	79.2	78.5
2013	78.0	77.8	79.6	80.1	81.0	81.6	82.0	82.2	82.3	82.0	82.7	83.1	81.0
2014	81.5	81.6	82.9	83.5	84.7	85.4	85.2	85.7	85.4	86.0	86.4	87.0	84.6
2015	85.5	86.1	87.3	87.7	89.1	90.5	90.2	90.2	90.6	91.9	92.3	92.9	89.5
2016	92.4	93.4	95.0	95.7	96.7	98.4	99.2	99.8	99.8	99.7	100.8	101.1	97.7
2017	99.6	100.3	100.8	101.8	103.3	104.6	104.1	100.3	98.9	99.8	99.8	100.2	101.1
2018	102.0	103.3	103.9	103.2	104.1	102.6	104.0	102.0	101.0	101.7	101.2	100.7	102.5

1. Employment by Industry: South Carolina, 2010–2018—*Continued*

(Numbers in thousands, not seasonally adjusted)

Industry and year	January	February	March	April	May	June	July	August	September	October	November	December	Annual average
Manufacturing													
2010	204.4	204.7	204.9	205.7	206.4	207.0	206.6	207.1	207.3	207.3	208.1	210.2	206.6
2011	208.9	211.0	212.9	214.0	214.4	215.7	215.7	216.3	216.3	216.1	216.9	218.3	214.7
2012	216.9	217.8	218.8	219.2	219.7	219.6	218.4	219.1	219.0	219.7	220.6	221.3	219.2
2013	220.2	221.9	222.7	222.5	223.3	223.8	222.4	223.3	223.9	224.4	225.0	225.5	223.2
2014	224.6	224.9	226.4	227.3	228.4	229.3	228.5	227.7	228.8	230.0	230.9	232.0	228.2
2015	231.1	232.3	232.4	232.6	233.3	234.5	233.6	233.8	234.5	233.6	234.8	235.1	233.5
2016	234.4	234.8	234.8	234.9	235.4	235.7	236.2	235.4	236.7	235.2	237.0	238.4	235.7
2017	238.1	239.4	240.0	238.9	239.8	241.5	241.7	241.2	242.2	241.2	243.0	244.4	241.0
2018	243.8	245.8	246.0	246.9	247.3	248.8	249.4	247.8	248.2	248.7	250.2	251.2	247.8
Trade, Transportation, and Utilities													
2010	338.8	337.8	341.4	343.5	345.8	347.3	347.1	347.7	345.2	347.6	353.1	355.7	345.9
2011	341.6	342.4	344.9	348.3	349.8	351.8	351.6	351.4	348.8	350.3	355.9	358.3	349.6
2012	347.4	346.3	349.4	351.1	353.7	355.9	355.3	355.2	354.1	356.4	364.5	365.6	354.6
2013	351.4	351.2	354.7	356.8	359.9	363.6	364.6	365.6	363.4	366.5	373.2	376.9	362.3
2014	363.4	361.7	366.1	368.9	372.3	376.0	374.3	374.8	373.2	376.5	384.4	388.5	373.3
2015	373.5	373.2	376.6	380.5	384.1	387.6	388.6	388.9	385.0	388.4	395.5	398.4	385.0
2016	385.2	386.0	387.4	390.6	393.4	394.8	396.1	395.9	393.8	393.6	402.3	405.2	393.7
2017	392.5	391.9	393.4	393.5	395.2	397.5	397.2	396.5	392.2	396.3	404.6	408.1	396.6
2018	397.6	398.0	399.7	401.2	405.2	408.4	407.9	407.6	403.3	407.8	417.7	421.4	406.3
Wholesale Trade													
2010	63.8	63.9	64.1	64.4	64.6	64.6	64.6	64.7	64.1	64.3	64.3	64.2	64.3
2011	63.3	64.0	64.1	64.4	64.5	64.6	64.6	64.6	64.3	64.2	64.3	64.6	64.3
2012	64.8	65.2	65.5	65.5	65.7	66.2	65.8	65.8	65.5	65.6	65.6	65.7	65.6
2013	65.4	65.7	66.1	66.3	66.6	66.9	66.5	66.8	66.5	66.5	66.8	66.9	66.4
2014	67.0	67.2	67.5	67.4	67.9	68.4	68.0	68.2	68.2	69.0	69.2	69.2	68.1
2015	69.4	69.7	70.2	70.4	70.7	70.7	70.5	70.6	70.4	70.8	70.9	71.3	70.5
2016	70.9	71.2	71.3	71.6	71.7	71.8	71.9	71.8	71.7	71.4	71.8	72.1	71.6
2017	71.5	71.9	72.2	71.7	71.9	72.3	72.2	72.1	71.5	71.0	71.2	71.4	71.7
2018	70.6	70.9	70.8	70.9	71.5	72.1	72.7	72.3	72.2	72.4	73.2	73.2	71.9
Retail Trade													
2010	217.5	216.4	219.1	220.7	222.5	223.6	223.1	223.5	221.6	223.3	228.3	230.5	222.5
2011	219.1	219.2	221.2	224.4	225.2	226.3	226.3	225.7	223.4	224.3	229.1	230.5	224.6
2012	221.2	219.7	222.3	223.7	225.7	226.8	226.9	226.5	225.4	227.0	234.5	234.5	226.2
2013	222.7	222.1	224.8	227.0	229.3	231.9	233.0	233.4	231.5	234.3	240.0	242.2	231.0
2014	230.3	228.9	232.3	233.9	235.8	238.2	237.3	237.1	235.4	237.2	243.7	246.1	236.4
2015	233.3	232.8	235.3	238.4	241.0	244.2	244.7	244.7	241.5	244.4	251.0	252.1	242.0
2016	241.0	241.6	242.8	245.2	247.1	247.5	248.1	247.7	245.6	245.1	252.4	253.3	246.5
2017	244.2	243.3	244.2	245.3	246.5	247.7	247.2	246.9	242.9	246.7	254.0	254.7	247.0
2018	247.8	247.9	249.4	250.6	253.8	254.6	252.3	251.4	248.0	251.0	258.4	259.3	252.0
Transportation and Utilities													
2010	57.5	57.5	58.2	58.4	58.7	59.1	59.4	59.5	59.5	60.0	60.5	61.0	59.1
2011	59.2	59.2	59.6	59.5	60.1	60.9	60.7	61.1	61.1	61.8	62.5	63.2	60.7
2012	61.4	61.4	61.6	61.9	62.3	62.9	62.6	62.9	63.2	63.8	64.4	65.4	62.8
2013	63.3	63.4	63.8	63.5	64.0	64.8	65.1	65.4	65.4	65.7	66.4	67.8	64.9
2014	66.1	65.6	66.3	67.6	68.6	69.4	69.0	69.5	69.6	70.3	71.5	73.2	68.9
2015	70.8	70.7	71.1	71.7	72.4	72.7	73.4	73.6	73.1	73.2	73.6	75.0	72.6
2016	73.3	73.2	73.3	73.8	74.6	75.5	76.1	76.4	76.5	77.1	78.1	79.8	75.6
2017	76.8	76.7	77.0	76.5	76.8	77.5	77.8	77.5	77.8	78.6	79.4	82.0	77.9
2018	79.2	79.2	79.5	79.7	79.9	81.7	82.9	83.9	83.1	84.4	86.1	88.9	82.4
Information													
2010	26.3	26.3	26.3	25.5	25.6	26.0	26.3	25.7	25.4	25.5	25.7	26.1	25.9
2011	26.0	25.7	25.9	25.7	25.7	25.8	25.8	25.7	25.3	26.0	26.1	26.1	25.8
2012	25.5	25.8	25.6	25.7	26.0	26.1	25.8	25.6	25.4	25.6	25.9	26.3	25.8
2013	26.1	26.4	26.4	26.7	26.7	26.5	26.6	26.3	26.2	26.2	26.4	26.4	26.4
2014	26.0	26.0	26.1	26.4	26.5	26.5	26.5	26.3	26.1	26.4	27.0	27.0	26.4
2015	26.6	26.6	26.6	26.6	26.9	26.8	27.0	26.9	26.7	26.8	27.8	27.3	26.9
2016	26.9	26.9	27.0	27.7	27.3	27.2	27.1	27.0	26.9	27.2	27.4	27.8	27.2
2017	27.3	27.5	27.7	27.4	27.8	27.9	27.4	27.5	27.5	27.4	27.5	27.7	27.6
2018	27.6	28.1	28.2	28.3	28.2	28.5	28.6	28.6	27.7	28.0	28.1	28.4	28.2

1. Employment by Industry: South Carolina, 2010–2018—Continued

(Numbers in thousands, not seasonally adjusted)

Industry and year	January	February	March	April	May	June	July	August	September	October	November	December	Annual average
Financial Activities													
2010	91.6	91.5	91.9	92.3	92.8	93.4	93.6	93.1	91.7	91.7	91.5	91.2	92.2
2011	89.9	89.8	90.1	90.9	91.7	92.2	92.6	92.6	91.7	91.7	92.0	92.0	91.4
2012	91.3	91.7	92.2	93.4	93.8	94.9	94.8	95.1	94.3	94.1	94.4	94.9	93.7
2013	93.4	94.0	94.8	95.6	96.4	97.3	97.5	97.7	96.6	96.4	96.4	96.5	96.1
2014	95.0	95.1	95.6	96.7	97.1	97.9	97.7	97.8	96.6	96.3	96.4	96.6	96.6
2015	95.5	95.7	96.1	97.0	97.7	98.7	98.8	99.0	98.1	98.7	98.9	99.3	97.8
2016	98.2	98.7	99.5	100.5	101.1	101.6	101.9	102.0	100.9	101.4	101.7	101.4	100.7
2017	100.2	100.5	101.2	101.5	102.2	103.2	103.5	103.6	102.4	102.6	102.5	102.8	102.2
2018	102.5	103.0	103.3	102.8	103.8	105.7	106.0	105.6	104.4	104.5	104.8	103.4	104.2
Professional and Business Services													
2010	200.0	202.8	205.5	214.5	216.0	218.0	219.2	221.3	221.0	222.6	223.1	223.0	215.6
2011	217.8	222.0	225.2	230.2	230.5	230.8	231.1	233.1	231.8	230.6	231.4	231.5	228.8
2012	227.4	230.3	234.0	237.3	238.5	239.6	236.7	239.1	236.1	235.6	239.8	240.0	236.2
2013	232.9	234.9	236.3	238.5	241.2	243.4	242.1	243.8	244.1	245.7	251.3	251.7	242.2
2014	242.9	244.0	250.8	253.0	255.3	254.5	253.1	255.0	255.5	257.2	264.0	263.2	254.0
2015	251.6	253.4	255.7	258.0	262.2	262.8	263.9	265.2	265.1	270.2	272.0	274.5	262.9
2016	259.2	262.9	263.8	270.2	270.4	269.8	269.3	270.8	271.6	272.7	278.3	277.0	269.7
2017	270.2	273.5	274.6	278.7	280.6	281.3	279.6	280.4	280.5	285.3	291.8	290.2	280.6
2018	286.1	289.3	291.1	291.8	296.0	293.5	287.3	292.8	289.3	298.3	298.6	300.8	292.9
Education and Health Services													
2010	206.1	208.2	208.4	210.1	210.6	208.5	208.5	209.9	210.6	213.2	213.6	213.4	210.1
2011	209.8	212.8	213.3	214.1	214.0	211.9	210.9	211.9	213.9	214.7	215.3	214.8	213.1
2012	212.7	214.9	215.3	214.6	215.0	212.6	211.9	213.4	216.3	217.8	218.4	218.1	215.1
2013	214.6	217.5	217.6	218.1	218.9	217.0	216.2	218.3	220.1	222.2	223.4	223.3	218.9
2014	221.4	222.9	224.5	227.4	227.3	225.2	224.7	227.0	228.8	231.5	232.5	232.5	227.1
2015	229.3	231.9	232.7	233.6	234.6	232.9	232.3	234.8	236.0	238.2	239.4	239.1	234.6
2016	235.8	238.4	239.6	240.4	241.0	238.8	239.1	241.3	243.8	243.4	244.7	244.6	240.9
2017	241.7	245.0	245.7	245.6	245.9	244.3	243.5	245.7	246.4	249.1	249.2	249.4	246.0
2018	248.0	250.8	251.5	251.9	251.6	250.4	250.8	253.5	255.2	257.3	257.3	257.0	252.9
Leisure and Hospitality													
2010	189.1	192.7	200.1	211.0	215.6	219.2	219.3	218.3	212.7	207.5	204.2	200.3	207.5
2011	190.2	195.0	203.7	214.7	221.0	223.5	222.1	222.1	214.8	209.9	207.6	204.1	210.7
2012	197.4	201.4	210.8	220.1	224.4	229.2	228.1	228.5	220.5	216.1	213.7	209.8	216.7
2013	202.6	206.8	213.5	225.1	231.1	236.3	235.6	234.6	227.7	222.8	220.7	216.7	222.8
2014	209.7	211.4	222.1	232.6	238.5	242.4	240.2	239.6	232.8	230.2	226.8	223.7	229.2
2015	218.3	222.5	231.3	240.7	246.6	250.9	251.6	249.7	241.3	239.9	237.3	234.0	238.7
2016	227.0	231.3	241.1	250.8	257.1	261.5	260.8	259.4	250.7	244.2	244.8	241.0	247.5
2017	234.8	240.1	248.2	257.3	263.0	268.4	267.1	265.9	254.1	253.7	251.6	246.6	254.2
2018	245.9	250.2	255.0	262.4	266.5	277.0	276.5	269.9	251.6	259.0	254.3	255.2	260.3
Other Services													
2010	67.4	67.7	68.4	68.8	69.0	69.2	68.7	68.4	68.6	68.7	68.5	68.3	68.5
2011	67.5	67.9	68.6	68.9	69.0	69.0	69.1	68.5	68.3	67.9	67.8	67.6	68.3
2012	67.7	67.9	69.0	69.0	69.5	69.9	69.9	69.7	69.4	69.6	69.8	69.7	69.3
2013	69.4	69.7	70.7	70.9	71.2	71.8	71.4	71.6	71.9	71.6	70.8	71.0	71.0
2014	70.2	70.4	71.9	71.9	72.5	72.8	72.4	72.5	72.3	72.5	72.6	72.4	72.0
2015	72.0	72.4	73.6	73.6	74.2	74.4	74.2	74.0	73.6	74.0	74.0	74.1	73.7
2016	73.3	73.6	74.3	74.6	74.8	75.0	75.1	75.0	75.1	74.7	75.1	75.2	74.7
2017	74.5	74.6	75.4	75.4	75.8	76.0	75.8	75.7	75.4	75.4	75.4	75.5	75.4
2018	76.0	76.7	77.0	77.4	77.5	77.7	77.1	77.8	76.9	76.1	75.3	75.6	76.8
Government													
2010	354.5	358.1	360.1	360.7	370.6	358.3	341.7	344.9	351.1	354.0	354.8	354.1	355.2
2011	349.1	352.3	353.6	353.8	352.6	347.3	332.5	335.7	348.2	351.3	352.5	351.9	348.4
2012	347.6	353.0	354.3	354.2	354.5	350.9	336.2	337.9	352.2	356.9	361.0	358.7	351.5
2013	352.0	356.5	358.1	358.9	358.0	352.1	337.5	339.0	352.8	357.4	359.0	358.0	353.3
2014	353.2	357.2	358.7	359.7	360.0	354.1	339.4	343.0	357.5	362.1	363.0	363.2	355.9
2015	357.5	362.1	363.0	364.1	364.1	358.0	344.4	348.1	361.7	365.3	366.7	367.7	360.2
2016	361.0	364.9	366.8	367.5	366.8	361.8	349.8	352.5	364.7	366.7	368.2	369.5	363.4
2017	363.3	366.9	369.0	369.0	368.8	364.2	353.2	355.7	367.3	370.3	372.6	372.1	366.0
2018	367.9	370.2	371.2	371.9	371.5	366.7	356.0	358.7	369.9	372.7	376.1	375.0	369.0

2. Average Weekly Hours by Selected Industry: South Carolina, 2014–2018

(Not seasonally adjusted)

Industry and year	January	February	March	April	May	June	July	August	September	October	November	December	Annual average
Total Private													
2014	34.6	33.4	34.7	34.5	34.5	34.9	34.6	34.6	34.5	34.3	34.7	34.6	34.5
2015	34.3	34.6	34.7	34.6	34.7	34.8	34.7	35.2	34.3	34.6	34.8	34.6	34.7
2016	34.4	34.4	34.6	34.6	34.8	34.6	34.4	34.4	34.4	34.2	34.5	34.5	34.5
2017	34.4	34.4	34.5	34.7	34.6	34.9	34.8	34.8	34.0	34.8	34.7	34.7	34.6
2018	34.0	34.6	34.7	35.0	34.6	34.7	34.9	34.7	33.5	34.5	34.7	34.8	34.6
Goods-Producing													
2014	41.3	38.6	39.4	39.2	40.0	40.4	39.7	40.1	40.1	39.7	40.6	40.4	40.0
2015	40.0	40.1	40.4	40.8	41.2	41.1	41.2	41.1	40.7	41.3	41.0	41.3	40.9
2016	40.7	40.8	42.0	41.4	41.7	41.7	40.3	40.5	41.0	40.7	41.1	41.1	41.1
2017	40.1	41.1	41.1	40.8	41.4	42.0	41.0	41.3	41.2	42.1	42.3	42.6	41.4
2018	41.7	41.9	42.3	42.2	41.8	42.2	41.8	41.7	40.3	41.3	41.8	42.0	41.8
Construction													
2014	40.3	35.8	39.3	38.3	39.5	39.6	39.0	39.0	38.6	38.3	39.1	39.3	38.9
2015	38.1	38.5	39.4	38.9	39.7	39.7	39.5	39.7	38.8	40.5	39.7	39.9	39.4
2016	38.8	39.1	40.6	39.3	40.5	40.7	40.0	39.9	39.6	39.7	40.2	39.6	39.8
2017	39.0	39.2	39.6	38.9	40.0	40.4	40.3	40.0	38.4	40.3	41.0	40.4	39.8
2018	39.6	39.7	40.1	40.1	39.8	39.9	39.9	39.4	37.2	39.1	38.7	39.5	39.4
Manufacturing													
2014	41.6	39.5	40.9	40.7	41.3	41.6	40.7	41.2	41.3	40.8	41.6	41.2	41.0
2015	41.2	41.1	41.1	41.9	42.0	41.9	42.1	41.8	41.7	41.6	41.7	42.0	41.7
2016	41.6	41.5	42.5	42.3	42.2	42.1	40.3	40.7	41.7	41.3	41.6	41.9	41.6
2017	40.6	41.7	41.6	41.6	41.9	42.6	41.2	41.8	42.5	43.0	43.0	43.8	42.1
2018	42.8	43.1	43.4	43.1	42.6	43.2	42.5	42.8	41.8	42.4	43.3	43.1	42.8
Trade, Transportation, and Utilities													
2014	34.0	33.0	33.8	33.9	34.1	34.5	34.5	34.3	34.7	34.3	35.0	35.0	34.3
2015	34.4	34.7	35.3	35.0	35.2	35.2	34.9	35.5	34.5	34.6	34.8	34.5	34.9
2016	34.4	34.3	34.0	34.3	34.3	34.1	34.3	34.4	34.5	33.7	33.7	34.0	34.2
2017	33.9	33.6	33.8	34.3	34.3	34.4	34.4	34.4	33.5	34.0	34.0	34.2	34.1
2018	33.2	33.6	34.0	34.4	34.2	34.1	34.5	34.3	33.2	34.2	34.1	33.9	34.0
Financial Activities													
2014	37.6	38.1	38.3	37.2	37.2	38.1	37.1	37.4	37.2	36.8	37.7	36.7	37.4
2015	36.7	37.7	37.4	36.8	36.7	37.0	37.2	38.0	36.9	37.1	38.2	37.0	37.2
2016	37.1	37.3	37.2	36.9	37.8	36.9	36.9	36.4	36.3	37.4	36.6	36.8	37.0
2017	37.7	36.7	36.6	37.6	36.6	36.8	37.6	36.7	36.7	37.9	37.2	37.4	37.1
2018	37.5	37.5	37.4	37.8	36.7	36.8	37.8	37.0	37.1	37.2	37.2	38.2	37.3
Professional and Business Services													
2014	36.9	35.3	38.0	37.8	37.9	38.2	37.6	37.8	37.5	37.5	37.8	37.2	37.5
2015	36.7	37.1	36.6	36.4	36.5	36.5	36.1	36.9	35.8	36.2	37.3	36.9	36.6
2016	36.1	36.5	36.1	36.4	36.8	36.2	35.8	36.1	36.0	36.3	36.6	36.6	36.3
2017	36.5	36.0	36.2	36.6	36.4	36.4	36.3	36.7	35.1	36.4	36.3	36.1	36.2
2018	35.3	36.3	36.5	37.3	36.9	36.9	37.4	37.2	35.6	36.1	36.7	37.0	36.6
Education and Health Services													
2014	32.6	31.9	32.7	32.4	32.3	32.1	32.5	32.6	32.4	32.6	32.9	33.1	32.5
2015	33.2	33.4	33.3	32.8	32.8	32.6	32.7	33.6	32.8	33.0	33.3	33.0	33.0
2016	32.9	32.5	32.8	32.8	33.0	32.6	32.7	32.6	32.6	32.6	32.8	32.7	32.7
2017	32.6	32.8	32.6	32.7	32.9	32.5	32.8	32.8	32.6	32.5	32.4	32.6	32.6
2018	31.9	32.1	31.9	32.0	32.1	32.1	31.7	31.9	31.8	32.0	32.2	31.9	32.0
Leisure and Hospitality													
2014	24.9	24.6	26.1	26.4	25.8	26.3	26.6	26.2	25.2	25.4	24.9	24.9	25.6
2015	24.6	25.1	25.7	26.0	25.8	26.4	26.7	26.6	25.2	25.0	25.0	24.7	25.6
2016	24.6	24.8	25.4	25.8	25.9	26.7	26.9	26.3	25.6	24.8	25.2	24.8	25.6
2017	24.5	24.9	25.5	26.1	25.4	26.4	26.9	26.4	24.8	25.9	25.6	25.1	25.7
2018	24.7	25.7	26.0	26.0	25.6	26.3	26.6	26.5	23.4	25.6	25.4	25.0	25.6
Other Services													
2014	31.2	28.9	31.0	31.4	31.0	30.3	31.1	30.9	31.1	31.2	30.5	30.6	30.8
2015	29.9	30.0	31.3	31.5	31.9	31.5	31.7	31.1	31.1	31.3	31.1	32.4	31.2
2016	32.7	33.1	33.1	34.4	33.2	33.6	34.4	33.9	34.7	34.5	33.8	33.8	33.8
2017	34.3	34.7	34.3	34.9	33.8	33.5	33.9	32.8	33.2	33.3	32.5	32.5	33.6
2018	33.0	33.0	32.7	33.9	33.0	33.3	33.4	32.8	31.5	32.2	32.8	32.5	32.8

3. Average Hourly Earnings by Selected Industry: South Carolina, 2014–2018

(Dollars, not seasonally adjusted)

Industry and year	January	February	March	April	May	June	July	August	September	October	November	December	Annual average
Total Private													
2014	21.06	21.73	21.19	20.80	20.68	20.78	20.64	20.76	21.01	21.07	21.47	21.39	21.05
2015	21.70	21.36	21.75	21.22	21.03	20.99	21.26	21.29	21.50	21.53	21.80	21.67	21.42
2016	21.87	21.79	22.17	21.93	21.87	22.07	21.93	21.95	22.24	22.53	22.49	22.46	22.11
2017	23.09	22.74	23.13	22.80	22.44	22.44	22.87	22.68	23.12	23.16	23.08	23.21	22.89
2018	23.89	23.85	23.86	23.99	23.61	23.46	23.72	23.54	24.64	24.14	24.37	24.51	23.96
Goods-Producing													
2014	22.19	22.97	22.30	22.20	21.87	22.07	22.25	22.19	22.26	22.23	22.48	22.85	22.32
2015	22.67	22.68	22.69	22.52	22.29	22.42	22.69	22.84	22.96	23.13	23.36	23.37	22.80
2016	23.39	23.33	23.55	23.47	23.47	23.59	24.20	24.04	24.33	24.02	24.08	24.27	23.81
2017	24.55	24.06	24.09	24.02	23.54	23.65	24.08	24.02	24.06	24.21	24.44	24.64	24.11
2018	24.96	24.90	24.87	25.32	25.33	25.37	25.75	25.75	26.10	26.43	26.29	26.78	25.65
Construction													
2014	20.14	21.09	20.38	19.98	20.10	20.40	20.55	20.72	20.95	20.97	20.90	20.74	20.57
2015	20.54	20.58	20.81	20.62	20.41	20.55	20.74	20.92	21.05	21.28	21.39	21.65	20.89
2016	21.68	21.72	22.15	21.79	21.76	21.98	22.60	22.57	23.08	23.16	22.98	22.76	22.37
2017	22.97	22.65	23.15	22.75	22.34	22.60	22.97	23.14	23.34	23.09	23.08	23.94	23.00
2018	23.87	24.31	24.65	24.32	24.62	24.41	24.45	24.79	25.13	25.59	25.35	25.54	24.74
Manufacturing													
2014	23.00	23.76	23.16	23.18	22.66	22.82	23.02	22.83	22.82	22.77	23.15	23.75	23.07
2015	23.56	23.57	23.50	23.35	23.11	23.26	23.59	23.75	23.86	24.03	24.34	24.25	23.68
2016	24.25	24.13	24.22	24.30	24.32	24.41	25.02	24.75	24.90	24.40	24.62	24.99	24.52
2017	25.33	24.87	24.60	24.72	24.22	24.25	24.70	24.50	24.43	24.79	25.15	24.91	24.71
2018	25.43	25.10	24.85	25.48	25.39	25.57	26.18	26.00	26.36	26.66	26.56	27.25	25.90
Trade, Transportation, and Utilities													
2014	20.39	20.89	20.87	19.57	19.37	19.60	19.14	19.50	19.73	20.02	20.12	19.57	19.89
2015	20.07	19.59	20.46	19.68	19.66	19.75	19.93	20.04	20.04	20.29	20.60	20.31	20.04
2016	20.53	20.27	21.07	20.38	20.40	20.11	20.37	20.13	20.33	20.69	20.69	20.57	20.46
2017	21.02	20.97	21.57	21.73	21.33	21.36	21.57	21.56	21.77	21.92	21.06	21.05	21.41
2018	21.35	21.48	22.15	22.15	21.54	21.87	21.75	21.71	22.87	22.25	22.67	22.23	22.00
Financial Activities													
2014	21.90	22.68	22.76	22.57	22.52	23.19	23.28	23.25	23.79	23.82	24.66	24.11	23.21
2015	24.95	25.20	25.10	25.01	24.56	24.31	24.84	24.58	24.54	24.31	25.17	25.07	24.80
2016	25.59	24.88	25.02	25.77	25.16	24.60	24.82	25.39	25.88	26.64	26.32	26.04	25.51
2017	26.73	25.75	24.99	26.09	25.73	25.75	26.19	26.26	26.93	27.19	27.22	27.04	26.33
2018	29.77	29.25	28.03	28.60	28.50	27.57	28.49	27.79	29.00	28.13	28.88	29.06	28.59
Professional and Business Services													
2014	23.57	24.64	23.69	23.34	23.45	23.24	23.21	23.17	23.20	23.06	23.17	22.75	23.36
2015	23.75	23.84	23.91	23.66	23.40	23.38	23.92	23.13	23.18	22.86	22.87	22.35	23.34
2016	22.78	22.97	22.88	23.50	23.60	23.36	23.79	23.74	24.22	24.50	24.28	24.05	23.65
2017	24.67	25.19	25.09	25.76	25.02	25.01	25.93	24.77	25.51	25.26	25.37	25.88	25.29
2018	26.23	25.85	26.04	26.29	25.82	25.63	26.58	25.78	27.20	26.08	26.45	26.68	26.22
Education and Health Services													
2014	24.10	24.67	24.19	24.62	24.48	24.79	24.83	24.94	25.40	25.36	25.89	25.94	24.94
2015	25.97	26.01	25.60	25.88	25.54	25.49	25.79	26.10	26.71	26.14	26.48	26.32	26.01
2016	26.23	26.42	25.94	26.18	25.77	25.88	26.05	25.91	25.75	26.10	26.36	26.00	26.05
2017	25.78	25.82	25.95	25.83	25.82	26.25	26.87	26.74	26.94	26.70	26.58	26.65	26.33
2018	27.09	27.02	26.53	26.20	25.56	25.75	25.56	25.09	25.98	26.22	26.08	26.14	26.10
Leisure and Hospitality													
2014	11.64	11.99	11.73	11.86	11.88	11.80	11.80	11.78	11.87	11.97	12.09	11.87	11.86
2015	11.90	12.02	12.09	12.07	12.02	11.89	11.88	12.02	12.05	12.28	12.22	12.40	12.07
2016	12.25	12.31	12.36	12.35	12.53	12.37	12.34	12.49	12.51	12.51	12.53	12.64	12.43
2017	12.58	12.48	12.47	12.78	12.83	12.55	12.48	12.53	12.57	12.72	12.73	12.82	12.63
2018	12.70	12.80	12.85	13.00	12.96	12.73	12.83	12.94	13.22	13.24	13.30	13.63	13.01
Other Services													
2014	16.43	16.75	16.16	15.95	15.69	15.51	14.56	15.04	14.92	14.98	15.46	15.65	15.58
2015	16.09	16.22	16.11	16.22	16.06	16.11	16.35	16.23	16.37	16.20	16.67	16.70	16.28
2016	17.18	17.36	17.14	17.53	18.00	17.97	18.14	17.81	17.78	18.26	19.29	19.69	18.02
2017	20.35	20.54	20.70	21.09	21.13	21.28	21.65	21.80	22.47	22.36	22.73	22.35	21.52
2018	23.50	23.31	23.33	22.72	23.24	22.30	23.29	23.35	23.85	23.49	23.94	24.90	23.42

4. Average Weekly Earnings by Selected Industry: South Carolina, 2014–2018

(Dollars, not seasonally adjusted)

Industry and year	January	February	March	April	May	June	July	August	September	October	November	December	Annual average
Total Private													
2014	728.68	725.78	735.29	717.60	713.46	725.22	714.14	718.30	724.85	722.70	745.01	740.09	726.23
2015	744.31	739.06	754.73	734.21	729.74	730.45	737.72	749.41	737.45	744.94	758.64	749.78	743.27
2016	752.33	749.58	767.08	758.78	761.08	763.62	754.39	755.08	765.06	770.53	775.91	774.87	762.80
2017	794.30	782.26	797.99	791.16	776.42	783.16	795.88	789.26	786.08	805.97	800.88	805.39	791.99
2018	812.26	825.21	827.94	839.65	816.91	814.06	827.83	816.84	825.44	832.83	845.64	852.95	829.02
Goods-Producing													
2014	916.45	886.64	878.62	870.24	874.80	891.63	883.33	889.82	892.63	882.53	912.69	923.14	892.80
2015	906.80	909.47	916.68	918.82	918.35	921.46	934.83	938.72	934.47	955.27	957.76	965.18	932.52
2016	951.97	951.86	989.10	971.66	978.70	983.70	975.26	973.62	997.53	977.61	989.69	997.50	978.59
2017	984.46	988.87	990.10	980.02	974.56	993.30	987.28	992.03	991.27	1,019.24	1,033.81	1,049.66	998.15
2018	1,040.83	1,043.31	1,052.00	1,068.50	1,058.79	1,070.61	1,076.35	1,073.78	1,051.83	1,091.56	1,098.92	1,124.76	1,072.17
Construction													
2014	811.64	755.02	800.93	765.23	793.95	807.84	801.45	808.08	808.67	803.15	817.19	815.08	800.17
2015	782.57	792.33	819.91	802.12	810.28	815.84	819.23	830.52	816.74	861.84	849.18	863.84	823.07
2016	841.18	849.25	899.29	856.35	881.28	894.59	904.00	900.54	913.97	919.45	923.80	901.30	890.33
2017	895.83	887.88	916.74	884.98	893.60	913.04	925.69	925.60	896.26	930.53	946.28	967.18	915.40
2018	945.25	965.11	988.47	975.23	979.88	973.96	975.56	976.73	934.84	1,000.57	981.05	1,008.83	974.76
Manufacturing													
2014	956.80	938.52	947.24	943.43	935.86	949.31	936.91	940.60	942.47	929.02	963.04	978.50	945.87
2015	970.67	968.73	965.85	978.37	970.62	974.59	993.14	992.75	994.96	999.65	1,014.98	1,018.50	987.46
2016	1,008.80	1,001.40	1,029.35	1,027.89	1,026.30	1,027.66	1,008.31	1,007.33	1,038.33	1,007.72	1,024.19	1,047.08	1,020.03
2017	1,028.40	1,037.08	1,023.36	1,028.35	1,014.82	1,033.05	1,017.64	1,024.10	1,038.28	1,065.97	1,081.45	1,091.06	1,040.29
2018	1,088.40	1,081.81	1,078.49	1,098.19	1,081.61	1,104.62	1,112.65	1,112.80	1,101.85	1,130.38	1,150.05	1,174.48	1,108.52
Trade, Transportation, and Utilities													
2014	693.26	689.37	705.41	663.42	660.52	676.20	660.33	668.85	684.63	686.69	704.20	684.95	682.23
2015	690.41	679.77	722.24	688.80	692.03	695.20	695.56	711.42	691.38	702.03	716.88	700.70	699.40
2016	706.23	695.26	716.38	699.03	699.72	685.75	698.69	692.47	701.39	697.25	697.25	699.38	699.73
2017	712.58	704.59	729.07	745.34	731.62	734.78	742.01	741.66	729.30	745.28	716.04	719.91	730.08
2018	708.82	721.73	753.10	761.96	736.67	745.77	750.38	744.65	759.28	760.95	773.05	753.60	748.00
Financial Activities													
2014	823.44	864.11	871.71	839.60	837.74	883.54	863.69	869.55	884.99	876.58	929.68	884.84	868.05
2015	915.67	950.04	938.74	920.37	901.35	899.47	924.05	934.04	905.53	901.90	961.49	927.59	922.56
2016	949.39	928.02	930.74	950.91	951.05	907.74	915.86	924.20	939.44	996.34	963.31	958.27	943.87
2017	1,007.72	945.03	914.63	980.98	941.72	947.60	984.74	963.74	988.33	1,030.50	1,012.58	1,011.30	976.84
2018	1,116.38	1,096.88	1,048.32	1,081.08	1,045.95	1,014.58	1,076.92	1,028.23	1,075.90	1,046.44	1,074.34	1,110.09	1,066.41
Professional and Business Services													
2014	869.73	869.79	900.22	882.25	888.76	887.77	872.70	875.83	870.00	864.75	875.83	846.30	876.00
2015	871.63	884.46	875.11	861.22	854.10	853.37	863.51	853.50	829.84	827.53	853.05	824.72	854.24
2016	822.36	838.41	825.97	855.40	868.48	845.63	851.68	857.01	871.92	889.35	888.65	880.23	858.50
2017	900.46	906.84	908.26	942.82	910.73	910.36	941.26	909.06	895.40	919.46	920.93	934.27	915.50
2018	925.92	938.36	950.46	980.62	952.76	945.75	994.09	959.02	968.32	941.49	970.72	987.16	959.65
Education and Health Services													
2014	785.66	786.97	791.01	797.69	790.70	795.76	806.98	813.04	822.96	826.74	851.78	858.61	810.55
2015	862.20	868.73	852.48	848.86	837.71	830.97	843.33	876.96	876.09	862.62	881.78	868.56	858.33
2016	862.97	858.65	850.83	858.70	850.41	843.69	851.84	844.67	839.45	850.86	864.61	850.20	851.84
2017	840.43	846.90	845.97	844.64	849.48	853.13	881.34	877.07	878.24	867.75	861.19	868.79	858.36
2018	864.17	867.34	846.31	838.40	820.48	826.58	810.25	800.37	826.16	839.04	839.78	833.87	835.20
Leisure and Hospitality													
2014	289.84	294.95	306.15	313.10	306.50	310.34	313.88	308.64	299.12	304.04	301.04	295.56	303.62
2015	292.74	301.70	310.71	313.82	310.12	313.90	317.20	319.73	303.66	307.00	305.50	306.28	308.99
2016	301.35	305.29	313.94	318.63	324.53	330.28	331.95	328.49	320.26	310.25	315.76	313.47	318.21
2017	308.21	310.75	317.99	333.56	325.88	331.32	335.71	330.79	311.74	329.45	325.89	321.78	324.59
2018	313.69	328.96	334.10	338.00	331.78	334.80	341.28	342.91	309.35	338.94	337.82	340.75	333.06
Other Services													
2014	512.62	484.08	500.96	500.83	486.39	469.95	452.82	464.74	464.01	467.38	471.53	478.89	479.86
2015	481.09	486.60	504.24	510.93	512.31	507.47	514.49	508.49	503.82	512.38	518.44	541.08	507.94
2016	561.79	574.62	567.33	603.03	597.60	603.79	624.02	603.76	616.97	629.67	652.00	665.52	609.08
2017	698.01	712.74	710.01	736.04	714.19	712.88	733.94	715.04	746.00	744.59	738.73	726.38	723.07
2018	775.50	769.23	762.89	770.21	766.92	742.59	777.89	765.88	751.28	756.38	785.23	809.25	768.18

SOUTH DAKOTA
At a Glance

Population:
  2010 census: 814,180
  2018 estimate: 882,235

Percent change in population:
  2010–2018: 8.4%

Percent change in total nonfarm employment:
  2010–2018: 8.9%

Industry with the largest growth in employment, 2010–2018 (percent):
  Manufacturing, 20.3%

Industry with the largest decline or smallest growth in employment, 2010–2018 (percent):
  Information, -13.8%

Civilian labor force:
  2010: 441,339
  2018: 459,459

Unemployment rate and rank among states (highest to lowest):
  2010: 5.0%, 49th
  2018: 3.0%, 41st

Over-the-year change in unemployment rates:
  2016–2017: 0.2%
  2017–2018: -0.2%

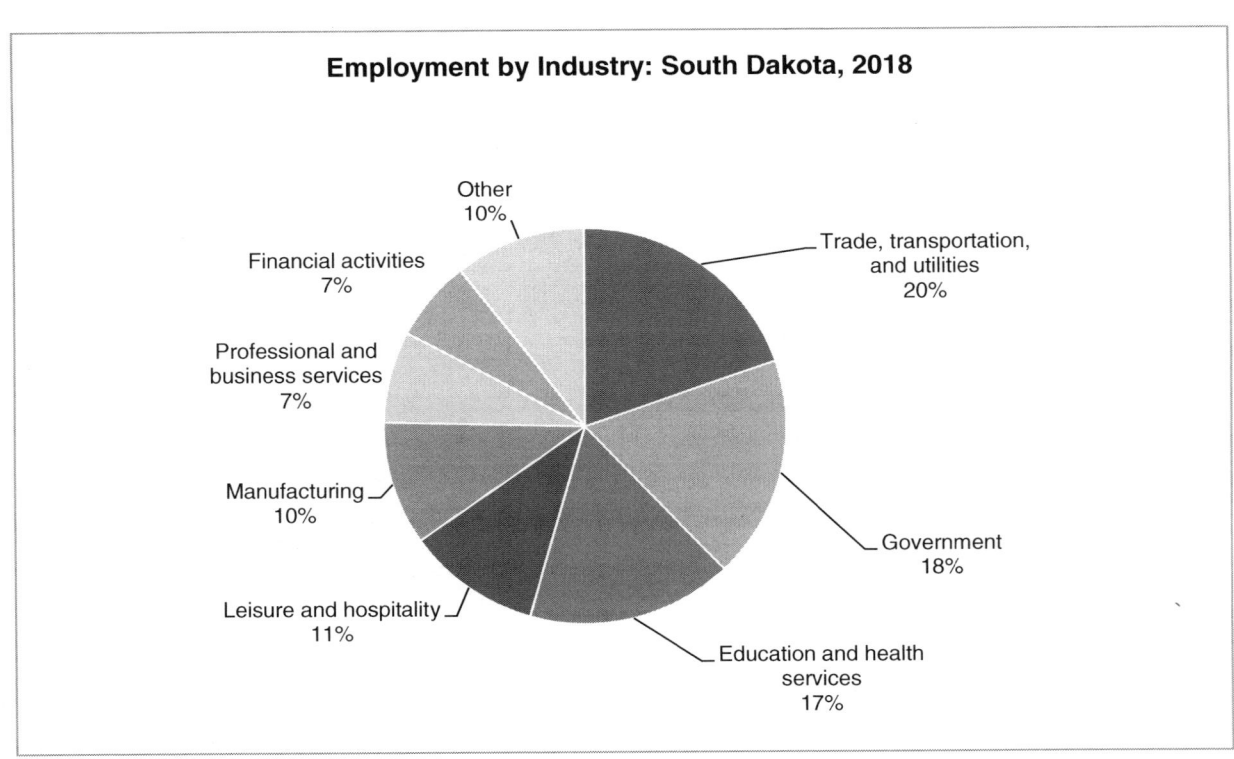

Employment by Industry: South Dakota, 2018

- Other 10%
- Financial activities 7%
- Professional and business services 7%
- Manufacturing 10%
- Leisure and hospitality 11%
- Trade, transportation, and utilities 20%
- Government 18%
- Education and health services 17%

1. Employment by Industry: South Dakota, 2010–2018

(Numbers in thousands, not seasonally adjusted)

Industry and year	January	February	March	April	May	June	July	August	September	October	November	December	Annual average
Total Nonfarm													
2010	388.2	389.2	392.0	399.6	407.3	413.0	409.0	411.6	407.8	408.6	407.1	405.2	403.2
2011	393.0	394.3	396.8	403.4	411.4	417.3	412.9	414.8	412.6	413.0	411.3	411.3	407.7
2012	399.9	400.6	404.8	411.3	418.9	424.6	419.1	420.8	418.7	418.1	417.2	415.6	414.1
2013	404.7	406.0	408.9	411.6	423.5	427.5	422.3	424.6	422.4	422.3	421.9	420.1	418.0
2014	410.4	411.8	414.1	419.5	429.2	434.0	429.5	431.4	429.1	428.1	426.0	425.8	424.1
2015	414.6	416.5	419.9	425.6	433.8	438.9	434.1	434.9	432.4	432.3	430.9	430.5	428.7
2016	418.5	420.4	423.3	429.5	437.1	442.2	438.6	439.5	436.9	435.7	434.6	432.5	432.4
2017	421.4	422.8	425.7	431.8	439.3	444.2	437.8	440.1	437.9	438.0	436.2	435.6	434.2
2018	425.0	427.0	429.8	431.8	443.4	448.4	443.0	445.5	443.4	443.3	443.3	442.8	438.9
Total Private													
2010	311.2	310.8	312.6	319.7	326.1	332.7	333.9	336.3	329.2	329.0	327.3	325.8	324.6
2011	315.4	315.4	317.7	324.0	331.5	337.3	338.6	341.4	335.3	334.3	332.5	332.3	329.6
2012	323.0	322.9	326.4	332.6	340.0	346.0	345.7	347.8	341.4	339.0	338.1	336.9	336.7
2013	327.8	327.7	330.5	333.6	344.7	350.1	349.7	351.3	344.5	343.6	343.0	341.7	340.7
2014	333.3	333.7	335.6	340.8	349.8	355.5	355.8	357.2	350.7	349.0	346.8	347.1	346.3
2015	337.9	338.6	341.5	346.9	354.1	359.9	360.0	361.3	354.3	353.4	351.7	351.4	350.9
2016	341.4	341.9	344.4	350.1	356.9	362.7	364.6	365.3	357.6	355.8	354.6	352.4	354.0
2017	343.2	343.4	346.0	352.0	358.2	363.9	363.2	365.0	358.1	357.6	355.8	355.4	355.2
2018	346.7	347.4	349.6	351.8	361.8	367.6	367.9	369.9	363.0	362.1	362.1	361.8	359.3
Goods Producing													
2010	53.2	52.8	53.2	56.3	57.9	60.1	61.2	61.3	60.5	60.7	59.9	58.0	57.9
2011	54.8	54.6	55.3	58.2	60.9	62.8	63.5	63.5	63.0	63.2	62.2	60.7	60.2
2012	58.4	58.2	59.2	61.5	63.3	65.0	65.1	64.9	64.0	63.6	62.9	61.4	62.3
2013	59.0	58.5	59.3	60.7	64.1	66.0	66.0	65.9	64.8	64.6	63.8	62.2	62.9
2014	59.8	59.8	60.5	62.5	65.2	67.2	67.6	67.5	66.7	66.7	65.6	64.7	64.5
2015	62.3	62.0	63.1	65.0	66.9	68.4	68.4	68.0	67.1	66.8	65.9	64.8	65.7
2016	61.8	61.6	62.7	64.6	66.6	69.4	70.0	68.9	67.6	67.1	66.2	64.6	65.9
2017	61.9	62.1	62.7	65.2	66.9	69.1	69.3	69.3	68.3	68.1	67.5	66.8	66.4
2018	64.0	64.1	64.8	66.1	68.8	70.8	71.2	71.0	70.4	70.0	69.7	68.9	68.3
Service-Providing													
2010	335.0	336.4	338.8	343.3	349.4	352.9	347.8	350.3	347.3	347.9	347.2	347.2	345.3
2011	338.2	339.7	341.5	345.2	350.5	354.5	349.4	351.3	349.6	349.8	349.1	350.6	347.5
2012	341.5	342.4	345.6	349.8	355.6	359.6	354.0	355.9	354.7	354.5	354.3	354.2	351.8
2013	345.7	347.5	349.6	350.9	359.4	361.5	356.3	358.7	357.6	357.7	358.1	357.9	355.1
2014	350.6	352.0	353.6	357.0	364.0	366.8	361.9	363.9	362.4	361.4	360.4	361.1	359.6
2015	352.3	354.5	356.8	360.6	366.9	370.5	365.7	366.9	365.3	365.5	365.0	365.7	363.0
2016	356.7	358.8	360.6	364.9	370.5	372.8	368.6	370.6	369.3	368.6	368.4	367.9	366.5
2017	359.5	360.7	363.0	366.6	372.4	375.1	368.5	370.8	369.6	369.9	368.7	368.8	367.8
2018	361.0	362.9	365.0	365.7	374.6	377.6	371.8	374.5	373.0	373.3	373.6	373.9	370.6
Mining and Logging													
2010	0.8	0.8	0.8	0.9	1.0	1.0	1.1	1.0	1.0	1.0	1.0	0.9	0.9
2011	0.8	0.8	0.8	0.9	1.0	1.1	1.1	1.1	1.1	1.0	1.0	0.9	1.0
2012	0.9	0.8	0.9	0.9	1.0	1.0	1.0	1.1	1.0	1.0	1.0	0.9	1.0
2013	0.8	0.8	0.8	0.9	1.0	1.0	1.0	1.0	1.0	0.9	0.9	0.9	0.9
2014	0.7	0.7	0.8	0.9	1.0	1.0	1.0	1.0	1.0	0.9	0.9	0.9	0.9
2015	0.8	0.8	0.8	0.9	1.0	1.0	1.0	1.0	1.0	1.0	1.0	0.9	0.9
2016	0.8	0.8	0.8	0.9	1.0	1.0	1.0	1.0	1.0	1.0	1.0	0.9	0.9
2017	0.8	0.8	0.9	1.0	1.0	1.1	1.1	1.1	1.0	1.0	1.0	0.9	1.0
2018	0.8	0.8	0.9	0.9	1.0	1.1	1.1	1.1	1.1	1.0	1.0	0.9	1.0
Construction													
2010	16.6	16.0	16.3	19.0	20.3	22.0	22.7	22.9	22.1	22.2	21.3	19.5	20.1
2011	16.6	16.2	16.5	18.8	20.7	22.2	22.7	22.6	22.1	22.1	20.9	19.6	20.1
2012	17.6	17.1	17.9	19.7	21.0	22.2	22.2	22.1	21.3	20.8	20.1	19.1	20.1
2013	17.0	16.6	17.2	18.5	21.4	22.8	23.1	23.2	22.4	22.1	21.5	20.0	20.5
2014	18.1	17.7	18.1	19.8	22.0	23.7	23.9	23.7	23.1	22.8	21.8	20.8	21.3
2015	18.7	18.6	19.7	21.6	23.2	24.5	24.8	24.4	23.5	23.2	22.4	21.4	22.2
2016	18.9	18.8	19.8	21.6	23.3	25.8	26.6	25.7	24.7	23.9	23.1	21.5	22.8
2017	19.2	19.1	19.6	21.8	23.1	24.5	24.6	24.5	23.8	23.5	22.8	22.0	22.4
2018	20.0	19.7	20.2	21.5	23.9	25.1	25.2	25.2	24.5	23.8	23.4	22.6	22.9

1. Employment by Industry: South Dakota, 2010–2018—*Continued*

(Numbers in thousands, not seasonally adjusted)

Industry and year	January	February	March	April	May	June	July	August	September	October	November	December	Annual average
Manufacturing													
2010	35.8	36.0	36.1	36.4	36.6	37.1	37.4	37.4	37.4	37.5	37.6	37.6	36.9
2011	37.4	37.6	38.0	38.5	39.2	39.5	39.7	39.8	39.8	40.1	40.3	40.2	39.2
2012	39.9	40.3	40.4	40.9	41.3	41.8	41.9	41.7	41.7	41.8	41.8	41.4	41.2
2013	41.2	41.1	41.3	41.3	41.7	42.2	41.9	41.7	41.4	41.6	41.4	41.3	41.5
2014	41.0	41.4	41.6	41.8	42.2	42.5	42.7	42.8	42.6	43.0	42.9	43.0	42.3
2015	42.8	42.6	42.6	42.5	42.7	42.9	42.6	42.6	42.6	42.6	42.5	42.5	42.6
2016	42.1	42.0	42.1	42.1	42.3	42.6	42.4	42.2	41.9	42.2	42.1	42.2	42.2
2017	41.9	42.2	42.2	42.4	42.8	43.5	43.6	43.7	43.5	43.6	43.7	43.9	43.1
2018	43.2	43.6	43.7	43.7	43.9	44.6	44.9	44.7	44.8	45.2	45.3	45.4	44.4
Trade, Transportation, and Utilities													
2010	78.7	78.0	78.5	79.6	80.7	81.6	81.4	81.8	80.2	81.0	81.9	82.2	80.5
2011	79.5	79.1	79.4	80.7	82.0	82.5	82.5	83.0	81.6	82.0	83.0	83.6	81.6
2012	81.0	80.2	80.9	81.8	83.3	84.0	83.6	84.1	82.9	83.0	84.2	84.4	82.8
2013	81.5	81.0	81.4	82.0	84.0	84.7	84.6	84.7	83.5	84.0	85.0	85.6	83.5
2014	83.4	83.1	83.4	84.3	85.7	86.8	87.1	87.4	85.9	86.1	86.9	87.6	85.6
2015	85.3	85.0	85.2	86.4	87.7	88.5	88.5	88.7	87.2	87.6	88.4	89.0	87.3
2016	86.6	86.3	86.5	87.5	88.7	89.2	89.3	89.3	87.3	87.6	88.6	88.6	88.0
2017	86.1	85.5	85.7	86.5	87.6	88.0	87.9	87.8	86.3	86.8	87.8	88.2	87.0
2018	85.4	84.9	85.1	85.1	87.2	87.5	87.5	87.6	86.4	86.7	88.9	89.1	86.8
Wholesale Trade													
2010	18.0	18.0	18.1	18.5	18.6	18.7	18.6	18.6	18.4	18.6	18.7	18.6	18.5
2011	18.3	18.3	18.5	18.7	19.1	19.1	19.1	19.0	18.8	19.0	19.0	19.1	18.8
2012	19.0	18.9	19.2	19.4	19.6	19.7	19.5	19.4	19.1	19.3	19.3	19.3	19.3
2013	19.2	19.2	19.4	19.6	20.2	20.2	20.1	19.9	19.6	19.8	20.0	20.0	19.8
2014	20.0	20.0	20.2	20.5	20.9	21.0	21.0	20.9	20.6	20.8	20.8	20.8	20.6
2015	20.6	20.6	20.8	21.0	21.3	21.3	21.2	21.1	20.8	21.0	21.0	21.0	21.0
2016	20.8	20.7	20.9	21.1	21.3	21.3	21.3	21.1	20.7	20.8	20.9	20.8	21.0
2017	20.5	20.4	20.7	20.9	21.1	21.1	21.0	20.9	20.5	20.7	20.7	20.8	20.8
2018	20.4	20.4	20.5	20.6	21.2	21.2	21.2	21.0	20.9	21.1	21.6	21.7	21.0
Retail Trade													
2010	48.5	47.9	48.2	48.7	49.5	50.2	50.3	50.6	49.1	49.7	50.5	50.9	49.5
2011	48.9	48.5	48.6	49.4	50.2	50.7	50.9	51.3	50.1	50.4	51.4	51.8	50.2
2012	49.8	49.1	49.4	50.2	51.2	51.7	51.6	52.2	51.0	51.0	52.2	52.4	51.0
2013	50.0	49.5	49.7	50.1	51.1	51.8	51.9	52.2	51.2	51.4	52.2	52.6	51.1
2014	50.7	50.3	50.4	50.9	51.6	52.6	53.0	53.2	52.0	51.9	52.8	53.3	51.9
2015	51.6	51.3	51.3	52.1	52.9	53.7	53.8	54.0	52.9	53.0	53.8	54.2	52.9
2016	52.5	52.4	52.4	53.2	54.0	54.6	54.8	54.9	53.3	53.5	54.4	54.4	53.7
2017	52.6	52.1	52.0	52.5	53.1	53.6	53.7	53.6	52.4	52.8	53.7	53.8	53.0
2018	51.8	51.5	51.6	51.4	52.5	52.8	53.0	53.1	51.9	52.0	53.7	53.6	52.4
Transportation and Utilities													
2010	12.2	12.1	12.2	12.4	12.6	12.7	12.5	12.6	12.7	12.7	12.7	12.7	12.5
2011	12.3	12.3	12.3	12.6	12.7	12.7	12.5	12.7	12.7	12.6	12.6	12.7	12.6
2012	12.2	12.2	12.3	12.2	12.5	12.6	12.5	12.5	12.8	12.7	12.7	12.7	12.5
2013	12.3	12.3	12.3	12.3	12.7	12.7	12.6	12.6	12.7	12.8	12.8	13.0	12.6
2014	12.7	12.8	12.8	12.9	13.2	13.2	13.1	13.3	13.3	13.4	13.3	13.5	13.1
2015	13.1	13.1	13.1	13.3	13.5	13.5	13.5	13.6	13.5	13.6	13.6	13.8	13.4
2016	13.3	13.2	13.2	13.2	13.4	13.3	13.2	13.3	13.3	13.3	13.3	13.4	13.3
2017	13.0	13.0	13.0	13.1	13.4	13.3	13.2	13.3	13.4	13.3	13.4	13.6	13.3
2018	13.2	13.0	13.0	13.1	13.5	13.5	13.3	13.5	13.6	13.6	13.6	13.8	13.4
Information													
2010	6.6	6.6	6.5	6.5	6.5	6.6	6.6	6.6	6.5	6.4	6.5	6.5	6.5
2011	6.4	6.4	6.4	6.3	6.4	6.5	6.5	6.5	6.4	6.4	6.3	6.3	6.4
2012	6.2	6.3	6.2	6.2	6.3	6.3	6.3	6.3	6.1	6.1	6.1	6.1	6.2
2013	6.0	6.0	6.0	6.0	6.1	6.1	6.1	6.2	6.0	5.9	6.0	6.0	6.0
2014	6.0	6.0	6.0	6.0	6.1	6.2	6.2	6.1	6.0	5.9	5.9	5.9	6.0
2015	5.8	5.8	5.8	5.9	5.9	5.9	5.9	6.0	5.8	5.8	5.8	5.9	5.9
2016	5.8	5.8	5.8	5.8	5.8	5.9	5.8	5.8	5.7	5.7	5.7	5.7	5.8
2017	5.8	5.7	5.7	5.6	5.8	5.8	5.8	5.8	5.7	5.7	5.7	5.7	5.7
2018	5.6	5.7	5.6	5.5	5.6	5.6	5.6	5.7	5.5	5.6	5.5	5.5	5.6

1. Employment by Industry: South Dakota, 2010–2018—*Continued*

(Numbers in thousands, not seasonally adjusted)

Industry and year	January	February	March	April	May	June	July	August	September	October	November	December	Annual average
Financial Activities													
2010	29.3	29.1	28.9	28.8	28.9	29.0	29.0	28.9	28.5	28.6	28.6	28.7	28.9
2011	28.3	28.3	28.3	28.1	28.1	28.3	28.1	28.1	27.9	27.9	27.9	28.2	28.1
2012	27.9	27.9	28.1	28.3	28.6	29.0	29.0	29.0	28.8	28.8	29.0	29.2	28.6
2013	29.1	29.3	29.4	29.4	29.7	30.1	30.0	30.0	29.8	29.8	30.0	30.1	29.7
2014	29.6	29.6	29.6	29.7	29.9	30.0	30.0	29.9	29.6	29.6	29.6	29.7	29.7
2015	29.4	29.3	29.4	29.4	29.6	29.9	30.1	29.9	29.7	29.7	29.7	29.8	29.7
2016	29.1	29.0	29.0	29.1	29.4	29.4	29.6	29.6	29.4	29.3	29.3	29.5	29.3
2017	29.0	28.9	29.0	29.1	29.3	29.5	29.5	29.5	29.3	29.3	29.3	29.4	29.3
2018	29.1	29.1	29.1	29.2	29.3	29.4	29.4	29.3	29.1	28.9	29.0	29.2	29.2
Professional and Business Services													
2010	26.3	26.5	26.7	27.7	27.8	28.0	28.3	28.4	27.9	28.2	28.0	28.2	27.7
2011	27.6	27.8	28.0	28.8	29.0	29.3	29.6	29.4	29.2	29.2	29.2	29.5	28.9
2012	28.4	28.5	28.8	29.3	29.4	29.8	30.0	30.1	29.7	29.4	29.3	29.3	29.3
2013	28.7	28.8	29.0	29.3	29.9	30.1	30.1	30.1	29.6	30.3	30.3	30.3	29.7
2014	29.6	29.6	29.6	30.5	31.0	31.3	31.4	31.1	30.5	30.5	30.5	30.5	30.5
2015	29.8	29.9	30.2	30.7	30.9	31.3	31.6	31.4	30.8	31.1	31.1	31.1	30.8
2016	30.4	30.6	30.6	31.4	31.7	32.1	32.2	32.0	31.4	31.5	31.6	31.7	31.4
2017	30.8	30.8	31.2	31.4	31.6	32.0	31.9	32.0	31.5	31.6	31.5	31.7	31.5
2018	31.1	31.5	31.7	31.9	32.3	32.9	33.3	33.3	32.8	33.0	33.5	34.0	32.6
Education and Health Services													
2010	63.5	63.8	64.1	64.2	64.6	64.5	64.3	64.1	64.5	65.0	65.2	65.6	64.5
2011	64.5	64.7	65.0	64.9	65.5	65.4	64.9	65.2	65.3	65.9	66.2	66.5	65.3
2012	65.6	65.9	66.3	67.1	67.5	67.6	66.9	66.9	67.3	67.6	68.0	68.1	67.1
2013	67.2	67.7	68.0	68.0	68.7	68.1	67.6	67.6	67.8	68.1	68.4	68.6	68.0
2014	67.7	68.1	68.3	68.4	68.9	68.6	68.0	67.9	68.1	68.4	68.5	69.0	68.3
2015	67.9	68.5	69.0	69.2	69.6	69.4	68.5	68.5	69.1	69.7	69.8	70.1	69.1
2016	69.1	69.6	70.0	70.1	70.5	69.9	69.8	70.0	70.6	70.8	71.2	71.5	70.3
2017	70.4	70.8	71.4	71.9	72.0	71.7	70.8	71.0	71.6	72.0	72.1	72.4	71.5
2018	72.1	72.3	72.7	72.5	73.1	72.8	71.9	72.5	72.8	73.4	73.4	74.2	72.8
Leisure and Hospitality													
2010	38.2	38.6	39.2	41.0	44.0	47.0	47.1	49.4	45.4	43.5	41.7	41.1	43.0
2011	38.9	39.2	39.8	41.4	43.9	46.5	47.5	49.6	46.2	43.9	42.0	41.7	43.4
2012	39.8	40.2	41.1	42.5	45.5	48.0	48.4	50.2	46.6	44.5	42.6	42.4	44.3
2013	40.4	40.5	41.4	42.1	45.8	48.5	48.8	50.5	46.9	44.9	43.4	42.9	44.7
2014	41.3	41.6	42.3	43.3	46.7	48.9	49.0	50.9	47.8	45.8	43.8	43.6	45.4
2015	41.5	42.1	42.8	44.1	47.2	49.8	50.2	52.1	48.4	46.4	44.8	44.4	46.2
2016	42.5	42.8	43.5	45.1	47.6	49.8	50.8	52.7	49.0	47.2	45.5	44.4	46.7
2017	42.9	43.3	43.9	45.7	48.2	50.5	50.8	52.6	48.7	47.4	45.3	44.6	47.0
2018	43.0	43.4	44.1	44.9	48.7	51.3	51.7	53.4	49.2	47.5	45.5	44.7	47.3
Other Services													
2010	15.4	15.4	15.5	15.6	15.7	15.9	16.0	15.8	15.7	15.6	15.5	15.5	15.6
2011	15.4	15.3	15.5	15.6	15.7	16.0	16.0	16.1	15.7	15.8	15.7	15.8	15.7
2012	15.7	15.7	15.8	15.9	16.1	16.3	16.4	16.3	16.0	16.0	16.0	16.0	16.0
2013	15.9	15.9	16.0	16.1	16.4	16.5	16.5	16.3	16.1	16.0	16.1	16.0	16.2
2014	15.9	15.9	15.9	16.1	16.3	16.5	16.5	16.4	16.1	16.0	16.0	16.1	16.1
2015	15.9	16.0	16.0	16.2	16.3	16.7	16.8	16.7	16.2	16.3	16.2	16.3	16.3
2016	16.1	16.2	16.3	16.5	16.6	17.0	17.1	17.0	16.6	16.6	16.5	16.4	16.6
2017	16.3	16.3	16.4	16.6	16.8	17.3	17.2	17.0	16.7	16.7	16.6	16.6	16.7
2018	16.4	16.4	16.5	16.6	16.8	17.3	17.3	17.1	16.8	17.0	16.6	16.2	16.8
Government													
2010	77.0	78.4	79.4	79.9	81.2	80.3	75.1	75.3	78.6	79.6	79.8	79.4	78.7
2011	77.6	78.9	79.1	79.4	79.9	80.0	74.3	73.4	77.3	78.7	78.8	79.0	78.0
2012	76.9	77.7	78.4	78.7	78.9	78.6	73.4	73.0	77.3	79.1	79.1	78.7	77.5
2013	76.9	78.3	78.4	78.0	78.8	77.4	72.6	73.3	77.9	78.7	78.9	78.4	77.3
2014	77.1	78.1	78.5	78.7	79.4	78.5	73.7	74.2	78.4	79.1	79.2	78.7	77.8
2015	76.7	77.9	78.4	78.7	79.7	79.0	74.1	73.6	78.1	78.9	79.2	79.1	77.8
2016	77.1	78.5	78.9	79.4	80.2	79.5	74.0	74.2	79.3	79.9	80.0	80.1	78.4
2017	78.2	79.4	79.7	79.8	81.1	80.3	74.6	75.1	79.8	80.4	80.4	80.2	79.1
2018	78.3	79.6	80.2	80.0	81.6	80.8	75.1	75.6	80.4	81.2	81.2	81.0	79.6

2. Average Weekly Hours by Selected Industry: South Dakota, 2014–2018

(Not seasonally adjusted)

Industry and year	January	February	March	April	May	June	July	August	September	October	November	December	Annual average
Total Private													
2014	33.7	34.5	34.6	34.1	34.5	35.1	34.4	34.6	34.2	34.3	34.3	34.0	34.4
2015	33.5	34.2	34.0	33.8	33.7	34.2	34.3	34.7	33.9	34.1	34.4	33.5	34.0
2016	33.6	33.4	33.6	33.9	34.5	34.6	34.4	34.1	34.1	34.5	34.0	33.1	34.0
2017	33.7	33.2	33.2	33.9	34.0	34.0	34.3	33.8	33.6	34.0	33.4	33.1	33.7
2018	33.2	33.1	33.0	33.3	33.7	34.2	34.4	33.8	34.4	33.4	33.6	34.0	33.7
Goods-Producing													
2014	39.8	40.6	40.3	40.8	41.4	40.8	40.4	40.7	40.3	40.9	39.9	39.9	40.5
2015	38.6	39.5	39.5	39.6	39.9	40.2	41.1	41.2	40.2	40.7	40.8	39.7	40.1
2016	39.9	39.5	39.7	40.8	41.3	41.2	41.5	41.6	41.2	42.0	41.7	39.5	40.8
2017	40.7	39.5	39.8	40.5	42.0	42.1	41.6	41.3	40.7	41.4	40.9	40.6	40.9
2018	40.5	39.9	39.5	39.5	39.9	41.3	41.5	40.8	41.7	40.2	40.9	41.0	40.6
Mining, Logging, and Construction													
2014	36.1	38.7	38.1	40.9	41.2	39.8	40.5	39.6	38.5	38.4	37.9	37.4	39.0
2015	36.5	36.9	37.8	38.1	38.3	40.0	41.4	41.3	40.4	41.2	39.6	37.9	39.3
2016	37.6	37.8	38.4	39.8	40.0	40.5	41.1	41.5	41.2	42.7	41.2	37.8	40.1
2017	37.8	38.5	37.8	38.9	42.1	42.3	42.3	41.6	41.3	42.3	40.7	39.9	40.6
2018	37.8	38.3	38.4	38.4	41.4	43.5	44.1	42.9	43.6	39.7	41.3	40.3	41.0
Manufacturing													
2014	41.5	41.5	41.3	40.7	41.4	41.3	40.4	41.3	41.4	42.2	41.1	41.3	41.3
2015	39.6	40.5	40.2	40.3	40.9	40.2	40.9	41.1	40.1	40.5	41.4	40.6	40.5
2016	40.9	40.2	40.3	41.3	42.1	41.6	41.6	41.6	41.1	41.6	42.0	40.6	41.2
2017	42.1	40.0	40.7	41.4	41.9	42.0	41.1	41.2	40.4	40.9	41.1	41.0	41.1
2018	41.8	40.6	40.1	40.1	39.0	40.1	40.0	39.6	40.6	40.4	40.8	41.4	40.4
Trade, Transportation, and Utilities													
2014	32.9	33.0	33.2	33.7	34.6	35.0	34.3	34.5	34.0	34.5	34.5	34.2	34.0
2015	33.6	34.3	34.2	33.9	34.1	34.5	34.3	34.7	34.0	33.8	34.2	33.1	34.1
2016	32.9	32.8	33.0	33.1	34.0	34.1	33.8	33.3	33.6	33.7	33.2	32.5	33.3
2017	32.8	32.5	32.5	33.4	33.8	34.0	34.4	33.7	33.7	33.7	33.1	32.9	33.4
2018	32.7	32.7	32.7	33.0	34.6	34.8	34.9	34.4	35.0	34.1	33.9	34.1	33.9
Professional and Business Services													
2014	35.6	37.1	36.5	35.9	35.8	36.1	34.9	35.2	35.0	34.9	35.7	35.6	35.7
2015	35.8	37.3	36.9	36.9	36.2	37.0	36.3	37.0	36.3	36.3	36.6	35.5	36.5
2016	35.9	36.1	36.2	36.7	38.0	37.4	36.6	36.8	36.9	37.6	36.8	35.8	36.7
2017	36.5	36.8	36.3	36.3	35.6	35.4	35.5	35.1	35.7	35.9	35.2	35.0	35.8
2018	34.3	35.3	35.8	36.1	36.1	36.0	35.6	35.1	36.3	36.0	35.8	35.9	35.7
Education and Health Services													
2014	31.2	32.3	32.9	31.4	31.2	32.8	31.7	32.8	32.3	31.7	32.3	32.2	32.1
2015	32.3	32.7	32.4	32.2	31.7	32.0	31.8	32.7	32.3	32.4	33.1	32.6	32.3
2016	32.7	32.2	32.1	32.1	32.0	32.1	32.3	31.9	32.1	32.5	31.7	31.8	32.1
2017	31.9	31.4	31.3	31.9	31.2	31.4	32.3	30.9	31.3	32.0	31.1	31.1	31.5
2018	31.5	31.4	30.7	31.3	31.0	31.3	31.7	31.6	31.6	30.5	30.7	31.5	31.2
Leisure and Hospitality													
2014	22.5	23.7	24.0	23.0	23.4	25.6	25.3	25.1	24.2	24.0	23.7	23.3	24.0
2015	22.6	24.0	23.9	23.1	23.4	25.0	25.5	26.1	24.5	24.1	24.2	23.5	24.2
2016	23.6	23.7	24.1	24.1	25.0	25.4	25.5	26.1	24.7	24.8	23.3	23.1	24.5
2017	23.9	23.7	23.9	24.3	24.0	25.6	26.1	25.9	24.5	23.9	22.9	22.7	24.3
2018	23.0	22.8	23.6	23.3	24.3	25.5	26.0	25.4	24.6	23.4	22.3	22.6	24.0

3. Average Hourly Earnings by Selected Industry: South Dakota, 2014–2018

(Dollars, not seasonally adjusted)

Industry and year	January	February	March	April	May	June	July	August	September	October	November	December	Annual average
Total Private													
2014	20.00	20.13	20.10	20.17	20.15	19.87	19.89	19.94	20.22	20.45	20.61	20.57	20.17
2015	20.94	20.93	20.88	20.91	20.99	20.72	20.68	20.79	21.04	21.32	21.23	21.39	20.98
2016	21.34	21.18	21.18	21.41	21.28	20.80	21.15	21.13	21.60	21.74	21.72	21.95	21.37
2017	22.13	22.21	22.04	22.10	21.83	21.56	21.67	21.66	22.02	22.12	21.97	22.20	21.95
2018	22.11	22.26	22.18	22.57	22.37	22.23	22.77	22.58	23.00	22.90	22.92	23.44	22.62
Goods-Producing													
2014	19.97	20.29	20.01	20.14	20.42	20.35	20.42	20.59	20.74	21.04	20.88	20.95	20.49
2015	21.85	21.77	21.60	21.63	21.49	21.55	21.31	21.58	21.54	21.96	21.78	22.05	21.67
2016	21.52	21.20	21.52	21.57	21.56	21.59	22.06	21.66	22.11	22.13	21.94	22.51	21.79
2017	22.84	22.61	22.67	22.49	22.65	22.36	22.29	22.29	22.30	22.31	22.02	22.41	22.43
2018	22.27	22.57	22.56	22.69	22.74	22.83	23.05	22.92	22.86	22.69	22.84	22.97	22.76
Mining, Logging, and Construction													
2014	20.99	21.28	21.15	20.98	21.27	20.38	20.90	21.42	21.99	22.52	21.11	22.03	21.34
2015	22.56	22.54	22.65	22.71	22.25	22.55	22.18	22.49	22.40	22.77	22.68	23.18	22.57
2016	22.83	22.89	22.82	22.74	22.96	22.82	23.02	22.89	23.13	23.59	23.31	24.30	23.11
2017	24.64	24.47	24.46	24.26	24.27	23.80	24.08	23.82	23.68	23.83	23.63	24.34	24.07
2018	25.12	25.17	24.90	25.25	24.70	24.87	24.93	25.22	25.23	25.23	25.31	25.92	25.15
Manufacturing													
2014	19.56	19.88	19.53	19.73	19.95	20.33	20.14	20.13	20.09	20.30	20.77	20.46	20.08
2015	21.55	21.45	21.12	21.09	21.09	20.96	20.78	21.04	21.04	21.49	21.31	21.50	21.20
2016	20.95	20.46	20.92	20.96	20.79	20.84	21.44	20.88	21.48	21.24	21.17	21.63	21.06
2017	22.07	21.76	21.86	21.60	21.74	21.51	21.20	21.39	21.49	21.42	21.15	21.43	21.55
2018	21.03	21.42	21.48	21.44	21.57	21.53	21.84	21.46	21.41	21.32	21.49	21.48	21.46
Trade, Transportation, and Utilities													
2014	19.26	19.43	19.32	19.55	19.65	19.32	19.39	19.36	19.42	19.50	19.87	19.91	19.50
2015	19.77	19.56	19.50	19.40	19.91	19.75	19.87	19.91	20.17	20.19	20.04	20.09	19.85
2016	20.14	19.96	19.82	20.38	20.47	19.70	20.15	20.24	20.42	20.53	20.62	20.69	20.26
2017	20.86	21.08	20.66	20.88	20.48	20.35	20.68	21.10	21.14	21.44	21.51	21.54	20.97
2018	21.60	21.52	21.23	21.57	21.28	21.27	21.96	21.86	22.29	21.97	22.09	22.52	21.77
Professional and Business Services													
2014	24.55	24.28	24.61	24.36	24.13	23.65	23.78	23.12	24.02	24.17	24.33	24.47	24.12
2015	24.42	24.43	24.69	24.68	24.23	24.05	24.57	24.73	24.80	24.96	24.98	24.64	24.60
2016	24.28	23.89	24.19	24.49	24.11	24.44	24.97	25.02	25.66	26.00	25.88	26.34	24.95
2017	26.09	26.48	26.85	27.00	27.18	27.18	27.32	26.87	27.27	26.88	26.99	27.05	26.93
2018	26.55	27.24	27.08	27.42	27.34	27.71	27.94	27.74	28.26	28.02	27.33	27.48	27.52
Education and Health Services													
2014	20.60	20.65	20.88	20.75	20.81	20.61	20.74	21.40	21.30	21.54	21.64	21.46	21.03
2015	21.81	22.31	22.08	22.12	22.42	22.04	22.08	22.42	22.73	22.99	22.76	22.81	22.38
2016	23.80	23.73	23.04	23.03	22.96	22.82	23.25	23.21	23.66	23.79	23.56	23.41	23.36
2017	23.68	23.44	23.14	22.90	22.47	22.32	22.18	22.12	22.36	22.17	22.11	22.24	22.59
2018	22.19	21.78	21.61	21.75	21.78	21.55	21.86	21.45	21.44	21.62	21.66	21.84	21.71
Leisure and Hospitality													
2014	12.50	12.39	12.50	12.45	12.26	11.97	11.88	11.98	12.32	12.52	12.56	12.76	12.32
2015	13.10	13.01	13.10	13.15	12.88	12.33	12.52	12.63	12.88	12.99	13.14	13.04	12.87
2016	13.27	13.16	13.27	13.25	13.18	12.91	13.04	13.05	13.52	13.40	13.51	13.52	13.25
2017	13.63	13.65	13.65	13.66	13.69	13.33	13.47	13.49	13.82	14.10	14.02	14.28	13.72
2018	14.19	14.35	14.42	14.33	14.07	13.79	13.83	13.94	14.01	14.04	14.18	14.62	14.12

4. Average Weekly Earnings by Selected Industry: South Dakota, 2014–2018

(Dollars, not seasonally adjusted)

Industry and year	January	February	March	April	May	June	July	August	September	October	November	December	Annual average
Total Private													
2014	674.00	694.49	695.46	687.80	695.18	697.44	684.22	689.92	691.52	701.44	706.92	699.38	693.85
2015	701.49	715.81	709.92	706.76	707.36	708.62	709.32	721.41	713.26	727.01	730.31	716.57	713.32
2016	717.02	707.41	711.65	725.80	734.16	719.68	727.56	720.53	736.56	750.03	738.48	726.55	726.58
2017	745.78	737.37	731.73	749.19	742.22	733.04	743.28	732.11	739.87	752.08	733.80	734.82	739.72
2018	734.05	736.81	731.94	751.58	753.87	760.27	783.29	763.20	791.20	764.86	770.11	796.96	762.29
Goods-Producing													
2014	794.81	823.77	806.40	821.71	845.39	830.28	824.97	838.01	835.82	860.54	833.11	835.91	829.85
2015	843.41	859.92	853.20	856.55	857.45	866.31	875.84	889.10	865.91	893.77	888.62	875.39	868.97
2016	858.65	837.40	854.34	880.06	890.43	889.51	915.49	901.06	910.93	929.46	914.90	889.15	889.03
2017	929.59	893.10	902.27	910.85	951.30	941.36	927.26	920.58	907.61	923.63	900.62	909.85	917.39
2018	901.94	900.54	891.12	896.26	907.33	942.88	956.58	935.14	953.26	912.14	934.16	941.77	924.06
Mining, Logging, and Construction													
2014	757.74	823.54	805.82	858.08	876.32	811.12	846.45	848.23	846.62	864.77	800.07	823.92	832.26
2015	823.44	831.73	856.17	865.25	852.18	902.00	918.25	928.84	904.96	938.12	898.13	878.52	887.00
2016	858.41	865.24	876.29	905.05	918.40	924.21	946.12	949.94	952.96	1,007.29	960.37	918.54	926.71
2017	931.39	942.10	924.59	943.71	1,021.77	1,006.74	1,018.58	990.91	977.98	1,008.01	961.74	971.17	977.24
2018	949.54	964.01	956.16	969.60	1,022.58	1,081.85	1,099.41	1,081.94	1,100.03	1,001.63	1,045.30	1,044.58	1,031.15
Manufacturing													
2014	811.74	825.02	806.59	803.01	825.93	839.63	813.66	831.37	831.73	856.66	853.65	845.00	829.30
2015	853.38	868.73	849.02	849.93	862.58	842.59	849.90	864.74	843.70	870.35	882.23	872.90	858.60
2016	856.86	822.49	843.08	865.65	875.26	866.94	891.90	868.61	882.83	883.58	889.14	878.18	867.67
2017	929.15	870.40	889.70	894.24	910.91	903.42	871.32	881.27	868.20	876.08	869.27	878.63	885.71
2018	879.05	869.65	861.35	859.74	841.23	863.35	873.60	849.82	869.25	861.33	876.79	889.27	866.98
Trade, Transportation, and Utilities													
2014	633.65	641.19	641.42	658.84	679.89	676.20	665.08	667.92	660.28	672.75	685.52	680.92	663.00
2015	664.27	670.91	666.90	657.66	678.93	681.38	681.54	690.88	685.78	682.42	685.37	664.98	676.89
2016	662.61	654.69	654.06	674.58	695.98	671.77	681.07	673.99	686.11	691.86	684.58	672.43	674.66
2017	684.21	685.10	671.45	697.39	692.22	691.90	711.39	711.07	712.42	722.53	711.98	708.67	700.40
2018	706.32	703.70	694.22	711.81	736.29	740.20	766.40	751.98	780.15	749.18	748.85	767.93	738.00
Professional and Business Services													
2014	873.98	900.79	898.27	874.52	863.85	853.77	829.92	813.82	840.70	843.53	868.58	871.13	861.08
2015	874.24	911.24	911.06	910.69	877.13	889.85	891.89	915.01	900.24	906.05	914.27	874.72	897.90
2016	871.65	862.43	875.68	898.78	916.18	914.06	913.90	920.74	946.85	977.60	952.38	942.97	915.67
2017	952.29	974.46	974.66	980.10	967.61	962.17	969.86	943.14	973.54	964.99	950.05	946.75	964.09
2018	910.67	961.57	969.46	989.86	986.97	997.56	994.66	973.67	1,025.84	1,008.72	978.41	986.53	982.46
Education and Health Services													
2014	642.72	667.00	686.95	651.55	649.27	676.01	657.46	701.92	687.99	682.82	698.97	691.01	675.06
2015	704.46	729.54	715.39	712.26	710.71	705.28	702.14	733.13	734.18	744.88	753.36	743.61	722.87
2016	778.26	764.11	739.58	739.26	734.72	732.52	750.98	740.40	759.49	773.18	746.85	744.44	749.86
2017	755.39	736.02	724.28	730.51	701.06	700.85	716.41	683.51	699.87	709.44	687.62	691.66	711.59
2018	698.99	683.89	663.43	680.78	675.18	674.52	692.96	677.82	677.50	659.41	664.96	687.96	677.35
Leisure and Hospitality													
2014	281.25	293.64	300.00	286.35	286.88	306.43	300.56	300.70	298.14	300.48	297.67	297.31	295.68
2015	296.06	312.24	313.09	303.77	301.39	308.25	319.26	329.64	315.56	313.06	317.99	306.44	311.45
2016	313.17	311.89	319.81	319.33	329.50	327.91	332.52	340.61	333.94	332.32	314.78	312.31	324.63
2017	325.76	323.51	326.24	331.94	328.56	341.25	351.57	349.39	338.59	336.99	321.06	324.16	333.40
2018	326.37	327.18	340.31	333.89	341.90	351.65	359.58	354.08	344.65	328.54	316.21	330.41	338.88

TENNESSEE
At a Glance

Population:
  2010 census: 6,346,105
  2018 estimate: 6,770,010

Percent change in population:
  2010–2018: 6.7%

Percent change in total nonfarm employment:
  2010–2018: 17.0%

Industry with the largest growth in employment, 2010–2018 (percent):
  Professional and business services, 35.3%

Industry with the largest decline or smallest growth in employment, 2010–2018 (percent):
  Information, 0.4%

Civilian labor force:
  2010: 3,090,795
  2018: 3,244,921

Unemployment rate and rank among states (highest to lowest):
  2010: 9.7%, 18th
  2018: 3.5%, 31st

Over-the-year change in unemployment rates:
  2016–2017: -0.9%
  2017–2018: -0.3%

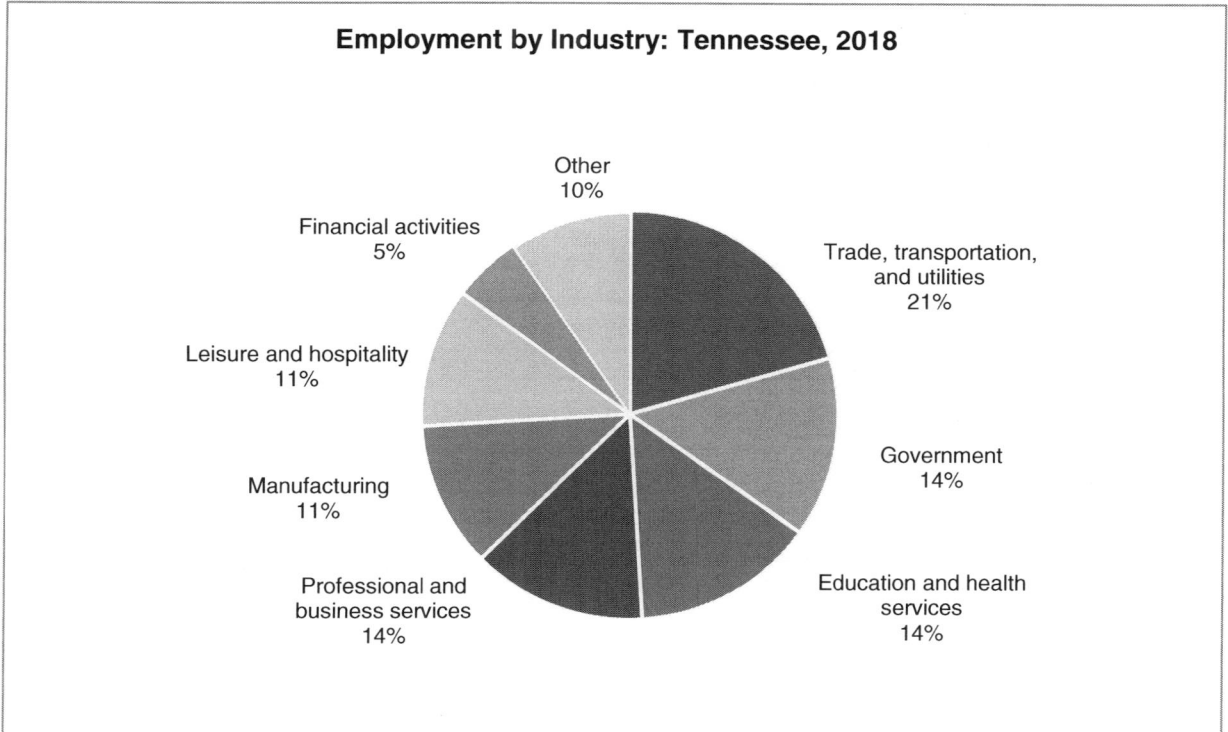

Employment by Industry: Tennessee, 2018

- Other 10%
- Financial activities 5%
- Leisure and hospitality 11%
- Manufacturing 11%
- Professional and business services 14%
- Education and health services 14%
- Government 14%
- Trade, transportation, and utilities 21%

1. Employment by Industry: Tennessee, 2010–2018

(Numbers in thousands, not seasonally adjusted)

Industry and year	January	February	March	April	May	June	July	August	September	October	November	December	Annual average
Total Nonfarm													
2010	2,556.9	2,562.3	2,584.9	2,614.8	2,637.8	2,613.1	2,600.4	2,619.3	2,635.3	2,645.4	2,657.1	2,655.2	2,615.2
2011	2,587.6	2,609.2	2,632.2	2,660.8	2,669.3	2,646.3	2,642.6	2,670.2	2,688.1	2,697.0	2,716.2	2,715.5	2,661.3
2012	2,649.0	2,667.2	2,698.8	2,715.3	2,724.7	2,705.7	2,687.6	2,714.7	2,734.0	2,745.3	2,766.3	2,768.8	2,714.8
2013	2,691.1	2,711.2	2,733.1	2,757.2	2,766.6	2,744.7	2,729.1	2,758.1	2,778.5	2,795.7	2,825.5	2,827.7	2,759.9
2014	2,752.4	2,764.4	2,791.5	2,815.2	2,824.8	2,800.2	2,792.3	2,825.3	2,847.5	2,863.5	2,890.5	2,897.3	2,822.1
2015	2,821.0	2,831.4	2,845.4	2,880.7	2,894.9	2,875.3	2,871.9	2,895.2	2,922.1	2,945.1	2,967.0	2,973.9	2,893.7
2016	2,897.9	2,914.4	2,938.0	2,963.0	2,963.0	2,944.6	2,940.3	2,967.9	2,997.9	3,003.2	3,025.2	3,028.4	2,965.3
2017	2,947.2	2,973.5	2,987.2	3,008.7	3,010.8	2,994.5	2,984.0	3,008.2	3,035.4	3,044.3	3,071.7	3,070.0	3,011.3
2018	2,988.3	3,015.4	3,034.7	3,052.2	3,061.6	3,044.3	3,029.7	3,063.9	3,087.3	3,102.8	3,126.2	3,117.0	3,060.3
Total Private													
2010	2,128.5	2,129.7	2,150.5	2,176.2	2,190.3	2,201.8	2,193.6	2,200.4	2,199.2	2,207.1	2,218.1	2,219.4	2,184.6
2011	2,158.5	2,174.9	2,196.7	2,225.9	2,236.3	2,246.3	2,246.5	2,255.8	2,258.6	2,263.5	2,281.8	2,283.8	2,235.7
2012	2,226.7	2,236.9	2,265.4	2,282.5	2,297.8	2,310.2	2,295.2	2,309.9	2,308.8	2,314.0	2,333.1	2,336.6	2,293.1
2013	2,273.0	2,284.1	2,304.4	2,320.2	2,334.9	2,346.7	2,335.3	2,351.6	2,351.4	2,361.1	2,390.7	2,393.4	2,337.2
2014	2,329.3	2,333.1	2,358.5	2,381.1	2,395.0	2,404.1	2,398.2	2,417.7	2,417.8	2,428.1	2,451.5	2,460.0	2,397.9
2015	2,395.6	2,398.6	2,412.9	2,447.0	2,465.4	2,478.1	2,477.2	2,486.4	2,489.9	2,506.9	2,528.5	2,536.8	2,468.6
2016	2,472.4	2,479.9	2,499.0	2,527.1	2,533.0	2,546.0	2,544.6	2,554.3	2,560.4	2,562.3	2,580.9	2,587.6	2,537.3
2017	2,520.4	2,535.7	2,548.6	2,569.2	2,576.5	2,592.0	2,584.2	2,593.7	2,595.6	2,601.3	2,626.6	2,627.2	2,580.9
2018	2,556.7	2,573.9	2,591.6	2,608.1	2,621.2	2,635.8	2,625.7	2,642.3	2,642.9	2,654.9	2,675.2	2,669.1	2,624.8
Goods Producing													
2010	391.3	389.5	394.2	400.5	402.7	407.4	406.2	407.8	407.8	406.7	405.8	404.4	402.0
2011	395.3	398.4	402.9	407.6	410.1	415.0	415.7	416.5	417.9	418.9	419.2	415.7	411.1
2012	407.9	409.9	415.3	417.6	420.5	424.9	422.8	426.3	425.3	424.0	424.1	423.0	420.1
2013	415.0	417.0	419.8	420.7	423.6	426.1	424.7	427.6	428.0	429.2	429.6	428.4	424.1
2014	422.4	424.0	427.6	429.7	432.8	434.2	434.2	438.3	438.3	439.2	441.2	442.3	433.7
2015	436.2	437.5	437.9	443.5	447.6	450.5	450.2	452.2	454.0	455.3	455.3	455.8	448.0
2016	450.3	451.0	455.4	457.7	459.5	463.4	464.1	464.9	465.8	464.9	465.5	467.3	460.8
2017	461.4	465.2	467.2	469.9	471.0	474.1	473.0	474.0	473.1	471.9	473.2	473.5	470.6
2018	467.5	469.7	473.2	476.0	477.9	482.3	482.5	485.0	486.0	486.9	487.0	484.6	479.9
Service-Providing													
2010	2,165.6	2,172.8	2,190.7	2,214.3	2,235.1	2,205.7	2,194.2	2,211.5	2,227.5	2,238.7	2,251.3	2,250.8	2,213.2
2011	2,192.3	2,210.8	2,229.3	2,253.2	2,259.2	2,231.3	2,226.9	2,253.7	2,270.2	2,278.1	2,297.0	2,299.8	2,250.2
2012	2,241.1	2,257.3	2,283.5	2,297.7	2,304.2	2,280.8	2,264.8	2,288.4	2,308.7	2,321.3	2,342.2	2,345.8	2,294.7
2013	2,276.1	2,294.2	2,313.3	2,336.5	2,343.0	2,318.6	2,304.4	2,330.5	2,350.5	2,366.5	2,395.9	2,399.3	2,335.7
2014	2,330.0	2,340.4	2,363.9	2,385.5	2,392.0	2,366.0	2,358.1	2,387.0	2,409.2	2,424.3	2,449.3	2,455.0	2,388.4
2015	2,384.8	2,393.9	2,407.5	2,437.2	2,447.3	2,424.8	2,421.7	2,443.0	2,468.1	2,489.8	2,511.7	2,518.1	2,445.7
2016	2,447.6	2,463.4	2,482.6	2,505.3	2,503.5	2,481.2	2,476.2	2,503.0	2,532.1	2,538.3	2,559.7	2,561.1	2,504.5
2017	2,485.8	2,508.3	2,520.0	2,538.8	2,539.8	2,520.4	2,511.0	2,534.2	2,562.3	2,572.4	2,598.5	2,596.5	2,540.7
2018	2,520.8	2,545.7	2,561.5	2,576.2	2,583.7	2,562.0	2,547.2	2,578.9	2,601.3	2,615.9	2,639.2	2,632.4	2,580.4
Mining and Logging													
2010	4.0	4.1	4.2	4.4	4.4	4.5	4.5	4.5	4.6	4.5	4.5	4.4	4.4
2011	4.1	4.2	4.4	4.4	4.4	4.7	4.5	4.6	4.6	4.5	4.4	4.4	4.4
2012	4.2	4.3	4.3	4.3	4.3	4.3	4.2	4.3	4.3	4.3	4.3	4.3	4.3
2013	4.2	4.3	4.4	4.4	4.4	4.4	4.3	4.4	4.3	4.3	4.2	4.2	4.3
2014	4.2	4.2	4.3	4.4	4.4	4.4	4.5	4.5	4.5	4.5	4.4	4.4	4.4
2015	4.3	4.5	4.4	4.6	4.6	4.6	4.5	4.5	4.5	4.5	4.5	4.5	4.5
2016	4.3	4.3	4.0	4.0	4.0	4.0	4.0	4.0	4.1	4.0	4.0	4.0	4.1
2017	4.0	4.1	4.0	4.1	4.2	4.3	4.2	4.2	4.3	4.2	4.3	4.3	4.2
2018	4.2	4.3	4.3	4.4	4.4	4.4	4.4	4.4	4.4	4.4	4.4	4.3	4.4
Construction													
2010	93.6	92.7	95.9	100.4	101.3	103.8	104.0	104.4	104.3	104.5	102.8	101.5	100.8
2011	93.8	95.6	98.8	102.6	103.9	106.7	107.6	108.5	109.8	109.5	108.4	106.3	104.3
2012	100.1	100.6	103.5	103.5	105.0	106.7	106.3	107.4	107.6	106.1	105.2	103.6	104.6
2013	98.0	99.3	100.8	102.3	104.3	105.5	105.5	105.9	106.1	106.4	105.6	103.8	103.6
2014	99.5	100.0	102.8	105.2	107.4	107.3	108.0	108.9	108.9	109.7	110.7	110.3	106.6
2015	105.8	106.4	106.9	110.6	113.1	114.4	115.4	115.3	116.2	117.4	116.2	114.9	112.7
2016	110.1	109.6	112.2	113.6	114.2	116.3	117.2	117.2	118.2	117.7	117.5	117.2	115.1
2017	113.7	115.6	117.4	119.4	120.7	122.1	122.2	122.8	122.5	122.0	122.2	121.5	120.2
2018	117.0	118.0	120.9	122.5	124.1	126.8	126.9	127.6	128.6	130.0	128.4	126.8	124.8

1. Employment by Industry: Tennessee, 2010–2018—*Continued*

(Numbers in thousands, not seasonally adjusted)

Industry and year	January	February	March	April	May	June	July	August	September	October	November	December	Annual average
Manufacturing													
2010	293.7	292.7	294.1	295.7	297.0	299.1	297.7	298.9	298.9	297.7	298.5	298.5	296.9
2011	297.4	298.6	299.7	300.6	301.8	303.6	303.6	303.4	303.5	304.9	306.4	305.0	302.4
2012	303.6	305.0	307.5	309.8	311.2	313.9	312.3	314.6	313.4	313.6	314.6	315.1	311.2
2013	312.8	313.4	314.6	314.0	314.9	316.2	314.9	317.3	317.6	318.5	319.8	320.4	316.2
2014	318.7	319.8	320.5	320.1	321.0	322.5	321.7	324.9	324.9	325.0	326.1	327.6	322.7
2015	326.1	326.6	326.6	328.3	329.9	331.5	330.3	332.4	333.3	333.4	334.6	336.4	330.8
2016	335.9	337.1	339.2	340.1	341.3	343.1	342.9	343.7	343.5	343.2	344.0	346.1	341.7
2017	343.7	345.5	345.8	346.4	346.1	347.7	346.6	347.0	346.3	345.7	346.7	347.7	346.3
2018	346.3	347.4	348.0	349.1	349.4	351.1	351.2	353.0	353.0	352.5	354.2	353.5	350.7
Trade, Transportation, and Utilities													
2010	544.7	542.1	545.6	548.6	550.6	552.1	552.7	554.3	552.5	556.7	566.5	571.2	553.1
2011	548.5	548.2	552.1	558.1	559.7	561.6	560.9	562.3	561.8	566.3	577.6	581.8	561.6
2012	563.0	559.7	566.0	568.5	571.3	572.2	570.7	572.4	574.0	576.7	589.8	593.5	573.2
2013	570.8	569.3	570.7	573.3	575.6	577.8	577.4	578.6	577.2	581.3	595.4	601.2	579.1
2014	575.4	573.6	578.0	582.0	583.4	585.9	586.3	588.9	588.6	593.8	606.7	611.2	587.8
2015	587.2	583.6	585.9	592.2	595.7	598.3	600.8	602.2	601.1	608.1	620.1	626.2	600.1
2016	605.0	603.8	606.1	611.0	611.7	613.0	615.2	615.9	615.2	619.0	632.3	635.2	615.3
2017	612.6	610.6	611.0	613.6	614.8	616.8	617.2	619.6	619.3	622.7	637.3	641.1	619.7
2018	618.0	616.3	618.9	619.8	623.6	625.2	625.0	626.8	626.2	630.1	648.5	648.2	627.2
Wholesale Trade													
2010	114.4	114.4	114.9	115.0	115.0	114.8	114.6	114.6	113.9	114.2	114.1	113.9	114.5
2011	113.2	113.7	114.3	115.3	115.8	116.2	116.0	116.1	116.2	116.2	116.8	116.9	115.6
2012	116.0	116.8	117.4	118.0	118.6	119.1	118.7	119.1	118.8	119.0	119.0	119.1	118.3
2013	117.4	117.7	118.2	118.5	118.7	119.0	118.8	118.8	118.8	118.4	118.8	118.8	118.5
2014	117.2	117.2	117.8	117.9	118.4	118.4	118.1	118.1	118.3	117.7	118.0	118.4	118.0
2015	117.0	117.1	117.1	117.3	117.7	117.9	117.7	117.6	117.5	117.2	117.2	117.5	117.4
2016	116.0	116.1	116.2	116.1	116.3	116.6	116.9	117.2	117.3	117.1	117.5	117.8	116.8
2017	116.8	117.5	117.7	117.7	118.2	118.4	118.2	118.3	118.3	118.4	118.9	119.0	118.1
2018	117.8	118.3	118.6	118.8	119.5	120.2	119.8	119.9	119.9	120.6	121.4	121.1	119.7
Retail Trade													
2010	302.1	299.8	302.4	304.7	306.1	307.1	306.1	307.0	304.1	307.6	316.3	319.2	306.9
2011	303.4	302.2	304.7	307.7	308.2	309.2	308.8	309.1	307.7	309.8	319.2	322.0	309.3
2012	308.3	304.7	309.3	310.8	312.2	312.7	311.9	311.3	310.6	313.6	324.7	325.6	313.0
2013	309.9	307.6	309.0	310.3	312.5	313.9	314.2	314.5	313.5	317.1	327.5	331.0	315.1
2014	314.4	312.6	315.0	317.5	318.6	320.5	320.7	321.2	319.9	322.6	332.7	335.6	320.9
2015	318.0	315.5	317.5	322.0	323.9	325.4	325.3	326.2	324.5	329.4	338.6	341.3	325.6
2016	327.3	326.9	329.0	332.3	332.7	332.9	333.8	333.8	332.8	335.3	344.9	346.4	334.0
2017	333.4	331.3	331.8	333.8	334.1	334.8	334.6	334.9	333.4	335.7	346.7	347.8	336.0
2018	333.3	332.2	333.8	335.1	337.1	337.4	336.1	336.2	334.5	336.7	350.1	349.1	337.6
Transportation and Utilities													
2010	128.2	127.9	128.3	128.9	129.5	130.2	132.0	132.7	134.5	134.9	136.1	138.1	131.8
2011	131.9	132.3	133.1	135.1	135.7	136.2	136.1	137.1	137.9	140.3	141.6	142.9	136.7
2012	138.7	138.2	139.3	139.7	140.5	140.4	140.1	142.0	144.6	144.1	146.1	148.8	141.9
2013	143.5	144.0	143.5	144.5	144.4	144.9	144.4	145.3	144.9	145.8	149.1	151.4	145.5
2014	143.8	143.8	145.2	146.6	146.4	147.0	147.5	149.6	150.4	153.5	156.0	157.2	148.9
2015	152.2	151.0	151.3	152.9	154.1	155.0	157.8	158.4	159.1	161.5	164.3	167.4	157.1
2016	161.7	160.8	160.9	162.6	162.7	163.5	164.5	164.9	165.1	166.6	169.9	171.0	164.5
2017	162.4	161.8	161.5	162.1	162.5	163.6	164.4	166.4	167.6	168.6	171.7	174.3	165.6
2018	166.9	165.8	166.5	165.9	167.0	167.6	169.1	170.7	171.8	172.8	177.0	178.0	169.9
Information													
2010	45.7	46.6	45.8	45.1	45.0	45.1	45.0	44.5	44.6	45.2	45.4	45.6	45.3
2011	44.6	44.4	44.3	44.4	44.4	44.2	43.9	44.1	43.5	43.2	43.6	43.4	44.0
2012	43.0	43.3	43.1	43.4	44.2	44.2	42.9	43.1	42.6	43.4	43.7	44.3	43.4
2013	43.7	44.1	44.3	44.0	44.5	45.1	44.5	44.4	43.9	44.0	44.7	44.6	44.3
2014	43.9	43.9	44.0	44.2	44.2	44.2	44.1	44.1	43.8	43.7	44.2	44.1	44.0
2015	43.6	43.7	43.8	44.1	44.4	44.9	44.8	45.0	44.7	44.8	45.8	45.8	44.6
2016	45.2	45.6	44.8	45.6	45.3	46.7	45.0	45.1	45.7	45.5	46.5	45.6	45.6
2017	45.2	45.9	45.5	45.4	45.9	47.5	45.8	45.9	45.6	46.5	47.7	46.0	46.1
2018	45.3	45.4	45.3	45.7	45.5	47.3	44.4	44.7	44.7	45.5	46.3	45.7	45.5

1. Employment by Industry: Tennessee, 2010–2018—*Continued*

(Numbers in thousands, not seasonally adjusted)

Industry and year	January	February	March	April	May	June	July	August	September	October	November	December	Annual average
Financial Activities													
2010	137.7	137.6	137.5	138.6	138.5	137.9	137.5	137.3	135.9	135.6	135.7	135.6	137.1
2011	134.8	134.7	134.7	136.2	136.9	136.8	137.3	137.6	137.1	137.1	137.6	137.7	136.5
2012	136.4	136.9	137.0	137.0	137.5	137.5	137.5	137.4	136.7	136.8	137.1	137.5	137.1
2013	136.0	135.9	136.2	137.4	138.1	138.8	140.0	140.3	140.0	140.6	141.5	141.9	138.9
2014	141.0	141.6	142.3	143.2	144.0	144.4	145.1	145.3	145.1	145.6	145.8	146.4	144.2
2015	145.4	145.8	145.9	146.5	147.3	148.2	148.8	149.1	148.6	149.6	150.1	151.0	148.0
2016	149.3	149.8	150.1	151.5	152.5	153.4	154.1	154.8	155.0	155.0	155.5	156.1	153.1
2017	154.9	156.0	156.6	157.4	158.3	159.6	159.7	160.1	159.7	161.0	160.4	160.6	158.7
2018	159.0	160.0	160.8	161.3	162.0	163.3	163.8	164.2	164.3	163.4	163.7	164.6	162.5
Professional and Business Services													
2010	295.3	297.6	301.1	304.1	311.6	310.4	305.2	308.8	311.8	315.5	318.0	318.7	308.2
2011	308.9	315.7	320.1	323.6	323.4	324.4	324.9	329.9	332.1	335.4	340.4	342.9	326.8
2012	327.4	331.5	335.5	338.9	342.0	344.5	338.8	344.9	346.4	349.9	355.3	355.9	342.6
2013	341.8	345.3	348.9	350.9	353.7	356.0	350.2	359.9	362.6	367.7	380.9	381.5	358.3
2014	365.2	364.1	367.7	374.3	377.9	378.8	374.2	383.7	384.4	389.3	397.3	401.3	379.9
2015	382.4	382.2	385.6	391.0	394.0	397.0	394.8	399.4	401.1	408.2	415.2	416.4	397.3
2016	397.8	398.2	400.6	406.3	405.9	407.6	405.1	410.4	412.6	414.7	416.9	421.1	408.1
2017	400.7	402.9	403.7	407.6	407.7	411.5	410.3	412.1	415.0	416.6	424.2	425.0	411.4
2018	405.6	410.8	410.9	414.3	415.8	418.0	412.5	418.3	419.9	422.6	425.9	427.7	416.9
Education and Health Services													
2010	368.1	370.0	371.9	375.7	373.5	372.2	373.7	375.2	379.0	382.3	383.0	383.1	375.6
2011	377.7	381.6	382.4	386.3	385.8	382.4	383.5	385.2	390.1	391.8	392.9	392.6	386.0
2012	389.0	392.9	395.0	395.2	393.9	392.1	391.3	394.4	399.5	400.8	401.6	401.6	395.6
2013	396.5	400.5	402.1	402.2	400.9	397.5	394.9	397.7	403.1	405.0	406.3	406.0	401.1
2014	401.2	404.0	406.1	405.3	403.3	400.4	400.0	403.3	409.5	411.8	412.1	412.4	405.8
2015	408.3	410.9	412.8	414.3	412.7	409.3	409.9	412.1	418.8	420.8	422.4	423.0	414.6
2016	416.5	420.8	422.4	423.5	422.1	417.9	419.0	422.5	428.5	430.6	431.7	431.2	423.9
2017	424.5	430.7	431.6	432.0	429.5	425.3	424.3	427.6	433.7	436.8	437.7	436.6	430.9
2018	429.9	436.0	437.2	436.2	434.0	430.1	429.5	433.9	439.1	442.2	440.3	439.1	435.6
Leisure and Hospitality													
2010	247.2	247.4	254.5	263.7	267.7	274.2	270.9	270.3	265.8	262.7	261.3	258.0	262.0
2011	249.0	251.5	259.0	268.2	273.7	278.0	276.8	277.0	273.8	268.8	268.2	267.4	267.6
2012	258.2	260.1	269.6	277.8	283.4	288.5	285.3	286.6	279.9	278.2	277.4	277.0	276.8
2013	266.2	268.3	277.8	285.8	292.0	297.6	296.4	296.7	290.7	287.8	286.7	284.9	285.9
2014	276.0	277.2	286.8	296.3	302.4	308.5	307.0	307.9	302.2	298.8	298.1	296.4	296.5
2015	287.4	289.2	294.8	307.9	315.0	320.1	318.5	317.9	313.1	311.4	310.8	309.8	308.0
2016	300.4	301.9	309.8	320.7	324.7	331.6	329.8	329.2	325.9	321.2	320.6	319.2	319.6
2017	310.1	312.5	320.1	329.4	334.6	340.9	338.0	338.9	333.6	330.4	330.2	328.4	328.9
2018	317.0	319.9	328.4	337.2	344.1	349.8	348.6	350.4	343.6	344.0	343.4	340.2	338.9
Other Services													
2010	98.5	98.9	99.9	99.9	100.7	102.5	102.4	102.2	101.8	102.4	102.4	102.8	101.2
2011	99.7	100.4	101.2	101.5	102.3	103.9	103.5	103.2	102.3	102.0	102.3	102.3	102.1
2012	101.8	102.6	103.9	104.1	105.0	106.3	105.9	104.8	104.4	104.2	104.1	103.8	104.2
2013	103.0	103.7	104.6	105.9	106.5	107.8	107.2	106.4	105.9	105.5	105.6	104.9	105.6
2014	104.2	104.7	106.0	106.1	107.0	107.7	107.3	106.2	105.9	105.9	106.1	105.9	106.1
2015	105.1	105.7	106.2	107.5	108.7	109.8	109.4	108.5	108.5	108.7	108.8	108.8	108.0
2016	107.9	108.8	109.8	110.8	111.3	112.4	112.3	111.5	111.7	111.4	111.9	111.9	111.0
2017	111.0	111.9	112.9	113.9	114.7	116.3	115.9	115.5	115.6	115.4	115.9	116.0	114.6
2018	114.4	115.8	116.9	117.6	118.3	119.8	119.4	119.0	119.1	120.2	120.1	119.0	118.3
Government													
2010	428.4	432.6	434.4	438.6	447.5	411.3	406.8	418.9	436.1	438.3	439.0	435.8	430.6
2011	429.1	434.3	435.5	434.0	433.0	400.0	396.1	414.4	429.5	433.5	434.4	431.7	425.5
2012	422.3	430.3	433.4	432.8	426.9	395.5	392.4	404.8	425.2	431.3	433.2	432.2	421.7
2013	418.1	427.1	428.7	437.0	431.7	398.0	393.8	406.5	427.1	434.6	434.8	434.3	422.6
2014	423.1	431.3	433.0	434.1	429.8	396.1	394.1	407.6	429.7	435.4	439.0	437.3	424.2
2015	425.4	432.8	432.5	433.7	429.5	397.2	394.7	408.8	432.2	438.2	438.5	437.1	425.1
2016	425.5	434.5	439.0	435.9	430.0	398.6	395.7	413.6	437.5	440.9	444.3	440.8	428.0
2017	426.8	437.8	438.6	439.5	434.3	402.5	399.8	414.5	439.8	443.0	445.1	442.8	430.4
2018	431.6	441.5	443.1	444.1	440.4	408.5	404.0	421.6	444.4	447.9	451.0	447.9	435.5

2. Average Weekly Hours by Selected Industry: Tennessee, 2014–2018

(Not seasonally adjusted)

Industry and year	January	February	March	April	May	June	July	August	September	October	November	December	Annual average
Total Private													
2014	34.8	35.0	35.6	35.2	35.3	35.7	35.2	35.4	35.1	34.9	35.6	35.3	35.3
2015	34.7	34.7	35.2	35.0	35.1	35.3	35.2	35.8	35.0	35.2	35.5	35.6	35.2
2016	35.1	35.0	35.3	35.4	35.8	35.6	35.5	35.5	35.4	35.8	35.5	35.6	35.5
2017	35.6	35.4	35.3	35.5	35.4	35.6	35.6	35.2	35.2	35.4	35.3	35.5	35.4
2018	33.9	35.0	35.2	35.8	35.4	35.7	35.8	35.3	35.9	35.5	35.3	35.6	35.4
Goods-Producing													
2014	40.2	39.8	41.4	41.1	41.5	41.6	40.8	41.5	41.3	40.3	41.8	41.8	41.1
2015	40.8	40.1	41.3	41.1	41.2	41.4	41.0	41.6	40.7	41.4	41.8	42.3	41.2
2016	41.5	40.9	41.6	42.0	42.5	42.4	42.3	42.8	42.9	42.4	43.2	43.2	42.3
2017	42.3	42.1	42.2	41.6	42.3	42.5	41.7	41.6	41.6	41.3	42.0	42.5	42.0
2018	39.7	41.6	42.4	42.6	42.0	42.6	41.7	41.6	41.6	41.5	41.5	41.3	41.7
Mining, Logging, and Construction													
2014	39.1	38.5	41.3	40.4	41.3	41.2	41.7	41.4	40.8	39.2	41.1	40.0	40.5
2015	37.7	37.5	37.5	38.4	40.2	40.2	40.3	39.8	38.4	40.2	39.7	40.5	39.2
2016	39.6	37.0	38.6	39.5	40.5	40.6	40.2	40.7	40.3	40.6	40.3	40.1	39.9
2017	38.9	39.5	39.5	40.4	40.8	41.3	42.0	41.1	40.8	41.5	42.0	41.8	40.8
2018	37.8	39.5	41.3	42.4	42.1	42.2	41.6	41.6	41.5	41.7	40.0	40.6	41.1
Manufacturing													
2014	40.6	40.2	41.5	41.4	41.5	41.7	40.5	41.5	41.5	40.7	42.1	42.4	41.3
2015	41.8	40.9	42.6	42.0	41.5	41.8	41.2	42.3	41.6	41.8	42.6	43.0	41.9
2016	42.1	42.2	42.7	42.8	43.2	43.1	43.0	43.5	43.8	43.1	44.2	44.3	43.2
2017	43.5	43.0	43.1	42.0	42.9	42.9	41.6	41.8	41.9	41.2	42.0	42.7	42.4
2018	40.3	42.4	42.8	42.7	42.0	42.8	41.7	41.6	41.7	41.5	42.0	41.6	41.9
Trade, Transportation, and Utilities													
2014	33.9	34.2	34.9	34.6	34.7	34.8	34.7	34.7	34.4	34.5	34.8	35.0	34.6
2015	34.0	33.9	34.8	34.6	34.6	34.8	34.7	34.9	34.7	34.3	34.6	35.0	34.6
2016	34.4	34.3	34.4	34.6	34.8	34.9	34.7	34.5	34.6	34.9	34.4	34.8	34.6
2017	34.6	34.2	34.1	34.4	34.3	34.4	34.4	34.3	34.4	34.4	34.3	34.8	34.4
2018	33.1	33.8	34.1	34.4	34.4	34.4	34.4	34.2	34.6	34.1	33.9	34.0	34.1
Information													
2014	36.8	38.0	38.5	37.9	37.7	38.0	37.2	37.6	37.4	37.9	38.4	36.5	37.7
2015	36.6	37.2	37.8	36.8	36.5	36.4	36.0	37.6	36.5	36.4	36.6	35.9	36.7
2016	35.1	35.5	35.9	37.1	37.0	36.1	36.5	36.5	37.0	37.2	36.4	37.0	36.4
2017	38.2	36.3	37.0	38.5	37.7	37.5	39.0	37.4	37.8	37.8	36.2	36.9	37.5
2018	36.4	37.0	37.1	38.2	37.1	37.4	38.8	38.0	39.0	38.0	37.9	38.0	37.7
Financial Activities													
2014	37.9	39.0	39.6	38.3	38.5	39.8	38.4	38.2	38.4	38.3	39.1	37.8	38.6
2015	37.4	38.4	38.7	37.8	37.6	37.6	37.6	38.1	37.1	37.0	37.5	37.0	37.6
2016	37.1	37.0	36.7	36.7	37.3	36.9	37.0	37.0	36.3	37.5	36.9	37.1	37.0
2017	37.9	37.4	37.2	38.1	37.2	37.5	38.7	37.5	37.7	38.7	38.0	38.1	37.8
2018	37.5	37.9	37.6	38.8	37.7	38.0	39.6	37.9	39.5	38.7	38.7	39.7	38.5
Professional and Business Services													
2014	36.0	36.1	36.2	36.2	36.4	36.6	35.9	35.9	35.7	35.2	35.9	35.6	36.0
2015	35.0	35.7	35.0	35.1	35.6	36.0	35.8	37.3	35.7	36.3	36.9	37.0	36.0
2016	36.5	36.3	36.5	36.7	37.3	36.9	36.7	36.6	36.4	37.4	36.5	36.5	36.7
2017	36.3	36.2	36.0	36.1	36.4	37.0	37.0	36.4	36.4	37.2	36.7	36.3	36.5
2018	35.0	35.9	36.2	37.0	36.5	37.4	37.9	37.5	38.1	37.6	37.2	37.4	37.0
Education and Health Services													
2014	34.5	34.5	34.7	34.2	34.1	34.5	34.3	34.5	34.4	34.2	34.9	34.7	34.5
2015	34.6	34.5	34.5	34.4	34.5	34.5	34.7	35.2	34.9	34.7	35.2	34.8	34.7
2016	34.9	34.9	34.9	34.7	35.1	34.8	34.9	34.8	35.0	34.9	34.8	34.8	34.9
2017	35.7	35.1	35.1	35.2	34.8	35.0	35.3	34.6	34.6	34.3	34.2	34.4	34.9
2018	33.6	34.3	34.0	35.1	34.6	34.5	35.4	34.4	35.5	34.5	34.5	35.4	34.6
Leisure and Hospitality													
2014	26.3	26.7	27.6	27.3	27.0	27.9	27.8	27.5	27.0	27.1	27.2	26.5	27.2
2015	25.9	25.9	26.6	27.0	26.7	27.3	27.2	27.1	26.5	26.9	26.7	26.6	26.7
2016	26.0	26.5	26.8	26.8	27.0	27.2	27.0	26.9	26.4	27.1	26.8	26.2	26.7
2017	26.3	26.7	26.7	27.4	26.8	27.4	27.3	26.7	26.5	27.1	26.7	26.5	26.8
2018	25.3	26.8	26.9	27.4	27.1	27.6	27.6	26.8	27.1	27.0	26.9	27.2	27.0
Other Services													
2014	32.4	32.9	32.5	32.3	32.4	33.3	32.8	33.4	32.4	32.5	32.6	32.9	32.7
2015	32.2	32.8	32.7	32.6	33.0	33.0	33.0	33.8	32.3	32.8	32.7	32.8	32.8
2016	31.7	31.9	32.2	32.7	33.0	32.2	32.4	32.1	31.8	32.2	32.1	32.7	32.2
2017	33.0	32.8	32.8	32.9	32.3	31.6	32.5	32.4	32.8	33.4	33.3	33.9	32.8
2018	30.9	31.9	32.3	33.3	32.9	32.6	32.1	32.4	33.2	32.8	32.4	31.8	32.4

3. Average Hourly Earnings by Selected Industry: Tennessee, 2014–2018

(Dollars, not seasonally adjusted)

Industry and year	January	February	March	April	May	June	July	August	September	October	November	December	Annual average
Total Private													
2014	20.76	20.98	20.80	20.77	20.76	20.80	20.68	20.74	20.74	20.69	20.90	20.47	20.76
2015	20.73	20.98	20.81	20.70	20.64	20.67	20.90	20.93	21.01	21.09	21.24	21.14	20.91
2016	21.46	21.33	21.35	21.38	21.67	21.54	21.79	21.71	22.09	22.28	22.21	22.66	21.80
2017	22.82	22.63	22.39	22.70	22.43	22.36	22.70	22.57	22.84	22.71	22.82	22.93	22.66
2018	23.13	23.07	22.97	23.19	23.04	23.20	23.37	23.45	23.86	23.58	23.79	24.13	23.40
Goods-Producing													
2014	21.18	21.42	20.98	21.01	20.88	21.20	21.34	21.10	21.03	21.05	21.26	21.19	21.14
2015	21.22	21.23	21.35	21.35	21.48	21.54	22.08	21.56	21.97	21.91	22.04	22.37	21.68
2016	22.55	22.52	22.47	22.59	22.98	23.02	23.40	23.25	23.85	23.63	23.96	24.42	23.24
2017	24.05	23.76	23.55	23.54	23.53	23.60	23.98	23.75	24.16	23.76	23.89	24.18	23.81
2018	24.14	24.09	24.02	24.28	24.12	24.14	24.58	24.63	24.91	24.83	24.95	25.16	24.49
Mining, Logging, and Construction													
2014	21.99	22.51	22.08	21.97	21.30	21.58	21.99	21.69	21.66	21.70	21.64	21.72	21.81
2015	21.92	22.10	22.48	22.08	22.01	22.45	22.44	22.19	22.49	22.67	23.16	23.49	22.47
2016	23.27	22.96	23.35	22.99	23.22	22.90	23.17	23.07	22.98	23.38	23.38	24.26	23.25
2017	24.07	23.88	23.94	24.20	24.09	23.98	24.26	24.04	24.38	24.10	24.75	24.69	24.21
2018	24.83	24.91	24.67	25.01	24.58	24.36	25.00	24.82	25.43	25.81	25.88	25.72	25.09
Manufacturing													
2014	20.93	21.08	20.61	20.69	20.74	21.07	21.11	20.90	20.82	20.83	21.13	21.02	20.91
2015	21.01	20.96	21.01	21.11	21.30	21.23	21.95	21.34	21.80	21.64	21.67	21.99	21.42
2016	22.32	22.39	22.20	22.46	22.90	23.06	23.48	23.31	24.13	23.71	24.15	24.47	23.23
2017	24.04	23.72	23.42	23.31	23.34	23.47	23.88	23.65	24.08	23.64	23.58	24.00	23.68
2018	23.92	23.82	23.79	24.02	23.95	24.06	24.43	24.56	24.71	24.45	24.62	24.96	24.27
Trade, Transportation, and Utilities													
2014	19.01	19.17	19.42	19.31	19.07	19.29	18.97	18.96	18.96	18.98	19.00	18.84	19.08
2015	19.37	19.37	19.12	19.41	19.07	19.20	19.25	19.05	19.10	19.11	19.13	18.90	19.17
2016	19.20	18.96	19.11	19.29	19.87	19.52	19.83	19.87	20.07	20.32	19.86	20.28	19.69
2017	20.57	20.43	20.35	20.66	20.43	20.30	20.62	20.47	20.58	20.47	20.33	20.44	20.47
2018	20.38	20.53	20.33	20.38	20.32	20.66	20.66	21.01	21.40	21.12	21.30	21.46	20.80
Information													
2014	25.82	25.16	25.26	24.72	24.64	25.57	25.54	25.70	25.74	26.10	26.44	26.49	25.60
2015	26.99	27.37	26.73	26.16	26.19	26.37	26.84	27.38	27.28	27.93	28.57	28.64	27.21
2016	29.31	28.68	27.81	27.90	28.79	28.22	28.84	28.57	29.12	30.02	29.91	30.98	29.02
2017	31.32	32.32	31.28	32.55	31.83	31.37	31.85	31.15	30.99	30.96	31.78	31.27	31.56
2018	31.30	32.02	31.28	31.09	31.09	30.92	31.02	30.46	31.06	30.65	30.87	30.73	31.04
Financial Activities													
2014	24.51	24.67	24.30	25.62	24.52	24.49	24.31	24.57	24.51	24.12	24.86	24.48	24.58
2015	25.06	25.85	25.30	25.39	25.69	25.63	25.94	27.07	25.84	26.12	26.47	26.29	25.89
2016	26.49	26.50	25.99	26.42	27.04	26.54	26.60	25.94	26.36	26.75	26.68	26.43	26.48
2017	27.06	27.55	26.61	27.82	27.18	27.18	27.72	27.82	27.97	28.57	28.64	28.30	27.71
2018	28.70	28.64	28.95	29.18	29.46	30.11	31.33	31.51	30.88	30.13	31.95	32.10	30.27
Professional and Business Services													
2014	25.64	26.12	25.88	25.46	26.49	26.24	25.90	25.90	25.80	25.40	25.65	23.54	25.66
2015	23.68	24.34	24.55	23.83	23.77	23.69	23.89	24.31	24.53	24.45	24.77	24.28	24.18
2016	24.91	24.90	25.35	24.79	24.94	25.17	25.29	25.10	25.83	26.23	26.02	26.91	25.46
2017	27.42	27.23	26.99	27.83	27.04	26.83	27.43	27.07	27.45	27.31	27.41	27.52	27.29
2018	27.76	27.48	27.52	28.00	27.31	27.72	27.69	27.52	28.04	27.36	27.78	28.62	27.74
Education and Health Services													
2014	21.00	21.23	21.15	21.27	21.27	21.20	21.18	21.38	21.42	21.50	21.45	21.49	21.30
2015	21.70	21.94	21.61	21.64	21.62	21.75	21.87	21.91	21.83	22.25	22.21	22.07	21.87
2016	22.53	22.23	22.22	22.49	22.36	22.36	22.59	22.45	22.45	22.69	22.67	23.12	22.51
2017	23.29	22.76	22.60	22.77	22.48	22.60	22.55	22.67	22.75	22.28	22.69	22.83	22.69
2018	23.36	23.22	23.14	23.52	23.65	23.56	23.21	23.16	23.78	23.64	23.69	23.84	23.48
Leisure and Hospitality													
2014	11.67	11.72	11.63	11.47	11.49	11.41	11.52	11.58	11.59	11.65	11.61	11.76	11.59
2015	11.77	11.94	11.87	11.87	11.89	12.02	12.15	12.13	12.35	12.33	12.36	12.38	12.09
2016	12.19	12.36	12.24	12.18	12.20	12.22	12.41	12.57	12.74	12.83	13.06	12.99	12.50
2017	12.88	13.08	12.97	12.90	13.06	12.87	13.00	13.31	13.67	13.72	13.92	14.13	13.29
2018	14.30	14.41	14.31	14.38	14.41	14.19	14.38	14.60	15.07	15.25	14.54	14.77	14.55
Other Services													
2014	20.00	20.35	20.18	19.67	19.19	19.21	19.52	20.14	19.91	20.02	21.29	20.24	19.97
2015	20.23	20.35	20.11	19.83	19.46	19.28	19.31	19.13	19.37	19.20	19.43	19.64	19.60
2016	19.52	19.56	19.51	19.57	19.85	19.34	19.55	19.64	19.98	19.61	19.83	19.60	19.60
2017	20.41	19.77	19.89	20.10	19.86	19.91	20.49	19.88	20.28	20.66	20.47	20.67	20.20
2018	21.13	20.70	20.54	20.51	20.49	20.59	20.82	20.79	21.36	21.10	21.54	22.55	21.01

4. Average Weekly Earnings by Selected Industry: Tennessee, 2014–2018

(Dollars, not seasonally adjusted)

Industry and year	January	February	March	April	May	June	July	August	September	October	November	December	Annual average
Total Private													
2014	722.45	734.30	740.48	731.10	732.83	742.56	727.94	734.20	727.97	722.08	744.04	722.59	732.83
2015	719.33	728.01	732.51	724.50	724.46	729.65	735.68	749.29	735.35	742.37	754.02	752.58	736.03
2016	753.25	746.55	753.66	756.85	775.79	766.82	773.55	770.71	781.99	797.62	788.46	806.70	773.90
2017	812.39	801.10	790.37	805.85	794.02	796.02	808.12	794.46	803.97	803.93	805.55	814.02	802.16
2018	784.11	807.45	808.54	830.20	815.62	828.24	836.65	827.79	856.57	837.09	839.79	859.03	828.36
Goods-Producing													
2014	851.44	852.52	868.57	863.51	866.52	881.92	870.67	875.65	868.54	848.32	888.67	885.74	868.85
2015	865.78	851.32	881.76	877.49	884.98	891.76	905.28	896.90	894.18	907.07	921.27	946.25	893.22
2016	935.83	921.07	934.75	948.78	976.65	976.05	989.82	995.10	1,023.17	1,001.91	1,035.07	1,054.94	983.05
2017	1,017.32	1,000.30	993.81	979.26	995.32	1,003.00	999.97	988.00	1,005.06	981.29	1,003.38	1,027.65	1,000.02
2018	958.36	1,002.14	1,018.45	1,034.33	1,013.04	1,028.36	1,024.99	1,024.61	1,036.26	1,030.45	1,035.43	1,039.11	1,021.23
Mining, Logging, and Construction													
2014	859.81	866.64	911.90	887.59	879.69	889.10	916.98	897.97	883.73	850.64	889.40	868.80	883.31
2015	826.38	828.75	843.00	847.87	884.80	902.49	904.33	883.16	863.62	911.33	919.45	951.35	880.82
2016	921.49	849.52	901.31	908.11	940.41	929.74	931.43	938.95	926.09	949.23	942.21	972.83	927.68
2017	936.32	943.26	945.63	977.68	982.87	990.37	1,018.92	988.04	994.70	1,000.15	1,039.50	1,032.04	987.77
2018	938.57	983.95	1,018.87	1,060.42	1,034.82	1,027.99	1,040.00	1,032.51	1,055.35	1,076.28	1,035.20	1,044.23	1,031.20
Manufacturing													
2014	849.76	847.42	855.32	856.57	860.71	878.62	854.96	867.35	864.03	847.78	889.57	891.25	863.58
2015	878.22	857.26	895.03	886.62	883.95	887.41	904.34	902.68	906.88	904.55	923.14	945.57	897.50
2016	939.67	944.86	947.94	961.29	989.28	993.89	1,009.64	1,013.99	1,056.89	1,021.90	1,067.43	1,084.02	1,003.54
2017	1,045.74	1,019.96	1,009.40	979.02	1,001.29	1,006.86	993.41	988.57	1,008.95	973.97	990.36	1,024.80	1,004.03
2018	963.98	1,009.97	1,018.21	1,025.65	1,005.90	1,029.77	1,018.73	1,021.70	1,030.41	1,014.68	1,034.04	1,038.34	1,016.91
Trade, Transportation, and Utilities													
2014	644.44	655.61	677.76	668.13	661.73	671.29	658.26	657.91	652.22	654.81	661.20	659.40	660.17
2015	658.58	656.64	665.38	671.59	659.82	668.16	667.98	664.85	662.77	655.47	661.90	661.50	663.28
2016	660.48	650.33	657.38	667.43	691.48	681.25	688.10	685.52	694.42	709.17	683.18	705.74	681.27
2017	711.72	698.71	693.94	710.70	700.75	698.32	709.33	702.12	707.95	704.17	697.32	711.31	704.17
2018	674.58	693.91	693.25	701.07	699.01	710.70	710.70	718.54	740.44	720.19	722.07	729.64	709.28
Information													
2014	950.18	956.08	972.51	936.89	928.93	971.66	950.09	966.32	962.68	989.19	1,015.30	966.89	965.12
2015	987.83	1,018.16	1,010.39	962.69	955.94	959.87	966.24	1,029.49	995.72	1,016.65	1,045.66	1,028.18	998.61
2016	1,028.78	1,018.14	998.38	1,035.09	1,065.23	1,018.74	1,052.66	1,042.81	1,077.44	1,116.74	1,088.72	1,146.26	1,056.33
2017	1,196.42	1,173.22	1,157.36	1,253.18	1,199.99	1,176.38	1,242.15	1,165.01	1,171.42	1,170.29	1,150.44	1,153.86	1,183.50
2018	1,139.32	1,184.74	1,160.49	1,187.64	1,153.44	1,156.41	1,203.58	1,157.48	1,211.34	1,164.70	1,169.97	1,167.74	1,170.21
Financial Activities													
2014	928.93	962.13	962.28	981.25	944.02	974.70	933.50	938.57	941.18	923.80	972.03	925.34	948.79
2015	937.24	992.64	979.11	959.74	965.94	963.69	975.34	1,031.37	958.66	966.44	992.63	972.73	973.46
2016	982.78	980.50	953.83	969.61	1,008.59	979.33	984.20	959.78	956.87	1,003.13	984.49	980.55	979.76
2017	1,025.57	1,030.37	989.89	1,059.94	1,011.10	1,019.25	1,072.76	1,043.25	1,054.47	1,105.66	1,088.32	1,078.23	1,047.44
2018	1,076.25	1,085.46	1,088.52	1,132.18	1,110.64	1,144.18	1,240.67	1,194.23	1,219.76	1,166.03	1,236.47	1,274.37	1,165.40
Professional and Business Services													
2014	923.04	942.93	936.86	921.65	964.24	960.38	929.81	929.81	921.06	894.08	920.84	838.02	923.76
2015	828.80	868.94	859.25	836.43	846.21	852.84	855.26	906.76	875.72	887.54	914.01	898.36	870.48
2016	909.22	903.87	925.28	909.79	930.26	928.77	928.14	918.66	940.21	981.00	949.73	982.22	934.38
2017	995.35	985.73	971.64	1,004.66	984.26	992.71	1,014.91	985.35	999.18	1,015.93	1,005.95	998.98	996.09
2018	971.60	986.53	996.22	1,036.00	996.82	1,036.73	1,049.45	1,032.00	1,068.32	1,028.74	1,033.42	1,070.39	1,026.38
Education and Health Services													
2014	724.50	732.44	733.91	727.43	725.31	731.40	726.47	737.61	736.85	735.30	748.61	745.70	734.85
2015	750.82	756.93	745.55	744.42	745.89	750.38	758.89	771.23	761.87	772.08	781.79	768.04	758.89
2016	786.30	775.83	775.48	780.40	784.84	778.13	788.39	781.26	785.75	791.88	788.92	804.58	785.60
2017	831.45	798.88	793.26	801.50	782.30	791.00	796.02	784.38	787.15	764.20	776.00	785.35	791.88
2018	784.90	796.45	786.76	825.55	818.29	812.82	821.63	796.70	844.19	815.58	817.31	843.94	812.41
Leisure and Hospitality													
2014	306.92	312.92	320.99	313.13	310.23	318.34	320.26	318.45	312.93	315.72	315.79	311.64	315.25
2015	304.84	309.25	315.74	320.49	317.46	328.15	330.48	328.72	327.28	331.68	330.01	329.31	322.80
2016	316.94	327.54	328.03	326.42	329.40	332.38	335.07	338.13	336.34	347.69	350.01	340.34	333.75
2017	338.74	349.24	346.30	353.46	350.01	352.64	354.90	355.38	362.26	371.81	371.66	374.45	356.17
2018	361.79	386.19	384.94	394.01	390.51	391.64	396.89	391.28	408.40	411.75	391.13	401.74	392.85
Other Services													
2014	648.00	669.52	655.85	635.34	621.76	639.69	640.26	672.68	645.08	650.65	694.05	665.90	653.02
2015	651.41	667.48	657.60	646.46	642.18	636.24	637.23	646.59	625.65	629.76	635.36	644.19	642.88
2016	618.78	623.96	628.22	639.94	655.05	622.75	621.43	627.56	624.55	643.36	629.48	648.44	631.12
2017	673.53	648.46	652.39	661.29	641.48	629.16	665.93	644.11	665.18	690.04	681.65	700.71	662.56
2018	652.92	660.33	663.44	682.98	674.12	671.23	668.32	673.60	709.15	692.08	697.90	717.09	680.72

TEXAS
At a Glance

Population:
  2010 census: 25,145,561
  2018 estimate: 28,701,845

Percent change in population:
  2010–2018: 14.1%

Percent change in total nonfarm employment:
  2010–2018: 20.5%

Industry with the largest growth in employment, 2010–2018 (percent):
  Professional and business services, 34.7%

Industry with the largest decline or smallest growth in employment, 2010–2018 (percent):
  Government, 3.2%

Civilian labor force:
  2010: 12,241,970
  2018: 13,848,080

Unemployment rate and rank among states (highest to lowest):
  2010: 8.1%, 32nd
  2018: 3.9%, 22nd

Over-the-year change in unemployment rates:
  2016–2017: -0.3%
  2017–2018: -0.4%

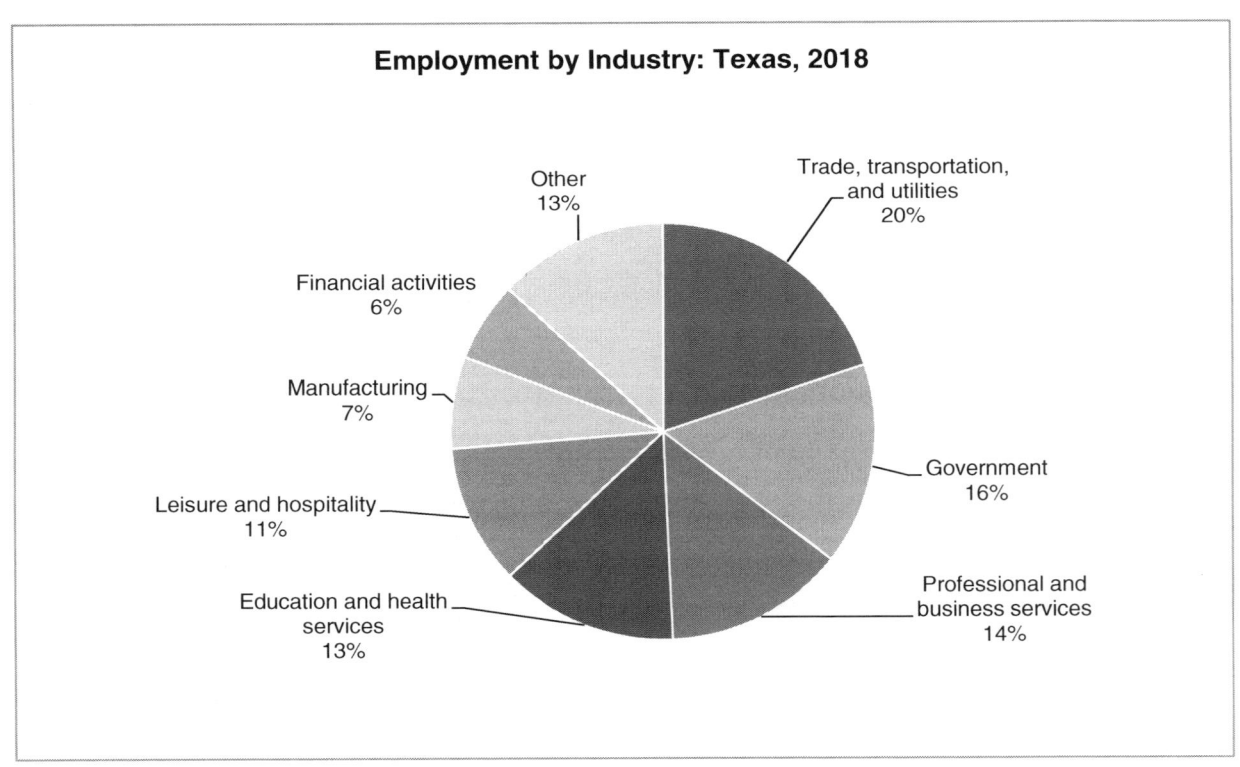

Employment by Industry: Texas, 2018

Other
13%

Trade, transportation, and utilities
20%

Financial activities
6%

Manufacturing
7%

Leisure and hospitality
11%

Education and health services
13%

Government
16%

Professional and business services
14%

1. Employment by Industry: Texas, 2010–2018

(Numbers in thousands, not seasonally adjusted)

Industry and year	January	February	March	April	May	June	July	August	September	October	November	December	Annual average
Total Nonfarm													
2010	10,156.8	10,210.0	10,299.8	10,347.8	10,437.4	10,441.9	10,324.2	10,352.4	10,393.0	10,476.7	10,519.5	10,548.0	10,375.6
2011	10,362.3	10,421.6	10,518.7	10,589.5	10,624.0	10,660.3	10,577.4	10,613.1	10,667.8	10,694.5	10,753.2	10,784.2	10,605.6
2012	10,621.4	10,713.9	10,800.8	10,852.3	10,918.1	10,964.7	10,866.8	10,931.4	10,975.5	11,046.2	11,130.4	11,157.5	10,914.9
2013	10,942.5	11,072.0	11,142.2	11,186.7	11,240.4	11,284.1	11,205.7	11,252.6	11,297.8	11,361.4	11,450.4	11,458.3	11,241.2
2014	11,273.3	11,368.4	11,441.5	11,520.9	11,593.0	11,636.0	11,558.6	11,606.0	11,651.2	11,760.0	11,836.4	11,879.2	11,593.7
2015	11,672.4	11,749.5	11,771.2	11,820.8	11,871.5	11,910.9	11,841.9	11,860.0	11,885.7	11,967.2	12,010.5	12,031.0	11,866.1
2016	11,830.9	11,908.6	11,923.4	11,987.2	12,018.9	12,028.3	11,974.6	11,996.0	12,044.7	12,100.2	12,168.0	12,181.0	12,013.5
2017	11,994.6	12,088.0	12,148.5	12,183.2	12,240.8	12,287.5	12,172.8	12,199.7	12,226.5	12,335.0	12,420.8	12,434.9	12,227.7
2018	12,222.4	12,342.2	12,400.5	12,427.6	12,498.0	12,551.4	12,475.6	12,524.9	12,531.6	12,651.0	12,704.1	12,711.0	12,503.4
Total Private													
2010	8,279.9	8,308.2	8,384.0	8,426.6	8,473.3	8,530.7	8,522.1	8,554.0	8,530.2	8,566.1	8,601.1	8,641.4	8,484.8
2011	8,477.5	8,519.4	8,614.8	8,691.2	8,722.5	8,794.0	8,804.9	8,851.9	8,849.9	8,847.4	8,901.6	8,942.1	8,751.4
2012	8,798.4	8,861.6	8,943.6	9,001.4	9,061.0	9,144.8	9,120.4	9,189.5	9,167.7	9,195.7	9,271.8	9,298.3	9,087.9
2013	9,113.5	9,210.0	9,273.9	9,323.7	9,372.3	9,448.7	9,439.8	9,495.5	9,469.4	9,491.6	9,569.4	9,583.6	9,399.3
2014	9,419.1	9,489.3	9,555.9	9,641.8	9,707.0	9,779.5	9,775.9	9,833.5	9,809.2	9,870.1	9,934.7	9,979.3	9,732.9
2015	9,799.7	9,850.1	9,868.2	9,922.5	9,965.9	10,029.0	10,033.4	10,056.3	10,013.6	10,051.9	10,083.1	10,102.6	9,981.4
2016	9,925.2	9,978.0	9,986.6	10,051.0	10,073.2	10,107.0	10,125.7	10,153.5	10,132.1	10,153.8	10,207.7	10,218.3	10,092.7
2017	10,063.5	10,124.9	10,177.7	10,215.7	10,269.4	10,345.2	10,312.7	10,349.2	10,311.8	10,375.9	10,448.1	10,463.7	10,288.2
2018	10,286.2	10,371.3	10,419.2	10,457.1	10,517.7	10,597.6	10,596.2	10,651.3	10,600.1	10,676.4	10,718.7	10,727.5	10,551.6
Goods Producing													
2010	1,558.6	1,557.9	1,570.5	1,574.7	1,581.4	1,592.0	1,599.9	1,605.6	1,603.3	1,606.7	1,602.9	1,604.7	1,588.2
2011	1,583.6	1,595.6	1,611.0	1,619.5	1,625.6	1,645.6	1,659.6	1,669.4	1,674.6	1,674.9	1,676.8	1,680.3	1,643.0
2012	1,668.7	1,684.2	1,699.4	1,708.7	1,718.4	1,734.8	1,737.2	1,748.4	1,747.2	1,754.3	1,753.8	1,752.1	1,725.6
2013	1,732.7	1,754.8	1,764.2	1,767.3	1,771.9	1,786.7	1,787.7	1,796.3	1,792.2	1,793.9	1,796.9	1,794.7	1,778.3
2014	1,781.9	1,801.6	1,810.0	1,828.6	1,842.9	1,855.9	1,863.7	1,875.3	1,875.1	1,887.2	1,890.5	1,895.9	1,850.7
2015	1,872.2	1,870.4	1,855.7	1,840.8	1,837.5	1,843.6	1,838.4	1,834.2	1,820.0	1,816.5	1,803.0	1,797.0	1,835.8
2016	1,774.9	1,777.7	1,765.9	1,765.0	1,759.0	1,761.3	1,762.0	1,758.4	1,756.2	1,756.3	1,748.5	1,746.9	1,761.0
2017	1,735.1	1,754.9	1,765.9	1,768.0	1,781.7	1,800.0	1,796.0	1,799.1	1,798.0	1,809.9	1,815.7	1,819.9	1,787.0
2018	1,800.1	1,825.9	1,837.2	1,843.1	1,855.8	1,875.8	1,876.1	1,888.8	1,885.1	1,898.1	1,903.1	1,910.0	1,866.6
Service-Providing													
2010	8,598.2	8,652.1	8,729.3	8,773.1	8,856.0	8,849.9	8,724.3	8,746.8	8,789.7	8,870.0	8,916.6	8,943.3	8,787.4
2011	8,778.7	8,826.0	8,907.7	8,970.0	8,998.4	9,014.7	8,917.8	8,943.7	8,993.2	9,019.6	9,076.4	9,103.9	8,962.5
2012	8,952.7	9,029.7	9,101.4	9,143.6	9,199.7	9,229.9	9,129.6	9,183.0	9,228.3	9,291.9	9,376.6	9,405.4	9,189.3
2013	9,209.8	9,317.2	9,378.0	9,419.4	9,468.5	9,497.4	9,418.0	9,456.3	9,505.6	9,567.5	9,653.5	9,663.6	9,462.9
2014	9,491.4	9,566.8	9,631.5	9,692.3	9,750.1	9,780.1	9,694.9	9,730.7	9,776.1	9,872.8	9,945.9	9,983.3	9,743.0
2015	9,800.2	9,879.1	9,915.5	9,980.0	10,034.0	10,067.3	10,003.5	10,025.8	10,065.7	10,150.7	10,207.5	10,234.0	10,030.3
2016	10,056.0	10,130.9	10,157.5	10,222.2	10,259.9	10,267.0	10,212.6	10,237.6	10,288.5	10,343.9	10,419.5	10,434.1	10,252.5
2017	10,259.5	10,333.1	10,382.6	10,415.2	10,459.1	10,487.5	10,376.8	10,400.6	10,428.5	10,525.1	10,605.1	10,615.0	10,440.7
2018	10,422.3	10,516.3	10,563.3	10,584.5	10,642.2	10,675.6	10,599.5	10,636.1	10,646.5	10,752.9	10,801.0	10,801.0	10,636.8
Mining and Logging													
2010	193.5	195.7	197.8	200.8	203.3	207.1	208.8	211.0	211.8	214.0	215.1	217.8	206.4
2011	218.3	220.9	223.9	227.7	229.9	235.7	240.7	244.6	246.6	250.9	253.1	256.6	237.4
2012	257.0	260.3	263.5	265.8	268.0	271.9	275.0	276.1	275.4	277.9	278.8	280.4	270.8
2013	279.0	281.4	282.9	285.0	286.6	290.1	292.2	293.9	293.2	293.7	294.7	295.7	289.0
2014	296.7	299.5	301.0	304.1	306.9	311.0	315.0	317.9	317.8	320.2	321.7	322.1	311.2
2015	314.6	302.4	292.5	280.4	273.9	271.8	266.7	263.7	257.6	252.5	247.5	245.5	272.4
2016	235.1	229.4	223.0	215.8	211.4	209.4	207.5	206.5	204.8	205.7	204.9	206.3	213.3
2017	208.8	212.6	214.2	216.7	220.0	222.9	224.9	226.3	227.1	228.5	230.0	232.3	222.0
2018	231.7	236.0	238.9	240.3	243.2	246.3	248.9	251.4	252.4	256.0	255.1	257.4	246.5
Construction													
2010	554.9	552.6	560.9	564.1	565.3	568.4	572.5	573.8	571.0	569.9	563.0	559.8	564.7
2011	543.6	549.6	557.8	559.2	560.4	567.5	571.9	575.0	576.8	572.3	569.2	565.8	564.1
2012	557.2	564.6	573.4	576.7	584.2	589.8	586.0	594.7	595.0	600.8	598.1	593.5	584.5
2013	583.2	599.2	606.8	607.7	611.6	618.3	617.8	624.0	622.5	624.2	623.9	619.9	613.3
2014	614.8	625.5	632.2	642.7	651.0	654.5	657.8	664.3	665.7	671.8	670.5	670.7	651.8
2015	662.3	673.6	673.4	675.4	681.2	688.1	691.7	694.2	691.4	697.6	691.0	688.7	684.1
2016	684.0	692.1	691.2	701.7	701.7	704.4	707.5	706.5	708.6	710.6	702.4	697.0	700.6
2017	688.5	699.7	707.3	706.1	714.4	721.1	714.2	714.1	713.8	722.7	723.5	720.6	712.2
2018	708.5	723.1	729.3	732.3	738.1	745.8	741.3	749.3	745.4	752.7	751.7	751.3	739.1

1. Employment by Industry: Texas, 2010–2018—*Continued*

(Numbers in thousands, not seasonally adjusted)

Industry and year	January	February	March	April	May	June	July	August	September	October	November	December	Annual average
Manufacturing													
2010	810.2	809.6	811.8	809.8	812.8	816.5	818.6	820.8	820.5	822.8	824.8	827.1	817.1
2011	821.7	825.1	829.3	832.6	835.3	842.4	847.0	849.8	851.2	851.7	854.5	857.9	841.5
2012	854.5	859.3	862.5	866.2	866.2	873.1	876.2	877.6	876.8	875.6	876.9	878.2	870.3
2013	870.5	874.2	874.5	874.6	873.7	878.3	877.7	878.4	876.5	876.0	878.3	879.1	876.0
2014	870.4	876.6	876.8	881.8	885.0	890.4	890.9	893.1	891.6	895.2	898.3	903.1	887.8
2015	895.3	894.4	889.8	885.0	882.4	883.7	880.0	876.3	871.0	866.4	864.5	862.8	879.3
2016	855.8	856.2	851.7	847.5	845.9	847.5	847.0	845.4	842.8	840.0	841.2	843.6	847.1
2017	837.8	842.6	844.4	845.2	847.3	856.0	856.9	858.7	857.1	858.7	862.2	867.0	852.8
2018	859.9	866.8	869.0	870.5	874.5	883.7	885.9	888.1	887.3	889.4	896.3	901.3	881.1
Trade, Transportation, and Utilities													
2010	2,005.5	1,995.1	2,009.0	2,012.7	2,023.1	2,031.7	2,032.9	2,044.8	2,037.2	2,051.8	2,085.9	2,113.6	2,036.9
2011	2,048.1	2,039.5	2,055.9	2,072.3	2,077.6	2,087.3	2,092.8	2,108.5	2,101.1	2,112.7	2,152.2	2,180.8	2,094.1
2012	2,118.0	2,110.1	2,121.0	2,130.2	2,141.9	2,155.9	2,158.1	2,173.0	2,164.2	2,178.7	2,232.3	2,251.3	2,161.2
2013	2,180.1	2,178.0	2,183.5	2,195.3	2,205.3	2,218.8	2,222.2	2,239.7	2,233.7	2,248.5	2,298.9	2,323.2	2,227.3
2014	2,253.8	2,247.3	2,253.4	2,264.1	2,274.6	2,291.2	2,295.1	2,312.3	2,307.5	2,329.0	2,379.2	2,413.5	2,301.8
2015	2,340.2	2,334.4	2,339.3	2,350.8	2,363.1	2,375.3	2,377.5	2,388.8	2,382.5	2,398.4	2,438.6	2,463.6	2,379.4
2016	2,388.8	2,381.5	2,381.8	2,390.4	2,392.3	2,400.7	2,407.9	2,418.2	2,408.3	2,427.0	2,479.6	2,499.7	2,414.7
2017	2,427.4	2,410.8	2,409.8	2,416.2	2,423.3	2,436.2	2,434.4	2,449.1	2,433.8	2,460.1	2,518.7	2,534.8	2,446.2
2018	2,459.2	2,448.4	2,448.7	2,454.0	2,464.8	2,473.2	2,475.1	2,487.3	2,482.0	2,505.8	2,558.1	2,566.4	2,485.3
Wholesale Trade													
2010	475.3	475.6	476.5	478.1	480.5	483.0	484.0	485.1	484.8	485.8	486.5	488.6	482.0
2011	485.2	488.4	491.4	495.5	498.7	501.9	503.3	505.4	507.5	509.0	510.1	513.5	500.8
2012	510.9	514.6	518.1	519.6	523.2	527.4	527.0	529.2	528.7	529.9	532.0	534.6	524.6
2013	531.2	535.1	537.5	537.5	539.4	542.5	543.3	544.9	544.7	546.9	549.3	550.5	541.9
2014	546.7	550.4	551.9	553.3	556.7	561.0	562.5	566.2	566.7	570.0	572.1	574.9	561.0
2015	571.8	573.8	573.8	573.3	574.0	575.3	575.1	575.5	573.3	570.8	569.6	569.1	573.0
2016	569.8	570.5	568.7	569.1	568.6	569.3	570.1	570.2	569.4	567.2	567.8	569.2	569.2
2017	566.0	568.0	569.7	572.4	575.5	580.4	580.0	582.0	581.0	581.9	583.3	585.9	577.2
2018	582.5	586.0	588.1	590.5	592.7	598.0	598.6	600.6	600.4	604.4	607.8	610.8	596.7
Retail Trade													
2010	1,119.2	1,108.6	1,119.3	1,120.4	1,126.7	1,130.6	1,129.3	1,138.2	1,129.3	1,142.0	1,173.7	1,193.1	1,135.9
2011	1,139.5	1,126.8	1,137.2	1,147.4	1,148.6	1,154.0	1,155.0	1,166.1	1,154.1	1,165.6	1,201.6	1,218.4	1,159.5
2012	1,168.2	1,154.2	1,158.3	1,165.2	1,171.1	1,177.4	1,180.2	1,189.4	1,180.9	1,194.5	1,241.9	1,252.0	1,186.1
2013	1,192.9	1,187.1	1,188.2	1,198.1	1,204.1	1,212.2	1,216.4	1,229.4	1,222.2	1,233.8	1,277.1	1,293.4	1,221.2
2014	1,237.2	1,230.4	1,232.5	1,238.1	1,240.7	1,250.4	1,252.4	1,261.0	1,253.1	1,265.5	1,307.1	1,325.2	1,257.8
2015	1,267.3	1,263.9	1,268.0	1,278.2	1,287.0	1,296.1	1,298.1	1,305.6	1,300.4	1,314.2	1,347.4	1,360.2	1,298.9
2016	1,304.8	1,299.6	1,301.9	1,309.4	1,310.8	1,315.4	1,320.1	1,328.6	1,314.5	1,331.9	1,372.8	1,381.1	1,324.2
2017	1,328.0	1,313.5	1,311.6	1,315.8	1,316.8	1,320.8	1,317.9	1,324.3	1,307.8	1,328.4	1,372.3	1,378.4	1,328.0
2018	1,327.4	1,313.8	1,311.4	1,314.2	1,319.9	1,320.4	1,322.4	1,328.9	1,320.9	1,331.9	1,368.8	1,368.8	1,329.1
Transportation and Utilities													
2010	411.0	410.9	413.2	414.2	415.9	418.1	419.6	421.5	423.1	424.0	425.7	431.9	419.1
2011	423.4	424.3	427.3	429.4	430.3	431.4	434.5	437.0	439.5	438.1	440.5	448.9	433.7
2012	438.9	441.3	444.6	445.4	447.6	451.1	450.9	454.4	454.6	454.3	458.4	464.7	450.5
2013	456.0	455.8	457.8	459.7	461.8	464.1	462.5	465.4	466.8	467.8	472.5	479.3	464.1
2014	469.9	466.5	469.0	472.7	477.2	479.8	480.2	485.1	487.7	493.5	500.0	513.4	482.9
2015	501.1	496.7	497.5	499.3	502.1	503.9	504.3	507.7	508.8	513.4	521.6	534.3	507.6
2016	514.2	511.4	511.2	511.9	512.9	516.0	517.7	519.4	524.4	527.9	539.0	549.4	521.3
2017	533.4	529.3	528.5	528.0	531.0	535.0	536.5	542.8	545.0	549.8	563.1	570.5	541.1
2018	549.3	548.6	549.2	549.3	552.2	554.8	554.1	557.8	560.7	569.5	581.5	586.8	559.5
Information													
2010	196.3	195.4	195.5	196.0	195.7	197.0	195.1	194.9	193.4	193.2	194.6	194.8	195.2
2011	194.1	193.7	194.1	194.4	195.3	196.0	197.1	196.1	194.8	194.7	195.9	196.5	195.2
2012	195.9	195.6	196.1	196.2	196.7	197.9	197.6	197.0	195.7	196.1	198.3	198.6	196.8
2013	196.4	196.9	197.7	199.0	200.4	201.9	202.3	202.4	200.2	201.3	203.7	204.6	200.6
2014	201.3	201.1	201.1	202.0	201.9	203.1	203.2	202.1	199.8	199.5	201.0	202.2	201.5
2015	198.2	197.7	197.8	199.8	201.0	201.8	202.4	201.9	199.3	199.6	201.6	203.1	200.4
2016	200.2	200.3	199.6	202.6	203.2	204.3	204.8	203.7	201.9	201.1	202.2	203.5	202.3
2017	201.6	202.0	203.5	203.3	203.0	204.2	204.2	203.2	201.0	202.6	203.8	205.2	203.1
2018	202.7	203.2	203.0	203.5	204.8	206.3	205.9	204.2	202.7	202.1	205.0	205.5	204.1

1. Employment by Industry: Texas, 2010–2018—*Continued*

(Numbers in thousands, not seasonally adjusted)

Industry and year	January	February	March	April	May	June	July	August	September	October	November	December	Annual average
Financial Activities													
2010	618.3	620.0	621.5	621.1	623.8	626.7	626.9	627.1	625.0	629.4	631.4	634.3	625.5
2011	629.1	631.5	634.5	636.2	637.5	641.3	644.0	645.0	645.7	647.2	648.0	651.4	641.0
2012	647.0	650.1	652.8	654.4	657.8	663.1	664.4	666.6	665.9	670.6	672.7	675.7	661.8
2013	668.5	673.0	675.9	677.1	680.1	685.3	689.2	690.7	689.2	691.6	693.7	694.3	684.1
2014	686.9	689.6	691.0	693.0	696.2	700.7	703.5	706.2	704.5	709.7	711.1	713.9	700.5
2015	707.5	709.9	711.0	712.9	715.7	720.7	723.2	724.1	722.5	725.4	726.4	727.7	718.9
2016	723.5	725.4	724.9	728.7	731.8	735.0	740.4	742.2	741.2	744.8	747.6	750.8	736.4
2017	745.6	748.8	750.6	753.2	756.6	762.9	765.3	766.5	767.7	771.5	770.9	773.2	761.1
2018	765.2	769.1	769.7	768.9	771.9	778.9	781.5	783.6	780.8	786.2	783.9	783.2	776.9
Professional and Business Services													
2010	1,241.7	1,251.4	1,264.3	1,275.4	1,277.2	1,287.3	1,291.1	1,299.5	1,300.3	1,313.6	1,316.6	1,322.8	1,286.8
2011	1,299.9	1,313.7	1,330.0	1,346.0	1,342.8	1,354.2	1,357.3	1,369.9	1,375.5	1,374.2	1,380.5	1,385.7	1,352.5
2012	1,366.0	1,382.6	1,397.9	1,408.9	1,415.7	1,426.8	1,424.2	1,445.2	1,443.1	1,450.3	1,461.7	1,458.8	1,423.4
2013	1,428.1	1,449.5	1,461.7	1,466.1	1,469.3	1,482.4	1,483.8	1,500.1	1,502.7	1,511.7	1,522.7	1,519.6	1,483.1
2014	1,491.0	1,507.6	1,522.0	1,540.5	1,547.2	1,556.1	1,560.3	1,576.9	1,575.6	1,593.6	1,599.0	1,598.9	1,555.7
2015	1,573.8	1,584.3	1,585.0	1,595.0	1,593.5	1,601.8	1,612.8	1,620.4	1,616.9	1,636.8	1,639.0	1,638.0	1,608.1
2016	1,608.1	1,619.3	1,618.0	1,634.0	1,627.3	1,631.1	1,645.4	1,653.1	1,655.4	1,663.2	1,667.1	1,656.7	1,639.9
2017	1,636.7	1,651.6	1,659.0	1,661.7	1,663.6	1,676.6	1,678.2	1,685.8	1,694.2	1,709.3	1,714.5	1,704.2	1,678.0
2018	1,683.3	1,705.1	1,710.4	1,715.9	1,720.1	1,736.2	1,743.8	1,757.8	1,748.9	1,761.8	1,761.2	1,750.1	1,732.9
Education and Health Services													
2010	1,351.3	1,362.1	1,371.3	1,376.4	1,382.3	1,380.5	1,375.7	1,383.5	1,390.6	1,398.2	1,399.6	1,402.0	1,381.1
2011	1,384.7	1,390.6	1,398.6	1,408.3	1,411.7	1,409.3	1,409.3	1,418.9	1,430.5	1,430.8	1,434.7	1,438.1	1,413.8
2012	1,417.8	1,430.4	1,436.6	1,436.2	1,441.9	1,440.9	1,433.4	1,450.5	1,460.0	1,466.3	1,471.7	1,476.2	1,446.8
2013	1,452.8	1,471.1	1,477.0	1,481.4	1,485.1	1,479.6	1,475.2	1,490.8	1,497.4	1,504.8	1,510.1	1,508.9	1,486.2
2014	1,489.3	1,502.2	1,506.1	1,514.1	1,520.7	1,514.0	1,509.3	1,524.8	1,531.5	1,543.6	1,550.0	1,552.5	1,521.5
2015	1,537.4	1,552.5	1,555.8	1,569.7	1,576.2	1,570.0	1,571.4	1,584.6	1,590.3	1,600.7	1,606.6	1,608.5	1,577.0
2016	1,589.8	1,605.1	1,606.6	1,615.0	1,620.6	1,610.3	1,616.8	1,634.4	1,643.7	1,649.3	1,654.3	1,657.2	1,625.3
2017	1,643.1	1,658.6	1,661.5	1,665.6	1,671.4	1,667.0	1,651.7	1,667.5	1,669.6	1,676.4	1,680.6	1,684.1	1,666.4
2018	1,665.4	1,682.5	1,684.1	1,687.6	1,693.3	1,690.6	1,689.1	1,705.1	1,706.1	1,718.2	1,718.5	1,720.6	1,696.8
Leisure and Hospitality													
2010	956.3	971.9	994.5	1,007.9	1,025.1	1,036.5	1,025.3	1,027.0	1,018.5	1,011.8	1,009.5	1,009.2	1,007.8
2011	983.4	996.8	1,028.7	1,045.8	1,061.4	1,074.3	1,061.4	1,064.2	1,055.5	1,043.0	1,042.9	1,039.9	1,041.4
2012	1,017.9	1,038.1	1,065.8	1,084.6	1,103.4	1,123.1	1,106.3	1,112.3	1,104.3	1,091.8	1,093.1	1,097.8	1,086.5
2013	1,072.2	1,098.0	1,122.3	1,141.0	1,160.5	1,177.2	1,165.2	1,165.2	1,153.3	1,140.6	1,142.1	1,139.3	1,139.7
2014	1,119.0	1,138.8	1,168.5	1,188.9	1,208.6	1,228.3	1,214.6	1,213.2	1,203.8	1,194.0	1,190.3	1,190.8	1,188.2
2015	1,165.7	1,191.6	1,212.2	1,237.8	1,259.4	1,279.4	1,272.4	1,271.6	1,262.8	1,253.8	1,249.4	1,248.1	1,242.0
2016	1,228.0	1,252.1	1,272.6	1,294.4	1,311.7	1,327.4	1,316.1	1,315.0	1,302.2	1,288.5	1,285.8	1,282.4	1,289.7
2017	1,260.7	1,278.9	1,304.8	1,320.6	1,341.0	1,358.9	1,350.6	1,348.1	1,321.5	1,317.9	1,315.0	1,316.3	1,319.5
2018	1,292.2	1,314.5	1,339.9	1,353.7	1,371.3	1,390.2	1,384.6	1,386.5	1,360.1	1,366.8	1,352.3	1,355.6	˙,355.6
Other Services													
2010	351.9	354.4	357.4	362.4	364.7	379.0	375.2	371.6	361.9	361.4	360.6	360.0	363.4
2011	354.6	358.0	362.0	368.7	370.6	386.0	383.4	379.9	372.2	369.9	370.6	369.4	370.4
2012	367.1	370.5	374.0	382.2	385.2	402.3	399.2	396.5	387.3	387.6	388.2	387.8	385.7
2013	382.7	388.7	391.6	396.5	399.7	416.8	414.2	410.3	400.7	399.2	401.3	399.0	400.1
2014	395.9	401.1	403.8	410.6	414.9	430.2	426.2	422.7	411.4	413.5	413.6	411.6	413.0
2015	404.7	409.3	411.4	415.7	419.5	436.4	435.3	430.7	419.3	420.7	418.5	416.6	419.8
2016	411.9	416.6	417.2	420.9	427.3	436.9	432.3	428.5	423.2	423.6	422.6	421.1	423.5
2017	413.3	419.3	422.6	427.1	428.8	439.4	432.3	429.9	426.0	428.2	428.9	426.0	426.8
2018	418.1	422.6	426.2	430.4	435.7	446.4	440.1	438.0	434.4	437.4	436.6	436.1	433.5
Government													
2010	1,876.9	1,901.8	1,915.8	1,921.2	1,964.1	1,911.2	1,802.1	1,798.4	1,862.8	1,910.6	1,918.4	1,906.6	1,890.8
2011	1,884.8	1,902.2	1,903.9	1,898.3	1,901.5	1,866.3	1,772.5	1,761.2	1,817.9	1,847.1	1,851.6	1,842.1	1,854.1
2012	1,823.0	1,852.3	1,857.2	1,850.9	1,857.1	1,819.9	1,746.4	1,741.9	1,807.8	1,850.5	1,858.6	1,859.2	1,827.1
2013	1,829.0	1,862.0	1,868.3	1,863.0	1,868.1	1,835.4	1,765.9	1,757.1	1,828.4	1,869.8	1,881.0	1,874.7	1,841.9
2014	1,854.2	1,879.1	1,885.6	1,879.1	1,886.0	1,856.5	1,782.7	1,772.5	1,842.0	1,889.9	1,901.7	1,899.9	1,860.8
2015	1,872.7	1,899.4	1,903.0	1,898.3	1,905.6	1,881.9	1,808.5	1,803.7	1,872.1	1,915.3	1,927.4	1,928.4	1,884.7
2016	1,905.7	1,930.6	1,936.8	1,936.2	1,945.7	1,921.3	1,848.9	1,842.5	1,912.6	1,946.4	1,960.3	1,962.7	1,920.8
2017	1,931.1	1,963.1	1,970.8	1,967.5	1,971.4	1,942.3	1,860.1	1,850.5	1,914.7	1,959.1	1,972.7	1,971.2	1,339.5
2018	1,936.2	1,970.9	1,981.3	1,970.5	1,980.3	1,953.8	1,879.4	1,873.6	1,931.5	1,974.6	1,985.4	1,983.5	1,951.8

2. Average Weekly Hours by Selected Industry: Texas, 2014–2018

(Not seasonally adjusted)

Industry and year	January	February	March	April	May	June	July	August	September	October	November	December	Annual average
Total Private													
2014	36.0	36.7	36.8	36.3	36.2	36.9	36.4	36.7	36.4	36.4	36.9	36.6	36.5
2015	36.1	36.8	36.5	36.0	35.9	36.2	36.2	36.6	35.4	35.7	36.4	35.9	36.1
2016	35.7	35.7	35.2	35.6	36.2	35.8	35.7	35.7	35.7	36.3	35.5	35.7	35.7
2017	35.9	35.4	35.5	35.7	35.6	35.8	36.3	35.8	36.1	36.5	36.0	35.9	35.9
2018	35.4	35.9	36.0	36.6	36.0	36.1	36.6	36.1	36.3	36.1	36.1	36.7	36.1
Goods-Producing													
2014	43.1	43.3	43.5	43.4	43.0	43.5	43.2	43.7	43.4	43.4	43.0	43.4	43.3
2015	42.7	42.7	41.5	41.9	41.4	42.8	42.7	42.8	40.7	42.3	42.4	42.5	42.2
2016	41.9	41.9	40.1	41.9	42.6	42.5	42.3	42.3	42.5	43.0	41.8	42.3	42.1
2017	41.9	41.8	42.0	41.3	42.9	42.9	43.2	42.3	43.8	43.8	43.0	42.9	42.7
2018	42.0	42.9	43.1	43.6	43.2	43.5	43.4	43.4	42.4	43.8	44.1	44.3	43.3
Construction													
2014	43.1	42.3	43.0	43.2	42.1	43.0	43.7	44.3	43.4	43.8	43.2	43.8	43.3
2015	43.1	43.4	40.9	42.2	41.0	43.3	42.9	43.0	39.7	42.1	42.2	42.4	42.2
2016	42.0	41.8	39.1	41.9	43.0	43.3	43.1	43.2	43.4	43.9	42.4	42.6	42.5
2017	42.2	42.1	42.0	40.2	42.8	42.8	43.0	42.2	43.8	43.8	43.1	42.7	42.6
2018	41.6	42.5	43.6	43.7	43.2	43.4	43.1	42.4	40.5	43.3	43.9	43.6	42.9
Manufacturing													
2014	43.1	43.8	43.7	43.3	43.4	43.6	42.5	42.9	42.9	42.6	42.0	42.4	43.0
2015	41.6	41.5	41.4	41.3	41.3	41.4	41.5	41.3	40.6	41.5	41.3	41.6	41.4
2016	41.0	41.5	40.9	41.5	41.7	41.6	41.2	41.1	41.5	41.6	40.7	41.7	41.3
2017	40.7	40.7	41.1	41.2	41.9	42.2	42.2	41.2	42.6	42.3	42.0	41.8	41.7
2018	41.0	41.9	41.5	42.3	42.1	42.5	42.3	43.4	43.1	43.3	43.3	44.0	42.6
Trade, Transportation, and Utilities													
2014	36.2	36.8	37.0	36.3	36.4	36.9	36.6	36.8	36.4	36.5	36.9	36.7	36.6
2015	35.8	36.7	36.6	35.9	36.0	36.0	36.3	36.6	35.9	35.9	36.4	36.2	36.2
2016	35.6	35.7	35.4	35.5	35.8	35.9	35.8	35.6	35.9	35.9	35.5	35.9	35.7
2017	35.4	35.4	35.3	36.0	35.7	35.9	36.3	35.9	36.0	36.3	36.0	36.0	35.9
2018	35.1	35.5	35.8	36.1	35.8	36.1	36.5	36.0	36.2	35.4	35.1	35.3	35.7
Financial Activities													
2014	37.5	38.5	38.3	37.4	37.2	38.6	37.7	37.6	37.7	37.8	39.5	38.0	38.0
2015	38.2	39.7	39.6	38.4	38.3	38.4	38.7	39.9	38.2	38.4	39.8	38.4	38.8
2016	38.8	38.7	38.5	38.7	40.0	38.4	38.5	38.5	38.4	40.0	38.5	38.4	38.8
2017	39.9	38.3	38.3	39.3	37.9	38.1	39.4	38.2	38.2	39.3	38.3	38.3	38.6
2018	38.2	38.3	37.8	39.1	37.7	37.9	39.2	38.1	39.2	38.1	38.4	39.3	38.4
Professional and Business Services													
2014	37.0	38.0	37.8	37.2	37.2	38.1	37.4	37.8	37.4	37.6	38.4	37.7	37.6
2015	36.9	37.9	37.9	37.3	37.2	37.5	37.4	37.6	36.3	36.8	37.6	36.9	37.3
2016	36.6	36.6	36.4	36.6	37.7	37.1	36.9	37.0	36.7	37.8	36.6	36.8	36.9
2017	37.5	36.8	36.7	37.6	37.2	37.3	37.9	37.2	37.1	37.7	36.8	36.5	37.2
2018	36.3	36.6	36.9	37.7	36.6	36.5	37.1	36.6	37.1	36.9	36.8	37.5	36.9
Education and Health Services													
2014	33.0	33.8	33.3	32.8	32.8	33.7	33.1	33.1	33.1	33.0	33.7	32.8	33.2
2015	32.8	33.3	33.0	33.0	32.6	32.6	32.6	33.3	32.5	32.4	33.3	32.5	32.8
2016	32.9	32.6	32.4	32.6	32.9	32.7	32.4	32.5	32.8	33.0	32.6	32.7	32.7
2017	33.6	32.5	32.3	31.9	31.6	31.7	32.4	31.8	32.2	32.7	32.6	32.5	32.3
2018	32.4	32.7	32.3	33.2	32.6	32.6	33.6	32.6	33.8	33.2	33.2	34.5	33.1
Leisure and Hospitality													
2014	27.5	28.2	29.1	28.1	28.1	28.6	28.0	28.5	27.6	27.9	28.3	28.2	28.2
2015	27.6	28.7	29.0	28.2	28.1	28.4	28.4	28.7	27.6	27.8	28.3	28.1	28.2
2016	27.8	28.4	28.4	28.0	28.7	28.6	28.6	28.6	28.1	28.8	28.5	28.1	28.4
2017	28.0	27.8	28.4	28.4	27.9	28.2	28.3	28.0	27.9	28.3	27.9	28.0	28.1
2018	27.2	27.8	28.3	28.2	28.1	28.2	28.3	28.2	28.1	27.8	27.9	28.3	28.0
Other Services													
2014	32.6	33.7	33.5	33.7	33.0	33.5	32.9	33.0	32.7	32.6	33.3	33.5	33.2
2015	32.8	34.1	33.3	32.6	32.7	32.2	32.3	33.6	32.5	32.6	34.0	33.8	33.0
2016	33.3	34.0	34.0	34.0	34.7	34.0	34.1	33.7	33.3	33.9	33.4	33.7	33.8
2017	33.9	33.3	33.6	32.8	33.2	32.9	32.9	33.3	33.0	34.0	33.3	33.2	33.3
2018	32.8	33.8	34.8	35.2	34.2	34.3	35.0	34.4	34.6	34.9	34.7	35.5	34.5

3. Average Hourly Earnings by Selected Industry: Texas, 2014–2018

(Dollars, not seasonally adjusted)

Industry and year	January	February	March	April	May	June	July	August	September	October	November	December	Annual average
Total Private													
2014	23.46	23.76	23.72	23.64	23.74	23.85	23.69	23.69	23.87	24.16	24.40	24.24	23.86
2015	24.46	24.66	24.57	24.39	24.36	24.25	24.21	24.59	24.44	24.56	24.67	24.42	24.46
2016	24.57	24.42	24.51	24.43	24.66	24.31	24.39	24.42	24.59	25.04	24.79	24.85	24.58
2017	25.34	25.16	25.12	25.60	25.24	25.02	25.54	25.20	25.45	25.79	25.57	25.66	25.39
2018	25.71	25.67	25.62	25.84	25.56	25.58	26.01	25.85	26.22	26.03	26.19	26.58	25.91
Goods-Producing													
2014	25.01	25.27	25.25	25.19	25.43	25.63	25.50	25.51	25.84	26.61	26.81	26.99	25.76
2015	26.90	27.16	27.34	27.07	27.10	26.82	26.63	26.96	26.96	26.94	27.16	27.18	27.02
2016	26.90	26.75	27.38	27.21	27.68	27.35	27.36	27.26	27.46	27.73	27.78	27.72	27.38
2017	27.90	27.55	27.61	27.83	27.61	27.53	28.01	27.77	27.94	28.31	28.29	28.75	27.93
2018	28.78	28.73	29.04	29.08	28.67	28.82	29.08	28.71	29.14	29.04	28.71	28.88	28.89
Construction													
2014	23.25	23.63	23.47	23.17	23.41	23.51	23.38	23.52	23.78	24.12	24.56	24.55	23.71
2015	24.75	25.05	25.22	25.02	25.25	24.95	24.43	24.82	24.65	24.80	24.99	25.05	24.91
2016	25.47	25.24	25.94	25.55	25.72	25.53	25.18	25.32	25.38	25.33	25.54	25.43	25.46
2017	25.38	25.15	25.23	25.23	25.47	25.72	26.19	26.18	26.37	26.76	26.72	27.29	25.99
2018	27.51	27.78	27.99	28.19	27.78	28.06	28.24	27.97	28.38	28.45	28.18	28.34	28.08
Manufacturing													
2014	25.29	25.33	25.53	25.58	25.89	26.13	26.05	25.97	26.31	26.37	26.38	26.81	25.97
2015	26.76	27.05	27.19	27.21	26.98	26.97	27.03	27.39	27.52	27.47	27.59	27.70	27.23
2016	27.80	27.61	28.04	28.23	28.80	28.37	28.75	28.40	28.58	29.00	29.01	28.75	28.44
2017	29.00	28.56	28.60	28.98	28.45	27.87	28.36	28.13	28.29	28.54	28.57	28.91	28.52
2018	28.88	28.31	28.60	28.75	28.53	28.54	28.85	28.35	28.64	28.57	28.52	28.45	28.58
Trade, Transportation, and Utilities													
2014	21.16	21.32	21.66	21.65	21.50	21.60	21.35	21.25	21.38	21.56	21.77	21.86	21.51
2015	22.11	22.41	22.34	22.47	22.29	22.29	22.34	22.70	22.62	22.54	22.35	22.26	22.39
2016	22.68	22.58	22.98	22.72	22.71	22.42	22.30	22.20	22.24	22.70	22.23	22.26	22.50
2017	22.91	22.47	22.27	22.76	22.27	22.04	22.48	22.05	22.41	22.68	22.46	22.33	22.43
2018	22.51	22.42	22.46	22.96	22.74	22.78	23.11	22.86	23.57	23.43	23.63	23.87	23.03
Financial Activities													
2014	25.74	26.25	26.62	26.26	26.48	26.95	26.44	26.52	26.61	27.00	27.69	27.10	26.65
2015	27.59	28.17	28.53	28.37	28.27	28.14	28.17	28.87	28.27	28.37	28.96	28.62	28.37
2016	29.00	28.80	28.97	28.77	29.34	28.57	29.06	29.04	29.11	30.18	29.76	29.80	29.21
2017	30.24	29.91	30.17	30.65	29.58	29.14	29.76	29.85	29.84	30.51	29.94	30.07	29.97
2018	30.35	30.68	30.69	30.19	29.96	29.81	30.74	30.78	31.18	30.46	30.70	31.31	30.58
Professional and Business Services													
2014	27.58	28.15	28.10	27.75	28.13	28.34	28.15	28.38	28.40	28.36	28.75	28.19	28.20
2015	28.66	28.98	28.53	28.20	28.21	28.29	28.49	29.27	28.86	28.91	29.29	28.83	28.71
2016	29.37	29.37	29.23	29.06	29.38	28.92	29.12	28.78	29.04	29.81	29.38	29.24	29.23
2017	30.04	29.67	29.81	30.44	29.71	29.43	30.10	29.28	29.66	30.17	29.78	29.82	29.83
2018	29.77	29.53	29.36	29.78	29.34	29.40	30.05	29.53	30.30	29.65	30.03	30.93	29.81
Education and Health Services													
2014	24.18	24.22	24.01	24.07	24.12	23.87	24.16	24.05	24.00	24.40	24.18	24.15	24.12
2015	24.31	24.43	24.51	24.15	24.31	24.15	24.22	24.29	24.26	24.71	24.57	24.58	24.38
2016	24.54	24.49	24.16	24.18	24.11	24.14	24.12	24.41	24.33	24.27	24.33	24.50	24.30
2017	24.55	25.33	25.21	25.27	25.66	25.37	25.47	25.69	25.57	25.59	25.88	25.70	25.44
2018	25.30	25.39	25.05	24.95	25.03	25.02	25.30	25.81	25.38	25.54	25.75	25.46	25.33
Leisure and Hospitality													
2014	12.25	12.40	12.23	12.27	12.38	12.36	12.29	12.32	12.55	12.62	12.65	12.74	12.42
2015	12.68	12.85	12.64	12.74	12.80	12.63	12.51	12.62	12.72	12.80	12.83	12.92	12.73
2016	12.88	12.92	12.86	12.88	12.89	12.73	12.76	12.76	12.89	12.97	12.99	13.23	12.90
2017	13.04	13.09	12.92	12.95	13.02	12.85	12.84	12.95	13.10	13.13	13.10	13.47	13.04
2018	13.32	13.33	13.25	13.50	13.44	13.45	13.56	13.64	13.83	13.93	14.11	14.45	13.65
Other Services													
2014	20.54	20.89	21.04	21.41	20.99	20.91	20.55	20.82	21.22	21.02	21.24	20.94	20.96
2015	21.21	20.86	20.98	20.55	20.40	20.09	19.61	19.62	19.49	19.47	19.40	19.31	20.07
2016	19.62	19.53	19.45	19.41	19.26	19.17	18.89	19.39	19.59	19.98	19.62	19.98	19.49
2017	20.42	20.48	20.49	21.19	20.61	20.91	21.25	21.04	21.33	21.91	21.49	21.83	21.08
2018	22.12	22.03	21.71	22.38	22.19	21.76	21.96	22.13	23.11	23.03	23.07	23.47	22.42

4. Average Weekly Earnings by Selected Industry: Texas, 2014–2018

(Dollars, not seasonally adjusted)

Industry and year	January	February	March	April	May	June	July	August	September	October	November	December	Annual average
Total Private													
2014	844.56	871.99	872.90	858.13	859.39	880.07	862.32	869.42	868.87	879.42	900.36	887.18	870.89
2015	883.01	907.49	896.81	878.04	874.52	877.85	876.40	899.99	865.18	876.79	897.99	876.68	883.01
2016	877.15	871.79	862.75	869.71	892.69	870.30	870.72	871.79	877.86	908.95	880.05	887.15	877.51
2017	909.71	890.66	891.76	913.92	898.54	895.72	927.10	902.16	918.75	941.34	920.52	921.19	911.50
2018	910.13	921.55	922.32	945.74	920.16	923.44	951.97	933.19	951.79	939.68	945.46	975.49	935.35
Goods-Producing													
2014	1,077.93	1,094.19	1,098.38	1,093.25	1,093.49	1,114.91	1,101.60	1,114.79	1,121.46	1,154.87	1,152.83	1,171.37	1,115.41
2015	1,148.63	1,159.73	1,134.61	1,134.23	1,121.94	1,147.90	1,137.10	1,153.89	1,097.27	1,139.56	1,151.58	1,155.15	1,140.24
2016	1,127.11	1,120.83	1,097.94	1,140.10	1,179.17	1,162.38	1,157.33	1,153.10	1,167.05	1,192.39	1,161.20	1,172.56	1,152.70
2017	1,169.01	1,151.59	1,159.62	1,149.38	1,184.47	1,181.04	1,210.03	1,174.67	1,223.77	1,239.98	1,216.47	1,233.38	1,192.61
2018	1,208.76	1,232.52	1,251.62	1,267.89	1,238.54	1,253.67	1,262.07	1,246.01	1,235.54	1,271.95	1,266.11	1,279.38	1,250.94
Construction													
2014	1,002.08	999.55	1,009.21	1,000.94	985.56	1,010.93	1,021.71	1,041.94	1,032.05	1,056.46	1,060.99	1,075.29	1,026.64
2015	1,066.73	1,087.17	1,031.50	1,055.84	1,035.25	1,080.34	1,048.05	1,067.26	978.61	1,044.08	1,054.58	1,062.12	1,051.20
2016	1,069.74	1,055.03	1,014.25	1,070.55	1,105.96	1,105.45	1,085.26	1,093.82	1,101.49	1,111.99	1,082.90	1,083.32	1,082.05
2017	1,071.04	1,058.82	1,059.66	1,014.25	1,090.12	1,100.82	1,126.17	1,104.80	1,155.01	1,172.09	1,151.63	1,165.28	1,107.17
2018	1,144.42	1,180.65	1,220.36	1,231.90	1,200.10	1,217.80	1,217.14	1,185.93	1,149.39	1,231.89	1,237.10	1,235.62	1,204.63
Manufacturing													
2014	1,090.00	1,109.45	1,115.66	1,107.61	1,123.63	1,139.27	1,107.13	1,114.11	1,128.70	1,123.36	1,107.96	1,136.74	1,116.71
2015	1,113.22	1,122.58	1,125.67	1,123.77	1,114.27	1,116.56	1,121.75	1,131.21	1,117.31	1,140.01	1,139.47	1,152.32	1,127.32
2016	1,139.80	1,145.82	1,146.84	1,171.55	1,200.96	1,180.19	1,184.50	1,167.24	1,186.07	1,206.40	1,180.71	1,198.88	1,174.57
2017	1,180.30	1,162.39	1,175.46	1,193.98	1,192.06	1,176.11	1,196.79	1,158.96	1,205.15	1,207.24	1,199.94	1,208.44	1,189.28
2018	1,184.08	1,186.19	1,186.90	1,216.13	1,201.11	1,212.95	1,220.36	1,230.39	1,234.38	1,237.08	1,234.92	1,251.80	1,217.51
Trade, Transportation, and Utilities													
2014	765.99	784.58	801.42	785.90	782.60	797.04	781.41	782.00	778.23	786.94	803.31	802.26	787.27
2015	791.54	822.45	817.64	806.67	802.44	802.44	810.94	830.82	812.06	809.19	813.54	805.81	810.52
2016	807.41	806.11	813.49	806.56	813.02	804.88	798.34	790.32	798.42	814.93	789.17	799.13	803.25
2017	811.01	795.44	786.13	819.36	795.04	791.24	816.02	791.60	806.76	823.28	808.56	803.88	805.24
2018	790.10	795.91	804.07	828.86	814.09	822.36	843.52	822.96	853.23	829.42	829.41	842.61	822.17
Financial Activities													
2014	965.25	1,010.63	1,019.55	982.12	985.06	1,040.27	996.79	997.15	1,003.20	1,020.60	1,093.76	1,029.80	1,012.70
2015	1,053.94	1,118.35	1,129.79	1,089.41	1,082.74	1,080.58	1,090.18	1,151.91	1,079.91	1,089.41	1,152.61	1,099.01	1,100.76
2016	1,125.20	1,114.56	1,115.35	1,113.40	1,173.60	1,097.09	1,118.81	1,118.04	1,117.82	1,207.20	1,145.76	1,144.32	1,133.35
2017	1,206.58	1,145.55	1,155.51	1,204.55	1,121.08	1,110.23	1,172.54	1,140.27	1,139.89	1,199.04	1,146.70	1,151.68	1,156.84
2018	1,159.37	1,175.04	1,160.08	1,180.43	1,129.49	1,129.80	1,205.01	1,172.72	1,222.26	1,160.53	1,178.88	1,230.48	1,174.27
Professional and Business Services													
2014	1,020.46	1,069.70	1,062.18	1,032.30	1,046.44	1,079.75	1,052.81	1,072.76	1,062.16	1,066.34	1,104.00	1,062.76	1,060.32
2015	1,057.55	1,098.34	1,081.29	1,051.86	1,049.41	1,060.88	1,065.53	1,100.55	1,047.62	1,063.89	1,101.30	1,063.83	1,070.88
2016	1,074.94	1,074.94	1,063.97	1,063.60	1,107.63	1,072.93	1,074.53	1,064.86	1,065.77	1,126.82	1,075.31	1,076.03	1,078.59
2017	1,126.50	1,091.86	1,094.03	1,144.54	1,105.21	1,097.74	1,140.79	1,089.22	1,100.39	1,137.41	1,095.90	1,088.43	1,109.68
2018	1,080.65	1,080.80	1,083.38	1,122.71	1,073.84	1,073.10	1,114.86	1,080.80	1,124.13	1,094.09	1,105.10	1,159.88	1,099.99
Education and Health Services													
2014	797.94	818.64	799.53	789.50	791.14	804.42	799.70	796.06	794.40	805.20	814.87	792.12	800.78
2015	797.37	813.52	808.83	796.95	792.51	787.29	789.57	808.86	788.45	800.60	818.18	798.85	799.66
2016	807.37	798.37	782.78	788.27	793.22	789.38	781.49	793.33	798.02	800.91	793.16	801.15	794.61
2017	824.88	823.23	814.28	806.11	810.86	804.23	825.23	816.94	823.35	836.79	843.69	835.25	821.71
2018	819.72	830.25	809.12	828.34	815.98	815.65	850.08	841.41	857.84	847.93	854.90	878.37	838.42
Leisure and Hospitality													
2014	336.88	349.68	355.89	344.79	347.88	353.50	344.12	351.12	346.38	352.10	358.00	359.27	350.24
2015	349.97	368.80	366.56	359.27	359.68	358.69	355.28	362.19	351.07	355.84	363.09	363.05	358.99
2016	358.06	366.93	365.22	360.64	369.94	364.08	364.94	364.94	362.21	373.54	370.22	371.76	366.36
2017	365.12	363.90	366.93	367.78	363.26	362.37	363.37	362.60	365.49	371.58	365.49	377.16	366.42
2018	362.30	370.57	374.98	380.70	377.66	379.29	383.75	384.65	388.62	387.25	393.67	408.94	382.20
Other Services													
2014	669.60	703.99	704.84	721.52	692.67	700.49	676.10	687.06	693.89	685.25	707.29	701.49	695.87
2015	695.69	711.33	698.63	669.93	667.08	646.90	633.40	659.23	633.43	634.72	659.60	652.68	662.31
2016	653.35	664.02	661.30	659.94	668.32	651.78	644.15	653.44	652.35	677.32	655.31	673.33	658.76
2017	692.24	681.98	688.46	695.03	684.25	687.94	699.13	700.63	703.89	744.94	715.62	724.76	701.96
2018	725.54	744.61	755.51	787.78	758.90	746.37	768.60	761.27	799.61	803.75	800.53	833.19	773.49

UTAH
At a Glance

Population:
  2010 census: 2,763,885
  2018 estimate: 3,161,105

Percent change in population:
  2010–2018: 14.4%

Percent change in total nonfarm employment:
  2010–2018: 28.2%

Industry with the largest growth in employment, 2010–2018 (percent):
  Construction, 60.2%

Industry with the largest decline or smallest growth in employment, 2010–2018 (percent):
  Mining and logging, -10.5%

Civilian labor force:
  2010: 1,356,097
  2018: 1,572,136

Unemployment rate and rank among states (highest to lowest):
  2010: 7.8%, 37th
  2018: 3.1%, 40th

Over-the-year change in unemployment rates:
  2016–2017: -0.1%
  2017–2018: -0.2%

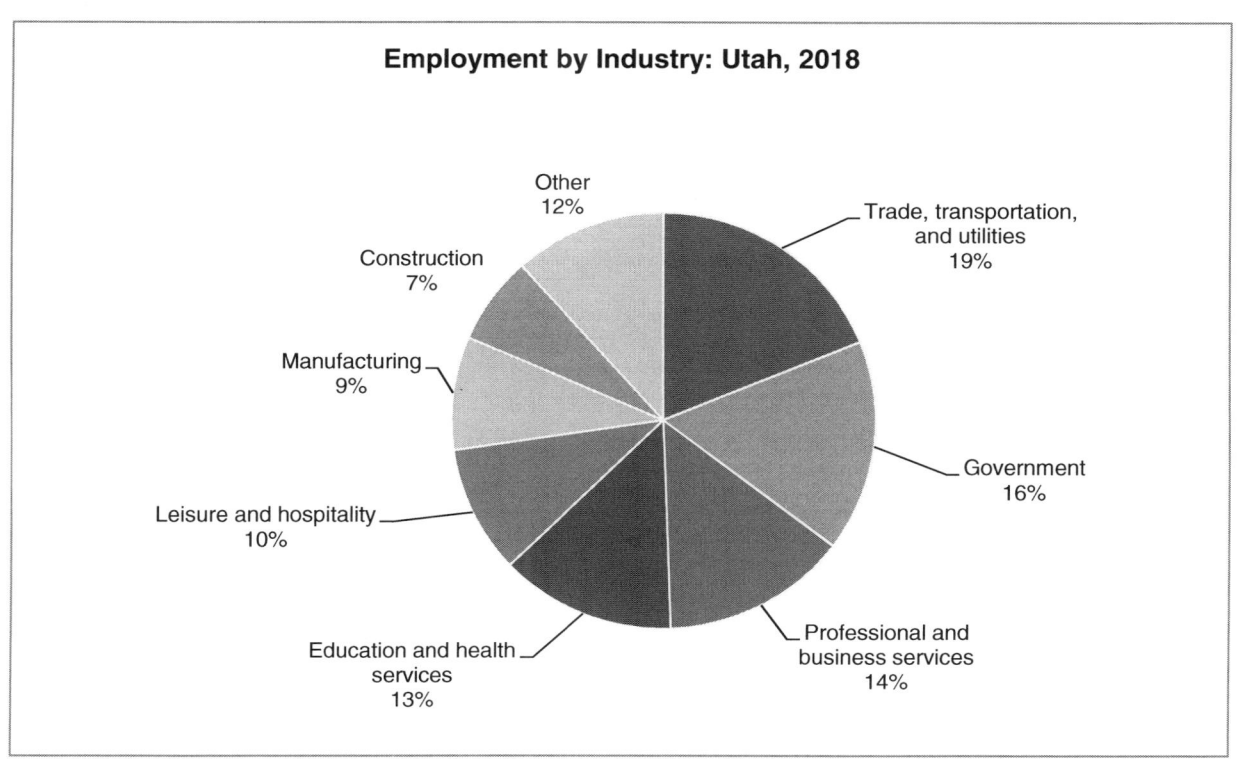

Employment by Industry: Utah, 2018

- Other 12%
- Construction 7%
- Manufacturing 9%
- Leisure and hospitality 10%
- Education and health services 13%
- Trade, transportation, and utilities 19%
- Government 16%
- Professional and business services 14%

1. Employment by Industry: Utah, 2010–2018

(Numbers in thousands, not seasonally adjusted)

Industry and year	January	February	March	April	May	June	July	August	September	October	November	December	Annual average
Total Nonfarm													
2010	1,159.6	1,159.7	1,168.8	1,182.1	1,183.9	1,187.2	1,171.9	1,179.0	1,193.0	1,198.4	1,201.3	1,204.5	1,182.5
2011	1,177.1	1,182.0	1,190.6	1,204.7	1,203.0	1,209.5	1,196.9	1,207.7	1,224.1	1,227.6	1,231.3	1,237.0	1,207.6
2012	1,212.0	1,218.6	1,229.2	1,246.4	1,251.3	1,257.5	1,237.2	1,249.2	1,264.9	1,272.2	1,281.8	1,283.7	1,250.3
2013	1,257.5	1,265.2	1,274.4	1,286.5	1,287.9	1,291.3	1,278.8	1,287.3	1,300.9	1,312.1	1,320.1	1,323.6	1,290.5
2014	1,293.8	1,301.4	1,309.6	1,320.8	1,323.6	1,328.2	1,312.2	1,325.1	1,342.3	1,352.7	1,358.7	1,364.3	1,327.7
2015	1,340.9	1,350.8	1,361.1	1,368.1	1,372.3	1,378.3	1,366.8	1,376.2	1,394.4	1,406.2	1,410.9	1,416.1	1,378.5
2016	1,388.2	1,399.9	1,410.0	1,420.3	1,421.0	1,426.5	1,418.2	1,426.2	1,446.6	1,452.3	1,455.1	1,455.8	1,426.7
2017	1,432.1	1,442.2	1,454.0	1,459.9	1,462.3	1,468.4	1,454.2	1,465.0	1,485.0	1,495.3	1,503.1	1,507.2	1,469.1
2018	1,479.0	1,493.9	1,501.2	1,506.8	1,512.2	1,516.2	1,503.7	1,516.6	1,533.5	1,542.0	1,544.2	1,549.1	1,516.5
Total Private													
2010	943.4	942.0	950.1	961.1	959.2	966.6	969.7	973.1	973.3	976.1	979.1	983.6	964.8
2011	958.2	960.8	967.9	980.5	978.4	986.8	992.3	999.1	1,001.8	1,003.3	1,007.3	1,013.5	987.5
2012	989.5	994.2	1,004.2	1,017.9	1,023.3	1,031.3	1,029.5	1,039.3	1,040.1	1,043.9	1,053.7	1,057.4	1,027.0
2013	1,032.9	1,038.8	1,047.8	1,057.9	1,057.4	1,063.7	1,068.8	1,075.9	1,073.6	1,081.0	1,089.4	1,093.6	1,065.1
2014	1,066.3	1,071.2	1,078.9	1,085.5	1,086.2	1,094.4	1,097.5	1,108.7	1,110.1	1,117.7	1,124.0	1,130.4	1,097.6
2015	1,108.9	1,115.8	1,125.0	1,130.2	1,132.6	1,142.9	1,148.9	1,157.1	1,158.3	1,166.7	1,172.2	1,177.6	1,144.7
2016	1,153.0	1,161.1	1,169.8	1,177.4	1,176.2	1,185.7	1,194.5	1,201.7	1,203.3	1,205.9	1,208.5	1,210.1	1,187.3
2017	1,189.5	1,196.0	1,207.1	1,211.3	1,211.3	1,224.7	1,228.9	1,236.5	1,237.8	1,244.8	1,252.5	1,256.5	1,224.7
2018	1,233.4	1,244.6	1,251.4	1,254.9	1,258.3	1,268.9	1,274.1	1,282.7	1,282.6	1,287.7	1,290.1	1,295.1	1,268.7
Goods Producing													
2010	180.4	178.5	179.8	183.5	186.2	188.6	190.1	191.7	191.8	192.1	190.8	188.5	186.8
2011	181.7	181.3	183.1	186.6	188.5	192.0	196.1	197.8	196.9	196.3	195.4	193.7	190.8
2012	188.9	189.6	192.0	195.2	199.8	202.3	202.9	204.6	203.4	203.2	202.6	201.4	198.8
2013	195.7	196.1	198.8	202.0	205.0	207.2	209.2	210.4	209.0	208.8	208.3	206.4	204.7
2014	202.1	202.9	205.5	208.2	212.1	214.2	215.1	216.3	215.8	216.8	216.3	215.1	211.7
2015	210.5	211.1	213.2	215.5	218.2	221.2	222.9	223.6	222.8	224.7	223.9	223.2	219.2
2016	217.7	219.2	221.8	224.5	226.3	228.1	230.5	230.8	230.1	230.3	229.8	228.0	226.4
2017	223.9	225.9	230.0	231.1	234.3	238.6	239.7	240.4	239.6	241.1	241.5	240.9	235.6
2018	237.4	239.8	241.9	243.5	246.3	250.1	250.7	251.1	249.9	252.2	249.6	247.0	246.6
Service-Providing													
2010	979.2	981.2	989.0	998.6	997.7	998.6	981.8	987.3	1,001.2	1,006.3	1,010.5	1,016.0	995.6
2011	995.4	1,000.7	1,007.5	1,018.1	1,014.5	1,017.5	1,000.8	1,009.9	1,027.2	1,031.3	1,035.9	1,043.3	1,016.8
2012	1,023.1	1,029.0	1,037.2	1,051.2	1,051.5	1,055.2	1,034.3	1,044.6	1,061.5	1,069.0	1,079.2	1,082.3	1,051.5
2013	1,061.8	1,069.1	1,075.6	1,084.5	1,082.9	1,084.1	1,069.6	1,076.9	1,091.9	1,103.3	1,111.8	1,117.2	1,085.7
2014	1,091.7	1,098.5	1,104.1	1,112.6	1,111.5	1,114.0	1,097.1	1,108.8	1,126.5	1,135.9	1,142.4	1,149.2	1,116.0
2015	1,130.4	1,139.7	1,147.9	1,152.6	1,154.1	1,157.1	1,143.9	1,152.6	1,171.6	1,181.5	1,187.0	1,192.9	1,159.3
2016	1,170.5	1,180.7	1,188.2	1,195.8	1,194.7	1,198.4	1,187.7	1,195.4	1,216.5	1,222.0	1,225.3	1,227.8	1,200.3
2017	1,208.2	1,216.3	1,224.0	1,228.8	1,228.0	1,229.8	1,214.5	1,224.6	1,245.4	1,254.2	1,261.6	1,266.3	1,233.5
2018	1,241.6	1,254.1	1,259.3	1,263.3	1,265.9	1,266.1	1,253.0	1,265.5	1,283.6	1,289.8	1,294.6	1,302.1	1,269.9
Mining and Logging													
2010	9.8	9.8	10.0	10.2	10.4	10.6	10.6	10.8	10.8	11.0	11.0	11.0	10.5
2011	10.8	10.9	11.1	11.3	11.4	11.7	12.0	12.1	12.3	12.3	12.2	12.2	11.7
2012	12.1	12.3	12.5	12.6	12.8	12.8	12.8	12.9	12.8	12.7	12.6	12.4	12.6
2013	12.1	12.0	12.1	12.2	12.3	12.4	12.4	12.4	12.4	12.2	12.2	12.1	12.2
2014	11.9	11.9	12.0	12.1	12.3	12.4	12.4	12.5	12.4	12.5	12.3	12.1	12.2
2015	11.7	11.1	10.9	10.6	10.6	10.5	10.4	10.3	10.1	10.0	9.8	9.5	10.5
2016	9.1	8.8	8.8	8.7	8.6	8.5	8.6	8.6	8.4	8.3	8.2	8.1	8.6
2017	8.1	8.2	8.4	8.5	8.6	8.9	8.9	8.9	8.8	9.0	9.1	8.9	8.7
2018	9.1	9.1	9.2	9.3	9.4	9.6	9.6	9.6	9.6	9.7	9.6	9.5	9.4
Construction													
2010	60.5	59.3	60.4	62.6	64.9	66.3	67.4	68.4	68.8	69.2	67.6	65.1	65.0
2011	59.5	58.8	60.0	62.5	64.0	66.5	69.4	70.6	69.8	68.9	68.0	66.1	65.3
2012	62.2	62.6	64.2	66.8	70.2	71.9	72.3	73.6	72.6	72.3	71.7	70.5	69.2
2013	66.2	66.6	68.8	71.3	74.0	75.6	77.3	78.1	77.1	77.0	76.3	74.1	73.5
2014	71.0	71.4	73.7	76.1	78.9	80.5	81.5	82.4	82.0	82.9	82.2	80.8	78.6
2015	76.8	77.8	79.8	82.0	84.0	86.4	87.9	88.6	88.2	89.3	88.6	88.2	84.8
2016	84.2	85.5	88.0	90.8	92.5	93.8	95.0	95.4	94.5	94.5	94.0	91.7	91.7
2017	88.5	89.7	93.0	94.3	96.9	100.2	101.1	101.8	101.3	102.1	101.6	100.7	97.6
2018	97.8	99.3	101.1	102.6	104.7	107.3	107.5	107.7	106.6	107.2	104.9	102.2	104.1

1. Employment by Industry: Utah, 2010–2018—*Continued*

(Numbers in thousands, not seasonally adjusted)

Industry and year	January	February	March	April	May	June	July	August	September	October	November	December	Annual average
Manufacturing													
2010	110.1	109.4	109.4	110.7	110.9	111.7	112.1	112.5	112.2	111.9	112.2	112.4	111.3
2011	111.4	111.6	112.0	112.8	113.1	113.8	114.7	115.1	114.8	115.1	115.2	115.4	113.8
2012	114.6	114.7	115.3	115.8	116.8	117.6	117.8	118.1	118.0	118.2	118.3	118.5	117.0
2013	117.4	117.5	117.9	118.5	118.7	119.2	119.5	119.9	119.5	119.6	119.8	120.2	119.0
2014	119.2	119.6	119.8	120.0	120.9	121.3	121.2	121.4	121.4	121.4	121.8	122.2	120.9
2015	122.0	122.2	122.5	122.9	123.6	124.3	124.6	124.7	124.5	125.4	125.5	125.5	124.0
2016	124.4	124.9	125.0	125.0	125.2	125.8	126.9	126.8	127.2	127.5	127.6	128.2	126.2
2017	127.3	128.0	128.6	128.3	128.8	129.5	129.7	129.7	129.5	130.0	130.8	131.3	129.3
2018	130.5	131.4	131.6	131.6	132.2	133.2	133.6	133.8	133.7	135.3	135.1	135.3	133.1
Trade, Transportation, and Utilities													
2010	225.8	224.4	225.2	226.0	227.1	227.8	227.8	229.1	228.1	229.4	234.0	235.8	228.4
2011	226.7	225.7	227.0	230.0	230.9	231.8	232.7	233.9	233.7	235.0	240.4	242.5	232.5
2012	234.1	233.2	234.9	237.1	239.0	240.4	240.1	240.9	241.2	242.8	249.8	250.5	240.3
2013	241.4	240.5	240.9	242.3	244.1	244.8	246.0	247.1	245.6	248.6	254.1	256.3	246.0
2014	245.9	245.4	246.3	247.8	249.6	251.0	250.9	252.9	253.0	255.8	261.9	264.5	252.1
2015	256.0	256.3	257.5	258.1	259.7	260.2	262.1	264.0	263.4	265.6	271.0	273.5	262.3
2016	264.2	264.5	266.5	266.8	268.3	269.3	270.3	271.8	271.7	272.6	278.5	280.9	270.5
2017	271.8	270.9	272.3	273.1	273.6	275.3	276.9	277.9	277.3	280.6	287.8	290.0	277.3
2018	278.7	278.4	279.9	280.4	282.8	284.3	286.2	287.8	288.4	289.6	294.9	297.8	285.8
Wholesale Trade													
2010	43.0	42.8	42.9	43.1	43.6	43.6	43.7	43.8	43.7	43.9	44.1	44.4	43.6
2011	44.0	44.3	44.6	44.9	45.2	45.4	45.5	45.7	45.6	45.7	45.8	46.0	45.2
2012	45.6	45.8	46.2	46.3	46.7	46.7	46.6	46.8	46.7	46.8	46.8	46.9	46.5
2013	46.9	47.0	47.0	47.3	47.5	47.4	47.5	47.6	47.3	47.3	47.4	47.5	47.3
2014	46.9	47.1	47.1	47.5	47.7	47.8	48.0	48.2	48.0	48.6	48.7	49.0	47.9
2015	48.2	48.5	48.6	49.0	49.3	49.3	49.5	49.5	49.1	49.0	49.0	49.0	49.0
2016	48.5	48.8	48.7	48.8	48.9	48.9	49.1	49.2	49.0	49.0	49.1	49.2	48.9
2017	48.8	49.0	49.2	49.3	49.6	49.9	50.1	50.1	49.9	50.3	50.4	50.6	49.8
2018	49.5	50.1	50.2	50.6	51.0	51.2	51.5	51.7	51.5	51.7	51.2	51.7	51.0
Retail Trade													
2010	136.5	135.2	135.7	136.3	136.9	137.2	136.9	137.7	136.7	137.6	141.4	142.1	137.5
2011	134.8	133.6	134.4	136.8	137.4	137.7	138.5	139.3	139.0	140.4	145.2	146.2	138.6
2012	139.1	138.1	139.1	140.5	141.7	142.9	143.4	143.7	143.6	145.1	151.7	151.5	143.4
2013	143.5	142.6	143.2	145.1	146.4	147.1	147.8	148.7	147.6	149.4	154.2	155.3	147.6
2014	147.3	146.8	147.5	148.6	149.9	150.7	151.3	152.7	152.5	154.1	159.0	160.5	151.7
2015	153.0	152.9	153.6	155.2	156.3	156.7	157.6	159.1	158.7	160.5	165.7	166.9	158.0
2016	159.7	159.8	161.6	161.7	162.7	163.9	164.3	165.4	165.1	166.1	171.0	171.8	164.4
2017	164.2	163.5	164.2	165.1	165.2	166.2	167.3	168.3	167.2	169.6	175.4	176.1	167.7
2018	168.4	167.4	168.6	168.9	170.6	171.3	173.0	173.9	173.0	174.2	178.8	180.2	172.4
Transportation and Utilities													
2010	46.3	46.4	46.6	46.6	46.6	47.0	47.2	47.6	47.7	47.9	48.5	49.3	47.3
2011	47.9	47.8	48.0	48.3	48.3	48.7	48.7	48.9	49.1	48.9	49.4	50.3	48.7
2012	49.4	49.3	49.6	50.3	50.6	50.8	50.1	50.4	50.9	50.9	51.3	52.1	50.5
2013	51.0	50.9	50.7	49.9	50.2	50.3	50.7	50.8	50.7	51.9	52.5	53.5	51.1
2014	51.7	51.5	51.7	51.7	52.0	52.5	51.6	52.0	52.5	53.1	54.2	55.0	52.5
2015	54.8	54.9	55.3	53.9	54.1	54.2	55.0	55.4	55.6	56.1	56.3	57.6	55.3
2016	56.0	55.9	56.2	56.3	56.7	56.5	56.9	57.2	57.6	57.5	58.4	59.9	57.1
2017	58.8	58.4	58.9	58.7	58.8	59.2	59.5	59.5	60.2	60.7	62.0	63.3	59.8
2018	60.8	60.9	61.1	60.9	61.2	61.8	61.7	62.2	63.9	63.7	64.9	65.9	62.4
Information													
2010	28.7	28.9	29.3	29.4	29.4	29.4	29.4	29.0	29.1	29.1	29.8	30.0	29.3
2011	28.9	29.2	29.2	29.2	29.5	29.6	29.6	29.8	29.6	29.9	30.7	30.9	29.7
2012	30.2	30.5	30.7	32.0	32.7	32.8	31.4	31.6	31.1	31.3	32.4	32.5	31.6
2013	33.2	33.3	33.4	32.0	32.4	32.5	32.5	32.8	32.2	32.3	33.2	33.4	32.8
2014	32.7	33.0	33.1	32.8	32.9	33.1	33.2	33.8	33.1	33.2	33.5	33.8	33.2
2015	33.0	33.4	33.5	33.6	34.2	34.5	34.9	35.4	35.0	35.5	36.3	36.3	34.6
2016	35.8	36.7	36.3	36.3	36.6	37.0	37.7	38.5	37.6	37.8	38.0	38.0	37.2
2017	38.1	38.8	38.4	38.1	38.3	38.7	38.1	38.7	38.3	38.8	38.8	38.3	38.5
2018	37.2	37.9	37.1	37.3	38.1	38.3	39.0	39.6	38.8	39.2	39.8	41.0	38.6

1. Employment by Industry: Utah, 2010–2018—*Continued*

(Numbers in thousands, not seasonally adjusted)

Industry and year	January	February	March	April	May	June	July	August	September	October	November	December	Annual average
Financial Activities													
2010	68.5	67.9	68.1	67.8	67.6	67.7	67.6	67.9	67.7	68.2	68.3	68.8	68.0
2011	67.4	67.6	67.7	68.0	67.8	68.2	68.2	68.4	68.0	68.4	68.5	69.3	68.1
2012	67.9	68.2	68.2	68.6	68.6	69.2	69.5	70.3	70.1	70.6	71.0	71.9	69.5
2013	70.6	71.1	71.3	71.8	71.8	72.8	73.6	74.1	73.6	73.7	74.1	74.8	72.8
2014	73.2	73.7	73.3	73.4	73.5	74.2	75.6	76.4	75.8	76.4	76.9	77.5	75.0
2015	77.1	77.6	77.9	78.0	78.2	78.7	79.4	79.6	79.4	80.0	80.2	80.9	78.9
2016	80.1	80.7	80.6	80.7	81.1	81.6	82.5	83.0	82.5	83.1	83.1	83.6	81.9
2017	82.7	83.0	82.9	82.9	83.3	84.3	84.5	85.0	84.5	85.4	85.6	86.2	84.2
2018	86.1	86.7	86.6	86.7	87.3	88.2	88.5	88.8	87.9	88.6	88.4	88.9	87.7
Professional and Business Services													
2010	144.5	145.3	148.3	151.4	153.2	154.8	156.0	155.5	154.9	156.6	156.6	157.0	152.8
2011	152.4	153.7	155.5	158.2	159.0	159.7	160.9	162.1	162.7	165.4	165.5	165.4	160.0
2012	159.3	161.2	163.2	165.9	167.9	169.0	169.4	172.0	171.6	174.3	174.7	174.2	168.6
2013	168.4	170.7	172.7	176.0	176.5	176.6	178.5	179.9	180.3	184.3	185.9	185.5	177.9
2014	179.3	179.2	180.3	182.1	183.4	184.6	185.4	188.3	188.8	191.6	191.8	192.9	185.6
2015	186.3	187.1	189.2	191.8	193.6	195.5	196.9	198.2	197.8	200.2	201.4	201.4	195.0
2016	195.6	196.0	197.7	200.1	201.2	202.5	205.4	206.8	205.5	207.2	206.1	205.0	202.4
2017	200.2	200.0	201.7	203.9	205.1	207.0	210.3	211.6	211.8	213.3	213.4	213.1	207.6
2018	207.6	210.0	211.9	213.2	214.8	216.7	217.8	218.8	218.2	217.7	218.0	216.4	215.1
Education and Health Services													
2010	154.6	155.3	156.0	156.4	152.1	151.4	150.7	151.7	157.1	158.6	158.9	158.4	155.1
2011	157.6	158.8	159.0	159.7	155.9	155.1	153.5	155.1	160.9	162.5	163.2	163.4	158.7
2012	162.2	163.2	164.0	165.7	161.6	161.0	158.9	161.4	166.8	168.9	170.3	170.4	164.5
2013	169.4	170.9	171.5	172.9	168.1	166.5	164.6	166.8	172.0	174.8	176.0	175.5	170.8
2014	173.2	175.1	176.0	174.4	170.8	169.1	168.0	170.2	175.9	178.4	180.3	179.7	174.3
2015	179.9	181.8	182.4	181.5	178.6	177.6	175.8	178.5	185.6	188.5	189.7	188.9	182.4
2016	188.2	190.1	190.4	191.3	187.1	186.1	184.5	187.1	195.3	196.7	197.9	196.3	190.9
2017	195.8	197.8	198.7	199.8	195.0	192.9	190.9	193.9	200.7	203.0	204.9	203.9	198.1
2018	203.7	205.8	206.0	206.4	201.0	197.8	196.6	199.7	206.7	208.9	210.0	208.2	204.2
Leisure and Hospitality													
2010	107.8	108.5	109.8	113.1	110.0	113.0	113.4	113.9	111.2	108.7	107.4	111.8	110.7
2011	110.5	111.2	113.0	115.1	112.7	116.0	116.4	116.9	115.4	111.5	109.4	114.1	113.5
2012	113.1	114.3	116.8	118.8	118.7	121.3	121.5	122.6	120.5	117.4	117.5	120.9	118.6
2013	119.0	120.5	123.1	124.2	122.3	126.6	127.2	127.6	124.5	122.1	121.3	125.2	123.6
2014	123.6	125.2	127.3	129.5	126.5	130.2	130.8	132.3	129.9	127.8	125.6	129.2	128.2
2015	128.1	130.1	132.6	133.3	131.7	136.1	137.4	138.3	135.6	133.5	130.9	134.6	133.5
2016	132.9	135.2	137.5	138.7	136.5	141.3	143.2	143.3	140.9	138.7	135.8	139.0	138.6
2017	137.8	140.2	143.3	142.4	141.4	146.8	147.0	147.9	145.4	142.5	140.4	143.9	143.3
2018	142.9	145.9	147.6	146.7	146.9	151.4	152.9	154.7	151.3	150.1	148.0	154.4	149.4
Other Services													
2010	33.1	33.2	33.6	33.5	33.6	33.9	34.7	34.3	33.4	33.4	33.3	33.3	33.6
2011	33.0	33.3	33.4	33.7	34.1	34.4	34.9	35.1	34.6	34.3	34.2	34.2	34.1
2012	33.8	34.0	34.4	34.6	35.0	35.3	35.8	35.9	35.4	35.4	35.4	35.6	35.1
2013	35.2	35.7	36.1	36.7	37.2	36.7	37.2	37.2	36.4	36.4	36.5	36.5	36.5
2014	36.3	36.7	37.1	37.3	37.4	38.0	38.5	38.5	37.8	37.7	37.7	37.7	37.6
2015	38.0	38.4	38.7	38.4	38.4	39.1	39.5	39.5	38.7	38.7	38.8	38.8	38.8
2016	38.5	38.7	39.0	39.0	39.1	39.8	40.4	40.4	39.7	39.5	39.3	39.3	39.4
2017	39.2	39.4	39.8	40.0	40.3	41.1	41.5	41.1	40.2	40.1	40.1	40.2	40.3
2018	39.8	40.1	40.4	40.7	41.1	42.1	42.4	42.2	41.4	41.4	41.4	41.4	41.2
Government													
2010	216.2	217.7	218.7	221.0	224.7	220.6	202.2	205.9	219.7	222.3	222.2	220.9	217.7
2011	218.9	221.2	222.7	224.2	224.6	222.7	204.6	208.6	222.3	224.3	224.0	223.5	220.1
2012	222.5	224.4	225.0	228.5	228.0	226.2	207.7	209.9	224.8	228.3	228.1	226.3	223.3
2013	224.6	226.4	226.6	228.6	230.5	227.6	210.0	211.4	227.3	231.1	230.7	230.0	225.4
2014	227.5	230.2	230.7	235.3	237.4	233.8	214.7	216.4	232.2	235.0	234.7	233.9	230.2
2015	232.0	235.0	236.1	237.9	239.7	235.4	217.9	219.1	236.1	239.5	238.7	238.5	233.8
2016	235.2	238.8	240.2	242.9	244.8	240.8	223.7	224.5	243.3	246.4	246.6	245.7	239.4
2017	242.6	246.2	246.9	248.6	251.0	243.7	225.3	228.5	247.2	250.5	250.6	250.7	244.3
2018	245.6	249.3	249.8	251.9	253.9	247.3	229.6	233.9	250.9	254.3	254.1	254.0	247.9

2. Average Weekly Hours by Selected Industry: Utah, 2014–2018

(Not seasonally adjusted)

Industry and year	January	February	March	April	May	June	July	August	September	October	November	December	Annual average
Total Private													
2014	34.8	35.5	35.7	34.8	35.1	35.9	35.2	35.4	35.2	35.3	35.6	34.7	35.2
2015	34.4	35.3	35.1	34.2	34.7	34.9	34.8	35.4	34.4	34.8	34.9	34.3	34.8
2016	34.0	34.2	34.3	34.4	35.3	34.8	34.8	34.9	34.5	35.4	34.8	34.8	34.7
2017	35.1	34.8	34.6	35.4	35.2	35.2	35.8	35.5	35.0	35.6	34.7	34.7	35.1
2018	34.4	34.7	34.7	35.5	35.0	35.2	35.6	35.0	35.4	34.3	34.3	34.9	34.9
Goods-Producing													
2014	39.3	39.2	40.0	40.2	39.9	40.3	39.9	39.7	39.6	40.2	39.3	38.8	39.7
2015	37.6	38.4	38.5	38.1	38.5	38.3	37.9	38.4	36.8	38.1	37.7	37.5	38.0
2016	36.3	37.0	37.7	38.0	38.0	38.1	37.6	38.0	37.8	38.6	38.1	38.1	37.8
2017	37.1	37.8	37.5	38.6	39.1	39.1	38.5	39.6	39.1	39.6	39.2	38.6	38.7
2018	37.9	38.3	38.2	38.4	38.9	39.4	39.2	39.7	39.5	39.0	39.1	39.2	38.9
Construction													
2014	38.3	38.1	39.4	40.1	39.7	40.1	39.7	39.9	39.5	40.5	39.1	38.3	39.4
2015	36.6	37.3	37.4	36.8	37.8	38.2	38.3	38.3	36.0	38.9	38.8	37.6	37.7
2016	35.1	35.9	37.2	38.1	37.7	37.9	37.9	38.4	38.2	38.8	37.8	36.7	37.5
2017	36.2	36.9	36.9	38.7	39.6	39.8	39.7	40.2	39.3	40.3	39.2	38.2	38.8
2018	37.5	37.8	37.9	37.8	38.7	39.6	39.9	40.5	40.1	39.4	39.3	39.0	39.0
Manufacturing													
2014	39.4	39.4	39.8	39.8	39.7	40.0	39.8	39.4	39.5	39.6	39.8	39.5	39.6
2015	38.6	39.3	39.4	39.2	39.3	38.6	38.3	39.1	37.9	38.1	37.3	37.6	38.6
2016	37.3	37.8	38.1	38.2	38.4	38.4	37.5	37.8	37.6	38.6	38.3	39.0	38.1
2017	37.6	38.5	37.9	38.6	38.7	38.7	37.6	39.2	38.8	39.1	39.1	38.6	38.5
2018	37.9	38.4	38.1	38.8	39.1	39.4	38.6	39.1	38.9	38.9	39.0	39.5	38.8
Trade, Transportation, and Utilities													
2014	32.9	34.2	34.5	33.6	34.8	34.9	34.3	34.5	34.3	33.9	34.8	34.1	34.2
2015	33.4	34.1	33.8	33.8	34.0	34.0	34.1	34.3	33.0	33.0	33.1	33.1	33.6
2016	32.2	32.8	32.5	33.0	33.8	33.3	33.4	33.6	32.8	33.9	32.8	33.7	33.2
2017	34.2	33.6	33.9	34.9	34.0	34.4	35.2	34.4	34.2	34.3	33.6	34.1	34.2
2018	33.0	32.9	32.8	33.6	32.9	33.2	33.5	32.7	33.3	32.1	31.7	33.1	32.9
Information													
2014	32.0	34.4	34.9	32.9	33.3	35.2	33.1	33.2	33.2	33.6	35.5	34.4	33.8
2015	34.8	36.0	36.0	34.5	34.6	34.5	34.6	36.3	33.6	34.3	35.9	34.5	34.9
2016	35.7	34.1	34.3	34.7	35.8	34.2	33.9	33.9	33.3	35.0	36.8	37.2	34.9
2017	38.6	36.5	36.5	37.0	36.7	34.8	36.4	34.7	34.0	36.4	34.4	34.6	35.9
2018	34.8	35.2	34.9	37.0	34.9	34.1	36.5	34.2	36.7	34.2	34.5	35.3	35.2
Financial Activities													
2014	36.5	36.2	36.9	35.7	35.7	36.9	36.2	36.4	36.3	36.4	37.7	36.1	36.4
2015	36.6	37.1	37.4	36.4	36.4	36.5	37.0	37.5	36.6	37.3	38.4	37.2	37.0
2016	37.6	37.2	37.2	37.3	38.0	37.5	37.1	37.4	37.3	38.2	37.6	37.8	37.5
2017	38.7	37.8	37.7	38.8	38.0	38.1	38.7	38.1	38.2	38.7	37.9	37.6	38.2
2018	37.3	36.6	36.4	37.3	36.2	36.6	37.3	37.0	37.7	37.2	37.4	37.7	37.1
Professional and Business Services													
2014	34.4	36.2	36.2	35.3	34.7	35.2	33.8	34.8	34.9	35.3	35.8	34.9	35.1
2015	34.0	35.2	35.5	34.7	35.0	35.7	35.1	36.2	35.3	35.2	35.7	35.1	35.2
2016	34.3	34.4	34.1	34.4	35.7	34.9	35.1	35.0	34.7	35.8	34.5	33.4	34.7
2017	34.4	33.9	33.8	35.4	35.0	35.3	36.2	36.2	35.5	36.7	35.2	35.7	35.3
2018	35.2	35.8	37.3	38.3	37.2	37.3	37.5	36.3	37.3	36.0	36.3	37.1	36.8
Education and Health Services													
2014	38.5	38.7	38.1	36.9	37.0	37.6	37.4	37.4	37.5	37.2	37.8	37.4	37.6
2015	37.7	38.1	37.1	35.9	36.1	36.8	37.1	37.3	37.4	37.7	38.2	37.7	37.3
2016	38.2	37.9	38.2	38.2	39.3	38.3	38.6	38.9	38.3	39.0	39.2	39.4	38.6
2017	39.4	39.7	39.1	38.6	38.9	38.7	39.0	38.8	38.1	38.5	38.5	38.6	38.8
2018	38.8	39.4	39.0	38.9	37.9	37.9	38.1	37.3	36.3	35.4	36.0	37.2	37.7
Leisure and Hospitality													
2014	25.5	26.2	26.1	24.6	25.0	26.6	26.1	26.6	25.5	25.3	24.7	24.0	25.5
2015	25.4	26.7	26.6	24.4	25.6	26.3	26.3	27.2	25.9	25.9	24.8	24.5	25.8
2016	25.2	25.7	25.3	24.2	25.5	25.8	25.3	25.1	24.3	25.4	23.9	24.3	25.0
2017	25.1	24.4	24.3	24.5	23.7	24.8	26.0	24.8	23.8	24.2	22.5	23.0	24.3
2018	23.7	24.2	23.9	23.3	23.6	24.4	25.2	24.5	24.9	23.6	22.7	23.3	23.9

3. Average Hourly Earnings by Selected Industry: Utah, 2014–2018

(Dollars, not seasonally adjusted)

Industry and year	January	February	March	April	May	June	July	August	September	October	November	December	Annual average
Total Private													
2014	23.40	23.54	23.59	23.66	23.35	23.40	23.47	23.47	23.56	23.59	24.34	23.66	23.59
2015	24.00	24.08	24.13	24.14	23.90	23.81	24.04	24.25	24.36	24.18	24.93	24.20	24.17
2016	24.45	24.24	24.11	24.43	24.40	24.17	24.28	24.17	24.75	24.66	25.04	24.37	24.42
2017	24.80	24.41	24.60	25.30	24.80	24.95	25.31	24.96	25.38	25.67	25.84	25.46	25.13
2018	25.41	25.35	25.35	25.94	25.72	25.56	26.00	25.64	26.28	25.93	26.03	26.36	25.80
Goods-Producing													
2014	23.91	23.86	23.86	24.02	24.24	24.04	24.01	24.10	24.17	24.38	23.84	24.04	24.04
2015	24.16	24.14	24.64	24.66	24.49	24.66	24.86	25.04	25.60	25.86	26.37	26.13	25.06
2016	26.21	26.00	26.03	26.07	26.49	26.16	26.04	26.08	26.26	26.31	26.44	26.42	26.21
2017	26.51	26.44	26.85	26.85	26.59	26.71	27.44	27.13	27.34	27.67	27.46	27.89	27.09
2018	27.70	27.37	27.28	27.14	26.61	26.68	27.03	26.80	26.64	26.60	27.07	27.20	27.00
Construction													
2014	23.99	24.06	24.07	24.01	24.04	23.93	24.04	24.18	24.09	24.30	24.06	24.58	24.12
2015	24.38	24.38	24.70	24.68	24.54	24.52	24.24	24.50	24.91	24.91	24.74	24.88	24.62
2016	25.46	24.94	24.74	24.67	25.52	25.14	25.26	25.24	25.35	25.38	25.07	25.35	25.18
2017	25.46	25.32	25.60	25.38	25.18	25.41	25.72	25.52	26.14	26.34	26.22	26.94	25.79
2018	26.63	27.00	26.61	26.75	26.22	26.51	26.99	27.14	26.87	27.04	27.72	28.09	26.97
Manufacturing													
2014	22.84	22.97	22.83	23.16	23.50	23.18	23.13	23.23	23.50	23.69	23.35	23.39	23.23
2015	23.69	23.69	24.27	24.34	24.16	24.37	24.83	24.83	25.48	25.59	26.10	25.54	24.74
2016	25.59	25.60	25.82	25.97	26.20	25.94	25.76	25.82	26.07	26.23	26.61	26.31	26.00
2017	26.44	26.50	27.00	27.23	27.00	26.94	27.71	26.97	26.97	27.35	27.18	27.47	27.07
2018	27.37	26.58	26.78	26.47	26.13	25.75	26.06	25.55	25.53	25.35	25.65	25.60	26.06
Trade, Transportation, and Utilities													
2014	22.25	23.05	23.32	23.66	22.10	22.59	23.05	23.26	22.79	22.92	23.21	22.81	22.92
2015	23.53	23.84	23.65	23.81	23.01	22.72	23.04	23.47	23.15	23.33	23.19	22.55	23.27
2016	23.15	22.87	21.92	22.75	22.57	22.34	22.77	22.20	22.80	23.00	22.49	22.19	22.58
2017	22.63	22.53	22.20	22.47	21.64	22.13	22.61	22.62	22.70	22.97	22.43	22.47	22.45
2018	22.94	22.95	22.42	22.99	22.79	22.77	23.66	23.31	24.00	23.54	23.11	23.25	23.15
Information													
2014	29.18	29.61	29.48	29.30	29.72	30.22	30.54	29.83	30.39	32.14	32.33	32.18	30.43
2015	32.88	31.90	32.62	32.38	31.37	32.12	32.43	32.69	32.75	33.18	33.78	33.63	32.66
2016	33.86	34.24	34.16	33.71	34.13	34.08	33.99	33.84	33.63	34.20	33.41	32.57	33.80
2017	33.73	32.12	32.65	34.50	33.76	35.50	34.00	33.29	34.82	35.28	35.41	34.92	34.15
2018	36.39	36.31	35.88	37.54	37.11	38.13	38.97	38.03	39.23	41.39	39.67	41.14	38.36
Financial Activities													
2014	28.06	28.02	27.75	27.50	27.81	27.71	27.20	27.38	27.14	26.36	27.31	26.93	27.42
2015	27.24	28.01	27.84	27.86	27.70	27.03	26.99	27.89	27.82	27.61	28.58	28.12	27.73
2016	27.99	28.77	29.33	28.94	28.70	28.25	28.19	28.34	28.78	29.46	29.58	28.90	28.77
2017	29.66	29.93	29.64	30.26	29.44	29.04	29.40	27.86	27.30	28.12	27.44	27.06	28.75
2018	27.28	27.80	27.63	28.20	28.13	27.63	27.36	28.03	28.19	27.33	27.13	27.54	27.69
Professional and Business Services													
2014	28.92	29.28	29.19	29.22	29.31	29.49	29.16	28.82	29.22	28.86	29.68	29.32	29.21
2015	29.32	29.65	29.40	28.51	28.48	28.05	28.13	28.94	28.82	29.16	30.14	30.13	29.06
2016	30.93	30.83	30.66	30.43	30.25	30.15	29.85	30.12	30.42	30.30	30.54	30.46	30.40
2017	31.08	30.35	30.75	32.04	31.10	31.29	31.82	31.19	32.23	31.72	31.58	31.81	31.43
2018	31.46	31.80	32.07	32.61	31.62	31.13	31.71	30.85	31.08	31.02	31.57	32.49	31.62
Education and Health Services													
2014	22.06	21.79	21.56	21.50	20.87	20.86	21.22	21.21	21.44	21.45	23.90	21.65	21.64
2015	22.33	22.28	22.27	22.48	22.62	22.84	23.31	22.91	22.99	22.89	25.22	23.28	22.97
2016	23.39	23.13	22.85	23.23	22.90	23.18	23.15	23.07	24.26	23.68	25.39	23.63	23.50
2017	24.20	23.31	23.67	24.07	23.42	24.16	24.34	23.87	25.39	24.07	26.08	24.59	24.27
2018	24.15	23.84	24.31	24.92	24.77	24.81	25.45	24.72	25.85	24.91	25.09	25.10	24.82
Leisure and Hospitality													
2014	12.88	12.97	13.22	12.55	12.55	12.46	12.60	12.74	12.88	13.09	13.15	13.33	12.86
2015	13.41	13.61	13.58	13.30	13.29	13.15	13.32	13.49	13.48	13.56	13.44	13.70	13.44
2016	13.83	13.93	13.90	13.65	13.50	13.19	13.32	13.14	13.14	13.26	13.43	13.84	13.52
2017	14.12	14.08	14.33	13.94	13.99	13.77	13.91	14.10	14.31	14.53	14.57	14.75	14.19
2018	14.93	14.92	15.01	14.86	14.84	14.50	14.66	14.64	14.90	14.98	15.30	15.49	14.91

4. Average Weekly Earnings by Selected Industry: Utah, 2014–2018

(Dollars, not seasonally adjusted)

Industry and year	January	February	March	April	May	June	July	August	September	October	November	December	Annual average
Total Private													
2014	814.32	835.67	842.16	823.37	819.59	840.06	826.14	830.84	829.31	832.73	866.50	821.00	830.37
2015	825.60	850.02	846.96	825.59	829.33	830.97	836.59	858.45	837.98	841.46	870.06	830.06	841.12
2016	831.30	829.01	826.97	840.39	861.32	841.12	844.94	843.53	853.88	872.96	871.39	848.08	847.37
2017	870.48	849.47	851.16	895.62	872.96	878.24	906.10	886.08	888.30	913.85	896.65	883.46	882.06
2018	874.10	879.65	879.65	920.87	900.20	899.71	925.60	897.40	930.31	889.40	892.83	919.96	900.42
Goods-Producing													
2014	939.66	935.31	954.40	965.60	967.18	968.81	958.00	956.77	957.13	980.08	936.91	932.75	954.39
2015	908.42	926.98	948.64	939.55	942.87	944.48	942.19	961.54	942.08	985.27	994.15	979.88	952.28
2016	951.42	962.00	981.33	990.66	1,006.62	996.70	979.10	991.04	992.63	1,015.57	1,007.36	1,006.60	990.74
2017	983.52	999.43	1,006.88	1,036.41	1,039.67	1,044.36	1,056.44	1,074.35	1,068.99	1,095.73	1,076.43	1,076.55	1,048.38
2018	1,049.83	1,048.27	1,042.10	1,042.18	1,035.13	1,051.19	1,059.58	1,063.96	1,052.28	1,037.40	1,058.44	1,066.24	1,050.30
Construction													
2014	918.82	916.69	948.36	962.80	954.39	959.59	954.39	964.78	951.56	984.15	940.75	941.41	950.33
2015	892.31	909.37	923.78	908.22	927.61	936.66	928.39	938.35	896.76	969.00	959.91	935.49	928.17
2016	893.65	895.35	920.33	939.93	962.10	952.81	957.35	969.22	968.37	984.74	947.65	930.35	944.25
2017	921.65	934.31	944.64	982.21	997.13	1,011.32	1,021.08	1,025.90	1,027.30	1,061.50	1,027.82	1,029.11	1,000.65
2018	998.63	1,020.60	1,008.52	1,011.15	1,014.71	1,049.80	1,076.90	1,099.17	1,077.49	1,065.38	1,089.40	1,095.51	1,051.83
Manufacturing													
2014	899.90	905.02	908.63	921.77	932.95	927.20	920.57	915.26	928.25	938.12	929.33	923.91	919.91
2015	914.43	931.02	956.24	954.13	949.49	940.68	950.99	970.85	965.69	974.98	973.53	960.30	954.96
2016	954.51	967.68	983.74	992.05	1,006.08	996.10	966.00	976.00	980.23	1,012.48	1,019.16	1,026.09	990.60
2017	994.14	1,020.25	1,023.30	1,051.08	1,044.90	1,042.58	1,041.90	1,057.22	1,046.44	1,069.39	1,062.74	1,060.34	1,042.20
2018	1,037.32	1,020.67	1,020.32	1,027.04	1,021.68	1,014.55	1,005.92	999.01	993.12	986.12	1,000.35	1,011.20	1,011.13
Trade, Transportation, and Utilities													
2014	732.03	788.31	804.54	794.98	769.08	788.39	790.62	802.47	781.70	776.99	807.71	777.82	783.86
2015	785.90	812.94	799.37	804.78	782.34	772.48	785.66	805.02	763.95	769.89	767.59	746.41	781.87
2016	745.43	750.14	712.40	750.75	762.87	743.92	760.52	745.92	747.84	779.70	737.67	747.80	749.66
2017	773.95	757.01	752.58	784.20	735.76	761.27	795.87	778.13	776.34	787.87	753.65	766.23	767.79
2018	757.02	755.06	735.38	772.46	749.79	755.96	792.61	762.24	799.20	755.63	732.59	769.58	761.64
Information													
2014	933.76	1,018.58	1,028.85	963.97	989.68	1,063.74	1,010.87	990.36	1,008.95	1,079.90	1,147.72	1,106.99	1,028.53
2015	1,144.22	1,148.40	1,174.32	1,117.11	1,085.40	1,108.14	1,122.08	1,186.65	1,100.40	1,138.07	1,212.70	1,160.24	1,139.83
2016	1,208.80	1,167.58	1,171.69	1,169.74	1,221.85	1,165.54	1,152.26	1,147.18	1,119.88	1,197.00	1,229.49	1,211.60	1,179.62
2017	1,301.98	1,172.38	1,191.73	1,276.50	1,238.99	1,235.40	1,237.60	1,155.16	1,183.88	1,284.19	1,218.10	1,208.23	1,225.99
2018	1,266.37	1,278.11	1,252.21	1,388.98	1,295.14	1,300.23	1,422.41	1,300.63	1,439.74	1,415.54	1,368.62	1,452.24	1,350.27
Financial Activities													
2014	1,024.19	1,014.32	1,023.98	981.75	992.82	1,022.50	984.64	996.63	985.18	959.50	1,029.59	972.17	998.09
2015	996.98	1,039.17	1,041.22	1,014.10	1,008.28	986.60	998.63	1,045.88	1,018.21	1,029.85	1,097.47	1,046.06	1,026.01
2016	1,052.42	1,070.24	1,091.08	1,079.46	1,090.60	1,059.38	1,045.85	1,059.92	1,073.49	1,125.37	1,112.21	1,092.42	1,078.88
2017	1,147.84	1,131.35	1,117.43	1,174.09	1,118.72	1,106.42	1,137.78	1,061.47	1,042.86	1,088.24	1,039.98	1,017.46	1,098.25
2018	1,017.54	1,017.48	1,005.73	1,051.86	1,018.31	1,011.26	1,020.53	1,037.11	1,062.76	1,016.68	1,014.66	1,038.26	1,027.30
Professional and Business Services													
2014	994.85	1,059.94	1,056.68	1,031.47	1,017.06	1,038.05	985.61	1,002.94	1,019.78	1,018.76	1,062.54	1,023.27	1,025.27
2015	996.88	1,043.68	1,043.70	989.30	996.80	1,001.39	987.36	1,047.63	1,017.35	1,026.43	1,076.00	1,057.56	1,022.91
2016	1,060.90	1,060.55	1,045.51	1,046.79	1,079.93	1,052.24	1,047.74	1,054.20	1,055.57	1,084.74	1,053.63	1,017.36	1,054.88
2017	1,069.15	1,028.87	1,039.35	1,134.22	1,088.50	1,104.54	1,151.88	1,129.08	1,144.17	1,164.12	1,111.62	1,135.62	1,109.48
2018	1,107.39	1,138.44	1,196.21	1,248.96	1,176.26	1,161.15	1,189.13	1,119.86	1,159.28	1,116.72	1,145.99	1,205.38	1,163.62
Education and Health Services													
2014	849.31	843.27	821.44	793.35	772.19	784.34	793.63	793.25	804.00	797.94	903.42	809.71	813.66
2015	841.84	848.87	826.22	807.03	816.58	840.51	864.80	854.54	859.83	862.95	963.40	877.66	856.78
2016	893.50	876.63	872.87	887.39	899.97	887.79	893.59	897.42	929.16	923.52	995.29	931.02	907.10
2017	953.48	925.41	925.50	929.10	911.04	934.99	949.26	926.16	967.36	926.70	1,004.08	949.17	941.68
2018	937.02	939.30	948.09	969.39	938.78	940.30	969.65	922.06	938.36	881.81	903.24	933.72	935.71
Leisure and Hospitality													
2014	328.44	339.81	345.04	308.73	313.75	331.44	328.86	338.88	328.44	331.18	324.81	319.92	327.93
2015	340.61	363.39	361.23	324.52	340.22	345.85	350.32	366.93	349.13	351.20	333.31	335.65	346.75
2016	348.52	358.00	351.67	330.33	344.25	340.30	337.00	329.81	324.41	336.80	320.98	336.31	338.00
2017	354.41	343.55	348.22	341.53	331.56	341.50	361.66	349.68	340.58	351.63	327.83	339.25	344.82
2018	353.84	361.06	358.74	346.24	350.22	353.80	369.43	358.68	371.01	353.53	347.31	360.92	356.35

VERMONT
At a Glance

Population:
  2010 census: 625,741
  2018 estimate: 626,299

Percent change in population:
  2010–2018: 0.1%

Percent change in total nonfarm employment:
  2010–2018: 5.9%

Industry with the largest growth in employment, 2010–2018 (percent):
  Professional and business services, 23.5%

Industry with the largest decline or smallest growth in employment, 2010–2018 (percent):
  Information, -20.4%

Civilian labor force:
  2010: 359,402
  2018: 346,061

Unemployment rate and rank among states (highest to lowest):
  2010: 6.1%, 46th
  2018: 2.7%, 47th

Over-the-year change in unemployment rates:
  2016–2017: -0.2%
  2017–2018: -0.3%

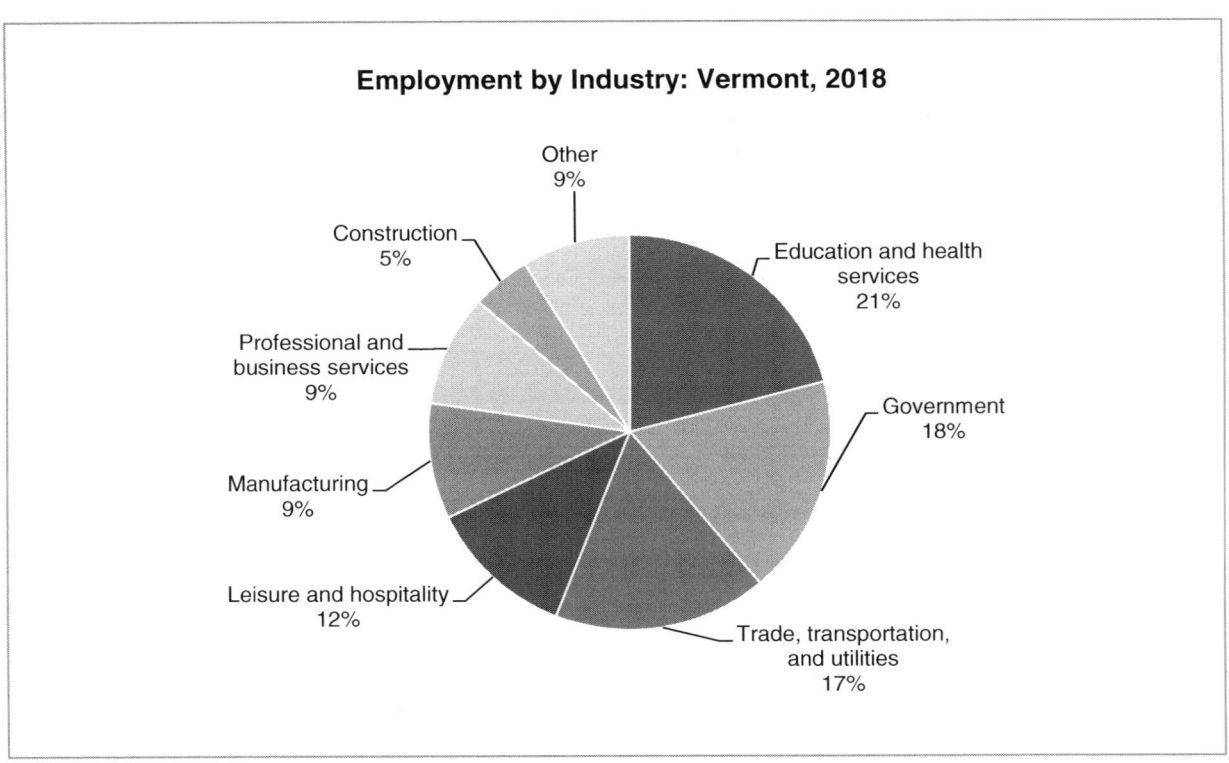

Employment by Industry: Vermont, 2018

- Other 9%
- Construction 5%
- Professional and business services 9%
- Manufacturing 9%
- Leisure and hospitality 12%
- Education and health services 21%
- Government 18%
- Trade, transportation, and utilities 17%

1. Employment by Industry: Vermont, 2010–2018

(Numbers in thousands, not seasonally adjusted)

Industry and year	January	February	March	April	May	June	July	August	September	October	November	December	Annual average
Total Nonfarm													
2010	293.7	296.2	295.2	295.6	297.5	297.5	294.0	294.2	299.7	305.3	301.5	305.6	298.0
2011	297.0	299.8	298.5	295.9	299.2	300.7	294.7	297.8	303.3	306.8	304.6	310.4	300.7
2012	300.9	303.0	303.6	299.2	304.0	304.8	299.9	302.2	307.6	308.3	308.0	312.5	304.5
2013	303.5	304.8	305.6	303.5	305.0	307.0	299.9	304.2	308.1	311.5	311.0	315.1	306.6
2014	306.7	308.4	307.8	304.4	308.3	310.6	304.7	308.4	311.7	314.0	313.3	317.3	309.6
2015	310.5	311.2	310.6	308.8	311.3	313.6	308.2	308.8	314.0	316.1	314.6	318.5	312.2
2016	310.3	312.4	310.9	309.0	311.7	314.1	310.7	310.9	315.8	317.2	315.7	319.8	313.2
2017	312.1	312.0	312.7	310.9	312.1	318.7	311.9	314.0	316.9	318.5	317.7	322.0	315.0
2018	310.9	314.3	313.8	310.1	311.3	315.6	315.0	316.5	316.7	319.5	319.3	322.5	315.5
Total Private													
2010	238.4	239.2	237.6	238.1	238.7	242.7	249.5	247.7	245.0	247.8	244.0	248.4	243.1
2011	241.8	242.8	241.5	238.8	241.6	246.5	250.2	250.8	248.1	249.1	246.8	252.3	245.9
2012	245.5	245.6	246.1	241.5	246.0	251.3	254.7	254.9	251.4	250.6	249.9	254.5	249.3
2013	247.3	247.5	248.0	245.6	248.0	253.3	254.8	255.9	252.1	253.2	252.6	256.9	251.3
2014	250.2	250.5	250.0	246.1	250.9	256.0	258.2	259.4	254.7	255.3	254.5	259.1	253.7
2015	253.4	253.0	252.5	250.5	254.0	258.8	261.4	260.5	257.3	257.8	256.3	260.6	256.3
2016	254.1	254.5	252.9	251.0	254.5	259.3	263.1	262.2	258.8	258.5	256.8	261.7	257.3
2017	255.9	254.1	254.7	252.7	255.6	262.5	263.4	263.4	259.5	259.6	259.1	263.5	258.7
2018	256.1	257.1	256.3	252.7	254.8	260.6	264.1	264.2	259.9	259.8	260.1	263.3	259.1
Goods Producing													
2010	41.9	41.7	41.6	43.8	45.5	46.1	47.1	47.0	46.4	46.7	45.9	44.7	44.9
2011	42.4	42.5	42.0	43.4	45.4	47.1	48.1	48.4	48.1	48.7	47.8	47.2	45.9
2012	44.3	44.0	44.4	45.8	47.4	48.4	48.9	48.7	48.3	48.0	47.3	46.7	46.9
2013	44.2	44.2	44.4	45.1	46.9	48.0	48.3	48.2	47.8	47.8	47.5	46.9	46.6
2014	44.3	44.3	44.1	44.6	46.9	48.2	48.9	48.9	48.0	48.0	47.6	47.3	46.8
2015	44.4	44.4	44.2	45.4	47.4	48.3	48.8	48.7	48.2	47.9	47.4	46.8	46.8
2016	44.2	43.8	43.6	45.2	46.6	47.7	48.0	47.8	47.1	47.1	46.4	45.7	46.1
2017	43.5	42.8	43.1	44.1	45.9	47.1	47.1	47.1	46.6	46.7	46.2	45.9	45.5
2018	43.3	43.3	43.5	44.5	46.1	47.0	47.7	47.6	46.9	46.7	46.6	45.4	45.7
Service-Providing													
2010	251.8	254.5	253.6	251.8	252.0	251.4	246.9	247.2	253.3	258.6	255.6	260.9	253.1
2011	254.6	257.3	256.5	252.5	253.8	253.6	246.6	249.4	255.2	258.1	256.8	263.2	254.8
2012	256.6	259.0	259.2	253.4	256.6	256.4	251.0	253.5	259.3	260.3	260.7	265.8	257.7
2013	259.3	260.6	261.2	258.4	258.1	259.0	251.6	256.0	260.3	263.7	263.5	268.2	260.0
2014	262.4	264.1	263.7	259.8	261.4	262.4	255.8	259.5	263.7	266.0	265.7	270.0	262.9
2015	266.1	266.8	266.4	263.4	263.9	265.3	259.4	260.1	265.8	268.2	267.2	271.7	265.4
2016	266.1	268.6	267.3	263.8	265.1	266.4	262.7	263.1	268.7	270.1	269.3	274.1	267.1
2017	268.6	269.2	269.6	266.8	266.2	271.6	264.8	266.9	270.3	271.8	271.5	276.1	269.5
2018	267.6	271.0	270.3	265.6	265.2	268.6	267.3	268.9	269.8	272.8	272.7	277.1	269.7
Mining and Logging													
2010	0.7	0.7	0.7	0.7	0.8	0.8	0.8	0.8	0.8	0.8	0.8	0.7	0.8
2011	0.7	0.7	0.7	0.7	0.8	0.8	0.8	0.8	0.8	0.8	0.8	0.8	0.8
2012	0.7	0.7	0.7	0.8	0.8	0.8	0.9	0.9	0.9	0.9	0.8	0.8	0.8
2013	0.7	0.7	0.7	0.7	0.8	0.8	0.8	0.8	0.8	0.8	0.8	0.8	0.8
2014	0.7	0.7	0.7	0.7	0.8	0.8	0.9	0.9	0.8	0.8	0.8	0.8	0.8
2015	0.7	0.8	0.8	0.8	0.8	0.9	0.9	0.9	0.9	0.9	0.8	0.8	0.8
2016	0.8	0.7	0.7	0.8	0.8	0.9	0.9	0.9	0.9	0.9	0.8	0.8	0.8
2017	0.7	0.7	0.7	0.7	0.8	0.8	0.8	0.8	0.8	0.8	0.8	0.8	0.8
2018	0.7	0.7	0.7	0.8	0.8	0.8	0.9	0.8	0.8	0.8	0.8	0.7	0.8
Construction													
2010	11.4	10.9	10.9	12.8	14.2	14.4	15.2	15.2	14.9	15.0	14.3	13.1	13.5
2011	11.5	11.1	11.0	12.2	13.8	15.0	15.9	16.0	16.0	16.4	15.5	14.5	14.1
2012	12.5	11.9	12.1	13.4	14.6	15.4	15.9	15.8	15.4	15.2	14.6	13.6	14.2
2013	12.1	11.7	12.0	12.7	14.3	15.0	15.4	15.6	15.5	15.5	15.1	14.2	14.1
2014	12.7	12.3	12.4	13.0	14.9	15.9	16.5	16.5	16.2	16.2	15.7	15.0	14.8
2015	13.2	12.8	12.8	13.9	15.7	16.3	16.8	16.7	16.4	16.2	15.8	15.1	15.1
2016	13.4	13.0	13.2	14.6	15.9	16.6	17.0	16.8	16.5	16.2	15.7	14.8	15.3
2017	13.5	13.0	13.1	14.1	15.6	16.4	16.6	16.6	16.3	16.3	15.7	15.0	15.2
2018	13.5	13.3	13.4	14.2	15.6	16.2	16.6	16.6	16.3	15.9	15.4	14.4	15.1

1. Employment by Industry: Vermont, 2010–2018—*Continued*

(Numbers in thousands, not seasonally adjusted)

Industry and year	January	February	March	April	May	June	July	August	September	October	November	December	Annual average
Manufacturing													
2010	29.8	30.1	30.0	30.3	30.5	30.9	31.1	31.0	30.7	30.9	30.8	30.9	30.6
2011	30.2	30.7	30.3	30.5	30.8	31.3	31.4	31.6	31.3	31.5	31.5	31.9	31.1
2012	31.1	31.4	31.6	31.6	32.0	32.2	32.1	32.0	32.0	31.9	31.9	32.3	31.8
2013	31.4	31.8	31.7	31.7	31.8	32.2	32.1	31.8	31.5	31.5	31.6	31.9	31.8
2014	30.9	31.3	31.0	30.9	31.2	31.5	31.5	31.5	31.0	31.0	31.1	31.5	31.2
2015	30.5	30.8	30.6	30.7	30.9	31.1	31.1	31.1	30.9	30.8	30.8	30.9	30.9
2016	30.0	30.1	29.7	29.8	29.9	30.2	30.1	30.1	29.8	30.0	29.9	30.1	30.0
2017	29.3	29.1	29.3	29.3	29.5	29.9	29.7	29.7	29.5	29.6	29.7	30.1	29.6
2018	29.1	29.3	29.4	29.5	29.7	30.0	30.2	30.2	29.8	30.0	30.4	30.3	29.8
Trade, Transportation, and Utilities													
2010	54.8	54.5	54.0	54.7	54.9	55.7	56.6	56.4	56.0	57.1	57.7	58.3	55.9
2011	55.6	55.2	54.9	54.8	55.3	56.0	55.8	55.9	55.5	56.3	57.0	57.9	55.9
2012	54.7	54.3	54.1	54.4	55.1	56.0	55.8	55.8	55.6	55.8	56.7	57.6	55.5
2013	54.8	54.2	54.3	54.3	55.0	56.0	55.4	55.7	55.3	56.0	56.8	57.7	55.5
2014	54.9	54.4	54.4	54.4	55.5	56.1	55.8	55.9	55.5	56.2	57.2	58.0	55.7
2015	55.3	54.7	54.6	54.5	55.2	56.0	55.6	55.4	55.0	55.7	56.4	57.4	55.5
2016	55.1	54.6	54.6	54.9	55.5	55.8	55.7	55.7	55.4	55.6	56.4	57.3	55.6
2017	55.2	54.1	54.1	54.6	55.0	55.8	55.1	55.3	54.7	55.3	56.0	56.7	55.2
2018	54.3	53.8	53.6	53.7	54.1	54.7	54.7	54.8	54.3	54.4	54.4	55.1	54.3
Wholesale Trade													
2010	9.2	9.2	9.2	9.3	9.3	9.4	9.6	9.6	9.5	9.6	9.7	9.5	9.4
2011	9.4	9.3	9.4	9.4	9.4	9.4	9.6	9.6	9.5	9.5	9.5	9.3	9.4
2012	9.1	9.0	9.1	9.2	9.2	9.3	9.3	9.3	9.2	9.2	9.3	9.2	9.2
2013	9.0	8.9	9.0	9.0	9.1	9.3	9.2	9.3	9.1	9.2	9.2	9.3	9.1
2014	9.1	9.0	9.1	9.1	9.3	9.3	9.3	9.4	9.3	9.3	9.3	9.3	9.2
2015	9.2	9.2	9.2	9.2	9.3	9.3	9.4	9.4	9.3	9.3	9.3	9.3	9.3
2016	9.3	9.3	9.3	9.5	9.6	9.5	9.5	9.5	9.4	9.3	9.3	9.3	9.4
2017	9.3	9.1	9.1	9.2	9.3	9.4	9.4	9.4	9.3	9.3	9.2	9.2	9.3
2018	8.9	8.9	9.0	9.0	9.1	9.1	9.1	9.2	9.1	9.2	9.3	9.3	9.1
Retail Trade													
2010	37.3	37.0	36.5	37.2	37.2	37.8	38.6	38.4	37.7	38.6	39.1	39.5	37.9
2011	37.5	37.3	36.9	37.0	37.4	37.9	38.0	38.2	37.2	37.8	38.4	39.3	37.7
2012	37.1	36.9	36.6	36.7	37.3	38.0	38.3	38.2	37.6	37.7	38.5	39.1	37.7
2013	37.1	36.8	36.6	36.9	37.4	38.1	38.1	38.2	37.5	37.9	38.5	39.2	37.7
2014	37.3	37.0	36.9	37.0	37.6	38.2	38.4	38.4	37.6	38.2	39.0	39.5	37.9
2015	37.7	37.3	37.2	37.2	37.7	38.3	38.4	38.2	37.4	38.0	38.6	39.2	37.9
2016	37.7	37.4	37.3	37.5	37.8	38.4	38.7	38.6	37.9	38.1	38.8	39.3	38.1
2017	37.9	37.1	37.1	37.5	37.7	38.3	38.1	38.2	37.4	38.0	38.6	38.9	37.9
2018	37.4	37.0	36.7	36.8	37.0	37.5	37.9	37.8	37.0	36.9	37.1	37.5	37.2
Transportation and Utilities													
2010	8.3	8.3	8.3	8.2	8.4	8.5	8.4	8.4	8.8	8.9	8.9	9.3	8.6
2011	8.7	8.6	8.6	8.4	8.5	8.7	8.2	8.1	8.8	9.0	9.1	9.3	8.7
2012	8.5	8.4	8.4	8.5	8.6	8.7	8.2	8.3	8.8	8.9	8.9	9.3	8.6
2013	8.7	8.5	8.7	8.4	8.5	8.6	8.1	8.2	8.7	8.9	9.1	9.2	8.6
2014	8.5	8.4	8.4	8.3	8.6	8.6	8.1	8.1	8.6	8.7	8.9	9.2	8.5
2015	8.4	8.2	8.2	8.1	8.2	8.4	7.8	7.8	8.3	8.4	8.5	8.9	8.3
2016	8.1	7.9	8.0	7.9	8.1	7.9	7.5	7.6	8.1	8.2	8.3	8.7	8.0
2017	8.0	7.9	7.9	7.9	8.0	8.1	7.6	7.7	8.0	8.0	8.2	8.6	8.0
2018	8.0	7.9	7.9	7.9	8.0	8.1	7.7	7.8	8.2	8.3	8.0	8.3	8.0
Information													
2010	5.4	5.4	5.4	5.4	5.4	5.4	5.3	5.3	5.3	5.3	5.3	5.3	5.4
2011	5.2	5.3	5.2	5.0	4.9	5.0	4.9	4.9	4.8	4.8	4.8	4.8	5.0
2012	4.7	4.7	4.7	4.6	4.7	4.7	4.7	4.7	4.7	4.7	4.7	4.8	4.7
2013	4.7	4.7	4.7	4.7	4.7	4.8	4.7	4.8	4.7	4.7	4.8	4.8	4.7
2014	4.8	4.8	4.9	4.8	4.8	4.9	4.8	4.8	4.8	4.8	4.4	4.4	4.8
2015	4.5	4.5	4.7	4.7	4.7	4.7	4.7	4.7	4.6	4.7	4.7	4.7	4.7
2016	4.6	4.6	4.7	4.6	4.7	4.6	4.6	4.6	4.7	4.6	4.6	4.6	4.6
2017	4.6	4.6	4.6	4.5	4.5	4.5	4.4	4.4	4.4	4.4	4.4	4.4	4.5
2018	4.3	4.3	4.4	4.3	4.3	4.4	4.3	4.3	4.2	4.2	4.3	4.3	4.3

1. Employment by Industry: Vermont, 2010–2018—*Continued*

(Numbers in thousands, not seasonally adjusted)

Industry and year	January	February	March	April	May	June	July	August	September	October	November	December	Annual average
Financial Activities													
2010	12.1	12.1	12.0	12.1	12.0	12.3	12.4	12.4	12.1	12.2	12.1	12.2	12.2
2011	12.1	12.0	12.0	11.9	12.0	12.3	12.3	12.3	12.1	12.1	12.0	12.1	12.1
2012	12.0	11.9	12.0	11.8	12.1	12.2	12.3	12.2	12.0	11.9	11.9	12.0	12.0
2013	11.8	11.8	11.8	11.8	12.1	12.3	12.3	12.3	12.1	12.1	12.0	12.1	12.0
2014	12.0	11.9	11.8	11.9	12.1	12.3	12.4	12.4	12.2	12.2	12.1	12.1	12.1
2015	12.0	12.0	11.8	11.9	12.1	12.2	12.3	12.3	12.0	12.1	11.9	11.9	12.0
2016	11.9	11.9	11.8	11.9	12.0	12.2	12.2	12.2	12.0	12.0	11.9	12.1	12.0
2017	11.9	11.9	11.9	11.9	12.0	12.2	12.3	12.3	12.1	12.1	12.0	12.1	12.1
2018	11.9	11.9	11.9	11.9	12.0	12.2	12.6	12.4	12.3	12.1	11.8	11.7	12.1
Professional and Business Services													
2010	21.9	21.9	22.0	23.1	23.2	23.6	24.4	24.4	24.1	24.5	24.0	23.7	23.4
2011	23.0	23.2	23.4	24.1	25.0	25.5	25.7	25.9	26.0	25.9	25.7	25.5	24.9
2012	24.7	24.9	25.2	26.1	26.2	26.9	26.9	27.0	26.5	26.4	26.2	26.0	26.1
2013	25.0	25.1	25.5	26.2	26.9	27.3	27.1	27.2	26.8	26.7	26.5	26.3	26.4
2014	25.2	25.4	25.6	26.0	26.9	27.6	27.5	27.4	27.1	27.2	26.9	26.7	26.6
2015	25.8	25.9	25.9	27.1	27.9	28.6	28.3	28.5	28.0	28.2	27.8	27.4	27.5
2016	26.3	26.5	26.6	27.5	28.0	28.6	29.0	29.1	28.5	28.5	28.0	27.8	27.9
2017	26.9	26.9	27.2	28.3	29.0	29.7	29.5	29.5	28.9	29.2	28.7	28.4	28.5
2018	27.6	27.7	27.8	28.4	29.1	29.8	29.9	30.1	29.3	29.0	28.8	28.7	28.9
Education and Health Services													
2010	58.1	59.0	59.2	59.7	58.9	58.2	59.5	58.5	59.4	60.0	59.5	59.7	59.1
2011	58.5	59.7	59.8	59.9	59.5	58.5	59.5	59.1	59.8	59.7	59.8	60.1	59.5
2012	59.5	60.2	60.8	60.4	60.2	59.6	61.0	61.0	60.7	61.5	61.4	61.8	60.7
2013	60.7	61.3	61.9	61.6	61.3	60.8	61.9	61.7	61.5	62.3	62.5	62.5	61.7
2014	61.9	61.9	62.3	62.1	62.1	62.0	62.6	62.5	62.2	62.9	63.0	63.3	62.4
2015	62.9	62.8	63.2	63.2	63.5	63.0	64.2	63.0	63.2	63.8	64.0	64.6	63.5
2016	63.7	64.1	64.2	64.7	64.4	63.6	65.0	64.1	64.4	64.9	65.1	65.6	64.5
2017	64.5	64.6	65.5	65.2	65.4	65.4	66.0	65.3	65.7	65.8	65.9	66.4	65.5
2018	65.1	66.0	66.2	66.0	65.7	65.4	66.2	65.5	65.9	67.0	66.9	67.4	66.1
Leisure and Hospitality													
2010	34.5	34.9	33.7	29.4	29.0	31.5	34.0	33.6	31.7	32.0	29.7	34.7	32.4
2011	35.3	35.2	34.5	29.8	29.5	32.0	33.7	34.2	31.7	31.5	29.7	34.6	32.6
2012	35.6	35.6	34.8	28.5	30.3	33.4	34.9	35.3	33.5	32.2	31.7	35.6	33.5
2013	36.3	36.4	35.6	31.9	31.1	33.8	34.8	35.7	33.7	33.5	32.5	36.5	34.3
2014	37.2	37.8	36.9	32.3	32.4	34.5	35.7	37.0	34.6	33.8	33.1	37.0	35.2
2015	38.4	38.7	37.9	33.5	33.0	35.5	36.9	37.4	35.9	35.0	33.8	37.4	36.1
2016	38.1	38.7	37.1	31.8	32.8	36.2	38.0	38.1	36.3	35.4	34.2	38.4	36.3
2017	39.4	39.3	38.3	34.1	33.7	37.5	38.7	39.2	36.9	35.9	35.8	39.5	37.4
2018	39.7	40.0	38.8	33.7	33.3	36.7	38.2	39.0	36.7	36.2	37.0	40.6	37.5
Other Services													
2010	9.7	9.7	9.7	9.9	9.8	9.9	10.2	10.1	10.0	10.0	9.8	9.8	9.9
2011	9.7	9.7	9.7	9.9	10.0	10.1	10.2	10.1	10.1	10.1	10.0	10.1	10.0
2012	10.0	10.0	10.1	9.9	10.0	10.1	10.2	10.2	10.1	10.1	10.0	10.0	10.1
2013	9.8	9.8	9.8	10.0	10.0	10.3	10.3	10.3	10.2	10.1	10.0	10.1	10.1
2014	9.9	10.0	10.0	10.0	10.2	10.4	10.5	10.5	10.3	10.2	10.2	10.3	10.2
2015	10.1	10.0	10.2	10.2	10.2	10.5	10.6	10.5	10.4	10.4	10.3	10.4	10.3
2016	10.2	10.3	10.3	10.4	10.5	10.6	10.6	10.6	10.4	10.4	10.2	10.2	10.4
2017	9.9	9.9	10.0	10.0	10.1	10.3	10.3	10.3	10.2	10.2	10.1	10.1	10.1
2018	9.9	10.1	10.1	10.2	10.2	10.4	10.5	10.5	10.3	10.2	10.3	10.1	10.2
Government													
2010	55.3	57.0	57.6	57.5	58.8	54.8	44.5	46.5	54.7	57.5	57.5	57.2	54.9
2011	55.2	57.0	57.0	57.1	57.6	54.2	44.5	47.0	55.2	57.7	57.8	58.1	54.9
2012	55.4	57.4	57.5	57.7	58.0	53.5	45.2	47.3	56.2	57.7	58.1	58.0	55.2
2013	56.2	57.3	57.6	57.9	57.0	53.7	45.1	48.3	56.0	58.3	58.4	58.2	55.3
2014	56.5	57.9	57.8	58.3	57.4	54.6	46.5	49.0	57.0	58.7	58.8	58.2	55.9
2015	57.1	58.2	58.1	58.3	57.3	54.8	46.8	48.3	56.7	58.3	58.3	57.9	55.8
2016	56.2	57.9	58.0	58.0	57.2	54.8	47.6	48.7	57.0	58.7	58.9	58.1	55.9
2017	56.2	57.9	58.0	58.2	56.5	56.2	48.5	50.6	57.4	58.9	58.6	58.5	56.3
2018	54.8	57.2	57.5	57.4	56.5	55.0	50.9	52.3	56.8	59.7	59.2	59.2	56.4

2. Average Weekly Hours by Selected Industry: Vermont, 2014–2018

(Not seasonally adjusted)

Industry and year	January	February	March	April	May	June	July	August	September	October	November	December	Annual average
Total Private													
2014	33.0	33.0	32.9	33.5	33.7	33.8	33.8	33.6	33.8	33.7	33.5	32.8	33.4
2015	32.9	33.0	33.0	33.1	33.5	33.6	33.8	33.8	33.5	33.6	33.3	32.9	33.3
2016	33.0	32.9	32.9	33.3	33.8	33.7	34.0	33.8	33.8	33.7	33.3	32.6	33.4
2017	33.4	32.9	32.6	33.4	33.5	33.7	34.2	33.9	33.7	33.8	33.3	32.9	33.5
2018	32.9	33.2	32.8	33.4	33.5	33.7	33.9	33.7	33.6	33.4	33.3	33.5	33.4
Goods-Producing													
2014	38.0	37.7	37.4	38.9	39.0	38.7	39.1	38.7	38.8	38.3	38.4	37.5	38.4
2015	37.3	37.0	37.4	37.5	37.9	37.8	37.9	37.9	37.0	37.8	38.0	38.2	37.6
2016	37.9	37.2	37.4	38.0	38.0	38.2	38.1	37.9	38.0	38.0	37.8	37.8	37.9
2017	38.5	37.9	37.4	38.2	38.4	38.5	38.7	38.2	38.5	38.8	38.3	37.2	38.2
2018	37.7	38.2	37.4	37.9	38.7	38.9	38.6	39.0	38.8	38.7	38.4	39.0	38.5
Construction													
2014	36.7	35.8	35.6	37.8	39.8	39.2	40.5	39.7	39.9	38.7	39.2	36.7	38.4
2015	35.9	35.4	36.4	36.5	37.1	37.1	37.9	37.6	36.7	37.7	37.4	38.2	37.1
2016	37.4	36.4	36.3	37.5	38.3	38.1	38.2	37.8	38.6	38.6	37.9	37.1	37.7
2017	37.5	36.4	35.7	37.0	38.5	38.9	39.1	38.5	38.8	38.5	37.6	36.8	37.9
2018	36.8	37.0	36.0	36.5	38.7	39.6	39.2	38.9	37.9	38.2	37.2	38.3	37.9
Manufacturing													
2014	38.8	38.8	38.4	39.5	38.6	38.4	38.2	38.1	38.2	38.2	37.9	38.0	38.4
2015	38.1	37.9	37.9	38.0	38.3	38.1	37.8	38.0	37.1	37.8	38.3	38.1	37.9
2016	38.1	37.6	38.0	38.1	37.6	38.1	37.8	37.8	37.4	37.4	37.5	38.0	37.8
2017	38.9	38.6	38.2	38.7	38.3	38.2	38.4	38.0	38.3	38.9	38.7	37.5	38.4
2018	38.2	38.9	38.2	38.7	38.7	38.5	38.2	39.0	39.3	38.9	38.9	39.2	38.7
Trade, Transportation, and Utilities													
2014	32.9	32.2	32.8	33.1	33.4	33.4	33.2	33.3	33.3	33.5	33.6	33.5	33.2
2015	33.4	33.2	33.6	33.2	33.6	33.6	34.0	33.9	33.9	34.0	34.0	33.6	33.7
2016	33.8	33.1	33.2	33.5	33.8	33.5	33.7	33.6	33.6	33.3	33.0	32.9	33.4
2017	33.0	32.5	32.3	33.1	33.2	33.2	33.6	33.2	33.1	32.9	33.2	33.0	33.0
2018	32.7	32.6	32.3	32.9	32.7	32.9	33.6	33.6	33.1	33.2	33.5	33.3	33.0
Professional and Business Services													
2014	35.3	35.1	35.2	34.9	35.3	35.4	35.3	35.6	35.7	35.3	35.9	35.2	35.4
2015	34.3	35.5	35.2	34.6	34.5	35.4	35.2	35.4	34.9	35.0	35.0	34.5	35.0
2016	34.5	34.8	35.0	35.4	36.0	35.7	35.2	35.0	35.1	35.6	35.0	34.4	35.1
2017	35.3	33.5	33.3	34.5	33.5	33.7	33.9	34.8	33.8	33.6	33.3	32.7	33.8
2018	32.9	32.6	32.4	33.6	33.4	33.2	33.7	32.8	33.0	32.7	31.8	32.8	32.9
Education and Health Services													
2014	33.1	33.0	32.9	32.9	32.8	33.0	33.2	32.9	33.2	33.1	33.2	33.0	33.0
2015	33.2	33.5	33.4	33.1	33.2	33.3	33.5	33.6	33.6	33.4	33.7	33.5	33.4
2016	33.7	33.6	33.6	33.5	33.7	33.6	33.9	33.8	34.2	33.6	33.7	33.2	33.7
2017	34.1	33.5	33.4	33.5	33.4	34.3	34.4	34.2	33.9	33.9	34.0	34.3	33.9
2018	34.0	33.9	34.0	34.3	34.0	34.2	34.1	34.2	34.0	33.4	33.7	33.4	33.9
Leisure and Hospitality													
2014	24.5	25.7	25.0	24.4	25.7	26.1	26.4	26.2	25.6	25.8	23.7	23.4	25.2
2015	24.6	25.4	24.4	24.9	25.7	25.9	26.4	26.5	25.8	25.9	23.3	23.4	25.2
2016	24.3	25.1	23.7	23.5	24.5	25.4	26.6	26.5	25.5	25.9	24.2	23.4	24.9
2017	24.9	25.5	24.1	24.3	25.7	26.3	27.1	27.1	25.9	26.4	23.6	23.9	25.4
2018	24.2	25.9	24.1	23.7	24.5	25.1	26.3	26.1	25.5	25.6	23.1	23.6	24.8

3. Average Hourly Earnings by Selected Industry: Vermont, 2014–2018

(Dollars, not seasonally adjusted)

Industry and year	January	February	March	April	May	June	July	August	September	October	November	December	Annual average
Total Private													
2014	23.08	23.07	23.11	23.15	22.88	23.11	22.85	23.02	23.36	23.43	23.57	23.41	23.17
2015	23.57	23.67	23.88	24.14	24.13	23.96	23.93	23.99	24.12	24.12	24.57	24.67	24.06
2016	24.64	24.40	24.31	24.46	24.40	24.06	23.95	23.85	24.33	24.58	24.67	24.54	24.34
2017	24.42	24.25	24.23	24.60	24.41	24.04	24.14	24.24	24.54	24.70	24.76	24.82	24.43
2018	25.05	24.97	25.08	25.39	25.21	25.13	25.21	25.07	25.61	25.84	26.12	26.00	25.39
Goods-Producing													
2014	22.12	22.23	22.41	22.47	22.21	22.30	22.26	22.33	22.40	22.34	22.43	22.88	22.36
2015	22.83	23.02	23.36	23.53	23.42	23.35	23.49	23.43	23.75	23.56	23.80	24.22	23.49
2016	24.19	24.25	24.25	24.03	24.13	24.08	23.97	23.99	24.16	24.18	24.48	24.64	24.19
2017	24.24	24.15	24.15	24.23	24.08	24.13	23.92	24.29	24.57	24.50	24.67	25.43	24.36
2018	25.11	25.20	25.42	24.89	24.96	24.96	24.94	24.89	25.00	25.31	25.25	25.49	25.11
Construction													
2014	22.29	22.92	22.91	22.98	21.67	22.02	21.80	22.19	22.28	22.45	22.52	23.07	22.38
2015	23.01	23.56	23.59	23.75	23.08	22.93	23.01	22.72	22.80	22.76	22.90	23.02	23.06
2016	22.99	23.61	23.41	23.25	23.12	22.97	22.94	22.54	23.08	23.30	23.75	23.75	23.21
2017	23.52	23.57	23.83	23.69	22.87	22.90	22.79	23.55	23.90	24.06	24.74	25.38	23.72
2018	25.16	25.19	25.63	25.13	24.91	24.53	24.39	24.44	24.78	25.16	25.78	26.46	25.09
Manufacturing													
2014	22.11	21.99	22.28	22.28	22.48	22.43	22.51	22.36	22.45	22.27	22.39	22.81	22.36
2015	22.78	22.78	23.30	23.34	23.56	23.59	23.81	23.88	24.41	24.13	24.44	25.10	23.76
2016	25.06	24.71	24.81	24.55	24.89	24.91	25.05	25.28	25.17	25.03	25.20	25.38	25.00
2017	24.89	24.71	24.58	24.73	24.90	24.98	24.80	24.89	25.13	24.91	24.73	25.57	24.90
2018	25.24	25.35	25.46	25.05	24.95	25.18	25.24	25.13	25.39	25.02	25.05	25.05	25.18
Trade, Transportation, and Utilities													
2014	19.02	18.75	19.04	19.07	18.97	19.07	19.07	19.29	19.40	19.13	19.42	19.59	19.16
2015	19.80	19.62	19.68	19.91	20.04	20.11	20.12	20.12	20.45	20.16	20.38	21.14	20.13
2016	21.01	20.54	20.54	20.63	20.66	20.45	20.55	20.63	20.64	20.70	20.79	20.79	20.66
2017	21.32	21.17	20.94	21.06	21.00	20.78	20.96	21.15	21.24	21.20	21.33	21.22	21.11
2018	21.60	21.52	21.45	21.47	21.67	21.81	21.69	21.70	22.12	22.19	22.28	22.06	21.80
Professional and Business Services													
2014	31.68	31.86	31.28	30.87	30.49	30.38	30.32	30.08	30.35	30.43	30.83	30.68	30.75
2015	30.95	31.45	31.60	31.37	30.93	30.08	31.02	31.02	30.69	30.51	31.02	31.04	30.96
2016	31.34	30.69	30.12	30.06	29.89	29.48	29.91	29.05	30.02	30.19	29.91	30.11	30.05
2017	30.06	31.16	30.89	31.41	30.40	30.04	30.56	30.04	29.96	29.92	29.76	30.71	30.40
2018	30.94	30.55	30.92	31.23	29.96	29.59	30.30	29.98	30.17	30.42	31.30	31.22	30.53
Education and Health Services													
2014	25.30	25.21	25.02	24.94	24.85	25.54	24.99	25.55	26.47	26.95	26.73	26.54	25.68
2015	27.01	27.25	27.50	27.52	27.33	27.19	26.92	26.89	27.03	27.64	28.29	28.76	27.45
2016	28.78	28.28	27.93	27.90	27.74	27.38	27.05	26.83	27.63	28.03	28.24	28.35	27.84
2017	27.39	27.09	27.09	27.00	27.25	26.39	26.43	26.42	26.90	27.11	27.14	26.98	26.93
2018	27.24	27.16	27.20	27.36	27.27	27.43	27.67	27.64	27.94	28.71	28.57	28.65	27.74
Leisure and Hospitality													
2014	15.18	15.18	15.02	15.38	15.23	15.09	15.24	15.37	15.45	15.76	15.59	15.31	15.31
2015	15.25	15.32	15.35	15.94	15.83	15.99	15.78	16.13	16.34	16.40	16.38	16.03	15.88
2016	15.92	16.04	16.20	16.38	16.42	16.08	16.03	16.15	16.75	17.09	17.02	16.45	16.37
2017	16.35	16.55	16.71	16.99	16.98	16.77	16.64	16.78	17.31	17.79	17.38	16.84	16.91
2018	16.88	17.14	17.19	17.84	18.01	17.77	17.83	18.06	18.51	19.10	18.43	17.64	17.85

4. Average Weekly Earnings by Selected Industry: Vermont, 2014–2018

(Dollars, not seasonally adjusted)

Industry and year	January	February	March	April	May	June	July	August	September	October	November	December	Annual average
Total Private													
2014	761.64	761.31	760.32	775.53	771.06	781.12	772.33	773.47	789.57	789.59	789.60	767.85	773.88
2015	775.45	781.11	788.04	799.03	808.36	805.06	808.83	810.86	808.02	810.43	818.18	811.64	801.20
2016	813.12	802.76	799.80	814.52	824.72	810.82	814.30	806.13	822.35	828.35	821.51	800.00	812.96
2017	815.63	797.83	789.90	821.64	817.74	810.15	825.59	821.74	827.00	834.86	824.51	816.58	818.41
2018	824.15	829.00	822.62	848.03	844.54	846.88	854.62	844.86	860.50	863.06	869.80	871.00	848.03
Goods-Producing													
2014	840.56	838.07	838.13	874.08	866.19	863.01	870.37	864.17	869.12	855.62	861.31	858.00	858.62
2015	851.56	851.74	873.66	882.38	887.62	882.63	890.27	888.00	878.75	890.57	904.40	925.20	883.22
2016	916.80	902.10	906.95	913.14	916.94	919.86	913.26	909.22	918.08	918.84	925.34	931.39	916.80
2017	933.24	915.29	903.21	925.59	924.67	929.01	925.70	927.88	945.95	950.60	944.86	946.00	930.55
2018	946.65	962.64	950.71	943.33	965.95	970.94	962.68	970.71	970.00	979.50	969.60	994.11	966.74
Construction													
2014	818.04	820.54	815.60	868.64	862.47	863.18	882.90	880.94	888.97	868.82	882.78	846.67	859.39
2015	826.06	834.02	858.68	866.88	856.27	850.70	872.08	854.27	836.76	858.05	856.46	879.36	855.53
2016	859.83	859.40	849.78	871.88	885.50	875.16	876.31	852.01	890.89	899.38	900.13	881.13	875.02
2017	882.00	857.95	850.73	876.53	880.50	890.81	891.09	906.68	927.32	926.31	930.22	933.98	898.99
2018	925.89	932.03	922.68	917.25	964.02	971.39	956.09	950.72	939.16	961.11	959.02	1,013.42	950.91
Manufacturing													
2014	857.87	853.21	855.55	880.06	867.73	861.31	859.88	851.92	857.59	850.71	848.58	866.78	858.62
2015	867.92	863.36	883.07	886.92	902.35	898.78	900.02	907.44	905.61	912.11	936.05	956.31	900.50
2016	954.79	929.10	942.78	935.36	935.86	949.07	946.89	955.58	941.36	936.12	945.00	964.44	945.00
2017	968.22	953.81	938.96	957.05	953.67	954.24	952.32	945.82	962.48	969.00	957.05	958.88	956.16
2018	964.17	986.12	972.57	969.44	965.57	969.43	964.17	980.07	987.61	987.67	973.28	981.96	974.47
Trade, Transportation, and Utilities													
2014	625.76	603.75	624.51	631.22	633.60	636.94	633.12	642.36	646.02	640.86	652.51	656.27	636.11
2015	661.32	651.38	661.25	661.01	673.34	675.70	684.08	682.07	693.26	685.44	692.92	710.30	678.38
2016	710.14	679.87	681.93	691.11	698.31	685.08	692.54	693.17	693.50	689.31	686.07	683.99	690.04
2017	703.56	688.03	676.36	697.09	697.20	689.90	704.26	702.18	703.04	697.48	708.16	700.26	696.63
2018	706.32	701.55	692.84	706.36	708.61	717.55	728.78	729.12	732.17	736.71	746.38	734.60	719.40
Professional and Business Services													
2014	1,118.30	1,118.29	1,101.06	1,077.36	1,076.30	1,075.45	1,070.30	1,070.85	1,083.50	1,074.18	1,106.80	1,079.94	1,088.55
2015	1,061.59	1,116.48	1,112.32	1,085.40	1,067.09	1,064.83	1,091.90	1,098.11	1,071.08	1,067.85	1,085.70	1,070.88	1,083.60
2016	1,081.23	1,068.01	1,054.20	1,064.12	1,076.04	1,052.44	1,052.83	1,016.75	1,053.70	1,074.76	1,046.85	1,035.78	1,054.76
2017	1,061.12	1,043.86	1,028.64	1,083.65	1,018.40	1,012.35	1,035.98	1,045.39	1,012.65	1,005.31	991.01	1,004.22	1,027.52
2018	1,017.93	995.93	1,001.81	1,049.33	1,000.66	982.39	1,021.11	983.34	995.61	994.73	995.34	1,024.02	1,004.44
Education and Health Services													
2014	837.43	831.93	823.16	820.53	815.08	842.82	829.67	840.60	878.80	892.05	887.44	875.82	847.44
2015	896.73	912.88	918.50	910.91	907.36	905.43	901.82	903.50	908.21	923.18	953.37	963.46	916.83
2016	969.89	950.21	938.45	934.65	934.84	919.97	917.00	906.85	944.95	941.81	951.69	941.22	938.21
2017	934.00	907.52	904.81	904.50	910.15	905.18	909.19	903.56	911.91	919.03	922.76	925.41	912.93
2018	926.16	920.72	924.80	938.45	927.18	938.11	943.55	945.29	949.96	958.91	962.81	956.91	940.39
Leisure and Hospitality													
2014	371.91	390.13	375.50	375.27	391.41	393.85	402.34	402.69	395.52	406.61	369.48	358.25	385.81
2015	375.15	389.13	374.54	396.91	406.83	414.14	416.59	427.45	421.57	424.76	381.65	375.10	400.18
2016	386.86	402.60	383.94	384.93	402.29	408.43	426.40	427.98	427.13	442.63	411.88	384.93	407.61
2017	407.12	422.03	402.71	412.86	436.39	441.05	450.94	454.74	448.33	469.66	410.17	402.48	429.51
2018	408.50	443.93	414.28	422.81	441.25	446.03	468.93	471.37	472.01	488.96	425.73	416.30	442.68

VIRGINIA
At a Glance

Population:
    2010 census: 8,001,024
    2018 estimate: 8,517,685

Percent change in population:
    2010–2018: 6.5%

Percent change in total nonfarm employment:
    2010–2018: 9.7%

Industry with the largest growth in employment, 2010–2018 (percent):
    Transportation and utilities, 19.7%

Industry with the largest decline or smallest growth in employment, 2010–2018 (percent):
    Mining and logging, -24.0%

Civilian labor force:
    2010: 4,157,658
    2018: 4,331,380

Unemployment rate and rank among states (highest to lowest):
    2010: 7.1%, 41st
    2018: 3.0%, 41st

Over-the-year change in unemployment rates:
    2016–2017: -0.4%
    2017–2018: -0.7%

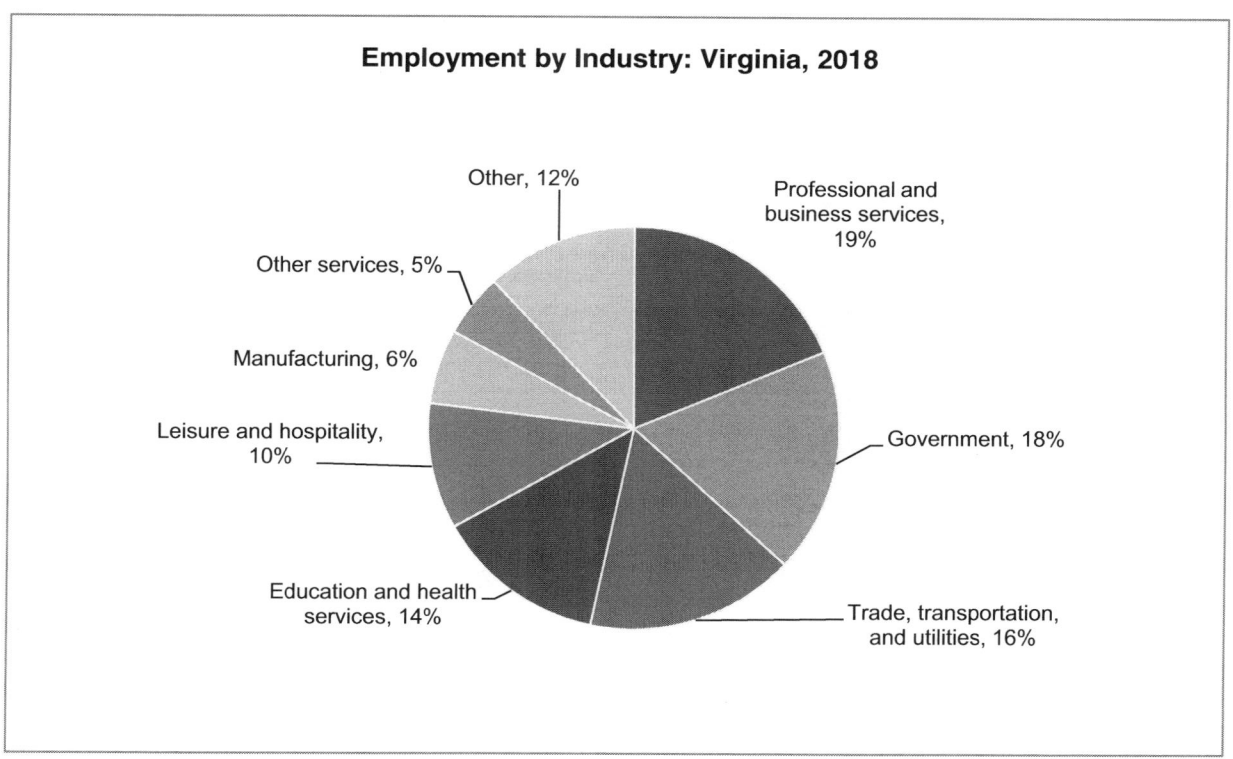

Employment by Industry: Virginia, 2018

- Other, 12%
- Professional and business services, 19%
- Other services, 5%
- Manufacturing, 6%
- Government, 18%
- Leisure and hospitality, 10%
- Education and health services, 14%
- Trade, transportation, and utilities, 16%

1. Employment by Industry: Virginia, 2010–2018

(Numbers in thousands, not seasonally adjusted)

Industry and year	January	February	March	April	May	June	July	August	September	October	November	December	Annual average
Total Nonfarm													
2010	3,560.4	3,545.3	3,587.9	3,642.7	3,673.1	3,691.7	3,677.9	3,664.6	3,654.2	3,677.6	3,690.5	3,689.7	3,646.3
2011	3,611.5	3,629.6	3,656.3	3,692.4	3,697.5	3,717.2	3,701.1	3,694.0	3,715.7	3,723.5	3,740.6	3,734.5	3,692.8
2012	3,659.3	3,676.5	3,703.9	3,728.1	3,738.6	3,759.1	3,724.7	3,737.7	3,750.8	3,772.9	3,790.2	3,788.3	3,735.8
2013	3,700.8	3,719.8	3,741.0	3,764.0	3,770.2	3,785.1	3,761.7	3,765.5	3,770.7	3,776.9	3,801.8	3,790.0	3,762.3
2014	3,710.4	3,710.5	3,736.7	3,783.7	3,801.5	3,814.7	3,787.6	3,792.4	3,798.7	3,811.1	3,828.7	3,824.9	3,783.4
2015	3,758.1	3,766.6	3,780.1	3,841.4	3,861.0	3,878.0	3,877.6	3,877.3	3,888.3	3,915.3	3,934.2	3,930.3	3,859.0
2016	3,836.1	3,851.1	3,876.6	3,917.8	3,918.3	3,939.5	3,916.0	3,919.9	3,930.7	3,945.6	3,965.9	3,956.2	3,914.5
2017	3,875.3	3,902.3	3,919.4	3,950.1	3,961.4	3,988.6	3,961.6	3,958.0	3,966.4	3,985.5	4,002.8	3,997.8	3,955.8
2018	3,925.2	3,951.5	3,971.1	4,001.4	4,013.8	4,037.3	4,013.8	4,008.6	4,005.1	4,018.1	4,035.7	4,025.6	4,000.6
Total Private													
2010	2,860.6	2,840.8	2,877.4	2,927.5	2,951.8	2,973.8	2,983.1	2,980.2	2,957.9	2,970.0	2,975.8	2,977.8	2,939.7
2011	2,905.1	2,911.0	2,934.3	2,969.3	2,979.8	3,002.3	3,018.1	3,014.9	3,002.4	2,999.7	3,011.4	3,006.4	2,979.6
2012	2,947.9	2,953.6	2,979.4	3,004.3	3,019.6	3,043.1	3,047.2	3,057.4	3,040.2	3,050.7	3,062.6	3,061.4	3,022.3
2013	2,990.9	2,997.7	3,017.7	3,038.6	3,049.1	3,070.2	3,077.2	3,084.6	3,061.4	3,060.5	3,079.9	3,069.7	3,049.8
2014	3,004.0	2,995.7	3,019.4	3,062.7	3,084.0	3,103.3	3,103.2	3,109.7	3,087.3	3,094.6	3,107.1	3,103.5	3,072.9
2015	3,051.7	3,047.9	3,062.7	3,119.7	3,143.7	3,165.5	3,193.3	3,196.3	3,178.7	3,195.5	3,209.9	3,206.8	3,147.6
2016	3,129.7	3,131.8	3,153.6	3,192.4	3,198.7	3,224.8	3,227.5	3,234.4	3,215.3	3,223.8	3,238.9	3,230.1	3,200.1
2017	3,165.5	3,179.7	3,196.2	3,222.9	3,239.1	3,269.2	3,271.2	3,270.6	3,247.8	3,262.4	3,273.7	3,271.0	3,239.1
2018	3,210.3	3,224.3	3,241.6	3,269.9	3,285.1	3,312.5	3,316.7	3,314.8	3,280.6	3,289.6	3,299.3	3,292.8	3,278.1
Goods Producing													
2010	414.2	407.9	415.4	424.7	428.3	429.4	431.7	430.7	429.2	428.1	425.9	423.2	424.1
2011	409.8	410.5	414.3	419.1	421.1	424.6	428.6	427.9	424.9	422.9	421.8	420.4	420.5
2012	411.6	410.9	414.7	416.6	418.6	422.1	425.1	424.7	423.0	421.8	420.6	419.7	419.1
2013	409.8	410.4	413.2	416.0	418.1	422.4	423.5	423.8	421.6	419.7	420.0	418.0	418.0
2014	409.1	407.9	412.0	418.5	422.0	425.6	425.4	425.8	424.7	424.5	424.1	422.1	420.1
2015	414.0	413.3	416.0	425.9	429.6	432.5	435.9	435.6	433.6	434.1	432.8	431.8	427.9
2016	421.0	419.2	422.6	426.4	428.4	432.2	433.4	432.9	432.9	435.1	434.5	432.6	429.3
2017	423.6	425.8	429.2	434.1	436.4	441.0	441.2	441.7	440.4	441.6	440.7	440.9	436.4
2018	431.6	435.1	438.5	442.5	445.5	449.5	452.8	452.5	449.6	448.5	449.3	449.3	445.4
Service-Providing													
2010	3,146.2	3,137.4	3,172.5	3,218.0	3,244.8	3,262.3	3,246.2	3,233.9	3,225.0	3,249.5	3,264.6	3,266.5	3,222.2
2011	3,201.7	3,219.1	3,242.0	3,273.3	3,276.4	3,292.6	3,272.5	3,266.1	3,290.8	3,300.6	3,318.8	3,314.1	3,272.3
2012	3,247.7	3,265.6	3,289.2	3,311.5	3,320.0	3,337.0	3,299.6	3,313.0	3,327.8	3,351.1	3,369.6	3,368.6	3,316.7
2013	3,291.0	3,309.4	3,327.8	3,348.0	3,352.1	3,362.7	3,338.2	3,341.7	3,349.1	3,357.2	3,381.8	3,372.0	3,344.3
2014	3,301.3	3,302.6	3,324.7	3,365.2	3,379.5	3,389.1	3,362.2	3,366.6	3,374.0	3,386.6	3,404.6	3,402.8	3,363.3
2015	3,344.1	3,353.3	3,364.1	3,415.5	3,431.4	3,445.5	3,441.7	3,441.7	3,454.7	3,481.2	3,501.4	3,498.5	3,431.1
2016	3,415.1	3,431.9	3,454.0	3,491.4	3,489.9	3,507.3	3,482.6	3,487.0	3,497.8	3,510.5	3,531.4	3,523.6	3,485.2
2017	3,451.7	3,476.5	3,490.2	3,516.0	3,525.0	3,547.6	3,520.4	3,516.3	3,526.0	3,543.9	3,562.1	3,556.9	3,519.4
2018	3,493.6	3,516.4	3,532.6	3,558.9	3,568.3	3,587.8	3,561.0	3,556.1	3,555.5	3,569.6	3,586.4	3,576.3	3,555.2
Mining and Logging													
2010	9.9	9.8	10.0	10.3	10.3	10.4	10.5	10.6	10.6	10.7	10.7	10.6	10.4
2011	10.7	10.6	10.7	10.7	10.8	10.9	11.0	11.1	11.2	11.1	11.2	11.2	10.9
2012	11.1	11.1	11.1	11.0	11.0	11.1	11.0	11.0	10.8	10.3	10.5	10.4	10.9
2013	10.2	10.1	10.1	10.1	10.1	10.2	9.8	9.8	9.7	9.9	9.8	9.9	10.0
2014	9.7	9.7	9.8	9.7	9.6	9.7	9.5	9.4	9.4	9.3	9.3	9.3	9.5
2015	9.4	9.3	9.2	9.2	9.1	9.0	9.1	9.1	8.8	8.6	8.5	8.5	9.0
2016	8.0	8.0	8.0	7.7	7.7	7.7	7.8	7.7	7.8	7.9	7.9	8.0	7.9
2017	7.9	8.0	8.0	7.9	7.9	8.0	8.0	8.1	8.1	7.9	7.9	7.9	8.0
2018	7.8	7.9	8.0	7.9	7.9	8.0	7.9	7.9	7.9	7.9	7.9	7.8	7.9
Construction													
2010	173.9	168.6	175.5	184.1	186.4	187.6	190.2	189.5	187.9	186.4	185.0	181.8	183.1
2011	171.7	172.0	174.5	178.2	179.5	181.5	184.3	183.7	180.9	179.7	178.5	177.3	178.5
2012	169.7	169.0	172.3	174.8	177.2	180.5	181.4	181.0	179.3	179.3	177.9	176.9	176.6
2013	169.7	170.3	172.8	175.6	177.4	180.5	181.7	182.1	180.6	178.3	178.4	175.6	176.9
2014	169.4	168.5	171.7	177.3	179.8	182.1	182.6	183.1	182.1	182.3	181.8	179.4	178.3
2015	173.3	173.0	175.2	183.6	186.8	188.5	191.0	190.8	189.1	190.0	188.7	187.7	184.8
2016	180.1	179.1	182.4	187.1	188.6	191.2	191.7	191.2	191.2	193.3	192.6	190.6	188.3
2017	183.9	185.1	187.8	191.7	194.2	197.5	197.4	197.8	196.9	197.5	196.2	195.9	193.5
2018	189.2	190.8	193.3	196.4	198.1	200.4	203.0	203.0	199.9	199.7	198.4	196.3	197.4

1. Employment by Industry: Virginia, 2010–2018—*Continued*

(Numbers in thousands, not seasonally adjusted)

Industry and year	January	February	March	April	May	June	July	August	September	October	November	December	Annual average
Manufacturing													
2010	230.4	229.5	229.9	230.3	231.6	231.4	231.0	230.6	230.7	231.0	230.2	230.8	230.6
2011	227.4	227.9	229.1	230.2	230.8	232.2	233.3	233.1	232.8	232.1	232.1	231.9	231.1
2012	230.8	230.8	231.3	230.8	230.4	230.5	232.7	232.7	232.9	232.2	232.2	232.4	231.6
2013	229.9	230.0	230.3	230.3	230.6	231.7	232.0	231.9	231.3	231.5	231.8	232.5	231.2
2014	230.0	229.7	230.5	231.5	232.6	233.8	233.3	233.3	233.2	232.9	233.0	233.4	232.3
2015	231.3	231.0	231.6	233.1	233.7	235.0	235.8	235.7	235.7	235.5	235.6	235.6	234.1
2016	232.9	232.1	232.2	231.6	232.1	233.3	233.9	234.0	233.9	233.9	234.0	234.0	233.2
2017	231.8	232.7	233.4	234.5	234.3	235.5	235.8	235.8	235.4	236.2	236.6	237.1	234.9
2018	234.6	236.4	237.2	238.2	239.5	241.1	241.9	241.6	241.8	240.9	243.0	245.2	240.1
Trade, Transportation, and Utilities													
2010	610.8	600.6	606.6	613.7	620.0	623.3	622.2	623.2	618.2	625.5	637.8	646.9	620.7
2011	619.2	614.0	616.5	622.7	625.9	628.7	629.0	630.1	626.2	629.7	644.2	652.7	628.2
2012	626.5	619.5	623.6	625.3	631.0	632.7	630.6	630.7	628.7	635.8	651.9	660.3	633.1
2013	626.3	620.4	622.6	626.0	630.7	634.5	635.2	636.0	632.7	637.7	653.1	660.7	634.7
2014	631.9	624.7	628.5	633.5	638.0	641.8	641.3	642.2	638.8	643.9	658.7	667.2	640.9
2015	639.2	632.8	634.2	641.2	647.4	651.8	657.5	658.5	655.5	660.2	674.7	680.8	652.8
2016	652.3	647.0	649.8	654.8	659.2	662.7	660.5	661.4	657.4	661.9	678.0	683.1	660.7
2017	656.3	649.8	650.7	654.4	658.9	663.5	662.0	662.1	658.5	661.9	677.7	681.9	661.5
2018	655.3	650.7	651.7	653.7	659.5	661.5	660.1	659.6	654.9	658.4	672.1	678.3	659.7
Wholesale Trade													
2010	107.5	107.2	107.8	109.0	109.6	109.8	110.3	110.5	110.1	110.8	111.1	111.3	109.6
2011	110.2	110.2	110.7	111.3	111.4	111.7	111.9	111.7	110.8	110.4	110.6	110.8	111.0
2012	109.6	109.9	110.5	110.7	111.2	111.6	111.6	111.7	111.3	111.2	111.3	111.3	111.0
2013	110.1	110.3	110.7	110.4	110.5	110.6	110.5	110.4	109.9	109.9	109.9	110.0	110.3
2014	109.0	109.0	109.5	109.9	110.5	110.6	110.6	110.6	109.9	109.7	109.9	110.1	109.9
2015	108.6	108.5	108.7	109.1	109.6	110.0	111.0	110.8	110.4	110.6	110.7	110.9	109.9
2016	109.3	109.1	109.4	110.2	110.5	110.6	110.5	110.4	110.2	110.4	110.5	110.8	110.2
2017	109.2	109.6	109.8	110.2	110.8	111.5	111.1	111.3	110.7	110.8	110.8	111.2	110.6
2018	109.5	109.7	109.8	110.1	110.2	111.0	110.8	110.7	110.0	109.9	109.9	110.9	110.2
Retail Trade													
2010	393.1	383.8	388.5	393.3	398.0	400.1	398.3	398.9	394.4	400.0	410.9	417.9	398.1
2011	396.1	391.4	393.0	397.8	400.3	402.0	401.2	402.2	399.8	403.8	417.4	423.9	402.4
2012	403.5	395.9	399.4	400.0	403.9	404.5	402.4	402.3	400.9	407.6	423.2	429.0	406.1
2013	401.2	396.3	397.6	400.8	404.6	407.4	407.5	408.1	405.5	410.2	423.9	428.8	407.7
2014	405.6	400.1	402.6	406.5	409.0	411.5	410.5	410.7	407.4	412.2	424.4	429.5	410.8
2015	407.6	402.4	403.8	408.6	413.0	415.8	417.7	418.5	416.1	420.1	432.0	434.6	415.9
2016	413.6	409.6	411.9	415.0	418.3	420.5	419.1	420.1	416.1	420.2	432.8	434.8	419.3
2017	415.9	409.9	410.9	413.4	416.0	419.2	418.3	417.5	413.5	416.9	430.4	431.5	417.8
2018	413.7	408.8	409.6	410.8	415.5	415.4	413.8	412.8	408.9	412.2	422.8	424.3	414.1
Transportation and Utilities													
2010	110.2	109.6	110.3	111.4	112.4	113.4	113.6	113.8	113.7	114.7	115.8	117.7	113.1
2011	112.9	112.4	112.8	113.6	114.2	115.0	115.9	116.2	115.6	115.5	116.2	118.0	114.9
2012	113.4	113.7	113.7	114.6	115.9	116.6	116.6	116.7	116.5	117.0	117.4	120.0	116.0
2013	115.0	113.8	114.3	114.8	115.6	116.5	117.2	117.5	117.3	117.6	119.3	121.9	116.7
2014	117.3	115.6	116.4	117.1	118.5	119.7	120.2	120.9	121.5	122.0	124.4	127.6	120.1
2015	123.0	121.9	121.7	123.5	124.8	126.0	128.8	129.2	129.0	129.5	132.0	135.3	127.1
2016	129.4	128.3	128.5	129.6	130.4	131.6	130.9	130.9	131.1	131.3	134.7	137.5	131.2
2017	131.2	130.3	130.0	130.8	132.1	132.8	132.6	133.3	134.3	134.2	136.5	139.2	133.1
2018	132.1	132.2	132.3	132.8	133.8	135.1	135.5	136.1	136.0	136.3	139.4	143.1	135.4
Information													
2010	77.4	76.8	76.7	75.8	75.8	76.0	75.9	75.8	75.6	75.6	75.5	75.7	76.1
2011	74.7	74.6	74.7	74.1	74.3	74.5	74.8	70.2	73.5	72.7	73.3	74.2	73.8
2012	71.4	72.1	72.6	71.2	71.9	72.9	71.7	72.9	70.3	70.5	72.2	71.0	71.7
2013	70.4	72.1	72.0	71.1	71.2	71.5	71.7	72.9	70.7	71.1	72.6	71.5	71.6
2014	72.3	70.9	71.0	70.9	72.4	71.4	71.5	72.4	70.4	70.9	70.1	70.1	71.2
2015	70.0	69.5	69.2	69.4	70.1	69.8	70.6	69.9	68.9	69.4	69.3	69.2	69.6
2016	68.6	68.8	68.0	68.6	66.2	69.1	69.2	68.9	68.5	67.6	67.6	68.3	68.3
2017	67.9	68.4	68.3	68.0	68.3	68.7	68.4	67.9	67.7	67.5	68.4	68.2	68.1
2018	67.4	68.1	67.5	67.9	68.4	68.6	68.0	67.4	66.1	65.8	65.6	65.0	67.2

1. Employment by Industry: Virginia, 2010–2018—*Continued*

(Numbers in thousands, not seasonally adjusted)

Industry and year	January	February	March	April	May	June	July	August	September	October	November	December	Annual average
Financial Activities													
2010	176.3	175.6	176.4	177.4	178.3	180.8	181.7	181.6	179.9	180.1	180.2	180.7	179.1
2011	178.4	178.6	179.0	180.9	182.0	183.7	185.4	185.4	184.2	183.8	184.2	185.3	182.6
2012	183.2	184.0	184.8	186.8	187.3	189.6	190.7	190.8	189.9	190.3	190.7	191.4	188.3
2013	189.2	189.7	190.4	191.4	192.1	193.9	194.8	194.6	193.0	193.4	193.6	193.9	192.5
2014	190.8	191.1	191.7	192.5	193.5	195.6	196.3	196.0	194.5	194.7	195.1	195.7	194.0
2015	194.1	194.8	195.2	195.9	197.3	198.9	200.2	200.0	198.5	199.1	199.1	199.6	197.7
2016	197.5	197.5	198.1	199.5	200.7	202.2	202.9	203.3	201.5	202.3	202.8	203.6	201.0
2017	201.2	202.0	202.3	202.7	204.3	206.7	207.7	207.3	205.7	206.6	206.8	207.4	205.1
2018	204.6	205.7	205.8	206.5	207.6	209.9	210.2	209.8	207.9	208.0	207.3	205.2	207.4
Professional and Business Services													
2010	631.5	631.3	636.3	648.8	648.6	652.7	657.7	658.5	655.3	661.8	662.8	661.8	650.6
2011	652.9	655.6	659.6	665.7	664.1	666.5	672.9	674.9	673.9	675.5	677.4	673.3	667.7
2012	664.5	667.1	671.1	675.9	675.9	679.3	682.0	685.6	682.1	687.8	686.7	685.2	678.6
2013	675.4	677.7	680.0	682.6	681.1	683.6	683.9	686.1	679.8	680.7	685.9	680.3	681.4
2014	668.9	668.5	670.9	681.2	683.4	685.3	687.2	688.2	682.5	688.0	693.1	690.4	682.3
2015	681.2	680.5	681.9	697.0	700.5	703.7	709.7	710.0	706.0	717.2	721.8	720.1	702.5
2016	700.4	702.9	705.1	712.3	711.2	715.9	719.5	722.1	719.5	724.0	726.4	725.8	715.4
2017	710.4	716.3	717.4	724.3	726.7	734.9	736.9	738.0	733.6	738.4	743.3	741.1	730.1
2018	730.6	736.8	739.2	746.7	748.9	754.8	756.6	757.7	748.8	754.4	756.9	751.4	748.6
Education and Health Services													
2010	454.8	454.6	458.5	462.1	463.2	460.3	462.6	461.4	464.3	471.4	472.8	471.4	463.1
2011	467.2	470.2	472.0	472.0	464.9	462.1	464.0	465.6	473.7	476.6	478.0	469.4	469.6
2012	473.7	477.0	478.8	480.8	473.3	472.1	472.3	478.1	486.2	491.5	493.1	487.5	480.4
2013	488.5	492.9	495.3	494.8	485.9	482.0	482.7	488.0	495.6	498.4	500.6	492.5	491.4
2014	494.1	495.2	497.0	502.3	494.2	491.0	490.7	495.0	501.8	505.6	506.2	499.5	497.7
2015	504.6	506.6	507.7	515.1	507.3	504.6	508.9	513.2	520.6	526.5	528.5	522.4	513.8
2016	523.8	526.2	527.8	531.6	521.9	518.4	516.0	522.7	527.7	532.5	534.3	524.9	525.7
2017	530.0	534.3	535.6	535.5	528.5	524.4	525.2	527.5	533.9	541.0	539.3	535.9	532.6
2018	539.1	542.5	543.5	545.2	534.3	533.4	533.7	535.5	544.3	548.8	549.4	543.8	541.1
Leisure and Hospitality													
2010	313.3	312.5	323.8	339.8	351.6	364.2	364.5	363.0	351.2	342.7	336.4	334.0	341.4
2011	319.9	323.5	333.0	346.9	359.2	371.8	372.0	370.7	357.4	350.0	344.0	342.4	349.2
2012	330.2	335.2	344.8	355.2	368.3	379.5	379.3	380.4	367.2	359.4	354.2	353.3	358.9
2013	340.4	342.9	351.7	363.2	375.4	386.1	387.9	387.0	373.6	365.3	360.0	358.9	366.0
2014	345.1	345.4	354.7	368.9	384.2	394.1	392.7	392.1	378.5	371.6	364.8	363.8	371.3
2015	354.7	356.4	363.0	380.0	394.6	405.5	410.3	409.4	397.8	390.9	385.4	384.9	386.1
2016	370.6	374.3	384.8	398.5	409.8	421.0	421.8	420.1	406.5	398.5	393.6	390.9	399.2
2017	376.9	383.4	391.8	404.1	415.6	427.0	426.3	424.2	407.7	404.5	397.3	395.5	404.5
2018	383.4	386.7	395.7	407.1	419.6	431.1	430.9	428.9	408.4	405.1	398.1	398.8	407.8
Other Services													
2010	182.3	181.5	183.7	185.2	186.0	187.1	186.8	186.0	184.2	184.8	184.4	184.1	184.7
2011	183.0	184.0	185.2	187.9	188.3	190.4	191.4	190.1	188.6	188.5	188.5	188.7	187.9
2012	186.8	187.8	189.0	192.5	193.3	194.9	195.5	194.2	192.8	193.6	193.2	193.0	192.2
2013	190.9	191.6	192.5	193.5	194.6	196.2	197.5	196.2	194.4	194.2	194.1	193.9	194.1
2014	191.8	192.0	193.6	194.9	196.3	198.5	198.1	198.0	196.1	195.4	195.0	194.7	195.4
2015	193.9	194.0	195.5	195.2	196.9	198.7	200.2	199.7	197.8	198.1	198.3	198.0	197.2
2016	195.5	195.9	197.4	200.7	201.3	203.3	204.2	203.0	201.3	201.9	201.7	200.9	200.6
2017	199.2	199.7	200.9	199.8	200.4	203.0	203.5	201.9	200.3	200.9	200.2	200.1	200.8
2018	198.3	198.7	199.7	200.3	201.3	203.7	204.4	203.4	200.6	200.6	200.6	201.0	201.1
Government													
2010	699.8	704.5	710.5	715.2	721.3	717.9	694.8	684.4	696.3	707.6	714.7	711.9	706.6
2011	706.4	718.6	722.0	723.1	717.7	714.9	683.0	679.1	713.3	723.8	729.2	728.1	713.3
2012	711.4	722.9	724.5	723.8	719.0	716.0	677.5	680.3	710.6	722.2	727.6	726.9	713.6
2013	709.9	722.1	723.3	725.4	721.1	714.9	684.5	680.9	709.3	716.4	721.9	720.3	712.5
2014	706.4	714.8	717.3	721.0	717.5	711.4	684.4	682.7	711.4	716.5	721.6	721.4	710.5
2015	706.4	718.7	717.4	721.7	717.3	712.5	684.3	681.0	709.6	719.8	724.3	723.5	711.4
2016	706.4	719.3	723.0	725.4	719.6	714.7	688.5	685.5	715.4	721.8	727.0	726.1	714.4
2017	709.8	722.6	723.2	727.2	722.3	719.4	690.4	687.4	718.6	723.1	729.1	726.8	716.7
2018	714.9	727.2	729.5	731.5	728.7	724.8	697.1	693.8	724.5	728.5	736.4	732.8	722.5

2. Average Weekly Hours by Selected Industry: Virginia, 2014–2018

(Not seasonally adjusted)

Industry and year	January	February	March	April	May	June	July	August	September	October	November	December	Annual average
Total Private													
2014	34.0	33.9	34.7	34.8	34.8	35.2	34.6	34.7	34.8	34.9	35.5	34.9	34.7
2015	34.6	35.1	35.3	35.3	35.3	35.1	35.1	35.6	35.0	35.0	35.4	35.0	35.1
2016	34.7	34.7	34.8	34.9	35.1	34.9	34.9	35.1	35.1	35.3	34.9	34.8	34.9
2017	34.7	34.5	34.2	34.7	34.2	34.5	34.9	34.3	34.6	34.9	34.7	34.8	34.6
2018	34.2	34.6	34.3	35.2	34.6	34.6	35.0	34.6	34.7	34.5	34.3	34.5	34.6
Goods-Producing													
2014	37.5	36.1	39.1	39.7	40.2	40.0	39.6	40.1	39.8	39.6	40.1	39.6	39.3
2015	38.7	38.8	39.3	40.0	40.6	40.6	40.0	40.5	39.8	40.4	40.1	40.4	39.9
2016	39.9	38.3	39.1	39.5	38.7	39.4	39.6	39.7	39.4	39.4	39.2	39.0	39.3
2017	38.7	37.4	36.7	37.3	37.2	38.4	38.6	37.8	38.5	38.7	39.2	39.4	38.2
2018	38.1	38.7	38.5	40.0	40.0	39.3	39.4	39.8	38.3	40.3	39.8	39.4	39.3
Construction													
2014	36.2	34.5	38.2	38.8	39.4	39.2	38.7	38.6	37.5	37.8	38.3	37.4	37.9
2015	35.5	36.6	37.5	38.4	39.7	39.8	38.8	39.1	37.3	38.7	37.8	38.0	38.1
2016	37.4	35.6	37.3	38.1	37.2	38.7	39.1	39.1	39.0	39.2	38.4	37.5	38.1
2017	36.5	38.0	36.4	38.5	37.4	39.0	39.1	37.9	38.8	38.6	39.0	39.6	38.3
2018	37.4	38.1	38.4	40.0	40.5	39.6	40.1	40.0	37.1	40.0	38.4	38.5	39.0
Manufacturing													
2014	40.0	38.8	41.2	41.5	41.7	41.3	41.0	41.6	42.0	41.3	41.9	41.8	41.2
2015	41.7	41.0	41.0	41.6	41.5	41.4	41.1	41.9	42.5	41.7	42.3	42.8	41.7
2016	42.1	40.6	40.7	40.7	39.9	39.9	40.0	40.1	39.7	39.4	39.7	40.3	40.3
2017	40.6	41.3	40.9	39.8	40.1	40.5	40.5	40.0	40.3	40.7	41.0	40.7	40.5
2018	40.1	40.4	39.7	40.9	40.3	39.8	39.4	40.2	40.0	40.4	41.4	40.4	40.2
Trade, Transportation, and Utilities													
2014	33.5	33.4	33.9	34.0	34.0	34.1	33.7	33.8	34.0	33.6	34.2	34.5	33.9
2015	33.7	33.7	33.8	33.9	34.4	34.0	34.3	34.3	34.3	34.0	34.0	34.2	34.1
2016	33.2	33.4	33.2	33.3	33.4	33.5	33.7	33.9	34.0	33.6	33.1	33.8	33.5
2017	32.9	33.1	33.3	33.7	33.4	33.1	33.5	33.3	33.6	33.2	33.3	33.5	33.3
2018	32.8	32.7	32.7	33.5	33.2	33.3	33.7	33.2	33.4	32.9	33.1	33.3	33.2
Financial Activities													
2014	36.8	37.2	36.8	36.5	36.4	37.6	36.6	36.9	37.0	37.3	39.0	37.7	37.2
2015	37.8	39.1	39.1	38.5	38.9	38.6	38.7	40.4	40.0	39.5	40.5	39.4	39.2
2016	39.6	39.5	39.0	38.2	38.3	37.9	38.2	39.2	38.8	39.7	39.2	38.5	38.8
2017	39.5	38.7	38.2	38.5	38.1	38.1	38.5	38.1	38.0	38.3	38.2	38.0	38.3
2018	37.7	38.4	38.4	39.4	38.2	38.4	38.6	37.6	39.3	38.0	38.2	39.1	38.4
Professional and Business Services													
2014	35.9	36.3	36.7	36.5	36.7	37.2	36.2	36.6	36.4	37.0	38.1	36.8	36.7
2015	36.4	37.4	37.7	37.2	37.2	36.9	36.8	37.9	36.6	36.6	37.9	37.3	37.2
2016	36.9	37.0	37.2	37.7	38.2	37.5	37.2	37.4	37.5	38.2	37.4	37.2	37.5
2017	37.7	37.5	37.1	38.0	36.8	37.8	38.0	37.4	37.9	38.4	37.7	37.5	37.7
2018	37.3	37.8	37.4	38.3	37.2	37.6	37.8	37.0	37.7	36.9	36.4	37.3	37.4
Education and Health Services													
2014	33.9	33.7	33.9	34.2	34.1	34.6	34.2	33.9	34.3	34.1	34.5	34.1	34.1
2015	34.2	34.6	34.3	34.2	34.2	34.2	34.1	34.5	34.2	34.3	34.7	33.7	34.3
2016	34.6	34.5	34.6	34.7	35.1	34.8	34.6	34.7	34.7	34.8	34.4	34.4	34.7
2017	34.6	34.0	33.8	34.1	33.9	33.7	34.0	33.4	33.9	34.1	33.6	34.0	33.9
2018	33.7	34.0	33.4	33.6	33.3	33.3	34.0	33.9	33.8	33.0	32.8	32.5	33.4
Leisure and Hospitality													
2014	25.5	25.5	26.5	26.9	26.8	27.0	26.9	26.7	26.5	26.3	26.5	25.9	26.4
2015	25.3	25.4	26.2	26.6	26.6	26.5	26.8	27.1	26.1	26.1	26.2	25.8	26.2
2016	24.7	25.6	25.9	26.3	26.4	26.4	26.7	26.5	26.4	26.8	26.7	26.2	26.2
2017	25.6	26.2	26.3	26.2	25.7	26.2	27.0	26.5	25.9	26.2	25.9	25.9	26.1
2018	25.1	25.9	25.9	26.3	26.0	26.4	26.6	26.6	25.7	26.3	25.6	25.5	26.0
Other Services													
2014	31.8	32.0	32.5	32.4	32.6	32.9	32.2	31.6	32.2	32.3	32.6	32.4	32.3
2015	32.4	32.4	32.5	32.5	31.9	32.7	32.7	32.4	31.8	32.1	32.8	32.4	32.4
2016	32.5	32.5	32.7	32.2	32.9	32.4	32.2	32.3	32.2	33.0	32.0	32.4	32.4
2017	32.6	32.2	32.1	33.1	32.0	32.0	32.6	31.7	31.4	32.6	31.8	32.5	32.2
2018	31.4	31.5	31.4	32.0	31.2	31.5	32.3	31.9	32.6	32.5	32.4	32.6	31.9

3. Average Hourly Earnings by Selected Industry: Virginia, 2014–2018

(Dollars, not seasonally adjusted)

Industry and year	January	February	March	April	May	June	July	August	September	October	November	December	Annual average
Total Private													
2014	25.82	25.29	25.60	25.18	25.04	25.27	25.02	25.18	25.25	25.32	25.64	25.47	25.34
2015	25.79	26.30	26.23	26.04	25.94	25.79	25.81	26.34	26.26	26.36	26.55	26.26	26.14
2016	26.64	26.63	26.71	26.89	27.20	26.76	27.03	26.64	27.08	27.55	27.13	27.29	26.96
2017	27.97	27.73	27.55	28.08	27.45	27.00	27.52	27.22	27.48	27.73	27.39	27.75	27.57
2018	28.09	27.87	27.97	28.26	27.97	28.05	28.46	28.28	29.07	28.53	28.65	29.46	28.39
Goods-Producing													
2014	23.35	23.75	23.06	23.20	23.16	23.22	23.19	23.11	23.19	23.41	23.60	23.47	23.30
2015	23.52	23.61	23.55	23.50	23.39	23.29	23.46	23.36	23.73	23.72	23.75	23.66	23.54
2016	23.96	24.19	24.06	24.35	24.42	24.60	24.98	24.82	24.98	25.08	24.77	24.78	24.59
2017	25.12	24.66	24.88	25.02	24.89	24.88	24.98	25.00	25.14	24.92	24.74	25.22	24.96
2018	25.19	25.01	25.08	24.98	25.01	24.84	24.75	25.24	25.29	25.70	25.47	26.31	25.24
Construction													
2014	24.82	25.23	23.99	24.29	24.25	23.95	23.88	24.08	24.15	24.07	24.04	24.20	24.23
2015	24.30	24.67	24.44	24.14	24.24	24.03	24.27	24.13	24.28	24.66	24.89	24.99	24.42
2016	25.47	25.76	25.69	26.02	25.82	25.88	26.04	26.12	26.13	26.17	25.92	25.87	25.92
2017	26.40	25.62	26.23	25.89	26.18	26.06	26.19	26.24	26.48	26.01	25.88	26.44	26.14
2018	26.30	26.27	26.15	25.96	26.16	25.72	25.90	26.44	26.36	26.68	26.12	27.30	26.28
Manufacturing													
2014	21.90	22.30	22.01	21.98	21.93	22.32	22.34	22.08	22.18	22.37	22.72	22.39	22.21
2015	22.47	22.36	22.40	22.69	22.37	22.36	22.49	22.43	22.60	22.20	22.12	21.92	22.37
2016	22.30	22.59	22.20	22.56	22.86	23.15	23.71	23.36	23.70	23.85	23.76	23.84	23.15
2017	24.09	23.76	23.54	24.15	23.65	23.72	23.83	23.83	23.86	23.88	23.73	24.06	23.84
2018	24.16	23.78	23.98	23.97	23.80	23.91	23.84	24.69	24.87	25.25	25.43	25.71	24.46
Trade, Transportation, and Utilities													
2014	19.76	20.70	20.15	20.15	20.33	20.35	20.36	20.24	20.20	20.01	20.05	19.34	20.13
2015	19.76	20.46	20.21	20.56	20.20	20.36	20.36	20.83	20.29	20.87	20.31	20.00	20.35
2016	20.71	20.04	20.35	21.24	20.87	20.95	21.47	20.98	21.34	21.77	21.30	21.37	21.04
2017	21.88	21.13	20.74	21.28	20.66	20.75	21.14	20.74	21.01	21.26	21.15	21.26	21.08
2018	21.51	21.60	21.62	21.98	21.60	21.94	22.63	22.61	23.54	23.10	22.87	23.89	22.42
Financial Activities													
2014	26.43	26.43	27.07	26.40	26.15	26.78	26.33	26.44	26.41	25.96	25.99	26.03	26.37
2015	25.79	26.29	26.33	26.53	26.69	26.74	26.70	27.10	26.53	26.71	27.13	26.73	26.61
2016	26.41	26.58	26.56	27.27	28.00	26.85	27.38	26.45	28.31	28.79	28.47	28.76	27.49
2017	28.74	28.91	28.59	29.43	29.06	29.50	30.20	29.36	30.09	30.39	29.67	30.11	29.51
2018	30.29	30.88	30.60	30.85	30.71	30.16	30.66	30.66	31.72	31.07	31.10	32.87	30.97
Professional and Business Services													
2014	34.86	35.71	35.33	34.29	33.87	34.33	33.81	33.88	33.65	33.84	34.58	34.28	34.36
2015	35.19	35.87	35.49	34.82	34.81	34.56	34.87	35.55	35.50	36.06	36.36	35.50	35.39
2016	35.73	35.99	36.12	36.07	37.03	36.08	36.44	36.25	36.31	37.10	36.56	37.49	36.44
2017	38.45	37.70	37.72	38.20	37.68	36.74	37.55	37.36	37.57	37.54	36.93	37.69	37.59
2018	37.89	37.17	37.37	37.50	37.46	37.78	38.33	38.04	39.11	38.05	38.99	39.49	38.10
Education and Health Services													
2014	24.32	24.86	24.37	24.23	24.17	24.27	24.36	24.64	24.84	24.56	24.62	25.29	24.54
2015	24.77	25.02	25.40	25.50	25.72	25.85	25.45	25.98	26.22	26.04	26.00	26.94	25.75
2016	25.70	25.96	26.14	25.62	26.02	25.97	26.31	26.17	26.51	26.90	27.06	27.04	26.28
2017	27.56	27.73	27.61	27.72	27.50	27.28	27.80	27.38	27.44	27.76	27.66	27.73	27.60
2018	27.91	27.51	27.80	27.99	27.66	27.47	27.32	26.74	26.90	26.74	26.84	26.61	27.29
Leisure and Hospitality													
2014	13.09	13.35	13.11	13.11	13.08	13.13	12.84	12.88	13.13	13.24	13.21	13.30	13.12
2015	13.32	13.44	13.39	13.34	13.27	13.06	12.93	12.83	13.12	13.27	13.34	13.40	13.22
2016	13.48	13.37	13.29	13.38	13.60	13.21	13.18	13.12	13.31	13.57	13.57	13.94	13.41
2017	13.93	13.80	14.01	14.21	14.25	13.76	13.80	13.77	13.87	14.00	14.13	14.27	13.98
2018	14.33	14.42	14.37	14.41	14.47	14.15	14.22	14.36	14.46	14.59	14.83	15.03	14.46
Other Services													
2014	25.81	25.88	25.89	25.78	25.61	25.68	25.24	25.10	25.12	25.42	25.61	26.17	25.61
2015	26.23	25.79	26.22	25.80	26.37	25.91	25.82	26.21	26.64	26.62	27.15	27.37	26.34
2016	27.75	27.29	27.49	27.52	27.64	27.66	26.75	26.71	27.47	27.70	27.35	27.35	27.39
2017	27.95	27.58	27.52	27.95	27.79	27.50	27.82	27.79	27.69	28.19	27.68	27.47	27.75
2018	27.84	27.69	28.16	28.58	27.82	27.89	28.39	28.47	29.24	29.26	29.32	30.93	28.64

4. Average Weekly Earnings by Selected Industry: Virginia, 2014–2018

(Dollars, not seasonally adjusted)

Industry and year	January	February	March	April	May	June	July	August	September	October	November	December	Annual average
Total Private													
2014	877.88	857.33	888.32	876.26	871.39	889.50	865.69	873.75	878.70	883.67	910.22	888.90	879.30
2015	892.33	923.13	925.92	919.21	915.68	905.23	905.93	937.70	919.10	922.60	939.87	919.10	917.51
2016	924.41	924.06	929.51	938.46	954.72	933.92	943.35	935.06	950.51	972.52	946.84	949.69	940.90
2017	970.56	956.69	942.21	974.38	938.79	931.50	960.45	933.65	950.81	967.78	950.43	965.70	953.92
2018	960.68	964.30	959.37	994.75	967.76	970.53	996.10	978.49	1,008.73	984.29	982.70	1,016.37	982.29
Goods-Producing													
2014	875.63	857.38	901.65	921.04	931.03	928.80	918.32	926.71	922.96	927.04	946.36	929.41	915.69
2015	910.22	916.07	925.52	940.00	949.63	945.57	938.40	946.08	944.45	958.29	952.38	955.86	939.25
2016	956.00	926.48	940.75	961.83	945.05	969.24	989.21	985.35	984.21	988.15	970.98	966.42	966.39
2017	972.14	922.28	913.10	933.25	925.91	955.39	964.23	945.00	967.89	964.40	969.81	993.67	953.47
2018	959.74	967.89	965.58	999.20	1,000.40	976.21	975.15	1,004.55	968.61	1,035.71	1,013.71	1,036.61	991.93
Construction													
2014	898.48	870.44	916.42	942.45	955.45	938.84	924.16	929.49	905.63	909.85	920.73	905.08	918.32
2015	862.65	902.92	916.50	926.98	962.33	956.39	941.68	943.48	905.64	954.34	940.84	949.62	930.40
2016	952.58	917.06	958.24	991.36	960.50	1,001.56	1,018.16	1,021.29	1,019.07	1,025.86	995.33	970.13	987.55
2017	963.60	973.56	954.77	996.77	979.13	1,016.34	1,024.03	994.50	1,027.42	1,003.99	1,009.32	1,047.02	1,001.16
2018	983.62	1,000.89	1,004.16	1,038.40	1,059.48	1,018.51	1,038.59	1,057.60	977.96	1,067.20	1,003.01	1,051.05	1,024.92
Manufacturing													
2014	876.00	865.24	906.81	912.17	914.48	921.82	915.94	918.53	931.56	923.88	951.97	935.90	915.05
2015	937.00	916.76	918.40	943.90	928.36	925.70	924.34	939.82	960.50	925.74	935.68	938.18	932.83
2016	938.83	917.15	903.54	918.19	912.11	923.69	948.40	936.74	940.89	939.69	943.27	960.75	932.95
2017	978.05	981.29	962.79	961.17	948.37	960.66	965.12	953.20	961.56	971.92	972.93	979.24	965.52
2018	968.82	960.71	952.01	980.37	959.14	951.62	939.30	992.54	994.80	1,020.10	1,052.80	1,038.68	983.29
Trade, Transportation, and Utilities													
2014	661.96	691.38	683.09	685.10	691.22	693.94	686.13	684.11	686.80	672.34	685.71	667.23	682.41
2015	665.91	689.50	683.10	696.98	694.88	692.24	698.35	714.47	695.95	709.58	690.54	684.00	693.94
2016	687.57	669.34	675.62	707.29	697.06	701.83	723.54	711.22	725.56	731.47	705.03	722.31	704.84
2017	719.85	699.40	690.64	717.14	690.04	686.83	708.19	690.64	705.94	705.83	704.30	712.21	701.96
2018	705.53	706.32	706.97	736.33	717.12	730.60	762.63	750.65	786.24	759.99	757.00	795.54	744.34
Financial Activities													
2014	972.62	983.20	996.18	963.60	951.86	1,006.93	963.68	975.64	977.17	968.31	1,013.61	981.33	980.96
2015	974.86	1,027.94	1,029.50	1,021.41	1,038.24	1,032.16	1,033.29	1,094.84	1,061.20	1,055.05	1,098.77	1,053.16	1,043.11
2016	1,045.84	1,049.91	1,035.84	1,041.71	1,072.40	1,017.62	1,045.92	1,036.84	1,098.43	1,142.96	1,116.02	1,107.26	1,066.61
2017	1,135.23	1,118.82	1,092.14	1,133.06	1,107.19	1,123.95	1,162.70	1,118.62	1,143.42	1,163.94	1,133.39	1,144.18	1,130.23
2018	1,141.93	1,185.79	1,175.04	1,215.49	1,173.12	1,158.14	1,183.48	1,152.82	1,246.60	1,180.66	1,188.02	1,285.22	1.189.25
Professional and Business Services													
2014	1,251.47	1,296.27	1,296.61	1,251.59	1,243.03	1,277.08	1,223.92	1,240.01	1,224.86	1,252.08	1,317.50	1,261.50	1,261.01
2015	1,280.92	1,341.54	1,337.97	1,295.30	1,294.93	1,275.26	1,283.22	1,347.35	1,299.30	1,319.80	1,378.04	1,324.15	1,316.51
2016	1,318.44	1,331.63	1,343.66	1,359.84	1,414.55	1,353.00	1,355.57	1,355.75	1,361.63	1,417.22	1,367.34	1,394.63	1,366.50
2017	1,449.57	1,413.75	1,399.41	1,451.60	1,386.62	1,388.77	1,426.90	1,397.26	1,423.90	1,441.54	1,392.26	1,413.38	1,417.14
2018	1,413.30	1,405.03	1,397.64	1,436.25	1,393.51	1,420.53	1,448.87	1,407.48	1,474.45	1,404.05	1,419.24	1,472.98	1,424.94
Education and Health Services													
2014	824.45	837.78	826.14	828.67	824.20	839.74	833.11	835.30	852.01	837.50	849.39	862.39	836.81
2015	847.13	865.69	871.22	872.10	879.62	884.07	867.85	896.31	896.72	893.17	902.20	907.88	883.23
2016	889.22	895.62	904.44	889.01	913.30	903.76	910.33	908.10	919.90	936.12	930.86	930.18	911.92
2017	953.58	942.82	933.22	945.25	932.25	919.34	945.20	914.49	930.22	946.62	929.38	942.82	935.64
2018	940.57	935.34	928.52	940.46	921.08	914.75	928.88	906.49	909.22	882.42	880.35	864.83	911.49
Leisure and Hospitality													
2014	333.80	340.43	347.42	352.66	350.54	354.51	345.40	343.90	347.95	348.21	350.07	344.47	346.37
2015	337.00	341.38	350.82	354.84	352.98	346.09	346.52	347.69	342.43	346.35	349.51	345.72	346.36
2016	332.96	342.27	344.21	351.89	359.04	348.74	351.91	347.68	351.38	363.68	362.32	365.23	351.34
2017	356.61	361.56	368.46	372.30	366.23	360.51	372.60	364.91	359.23	366.80	365.97	369.59	364.88
2018	359.68	373.48	372.18	378.98	376.22	373.56	378.25	381.98	371.62	383.72	379.65	383.27	375.96
Other Services													
2014	820.76	828.16	841.43	835.27	834.89	844.87	812.73	793.16	808.86	821.07	834.89	847.91	827.20
2015	849.85	835.60	852.15	838.50	841.20	847.26	844.31	849.20	847.15	854.50	890.52	886.79	853.42
2016	901.88	886.93	898.92	886.14	909.36	896.18	861.35	862.73	884.53	914.10	875.20	886.14	887.44
2017	911.17	888.08	883.39	925.15	889.28	880.00	906.93	880.94	869.47	918.99	880.22	892.78	893.55
2018	874.18	872.24	884.22	914.56	867.98	878.54	917.00	908.19	953.22	950.95	949.97	1,008.32	913.62

WASHINGTON
At a Glance

Population:
  2010 census: 6,724,540
  2018 estimate: 7,535,591

Percent change in population:
  2010–2018: 12.1%

Percent change in total nonfarm employment:
  2010–2018: 20.1%

Industry with the largest growth in employment, 2010–2018 (percent):
  Construction, 51.8%

Industry with the largest decline or smallest growth in employment, 2010–2018 (percent):
  Government, 6.7%

Civilian labor force:
  2010: 3,511,326
  2018: 3,793,095

Unemployment rate and rank among states (highest to lowest):
  2010: 10.0%, 17th
  2018: 4.5%, 10th

Over-the-year change in unemployment rates:
  2016–2017: -0.6%
  2017–2018: -0.2%

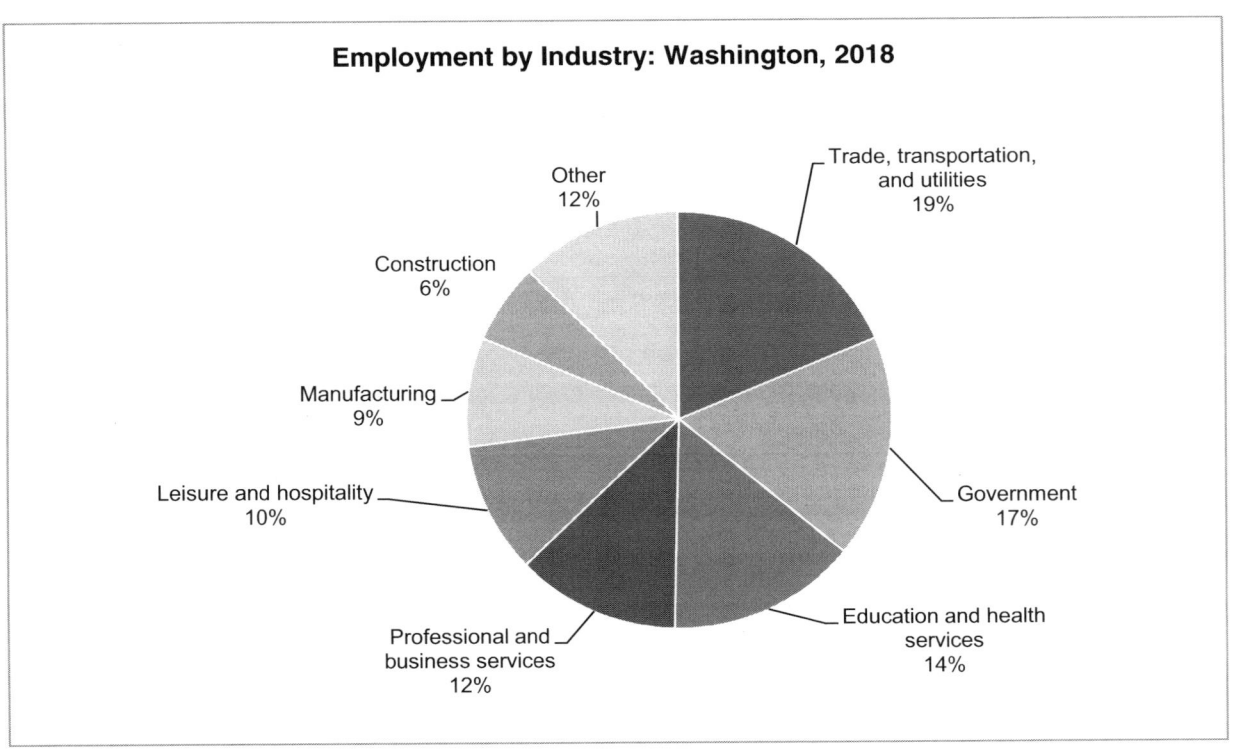

Employment by Industry: Washington, 2018

- Other 12%
- Trade, transportation, and utilities 19%
- Construction 6%
- Government 17%
- Manufacturing 9%
- Leisure and hospitality 10%
- Education and health services 14%
- Professional and business services 12%

1. Employment by Industry: Washington, 2010–2018

(Numbers in thousands, not seasonally adjusted)

Industry and year	January	February	March	April	May	June	July	August	September	October	November	December	Annual average
Total Nonfarm													
2010	2,777.4	2,784.9	2,802.1	2,827.6	2,853.8	2,859.9	2,847.7	2,829.2	2,849.5	2,872.4	2,870.4	2,859.1	2,836.2
2011	2,807.6	2,820.2	2,832.3	2,862.7	2,880.6	2,893.8	2,889.0	2,878.0	2,895.8	2,905.8	2,908.6	2,895.7	2,872.5
2012	2,840.3	2,854.8	2,876.8	2,898.1	2,926.6	2,945.9	2,932.1	2,928.1	2,943.7	2,964.8	2,969.3	2,955.0	2,919.6
2013	2,906.7	2,924.6	2,939.0	2,960.6	2,990.3	3,001.8	2,993.0	2,994.6	3,012.1	3,027.4	3,033.6	3,024.1	2,984.0
2014	2,985.8	2,993.0	3,011.0	3,027.1	3,052.1	3,070.1	3,072.3	3,073.8	3,091.0	3,097.7	3,105.8	3,107.1	3,057.2
2015	3,061.9	3,074.2	3,096.1	3,121.3	3,148.1	3,171.5	3,163.4	3,158.0	3,177.9	3,183.9	3,191.4	3,189.2	3,144.7
2016	3,153.7	3,172.6	3,190.8	3,223.9	3,249.6	3,265.8	3,261.1	3,255.8	3,281.9	3,279.7	3,291.0	3,287.3	3,242.8
2017	3,234.6	3,251.5	3,277.0	3,300.0	3,330.8	3,355.7	3,341.3	3,331.6	3,351.2	3,354.1	3,363.8	3,362.1	3,321.1
2018	3,325.6	3,340.8	3,365.1	3,382.9	3,413.3	3,433.2	3,420.5	3,422.8	3,428.1	3,449.2	3,446.5	3,444.5	3,406.0
Total Private													
2010	2,226.0	2,229.8	2,245.4	2,266.4	2,281.4	2,299.4	2,312.0	2,313.8	2,319.2	2,318.3	2,312.1	2,310.6	2,286.2
2011	2,258.0	2,267.1	2,278.8	2,307.1	2,323.5	2,344.4	2,360.0	2,367.3	2,372.4	2,357.7	2,357.6	2,354.4	2,329.0
2012	2,297.9	2,309.0	2,328.2	2,347.0	2,374.1	2,399.3	2,406.1	2,419.3	2,418.4	2,415.1	2,415.7	2,411.2	2,378.4
2013	2,360.8	2,374.5	2,388.2	2,407.4	2,435.8	2,453.9	2,467.7	2,483.1	2,483.3	2,477.0	2,479.2	2,477.7	2,440.7
2014	2,436.4	2,440.3	2,455.8	2,468.7	2,492.1	2,516.0	2,537.4	2,552.1	2,550.3	2,536.6	2,542.8	2,550.7	2,506.6
2015	2,502.1	2,510.8	2,529.5	2,550.9	2,576.0	2,604.9	2,616.9	2,624.9	2,623.6	2,613.4	2,617.5	2,622.5	2,582.8
2016	2,581.6	2,596.1	2,612.6	2,642.1	2,663.3	2,688.2	2,701.1	2,709.8	2,713.6	2,693.2	2,700.4	2,703.6	2,667.1
2017	2,652.4	2,664.5	2,686.8	2,706.2	2,732.8	2,764.6	2,766.5	2,776.2	2,776.1	2,758.6	2,766.0	2,772.2	2,735.2
2018	2,735.0	2,747.6	2,770.0	2,785.2	2,812.7	2,840.7	2,848.0	2,865.3	2,854.3	2,857.3	2,855.4	2,860.8	2,819.4
Goods Producing													
2010	393.8	392.8	394.4	397.8	401.8	407.2	414.8	417.1	418.2	415.5	407.3	400.6	405.1
2011	391.0	393.6	396.4	402.0	407.2	414.2	422.1	426.7	428.9	424.9	418.3	412.4	411.5
2012	402.5	404.2	409.6	413.9	420.5	429.6	436.3	442.2	442.0	441.2	436.0	430.7	425.7
2013	422.8	426.3	429.6	432.3	439.0	445.9	452.4	457.3	457.3	453.5	447.8	442.0	442.2
2014	436.8	436.9	441.5	443.3	449.2	456.9	466.0	470.2	469.9	466.6	462.3	461.5	455.1
2015	456.3	457.4	461.7	465.0	469.7	477.3	483.7	484.3	482.7	479.1	473.7	471.6	471.9
2016	467.1	470.7	473.1	478.7	482.9	487.8	494.3	495.1	494.4	488.5	484.5	481.5	483.2
2017	473.6	476.6	481.3	485.1	489.6	498.2	498.8	500.2	500.4	495.5	492.0	490.7	490.2
2018	484.7	489.3	495.0	498.7	505.2	512.0	516.6	520.1	519.2	521.3	515.8	516.0	507.8
Service-Providing													
2010	2,383.6	2,392.1	2,407.7	2,429.8	2,452.0	2,452.7	2,432.9	2,412.1	2,431.3	2,456.9	2,463.1	2,458.5	2,431.1
2011	2,416.6	2,426.6	2,435.9	2,460.7	2,473.4	2,479.6	2,466.9	2,451.3	2,466.9	2,480.9	2,490.3	2,483.3	2,461.0
2012	2,437.8	2,450.6	2,467.2	2,484.2	2,506.1	2,516.3	2,495.8	2,485.9	2,501.7	2,523.6	2,533.3	2,524.3	2,493.9
2013	2,483.9	2,498.3	2,509.4	2,528.3	2,551.3	2,555.9	2,540.6	2,537.3	2,554.8	2,573.9	2,585.8	2,582.1	2,541.8
2014	2,549.0	2,556.1	2,569.5	2,583.8	2,602.9	2,613.2	2,606.3	2,603.6	2,621.1	2,631.1	2,643.5	2,645.6	2,602.1
2015	2,605.6	2,616.8	2,634.4	2,656.3	2,678.4	2,694.2	2,679.7	2,673.7	2,695.2	2,704.8	2,717.7	2,717.6	2,672.9
2016	2,686.6	2,701.9	2,717.7	2,745.2	2,766.7	2,778.0	2,766.8	2,760.7	2,787.5	2,791.2	2,806.5	2,805.8	2,759.6
2017	2,761.0	2,774.9	2,795.7	2,814.9	2,841.2	2,857.5	2,842.5	2,831.4	2,850.8	2,858.6	2,871.8	2,871.4	2,831.0
2018	2,840.9	2,851.5	2,870.1	2,884.2	2,908.1	2,921.2	2,903.9	2,902.7	2,908.9	2,927.9	2,930.7	2,928.5	2,898.2
Mining and Logging													
2010	5.4	5.5	5.5	5.6	5.9	6.1	6.2	6.3	6.3	6.2	5.9	5.7	5.9
2011	5.6	5.7	5.7	5.7	5.8	6.1	6.2	6.3	6.2	6.3	6.1	6.0	6.0
2012	5.7	5.6	5.6	5.6	5.7	6.0	6.1	6.2	6.2	6.2	6.0	5.9	5.9
2013	5.7	5.8	5.8	5.8	6.0	6.2	6.3	6.4	6.4	6.4	6.3	6.2	6.1
2014	6.0	6.1	6.1	5.9	6.1	6.2	6.4	6.5	6.4	6.4	6.3	6.3	6.2
2015	6.3	6.3	6.2	6.2	6.3	6.4	6.5	6.4	6.3	6.5	6.3	6.3	6.3
2016	6.1	6.2	6.0	6.1	6.3	6.4	6.5	6.5	6.5	6.4	6.2	6.1	6.3
2017	5.9	6.0	5.9	6.0	6.2	6.4	6.4	6.4	6.4	6.3	6.2	6.3	6.2
2018	6.1	6.1	6.1	6.2	6.3	6.5	6.5	6.5	6.5	6.5	6.3	6.2	6.3
Construction													
2010	134.7	133.9	135.5	137.3	140.0	142.2	146.8	148.6	147.7	146.2	140.4	135.2	140.7
2011	127.3	127.8	129.3	132.8	136.3	139.4	142.5	144.5	144.5	142.0	137.2	133.4	136.4
2012	125.6	126.9	130.2	133.7	137.6	141.6	144.7	148.1	147.4	147.6	144.2	141.6	139.1
2013	135.2	137.4	139.9	143.0	147.7	150.8	155.2	159.0	158.7	157.1	154.1	149.9	149.0
2014	146.8	146.3	150.4	151.6	155.8	160.0	165.5	169.2	169.5	168.3	166.4	165.8	159.6
2015	162.3	163.3	166.2	169.9	173.5	176.4	179.8	180.3	179.1	178.2	175.3	174.3	173.2
2016	171.8	174.7	177.6	182.3	185.4	188.5	193.0	195.1	195.4	193.1	191.9	190.4	186.6
2017	184.8	187.7	192.2	195.1	199.4	204.3	205.3	207.5	208.1	206.0	204.1	202.7	199.8
2018	198.8	201.6	205.7	209.1	213.2	217.0	218.7	222.1	220.6	223.0	217.1	216.0	213.6

1. Employment by Industry: Washington, 2010–2018—*Continued*

(Numbers in thousands, not seasonally adjusted)

Industry and year	January	February	March	April	May	June	July	August	September	October	November	December	Annual average
Manufacturing													
2010	253.7	253.4	253.4	254.9	255.9	258.9	261.8	262.2	264.2	263.1	261.0	259.7	258.5
2011	258.1	260.1	261.4	263.5	265.1	268.7	273.4	275.9	278.2	276.6	275.0	273.0	269.1
2012	271.2	271.7	273.8	274.6	277.2	282.0	285.5	287.9	288.4	287.4	285.8	283.2	280.7
2013	281.9	283.1	283.9	283.5	285.3	288.9	290.9	291.9	292.2	290.0	287.4	285.9	287.1
2014	284.0	284.5	285.0	285.8	287.3	290.7	294.1	294.5	294.0	291.9	289.6	289.4	289.2
2015	287.7	287.8	289.3	288.9	289.9	294.5	297.4	297.6	297.3	294.4	292.1	291.0	292.3
2016	289.2	289.8	289.5	290.3	291.2	292.9	294.8	293.5	292.5	289.0	286.4	285.0	290.3
2017	282.9	282.9	283.2	284.0	284.0	287.5	287.1	286.3	285.9	283.2	281.7	281.7	284.2
2018	279.8	281.6	283.2	283.4	285.7	288.5	291.4	291.5	292.1	291.8	292.4	293.8	287.9
Trade, Transportation, and Utilities													
2010	506.7	502.8	505.3	509.6	512.9	516.6	518.4	518.1	517.5	521.6	528.8	532.8	515.9
2011	511.5	508.8	511.1	514.8	519.3	523.9	529.1	530.2	529.3	530.1	538.8	541.5	524.0
2012	521.0	517.8	520.7	523.0	530.0	536.6	539.5	541.2	540.2	542.7	552.1	553.9	534.9
2013	534.4	532.6	533.3	536.5	544.4	548.8	553.5	556.7	555.5	559.7	570.0	573.5	549.9
2014	554.3	550.7	551.9	554.8	561.0	567.4	573.1	576.9	576.5	577.5	588.1	593.0	568.8
2015	572.1	569.8	573.5	576.4	582.5	589.5	591.3	594.3	593.5	593.4	603.6	607.3	587.3
2016	586.8	585.1	588.7	594.3	600.3	608.7	612.1	614.1	612.3	613.8	624.6	628.4	605.8
2017	609.3	605.6	609.4	613.0	619.8	626.6	630.8	632.6	631.4	630.5	641.7	644.7	624.6
2018	629.8	624.0	626.5	627.1	633.1	639.2	641.4	644.4	641.3	641.0	651.6	653.4	637.7
Wholesale Trade													
2010	117.5	117.7	118.3	119.8	120.0	120.1	120.4	119.9	119.8	120.8	120.6	119.5	119.5
2011	118.3	118.7	119.4	120.1	121.2	121.7	122.3	122.1	121.9	122.6	122.4	121.5	121.0
2012	120.3	120.7	121.4	122.2	123.1	124.2	124.3	124.8	124.3	125.1	124.8	124.1	123.3
2013	122.7	123.8	124.2	124.8	125.6	126.4	127.5	127.5	127.4	128.3	128.1	127.2	126.1
2014	126.3	126.7	127.0	127.2	128.1	129.2	131.1	131.0	131.2	131.0	130.9	130.4	129.2
2015	128.8	129.4	129.8	130.4	131.0	132.4	132.4	132.5	132.3	132.0	132.0	131.9	131.2
2016	129.8	130.3	130.7	131.7	132.0	132.8	133.1	133.3	133.1	132.8	132.8	132.6	132.1
2017	131.1	131.6	132.0	132.5	133.3	134.1	134.3	133.8	134.1	134.2	134.2	134.2	133.3
2018	133.4	134.1	135.0	135.5	136.4	137.5	137.7	137.8	137.3	137.5	136.5	135.4	136.2
Retail Trade													
2010	303.0	299.4	300.8	302.9	305.4	308.1	308.7	309.3	308.0	311.0	319.1	322.8	308.2
2011	306.3	303.3	303.8	306.0	309.0	312.2	314.1	315.7	314.1	316.3	325.1	327.3	312.8
2012	311.2	307.5	309.1	310.4	315.0	319.1	321.7	322.5	321.7	324.2	333.9	335.3	319.3
2013	320.1	317.0	317.8	320.4	326.1	329.3	332.1	334.4	332.8	336.0	345.9	349.2	330.1
2014	332.9	329.4	330.5	332.2	336.2	340.4	343.3	346.0	344.8	346.4	356.8	359.8	341.6
2015	343.5	341.0	343.9	346.7	350.9	354.6	355.9	358.6	357.7	357.6	366.5	367.9	353.7
2016	353.7	352.1	354.3	357.2	361.5	366.8	369.0	370.3	368.1	370.2	378.8	380.4	365.2
2017	367.7	364.4	367.4	370.5	375.5	380.1	384.1	385.1	383.4	382.5	391.8	392.5	378.8
2018	382.2	377.3	378.5	378.8	383.2	386.4	389.1	391.0	388.5	387.6	396.1	395.9	386.2
Transportation and Utilities													
2010	86.2	85.7	86.2	86.9	87.5	88.4	89.3	88.9	89.7	89.8	89.1	90.5	88.2
2011	86.9	86.8	87.9	88.7	89.1	90.0	92.7	92.4	93.3	91.2	91.3	92.7	90.3
2012	89.5	89.6	90.2	90.4	91.9	93.3	93.5	93.9	94.2	93.4	94.5	94.5	92.3
2013	91.6	91.8	91.3	91.3	92.7	93.1	93.9	94.8	95.3	95.4	96.0	97.1	93.7
2014	95.1	94.6	94.4	95.4	96.7	97.8	98.7	99.9	100.5	100.1	100.4	102.8	98.0
2015	99.8	99.4	99.8	99.3	100.6	102.5	103.0	103.2	103.5	103.8	105.1	107.5	102.3
2016	103.3	102.7	103.7	105.4	106.8	109.1	110.0	110.5	111.1	110.8	113.0	115.4	108.5
2017	110.5	109.6	110.0	110.0	111.0	112.4	112.4	113.7	113.9	113.8	115.7	118.0	112.6
2018	114.2	112.6	113.0	112.8	113.5	115.3	114.6	115.6	115.5	115.9	119.0	122.1	115.3
Information													
2010	102.2	102.4	102.4	101.7	102.5	103.6	103.8	104.2	103.7	102.8	103.3	103.8	103.0
2011	102.9	103.4	103.1	103.3	103.6	104.8	105.7	106.0	104.9	104.0	104.5	104.3	104.2
2012	104.0	104.4	104.0	103.8	104.6	105.9	106.0	106.0	104.5	103.9	104.4	104.9	104.7
2013	104.0	104.7	104.4	104.7	105.6	106.5	107.7	108.2	107.1	106.3	107.2	107.3	106.1
2014	106.9	107.1	107.2	107.6	108.7	110.6	112.3	113.1	112.1	110.2	110.7	110.5	109.8
2015	110.0	110.9	111.1	111.3	112.5	114.3	116.4	117.5	116.8	116.1	117.1	117.4	114.3
2016	116.8	117.8	118.3	119.0	119.8	122.5	123.8	124.6	124.0	122.7	123.5	123.6	121.4
2017	123.0	123.5	124.0	123.7	124.9	127.3	128.3	129.2	128.6	127.4	127.6	128.1	126.3
2018	127.6	128.7	129.4	130.2	131.2	135.2	136.8	137.8	137.0	137.9	137.1	138.2	133.9

1. Employment by Industry: Washington, 2010–2018—*Continued*

(Numbers in thousands, not seasonally adjusted)

Industry and year	January	February	March	April	May	June	July	August	September	October	November	December	Annual average
Financial Activities													
2010	137.4	137.0	137.2	137.7	137.7	138.2	139.1	139.2	138.8	138.4	138.0	138.5	138.1
2011	136.8	136.9	137.0	137.7	137.7	138.7	139.2	139.4	139.2	138.1	138.5	138.6	138.2
2012	137.0	137.7	138.3	139.0	140.2	140.9	142.2	142.1	141.1	140.9	141.0	141.3	140.1
2013	140.8	141.2	142.0	142.4	143.5	144.4	145.7	145.8	145.0	144.6	144.5	145.0	143.7
2014	143.5	143.7	144.2	144.6	144.4	145.4	146.7	147.2	146.3	145.8	145.7	146.3	145.3
2015	145.4	145.8	145.9	146.8	147.7	148.6	149.7	150.0	149.2	148.1	148.1	148.3	147.8
2016	147.8	148.0	148.5	149.4	150.4	151.5	153.4	153.7	153.0	151.9	151.8	152.3	151.0
2017	150.9	151.8	152.4	152.1	153.8	155.1	155.7	156.4	155.9	154.3	154.7	154.9	154.0
2018	155.0	155.6	156.4	156.6	158.1	159.2	159.6	160.0	158.7	159.4	158.9	159.0	158.0
Professional and Business Services													
2010	313.7	315.8	319.9	324.0	324.7	327.9	332.9	331.7	333.2	335.3	333.6	334.2	327.2
2011	326.9	330.0	332.5	339.7	339.5	342.0	346.2	345.9	347.7	345.5	345.1	344.2	340.4
2012	336.2	339.4	342.2	347.5	350.2	354.3	353.9	357.6	358.1	359.5	358.6	356.4	351.2
2013	350.0	353.2	355.6	360.5	362.0	364.6	365.6	370.0	371.1	370.7	368.3	367.3	363.2
2014	360.9	362.3	365.4	367.5	368.8	372.6	376.7	379.4	379.7	379.5	380.8	381.4	372.9
2015	372.9	374.7	378.7	383.6	386.1	389.8	392.7	394.5	396.0	394.8	395.6	396.4	388.0
2016	388.9	391.1	394.2	398.5	400.4	403.5	405.7	407.0	409.9	406.0	407.0	405.6	401.5
2017	399.3	401.7	405.9	409.8	413.0	417.6	419.0	421.1	421.1	417.7	417.3	417.0	413.4
2018	411.5	414.9	419.7	421.0	423.6	428.8	430.5	435.0	433.3	431.1	428.4	425.8	425.3
Education and Health Services													
2010	418.2	423.1	425.1	426.6	427.5	424.1	417.9	417.0	423.8	431.0	432.2	430.8	424.8
2011	427.7	431.4	432.9	433.1	433.2	430.3	425.3	424.5	430.3	435.2	436.7	436.2	431.4
2012	429.3	434.2	436.5	436.1	437.3	433.5	426.7	426.6	431.8	437.0	438.6	437.5	433.8
2013	431.8	437.5	438.4	438.6	439.2	433.6	429.4	428.8	435.5	442.3	444.0	443.8	436.9
2014	440.7	446.1	445.8	445.6	446.6	441.7	438.3	437.3	442.9	446.4	447.8	448.7	444.0
2015	442.9	447.5	448.2	449.9	449.7	447.6	441.5	440.7	447.0	454.1	455.9	456.6	448.5
2016	455.6	461.3	462.7	465.3	465.7	462.4	455.6	457.2	464.7	468.6	471.0	472.0	463.5
2017	465.8	472.1	474.1	474.5	475.8	473.4	467.5	470.0	477.4	483.3	486.3	486.6	475.6
2018	483.0	489.6	491.6	491.9	492.8	488.0	483.2	485.5	491.2	499.5	502.5	503.3	491.8
Leisure and Hospitality													
2010	251.4	252.8	257.5	264.7	269.3	275.3	277.6	279.0	277.8	267.6	262.7	263.8	266.6
2011	256.2	257.1	259.6	268.8	274.3	280.4	281.7	284.1	282.8	270.9	267.3	268.4	271.0
2012	260.5	263.0	267.4	273.3	280.1	286.3	288.5	290.9	289.0	278.6	274.2	276.1	277.3
2013	269.0	270.4	275.4	282.2	290.7	298.0	300.0	302.9	299.7	288.1	285.4	287.3	287.4
2014	282.4	282.3	287.4	292.8	299.8	306.5	308.1	311.8	308.3	296.7	293.6	295.1	297.1
2015	290.2	292.0	296.5	303.3	312.2	321.3	324.3	326.5	322.9	313.0	308.9	310.3	310.1
2016	304.4	307.3	311.4	319.6	325.4	332.3	336.7	338.3	336.9	324.1	320.3	322.3	323.3
2017	314.1	315.9	321.3	328.9	335.5	344.2	344.6	345.1	341.2	330.0	327.0	330.4	331.5
2018	324.9	326.3	331.3	339.2	346.7	354.2	355.7	358.2	351.1	343.5	337.9	341.6	342.6
Other Services													
2010	102.6	103.1	103.6	104.3	105.0	106.5	107.5	107.5	106.2	106.1	106.2	106.1	105.4
2011	105.0	105.9	106.2	107.7	108.7	110.1	110.7	110.5	109.3	109.0	108.4	108.8	108.4
2012	107.4	108.3	109.5	110.4	111.2	112.2	113.0	112.7	111.7	111.3	110.8	110.4	110.7
2013	108.0	108.6	109.5	110.2	111.4	112.1	113.4	113.4	112.1	111.8	112.0	111.5	111.2
2014	110.9	111.2	112.4	112.5	113.6	114.9	116.2	116.2	114.6	113.9	113.8	114.2	113.7
2015	112.3	112.7	113.9	114.6	115.6	116.5	117.3	117.1	115.5	114.8	114.6	114.6	115.0
2016	114.2	114.8	115.7	117.3	118.4	119.5	119.5	119.8	118.4	117.6	117.7	117.9	117.6
2017	116.4	117.3	118.4	119.1	120.4	122.2	121.8	121.6	120.1	119.9	119.4	119.8	119.7
2018	118.5	119.2	120.1	120.5	122.0	124.1	124.2	124.3	122.5	123.6	123.2	123.5	122.1
Government													
2010	551.4	555.1	556.7	561.2	572.4	560.5	535.7	515.4	530.3	554.1	558.3	548.5	550.0
2011	549.6	553.1	553.5	555.6	557.1	549.4	529.0	510.7	523.4	548.1	551.0	541.3	543.5
2012	542.4	545.8	548.6	551.1	552.5	546.6	526.0	508.8	525.3	549.7	553.6	543.8	541.2
2013	545.9	550.1	550.8	553.2	554.5	547.9	525.3	511.5	528.8	550.4	554.4	546.4	543.3
2014	549.4	552.7	555.2	558.4	560.0	554.1	534.9	521.7	540.7	561.1	563.0	556.4	550.6
2015	559.8	563.4	566.6	570.4	572.1	566.6	546.5	533.1	554.3	570.5	573.9	566.7	562.0
2016	572.1	576.5	578.2	581.8	586.3	577.6	560.0	546.0	568.3	586.5	590.6	583.7	575.6
2017	582.2	587.0	590.2	593.8	598.0	591.1	574.8	555.4	575.1	595.5	597.8	589.9	585.9
2018	590.6	593.2	595.1	597.7	600.6	592.5	572.5	557.5	573.8	591.9	591.1	583.7	586.7

2. Average Weekly Hours by Selected Industry: Washington, 2014–2018

(Not seasonally adjusted)

Industry and year	January	February	March	April	May	June	July	August	September	October	November	December	Annual average
Total Private													
2014	33.4	34.7	34.8	33.9	34.0	34.9	34.0	34.3	34.1	33.9	34.9	33.9	34.2
2015	33.6	34.7	34.7	34.0	34.0	34.2	34.3	35.3	34.3	34.3	35.1	34.0	34.4
2016	34.0	34.2	34.1	34.4	35.2	34.5	34.6	34.9	34.6	35.4	34.5	34.4	34.6
2017	34.9	34.2	34.3	35.4	34.5	34.6	35.5	34.8	34.6	35.5	34.5	34.6	34.8
2018	34.4	34.7	34.5	35.6	34.7	34.8	35.3	34.6	35.5	34.4	34.3	35.3	34.8
Goods-Producing													
2014	39.2	39.5	39.7	39.4	39.5	39.9	39.3	39.8	40.0	40.1	40.3	39.9	39.7
2015	39.5	39.8	39.8	39.6	39.8	40.1	39.9	40.3	39.2	40.1	39.9	39.5	39.8
2016	39.2	39.2	39.4	39.5	39.9	39.5	39.5	39.6	39.5	39.8	39.5	39.2	39.5
2017	38.7	38.5	39.1	39.5	39.5	39.7	39.6	39.9	39.7	40.4	39.6	39.8	39.5
2018	39.2	39.6	39.4	40.3	39.9	40.0	39.6	39.9	40.0	40.1	40.2	40.6	39.9
Construction													
2014	36.3	36.1	36.6	36.9	37.0	37.9	37.8	38.3	38.5	38.1	38.2	37.8	37.5
2015	37.8	38.1	37.9	37.9	38.1	38.5	38.3	38.8	36.3	37.9	37.5	36.7	37.8
2016	36.6	36.9	37.2	37.5	38.2	37.6	37.6	38.1	37.7	37.4	37.4	36.9	37.4
2017	36.0	35.7	36.8	37.4	37.8	38.3	38.4	38.5	38.0	38.8	37.5	37.5	37.6
2018	36.7	36.9	37.0	38.2	38.3	38.3	38.2	38.5	38.1	38.4	38.0	38.4	37.9
Manufacturing													
2014	40.4	40.8	40.9	40.4	40.5	40.7	40.0	40.5	40.8	41.1	41.4	41.0	40.7
2015	40.4	40.7	40.8	40.6	40.7	41.0	40.8	41.1	40.7	41.2	41.1	40.9	40.8
2016	40.5	40.3	40.4	40.4	40.6	40.3	40.3	40.2	40.3	41.0	40.6	40.4	40.4
2017	40.1	39.9	40.2	40.5	40.4	40.4	40.3	40.7	40.7	41.3	40.8	41.1	40.5
2018	40.5	41.0	40.7	41.5	40.9	41.1	40.5	40.8	41.1	41.1	41.3	41.7	41.0
Trade, Transportation, and Utilities													
2014	33.5	35.0	35.1	34.5	34.7	35.5	34.9	35.1	35.0	34.4	35.6	34.8	34.8
2015	34.2	35.3	35.3	34.7	35.2	35.2	35.2	36.4	35.9	35.1	36.0	35.0	35.3
2016	34.9	35.4	35.2	35.9	36.6	35.6	35.8	35.9	35.7	36.3	35.3	35.9	35.7
2017	35.5	35.2	35.0	36.0	35.5	35.6	36.3	35.6	35.6	36.0	35.2	35.3	35.6
2018	34.9	35.1	35.0	35.9	35.3	35.3	36.0	35.3	35.7	34.5	34.5	35.2	35.2
Information													
2014	38.8	42.0	41.6	38.6	38.4	41.6	38.4	38.3	39.4	38.4	41.6	38.4	39.6
2015	38.1	41.3	41.3	38.3	38.2	38.2	38.2	41.0	37.9	37.9	41.2	37.7	39.1
2016	38.1	38.0	38.0	38.2	41.0	38.0	38.6	37.9	37.8	41.0	38.2	37.3	38.5
2017	41.2	37.7	37.7	40.8	37.9	38.1	41.4	37.9	37.9	41.4	37.8	38.6	39.0
2018	37.6	37.8	38.3	41.2	37.9	38.4	41.6	38.1	41.5	38.2	38.3	41.3	39.2
Financial Activities													
2014	34.6	36.3	36.2	35.0	35.1	35.9	34.4	34.8	34.8	34.7	36.0	34.9	35.2
2015	35.0	36.6	36.6	35.3	35.1	35.2	35.0	36.7	35.1	35.4	37.1	35.7	35.7
2016	35.7	35.9	35.7	36.0	37.1	36.0	35.4	35.8	35.7	37.0	35.7	35.3	35.9
2017	36.8	35.7	35.4	37.1	35.4	35.8	36.6	35.3	35.7	36.7	35.4	35.3	35.9
2018	35.2	35.8	35.6	37.2	36.2	36.2	37.6	36.2	37.9	36.4	36.6	37.8	36.6
Professional and Business Services													
2014	34.7	36.4	36.6	35.8	35.7	36.7	35.4	35.7	35.7	35.7	36.6	35.3	35.9
2015	35.0	36.4	36.4	35.5	35.3	35.5	35.2	36.5	35.6	35.7	36.5	35.2	35.7
2016	35.4	35.8	35.7	36.0	36.9	35.9	35.8	36.0	35.7	36.6	35.7	35.6	35.9
2017	36.3	35.6	35.8	36.9	35.6	35.7	36.8	35.8	35.8	36.9	36.0	35.7	36.1
2018	35.9	36.2	36.2	37.1	36.1	36.4	37.3	36.4	37.8	36.7	36.2	37.4	36.6
Education and Health Services													
2014	31.7	32.8	32.8	31.8	32.0	32.7	31.7	31.9	32.0	32.0	33.2	32.4	32.3
2015	32.5	33.4	33.1	32.4	32.3	32.5	32.9	33.7	33.1	32.9	33.8	32.5	32.9
2016	33.1	32.6	32.5	32.6	33.4	33.8	34.1	34.6	34.3	34.7	34.0	33.9	33.6
2017	34.9	34.0	33.9	34.7	33.9	34.0	34.9	34.6	34.2	35.1	34.2	34.3	34.4
2018	34.9	34.5	34.3	35.2	34.2	34.1	33.0	32.5	33.7	32.3	32.7	33.5	33.7
Leisure and Hospitality													
2014	24.1	25.3	25.2	24.4	24.2	25.4	25.1	25.7	24.7	23.8	24.7	23.7	24.7
2015	22.8	24.2	24.3	24.0	24.0	24.5	25.0	26.3	24.8	24.6	25.1	24.1	24.5
2016	23.8	24.3	24.2	24.5	25.5	24.7	25.1	25.6	25.1	25.6	24.6	24.2	24.8
2017	25.0	24.6	24.7	26.2	25.1	25.2	26.5	25.8	25.1	25.6	24.8	24.7	25.3
2018	24.4	25.2	24.6	26.0	25.4	25.7	27.0	26.2	26.6	25.7	24.6	25.9	25.6
Other Services													
2014	30.5	31.3	31.7	30.5	30.4	31.3	30.6	30.6	28.2	28.1	29.3	27.6	30.0
2015	28.1	29.8	29.4	28.5	28.6	28.8	29.0	29.7	27.7	27.5	28.8	27.7	28.6
2016	27.9	28.7	28.6	28.8	29.6	28.3	28.7	29.6	28.2	29.2	28.2	28.2	28.7
2017	28.8	28.5	28.4	29.9	28.4	28.4	29.9	29.6	28.6	29.2	28.2	28.8	28.9
2018	28.0	28.4	28.6	29.4	28.2	28.2	29.6	29.0	29.1	28.7	28.0	29.7	28.7

3. Average Hourly Earnings by Selected Industry: Washington, 2014–2018

(Dollars, not seasonally adjusted)

Industry and year	January	February	March	April	May	June	July	August	September	October	November	December	Annual average
Total Private													
2014	28.16	28.25	28.31	28.22	28.14	28.35	28.21	28.19	28.71	28.67	29.12	29.07	28.45
2015	29.50	29.54	29.53	29.38	29.38	29.15	29.12	29.44	29.79	30.00	30.39	30.28	29.63
2016	30.39	30.33	30.30	30.24	30.36	29.97	30.02	29.81	30.43	30.84	30.59	30.65	30.33
2017	31.41	31.15	31.07	31.48	31.04	30.98	31.37	31.07	31.60	31.84	31.69	31.89	31.39
2018	31.99	32.25	32.25	32.62	32.23	32.38	32.64	32.43	33.40	33.10	33.48	33.99	32.74
Goods-Producing													
2014	32.49	32.30	32.70	32.68	32.66	32.69	32.52	32.42	32.53	32.50	32.44	32.66	32.55
2015	32.48	32.61	32.90	32.82	32.80	32.73	32.46	32.58	32.80	32.71	32.80	33.37	32.75
2016	33.06	33.24	33.62	33.58	33.48	33.40	33.36	33.55	33.78	33.69	33.95	34.21	33.58
2017	34.42	34.51	34.75	34.62	34.47	34.62	34.71	34.72	35.18	35.22	35.64	35.80	34.89
2018	35.74	35.63	35.85	36.01	35.97	36.17	36.28	36.34	36.61	36.55	36.89	37.10	36.27
Construction													
2014	30.29	30.42	30.32	30.34	30.60	31.04	30.82	31.11	31.52	31.49	31.60	31.56	30.96
2015	31.32	31.52	31.27	31.41	31.50	31.91	31.60	31.75	31.79	31.55	31.62	32.16	31.62
2016	31.46	31.64	31.99	31.71	31.61	31.74	31.98	32.31	32.56	32.66	32.85	32.79	32.12
2017	32.97	33.17	33.23	32.74	32.70	32.81	32.67	33.06	33.35	33.75	33.89	33.83	33.19
2018	33.94	34.03	34.37	34.83	35.00	34.87	35.14	35.44	35.20	34.90	35.57	35.50	34.92
Manufacturing													
2014	33.40	33.10	33.70	33.67	33.56	33.46	33.32	33.05	33.03	32.97	32.84	33.19	33.27
2015	33.07	33.18	33.71	33.54	33.48	33.17	32.94	33.06	33.30	33.32	33.40	33.83	33.33
2016	33.68	33.93	34.32	34.46	34.39	34.23	34.02	34.17	34.42	34.24	34.52	34.93	34.27
2017	35.15	35.20	35.56	35.63	35.43	35.67	35.88	35.69	36.22	36.09	36.62	36.87	35.84
2018	36.77	36.53	37.03	37.02	36.86	37.14	37.16	37.07	37.50	37.53	37.62	37.93	37.19
Trade, Transportation, and Utilities													
2014	22.72	23.05	23.01	23.10	23.06	23.33	22.99	23.37	23.57	23.52	24.28	23.66	23.32
2015	24.56	24.55	24.50	24.75	24.71	24.69	24.83	25.43	26.31	26.59	26.81	26.36	25.36
2016	26.61	26.28	26.16	26.17	26.08	25.60	25.56	25.16	25.30	25.70	25.17	24.86	25.71
2017	25.91	25.36	25.21	26.02	25.47	25.54	25.99	25.38	25.44	25.63	25.31	25.35	25.55
2018	25.18	25.25	25.24	25.65	25.24	25.38	25.50	25.43	26.06	25.78	25.78	26.03	25.55
Information													
2014	54.64	55.19	55.57	55.46	55.22	55.28	54.61	54.69	59.33	54.28	54.85	54.77	55.33
2015	56.22	55.92	56.27	55.88	56.36	55.97	55.96	57.74	59.72	58.88	60.42	58.73	57.37
2016	59.11	59.24	58.79	58.37	59.88	58.56	58.15	58.81	61.33	61.91	61.09	60.85	59.70
2017	60.62	60.80	61.14	62.89	61.31	60.42	60.14	59.94	63.81	61.84	61.89	61.49	61.36
2018	62.49	62.63	62.58	63.72	61.88	62.42	61.33	61.12	66.08	64.85	65.09	65.87	63.38
Financial Activities													
2014	28.76	28.62	28.90	28.44	28.43	28.64	28.61	28.38	28.60	28.54	29.15	28.54	28.64
2015	29.21	29.15	29.33	29.40	29.82	28.67	29.83	29.37	28.81	29.39	28.97	28.65	29.22
2016	29.62	29.36	29.47	30.18	30.54	30.61	31.12	31.33	32.05	32.68	32.25	32.86	31.02
2017	33.88	32.51	32.40	33.13	32.57	32.63	33.52	32.92	33.18	33.98	34.02	34.14	33.24
2018	34.31	35.34	34.88	35.34	35.37	35.41	35.81	36.27	36.14	35.77	37.03	37.34	35.77
Professional and Business Services													
2014	32.88	32.95	32.70	32.49	32.35	32.56	32.60	32.29	32.51	32.78	33.40	33.23	32.73
2015	33.71	33.92	33.65	33.27	33.38	33.06	32.95	32.83	32.74	33.13	33.69	33.78	33.34
2016	33.84	33.99	33.93	33.50	33.80	33.53	33.61	33.20	33.76	34.54	34.04	34.33	33.84
2017	35.45	35.10	34.80	35.37	34.87	34.80	35.53	34.91	35.24	36.01	35.61	36.05	35.32
2018	36.35	36.57	36.63	37.02	36.50	36.71	37.35	36.74	37.86	37.33	37.84	38.78	37.15
Education and Health Services													
2014	25.25	25.40	25.46	25.58	25.55	25.93	26.56	26.42	26.34	27.12	27.64	28.43	26.31
2015	28.46	28.32	28.13	28.11	28.11	27.81	27.60	27.99	28.26	28.39	28.71	28.72	28.22
2016	28.42	28.46	28.09	28.25	28.06	27.52	27.84	27.44	28.76	28.79	28.79	29.03	28.29
2017	29.03	29.58	29.20	29.18	29.17	28.90	29.29	29.80	29.93	29.81	29.88	30.08	29.49
2018	30.02	30.87	30.56	30.56	30.61	30.53	30.90	30.81	31.71	31.38	31.74	32.16	30.98
Leisure and Hospitality													
2014	15.41	15.58	15.57	15.72	15.44	15.37	15.20	15.27	15.54	15.77	15.73	16.09	15.55
2015	15.95	16.04	16.15	15.98	15.97	15.91	15.80	15.85	16.01	16.12	16.16	16.48	16.03
2016	16.68	16.76	16.74	16.76	16.81	16.84	16.78	16.77	17.00	17.11	17.32	17.63	16.93
2017	17.88	18.10	18.30	18.46	18.50	18.43	18.27	18.32	18.75	18.88	19.01	19.63	18.54
2018	19.57	19.75	19.74	19.95	19.95	19.87	19.73	19.85	19.84	19.93	20.68	21.12	20.00
Other Services													
2014	22.85	21.80	21.71	21.40	21.80	21.50	20.96	21.21	22.50	22.60	23.22	23.67	22.07
2015	23.78	23.42	23.09	23.02	22.81	22.94	23.01	23.45	23.97	24.13	25.35	25.95	23.73
2016	25.95	25.49	25.75	25.95	26.30	26.03	25.98	25.48	25.90	26.42	26.18	26.61	26.00
2017	27.92	27.07	26.70	27.02	26.42	26.00	26.19	25.52	26.84	26.92	26.67	26.82	26.66
2018	28.10	27.65	27.27	28.41	28.04	27.79	28.28	27.03	28.13	28.72	28.63	29.61	28.15

4. Average Weekly Earnings by Selected Industry: Washington, 2014–2018

(Dollars, not seasonally adjusted)

Industry and year	January	February	March	April	May	June	July	August	September	October	November	December	Annual average
Total Private													
2014	940.54	980.28	985.19	956.66	956.76	989.42	959.14	966.92	979.01	971.91	1,016.29	985.47	972.99
2015	991.20	1,025.04	1,024.69	998.92	998.92	996.93	998.82	1,039.23	1,021.80	1,029.00	1,066.69	1,029.52	1,019.27
2016	1,033.26	1,037.29	1,033.23	1,040.26	1,068.67	1,033.97	1,038.69	1,040.37	1,052.88	1,091.74	1,055.36	1,054.36	1,049.42
2017	1,096.21	1,065.33	1,065.70	1,114.39	1,070.88	1,071.91	1,113.64	1,081.24	1,093.36	1,130.32	1,093.31	1,103.39	1,092.37
2018	1,100.46	1,119.08	1,112.63	1,161.27	1,118.38	1,126.82	1,152.19	1,122.08	1,185.70	1,138.64	1,148.36	1,199.85	1,139.35
Goods-Producing													
2014	1,273.61	1,275.85	1,298.19	1,287.59	1,290.07	1,304.33	1,278.04	1,290.32	1,301.20	1,303.25	1,307.33	1,303.13	1,292.24
2015	1,282.96	1,297.88	1,309.42	1,299.67	1,305.44	1,312.47	1,295.15	1,312.97	1,285.76	1,311.67	1,308.72	1,318.12	1,303.45
2016	1,295.95	1,303.01	1,324.63	1,326.41	1,335.85	1,319.30	1,317.72	1,328.58	1,334.31	1,340.86	1,341.03	1,341.03	1,326.41
2017	1,332.05	1,328.64	1,358.73	1,367.49	1,361.57	1,374.41	1,374.52	1,385.33	1,396.65	1,422.89	1,411.34	1,424.84	1,378.16
2018	1,401.01	1,410.95	1,412.49	1,451.20	1,435.20	1,446.80	1,436.69	1,449.97	1,464.40	1,465.66	1,482.98	1,506.26	1,447.17
Construction													
2014	1,099.53	1,098.16	1,109.71	1,119.55	1,132.20	1,176.42	1,165.00	1,191.51	1,213.52	1,199.77	1,207.12	1,192.97	1,161.00
2015	1,183.90	1,200.91	1,185.13	1,190.44	1,200.15	1,228.54	1,210.28	1,231.90	1,153.98	1,195.75	1,185.75	1,180.27	1,195.24
2016	1,151.44	1,167.52	1,190.03	1,189.13	1,207.50	1,193.42	1,202.45	1,231.01	1,227.51	1,221.48	1,228.59	1,209.95	1,201.29
2017	1,186.92	1,184.17	1,222.86	1,224.48	1,236.06	1,256.62	1,254.53	1,272.81	1,267.30	1,309.50	1,270.88	1,268.63	1,247.94
2018	1,245.60	1,255.71	1,271.69	1,330.51	1,340.50	1,335.52	1,342.35	1,364.44	1,341.12	1,340.16	1,351.66	1,363.20	1,323.47
Manufacturing													
2014	1,349.36	1,350.48	1,378.33	1,360.27	1,359.18	1,361.82	1,332.80	1,338.53	1,347.62	1,355.07	1,359.58	1,360.79	1,354.09
2015	1,336.03	1,350.43	1,375.37	1,361.72	1,362.64	1,359.97	1,343.95	1,358.77	1,355.31	1,372.78	1,372.74	1,383.65	1,359.86
2016	1,364.04	1,367.38	1,386.53	1,392.18	1,396.23	1,379.47	1,371.01	1,373.63	1,387.13	1,403.84	1,401.51	1,411.17	1,384.51
2017	1,409.52	1,404.48	1,429.51	1,443.02	1,431.37	1,441.07	1,445.96	1,452.58	1,474.15	1,490.52	1,494.10	1,515.36	1,451.52
2018	1,489.19	1,497.73	1,507.12	1,536.33	1,507.57	1,526.45	1,504.98	1,512.46	1,541.25	1,542.48	1,553.71	1,581.68	1,524.79
Trade, Transportation, and Utilities													
2014	761.12	806.75	807.65	796.95	800.18	828.22	802.35	820.29	824.95	809.09	864.37	823.37	811.54
2015	839.95	866.62	864.85	858.83	869.79	869.09	874.02	925.65	944.53	933.31	965.16	922.60	895.21
2016	928.69	930.31	920.83	939.50	954.53	911.36	915.05	903.24	903.21	932.91	888.50	892.47	917.85
2017	919.81	892.67	882.35	936.72	904.19	909.22	943.44	903.53	905.66	922.68	890.91	894.86	909.58
2018	878.78	886.28	883.40	920.84	890.97	895.91	918.00	897.68	930.34	889.41	889.41	916.26	899.36
Information													
2014	2,120.03	2,317.98	2,311.71	2,140.76	2,120.45	2,299.65	2,097.02	2,094.63	2,337.60	2,084.35	2,281.76	2,103.17	2,191.07
2015	2,141.98	2,309.50	2,323.95	2,140.20	2,152.95	2,138.05	2,137.67	2,367.34	2,263.39	2,231.55	2,489.30	2,214.12	2,243.17
2016	2,252.09	2,251.12	2,234.02	2,229.73	2,455.08	2,225.28	2,244.59	2,228.90	2,318.27	2,538.31	2,333.64	2,269.71	2,298.45
2017	2,497.54	2,292.16	2,304.98	2,565.91	2,323.65	2,302.00	2,489.80	2,271.73	2,418.40	2,560.18	2,339.44	2,373.51	2,393.04
2018	2,349.62	2,367.41	2,396.81	2,625.26	2,345.25	2,396.93	2,551.33	2,328.67	2,742.32	2,477.27	2,492.95	2,720.43	2,484.50
Financial Activities													
2014	995.10	1,038.91	1,046.18	995.40	997.89	1,028.18	984.18	987.62	995.28	990.34	1,049.40	996.05	1,008.13
2015	1,022.35	1,066.89	1,073.48	1,037.82	1,046.68	1,009.18	1,044.05	1,077.88	1,011.23	1,040.41	1,074.79	1,022.81	1,043.15
2016	1,057.43	1,054.02	1,052.08	1,086.48	1,133.03	1,101.96	1,101.65	1,121.61	1,144.19	1,209.16	1,151.33	1,159.96	1,113.62
2017	1,246.78	1,160.61	1,146.96	1,229.12	1,152.98	1,168.15	1,226.83	1,162.08	1,184.53	1,247.07	1,204.31	1,205.14	1,193.32
2018	1,207.71	1,265.17	1,241.73	1,314.65	1,280.39	1,281.84	1,346.46	1,312.97	1,369.71	1,302.03	1,355.30	1,411.45	1,309.18
Professional and Business Services													
2014	1,140.94	1,199.38	1,196.82	1,163.14	1,154.90	1,194.95	1,154.04	1,152.75	1,160.61	1,170.25	1,222.44	1,173.02	1,175.01
2015	1,179.85	1,234.69	1,224.86	1,181.09	1,178.31	1,173.63	1,159.84	1,198.30	1,165.54	1,182.74	1,229.69	1,189.06	1,190.24
2016	1,197.94	1,216.84	1,211.30	1,206.00	1,247.22	1,203.73	1,203.24	1,195.20	1,205.23	1,264.16	1,215.23	1,222.15	1,214.86
2017	1,286.84	1,249.56	1,245.84	1,305.15	1,241.37	1,242.36	1,307.50	1,249.78	1,261.59	1,328.77	1,281.96	1,286.99	1,275.05
2018	1,304.97	1,323.83	1,326.01	1,373.44	1,317.65	1,336.24	1,393.16	1,337.34	1,431.11	1,370.01	1,369.81	1,450.37	1,359.69
Education and Health Services													
2014	800.43	833.12	835.09	813.44	817.60	847.91	841.95	842.80	842.88	867.84	917.65	921.13	849.81
2015	924.95	945.89	931.10	910.76	907.95	903.83	908.04	943.26	935.41	934.03	970.40	933.40	928.44
2016	940.70	927.80	912.93	920.95	937.20	930.18	949.34	949.42	986.47	999.01	978.86	984.12	950.54
2017	1,013.15	1,005.72	989.88	1,012.55	988.86	982.60	1,022.22	1,031.08	1,023.61	1,046.33	1,021.90	1,031.74	1,014.46
2018	1,047.70	1,065.02	1,048.21	1,075.71	1,046.86	1,041.07	1,019.70	1,001.33	1,068.63	1,013.57	1,037.90	1,077.36	1,044.03
Leisure and Hospitality													
2014	371.38	394.17	392.36	383.57	373.65	390.40	381.52	392.44	383.84	375.33	388.53	381.33	384.09
2015	363.66	388.17	392.45	383.52	383.28	389.80	395.00	416.86	397.05	396.55	405.62	397.17	392.74
2016	396.98	407.27	405.11	410.62	428.66	415.95	421.18	429.31	426.70	438.02	426.07	426.65	419.86
2017	447.00	445.26	452.01	483.65	464.35	464.44	484.16	472.66	470.63	483.33	471.45	484.86	469.06
2018	477.51	497.70	485.60	518.70	506.73	510.66	532.71	520.07	527.74	512.20	508.73	547.01	512.00
Other Services													
2014	696.93	682.34	688.21	652.70	662.72	672.95	641.38	649.03	634.50	635.06	680.35	653.29	662.10
2015	668.22	697.92	678.85	656.07	652.37	660.67	667.29	696.47	663.97	663.58	730.08	718.82	678.68
2016	724.01	731.56	736.45	747.36	778.48	736.65	745.63	754.21	730.38	771.46	738.28	750.40	746.20
2017	804.10	771.50	758.28	807.90	750.33	738.40	783.08	755.39	767.62	786.06	752.09	772.42	770.47
2018	786.80	785.26	779.92	835.25	790.73	783.68	837.09	783.87	818.58	824.26	801.64	879.42	807.91

WEST VIRGINIA
At a Glance

Population:
    2010 census: 1,852,994
    2018 estimate: 1,805,832

Percent change in population:
    2010–2018: -2.5%

Percent change in total nonfarm employment:
    2010–2018: 1.3%

Industry with the largest growth in employment, 2010–2018 (percent):
    Construction, 25.3%

Industry with the largest decline or smallest growth in employment, 2010–2018 (percent):
    Mining and logging, -24.9%

Civilian labor force:
    2010: 811,125
    2018: 783,344

Unemployment rate and rank among states (highest to lowest):
    2010: 8.7%, 24th
    2018: 5.3%, 3rd

Over-the-year change in unemployment rates:
    2016–2017: -0.9%
    2017–2018: 0.1%

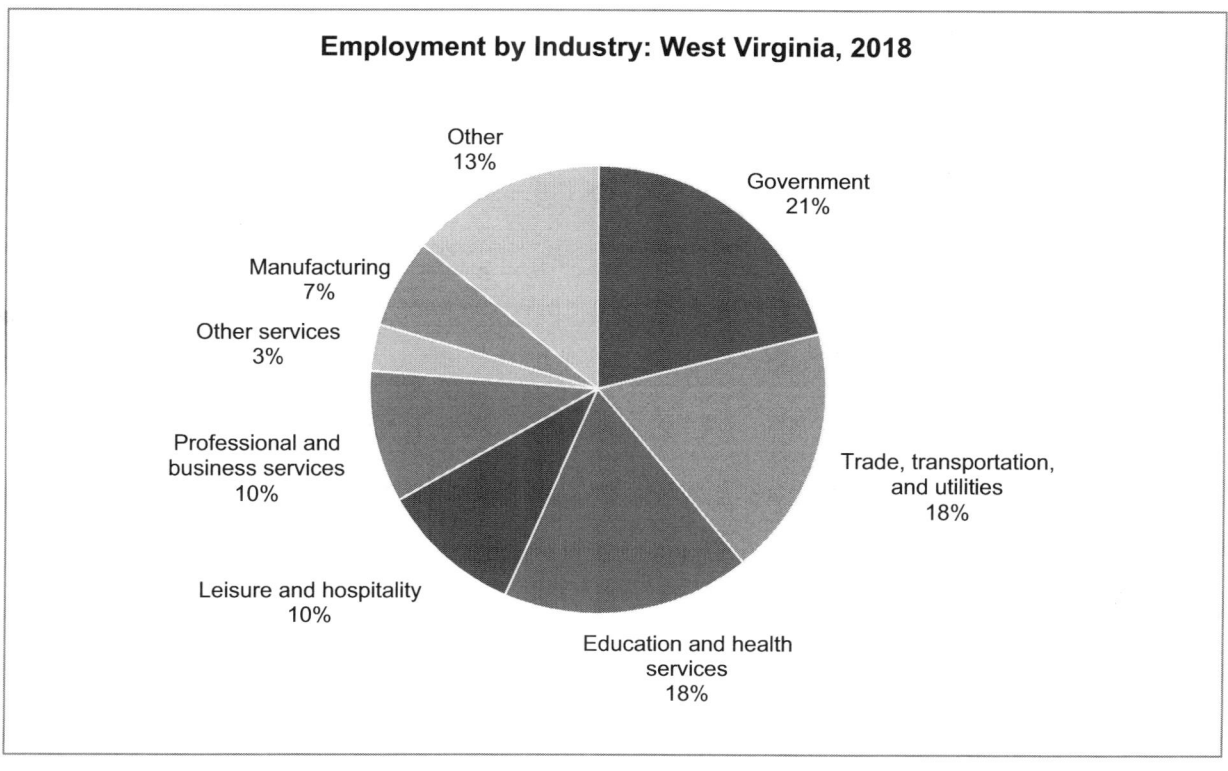

Employment by Industry: West Virginia, 2018

- Other 13%
- Government 21%
- Manufacturing 7%
- Other services 3%
- Professional and business services 10%
- Trade, transportation, and utilities 18%
- Leisure and hospitality 10%
- Education and health services 18%

1. Employment by Industry: West Virginia, 2010–2018

(Numbers in thousands, not seasonally adjusted)

Industry and year	January	February	March	April	May	June	July	August	September	October	November	December	Annual average
Total Nonfarm													
2010	694.2	696.1	708.3	715.2	732.0	721.1	716.8	717.7	722.9	726.0	727.9	724.1	716.9
2011	702.7	707.1	715.3	724.7	728.7	722.2	718.1	722.9	734.6	737.1	740.7	739.9	724.5
2012	720.3	723.4	731.6	736.8	750.7	731.4	724.4	727.6	738.9	740.6	741.4	740.8	734.0
2013	719.4	721.5	728.0	733.5	739.8	732.9	725.7	729.1	734.9	737.7	741.4	738.3	731.9
2014	714.3	713.6	722.7	731.0	747.1	721.7	717.8	723.9	735.4	741.3	742.3	740.3	729.3
2015	718.4	716.4	720.7	728.1	733.6	726.0	718.1	720.0	729.0	734.0	735.2	733.8	726.1
2016	708.3	706.0	714.5	719.7	729.4	712.7	706.6	709.1	719.8	722.0	733.6	721.3	716.9
2017	702.6	704.2	710.6	713.5	718.4	715.8	709.7	712.5	721.9	726.4	727.2	723.3	715.5
2018	705.7	707.4	713.6	721.0	734.7	727.8	723.5	727.9	733.6	740.3	740.5	736.0	726.0
Total Private													
2010	544.7	543.4	552.2	560.3	562.8	567.7	569.7	571.0	571.9	572.2	573.1	569.9	563.2
2011	552.6	555.0	560.9	569.4	573.3	575.5	577.0	580.0	580.7	581.3	584.4	584.0	572.8
2012	566.9	568.7	574.5	580.6	583.7	584.6	582.5	584.5	585.5	584.4	583.7	583.4	580.3
2013	565.5	566.7	571.4	577.2	582.2	581.2	580.8	582.6	582.3	581.3	584.4	582.0	578.1
2014	561.5	560.2	566.9	574.8	580.1	580.8	578.6	581.1	582.4	584.5	585.3	584.0	576.7
2015	565.8	562.7	565.9	572.6	577.7	576.1	573.8	574.2	575.0	576.4	577.0	575.6	572.7
2016	553.6	550.7	556.7	561.8	561.9	560.0	560.3	561.2	564.9	564.5	566.5	564.3	560.5
2017	548.0	548.3	552.5	556.8	561.7	565.4	564.7	566.4	568.3	570.5	571.9	568.6	561.9
2018	554.1	554.2	559.5	565.8	571.7	577.1	579.0	581.5	582.1	587.0	586.1	583.2	573.4
Goods Producing													
2010	104.8	104.0	107.5	110.9	111.6	113.6	115.2	115.8	116.3	116.5	115.6	112.2	112.0
2011	107.7	108.5	110.7	114.1	115.8	117.9	118.9	119.7	120.0	120.3	120.5	119.6	116.1
2012	115.8	115.8	117.4	119.0	119.6	121.1	119.8	119.4	119.3	119.1	116.9	115.5	118.2
2013	110.7	110.5	111.8	114.5	116.4	116.2	117.1	117.3	116.7	115.9	115.0	112.0	114.5
2014	106.9	105.9	108.5	111.7	113.6	114.2	114.0	114.4	114.8	114.8	112.5	110.1	111.8
2015	105.4	104.0	105.2	107.4	109.4	108.5	107.5	107.4	106.7	106.2	104.0	101.9	106.1
2016	95.8	94.2	96.7	98.4	97.2	97.8	98.2	98.1	98.5	98.3	97.5	96.4	97.3
2017	93.0	93.6	95.5	98.1	99.6	101.9	102.3	102.5	104.0	104.3	103.4	102.1	100.0
2018	97.6	97.9	101.0	104.7	108.3	112.5	115.6	117.0	118.0	119.3	119.0	117.9	110.7
Service-Providing													
2010	589.4	592.1	600.8	604.3	620.4	607.5	601.6	601.9	606.6	609.5	612.3	611.9	604.9
2011	595.0	598.6	604.6	610.6	612.9	604.3	599.2	603.2	614.6	616.8	620.2	620.3	608.4
2012	604.5	607.6	614.2	617.8	631.1	610.3	604.6	608.2	619.6	621.5	624.5	625.3	615.8
2013	608.7	611.0	616.2	619.0	623.4	616.7	608.6	611.8	618.2	621.8	626.4	626.3	617.3
2014	607.4	607.7	614.2	619.3	633.5	607.5	603.8	609.5	620.6	626.5	629.8	630.2	617.5
2015	613.0	612.4	615.5	620.7	624.2	617.5	610.6	612.6	622.3	627.8	631.2	631.9	620.0
2016	612.5	611.8	617.8	621.3	632.2	614.9	608.4	611.0	621.3	623.7	636.1	624.9	619.7
2017	609.6	610.6	615.1	615.4	618.8	613.9	607.4	610.0	617.9	622.1	623.8	621.2	615.5
2018	608.1	609.5	612.6	616.3	626.4	615.3	607.9	610.9	615.6	621.0	621.5	618.1	615.3
Mining and Logging													
2010	28.2	28.4	28.8	29.2	29.4	30.1	30.5	30.9	31.1	31.2	31.6	31.6	30.1
2011	31.6	32.0	32.2	32.6	32.9	33.7	33.8	34.4	34.8	35.0	35.3	35.7	33.7
2012	35.2	34.9	34.7	34.0	33.7	33.7	33.1	33.0	32.8	32.6	32.5	32.2	33.5
2013	31.6	31.6	31.7	31.9	32.1	32.3	31.9	32.0	31.6	31.6	31.4	31.1	31.7
2014	30.1	30.2	30.5	30.6	30.5	30.6	30.1	30.2	30.1	30.0	29.8	29.0	30.1
2015	28.5	27.8	27.6	27.3	27.0	26.0	25.5	24.9	24.9	24.7	24.0	23.3	26.0
2016	21.7	21.4	21.2	20.8	19.9	19.8	19.5	19.6	19.6	20.0	20.2	20.5	20.4
2017	20.5	20.9	21.2	21.4	21.6	22.0	22.2	22.1	22.2	22.6	22.6	22.5	21.8
2018	21.9	21.9	22.1	22.5	22.7	22.7	23.2	22.9	22.9	22.8	22.3	22.9	22.6
Construction													
2010	28.3	27.5	30.3	32.8	33.0	34.0	35.0	35.1	35.8	36.0	34.6	31.1	32.8
2011	27.4	27.7	29.2	32.2	33.4	34.2	35.1	35.5	35.6	35.8	35.6	34.3	33.0
2012	31.3	31.6	33.3	35.6	36.4	37.6	37.3	37.9	38.2	37.7	35.9	34.3	35.6
2013	31.0	30.9	32.0	34.5	35.9	35.2	36.3	36.6	36.4	35.9	35.1	32.5	34.4
2014	29.1	28.4	30.3	33.4	35.1	35.4	35.6	36.1	36.8	36.9	35.0	33.2	33.8
2015	29.3	28.6	29.8	32.6	34.6	34.4	34.2	34.7	34.2	33.9	32.4	31.0	32.5
2016	27.1	26.2	28.7	30.7	30.4	30.9	31.5	31.7	32.0	31.7	30.7	29.0	30.1
2017	26.2	26.2	27.7	29.9	31.2	32.8	33.2	33.7	35.1	35.1	34.2	32.8	31.5
2018	29.4	29.6	32.1	35.3	38.5	42.8	45.4	46.9	48.0	48.8	48.7	47.2	41.1

1. Employment by Industry: West Virginia, 2010–2018—*Continued*

(Numbers in thousands, not seasonally adjusted)

Industry and year	January	February	March	April	May	June	July	August	September	October	November	December	Annual average
Manufacturing													
2010	48.3	48.1	48.4	48.9	49.2	49.5	49.7	49.8	49.4	49.3	49.4	49.5	49.1
2011	48.7	48.8	49.3	49.3	49.5	50.0	50.0	49.8	49.6	49.5	49.6	49.6	49.5
2012	49.3	49.3	49.4	49.4	49.5	49.8	49.4	48.5	48.3	48.8	48.5	49.0	49.1
2013	48.1	48.0	48.1	48.1	48.4	48.7	48.9	48.7	48.7	48.4	48.5	48.4	48.4
2014	47.7	47.3	47.7	47.7	48.0	48.2	48.3	48.1	47.9	47.9	47.7	47.9	47.9
2015	47.6	47.6	47.8	47.5	47.8	48.1	47.8	47.8	47.6	47.6	47.6	47.6	47.7
2016	47.0	46.6	46.8	46.9	46.9	47.1	47.2	46.8	46.9	46.6	46.6	46.9	46.9
2017	46.3	46.5	46.6	46.8	46.8	47.1	46.9	46.7	46.7	46.6	46.6	46.8	46.7
2018	46.3	46.4	46.8	46.9	47.1	47.0	47.0	47.2	47.1	47.7	48.0	47.8	47.1
Trade, Transportation, and Utilities													
2010	132.5	131.1	132.5	133.2	134.4	134.8	134.7	134.7	134.1	135.8	138.8	139.1	134.6
2011	133.4	132.5	133.1	134.4	134.8	135.1	135.2	135.7	135.5	136.1	139.1	139.6	135.4
2012	134.4	132.9	133.7	134.0	134.7	135.0	134.9	135.4	135.5	136.3	139.7	140.2	135.6
2013	134.2	133.2	133.4	134.0	134.7	135.4	135.1	135.1	135.1	136.4	140.8	141.1	135.7
2014	133.8	132.5	132.6	133.8	134.5	135.0	134.1	134.8	134.5	136.8	140.8	141.2	135.4
2015	133.7	132.4	132.8	134.0	135.0	135.2	134.9	134.5	134.8	136.4	140.1	140.7	135.4
2016	132.7	131.4	132.1	133.1	133.1	132.7	132.6	132.8	133.4	134.0	137.9	138.4	133.7
2017	130.9	129.0	129.1	129.2	129.9	130.4	130.0	130.2	131.0	133.1	136.7	135.6	131.3
2018	130.2	128.2	128.5	128.5	129.7	129.7	128.9	128.8	129.2	131.2	133.7	133.4	130.0
Wholesale Trade													
2010	22.4	22.3	22.5	22.7	22.7	22.8	22.9	22.9	23.0	23.3	23.4	23.3	22.9
2011	22.7	22.6	22.8	23.1	23.2	23.1	23.1	23.2	23.3	23.4	23.6	23.6	23.1
2012	23.1	22.9	23.1	23.1	23.1	23.1	23.0	23.0	23.1	23.3	23.7	23.5	23.2
2013	22.7	22.7	22.6	22.7	22.7	22.8	22.8	22.9	22.9	22.8	22.8	22.9	22.8
2014	22.4	22.4	22.4	22.5	22.6	22.6	22.6	22.7	22.7	22.8	22.9	22.9	22.6
2015	22.4	22.3	22.3	22.4	22.3	22.3	22.2	22.1	22.0	22.1	22.1	22.0	22.2
2016	21.3	21.1	21.0	21.2	21.1	21.0	21.2	21.1	21.1	21.1	21.1	21.1	21.1
2017	20.5	20.4	20.5	20.6	20.6	20.9	20.7	20.7	20.6	20.6	20.7	20.7	20.6
2018	20.3	20.2	20.3	20.3	20.4	20.5	20.2	20.2	20.2	20.3	20.1	19.9	20.2
Retail Trade													
2010	85.3	84.0	84.9	85.4	86.3	86.5	86.5	86.5	85.9	87.2	90.1	90.2	86.6
2011	85.7	84.8	85.3	86.5	86.8	87.1	87.1	87.5	87.1	87.6	90.4	90.7	87.2
2012	86.7	85.4	86.1	86.4	87.1	87.3	87.4	87.8	87.6	88.2	91.1	91.4	87.7
2013	86.9	85.9	86.2	86.7	87.3	87.8	87.5	87.2	87.1	87.9	90.5	91.0	87.7
2014	86.2	85.2	85.4	86.4	86.9	87.2	86.4	86.9	86.3	86.5	89.3	89.7	86.9
2015	85.4	84.6	85.0	86.0	86.8	86.8	87.0	86.9	86.9	87.6	89.8	90.1	86.9
2016	85.9	85.5	86.1	86.8	87.1	86.8	86.6	86.8	86.8	86.7	89.0	89.0	86.9
2017	85.2	83.7	83.8	84.1	84.6	84.5	84.3	84.3	84.3	85.2	87.6	87.2	84.9
2018	83.3	82.5	82.7	82.8	83.6	83.2	82.7	82.3	81.7	82.2	83.5	82.8	82.8
Transportation and Utilities													
2010	24.8	24.8	25.1	25.1	25.4	25.5	25.3	25.3	25.2	25.3	25.3	25.6	25.2
2011	25.0	25.1	25.0	24.8	24.8	24.9	25.0	25.0	25.1	25.1	25.1	25.3	25.0
2012	24.6	24.6	24.5	24.5	24.5	24.6	24.5	24.6	24.8	24.8	24.9	25.3	24.7
2013	24.6	24.6	24.6	24.6	24.7	24.8	24.8	25.0	25.1	25.7	27.5	27.2	25.3
2014	25.2	24.9	24.8	24.9	25.0	25.2	25.1	25.2	25.5	27.5	28.6	28.6	25.9
2015	25.9	25.5	25.5	25.6	25.9	26.1	25.7	25.5	25.9	26.7	28.2	28.6	26.3
2016	25.5	24.8	25.0	25.1	24.9	24.9	24.8	24.9	25.5	26.2	27.8	28.3	25.6
2017	25.2	24.9	24.8	24.5	24.7	25.0	25.0	25.2	26.1	27.3	28.4	27.7	25.7
2018	26.6	25.5	25.5	25.4	25.7	26.0	26.0	26.3	27.3	28.7	30.1	30.7	27.0
Information													
2010	10.1	10.0	10.0	9.8	10.1	10.3	10.7	10.6	10.5	10.5	10.5	10.6	10.3
2011	10.4	10.4	10.4	10.3	10.2	10.2	10.2	10.2	10.0	10.0	9.9	9.9	10.2
2012	9.5	9.5	9.5	9.6	9.6	9.7	9.6	9.6	9.6	9.6	9.6	9.5	9.6
2013	9.3	9.4	9.5	9.5	9.6	9.6	9.7	9.7	9.7	9.7	9.8	9.8	9.6
2014	9.6	9.6	9.7	9.6	9.6	9.6	9.6	9.6	9.6	9.5	9.6	9.7	9.6
2015	9.6	9.6	9.7	9.7	9.8	9.7	9.7	9.7	9.6	9.7	9.7	9.7	9.7
2016	9.6	9.6	9.6	9.5	9.5	9.5	9.5	9.5	9.5	9.5	9.6	9.5	9.5
2017	9.2	8.9	8.9	8.7	8.7	8.7	8.6	8.5	8.5	8.4	8.4	8.4	8.7
2018	8.4	8.3	7.4	8.3	8.4	8.4	8.1	8.1	8.1	8.2	8.0	8.1	8.2

1. Employment by Industry: West Virginia, 2010–2018—*Continued*

(Numbers in thousands, not seasonally adjusted)

Industry and year	January	February	March	April	May	June	July	August	September	October	November	December	Annual average
Financial Activities													
2010	29.8	29.9	30.1	30.3	30.3	30.6	30.3	30.2	30.1	30.3	30.3	30.2	30.2
2011	29.7	29.4	29.3	29.4	29.5	29.6	29.8	29.7	29.6	29.8	29.7	29.8	29.6
2012	29.4	29.6	29.7	29.9	30.0	30.1	30.1	30.3	30.2	30.0	30.0	30.3	30.0
2013	29.9	30.0	30.3	30.4	30.4	30.3	30.4	30.3	30.3	30.4	30.4	30.6	30.3
2014	30.1	30.0	30.2	29.9	30.0	29.9	29.9	29.8	29.6	29.5	29.5	29.5	29.8
2015	29.1	29.0	29.1	29.5	29.6	29.6	29.6	29.5	29.4	29.5	29.4	29.4	29.4
2016	29.2	29.2	29.3	29.1	29.2	29.1	29.1	29.0	29.0	28.9	28.9	29.0	29.1
2017	28.6	28.7	28.9	28.8	29.0	29.0	28.8	28.8	28.8	28.8	28.7	28.8	28.8
2018	28.8	29.0	29.1	29.0	29.2	29.4	29.2	29.2	29.2	29.3	29.0	29.1	29.1
Professional and Business Services													
2010	59.7	59.5	60.2	61.4	60.4	61.0	61.8	61.8	61.5	61.9	61.9	62.0	61.1
2011	61.3	61.9	62.5	63.5	62.8	63.2	63.7	64.2	64.4	64.6	65.2	65.2	63.5
2012	63.4	63.7	63.9	65.2	65.0	65.1	64.7	65.2	64.9	65.1	64.7	64.7	64.6
2013	63.4	63.9	64.5	65.0	65.2	65.3	65.3	65.9	65.2	64.6	65.0	64.5	64.8
2014	63.6	63.9	64.6	66.1	66.6	67.3	67.7	68.2	67.9	68.8	68.9	69.3	66.9
2015	67.0	66.5	66.5	67.0	66.7	67.3	67.4	67.9	67.0	67.4	67.2	66.9	67.1
2016	64.4	64.7	65.2	65.9	65.2	65.5	66.8	66.5	66.0	66.6	66.4	65.6	65.7
2017	64.8	65.4	65.9	66.2	66.6	67.2	67.3	67.5	67.5	67.6	67.9	67.5	66.8
2018	66.4	67.2	68.1	68.8	68.8	69.4	69.8	70.2	69.9	70.1	70.0	68.6	68.9
Education and Health Services													
2010	115.2	116.7	117.7	118.1	117.8	117.0	116.8	117.0	119.5	119.2	119.6	119.6	117.9
2011	116.9	118.7	119.5	120.4	120.8	118.9	118.4	119.1	121.3	122.1	122.7	122.8	120.1
2012	119.6	121.5	122.4	123.4	123.6	121.4	120.9	121.7	124.6	124.4	124.5	124.8	122.7
2013	121.3	123.2	123.6	123.7	124.0	121.4	120.4	121.4	124.2	124.4	124.8	125.1	123.1
2014	122.0	122.5	123.7	124.3	124.6	122.2	121.0	121.9	125.0	125.1	125.5	125.7	123.6
2015	124.8	125.3	125.5	126.0	126.5	123.6	122.2	123.0	126.6	127.5	128.0	128.2	125.6
2016	125.7	125.6	126.2	127.2	127.4	123.8	122.8	123.9	128.2	128.0	128.5	128.5	126.3
2017	126.9	127.4	127.5	127.6	127.6	126.0	125.8	126.9	128.2	128.8	128.9	128.8	127.5
2018	127.4	128.0	128.4	128.1	128.0	126.9	126.3	127.6	128.5	129.7	129.5	129.6	128.2
Leisure and Hospitality													
2010	67.7	67.4	69.3	71.5	73.0	75.0	75.1	75.8	74.8	72.9	71.4	71.2	72.1
2011	68.6	68.9	70.5	72.4	74.3	75.5	75.6	76.3	74.8	73.2	72.1	72.0	72.9
2012	69.9	70.7	72.7	74.0	75.7	76.7	77.1	77.6	76.2	74.6	73.0	73.2	74.3
2013	71.7	71.5	72.9	74.3	76.3	77.4	77.2	77.4	75.6	74.5	73.2	73.6	74.6
2014	70.5	70.8	72.4	73.9	75.8	77.1	76.9	77.1	75.7	74.7	73.3	73.4	74.3
2015	71.3	71.0	72.1	74.1	75.8	77.1	77.4	77.2	76.0	74.9	73.9	74.1	74.6
2016	71.8	71.6	72.9	74.0	75.7	76.9	76.7	76.8	75.8	74.7	73.3	72.5	74.4
2017	70.3	71.0	72.3	73.7	75.6	77.2	77.1	77.2	75.6	74.9	73.5	73.1	74.3
2018	71.5	71.7	72.5	73.7	74.9	76.2	76.5	76.1	74.9	74.6	72.9	72.4	74.0
Other Services													
2010	24.9	24.8	24.9	25.1	25.2	25.4	25.1	25.1	25.1	25.1	25.0	25.0	25.1
2011	24.6	24.7	24.9	24.9	25.1	25.1	25.2	25.1	25.1	25.2	25.2	25.1	25.0
2012	24.9	25.0	25.2	25.5	25.5	25.5	25.4	25.3	25.2	25.3	25.3	25.2	25.3
2013	25.0	25.0	25.4	25.8	25.6	25.6	25.6	25.5	25.5	25.4	25.4	25.3	25.4
2014	25.0	25.0	25.2	25.5	25.4	25.5	25.4	25.3	25.3	25.3	25.2	25.1	25.3
2015	24.9	24.9	25.0	24.9	24.9	25.1	25.1	25.0	24.9	24.8	24.7	24.7	24.9
2016	24.4	24.4	24.7	24.6	24.6	24.7	24.6	24.6	24.5	24.5	24.4	24.4	24.5
2017	24.3	24.3	24.4	24.5	24.7	25.0	24.8	24.8	24.7	24.6	24.4	24.3	24.6
2018	23.8	23.9	24.5	24.7	24.4	24.6	24.6	24.5	24.3	24.6	24.0	24.1	24.3
Government													
2010	149.5	152.7	156.1	154.9	169.2	153.4	147.1	146.7	151.0	153.8	154.8	154.2	153.6
2011	150.1	152.1	154.4	155.3	155.4	146.7	141.1	142.9	153.9	155.8	156.3	155.9	151.7
2012	153.4	154.7	157.1	156.2	167.0	146.8	141.9	143.1	153.4	156.2	157.7	157.4	153.7
2013	153.9	154.8	156.6	156.3	157.6	151.7	144.9	146.5	152.6	156.4	157.0	156.3	153.7
2014	152.8	153.4	155.8	156.2	167.0	140.9	139.2	142.8	153.0	156.8	157.0	156.3	152.6
2015	152.6	153.7	154.8	155.5	155.9	149.9	144.3	145.8	154.0	157.6	158.2	158.2	153.4
2016	154.7	155.3	157.8	157.9	167.5	152.7	146.3	147.9	154.9	157.5	167.1	157.0	156.4
2017	154.6	155.9	158.1	156.7	156.7	150.4	145.0	146.1	153.6	155.9	155.3	154.7	153.6
2018	151.6	153.2	154.1	155.2	163.0	150.7	144.5	146.4	151.5	153.3	154.4	152.8	152.6

2. Average Weekly Hours by Selected Industry: West Virginia, 2014–2018

(Not seasonally adjusted)

Industry and year	January	February	March	April	May	June	July	August	September	October	November	December	Annual average
Total Private													
2014	33.9	34.0	34.4	34.7	34.7	35.4	35.4	35.4	35.3	35.1	35.3	35.1	34.9
2015	34.4	34.2	34.6	34.7	35.0	34.9	35.0	35.2	34.7	35.0	35.0	34.6	34.8
2016	34.3	34.4	34.9	35.1	34.9	35.3	35.3	35.2	35.2	35.5	35.3	35.3	35.1
2017	35.3	35.2	35.1	35.4	35.4	35.8	36.1	35.8	35.8	35.7	35.5	35.5	35.5
2018	34.9	35.1	35.2	35.5	35.4	35.8	35.9	35.7	35.8	35.4	35.3	35.6	35.5
Goods-Producing													
2014	38.7	39.4	39.7	40.3	40.0	41.8	41.6	41.8	41.6	41.4	40.5	41.4	40.7
2015	39.4	38.9	39.6	39.9	41.3	40.5	40.0	41.0	39.2	41.1	39.8	40.0	40.1
2016	39.3	39.1	40.2	40.5	39.4	40.4	39.8	40.6	40.6	41.3	41.3	40.5	40.2
2017	40.4	40.9	40.4	41.2	41.0	41.6	41.3	41.6	41.6	41.7	41.2	41.3	41.2
2018	40.3	40.8	40.8	41.5	41.7	42.0	41.5	42.1	41.9	42.1	41.6	42.1	41.6
Mining and Logging													
2014	43.7	44.0	44.3	45.6	44.3	47.0	47.0	46.9	46.4	46.3	46.2	48.9	45.9
2015	47.6	44.6	46.3	46.2	45.8	45.3	45.8	46.0	43.2	46.3	46.9	46.0	45.8
2016	45.8	44.4	46.0	46.5	45.5	43.9	44.1	46.1	46.4	48.4	46.6	44.8	45.7
2017	44.5	43.8	42.2	42.3	43.0	42.4	42.8	43.3	43.3	43.3	43.5	43.9	43.2
2018	43.7	44.1	43.2	43.0	42.6	42.5	41.6	43.3	43.8	42.8	43.7	44.8	43.3
Construction													
2014	37.6	37.3	37.7	39.1	38.0	39.7	39.8	40.0	39.3	38.6	37.0	38.0	38.6
2015	36.2	35.7	36.8	37.3	39.2	39.1	38.5	40.1	38.1	40.7	37.4	38.9	38.2
2016	37.3	36.6	38.6	38.9	38.3	41.0	40.2	40.5	40.6	40.7	40.3	38.9	39.4
2017	37.7	39.1	38.2	41.3	40.7	42.7	41.9	41.7	42.1	41.8	41.6	41.3	41.0
2018	39.7	39.3	39.9	41.9	42.5	42.7	42.6	42.1	41.1	42.0	40.8	41.5	41.5
Manufacturing													
2014	36.3	37.7	38.1	37.7	38.6	39.9	39.6	39.9	40.4	40.4	39.4	39.2	38.9
2015	36.5	37.5	37.5	38.1	40.2	39.0	37.9	39.1	37.9	38.8	37.9	37.8	38.2
2016	37.4	37.9	38.5	39.0	37.5	38.5	37.7	38.4	38.2	38.6	39.5	39.7	38.4
2017	40.1	40.7	40.8	40.7	40.3	40.5	40.1	40.6	40.4	40.7	39.7	40.2	40.4
2018	39.1	40.2	40.2	40.4	40.5	41.2	40.5	41.4	41.6	41.9	41.4	41.4	40.8
Trade, Transportation, and Utilities													
2014	33.7	33.3	33.6	34.0	34.4	34.1	34.4	34.9	34.9	34.8	35.0	34.9	34.3
2015	34.2	34.7	35.3	35.5	36.0	35.9	35.7	36.0	35.7	35.8	35.7	35.1	35.5
2016	34.4	34.8	34.9	35.2	35.1	35.1	35.4	35.4	35.5	35.6	35.6	35.9	35.2
2017	35.4	35.2	35.3	35.1	35.5	36.0	36.0	36.0	35.7	35.1	35.2	34.9	35.4
2018	33.7	33.7	33.9	34.2	34.1	34.9	34.6	34.6	34.4	34.1	34.1	33.6	34.2
Financial Activities													
2014	35.3	35.6	35.2	34.5	34.7	35.3	34.7	35.5	35.5	35.5	36.2	34.3	35.2
2015	35.5	35.9	35.8	36.1	36.1	36.6	36.0	37.0	35.6	36.2	36.6	36.1	36.1
2016	35.7	35.9	35.0	35.5	35.7	36.3	35.9	35.3	34.6	36.2	35.9	36.0	35.7
2017	36.5	35.9	35.8	36.1	35.7	35.6	36.2	35.7	35.5	36.2	35.5	35.9	35.9
2018	35.1	35.2	36.1	36.1	35.6	35.5	35.6	34.8	35.4	35.0	34.5	36.0	35.4
Professional and Business Services													
2014	34.5	34.1	34.5	34.9	35.3	36.1	36.7	36.3	36.6	36.2	36.5	35.5	35.6
2015	35.0	34.2	35.2	34.2	34.9	34.6	35.4	35.3	35.4	35.7	36.5	36.5	35.2
2016	35.5	35.5	36.1	36.4	36.6	36.7	36.6	36.5	36.5	38.0	37.2	37.4	36.6
2017	37.1	37.2	37.1	37.5	36.6	36.9	37.8	36.8	37.1	36.6	36.3	36.2	36.9
2018	35.9	36.5	36.4	37.1	36.5	37.2	37.7	37.6	38.2	37.6	37.0	37.4	37.1
Education and Health Services													
2014	34.8	34.7	35.0	34.9	34.9	35.4	35.3	35.0	35.1	34.8	35.3	35.2	35.0
2015	35.0	34.5	34.5	34.7	34.8	34.8	35.1	35.0	34.9	34.5	34.9	34.8	34.8
2016	35.0	35.0	35.3	35.5	35.7	35.9	36.3	35.7	35.7	35.6	35.3	35.5	35.5
2017	36.0	35.4	35.5	35.8	35.9	36.1	36.5	36.0	36.0	36.0	35.8	35.8	35.9
2018	36.2	36.2	36.1	36.3	36.0	36.2	36.4	35.5	35.5	35.1	35.5	35.3	35.9
Leisure and Hospitality													
2014	24.8	25.3	26.1	26.8	26.4	26.9	27.1	26.7	26.2	25.9	25.8	25.7	26.2
2015	25.0	25.2	25.8	26.0	26.3	26.7	27.0	26.8	26.4	26.4	26.5	25.9	26.2
2016	25.4	26.1	27.1	26.8	26.8	27.3	27.3	27.0	26.5	26.1	26.0	25.5	26.5
2017	25.0	25.7	25.6	25.5	25.9	26.6	26.9	27.0	26.8	26.4	26.3	26.3	26.2
2018	25.4	26.2	26.8	26.9	27.1	27.3	27.8	27.6	27.4	27.0	26.6	26.8	26.9
Other Services													
2014	31.4	30.8	32.3	31.4	31.4	32.3	32.7	33.0	31.6	32.7	33.5	32.6	32.2
2015	32.1	32.1	32.1	32.5	31.7	32.1	32.2	32.4	32.0	32.3	32.9	32.4	32.2
2016	31.6	32.4	31.9	32.5	32.7	33.3	32.1	32.2	32.9	33.8	33.6	33.2	32.7
2017	33.0	32.8	33.4	32.9	33.5	33.7	33.4	33.4	33.6	33.7	33.3	33.6	33.3
2018	33.5	33.2	33.6	33.5	33.1	33.3	34.1	34.1	34.1	32.9	33.6	33.4	33.5

3. Average Hourly Earnings by Selected Industry: West Virginia, 2014–2018

(Dollars, not seasonally adjusted)

Industry and year	January	February	March	April	May	June	July	August	September	October	November	December	Annual average
Total Private													
2014	20.68	20.84	20.62	20.65	20.47	20.48	20.63	20.52	20.63	20.66	20.56	20.51	20.60
2015	20.91	20.88	20.80	20.67	20.65	20.60	20.70	20.84	20.89	20.86	21.03	20.83	20.80
2016	21.13	21.16	20.97	20.92	20.71	20.62	20.89	20.86	21.05	21.24	21.15	21.09	20.98
2017	21.41	21.44	21.56	21.53	21.42	21.50	21.74	21.76	22.00	22.18	22.27	22.26	21.76
2018	22.69	22.67	22.47	22.93	22.74	22.70	23.03	23.01	23.27	23.44	23.44	23.71	23.01
Goods-Producing													
2014	25.49	25.18	25.26	25.18	24.94	24.94	25.03	24.78	24.82	24.67	24.66	24.83	24.97
2015	24.96	24.71	24.84	24.90	24.65	24.73	24.56	24.82	25.26	24.99	25.28	25.09	24.89
2016	25.16	24.99	25.11	25.15	25.00	25.21	25.32	25.30	25.28	25.69	25.19	25.24	25.22
2017	25.15	25.45	25.02	25.44	25.45	25.53	25.75	25.90	26.06	26.16	25.94	25.98	25.67
2018	25.38	25.10	25.03	25.33	25.23	25.69	26.06	25.87	26.15	26.30	26.61	26.94	25.85
Mining and Logging													
2014	31.84	31.22	31.04	30.76	30.58	30.32	30.08	30.09	29.78	29.29	29.10	29.22	30.26
2015	29.89	29.86	30.10	29.68	29.78	29.71	29.48	29.31	30.16	29.38	29.47	28.87	29.65
2016	29.72	29.23	29.26	28.49	28.40	28.52	27.79	28.35	28.33	28.75	27.84	28.47	28.61
2017	28.35	29.20	29.07	28.85	28.99	28.03	28.37	28.80	28.84	28.95	29.04	28.52	28.75
2018	27.74	27.22	27.32	27.65	27.70	28.29	28.72	28.81	28.84	29.45	29.39	29.84	28.43
Construction													
2014	24.25	24.00	24.56	24.65	24.35	24.55	24.76	24.57	24.43	24.38	24.55	24.93	24.51
2015	24.26	23.80	24.18	24.90	24.47	25.16	24.30	24.97	25.00	25.36	25.12	25.43	24.78
2016	24.60	24.95	25.67	26.36	25.96	26.03	26.51	25.82	25.98	26.12	25.60	25.08	25.76
2017	24.77	25.71	25.15	25.75	25.82	26.61	26.62	26.98	26.90	27.04	27.00	27.03	26.38
2018	26.29	26.58	26.16	26.33	26.51	26.78	27.07	27.12	27.10	27.42	28.00	28.48	27.08
Manufacturing													
2014	21.44	21.39	21.39	21.24	21.24	21.20	21.50	21.03	21.54	21.57	21.49	21.45	21.37
2015	21.54	21.65	21.50	21.58	21.48	21.29	21.57	21.94	22.52	21.99	22.77	22.62	21.87
2016	22.92	22.74	22.52	22.59	22.60	23.06	23.28	23.40	23.22	23.74	23.55	23.74	23.12
2017	23.77	23.50	23.04	23.61	23.46	23.51	23.79	23.63	23.97	24.03	23.48	23.89	23.64
2018	23.55	23.09	23.09	23.36	22.89	23.38	23.69	23.11	23.82	23.62	23.85	23.92	23.45
Trade, Transportation, and Utilities													
2014	18.17	18.57	18.40	18.75	18.69	18.66	18.56	18.60	18.72	18.82	18.31	17.93	18.51
2015	18.44	18.64	18.39	18.54	18.27	18.53	18.66	18.73	18.88	19.04	18.94	18.72	18.65
2016	19.23	18.85	19.42	19.78	19.40	19.42	19.77	19.49	19.80	20.07	19.78	19.45	19.54
2017	19.64	20.00	20.12	20.16	19.94	19.64	19.62	19.55	19.90	20.07	19.85	19.85	19.86
2018	20.29	20.35	20.09	20.43	20.37	20.00	20.05	20.10	20.23	20.17	19.72	19.78	20.13
Financial Activities													
2014	19.83	19.76	19.85	19.93	20.04	20.61	20.47	20.61	20.44	20.92	20.67	20.34	20.29
2015	20.37	20.39	20.20	20.95	20.60	19.83	21.86	22.73	21.84	21.28	22.27	21.35	21.15
2016	21.24	21.74	21.64	21.27	21.23	20.41	20.45	20.60	21.49	21.97	22.19	22.03	21.35
2017	22.26	21.90	22.22	22.74	22.00	21.55	22.10	22.01	22.22	22.38	23.04	22.55	22.25
2018	23.09	23.41	23.18	23.77	23.55	23.31	24.05	24.19	24.87	24.83	24.62	24.98	23.99
Professional and Business Services													
2014	21.05	21.35	21.15	21.02	20.52	20.48	20.54	20.30	20.38	20.36	20.45	20.07	20.62
2015	20.17	20.18	20.10	20.18	19.94	19.96	20.00	20.28	20.47	20.33	20.85	19.98	20.21
2016	20.23	20.31	20.08	20.41	20.48	20.46	20.82	20.89	20.87	21.16	21.12	21.56	20.71
2017	21.51	21.43	21.90	21.76	22.15	22.11	22.02	22.23	22.42	22.98	22.92	23.05	22.21
2018	23.70	24.00	23.96	24.26	24.32	24.27	24.59	24.52	24.83	24.73	24.59	24.97	24.41
Education and Health Services													
2014	21.70	22.03	21.46	21.57	21.38	21.31	21.83	21.55	21.59	21.52	21.56	21.63	21.59
2015	22.45	22.54	22.49	22.22	22.38	22.23	22.48	22.33	22.20	22.18	22.33	22.34	22.35
2016	22.83	23.10	22.16	21.70	21.58	21.36	22.05	22.05	22.18	22.06	22.21	22.12	22.11
2017	22.72	22.50	22.93	22.85	22.59	22.61	23.09	23.01	23.13	23.17	23.16	23.02	22.90
2018	23.91	23.91	23.80	24.32	24.10	24.14	24.62	24.78	24.88	25.11	25.58	25.71	24.57
Leisure and Hospitality													
2014	10.78	10.69	10.61	10.44	10.61	10.45	10.47	10.54	10.66	10.78	10.76	10.91	10.64
2015	11.24	11.27	11.30	11.17	11.09	11.10	11.07	11.14	11.28	11.36	11.29	11.42	11.22
2016	11.55	11.67	11.65	11.64	11.75	11.55	11.60	11.69	11.83	11.96	11.93	11.92	11.73
2017	11.92	11.99	11.94	11.86	12.11	11.92	12.09	12.03	12.28	12.31	12.45	12.53	12.12
2018	12.66	12.54	12.54	12.58	12.46	12.48	12.56	12.51	12.39	12.56	12.62	12.53	12.53
Other Services													
2014	19.22	20.06	20.25	20.22	20.06	20.20	20.20	20.47	20.71	21.00	20.91	21.02	20.37
2015	21.47	20.91	21.12	20.92	20.60	20.58	20.87	20.89	20.67	20.50	20.31	20.32	20.76
2016	20.41	20.63	20.67	20.57	20.19	20.09	20.60	20.81	20.69	20.29	20.62	20.33	20.49
2017	20.50	20.49	20.49	20.60	20.36	19.92	20.21	20.62	20.47	20.45	20.47	20.36	20.41
2018	20.62	20.55	20.22	20.15	20.43	19.85	19.99	19.87	19.77	20.03	20.48	20.84	20.23

4. Average Weekly Earnings by Selected Industry: West Virginia, 2014–2018

(Dollars, not seasonally adjusted)

Industry and year	January	February	March	April	May	June	July	August	September	October	November	December	Annual average
Total Private													
2014	701.05	708.56	709.33	716.56	710.31	724.99	730.30	726.41	728.24	725.17	725.77	719.90	718.94
2015	719.30	714.10	719.68	717.25	722.75	718.94	724.50	733.57	724.88	730.10	736.05	720.72	723.84
2016	724.76	727.90	731.85	734.29	722.78	727.89	737.42	734.27	740.96	754.02	746.60	744.48	736.40
2017	755.77	754.69	756.76	762.16	758.27	769.70	784.81	779.01	787.60	791.83	790.59	790.23	772.48
2018	791.88	795.72	790.94	814.02	805.00	812.66	826.78	821.46	833.07	829.78	827.43	844.08	816.86
Goods-Producing													
2014	986.46	992.09	1,002.82	1,014.75	997.60	1,042.49	1,041.25	1,035.80	1,032.51	1,021.34	998.73	1,027.96	1,016.28
2015	983.42	961.22	983.66	993.51	1,018.05	1,001.57	982.40	1,017.62	990.19	1,027.09	1,006.14	1,003.60	998.09
2016	988.79	977.11	1,009.42	1,018.58	985.00	1,018.48	1,007.74	1,027.18	1,026.37	1,061.00	1,040.35	1,022.22	1,013.84
2017	1,016.06	1,040.91	1,010.81	1,048.13	1,043.45	1,062.05	1,063.48	1,077.44	1,084.10	1,090.87	1,068.73	1,072.97	1,057.60
2018	1,022.81	1,024.08	1,021.22	1,051.20	1,052.09	1,078.98	1,081.49	1,089.13	1,095.69	1,107.23	1,106.98	1,134.17	1,075.36
Mining and Logging													
2014	1,391.41	1,373.68	1,375.07	1,402.66	1,354.69	1,425.04	1,413.76	1,411.22	1,381.79	1,356.13	1,344.42	1,428.86	1,388.93
2015	1,422.76	1,331.76	1,393.63	1,371.22	1,363.92	1,345.86	1,350.18	1,348.26	1,302.91	1,360.29	1,382.14	1,328.02	1,357.97
2016	1,361.18	1,297.81	1,345.96	1,324.79	1,292.20	1,252.03	1,225.54	1,306.94	1,314.51	1,391.50	1,297.34	1,275.46	1,307.48
2017	1,261.58	1,278.96	1,226.75	1,220.36	1,246.57	1,188.47	1,214.24	1,247.04	1,248.77	1,253.54	1,263.24	1,252.03	1,242.00
2018	1,212.24	1,200.40	1,180.22	1,188.95	1,180.02	1,202.33	1,194.75	1,247.47	1,263.19	1,260.46	1,284.34	1,336.83	1,231.02
Construction													
2014	911.80	895.20	925.91	963.82	925.30	974.64	985.45	982.80	960.10	941.07	908.35	947.34	946.09
2015	878.21	849.66	889.82	928.77	959.22	983.76	935.55	1,001.30	952.50	1,032.15	939.49	989.23	946.60
2016	917.58	913.17	990.86	1,025.40	994.27	1,067.23	1,065.70	1,045.71	1,054.79	1,063.08	1,031.68	975.61	1,014.94
2017	933.83	1,005.26	960.73	1,063.48	1,050.87	1,136.25	1,115.38	1,125.07	1,132.49	1,130.27	1,123.20	1,116.34	1,081.58
2018	1,043.71	1,044.59	1,043.78	1,103.23	1,126.68	1,143.51	1,153.18	1,141.75	1,113.81	1,151.64	1,142.40	1,181.92	1,123.82
Manufacturing													
2014	778.27	806.40	814.96	800.75	819.86	845.88	851.40	839.10	870.22	871.43	846.71	840.84	831.29
2015	786.21	811.88	806.25	822.20	863.50	830.31	817.50	857.85	853.51	853.21	862.98	855.04	835.43
2016	857.21	861.85	867.02	881.01	847.50	887.81	877.66	898.56	887.00	916.36	930.23	942.48	887.81
2017	953.18	956.45	940.03	960.93	945.44	952.16	953.98	959.38	968.39	978.02	932.16	960.38	955.06
2018	920.81	928.22	928.22	943.74	927.05	963.26	959.45	956.75	990.91	989.68	987.39	990.29	956.76
Trade, Transportation, and Utilities													
2014	612.33	618.38	618.24	637.50	642.94	636.31	638.46	649.14	653.33	654.94	640.85	625.76	634.89
2015	630.65	646.81	649.17	658.17	657.72	665.23	666.16	674.28	674.02	681.63	676.16	657.07	662.08
2016	661.51	655.98	677.76	696.26	680.94	681.64	699.86	689.95	702.90	714.49	704.17	698.26	687.81
2017	695.26	704.00	710.24	707.62	707.87	707.04	706.32	703.80	710.43	704.46	698.72	692.77	703.04
2018	683.77	685.80	681.05	698.71	694.62	698.00	693.73	695.46	695.91	687.80	672.45	664.61	688.45
Financial Activities													
2014	700.00	703.46	698.72	687.59	695.39	727.53	710.31	731.66	725.62	742.66	748.25	697.66	714.21
2015	723.14	732.00	723.16	756.30	743.66	725.78	786.96	841.01	777.50	770.34	815.08	770.74	763.52
2016	758.27	780.47	757.40	755.09	757.91	740.88	734.16	727.18	743.55	795.31	796.62	793.08	762.20
2017	812.49	786.21	795.48	820.91	785.40	767.18	800.02	785.76	788.81	810.16	817.92	809.55	798.78
2018	810.46	824.03	836.80	858.10	838.38	827.51	856.18	841.81	880.40	869.05	849.39	899.28	849.25
Professional and Business Services													
2014	726.23	728.04	729.68	733.60	724.36	739.33	753.82	736.89	745.91	737.03	746.43	712.49	734.07
2015	705.95	690.16	707.52	690.16	695.91	690.62	708.00	715.88	724.64	725.78	761.03	729.27	711.39
2016	718.17	721.01	724.89	742.92	749.57	750.88	762.01	762.49	761.76	804.08	785.66	806.34	757.99
2017	798.02	797.20	812.49	816.00	810.69	815.86	832.36	818.06	831.78	841.07	832.00	834.41	819.55
2018	850.83	876.00	872.14	900.05	887.68	902.84	927.04	921.95	948.51	929.85	909.83	933.88	905.61
Education and Health Services													
2014	755.16	764.44	751.10	752.79	746.16	754.37	770.60	754.25	757.81	748.90	761.07	761.38	755.65
2015	785.75	777.63	775.91	771.03	778.82	773.60	789.05	781.55	774.78	765.21	779.32	777.43	777.78
2016	799.05	808.50	782.25	770.35	770.41	766.82	800.42	787.19	791.83	785.34	784.01	785.26	784.91
2017	817.92	796.50	814.02	818.03	810.98	816.22	842.79	828.36	832.68	834.12	829.13	824.12	822.11
2018	865.54	865.54	859.18	882.82	867.60	873.87	896.17	879.69	883.24	881.36	908.09	907.56	882.06
Leisure and Hospitality													
2014	267.34	270.46	276.92	279.79	280.10	281.11	283.74	281.42	279.29	279.20	277.61	280.39	278.77
2015	281.00	284.00	291.54	290.42	291.67	296.37	298.89	298.55	297.79	299.90	299.19	295.78	293.96
2016	293.37	304.59	315.72	311.95	314.90	315.32	316.68	315.63	313.50	312.16	310.18	303.96	310.85
2017	298.00	308.14	305.66	302.43	313.65	317.07	325.22	324.81	329.10	324.98	327.44	329.54	317.54
2018	321.56	328.55	336.07	338.40	337.67	340.70	349.17	345.28	339.49	339.12	335.69	335.80	337.06
Other Services													
2014	603.51	617.85	654.08	634.91	629.88	652.46	660.54	675.51	654.44	686.70	700.49	685.25	655.91
2015	689.19	671.21	677.95	679.90	653.02	660.62	672.01	676.84	661.44	662.15	668.20	658.37	668.47
2016	644.96	668.41	659.37	668.53	660.21	669.00	661.26	670.08	680.70	685.80	692.83	674.96	670.02
2017	676.50	672.07	684.37	677.74	682.06	671.30	675.01	688.71	687.79	689.17	681.65	684.10	679.65
2018	690.77	682.26	679.39	675.03	676.23	661.01	681.66	677.57	674.16	658.99	688.13	696.06	677.71

WISCONSIN
At a Glance

Population:
  2010 census: 5,686,986
  2018 estimate: 5,813,568

Percent change in population:
  2010–2018: 2.2%

Percent change in total nonfarm employment:
  2010–2018: 9.0%

Industry with the largest growth in employment, 2010–2018 (percent):
  Mining and logging, 65.5%

Industry with the largest decline or smallest growth in employment, 2010–2018 (percent):
  Government, -2.8%

Civilian labor force:
  2010: 3,081,512
  2018: 3,133,294

Unemployment rate and rank among states (highest to lowest):
  2010: 8.7%, 24th
  2018: 3.0%, 41st

Over-the-year change in unemployment rates:
  2016–2017: -0.7%
  2017–2018: -0.3%

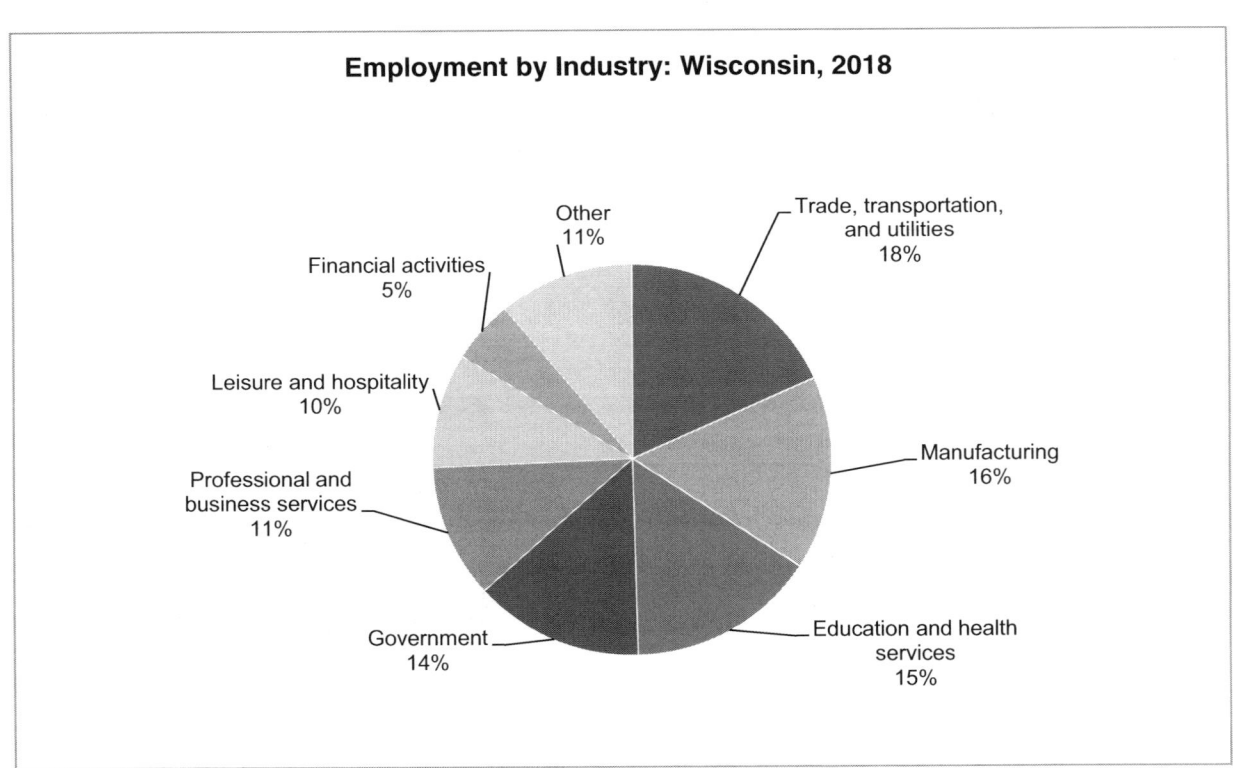

Employment by Industry: Wisconsin, 2018

- Other 11%
- Trade, transportation, and utilities 18%
- Financial activities 5%
- Manufacturing 16%
- Leisure and hospitality 10%
- Professional and business services 11%
- Government 14%
- Education and health services 15%

1. Employment by Industry: Wisconsin, 2010–2018

(Numbers in thousands, not seasonally adjusted)

Industry and year	January	February	March	April	May	June	July	August	September	October	November	December	Annual average
Total Nonfarm													
2010	2,646.3	2,651.0	2,665.4	2,710.9	2,743.2	2,762.0	2,740.6	2,744.6	2,747.0	2,767.6	2,768.3	2,753.2	2,725.0
2011	2,676.8	2,683.6	2,699.6	2,737.0	2,766.6	2,784.4	2,770.9	2,771.2	2,782.4	2,786.0	2,785.9	2,777.4	2,751.8
2012	2,690.1	2,704.3	2,732.7	2,768.8	2,802.3	2,820.2	2,787.8	2,794.4	2,805.4	2,818.9	2,827.0	2,814.6	2,780.5
2013	2,716.8	2,746.2	2,760.2	2,779.6	2,822.3	2,844.7	2,821.2	2,830.1	2,840.8	2,849.8	2,853.2	2,847.0	2,809.3
2014	2,761.8	2,778.6	2,792.2	2,827.8	2,863.1	2,888.3	2,867.2	2,880.1	2,881.7	2,892.6	2,902.9	2,891.0	2,852.3
2015	2,804.8	2,824.3	2,838.1	2,877.4	2,905.4	2,927.3	2,911.0	2,912.9	2,915.5	2,929.5	2,928.4	2,929.0	2,892.0
2016	2,847.9	2,868.6	2,878.4	2,921.9	2,936.9	2,955.6	2,946.7	2,952.2	2,945.6	2,953.9	2,963.8	2,945.3	2,926.4
2017	2,870.3	2,890.5	2,903.0	2,936.6	2,962.9	2,987.4	2,968.9	2,965.2	2,964.4	2,974.6	2,978.0	2,973.4	2,947.9
2018	2,900.6	2,925.4	2,935.8	2,953.8	2,984.3	3,013.2	2,990.9	2,993.0	2,981.1	2,992.5	2,999.7	2,987.9	2,971.5
Total Private													
2010	2,231.0	2,225.9	2,237.8	2,275.5	2,305.7	2,340.6	2,350.7	2,360.4	2,335.8	2,338.7	2,334.4	2,326.7	2,305.3
2011	2,264.6	2,257.0	2,271.4	2,306.2	2,338.0	2,372.9	2,384.1	2,390.5	2,373.7	2,366.9	2,363.9	2,355.2	2,337.0
2012	2,294.3	2,292.9	2,312.9	2,341.5	2,373.5	2,411.5	2,409.5	2,415.8	2,398.7	2,396.7	2,397.3	2,391.6	2,369.7
2013	2,321.9	2,325.9	2,340.6	2,356.9	2,405.4	2,440.5	2,443.0	2,454.4	2,431.9	2,427.5	2,429.7	2,424.8	2,400.2
2014	2,356.6	2,360.5	2,373.4	2,403.2	2,445.2	2,482.6	2,486.4	2,495.7	2,471.3	2,470.1	2,471.9	2,468.2	2,440.4
2015	2,401.8	2,404.3	2,419.2	2,450.7	2,488.0	2,523.3	2,530.7	2,535.7	2,509.6	2,511.0	2,509.1	2,508.3	2,482.6
2016	2,444.8	2,449.5	2,460.2	2,494.9	2,521.7	2,551.9	2,563.4	2,565.1	2,537.5	2,533.2	2,530.6	2,522.0	2,514.6
2017	2,469.4	2,473.5	2,489.4	2,513.3	2,546.2	2,587.9	2,587.6	2,588.7	2,559.5	2,556.3	2,557.7	2,557.0	2,540.5
2018	2,503.0	2,508.0	2,521.1	2,532.0	2,567.6	2,611.2	2,609.0	2,611.5	2,576.8	2,575.8	2,577.9	2,570.5	2,563.7
Goods Producing													
2010	504.3	500.9	504.8	517.6	526.3	540.1	546.3	548.7	542.8	540.1	536.8	527.9	528.1
2011	515.1	512.5	517.4	529.2	540.0	554.5	561.1	562.1	555.4	551.7	549.2	541.4	540.8
2012	529.5	527.2	533.1	544.4	551.6	566.9	571.5	571.6	563.9	562.2	558.0	552.9	552.7
2013	539.5	537.6	541.0	545.3	559.4	573.1	577.7	579.3	570.9	569.0	566.3	558.0	559.8
2014	546.2	544.6	549.4	559.1	571.7	585.9	593.5	594.2	585.9	583.3	580.0	574.4	572.4
2015	561.8	560.2	563.4	573.4	582.2	595.2	600.2	598.6	589.3	585.9	582.5	577.2	580.8
2016	563.8	561.6	565.6	574.7	581.5	594.3	598.8	597.9	588.9	586.2	583.2	576.5	581.1
2017	566.6	566.2	571.0	580.4	588.7	603.9	607.8	606.7	598.0	596.1	593.5	590.0	589.1
2018	580.9	580.9	585.6	591.4	601.4	618.0	621.6	621.8	612.4	611.5	606.4	598.1	602.5
Service-Providing													
2010	2,142.0	2,150.1	2,160.6	2,193.3	2,216.9	2,221.9	2,194.3	2,195.9	2,204.2	2,227.5	2,231.5	2,225.3	2,197.0
2011	2,161.7	2,171.1	2,182.2	2,207.8	2,226.6	2,229.9	2,209.8	2,209.1	2,227.0	2,234.3	2,236.7	2,236.0	2,211.0
2012	2,160.6	2,177.1	2,199.6	2,224.4	2,250.7	2,253.3	2,216.3	2,222.8	2,241.5	2,256.7	2,269.0	2,261.7	2,227.8
2013	2,177.3	2,208.6	2,219.2	2,234.3	2,262.9	2,271.6	2,243.5	2,250.8	2,269.9	2,280.8	2,286.9	2,289.0	2,249.6
2014	2,215.6	2,234.0	2,242.8	2,268.7	2,291.4	2,302.4	2,273.7	2,285.9	2,295.8	2,309.3	2,322.9	2,316.6	2,279.9
2015	2,243.0	2,264.1	2,274.7	2,304.0	2,323.2	2,332.1	2,310.8	2,314.3	2,326.2	2,343.6	2,345.9	2,351.8	2,311.1
2016	2,284.1	2,307.0	2,312.8	2,347.2	2,355.4	2,361.3	2,347.9	2,354.3	2,356.7	2,367.7	2,380.6	2,368.8	2,345.3
2017	2,303.7	2,324.3	2,332.0	2,356.2	2,374.2	2,383.5	2,361.1	2,358.5	2,366.4	2,378.5	2,384.5	2,383.4	2,358.9
2018	2,319.7	2,344.5	2,350.2	2,362.4	2,382.9	2,395.2	2,369.3	2,371.2	2,368.7	2,381.0	2,393.3	2,389.8	2,369.0
Mining and Logging													
2010	2.4	2.4	2.5	2.8	3.1	3.2	3.3	3.3	3.2	3.2	3.1	2.7	2.9
2011	2.5	2.5	2.6	2.7	3.0	3.3	3.3	3.3	3.4	3.4	3.4	3.1	3.0
2012	2.9	2.9	3.1	3.4	3.6	3.7	3.8	3.8	3.8	3.7	3.6	3.4	3.5
2013	3.2	3.2	3.2	3.4	3.8	4.0	4.0	4.1	4.0	4.0	3.9	3.6	3.7
2014	3.4	3.5	3.5	3.8	4.1	4.3	4.4	4.5	4.4	4.5	4.4	4.2	4.1
2015	3.9	4.0	4.0	4.2	4.4	4.5	4.4	4.3	4.2	4.2	4.1	3.9	4.2
2016	3.5	3.5	3.6	3.7	3.9	3.9	3.9	3.9	3.8	3.9	3.8	3.6	3.8
2017	3.5	3.6	3.9	4.2	4.4	4.6	4.7	4.8	4.7	4.7	4.6	4.4	4.3
2018	4.3	4.4	4.6	4.6	4.8	5.1	5.1	5.1	4.9	4.8	4.8	4.5	4.8
Construction													
2010	82.1	79.9	81.6	92.1	97.1	101.7	103.6	103.9	102.1	102.3	98.5	90.0	94.6
2011	79.2	76.8	79.5	87.7	95.1	100.5	102.8	103.0	101.0	100.3	97.3	89.6	92.7
2012	79.7	78.0	81.5	90.4	95.3	100.6	101.9	102.3	100.5	101.2	98.3	93.1	93.6
2013	83.6	82.9	85.2	89.4	101.0	106.3	108.8	110.2	107.6	107.2	104.4	96.1	98.6
2014	87.1	86.2	89.1	96.2	105.2	111.7	114.1	115.1	113.0	112.5	109.4	103.1	103.6
2015	94.4	93.2	95.5	105.7	112.7	117.7	120.1	119.4	116.6	116.2	113.3	108.0	109.4
2016	98.3	98.1	101.0	109.5	114.8	119.8	122.2	122.3	119.7	119.0	116.8	109.4	112.6
2017	102.0	102.3	104.6	113.1	120.0	125.5	127.8	127.3	124.7	123.9	121.3	116.2	117.4
2018	108.2	108.0	111.5	117.0	124.9	131.7	132.2	132.2	129.2	129.1	124.2	118.3	122.2

1. Employment by Industry: Wisconsin, 2010–2018—*Continued*

(Numbers in thousands, not seasonally adjusted)

Industry and year	January	February	March	April	May	June	July	August	September	October	November	December	Annual average
Manufacturing													
2010	419.8	418.6	420.7	422.7	426.1	435.2	439.4	441.5	437.5	434.6	435.2	435.2	430.5
2011	433.4	433.2	435.3	438.8	441.9	450.7	455.0	455.8	451.0	448.0	448.5	448.7	445.0
2012	446.9	446.3	448.5	450.6	452.7	462.6	465.8	465.5	459.6	457.3	456.1	456.4	455.7
2013	452.7	451.5	452.6	452.5	454.6	462.8	464.9	465.0	459.3	457.8	458.0	458.3	457.5
2014	455.7	454.9	456.8	459.1	462.4	469.9	475.0	474.6	468.5	466.3	466.2	467.1	464.7
2015	463.5	463.0	463.9	463.5	465.1	473.0	475.7	474.9	468.5	465.5	465.1	465.3	467.3
2016	462.0	460.0	461.0	461.5	462.8	470.6	472.7	471.7	465.4	463.3	462.6	463.5	464.8
2017	461.1	460.3	462.5	463.1	464.3	473.8	475.3	474.6	468.6	467.5	467.6	469.4	467.3
2018	468.4	468.5	469.5	469.8	471.7	481.2	484.3	484.5	478.3	477.6	477.4	475.3	475.5
Trade, Transportation, and Utilities													
2010	501.1	494.2	496.1	501.4	507.3	511.9	507.7	508.6	506.9	514.5	521.3	523.7	507.9
2011	502.0	495.3	497.4	503.6	508.4	511.8	511.2	512.4	511.8	516.5	525.2	527.6	510.3
2012	505.2	498.3	500.4	503.1	510.9	514.4	511.3	512.9	511.5	516.9	528.7	530.2	512.0
2013	507.2	502.2	504.1	508.3	516.7	522.0	518.5	520.6	517.6	522.4	532.8	536.6	517.4
2014	513.1	509.0	511.6	516.9	523.9	528.8	526.2	527.2	524.0	528.1	539.1	542.5	524.2
2015	519.1	513.9	517.1	520.7	528.8	534.2	533.4	535.6	534.3	538.8	547.5	550.0	531.1
2016	529.8	526.2	527.9	534.0	539.3	541.8	542.4	542.3	538.6	542.5	551.6	554.8	539.3
2017	536.2	531.3	532.6	535.2	541.7	544.5	543.0	544.2	539.9	543.9	555.3	559.2	542.3
2018	539.0	534.1	536.3	537.3	543.8	546.5	545.7	546.8	540.3	541.5	553.6	554.0	543.2
Wholesale Trade													
2010	111.2	110.6	110.8	112.5	113.3	114.6	115.2	115.0	112.9	113.9	113.9	113.9	113.2
2011	112.4	112.1	112.6	114.2	115.3	116.7	117.8	117.3	115.9	116.3	116.3	116.5	115.3
2012	115.0	114.8	115.5	116.8	117.5	119.0	119.0	118.3	116.8	117.1	117.3	117.5	117.1
2013	117.1	116.9	117.2	118.4	119.8	121.1	121.1	120.7	119.0	119.1	119.1	119.3	119.1
2014	117.4	117.4	118.2	119.4	120.7	122.1	122.4	122.1	120.2	120.2	120.3	120.6	120.1
2015	119.5	119.2	119.8	121.1	122.4	124.1	124.5	124.1	122.2	122.9	123.1	123.3	122.2
2016	121.8	121.7	122.2	123.6	124.4	125.6	126.2	125.7	123.9	123.6	123.6	124.2	123.9
2017	122.6	122.5	123.0	123.8	125.3	127.0	127.1	127.1	125.2	125.8	126.1	126.7	125.2
2018	125.3	125.2	125.7	126.4	127.6	129.7	129.4	129.2	127.2	127.3	128.8	128.1	127.5
Retail Trade													
2010	289.5	283.1	284.4	286.5	290.8	293.7	292.5	293.9	290.8	296.6	303.9	306.2	292.7
2011	289.8	283.8	285.1	288.7	291.4	294.2	294.7	296.3	293.4	297.4	306.3	308.3	294.1
2012	291.3	284.7	286.0	287.5	292.0	294.8	293.9	295.8	292.6	297.4	308.9	309.6	294.5
2013	291.3	286.4	287.6	290.5	295.8	300.2	299.8	301.2	297.2	301.3	311.3	314.4	298.1
2014	296.4	292.2	293.7	297.1	301.1	304.7	304.8	305.3	300.8	304.4	314.2	316.1	302.6
2015	298.3	293.7	295.6	297.3	302.4	305.8	306.2	307.5	304.3	307.7	315.9	316.6	304.3
2016	302.9	299.4	300.6	304.2	307.5	309.8	311.5	311.3	306.1	309.7	317.7	318.9	308.3
2017	306.4	302.3	303.0	304.6	307.5	310.1	310.0	310.0	304.5	307.0	317.0	318.9	308.4
2018	304.3	299.9	301.3	301.4	305.5	307.4	308.4	308.4	301.1	301.7	312.2	312.0	305.3
Transportation and Utilities													
2010	100.4	100.5	100.9	102.4	103.2	103.6	100.0	99.7	103.2	104.0	103.5	103.6	102.1
2011	99.8	99.4	99.7	100.7	101.7	100.9	98.7	98.8	102.5	102.8	102.6	102.8	100.9
2012	98.9	98.8	98.9	98.8	101.4	100.6	98.4	98.8	102.1	102.4	102.5	103.1	100.4
2013	98.8	98.9	99.3	99.4	101.1	100.7	97.6	98.7	101.4	102.0	102.4	102.9	100.3
2014	99.3	99.4	99.7	100.4	102.1	102.0	99.0	99.8	103.0	103.5	104.6	105.8	101.6
2015	101.3	101.0	101.7	102.3	104.0	104.3	102.7	104.0	107.8	108.2	108.5	110.1	104.7
2016	105.1	105.1	105.1	106.2	107.4	106.4	104.7	105.3	108.6	109.2	110.3	111.7	107.1
2017	107.2	106.5	106.6	106.8	108.9	107.4	105.9	107.1	110.2	111.1	112.2	113.6	108.6
2018	109.4	109.0	109.3	109.5	110.7	109.4	107.9	109.2	112.0	112.5	112.6	113.9	110.5
Information													
2010	46.6	46.2	46.1	45.9	46.1	46.7	47.2	47.2	46.8	46.6	47.4	47.4	46.7
2011	46.9	46.6	46.5	46.6	46.5	46.4	47.2	47.2	46.8	46.7	47.3	47.1	46.8
2012	46.4	46.0	45.8	45.9	45.9	46.5	46.8	47.1	46.5	46.6	47.2	47.0	46.5
2013	46.9	46.7	46.5	46.7	47.2	47.2	47.7	48.0	47.1	47.4	47.8	47.9	47.3
2014	47.5	47.4	47.1	47.2	47.6	47.7	48.4	48.8	47.8	48.5	48.8	48.8	48.0
2015	48.5	48.2	47.9	48.0	48.3	48.4	49.7	50.0	49.1	49.6	49.8	49.7	48.9
2016	49.2	49.1	48.9	49.0	49.0	49.0	49.5	49.8	48.7	48.8	49.0	49.0	49.1
2017	48.7	48.4	48.1	47.7	47.8	47.9	48.2	48.0	47.5	47.1	47.5	47.5	47.9
2018	47.4	47.0	46.8	46.7	46.7	47.0	47.6	47.5	47.0	47.6	48.0	48.3	47.3

1. Employment by Industry: Wisconsin, 2010–2018—*Continued*

(Numbers in thousands, not seasonally adjusted)

Industry and year	January	February	March	April	May	June	July	August	September	October	November	December	Annual average
Financial Activities													
2010	152.1	151.7	151.9	152.1	152.3	153.3	153.5	153.2	151.6	151.5	151.3	151.9	152.2
2011	150.2	149.8	149.9	150.3	150.7	151.8	152.3	152.1	151.0	150.6	150.3	150.8	150.8
2012	150.1	149.8	150.0	150.1	150.8	152.2	152.5	152.5	150.8	150.7	150.4	150.9	150.9
2013	149.4	149.2	149.5	149.4	150.3	151.9	152.6	152.4	150.6	150.3	150.0	150.5	150.5
2014	147.9	147.8	148.2	148.9	149.7	151.5	152.0	152.3	150.8	150.0	150.0	150.9	150.0
2015	149.6	149.5	149.7	150.0	151.1	152.8	153.5	153.1	151.2	151.1	151.0	151.6	151.2
2016	150.0	149.8	150.0	150.7	151.3	153.1	154.4	154.3	152.5	152.2	152.1	152.5	151.9
2017	151.7	151.7	152.2	152.1	152.6	154.6	155.0	154.8	152.9	152.4	152.0	152.4	152.9
2018	151.3	151.1	151.2	151.5	152.0	154.4	154.7	154.7	152.8	153.6	153.5	154.0	152.9
Professional and Business Services													
2010	256.2	259.7	260.0	269.5	271.2	275.1	279.1	283.3	281.7	285.7	286.3	286.4	274.5
2011	277.4	277.8	280.7	284.0	284.9	290.9	291.5	294.1	294.2	294.2	293.9	291.3	287.9
2012	282.9	284.4	288.3	291.9	293.1	298.4	297.4	299.0	299.1	300.6	301.7	297.8	294.6
2013	287.8	291.5	295.0	294.9	299.8	304.8	306.9	309.3	307.7	307.8	309.2	308.0	301.9
2014	298.2	299.4	299.3	302.5	306.4	310.0	311.5	314.3	312.3	315.5	315.5	311.8	308.1
2015	302.8	303.6	304.4	310.9	313.4	316.8	321.1	324.0	320.2	323.0	322.1	322.3	315.4
2016	314.9	316.2	315.9	321.8	321.5	324.6	327.2	328.4	326.1	326.3	325.7	322.9	322.6
2017	314.6	315.3	318.5	322.7	324.9	329.1	331.6	332.3	329.5	330.8	330.6	330.0	325.8
2018	321.0	323.8	324.1	326.6	328.7	332.5	331.0	331.0	326.6	326.8	325.3	324.1	326.8
Education and Health Services													
2010	405.4	407.5	409.3	406.5	407.1	406.1	405.5	406.0	406.2	409.5	410.5	411.0	407.6
2011	405.2	407.5	408.4	410.4	411.6	408.2	406.9	407.4	412.8	415.9	416.7	418.1	410.8
2012	410.1	415.6	418.2	418.4	419.3	416.2	410.6	413.3	420.2	425.1	425.8	427.1	418.3
2013	416.7	423.4	424.8	425.0	425.5	422.0	416.1	419.3	425.4	429.6	430.7	431.0	424.1
2014	422.8	429.3	430.7	431.4	431.5	429.3	423.2	425.7	431.7	435.1	436.9	438.1	430.5
2015	427.6	434.8	436.7	437.0	437.6	434.8	429.4	430.6	436.5	441.4	442.9	444.8	436.2
2016	435.9	443.3	444.7	446.6	446.2	442.8	439.2	440.3	447.1	449.9	450.9	451.0	444.8
2017	443.1	450.3	451.5	452.3	452.0	450.8	443.7	445.1	452.2	455.5	457.2	458.2	451.0
2018	449.7	456.1	457.4	456.8	455.7	455.6	448.6	450.7	456.5	461.0	462.2	463.2	456.1
Leisure and Hospitality													
2010	230.8	230.7	233.6	245.4	258.1	268.8	273.1	275.4	262.8	253.0	244.1	241.2	251.4
2011	232.7	232.4	235.0	245.1	258.4	270.3	275.1	276.7	264.3	253.8	244.3	241.0	252.4
2012	234.4	235.4	240.4	250.2	263.9	276.5	280.2	280.6	269.0	256.6	247.8	247.6	256.9
2013	238.8	239.6	243.2	250.4	268.6	279.8	284.5	286.6	273.8	262.5	253.6	252.6	261.2
2014	242.5	243.8	246.8	255.8	271.8	284.5	286.3	287.5	273.8	264.4	256.3	255.2	264.1
2015	247.3	248.5	253.1	262.8	277.9	290.9	293.5	294.4	280.7	272.8	265.3	263.4	270.9
2016	254.3	256.4	259.2	268.6	283.1	295.1	300.1	300.5	284.8	276.7	267.6	264.5	275.9
2017	259.8	261.1	265.2	271.8	286.6	303.3	305.4	305.0	287.8	279.1	270.7	268.0	280.3
2018	263.6	264.8	268.6	270.5	287.0	302.9	306.6	305.8	289.1	281.5	275.6	274.9	282.6
Other Services													
2010	134.5	135.0	136.0	137.1	137.3	138.6	138.3	138.0	137.0	137.8	136.7	137.2	137.0
2011	135.1	135.1	136.1	137.0	137.5	139.0	138.8	138.5	137.4	137.5	137.0	137.9	137.2
2012	135.7	136.2	136.7	137.5	138.0	140.4	139.2	138.8	137.7	138.0	137.7	138.1	137.8
2013	135.6	135.7	136.5	136.9	137.9	139.7	139.0	138.9	138.8	138.5	139.3	140.2	138.1
2014	138.4	139.2	140.3	141.4	142.6	144.9	145.3	145.7	145.0	145.2	145.3	146.5	143.3
2015	145.1	145.6	146.9	147.9	148.7	150.2	149.9	149.4	148.3	148.4	148.0	149.3	148.1
2016	146.9	146.9	148.0	149.5	149.8	151.2	151.8	151.6	150.8	150.6	150.5	150.8	149.9
2017	148.7	149.2	150.3	151.1	151.9	153.8	152.9	152.6	151.7	151.4	150.9	151.7	151.4
2018	150.1	150.2	151.1	151.2	152.3	154.3	153.2	153.2	152.1	152.3	153.3	153.9	152.3
Government													
2010	415.3	425.1	427.6	435.4	437.5	421.4	389.9	384.2	411.2	428.9	433.9	426.5	419.7
2011	412.2	426.6	428.2	430.8	428.6	411.5	386.8	380.7	408.7	419.1	422.0	422.2	414.8
2012	395.8	411.4	419.8	427.3	428.8	408.7	378.3	378.6	406.7	422.2	429.7	423.0	410.9
2013	394.9	420.3	419.6	422.7	416.9	404.2	378.2	375.7	408.9	422.3	423.5	422.2	409.1
2014	405.2	418.1	418.8	424.6	417.9	405.7	380.8	384.4	410.4	422.5	431.0	422.8	411.9
2015	403.0	420.0	418.9	426.7	417.4	404.0	380.3	377.2	405.9	418.5	419.3	420.7	409.3
2016	403.1	419.1	418.2	427.0	415.2	403.7	383.3	387.1	408.1	420.7	433.2	423.3	411.8
2017	400.9	417.0	413.6	423.3	416.7	399.5	381.3	376.5	404.9	418.3	420.3	416.4	407.4
2018	397.6	417.4	414.7	421.8	416.7	402.0	381.9	381.5	404.3	416.7	421.8	417.4	407.8

2. Average Weekly Hours by Selected Industry: Wisconsin, 2014–2018

(Not seasonally adjusted)

Industry and year	January	February	March	April	May	June	July	August	September	October	November	December	Annual average
Total Private													
2014	33.0	33.8	33.9	33.5	33.7	34.2	33.9	34.0	34.1	34.0	34.1	33.8	33.8
2015	33.4	33.7	33.8	33.4	33.6	33.7	33.8	34.1	33.6	33.7	34.0	33.6	33.7
2016	33.1	33.1	33.3	33.4	33.6	33.6	33.8	33.8	33.6	34.0	33.7	33.4	33.5
2017	33.6	33.3	33.3	33.8	33.5	33.8	34.2	33.9	33.8	34.1	33.8	33.8	33.7
2018	33.4	33.6	33.4	33.5	33.5	33.8	34.1	33.8	33.9	33.3	33.0	33.5	33.6
Goods-Producing													
2014	38.9	39.6	40.0	39.8	40.4	40.8	40.6	41.0	41.3	40.9	41.0	40.8	40.4
2015	40.3	39.8	40.0	40.3	40.9	40.7	40.7	41.0	40.6	41.3	41.1	40.6	40.6
2016	39.7	39.3	39.9	40.0	40.1	40.2	40.6	40.2	40.6	40.8	41.1	40.0	40.2
2017	39.8	39.7	40.1	40.0	40.4	40.2	40.5	40.8	40.8	40.8	40.6	40.3	40.3
2018	39.9	39.7	39.6	39.7	40.2	40.3	40.3	40.3	40.3	39.5	39.0	39.8	39.9
Construction													
2014	36.3	36.7	37.5	38.6	40.5	41.1	41.0	41.2	41.0	40.4	39.7	39.0	39.6
2015	37.9	36.0	37.8	38.6	39.7	38.6	39.0	39.7	38.4	40.7	39.0	38.6	38.7
2016	37.0	37.4	38.2	39.4	39.0	40.2	40.1	40.4	40.2	40.3	40.1	37.5	39.2
2017	37.7	37.9	38.1	39.3	40.2	39.6	39.0	40.0	40.0	40.2	39.4	38.2	39.2
2018	37.7	38.0	37.7	38.3	39.2	40.2	40.5	40.3	40.3	38.7	38.4	39.2	39.1
Manufacturing													
2014	39.4	40.1	40.4	39.9	40.3	40.7	40.4	40.8	41.2	40.9	41.2	41.1	40.5
2015	40.7	40.5	40.3	40.6	41.0	41.1	41.0	41.3	40.5	40.7	41.0	40.5	40.8
2016	39.8	39.3	39.9	39.8	40.1	39.9	40.3	39.7	40.3	40.5	41.0	40.4	40.1
2017	40.1	40.0	40.4	40.0	40.2	40.2	40.7	40.8	40.9	40.9	40.9	40.8	40.5
2018	40.4	40.1	40.0	40.0	40.5	40.4	40.2	40.4	40.3	39.8	39.3	39.9	40.1
Trade, Transportation, and Utilities													
2014	31.8	32.8	32.8	32.8	33.1	33.2	33.1	33.3	33.4	33.4	33.5	33.9	33.1
2015	33.2	33.8	33.9	33.4	33.9	33.8	34.0	34.0	33.5	33.4	33.7	33.6	33.7
2016	32.3	32.3	32.3	32.9	32.9	33.2	33.3	33.2	32.9	32.9	32.4	32.6	32.8
2017	32.1	31.9	32.0	32.6	32.4	32.9	33.3	33.0	33.0	33.1	33.5	33.5	32.8
2018	32.8	32.7	32.8	32.7	32.9	33.0	33.2	32.5	32.6	32.0	32.3	32.5	32.7
Financial Activities													
2014	37.1	38.0	38.1	37.0	37.0	38.5	37.2	37.1	36.9	37.1	38.1	37.1	37.4
2015	36.7	37.6	37.9	36.5	36.5	36.3	36.0	37.8	37.1	36.8	37.9	37.2	37.0
2016	37.4	37.3	37.9	37.4	36.8	36.8	36.5	37.3	36.8	38.1	37.5	37.4	37.4
2017	37.9	36.2	36.3	37.8	36.4	37.2	37.5	37.4	36.7	37.9	37.2	37.5	37.2
2018	37.3	37.9	37.3	38.1	37.2	37.8	38.1	37.9	38.4	37.8	37.6	38.1	37.8
Professional and Business Services													
2014	34.1	35.4	35.7	34.9	34.9	35.6	34.8	34.7	34.8	35.0	35.0	34.6	35.0
2015	34.1	34.6	34.8	34.1	34.5	34.6	34.4	34.8	34.0	34.4	35.1	34.3	34.5
2016	34.2	34.9	35.0	34.6	35.1	35.2	34.9	35.1	34.9	35.6	34.8	34.6	34.9
2017	35.1	35.0	34.9	35.7	35.3	36.1	36.2	35.4	35.3	35.7	35.4	35.1	35.4
2018	34.7	35.2	35.1	35.4	34.6	35.3	35.7	35.3	35.1	34.8	34.6	35.0	35.1
Education and Health Services													
2014	31.5	31.7	31.7	31.4	31.5	31.6	31.3	31.3	31.4	31.5	31.8	31.4	31.5
2015	31.2	31.4	31.2	30.9	30.9	30.8	30.9	31.1	31.0	30.8	31.0	30.9	31.0
2016	30.9	30.8	30.8	31.1	31.6	31.2	31.5	31.3	31.2	31.5	31.3	31.4	31.2
2017	32.1	31.6	31.6	32.0	31.5	31.6	32.2	31.5	31.6	31.6	31.3	31.7	31.7
2018	31.4	31.3	31.2	31.3	31.3	31.5	31.7	31.7	31.8	31.1	31.1	31.5	31.4
Leisure and Hospitality													
2014	21.4	22.5	22.5	21.9	22.1	22.9	23.4	23.4	22.8	22.6	22.6	22.0	22.5
2015	21.8	22.5	22.4	22.1	22.0	22.7	22.9	23.2	22.1	22.0	21.8	21.8	22.3
2016	21.2	22.0	21.7	21.8	22.4	22.7	23.2	23.3	22.4	22.3	21.9	21.2	22.2
2017	21.7	22.0	22.0	21.8	21.9	22.9	23.3	22.8	22.3	22.4	21.7	21.4	22.2
2018	21.4	22.1	21.8	21.3	22.0	22.7	23.4	22.8	22.1	21.9	20.7	21.3	22.0
Other Services													
2014	30.6	30.6	30.4	29.6	29.0	30.1	29.2	29.5	29.1	28.7	27.9	28.1	29.4
2015	27.6	27.6	28.1	27.1	27.2	29.0	29.2	29.5	27.8	27.7	28.0	27.8	28.1
2016	28.3	27.7	27.4	27.7	28.0	28.5	28.7	28.6	27.8	28.5	28.4	28.3	28.2
2017	28.2	27.9	27.2	27.8	27.2	27.8	27.6	27.7	26.6	26.9	27.0	27.0	27.4
2018	26.4	26.9	26.5	27.3	27.2	27.7	28.8	28.8	29.0	29.0	28.0	28.1	27.8

3. Average Hourly Earnings by Selected Industry: Wisconsin, 2014–2018

(Dollars, not seasonally adjusted)

Industry and year	January	February	March	April	May	June	July	August	September	October	November	December	Annual average
Total Private													
2014	23.48	23.59	23.45	23.57	23.23	23.11	22.99	22.91	23.11	23.08	23.23	23.21	23.24
2015	23.57	23.60	23.54	23.52	23.40	23.09	23.11	23.25	23.38	23.60	23.69	23.81	23.46
2016	23.98	23.91	23.86	23.99	24.09	23.76	23.96	23.91	23.84	24.28	24.31	24.43	24.03
2017	24.68	24.40	24.50	24.95	24.40	24.15	24.53	24.39	24.87	25.21	25.15	25.57	24.73
2018	25.96	25.85	25.86	26.42	25.94	25.61	25.76	25.62	26.06	25.95	25.97	26.19	25.93
Goods-Producing													
2014	23.87	23.90	23.94	24.11	23.96	23.94	23.85	23.92	24.10	24.23	24.34	24.67	24.07
2015	24.44	24.53	24.61	24.73	24.62	24.38	24.48	24.55	24.48	24.66	24.63	25.08	24.60
2016	24.74	24.73	24.53	24.76	24.78	24.96	25.20	25.23	25.44	25.74	25.54	25.78	25.13
2017	25.73	25.49	25.46	25.87	25.70	25.55	25.95	25.80	26.08	26.12	26.31	26.75	25.91
2018	26.83	26.73	26.56	27.19	26.80	26.76	27.02	26.91	27.18	27.33	27.27	27.72	27.03
Construction													
2014	27.33	26.85	27.08	26.58	25.75	26.03	26.15	26.69	27.08	27.28	26.89	27.39	26.73
2015	27.37	27.26	27.77	27.99	27.91	27.67	27.64	27.82	27.36	27.65	27.72	27.91	27.68
2016	28.19	27.76	27.69	27.77	27.52	28.10	28.56	27.89	28.20	28.07	27.88	28.55	28.02
2017	27.99	27.92	28.28	27.69	28.13	28.01	28.54	28.97	28.67	28.71	28.17	29.04	28.36
2018	29.14	29.29	29.25	29.93	29.66	29.62	29.65	30.15	30.74	31.07	30.22	31.38	30.04
Manufacturing													
2014	23.03	23.18	23.18	23.43	23.36	23.24	23.13	23.10	23.27	23.39	23.66	24.02	23.33
2015	23.79	23.96	23.92	23.94	23.79	23.54	23.64	23.62	23.71	23.81	23.80	24.37	23.82
2016	23.96	24.00	23.76	23.90	24.02	23.98	24.15	24.37	24.58	25.02	24.83	25.06	24.31
2017	25.15	24.87	24.75	25.36	25.16	24.98	25.34	24.96	25.38	25.43	25.86	26.21	25.29
2018	26.31	26.15	25.95	26.53	26.09	25.94	26.26	25.93	26.10	26.23	26.42	26.69	26.22
Trade, Transportation, and Utilities													
2014	19.69	19.89	19.94	20.15	19.99	20.09	20.35	19.97	20.15	20.18	20.25	19.93	20.05
2015	20.68	20.84	20.65	20.96	20.64	20.38	20.57	20.63	20.71	20.57	20.41	20.44	20.62
2016	20.93	20.87	20.92	21.16	21.23	21.08	21.15	20.82	21.32	21.48	21.55	21.53	21.17
2017	21.68	21.43	21.53	21.93	22.12	22.07	22.23	22.23	22.79	22.84	22.35	22.63	22.16
2018	23.33	23.33	23.12	23.59	23.07	23.23	22.98	23.09	23.44	23.20	22.92	23.09	23.20
Financial Activities													
2014	28.61	29.49	28.81	29.00	28.12	28.26	28.00	28.37	28.55	28.22	28.89	29.22	28.63
2015	29.60	29.91	29.75	29.33	29.98	29.31	29.79	29.54	29.21	29.91	29.49	29.38	29.60
2016	30.43	30.25	29.98	30.22	30.22	29.31	29.82	29.81	30.36	30.24	30.24	30.33	30.10
2017	31.41	31.23	31.61	32.32	31.50	30.58	31.50	31.04	31.53	32.43	32.14	33.29	31.72
2018	34.35	34.06	34.42	34.71	34.05	32.86	33.48	33.04	33.18	32.48	33.41	33.47	33.62
Professional and Business Services													
2014	29.69	29.80	29.13	29.54	28.76	28.50	28.05	27.66	27.26	27.11	27.09	26.71	28.26
2015	27.13	26.82	26.86	26.16	25.96	25.80	25.51	25.78	26.04	26.46	26.94	26.96	26.36
2016	27.06	27.12	26.93	27.29	27.79	27.44	27.21	27.27	27.40	28.08	28.20	28.27	27.51
2017	27.39	26.86	27.39	28.34	27.68	27.86	28.35	27.79	27.98	28.52	28.33	28.19	27.90
2018	28.63	28.64	28.70	29.28	29.31	28.90	29.27	28.89	29.02	28.46	28.20	28.55	28.82
Education and Health Services													
2014	24.32	24.16	24.22	24.12	24.06	24.01	23.95	24.06	24.61	24.17	24.28	24.50	24.21
2015	24.93	24.67	24.52	24.57	24.59	24.39	24.29	24.56	24.73	24.86	25.06	25.15	24.70
2016	25.06	24.93	25.00	24.66	24.90	24.71	25.26	25.33	25.36	25.71	26.01	25.75	25.23
2017	26.00	26.21	26.03	26.17	26.11	25.90	26.12	25.83	26.11	26.42	26.53	26.67	26.18
2018	27.03	26.88	26.96	27.24	26.66	26.37	26.37	25.95	26.50	26.59	26.76	26.56	26.66
Leisure and Hospitality													
2014	12.23	12.29	12.25	12.39	12.26	11.96	11.80	12.00	12.09	12.49	12.59	12.59	12.23
2015	12.73	13.03	12.95	13.13	13.01	12.72	12.70	12.69	13.02	13.43	13.52	13.49	13.02
2016	13.43	13.59	13.58	13.68	13.49	13.02	13.08	12.99	13.50	13.84	13.73	14.00	13.47
2017	13.97	14.02	14.14	14.21	14.07	13.47	13.25	13.39	13.75	14.04	14.06	14.44	13.88
2018	14.13	14.27	14.49	14.76	14.50	14.32	14.18	14.38	14.73	14.96	14.97	15.06	14.55
Other Services													
2014	20.80	20.55	20.19	19.99	19.96	19.31	19.10	19.02	19.05	18.81	19.04	18.51	19.53
2015	19.39	19.56	19.47	19.61	19.65	19.20	19.01	19.19	19.48	18.75	19.17	19.27	19.31
2016	19.09	18.93	19.09	18.95	19.10	18.62	19.06	18.91	19.35	19.81	19.88	20.37	19.27
2017	20.52	20.77	20.39	20.35	20.08	19.36	19.80	19.84	20.37	20.71	20.14	21.02	20.27
2018	21.39	20.93	21.01	21.77	21.72	21.74	21.49	21.25	21.81	21.74	21.32	21.81	21.50

4. Average Weekly Earnings by Selected Industry: Wisconsin, 2014–2018

(Dollars, not seasonally adjusted)

Industry and year	January	February	March	April	May	June	July	August	September	October	November	December	Annual average
Total Private													
2014	774.84	797.34	794.96	789.60	782.85	790.36	779.36	778.94	788.05	784.72	792.14	784.50	785.51
2015	787.24	795.32	795.65	785.57	786.24	778.13	781.12	792.83	785.57	795.32	805.46	800.02	790.60
2016	793.74	791.42	794.54	801.27	809.42	798.34	809.85	808.16	801.02	825.52	819.25	815.96	805.01
2017	829.25	812.52	815.85	843.31	817.40	816.27	838.93	826.82	840.61	859.66	850.07	864.27	833.40
2018	867.06	868.56	863.72	885.07	868.99	865.62	878.42	865.96	883.43	864.14	857.01	877.37	871.25
Goods-Producing													
2014	928.54	946.44	957.60	959.58	967.98	976.75	968.31	980.72	995.33	991.01	997.94	1,006.54	972.43
2015	984.93	976.29	984.40	996.62	1,006.96	992.27	996.34	1,006.55	993.89	1,018.46	1,012.29	1,018.25	998.76
2016	982.18	971.89	978.75	990.40	993.68	1,003.39	1,023.12	1,014.25	1,032.86	1,050.19	1,049.69	1,031.20	1,010.23
2017	1,024.05	1,011.95	1,020.95	1,034.80	1,038.28	1,027.11	1,050.98	1,052.64	1,064.06	1,065.70	1,068.19	1,078.03	1,044.17
2018	1,070.52	1,061.18	1,051.78	1,079.44	1,077.36	1,078.43	1,088.91	1,084.47	1,095.35	1,079.54	1,063.53	1,103.26	1,078.50
Construction													
2014	992.08	985.40	1,015.50	1,025.99	1,042.88	1,069.83	1,072.15	1,099.63	1,110.28	1,102.11	1,067.53	1,068.21	1,058.51
2015	1,037.32	981.36	1,049.71	1,080.41	1,108.03	1,068.06	1,077.96	1,104.45	1,050.62	1,125.36	1,081.08	1,077.33	1,071.22
2016	1,043.03	1,038.22	1,057.76	1,094.14	1,073.28	1,129.62	1,145.26	1,126.76	1,133.64	1,131.22	1,117.99	1,070.63	1,098.38
2017	1,055.22	1,058.17	1,077.47	1,088.22	1,130.83	1,109.20	1,113.06	1,158.80	1,146.80	1,154.14	1,109.90	1,109.33	1,111.71
2018	1,098.58	1,113.02	1,102.73	1,146.32	1,162.67	1,190.72	1,200.83	1,215.05	1,238.82	1,202.41	1,160.45	1,230.10	1,174.56
Manufacturing													
2014	907.38	929.52	936.47	934.86	941.41	945.87	934.45	942.48	958.72	956.65	974.79	987.22	944.87
2015	968.25	970.38	963.98	971.96	975.39	967.49	969.24	975.51	960.26	969.07	975.80	986.99	971.86
2016	953.61	943.20	948.02	951.22	963.20	956.80	973.25	967.49	990.57	1,013.31	1,018.03	1,012.42	974.83
2017	1,008.52	994.80	999.90	1,014.40	1,011.43	1,004.20	1,031.34	1,018.37	1,038.04	1,040.09	1,057.67	1,069.37	1,024.25
2018	1,062.92	1,048.62	1,038.00	1,061.20	1,056.65	1,047.98	1,055.65	1,047.57	1,051.83	1,043.95	1,038.31	1,064.93	1,051.42
Trade, Transportation, and Utilities													
2014	626.14	652.39	654.03	660.92	661.67	666.99	673.59	665.00	673.01	674.01	678.38	675.63	663.66
2015	686.58	704.39	700.04	700.06	699.70	688.84	699.38	701.42	693.79	687.04	687.82	686.78	694.89
2016	676.04	674.10	675.72	696.16	698.47	699.86	704.30	691.22	701.43	706.69	698.22	701.88	694.38
2017	695.93	683.62	688.96	714.92	716.69	726.10	740.26	733.59	752.07	756.00	748.73	758.11	726.85
2018	765.22	762.89	758.34	771.39	759.00	766.59	762.94	750.43	764.14	742.40	740.32	750.43	758.64
Financial Activities													
2014	1,061.43	1,120.62	1,097.66	1,073.00	1,040.44	1,088.01	1,041.60	1,052.53	1,053.50	1,046.96	1,100.71	1,084.06	1,070.76
2015	1,086.32	1,124.62	1,127.53	1,070.55	1,094.27	1,063.95	1,072.44	1,116.61	1,083.69	1,100.69	1,117.67	1,092.94	1,095.20
2016	1,138.08	1,128.33	1,136.24	1,130.23	1,157.43	1,078.61	1,088.43	1,111.91	1,117.25	1,152.14	1,134.00	1,134.34	1,125.74
2017	1,190.44	1,130.53	1,147.44	1,221.70	1,146.60	1,137.58	1,181.25	1,160.90	1,157.15	1,229.10	1,195.61	1,248.38	1,179.98
2018	1,281.26	1,290.87	1,283.87	1,322.45	1,266.66	1,242.11	1,275.59	1,252.22	1,274.11	1,227.74	1,256.22	1,275.21	1,270.84
Professional and Business Services													
2014	1,012.43	1,054.92	1,039.94	1,030.95	1,003.72	1,014.60	976.14	959.80	948.65	948.85	948.15	924.17	989.10
2015	925.13	927.97	934.73	892.06	895.62	892.68	877.54	897.14	885.36	910.22	945.59	924.73	909.42
2016	925.45	946.49	942.55	944.23	975.43	965.89	949.63	957.18	956.26	999.65	981.36	978.14	960.10
2017	961.39	940.10	955.91	1,011.74	977.10	1,005.75	1,026.27	983.77	987.69	1,018.16	1,002.88	989.47	987.66
2018	993.46	1,008.13	1,007.37	1,036.51	1,014.13	1,020.17	1,044.94	1,019.82	1,018.60	990.41	975.72	999.25	1,011.58
Education and Health Services													
2014	766.08	765.87	767.77	757.37	757.89	758.72	749.64	753.08	772.75	761.36	772.10	769.30	762.62
2015	777.82	774.64	765.02	759.21	759.83	751.21	750.56	763.82	766.63	765.69	776.86	777.14	765.70
2016	774.35	767.84	770.00	766.93	786.84	770.95	795.69	792.83	791.23	809.87	814.11	808.55	787.18
2017	834.60	828.24	822.55	837.44	822.47	818.44	841.06	813.65	825.08	834.87	830.39	845.44	829.91
2018	848.74	841.34	841.15	852.61	834.46	830.66	835.93	822.62	842.70	826.95	832.24	836.64	837.12
Leisure and Hospitality													
2014	261.72	276.53	275.63	271.34	270.95	273.88	276.12	280.80	275.65	282.27	284.53	276.98	275.18
2015	277.51	293.18	290.08	290.17	286.22	288.74	290.83	294.41	287.74	295.46	294.74	294.08	290.35
2016	284.72	298.98	294.69	298.22	302.18	295.55	303.46	302.67	302.40	308.63	300.69	296.80	299.03
2017	303.15	308.44	311.08	309.78	308.13	308.46	308.73	305.29	306.63	314.50	305.10	309.02	308.14
2018	302.38	315.37	315.88	314.39	319.00	325.06	331.81	327.86	325.53	327.62	309.88	320.78	320.10
Other Services													
2014	636.48	628.83	613.78	591.70	578.84	581.23	557.72	561.09	554.36	539.85	531.22	520.13	574.18
2015	535.16	539.86	547.11	531.43	534.48	556.80	555.09	566.11	541.54	519.38	536.76	535.71	542.61
2016	540.25	524.36	523.07	524.92	534.80	530.67	547.02	540.83	537.93	564.59	564.59	576.47	543.41
2017	578.66	579.48	554.61	565.73	546.18	538.21	546.48	549.57	541.84	557.10	543.78	567.54	555.40
2018	564.70	563.02	556.77	594.32	590.78	602.20	618.91	612.00	632.49	630.46	596.96	612.86	597.70

WYOMING
At a Glance

Population:
  2010 census: 563,626
  2018 estimate: 577,737

Percent change in population:
  2010–2018: 2.5%

Percent change in total nonfarm employment:
  2010–2018: 0.4%

Industry with the largest growth in employment, 2010–2018 (percent):
  Other services, 16.3%

Industry with the largest decline or smallest growth in employment, 2010–2018 (percent):
  Mining and logging, -17.9%

Civilian labor force:
  2010: 303,297
  2018: 289,574

Unemployment rate and rank among states (highest to lowest):
  2010: 6.4%, 45th
  2018: 4.1%, 16th

Over-the-year change in unemployment rates:
  2016–2017: -1.1%
  2017–2018: -0.1%

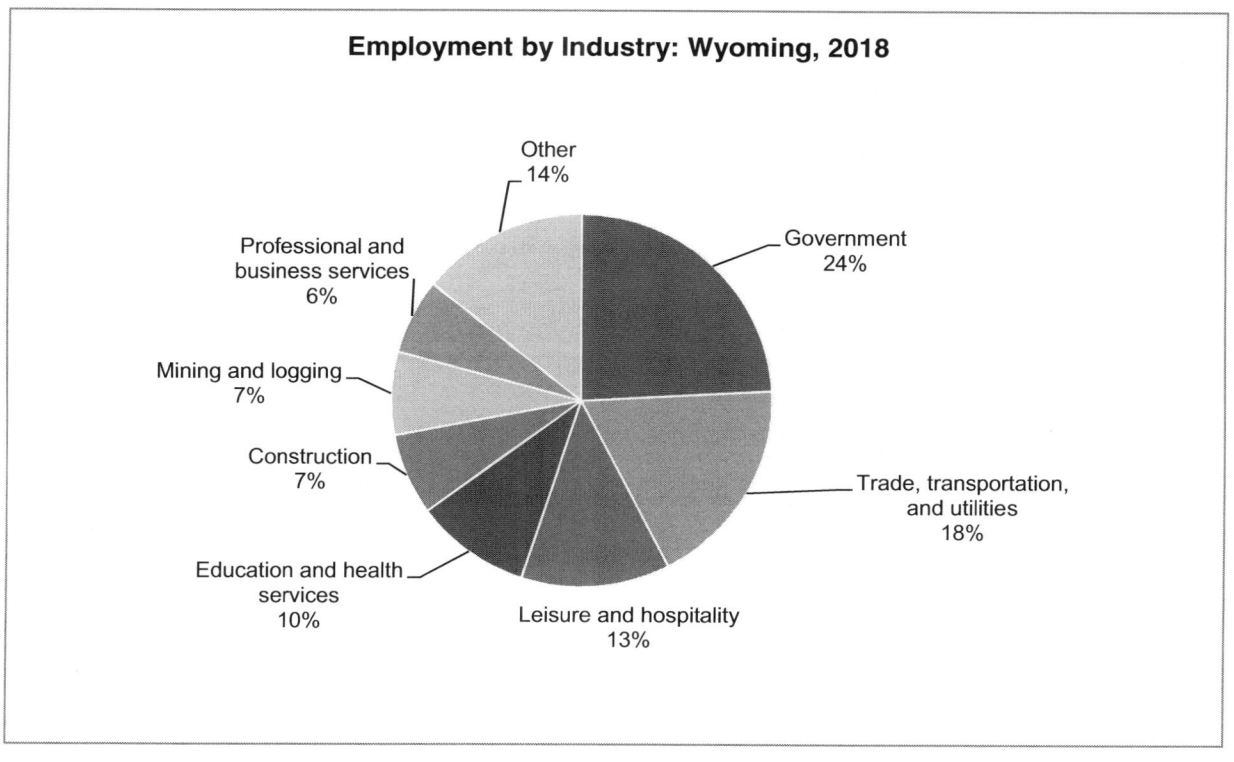

Employment by Industry: Wyoming, 2018

- Other 14%
- Government 24%
- Professional and business services 6%
- Mining and logging 7%
- Construction 7%
- Education and health services 10%
- Leisure and hospitality 13%
- Trade, transportation, and utilities 18%

1. Employment by Industry: Wyoming, 2010–2018

(Numbers in thousands, not seasonally adjusted)

Industry and year	January	February	March	April	May	June	July	August	September	October	November	December	Annual average
Total Nonfarm													
2010	272.7	273.8	275.9	278.5	286.4	292.9	289.1	290.7	293.3	290.6	284.3	284.6	284.4
2011	276.2	277.8	280.1	281.3	288.8	296.9	296.9	297.5	299.2	295.5	290.3	291.7	289.4
2012	283.2	284.6	286.7	287.8	294.2	300.8	299.2	299.2	299.1	296.1	291.0	291.9	292.8
2013	283.9	284.5	287.0	287.6	295.2	303.2	301.5	301.0	300.1	298.2	292.4	293.2	294.0
2014	286.7	287.6	289.6	291.4	300.0	307.4	306.9	305.8	305.5	304.2	296.4	298.8	298.4
2015	291.6	291.8	292.8	293.2	298.7	303.9	303.5	302.7	302.1	299.6	291.2	291.5	296.9
2016	283.1	282.4	283.2	282.7	288.1	293.6	291.6	290.6	289.1	285.8	279.7	280.4	285.9
2017	274.1	275.1	277.0	277.8	285.5	292.1	290.5	291.1	290.6	286.4	280.7	282.0	283.6
2018	276.1	276.4	278.2	279.4	286.5	293.0	292.6	292.5	291.4	289.0	285.0	286.0	285.5
Total Private													
2010	202.6	202.2	203.2	206.4	211.4	219.1	223.2	224.9	221.5	217.8	211.9	212.2	213.0
2011	205.6	205.6	207.3	208.6	214.8	223.6	227.8	229.0	226.7	222.3	217.5	218.7	217.3
2012	211.9	211.6	213.3	215.2	219.9	227.7	229.7	230.9	226.5	222.6	217.9	218.6	220.5
2013	212.3	211.8	213.8	214.8	221.3	230.2	233.3	233.0	228.2	225.5	220.2	220.8	222.1
2014	216.1	215.8	217.0	219.5	227.0	235.8	238.5	238.6	234.2	232.0	224.8	226.9	227.2
2015	221.8	220.8	220.8	221.6	225.7	232.2	235.8	234.8	230.1	226.6	218.7	218.9	225.7
2016	212.5	210.5	210.6	210.7	214.8	221.3	223.9	222.8	217.9	214.2	208.4	208.9	214.7
2017	204.7	204.2	205.5	206.8	213.3	221.3	224.0	224.3	220.6	216.0	210.8	212.1	213.6
2018	208.4	207.3	208.6	209.8	216.1	223.7	227.0	226.5	222.1	218.7	215.0	216.2	216.6
Goods Producing													
2010	52.3	51.9	52.5	54.2	55.8	56.9	58.3	59.7	59.3	59.7	57.9	56.1	56.2
2011	52.9	52.7	53.2	54.5	56.5	58.5	59.9	60.7	61.3	61.6	60.7	59.4	57.7
2012	56.1	55.7	56.4	58.3	59.2	59.8	59.9	60.6	60.4	60.1	58.8	57.4	58.6
2013	55.1	54.6	55.2	56.0	58.1	59.6	60.3	60.5	59.5	60.0	59.1	58.5	58.0
2014	56.7	56.6	57.1	58.6	61.4	63.3	63.8	63.7	63.5	63.5	61.7	60.8	60.9
2015	58.3	57.4	56.7	57.1	57.3	57.3	58.2	58.2	57.5	57.4	54.9	53.1	57
2016	50.2	49.0	48.7	49.5	49.6	49.5	50.1	50.0	49.3	49.1	48.4	47.3	49.2
2017	45.2	45.2	45.8	47.5	48.9	49.8	50.3	50.6	50.7	50.4	49.9	49.1	48.6
2018	47.6	47.2	47.7	48.7	49.8	51.2	52.0	52.9	52.4	53.3	53.2	52.3	50.7
Service-Providing													
2010	220.4	221.9	223.4	224.3	230.6	236.0	230.8	231.0	234.0	230.9	226.4	228.5	228.2
2011	223.3	225.1	226.9	226.8	232.3	238.4	237.0	236.8	237.9	233.9	229.6	232.3	231.7
2012	227.1	228.9	230.3	229.5	235.0	241.0	239.3	238.6	238.7	236.0	232.2	234.5	234.3
2013	228.8	229.9	231.8	231.6	237.1	243.6	241.2	240.5	240.6	238.2	233.3	234.7	235.9
2014	230.0	231.0	232.5	232.8	238.6	244.1	243.1	242.1	242.0	240.7	234.7	238.0	237.5
2015	233.3	234.4	236.1	236.1	241.4	246.6	245.3	244.5	244.6	242.2	236.3	238.4	239.9
2016	232.9	233.4	234.5	233.2	238.5	244.1	241.5	240.6	239.8	236.7	231.3	233.1	236.6
2017	228.9	229.9	231.2	230.3	236.6	242.3	240.2	240.5	239.9	236.0	230.8	232.9	235.0
2018	228.5	229.2	230.5	230.7	236.7	241.8	240.6	239.6	239.0	235.7	231.8	233.7	234.8
Mining and Logging													
2010	24.0	24.0	24.1	24.2	24.6	25.1	25.6	25.9	25.8	26.1	26.3	26.5	25.2
2011	26.2	26.2	26.3	26.4	26.7	27.3	27.8	28.1	28.2	28.5	28.6	28.8	27.4
2012	28.3	28.3	28.1	27.8	27.8	28.1	27.8	27.7	27.3	27.4	27.4	27.3	27.8
2013	26.6	26.5	26.5	26.4	26.3	26.6	26.8	26.9	26.7	26.8	26.8	27.0	26.7
2014	26.9	26.8	26.9	26.9	27.0	27.4	27.6	27.8	27.7	27.8	27.9	27.9	27.4
2015	27.4	26.6	25.7	24.5	23.8	23.4	23.4	23.2	22.8	22.8	22.0	21.7	23.9
2016	21.2	20.5	19.8	19.0	18.3	18.1	18.1	18.0	18.0	18.3	18.4	18.6	18.9
2017	18.5	18.7	18.9	19.1	19.4	19.7	19.8	20.0	20.1	20.4	20.6	20.7	19.7
2018	20.6	20.5	20.6	20.3	20.2	20.5	20.8	21.0	20.9	21.0	20.8	20.8	20.7
Construction													
2010	19.7	19.5	19.9	21.6	22.8	23.2	24.0	24.9	24.6	24.5	22.4	20.5	22.3
2011	17.9	17.8	18.3	19.3	20.9	22.1	23.0	23.3	23.8	23.5	22.5	21.0	21.1
2012	18.6	18.2	19.2	21.5	22.3	22.4	22.7	23.6	23.7	23.1	21.8	20.6	21.5
2013	19.1	18.8	19.6	20.5	22.6	23.5	23.9	24.0	23.1	23.2	22.4	21.6	21.9
2014	20.2	20.3	20.6	22.3	24.8	26.1	26.3	26.0	25.9	25.6	23.7	22.8	23.7
2015	21.0	21.0	21.5	23.1	23.8	24.2	25.0	25.2	24.9	24.7	23.1	21.7	23.3
2016	19.6	19.3	19.8	21.5	22.3	22.2	22.7	22.7	22.1	21.5	20.6	19.4	21.1
2017	17.5	17.4	17.7	19.4	20.4	20.8	21.0	21.0	21.0	20.3	19.5	18.7	19.6
2018	17.4	17.2	17.7	19.0	20.2	21.0	21.5	22.1	21.5	22.1	22.1	21.2	20.3

1. Employment by Industry: Wyoming, 2010–2018—*Continued*

(Numbers in thousands, not seasonally adjusted)

Industry and year	January	February	March	April	May	June	July	August	September	October	November	December	Annual average
Manufacturing													
2010	8.6	8.4	8.5	8.4	8.4	8.6	8.7	8.9	8.9	9.1	9.2	9.1	8.7
2011	8.8	8.7	8.6	8.8	8.9	9.1	9.1	9.3	9.3	9.6	9.6	9.6	9.1
2012	9.2	9.2	9.1	9.0	9.1	9.3	9.4	9.3	9.4	9.7	9.6	9.5	9.3
2013	9.4	9.3	9.1	9.1	9.2	9.5	9.6	9.6	9.7	10.0	9.9	9.9	9.5
2014	9.6	9.5	9.6	9.4	9.6	9.8	9.9	9.9	9.9	10.1	10.1	10.1	9.8
2015	9.9	9.8	9.5	9.5	9.7	9.7	9.8	9.8	9.8	9.9	9.8	9.7	9.7
2016	9.4	9.2	9.1	9.0	9.0	9.2	9.3	9.3	9.2	9.3	9.4	9.3	9.2
2017	9.2	9.1	9.2	9.0	9.1	9.3	9.5	9.6	9.6	9.7	9.8	9.7	9.4
2018	9.6	9.5	9.4	9.4	9.4	9.7	9.7	9.8	10.0	10.2	10.3	10.3	9.8
Trade, Transportation, and Utilities													
2010	50.6	50.3	50.2	50.8	51.5	52.8	53.1	53.0	52.4	52.0	52.1	52.6	51.8
2011	50.7	50.6	50.8	51.3	52.2	53.4	54.0	54.0	53.5	52.8	53.1	53.5	52.5
2012	52.0	51.7	52.0	52.4	53.3	54.3	54.6	54.6	53.7	53.4	53.7	54.3	53.3
2013	52.2	52.1	52.4	52.5	53.9	55.1	55.6	55.5	54.4	54.3	54.5	54.9	54.0
2014	53.3	53.0	53.2	53.5	54.6	55.8	56.2	56.4	55.4	55.5	55.6	56.4	54.9
2015	55.0	54.7	55.1	55.1	55.7	56.9	57.2	56.9	55.8	55.5	55.5	55.9	55.8
2016	54.3	53.6	53.4	52.9	53.4	54.4	54.7	54.3	53.2	52.9	52.8	52.8	53.6
2017	51.3	50.8	50.8	50.8	51.7	53.0	53.6	53.5	52.6	51.8	51.9	52.2	52.0
2018	51.0	50.5	50.6	50.9	51.7	52.9	53.4	53.1	52.3	52.0	52.5	53.4	52.0
Wholesale Trade													
2010	8.3	8.3	8.3	8.3	8.4	8.5	8.4	8.4	8.4	8.4	8.5	8.5	8.4
2011	8.4	8.5	8.5	8.6	8.7	8.8	8.8	8.8	8.8	8.8	8.9	8.9	8.7
2012	8.9	8.9	9.0	9.2	9.2	9.2	9.1	9.1	9.0	9.0	9.0	9.1	9.1
2013	8.9	8.9	9.0	9.0	9.1	9.1	9.1	9.1	9.1	9.2	9.2	9.2	9.1
2014	9.2	9.2	9.2	9.3	9.4	9.5	9.5	9.5	9.4	9.5	9.5	9.6	9.4
2015	9.5	9.5	9.6	9.5	9.5	9.5	9.4	9.3	9.2	9.2	9.1	9.1	9.4
2016	9.0	8.9	8.8	8.6	8.5	8.3	8.3	8.2	8.1	8.1	8.0	8.0	8.4
2017	7.9	7.9	8.0	8.0	8.0	8.1	8.1	8.1	8.1	8.0	8.0	8.0	8.0
2018	8.0	8.0	8.1	8.1	8.1	8.2	8.3	8.3	8.2	8.2	8.2	8.2	8.2
Retail Trade													
2010	28.8	28.7	28.7	28.9	29.5	30.3	30.5	30.2	29.6	29.3	29.3	29.6	29.5
2011	28.2	27.9	28.1	28.4	29.0	29.9	30.4	30.3	29.8	29.3	29.5	29.7	29.2
2012	28.5	28.2	28.3	28.5	29.3	30.3	30.6	30.5	29.8	29.6	29.9	30.1	29.5
2013	28.5	28.3	28.5	28.6	29.7	30.7	31.1	30.9	30.0	29.8	30.0	30.2	29.7
2014	28.7	28.5	28.7	28.9	29.7	30.6	30.9	30.9	30.1	30.1	30.1	30.5	29.8
2015	29.3	29.3	29.6	30.0	30.7	31.6	32.1	31.9	31.2	31.1	31.2	31.4	30.8
2016	30.2	30.0	30.0	30.0	30.6	31.6	31.8	31.6	30.8	30.6	30.5	30.4	30.7
2017	29.3	28.8	28.7	28.8	29.6	30.7	31.1	31.0	30.1	29.4	29.6	29.5	29.7
2018	28.5	28.2	28.2	28.5	29.3	30.2	30.5	30.2	29.6	29.5	29.7	30.0	29.4
Transportation and Utilities													
2010	13.5	13.3	13.2	13.6	13.6	14.0	14.2	14.4	14.4	14.3	14.3	14.5	13.9
2011	14.1	14.2	14.2	14.3	14.5	14.7	14.8	14.9	14.9	14.7	14.7	14.9	14.6
2012	14.6	14.6	14.7	14.7	14.8	14.8	14.9	15.0	14.9	14.8	14.8	15.1	14.8
2013	14.8	14.9	14.9	14.9	15.1	15.3	15.4	15.5	15.3	15.3	15.3	15.5	15.2
2014	15.4	15.3	15.3	15.3	15.5	15.7	15.8	16.0	15.9	15.9	16.0	16.3	15.7
2015	16.2	15.9	15.9	15.6	15.5	15.8	15.7	15.7	15.4	15.2	15.2	15.4	15.6
2016	15.1	14.7	14.6	14.3	14.3	14.5	14.6	14.5	14.3	14.2	14.3	14.4	14.5
2017	14.1	14.1	14.1	14.0	14.1	14.2	14.4	14.4	14.4	14.4	14.3	14.7	14.3
2018	14.5	14.3	14.3	14.3	14.3	14.5	14.6	14.6	14.5	14.3	14.6	15.2	14.5
Information													
2010	3.9	3.9	3.9	3.9	3.9	3.9	3.9	3.9	3.9	3.8	3.8	3.8	3.9
2011	3.8	3.8	3.8	3.8	3.9	3.9	3.9	3.9	3.8	3.8	3.8	3.9	3.8
2012	3.9	3.9	3.9	3.9	3.9	4.0	4.0	4.0	3.9	3.8	3.9	3.9	3.9
2013	3.8	3.8	3.8	3.7	3.8	3.8	3.8	3.8	3.8	3.8	3.8	3.8	3.8
2014	3.8	3.7	3.7	3.7	3.8	3.8	3.8	3.8	3.8	3.8	3.8	3.8	3.8
2015	3.8	3.8	3.8	3.8	3.8	3.8	3.8	3.8	3.8	3.7	3.7	3.8	3.8
2016	3.8	3.8	3.7	3.7	3.7	3.8	3.8	3.8	3.7	3.7	3.7	3.7	3.7
2017	3.7	3.7	3.7	3.7	3.7	3.7	3.7	3.7	3.7	3.6	3.6	3.7	3.7
2018	3.6	3.6	3.6	3.6	3.6	3.6	3.6	3.5	3.5	3.5	3.5	3.5	3.6

1. Employment by Industry: Wyoming, 2010–2018—*Continued*

(Numbers in thousands, not seasonally adjusted)

Industry and year	January	February	March	April	May	June	July	August	September	October	November	December	Annual average
Financial Activities													
2010	10.7	10.7	10.7	10.8	10.9	10.9	10.9	10.8	10.7	10.8	10.7	10.8	10.8
2011	10.7	10.6	10.6	10.7	10.7	10.8	10.8	10.9	10.8	10.7	10.7	10.7	10.7
2012	10.6	10.6	10.7	10.6	10.7	10.9	10.9	11.0	10.8	10.9	10.8	10.8	10.8
2013	10.9	10.9	10.9	11.0	11.1	11.3	11.4	11.4	11.3	11.2	11.2	11.2	11.2
2014	11.0	11.0	11.0	11.0	11.2	11.4	11.4	11.5	11.4	11.4	11.3	11.4	11.3
2015	11.2	11.2	11.1	11.1	11.0	11.1	11.3	11.2	11.1	11.0	11.0	11.0	11.1
2016	10.9	10.9	10.8	10.8	10.8	11.0	11.0	10.9	10.8	10.7	10.7	10.8	10.8
2017	10.7	10.7	10.7	10.7	10.8	11.1	11.0	11.0	11.0	11.0	10.9	11.1	10.9
2018	10.9	10.9	10.9	11.0	11.1	11.2	11.3	11.3	11.1	10.9	10.8	11.0	11.0
Professional and Business Services													
2010	16.1	15.9	16.2	16.9	17.3	18.0	18.4	18.7	18.1	17.6	17.1	16.8	17.3
2011	16.5	16.5	16.7	17.2	17.9	18.6	18.9	19.3	18.6	18.3	18.0	17.8	17.9
2012	17.2	17.3	17.4	17.8	18.1	19.0	18.8	19.1	18.5	18.3	17.8	17.7	18.1
2013	17.0	17.1	17.3	17.9	18.4	19.1	19.2	19.1	18.6	18.6	18.4	17.8	18.2
2014	17.2	17.5	17.6	18.2	18.8	19.3	19.6	19.5	19.0	19.0	18.4	18.3	18.5
2015	17.6	17.7	17.7	18.3	18.8	19.2	19.7	19.7	19.1	18.8	18.3	18.0	18.6
2016	17.1	17.0	17.0	17.6	18.0	18.5	18.8	18.8	18.3	18.1	17.5	17.6	17.9
2017	17.2	17.2	17.3	17.7	18.2	18.7	19.1	19.2	18.8	18.5	18.0	17.9	18.2
2018	17.4	17.2	17.5	18.1	18.7	19.2	19.7	19.7	19.4	19.0	19.0	19.0	18.7
Education and Health Services													
2010	26.1	26.3	26.4	26.4	26.4	25.8	25.7	25.9	26.7	27.0	27.1	26.9	26.4
2011	26.9	27.2	27.4	27.0	27.1	26.1	25.8	26.1	26.9	26.9	26.6	26.9	26.7
2012	26.5	26.7	26.7	26.6	26.7	26.0	25.8	26.2	26.9	26.9	27.0	27.1	26.6
2013	26.8	26.8	27.2	27.1	27.1	26.5	26.2	26.5	27.1	27.1	27.1	27.1	26.9
2014	27.0	27.0	27.1	27.2	27.3	26.5	26.2	26.4	27.0	27.5	26.9	26.9	26.9
2015	26.9	26.9	27.0	27.3	27.4	26.6	26.5	26.6	27.4	28.0	27.4	27.7	27.1
2016	27.4	27.7	28.0	28.1	28.0	27.2	27.1	27.0	27.8	28.0	27.8	27.7	27.7
2017	27.7	27.8	27.9	27.8	28.0	27.4	26.9	27.1	28.0	28.0	27.9	28.2	27.7
2018	28.3	28.4	28.6	28.4	28.5	27.7	27.5	27.5	28.3	28.5	28.2	28.0	28.2
Leisure and Hospitality													
2010	29.4	29.6	29.6	29.4	31.6	36.7	38.5	38.5	36.1	32.6	28.9	30.8	32.6
2011	29.8	29.8	30.2	29.3	31.7	37.1	39.1	38.9	36.7	33.1	29.6	31.5	33.1
2012	30.6	30.7	31.1	30.4	32.7	38.1	40.1	39.8	36.8	33.9	30.7	32.1	33.9
2013	31.3	31.3	31.7	31.1	33.4	39.0	40.9	40.5	38.0	34.8	31.0	32.5	34.6
2014	32.1	32.1	32.3	31.9	34.3	39.9	41.6	41.5	38.4	35.5	31.4	33.5	35.4
2015	33.2	33.2	33.4	32.9	35.5	40.8	42.5	42.0	39.2	36.0	31.8	33.3	36.2
2016	32.8	32.6	32.9	32.0	35.1	40.8	42.3	42.0	38.8	35.8	31.7	33.2	35.8
2017	33.1	33.0	33.4	32.5	35.7	41.0	42.7	42.6	39.4	36.3	32.4	33.7	36.3
2018	33.5	33.4	33.5	32.9	36.3	41.2	42.8	42.0	38.8	34.7	31.1	32.6	36.1
Other Services													
2010	13.5	13.6	13.7	14.0	14.0	14.1	14.4	14.4	14.3	14.3	14.3	14.4	14.1
2011	14.3	14.4	14.6	14.8	14.8	15.2	15.4	15.2	15.1	15.1	15.0	15.0	14.9
2012	15.0	15.0	15.1	15.2	15.3	15.6	15.6	15.6	15.5	15.3	15.2	15.3	15.3
2013	15.2	15.2	15.3	15.5	15.5	15.8	15.9	15.7	15.5	15.7	15.1	15.0	15.5
2014	15.0	14.9	15.0	15.4	15.6	15.8	15.9	15.8	15.7	15.8	15.7	15.8	15.5
2015	15.8	15.9	16.0	16.0	16.2	16.5	16.6	16.4	16.2	16.2	16.1	16.1	16.2
2016	16.0	15.9	16.1	16.1	16.2	16.1	16.1	16.0	16.0	15.9	15.8	15.8	16.0
2017	15.8	15.8	15.9	16.1	16.3	16.6	16.7	16.6	16.4	16.4	16.2	16.2	16.3
2018	16.1	16.1	16.2	16.2	16.4	16.7	16.7	16.5	16.3	16.8	16.7	16.4	16.4
Government													
2010	70.1	71.6	72.7	72.1	75.0	73.8	65.9	65.8	71.8	72.8	72.4	72.4	71.4
2011	70.6	72.2	72.8	72.7	74.0	73.3	69.1	68.5	72.5	73.2	72.8	73.0	72.1
2012	71.3	73.0	73.4	72.6	74.3	73.1	69.5	68.3	72.6	73.5	73.1	73.3	72.3
2013	71.6	72.7	73.2	72.8	73.9	73.0	68.2	68.0	71.9	72.7	72.2	72.4	71.9
2014	70.6	71.8	72.6	71.9	73.0	71.6	68.4	67.2	71.3	72.2	71.6	71.9	71.2
2015	69.8	71.0	72.0	71.6	73.0	71.7	67.7	67.9	72.0	73.0	72.5	72.6	71.2
2016	70.6	71.9	72.6	72.0	73.3	72.3	67.7	67.8	71.2	71.6	71.3	71.5	71.2
2017	69.4	70.9	71.5	71.0	72.2	70.8	66.5	66.8	70.0	70.4	69.9	69.9	69.9
2018	67.7	69.1	69.6	69.6	70.4	69.3	65.6	66.0	69.3	70.3	70.0	69.8	68.9

2. Average Weekly Hours by Selected Industry: Wyoming, 2014–2018

(Not seasonally adjusted)

Industry and year	January	February	March	April	May	June	July	August	September	October	November	December	Annual average
Total Private													
2014	34.9	36.3	35.9	35.4	35.2	36.3	35.4	36.2	35.6	35.8	35.6	35.1	35.6
2015	34.7	35.9	35.4	34.9	35.3	35.8	35.6	36.3	34.5	34.4	34.8	33.4	35.1
2016	33.5	33.4	33.3	32.1	33.1	32.9	33.2	33.7	33.3	34.0	33.2	32.5	33.2
2017	33.5	33.0	33.0	34.4	34.0	34.6	35.3	34.8	34.3	35.2	34.6	33.7	34.2
2018	33.8	33.8	34.2	34.7	34.2	34.9	35.3	35.4	36.0	34.9	35.5	36.0	34.9
Goods-Producing													
2014	40.5	41.9	41.7	42.3	41.6	42.2	40.7	42.7	41.5	42.6	40.5	41.6	41.7
2015	40.2	40.6	40.0	40.0	41.4	41.5	41.5	41.9	39.7	41.6	41.3	39.8	40.8
2016	39.2	38.4	39.4	40.0	40.4	39.8	40.0	41.4	40.8	41.5	41.2	38.7	40.1
2017	38.7	39.2	39.3	41.0	41.5	41.8	41.2	41.1	40.2	41.4	41.4	39.4	40.6
2018	40.2	39.7	40.4	41.2	41.7	42.4	42.2	42.7	42.7	41.9	43.4	44.0	41.9
Mining and Logging													
2014	45.1	46.2	45.7	45.8	44.9	44.0	43.3	45.0	44.2	45.3	44.5	46.3	45.0
2015	43.8	44.5	44.0	42.9	44.0	42.5	42.8	43.0	41.7	42.6	43.1	42.5	43.2
2016	41.7	41.5	41.4	41.5	40.0	40.5	41.7	42.9	42.6	43.7	43.1	41.6	41.9
2017	42.0	41.0	41.8	42.2	44.1	45.1	44.3	43.6	42.5	43.8	45.9	44.2	43.4
2018	44.0	43.2	43.9	44.9	43.8	45.0	45.9	45.7	46.9	44.5	46.7	49.4	45.3
Construction													
2014	38.3	39.9	39.6	40.7	40.5	42.0	40.0	42.5	41.0	42.3	39.2	40.5	40.6
2015	39.0	39.3	38.8	39.3	40.7	41.6	41.3	41.8	39.9	42.0	41.0	39.2	40.4
2016	37.7	36.7	38.6	39.1	40.5	39.3	39.3	41.2	40.3	40.5	40.4	38.3	39.3
2017	37.7	39.9	39.3	42.1	41.6	41.1	40.4	40.4	39.3	40.8	39.4	39.0	40.1
2018	38.0	37.6	38.5	39.4	41.5	43.1	42.5	43.6	42.6	42.7	44.3	43.3	41.6
Trade, Transportation, and Utilities													
2014	35.4	36.1	36.3	35.3	35.2	35.4	35.1	35.4	35.2	35.0	35.5	34.5	35.4
2015	34.9	36.1	35.7	35.0	35.0	36.0	35.6	35.8	35.2	34.6	34.6	33.8	35.2
2016	33.4	33.7	33.3	34.1	34.4	34.4	34.5	34.7	34.5	34.9	34.0	34.7	34.2
2017	35.1	33.8	34.0	35.1	34.3	34.7	35.9	34.9	34.6	35.7	35.2	35.0	34.8
2018	33.9	34.1	34.4	35.5	35.8	35.8	36.4	36.1	36.6	35.8	35.9	36.6	35.6
Professional and Business Services													
2014	34.0	35.7	34.8	34.5	34.6	36.4	36.1	36.1	35.7	35.7	35.6	35.0	35.4
2015	34.0	35.1	34.9	35.4	35.1	35.4	35.4	36.8	34.9	34.2	34.8	33.4	35.0
2016	33.5	34.4	33.9	34.6	35.2	34.8	34.4	35.4	34.5	34.6	33.9	33.3	34.4
2017	35.0	33.8	32.9	35.2	34.9	35.2	35.8	34.9	35.3	35.8	34.6	33.9	34.7
2018	32.9	33.3	33.3	34.0	33.4	34.3	34.0	34.3	33.6	32.7	33.2	32.2	33.4
Education and Health Services													
2014	33.4	35.1	34.2	33.6	33.7	34.5	33.4	32.9	33.4	33.0	33.5	33.4	33.7
2015	33.4	35.1	34.6	33.8	33.8	34.2	33.3	34.6	33.6	33.6	34.9	33.1	34.0
2016	33.9	34.2	34.2	34.3	35.4	35.4	35.3	35.0	35.2	36.2	35.2	34.7	34.9
2017	35.7	35.3	34.4	35.5	33.7	33.9	34.7	33.6	34.5	34.7	34.3	33.6	34.5
2018	33.6	34.1	34.1	34.9	33.1	33.3	33.8	33.3	34.7	33.4	33.0	34.1	33.8
Leisure and Hospitality													
2014	24.9	26.1	26.4	24.6	25.6	28.7	28.5	28.7	27.4	26.4	26.4	25.7	26.7
2015	26.1	27.4	27.2	25.9	26.7	28.6	29.5	30.2	28.3	25.2	25.0	24.5	27.2
2016	25.2	25.3	25.2	24.9	26.9	27.3	27.9	28.0	26.2	24.6	23.5	23.0	25.8
2017	24.5	24.5	24.7	23.5	24.5	27.4	28.7	28.7	26.9	25.6	24.1	24.4	25.8
2018	25.4	25.5	25.8	24.1	23.9	27.0	28.0	26.8	26.4	23.5	22.8	23.6	25.4
Other Services													
2014	35.4	35.6	35.0	35.6	33.9	35.4	35.0	34.8	34.5	33.3	32.2	30.6	34.3
2015	31.4	32.9	31.8	31.3	30.0	30.3	29.8	30.5	29.3	28.4	28.8	26.7	30.1
2016	26.2	27.0	26.4	26.4	27.2	27.2	27.7	26.8	27.1	29.0	27.1	26.7	27.1
2017	27.9	27.9	27.8	29.1	27.4	28.3	29.6	28.8	29.1	29.8	28.8	28.4	28.6
2018	28.0	29.0	28.2	29.3	29.1	30.3	31.9	32.2	31.8	31.3	29.4	30.4	30.1

3. Average Hourly Earnings by Selected Industry: Wyoming, 2014–2018

(Dollars, not seasonally adjusted)

Industry and year	January	February	March	April	May	June	July	August	September	October	November	December	Annual average
Total Private													
2014	23.31	23.24	23.39	23.37	23.27	22.70	22.61	22.90	23.33	23.25	23.48	23.28	23.17
2015	23.26	23.24	23.29	23.22	23.04	22.60	22.69	22.97	23.21	23.33	23.38	23.22	23.11
2016	23.01	23.16	23.21	23.49	23.27	22.65	22.72	22.83	23.25	23.76	23.77	23.65	23.22
2017	23.60	23.66	23.62	24.21	24.08	23.37	23.55	23.30	24.09	24.27	24.08	24.53	23.86
2018	24.71	24.73	24.78	25.22	25.23	24.97	25.06	25.15	25.79	26.00	26.50	26.36	25.39
Goods-Producing													
2014	28.19	27.71	28.00	27.83	27.83	26.93	27.19	27.26	27.88	27.68	27.89	27.69	27.66
2015	27.85	27.58	27.58	27.69	27.54	27.39	27.56	27.77	27.91	27.77	28.03	28.49	27.76
2016	28.55	28.63	28.65	28.47	28.64	27.99	27.95	28.09	28.47	28.77	28.39	28.57	28.43
2017	28.72	28.43	28.42	28.76	28.82	28.01	28.10	28.22	28.94	28.96	28.39	29.32	28.59
2018	29.68	29.29	29.37	29.64	29.71	29.21	29.13	29.37	29.97	29.98	30.22	30.06	29.65
Mining and Logging													
2014	35.13	33.85	33.93	33.72	33.83	33.37	33.82	33.75	34.85	34.04	33.71	34.20	34.02
2015	34.85	34.16	34.36	34.47	34.40	35.04	35.31	36.07	36.34	35.24	35.00	35.69	35.04
2016	36.30	35.79	35.89	35.35	35.77	35.87	34.82	34.14	35.14	35.54	34.95	35.10	35.40
2017	36.04	35.93	35.65	35.86	34.87	34.38	34.52	34.43	35.32	35.36	33.94	35.39	35.11
2018	35.05	34.16	34.06	34.38	34.68	33.92	33.62	33.79	34.36	34.99	34.74	33.60	34.27
Construction													
2014	25.54	25.45	26.19	26.24	26.34	24.96	24.99	24.98	25.30	25.31	25.32	24.99	25.44
2015	25.21	25.14	25.15	25.68	25.50	24.96	25.20	25.28	25.13	25.69	25.92	25.97	25.40
2016	25.31	25.48	25.70	25.78	26.48	25.05	25.32	26.23	25.89	26.17	25.84	26.06	25.79
2017	25.64	25.07	25.24	25.59	26.14	25.43	25.35	25.72	26.40	26.27	26.65	27.22	25.90
2018	27.59	27.36	27.57	27.95	28.06	27.16	26.99	27.36	28.03	28.13	28.20	28.24	27.73
Trade, Transportation, and Utilities													
2014	21.94	22.28	22.33	22.39	21.89	21.68	21.43	21.58	21.79	21.52	21.79	21.55	21.84
2015	21.33	21.51	21.95	21.71	21.30	21.10	21.31	21.60	20.91	20.65	20.75	20.39	21.21
2016	20.62	20.63	21.05	21.15	21.31	20.77	20.98	21.17	21.56	21.69	21.81	21.59	21.19
2017	21.96	22.04	22.03	22.68	22.21	22.07	22.41	22.01	22.18	22.20	22.08	22.19	22.17
2018	22.36	22.32	22.54	23.11	22.51	22.46	22.43	22.32	23.19	22.93	23.25	23.28	22.73
Professional and Business Services													
2014	26.07	25.80	25.92	26.16	26.05	25.68	25.88	26.39	26.67	26.67	26.81	26.98	26.26
2015	27.52	27.27	27.23	27.03	26.63	26.10	26.03	26.12	27.55	27.16	26.39	26.38	26.77
2016	25.83	25.77	25.86	26.10	25.93	25.90	25.90	26.15	26.53	27.40	27.17	27.71	26.35
2017	27.42	27.36	26.87	27.02	26.74	26.59	26.71	26.38	26.57	26.71	26.78	27.47	26.87
2018	27.93	28.05	27.16	28.09	28.07	27.79	27.72	27.51	28.90	29.14	29.77	30.08	28.35
Education and Health Services													
2014	21.91	21.65	21.68	21.30	21.36	21.15	21.34	21.43	21.86	21.45	21.97	22.17	21.61
2015	22.37	22.87	22.83	22.65	22.68	22.65	22.85	22.94	22.82	22.60	22.71	22.42	22.70
2016	22.05	22.16	21.96	21.97	22.18	21.91	22.19	22.11	22.03	22.30	21.99	22.14	22.08
2017	22.41	22.64	22.47	22.72	23.24	23.52	23.91	23.76	23.80	24.36	23.53	24.28	23.38
2018	24.06	23.61	23.62	23.41	24.00	24.35	25.11	24.79	24.50	25.15	25.33	24.90	24.39
Leisure and Hospitality													
2014	13.15	13.25	13.33	12.93	12.93	12.99	13.02	13.33	13.48	13.53	13.84	14.11	13.31
2015	14.06	14.30	14.14	13.91	13.56	13.44	13.46	13.70	13.68	14.21	14.21	14.44	13.72
2016	13.98	14.15	14.17	14.07	13.52	13.68	13.89	13.90	14.26	14.21	14.21	14.44	14.02
2017	14.98	15.10	14.89	14.69	14.33	14.22	14.33	14.43	14.86	14.73	14.76	15.10	14.67
2018	16.03	16.08	16.15	15.59	15.60	15.34	15.43	15.66	15.63	15.44	15.42	15.95	15.68
Other Services													
2014	19.47	19.65	19.57	19.26	20.04	19.78	19.06	19.21	19.39	19.13	19.17	19.26	19.42
2015	19.93	20.89	20.72	20.07	21.27	19.96	20.84	21.65	20.65	20.01	20.53	20.68	20.60
2016	20.71	20.76	20.72	20.22	21.07	20.27	20.75	21.60	21.97	22.76	22.11	22.54	21.30
2017	21.96	21.76	21.90	22.32	22.65	21.51	21.45	21.57	21.61	21.88	21.02	21.77	21.78
2018	21.40	21.19	21.73	22.00	22.37	22.67	22.11	22.51	22.13	21.69	21.25	21.73	21.91

4. Average Weekly Earnings by Selected Industry: Wyoming, 2014–2018

(Dollars, not seasonally adjusted)

Industry and year	January	February	March	April	May	June	July	August	September	October	November	December	Annual average
Total Private													
2014	813.52	843.61	839.70	827.30	819.10	824.01	800.39	828.98	830.55	832.35	835.89	817.13	824.85
2015	807.12	834.32	824.47	810.38	813.31	809.08	807.76	833.81	800.75	802.55	813.62	775.55	811.16
2016	770.84	773.54	772.89	754.03	770.24	745.19	754.30	769.37	774.23	807.84	789.16	768.63	770.90
2017	790.60	780.78	779.46	832.82	818.72	808.60	831.32	810.84	826.29	854.30	833.17	826.66	816.01
2018	835.20	835.87	847.48	875.13	862.87	871.45	884.62	890.31	928.44	907.40	940.75	948.96	886.11
Goods-Producing													
2014	1,141.70	1,161.05	1,167.60	1,177.21	1,157.73	1,136.45	1,106.63	1,164.00	1,157.02	1,179.17	1,129.55	1,151.90	1,153.42
2015	1,119.57	1,119.75	1,103.20	1,107.60	1,140.16	1,136.69	1,143.74	1,163.56	1,108.03	1,155.23	1,157.64	1,133.90	1,132.61
2016	1,119.16	1,099.39	1,128.81	1,138.80	1,157.06	1,114.00	1,118.00	1,162.93	1,161.58	1,193.96	1,169.67	1,105.66	1,140.04
2017	1,111.46	1,114.46	1,116.91	1,179.16	1,196.03	1,170.82	1,157.72	1,159.84	1,163.39	1,198.94	1,175.35	1,155.21	1,160.75
2018	1,193.14	1,162.81	1,186.55	1,221.17	1,238.91	1,238.50	1,229.29	1,254.10	1,279.72	1,256.16	1,311.55	1,322.64	1,242.34
Mining and Logging													
2014	1,584.36	1,563.87	1,550.60	1,544.38	1,518.97	1,468.28	1,464.41	1,518.75	1,540.37	1,542.01	1,500.10	1,583.46	1,530.90
2015	1,526.43	1,520.12	1,511.84	1,478.76	1,513.60	1,489.20	1,511.27	1,551.01	1,515.38	1,501.22	1,508.50	1,516.83	1,513.73
2016	1,513.71	1,485.29	1,485.85	1,467.03	1,430.80	1,452.74	1,451.99	1,464.61	1,496.96	1,553.10	1,506.35	1,460.16	1,483.26
2017	1,513.68	1,473.13	1,490.17	1,513.29	1,537.77	1,550.54	1,529.24	1,501.15	1,501.10	1,548.77	1,557.85	1,564.24	1,523.77
2018	1,542.20	1,475.71	1,495.23	1,543.66	1,518.98	1,526.40	1,543.16	1,544.20	1,611.48	1,557.06	1,622.36	1,659.84	1,552.43
Construction													
2014	978.18	1,015.46	1,037.12	1,067.97	1,066.77	1,048.32	999.60	1,061.65	1,037.30	1,070.61	992.54	1,012.10	1,032.86
2015	983.19	988.00	975.82	1,009.22	1,037.85	1,038.34	1,040.76	1,056.70	1,002.69	1,078.98	1,062.72	1,018.02	1,026.16
2016	954.19	935.12	992.02	1,008.00	1,072.44	984.47	995.08	1,080.68	1,043.37	1,059.89	1,043.94	998.10	1,013.55
2017	966.63	1,000.29	991.93	1,077.34	1,087.42	1,045.17	1,024.14	1,039.09	1,037.52	1,071.82	1,050.01	1,061.58	1,038.59
2018	1,048.42	1,028.74	1,061.45	1,101.23	1,164.49	1,170.60	1,147.08	1,192.90	1,194.08	1,201.15	1,249.26	1,222.79	1,153.57
Trade, Transportation, and Utilities													
2014	776.68	804.31	810.58	790.37	770.53	767.47	752.19	763.93	767.01	753.20	773.55	743.48	773.14
2015	744.42	776.51	783.62	759.85	745.50	759.60	758.64	773.28	736.03	714.49	717.95	689.18	746.59
2016	688.71	695.23	700.97	721.22	733.06	714.49	723.81	734.60	743.82	756.98	741.54	749.17	724.70
2017	770.80	744.95	749.02	796.07	761.80	765.83	804.52	768.15	767.43	792.54	777.22	776.65	771.52
2018	758.00	761.11	775.38	820.41	805.86	804.07	816.45	805.75	848.75	820.89	834.68	852.05	809.19
Professional and Business Services													
2014	886.38	921.06	902.02	902.52	901.33	934.75	934.27	952.68	952.12	952.12	954.44	944.30	929.60
2015	935.68	957.18	950.33	956.86	934.71	923.94	921.46	961.22	961.50	928.87	918.37	881.09	936.95
2016	865.31	886.49	876.65	903.06	912.74	901.32	890.96	925.71	915.29	948.04	921.06	922.74	906.44
2017	959.70	924.77	884.02	951.10	933.23	935.97	956.22	920.66	937.92	956.22	926.59	931.23	932.39
2018	918.90	934.07	904.43	955.06	937.54	953.20	942.48	943.59	971.04	952.88	988.36	968.58	946.89
Education and Health Services													
2014	731.79	759.92	741.46	715.68	719.83	729.68	712.76	705.05	730.12	707.85	736.00	740.48	728.26
2015	747.16	802.74	789.92	765.57	766.58	774.63	760.91	793.72	766.75	759.36	792.58	742.10	771.80
2016	747.50	757.87	751.03	753.57	785.17	775.61	783.31	773.85	775.46	807.26	774.05	768.26	770.59
2017	800.04	799.19	772.97	806.56	783.19	797.33	829.68	798.34	821.10	845.29	807.08	815.81	806.61
2018	808.42	805.10	805.44	817.01	794.40	810.86	848.72	825.51	850.15	840.01	835.89	849.09	824.38
Leisure and Hospitality													
2014	327.44	345.83	351.91	318.08	331.01	372.81	371.07	382.57	369.35	357.19	365.38	362.63	355.38
2015	366.97	391.82	384.61	360.27	362.05	384.38	394.12	406.49	387.71	344.74	340.75	336.63	373.18
2016	352.30	358.00	357.08	350.34	363.69	373.46	387.53	389.20	373.61	349.57	333.94	332.12	361.72
2017	367.01	369.95	367.78	345.22	351.09	389.63	411.27	414.14	399.73	377.09	355.72	368.44	378.49
2018	407.16	410.04	416.67	375.72	372.84	414.18	432.04	419.69	412.63	362.84	351.58	376.42	398.27
Other Services													
2014	689.24	699.54	684.95	685.66	679.36	700.21	667.10	668.51	668.96	637.03	617.27	589.36	666.11
2015	625.80	687.28	658.90	628.19	638.10	604.79	621.03	660.33	605.05	568.28	591.26	552.16	620.06
2016	542.60	560.52	547.01	533.81	573.10	551.34	574.78	578.88	595.39	660.04	599.18	601.82	577.23
2017	612.68	607.10	608.82	649.51	620.61	608.73	634.92	621.22	628.85	652.02	605.38	618.27	622.91
2018	599.20	614.51	612.79	644.60	650.97	686.90	705.31	724.82	703.73	678.90	624.75	660.59	659.49

PART B

METROPOLITAN STATISTICAL AREA (MSA) DATA

METROPOLITAN STATISTICAL AREA (MSA) NOTES

Part B provides employment data for the 75 largest metropolitan statistical areas (MSAs) and New England city and town areas (NECTAs) in the United States from 2010 through 2018. As mentioned in the technical notes, all employment data are for MSAs unless otherwise noted. NECTAs are similar to MSAs but are defined by cities and towns rather than counties in the New England region.

According to the 2018 estimates from the Census Bureau, New York-Newark-Jersey City, NY-NJ-PA metro area, was the largest MSA in the United States—with a population of 19,979,477. Los Angeles-Long Beach-Anaheim, CA followed with a population of 13,291,486. Although the New York area was the most populated MSA, it was not among the fastest growing 75 largest MSAs. The fastest growing MSAs between 2017 and 2018 was Austin–Round Rock–San Marcos, TX with a growth rate of 2.5 percent followed by Orlando-Kissimmee-Sanford, FL with a growth rate of 2.4 percent and Las Vegas-Henderson-Paradise, NV, with a growth rate of 2.2 percent. MSAs in the South and West typically had higher growth rates. Six MSAs among the 75 largest experienced a decline in growth.

Austin-Round Rock, TX was also the fastest growing MSA in terms of total nonfarm employment. Total nonfarm employment grew 36.1 percent there from 2010 to 2018 while it grew 32.7 percent in Nashville-Davidson—Murfreesboro—Franklin, TN. Two of the top five fastest growing MSAs were in Florida. Total nonfarm employment grew 30.4 percent in Orlando-Kissimmee-Sanford, FL and 29.8 percent in North Port-Sarasota-Bradenton, FL. Total nonfarm employment increased in all of the 75 largest MSAs from 2010 to 2018.

Among the 75 largest MSAs, the unemployment rate increased in two MSAs, remained stable in three other MSAs, and declined in seventy MSAs between 2017 and 2018. Denver-Aurora-Lakewood, CO, experienced the greatest increase in unemployment growing from 2.6 percent to 3.2 percent in just one year. Bakersfield, CA experienced the greatest decline in unemployment from 2017 to 2018 dropping 1.2 percent but still had the highest unemployment rate at 8.0 percent. Among all places with a population of one million or more, Cleveland-Elyria, OH had the highest unemployment rate at 5.1 percent followed by Las Vegas-Henderson-Paradise, NV at 4.8 percent and New Orleans-Metairie, LA at 4.6 percent.

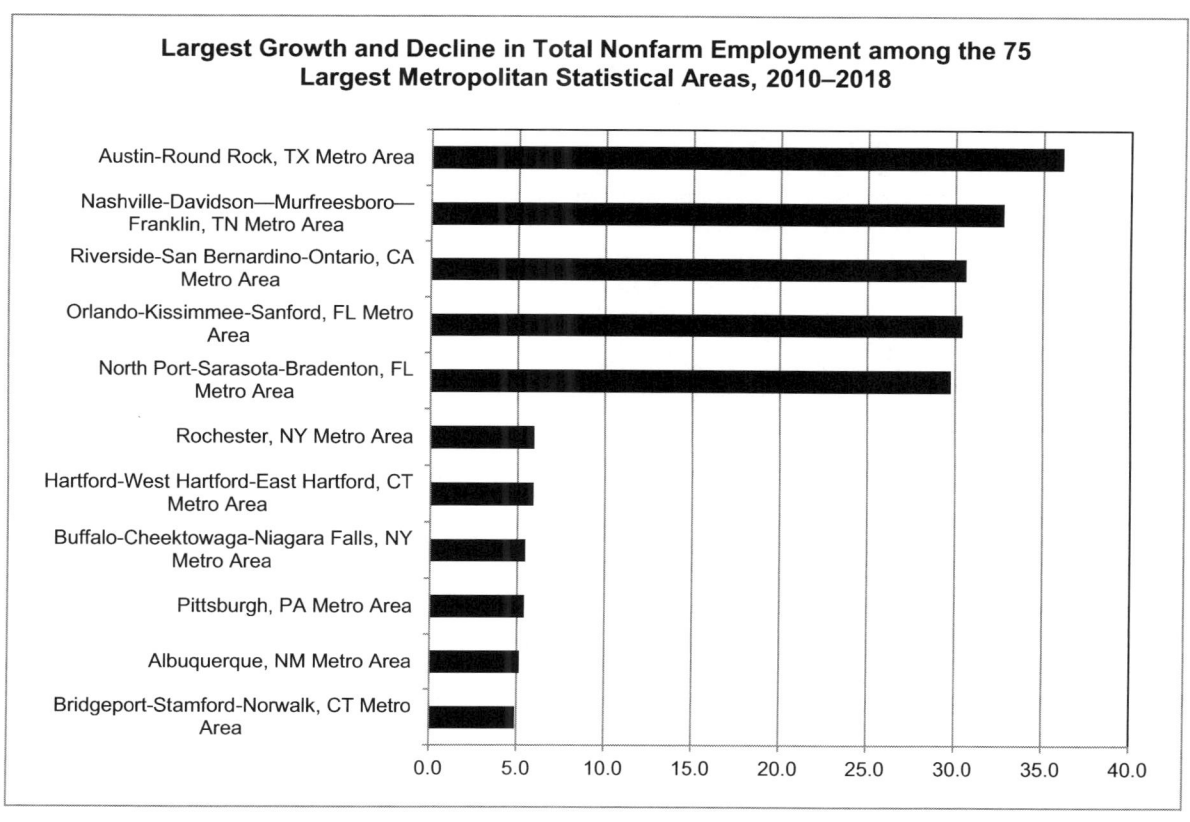

Largest Growth and Decline in Total Nonfarm Employment among the 75 Largest Metropolitan Statistical Areas, 2010–2018

Metropolitan Statistical Areas: Employment and Unemployment Rates

(Seventy-five largest MSAs; ranked by population)

Rank	Metropolitan statistical area	2018 Census population estimates[1]	Total nonfarm employment		Percent change in total nonfarm employment, 2010–2018	Unemployment rates	
			2010	2018		2017	2018
1	New York-Newark-Jersey City, NY-NJ-PA Metro Area	19,979,477	8,599.2	9,829.2	14.3	4.5	4.0
2	Los Angeles-Long Beach-Anaheim, CA Metro Area	13,291,486	5,296.2	6,159.4	16.3	4.5	4.2
3	Chicago-Naperville-Elgin, IL-IN-WI Metro Area	9,498,716	4,244.5	4,745.4	11.8	4.8	4.0
4	Dallas-Fort Worth-Arlington, TX Metro Area	7,539,711	2,929.4	3,683.2	25.7	3.7	3.5
5	Houston-The Woodlands-Sugar Land, TX Metro Area	6,997,384	2,567.3	3,084.7	20.2	5.0	4.3
6	Washington-Arlington-Alexandria, DC-VA-MD-WV Metro Area	6,249,950	2,981.0	3,302.0	10.8	3.7	3.3
7	Miami-Fort Lauderdale-West Palm Beach, FL Metro Area	6,198,782	2,195.3	2,680.6	22.1	4.3	3.6
8	Philadelphia-Camden-Wilmington, PA-NJ-DE-MD Metro Area	6,096,372	2,695.7	2,938.6	9.0	4.7	4.2
9	Atlanta-Sandy Springs-Roswell, GA Metro Area	5,949,951	2,276.0	2,785.9	22.4	4.5	3.8
10	Boston-Cambridge-Newton, MA-NH Metro Area	4,875,390	1,617.3	1,871.0	15.7	3.4	3.0
11	Phoenix-Mesa-Scottsdale, AZ Metro Area	4,857,962	1,691.6	2,107.3	24.6	4.3	4.2
12	San Francisco-Oakland-Hayward, CA Metro Area	4,729,484	1,926.7	2,440.8	26.7	3.3	2.7
13	Riverside-San Bernardino-Ontario, CA Metro Area	4,622,361	1,151.5	1,504.2	30.6	5.1	4.2
14	Detroit-Warren-Dearborn, MI Metro Area	4,326,442	1,735.9	2,031.5	17.0	4.6	4.3
15	Seattle-Tacoma-Bellevue, WA Metro Area	3,939,363	1,667.4	2,047.2	22.8	4.1	3.9
16	Minneapolis-St. Paul-Bloomington, MN-WI Metro Area	3,629,190	1,749.8	2,011.1	14.9	3.1	2.7
17	San Diego-Carlsbad, CA Metro Area	3,343,364	1,240.7	1,484.6	19.7	4.0	3.3
18	Tampa-St. Petersburg-Clearwater, FL Metro Area	3,142,663	1,105.9	1,351.7	22.2	4.0	3.5
19	Denver-Aurora-Lakewood, CO Metro Area	2,932,415	1,193.9	1,501.0	25.7	2.6	3.2
20	St. Louis, MO-IL Metro Area	2,805,465	1,283.9	1,385.3	7.9	3.8	3.4
21	Baltimore-Columbia-Towson, MD Metro Area	2,802,789	1,272.8	1,414.4	11.1	4.4	4.0
22	Orlando-Kissimmee-Sanford, FL Metro Area	2,572,962	992.6	1,294.6	30.4	3.9	3.3
23	Charlotte-Concord-Gastonia, NC-SC Metro Area	2,569,213	954.2	1,206.1	26.4	4.3	3.6
24	San Antonio-New Braunfels, TX Metro Area	2,518,036	855.0	1,056.8	23.6	3.5	3.3
25	Portland-Vancouver-Hillsboro, OR-WA Metro Area	2,478,810	979.7	1,196.1	22.1	3.9	3.9
26	Sacramento--Roseville--Arden-Arcade, CA Metro Area	2,345,210	831.4	999.5	20.2	4.5	3.7
27	Pittsburgh, PA Metro Area	2,324,743	1,125.6	1,186.2	5.4	5.0	4.3
28	Las Vegas-Henderson-Paradise, NV Metro Area	2,231,647	803.7	1,006.7	25.3	5.3	4.8
29	Cincinnati, OH-KY-IN Metro Area	2,190,209	981.7	1,108.4	12.9	4.3	4.0
30	Austin-Round Rock, TX Metro Area	2,168,316	785.5	1,069.1	36.1	3.1	2.9
31	Kansas City, MO-KS Metro Area	2,143,651	966.2	1,096.5	13.5	3.8	3.4
32	Columbus, OH Metro Area	2,106,541	920.3	1,099.5	19.5	4.1	3.8
33	Cleveland-Elyria, OH Metro Area	2,057,009	990.9	1,067.4	7.7	5.6	5.1
34	Indianapolis-Carmel-Anderson, IN Metro Area	2,048,703	912.3	1,070.8	17.4	3.3	3.2
35	San Jose-Sunnyvale-Santa Clara, CA Metro Area	1,999,107	873.7	1,125.2	28.8	3.3	2.7
36	Nashville-Davidson--Murfreesboro--Franklin, TN Metro Area	1,930,961	762.5	1,012.1	32.7	2.9	2.7
37	Virginia Beach-Norfolk-Newport News, VA-NC Metro Area	1,728,733	737.1	790.5	7.2	4.1	3.3
38	Providence-Warwick, RI-MA Metro Area	1,621,337	540.9	592.1	9.5	4.4	4.1
39	Milwaukee-Waukesha-West Allis, WI Metro Area	1,576,113	808.5	873.5	8.0	3.5	3.2
40	Jacksonville, FL Metro Area	1,534,701	579.9	708.4	22.2	4.0	3.4
41	Oklahoma City, OK Metro Area	1,396,445	566.9	649.6	14.6	3.8	3.1
42	Raleigh, NC Metro Area	1,362,540	500.1	632.8	26.5	3.9	3.4
43	Memphis, TN-MS-AR Metro Area	1,350,620	592.4	648.6	9.5	4.3	4.1
44	Richmond, VA Metro Area	1,306,172	591.7	677.6	14.5	3.9	3.2
45	Louisville/Jefferson County, KY-IN Metro Area	1,297,301	580.4	669.5	15.4	4.1	3.9
46	New Orleans-Metairie, LA Metro Area	1,270,399	533.0	577.4	8.3	4.8	4.6
47	Salt Lake City, UT Metro Area	1,222,540	587.3	732.9	24.8	3.1	3.0
48	Hartford-West Hartford-East Hartford, CT Metro Area	1,206,300	549.5	581.9	5.9	4.7	4.1
49	Birmingham-Hoover, AL Metro Area	1,151,801	496.6	538.5	8.4	4.1	3.5
50	Buffalo-Cheektowaga-Niagara Falls, NY Metro Area	1,130,152	535.0	564.1	5.4	5.3	4.6
51	Rochester, NY Metro Area	1,071,082	508.5	538.6	5.9	4.9	4.2
52	Grand Rapids-Wyoming, MI Metro Area	1,069,405	454.7	564.5	24.1	3.5	3.0
53	Tucson, AZ Metro Area	1,039,073	353.3	381.5	8.0	4.5	4.5
54	Fresno, CA Metro Area	994,400	290.5	353.4	21.7	8.5	7.5
55	Tulsa, OK Metro Area	993,797	413.5	454.8	10.0	4.4	3.5

Metropolitan Statistical Areas: Employment and Unemployment Rates—*Continued*

(Seventy-five largest MSAs; ranked by population)

Rank	Metropolitan statistical area	2018 Census population estimates[1]	Total nonfarm employment		Percent change in total nonfarm employment, 2010–2018	Unemployment rates	
			2010	2018		2017	2018
56	Urban Honolulu, HI Metro Area	980,080	434.4	477.7	10.0	2.3	2.3
57	Worcester, MA-CT Metro Area	947,866	260.2	286.9	10.3	4.0	3.6
58	Bridgeport-Stamford-Norwalk, CT Metro Area	943,823	389.1	408.1	4.9	4.7	4.1
59	Omaha-Council Bluffs, NE-IA Metro Area	942,198	459.1	502.4	9.4	3.0	2.9
60	Albuquerque, NM Metro Area	915,927	373.6	392.8	5.1	5.4	4.7
61	Greenville-Anderson-Mauldin, SC Metro Area	906,626	354.5	424.9	19.9	3.8	3.1
62	Bakersfield, CA Metro Area	896,764	230.4	266.9	15.8	9.2	8.0
63	Knoxville, TN Metro Area	883,309	358.2	399.7	11.6	3.6	3.3
64	Albany-Schenectady-Troy, NY Metro Area	883,169	433.4	471.9	8.9	4.3	3.8
65	McAllen-Edinburg-Mission, TX Metro Area	865,939	220.7	264.2	19.7	7.5	6.6
66	New Haven-Milford, CT Metro Area	857,620	265.1	285.4	7.7	4.7	4.0
67	Oxnard-Thousand Oaks-Ventura, CA Metro Area	850,967	278.1	308.9	11.1	4.5	3.8
68	El Paso, TX Metro Area	845,553	280.8	317.3	13.0	4.6	4.2
69	Allentown-Bethlehem-Easton, PA-NJ Metro Area	842,913	333.6	374.3	12.2	4.9	4.5
70	Columbia, SC Metro Area	832,666	346.2	401.1	15.9	4.1	2.3
71	Baton Rouge, LA Metro Area	831,310	365.0	410.1	12.4	4.5	4.4
72	North Port-Sarasota-Bradenton, FL Metro Area	821,573	237.3	307.9	29.8	4.0	3.4
73	Dayton, OH Metro Area	806,548	360.7	390.0	8.1	4.6	4.3
74	Charleston-North Charleston, SC Metro Area	787,643	287.4	366.0	27.3	3.7	2.9
75	Greensboro-High Point, NC Metro Area	767,711	336.6	360.2	7.0	4.7	4.1

Employment by Industry: New York-Newark-Jersey City, NY-NJ-PA, 2010–2018

(Numbers in thousands, not seasonally adjusted)

Industry and year	January	February	March	April	May	June	July	August	September	October	November	December	Annual average
Total Nonfarm													
2010	8,392.5	8,416.3	8,486.3	8,597.0	8,674.4	8,712.5	8,594.6	8,549.7	8,577.8	8,689.3	8,735.8	8,764.4	8,599.2
2011	8,487.7	8,531.5	8,594.2	8,698.7	8,740.0	8,795.0	8,736.3	8,686.2	8,729.9	8,808.3	8,868.0	8,896.9	8,714.4
2012	8,627.2	8,692.0	8,767.1	8,808.7	8,889.2	8,946.6	8,837.3	8,810.9	8,860.3	8,954.9	8,960.6	9,037.5	8,849.4
2013	8,740.1	8,795.8	8,871.9	8,962.1	9,021.0	9,075.1	9,015.4	8,973.7	9,009.4	9,133.8	9,206.7	9,222.5	9,002.3
2014	8,904.5	8,956.0	9,030.6	9,134.3	9,216.6	9,269.1	9,214.7	9,177.7	9,203.7	9,325.5	9,398.4	9,430.5	9,188.5
2015	9,117.1	9,164.7	9,232.7	9,323.7	9,409.1	9,462.6	9,416.1	9,371.5	9,387.9	9,524.0	9,587.3	9,609.0	9,383.8
2016	9,294.5	9,350.4	9,429.2	9,520.4	9,551.9	9,625.2	9,579.8	9,534.1	9,565.6	9,658.3	9,725.1	9,756.2	9,549.2
2017	9,458.9	9,523.4	9,574.3	9,632.6	9,729.7	9,813.2	9,731.3	9,682.1	9,710.9	9,821.2	9,893.4	9,920.5	9,707.6
2018	9,581.4	9,671.0	9,722.6	9,792.1	9,868.4	9,949.8	9,859.7	9,803.8	9,811.5	9,923.1	9,980.7	9,985.7	9,829.2
Total Private													
2010	7,039.2	7,049.0	7,111.5	7,212.2	7,255.4	7,312.1	7,259.9	7,253.5	7,268.9	7,339.2	7,380.3	7,413.5	7,241.2
2011	7,168.0	7,194.6	7,253.2	7,350.0	7,398.5	7,452.5	7,417.5	7,390.8	7,436.6	7,476.6	7,528.8	7,563.1	7,385.9
2012	7,331.4	7,370.9	7,437.1	7,480.0	7,561.8	7,617.9	7,545.0	7,547.6	7,580.4	7,633.1	7,639.0	7,711.3	7,538.0
2013	7,447.9	7,477.4	7,548.5	7,636.0	7,695.7	7,754.1	7,724.4	7,713.5	7,734.6	7,811.2	7,876.9	7,896.6	7,693.1
2014	7,619.3	7,646.1	7,712.6	7,806.5	7,891.9	7,948.7	7,920.7	7,910.1	7,919.0	8,003.2	8,064.6	8,100.2	7,878.6
2015	7,828.8	7,851.1	7,911.7	7,995.1	8,080.3	8,136.4	8,112.6	8,092.2	8,094.9	8,198.8	8,249.0	8,273.1	8,068.7
2016	7,996.2	8,028.0	8,096.6	8,184.7	8,216.5	8,291.7	8,272.9	8,252.8	8,264.3	8,326.3	8,385.0	8,417.6	8,227.7
2017	8,153.1	8,193.7	8,238.4	8,297.0	8,394.4	8,475.1	8,417.4	8,400.0	8,410.5	8,488.0	8,554.0	8,582.0	8,383.6
2018	8,282.7	8,345.9	8,393.3	8,457.9	8,530.8	8,610.9	8,544.1	8,514.3	8,506.4	8,583.5	8,632.6	8,640.2	8,503.6
Goods Producing													
2010	664.1	658.4	668.4	687.1	691.4	697.5	698.0	699.9	697.5	695.9	694.8	685.4	686.5
2011	650.1	649.4	660.6	675.8	685.8	693.0	697.8	701.4	699.4	698.6	698.3	692.4	683.6
2012	665.4	664.1	672.6	681.2	687.6	694.8	696.4	699.6	698.2	700.1	696.9	700.2	688.1
2013	675.3	673.4	682.7	698.7	705.6	711.9	715.2	720.7	719.0	722.8	722.2	712.0	705.0
2014	682.4	677.3	690.0	709.0	720.4	728.8	735.2	737.6	736.6	739.6	739.9	732.9	719.1
2015	702.1	695.9	707.3	728.3	740.7	749.1	754.3	756.8	752.8	759.7	758.9	753.4	738.3
2016	727.4	723.2	736.3	750.1	756.7	763.9	768.1	770.7	766.1	767.9	766.9	761.0	754.9
2017	734.4	736.0	741.2	756.4	768.0	776.5	777.6	778.8	775.7	778.4	779.0	772.5	764.5
2018	740.0	748.2	753.7	765.9	775.5	784.9	783.3	783.1	780.2	780.8	780.3	776.5	771.0
Service-Providing													
2010	7,728.4	7,757.9	7,817.9	7,909.9	7,983.0	8,015.0	7,896.6	7,849.8	7,880.3	7,993.4	8,041.0	8,079.0	7,912.7
2011	7,837.6	7,882.1	7,933.6	8,022.9	8,054.2	8,102.0	8,038.5	7,984.8	8,030.5	8,109.7	8,169.7	8,204.5	8,030.8
2012	7,961.8	8,027.9	8,094.5	8,127.5	8,201.6	8,251.8	8,140.9	8,111.3	8,162.1	8,254.8	8,263.7	8,337.3	8,161.3
2013	8,064.8	8,122.4	8,189.2	8,263.4	8,315.4	8,363.2	8,300.2	8,253.0	8,290.4	8,411.0	8,484.5	8,510.5	8,297.3
2014	8,222.1	8,278.7	8,340.6	8,425.3	8,496.2	8,540.3	8,479.5	8,440.1	8,467.1	8,585.9	8,658.5	8,697.6	8,469.3
2015	8,415.0	8,468.8	8,525.4	8,595.4	8,668.4	8,713.5	8,661.8	8,614.7	8,635.1	8,764.3	8,828.4	8,855.6	8,645.5
2016	8,567.1	8,627.2	8,692.9	8,770.3	8,795.2	8,861.3	8,811.7	8,763.4	8,799.5	8,890.4	8,958.2	8,995.2	8,794.4
2017	8,724.5	8,787.4	8,833.1	8,876.2	8,961.7	9,036.7	8,953.7	8,903.3	8,935.2	9,042.8	9,114.4	9,148.0	8,943.1
2018	8,841.4	8,922.8	8,968.9	9,026.2	9,092.9	9,164.9	9,076.4	9,020.7	9,031.3	9,142.3	9,200.4	9,209.2	9,058.1
Mining, Logging, and Construction													
2010	286.5	281.1	289.5	306.7	310.0	313.8	317.4	319.4	316.8	314.7	313.6	304.1	306.1
2011	276.4	275.4	285.7	300.4	309.4	314.7	321.7	324.2	321.4	321.0	320.4	314.9	307.1
2012	293.8	291.8	298.4	308.1	312.5	317.5	321.8	324.5	321.8	323.5	322.2	324.9	313.4
2013	307.6	304.5	311.7	326.7	332.4	336.8	342.6	346.9	344.7	348.3	347.4	337.4	332.3
2014	315.2	309.9	321.9	341.0	351.1	357.4	366.1	368.2	367.6	370.7	370.5	363.8	350.3
2015	338.3	332.0	342.0	363.2	373.9	379.7	385.7	388.2	383.9	390.3	389.5	383.4	370.8
2016	362.7	357.3	369.3	384.6	390.5	395.2	400.7	403.4	400.1	400.5	399.3	392.9	388.0
2017	372.2	373.3	377.7	393.5	403.1	408.8	412.3	414.4	412.4	414.7	414.5	407.9	400.4
2018	380.7	387.7	392.9	405.0	413.6	419.7	420.9	420.9	419.5	418.5	417.5	412.6	409.1
Manufacturing													
2010	377.6	377.3	378.9	380.4	381.4	383.7	380.6	380.5	380.7	381.2	381.2	381.3	380.4
2011	373.7	374.0	374.9	375.4	376.4	378.3	376.1	377.2	378.0	377.6	377.9	377.5	376.4
2012	371.6	372.3	374.2	373.1	375.1	377.3	374.6	375.1	376.4	376.6	374.7	375.3	374.7
2013	367.7	368.9	371.0	372.0	373.2	375.1	372.6	373.8	374.3	374.5	374.8	374.6	372.7
2014	367.2	367.4	368.1	368.0	369.3	371.4	369.1	369.4	369.0	368.9	369.4	369.1	368.9
2015	363.8	363.9	365.3	365.1	366.8	369.4	368.6	368.6	368.9	369.4	369.4	370.0	367.4
2016	364.7	365.9	367.0	365.5	366.2	368.7	367.4	367.3	366.0	367.4	367.6	368.1	366.8
2017	362.2	362.7	363.5	362.9	364.9	367.7	365.3	364.4	363.3	363.7	364.5	364.6	364.1
2018	359.3	360.5	360.8	360.9	361.9	365.2	362.4	362.2	360.7	362.3	362.8	363.9	361.9

Employment by Industry: New York-Newark-Jersey City, NY-NJ-PA, 2010–2018—*Continued*

(Numbers in thousands, not seasonally adjusted)

Industry and year	January	February	March	April	May	June	July	August	September	October	November	December	Annual average
Trade, Transportation, and Utilities													
2010	1,566.4	1,547.5	1,553.7	1,568.2	1,579.3	1,598.9	1,576.8	1,575.9	1,588.6	1,606.2	1,634.9	1,661.7	1,588.2
2011	1,593.9	1,576.4	1,580.9	1,593.6	1,603.5	1,622.7	1,600.3	1,600.3	1,616.1	1,627.8	1,663.3	1,691.5	1,614.2
2012	1,628.9	1,609.6	1,616.5	1,613.5	1,634.6	1,652.7	1,617.6	1,620.7	1,637.8	1,650.7	1,682.8	1,711.9	1,639.8
2013	1,634.3	1,611.6	1,624.5	1,635.5	1,649.3	1,670.5	1,654.1	1,651.3	1,667.3	1,681.7	1,725.6	1,747.5	1,662.8
2014	1,671.8	1,650.9	1,658.6	1,666.7	1,682.5	1,700.6	1,684.1	1,683.4	1,696.4	1,713.4	1,753.6	1,780.5	1,695.2
2015	1,702.8	1,682.6	1,686.3	1,691.6	1,709.6	1,728.4	1,706.2	1,703.9	1,714.1	1,728.1	1,765.3	1,781.2	1,716.7
2016	1,708.9	1,692.2	1,695.8	1,705.4	1,712.7	1,727.5	1,709.3	1,705.1	1,717.1	1,735.5	1,774.0	1,799.8	1,723.6
2017	1,729.6	1,706.9	1,707.8	1,710.9	1,729.3	1,746.7	1,727.0	1,724.0	1,735.6	1,747.3	1,793.6	1,816.7	1,739.6
2018	1,742.1	1,720.2	1,719.6	1,719.9	1,734.5	1,749.5	1,725.3	1,717.5	1,727.5	1,746.1	1,787.3	1,802.0	1,741.0
Wholesale Trade													
2010	399.7	398.8	400.4	401.3	402.7	405.8	405.2	404.7	404.8	405.9	407.2	409.0	403.8
2011	402.5	401.4	403.4	405.1	406.2	409.1	408.4	408.7	407.5	407.9	408.2	411.1	406.6
2012	407.0	408.4	409.9	409.6	411.1	414.2	411.6	411.2	410.3	411.4	411.4	413.8	410.8
2013	406.1	406.5	407.6	410.0	411.5	415.1	415.2	414.8	413.7	414.3	415.6	417.0	412.3
2014	410.0	410.2	411.6	413.3	415.0	417.4	417.9	417.1	416.4	417.3	419.2	420.7	415.5
2015	414.1	414.2	415.6	416.2	418.0	421.0	421.1	420.5	418.6	419.6	420.1	421.1	418.3
2016	414.3	414.8	414.9	414.6	414.6	416.6	416.4	415.8	413.9	414.1	414.6	416.3	415.1
2017	409.3	409.7	410.3	411.6	413.8	417.1	416.1	415.4	414.1	413.0	414.7	416.6	413.5
2018	409.7	410.1	410.9	410.2	412.0	415.0	414.7	412.7	411.8	410.6	410.3	410.7	411.6
Retail Trade													
2010	855.9	840.1	844.2	855.4	863.7	877.8	873.8	874.8	869.5	884.6	909.1	928.3	873.1
2011	877.7	863.0	864.2	873.0	879.8	893.1	889.5	890.9	889.3	900.3	930.8	951.7	891.9
2012	905.3	885.0	888.6	890.5	902.5	914.5	906.9	906.8	905.9	917.7	947.7	966.0	911.5
2013	911.2	895.7	900.7	906.7	917.1	932.7	931.4	932.8	930.1	941.7	979.4	995.1	931.2
2014	936.8	920.1	924.2	930.4	939.8	953.3	951.3	953.3	949.0	961.7	993.6	1,012.0	952.1
2015	952.3	934.7	936.2	939.0	951.0	963.6	957.2	956.8	951.7	961.2	991.8	998.9	957.9
2016	948.2	932.3	934.0	940.3	946.5	957.8	955.4	954.4	948.2	960.5	991.4	1,006.6	956.3
2017	957.4	937.2	936.5	940.8	950.3	960.4	956.5	954.5	947.2	957.1	990.4	1,001.5	957.5
2018	953.8	936.7	935.2	935.7	944.8	954.1	947.3	943.6	935.6	949.4	982.0	988.4	950.6
Transportation and Utilities													
2010	310.8	308.6	309.1	311.5	312.9	315.3	297.8	296.4	314.3	315.7	318.6	324.4	311.3
2011	313.7	312.0	313.3	315.5	317.5	320.5	302.4	300.7	319.3	319.6	324.3	328.7	315.6
2012	316.6	316.2	318.0	313.4	321.0	324.0	299.1	302.7	321.6	321.6	323.7	332.1	317.5
2013	317.0	309.4	316.2	318.8	320.7	322.7	307.5	303.7	323.5	325.7	330.6	335.4	319.3
2014	325.0	320.6	322.8	323.0	327.7	329.9	314.9	313.0	331.0	334.4	340.8	347.8	327.6
2015	336.4	333.7	334.5	336.4	340.6	343.8	327.9	326.6	343.8	347.3	353.4	361.2	340.5
2016	346.4	345.1	346.9	350.5	351.6	353.1	337.5	334.9	355.0	360.9	368.0	376.9	352.2
2017	362.9	360.0	361.0	358.5	365.2	369.2	354.4	354.1	374.3	377.2	388.5	398.6	368.7
2018	378.6	373.4	373.5	374.0	377.7	380.4	363.3	361.2	380.1	386.1	395.0	402.9	378.9
Information													
2010	268.3	268.5	269.6	269.5	270.7	272.8	272.8	273.3	272.9	274.7	274.3	278.4	272.2
2011	269.6	270.7	272.4	275.0	275.5	277.1	278.9	262.0	278.4	276.1	277.5	279.5	274.4
2012	274.7	276.0	277.5	277.7	279.5	281.5	278.9	278.6	277.0	278.7	279.6	280.0	278.3
2013	272.2	274.0	275.4	277.0	279.2	282.0	281.6	284.3	282.1	283.7	287.1	286.2	280.4
2014	278.3	281.2	282.2	280.9	281.8	285.3	283.7	284.9	282.3	284.6	284.4	286.8	283.0
2015	279.9	281.4	282.0	280.7	281.8	284.7	286.7	285.1	284.1	288.2	289.7	290.6	284.6
2016	279.9	280.9	282.5	284.4	271.4	286.5	292.1	290.9	288.8	290.3	291.3	293.0	286.0
2017	282.3	286.5	287.4	284.1	286.0	290.5	291.6	293.7	293.6	294.4	297.1	297.9	290.4
2018	282.4	290.6	292.4	287.6	289.9	296.1	295.1	296.0	293.4	294.7	295.6	292.0	292.2
Financial Activities													
2010	725.6	726.1	728.2	728.3	730.1	740.0	741.9	742.9	737.0	736.6	738.9	743.1	734.9
2011	733.5	734.6	735.8	737.2	739.1	750.1	753.2	754.2	745.7	742.9	743.2	746.0	743.0
2012	736.4	738.5	739.3	737.4	739.2	748.8	749.7	748.1	739.7	741.2	740.4	746.1	742.1
2013	732.2	734.5	734.0	734.4	735.4	745.9	749.6	749.2	740.7	742.4	744.5	748.8	741.0
2014	737.4	739.2	741.2	740.6	744.1	756.6	760.1	759.3	750.1	750.9	752.7	757.8	749.2
2015	746.1	747.4	748.5	748.7	751.9	764.3	770.3	770.1	760.2	763.3	764.2	768.0	758.6
2016	759.0	759.4	759.7	759.2	762.4	773.1	778.1	778.3	765.6	766.3	767.8	772.6	766.8
2017	761.9	764.6	766.8	764.2	768.2	782.1	785.4	785.3	775.0	777.1	778.7	783.3	774.4
2018	769.4	772.8	773.4	773.7	776.7	791.7	795.0	794.4	782.7	780.6	778.4	779.0	780.7

Employment by Industry: New York-Newark-Jersey City, NY-NJ-PA, 2010–2018—*Continued*

(Numbers in thousands, not seasonally adjusted)

Industry and year	January	February	March	April	May	June	July	August	September	October	November	December	Annual average
Professional and Business Services													
2010	1,234.4	1,240.7	1,252.6	1,278.7	1,282.6	1,300.3	1,296.6	1,298.7	1,293.7	1,305.1	1,310.7	1,313.0	1,283.9
2011	1,277.6	1,283.0	1,295.5	1,317.9	1,321.6	1,340.5	1,344.2	1,345.9	1,343.4	1,348.1	1,357.4	1,356.9	1,327.7
2012	1,312.9	1,321.6	1,337.4	1,353.0	1,363.3	1,381.6	1,377.9	1,387.2	1,385.1	1,394.0	1,401.4	1,409.0	1,368.7
2013	1,356.2	1,362.2	1,376.2	1,390.2	1,398.3	1,416.6	1,421.8	1,425.3	1,417.0	1,425.0	1,430.9	1,432.8	1,404.4
2014	1,381.7	1,390.1	1,396.6	1,423.8	1,434.3	1,449.2	1,456.9	1,458.5	1,448.5	1,461.4	1,469.9	1,472.3	1,436.9
2015	1,427.8	1,435.5	1,446.6	1,469.5	1,478.5	1,496.2	1,501.1	1,501.6	1,493.1	1,511.2	1,515.6	1,514.4	1,482.6
2016	1,465.3	1,472.9	1,487.0	1,507.6	1,512.4	1,532.5	1,537.6	1,539.8	1,536.2	1,540.2	1,548.2	1,549.0	1,519.1
2017	1,498.7	1,507.8	1,515.6	1,529.6	1,544.7	1,567.6	1,563.9	1,560.6	1,557.9	1,565.7	1,574.9	1,576.0	1,546.9
2018	1,520.5	1,531.7	1,541.2	1,559.9	1,572.4	1,596.5	1,586.5	1,586.9	1,579.2	1,588.8	1,597.3	1,582.7	1,570.3
Education and Health Services													
2010	1,574.6	1,601.0	1,614.2	1,618.4	1,613.1	1,586.8	1,554.5	1,546.5	1,582.0	1,627.3	1,639.9	1,642.9	1,600.1
2011	1,601.5	1,632.4	1,644.0	1,649.8	1,645.7	1,611.1	1,580.8	1,572.3	1,616.5	1,652.1	1,662.5	1,670.1	1,628.2
2012	1,626.7	1,662.8	1,676.5	1,676.4	1,680.9	1,648.2	1,613.8	1,605.7	1,655.8	1,689.6	1,685.4	1,700.0	1,660.2
2013	1,656.8	1,692.6	1,706.1	1,719.6	1,715.3	1,676.7	1,648.4	1,638.8	1,684.1	1,736.5	1,751.2	1,754.0	1,698.3
2014	1,700.1	1,732.4	1,750.5	1,760.9	1,761.6	1,730.2	1,704.4	1,699.1	1,739.3	1,791.4	1,808.4	1,814.4	1,749.4
2015	1,762.2	1,796.8	1,812.0	1,820.8	1,817.8	1,783.7	1,755.6	1,744.9	1,782.7	1,845.9	1,862.5	1,869.0	1,804.5
2016	1,816.4	1,853.3	1,867.4	1,878.0	1,872.1	1,841.9	1,814.2	1,805.4	1,853.7	1,901.9	1,916.8	1,923.7	1,862.1
2017	1,875.9	1,916.6	1,929.4	1,930.7	1,932.6	1,905.4	1,866.9	1,858.3	1,907.9	1,964.8	1,979.3	1,985.4	1,921.1
2018	1,932.7	1,981.4	1,993.2	2,002.6	2,000.1	1,967.3	1,938.0	1,926.2	1,970.2	2,027.7	2,043.5	2,056.5	1,986.6
Leisure and Hospitality													
2010	646.4	647.7	663.0	695.9	719.0	743.0	748.3	747.0	730.6	722.1	715.4	716.2	707.9
2011	676.2	680.9	694.7	725.9	749.2	775.4	781.6	777.0	759.8	751.9	747.1	745.2	738.7
2012	709.4	720.2	736.0	756.5	787.8	815.7	819.6	818.7	797.9	787.7	763.5	771.5	773.7
2013	736.5	742.8	761.4	789.8	819.4	851.8	856.8	848.3	831.3	823.6	818.5	817.7	808.2
2014	776.6	782.1	798.0	824.3	862.0	888.8	889.6	882.2	862.4	855.4	847.5	846.0	842.9
2015	805.8	808.8	824.3	849.1	888.3	913.2	923.8	916.4	896.5	887.5	876.7	879.1	872.5
2016	829.5	834.0	853.9	880.8	906.9	940.6	950.0	941.5	917.4	902.4	897.9	896.4	895.9
2017	856.2	861.5	875.2	902.4	942.7	978.0	980.8	977.8	945.0	937.3	927.8	925.6	925.9
2018	879.8	883.3	900.3	924.6	954.2	992.2	993.8	985.2	951.5	936.2	921.4	920.3	936.9
Other Services													
2010	359.4	359.1	361.8	366.1	369.2	372.8	371.0	369.3	366.6	371.3	371.4	372.8	367.6
2011	365.6	367.2	369.3	374.8	378.1	382.6	380.7	377.7	377.3	379.1	379.5	381.5	376.1
2012	377.0	378.1	381.3	384.3	388.9	394.6	391.1	389.0	388.9	391.1	389.0	392.6	387.2
2013	384.4	386.3	388.2	390.8	393.2	398.7	396.9	395.6	393.1	395.5	396.9	397.6	393.1
2014	391.0	392.9	395.5	400.3	405.2	409.2	406.7	405.1	403.4	406.5	408.2	409.5	402.8
2015	402.1	402.7	404.7	406.4	411.7	416.8	414.6	413.4	411.4	414.9	416.1	417.4	411.0
2016	409.8	412.1	414.0	419.2	421.9	425.7	423.5	421.1	419.4	421.8	422.1	422.1	419.4
2017	414.1	413.8	415.0	418.7	422.9	428.3	424.2	421.5	419.8	423.0	423.6	424.6	420.8
2018	415.8	417.7	419.5	423.7	427.5	432.7	427.1	425.0	421.7	428.6	428.8	431.2	424.9
Government													
2010	1,353.3	1,367.3	1,374.8	1,384.8	1,419.0	1,400.4	1,334.7	1,296.2	1,308.9	1,350.1	1,355.5	1,350.9	1,358.0
2011	1,319.7	1,336.9	1,341.0	1,348.7	1,341.5	1,342.5	1,318.8	1,295.4	1,293.3	1,331.7	1,339.2	1,333.8	1,328.5
2012	1,295.8	1,321.1	1,330.0	1,328.7	1,327.4	1,328.7	1,292.3	1,263.3	1,279.9	1,321.8	1,321.6	1,326.2	1,311.4
2013	1,292.2	1,318.4	1,323.4	1,326.1	1,325.3	1,321.0	1,291.0	1,260.2	1,274.8	1,322.6	1,329.8	1,325.9	1,309.2
2014	1,285.2	1,309.9	1,318.0	1,327.8	1,324.7	1,320.4	1,294.0	1,267.6	1,284.7	1,322.3	1,333.8	1,330.3	1,309.9
2015	1,288.3	1,313.6	1,321.0	1,328.6	1,328.8	1,326.2	1,303.5	1,279.3	1,293.0	1,325.2	1,338.3	1,335.9	1,315.1
2016	1,298.3	1,322.4	1,332.6	1,335.7	1,335.4	1,333.5	1,306.9	1,281.3	1,301.3	1,332.0	1,340.1	1,338.6	1,321.5
2017	1,305.8	1,329.7	1,335.9	1,335.6	1,335.3	1,338.1	1,313.9	1,282.1	1,300.4	1,333.2	1,339.4	1,338.5	1,324.0
2018	1,298.7	1,325.1	1,329.3	1,334.2	1,337.6	1,338.9	1,315.6	1,289.5	1,305.1	1,339.6	1,348.1	1,345.5	1,325.6

Employment by Industry: Los Angeles-Long Beach-Anaheim, CA, 2010–2018

(Numbers in thousands, not seasonally adjusted)

Industry and year	January	February	March	April	May	June	July	August	September	October	November	December	Annual average
Total Nonfarm													
2010	5,238.1	5,248.0	5,269.4	5,304.8	5,328.4	5,325.5	5,254.6	5,243.3	5,271.6	5,335.7	5,356.6	5,378.5	5,296.2
2011	5,277.1	5,302.8	5,322.6	5,326.7	5,336.4	5,337.9	5,289.0	5,285.0	5,329.6	5,371.1	5,407.4	5,429.9	5,334.6
2012	5,334.1	5,372.5	5,407.6	5,446.4	5,473.3	5,482.7	5,423.2	5,435.2	5,471.0	5,521.5	5,577.3	5,597.8	5,461.9
2013	5465.5	5509.7	5530.4	5557.2	5577.4	5581.7	5529.2	5556.9	5583.8	5640.7	5697.8	5713.1	5578.6
2014	5,602.6	5,629.5	5,653.7	5,663.4	5,687.2	5,680.0	5,617.2	5,665.0	5,700.0	5,755.4	5,799.6	5,817.2	5,689.2
2015	5,705.6	5,748.5	5,772.8	5,791.9	5,806.0	5,811.6	5,788.1	5,808.6	5,848.9	5,933.1	5,967.2	5,980.8	5,830.3
2016	5,883.2	5,925.5	5,925.5	5,976.4	5,987.9	5,955.6	5,929.9	5,946.0	5,986.3	6,047.5	6,086.4	6,098.2	5,979.0
2017	5,957.3	6,002.4	6,020.1	6,032.8	6,057.2	6,057.8	6,009.4	6,032.9	6,081.8	6,147.8	6,182.0	6,201.9	6,065.3
2018	6,086.7	6,128.2	6,140.8	6,146.7	6,151.0	6,157.1	6,100.3	6,131.3	6,155.6	6,217.4	6,247.2	6,251.0	6,159.4
Total Private													
2010	4,497.0	4,504.2	4,520.7	4,547.9	4,557.6	4,568.4	4,553.7	4,566.5	4,577.3	4,608.2	4,623.0	4,647.8	4,564.4
2011	4,552.3	4,575.0	4,588.2	4,593.5	4,602.2	4,603.3	4,610.9	4,622.5	4,641.9	4,655.3	4,683.2	4,710.3	4,619.9
2012	4,624.6	4,654.0	4,683.3	4,724.5	4,748.8	4,759.5	4,755.1	4,775.4	4,786.5	4,818.0	4,867.4	4,889.5	4,757.2
2013	4,767.3	4,802.4	4,816.5	4,846.1	4,864.0	4,868.6	4,867.5	4,891.8	4,898.6	4,935.5	4,985.1	5,001.1	4,878.7
2014	4,900.3	4,922.2	4,936.5	4,945.1	4,963.8	4,961.4	4,951.6	4,990.8	4,999.8	5,035.9	5,072.6	5,090.1	4,980.8
2015	4986.6	5021.8	5040.3	5055.5	5072.3	5075.7	5101.4	5121.9	5132.5	5194.4	5224.5	5237.4	5105.4
2016	5,150.6	5,184.7	5,179.1	5,229.0	5,237.4	5,215.0	5,234.3	5,249.5	5,257.8	5,298.9	5,333.2	5,343.8	5,242.8
2017	5,212.5	5,250.9	5,262.1	5,274.9	5,294.9	5,297.3	5,306.7	5,329.2	5,347.0	5,392.2	5,419.6	5,440.6	5,319.0
2018	5,336.5	5,370.1	5,379.3	5,384.6	5,386.7	5,393.8	5,391.7	5,420.7	5,418.3	5,457.5	5,482.2	5,487.1	5,409.0
Goods Producing													
2010	702.3	700.8	703.4	705.5	708.4	711.8	710.8	711.0	707.8	708.0	706.7	704.3	706.7
2011	694.8	696.5	700.0	702.7	706.4	709.1	713.2	714.1	712.8	709.4	709.5	708.3	706.4
2012	704.1	706.0	709.7	712.3	715.9	721.4	724.0	724.6	724.1	723.7	725.1	724.3	717.9
2013	717.7	723.5	724.7	725.3	728.1	733.2	735.5	738.1	736.4	738.2	739.7	738.1	731.5
2014	726.6	732.4	733.6	729.9	733.4	735.5	735.7	739.6	738.6	738.2	738.6	736.9	734.9
2015	734.3	735.9	738.6	739.6	742.9	746.7	753.1	755.7	752.7	755.6	755.6	755.2	747.2
2016	746.6	751.3	749.2	753.0	753.4	752.4	756.2	756.5	755.4	754.5	754.1	753.6	753.0
2017	740.4	744.7	748.8	749.3	751.4	755.4	757.0	758.9	756.8	757.5	757.1	758.3	753.0
2018	747.5	754.8	754.0	755.5	756.7	759.5	761.8	764.6	762.3	761.3	761.5	756.1	758.0
Service-Providing													
2010	4,535.8	4,547.2	4,566.0	4,599.3	4,620.0	4,613.7	4,543.8	4,532.3	4,563.8	4,627.7	4,649.9	4,674.2	4,589.5
2011	4,582.3	4,606.3	4,622.6	4,624.0	4,630.0	4,628.8	4,575.8	4,570.9	4,616.8	4,661.7	4,697.9	4,721.6	4,628.2
2012	4,630.0	4,666.5	4,697.9	4,734.1	4,757.4	4,761.3	4,699.2	4,710.6	4,746.9	4,797.8	4,852.2	4,873.5	4,744.0
2013	4,747.8	4,786.2	4,805.7	4,831.9	4,849.3	4,848.5	4,793.7	4,818.8	4,847.4	4,902.5	4,958.1	4,975.0	4,847.1
2014	4,876.0	4,897.1	4,920.1	4,933.5	4,953.8	4,944.5	4,881.5	4,925.4	4,961.4	5,017.2	5,061.0	5,080.3	4,954.3
2015	4971.3	5012.6	5034.2	5052.3	5063.1	5064.9	5035.0	5052.9	5096.2	5177.5	5211.6	5225.6	5,083.1
2016	5,136.6	5,174.2	5,176.3	5,223.4	5,234.5	5,203.2	5,173.7	5,189.5	5,230.9	5,293.0	5,332.3	5,344.6	5,226.0
2017	5,216.9	5,257.7	5,271.3	5,283.5	5,305.8	5,302.4	5,252.4	5,274.0	5,325.0	5,390.3	5,424.9	5,443.6	5,312.3
2018	5,339.2	5,373.4	5,386.8	5,391.2	5,394.3	5,397.6	5,338.5	5,366.7	5,393.3	5,456.1	5,485.7	5,494.9	5,401.5
Mining and Logging													
2010	3.3	3.4	3.4	3.4	3.4	3.4	3.4	3.4	3.3	3.3	3.3	3.3	3.4
2011	3.2	3.2	3.2	3.3	3.3	3.3	3.3	3.3	3.3	3.4	3.5	3.5	3.3
2012	3.5	3.5	3.5	3.5	3.5	3.5	3.6	3.6	3.6	3.7	3.7	3.8	3.6
2013	3.9	3.8	3.7	3.8	3.8	3.8	3.8	3.9	3.8	3.8	3.8	3.8	3.8
2014	3.7	3.7	3.6	3.6	3.7	3.7	3.6	3.6	3.6	3.7	3.6	3.6	3.6
2015	3.6	3.5	3.5	3.4	3.3	3.3	3.3	3.2	3.2	3.1	3.1	3	3.3
2016	3.0	3.0	2.9	2.8	2.7	2.7	2.7	2.8	2.7	2.7	2.7	2.6	2.8
2017	2.5	2.5	2.5	2.6	2.6	2.6	2.5	2.5	2.5	2.4	2.4	2.5	2.5
2018	2.5	2.4	2.4	2.4	2.4	2.5	2.4	2.4	2.5	2.4	2.4	2.5	2.4
Construction													
2010	171.3	169.6	171.0	172.5	173.4	174.1	173.7	174.6	172.8	173.4	173.3	171.2	172.6
2011	167.2	167.8	169.4	171.1	173.5	175.2	178.1	179.8	179.3	177.3	177.3	175.7	174.3
2012	173.8	173.8	175.1	175.0	177.5	181.0	183.7	184.7	184.8	184.9	186.0	185.4	180.5
2013	183.6	185.9	187.4	188.2	190.5	193.9	195.9	198.0	197.0	199.1	199.1	197.3	193.0
2014	193.4	196.2	198.0	197.3	200.2	201.4	202.2	205.8	205.6	206.7	207.6	204.9	201.6
2015	205.6	206.3	209.5	211	213.5	216.5	221.4	224.6	223.2	227.5	227.8	226.8	217.8
2016	223.5	226.1	225.7	229.4	230.2	230.3	234.4	235.6	235.1	236.3	234.8	233.7	231.3
2017	224.5	229.5	233.9	236.8	238.6	241.3	244.2	246.2	245.8	247.5	246.7	246.8	240.2
2018	242.5	247.8	246.7	249.4	250.6	252.0	254.0	257.7	256.5	258.9	257.6	250.9	252.1

Employment by Industry: Los Angeles-Long Beach-Anaheim, CA, 2010–2018—*Continued*

(Numbers in thousands, not seasonally adjusted)

Industry and year	January	February	March	April	May	June	July	August	September	October	November	December	Annual average
Manufacturing													
2010	527.7	527.8	529.0	529.6	531.6	534.3	533.7	533.0	531.7	531.3	530.1	529.8	530.8
2011	524.4	525.5	527.4	528.3	529.6	530.6	531.8	531.0	530.2	528.7	528.7	529.1	528.8
2012	526.8	528.7	531.1	533.8	534.9	536.9	536.7	536.3	535.7	535.1	535.4	535.1	533.9
2013	530.2	533.8	533.6	533.3	533.8	535.5	535.8	536.2	535.6	535.3	536.8	537.0	534.7
2014	529.5	532.5	532.0	529.0	529.5	530.4	529.9	530.2	529.4	527.8	527.4	528.4	529.7
2015	525.1	526.1	525.6	525.2	526.1	526.9	528.4	527.9	526.3	525	524.7	525.4	526.1
2016	520.1	522.2	520.6	520.8	520.5	519.4	519.1	518.1	517.6	515.5	516.6	517.3	519.0
2017	513.4	512.7	512.4	509.9	510.2	511.5	510.3	510.2	508.5	507.6	508.0	509.0	510.3
2018	502.5	504.6	504.9	503.7	503.7	505.0	505.4	504.5	503.3	500.0	501.5	502.7	503.5
Trade, Transportation, and Utilities													
2010	981.5	975.3	973.7	979.3	984.2	986.2	984.0	986.9	985.1	993.8	1,011.1	1,024.9	988.8
2011	992.4	988.9	986.4	990.4	992.9	994.1	996.7	1,000.3	999.5	1,003.9	1,026.9	1,040.0	1,001.0
2012	1,009.0	998.8	999.8	1,006.6	1,011.2	1,015.1	1,014.9	1,017.2	1,018.3	1,024.5	1,055.4	1,064.6	1,019.6
2013	1,028.9	1,023.1	1,019.6	1,021.6	1,027.0	1,030.6	1,032.6	1,036.1	1,033.7	1,042.4	1,073.9	1,085.1	1,037.9
2014	1,049.6	1,041.3	1,039.0	1,041.2	1,046.2	1,050.0	1,051.3	1,057.1	1,057.4	1,066.9	1,096.2	1,108.9	1,058.8
2015	1071.8	1063.4	1066	1062.8	1067.5	1068.7	1075	1079.4	1078.7	1088.1	1113.1	1121.4	1079.7
2016	1,087.5	1,078.6	1,077.8	1,083.0	1,084.8	1,082.0	1,091.9	1,095.6	1,093.0	1,098.4	1,122.4	1,133.5	1,094.0
2017	1,102.5	1,087.3	1,091.8	1,093.9	1,095.8	1,096.8	1,099.9	1,102.6	1,103.3	1,112.7	1,139.4	1,149.2	1,106.3
2018	1,113.4	1,101.6	1,102.6	1,102.0	1,103.0	1,102.6	1,107.3	1,111.0	1,109.2	1,116.2	1,139.6	1,149.2	1,113.1
Wholesale Trade													
2010	273.5	274.0	274.4	276.4	277.6	277.9	277.4	277.6	277.3	279.2	279.0	279.7	277.0
2011	277.2	278.2	278.1	279.5	279.7	279.3	279.2	279.4	279.9	279.7	279.6	280.7	279.2
2012	277.9	278.7	279.4	283.9	285.1	286.0	285.6	286.7	286.5	288.0	289.0	290.8	284.8
2013	288.5	290.1	291.5	292.5	293.1	294.4	293.9	294.3	293.8	295.1	296.5	298.1	293.5
2014	295.5	297.0	297.3	296.4	297.4	297.7	298.0	299.6	299.8	300.7	301.9	302.7	298.7
2015	298.8	300.3	300.3	300.2	300.7	300.8	302	302.2	301.4	302.5	303	303.2	301.3
2016	299.8	300.6	299.1	300.6	300.6	299.4	302.3	302.3	301.3	300.6	300.7	301.4	300.7
2017	297.8	298.7	299.8	299.9	300.7	301.1	300.6	300.5	300.3	301.4	302.2	303.3	300.5
2018	300.7	302.1	302.2	302.1	302.8	302.9	303.3	303.3	302.4	303.0	304.2	305.6	302.9
Retail Trade													
2010	528.0	520.9	519.8	522.9	524.0	525.1	525.0	527.2	525.5	530.4	548.2	559.1	529.7
2011	533.9	527.5	526.3	527.0	529.0	530.8	533.6	535.8	535.5	539.6	561.9	571.8	537.7
2012	547.1	536.3	535.7	535.6	538.5	540.0	540.8	542.7	543.2	548.0	577.1	581.9	547.2
2013	551.0	543.2	541.2	542.1	544.5	547.1	547.7	549.8	548.6	555.3	583.1	591.2	553.7
2014	560.9	551.2	550.4	552.8	554.5	557.6	558.4	562.0	560.8	567.3	593.7	602.2	564.3
2015	573.4	565.3	563.8	562.1	564.8	565.4	568.8	571.6	570.5	577.4	598.7	604.4	573.9
2016	577.5	569.6	567.8	569.4	570.1	568.3	571.8	574.1	572.3	579.5	600.1	605.6	577.2
2017	583.0	571.4	569.6	571.2	571.2	571.4	573.4	575.1	574.9	581.0	604.3	608.4	579.6
2018	584.2	574.1	572.3	570.7	571.3	570.2	572.5	574.4	572.6	577.2	596.7	601.6	578.2
Transportation and Utilities													
2010	180.0	180.4	179.5	180.0	182.6	183.2	181.6	182.1	182.3	184.2	183.9	186.1	182.2
2011	181.3	183.2	182.0	183.9	184.2	184.0	183.9	185.1	184.1	184.6	185.4	187.5	184.1
2012	184.0	183.8	184.7	187.1	187.6	189.1	188.5	187.8	188.6	188.5	189.3	191.9	187.6
2013	189.4	189.8	186.9	187.0	189.4	189.1	191.0	192.0	191.3	192.0	194.3	195.8	190.7
2014	193.2	193.1	191.3	192.0	194.3	194.7	194.9	195.5	196.8	198.9	200.6	204.0	195.8
2015	199.6	197.8	201.9	200.5	202	202.5	204.2	205.6	206.8	208.2	211.4	213.8	204.5
2016	210.2	208.4	210.9	213.0	214.1	214.3	217.8	219.2	219.4	218.3	221.6	226.5	216.1
2017	221.7	217.2	222.4	222.8	223.9	224.3	225.9	227.0	228.1	230.3	232.9	237.5	226.2
2018	228.5	225.4	228.1	229.2	228.9	229.5	231.5	233.3	234.2	236.0	238.7	242.0	232.1
Information													
2010	209.4	209.9	213.6	208.1	208.8	212.1	213.0	217.9	219.9	213.8	216.2	222.6	213.8
2011	216.5	215.7	216.9	212.9	211.7	211.6	211.2	213.6	211.8	213.1	210.5	213.8	213.3
2012	207.9	208.4	210.6	215.6	212.5	210.0	213.9	216.3	213.2	217.3	221.6	224.8	214.3
2013	216.0	217.7	219.4	219.2	218.0	219.6	215.6	219.3	221.5	224.0	227.6	226.5	220.4
2014	221.9	219.8	221.6	224.0	219.8	218.7	217.2	223.1	224.2	226.8	225.5	225.8	222.4
2015	219.1	227.6	230.4	229.2	227.6	231.3	228.1	232.5	235.3	242.1	244.4	242.6	232.5
2016	249.3	256.1	254.8	263.1	265.8	256.9	251.5	254.8	252.6	249.9	255.3	253.6	255.3
2017	237.6	258.4	239.5	237.1	236.8	234.2	231.9	236.2	242.9	246.4	246.8	252.6	241.7
2018	245.9	255.2	252.3	238.0	233.9	238.4	231.8	240.3	242.3	251.7	250.4	248.7	244.1

Employment by Industry: Los Angeles-Long Beach-Anaheim, CA, 2010–2018—*Continued*

(Numbers in thousands, not seasonally adjusted)

Industry and year	January	February	March	April	May	June	July	August	September	October	November	December	Annual average
Financial Activities													
2010	312.3	312.7	313.4	313.7	313.6	314.9	315.4	315.3	315.0	315.8	316.2	318.5	314.7
2011	314.6	314.8	315.5	313.3	313.5	314.8	315.2	315.7	314.7	315.8	315.7	317.9	315.1
2012	313.6	314.9	316.4	318.5	319.7	321.5	322.9	323.2	322.9	324.7	325.7	327.9	321.0
2013	324.2	325.3	325.7	326.3	326.8	327.4	328.0	327.1	324.6	326.9	327.0	327.3	326.4
2014	322.0	322.5	322.1	322.9	324.8	326.0	325.3	326.0	324.3	326.5	328.6	330.4	325.1
2015	325.3	326.9	327.3	328.6	330.3	331.4	334.2	334.8	333.4	336.6	336.6	338.1	332
2016	333.3	334.6	334.0	336.7	337.3	336.9	339.9	339.6	337.8	340.1	341.0	342.4	337.8
2017	337.8	338.2	338.0	339.5	341.0	341.3	342.6	341.9	340.7	343.5	343.4	345.5	341.1
2018	340.8	341.9	341.4	341.8	342.7	343.3	344.1	343.4	340.1	340.6	342.1	342.8	342.1
Professional and Business Services													
2010	748.0	753.4	755.4	761.3	761.1	766.2	762.6	767.6	766.0	786.5	784.9	785.4	766.5
2011	766.9	775.0	776.7	774.1	774.5	778.7	784.2	786.8	792.8	798.5	800.9	805.0	784.5
2012	786.6	800.3	808.7	813.8	818.0	824.3	822.6	827.9	831.3	841.8	850.1	852.7	823.2
2013	825.1	836.0	839.2	843.1	845.4	846.5	851.0	860.0	860.5	869.0	878.2	878.1	852.7
2014	858.7	863.0	865.7	862.6	863.1	861.9	861.3	869.0	867.6	874.9	880.0	882.0	867.5
2015	858.8	866.1	867.6	872.2	870.2	871.9	879.6	881.8	881.1	898.2	899.8	899.4	878.9
2016	883.1	890.6	883.6	891.6	888.4	889.2	897.6	900.4	903.5	912.6	918.9	916.2	898.0
2017	887.6	895.4	898.1	896.5	899.3	904.6	916.5	921.2	923.6	930.5	934.2	934.3	911.8
2018	914.4	920.8	924.9	928.5	925.2	932.8	938.5	943.9	943.2	952.6	952.5	947.8	935.4
Education and Health Services													
2010	834.8	842.4	846.0	849.5	845.2	834.3	823.3	825.5	842.9	851.4	854.6	856.4	842.2
2011	844.0	855.7	859.2	857.1	854.1	842.1	830.9	832.8	849.2	859.6	864.6	869.7	851.6
2012	857.5	873.6	877.9	882.7	884.5	874.1	863.5	871.4	882.8	892.8	896.7	900.7	879.9
2013	873.9	885.8	889.8	900.8	898.1	882.9	874.1	881.1	892.3	903.5	907.8	913.1	891.9
2014	899.1	911.5	915.2	916.6	916.5	903.9	894.6	906.3	920.2	932.8	936.4	937.5	915.9
2015	922.4	937	939.4	941.9	943	929.8	928	934.9	950.2	965.6	971.1	974.1	944.8
2016	958.5	971.3	973.7	980.5	980.5	968.1	959.9	963.9	978.2	999.9	1,004.3	1,007.6	978.9
2017	994.1	1,006.6	1,012.7	1,013.9	1,017.0	1,004.9	998.5	1,005.4	1,022.4	1,038.3	1,041.8	1,042.1	1,016.5
2018	1,033.9	1,045.4	1,047.8	1,051.5	1,051.1	1,040.0	1,030.0	1,039.7	1,051.2	1,060.8	1,063.5	1,068.5	1,048.6
Leisure and Hospitality													
2010	532.8	534.3	538.6	551.0	556.0	561.6	564.4	563.7	560.5	558.2	553.6	557.1	552.7
2011	546.7	550.4	554.8	563.5	568.9	572.3	578.3	579.0	578.9	573.0	573.5	573.4	567.7
2012	565.5	569.6	576.5	589.3	599.5	605.0	606.4	608.3	605.9	603.8	604.0	606.3	595.0
2013	595.5	602.6	608.6	618.6	628.8	636.0	639.3	638.6	636.9	638.4	637.4	639.6	626.7
2014	630.1	636.9	643.4	650.3	661.4	665.6	668.5	671.5	668.2	670.0	667.8	669.2	658.6
2015	659	667.1	672.4	682	690.1	695.5	702.8	703.2	700.2	706	701.7	705.4	690.5
2016	693.7	700.6	705.0	717.6	723.2	726.5	732.9	734.7	731.8	735.9	730.8	731.4	722.0
2017	712.3	717.9	728.8	738.7	746.7	752.8	754.1	756.6	749.9	754.9	749.2	750.2	742.7
2018	734.6	742.3	747.9	757.0	762.7	765.2	766.9	766.7	759.1	761.3	758.4	760.4	756.9
Other Services													
2010	175.9	175.4	176.6	179.5	180.3	181.3	180.2	178.6	180.1	180.7	179.7	178.6	178.9
2011	176.4	178.0	178.7	179.5	180.2	180.6	181.2	180.2	182.2	182.0	181.6	182.2	180.2
2012	180.4	182.4	183.7	185.7	187.5	188.1	186.9	186.5	188.0	189.4	188.8	188.2	186.3
2013	186.0	188.4	189.5	191.2	191.8	192.4	191.4	191.5	192.7	193.1	193.5	193.3	191.2
2014	192.3	194.8	195.9	197.6	198.6	199.8	197.7	198.2	199.3	199.8	199.5	199.4	197.7
2015	195.9	197.8	198.6	199.2	200.7	200.4	200.6	199.6	200.9	202.2	202.2	201.2	199.9
2016	198.6	201.6	201.0	203.5	204.0	203.0	204.4	204.0	205.5	207.6	206.4	205.5	203.8
2017	200.2	202.4	204.4	206.0	206.9	207.3	206.2	206.4	207.4	208.4	207.7	208.4	206.0
2018	206.0	208.1	208.4	210.3	211.4	212.0	211.3	211.1	210.9	213.0	214.2	213.6	210.9
Government													
2010	741.1	743.8	748.7	756.9	770.8	757.1	700.9	676.8	694.3	727.5	733.6	730.7	731.9
2011	724.8	727.8	734.4	733.2	734.2	734.6	678.1	662.5	687.7	715.8	724.2	719.6	714.7
2012	709.5	718.5	724.3	721.9	724.5	723.2	668.1	659.8	684.5	703.5	709.9	708.3	704.7
2013	698.2	707.3	713.9	711.1	713.4	713.1	661.7	665.1	685.2	705.2	712.7	712.0	699.9
2014	702.3	707.3	717.2	718.3	723.4	718.6	665.6	674.2	700.2	719.5	727.0	727.1	708.4
2015	719.0	726.7	732.5	736.4	733.7	735.9	686.7	686.7	716.4	738.7	742.7	743.4	724.9
2016	732.6	740.8	746.4	747.4	750.5	740.6	695.6	696.5	728.5	748.6	753.2	754.4	736.3
2017	744.8	751.5	758.0	757.9	762.3	760.5	702.7	703.7	734.8	755.6	762.4	761.3	746.3
2018	750.2	758.1	761.5	762.1	764.3	763.3	708.6	710.6	737.3	759.9	765.0	763.9	750.4

Employment by Industry: Chicago-Naperville-Elgin, IL-IN-WI, 2010–2018

(Numbers in thousands, not seasonally adjusted)

Industry and year	January	February	March	April	May	June	July	August	September	October	November	December	Annual average
Total Nonfarm													
2010	4,139.4	4,147.8	4,169.1	4,222.2	4,276.9	4,290.6	4,247.9	4,256.9	4,266.2	4,300.5	4,312.6	4,304.0	4,244.5
2011	4,183.9	4,193.7	4,224.8	4,283.2	4,316.3	4,341.9	4,326.9	4,335.0	4,349.4	4,361.4	4,375.0	4,365.6	4,304.8
2012	4,252.8	4,264.1	4,298.8	4,346.1	4,388.7	4,420.6	4,393.6	4,406.2	4,419.7	4,430.0	4,449.5	4,443.7	4,376.2
2013	4,316.3	4,338.4	4,366.9	4,403.1	4,460.1	4,492.7	4,465.1	4,479.5	4,483.8	4,497.1	4,514.3	4,516.0	4,444.4
2014	4,376.3	4,390.8	4,423.1	4,477.4	4,534.0	4,563.6	4,536.5	4,545.0	4,542.3	4,571.4	4,583.9	4,586.5	4,510.9
2015	4,451.1	4,467.2	4,495.8	4,562.2	4,621.5	4,651.7	4,632.6	4,631.7	4,632.4	4,664.3	4,670.4	4,676.0	4,596.4
2016	4,543.5	4,552.7	4,578.3	4,636.9	4,670.3	4,703.7	4,695.8	4,693.9	4,693.1	4,713.9	4,726.5	4,717.5	4,660.5
2017	4,586.7	4,600.1	4,634.7	4,666.0	4,716.2	4,757.6	4,727.3	4,730.1	4,726.7	4,745.0	4,762.1	4,755.0	4,700.6
2018	4,620.3	4,636.6	4,678.3	4,698.4	4,751.1	4,792.2	4,781.5	4,782.9	4,773.8	4,806.1	4,820.0	4,803.2	4,745.4
Total Private													
2010	3,578.2	3,579.1	3,599.9	3,648.4	3,685.5	3,713.3	3,699.4	3,714.8	3,708.7	3,734.9	3,745.6	3,745.0	3,679.4
2011	3,635.1	3,637.1	3,666.0	3,722.3	3,752.5	3,785.4	3,783.9	3,798.9	3,797.0	3,804.7	3,815.9	3,811.6	3,750.9
2012	3,710.2	3,712.5	3,744.1	3,790.6	3,829.5	3,865.6	3,856.4	3,871.8	3,870.0	3,875.2	3,893.4	3,891.2	3,825.9
2013	3,775.4	3,787.8	3,813.9	3,850.0	3,901.8	3,937.0	3,928.9	3,943.5	3,934.2	3,947.3	3,961.9	3,964.7	3,895.5
2014	3,841.7	3,848.2	3,876.9	3,928.9	3,978.6	4,012.8	4,000.8	4,012.0	3,994.5	4,019.6	4,032.5	4,034.7	3,965.1
2015	3,913.7	3,920.2	3,946.4	4,010.0	4,063.5	4,097.2	4,095.7	4,097.9	4,083.3	4,110.0	4,118.4	4,122.1	4,048.2
2016	4,005.2	4,007.7	4,028.4	4,087.3	4,116.8	4,145.9	4,154.2	4,156.9	4,138.9	4,164.3	4,175.6	4,159.5	4,111.7
2017	4,048.4	4,054.4	4,085.3	4,117.7	4,163.0	4,199.6	4,187.6	4,195.6	4,174.3	4,196.8	4,212.6	4,204.7	4,153.3
2018	4,084.2	4,094.0	4,129.2	4,152.5	4,198.5	4,236.9	4,243.1	4,247.1	4,221.1	4,256.1	4,266.5	4,249.3	4,198.2
Goods Producing													
2010	528.4	526.9	533.7	546.8	554.3	560.7	556.1	565.6	563.3	567.5	563.9	553.5	551.7
2011	533.5	532.0	540.7	554.6	563.4	570.2	572.8	574.5	570.8	569.9	566.9	557.9	558.9
2012	538.6	537.1	545.5	556.1	563.1	571.5	574.1	575.3	574.2	571.8	567.7	562.4	561.5
2013	540.2	541.4	547.0	553.3	564.0	572.0	572.8	573.9	571.3	571.9	570.3	561.1	561.6
2014	539.1	540.8	548.2	559.4	569.6	578.6	580.5	581.1	579.3	583.5	582.3	576.4	568.2
2015	555.1	554.5	563.0	574.6	584.1	593.2	594.1	594.0	592.7	592.9	591.5	584.2	581.2
2016	563.1	564.4	572.6	586.4	591.5	598.0	598.9	598.4	595.7	597.1	595.2	582.8	587.0
2017	564.7	566.6	574.1	583.9	593.8	602.1	603.3	603.6	602.3	601.6	599.6	592.3	590.7
2018	573.1	575.5	586.3	595.3	605.6	614.5	615.4	615.3	612.7	616.6	610.0	598.9	601.6
Service-Providing													
2010	3,611.0	3,620.9	3,635.4	3,675.4	3,722.6	3,729.9	3,691.8	3,691.3	3,702.9	3,733.0	3,748.7	3,750.5	3,692.8
2011	3,650.4	3,661.7	3,684.1	3,728.6	3,752.9	3,771.7	3,754.1	3,760.5	3,778.6	3,791.5	3,808.1	3,807.7	3,745.8
2012	3,714.2	3,727.0	3,753.3	3,790.0	3,825.6	3,849.1	3,819.5	3,830.9	3,845.5	3,858.2	3,881.8	3,881.3	3,814.7
2013	3,776.1	3,797.0	3,819.9	3,849.8	3,896.1	3,920.7	3,892.3	3,905.6	3,912.5	3,925.2	3,944.0	3,954.9	3,882.8
2014	3,837.2	3,850.0	3,874.9	3,918.0	3,964.4	3,985.0	3,956.0	3,963.9	3,963.0	3,987.9	4,001.6	4,010.1	3,942.7
2015	3,896.0	3,912.7	3,932.8	3,987.6	4,037.4	4,058.5	4,038.5	4,037.7	4,039.7	4,071.4	4,078.9	4,091.8	4,015.3
2016	3,980.4	3,988.3	4,005.7	4,050.5	4,078.8	4,105.7	4,096.9	4,095.5	4,097.4	4,116.8	4,131.3	4,134.7	4,073.5
2017	4,022.0	4,033.5	4,060.6	4,082.1	4,122.4	4,155.5	4,124.0	4,126.5	4,124.4	4,143.4	4,162.5	4,162.7	4,110.0
2018	4,047.2	4,061.1	4,092.0	4,103.1	4,145.5	4,177.7	4,166.1	4,167.6	4,161.1	4,189.5	4,210.0	4,204.3	4,143.8
Mining and Logging													
2010	1.2	1.2	1.3	1.5	1.5	1.6	1.6	1.6	1.7	1.6	1.6	1.5	1.5
2011	1.2	1.2	1.3	1.5	1.5	1.5	1.6	1.5	1.5	1.5	1.5	1.3	1.4
2012	1.2	1.2	1.2	1.3	1.4	1.5	1.5	1.5	1.5	1.5	1.5	1.3	1.4
2013	1.2	1.2	1.2	1.3	1.6	1.6	1.5	1.5	1.5	1.5	1.6	1.3	1.4
2014	1.2	1.2	1.2	1.4	1.5	1.6	1.6	1.6	1.6	1.6	1.6	1.6	1.5
2015	1.3	1.3	1.5	1.6	1.6	1.5	1.5	1.6	1.6	1.6	1.7	1.7	1.5
2016	1.4	1.5	1.6	1.6	1.6	1.6	1.6	1.6	1.6	1.6	1.6	1.5	1.6
2017	1.3	1.3	1.4	1.6	1.6	1.7	1.6	1.7	1.6	1.6	1.6	1.6	1.6
2018	1.3	1.4	1.5	1.6	1.7	1.7	1.7	1.7	1.6	1.6	1.6	1.5	1.6
Construction													
2010	128.2	126.6	132.3	144.1	149.7	153.7	149.9	157.5	155.4	157.2	152.9	141.9	145.8
2011	125.8	124.2	130.5	142.2	150.1	154.3	157.7	159.5	157.3	155.8	153.2	144.3	146.2
2012	128.6	126.7	133.3	142.7	148.4	154.0	157.3	158.4	158.4	158.0	153.5	146.9	147.2
2013	129.9	130.5	135.5	143.1	152.7	157.3	160.2	160.5	160.0	160.6	157.8	148.7	149.7
2014	130.6	132.1	137.7	148.8	157.6	163.7	167.0	167.5	167.0	169.6	166.9	160.0	155.7
2015	141.8	141.5	148.5	161.0	168.4	173.1	174.8	175.2	174.7	176.7	174.7	166.4	164.7
2016	149.0	149.3	156.5	168.6	172.9	177.5	179.9	180.6	180.4	182.3	179.2	166.4	170.2
2017	151.8	152.8	159.0	169.2	177.8	181.8	183.4	184.0	184.3	184.4	181.1	172.3	173.5
2018	156.7	157.1	166.6	174.2	182.8	189.3	189.2	189.6	189.2	191.1	184.7	172.9	178.6

Employment by Industry: Chicago-Naperville-Elgin, IL-IN-WI, 2010–2018—*Continued*

(Numbers in thousands, not seasonally adjusted)

Industry and year	January	February	March	April	May	June	July	August	September	October	November	December	Annual average
Manufacturing													
2010	399.0	399.1	400.1	401.2	403.1	405.4	404.6	406.5	406.2	408.7	409.4	410.1	404.5
2011	406.5	406.6	408.9	410.9	411.8	414.4	413.5	413.5	412.0	412.6	412.2	412.3	411.3
2012	408.8	409.2	411.0	412.1	413.3	416.0	415.3	415.4	414.3	412.3	412.7	414.2	412.9
2013	409.1	409.7	410.3	408.9	409.7	413.1	411.1	411.9	409.8	409.8	410.9	411.1	410.5
2014	407.3	407.5	409.3	409.2	410.5	413.3	411.9	412.0	410.7	412.3	413.8	414.8	411.1
2015	412.0	411.7	413.0	412.0	414.1	418.6	417.8	417.2	416.4	414.6	415.1	416.1	414.9
2016	412.7	413.6	414.5	416.2	417.0	418.9	417.4	416.2	413.7	413.2	414.4	414.9	415.2
2017	411.6	412.5	413.7	413.1	414.4	418.6	418.3	417.9	416.4	415.6	416.9	418.4	415.6
2018	415.1	417.0	418.2	419.5	421.1	423.5	424.5	424.0	421.9	423.9	423.7	424.5	421.4
Trade, Transportation, and Utilities													
2010	841.1	833.3	835.6	841.6	849.1	854.3	851.2	853.4	850.6	859.1	874.8	886.4	852.5
2011	855.0	846.9	849.7	858.0	863.9	869.9	867.2	871.2	871.3	877.4	893.8	904.7	869.1
2012	871.9	861.9	866.9	869.4	877.1	882.2	881.1	883.5	882.4	889.8	911.3	917.4	882.9
2013	881.7	873.8	877.1	881.6	891.2	898.6	895.8	899.0	895.9	901.5	919.7	932.2	895.7
2014	892.5	883.5	888.8	893.8	903.7	911.4	907.9	910.5	908.5	915.4	934.6	946.2	908.1
2015	908.3	901.9	906.4	913.6	924.4	933.1	931.5	933.0	932.5	939.3	956.3	965.8	928.8
2016	927.4	921.0	923.8	932.0	936.7	941.4	941.9	942.9	938.1	950.8	967.3	980.8	942.0
2017	941.7	932.5	934.6	935.1	940.2	947.7	942.5	943.4	941.1	950.3	972.1	981.7	946.9
2018	945.0	934.6	938.1	938.7	945.9	951.9	952.1	950.1	944.6	957.0	978.3	987.2	952.0
Wholesale Trade													
2010	223.7	222.9	224.0	225.4	226.7	227.7	227.9	228.1	226.6	227.4	227.6	228.3	226.4
2011	226.6	226.6	227.4	228.9	229.8	231.7	231.8	231.9	230.9	230.9	231.3	232.6	230.0
2012	231.3	231.2	232.5	233.4	234.6	236.7	236.1	236.1	235.3	235.9	236.4	237.1	234.7
2013	234.4	234.7	236.0	236.9	238.2	240.6	240.1	239.5	239.0	238.6	239.2	240.6	238.2
2014	236.3	237.1	237.8	237.7	239.1	240.3	239.4	239.1	237.5	238.6	239.3	240.2	238.5
2015	237.6	237.4	238.7	240.1	242.2	243.7	243.4	242.5	241.1	240.5	240.7	241.6	240.8
2016	236.6	236.7	237.1	238.7	239.1	241.0	240.9	240.5	238.9	239.9	240.5	241.4	239.3
2017	238.0	238.6	239.4	240.4	241.9	244.1	243.4	242.6	241.6	242.8	242.7	244.2	241.6
2018	241.4	242.2	243.3	243.1	244.1	245.9	246.3	245.6	244.5	245.8	248.1	249.9	245.0
Retail Trade													
2010	431.8	424.6	425.7	428.3	433.2	437.9	437.1	437.2	432.4	438.7	452.8	461.1	436.7
2011	437.1	428.9	430.3	435.2	438.8	443.4	442.5	444.8	442.1	447.9	463.1	470.6	443.7
2012	444.6	435.0	437.4	437.2	441.8	446.3	445.9	446.0	442.9	449.1	468.8	471.5	447.2
2013	446.4	438.0	439.4	440.6	447.6	454.1	452.5	453.2	449.6	455.4	471.1	479.7	452.3
2014	451.0	441.7	444.6	448.4	454.0	460.6	459.7	459.4	456.5	462.3	477.7	484.0	458.3
2015	456.9	450.6	453.3	456.6	462.4	469.0	468.1	467.8	465.8	470.9	485.1	489.1	466.3
2016	464.9	458.5	460.1	464.5	467.3	471.9	472.0	471.2	464.9	471.4	484.4	490.4	470.1
2017	467.9	459.8	459.7	461.1	462.5	467.8	465.1	463.0	456.9	462.7	479.2	483.8	465.8
2018	459.2	449.5	451.8	451.8	456.5	460.1	458.9	455.9	449.6	458.2	473.1	475.6	458.4
Transportation and Utilities													
2010	185.6	185.8	185.9	187.9	189.2	188.7	186.2	188.1	191.6	193.0	194.4	197.0	189.5
2011	191.3	191.4	192.0	193.9	195.3	194.8	192.9	194.5	198.3	198.6	199.4	201.5	195.3
2012	196.0	195.7	197.0	198.8	200.7	199.2	199.1	201.4	204.2	204.8	206.1	208.8	201.0
2013	200.9	201.1	201.7	204.1	205.4	203.9	203.2	206.3	207.3	207.5	209.4	211.9	205.2
2014	205.2	204.7	206.4	207.7	210.6	210.5	208.8	212.0	214.5	214.5	217.6	222.0	211.2
2015	213.8	213.9	214.4	216.9	219.8	220.4	220.0	222.7	225.6	227.9	230.5	235.1	221.8
2016	225.9	225.8	226.6	228.8	230.3	228.5	229.0	231.2	234.3	239.5	242.4	249.0	232.6
2017	235.8	234.1	235.5	233.6	235.8	235.8	234.0	237.8	242.6	244.8	250.2	253.7	239.5
2018	244.4	242.9	243.0	243.8	245.3	245.9	246.9	248.6	250.5	253.0	257.1	261.7	248.6
Information													
2010	81.5	80.7	80.4	80.3	80.3	80.6	80.4	80.3	79.4	80.1	80.0	79.9	80.3
2011	79.4	79.2	79.0	79.3	79.5	80.3	80.8	80.5	79.8	80.2	80.7	80.5	79.9
2012	80.5	80.3	80.1	80.5	81.0	80.8	80.8	80.5	79.9	80.5	81.1	81.0	80.6
2013	79.9	79.9	79.5	80.0	80.3	80.6	80.2	79.7	79.1	79.3	79.7	79.8	79.8
2014	78.6	78.8	79.4	79.8	79.6	80.2	80.2	80.2	78.9	79.9	79.9	80.1	79.6
2015	79.4	79.2	78.6	80.1	80.7	80.3	79.8	79.7	78.6	79.3	79.5	79.6	79.6
2016	78.2	77.7	77.8	77.9	78.1	78.2	78.2	79.3	78.4	81.8	82.1	81.2	79.1
2017	80.5	80.5	80.6	79.2	79.9	79.9	79.0	79.5	77.9	77.7	77.8	77.6	79.2
2018	77.4	76.9	77.1	77.3	77.3	77.7	79.0	78.8	77.0	77.4	75.9	76.2	77.3

Employment by Industry: Chicago-Naperville-Elgin, IL-IN-WI, 2010–2018—*Continued*

(Numbers in thousands, not seasonally adjusted)

Industry and year	January	February	March	April	May	June	July	August	September	October	November	December	Annual average
Financial Activities													
2010	290.9	290.4	290.5	289.9	290.0	292.2	291.4	290.9	288.0	289.2	288.7	289.1	290.1
2011	285.2	284.7	284.7	285.0	285.4	288.0	289.5	289.5	287.6	288.4	288.2	288.3	287.0
2012	285.3	285.7	286.0	286.9	288.2	291.2	292.1	292.5	290.5	290.2	289.8	290.8	289.1
2013	288.2	288.6	288.3	289.1	289.9	293.6	293.6	293.0	291.4	292.0	291.3	292.1	290.9
2014	288.8	288.1	288.1	288.7	290.7	293.6	294.4	295.4	292.2	293.0	292.5	293.7	291.6
2015	291.3	291.4	291.3	293.1	295.4	299.2	300.3	300.7	297.1	298.8	298.3	299.4	296.4
2016	296.3	296.9	297.2	298.8	300.0	303.0	305.7	306.1	303.0	304.3	304.0	304.8	301.7
2017	302.3	302.5	303.3	304.4	305.8	310.0	312.8	312.6	309.2	310.0	309.6	310.7	307.8
2018	305.9	306.1	307.0	307.5	308.8	313.2	315.5	315.7	311.9	313.4	314.1	313.8	311.1
Professional and Business Services													
2010	653.9	656.8	658.0	678.4	683.0	691.8	694.0	699.3	697.5	705.8	705.4	703.7	685.6
2011	679.3	683.4	687.7	706.3	706.9	717.0	721.5	726.8	726.9	730.5	730.9	724.8	711.8
2012	704.9	706.6	714.0	732.3	739.7	750.9	750.0	757.8	759.5	760.9	764.3	760.0	741.7
2013	733.1	739.6	745.4	758.9	771.3	781.4	784.4	792.2	791.0	800.1	802.0	799.9	774.9
2014	765.4	770.6	775.1	790.8	800.4	809.1	807.3	812.8	809.1	817.1	817.3	810.9	798.8
2015	780.5	783.7	785.4	803.9	812.1	819.4	827.3	826.2	822.2	832.7	830.0	827.3	812.6
2016	801.4	801.6	801.5	813.9	814.8	823.8	831.9	834.6	833.4	837.4	838.2	828.8	821.8
2017	799.0	800.9	807.2	815.3	824.2	835.3	836.3	840.6	837.1	845.0	848.0	841.2	827.5
2018	807.4	815.6	817.6	820.4	827.6	839.9	848.6	854.5	852.8	859.4	862.0	849.4	837.9
Education and Health Services													
2010	621.5	629.7	632.8	634.5	636.4	629.9	624.2	621.8	633.3	643.4	648.1	648.5	633.7
2011	640.1	648.2	651.1	650.7	650.6	644.8	638.1	637.5	652.5	659.3	662.2	664.5	650.0
2012	652.5	662.7	663.4	665.4	665.0	659.9	651.6	651.3	666.1	671.1	674.4	674.8	663.2
2013	664.0	675.9	677.9	676.1	676.7	668.9	658.9	662.0	674.6	680.8	684.7	685.1	673.8
2014	676.2	684.7	686.5	690.3	691.3	682.7	675.3	677.9	686.1	693.7	697.1	699.3	686.8
2015	688.3	695.9	699.7	704.2	707.0	698.4	692.7	692.3	700.8	710.7	712.8	712.8	701.3
2016	704.6	712.1	713.6	718.0	719.4	711.5	707.1	706.3	714.9	722.2	723.8	722.6	714.7
2017	714.3	723.7	726.8	727.0	728.1	718.4	710.9	711.7	720.8	730.2	733.2	731.7	723.1
2018	721.3	731.6	735.2	734.2	735.0	726.0	719.8	719.9	729.9	743.0	747.7	744.5	732.3
Leisure and Hospitality													
2010	369.5	370.0	376.5	389.9	404.1	413.7	413.0	414.4	408.6	400.6	395.1	393.8	395.8
2011	375.7	375.1	384.0	398.6	411.2	421.6	421.1	426.5	417.1	408.8	403.5	400.1	403.6
2012	388.3	389.4	398.2	410.7	424.4	435.2	434.3	439.5	427.0	421.2	414.7	414.6	416.5
2013	400.4	400.0	409.0	420.6	436.7	448.3	448.0	448.2	437.5	429.6	422.4	421.7	426.9
2014	410.2	409.8	417.4	432.2	447.3	458.5	456.7	457.9	446.4	442.5	434.4	433.4	437.2
2015	418.8	420.8	427.9	446.3	464.5	475.8	473.2	475.7	465.1	461.4	454.9	457.4	453.5
2016	441.0	440.4	447.4	465.1	480.4	492.5	493.1	492.2	480.3	475.4	470.0	462.8	470.1
2017	452.1	453.7	463.0	476.5	493.7	506.8	504.0	505.9	489.9	484.9	475.3	471.2	481.4
2018	458.8	457.7	470.1	481.4	499.2	512.8	511.6	512.7	494.8	491.1	480.3	479.7	487.5
Other Services													
2010	191.4	191.3	192.4	187.0	188.3	190.1	189.1	189.1	188.0	189.2	189.6	190.1	189.6
2011	186.9	187.6	189.1	189.8	191.6	193.6	192.9	192.4	191.0	190.2	189.7	190.8	190.5
2012	188.2	188.8	190.0	189.3	191.0	193.9	192.4	191.4	190.4	189.7	190.1	190.2	190.5
2013	187.9	188.6	189.7	190.4	191.7	193.6	195.2	195.5	193.4	192.1	191.8	192.8	191.9
2014	190.9	191.9	193.4	193.9	196.0	198.7	198.5	196.2	194.0	194.5	194.4	194.7	194.8
2015	192.0	192.8	194.1	194.2	195.3	197.8	196.8	196.3	194.3	194.9	195.1	195.6	194.9
2016	193.2	193.6	194.5	195.2	195.9	197.5	197.4	197.1	195.1	195.3	195.0	195.7	195.5
2017	193.8	194.0	195.7	196.3	197.3	199.4	198.8	198.3	196.0	197.1	197.0	198.3	196.8
2018	195.3	196.0	197.8	197.7	199.1	200.9	201.1	200.1	197.4	198.2	198.2	199.6	198.5
Government													
2010	561.2	568.7	569.2	573.8	591.4	577.3	548.5	542.1	557.5	565.6	567.0	559.0	565.1
2011	548.8	556.6	558.8	560.9	563.8	556.5	543.0	536.1	552.4	556.7	559.1	554.0	553.9
2012	542.6	551.6	554.7	555.5	559.2	555.0	537.2	534.4	549.7	554.8	556.1	552.5	550.3
2013	540.9	550.6	553.0	553.1	558.3	555.7	536.2	536.0	549.6	549.8	552.4	551.3	548.9
2014	534.6	542.6	546.2	548.5	555.4	550.8	535.7	533.0	547.8	551.8	551.4	551.8	545.8
2015	537.4	547.0	549.4	552.2	558.0	554.5	536.9	533.8	549.1	554.3	552.0	553.9	548.2
2016	538.3	545.0	549.9	549.6	553.5	557.8	541.6	537.0	554.2	549.6	550.9	558.0	548.8
2017	538.3	545.7	549.4	548.3	553.2	558.0	539.7	534.5	552.4	548.2	549.5	550.3	547.3
2018	536.1	542.6	549.1	545.9	552.6	555.3	538.4	535.8	552.7	550.0	553.5	553.9	547.2

Employment by Industry: Dallas-Fort Worth-Arlington, TX, 2010–2018

(Numbers in thousands, not seasonally adjusted)

Industry and year	January	February	March	April	May	June	July	August	September	October	November	December	Annual average
Total Nonfarm													
2010	2,867.3	2,878.4	2,901.9	2,914.6	2,939.4	2,948.1	2,923.9	2,930.6	2,934.1	2,962.8	2,970.9	2,981.1	2,929.4
2011	2,927.2	2,941.2	2,968.8	2,992.2	3,004.3	3,019.6	3,004.4	3,015.5	3,026.9	3,034.7	3,047.6	3,055.0	3,003.1
2012	3,003.5	3,026.6	3,049.9	3,064.9	3,082.3	3,098.9	3,070.5	3,090.5	3,098.7	3,115.9	3,139.4	3,147.0	3,082.3
2013	3,078.2	3,107.5	3,127.5	3,144.1	3,165.7	3,186.1	3,169.8	3,189.5	3,199.2	3,213.9	3,240.6	3,242.5	3,172.1
2014	3,184.8	3,209.9	3,231.7	3,255.4	3,278.4	3,298.4	3,279.8	3,298.0	3,306.5	3,335.4	3,358.8	3,374.5	3,284.3
2015	3,319.1	3,341.7	3,347.2	3,373.3	3,394.7	3,413.8	3,403.4	3,414.8	3,418.3	3,445.2	3,459.4	3,471.8	3,400.2
2016	3,421.5	3,446.6	3,453.7	3,482.3	3,497.6	3,507.6	3,498.6	3,513.1	3,528.0	3,544.7	3,570.4	3,579.3	3,503.6
2017	3,523.5	3,545.0	3,557.5	3,572.1	3,588.3	3,609.4	3,583.4	3,598.6	3,608.6	3,637.2	3,666.5	3,666.5	3,596.4
2018	3,603.4	3,628.1	3,639.5	3,649.0	3,673.0	3,695.0	3,679.1	3,695.1	3,697.9	3,729.9	3,749.7	3,759.2	3,683.2
Total Private													
2010	2,466.6	2,470.8	2,492.7	2,505.5	2,518.7	2,536.5	2,534.3	2,544.5	2,537.8	2,553.1	2,560.6	2,571.9	2,524.4
2011	2,522.9	2,532.7	2,559.7	2,581.3	2,592.0	2,613.9	2,617.5	2,630.7	2,629.9	2,631.6	2,644.4	2,653.6	2,600.9
2012	2,607.8	2,625.8	2,648.5	2,663.6	2,678.7	2,704.2	2,692.7	2,712.2	2,704.2	2,712.6	2,735.8	2,742.2	2,685.7
2013	2,680.5	2,703.6	2,722.1	2,738.0	2,758.7	2,785.3	2,784.0	2,803.1	2,799.8	2,805.3	2,829.8	2,831.7	2,770.2
2014	2,781.2	2,799.3	2,818.9	2,842.4	2,863.4	2,890.8	2,889.7	2,906.1	2,900.8	2,919.3	2,940.7	2,955.7	2,875.7
2015	2,907.1	2,922.9	2,928.2	2,954.3	2,973.9	2,998.1	3,006.0	3,016.5	3,004.9	3,022.6	3,034.1	3,044.9	2,984.5
2016	3,000.6	3,020.2	3,026.1	3,054.2	3,067.2	3,084.0	3,092.4	3,104.6	3,103.3	3,114.4	3,137.4	3,144.5	3,079.1
2017	3,095.5	3,109.6	3,120.1	3,133.5	3,148.3	3,177.8	3,171.3	3,185.4	3,180.2	3,198.0	3,223.5	3,225.1	3,164.0
2018	3,170.1	3,186.0	3,195.1	3,206.6	3,228.1	3,257.6	3,260.3	3,275.2	3,262.2	3,284.3	3,300.6	3,311.4	3,244.8
Goods Producing													
2010	408.7	406.1	409.8	411.6	413.7	417.9	418.6	419.7	418.0	416.8	416.1	416.4	414.5
2011	409.2	411.4	415.4	417.6	419.1	424.5	427.3	428.7	427.8	425.9	426.5	426.9	421.7
2012	423.1	426.7	429.6	431.0	431.2	436.5	439.1	440.6	439.4	438.2	439.2	439.6	434.5
2013	433.3	436.2	439.6	439.7	442.2	446.7	448.0	449.5	448.4	445.5	446.2	444.3	443.3
2014	440.4	445.3	447.4	451.8	455.5	458.9	460.8	461.8	461.0	461.9	463.2	465.1	456.1
2015	460.9	462.2	460.0	462.2	463.0	466.7	468.2	467.5	464.5	464.2	463.1	462.4	463.7
2016	460.8	464.1	463.5	467.4	467.1	470.7	473.2	473.4	472.6	472.2	472.2	473.4	469.2
2017	471.0	475.7	478.3	479.5	481.4	488.6	488.7	488.2	487.1	488.0	488.4	489.4	483.7
2018	484.2	488.4	490.7	491.6	494.2	501.4	503.1	504.1	502.4	504.8	507.3	509.5	498.5
Service-Providing													
2010	2,458.6	2,472.3	2,492.1	2,503.0	2,525.7	2,530.2	2,505.3	2,510.9	2,516.1	2,546.0	2,554.8	2,564.7	2,515.0
2011	2,518.0	2,529.8	2,553.4	2,574.6	2,585.2	2,595.1	2,577.1	2,586.8	2,599.1	2,608.8	2,621.1	2,628.1	2,581.4
2012	2,580.4	2,599.9	2,620.3	2,633.9	2,651.1	2,662.4	2,631.4	2,649.9	2,659.3	2,677.7	2,700.2	2,707.4	2,647.8
2013	2,644.9	2,671.3	2,687.9	2,704.4	2,723.5	2,739.4	2,721.8	2,740.0	2,750.8	2,768.4	2,794.4	2,798.2	2,728.8
2014	2,744.4	2,764.6	2,784.3	2,803.6	2,822.9	2,839.5	2,819.0	2,836.2	2,845.5	2,873.5	2,895.6	2,909.4	2,828.2
2015	2,858.2	2,879.5	2,887.2	2,911.1	2,931.7	2,947.1	2,935.2	2,947.3	2,953.8	2,981.0	2,996.3	3,009.4	2,936.5
2016	2,960.7	2,982.5	2,990.2	3,014.9	3,030.5	3,036.9	3,025.4	3,039.7	3,055.4	3,072.5	3,098.2	3,105.9	3,034.4
2017	3,052.5	3,069.3	3,079.2	3,092.6	3,106.9	3,120.8	3,094.7	3,110.4	3,121.5	3,149.2	3,178.1	3,177.1	3,112.7
2018	3,119.2	3,139.7	3,148.8	3,157.4	3,178.8	3,193.6	3,176.0	3,191.0	3,195.5	3,225.1	3,242.4	3,249.7	3,184.8
Mining, Logging, and Construction													
2010	155.1	154.1	157.4	158.8	159.8	162.4	163.4	164.1	162.8	161.9	160.8	160.6	160.1
2011	156.1	157.3	160.0	161.2	162.1	165.1	167.1	168.1	167.0	165.3	165.5	165.9	163.4
2012	163.7	166.0	168.3	169.5	172.4	175.6	175.6	176.9	176.1	175.7	176.6	176.3	172.7
2013	172.6	174.9	177.6	178.2	180.4	183.3	185.4	187.1	186.7	184.7	185.2	183.5	181.6
2014	183.6	184.9	187.2	190.3	193.1	195.6	197.2	197.9	197.9	198.7	199.1	199.4	193.7
2015	197.0	197.7	196.1	197.9	198.3	200.9	201.9	201.5	199.8	200.6	199.5	198.9	199.2
2016	197.9	200.0	199.6	203.7	203.1	205.3	206.5	207.0	207.1	206.5	205.9	206.0	204.1
2017	205.1	208.0	210.1	211.0	212.5	216.3	216.0	215.5	215.1	215.5	215.5	215.2	213.0
2018	211.6	213.9	215.6	216.8	218.5	222.4	223.1	223.9	222.4	223.2	224.6	225.5	220.1
Manufacturing													
2010	253.6	252.0	252.4	252.8	253.9	255.5	255.2	255.6	255.2	254.9	255.3	255.8	254.4
2011	253.1	254.1	255.4	256.4	257.0	259.4	260.2	260.6	260.8	260.6	261.0	261.0	258.3
2012	259.4	260.7	261.3	261.5	258.8	260.9	263.5	263.7	263.3	262.5	262.6	263.3	261.8
2013	260.7	261.3	262.0	261.5	261.8	263.4	262.6	262.4	261.7	260.8	261.0	260.8	261.7
2014	256.8	260.4	260.2	261.5	262.4	263.3	263.6	263.9	263.1	263.2	264.1	265.7	262.4
2015	263.9	264.5	263.9	264.3	264.7	265.8	266.3	266.0	264.7	263.6	263.6	263.5	264.6
2016	262.9	264.1	263.9	263.7	264.0	265.4	266.7	266.4	265.5	265.7	266.3	267.4	265.2
2017	265.9	267.7	268.2	268.5	268.9	272.3	272.7	272.7	272.0	272.5	272.9	274.2	270.7
2018	272.6	274.5	275.1	274.8	275.7	279.0	280.0	280.2	280.0	281.6	282.7	284.0	278.4

Employment by Industry: Dallas-Fort Worth-Arlington, TX, 2010–2018—*Continued*

(Numbers in thousands, not seasonally adjusted)

Industry and year	January	February	March	April	May	June	July	August	September	October	November	December	Annual average
Trade, Transportation, and Utilities													
2010	598.1	594.6	599.2	600.1	603.5	605.6	605.6	608.2	606.0	611.0	621.1	627.7	606.7
2011	608.4	606.1	610.8	615.8	617.2	619.5	621.1	625.8	624.7	627.7	638.5	645.8	621.8
2012	626.7	625.1	628.7	629.7	633.7	637.8	638.0	642.5	640.2	643.7	659.5	664.9	639.2
2013	642.0	641.1	642.9	645.9	649.6	654.7	655.4	661.5	660.0	665.7	682.1	688.6	657.5
2014	665.6	663.1	666.5	668.6	673.5	680.2	681.7	687.3	687.3	695.0	711.1	723.2	683.6
2015	703.1	701.7	703.4	708.6	713.9	719.8	722.2	727.5	726.3	732.9	745.5	755.1	721.7
2016	732.6	731.2	731.6	735.5	737.4	741.7	745.2	749.5	748.0	756.4	775.0	784.0	747.3
2017	759.6	752.6	751.6	752.5	754.7	762.1	762.8	770.3	768.0	776.4	798.3	803.1	767.7
2018	775.2	769.2	768.5	770.5	775.1	778.7	780.9	785.5	785.1	792.6	813.1	816.4	784.2
Wholesale Trade													
2010	163.4	163.3	163.9	163.6	164.4	164.7	165.5	165.6	165.3	166.0	166.2	166.8	164.9
2011	165.1	166.4	166.9	167.7	168.7	169.2	169.3	169.8	170.1	170.5	170.8	171.8	168.9
2012	170.2	171.5	172.4	173.1	174.4	175.4	175.4	176.1	176.0	175.5	176.4	177.2	174.5
2013	175.6	176.5	177.2	177.5	178.1	179.1	179.2	179.7	179.3	180.5	181.7	182.2	178.9
2014	179.8	180.7	181.5	181.6	182.4	183.8	184.7	185.6	185.5	186.5	186.8	187.6	183.9
2015	187.7	188.8	189.1	189.4	190.4	191.3	191.9	192.6	192.0	190.7	190.3	190.2	190.4
2016	192.7	193.5	193.1	193.5	193.6	194.1	194.9	195.1	194.4	193.8	193.9	194.4	193.9
2017	192.8	192.9	192.7	192.8	193.9	195.7	195.7	196.6	196.3	196.7	196.8	197.8	195.1
2018	197.1	198.0	198.1	199.1	200.0	201.7	201.7	202.3	202.2	203.3	203.5	205.0	201.0
Retail Trade													
2010	300.4	297.2	300.5	302.2	304.4	305.5	304.4	306.5	304.0	308.0	316.8	322.0	306.0
2011	306.3	302.2	305.4	309.1	309.5	311.1	312.5	316.1	313.5	317.0	326.7	331.6	313.4
2012	316.6	312.7	314.4	314.7	316.5	318.5	318.4	321.1	318.2	322.4	335.9	338.1	320.6
2013	321.6	319.6	319.9	322.0	324.0	326.9	327.3	331.9	330.2	334.1	347.5	351.3	329.7
2014	334.0	331.3	332.8	333.9	335.5	339.2	339.3	342.4	340.1	344.7	357.8	363.8	341.2
2015	347.6	346.0	346.5	350.1	352.5	355.8	357.3	359.4	357.6	363.1	373.0	378.0	357.2
2016	359.9	358.0	358.5	361.4	362.0	363.8	366.3	368.9	364.5	370.9	383.0	387.4	367.1
2017	371.2	366.4	366.3	367.8	368.0	371.4	371.0	373.9	369.8	375.7	390.9	393.0	373.8
2018	375.1	370.0	369.6	370.3	372.5	373.3	375.5	377.8	375.2	377.2	391.7	392.3	376.7
Transportation and Utilities													
2010	134.3	134.1	134.8	134.3	134.7	135.4	135.7	136.1	136.7	137.0	138.1	138.9	135.8
2011	137.0	137.5	138.5	139.0	139.0	139.2	139.3	139.9	141.1	140.2	141.0	142.4	139.5
2012	139.9	140.9	141.9	141.9	142.8	143.9	144.2	145.3	146.0	145.8	147.2	149.6	144.1
2013	144.8	145.0	145.8	146.4	147.5	148.7	148.9	149.9	150.5	151.1	152.9	155.1	148.9
2014	151.8	151.1	152.2	153.1	155.6	157.2	157.7	159.3	161.7	163.8	166.5	171.8	158.5
2015	167.8	166.9	167.8	169.1	171.0	172.7	173.0	175.5	176.7	179.1	182.2	186.9	174.1
2016	180.0	179.7	180.0	180.6	181.8	183.8	184.0	185.5	189.1	191.7	198.1	202.2	186.4
2017	195.6	193.3	192.6	191.9	192.8	195.0	196.1	199.8	201.9	204.0	210.6	212.3	198.8
2018	203.0	201.2	200.8	201.1	202.6	203.7	203.7	205.4	207.7	212.1	217.9	219.1	206.5
Information													
2010	81.3	80.9	80.9	81.4	81.1	81.7	81.1	81.1	80.4	80.2	80.5	80.4	80.9
2011	80.5	80.3	80.3	80.1	80.4	80.7	80.9	80.5	80.0	80.3	80.6	80.8	80.5
2012	79.6	79.5	79.5	79.6	79.6	80.0	79.4	79.2	78.8	79.2	80.2	80.1	79.6
2013	79.8	80.1	79.9	80.4	81.1	81.3	81.7	81.8	80.9	81.5	82.1	82.5	81.1
2014	82.1	81.9	81.5	81.7	82.2	82.7	82.5	82.1	81.1	80.4	80.8	81.0	81.7
2015	79.8	79.6	79.8	80.3	80.5	80.6	81.6	81.7	80.8	80.9	81.5	82.4	80.8
2016	81.5	81.6	81.6	83.0	82.9	83.5	84.0	84.1	83.6	82.8	83.4	83.8	83.0
2017	83.5	83.7	84.6	84.1	83.9	84.4	84.4	84.1	83.0	82.7	83.3	83.7	83.8
2018	83.1	83.9	83.6	83.1	83.6	84.6	83.8	83.1	81.8	81.9	82.7	82.5	83.1
Financial Activities													
2010	231.7	232.3	232.9	232.9	233.6	234.3	235.1	235.3	234.9	236.5	236.7	238.1	234.5
2011	237.0	237.9	239.0	238.9	238.9	240.8	241.8	242.5	242.6	243.4	244.0	245.7	241.0
2012	243.8	245.3	246.5	247.2	248.4	250.6	250.5	250.7	250.8	252.5	253.7	255.2	249.6
2013	253.1	255.0	256.8	256.9	258.6	261.0	262.8	263.3	262.7	263.0	263.8	264.3	260.1
2014	261.6	262.5	263.1	264.1	264.1	265.9	267.8	268.4	267.5	269.6	270.0	270.7	266.3
2015	268.9	269.9	270.3	271.2	272.1	273.9	275.3	275.7	275.8	276.1	276.8	277.4	273.6
2016	277.3	278.4	278.7	280.6	282.0	283.2	285.0	285.8	286.5	288.0	289.1	290.5	283.8
2017	288.3	290.0	291.2	293.2	294.3	296.6	297.6	298.1	300.1	300.4	299.4	300.0	295.8
2018	298.2	299.5	299.5	298.3	299.6	302.2	303.0	303.7	303.2	304.7	304.6	305.0	301.8

Employment by Industry: Dallas-Fort Worth-Arlington, TX, 2010–2018—*Continued*

(Numbers in thousands, not seasonally adjusted)

Industry and year	January	February	March	April	May	June	July	August	September	October	November	December	Annual average
Professional and Business Services													
2010	425.6	428.4	431.9	437.3	438.2	441.5	443.5	448.0	449.8	454.6	456.2	457.9	442.7
2011	448.9	452.8	457.7	463.5	463.5	467.2	468.6	473.3	475.8	476.2	478.6	477.8	467.0
2012	469.5	474.9	480.2	484.6	488.3	491.4	486.4	495.3	494.3	499.2	504.0	499.6	489.0
2013	487.2	493.4	496.7	498.6	502.0	507.3	507.7	515.3	518.3	522.0	526.3	523.7	508.2
2014	514.1	519.7	524.1	530.8	534.0	537.6	539.2	545.0	545.4	550.8	554.2	553.4	537.4
2015	546.5	550.0	550.2	555.0	556.7	558.6	563.3	566.1	564.1	572.7	573.1	572.7	560.8
2016	565.7	570.5	569.2	576.2	577.0	579.4	584.7	589.2	590.5	593.0	596.6	591.7	582.0
2017	583.6	588.3	587.0	588.9	591.3	593.7	594.7	598.3	599.5	607.1	610.5	602.9	595.5
2018	598.1	604.0	604.6	609.2	613.4	617.5	622.4	627.4	624.6	631.6	625.4	622.4	616.7
Education and Health Services													
2010	347.7	350.7	354.2	356.6	358.0	356.9	356.2	358.6	360.4	363.7	364.0	365.7	357.7
2011	360.8	361.8	365.7	368.2	369.8	369.8	369.6	371.7	375.3	375.4	376.1	378.1	370.2
2012	372.4	376.0	378.2	378.2	378.5	377.6	376.1	379.3	381.0	381.9	382.7	384.0	378.8
2013	376.9	381.5	383.0	385.7	387.1	385.7	384.2	388.7	391.0	392.7	394.7	395.0	387.2
2014	390.1	394.0	395.7	396.3	398.3	397.6	395.7	400.8	403.0	405.8	408.1	409.7	399.6
2015	403.5	407.7	408.6	412.6	415.9	414.9	414.7	418.4	419.2	422.2	424.1	425.6	415.6
2016	420.8	424.8	425.6	426.8	428.9	426.0	426.3	430.2	433.0	434.4	435.8	436.6	429.1
2017	434.4	439.0	440.3	441.6	442.7	442.4	438.3	442.4	444.6	446.1	447.5	448.8	442.3
2018	443.7	447.5	448.2	448.9	450.6	450.2	449.6	453.0	453.3	455.7	454.7	457.9	451.1
Leisure and Hospitality													
2010	271.5	275.0	280.4	283.1	287.1	290.6	287.0	287.8	285.3	287.1	283.3	283.4	283.5
2011	276.1	279.3	286.7	292.5	297.1	300.7	297.3	298.6	295.7	295.6	293.3	292.1	292.1
2012	285.8	290.5	297.2	304.5	308.7	314.9	308.5	311.1	309.2	306.7	305.5	308.1	304.2
2013	298.3	304.7	311.1	318.4	324.0	329.6	325.6	325.4	323.1	320.9	320.4	319.8	318.4
2014	313.0	317.7	324.7	332.5	337.5	344.3	339.1	339.1	337.5	337.2	334.8	334.7	332.7
2015	327.5	333.5	337.1	347.8	353.5	360.1	357.9	358.1	356.3	355.2	351.7	351.6	349.2
2016	345.3	351.6	357.4	365.1	370.5	374.7	370.5	370.3	368.6	367.5	364.8	364.1	364.2
2017	357.5	361.4	366.9	372.7	378.4	384.2	381.0	381.0	376.0	375.3	374.2	375.7	373.7
2018	368.5	373.5	378.7	382.4	388.0	395.2	391.1	392.6	386.9	387.9	387.4	393.7	385.5
Other Services													
2010	102.0	102.8	103.4	102.5	103.5	108.0	107.2	105.8	103.0	103.2	102.7	102.3	103.9
2011	102.0	103.1	104.1	104.7	106.0	110.7	110.9	109.6	108.0	107.1	106.8	106.4	106.6
2012	106.9	107.8	108.6	108.8	110.3	115.4	114.7	113.5	110.5	111.2	111.0	110.7	110.8
2013	109.9	111.6	112.1	112.4	114.1	119.0	118.6	117.6	115.4	114.0	114.2	113.5	114.4
2014	114.3	115.1	115.9	116.6	118.3	123.6	122.9	121.6	118.0	118.6	118.5	117.9	118.4
2015	116.9	118.3	118.8	116.6	118.3	123.5	122.8	121.5	117.9	118.4	118.3	117.7	119.1
2016	116.6	118.0	118.5	119.6	121.4	124.8	123.5	122.1	120.5	120.1	120.5	120.4	120.5
2017	117.6	118.9	120.2	121.0	121.6	125.8	123.8	123.0	121.9	122.0	121.9	121.5	121.6
2018	119.1	120.0	121.3	122.6	123.6	127.8	126.4	125.8	124.9	125.1	125.4	124.0	123.8
Government													
2010	400.7	407.6	409.2	409.1	420.7	411.6	389.6	386.1	396.3	409.7	410.3	409.2	405.0
2011	404.3	408.5	409.1	410.9	412.3	405.7	386.9	384.8	397.0	403.1	403.2	401.4	402.3
2012	395.7	400.8	401.4	401.3	403.6	394.7	377.8	378.3	394.5	403.3	403.6	404.8	396.7
2013	397.7	403.9	405.4	406.1	407.0	400.8	385.8	386.4	399.4	408.6	410.8	410.8	401.9
2014	403.6	410.6	412.8	413.0	415.0	407.6	390.1	391.9	405.7	416.1	418.1	418.8	408.6
2015	412.0	418.8	419.0	419.0	420.8	415.7	397.4	398.3	413.4	422.6	425.3	426.9	415.8
2016	420.9	426.4	427.6	428.1	430.4	423.6	406.2	408.5	424.7	430.3	433.0	434.8	424.5
2017	428.0	435.4	437.4	438.6	440.0	431.6	412.1	413.2	428.4	439.2	443.0	441.4	432.4
2018	433.3	442.1	444.4	442.4	444.9	437.4	418.8	419.9	435.7	445.6	449.1	447.8	438.5

Employment by Industry: Houston-The Woodlands-Sugar Land, TX, 2010–2018

(Numbers in thousands, not seasonally adjusted)

Industry and year	January	February	March	April	May	June	July	August	September	October	November	December	Annual average
Total Nonfarm													
2010	2,513.3	2,527.2	2,544.0	2,559.2	2,578.5	2,583.0	2,566.2	2,569.3	2,574.1	2,587.3	2,597.9	2,608.0	2,567.3
2011	2,566.4	2,582.3	2,604.5	2,625.4	2,631.5	2,647.8	2,634.2	2,641.2	2,655.2	2,659.6	2,675.1	2,690.9	2,634.5
2012	2,650.4	2,675.2	2,700.1	2,713.1	2,733.0	2,751.4	2,735.6	2,751.2	2,763.3	2,778.1	2,797.7	2,808.4	2,738.1
2013	2,759.4	2,796.3	2,812.9	2,824.0	2,837.4	2,851.6	2,839.6	2,845.1	2,854.5	2,872.3	2,889.7	2,898.4	2,840.1
2014	2,851.9	2,881.1	2,898.3	2,916.0	2,935.5	2,947.5	2,936.9	2,946.6	2,957.7	2,984.4	3,000.4	3,015.1	2,939.3
2015	2,964.7	2,984.7	2,988.8	2,989.8	2,997.3	3,003.3	2,986.9	2,984.6	2,988.1	3,006.5	3,006.8	3,012.6	2,992.8
2016	2,971.9	2,987.3	2,987.6	2,996.5	2,999.1	2,998.5	2,983.2	2,978.7	2,986.9	2,998.7	3,007.0	3,010.2	2,992.1
2017	2,965.0	2,991.3	3,009.8	3,014.6	3,030.0	3,040.7	3,007.3	3,009.9	3,006.4	3,038.8	3,059.0	3,064.4	3,019.8
2018	3,009.5	3,047.7	3,064.2	3,065.1	3,083.8	3,099.2	3,075.7	3,085.0	3,089.2	3,121.7	3,137.6	3,137.7	3,084.7
Total Private													
2010	2,132.6	2,138.4	2,153.5	2,165.9	2,176.1	2,193.3	2,194.5	2,200.7	2,192.0	2,197.8	2,206.5	2,218.9	2,180.9
2011	2,180.1	2,192.6	2,214.2	2,234.6	2,243.2	2,267.6	2,270.4	2,283.7	2,283.3	2,282.6	2,298.0	2,314.8	2,255.4
2012	2,281.2	2,299.1	2,323.2	2,335.9	2,355.2	2,382.7	2,379.8	2,397.9	2,393.6	2,401.2	2,418.9	2,429.1	2,366.5
2013	2,389.5	2,417.0	2,432.8	2,442.8	2,455.4	2,477.6	2,479.4	2,491.2	2,478.1	2,487.8	2,503.0	2,512.0	2,463.9
2014	2,474.3	2,494.2	2,510.6	2,528.4	2,547.1	2,563.9	2,569.4	2,584.6	2,575.9	2,593.8	2,607.0	2,622.4	2,556.0
2015	2,580.3	2,591.8	2,594.6	2,596.6	2,603.3	2,614.7	2,614.0	2,616.1	2,600.2	2,608.8	2,606.6	2,612.3	2,603.3
2016	2,578.3	2,585.7	2,584.6	2,591.7	2,592.6	2,596.6	2,597.5	2,598.4	2,587.8	2,591.7	2,596.5	2,597.8	2,591.6
2017	2,564.5	2,580.4	2,596.0	2,601.8	2,616.1	2,632.1	2,618.1	2,625.8	2,603.6	2,627.5	2,643.6	2,648.1	2,613.1
2018	2,605.1	2,631.9	2,646.8	2,650.4	2,666.6	2,687.3	2,682.0	2,696.3	2,681.8	2,703.3	2,716.5	2,715.6	2,673.6
Goods Producing													
2010	465.6	465.6	467.0	468.3	470.2	472.8	474.3	475.8	475.7	477.2	475.6	475.7	472.0
2011	470.0	476.1	479.2	481.8	482.6	490.6	494.9	498.8	502.3	504.5	504.9	507.0	491.1
2012	502.0	508.4	514.5	516.4	520.4	526.1	526.2	530.5	532.6	538.7	537.7	538.2	524.3
2013	533.4	543.0	545.0	546.6	547.5	552.7	551.9	553.8	551.9	554.8	554.2	555.1	549.2
2014	551.8	559.3	560.8	564.5	568.6	571.0	573.3	577.5	578.8	583.3	584.8	587.3	571.8
2015	579.6	579.3	575.3	567.8	565.5	565.3	562.1	558.7	554.4	554.5	546.3	542.4	562.6
2016	537.6	537.8	533.4	530.7	527.1	523.9	520.4	515.8	514.8	515.9	509.8	506.7	522.8
2017	503.3	509.1	512.1	510.9	514.8	515.8	510.0	511.7	510.5	516.6	516.7	516.0	512.3
2018	508.9	518.2	522.1	523.0	526.7	530.8	528.4	534.2	535.2	540.4	542.5	539.7	529.2
Service-Providing													
2010	2,047.7	2,061.6	2,077.0	2,090.9	2,108.3	2,110.2	2,091.9	2,093.5	2,098.4	2,110.1	2,122.3	2,132.3	2,095.4
2011	2,096.4	2,106.2	2,125.3	2,143.6	2,148.9	2,157.2	2,139.3	2,142.4	2,152.9	2,155.1	2,170.2	2,183.9	2,143.5
2012	2,148.4	2,166.8	2,185.6	2,196.7	2,212.6	2,225.3	2,209.4	2,220.7	2,230.7	2,239.4	2,260.0	2,270.2	2,213.8
2013	2,226.0	2,253.3	2,267.9	2,277.4	2,289.9	2,298.9	2,287.7	2,291.3	2,302.6	2,317.5	2,335.5	2,343.3	2,290.9
2014	2,300.1	2,321.8	2,337.5	2,351.5	2,366.9	2,376.5	2,363.6	2,369.1	2,378.9	2,401.1	2,415.6	2,427.8	2,367.5
2015	2,385.1	2,405.4	2,413.5	2,422.0	2,431.8	2,438.0	2,424.8	2,425.9	2,433.7	2,452.0	2,460.5	2,470.2	2,430.2
2016	2,434.3	2,449.5	2,454.2	2,465.8	2,472.0	2,474.6	2,462.8	2,462.9	2,472.1	2,482.8	2,497.2	2,503.5	2,469.3
2017	2,461.7	2,482.2	2,497.7	2,503.7	2,515.2	2,524.9	2,497.3	2,498.2	2,495.9	2,522.2	2,542.3	2,548.4	2,507.5
2018	2,500.6	2,529.5	2,542.1	2,542.1	2,557.1	2,568.4	2,547.3	2,550.8	2,554.0	2,581.3	2,595.1	2,598.0	2,555.5
Mining and Logging													
2010	79.3	79.6	79.8	81.1	81.9	83.6	83.8	84.4	84.2	84.8	85.3	85.7	82.8
2011	85.4	86.4	86.9	87.9	88.2	91.0	92.7	94.1	94.3	95.7	96.3	97.6	91.4
2012	96.4	97.2	98.3	98.9	98.9	100.3	102.1	102.1	102.1	102.9	103.2	104.1	100.5
2013	103.9	104.5	105.0	106.1	106.6	108.1	109.5	109.9	109.2	110.2	110.5	110.7	107.9
2014	109.7	110.5	110.1	110.2	110.8	111.5	112.6	112.7	112.3	111.9	112.8	113.0	111.5
2015	111.3	107.5	105.0	102.5	100.6	99.9	99.1	97.5	95.6	94.9	92.4	91.2	99.8
2016	89.5	88.0	86.1	83.5	81.7	81.1	79.3	78.6	77.3	77.4	76.0	75.7	81.2
2017	76.1	77.0	76.7	76.9	77.8	77.7	77.7	77.8	77.3	77.9	77.7	77.9	77.4
2018	77.1	77.9	78.4	77.6	78.3	78.6	78.6	79.2	80.0	81.4	81.3	81.0	79.1
Construction													
2010	172.2	171.5	172.4	173.2	173.9	173.9	174.5	175.0	174.9	175.2	172.4	171.0	173.3
2011	165.9	169.6	170.8	170.9	170.7	173.3	174.5	175.9	178.0	177.7	176.1	174.5	173.2
2012	171.7	175.3	178.2	178.0	180.6	181.8	179.5	183.8	184.9	190.2	188.1	186.7	181.6
2013	183.6	190.8	191.6	192.0	192.3	193.9	192.0	193.4	192.5	194.2	192.5	192.1	191.7
2014	191.5	196.9	198.3	202.2	204.4	203.7	204.0	207.5	209.4	212.4	211.1	211.8	204.4
2015	208.8	214.4	214.9	214.4	216.2	217.8	218.2	219.1	219.0	222.6	218.9	217.4	216.8
2016	216.5	219.5	219.5	222.1	222.0	220.0	219.3	216.9	218.5	220.9	216.6	213.3	218.8
2017	210.1	214.2	216.4	215.6	217.8	216.9	211.0	211.6	211.6	216.9	216.0	213.9	214.3
2018	209.9	216.6	218.9	220.0	221.7	222.6	219.4	223.5	223.9	227.1	226.8	222.9	221.1

Employment by Industry: Houston-The Woodlands-Sugar Land, TX, 2010–2018—Continued

(Numbers in thousands, not seasonally adjusted)

Industry and year	January	February	March	April	May	June	July	August	September	October	November	December	Annual average
Manufacturing													
2010	214.1	214.5	214.8	214.0	214.4	215.3	216.0	216.4	216.6	217.2	217.9	219.0	215.9
2011	218.7	220.1	221.5	223.0	223.7	226.3	227.7	228.8	230.0	231.1	232.5	234.9	226.5
2012	233.9	235.9	238.0	239.5	240.9	244.0	244.6	244.6	245.6	245.6	246.4	247.4	242.2
2013	245.9	247.7	248.4	248.5	248.6	250.7	250.4	250.5	250.2	250.4	251.2	252.3	249.6
2014	250.6	251.9	252.4	252.1	253.4	255.8	256.7	257.3	257.1	259.0	260.9	262.5	255.8
2015	259.5	257.4	255.4	250.9	248.7	247.6	244.8	242.1	239.8	237.0	235.0	233.8	246.0
2016	231.6	230.3	227.8	225.1	223.4	222.8	221.8	220.3	219.0	217.6	217.2	217.7	222.9
2017	217.1	217.9	219.0	218.4	219.2	221.2	221.3	222.3	221.6	221.8	223.0	224.2	220.6
2018	221.9	223.7	224.8	225.4	226.7	229.6	230.4	231.5	231.3	231.9	234.4	235.8	229.0
Trade, Transportation, and Utilities													
2010	515.8	513.4	516.5	516.9	518.7	522.2	522.6	525.8	523.4	526.6	535.5	545.0	523.5
2011	527.8	525.5	529.7	533.7	534.7	538.6	538.9	543.1	540.3	543.5	554.7	564.8	539.6
2012	546.5	544.3	547.5	549.4	552.5	556.4	556.8	561.1	558.1	561.9	575.8	581.4	557.6
2013	564.2	563.5	565.4	568.0	570.1	573.9	575.3	580.0	576.5	578.8	591.2	599.0	575.5
2014	584.3	582.3	583.5	585.0	587.6	591.4	593.0	598.0	594.9	599.5	611.8	621.4	594.4
2015	603.4	601.8	602.1	603.8	606.7	608.2	608.5	611.0	607.9	610.8	619.9	625.9	609.2
2016	608.6	606.2	605.5	605.5	604.9	607.1	608.0	609.2	604.9	609.9	621.4	627.8	609.9
2017	611.1	607.7	607.8	608.9	611.3	614.0	612.4	614.9	607.6	617.1	630.9	636.2	615.0
2018	619.2	617.4	618.1	617.7	620.4	622.6	622.3	624.2	621.8	628.7	641.2	644.7	624.9
Wholesale Trade													
2010	133.4	133.6	134.2	134.3	134.8	135.6	135.9	136.2	136.2	136.0	136.2	136.8	135.3
2011	136.6	137.4	138.3	139.4	140.2	141.2	141.9	142.7	143.5	143.9	144.7	145.9	141.3
2012	145.2	146.3	147.3	147.5	148.7	150.2	150.2	151.1	151.2	151.7	152.4	153.0	149.6
2013	151.9	153.5	154.3	154.4	155.3	156.5	157.1	158.1	158.5	158.7	159.7	160.1	156.5
2014	159.2	160.7	161.4	161.4	162.8	164.3	164.5	166.2	166.8	167.6	168.4	169.6	164.4
2015	168.4	169.4	169.4	168.7	168.3	168.1	167.4	167.7	166.8	166.8	166.3	166.1	167.8
2016	165.4	165.5	164.4	162.9	162.4	162.1	162.0	161.8	161.4	160.2	160.5	160.9	162.5
2017	159.7	160.5	161.2	162.6	163.8	165.4	164.4	165.0	164.1	164.5	165.1	165.8	163.5
2018	164.6	165.9	166.8	167.1	167.7	169.0	169.2	169.8	169.7	171.4	172.0	172.6	168.8
Retail Trade													
2010	260.5	258.1	260.2	260.0	261.2	263.1	262.5	264.9	262.3	265.7	274.1	279.4	264.3
2011	266.7	263.6	266.3	268.8	269.1	271.5	270.2	273.3	269.4	272.7	282.3	287.0	271.7
2012	274.2	270.6	271.6	272.8	274.6	276.4	276.8	279.6	276.9	280.4	292.0	295.4	278.4
2013	280.4	278.5	279.1	281.4	282.6	284.7	285.8	288.4	284.9	287.0	297.5	302.6	286.1
2014	290.4	288.2	288.2	288.9	289.3	291.2	292.1	294.1	290.8	292.9	302.7	307.3	293.0
2015	293.6	292.1	292.8	294.5	297.5	299.8	300.6	302.6	300.6	303.4	311.9	315.3	300.4
2016	302.9	301.4	302.2	303.2	303.6	305.5	306.0	308.0	303.6	309.1	318.8	321.6	307.2
2017	310.6	306.9	306.0	305.9	306.2	307.0	305.8	306.8	300.6	308.1	318.5	320.4	308.6
2018	310.0	306.6	305.9	304.8	306.2	306.6	306.0	306.9	304.0	306.4	314.5	314.6	307.7
Transportation and Utilities													
2010	121.9	121.7	122.1	122.6	122.7	123.5	124.2	124.7	124.9	124.9	125.2	128.8	123.9
2011	124.5	124.5	125.1	125.5	125.4	125.9	126.8	127.1	127.4	126.9	127.7	131.9	126.6
2012	127.1	127.4	128.6	129.1	129.2	129.8	129.8	130.4	130.0	129.8	131.4	133.0	129.6
2013	131.9	131.5	132.0	132.2	132.2	132.7	132.4	133.5	133.1	133.1	134.0	136.3	132.9
2014	134.7	133.4	133.9	134.7	135.5	135.9	136.4	137.7	137.3	139.0	140.7	144.5	137.0
2015	141.4	140.3	139.9	140.6	140.9	140.3	140.5	140.7	140.5	140.6	141.7	144.5	141.0
2016	140.3	139.3	138.9	139.4	138.9	139.5	140.0	139.4	139.9	140.6	142.1	145.3	140.3
2017	140.8	140.3	140.6	140.4	141.3	141.6	142.2	143.1	142.9	144.5	147.3	150.0	142.9
2018	144.6	144.9	145.4	145.8	146.5	147.0	147.1	147.5	148.1	150.9	154.7	157.5	148.3
Information													
2010	33.2	32.9	32.7	32.6	32.5	33.1	32.5	32.5	32.1	32.2	32.4	32.5	32.6
2011	32.5	32.4	32.2	32.2	32.4	32.5	32.3	32.2	32.0	31.8	31.8	31.9	32.2
2012	31.7	31.7	31.7	31.7	31.9	32.4	32.7	32.9	32.8	32.3	32.6	32.7	32.3
2013	32.2	32.4	32.7	32.7	32.9	33.4	33.4	33.4	33.0	33.5	33.6	33.7	33.1
2014	33.0	32.9	32.9	32.9	32.8	33.0	32.8	32.5	31.9	31.9	32.0	32.2	32.6
2015	32.0	32.0	32.0	32.3	32.3	32.5	32.6	32.4	31.8	31.5	31.7	32.1	32.1
2016	32.2	32.2	32.1	32.5	32.7	33.1	33.1	32.8	32.3	32.2	32.3	32.7	32.5
2017	32.3	32.2	32.5	32.5	32.5	32.6	32.6	32.2	31.3	31.2	31.5	32.0	32.1
2018	31.7	31.7	31.7	31.5	31.7	31.9	31.8	31.5	31.3	31.3	31.7	31.8	31.6

Employment by Industry: Houston-The Woodlands-Sugar Land, TX, 2010–2018—*Continued*

(Numbers in thousands, not seasonally adjusted)

Industry and year	January	February	March	April	May	June	July	August	September	October	November	December	Annual average
Financial Activities													
2010	137.3	137.5	137.8	137.6	137.7	138.4	138.5	138.6	137.6	138.3	138.6	139.0	138.1
2011	138.0	138.2	138.7	138.6	138.9	139.4	140.0	140.1	140.7	141.0	140.8	140.8	139.6
2012	139.5	140.2	140.7	141.2	142.0	143.1	143.1	143.3	142.6	143.9	144.0	144.5	142.3
2013	142.3	143.5	143.2	143.7	144.3	145.6	146.4	146.6	146.3	147.0	146.8	146.9	145.2
2014	145.2	146.0	145.9	146.7	147.7	148.4	149.0	149.6	149.1	150.3	150.2	150.7	148.2
2015	149.2	149.8	150.1	150.5	151.1	151.5	152.1	152.3	151.8	153.1	153.1	153.4	151.5
2016	153.6	154.0	153.9	154.6	154.9	155.6	157.2	157.4	157.0	157.4	157.9	158.3	156.0
2017	157.5	158.1	158.4	158.6	159.3	160.7	161.3	161.5	160.8	162.8	162.7	163.0	160.4
2018	161.7	162.7	162.7	163.3	164.0	165.3	165.3	165.7	164.5	165.2	164.3	164.1	164.1
Professional and Business Services													
2010	362.2	364.9	368.1	373.2	374.6	378.8	381.0	382.0	381.1	382.5	383.2	385.1	376.4
2011	379.7	384.1	389.0	395.4	395.9	401.2	403.6	406.7	407.1	405.5	406.9	410.3	398.8
2012	407.5	412.4	417.8	421.0	424.0	430.5	432.0	436.4	435.7	434.7	437.7	439.4	427.4
2013	432.5	438.5	443.8	443.9	444.8	449.8	450.8	453.1	451.3	454.2	455.1	455.2	447.8
2014	446.5	450.6	455.7	459.8	463.1	466.6	468.7	473.4	472.0	475.9	475.5	476.5	465.4
2015	469.4	472.0	471.6	472.9	472.1	475.2	476.9	477.7	474.4	477.7	475.8	476.5	474.4
2016	470.6	471.2	470.3	473.7	471.2	471.4	475.2	475.8	475.2	476.0	474.5	471.8	473.1
2017	468.6	473.1	477.3	477.9	478.3	484.1	484.6	485.7	486.5	488.2	487.7	486.2	481.5
2018	480.6	487.0	489.5	488.1	489.6	497.2	496.4	499.5	494.9	498.5	502.3	500.5	493.7
Education and Health Services													
2010	302.5	304.6	306.3	308.0	309.5	308.7	308.8	310.4	311.6	313.2	313.6	313.8	309.3
2011	309.8	311.0	312.3	314.1	315.1	314.7	314.4	316.3	318.4	318.6	320.6	321.5	315.6
2012	318.0	320.9	322.7	323.6	325.6	326.0	325.1	328.8	330.9	332.7	333.6	334.6	326.9
2013	330.4	334.3	335.2	336.4	338.0	337.2	337.0	341.3	342.1	345.2	346.7	345.9	339.1
2014	341.8	344.5	345.2	347.8	349.2	347.3	348.9	352.7	354.0	358.5	359.7	360.3	350.8
2015	358.0	361.6	362.8	363.9	364.9	362.8	364.5	367.5	368.9	371.5	372.4	372.6	366.0
2016	369.4	372.5	372.6	374.3	375.5	374.0	375.7	380.1	381.4	382.4	383.4	384.1	377.1
2017	379.3	382.9	383.4	385.2	387.0	386.0	383.5	386.5	384.7	387.4	388.8	389.7	385.4
2018	384.7	389.5	390.6	391.1	392.6	392.2	392.5	396.4	396.7	397.8	399.4	398.6	393.5
Leisure and Hospitality													
2010	224.0	226.8	232.6	235.9	238.8	241.7	238.8	239.1	236.8	234.9	235.4	235.6	235.0
2011	230.5	232.8	240.5	243.9	247.7	250.6	246.5	246.4	242.6	244.0	244.0	243.1	243.1
2012	241.4	245.7	253.1	254.8	259.9	265.1	260.7	262.3	260.7	257.5	259.1	259.7	256.7
2013	255.8	262.1	267.7	270.1	275.4	278.1	277.3	277.5	273.6	271.2	272.7	273.9	271.3
2014	269.1	274.4	282.2	285.0	290.6	294.8	292.3	290.9	287.9	286.2	286.0	287.3	285.6
2015	282.8	288.3	294.0	298.7	303.1	307.6	305.7	306.3	303.4	301.2	300.1	302.3	299.5
2016	300.0	304.4	309.6	312.6	317.6	320.7	317.8	318.0	313.5	308.4	308.8	309.0	311.7
2017	306.4	309.1	315.5	316.4	322.1	326.5	323.7	323.5	312.9	313.4	314.5	315.2	316.6
2018	310.7	316.1	322.1	324.3	329.3	332.7	333.3	332.9	325.7	327.6	321.7	323.5	325.0
Other Services													
2010	92.0	92.7	92.5	93.4	94.1	97.6	98.0	96.5	93.7	92.9	92.2	92.2	94.0
2011	91.8	92.5	92.6	94.9	95.9	100.0	99.8	98.6	96.1	95.1	94.3	94.5	95.5
2012	94.6	95.5	95.2	97.8	98.9	103.1	103.2	102.6	100.2	99.5	98.4	98.6	99.0
2013	98.7	99.7	99.8	101.4	102.4	106.9	107.3	105.5	103.4	103.1	102.7	102.3	102.8
2014	102.6	104.2	104.4	106.7	107.5	111.4	111.4	110.0	107.3	108.2	107.0	106.7	107.3
2015	105.9	107.0	106.7	106.7	107.6	111.6	111.6	110.2	107.6	108.5	107.3	107.1	108.2
2016	106.3	107.4	107.2	107.8	108.7	110.8	110.1	109.3	108.7	109.5	108.4	107.4	108.5
2017	106.0	108.2	109.0	111.4	110.8	112.4	110.0	109.8	109.3	110.8	110.8	109.8	109.9
2018	107.6	109.3	110.0	111.4	112.3	114.6	112.0	111.9	111.7	113.8	113.4	112.7	111.7
Government													
2010	380.7	388.8	390.5	393.3	402.4	389.7	371.7	368.6	382.1	389.5	391.4	389.1	386.5
2011	386.3	389.7	390.3	390.8	388.3	380.2	363.8	357.5	371.9	377.0	377.1	376.1	379.1
2012	369.2	376.1	376.9	377.2	377.8	368.7	355.8	353.3	369.7	376.9	378.8	379.3	371.6
2013	369.9	379.3	380.1	381.2	382.0	374.0	360.2	353.9	376.4	384.5	386.7	386.4	376.2
2014	377.6	386.9	387.7	387.6	388.4	383.6	367.5	362.0	381.8	390.6	393.4	392.7	383.3
2015	384.4	392.9	394.2	393.2	394.0	388.6	372.9	368.5	387.9	397.7	400.2	400.3	389.6
2016	393.6	401.6	403.0	404.8	406.5	401.9	385.7	380.3	399.1	407.0	410.5	412.4	400.5
2017	400.5	410.9	413.8	412.8	413.9	408.6	389.2	384.1	402.8	411.3	415.4	416.3	406.6
2018	404.4	415.8	417.4	414.7	417.2	411.9	393.7	388.7	407.4	418.4	421.1	422.1	411.1

Employment by Industry: Washington-Arlington-Alexandria, DC-VA-MD-WV, 2010–2018

(Numbers in thousands, not seasonally adjusted)

Industry and year	January	February	March	April	May	June	July	August	September	October	November	December	Annual average
Total Nonfarm													
2010	2,916.5	2,893.3	2,939.7	2,977.0	3,001.9	3,015.6	3,013.3	2,980.6	2,985.8	3,006.6	3,017.6	3,023.6	2,981.0
2011	2,964.4	2,973.5	2,995.8	3,022.2	3,023.3	3,041.2	3,048.3	3,022.1	3,038.7	3,043.7	3,053.8	3,058.1	3,023.8
2012	2,995.4	3,009.0	3,036.2	3,050.4	3,064.4	3,081.4	3,070.9	3,058.9	3,069.9	3,089.9	3,102.8	3,101.7	3,060.9
2013	3,041.2	3,053.8	3,069.7	3,084.9	3,097.2	3,102.3	3,097.4	3,081.9	3,090.3	3,093.4	3,113.8	3,106.1	3,086.0
2014	3,041.9	3,048.5	3,065.8	3,093.2	3,113.5	3,131.4	3,115.9	3,103.5	3,112.6	3,128.0	3,140.5	3,138.1	3,102.7
2015	3,088.0	3,100.6	3,108.2	3,138.6	3,158.7	3,178.5	3,179.8	3,161.2	3,169.3	3,195.6	3,209.1	3,211.6	3,158.3
2016	3,144.0	3,155.4	3,174.7	3,212.4	3,217.4	3,234.6	3,233.4	3,222.1	3,231.1	3,247.1	3,265.9	3,264.3	3,216.9
2017	3,206.2	3,227.0	3,243.9	3,259.6	3,274.3	3,296.8	3,279.3	3,263.0	3,266.2	3,288.3	3,302.4	3,293.1	3,266.7
2018	3,244.3	3,268.9	3,278.8	3,300.4	3,314.7	3,334.0	3,318.8	3,301.1	3,301.4	3,313.2	3,323.8	3,324.6	3,302.0
Total Private													
2010	2,237.1	2,211.3	2,251.3	2,287.2	2,300.8	2,318.4	2,311.8	2,307.5	2,297.4	2,309.5	2,316.7	2,324.8	2,289.5
2011	2,277.4	2,279.1	2,297.6	2,326.4	2,326.1	2,346.0	2,359.7	2,351.2	2,344.7	2,347.8	2,358.1	2,361.9	2,331.3
2012	2,311.0	2,316.4	2,338.4	2,355.3	2,368.5	2,387.8	2,388.6	2,390.5	2,379.7	2,390.6	2,402.1	2,401.7	2,369.2
2013	2,353.7	2,358.6	2,372.4	2,387.3	2,397.9	2,407.5	2,417.3	2,415.7	2,402.3	2,399.5	2,416.2	2,411.1	2,395.0
2014	2,364.7	2,362.8	2,378.9	2,406.0	2,422.2	2,441.1	2,441.8	2,440.3	2,423.8	2,433.8	2,443.6	2,443.5	2,416.9
2015	2,406.0	2,407.4	2,414.5	2,446.9	2,464.2	2,483.2	2,500.4	2,495.6	2,478.2	2,503.9	2,514.0	2,515.5	2,469.2
2016	2,458.6	2,464.0	2,479.6	2,512.5	2,516.6	2,535.9	2,548.4	2,545.8	2,531.4	2,543.0	2,557.7	2,556.6	2,520.8
2017	2,510.8	2,521.3	2,535.3	2,553.8	2,565.3	2,590.6	2,592.9	2,586.4	2,566.9	2,584.4	2,595.0	2,589.9	2,566.1
2018	2,550.8	2,563.2	2,572.6	2,592.9	2,605.0	2,628.3	2,631.4	2,623.8	2,602.8	2,609.1	2,616.2	2,620.5	2,601.4
Goods Producing													
2010	189.7	181.6	189.4	195.3	197.1	198.5	200.4	200.3	198.8	197.6	196.8	195.0	195.0
2011	188.5	187.8	189.6	194.1	195.7	198.3	201.6	201.0	198.1	196.6	196.2	196.3	195.3
2012	189.9	189.4	192.1	194.5	195.5	199.4	201.2	200.6	199.3	199.4	198.5	197.5	196.4
2013	191.6	191.0	192.7	195.2	197.8	200.3	201.6	202.4	200.2	198.8	199.8	197.1	197.4
2014	192.1	190.8	193.5	198.7	201.1	203.9	203.3	204.4	202.7	203.3	203.2	201.3	199.9
2015	194.1	193.9	195.0	200.7	203.5	205.8	208.5	209.2	208.1	211.2	211.8	211.2	204.4
2016	204.0	202.9	206.5	210.0	212.0	214.0	213.7	213.5	213.1	215.2	215.0	214.9	211.2
2017	207.7	209.0	210.6	214.2	215.4	218.2	218.3	218.0	216.8	216.7	215.8	214.8	214.6
2018	209.2	210.6	212.0	214.0	215.3	218.1	220.7	220.6	218.6	218.1	218.2	216.7	216.0
Service-Providing													
2010	2,726.8	2,711.7	2,750.3	2,781.7	2,804.8	2,817.1	2,812.9	2,780.3	2,787.0	2,809.0	2,820.8	2,828.6	2,785.9
2011	2,775.9	2,785.7	2,806.2	2,828.1	2,827.6	2,842.9	2,846.7	2,821.1	2,840.6	2,847.1	2,857.6	2,861.8	2,828.4
2012	2,805.5	2,819.6	2,844.1	2,855.9	2,868.9	2,882.0	2,869.7	2,858.3	2,870.6	2,890.5	2,904.3	2,904.2	2,864.5
2013	2,849.6	2,862.8	2,877.0	2,889.7	2,899.4	2,902.0	2,895.8	2,879.5	2,890.1	2,894.6	2,914.0	2,909.0	2,888.6
2014	2,849.8	2,857.7	2,872.3	2,894.5	2,912.4	2,927.5	2,912.6	2,899.1	2,909.9	2,924.7	2,937.3	2,936.8	2,902.9
2015	2,893.9	2,906.7	2,913.2	2,937.9	2,955.2	2,972.7	2,971.3	2,952.0	2,961.2	2,984.4	2,997.3	3,000.4	2,953.9
2016	2,940.0	2,952.5	2,968.2	3,002.4	3,005.4	3,020.6	3,019.7	3,008.6	3,018.0	3,031.9	3,050.9	3,049.4	3,005.6
2017	2,998.5	3,018.0	3,033.3	3,045.4	3,058.9	3,078.6	3,061.0	3,045.0	3,049.4	3,071.6	3,086.6	3,078.3	3,052.1
2018	3,035.1	3,058.3	3,066.8	3,086.4	3,099.4	3,115.9	3,098.1	3,080.5	3,082.8	3,095.1	3,105.6	3,107.9	3,086.0
Mining, Logging, and Construction													
2010	135.0	128.0	135.3	141.0	142.6	143.8	146.2	146.4	145.3	143.9	143.1	141.3	141.0
2011	135.4	135.2	137.0	141.5	143.0	145.4	148.9	148.5	146.2	144.7	144.2	143.8	142.8
2012	138.1	138.6	141.0	143.3	144.4	147.8	149.5	149.1	148.1	148.5	147.2	146.4	145.2
2013	141.1	141.0	142.6	145.0	147.4	149.7	151.0	151.8	150.2	148.3	148.8	145.9	146.9
2014	141.9	140.7	143.1	146.8	149.1	151.5	151.1	152.0	150.6	150.8	150.1	148.1	148.0
2015	142.0	141.7	142.6	147.7	150.3	152.2	154.5	155.0	154.1	157.1	157.2	156.7	150.9
2016	151.1	149.9	153.3	156.2	157.7	159.5	158.9	158.9	158.7	160.7	159.9	159.7	157.1
2017	153.5	154.6	156.0	159.5	160.6	163.0	163.0	162.7	161.9	161.6	160.6	159.5	159.7
2018	154.8	156.1	157.3	158.9	160.0	162.0	164.5	164.6	163.1	162.9	163.0	161.5	160.7

Employment by Industry: Washington-Arlington-Alexandria, DC-VA-MD-WV, 2010–2018—*Continued*

(Numbers in thousands, not seasonally adjusted)

Industry and year	January	February	March	April	May	June	July	August	September	October	November	December	Annual average
Manufacturing													
2010	54.7	53.6	54.1	54.3	54.5	54.7	54.2	53.9	53.5	53.7	53.7	53.7	54.1
2011	53.1	52.6	52.6	52.6	52.7	52.9	52.7	52.5	51.9	51.9	52.0	52.5	52.5
2012	51.8	50.8	51.1	51.2	51.1	51.6	51.7	51.5	51.2	50.9	51.3	51.1	51.3
2013	50.5	50.0	50.1	50.2	50.4	50.6	50.6	50.6	50.0	50.5	51.0	51.2	50.5
2014	50.2	50.1	50.4	51.9	52.0	52.4	52.2	52.4	52.1	52.5	53.1	53.2	51.9
2015	52.1	52.2	52.4	53.0	53.2	53.6	54.0	54.2	54.0	54.1	54.6	54.5	53.5
2016	52.9	53.0	53.2	53.8	54.3	54.5	54.8	54.6	54.3	54.5	55.1	55.2	54.2
2017	54.2	54.4	54.6	54.7	54.8	55.2	55.3	55.3	54.9	55.1	55.2	55.3	54.9
2018	54.4	54.5	54.7	55.1	55.3	56.1	56.2	56.0	55.5	55.2	55.2	55.2	55.3
Trade, Transportation, and Utilities													
2010	375.8	366.0	372.4	375.5	379.3	383.1	381.2	381.6	379.1	384.6	393.1	400.7	381.0
2011	382.3	377.4	379.0	382.7	384.1	386.8	387.3	387.3	385.1	389.3	398.1	405.2	387.1
2012	387.3	382.8	385.1	384.6	388.4	391.0	389.2	389.0	387.5	391.0	402.1	407.4	390.5
2013	388.3	383.0	384.9	385.9	388.8	391.7	392.0	392.2	390.0	393.6	404.3	411.1	392.2
2014	392.1	386.5	389.0	391.3	394.8	398.1	397.8	397.7	395.4	399.2	409.0	416.5	397.3
2015	398.3	392.1	392.8	394.7	399.4	402.6	403.7	403.3	401.4	405.6	415.1	421.3	402.5
2016	400.2	395.5	397.3	400.4	403.7	405.6	406.1	405.4	402.8	406.7	417.3	423.3	405.4
2017	405.0	399.4	400.6	403.0	405.5	408.9	407.6	407.5	403.9	407.4	418.8	423.0	407.6
2018	406.3	401.6	401.5	402.4	405.1	407.5	406.8	405.9	404.8	405.2	413.7	418.6	406.6
Wholesale Trade													
2010	62.9	62.6	62.9	62.6	62.8	62.9	62.8	62.8	62.4	62.8	62.6	62.9	62.8
2011	62.6	62.6	62.8	62.8	62.7	62.6	62.8	62.8	62.2	62.6	62.3	62.5	62.6
2012	62.1	62.4	62.7	61.8	62.5	62.8	62.8	63.1	62.8	63.0	63.1	63.0	62.7
2013	62.8	62.9	63.0	62.7	62.7	62.8	62.6	62.4	62.0	62.4	62.5	62.6	62.6
2014	61.8	61.8	62.1	61.8	62.2	62.2	62.2	62.2	61.7	61.4	61.4	61.4	61.9
2015	60.9	60.7	60.7	60.4	60.7	60.8	61.5	61.2	60.9	61.1	61.1	61.3	60.9
2016	61.0	60.7	60.6	61.2	61.5	61.6	62.3	62.4	62.1	62.5	62.4	62.3	61.7
2017	62.2	62.4	62.2	62.3	62.6	62.8	62.7	62.7	62.2	62.4	62.5	62.4	62.5
2018	62.4	62.6	62.4	62.3	62.4	63.1	62.9	63.1	63.1	63.3	63.4	63.9	62.9
Retail Trade													
2010	252.9	244.1	249.4	252.5	255.5	258.2	257.1	257.4	255.4	260.6	268.1	273.1	257.0
2011	258.4	254.2	255.2	258.5	259.8	261.9	261.5	261.7	260.7	264.2	272.8	277.7	262.2
2012	263.6	258.7	260.8	260.5	263.0	264.7	263.4	262.9	262.1	265.2	275.4	278.2	264.9
2013	263.7	259.6	260.8	262.3	264.7	266.8	267.4	267.5	266.2	269.7	278.8	282.8	267.5
2014	268.3	264.0	265.7	267.9	270.2	272.8	272.8	272.5	270.7	274.6	282.8	287.4	272.5
2015	273.8	269.5	270.3	272.1	275.5	278.1	278.3	277.9	276.7	280.9	288.8	291.5	277.8
2016	275.9	271.8	273.6	275.1	277.5	278.6	278.5	278.3	275.6	279.4	287.9	290.7	278.6
2017	277.3	272.2	273.3	274.9	276.4	278.8	277.6	277.6	274.3	277.9	287.6	288.8	278.1
2018	276.6	272.2	272.2	272.6	274.9	275.4	275.6	274.7	273.2	273.8	280.0	280.0	275.1
Transportation and Utilities													
2010	60.0	59.3	60.1	60.4	61.0	62.0	61.3	61.4	61.3	61.2	62.4	64.7	61.3
2011	61.3	60.6	61.0	61.4	61.6	62.3	63.0	62.8	62.2	62.5	63.0	65.0	62.2
2012	61.6	61.7	61.6	62.3	62.9	63.5	63.0	63.0	62.6	62.8	63.6	66.2	62.9
2013	61.8	60.5	61.1	60.9	61.4	62.1	62.0	62.3	61.8	61.5	63.0	65.7	62.0
2014	62.0	60.7	61.2	61.6	62.4	63.1	62.8	63.0	63.0	63.2	64.8	67.7	63.0
2015	63.6	61.9	61.8	62.2	63.2	63.7	63.9	64.2	63.8	63.6	65.2	68.5	63.8
2016	63.3	63.0	63.1	64.1	64.7	65.4	65.3	64.7	65.1	64.8	67.0	70.3	65.1
2017	65.5	64.8	65.1	65.8	66.5	67.3	67.3	67.2	67.4	67.1	68.7	71.8	67.0
2018	67.3	66.8	66.9	67.5	67.8	69.0	68.3	68.1	68.5	68.1	70.3	74.7	68.6
Information													
2010	80.5	80.0	80.2	79.7	79.6	80.6	80.9	80.8	81.9	81.8	81.3	83.1	80.9
2011	80.1	80.7	81.0	82.0	80.0	81.8	81.6	76.2	80.2	77.3	78.5	79.8	79.9
2012	76.1	77.3	78.1	76.3	77.1	78.8	77.9	79.1	77.0	76.8	78.4	77.3	77.5
2013	76.5	78.0	77.9	76.5	77.2	77.2	77.6	78.7	76.6	76.7	78.5	77.3	77.4
2014	79.1	77.8	77.8	77.9	79.3	78.5	78.5	79.3	77.3	78.1	77.4	77.4	78.2
2015	77.7	77.0	76.6	77.0	77.2	76.5	76.9	76.1	75.1	76.3	76.1	76.1	76.6
2016	75.0	75.4	74.4	74.7	71.8	74.7	74.9	74.5	74.2	73.7	73.8	74.2	74.3
2017	73.6	74.4	74.1	74.0	74.0	74.6	74.4	74.1	73.9	73.6	74.3	74.5	74.1
2018	73.8	74.7	74.1	74.5	74.8	75.7	75.0	74.5	73.6	74.2	74.1	74.6	74.5

Employment by Industry: Washington-Arlington-Alexandria, DC-VA-MD-WV, 2010–2018—*Continued*

(Numbers in thousands, not seasonally adjusted)

Industry and year	January	February	March	April	May	June	July	August	September	October	November	December	Annual average
Financial Activities													
2010	144.9	144.2	145.2	145.0	145.8	147.2	147.1	146.5	145.0	146.2	146.3	146.5	145.8
2011	144.0	144.0	144.3	145.5	145.7	146.4	146.7	146.2	145.5	145.9	145.6	146.2	145.5
2012	144.7	145.0	145.5	146.2	146.5	147.8	148.0	147.6	147.2	147.8	147.9	148.5	146.9
2013	147.3	147.6	148.3	148.6	148.9	150.3	150.8	150.5	149.2	149.9	150.1	150.6	149.3
2014	148.5	148.2	148.6	148.7	149.3	150.7	151.2	150.7	149.7	150.1	150.2	150.6	149.7
2015	150.0	150.2	150.5	149.9	150.7	152.1	153.0	152.5	151.1	152.0	151.8	152.1	151.3
2016	150.8	150.9	151.1	152.3	152.8	153.9	155.0	155.0	154.0	154.6	154.7	155.5	153.4
2017	154.2	154.9	155.2	155.3	156.5	158.1	158.9	158.3	157.1	157.8	158.0	158.3	156.9
2018	157.3	157.9	158.0	158.6	159.3	160.9	160.9	160.2	159.1	157.9	155.8	155.1	158.4
Professional and Business Services													
2010	667.5	667.1	674.4	685.0	685.6	691.7	689.3	687.5	681.9	688.9	689.0	689.8	683.1
2011	683.4	685.9	691.0	694.4	693.1	698.3	705.6	705.1	699.5	703.4	703.7	702.1	697.1
2012	691.8	694.7	701.0	708.3	708.6	715.1	717.4	718.7	710.6	716.4	717.1	714.0	709.5
2013	704.4	708.1	710.3	710.3	708.4	711.3	715.3	714.7	706.4	705.3	706.8	702.7	708.7
2014	693.5	696.2	697.9	704.5	707.1	711.5	715.3	713.6	707.0	711.3	711.9	710.2	706.7
2015	706.9	708.7	709.6	718.7	721.2	725.9	732.1	730.4	722.4	731.5	731.9	729.9	722.4
2016	721.5	724.0	726.8	735.5	734.5	740.1	746.1	745.6	737.9	742.0	742.4	739.8	736.4
2017	734.0	735.8	737.9	741.9	742.8	752.1	755.7	753.8	745.3	751.5	753.1	749.5	746.1
2018	746.5	751.4	753.4	758.1	760.3	768.3	772.0	770.6	761.6	764.7	762.5	764.9	761.2
Education and Health Services													
2010	358.3	356.3	361.9	367.0	367.2	360.7	358.3	357.7	365.6	367.2	369.2	369.2	363.2
2011	370.1	372.0	373.9	377.3	371.4	368.3	370.3	369.1	379.1	380.8	382.2	379.8	374.5
2012	378.2	380.7	382.2	384.1	381.8	374.9	372.9	374.6	386.4	391.0	392.0	390.8	382.5
2013	387.6	391.2	392.9	396.2	393.0	382.8	385.3	384.9	396.6	398.4	400.1	397.3	392.2
2014	394.1	397.1	398.8	401.2	396.7	393.8	392.7	394.0	401.2	405.3	407.3	405.2	399.0
2015	402.4	407.9	407.5	412.9	408.0	404.8	408.2	408.4	415.5	425.3	427.5	424.3	412.7
2016	418.5	424.5	425.3	429.2	422.5	416.6	419.3	419.9	425.7	430.3	432.0	427.6	424.3
2017	425.2	431.0	431.9	432.4	427.7	425.5	425.4	425.5	433.1	440.1	441.2	437.7	431.4
2018	436.0	442.7	442.6	445.6	440.3	436.6	435.4	435.9	442.6	445.5	450.9	449.4	442.0
Leisure and Hospitality													
2010	243.9	240.4	249.7	260.5	265.9	274.8	273.5	272.9	266.8	264.0	261.9	261.1	261.3
2011	251.5	252.7	259.4	268.8	274.3	282.8	282.2	283.2	275.5	272.8	271.4	269.8	270.4
2012	262.0	264.3	271.3	278.6	287.0	295.9	295.1	295.2	287.1	283.7	281.4	280.7	281.9
2013	274.6	275.8	281.3	289.4	297.7	306.5	306.4	304.7	296.5	290.6	289.8	288.4	291.8
2014	280.1	280.6	286.6	296.3	305.6	314.1	312.6	311.1	302.4	299.0	297.1	295.1	298.4
2015	290.4	291.2	295.6	305.4	315.3	324.9	326.2	325.0	315.4	312.2	309.9	310.7	310.2
2016	300.3	302.0	308.6	318.7	325.9	334.7	334.2	332.6	324.5	319.7	320.3	318.4	320.0
2017	308.9	312.5	319.0	327.0	336.7	344.3	343.1	341.3	331.2	330.0	326.7	324.8	328.8
2018	315.4	317.6	323.8	331.8	341.2	350.4	349.3	346.0	334.5	334.9	332.1	332.9	334.2
Other Services													
2010	176.5	175.7	178.1	179.2	180.3	181.8	181.1	180.2	178.3	179.2	179.1	179.4	179.1
2011	177.5	178.6	179.4	181.6	181.8	183.3	184.4	183.1	181.7	181.7	182.4	182.7	181.5
2012	181.0	182.2	183.1	182.7	183.6	184.9	186.9	185.7	184.6	184.5	184.7	185.5	184.1
2013	183.4	183.9	184.1	185.2	186.1	187.4	188.3	187.6	186.8	186.2	186.8	186.6	186.0
2014	185.2	185.6	186.7	187.4	188.3	190.5	190.4	189.5	188.1	187.5	187.5	187.2	187.8
2015	186.2	186.4	186.9	187.6	188.9	190.6	191.8	190.7	189.2	189.8	189.9	189.9	189.0
2016	188.3	188.8	189.6	191.7	193.4	196.3	199.1	199.3	199.2	200.8	202.2	202.9	196.0
2017	202.2	204.3	206.0	206.0	206.7	208.9	209.5	207.9	205.6	207.3	207.1	207.3	206.6
2018	206.3	206.7	207.2	207.9	208.7	210.8	211.3	210.1	208.0	208.6	208.9	208.3	208.6
Government													
2010	679.4	682.0	688.4	689.8	701.1	697.2	701.5	673.1	688.4	697.1	700.9	698.8	691.5
2011	687.0	694.4	698.2	695.8	697.2	695.2	688.6	670.9	694.0	695.9	695.7	696.2	692.4
2012	684.4	692.6	697.8	695.1	695.9	693.6	682.3	668.4	690.2	699.3	700.7	700.0	691.7
2013	687.5	695.2	697.3	697.6	699.3	694.8	680.1	666.2	688.0	693.9	697.6	695.0	691.0
2014	677.2	685.7	686.9	687.2	691.3	690.3	674.1	663.2	688.8	694.2	696.9	694.6	685.9
2015	682.0	693.2	693.7	691.7	694.5	695.3	679.4	665.6	691.1	691.7	695.1	696.1	689.1
2016	685.4	691.4	695.1	699.9	700.8	698.7	685.0	676.3	699.7	704.1	708.2	707.7	696.0
2017	695.4	705.7	708.6	705.8	709.0	706.2	686.4	676.6	699.3	703.9	707.4	703.2	700.6
2018	693.5	705.7	706.2	707.5	709.7	705.7	687.4	677.3	698.6	704.1	707.6	704.1	700.6

Employment by Industry: Miami-Fort Lauderdale-West Palm Beach, 2010–2018

(Numbers in thousands, not seasonally adjusted)

Industry and year	January	February	March	April	May	June	July	August	September	October	November	December	Annual average
Total Nonfarm													
2010	2,180.6	2,192.5	2,199.9	2,199.4	2,207.8	2,172.4	2,150.5	2,178.9	2,181.4	2,203.3	2,229.5	2,247.2	2,195.3
2011	2,212.0	2,224.4	2,230.5	2,242.8	2,237.2	2,202.8	2,186.7	2,217.7	2,231.3	2,249.4	2,277.8	2,297.3	2,234.2
2012	2,261.4	2,274.4	2,286.9	2,289.0	2,290.4	2,259.5	2,237.8	2,267.9	2,279.9	2,306.7	2,338.4	2,350.9	2,286.9
2013	2,313.8	2,333.6	2,344.8	2,345.6	2,348.1	2,320.0	2,303.4	2,336.3	2,346.4	2,367.9	2,407.7	2,423.1	2,349.2
2014	2,383.6	2,401.9	2,413.3	2,421.1	2,425.4	2,395.9	2,380.5	2,416.6	2,429.7	2,460.0	2,498.2	2,514.1	2,428.4
2015	2,472.6	2,487.7	2,499.0	2,501.5	2,505.8	2,475.4	2,465.5	2,499.4	2,506.1	2,544.8	2,577.4	2,593.7	2,510.7
2016	2,552.5	2,570.5	2,577.7	2,590.0	2,586.0	2,549.1	2,544.0	2,572.3	2,584.7	2,603.9	2,638.3	2,651.5	2,585.0
2017	2,614.6	2,630.4	2,640.2	2,637.5	2,643.8	2,610.9	2,594.4	2,620.9	2,564.8	2,642.3	2,677.0	2,691.9	2,630.7
2018	2,651.4	2,672.1	2,680.2	2,676.0	2,677.6	2,644.4	2,635.9	2,672.7	2,675.0	2,705.6	2,735.0	2,740.7	2,680.6
Total Private													
2010	1,862.3	1,873.7	1,881.2	1,879.6	1,878.6	1,876.8	1,861.4	1,868.7	1,869.9	1,889.7	1,915.4	1,933.8	1,882.6
2011	1,899.9	1,910.8	1,918.4	1,930.8	1,927.1	1,919.2	1,906.2	1,914.2	1,924.8	1,939.7	1,969.6	1,988.6	1,929.1
2012	1,956.1	1,967.8	1,981.3	1,983.4	1,985.7	1,980.1	1,961.1	1,969.7	1,977.5	2,001.2	2,032.8	2,045.5	1,986.9
2013	2,010.5	2,027.4	2,038.3	2,039.4	2,042.0	2,039.7	2,025.5	2,037.7	2,043.0	2,062.8	2,100.4	2,117.6	2,048.7
2014	2,079.6	2,096.0	2,106.6	2,114.4	2,119.4	2,115.5	2,102.9	2,118.4	2,127.8	2,155.0	2,191.5	2,209.2	2,128.0
2015	2,169.5	2,182.7	2,192.7	2,194.4	2,198.9	2,193.9	2,185.9	2,199.7	2,202.1	2,237.1	2,269.6	2,287.2	2,209.5
2016	2,247.0	2,262.7	2,269.5	2,279.5	2,276.4	2,263.6	2,259.3	2,268.6	2,274.5	2,292.9	2,325.7	2,340.8	2,280.0
2017	2,304.0	2,317.8	2,326.3	2,325.0	2,330.1	2,322.1	2,307.3	2,314.6	2,254.4	2,329.2	2,363.3	2,378.7	2,322.7
2018	2,337.6	2,356.9	2,363.7	2,360.3	2,361.8	2,351.9	2,346.1	2,359.9	2,360.7	2,389.5	2,416.9	2,424.2	2,369.1
Goods Producing													
2010	164.5	165.1	165.0	164.6	165.0	166.0	165.5	166.0	165.7	165.3	164.8	164.6	165.2
2011	160.2	160.9	160.9	161.3	161.5	162.3	161.4	162.3	163.1	163.3	163.9	163.9	162.1
2012	161.1	161.5	162.5	161.6	162.9	164.2	163.3	165.6	166.3	166.7	167.8	167.8	164.3
2013	163.8	165.9	167.1	167.0	169.5	171.1	171.9	174.5	175.1	175.9	177.2	177.6	171.4
2014	175.0	177.4	178.8	179.8	182.2	184.0	184.8	187.0	188.0	189.8	190.4	190.9	184.0
2015	188.9	191.3	193.0	193.9	196.3	198.3	198.6	200.6	201.6	205.5	206.5	207.2	198.5
2016	204.1	206.4	207.4	209.2	210.1	210.7	212.1	213.6	214.6	215.2	217.0	217.0	211.5
2017	213.9	216.5	218.1	218.1	219.6	220.9	219.6	220.9	212.1	221.6	222.4	223.0	218.9
2018	220.0	223.0	224.4	225.1	226.3	228.4	228.3	229.4	231.2	233.5	234.3	232.5	228.0
Service-Providing													
2010	2,016.1	2,027.4	2,034.9	2,034.8	2,042.8	2,006.4	1,985.0	2,012.9	2,015.7	2,038.0	2,064.7	2,082.6	2,030.1
2011	2,051.8	2,063.5	2,069.6	2,081.5	2,075.7	2,040.5	2,025.3	2,055.4	2,068.2	2,086.1	2,113.9	2,133.4	2,072.1
2012	2,100.3	2,112.9	2,124.4	2,127.4	2,127.5	2,095.3	2,074.5	2,102.3	2,113.6	2,140.0	2,170.6	2,183.1	2,122.7
2013	2,150.0	2,167.7	2,177.7	2,178.6	2,178.6	2,148.9	2,131.5	2,161.8	2,171.3	2,192.0	2,230.5	2,245.5	2,177.8
2014	2,208.6	2,224.5	2,234.5	2,241.3	2,243.2	2,211.9	2,195.7	2,229.6	2,241.7	2,270.2	2,307.8	2,323.2	2,244.4
2015	2,283.7	2,296.4	2,306.0	2,307.6	2,309.5	2,277.1	2,266.9	2,298.8	2,304.5	2,339.3	2,370.9	2,386.5	2,312.3
2016	2,348.4	2,364.1	2,370.3	2,380.8	2,375.9	2,338.4	2,331.9	2,358.7	2,370.1	2,388.7	2,421.3	2,434.5	2,373.6
2017	2,400.7	2,413.9	2,422.1	2,419.4	2,424.2	2,390.0	2,374.8	2,400.0	2,352.7	2,420.7	2,454.6	2,468.9	2,411.8
2018	2,431.4	2,449.1	2,455.8	2,450.9	2,451.3	2,416.0	2,407.6	2,443.3	2,443.8	2,472.1	2,500.7	2,508.2	2,452.5
Mining and Logging													
2010	0.5	0.5	0.5	0.5	0.5	0.6	0.6	0.6	0.5	0.6	0.6	0.6	0.6
2011	0.6	0.6	0.7	0.7	0.7	0.7	0.6	0.6	0.5	0.6	0.6	0.6	0.6
2012	0.6	0.6	0.6	0.6	0.7	0.7	0.6	0.6	0.6	0.6	0.6	0.6	0.6
2013	0.6	0.6	0.6	0.6	0.6	0.5	0.6	0.6	0.6	0.6	0.6	0.6	0.6
2014	0.6	0.6	0.6	0.6	0.6	0.6	0.6	0.6	0.6	0.6	0.6	0.6	0.6
2015	0.6	0.6	0.6	0.6	0.6	0.6	0.6	0.6	0.6	0.6	0.6	0.6	0.6
2016	0.7	0.7	0.7	0.7	0.7	0.7	0.7	0.7	0.7	0.7	0.7	0.7	0.7
2017	0.7	0.7	0.7	0.7	0.7	0.7	0.7	0.7	0.7	0.7	0.7	0.7	0.7
2018	0.7	0.7	0.7	0.7	0.7	0.7	0.7	0.7	0.7	0.7	0.7	0.7	0.7
Construction													
2010	88.0	88.4	88.4	88.3	88.6	89.0	89.3	89.4	89.5	88.7	87.8	87.2	88.6
2011	84.2	84.6	84.7	84.7	84.4	84.8	84.8	85.2	86.1	85.8	86.1	85.8	85.1
2012	83.6	83.6	84.3	84.3	85.2	86.5	86.4	88.1	88.8	88.9	89.5	89.5	86.6
2013	87.4	88.6	89.4	89.7	91.6	92.6	93.5	95.6	96.2	96.4	96.9	97.1	92.9
2014	94.8	96.6	98.0	99.1	100.8	102.3	103.0	104.6	105.2	106.4	106.5	106.8	102.0
2015	105.3	107.1	108.2	109.2	110.7	112.3	112.9	114.3	115.3	118.1	118.8	119.1	112.6
2016	116.3	118.0	119.0	120.8	121.8	122.5	124.0	124.9	125.7	126.1	127.2	127.2	122.8
2017	125.4	127.3	128.4	128.5	129.6	130.8	130.8	131.7	124.8	132.5	132.7	133.1	129.6
2018	131.3	133.5	134.6	135.3	136.3	138.1	138.2	138.9	140.2	141.3	141.6	140.1	137.5

Employment by Industry: Miami-Fort Lauderdale-West Palm Beach, 2010–2018—*Continued*

(Numbers in thousands, not seasonally adjusted)

Industry and year	January	February	March	April	May	June	July	August	September	October	November	December	Annual average
Manufacturing													
2010	76.0	76.2	76.1	75.8	75.9	76.4	75.6	76.0	75.7	76.0	76.4	76.8	76.1
2011	75.4	75.7	75.5	75.9	76.4	76.8	76.0	76.5	76.5	76.9	77.2	77.5	76.4
2012	76.9	77.3	77.6	76.7	77.0	77.0	76.3	76.9	76.9	77.2	77.7	77.7	77.1
2013	75.8	76.7	77.1	76.7	77.3	78.0	77.8	78.3	78.3	78.9	79.7	79.9	77.9
2014	79.6	80.2	80.2	80.1	80.8	81.1	81.2	81.8	82.2	82.8	83.3	83.5	81.4
2015	83.0	83.6	84.2	84.1	85.0	85.4	85.1	85.7	85.7	86.8	87.1	87.5	85.3
2016	87.1	87.7	87.7	87.7	87.6	87.5	87.4	88.0	88.2	88.4	89.1	89.1	88.0
2017	87.8	88.5	89.0	88.9	89.3	89.4	88.1	88.5	86.6	88.4	89.0	89.2	88.6
2018	88.0	88.8	89.1	89.1	89.3	89.6	89.4	89.8	90.3	91.5	92.0	91.7	89.9
Trade, Transportation, and Utilities													
2010	500.0	498.7	499.4	500.8	502.3	502.1	498.4	500.3	499.8	506.8	519.4	527.5	504.6
2011	511.4	510.6	511.7	515.0	514.9	515.1	514.9	517.1	519.0	525.1	538.3	546.3	520.0
2012	532.3	531.1	532.4	533.2	534.8	533.4	530.0	530.7	532.6	537.9	552.9	558.1	536.6
2013	543.5	542.4	543.2	543.7	545.3	546.4	543.0	545.2	546.3	552.5	570.0	578.9	550.0
2014	558.0	557.9	558.3	559.5	560.7	561.0	559.1	563.0	563.9	571.8	589.8	598.8	566.8
2015	580.5	578.5	579.7	579.0	579.5	580.5	577.7	580.3	578.1	586.1	601.7	609.5	584.3
2016	588.7	587.3	587.7	589.3	589.8	587.7	588.0	588.6	588.1	591.6	608.9	616.8	592.7
2017	598.3	595.0	595.9	594.4	595.1	594.2	592.9	593.6	580.0	596.4	616.1	623.6	598.0
2018	606.5	604.8	603.6	603.0	604.1	604.3	602.4	603.6	604.7	610.1	625.4	630.1	608.6
Wholesale Trade													
2010	131.6	132.2	132.2	132.3	132.9	132.1	131.0	131.2	131.2	132.1	133.0	133.9	132.1
2011	131.8	132.8	133.0	134.0	133.6	133.4	133.0	133.3	133.8	135.2	136.1	137.8	134.0
2012	136.5	137.5	138.4	139.0	139.3	138.6	137.8	137.8	138.2	139.0	139.9	141.0	138.6
2013	139.1	140.2	140.2	139.9	140.5	140.1	139.0	139.4	139.8	140.3	141.4	142.3	140.2
2014	140.9	141.9	141.7	141.8	142.3	141.6	140.9	141.7	142.1	143.3	144.9	145.7	142.4
2015	144.3	144.8	144.8	144.4	144.6	144.1	143.2	143.4	143.2	144.9	145.6	146.2	144.5
2016	144.7	145.4	145.5	145.9	146.1	145.0	144.4	144.3	144.5	144.5	146.1	147.1	145.3
2017	145.4	145.8	146.3	145.8	146.5	145.8	145.0	144.9	143.4	144.9	145.7	146.6	145.5
2018	146.4	147.3	147.5	147.9	148.0	147.7	147.3	147.3	147.4	148.0	148.3	148.2	147.6
Retail Trade													
2010	280.2	278.2	278.7	280.0	281.5	282.2	280.0	281.7	281.1	286.5	296.6	302.2	284.1
2011	290.2	287.7	288.3	290.3	290.8	291.0	291.3	293.1	294.4	298.6	309.5	314.1	294.9
2012	303.0	299.9	300.1	300.3	301.7	301.0	298.8	299.5	300.7	304.0	316.9	319.2	303.8
2013	308.8	306.2	306.7	307.4	308.6	309.7	308.4	310.1	310.4	315.1	330.2	336.2	313.2
2014	319.2	317.6	317.9	318.9	319.7	320.5	319.6	322.3	322.4	328.5	342.7	348.8	324.8
2015	334.0	331.7	332.3	331.8	332.3	333.5	331.2	333.3	330.9	335.7	348.1	352.6	335.6
2016	335.7	333.3	333.2	334.3	335.1	334.2	335.0	336.3	335.0	338.1	351.6	355.8	338.1
2017	340.9	337.3	337.0	336.2	336.2	335.6	335.2	335.9	325.1	337.0	352.8	355.9	338.8
2018	342.7	339.7	338.1	337.2	337.6	337.5	335.9	336.7	337.0	340.3	351.9	354.4	340.8
Transportation and Utilities													
2010	88.2	88.3	88.5	88.5	87.9	87.8	87.4	87.4	87.5	88.2	89.8	91.4	88.4
2011	89.4	90.1	90.4	90.7	90.5	90.7	90.6	90.7	90.8	91.3	92.7	94.4	91.0
2012	92.8	93.7	93.9	93.9	93.8	93.8	93.4	93.4	93.7	94.9	96.1	97.9	94.3
2013	95.6	96.0	96.3	96.4	96.2	96.6	95.6	95.7	96.1	97.1	98.4	100.4	96.7
2014	97.9	98.4	98.7	98.8	98.7	98.9	98.6	99.0	99.4	100.0	102.2	104.3	99.6
2015	102.2	102.0	102.6	102.8	102.6	102.9	103.3	103.6	104.0	105.5	108.0	110.7	104.2
2016	108.3	108.6	109.0	109.1	108.6	108.5	108.6	108.0	108.6	109.0	111.2	113.9	109.3
2017	112.0	111.9	112.6	112.4	112.4	112.8	112.7	112.8	111.5	114.5	117.6	121.1	113.7
2018	117.4	117.8	118.0	117.9	118.5	119.1	119.2	119.6	120.3	121.8	125.2	127.5	120.2
Information													
2010	43.1	43.1	43.5	43.4	43.6	43.7	43.6	43.8	43.5	43.9	44.0	44.1	43.6
2011	43.9	43.9	44.0	43.9	43.9	43.9	43.8	44.2	44.2	44.3	44.6	44.7	44.1
2012	44.7	44.7	45.1	45.1	45.1	44.9	45.0	45.1	44.8	45.9	45.9	46.1	45.2
2013	45.5	45.6	46.2	45.9	46.1	46.2	46.4	46.6	46.6	47.2	47.3	47.6	46.4
2014	47.3	47.5	47.2	47.5	47.5	48.2	48.1	47.7	47.6	47.8	48.5	48.5	47.8
2015	47.6	47.5	47.9	47.6	48.3	48.2	48.1	48.6	48.2	48.5	48.5	48.8	48.2
2016	48.6	49.2	49.1	49.2	49.8	49.9	49.8	50.4	49.2	49.9	50.5	50.5	49.7
2017	50.8	52.1	52.0	51.3	52.0	51.6	50.7	51.3	49.6	50.1	51.2	51.3	51.2
2018	50.3	51.6	51.6	50.6	50.8	50.8	50.5	51.9	50.5	51.1	51.7	51.7	51.1

Employment by Industry: Miami-Fort Lauderdale-West Palm Beach, 2010–2018—*Continued*

(Numbers in thousands, not seasonally adjusted)

Industry and year	January	February	March	April	May	June	July	August	September	October	November	December	Annual average
Financial Activities													
2010	151.9	152.5	152.9	152.5	152.8	153.6	153.4	153.4	152.8	154.3	155.3	156.4	153.5
2011	153.6	154.0	154.5	155.8	156.2	156.0	156.4	157.0	157.3	158.5	159.2	160.6	156.6
2012	158.7	159.4	160.0	161.0	161.5	161.8	161.7	162.0	161.4	163.3	164.1	165.1	161.7
2013	162.6	163.0	163.6	164.0	164.2	165.0	164.9	165.0	165.0	166.5	167.3	168.6	165.0
2014	166.3	167.1	167.5	168.5	169.5	169.7	169.8	169.9	170.1	172.6	173.7	174.7	170.0
2015	172.9	173.8	174.0	174.4	174.8	175.3	176.1	176.4	175.7	177.7	178.5	179.3	175.7
2016	176.0	176.9	177.0	177.4	177.8	177.4	177.6	177.6	177.7	178.9	179.7	181.5	178.0
2017	180.0	180.6	180.9	180.4	180.8	181.0	181.0	181.0	179.9	182.8	182.6	184.0	181.3
2018	181.1	182.2	182.6	183.5	183.7	184.0	184.5	184.4	184.2	185.8	186.1	187.7	184.2
Professional and Business Services													
2010	319.7	324.3	326.0	323.9	322.2	323.2	322.9	324.8	325.2	329.4	332.5	336.9	325.9
2011	331.5	336.3	337.7	340.6	338.6	337.4	336.1	336.9	338.7	342.7	346.6	350.1	339.4
2012	341.3	345.8	349.0	350.6	350.4	351.3	349.5	350.8	352.7	361.2	366.1	368.3	353.1
2013	360.8	366.5	368.6	368.9	369.0	368.3	368.2	370.4	370.5	375.9	381.6	383.3	371.0
2014	376.6	380.3	381.9	385.5	387.1	385.8	385.6	388.8	390.5	397.5	402.5	406.0	389.0
2015	394.1	398.4	398.7	400.3	402.1	400.3	402.2	404.8	405.2	415.0	419.2	421.3	405.1
2016	414.1	417.8	417.7	421.4	419.8	417.8	419.5	422.8	422.4	430.8	434.8	433.8	422.7
2017	428.6	431.6	431.6	433.7	434.7	434.4	434.6	435.4	423.4	440.5	444.7	445.1	434.9
2018	436.5	440.0	441.5	442.6	443.4	442.2	444.1	446.8	444.9	453.6	454.6	455.9	445.5
Education and Health Services													
2010	332.6	334.8	335.3	335.5	337.0	335.4	331.6	332.8	335.2	338.2	340.1	340.7	335.8
2011	338.6	341.4	341.7	344.3	343.7	340.6	334.7	336.4	340.6	342.1	343.7	343.8	341.0
2012	339.2	342.3	343.8	343.2	343.1	340.4	334.6	338.6	342.0	343.7	345.3	344.8	341.8
2013	341.9	345.5	346.5	347.9	348.1	345.8	339.8	344.1	346.9	348.7	351.2	352.1	346.5
2014	349.0	352.4	353.0	355.2	355.7	353.6	349.4	354.9	358.9	361.2	362.9	364.1	355.9
2015	360.6	363.7	364.9	366.3	368.4	365.8	361.6	364.7	369.4	373.9	376.4	376.8	367.7
2016	374.3	377.0	377.7	381.4	381.7	378.2	376.0	379.2	384.3	386.9	388.7	390.7	381.3
2017	387.0	391.0	392.2	393.7	395.7	391.6	386.6	390.6	387.8	397.2	399.1	400.0	392.7
2018	394.9	399.1	399.9	399.5	399.4	395.3	391.8	397.9	401.0	407.5	407.7	408.5	400.2
Leisure and Hospitality													
2010	249.0	252.9	256.5	256.1	253.5	250.9	245.5	247.0	247.4	250.6	257.3	261.3	252.3
2011	259.2	261.7	265.3	266.4	264.5	261.0	255.6	256.6	257.6	258.5	266.8	272.1	262.1
2012	272.0	275.3	280.0	279.5	278.7	275.0	269.0	269.4	269.8	273.6	281.1	285.3	275.7
2013	283.0	287.9	291.8	290.3	288.3	285.3	280.2	280.8	280.9	283.3	291.9	294.8	286.5
2014	292.8	297.4	303.0	301.5	299.7	296.6	289.7	290.5	291.8	296.0	304.0	306.1	297.4
2015	305.4	309.0	313.4	311.4	308.4	304.3	301.1	303.7	302.9	308.8	315.7	320.6	308.7
2016	318.4	324.1	328.2	326.8	323.0	317.7	312.7	313.4	315.1	316.2	322.1	326.7	320.4
2017	322.9	327.5	331.8	329.9	328.6	325.3	319.3	319.7	302.9	318.3	324.2	328.0	323.2
2018	326.3	333.1	336.4	332.4	330.5	323.8	321.3	323.1	321.3	324.2	332.6	333.3	328.2
Other Services													
2010	101.5	102.3	102.6	102.8	102.2	101.9	100.5	100.6	100.3	101.2	102.0	102.3	101.7
2011	101.5	102.0	102.6	103.5	103.8	102.9	103.3	103.7	104.3	105.2	106.5	107.1	103.9
2012	106.8	107.7	108.5	109.2	109.2	109.1	108.0	107.5	107.9	108.9	109.6	110.0	108.5
2013	109.4	110.6	111.3	111.7	111.5	111.6	111.1	111.1	111.7	112.8	113.9	114.7	111.8
2014	114.6	116.0	116.9	116.9	117.0	116.6	116.4	116.6	117.0	118.3	119.7	120.1	117.2
2015	119.5	120.5	121.1	121.5	121.1	121.2	120.5	120.6	121.0	121.6	123.1	123.7	121.3
2016	122.8	124.0	124.7	124.8	124.4	124.2	123.6	123.0	123.1	123.4	124.0	123.8	123.8
2017	122.5	123.5	123.8	123.5	123.6	123.1	122.6	122.1	118.7	122.3	123.0	123.7	122.7
2018	122.0	123.1	123.7	123.6	123.6	123.1	123.2	122.8	122.9	123.7	124.5	124.5	123.4
Government													
2010	318.3	318.8	318.7	319.8	329.2	295.6	289.1	310.2	311.5	313.6	314.1	313.4	312.7
2011	312.1	313.6	312.1	312.0	310.1	283.6	280.5	303.5	306.5	309.7	308.2	308.7	305.1
2012	305.3	306.6	305.6	305.6	304.7	279.4	276.7	298.2	302.4	305.5	305.6	305.4	300.1
2013	303.3	306.2	306.5	306.2	306.1	280.3	277.9	298.6	303.4	305.1	307.3	305.5	300.5
2014	304.0	305.9	306.7	306.7	306.0	280.4	277.6	298.2	301.9	305.0	306.7	304.9	300.3
2015	303.1	305.0	306.3	307.1	306.9	281.5	279.6	299.7	304.0	307.7	307.8	306.5	301.3
2016	305.5	307.8	308.2	310.5	309.6	285.5	284.7	303.7	310.2	311.0	312.6	310.7	305.0
2017	310.6	312.6	313.9	312.5	313.7	288.8	287.1	306.3	310.4	313.1	313.7	313.2	308.0
2018	313.8	315.2	316.5	315.7	315.8	292.5	289.8	312.8	314.3	316.1	318.1	316.5	311.4

Employment by Industry: Philadelphia-Camden-Wilmington, 2010–2018

(Numbers in thousands, not seasonally adjusted)

Industry and year	January	February	March	April	May	June	July	August	September	October	November	December	Annual average
Total Nonfarm													
2010	2,647.1	2,645.9	2,666.5	2,700.6	2,723.8	2,721.4	2,683.6	2,672.7	2,691.1	2,723.0	2,735.3	2,737.7	2,695.7
2011	2,662.0	2,673.5	2,694.4	2,724.5	2,725.4	2,724.0	2,685.4	2,675.1	2,704.6	2,725.3	2,739.3	2,740.4	2,706.2
2012	2,668.3	2,684.3	2,710.1	2,723.7	2,735.2	2,737.1	2,698.4	2,696.4	2,724.0	2,750.6	2,767.0	2,767.4	2,721.9
2013	2,689.7	2,708.4	2,728.5	2,750.1	2,758.6	2,761.8	2,719.7	2,717.5	2,746.7	2,770.5	2,791.3	2,783.8	2,743.9
2014	2,712.3	2,717.3	2,741.3	2,775.4	2,789.6	2,794.5	2,754.2	2,752.7	2,787.5	2,816.4	2,835.1	2,835.7	2,776.0
2015	2,753.1	2,766.0	2,780.8	2,817.0	2,835.8	2,839.3	2,801.0	2,795.8	2,826.2	2,858.9	2,875.2	2,877.3	2,818.9
2016	2,795.2	2,809.3	2,833.2	2,866.7	2,873.5	2,876.2	2,854.2	2,848.3	2,885.4	2,905.3	2,919.1	2,922.5	2,865.7
2017	2,851.7	2,864.0	2,877.2	2,903.2	2,920.0	2,919.7	2,887.5	2,885.4	2,917.2	2,941.5	2,959.8	2,959.2	2,907.2
2018	2,880.2	2,900.0	2,909.7	2,936.7	2,948.3	2,954.6	2,921.8	2,919.0	2,949.9	2,975.4	2,982.3	2,984.7	2,938.6
Total Private													
2010	2,290.5	2,283.3	2,301.8	2,333.9	2,351.4	2,355.0	2,349.6	2,344.6	2,343.6	2,366.0	2,374.9	2,377.3	2,339.3
2011	2,310.6	2,317.5	2,336.5	2,365.5	2,371.1	2,373.7	2,364.7	2,358.2	2,366.6	2,377.9	2,389.9	2,391.0	2,360.3
2012	2,329.1	2,338.0	2,362.5	2,376.2	2,390.3	2,397.1	2,384.6	2,384.2	2,390.9	2,406.8	2,421.4	2,421.8	2,383.6
2013	2,353.3	2,364.8	2,383.1	2,405.4	2,414.3	2,423.0	2,408.9	2,409.3	2,416.0	2,429.9	2,448.4	2,442.5	2,408.2
2014	2,379.1	2,377.3	2,400.0	2,433.0	2,448.8	2,457.0	2,444.0	2,445.1	2,456.4	2,476.9	2,493.9	2,496.2	2,442.3
2015	2,421.3	2,428.4	2,440.6	2,476.0	2,495.7	2,503.1	2,492.4	2,487.9	2,494.9	2,522.3	2,536.1	2,538.9	2,486.5
2016	2,465.5	2,473.5	2,494.7	2,528.7	2,536.7	2,544.1	2,543.9	2,539.0	2,552.8	2,567.1	2,578.7	2,582.6	2,533.9
2017	2,519.7	2,525.9	2,537.2	2,564.2	2,581.7	2,586.2	2,575.6	2,572.3	2,583.3	2,602.5	2,618.8	2,618.4	2,573.8
2018	2,547.6	2,560.9	2,569.4	2,596.5	2,610.2	2,619.7	2,609.0	2,604.5	2,613.0	2,632.3	2,637.2	2,640.0	2,603.4
Goods Producing													
2010	279.9	275.7	280.1	286.9	289.5	292.3	293.0	292.8	290.6	291.3	290.1	287.2	287.5
2011	276.7	275.5	281.4	287.4	288.3	290.7	291.8	292.0	290.1	290.2	288.7	285.2	286.5
2012	276.8	276.6	279.5	281.4	282.2	285.7	286.0	286.4	285.6	284.9	282.9	281.6	282.5
2013	274.3	274.0	277.9	281.8	283.0	286.2	286.6	288.5	286.9	287.1	286.1	280.8	282.8
2014	274.8	273.4	279.1	283.6	286.7	289.4	290.7	290.8	289.4	289.7	289.5	287.1	285.4
2015	279.0	279.3	281.6	289.0	292.5	295.2	296.8	297.3	296.0	295.5	294.3	292.8	290.8
2016	284.7	284.0	288.5	292.0	294.3	297.7	299.3	299.4	298.2	299.2	297.7	296.5	294.3
2017	289.9	290.7	291.8	296.6	299.9	302.1	302.3	301.7	299.7	299.7	299.6	297.6	297.6
2018	289.2	290.5	292.9	298.1	299.7	303.3	304.1	304.5	302.9	303.6	304.2	302.9	299.7
Service-Providing													
2010	2,367.2	2,370.2	2,386.4	2,413.7	2,434.3	2,429.1	2,390.6	2,379.9	2,400.5	2,431.7	2,445.2	2,450.5	2,408.3
2011	2,385.3	2,398.0	2,413.0	2,437.1	2,437.1	2,433.3	2,393.6	2,383.1	2,414.5	2,435.1	2,450.6	2,455.2	2,419.7
2012	2,391.5	2,407.7	2,430.6	2,442.3	2,453.0	2,451.4	2,412.4	2,410.0	2,438.4	2,465.7	2,484.1	2,485.8	2,439.4
2013	2,415.4	2,434.4	2,450.6	2,468.3	2,475.6	2,475.6	2,433.1	2,429.0	2,459.8	2,483.4	2,505.2	2,503.0	2,461.1
2014	2,437.5	2,443.9	2,462.2	2,491.8	2,502.9	2,505.1	2,463.5	2,461.9	2,498.1	2,526.7	2,545.6	2,548.6	2,490.7
2015	2,474.1	2,486.7	2,499.2	2,528.0	2,543.3	2,544.1	2,504.2	2,498.5	2,530.2	2,563.4	2,580.9	2,584.5	2,528.1
2016	2,510.5	2,525.3	2,544.7	2,574.7	2,579.2	2,578.5	2,554.9	2,548.9	2,587.2	2,606.1	2,621.4	2,626.0	2,571.5
2017	2,561.8	2,573.3	2,585.4	2,606.6	2,620.1	2,617.6	2,585.2	2,583.7	2,617.5	2,641.8	2,660.2	2,661.6	2,609.6
2018	2,591.0	2,609.5	2,616.8	2,638.6	2,648.6	2,651.3	2,617.7	2,614.5	2,647.0	2,671.8	2,678.1	2,681.8	2,638.9
Mining, Logging, and Construction													
2010	92.0	89.1	93.5	99.5	101.7	103.2	104.6	104.6	103.1	103.8	102.8	99.3	99.8
2011	90.6	90.0	95.2	100.9	101.6	103.2	104.9	105.2	104.4	104.6	103.3	100.0	100.3
2012	93.4	93.5	96.0	98.2	98.9	101.4	102.3	102.9	103.0	102.6	101.3	99.9	99.5
2013	94.3	94.1	98.2	101.5	102.4	104.4	105.4	107.0	105.8	106.0	104.7	99.3	101.9
2014	95.3	94.0	99.1	104.2	106.0	107.9	109.5	109.4	108.8	109.1	108.5	105.5	104.8
2015	99.1	99.3	101.4	108.8	111.4	113.4	115.0	115.7	115.2	115.4	114.0	112.1	110.1
2016	106.0	104.9	109.6	112.7	114.3	116.3	118.0	118.3	117.8	118.7	117.1	115.0	114.1
2017	110.3	111.1	112.0	116.1	118.9	119.6	119.9	119.6	118.7	118.7	117.8	115.5	116.5
2018	108.8	110.3	112.9	117.7	118.4	120.6	121.3	121.8	121.1	121.5	122.1	121.2	118.1
Manufacturing													
2010	187.9	186.6	186.6	187.4	187.8	189.1	188.4	188.2	187.5	187.5	187.3	187.9	187.7
2011	186.1	185.5	186.2	186.5	186.7	187.5	186.9	186.8	185.7	185.6	185.4	185.2	186.2
2012	183.4	183.1	183.5	183.2	183.3	184.3	183.7	183.5	182.6	182.3	181.6	181.7	183.0
2013	180.0	179.9	179.7	180.3	180.6	181.8	181.2	181.5	181.1	181.1	181.4	181.5	180.8
2014	179.5	179.4	180.0	179.4	180.7	181.5	181.2	181.4	180.6	180.6	181.0	181.6	180.6
2015	179.9	180.0	180.2	180.2	181.1	181.8	181.8	181.6	180.8	180.1	180.3	180.7	180.7
2016	178.7	179.1	178.9	179.3	180.0	181.4	181.3	181.1	180.4	180.5	180.6	181.5	180.2
2017	179.6	179.6	179.8	180.5	181.0	182.5	182.4	182.1	181.0	181.0	181.8	182.1	181.1
2018	180.4	180.2	180.0	180.4	181.3	182.7	182.8	182.7	181.8	182.1	182.1	181.7	181.5

Employment by Industry: Philadelphia-Camden-Wilmington, 2010–2018—*Continued*

(Numbers in thousands, not seasonally adjusted)

Industry and year	January	February	March	April	May	June	July	August	September	October	November	December	Annual average
Trade, Transportation, and Utilities													
2010	495.1	486.0	489.5	492.6	497.5	500.2	494.1	492.7	493.7	499.2	508.9	517.7	497.3
2011	496.5	491.3	492.2	496.1	497.9	499.1	493.8	493.1	495.4	499.2	510.8	518.4	498.7
2012	498.0	492.8	496.4	495.9	501.7	502.3	497.8	497.8	499.2	504.4	518.3	523.0	502.3
2013	501.4	496.2	498.1	499.8	503.4	506.0	501.3	502.0	503.4	508.3	521.5	528.3	505.8
2014	505.6	499.8	503.4	505.6	509.7	513.0	506.6	507.1	508.0	513.5	527.0	534.0	511.1
2015	508.1	502.6	504.4	508.3	513.1	516.9	510.8	511.1	511.8	517.5	530.5	536.9	514.3
2016	512.3	507.3	509.2	511.7	515.5	516.7	514.6	514.5	515.7	520.5	533.3	540.4	517.6
2017	518.6	510.9	510.7	513.0	516.5	518.3	514.3	516.0	517.9	523.2	536.9	542.7	519.9
2018	520.6	515.2	515.8	518.2	522.7	525.0	521.8	519.4	521.0	525.9	535.7	539.7	523.4
Wholesale Trade													
2010	117.6	116.9	117.4	118.0	118.4	118.7	118.8	118.5	117.8	118.1	117.9	118.2	118.0
2011	117.2	117.2	117.8	118.7	118.9	119.4	119.7	119.6	119.1	119.2	119.2	119.6	118.8
2012	117.6	117.8	118.7	118.7	119.0	119.7	119.3	119.1	118.3	118.4	118.2	118.7	118.6
2013	117.1	117.1	117.7	118.1	118.6	119.1	118.5	118.2	118.0	117.5	117.9	118.0	118.0
2014	116.5	116.6	117.2	117.2	117.7	118.6	117.7	117.3	116.3	116.1	116.5	116.7	117.0
2015	114.0	113.9	113.9	114.5	115.2	115.8	115.4	115.5	114.6	114.6	114.5	114.6	114.7
2016	113.4	113.3	113.2	113.3	113.8	113.9	114.4	114.2	113.6	113.6	113.6	113.6	113.7
2017	113.4	112.9	113.2	113.9	114.4	115.3	115.2	115.5	115.1	115.4	115.8	116.2	114.7
2018	116.0	116.2	116.5	117.1	117.7	118.3	118.5	118.4	117.5	117.7	117.2	117.3	117.4
Retail Trade													
2010	287.0	278.9	282.1	284.0	288.1	290.1	288.3	288.0	285.0	289.8	299.1	305.1	288.8
2011	288.5	283.4	283.4	286.0	287.0	287.8	285.8	286.2	284.3	288.1	298.8	304.2	288.6
2012	289.8	284.0	286.4	287.0	291.0	291.6	290.6	291.3	288.9	292.9	305.9	308.4	292.3
2013	292.0	286.9	287.8	288.6	291.1	293.3	292.5	293.5	291.0	295.3	306.6	311.4	294.2
2014	294.0	288.8	291.1	292.6	295.4	297.7	296.5	297.3	294.5	298.9	310.1	314.5	297.6
2015	296.4	291.1	292.6	295.0	298.7	301.7	298.8	299.0	296.0	300.3	311.0	314.1	299.6
2016	297.3	292.9	294.7	296.5	299.3	300.9	301.1	301.1	296.8	300.3	309.2	312.9	300.3
2017	298.3	293.1	292.6	294.9	296.5	297.7	296.9	296.7	293.4	296.9	307.4	310.2	297.9
2018	295.6	291.1	291.4	292.9	296.1	297.5	296.4	294.7	292.0	294.2	303.0	303.9	295.7
Transportation and Utilities													
2010	90.5	90.2	90.0	90.6	91.0	91.4	87.0	86.2	90.9	91.3	91.9	94.4	90.5
2011	90.8	90.7	91.0	91.4	92.0	91.9	88.3	87.3	92.0	91.9	92.8	94.6	91.2
2012	90.6	91.0	91.3	90.2	91.7	91.0	87.9	87.4	92.0	93.1	94.2	95.9	91.4
2013	92.3	92.2	92.6	93.1	93.7	93.6	90.3	90.3	94.4	95.5	97.0	98.9	93.7
2014	95.1	94.4	95.1	95.8	96.6	96.7	92.4	92.5	97.2	98.5	100.4	102.8	96.5
2015	97.7	97.6	97.9	98.8	99.2	99.4	96.6	96.6	101.2	102.6	105.0	108.2	100.1
2016	101.6	101.1	101.3	101.9	102.4	101.9	99.1	99.2	105.3	106.6	110.5	113.9	103.7
2017	106.9	104.9	104.9	104.2	105.6	105.3	102.2	103.8	109.4	110.9	113.7	116.3	107.3
2018	109.0	107.9	107.9	108.2	108.9	109.2	106.9	106.3	111.5	114.0	115.5	118.5	110.3
Information													
2010	51.8	51.4	51.7	51.9	51.8	52.5	52.3	51.9	52.0	51.2	51.1	51.4	51.8
2011	50.3	50.3	50.1	50.7	50.5	50.9	50.8	47.8	51.0	50.4	50.8	50.2	50.3
2012	49.7	49.5	49.9	49.5	49.5	49.8	49.9	50.4	49.6	49.2	50.1	49.5	49.7
2013	49.2	49.3	49.1	48.4	48.2	48.0	48.0	48.1	47.2	47.3	47.2	47.4	48.1
2014	46.6	46.5	46.2	46.5	46.3	46.7	46.6	46.6	46.3	46.4	46.4	46.8	46.5
2015	45.9	46.2	46.4	46.2	46.1	46.6	46.8	46.9	46.6	46.4	46.6	47.1	46.5
2016	46.3	46.3	46.2	46.6	44.5	47.1	47.3	47.1	46.3	46.4	46.5	46.7	46.4
2017	46.6	46.8	46.5	46.8	47.4	47.7	47.4	47.3	46.6	47.1	47.4	47.8	47.1
2018	47.5	48.1	48.0	48.8	48.6	49.4	48.7	48.5	48.1	48.7	48.6	48.4	48.5
Financial Activities													
2010	200.4	199.8	199.7	199.6	200.3	201.0	201.6	201.4	200.0	200.3	200.5	201.5	200.5
2011	199.6	198.9	198.9	198.9	198.8	199.7	200.6	200.1	199.2	198.7	198.4	199.3	199.3
2012	198.1	198.0	198.5	198.6	199.5	201.1	202.0	202.1	200.8	200.9	201.5	202.4	200.3
2013	201.7	202.5	202.5	202.9	203.0	204.7	205.1	204.8	202.9	202.5	202.8	203.3	203.2
2014	201.7	201.5	201.6	202.2	203.2	205.4	205.9	206.0	204.6	205.1	205.7	207.0	204.2
2015	205.3	205.9	206.3	207.0	208.0	210.0	210.9	210.3	209.0	209.0	209.5	210.2	208.5
2016	209.2	209.5	209.8	210.2	210.7	213.0	213.5	213.8	212.2	212.4	213.1	213.7	211.8
2017	212.1	212.5	212.8	212.6	213.6	216.2	216.7	216.8	215.1	214.7	215.0	215.1	214.4
2018	214.5	215.2	215.2	215.4	216.0	218.0	218.2	217.6	215.9	216.1	216.6	216.7	216.3

Employment by Industry: Philadelphia-Camden-Wilmington, 2010–2018—*Continued*

(Numbers in thousands, not seasonally adjusted)

Industry and year	January	February	March	April	May	June	July	August	September	October	November	December	Annual average
Professional and Business Services													
2010	398.3	399.2	401.4	409.8	411.6	413.7	413.0	413.2	411.8	416.1	417.4	417.1	410.2
2011	408.5	408.4	412.3	420.8	419.9	422.6	420.2	420.3	421.4	424.1	425.3	424.2	419.0
2012	412.1	413.5	418.5	423.4	424.7	428.1	426.3	427.5	429.5	433.9	435.6	433.1	425.5
2013	419.5	421.8	426.8	432.7	434.5	438.0	433.6	434.6	434.6	439.3	443.3	439.3	433.2
2014	427.2	425.9	429.8	440.4	443.1	445.4	440.3	441.6	445.9	451.0	455.0	454.1	441.6
2015	438.4	438.2	440.4	449.3	453.7	454.9	453.0	452.0	453.4	464.1	467.6	464.8	452.5
2016	449.3	449.4	454.2	462.5	463.8	465.9	466.1	463.3	467.2	469.0	470.8	471.7	462.8
2017	456.6	455.3	458.6	465.2	469.3	471.8	467.4	466.4	470.6	475.1	477.8	476.4	467.5
2018	459.9	460.8	462.0	465.1	467.9	470.8	467.6	467.0	468.8	474.8	471.6	470.1	467.2
Education and Health Services													
2010	542.2	551.5	551.4	553.7	551.8	540.7	539.9	537.3	546.8	560.8	562.0	559.5	549.8
2011	547.3	560.9	561.3	561.9	558.3	547.6	546.0	544.0	556.8	565.2	568.1	567.9	557.1
2012	557.0	569.6	572.1	572.9	568.8	557.5	553.1	550.4	566.1	576.7	578.1	576.2	566.5
2013	565.1	577.8	579.3	579.6	573.8	564.1	560.9	559.0	577.1	586.1	590.9	586.7	575.0
2014	577.4	587.3	588.9	594.7	589.3	579.2	577.5	576.4	593.9	603.7	607.5	603.9	590.0
2015	594.2	605.7	604.5	610.1	605.2	594.9	592.1	588.8	605.3	616.7	619.4	617.1	604.5
2016	607.0	619.1	620.0	628.6	623.0	611.2	611.1	609.5	629.5	637.4	639.4	637.7	622.8
2017	629.5	642.4	642.4	645.9	641.0	627.8	625.9	623.6	643.4	653.4	656.5	655.2	640.6
2018	642.4	656.9	655.3	660.2	655.2	644.1	640.6	640.3	659.7	668.8	670.8	671.1	655.5
Leisure and Hospitality													
2010	206.3	204.1	211.0	221.4	229.8	234.4	236.4	236.1	230.4	228.4	226.1	224.0	224.0
2011	213.9	214.2	221.5	230.0	237.2	241.4	240.9	240.9	233.7	231.2	229.0	226.9	230.1
2012	219.0	219.7	228.6	234.8	243.1	250.1	248.3	248.6	240.3	237.2	235.4	236.1	236.8
2013	223.6	224.5	230.2	240.2	247.8	253.8	254.0	253.4	246.7	242.2	239.9	240.5	241.4
2014	231.2	229.1	236.1	244.1	253.0	258.6	258.2	259.0	252.0	250.6	245.9	246.7	247.0
2015	235.1	235.0	240.8	249.5	259.2	265.2	263.7	263.7	256.3	256.0	250.8	252.2	252.3
2016	240.3	240.9	248.5	258.0	265.0	271.0	271.1	271.0	264.9	262.2	258.3	257.0	259.0
2017	248.2	249.4	255.8	264.7	273.3	280.1	280.4	279.7	271.0	269.8	265.9	264.0	266.9
2018	254.9	255.6	260.9	270.0	278.3	285.7	285.3	285.0	275.5	272.7	267.9	269.5	271.8
Other Services													
2010	116.5	115.6	117.0	118.0	119.1	120.2	119.3	119.2	118.3	118.7	118.8	118.9	118.3
2011	117.8	118.0	118.8	119.7	120.2	121.7	120.6	120.0	119.0	118.9	118.8	118.9	119.4
2012	118.4	118.3	119.0	119.7	120.8	122.5	121.2	121.0	119.8	119.6	119.5	119.9	120.0
2013	118.5	118.7	119.2	120.0	120.6	122.2	119.4	118.9	117.2	117.1	116.7	116.2	118.7
2014	114.6	113.8	114.9	115.9	117.5	119.3	118.2	117.6	116.3	116.9	116.9	116.6	116.5
2015	115.3	115.5	116.2	116.6	117.9	119.4	118.3	117.8	116.5	117.1	117.4	117.8	117.2
2016	116.4	117.0	118.3	119.1	119.9	121.5	120.9	120.4	118.8	120.0	119.6	118.9	119.2
2017	118.2	117.9	118.6	119.4	120.7	122.2	121.2	120.8	119.0	119.5	119.7	119.6	119.7
2018	118.6	118.6	119.3	120.7	121.8	123.4	122.7	122.2	121.1	121.7	121.8	121.6	121.1
Government													
2010	356.6	362.6	364.7	366.7	372.4	366.4	334.0	328.1	347.5	357.0	360.4	360.4	356.4
2011	351.4	356.0	357.9	359.0	354.3	350.3	320.7	316.9	338.0	347.4	349.4	349.4	345.9
2012	339.2	346.3	347.6	347.5	344.9	340.0	313.8	312.2	333.1	343.8	345.6	345.6	338.3
2013	336.4	343.6	345.4	344.7	344.3	338.8	310.8	308.2	330.7	340.6	342.9	341.3	335.6
2014	333.2	340.0	341.3	342.4	340.8	337.5	310.2	307.6	331.1	339.5	341.2	339.5	333.7
2015	331.8	337.6	340.2	341.0	340.1	336.2	308.6	307.9	331.3	336.6	339.1	338.4	332.4
2016	329.7	335.8	338.5	338.0	336.8	332.1	310.3	309.3	332.6	338.2	340.4	339.9	331.8
2017	332.0	338.1	340.0	339.0	338.3	333.5	311.9	313.1	333.9	339.0	341.0	340.8	333.4
2018	332.6	339.1	340.3	340.2	338.1	334.9	312.8	314.5	336.9	343.1	345.1	344.7	335.2

Employment by Industry: Atlanta-Sandy Springs-Roswell, GA, 2010–2018

(Numbers in thousands, not seasonally adjusted)

Industry and year	January	February	March	April	May	June	July	August	September	October	November	December	Annual average
Total Nonfarm													
2010	2,236.1	2,243.6	2,255.5	2,272.9	2,291.2	2,282.3	2,275.0	2,280.4	2,272.8	2,295.7	2,305.0	2,301.5	2,276.0
2011	2,248.1	2,283.4	2,299.6	2,314.5	2,322.8	2,311.5	2,305.8	2,318.6	2,318.1	2,331.0	2,343.7	2,343.2	2,311.7
2012	2,304.8	2,316.9	2,331.9	2,350.0	2,362.8	2,360.3	2,343.0	2,361.3	2,353.7	2,375.9	2,397.2	2,392.8	2,354.2
2013	2,357.1	2,372.9	2,382.2	2,401.2	2,410.9	2,409.2	2,401.9	2,424.6	2,424.2	2,448.3	2,468.8	2,470.4	2,414.3
2014	2,428.3	2,431.2	2,462.7	2,483.2	2,502.9	2,501.3	2,499.7	2,525.7	2,519.9	2,542.6	2,566.4	2,574.7	2,503.2
2015	2,520.0	2,534.7	2,546.4	2,559.1	2,579.9	2,584.2	2,576.3	2,592.9	2,591.1	2,620.4	2,635.4	2,645.7	2,582.2
2016	2,602.4	2,616.0	2,623.4	2,649.8	2,662.3	2,663.2	2,659.6	2,677.1	2,682.6	2,696.4	2,719.4	2,725.6	2,664.8
2017	2,667.2	2,683.9	2,700.4	2,708.4	2,721.5	2,729.4	2,717.5	2,740.7	2,735.0	2,760.9	2,782.0	2,782.5	2,727.5
2018	2,725.3	2,743.0	2,759.3	2,767.6	2,783.5	2,789.3	2,781.6	2,805.6	2,798.1	2,815.7	2,826.7	2,835.3	2,785.9
Total Private													
2010	1,899.3	1,904.8	1,915.6	1,932.4	1,945.4	1,945.2	1,952.1	1,955.3	1,945.5	1,967.1	1,972.4	1,973.2	1,942.4
2011	1,923.6	1,955.4	1,970.0	1,986.9	1,995.0	1,990.5	1,994.5	2,001.8	1,996.4	2,007.6	2,017.4	2,018.6	1,988.1
2012	1,982.9	1,992.7	2,004.2	2,023.5	2,037.7	2,039.1	2,035.7	2,046.0	2,034.5	2,054.3	2,070.8	2,070.6	2,032.7
2013	2,036.8	2,050.5	2,059.5	2,076.6	2,088.8	2,093.8	2,097.8	2,112.0	2,106.4	2,126.7	2,143.9	2,146.9	2,095.0
2014	2,111.1	2,111.8	2,140.5	2,160.3	2,179.1	2,184.3	2,192.8	2,207.5	2,198.5	2,219.1	2,238.6	2,250.2	2,182.8
2015	2,197.9	2,209.9	2,221.2	2,234.0	2,256.0	2,265.0	2,267.1	2,273.3	2,267.8	2,293.6	2,305.8	2,317.9	2,259.1
2016	2,276.9	2,288.2	2,295.9	2,321.1	2,333.6	2,337.4	2,348.0	2,352.4	2,353.6	2,365.4	2,384.6	2,393.3	2,337.5
2017	2,338.7	2,351.7	2,367.7	2,375.8	2,390.2	2,400.7	2,400.4	2,412.7	2,401.3	2,425.9	2,444.7	2,447.1	2,396.4
2018	2,391.6	2,406.8	2,422.4	2,430.9	2,445.1	2,456.9	2,459.4	2,471.6	2,461.4	2,478.0	2,487.5	2,496.3	2,450.7
Goods Producing													
2010	235.1	235.1	235.3	236.2	237.7	238.2	239.9	239.7	238.8	239.8	239.1	237.3	237.7
2011	229.7	236.0	237.9	240.2	241.0	241.5	242.5	242.0	240.4	240.8	239.9	238.4	239.2
2012	234.8	235.8	236.1	237.3	238.2	238.6	239.3	239.7	239.3	240.6	241.2	240.1	238.4
2013	237.5	238.7	240.4	240.3	242.5	243.9	246.0	246.8	247.4	248.3	249.7	249.0	244.2
2014	247.0	248.0	250.5	252.6	254.9	256.8	258.5	260.0	260.3	262.6	262.3	263.0	256.4
2015	260.7	262.8	263.1	265.1	266.9	269.1	270.0	270.8	271.8	273.7	273.3	275.1	268.5
2016	272.4	274.6	276.4	278.2	279.5	281.5	284.1	284.9	285.8	286.2	287.3	288.1	281.6
2017	286.0	287.9	288.8	288.0	289.7	291.9	291.8	292.1	292.2	293.1	293.4	294.9	290.8
2018	291.8	294.7	296.9	296.5	298.3	300.4	300.4	301.3	301.9	303.2	302.1	304.4	299.3
Service-Providing													
2010	2,001.0	2,008.5	2,020.2	2,036.7	2,053.5	2,044.1	2,035.1	2,040.7	2,034.0	2,055.9	2,065.9	2,064.2	2,038.3
2011	2,018.4	2,047.4	2,061.7	2,074.3	2,081.8	2,070.0	2,063.3	2,076.6	2,077.7	2,090.2	2,103.8	2,104.8	2,072.5
2012	2,070.0	2,081.1	2,095.8	2,112.7	2,124.6	2,121.7	2,103.7	2,121.6	2,114.4	2,135.3	2,156.0	2,152.7	2,115.8
2013	2,119.6	2,134.2	2,141.8	2,160.9	2,168.4	2,165.3	2,155.9	2,177.8	2,176.8	2,200.0	2,219.1	2,221.4	2,170.1
2014	2,181.3	2,183.2	2,212.2	2,230.6	2,248.0	2,244.5	2,241.2	2,265.7	2,259.6	2,280.0	2,304.1	2,311.7	2,246.8
2015	2,259.3	2,271.9	2,283.3	2,294.0	2,313.0	2,315.1	2,306.3	2,322.1	2,319.3	2,346.7	2,362.1	2,370.6	2,313.6
2016	2,330.0	2,341.4	2,347.0	2,371.6	2,382.8	2,381.7	2,375.5	2,392.2	2,396.8	2,410.2	2,432.1	2,437.5	2,383.2
2017	2,381.2	2,396.0	2,411.6	2,420.4	2,431.8	2,437.5	2,425.7	2,448.6	2,442.8	2,467.8	2,488.6	2,487.6	2,436.6
2018	2,433.5	2,448.3	2,462.4	2,471.1	2,485.2	2,488.9	2,481.2	2,504.3	2,496.2	2,512.5	2,524.6	2,530.9	2,486.6
Mining, Logging, and Construction													
2010	92.4	92.8	92.6	93.6	94.1	94.0	94.6	94.4	93.9	94.0	93.2	91.0	93.4
2011	85.4	89.5	91.2	92.8	92.8	93.1	93.5	93.2	92.5	92.6	91.3	89.8	91.5
2012	86.6	87.5	87.6	88.3	88.2	88.4	89.0	89.3	88.9	89.9	90.4	89.1	88.6
2013	86.9	88.0	89.7	89.8	91.6	92.8	94.6	95.5	96.0	96.8	97.9	96.9	93.0
2014	95.8	96.9	98.7	99.9	101.2	102.6	104.1	105.0	105.4	107.0	106.3	106.2	102.4
2015	104.1	105.6	105.5	107.9	108.6	109.9	110.1	110.6	110.9	112.4	111.4	112.2	109.1
2016	110.2	111.9	112.9	114.0	115.1	116.6	118.7	119.1	119.9	120.0	120.3	120.3	116.6
2017	117.7	119.3	119.5	120.2	121.7	123.1	122.5	122.5	123.0	123.3	122.9	123.6	121.6
2018	120.8	122.9	124.7	125.3	126.6	128.2	128.6	129.2	129.5	130.3	129.9	131.5	127.3
Manufacturing													
2010	142.7	142.3	142.7	142.6	143.6	144.2	145.3	145.3	144.9	145.8	145.9	146.3	144.3
2011	144.3	146.5	146.7	147.4	148.2	148.4	149.0	148.8	147.9	148.2	148.6	148.6	147.7
2012	148.2	148.3	148.5	149.0	150.0	150.2	150.3	150.4	150.4	150.7	150.8	151.0	149.8
2013	150.6	150.7	150.7	150.5	150.9	151.1	151.4	151.3	151.4	151.5	151.8	152.1	151.2
2014	151.2	151.1	151.8	152.7	153.7	154.2	154.4	155.0	154.9	155.6	156.0	156.8	154.0
2015	156.6	157.2	157.6	157.2	158.3	159.2	159.9	160.2	160.9	161.3	161.9	162.9	159.4
2016	162.2	162.7	163.5	164.2	164.4	164.9	165.4	165.8	165.9	166.2	167.0	167.8	165.0
2017	168.3	168.6	169.3	167.8	168.0	168.8	169.3	169.6	169.2	169.8	170.5	171.3	169.2
2018	171.0	171.8	172.2	171.2	171.7	172.2	171.8	172.1	172.4	172.9	172.2	172.9	172.0

Employment by Industry: Atlanta-Sandy Springs-Roswell, GA, 2010–2018—*Continued*

(Numbers in thousands, not seasonally adjusted)

Industry and year	January	February	March	April	May	June	July	August	September	October	November	December	Annual average
Trade, Transportation, and Utilities													
2010	507.0	505.1	506.1	506.7	509.9	510.8	511.8	512.7	509.1	517.3	525.1	529.4	512.6
2011	509.2	512.8	515.2	518.5	520.3	520.1	520.9	521.7	519.3	524.8	533.6	536.7	521.1
2012	521.5	519.3	521.2	524.2	526.9	526.5	526.8	526.9	524.6	529.6	542.3	543.7	527.8
2013	527.0	525.5	525.4	526.9	529.8	530.7	533.6	535.9	534.2	539.3	551.1	556.7	534.7
2014	540.0	536.2	540.2	544.7	547.2	547.6	550.7	551.7	549.8	558.9	572.8	579.7	551.6
2015	560.8	558.1	559.8	561.6	564.7	566.0	566.7	567.4	565.8	573.9	586.3	591.5	568.6
2016	574.3	571.3	572.5	573.3	575.7	576.2	578.4	577.8	577.3	583.5	598.6	606.3	580.4
2017	584.0	581.8	584.3	584.4	585.7	587.7	589.4	590.2	589.3	595.0	612.2	615.8	591.7
2018	594.1	593.7	595.6	597.8	599.8	602.0	603.1	603.1	603.0	603.6	617.0	620.3	602.8
Wholesale Trade													
2010	138.5	139.0	138.7	139.3	139.7	139.7	139.6	139.5	138.3	139.6	139.5	139.0	139.2
2011	137.9	138.9	139.1	139.9	140.3	139.9	140.8	141.1	140.2	141.2	141.4	141.0	140.1
2012	140.1	140.9	140.9	141.6	142.1	141.8	142.7	142.7	141.2	142.2	142.5	142.4	141.8
2013	140.7	141.4	141.0	141.5	141.8	141.8	142.1	142.3	141.5	143.1	143.8	144.1	142.1
2014	144.0	144.5	144.6	144.8	145.3	145.3	146.1	146.5	146.2	147.1	148.1	148.6	145.9
2015	147.7	148.2	148.5	148.7	149.3	149.2	148.8	148.9	148.3	149.8	149.8	149.7	148.9
2016	148.1	148.0	148.3	148.8	149.0	148.9	149.2	148.8	148.5	148.4	148.7	149.3	148.7
2017	148.5	149.1	149.5	148.9	148.9	149.4	149.7	149.2	149.3	149.3	150.1	150.9	149.4
2018	150.1	151.2	151.5	151.8	152.4	153.7	153.8	153.5	153.7	152.9	154.5	155.4	152.9
Retail Trade													
2010	247.2	245.0	246.0	247.1	248.8	249.3	249.8	250.1	247.8	253.0	260.1	263.1	250.6
2011	248.8	250.0	251.2	253.7	254.3	254.2	254.3	254.6	253.1	257.4	265.3	267.4	255.4
2012	256.3	253.9	255.3	256.5	258.2	258.0	257.6	257.5	256.8	260.3	271.7	271.7	259.5
2013	259.3	258.2	258.7	259.9	261.9	262.9	264.6	266.4	265.8	269.3	278.9	282.6	265.7
2014	268.3	264.7	266.8	268.3	269.6	270.4	271.3	271.5	270.4	275.4	287.4	290.9	272.9
2015	274.7	273.4	275.2	277.3	278.8	280.0	279.6	280.0	279.2	283.6	294.2	296.4	281.0
2016	282.1	280.2	281.8	283.3	284.4	284.1	285.4	284.7	284.1	289.0	299.9	302.2	286.8
2017	288.1	286.1	287.1	287.7	288.0	288.7	289.2	289.3	286.9	291.2	303.4	304.2	290.8
2018	289.8	287.9	288.9	289.5	290.5	289.9	290.4	289.3	288.8	291.1	300.3	300.9	291.4
Transportation and Utilities													
2010	121.3	121.1	121.4	120.3	121.4	121.8	122.4	123.1	123.0	124.7	125.5	127.3	122.8
2011	122.5	123.9	124.9	124.9	125.7	126.0	125.8	126.0	126.0	126.2	126.9	128.3	125.6
2012	125.1	124.5	125.0	126.1	126.6	126.7	126.5	126.7	126.6	127.1	128.1	129.6	126.6
2013	127.0	125.9	125.7	125.5	126.1	126.0	126.9	127.2	126.9	126.9	128.4	130.0	126.9
2014	127.7	127.0	128.8	131.6	132.3	131.9	133.3	133.7	133.2	136.4	137.3	140.2	132.8
2015	138.4	136.5	136.1	135.6	136.6	136.8	138.3	138.5	138.3	140.5	142.3	145.4	138.6
2016	144.1	143.1	142.4	141.2	142.3	143.2	143.8	144.3	144.7	146.1	150.0	154.8	145.0
2017	147.4	146.6	147.7	147.8	148.8	149.6	150.5	151.7	153.1	154.5	158.7	160.7	151.4
2018	154.2	154.6	155.2	156.5	156.9	158.4	158.9	160.3	160.5	159.6	162.2	164.0	158.4
Information													
2010	75.5	75.6	75.8	76.5	77.0	76.6	76.8	76.6	76.0	76.2	76.7	76.9	76.4
2011	78.3	78.4	78.9	79.1	78.9	78.3	79.0	79.3	79.0	79.5	81.0	79.2	79.1
2012	78.9	80.1	79.9	79.6	80.5	80.3	80.9	81.3	81.1	82.5	82.9	82.9	80.9
2013	81.4	82.4	82.5	83.1	83.6	82.8	84.0	84.4	84.4	86.6	86.4	86.2	84.0
2014	86.6	86.9	87.8	88.4	88.7	89.4	89.6	89.6	89.1	91.3	91.9	92.0	89.3
2015	89.2	90.0	90.7	91.6	93.6	93.9	96.1	93.9	92.4	96.9	97.8	98.1	93.7
2016	93.9	96.1	95.2	98.0	97.3	97.7	99.7	97.6	98.8	98.9	101.1	99.3	97.8
2017	99.5	101.5	101.5	100.3	101.2	100.8	99.8	102.6	100.3	104.5	103.8	103.1	101.6
2018	98.8	99.7	97.6	98.1	97.9	97.8	97.4	99.2	99.3	99.6	98.7	97.5	98.5
Financial Activities													
2010	148.6	148.5	148.3	148.2	148.6	148.5	148.4	148.9	148.2	149.7	149.9	150.3	148.8
2011	149.5	150.1	150.4	150.8	151.0	151.1	151.3	151.8	151.8	152.5	152.7	152.9	151.3
2012	152.8	153.3	153.7	153.7	153.5	153.8	154.0	154.1	153.2	154.6	155.6	155.7	154.0
2013	153.7	154.3	154.9	155.7	156.2	156.6	156.8	157.3	156.3	157.6	158.8	158.6	156.4
2014	156.7	157.0	157.5	157.9	158.5	159.1	159.5	160.0	159.0	160.7	160.9	161.1	159.0
2015	160.0	160.4	160.8	161.5	162.0	162.4	162.8	162.4	161.7	163.3	163.5	163.6	162.0
2016	163.6	163.6	163.6	164.7	165.9	166.4	167.9	168.1	167.9	168.9	169.1	169.3	166.6
2017	167.2	168.0	168.8	169.1	170.4	171.6	171.9	171.9	171.8	173.6	173.4	173.7	171.0
2018	171.2	172.8	172.9	173.5	173.8	175.0	175.4	175.3	174.9	175.4	174.8	175.5	174.2

Employment by Industry: Atlanta-Sandy Springs-Roswell, GA, 2010–2018—*Continued*

(Numbers in thousands, not seasonally adjusted)

Industry and year	January	February	March	April	May	June	July	August	September	October	November	December	Annual average
Professional and Business Services													
2010	374.8	377.5	380.8	387.8	388.9	390.3	392.6	392.1	390.5	397.4	397.0	397.2	388.9
2011	390.4	401.0	404.2	404.2	403.7	404.0	405.2	408.2	408.9	411.5	412.4	414.2	405.7
2012	404.0	408.2	410.9	415.7	419.0	423.3	420.0	423.4	420.5	426.8	430.2	430.2	419.4
2013	423.2	430.5	432.4	435.8	436.6	440.6	439.5	443.4	443.5	450.1	453.5	452.1	440.1
2014	445.5	447.4	458.1	458.2	462.8	466.0	469.7	473.9	472.7	476.6	479.9	480.7	466.0
2015	467.3	472.0	474.9	474.1	481.1	483.9	484.4	486.0	485.5	490.8	489.5	491.7	481.8
2016	483.3	487.2	487.9	493.7	494.2	494.3	499.3	502.0	503.9	505.3	506.1	508.1	497.1
2017	494.7	498.5	502.1	504.4	504.9	508.9	512.1	515.2	512.7	519.7	523.7	522.7	510.0
2018	508.5	512.4	517.1	517.5	518.0	521.0	522.3	528.4	525.5	536.1	538.4	539.3	523.7
Education and Health Services													
2010	257.0	259.5	260.6	261.3	262.9	259.5	261.1	264.4	264.5	268.7	268.6	268.3	263.0
2011	263.7	267.8	268.7	273.7	273.4	268.9	269.4	273.5	275.1	278.9	279.1	279.9	272.7
2012	278.1	281.0	282.3	284.4	285.1	281.0	280.0	285.7	286.8	289.8	290.1	290.5	284.6
2013	289.8	292.5	293.1	295.4	296.1	292.3	290.7	296.4	297.8	300.9	303.1	303.4	296.0
2014	300.3	301.0	303.8	305.5	307.1	303.3	302.7	309.4	310.4	311.7	313.3	314.6	306.9
2015	312.9	314.8	315.3	316.3	318.0	315.2	314.2	319.5	321.2	326.8	328.4	329.2	319.3
2016	327.3	330.5	330.8	332.8	333.6	329.5	329.7	334.7	336.4	339.9	340.5	340.4	333.8
2017	335.7	338.5	340.3	340.4	341.5	338.0	337.0	342.2	343.4	346.0	347.2	347.3	341.5
2018	346.0	348.6	350.1	351.5	353.2	349.9	351.0	357.6	357.1	359.9	360.4	361.2	353.9
Leisure and Hospitality													
2010	209.5	211.2	216.3	222.3	226.2	227.7	227.1	226.9	224.8	223.5	221.6	220.5	221.5
2011	211.2	216.1	221.4	227.8	233.4	233.4	232.9	232.4	229.4	227.2	226.3	225.7	226.4
2012	221.8	223.5	228.5	235.7	241.1	241.8	240.6	241.2	236.1	236.6	234.7	234.7	234.7
2013	231.8	233.7	238.2	245.6	249.9	252.5	253.0	253.8	249.4	250.4	247.9	248.1	246.2
2014	243.0	243.0	249.9	258.7	265.1	266.7	266.6	267.3	262.5	262.9	262.8	264.4	259.4
2015	253.3	257.2	261.7	267.8	273.2	277.3	275.1	276.2	273.1	272.4	271.4	272.5	269.3
2016	266.7	268.9	273.4	282.8	289.2	292.4	289.5	288.6	285.7	284.6	283.9	284.0	282.5
2017	274.6	277.8	283.6	289.9	296.2	300.4	297.6	298.3	292.3	295.4	292.8	291.7	290.9
2018	284.0	286.9	293.5	296.4	303.2	308.6	307.2	304.9	298.6	300.4	298.7	301.3	298.6
Other Services													
2010	91.8	92.3	92.4	93.4	94.2	93.6	94.4	94.0	93.6	94.5	94.4	93.3	93.5
2011	91.6	93.2	93.3	92.6	93.3	93.2	93.3	92.9	92.5	92.4	92.4	91.6	92.7
2012	91.0	91.5	91.6	92.9	93.4	93.8	94.1	93.7	92.9	93.8	93.8	92.8	92.9
2013	92.4	92.9	92.6	93.8	94.1	94.4	94.2	94.0	93.4	93.5	93.4	92.8	93.5
2014	92.0	92.3	92.7	94.3	94.8	95.4	95.5	95.6	94.7	94.4	94.7	94.7	94.3
2015	93.7	94.6	94.9	96.0	96.5	97.2	97.8	97.1	96.3	95.8	95.6	96.2	96.0
2016	95.4	96.0	96.1	97.6	98.2	99.4	99.4	98.7	97.8	98.1	98.0	97.8	97.7
2017	97.0	97.7	98.3	99.3	100.6	101.4	100.8	100.2	99.3	98.6	98.2	97.9	99.1
2018	97.2	98.0	98.7	99.6	100.9	102.2	102.6	101.8	101.1	99.8	97.4	96.8	99.7
Government													
2010	336.8	338.8	339.9	340.5	345.8	337.1	322.9	325.1	327.3	328.6	332.6	328.3	333.6
2011	324.5	328.0	329.6	327.6	327.8	321.0	311.3	316.8	321.7	323.4	326.3	324.6	323.6
2012	321.9	324.2	327.7	326.5	325.1	321.2	307.3	315.3	319.2	321.6	326.4	322.2	321.6
2013	320.3	322.4	322.7	324.6	322.1	315.4	304.1	312.6	317.8	321.6	324.9	323.5	319.3
2014	317.2	319.4	322.2	322.9	323.8	317.0	306.9	318.2	321.4	323.5	327.8	324.5	320.4
2015	322.1	324.8	325.2	325.1	323.9	319.2	309.2	319.6	323.3	326.8	329.6	327.8	323.1
2016	325.5	327.8	327.5	328.7	328.7	325.8	311.6	324.7	329.0	331.0	334.8	332.3	327.3
2017	328.5	332.2	332.7	332.6	331.3	328.7	317.1	328.0	333.7	335.0	337.3	335.4	331.0
2018	333.7	336.2	336.9	336.7	338.4	332.4	322.2	334.0	336.7	337.7	339.2	339.0	335.3

Employment by Industry: Boston-Cambridge-Newton, MA NECTA Division, 2010–2018

(Numbers in thousands, not seasonally adjusted)

Industry and year	January	February	March	April	May	June	July	August	September	October	November	December	Annual average
Total Nonfarm													
2010	1,587.1	1,591.1	1,596.9	1,615.6	1,625.0	1,622.7	1,616.9	1,611.0	1,618.7	1,637.7	1,641.4	1,643.4	1,617.3
2011	1,601.5	1,607.0	1,615.1	1,639.0	1,642.3	1,646.2	1,649.0	1,642.9	1,655.3	1,666.7	1,671.1	1,672.3	1,642.4
2012	1,631.4	1,636.7	1,647.4	1,661.9	1,669.7	1,683.3	1,677.0	1,673.4	1,682.0	1,695.8	1,703.1	1,700.8	1,671.9
2013	1,660.0	1,664.4	1,676.7	1,701.3	1,710.4	1,721.4	1,707.5	1,705.8	1,711.4	1,729.3	1,737.1	1,734.1	1,705.0
2014	1,687.3	1,697.5	1,706.9	1,731.8	1,742.3	1,751.8	1,746.5	1,738.7	1,747.7	1,767.7	1,776.2	1,777.4	1,739.3
2015	1,727.2	1,728.3	1,743.7	1,771.5	1,785.7	1,795.4	1,793.0	1,784.5	1,781.6	1,806.1	1,812.4	1,812.7	1,778.5
2016	1,764.0	1,774.7	1,785.9	1,811.6	1,819.7	1,829.1	1,835.8	1,829.2	1,829.8	1,838.5	1,845.1	1,846.8	1,817.5
2017	1,799.8	1,807.9	1,816.8	1,840.7	1,849.8	1,867.6	1,856.6	1,849.7	1,850.8	1,864.1	1,871.4	1,870.5	1,845.5
2018	1,824.7	1,841.7	1,848.2	1,866.1	1,877.5	1,895.9	1,883.8	1,875.1	1,875.2	1,889.4	1,890.6	1,883.5	1,871.0
Total Private													
2010	1,393.2	1,396.1	1,401.4	1,418.9	1,423.6	1,424.9	1,431.0	1,427.7	1,426.1	1,442.5	1,444.7	1,447.1	1,423.1
2011	1,408.1	1,411.7	1,419.8	1,444.2	1,447.1	1,451.7	1,465.0	1,461.4	1,462.8	1,473.3	1,477.4	1,477.4	1,450.0
2012	1,438.9	1,442.3	1,452.2	1,468.2	1,475.8	1,489.5	1,492.9	1,491.1	1,489.9	1,502.7	1,507.9	1,506.6	1,479.8
2013	1,469.5	1,470.8	1,482.9	1,506.2	1,514.8	1,526.4	1,524.4	1,524.6	1,518.8	1,532.8	1,538.9	1,536.5	1,512.2
2014	1,492.9	1,499.9	1,509.0	1,531.8	1,542.6	1,552.9	1,559.3	1,553.6	1,551.5	1,568.9	1,574.8	1,577.3	1,542.9
2015	1,531.6	1,530.8	1,544.5	1,571.7	1,586.4	1,596.4	1,605.5	1,601.1	1,587.0	1,608.6	1,613.6	1,613.5	1,582.6
2016	1,568.3	1,576.5	1,585.1	1,612.3	1,619.5	1,629.4	1,645.7	1,642.2	1,631.2	1,639.3	1,643.7	1,646.4	1,620.0
2017	1,603.2	1,609.5	1,618.4	1,641.6	1,650.0	1,668.2	1,670.6	1,666.1	1,655.0	1,666.5	1,672.4	1,671.6	1,649.4
2018	1,629.3	1,643.4	1,650.5	1,667.9	1,678.1	1,695.2	1,697.4	1,691.2	1,678.5	1,690.2	1,689.7	1,682.8	1,674.5
Goods Producing													
2010	124.9	123.4	123.9	126.8	129.2	131.4	133.2	133.0	131.9	131.9	131.5	130.5	129.3
2011	125.1	124.1	125.0	128.5	130.3	132.5	134.3	134.3	132.1	131.4	130.6	129.5	129.8
2012	126.0	124.8	125.9	129.1	130.8	134.0	136.0	135.9	134.8	135.4	135.1	134.4	131.9
2013	130.0	128.8	130.1	133.2	136.6	138.9	139.9	140.1	138.8	138.3	137.6	136.7	135.8
2014	132.4	131.3	132.0	134.6	137.8	140.3	142.3	142.2	140.8	140.7	141.1	140.9	138.0
2015	137.0	135.5	136.7	140.7	143.9	146.7	147.4	147.5	145.2	146.0	145.8	145.0	143.1
2016	141.7	139.4	140.6	143.6	145.7	148.2	149.8	149.5	148.1	147.7	147.2	146.6	145.7
2017	141.5	140.0	140.4	143.8	145.9	148.9	150.8	151.2	149.8	149.9	149.8	148.7	146.7
2018	144.9	144.8	145.7	148.6	151.3	154.6	155.4	154.5	153.4	154.1	151.5	150.6	150.8
Service-Providing													
2010	1,462.2	1,467.7	1,473.0	1,488.8	1,495.8	1,491.3	1,483.7	1,478.0	1,486.8	1,505.8	1,509.9	1,512.9	1,488.0
2011	1,476.4	1,482.9	1,490.1	1,510.5	1,512.0	1,513.7	1,514.7	1,508.6	1,523.2	1,535.3	1,540.5	1,542.8	1,512.6
2012	1,505.4	1,511.9	1,521.5	1,532.8	1,538.9	1,549.3	1,541.0	1,537.5	1,547.2	1,560.4	1,568.0	1,566.4	1,540.0
2013	1,530.0	1,535.6	1,546.6	1,568.1	1,573.8	1,582.5	1,567.6	1,565.7	1,572.6	1,591.0	1,599.5	1,597.4	1,569.2
2014	1,554.9	1,566.2	1,574.9	1,597.2	1,604.5	1,611.5	1,604.2	1,596.5	1,606.9	1,627.0	1,635.1	1,636.5	1,601.3
2015	1,590.2	1,592.8	1,607.0	1,630.8	1,641.8	1,648.7	1,645.6	1,637.0	1,636.4	1,660.1	1,666.6	1,667.7	1,635.4
2016	1,622.3	1,635.3	1,645.3	1,668.0	1,674.0	1,680.9	1,686.0	1,679.7	1,681.7	1,690.8	1,697.9	1,700.2	1,671.8
2017	1,658.3	1,667.9	1,676.4	1,696.9	1,703.9	1,718.7	1,705.8	1,698.5	1,701.0	1,714.2	1,721.6	1,721.8	1,698.8
2018	1,679.8	1,696.9	1,702.5	1,717.5	1,726.2	1,741.3	1,728.4	1,720.6	1,721.8	1,735.3	1,739.1	1,732.9	1,720.2
Mining, Logging, and Construction													
2010	43.8	42.5	43.2	46.0	47.9	49.4	51.0	50.8	50.0	49.3	48.8	47.5	47.5
2011	43.5	42.6	43.4	46.7	48.8	50.5	52.2	52.4	51.1	50.4	49.7	48.7	48.3
2012	45.2	44.1	45.1	47.9	49.5	51.7	53.9	54.1	53.4	53.8	53.5	52.4	50.4
2013	49.1	48.3	49.3	52.2	55.1	56.8	58.3	58.5	57.6	57.1	56.4	55.2	54.5
2014	52.0	51.2	51.7	54.6	57.7	59.6	61.5	61.6	60.7	60.9	61.0	60.5	57.8
2015	57.3	55.6	56.7	60.9	63.8	65.6	66.6	66.8	65.5	66.1	65.9	65.2	63.0
2016	62.6	60.9	62.0	65.1	67.0	68.7	70.0	69.5	68.5	68.2	67.7	66.9	66.4
2017	62.3	61.0	61.9	64.9	66.9	69.0	70.6	71.1	70.3	70.4	70.3	68.9	67.3
2018	65.7	66.0	66.8	70.0	72.4	74.5	74.7	74.1	73.7	73.8	72.3	70.1	71.2
Manufacturing													
2010	81.1	80.9	80.7	80.8	81.3	82.0	82.2	82.2	81.9	82.6	82.7	83.0	81.8
2011	81.6	81.5	81.6	81.8	81.5	82.0	82.1	81.9	81.0	81.0	80.9	80.8	81.5
2012	80.8	80.7	80.8	81.2	81.3	82.3	82.1	81.8	81.4	81.6	81.6	82.0	81.5
2013	80.9	80.5	80.8	81.0	81.5	82.1	81.6	81.6	81.2	81.2	81.2	81.5	81.3
2014	80.4	80.1	80.3	80.0	80.1	80.7	80.8	80.6	80.1	79.8	80.1	80.4	80.3
2015	79.7	79.9	80.0	79.8	80.1	81.1	80.8	80.7	79.7	79.9	79.9	79.8	80.1
2016	79.1	78.5	78.6	78.5	78.7	79.5	79.8	80.0	79.6	79.5	79.5	79.7	79.3
2017	79.2	79.0	78.5	78.9	79.0	79.9	80.2	80.1	79.5	79.5	79.5	79.8	79.4
2018	79.2	78.8	78.9	78.6	78.9	80.1	80.7	80.4	79.7	80.3	79.2	80.5	79.6

Employment by Industry: Boston-Cambridge-Newton, MA NECTA Division, 2010–2018—*Continued*

(Numbers in thousands, not seasonally adjusted)

Industry and year	January	February	March	April	May	June	July	August	September	October	November	December	Annual average
Trade, Transportation, and Utilities													
2010	226.3	223.0	223.2	225.3	227.3	229.2	227.4	226.8	226.3	229.7	232.6	236.6	227.8
2011	227.9	225.0	225.2	228.3	229.3	231.9	231.2	231.0	231.3	233.4	236.5	239.6	230.9
2012	230.8	226.5	227.1	227.5	230.3	233.6	231.2	230.7	230.8	234.2	238.9	240.9	231.9
2013	233.3	229.5	230.3	232.1	234.4	238.2	236.2	236.4	236.5	238.4	242.2	245.9	236.1
2014	238.5	235.2	235.6	237.0	239.5	242.7	239.8	236.9	240.4	243.9	248.2	251.8	240.8
2015	243.4	237.8	239.5	242.2	245.0	248.9	247.5	247.1	245.9	249.0	252.1	255.1	246.1
2016	246.9	243.4	243.9	246.4	248.7	252.6	251.4	250.8	249.7	250.3	253.4	257.3	249.6
2017	249.7	245.3	245.8	248.4	250.7	254.8	252.3	251.4	250.7	252.3	256.5	259.7	251.5
2018	251.5	247.9	247.0	248.1	250.8	255.3	252.2	251.3	250.3	252.2	256.2	258.4	251.8
Wholesale Trade													
2010	53.1	53.0	53.1	52.9	53.3	53.6	53.9	53.7	53.2	53.4	53.4	53.5	53.3
2011	52.8	52.7	52.9	53.5	53.4	53.5	54.0	53.9	53.3	53.5	53.3	53.3	53.3
2012	52.8	52.6	52.7	53.0	53.2	53.7	54.0	54.0	53.4	54.2	54.9	54.9	53.6
2013	54.6	54.5	54.7	55.0	55.0	55.5	56.1	56.1	55.7	56.0	56.0	56.0	55.4
2014	55.7	55.6	55.6	56.0	56.2	56.7	56.8	56.6	56.2	56.5	56.7	56.7	56.3
2015	56.2	55.9	55.9	56.6	56.9	57.6	58.5	58.3	57.8	58.2	58.4	58.5	57.4
2016	57.8	57.8	57.7	58.2	58.3	58.8	59.9	59.8	59.1	59.3	59.3	59.3	58.8
2017	58.9	58.8	58.9	59.0	59.3	59.9	60.0	59.8	59.0	59.0	59.0	59.1	59.2
2018	58.1	58.3	58.5	58.3	58.4	59.2	59.1	58.9	58.4	58.7	58.9	58.6	58.6
Retail Trade													
2010	135.2	132.1	132.2	134.0	135.0	136.3	136.0	136.2	134.6	137.7	141.0	144.2	136.2
2011	137.4	134.6	134.4	135.8	136.4	138.1	138.2	138.8	137.7	140.1	143.6	146.4	138.5
2012	139.2	135.1	135.5	135.5	137.5	139.6	138.4	138.6	137.2	140.0	144.6	145.9	138.9
2013	140.0	136.3	136.7	137.7	139.2	141.4	140.5	141.3	139.8	141.4	145.5	148.6	140.7
2014	142.4	139.3	139.3	140.3	141.8	143.9	142.6	140.7	142.1	145.5	149.6	152.2	143.3
2015	146.0	141.2	142.3	143.5	145.2	147.5	146.6	146.8	144.1	146.9	150.3	152.5	146.1
2016	146.5	143.4	143.6	144.9	146.3	148.9	148.3	148.7	145.9	147.0	150.2	153.3	147.3
2017	147.5	143.6	143.9	145.5	146.6	149.0	148.6	148.5	145.9	147.8	152.0	154.1	147.8
2018	148.8	145.3	144.2	144.8	146.7	149.5	149.1	148.7	146.1	147.6	151.2	153.0	147.9
Transportation and Utilities													
2010	38.0	37.9	37.9	38.4	39.0	39.3	37.5	36.9	38.5	38.6	38.2	38.9	38.3
2011	37.7	37.7	37.9	39.0	39.5	40.3	39.0	38.3	40.3	39.8	39.6	39.9	39.1
2012	38.8	38.8	38.9	39.0	39.6	40.3	38.8	38.1	40.2	40.0	39.4	40.1	39.3
2013	38.7	38.7	38.9	39.4	40.2	41.3	39.6	39.0	41.0	41.0	40.7	41.3	40.0
2014	40.4	40.3	40.7	40.7	41.5	42.1	40.4	39.6	42.1	41.9	41.9	42.9	41.2
2015	41.2	40.7	41.3	42.1	42.9	43.8	42.4	42.0	44.0	43.9	43.4	44.1	42.7
2016	42.6	42.2	42.6	43.3	44.1	44.9	43.2	42.3	44.7	44.0	43.9	44.7	43.5
2017	43.3	42.9	43.0	43.9	44.8	45.9	43.7	43.1	45.8	45.5	45.5	46.5	44.5
2018	44.6	44.3	44.3	45.0	45.7	46.6	44.0	43.7	45.8	45.9	46.1	46.8	45.2
Information													
2010	53.7	53.5	53.6	53.9	54.0	54.6	54.2	54.0	53.4	53.0	53.2	53.4	53.7
2011	53.0	53.1	53.3	53.4	53.9	54.6	55.8	54.2	55.4	55.7	55.8	56.1	54.5
2012	54.0	54.0	54.0	54.4	54.5	55.9	56.7	56.0	54.3	54.5	54.4	54.2	54.7
2013	53.9	53.8	53.7	54.5	54.7	55.8	56.1	55.9	55.3	55.1	56.4	55.3	55.0
2014	54.5	54.7	54.7	55.1	55.3	56.3	56.4	56.3	55.8	56.0	56.0	56.3	55.6
2015	56.2	56	56.4	56.5	56.6	57.5	58	57.8	57.2	57.6	57.5	57.7	57.1
2016	57.6	57.4	57.5	58.1	57.1	58.7	59.4	59.7	59.0	59.3	59.3	59.6	58.6
2017	59.0	59.2	59.4	59.5	59.6	60.3	60.6	60.4	59.9	60.1	60.2	60.3	59.9
2018	59.8	60.2	60.0	59.8	59.5	60.7	61.0	61.2	60.3	60.9	61.5	61.8	60.6

Employment by Industry: Boston-Cambridge-Newton, MA NECTA Division, 2010–2018—*Continued*

(Numbers in thousands, not seasonally adjusted)

Industry and year	January	February	March	April	May	June	July	August	September	October	November	December	Annual average
Financial Activities													
2010	144.8	144.5	144.2	143.9	144.4	145.5	146.6	146.3	144.5	144.3	144.1	145.1	144.9
2011	143.4	142.8	142.6	143.0	143.5	144.6	146.1	146.3	144.7	144.0	143.8	144.2	144.1
2012	143.0	143.2	143.1	143.1	143.8	145.7	146.1	146.3	144.2	144.2	144.1	144.6	144.3
2013	143.0	143.5	143.8	143.6	144.0	145.6	146.3	146.8	144.5	144.4	144.6	145.0	144.6
2014	143.4	143.5	143.5	143.9	144.7	146.7	147.3	147.4	145.7	146.5	146.8	147.5	145.6
2015	146.2	146.2	146.1	146.4	147.2	148.9	151.9	152.4	149.5	151	151.4	151.8	149.1
2016	150.5	150.9	150.7	151.3	152.0	153.8	156.3	156.3	153.4	153.2	153.2	154.2	153.0
2017	152.2	152.7	152.3	152.2	153.0	155.5	155.7	155.8	153.2	153.5	153.3	154.1	153.6
2018	152.2	152.7	152.6	153.2	153.2	155.5	155.9	155.7	153.2	153.2	152.8	152.6	153.6
Professional and Business Services													
2010	288.5	289.0	289.8	294.8	294.7	297.2	299.2	298.8	295.6	298.7	298.8	299.1	295.4
2011	294.8	294.9	295.8	303.4	303.6	306.6	310.3	308.8	307.2	309.7	310.4	311.1	304.7
2012	303.5	303.9	306.5	312.4	313.7	319.2	320.9	320.9	319.1	322.0	323.1	322.9	315.7
2013	316.0	317.8	319.5	326.5	328.0	332.6	334.2	334.0	330.8	333.9	335.5	334.9	328.6
2014	327.1	327.1	327.9	334.2	336.2	340.7	343.1	343.0	339.9	342.3	342.9	342.9	337.3
2015	336.1	335.6	337.7	345.7	348.4	353.2	355.7	355.2	350.3	354.4	355.3	354.8	348.5
2016	345.4	347.4	348.9	356.9	357.8	363.0	368.0	367.5	362.9	365.8	366.6	366.5	359.7
2017	358.6	359.9	362.1	367.9	368.7	375.4	377.3	376.2	371.5	373.6	375.7	374.3	370.1
2018	367.7	370.1	372.1	377.4	379.3	386.0	389.2	388.9	383.1	386.1	388.1	385.0	381.1
Education and Health Services													
2010	357.7	366.8	368.4	365.8	359.5	346.9	350.1	348.3	359.7	368.3	370.9	370.1	361.0
2011	359.9	369.0	370.9	370.7	364.9	353.1	356.3	355.3	366.2	374.7	378.1	377.4	366.4
2012	368.2	377.2	378.8	377.2	371.8	361.5	362.6	361.5	372.2	380.7	383.7	382.9	373.2
2013	373.8	380.1	382.5	385.5	380.0	370.4	368.8	366.3	374.3	383.3	386.1	385.3	378.0
2014	372.9	384.8	386.6	391.8	386.6	376.1	379.5	377.0	384.8	395.2	398.9	397.8	386.0
2015	382.2	393.4	396.4	401.3	397.9	386.6	388.3	385.7	392.4	403.1	406.1	404.3	394.8
2016	391.0	403.6	404.6	407.8	404.3	391.7	397.1	394.7	403.2	409.7	413.1	412.0	402.7
2017	400.2	412.1	413.6	416.9	413.4	404.3	405.2	402.9	410.7	417.2	419.9	419.3	411.3
2018	406.3	419.1	421.0	423.8	420.5	410.3	412.6	409.5	418.4	425.9	428.2	425.5	418.4
Leisure and Hospitality													
2010	138.0	136.7	138.6	147.1	152.3	156.3	156.0	156.4	152.7	154.5	151.2	149.8	149.1
2011	142.5	140.7	144.1	152.8	157.0	162.1	163.9	164.7	161.4	159.8	157.3	154.8	155.1
2012	150.0	149.0	152.0	159.1	164.7	171.2	171.0	171.9	168.1	165.4	162.4	160.8	162.1
2013	154.8	152.6	157.1	164.4	170.4	176.9	174.7	177.1	172.7	173.5	170.5	167.7	167.7
2014	159.7	158.8	163.3	169.0	175.5	181.1	181.6	181.9	177.3	177.3	174.0	173.2	172.7
2015	165.3	161.9	165.8	172.7	180.5	185.7	187.3	186.5	179.9	180.8	178.8	178.3	177
2016	170.2	169.4	172.9	181.4	186.7	192.6	193.9	194.4	187.9	186.1	183.7	183.2	183.5
2017	176.2	174.4	178.1	186.1	191.2	199.2	198.6	198.3	191.8	192.5	189.4	187.8	188.6
2018	180.0	181.5	184.6	188.6	194.5	201.4	200.2	199.3	191.8	189.6	183.2	180.8	189.6
Other Services													
2010	59.3	59.2	59.7	61.3	62.2	63.8	64.3	64.1	62.0	62.1	62.4	62.5	61.9
2011	61.5	62.1	62.9	64.1	64.6	66.3	67.1	66.8	64.5	64.6	64.9	64.7	64.5
2012	63.4	63.7	64.8	65.4	66.2	68.4	68.4	67.9	66.4	66.3	66.2	65.9	66.1
2013	64.7	64.7	65.9	66.4	66.7	68.0	68.2	68.0	65.9	65.9	66.0	65.7	66.3
2014	64.4	64.5	65.4	66.2	67.0	69.0	69.3	68.9	66.8	67.0	66.9	66.9	66.9
2015	65.2	64.4	65.9	66.2	66.9	68.9	69.4	68.9	66.6	66.7	66.6	66.5	66.9
2016	65.0	65.0	66.0	66.8	67.2	68.8	69.8	69.3	67.0	67.2	67.2	67.0	67.2
2017	65.8	65.9	66.7	66.8	67.5	69.8	70.1	69.9	67.4	67.4	67.6	67.4	67.7
2018	66.9	67.1	67.5	68.4	69.0	71.4	70.9	70.8	68.0	68.2	68.2	68.1	68.7
Government													
2010	193.9	195.0	195.5	196.7	201.4	197.8	185.9	183.3	192.6	195.2	196.7	196.3	194.2
2011	193.4	195.3	195.3	194.8	195.2	194.5	184.0	181.5	192.5	193.4	193.7	194.9	192.4
2012	192.5	194.4	195.2	193.7	193.9	193.8	184.1	182.3	192.1	193.1	195.2	194.2	192.0
2013	190.5	193.6	193.8	195.1	195.6	195.0	183.1	181.2	192.6	196.5	198.2	197.6	192.7
2014	194.4	197.6	197.9	200.0	199.7	198.9	187.2	185.1	196.2	198.8	201.4	200.1	196.4
2015	195.6	197.5	199.2	199.8	199.3	199.0	187.5	183.4	194.6	197.5	198.8	199.2	196.0
2016	195.7	198.2	200.8	199.3	200.2	199.7	190.1	187.0	198.6	199.2	201.4	200.4	197.6
2017	196.6	198.4	198.4	199.1	199.8	199.4	186.0	183.6	195.8	197.6	199.0	198.9	196.1
2018	195.4	198.3	197.7	198.2	199.4	200.7	186.4	183.9	196.7	199.2	200.9	200.7	196.5

Employment by Industry: Phoenix-Mesa-Scartsdale, AZ, 2010–2018

(Numbers in thousands, not seasonally adjusted)

Industry and year	January	February	March	April	May	June	July	August	September	October	November	December	Annual average
Total Nonfarm													
2010	1,676.7	1,689.3	1,699.4	1,704.4	1,708.6	1,664.8	1,647.5	1,670.1	1,681.6	1,705.9	1,723.0	1,728.3	1,691.6
2011	1,692.9	1,707.9	1,718.2	1,727.0	1,724.0	1,680.0	1,665.3	1,702.1	1,724.8	1,738.5	1,758.4	1,761.9	1,716.8
2012	1,731.5	1,746.1	1,758.9	1,760.1	1,757.7	1,726.9	1,706.9	1,746.9	1,768.6	1,785.9	1,809.4	1,817.2	1,759.7
2013	1,779.1	1,797.2	1,806.8	1,812.4	1,810.7	1,776.5	1,761.3	1,798.1	1,816.6	1,838.0	1,864.8	1,869.7	1,810.9
2014	1,827.5	1,842.1	1,849.3	1,854.6	1,843.0	1,812.6	1,796.2	1,837.2	1,855.4	1,883.3	1,907.8	1,918.6	1,852.3
2015	1878.6	1896.9	1902.2	1910.7	1904.1	1870.7	1864.9	1900	1922.5	1956.3	1981.6	1984.6	1914.4
2016	1,944.9	1,965.9	1,972.8	1,982.0	1,971.2	1,932.0	1,931.8	1,968.7	1,994.8	2,013.4	2,033.5	2,036.8	1,979.0
2017	1,999.6	2,019.6	2,027.7	2,040.1	2,028.6	2,003.6	1,988.6	2,028.2	2,051.6	2,076.3	2,101.7	2,105.0	2,039.2
2018	2,069.5	2,093.2	2,101.2	2,101.3	2,094.5	2,061.8	2,056.9	2,102.8	2,122.5	2,145.1	2,169.3	2,169.5	2,107.3
Total Private													
2010	1,438.4	1,444.7	1,456.1	1,460.3	1,457.8	1,450.2	1,440.5	1,446.9	1,445.6	1,467.3	1,483.0	1,491.1	1,456.8
2011	1,460.4	1,469.6	1,480.0	1,488.3	1,485.6	1,477.1	1,472.9	1,483.1	1,490.6	1,501.2	1,520.2	1,528.0	1,488.1
2012	1,500.4	1,508.5	1,521.0	1,521.6	1,524.2	1,520.3	1,510.4	1,525.7	1,531.1	1,546.9	1,569.0	1,577.7	1,529.7
2013	1,544.4	1,557.3	1,567.6	1,572.5	1,574.0	1,569.3	1,563.4	1,577.2	1,578.8	1,597.1	1,623.8	1,631.0	1,579.7
2014	1,592.3	1,601.8	1,609.5	1,613.9	1,611.9	1,605.1	1,598.0	1,613.3	1,614.7	1,638.1	1,662.4	1,674.9	1,619.7
2015	1643.3	1653.4	1659.3	1668.2	1668.3	1663.1	1664.7	1677.9	1682.6	1711.2	1735.1	1742.5	1680.8
2016	1,710.7	1,722.5	1,729.5	1,738.0	1,734.2	1,721.8	1,728.2	1,741.7	1,750.5	1,767.4	1,786.1	1,791.9	1,743.5
2017	1,762.2	1,773.6	1,781.9	1,793.4	1,791.0	1,786.6	1,781.0	1,796.8	1,806.6	1,828.5	1,853.1	1,860.3	1,801.3
2018	1,831.1	1,846.8	1,854.9	1,855.4	1,853.4	1,846.2	1,847.8	1,866.2	1,874.8	1,897.2	1,921.0	1,924.7	1,868.3
Goods Producing													
2010	194.2	194.2	194.7	196.1	196.0	196.9	197.1	196.8	196.0	197.6	197.0	196.6	196.1
2011	193.4	193.2	194.4	196.5	198.1	199.8	201.8	202.2	202.3	202.1	202.1	202.4	199.0
2012	200.7	201.6	204.0	205.1	206.6	209.6	210.3	212.2	212.4	212.8	212.3	211.4	208.3
2013	208.0	209.6	211.0	211.7	213.6	216.4	216.7	217.0	216.0	216.8	216.6	215.9	214.1
2014	214.5	215.9	215.9	217.4	218.0	218.2	217.9	217.8	216.5	217.8	218.3	218.6	217.2
2015	216.1	217.7	218.3	220.2	221.3	222.6	223.6	224	223.5	225.3	225.4	226.3	222
2016	224.0	226.4	226.7	227.3	227.8	230.1	231.3	231.7	230.9	230.1	230.1	231.4	229.0
2017	230.1	231.9	232.9	235.0	237.3	241.5	242.6	243.6	244.7	246.3	247.7	248.6	240.2
2018	246.5	249.5	251.2	251.3	251.8	255.8	257.3	258.1	258.5	261.4	264.0	265.5	255.9
Service-Providing													
2010	1,482.5	1,495.1	1,504.7	1,508.3	1,512.6	1,467.9	1,450.4	1,473.3	1,485.6	1,508.3	1,526.0	1,531.7	1,495.5
2011	1,499.5	1,514.7	1,523.8	1,530.5	1,525.9	1,480.2	1,463.5	1,499.9	1,522.5	1,536.4	1,556.3	1,559.5	1,517.7
2012	1,530.8	1,544.5	1,554.9	1,555.0	1,551.1	1,517.3	1,496.6	1,534.7	1,556.2	1,573.1	1,597.1	1,605.8	1,551.4
2013	1,571.1	1,587.6	1,595.8	1,600.7	1,597.1	1,560.1	1,544.6	1,581.1	1,600.6	1,621.2	1,648.2	1,653.8	1,596.8
2014	1,613.0	1,626.2	1,633.4	1,637.2	1,625.0	1,594.4	1,578.3	1,619.4	1,638.9	1,665.5	1,689.5	1,700.0	1,635.1
2015	1,662.5	1,679.2	1,683.9	1,690.5	1,682.8	1,648.1	1,641.3	1,676.0	1,699.0	1,731.0	1,756.2	1,758.3	1,692.4
2016	1,720.9	1,739.5	1,746.1	1,754.7	1,743.4	1,701.9	1,700.5	1,737.0	1,763.9	1,783.3	1,803.4	1,805.4	1,750.0
2017	1,769.5	1,787.7	1,794.8	1,805.1	1,791.3	1,762.1	1,746.0	1,784.6	1,806.9	1,830.0	1,854.0	1,856.4	1,799.0
2018	1,823.0	1,843.7	1,850.0	1,850.0	1,842.7	1,806.0	1,799.6	1,844.7	1,864.0	1,883.7	1,905.3	1,904.0	1,851.4
Mining and Logging													
2010	3.0	3.0	3.0	3.0	3.1	3.0	3.0	3.0	3.0	3.0	3.1	3.1	3.0
2011	3.2	3.2	3.2	3.1	3.2	3.2	3.2	3.2	3.2	3.4	3.4	3.4	3.2
2012	3.4	3.4	3.4	3.4	3.4	3.5	3.6	3.6	3.7	3.6	3.6	3.6	3.5
2013	3.6	3.6	3.6	3.6	3.6	3.8	3.8	3.7	3.6	3.5	3.5	3.5	3.6
2014	3.4	3.4	3.4	3.4	3.4	3.4	3.4	3.4	3.4	3.4	3.4	3.4	3.4
2015	3.4	3.4	3.4	3.3	3.4	3.4	3.5	3.4	3.3	3.2	3.2	3.2	3.3
2016	3.2	3.2	3.2	3.2	3.2	3.3	3.3	3.3	3.2	3.2	3.2	3.2	3.2
2017	3.1	3.1	3.1	3.2	3.2	3.3	3.3	3.4	3.3	3.4	3.4	3.4	3.3
2018	3.4	3.5	3.5	3.5	3.5	3.6	3.6	3.7	3.7	3.7	3.7	3.8	3.6
Construction													
2010	81.1	81.3	81.8	82.7	82.2	83.1	83.2	83.1	82.3	83.4	82.6	81.5	82.4
2011	79.2	78.9	80.0	81.5	82.4	83.9	85.3	85.6	85.8	85.2	84.5	83.9	83.0
2012	82.5	83.0	84.8	85.5	86.5	88.5	89.4	90.9	91.3	91.9	91.5	90.2	88.0
2013	87.8	89.1	90.6	91.4	92.9	95.1	95.3	96.2	95.6	96.2	95.8	94.9	93.4
2014	93.8	94.4	94.4	95.7	96.0	96.1	95.9	95.6	94.7	95.9	96.0	95.8	95.4
2015	94.8	96	96.7	97.9	98.6	99.2	99.6	100	100	101.6	101.5	101.7	99
2016	100.4	102.3	103.2	103.9	104.3	105.9	107.6	107.9	107.3	107.4	106.8	107.1	105.3
2017	106.8	108.1	109.6	110.8	112.3	114.9	115.5	116.1	116.7	117.9	118.4	119.0	113.8
2018	117.8	119.8	121.1	121.5	122.1	124.2	125.3	126.0	126.3	128.5	129.9	130.6	124.4

Employment by Industry: Phoenix-Mesa-Scartsdale, AZ, 2010–2018—*Continued*

(Numbers in thousands, not seasonally adjusted)

Industry and year	January	February	March	April	May	June	July	August	September	October	November	December	Annual average
Manufacturing													
2010	110.1	109.9	109.9	110.4	110.7	110.8	110.9	110.7	110.7	111.2	111.3	112.0	110.7
2011	111.0	111.1	111.2	111.9	112.5	112.7	113.3	113.4	113.3	113.5	114.2	115.1	112.8
2012	114.8	115.2	115.8	116.2	116.7	117.6	117.3	117.7	117.4	117.3	117.2	117.6	116.7
2013	116.6	116.9	116.8	116.7	117.1	117.5	117.6	117.1	116.8	117.1	117.3	117.5	117.1
2014	117.3	118.1	118.1	118.3	118.6	118.7	118.6	118.8	118.4	118.5	118.9	119.4	118.5
2015	117.9	118.3	118.2	119	119.3	120	120.5	120.6	120.2	120.5	120.7	121.4	119.7
2016	120.4	120.9	120.3	120.2	120.3	120.9	120.4	120.5	120.4	119.5	120.1	121.1	120.4
2017	120.2	120.7	120.2	121.0	121.8	123.3	123.8	124.1	124.7	125.0	125.9	126.2	123.1
2018	125.3	126.2	126.6	126.3	126.2	128.0	128.4	128.4	128.5	129.2	130.4	131.1	127.9
Trade, Transportation, and Utilities													
2010	344.2	343.6	343.9	344.2	344.2	342.1	340.1	340.0	337.8	342.4	350.3	354.4	343.9
2011	343.8	343.7	344.4	346.4	346.0	345.1	344.6	345.2	345.3	349.9	359.3	361.3	347.9
2012	349.8	347.6	348.8	348.9	349.8	348.5	347.6	347.4	348.2	352.5	363.5	366.2	351.6
2013	350.2	349.2	348.8	349.6	350.7	350.2	350.6	352.1	353.0	357.5	368.5	373.8	354.5
2014	359.7	358.6	358.8	359.1	358.9	359.1	359.0	360.9	361.0	366.1	376.8	382.5	363.4
2015	368.7	368.3	369.1	369.6	370	371.1	371.8	374.1	375.7	382.1	393	394.8	375.7
2016	379.5	379.4	380.1	381.2	381.1	379.8	382.0	382.9	383.1	390.7	401.6	405.1	385.5
2017	390.2	388.5	387.6	388.0	387.9	388.1	389.1	390.3	390.5	396.7	410.3	411.6	393.2
2018	399.7	396.8	397.1	397.2	398.5	398.9	401.2	402.6	404.9	407.3	420.1	420.6	403.7
Wholesale Trade													
2010	78.4	78.7	78.9	78.8	78.7	78.6	78.4	78.2	77.6	77.7	77.8	77.8	78.3
2011	77.1	77.7	77.7	78.1	78.0	78.0	77.7	77.5	77.3	77.4	77.4	77.3	77.6
2012	76.9	77.2	77.6	77.4	77.4	77.6	77.7	77.6	77.6	77.8	77.8	77.8	77.5
2013	76.7	77.4	77.2	77.4	77.3	77.4	77.3	77.4	77.1	77.6	77.7	78.0	77.4
2014	76.6	76.9	77.1	76.8	77.0	76.8	76.9	77.1	76.9	76.8	76.7	77.3	76.9
2015	76	76.1	76.2	76.5	76.6	76.7	76.7	76.9	77	77.3	77.4	77.4	76.7
2016	76.9	77.2	76.9	77.4	77.4	77.3	78.1	77.8	77.7	78.8	78.7	79.0	77.8
2017	78.1	78.5	78.5	78.3	78.4	78.4	78.4	78.6	78.6	79.1	79.2	79.3	78.6
2018	79.1	79.3	79.6	79.8	80.3	80.3	81.9	82.3	82.6	82.9	83.7	84.1	81.3
Retail Trade													
2010	204.7	203.7	204.0	205.0	204.9	202.9	201.5	201.2	199.5	202.9	210.0	212.4	204.4
2011	204.1	203.3	203.9	204.9	204.4	203.1	203.1	203.6	203.4	206.9	215.6	216.6	206.1
2012	207.1	204.5	204.9	205.7	206.2	204.8	203.5	203.3	204.0	207.7	218.4	219.8	207.5
2013	206.0	204.5	204.8	205.8	206.3	205.9	206.6	207.7	208.5	211.6	221.8	225.3	209.6
2014	214.0	212.9	212.6	213.7	213.1	213.3	213.4	214.3	214.5	218.7	228.5	231.8	216.7
2015	220.5	219.3	219.6	220.6	220.7	221.6	220.9	221.8	222.7	227.7	236.6	237.3	224.1
2016	225.1	224.4	224.4	224.5	224.5	223.8	224.4	225.3	225.7	231.0	240.1	241.6	227.9
2017	230.4	228.9	228.9	229.3	229.2	229.3	230.0	230.5	230.1	233.8	244.4	243.6	232.4
2018	234.4	231.9	231.9	231.2	231.8	231.8	231.5	232.4	233.7	234.5	244.9	243.9	234.5
Transportation and Utilities													
2010	61.1	61.2	61.0	60.4	60.6	60.6	60.2	60.6	60.7	61.8	62.5	64.2	61.2
2011	62.6	62.7	62.8	63.4	63.6	64.0	63.8	64.1	64.6	65.6	66.3	67.4	64.2
2012	65.8	65.9	66.3	65.8	66.2	66.1	66.4	66.5	66.6	67.0	67.3	68.6	66.5
2013	67.5	67.3	66.8	66.4	67.1	66.9	66.7	67.0	67.4	68.3	69.0	70.5	67.6
2014	69.1	68.8	69.1	68.6	68.8	69.0	68.7	69.5	69.6	70.6	71.6	73.4	69.7
2015	72.2	72.9	73.3	72.5	72.7	72.8	74.2	75.4	76	77.1	79	80.1	74.9
2016	77.5	77.8	78.8	79.3	79.2	78.7	79.5	79.8	79.7	80.9	82.8	84.5	79.9
2017	81.7	81.1	80.2	80.4	80.3	80.4	80.7	81.2	81.8	83.8	86.7	88.7	82.3
2018	86.2	85.6	85.6	86.2	86.4	86.8	87.8	87.9	88.6	89.9	91.5	92.6	87.9
Information													
2010	28.4	28.7	28.9	28.9	28.7	29.0	28.3	28.2	28.0	27.7	28.3	28.9	28.5
2011	28.7	28.6	28.9	29.2	29.2	29.4	29.7	29.7	29.6	30.0	30.8	30.9	29.6
2012	30.9	31.2	31.5	31.8	32.3	32.3	32.4	32.7	32.3	32.4	33.4	33.6	32.2
2013	33.3	33.8	34.2	34.2	34.8	34.5	34.7	34.8	34.3	34.6	35.2	35.1	34.5
2014	35.0	35.0	35.4	35.8	36.2	36.6	37.0	36.8	36.0	36.4	36.6	36.9	36.1
2015	36.7	37.8	37	37.5	37.9	37.7	37.5	36.9	36.2	36.3	36.8	36.8	37.1
2016	37.2	37.7	37.2	37.6	37.9	37.8	37.6	36.9	36.4	36.7	36.7	36.8	37.2
2017	36.4	37.0	37.1	37.9	38.1	38.1	38.0	37.9	37.4	37.8	37.9	38.4	37.7
2018	38.6	39.1	38.7	38.8	39.0	38.8	38.8	38.6	38.0	38.5	38.9	39.1	38.7

Employment by Industry: Phoenix-Mesa-Scartsdale, AZ, 2010–2018—*Continued*

(Numbers in thousands, not seasonally adjusted)

Industry and year	January	February	March	April	May	June	July	August	September	October	November	December	Annual average
Financial Activities													
2010	139.3	139.9	140.8	139.6	139.6	139.7	140.2	140.7	140.2	142.3	142.9	144.1	140.8
2011	142.1	142.9	143.7	144.4	144.3	144.8	145.3	145.8	146.0	146.4	147.2	148.8	145.1
2012	147.2	149.0	149.3	149.0	149.1	149.1	149.3	150.2	150.5	152.3	153.6	154.5	150.3
2013	153.3	155.9	156.0	156.9	157.5	158.0	158.1	158.6	158.6	160.9	162.1	162.5	158.2
2014	160.7	161.6	161.1	160.5	160.7	160.7	160.5	161.1	161.1	162.8	163.9	164.2	161.6
2015	163.1	164.5	164.9	165.2	165.8	166.4	167.4	168.4	168.6	171	172.5	173.7	167.6
2016	172.6	174.0	174.6	175.9	175.9	176.2	177.8	178.8	179.6	181.3	182.9	183.7	177.8
2017	182.8	183.3	184.2	184.6	184.9	185.9	187.1	187.9	188.7	189.9	191.0	191.4	186.8
2018	190.5	191.6	191.4	191.8	191.7	192.3	193.1	193.3	193.6	194.5	193.5	193.9	192.6
Professional and Business Services													
2010	263.0	264.1	267.7	270.3	269.3	268.6	266.8	267.5	266.9	273.3	274.8	278.6	269.2
2011	270.2	273.2	274.7	276.3	273.3	272.5	272.6	274.3	274.9	278.0	280.8	284.9	275.5
2012	276.2	277.5	279.4	280.4	280.8	282.8	282.1	285.2	285.0	289.3	294.6	298.1	284.3
2013	292.8	291.9	294.7	296.6	297.0	299.5	298.5	300.0	298.7	304.6	312.7	314.3	300.1
2014	299.4	299.1	301.1	303.8	304.1	304.9	304.7	307.5	307.5	314.7	321.4	325.3	307.8
2015	314.3	313.7	313.5	317.3	317.1	318.2	320.1	321.5	322.3	330.3	336.9	340	322.1
2016	330.3	330.8	331.6	335.3	333.3	330.2	335.6	337.2	339.6	342.3	344.5	345.1	336.3
2017	338.2	338.4	338.3	340.7	339.3	338.1	336.5	339.5	342.1	347.6	352.0	354.7	342.1
2018	346.5	349.2	350.0	349.6	348.9	349.8	351.1	355.2	355.6	361.4	366.4	366.2	354.2
Education and Health Services													
2010	236.2	237.3	238.5	238.5	239.4	237.4	236.8	241.5	243.1	247.5	249.1	248.0	241.1
2011	244.8	246.5	247.4	248.3	249.3	244.8	244.1	249.4	252.6	254.2	255.9	256.8	249.5
2012	253.9	256.3	256.9	257.1	257.2	253.8	251.0	257.2	259.3	261.2	262.8	264.2	257.6
2013	259.3	261.9	263.8	263.9	263.0	258.6	256.8	262.9	264.9	265.4	267.8	267.9	263.0
2014	265.8	267.8	268.3	269.2	269.0	265.8	265.0	271.6	273.4	276.6	278.7	280.2	271.0
2015	276.8	280.1	280.6	282.2	282.2	278.8	279.6	285.7	287.3	291.9	293.8	294.2	284.4
2016	290.8	292.7	293.6	295.3	293.9	289.5	290.3	297.0	301.0	302.9	305.4	306.6	296.6
2017	303.6	307.2	308.3	310.2	309.3	305.9	304.3	311.0	314.5	317.8	319.9	321.1	311.1
2018	318.1	322.1	323.1	324.0	322.2	314.4	315.2	324.5	328.0	333.0	335.2	335.9	324.6
Leisure and Hospitality													
2010	169.2	172.4	176.9	179.0	176.5	172.2	167.8	169.2	170.8	173.2	176.7	176.4	173.4
2011	173.7	176.9	181.7	182.4	180.4	175.9	171.1	173.3	176.8	177.8	181.4	180.7	177.7
2012	180.1	183.5	188.9	187.2	185.7	181.2	175.7	179.2	181.4	184.1	185.9	186.7	183.3
2013	185.1	190.7	195.2	195.6	193.2	188.1	184.6	188.7	190.1	193.4	196.7	197.3	191.6
2014	194.2	200.0	204.7	204.1	201.1	196.1	191.0	195.1	196.4	200.1	203.1	203.8	199.1
2015	204.8	207.7	212.2	212.9	210.4	204.7	201.4	204.3	205.6	210.3	212.2	212.2	208.2
2016	211.7	216.0	219.9	219.7	217.8	212.2	208.5	212.3	214.5	217.6	218.7	217.7	215.6
2017	216.2	221.7	227.7	229.8	226.6	221.6	216.7	220.2	222.0	225.2	226.4	226.8	223.4
2018	224.1	230.3	235.0	233.4	231.6	226.4	221.7	224.7	226.5	230.4	231.7	233.2	229.1
Other Services													
2010	63.9	64.5	64.7	63.7	64.1	64.3	63.4	63.0	62.8	63.3	63.9	64.1	63.8
2011	63.7	64.6	64.8	64.8	65.0	64.8	63.7	63.2	63.1	62.8	62.7	62.2	63.8
2012	61.6	61.8	62.2	62.1	62.7	63.0	62.0	61.6	62.0	62.3	62.9	63.0	62.3
2013	62.4	64.3	63.9	64.0	64.2	64.0	63.4	63.1	63.2	63.9	64.2	64.2	63.7
2014	63.0	63.8	64.2	64.0	63.9	63.7	62.9	62.5	62.8	63.6	63.6	63.4	63.5
2015	62.8	63.6	63.7	63.3	63.6	63.6	63.3	63.0	63.4	64.0	64.5	64.5	63.6
2016	64.6	65.5	65.8	65.7	66.5	66.0	65.1	64.9	65.4	65.8	66.2	65.5	65.6
2017	64.7	65.6	65.8	67.2	67.6	67.4	66.7	66.4	66.7	67.2	67.9	67.7	66.7
2018	67.1	68.2	68.4	69.3	69.7	69.8	69.4	69.2	69.7	70.7	71.2	70.3	69.4
Government													
2010	238.3	244.6	243.3	244.1	250.8	214.6	207.0	223.2	236.0	238.6	240.0	237.2	234.8
2011	232.5	238.3	238.2	238.7	238.4	202.9	192.4	219.0	234.2	237.3	238.2	233.9	228.7
2012	231.1	237.6	237.9	238.5	233.5	206.6	196.5	221.2	237.5	239.0	240.4	239.5	229.9
2013	234.7	239.9	239.2	239.9	236.7	207.2	197.9	220.9	237.8	240.9	241.0	238.7	231.2
2014	235.2	240.3	239.8	240.7	231.1	207.5	198.2	223.9	240.7	245.2	245.4	243.7	232.6
2015	235.3	243.5	242.9	242.5	235.8	207.6	200.2	222.1	239.9	245.1	246.5	242.1	233.6
2016	234.2	243.4	243.3	244.0	237.0	210.2	203.6	227.0	244.3	246.0	247.4	244.9	235.4
2017	237.4	246.0	245.8	246.7	237.6	217.0	207.6	231.4	245.0	247.8	248.6	244.7	238.0
2018	238.4	246.4	246.3	245.9	241.1	215.6	209.1	236.6	247.7	247.9	248.3	244.8	239.0

Employment by Industry: San Francisco-Oakland-Hayward, CA, 2010–2018

(Numbers in thousands, not seasonally adjusted)

Industry and year	January	February	March	April	May	June	July	August	September	October	November	December	Annual average
Total Nonfarm													
2010	1,901.0	1,903.5	1,911.4	1,925.5	1,937.5	1,939.6	1,920.1	1,913.6	1,929.6	1,942.6	1,945.3	1,950.5	1,926.7
2011	1,918.5	1,926.6	1,931.8	1,950.6	1,958.6	1,960.8	1,959.4	1,963.3	1,974.1	1,987.1	1,995.7	2,001.4	1,960.7
2012	1,967.7	1,981.2	1,993.2	2,017.6	2,032.9	2,043.8	2,037.3	2,044.2	2,049.1	2,066.0	2,080.3	2,087.9	2,033.4
2013	2,045.0	2,062.7	2,074.2	2,087.4	2,098.5	2,100.1	2,095.3	2,105.7	2,107.4	2,127.3	2,145.5	2,148.9	2,099.8
2014	2,110.4	2,127.2	2,137.1	2,152.0	2,165.3	2,171.1	2,166.0	2,176.1	2,179.7	2,197.3	2,214.0	2,221.8	2,168.2
2015	2,189.4	2,202.6	2,217.9	2,231.5	2,243.1	2,251.5	2,258.3	2,268.1	2,269.7	2,292.0	2,303.2	2,310.3	2,253.1
2016	2,276.6	2,294.9	2,300.2	2,322.6	2,328.1	2,333.2	2,337.6	2,343.1	2,348.1	2,365.4	2,376.2	2,377.6	2,333.6
2017	2,336.7	2,353.6	2,368.4	2,371.5	2,383.0	2,395.1	2,384.7	2,387.2	2,391.3	2,409.1	2,422.0	2,427.4	2,385.8
2018	2,385.4	2,406.4	2,416.9	2,426.6	2,436.1	2,450.0	2,440.2	2,449.7	2,447.3	2,461.0	2,479.2	2,490.3	2,440.8
Total Private													
2010	1,601.0	1,601.5	1,607.9	1,616.5	1,622.2	1,628.8	1,633.8	1,630.9	1,630.8	1,640.4	1,640.0	1,646.9	1,625.1
2011	1,617.5	1,622.9	1,625.7	1,643.9	1,651.7	1,655.6	1,669.0	1,673.0	1,681.1	1,687.4	1,694.9	1,702.7	1,660.5
2012	1,671.5	1,682.1	1,691.4	1,715.6	1,730.6	1,742.7	1,746.6	1,755.4	1,756.7	1,769.2	1,778.8	1,787.9	1,735.7
2013	1,749.3	1,764.9	1,772.5	1,784.8	1,795.9	1,802.1	1,807.8	1,817.1	1,813.4	1,827.3	1,842.7	1,850.2	1,802.3
2014	1,811.5	1,826.1	1,834.8	1,846.4	1,858.5	1,866.4	1,870.9	1,882.4	1,880.6	1,891.6	1,904.5	1,913.2	1,865.6
2015	1,883.6	1,895.6	1,907.5	1,919.0	1,930.1	1,940.8	1,958.4	1,965.6	1,962.5	1,979.6	1,988.2	1,996.7	1,944.0
2016	1,964.3	1,980.3	1,982.5	2,003.6	2,007.3	2,015.9	2,032.7	2,035.1	2,032.5	2,043.6	2,052.1	2,054.6	2,017.0
2017	2,017.7	2,032.7	2,044.9	2,047.9	2,057.4	2,073.3	2,076.8	2,078.4	2,073.9	2,085.3	2,096.2	2,102.8	2,065.6
2018	2,064.6	2,083.2	2,091.5	2,100.5	2,108.9	2,124.0	2,131.4	2,137.3	2,127.9	2,135.4	2,151.4	2,164.2	2,118.4
Goods Producing													
2010	196.4	194.7	196.4	192.4	194.7	196.2	198.4	198.8	197.2	197.6	196.0	194.7	196.1
2011	192.6	192.3	190.4	193.0	195.0	196.9	202.0	202.8	201.8	201.9	200.8	199.9	197.5
2012	196.1	196.4	196.4	198.0	202.1	205.2	208.3	208.8	209.3	209.3	208.4	207.4	203.8
2013	203.7	205.6	206.4	207.2	208.8	211.3	214.2	216.2	215.7	216.7	216.8	214.6	211.4
2014	211.4	213.3	213.9	215.5	217.7	220.6	223.6	225.6	225.9	225.9	226.7	224.6	220.4
2015	225.3	226.5	228.8	227.5	229.9	232.9	237.4	239.2	239.6	241.2	241.2	240.2	234.1
2016	238.3	240.5	239.3	242.9	243.9	246.8	251.8	252.9	253.4	254.1	253.2	251.3	247.4
2017	247.8	250.0	252.6	252.4	255.9	259.0	263.1	263.4	263.2	264.1	264.2	263.6	258.3
2018	261.0	265.6	265.1	267.8	268.7	271.5	274.8	274.3	273.6	273.0	273.3	272.1	270.1
Service-Providing													
2010	1,704.6	1,708.8	1,715.0	1,733.1	1,742.8	1,743.4	1,721.7	1,714.8	1,732.4	1,745.0	1,749.3	1,755.8	1,730.6
2011	1,725.9	1,734.3	1,741.4	1,757.6	1,763.6	1,763.9	1,757.4	1,760.5	1,772.3	1,785.2	1,794.9	1,801.5	1,763.2
2012	1,771.6	1,784.8	1,796.8	1,819.6	1,830.8	1,838.6	1,829.0	1,835.4	1,839.8	1,856.7	1,871.9	1,880.5	1,829.6
2013	1,841.3	1,857.1	1,867.8	1,880.2	1,889.7	1,888.8	1,881.1	1,889.5	1,891.7	1,910.6	1,928.8	1,934.3	1,888.4
2014	1,899.0	1,913.9	1,923.2	1,936.5	1,947.6	1,950.5	1,942.4	1,950.5	1,953.8	1,971.4	1,987.3	1,997.2	1,947.8
2015	1,964.1	1,976.1	1,989.1	2,004.0	2,013.2	2,018.6	2,020.9	2,028.9	2,030.1	2,050.8	2,062.0	2,070.1	2,019.0
2016	2,038.3	2,054.4	2,060.9	2,079.7	2,084.2	2,086.4	2,085.8	2,090.2	2,094.7	2,111.3	2,123.0	2,126.3	2,086.3
2017	2,088.9	2,103.6	2,115.8	2,119.1	2,127.1	2,136.1	2,121.6	2,123.8	2,128.1	2,145.0	2,157.8	2,163.8	2,127.6
2018	2,124.4	2,140.8	2,151.8	2,158.8	2,167.4	2,178.5	2,165.4	2,175.4	2,173.7	2,188.0	2,205.9	2,218.2	2,170.7
Mining and Logging													
2010	0.8	0.8	0.8	0.8	0.8	0.8	0.8	0.9	0.9	0.8	0.7	0.7	0.8
2011	0.8	0.8	0.8	0.8	0.8	0.8	0.7	0.7	0.6	0.7	0.6	0.6	0.7
2012	0.6	0.6	0.6	0.6	0.6	0.6	0.6	0.7	0.6	0.6	0.6	0.6	0.6
2013	0.5	0.5	0.5	0.6	0.5	0.5	0.5	0.5	0.5	0.5	0.4	0.4	0.5
2014	0.5	0.5	0.5	0.4	0.4	0.4	0.5	0.5	0.5	0.5	0.5	0.4	0.5
2015	0.5	0.4	0.4	0.4	0.4	0.4	0.4	0.4	0.4	0.4	0.4	0.4	0.4
2016	0.4	0.4	0.4	0.4	0.4	0.4	0.4	0.4	0.4	0.4	0.4	0.3	0.4
2017	0.3	0.3	0.3	0.3	0.3	0.3	0.3	0.3	0.3	0.3	0.3	0.3	0.3
2018	0.3	0.3	0.3	0.3	0.3	0.3	0.3	0.3	0.3	0.3	0.3	0.3	0.3
Construction													
2010	77.8	76.0	77.4	77.5	79.0	80.0	81.6	81.9	80.4	80.9	79.0	77.6	79.1
2011	75.5	75.2	73.1	75.4	77.2	78.8	83.1	84.3	84.7	84.8	83.9	83.0	79.9
2012	80.3	80.5	79.9	80.9	84.4	87.1	89.7	90.2	90.7	91.2	90.6	89.6	86.3
2013	87.2	88.6	88.9	89.5	90.7	92.6	94.9	96.0	95.5	96.7	96.3	94.1	92.6
2014	91.7	93.2	93.4	94.4	96.0	98.1	100.0	101.3	101.1	100.4	100.4	97.9	97.3
2015	99.7	100.7	102.4	100.9	102.6	104.2	107.0	108.5	108.5	109.8	110.1	108.7	105.3
2016	106.9	108.9	107.4	110.7	111.3	112.8	116.2	116.8	117.3	118.6	117.3	114.9	113.3
2017	111.6	113.0	114.4	115.1	117.2	119.0	121.4	121.3	121.3	121.9	122.2	121.0	118.3
2018	118.6	122.5	121.6	123.7	124.4	126.3	127.8	127.4	127.8	128.1	129.0	127.0	125.4

Employment by Industry: San Francisco-Oakland-Hayward, CA, 2010–2018—*Continued*

(Numbers in thousands, not seasonally adjusted)

Industry and year	January	February	March	April	May	June	July	August	September	October	November	December	Annual average
Manufacturing													
2010	117.8	117.9	118.2	114.1	114.9	115.4	116.0	116.0	115.9	115.9	116.3	116.4	116.2
2011	116.3	116.3	116.5	116.8	117.0	117.3	118.2	117.8	116.5	116.4	116.3	116.3	116.8
2012	115.2	115.3	115.9	116.5	117.1	117.5	118.0	117.9	118.0	117.5	117.2	117.2	116.9
2013	116.0	116.5	117.0	117.1	117.6	118.2	118.8	119.7	119.7	119.5	120.1	120.1	118.4
2014	119.2	119.6	120.0	120.7	121.3	122.1	123.1	123.8	124.3	125.0	125.8	126.3	122.6
2015	125.1	125.4	126.0	126.2	126.9	128.3	130.0	130.3	130.7	131.0	130.7	131.1	128.5
2016	131.0	131.2	131.5	131.8	132.2	133.6	135.2	135.7	135.7	135.1	135.5	136.1	133.7
2017	135.9	136.7	137.9	137.0	138.4	139.7	141.4	141.8	141.6	141.9	141.7	142.3	139.7
2018	142.1	142.8	143.2	143.8	144.0	144.9	146.7	146.6	145.5	144.6	144.0	144.8	144.4
Trade, Transportation, and Utilities													
2010	315.1	311.5	310.6	311.1	312.1	313.3	312.2	312.5	311.8	313.7	319.9	325.8	314.1
2011	313.4	310.9	310.3	312.8	313.9	314.7	316.7	317.6	317.1	318.7	327.1	332.1	317.1
2012	321.3	317.0	317.4	321.1	323.3	324.6	326.2	327.5	327.1	329.9	340.5	345.4	326.8
2013	333.0	330.2	329.5	329.5	331.4	333.5	335.0	336.3	335.8	339.7	349.3	355.7	336.6
2014	342.3	339.1	339.4	339.8	341.5	343.3	344.9	347.1	345.1	347.9	357.3	363.8	346.0
2015	352.8	349.5	349.7	350.4	352.3	354.0	357.4	358.6	357.4	360.1	368.3	373.6	357.0
2016	362.6	360.9	359.8	361.6	361.6	362.4	366.9	368.2	366.3	369.2	377.4	383.5	366.7
2017	373.1	369.0	368.4	369.1	369.0	371.1	372.3	373.7	371.6	374.9	384.2	390.1	373.9
2018	377.7	374.5	374.5	373.1	374.3	375.7	378.5	379.6	377.4	376.9	388.9	394.5	378.8
Wholesale Trade													
2010	64.0	63.9	63.7	64.3	64.5	64.7	64.5	64.3	64.1	64.6	64.5	64.4	64.3
2011	64.1	64.2	64.4	65.0	65.4	65.5	66.1	66.2	66.3	66.5	66.8	67.0	65.6
2012	66.1	66.3	66.5	67.6	68.2	68.4	69.1	69.2	69.0	69.4	69.6	69.9	68.3
2013	69.7	69.7	69.6	69.9	70.2	70.7	71.2	71.3	71.3	71.5	71.8	72.5	70.8
2014	71.5	71.7	71.7	71.7	72.0	72.2	72.7	72.9	72.7	73.2	73.5	73.9	72.5
2015	73.8	74.1	74.1	74.4	74.7	74.9	75.7	75.8	75.5	75.9	76.1	76.4	75.1
2016	75.8	76.0	75.9	76.2	76.3	76.4	77.7	77.8	77.3	77.5	77.4	77.6	76.8
2017	77.1	77.4	77.3	77.6	78.0	78.3	78.7	78.5	77.8	78.1	78.2	78.4	78.0
2018	77.6	77.7	77.4	77.3	77.5	77.3	77.8	77.9	77.3	77.6	77.6	77.8	77.6
Retail Trade													
2010	188.5	184.9	184.4	184.9	185.8	186.3	186.1	186.6	185.7	187.2	193.2	197.6	187.6
2011	187.7	185.1	184.6	185.5	186.0	186.6	187.7	188.4	187.7	189.2	196.8	200.1	188.8
2012	192.3	188.1	187.7	189.3	190.7	191.3	192.5	193.2	192.8	195.1	204.5	207.9	193.8
2013	197.4	194.6	194.3	193.5	194.8	196.3	197.0	198.0	197.1	199.8	208.4	212.2	198.6
2014	202.5	198.7	199.0	199.2	199.9	201.2	202.1	203.4	201.4	203.6	211.8	215.4	203.2
2015	206.5	203.2	203.2	203.1	204.0	204.6	206.5	207.0	206.1	207.1	214.0	217.0	206.9
2016	208.9	206.7	205.9	206.3	206.2	206.4	208.2	208.7	207.1	208.8	215.2	218.2	208.9
2017	211.1	207.5	207.0	207.7	207.5	208.3	208.8	209.6	208.0	209.7	217.2	219.8	210.2
2018	211.8	209.3	208.9	208.0	208.4	208.8	210.4	210.7	209.0	208.9	217.5	220.1	211.0
Transportation and Utilities													
2010	62.6	62.7	62.5	61.9	61.8	62.3	61.6	61.6	62.0	61.9	62.2	63.8	62.2
2011	61.6	61.6	61.3	62.3	62.5	62.6	62.9	63.0	63.1	63.0	63.5	65.0	62.7
2012	62.9	62.6	63.2	64.2	64.4	64.9	64.6	65.1	65.3	65.4	66.4	67.6	64.7
2013	65.9	65.9	65.6	66.1	66.4	66.5	66.8	67.0	67.4	68.4	69.1	71.0	67.2
2014	68.3	68.7	68.7	68.9	69.6	69.9	70.1	70.8	71.0	71.1	72.0	74.5	70.3
2015	72.5	72.2	72.4	72.9	73.6	74.5	75.2	75.8	75.8	77.1	78.2	80.2	75.0
2016	77.9	78.2	78.0	79.1	79.1	79.6	81.0	81.7	81.9	82.9	84.8	87.7	81.0
2017	84.9	84.1	84.1	83.8	83.5	84.5	84.8	85.6	85.8	87.1	88.8	91.9	85.7
2018	88.3	87.5	88.2	87.8	88.4	89.6	90.3	91.0	91.1	90.4	93.8	96.6	90.3
Information													
2010	63.7	63.5	63.5	63.0	63.3	63.8	63.8	63.6	63.0	63.3	63.6	64.0	63.5
2011	64.1	64.6	65.1	65.4	65.9	66.7	67.5	68.0	67.9	68.5	69.0	69.2	66.8
2012	69.8	70.3	70.6	71.5	72.0	73.0	73.4	73.7	73.6	73.7	74.4	75.0	72.6
2013	73.2	73.9	73.7	74.4	74.9	76.0	76.7	76.8	76.1	76.6	78.1	77.9	75.7
2014	77.2	77.9	78.7	79.0	79.9	81.0	82.4	83.3	82.9	83.9	84.7	85.9	81.4
2015	85.9	87.0	87.8	89.2	90.3	92.3	93.9	94.5	94.0	94.6	95.3	95.8	91.7
2016	96.3	97.2	98.3	98.8	99.2	101.4	102.5	103.0	102.9	101.1	102.9	102.3	100.5
2017	103.0	103.5	104.5	104.2	104.6	108.0	110.0	110.0	109.2	109.7	110.1	111.4	107.4
2018	110.8	112.0	112.7	112.8	113.7	117.4	118.7	119.2	118.2	117.6	117.7	119.1	115.8

Employment by Industry: San Francisco-Oakland-Hayward, CA, 2010–2018—*Continued*

(Numbers in thousands, not seasonally adjusted)

Industry and year	January	February	March	April	May	June	July	August	September	October	November	December	Annual average
Financial Activities													
2010	120.6	121.0	121.1	121.2	121.5	121.5	122.0	121.9	121.8	121.6	121.2	122.0	121.5
2011	120.1	120.5	120.5	120.6	120.8	121.3	121.9	122.2	122.4	122.3	122.3	123.0	121.5
2012	122.3	123.1	123.4	124.2	124.8	125.7	126.0	126.4	125.8	126.6	126.3	127.2	125.2
2013	126.9	127.8	127.8	128.4	129.0	129.5	130.2	130.5	129.9	130.2	130.3	130.9	129.3
2014	129.5	130.0	130.1	130.0	130.7	131.3	132.3	132.6	132.1	132.6	132.9	133.4	131.5
2015	132.6	133.4	133.7	133.3	134.3	135.6	137.2	137.5	136.5	137.9	138.0	138.8	135.7
2016	137.9	138.5	138.5	139.5	139.9	140.4	141.9	141.5	140.7	140.7	141.0	141.2	140.1
2017	139.2	139.9	140.0	140.2	140.6	141.3	141.6	141.3	140.4	140.8	141.1	141.5	140.7
2018	139.7	140.3	140.0	140.7	140.9	142.2	142.4	142.9	141.4	141.9	142.1	142.3	141.4
Professional and Business Services													
2010	347.1	348.9	351.1	353.4	352.9	356.3	359.8	359.8	359.4	361.3	361.2	361.4	356.1
2011	359.6	361.7	363.6	367.8	368.8	371.2	376.7	378.8	381.1	383.0	384.7	386.1	373.6
2012	382.8	385.7	388.7	395.8	397.5	402.3	403.6	406.8	406.5	411.5	412.1	412.6	400.5
2013	407.4	410.0	412.1	415.8	415.7	417.7	421.3	424.4	421.5	425.3	427.4	429.1	419.0
2014	425.0	428.1	430.4	432.4	435.5	436.5	438.2	442.4	440.7	443.4	444.8	446.8	437.0
2015	441.0	443.8	446.8	451.0	450.5	453.1	459.4	462.2	459.5	464.6	464.9	466.1	455.2
2016	460.1	463.4	463.4	467.9	466.6	469.9	474.4	474.8	472.3	474.1	474.9	472.9	469.6
2017	467.7	471.0	473.0	473.3	474.3	479.4	482.0	483.1	480.6	483.7	484.4	485.3	478.2
2018	478.9	482.7	485.0	488.3	489.4	493.4	496.9	500.7	497.6	504.2	504.9	506.9	494.1
Education and Health Services													
2010	289.4	292.0	293.8	294.7	295.1	291.5	290.1	286.8	291.7	294.8	294.7	295.4	292.5
2011	291.2	294.1	294.7	295.9	295.4	290.5	288.2	287.2	293.3	296.5	297.3	298.3	293.6
2012	292.9	300.0	302.6	304.2	305.0	302.3	300.5	300.6	304.2	307.0	308.7	310.5	303.2
2013	303.7	311.5	314.0	314.9	316.5	312.9	309.6	309.9	312.2	316.6	318.7	319.1	313.3
2014	311.0	318.1	319.4	320.9	320.9	317.7	314.3	314.1	317.6	322.2	324.4	324.3	318.7
2015	320.0	325.2	326.4	328.1	328.7	326.9	326.6	325.8	329.0	334.5	335.8	336.6	328.6
2016	329.7	335.5	337.7	339.9	340.3	337.5	337.2	335.6	340.8	347.1	347.9	348.9	339.8
2017	341.9	348.6	351.4	349.5	350.3	347.9	342.9	342.9	347.8	351.7	353.1	353.5	348.5
2018	347.8	354.0	356.6	355.8	356.7	355.5	351.0	352.1	354.6	359.0	361.2	363.4	355.6
Leisure and Hospitality													
2010	197.9	198.7	199.7	208.0	209.2	212.3	213.6	214.4	213.3	214.2	210.4	210.5	208.5
2011	204.3	206.3	208.3	213.8	217.4	219.5	220.4	221.3	222.1	220.7	218.0	218.4	215.9
2012	212.4	214.8	216.8	224.3	228.1	231.2	230.8	233.9	232.3	232.9	230.2	231.2	226.6
2013	224.6	227.8	230.5	234.9	239.7	240.8	240.5	242.6	241.8	241.5	241.3	242.0	237.3
2014	235.1	238.6	241.4	245.9	249.2	252.8	252.4	254.5	253.6	252.8	251.0	251.9	248.3
2015	244.4	247.8	251.5	256.3	260.1	261.9	262.6	264.3	263.2	262.5	260.8	261.7	258.1
2016	255.9	260.4	261.5	267.6	270.2	271.3	271.8	273.1	270.6	271.2	269.1	268.7	267.6
2017	260.0	265.1	268.7	271.9	275.2	278.5	277.0	276.3	273.9	273.1	271.9	270.3	271.8
2018	263.0	267.3	270.4	274.0	276.7	279.2	279.3	279.4	276.8	273.8	274.9	277.7	274.4
Other Services													
2010	70.8	71.2	71.7	72.7	73.4	73.9	73.9	73.1	72.6	73.9	73.0	73.1	72.8
2011	72.2	72.5	72.8	74.6	74.5	74.8	75.6	75.1	75.4	75.8	75.7	75.7	74.6
2012	73.9	74.8	75.5	76.5	77.8	78.4	77.8	77.7	77.9	78.3	78.2	78.6	77.1
2013	76.8	78.1	78.5	79.7	79.9	80.4	80.3	80.4	80.4	80.7	80.8	80.9	79.7
2014	80.0	81.0	81.5	82.9	83.1	83.2	82.8	82.8	82.7	82.9	82.7	82.5	82.3
2015	81.6	82.4	82.8	83.2	84.0	84.1	83.9	83.5	83.3	84.2	83.9	83.9	83.4
2016	83.5	83.9	84.0	85.4	85.6	86.2	86.2	86.0	85.5	86.1	85.7	85.8	85.3
2017	85.0	85.6	86.3	87.3	87.5	88.1	87.9	87.7	87.2	87.3	87.2	87.1	87.0
2018	85.7	86.8	87.2	88.0	88.5	89.1	89.8	89.1	88.3	89.0	88.4	88.2	88.2
Government													
2010	300.0	302.0	303.5	309.0	315.3	310.8	286.3	282.7	298.8	302.2	305.3	303.6	301.6
2011	301.0	303.7	306.1	306.7	306.9	305.2	290.4	290.3	293.0	299.7	300.8	298.7	300.2
2012	296.2	299.1	301.8	302.0	302.3	301.1	290.7	288.8	292.4	296.8	301.5	300.0	297.7
2013	295.7	297.8	301.7	302.6	302.6	298.0	287.5	288.6	294.0	300.0	302.9	298.7	297.5
2014	298.9	301.1	302.3	305.6	306.8	304.7	295.1	293.7	299.1	305.7	309.5	308.6	302.6
2015	305.8	307.0	310.4	312.5	313.0	310.7	299.9	302.5	307.2	312.4	315.0	313.6	309.2
2016	312.3	314.6	317.7	319.0	320.8	317.3	304.9	308.0	315.6	321.8	324.1	323.0	316.6
2017	319.0	320.9	323.5	323.6	325.6	321.8	307.9	308.8	317.4	323.8	325.8	324.6	320.2
2018	320.8	323.2	325.4	326.1	327.2	326.0	308.8	312.4	319.4	325.6	327.8	326.1	322.4

Employment by Industry: Riverside-San Bernardino-Ontario, CA, 2010–2018

(Numbers in thousands, not seasonally adjusted)

Industry and year	January	February	March	April	May	June	July	August	September	October	November	December	Annual average
Total Nonfarm													
2010	1,142.8	1,143.9	1,150.3	1,158.4	1,162.1	1,158.8	1,131.9	1,139.0	1,139.9	1,153.6	1,167.3	1,169.4	1,151.5
2011	1,145.4	1,149.8	1,154.3	1,158.2	1,157.9	1,152.0	1,135.9	1,143.8	1,150.1	1,161.6	1,176.9	1,177.2	1,155.3
2012	1,166.0	1,168.2	1,173.9	1,183.8	1,187.3	1,186.3	1,167.3	1,177.6	1,182.7	1,201.8	1,219.8	1,217.2	1,186.0
2013	1,208.6	1,215.4	1,221.8	1,227.2	1,231.0	1,230.2	1,211.1	1,226.2	1,235.0	1,253.3	1,274.4	1,276.0	1,234.2
2014	1,258.3	1,264.6	1,272.1	1,280.8	1,283.2	1,282.2	1,266.6	1,282.5	1,293.3	1,313.7	1,341.5	1,345.7	1,290.4
2015	1,324.1	1,326.2	1,333.4	1,340.0	1,344.7	1,343.3	1,335.3	1,348.0	1,353.5	1,382.0	1,407.1	1,414.7	1,354.4
2016	1,383.1	1,382.1	1,386.2	1,397.6	1,397.9	1,391.8	1,385.1	1,395.0	1,403.2	1,426.1	1,444.0	1,446.8	1,403.2
2017	1,424.4	1,426.4	1,439.0	1,440.9	1,448.9	1,448.9	1,434.7	1,447.2	1,458.6	1,480.4	1,505.3	1,504.1	1,454.9
2018	1,482.7	1,488.6	1,494.2	1,499.3	1,502.0	1,502.9	1,487.4	1,492.9	1,502.6	1,518.8	1,538.9	1,539.5	1,504.2
Total Private													
2010	906.0	906.5	910.6	916.6	917.4	917.2	910.4	913.0	914.2	920.5	933.6	939.4	917.1
2011	914.1	918.2	920.9	924.8	924.3	921.2	921.9	926.0	930.1	933.7	947.8	950.4	927.8
2012	937.9	940.1	944.3	954.0	957.2	960.2	958.1	962.6	966.0	975.3	990.8	990.2	961.4
2013	981.7	988.2	993.2	998.7	1,001.4	1,002.4	1,000.1	1,009.6	1,014.0	1,025.7	1,044.8	1,048.5	1,009.0
2014	1,029.9	1,036.0	1,040.5	1,048.0	1,050.5	1,050.8	1,051.5	1,062.2	1,068.5	1,081.5	1,107.4	1,112.7	1,061.6
2015	1091.7	1092.9	1097.3	1103.6	1107.5	1108.9	1115.9	1122.5	1123.9	1144.7	1167.5	1176.4	1121.1
2016	1,143.3	1,142.9	1,143.0	1,153.1	1,153.0	1,147.6	1,153.7	1,159.2	1,163.2	1,179.7	1,194.9	1,197.6	1,160.9
2017	1,175.2	1,177.1	1,186.8	1,189.6	1,195.0	1,195.6	1,195.3	1,205.0	1,209.0	1,224.6	1,246.9	1,246.6	1,203.9
2018	1,225.0	1,231.0	1,233.8	1,238.6	1,240.5	1,240.8	1,242.3	1,246.7	1,250.0	1,258.5	1,275.5	1,276.6	1,246.6
Goods Producing													
2010	144.6	144.0	145.0	146.6	147.6	148.0	146.9	147.5	146.4	145.4	145.3	144.3	146.0
2011	140.5	142.0	142.9	144.6	145.6	146.3	147.6	148.0	148.0	146.8	146.4	145.1	145.3
2012	144.1	144.8	146.1	147.2	149.7	152.2	153.1	154.5	154.3	154.7	153.9	153.2	150.7
2013	151.9	154.0	155.3	155.4	156.6	157.6	159.7	161.5	161.8	163.4	163.7	163.2	158.7
2014	163.3	164.7	165.8	166.5	168.4	169.8	172.1	174.7	174.9	174.5	175.0	173.8	170.3
2015	173.9	176.1	177.8	178.6	180.6	182.8	186.4	188.6	187.3	189	188.7	187.7	183.1
2016	185.8	187.2	188.3	190.6	191.3	192.0	194.3	195.3	194.4	194.2	192.7	192.7	191.6
2017	186.1	189.3	192.6	195.7	197.6	200.0	200.3	201.7	201.8	202.3	202.1	201.7	197.6
2018	199.4	203.3	203.8	205.9	207.8	210.0	210.3	211.2	210.6	210.2	208.7	206.3	207.3
Service-Providing													
2010	998.2	999.9	1,005.3	1,011.8	1,014.5	1,010.8	985.0	991.5	993.5	1,008.2	1,022.0	1,025.1	1,005.5
2011	1,004.9	1,007.8	1,011.4	1,013.6	1,012.3	1,005.7	988.3	995.8	1,002.1	1,014.8	1,030.5	1,032.1	1,009.9
2012	1,021.9	1,023.4	1,027.8	1,036.6	1,037.6	1,034.1	1,014.2	1,023.1	1,028.4	1,047.1	1,065.9	1,064.0	1,035.3
2013	1,056.7	1,061.4	1,066.5	1,071.8	1,074.4	1,072.6	1,051.4	1,064.7	1,073.2	1,089.9	1,110.7	1,112.8	1,075.5
2014	1,095.0	1,099.9	1,106.3	1,114.3	1,114.8	1,112.4	1,094.5	1,107.8	1,118.4	1,139.2	1,166.5	1,171.9	1,120.1
2015	1150.2	1150.1	1155.6	1161.4	1164.1	1160.5	1148.9	1159.4	1166.2	1193.0	1218.4	1227.0	1,171.2
2016	1,197.3	1,194.9	1,197.9	1,207.0	1,206.6	1,199.8	1,190.8	1,199.7	1,208.8	1,231.9	1,251.3	1,254.1	1,211.7
2017	1,238.3	1,237.1	1,246.4	1,245.2	1,251.3	1,248.9	1,234.4	1,245.5	1,256.8	1,278.1	1,303.2	1,302.4	1,257.3
2018	1,283.3	1,285.3	1,290.4	1,293.4	1,294.2	1,292.9	1,277.1	1,281.7	1,292.0	1,308.6	1,330.2	1,333.2	1,296.9
Mining and Logging													
2010	1.0	1.0	1.0	1.0	1.0	1.0	1.0	1.0	1.0	1.0	1.0	1.0	1.0
2011	1.0	1.0	1.0	1.0	1.0	1.0	1.0	1.1	1.1	1.1	1.1	1.1	1.0
2012	1.1	1.2	1.2	1.2	1.2	1.2	1.2	1.2	1.2	1.2	1.2	1.2	1.2
2013	1.2	1.2	1.2	1.2	1.2	1.2	1.2	1.2	1.2	1.2	1.2	1.2	1.2
2014	1.2	1.3	1.3	1.3	1.3	1.3	1.3	1.3	1.3	1.3	1.3	1.3	1.3
2015	1.3	1.3	1.4	1.4	1.4	1.4	1.4	1.3	1.3	1.1	1.1	1	1.3
2016	0.9	0.9	0.9	0.9	0.9	0.9	0.9	0.9	0.9	1.0	1.0	1.0	0.9
2017	1.0	1.0	0.9	0.9	0.9	0.9	0.9	0.9	1.0	1.0	1.1	1.1	1.0
2018	1.1	1.1	1.1	1.2	1.2	1.2	1.2	1.2	1.2	1.2	1.1	1.2	1.2
Construction													
2010	59.0	58.5	59.8	60.5	61.2	61.3	60.4	60.7	59.7	58.8	58.8	57.7	59.7
2011	55.6	56.9	57.3	58.6	59.1	59.4	60.8	61.0	61.0	60.5	60.0	58.7	59.1
2012	58.0	58.0	58.8	59.3	61.1	63.5	64.4	65.7	65.8	66.1	65.7	65.2	62.6
2013	64.7	66.4	67.1	67.5	68.1	68.9	70.9	72.4	72.7	74.0	74.1	73.5	70.0
2014	72.9	73.6	74.5	75.1	76.3	77.2	79.3	81.4	81.2	80.4	80.3	78.8	77.6
2015	78.7	80.3	81.4	82	83.4	85.1	88.2	90.2	89.1	90.5	90.1	88.9	85.7
2016	87.7	88.7	89.4	91.1	91.5	92.1	93.8	94.9	94.3	94.3	92.8	92.8	92.0
2017	86.7	89.7	92.6	95.7	97.4	99.3	100.0	101.4	101.7	102.0	101.5	100.8	97.4
2018	98.8	101.7	101.7	103.6	105.3	106.9	107.6	108.2	107.7	106.7	106.2	103.7	104.8

Employment by Industry: Riverside-San Bernardino-Ontario, CA, 2010–2018—*Continued*

(Numbers in thousands, not seasonally adjusted)

Industry and year	January	February	March	April	May	June	July	August	September	October	November	December	Annual average
Manufacturing													
2010	84.6	84.5	84.2	85.1	85.4	85.7	85.5	85.8	85.7	85.6	85.5	85.6	85.3
2011	83.9	84.1	84.6	85.0	85.5	85.9	85.8	85.9	85.9	85.2	85.3	85.3	85.2
2012	85.0	85.6	86.1	86.7	87.4	87.5	87.5	87.6	87.3	87.4	87.0	86.8	86.8
2013	86.0	86.4	87.0	86.7	87.3	87.5	87.6	87.9	87.9	88.2	88.4	88.5	87.5
2014	89.2	89.8	90.0	90.1	90.8	91.3	91.5	92.0	92.4	92.8	93.4	93.7	91.4
2015	93.9	94.5	95	95.2	95.8	96.3	96.8	97.1	96.9	97.4	97.5	97.8	96.2
2016	97.2	97.6	98.0	98.6	98.9	99.0	99.6	99.5	99.2	98.9	98.9	98.9	98.7
2017	98.4	98.6	99.1	99.1	99.3	99.8	99.4	99.4	99.1	99.3	99.5	99.8	99.2
2018	99.5	100.5	101.0	101.1	101.3	101.9	101.5	101.8	101.7	102.3	101.4	101.4	101.3
Trade, Transportation, and Utilities													
2010	267.9	265.8	265.9	266.7	267.8	268.2	267.0	267.1	268.0	271.1	279.7	282.9	269.8
2011	272.6	270.6	270.2	271.3	272.2	272.1	272.7	273.9	275.0	277.2	287.5	289.9	275.4
2012	281.7	278.2	278.8	282.1	283.7	284.4	284.7	286.4	287.9	291.5	304.4	305.1	287.4
2013	293.2	291.8	292.0	292.7	294.6	295.4	295.4	298.0	298.4	303.9	317.6	320.9	299.5
2014	306.7	304.9	304.8	306.9	308.8	309.7	309.6	313.9	316.3	321.5	335.3	338.9	314.8
2015	324.9	322.5	323.2	323.7	326.5	326.8	331	334.3	335.3	341	352.6	355.1	333.1
2016	340.3	338.6	338.9	341.1	341.2	338.7	343.2	345.6	346.5	356.5	371.2	373.3	347.9
2017	359.9	354.7	355.2	355.3	357.4	357.8	361.4	365.7	366.6	371.9	390.1	390.1	365.5
2018	374.3	370.4	369.5	371.7	374.0	375.4	375.2	376.3	378.4	381.6	394.2	398.7	378.3
Wholesale Trade													
2010	47.8	47.9	47.9	48.2	48.3	48.5	48.3	48.1	48.1	48.4	48.2	48.3	48.2
2011	48.0	48.3	48.4	48.5	48.6	48.6	48.7	48.8	48.9	49.0	49.0	49.0	48.7
2012	48.9	49.1	49.5	51.2	51.6	52.0	52.2	52.7	53.0	53.4	53.4	53.5	51.7
2013	54.0	54.4	55.0	55.0	55.3	55.6	55.9	56.4	56.4	56.5	57.0	57.3	55.7
2014	56.8	57.1	57.4	57.9	58.3	58.2	58.3	58.1	58.3	58.8	59.1	59.2	58.1
2015	58.7	59	59.1	60.2	60.6	60.4	60.9	61.1	61.3	61.8	61.6	61.7	60.5
2016	61.3	61.4	61.4	61.5	61.7	61.6	62.0	62.3	62.2	61.8	61.2	61.3	61.6
2017	61.1	61.3	61.7	62.2	62.4	62.4	62.5	63.0	63.1	63.7	63.7	63.8	62.6
2018	63.5	63.9	64.2	64.8	65.5	65.2	65.2	65.3	65.1	64.6	65.8	65.5	64.9
Retail Trade													
2010	154.9	153.1	153.3	153.9	154.2	154.0	153.3	153.2	153.1	155.6	163.1	165.3	155.6
2011	157.4	155.1	154.6	155.6	155.9	155.7	156.4	157.2	157.2	159.1	168.5	170.3	158.6
2012	162.7	158.9	158.5	159.8	160.1	159.4	159.7	160.1	160.2	162.5	173.9	173.4	162.4
2013	163.4	161.3	160.7	161.1	162.2	162.5	162.4	163.0	162.4	165.5	176.2	178.5	164.9
2014	167.8	165.6	165.6	166.5	166.5	166.7	166.9	168.1	167.8	170.3	180.4	182.6	169.6
2015	172.4	170	169.9	170.2	171.6	171.4	172.6	173.4	173	176.4	185.6	186.8	174.4
2016	177.4	175.2	175.1	175.7	175.8	174.6	176.2	176.9	176.2	179.1	188.1	188.9	178.3
2017	182.8	179.0	178.6	179.0	178.7	178.1	178.6	178.9	178.0	180.0	189.4	189.5	180.9
2018	181.2	178.3	177.7	178.4	179.0	178.6	178.7	179.2	179.2	180.3	188.3	191.2	180.8
Transportation and Utilities													
2010	65.2	64.8	64.7	64.6	65.3	65.7	65.4	65.8	66.8	67.1	68.4	69.3	66.1
2011	67.2	67.2	67.2	67.2	67.7	67.8	67.6	67.9	68.9	69.1	70.0	70.6	68.2
2012	70.1	70.2	70.8	71.1	72.0	73.0	72.8	73.6	74.7	75.6	77.1	78.2	73.3
2013	75.8	76.1	76.3	76.6	77.1	77.3	77.1	78.6	79.6	81.9	84.4	85.1	78.8
2014	82.1	82.2	81.8	82.5	84.0	84.8	84.4	87.7	90.2	92.4	95.8	97.1	87.1
2015	93.8	93.5	94.2	93.3	94.3	95	97.5	99.8	101	102.8	105.4	106.6	98.1
2016	101.6	102.0	102.4	103.9	103.7	102.5	105.0	106.4	108.1	115.6	121.9	123.1	108.0
2017	116.0	114.4	114.9	114.1	116.3	117.3	120.3	123.8	125.5	128.2	137.0	136.8	122.1
2018	129.6	128.2	127.6	128.5	129.5	131.6	131.3	131.8	134.1	136.7	140.1	142.0	132.6
Information													
2010	14.2	14.2	14.3	14.2	14.2	14.3	14.2	14.1	13.8	13.6	13.6	13.5	14.0
2011	12.9	12.7	12.5	12.4	12.3	12.3	12.4	12.2	11.8	11.7	11.6	11.6	12.2
2012	12.0	11.9	11.8	11.7	11.7	11.8	11.8	11.6	11.5	11.5	11.6	11.7	11.7
2013	11.6	11.6	11.5	11.5	11.6	11.6	11.6	11.5	11.4	11.5	11.5	11.5	11.5
2014	11.5	11.4	11.3	11.3	11.3	11.4	11.2	11.1	11.0	11.1	11.2	11.3	11.3
2015	11.3	11.3	11.3	11.5	11.5	11.2	11.4	11.4	11.2	11.5	11.6	11.7	11.4
2016	11.5	11.4	11.4	11.6	11.7	11.6	11.7	11.5	11.4	11.2	11.3	11.3	11.5
2017	11.3	11.2	11.3	11.3	11.2	11.2	11.6	11.4	11.2	11.3	11.1	11.3	11.3
2018	11.1	11.0	11.1	11.2	11.2	11.2	11.2	11.3	11.1	11.2	11.2	11.2	11.2

Employment by Industry: Riverside-San Bernardino-Ontario, CA, 2010–2018—*Continued*

(Numbers in thousands, not seasonally adjusted)

Industry and year	January	February	March	April	May	June	July	August	September	October	November	December	Annual average
Financial Activities													
2010	40.7	40.8	41.0	41.0	40.6	40.6	40.4	40.3	40.6	40.8	40.6	40.8	40.7
2011	40.1	40.3	40.1	40.1	39.9	39.9	39.6	39.6	39.5	39.7	39.7	39.8	39.9
2012	39.5	39.7	40.0	40.6	40.7	40.6	40.7	40.8	41.0	41.2	41.5	41.6	40.7
2013	41.2	41.4	41.4	41.7	42.0	42.0	41.9	42.0	41.9	42.1	42.2	42.3	41.8
2014	42.0	42.0	42.0	43.1	43.2	43.1	43.0	43.0	42.9	43.2	43.4	43.5	42.9
2015	43.3	43.5	43.6	43.9	44	43.9	44.1	44	43.7	44.5	44.4	44.6	44
2016	44.6	44.4	44.1	44.5	44.6	44.5	44.8	44.8	44.6	44.8	44.8	44.7	44.6
2017	44.3	44.2	44.1	44.6	44.6	44.1	44.1	44.1	43.9	44.3	44.2	44.2	44.2
2018	44.1	44.2	43.9	43.8	43.9	43.6	43.5	43.4	43.1	43.5	43.7	43.2	43.7
Professional and Business Services													
2010	118.6	119.6	120.4	121.7	122.0	122.9	123.4	124.9	124.9	127.3	127.6	128.1	123.5
2011	122.7	124.9	125.3	125.4	124.0	123.2	124.5	127.2	127.8	128.0	127.8	126.6	125.6
2012	124.6	126.5	125.7	128.0	126.7	128.0	127.1	127.5	127.0	129.7	128.3	125.8	127.1
2013	126.4	129.5	128.8	131.5	130.3	130.9	131.9	134.3	135.2	135.7	135.3	133.7	132.0
2014	130.7	133.1	133.9	136.2	134.3	134.9	136.2	137.8	139.7	144.1	151.3	152.6	138.7
2015	145.2	142.7	141.8	144	143.2	144.2	144.1	144	144.3	152.1	159.9	163.8	147.4
2016	149.4	145.8	142.4	143.1	142.0	142.3	143.2	144.0	146.5	147.3	146.0	146.8	144.9
2017	145.5	145.7	147.2	144.1	143.9	145.0	144.6	146.2	147.9	150.1	151.4	150.9	146.9
2018	147.7	149.3	149.6	149.6	148.2	147.8	149.5	150.9	152.2	154.9	154.2	153.8	150.6
Education and Health Services													
2010	160.5	161.7	161.9	162.4	162.1	161.1	159.9	160.8	161.9	163.1	165.0	165.4	162.2
2011	162.9	165.2	165.5	166.7	165.9	164.4	163.8	164.3	167.1	168.6	169.8	170.5	166.2
2012	170.4	172.2	173.3	173.5	173.6	173.2	171.7	172.7	175.2	178.2	179.2	180.0	174.4
2013	184.4	185.9	187.4	187.8	188.2	188.1	185.3	187.2	189.5	191.7	193.4	193.5	188.5
2014	191.4	193.4	194.3	195.5	195.1	194.2	193.3	195.5	197.1	199.5	200.4	200.9	195.9
2015	201.6	203.4	203.7	204.8	204.6	204.1	204.8	206.3	208.3	210.6	211.5	212.4	206.3
2016	210.6	212.4	212.7	216.0	215.5	213.8	212.8	214.8	216.6	221.2	221.7	220.3	215.7
2017	220.3	222.0	222.9	225.0	225.5	224.5	223.3	226.1	227.9	233.6	234.5	234.3	226.7
2018	234.8	237.0	238.0	238.2	238.2	237.6	239.0	240.2	241.5	243.8	245.6	246.2	240.0
Leisure and Hospitality													
2010	122.4	122.9	124.1	125.2	124.2	122.9	120.2	120.1	120.6	121.1	123.6	126.1	122.8
2011	124.4	124.0	125.8	125.2	125.0	123.6	122.2	121.4	121.5	122.2	125.6	127.5	124.0
2012	126.8	127.6	129.1	130.6	130.5	129.2	128.5	128.4	128.3	128.6	131.9	133.1	129.4
2013	133.2	133.8	135.7	137.0	137.0	135.5	133.4	133.7	134.3	135.7	139.2	141.7	135.9
2014	142.2	143.9	145.3	144.8	145.8	144.3	143.2	143.0	143.4	144.9	147.8	148.8	144.8
2015	148.8	150.1	152.2	152.6	152.8	151.6	149.7	149.9	149.8	151.6	154.5	156.9	151.7
2016	157.1	158.7	160.5	161.3	161.8	159.9	159.3	158.7	158.4	159.6	162.5	164.0	160.2
2017	163.5	165.4	168.5	167.8	168.8	167.0	164.3	164.0	164.2	165.4	168.0	169.0	166.3
2018	168.4	170.1	172.1	172.0	171.1	169.1	167.9	167.5	167.5	168.0	173.0	173.0	170.0
Other Services													
2010	37.1	37.5	38.0	38.8	38.9	39.2	38.4	38.2	38.0	38.1	38.2	38.3	38.2
2011	38.0	38.5	38.6	39.1	39.4	39.4	39.1	39.4	39.4	39.5	39.4	39.4	39.1
2012	38.8	39.2	39.5	40.3	40.6	40.8	40.5	40.7	40.8	39.9	40.0	39.7	40.1
2013	39.8	40.2	41.1	41.1	41.1	41.3	40.9	41.4	41.5	41.7	41.9	41.7	41.1
2014	42.1	42.6	43.1	43.7	43.6	43.4	42.9	43.2	43.2	42.7	43.0	42.9	43.0
2015	42.7	43.3	43.7	44.5	44.3	44.3	44.4	44.0	44.0	44.4	44.3	44.2	44.0
2016	44.0	44.4	44.7	44.9	44.9	44.8	44.4	44.5	44.8	44.9	44.7	44.5	44.6
2017	44.3	44.6	45.0	45.8	46.0	46.0	45.7	45.8	45.5	45.7	45.5	45.1	45.4
2018	45.2	45.7	45.8	46.2	46.1	46.1	45.7	45.9	45.6	45.3	44.9	44.2	45.6
Government													
2010	236.8	237.4	239.7	241.8	244.7	241.6	221.5	226.0	225.7	233.1	233.7	230.0	234.3
2011	231.3	231.6	233.4	233.4	233.6	230.8	214.0	217.8	220.0	227.9	229.1	226.8	227.5
2012	228.1	228.1	229.6	229.8	230.1	226.1	209.2	215.0	216.7	226.5	229.0	227.0	224.6
2013	226.9	227.2	228.6	228.5	229.6	227.8	211.0	216.6	221.0	227.6	229.6	227.5	225.2
2014	228.4	228.6	231.6	232.8	232.7	231.4	215.1	220.3	224.8	232.2	234.1	233.0	228.8
2015	232.4	233.3	236.1	236.4	237.2	234.4	219.4	225.5	229.6	237.3	239.6	238.3	233.3
2016	239.8	239.2	243.2	244.5	244.9	244.2	231.4	235.8	240.0	246.4	249.1	249.2	242.3
2017	249.2	249.3	252.2	251.3	253.9	253.3	239.4	242.2	249.6	255.8	258.4	257.5	251.0
2018	257.7	257.6	260.4	260.7	261.5	262.1	245.1	246.2	252.6	260.3	263.4	262.9	257.5

Employment by Industry: Detroit-Warren-Dearborn, MI, 2010–2018

(Numbers in thousands, not seasonally adjusted)

Industry and year	January	February	March	April	May	June	July	August	September	October	November	December	Annual average
Total Nonfarm													
2010	1,694.1	1,698.2	1,701.5	1,725.6	1,749.8	1,757.6	1,723.2	1,727.1	1,750.0	1,766.7	1,770.3	1,767.2	1,735.9
2011	1,730.8	1,739.0	1,750.9	1,775.0	1,793.0	1,800.0	1,769.9	1,785.4	1,805.3	1,820.0	1,826.9	1,821.5	1,784.8
2012	1,790.5	1,797.4	1,811.8	1,817.4	1,840.1	1,849.1	1,821.4	1,834.5	1,842.5	1,855.5	1,863.6	1,862.6	1,832.2
2013	1,825.4	1,834.2	1,844.8	1,851.1	1,879.3	1,889.1	1,844.6	1,866.3	1,877.5	1,893.3	1,898.0	1,891.6	1,866.3
2014	1,847.2	1,862.1	1,870.9	1,872.7	1,904.6	1,924.2	1,892.4	1,901.7	1,903.9	1,921.2	1,932.2	1,934.2	1,897.3
2015	1,893.1	1,896.3	1,904.0	1,918.3	1,949.8	1,960.9	1,930.3	1,938.9	1,945.7	1,960.4	1,968.4	1,966.0	1,936.0
2016	1,931.1	1,932.6	1,938.7	1,962.9	1,983.3	1,996.5	1,973.5	1,976.2	1,988.4	1,996.5	2,012.7	2,002.8	1,974.6
2017	1,968.4	1,971.4	1,978.8	1,992.8	2,018.2	2,034.5	1,995.4	2,009.8	2,013.7	2,021.3	2,034.7	2,026.8	2,005.5
2018	1,989.7	1,997.6	2,010.4	2,018.9	2,043.5	2,061.2	2,027.0	2,039.9	2,038.2	2,050.9	2,052.7	2,047.6	2,031.5
Total Private													
2010	1,484.5	1,484.5	1,487.2	1,509.7	1,530.9	1,543.9	1,529.2	1,538.0	1,547.1	1,559.4	1,563.6	1,562.1	1,528.3
2011	1,531.6	1,535.5	1,547.3	1,571.4	1,592.0	1,600.4	1,586.6	1,603.2	1,607.8	1,619.4	1,625.3	1,622.1	1,586.9
2012	1,596.1	1,599.2	1,613.3	1,619.4	1,643.9	1,653.3	1,642.7	1,656.0	1,649.3	1,661.0	1,668.C	1,668.8	1,639.3
2013	1,636.8	1,642.1	1,652.8	1,659.6	1,690.1	1,700.1	1,671.8	1,695.0	1,691.1	1,703.9	1,708.3	1,703.7	1,679.6
2014	1,663.5	1,674.3	1,682.6	1,683.7	1,717.8	1,737.8	1,721.5	1,732.1	1,720.7	1,733.2	1,742.6	1,747.6	1,713.1
2015	1,711.1	1,710.5	1,717.3	1,730.8	1,763.0	1,775.6	1,760.8	1,771.0	1,763.1	1,773.7	1,780.5	1,779.6	1,753.1
2016	1,748.9	1,746.6	1,750.5	1,775.2	1,798.1	1,811.0	1,801.3	1,804.7	1,802.8	1,808.7	1,822.3	1,814.7	1,790.4
2017	1,784.3	1,784.7	1,790.8	1,804.5	1,829.9	1,846.3	1,821.9	1,837.8	1,826.5	1,831.4	1,844.0	1,837.5	1,820.0
2018	1,804.6	1,809.1	1,819.5	1,829.1	1,853.8	1,871.9	1,853.2	1,866.9	1,851.9	1,860.5	1,860.9	1,857.6	1,844.9
Goods Producing													
2010	217.3	215.2	215.2	222.7	228.8	234.2	232.9	231.7	240.9	242.0	240.7	237.8	230.0
2011	232.4	233.9	236.2	244.6	251.3	257.2	254.1	260.6	262.0	262.8	263.7	262.1	251.7
2012	256.9	256.0	259.1	260.0	267.4	271.4	271.2	274.1	274.2	275.1	274.4	272.5	267.7
2013	267.6	267.9	269.8	272.0	280.5	284.4	277.0	286.1	286.9	288.5	287.9	280.8	279.1
2014	274.9	280.5	282.0	278.6	290.1	301.7	297.9	302.9	299.1	301.7	304.0	303.8	293.1
2015	294.8	294.3	295.4	300.0	308.9	314.3	310.6	314.6	314.4	312.4	313.7	310.2	307.0
2016	306.0	302.6	303.0	313.4	318.7	323.0	317.6	318.8	321.5	321.3	325.2	318.6	315.8
2017	316.1	316.5	315.8	321.6	329.0	333.8	323.1	333.4	329.4	330.9	332.1	327.2	325.7
2018	320.6	324.5	327.5	330.5	336.1	341.4	336.6	342.0	340.7	341.1	339.7	337.4	334.8
Service-Providing													
2010	1,476.8	1,483.0	1,486.3	1,502.9	1,521.0	1,523.4	1,490.3	1,495.4	1,509.1	1,524.7	1,529.6	1,529.4	1,506.0
2011	1,498.4	1,505.1	1,514.7	1,530.4	1,541.7	1,542.8	1,515.8	1,524.8	1,543.3	1,557.2	1,563.2	1,559.4	1,533.1
2012	1,533.6	1,541.4	1,552.7	1,557.4	1,572.7	1,577.7	1,550.2	1,560.4	1,568.3	1,580.4	1,589.2	1,590.1	1,564.5
2013	1,557.8	1,566.3	1,575.0	1,579.1	1,598.8	1,604.7	1,567.6	1,580.2	1,590.6	1,604.8	1,610.1	1,610.8	1,587.2
2014	1,572.3	1,581.6	1,588.9	1,594.1	1,614.5	1,622.5	1,594.5	1,598.8	1,604.8	1,619.5	1,628.2	1,630.4	1,604.2
2015	1,598.3	1,602.0	1,608.6	1,618.3	1,640.9	1,646.6	1,619.7	1,624.3	1,631.3	1,648.0	1,654.7	1,655.8	1,629.0
2016	1,625.1	1,630.0	1,635.7	1,649.5	1,664.6	1,673.5	1,655.9	1,657.4	1,666.9	1,675.2	1,687.5	1,684.2	1,658.8
2017	1,652.3	1,654.9	1,663.0	1,671.2	1,689.2	1,700.7	1,672.3	1,676.4	1,684.3	1,690.4	1,702.6	1,699.6	1,679.7
2018	1,669.1	1,673.1	1,682.9	1,688.4	1,707.4	1,719.8	1,690.4	1,697.9	1,697.5	1,709.8	1,713.0	1,710.2	1,696.6
Mining, Logging, and Construction													
2010	43.9	42.6	44.3	47.9	51.6	53.7	56.2	56.8	56.2	56.6	55.3	52.3	51.5
2011	47.4	46.2	47.3	50.3	54.7	58.6	60.4	60.6	59.7	59.0	57.8	55.2	54.8
2012	51.0	49.1	50.3	52.9	56.4	59.1	59.9	60.0	60.0	59.7	58.4	55.8	56.1
2013	52.2	50.7	51.8	53.3	59.6	61.1	62.7	62.6	61.6	61.9	60.7	57.9	58.0
2014	53.1	52.6	52.9	55.3	62.2	65.5	66.3	67.9	68.0	67.7	66.1	63.4	61.8
2015	58.0	56.9	58.3	62.1	67.3	70.2	70.3	70.5	69.6	70.2	68.8	65.9	65.7
2016	61.1	60.0	61.3	65.7	70.4	71.8	72.9	73.0	72.8	72.9	71.7	66.8	68.4
2017	64.0	63.2	64.4	68.5	74.2	76.7	77.5	77.9	77.1	76.7	75.0	70.4	72.1
2018	66.3	66.0	67.5	70.5	76.6	79.3	79.6	79.9	77.8	78.1	76.5	74.7	74.4
Manufacturing													
2010	173.4	172.6	170.9	174.8	177.2	180.5	176.7	174.9	184.7	185.4	185.4	185.5	178.5
2011	185.0	187.7	188.9	194.3	196.6	198.6	193.7	200.0	202.3	203.8	205.9	206.9	197.0
2012	205.9	206.9	208.8	207.1	211.0	212.3	211.3	214.1	214.2	215.4	216.0	216.7	211.6
2013	215.4	217.2	218.0	218.7	220.9	223.3	214.3	223.5	225.3	226.6	227.2	222.9	221.1
2014	221.8	227.9	229.1	223.3	227.9	236.2	231.6	235.0	231.1	234.0	237.9	240.4	231.4
2015	236.8	237.4	237.1	237.9	241.6	244.1	240.3	244.1	244.8	242.2	244.9	244.3	241.3
2016	244.9	242.6	241.7	247.7	248.3	251.2	244.7	245.8	248.7	248.4	253.5	251.8	247.4
2017	252.1	253.3	251.4	253.1	254.8	257.1	245.6	255.5	252.3	254.2	257.1	256.8	253.6
2018	254.3	258.5	260.0	260.0	259.5	262.1	257.0	262.1	262.9	263.0	263.2	262.7	260.4

Employment by Industry: Detroit-Warren-Dearborn, MI, 2010–2018—*Continued*

(Numbers in thousands, not seasonally adjusted)

Industry and year	January	February	March	April	May	June	July	August	September	October	November	December	Annual average
Trade, Transportation, and Utilities													
2010	320.3	317.3	318.7	321.8	325.8	327.8	325.9	327.5	325.9	332.1	337.9	341.4	326.9
2011	328.0	325.0	326.0	329.0	332.7	334.4	333.4	334.7	334.4	337.7	345.5	348.6	334.1
2012	337.6	334.3	335.8	334.7	339.5	341.3	338.9	340.2	339.1	343.2	352.9	354.3	341.0
2013	340.8	338.3	339.0	339.1	344.4	347.5	345.6	347.5	345.9	349.1	356.9	361.4	346.3
2014	348.0	346.3	346.9	349.1	353.8	355.8	353.6	354.6	352.7	357.1	365.3	369.8	354.4
2015	355.2	352.4	352.8	354.4	359.3	361.1	358.6	359.6	357.2	360.6	369.4	373.4	359.5
2016	360.1	357.5	357.7	359.6	363.8	365.2	364.3	365.4	363.8	366.8	375.3	378.3	364.8
2017	366.1	362.7	363.4	364.6	367.7	370.1	367.7	368.9	367.5	371.9	381.1	383.7	369.6
2018	370.1	366.9	367.5	368.4	373.4	375.8	374.4	376.4	374.4	378.4	386.3	388.8	375.1
Wholesale Trade													
2010	76.0	76.3	76.5	77.1	77.8	78.3	78.2	78.8	78.5	79.3	79.5	79.9	78.0
2011	78.9	78.9	79.3	80.3	80.6	80.8	81.1	81.3	80.9	81.1	81.6	81.6	80.5
2012	81.4	81.7	81.9	81.9	82.8	83.2	83.1	83.3	82.9	83.4	83.4	83.6	82.7
2013	83.1	83.2	83.5	83.3	83.9	84.4	84.0	84.0	83.6	83.3	83.3	83.7	83.6
2014	83.1	83.2	83.2	83.2	84.3	84.7	84.1	84.3	83.8	83.7	84.0	84.4	83.8
2015	83.3	83.6	83.6	83.9	84.6	84.9	84.7	84.8	84.0	84.0	84.1	84.3	84.2
2016	83.3	83.7	83.4	84.1	84.8	85.2	84.9	85.2	84.7	84.9	85.2	85.5	84.6
2017	85.0	85.3	85.5	85.3	85.9	86.4	85.8	86.0	85.5	85.5	85.4	85.9	85.6
2018	85.9	86.1	86.2	86.4	87.0	87.6	87.3	87.2	86.7	86.5	87.1	87.5	86.8
Retail Trade													
2010	190.6	187.5	188.2	191.0	193.9	194.8	193.7	194.2	192.3	196.7	201.8	204.1	194.1
2011	192.9	190.1	190.6	192.6	194.9	195.5	195.1	195.8	195.3	198.4	205.2	207.5	196.2
2012	197.2	193.5	194.6	194.1	197.2	198.0	196.7	197.3	196.0	199.0	208.3	208.8	198.4
2013	197.3	194.4	194.9	195.4	199.2	201.3	200.9	201.9	200.4	203.0	210.0	212.7	201.0
2014	201.0	199.1	199.7	201.7	204.8	206.2	204.9	205.5	204.0	208.3	215.7	217.6	205.7
2015	205.0	203.0	203.8	204.3	207.8	208.9	207.2	208.3	206.3	209.3	216.5	218.5	208.2
2016	208.0	205.9	206.5	207.7	210.8	211.6	211.1	211.9	209.7	212.3	219.0	220.9	211.3
2017	211.2	208.5	208.9	210.0	211.9	213.1	212.0	212.3	210.6	213.5	220.5	220.6	212.8
2018	210.9	207.8	208.0	208.2	211.8	212.5	212.3	212.7	209.5	212.5	218.4	219.4	212.0
Transportation and Utilities													
2010	53.7	53.5	54.0	53.7	54.1	54.7	54.0	54.5	55.1	56.1	56.6	57.4	54.8
2011	56.2	56.0	56.1	56.1	57.2	58.1	57.2	57.6	58.2	58.2	58.7	59.5	57.4
2012	59.0	59.1	59.3	58.7	59.5	60.1	59.1	59.6	60.2	60.8	61.2	61.9	59.9
2013	60.4	60.7	60.6	60.4	61.3	61.8	60.7	61.6	61.9	62.8	63.6	65.0	61.7
2014	63.9	64.0	64.0	64.2	64.7	64.9	64.6	64.8	64.9	65.1	65.6	67.8	64.9
2015	66.9	65.8	65.4	66.2	66.9	67.3	66.7	66.5	66.9	67.3	68.8	70.6	67.1
2016	68.8	67.9	67.8	67.8	68.2	68.4	68.3	68.3	69.4	69.6	71.1	71.9	69.0
2017	69.9	68.9	69.0	69.3	69.9	70.6	69.9	70.6	71.4	72.9	75.2	77.2	71.2
2018	73.3	73.0	73.3	73.8	74.6	75.7	74.8	76.5	78.2	79.4	80.8	81.9	76.3
Information													
2010	26.9	26.8	26.7	26.8	27.0	27.2	26.8	28.6	28.4	26.4	26.3	26.5	27.0
2011	26.4	26.1	26.1	25.8	26.0	26.0	26.1	26.2	26.0	26.7	26.7	26.6	26.2
2012	26.8	26.6	26.7	26.3	26.5	26.3	26.6	27.0	26.2	26.4	26.6	26.6	26.6
2013	26.7	26.7	26.8	27.4	27.6	27.9	27.6	27.6	27.1	27.0	27.2	27.2	27.2
2014	27.5	27.2	27.4	27.8	27.8	28.3	28.8	28.6	27.6	28.2	28.2	27.9	27.9
2015	27.2	27.0	27.0	26.8	27.3	27.7	28.3	27.7	27.6	27.3	27.5	27.1	27.4
2016	27.5	27.4	27.6	27.9	28.2	28.6	29.1	28.6	28.4	27.7	28.2	27.9	28.1
2017	27.2	27.2	27.6	27.3	27.5	27.7	27.8	27.6	27.6	27.4	27.6	27.9	27.5
2018	27.1	26.7	26.7	26.5	26.8	27.0	27.5	27.6	27.2	27.0	27.2	27.2	27.0

Employment by Industry: Detroit-Warren-Dearborn, MI, 2010–2018—*Continued*

(Numbers in thousands, not seasonally adjusted)

Industry and year	January	February	March	April	May	June	July	August	September	October	November	December	Annual average
Financial Activities													
2010	95.1	94.9	94.2	93.8	95.0	96.1	96.4	96.8	95.7	96.0	96.3	96.9	95.6
2011	96.5	96.7	97.3	97.9	98.1	98.8	99.2	99.5	98.0	97.6	97.6	97.8	97.9
2012	97.3	97.6	98.1	98.1	98.9	100.3	101.4	101.9	100.1	100.4	100.8	101.7	99.7
2013	101.6	102.0	102.5	102.7	103.6	105.6	106.3	106.5	104.2	104.1	104.1	104.3	104.0
2014	103.4	103.4	103.3	103.1	104.6	106.1	106.0	106.3	104.5	104.5	104.6	105.1	104.6
2015	104.5	104.6	104.8	105.7	107.1	109.0	109.1	109.4	108.1	108.4	108.7	109.0	107.4
2016	109.1	109.3	109.4	110.3	111.6	113.6	114.1	114.1	113.0	113.1	113.3	113.8	112.1
2017	114.2	114.1	114.2	114.9	115.6	117.4	117.5	117.2	115.5	114.6	115.0	114.9	115.4
2018	114.8	114.8	114.8	115.0	116.1	117.7	117.8	117.6	116.0	115.0	115.7	116.1	116.0
Professional and Business Services													
2010	301.9	304.6	304.0	310.7	313.7	316.0	310.6	315.2	320.4	325.6	326.7	324.1	314.5
2011	323.1	325.4	329.3	335.3	338.8	336.9	330.3	337.3	343.1	349.5	349.8	344.4	336.9
2012	342.8	346.4	349.4	353.9	358.9	356.6	352.0	357.5	358.7	364.0	363.4	361.8	355.5
2013	357.6	360.8	364.5	365.5	373.0	372.7	358.4	368.2	371.4	376.3	375.6	373.4	368.1
2014	364.2	367.6	369.1	367.7	375.3	376.4	369.7	372.9	374.1	377.3	377.2	376.5	372.3
2015	375.5	377.1	377.8	382.4	388.0	387.7	379.9	382.6	385.2	388.9	387.5	384.9	383.1
2016	379.9	380.5	380.0	386.4	390.6	392.4	388.8	390.0	391.9	395.5	396.5	392.5	388.8
2017	386.5	387.1	389.3	392.6	397.9	400.2	392.5	395.4	395.2	396.2	397.6	393.2	393.6
2018	391.1	393.3	395.6	397.7	402.6	405.9	397.5	401.8	400.1	404.3	401.4	398.2	399.1
Education and Health Services													
2010	281.3	283.9	284.7	283.9	284.8	283.7	282.2	282.2	283.5	288.4	289.4	289.3	284.8
2011	285.8	287.8	288.8	291.4	291.9	290.3	289.5	289.9	291.8	294.7	295.7	296.4	291.2
2012	292.2	295.5	296.7	295.3	296.1	295.5	293.8	294.4	294.6	297.9	298.8	299.9	295.9
2013	295.4	298.2	298.8	298.3	298.8	297.9	295.2	296.0	297.7	300.3	301.2	301.2	298.3
2014	296.2	299.8	300.7	299.2	300.0	299.0	296.7	297.2	298.3	301.8	303.3	304.2	299.7
2015	299.2	301.4	302.6	301.3	303.0	302.8	301.6	304.2	302.5	309.2	309.4	310.3	304.0
2016	306.0	308.5	309.0	309.8	311.0	309.8	309.7	309.2	310.6	312.8	314.0	314.4	310.4
2017	309.7	312.1	312.6	312.4	314.1	314.0	312.2	312.6	313.7	316.0	317.3	317.5	313.7
2018	314.7	316.8	317.8	317.8	318.1	317.9	316.5	316.6	316.0	320.1	320.7	320.6	317.8
Leisure and Hospitality													
2010	162.8	163.0	164.9	171.8	177.1	179.9	176.6	178.8	176.0	173.2	171.1	171.0	172.2
2011	165.5	166.9	169.7	173.4	178.6	181.5	179.2	180.0	177.9	175.7	172.0	171.5	174.3
2012	168.6	168.7	172.5	175.3	180.2	184.3	181.7	183.1	179.1	177.1	174.6	175.6	176.7
2013	171.1	171.7	174.2	177.8	184.8	186.1	184.2	185.3	180.7	181.5	178.3	178.3	179.5
2014	172.9	173.0	176.5	181.5	188.9	192.7	190.8	191.7	187.1	185.2	183.1	183.5	183.9
2015	179.7	178.6	181.7	185.2	193.5	196.2	195.6	195.6	191.4	190.2	187.9	188.0	188.6
2016	185.0	185.5	188.2	192.4	198.0	201.7	201.3	202.0	197.1	195.4	193.6	193.3	194.5
2017	189.9	190.3	192.9	196.9	202.9	207.0	205.6	207.1	202.2	199.1	197.8	197.8	199.1
2018	192.1	191.7	194.8	198.0	204.6	209.4	207.4	208.6	202.0	199.2	194.8	194.0	199.7
Other Services													
2010	78.9	78.8	78.8	78.2	78.7	79.0	77.8	77.2	76.3	75.7	75.2	75.1	77.5
2011	73.9	73.7	73.9	74.0	74.6	75.3	74.8	75.0	74.6	74.7	74.3	74.7	74.5
2012	73.9	74.1	75.0	75.8	76.4	77.6	77.1	77.8	77.3	76.9	76.5	76.4	76.2
2013	76.0	76.5	77.2	76.8	77.4	78.0	77.5	77.8	77.2	77.1	77.1	77.1	77.1
2014	76.4	76.5	76.7	76.7	77.3	77.8	78.0	77.9	77.3	77.4	76.9	76.8	77.1
2015	75.0	75.1	75.2	75.0	75.9	76.8	77.1	77.3	76.7	76.7	76.4	76.7	76.2
2016	75.3	75.3	75.6	75.4	76.2	76.7	76.4	76.6	76.5	76.1	76.2	75.9	76.0
2017	74.6	74.7	75.0	74.2	75.2	76.1	75.5	75.6	75.4	75.3	75.5	75.3	75.2
2018	74.1	74.4	74.8	75.2	76.1	76.8	75.5	76.3	75.5	75.4	75.1	75.3	75.4
Government													
2010	209.6	213.7	214.3	215.9	218.9	213.7	194.0	189.1	202.9	207.3	206.7	205.1	207.6
2011	199.2	203.5	203.6	203.6	201.0	199.6	183.3	182.2	197.5	200.6	201.6	199.4	197.9
2012	194.4	198.2	198.5	198.0	196.2	195.8	178.7	178.5	193.2	194.5	195.6	193.8	193.0
2013	188.6	192.1	192.0	191.5	189.2	189.0	172.8	171.3	186.4	189.4	189.7	187.9	186.7
2014	183.7	187.8	188.3	189.0	186.8	186.4	170.9	169.6	183.2	188.0	189.6	186.6	184.2
2015	182.0	185.8	186.7	187.5	186.8	185.3	169.5	167.9	182.6	186.7	187.9	186.4	182.9
2016	182.2	186.0	188.2	187.7	185.2	185.5	172.2	171.5	185.6	187.8	190.4	188.1	184.2
2017	184.1	186.7	188.0	188.3	188.3	188.2	173.5	172.0	187.2	189.9	190.7	189.3	185.5
2018	185.1	188.5	190.9	189.8	189.7	189.3	173.8	173.0	186.3	190.4	191.8	190.0	186.6

Employment by Industry: Seattle-Tacoma-Bellevue, WA, 2010–2018

(Numbers in thousands, not seasonally adjusted)

Industry and year	January	February	March	April	May	June	July	August	September	October	November	December	Annual average
Total Nonfarm													
2010	1,637.2	1,639.4	1,646.6	1,658.8	1,671.7	1,678.7	1,675.5	1,664.6	1,675.6	1,684.1	1,688.4	1,688.1	1,667.4
2011	1,656.8	1,664.7	1,669.5	1,684.4	1,693.4	1,704.0	1,705.6	1,698.6	1,706.9	1,712.0	1,719.7	1,719.1	1,694.6
2012	1,689.0	1,697.5	1,708.0	1,718.1	1,734.3	1,746.8	1,743.0	1,739.5	1,747.3	1,756.3	1,766.3	1,764.1	1,734.2
2013	1,738.2	1,747.9	1,754.2	1,764.7	1,780.6	1,790.5	1,790.4	1,790.3	1,797.1	1,803.2	1,813.7	1,814.6	1,782.1
2014	1,792.6	1,795.8	1,803.6	1,810.0	1,824.6	1,836.4	1,844.6	1,845.8	1,850.9	1,853.4	1,862.2	1,867.8	1,832.3
2015	1,842.6	1,847.8	1,859.1	1,868.5	1,882.5	1,901.3	1,902.8	1,901.7	1,910.2	1,910.7	1,919.2	1,923.1	1,889.1
2016	1,898.3	1,910.6	1,919.1	1,935.2	1,950.1	1,963.4	1,964.5	1,963.1	1,971.9	1,968.5	1,978.9	1,983.6	1,950.6
2017	1,954.5	1,962.2	1,974.9	1,982.8	1,999.1	2,015.8	2,011.8	2,008.0	2,011.1	2,012.1	2,022.0	2,027.6	1,998.5
2018	2,006.8	2,011.3	2,021.9	2,029.7	2,045.4	2,059.0	2,058.2	2,059.4	2,056.5	2,067.2	2,073.7	2,076.7	2,047.2
Total Private													
2010	1,372.5	1,373.2	1,380.3	1,390.4	1,397.5	1,408.1	1,415.2	1,416.2	1,417.8	1,419.4	1,421.3	1,426.4	1,403.2
2011	1,393.9	1,400.3	1,405.2	1,419.9	1,427.7	1,441.1	1,449.5	1,453.7	1,456.5	1,450.2	1,456.7	1,460.2	1,434.6
2012	1,428.6	1,436.0	1,444.9	1,454.5	1,470.1	1,485.1	1,487.2	1,495.1	1,494.6	1,493.5	1,501.5	1,504.0	1,474.6
2013	1,476.5	1,484.2	1,490.3	1,500.2	1,515.4	1,527.4	1,535.0	1,543.9	1,542.3	1,539.1	1,547.9	1,552.3	1,521.2
2014	1,528.4	1,530.6	1,537.2	1,542.4	1,556.2	1,569.7	1,584.0	1,594.1	1,590.6	1,585.0	1,592.4	1,601.1	1,567.6
2015	1,573.9	1,577.5	1,587.2	1,595.1	1,609.0	1,627.8	1,637.4	1,643.7	1,642.6	1,637.0	1,643.3	1,651.1	1,618.8
2016	1,626.3	1,634.7	1,643.0	1,657.1	1,670.2	1,686.0	1,693.8	1,700.6	1,700.2	1,689.1	1,697.0	1,704.4	1,675.2
2017	1,675.6	1,681.3	1,692.3	1,699.4	1,714.2	1,732.8	1,734.8	1,740.6	1,738.2	1,728.5	1,738.0	1,747.4	1,718.6
2018	1,725.7	1,730.1	1,740.6	1,746.5	1,761.9	1,780.4	1,785.1	1,796.2	1,786.4	1,787.6	1,795.4	1,802.5	1,769.9
Goods Producing													
2010	247.9	246.8	246.6	247.5	248.5	251.0	254.8	255.7	255.5	254.4	251.5	249.5	250.8
2011	245.1	246.2	247.2	249.6	251.8	255.9	260.5	262.3	263.8	262.4	260.7	260.2	255.5
2012	255.9	257.1	258.9	260.8	264.1	269.2	272.3	275.5	275.9	275.2	274.2	272.8	267.7
2013	270.3	271.9	273.2	273.9	276.4	280.1	283.0	285.8	285.1	282.9	281.3	280.2	278.7
2014	277.0	277.5	278.9	279.2	282.0	285.4	290.1	292.1	291.7	291.1	290.3	290.6	285.5
2015	288.5	289.2	291.4	291.6	293.7	297.6	301.5	301.7	301.3	299.1	297.3	297.5	295.9
2016	295.1	297.0	297.7	299.8	301.6	303.6	306.3	305.9	305.4	301.8	300.5	299.6	301.2
2017	295.9	296.4	297.8	298.8	299.6	303.1	302.8	302.8	302.7	300.0	299.6	299.9	300.0
2018	297.1	298.7	301.2	302.2	305.1	308.3	310.2	312.2	312.0	312.6	313.8	314.3	307.3
Service-Providing													
2010	1389.3	1392.6	1400.0	1411.3	1423.2	1427.7	1420.7	1408.9	1420.1	1429.7	1436.9	1438.6	1416.6
2011	1411.7	1418.5	1422.3	1434.8	1441.6	1448.1	1445.1	1436.3	1443.1	1449.6	1459.0	1458.9	1439.1
2012	1433.1	1440.4	1449.1	1457.3	1470.2	1477.6	1470.7	1464.0	1471.4	1481.1	1492.1	1491.3	1466.5
2013	1467.9	1476.0	1481.0	1490.8	1504.2	1510.4	1507.4	1504.5	1512.0	1520.3	1532.4	1534.4	1503.4
2014	1515.6	1518.3	1524.7	1530.8	1542.6	1551.0	1554.5	1553.7	1559.2	1562.3	1571.9	1577.2	1546.8
2015	1554.1	1558.6	1567.7	1576.9	1588.8	1603.7	1601.3	1600.0	1608.9	1611.6	1621.9	1625.6	1593.3
2016	1603.2	1613.6	1621.4	1635.4	1648.5	1659.8	1658.2	1657.2	1666.5	1666.7	1678.4	1684.0	1649.4
2017	1658.6	1665.8	1677.1	1684.0	1699.5	1712.7	1709.0	1705.2	1708.4	1712.1	1722.4	1727.7	1698.5
2018	1709.7	1712.6	1720.7	1727.5	1740.3	1750.7	1748.0	1747.2	1744.5	1754.6	1759.9	1762.4	1739.8
Mining and Logging													
2010	1.0	1.1	1.0	1.0	1.1	1.1	1.1	1.1	1.1	1.1	1.0	1.0	1.1
2011	1.0	1.0	1.0	1.0	1.0	1.0	1.0	1.0	1.0	1.1	1.1	1.1	1.0
2012	1.0	1.0	1.0	1.0	1.0	1.0	1.0	1.1	1.0	1.1	1.0	1.0	1.0
2013	1.0	1.0	1.0	1.0	1.0	1.1	1.0	1.1	1.1	1.0	1.0	1.0	1.0
2014	1.0	1.0	1.0	1.0	1.0	1.0	1.0	1.0	1.0	1.1	1.1	1.1	1.0
2015	1.1	1.1	1.0	1.1	1.1	1.1	1.1	1.1	1.1	1.2	1.1	1.1	1.1
2016	1.0	1.0	1.0	1.1	1.1	1.1	1.1	1.1	1.1	1.1	1.1	1.1	1.1
2017	1.1	1.1	1.0	1.1	1.1	1.1	1.1	1.1	1.1	1.1	1.1	1.1	1.1
2018	1.1	1.1	1.1	1.1	1.1	1.1	1.1	1.1	1.1	1.1	1.1	1.1	1.1
Construction													
2010	80.4	79.6	79.9	80.6	81.9	82.9	85.6	86.6	85.9	85.1	81.8	79.7	82.5
2011	75.5	75.3	75.5	76.6	78.2	80.1	82.2	83.2	83.4	82.2	79.9	79.0	79.3
2012	75.0	76.1	76.8	78.4	80.6	83.2	85.1	87.2	87.4	87.3	85.9	85.1	82.3
2013	82.5	83.9	84.6	85.7	88.0	89.9	92.6	95.0	94.6	93.7	92.6	91.1	89.5
2014	89.4	89.6	91.2	91.4	93.8	96.1	99.1	101.3	101.7	102.0	101.5	101.6	96.6
2015	99.8	100.5	102.0	103.4	105.1	107.3	109.5	109.9	109.5	109.4	108.0	108.1	106.0
2016	106.5	108.5	109.4	111.4	113.0	115.0	117.0	118.3	118.3	117.2	116.8	116.4	114.0
2017	113.8	114.9	116.5	117.1	119.0	121.8	122.2	123.2	123.7	122.6	121.7	121.8	119.9
2018	120.0	121.3	123.0	124.0	126.1	128.0	129.1	131.1	130.0	131.5	130.5	129.9	127.0

Employment by Industry: Seattle-Tacoma-Bellevue, WA, 2010–2018—*Continued*

(Numbers in thousands, not seasonally adjusted)

Industry and year	January	February	March	April	May	June	July	August	September	October	November	December	Annual average
Manufacturing													
2010	166.5	166.1	165.7	165.9	165.5	167.0	168.1	168.0	168.5	168.2	168.7	168.8	167.3
2011	168.6	169.9	170.7	172.0	172.6	174.8	177.3	178.1	179.4	179.1	179.7	180.1	175.2
2012	179.9	180.0	181.1	181.4	182.5	185.0	186.2	187.2	187.5	186.8	187.3	186.7	184.3
2013	186.8	187.0	187.6	187.2	187.4	189.1	189.4	189.7	189.4	188.2	187.7	188.1	188.1
2014	186.6	186.9	186.7	186.8	187.2	188.3	190.0	189.8	189.0	188.0	187.7	187.9	187.9
2015	187.6	187.6	188.4	187.1	187.5	189.2	190.9	190.7	190.7	188.5	188.2	188.3	188.7
2016	187.6	187.5	187.3	187.3	187.5	187.5	188.2	186.5	186.0	183.5	182.6	182.1	186.1
2017	181.0	180.4	180.3	180.6	179.5	180.2	179.5	178.5	177.9	176.3	176.8	177.0	179.0
2018	176.0	176.3	177.1	177.1	177.9	179.2	180.0	180.0	180.9	180.0	182.2	183.3	179.2
Trade, Transportation, and Utilities													
2010	297.1	295.0	295.4	297.0	298.8	301.3	302.4	303.1	302.0	304.2	308.8	314.1	301.6
2011	301.7	300.6	301.4	302.8	305.2	308.1	310.5	311.6	310.3	310.3	316.2	319.6	308.2
2012	308.6	306.6	307.8	308.8	312.8	316.9	319.5	320.3	319.0	320.0	326.8	329.2	316.4
2013	319.3	317.4	317.9	319.0	323.5	326.7	329.7	331.6	330.4	332.0	339.6	343.1	327.5
2014	333.6	331.4	331.4	332.2	336.3	340.4	344.0	346.3	345.4	345.9	352.8	357.3	341.4
2015	346.9	344.9	346.3	346.7	350.4	354.9	356.4	358.4	357.7	357.3	364.0	368.4	354.4
2016	356.1	354.6	356.5	359.4	363.4	368.7	371.9	373.6	371.9	372.6	380.2	384.6	367.8
2017	374.6	372.2	374.1	375.0	380.1	384.9	388.1	390.0	388.5	387.5	395.1	398.8	384.1
2018	389.6	385.6	385.9	385.5	388.5	392.6	394.2	395.7	393.3	393.3	399.4	402.4	392.2
Wholesale Trade													
2010	76.1	76.2	76.4	76.8	76.9	76.9	77.0	77.0	76.7	76.9	76.9	76.9	76.7
2011	76.4	76.7	76.9	77.3	77.6	77.8	78.0	78.0	77.8	77.5	77.5	77.7	77.4
2012	77.1	77.3	77.5	78.0	78.3	78.7	79.2	79.7	79.2	79.0	79.1	79.4	78.5
2013	78.9	79.5	79.8	79.7	79.9	80.6	81.0	81.2	81.1	80.6	81.0	81.1	80.4
2014	80.8	81.0	80.9	80.6	81.1	81.6	82.5	82.6	82.7	82.1	82.3	82.7	81.7
2015	81.9	82.1	82.5	82.3	82.8	83.4	83.5	83.8	83.6	83.1	83.3	83.7	83.0
2016	82.4	82.5	82.8	83.0	83.3	83.7	84.0	84.2	84.0	83.6	84.0	84.3	83.5
2017	83.8	84.1	84.4	84.4	84.9	85.5	85.5	85.6	85.6	85.4	85.7	86.1	85.1
2018	85.4	85.8	86.2	86.4	86.6	87.1	87.3	87.6	87.2	86.7	86.4	86.2	86.6
Retail Trade													
2010	165.0	163.0	163.1	164.2	165.5	167.2	167.6	168.3	167.5	169.6	174.3	177.9	167.8
2011	168.3	166.7	166.5	167.1	169.0	171.1	172.3	173.4	172.1	173.3	178.8	181.1	171.6
2012	172.6	170.2	170.9	171.2	173.9	176.7	178.7	178.9	178.4	180.2	186.5	188.0	177.2
2013	180.3	178.2	178.3	179.3	182.7	184.9	187.2	188.6	187.4	189.7	196.1	198.8	186.0
2014	190.2	188.1	188.2	188.4	191.0	193.9	195.9	197.4	196.3	197.5	203.8	206.4	194.8
2015	198.7	196.8	197.8	198.5	200.9	203.8	204.6	206.2	205.7	205.2	210.8	212.8	203.5
2016	204.3	203.2	204.3	205.2	207.8	211.3	213.5	214.4	212.6	214.0	219.4	221.7	211.0
2017	215.3	213.4	214.8	216.2	219.9	223.3	226.4	227.2	225.5	224.6	230.3	231.8	222.4
2018	226.4	223.2	223.0	222.5	225.0	227.4	229.1	230.1	228.5	227.7	233.0	233.8	227.5
Transportation and Utilities													
2010	56.0	55.8	55.9	56.0	56.4	57.2	57.8	57.8	57.8	57.7	57.6	59.3	57.1
2011	57.0	57.2	58.0	58.4	58.6	59.2	60.2	60.2	60.4	59.5	59.9	60.8	59.1
2012	58.9	59.1	59.4	59.6	60.6	61.5	61.6	61.7	61.4	60.8	61.2	61.8	60.6
2013	60.1	59.7	59.8	60.0	60.9	61.2	61.5	61.8	61.9	61.7	62.5	63.2	61.2
2014	62.6	62.3	62.3	63.2	64.2	64.9	65.6	66.3	66.4	66.3	66.7	68.2	64.9
2015	66.3	66.0	66.0	65.9	66.7	67.7	68.3	68.4	68.4	69.0	69.9	71.9	67.9
2016	69.4	68.9	69.4	71.2	72.3	73.7	74.4	75.0	75.3	75.0	76.8	78.6	73.3
2017	75.5	74.7	74.9	74.4	75.3	76.1	76.2	77.2	77.4	77.5	79.1	80.9	76.6
2018	77.8	76.6	76.7	76.6	76.9	78.1	77.8	78.0	77.6	78.9	80.0	82.4	78.1
Information													
2010	86.7	86.9	86.8	86.5	87.1	88.1	88.3	88.8	88.7	87.9	88.3	88.7	87.7
2011	87.3	88.0	87.7	87.8	88.0	89.2	90.0	90.4	89.6	88.9	89.2	88.9	88.8
2012	88.8	89.3	88.9	88.8	89.6	90.6	90.7	90.9	89.6	89.1	89.6	89.4	89.6
2013	88.9	89.7	89.2	89.6	90.2	91.0	92.4	93.0	92.1	91.5	92.3	92.3	91.0
2014	92.0	92.2	92.4	92.8	93.3	94.9	96.6	97.6	96.8	95.0	95.4	95.1	94.5
2015	93.6	94.5	94.7	94.6	95.5	97.2	99.4	100.4	99.6	99.4	100.2	100.3	97.5
2016	99.9	100.9	101.4	101.9	102.8	105.5	107.2	108.2	107.6	107.1	107.9	108.1	104.9
2017	107.8	108.3	108.8	108.8	109.5	111.8	113.0	114.0	113.3	112.6	112.8	113.2	111.2
2018	112.3	113.3	113.9	114.9	115.9	119.6	121.3	122.4	121.6	122.0	120.9	121.5	118.3

Employment by Industry: Seattle-Tacoma-Bellevue, WA, 2010–2018—*Continued*

(Numbers in thousands, not seasonally adjusted)

Industry and year	January	February	March	April	May	June	July	August	September	October	November	December	Annual average
Financial Activities													
2010	91.9	91.7	91.7	92.4	92.2	92.3	92.9	92.3	92.0	91.9	91.6	91.9	92.1
2011	90.7	90.9	90.7	91.1	90.7	91.0	91.1	90.9	90.6	90.2	90.4	90.2	90.7
2012	89.1	89.3	89.5	89.7	90.3	90.8	91.5	91.3	90.9	91.0	91.3	91.5	90.5
2013	91.3	91.7	92.2	92.7	93.3	93.5	94.3	94.4	93.8	93.7	93.8	94.2	93.2
2014	93.2	93.3	93.6	93.8	94.1	94.6	95.4	95.7	95.1	95.0	95.1	95.4	94.5
2015	94.7	94.9	94.9	95.3	95.7	96.2	97.0	97.0	96.5	96.0	96.2	96.3	95.9
2016	95.8	96.1	96.2	96.5	97.0	97.3	98.6	98.8	98.2	97.5	97.7	98.0	97.3
2017	96.9	97.5	97.9	97.9	98.9	99.7	100.0	100.4	100.0	99.2	99.7	100.0	99.0
2018	99.9	100.2	100.8	100.8	101.8	102.2	102.2	102.4	101.6	101.3	101.7	101.2	101.3
Professional and Business Services													
2010	212.2	213.3	216.1	218.7	219.3	220.9	223.9	223.1	224.0	225.2	225.2	225.9	220.7
2011	220.4	222.6	224.0	228.1	228.0	229.5	232.6	233.2	234.0	234.4	234.8	234.7	229.7
2012	229.0	231.4	232.7	236.6	238.7	240.9	239.9	242.7	242.8	243.3	245.0	244.8	239.1
2013	240.5	242.6	243.0	245.3	247.2	249.3	249.6	252.1	252.4	253.0	253.8	253.5	248.5
2014	249.0	249.6	251.3	252.1	253.1	255.1	258.7	261.3	261.0	262.1	262.9	264.2	256.7
2015	258.7	259.4	261.8	264.3	265.9	268.8	271.2	273.5	274.1	273.9	274.9	276.5	268.6
2016	270.9	272.4	274.6	276.8	277.8	280.1	281.1	282.9	284.2	282.4	283.2	283.5	279.2
2017	278.7	279.9	282.0	283.9	285.8	288.2	289.0	290.3	289.9	289.3	290.1	290.7	286.5
2018	287.1	288.7	291.3	291.3	292.7	296.2	298.0	301.3	298.9	297.0	297.5	297.8	294.8
Education and Health Services													
2010	228.0	230.0	231.1	231.6	232.4	230.9	227.2	226.8	230.6	235.8	237.3	236.0	231.5
2011	235.0	237.5	238.2	238.6	238.6	237.4	234.2	233.6	236.8	240.0	242.0	240.9	237.7
2012	238.2	240.9	242.5	241.8	242.8	240.9	236.2	235.9	238.8	242.4	244.0	243.8	240.7
2013	239.7	243.5	244.1	244.8	244.7	242.0	239.2	239.1	242.7	246.5	248.1	248.1	243.5
2014	246.2	249.4	249.2	249.0	249.6	247.0	245.3	244.9	247.4	249.5	250.4	251.1	248.3
2015	248.1	250.2	250.6	251.8	251.9	251.0	247.5	247.1	250.4	254.3	255.9	256.2	251.3
2016	255.9	259.2	260.1	261.2	261.5	259.9	256.0	257.4	260.8	263.2	264.5	264.9	260.4
2017	261.9	265.4	266.5	265.6	266.4	265.5	262.2	263.2	266.7	270.6	272.4	272.5	266.6
2018	271.8	275.0	275.8	275.8	276.7	274.8	272.0	273.4	275.9	279.7	281.5	281.7	276.2
Leisure and Hospitality													
2010	147.4	148.0	150.8	154.5	156.4	159.9	161.2	161.8	161.5	156.1	154.5	156.4	155.7
2011	150.7	151.2	152.4	157.5	160.3	164.0	163.9	165.2	165.6	158.7	158.1	160.1	159.0
2012	154.4	156.1	158.7	161.8	165.2	168.4	169.0	170.7	170.2	164.5	163.5	165.6	164.0
2013	161.2	161.6	164.5	168.3	172.8	177.0	178.1	179.5	178.1	171.7	171.1	173.2	171.4
2014	170.1	169.7	172.3	175.2	178.8	182.5	183.3	185.5	183.6	177.1	175.9	177.5	177.6
2015	174.8	175.5	177.8	181.2	185.7	191.0	192.9	194.1	192.5	186.6	184.6	185.4	185.2
2016	182.7	184.1	185.7	189.8	193.1	197.4	199.5	200.3	199.7	192.3	190.6	193.2	192.4
2017	188.7	190.1	193.1	197.1	200.7	205.2	205.5	205.8	204.1	196.6	195.6	199.0	198.5
2018	195.9	196.3	198.9	203.3	207.5	211.4	211.9	213.3	208.7	207.4	205.7	208.1	205.7
Other Services													
2010	61.3	61.5	61.8	62.2	62.8	63.7	64.5	64.6	63.5	63.9	64.1	63.9	63.2
2011	63.0	63.3	63.6	64.4	65.1	66.0	66.7	66.5	65.8	65.3	65.3	65.6	65.1
2012	64.6	65.3	65.9	66.2	66.6	67.4	68.1	67.8	67.4	67.0	67.1	66.9	66.7
2013	65.3	65.8	66.2	66.6	67.3	67.8	68.7	68.4	67.7	67.8	67.9	67.7	67.3
2014	67.3	67.5	68.1	68.1	69.0	69.8	70.6	70.7	69.6	69.3	69.6	69.9	69.1
2015	68.6	68.9	69.7	69.6	70.2	71.1	71.5	71.5	70.5	70.4	70.2	70.5	70.2
2016	69.9	70.4	70.8	71.7	73.0	73.5	73.2	73.5	72.4	72.2	72.4	72.5	72.1
2017	71.1	71.5	72.1	72.3	73.2	74.4	74.2	74.1	73.0	72.7	72.7	73.3	72.9
2018	72.0	72.3	72.8	72.7	73.7	75.3	75.3	75.5	74.4	74.3	74.9	75.5	74.1
Government													
2010	264.7	266.2	266.3	268.4	274.2	270.6	260.3	248.4	257.8	264.7	267.1	261.7	264.2
2011	262.9	264.4	264.3	264.5	265.7	262.9	256.1	244.9	250.4	261.8	263.0	258.9	260.0
2012	260.4	261.5	263.1	263.6	264.2	261.7	255.8	244.4	252.7	262.8	264.8	260.1	259.6
2013	261.7	263.7	263.9	264.5	265.2	263.1	255.4	246.4	254.8	264.1	265.8	262.3	260.9
2014	264.2	265.2	266.4	267.6	268.4	266.7	260.6	251.7	260.3	268.4	269.8	266.7	264.7
2015	268.7	270.3	271.9	273.4	273.5	273.5	265.4	258.0	267.6	273.7	275.9	272.0	270.3
2016	272.0	275.9	276.1	278.1	279.9	277.4	270.7	262.5	271.7	279.4	281.9	279.2	275.4
2017	278.9	280.9	282.6	283.4	284.9	283.0	277.0	267.4	272.9	283.6	284.0	280.2	279.9
2018	281.1	281.2	281.3	283.2	283.5	278.6	273.1	263.2	270.1	279.6	278.3	274.2	277.3

Employment by Industry: Minneapolis-St. Paul-Bloomington, MN-WI, 2010–2018

(Numbers in thousands, not seasonally adjusted)

Industry and year	January	February	March	April	May	June	July	August	September	October	November	December	Annual average
Total Nonfarm													
2010	1,704.4	1,704.2	1,709.4	1,745.0	1,765.6	1,773.4	1,751.9	1,753.0	1,758.8	1,777.9	1,779.8	1,774.3	1,749.8
2011	1,738.8	1,743.0	1,749.2	1,782.1	1,802.2	1,808.1	1,779.5	1,798.2	1,814.8	1,821.1	1,822.5	1,819.8	1,790.0
2012	1,776.6	1,780.9	1,789.8	1,812.1	1,829.8	1,840.3	1,814.0	1,823.0	1,839.2	1,849.9	1,853.4	1,846.1	1,821.3
2013	1,813.0	1,821.2	1,824.4	1,841.8	1,868.4	1,879.4	1,851.3	1,863.9	1,879.9	1,891.9	1,893.1	1,888.0	1,859.7
2014	1,842.8	1,847.7	1,849.6	1,874.6	1,902.3	1,916.3	1,899.3	1,905.4	1,907.4	1,919.5	1,923.2	1,919.7	1,892.3
2015	1,875.8	1,882.3	1,886.8	1,917.1	1,942.0	1,954.2	1,938.7	1,940.9	1,938.7	1,955.0	1,956.3	1,951.6	1,928.3
2016	1,909.6	1,915.7	1,916.6	1,951.2	1,967.3	1,973.4	1,973.4	1,979.0	1,980.0	1,986.3	1,987.6	1,980.0	1,960.0
2017	1,951.2	1,955.1	1,959.8	1,979.4	1,996.9	2,013.7	2,000.3	2,003.0	2,003.4	2,012.5	2,014.4	2,006.6	1,991.4
2018	1,980.4	1,983.5	1,976.4	1,993.1	2,021.4	2,033.6	2,026.8	2,027.4	2,021.0	2,031.1	2,027.4	2,010.9	2,011.1
Total Private													
2010	1,461.9	1,457.0	1,462.1	1,495.1	1,511.9	1,524.3	1,527.1	1,531.2	1,520.0	1,531.1	1,531.3	1,526.9	1,506.7
2011	1,497.0	1,495.4	1,502.8	1,535.5	1,554.4	1,565.8	1,571.2	1,579.7	1,579.3	1,578.5	1,579.6	1,577.4	1,551.4
2012	1,539.4	1,539.2	1,547.8	1,568.1	1,585.4	1,599.2	1,598.1	1,604.8	1,600.0	1,605.2	1,606.7	1,601.0	1,582.9
2013	1,572.9	1,575.5	1,579.7	1,594.3	1,621.0	1,637.0	1,636.5	1,646.5	1,637.6	1,642.9	1,642.3	1,639.7	1,618.8
2014	1,599.5	1,599.0	1,601.7	1,625.3	1,652.7	1,670.3	1,671.7	1,679.3	1,665.4	1,669.7	1,671.9	1,670.8	1,648.1
2015	1,631.5	1,633.6	1,639.8	1,668.3	1,693.2	1,708.3	1,710.4	1,714.6	1,697.0	1,706.1	1,706.7	1,702.9	1,684.4
2016	1,664.9	1,667.7	1,669.2	1,704.2	1,720.7	1,730.3	1,744.6	1,749.7	1,735.4	1,736.3	1,736.9	1,733.1	1,716.1
2017	1,703.0	1,704.0	1,710.1	1,730.5	1,748.7	1,766.5	1,767.8	1,771.4	1,754.8	1,757.5	1,759.0	1,755.4	1,744.1
2018	1,728.4	1,728.2	1,723.9	1,740.1	1,769.4	1,784.2	1,790.5	1,793.3	1,774.1	1,777.6	1,773.1	1,760.7	1,762.0
Goods Producing													
2010	220.9	217.5	217.8	226.7	232.2	237.8	241.4	241.5	239.4	239.3	236.6	231.8	231.9
2011	225.7	224.6	226.2	232.7	239.7	245.7	248.8	250.7	248.4	248.1	244.9	240.1	239.6
2012	231.7	231.0	234.2	240.5	245.8	252.1	254.4	255.6	252.7	252.3	248.8	244.3	245.3
2013	238.1	237.8	239.6	243.7	252.6	258.5	260.7	263.2	261.0	260.5	258.1	252.9	252.2
2014	245.7	245.0	247.0	252.3	261.6	268.7	271.1	272.8	269.3	269.7	266.4	263.4	261.1
2015	255.6	255.7	257.8	266.8	273.2	279.5	282.4	282.8	278.3	278.9	275.1	269.8	271.3
2016	260.9	260.3	262.3	271.1	276.3	281.1	284.8	284.7	281.1	280.2	276.4	269.5	274.1
2017	263.1	263.4	265.9	271.4	277.8	284.1	286.4	286.7	282.3	283.2	279.2	274.0	276.5
2018	267.8	266.8	268.1	271.9	281.7	289.8	292.6	292.9	289.7	289.1	284.6	277.3	281.0
Service-Providing													
2010	1,483.5	1,486.7	1,491.6	1,518.3	1,533.4	1,535.6	1,510.5	1,511.5	1,519.4	1,538.6	1,543.2	1,542.5	1,517.9
2011	1,513.1	1,518.4	1,523.0	1,549.4	1,562.5	1,562.4	1,530.7	1,547.5	1,566.4	1,573.0	1,577.7	1,579.7	1,550.3
2012	1,544.9	1,549.9	1,555.6	1,571.6	1,584.0	1,588.2	1,559.6	1,567.4	1,586.5	1,597.6	1,604.6	1,601.8	1,576.0
2013	1,574.9	1,583.4	1,584.8	1,598.1	1,615.8	1,620.9	1,590.6	1,600.7	1,618.9	1,631.4	1,635.0	1,635.1	1,607.5
2014	1,597.1	1,602.7	1,602.6	1,622.3	1,640.7	1,647.6	1,628.2	1,632.6	1,638.1	1,649.8	1,656.8	1,656.3	1,631.2
2015	1,620.2	1,626.6	1,629.0	1,650.3	1,668.8	1,674.7	1,656.3	1,658.1	1,660.4	1,676.1	1,681.2	1,681.8	1,657.0
2016	1,648.7	1,655.4	1,654.3	1,680.1	1,691.0	1,692.3	1,688.6	1,694.3	1,698.9	1,706.1	1,711.2	1,710.5	1,686.0
2017	1,688.1	1,691.7	1,693.9	1,708.0	1,719.1	1,729.6	1,713.9	1,716.3	1,721.1	1,729.3	1,735.2	1,732.6	1,714.9
2018	1,712.6	1,716.7	1,708.3	1,721.2	1,739.7	1,743.8	1,734.2	1,734.5	1,731.3	1,742.0	1,742.8	1,733.6	1,730.1
Mining, Logging, and Construction													
2010	48.3	45.7	45.8	52.4	56.2	59.5	61.7	61.9	60.8	60.6	58.0	53.0	55.3
2011	48.5	47.8	49.1	53.8	59.1	62.8	64.4	65.7	64.7	64.0	61.2	56.7	58.2
2012	50.4	50.0	52.3	57.7	61.7	65.4	67.1	68.0	66.6	66.0	62.8	58.7	60.6
2013	53.7	53.9	55.3	59.1	66.8	70.4	72.7	74.8	74.0	73.2	70.4	65.1	65.8
2014	59.3	58.7	60.1	64.7	72.4	76.6	78.4	79.4	77.7	77.2	73.6	70.0	70.7
2015	64.1	64.2	65.7	73.5	79.0	82.8	84.9	85.4	82.8	82.5	78.8	73.8	76.5
2016	66.5	66.2	67.7	75.8	80.5	83.4	85.1	85.1	83.8	83.0	80.0	74.0	77.6
2017	69.0	69.3	71.3	76.7	82.7	86.6	87.9	88.2	86.2	86.0	82.3	78.0	80.4
2018	72.0	71.4	72.3	75.2	84.0	88.9	90.6	90.9	89.3	88.3	85.0	77.8	82.1
Manufacturing													
2010	172.6	171.8	172.0	174.3	176.0	178.3	179.7	179.6	178.6	178.7	178.6	178.8	176.6
2011	177.2	176.8	177.1	178.9	180.6	182.9	184.4	185.0	183.7	184.1	183.7	183.4	181.5
2012	181.3	181.0	181.9	182.8	184.1	186.7	187.3	187.6	186.1	186.3	186.0	185.6	184.7
2013	184.4	183.9	184.3	184.6	185.8	188.1	188.0	188.4	187.0	187.3	187.7	187.8	186.4
2014	186.4	186.3	186.9	187.6	189.2	192.1	192.7	193.4	191.6	192.5	192.8	193.4	190.4
2015	191.5	191.5	192.1	193.3	194.2	196.7	197.5	197.4	195.5	196.4	196.3	196.0	194.9
2016	194.4	194.1	194.6	195.3	195.8	197.7	199.7	199.6	197.3	197.2	196.4	195.5	196.5
2017	194.1	194.1	194.6	194.7	195.1	197.5	198.5	198.5	196.1	197.2	196.9	196.0	196.1
2018	195.8	195.4	195.8	196.7	197.7	200.9	202.0	202.0	200.4	200.8	199.6	199.5	198.9

Employment by Industry: Minneapolis-St. Paul-Bloomington, MN-WI, 2010–2018—*Continued*

(Numbers in thousands, not seasonally adjusted)

Industry and year	January	February	March	April	May	June	July	August	September	October	November	December	Annual average
Trade, Transportation, and Utilities													
2010	317.1	313.0	313.9	318.1	321.1	324.0	321.5	320.7	319.6	322.6	328.1	330.7	320.9
2011	319.0	315.8	316.9	323.4	326.3	327.5	327.9	328.1	328.3	329.7	335.5	338.8	326.4
2012	327.5	322.5	324.0	327.7	331.6	333.3	330.6	331.0	329.5	332.6	340.2	340.9	331.0
2013	331.1	327.3	327.5	329.7	334.6	337.9	335.7	338.0	335.9	338.4	344.5	347.9	335.7
2014	335.5	332.0	332.3	336.8	340.8	343.7	342.6	343.6	339.5	342.9	349.2	354.0	341.1
2015	340.5	337.3	338.1	343.0	347.5	351.3	349.1	349.9	346.0	349.5	355.7	358.9	347.2
2016	346.5	344.4	344.6	349.7	353.3	354.5	356.1	356.9	352.6	355.2	360.8	365.6	353.4
2017	355.7	352.5	352.1	355.1	358.4	361.2	360.4	360.4	356.5	359.0	366.2	370.4	359.0
2018	359.2	356.1	355.4	356.6	361.3	362.6	363.1	362.6	358.5	362.4	370.9	372.1	361.7
Wholesale Trade													
2010	87.0	86.7	86.9	87.6	88.1	89.1	89.2	88.9	87.6	88.2	88.1	88.1	88.0
2011	87.8	87.8	88.0	89.5	90.0	90.4	91.4	91.5	90.5	90.4	90.4	90.6	89.9
2012	90.2	90.0	90.5	91.6	92.3	93.3	93.4	92.9	91.8	91.8	91.9	92.0	91.8
2013	91.5	91.5	91.7	92.0	92.7	93.6	93.8	93.6	92.6	92.7	92.8	92.8	92.6
2014	92.3	92.2	92.4	92.9	93.9	94.8	95.0	94.9	93.7	93.9	94.1	94.4	93.7
2015	93.0	93.0	93.2	94.1	94.5	95.5	96.0	95.6	94.1	94.3	94.4	94.4	94.3
2016	93.0	93.1	93.0	94.2	94.7	94.7	95.6	95.4	94.2	93.7	93.7	94.0	94.1
2017	93.7	93.6	93.7	93.5	94.2	95.0	95.5	95.2	93.9	94.2	94.3	94.6	94.3
2018	93.6	93.7	93.9	94.3	95.0	96.0	95.6	95.6	94.3	93.8	94.7	95.4	94.7
Retail Trade													
2010	169.0	165.6	166.0	169.2	171.3	173.3	172.1	172.6	169.8	171.7	176.4	178.3	171.3
2011	169.2	166.0	166.4	170.6	172.8	174.3	174.5	175.3	173.6	174.8	180.5	182.7	173.4
2012	174.0	169.5	170.3	172.6	175.2	176.9	175.6	176.2	174.0	176.6	183.6	183.9	175.7
2013	176.3	172.4	172.6	174.4	177.6	180.7	179.8	181.2	178.3	179.5	185.0	187.7	178.8
2014	178.2	175.2	175.3	178.2	180.8	183.4	183.4	184.0	179.6	182.0	187.7	190.7	181.5
2015	181.4	178.2	178.6	181.4	185.2	188.7	187.5	188.6	184.4	186.4	192.0	193.6	185.5
2016	185.2	183.2	183.5	186.4	188.8	190.5	192.4	192.4	186.6	189.0	193.5	195.5	188.9
2017	188.2	185.4	185.3	188.2	190.1	192.1	192.2	192.4	187.2	189.0	194.8	197.0	190.2
2018	190.1	187.1	186.3	186.8	190.9	192.9	193.6	193.3	188.7	192.2	198.9	198.6	191.6
Transportation and Utilities													
2010	61.1	60.7	61.0	61.3	61.7	61.6	60.2	59.2	62.2	62.7	63.6	64.3	61.6
2011	62.0	62.0	62.5	63.3	63.5	62.8	62.0	61.3	64.2	64.5	64.6	65.5	63.2
2012	63.3	63.0	63.2	63.5	64.1	63.1	61.6	61.9	63.7	64.2	64.7	65.0	63.4
2013	63.3	63.4	63.2	63.3	64.3	63.6	62.1	63.2	65.0	66.2	66.7	67.4	64.3
2014	65.0	64.6	64.6	65.7	66.1	65.5	64.2	64.7	66.2	67.0	67.4	68.9	65.8
2015	66.1	66.1	66.3	67.5	67.8	67.1	65.6	65.7	67.5	68.8	69.3	70.9	67.4
2016	68.3	68.1	68.1	69.1	69.8	69.3	68.1	69.1	71.8	72.5	73.6	76.1	70.3
2017	73.8	73.5	73.1	73.4	74.1	74.1	72.7	72.8	75.4	75.8	77.1	78.8	74.6
2018	75.5	75.3	75.2	75.5	75.4	73.7	73.9	73.7	75.5	76.4	77.3	78.1	75.5
Information													
2010	40.3	40.3	40.3	40.4	40.1	40.2	40.7	40.7	40.3	40.4	40.3	40.2	40.4
2011	40.6	40.2	40.0	40.7	40.6	40.8	41.3	41.6	41.2	41.1	41.0	41.1	40.9
2012	40.0	40.1	40.2	40.6	40.9	40.8	40.9	41.0	40.7	40.9	40.8	40.9	40.7
2013	40.2	40.2	40.2	40.3	40.2	40.3	40.8	40.5	40.0	39.9	40.0	40.2	40.2
2014	39.6	39.6	39.4	39.4	39.4	39.8	40.1	39.9	39.2	39.4	39.3	39.6	39.6
2015	38.7	38.5	38.5	38.4	38.5	38.8	39.0	38.9	38.1	38.0	38.1	37.9	38.5
2016	37.6	37.6	37.6	37.7	37.8	37.8	38.2	38.6	38.7	38.2	38.2	38.2	38.0
2017	38.1	38.0	38.1	38.1	38.0	38.2	38.2	38.6	37.9	37.8	38.1	38.2	38.1
2018	37.9	38.0	37.6	37.6	37.6	37.9	38.1	38.3	37.3	37.2	37.4	37.4	37.7

Employment by Industry: Minneapolis-St. Paul-Bloomington, MN-WI, 2010–2018—*Continued*

(Numbers in thousands, not seasonally adjusted)

Industry and year	January	February	March	April	May	June	July	August	September	October	November	December	Annual average
Financial Activities													
2010	129.4	129.3	129.1	129.7	130.1	131.4	132.0	132.3	131.5	132.4	132.8	133.2	131.1
2011	132.6	132.6	132.7	132.1	132.4	132.9	133.5	133.6	132.7	132.3	132.3	132.4	132.7
2012	133.1	133.4	133.6	134.1	134.8	136.2	136.2	136.2	135.3	136.3	136.5	136.7	135.2
2013	136.4	136.7	136.8	136.9	137.4	138.8	139.2	139.4	137.8	138.1	138.1	138.3	137.8
2014	137.2	137.1	137.0	136.4	136.9	138.5	138.7	138.5	136.9	137.4	137.5	138.0	137.5
2015	138.6	138.8	138.9	139.8	140.9	142.3	143.5	143.6	141.5	142.1	142.3	142.5	141.2
2016	141.4	141.8	141.8	142.9	143.3	144.4	146.2	146.4	145.2	145.8	145.8	146.3	144.3
2017	145.6	145.8	145.9	146.3	146.8	148.7	149.5	149.4	147.7	148.0	147.9	148.5	147.5
2018	147.6	148.0	148.1	149.0	149.3	151.0	152.1	152.0	150.2	150.2	150.0	149.3	149.7
Professional and Business Services													
2010	262.6	263.5	263.2	270.8	273.0	276.1	280.0	281.6	278.5	282.2	283.3	282.8	274.8
2011	276.5	277.1	278.7	286.4	287.6	290.5	295.6	298.0	298.2	299.8	300.0	300.0	290.7
2012	291.0	291.4	292.0	294.2	295.8	298.4	300.2	302.3	300.9	303.6	303.0	302.6	298.0
2013	295.5	298.2	298.1	299.8	301.7	305.5	306.7	308.5	306.8	311.0	309.6	309.3	304.2
2014	300.5	301.2	300.7	304.4	307.9	311.2	313.9	315.2	313.0	316.1	318.4	314.8	309.8
2015	307.1	308.0	307.5	314.7	317.4	318.2	320.1	320.3	316.1	321.6	321.9	320.1	316.1
2016	312.2	314.2	311.5	319.5	320.1	321.6	325.7	326.2	325.2	328.5	326.6	325.8	321.4
2017	318.9	318.1	318.5	322.3	323.4	325.0	326.5	327.4	324.8	328.4	329.2	326.2	324.1
2018	322.3	322.4	318.0	322.9	325.6	326.2	329.8	330.6	326.7	331.3	329.0	325.8	325.9
Education and Health Services													
2010	267.7	270.4	272.2	275.6	276.1	272.2	268.6	269.8	271.8	277.2	278.6	277.8	273.2
2011	276.3	278.9	279.3	284.2	283.5	279.3	276.1	277.3	282.0	285.4	286.6	287.2	281.3
2012	283.7	287.6	287.9	289.2	289.2	284.8	282.7	283.8	290.1	293.9	295.1	294.5	288.5
2013	294.1	297.8	297.6	299.9	301.2	296.7	294.5	296.3	300.1	303.7	305.4	304.9	299.4
2014	300.6	303.8	304.0	306.7	307.4	303.5	301.6	303.5	307.7	310.6	311.7	312.0	306.1
2015	306.7	310.8	311.8	312.6	314.1	310.3	308.7	310.0	314.7	317.3	318.9	318.7	312.9
2016	316.3	319.3	319.2	323.7	323.8	319.1	319.1	321.4	322.8	323.5	328.7	328.8	322.1
2017	325.3	329.4	329.6	332.5	332.5	330.6	328.1	329.1	333.1	335.2	336.8	336.7	331.6
2018	333.0	336.4	336.8	338.9	339.8	337.0	334.3	335.3	338.0	339.8	338.8	336.4	337.0
Leisure and Hospitality													
2010	148.5	147.4	149.3	157.2	162.7	164.8	165.0	166.5	162.6	159.7	155.0	153.9	157.7
2011	150.5	150.1	152.5	158.7	166.7	170.6	168.8	170.8	169.7	163.9	161.0	159.6	161.9
2012	155.2	155.8	158.3	163.7	168.9	173.6	173.6	175.3	172.5	167.1	164.0	162.9	165.9
2013	160.0	159.8	161.7	165.9	174.1	179.2	179.2	180.5	176.7	172.9	168.4	168.0	170.5
2014	163.1	163.1	163.8	170.6	179.2	184.2	183.0	185.0	180.2	174.0	170.0	170.1	173.9
2015	167.1	167.1	169.2	174.2	182.5	187.7	187.6	188.9	183.8	179.4	175.5	175.7	178.2
2016	172.6	172.2	173.9	180.1	186.5	191.5	193.4	194.3	189.0	184.7	180.3	179.1	183.1
2017	177.2	177.7	180.2	184.8	191.5	197.2	197.7	198.7	192.7	186.7	182.9	182.9	187.5
2018	182.5	182.4	182.1	185.1	195.4	199.5	199.8	201.2	195.2	189.4	184.3	184.1	190.1
Other Services													
2010	75.4	75.6	76.3	76.6	76.6	77.8	77.9	78.1	76.3	77.3	76.6	76.5	76.8
2011	75.8	76.1	76.5	77.3	77.6	78.5	79.2	79.6	78.8	78.2	78.3	78.2	77.8
2012	77.2	77.4	77.6	78.1	78.4	80.0	79.5	79.6	78.3	78.5	78.3	78.2	78.4
2013	77.5	77.7	78.2	78.1	79.2	80.1	79.7	80.1	79.3	78.4	78.2	78.2	78.7
2014	77.3	77.2	77.5	78.7	79.5	80.7	80.7	80.8	79.6	79.6	79.4	78.9	79.2
2015	77.2	77.4	78.0	78.8	79.1	80.2	80.0	80.2	78.5	79.3	79.2	79.3	78.9
2016	77.4	77.9	78.3	79.5	79.6	80.3	81.1	81.2	80.8	80.2	80.1	79.8	79.7
2017	79.1	79.1	79.8	80.0	80.3	81.5	81.0	81.1	79.8	79.2	78.7	78.5	79.8
2018	78.1	78.1	77.8	78.1	78.7	80.2	80.7	80.4	78.5	78.2	78.1	78.3	78.8
Government													
2010	242.5	247.2	247.3	249.9	253.7	249.1	224.8	221.8	238.8	246.8	248.5	247.4	243.2
2011	241.8	247.6	246.4	246.6	247.8	242.3	208.3	218.5	235.5	242.6	243.0	242.4	238.6
2012	237.2	241.7	242.0	244.0	244.4	241.1	215.9	218.2	239.2	244.7	246.7	245.1	238.4
2013	240.1	245.7	244.7	247.5	247.4	242.4	214.8	217.4	242.3	249.0	250.8	248.3	240.9
2014	243.3	248.7	247.9	249.3	249.6	246.0	227.6	226.1	242.0	249.8	251.3	248.9	244.2
2015	244.3	248.7	247.0	248.8	248.8	245.9	228.3	226.3	241.7	248.9	249.6	248.7	243.9
2016	244.7	248.0	247.4	247.0	246.6	243.1	228.8	229.3	244.6	250.0	250.7	246.9	243.9
2017	248.2	251.1	249.7	248.9	248.2	247.2	232.5	231.6	248.6	255.0	255.4	251.2	247.3
2018	252.0	255.3	252.5	253.0	252.0	249.4	236.3	234.1	246.9	253.5	254.3	250.2	249.1

Employment by Industry: San Diego-Carlsbad, CA, 2010–2018

(Numbers in thousands, not seasonally adjusted)

Industry and year	January	February	March	April	May	June	July	August	September	October	November	December	Annual average
Total Nonfarm													
2010	1,217.4	1,220.9	1,226.0	1,239.3	1,250.4	1,252.3	1,240.8	1,243.5	1,241.9	1,247.4	1,252.0	1,256.2	1,240.7
2011	1,233.6	1,241.3	1,245.0	1,247.9	1,250.5	1,254.4	1,244.1	1,247.1	1,251.3	1,256.8	1,266.3	1,269.2	1,250.6
2012	1,245.0	1,254.0	1,261.1	1,278.8	1,288.1	1,296.1	1,280.8	1,286.9	1,287.0	1,297.9	1,309.6	1,312.7	1,283.2
2013	1,288.6	1,296.9	1,304.3	1,309.6	1,314.8	1,320.9	1,309.8	1,315.0	1,315.6	1,331.2	1,343.0	1,345.3	1,316.3
2014	1,315.1	1,324.8	1,331.7	1,335.5	1,342.3	1,349.9	1,338.3	1,346.8	1,346.9	1,359.3	1,372.7	1,375.4	1,344.9
2015	1,352.5	1,358.7	1,365.5	1,371.5	1,382.0	1,386.1	1,386.2	1,389.4	1,389.6	1,406.1	1,416.1	1,416.5	1,385.0
2016	1,391.6	1,402.2	1,402.3	1,416.8	1,421.9	1,422.9	1,420.6	1,425.4	1,428.5	1,440.1	1,450.5	1,451.4	1,422.9
2017	1,425.1	1,433.7	1,437.4	1,445.9	1,451.4	1,459.8	1,445.7	1,449.9	1,454.1	1,468.6	1,478.5	1,480.5	1,452.6
2018	1,459.9	1,469.9	1,473.9	1,480.0	1,485.0	1,491.6	1,480.3	1,485.3	1,484.4	1,495.4	1,503.8	1,505.9	1,484.6
Total Private													
2010	992.8	995.2	998.6	1,004.5	1,009.7	1,014.3	1,015.2	1,019.7	1,014.3	1,015.5	1,018.7	1,024.0	1,010.2
2011	1,003.5	1,008.4	1,011.2	1,014.1	1,017.8	1,020.8	1,024.4	1,029.9	1,028.1	1,027.2	1,035.2	1,039.4	1,021.7
2012	1,018.3	1,024.6	1,030.2	1,048.0	1,056.8	1,064.0	1,062.7	1,067.9	1,064.0	1,068.5	1,077.5	1,081.5	1,055.3
2013	1,061.0	1,066.9	1,071.9	1,077.7	1,082.5	1,086.9	1,089.3	1,094.1	1,089.7	1,099.9	1,109.1	1,112.2	1,086.8
2014	1,085.8	1,092.4	1,097.3	1,100.8	1,107.1	1,112.2	1,116.0	1,123.5	1,119.8	1,125.4	1,136.1	1,139.3	1,113.0
2015	1,118.0	1,122.9	1,127.9	1,133.3	1,142.4	1,147.3	1,158.8	1,162.5	1,158.0	1,166.8	1,173.8	1,174.7	1,148.9
2016	1,153.2	1,161.1	1,159.4	1,173.1	1,177.0	1,177.5	1,189.4	1,191.1	1,188.8	1,193.3	1,201.4	1,202.0	1,180.6
2017	1,178.5	1,184.2	1,187.6	1,195.3	1,200.3	1,207.9	1,212.5	1,216.2	1,212.4	1,220.9	1,228.7	1,230.7	1,206.3
2018	1,212.6	1,220.7	1,223.5	1,228.8	1,233.0	1,238.2	1,247.1	1,250.4	1,240.5	1,245.0	1,250.8	1,253.4	1,237.0
Goods Producing													
2010	150.9	149.8	150.8	152.2	152.6	152.5	152.3	152.7	151.5	150.8	150.8	151.0	151.5
2011	150.1	150.5	150.9	151.1	151.7	152.7	152.8	153.7	153.2	153.2	152.8	152.9	152.1
2012	150.7	151.0	152.1	153.8	155.3	156.7	157.3	158.1	157.6	158.0	159.0	158.8	155.7
2013	157.2	158.1	158.7	159.5	159.6	160.8	161.8	162.6	162.1	162.7	163.6	163.8	160.9
2014	162.1	162.6	162.9	164.0	165.2	165.9	167.7	168.9	169.0	170.3	171.0	171.1	166.7
2015	169.9	170.7	172.3	173.1	175.0	176.4	179.3	180.9	180.4	180.8	181.0	181.6	176.8
2016	180.5	181.8	181.7	183.0	183.7	184.6	187.1	187.2	186.5	187.5	187.9	188.2	185.0
2017	183.3	185.1	186.2	186.7	187.2	189.2	190.7	191.6	192.3	193.0	192.3	193.3	189.2
2018	192.8	194.9	194.6	195.6	197.0	198.4	199.9	200.2	199.3	198.1	198.0	198.0	197.2
Service-Providing													
2010	1,066.5	1,071.1	1,075.2	1,087.1	1,097.8	1,099.8	1,088.5	1,090.8	1,090.4	1,096.6	1,101.2	1,105.2	1,089.2
2011	1,083.5	1,090.8	1,094.1	1,096.8	1,098.8	1,101.7	1,091.3	1,093.4	1,098.1	1,103.6	1,113.5	1,116.3	1,098.5
2012	1,094.3	1,103.0	1,109.0	1,125.0	1,132.8	1,139.4	1,123.5	1,128.8	1,129.4	1,139.9	1,150.6	1,153.9	1,127.5
2013	1,131.4	1,138.8	1,145.6	1,150.1	1,155.2	1,160.1	1,148.0	1,152.4	1,153.5	1,168.5	1,179.4	1,181.5	1,155.4
2014	1,153.0	1,162.2	1,168.8	1,171.5	1,177.1	1,184.0	1,170.6	1,177.9	1,177.9	1,189.0	1,201.7	1,204.3	1,178.2
2015	1,182.6	1,188.0	1,193.2	1,198.4	1,207.0	1,209.7	1,206.9	1,208.5	1,209.2	1,225.3	1,235.1	1,234.9	1,208.2
2016	1,211.1	1,220.4	1,220.6	1,233.8	1,238.2	1,238.3	1,233.5	1,238.2	1,242.0	1,252.6	1,262.6	1,263.2	1,237.9
2017	1,241.8	1,248.6	1,251.2	1,259.2	1,264.2	1,270.6	1,255.0	1,258.3	1,261.8	1,275.6	1,286.2	1,287.2	1,263.3
2018	1,267.1	1,275.0	1,279.3	1,284.4	1,288.0	1,293.2	1,280.4	1,285.1	1,285.1	1,297.3	1,305.8	1,307.9	1,287.4
Mining and Logging													
2010	0.3	0.3	0.4	0.3	0.4	0.4	0.4	0.4	0.4	0.4	0.4	0.4	0.4
2011	0.4	0.4	0.4	0.4	0.4	0.4	0.4	0.4	0.4	0.3	0.3	0.3	0.4
2012	0.3	0.3	0.3	0.4	0.4	0.4	0.3	0.4	0.3	0.3	0.4	0.4	0.4
2013	0.3	0.3	0.3	0.3	0.3	0.3	0.3	0.3	0.3	0.3	0.3	0.3	0.3
2014	0.4	0.4	0.3	0.4	0.4	0.4	0.4	0.4	0.4	0.4	0.4	0.4	0.4
2015	0.4	0.3	0.3	0.3	0.3	0.3	0.3	0.3	0.3	0.3	0.3	0.3	0.3
2016	0.3	0.3	0.3	0.3	0.3	0.3	0.3	0.3	0.3	0.3	0.3	0.3	0.3
2017	0.3	0.3	0.3	0.3	0.3	0.3	0.3	0.3	0.3	0.3	0.3	0.3	0.3
2018	0.3	0.3	0.3	0.3	0.4	0.4	0.4	0.4	0.3	0.3	0.3	0.3	0.3
Construction													
2010	55.8	54.8	55.2	55.8	56.2	56.2	56.2	56.3	55.4	54.6	54.5	54.2	55.4
2011	53.7	54.2	54.4	54.7	55.1	55.5	55.8	56.6	56.0	56.1	55.6	55.2	55.2
2012	54.2	54.2	55.2	56.0	57.0	58.1	57.8	58.2	58.0	58.3	58.9	58.4	57.0
2013	58.0	58.6	59.0	59.9	60.2	61.5	62.0	62.8	62.2	62.4	62.9	62.7	61.0
2014	61.4	61.7	61.9	62.2	63.1	63.3	64.5	65.4	65.4	66.1	66.3	65.8	63.9
2015	65.1	65.6	66.5	67.4	68.8	69.6	71.5	72.7	72.5	72.9	73.0	73.4	69.9
2016	72.7	73.9	73.8	74.8	75.4	75.9	77.7	78.3	77.9	78.0	78.4	78.6	76.3
2017	75.0	76.6	77.7	78.0	78.4	79.6	79.8	80.8	82.0	82.5	82.0	82.1	79.5
2018	81.8	83.6	83.0	83.8	84.6	85.0	85.9	86.4	86.2	83.9	83.3	83.1	84.2

Employment by Industry: San Diego-Carlsbad, CA, 2010–2018—*Continued*

(Numbers in thousands, not seasonally adjusted)

Industry and year	January	February	March	April	May	June	July	August	September	October	November	December	Annual average
Manufacturing													
2010................	94.8	94.7	95.2	96.1	96.0	95.9	95.7	96.0	95.7	95.8	95.9	96.4	95.7
2011................	96.0	95.9	96.1	96.0	96.2	96.8	96.6	96.7	96.8	96.8	96.9	97.4	96.5
2012................	96.2	96.5	96.6	97.4	97.9	98.2	99.2	99.5	99.3	99.4	99.7	100.0	98.3
2013................	98.9	99.2	99.4	99.3	99.1	99.0	99.5	99.5	99.6	100.0	100.4	100.8	99.6
2014................	100.3	100.5	100.7	101.4	101.7	102.2	102.8	103.1	103.2	103.8	104.3	104.9	102.4
2015................	104.4	104.8	105.5	105.4	105.9	106.5	107.5	107.9	107.6	107.6	107.7	107.9	106.6
2016................	107.5	107.6	107.6	107.9	108.0	108.4	109.1	108.6	108.3	109.2	109.2	109.3	108.4
2017................	108.0	108.2	108.2	108.4	108.5	109.3	110.6	110.5	110.0	110.2	110.0	110.9	109.4
2018................	110.7	111.0	111.3	111.5	112.0	113.0	113.6	113.4	112.8	113.9	114.4	114.6	112.7
Trade, Transportation, and Utilities													
2010................	196.7	195.2	194.4	195.8	196.8	197.8	198.6	199.5	198.8	200.4	206.1	209.5	199.1
2011................	200.2	198.1	197.7	199.0	199.7	200.6	202.2	203.1	203.4	204.5	211.0	214.0	202.8
2012................	206.4	204.1	203.8	206.2	207.8	208.7	208.9	209.3	209.6	211.5	220.5	222.3	209.9
2013................	212.3	210.6	210.5	210.7	212.0	212.4	212.8	213.4	212.3	215.1	223.0	225.6	214.2
2014................	215.2	213.8	212.5	212.3	213.2	214.4	214.7	215.4	214.9	216.5	224.2	226.8	216.2
2015................	217.2	215.9	214.9	215.4	216.8	217.0	219.3	219.0	218.6	221.2	227.2	228.6	219.3
2016................	219.0	218.3	216.7	218.4	218.4	217.7	219.6	220.6	219.1	222.6	229.4	230.9	220.9
2017................	223.9	221.7	220.4	221.8	222.3	222.3	223.7	224.0	223.4	225.8	232.7	234.8	224.7
2018................	225.7	223.6	222.6	222.9	224.1	223.9	224.2	225.0	223.6	224.6	229.9	233.5	225.3
Wholesale Trade													
2010................	40.5	40.7	40.5	41.2	41.5	41.8	42.0	42.3	42.3	43.1	43.5	43.8	41.9
2011................	42.5	42.9	42.8	43.1	43.2	43.2	43.3	43.4	43.4	43.7	43.9	43.9	43.3
2012................	43.7	44.3	44.2	45.1	45.6	45.4	45.7	45.9	45.7	46.2	46.5	46.3	45.4
2013................	45.9	46.5	46.3	45.7	46.1	45.5	45.2	45.2	45.0	45.9	46.0	45.9	45.8
2014................	44.9	45.6	45.2	45.0	45.0	45.1	44.7	44.8	44.6	44.3	44.5	44.6	44.9
2015................	43.4	44.3	43.8	44.0	44.1	43.7	44.2	44.0	43.9	44.5	44.5	44.3	44.1
2016................	43.7	44.2	43.4	43.9	43.6	43.2	43.6	43.5	43.2	44.0	44.1	44.1	43.7
2017................	43.4	44.0	42.7	44.0	44.0	43.8	44.1	43.9	43.7	44.1	44.1	44.2	43.8
2018................	43.4	43.8	43.4	43.7	44.3	43.8	43.8	43.9	43.6	43.3	43.3	43.7	43.7
Retail Trade													
2010................	130.0	128.4	127.8	128.3	128.7	129.3	129.8	130.4	129.8	130.9	136.1	138.7	130.7
2011................	131.6	129.5	129.1	130.1	130.7	131.4	132.8	133.4	133.6	134.8	141.0	143.3	133.4
2012................	136.4	133.4	133.0	134.2	135.0	135.6	135.5	135.8	136.2	137.9	146.3	147.5	137.2
2013................	139.2	137.0	137.0	137.5	138.4	139.4	140.1	140.9	140.4	142.6	150.1	152.5	141.3
2014................	143.6	141.5	140.9	140.9	141.4	142.2	142.8	143.7	143.2	145.0	152.3	154.1	144.3
2015................	146.2	144.1	143.6	143.9	145.0	145.1	146.3	146.2	145.8	147.9	153.5	154.4	146.8
2016................	146.4	145.3	144.5	145.6	145.7	145.1	146.0	146.9	145.7	148.3	154.6	155.6	147.5
2017................	149.6	146.8	146.3	146.7	146.7	146.6	147.5	148.0	147.5	149.3	155.7	156.7	149.0
2018................	149.5	147.2	146.5	146.1	146.6	146.2	147.1	147.5	146.3	147.8	152.4	154.8	148.2
Transportation and Utilities													
2010................	26.2	26.1	26.1	26.3	26.6	26.7	26.8	26.8	26.7	26.4	26.5	27.0	26.5
2011................	26.1	25.7	25.8	25.8	25.8	26.0	26.1	26.3	26.4	26.0	26.1	26.8	26.1
2012................	26.3	26.4	26.6	26.9	27.2	27.7	27.7	27.6	27.7	27.4	27.7	28.5	27.3
2013................	27.2	27.1	27.2	27.5	27.5	27.5	27.5	27.3	26.9	26.6	26.9	27.2	27.2
2014................	26.7	26.7	26.4	26.4	26.8	27.1	27.2	26.9	27.1	27.2	27.4	28.1	27.0
2015................	27.6	27.5	27.5	27.5	27.7	28.2	28.8	28.8	28.9	28.8	29.2	29.9	28.4
2016................	28.9	28.8	28.8	28.9	29.1	29.4	30.0	30.2	30.2	30.3	30.7	31.2	29.7
2017................	30.9	30.9	31.4	31.1	31.6	31.9	32.1	32.1	32.2	32.4	32.9	33.9	32.0
2018................	32.8	32.6	32.7	33.1	33.2	33.9	33.3	33.6	33.7	33.5	34.2	35.0	33.5
Information													
2010................	26.0	25.7	25.6	25.5	25.5	25.7	25.5	25.4	25.1	25.0	25.0	24.9	25.4
2011................	24.8	24.8	24.7	24.6	24.6	24.5	24.7	24.7	24.7	24.7	24.6	24.7	24.7
2012................	24.9	24.8	24.8	25.1	25.1	25.2	25.0	24.9	24.7	24.7	24.8	24.9	24.9
2013................	24.6	24.4	24.4	24.3	24.5	24.6	24.5	24.6	24.5	24.6	24.8	24.9	24.6
2014................	24.5	24.8	24.6	24.6	24.6	24.5	24.6	24.6	24.5	24.5	24.3	24.3	24.5
2015................	23.8	23.8	23.7	23.8	23.9	23.9	24.1	24.0	23.7	23.8	23.7	23.8	23.8
2016................	23.9	23.7	23.4	23.5	23.3	23.5	24.0	24.0	23.8	23.7	23.8	24.0	23.7
2017................	23.8	23.9	23.8	23.8	23.9	24.1	24.3	24.1	24.0	24.0	24.0	24.1	24.0
2018................	24.1	24.0	24.0	24.2	24.1	24.1	24.2	24.0	23.7	24.0	23.9	24.0	24.0

Employment by Industry: San Diego-Carlsbad, CA, 2010–2018—*Continued*

(Numbers in thousands, not seasonally adjusted)

Industry and year	January	February	March	April	May	June	July	August	September	October	November	December	Annual average
Financial Activities													
2010	66.9	67.2	67.2	67.0	66.8	67.0	67.3	67.1	66.8	67.7	67.5	67.6	67.2
2011	66.8	67.1	66.7	67.0	66.9	67.2	67.7	67.4	67.6	68.0	67.9	68.7	67.4
2012	68.0	68.3	68.6	69.5	69.6	70.0	70.7	70.6	70.1	70.6	71.0	71.2	69.9
2013	70.6	70.9	71.0	71.1	71.3	71.2	71.5	71.3	70.7	70.9	70.5	70.5	71.0
2014	69.3	69.5	69.5	69.1	69.4	69.5	70.3	70.2	69.5	69.7	69.8	69.9	69.6
2015	70.1	70.1	70.2	70.8	71.2	71.2	72.4	72.0	71.3	72.5	72.4	72.4	71.4
2016	71.5	71.7	71.6	72.7	72.9	72.9	73.9	73.8	73.4	74.0	73.8	73.7	73.0
2017	73.4	73.3	73.3	73.8	74.2	74.5	75.6	75.2	74.9	75.7	75.8	76.0	74.6
2018	75.4	75.7	75.4	75.9	76.1	75.9	76.6	76.4	75.4	76.1	76.1	76.0	75.9
Professional and Business Services													
2010	197.7	199.3	198.8	200.9	201.5	203.2	204.7	206.5	206.1	206.6	205.8	207.1	203.2
2011	203.1	204.5	205.1	204.3	203.2	203.4	204.7	206.4	204.8	205.2	205.9	206.6	204.8
2012	202.3	205.4	206.1	211.2	211.6	213.1	211.6	213.0	211.6	214.3	213.9	215.6	210.8
2013	213.1	215.5	215.9	215.4	216.2	216.8	218.2	219.1	219.2	223.9	224.4	224.6	218.5
2014	218.1	221.0	221.8	219.2	219.9	220.8	221.5	223.3	222.8	225.8	226.8	227.3	222.4
2015	223.7	225.3	225.4	226.0	226.5	228.1	230.6	231.6	229.9	234.3	235.3	234.7	229.3
2016	231.6	233.3	231.6	234.0	233.7	233.1	236.7	236.3	236.2	235.5	235.7	236.1	234.5
2017	233.0	235.0	235.2	235.9	235.9	237.4	239.2	240.5	239.8	243.3	245.3	245.0	238.8
2018	243.5	247.0	247.8	248.0	247.3	247.6	250.2	250.8	249.2	251.8	252.5	249.7	248.8
Education and Health Services													
2010	163.1	164.9	165.7	164.8	165.3	164.5	161.9	162.4	163.9	165.5	166.1	166.6	164.6
2011	165.9	167.8	168.5	167.7	168.2	167.4	165.3	165.7	168.0	168.8	170.8	171.0	167.9
2012	168.8	170.8	172.3	174.6	176.0	175.2	173.0	173.6	175.7	177.8	178.3	178.9	174.6
2013	179.2	180.6	182.0	182.7	182.2	180.3	177.2	178.3	180.1	183.3	183.7	183.4	181.1
2014	181.7	183.1	184.7	187.3	186.7	185.4	182.6	183.9	186.9	189.2	190.6	190.9	186.1
2015	189.2	189.8	191.5	192.2	192.6	191.5	190.5	191.6	193.8	195.9	196.3	197.4	192.7
2016	195.2	197.4	197.0	199.6	199.8	198.1	195.9	196.5	198.9	201.0	202.4	203.0	198.7
2017	200.8	202.9	203.7	204.3	204.4	203.9	200.4	203.0	204.4	207.2	208.1	208.3	204.3
2018	206.4	207.7	208.6	209.6	209.2	208.1	209.1	211.5	212.4	213.2	214.4	215.2	210.5
Leisure and Hospitality													
2010	146.0	147.0	149.4	152.9	155.1	157.0	158.4	159.7	156.3	153.2	151.5	151.5	153.2
2011	146.9	148.8	150.7	152.6	155.0	156.7	158.9	160.9	158.2	154.5	154.4	154.1	154.3
2012	150.0	151.9	153.8	158.3	161.5	164.7	166.6	169.1	165.3	161.8	160.9	160.9	160.4
2013	156.3	158.5	161.2	165.3	167.6	170.9	173.3	174.8	170.9	169.5	169.0	169.5	167.2
2014	164.9	166.9	170.3	172.9	176.0	179.5	181.9	184.5	179.2	176.5	176.8	176.6	175.5
2015	172.7	175.2	177.7	179.3	183.2	185.7	188.4	189.1	186.2	184.4	184.2	182.7	182.4
2016	178.4	180.9	183.9	187.6	190.6	192.9	197.0	197.5	195.8	194.0	194.0	191.9	190.4
2017	187.1	188.4	190.9	194.2	197.0	200.3	202.2	202.1	197.8	196.8	195.5	194.7	195.6
2018	190.5	193.2	195.8	197.7	200.1	204.3	206.8	206.6	201.6	201.2	199.7	200.9	199.9
Other Services													
2010	45.5	46.1	46.7	45.4	46.1	46.6	46.5	46.4	45.8	46.3	45.9	45.8	46.1
2011	45.7	46.8	46.9	47.8	48.5	48.3	48.1	48.0	48.2	48.3	47.8	47.4	47.7
2012	47.2	48.3	48.7	49.3	49.9	50.4	49.6	49.3	49.4	49.8	49.1	48.9	49.2
2013	47.7	48.3	48.2	48.7	49.1	49.9	50.0	50.0	49.9	49.9	50.1	49.9	49.3
2014	50.0	50.7	51.0	51.4	52.1	52.2	52.7	52.7	53.0	52.9	52.6	52.4	52.0
2015	51.4	52.1	52.2	52.7	53.2	53.5	54.2	54.3	54.1	53.9	53.7	53.5	53.2
2016	53.1	54.0	53.5	54.3	54.6	54.7	55.2	55.2	55.1	55.0	54.4	54.2	54.4
2017	53.2	53.9	54.1	54.8	55.4	56.2	56.4	55.7	55.8	55.1	55.0	54.5	55.0
2018	54.2	54.6	54.7	54.9	55.1	55.9	56.1	55.9	55.3	56.0	56.3	56.1	55.4
Government													
2010	224.6	225.7	227.4	234.8	240.7	238.0	225.6	223.8	227.6	231.9	233.3	232.2	230.5
2011	230.1	232.9	233.8	233.8	232.7	233.6	219.7	217.2	223.2	229.6	231.1	229.8	229.0
2012	226.7	229.4	230.9	230.8	231.3	232.1	218.1	219.0	223.0	229.4	232.1	231.2	227.8
2013	227.6	230.0	232.4	231.9	232.3	234.0	220.5	220.9	225.9	231.3	233.9	233.1	229.5
2014	229.3	232.4	234.4	234.7	235.2	237.7	222.3	223.3	227.1	233.9	236.6	236.1	231.9
2015	234.5	235.8	237.6	238.2	239.6	238.8	227.4	226.9	231.6	239.3	242.3	241.8	236.2
2016	238.4	241.1	242.9	243.7	244.9	245.4	231.2	234.3	239.7	246.8	249.1	249.4	242.2
2017	246.6	249.5	249.8	250.6	251.1	251.9	233.2	233.7	241.7	247.7	249.8	249.8	246.3
2018	247.3	249.2	250.4	251.2	252.0	253.4	233.2	234.9	243.9	250.4	253.0	252.5	247.6

Employment by Industry: Tampa-St. Petersburg-Clearwater, FL, 2010–2018

(Numbers in thousands, not seasonally adjusted)

Industry and year	January	February	March	April	May	June	July	August	September	October	November	December	Annual average
Total Nonfarm													
2010	1,089.8	1,098.8	1,107.2	1,106.9	1,113.1	1,100.3	1,093.0	1,103.5	1,102.2	1,113.7	1,118.9	1,123.7	1,105.9
2011	1,106.5	1,115.2	1,123.3	1,127.0	1,123.2	1,110.5	1,107.5	1,121.5	1,128.5	1,132.2	1,139.8	1,145.2	1,123.4
2012	1,132.1	1,140.7	1,148.3	1,153.0	1,152.0	1,139.9	1,132.2	1,146.6	1,147.0	1,155.1	1,165.8	1,172.1	1,148.7
2013	1,154.9	1,165.4	1,173.9	1,177.3	1,178.6	1,166.5	1,162.7	1,176.8	1,177.0	1,185.6	1,198.5	1,200.7	1,176.5
2014	1,181.7	1,190.3	1,200.4	1,207.9	1,210.9	1,198.7	1,195.2	1,209.7	1,211.7	1,221.7	1,234.3	1,239.3	1,208.5
2015	1,222.1	1,234.1	1,241.7	1,246.7	1,248.6	1,238.6	1,235.8	1,248.7	1,251.3	1,269.8	1,285.3	1,288.1	1,250.9
2016	1,270.3	1,281.3	1,287.2	1,297.7	1,295.4	1,280.6	1,281.0	1,292.1	1,298.0	1,309.9	1,320.8	1,324.5	1,294.9
2017	1,307.8	1,315.5	1,320.2	1,322.2	1,320.4	1,311.9	1,305.8	1,319.6	1,302.5	1,333.8	1,347.5	1,349.2	1,321.4
2018	1,331.4	1,343.8	1,349.0	1,350.4	1,348.9	1,339.3	1,335.3	1,353.4	1,354.8	1,363.8	1,373.9	1,375.8	1,351.7
Total Private													
2010	935.3	941.4	950.2	950.5	951.8	952.3	946.4	949.6	946.5	957.3	962.2	968.5	951.0
2011	951.6	957.8	966.2	970.7	968.7	966.2	964.9	969.7	973.3	976.8	984.8	990.1	970.1
2012	977.5	985.6	993.5	997.3	997.3	995.8	989.4	995.7	994.2	1,001.9	1,011.6	1,018.3	996.5
2013	1,000.6	1,009.9	1,018.5	1,021.9	1,025.1	1,023.4	1,020.8	1,025.9	1,024.3	1,030.9	1,043.5	1,046.3	1,024.3
2014	1,028.8	1,036.9	1,044.7	1,051.9	1,055.4	1,054.1	1,051.9	1,058.6	1,058.1	1,066.3	1,079.1	1,084.0	1,055.8
2015	1,068.3	1,078.5	1,086.4	1,090.7	1,093.5	1,094.2	1,092.1	1,096.7	1,097.7	1,112.6	1,127.5	1,132.1	1,097.5
2016	1,114.1	1,123.2	1,129.7	1,139.4	1,138.3	1,134.3	1,135.5	1,138.7	1,141.3	1,150.8	1,161.4	1,165.4	1,139.3
2017	1,150.0	1,155.2	1,160.5	1,162.8	1,163.0	1,163.3	1,160.5	1,166.1	1,145.7	1,174.6	1,188.3	1,190.0	1,165.0
2018	1,174.0	1,184.1	1,189.6	1,191.0	1,191.7	1,191.0	1,189.1	1,199.5	1,197.4	1,205.7	1,215.9	1,218.2	1,195.6
Goods Producing													
2010	110.7	110.7	110.8	110.4	111.6	111.7	112.0	111.9	111.0	110.8	110.4	110.2	111.0
2011	108.4	109.0	110.2	111.0	111.6	111.9	112.4	112.3	113.1	112.6	112.5	112.6	111.5
2012	110.7	111.8	112.6	112.9	113.8	114.8	114.3	115.1	114.3	114.7	115.1	115.2	113.8
2013	112.7	113.5	114.7	116.2	116.7	117.6	117.6	118.4	118.5	119.2	120.2	119.9	117.1
2014	117.7	118.9	120.0	121.1	122.6	123.4	123.3	123.9	123.8	124.1	123.8	123.9	122.2
2015	122.4	123.2	124.4	125.1	126.1	127.5	128.0	128.8	129.3	130.7	131.5	131.2	127.4
2016	130.0	131.4	132.8	134.3	135.2	135.8	136.3	136.5	137.3	138.4	138.2	138.6	135.4
2017	136.9	138.2	139.2	139.3	139.7	141.5	141.1	142.1	138.4	142.3	142.5	142.7	140.3
2018	141.4	143.3	144.3	144.5	144.5	145.9	146.0	146.6	146.7	147.8	145.5	146.5	145.3
Service-Providing													
2010	979.1	988.1	996.4	996.5	1,001.5	988.6	981.0	991.6	991.2	1,002.9	1,008.5	1,013.5	994.9
2011	998.1	1,006.2	1,013.1	1,016.0	1,011.6	998.6	995.1	1,009.2	1,015.4	1,019.6	1,027.3	1,032.6	1,011.9
2012	1,021.4	1,028.9	1,035.7	1,040.1	1,038.2	1,025.1	1,017.9	1,031.5	1,032.7	1,040.4	1,050.7	1,056.9	1,035.0
2013	1,042.2	1,051.9	1,059.2	1,061.1	1,061.9	1,048.9	1,045.1	1,058.4	1,058.5	1,066.4	1,078.3	1,080.8	1,059.4
2014	1,064.0	1,071.4	1,080.4	1,086.8	1,088.3	1,075.3	1,071.9	1,085.8	1,087.9	1,097.6	1,110.5	1,115.4	1,086.3
2015	1,099.7	1,110.9	1,117.3	1,121.6	1,122.5	1,111.1	1,107.8	1,119.9	1,122.0	1,139.1	1,153.8	1,156.9	1,123.6
2016	1,140.3	1,149.9	1,154.4	1,163.4	1,160.2	1,144.8	1,144.7	1,155.6	1,160.7	1,171.5	1,182.6	1,185.9	1,159.5
2017	1,170.9	1,177.3	1,181.0	1,182.9	1,180.7	1,170.4	1,164.7	1,177.5	1,164.1	1,191.5	1,205.0	1,206.5	1,181.0
2018	1,190.0	1,200.5	1,204.7	1,205.9	1,204.4	1,193.4	1,189.3	1,206.8	1,208.1	1,216.0	1,228.4	1,229.3	1,206.4
Mining and Logging													
2010	0.5	0.5	0.4	0.4	0.4	0.4	0.4	0.4	0.4	0.4	0.4	0.4	0.4
2011	0.4	0.4	0.4	0.4	0.4	0.4	0.4	0.4	0.4	0.4	0.5	0.5	0.4
2012	0.5	0.5	0.5	0.5	0.5	0.5	0.5	0.5	0.4	0.5	0.5	0.5	0.5
2013	0.4	0.4	0.5	0.5	0.4	0.4	0.5	0.4	0.4	0.4	0.4	0.4	0.4
2014	0.4	0.4	0.4	0.4	0.4	0.4	0.4	0.4	0.4	0.4	0.4	0.4	0.4
2015	0.3	0.3	0.4	0.4	0.4	0.4	0.4	0.4	0.3	0.3	0.3	0.3	0.4
2016	0.3	0.3	0.3	0.3	0.3	0.3	0.3	0.3	0.3	0.3	0.2	0.3	0.3
2017	0.3	0.3	0.3	0.3	0.3	0.3	0.3	0.3	0.3	0.3	0.3	0.3	0.3
2018	0.3	0.3	0.3	0.3	0.3	0.3	0.3	0.3	0.3	0.3	0.3	0.3	0.3
Construction													
2010	52.4	52.4	52.6	52.2	52.7	52.7	53.0	52.7	52.2	52.4	51.6	51.4	52.4
2011	50.1	50.5	51.3	52.0	52.5	52.5	52.8	52.6	53.3	53.2	52.9	52.9	52.2
2012	51.3	52.0	52.6	52.8	53.6	54.4	54.0	54.5	54.5	54.7	55.0	55.1	53.7
2013	53.4	54.0	54.8	55.5	56.2	56.8	56.8	57.4	57.6	58.0	58.8	58.5	56.5
2014	56.8	57.8	58.5	59.6	60.5	61.4	61.5	61.9	61.8	61.9	61.7	61.8	60.4
2015	60.9	61.6	62.4	63.2	63.9	64.8	64.9	65.5	66.0	67.1	67.6	67.4	64.6
2016	66.5	67.6	68.3	69.4	70.1	70.5	70.7	70.9	71.7	72.7	72.4	72.5	70.3
2017	70.9	71.9	72.5	72.9	73.2	74.5	74.3	75.0	72.2	75.3	75.3	75.3	73.6
2018	74.7	76.3	77.1	77.4	77.2	78.4	78.5	78.8	79.1	79.5	77.0	77.7	77.6

Employment by Industry: Tampa-St. Petersburg-Clearwater, FL, 2010–2018—*Continued*

(Numbers in thousands, not seasonally adjusted)

Industry and year	January	February	March	April	May	June	July	August	September	October	November	December	Annual average
Manufacturing													
2010	57.8	57.8	57.8	57.8	58.5	58.6	58.6	58.8	58.4	58.0	58.4	58.4	58.2
2011	57.9	58.1	58.5	58.6	58.7	59.0	59.2	59.3	59.4	59.0	59.1	59.2	58.8
2012	58.9	59.3	59.5	59.6	59.7	59.9	59.8	60.1	59.4	59.5	59.6	59.6	59.6
2013	58.9	59.1	59.4	60.2	60.1	60.4	60.3	60.6	60.5	60.8	61.0	61.0	60.2
2014	60.5	60.7	61.1	61.1	61.7	61.6	61.4	61.6	61.6	61.8	61.7	61.7	61.4
2015	61.2	61.3	61.6	61.5	61.8	62.3	62.7	62.9	63.0	63.3	63.6	63.5	62.4
2016	63.2	63.5	64.2	64.6	64.8	65.0	65.3	65.3	65.3	65.4	65.6	65.8	64.8
2017	65.7	66.0	66.4	66.1	66.2	66.7	66.5	66.8	65.9	66.7	66.9	67.1	66.4
2018	66.4	66.7	66.9	66.8	67.0	67.2	67.2	67.5	67.3	68.0	68.2	68.5	67.3
Trade, Transportation, and Utilities													
2010	206.0	205.9	206.7	207.1	208.2	208.2	206.9	207.5	207.4	209.9	214.2	218.1	208.8
2011	210.3	209.8	210.9	211.3	211.7	210.7	211.1	212.2	212.5	213.6	218.8	222.1	212.9
2012	217.1	216.7	216.1	216.7	217.5	216.5	216.0	216.6	216.7	218.2	224.4	226.8	218.3
2013	220.1	219.9	219.7	219.6	220.6	220.5	219.8	220.6	220.6	222.9	229.7	232.5	222.2
2014	226.0	226.8	227.3	228.6	229.4	229.2	228.7	229.7	230.6	232.9	241.1	245.2	231.3
2015	236.4	236.0	236.8	236.3	237.1	237.8	236.6	237.4	237.2	241.5	248.0	251.6	239.4
2016	244.2	244.7	244.6	245.7	245.8	244.1	244.3	244.5	244.3	246.8	254.5	256.7	246.7
2017	248.3	246.7	245.5	245.1	245.4	244.8	244.4	245.5	240.5	246.2	254.5	257.1	247.0
2018	249.6	248.6	248.1	247.9	248.0	246.9	247.2	247.4	246.5	247.8	254.7	255.5	249.0
Wholesale Trade													
2010	45.1	45.2	45.6	45.5	45.9	45.6	45.0	45.0	44.9	45.3	45.2	45.7	45.3
2011	44.9	44.9	45.2	45.2	45.6	45.3	45.5	45.8	46.1	46.2	46.6	47.2	45.7
2012	47.5	47.8	47.6	47.6	47.9	47.6	47.1	47.4	47.5	47.6	48.4	48.2	47.7
2013	48.1	48.2	48.3	47.9	48.2	47.8	47.6	47.9	47.8	48.1	48.7	48.8	48.1
2014	48.6	49.0	49.2	49.4	49.7	49.5	49.5	49.7	49.7	49.9	50.4	50.9	49.6
2015	50.1	50.1	50.4	50.2	50.4	50.1	50.2	50.3	50.3	50.8	51.1	51.3	50.4
2016	50.7	50.8	50.8	51.2	51.2	50.8	51.2	51.4	51.5	51.8	52.2	52.6	51.4
2017	51.8	52.2	52.2	51.8	52.0	51.9	51.9	52.0	51.5	52.2	52.5	52.8	52.1
2018	52.8	52.9	53.1	52.9	53.1	53.1	53.3	53.4	53.4	53.2	53.4	53.2	53.2
Retail Trade													
2010	136.1	135.9	136.4	136.7	137.2	137.7	136.9	137.5	137.5	139.3	143.5	145.8	138.4
2011	140.0	139.6	140.2	140.7	140.5	139.8	139.8	140.6	140.5	141.5	146.0	147.6	141.4
2012	143.3	142.5	142.1	142.6	143.0	142.3	142.3	142.9	142.8	144.2	149.3	151.0	144.0
2013	145.2	144.6	144.3	144.5	145.2	145.3	145.1	145.6	145.7	147.6	153.2	155.1	146.8
2014	149.5	149.7	149.8	150.8	151.1	151.1	150.6	151.4	152.2	154.1	161.3	163.6	152.9
2015	157.0	156.8	157.2	156.9	157.4	158.3	157.1	157.8	157.6	161.0	166.5	168.8	159.4
2016	163.0	163.8	163.8	164.5	164.4	163.3	162.8	162.9	162.6	164.5	171.0	172.3	164.9
2017	165.8	163.9	162.9	163.1	163.0	162.6	162.3	163.5	159.5	164.0	171.1	172.6	164.5
2018	166.1	165.5	164.5	164.6	164.2	163.0	163.0	163.2	162.0	163.0	168.8	169.0	164.7
Transportation and Utilities													
2010	24.8	24.8	24.7	24.9	25.1	24.9	25.0	25.0	25.0	25.3	25.5	26.6	25.1
2011	25.4	25.3	25.5	25.4	25.6	25.6	25.8	25.8	25.9	25.9	26.2	27.3	25.8
2012	26.3	26.4	26.4	26.5	26.6	26.6	26.6	26.3	26.4	26.4	26.7	27.6	26.6
2013	26.8	27.1	27.1	27.2	27.2	27.4	27.1	27.1	27.1	27.2	27.8	28.6	27.3
2014	27.9	28.1	28.3	28.4	28.6	28.6	28.6	28.6	28.7	28.9	29.4	30.7	28.7
2015	29.3	29.1	29.2	29.2	29.3	29.4	29.3	29.3	29.3	29.7	30.4	31.5	29.6
2016	30.5	30.1	30.0	30.0	30.2	30.0	30.3	30.2	30.2	30.5	31.3	31.8	30.4
2017	30.7	30.6	30.4	30.2	30.4	30.3	30.2	30.0	29.5	30.0	30.9	31.7	30.4
2018	30.7	30.2	30.5	30.4	30.7	30.8	30.9	30.8	31.1	31.6	32.5	33.3	31.1
Information													
2010	26.0	26.0	26.0	25.8	25.8	25.7	25.7	25.6	25.5	25.5	25.6	25.6	25.7
2011	25.8	25.9	25.7	25.6	25.7	25.8	26.0	25.9	25.9	26.0	26.1	26.2	25.9
2012	25.8	25.7	25.7	25.7	25.6	25.8	25.7	25.6	25.6	25.9	25.9	25.9	25.7
2013	26.1	26.1	26.2	26.2	26.3	26.4	26.1	26.1	25.9	25.9	26.0	26.0	26.1
2014	25.5	25.6	25.4	25.5	25.5	25.6	25.6	25.5	25.4	25.7	25.7	25.6	25.6
2015	25.5	25.6	25.4	25.5	25.6	25.7	26.0	25.8	25.9	26.0	26.2	26.4	25.8
2016	25.6	25.6	25.5	25.3	25.4	25.5	25.9	25.7	25.5	25.3	25.6	25.6	25.5
2017	25.4	25.2	25.4	25.0	25.1	25.1	25.1	25.1	24.6	24.8	25.3	25.3	25.1
2018	25.1	25.5	25.1	25.4	25.6	25.6	25.5	25.5	25.5	25.7	26.0	26.0	25.5

Employment by Industry: Tampa-St. Petersburg-Clearwater, FL, 2010–2018—*Continued*

(Numbers in thousands, not seasonally adjusted)

Industry and year	January	February	March	April	May	June	July	August	September	October	November	December	Annual average
Financial Activities													
2010	89.4	89.3	89.5	89.2	89.2	89.4	89.2	89.6	89.2	89.7	89.8	90.6	89.5
2011	89.8	90.1	90.4	90.6	90.6	91.1	91.4	92.3	93.1	93.6	93.6	94.3	91.7
2012	93.5	94.0	94.6	94.7	95.0	95.6	95.7	96.1	96.3	97.0	97.7	98.3	95.7
2013	97.8	98.6	99.2	99.0	99.4	100.0	100.3	100.6	100.3	100.5	101.1	101.5	99.9
2014	100.4	100.7	101.2	101.2	101.5	101.8	102.4	102.6	102.7	102.5	103.0	103.2	101.9
2015	102.4	102.6	102.8	103.0	103.4	103.6	104.5	104.8	104.5	105.2	106.2	106.3	104.1
2016	105.4	105.5	105.8	106.4	106.5	107.0	108.3	108.7	108.8	109.4	109.7	110.8	107.7
2017	110.1	110.6	110.8	111.5	111.5	112.3	113.4	113.4	113.1	114.4	114.9	115.3	112.6
2018	114.4	115.2	115.5	115.4	115.7	116.4	116.7	117.5	117.5	118.8	120.5	121.3	117.1
Professional and Business Services													
2010	167.4	170.2	172.5	172.5	172.5	174.5	174.1	176.2	174.9	179.2	179.6	180.9	174.5
2011	177.9	180.1	181.0	182.4	181.0	181.8	182.7	184.2	184.0	184.5	186.5	188.3	182.9
2012	186.2	188.8	190.7	191.3	190.7	190.4	190.1	192.0	190.6	193.3	195.0	196.7	191.3
2013	192.5	196.0	197.3	197.9	199.4	198.4	199.2	200.3	199.1	200.1	201.7	201.6	198.6
2014	198.4	200.4	200.7	201.9	203.2	203.1	204.1	206.9	205.3	209.1	211.4	211.8	204.7
2015	210.5	213.8	214.3	215.6	216.5	216.8	218.6	220.0	218.8	222.2	225.2	226.2	218.2
2016	224.0	226.3	227.2	230.3	229.8	229.0	230.5	230.7	230.6	233.1	234.1	233.9	230.0
2017	233.0	232.8	233.2	234.5	234.6	234.8	235.5	236.2	232.2	239.7	242.7	240.5	235.8
2018	237.2	238.5	238.7	239.7	240.0	241.1	242.3	244.9	243.8	245.7	250.0	249.9	242.7
Education and Health Services													
2010	176.4	177.3	179.3	178.5	178.1	177.2	175.8	176.1	176.8	179.5	180.4	180.6	178.0
2011	179.0	180.1	181.1	182.5	181.6	179.7	178.6	179.8	181.0	182.0	182.9	182.8	180.9
2012	180.7	182.0	182.9	183.5	183.1	182.0	179.2	181.1	182.1	183.1	183.7	184.2	182.3
2013	182.2	183.6	185.0	185.4	185.2	183.4	181.7	183.6	184.5	186.5	187.6	187.1	184.7
2014	185.1	186.3	187.6	188.4	188.5	186.8	185.5	188.0	188.8	191.0	192.1	192.4	188.4
2015	190.2	192.4	192.8	194.4	194.5	193.6	191.6	193.3	195.1	198.6	199.7	199.8	194.7
2016	196.7	197.9	198.3	200.3	199.7	197.2	196.8	198.9	200.5	203.0	203.5	204.2	199.8
2017	202.6	204.4	205.3	205.9	205.5	204.0	202.3	204.9	203.4	207.7	208.1	208.7	205.2
2018	207.7	209.4	209.8	210.5	209.9	208.6	207.1	211.3	212.2	213.4	213.0	212.6	210.5
Leisure and Hospitality													
2010	117.8	120.0	123.3	124.8	124.1	123.1	120.7	121.0	120.3	120.6	120.5	120.7	121.4
2011	119.1	121.2	124.8	125.2	124.5	123.7	121.5	122.1	123.0	123.8	123.8	123.2	123.0
2012	123.1	125.9	129.8	131.3	130.4	129.5	127.5	128.3	127.5	128.5	128.4	129.7	128.3
2013	128.1	130.8	134.7	135.3	135.0	134.3	133.6	133.6	132.7	133.0	134.0	134.4	133.3
2014	132.7	134.7	138.7	141.6	141.2	140.6	138.9	138.7	138.3	137.8	138.9	138.7	138.4
2015	138.2	142.0	146.7	147.5	146.9	145.6	143.8	143.3	143.5	144.7	146.7	146.4	144.6
2016	144.0	147.4	151.0	152.3	151.0	150.5	148.5	148.5	148.7	149.0	150.0	149.8	149.2
2017	148.7	151.9	155.7	155.8	155.3	154.7	153.0	153.2	148.7	153.6	154.1	154.0	153.2
2018	152.6	157.0	161.2	160.7	160.9	159.3	157.5	159.5	158.6	159.0	158.6	159.6	158.7
Other Services													
2010	41.6	42.0	42.1	42.2	42.3	42.5	42.0	41.7	41.4	42.1	41.7	41.8	42.0
2011	41.3	41.6	42.1	42.1	42.0	41.5	41.2	40.9	40.7	40.7	40.6	40.6	41.3
2012	40.4	40.7	41.1	41.2	41.2	41.2	40.9	40.9	41.1	41.2	41.4	41.5	41.1
2013	41.1	41.4	41.7	42.3	42.5	42.8	42.5	42.7	42.7	42.8	43.2	43.3	42.4
2014	43.0	43.5	43.8	43.6	43.5	43.6	43.4	43.3	43.2	43.2	43.1	43.2	43.4
2015	42.7	42.9	43.2	43.3	43.4	43.6	43.0	43.3	43.4	43.7	44.0	44.2	43.4
2016	44.2	44.4	44.5	44.8	44.9	45.2	44.9	45.2	45.6	45.8	45.8	45.8	45.1
2017	45.0	45.4	45.4	45.7	45.9	46.1	45.7	45.7	44.8	45.9	46.2	46.4	45.7
2018	46.0	46.6	46.9	46.9	47.1	47.2	46.8	46.8	46.6	47.5	47.6	46.8	46.9
Government													
2010	154.5	157.4	157.0	156.4	161.3	148.0	146.6	153.9	155.7	156.4	156.7	155.2	154.9
2011	154.9	157.4	157.1	156.3	154.5	144.3	142.6	151.8	155.2	155.4	155.0	155.1	153.3
2012	154.6	155.1	154.8	155.7	154.7	144.1	142.8	150.9	152.8	153.2	154.2	153.8	152.2
2013	154.3	155.5	155.4	155.4	153.5	143.1	141.9	150.9	152.7	154.7	155.0	154.4	152.2
2014	152.9	153.4	155.7	156.0	155.5	144.6	143.3	151.1	153.6	155.4	155.2	155.3	152.7
2015	153.8	155.6	155.3	156.0	155.1	144.4	143.7	152.0	153.6	157.2	157.8	156.0	153.4
2016	156.2	158.1	157.5	158.3	157.1	146.3	145.5	153.4	156.7	159.1	159.4	159.1	155.6
2017	157.8	160.3	159.7	159.4	157.4	148.6	145.3	153.5	156.8	159.2	159.2	159.2	156.4
2018	157.4	159.7	159.4	159.4	157.2	148.3	146.2	153.9	157.4	158.1	158.0	157.6	156.1

Employment by Industry: Denver-Aurora-Lakewood, CO, 2010–2018

(Numbers in thousands, not seasonally adjusted)

Industry and year	January	February	March	April	May	June	July	August	September	October	November	December	Annual average
Total Nonfarm													
2010	1,162.3	1,167.6	1,175.0	1,186.2	1,200.0	1,207.1	1,203.0	1,203.5	1,199.9	1,206.7	1,208.2	1,207.5	1,193.9
2011	1,180.9	1,184.4	1,192.1	1,208.4	1,218.0	1,227.0	1,219.5	1,224.4	1,225.2	1,226.5	1,231.4	1,233.2	1,214.3
2012	1,208.0	1,213.3	1,225.0	1,236.8	1,249.0	1,263.0	1,256.6	1,258.8	1,260.1	1,270.0	1,276.4	1,277.0	1,249.5
2013	1,251.1	1,260.0	1,270.2	1,282.1	1,294.7	1,307.1	1,302.9	1,310.6	1,309.4	1,318.5	1,324.0	1,323.9	1,296.2
2014	1,299.6	1,305.5	1,314.3	1,330.7	1,344.5	1,355.3	1,351.5	1,363.4	1,362.9	1,373.9	1,374.9	1,380.1	1,346.4
2015	1357	1365.1	1370.6	1384.9	1396.2	1408.9	1405.4	1411.1	1410.5	1416.4	1421.4	1424.3	1397.7
2016	1,399.0	1,405.4	1,411.8	1,425.9	1,431.8	1,445.3	1,444.4	1,447.5	1,445.9	1,448.7	1,451.6	1,451.4	1,434.1
2017	1,425.0	1,432.1	1,441.1	1,452.0	1,463.0	1,478.8	1,474.4	1,477.6	1,474.5	1,480.5	1,487.5	1,490.7	1,464.8
2018	1,464.3	1,471.0	1,480.4	1,493.1	1,502.5	1,519.0	1,516.1	1,518.1	1,508.1	1,513.5	1,510.1	1,516.0	1,501.0
Total Private													
2010	990.4	990.0	996.2	1,006.4	1,014.8	1,026.9	1,030.2	1,032.1	1,021.3	1,025.6	1,026.7	1,028.0	1,015.7
2011	1,007.0	1,005.1	1,012.1	1,027.0	1,035.1	1,046.5	1,047.9	1,053.0	1,046.6	1,046.3	1,050.9	1,053.7	1,035.9
2012	1,034.1	1,034.1	1,044.1	1,055.0	1,065.6	1,080.5	1,083.2	1,086.4	1,080.2	1,088.5	1,093.2	1,095.4	1,070.0
2013	1,074.9	1,078.0	1,087.0	1,097.5	1,109.1	1,123.0	1,127.1	1,133.5	1,123.9	1,129.8	1,135.6	1,137.5	1,113.1
2014	1,118.4	1,120.5	1,128.2	1,143.8	1,156.3	1,168.7	1,176.0	1,183.5	1,175.3	1,182.4	1,182.5	1,190.2	1,160.5
2015	1171.5	1175.4	1180.1	1192.7	1202.2	1216.8	1223	1225.2	1216.2	1221.5	1225.4	1229.4	1206.6
2016	1,208.4	1,210.4	1,215.8	1,228.6	1,234.3	1,248.2	1,256.9	1,256.3	1,248.6	1,250.8	1,251.8	1,253.2	1,238.6
2017	1,230.2	1,233.0	1,240.6	1,252.7	1,261.7	1,279.3	1,282.0	1,283.0	1,274.2	1,279.9	1,286.5	1,290.1	1,266.1
2018	1,267.5	1,270.2	1,278.0	1,289.3	1,296.9	1,313.7	1,317.2	1,316.9	1,304.3	1,310.7	1,307.7	1,314.6	1,298.9
Goods Producing													
2010	127.8	127.2	128.0	129.9	131.1	133.3	134.4	133.9	132.2	132.3	131.1	130.2	131.0
2011	126.1	125.4	127.5	130.6	131.0	133.9	134.9	135.5	134.8	134.7	134.1	132.8	131.8
2012	130.0	130.0	131.7	133.5	135.5	138.6	139.4	139.9	139.5	140.7	140.2	139.3	136.5
2013	136.6	137.3	139.2	140.3	143.4	146.4	147.4	148.7	147.7	149.0	149.2	148.5	144.5
2014	146.6	147.3	149.3	152.3	154.9	157.6	159.4	160.3	160.0	160.6	160.1	160.5	155.7
2015	157.8	158.6	159.5	160.8	162.3	164.8	165.6	165.4	164.8	165.3	164.8	164.3	162.8
2016	161.5	162.1	163.8	165.0	165.5	168.1	169.0	168.6	168.2	168.7	168.0	167.6	166.3
2017	164.2	165.4	167.2	168.3	169.5	173.0	173.8	174.4	173.8	174.8	174.6	174.2	171.1
2018	171.7	173.3	175.7	176.8	177.3	180.7	180.6	180.6	179.5	179.6	177.9	178.9	177.7
Service-Providing													
2010	1,034.5	1,040.4	1,047.0	1,056.3	1,068.9	1,073.8	1,068.6	1,069.6	1,067.7	1,074.4	1,077.1	1,077.3	1,063.0
2011	1,054.8	1,059.0	1,064.6	1,077.8	1,087.0	1,093.1	1,084.6	1,088.9	1,090.4	1,091.8	1,097.3	1,100.4	1,082.5
2012	1,078.0	1,083.3	1,093.3	1,103.3	1,113.5	1,124.4	1,117.2	1,118.9	1,120.6	1,129.3	1,136.2	1,137.7	1,113.0
2013	1,114.5	1,122.7	1,131.0	1,141.8	1,151.3	1,160.7	1,155.5	1,161.9	1,161.7	1,169.5	1,174.8	1,175.4	1,151.7
2014	1,153.0	1,158.2	1,165.0	1,178.4	1,189.6	1,197.7	1,192.1	1,203.1	1,202.9	1,213.3	1,214.8	1,219.6	1,190.6
2015	1199.2	1206.5	1211.1	1224.1	1233.9	1244.1	1239.8	1245.7	1245.7	1251.1	1256.6	1260.0	1,234.8
2016	1,237.5	1,243.3	1,248.0	1,260.9	1,266.3	1,277.2	1,275.4	1,278.9	1,277.7	1,280.0	1,283.6	1,283.8	1,267.7
2017	1,260.8	1,266.7	1,273.9	1,283.7	1,293.5	1,305.8	1,300.6	1,303.2	1,300.7	1,305.7	1,312.9	1,316.5	1,293.7
2018	1,292.6	1,297.7	1,304.7	1,316.3	1,325.2	1,338.3	1,335.5	1,337.5	1,328.6	1,333.9	1,332.2	1,337.1	1,323.3
Mining, Logging, and Construction													
2010	67.5	66.9	67.6	69.4	70.0	71.7	72.7	72.1	70.7	70.8	69.6	68.7	69.8
2011	64.9	64.3	66.0	68.8	68.9	71.4	72.3	72.7	72.0	72.3	71.6	70.4	69.6
2012	68.1	67.9	69.2	70.8	72.5	75.0	75.5	76.1	75.7	76.8	76.3	75.5	73.3
2013	73.3	73.9	75.4	76.7	79.6	82.1	83.2	84.4	83.6	85.0	85.1	84.3	80.6
2014	83.0	83.5	85.3	87.7	89.9	92.1	93.5	94.2	93.9	94.2	93.4	93.5	90.4
2015	91.2	91.8	92.4	93.5	94.6	96.3	96.9	96.7	96.2	96.8	95.9	95.4	94.8
2016	92.8	93.4	95.1	96.3	96.7	98.8	99.4	99.3	99.1	99.5	99.0	98.2	97.3
2017	95.8	96.9	98.5	99.6	100.5	103.2	104.1	104.9	104.6	105.8	105.6	104.9	102.0
2018	102.9	104.4	106.2	107.3	107.9	110.4	110.5	110.6	109.8	109.8	108.1	108.0	108.0
Manufacturing													
2010	60.3	60.3	60.4	60.5	61.1	61.6	61.7	61.8	61.5	61.5	61.5	61.5	61.1
2011	61.2	61.1	61.5	61.8	62.1	62.5	62.6	62.8	62.8	62.4	62.5	62.4	62.1
2012	61.9	62.1	62.5	62.7	63.0	63.6	63.9	63.8	63.8	63.9	63.9	63.8	63.2
2013	63.3	63.4	63.8	63.6	63.8	64.3	64.2	64.3	64.1	64.0	64.1	64.2	63.9
2014	63.6	63.8	64.0	64.6	65.0	65.5	65.9	66.1	66.1	66.4	66.7	67.0	65.4
2015	66.6	66.8	67.1	67.3	67.7	68.5	68.7	68.7	68.6	68.5	68.9	68.9	68
2016	68.7	68.7	68.7	68.7	68.8	69.3	69.6	69.3	69.1	69.2	69.0	69.4	69.0
2017	68.4	68.5	68.7	68.7	69.0	69.8	69.7	69.5	69.2	69.0	69.0	69.3	69.1
2018	68.8	68.9	69.5	69.5	69.4	70.3	70.1	70.0	69.7	69.8	69.8	70.9	69.7

Employment by Industry: Denver-Aurora-Lakewood, CO, 2010–2018—*Continued*

(Numbers in thousands, not seasonally adjusted)

Industry and year	January	February	March	April	May	June	July	August	September	October	November	December	Annual average
Trade, Transportation, and Utilities													
2010	224.9	223.8	224.0	224.9	226.4	228.1	228.7	229.1	227.6	229.5	232.8	235.2	227.9
2011	226.3	224.5	225.3	227.4	228.8	230.0	230.8	231.2	229.9	231.6	236.0	238.0	230.0
2012	230.9	228.9	229.8	231.0	232.7	234.9	235.6	235.6	235.5	238.3	243.9	246.4	235.3
2013	238.1	236.7	237.6	238.4	240.4	242.0	242.9	244.4	243.3	244.9	250.2	253.1	242.7
2014	245.2	244.3	244.7	246.3	248.1	250.6	250.8	251.7	250.2	252.5	257.5	261.3	250.3
2015	253.4	252.2	252.5	253.7	254.6	257.1	258.4	258.7	257	259.8	264.5	268.2	257.5
2016	259.5	258.0	258.1	259.1	260.1	261.5	263.1	262.9	261.6	263.3	268.2	272.2	262.3
2017	264.3	262.5	262.4	263.2	264.1	266.4	267.0	267.3	266.4	268.9	275.9	279.5	267.3
2018	271.5	268.4	268.8	269.1	270.4	272.4	273.6	274.2	272.7	274.6	280.2	282.9	273.2
Wholesale Trade													
2010	60.8	60.6	60.7	60.9	61.0	61.4	61.6	61.6	61.4	61.6	61.6	61.7	61.2
2011	61.2	61.3	61.6	61.9	62.1	62.3	62.5	62.6	62.4	62.3	62.3	62.3	62.1
2012	61.9	62.1	62.5	62.9	63.1	63.6	63.9	64.0	63.9	64.2	64.2	64.6	63.4
2013	63.8	64.2	64.5	64.6	64.9	65.4	65.4	65.6	65.4	65.6	65.8	65.9	65.1
2014	65.6	66.1	66.3	66.8	67.1	67.5	68.0	68.4	68.1	68.6	68.9	69.3	67.6
2015	68.7	69.1	69.2	69.2	69.5	69.8	70.1	70.4	70.1	70.7	70.8	70.9	69.9
2016	70.5	70.6	70.7	71.0	70.9	70.9	71.4	71.2	71.2	71.2	71.3	71.4	71.0
2017	71.2	71.4	71.7	71.7	71.8	72.3	72.5	72.6	72.5	72.6	72.5	72.6	72.1
2018	72.4	72.6	72.7	72.8	73.0	73.5	73.9	73.7	73.4	73.3	74.0	73.3	73.2
Retail Trade													
2010	117.9	116.7	117.1	118.2	119.6	120.8	121.4	121.7	120.4	121.7	124.7	125.9	120.5
2011	119.4	117.9	118.4	119.9	121.0	121.9	122.2	122.7	121.9	123.2	127.1	128.4	122.0
2012	122.7	120.4	121.1	121.8	123.3	124.6	124.7	124.6	124.5	125.7	130.6	131.9	124.7
2013	125.3	123.6	124.0	124.7	126.3	127.5	128.3	129.2	128.3	129.3	133.6	135.4	128.0
2014	128.8	127.4	127.9	128.7	129.8	131.6	131.5	131.8	130.7	132.3	136.2	138.4	131.3
2015	131.8	130.6	131.4	132.2	133.2	135.1	135.6	135.9	134.5	136.5	140.3	142.2	134.9
2016	135.3	134.2	134.7	135.0	136.0	137.3	137.7	137.4	136.0	137.6	141.5	143.3	137.2
2017	137.0	135.3	135.6	136.5	137.0	138.3	138.5	138.4	136.7	138.3	143.4	145.0	138.3
2018	139.5	137.1	137.3	137.4	138.4	139.2	140.0	139.7	137.7	138.6	142.7	143.2	139.2
Transportation and Utilities													
2010	46.2	46.5	46.2	45.8	45.8	45.9	45.7	45.8	45.8	46.2	46.5	47.6	46.2
2011	45.7	45.3	45.3	45.6	45.7	45.8	46.1	45.9	45.6	46.1	46.6	47.3	45.9
2012	46.3	46.4	46.2	46.3	46.3	46.7	47.0	47.0	47.1	48.4	49.1	49.9	47.2
2013	49.0	48.9	49.1	49.1	49.2	49.1	49.2	49.6	49.6	50.0	50.8	51.8	49.6
2014	50.8	50.8	50.5	50.8	51.2	51.5	51.3	51.5	51.4	51.6	52.4	53.6	51.5
2015	52.9	52.5	51.9	52.3	51.9	52.2	52.7	52.4	52.4	52.6	53.4	55.1	52.7
2016	53.7	53.2	52.7	53.1	53.2	53.3	54.0	54.3	54.4	54.5	55.4	57.5	54.1
2017	56.1	55.8	55.1	55.0	55.3	55.8	56.0	56.3	57.2	58.0	60.0	61.9	56.9
2018	59.6	58.7	58.8	58.9	59.0	59.7	59.7	60.8	61.6	62.7	63.5	66.4	60.8
Information													
2010	43.9	43.7	43.7	43.4	43.5	43.8	43.8	43.8	43.7	43.8	44.2	44.2	43.8
2011	44.0	44.0	43.6	43.9	43.8	43.8	43.6	43.6	43.5	43.4	43.5	43.4	43.7
2012	43.3	43.4	43.4	43.2	43.3	43.5	43.3	43.3	43.3	43.4	43.6	43.7	43.4
2013	43.8	44.2	44.2	44.2	44.4	44.9	45.0	44.9	44.5	44.4	44.7	44.7	44.5
2014	44.8	45.0	44.9	44.9	45.0	45.7	46.3	46.2	45.2	45.3	45.2	45.6	45.3
2015	45.6	45.9	46	45.8	46	46.4	46.7	46.6	46.1	45.8	46.1	46.3	46.1
2016	45.9	46.3	46.3	46.5	46.6	47.1	47.5	47.4	46.6	46.7	46.9	46.9	46.7
2017	46.5	46.4	46.5	46.4	46.7	47.5	47.6	47.7	47.5	48.0	48.7	48.9	47.4
2018	49.3	49.5	49.6	50.1	50.2	50.8	50.9	50.4	50.1	49.9	49.9	49.8	50.0
Financial Activities													
2010	90.5	90.4	90.4	90.5	90.5	90.9	91.2	91.2	90.8	91.0	90.9	91.4	90.8
2011	90.2	90.1	90.1	90.2	90.3	90.9	90.9	91.1	90.9	90.7	91.1	91.7	90.7
2012	90.7	90.8	91.3	91.5	92.0	92.8	93.0	93.4	93.2	94.1	94.1	94.9	92.7
2013	93.9	94.5	94.9	95.3	95.6	96.5	96.7	96.9	96.6	96.8	96.9	97.1	96.0
2014	95.7	96.0	96.2	96.8	97.5	97.9	98.6	99.0	98.7	99.5	99.9	100.7	98.0
2015	99.7	100.2	100.6	101	101.8	102.7	103.5	103.8	103.4	104	104.3	104.7	102.5
2016	104.2	104.3	104.5	105.0	105.4	106.3	107.0	107.0	106.7	107.2	107.4	107.7	106.1
2017	106.9	107.4	107.6	108.2	108.7	109.5	109.5	109.6	109.1	109.9	109.9	110.5	108.9
2018	109.4	109.8	110.1	110.6	111.1	111.8	111.9	111.7	111.2	109.9	109.0	109.6	110.5

Employment by Industry: Denver-Aurora-Lakewood, CO, 2010–2018—*Continued*

(Numbers in thousands, not seasonally adjusted)

Industry and year	January	February	March	April	May	June	July	August	September	October	November	December	Annual average
Professional and Business Services													
2010	197.1	198.0	200.0	203.4	205.1	207.4	208.3	208.7	205.5	207.4	207.3	206.5	204.6
2011	204.2	204.4	205.2	210.6	212.5	213.8	214.3	215.9	214.8	215.1	216.7	217.0	212.0
2012	212.5	213.4	216.2	220.1	222.1	225.4	226.3	227.9	226.6	229.3	229.2	228.3	223.1
2013	223.9	225.5	227.6	230.9	232.5	235.3	236.0	237.9	235.6	237.7	237.5	237.2	233.1
2014	232.3	233.0	234.6	238.8	240.5	243.3	245.1	248.6	247.0	249.5	246.9	247.8	242.3
2015	243.5	244.8	245.7	249.2	250.9	253.1	254.6	255.8	253.8	255.5	254.5	254.4	251.3
2016	249.7	250.6	251.6	256.0	256.1	259.0	262.0	261.7	260.5	261.5	261.0	259.7	257.5
2017	254.1	255.6	257.7	261.4	262.6	266.0	267.5	267.9	266.5	268.1	268.2	266.9	263.5
2018	261.3	263.5	264.9	269.4	270.6	273.6	276.9	276.6	273.9	278.0	277.2	277.0	271.9
Education and Health Services													
2010	139.6	140.9	141.7	142.1	142.7	142.7	142.2	143.0	143.4	144.5	145.5	145.7	142.8
2011	144.8	145.9	146.4	147.0	147.5	147.4	146.9	148.4	148.8	150.0	150.5	151.9	148.0
2012	150.6	152.0	152.5	152.8	153.0	152.8	152.7	153.2	153.7	155.3	156.0	156.9	153.5
2013	155.8	157.2	157.7	159.1	159.1	158.8	159.2	160.4	161.1	162.8	164.1	164.6	160.0
2014	163.1	164.7	165.4	167.4	167.9	167.0	167.1	168.5	169.2	171.4	172.1	172.7	168.0
2015	172.6	174.3	174.7	176.7	176.9	176.4	176.8	177.5	177.8	180.3	181.2	181.3	177.2
2016	180.0	181.2	181.6	183.6	183.3	182.6	183.0	183.2	183.5	183.5	183.2	183.0	182.6
2017	181.3	182.2	182.9	185.7	186.2	186.0	185.6	186.1	185.2	186.3	186.8	187.2	185.1
2018	185.4	187.3	187.7	188.5	188.9	188.7	188.3	189.0	188.4	191.5	190.6	191.5	188.8
Leisure and Hospitality													
2010	119.5	119.1	121.4	125.3	128.2	132.9	133.6	134.3	130.6	129.8	127.4	127.4	127.5
2011	124.0	123.5	126.4	129.2	132.7	137.7	137.6	138.1	135.2	132.4	130.6	130.3	131.5
2012	127.5	127.0	130.2	133.7	137.6	142.3	142.7	142.8	138.4	137.2	136.2	136.0	136.0
2013	132.7	132.9	135.7	139.0	142.7	147.9	148.6	149.0	144.3	143.4	142.1	141.5	141.7
2014	139.2	139.0	141.8	145.4	150.1	153.7	155.1	155.4	152.0	149.9	147.5	148.5	148.1
2015	145.6	146.3	147.7	152	156	161.9	162.6	162.6	158.9	156.4	155.8	155.8	155.1
2016	153.1	153.2	155.0	158.3	161.8	167.2	168.6	168.6	164.8	163.0	160.6	160.1	161.2
2017	157.5	157.5	160.1	163.3	167.3	173.6	173.9	172.8	168.9	167.1	165.5	165.9	166.1
2018	162.6	161.8	164.1	167.6	170.5	177.1	176.7	176.1	170.4	168.0	163.9	165.1	168.7
Other Services													
2010	47.1	46.9	47.0	46.9	47.3	47.8	48.0	48.1	47.5	47.3	47.5	47.4	47.4
2011	47.4	47.3	47.6	48.1	48.5	49.0	48.9	49.2	48.7	48.4	48.4	48.6	48.3
2012	48.6	48.6	49.0	49.2	49.4	50.2	50.2	50.3	50.0	50.2	50.0	49.9	49.6
2013	50.1	49.7	50.1	50.3	51.0	51.2	51.3	51.3	50.8	50.8	50.9	50.8	50.7
2014	51.5	51.2	51.3	51.9	52.3	52.9	53.6	53.8	53.0	53.7	53.3	53.1	52.6
2015	53.3	53.1	53.4	53.5	53.7	54.4	54.8	54.8	54.4	54.4	54.2	54.4	54.0
2016	54.5	54.7	54.9	55.1	55.5	56.4	56.7	56.9	56.7	56.9	56.5	56.0	55.9
2017	55.4	56.0	56.2	56.2	56.6	57.3	57.1	57.2	56.8	56.8	56.9	57.0	56.6
2018	56.3	56.6	57.1	57.2	57.9	58.6	58.3	58.3	58.1	59.2	59.0	59.8	58.0
Government													
2010	171.9	177.6	178.8	179.8	185.2	180.2	172.8	171.4	178.6	181.1	181.5	179.5	178.2
2011	173.9	179.3	180.0	181.4	182.9	180.5	171.6	171.4	178.6	180.2	180.5	179.5	178.3
2012	173.9	179.2	180.9	181.8	183.4	182.5	173.4	172.4	179.9	181.5	183.2	181.6	179.5
2013	176.2	182.0	183.2	184.6	185.6	184.1	175.8	177.1	185.5	188.7	188.4	186.4	183.1
2014	181.2	185.0	186.1	186.9	188.2	186.6	175.5	179.9	187.6	191.5	192.4	189.9	185.9
2015	185.5	189.7	190.5	192.2	194.0	192.1	182.4	185.9	194.3	194.9	196.0	194.9	191.0
2016	190.6	195.0	196.0	197.3	197.5	197.1	187.5	191.2	197.3	197.9	199.8	198.2	195.5
2017	194.8	199.1	200.5	199.3	201.3	199.5	192.4	194.6	200.3	200.6	201.0	200.6	198.7
2018	196.8	200.8	202.4	203.8	205.6	205.3	198.9	201.2	203.8	202.8	202.4	201.4	202.1

Employment by Industry: St. Louis, MO, 2010–2018

(Numbers in thousands, not seasonally adjusted)

Industry and year	January	February	March	April	May	June	July	August	September	October	November	December	Annual average
Total Nonfarm													
2010	1,258.9	1,264.5	1,275.6	1,288.4	1,297.2	1,293.8	1,270.7	1,283.0	1,288.8	1,296.6	1,295.5	1,293.3	1,283.9
2011	1,269.5	1,272.1	1,285.2	1,306.3	1,311.4	1,307.4	1,288.0	1,296.6	1,304.7	1,305.8	1,304.3	1,304.8	1,296.3
2012	1,273.0	1,278.5	1,290.7	1,303.1	1,311.1	1,307.6	1,283.6	1,292.8	1,300.5	1,307.4	1,307.7	1,309.8	1,297.2
2013	1,278.9	1,285.8	1,292.8	1,310.0	1,320.3	1,316.3	1,295.8	1,305.2	1,313.8	1,319.9	1,320.6	1,322.2	1,306.8
2014	1,284.8	1,295.0	1,304.1	1,328.7	1,336.5	1,331.9	1,311.8	1,322.3	1,328.7	1,343.4	1,342.2	1,343.3	1,322.7
2015	1,312.2	1,317.9	1,324.1	1,346.7	1,359.0	1,358.0	1,340.8	1,348.9	1,357.7	1,369.2	1,370.4	1,371.4	1,348.0
2016	1,333.7	1,342.2	1,350.1	1,371.9	1,377.6	1,377.3	1,356.5	1,366.1	1,376.1	1,382.8	1,382.0	1,378.5	1,366.2
2017	1,349.2	1,361.4	1,366.4	1,383.4	1,390.4	1,395.3	1,373.0	1,379.3	1,386.3	1,390.2	1,393.4	1,391.7	1,380.0
2018	1,357.5	1,367.1	1,373.5	1,386.0	1,393.1	1,396.1	1,378.5	1,385.7	1,390.6	1,396.8	1,399.6	1,398.7	1,385.3
Total Private													
2010	1,089.4	1,092.2	1,103.2	1,113.8	1,118.7	1,126.2	1,125.6	1,126.8	1,120.5	1,126.5	1,125.2	1,123.7	1,116.0
2011	1,103.1	1,104.0	1,116.4	1,136.3	1,140.7	1,145.4	1,146.1	1,146.2	1,137.7	1,138.5	1,137.0	1,137.4	1,132.4
2012	1,110.1	1,112.8	1,124.1	1,135.5	1,142.6	1,147.6	1,144.1	1,144.8	1,137.0	1,142.8	1,143.2	1,145.0	1,135.8
2013	1,118.5	1,122.4	1,128.7	1,141.3	1,151.0	1,155.5	1,156.2	1,157.1	1,149.9	1,154.9	1,155.1	1,156.5	1,145.6
2014	1,123.7	1,130.6	1,139.1	1,164.7	1,171.8	1,175.6	1,176.1	1,178.3	1,169.4	1,180.6	1,180.2	1,181.0	1,164.3
2015	1,154.9	1,157.0	1,163.0	1,185.3	1,196.6	1,200.5	1,204.2	1,203.9	1,197.1	1,205.5	1,207.0	1,207.8	1,190.2
2016	1,175.8	1,180.8	1,188.5	1,209.9	1,214.2	1,218.8	1,219.4	1,220.3	1,214.5	1,220.3	1,219.4	1,215.6	1,208.1
2017	1,192.0	1,201.0	1,206.1	1,223.4	1,230.0	1,237.8	1,236.8	1,239.0	1,230.6	1,233.5	1,237.4	1,236.2	1,225.3
2018	1,207.2	1,213.7	1,220.2	1,232.8	1,239.8	1,245.4	1,248.0	1,246.8	1,236.8	1,241.8	1,244.0	1,243.6	1,235.0
Goods Producing													
2010	161.3	160.4	163.9	166.2	166.9	170.7	170.9	170.6	170.2	171.1	169.7	168.2	167.5
2011	165.3	165.4	169.3	172.6	173.9	176.2	177.1	176.2	174.0	171.7	169.3	168.2	171.6
2012	162.2	161.8	164.4	166.6	168.6	170.8	171.4	171.3	169.4	169.2	167.5	167.0	167.5
2013	162.3	162.9	163.8	166.5	169.4	173.0	173.4	173.0	171.8	171.5	169.9	168.0	168.8
2014	161.5	163.4	166.7	170.1	172.6	175.4	176.6	176.5	176.1	176.0	174.1	173.4	171.9
2015	168.4	168.3	170.5	174.3	177.2	179.4	180.7	180.7	180.2	180.5	178.6	179.3	176.5
2016	173.9	173.4	175.9	178.9	179.9	183.2	183.1	182.8	182.4	183.3	182.6	181.7	180.1
2017	176.2	177.9	178.6	180.1	181.6	184.8	184.2	184.5	183.3	182.9	182.0	182.4	181.5
2018	176.1	178.3	180.4	181.9	184.1	187.0	187.3	187.2	187.0	189.2	186.9	187.4	184.4
Service-Providing													
2010	1,097.6	1,104.1	1,111.7	1,122.2	1,130.3	1,123.1	1,099.8	1,112.4	1,118.6	1,125.5	1,125.8	1,125.1	1,116.4
2011	1,104.2	1,106.7	1,115.9	1,133.7	1,137.5	1,131.2	1,110.9	1,120.4	1,130.7	1,134.1	1,135.0	1,136.6	1,124.7
2012	1,110.8	1,116.7	1,126.3	1,136.5	1,142.5	1,136.8	1,112.2	1,121.5	1,131.1	1,138.2	1,140.2	1,142.8	1,129.6
2013	1,116.6	1,122.9	1,129.0	1,143.5	1,150.9	1,143.3	1,122.4	1,132.2	1,142.0	1,148.4	1,150.7	1,154.2	1,138.0
2014	1,123.3	1,131.6	1,137.4	1,158.6	1,163.9	1,156.5	1,135.2	1,145.8	1,152.6	1,167.4	1,168.1	1,169.9	1,150.9
2015	1,143.8	1,149.6	1,153.6	1,172.4	1,181.8	1,178.6	1,160.1	1,168.2	1,177.5	1,188.7	1,191.8	1,192.1	1,171.5
2016	1,159.8	1,168.8	1,174.2	1,193.0	1,197.7	1,194.1	1,173.4	1,183.3	1,193.7	1,199.5	1,199.4	1,196.8	1,186.1
2017	1,173.0	1,183.5	1,187.8	1,203.3	1,208.8	1,210.5	1,188.8	1,194.8	1,203.0	1,207.3	1,211.4	1,209.3	1,198.5
2018	1,181.4	1,188.8	1,193.1	1,204.1	1,209.0	1,209.1	1,191.2	1,198.5	1,203.6	1,207.6	1,212.7	1,211.3	1,200.9
Mining, Logging, and Construction													
2010	54.9	53.9	57.1	59.2	59.5	62.2	62.5	62.2	61.8	61.8	60.4	58.4	59.5
2011	56.5	56.5	59.8	62.9	63.9	65.2	65.4	64.7	62.7	60.5	58.6	57.0	61.1
2012	51.9	51.4	53.5	55.7	57.3	58.8	59.6	60.0	59.5	58.9	57.5	56.9	56.8
2013	52.3	52.4	53.6	56.4	59.0	61.7	62.9	62.2	61.3	60.6	59.1	57.1	58.2
2014	52.9	52.1	55.8	58.3	59.8	61.4	62.5	62.5	62.4	62.2	60.5	59.6	59.2
2015	55.5	55.3	57.4	60.8	63.0	64.0	64.8	65.6	65.4	66.1	64.4	64.7	62.3
2016	60.9	59.4	62.1	65.1	66.0	68.3	68.1	68.1	68.0	68.4	67.9	66.9	65.8
2017	62.8	63.6	64.6	65.8	67.0	68.8	68.8	68.9	68.2	68.0	67.1	66.7	66.7
2018	61.1	62.3	64.7	65.8	67.6	69.3	69.6	69.5	69.4	70.0	67.3	67.3	67.0
Manufacturing													
2010	106.4	106.5	106.8	107.0	107.4	108.5	108.4	108.4	108.4	109.3	109.3	109.8	108.0
2011	108.8	108.9	109.5	109.7	110.0	111.0	111.7	111.5	111.3	111.2	110.7	111.2	110.5
2012	110.3	110.4	110.9	110.9	111.3	112.0	111.8	111.3	109.9	110.3	110.0	110.1	110.8
2013	110.0	110.5	110.2	110.1	110.4	111.3	110.5	110.8	110.5	110.9	110.8	110.9	110.6
2014	108.6	111.3	110.9	111.8	112.8	114.0	114.1	114.0	113.7	113.8	113.6	113.8	112.7
2015	112.9	113.0	113.1	113.5	114.2	115.4	115.9	115.1	114.8	114.4	114.2	114.6	114.3
2016	113.0	114.0	113.8	113.8	113.9	114.9	115.0	114.7	114.4	114.9	114.7	114.8	114.3
2017	113.4	114.3	114.0	114.3	114.6	116.0	115.4	115.6	115.1	114.9	114.9	115.7	114.9
2018	115.0	116.0	115.7	116.1	116.5	117.7	117.7	117.7	117.6	119.2	119.6	120.1	117.4

Employment by Industry: St. Louis, MO, 2010–2018—*Continued*

(Numbers in thousands, not seasonally adjusted)

Industry and year	January	February	March	April	May	June	July	August	September	October	November	December	Annual average
Trade, Transportation, and Utilities													
2010	238.6	236.2	237.8	238.4	240.0	240.2	238.9	240.3	238.9	239.9	243.5	246.3	239.9
2011	239.5	237.7	239.0	241.8	242.8	242.7	241.8	242.7	241.6	242.0	246.6	248.8	242.3
2012	240.6	238.5	240.0	242.0	243.5	243.4	242.5	243.7	243.4	245.3	250.6	252.4	243.8
2013	242.5	239.8	240.2	242.5	244.2	244.5	243.8	245.4	244.6	246.8	252.0	255.3	245.1
2014	244.7	242.7	244.1	246.6	248.3	249.6	248.1	249.4	248.5	251.1	256.6	259.7	249.1
2015	249.1	246.7	248.0	249.8	251.9	252.5	252.3	253.3	252.5	254.6	259.6	262.5	252.7
2016	252.5	250.9	251.7	253.9	255.0	254.4	255.2	254.4	253.7	254.6	259.4	262.1	254.8
2017	253.3	251.7	252.5	255.3	256.2	256.8	258.1	259.2	259.8	260.5	266.9	269.5	258.3
2018	259.8	257.6	258.1	258.6	260.5	260.1	260.0	260.0	259.2	259.5	266.4	267.7	260.6
Wholesale Trade													
2010	58.0	57.9	58.3	60.0	60.0	60.0	59.7	59.3	59.0	59.0	58.8	59.0	59.1
2011	58.6	58.6	58.7	59.0	59.1	59.5	59.8	59.7	59.4	59.4	59.5	59.5	59.2
2012	59.1	59.2	59.5	60.1	60.4	60.8	60.6	60.9	60.4	60.5	60.4	60.6	60.2
2013	59.5	59.4	59.5	59.8	60.3	60.6	60.6	60.7	60.5	60.9	61.1	61.3	60.4
2014	60.5	60.6	60.8	61.2	61.5	61.9	62.1	62.1	61.5	61.6	61.8	61.9	61.5
2015	60.8	60.6	60.8	60.4	60.9	61.1	62.0	61.3	60.9	61.0	61.1	61.2	61.0
2016	60.6	60.5	60.3	60.9	61.0	61.3	62.1	61.2	61.6	60.6	60.7	60.8	61.0
2017	60.5	60.7	60.7	60.8	61.2	61.7	62.1	61.6	62.0	62.2	62.6	63.2	61.6
2018	62.3	62.3	62.4	62.7	63.1	63.3	63.8	63.3	63.3	63.4	64.4	64.3	63.2
Retail Trade													
2010	135.3	133.2	134.3	134.9	136.3	137.5	136.9	136.9	135.4	136.3	140.0	142.1	136.6
2011	136.7	134.8	135.7	137.7	138.3	138.9	138.6	138.4	137.0	137.5	141.9	143.4	138.2
2012	137.2	134.9	136.0	136.9	137.6	138.3	137.9	137.2	136.9	138.7	143.7	144.5	138.3
2013	137.7	135.3	135.4	137.0	138.1	139.3	138.7	138.8	137.8	139.7	144.2	146.4	139.0
2014	138.2	136.2	137.3	138.9	139.9	141.6	140.7	140.6	139.4	141.4	146.2	147.9	140.7
2015	140.2	138.3	139.3	141.0	142.2	143.7	142.9	143.4	142.2	144.3	148.4	150.0	143.0
2016	142.6	141.4	142.1	143.3	144.1	144.5	144.6	143.7	141.9	143.6	147.7	148.9	144.0
2017	142.6	140.9	141.8	142.7	142.9	143.7	143.6	143.1	141.3	142.7	147.2	148.1	143.4
2018	141.8	140.0	140.5	141.2	142.5	142.6	142.6	142.0	140.6	141.1	145.7	146.0	142.2
Transportation and Utilities													
2010	45.3	45.1	45.2	43.5	43.7	42.7	42.3	44.1	44.5	44.6	44.7	45.2	44.2
2011	44.2	44.3	44.6	45.1	45.4	44.3	43.4	44.6	45.2	45.1	45.2	45.9	44.8
2012	44.3	44.4	44.5	45.0	45.5	44.3	44.0	45.6	46.1	46.1	46.5	47.3	45.3
2013	45.3	45.1	45.3	45.7	45.8	44.6	44.5	45.9	46.3	46.2	46.7	47.6	45.8
2014	46.0	45.9	46.0	46.5	46.9	46.1	45.3	46.7	47.6	48.1	48.6	49.9	47.0
2015	48.1	47.8	47.9	48.4	48.8	47.7	47.4	48.6	49.4	49.3	50.1	51.3	48.7
2016	49.3	49.0	49.3	49.7	49.9	48.6	48.5	49.5	50.2	50.4	51.0	52.4	49.8
2017	50.2	50.1	50.0	51.8	52.1	51.4	52.4	54.5	56.5	55.6	57.1	58.2	53.3
2018	55.7	55.3	55.2	54.7	54.9	54.2	53.6	54.7	55.3	55.0	56.3	57.4	55.2
Information													
2010	29.8	29.6	29.6	31.6	31.3	31.8	31.4	31.4	31.1	30.9	30.8	31.0	30.9
2011	30.4	30.3	30.1	30.9	31.1	31.3	31.6	31.5	31.3	30.9	30.9	30.8	30.9
2012	30.6	30.5	30.4	30.0	30.2	30.2	30.3	30.1	29.7	29.3	29.2	29.2	30.0
2013	29.1	29.2	29.2	29.1	29.4	29.4	29.3	29.2	28.9	28.8	28.7	28.9	29.1
2014	28.2	28.1	28.3	28.6	28.9	29.2	29.3	29.2	28.9	28.6	28.7	28.7	28.7
2015	28.6	28.6	28.6	28.7	28.8	29.0	29.0	28.9	28.5	28.4	28.4	28.6	28.7
2016	28.5	28.4	28.5	28.6	28.8	28.9	28.8	28.8	28.6	28.3	28.2	28.2	28.6
2017	28.1	27.9	27.9	27.9	28.2	28.3	28.4	28.4	28.0	27.8	27.8	28.0	28.1
2018	27.8	27.9	28.0	28.1	28.2	28.3	28.2	27.9	27.7	27.4	27.9	27.6	27.9

Employment by Industry: St. Louis, MO, 2010–2018—*Continued*

(Numbers in thousands, not seasonally adjusted)

Industry and year	January	February	March	April	May	June	July	August	September	October	November	December	Annual average
Financial Activities													
2010	79.0	79.0	79.1	80.4	80.5	81.0	81.8	81.8	81.4	82.3	82.2	82.2	80.9
2011	81.3	81.2	81.4	82.7	82.9	82.8	83.7	83.9	83.4	84.0	84.1	84.2	83.0
2012	83.6	84.0	84.6	85.1	85.4	85.7	85.9	86.1	85.7	86.7	87.0	86.9	85.6
2013	84.8	85.1	85.3	85.5	86.3	86.8	86.9	86.8	86.3	86.7	86.8	86.5	86.2
2014	85.5	85.6	85.5	85.9	86.3	86.4	86.8	86.7	86.0	86.4	86.7	86.7	86.2
2015	85.7	85.6	85.7	86.3	86.8	87.3	87.7	87.6	86.7	87.2	87.4	87.5	86.8
2016	86.2	86.2	86.3	86.5	86.8	87.1	87.5	87.4	87.1	87.6	87.6	87.8	87.0
2017	87.4	87.6	88.0	88.4	88.8	89.5	89.7	89.6	89.0	89.0	88.7	88.9	88.7
2018	89.0	89.1	88.9	89.3	89.4	90.0	91.2	90.8	90.3	90.5	91.1	90.6	90.0
Professional and Business Services													
2010	179.0	181.1	182.5	187.8	187.2	188.1	189.1	189.4	188.3	190.1	189.8	189.0	186.8
2011	187.1	187.9	190.0	194.2	192.6	192.9	192.6	192.2	191.4	191.7	191.5	190.8	191.2
2012	186.4	187.2	189.1	193.3	192.8	193.9	191.6	191.5	190.7	192.3	192.9	193.0	191.2
2013	189.5	191.3	194.1	197.8	198.3	199.0	200.0	201.1	200.4	201.7	202.0	202.7	198.2
2014	197.0	198.9	201.0	206.1	204.9	205.6	203.3	204.5	204.3	206.2	205.7	206.0	203.6
2015	200.7	202.1	203.5	207.0	208.0	207.5	208.9	209.6	209.1	210.1	210.8	210.7	207.3
2016	205.3	207.3	208.4	213.6	212.8	213.2	212.1	213.1	212.2	213.5	212.6	210.7	211.2
2017	207.0	209.0	210.9	213.6	212.9	214.7	213.8	214.7	213.4	214.1	215.2	212.3	212.6
2018	208.9	210.3	212.1	214.5	214.1	216.1	216.6	217.4	215.5	217.0	216.4	213.9	214.4
Education and Health Services													
2010	220.5	223.4	223.8	224.9	224.8	223.7	222.2	222.3	225.3	229.0	229.7	229.3	224.9
2011	227.4	229.9	230.3	231.7	231.3	229.7	229.6	229.7	232.9	235.1	236.6	236.6	231.7
2012	234.3	237.4	237.7	234.1	233.0	230.8	230.7	230.4	233.6	235.6	235.6	236.1	234.1
2013	233.1	236.8	236.0	232.9	230.9	227.6	228.0	227.7	229.9	232.4	233.0	232.1	231.7
2014	229.3	233.9	231.6	236.6	234.2	230.6	232.9	232.7	234.6	239.6	240.3	238.2	234.5
2015	238.1	240.5	238.5	244.7	243.1	240.5	242.6	241.5	243.0	248.1	248.4	246.2	242.9
2016	242.9	247.3	246.3	249.7	247.7	244.1	246.6	247.3	249.0	252.8	252.8	250.5	248.1
2017	248.7	253.1	250.9	256.0	255.0	250.9	251.8	251.9	253.4	257.3	257.7	256.4	253.6
2018	251.5	256.2	253.7	257.7	255.5	250.9	253.1	252.3	253.3	256.5	256.1	256.0	254.4
Leisure and Hospitality													
2010	127.3	128.5	131.9	139.1	142.5	145.0	145.7	145.4	140.5	138.0	134.3	132.5	137.6
2011	127.7	127.2	131.3	136.4	140.0	143.0	142.9	143.5	137.0	137.3	132.3	132.2	135.9
2012	127.4	128.3	132.4	139.0	143.2	146.5	145.5	145.7	139.2	139.1	135.2	135.3	138.1
2013	131.8	131.9	134.5	141.5	146.4	148.4	148.3	147.3	142.3	140.9	136.6	136.8	140.6
2014	131.7	131.9	135.2	143.5	148.9	150.4	150.6	151.2	143.9	145.6	141.4	141.4	143.0
2015	137.7	138.3	140.8	146.9	153.0	155.6	154.6	154.4	150.0	149.1	146.4	145.4	147.7
2016	139.5	140.2	144.1	150.8	154.8	158.0	156.0	156.3	152.0	150.3	146.0	144.2	149.4
2017	141.0	143.1	145.9	150.5	155.6	160.0	158.1	158.3	152.4	150.7	148.2	147.5	150.9
2018	143.6	143.9	148.0	151.8	156.9	160.8	159.5	159.4	153.2	151.2	149.3	150.5	152.3
Other Services													
2010	53.9	54.0	54.6	45.4	45.5	45.7	45.6	45.6	44.8	45.2	45.2	45.2	47.6
2011	44.4	44.4	45.0	46.0	46.1	46.8	46.8	46.5	46.1	45.8	45.7	45.8	45.8
2012	45.0	45.1	45.5	45.4	45.9	46.3	46.2	46.0	45.3	45.3	45.2	45.1	45.5
2013	45.4	45.4	45.6	45.5	46.1	46.8	46.5	46.6	45.7	46.1	46.1	46.2	46.0
2014	45.8	46.1	46.7	47.3	47.7	48.4	48.5	48.1	47.1	47.1	46.7	46.9	47.2
2015	46.6	46.9	47.4	47.6	47.8	48.7	48.4	47.9	47.1	47.5	47.4	47.6	47.6
2016	47.0	47.1	47.3	47.9	48.4	49.9	50.1	50.2	49.5	49.9	50.2	50.4	49.0
2017	50.3	50.7	51.4	51.6	51.7	52.8	52.7	52.4	51.3	51.2	50.9	51.2	51.5
2018	50.5	50.4	51.0	50.9	51.1	52.2	52.1	51.8	50.6	50.5	49.9	49.9	50.9
Government													
2010	169.5	172.3	172.4	174.6	178.5	167.6	145.1	156.2	168.3	170.1	170.3	169.6	167.9
2011	166.4	168.1	168.8	170.0	170.7	162.0	141.9	150.4	167.0	167.3	167.3	167.4	163.9
2012	162.9	165.7	166.6	167.6	168.5	160.0	139.5	148.0	163.5	164.6	164.5	164.8	161.4
2013	160.4	163.4	164.1	168.7	169.3	160.8	139.6	148.1	163.9	165.0	165.5	165.7	161.2
2014	161.1	164.4	165.0	164.0	164.7	156.3	135.7	144.0	159.3	162.8	162.0	162.3	158.5
2015	157.3	160.9	161.1	161.4	162.4	157.5	136.6	145.0	160.6	163.7	163.4	163.6	157.8
2016	157.9	161.4	161.6	162.0	163.4	158.5	137.1	145.8	161.6	162.5	162.6	162.9	158.1
2017	157.2	160.4	160.3	160.0	160.4	157.5	136.2	140.3	155.7	156.7	156.0	155.5	154.7
2018	150.3	153.4	153.3	153.2	153.3	150.7	130.5	138.9	153.8	155.0	155.6	155.1	150.3

Employment by Industry: Baltimore-Columbia-Towson, MD, 2010–2018

(Numbers in thousands, not seasonally adjusted)

Industry and year	January	February	March	April	May	June	July	August	September	October	November	December	Annual average
Total Nonfarm													
2010	1,241.1	1,228.8	1,259.0	1,277.9	1,286.0	1,288.3	1,275.7	1,273.8	1,275.1	1,287.3	1,289.8	1,290.6	1,272.8
2011	1,255.6	1,263.9	1,277.8	1,295.0	1,300.5	1,302.3	1,295.7	1,294.8	1,301.2	1,308.8	1,314.0	1,316.8	1,293.9
2012	1,284.2	1,290.3	1,302.9	1,311.6	1,320.1	1,323.0	1,312.2	1,313.3	1,321.3	1,328.2	1,333.8	1,336.6	1,314.8
2013	1,303.7	1,310.8	1,323.1	1,331.2	1,340.7	1,344.6	1,333.3	1,332.6	1,337.5	1,341.8	1,349.4	1,345.6	1,332.9
2014	1,305.6	1,309.8	1,322.0	1,342.0	1,351.8	1,354.1	1,342.1	1,346.1	1,351.5	1,359.0	1,364.9	1,365.4	1,342.9
2015	1,325.5	1,331.8	1,340.0	1,360.9	1,373.8	1,374.2	1,371.9	1,370.9	1,371.3	1,386.9	1,392.1	1,394.5	1,366.2
2016	1,352.2	1,355.6	1,367.2	1,385.5	1,392.7	1,393.3	1,386.4	1,386.7	1,392.5	1,399.3	1,407.1	1,407.2	1,385.5
2017	1,365.8	1,372.8	1,380.8	1,393.8	1,404.3	1,408.8	1,403.7	1,402.4	1,405.8	1,414.3	1,421.9	1,419.3	1,399.5
2018	1,383.8	1,392.7	1,401.7	1,413.4	1,423.3	1,426.3	1,413.6	1,412.9	1,413.3	1,424.6	1,433.3	1,434.0	1,414.4
Total Private													
2010	1,013.7	996.4	1,022.5	1,039.6	1,046.2	1,053.7	1,050.1	1,049.2	1,045.8	1,050.2	1,051.1	1,054.2	1,039.4
2011	1,026.0	1,028.2	1,038.6	1,054.8	1,062.2	1,068.8	1,071.7	1,070.1	1,069.1	1,068.9	1,075.3	1,077.7	1,059.3
2012	1,055.6	1,055.1	1,064.9	1,074.4	1,084.4	1,094.5	1,091.5	1,093.6	1,092.7	1,091.9	1,097.5	1,100.8	1,083.1
2013	1,075.7	1,077.2	1,087.2	1,095.7	1,105.7	1,115.1	1,113.6	1,113.8	1,110.3	1,109.8	1,115.4	1,113.1	1,102.7
2014	1,081.4	1,079.1	1,089.6	1,107.5	1,120.0	1,126.9	1,125.6	1,128.4	1,124.9	1,126.5	1,130.9	1,133.1	1,114.5
2015	1,101.8	1,102.6	1,108.5	1,129.2	1,142.5	1,148.7	1,154.8	1,153.8	1,147.2	1,156.4	1,160.5	1,162.9	1,139.1
2016	1,129.8	1,128.3	1,137.3	1,154.4	1,161.7	1,168.0	1,170.0	1,170.7	1,168.4	1,170.1	1,177.0	1,176.3	1,159.3
2017	1,142.8	1,144.9	1,151.7	1,163.8	1,174.2	1,183.4	1,188.4	1,187.8	1,183.2	1,185.8	1,192.0	1,190.0	1,174.0
2018	1,161.5	1,164.4	1,172.0	1,183.4	1,192.9	1,200.0	1,200.6	1,199.1	1,190.4	1,194.7	1,202.0	1,203.2	1,188.7
Goods Producing													
2010	129.4	124.8	128.5	132.0	132.8	134.4	134.3	134.3	133.3	132.7	132.3	132.0	131.7
2011	128.7	128.2	129.5	132.1	132.8	134.2	134.9	134.6	133.0	132.5	132.0	131.6	132.0
2012	128.5	127.3	128.3	129.2	129.5	131.3	131.8	131.8	130.0	129.5	129.7	129.3	129.7
2013	125.9	125.1	126.0	127.9	128.6	130.2	130.9	131.1	130.1	129.4	129.1	127.4	128.5
2014	124.0	122.9	124.7	127.6	129.2	130.7	131.0	131.3	130.5	130.0	129.7	129.1	128.4
2015	125.3	124.6	125.6	128.2	129.9	131.7	133.3	133.7	133.0	133.4	132.7	132.6	130.3
2016	129.4	127.8	130.0	132.9	133.5	135.1	135.8	135.7	134.7	134.1	133.8	133.4	133.0
2017	129.9	130.2	131.0	132.4	133.8	136.0	136.4	136.8	136.0	136.0	136.3	136.2	134.3
2018	132.5	133.2	134.4	136.4	137.1	138.6	139.7	139.7	138.4	139.0	138.9	139.3	137.3
Service-Providing													
2010	1,111.7	1,104.0	1,130.5	1,145.9	1,153.2	1,153.9	1,141.4	1,139.5	1,141.8	1,154.6	1,157.5	1,158.6	1,141.1
2011	1,126.9	1,135.7	1,148.3	1,162.9	1,167.7	1,168.1	1,160.8	1,160.2	1,168.2	1,176.3	1,182.0	1,185.2	1,161.9
2012	1,155.7	1,163.0	1,174.6	1,182.4	1,190.6	1,191.7	1,180.4	1,181.5	1,191.3	1,198.7	1,204.1	1,207.3	1,185.1
2013	1,177.8	1,185.7	1,197.1	1,203.3	1,212.1	1,214.4	1,202.4	1,201.5	1,207.4	1,212.4	1,220.3	1,218.2	1,204.4
2014	1,181.6	1,186.9	1,197.3	1,214.4	1,222.6	1,223.4	1,211.1	1,214.8	1,221.0	1,229.0	1,235.2	1,236.3	1,214.5
2015	1,200.2	1,207.2	1,214.4	1,232.7	1,243.9	1,242.5	1,238.6	1,237.2	1,238.3	1,253.5	1,259.4	1,261.9	1,235.8
2016	1,222.8	1,227.8	1,237.2	1,252.6	1,259.2	1,258.2	1,250.6	1,251.0	1,257.8	1,265.2	1,273.3	1,273.8	1,252.5
2017	1,235.9	1,242.6	1,249.8	1,261.4	1,270.5	1,272.8	1,267.3	1,265.6	1,269.8	1,278.3	1,285.6	1,283.1	1,265.2
2018	1,251.3	1,259.5	1,267.3	1,277.0	1,286.2	1,287.7	1,273.9	1,273.2	1,274.9	1,285.6	1,294.4	1,294.7	1,277.1
Mining, Logging, and Construction													
2010	65.3	61.7	65.0	68.2	68.9	70.1	69.9	70.0	69.5	69.3	69.2	68.6	68.0
2011	64.8	64.3	65.5	67.7	68.5	69.8	70.7	70.6	69.9	69.9	69.6	69.2	68.4
2012	66.4	65.6	66.7	67.8	68.2	69.4	69.9	70.1	69.9	69.7	69.9	69.5	68.6
2013	66.9	66.2	67.2	69.4	70.2	71.5	72.3	72.6	72.2	71.9	72.0	70.4	70.2
2014	68.0	67.1	68.8	71.4	73.0	74.2	74.7	75.0	74.5	74.0	73.7	73.2	72.3
2015	69.8	69.2	70.4	73.3	74.8	76.0	77.1	77.5	77.3	77.8	77.2	76.8	74.8
2016	74.3	72.9	75.0	77.4	77.9	79.1	79.7	79.5	78.9	78.4	78.2	77.6	77.4
2017	74.8	74.8	75.3	76.5	77.9	79.7	80.1	80.5	80.0	79.9	80.0	80.1	78.3
2018	76.8	77.5	78.8	80.1	80.9	82.0	82.6	82.5	81.6	81.5	81.6	81.8	80.6
Manufacturing													
2010	64.1	63.1	63.5	63.8	63.9	64.3	64.4	64.3	63.8	63.4	63.1	63.4	63.8
2011	63.9	63.9	64.0	64.4	64.3	64.4	64.2	64.0	63.1	62.6	62.4	62.4	63.6
2012	62.1	61.7	61.6	61.4	61.3	61.9	61.9	61.7	60.1	59.8	59.8	59.8	61.1
2013	59.0	58.9	58.8	58.5	58.4	58.7	58.6	58.5	57.9	57.5	57.1	57.0	58.2
2014	56.0	55.8	55.9	56.2	56.2	56.5	56.3	56.3	56.0	56.0	56.0	55.9	56.1
2015	55.5	55.4	55.2	54.9	55.1	55.7	56.2	56.2	55.7	55.6	55.5	55.8	55.6
2016	55.1	54.9	55.0	55.5	55.6	56.0	56.1	56.2	55.8	55.7	55.6	55.8	55.6
2017	55.1	55.4	55.7	55.9	55.9	56.3	56.3	56.3	56.0	56.1	56.3	56.1	56.0
2018	55.7	55.7	55.6	56.3	56.2	56.6	57.1	57.2	56.8	57.5	57.3	57.5	56.6

Employment by Industry: Baltimore-Columbia-Towson, MD, 2010–2018—*Continued*

(Numbers in thousands, not seasonally adjusted)

Industry and year	January	February	March	April	May	June	July	August	September	October	November	December	Annual average
Trade, Transportation, and Utilities													
2010	220.9	215.5	220.3	224.1	225.1	225.8	224.3	224.3	223.9	227.5	231.0	234.4	224.8
2011	225.5	223.6	225.1	227.8	229.1	229.9	228.8	229.4	229.5	230.9	236.2	239.8	229.6
2012	230.1	227.5	229.5	230.5	232.1	232.8	230.9	230.9	232.2	233.2	238.9	241.8	232.5
2013	233.8	231.1	232.2	232.7	234.7	235.5	233.9	233.7	234.0	234.9	240.4	243.7	235.1
2014	232.4	228.6	230.6	232.7	234.5	236.1	235.0	235.5	235.6	238.2	244.9	248.7	236.1
2015	237.1	234.9	235.3	238.9	240.9	243.3	242.8	242.4	242.6	246.9	251.7	255.2	242.7
2016	243.7	241.3	242.3	244.6	245.5	246.4	244.8	245.6	246.0	247.5	253.4	255.5	246.4
2017	244.8	241.3	241.2	243.2	244.6	246.2	245.5	245.9	246.0	248.5	257.1	257.5	246.8
2018	246.0	243.0	243.0	244.3	245.6	247.3	244.7	244.5	244.6	246.5	250.5	252.7	246.1
Wholesale Trade													
2010	49.7	49.5	49.9	50.4	50.6	50.5	50.6	50.5	50.1	50.5	50.5	50.7	50.3
2011	50.3	50.5	50.7	51.1	51.3	51.4	51.4	51.3	51.1	50.9	50.8	50.9	51.0
2012	50.5	50.5	50.9	51.5	51.9	52.2	52.0	51.9	51.7	51.7	51.7	51.9	51.5
2013	51.2	51.4	51.5	51.8	51.9	52.0	51.5	51.3	51.2	50.7	50.8	50.9	51.4
2014	50.1	50.0	50.0	50.5	50.8	51.0	51.1	51.0	50.7	51.3	51.4	52.0	50.8
2015	51.2	51.2	51.2	51.8	51.9	52.1	52.3	52.1	51.9	52.3	52.2	52.2	51.9
2016	51.8	51.7	51.7	52.4	52.4	52.4	51.9	52.1	51.7	51.6	51.5	51.7	51.9
2017	51.3	51.1	51.3	51.8	52.0	52.4	52.3	52.3	52.1	52.3	52.3	52.5	52.0
2018	51.8	51.8	51.6	52.1	52.3	52.7	52.7	52.7	52.5	52.8	52.4	51.9	52.3
Retail Trade													
2010	130.1	125.7	129.0	130.5	131.7	132.3	132.0	132.1	130.9	133.4	137.1	139.7	132.0
2011	132.4	130.5	131.6	132.5	133.5	134.2	133.4	134.0	133.3	135.4	140.1	143.0	134.5
2012	135.1	132.5	134.0	133.9	134.9	135.2	134.5	134.6	134.5	135.7	140.5	142.4	135.7
2013	137.1	134.9	135.5	135.7	136.9	137.7	137.7	137.9	136.7	137.8	142.6	144.6	137.9
2014	136.7	134.1	135.2	136.4	137.2	138.4	138.4	138.7	137.5	139.1	143.6	146.1	138.5
2015	137.9	135.6	136.3	137.8	138.9	140.3	139.8	139.7	138.4	140.6	144.6	146.6	139.7
2016	139.8	137.5	138.7	138.4	139.2	140.0	139.1	139.6	138.3	139.3	143.1	144.9	139.8
2017	137.8	135.3	135.3	136.0	136.6	137.1	136.8	136.8	135.7	137.0	142.4	143.1	137.5
2018	135.4	133.1	133.4	134.2	135.0	135.4	135.0	134.8	133.4	134.5	138.0	138.8	135.1
Transportation and Utilities													
2010	41.1	40.3	41.4	43.2	42.8	43.0	41.7	41.7	42.9	43.6	43.4	44.0	42.4
2011	42.8	42.6	42.8	44.2	44.3	44.3	44.0	44.1	45.1	44.6	45.3	45.9	44.2
2012	44.5	44.5	44.6	45.1	45.3	45.4	44.4	44.4	46.0	45.8	46.7	47.5	45.4
2013	45.5	44.8	45.2	45.2	45.9	45.8	44.7	44.5	46.1	46.4	47.0	48.2	45.8
2014	45.6	44.5	45.4	45.8	46.5	46.7	45.5	45.8	47.4	47.8	49.9	50.6	46.8
2015	48.0	48.1	47.8	49.3	50.1	50.9	50.7	50.6	52.3	54.0	54.9	56.4	51.1
2016	52.1	52.1	51.9	53.8	53.9	54.0	53.8	53.9	56.0	56.6	58.8	58.9	54.7
2017	55.7	54.9	54.6	55.4	56.0	56.7	56.4	56.8	58.2	59.2	62.4	61.9	57.4
2018	58.8	58.1	58.0	58.0	58.3	59.2	57.0	57.0	58.7	59.2	60.1	62.0	58.7
Information													
2010	19.4	19.8	21.1	20.8	20.9	21.3	20.0	19.3	19.3	18.9	18.5	19.3	19.9
2011	17.7	18.1	18.2	17.7	17.8	17.5	17.5	16.6	17.1	17.2	17.6	17.3	17.5
2012	17.1	17.1	17.1	16.7	16.7	17.2	17.2	17.2	17.1	16.8	16.9	17.6	17.1
2013	17.0	16.9	16.9	16.6	16.7	16.8	17.0	17.0	16.8	16.9	17.0	17.0	16.9
2014	16.8	16.3	16.4	16.2	16.5	16.2	16.5	16.8	16.2	16.6	16.4	16.4	16.4
2015	16.1	16.0	16.2	16.6	16.8	16.7	17.1	17.0	16.7	17.0	17.1	17.0	16.7
2016	16.3	16.5	16.6	17.3	16.7	17.7	17.6	17.5	17.2	17.2	17.3	17.5	17.1
2017	17.3	17.6	17.6	17.6	17.6	17.8	17.6	17.5	17.3	17.5	17.4	17.5	17.5
2018	17.0	17.2	17.1	17.4	17.4	17.6	17.5	17.5	17.0	17.2	17.4	17.4	17.3
Financial Activities													
2010	72.5	72.0	72.4	72.5	72.6	73.2	73.4	73.4	73.1	73.6	73.6	74.0	73.0
2011	73.1	73.1	73.5	73.7	73.6	73.8	73.9	73.6	73.2	73.2	73.2	73.1	73.4
2012	73.0	73.0	72.8	72.8	73.1	73.7	74.1	74.4	74.2	74.2	74.7	74.8	73.7
2013	74.4	74.4	74.5	74.9	75.2	75.9	76.2	76.1	75.8	75.6	75.8	75.8	75.4
2014	75.0	75.1	74.7	75.6	75.9	76.6	76.8	77.0	76.5	76.7	76.7	76.9	76.1
2015	76.3	76.5	76.4	76.7	77.0	77.8	78.2	78.5	77.5	77.9	78.2	78.6	77.5
2016	77.9	78.1	77.9	78.5	78.9	79.2	79.7	80.0	79.7	79.9	80.1	80.2	79.2
2017	79.8	80.0	80.3	80.4	80.7	81.8	83.1	83.3	82.6	82.3	80.8	80.7	81.3
2018	80.1	80.2	80.0	80.2	80.0	80.4	80.6	80.2	79.3	79.7	79.9	79.4	80.0

Employment by Industry: Baltimore-Columbia-Towson, MD, 2010–2018—*Continued*

(Numbers in thousands, not seasonally adjusted)

Industry and year	January	February	March	April	May	June	July	August	September	October	November	December	Annual average
Professional and Business Services													
2010	177.5	175.2	180.3	184.2	184.6	187.6	186.5	187.6	186.6	189.3	188.7	188.6	184.7
2011	183.8	183.8	186.3	192.0	193.3	196.1	198.1	199.8	200.7	202.1	203.5	203.9	195.3
2012	199.5	199.4	201.7	203.9	206.5	208.3	207.9	211.3	211.6	211.7	213.4	212.4	207.3
2013	207.4	208.7	211.5	212.4	214.2	217.5	216.8	219.3	219.3	218.6	220.1	217.8	215.3
2014	212.5	213.4	215.4	220.0	221.9	223.5	223.6	224.7	223.5	223.8	223.7	223.2	220.8
2015	216.9	217.5	219.0	223.4	225.2	226.4	229.4	230.9	228.1	232.5	232.4	231.0	226.1
2016	225.6	225.2	226.5	230.3	231.7	233.6	234.0	236.2	234.8	235.1	236.1	234.2	231.9
2017	226.0	226.1	227.5	231.2	232.8	234.7	234.7	235.3	234.5	234.3	234.5	233.7	232.1
2018	230.1	230.6	232.5	235.3	237.3	238.3	240.2	241.5	239.3	237.6	241.1	239.9	237.0
Education and Health Services													
2010	234.7	232.9	237.3	238.4	238.0	236.3	236.5	234.8	237.3	239.9	240.9	240.8	237.3
2011	238.1	241.7	242.0	242.4	241.7	239.9	240.5	239.2	242.1	244.5	245.1	244.6	241.8
2012	243.0	245.5	246.3	247.2	246.5	246.0	245.4	244.4	247.1	249.6	249.9	251.4	246.9
2013	247.5	250.7	252.1	252.5	252.0	250.5	249.9	249.1	251.3	254.3	255.1	254.8	251.7
2014	250.0	252.0	253.3	254.1	253.9	253.0	252.2	251.9	254.7	256.2	257.5	257.9	253.9
2015	253.9	256.6	256.9	261.6	261.5	259.6	259.8	258.1	261.0	264.1	265.5	265.6	260.4
2016	260.1	262.5	264.0	265.6	265.2	262.0	264.7	262.7	266.3	269.7	270.8	270.9	265.4
2017	265.1	269.0	270.5	271.2	271.0	268.6	274.0	272.9	275.2	278.4	279.0	278.9	272.8
2018	275.5	278.6	279.8	280.4	279.9	278.2	278.3	276.8	278.8	284.6	285.7	286.1	280.2
Leisure and Hospitality													
2010	104.8	102.5	107.4	112.2	116.4	119.1	119.0	119.7	116.7	112.9	110.6	109.8	112.6
2011	104.5	105.0	108.8	113.4	118.1	121.1	121.9	121.1	118.5	113.7	113.0	112.4	114.3
2012	110.1	111.0	114.5	118.7	124.6	129.1	128.2	128.2	125.3	122.0	119.4	118.7	120.8
2013	115.5	115.8	119.1	123.5	129.0	133.0	133.4	133.0	128.6	126.5	124.3	123.4	125.4
2014	118.5	118.8	122.2	127.9	134.7	136.9	136.8	138.1	134.8	132.4	129.6	128.6	129.9
2015	124.8	125.2	127.7	132.3	139.4	141.1	142.0	141.4	137.1	133.8	132.1	132.3	134.1
2016	126.5	126.8	129.8	134.7	139.4	142.9	142.0	142.0	138.8	135.7	134.5	133.9	135.6
2017	129.7	130.3	132.9	136.9	142.4	146.1	144.9	144.5	140.1	137.3	135.2	133.6	137.8
2018	128.9	130.1	133.3	137.2	143.1	146.8	146.8	146.5	141.1	137.5	135.5	135.7	138.5
Other Services													
2010	54.5	53.7	55.2	55.4	55.8	56.0	56.1	55.8	55.6	55.4	55.5	55.3	55.4
2011	54.6	54.7	55.2	55.7	55.8	56.3	56.1	55.8	55.0	54.8	54.7	55.0	55.3
2012	54.3	54.3	54.7	55.4	55.4	56.1	56.0	55.4	55.2	54.9	54.6	54.8	55.1
2013	54.2	54.5	54.9	55.2	55.3	55.7	55.5	54.5	54.4	53.6	53.6	53.2	54.6
2014	52.2	52.0	52.3	53.4	53.4	53.9	53.7	53.1	53.1	52.6	52.4	52.3	52.9
2015	51.4	51.3	51.4	51.5	51.8	52.1	52.2	51.8	51.2	50.8	50.8	50.6	51.4
2016	50.3	50.1	50.2	50.5	50.8	51.1	51.4	51.0	50.9	50.9	51.0	50.7	50.7
2017	50.2	50.4	50.7	50.9	51.3	52.2	52.2	51.6	51.5	51.5	51.7	51.9	51.3
2018	51.4	51.5	51.9	52.2	52.5	52.8	52.8	52.4	51.9	52.6	53.0	52.7	52.3
Government													
2010	227.4	232.4	236.5	238.3	239.8	234.6	225.6	224.6	229.3	237.1	238.7	236.4	233.4
2011	229.6	235.7	239.2	240.2	238.3	233.5	224.0	224.7	232.1	239.9	238.7	239.1	234.6
2012	228.6	235.2	238.0	237.2	235.7	228.5	220.7	219.7	228.6	236.3	236.3	235.8	231.7
2013	228.0	233.6	235.9	235.5	235.0	229.5	219.7	218.8	227.2	232.0	234.0	232.5	230.1
2014	224.2	230.7	232.4	234.5	231.8	227.2	216.5	217.7	226.6	232.5	234.0	232.3	228.4
2015	223.7	229.2	231.5	231.7	231.3	225.5	217.1	217.1	224.1	230.5	231.6	231.6	227.1
2016	222.4	227.3	229.9	231.1	231.0	225.3	216.4	216.0	224.1	229.2	230.1	230.9	226.1
2017	223.0	227.9	229.1	230.0	230.1	225.4	215.3	214.6	222.6	228.5	229.9	229.3	225.5
2018	222.3	228.3	229.7	230.0	230.4	226.3	213.0	213.8	222.9	229.9	231.3	230.8	225.7

Employment by Industry: Orlando-Kissimmee-Sanford, FL, 2010–2018

(Numbers in thousands, not seasonally adjusted)

Industry and year	January	February	March	April	May	June	July	August	September	October	November	December	Annual average
Total Nonfarm													
2010	976.4	982.4	989.9	996.0	1,000.9	989.2	984.3	994.0	989.9	998.0	1,004.5	1,005.6	992.6
2011	989.5	996.2	1,002.5	1,007.5	1,007.0	995.5	993.8	1,004.3	1,009.7	1,012.2	1,022.8	1,025.0	1,005.5
2012	1,011.3	1,021.2	1,031.0	1,030.6	1,031.2	1,021.3	1,018.0	1,029.0	1,031.4	1,043.6	1,056.4	1,057.0	1,031.8
2013	1,037.1	1,051.3	1,059.1	1,059.6	1,063.7	1,056.9	1,054.0	1,069.4	1,069.4	1,079.0	1,092.9	1,094.7	1,065.6
2014	1,082.3	1,091.4	1,100.3	1,102.8	1,109.0	1,100.6	1,098.4	1,114.3	1,113.7	1,122.1	1,134.2	1,137.8	1,108.9
2015	1,122.3	1,135.0	1,142.0	1,150.0	1,156.2	1,148.8	1,148.4	1,162.1	1,164.1	1,177.9	1,190.7	1,196.3	1,157.8
2016	1,178.3	1,189.6	1,196.6	1,203.4	1,206.5	1,195.3	1,199.8	1,212.4	1,217.4	1,224.6	1,237.8	1,241.4	1,208.6
2017	1,226.6	1,237.1	1,242.2	1,245.4	1,248.3	1,239.9	1,235.6	1,248.8	1,234.6	1,268.0	1,282.9	1,287.7	1,249.8
2018	1,267.9	1,279.9	1,287.5	1,289.2	1,290.3	1,280.7	1,279.4	1,295.8	1,295.3	1,311.9	1,328.2	1,329.5	1,294.6
Total Private													
2010	859.8	865.6	872.9	878.1	880.2	881.2	877.8	877.4	873.6	880.3	886.7	889.1	876.9
2011	873.2	878.2	884.3	890.1	890.4	889.8	889.1	889.4	893.4	894.6	904.7	907.8	890.4
2012	893.7	901.8	911.1	912.4	914.0	914.8	912.0	911.9	914.2	925.0	937.0	938.6	915.5
2013	919.4	931.9	939.3	939.7	944.7	949.0	946.9	951.0	951.5	960.4	973.7	976.2	948.6
2014	963.4	972.2	980.9	982.4	989.3	991.8	990.1	994.8	994.5	1,000.8	1,012.7	1,016.4	990.8
2015	1,001.1	1,013.0	1,019.5	1,027.3	1,034.8	1,038.4	1,038.0	1,040.2	1,042.9	1,054.6	1,067.2	1,073.4	1,037.5
2016	1,054.8	1,065.7	1,072.0	1,078.3	1,081.7	1,080.9	1,085.2	1,087.2	1,092.5	1,098.7	1,110.8	1,115.2	1,085.3
2017	1,101.2	1,110.5	1,115.3	1,118.3	1,121.8	1,123.9	1,119.2	1,122.3	1,108.7	1,139.4	1,152.8	1,158.2	1,124.3
2018	1,138.7	1,150.2	1,157.4	1,159.3	1,161.8	1,162.7	1,160.0	1,166.0	1,166.6	1,181.8	1,196.8	1,199.0	1,166.7
Goods Producing													
2010	84.8	85.2	85.7	86.2	86.3	86.9	87.0	86.4	86.0	85.4	84.7	84.3	85.7
2011	83.1	83.3	83.1	83.0	83.1	83.0	83.3	83.4	83.8	83.3	83.5	83.5	83.3
2012	82.7	83.2	83.6	82.4	83.1	83.4	84.2	84.9	85.3	86.0	86.4	85.9	84.3
2013	85.1	86.2	87.0	87.9	88.7	89.4	90.0	91.0	91.4	91.7	92.2	92.3	89.4
2014	91.9	93.0	93.3	94.0	94.7	95.5	96.2	96.9	97.3	97.9	98.2	97.6	95.5
2015	97.1	98.1	98.8	99.7	100.8	101.9	102.7	103.0	103.5	105.5	106.0	106.5	102.0
2016	106.2	107.3	107.7	108.9	109.7	110.9	112.2	112.7	113.5	112.7	113.7	113.8	110.8
2017	113.7	115.5	116.7	116.4	117.6	119.2	119.5	120.1	117.9	121.2	122.4	123.1	118.6
2018	123.5	125.6	126.6	126.8	127.6	128.6	129.0	130.1	129.9	132.0	131.9	132.1	128.6
Service-Providing													
2010	891.6	897.2	904.2	909.8	914.6	902.3	897.3	907.6	903.9	912.6	919.8	921.3	906.9
2011	906.4	912.9	919.4	924.5	923.9	912.5	910.5	920.9	925.9	928.9	939.3	941.5	922.2
2012	928.6	938.0	947.4	948.2	948.1	937.9	933.8	944.1	946.1	957.6	970.0	971.1	947.6
2013	952.0	965.1	972.1	971.7	975.0	967.5	964.0	978.4	978.0	987.3	1,000.7	1,002.4	976.2
2014	990.4	998.4	1,007.0	1,008.8	1,014.3	1,005.1	1,002.2	1,017.4	1,016.4	1,024.2	1,036.0	1,040.2	1,013.4
2015	1,025.2	1,036.9	1,043.2	1,050.3	1,055.4	1,046.9	1,045.7	1,059.1	1,060.6	1,072.4	1,084.7	1,089.8	1,055.9
2016	1,072.1	1,082.3	1,088.9	1,094.5	1,096.8	1,084.4	1,087.6	1,099.7	1,103.9	1,111.9	1,124.1	1,127.6	1,097.8
2017	1,112.9	1,121.6	1,125.5	1,129.0	1,130.7	1,120.7	1,116.1	1,128.7	1,116.7	1,146.8	1,160.5	1,164.6	1,131.2
2018	1,144.4	1,154.3	1,160.9	1,162.4	1,162.7	1,152.1	1,150.4	1,165.7	1,165.4	1,179.9	1,196.3	1,197.4	1,166.0
Mining, Logging, and Construction													
2010	47.5	48.0	48.2	48.6	48.2	48.7	48.4	48.1	47.7	47.2	46.4	45.8	47.7
2011	44.9	45.0	44.9	44.7	44.9	45.0	45.4	45.5	45.9	45.6	45.7	45.7	45.3
2012	44.7	45.1	45.3	44.2	44.9	45.2	46.1	47.1	47.7	48.3	48.6	48.2	46.3
2013	47.7	48.6	49.4	49.8	50.5	51.1	51.7	52.7	52.9	53.2	53.5	53.6	51.2
2014	53.2	54.1	54.5	54.7	55.2	55.8	56.2	56.9	57.3	57.8	58.1	57.4	55.9
2015	57.1	57.9	58.4	59.0	60.0	60.9	61.6	62.1	62.5	63.6	64.2	64.6	61.0
2016	64.7	65.7	65.9	66.8	67.5	68.3	69.3	69.7	70.5	69.9	70.6	70.6	68.3
2017	70.6	71.9	72.9	72.7	73.7	74.7	74.6	75.2	73.6	76.3	77.2	77.6	74.3
2018	78.2	80.1	80.7	80.9	81.4	82.0	82.4	83.4	83.3	85.0	84.9	85.0	82.3
Manufacturing													
2010	37.3	37.2	37.5	37.6	38.1	38.2	38.6	38.3	38.3	38.2	38.3	38.5	38.0
2011	38.2	38.3	38.2	38.3	38.2	38.0	37.9	37.9	37.9	37.7	37.8	37.8	38.0
2012	38.0	38.1	38.3	38.2	38.2	38.2	38.1	37.8	37.6	37.7	37.8	37.7	38.0
2013	37.4	37.6	37.6	38.1	38.2	38.3	38.3	38.3	38.5	38.5	38.7	38.7	38.2
2014	38.7	38.9	38.8	39.3	39.5	39.7	40.0	40.0	40.0	40.1	40.1	40.2	39.6
2015	40.0	40.2	40.4	40.7	40.8	41.0	41.1	40.9	41.0	41.9	41.8	41.9	41.0
2016	41.5	41.6	41.8	42.1	42.2	42.6	42.9	43.0	43.0	42.8	43.1	43.2	42.5
2017	43.1	43.6	43.8	43.7	43.9	44.5	44.9	44.9	44.3	44.9	45.2	45.5	44.4
2018	45.3	45.5	45.9	45.9	46.2	46.6	46.6	46.7	46.6	47.0	47.0	47.1	46.4

Employment by Industry: Orlando-Kissimmee-Sanford, FL, 2010–2018—*Continued*

(Numbers in thousands, not seasonally adjusted)

Industry and year	January	February	March	April	May	June	July	August	September	October	November	December	Annual average
Trade, Transportation, and Utilities													
2010	182.6	182.7	182.6	183.8	184.4	185.0	184.9	185.6	185.0	187.0	192.5	195.3	186.0
2011	188.7	188.3	188.5	189.2	189.5	189.4	190.3	191.3	191.2	193.3	199.7	201.8	191.8
2012	195.8	194.7	196.0	195.5	196.2	196.2	196.4	196.7	196.2	198.2	205.7	207.3	197.9
2013	199.9	199.4	199.9	199.9	201.1	202.2	203.1	204.0	204.4	206.1	214.0	216.6	204.2
2014	209.5	209.6	210.3	209.6	210.1	210.5	210.6	211.7	211.5	213.4	221.3	224.3	212.7
2015	216.2	216.2	216.5	217.3	218.1	219.5	219.6	221.0	220.6	222.4	229.6	233.5	220.9
2016	223.6	223.4	224.1	224.5	225.4	225.2	225.6	226.6	227.1	228.9	236.3	239.9	227.6
2017	231.4	229.8	230.1	230.7	231.0	231.0	230.7	231.3	228.6	234.1	243.7	245.5	233.2
2018	237.8	236.4	236.7	236.7	237.4	236.8	237.4	237.9	238.1	241.0	247.6	248.9	239.4
Wholesale Trade													
2010	38.2	38.6	38.4	38.5	38.5	38.2	37.9	37.8	37.8	37.9	37.8	37.8	38.1
2011	38.3	38.4	38.3	38.2	38.2	38.1	38.1	38.0	38.0	38.0	38.1	38.3	38.2
2012	38.2	38.2	38.5	38.6	38.5	38.7	38.8	39.0	38.9	39.1	39.4	39.3	38.8
2013	38.9	39.3	39.5	39.5	39.7	39.7	39.7	39.8	40.1	40.4	40.8	40.9	39.9
2014	40.5	40.9	41.1	41.2	41.6	41.7	41.9	42.1	42.2	42.4	42.5	42.7	41.7
2015	42.6	42.8	42.9	43.0	43.2	43.3	43.4	43.4	43.4	43.3	43.5	43.8	43.2
2016	43.3	43.6	43.6	43.9	44.0	43.8	43.4	43.5	43.8	43.5	43.8	44.0	43.7
2017	43.2	43.3	43.6	43.5	43.6	43.7	43.9	43.9	43.7	44.0	44.3	44.6	43.8
2018	44.3	44.4	44.4	44.4	44.5	44.5	44.7	45.0	45.0	45.8	45.8	46.6	45.0
Retail Trade													
2010	115.1	114.4	114.5	115.6	116.1	117.2	117.4	118.2	117.6	119.5	124.7	126.8	118.1
2011	120.9	120.4	120.3	121.0	121.3	121.3	122.2	123.2	123.0	124.7	130.6	131.8	123.4
2012	126.8	125.6	126.4	126.0	126.8	126.6	126.8	127.0	126.8	128.3	135.2	136.4	128.2
2013	130.4	129.5	129.6	129.5	130.1	131.0	132.2	132.8	132.7	134.2	141.1	143.4	133.0
2014	137.4	136.9	137.1	136.6	136.7	137.0	136.7	137.4	137.2	138.6	145.6	147.3	138.7
2015	140.4	140.2	140.4	140.7	140.8	141.5	141.4	142.5	142.1	143.3	149.2	151.3	142.8
2016	143.6	143.2	143.4	143.4	143.9	143.9	144.5	145.4	145.4	147.1	153.5	155.2	146.0
2017	149.1	147.8	147.5	148.1	148.0	147.9	147.3	147.7	145.4	149.5	157.5	158.1	149.5
2018	151.3	150.0	150.2	150.0	150.3	149.8	150.1	150.1	150.1	152.1	157.5	156.6	151.5
Transportation and Utilities													
2010	29.3	29.7	29.7	29.7	29.8	29.6	29.6	29.6	29.6	29.6	30.0	30.7	29.7
2011	29.5	29.5	29.9	30.0	30.0	30.0	30.0	30.1	30.2	30.6	31.0	31.7	30.2
2012	30.8	30.9	31.1	30.9	30.9	30.9	30.8	30.7	30.5	30.8	31.1	31.6	30.9
2013	30.6	30.6	30.8	30.9	31.3	31.5	31.2	31.4	31.6	31.5	32.1	32.3	31.3
2014	31.6	31.8	32.1	31.8	31.8	31.8	32.0	32.2	32.1	32.4	33.2	34.3	32.3
2015	33.2	33.2	33.2	33.6	34.1	34.7	34.8	35.1	35.1	35.8	36.9	38.4	34.8
2016	36.7	36.6	37.1	37.2	37.5	37.5	37.7	37.7	37.9	38.3	39.0	40.7	37.8
2017	39.1	38.7	39.0	39.1	39.4	39.4	39.5	39.7	39.5	40.6	41.9	42.8	39.9
2018	42.2	42.0	42.1	42.3	42.6	42.5	42.6	42.8	43.0	43.1	44.3	45.7	42.9
Information													
2010	23.9	23.8	23.9	23.8	23.6	23.7	23.7	23.9	23.7	23.7	23.9	23.9	23.8
2011	23.8	23.9	23.9	23.9	24.0	24.0	24.2	24.1	24.1	23.9	24.2	24.1	24.0
2012	23.9	23.9	23.8	23.6	23.5	23.5	23.6	23.5	23.3	23.6	23.5	23.5	23.6
2013	23.2	23.5	23.4	23.4	23.5	23.7	23.7	23.7	23.6	23.6	23.7	23.7	23.6
2014	23.7	23.6	23.8	23.7	23.9	24.1	23.9	23.8	23.7	23.8	24.2	24.2	23.9
2015	24.3	24.3	24.2	24.1	24.2	24.2	23.9	23.7	23.5	23.8	24.0	24.0	24.0
2016	24.0	24.0	23.9	24.0	24.1	24.0	24.3	24.3	24.0	24.1	24.4	24.3	24.1
2017	24.1	24.4	24.2	24.2	24.6	24.5	24.2	24.3	24.1	24.4	24.8	25.1	24.4
2018	25.1	25.9	25.4	25.0	25.2	25.1	25.2	25.1	24.9	25.2	25.5	25.5	25.3
Financial Activities													
2010	64.1	64.4	64.7	64.6	65.0	65.6	65.5	65.6	65.0	65.7	65.6	65.9	65.1
2011	65.5	65.8	66.1	65.7	65.7	65.5	65.9	65.9	66.1	65.8	66.0	66.2	65.9
2012	65.9	66.3	66.7	66.7	67.0	67.2	67.4	67.4	67.3	68.1	68.5	68.6	67.3
2013	68.0	68.5	68.9	69.1	69.3	69.9	69.8	70.2	70.1	70.8	71.2	71.1	69.7
2014	70.1	70.4	70.5	70.2	70.5	70.4	70.3	70.5	70.2	70.5	70.5	70.5	70.4
2015	70.0	70.2	70.5	70.5	70.9	71.0	71.2	71.4	71.3	72.0	72.5	72.7	71.2
2016	72.7	72.9	73.0	73.0	73.1	73.2	73.1	73.3	73.1	74.0	74.1	74.5	73.3
2017	73.3	73.6	73.7	74.0	74.3	74.5	74.2	74.3	74.1	74.7	74.9	75.2	74.2
2018	74.7	75.3	75.5	75.8	75.8	75.9	75.8	75.9	75.9	75.8	77.4	77.1	75.9

Employment by Industry: Orlando-Kissimmee-Sanford, FL, 2010–2018—*Continued*

(Numbers in thousands, not seasonally adjusted)

Industry and year	January	February	March	April	May	June	July	August	September	October	November	December	Annual average
Professional and Business Services													
2010	161.4	161.7	163.1	163.8	163.5	162.3	160.0	160.1	159.8	160.0	159.8	159.1	161.2
2011	157.5	158.9	159.5	161.8	161.9	161.6	160.6	161.5	163.7	164.1	166.2	165.9	161.9
2012	164.8	167.9	169.9	169.8	170.4	168.9	166.2	167.0	168.2	172.1	173.7	173.3	169.4
2013	169.6	173.2	174.4	174.8	176.3	176.4	174.0	175.3	175.8	178.2	180.4	179.8	175.7
2014	179.5	180.8	182.2	182.0	184.7	184.1	183.0	184.7	183.8	185.3	186.8	185.7	183.6
2015	185.4	187.7	189.7	193.6	196.1	196.2	196.9	196.2	196.7	199.6	201.1	200.4	195.0
2016	198.4	200.4	203.0	205.3	205.6	206.3	208.9	209.4	210.5	213.6	214.8	214.5	207.6
2017	215.7	218.2	219.0	219.2	220.4	221.1	219.2	218.7	215.0	226.1	227.0	227.5	220.6
2018	224.0	225.6	228.1	229.2	230.0	231.3	229.7	231.5	230.9	236.9	242.2	243.9	231.9
Education and Health Services													
2010	120.0	120.2	120.7	121.3	121.7	120.8	120.2	120.7	120.3	121.5	122.0	121.1	120.9
2011	121.1	121.9	122.2	123.4	123.6	122.6	122.9	123.7	124.6	124.9	125.6	125.9	123.5
2012	124.3	125.1	125.8	128.4	128.5	127.9	127.6	128.3	129.3	130.5	130.9	131.1	128.1
2013	129.7	130.9	131.4	131.4	131.6	130.6	129.2	131.3	131.6	132.6	133.5	133.3	131.4
2014	132.3	133.5	134.2	135.1	136.0	134.7	133.5	135.8	136.8	138.2	139.2	139.8	135.8
2015	139.1	140.6	141.4	142.7	143.8	142.7	141.1	143.2	144.5	146.1	146.8	146.8	143.2
2016	145.7	146.9	147.1	148.6	148.7	146.9	146.4	147.6	149.2	150.2	150.9	151.4	148.3
2017	150.6	151.4	151.5	152.3	152.3	150.6	149.7	152.3	151.5	154.1	154.7	155.6	152.2
2018	153.8	155.1	155.7	155.8	155.8	153.8	153.0	155.8	156.5	158.9	159.5	159.2	156.1
Leisure and Hospitality													
2010	184.7	189.2	193.6	195.7	196.8	198.0	197.7	196.6	195.5	198.6	199.9	201.4	195.6
2011	195.7	198.2	202.8	205.1	204.9	206.5	205.4	203.7	204.5	204.2	204.8	206.1	203.5
2012	202.2	206.4	210.7	211.2	210.5	212.6	211.7	209.3	209.8	211.3	213.1	213.5	210.2
2013	208.7	214.9	218.8	217.4	218.3	220.7	221.1	219.5	218.5	221.1	222.1	222.6	218.6
2014	219.2	223.9	229.0	230.1	231.4	234.6	234.9	233.5	233.0	233.2	233.8	235.4	231.0
2015	229.8	236.3	238.6	239.0	240.0	242.0	241.6	240.3	241.2	243.1	244.6	246.6	240.3
2016	240.9	247.0	248.9	249.6	250.6	250.2	250.7	249.5	251.1	251.5	252.4	252.4	249.6
2017	248.5	253.6	256.4	257.6	257.7	259.1	258.0	257.6	254.5	261.0	261.3	261.9	257.3
2018	256.0	262.3	265.1	265.9	266.0	267.1	266.2	265.8	266.6	267.6	268.2	267.6	265.4
Other Services													
2010	38.3	38.4	38.6	38.9	38.9	38.9	38.8	38.5	38.3	38.4	38.3	38.1	38.5
2011	37.8	37.9	38.2	38.0	37.7	37.2	36.5	35.8	35.4	35.1	34.7	34.3	36.6
2012	34.1	34.3	34.6	34.8	34.8	35.1	34.9	34.8	34.8	35.2	35.2	35.4	34.8
2013	35.2	35.3	35.5	35.8	35.9	36.1	36.0	36.0	36.1	36.3	36.6	36.8	36.0
2014	37.2	37.4	37.6	37.7	38.0	37.9	37.7	37.9	38.2	38.5	38.7	38.9	38.0
2015	39.2	39.6	39.8	40.4	40.9	40.9	41.0	41.4	41.6	42.1	42.6	42.9	41.0
2016	43.3	43.8	44.3	44.4	44.5	44.2	44.0	43.8	44.0	43.7	44.2	44.4	44.1
2017	43.9	44.0	43.7	43.9	43.9	43.9	43.7	43.7	43.0	43.8	44.0	44.3	43.8
2018	43.8	44.0	44.3	44.1	44.0	44.1	43.7	43.9	43.8	44.4	44.5	44.7	44.1
Government													
2010	116.6	116.8	117.0	117.9	120.7	108.0	106.5	116.6	116.3	117.7	117.8	116.5	115.7
2011	116.3	118.0	118.2	117.4	116.6	105.7	104.7	114.9	116.3	117.6	118.1	117.2	115.1
2012	117.6	119.4	119.9	118.2	117.2	106.5	106.0	117.1	117.2	118.6	119.4	118.4	116.3
2013	117.7	119.4	119.8	119.9	119.0	107.9	107.1	118.4	117.9	118.6	119.2	118.5	117.0
2014	118.9	119.2	119.4	120.4	119.7	108.8	108.3	119.5	119.2	121.3	121.5	121.4	118.1
2015	121.2	122.0	122.5	122.7	121.4	110.4	110.4	121.9	121.2	123.3	123.5	122.9	120.3
2016	123.5	123.9	124.6	125.1	124.8	114.4	114.6	125.2	124.9	125.9	127.0	126.2	123.3
2017	125.4	126.6	126.9	127.1	126.5	116.0	116.4	126.5	125.9	128.6	130.1	129.5	125.5
2018	129.2	129.7	130.1	129.9	128.5	118.0	119.4	129.8	128.7	130.1	131.4	130.5	127.9

Employment by Industry: Charlotte-Concord-Gastonia, NC-SC, 2010–2018

(Numbers in thousands, not seasonally adjusted)

Industry and year	January	February	March	April	May	June	July	August	September	October	November	December	Annual average
Total Nonfarm													
2010	933.9	936.6	946.3	953.2	963.3	955.2	932.6	954.7	957.7	969.5	973.3	974.2	954.2
2011	952.1	962.4	970.7	976.5	980.2	975.9	955.0	979.8	983.5	989.1	996.3	996.9	976.5
2012	981.7	987.1	998.2	1,001.7	1,010.8	1,000.4	982.6	1,004.1	1,009.2	1,019.6	1,025.9	1,027.5	1,004.1
2013	1,005.8	1,012.5	1,021.0	1,026.4	1,033.6	1,024.5	1,008.0	1,028.4	1,032.7	1,046.9	1,054.0	1,057.6	1,029.3
2014	1,040.2	1,039.0	1,053.0	1,061.7	1,071.4	1,065.2	1,047.5	1,066.3	1,072.0	1,087.7	1,094.0	1,099.3	1,066.4
2015	1,078.9	1,086.1	1,092.0	1,099.4	1,112.3	1,111.7	1,093.4	1,109.1	1,113.1	1,130.2	1,136.5	1,143.3	1,108.8
2016	1,120.4	1,125.6	1,134.9	1,144.8	1,149.9	1,147.9	1,135.1	1,148.3	1,157.8	1,166.0	1,171.2	1,173.1	1,147.9
2017	1,153.3	1,159.2	1,167.8	1,171.2	1,181.0	1,182.5	1,165.0	1,180.8	1,184.0	1,192.3	1,196.9	1,198.4	1,177.7
2018	1,179.4	1,187.1	1,194.8	1,201.3	1,210.4	1,213.3	1,196.8	1,211.7	1,210.8	1,221.2	1,224.0	1,222.2	1,206.1
Total Private													
2010	789.2	790.6	799.1	805.6	811.8	815.6	815.7	818.5	817.9	823.8	826.9	827.6	811.9
2011	808.7	817.8	825.2	830.4	834.1	839.1	838.9	842.1	843.1	844.5	848.8	849.8	835.2
2012	836.8	840.9	850.6	853.5	861.7	866.7	864.8	866.5	865.5	869.6	874.5	876.5	860.6
2013	857.0	862.7	869.9	875.2	881.9	888.1	887.6	891.0	889.3	895.2	901.2	905.2	883.7
2014	890.8	889.1	902.1	909.5	918.6	924.5	924.7	927.6	927.6	935.2	940.3	946.1	919.7
2015	928.7	934.7	939.8	946.7	959.3	966.6	968.1	968.6	967.2	977.0	982.1	988.5	960.6
2016	971.0	974.8	982.9	992.8	997.3	1,001.4	1,005.7	1,006.5	1,005.1	1,011.6	1,015.5	1,017.9	998.5
2017	1,000.3	1,004.8	1,012.4	1,015.1	1,024.9	1,032.6	1,032.8	1,036.2	1,028.8	1,036.2	1,040.3	1,041.8	1,025.5
2018	1,024.4	1,031.0	1,038.1	1,044.6	1,053.4	1,063.0	1,063.8	1,067.4	1,057.9	1,067.2	1,069.4	1,067.5	1,054.0
Goods Producing													
2010	136.2	136.0	136.6	137.4	137.6	138.2	138.3	137.9	137.3	137.1	137.3	136.9	137.2
2011	132.6	134.7	135.4	136.7	137.6	138.7	140.1	140.5	140.8	140.5	140.9	140.8	138.3
2012	140.6	141.6	143.1	143.5	144.7	145.8	145.7	145.7	145.5	144.3	145.8	146.3	144.4
2013	144.7	146.0	147.4	147.1	147.4	148.6	148.8	148.9	148.6	148.5	148.8	149.0	147.8
2014	147.5	147.6	149.6	150.3	151.9	152.9	153.5	154.1	154.4	155.1	156.0	156.8	152.5
2015	155.6	156.5	157.1	158.5	160.0	161.6	162.4	162.8	163.3	163.4	163.8	164.3	160.8
2016	163.8	164.8	165.5	166.5	165.6	165.8	166.7	166.1	166.0	165.8	165.8	166.3	165.7
2017	163.7	164.9	165.4	166.6	167.5	169.3	170.2	170.1	169.7	169.5	169.7	170.3	168.1
2018	169.1	170.4	171.7	172.9	173.9	175.8	176.1	176.3	175.9	174.5	174.4	173.8	173.7
Service-Providing													
2010	797.7	800.6	809.7	815.8	825.7	817.0	794.3	816.8	820.4	832.4	836.0	837.3	817.0
2011	819.5	827.7	835.3	839.8	842.6	837.2	814.9	839.3	842.7	848.6	855.4	856.1	838.3
2012	841.1	845.5	855.1	858.2	866.1	854.6	836.9	858.4	863.7	875.3	880.1	881.2	859.7
2013	861.1	866.5	873.6	879.3	886.2	875.9	859.2	879.5	884.1	898.4	905.2	908.6	881.5
2014	892.7	891.4	903.4	911.4	919.5	912.3	894.0	912.2	917.6	932.6	938.0	942.5	914.0
2015	923.3	929.6	934.9	940.9	952.3	950.1	931.0	946.3	949.8	966.8	972.7	979.0	948.1
2016	956.6	960.8	969.4	978.3	984.3	982.1	968.4	982.2	991.8	1,000.2	1,005.4	1,006.8	982.2
2017	989.6	994.3	1,002.4	1,004.6	1,013.5	1,013.2	994.8	1,010.7	1,014.3	1,022.8	1,027.2	1,028.1	1,009.6
2018	1,010.3	1,016.7	1,023.1	1,028.4	1,036.5	1,037.5	1,020.7	1,035.4	1,034.9	1,046.7	1,049.6	1,048.4	1,032.4
Mining, Logging, and Construction													
2010	45.1	44.7	45.3	46.0	46.0	46.6	46.4	46.1	45.7	45.6	45.7	45.2	45.7
2011	41.7	43.4	43.8	44.7	45.1	45.5	46.1	46.0	45.9	45.6	45.5	45.2	44.9
2012	44.7	45.0	46.0	46.2	46.7	47.4	47.2	47.1	46.9	46.9	47.1	47.2	46.5
2013	46.2	46.8	48.0	48.6	48.8	49.3	49.7	50.0	50.1	50.5	50.7	50.5	49.1
2014	49.4	49.5	50.9	51.2	52.1	52.6	53.0	53.3	53.4	54.0	54.2	54.3	52.3
2015	53.1	53.4	53.8	54.6	55.7	56.4	57.1	57.2	57.8	58.1	58.1	58.2	56.1
2016	57.8	58.6	59.8	60.7	60.9	61.3	61.5	61.5	61.5	61.7	61.6	61.4	60.7
2017	59.3	60.0	60.2	60.8	61.3	62.0	62.8	62.7	62.9	63.1	63.0	63.0	61.8
2018	62.2	62.7	63.3	64.0	64.5	65.2	65.4	65.8	65.6	64.7	64.6	64.0	64.3
Manufacturing													
2010	91.1	91.3	91.3	91.4	91.6	91.6	91.9	91.8	91.6	91.5	91.6	91.7	91.5
2011	90.9	91.3	91.6	92.0	92.5	93.2	94.0	94.5	94.9	94.9	95.4	95.6	93.4
2012	95.9	96.6	97.1	97.3	98.0	98.4	98.5	98.6	98.6	97.4	98.7	99.1	97.9
2013	98.5	99.2	99.4	98.5	98.6	99.3	99.1	98.9	98.5	98.0	98.1	98.5	98.7
2014	98.1	98.1	98.7	99.1	99.8	100.3	100.5	100.8	101.0	101.1	101.8	102.5	100.2
2015	102.5	103.1	103.3	103.9	104.3	105.2	105.3	105.6	105.5	105.3	105.7	106.1	104.7
2016	106.0	106.2	105.7	105.8	104.7	104.5	105.2	104.6	104.5	104.1	104.2	104.9	105.0
2017	104.4	104.9	105.2	105.8	106.2	107.3	107.4	107.4	106.8	106.4	106.7	107.3	106.3
2018	106.9	107.7	108.4	108.9	109.4	110.6	110.7	110.5	110.3	109.8	109.8	109.8	109.4

Employment by Industry: Charlotte-Concord-Gastonia, NC-SC, 2010–2018—*Continued*

(Numbers in thousands, not seasonally adjusted)

Industry and year	January	February	March	April	May	June	July	August	September	October	November	December	Annual average
Trade, Transportation, and Utilities													
2010	193.3	192.2	193.9	194.1	195.4	195.7	195.8	196.5	195.5	197.3	200.7	202.3	196.1
2011	195.8	195.7	197.3	197.6	198.2	198.2	199.3	199.7	199.0	200.8	204.5	206.2	199.4
2012	200.9	200.0	201.6	202.5	203.8	204.9	205.1	205.3	205.3	206.9	211.8	213.2	205.1
2013	205.7	205.1	206.4	206.5	207.9	208.7	209.6	210.4	209.9	212.1	217.2	220.4	210.0
2014	213.2	211.4	213.7	213.7	215.2	216.8	216.3	216.9	217.3	220.3	225.9	228.9	217.5
2015	220.3	219.8	221.0	223.0	224.6	226.1	225.9	226.4	225.8	228.9	234.0	237.2	226.1
2016	229.5	229.2	229.8	230.5	231.7	231.7	233.6	234.2	234.1	236.6	242.4	246.6	234.2
2017	236.7	235.1	235.8	235.5	236.9	238.1	237.8	238.7	237.4	239.3	244.7	247.0	238.6
2018	239.0	238.6	239.7	240.4	241.8	242.9	244.1	244.1	243.0	244.8	251.3	251.9	243.5
Wholesale Trade													
2010	47.8	47.9	48.1	47.9	47.9	47.7	48.0	48.1	47.8	48.1	48.0	48.1	48.0
2011	47.7	48.0	48.2	47.8	47.9	47.9	48.2	48.3	48.3	48.5	48.6	48.8	48.2
2012	48.5	48.6	48.9	49.0	49.2	49.4	49.5	49.5	49.4	49.4	49.5	49.7	49.2
2013	49.1	49.5	49.7	49.6	49.7	49.9	50.2	50.4	50.3	50.8	51.0	51.3	50.1
2014	51.2	51.2	51.6	51.4	51.6	51.9	51.9	52.2	52.2	52.3	52.7	52.9	51.9
2015	52.3	52.6	53.0	53.0	53.4	53.7	53.8	53.9	53.9	54.2	54.4	54.8	53.6
2016	54.7	54.9	55.1	55.7	56.0	56.0	56.7	56.7	56.8	56.9	57.1	57.4	56.2
2017	56.5	57.1	57.2	57.1	57.3	57.5	56.5	56.4	56.1	55.8	56.0	56.0	56.6
2018	55.9	56.1	56.2	56.1	56.3	56.6	57.3	57.5	57.2	57.3	57.9	57.5	56.8
Retail Trade													
2010	105.5	104.4	105.6	105.9	106.9	107.2	107.0	107.8	106.9	108.2	111.3	112.6	107.4
2011	107.0	106.6	107.5	108.0	108.4	108.4	109.1	109.3	108.5	110.0	113.3	114.4	109.2
2012	110.4	109.4	110.4	111.1	112.2	112.7	112.8	112.9	112.8	114.4	118.8	119.4	113.1
2013	113.5	112.8	113.4	113.7	114.6	115.1	115.6	115.9	115.4	116.9	121.0	123.0	115.9
2014	116.7	115.3	116.6	116.8	117.4	118.2	117.9	118.1	117.7	120.2	124.6	126.3	118.8
2015	120.0	119.3	119.8	121.0	121.7	122.6	122.2	122.6	121.9	124.3	128.2	129.4	122.8
2016	123.2	123.2	123.5	124.1	124.7	124.5	125.3	125.7	125.4	127.4	130.9	132.0	125.8
2017	126.0	124.9	125.3	124.7	125.5	125.8	125.8	126.1	125.3	127.1	131.2	131.9	126.6
2018	126.4	125.8	126.5	126.8	127.6	127.9	127.5	127.0	125.6	127.0	130.6	131.4	127.5
Transportation and Utilities													
2010	40.0	39.9	40.2	40.3	40.6	40.8	40.8	40.6	40.8	41.0	41.4	41.6	40.7
2011	41.1	41.1	41.6	41.8	41.9	41.9	42.0	42.1	42.2	42.3	42.6	43.0	42.0
2012	42.0	42.0	42.3	42.4	42.4	42.8	42.8	42.9	43.1	43.1	43.5	44.1	42.8
2013	43.1	42.8	43.3	43.2	43.6	43.7	43.8	44.1	44.2	44.4	45.2	46.1	44.0
2014	45.3	44.9	45.5	45.5	46.2	46.7	46.5	46.6	47.4	47.8	48.6	49.7	46.7
2015	48.0	47.9	48.2	49.0	49.5	49.8	49.9	49.9	50.0	50.4	51.4	53.0	49.8
2016	51.6	51.1	51.2	50.7	51.0	51.2	51.6	51.8	51.9	52.3	54.4	57.2	52.2
2017	54.2	53.1	53.3	53.7	54.1	54.8	55.5	56.2	56.0	56.4	57.5	59.1	55.3
2018	56.7	56.7	57.0	57.5	57.9	58.4	59.3	59.6	60.2	60.5	62.8	63.0	59.1
Information													
2010	22.2	22.1	22.3	22.2	22.3	22.5	22.4	22.5	22.6	22.6	22.8	22.8	22.4
2011	22.6	22.6	22.6	22.7	22.5	22.8	22.9	23.0	23.2	23.1	23.2	23.1	22.9
2012	23.0	23.1	23.2	23.1	23.1	23.3	23.4	23.3	23.2	23.1	23.2	23.2	23.2
2013	23.3	23.3	23.3	23.3	23.7	23.8	23.9	24.0	23.9	24.1	24.2	24.5	23.8
2014	24.2	24.3	24.3	24.1	24.4	24.6	24.7	24.7	24.7	25.1	25.3	25.5	24.7
2015	25.6	25.7	25.8	25.7	26.1	26.3	26.7	26.7	26.4	26.6	26.7	26.9	26.3
2016	27.1	27.1	26.9	27.2	27.3	27.6	27.6	27.5	27.3	27.5	27.7	27.8	27.4
2017	27.5	27.5	27.8	27.1	27.3	27.6	27.9	27.9	28.0	28.4	28.7	28.9	27.9
2018	28.8	29.0	29.2	28.9	29.0	29.4	29.6	29.4	29.4	29.5	29.7	29.8	29.3
Financial Activities													
2010	73.1	73.7	73.9	73.5	73.7	74.1	74.0	74.2	74.7	75.2	75.5	75.6	74.3
2011	75.7	76.1	76.1	75.3	75.7	76.2	75.3	75.5	75.1	75.8	76.0	76.3	75.8
2012	75.8	76.2	76.4	76.0	76.2	76.6	76.5	76.6	76.5	76.8	77.2	77.5	76.5
2013	77.1	77.4	77.1	78.0	78.2	78.6	78.8	78.7	78.5	78.8	78.9	79.0	78.3
2014	79.2	79.1	79.4	79.6	79.9	80.6	81.2	81.3	81.3	81.7	82.1	82.4	80.7
2015	82.1	82.4	82.7	82.8	83.3	84.0	84.7	84.6	84.5	85.9	86.2	86.3	84.1
2016	86.3	86.6	87.1	87.4	87.6	88.2	89.1	89.4	89.0	89.4	89.5	89.9	88.3
2017	90.1	90.3	90.5	90.6	91.1	92.0	92.6	92.9	92.5	93.5	93.8	94.1	92.0
2018	93.8	94.2	94.5	94.5	94.9	95.6	95.7	96.2	95.8	96.7	96.5	96.6	95.4

Employment by Industry: Charlotte-Concord-Gastonia, NC-SC, 2010–2018—*Continued*

(Numbers in thousands, not seasonally adjusted)

Industry and year	January	February	March	April	May	June	July	August	September	October	November	December	Annual average
Professional and Business Services													
2010	138.8	139.9	142.8	145.0	145.7	146.7	147.6	149.1	149.7	152.7	152.5	152.9	147.0
2011	149.3	153.6	155.1	157.1	156.4	157.4	156.9	157.5	159.4	159.2	159.6	159.1	156.7
2012	156.2	157.8	159.8	160.5	161.3	162.2	159.9	161.0	161.6	163.9	162.7	162.2	160.8
2013	157.3	159.3	160.8	163.5	164.0	165.2	165.8	167.6	168.3	171.4	172.1	171.5	165.6
2014	170.0	170.8	173.8	177.2	177.8	179.0	179.3	180.0	180.7	182.9	182.5	183.9	178.2
2015	179.9	182.5	183.0	183.8	185.6	186.4	187.2	188.4	189.8	192.0	192.8	193.1	187.0
2016	188.2	189.3	191.9	195.6	195.5	196.9	198.5	198.9	199.4	200.6	200.9	199.7	196.3
2017	197.0	199.0	201.7	202.0	202.3	203.2	203.5	204.0	202.1	204.2	204.9	202.9	202.2
2018	200.2	201.5	202.5	204.5	204.9	207.5	207.2	209.7	209.0	212.8	210.4	208.1	206.5
Education and Health Services													
2010	99.7	100.4	100.4	101.7	101.8	100.9	101.1	101.7	101.8	103.5	104.1	104.2	101.8
2011	103.3	104.4	104.5	104.3	103.8	103.0	102.8	103.7	104.9	105.7	106.2	106.6	104.4
2012	105.4	106.6	106.3	105.5	105.8	105.2	104.6	105.1	106.0	108.1	108.3	109.0	106.3
2013	106.2	107.7	107.2	107.4	107.8	107.3	106.2	107.1	108.4	108.6	109.4	110.0	107.8
2014	108.3	108.8	109.5	109.4	109.9	109.1	109.2	110.1	111.2	112.4	113.2	113.4	110.4
2015	112.4	113.5	113.6	113.7	114.6	113.5	113.0	112.7	113.7	116.0	116.4	116.6	114.1
2016	115.1	115.7	116.2	117.0	116.8	115.7	116.4	116.9	118.3	119.6	119.5	119.3	117.2
2017	119.3	120.5	120.1	120.2	120.6	120.1	119.0	120.0	121.7	123.0	122.6	122.9	120.8
2018	121.0	123.2	123.1	123.5	123.8	122.9	121.9	123.0	124.0	126.2	125.9	126.1	123.7
Leisure and Hospitality													
2010	95.4	95.7	98.2	100.9	104.1	106.0	104.9	104.8	104.3	103.2	101.7	100.5	101.6
2011	97.0	97.9	101.2	103.6	106.6	109.2	108.1	108.6	107.4	105.9	104.9	104.1	104.5
2012	101.6	102.2	106.4	108.4	112.4	114.2	114.6	114.4	112.2	111.3	110.1	109.5	109.8
2013	107.1	107.8	110.7	112.4	116.3	119.3	117.9	117.7	115.2	115.3	113.4	114.4	114.0
2014	112.3	111.2	115.1	118.1	122.3	124.3	123.1	123.0	120.7	120.3	118.0	117.7	118.8
2015	115.9	117.1	119.3	121.3	126.7	130.3	129.6	128.4	125.5	126.0	124.0	125.8	124.2
2016	122.9	123.9	127.1	130.0	133.7	136.5	134.7	134.5	132.0	132.9	130.6	129.3	130.7
2017	126.7	128.1	131.4	133.6	139.4	141.8	141.9	142.9	137.9	138.3	135.8	135.4	136.1
2018	132.4	133.9	137.0	139.2	143.9	147.4	147.9	147.3	140.0	141.1	140.0	139.5	140.8
Other Services													
2010	30.5	30.6	31.0	30.8	31.2	31.5	31.6	31.8	32.0	32.2	32.3	32.4	31.5
2011	32.4	32.8	33.0	33.1	33.3	33.6	33.5	33.6	33.3	33.5	33.5	33.6	33.3
2012	33.3	33.4	33.8	34.0	34.4	34.5	35.0	35.1	35.2	35.2	35.4	35.6	34.6
2013	35.6	36.1	37.0	37.0	36.6	36.6	36.6	36.6	36.5	36.4	37.2	36.4	36.6
2014	36.1	35.9	36.7	37.1	37.2	37.2	37.4	37.5	37.3	37.4	37.3	37.5	37.1
2015	36.9	37.2	37.3	37.9	38.4	38.4	38.6	38.6	38.2	38.2	38.2	38.3	38.0
2016	38.1	38.2	38.4	38.6	39.1	39.0	39.1	39.0	39.0	39.2	39.1	39.0	38.8
2017	39.3	39.4	39.7	39.5	39.8	40.5	39.9	39.7	39.5	40.0	40.1	40.3	39.8
2018	40.1	40.2	40.4	40.7	41.2	41.5	41.3	41.4	40.8	41.6	41.2	41.7	41.0
Government													
2010	144.7	146.0	147.2	147.6	151.5	139.6	116.9	136.2	139.8	145.7	146.4	146.6	142.4
2011	143.4	144.6	145.5	146.1	146.1	136.8	116.1	137.7	140.4	144.6	147.5	147.1	141.3
2012	144.9	146.2	147.6	148.2	149.1	133.7	117.8	137.6	143.7	150.0	151.4	151.0	143.4
2013	148.8	149.8	151.1	151.2	151.7	136.4	120.4	137.4	143.4	151.7	152.8	152.4	145.6
2014	149.4	149.9	150.9	152.2	152.8	140.7	122.8	138.7	144.4	152.5	153.7	153.2	146.8
2015	150.2	151.4	152.2	152.7	153.0	145.1	125.3	140.5	145.9	153.2	154.4	154.8	148.2
2016	149.4	150.8	152.0	152.0	152.6	146.5	129.4	141.8	152.7	154.4	155.7	155.2	149.4
2017	153.0	154.4	155.4	156.1	156.1	149.9	132.2	144.6	155.2	156.1	156.6	156.6	152.2
2018	155.0	156.1	156.7	156.7	157.0	150.3	133.0	144.3	152.9	154.0	154.6	154.7	152.1

Employment by Industry: San Antonio-New Braunfels, TX, 2010–2018

(Numbers in thousands, not seasonally adjusted)

Industry and year	January	February	March	April	May	June	July	August	September	October	November	December	Annual average
Total Nonfarm													
2010	836.4	844.4	851.3	855.5	863.0	862.7	851.6	853.2	853.8	861.1	862.5	864.8	855.0
2011	849.7	856.8	865.0	871.0	874.5	875.6	871.4	873.4	876.1	877.5	880.6	883.1	871.2
2012	867.8	876.2	883.4	888.4	894.0	898.8	891.5	898.5	899.8	903.9	909.1	912.2	893.6
2013	894.7	906.0	912.1	917.6	922.5	928.6	924.4	926.6	929.2	932.5	938.3	939.0	922.6
2014	923.6	932.5	940.2	948.3	955.2	960.6	955.7	958.0	959.6	969.5	974.8	976.1	954.5
2015	962.5	972.0	976.0	981.7	988.1	991.1	987.3	988.5	992.6	999.0	1,005.1	1,005.4	987.4
2016	993.4	1,001.6	1,006.0	1,012.0	1,015.6	1,018.0	1,016.4	1,019.0	1,023.6	1,026.5	1,033.8	1,035.1	1,016.8
2017	1,021.1	1,027.0	1,032.8	1,034.7	1,038.5	1,045.0	1,037.4	1,039.3	1,043.5	1,045.4	1,050.8	1,052.2	1,039.0
2018	1,034.6	1,043.2	1,049.6	1,054.4	1,057.6	1,064.1	1,056.7	1,060.6	1,058.9	1,063.2	1,068.5	1,070.4	1,056.8
Total Private													
2010	675.6	680.6	686.6	689.7	694.5	698.5	695.9	695.5	690.8	694.2	695.8	698.6	691.4
2011	686.5	691.1	699.8	705.6	709.0	712.7	714.9	717.1	714.8	713.6	717.0	719.4	708.5
2012	706.7	713.1	720.2	724.7	730.7	739.2	737.5	742.3	737.8	739.7	744.8	747.9	732.1
2013	732.8	741.8	747.9	752.7	757.9	766.3	766.6	768.8	766.1	766.5	772.1	773.3	759.4
2014	760.3	767.0	774.6	782.4	789.7	797.5	797.9	799.8	795.3	801.3	806.0	807.9	790.0
2015	795.7	803.4	807.6	812.8	819.1	825.7	826.8	827.6	824.1	829.1	833.5	834.1	820.0
2016	823.1	830.0	834.5	841.8	845.0	849.8	853.3	855.4	853.1	855.2	861.5	862.8	847.1
2017	849.9	854.1	859.5	862.1	865.7	875.1	873.0	874.5	872.7	873.5	877.6	879.0	868.1
2018	862.7	870.4	875.9	881.0	883.8	893.6	891.8	895.6	888.3	891.2	895.2	896.9	885.5
Goods Producing													
2010	91.3	90.7	91.1	91.8	91.9	91.9	92.1	91.7	90.9	91.2	90.7	90.7	91.3
2011	89.2	89.3	90.1	90.9	91.1	91.8	92.3	92.0	91.6	91.2	91.1	90.6	90.9
2012	90.2	90.5	90.9	91.7	92.1	93.3	93.5	94.0	93.5	93.9	94.2	94.2	92.7
2013	93.2	93.6	94.4	95.4	95.9	97.1	97.7	97.8	97.6	97.5	97.8	97.6	96.3
2014	97.0	97.8	98.4	99.4	100.3	101.4	102.0	102.6	102.7	104.2	104.7	105.1	101.3
2015	104.1	104.8	104.4	105.1	105.4	106.2	106.5	106.3	105.3	105.9	105.7	105.5	105.4
2016	104.7	105.3	105.0	104.9	104.7	104.9	105.9	105.8	105.9	105.4	105.3	105.5	105.3
2017	104.8	105.7	106.1	106.4	106.9	108.3	108.2	109.2	109.4	109.7	110.2	111.0	108.0
2018	110.5	111.5	111.9	111.9	112.3	113.8	114.5	114.9	114.0	114.9	113.5	113.5	113.1
Service-Providing													
2010	745.1	753.7	760.2	763.7	771.1	770.8	759.5	761.5	762.9	769.9	771.9	774.1	763.7
2011	760.5	767.5	774.9	780.1	783.4	783.8	779.1	781.4	784.5	786.3	789.5	792.5	780.3
2012	777.6	785.7	792.5	796.7	801.9	805.5	798.0	804.5	806.3	810.0	814.9	818.0	801.0
2013	801.5	812.4	817.7	822.2	826.6	831.5	826.7	828.8	831.6	835.0	840.5	841.4	826.3
2014	826.6	834.7	841.8	848.9	854.9	859.2	853.7	855.4	856.9	865.3	870.1	871.0	853.2
2015	858.4	867.2	871.6	876.6	882.7	884.9	880.8	882.2	887.3	893.1	899.4	899.9	882.0
2016	888.7	896.3	901.0	907.1	910.9	913.1	910.5	913.2	917.7	921.1	928.5	929.6	911.5
2017	916.3	921.3	926.7	928.3	931.6	936.7	929.2	930.1	934.1	935.7	940.6	941.2	931.0
2018	924.1	931.7	937.7	942.5	945.3	950.3	942.2	945.7	944.9	948.3	955.0	956.9	943.7
Mining and Logging													
2010	3.0	3.0	2.9	3.0	3.0	3.1	3.0	3.0	3.0	3.0	2.9	2.9	3.0
2011	2.9	2.9	2.9	3.0	3.0	3.1	3.3	3.3	3.3	3.4	3.4	3.5	3.2
2012	3.5	3.6	3.7	4.0	4.0	4.2	4.4	4.5	4.6	4.7	4.8	4.9	4.2
2013	5.0	5.1	5.2	5.5	5.7	5.8	6.3	6.3	6.3	6.8	6.8	6.9	6.0
2014	7.5	7.7	7.9	8.2	8.4	8.7	8.6	8.8	8.9	9.3	9.5	9.6	8.6
2015	9.4	9.4	8.9	8.8	8.6	8.6	8.6	8.4	8.0	7.9	7.8	7.8	8.5
2016	7.5	7.4	7.2	7.0	6.8	6.7	6.8	6.7	6.7	6.7	6.9	7.0	7.0
2017	6.8	7.0	7.1	7.3	7.5	7.9	8.0	8.1	8.1	8.4	8.5	8.7	7.8
2018	9.1	9.1	9.3	9.8	9.9	10.2	10.4	10.5	10.3	10.4	10.3	10.5	10.0
Construction													
2010	45.1	44.4	44.9	45.1	44.9	44.4	44.7	44.1	43.2	43.1	42.5	42.4	44.1
2011	41.0	41.1	42.0	42.3	42.4	42.6	42.8	42.6	42.1	41.6	41.3	40.6	41.9
2012	40.5	40.6	40.8	40.8	41.3	42.1	42.3	42.8	42.3	42.4	42.5	42.3	41.7
2013	41.7	42.1	43.1	43.5	43.9	44.8	44.9	45.1	44.8	44.7	44.7	44.3	44.0
2014	43.7	44.2	44.7	45.2	45.7	46.2	46.9	47.2	47.2	47.9	48.2	48.4	46.3
2015	48.0	48.5	48.7	49.3	49.8	50.3	51.0	51.2	50.6	50.7	50.5	50.2	49.9
2016	50.0	50.4	50.4	50.4	50.5	50.7	51.2	51.2	51.2	51.0	50.3	50.3	50.6
2017	50.1	50.5	50.8	50.8	51.2	51.7	51.4	51.9	52.0	51.7	51.8	52.0	51.3
2018	51.9	52.6	52.6	52.7	52.9	53.7	53.6	53.9	53.0	53.7	52.2	52.6	53.0

Employment by Industry: San Antonio-New Braunfels, TX, 2010–2018—*Continued*

(Numbers in thousands, not seasonally adjusted)

Industry and year	January	February	March	April	May	June	July	August	September	October	November	December	Annual average
Manufacturing													
2010	43.2	43.3	43.3	43.7	44.0	44.4	44.4	44.6	44.7	45.1	45.3	45.4	44.3
2011	45.3	45.3	45.2	45.6	45.7	46.1	46.2	46.1	46.2	46.2	46.4	46.5	45.9
2012	46.2	46.3	46.4	46.9	46.8	47.0	46.8	46.7	46.6	46.8	46.9	47.0	46.7
2013	46.5	46.4	46.1	46.4	46.3	46.5	46.5	46.4	46.5	46.0	46.3	46.4	46.4
2014	45.8	45.9	45.8	46.0	46.2	46.5	46.5	46.6	46.6	47.0	47.0	47.1	46.4
2015	46.7	46.9	46.8	47.0	47.0	47.3	46.9	46.7	46.7	47.3	47.4	47.5	47.0
2016	47.2	47.5	47.4	47.5	47.4	47.5	47.9	47.9	48.0	47.7	48.1	48.2	47.7
2017	47.9	48.2	48.2	48.3	48.2	48.7	48.8	49.2	49.3	49.6	49.9	50.3	48.9
2018	49.5	49.8	50.0	49.4	49.5	49.9	50.5	50.5	50.7	50.8	51.0	50.4	50.2
Trade, Transportation, and Utilities													
2010	143.0	142.0	142.4	142.9	143.3	143.6	143.3	144.6	143.6	145.0	147.2	149.0	144.2
2011	144.8	143.6	144.4	145.4	145.6	146.0	146.5	147.8	147.2	148.6	151.5	153.2	147.1
2012	148.8	148.0	148.4	149.1	149.7	150.7	150.7	151.8	151.7	153.4	157.6	158.5	151.5
2013	153.6	153.5	153.6	154.6	155.5	156.3	156.6	158.6	158.6	160.5	164.1	166.3	157.7
2014	161.4	161.1	161.4	162.6	163.2	164.5	164.9	166.0	166.3	168.7	172.3	174.6	165.6
2015	169.2	168.4	168.8	170.0	171.1	172.2	172.9	173.8	174.3	176.2	179.1	180.8	173.1
2016	174.7	174.5	174.9	175.7	176.4	177.6	178.0	179.0	179.0	180.5	185.1	185.8	178.4
2017	180.7	179.0	178.7	179.2	179.6	180.1	179.6	181.0	180.2	181.4	185.9	186.7	181.0
2018	180.3	179.2	178.5	179.1	179.5	179.8	179.2	180.2	179.7	181.1	185.9	184.9	180.6
Wholesale Trade													
2010	28.5	28.5	27.8	28.7	28.8	29.0	28.9	29.0	29.0	29.3	29.2	29.2	28.8
2011	28.8	28.9	29.2	29.4	29.5	29.7	29.8	29.9	29.8	30.0	30.1	30.0	29.6
2012	30.1	30.2	30.4	30.5	30.6	30.9	30.9	31.1	30.8	31.1	31.0	31.0	30.7
2013	31.3	31.6	31.3	31.2	31.4	31.6	31.5	31.7	31.8	31.7	31.9	31.9	31.6
2014	31.7	32.1	32.2	32.2	32.3	32.6	32.7	32.8	33.0	33.3	33.6	33.7	32.7
2015	33.7	33.9	34.0	33.8	34.1	34.2	34.2	34.2	34.2	34.3	34.3	34.2	34.1
2016	34.3	34.4	34.4	34.5	34.5	34.6	34.8	34.8	34.9	34.8	34.8	34.9	34.6
2017	34.8	35.0	35.1	35.1	35.3	35.4	35.3	35.3	35.3	35.3	35.5	35.7	35.3
2018	35.5	35.7	35.7	35.9	35.9	36.0	35.8	36.0	35.9	36.0	36.1	36.4	35.9
Retail Trade													
2010	94.7	93.9	94.7	94.3	94.6	94.7	94.5	95.7	94.6	95.6	97.8	99.4	95.4
2011	95.6	94.3	94.7	95.4	95.4	95.5	95.8	96.8	96.0	97.2	99.9	101.2	96.5
2012	97.4	96.4	96.4	96.9	97.2	97.6	97.6	98.3	98.4	99.8	103.8	104.2	98.7
2013	99.3	99.0	99.3	100.1	100.6	100.9	101.6	102.9	102.7	104.5	107.3	108.9	102.3
2014	104.4	104.0	103.9	104.7	104.8	105.7	105.8	106.5	106.6	108.1	110.9	112.1	106.5
2015	107.4	106.8	106.9	108.3	108.9	109.6	110.1	110.9	111.3	113.0	115.2	116.1	110.4
2016	111.9	111.8	112.2	112.7	113.1	113.4	113.9	115.0	114.2	115.6	118.6	118.7	114.3
2017	115.0	113.6	113.5	114.1	114.1	114.0	114.0	114.8	113.7	114.8	117.7	118.1	114.8
2018	113.9	113.0	112.4	112.7	113.1	113.0	112.8	113.6	113.4	114.4	118.3	117.5	114.0
Transportation and Utilities													
2010	19.8	19.6	19.9	19.9	19.9	19.9	19.9	19.9	20.0	20.1	20.2	20.4	20.0
2011	20.4	20.4	20.5	20.6	20.7	20.8	20.9	21.1	21.4	21.4	21.5	22.0	21.0
2012	21.3	21.4	21.6	21.7	21.9	22.2	22.2	22.4	22.5	22.5	22.8	23.3	22.2
2013	23.0	22.9	23.0	23.3	23.5	23.8	23.7	24.0	24.1	24.3	24.9	25.5	23.8
2014	25.3	25.0	25.3	25.7	26.1	26.2	26.4	26.7	26.7	27.3	27.8	28.8	26.4
2015	28.1	27.7	27.9	27.9	28.1	28.4	28.6	28.7	28.8	28.9	29.6	30.5	28.6
2016	28.5	28.3	28.3	28.5	28.8	29.6	29.3	29.2	29.9	30.1	31.7	32.2	29.5
2017	30.9	30.4	30.1	30.0	30.2	30.7	30.3	30.9	31.2	31.3	32.7	32.9	31.0
2018	30.9	30.5	30.4	30.5	30.5	30.8	30.6	30.6	30.4	30.7	31.5	31.0	30.7
Information													
2010	18.5	18.6	18.9	19.5	19.3	19.0	18.7	18.5	18.3	18.1	18.3	18.4	18.7
2011	18.6	18.6	19.0	19.3	19.3	18.9	19.7	19.5	19.3	19.3	19.5	19.7	19.2
2012	19.7	19.7	20.1	20.3	20.3	20.3	20.3	20.4	20.3	20.2	20.6	20.5	20.2
2013	20.4	20.6	20.9	21.5	21.6	21.6	21.6	21.5	21.2	21.2	21.7	21.5	21.3
2014	20.8	20.8	21.0	21.6	21.7	21.5	21.6	21.4	21.4	21.4	21.5	21.8	21.4
2015	21.0	21.0	21.1	21.5	22.0	22.0	21.6	21.4	21.0	21.3	21.4	21.5	21.4
2016	21.1	21.2	21.1	21.4	21.5	21.3	21.3	20.9	20.7	21.0	20.8	21.1	21.1
2017	20.6	20.9	20.9	21.4	21.1	20.9	20.6	20.6	20.4	20.5	20.6	20.8	20.8
2018	20.6	20.8	20.9	21.3	21.3	21.3	20.9	20.8	20.7	20.7	20.9	20.9	20.9

Employment by Industry: San Antonio-New Braunfels, TX, 2010–2018—*Continued*

(Numbers in thousands, not seasonally adjusted)

Industry and year	January	February	March	April	May	June	July	August	September	October	November	December	Annual average
Financial Activities													
2010	66.8	67.4	67.6	67.5	68.2	68.8	68.6	68.5	68.1	69.0	69.4	69.8	68.3
2011	69.2	70.0	70.4	70.6	70.8	71.2	71.9	71.5	71.2	71.5	71.5	71.9	71.0
2012	71.9	72.3	72.5	72.8	73.2	73.8	74.4	74.6	74.6	75.2	75.7	76.3	73.9
2013	75.7	76.6	77.0	77.2	77.4	78.0	78.4	78.3	78.1	78.1	78.6	78.6	77.7
2014	78.4	78.7	78.8	79.5	80.0	81.0	81.1	81.3	81.2	81.6	82.1	82.4	80.5
2015	82.5	82.7	82.7	83.1	83.6	84.4	84.8	84.8	84.7	85.5	85.9	86.2	84.2
2016	86.4	87.0	87.0	87.2	87.6	88.4	88.7	88.5	88.2	88.8	89.5	90.0	88.1
2017	89.8	90.4	90.3	89.9	90.0	90.8	90.8	90.6	90.3	90.5	90.8	90.8	90.4
2018	90.5	91.2	90.7	90.8	90.9	91.9	91.9	91.9	91.8	92.5	92.6	92.9	91.6
Professional and Business Services													
2010	104.7	105.5	105.9	104.8	104.3	104.8	103.4	103.7	103.4	104.6	104.6	104.6	104.5
2011	103.9	105.0	106.1	106.4	105.7	106.0	105.6	107.0	108.0	107.4	107.6	108.5	106.4
2012	106.3	107.7	108.5	109.0	109.3	110.1	110.3	112.6	112.6	112.4	113.2	114.4	110.5
2013	111.6	113.3	114.1	113.8	113.2	114.7	114.9	115.6	116.7	116.7	117.6	117.6	115.0
2014	115.6	117.5	118.4	120.7	120.7	121.5	121.6	122.8	122.4	123.8	124.2	123.0	121.0
2015	123.2	124.6	125.2	125.3	124.5	124.5	124.7	124.6	125.2	126.8	127.1	127.1	125.2
2016	127.5	127.7	128.5	130.2	128.7	128.9	130.7	132.1	133.3	134.2	134.4	134.0	130.9
2017	132.9	133.1	133.7	133.4	133.4	135.3	135.2	135.8	138.8	139.9	139.3	138.2	135.8
2018	136.1	137.5	139.0	140.5	139.5	140.9	141.2	142.8	142.1	140.5	141.4	144.0	140.5
Education and Health Services													
2010	125.5	127.5	128.1	128.5	129.1	129.3	128.8	129.1	130.2	131.4	131.6	131.9	129.3
2011	130.1	131.1	131.9	133.1	133.4	132.7	132.7	134.2	136.1	136.2	136.5	137.1	133.8
2012	134.7	136.3	137.1	136.8	137.6	137.7	135.3	137.0	137.2	137.7	138.2	138.7	137.0
2013	135.8	137.5	138.2	138.8	139.5	139.4	138.2	139.9	140.8	141.0	141.5	142.2	139.4
2014	140.5	142.0	142.9	143.1	144.4	144.5	144.3	145.4	145.9	146.9	147.1	147.4	144.5
2015	146.1	148.0	148.7	149.5	150.0	149.5	148.9	150.4	151.0	151.8	153.3	153.9	150.1
2016	152.1	153.6	154.8	155.4	156.3	155.1	155.2	157.0	158.5	159.5	160.9	161.3	156.6
2017	159.9	160.5	160.9	160.4	160.6	161.0	159.5	160.6	161.6	161.8	162.4	162.9	161.0
2018	161.2	162.5	163.3	163.3	164.4	165.4	163.7	165.2	166.1	167.2	166.7	166.1	164.6
Leisure and Hospitality													
2010	94.3	97.1	100.5	102.4	105.7	107.3	107.3	106.0	103.3	102.0	101.3	101.2	102.4
2011	98.9	101.3	105.6	107.3	110.2	112.2	112.1	111.3	108.1	106.4	106.0	105.6	107.1
2012	102.4	105.6	109.2	111.6	114.8	118.0	117.7	116.9	113.3	112.3	110.5	110.8	111.9
2013	108.4	112.0	114.8	116.4	119.3	122.5	122.0	120.6	117.2	115.6	114.8	114.2	116.5
2014	111.6	113.8	118.3	120.0	123.4	125.7	125.1	123.3	119.1	118.4	117.6	117.7	119.5
2015	114.1	117.9	120.6	122.8	126.4	129.4	130.1	129.2	126.2	125.2	124.3	123.0	124.1
2016	120.9	124.5	126.9	130.2	132.4	135.3	135.9	134.6	130.5	128.8	128.0	127.8	129.7
2017	124.7	127.4	131.7	133.6	136.0	139.6	140.5	138.4	133.9	131.8	130.0	130.8	133.2
2018	126.3	129.9	133.5	135.7	137.1	140.8	141.4	140.9	135.7	136.1	135.7	136.5	135.8
Other Services													
2010	31.5	31.8	32.1	32.3	32.7	33.8	33.7	33.4	33.0	32.9	32.7	33.0	32.7
2011	31.8	32.2	32.3	32.6	32.9	33.9	34.1	33.8	33.3	33.0	33.3	32.8	33.0
2012	32.7	33.0	33.5	33.4	33.7	35.3	35.3	35.0	34.6	34.6	34.8	34.5	34.2
2013	34.1	34.7	34.9	35.0	35.5	36.7	37.0	36.5	35.9	35.9	36.0	35.3	35.6
2014	35.0	35.3	35.4	35.5	36.0	37.4	37.3	37.0	36.3	36.3	36.5	35.9	36.2
2015	35.5	36.0	36.1	35.5	36.1	37.5	37.3	37.1	36.4	36.4	36.7	36.1	36.4
2016	35.7	36.2	36.3	36.8	37.4	38.3	37.6	37.5	37.0	37.0	37.5	37.3	37.1
2017	36.5	37.1	37.2	37.8	38.1	39.1	38.6	38.3	38.1	37.9	38.4	37.8	37.9
2018	37.2	37.8	38.1	38.4	38.8	39.7	39.0	38.9	38.2	38.2	38.5	38.1	38.4
Government													
2010	160.8	163.8	164.7	165.8	168.5	164.2	155.7	157.7	163.0	166.9	166.8	166.2	163.7
2011	163.2	165.7	165.2	165.4	165.5	162.9	156.5	156.3	161.3	163.9	163.6	163.7	162.8
2012	161.1	163.1	163.2	163.7	163.3	159.6	154.0	156.2	162.0	164.2	164.3	164.3	161.6
2013	161.9	164.2	164.2	164.9	164.6	162.3	157.8	157.8	163.1	166.0	166.2	165.7	163.2
2014	163.3	165.5	165.6	165.9	165.5	163.1	157.8	158.2	164.3	168.2	168.8	168.2	164.5
2015	166.8	168.6	168.4	168.9	169.0	165.4	160.5	160.9	168.5	169.9	171.6	171.3	167.5
2016	170.3	171.6	171.5	170.2	170.6	168.2	163.1	163.6	170.5	171.3	172.3	172.3	169.6
2017	171.2	172.9	173.3	172.6	172.8	169.9	164.4	164.8	170.8	171.9	173.2	173.2	170.9
2018	171.9	172.8	173.7	173.4	173.8	170.5	164.9	165.0	170.6	172.0	173.3	173.5	171.3

Employment by Industry: Portland-Vancouver-Hillsboro, OR-WA, 2010–2018

(Numbers in thousands, not seasonally adjusted)

Industry and year	January	February	March	April	May	June	July	August	September	October	November	December	Annual average
Total Nonfarm													
2010	959.2	963.3	968.0	976.2	982.4	984.5	974.2	974.6	981.5	996.4	998.2	997.8	979.7
2011	977.5	984.4	988.1	998.3	1,000.3	1,001.2	995.3	995.9	1,002.0	1,012.2	1,016.9	1,016.9	999.1
2012	998.5	1,005.4	1,010.1	1,016.9	1,023.2	1,025.1	1,017.0	1,018.9	1,023.1	1,034.9	1,038.4	1,036.8	1,020.7
2013	1,014.6	1,024.6	1,029.0	1,039.1	1,046.1	1,048.6	1,040.7	1,046.1	1,052.3	1,063.1	1,069.4	1,067.7	1,045.1
2014	1,050.6	1,054.4	1,062.1	1,069.8	1,076.1	1,079.3	1,072.3	1,076.7	1,084.2	1,093.1	1,098.6	1,101.8	1,076.6
2015	1,083.7	1,092.6	1,097.8	1,105.4	1,110.1	1,113.8	1,110.8	1,114.4	1,119.7	1,131.4	1,134.6	1,137.7	1,112.7
2016	1,118.2	1,128.9	1,133.5	1,143.3	1,146.8	1,148.7	1,141.8	1,145.3	1,151.8	1,160.7	1,165.8	1,163.4	1,145.7
2017	1,138.6	1,156.2	1,163.8	1,172.3	1,176.8	1,182.8	1,174.2	1,176.5	1,181.5	1,188.7	1,194.4	1,195.6	1,175.1
2018	1,172.8	1,181.0	1,187.2	1,189.6	1,193.7	1,198.5	1,195.2	1,196.0	1,202.8	1,209.8	1,213.4	1,213.7	1,196.1
Total Private													
2010	810.6	813.3	817.6	826.6	829.0	831.2	834.6	837.3	842.0	848.0	847.8	849.9	832.3
2011	829.2	835.1	838.9	847.4	848.9	852.3	858.2	861.1	864.9	865.4	868.5	870.2	853.3
2012	852.0	857.4	862.1	869.0	874.0	876.7	880.2	884.2	885.9	888.6	890.6	890.5	875.9
2013	869.5	877.3	881.9	891.6	897.7	900.0	905.9	912.1	915.7	917.4	921.8	920.9	901.0
2014	904.3	906.9	914.0	920.7	925.7	930.1	935.2	939.4	943.6	943.6	947.1	950.9	930.1
2015	933.3	940.5	945.5	952.6	956.9	962.0	969.8	973.1	975.9	978.2	979.9	983.6	962.6
2016	965.4	974.1	978.0	986.9	989.0	992.0	996.6	1,001.4	1,003.9	1,004.8	1,008.3	1,006.7	992.3
2017	984.6	998.9	1,005.0	1,013.0	1,016.8	1,022.4	1,024.3	1,027.3	1,030.1	1,030.5	1,034.5	1,036.0	1,018.6
2018	1,022.9	1,029.2	1,035.0	1,037.1	1,040.9	1,045.7	1,052.8	1,056.2	1,057.3	1,058.4	1,059.7	1,060.7	1,046.3
Goods Producing													
2010	149.5	148.8	149.8	150.7	151.9	153.6	157.0	157.7	157.8	158.4	155.9	155.2	153.9
2011	151.9	153.2	154.5	156.5	158.0	160.3	163.1	164.2	163.8	163.4	162.0	161.6	159.4
2012	159.0	159.5	160.2	161.1	163.7	165.5	168.5	169.4	168.1	167.4	165.0	163.4	164.2
2013	161.3	162.3	163.3	165.6	167.7	170.0	172.3	173.8	173.5	173.8	172.6	171.2	169.0
2014	170.5	170.3	172.2	172.7	174.3	176.0	178.3	178.8	178.1	176.8	175.4	175.4	174.9
2015	174.1	174.7	175.7	176.6	178.1	180.4	183.2	183.8	183.3	183.8	182.1	182.2	179.8
2016	180.6	182.2	183.2	184.3	185.7	186.4	188.7	190.3	188.9	188.7	187.0	186.3	186.0
2017	183.0	185.7	187.2	189.1	191.4	194.2	196.1	196.9	196.4	196.7	195.7	196.2	192.4
2018	193.9	195.3	196.5	197.2	199.2	201.8	205.7	206.5	205.7	205.9	203.8	203.7	201.3
Service-Providing													
2010	809.7	814.5	818.2	825.5	830.5	830.9	817.2	816.9	823.7	838.0	842.3	842.6	825.8
2011	825.6	831.2	833.6	841.8	842.3	840.9	832.2	831.7	838.2	848.8	854.9	855.3	839.7
2012	839.5	845.9	849.9	855.8	859.5	859.6	848.5	849.5	855.0	867.5	873.4	873.4	856.5
2013	853.3	862.3	865.7	873.5	878.4	878.6	868.4	872.3	878.8	889.3	896.8	896.5	876.2
2014	880.1	884.1	889.9	897.1	901.8	903.3	894.0	897.9	906.1	916.3	923.2	926.4	901.7
2015	909.6	917.9	922.1	928.8	932.0	933.4	927.6	930.6	936.4	947.6	952.5	955.5	932.8
2016	937.6	946.7	950.3	959.0	961.1	962.3	953.1	955.0	962.9	972.0	978.8	977.1	959.7
2017	955.6	970.5	976.6	983.2	985.4	988.6	978.1	979.6	985.1	992.0	998.7	999.4	982.7
2018	978.9	985.7	990.7	992.4	994.5	996.7	989.5	989.5	997.1	1,003.9	1,009.6	1,010.0	994.9
Mining and Logging													
2010	1.0	1.0	1.1	1.0	1.1	1.1	1.1	1.1	1.1	1.1	1.1	1.0	1.1
2011	0.9	1.0	1.0	1.0	1.1	1.1	1.1	1.1	1.1	1.1	1.1	1.0	1.1
2012	0.9	0.9	0.9	0.9	1.0	1.0	1.0	1.0	1.0	1.0	1.0	1.0	1.0
2013	1.0	1.0	1.0	1.0	1.0	1.1	1.1	1.1	1.1	1.2	1.2	1.1	1.1
2014	1.1	1.1	1.1	1.2	1.2	1.2	1.2	1.3	1.3	1.2	1.2	1.2	1.2
2015	1.2	1.2	1.2	1.3	1.2	1.3	1.3	1.3	1.3	1.3	1.3	1.3	1.3
2016	1.3	1.3	1.3	1.3	1.3	1.3	1.4	1.4	1.3	1.4	1.3	1.3	1.3
2017	1.3	1.3	1.3	1.3	1.3	1.4	1.4	1.4	1.3	1.3	1.3	1.4	1.3
2018	1.3	1.3	1.3	1.4	1.4	1.4	1.4	1.4	1.4	1.4	1.4	1.4	1.4
Construction													
2010	43.2	42.8	43.4	44.1	44.8	45.6	47.8	48.4	48.3	48.1	45.8	45.3	45.6
2011	42.8	43.3	44.2	45.6	46.4	47.7	49.4	50.1	50.0	49.6	48.2	48.0	47.1
2012	46.2	46.3	46.7	47.3	49.0	49.7	51.3	52.5	51.4	50.8	48.8	47.7	49.0
2013	46.4	47.0	48.1	49.8	51.8	52.8	54.7	55.6	55.5	55.7	55.0	54.0	52.2
2014	53.6	53.2	54.7	54.9	55.8	56.7	57.7	58.0	57.2	55.8	54.8	54.3	55.6
2015	53.3	53.5	53.8	54.2	55.1	56.2	57.7	58.6	58.3	58.9	57.8	57.4	56.2
2016	56.6	57.9	58.5	60.0	61.1	61.9	63.9	65.0	64.9	64.4	63.7	63.1	61.8
2017	61.1	63.2	64.2	65.5	67.0	68.5	69.7	70.7	70.6	70.1	69.3	69.3	67.4
2018	67.8	68.7	69.4	69.7	71.2	72.4	75.2	76.1	75.4	75.3	73.3	72.8	72.3

Employment by Industry: Portland-Vancouver-Hillsboro, OR-WA, 2010–2018—*Continued*

(Numbers in thousands, not seasonally adjusted)

Industry and year	January	February	March	April	May	June	July	August	September	October	November	December	Annual average
Manufacturing													
2010	105.3	105.0	105.3	105.6	106.0	106.9	108.1	108.2	108.4	109.2	109.0	108.9	107.2
2011	108.2	108.9	109.3	109.9	110.5	111.5	112.6	113.0	112.7	112.7	112.7	112.6	111.2
2012	111.9	112.3	112.6	112.9	113.7	114.8	116.2	115.9	115.7	115.6	115.2	114.7	114.3
2013	113.9	114.3	114.2	114.8	114.9	116.1	116.5	117.1	116.9	116.9	116.4	116.1	115.7
2014	115.8	116.0	116.4	116.6	117.3	118.1	119.4	119.5	119.6	119.8	119.4	119.9	118.2
2015	119.6	120.0	120.7	121.1	121.8	122.9	124.2	123.9	123.7	123.6	123.0	123.5	122.3
2016	122.7	123.0	123.4	123.0	123.3	123.2	123.4	123.9	122.7	122.9	122.0	121.9	123.0
2017	120.6	121.2	121.7	122.3	123.1	124.3	125.0	124.8	124.5	125.3	125.1	125.5	123.6
2018	124.8	125.3	125.8	126.1	126.6	128.0	129.1	129.0	128.9	129.2	129.1	129.5	127.6
Trade, Transportation, and Utilities													
2010	182.0	180.5	180.6	181.8	182.6	183.5	184.4	184.8	184.9	186.3	189.5	191.9	184.4
2011	184.7	183.5	183.4	184.7	185.9	186.8	187.9	187.7	188.0	188.5	192.4	194.1	187.3
2012	187.2	185.8	186.2	187.5	189.4	190.9	190.8	191.2	190.9	192.0	197.1	198.9	190.7
2013	191.3	191.0	191.1	192.2	193.9	194.5	195.9	196.7	196.8	197.2	201.6	203.3	195.5
2014	197.2	195.6	195.7	196.7	198.4	199.7	201.3	202.4	202.6	203.3	207.6	210.5	200.9
2015	203.5	202.4	202.8	203.4	204.8	206.2	207.3	208.3	208.5	209.0	212.1	214.6	206.9
2016	207.2	206.1	206.1	207.0	207.6	209.1	209.9	210.7	210.5	211.0	216.1	218.0	209.9
2017	211.9	211.4	211.6	211.9	213.0	213.8	214.6	215.4	215.4	216.1	220.9	223.1	214.9
2018	215.2	212.8	212.8	212.9	214.5	215.5	217.2	218.1	218.6	220.7	223.7	224.7	217.2
Wholesale Trade													
2010	47.9	48.0	47.9	48.7	49.2	49.2	49.6	49.6	49.3	49.7	49.7	49.7	49.0
2011	48.9	49.3	49.1	50.0	50.5	50.5	50.9	50.9	50.6	50.8	50.7	50.5	50.2
2012	50.1	50.4	50.5	51.5	52.0	51.9	52.3	52.3	52.0	52.1	52.4	52.4	51.7
2013	51.5	52.1	52.0	52.3	52.8	52.7	53.4	53.3	53.2	52.8	53.3	53.2	52.7
2014	52.5	52.7	52.5	52.6	52.8	52.9	53.4	53.5	53.4	53.2	53.4	53.6	53.0
2015	53.0	53.5	53.4	53.5	53.8	53.9	54.5	54.5	54.4	54.3	54.5	54.7	54.0
2016	53.7	54.1	54.0	54.4	54.3	54.6	54.9	55.1	54.8	54.8	55.2	55.5	54.6
2017	54.8	55.5	55.4	55.7	56.2	56.3	56.4	56.6	56.3	56.0	56.3	56.5	56.0
2018	55.7	56.1	56.0	56.1	56.5	56.6	57.1	57.2	57.0	57.8	57.5	57.8	56.8
Retail Trade													
2010	100.9	99.6	99.8	99.8	100.2	100.9	102.0	102.4	101.9	102.8	106.0	107.6	102.0
2011	102.2	100.9	100.9	101.2	101.7	102.6	103.6	103.5	103.1	103.8	107.4	108.8	103.3
2012	103.6	101.9	101.9	102.5	103.6	104.9	105.4	105.6	105.0	105.9	110.2	111.4	105.2
2013	106.1	105.1	105.2	105.8	107.0	107.7	109.0	109.7	109.2	109.9	113.4	114.6	108.6
2014	109.8	108.1	108.5	109.2	110.5	111.5	113.1	113.7	113.4	113.9	117.5	119.0	112.4
2015	113.6	112.3	112.7	113.7	114.5	115.1	116.6	117.3	116.9	117.3	119.7	120.8	115.9
2016	115.8	114.9	115.0	115.2	115.8	116.9	117.9	118.2	117.6	118.0	120.8	121.4	117.3
2017	117.5	116.9	117.1	117.4	117.6	118.1	119.4	119.7	119.3	119.9	123.0	123.8	119.1
2018	119.4	117.4	117.4	117.5	118.3	118.9	120.2	120.4	119.6	120.9	122.9	122.8	119.6
Transportation and Utilities													
2010	33.2	32.9	32.9	33.3	33.2	33.4	32.8	32.8	33.7	33.8	33.8	34.6	33.4
2011	33.6	33.3	33.4	33.5	33.7	33.7	33.4	33.3	34.3	33.9	34.3	34.8	33.8
2012	33.5	33.5	33.8	33.5	33.8	34.1	33.1	33.3	33.9	34.0	34.5	35.1	33.8
2013	33.7	33.8	33.9	34.1	34.1	34.1	33.5	33.7	34.4	34.5	34.9	35.5	34.2
2014	34.9	34.8	34.7	34.9	35.1	35.3	34.8	35.2	35.8	36.2	36.7	37.9	35.5
2015	36.9	36.6	36.7	36.2	36.5	37.2	36.2	36.5	37.2	37.4	37.9	39.1	37.0
2016	37.7	37.1	37.1	37.4	37.5	37.6	37.1	37.4	38.1	38.2	40.1	41.1	38.0
2017	39.6	39.0	39.1	38.8	39.2	39.4	38.8	39.1	39.8	40.2	41.6	42.8	39.8
2018	40.1	39.3	39.4	39.3	39.7	40.0	39.9	40.5	42.0	42.0	43.3	44.1	40.8
Information													
2010	23.1	23.2	23.3	23.2	23.7	23.7	23.2	23.5	23.4	23.1	23.5	23.4	23.4
2011	23.4	23.4	23.7	23.5	23.4	23.2	23.5	23.6	23.3	23.3	23.5	23.4	23.4
2012	23.1	23.4	23.8	24.0	23.9	24.2	24.4	24.1	24.0	24.4	24.5	24.3	24.0
2013	23.9	23.9	24.0	24.0	23.9	23.8	23.9	24.1	24.2	24.3	24.4	24.4	24.1
2014	23.6	23.7	24.0	24.1	24.0	24.3	24.7	24.7	24.7	24.6	24.7	24.8	24.3
2015	24.3	24.6	24.7	24.6	24.8	24.9	25.5	25.8	25.4	25.2	25.4	25.7	25.1
2016	25.2	25.5	25.6	25.7	26.1	26.1	25.9	26.2	27.1	26.7	26.5	26.4	26.1
2017	26.3	26.8	26.6	26.5	26.0	25.8	25.5	25.8	25.8	25.2	25.2	24.9	25.9
2018	24.7	25.1	25.4	25.3	25.0	25.0	25.7	25.4	25.4	25.6	25.4	25.7	25.3

Employment by Industry: Portland-Vancouver-Hillsboro, OR-WA, 2010–2018—*Continued*

(Numbers in thousands, not seasonally adjusted)

Industry and year	January	February	March	April	May	June	July	August	September	October	November	December	Annual average
Financial Activities													
2010	62.4	62.2	62.1	62.5	62.3	62.6	62.7	62.6	62.4	62.5	62.2	62.5	62.4
2011	61.8	61.8	61.6	61.7	61.8	62.0	62.2	62.2	61.9	61.8	62.0	62.1	61.9
2012	61.8	61.9	61.9	62.2	62.2	62.4	63.0	63.1	62.8	62.9	62.9	63.2	62.5
2013	62.4	62.5	62.6	63.1	63.5	63.7	64.6	64.5	64.3	64.3	64.2	64.2	63.7
2014	63.3	63.2	63.2	63.5	63.8	64.2	64.8	65.1	65.0	65.2	65.2	65.4	64.3
2015	65.2	65.3	65.2	65.9	66.3	66.6	67.4	67.5	67.1	67.5	67.4	67.8	66.6
2016	66.8	66.7	66.6	67.5	67.8	68.3	69.1	69.5	69.1	69.5	69.8	69.8	68.4
2017	69.0	69.2	69.6	69.9	70.4	70.8	71.8	71.8	71.1	71.7	71.8	71.6	70.7
2018	70.9	71.1	71.3	71.6	71.9	72.0	73.3	73.2	72.4	71.9	72.1	72.5	72.0
Professional and Business Services													
2010	130.1	131.4	133.0	135.8	135.4	136.3	137.8	139.0	139.0	140.5	140.0	140.1	136.5
2011	136.6	138.1	139.2	141.5	141.4	142.3	144.7	145.4	145.8	145.9	146.1	146.4	142.8
2012	144.2	145.0	146.1	147.5	147.9	149.0	150.3	151.5	151.0	152.2	151.6	151.5	149.0
2013	148.4	149.8	151.7	154.1	154.8	156.1	158.5	160.1	159.9	160.7	160.7	160.7	156.3
2014	157.7	158.8	160.4	162.5	163.3	164.9	166.4	167.8	168.2	168.3	168.0	168.3	164.6
2015	164.9	166.5	168.2	170.6	171.2	172.2	174.2	175.0	174.7	175.4	174.8	174.9	171.9
2016	172.3	174.1	175.1	177.1	177.1	178.2	179.2	180.0	178.8	179.5	179.1	178.0	177.4
2017	175.1	178.1	179.3	181.6	182.0	183.8	183.3	183.8	183.7	183.5	183.1	182.9	181.7
2018	181.0	182.6	183.9	183.6	183.7	184.5	185.0	186.4	185.6	185.1	185.0	181.3	184.0
Education and Health Services													
2010	139.5	142.3	143.2	144.0	142.9	139.6	137.3	137.0	142.3	146.2	147.2	147.2	142.4
2011	144.5	147.3	147.8	148.1	146.3	143.4	140.9	141.2	146.2	149.3	150.2	149.8	146.3
2012	146.3	150.1	150.7	151.4	149.3	145.8	142.9	143.5	148.5	151.2	152.2	151.8	148.6
2013	147.7	151.8	151.9	153.3	152.2	148.3	145.4	146.6	151.6	155.3	156.4	155.8	151.4
2014	152.6	155.4	156.2	156.8	155.2	152.8	150.1	149.9	155.3	158.2	159.6	159.5	155.1
2015	156.3	160.3	160.6	161.3	159.2	156.9	155.0	154.9	160.3	163.1	164.2	163.8	159.7
2016	161.2	165.1	165.4	166.1	163.7	160.6	158.7	159.7	165.2	168.4	169.3	168.2	164.3
2017	164.1	169.9	170.9	171.2	169.4	166.3	163.8	164.8	170.6	173.0	174.0	173.4	169.3
2018	176.9	180.7	181.6	180.9	179.0	176.6	174.1	175.1	180.2	182.6	183.6	184.5	179.7
Leisure and Hospitality													
2010	90.1	90.8	91.3	94.0	95.3	96.4	97.1	97.7	97.2	95.7	94.8	94.8	94.6
2011	91.9	93.0	93.7	96.2	96.8	98.8	100.1	100.8	100.0	97.3	96.5	97.0	96.8
2012	94.7	95.6	97.0	98.7	100.4	101.9	103.3	104.4	103.8	101.5	100.7	101.0	100.3
2013	98.3	99.5	100.7	102.6	104.5	106.6	107.8	108.8	108.2	104.9	104.6	104.4	104.2
2014	102.5	102.9	104.9	106.9	108.5	109.6	111.0	112.0	111.1	108.7	108.2	108.6	107.9
2015	107.0	108.3	109.8	111.3	113.4	115.5	117.4	117.8	116.9	114.4	113.9	114.6	113.4
2016	112.1	113.8	115.1	117.6	119.1	121.2	123.1	122.8	122.0	119.0	118.6	118.6	118.6
2017	115.4	117.2	118.8	121.4	123.0	126.0	127.1	126.7	125.3	122.7	122.2	122.3	122.3
2018	119.4	120.3	121.8	123.7	125.4	127.8	128.8	128.8	127.1	123.6	123.3	125.3	124.6
Other Services													
2010	33.9	34.1	34.3	34.6	34.9	35.5	35.1	35.0	35.0	35.3	34.7	34.8	34.8
2011	34.4	34.8	35.0	35.2	35.3	35.5	35.8	36.0	35.9	35.9	35.8	35.8	35.5
2012	35.7	36.1	36.2	36.6	37.2	37.0	37.0	37.0	36.8	37.0	36.6	36.4	36.6
2013	36.2	36.5	36.6	36.7	37.2	37.0	37.5	37.5	37.2	36.9	37.3	36.9	37.0
2014	36.9	37.0	37.4	37.5	38.2	38.6	38.6	38.7	38.6	38.5	38.4	38.4	38.1
2015	38.0	38.4	38.5	38.9	39.1	39.3	39.8	40.0	39.7	39.8	40.0	40.0	39.3
2016	40.0	40.6	40.9	41.6	41.9	42.1	42.0	42.2	42.3	42.0	41.9	41.4	41.6
2017	39.8	40.6	41.0	41.4	41.6	41.7	42.1	42.1	41.8	41.6	41.6	41.6	41.4
2018	40.9	41.3	41.7	41.9	42.2	42.5	43.0	42.7	42.3	43.0	42.8	43.0	42.3
Government													
2010	148.6	150.0	150.4	149.6	153.4	153.3	139.6	137.3	139.5	148.4	150.4	147.9	147.4
2011	148.3	149.3	149.2	150.9	151.4	148.9	137.1	134.8	137.1	146.8	148.4	146.7	145.7
2012	146.5	148.0	148.0	147.9	149.2	148.4	136.8	134.7	137.2	146.3	147.8	146.3	144.8
2013	145.1	147.3	147.1	147.5	148.4	148.6	134.8	134.0	136.6	145.7	147.6	146.8	144.1
2014	146.3	147.5	148.1	149.1	150.4	149.2	137.1	137.3	140.6	149.5	151.5	150.9	146.5
2015	150.4	152.1	152.3	152.8	153.2	151.8	141.0	141.3	143.8	153.2	154.7	154.1	150.1
2016	152.8	154.8	155.5	156.4	157.8	156.7	145.2	143.9	147.9	155.9	157.5	156.7	153.4
2017	154.0	157.3	158.8	159.3	160.0	160.4	149.9	149.2	151.4	158.2	159.9	159.6	156.5
2018	149.9	151.8	152.2	152.5	152.8	152.8	142.4	139.8	145.5	151.4	153.7	153.0	149.8

Employment by Industry: Sacramento—Roseville—Arden-Arcade, CA, 2010–2018

(Numbers in thousands, not seasonally adjusted)

Industry and year	January	February	March	April	May	June	July	August	September	October	November	December	Annual average
Total Nonfarm													
2010	827.0	826.6	829.6	834.1	839.5	841.0	828.2	825.6	827.1	832.7	833.5	831.3	831.4
2011	819.8	822.3	823.9	827.8	829.4	830.9	822.2	826.8	831.0	835.4	839.7	837.2	828.9
2012	825.7	831.3	835.3	845.6	850.7	858.5	844.7	848.1	848.1	853.8	860.5	857.9	846.7
2013	854.1	860.1	863.7	865.8	869.6	872.9	863.1	868.3	870.4	875.8	883.8	882.6	869.2
2014	872.0	875.6	879.9	885.0	890.7	897.5	884.6	890.4	892.0	898.9	905.7	902.8	889.6
2015	896.5	898.6	904.8	910.0	914.5	920.6	918.3	920.4	921.2	931.7	937.2	939.4	917.8
2016	929.8	935.9	936.3	945.3	948.8	952.4	950.1	953.2	952.5	957.7	962.4	963.1	949.0
2017	946.5	950.8	957.1	962.7	968.7	975.6	967.4	969.7	971.6	982.1	986.4	990.0	969.1
2018	978.2	984.1	985.9	992.8	998.6	1,005.0	998.9	1,003.4	1,000.8	1,009.4	1,017.0	1,020.2	999.5
Total Private													
2010	596.0	594.6	596.0	597.7	599.4	603.9	605.5	606.3	603.0	602.7	602.7	605.3	601.1
2011	592.5	593.2	593.6	596.9	599.9	602.6	608.1	611.8	611.8	610.2	614.5	616.2	604.3
2012	604.0	607.4	609.1	619.1	624.1	630.8	632.3	635.2	632.1	631.6	637.4	639.1	625.2
2013	633.4	637.6	639.0	641.0	643.6	646.5	648.3	652.2	651.0	651.7	656.5	658.9	646.6
2014	646.7	648.1	651.3	654.1	659.2	664.4	666.0	670.1	668.5	667.2	672.2	674.3	661.8
2015	665.6	667.0	671.4	675.8	680.7	685.5	693.6	694.5	692.8	696.6	700.5	705.6	685.8
2016	695.8	701.4	699.7	708.7	711.2	714.4	721.0	723.4	721.2	722.0	725.5	727.2	714.3
2017	711.8	715.7	719.8	725.6	730.6	737.4	738.9	741.7	740.4	744.8	747.9	752.2	733.9
2018	741.0	745.9	745.9	752.8	757.7	763.3	769.2	772.0	768.2	769.8	776.9	782.2	762.1
Goods Producing													
2010	69.9	68.7	69.5	70.3	71.4	73.1	73.9	74.9	73.9	73.1	71.5	69.8	71.7
2011	67.1	67.0	66.6	68.2	69.6	70.9	72.6	74.1	74.5	74.1	72.3	70.3	70.6
2012	68.3	68.2	67.4	69.2	71.8	73.9	75.7	77.0	77.0	76.1	74.8	73.9	72.8
2013	72.4	73.6	74.2	75.6	77.2	78.6	80.0	81.9	81.9	81.0	79.7	78.7	77.9
2014	76.8	77.2	77.4	78.6	80.9	82.3	83.7	85.1	85.0	84.2	83.7	81.3	81.4
2015	80.9	81.1	82.4	84.0	85.8	87.7	89.6	90.6	90.9	91.5	90.7	90.0	87.1
2016	86.9	87.9	87.3	90.2	91.6	92.6	94.8	95.6	95.5	93.9	92.9	90.5	91.6
2017	87.0	88.1	90.3	91.5	94.4	96.6	97.7	98.7	99.3	99.5	97.5	97.5	94.8
2018	94.2	95.8	94.5	97.0	99.1	101.8	103.6	105.1	105.2	103.1	101.6	101.7	100.2
Service-Providing													
2010	757.1	757.9	760.1	763.8	768.1	767.9	754.3	750.7	753.2	759.6	762.0	761.5	759.7
2011	752.7	755.3	757.3	759.6	759.8	760.0	749.6	752.7	756.5	761.3	767.4	766.9	758.3
2012	757.4	763.1	767.9	776.4	778.9	784.6	769.0	771.1	771.1	777.7	785.7	784.0	773.9
2013	781.7	786.5	789.5	790.2	792.4	794.3	783.1	786.4	788.5	794.8	804.1	803.9	791.3
2014	795.2	798.4	802.5	806.4	809.8	815.2	800.9	805.3	807.0	814.7	822.0	821.5	808.2
2015	815.6	817.5	822.4	826.0	828.7	832.9	828.7	829.8	830.3	840.2	846.5	849.4	830.7
2016	842.9	848.0	849.0	855.1	857.2	859.8	855.3	857.6	857.0	863.8	869.5	872.6	857.3
2017	859.5	862.7	866.8	871.2	874.3	879.0	869.7	871.0	872.3	882.6	888.9	892.5	874.2
2018	884.0	888.3	891.4	895.8	899.5	903.2	895.3	898.3	895.6	906.3	915.4	918.5	899.3
Mining and Logging													
2010	0.3	0.3	0.4	0.4	0.4	0.5	0.5	0.5	0.5	0.5	0.5	0.5	0.4
2011	0.4	0.4	0.4	0.4	0.4	0.4	0.4	0.5	0.5	0.5	0.5	0.4	0.4
2012	0.4	0.4	0.4	0.3	0.4	0.4	0.4	0.4	0.4	0.4	0.4	0.4	0.4
2013	0.3	0.3	0.3	0.3	0.4	0.4	0.4	0.4	0.4	0.4	0.4	0.4	0.4
2014	0.3	0.4	0.3	0.4	0.4	0.5	0.4	0.5	0.4	0.5	0.5	0.4	0.4
2015	0.4	0.4	0.4	0.4	0.4	0.4	0.5	0.5	0.5	0.5	0.4	0.4	0.4
2016	0.4	0.4	0.4	0.4	0.4	0.4	0.5	0.5	0.5	0.5	0.5	0.4	0.4
2017	0.4	0.4	0.4	0.4	0.4	0.5	0.5	0.5	0.5	0.5	0.4	0.4	0.4
2018	0.4	0.4	0.4	0.4	0.5	0.5	0.5	0.5	0.5	0.5	0.5	0.5	0.5
Construction													
2010	37.2	36.2	36.8	37.6	38.6	40.0	40.5	40.6	39.5	39.3	38.3	36.5	38.4
2011	34.4	34.2	33.6	35.1	36.3	37.3	39.3	39.6	39.6	39.3	38.5	36.4	37.0
2012	34.8	34.7	34.0	35.5	37.8	39.5	40.8	41.4	41.3	41.5	40.7	39.9	38.5
2013	38.8	39.8	40.6	41.6	43.0	44.3	45.4	46.4	46.2	46.1	44.9	43.7	43.4
2014	42.3	42.3	42.6	43.5	45.6	46.6	47.5	48.0	47.9	47.9	47.4	45.1	45.6
2015	45.0	45.2	46.2	47.6	49.3	50.9	52.2	52.8	52.9	54.4	53.9	53.2	50.3
2016	50.3	51.3	50.6	53.8	54.9	56.2	57.8	58.2	58.0	57.5	56.8	54.7	55.0
2017	51.5	52.5	55.2	56.0	58.5	60.5	61.3	61.9	62.1	62.7	61.1	61.0	58.7
2018	59.0	60.5	59.1	61.2	63.0	65.0	66.3	67.6	67.7	66.0	64.2	64.0	63.6

Employment by Industry: Sacramento—Roseville—Arden-Arcade, CA, 2010–2018—*Continued*

(Numbers in thousands, not seasonally adjusted)

Industry and year	January	February	March	April	May	June	July	August	September	October	November	December	Annual average
Manufacturing													
2010	32.4	32.2	32.3	32.3	32.4	32.6	32.9	33.8	33.9	33.3	32.7	32.8	32.8
2011	32.3	32.4	32.6	32.7	32.9	33.2	32.9	34.0	34.4	34.3	33.3	33.5	33.2
2012	33.1	33.1	33.0	33.4	33.6	34.0	34.5	35.2	35.3	34.2	33.7	33.6	33.9
2013	33.3	33.5	33.3	33.7	33.8	33.9	34.2	35.1	35.3	34.5	34.4	34.6	34.1
2014	34.2	34.5	34.5	34.7	34.9	35.2	35.8	36.6	36.7	35.8	35.8	35.8	35.4
2015	35.5	35.5	35.8	36.0	36.1	36.4	36.9	37.3	37.5	36.6	36.4	36.4	36.4
2016	36.2	36.2	36.3	36.0	36.3	36.0	36.5	36.9	37.0	35.9	35.6	35.4	36.2
2017	35.1	35.2	34.7	35.1	35.5	35.6	35.9	36.3	36.7	36.3	36.0	36.1	35.7
2018	34.8	34.9	35.0	35.4	35.6	36.3	36.8	37.0	37.0	36.6	36.9	37.2	36.1
Trade, Transportation, and Utilities													
2010	132.1	130.0	130.0	130.6	131.1	131.2	131.5	132.1	131.8	133.1	135.8	137.8	132.3
2011	132.2	130.8	130.7	131.0	131.7	132.4	133.1	133.7	133.9	135.5	139.7	141.5	133.9
2012	135.5	133.9	134.3	136.4	137.3	138.4	138.5	139.1	139.3	140.0	144.6	146.0	138.6
2013	140.0	138.8	138.8	139.0	139.6	140.2	140.7	140.6	140.4	142.0	146.9	148.2	141.3
2014	141.7	140.3	140.4	140.4	140.9	141.8	142.4	143.2	142.7	143.7	148.3	150.3	143.0
2015	144.2	142.7	143.0	144.1	145.2	145.3	146.6	147.3	147.4	149.2	153.9	155.1	147.0
2016	149.5	148.5	148.2	149.6	150.3	150.5	151.9	152.6	151.9	153.1	158.0	158.5	151.9
2017	152.9	150.9	150.6	151.6	152.2	152.7	153.3	154.2	153.8	157.1	161.7	162.8	154.5
2018	157.8	156.3	156.2	157.2	157.9	158.6	160.6	160.7	160.2	160.5	165.2	167.2	159.9
Wholesale Trade													
2010	22.7	22.5	22.3	22.6	22.6	22.4	22.3	22.3	22.3	22.5	22.5	22.6	22.5
2011	22.5	22.4	22.5	23.0	23.2	23.4	23.4	23.4	23.6	24.0	24.3	24.5	23.4
2012	24.2	24.5	24.9	25.2	25.2	25.3	25.0	24.9	24.8	24.8	24.8	24.9	24.9
2013	24.5	24.5	24.5	24.6	24.5	24.6	24.7	24.4	24.4	24.6	24.7	24.6	24.6
2014	24.4	24.4	24.3	24.2	24.1	24.2	24.1	24.0	24.0	23.9	24.0	24.0	24.1
2015	24.1	24.0	23.9	24.2	24.3	24.3	24.5	24.4	24.4	24.9	25.0	25.0	24.4
2016	25.0	25.0	24.9	25.3	25.3	25.3	25.7	25.8	25.6	25.7	25.8	26.0	25.5
2017	25.8	26.0	25.9	26.1	26.2	26.5	26.6	26.6	26.6	26.8	27.1	27.4	26.5
2018	27.8	28.0	28.1	28.2	28.2	28.4	29.0	29.0	28.9	28.9	28.7	28.9	28.5
Retail Trade													
2010	87.2	85.6	85.7	86.4	86.9	87.1	87.6	88.1	88.0	89.0	91.7	93.2	88.0
2011	89.0	87.7	87.3	87.2	87.5	87.9	88.6	89.0	89.1	90.2	94.0	95.3	89.4
2012	90.7	88.7	88.8	89.7	90.3	90.9	91.2	91.8	91.9	92.6	97.0	97.8	91.8
2013	92.9	91.7	91.7	91.8	92.4	92.7	93.2	93.3	93.0	94.4	98.8	99.7	93.8
2014	94.5	93.2	93.4	93.3	93.6	94.2	94.7	95.2	94.7	95.8	99.8	101.1	95.3
2015	96.2	94.9	95.2	95.9	96.8	96.8	97.4	97.9	98.0	99.2	103.3	103.9	98.0
2016	99.5	98.7	98.4	99.0	99.2	99.1	99.9	100.4	99.9	101.1	105.1	105.1	100.5
2017	101.2	99.3	98.9	100.0	100.4	100.4	100.7	101.4	101.0	102.2	105.4	105.5	101.4
2018	101.6	100.1	99.9	100.5	101.0	101.1	102.4	102.4	101.8	102.5	106.5	107.7	102.3
Transportation and Utilities													
2010	22.2	21.9	22.0	21.6	21.6	21.7	21.6	21.7	21.5	21.6	21.6	22.0	21.8
2011	20.7	20.7	20.9	20.8	21.0	21.1	21.1	21.3	21.2	21.3	21.4	21.7	21.1
2012	20.6	20.7	20.6	21.5	21.8	22.2	22.3	22.4	22.6	22.6	22.8	23.3	22.0
2013	22.6	22.6	22.6	22.6	22.7	22.9	22.8	22.9	23.0	23.0	23.4	23.9	22.9
2014	22.8	22.7	22.7	22.9	23.2	23.4	23.6	24.0	24.0	24.0	24.5	25.2	23.6
2015	23.9	23.8	23.9	24.0	24.1	24.2	24.7	25.0	25.0	25.1	25.6	26.2	24.6
2016	25.0	24.8	24.9	25.3	25.8	26.1	26.3	26.4	26.4	26.3	27.1	27.4	26.0
2017	25.9	25.6	25.8	25.5	25.6	25.8	26.0	26.2	26.2	28.1	29.2	29.9	26.7
2018	28.4	28.2	28.2	28.5	28.7	29.1	29.2	29.3	29.5	29.1	30.0	30.6	29.1
Information													
2010	17.8	17.7	17.4	17.3	17.2	17.6	17.1	16.9	16.7	16.7	17.0	17.0	17.2
2011	16.9	16.8	16.8	16.7	16.6	16.5	16.4	16.2	15.9	15.9	15.7	15.6	16.3
2012	15.6	15.6	15.6	15.7	15.7	15.8	15.7	15.5	15.3	15.3	15.5	15.6	15.6
2013	15.3	15.3	15.0	15.1	15.0	15.0	14.9	14.7	14.4	14.2	14.2	14.1	14.8
2014	13.8	13.7	13.6	13.7	13.8	13.9	14.0	14.0	13.8	13.9	14.0	14.2	13.9
2015	14.2	14.2	14.1	14.2	14.2	14.3	14.3	14.1	14.0	14.0	13.9	14.1	14.1
2016	14.0	14.0	13.9	13.9	13.9	13.8	13.7	13.7	13.5	13.4	13.6	13.6	13.8
2017	13.4	12.7	12.6	12.3	12.3	12.3	12.4	12.4	12.2	12.2	12.3	12.5	12.5
2018	12.2	12.3	12.3	12.4	12.4	12.3	12.5	12.3	12.2	12.2	12.1	12.2	12.3

Employment by Industry: Sacramento—Roseville—Arden-Arcade, CA, 2010–2018—*Continued*

(Numbers in thousands, not seasonally adjusted)

Industry and year	January	February	March	April	May	June	July	August	September	October	November	December	Annual average
Financial Activities													
2010	50.0	49.6	49.6	49.1	48.8	48.9	48.4	48.2	48.0	47.7	46.6	46.6	48.5
2011	46.5	46.2	46.3	46.6	46.8	46.8	47.2	47.4	47.2	46.9	46.8	46.8	46.8
2012	47.1	47.2	47.4	47.8	47.9	48.3	48.8	48.8	48.7	48.9	48.9	49.3	48.3
2013	49.1	49.3	49.3	49.6	49.6	49.8	50.2	50.1	49.6	49.2	48.9	49.1	49.5
2014	48.7	48.5	48.3	48.3	48.6	48.9	49.1	49.2	49.2	49.7	49.7	50.0	49.0
2015	49.9	50.1	50.4	50.4	50.7	51.0	51.8	51.4	51.0	51.3	51.4	51.4	50.9
2016	51.1	51.2	51.2	51.4	51.5	51.5	52.3	52.3	52.1	52.2	52.1	52.2	51.8
2017	51.9	52.0	52.0	51.9	52.1	52.3	52.9	52.9	52.5	52.7	52.6	52.8	52.4
2018	53.6	53.5	53.4	54.0	53.9	54.1	54.2	53.9	53.6	54.0	54.2	54.8	53.9
Professional and Business Services													
2010	98.9	100.6	100.9	101.6	101.7	103.0	103.8	103.8	103.3	104.0	103.3	102.8	102.3
2011	100.5	102.3	101.5	102.7	102.9	103.3	105.4	106.7	106.3	106.9	107.2	107.2	104.4
2012	104.0	106.4	106.0	110.0	111.6	113.1	114.1	114.9	112.5	114.3	114.1	113.1	111.2
2013	112.3	113.9	113.1	112.7	113.2	114.2	113.9	115.7	116.2	117.2	117.2	116.6	114.7
2014	114.4	116.7	117.2	117.8	118.3	118.8	118.7	119.8	119.9	119.0	119.4	119.4	118.3
2015	116.6	117.5	117.8	118.5	118.7	119.5	122.0	122.7	121.8	122.8	122.6	123.1	120.3
2016	123.8	125.8	124.9	127.5	127.6	128.0	129.2	130.4	129.2	130.9	130.2	130.1	128.1
2017	127.2	128.8	128.9	128.8	130.0	130.8	131.1	131.5	131.0	132.8	133.6	133.1	130.6
2018	131.1	132.9	133.0	134.7	135.9	136.2	135.9	137.2	136.7	137.6	139.1	138.6	135.7
Education and Health Services													
2010	120.1	120.0	120.1	121.2	121.8	120.7	119.6	119.6	120.2	121.2	121.8	121.8	120.7
2011	121.1	121.2	121.7	122.5	123.0	122.0	121.2	121.8	123.0	123.2	124.3	124.4	122.5
2012	124.5	125.3	126.6	126.3	127.0	126.1	123.8	124.1	125.6	125.1	126.7	126.2	125.6
2013	129.0	130.1	130.8	131.3	132.1	129.8	128.7	129.6	130.5	131.6	132.2	132.3	130.7
2014	132.3	131.8	132.9	133.5	135.1	133.8	132.8	134.0	135.2	136.1	136.7	137.0	134.3
2015	136.9	137.4	138.6	139.7	140.5	139.5	139.5	139.5	140.6	142.5	142.7	143.6	140.1
2016	142.6	144.3	144.0	144.9	145.7	145.1	144.2	144.5	146.2	148.0	148.5	149.6	145.6
2017	147.5	149.0	150.1	153.2	153.3	153.6	151.8	153.4	155.0	155.3	155.4	156.2	152.8
2018	155.8	157.1	157.7	158.0	159.0	158.4	158.6	160.2	160.6	161.7	163.7	163.2	159.5
Leisure and Hospitality													
2010	79.5	80.2	80.6	79.3	78.9	80.7	82.4	82.1	80.4	78.5	78.6	81.7	80.2
2011	80.5	81.2	82.2	80.9	80.9	82.3	83.6	83.4	82.4	79.7	80.6	82.5	81.7
2012	80.9	82.7	83.3	84.9	83.7	85.7	86.9	86.9	85.1	83.3	84.2	86.5	84.5
2013	87.0	87.9	88.8	88.7	87.7	89.6	90.7	90.3	88.6	87.1	88.0	90.5	88.7
2014	89.8	90.4	91.6	91.6	91.0	93.9	94.5	94.2	92.1	90.1	90.1	92.0	91.8
2015	93.1	94.0	94.8	93.9	94.4	96.9	98.2	97.5	95.8	94.1	94.3	97.4	95.4
2016	97.4	98.7	99.2	99.9	99.0	100.8	102.4	102.2	100.7	98.3	98.1	101.0	99.8
2017	100.6	102.3	103.1	103.6	103.2	105.5	106.3	105.1	102.8	101.6	101.5	104.1	103.3
2018	103.3	104.7	105.4	105.6	105.1	107.2	108.9	107.8	105.2	105.6	106.7	110.6	106.3
Other Services													
2010	27.7	27.8	27.9	28.3	28.5	28.7	28.8	28.7	28.7	28.4	28.1	27.8	28.3
2011	27.7	27.7	27.8	28.3	28.4	28.4	28.6	28.5	28.6	28.0	27.9	27.9	28.2
2012	28.1	28.1	28.5	28.8	29.1	29.5	28.8	28.9	28.6	28.6	28.6	28.5	28.7
2013	28.3	28.7	29.0	29.0	29.2	29.3	29.2	29.3	29.4	29.4	29.4	29.4	29.1
2014	29.2	29.5	29.9	30.2	30.6	31.0	30.8	30.6	30.6	30.5	30.3	30.1	30.3
2015	29.8	30.0	30.3	31.0	31.2	31.3	31.6	31.4	31.3	31.2	31.0	30.9	30.9
2016	30.5	31.0	31.0	31.3	31.6	32.1	32.5	32.1	32.1	32.2	32.1	31.7	31.7
2017	31.3	31.9	32.2	32.7	33.1	33.6	33.4	33.5	33.8	33.6	33.3	33.2	33.0
2018	33.0	33.3	33.4	33.9	34.4	34.7	34.9	34.8	34.5	35.1	34.3	33.9	34.2
Government													
2010	231.0	232.0	233.6	236.4	240.1	237.1	222.7	219.3	224.1	230.0	230.8	226.0	230.3
2011	227.3	229.1	230.3	230.9	229.5	228.3	214.1	215.0	219.2	225.2	225.2	221.0	224.6
2012	221.7	223.9	226.2	226.5	226.6	227.7	212.4	212.9	216.0	222.2	223.1	218.8	221.5
2013	220.7	222.5	224.7	224.8	226.0	226.4	214.8	216.1	219.4	224.1	227.3	223.7	222.5
2014	225.3	227.5	228.6	230.9	231.5	233.1	218.6	220.3	223.5	231.7	233.5	228.5	227.8
2015	230.9	231.6	233.4	234.2	233.8	235.1	224.7	225.9	228.4	235.1	236.7	233.8	232.0
2016	234.0	234.5	236.6	236.6	237.6	238.0	229.1	229.8	231.3	235.7	236.9	235.9	234.7
2017	234.7	235.1	237.3	237.1	238.1	238.2	228.5	228.0	231.2	237.3	238.5	237.8	235.2
2018	237.2	238.2	240.0	240.0	240.9	241.7	229.7	231.4	232.6	239.6	240.1	238.0	237.5

Employment by Industry: Pittsburgh, PA, 2010–2018

(Numbers in thousands, not seasonally adjusted)

Industry and year	January	February	March	April	May	June	July	August	September	October	November	December	Annual average
Total Nonfarm													
2010	1,090.9	1,088.7	1,103.0	1,122.2	1,134.2	1,142.4	1,130.4	1,127.5	1,135.7	1,143.5	1,144.7	1,143.8	1,125.6
2011	1,116.5	1,118.4	1,128.4	1,143.1	1,153.0	1,160.7	1,144.3	1,140.4	1,153.6	1,160.6	1,163.2	1,160.0	1,145.2
2012	1,130.5	1,137.7	1,151.1	1,160.8	1,168.8	1,171.1	1,154.9	1,150.4	1,160.1	1,169.5	1,170.9	1,165.7	1,157.6
2013	1,133.7	1,140.9	1,148.1	1,158.5	1,168.1	1,170.0	1,157.1	1,152.7	1,161.7	1,167.8	1,168.0	1,164.3	1,157.6
2014	1,134.1	1,135.2	1,144.4	1,160.2	1,171.2	1,173.1	1,158.4	1,156.3	1,166.0	1,172.5	1,172.2	1,170.2	1,159.5
2015	1,139.7	1,139.7	1,146.1	1,161.9	1,172.3	1,171.8	1,161.9	1,160.5	1,167.4	1,172.6	1,175.4	1,169.6	1,161.6
2016	1,140.1	1,142.6	1,151.1	1,166.5	1,171.6	1,169.1	1,162.5	1,158.6	1,168.0	1,172.7	1,176.5	1,169.7	1,162.4
2017	1,143.4	1,150.9	1,157.3	1,172.9	1,181.7	1,180.4	1,171.9	1,170.9	1,183.1	1,189.3	1,190.7	1,186.4	1,173.2
2018	1,158.8	1,167.6	1,173.9	1,185.9	1,193.1	1,190.9	1,184.6	1,181.3	1,191.9	1,201.8	1,205.3	1,199.6	1,186.2
Total Private													
2010	965.2	959.1	972.4	990.8	1000.9	1011.3	1010.2	1009.7	1008.5	1013.3	1014.2	1013.7	997.4
2011	989.9	989.1	998.4	1013.6	1025.2	1034.8	1028.9	1027.1	1032.0	1036.0	1037.5	1034.5	1020.6
2012	1011.0	1013.5	1026.6	1036.5	1044.6	1049.9	1042.3	1038.7	1040.1	1046.9	1047.2	1042.4	1036.6
2013	1015.3	1018.1	1025.2	1035.5	1044.5	1050.9	1046.6	1042.6	1042.7	1046.9	1045.8	1042.6	1038.1
2014	1016.1	1014.9	1023.9	1039.1	1049.5	1055.2	1049.0	1047.7	1048.4	1052.5	1051.3	1049.5	1041.5
2015	1023.6	1020.5	1026.7	1041.6	1052.1	1054.6	1052.6	1051.8	1050.3	1054.3	1055.9	1051.3	1044.6
2016	1025.2	1024.7	1032.3	1047.8	1052.5	1053.2	1052.7	1050.4	1050.9	1054.3	1057.4	1051.0	1046.0
2017	1029.6	1032.6	1038.7	1054.3	1062.8	1065.1	1063.0	1063.5	1066.3	1071.6	1072.4	1069.2	1057.4
2018	1045.9	1050.5	1056.4	1068.2	1076.8	1076.0	1076.4	1074.9	1076.6	1085.4	1087.6	1082.9	1071.5
Goods Producing													
2010	134.0	131.9	136.6	142.8	145.3	147.3	149.1	148.9	147.8	147.7	146.9	143.6	143.5
2011	137.9	137.8	141.7	146.0	149.3	152.1	153.6	154.1	154.3	154.7	153.3	150.5	148.8
2012	145.5	145.7	148.3	153.1	155.5	157.7	158.1	157.8	157.7	158.6	155.5	151.9	153.8
2013	146.2	146.4	148.7	152.5	155.3	157.0	157.6	157.4	156.7	156.5	153.9	150.1	153.2
2014	146.0	144.9	148.1	153.2	156.1	159.1	159.4	159.5	158.9	158.5	155.9	152.8	154.4
2015	147.4	145.9	148.0	152.8	155.5	157.7	158.9	158.8	157.5	155.7	153.5	150.1	153.5
2016	143.9	141.8	145.6	149.8	151.5	152.4	153.1	152.2	150.9	150.7	149.2	146.2	148.9
2017	142.0	142.4	144.7	150.3	153.7	156.6	157.8	157.9	157.7	157.8	156.0	153.6	152.5
2018	147.9	148.0	150.8	154.0	157.7	160.5	161.5	161.7	161.1	162.1	160.7	157.8	157.0
Service-Providing													
2010	956.9	956.8	966.4	979.4	988.9	995.1	981.3	978.6	987.9	995.8	997.8	1,000.2	982.1
2011	978.6	980.6	986.7	997.1	1,003.7	1,008.6	990.7	986.3	999.3	1,005.9	1,009.9	1,009.5	996.4
2012	985.0	992.0	1,002.8	1,007.7	1,013.3	1,013.4	996.8	992.6	1,002.4	1,010.9	1,015.4	1,013.8	1,003.8
2013	987.5	994.5	999.4	1,006.0	1,012.8	1,013.0	999.5	995.3	1,005.0	1,011.3	1,014.1	1,014.2	1,004.4
2014	988.1	990.3	996.3	1,007.0	1,015.1	1,014.0	999.0	996.8	1,007.1	1,014.0	1,016.3	1,017.4	1,005.1
2015	992.3	993.8	998.1	1,009.1	1,016.8	1,014.1	1,003.0	1,001.7	1,009.9	1,016.9	1,021.9	1,019.5	1,008.1
2016	996.2	1,000.8	1,005.5	1,016.7	1,020.1	1,016.7	1,009.4	1,006.4	1,017.1	1,022.0	1,027.3	1,023.5	1,013.5
2017	1,001.4	1,008.5	1,012.6	1,022.6	1,028.0	1,023.8	1,014.1	1,013.0	1,025.4	1,031.5	1,034.7	1,032.8	1,020.7
2018	1,010.9	1,019.6	1,023.1	1,031.9	1,035.4	1,030.4	1,023.1	1,019.6	1,030.8	1,039.7	1,044.6	1,041.8	1,029.2
Mining and Logging													
2010	5.9	6.0	6.2	6.4	6.5	6.7	7.0	7.1	7.3	7.2	7.3	7.5	6.8
2011	7.6	7.8	7.9	8.3	8.4	8.7	8.9	9.0	9.1	9.2	9.4	9.6	8.7
2012	9.6	9.7	9.7	9.8	9.9	10.1	10.1	10.1	10.1	10.1	10.1	10.1	10.0
2013	10.1	10.3	10.4	10.7	10.8	10.8	10.9	10.9	10.9	11.0	10.9	11.1	10.7
2014	11.2	11.1	11.3	11.5	11.7	11.9	12.0	12.1	12.1	12.2	12.3	12.3	11.8
2015	12.1	12.1	12.0	11.6	11.5	11.4	11.4	11.1	10.9	10.5	10.2	10.2	11.3
2016	9.9	9.4	9.1	8.8	8.8	8.6	8.5	8.5	8.5	8.6	8.8	8.9	8.9
2017	8.8	9.1	9.3	9.5	9.8	10.1	10.3	10.3	10.4	10.5	10.6	10.5	9.9
2018	10.4	10.5	10.5	10.7	10.9	11.1	11.1	11.1	11.0	11.0	11.0	11.0	10.9
Construction													
2010	41.7	40.0	44.0	49.7	51.9	52.6	53.9	53.6	52.7	52.4	51.2	47.5	49.3
2011	42.6	42.3	45.7	49.3	52.2	54.1	55.1	55.6	55.8	56.2	54.5	51.4	51.2
2012	47.1	47.2	49.6	54.1	55.8	57.1	57.4	57.0	57.4	58.3	55.1	51.8	54.0
2013	46.6	46.9	49.0	52.4	55.1	56.1	56.9	56.9	56.6	56.3	53.7	49.6	53.0
2014	46.5	45.6	48.1	53.2	55.9	58.0	58.5	58.2	58.2	57.9	55.1	51.7	53.9
2015	47.2	46.0	47.9	52.9	55.8	57.4	58.8	59.4	59.1	59.0	57.1	53.8	54.5
2016	48.6	47.4	50.6	55.2	56.7	57.3	57.9	57.4	56.9	56.7	55.0	51.5	54.3
2017	47.8	47.9	50.1	55.4	58.4	60.4	61.4	61.6	61.8	61.7	59.6	56.7	56.9
2018	51.8	51.9	54.3	57.3	60.3	62.1	63.0	63.0	63.3	64.2	63.1	60.1	59.5

Employment by Industry: Pittsburgh, PA, 2010–2018—*Continued*

(Numbers in thousands, not seasonally adjusted)

Industry and year	January	February	March	April	May	June	July	August	September	October	November	December	Annual average
Manufacturing													
2010	86.4	85.9	86.4	86.7	86.9	88.0	88.2	88.2	87.8	88.1	88.4	88.6	87.5
2011	87.7	87.7	88.1	88.4	88.7	89.3	89.6	89.5	89.4	89.3	89.4	89.5	88.9
2012	88.8	88.8	89.0	89.2	89.8	90.5	90.6	90.7	90.2	90.2	90.3	90.0	89.8
2013	89.5	89.2	89.3	89.4	89.4	90.1	89.8	89.6	89.2	89.2	89.3	89.4	89.5
2014	88.3	88.2	88.7	88.5	88.5	89.2	88.9	89.2	88.6	88.4	88.5	88.8	88.7
2015	88.1	87.8	88.1	88.3	88.2	88.9	88.7	88.3	87.5	86.2	86.2	86.1	87.7
2016	85.4	85.0	85.9	85.8	86.0	86.5	86.7	86.3	85.5	85.4	85.4	85.8	85.8
2017	85.4	85.4	85.3	85.4	85.5	86.1	86.1	86.0	85.5	85.6	85.8	86.4	85.7
2018	85.7	85.6	86.0	86.0	86.5	87.3	87.4	87.6	86.8	86.9	86.6	86.7	86.6
Trade, Transportation, and Utilities													
2010	211.2	207.6	209.6	211.1	213.5	214.9	211.8	212.0	213.3	216.6	220.3	223.7	213.8
2011	214.9	212.7	213.3	215.2	217.0	216.7	214.0	214.0	215.8	217.6	222.1	224.8	216.5
2012	216.6	214.5	216.2	216.3	217.6	216.7	213.3	212.4	214.0	216.1	221.2	222.8	216.5
2013	213.7	211.1	211.8	211.9	214.2	214.2	211.6	212.2	213.2	215.0	219.9	222.9	214.3
2014	213.2	210.5	211.5	213.1	215.8	216.8	212.7	212.9	214.4	216.5	221.0	224.6	215.3
2015	215.7	212.0	212.4	213.2	216.1	216.3	213.2	213.0	213.2	215.3	219.7	222.9	215.3
2016	213.2	210.7	210.9	211.9	214.0	213.0	210.6	210.0	210.9	212.3	217.0	220.2	212.9
2017	211.7	209.3	209.3	210.5	211.8	210.8	208.8	208.3	210.3	211.8	216.7	218.8	211.5
2018	210.6	208.8	208.6	209.0	211.5	211.1	208.7	207.9	209.5	211.1	216.0	217.2	210.8
Wholesale Trade													
2010	44.9	44.5	44.9	45.5	45.7	46.0	46.3	46.4	46.1	46.6	46.4	46.6	45.8
2011	46.1	46.2	46.4	46.9	47.1	46.9	46.8	46.9	46.4	46.5	46.4	46.4	46.6
2012	46.0	46.2	46.5	46.6	46.4	46.4	46.1	45.8	45.4	45.4	45.2	45.2	45.9
2013	44.5	44.4	44.6	44.6	44.8	45.0	45.0	45.0	44.7	44.7	44.6	44.8	44.7
2014	44.4	44.3	44.3	44.3	44.7	45.0	45.1	44.8	44.6	44.8	44.8	44.9	44.7
2015	44.3	44.1	44.0	44.0	44.3	44.4	44.5	44.3	43.8	44.1	44.0	44.0	44.2
2016	43.3	43.3	43.2	43.2	43.3	43.3	43.2	43.0	42.6	42.5	42.4	42.4	43.0
2017	41.9	42.1	42.2	42.2	42.5	42.7	42.8	42.7	42.4	42.4	42.3	42.5	42.4
2018	41.9	42.0	41.9	42.2	42.5	42.9	43.0	42.9	42.6	42.9	43.2	43.9	42.7
Retail Trade													
2010	124.7	121.8	123.1	123.7	125.6	126.6	126.5	126.6	124.6	126.7	130.4	132.6	126.1
2011	126.0	123.7	124.1	125.2	126.7	127.3	127.5	127.9	126.1	127.5	131.6	133.5	127.3
2012	127.2	124.9	126.0	126.2	127.4	128.1	127.4	127.0	125.3	127.0	132.0	132.8	127.6
2013	125.9	123.7	124.0	124.2	125.9	127.0	126.6	126.9	124.9	126.5	130.7	132.7	126.6
2014	125.2	122.9	123.7	124.6	126.5	127.7	126.7	127.1	125.0	126.5	130.3	132.7	126.6
2015	125.9	123.0	123.4	124.0	126.0	126.9	126.6	126.6	124.2	125.9	129.7	131.8	126.2
2016	125.1	123.2	123.6	124.5	126.1	126.4	126.2	126.0	123.4	124.6	128.6	130.4	125.7
2017	124.9	122.3	122.2	123.1	123.6	124.2	123.8	123.4	121.6	122.9	127.0	127.8	123.9
2018	122.2	120.5	120.3	120.3	122.0	122.6	122.2	121.5	119.7	120.1	123.3	123.2	121.5
Transportation and Utilities													
2010	41.6	41.3	41.6	41.9	42.2	42.3	39.0	39.0	42.6	43.3	43.5	44.5	41.9
2011	42.8	42.8	42.8	43.1	43.2	42.5	39.7	39.2	43.3	43.6	44.1	44.9	42.7
2012	43.4	43.4	43.7	43.5	43.8	42.2	39.8	39.6	43.3	43.7	44.0	44.8	42.9
2013	43.3	43.0	43.2	43.1	43.5	42.2	40.0	40.3	43.6	43.8	44.6	45.4	43.0
2014	43.6	43.3	43.5	44.2	44.6	44.1	40.9	41.0	44.8	45.2	45.9	47.0	44.0
2015	45.5	44.9	45.0	45.2	45.8	45.0	42.1	42.1	45.2	45.3	46.0	47.1	44.9
2016	44.8	44.2	44.1	44.2	44.6	43.3	41.2	41.0	44.9	45.2	46.0	47.4	44.2
2017	44.9	44.9	44.9	45.2	45.7	43.9	42.2	42.2	46.3	46.5	47.4	48.5	45.2
2018	46.5	46.3	46.4	46.5	47.0	45.6	43.5	43.5	47.2	48.1	49.5	50.1	46.7
Information													
2010	18.8	18.7	18.4	18.5	18.6	19.0	19.0	18.7	18.9	18.3	18.4	18.5	18.7
2011	18.4	18.4	18.5	18.7	18.9	19.1	19.0	17.5	18.7	18.8	19.1	18.5	18.6
2012	18.4	18.4	18.7	18.7	19.8	19.2	19.1	19.1	18.9	18.9	18.9	18.7	18.9
2013	18.8	18.4	18.4	18.3	18.6	18.6	18.9	18.8	18.8	20.0	19.2	19.3	18.8
2014	18.3	18.3	18.4	19.1	18.6	18.6	18.7	18.7	18.6	18.4	18.4	18.4	18.5
2015	18.1	18.3	18.3	18.2	18.5	18.7	18.7	18.9	18.6	18.5	18.4	18.4	18.5
2016	18.0	18.0	18.0	18.4	17.4	18.9	19.0	19.1	18.8	18.9	18.8	18.5	18.5
2017	18.4	18.8	18.4	18.5	18.9	19.5	19.0	19.7	19.0	18.8	18.8	18.8	18.9
2018	18.5	19.3	19.1	19.7	19.4	19.5	19.5	19.3	19.9	20.0	19.9	19.7	19.5

Employment by Industry: Pittsburgh, PA, 2010–2018—*Continued*

(Numbers in thousands, not seasonally adjusted)

Industry and year	January	February	March	April	May	June	July	August	September	October	November	December	Annual average
Financial Activities													
2010	67.6	67.4	67.7	68.0	68.4	68.9	69.0	69.0	68.2	68.3	68.3	68.5	68.3
2011	68.6	68.4	68.5	68.8	69.3	70.1	70.4	70.4	69.7	69.9	70.1	70.3	69.5
2012	69.9	70.0	70.3	70.3	70.7	71.7	71.8	71.8	71.0	71.1	71.3	71.3	70.9
2013	70.8	70.9	71.0	71.1	71.3	71.9	71.8	71.9	70.9	71.0	71.1	70.8	71.2
2014	70.9	70.7	70.5	70.3	70.8	71.2	71.3	71.0	69.9	70.0	70.2	70.1	70.6
2015	69.4	69.5	69.5	69.7	70.4	71.0	71.2	71.2	70.4	70.6	70.9	70.8	70.4
2016	70.3	70.5	70.4	70.7	71.2	71.9	72.3	72.5	71.9	72.0	72.2	72.4	71.5
2017	72.1	72.6	72.5	72.6	73.1	73.8	74.2	73.9	73.2	73.4	73.5	73.6	73.2
2018	73.4	73.7	73.7	74.0	74.5	75.5	75.8	75.7	75.0	74.8	75.6	75.6	74.8
Professional and Business Services													
2010	151.4	151.5	153.1	157.0	157.8	160.0	161.0	161.1	160.1	161.5	162.4	161.8	158.2
2011	160.1	160.4	161.5	164.6	166.1	167.4	167.7	167.8	167.9	169.8	169.7	168.5	166.0
2012	167.4	168.0	170.4	172.4	173.3	174.7	174.1	173.4	172.4	174.3	174.3	173.5	172.4
2013	171.0	172.6	174.1	175.8	176.9	177.8	177.9	177.1	175.5	176.1	175.5	174.2	175.4
2014	171.2	172.1	173.2	176.4	177.9	178.8	179.1	179.5	178.2	179.4	179.9	178.9	177.1
2015	176.5	176.9	177.8	180.5	181.7	182.2	182.8	182.2	181.2	183.5	183.7	182.3	180.9
2016	179.3	179.0	179.7	182.8	182.3	183.2	182.8	182.3	182.3	183.6	184.0	182.0	181.9
2017	179.0	178.9	179.6	182.2	182.7	183.4	183.0	182.8	182.3	183.2	182.7	181.0	181.7
2018	178.3	179.4	180.2	182.6	183.5	184.1	184.3	183.6	182.5	183.2	182.9	182.2	182.2
Education and Health Services													
2010	234.3	234.7	236.0	236.4	234.9	234.8	233.8	231.7	236.7	240.1	239.8	239.6	236.1
2011	238.2	240.1	240.6	240.6	238.6	239.1	235.9	234.4	240.3	243.2	244.1	243.2	239.9
2012	240.1	243.5	245.1	244.1	240.7	237.8	235.6	233.1	239.7	243.7	244.5	242.4	240.9
2013	239.6	243.4	243.3	243.4	238.5	237.1	235.2	231.9	239.4	242.9	244.0	242.7	240.1
2014	240.3	242.3	243.3	243.9	240.1	237.2	235.6	232.3	240.3	243.8	244.6	242.7	240.5
2015	239.7	241.0	241.3	242.6	238.6	234.1	233.5	232.3	239.6	243.6	244.4	241.8	239.4
2016	240.8	244.5	244.4	246.3	242.5	236.9	237.5	236.6	244.7	247.8	249.2	247.0	243.2
2017	245.8	249.7	250.4	251.5	248.4	242.4	242.9	242.2	251.3	255.7	256.7	255.6	249.4
2018	253.6	258.2	258.5	259.7	255.9	248.9	249.6	249.9	257.7	261.4	261.9	259.4	256.2
Leisure and Hospitality													
2010	97.6	97.3	100.3	106.2	111.0	114.2	114.1	115.9	112.5	109.7	107.1	106.9	107.7
2011	101.5	100.8	103.4	108.6	114.3	117.8	115.9	116.7	114.0	110.8	107.9	107.4	109.9
2012	102.4	102.5	106.1	109.9	115.0	119.0	117.4	118.9	114.8	112.9	110.5	110.8	111.7
2013	105.2	105.2	107.6	111.8	118.5	122.1	121.4	121.4	117.0	114.7	111.7	111.9	114.0
2014	106.3	106.1	108.5	112.8	119.8	121.9	120.0	121.8	117.2	115.2	110.9	111.4	114.3
2015	106.9	106.9	108.8	113.8	119.9	122.6	122.0	123.4	119.1	116.6	114.8	114.4	115.8
2016	109.5	110.0	112.6	116.9	122.3	124.8	125.2	126.1	120.9	118.2	116.7	114.5	118.1
2017	110.8	111.0	113.7	118.3	123.2	126.8	125.4	126.9	122.1	120.3	117.5	117.4	119.5
2018	113.9	113.3	115.5	118.9	123.7	125.2	125.4	125.7	120.8	122.0	119.8	119.8	120.3
Other Services													
2010	50.3	50.0	50.7	50.8	51.4	52.2	52.4	52.4	51.0	51.1	51.0	51.1	51.2
2011	50.3	50.5	50.9	51.1	51.7	52.5	52.4	52.2	51.3	51.2	51.2	51.3	51.4
2012	50.7	50.9	51.5	51.7	52.0	53.1	52.9	52.2	51.6	51.3	51.0	51.0	51.7
2013	50.0	50.1	50.3	50.7	51.2	52.2	52.2	51.9	51.2	50.7	50.5	50.7	51.0
2014	49.9	50.0	50.4	50.3	50.8	51.6	52.2	52.0	50.9	50.7	50.4	50.6	50.8
2015	49.9	50.0	50.6	50.8	51.4	52.0	52.3	52.0	50.7	50.5	50.5	50.6	50.9
2016	50.2	50.2	50.7	51.0	51.3	52.1	52.2	51.6	50.5	50.8	50.3	50.2	50.9
2017	49.8	49.9	50.1	50.4	51.0	51.8	51.9	51.8	50.4	50.6	50.5	50.4	50.7
2018	49.7	49.8	50.0	50.3	50.6	51.2	51.6	51.1	50.1	50.8	50.8	51.2	50.6
Government													
2010	125.7	129.6	130.6	131.4	133.3	131.1	120.2	117.8	127.2	130.2	130.5	130.1	128.1
2011	126.6	129.3	130.0	129.5	127.8	125.9	115.4	113.3	121.6	124.6	125.7	125.5	124.6
2012	119.5	124.2	124.5	124.3	124.2	121.2	112.6	111.7	120.0	122.6	123.7	123.3	121.0
2013	118.4	122.8	122.9	123.0	123.6	119.1	110.5	110.1	119.0	120.9	122.2	121.7	119.5
2014	118.0	120.3	120.5	121.1	121.3	117.9	109.4	108.6	117.6	120.0	120.9	120.7	118.0
2015	116.1	119.2	119.4	120.3	120.2	117.2	109.3	108.7	117.1	118.3	119.5	118.3	117.0
2016	114.9	117.9	118.8	118.7	119.1	115.9	109.8	108.2	117.1	118.4	119.1	118.7	116.4
2017	113.8	118.3	118.6	118.6	118.9	115.3	108.9	107.4	116.8	117.7	118.3	117.2	115.8
2018	112.9	117.1	117.5	117.7	116.3	114.9	108.2	106.4	115.3	116.4	117.7	116.7	114.8

Employment by Industry: Las Vegas-Henderson-Paradise, NV, 2010–2018

(Numbers in thousands, not seasonally adjusted)

Industry and year	January	February	March	April	May	June	July	August	September	October	November	December	Annual average
Total Nonfarm													
2010	798.2	798.8	799.4	808.2	811.7	807.7	800.7	799.4	799.8	806.4	807.9	805.6	803.7
2011	797.2	797.2	803.5	810.3	811.3	807.5	804.5	803.8	811.5	817.6	818.4	816.5	808.3
2012	808.7	810.5	815.8	821.9	827.7	826.7	818.9	822.7	830.8	837.8	842.3	838.5	825.2
2013	831.1	832.4	839.5	846.7	850.5	851.0	845.1	849.3	853.8	861.7	867.8	865.6	849.5
2014	858.5	862.9	871.3	878.3	884.7	881.0	874.4	885.0	892.8	903.2	905.4	905.5	883.6
2015	898.1	900.3	908.1	915.3	919.3	915.4	910.0	918.1	924.7	935.3	941.4	941.8	919.0
2016	926.4	930.1	937.5	946.0	947.4	946.3	946.9	950.0	961.1	964.5	969.4	967.0	949.4
2017	959.5	961.9	972.8	968.6	976.5	972.1	971.0	975.1	985.0	992.2	997.3	997.4	977.5
2018	983.3	990.0	998.0	999.2	1,006.2	1,001.4	1,002.2	1,010.6	1,016.9	1,026.1	1,023.0	1,023.3	1,006.7
Total Private													
2010	702.6	700.6	701.0	709.5	710.8	712.4	707.5	708.2	704.0	709.6	711.0	708.8	707.2
2011	702.0	700.4	706.6	713.6	715.0	717.4	715.5	714.7	718.2	723.0	723.8	721.0	714.3
2012	716.1	716.0	720.1	726.3	731.9	735.3	729.6	734.0	736.4	742.4	746.0	741.3	731.3
2013	736.7	737.0	743.3	750.2	754.1	758.3	755.6	758.2	758.6	764.8	770.0	766.9	754.5
2014	762.7	765.6	772.9	780.4	786.5	788.4	783.5	793.1	795.9	805.0	806.7	806.0	787.2
2015	801.1	802.1	808.7	815.9	820.1	819.8	817.4	824.2	825.5	836.3	840.7	839.8	821.0
2016	827.3	829.5	835.5	844.9	846.3	850.9	852.0	854.6	859.7	863.3	866.8	863.4	849.5
2017	859.8	859.4	869.3	867.3	874.2	875.8	873.6	875.9	879.8	889.3	892.9	892.0	875.8
2018	882.6	885.9	892.9	896.6	902.6	903.4	905.5	912.3	912.5	920.7	917.7	917.2	904.2
Goods Producing													
2010	66.8	65.3	64.6	66.8	66.7	66.3	65.2	65.0	63.6	63.0	61.7	60.1	64.6
2011	57.7	57.5	57.2	57.6	57.1	57.2	57.9	58.6	58.0	58.0	57.2	57.0	57.6
2012	54.8	54.7	55.1	55.6	56.6	57.8	58.0	59.5	60.0	60.5	61.0	61.0	57.9
2013	59.3	59.8	60.4	61.2	61.1	61.9	62.0	63.4	63.3	64.2	64.4	64.1	62.1
2014	63.7	64.2	64.4	65.3	65.8	66.0	66.9	68.6	68.9	69.6	69.4	69.6	66.9
2015	69.8	70.3	70.4	70.9	72.1	72.7	72.6	74.0	74.3	76.0	76.4	77.0	73.0
2016	75.6	75.6	75.5	75.5	75.3	76.9	77.7	78.4	78.9	79.1	79.0	79.4	77.2
2017	79.4	80.1	81.9	81.5	81.9	83.0	82.5	82.4	83.5	84.2	84.0	84.0	82.4
2018	83.7	84.7	85.3	86.7	87.3	88.8	89.4	91.0	90.9	91.1	91.0	92.0	88.5
Service-Providing													
2010	731.4	733.5	734.8	741.4	745.0	741.4	735.5	734.4	736.2	743.4	746.2	745.5	739.1
2011	739.5	739.7	746.3	752.7	754.2	750.3	746.6	745.2	753.5	759.6	761.2	759.5	750.7
2012	753.9	755.8	760.7	766.3	771.1	768.9	760.9	763.2	770.8	777.3	781.3	777.5	767.3
2013	771.8	772.6	779.1	785.5	789.4	789.1	783.1	785.9	790.5	797.5	803.4	801.5	787.5
2014	794.8	798.7	806.9	813.0	818.9	815.0	807.5	816.4	823.9	833.6	836.0	835.9	816.7
2015	828.3	830.0	837.7	844.4	847.2	842.7	837.4	844.1	850.4	859.3	865.0	864.8	845.9
2016	850.8	854.5	862.0	870.5	872.1	869.4	869.2	871.6	882.2	885.4	890.4	887.6	872.1
2017	880.1	881.8	890.9	887.1	894.6	889.1	888.5	892.7	901.5	908.0	913.3	913.4	895.1
2018	899.6	905.3	912.7	912.5	918.9	912.6	912.8	919.6	926.0	935.0	932.0	931.3	918.2
Mining, Logging, and Construction													
2010	47.1	45.8	45.2	47.1	47.1	46.7	45.7	45.7	44.2	43.6	42.2	40.7	45.1
2011	38.3	38.1	37.7	38.0	37.6	37.5	38.2	38.6	38.0	37.9	37.2	36.9	37.8
2012	35.1	35.1	35.3	35.6	36.5	37.3	37.6	39.0	39.6	40.1	40.5	40.5	37.7
2013	39.1	39.5	40.0	40.6	40.3	41.0	41.1	42.5	42.5	43.3	43.4	42.9	41.4
2014	42.7	43.3	43.5	44.3	44.7	44.9	45.8	47.4	47.7	48.2	48.0	48.2	45.7
2015	48.5	49.0	48.9	49.5	50.5	50.9	51.0	52.5	52.7	54.3	54.5	55.1	51.5
2016	53.9	53.8	53.6	53.7	53.4	54.8	55.5	56.1	56.5	56.6	56.5	56.7	55.1
2017	56.9	57.5	59.1	58.5	58.9	59.8	59.2	59.2	60.2	60.8	60.4	60.3	59.2
2018	60.1	60.9	61.3	62.5	63.1	64.3	64.8	66.2	66.0	65.9	66.0	66.9	64.0
Manufacturing													
2010	19.7	19.5	19.4	19.7	19.6	19.6	19.5	19.3	19.4	19.4	19.5	19.4	19.5
2011	19.4	19.4	19.5	19.6	19.5	19.7	19.7	20.0	20.0	20.1	20.0	20.1	19.8
2012	19.7	19.6	19.8	20.0	20.1	20.5	20.4	20.5	20.4	20.4	20.5	20.5	20.2
2013	20.2	20.3	20.4	20.6	20.8	20.9	20.9	20.9	20.8	20.9	21.0	21.2	20.7
2014	21.0	20.9	20.9	21.0	21.1	21.1	21.1	21.2	21.2	21.4	21.4	21.4	21.1
2015	21.3	21.3	21.5	21.4	21.6	21.8	21.6	21.5	21.6	21.7	21.9	21.9	21.6
2016	21.7	21.8	21.9	21.8	21.9	22.1	22.2	22.3	22.4	22.5	22.5	22.7	22.2
2017	22.5	22.6	22.8	23.0	23.0	23.2	23.3	23.2	23.3	23.4	23.6	23.7	23.1
2018	23.6	23.8	24.0	24.2	24.2	24.5	24.6	24.8	24.9	25.2	25.0	25.1	24.5

Employment by Industry: Las Vegas-Henderson-Paradise, NV, 2010–2018—*Continued*

(Numbers in thousands, not seasonally adjusted)

Industry and year	January	February	March	April	May	June	July	August	September	October	November	December	Annual average
Trade, Transportation, and Utilities													
2010	146.3	144.7	144.7	145.1	145.7	146.5	146.8	147.2	146.8	148.3	151.7	152.8	147.2
2011	147.0	145.5	146.1	147.4	147.7	148.3	149.0	149.5	149.6	151.9	156.1	156.6	149.6
2012	152.2	150.2	151.1	151.8	152.7	153.2	153.2	153.3	153.8	154.5	160.0	159.7	153.8
2013	154.6	152.5	151.6	152.3	154.6	155.4	156.1	156.7	157.2	158.9	163.9	165.3	156.6
2014	159.1	157.8	158.4	159.1	159.9	160.7	161.0	161.9	162.7	165.4	170.2	171.6	162.3
2015	166.0	164.4	165.6	166.4	167.4	167.6	167.7	168.4	168.9	170.7	175.1	175.5	168.6
2016	167.0	166.4	166.8	168.1	168.8	169.0	169.7	170.4	170.9	172.2	177.6	177.9	170.4
2017	172.2	170.6	170.5	170.5	171.7	172.3	172.8	174.4	175.0	177.4	183.9	185.5	174.7
2018	177.3	175.7	175.9	176.0	177.2	178.0	178.8	179.7	179.9	180.8	184.0	186.9	179.2
Wholesale Trade													
2010	20.2	20.1	20.2	20.2	20.3	20.4	20.3	20.3	20.2	20.4	20.3	20.3	20.3
2011	20.0	19.9	20.0	20.1	20.0	20.1	20.1	20.0	19.9	20.0	19.9	19.9	20.0
2012	19.7	19.7	19.8	19.8	19.9	20.0	20.0	20.0	20.0	20.0	20.0	20.1	19.9
2013	19.9	19.9	19.9	20.0	20.1	20.2	20.4	20.5	20.5	20.5	20.6	20.7	20.3
2014	20.5	20.7	20.7	20.7	20.7	20.7	20.9	20.9	20.9	21.0	21.0	21.1	20.8
2015	21.0	21.0	21.0	21.0	21.1	21.1	21.2	21.2	21.3	21.4	21.5	21.5	21.2
2016	21.0	21.1	20.9	21.1	21.2	21.2	21.4	21.4	21.5	21.5	21.6	21.7	21.3
2017	21.7	21.8	21.9	22.1	22.3	22.5	22.5	22.5	22.5	22.5	22.6	22.6	22.3
2018	22.5	22.5	22.7	22.9	23.0	23.2	23.6	23.7	23.7	23.7	23.7	23.8	23.3
Retail Trade													
2010	91.6	90.2	90.3	90.7	91.1	91.6	92.1	92.5	92.2	93.5	96.8	97.6	92.5
2011	92.7	91.3	91.6	92.2	92.7	93.0	93.4	94.1	94.2	95.9	100.1	100.6	94.3
2012	96.6	94.8	95.5	96.0	96.4	96.8	96.6	96.8	97.2	98.2	103.6	103.0	97.6
2013	98.1	96.4	96.4	96.8	97.9	98.4	98.9	99.5	99.7	101.1	105.8	106.9	99.7
2014	101.3	99.8	100.2	100.5	101.1	101.6	101.7	102.5	103.0	105.4	110.0	110.9	103.2
2015	105.3	104.0	104.8	105.4	105.9	106.0	105.9	106.6	106.5	108.2	112.1	112.1	106.9
2016	105.5	104.7	105.1	105.6	106.0	106.2	106.3	107.0	107.1	108.8	113.5	113.2	107.4
2017	107.7	106.3	106.1	106.0	106.8	106.8	106.8	107.2	107.5	109.3	114.6	114.9	108.3
2018	108.7	107.4	107.1	106.9	107.8	108.2	108.8	109.5	109.7	110.0	112.3	113.2	109.1
Transportation and Utilities													
2010	34.5	34.4	34.2	34.2	34.3	34.5	34.4	34.4	34.4	34.4	34.6	34.9	34.4
2011	34.3	34.3	34.5	35.1	35.0	35.2	35.5	35.4	35.5	36.0	36.1	36.1	35.3
2012	35.9	35.7	35.8	36.0	36.4	36.4	36.6	36.5	36.6	36.3	36.4	36.6	36.3
2013	36.6	36.2	35.3	35.5	36.6	36.8	36.8	36.7	37.0	37.3	37.5	37.7	36.7
2014	37.3	37.3	37.5	37.9	38.1	38.4	38.4	38.5	38.8	39.0	39.2	39.6	38.3
2015	39.7	39.4	39.8	40.0	40.4	40.5	40.6	40.6	41.1	41.1	41.5	41.9	40.6
2016	40.5	40.6	40.8	41.4	41.6	41.6	42.0	42.0	42.3	41.9	42.5	43.0	41.7
2017	42.8	42.5	42.5	42.4	42.6	43.0	43.5	44.7	45.0	45.6	46.7	48.0	44.1
2018	46.1	45.8	46.1	46.2	46.4	46.6	46.4	46.5	46.5	47.1	48.0	49.9	46.8
Information													
2010	9.0	9.0	8.9	9.3	9.1	9.1	9.4	9.2	9.0	9.1	9.4	9.3	9.2
2011	9.2	9.0	9.1	9.4	9.4	9.4	9.2	9.1	9.5	9.8	9.1	9.6	9.3
2012	9.1	9.2	9.4	9.4	9.5	9.5	9.2	9.5	9.6	10.2	11.3	9.9	9.7
2013	9.1	9.3	9.5	9.7	9.8	10.8	10.1	9.8	9.8	9.9	10.1	10.1	9.8
2014	9.8	9.9	9.7	10.9	11.7	12.2	10.3	10.1	10.4	10.5	10.9	10.7	10.6
2015	10.4	10.7	10.6	10.5	10.5	10.9	10.2	10.4	10.2	10.6	11.3	11.0	10.6
2016	11.0	11.1	10.7	11.6	11.4	11.5	11.1	10.7	10.8	11.0	10.8	10.6	11.0
2017	11.2	10.9	10.9	11.6	11.9	12.3	11.1	11.5	11.1	11.5	11.8	11.4	11.4
2018	11.1	11.3	11.2	12.4	12.7	12.2	11.1	11.3	11.0	11.1	11.4	11.1	11.5
Financial Activities													
2010	40.3	39.9	40.0	40.5	40.3	40.1	40.2	39.9	39.8	40.3	40.2	40.3	40.2
2011	39.8	39.6	39.8	40.0	39.9	40.0	39.9	39.7	40.0	40.2	40.2	40.5	40.0
2012	40.2	40.3	40.6	41.4	41.7	41.9	41.8	42.0	42.2	42.8	42.8	42.9	41.7
2013	42.5	42.9	43.6	43.3	43.7	43.5	43.0	43.0	42.9	43.4	43.6	43.8	43.3
2014	42.8	42.9	43.0	43.0	43.5	43.4	43.1	43.6	43.7	44.4	44.5	44.7	43.6
2015	44.3	44.8	45.0	45.5	46.1	45.7	46.1	46.1	46.3	47.3	47.3	47.9	46.0
2016	47.3	47.5	47.7	48.3	48.6	48.3	48.4	48.6	48.8	49.1	49.2	49.3	48.4
2017	49.1	49.7	49.5	50.0	50.8	50.6	51.3	51.3	51.4	51.9	51.9	52.0	50.8
2018	51.7	52.3	52.6	52.6	53.1	52.9	53.2	53.2	53.0	53.3	53.4	54.0	52.9

Employment by Industry: Las Vegas-Henderson-Paradise, NV, 2010–2018—*Continued*

(Numbers in thousands, not seasonally adjusted)

Industry and year	January	February	March	April	May	June	July	August	September	October	November	December	Annual average
Professional and Business Services													
2010	100.4	99.2	98.7	99.7	99.8	100.4	98.3	100.5	98.5	100.9	100.7	99.5	99.7
2011	102.8	101.2	101.5	101.9	101.7	101.9	101.1	101.2	102.9	104.2	103.9	102.7	102.3
2012	107.3	106.6	105.2	106.1	106.2	106.7	103.5	107.0	108.0	109.7	108.5	106.9	106.8
2013	111.6	110.2	111.4	112.6	112.7	111.6	108.9	111.2	110.3	113.4	113.6	111.7	111.6
2014	115.5	115.6	116.5	116.8	116.9	116.9	113.6	117.5	118.3	123.1	121.8	120.6	117.8
2015	124.8	123.1	124.3	126.7	126.3	124.5	123.5	127.1	127.1	130.9	131.3	130.4	126.7
2016	130.9	129.5	131.4	133.3	132.4	134.2	133.2	134.0	136.6	139.0	137.9	135.4	134.0
2017	139.3	136.3	139.8	136.0	137.5	137.3	137.3	137.7	138.6	143.4	142.2	140.9	138.9
2018	143.1	142.2	142.5	142.4	143.2	142.2	144.7	148.2	147.6	151.1	147.8	146.2	145.1
Education and Health Services													
2010	68.3	68.6	69.1	69.7	69.8	69.7	69.1	69.3	69.6	70.7	71.1	71.3	69.7
2011	70.8	71.4	71.9	72.5	72.5	72.7	72.3	72.7	73.0	73.7	74.0	74.4	72.7
2012	73.9	74.6	74.6	75.2	75.8	75.4	74.9	76.0	75.9	76.8	76.8	77.2	75.6
2013	76.7	77.8	78.3	78.8	78.9	79.0	78.9	79.5	80.0	80.5	80.9	80.9	79.2
2014	80.2	80.9	81.4	81.5	81.8	82.0	81.8	82.5	82.8	83.9	84.1	84.3	82.3
2015	83.5	84.3	84.8	85.2	85.5	86.1	86.3	87.2	87.8	89.2	89.3	89.6	86.6
2016	88.6	89.6	89.8	90.2	90.7	90.8	91.2	92.1	92.7	93.8	94.5	94.8	91.6
2017	93.7	94.7	95.2	95.6	96.2	96.3	95.2	97.0	97.9	99.0	99.5	100.0	96.7
2018	99.4	100.5	101.1	101.3	102.0	101.9	101.3	102.9	103.8	104.0	103.3	104.6	102.2
Leisure and Hospitality													
2010	248.9	251.2	252.0	255.1	256.0	256.9	255.0	253.5	253.2	253.6	253.1	252.6	253.4
2011	252.0	253.2	257.8	261.4	263.2	264.2	262.4	260.3	261.8	261.9	260.1	256.9	259.6
2012	255.4	257.2	260.6	263.0	265.1	266.2	264.5	262.1	262.2	262.8	261.5	259.8	261.7
2013	259.2	260.6	264.3	267.7	268.5	271.2	271.7	269.8	270.5	269.9	268.9	266.4	267.4
2014	267.2	269.8	274.6	278.4	281.1	281.3	280.8	283.0	283.1	281.7	280.0	278.9	278.3
2015	276.9	278.9	282.1	284.4	285.5	285.1	283.7	283.5	283.4	283.9	282.1	280.1	282.5
2016	278.4	280.5	283.4	287.3	288.4	289.4	289.3	289.0	289.0	286.6	286.1	285.2	286.1
2017	284.2	286.4	290.6	290.8	292.9	292.5	291.5	289.8	290.5	290.1	287.9	286.6	289.5
2018	284.9	287.7	292.6	293.2	294.8	294.5	294.4	293.1	293.1	296.1	293.9	289.7	292.3
Other Services													
2010	22.6	22.7	23.0	23.3	23.4	23.4	23.5	23.6	23.5	23.7	23.1	22.9	23.2
2011	22.7	23.0	23.2	23.4	23.5	23.7	23.7	23.6	23.4	23.3	23.2	23.3	23.3
2012	23.2	23.2	23.5	23.8	24.3	24.6	24.5	24.6	24.7	25.1	24.1	23.9	24.1
2013	23.7	23.9	24.2	24.6	24.8	24.9	24.9	24.8	24.6	24.6	24.6	24.6	24.5
2014	24.4	24.5	24.9	25.4	25.8	25.9	26.0	25.9	26.0	26.4	25.8	25.6	25.6
2015	25.4	25.6	25.9	26.3	26.7	27.2	27.3	27.5	27.5	27.7	27.9	28.3	26.9
2016	28.5	29.3	30.2	30.6	30.7	30.8	31.4	31.4	32.0	32.5	31.7	30.8	30.8
2017	30.7	30.7	30.9	31.3	31.3	31.5	31.9	31.8	31.8	31.8	31.7	31.6	31.4
2018	31.4	31.5	31.7	32.0	32.3	32.9	32.6	32.9	33.2	33.2	32.9	32.7	32.4
Government													
2010	95.6	98.2	98.4	98.7	100.9	95.3	93.2	91.2	95.8	96.8	96.9	96.8	96.5
2011	95.2	96.8	96.9	96.7	96.3	90.1	89.0	89.1	93.3	94.6	94.6	95.5	94.0
2012	92.6	94.5	95.7	95.6	95.8	91.4	89.3	88.7	94.4	95.4	96.3	97.2	93.9
2013	94.4	95.4	96.2	96.5	96.4	92.7	89.5	91.1	95.2	96.9	97.8	98.7	95.1
2014	95.8	97.3	98.4	97.9	98.2	92.6	90.9	91.9	96.9	98.2	98.7	99.5	96.4
2015	97.0	98.2	99.4	99.4	99.2	95.6	92.6	93.9	99.2	99.0	100.7	102.0	98.0
2016	99.1	100.6	102.0	101.1	101.1	95.4	94.9	95.4	101.4	101.2	102.6	103.6	99.9
2017	99.7	102.5	103.5	101.3	102.3	96.3	97.4	99.2	105.2	102.9	104.4	105.4	101.7
2018	100.7	104.1	105.1	102.6	103.6	98.0	96.7	98.3	104.4	105.4	105.3	106.1	102.5

Employment by Industry: Cincinnati, OH-KY-IN, 2010–2018

(Numbers in thousands, not seasonally adjusted)

Industry and year	January	February	March	April	May	June	July	August	September	October	November	December	Annual average
Total Nonfarm													
2010	959.9	960.3	970.9	985.7	995.7	989.1	978.0	983.2	983.7	990.4	992.2	990.7	981.7
2011	964.9	968.5	978.1	993.4	999.8	994.6	992.4	1,000.6	1,001.4	1,003.0	1,005.5	1,004.9	992.3
2012	979.5	986.6	996.5	1,008.5	1,019.3	1,016.5	1,006.5	1,012.9	1,016.9	1,021.9	1,021.0	1,018.1	1,008.7
2013	990.8	1,000.1	1,006.8	1,026.3	1,036.8	1,031.4	1,021.3	1,031.8	1,035.2	1,038.6	1,041.4	1,036.9	1,024.8
2014	1,009.1	1,015.2	1,027.6	1,042.0	1,054.7	1,047.6	1,040.5	1,049.0	1,048.7	1,053.4	1,057.5	1,058.8	1,042.0
2015	1,030.5	1,032.4	1,042.1	1,057.8	1,070.6	1,068.8	1,063.3	1,068.1	1,068.7	1,073.4	1,077.5	1,078.4	1,061.0
2016	1,051.7	1,055.1	1,066.5	1,079.3	1,088.4	1,083.2	1,082.2	1,085.0	1,087.8	1,091.5	1,094.7	1,094.3	1,080.0
2017	1,068.6	1,074.5	1,082.1	1,093.2	1,101.8	1,103.8	1,094.4	1,098.8	1,099.6	1,103.7	1,107.6	1,109.9	1,094.8
2018	1,081.6	1,086.9	1,093.8	1,102.9	1,113.3	1,116.5	1,110.0	1,113.4	1,115.2	1,121.9	1,122.3	1,122.6	1,108.4
Total Private													
2010	827.1	825.1	834.7	848.4	855.9	860.0	858.7	859.3	853.7	857.6	857.7	856.5	849.6
2011	834.4	835.6	844.3	859.3	866.9	870.6	874.1	875.5	871.1	870.1	873.0	875.3	862.5
2012	853.6	854.5	863.2	874.9	885.2	891.8	888.4	890.7	887.2	889.5	888.1	889.3	879.7
2013	864.4	867.7	874.8	891.1	902.5	907.2	904.9	906.6	903.2	905.3	907.8	908.0	895.3
2014	882.8	883.3	895.4	908.2	920.1	923.2	921.9	924.8	917.5	920.9	925.0	927.2	912.5
2015	902.7	901.5	910.1	925.3	937.1	943.5	943.0	943.0	938.3	941.6	945.3	946.9	931.5
2016	924.1	924.0	934.3	946.3	954.4	958.2	959.8	959.0	956.1	958.5	961.4	961.8	949.8
2017	939.6	942.2	948.7	959.3	968.3	976.3	972.9	973.8	967.7	970.3	973.8	977.0	964.2
2018	952.4	954.6	961.1	970.4	980.8	990.3	989.7	989.9	984.4	990.3	990.4	992.2	978.9
Goods Producing													
2010	135.1	133.6	135.8	138.7	139.8	140.6	141.6	141.7	141.6	142.3	141.6	139.5	139.3
2011	135.6	135.7	137.4	140.2	141.8	143.2	144.6	144.8	144.7	144.7	144.2	143.8	141.7
2012	139.7	139.4	140.8	142.7	144.2	146.1	146.2	146.1	145.4	144.9	144.4	143.7	143.6
2013	139.5	139.0	139.4	142.4	145.0	146.6	147.4	147.2	147.6	148.1	148.2	146.9	144.8
2014	143.6	143.7	146.6	149.5	152.2	153.6	153.7	154.4	153.8	154.5	154.5	153.8	151.2
2015	149.9	149.8	151.0	154.2	156.7	158.8	158.6	159.3	158.3	159.4	159.5	159.1	156.2
2016	155.1	154.9	157.0	159.2	160.5	162.0	162.7	162.4	162.0	161.6	161.8	161.2	160.0
2017	158.5	159.4	160.8	162.3	164.3	166.0	165.5	166.1	165.4	165.7	165.5	165.0	163.7
2018	160.2	161.5	163.4	165.0	166.5	168.1	168.8	168.5	168.2	169.4	169.7	168.7	166.5
Service-Providing													
2010	824.8	826.7	835.1	847.0	855.9	848.5	836.4	841.5	842.1	848.1	850.6	851.2	842.3
2011	829.3	832.8	840.7	853.2	858.0	851.4	847.8	855.8	856.7	858.3	861.3	861.1	850.5
2012	839.8	847.2	855.7	865.8	875.1	870.4	860.3	866.8	871.5	877.0	876.6	874.4	865.1
2013	851.3	861.1	867.4	883.9	891.8	884.8	873.9	884.6	887.6	890.5	893.2	890.0	880.0
2014	865.5	871.5	881.0	892.5	902.5	894.0	886.8	894.6	894.9	898.9	903.0	905.0	890.9
2015	880.6	882.6	891.1	903.6	913.9	910.0	904.7	908.8	910.4	914.0	918.0	919.3	904.8
2016	896.6	900.2	909.5	920.1	927.9	921.2	919.5	922.6	925.8	929.9	932.9	933.1	919.9
2017	910.1	915.1	921.3	930.9	937.5	937.8	928.9	932.7	934.2	938.0	942.1	944.9	931.1
2018	921.4	925.4	930.4	937.9	946.8	948.4	941.2	944.9	947.0	952.5	952.6	953.9	941.9
Mining, Logging, and Construction													
2010	32.9	31.8	33.3	35.8	36.6	37.3	38.1	38.3	37.9	38.8	38.1	36.4	36.3
2011	33.3	33.3	34.6	36.8	37.9	38.7	39.8	40.1	39.8	39.8	39.0	38.4	37.6
2012	35.4	34.9	36.1	37.9	38.8	39.6	39.7	39.9	39.8	39.4	39.0	38.0	38.2
2013	35.2	34.8	35.4	37.3	38.7	39.7	40.2	40.5	41.0	41.1	40.6	39.1	38.6
2014	36.5	36.0	38.0	40.2	42.0	42.5	42.8	43.3	43.1	43.2	42.9	41.8	41.0
2015	38.6	38.5	39.3	41.7	43.6	44.6	44.5	45.0	44.7	45.6	45.6	44.6	43.0
2016	41.4	41.2	43.3	45.2	45.9	46.7	47.1	47.0	47.0	47.0	46.9	45.9	45.4
2017	42.9	43.4	44.6	46.3	47.9	48.7	48.8	49.0	49.0	49.1	48.5	47.5	47.1
2018	43.2	44.2	45.8	47.6	48.7	49.2	49.3	49.0	49.1	49.7	49.5	48.8	47.8
Manufacturing													
2010	102.2	101.8	102.5	102.9	103.2	103.3	103.5	103.4	103.7	103.5	103.5	103.1	103.1
2011	102.3	102.4	102.8	103.4	103.9	104.5	104.8	104.7	104.9	104.9	105.2	105.4	104.1
2012	104.3	104.5	104.7	104.8	105.4	106.5	106.5	106.2	105.6	105.5	105.4	105.7	105.4
2013	104.3	104.2	104.0	105.1	106.3	106.9	107.2	106.7	106.6	107.0	107.6	107.8	106.1
2014	107.1	107.7	108.6	109.3	110.2	111.1	110.9	111.1	110.7	111.3	111.6	112.0	110.1
2015	111.3	111.3	111.7	112.5	113.1	114.2	114.1	114.3	113.6	113.8	113.9	114.5	113.2
2016	113.7	113.7	113.7	114.0	114.6	115.3	115.6	115.4	115.0	114.6	114.9	115.3	114.7
2017	115.6	116.0	116.2	116.0	116.4	117.3	116.7	117.1	116.4	116.6	117.0	117.5	116.6
2018	117.0	117.3	117.6	117.4	117.8	118.9	119.5	119.5	119.1	119.7	120.2	119.9	118.7

Employment by Industry: Cincinnati, OH-KY-IN, 2010–2018—*Continued*

(Numbers in thousands, not seasonally adjusted)

Industry and year	January	February	March	April	May	June	July	August	September	October	November	December	Annual average
Trade, Transportation, and Utilities													
2010	192.7	191.9	192.9	193.9	195.5	195.5	193.9	194.1	193.0	195.6	199.6	200.7	194.9
2011	192.3	191.3	192.2	194.0	194.8	195.3	196.1	197.0	197.0	198.9	203.8	205.4	196.5
2012	196.2	194.9	196.4	197.4	199.6	199.7	198.6	199.4	199.3	201.0	204.7	205.4	199.4
2013	197.6	196.4	197.5	199.0	200.9	201.0	199.6	200.4	199.3	201.5	206.3	207.8	200.6
2014	199.0	198.2	199.1	200.6	202.0	202.6	201.8	203.3	201.8	205.3	209.2	211.1	202.8
2015	202.8	201.7	202.9	204.6	206.3	206.8	206.2	206.8	205.8	208.8	213.3	216.0	206.8
2016	207.6	206.5	207.2	208.3	209.5	209.1	209.6	210.7	210.3	212.8	216.5	218.5	210.6
2017	209.2	208.3	208.7	210.9	212.8	212.8	213.1	214.0	213.9	215.6	221.1	223.2	213.6
2018	218.1	215.3	215.3	216.2	218.0	218.7	219.3	219.0	219.1	222.6	226.3	225.6	219.5
Wholesale Trade													
2010	54.6	54.6	54.6	54.4	54.6	54.9	54.6	54.5	54.0	54.3	54.4	54.3	54.5
2011	54.3	54.4	54.7	55.1	55.3	55.4	55.7	55.8	55.9	55.7	55.8	55.8	55.3
2012	55.9	55.9	56.3	56.8	57.1	57.8	57.5	57.7	57.5	57.8	57.7	58.0	57.2
2013	58.1	58.3	58.5	58.7	59.0	59.1	59.0	58.9	58.8	58.6	58.8	58.9	58.7
2014	57.8	58.3	58.3	58.6	58.8	59.0	59.1	59.2	58.9	59.0	59.2	59.4	58.8
2015	58.8	59.0	59.2	59.3	59.8	60.1	59.8	59.9	59.3	59.6	59.9	60.1	59.6
2016	60.0	60.2	60.2	60.2	60.5	60.6	60.3	60.4	60.2	60.1	59.8	59.9	60.2
2017	58.9	58.7	58.6	58.9	59.2	59.6	59.5	59.5	59.1	59.0	59.2	59.6	59.2
2018	58.7	58.9	58.9	59.2	59.5	60.0	59.9	60.0	59.7	60.1	60.4	59.8	59.6
Retail Trade													
2010	99.6	98.9	99.9	100.9	102.0	101.5	101.4	101.3	100.4	102.2	105.4	106.1	101.6
2011	100.0	99.1	99.4	100.6	101.0	101.5	101.6	101.5	100.4	102.1	105.6	106.7	101.6
2012	100.3	99.0	100.1	100.9	102.3	102.2	101.8	101.7	101.5	103.3	107.0	107.3	102.3
2013	101.3	100.1	100.9	102.1	103.5	103.8	103.1	103.5	102.2	104.0	107.5	108.4	103.4
2014	102.3	101.2	101.7	103.1	104.0	104.4	103.9	104.5	103.3	105.9	109.1	110.1	104.5
2015	103.7	102.8	103.5	104.7	105.4	105.8	105.3	105.4	104.9	107.1	110.8	112.4	106.0
2016	106.0	104.9	105.5	106.4	107.0	106.7	107.3	107.7	107.1	109.3	112.3	113.0	107.8
2017	107.1	106.3	106.4	107.8	108.6	108.2	108.5	108.5	108.2	110.0	113.9	114.4	109.0
2018	110.0	107.7	107.3	107.6	108.8	108.4	109.0	108.2	108.3	109.4	113.2	112.9	109.2
Transportation and Utilities													
2010	38.5	38.4	38.4	38.6	38.9	39.1	37.9	38.3	38.6	39.1	39.8	40.3	38.8
2011	38.0	37.8	38.1	38.3	38.5	38.4	38.8	39.7	40.7	41.1	42.4	42.9	39.6
2012	40.0	40.0	40.0	39.7	40.2	39.7	39.3	40.0	40.3	39.9	40.0	40.1	39.9
2013	38.2	38.0	38.1	38.2	38.4	38.1	37.5	38.0	38.3	38.9	40.0	40.5	38.5
2014	38.9	38.7	39.1	38.9	39.2	39.2	38.8	39.6	39.6	40.4	40.9	41.6	39.6
2015	40.3	39.9	40.2	40.6	41.1	40.9	41.1	41.5	41.6	42.1	42.6	43.5	41.3
2016	41.6	41.4	41.5	41.7	42.0	41.8	42.0	42.6	43.0	43.4	44.4	45.6	42.6
2017	43.2	43.3	43.7	44.2	45.0	45.0	45.1	46.0	46.6	46.6	48.0	49.2	45.5
2018	49.4	48.7	49.1	49.4	49.7	50.3	50.4	50.8	51.1	53.1	52.7	52.9	50.6
Information													
2010	14.2	14.0	14.0	13.9	14.0	14.0	14.2	14.2	14.1	14.0	14.1	14.0	14.1
2011	13.9	13.9	13.8	13.8	13.9	14.0	14.0	14.1	14.0	13.8	14.0	13.9	13.9
2012	13.9	13.9	13.8	13.7	13.8	13.9	13.9	13.8	13.7	14.0	14.1	14.2	13.9
2013	14.1	14.2	14.1	14.1	14.1	14.1	14.0	13.9	13.6	13.5	13.5	13.5	13.9
2014	13.3	13.3	13.4	13.6	13.7	13.5	13.6	13.7	13.4	13.3	13.5	13.7	13.5
2015	13.5	13.5	13.6	13.6	13.5	13.7	13.5	13.8	13.5	13.9	14.0	14.2	13.7
2016	14.1	14.2	14.2	14.1	14.2	14.2	14.3	14.2	14.0	14.0	14.0	14.0	14.1
2017	13.9	14.1	13.9	13.9	14.0	14.1	14.2	14.0	13.8	13.6	13.8	13.7	13.9
2018	13.7	13.9	13.9	13.9	14.0	14.1	14.1	14.2	13.9	13.9	13.9	13.9	14.0
Financial Activities													
2010	61.5	61.3	61.3	62.1	62.3	62.6	63.3	63.3	63.1	63.1	63.2	63.5	62.6
2011	63.3	63.3	63.3	63.2	63.4	63.5	63.2	63.2	63.0	62.9	63.1	63.4	63.2
2012	63.4	63.3	63.4	63.6	64.0	64.5	64.6	64.5	64.5	64.5	64.7	65.2	64.2
2013	64.4	64.6	64.9	65.2	65.6	66.2	66.5	66.7	66.2	66.0	66.2	66.2	65.7
2014	65.6	65.7	65.8	66.1	66.8	67.4	67.8	67.8	67.2	67.2	67.9	67.8	66.9
2015	67.4	67.6	67.8	68.1	68.8	69.5	69.8	70.1	69.6	69.9	70.2	70.3	69.1
2016	70.4	70.8	70.8	71.3	71.8	72.4	73.2	73.3	72.9	73.2	73.5	73.9	72.3
2017	73.5	73.6	73.6	73.7	73.9	74.4	74.2	74.2	73.4	73.8	73.7	73.8	73.8
2018	73.2	73.5	73.2	73.8	74.1	74.7	75.1	74.8	73.9	74.0	74.4	75.4	74.2

Employment by Industry: Cincinnati, OH-KY-IN, 2010–2018—*Continued*

(Numbers in thousands, not seasonally adjusted)

Industry and year	January	February	March	April	May	June	July	August	September	October	November	December	Annual average
Professional and Business Services													
2010	143.7	143.7	145.3	148.4	148.1	149.5	149.5	150.2	149.7	151.6	151.4	150.9	148.5
2011	149.0	149.4	151.2	154.1	153.2	153.6	156.2	157.0	156.9	157.6	158.7	158.8	154.6
2012	156.3	156.1	157.6	160.4	160.5	161.4	161.6	163.3	163.3	164.1	162.8	162.6	160.8
2013	157.1	158.0	159.3	162.9	163.0	164.1	164.0	165.6	166.0	166.4	166.9	167.8	163.4
2014	162.1	161.8	163.8	166.5	166.6	166.4	167.4	168.8	168.4	168.7	170.3	170.3	166.8
2015	165.2	164.2	164.9	168.0	167.7	169.2	169.6	169.9	168.9	169.9	170.0	169.6	168.1
2016	165.3	164.2	165.7	169.2	168.0	168.4	169.0	169.7	169.8	170.8	171.4	170.9	168.5
2017	166.2	165.1	165.5	168.6	167.5	169.7	169.5	169.8	168.4	170.5	172.1	171.4	168.7
2018	165.7	166.0	167.2	168.3	168.7	171.6	172.2	172.6	173.0	175.7	174.4	176.0	171.0
Education and Health Services													
2010	144.7	145.6	146.6	148.3	148.6	146.7	146.1	146.1	147.2	148.7	149.2	149.2	147.3
2011	146.4	147.6	148.2	150.1	151.2	149.4	148.6	148.8	150.0	150.7	151.0	151.2	149.4
2012	149.4	151.0	151.6	152.5	153.3	152.0	150.3	150.8	152.8	154.1	154.7	154.5	152.3
2013	152.4	154.1	154.7	156.3	157.5	156.1	155.2	155.5	157.1	158.0	159.6	158.9	156.3
2014	157.3	158.1	159.2	159.3	160.5	158.9	158.0	158.6	159.9	160.3	161.7	161.8	159.5
2015	159.4	159.7	160.9	161.7	162.6	160.8	159.7	160.2	161.7	163.2	164.4	163.9	161.5
2016	161.5	162.6	163.9	164.2	165.0	162.5	160.9	161.3	163.2	164.0	164.8	164.4	163.2
2017	163.2	164.4	165.1	165.3	166.4	165.1	162.7	162.8	164.4	165.6	166.1	166.6	164.8
2018	164.1	166.0	166.1	166.6	167.5	166.2	164.3	165.3	167.1	168.5	169.8	168.5	166.7
Leisure and Hospitality													
2010	93.9	93.9	97.2	102.3	106.9	110.1	109.0	108.7	104.5	101.8	98.3	98.5	102.1
2011	94.1	94.8	98.2	103.7	108.1	111.3	111.3	110.8	106.2	102.7	99.7	100.4	103.4
2012	96.9	98.3	101.7	106.1	110.9	114.6	113.7	113.3	109.0	107.5	103.3	104.1	106.6
2013	100.1	102.0	105.2	111.3	116.4	118.9	118.2	117.5	113.9	112.5	108.1	107.9	111.0
2014	103.6	104.2	108.8	113.6	119.0	121.3	120.3	119.0	114.6	112.8	109.2	109.9	113.0
2015	106.6	107.2	110.8	116.5	122.4	125.2	125.9	123.3	121.4	116.9	114.2	113.9	117.0
2016	110.4	110.9	115.2	119.1	124.2	128.5	128.6	126.1	122.7	120.2	117.5	116.8	120.0
2017	112.9	114.8	118.1	121.7	126.2	130.6	130.7	130.1	125.8	123.0	119.4	120.9	122.9
2018	115.7	116.5	119.8	124.4	129.7	134.3	133.6	133.3	127.3	123.9	120.3	123.2	125.2
Other Services													
2010	41.3	41.1	41.6	40.8	40.7	41.0	41.1	41.0	40.5	40.5	40.3	40.2	40.8
2011	39.8	39.6	40.0	40.2	40.5	40.3	40.1	39.8	39.3	38.8	38.5	38.4	39.6
2012	37.8	37.6	37.9	38.5	38.9	39.6	39.5	39.5	39.2	39.4	39.4	39.6	38.9
2013	39.2	39.4	39.7	39.9	40.0	40.2	40.0	39.8	39.5	39.3	39.0	39.0	39.6
2014	38.3	38.3	38.7	39.0	39.3	39.5	39.3	39.2	38.4	38.8	38.7	38.8	38.9
2015	37.9	37.8	38.2	38.6	39.1	39.5	39.7	39.6	39.1	39.6	39.7	39.9	39.1
2016	39.7	39.9	40.3	40.9	41.2	41.1	41.5	41.3	41.2	41.9	41.9	42.1	41.1
2017	42.2	42.5	43.0	42.9	43.2	43.6	43.0	42.8	42.6	42.5	42.1	42.4	42.7
2018	41.7	41.9	42.2	42.2	42.3	42.6	42.3	42.2	41.9	42.3	41.6	40.9	42.0
Government													
2010	132.8	135.2	136.2	137.3	139.8	129.1	119.3	123.9	130.0	132.8	134.5	134.2	132.1
2011	130.5	132.9	133.8	134.1	132.9	124.0	118.3	125.1	130.3	132.9	132.5	129.6	129.7
2012	125.9	132.1	133.3	133.6	134.1	124.7	118.1	122.2	129.7	132.4	132.9	128.8	129.0
2013	126.4	132.4	132.0	135.2	134.3	124.2	116.4	125.2	132.0	133.3	133.6	128.9	129.5
2014	126.3	131.9	132.2	133.8	134.6	124.4	118.6	124.2	131.2	132.5	132.5	131.6	129.5
2015	127.8	130.9	132.0	132.5	133.5	125.3	120.3	125.1	130.4	131.8	132.2	131.5	129.4
2016	127.6	131.1	132.2	133.0	134.0	125.0	122.4	126.0	131.7	133.0	133.3	132.5	130.2
2017	129.0	132.3	133.4	133.9	133.5	127.5	121.5	125.0	131.9	133.4	133.8	132.9	130.7
2018	129.2	132.3	132.7	132.5	132.5	126.2	120.3	123.5	130.8	131.6	131.9	130.4	129.5

Employment by Industry: Austin-Round Rock, TX, 2010–2018

(Numbers in thousands, not seasonally adjusted)

Industry and year	January	February	March	April	May	June	July	August	September	October	November	December	Annual average
Total Nonfarm													
2010	765.7	771.5	780.1	783.6	788.6	790.8	777.7	780.7	787.0	796.5	801.9	801.9	785.5
2011	789.3	797.4	804.6	812.8	814.2	815.7	804.5	809.2	818.3	820.9	827.2	828.5	811.9
2012	819.2	825.9	832.8	837.5	842.5	847.1	835.7	841.7	852.0	859.5	870.0	869.0	844.4
2013	855.3	864.9	871.7	878.5	883.7	888.8	878.6	881.7	892.1	897.9	908.3	907.3	884.1
2014	895.3	905.8	913.6	918.5	922.9	928.3	917.7	919.7	928.0	936.7	944.1	945.8	923.0
2015	933.4	943.5	949.9	955.8	962.2	969.1	960.6	962.5	970.6	979.7	985.6	987.0	963.3
2016	975.0	984.8	988.9	995.9	999.0	1,003.7	999.6	999.9	1,007.6	1,015.4	1,020.5	1,020.6	1,000.9
2017	1,009.1	1,018.5	1,024.7	1,029.9	1,035.9	1,040.4	1,030.8	1,031.1	1,037.6	1,049.2	1,054.2	1,055.2	1,034.7
2018	1,043.3	1,054.3	1,060.2	1,062.9	1,070.1	1,076.7	1,069.9	1,072.7	1,073.6	1,079.9	1,083.2	1,082.0	1,069.1
Total Private													
2010	592.7	596.2	602.1	606.3	609.3	613.4	614.5	617.4	615.7	622.0	626.1	628.3	612.0
2011	616.8	621.4	628.5	636.2	637.9	641.2	643.6	648.7	648.9	650.9	655.8	658.9	640.7
2012	648.5	653.2	659.9	664.1	669.0	675.7	675.6	682.5	682.5	688.0	696.0	697.3	674.4
2013	682.8	689.9	696.2	702.8	707.7	714.4	715.0	720.3	720.4	725.0	733.2	734.4	711.8
2014	721.7	729.9	737.1	742.5	746.3	753.5	753.5	757.6	755.7	761.6	768.1	770.1	749.8
2015	757.6	766.3	772.4	778.1	784.1	792.3	794.1	797.9	795.8	802.4	807.8	809.2	788.2
2016	797.7	806.3	808.4	816.0	818.1	823.8	829.2	831.7	830.4	835.0	838.6	838.7	822.8
2017	827.1	835.0	840.3	846.4	851.8	857.6	858.5	861.4	859.3	866.4	871.4	872.8	854.0
2018	860.9	870.1	874.8	878.0	884.0	891.0	894.6	899.0	894.3	896.6	900.2	899.3	886.9
Goods Producing													
2010	90.7	90.7	91.4	92.4	92.3	93.4	94.2	95.1	94.6	95.0	94.8	94.6	93.3
2011	93.3	93.6	94.3	94.3	94.5	95.5	96.0	96.2	95.9	96.0	95.9	96.0	95.1
2012	95.3	96.3	97.1	97.5	98.3	100.1	100.6	101.5	101.2	101.2	100.8	100.7	99.2
2013	99.7	100.3	101.1	102.2	103.0	103.9	104.1	104.6	104.4	104.7	105.3	105.6	103.2
2014	104.5	105.7	106.4	106.7	107.7	109.0	109.5	109.8	109.0	108.7	108.9	109.1	107.9
2015	108.7	109.6	109.9	109.7	110.0	111.5	112.3	112.5	111.3	111.7	111.7	111.7	110.9
2016	111.5	112.6	112.7	113.4	113.8	115.0	116.5	116.5	115.6	115.9	115.8	115.8	114.6
2017	114.6	115.7	116.6	117.8	119.0	120.7	121.3	121.4	120.8	121.3	121.7	121.9	119.4
2018	120.9	122.2	122.8	123.5	124.3	125.9	126.5	127.1	126.0	124.6	124.2	125.0	124.4
Service-Providing													
2010	675.0	680.8	688.7	691.2	696.3	697.4	683.5	685.6	692.4	701.5	707.1	707.3	692.2
2011	696.0	703.8	710.3	718.5	719.7	720.2	708.5	713.0	722.4	724.9	731.3	732.5	716.8
2012	723.9	729.6	735.7	740.0	744.2	747.0	735.1	740.2	750.8	758.3	769.2	768.3	745.2
2013	755.6	764.6	770.6	776.3	780.7	784.9	774.5	777.1	787.7	793.2	803.0	801.7	780.8
2014	790.8	800.1	807.2	811.8	815.2	819.3	808.2	809.9	819.0	828.0	835.2	836.7	815.1
2015	824.7	833.9	840.0	846.1	852.2	857.6	848.3	850.0	859.3	868.0	873.9	875.3	852.4
2016	863.5	872.2	876.2	882.5	885.2	888.7	883.1	883.4	892.0	899.5	904.7	904.8	886.3
2017	894.5	902.8	908.1	912.1	916.9	919.7	909.5	909.7	916.8	927.9	932.5	933.3	915.3
2018	922.4	932.1	937.4	939.4	945.8	950.8	943.4	945.6	947.6	955.3	959.0	957.0	944.7
Mining, Logging, and Construction													
2010	38.6	38.4	39.1	40.2	40.0	40.7	41.5	42.0	41.4	41.5	41.1	40.8	40.4
2011	39.8	39.8	40.1	39.7	39.6	40.2	40.3	40.4	40.4	40.1	40.0	40.1	40.0
2012	40.0	40.5	41.2	41.6	42.1	43.2	43.4	44.0	44.0	44.0	43.8	44.0	42.7
2013	43.4	44.1	44.9	45.4	46.1	46.3	46.4	46.8	46.9	47.0	47.2	47.4	46.0
2014	46.9	47.8	48.5	49.3	50.3	51.2	51.9	52.4	52.3	52.4	52.7	52.9	50.7
2015	52.9	53.8	54.1	54.2	54.6	55.4	56.1	56.4	56.0	56.5	56.6	56.8	55.3
2016	56.4	57.3	57.5	58.0	58.2	58.8	59.9	59.9	59.7	59.9	59.8	59.8	58.8
2017	58.9	59.7	60.4	61.1	62.1	63.1	63.4	63.3	63.0	63.3	63.3	63.3	62.1
2018	62.4	63.1	63.5	64.0	64.4	65.1	65.4	65.8	65.2	63.9	62.9	63.4	64.1
Manufacturing													
2010	52.1	52.3	52.3	52.2	52.3	52.7	52.7	53.1	53.2	53.5	53.7	53.8	52.8
2011	53.5	53.8	54.2	54.6	54.9	55.3	55.7	55.8	55.5	55.9	55.9	55.9	55.1
2012	55.3	55.8	55.9	55.9	56.2	56.9	57.2	57.5	57.2	57.2	57.0	56.7	56.6
2013	56.3	56.2	56.2	56.8	56.9	57.6	57.7	57.8	57.5	57.7	58.1	58.2	57.3
2014	57.6	57.9	57.9	57.4	57.4	57.8	57.6	57.4	56.7	56.3	56.2	56.2	57.2
2015	55.8	55.8	55.8	55.5	55.4	56.1	56.2	56.1	55.3	55.2	55.1	54.9	55.6
2016	55.1	55.3	55.2	55.4	55.6	56.2	56.6	56.6	55.9	56.0	56.0	56.0	55.8
2017	55.7	56.0	56.2	56.7	56.9	57.6	57.9	58.1	57.8	58.0	58.4	58.6	57.3
2018	58.5	59.1	59.3	59.5	59.9	60.8	61.1	61.3	60.8	60.7	61.3	61.6	60.3

Employment by Industry: Austin-Round Rock, TX, 2010–2018—*Continued*

(Numbers in thousands, not seasonally adjusted)

Industry and year	January	February	March	April	May	June	July	August	September	October	November	December	Annual average
Trade, Transportation, and Utilities													
2010	130.3	129.3	129.8	131.0	131.3	131.7	131.9	133.0	132.6	134.2	137.5	139.8	132.7
2011	135.2	134.7	135.8	136.6	136.9	136.7	137.7	139.2	138.9	140.4	143.5	145.9	138.5
2012	141.0	140.4	140.9	141.7	142.4	143.0	143.1	144.9	144.1	145.7	150.4	151.8	144.1
2013	146.9	146.7	146.6	147.9	148.7	150.3	150.8	152.1	151.9	153.5	157.9	160.0	151.1
2014	155.0	154.4	154.4	154.8	154.9	156.0	156.0	156.9	156.6	158.3	162.1	164.3	157.0
2015	158.9	158.6	159.1	159.5	160.6	162.2	162.9	164.2	164.2	165.6	169.3	172.1	163.1
2016	166.7	166.6	166.9	167.4	167.5	168.4	169.7	170.9	170.7	172.3	175.9	178.0	170.1
2017	172.8	171.8	171.8	172.7	173.1	173.7	174.2	175.2	174.2	176.1	180.1	182.1	174.8
2018	176.7	176.3	176.5	176.9	177.6	178.5	179.1	180.0	179.8	182.5	185.8	187.7	179.8
Wholesale Trade													
2010	35.6	35.6	35.7	36.2	36.3	36.5	36.6	36.7	36.5	37.1	37.3	37.5	36.5
2011	37.5	37.8	38.1	38.3	38.5	38.7	39.0	39.1	39.5	40.1	40.3	40.5	39.0
2012	40.0	40.2	40.4	40.5	40.8	41.0	40.9	41.1	40.8	40.8	41.0	41.2	40.7
2013	41.4	41.7	41.9	41.9	41.8	42.5	42.6	42.8	42.6	43.0	43.1	43.3	42.4
2014	43.0	43.2	43.0	43.1	43.2	43.6	43.8	43.9	44.0	44.3	44.6	44.8	43.7
2015	45.1	45.3	45.4	45.4	45.6	46.1	46.5	47.0	46.9	47.0	47.4	47.6	46.3
2016	47.1	47.3	47.4	48.0	47.9	48.0	48.0	48.0	47.9	47.7	47.3	47.3	47.7
2017	47.6	47.6	47.8	48.1	48.1	48.3	48.7	48.8	48.8	48.6	48.7	48.7	48.3
2018	48.4	48.6	48.9	49.1	49.2	50.1	50.6	50.9	50.9	51.8	52.2	52.7	50.3
Retail Trade													
2010	81.9	80.9	81.2	81.9	82.1	82.4	82.7	83.5	83.0	84.1	87.0	88.6	83.3
2011	84.2	83.5	84.2	84.8	84.8	84.9	85.4	86.3	85.5	86.6	89.4	91.0	85.9
2012	87.1	86.2	86.5	87.3	87.7	88.2	88.5	89.6	89.0	90.7	94.9	95.7	89.3
2013	91.2	90.9	90.7	91.6	92.2	92.9	93.6	94.3	94.1	95.3	99.2	100.6	93.9
2014	96.4	95.9	96.0	96.2	96.2	96.8	97.1	97.6	96.9	98.2	101.5	102.7	97.6
2015	97.8	97.6	97.9	98.1	98.8	99.8	100.2	100.7	100.7	101.7	104.7	106.2	100.4
2016	102.0	102.0	102.3	102.4	102.4	103.0	103.4	104.1	103.8	105.0	108.4	109.6	104.0
2017	105.1	104.6	104.5	104.6	105.0	105.2	105.2	105.5	104.6	106.3	109.4	110.6	105.9
2018	106.6	106.1	105.9	106.2	106.6	106.6	106.9	107.2	106.9	108.4	111.0	112.2	107.6
Transportation and Utilities													
2010	12.8	12.8	12.9	12.9	12.9	12.8	12.6	12.8	13.1	13.0	13.2	13.7	13.0
2011	13.5	13.4	13.5	13.5	13.6	13.1	13.3	13.8	13.9	13.7	13.8	14.4	13.6
2012	13.9	14.0	14.0	13.9	13.9	13.8	13.7	14.2	14.3	14.2	14.5	14.9	14.1
2013	14.3	14.1	14.0	14.4	14.7	14.9	14.6	15.0	15.2	15.2	15.6	16.1	14.8
2014	15.6	15.3	15.4	15.5	15.5	15.6	15.1	15.4	15.7	15.8	16.0	16.8	15.6
2015	16.0	15.7	15.8	16.0	16.2	16.3	16.2	16.5	16.6	16.9	17.2	18.3	16.5
2016	17.6	17.3	17.2	17.0	17.2	17.4	18.3	18.8	19.0	19.6	20.2	21.1	18.4
2017	20.1	19.6	19.5	20.0	20.0	20.2	20.3	20.9	20.8	21.2	22.0	22.8	20.6
2018	21.7	21.6	21.7	21.6	21.8	21.8	21.6	21.9	22.0	22.3	22.6	22.8	22.0
Information													
2010	19.5	19.6	19.6	19.6	19.7	19.8	19.9	20.0	20.0	20.1	20.3	20.5	19.9
2011	20.1	20.2	20.3	20.4	20.6	20.8	21.2	21.3	21.4	21.4	21.8	21.9	21.0
2012	22.0	21.9	22.1	22.1	22.3	22.6	23.0	23.1	23.0	23.3	23.6	23.8	22.7
2013	23.1	23.2	23.7	23.4	23.4	23.9	24.1	24.3	24.1	24.1	24.7	25.0	23.9
2014	24.3	24.3	24.4	25.0	24.5	25.2	25.6	25.7	25.7	26.0	26.5	27.1	25.4
2015	26.7	26.7	26.9	27.3	27.5	28.0	27.8	28.0	28.0	28.2	28.8	28.9	27.7
2016	28.8	29.0	28.7	28.7	28.8	29.1	29.0	29.0	28.8	29.1	29.1	29.4	29.0
2017	29.4	29.5	29.8	29.8	30.0	30.5	30.9	30.8	31.1	32.1	32.0	32.2	30.7
2018	32.3	31.9	32.1	32.4	32.9	33.0	33.3	33.4	33.4	33.5	33.9	34.3	33.0
Financial Activities													
2010	43.1	43.2	43.3	43.2	43.4	43.4	43.4	43.4	43.1	43.5	43.6	43.7	43.4
2011	43.5	43.7	44.1	44.5	44.7	44.9	45.2	45.3	45.2	45.4	45.6	46.0	44.8
2012	45.7	45.9	46.2	46.3	46.7	47.1	47.0	47.4	47.4	48.0	48.1	48.3	47.0
2013	47.9	48.2	48.3	48.7	49.0	49.3	49.7	49.8	49.8	50.3	50.4	50.7	49.3
2014	50.7	51.1	51.3	51.4	51.7	52.1	52.0	52.2	51.9	52.4	52.5	53.0	51.9
2015	52.4	52.9	52.9	53.6	53.9	54.2	54.4	54.6	54.3	54.9	55.1	55.5	54.1
2016	55.1	55.5	55.8	56.1	56.3	56.9	57.5	57.9	57.6	58.0	58.1	58.7	57.0
2017	58.3	58.7	59.1	59.5	59.8	60.5	60.8	60.9	60.8	61.2	61.1	61.8	60.2
2018	61.2	61.7	61.9	62.0	62.5	63.0	64.0	64.4	63.8	63.5	63.6	63.6	62.9

Employment by Industry: Austin-Round Rock, TX, 2010–2018—*Continued*

(Numbers in thousands, not seasonally adjusted)

Industry and year	January	February	March	April	May	June	July	August	September	October	November	December	Annual average
Professional and Business Services													
2010	109.2	110.3	112.0	112.2	112.9	114.0	114.1	114.6	114.7	117.0	117.1	117.6	113.8
2011	116.6	118.2	119.6	121.1	120.9	122.0	122.5	123.9	124.7	125.0	125.6	126.3	122.2
2012	124.8	125.9	127.7	127.8	128.5	129.8	130.9	132.9	133.3	134.7	136.0	135.3	130.6
2013	132.4	134.5	136.2	138.1	139.0	140.1	141.2	143.3	143.9	145.2	146.4	145.9	140.5
2014	143.8	146.5	149.1	150.4	150.9	151.8	152.4	153.9	153.7	156.1	156.7	156.5	151.8
2015	154.9	157.2	159.1	160.0	160.9	162.6	164.3	165.1	165.1	167.4	168.0	166.7	162.6
2016	165.0	167.4	167.8	169.9	169.9	171.1	172.6	173.2	172.7	174.0	174.7	173.2	171.0
2017	171.4	173.8	175.3	175.6	176.5	178.4	178.6	179.5	179.7	181.0	181.1	180.5	177.6
2018	179.4	182.4	183.0	183.3	184.5	186.7	188.9	190.3	190.3	191.0	190.9	188.0	186.6
Education and Health Services													
2010	84.5	86.0	86.4	87.4	87.8	87.3	87.8	88.2	88.6	89.8	90.1	89.7	87.8
2011	88.7	89.8	90.1	92.2	92.5	91.9	92.6	94.3	95.0	95.4	96.1	95.9	92.9
2012	95.0	96.4	97.0	97.2	97.7	97.5	96.8	98.3	99.4	100.1	100.7	100.6	98.1
2013	99.7	101.3	101.3	102.4	102.6	102.0	101.3	102.7	103.4	104.3	104.9	104.4	102.5
2014	102.9	104.6	104.9	106.2	106.7	106.1	105.3	106.5	107.0	108.5	109.5	109.1	106.4
2015	107.7	109.7	109.9	111.6	112.1	111.5	110.7	112.2	112.5	113.8	114.0	113.7	111.6
2016	113.4	114.9	114.2	114.6	114.7	113.6	115.0	116.4	116.9	118.1	117.6	117.4	115.6
2017	117.9	119.7	119.6	120.8	121.0	119.5	119.4	121.0	120.9	122.4	122.7	122.3	120.6
2018	122.1	124.4	123.7	124.5	124.4	123.2	124.0	125.8	125.2	128.0	127.7	126.9	125.0
Leisure and Hospitality													
2010	80.7	82.1	83.9	85.3	86.6	87.4	86.4	86.6	86.5	86.8	87.2	86.9	85.5
2011	84.8	86.2	88.6	91.3	91.9	92.2	90.9	91.5	91.7	91.0	91.1	90.6	90.2
2012	88.8	90.2	92.2	94.1	95.3	96.3	94.4	94.9	95.3	95.9	97.1	97.2	94.3
2013	94.5	96.5	99.2	100.1	101.6	103.1	101.7	101.9	102.3	102.1	102.4	101.6	100.6
2014	100.3	102.6	105.1	106.4	107.8	109.6	108.6	108.9	109.3	108.8	109.3	108.6	107.1
2015	106.8	109.7	112.2	114.8	117.0	118.5	117.6	117.5	117.8	118.0	118.2	118.1	115.5
2016	115.7	118.3	119.8	122.3	122.9	124.4	123.9	123.3	124.0	123.3	123.2	122.3	122.0
2017	119.5	121.9	123.8	125.4	127.3	127.9	127.3	127.0	126.7	127.1	127.2	126.9	125.7
2018	124.1	126.5	129.5	130.2	131.9	133.7	132.0	131.4	129.8	128.1	128.9	128.7	129.6
Other Services													
2010	34.7	35.0	35.7	35.2	35.3	36.4	36.8	36.5	35.6	35.6	35.5	35.5	35.7
2011	34.6	35.0	35.7	35.8	35.9	37.2	37.5	37.0	36.1	36.3	36.2	36.3	36.1
2012	35.9	36.2	36.7	37.4	37.8	39.3	39.8	39.5	38.8	39.1	39.3	39.6	38.3
2013	38.6	39.2	39.8	40.0	40.4	41.8	42.1	41.6	40.6	40.8	41.2	41.2	40.6
2014	40.2	40.7	41.5	41.6	42.1	43.7	44.1	43.7	42.5	42.8	42.6	42.4	42.3
2015	41.5	41.9	42.4	41.6	42.1	43.8	44.1	43.8	42.6	42.8	42.7	42.5	42.7
2016	41.5	42.0	42.5	43.6	44.2	45.3	45.0	44.5	44.1	44.3	44.2	43.9	43.8
2017	43.2	43.9	44.3	44.8	45.1	46.4	46.0	45.6	45.1	45.2	45.5	45.1	45.0
2018	44.2	44.7	45.3	45.2	45.9	47.0	46.8	46.6	46.0	45.4	45.2	45.1	45.6
Government													
2010	173.0	175.3	178.0	177.3	179.3	177.4	163.2	163.3	171.3	174.5	175.8	173.6	173.5
2011	172.5	176.0	176.1	176.6	176.3	174.5	160.9	160.5	169.4	170.0	171.4	169.6	171.2
2012	170.7	172.7	172.9	173.4	173.5	171.4	160.1	159.2	169.5	171.5	174.0	171.7	170.1
2013	172.5	175.0	175.5	175.7	176.0	174.4	163.6	161.4	171.7	172.9	175.1	172.9	172.2
2014	173.6	175.9	176.5	176.0	176.6	174.8	164.2	162.1	172.3	175.1	176.0	175.7	173.2
2015	175.8	177.2	177.5	177.7	178.1	176.8	166.5	164.6	174.8	177.3	177.8	177.8	175.2
2016	177.3	178.5	180.5	179.9	180.9	179.9	170.4	168.2	177.2	180.4	181.9	181.9	178.1
2017	182.0	183.5	184.4	183.5	184.1	182.8	172.3	169.7	178.3	182.8	182.8	182.4	180.7
2018	182.4	184.2	185.4	184.9	186.1	185.7	175.3	173.7	179.3	183.3	183.0	182.7	182.2

Employment by Industry: Kansas City, MO-KS, 2010–2018

(Numbers in thousands, not seasonally adjusted)

Industry and year	January	February	March	April	May	June	July	August	September	October	November	December	Annual average
Total Nonfarm													
2010	941.9	944.7	953.1	972.5	978.9	979.7	960.1	961.0	971.6	977.2	977.1	976.7	966.2
2011	950.4	953.2	965.8	976.4	981.7	982.1	971.8	971.5	980.9	985.4	990.0	989.0	974.9
2012	968.3	973.4	984.2	992.5	998.3	1,000.5	984.3	991.8	993.5	999.6	1,002.3	998.6	990.6
2013	977.5	981.0	987.7	1,000.6	1,007.3	1,011.6	996.1	1,002.6	1,009.6	1,014.5	1,014.5	1,014.2	1,001.4
2014	989.4	995.3	1,005.9	1,019.7	1,028.1	1,032.2	1,018.2	1,023.7	1,026.8	1,036.0	1,038.4	1,039.7	1,021.1
2015	1,016.8	1,023.7	1,031.9	1,042.0	1,050.8	1,055.2	1,045.1	1,045.4	1,051.5	1,060.6	1,060.4	1,062.4	1,045.5
2016	1,042.6	1,046.3	1,052.3	1,068.6	1,069.7	1,071.7	1,062.9	1,068.2	1,078.2	1,083.0	1,084.3	1,083.3	1,067.6
2017	1,059.5	1,065.7	1,072.3	1,082.6	1,086.0	1,091.0	1,081.4	1,083.6	1,093.9	1,096.3	1,101.6	1,102.8	1,084.7
2018	1,074.2	1,079.9	1,083.9	1,094.2	1,096.8	1,105.0	1,095.5	1,096.7	1,104.4	1,109.4	1,110.8	1,106.9	1,096.5
Total Private													
2010	792.2	791.8	798.7	816.1	819.9	823.7	822.7	824.7	821.3	826.8	826.5	826.8	815.9
2011	802.2	802.7	812.7	822.6	828.5	831.1	833.2	834.7	833.1	836.9	841.2	840.2	826.6
2012	822.7	824.1	833.7	841.3	846.7	852.8	848.7	852.6	846.2	850.8	853.5	850.2	843.6
2013	832.9	832.8	838.8	849.4	856.6	864.0	862.1	867.5	862.1	867.8	867.9	867.8	855.8
2014	845.9	848.7	858.3	871.7	879.0	885.2	883.5	889.5	879.9	888.6	891.1	893.4	876.2
2015	871.0	875.6	882.4	892.0	901.0	907.9	909.8	909.1	903.0	912.3	911.9	915.0	899.3
2016	895.1	896.8	902.4	917.3	919.7	923.9	926.2	930.0	927.3	932.7	934.2	934.2	920.0
2017	910.9	914.8	921.0	930.8	934.8	940.6	941.6	942.5	941.6	942.9	948.2	949.6	934.9
2018	921.5	925.0	928.3	938.5	941.6	950.2	952.2	952.5	947.0	951.3	952.6	948.7	942.5
Goods Producing													
2010	103.3	102.9	105.1	108.6	108.9	110.7	109.7	111.8	111.3	111.5	110.3	108.8	108.6
2011	102.5	101.6	104.6	107.1	108.0	109.2	109.2	107.4	108.9	108.9	108.8	107.9	107.0
2012	104.7	104.2	106.6	107.7	107.9	109.9	109.3	110.1	109.9	109.4	109.0	106.7	108.0
2013	105.3	104.8	106.9	108.5	110.7	112.6	110.4	112.5	113.0	113.0	113.0	111.4	110.2
2014	106.6	109.3	111.9	114.5	115.1	117.3	116.4	118.1	117.2	117.9	118.2	118.3	115.1
2015	113.2	115.6	118.0	117.1	120.5	122.2	121.7	121.6	122.4	123.3	122.5	122.2	120.0
2016	119.0	119.5	122.3	125.2	125.7	128.1	126.7	128.2	127.9	128.0	127.5	126.2	125.4
2017	122.1	123.3	124.8	126.0	126.6	129.2	129.1	126.5	127.9	124.8	126.4	126.3	126.1
2018	120.0	123.0	124.6	125.6	123.9	128.9	129.9	129.5	129.1	128.0	127.9	127.1	126.5
Service-Providing													
2010	838.6	841.8	848.0	863.9	870.0	869.0	850.4	849.2	860.3	865.7	866.8	867.9	857.6
2011	847.9	851.6	861.2	869.3	873.7	872.9	862.6	864.1	872.0	876.5	881.2	881.1	867.8
2012	863.6	869.2	877.6	884.8	890.4	890.6	875.0	881.7	883.6	890.2	893.3	891.9	882.7
2013	872.2	876.2	880.8	892.1	896.6	899.0	885.7	890.1	896.6	901.5	901.5	902.8	891.3
2014	882.8	886.0	894.0	905.2	913.0	914.9	901.8	905.6	909.6	918.1	920.2	921.4	906.1
2015	903.6	908.1	913.9	924.9	930.3	933.0	923.4	923.8	929.1	937.3	937.9	940.2	925.5
2016	923.6	926.8	930.0	943.4	944.0	943.6	936.2	940.0	950.3	955.0	956.8	957.1	942.2
2017	937.4	942.4	947.5	956.6	959.4	961.8	952.3	957.1	966.0	971.5	975.2	976.5	958.6
2018	954.2	956.9	959.3	968.6	972.9	976.1	965.6	967.2	975.3	981.4	982.9	979.8	970.0
Mining, Logging, and Construction													
2010	33.8	33.5	35.7	38.8	38.8	40.1	40.8	40.8	40.2	40.5	39.5	37.9	38.4
2011	33.1	32.4	35.1	37.4	38.1	38.9	39.4	39.2	38.9	38.7	38.6	37.6	37.3
2012	35.3	34.8	36.7	38.0	39.4	40.4	40.6	40.6	40.2	40.0	39.6	39.1	38.7
2013	36.6	37.2	37.9	39.7	41.6	42.8	43.7	43.4	43.0	43.2	42.7	41.1	41.1
2014	39.0	38.4	41.0	42.6	43.9	44.7	45.9	45.1	44.3	44.5	44.4	44.4	43.2
2015	42.1	42.3	43.5	45.3	45.5	46.4	47.2	47.1	46.6	47.0	46.1	45.6	45.4
2016	43.1	43.4	45.5	47.9	48.2	50.1	50.3	50.2	50.2	50.4	49.6	48.6	48.1
2017	46.3	46.9	47.9	48.9	49.6	51.4	51.5	50.9	50.5	50.9	50.3	49.6	49.6
2018	45.9	46.5	48.1	49.2	50.3	51.7	52.1	51.5	51.4	50.4	49.8	48.4	49.6
Manufacturing													
2010	69.5	69.4	69.4	69.8	70.1	70.6	68.9	71.0	71.1	71.0	70.8	70.9	70.2
2011	69.4	69.2	69.5	69.7	69.9	70.3	69.8	68.2	70.0	70.2	70.2	70.3	69.7
2012	69.4	69.4	69.9	69.7	68.5	69.5	68.7	69.5	69.7	69.4	69.4	67.6	69.2
2013	68.7	67.6	69.0	68.8	69.1	69.8	66.7	69.1	70.0	69.8	70.3	70.3	69.1
2014	67.6	70.9	70.9	71.9	71.2	72.6	70.5	73.0	72.9	73.4	73.8	73.9	71.9
2015	71.1	73.3	74.5	71.8	75.0	75.8	74.5	74.5	75.8	76.3	76.4	76.6	74.6
2016	75.9	76.1	76.8	77.3	77.5	78.0	76.4	78.0	77.7	77.6	77.9	77.6	77.2
2017	75.8	76.4	76.9	77.1	77.0	77.8	77.6	75.6	77.4	73.9	76.1	76.7	76.5
2018	74.1	76.5	76.5	76.4	73.6	77.2	77.8	78.0	77.7	77.6	78.1	78.7	76.9

Employment by Industry: Kansas City, MO-KS, 2010–2018—*Continued*

(Numbers in thousands, not seasonally adjusted)

Industry and year	January	February	March	April	May	June	July	August	September	October	November	December	Annual average
Trade, Transportation, and Utilities													
2010	186.4	184.8	185.5	188.0	189.4	189.9	189.6	189.9	189.3	191.7	194.7	195.7	189.6
2011	189.0	187.7	189.1	191.1	192.0	191.7	191.8	192.5	192.1	193.3	197.2	198.2	192.1
2012	192.6	190.5	191.8	192.5	194.0	194.5	193.1	193.4	192.9	194.3	198.2	198.4	193.9
2013	191.9	190.5	191.1	192.8	193.8	194.9	195.1	195.8	195.0	197.6	201.5	202.9	195.2
2014	196.5	194.3	196.8	198.4	199.9	200.8	200.4	201.3	199.6	201.9	205.5	207.3	200.2
2015	201.2	199.9	200.4	202.0	204.0	205.5	204.6	204.6	203.6	206.2	209.4	211.5	204.4
2016	204.2	203.6	204.3	206.0	207.3	207.6	208.2	208.9	207.8	210.2	215.0	217.7	208.4
2017	209.7	208.6	208.6	209.8	210.9	211.2	211.7	213.9	213.8	215.4	222.0	223.2	213.2
2018	215.2	213.0	212.5	214.2	215.6	216.0	216.6	217.4	216.0	217.1	222.7	222.6	216.6
Wholesale Trade													
2010	45.2	45.1	45.2	46.5	46.5	46.5	46.6	46.3	46.0	46.3	46.2	46.1	46.0
2011	45.6	45.6	45.7	46.1	46.5	46.5	46.7	46.6	46.6	46.0	46.2	46.4	46.2
2012	46.4	46.3	46.6	46.6	46.8	47.1	47.1	47.0	46.7	46.7	46.7	46.7	46.7
2013	46.0	46.2	46.1	46.3	46.4	46.6	47.5	47.5	47.2	47.7	47.7	47.9	46.9
2014	47.5	47.3	48.2	48.2	48.5	48.8	48.7	48.6	48.3	48.7	48.5	48.6	48.3
2015	48.4	48.5	48.3	48.3	48.4	48.7	48.5	48.4	47.9	48.4	48.2	48.2	48.4
2016	47.7	47.7	47.8	48.4	48.7	48.7	49.1	49.0	48.9	49.1	49.1	49.3	48.6
2017	49.0	49.2	49.4	49.7	50.0	50.2	50.4	50.4	50.1	50.1	50.3	50.4	49.9
2018	50.1	50.1	50.3	50.5	50.6	51.0	51.5	51.7	51.5	51.6	51.7	51.7	51.0
Retail Trade													
2010	100.1	98.8	99.3	100.9	102.0	102.5	102.1	102.2	101.3	102.8	105.7	106.5	102.0
2011	101.5	100.1	101.2	102.5	103.1	103.4	103.4	103.6	102.7	104.0	107.5	107.9	103.4
2012	103.1	101.5	102.5	102.9	104.0	104.2	103.9	103.4	103.2	104.0	107.7	107.9	104.0
2013	102.8	101.3	102.0	103.2	103.9	104.9	104.8	104.7	104.1	105.6	108.8	110.1	104.7
2014	104.9	103.0	104.2	105.5	106.3	107.1	107.3	107.1	105.9	107.3	110.7	111.8	106.8
2015	106.5	105.2	105.9	107.4	108.9	110.4	110.0	109.6	108.4	110.3	113.1	114.1	109.2
2016	109.1	108.6	109.2	110.3	111.1	111.8	112.3	112.3	110.6	112.0	115.5	116.9	111.6
2017	111.8	110.5	110.6	111.3	111.9	112.4	112.4	112.2	110.4	111.8	115.7	116.4	112.3
2018	111.3	109.8	109.8	110.7	111.6	112.2	112.4	111.8	110.3	110.8	114.7	115.0	111.7
Transportation and Utilities													
2010	41.1	40.9	41.0	40.6	40.9	40.9	40.9	41.4	42.0	42.6	42.8	43.1	41.5
2011	41.9	42.0	42.2	42.5	42.4	41.8	41.7	42.3	42.8	43.3	43.5	43.9	42.5
2012	43.1	42.7	42.7	43.0	43.2	43.2	42.1	43.0	43.0	43.6	43.8	43.8	43.1
2013	43.1	43.0	43.0	43.3	43.5	43.4	42.8	43.6	43.7	44.3	45.0	44.9	43.6
2014	44.1	44.0	44.4	44.7	45.1	44.9	44.4	45.6	45.4	45.9	46.3	46.9	45.1
2015	46.3	46.2	46.2	46.3	46.7	46.4	46.1	46.6	47.3	47.5	48.1	49.2	46.9
2016	47.4	47.3	47.3	47.3	47.5	47.1	46.8	47.6	48.3	49.1	50.4	51.5	48.1
2017	48.9	48.9	48.6	48.8	49.0	48.6	48.9	51.3	53.3	53.5	56.0	56.4	51.0
2018	53.8	53.1	52.4	53.0	53.4	52.8	52.7	53.9	54.2	54.7	56.3	55.9	53.9
Information													
2010	28.4	27.9	28.0	28.7	28.5	28.0	27.4	27.0	26.6	26.4	26.2	25.8	27.4
2011	24.7	24.6	24.5	24.6	24.6	24.6	24.6	24.6	24.6	24.5	24.6	24.8	24.6
2012	24.7	24.6	24.6	24.7	24.7	24.8	24.6	24.8	24.4	24.7	24.7	24.8	24.7
2013	24.4	24.5	24.3	24.3	24.4	24.6	24.7	24.7	24.3	24.3	24.4	24.2	24.4
2014	24.2	24.1	23.9	23.3	23.1	23.1	22.8	22.4	21.8	21.5	21.4	21.3	22.7
2015	21.0	20.8	20.9	20.9	20.8	20.7	20.9	20.6	20.2	20.0	20.1	20.1	20.6
2016	19.9	19.9	19.7	18.8	18.8	18.8	18.9	18.8	18.5	18.5	18.6	18.7	19.0
2017	18.0	18.1	18.1	18.1	17.9	17.9	17.8	17.6	17.4	17.2	17.3	17.2	17.7
2018	17.5	17.4	17.5	17.5	17.4	17.2	17.1	16.7	16.5	16.4	16.6	16.4	17.0
Financial Activities													
2010	72.5	72.7	72.8	73.5	73.8	73.8	73.7	73.3	72.8	73.1	73.1	73.2	73.2
2011	72.5	72.7	72.8	73.2	73.9	73.9	73.9	73.9	73.5	75.0	75.1	75.0	73.8
2012	75.4	75.9	76.3	76.4	76.4	76.7	77.0	77.1	76.3	76.6	76.7	76.6	76.5
2013	76.9	77.2	76.8	76.5	76.6	77.3	77.6	77.2	76.6	76.1	76.2	76.0	76.8
2014	75.0	75.2	75.4	76.0	76.3	76.7	76.9	77.1	76.6	77.0	77.0	77.1	76.4
2015	76.8	77.2	77.4	77.7	78.1	78.6	79.4	79.4	78.5	79.0	79.2	79.3	78.4
2016	80.1	80.3	80.3	81.4	81.4	81.6	82.1	81.9	81.3	81.3	81.4	81.2	81.2
2017	80.8	81.1	81.2	81.9	82.3	83.0	82.8	82.5	81.9	82.5	82.4	82.4	82.1
2018	80.3	80.5	80.1	80.3	80.4	81.0	80.2	80.0	79.3	79.2	79.1	79.3	80.0

Employment by Industry: Kansas City, MO-KS, 2010–2018—*Continued*

(Numbers in thousands, not seasonally adjusted)

Industry and year	January	February	March	April	May	June	July	August	September	October	November	December	Annual average
Professional and Business Services													
2010	145.5	145.5	147.0	153.5	152.7	153.0	153.7	153.6	152.8	155.0	155.1	156.3	152.0
2011	152.8	154.0	155.9	158.2	158.1	158.6	159.2	160.1	160.2	160.8	162.3	161.8	158.5
2012	158.6	160.0	162.0	164.5	164.7	166.5	166.4	166.8	167.1	169.9	169.8	169.2	165.5
2013	164.6	165.7	167.5	170.9	170.3	172.3	172.0	173.6	172.4	173.9	173.9	174.4	171.0
2014	169.4	170.6	171.6	174.8	174.8	177.3	178.6	180.2	178.5	181.5	183.1	184.2	177.1
2015	177.0	178.4	179.7	182.5	183.0	184.6	185.7	185.6	184.9	187.9	187.2	188.0	183.7
2016	182.0	183.1	183.2	186.2	185.0	186.5	189.2	190.7	191.3	192.1	192.0	191.3	187.7
2017	184.5	185.7	187.8	191.5	190.5	192.9	194.6	194.8	194.5	195.3	195.3	194.6	191.8
2018	188.3	189.5	190.7	193.7	193.8	195.5	197.2	196.8	195.7	197.6	197.2	195.0	194.3
Education and Health Services													
2010	127.7	128.8	128.9	127.9	128.3	128.2	128.8	128.8	129.9	131.3	131.7	132.2	129.4
2011	130.1	131.5	132.0	131.6	131.8	130.8	131.2	132.4	133.4	135.1	135.7	135.9	132.6
2012	132.9	134.1	134.4	134.4	135.1	134.6	133.4	134.5	134.2	135.8	136.5	137.1	134.8
2013	135.0	135.8	135.1	136.9	137.9	136.7	136.5	137.4	137.3	140.2	140.4	140.3	137.5
2014	138.3	139.3	139.0	142.0	142.9	142.3	142.0	142.4	142.6	144.6	145.1	145.1	142.1
2015	144.0	145.4	144.7	146.6	146.7	146.1	147.4	147.0	146.8	148.6	149.0	148.5	146.7
2016	147.0	147.5	147.3	149.0	148.8	146.2	147.0	146.8	149.0	150.9	150.9	150.2	148.4
2017	149.4	150.8	150.6	152.2	152.3	150.2	150.6	151.0	152.8	154.6	154.8	154.5	152.0
2018	153.1	154.3	153.9	154.7	154.9	153.4	153.6	153.8	155.5	159.5	159.2	160.0	155.5
Leisure and Hospitality													
2010	85.1	85.8	88.0	92.1	94.5	96.1	95.6	96.2	95.0	93.9	91.5	90.9	92.1
2011	86.9	87.0	89.9	92.7	95.9	97.9	98.8	99.4	96.3	95.0	93.3	92.4	93.8
2012	90.2	91.1	94.1	97.2	100.0	102.1	101.4	102.6	98.5	97.4	96.1	94.9	97.1
2013	92.7	92.3	95.0	97.7	100.9	103.4	103.5	103.9	101.4	100.8	96.7	96.7	98.8
2014	94.7	94.5	97.9	101.7	105.5	106.5	105.1	106.8	102.7	103.1	100.0	99.3	101.5
2015	97.1	97.6	100.3	103.9	106.4	108.5	108.3	108.4	105.2	105.3	102.7	103.6	103.9
2016	101.1	101.0	103.2	107.4	109.3	111.6	110.2	111.2	108.2	108.2	105.2	105.6	106.9
2017	103.4	104.2	106.9	108.9	111.6	113.4	112.3	113.6	110.8	110.1	107.2	108.7	109.3
2018	104.9	105.0	106.8	109.8	112.9	115.1	114.4	115.4	112.4	110.6	107.2	105.6	110.0
Other Services													
2010	43.3	43.4	43.4	43.8	43.8	44.0	44.2	44.1	43.6	43.9	43.9	43.9	43.8
2011	43.7	43.6	43.9	44.1	44.2	44.4	44.5	44.4	44.1	44.3	44.2	44.2	44.1
2012	43.6	43.7	43.9	43.9	43.9	43.7	43.5	43.3	42.9	42.7	42.5	42.5	43.3
2013	42.1	42.0	42.1	41.8	42.0	42.2	42.3	42.4	42.1	41.9	41.8	41.9	42.1
2014	41.2	41.4	41.8	41.0	41.4	41.2	41.3	41.2	40.9	41.1	40.8	40.8	41.2
2015	40.7	40.7	41.0	41.3	41.5	41.7	41.8	41.9	41.4	42.0	41.8	41.8	41.5
2016	41.8	41.9	42.1	43.3	43.4	43.5	43.9	43.5	43.3	43.5	43.6	43.3	43.1
2017	43.0	43.0	43.0	42.4	42.7	42.8	42.7	42.6	42.5	43.0	42.8	42.7	42.8
2018	42.2	42.3	42.2	42.7	42.7	43.1	43.2	42.9	42.5	42.9	42.7	42.7	42.7
Government													
2010	149.7	152.9	154.4	156.4	159.0	156.0	137.4	136.3	150.3	150.4	150.6	149.9	150.3
2011	148.2	150.5	153.1	153.8	153.2	151.0	138.6	136.8	147.8	148.5	148.8	148.8	148.3
2012	145.6	149.3	150.5	151.2	151.6	147.7	135.6	139.2	147.3	148.8	148.8	148.4	147.0
2013	144.6	148.2	148.9	151.2	150.7	147.6	134.0	135.1	147.5	146.7	146.6	146.4	145.6
2014	143.5	146.6	147.6	148.0	149.1	147.0	134.7	134.2	146.9	147.4	147.3	146.3	144.9
2015	145.8	148.1	149.5	150.0	149.8	147.3	135.3	136.3	148.5	148.3	148.5	147.4	146.2
2016	147.5	149.5	149.9	151.3	150.0	147.8	136.7	138.2	150.9	150.3	150.1	149.1	147.6
2017	148.6	150.9	151.3	151.8	151.2	150.4	139.8	141.1	152.3	153.4	153.4	153.2	149.8
2018	152.7	154.9	155.6	155.7	155.2	154.8	143.3	144.2	157.4	158.1	158.2	158.2	154.0

Employment by Industry: Columbus, OH, 2010–2018

(Numbers in thousands, not seasonally adjusted)

Industry and year	January	February	March	April	May	June	July	August	September	October	November	December	Annual average
Total Nonfarm													
2010	900.0	901.3	906.7	919.2	927.4	921.1	915.9	918.7	923.3	933.8	938.3	937.7	920.3
2011	912.2	917.0	922.6	939.2	945.9	939.5	938.6	942.6	951.9	958.0	964.9	964.1	941.4
2012	940.9	947.7	953.0	961.7	971.6	968.9	960.4	963.6	973.1	987.3	994.8	993.2	968.0
2013	966.4	968.6	972.2	986.7	997.1	989.8	986.4	992.0	997.0	1,007.2	1,018.2	1,018.1	991.6
2014	987.6	990.0	993.7	1,009.8	1,021.3	1,013.8	1,012.4	1,020.2	1,025.6	1,034.8	1,044.9	1,045.3	1,016.6
2015	1,015.3	1,017.0	1,019.8	1,032.3	1,043.7	1,043.4	1,041.8	1,046.7	1,044.2	1,056.5	1,063.5	1,063.4	1,040.6
2016	1,039.1	1,042.1	1,047.4	1,056.2	1,065.4	1,063.5	1,063.0	1,068.0	1,070.1	1,080.3	1,090.2	1,086.8	1,064.3
2017	1,062.6	1,065.5	1,068.5	1,079.1	1,089.0	1,090.3	1,085.5	1,089.8	1,087.6	1,098.7	1,107.0	1,101.4	1,085.4
2018	1,077.9	1,081.4	1,082.5	1,090.9	1,102.1	1,103.8	1,101.9	1,106.6	1,103.5	1,113.5	1,114.5	1,115.2	1,099.5
Total Private													
2010	735.1	733.9	738.8	749.3	754.0	757.0	760.4	763.4	759.3	764.7	768.7	767.8	754.4
2011	748.5	751.1	755.6	769.4	775.2	776.8	782.5	785.7	786.0	790.6	796.2	796.8	776.2
2012	776.9	780.9	786.5	795.4	803.0	808.8	807.5	809.9	808.3	818.2	824.6	824.3	803.7
2013	803.2	803.3	807.1	819.6	828.8	832.0	832.3	836.1	832.5	839.8	848.7	849.2	827.7
2014	824.3	824.1	828.1	841.8	851.9	855.7	856.7	863.2	857.8	865.6	875.4	876.7	851.8
2015	849.3	848.5	851.4	862.9	873.4	878.9	880.2	882.9	875.1	885.0	891.6	891.8	872.6
2016	869.1	868.9	874.4	882.6	893.2	896.4	899.4	903.1	897.8	904.8	913.3	911.6	892.9
2017	888.2	889.3	892.7	902.2	912.9	919.1	917.8	919.1	912.0	920.9	928.0	924.7	910.6
2018	901.6	903.9	905.7	913.1	924.5	931.3	931.6	932.2	926.3	935.2	935.6	937.1	923.2
Goods Producing													
2010	89.8	88.9	89.8	92.1	93.7	94.8	95.6	95.8	95.6	96.1	95.6	94.2	93.5
2011	90.8	90.8	91.9	94.4	95.6	97.0	98.6	99.0	98.4	98.5	98.3	97.1	95.9
2012	94.3	94.7	95.7	97.5	99.0	100.3	101.2	101.3	100.8	100.7	100.5	99.5	98.8
2013	97.2	97.3	98.3	100.3	102.5	104.1	104.3	104.5	104.1	104.3	104.4	103.1	102.0
2014	99.5	99.3	100.7	102.9	104.9	106.1	106.8	107.0	106.5	106.4	107.1	105.2	104.4
2015	102.5	102.8	103.4	105.8	108.4	109.2	109.9	110.0	109.2	109.3	109.7	108.5	107.4
2016	104.9	105.3	107.1	108.6	110.0	111.1	111.2	111.1	110.2	110.3	110.5	109.0	109.1
2017	106.7	107.5	109.0	111.1	113.6	114.8	114.9	114.7	113.7	114.1	114.2	113.0	112.3
2018	110.0	110.6	111.5	113.3	115.8	117.1	118.0	118.1	117.3	116.7	116.8	117.6	115.2
Service-Providing													
2010	810.2	812.4	816.9	827.1	833.7	826.3	820.3	822.9	827.7	837.7	842.7	843.5	826.8
2011	821.4	826.2	830.7	844.8	850.3	842.5	840.0	843.6	853.5	859.5	866.6	867.0	845.5
2012	846.6	853.0	857.3	864.2	872.6	868.6	859.2	862.3	872.3	886.6	894.3	893.7	869.2
2013	869.2	871.3	873.9	886.4	894.6	885.7	882.1	887.5	892.9	902.9	913.8	915.0	889.6
2014	888.1	890.7	893.0	906.9	916.4	907.7	905.6	913.2	919.1	928.4	937.8	940.1	912.3
2015	912.8	914.2	916.4	926.5	935.3	934.2	931.9	936.7	935.0	947.2	953.8	954.9	933.2
2016	934.2	936.8	940.3	947.6	955.4	952.4	951.8	956.9	959.9	970.0	979.7	977.8	955.2
2017	955.9	958.0	959.5	968.0	975.4	975.5	970.6	975.1	973.9	984.6	992.8	988.4	973.1
2018	967.9	970.8	971.0	977.6	986.3	986.7	983.9	988.5	986.2	996.8	997.7	997.6	984.3
Mining, Logging, and Construction													
2010	25.5	24.6	25.4	27.5	28.8	29.7	30.5	30.6	30.5	30.7	30.1	28.6	28.5
2011	26.0	25.9	26.7	28.6	29.7	30.7	32.2	32.4	32.0	31.7	31.1	30.0	29.8
2012	27.8	27.8	28.6	30.0	31.2	32.0	32.7	32.8	32.4	32.3	31.5	30.5	30.8
2013	28.6	28.6	29.4	31.2	33.1	34.3	34.6	35.0	34.6	34.7	34.4	32.7	32.6
2014	30.5	30.2	31.7	33.5	35.1	36.3	36.5	36.6	36.2	36.1	35.6	34.3	34.4
2015	31.6	31.8	32.6	34.4	36.5	37.4	37.7	37.9	37.6	37.6	37.0	35.9	35.7
2016	33.4	33.5	35.1	37.1	38.4	39.5	39.6	39.6	39.0	38.9	38.4	37.1	37.5
2017	35.2	35.8	37.4	39.2	41.2	42.3	42.3	42.3	41.8	41.4	40.8	39.5	39.9
2018	37.2	37.8	39.0	40.4	42.4	43.5	44.1	44.1	43.7	43.4	42.7	42.0	41.7
Manufacturing													
2010	64.3	64.3	64.4	64.6	64.9	65.1	65.1	65.2	65.1	65.4	65.5	65.6	65.0
2011	64.8	64.9	65.2	65.8	65.9	66.3	66.4	66.6	66.4	66.8	67.2	67.1	66.1
2012	66.5	66.9	67.1	67.5	67.8	68.3	68.5	68.5	68.4	68.4	69.0	69.0	68.0
2013	68.6	68.7	68.9	69.1	69.4	69.8	69.7	69.5	69.5	69.6	70.0	70.4	69.4
2014	69.0	69.1	69.0	69.4	69.8	69.8	70.3	70.4	70.3	70.3	71.5	70.9	70.0
2015	70.9	71.0	70.8	71.4	71.9	71.8	72.2	72.1	71.6	71.7	72.7	72.6	71.7
2016	71.5	71.8	72.0	71.5	71.6	71.6	71.6	71.5	71.2	71.4	72.1	71.9	71.6
2017	71.5	71.7	71.6	71.9	72.4	72.5	72.6	72.4	71.9	72.7	73.4	73.5	72.3
2018	72.8	72.8	72.5	72.9	73.4	73.6	73.9	74.0	73.6	73.3	74.1	75.6	73.5

Employment by Industry: Columbus, OH, 2010–2018—*Continued*

(Numbers in thousands, not seasonally adjusted)

Industry and year	January	February	March	April	May	June	July	August	September	October	November	December	Annual average
Trade, Transportation, and Utilities													
2010	176.9	174.6	174.8	175.5	177.2	177.4	176.6	177.4	176.6	179.6	183.2	185.5	177.9
2011	177.8	177.4	177.3	179.9	180.6	180.6	181.4	182.0	181.4	184.3	188.5	191.4	181.9
2012	182.9	181.3	181.4	182.0	183.7	184.1	183.9	184.0	183.8	187.1	192.2	193.8	185.0
2013	184.5	182.5	182.4	183.8	185.3	186.3	186.8	187.0	186.3	189.8	195.4	197.4	187.3
2014	187.1	185.2	185.1	187.3	189.3	190.3	190.8	192.2	191.9	195.9	202.2	205.2	191.9
2015	194.7	192.9	193.0	194.1	195.4	195.7	196.2	196.8	195.9	199.4	204.7	207.1	197.2
2016	198.6	196.7	196.4	196.6	198.8	198.6	199.9	200.5	201.1	205.2	212.5	217.3	201.9
2017	206.0	202.5	202.3	203.3	204.9	205.7	206.0	206.5	204.9	209.2	215.8	216.6	207.0
2018	207.2	204.9	204.1	204.6	206.7	207.4	208.0	207.8	207.5	208.4	211.0	212.0	207.5
Wholesale Trade													
2010	36.8	36.9	36.8	37.1	37.3	37.4	37.2	37.3	37.0	37.0	37.1	36.9	37.1
2011	36.9	37.0	37.0	37.3	37.5	37.4	37.4	37.5	37.2	37.4	37.4	37.5	37.3
2012	37.6	37.8	37.7	37.9	38.1	38.2	38.4	38.4	38.2	38.2	38.3	38.2	38.1
2013	38.0	38.1	38.1	38.5	38.7	38.6	38.8	39.1	38.8	39.2	39.4	39.4	38.7
2014	39.8	40.2	40.4	40.6	41.1	41.0	41.2	41.3	41.1	41.1	41.4	41.5	40.9
2015	40.8	40.9	41.1	41.2	41.4	41.2	41.3	41.4	41.0	41.3	41.5	41.7	41.2
2016	41.3	41.4	41.5	41.1	41.4	41.3	41.6	41.6	41.3	41.3	41.2	41.3	41.4
2017	40.9	40.9	40.6	40.7	41.0	41.2	41.1	41.1	40.7	40.7	40.8	40.6	40.9
2018	40.6	40.9	41.0	41.3	41.7	41.9	42.0	41.9	41.5	41.5	41.6	42.2	41.5
Retail Trade													
2010	96.2	94.5	94.9	95.9	96.9	97.1	97.0	97.6	96.9	99.4	102.1	103.9	97.7
2011	97.2	96.7	96.7	98.5	98.7	98.8	99.6	100.0	99.3	101.3	104.6	106.8	99.9
2012	99.7	98.3	98.5	99.2	100.2	100.1	99.6	99.8	99.4	101.7	105.7	106.4	100.7
2013	100.0	98.4	98.3	99.5	100.5	100.9	101.3	101.3	100.8	103.4	107.3	108.4	101.7
2014	100.3	99.0	98.5	100.4	100.8	101.5	101.6	102.4	101.5	104.2	108.2	109.4	102.3
2015	101.9	100.7	100.8	101.3	102.1	102.1	102.4	102.5	101.5	103.1	106.5	107.3	102.7
2016	102.6	101.4	101.0	101.7	102.8	102.7	103.4	103.7	102.8	104.2	107.4	108.6	103.5
2017	103.4	102.3	102.2	102.7	103.2	103.1	103.1	102.9	101.2	103.7	107.2	107.6	103.6
2018	102.9	101.6	101.3	101.3	103.0	102.4	103.1	102.8	101.9	102.2	104.4	103.5	102.5
Transportation and Utilities													
2010	43.9	43.2	43.1	42.5	43.0	42.9	42.4	42.5	42.7	43.2	44.0	44.7	43.2
2011	43.7	43.7	43.6	44.1	44.4	44.4	44.4	44.5	44.9	45.6	46.5	47.1	44.7
2012	45.6	45.2	45.2	44.9	45.4	45.8	45.9	45.8	46.2	47.2	48.2	49.2	46.2
2013	46.5	46.0	46.0	45.8	46.1	46.8	46.7	46.6	46.7	47.2	48.7	49.6	46.9
2014	47.0	46.0	46.2	46.3	47.4	47.8	48.0	48.5	49.3	50.6	52.6	54.3	48.7
2015	52.0	51.3	51.1	51.6	51.9	52.4	52.5	52.9	53.4	55.0	56.7	58.1	53.2
2016	54.7	53.9	53.9	53.8	54.6	54.6	54.9	55.2	57.0	59.7	63.9	67.4	57.0
2017	61.7	59.3	59.5	59.9	60.7	61.4	61.8	62.5	63.0	64.8	67.8	68.4	62.6
2018	63.7	62.4	61.8	62.0	62.0	63.1	62.9	63.1	64.1	64.7	65.0	66.3	63.4
Information													
2010	16.9	16.9	16.8	16.6	16.7	16.7	16.8	16.8	16.7	16.6	16.9	16.9	16.8
2011	16.7	16.7	16.6	16.9	17.0	17.0	17.1	17.1	16.8	16.9	16.9	17.0	16.9
2012	16.7	16.8	16.8	16.9	17.0	17.3	17.4	17.3	17.3	17.4	17.6	17.8	17.2
2013	18.0	18.3	18.5	18.7	18.6	18.7	18.8	18.8	18.6	18.5	18.5	18.5	18.5
2014	18.2	18.2	18.1	18.1	17.8	17.7	17.5	17.3	16.8	16.6	16.9	17.0	17.5
2015	16.6	16.8	16.8	17.1	17.0	17.2	17.0	16.9	16.8	16.8	17.0	17.0	16.9
2016	16.7	16.8	16.7	16.5	16.7	17.0	17.0	17.0	17.1	17.1	17.3	17.2	16.9
2017	17.0	17.3	17.2	17.5	17.6	17.5	17.6	17.7	17.5	17.3	17.5	17.5	17.4
2018	17.3	17.5	17.3	17.4	17.4	17.5	17.4	17.5	17.2	17.2	17.3	17.3	17.4

Employment by Industry: Columbus, OH, 2010–2018—*Continued*

(Numbers in thousands, not seasonally adjusted)

Industry and year	January	February	March	April	May	June	July	August	September	October	November	December	Annual average
Financial Activities													
2010	68.6	68.6	68.5	69.3	69.2	69.4	69.8	69.7	69.3	69.8	69.9	70.0	69.3
2011	70.1	70.1	70.2	70.0	70.5	70.7	70.9	71.4	71.9	72.1	72.1	72.0	71.0
2012	72.3	72.5	72.9	72.9	73.5	74.0	74.2	74.3	74.0	74.3	74.8	74.9	73.7
2013	74.8	75.2	75.4	75.4	75.8	76.0	75.9	76.0	75.2	75.0	75.2	75.1	75.4
2014	75.2	75.3	75.2	75.3	76.1	76.5	77.0	77.5	77.1	77.6	78.1	78.1	76.6
2015	78.0	78.3	78.2	78.5	79.2	79.6	80.3	80.6	79.7	80.2	80.4	80.3	79.4
2016	81.2	81.6	81.6	82.2	82.7	82.7	83.2	83.4	83.0	83.6	83.9	84.3	82.8
2017	84.2	84.3	84.4	84.7	84.9	85.3	85.3	85.2	84.6	85.1	85.1	85.3	84.9
2018	85.2	85.7	85.2	85.6	86.0	86.5	86.8	86.8	86.1	87.0	86.1	86.4	86.1
Professional and Business Services													
2010	141.7	142.0	142.8	146.4	145.7	147.0	148.6	149.9	147.9	149.5	150.3	150.3	146.8
2011	146.2	146.6	148.0	150.4	149.9	150.7	152.8	153.7	154.2	155.5	157.2	157.5	151.9
2012	153.3	154.3	155.7	157.4	157.4	158.8	158.9	160.1	159.8	163.4	165.5	165.8	159.2
2013	160.0	159.4	159.8	163.0	164.1	165.3	166.3	167.4	167.3	170.1	173.0	174.3	165.8
2014	169.3	168.9	169.6	172.7	173.1	174.6	175.7	177.9	177.3	179.8	182.7	183.8	175.5
2015	173.7	171.5	171.8	174.5	175.1	177.0	178.4	179.0	176.6	181.0	182.3	181.3	176.9
2016	175.1	174.3	175.6	178.1	179.1	181.2	183.0	184.2	182.7	183.5	185.2	183.6	180.5
2017	177.1	176.6	176.5	177.4	179.1	181.1	180.5	181.0	180.4	182.5	184.7	183.3	180.0
2018	177.9	178.0	178.2	179.4	180.5	182.7	183.2	183.6	182.3	184.9	185.8	184.4	181.7
Education and Health Services													
2010	124.0	125.1	126.3	126.6	126.4	124.4	125.3	126.4	128.0	129.0	129.5	128.9	126.7
2011	128.0	129.6	129.8	132.2	132.7	129.8	130.6	131.3	134.6	135.6	136.3	136.2	132.2
2012	135.0	137.3	137.4	139.2	138.9	137.3	135.1	136.0	137.1	139.5	140.0	139.4	137.7
2013	138.6	139.7	139.1	141.4	141.6	138.8	138.0	140.1	140.7	143.3	144.4	144.4	140.8
2014	142.8	144.9	145.0	147.8	147.7	145.3	144.2	145.7	146.4	148.4	149.1	148.8	146.3
2015	148.2	149.7	149.6	151.2	152.2	151.7	150.4	151.3	151.2	152.9	153.5	153.9	151.3
2016	152.9	154.2	154.8	155.5	156.7	154.5	154.4	155.8	155.8	158.1	158.4	157.4	155.7
2017	157.6	159.2	159.6	161.8	162.3	161.5	160.4	161.0	162.0	164.0	164.2	163.2	161.4
2018	162.3	163.8	164.0	165.0	165.6	164.9	163.0	163.4	164.9	168.8	170.8	172.2	165.7
Leisure and Hospitality													
2010	81.6	82.1	83.9	87.0	89.2	91.2	91.2	91.1	89.3	88.0	87.3	86.1	87.3
2011	83.7	84.5	86.4	89.9	93.0	94.9	94.6	94.8	92.8	91.4	90.8	89.7	90.5
2012	86.6	87.9	90.3	92.7	96.4	99.1	98.4	99.0	97.6	96.7	95.6	94.8	94.6
2013	92.6	93.2	95.7	98.7	102.3	104.1	103.5	103.8	102.0	100.5	99.3	98.1	99.5
2014	93.9	93.9	95.7	98.8	103.6	105.3	104.5	105.2	101.8	100.7	99.3	98.8	100.1
2015	95.9	96.6	98.3	101.1	105.3	107.4	106.4	106.7	104.6	104.2	103.0	103.0	102.7
2016	99.3	99.5	101.5	103.9	107.7	109.3	109.0	109.0	106.3	105.0	103.8	102.4	104.7
2017	99.4	101.5	103.1	105.5	109.3	111.1	110.9	110.9	108.0	107.6	105.6	104.8	106.5
2018	101.0	102.5	104.4	106.5	111.0	112.7	112.6	112.6	109.2	110.3	106.3	105.9	107.9
Other Services													
2010	35.6	35.7	35.9	35.8	35.9	36.1	36.5	36.3	35.9	36.1	36.0	35.9	36.0
2011	35.2	35.4	35.4	35.7	35.9	36.1	36.5	36.4	35.9	36.3	36.1	35.9	35.9
2012	35.8	36.1	36.3	36.8	37.1	37.9	38.4	37.9	37.9	39.1	38.4	38.3	37.5
2013	37.5	37.7	37.9	38.3	38.6	38.7	38.7	38.5	38.3	38.3	38.5	38.3	38.3
2014	38.3	38.4	38.7	38.9	39.4	39.9	40.2	40.4	40.0	40.2	40.0	39.8	39.5
2015	39.7	39.9	40.3	40.6	40.8	41.1	41.6	41.6	41.1	41.2	41.0	40.7	40.8
2016	40.4	40.5	40.7	41.2	41.5	42.0	41.7	42.1	41.6	42.0	41.7	40.4	41.3
2017	40.2	40.4	40.6	40.9	41.2	42.1	42.2	42.1	40.9	41.1	40.9	41.0	41.1
2018	40.7	40.9	41.0	41.3	41.5	42.5	42.6	42.4	41.8	41.9	41.5	41.3	41.6
Government													
2010	164.9	167.4	167.9	169.9	173.4	164.1	155.5	155.3	164.0	169.1	169.6	169.9	165.9
2011	163.7	165.9	167.0	169.8	170.7	162.7	156.1	156.9	165.9	167.4	168.7	167.3	165.2
2012	164.0	166.8	166.5	166.3	168.6	160.1	152.9	153.7	164.8	169.1	170.2	168.9	164.3
2013	163.2	165.3	165.1	167.1	168.3	157.8	154.1	155.9	164.5	167.4	169.5	168.9	163.9
2014	163.3	165.9	165.6	168.0	169.4	158.1	155.7	157.0	167.8	169.2	169.5	168.6	164.8
2015	166.0	168.5	168.4	169.4	170.3	164.5	161.6	163.8	169.1	171.5	171.9	171.6	168.1
2016	170.0	173.2	173.0	173.6	172.2	167.1	163.6	164.9	172.3	175.5	176.9	175.2	171.5
2017	174.4	176.2	175.8	176.9	176.1	171.2	167.7	170.7	175.6	177.8	179.0	176.7	174.8
2018	176.3	177.5	176.8	177.8	177.6	172.5	170.3	174.4	177.2	178.3	178.9	178.1	176.3

Employment by Industry: Cleveland-Elyria, OH, 2010–2018

(Numbers in thousands, not seasonally adjusted)

Industry and year	January	February	March	April	May	June	July	August	September	October	November	December	Annual average
Total Nonfarm													
2010	969.1	969.7	972.8	986.2	998.5	1,000.0	996.2	995.7	995.4	1,002.1	1,003.5	1,001.5	990.9
2011	971.4	977.5	981.8	998.8	1,006.3	1,007.9	1,008.9	1,011.8	1,007.4	1,009.9	1,016.5	1,015.1	1,001.1
2012	987.1	994.5	1,002.9	1,016.2	1,027.3	1,032.9	1,025.8	1,025.5	1,023.8	1,031.4	1,034.9	1,032.0	1,019.5
2013	1,002.2	1,004.9	1,009.9	1,023.9	1,037.2	1,042.7	1,033.4	1,040.0	1,032.8	1,040.5	1,044.7	1,043.5	1,029.6
2014	1,011.0	1,012.1	1,017.7	1,031.5	1,044.9	1,048.8	1,039.6	1,044.8	1,039.3	1,047.9	1,050.4	1,051.3	1,036.6
2015	1,018.5	1,022.1	1,024.5	1,041.6	1,056.8	1,058.6	1,052.8	1,054.3	1,045.9	1,055.3	1,056.6	1,057.3	1,045.4
2016	1,033.6	1,036.0	1,040.8	1,053.3	1,063.6	1,064.2	1,063.6	1,064.3	1,056.1	1,062.6	1,065.0	1,060.6	1,055.3
2017	1,033.5	1,037.9	1,041.9	1,055.0	1,066.8	1,073.1	1,065.6	1,067.4	1,061.3	1,068.6	1,068.0	1,065.7	1,058.7
2018	1,042.2	1,047.4	1,051.6	1,062.0	1,074.1	1,080.4	1,077.5	1,079.4	1,069.7	1,075.9	1,076.2	1,072.5	1,067.4
Total Private													
2010	831.4	829.3	832.9	845.7	853.9	859.0	861.7	863.6	860.4	863.2	864.5	863.4	852.4
2011	838.8	840.5	844.3	860.4	868.2	870.6	877.4	881.7	874.1	875.1	880.3	879.2	865.9
2012	855.2	858.7	866.5	879.5	889.4	896.2	894.2	895.3	889.7	895.9	899.4	897.3	884.8
2013	868.9	870.8	876.2	889.3	900.8	908.1	904.8	909.7	900.4	906.2	909.7	908.8	896.1
2014	879.0	878.6	884.2	897.1	908.4	913.7	910.2	913.8	906.0	912.3	914.7	916.2	902.9
2015	885.7	888.0	891.8	906.4	919.5	922.2	922.6	921.9	912.1	918.7	920.0	920.7	910.8
2016	899.3	900.0	904.8	916.0	924.7	926.7	930.3	929.7	921.3	924.9	927.0	923.3	919.0
2017	898.1	901.0	905.3	917.8	928.0	934.9	933.1	933.1	925.5	930.4	929.9	928.3	922.1
2018	906.6	909.8	913.8	923.9	934.0	941.5	944.0	944.5	933.8	938.4	937.6	934.7	930.2
Goods Producing													
2010	142.1	141.6	143.1	145.1	148.4	150.9	150.6	151.8	151.2	151.9	151.1	149.0	148.1
2011	145.2	145.2	146.4	149.8	152.0	152.9	156.3	158.4	156.2	156.8	158.4	157.3	152.9
2012	150.4	151.6	153.4	156.1	158.1	160.2	159.4	160.0	159.4	158.5	159.5	158.5	157.1
2013	153.6	153.4	154.3	156.4	158.8	160.6	158.4	161.6	160.8	160.9	161.7	158.7	158.3
2014	154.1	153.6	155.2	157.6	160.2	162.4	161.0	163.3	162.6	163.0	162.9	161.6	159.8
2015	156.3	156.2	157.3	160.3	162.2	163.4	163.1	162.7	161.0	160.8	160.2	158.9	160.2
2016	155.3	154.3	155.1	157.0	158.2	159.1	159.1	158.9	157.3	157.4	157.3	155.3	157.0
2017	152.0	152.2	153.8	155.7	158.0	160.5	161.1	161.0	159.9	160.2	160.2	158.7	157.8
2018	155.3	156.2	157.2	159.6	162.5	164.9	165.6	165.6	164.0	164.4	163.9	163.8	161.9
Service-Providing													
2010	827.0	828.1	829.7	841.1	850.1	849.1	845.6	843.9	844.2	850.2	852.4	852.5	842.8
2011	826.2	832.3	835.4	849.0	854.3	855.0	852.6	853.4	851.2	853.1	858.1	857.8	848.2
2012	836.7	842.9	849.5	860.1	869.2	872.7	866.4	865.5	864.4	872.9	875.4	873.5	862.4
2013	848.6	851.5	855.6	867.5	878.4	882.1	875.0	878.4	872.0	879.6	883.0	884.8	871.4
2014	856.9	858.5	862.5	873.9	884.7	886.4	878.6	881.5	876.7	884.9	887.5	889.7	876.8
2015	862.2	865.9	867.2	881.3	894.6	895.2	889.7	891.6	884.9	894.5	896.4	898.4	885.2
2016	878.3	881.7	885.7	896.3	905.4	905.1	904.5	905.4	898.8	905.2	907.7	905.3	898.3
2017	881.5	885.7	888.1	899.3	908.8	912.6	904.5	906.4	901.4	908.4	907.8	907.0	901.0
2018	886.9	891.2	894.4	902.4	911.6	915.5	911.9	913.8	905.7	911.5	912.3	908.7	905.5
Mining, Logging, and Construction													
2010	27.3	26.6	27.9	30.2	31.9	33.4	34.7	34.6	34.1	34.2	33.3	30.8	31.6
2011	27.6	27.2	28.1	30.3	32.1	33.6	35.8	36.3	36.2	36.1	35.7	34.4	32.8
2012	30.0	29.3	30.4	32.6	34.4	35.4	36.1	35.7	35.0	35.5	35.2	33.9	33.6
2013	30.0	29.7	30.4	32.4	34.7	35.8	36.2	36.9	36.9	38.0	37.2	34.1	34.4
2014	30.3	30.2	31.5	33.9	36.1	37.4	38.0	38.4	38.1	38.4	37.7	35.9	35.5
2015	31.7	31.3	32.3	35.4	37.1	37.9	38.2	38.2	37.6	37.7	37.3	35.7	35.9
2016	32.9	32.5	33.6	35.7	36.9	37.7	37.9	37.8	37.2	37.2	36.7	34.6	35.9
2017	31.9	32.1	33.2	35.3	37.3	38.8	39.1	39.2	38.8	39.0	38.2	36.3	36.6
2018	33.3	33.6	34.5	36.6	39.0	40.4	41.1	41.0	40.4	41.4	41.4	40.6	38.6
Manufacturing													
2010	114.8	115.0	115.2	114.9	116.5	117.5	115.9	117.2	117.1	117.7	117.8	118.2	116.5
2011	117.6	118.0	118.3	119.5	119.9	119.3	120.5	122.1	120.0	120.7	122.7	122.9	120.1
2012	120.4	122.3	123.0	123.5	123.7	124.8	123.3	124.3	124.4	123.0	124.3	124.6	123.5
2013	123.6	123.7	123.9	124.0	124.1	124.8	122.2	124.7	123.9	122.9	124.5	124.6	123.9
2014	123.8	123.4	123.7	123.7	124.1	125.0	123.0	124.9	124.5	124.6	125.2	125.7	124.3
2015	124.6	124.9	125.0	124.9	125.1	125.5	124.9	124.5	123.4	123.1	122.9	123.2	124.3
2016	122.4	121.8	121.5	121.3	121.3	121.4	121.2	121.1	120.1	120.2	120.6	120.7	121.1
2017	120.1	120.1	120.6	120.4	120.7	121.7	122.0	121.8	121.1	121.2	122.0	122.4	121.2
2018	122.0	122.6	122.7	123.0	123.5	124.5	124.5	124.6	123.6	123.0	122.5	123.2	123.3

Employment by Industry: Cleveland-Elyria, OH, 2010–2018—*Continued*

(Numbers in thousands, not seasonally adjusted)

Industry and year	January	February	March	April	May	June	July	August	September	October	November	December	Annual average
Trade, Transportation, and Utilities													
2010	174.3	172.3	172.5	173.5	174.9	176.4	176.8	177.3	175.4	176.8	179.5	182.1	176.0
2011	174.0	172.9	173.4	175.6	176.8	177.6	177.7	178.2	176.4	178.3	181.9	184.5	177.3
2012	177.8	176.4	177.8	179.0	181.1	181.7	181.1	180.7	179.7	181.5	185.5	187.1	180.8
2013	179.1	177.2	177.8	179.5	181.9	182.8	181.7	182.0	180.4	182.1	186.5	188.5	181.6
2014	180.3	178.7	178.8	180.7	183.1	183.8	182.4	182.9	180.7	182.7	186.7	189.2	182.5
2015	181.6	179.6	180.2	182.1	184.4	185.0	184.4	184.7	182.6	184.2	188.8	190.8	184.0
2016	184.5	182.9	183.4	183.6	185.2	185.3	184.7	185.1	182.4	183.3	186.8	189.0	184.7
2017	181.4	179.4	179.5	180.8	182.2	182.9	182.0	182.3	180.4	181.9	185.9	187.6	182.2
2018	180.4	178.6	178.9	179.5	181.5	182.1	182.1	182.4	180.4	182.8	187.3	189.4	182.1
Wholesale Trade													
2010	46.2	46.1	45.9	46.1	46.2	46.5	47.1	47.1	46.7	46.7	46.7	46.8	46.5
2011	47.1	47.1	47.1	47.5	47.8	48.0	48.3	48.3	47.9	48.3	48.4	48.7	47.9
2012	48.6	48.6	48.8	49.0	49.4	49.7	49.7	49.6	49.3	49.5	49.6	49.7	49.3
2013	48.9	48.8	49.0	49.2	49.5	49.8	49.5	49.5	49.2	49.9	50.1	50.3	49.5
2014	49.6	49.5	49.7	49.8	50.4	50.6	50.7	50.8	50.4	50.7	50.8	51.2	50.4
2015	50.3	50.4	50.6	50.6	50.9	51.2	51.3	51.2	50.7	50.9	51.1	51.0	50.9
2016	51.2	51.2	51.4	51.3	51.5	51.7	51.7	51.6	51.1	51.2	51.3	51.5	51.4
2017	50.8	50.6	50.6	50.7	51.0	51.5	51.6	51.6	51.3	51.5	51.6	51.8	51.2
2018	51.4	51.5	51.6	51.8	52.0	52.4	53.1	52.9	52.7	52.9	53.5	54.6	52.5
Retail Trade													
2010	99.1	97.3	97.7	98.4	99.6	100.5	100.4	100.7	99.3	100.6	103.4	105.5	100.2
2011	98.3	97.3	97.7	99.2	99.9	100.4	100.3	100.6	99.1	100.4	103.9	105.6	100.2
2012	100.2	98.7	99.8	100.5	101.8	102.0	101.4	100.8	100.1	101.6	105.0	106.0	101.5
2013	100.4	98.7	99.2	100.2	101.9	102.4	102.1	102.1	100.7	101.7	105.3	106.5	101.8
2014	100.3	99.0	99.1	100.4	101.8	102.3	101.4	101.6	99.9	101.4	104.7	105.9	101.5
2015	100.5	98.9	99.4	100.9	102.4	102.7	102.2	102.4	100.8	102.1	105.7	107.2	102.1
2016	102.3	100.9	101.3	101.4	102.5	102.5	102.1	102.3	100.1	101.1	104.1	105.6	102.2
2017	100.3	98.4	98.7	99.7	100.6	100.8	100.0	100.1	98.4	99.7	103.2	104.2	100.3
2018	99.1	97.2	97.5	97.8	99.1	99.2	98.8	98.9	97.0	97.0	100.4	100.6	98.6
Transportation and Utilities													
2010	29.0	28.9	28.9	29.0	29.1	29.4	29.3	29.5	29.4	29.5	29.4	29.8	29.3
2011	28.6	28.5	28.6	28.9	29.1	29.2	29.1	29.3	29.4	29.6	29.6	30.2	29.2
2012	29.0	29.1	29.2	29.5	29.9	30.0	30.0	30.3	30.3	30.4	30.9	31.4	30.0
2013	29.8	29.7	29.6	30.1	30.5	30.6	30.1	30.4	30.5	30.5	31.1	31.7	30.4
2014	30.4	30.2	30.0	30.5	30.9	30.9	30.3	30.5	30.4	30.6	31.2	32.1	30.7
2015	30.8	30.3	30.2	30.6	31.1	31.1	30.9	31.1	31.1	31.2	32.0	32.6	31.1
2016	31.0	30.8	30.7	30.9	31.2	31.1	30.9	31.2	31.2	31.0	31.4	31.9	31.1
2017	30.3	30.4	30.2	30.4	30.6	30.6	30.4	30.6	30.7	30.7	31.1	31.6	30.6
2018	29.9	29.9	29.8	29.9	30.4	30.5	30.2	30.6	30.7	32.9	33.4	34.2	31.0
Information													
2010	16.0	15.9	15.8	15.8	15.9	15.8	15.8	15.9	15.5	15.6	15.6	15.7	15.8
2011	15.4	15.3	15.2	15.3	15.4	15.4	15.5	15.5	15.5	15.4	15.5	15.5	15.4
2012	15.5	15.3	15.3	15.3	15.3	15.4	15.5	15.4	15.2	15.2	15.3	15.2	15.3
2013	14.9	15.0	15.0	15.0	15.1	15.3	15.4	15.3	15.2	15.1	15.0	15.3	15.1
2014	14.7	14.6	14.6	14.6	14.6	14.6	14.7	14.6	14.5	14.5	14.4	14.6	14.6
2015	14.3	14.3	14.3	14.4	14.3	14.3	14.4	14.3	14.1	14.1	14.2	14.3	14.3
2016	14.0	14.0	14.0	14.1	14.1	14.2	14.2	14.3	14.1	14.0	14.2	14.0	14.1
2017	13.9	13.8	13.8	13.9	13.9	14.1	14.0	14.1	14.0	13.8	13.9	13.9	13.9
2018	13.9	13.8	13.8	13.6	13.8	14.2	13.8	13.7	13.6	13.5	13.6	13.6	13.7
Financial Activities													
2010	64.4	64.3	64.1	64.5	64.6	64.8	65.1	65.0	64.3	64.7	64.6	64.6	64.6
2011	64.4	64.3	64.0	64.1	63.9	63.7	63.5	63.2	62.7	62.5	62.4	62.2	63.4
2012	61.8	61.8	61.9	62.2	62.5	62.7	63.1	63.1	62.6	62.9	63.0	63.0	62.6
2013	62.4	62.5	62.4	63.1	63.2	63.9	64.3	64.7	64.2	64.6	64.8	64.9	63.8
2014	64.0	64.3	64.5	64.5	64.7	65.2	64.9	64.9	64.2	64.5	64.8	64.9	64.6
2015	64.3	64.5	64.5	65.0	65.1	65.7	65.5	65.3	64.7	65.0	65.1	64.8	65.0
2016	64.5	64.5	64.4	64.8	65.0	65.5	66.0	66.0	65.6	66.0	66.2	66.3	65.4
2017	65.9	66.1	66.1	66.2	66.5	67.1	67.3	67.3	66.8	67.0	67.0	66.8	66.7
2018	66.6	66.9	66.6	66.6	67.0	67.5	68.1	68.0	67.1	66.9	66.9	66.2	67.0

Employment by Industry: Cleveland-Elyria, OH, 2010–2018—*Continued*

(Numbers in thousands, not seasonally adjusted)

Industry and year	January	February	March	April	May	June	July	August	September	October	November	December	Annual average
Professional and Business Services													
2010	127.9	127.6	128.0	132.9	133.8	135.4	136.3	136.6	136.1	136.3	136.6	136.3	133.7
2011	132.9	134.3	135.4	140.3	141.0	142.3	144.9	146.2	144.8	144.9	144.8	143.7	141.3
2012	139.3	140.5	141.9	144.2	145.5	146.9	147.9	148.4	146.2	149.1	149.0	146.3	145.4
2013	140.2	141.7	143.3	147.3	149.3	151.2	150.8	152.5	149.1	151.7	151.4	150.6	148.3
2014	145.1	145.8	146.6	150.5	151.9	152.7	152.8	154.2	151.7	153.1	152.9	151.3	150.7
2015	145.8	146.6	146.9	149.6	152.8	153.3	154.3	154.3	150.6	153.6	151.9	150.2	150.8
2016	147.3	147.6	148.3	152.8	153.9	155.2	157.0	156.6	155.0	155.6	155.0	152.5	153.1
2017	149.3	150.4	150.5	154.5	156.0	158.5	158.3	159.0	156.6	158.1	156.5	154.5	155.2
2018	152.5	153.6	154.1	157.4	158.1	159.9	161.8	162.4	158.9	158.9	157.7	153.6	157.4
Education and Health Services													
2010	185.4	186.7	186.8	186.5	185.5	182.7	183.1	182.6	187.2	189.0	189.5	188.8	186.2
2011	185.2	187.0	186.8	188.2	188.4	185.7	184.9	184.9	187.5	189.3	189.8	189.6	187.3
2012	187.5	190.6	190.7	192.2	192.8	191.3	189.2	189.5	193.0	195.7	195.7	194.8	191.9
2013	191.5	193.9	193.9	193.8	193.3	192.6	192.1	192.4	193.7	195.9	196.8	196.7	193.9
2014	191.4	192.7	193.3	194.0	193.7	192.4	192.0	191.7	194.0	197.2	197.8	197.8	194.0
2015	193.1	195.5	195.7	197.1	197.4	195.6	195.6	195.4	197.9	200.7	201.1	202.2	197.3
2016	198.0	200.8	201.6	201.9	201.6	199.2	199.8	200.0	202.9	204.3	204.7	204.4	201.6
2017	198.9	201.6	202.2	203.0	203.1	201.4	200.2	200.2	202.7	204.2	204.6	204.2	202.2
2018	200.5	203.2	203.3	203.5	203.1	202.0	201.4	201.7	203.8	205.5	206.4	205.5	203.3
Leisure and Hospitality													
2010	80.2	80.0	81.4	86.0	89.5	91.4	92.3	92.9	89.5	87.5	86.3	85.4	86.9
2011	80.8	80.7	82.3	86.3	89.9	92.2	93.4	94.3	90.6	87.4	87.2	86.3	87.6
2012	83.2	82.7	85.4	90.4	93.8	97.2	97.3	97.7	93.7	93.2	91.7	92.6	91.6
2013	87.9	88.0	90.3	94.5	99.3	101.7	102.2	101.2	97.6	96.3	93.9	94.5	95.6
2014	90.2	89.7	91.9	95.7	100.2	102.6	102.5	102.3	99.0	97.6	95.6	96.9	97.0
2015	91.4	92.2	93.8	98.2	103.2	104.6	105.2	105.2	101.7	100.7	99.1	99.6	99.6
2016	95.9	96.1	98.1	101.7	106.3	107.8	108.8	108.5	104.3	104.4	103.1	102.2	103.1
2017	97.5	98.3	100.1	104.3	108.7	110.5	110.3	109.5	106.1	105.9	102.4	103.0	104.7
2018	98.3	98.2	100.5	104.1	108.3	111.0	111.0	110.6	106.5	106.6	102.7	103.5	105.1
Other Services													
2010	41.1	40.9	41.2	41.4	41.3	41.6	41.7	41.5	41.2	41.4	41.3	41.5	41.3
2011	40.9	40.8	40.8	40.8	40.8	40.8	41.2	41.0	40.4	40.5	40.3	40.1	40.7
2012	39.7	39.8	40.1	40.1	40.3	40.8	40.7	40.5	39.9	39.8	39.7	39.8	40.1
2013	39.3	39.1	39.2	39.7	39.9	40.0	39.9	40.0	39.4	39.6	39.6	39.6	39.6
2014	39.2	39.2	39.3	39.5	40.0	40.0	39.9	39.9	39.3	39.7	39.6	39.9	39.6
2015	38.9	39.1	39.1	39.7	40.1	40.3	40.1	40.0	39.5	39.6	39.6	39.9	39.7
2016	39.8	39.8	39.9	40.1	40.4	40.4	40.7	40.3	39.7	39.9	39.7	39.6	40.0
2017	39.2	39.2	39.3	39.4	39.6	39.9	39.9	39.7	39.0	39.3	39.4	39.6	39.5
2018	39.1	39.3	39.4	39.6	39.7	39.9	40.2	40.1	39.5	39.8	39.1	39.1	39.6
Government													
2010	137.7	140.4	139.9	140.5	144.6	141.0	134.5	132.1	135.0	138.9	139.0	138.1	138.5
2011	132.6	137.0	137.5	138.4	138.1	137.3	131.5	130.1	133.3	134.8	136.2	135.9	135.2
2012	131.9	135.8	136.4	136.7	137.9	136.7	131.6	130.2	134.1	135.5	135.5	134.7	134.8
2013	133.3	134.1	133.7	134.6	136.4	134.6	128.6	130.3	132.4	134.3	135.0	134.7	133.5
2014	132.0	133.5	133.5	134.4	136.5	135.1	129.4	131.0	133.3	135.6	135.7	135.1	133.8
2015	132.8	134.1	132.7	135.2	137.3	136.4	130.2	132.4	133.8	136.6	136.6	136.6	134.6
2016	134.3	136.0	136.0	137.3	138.9	137.5	133.3	134.6	134.8	137.7	138.0	137.3	136.3
2017	135.4	136.9	136.6	137.2	138.8	138.2	132.5	134.3	135.8	138.2	138.1	137.4	136.6
2018	135.6	137.6	137.8	138.1	140.1	138.9	133.5	134.9	135.9	137.5	138.6	137.8	137.2

Employment by Industry: Indianapolis-Carmel-Anderson, 2010–2018

(Numbers in thousands, not seasonally adjusted)

Industry and year	January	February	March	April	May	June	July	August	September	October	November	December	Annual average
Total Nonfarm													
2010	888.9	889.0	898.4	913.0	922.1	915.9	907.2	918.7	916.7	925.7	927.0	924.5	912.3
2011	900.8	902.5	913.0	925.7	933.6	924.5	924.9	936.2	943.2	946.0	948.2	950.4	929.1
2012	926.7	937.0	942.6	949.4	959.4	955.9	947.8	963.4	968.1	969.4	972.7	971.8	955.4
2013	944.5	951.7	959.1	966.9	975.5	972.9	964.8	984.5	986.9	990.0	1,002.8	1,000.3	975.0
2014	963.4	966.6	977.1	987.8	1,000.5	996.0	985.1	1,002.0	1,001.3	1,005.1	1,017.5	1,018.8	993.4
2015	987.0	990.4	1,000.1	1,011.7	1,023.4	1,022.1	1,014.1	1,029.2	1,028.3	1,034.1	1,042.7	1,045.3	1,019.0
2016	1,014.7	1,020.2	1,029.4	1,037.9	1,047.7	1,042.4	1,041.9	1,054.4	1,057.0	1,052.8	1,060.7	1,057.9	1,043.1
2017	1,031.5	1,035.7	1,045.2	1,054.4	1,063.9	1,065.3	1,052.4	1,066.9	1,067.9	1,069.3	1,077.3	1,078.4	1,059.0
2018	1,049.1	1,052.5	1,062.0	1,063.7	1,076.3	1,076.4	1,065.1	1,080.3	1,079.3	1,081.6	1,084.3	1,079.1	1,070.8
Total Private													
2010	757.9	756.0	765.2	779.8	785.3	789.2	788.3	793.3	787.7	794.7	795.7	794.1	782.3
2011	771.4	772.3	782.4	795.1	802.6	802.6	807.9	812.8	815.1	816.9	819.0	820.8	801.6
2012	799.4	807.2	813.6	821.1	830.0	835.7	833.0	838.4	839.2	840.7	843.9	843.3	828.8
2013	819.6	823.0	829.9	838.2	846.5	853.0	852.7	858.4	858.5	861.4	873.0	870.7	848.7
2014	836.9	837.1	846.8	858.0	870.0	871.5	869.1	874.2	872.2	876.3	887.5	888.1	865.6
2015	858.1	860.4	869.7	881.5	892.4	897.4	896.8	901.0	897.2	904.2	911.4	913.1	890.3
2016	884.1	888.2	896.4	907.6	916.6	919.9	922.6	924.1	924.4	922.1	928.2	925.3	913.3
2017	899.9	903.3	912.3	922.4	930.5	938.9	932.7	935.3	934.1	936.4	942.6	943.5	927.7
2018	916.6	918.6	927.9	930.0	941.0	947.9	944.4	947.5	944.2	946.7	948.1	943.2	938.0
Goods Producing													
2010	120.5	119.4	121.7	124.6	125.9	127.6	128.1	128.1	126.7	126.2	124.9	122.7	124.7
2011	118.2	117.7	120.0	122.5	124.4	127.1	128.2	129.0	129.1	129.3	127.7	126.7	125.0
2012	124.1	123.9	125.8	128.3	130.1	132.7	133.1	133.5	131.8	131.4	129.6	128.7	129.4
2013	126.1	126.2	126.6	128.7	130.6	133.3	133.6	133.8	133.3	133.7	133.2	131.4	130.9
2014	126.6	121.1	128.3	130.4	132.0	134.6	135.7	135.7	134.9	134.4	134.1	133.3	132.2
2015	129.0	129.1	130.6	132.8	134.9	137.4	138.2	138.8	138.1	137.6	137.4	136.8	135.1
2016	132.6	132.7	134.9	137.6	139.7	142.3	142.8	142.7	142.3	142.0	141.7	140.9	139.4
2017	137.6	138.6	140.7	142.7	143.8	146.5	146.0	146.0	145.4	144.4	143.6	143.5	143.2
2018	139.2	138.3	139.5	140.9	142.3	145.4	146.0	146.6	145.5	145.2	145.2	145.1	143.3
Service-Providing													
2010	768.4	769.6	776.7	788.4	796.2	788.3	779.1	790.6	790.0	799.5	802.1	801.8	787.6
2011	782.6	784.8	793.0	803.2	809.2	797.4	796.7	807.2	814.1	816.7	820.5	823.7	804.1
2012	802.6	813.1	816.8	821.1	829.3	823.2	814.7	829.9	836.3	838.0	843.1	843.1	825.9
2013	818.4	825.5	832.5	838.2	844.9	839.6	831.2	850.7	853.6	856.3	869.6	868.9	844.1
2014	836.8	840.5	848.8	857.4	868.5	861.4	849.4	866.3	866.4	870.7	883.4	885.5	861.3
2015	858.0	861.3	869.5	878.9	888.5	884.7	875.9	890.4	890.2	896.5	905.3	908.5	884.0
2016	882.1	887.5	894.5	900.3	908.0	900.1	899.1	911.7	914.7	910.8	919.0	917.0	903.7
2017	893.9	897.1	904.5	911.7	920.1	918.8	906.4	920.9	922.5	924.9	933.7	934.9	915.8
2018	909.9	914.2	922.5	922.8	934.0	931.0	919.1	933.7	933.8	936.4	939.1	934.0	927.5
Mining and Logging													
2010	0.7	0.7	0.7	0.7	0.7	0.7	0.7	0.7	0.7	0.7	0.7	0.7	0.7
2011	0.5	0.5	0.6	0.6	0.7	0.7	0.7	0.7	0.6	0.6	0.6	0.6	0.6
2012	0.6	0.6	0.6	0.6	0.6	0.6	0.6	0.6	0.6	0.6	0.6	0.6	0.6
2013	0.6	0.6	0.6	0.6	0.6	0.6	0.6	0.6	0.6	0.6	0.6	0.6	0.6
2014	0.5	0.5	0.6	0.6	0.6	0.6	0.7	0.6	0.6	0.6	0.6	0.6	0.6
2015	0.6	0.6	0.6	0.6	0.6	0.7	0.6	0.6	0.6	0.7	0.7	0.6	0.6
2016	0.6	0.6	0.7	0.7	0.7	0.7	0.7	0.7	0.7	0.7	0.7	0.7	0.7
2017	0.6	0.7	0.7	0.7	0.7	0.7	0.7	0.7	0.7	0.7	0.7	0.7	0.7
2018	0.7	0.7	0.7	0.7	0.7	0.7	0.7	0.7	0.7	0.7	0.7	0.7	0.7
Construction													
2010	35.5	34.5	36.4	39.3	40.5	41.8	42.4	42.2	41.2	41.2	40.4	38.2	39.5
2011	35.3	34.9	36.6	38.9	40.5	42.5	43.6	44.1	44.2	44.3	43.6	42.3	40.9
2012	39.6	39.4	40.7	42.8	44.1	45.4	45.9	45.8	44.8	44.6	43.8	42.8	43.3
2013	39.7	39.7	40.1	42.1	43.9	45.8	46.3	46.1	46.0	46.7	46.4	44.3	43.9
2014	40.0	39.4	41.0	42.9	44.0	45.9	46.5	46.3	45.9	45.3	45.2	43.8	43.9
2015	40.2	40.1	41.3	43.6	45.6	47.1	47.8	48.1	47.9	48.0	47.8	46.9	45.4
2016	43.1	43.2	45.0	47.7	49.5	51.0	51.1	50.8	50.8	51.1	50.6	49.1	48.6
2017	45.8	46.5	48.3	50.4	51.1	52.9	52.9	53.0	52.7	51.8	51.0	50.3	50.6
2018	46.6	46.7	48.1	49.6	50.9	52.5	53.1	53.2	52.8	52.5	52.5	51.9	50.9

Employment by Industry: Indianapolis-Carmel-Anderson, 2010–2018—*Continued*

(Numbers in thousands, not seasonally adjusted)

Industry and year	January	February	March	April	May	June	July	August	September	October	November	December	Annual average
Manufacturing													
2010	84.3	84.2	84.6	84.6	84.7	85.1	85.0	85.2	84.8	84.3	83.8	83.8	84.5
2011	82.4	82.3	82.8	83.0	83.2	83.9	83.9	84.2	84.3	84.4	83.5	83.8	83.5
2012	83.9	83.9	84.5	84.9	85.4	86.7	86.6	87.1	86.4	86.2	85.2	85.3	85.5
2013	85.8	85.9	85.9	86.0	86.1	86.9	86.7	87.1	86.7	86.4	86.2	86.5	86.4
2014	86.1	86.2	86.7	86.9	87.4	88.1	88.5	88.8	88.4	88.5	88.3	88.9	87.7
2015	88.2	88.4	88.7	88.6	88.7	89.6	89.8	90.1	89.6	88.9	88.9	89.3	89.1
2016	88.9	88.9	89.2	89.2	89.5	90.6	91.0	91.2	90.8	90.2	90.4	91.1	90.1
2017	91.2	91.4	91.7	91.6	92.0	92.9	92.4	92.3	92.0	91.9	91.9	92.5	92.0
2018	91.9	90.9	90.7	90.6	90.7	92.2	92.2	92.7	92.0	92.0	92.0	92.5	91.7
Trade, Transportation, and Utilities													
2010	189.9	187.8	189.5	191.1	192.9	193.8	193.9	194.5	192.6	195.4	198.6	200.0	193.3
2011	192.5	191.6	192.3	194.7	196.6	197.2	197.5	198.0	196.7	199.0	202.6	203.8	196.9
2012	196.6	195.7	196.9	198.1	200.7	202.0	201.5	201.3	201.5	203.7	208.3	209.6	201.3
2013	201.1	200.9	201.7	203.5	205.7	207.3	206.2	206.8	207.0	208.8	213.6	214.8	206.5
2014	205.5	204.8	205.6	206.5	208.8	209.8	210.0	210.1	210.0	210.9	214.8	216.6	209.5
2015	208.5	207.8	209.0	210.5	213.2	214.6	215.6	216.7	215.8	218.4	222.7	225.8	214.9
2016	217.7	217.5	218.5	218.2	219.9	220.3	222.1	222.3	222.2	222.6	226.9	228.5	221.4
2017	220.7	219.4	220.0	220.8	222.2	224.2	222.6	223.1	222.6	224.2	229.3	230.7	223.3
2018	221.8	220.7	221.9	221.4	224.4	226.3	226.0	225.9	226.2	227.7	229.7	229.1	225.1
Wholesale Trade													
2010	44.9	44.7	45.0	45.1	45.1	45.2	45.6	45.6	45.2	45.4	45.2	45.2	45.2
2011	45.1	45.3	45.3	45.8	46.1	46.2	46.4	46.4	46.1	46.2	46.3	46.3	46.0
2012	45.7	45.7	45.8	46.1	46.4	46.5	46.7	46.4	46.3	46.4	46.2	46.3	46.2
2013	45.7	46.0	46.2	46.5	46.6	46.9	47.1	46.7	46.5	46.5	46.6	46.6	46.5
2014	46.1	46.1	46.3	46.4	46.7	46.9	47.1	46.9	46.7	46.7	46.7	46.8	46.6
2015	46.5	46.6	46.7	46.9	47.1	47.1	47.4	47.4	47.1	47.4	47.5	47.6	47.1
2016	47.7	47.7	47.9	48.1	48.4	48.5	48.8	48.4	48.2	48.1	48.3	48.4	48.2
2017	48.5	48.6	48.6	48.5	48.8	49.2	49.1	49.3	48.8	48.8	49.0	48.9	48.8
2018	48.7	48.8	49.1	49.1	49.4	49.6	49.9	49.7	49.6	50.3	50.5	50.3	49.6
Retail Trade													
2010	93.5	91.9	92.8	93.6	95.0	95.5	95.3	95.3	93.6	95.6	98.4	99.2	95.0
2011	93.4	92.1	92.7	93.9	95.2	95.3	95.3	95.6	94.4	95.7	98.4	99.3	95.1
2012	94.7	93.4	94.3	95.0	96.7	97.0	96.4	95.8	95.8	96.9	100.4	100.6	96.4
2013	94.9	94.3	94.6	95.8	97.3	98.2	97.4	97.7	97.5	98.7	101.5	102.1	97.5
2014	95.8	95.2	95.9	97.0	98.5	99.1	98.9	98.9	98.9	99.5	102.5	103.3	98.6
2015	98.0	97.4	98.0	99.1	100.6	101.2	101.4	101.7	100.9	102.4	105.1	106.1	101.0
2016	100.4	100.3	100.9	101.4	102.5	102.8	102.7	102.7	102.6	103.8	106.7	107.0	102.8
2017	103.1	102.1	102.7	104.1	105.1	105.4	104.0	103.8	103.2	104.2	107.4	107.7	104.4
2018	102.8	101.8	102.8	102.2	104.2	105.2	104.5	104.2	104.1	104.4	106.5	105.0	104.0
Transportation and Utilities													
2010	51.5	51.2	51.7	52.4	52.8	53.1	53.0	53.6	53.8	54.4	55.0	55.6	53.2
2011	54.0	54.2	54.3	55.0	55.3	55.7	55.8	56.0	56.2	57.1	57.9	58.2	55.8
2012	56.2	56.6	56.8	57.0	57.6	58.5	58.4	59.1	59.4	60.4	61.7	62.7	58.7
2013	60.5	60.6	60.9	61.2	61.8	62.2	61.7	62.4	63.0	63.6	65.5	66.1	62.5
2014	63.6	63.5	63.4	63.1	63.6	63.8	64.0	64.3	64.4	64.7	65.6	66.5	64.2
2015	64.0	63.8	64.3	64.5	65.5	66.3	66.8	67.6	67.8	68.6	70.1	72.1	66.8
2016	69.6	69.5	69.7	68.7	69.0	69.0	70.6	71.2	71.4	70.7	71.9	73.1	70.4
2017	69.1	68.7	68.7	68.2	68.3	69.6	69.5	70.0	70.6	71.2	72.9	74.1	70.1
2018	70.3	70.1	70.0	70.1	70.8	71.5	71.6	72.0	72.5	73.0	72.7	73.8	71.5
Information													
2010	15.7	15.7	15.6	15.7	15.9	16.1	15.9	15.8	15.5	15.4	15.4	15.3	15.7
2011	15.0	14.9	15.0	15.0	15.2	15.4	15.4	15.5	15.5	15.5	15.6	15.6	15.3
2012	16.0	16.1	16.1	16.1	16.2	16.5	16.4	16.4	16.3	16.6	16.6	16.5	16.3
2013	16.6	16.6	16.7	16.8	16.8	17.1	17.2	17.0	16.8	16.9	16.9	16.9	16.9
2014	16.8	16.8	16.9	17.0	17.2	17.4	17.5	17.2	16.9	16.7	16.7	16.7	17.0
2015	16.8	16.8	16.7	16.6	16.7	16.8	16.8	16.5	16.3	16.1	16.2	16.2	16.5
2016	16.1	16.1	16.1	16.0	16.1	16.2	16.0	15.9	15.8	15.9	15.7	15.7	16.0
2017	16.0	16.0	16.1	15.8	15.7	15.5	15.1	14.9	14.6	14.6	14.7	14.7	15.3
2018	14.2	14.1	14.1	13.9	13.9	13.8	13.5	13.4	13.3	13.2	13.2	13.2	13.7

Employment by Industry: Indianapolis-Carmel-Anderson, 2010–2018—*Continued*

(Numbers in thousands, not seasonally adjusted)

Industry and year	January	February	March	April	May	June	July	August	September	October	November	December	Annual average
Financial Activities													
2010	59.1	58.9	59.0	59.1	59.3	59.8	60.3	60.2	59.7	60.1	60.1	60.2	59.7
2011	59.8	59.9	60.1	60.0	60.3	60.7	60.8	60.5	60.2	60.3	60.2	60.4	60.3
2012	60.0	60.0	60.1	60.1	60.4	60.8	60.8	60.6	60.1	60.1	60.0	60.2	60.3
2013	59.7	59.6	59.6	59.9	60.4	61.1	61.1	61.0	60.6	60.7	60.8	61.0	60.5
2014	59.8	59.9	60.2	60.4	60.9	61.3	61.5	61.6	61.4	61.7	61.9	62.0	61.1
2015	61.6	61.9	62.2	62.5	63.1	63.7	63.9	64.2	63.9	64.3	64.5	64.7	63.4
2016	64.2	64.3	64.5	65.0	65.4	65.9	66.3	66.1	65.8	66.1	65.9	66.0	65.5
2017	65.4	65.6	65.6	66.0	66.3	67.2	67.5	67.7	67.6	67.9	68.2	68.6	67.0
2018	67.9	68.3	68.6	68.8	69.3	70.0	70.1	69.8	69.2	69.8	68.9	68.1	69.1
Professional and Business Services													
2010	119.6	118.9	120.7	125.9	125.7	127.0	127.6	129.4	127.3	131.0	131.3	132.2	126.4
2011	127.2	126.7	129.2	132.8	132.9	131.9	134.5	136.6	137.3	138.4	139.0	140.7	133.9
2012	133.5	137.2	137.5	139.1	140.5	143.5	142.9	145.4	145.1	145.7	146.8	145.7	141.9
2013	140.0	139.5	141.7	144.1	144.9	146.9	148.8	152.0	152.0	153.0	160.9	159.3	148.6
2014	150.3	147.5	150.0	154.7	157.3	156.3	154.8	158.6	158.7	162.2	169.8	168.9	157.4
2015	156.9	156.1	158.9	163.7	165.8	166.4	165.6	166.1	164.9	169.4	172.8	172.2	164.9
2016	162.1	161.7	163.1	167.2	168.2	168.3	169.4	170.1	170.0	169.7	172.1	170.6	167.7
2017	161.3	161.3	163.9	167.0	167.8	170.6	169.3	171.1	171.1	172.6	174.6	174.9	168.8
2018	167.8	167.5	169.8	169.8	171.2	173.0	171.9	174.4	173.4	172.1	176.3	174.2	171.8
Education and Health Services													
2010	128.9	131.0	131.5	132.5	131.4	128.8	127.5	128.9	133.1	134.5	134.8	134.5	131.5
2011	132.9	135.1	135.5	136.8	136.2	132.6	133.3	134.3	140.2	139.5	139.6	139.8	136.3
2012	138.1	141.3	141.7	141.3	140.2	136.7	135.9	137.6	143.6	143.4	143.7	144.0	140.6
2013	141.2	144.6	145.0	144.5	143.0	140.2	139.7	141.1	144.6	145.1	145.3	145.2	143.3
2014	141.5	144.2	144.7	144.7	144.2	140.9	140.0	140.6	143.8	144.2	144.7	145.0	143.2
2015	143.3	145.6	145.9	147.3	146.4	144.4	144.2	145.0	147.8	149.1	149.5	149.3	146.5
2016	147.7	150.4	150.8	152.2	152.0	150.0	149.8	150.8	154.1	153.7	154.5	153.6	151.6
2017	152.4	154.5	155.4	156.1	157.0	156.0	154.4	154.6	157.8	158.0	158.3	158.0	156.0
2018	157.2	159.7	160.9	160.5	160.6	158.8	157.2	157.9	161.2	163.4	163.2	163.0	160.3
Leisure and Hospitality													
2010	85.6	85.8	88.1	91.7	94.7	96.0	94.9	96.6	93.3	92.5	91.0	89.8	91.7
2011	86.7	87.2	90.5	93.4	96.8	97.0	97.1	97.9	95.6	94.6	93.9	93.5	93.7
2012	91.0	92.5	94.8	97.3	100.7	101.6	100.5	101.8	99.6	98.4	97.5	97.3	97.8
2013	93.8	94.1	96.5	99.2	103.1	103.9	103.0	103.8	101.7	100.5	99.3	98.8	99.8
2014	93.8	94.7	97.4	100.7	105.4	106.2	104.8	106.1	102.7	102.6	101.7	101.9	101.5
2015	98.5	99.4	102.3	104.6	108.3	109.4	107.7	109.2	106.4	105.5	104.1	104.0	105.0
2016	100.1	101.6	104.2	106.8	110.3	111.3	110.6	110.9	109.3	107.4	106.6	105.3	107.0
2017	102.4	103.6	105.8	108.5	111.6	112.1	111.4	112.2	109.7	109.3	108.4	107.5	108.5
2018	103.6	104.6	107.4	108.7	112.8	113.2	112.7	113.1	109.5	109.1	105.1	103.9	108.6
Other Services													
2010	38.6	38.5	39.1	39.2	39.5	40.1	40.1	39.8	39.5	39.6	39.6	39.4	39.4
2011	39.1	39.2	39.8	39.9	40.2	40.7	41.1	41.0	40.5	40.3	40.4	40.3	40.2
2012	40.1	40.5	40.7	40.8	41.2	41.9	41.9	41.8	41.2	41.4	41.4	41.3	41.2
2013	41.1	41.5	42.1	41.5	42.0	43.2	43.1	42.9	42.5	42.7	43.0	43.3	42.4
2014	42.6	43.1	43.7	43.6	44.2	45.0	44.8	44.3	43.8	43.6	43.8	43.7	43.9
2015	43.5	43.7	44.1	43.5	44.0	44.7	44.8	44.5	44.0	43.8	44.2	44.1	44.1
2016	43.6	43.9	44.3	44.6	45.0	45.6	45.6	45.3	44.9	44.7	44.8	44.7	44.8
2017	44.1	44.3	44.8	45.5	46.1	46.8	46.4	45.7	45.3	45.4	45.5	45.6	45.5
2018	44.9	45.4	45.7	46.0	46.5	47.4	47.0	46.4	45.9	46.2	46.5	46.6	46.2
Government													
2010	131.0	133.0	133.2	133.2	136.8	126.7	118.9	125.4	129.0	131.0	131.3	130.4	130.0
2011	129.4	130.2	130.6	130.6	131.0	121.9	117.0	123.4	128.1	129.1	129.2	129.6	127.5
2012	127.3	129.8	129.0	128.3	129.4	120.2	114.8	125.0	128.9	128.7	128.8	128.5	126.6
2013	124.9	128.7	129.2	128.7	129.0	119.9	112.1	126.1	128.4	128.6	129.8	129.6	126.3
2014	126.5	129.5	130.3	129.8	130.5	124.5	116.0	127.8	129.1	128.8	130.0	130.7	127.8
2015	128.9	130.0	130.4	130.2	131.0	124.7	117.3	128.2	131.1	129.9	131.3	132.2	128.8
2016	130.6	132.0	133.0	130.3	131.1	122.5	119.3	130.3	132.6	130.7	132.5	132.6	129.8
2017	131.6	132.4	132.9	132.0	133.4	126.4	119.7	131.6	133.8	132.9	134.7	134.9	131.4
2018	132.5	133.9	134.1	133.7	135.3	128.5	120.7	132.8	135.1	134.9	136.2	135.9	132.8

Employment by Industry: San Jose-Sunnyvale-Santa Clara, CA, 2010–2018

(Numbers in thousands, not seasonally adjusted)

Industry and year	January	February	March	April	May	June	July	August	September	October	November	December	Annual average
Total Nonfarm													
2010	858.3	859.7	863.8	871.2	877.9	879.8	868.2	869.2	873.1	884.3	888.6	890.8	873.7
2011	876.8	882.2	885.8	889.6	893.0	898.8	889.3	893.0	899.1	907.9	910.4	913.5	895.0
2012	900.9	907.2	913.8	922.4	928.4	936.8	926.3	931.8	935.5	945.6	951.2	954.0	929.5
2013	939.9	948.4	953.1	958.1	964.3	970.3	959.3	968.9	972.9	980.2	989.9	993.4	966.6
2014	981.4	989.0	994.0	999.4	1,005.4	1,011.2	1,001.7	1,011.2	1,014.5	1,022.4	1,027.0	1,029.6	1,007.2
2015	1,018.6	1,023.8	1,028.1	1,035.7	1,042.8	1,050.2	1,046.6	1,052.3	1,052.2	1,065.8	1,067.5	1,068.1	1,046.0
2016	1,057.9	1,063.8	1,064.2	1,075.4	1,079.9	1,085.9	1,081.9	1,084.5	1,082.1	1,090.1	1,095.8	1,097.2	1,079.9
2017	1,081.2	1,088.0	1,094.1	1,097.7	1,103.3	1,112.6	1,108.5	1,109.4	1,105.6	1,114.8	1,121.0	1,122.2	1,104.9
2018	1,100.8	1,110.1	1,113.0	1,117.2	1,125.0	1,134.4	1,127.8	1,129.7	1,126.0	1,132.9	1,141.9	1,143.9	1,125.2
Total Private													
2010	762.3	763.5	766.2	771.8	777.0	783.2	783.2	785.7	783.2	788.9	791.6	794.7	779.3
2011	782.2	786.9	790.1	793.1	796.2	802.6	808.0	810.6	808.2	814.1	816.0	819.1	802.3
2012	809.2	814.3	819.8	828.2	834.2	841.9	845.2	848.7	845.3	852.1	857.1	860.7	838.1
2013	847.3	854.4	860.0	863.8	868.6	875.9	880.7	885.5	881.6	886.1	894.5	899.2	874.8
2014	886.9	893.4	898.2	902.5	908.4	917.0	919.4	925.1	922.3	927.2	931.1	934.4	913.8
2015	924.8	929.2	934.0	940.9	947.6	955.5	962.9	965.0	960.6	971.0	972.0	972.9	953.0
2016	964.3	969.5	968.8	979.8	983.5	989.9	996.6	996.2	989.2	994.1	997.9	999.4	985.8
2017	985.4	992.2	997.3	1,000.2	1,005.3	1,015.9	1,020.5	1,019.8	1,011.6	1,017.2	1,022.4	1,024.2	1,009.3
2018	1,004.4	1,013.3	1,014.7	1,018.5	1,025.9	1,035.6	1,038.2	1,038.8	1,031.0	1,034.3	1,041.7	1,044.2	1,028.4
Goods Producing													
2010	182.6	182.2	182.9	183.2	184.4	187.1	188.6	190.1	189.4	189.2	187.7	186.8	186.2
2011	184.8	185.3	186.1	187.9	188.8	191.2	193.5	194.6	193.0	191.3	189.2	188.9	189.6
2012	188.1	188.4	189.1	190.9	193.1	196.4	197.1	197.9	196.4	195.0	194.3	194.0	193.4
2013	190.9	191.4	192.3	193.1	194.0	196.9	199.9	201.2	200.3	197.9	198.2	198.4	196.2
2014	196.2	197.2	198.0	198.2	200.0	202.6	204.1	206.6	206.1	203.6	203.8	204.1	201.7
2015	201.9	203.4	204.6	205.9	207.4	210.5	212.7	213.8	212.6	212.6	211.2	211.1	209.0
2016	210.1	211.0	211.0	213.3	214.2	216.6	220.0	219.9	218.0	216.3	215.7	215.2	215.1
2017	213.5	214.0	211.8	211.4	212.8	216.0	218.6	219.3	218.6	218.3	218.2	218.9	216.0
2018	216.6	218.0	218.2	219.8	220.5	223.5	224.8	225.4	224.4	224.2	223.6	223.9	221.9
Service-Providing													
2010	675.7	677.5	680.9	688.0	693.5	692.7	679.6	679.1	683.7	695.1	700.9	704.0	687.6
2011	692.0	696.9	699.7	701.7	704.2	707.6	695.8	698.4	706.1	716.6	721.2	724.6	705.4
2012	712.8	718.8	724.7	731.5	735.3	740.4	729.2	733.9	739.1	750.6	756.9	760.0	736.1
2013	749.0	757.0	760.8	765.0	770.3	773.4	759.4	767.7	772.6	782.3	791.7	795.0	770.4
2014	785.2	791.8	796.0	801.2	805.4	808.6	797.6	804.6	808.4	818.8	823.2	825.5	805.5
2015	816.7	820.4	823.5	829.8	835.4	839.7	833.9	838.5	839.6	853.2	856.3	857.0	837.0
2016	847.8	852.8	853.2	862.1	865.7	869.3	861.9	864.6	864.1	873.8	880.1	882.0	864.8
2017	867.7	874.0	882.3	886.3	890.5	896.6	889.9	890.1	887.0	896.5	902.8	903.3	888.9
2018	884.2	892.1	894.8	897.4	904.5	910.9	903.0	904.3	901.6	908.7	918.3	920.0	903.3
Mining and Logging													
2010	0.2	0.2	0.2	0.2	0.2	0.2	0.2	0.2	0.2	0.2	0.2	0.2	0.2
2011	0.2	0.2	0.2	0.2	0.2	0.2	0.2	0.2	0.2	0.2	0.2	0.2	0.2
2012	0.2	0.2	0.2	0.2	0.2	0.2	0.2	0.3	0.3	0.3	0.3	0.2	0.2
2013	0.2	0.2	0.2	0.2	0.3	0.3	0.3	0.3	0.3	0.3	0.3	0.3	0.3
2014	0.3	0.3	0.3	0.3	0.3	0.3	0.3	0.3	0.3	0.3	0.3	0.3	0.3
2015	0.2	0.2	0.2	0.2	0.2	0.2	0.3	0.3	0.3	0.2	0.2	0.2	0.2
2016	0.2	0.3	0.3	0.3	0.3	0.3	0.3	0.3	0.3	0.3	0.3	0.3	0.3
2017	0.2	0.2	0.3	0.2	0.2	0.3	0.2	0.2	0.2	0.2	0.2	0.2	0.2
2018	0.2	0.2	0.2	0.2	0.2	0.2	0.2	0.2	0.2	0.2	0.2	0.2	0.2
Construction													
2010	31.5	31.0	31.3	31.9	32.3	33.1	33.6	33.5	33.3	33.0	32.2	31.8	32.4
2011	30.0	29.9	30.3	30.3	30.6	31.3	33.0	33.3	33.6	33.2	33.0	32.8	31.8
2012	32.1	32.3	32.5	33.4	34.9	35.8	36.0	36.1	35.9	36.2	36.2	36.2	34.8
2013	35.1	35.6	35.9	36.1	36.5	37.4	39.0	39.4	38.8	38.7	38.6	38.8	37.5
2014	37.5	37.7	37.8	38.1	38.6	39.7	40.9	41.4	41.4	41.2	41.1	40.7	39.7
2015	40.4	41.1	41.8	42.8	43.1	44.2	45.1	45.9	45.5	46.4	45.7	45.3	43.9
2016	45.1	45.8	45.6	47.5	48.0	48.8	50.4	50.6	50.4	49.8	48.9	48.2	48.3
2017	47.1	47.2	48.2	48.6	49.0	49.9	50.6	50.8	50.4	50.5	50.1	49.7	49.3
2018	48.8	49.2	48.7	49.3	49.2	50.0	50.3	50.6	50.4	49.1	48.5	48.8	49.4

Employment by Industry: San Jose-Sunnyvale-Santa Clara, CA, 2010–2018—*Continued*

(Numbers in thousands, not seasonally adjusted)

Industry and year	January	February	March	April	May	June	July	August	September	October	November	December	Annual average
Manufacturing													
2010	150.9	151.0	151.4	151.1	151.9	153.8	154.8	156.4	155.9	156.0	155.3	154.8	153.6
2011	154.6	155.2	155.6	157.4	158.0	159.7	160.3	161.1	159.2	157.9	156.0	155.9	157.6
2012	155.8	155.9	156.4	157.3	158.0	160.4	160.9	161.5	160.2	158.5	157.8	157.6	158.4
2013	155.6	155.6	156.2	156.8	157.2	159.2	160.6	161.5	161.2	158.9	159.3	159.3	158.5
2014	158.4	159.2	159.9	159.8	161.1	162.6	162.9	164.9	164.4	162.1	162.4	163.1	161.7
2015	161.3	162.1	162.6	162.9	164.1	166.1	167.3	167.6	166.8	166.0	165.3	165.6	164.8
2016	164.8	164.9	165.1	165.5	165.9	167.5	169.3	169.0	167.3	166.2	166.5	166.7	166.6
2017	166.2	166.6	163.3	162.6	163.6	165.8	167.8	168.3	168.0	167.6	167.9	169.0	166.4
2018	167.6	168.6	169.3	170.3	171.1	173.3	174.3	174.6	173.8	174.9	174.9	174.9	172.3
Trade, Transportation, and Utilities													
2010	123.6	122.2	121.8	122.2	123.0	123.6	124.1	124.7	124.3	124.7	128.5	130.6	124.4
2011	125.1	123.9	123.4	123.9	124.2	125.0	125.9	126.5	126.4	127.9	132.1	134.4	126.6
2012	128.9	127.1	126.7	127.8	128.4	129.3	130.4	130.8	130.1	131.5	136.8	138.3	130.5
2013	132.4	131.2	131.0	131.1	131.3	132.5	133.2	133.5	132.8	133.7	138.3	140.3	133.4
2014	134.5	133.0	133.1	133.4	133.5	134.5	135.0	135.6	134.8	135.5	140.0	142.1	135.4
2015	136.8	134.8	134.5	134.3	134.7	135.4	136.5	137.1	136.6	138.5	141.7	143.2	137.0
2016	137.1	136.2	135.5	135.1	135.1	135.3	136.7	136.6	135.5	135.5	138.8	140.9	136.5
2017	134.7	133.1	132.8	132.9	133.0	133.8	133.9	134.2	133.1	133.0	136.6	138.3	134.1
2018	133.7	132.8	132.4	131.9	132.2	133.1	134.1	134.0	133.2	133.7	137.9	138.5	134.0
Wholesale Trade													
2010	34.1	34.1	34.1	34.2	34.4	34.5	34.8	34.7	34.8	34.5	34.4	34.4	34.4
2011	34.1	34.0	33.8	33.5	33.4	33.3	33.5	33.3	33.1	33.3	33.1	33.3	33.5
2012	33.5	33.8	33.5	33.9	34.0	34.2	34.8	34.9	34.6	35.4	35.4	35.4	34.5
2013	35.4	35.5	35.6	35.7	35.6	35.7	36.0	36.0	35.8	35.6	35.8	35.9	35.7
2014	35.8	35.7	35.8	35.6	35.5	35.7	35.9	35.9	35.7	35.8	36.0	36.0	35.8
2015	35.4	35.5	35.4	35.4	35.7	35.8	36.0	35.9	35.7	36.7	36.1	36.1	35.8
2016	35.7	35.7	35.7	35.7	35.6	35.4	35.5	35.4	35.0	34.5	34.3	34.3	35.2
2017	33.5	33.4	33.3	33.3	33.1	33.1	32.9	32.8	32.6	32.5	32.3	32.2	32.9
2018	32.1	32.1	31.9	31.8	31.9	32.0	31.9	31.8	31.5	31.5	31.3	30.9	31.7
Retail Trade													
2010	77.7	76.4	76.0	76.3	76.6	77.0	77.2	77.8	77.2	78.1	82.0	83.8	78.0
2011	79.2	78.0	77.7	78.4	78.7	79.5	80.2	81.1	81.1	82.5	86.8	88.5	81.0
2012	83.1	81.1	81.0	81.5	81.9	82.3	82.7	82.8	82.3	82.9	88.1	89.2	83.2
2013	83.8	82.3	82.0	82.0	82.3	83.2	83.4	83.7	83.0	83.8	87.9	89.2	83.9
2014	84.6	83.3	83.2	83.8	83.8	84.4	84.7	85.3	84.8	85.3	89.4	90.8	85.3
2015	86.5	85.2	85.0	84.7	84.8	85.3	86.0	86.6	86.3	87.1	90.4	91.2	86.6
2016	86.4	85.6	85.0	84.5	84.5	84.6	85.7	85.7	85.0	85.3	88.1	89.2	85.8
2017	85.7	84.4	84.3	84.4	84.7	85.3	85.8	86.0	85.1	85.3	88.9	89.8	85.8
2018	86.4	85.3	85.1	84.6	84.7	85.4	86.3	86.2	85.5	85.8	89.4	90.3	86.3
Transportation and Utilities													
2010	11.8	11.7	11.7	11.7	12.0	12.1	12.1	12.2	12.3	12.1	12.1	12.4	12.0
2011	11.8	11.9	11.9	12.0	12.1	12.2	12.2	12.1	12.2	12.1	12.2	12.6	12.1
2012	12.3	12.2	12.2	12.4	12.5	12.8	12.9	13.1	13.2	13.2	13.3	13.7	12.8
2013	13.2	13.4	13.4	13.4	13.4	13.6	13.8	13.8	14.0	14.3	14.6	15.2	13.8
2014	14.1	14.0	14.1	14.0	14.2	14.4	14.4	14.4	14.3	14.4	14.6	15.3	14.4
2015	14.9	14.1	14.1	14.2	14.2	14.3	14.5	14.6	14.6	14.7	15.2	15.9	14.6
2016	15.0	14.9	14.8	14.9	15.0	15.3	15.5	15.5	15.5	15.7	16.4	17.4	15.5
2017	15.5	15.3	15.2	15.2	15.2	15.4	15.2	15.4	15.4	15.2	15.4	16.3	15.4
2018	15.2	15.4	15.4	15.5	15.6	15.7	15.9	16.0	16.2	16.4	17.2	17.3	16.0
Information													
2010	43.0	43.4	43.0	43.6	44.2	45.4	46.3	46.6	46.2	46.5	47.1	47.2	45.2
2011	47.7	48.2	48.2	48.3	48.8	50.2	51.0	51.0	50.4	50.4	50.4	50.6	49.6
2012	50.3	50.7	50.9	51.4	51.7	52.6	53.6	53.3	53.0	53.1	53.2	53.5	52.3
2013	54.3	54.5	54.8	54.8	54.9	56.7	58.0	57.8	57.1	57.8	58.4	59.0	56.5
2014	59.1	60.0	60.8	61.1	61.8	64.0	66.1	65.5	64.8	65.3	65.4	65.8	63.3
2015	66.4	66.3	66.5	66.7	66.9	69.4	71.0	69.8	69.0	69.4	69.5	69.7	68.4
2016	72.4	72.4	72.1	72.4	73.2	75.9	76.0	75.6	74.9	76.4	77.6	78.0	74.7
2017	78.5	79.3	80.5	81.5	82.3	86.1	88.5	88.4	87.5	87.1	87.8	88.4	84.7
2018	86.9	87.4	87.9	88.3	89.5	93.4	94.8	94.5	93.5	93.9	94.7	95.2	91.7

Employment by Industry: San Jose-Sunnyvale-Santa Clara, CA, 2010–2018—*Continued*

(Numbers in thousands, not seasonally adjusted)

Industry and year	January	February	March	April	May	June	July	August	September	October	November	December	Annual average
Financial Activities													
2010	30.8	30.9	31.5	30.2	30.5	30.8	30.9	31.0	30.9	31.3	31.7	31.7	31.0
2011	31.6	31.7	31.7	31.9	32.0	32.3	32.5	32.5	32.5	32.8	33.1	33.2	32.3
2012	32.7	32.6	32.9	32.9	33.2	33.4	33.5	33.4	33.3	33.6	33.7	33.6	33.2
2013	32.6	32.9	33.3	33.5	33.8	33.8	33.9	33.9	33.7	34.1	34.2	34.2	33.7
2014	33.6	33.8	34.0	34.0	34.2	34.6	34.4	34.2	34.2	34.2	34.2	34.2	34.1
2015	34.0	34.0	33.8	34.1	34.4	34.7	34.9	34.9	34.7	35.3	35.3	35.0	34.6
2016	35.0	35.1	35.1	35.4	35.4	35.5	36.0	36.0	35.8	35.9	36.1	36.2	35.6
2017	35.8	35.9	35.9	36.3	36.2	36.4	36.4	36.2	35.8	36.1	36.1	36.1	36.1
2018	36.3	36.5	36.4	36.7	36.9	37.1	37.4	37.3	37.0	37.6	37.7	38.0	37.1
Professional and Business Services													
2010	160.9	161.9	162.8	164.3	164.7	166.4	167.2	167.7	167.0	168.5	168.6	169.5	165.8
2011	167.7	168.9	170.1	170.4	170.0	171.7	174.5	175.1	174.3	174.8	174.5	175.1	172.3
2012	174.1	176.3	178.1	181.1	181.6	184.1	187.3	188.6	187.7	189.5	190.3	192.4	184.3
2013	190.3	192.7	194.2	193.9	194.4	196.7	200.1	202.2	200.7	201.2	203.4	205.1	197.9
2014	203.2	204.7	205.3	206.1	206.3	209.2	211.1	213.1	212.5	214.8	216.1	217.2	210.0
2015	215.4	216.6	217.8	220.4	221.5	223.2	227.3	228.3	227.1	229.5	230.6	230.8	224.0
2016	228.2	230.1	229.3	233.0	232.2	233.4	236.0	236.2	233.1	235.1	234.9	234.6	233.0
2017	230.6	232.4	236.4	237.6	237.1	239.1	241.3	240.8	237.7	238.6	238.7	238.4	237.4
2018	233.3	234.7	234.0	235.3	236.2	238.5	239.8	239.8	237.2	238.5	240.1	239.7	237.3
Education and Health Services													
2010	124.9	125.9	126.0	128.3	128.8	128.4	125.6	125.4	124.8	128.3	129.0	129.7	127.1
2011	128.5	130.3	130.7	129.5	130.0	129.1	125.9	126.4	126.8	131.8	133.5	133.8	129.7
2012	133.6	136.7	137.3	137.3	137.7	136.8	133.2	134.6	134.4	139.2	140.6	140.7	136.8
2013	140.4	142.7	143.5	144.1	145.1	143.8	140.5	141.9	141.9	146.1	147.9	147.7	143.8
2014	148.0	149.6	150.1	150.8	151.5	150.3	147.0	147.8	148.0	152.7	152.3	152.0	150.0
2015	153.1	154.8	155.6	156.1	157.1	156.2	154.4	154.9	154.7	159.5	159.9	159.7	156.3
2016	159.3	161.6	161.9	163.3	164.0	163.1	160.9	160.5	160.7	164.4	165.7	165.1	162.5
2017	166.3	169.0	169.9	168.8	169.9	169.3	166.8	166.4	165.7	170.4	171.7	171.9	168.8
2018	170.0	172.9	173.9	172.3	173.2	172.8	170.1	171.1	170.2	174.4	175.7	175.8	172.7
Leisure and Hospitality													
2010	71.9	72.1	73.0	75.9	77.2	77.0	76.7	76.5	76.6	76.2	74.7	75.1	75.2
2011	72.7	74.3	75.6	76.7	77.7	78.4	79.8	79.9	80.2	80.4	78.3	78.4	77.7
2012	77.4	78.3	80.4	82.0	83.5	84.1	84.9	85.2	85.6	85.3	83.4	83.5	82.8
2013	81.7	83.9	85.8	87.9	89.4	89.8	89.5	89.6	89.6	89.7	88.4	88.9	87.9
2014	86.8	89.3	90.9	92.4	94.4	94.9	95.1	95.7	95.4	94.4	92.6	92.6	92.9
2015	91.0	92.9	94.6	96.6	98.4	99.0	98.9	99.0	98.9	99.0	96.6	96.3	96.8
2016	95.6	96.1	97.0	99.9	101.7	102.4	103.0	103.4	103.3	102.3	101.0	101.4	100.6
2017	97.9	100.0	101.3	102.5	104.6	105.9	106.1	105.6	104.3	104.7	104.5	103.5	103.4
2018	99.5	102.2	103.1	105.1	108.1	107.8	107.8	107.7	106.7	103.7	103.7	104.4	105.0
Other Services													
2010	24.6	24.9	25.2	24.1	24.2	24.5	23.8	23.7	24.0	24.2	24.3	24.1	24.3
2011	24.1	24.3	24.3	24.5	24.7	24.7	24.9	24.6	24.6	24.7	24.9	24.7	24.6
2012	24.1	24.2	24.4	24.8	25.0	25.2	25.2	24.9	24.8	24.9	24.8	24.7	24.8
2013	24.7	25.1	25.1	25.4	25.7	25.7	25.6	25.4	25.5	25.6	25.7	25.6	25.4
2014	25.5	25.8	26.0	26.5	26.7	26.9	26.6	26.6	26.5	26.7	26.7	26.4	26.4
2015	26.2	26.4	26.6	26.8	27.2	27.1	27.2	27.2	27.0	27.2	27.2	27.1	26.9
2016	26.6	27.0	26.9	27.4	27.7	27.7	28.0	28.0	27.9	28.2	28.1	28.0	27.6
2017	28.1	28.5	28.7	29.2	29.4	29.3	28.9	28.9	28.9	29.0	28.8	28.7	28.9
2018	28.1	28.8	28.8	29.1	29.3	29.4	29.4	29.0	28.8	28.3	28.3	28.7	28.8
Government													
2010	96.0	96.2	97.6	99.4	100.9	96.6	85.0	83.5	89.9	95.4	97.0	96.1	94.5
2011	94.6	95.3	95.7	96.5	96.8	96.2	81.3	82.4	90.9	93.8	94.4	94.4	92.7
2012	91.7	92.9	94.0	94.2	94.2	94.9	81.1	83.1	90.2	93.5	94.1	93.3	91.4
2013	92.6	94.0	93.1	94.3	95.7	94.4	78.6	83.4	91.3	94.1	95.4	94.2	91.8
2014	94.5	95.6	95.8	96.9	97.0	94.2	82.3	86.1	92.2	95.2	95.9	95.2	93.4
2015	93.8	94.6	94.1	94.8	95.2	94.7	83.7	87.3	91.6	94.8	95.5	95.2	92.9
2016	93.6	94.3	95.4	95.6	96.4	96.0	85.3	88.3	92.9	96.0	97.9	97.8	94.1
2017	95.8	95.8	96.8	97.5	98.0	96.7	88.0	89.6	94.0	97.6	98.6	98.0	95.5
2018	96.4	96.8	98.3	98.7	99.1	98.8	89.6	90.9	95.0	98.6	100.2	99.7	96.8

Employment by Industry: Nashville-Davidson—Murfreesboro—Franklin, TN, 2010–2018

(Numbers in thousands, not seasonally adjusted)

Industry and year	January	February	March	April	May	June	July	August	September	October	November	December	Annual average
Total Nonfarm													
2010	742.3	745.0	751.5	760.2	766.8	758.4	752.6	761.0	770.7	777.4	781.8	782.2	762.5
2011	759.8	765.8	773.1	781.5	785.6	779.5	780.8	790.4	796.4	801.5	808.6	810.5	786.1
2012	791.4	798.0	809.0	811.2	814.9	811.0	807.0	818.6	825.0	830.8	839.5	841.3	816.5
2013	817.6	827.1	833.1	841.0	845.1	840.9	837.1	849.7	855.0	863.0	871.4	872.4	846.1
2014	850.9	857.8	862.3	874.6	879.6	873.3	870.5	885.6	891.6	899.8	907.2	909.8	880.3
2015	886.4	891.9	896.7	907.0	913.1	908.8	907.6	917.8	925.0	934.6	941.3	945.0	914.6
2016	923.1	929.0	936.3	943.9	945.2	942.4	943.6	953.4	962.7	967.1	974.9	977.1	949.9
2017	954.9	964.1	968.7	975.5	977.2	976.3	975.0	985.0	993.4	998.8	1,008.9	1,006.7	982.0
2018	985.1	994.4	1,000.2	1,004.9	1,007.4	1,007.4	1,002.1	1,016.5	1,024.6	1,028.4	1,038.7	1,036.0	1,012.1
Total Private													
2010	630.8	631.6	637.7	645.7	650.5	654.3	651.2	653.9	655.6	661.8	666.6	667.4	650.6
2011	648.0	653.7	660.4	668.2	672.5	676.1	677.3	681.2	683.6	688.4	695.2	697.4	675.2
2012	680.5	685.2	695.4	698.6	703.9	709.7	706.6	711.7	714.2	719.0	726.8	728.7	706.7
2013	707.8	714.9	720.7	727.1	732.4	738.5	735.3	741.4	742.5	748.9	757.3	758.5	735.4
2014	739.5	743.8	748.2	760.6	765.5	770.0	767.8	776.3	777.9	784.7	790.2	794.3	768.2
2015	774.1	776.5	781.3	791.8	798.5	804.0	803.3	806.8	809.4	816.8	823.9	827.6	801.2
2016	809.4	812.9	818.1	827.1	830.2	836.5	837.7	840.2	844.7	849.3	856.2	858.5	835.1
2017	838.9	845.6	849.8	856.8	859.7	868.3	867.4	870.5	874.3	878.9	888.4	885.8	865.4
2018	867.1	873.9	879.5	884.3	888.2	897.5	893.0	900.7	903.6	905.9	915.6	912.5	893.5
Goods Producing													
2010	92.2	91.6	92.5	94.4	94.7	96.0	95.8	96.5	96.6	97.0	96.4	96.3	95.0
2011	93.5	94.4	95.9	97.8	98.0	99.0	99.2	99.5	100.1	100.7	100.7	101.1	98.3
2012	98.8	100.1	101.9	102.1	102.8	104.1	104.4	105.2	106.0	105.3	105.8	105.9	103.5
2013	104.2	105.2	106.0	106.5	107.6	108.8	108.9	109.7	110.0	110.6	110.6	110.9	108.3
2014	109.7	110.2	111.1	111.8	113.0	113.2	113.0	114.7	114.3	115.0	115.9	116.6	113.2
2015	114.8	115.7	115.7	117.6	118.9	119.5	118.8	119.5	120.0	119.7	119.7	119.4	118.3
2016	118.6	119.1	120.0	120.3	121.3	122.6	123.9	123.6	123.9	124.3	124.9	126.4	122.4
2017	125.0	126.0	126.3	127.5	127.5	128.6	128.7	128.4	128.6	127.9	128.5	128.1	127.6
2018	127.0	127.6	128.7	129.1	129.6	131.6	130.7	131.5	132.2	132.2	133.0	131.1	130.4
Service-Providing													
2010	650.1	653.4	659.0	665.8	672.1	662.4	656.8	664.5	674.1	680.4	685.4	685.9	667.5
2011	666.3	671.4	677.2	683.7	687.6	680.5	681.6	690.9	696.3	700.8	707.9	709.4	687.8
2012	692.6	697.9	707.1	709.1	712.1	706.9	702.6	713.4	719.0	725.5	733.7	735.4	712.9
2013	713.4	721.9	727.1	734.5	737.5	732.1	728.2	740.0	745.0	752.4	760.8	761.5	737.9
2014	741.2	747.6	751.2	762.8	766.6	760.1	757.5	770.9	777.3	784.8	791.3	793.2	767.0
2015	771.6	776.2	781.0	789.4	794.2	789.3	788.8	798.3	805.0	814.9	821.6	825.6	796.3
2016	804.5	809.9	816.3	823.6	823.9	819.8	819.7	829.8	838.8	842.8	850.0	850.7	827.5
2017	829.9	838.1	842.4	848.0	849.7	847.7	846.3	856.6	864.8	870.9	880.4	878.6	854.5
2018	858.1	866.8	871.5	875.8	877.8	875.8	871.4	885.0	892.4	896.2	905.7	904.9	881.8
Mining, Logging, and Construction													
2010	29.0	28.7	29.6	31.5	31.7	32.7	32.8	33.1	33.0	33.4	32.5	32.1	31.7
2011	29.5	30.1	31.3	32.8	32.9	33.8	33.7	33.9	34.2	33.8	33.5	33.1	32.7
2012	31.9	32.3	33.6	33.2	33.4	33.6	33.4	33.7	34.0	33.1	32.6	32.3	33.1
2013	31.0	31.8	32.5	33.0	33.7	34.3	34.2	34.2	34.2	34.2	33.4	33.3	33.3
2014	32.5	32.8	34.1	34.8	35.6	35.4	35.8	36.2	35.9	36.4	36.8	37.1	35.3
2015	36.2	36.8	37.2	38.7	39.7	40.1	40.4	40.0	40.3	40.3	40.1	39.3	39.1
2016	38.2	38.2	38.5	38.9	39.5	40.4	41.0	40.9	41.1	41.3	41.6	41.7	40.1
2017	40.4	41.1	41.9	42.8	43.3	43.9	43.9	44.1	44.1	43.8	44.3	44.1	43.1
2018	43.2	43.6	44.6	45.3	45.7	47.0	46.9	47.2	47.6	47.9	48.7	47.3	46.3
Manufacturing													
2010	63.2	62.9	62.9	62.9	63.0	63.3	63.0	63.4	63.6	63.6	63.9	64.2	63.3
2011	64.0	64.3	64.6	65.0	65.1	65.2	65.5	65.6	65.9	66.9	67.2	68.0	65.6
2012	66.9	67.8	68.3	68.9	69.4	70.5	71.0	71.5	72.0	72.2	73.2	73.6	70.4
2013	73.2	73.4	73.5	73.5	73.9	74.5	74.7	75.5	75.8	76.4	77.2	77.6	74.9
2014	77.2	77.4	77.0	77.0	77.4	77.8	77.2	78.5	78.4	78.6	79.1	79.5	77.9
2015	78.6	78.9	78.5	78.9	79.2	79.4	78.4	79.5	79.7	79.4	79.6	80.1	79.2
2016	80.4	80.9	81.5	81.4	81.8	82.2	82.9	82.7	82.8	83.0	83.3	84.7	82.3
2017	84.6	84.9	84.4	84.7	84.2	84.7	84.8	84.3	84.5	84.1	84.2	84.0	84.5
2018	83.8	84.0	84.1	83.8	83.9	84.6	83.8	84.3	84.6	84.3	84.3	83.8	84.1

Employment by Industry: Nashville-Davidson—Murfreesboro—Franklin, TN, 2010–2018—*Continued*

(Numbers in thousands, not seasonally adjusted)

Industry and year	January	February	March	April	May	June	July	August	September	October	November	December	Annual average
Trade, Transportation, and Utilities													
2010	150.3	149.4	150.1	150.8	151.1	152.2	151.9	152.7	152.3	154.5	157.6	159.4	152.7
2011	152.8	152.9	154.1	155.6	156.2	156.5	156.8	157.1	157.5	159.6	163.4	164.8	157.3
2012	159.0	158.2	160.1	160.7	161.6	161.6	161.4	162.1	162.9	164.9	169.8	170.9	162.8
2013	162.6	162.4	163.1	165.0	165.9	166.9	166.3	167.3	167.0	169.2	174.5	177.1	167.3
2014	167.3	166.8	167.7	170.6	171.3	172.1	171.9	172.9	173.1	176.0	179.8	181.8	172.6
2015	173.1	171.6	172.0	173.4	174.4	175.0	175.0	175.9	175.9	178.6	182.9	185.1	176.1
2016	178.2	177.1	177.3	178.5	178.8	179.5	180.8	181.3	181.6	184.6	189.2	190.7	181.5
2017	182.6	182.2	182.6	183.7	184.2	185.6	186.0	187.4	188.1	190.8	196.5	197.2	187.2
2018	190.1	189.6	190.2	190.6	191.7	192.4	193.5	194.6	194.8	196.2	203.3	203.2	194.2
Wholesale Trade													
2010	36.1	36.1	36.2	36.3	36.4	36.4	36.5	36.7	36.6	37.1	37.1	37.3	36.6
2011	36.9	37.2	37.5	37.5	37.7	37.8	37.9	38.0	38.2	38.5	38.7	38.9	37.9
2012	38.6	38.8	39.0	39.1	39.4	39.5	39.7	40.0	40.0	40.2	40.4	40.5	39.6
2013	39.8	40.1	40.5	40.7	40.8	41.0	41.2	41.1	41.0	41.1	41.3	41.1	40.8
2014	40.2	40.1	40.3	40.3	40.4	40.4	40.4	40.4	40.5	40.6	40.5	40.6	40.4
2015	39.6	39.7	39.7	39.6	39.6	39.6	39.6	39.5	39.6	39.8	39.8	39.7	39.7
2016	38.8	38.7	38.6	38.6	38.7	38.8	39.2	39.5	39.7	40.0	40.1	40.3	39.3
2017	39.9	40.1	40.2	40.3	40.4	40.6	40.6	40.8	41.0	41.2	41.4	41.4	40.7
2018	41.2	41.3	41.4	41.4	41.6	41.9	42.1	42.3	42.3	42.4	42.4	41.9	41.9
Retail Trade													
2010	85.4	84.7	85.1	85.8	85.9	86.6	86.1	86.5	85.7	86.8	89.3	90.5	86.5
2011	86.6	86.5	87.1	88.1	88.2	88.5	88.5	88.5	88.4	89.1	91.9	93.0	88.7
2012	88.9	87.8	89.1	89.1	89.3	89.2	88.7	88.5	88.3	89.2	92.5	92.8	89.5
2013	88.0	87.1	87.4	88.7	89.4	89.7	89.4	89.8	89.4	90.7	93.5	94.6	89.8
2014	90.0	89.6	90.1	92.8	93.4	93.9	93.6	93.8	93.6	94.7	97.5	98.7	93.5
2015	94.0	93.0	93.3	94.1	94.8	95.1	95.0	95.0	94.4	95.6	98.5	99.6	95.2
2016	95.4	95.1	95.5	96.1	96.3	96.7	96.9	97.0	96.8	97.7	100.5	101.5	97.1
2017	97.7	97.2	97.3	98.1	98.4	99.0	99.3	99.4	99.0	99.7	103.3	104.1	99.4
2018	99.8	99.7	100.1	100.5	101.1	101.3	101.0	101.1	100.5	100.8	105.9	106.3	101.5
Transportation and Utilities													
2010	28.8	28.6	28.8	28.7	28.8	29.2	29.3	29.5	30.0	30.6	31.2	31.6	29.6
2011	29.3	29.2	29.5	30.0	30.3	30.2	30.4	30.6	30.9	32.0	32.8	32.9	30.7
2012	31.5	31.6	32.0	32.5	32.9	32.9	33.0	33.6	34.6	35.5	36.9	37.6	33.7
2013	34.8	35.2	35.2	35.6	35.7	36.2	35.7	36.4	36.6	37.4	39.7	41.4	36.7
2014	37.1	37.1	37.3	37.5	37.5	37.8	37.9	38.7	39.0	40.7	41.8	42.5	38.7
2015	39.5	38.9	39.0	39.7	40.0	40.3	40.4	41.4	41.9	43.2	44.6	45.8	41.2
2016	44.0	43.3	43.2	43.8	43.8	44.0	44.7	44.8	45.1	46.9	48.6	48.9	45.1
2017	45.0	44.9	45.1	45.3	45.4	46.0	46.1	47.2	48.1	49.9	51.8	51.7	47.2
2018	49.1	48.6	48.7	48.7	49.0	49.2	50.4	51.2	52.0	53.0	55.0	55.0	50.8
Information													
2010	19.9	19.9	20.0	19.9	19.8	19.9	19.8	19.5	19.5	19.8	19.8	19.8	19.8
2011	19.4	19.3	19.3	19.4	19.6	19.7	19.7	20.1	19.8	20.1	20.4	20.5	19.8
2012	20.3	20.5	20.4	20.5	21.3	21.5	20.4	20.6	20.4	20.6	20.6	20.7	20.7
2013	20.4	20.7	20.8	20.6	21.0	21.6	20.9	21.0	20.7	20.8	21.2	21.1	20.9
2014	20.5	20.5	20.6	20.6	20.7	20.8	20.6	20.6	20.4	20.6	20.6	20.5	20.6
2015	20.4	20.5	20.5	20.6	21.1	21.7	21.6	22.1	21.9	22.3	23.0	22.9	21.6
2016	22.7	22.9	22.4	22.4	22.4	23.8	22.2	22.3	23.1	23.1	23.9	22.8	22.8
2017	22.5	23.4	22.7	22.7	23.1	24.7	23.0	23.0	22.9	24.0	25.1	23.2	23.4
2018	23.1	23.4	23.2	23.2	23.0	24.9	22.5	23.0	23.0	23.4	23.9	23.7	23.4

Employment by Industry: Nashville-Davidson—Murfreesboro—Franklin, TN, 2010–2018—*Continued*

(Numbers in thousands, not seasonally adjusted)

Industry and year	January	February	March	April	May	June	July	August	September	October	November	December	Annual average
Financial Activities													
2010	47.6	47.7	47.6	48.1	48.4	48.4	48.5	48.8	48.5	48.9	49.1	49.2	48.4
2011	48.4	48.5	48.5	49.3	49.8	49.5	49.7	50.0	50.0	50.2	50.5	50.4	49.6
2012	49.8	50.2	50.2	50.3	50.6	51.0	51.1	51.5	51.5	51.6	51.9	52.4	51.0
2013	52.1	52.4	52.8	53.4	53.7	53.7	54.4	54.2	54.0	54.4	54.7	54.7	53.7
2014	54.7	55.0	55.2	55.8	56.3	56.6	57.0	57.4	57.5	57.8	57.9	58.3	56.6
2015	57.9	58.3	58.6	58.9	59.2	59.6	59.9	60.0	59.9	60.5	60.7	61.1	59.6
2016	60.5	61.0	61.1	61.9	62.5	63.0	63.4	63.8	63.9	64.0	64.1	64.5	62.8
2017	63.9	64.7	65.2	65.5	65.9	66.5	66.6	66.9	66.7	67.9	67.0	66.9	66.1
2018	66.4	66.9	67.3	67.4	67.9	68.4	68.8	69.1	69.2	69.0	68.9	69.1	68.2
Professional and Business Services													
2010	94.0	94.8	96.2	98.1	102.6	102.4	100.8	101.4	103.3	103.4	105.1	105.3	100.6
2011	101.3	103.6	105.0	106.1	107.1	109.5	109.4	111.0	111.8	112.6	114.0	114.0	108.8
2012	109.8	111.5	114.6	114.8	116.1	118.5	118.0	119.8	120.9	122.4	124.0	123.7	117.8
2013	118.7	120.7	121.9	121.6	122.8	125.2	124.5	127.8	129.0	131.5	133.7	132.6	125.8
2014	129.2	130.3	129.8	133.4	134.6	137.0	135.4	139.8	140.3	142.4	142.9	144.3	136.6
2015	138.5	139.1	141.3	143.6	144.4	147.6	148.2	149.6	150.2	152.7	153.5	154.0	146.9
2016	150.0	150.6	151.8	154.7	154.7	156.5	155.8	156.8	157.3	158.8	158.4	158.3	155.3
2017	154.4	154.9	155.8	158.1	158.1	161.2	161.8	161.8	162.8	163.3	165.3	164.9	160.2
2018	160.8	162.5	163.0	164.0	164.4	167.0	164.4	167.2	167.8	168.9	170.2	171.2	166.0
Education and Health Services													
2010	119.7	120.5	121.0	122.6	121.4	120.9	122.5	122.6	124.5	125.3	125.6	125.3	122.7
2011	123.9	125.3	125.4	126.2	125.6	124.4	125.0	125.3	126.9	127.6	128.2	128.4	126.0
2012	127.6	128.8	129.3	129.6	128.5	128.3	127.9	128.8	130.9	131.1	131.7	131.4	129.5
2013	130.2	131.8	132.3	133.2	132.4	131.8	131.0	132.0	134.2	134.0	133.9	133.9	132.6
2014	133.2	134.2	134.8	136.0	135.3	134.4	134.5	135.4	137.7	138.5	138.5	138.8	135.9
2015	138.1	139.1	139.4	140.4	140.3	138.7	139.4	139.7	142.6	143.2	144.2	144.5	140.8
2016	142.1	143.7	144.5	144.9	144.8	143.2	144.3	145.3	148.2	148.3	148.9	148.8	145.6
2017	146.9	148.7	149.2	149.5	148.7	146.5	147.1	147.9	151.1	151.5	151.9	151.6	149.2
2018	150.2	152.1	152.6	153.0	151.9	150.4	150.5	152.1	154.7	154.8	154.8	154.8	152.7
Leisure and Hospitality													
2010	76.5	76.8	79.1	80.7	81.1	82.4	79.9	80.3	78.9	80.5	80.4	79.2	79.7
2011	75.9	76.4	78.6	80.5	82.5	83.0	83.2	84.1	83.7	83.8	83.9	84.1	81.6
2012	81.3	81.7	84.3	85.9	88.0	88.9	87.8	88.5	86.6	87.9	87.7	88.2	86.4
2013	84.3	85.9	87.7	90.4	92.3	93.3	92.4	92.7	91.2	92.0	92.1	91.9	90.5
2014	88.8	90.4	92.3	95.4	97.1	98.4	97.9	98.6	97.8	97.4	97.4	97.0	95.7
2015	94.5	95.4	96.8	100.0	102.3	103.5	102.3	102.4	101.2	102.0	102.0	102.4	100.4
2016	99.5	100.3	102.4	105.5	106.5	108.3	107.6	107.6	107.2	106.7	107.1	107.2	105.5
2017	104.2	105.9	107.9	109.5	111.5	113.7	113.0	113.9	112.9	112.3	112.8	112.4	110.8
2018	108.7	110.5	112.8	115.1	117.4	119.7	119.8	120.4	119.2	118.3	118.8	116.6	116.4
Other Services													
2010	30.6	30.9	31.2	31.1	31.4	32.1	32.0	32.1	32.0	32.4	32.6	32.9	31.8
2011	32.8	33.3	33.6	33.3	33.7	34.5	34.3	34.1	33.8	33.8	34.1	34.1	33.8
2012	33.9	34.2	34.6	34.7	35.0	35.8	35.6	35.2	35.0	35.2	35.3	35.5	35.0
2013	35.3	35.8	36.1	36.4	36.7	37.2	36.9	36.7	36.4	36.4	36.6	36.3	36.4
2014	36.1	36.4	36.7	37.0	37.2	37.5	37.5	36.9	36.8	37.0	37.2	37.0	36.9
2015	36.8	36.8	37.0	37.3	37.9	38.4	38.1	37.6	37.7	37.8	37.9	38.2	37.6
2016	37.8	38.2	38.6	38.9	39.2	39.6	39.7	39.5	39.5	39.5	39.7	39.8	39.2
2017	39.4	39.8	40.1	40.3	40.7	41.5	41.2	41.2	41.2	41.2	41.3	41.5	40.8
2018	40.8	41.3	41.7	41.9	42.3	43.1	42.8	42.8	42.7	43.1	42.7	42.8	42.3
Government													
2010	111.5	113.4	113.8	114.5	116.3	104.1	101.4	107.1	115.1	115.6	115.2	114.8	111.9
2011	111.8	112.1	112.7	113.3	113.1	103.4	103.5	109.2	112.8	113.1	113.4	113.1	111.0
2012	110.9	112.8	113.6	112.6	111.0	101.3	100.4	106.9	110.8	111.8	112.7	112.6	109.8
2013	109.8	112.2	112.4	113.9	112.7	102.4	101.8	108.3	112.5	114.1	114.1	113.9	110.7
2014	111.4	114.0	114.1	114.0	114.1	103.3	102.7	109.3	113.7	115.1	117.0	115.5	112.0
2015	112.3	115.4	115.4	115.2	114.6	104.8	104.3	111.0	115.6	117.8	117.4	117.4	113.4
2016	113.7	116.1	118.2	116.8	115.0	105.9	105.9	113.2	118.0	117.8	118.7	118.6	114.8
2017	116.0	118.5	118.9	118.7	117.5	108.0	107.6	114.5	119.1	119.9	120.5	120.9	116.7
2018	118.0	120.5	120.7	120.6	119.2	109.9	109.1	115.8	121.0	122.5	123.1	123.5	118.7

Employment by Industry: Virginia Beach-Norfolk-Newport News, VA-NC, 2010–2018

(Numbers in thousands, not seasonally adjusted)

Industry and year	January	February	March	April	May	June	July	August	September	October	November	December	Annual average
Total Nonfarm													
2010	720.6	720.1	727.5	738.1	743.6	748.4	744.6	744.5	739.7	740.1	739.5	738.8	737.1
2011	720.8	722.5	730.7	739.8	743.3	751.0	749.4	749.0	745.5	742.9	743.4	743.5	740.2
2012	728.5	731.7	738.1	744.7	747.0	754.4	751.3	753.0	748.7	753.5	755.3	755.7	746.8
2013	740.2	742.6	748.6	755.0	758.4	765.1	763.6	765.4	758.6	758.7	760.2	760.2	756.4
2014	742.6	742.3	748.7	758.2	762.7	768.1	764.8	767.3	760.8	760.3	761.4	761.4	758.2
2015	747.9	748.4	752.1	763.5	767.7	773.7	774.9	776.4	771.4	774.1	775.5	775.2	766.7
2016	755.3	757.0	763.0	772.5	772.6	780.3	777.4	779.1	776.3	777.5	780.1	778.1	772.4
2017	760.8	768.4	773.5	782.2	784.0	792.7	788.6	788.9	785.0	786.5	789.7	791.4	782.6
2018	772.8	779.5	786.8	792.8	796.5	803.7	798.4	798.0	787.2	789.8	791.1	789.1	790.5
Total Private													
2010	559.9	558.5	565.2	575.2	578.5	584.1	587.1	586.5	578.9	578.0	577.0	576.7	575.5
2011	559.8	560.7	568.0	576.9	580.7	588.0	590.1	589.1	583.2	579.0	577.7	578.0	577.6
2012	565.5	567.6	574.5	581.0	583.6	590.7	592.4	593.8	587.4	590.1	590.4	591.6	584.1
2013	578.8	579.6	585.5	592.0	596.0	603.0	605.2	606.6	598.2	596.8	597.4	597.1	594.7
2014	582.6	581.5	587.5	596.7	602.1	608.1	608.0	609.6	601.8	600.7	600.6	600.4	598.3
2015	589.0	587.9	592.2	602.2	607.4	613.4	618.5	620.1	614.0	613.3	613.2	613.3	607.0
2016	596.7	596.6	601.7	611.3	612.3	619.9	621.2	622.5	617.3	616.4	617.7	615.8	612.5
2017	601.6	607.4	612.6	620.8	624.0	631.9	632.1	632.2	626.0	625.7	626.7	628.9	622.5
2018	613.8	618.4	625.2	631.1	635.5	642.3	642.7	642.7	629.1	630.7	630.5	628.1	630.8
Goods Producing													
2010	88.0	87.7	88.4	89.4	89.7	89.3	89.6	89.4	89.0	88.7	88.5	87.8	88.8
2011	85.7	85.7	86.7	86.6	87.3	87.6	88.3	88.3	87.8	86.9	86.8	86.7	87.0
2012	86.6	86.8	87.3	86.8	86.4	86.7	89.6	89.6	89.8	89.6	89.6	89.6	88.2
2013	88.2	88.6	88.8	89.0	89.2	89.8	90.4	90.4	90.1	89.5	89.7	89.8	89.5
2014	88.4	88.3	88.7	89.4	89.8	90.4	90.5	90.3	89.8	89.7	89.8	89.7	89.6
2015	88.5	88.2	88.6	89.9	90.0	90.6	91.4	91.0	90.5	90.7	90.2	90.0	90.0
2016	88.0	87.2	87.2	86.8	86.8	87.6	88.5	88.6	88.8	89.0	89.3	89.3	88.1
2017	88.3	88.9	89.4	89.8	90.2	90.8	90.8	91.0	90.9	91.5	92.0	92.5	90.5
2018	91.2	92.5	93.2	94.0	94.7	95.7	96.2	96.3	95.0	94.8	95.2	95.9	94.6
Service-Providing													
2010	632.6	632.4	639.1	648.7	653.9	659.1	655.0	655.1	650.7	651.4	651.0	651.0	648.3
2011	635.1	636.8	644.0	653.2	656.0	663.4	661.1	660.7	657.7	656.0	656.6	656.8	653.1
2012	641.9	644.9	650.8	657.9	660.6	667.7	661.7	663.4	658.9	663.9	665.7	666.1	658.6
2013	652.0	654.0	659.8	666.0	669.2	675.3	673.2	675.0	668.5	669.2	670.5	670.4	666.9
2014	654.2	654.0	660.0	668.8	672.9	677.7	674.3	677.0	671.0	670.6	671.6	671.7	668.7
2015	659.4	660.2	663.5	673.6	677.7	683.1	683.5	685.4	680.9	683.4	685.3	685.2	676.8
2016	667.3	669.8	675.8	685.7	685.8	692.7	688.9	690.5	687.5	688.5	690.8	688.8	684.3
2017	672.5	679.5	684.1	692.4	693.8	701.9	697.8	697.9	694.1	695.0	697.7	698.9	692.1
2018	681.6	687.0	693.6	698.8	701.8	708.0	702.2	701.7	692.2	695.0	695.9	693.2	695.9
Mining, Logging, and Construction													
2010	35.8	35.5	36.2	37.1	37.5	37.4	37.8	37.7	37.3	36.9	36.8	36.3	36.9
2011	34.8	34.9	35.1	35.5	35.6	35.7	35.6	35.5	35.0	34.6	34.5	34.4	35.1
2012	33.4	33.5	33.8	34.2	34.7	35.4	35.5	35.3	34.6	34.9	34.6	34.5	34.5
2013	33.9	34.1	34.4	34.4	34.7	35.2	35.4	35.4	35.1	34.6	34.7	34.5	34.7
2014	33.6	33.3	33.6	34.1	34.4	34.9	35.1	35.2	34.9	34.8	34.8	34.8	34.5
2015	34.1	34.1	34.4	35.6	36.0	36.4	37.1	37.0	36.6	36.9	36.8	36.8	36.0
2016	35.6	35.5	35.8	35.7	35.6	36.1	36.7	36.6	36.7	36.9	37.1	37.1	36.3
2017	36.3	36.7	37.0	37.2	37.6	38.1	37.8	38.0	37.6	37.8	37.9	38.0	37.5
2018	36.8	37.3	37.6	37.9	38.2	38.6	38.9	38.8	37.9	37.6	37.7	38.0	37.9
Manufacturing													
2010	52.2	52.2	52.2	52.3	52.2	51.9	51.8	51.7	51.7	51.8	51.7	51.5	51.9
2011	50.9	50.8	51.6	51.1	51.7	51.9	52.7	52.8	52.8	52.3	52.3	52.3	51.9
2012	53.2	53.3	53.5	52.6	51.7	51.3	54.1	54.3	55.2	54.7	55.0	55.1	53.7
2013	54.3	54.5	54.4	54.6	54.5	54.6	55.0	55.0	55.0	54.9	55.0	55.3	54.8
2014	54.8	55.0	55.1	55.3	55.4	55.5	55.4	55.1	54.9	54.9	55.0	54.9	55.1
2015	54.4	54.1	54.2	54.3	54.0	54.2	54.3	54.0	53.9	53.8	53.4	53.2	54.0
2016	52.4	51.7	51.4	51.1	51.2	51.5	51.8	52.0	52.1	52.1	52.2	52.2	51.8
2017	52.0	52.2	52.4	52.6	52.6	52.7	53.0	53.0	53.3	53.7	54.1	54.5	53.0
2018	54.4	55.2	55.6	56.1	56.5	57.1	57.3	57.5	57.1	57.2	57.5	57.9	56.6

Employment by Industry: Virginia Beach-Norfolk-Newport News, VA-NC, 2010–2018—*Continued*

(Numbers in thousands, not seasonally adjusted)

Industry and year	January	February	March	April	May	June	July	August	September	October	November	December	Annual average
Trade, Transportation, and Utilities													
2010	125.7	124.2	125.2	126.6	128.0	128.4	128.6	128.6	127.1	128.5	130.9	132.3	127.8
2011	126.2	125.2	125.7	127.0	127.5	128.3	127.8	127.9	126.6	127.2	129.9	131.4	127.6
2012	125.5	124.3	125.2	126.0	127.2	128.0	127.5	126.9	125.6	127.4	130.6	131.6	127.2
2013	125.6	124.4	124.9	125.5	126.8	127.9	128.5	128.9	127.8	128.5	131.8	133.1	127.8
2014	126.4	125.3	125.6	126.7	127.7	128.8	129.0	129.5	128.8	129.9	133.5	134.7	128.8
2015	128.5	127.5	127.7	128.5	129.8	130.9	131.9	132.0	130.8	131.5	135.1	136.1	130.9
2016	130.0	129.2	129.8	131.3	132.8	133.8	133.4	133.8	133.3	134.1	137.6	137.6	133.1
2017	131.3	130.6	131.0	131.9	133.1	134.7	134.0	134.1	133.2	133.5	136.9	137.0	133.4
2018	130.1	129.4	129.6	129.7	131.8	131.6	131.3	131.2	129.4	130.5	132.8	132.5	130.8
Wholesale Trade													
2010	20.7	20.6	20.6	20.9	20.9	20.9	21.0	21.0	20.9	20.9	21.0	20.9	20.9
2011	20.6	20.5	20.6	20.6	20.7	20.7	20.6	20.5	20.3	20.2	20.1	20.3	20.5
2012	20.1	20.1	20.1	20.0	20.0	20.1	20.1	20.0	19.8	19.9	19.9	19.9	20.0
2013	19.4	19.4	19.4	19.3	19.4	19.4	19.5	19.6	19.5	19.5	19.5	19.6	19.5
2014	19.4	19.5	19.4	19.5	19.6	19.4	19.4	19.4	19.3	19.3	19.4	19.5	19.4
2015	19.2	19.2	19.1	19.2	19.2	19.3	19.4	19.3	19.3	19.3	19.3	19.4	19.3
2016	19.0	19.0	18.9	18.9	19.0	19.1	19.1	19.0	18.9	18.8	18.9	19.0	19.0
2017	18.9	18.8	18.8	19.0	19.0	19.1	19.0	18.9	18.8	18.9	18.8	19.0	18.9
2018	18.5	18.6	18.6	18.6	18.7	18.8	18.8	18.8	18.7	18.6	18.7	18.8	18.7
Retail Trade													
2010	82.8	81.6	82.5	83.4	84.4	84.7	84.4	84.5	83.0	83.8	86.0	87.4	84.0
2011	82.6	81.9	82.3	83.4	84.2	84.9	84.6	84.7	83.5	84.1	86.7	88.0	84.2
2012	83.3	81.9	82.8	83.4	84.3	84.8	84.4	84.0	82.9	84.3	87.6	88.4	84.3
2013	83.8	83.0	83.5	84.0	84.9	85.7	85.9	86.2	85.2	85.8	88.7	89.9	85.6
2014	84.1	83.1	83.4	84.4	85.1	86.1	86.2	86.7	86.0	87.2	90.1	90.8	86.1
2015	86.0	84.9	85.3	85.9	86.9	87.6	88.0	88.2	87.2	87.5	90.6	91.1	87.4
2016	86.6	86.0	86.6	87.7	88.6	89.2	88.8	89.2	88.7	89.3	92.0	91.7	88.7
2017	87.0	86.4	86.8	87.4	88.3	89.6	89.3	89.3	88.5	88.6	91.8	91.4	88.7
2018	86.5	85.7	85.9	86.1	87.7	87.1	86.6	86.3	84.9	86.3	88.2	87.7	86.6
Transportation and Utilities													
2010	22.2	22.0	22.1	22.3	22.7	22.8	23.2	23.1	23.2	23.8	23.9	24.0	22.9
2011	23.0	22.8	22.8	23.0	22.6	22.7	22.6	22.7	22.8	22.9	23.1	23.1	22.8
2012	22.1	22.3	22.3	22.6	22.9	23.1	23.0	22.9	22.9	23.2	23.1	23.3	22.8
2013	22.4	22.0	22.0	22.2	22.5	22.8	23.1	23.1	23.1	23.2	23.6	23.6	22.8
2014	22.9	22.7	22.8	22.8	23.0	23.3	23.4	23.4	23.5	23.4	24.1	24.4	23.3
2015	23.3	23.4	23.3	23.4	23.7	24.0	24.5	24.5	24.3	24.7	25.2	25.6	24.2
2016	24.4	24.2	24.3	24.7	25.2	25.5	25.5	25.6	25.7	26.0	26.7	26.9	25.4
2017	25.4	25.4	25.4	25.5	25.8	26.0	25.7	25.9	25.9	26.0	26.3	26.6	25.8
2018	25.1	25.1	25.1	25.0	25.4	25.7	25.9	26.1	25.8	25.6	25.9	26.0	25.6
Information													
2010	12.6	12.4	12.5	12.3	12.4	12.4	12.2	12.2	12.0	11.8	11.8	11.7	12.2
2011	11.6	11.5	11.6	11.6	11.7	11.8	11.9	10.9	11.6	11.4	11.4	11.6	11.6
2012	11.6	11.6	11.7	11.7	11.8	11.8	11.5	11.7	11.3	11.4	11.6	11.6	11.6
2013	11.5	11.6	11.6	11.4	11.6	11.6	11.6	11.6	11.3	11.3	11.4	11.2	11.5
2014	11.2	10.9	10.9	10.8	11.2	11.0	11.0	11.1	10.8	10.8	10.8	10.8	10.9
2015	10.8	10.7	10.7	10.8	11.0	11.0	11.2	11.0	10.8	11.0	11.1	11.1	10.9
2016	11.3	11.3	11.1	11.4	10.7	11.5	11.4	11.2	11.0	11.0	11.0	11.2	11.2
2017	11.2	11.3	11.2	11.2	11.3	11.4	11.4	11.2	11.0	10.9	11.0	11.2	11.2
2018	10.8	11.0	11.0	11.0	11.1	11.1	10.9	10.9	10.4	10.4	10.4	10.3	10.8
Financial Activities													
2010	36.1	35.9	35.9	36.2	36.2	37.1	37.3	37.4	36.8	36.2	36.2	36.1	36.5
2011	36.0	36.1	36.1	36.9	37.0	37.6	37.9	37.6	37.0	36.6	36.5	36.9	36.9
2012	36.4	36.7	36.8	37.3	37.1	37.9	38.3	38.2	37.8	37.7	37.6	37.7	37.5
2013	37.1	37.1	37.2	37.8	38.0	38.6	38.7	38.5	38.0	37.7	37.7	37.8	37.9
2014	36.9	37.0	37.2	37.5	37.9	38.4	38.6	38.5	38.2	37.7	37.6	37.8	37.8
2015	37.6	37.8	37.8	37.6	37.9	38.4	38.7	38.6	38.2	37.9	37.5	37.6	38.0
2016	37.0	36.8	37.0	37.5	37.8	38.5	38.6	38.5	38.0	37.9	37.7	37.8	37.8
2017	37.0	37.2	37.2	37.3	37.7	38.4	38.7	38.7	38.5	38.2	38.2	38.3	38.0
2018	38.4	38.4	38.6	38.5	38.9	39.5	39.4	39.4	38.7	38.6	38.7	38.6	38.8

Employment by Industry: Virginia Beach-Norfolk-Newport News, VA-NC, 2010–2018—*Continued*

(Numbers in thousands, not seasonally adjusted)

Industry and year	January	February	March	April	May	June	July	August	September	October	November	December	Annual average
Professional and Business Services													
2010	96.8	96.3	96.5	97.8	96.6	97.5	98.9	99.0	98.7	98.7	99.0	99.0	97.9
2011	96.5	96.5	96.9	98.0	97.7	98.6	99.5	100.4	100.7	99.5	99.3	99.0	98.6
2012	97.6	98.2	98.6	99.3	98.7	99.7	99.6	100.4	99.9	101.5	101.4	101.7	99.7
2013	101.3	101.7	102.2	102.7	102.3	103.1	103.2	103.8	102.1	102.6	102.9	102.3	102.5
2014	101.6	102.1	103.1	104.9	104.5	105.5	105.5	106.1	104.9	105.5	104.9	104.3	104.4
2015	102.8	103.0	103.3	104.7	104.8	105.4	106.3	107.0	106.0	106.0	105.5	105.2	105.0
2016	102.2	102.9	102.5	104.1	103.1	104.5	105.4	105.9	105.4	105.6	105.8	105.3	104.4
2017	103.9	106.5	107.4	109.3	108.5	110.1	110.0	110.5	110.5	109.9	110.5	111.2	109.0
2018	109.4	111.7	113.0	114.7	114.0	115.5	115.1	115.5	113.2	115.5	115.4	113.1	113.8
Education and Health Services													
2010	93.4	93.8	94.7	95.0	93.9	93.3	93.7	94.1	94.7	96.5	96.8	96.9	94.7
2011	96.3	97.1	97.7	98.4	97.3	97.0	97.3	97.6	99.1	99.5	99.7	98.4	98.0
2012	98.8	99.6	99.9	100.4	99.1	99.2	98.6	99.6	101.2	102.9	103.3	102.5	100.4
2013	102.9	103.6	103.8	104.7	103.0	103.0	102.4	103.9	105.2	106.0	106.6	105.3	104.2
2014	105.1	105.3	105.3	106.2	104.7	104.1	103.8	105.0	106.0	106.4	106.4	105.3	105.3
2015	106.6	106.9	107.0	108.8	107.3	106.8	107.5	108.8	110.2	111.4	111.8	110.3	108.6
2016	110.3	110.7	111.1	112.2	110.2	109.3	108.8	110.0	111.6	112.3	112.4	110.7	110.8
2017	110.9	112.1	112.4	112.7	111.0	110.4	110.3	111.2	112.1	113.7	113.5	113.3	112.0
2018	113.0	114.3	114.8	114.4	112.2	112.2	112.3	113.0	113.8	114.0	113.8	113.2	113.4
Leisure and Hospitality													
2010	74.0	74.9	78.2	83.7	87.2	91.5	92.0	91.1	86.3	83.2	79.6	79.1	83.4
2011	74.0	74.9	79.1	83.6	87.2	91.8	92.0	91.0	85.3	82.9	79.3	79.3	83.4
2012	75.0	76.1	80.3	83.7	87.4	91.2	91.3	91.3	86.2	83.6	80.4	81.1	84.0
2013	76.8	77.0	81.2	84.7	88.7	92.3	93.6	93.0	87.6	85.3	81.5	81.9	85.3
2014	77.9	77.4	81.1	85.3	90.0	93.3	93.0	92.5	87.0	84.9	81.9	82.3	85.6
2015	78.9	78.5	81.5	86.3	90.6	94.0	95.2	95.4	91.6	88.8	86.0	87.0	87.8
2016	82.4	83.1	87.2	91.7	94.4	98.1	98.5	98.0	93.0	90.2	87.6	87.9	91.0
2017	83.2	84.9	87.8	92.7	96.1	99.6	100.3	99.2	93.8	92.1	88.9	89.7	92.4
2018	85.6	85.8	89.3	93.0	96.7	100.1	100.9	99.9	92.8	91.1	88.6	89.0	92.7
Other Services													
2010	33.3	33.3	33.8	34.2	34.5	34.6	34.8	34.7	34.3	34.4	34.2	33.8	34.2
2011	33.5	33.7	34.2	34.8	35.0	35.3	35.4	35.4	35.1	35.0	34.8	34.7	34.7
2012	34.0	34.3	34.7	35.8	35.9	36.2	36.0	36.1	35.6	36.0	35.9	35.8	35.5
2013	35.4	35.6	35.8	36.2	36.4	36.7	36.8	36.5	36.1	35.9	35.8	35.7	36.1
2014	35.1	35.2	35.6	35.9	36.3	36.6	36.6	36.6	36.3	35.8	35.6	35.5	35.9
2015	35.3	35.3	35.6	35.6	36.0	36.3	36.3	36.3	35.9	36.0	36.0	36.0	35.9
2016	35.5	35.4	35.8	36.3	36.5	36.6	36.6	36.5	36.2	36.3	36.3	36.0	36.2
2017	35.8	35.9	36.2	35.9	36.1	36.5	36.6	36.3	36.0	35.9	35.7	35.7	36.1
2018	35.3	35.3	35.7	35.8	36.1	36.6	36.6	36.5	35.8	35.8	35.6	35.5	35.9
Government													
2010	160.7	161.6	162.3	162.9	165.1	164.3	157.5	158.0	160.8	162.1	162.5	162.1	161.7
2011	161.0	161.8	162.7	162.9	162.6	163.0	159.3	159.9	162.3	163.9	165.7	165.5	162.6
2012	163.0	164.1	163.6	163.7	163.4	163.7	158.9	159.2	161.3	163.4	164.9	164.1	162.8
2013	161.4	163.0	163.1	163.0	162.4	162.1	158.4	158.8	160.4	161.9	162.8	163.1	161.7
2014	160.0	160.8	161.2	161.5	160.6	160.0	156.8	157.7	159.0	159.6	160.8	161.0	159.9
2015	158.9	160.5	159.9	161.3	160.3	160.3	156.4	156.3	157.4	160.8	162.3	161.9	159.7
2016	158.6	160.4	161.3	161.2	160.3	160.4	156.2	156.6	159.0	161.1	162.4	162.3	160.0
2017	159.2	161.0	160.9	161.4	160.0	160.8	156.5	156.7	159.0	160.8	163.0	162.5	160.2
2018	159.0	161.1	161.6	161.7	161.0	161.4	155.7	155.3	158.1	159.1	160.6	161.0	159.6

Employment by Industry: Providence-Warwick, RI-MA NECTA, 2010–2018

(Numbers in thousands, not seasonally adjusted)

Industry and year	January	February	March	April	May	June	July	August	September	October	November	December	Annual average
Total Nonfarm													
2010	524.3	526.5	530.6	538.8	547.3	547.3	540.2	541.3	546.9	549.1	550.6	548.2	540.9
2011	527.8	531.1	533.5	544.9	550.7	552.5	543.4	542.6	550.2	552.9	553.2	550.5	544.4
2012	532.8	537.0	541.0	548.4	555.6	557.2	546.9	549.4	557.1	558.1	558.4	558.7	550.1
2013	539.8	541.3	545.4	554.9	563.3	567.0	556.9	557.9	565.1	568.9	568.4	566.6	558.0
2014	548.2	550.8	554.1	565.1	573.7	574.8	566.3	566.8	575.3	578.4	579.8	579.1	567.7
2015	558.4	556.4	561.0	573.0	582.3	583.7	576.7	574.9	581.8	586.8	588.1	587.5	575.9
2016	566.9	569.9	575.0	582.5	588.3	591.3	583.3	581.8	587.3	590.7	591.4	589.9	583.2
2017	571.6	573.9	576.8	586.0	593.4	597.2	588.8	589.8	593.1	596.1	596.8	596.2	588.3
2018	574.6	579.7	582.2	590.5	598.9	601.3	592.9	592.0	596.4	600.6	598.9	597.7	592.1
Total Private													
2010	452.8	455.0	458.4	466.6	473.1	474.8	473.9	475.2	477.3	477.8	478.5	476.4	470.0
2011	456.8	460.0	461.8	473.3	478.9	481.1	478.4	477.5	480.9	482.2	482.3	479.5	474.4
2012	462.6	466.4	470.3	477.5	483.9	487.0	482.2	484.4	487.9	487.4	487.1	487.5	480.4
2013	469.2	471.1	474.7	484.1	491.5	496.1	491.2	493.0	495.5	497.6	496.9	494.7	488.0
2014	477.4	479.8	482.9	493.6	501.2	503.2	500.6	501.7	505.0	506.9	507.6	507.3	497.3
2015	487.2	485.3	489.8	501.5	510.2	512.4	511.1	510.1	512.4	515.5	516.7	515.8	505.7
2016	495.8	498.8	503.2	511.1	516.3	519.7	517.1	516.2	517.1	519.0	519.2	517.9	512.6
2017	500.1	502.4	504.9	514.4	521.1	525.3	522.3	523.7	522.4	523.8	524.8	523.7	517.4
2018	502.5	507.6	510.0	518.5	525.4	528.5	526.0	525.8	525.1	527.6	525.6	524.3	520.6
Goods Producing													
2010	67.0	66.6	67.0	69.0	70.7	71.7	71.3	72.5	72.2	72.1	72.0	70.9	70.3
2011	67.2	66.6	67.1	69.5	70.7	71.8	71.3	72.1	71.8	71.7	71.4	70.4	70.1
2012	67.3	66.9	67.7	69.4	70.2	71.5	70.6	71.7	71.4	71.5	71.2	70.9	70.0
2013	67.5	66.7	67.9	69.6	71.3	72.3	71.1	72.6	72.6	72.5	72.6	71.7	70.7
2014	68.9	68.1	68.6	71.1	72.9	73.9	73.0	74.0	73.9	73.9	73.9	73.4	72.1
2015	70.3	69.1	69.7	72.0	73.7	74.6	74.6	75.3	74.9	75.1	75.3	74.8	73.3
2016	71.4	70.8	71.8	73.4	74.6	75.5	75.1	75.6	75.1	75.2	74.9	74.0	74.0
2017	71.2	70.7	71.0	73.5	74.7	75.9	75.5	76.2	75.7	76.0	75.9	75.4	74.3
2018	72.1	72.9	73.3	74.8	76.1	77.0	76.1	76.7	76.5	76.1	75.7	75.3	75.2
Service-Providing													
2010	457.3	459.9	463.6	469.8	476.6	475.6	468.9	468.8	474.7	477.0	478.6	477.3	470.7
2011	460.6	464.5	466.4	475.4	480.0	480.7	472.1	470.5	478.4	481.2	481.8	480.1	474.3
2012	465.5	470.1	473.3	479.0	485.4	485.7	476.3	477.7	485.7	486.6	487.2	487.8	480.0
2013	472.3	474.6	477.5	485.3	492.0	494.7	485.8	485.3	492.5	496.4	495.8	494.9	487.3
2014	479.3	482.7	485.5	494.0	500.8	500.9	493.3	492.8	501.4	504.5	505.9	505.7	495.6
2015	488.1	487.3	491.3	501.0	508.6	509.1	502.1	499.6	506.9	511.7	512.8	512.7	502.6
2016	495.5	499.1	503.2	509.1	513.7	515.8	508.2	506.2	512.2	515.5	516.5	515.9	509.2
2017	500.4	503.2	505.8	512.5	518.7	521.3	513.3	513.6	517.4	520.1	520.9	520.8	514.0
2018	502.5	506.8	508.9	515.7	522.8	524.3	516.8	515.3	519.9	524.5	523.2	522.4	516.9
Mining and Logging													
2010	0.1	0.1	0.1	0.2	0.2	0.2	0.2	0.2	0.2	0.2	0.2	0.2	0.2
2011	0.1	0.1	0.1	0.2	0.2	0.2	0.2	0.2	0.2	0.2	0.2	0.2	0.2
2012	0.1	0.1	0.1	0.2	0.2	0.2	0.2	0.2	0.2	0.2	0.2	0.2	0.2
2013	0.1	0.1	0.1	0.2	0.2	0.2	0.2	0.2	0.2	0.2	0.2	0.2	0.2
2014	0.1	0.1	0.1	0.2	0.2	0.2	0.2	0.2	0.2	0.2	0.2	0.2	0.2
2015	0.2	0.2	0.2	0.2	0.2	0.2	0.2	0.2	0.2	0.2	0.2	0.2	0.2
2016	0.2	0.2	0.2	0.2	0.2	0.2	0.2	0.2	0.2	0.2	0.2	0.2	0.2
2017	0.2	0.2	0.2	0.2	0.2	0.2	0.2	0.2	0.2	0.2	0.2	0.2	0.2
2018	0.1	0.2	0.2	0.2	0.2	0.2	0.2	0.2	0.2	0.2	0.2	0.2	0.2
Construction													
2010	16.8	16.3	16.8	18.8	20.1	20.7	21.4	21.6	21.0	20.8	20.6	19.5	19.5
2011	16.6	16.0	16.4	18.5	19.7	20.5	21.2	21.1	20.8	20.8	20.7	19.8	19.3
2012	17.6	17.0	17.8	19.3	19.9	20.8	21.2	21.1	20.8	20.8	20.5	20.1	19.7
2013	17.4	16.9	17.6	19.2	20.6	21.2	21.8	21.9	21.8	21.7	21.4	20.3	20.2
2014	18.2	17.5	17.9	20.0	21.4	22.0	22.4	22.3	22.2	22.2	22.0	21.3	20.8
2015	18.7	17.7	18.2	20.3	21.8	22.4	23.1	23.2	23.0	23.1	23.1	22.7	21.4
2016	20.2	19.6	20.4	22.2	23.4	23.9	24.4	24.5	24.3	24.3	23.9	22.9	22.8
2017	20.7	20.3	20.4	22.6	23.7	24.5	24.9	25.0	24.6	24.7	24.5	23.7	23.3
2018	21.0	21.6	21.8	23.7	24.9	25.6	25.7	25.7	25.6	25.4	25.0	24.6	24.2

Employment by Industry: Providence-Warwick, RI-MA NECTA, 2010–2018—*Continued*

(Numbers in thousands, not seasonally adjusted)

Industry and year	January	February	March	April	May	June	July	August	September	October	November	December	Annual average
Manufacturing													
2010	50.1	50.2	50.1	50.0	50.4	50.8	49.7	50.7	51.0	51.1	51.2	51.2	50.5
2011	50.5	50.5	50.6	50.8	50.8	51.1	49.9	50.8	50.8	50.7	50.5	50.4	50.6
2012	49.6	49.8	49.8	49.9	50.1	50.5	49.2	50.4	50.4	50.5	50.5	50.6	50.1
2013	50.0	49.7	50.2	50.2	50.5	50.9	49.1	50.5	50.6	50.6	51.0	51.2	50.4
2014	50.6	50.5	50.6	50.9	51.3	51.7	50.4	51.5	51.5	51.5	51.7	51.9	51.2
2015	51.4	51.2	51.3	51.5	51.7	52.0	51.3	51.9	51.7	51.8	52.0	51.9	51.6
2016	51.0	51.0	51.2	51.0	51.0	51.4	50.5	50.9	50.6	50.7	50.8	50.9	50.9
2017	50.3	50.2	50.4	50.7	50.8	51.2	50.4	51.0	50.9	51.1	51.2	51.5	50.8
2018	51.0	51.1	51.3	50.9	51.0	51.2	50.2	50.8	50.7	50.5	50.5	50.5	50.8
Trade, Transportation, and Utilities													
2010	93.5	92.6	93.0	92.5	93.2	94.4	93.2	93.4	94.3	95.2	96.9	97.8	94.2
2011	93.6	93.0	92.7	94.0	94.9	95.5	94.2	94.3	95.5	96.5	98.5	99.7	95.2
2012	95.4	94.3	94.5	94.9	96.1	97.0	94.9	95.2	96.3	97.0	99.0	99.5	96.2
2013	94.5	93.7	93.6	94.5	95.7	96.6	95.0	95.3	96.2	97.2	99.0	100.3	96.0
2014	95.7	95.1	94.8	95.8	96.9	97.8	96.1	96.3	97.5	99.0	101.2	102.7	97.4
2015	98.1	96.8	96.6	97.8	98.8	99.9	98.3	98.4	99.3	100.0	102.4	103.7	99.2
2016	98.9	98.3	98.0	98.3	99.2	100.0	98.5	98.5	99.3	101.0	103.7	105.3	99.9
2017	100.4	99.2	99.0	99.7	101.0	101.8	100.6	100.6	101.6	103.1	105.5	106.7	101.6
2018	102.1	100.8	100.6	100.9	102.1	102.8	101.4	101.0	101.6	102.6	105.5	106.5	102.3
Wholesale Trade													
2010	19.4	19.4	19.4	19.4	19.7	19.8	19.8	19.8	19.8	19.8	19.9	19.9	19.7
2011	19.5	19.6	19.1	19.3	19.4	19.5	19.7	19.6	19.7	19.7	19.8	20.0	19.6
2012	19.8	19.9	20.0	20.0	20.1	20.3	20.2	20.2	20.1	20.1	20.1	20.0	20.1
2013	19.7	19.7	19.8	19.8	20.0	20.1	20.0	20.1	20.0	20.1	20.1	20.1	20.0
2014	19.8	19.9	19.8	19.8	20.0	20.0	20.1	20.2	20.1	20.2	20.3	20.3	20.0
2015	20.1	20.1	20.0	20.2	20.2	20.3	20.2	20.2	20.1	20.0	20.2	20.2	20.2
2016	19.7	19.8	19.7	20.0	20.0	20.0	19.9	20.0	19.9	19.8	19.8	19.9	19.9
2017	19.6	19.6	19.7	19.6	19.7	19.8	19.8	19.8	19.6	19.7	19.8	19.8	19.7
2018	19.6	19.6	19.6	19.7	19.7	19.8	19.7	19.7	19.5	19.7	19.7	19.5	19.7
Retail Trade													
2010	62.2	61.2	61.6	60.8	61.0	61.8	61.8	62.0	61.6	62.4	64.0	64.7	62.1
2011	61.6	60.9	61.1	61.8	62.4	62.7	62.4	62.8	62.4	63.4	65.3	65.9	62.7
2012	62.6	61.5	61.6	61.9	62.7	63.2	62.6	62.7	62.7	63.4	65.4	65.7	63.0
2013	62.1	61.2	61.0	61.6	62.4	63.0	62.7	62.8	62.6	63.5	65.2	66.0	62.8
2014	62.8	62.1	61.9	62.7	63.4	63.9	63.4	63.3	63.3	64.7	66.6	67.6	63.8
2015	64.2	63.0	63.1	63.7	64.4	65.3	65.0	65.1	64.8	65.5	67.6	68.4	65.0
2016	65.2	64.4	64.4	64.3	64.9	65.3	65.1	65.1	64.6	65.1	66.8	67.2	65.2
2017	64.2	63.1	62.9	63.9	64.7	65.0	64.7	64.8	64.4	65.4	67.1	67.4	64.8
2018	64.5	63.8	63.3	63.8	64.8	65.1	64.9	64.8	64.3	65.2	66.8	67.7	64.9
Transportation and Utilities													
2010	11.9	12.0	12.0	12.3	12.5	12.8	11.6	11.6	12.9	13.0	13.0	13.2	12.4
2011	12.5	12.5	12.5	12.9	13.1	13.3	12.1	11.9	13.4	13.4	13.4	13.8	12.9
2012	13.0	12.9	12.9	13.0	13.3	13.5	12.1	12.3	13.5	13.5	13.5	13.8	13.1
2013	12.7	12.8	12.8	13.1	13.3	13.5	12.3	12.4	13.6	13.6	13.7	14.2	13.2
2014	13.1	13.1	13.1	13.3	13.5	13.9	12.6	12.8	14.1	14.1	14.3	14.8	13.6
2015	13.8	13.7	13.5	13.9	14.2	14.3	13.1	13.1	14.4	14.5	14.6	15.1	14.0
2016	14.0	14.1	13.9	14.0	14.3	14.7	13.5	13.4	14.8	16.1	17.1	18.2	14.8
2017	16.6	16.5	16.4	16.2	16.6	17.0	16.1	16.0	17.6	18.0	18.6	19.5	17.1
2018	18.0	17.4	17.7	17.4	17.6	17.9	16.8	16.5	17.8	17.7	19.0	19.3	17.8
Information													
2010	9.6	9.7	9.8	9.6	9.6	9.6	9.7	10.0	10.1	9.9	9.9	9.9	9.8
2011	9.4	9.3	9.4	9.9	10.1	10.0	9.8	8.8	9.5	9.4	9.5	9.6	9.6
2012	9.3	9.3	9.4	9.2	9.0	9.2	8.9	9.0	8.8	8.8	8.8	8.8	9.0
2013	8.8	8.8	8.6	8.4	8.6	8.6	8.4	8.5	8.3	8.3	8.4	8.4	8.5
2014	8.5	8.3	8.3	8.3	8.4	8.3	8.4	8.5	8.3	8.2	8.2	8.3	8.3
2015	8.0	7.9	8.0	8.1	8.1	7.9	8.0	7.9	8.0	8.1	7.3	7.2	7.9
2016	7.2	7.3	7.2	7.4	6.5	7.4	7.5	7.3	7.4	7.3	7.3	7.3	7.3
2017	7.3	7.5	7.4	7.4	7.5	7.6	7.4	7.4	7.4	7.3	7.4	7.3	7.4
2018	7.1	7.2	7.2	7.1	7.0	7.1	7.0	7.2	7.2	7.3	7.5	7.3	7.2

Employment by Industry: Providence-Warwick, RI-MA NECTA, 2010–2018—*Continued*

(Numbers in thousands, not seasonally adjusted)

Industry and year	January	February	March	April	May	June	July	August	September	October	November	December	Annual average
Financial Activities													
2010	34.3	34.3	34.5	34.4	34.6	34.7	34.8	34.7	34.8	35.0	35.1	35.2	34.7
2011	34.6	34.7	34.8	34.9	34.8	35.4	35.0	35.1	35.1	35.1	35.4	35.3	35.0
2012	35.1	35.3	35.5	35.6	35.9	36.1	36.1	36.0	36.1	36.1	36.2	36.2	35.9
2013	35.9	36.2	36.4	36.4	36.4	36.6	36.7	36.5	36.3	36.4	36.4	36.6	36.4
2014	36.2	36.1	36.2	36.6	36.7	36.9	37.0	36.8	36.7	36.7	36.7	36.7	36.6
2015	36.4	36.6	36.8	37.1	37.3	37.5	37.4	37.3	37.6	38.2	38.7	38.8	37.5
2016	37.9	38.1	38.2	38.0	38.0	38.4	38.4	38.4	38.3	38.3	38.4	38.4	38.2
2017	38.1	38.2	38.2	38.3	38.5	38.8	38.7	38.8	38.7	38.5	38.7	38.6	38.5
2018	38.1	38.2	38.1	38.2	38.1	38.3	38.2	38.1	37.7	37.8	37.7	37.6	38.0
Professional and Business Services													
2010	55.0	55.3	56.2	59.5	59.6	60.4	60.2	60.1	60.2	60.5	60.3	59.2	58.9
2011	56.9	57.4	57.6	59.7	60.0	60.4	60.2	60.7	61.4	61.4	61.2	59.7	59.7
2012	57.8	58.1	59.2	61.3	61.7	62.6	62.1	62.5	62.4	62.3	62.4	62.1	61.2
2013	59.9	60.5	60.8	63.6	64.3	65.8	64.9	65.7	65.8	66.7	66.3	65.5	64.2
2014	62.6	63.5	63.9	66.7	67.3	68.1	68.1	68.7	68.9	69.8	69.9	69.4	67.2
2015	64.9	65.1	65.7	69.0	70.2	70.6	70.7	70.6	70.4	71.1	71.5	71.0	69.2
2016	68.5	68.6	69.2	71.5	72.0	72.7	73.0	73.3	73.4	73.7	73.5	72.9	71.9
2017	70.3	71.0	71.1	73.7	74.0	75.2	75.8	76.0	75.7	76.0	75.7	75.0	74.1
2018	71.7	72.1	72.7	75.2	75.8	76.5	76.5	77.0	76.6	76.4	76.6	76.0	75.3
Education and Health Services													
2010	116.0	118.6	119.6	119.4	119.6	114.9	114.2	114.4	118.3	120.3	121.0	121.1	118.1
2011	116.9	120.2	120.7	121.8	121.8	117.2	116.0	115.2	119.0	122.1	122.1	121.4	119.5
2012	118.0	121.8	122.4	121.5	122.0	117.6	116.0	116.3	122.0	123.3	123.2	124.0	120.7
2013	120.9	123.2	123.8	123.9	123.6	120.4	119.1	118.8	123.3	125.7	125.9	124.4	122.8
2014	121.9	124.1	125.1	125.6	125.1	120.8	120.2	119.7	124.5	126.5	127.0	126.9	124.0
2015	123.4	124.6	126.0	126.6	126.1	122.6	121.8	120.8	125.3	127.7	128.2	127.5	125.1
2016	123.3	126.6	127.6	127.9	127.9	122.7	121.7	121.1	125.1	127.5	127.5	127.1	125.5
2017	124.0	126.3	127.9	128.5	128.2	123.6	122.3	122.4	125.4	126.6	127.3	127.3	125.8
2018	122.3	126.1	126.8	127.7	127.4	123.1	122.5	121.8	126.2	129.9	130.5	130.1	126.2
Leisure and Hospitality													
2010	52.6	52.9	53.3	57.1	60.3	63.3	64.0	63.7	62.0	59.5	57.9	56.9	58.6
2011	53.4	53.9	54.4	58.1	60.9	64.4	64.7	64.3	62.8	60.5	58.5	57.6	59.5
2012	54.6	55.5	56.3	59.7	62.9	66.2	66.4	66.4	64.4	62.3	60.1	59.6	61.2
2013	56.1	56.4	57.7	61.2	64.8	68.3	68.1	68.0	66.2	64.3	61.7	61.1	62.8
2014	57.6	58.4	59.5	62.9	66.8	69.5	69.4	69.4	68.0	65.9	63.7	62.8	64.5
2015	59.6	58.9	60.2	64.0	68.6	71.2	71.5	71.2	69.6	68.0	65.9	65.4	66.2
2016	61.7	62.2	64.0	67.1	70.3	74.2	73.6	73.0	71.0	68.7	66.5	65.4	68.1
2017	61.9	62.6	63.3	66.0	69.7	73.9	73.2	73.6	70.6	69.0	66.9	66.0	68.1
2018	62.6	63.6	64.4	67.5	71.5	75.2	75.3	75.1	71.8	69.3	64.6	63.7	68.7
Other Services													
2010	24.8	25.0	25.0	25.1	25.5	25.8	26.5	26.4	25.4	25.3	25.4	25.4	25.5
2011	24.8	24.9	25.1	25.4	25.7	26.4	27.2	27.0	25.8	25.5	25.7	25.8	25.8
2012	25.1	25.2	25.3	25.9	26.1	26.8	27.2	27.3	26.5	26.1	26.2	26.4	26.2
2013	25.6	25.6	25.9	26.5	26.8	27.5	27.9	27.6	26.8	26.5	26.6	26.7	26.7
2014	26.0	26.2	26.5	26.6	27.1	27.9	28.4	28.3	27.2	26.9	27.0	27.1	27.1
2015	26.5	26.3	26.8	26.9	27.4	28.1	28.8	28.6	27.3	27.3	27.4	27.4	27.4
2016	26.9	26.9	27.2	27.5	27.8	28.8	29.3	29.0	27.5	27.3	27.4	27.5	27.8
2017	26.9	26.9	27.0	27.3	27.5	28.5	28.8	28.7	27.3	27.3	27.4	27.4	27.6
2018	26.5	26.7	26.9	27.1	27.4	28.5	29.0	28.9	27.5	28.2	27.5	27.8	27.7
Government													
2010	71.5	71.5	72.2	72.2	74.2	72.5	66.3	66.1	69.6	71.3	72.1	71.8	70.9
2011	71.0	71.1	71.7	71.6	71.8	71.4	65.0	65.1	69.3	70.7	70.9	71.0	70.1
2012	70.2	70.6	70.7	70.9	71.7	70.2	64.7	65.0	69.2	70.7	71.3	71.2	69.7
2013	70.6	70.2	70.7	70.8	71.8	70.9	65.7	64.9	69.6	71.3	71.5	71.9	70.0
2014	70.8	71.0	71.2	71.5	72.5	71.6	65.7	65.1	70.3	71.5	72.2	71.8	70.4
2015	71.2	71.1	71.2	71.5	72.1	71.3	65.6	64.8	69.4	71.3	71.4	71.7	70.2
2016	71.1	71.1	71.8	71.4	72.0	71.6	66.2	65.6	70.2	71.7	72.2	72.0	70.6
2017	71.5	71.5	71.9	71.6	72.3	71.9	66.5	66.1	70.7	72.3	72.0	72.5	70.9
2018	72.1	72.1	72.2	72.0	73.5	72.8	66.9	66.2	71.3	73.0	73.3	73.4	71.6

Employment by Industry: Milwaukee-Waukesha-West Allis, WI, 2010–2018

(Numbers in thousands, not seasonally adjusted)

Industry and year	January	February	March	April	May	June	July	August	September	October	November	December	Annual average
Total Nonfarm													
2010	793.3	792.8	795.4	804.2	812.0	813.6	811.0	812.7	811.0	817.8	820.2	817.4	808.5
2011	798.9	800.5	804.3	811.8	816.3	820.2	817.5	819.0	818.8	819.4	822.3	818.7	814.0
2012	799.8	803.0	809.8	815.8	825.4	828.3	821.9	824.8	826.2	830.8	835.2	832.3	821.1
2013	808.9	816.7	820.7	826.3	835.9	840.3	835.6	837.5	842.1	843.0	846.3	846.1	833.3
2014	822.3	829.1	830.8	837.2	844.0	851.8	846.3	853.7	852.4	853.8	859.5	858.1	844.9
2015	831.4	839.3	842.5	852.1	859.4	865.0	859.2	864.7	862.0	865.8	867.4	867.3	856.3
2016	845.9	852.6	854.2	863.9	866.1	869.8	865.6	870.8	867.8	868.9	871.1	868.8	863.8
2017	847.8	854.3	859.9	863.8	870.6	876.2	869.8	873.3	869.9	873.5	875.0	878.4	867.7
2018	857.7	864.1	867.4	869.7	874.9	881.9	876.0	879.6	874.6	879.0	878.9	878.1	873.5
Total Private													
2010	701.6	701.2	703.4	712.6	718.0	722.3	726.1	728.7	723.0	727.5	728.4	727.3	718.3
2011	710.0	707.7	712.0	720.2	725.3	729.5	730.3	732.4	730.9	732.9	733.8	729.9	724.6
2012	714.0	715.8	721.0	725.7	734.4	739.0	738.6	739.8	739.4	742.2	744.0	743.4	733.1
2013	724.2	728.6	732.6	738.3	748.2	753.0	753.8	754.1	754.7	755.3	758.4	758.5	746.6
2014	737.3	741.9	743.2	749.8	756.8	764.0	764.3	767.6	764.9	766.4	770.7	770.8	758.1
2015	748.3	751.8	755.2	763.8	771.8	778.2	776.9	780.8	775.1	778.7	780.4	779.9	770.1
2016	760.4	765.0	766.6	774.9	778.5	783.8	784.9	786.5	781.1	780.6	781.3	780.1	777.0
2017	763.1	766.6	772.2	775.5	782.8	790.6	789.2	790.1	784.4	786.3	787.6	790.8	781.6
2018	773.4	777.3	780.7	781.8	787.7	796.9	795.1	797.3	789.7	791.8	790.1	790.7	787.7
Goods Producing													
2010	135.2	133.7	134.0	136.8	138.0	140.5	142.3	143.0	141.6	141.7	140.9	139.1	138.9
2011	136.7	135.9	137.1	140.1	141.7	144.9	145.8	146.2	144.7	144.5	144.1	142.4	142.0
2012	139.8	139.1	140.1	142.4	143.7	146.6	147.5	147.0	145.5	145.3	144.7	143.7	143.8
2013	141.5	141.0	141.6	143.2	145.7	148.3	148.9	149.4	147.6	147.6	147.1	145.1	145.6
2014	142.6	142.4	143.5	145.4	147.7	149.9	151.9	152.4	150.8	149.9	149.9	148.7	147.9
2015	146.3	145.7	146.7	148.6	150.3	152.5	153.2	153.1	151.3	150.9	150.2	149.1	149.8
2016	146.3	146.0	146.5	148.2	149.2	151.4	152.0	152.0	150.0	149.5	149.0	147.5	149.0
2017	145.2	145.2	146.0	147.5	149.1	151.4	151.9	151.6	149.7	149.7	149.5	149.1	148.8
2018	146.7	146.7	147.7	148.9	150.7	153.7	154.7	154.8	153.0	152.8	152.4	150.3	151.0
Service-Providing													
2010	658.1	659.1	661.4	667.4	674.0	673.1	668.7	669.7	669.4	676.1	679.3	678.3	669.6
2011	662.2	664.6	667.2	671.7	674.6	675.3	671.7	672.8	674.1	674.9	678.2	676.3	672.0
2012	660.0	663.9	669.7	673.4	681.7	681.7	674.4	677.8	680.7	685.5	690.5	688.6	677.3
2013	667.4	675.7	679.1	683.1	690.2	692.0	686.7	688.1	694.5	695.4	699.2	701.0	687.7
2014	679.7	686.7	687.3	691.8	696.3	701.9	694.4	701.3	701.6	703.9	709.6	709.4	697.0
2015	685.1	693.6	695.8	703.5	709.1	712.5	706.0	711.6	710.7	714.9	717.2	718.2	706.5
2016	699.6	706.6	707.7	715.7	716.9	718.4	713.6	718.8	717.8	719.4	722.1	721.3	714.8
2017	702.6	709.1	713.9	716.3	721.5	724.8	717.9	721.7	720.2	723.8	725.5	729.3	718.9
2018	711.0	717.4	719.7	720.8	724.2	728.2	721.3	724.8	721.6	726.2	726.5	727.8	722.5
Mining and Logging													
2010	0.3	0.3	0.3	0.4	0.4	0.4	0.4	0.4	0.4	0.4	0.3	0.3	0.4
2011	0.3	0.3	0.3	0.3	0.3	0.4	0.4	0.4	0.4	0.4	0.4	0.3	0.4
2012	0.3	0.3	0.3	0.4	0.4	0.4	0.4	0.4	0.4	0.4	0.4	0.3	0.4
2013	0.3	0.3	0.3	0.4	0.4	0.4	0.4	0.4	0.4	0.4	0.4	0.4	0.4
2014	0.3	0.3	0.3	0.4	0.4	0.4	0.5	0.4	0.4	0.4	0.4	0.4	0.4
2015	0.4	0.4	0.4	0.4	0.5	0.5	0.5	0.5	0.5	0.5	0.5	0.4	0.5
2016	0.4	0.4	0.4	0.4	0.5	0.5	0.5	0.5	0.5	0.5	0.5	0.4	0.5
2017	0.4	0.4	0.4	0.4	0.4	0.5	0.5	0.5	0.5	0.4	0.4	0.4	0.4
2018	0.4	0.4	0.4	0.4	0.5	0.5	0.5	0.5	0.5	0.5	0.4	0.4	0.5
Construction													
2010	23.3	22.5	22.8	25.2	26.2	27.4	27.9	28.2	27.5	27.2	26.2	24.2	25.7
2011	21.6	21.0	21.6	23.8	25.2	26.4	26.7	26.8	26.4	26.2	25.6	23.6	24.6
2012	20.8	20.5	21.2	23.1	24.2	25.4	25.8	25.7	25.3	25.2	24.7	23.4	23.8
2013	21.6	21.6	22.1	23.1	25.8	26.9	27.8	28.3	27.7	27.7	27.2	25.2	25.4
2014	23.2	23.0	23.8	25.6	27.6	28.8	29.7	30.2	29.8	29.4	29.0	27.5	27.3
2015	25.3	25.0	25.7	27.7	29.3	30.4	30.9	30.9	30.2	30.2	29.7	28.6	28.7
2016	26.4	26.4	27.0	28.7	29.9	31.2	31.7	31.8	31.3	31.0	30.7	29.0	29.6
2017	27.4	27.4	28.0	29.7	31.4	32.5	33.1	33.0	32.3	32.4	31.9	30.8	30.8
2018	28.9	28.9	29.7	31.0	32.6	34.1	34.5	34.5	33.8	33.9	33.5	30.8	32.2

Employment by Industry: Milwaukee-Waukesha-West Allis, WI, 2010–2018—*Continued*

(Numbers in thousands, not seasonally adjusted)

Industry and year	January	February	March	April	May	June	July	August	September	October	November	December	Annual average
Manufacturing													
2010	111.6	110.9	110.9	111.2	111.4	112.7	114.0	114.4	113.7	114.1	114.4	114.6	112.8
2011	114.8	114.6	115.2	116.0	116.2	118.1	118.7	119.0	117.9	117.9	118.1	118.5	117.1
2012	118.7	118.3	118.6	118.9	119.1	120.8	121.3	120.9	119.8	119.7	119.6	120.0	119.6
2013	119.6	119.1	119.2	119.7	119.5	121.0	120.7	120.7	119.5	119.5	119.5	119.5	119.8
2014	119.1	119.1	119.4	119.4	119.7	120.7	121.7	121.8	120.6	120.1	120.5	120.8	120.2
2015	120.6	120.3	120.6	120.5	120.5	121.6	121.8	121.7	120.6	120.2	120.0	120.1	120.7
2016	119.5	119.2	119.1	119.1	118.8	119.7	119.8	119.7	118.2	118.0	117.8	118.1	118.9
2017	117.4	117.4	117.6	117.4	117.3	118.4	118.3	118.1	116.9	116.9	117.2	117.9	117.6
2018	117.4	117.4	117.6	117.5	117.6	119.1	119.7	119.8	118.7	118.4	118.5	119.1	118.4
Trade, Transportation, and Utilities													
2010	140.8	138.4	138.6	138.9	140.3	141.1	139.7	140.1	140.5	143.7	144.9	145.6	141.1
2011	140.8	139.1	139.9	140.7	141.5	141.8	141.3	141.7	142.4	144.6	145.9	146.2	142.2
2012	141.9	140.2	140.5	139.6	142.2	142.8	141.7	142.3	142.4	144.0	146.7	147.3	142.6
2013	141.6	140.6	140.9	141.6	143.4	144.4	143.0	143.2	143.2	144.2	146.7	148.0	143.4
2014	142.2	141.3	141.9	142.9	144.0	145.4	143.8	144.2	143.3	144.3	147.2	148.1	144.1
2015	142.9	141.5	141.8	142.5	144.0	145.4	144.5	145.5	144.8	146.1	148.7	148.9	144.7
2016	144.2	143.5	143.7	144.8	145.4	146.0	145.9	146.3	144.9	146.3	148.5	149.3	145.7
2017	145.2	143.8	144.1	143.9	145.4	145.6	145.8	146.6	145.1	146.3	149.3	150.5	146.0
2018	146.9	145.4	146.0	146.0	147.1	147.0	147.7	148.2	145.6	146.8	149.2	149.8	147.1
Wholesale Trade													
2010	37.4	37.2	37.1	37.0	37.2	37.5	37.7	37.7	37.3	37.7	37.7	37.6	37.4
2011	37.2	37.1	37.3	37.5	37.7	37.9	38.4	38.4	38.1	38.6	38.5	38.3	37.9
2012	38.0	38.1	38.3	38.3	38.5	38.8	38.8	38.8	38.3	38.5	38.5	38.7	38.5
2013	38.0	38.0	38.0	38.1	38.2	38.5	38.4	38.5	38.1	38.0	37.9	38.0	38.1
2014	37.6	37.6	37.7	38.0	38.1	38.4	38.4	38.3	37.9	38.0	38.1	38.2	38.0
2015	38.0	37.9	38.1	38.3	38.5	38.9	39.0	39.1	38.5	38.6	38.6	38.7	38.5
2016	38.3	38.4	38.4	38.4	38.5	38.7	38.9	38.9	38.4	38.4	38.3	38.5	38.5
2017	38.3	38.2	38.3	38.2	38.3	38.7	38.7	38.8	38.3	38.3	38.3	38.6	38.4
2018	38.2	38.2	38.3	38.4	38.4	39.1	39.2	39.2	38.7	38.7	38.5	39.2	38.7
Retail Trade													
2010	75.6	73.7	74.1	74.5	75.5	75.8	75.5	75.8	75.4	77.7	78.7	79.3	76.0
2011	75.8	74.2	74.7	75.3	75.7	76.2	76.1	76.6	76.1	77.8	79.1	79.7	76.4
2012	76.4	74.6	74.8	74.8	75.9	76.6	76.5	77.0	76.6	77.9	80.5	80.7	76.9
2013	76.8	75.8	76.0	76.7	78.0	78.8	78.7	78.8	78.2	79.2	81.4	82.4	78.4
2014	78.3	77.3	77.8	78.3	79.0	80.0	79.7	79.9	78.4	79.0	81.6	82.1	79.3
2015	78.3	77.1	77.2	77.5	78.4	79.5	79.7	80.3	79.2	80.3	82.7	82.6	79.4
2016	79.7	78.9	79.1	79.8	80.3	81.1	81.5	81.6	79.8	80.9	82.9	83.2	80.7
2017	80.8	79.4	79.5	79.8	80.4	81.1	81.4	81.6	79.7	80.7	83.5	83.9	81.0
2018	80.4	79.0	79.3	79.1	80.0	80.2	80.7	80.5	77.7	77.8	79.7	79.4	79.5
Transportation and Utilities													
2010	27.8	27.5	27.4	27.4	27.6	27.8	26.5	26.6	27.8	28.3	28.5	28.7	27.7
2011	27.8	27.8	27.9	27.9	28.1	27.7	26.8	26.7	28.2	28.2	28.3	28.2	27.8
2012	27.5	27.5	27.4	26.5	27.8	27.4	26.4	26.5	27.5	27.6	27.7	27.9	27.3
2013	26.8	26.8	26.9	26.8	27.2	27.1	25.9	25.9	26.9	27.0	27.4	27.6	26.9
2014	26.3	26.4	26.4	26.6	26.9	27.0	25.7	26.0	27.0	27.3	27.5	27.8	26.7
2015	26.6	26.5	26.5	26.7	27.1	27.0	25.8	26.1	27.1	27.2	27.4	27.6	26.8
2016	26.2	26.2	26.2	26.6	26.6	26.2	25.5	25.8	26.7	27.0	27.3	27.6	26.5
2017	26.1	26.2	26.3	25.9	26.7	25.8	25.7	26.2	27.1	27.3	27.5	28.0	26.6
2018	28.3	28.2	28.4	28.5	28.7	27.7	27.8	28.5	29.2	30.3	31.0	31.2	29.0
Information													
2010	15.8	15.7	15.7	15.7	15.6	15.8	16.0	15.9	15.7	15.4	15.9	15.8	15.8
2011	15.7	15.7	15.6	15.6	15.6	15.6	15.5	15.6	15.5	15.4	15.4	15.3	15.5
2012	15.1	15.0	14.9	14.9	14.8	15.0	15.0	15.0	14.9	15.0	15.0	14.8	15.0
2013	14.8	14.7	14.6	14.9	15.0	15.0	15.0	15.0	14.9	14.7	14.8	14.6	14.8
2014	14.4	14.5	14.5	14.5	14.5	14.5	14.7	14.6	14.4	14.5	14.6	14.6	14.5
2015	14.4	14.3	14.2	14.2	14.3	14.4	14.3	14.4	14.3	14.5	14.6	14.6	14.4
2016	14.4	14.4	14.4	14.3	14.2	14.3	14.2	14.1	13.9	13.9	13.9	13.9	14.2
2017	14.0	14.0	13.9	13.7	13.7	13.8	13.7	13.6	13.4	13.3	13.4	13.5	13.7
2018	13.5	13.5	13.5	13.4	13.5	13.6	13.6	13.5	13.3	13.4	13.4	13.5	13.5

Employment by Industry: Milwaukee-Waukesha-West Allis, WI, 2010–2018—*Continued*

(Numbers in thousands, not seasonally adjusted)

Industry and year	January	February	March	April	May	June	July	August	September	October	November	December	Annual average
Financial Activities													
2010	54.0	54.0	54.2	54.1	54.0	54.1	54.3	54.2	53.7	53.8	53.7	54.0	54.0
2011	52.9	52.8	52.9	52.9	52.9	53.3	53.2	52.9	52.7	52.5	52.5	51.9	52.8
2012	51.9	51.8	51.9	51.8	52.0	52.4	52.5	52.4	51.7	51.9	51.7	51.9	52.0
2013	51.4	51.4	51.4	51.8	52.0	52.5	53.0	52.5	52.1	52.1	51.9	52.1	52.0
2014	51.2	51.1	51.3	51.3	51.5	52.1	52.3	52.4	51.9	51.7	51.8	52.1	51.7
2015	51.7	51.5	51.7	51.9	52.1	52.7	53.0	52.7	51.7	51.5	51.3	51.6	52.0
2016	51.0	50.8	51.0	50.9	50.9	51.5	51.9	51.7	51.2	51.2	51.1	51.1	51.2
2017	51.2	51.2	51.5	51.4	51.4	51.9	51.8	51.8	51.0	50.8	50.6	50.8	51.3
2018	50.4	50.3	50.5	50.5	50.7	51.6	51.8	51.8	51.2	51.8	51.9	51.8	51.2
Professional and Business Services													
2010	102.6	103.9	102.9	106.5	107.1	108.6	111.1	112.6	112.1	113.5	114.5	114.7	109.2
2011	111.6	111.8	113.1	113.1	112.7	115.3	115.2	116.6	116.5	116.0	116.8	115.7	114.5
2012	114.0	114.8	116.4	116.7	117.6	119.8	119.2	120.1	121.1	121.5	122.0	121.0	118.7
2013	117.4	119.1	121.2	120.5	121.6	123.2	124.0	124.1	125.0	124.1	125.1	125.5	122.6
2014	120.7	121.9	121.3	121.5	123.0	124.4	124.5	126.3	126.1	126.9	127.4	126.4	124.2
2015	121.0	121.7	120.9	123.3	124.4	126.0	126.9	128.6	127.2	128.1	127.9	126.6	125.2
2016	124.1	124.9	124.4	126.2	125.8	127.4	128.4	129.1	128.5	127.6	127.5	127.2	126.8
2017	122.9	123.2	125.2	125.6	126.3	128.3	129.0	129.3	128.8	129.8	129.7	130.8	127.4
2018	125.7	127.2	126.5	126.9	127.1	129.2	127.9	128.6	126.8	125.2	123.6	123.3	126.5
Education and Health Services													
2010	146.2	147.9	148.9	148.4	148.3	146.4	146.0	145.6	145.7	147.5	147.8	147.7	147.2
2011	144.1	144.9	145.2	146.1	146.6	143.3	142.1	141.6	145.4	147.3	147.9	148.0	145.2
2012	143.1	146.4	147.9	148.8	149.1	145.8	144.3	145.2	149.0	151.7	152.0	152.4	148.0
2013	147.8	151.7	151.9	153.0	152.9	150.2	148.8	149.7	154.0	156.8	157.3	157.4	152.6
2014	153.2	157.1	157.4	158.0	157.5	155.3	154.1	155.2	159.0	161.0	162.2	162.6	157.7
2015	156.8	161.5	162.5	162.9	163.2	160.5	158.8	159.6	163.3	165.9	166.5	167.6	162.4
2016	162.0	166.5	167.0	167.9	167.4	164.8	163.4	163.7	167.8	169.0	169.6	169.2	166.5
2017	164.0	168.2	168.9	169.1	168.8	167.0	164.8	165.5	169.5	171.0	171.5	171.8	168.3
2018	167.0	171.2	172.0	171.5	170.6	169.1	166.5	167.6	171.3	173.5	173.6	175.2	170.8
Leisure and Hospitality													
2010	63.3	63.4	64.4	67.1	69.9	70.7	71.7	72.4	69.6	68.0	67.0	66.7	67.9
2011	65.0	64.5	65.1	68.2	70.7	71.6	73.3	74.0	70.7	69.4	68.3	67.4	69.0
2012	66.2	66.6	67.4	69.6	72.9	73.8	75.8	75.4	72.8	70.6	69.8	70.1	70.9
2013	68.2	68.6	69.3	71.1	75.2	76.5	78.1	77.4	75.2	73.4	73.0	73.1	73.3
2014	71.1	71.6	71.2	73.3	75.6	78.4	78.7	78.0	75.2	73.8	73.2	73.6	74.5
2015	70.8	71.0	72.3	75.0	77.9	80.7	79.8	80.6	76.8	76.2	75.8	75.7	76.1
2016	73.3	73.9	74.3	76.7	79.7	82.1	82.4	82.9	78.5	77.0	75.7	75.8	77.7
2017	74.8	75.1	76.5	77.7	81.3	85.0	84.8	84.3	79.9	78.7	77.1	77.6	79.4
2018	76.8	76.7	77.9	77.9	81.0	85.0	85.4	85.2	81.5	81.0	78.9	79.7	80.6
Other Services													
2010	43.7	44.2	44.7	45.1	44.8	45.1	45.0	44.9	44.1	43.9	43.7	43.7	44.4
2011	43.2	43.0	43.1	43.5	43.6	43.7	43.9	43.8	43.0	43.2	42.9	43.0	43.3
2012	42.0	41.9	41.9	41.9	42.1	42.8	42.6	42.4	42.0	42.2	42.1	42.2	42.2
2013	41.5	41.5	41.7	42.2	42.4	42.9	43.0	42.8	42.7	42.4	42.5	42.7	42.4
2014	41.9	42.0	42.1	42.9	43.0	44.0	44.3	44.5	44.2	44.3	44.4	44.7	43.5
2015	44.4	44.6	45.1	45.4	45.6	46.0	46.4	46.3	45.7	45.5	45.4	45.8	45.5
2016	45.1	45.0	45.3	45.9	45.9	46.3	46.7	46.7	46.3	46.1	46.0	46.1	46.0
2017	45.8	45.9	46.1	46.6	46.8	47.6	47.4	47.4	47.0	46.7	46.5	46.7	46.7
2018	46.4	46.3	46.6	46.7	47.0	47.7	47.5	47.6	47.0	47.3	47.1	47.1	47.0
Government													
2010	91.7	91.6	92.0	91.6	94.0	91.3	84.9	84.0	88.0	90.3	91.8	90.1	90.1
2011	88.9	92.8	92.3	91.6	91.0	90.7	87.2	86.6	87.9	86.5	88.5	88.8	89.4
2012	85.8	87.2	88.8	90.1	91.0	89.3	83.3	85.0	86.8	88.6	91.2	88.9	88.0
2013	84.7	88.1	88.1	88.0	87.7	87.3	81.8	83.4	87.4	87.7	87.9	87.6	86.6
2014	85.0	87.2	87.6	87.4	87.2	87.8	82.0	86.1	87.5	87.4	88.8	87.3	86.8
2015	83.1	87.5	87.3	88.3	87.6	86.8	82.3	83.9	86.9	87.1	87.0	87.4	86.3
2016	85.5	87.6	87.6	89.0	87.6	86.0	80.7	84.3	86.7	88.3	89.8	88.7	86.8
2017	84.7	87.7	87.7	88.3	87.8	85.6	80.6	83.2	85.5	87.2	87.4	87.6	86.1
2018	84.3	86.8	86.7	87.9	87.2	85.0	80.9	82.3	84.9	87.2	88.8	87.4	85.8

Employment by Industry: Jacksonville, FL, 2010–2018

(Numbers in thousands, not seasonally adjusted)

Industry and year	January	February	March	April	May	June	July	August	September	October	November	December	Annual average
Total Nonfarm													
2010	571.0	573.9	576.9	578.9	583.0	576.3	575.1	578.2	579.8	585.5	589.6	590.5	579.9
2011	580.3	583.9	588.4	589.9	589.9	582.9	578.7	583.1	584.9	587.6	591.1	592.7	586.1
2012	584.2	588.9	593.3	595.5	597.9	592.8	588.3	593.6	594.0	598.4	602.7	604.1	594.5
2013	592.1	599.2	603.7	605.8	607.8	604.1	604.0	609.7	610.5	614.6	620.0	623.2	607.9
2014	608.7	613.7	617.4	621.4	624.1	619.2	617.4	624.8	624.2	634.0	638.8	643.6	623.9
2015	630.0	636.8	641.3	643.7	645.8	641.4	640.7	646.6	647.0	655.9	660.8	663.5	646.1
2016	651.0	656.3	660.5	666.4	668.3	662.4	665.0	671.1	673.5	676.1	684.3	685.0	668.3
2017	675.1	679.7	682.5	685.9	688.9	684.3	685.4	690.7	682.3	699.8	709.7	711.3	689.6
2018	699.6	704.1	707.8	706.8	709.8	705.5	702.1	710.4	710.4	710.2	713.7	720.2	708.4
Total Private													
2010	494.0	496.4	499.5	501.0	502.6	502.2	501.5	502.2	502.9	507.8	511.3	512.7	502.8
2011	502.5	505.7	510.2	511.7	511.9	509.5	506.5	507.4	509.0	511.1	514.4	516.0	509.7
2012	508.7	512.4	516.7	520.1	522.5	521.7	517.7	519.8	519.3	522.7	527.0	528.8	519.8
2013	518.1	523.8	528.3	530.4	532.5	533.7	534.5	536.8	536.8	540.3	545.1	548.2	534.0
2014	535.9	539.1	542.6	546.2	549.1	549.0	547.7	551.6	550.0	559.2	563.8	568.2	550.2
2015	556.9	561.5	565.7	568.1	570.5	570.8	570.5	572.7	572.2	580.1	584.6	587.1	571.7
2016	576.2	580.2	584.0	589.9	591.9	590.6	593.3	595.9	597.0	599.7	607.4	607.5	592.8
2017	599.6	602.5	604.9	608.6	611.3	611.3	613.1	615.0	605.7	622.7	632.0	633.6	613.4
2018	623.6	626.8	629.5	629.6	631.9	631.9	628.9	633.7	632.9	632.1	635.1	640.8	631.4
Goods Producing													
2010	56.3	56.1	56.5	56.7	56.7	56.9	57.2	56.8	56.9	56.7	56.6	56.0	56.6
2011	54.1	54.1	54.7	55.0	54.8	54.9	55.4	55.6	55.3	54.9	55.1	54.9	54.9
2012	54.1	54.2	54.6	55.2	55.3	55.9	55.9	56.0	56.2	56.4	56.6	56.5	55.6
2013	56.1	56.6	57.5	57.4	57.5	58.1	58.4	58.3	58.6	58.5	59.0	59.0	57.9
2014	58.4	58.8	59.1	59.5	60.1	60.6	60.9	61.3	61.3	62.0	62.4	62.5	60.6
2015	62.4	63.2	63.9	64.1	64.5	65.0	64.9	64.8	64.6	65.6	65.7	66.0	64.6
2016	66.0	66.5	67.0	68.0	68.5	69.3	69.6	69.2	69.8	69.8	70.6	70.9	68.8
2017	71.1	71.7	72.1	72.7	73.3	74.0	74.2	74.3	71.7	74.3	74.6	74.8	73.2
2018	75.9	77.5	78.6	78.4	78.4	78.3	76.3	76.9	75.9	76.1	76.2	77.3	77.2
Service-Providing													
2010	514.7	517.8	520.4	522.2	526.3	519.4	517.9	521.4	522.9	528.8	533.0	534.5	523.3
2011	526.2	529.8	533.7	534.9	535.1	528.0	523.3	527.5	529.6	532.7	536.0	537.8	531.2
2012	530.1	534.7	538.7	540.3	542.6	536.9	532.4	537.6	537.8	542.0	546.1	547.6	538.9
2013	536.0	542.6	546.2	548.4	550.3	546.0	545.6	551.4	551.9	556.1	561.0	564.2	550.0
2014	550.3	554.9	558.3	561.9	564.0	558.6	556.5	563.5	562.9	572.0	576.4	581.1	563.4
2015	567.6	573.6	577.4	579.6	581.3	576.4	575.8	581.8	582.4	590.3	595.1	597.5	581.6
2016	585.0	589.8	593.5	598.4	599.8	593.1	595.4	601.9	603.7	606.3	613.7	614.1	599.6
2017	604.0	608.0	610.4	613.2	615.6	610.3	611.2	616.4	610.6	625.5	635.1	636.5	616.4
2018	623.7	626.6	629.2	628.4	631.4	627.2	625.8	633.5	634.5	634.1	637.5	642.9	631.2
Mining and Logging													
2010	0.3	0.3	0.3	0.3	0.3	0.4	0.3	0.3	0.3	0.4	0.4	0.4	0.3
2011	0.3	0.3	0.3	0.3	0.3	0.3	0.3	0.3	0.3	0.3	0.3	0.3	0.3
2012	0.3	0.3	0.3	0.3	0.3	0.3	0.3	0.3	0.3	0.4	0.4	0.4	0.3
2013	0.4	0.4	0.4	0.4	0.4	0.4	0.4	0.4	0.4	0.4	0.4	0.4	0.4
2014	0.4	0.4	0.4	0.4	0.4	0.4	0.4	0.4	0.4	0.4	0.4	0.4	0.4
2015	0.4	0.4	0.4	0.4	0.4	0.4	0.4	0.4	0.4	0.4	0.4	0.4	0.4
2016	0.4	0.4	0.4	0.4	0.4	0.4	0.4	0.4	0.4	0.4	0.4	0.4	0.4
2017	0.5	0.4	0.5	0.4	0.4	0.4	0.4	0.4	0.4	0.4	0.4	0.4	0.4
2018	0.4	0.4	0.4	0.4	0.4	0.4	0.4	0.4	0.4	0.4	0.4	0.4	0.4
Construction													
2010	28.3	28.3	28.9	29.2	29.1	29.2	29.4	29.1	29.0	28.6	28.4	27.8	28.8
2011	26.4	26.4	27.0	27.2	27.0	27.2	27.6	27.7	27.6	27.2	27.3	27.0	27.1
2012	26.1	26.2	26.6	27.0	27.0	27.5	27.6	27.9	28.0	28.1	28.2	28.3	27.4
2013	27.7	28.3	29.1	29.1	29.2	29.7	30.1	30.2	30.5	30.6	31.0	30.9	29.7
2014	30.4	31.0	31.4	31.6	31.9	32.2	32.5	32.7	32.7	33.0	33.2	33.3	32.2
2015	33.1	33.8	34.4	34.5	34.9	35.3	35.3	35.3	35.3	36.3	36.6	36.9	35.1
2016	36.6	37.1	37.7	38.4	38.7	39.2	39.2	38.9	39.4	39.5	40.1	40.2	38.8
2017	40.1	40.4	40.7	41.2	41.7	42.1	42.5	42.7	41.3	42.9	43.1	43.2	41.8
2018	44.5	45.8	46.8	46.8	46.6	46.3	44.4	45.0	44.7	44.2	44.1	45.0	45.4

Employment by Industry: Jacksonville, FL, 2010–2018—*Continued*

(Numbers in thousands, not seasonally adjusted)

Industry and year	January	February	March	April	May	June	July	August	September	October	November	December	Annual average
Manufacturing													
2010	27.7	27.5	27.3	27.2	27.3	27.3	27.5	27.4	27.6	27.7	27.8	27.8	27.5
2011	27.4	27.4	27.4	27.5	27.5	27.4	27.5	27.6	27.4	27.4	27.5	27.6	27.5
2012	27.7	27.7	27.7	27.9	28.0	28.1	28.0	27.8	27.9	27.9	28.0	27.8	27.9
2013	28.0	27.9	28.0	27.9	27.9	28.0	27.9	27.7	27.7	27.5	27.6	27.7	27.8
2014	27.6	27.4	27.3	27.5	27.8	28.0	28.0	28.2	28.2	28.6	28.8	28.8	28.0
2015	28.9	29.0	29.1	29.2	29.2	29.3	29.2	29.1	28.9	28.9	28.7	28.7	29.0
2016	29.0	29.0	28.9	29.2	29.4	29.7	30.0	29.9	30.0	29.9	30.1	30.3	29.6
2017	30.5	30.9	30.9	31.1	31.2	31.5	31.3	31.2	30.0	31.0	31.1	31.2	31.0
2018	31.0	31.3	31.4	31.2	31.4	31.6	31.5	31.5	30.8	31.5	31.7	31.9	31.4
Trade, Transportation, and Utilities													
2010	123.8	123.0	123.3	123.2	123.2	123.2	122.7	123.4	122.8	124.0	126.2	127.7	123.9
2011	122.5	122.7	123.1	123.7	123.1	123.2	123.2	123.3	122.9	122.9	125.3	126.2	123.5
2012	124.1	124.1	124.7	124.6	125.0	124.9	123.7	124.5	124.7	124.9	127.7	128.8	125.1
2013	125.1	125.1	125.8	126.7	126.8	126.6	126.8	127.2	126.8	128.4	131.1	133.2	127.5
2014	127.7	127.8	127.6	128.2	128.6	128.5	128.7	130.1	129.9	132.8	136.3	138.2	130.4
2015	133.1	133.1	133.0	132.9	133.5	133.5	133.7	135.1	135.0	135.7	138.9	140.1	134.8
2016	135.5	135.7	135.9	136.5	136.8	136.4	137.2	138.0	137.5	137.6	140.9	142.3	137.5
2017	139.3	138.9	138.7	139.3	139.3	139.2	139.5	140.0	140.1	145.1	152.7	154.5	142.2
2018	150.0	148.8	148.8	148.6	149.3	149.5	149.1	150.2	150.6	150.6	153.8	155.0	150.4
Wholesale Trade													
2010	25.2	25.1	25.0	25.0	25.1	25.2	25.4	25.4	25.2	25.1	25.0	25.0	25.1
2011	24.3	24.5	24.5	24.4	24.4	24.3	24.3	24.2	24.1	24.1	24.0	24.0	24.3
2012	24.1	24.2	24.5	24.4	24.5	24.4	24.6	24.5	24.4	24.4	24.4	24.5	24.4
2013	24.3	24.4	24.5	24.7	24.7	24.7	24.5	24.3	24.1	24.2	24.1	24.0	24.4
2014	23.7	23.8	23.7	23.5	23.7	23.7	23.6	23.7	23.6	23.9	23.9	23.9	23.7
2015	23.9	23.9	23.8	24.1	24.4	24.6	24.8	25.1	25.4	25.4	25.6	25.8	24.7
2016	25.3	25.7	25.8	25.4	25.5	25.3	25.5	25.6	25.4	25.2	25.2	25.2	25.4
2017	25.1	25.2	25.2	25.1	25.2	25.2	25.0	25.0	24.6	24.7	24.9	24.9	25.0
2018	25.2	25.2	25.1	25.3	25.5	25.5	25.6	25.7	25.9	25.4	25.8	26.1	25.5
Retail Trade													
2010	68.8	68.2	68.5	68.5	68.4	68.3	67.9	68.1	67.7	68.6	70.7	71.3	68.8
2011	67.9	67.8	68.3	68.4	68.5	68.8	68.7	68.9	68.7	69.0	71.3	71.8	69.0
2012	69.6	69.5	69.9	69.9	70.3	70.2	69.1	69.5	69.6	69.8	72.2	72.6	70.2
2013	70.1	69.8	70.2	70.5	70.8	71.1	71.5	71.4	71.0	72.2	75.0	75.5	71.6
2014	71.9	71.7	71.6	71.9	72.1	72.1	72.5	73.1	73.2	75.3	78.7	79.5	73.6
2015	75.4	75.3	75.3	74.6	75.0	75.2	75.3	75.8	75.2	75.7	78.3	78.8	75.8
2016	75.7	75.7	75.9	76.5	76.8	76.6	77.6	78.0	77.6	77.7	80.7	81.5	77.5
2017	79.0	78.6	78.2	78.7	78.8	78.8	79.1	79.5	80.4	84.2	91.1	91.3	81.5
2018	87.0	86.0	85.9	86.0	86.4	86.4	86.0	86.3	86.2	87.3	89.3	89.5	86.9
Transportation and Utilities													
2010	29.8	29.7	29.8	29.7	29.7	29.7	29.4	29.9	29.9	30.3	30.5	31.4	30.0
2011	30.3	30.4	30.5	30.9	30.2	30.1	30.2	30.2	30.1	29.8	30.0	30.4	30.3
2012	30.4	30.4	30.3	30.3	30.2	30.3	30.0	30.5	30.7	30.7	31.1	31.7	30.6
2013	30.7	30.9	31.1	31.5	31.3	30.8	30.8	31.5	31.7	32.0	32.0	33.7	31.5
2014	32.1	32.3	32.3	32.8	32.8	32.7	32.6	33.3	33.1	33.6	33.7	34.8	33.0
2015	33.8	33.9	33.9	34.2	34.1	33.7	33.6	34.2	34.4	34.6	35.0	35.5	34.2
2016	34.5	34.3	34.2	34.6	34.5	34.5	34.1	34.4	34.5	34.7	35.0	35.6	34.6
2017	35.2	35.1	35.3	35.5	35.3	35.2	35.4	35.5	35.1	36.2	36.7	38.3	35.7
2018	37.8	37.6	37.8	37.3	37.4	37.6	37.5	38.2	38.5	37.9	38.7	39.4	38.0
Information													
2010	10.3	10.3	10.5	10.5	10.3	10.3	10.2	10.2	10.1	10.1	10.1	9.9	10.2
2011	9.8	9.7	9.7	9.8	9.8	9.7	9.7	9.7	9.6	9.6	9.7	9.6	9.7
2012	9.4	9.4	9.3	9.4	9.4	9.3	9.3	9.2	9.0	9.2	9.2	9.2	9.3
2013	9.1	9.1	9.1	9.1	9.2	9.2	9.3	9.3	9.2	9.3	9.3	9.4	9.2
2014	9.3	9.3	9.3	9.3	9.3	9.3	9.3	9.3	9.2	9.1	9.2	9.2	9.3
2015	9.2	9.2	9.2	9.2	9.2	9.3	9.4	9.5	9.4	9.5	9.5	9.6	9.4
2016	9.3	9.4	9.4	9.5	9.6	9.5	9.5	9.5	9.5	9.4	9.5	9.5	9.5
2017	9.3	9.4	9.3	9.3	9.4	9.4	9.5	9.4	9.3	9.2	9.3	9.3	9.3
2018	9.2	9.3	9.3	9.4	9.5	9.5	9.4	9.4	9.3	9.4	9.4	9.4	9.4

Employment by Industry: Jacksonville, FL, 2010–2018—*Continued*

(Numbers in thousands, not seasonally adjusted)

Industry and year	January	February	March	April	May	June	July	August	September	October	November	December	Annual average
Financial Activities													
2010	54.9	55.0	55.0	54.8	55.1	55.4	55.9	55.9	55.9	56.4	56.9	57.3	55.7
2011	57.0	57.3	57.8	57.8	57.7	58.0	57.9	58.0	58.5	58.4	58.3	59.0	58.0
2012	58.6	59.2	59.5	59.5	59.8	60.0	60.1	60.1	60.2	60.8	61.2	61.4	60.0
2013	60.8	61.1	61.1	61.2	61.2	61.6	61.7	61.7	61.6	61.7	61.9	62.0	61.5
2014	61.0	60.9	61.2	61.1	61.0	60.8	61.0	60.7	60.3	60.7	60.9	60.9	60.9
2015	61.2	61.2	61.3	61.0	61.0	61.1	61.0	61.2	61.4	62.3	62.5	62.5	61.5
2016	62.5	62.9	62.9	63.4	63.8	63.9	64.1	64.4	65.1	65.4	65.8	66.5	64.2
2017	66.2	66.4	66.8	67.0	67.1	67.2	67.0	67.2	66.9	67.5	67.8	67.8	67.1
2018	67.1	67.2	67.3	66.9	66.9	67.2	67.1	67.2	66.8	67.0	66.7	66.6	67.0
Professional and Business Services													
2010	79.5	81.0	81.5	81.3	81.9	81.8	81.5	82.2	83.6	86.0	86.2	86.2	82.7
2011	85.7	87.6	88.4	88.4	89.0	87.8	85.2	85.5	87.7	89.2	90.2	90.3	87.9
2012	89.2	90.4	90.9	92.5	93.4	92.3	89.8	90.6	90.3	91.6	92.0	91.7	91.2
2013	89.2	90.9	92.3	92.6	93.9	94.1	94.4	95.3	95.7	97.5	97.6	97.8	94.3
2014	95.1	95.5	95.9	97.1	98.3	97.8	97.4	98.7	99.1	101.3	102.3	103.2	98.5
2015	99.6	100.6	100.9	101.8	101.9	100.7	100.6	99.6	99.3	101.9	102.5	102.4	101.0
2016	99.4	99.5	100.6	102.3	102.1	101.2	102.5	102.9	102.9	106.1	106.9	105.7	102.7
2017	103.8	103.4	104.1	104.5	104.7	105.1	106.4	106.7	104.9	109.5	109.6	109.7	106.0
2018	106.4	107.1	107.1	107.1	108.0	108.4	108.8	109.5	109.4	107.6	107.3	109.0	108.0
Education and Health Services													
2010	84.5	85.0	85.2	85.4	85.5	84.9	84.6	84.8	85.5	87.5	87.9	88.0	85.7
2011	87.1	87.6	87.7	87.4	87.4	86.4	86.3	86.8	88.1	89.2	89.5	89.8	87.8
2012	87.6	88.4	88.7	88.7	89.0	88.6	88.2	88.9	90.0	90.5	90.8	91.3	89.2
2013	90.0	91.4	91.4	90.8	91.0	90.7	90.0	90.6	91.3	92.1	92.7	93.0	91.3
2014	91.4	92.5	92.8	93.4	93.3	92.4	92.2	93.2	93.7	95.1	95.3	96.0	93.4
2015	95.0	95.7	96.4	96.7	96.9	96.3	96.2	97.4	98.4	100.4	100.9	101.0	97.6
2016	99.7	100.9	101.2	102.4	102.7	101.7	101.9	103.0	103.7	104.6	104.8	104.6	102.6
2017	103.4	104.7	104.8	105.4	105.7	104.7	104.4	105.5	104.9	107.0	107.5	107.3	105.4
2018	106.1	107.0	107.4	107.4	107.2	106.4	105.5	106.9	108.2	109.4	109.4	109.4	107.5
Leisure and Hospitality													
2010	61.8	63.0	64.4	66.0	66.8	66.5	66.4	66.0	65.4	64.2	64.5	64.9	65.0
2011	63.8	64.1	65.8	67.1	68.0	67.7	67.1	67.2	66.0	66.3	66.1	66.3	66.3
2012	65.7	66.6	68.7	69.7	70.1	70.2	70.3	70.1	68.6	69.0	69.3	69.7	69.0
2013	67.8	69.5	70.9	72.2	72.4	72.7	73.1	73.5	72.9	71.9	72.4	72.7	71.8
2014	71.9	73.0	75.2	75.8	76.6	77.7	76.5	76.5	74.7	76.2	75.5	76.3	75.5
2015	74.5	76.4	78.7	80.0	80.7	81.8	81.3	81.6	80.6	80.9	80.7	81.4	79.9
2016	79.6	80.7	82.1	82.7	83.2	83.3	83.1	83.6	83.2	81.9	83.8	82.9	82.5
2017	81.8	83.0	84.0	85.4	86.4	86.1	86.4	86.4	82.8	84.6	84.9	84.4	84.7
2018	83.3	84.1	85.1	85.7	86.4	85.9	85.7	86.7	85.9	85.0	85.2	87.1	85.5
Other Services													
2010	22.9	23.0	23.1	23.1	23.1	23.2	23.0	22.9	22.7	22.9	22.9	22.7	23.0
2011	22.5	22.6	22.8	22.5	22.1	21.8	21.7	21.3	20.9	20.6	20.2	19.9	21.6
2012	20.0	20.1	20.3	20.5	20.5	20.5	20.4	20.4	20.3	20.3	20.2	20.2	20.3
2013	20.0	20.1	20.2	20.4	20.5	20.7	20.8	20.9	20.7	20.9	21.1	21.1	20.6
2014	21.1	21.3	21.5	21.8	21.9	21.9	21.7	21.8	21.8	22.0	21.9	21.9	21.7
2015	21.9	22.1	22.3	22.4	22.8	23.1	23.4	23.5	23.5	23.8	23.9	24.1	23.1
2016	24.2	24.6	24.9	25.1	25.2	25.3	25.4	25.3	25.3	24.9	25.1	25.1	25.0
2017	24.7	25.0	25.1	25.0	25.4	25.6	25.7	25.5	25.1	25.5	25.6	25.8	25.3
2018	25.6	25.8	25.9	26.1	26.2	26.7	27.0	26.9	26.8	27.0	27.1	27.0	26.5
Government													
2010	77.0	77.5	77.4	77.9	80.4	74.1	73.6	76.0	76.9	77.7	78.3	77.8	77.1
2011	77.8	78.2	78.2	78.2	78.0	73.4	72.2	75.7	75.9	76.5	76.7	76.7	76.5
2012	75.5	76.5	76.6	75.4	75.4	71.1	70.6	73.8	74.7	75.7	75.7	75.3	74.7
2013	74.0	75.4	75.4	75.4	75.3	70.4	69.5	72.9	73.7	74.3	74.9	75.0	73.9
2014	72.8	74.6	74.8	75.2	75.0	70.2	69.7	73.2	74.2	74.8	75.0	75.4	73.7
2015	73.1	75.3	75.6	75.6	75.3	70.6	70.2	73.9	74.8	75.8	76.2	76.4	74.4
2016	74.8	76.1	76.5	76.5	76.4	71.8	71.7	75.2	76.5	76.4	76.9	77.5	75.5
2017	75.5	77.2	77.6	77.3	77.6	73.0	72.3	75.7	76.6	77.1	77.7	77.7	76.3
2018	76.0	77.3	78.3	77.2	77.9	73.6	73.2	76.7	77.5	78.1	78.6	79.4	77.0

Employment by Industry: Oklahoma City, OK, 2010–2018

(Numbers in thousands, not seasonally adjusted)

Industry and year	January	February	March	April	May	June	July	August	September	October	November	December	Annual average
Total Nonfarm													
2010	552.5	555.3	561.9	566.1	569.3	566.6	560.3	564.5	571.3	575.6	578.5	580.8	566.9
2011	564.6	567.7	575.5	582.0	582.2	579.0	574.4	577.7	586.6	587.4	590.8	593.7	580.1
2012	579.5	586.1	592.2	596.1	597.7	595.7	584.8	590.4	597.0	602.9	606.4	607.0	594.7
2013	593.2	600.2	604.7	607.7	611.7	608.4	602.2	607.4	612.4	615.9	621.6	619.1	608.7
2014	604.7	609.8	615.1	618.7	622.1	618.9	613.9	619.3	626.0	629.7	633.1	634.8	620.5
2015	621.5	626.5	627.7	630.1	631.8	629.8	625.0	628.6	632.9	635.1	637.5	638.0	630.4
2016	623.1	628.8	629.1	633.2	632.0	626.9	622.9	627.2	632.7	631.9	634.8	634.9	629.8
2017	617.4	624.6	629.8	634.1	635.1	636.0	631.7	635.3	643.0	644.1	648.3	649.1	635.7
2018	634.2	640.2	644.5	647.0	649.7	649.0	645.4	648.8	655.8	659.0	661.4	660.3	649.6
Total Private													
2010	432.6	432.5	437.9	441.7	443.1	445.7	445.2	447.9	449.0	451.9	454.4	456.3	444.9
2011	445.5	444.9	451.9	458.1	458.2	459.8	460.0	462.5	463.5	462.7	465.6	468.0	458.4
2012	459.4	462.6	467.7	471.1	472.8	475.8	471.3	474.3	473.9	476.6	479.5	480.9	472.2
2013	471.7	474.2	478.1	480.6	483.8	485.7	484.7	487.7	487.9	488.9	493.7	492.1	484.1
2014	483.2	483.9	488.8	492.3	494.7	496.5	496.8	499.8	500.3	501.6	504.6	506.9	495.8
2015	498.0	498.5	499.3	501.5	502.4	505.4	505.6	507.0	505.3	504.5	506.3	507.2	503.4
2016	496.7	498.1	497.8	501.2	500.3	500.2	501.1	502.9	502.5	501.1	503.7	504.5	500.8
2017	492.0	494.9	499.3	503.6	504.9	509.4	509.6	511.4	513.7	513.9	517.7	518.9	507.4
2018	508.3	510.5	514.3	516.9	519.2	522.1	522.8	524.3	525.3	527.2	529.0	528.2	520.7
Goods Producing													
2010	67.6	67.2	68.1	69.2	69.7	70.6	70.9	71.4	71.6	73.1	72.9	73.6	70.5
2011	72.3	72.2	73.5	74.9	75.3	76.3	77.0	77.1	77.2	77.4	77.7	78.7	75.8
2012	78.0	78.6	80.0	81.0	81.6	83.1	82.6	82.8	82.5	83.1	83.1	83.2	81.6
2013	82.7	82.9	83.4	83.7	84.3	85.4	85.2	85.2	84.9	85.2	85.5	85.4	84.5
2014	84.0	84.1	85.4	85.7	86.6	87.8	88.3	89.0	89.3	89.8	89.9	90.2	87.5
2015	89.8	89.1	88.1	86.7	86.2	86.4	87.3	87.1	86.2	85.0	84.1	83.6	86.6
2016	82.3	82.2	81.0	80.9	80.4	80.2	80.3	80.0	79.6	79.0	79.1	79.9	80.4
2017	78.1	79.0	79.5	79.9	80.5	81.9	82.3	82.7	83.4	83.2	83.8	84.3	81.6
2018	82.7	83.7	84.5	84.9	85.2	86.7	86.6	86.8	86.9	87.2	87.6	88.0	85.9
Service-Providing													
2010	484.9	488.1	493.8	496.9	499.6	496.0	489.4	493.1	499.7	502.5	505.6	507.2	496.4
2011	492.3	495.5	502.0	507.1	506.9	502.7	497.4	500.6	509.4	510.0	513.1	515.0	504.3
2012	501.5	507.5	512.2	515.1	516.1	512.6	502.2	507.6	514.5	519.8	523.3	523.8	513.0
2013	510.5	517.3	521.3	524.0	527.4	523.0	517.0	522.2	527.5	530.7	536.1	533.7	524.2
2014	520.7	525.7	529.7	533.0	535.5	531.1	525.6	530.3	536.7	539.9	543.2	544.6	533.0
2015	531.7	537.4	539.6	543.4	545.6	543.4	537.7	541.5	546.7	550.1	553.4	554.4	543.7
2016	540.8	546.6	548.1	552.3	551.6	546.7	542.6	547.2	553.1	552.9	555.7	555.0	549.4
2017	539.3	545.6	550.3	554.2	554.6	554.1	549.4	552.6	559.6	560.9	564.5	564.8	554.2
2018	551.5	556.5	560.0	562.1	564.5	562.3	558.8	562.0	568.9	571.8	573.8	572.3	563.7
Mining, Logging, and Construction													
2010	37.0	36.7	37.6	38.5	38.9	39.7	40.1	40.4	40.4	41.6	41.2	41.7	39.5
2011	40.9	40.6	41.6	42.4	42.7	43.5	43.9	43.7	43.7	43.7	43.8	44.4	42.9
2012	43.8	44.2	45.4	46.3	46.8	48.0	47.6	47.6	47.2	47.4	47.2	47.2	46.6
2013	46.9	47.0	47.4	47.5	47.9	48.8	48.5	48.5	48.4	48.3	48.4	48.3	48.0
2014	47.3	47.0	48.3	48.6	49.3	50.2	50.8	51.3	51.5	51.8	51.8	51.8	50.0
2015	51.3	50.6	49.9	48.9	48.6	49.0	49.8	49.7	49.1	48.3	47.8	47.3	49.2
2016	46.4	46.1	45.7	46.0	45.7	45.7	46.0	45.8	45.6	45.6	45.6	46.2	45.9
2017	45.2	45.9	46.6	46.8	47.3	48.4	48.8	49.1	49.7	49.5	49.9	50.3	48.1
2018	49.3	49.9	50.7	51.1	51.4	52.6	52.7	52.9	52.9	53.2	53.4	54.1	52.0
Manufacturing													
2010	30.6	30.5	30.5	30.7	30.8	30.9	30.8	31.0	31.2	31.5	31.7	31.9	31.0
2011	31.4	31.6	31.9	32.5	32.6	32.8	33.1	33.4	33.5	33.7	33.9	34.3	32.9
2012	34.2	34.4	34.6	34.7	34.8	35.1	35.0	35.2	35.3	35.7	35.9	36.0	35.1
2013	35.8	35.9	36.0	36.2	36.4	36.6	36.7	36.7	36.5	36.9	37.1	37.1	36.5
2014	36.7	37.1	37.1	37.1	37.3	37.6	37.5	37.7	37.8	38.0	38.1	38.4	37.5
2015	38.5	38.5	38.2	37.8	37.6	37.4	37.5	37.4	37.1	36.7	36.3	36.3	37.4
2016	35.9	36.1	35.3	34.9	34.7	34.5	34.3	34.2	34.0	33.4	33.5	33.7	34.5
2017	32.9	33.1	32.9	33.1	33.2	33.5	33.5	33.6	33.7	33.7	33.9	34.0	33.4
2018	33.4	33.8	33.8	33.8	33.8	34.1	33.9	33.9	34.0	34.0	34.2	33.9	33.9

Employment by Industry: Oklahoma City, OK, 2010–2018—*Continued*

(Numbers in thousands, not seasonally adjusted)

Industry and year	January	February	March	April	May	June	July	August	September	October	November	December	Annual average
Trade, Transportation, and Utilities													
2010	94.8	94.3	95.5	95.8	96.3	97.1	97.3	97.5	97.0	98.2	100.1	101.5	97.1
2011	97.8	97.4	98.7	99.1	99.0	99.3	99.6	100.4	100.3	100.5	102.6	103.7	99.9
2012	100.3	100.1	100.8	101.4	102.1	102.4	102.2	102.6	102.9	104.0	106.7	107.8	102.8
2013	103.5	103.9	104.7	105.2	106.1	106.5	106.6	107.3	107.4	108.3	111.0	111.9	106.9
2014	108.1	107.3	107.8	107.7	108.2	108.9	108.8	109.4	109.6	110.3	112.6	114.3	109.4
2015	109.9	109.6	109.9	110.6	111.0	112.0	111.8	112.0	111.7	112.1	114.5	115.7	111.7
2016	110.9	110.7	111.1	111.6	111.7	111.5	111.5	111.8	111.7	111.9	114.6	114.7	112.0
2017	110.5	109.7	109.9	110.4	110.3	110.7	110.8	111.2	111.3	112.2	115.3	115.9	111.5
2018	111.8	110.6	110.8	110.8	111.4	111.8	112.0	112.4	113.0	113.8	115.6	116.4	112.5
Wholesale Trade													
2010	20.0	20.0	20.0	20.1	20.2	20.3	20.5	20.6	20.6	20.9	20.9	21.1	20.4
2011	21.0	21.0	21.2	21.3	21.3	21.5	21.5	21.4	21.5	21.6	21.6	21.8	21.4
2012	22.0	22.2	22.2	22.1	22.3	22.5	22.6	22.7	22.6	22.9	23.2	23.4	22.6
2013	23.4	23.5	23.6	23.5	23.7	23.9	23.7	23.7	23.8	23.9	24.1	24.1	23.7
2014	24.0	23.9	23.9	24.0	24.1	24.3	24.2	24.4	24.5	24.8	24.8	24.9	24.3
2015	24.7	24.7	24.6	24.4	24.4	24.5	24.5	24.4	24.4	24.3	24.3	24.3	24.5
2016	23.9	24.0	24.0	24.1	24.0	23.8	23.9	23.8	23.7	23.7	23.7	23.5	23.8
2017	23.4	23.5	23.6	23.7	23.8	23.9	23.8	23.9	23.9	24.5	24.5	24.6	23.9
2018	23.8	23.7	23.6	23.7	23.8	24.1	24.3	24.2	24.5	24.8	24.7	25.2	24.2
Retail Trade													
2010	58.7	58.2	59.2	59.3	59.7	60.2	60.1	60.2	59.6	60.6	62.4	63.0	60.1
2011	60.1	59.6	60.5	60.9	60.7	60.5	60.8	61.6	61.3	61.3	63.3	63.9	61.2
2012	60.9	60.5	61.2	61.8	62.0	62.1	61.6	61.9	62.2	63.0	65.3	66.0	62.4
2013	62.0	61.8	62.4	63.0	63.6	63.6	63.9	64.5	64.6	65.3	67.6	68.4	64.2
2014	65.0	64.6	64.8	65.0	65.1	65.5	65.6	65.9	66.0	66.3	68.4	69.4	66.0
2015	65.9	65.8	66.2	66.9	67.0	67.7	67.6	67.9	67.6	68.2	70.2	70.8	67.7
2016	67.2	67.1	67.5	67.9	68.0	67.9	67.8	68.2	68.2	68.4	70.5	70.1	68.2
2017	66.7	65.9	65.9	66.4	66.0	66.2	66.1	66.3	66.2	66.4	68.9	69.0	66.7
2018	66.3	65.4	65.5	65.5	65.7	65.5	65.5	65.9	66.1	66.5	68.0	68.0	66.2
Transportation and Utilities													
2010	16.1	16.1	16.3	16.4	16.4	16.6	16.7	16.7	16.8	16.7	16.8	17.4	16.6
2011	16.7	16.8	17.0	16.9	17.0	17.3	17.3	17.4	17.5	17.6	17.7	18.0	17.3
2012	17.4	17.4	17.4	17.5	17.8	17.8	18.0	18.0	18.1	18.1	18.2	18.4	17.8
2013	18.1	18.6	18.7	18.7	18.8	19.0	19.0	19.1	19.0	19.1	19.3	19.4	18.9
2014	19.1	18.8	19.1	18.7	19.0	19.1	19.0	19.1	19.1	19.2	19.4	20.0	19.1
2015	19.3	19.1	19.1	19.3	19.6	19.8	19.7	19.7	19.7	19.6	20.0	20.6	19.6
2016	19.8	19.6	19.6	19.6	19.7	19.8	19.8	19.8	19.8	19.8	20.4	21.1	19.9
2017	20.4	20.3	20.4	20.3	20.5	20.6	20.9	21.0	21.2	21.3	21.9	22.3	20.9
2018	21.7	21.5	21.7	21.6	21.9	22.2	22.2	22.3	22.4	22.5	22.9	23.2	22.2
Information													
2010	10.2	10.1	9.9	9.8	9.7	9.6	9.5	9.3	9.2	9.1	9.2	9.1	9.6
2011	9.2	9.1	8.9	9.0	9.0	9.0	9.0	8.9	8.9	9.0	9.0	9.0	9.0
2012	8.9	8.9	8.8	8.7	8.7	8.6	8.7	8.5	8.3	8.4	8.4	8.3	8.6
2013	8.1	8.1	8.0	8.2	8.2	8.2	8.2	8.2	8.2	8.2	8.4	8.3	8.2
2014	8.1	8.1	8.1	8.1	8.1	8.1	8.2	8.2	8.2	8.1	8.2	8.1	8.1
2015	8.1	8.0	8.1	8.1	8.3	8.3	8.3	8.3	8.3	8.4	8.4	8.5	8.3
2016	8.2	8.3	8.3	8.2	8.2	8.2	8.1	8.1	8.0	8.0	8.1	8.2	8.2
2017	7.8	7.8	7.8	7.8	7.8	7.7	7.7	7.6	7.5	7.5	7.5	7.5	7.7
2018	7.3	7.4	7.4	7.3	7.4	7.4	7.4	7.4	7.3	7.3	7.3	7.3	7.4
Financial Activities													
2010	31.1	31.1	31.2	30.9	31.0	31.1	31.0	31.0	30.8	30.9	31.0	31.2	31.0
2011	30.3	30.4	30.5	30.7	30.7	30.8	30.9	31.0	30.9	31.2	31.3	31.5	30.9
2012	31.2	31.4	31.5	31.6	31.8	32.0	31.8	31.9	31.7	31.9	32.1	32.4	31.8
2013	32.2	32.3	32.2	32.1	32.2	32.3	32.4	32.5	32.4	32.6	32.8	32.9	32.4
2014	32.5	32.7	32.9	32.9	33.1	33.2	33.3	33.4	33.2	33.3	33.5	33.9	33.2
2015	33.4	33.5	33.4	33.4	33.5	33.5	33.5	33.4	33.2	33.3	33.3	33.4	33.4
2016	32.8	33.0	32.9	32.9	32.9	33.0	33.4	33.4	33.3	33.4	33.4	33.6	33.2
2017	32.9	33.0	33.2	33.2	33.2	33.4	33.3	33.4	33.3	33.3	33.3	33.6	33.3
2018	32.9	32.9	33.1	33.1	33.2	33.4	33.5	33.5	33.4	33.5	33.9	33.8	33.4

Employment by Industry: Oklahoma City, OK, 2010–2018—*Continued*

(Numbers in thousands, not seasonally adjusted)

Industry and year	January	February	March	April	May	June	July	August	September	October	November	December	Annual average
Professional and Business Services													
2010	69.7	70.3	71.2	71.8	71.7	72.8	73.5	74.7	74.9	75.6	75.9	75.9	73.2
2011	73.9	73.8	74.8	76.4	76.2	75.8	76.0	76.8	76.3	76.4	76.3	76.9	75.8
2012	75.4	76.5	77.0	77.1	76.4	77.6	76.3	77.3	76.3	77.5	77.4	76.8	76.8
2013	75.7	76.2	77.5	77.5	77.4	78.0	77.5	78.2	77.7	78.4	79.2	78.1	77.6
2014	76.9	77.0	77.8	78.2	78.2	78.3	78.9	79.7	79.1	79.9	80.5	80.1	78.7
2015	78.9	78.9	78.8	79.4	79.2	79.7	79.9	80.4	79.7	80.1	80.3	80.7	79.7
2016	79.2	79.3	79.0	79.7	79.2	79.3	79.3	80.1	80.4	80.5	79.9	79.8	79.6
2017	78.1	78.4	79.5	80.4	80.1	81.8	82.8	83.1	83.5	83.4	83.6	83.4	81.5
2018	82.7	83.4	84.0	84.6	84.2	85.4	86.0	86.2	86.6	86.3	85.7	84.8	85.0
Education and Health Services													
2010	82.0	82.4	82.7	83.4	83.2	83.0	82.2	82.8	83.8	84.3	84.4	84.3	83.2
2011	82.6	82.6	83.5	84.1	84.2	84.3	83.8	84.5	85.5	85.4	86.0	86.0	84.4
2012	84.5	85.2	85.8	86.4	86.6	86.5	85.4	86.5	87.3	87.4	87.7	88.0	86.4
2013	86.9	87.3	87.7	87.9	88.1	87.7	86.9	87.7	88.3	88.9	89.3	88.7	88.0
2014	87.7	88.1	88.6	89.4	89.3	88.8	88.2	88.5	89.1	89.5	89.6	89.9	88.9
2015	89.2	89.7	89.9	90.5	90.5	90.4	89.9	90.3	91.2	91.6	91.6	91.5	90.5
2016	90.7	91.0	90.9	91.3	91.0	90.3	90.9	91.3	91.8	91.3	91.7	91.7	91.2
2017	89.7	90.6	91.0	92.3	92.4	92.2	91.7	92.1	92.8	93.2	93.2	93.2	92.0
2018	91.9	92.6	92.7	92.8	93.0	92.3	92.9	93.5	93.8	94.4	94.6	93.9	93.2
Leisure and Hospitality													
2010	54.7	54.6	56.6	58.0	58.7	58.6	58.2	58.6	59.1	58.0	58.1	57.9	57.6
2011	57.0	57.0	59.5	61.2	60.8	61.3	60.9	61.1	61.6	60.1	59.9	59.6	60.0
2012	58.6	59.3	61.2	62.1	62.8	62.7	61.7	62.4	62.8	62.4	62.3	62.6	61.7
2013	60.9	61.7	62.8	64.0	65.3	65.1	65.2	65.9	66.3	64.6	64.6	63.8	64.2
2014	63.0	63.5	64.8	66.6	67.1	67.0	66.6	67.3	67.4	66.2	65.8	65.8	65.9
2015	64.2	65.0	66.0	67.6	68.4	69.5	69.3	70.0	69.5	68.7	68.8	68.5	68.0
2016	67.2	68.0	69.1	70.5	70.6	71.0	70.8	71.5	70.9	70.3	70.0	69.5	70.0
2017	68.0	69.1	70.7	71.8	72.5	73.1	72.5	72.9	73.2	72.5	72.3	72.2	71.7
2018	70.4	71.1	72.7	74.3	75.6	75.5	75.0	75.2	75.0	75.5	75.1	74.7	74.2
Other Services													
2010	22.5	22.5	22.7	22.8	22.8	22.9	22.6	22.6	22.6	22.7	22.8	22.8	22.7
2011	22.4	22.4	22.5	22.7	23.0	23.0	22.8	22.7	22.8	22.7	22.8	22.6	22.7
2012	22.5	22.6	22.6	22.8	22.8	22.9	22.6	22.3	22.1	21.9	21.8	21.8	22.4
2013	21.7	21.8	21.8	22.0	22.2	22.5	22.7	22.7	22.7	22.7	22.9	23.0	22.4
2014	22.9	23.1	23.4	23.7	24.1	24.4	24.5	24.3	24.4	24.5	24.5	24.6	24.0
2015	24.5	24.7	25.1	25.2	25.3	25.6	25.6	25.5	25.5	25.3	25.3	25.3	25.2
2016	25.4	25.6	25.5	26.1	26.3	26.7	26.8	26.7	26.8	26.7	26.9	27.1	26.4
2017	26.9	27.3	27.7	27.8	28.1	28.6	28.5	28.4	28.7	28.6	28.7	28.8	28.2
2018	28.6	28.8	29.1	29.1	29.2	29.6	29.4	29.3	29.3	29.2	29.2	29.3	29.2
Government													
2010	119.9	122.8	124.0	124.4	126.2	120.9	115.1	116.6	122.3	123.7	124.1	124.5	122.0
2011	119.1	122.8	123.6	123.9	124.0	119.2	114.4	115.2	123.1	124.7	125.2	125.7	121.7
2012	120.1	123.5	124.5	125.0	124.9	119.9	113.5	116.1	123.1	126.3	126.9	126.1	122.5
2013	121.5	126.0	126.6	127.1	127.9	122.7	117.5	119.7	124.5	127.0	127.9	127.0	124.6
2014	121.5	125.9	126.3	126.4	127.4	122.4	117.1	119.5	125.7	128.1	128.5	127.9	124.7
2015	123.5	128.0	128.4	128.6	129.4	124.4	119.4	121.6	127.6	130.6	131.2	130.8	127.0
2016	126.4	130.7	131.3	132.0	131.7	126.7	121.8	124.3	130.2	130.8	131.1	130.4	129.0
2017	125.4	129.7	130.5	130.5	130.2	126.6	122.1	123.9	129.3	130.2	130.6	130.2	128.3
2018	125.9	129.7	130.2	130.1	130.5	126.9	122.6	124.5	130.5	131.8	132.4	132.1	128.9

Employment by Industry: Raleigh, NC, 2010–2018

(Numbers in thousands, not seasonally adjusted)

Industry and year	January	February	March	April	May	June	July	August	September	October	November	December	Annual average
Total Nonfarm													
2010	487.5	487.9	492.2	497.6	502.2	502.4	500.6	503.3	502.9	506.8	509.0	508.4	500.1
2011	498.8	502.7	505.7	508.3	509.8	509.2	507.5	511.2	512.2	515.1	517.5	517.0	509.6
2012	512.2	514.4	518.3	522.7	525.8	526.1	524.7	529.8	528.9	531.9	535.4	534.6	525.4
2013	525.5	530.2	533.6	535.3	537.7	537.6	536.5	545.1	547.9	549.9	553.9	553.8	540.6
2014	544.3	544.0	550.0	555.2	559.6	562.3	557.4	563.8	564.7	571.6	574.8	575.1	560.2
2015	563.8	567.5	570.1	575.6	579.3	581.9	578.1	584.5	585.2	590.6	594.2	594.9	580.5
2016	585.8	588.9	591.8	596.9	599.5	601.3	598.4	602.8	604.0	608.1	612.8	611.2	600.1
2017	599.4	605.4	608.0	609.3	615.0	617.1	616.8	623.9	621.1	626.0	630.5	630.4	616.9
2018	619.6	625.0	627.9	632.7	638.0	639.7	632.3	640.5	631.0	635.5	636.5	635.4	632.8
Total Private													
2010	395.4	395.0	398.7	402.6	405.3	407.8	410.2	411.1	408.9	412.3	415.0	414.7	406.4
2011	406.1	409.2	411.9	414.9	416.5	419.1	421.2	421.8	420.6	422.2	424.8	426.3	417.9
2012	420.9	421.9	425.8	430.6	434.3	436.3	438.7	440.0	437.1	439.0	442.4	443.3	434.2
2013	434.0	437.3	440.4	442.6	446.3	449.5	450.8	454.9	454.5	454.9	458.7	460.3	448.7
2014	451.2	450.4	455.9	460.3	465.6	469.7	469.8	472.6	470.0	474.5	477.4	479.6	466.4
2015	469.1	471.5	474.2	479.6	485.1	489.0	490.2	492.9	489.7	494.0	497.1	499.2	486.0
2016	490.9	492.1	494.9	500.2	504.6	507.4	510.0	511.1	508.2	510.7	514.4	514.8	504.9
2017	503.9	507.7	510.1	511.7	518.2	522.5	527.5	528.4	523.2	527.3	530.5	531.7	520.2
2018	522.2	525.8	528.4	533.0	538.7	543.1	540.8	543.5	532.8	536.3	536.0	536.3	534.7
Goods Producing													
2010	56.9	56.6	57.1	57.4	58.0	58.5	59.2	59.3	59.1	59.2	58.9	58.6	58.2
2011	57.4	58.1	58.7	58.7	59.0	59.5	59.9	59.6	59.3	59.0	59.0	59.2	59.0
2012	58.9	59.1	59.6	59.7	60.3	60.9	61.5	61.6	61.4	61.2	61.1	61.1	60.5
2013	59.8	60.1	60.5	60.5	60.9	61.6	61.9	62.3	62.2	62.4	62.6	62.9	61.5
2014	61.9	61.9	63.0	62.8	63.7	64.7	65.4	65.8	65.6	65.7	65.6	65.5	64.3
2015	65.2	65.7	65.9	66.5	67.4	68.2	68.4	68.4	67.9	68.2	68.0	68.3	67.3
2016	68.0	68.2	68.5	69.0	69.4	70.2	70.5	70.5	70.3	70.6	70.9	71.0	69.8
2017	70.4	71.3	71.7	71.7	72.1	73.2	74.0	74.0	73.8	74.1	74.0	74.3	72.9
2018	73.2	74.2	74.8	75.6	76.4	77.7	77.0	77.0	76.2	76.1	75.8	76.2	75.9
Service-Providing													
2010	430.6	431.3	435.1	440.2	444.2	443.9	441.4	444.0	443.8	447.6	450.1	449.8	441.8
2011	441.4	444.6	447.0	449.6	450.8	449.7	447.6	451.6	452.9	456.1	458.5	457.8	450.6
2012	453.3	455.3	458.7	463.0	465.5	465.2	463.2	468.2	467.5	470.7	474.3	473.5	464.9
2013	465.7	470.1	473.1	474.8	476.8	476.0	474.6	482.8	485.7	487.5	491.3	490.9	479.1
2014	482.4	482.1	487.0	492.4	495.9	497.6	492.0	498.0	499.1	505.9	509.2	509.6	495.9
2015	498.6	501.8	504.2	509.1	511.9	513.7	509.7	516.1	517.3	522.4	526.2	526.6	513.1
2016	517.8	520.7	523.3	527.9	530.1	531.1	527.9	532.3	533.7	537.5	541.9	540.2	530.4
2017	529.0	534.1	536.3	537.6	542.9	543.9	542.8	549.9	547.3	551.9	556.5	556.1	544.0
2018	546.4	550.8	553.1	557.1	561.6	562.0	555.3	563.5	554.8	559.4	560.7	559.2	557.0
Mining, Logging, and Construction													
2010	27.0	26.8	27.3	27.7	28.1	28.4	29.0	29.1	28.9	28.9	28.6	28.1	28.2
2011	27.2	27.8	28.2	28.0	28.3	28.8	29.3	29.1	28.9	28.7	28.6	28.6	28.5
2012	28.4	28.6	29.1	29.2	29.6	30.0	30.5	30.5	30.4	30.3	30.2	30.2	29.8
2013	29.0	29.3	29.6	29.6	30.1	30.4	30.4	30.6	30.5	30.9	30.9	30.8	30.2
2014	30.1	30.0	30.9	30.9	31.5	31.9	32.5	32.6	32.4	32.3	32.0	31.8	31.6
2015	31.6	31.8	32.1	32.7	33.4	33.8	34.3	34.1	33.8	34.1	34.0	34.1	33.3
2016	33.7	33.7	34.1	34.7	35.1	35.4	35.6	35.7	35.8	36.2	36.4	36.5	35.2
2017	35.7	36.4	36.8	37.0	37.4	38.2	38.8	38.7	38.6	38.7	38.9	38.9	37.8
2018	38.0	38.6	39.0	39.7	40.3	41.1	40.8	40.7	40.2	40.2	39.8	40.1	39.9
Manufacturing													
2010	29.9	29.8	29.8	29.7	29.9	30.1	30.2	30.2	30.2	30.3	30.3	30.5	30.1
2011	30.2	30.3	30.5	30.7	30.7	30.7	30.6	30.5	30.4	30.3	30.4	30.6	30.5
2012	30.5	30.5	30.5	30.5	30.7	30.9	31.0	31.1	31.0	30.9	30.9	30.9	30.8
2013	30.8	30.8	30.9	30.9	30.8	31.2	31.5	31.7	31.7	31.5	31.7	32.1	31.3
2014	31.8	31.9	32.1	31.9	32.2	32.8	32.9	33.2	33.2	33.4	33.6	33.7	32.7
2015	33.6	33.9	33.8	33.8	34.0	34.4	34.1	34.3	34.1	34.1	34.0	34.2	34.0
2016	34.3	34.5	34.4	34.3	34.3	34.8	34.9	34.8	34.5	34.4	34.5	34.5	34.5
2017	34.7	34.9	34.9	34.7	34.7	35.0	35.2	35.3	35.2	35.4	35.1	35.4	35.0
2018	35.2	35.6	35.8	35.9	36.1	36.6	36.2	36.3	36.0	35.9	36.0	36.1	36.0

Employment by Industry: Raleigh, NC, 2010–2018—*Continued*

(Numbers in thousands, not seasonally adjusted)

Industry and year	January	February	March	April	May	June	July	August	September	October	November	December	Annual average
Trade, Transportation, and Utilities													
2010	85.4	84.8	85.1	85.5	86.1	86.5	86.6	86.9	85.8	87.0	89.2	90.7	86.6
2011	86.9	86.8	87.3	88.1	88.3	88.5	88.8	89.0	89.1	89.4	91.8	92.9	88.9
2012	90.6	89.8	90.6	90.4	91.3	91.5	91.6	91.4	91.3	91.8	94.3	94.8	91.6
2013	91.1	90.5	91.2	91.0	91.8	92.4	92.2	92.8	92.9	94.1	96.7	98.0	92.9
2014	95.1	94.5	95.4	96.2	96.9	97.4	97.4	98.0	97.8	99.2	102.2	104.0	97.8
2015	99.6	99.5	100.1	101.2	101.8	102.3	102.5	103.1	102.6	103.9	106.6	107.6	102.6
2016	103.7	103.6	104.4	105.4	106.3	106.5	106.6	106.8	106.5	107.2	109.6	111.5	106.5
2017	106.7	106.6	107.1	107.2	108.1	108.5	109.7	110.1	109.2	110.4	113.5	114.7	109.3
2018	110.6	110.3	110.4	110.5	111.1	111.2	111.2	111.5	109.7	110.3	113.5	114.6	111.2
Wholesale Trade													
2010	19.4	19.5	19.4	19.6	19.6	19.7	19.8	20.0	19.8	19.9	20.0	20.0	19.7
2011	20.1	20.2	20.2	20.6	20.7	20.7	21.1	21.2	21.5	21.2	21.4	21.5	20.9
2012	21.7	21.9	22.1	22.1	22.2	22.1	22.5	22.5	22.5	22.1	22.0	21.9	22.1
2013	21.6	21.7	21.7	21.4	21.5	21.7	21.4	21.5	21.5	21.5	21.5	21.5	21.5
2014	21.5	21.6	21.7	21.8	21.9	22.0	22.2	22.5	22.5	22.7	22.8	22.9	22.2
2015	22.8	22.9	22.9	23.0	23.0	23.1	23.3	23.4	23.3	23.3	23.4	23.4	23.2
2016	23.7	23.9	24.0	24.0	24.2	24.2	24.4	24.6	24.6	24.6	24.6	24.8	24.3
2017	24.5	24.7	24.8	25.0	25.2	25.3	26.2	26.3	26.2	26.2	26.1	26.3	25.6
2018	26.0	26.2	26.3	26.2	26.3	26.5	26.5	26.6	26.4	25.8	26.1	25.9	26.2
Retail Trade													
2010	56.2	55.5	55.9	55.9	56.5	56.7	56.7	56.8	56.1	57.1	59.2	60.5	56.9
2011	57.2	57.0	57.4	57.5	57.6	57.7	57.6	57.7	57.4	58.2	60.4	61.1	58.1
2012	58.8	57.9	58.4	58.3	58.9	59.1	58.9	58.8	58.7	59.6	62.1	62.4	59.3
2013	59.3	58.8	59.4	59.5	60.1	60.4	60.5	60.9	60.9	61.9	64.3	65.2	60.9
2014	62.0	61.5	62.1	62.9	63.3	63.7	63.6	63.8	63.5	64.8	67.4	68.5	63.9
2015	65.0	64.7	65.3	66.1	66.6	67.0	67.1	67.4	67.0	68.3	70.6	71.0	67.2
2016	67.5	67.3	67.9	68.9	69.4	69.5	69.5	69.5	69.0	69.8	72.0	73.0	69.4
2017	69.4	69.2	69.4	69.4	69.8	70.0	70.6	70.6	69.7	70.7	73.6	73.8	70.5
2018	70.8	70.3	70.3	70.4	70.8	70.6	70.8	70.9	69.2	70.4	72.9	74.0	71.0
Transportation and Utilities													
2010	9.8	9.8	9.8	10.0	10.0	10.1	10.1	10.1	9.9	10.0	10.0	10.2	10.0
2011	9.6	9.6	9.7	10.0	10.0	10.1	10.1	10.1	10.2	10.0	10.0	10.3	10.0
2012	10.1	10.0	10.1	10.0	10.2	10.3	10.2	10.1	10.1	10.1	10.2	10.5	10.2
2013	10.2	10.0	10.1	10.1	10.2	10.3	10.3	10.4	10.5	10.7	10.9	11.3	10.4
2014	11.6	11.4	11.6	11.5	11.7	11.7	11.6	11.7	11.8	11.7	12.0	12.6	11.7
2015	11.8	11.9	11.9	12.1	12.2	12.2	12.1	12.3	12.3	12.3	12.6	13.2	12.2
2016	12.5	12.4	12.5	12.5	12.7	12.8	12.7	12.7	12.9	12.8	13.0	13.7	12.8
2017	12.8	12.7	12.9	12.8	13.1	13.2	12.9	13.2	13.3	13.5	13.8	14.6	13.2
2018	13.8	13.8	13.8	13.9	14.0	14.1	13.9	14.0	14.1	14.1	14.5	14.7	14.1
Information													
2010	16.5	16.5	16.6	16.6	16.5	16.7	16.8	16.8	16.7	16.7	16.9	16.9	16.7
2011	16.9	17.0	17.0	17.1	17.1	17.4	17.5	17.7	17.5	17.6	17.8	17.8	17.4
2012	17.7	17.7	17.7	17.5	17.5	17.7	17.7	17.7	17.5	17.6	17.6	17.7	17.6
2013	17.7	17.8	17.8	17.8	17.9	18.0	18.2	18.2	18.0	17.9	18.1	18.2	18.0
2014	18.2	18.2	18.3	18.3	18.5	18.8	19.0	19.3	19.1	19.1	19.1	19.3	18.8
2015	19.2	19.3	19.3	19.3	19.4	19.7	19.9	20.0	20.0	20.2	20.3	20.4	19.8
2016	20.5	20.7	20.8	20.8	20.9	21.2	21.5	21.4	21.2	21.2	21.3	21.4	21.1
2017	21.2	21.4	21.4	21.5	21.6	21.8	22.0	21.9	21.7	21.5	21.6	21.7	21.6
2018	21.7	21.9	21.9	22.0	22.2	22.4	22.2	22.2	22.0	22.0	22.1	22.2	22.1
Financial Activities													
2010	26.4	26.4	26.4	26.3	26.4	26.4	26.6	26.6	26.8	26.7	26.9	27.0	26.6
2011	26.4	26.4	26.4	26.3	26.3	26.3	26.3	26.4	26.2	26.2	26.1	26.2	26.3
2012	25.8	26.1	26.2	26.4	26.4	26.5	26.4	26.3	26.2	26.7	26.6	26.7	26.4
2013	26.5	26.4	26.6	26.9	27.0	27.1	27.1	27.2	27.1	27.4	27.5	27.7	27.0
2014	27.2	27.3	27.3	27.5	27.7	27.9	27.9	28.0	27.9	28.2	28.2	28.5	27.8
2015	28.2	28.5	28.7	29.2	29.7	30.0	30.1	30.2	30.1	30.4	30.5	30.6	29.7
2016	30.5	30.6	30.5	30.7	30.7	30.8	31.1	31.1	30.9	31.0	31.0	30.9	30.8
2017	30.7	30.9	30.9	31.2	31.4	31.7	31.9	32.0	31.9	32.2	32.2	32.4	31.6
2018	32.2	32.2	32.2	32.7	32.8	33.1	33.2	33.3	33.0	33.3	33.1	33.4	32.9

Employment by Industry: Raleigh, NC, 2010–2018—*Continued*

(Numbers in thousands, not seasonally adjusted)

Industry and year	January	February	March	April	May	June	July	August	September	October	November	December	Annual average
Professional and Business Services													
2010	82.1	82.3	83.1	84.7	85.1	86.1	86.6	86.7	86.8	89.6	89.7	89.7	86.0
2011	88.1	89.0	88.9	90.1	90.4	91.5	92.1	91.9	92.6	93.0	93.2	93.5	91.2
2012	92.5	92.5	93.1	96.1	96.2	97.3	98.9	99.1	98.4	99.1	99.9	99.9	96.9
2013	98.6	101.1	101.5	101.5	102.5	102.6	104.1	106.3	106.4	105.9	106.4	105.6	103.5
2014	103.7	103.2	104.4	106.0	107.2	108.1	108.2	109.1	108.3	109.8	109.6	109.6	107.3
2015	106.0	106.6	107.0	107.8	108.8	109.5	109.9	111.0	110.4	111.7	111.9	111.9	109.4
2016	109.5	109.3	109.4	110.0	111.3	112.2	113.3	113.5	113.7	114.3	114.1	113.0	112.0
2017	111.0	111.8	111.6	112.1	113.7	115.8	117.6	117.7	116.6	117.1	117.9	117.4	115.0
2018	115.6	116.6	117.2	118.4	119.3	120.7	121.7	122.3	119.3	121.5	118.3	117.9	119.1
Education and Health Services													
2010	59.6	60.1	60.5	61.3	61.4	60.3	60.3	60.7	60.6	61.0	61.2	60.7	60.6
2011	60.7	61.5	61.6	61.1	61.3	60.6	60.5	60.8	61.0	62.2	62.3	62.1	61.3
2012	62.1	62.8	63.4	63.2	63.8	62.9	62.7	63.3	63.7	64.5	64.7	64.8	63.5
2013	63.5	64.2	64.4	64.6	64.9	64.1	64.2	65.1	65.6	65.7	65.9	65.9	64.8
2014	64.9	65.5	66.0	66.1	66.7	65.8	66.0	66.8	66.9	67.9	68.3	68.2	66.6
2015	67.5	68.1	68.3	69.0	69.4	68.8	69.0	70.0	70.1	71.1	71.3	71.5	69.5
2016	71.0	71.7	72.2	72.6	73.0	71.9	72.2	73.1	73.1	74.1	74.5	74.5	72.8
2017	73.8	74.7	74.9	75.3	76.0	74.5	75.3	76.3	76.2	77.6	77.6	77.5	75.8
2018	76.9	77.6	77.8	78.6	79.0	78.3	77.9	78.8	78.2	78.2	78.9	78.9	78.3
Leisure and Hospitality													
2010	47.4	47.3	48.6	49.7	50.6	51.9	52.7	52.9	52.4	50.9	51.4	50.7	50.5
2011	49.5	50.2	51.5	53.1	53.6	54.3	55.1	55.4	54.2	53.8	53.7	53.9	53.2
2012	52.5	53.0	54.2	55.9	56.9	57.5	57.7	58.1	56.1	55.8	55.9	56.5	55.8
2013	55.1	55.2	56.1	57.8	58.5	60.5	60.4	60.5	59.9	59.1	59.2	59.8	58.5
2014	58.0	57.6	58.9	60.7	61.7	63.5	62.5	62.3	61.4	61.5	61.3	61.8	60.9
2015	61.0	61.3	62.2	63.5	65.2	66.9	66.6	66.6	65.2	65.1	65.1	65.5	64.5
2016	64.1	64.4	65.3	67.7	68.9	70.3	70.1	70.0	68.1	67.7	68.5	68.5	67.8
2017	66.5	67.4	68.6	68.7	71.1	72.5	72.5	72.1	69.8	69.9	69.4	69.4	69.8
2018	67.9	68.7	69.6	70.6	73.1	74.6	72.6	73.3	69.9	70.1	69.6	68.6	70.7
Other Services													
2010	21.1	21.0	21.3	21.1	21.2	21.4	21.4	21.2	20.7	21.2	20.8	20.4	21.1
2011	20.2	20.2	20.5	20.4	20.5	21.0	21.0	21.0	20.7	21.0	20.9	20.7	20.7
2012	20.8	20.9	21.0	21.4	21.9	22.0	22.2	22.5	22.5	22.3	22.3	21.8	21.8
2013	21.7	22.0	22.3	22.5	22.8	23.2	22.7	22.5	22.4	22.4	22.3	22.2	22.4
2014	22.2	22.2	22.6	22.7	23.2	23.5	23.4	23.3	23.0	23.1	23.1	22.7	22.9
2015	22.4	22.5	22.7	23.1	23.4	23.6	23.8	23.6	23.4	23.4	23.4	23.4	23.2
2016	23.6	23.6	23.8	24.0	24.1	24.3	24.7	24.7	24.4	24.6	24.5	24.0	24.2
2017	23.6	23.6	23.9	24.0	24.2	24.5	24.5	24.3	24.0	24.5	24.3	24.3	24.1
2018	24.1	24.3	24.5	24.6	24.8	25.1	25.0	25.1	24.5	24.8	24.7	24.5	24.7
Government													
2010	92.1	92.9	93.5	95.0	96.9	94.6	90.4	92.2	94.0	94.5	94.0	93.7	93.7
2011	92.7	93.5	93.8	93.4	93.3	90.1	86.3	89.4	91.6	92.9	92.7	90.7	91.7
2012	91.3	92.5	92.5	92.1	91.5	89.8	86.0	89.8	91.8	92.9	93.0	91.3	91.2
2013	91.5	92.9	93.2	92.7	91.4	88.1	85.7	90.2	93.4	95.0	95.2	93.5	91.9
2014	93.1	93.6	94.1	94.9	94.0	92.6	87.6	91.2	94.7	97.1	97.4	95.5	93.8
2015	94.7	96.0	95.9	96.0	94.2	92.9	87.9	91.6	95.5	96.6	97.1	95.7	94.5
2016	94.9	96.8	96.9	96.7	94.9	93.9	88.4	91.7	95.8	97.4	98.4	96.4	95.2
2017	95.5	97.7	97.9	97.6	96.8	94.6	89.3	95.5	97.9	98.7	100.0	98.7	96.7
2018	97.4	99.2	99.5	99.7	99.3	96.6	91.5	97.0	98.2	99.2	100.5	99.1	98.1

Employment by Industry: Memphis, TN-MS-AR, 2010–2018

(Numbers in thousands, not seasonally adjusted)

Industry and year	January	February	March	April	May	June	July	August	September	October	November	December	Annual average
Total Nonfarm													
2010	584.4	586.5	590.9	592.0	597.9	592.5	588.6	591.8	589.8	596.2	599.1	598.5	592.4
2011	584.4	586.3	589.9	595.6	596.4	592.0	592.7	596.6	598.0	600.5	606.6	607.1	595.5
2012	590.6	595.0	598.5	600.4	603.1	600.8	598.7	603.9	605.5	609.4	618.1	618.8	603.6
2013	599.5	604.2	606.5	610.5	611.8	606.9	600.9	605.5	607.4	609.3	620.7	622.2	608.8
2014	604.0	605.4	609.0	617.5	617.5	614.0	609.9	616.8	617.8	622.3	630.5	632.9	616.5
2015	614.1	617.5	618.2	622.0	623.8	621.8	626.3	629.8	631.1	636.9	646.0	650.5	628.2
2016	628.8	631.4	633.1	637.4	636.0	632.3	633.6	638.4	641.4	643.9	650.7	652.0	638.3
2017	630.6	635.1	637.1	640.0	639.7	638.3	635.6	640.9	643.0	647.0	655.0	655.9	641.5
2018	634.7	639.7	642.5	644.6	647.1	645.1	642.7	649.5	651.2	655.7	665.0	664.8	648.6
Total Private													
2010	499.6	499.5	503.6	504.5	508.5	509.6	506.1	507.2	503.8	508.6	511.5	512.4	506.2
2011	499.0	499.4	503.2	508.7	510.7	512.4	513.4	513.6	513.2	515.2	520.9	522.4	511.0
2012	506.4	509.2	512.6	514.1	518.2	520.6	518.0	520.9	520.2	523.7	531.9	533.6	519.1
2013	515.6	518.0	520.6	523.7	527.3	528.1	522.8	524.6	524.3	525.8	536.6	539.7	525.6
2014	522.0	522.1	525.5	533.4	535.5	536.8	532.8	536.6	535.2	539.1	547.0	550.2	534.7
2015	532.4	533.3	534.1	538.7	542.9	545.7	550.2	550.7	548.9	553.5	562.5	568.4	546.8
2016	547.9	548.7	549.9	555.2	556.1	557.1	557.9	559.3	558.6	560.4	566.8	569.2	557.3
2017	548.7	551.3	553.4	556.0	557.7	560.8	557.8	560.1	558.0	562.3	569.7	572.0	559.0
2018	551.3	554.4	557.0	560.0	563.9	566.4	564.0	567.3	565.7	569.7	578.4	579.7	564.8
Goods Producing													
2010	60.3	60.6	61.5	61.7	62.2	62.7	62.8	62.7	62.4	61.4	61.7	61.4	61.8
2011	60.6	60.2	60.6	61.2	61.9	62.9	63.3	63.1	62.8	61.5	62.3	62.0	61.9
2012	61.0	61.0	61.7	62.3	63.0	63.8	63.7	64.0	62.8	62.2	63.0	62.5	62.6
2013	61.7	61.7	62.2	62.4	63.0	63.4	63.1	62.6	62.3	61.9	62.1	61.9	62.4
2014	62.0	61.9	61.8	62.8	63.4	63.3	63.7	63.8	63.5	63.5	63.6	63.9	63.1
2015	62.7	62.9	63.2	63.9	64.5	65.3	66.2	65.4	65.2	65.2	65.2	65.2	64.6
2016	64.2	64.0	63.8	64.9	65.1	65.5	66.1	65.4	65.0	64.5	64.6	64.8	64.8
2017	64.4	64.7	65.2	65.7	65.9	66.5	66.3	66.6	66.2	65.9	65.8	65.9	65.8
2018	64.7	65.2	65.6	66.5	67.0	68.0	68.8	69.0	68.7	68.1	67.8	67.9	67.3
Service-Providing													
2010	524.1	525.9	529.4	530.3	535.7	529.8	525.8	529.1	527.4	534.8	537.4	537.1	530.6
2011	523.8	526.1	529.3	534.4	534.5	529.1	529.4	533.5	535.2	539.0	544.3	545.1	533.6
2012	529.6	534.0	536.8	538.1	540.1	537.0	535.0	539.9	542.7	547.2	555.1	556.3	541.0
2013	537.8	542.5	544.3	548.1	548.8	543.5	537.8	542.9	545.1	547.4	558.6	560.3	546.4
2014	542.0	543.5	547.2	554.7	554.1	550.7	546.2	553.0	554.3	558.8	566.9	569.0	553.4
2015	551.4	554.6	555.0	558.1	559.3	556.5	560.1	564.4	565.9	571.7	580.8	585.3	563.6
2016	564.6	567.4	569.3	572.5	570.9	566.8	567.5	573.0	576.4	579.4	586.1	587.2	573.4
2017	566.2	570.4	571.9	574.3	573.8	571.8	569.3	574.3	576.8	581.1	589.2	590.0	575.8
2018	570.0	574.5	576.9	578.1	580.1	577.1	573.9	580.5	582.5	587.6	597.2	596.9	581.3
Mining, Logging, and Construction													
2010	19.0	18.8	19.3	19.2	19.4	19.8	19.8	19.9	19.7	19.4	19.1	18.9	19.4
2011	18.1	18.2	18.6	19.0	19.4	20.2	20.7	20.8	20.9	20.8	20.7	20.6	19.8
2012	19.6	19.5	20.0	20.4	20.9	21.4	21.3	21.5	21.3	20.8	20.7	20.6	20.7
2013	19.8	19.8	20.0	20.2	20.7	21.0	20.9	20.9	20.7	20.5	20.7	20.5	20.5
2014	20.5	20.3	19.9	21.0	21.4	21.1	21.1	21.2	21.1	21.4	21.5	21.4	21.0
2015	20.6	20.6	20.5	21.0	21.2	21.6	22.5	22.4	22.3	22.3	22.3	22.0	21.6
2016	21.2	21.0	20.9	21.5	21.5	21.8	22.4	22.0	22.1	21.9	22.0	21.9	21.7
2017	21.7	22.1	22.5	22.6	22.8	23.1	23.2	23.3	23.4	23.3	23.1	22.9	22.8
2018	21.8	22.3	22.6	22.8	23.1	23.7	23.9	24.0	24.3	24.4	24.0	23.9	23.4
Manufacturing													
2010	41.3	41.8	42.2	42.5	42.8	42.9	43.0	42.8	42.7	42.0	42.6	42.5	42.4
2011	42.5	42.0	42.0	42.2	42.5	42.7	42.6	42.3	41.9	40.7	41.6	41.4	42.0
2012	41.4	41.5	41.7	41.9	42.1	42.4	42.4	42.5	41.5	41.4	42.3	41.9	41.9
2013	41.9	41.9	42.2	42.2	42.3	42.4	42.2	41.7	41.6	41.4	41.4	41.4	41.9
2014	41.5	41.6	41.9	41.8	42.0	42.2	42.6	42.6	42.4	42.1	42.1	42.5	42.1
2015	42.1	42.3	42.7	42.9	43.3	43.7	43.7	43.0	42.9	42.9	42.9	43.2	43.0
2016	43.0	43.0	42.9	43.4	43.6	43.7	43.7	43.4	42.9	42.6	42.6	42.9	43.1
2017	42.7	42.6	42.7	43.1	43.1	43.4	43.1	43.3	42.8	42.6	42.7	43.0	42.9
2018	42.9	42.9	43.0	43.7	43.9	44.3	44.9	45.0	44.4	43.7	43.8	44.0	43.9

Employment by Industry: Memphis, TN-MS-AR, 2010–2018—*Continued*

(Numbers in thousands, not seasonally adjusted)

Industry and year	January	February	March	April	May	June	July	August	September	October	November	December	Annual average
Trade, Transportation, and Utilities													
2010	157.4	156.7	157.0	158.1	158.3	158.5	158.7	158.7	157.2	158.8	161.1	162.5	158.6
2011	157.1	156.4	156.8	158.3	159.0	159.4	160.0	159.4	159.8	161.6	164.3	165.3	159.8
2012	160.2	159.4	160.1	160.1	161.2	161.5	161.4	161.4	161.6	162.3	166.2	167.5	161.9
2013	161.8	161.4	161.0	161.8	161.8	162.1	162.3	161.6	160.9	161.8	165.5	166.9	162.4
2014	160.9	160.8	161.7	163.2	163.1	163.9	163.8	163.9	164.1	166.1	169.9	170.5	164.3
2015	164.8	163.7	163.8	164.5	165.5	166.7	170.1	168.7	168.4	170.2	175.4	178.1	168.3
2016	171.0	170.6	170.7	172.0	172.3	173.7	174.7	173.9	173.7	176.0	179.3	180.6	174.0
2017	173.6	173.0	172.8	173.1	173.3	174.3	174.8	174.2	173.7	174.7	179.0	180.5	174.8
2018	173.7	172.6	172.8	172.7	173.8	174.8	174.7	174.3	174.3	175.8	182.6	182.6	175.4
Wholesale Trade													
2010	31.8	31.8	31.8	32.6	32.5	32.6	32.5	32.6	32.3	32.4	32.5	32.6	32.3
2011	32.4	32.4	32.4	32.6	32.7	32.8	32.9	32.9	32.9	32.9	33.0	32.8	32.7
2012	32.8	33.0	33.0	33.1	33.4	33.5	33.5	33.5	33.4	33.4	33.6	33.6	33.3
2013	33.1	33.2	33.3	33.5	33.5	33.6	33.5	33.6	33.6	33.3	33.3	33.4	33.4
2014	32.9	33.1	33.2	33.2	33.3	33.5	33.3	33.2	33.2	33.0	33.3	33.5	33.2
2015	33.3	33.3	33.2	33.5	33.7	33.8	34.3	34.5	34.7	34.8	35.2	35.5	34.2
2016	34.6	34.8	34.8	34.8	34.9	35.1	35.2	35.3	35.3	35.3	35.4	35.7	35.1
2017	35.7	35.8	35.9	35.4	35.5	35.6	35.5	35.4	35.3	35.2	35.2	35.1	35.5
2018	34.8	34.9	34.8	34.9	35.1	35.2	35.0	35.0	35.1	35.3	35.8	36.6	35.2
Retail Trade													
2010	64.6	64.1	64.5	64.4	64.6	64.5	64.7	64.1	63.0	63.9	65.8	66.6	64.6
2011	62.5	61.8	61.9	62.6	62.8	62.7	62.8	62.2	61.9	62.7	65.3	66.0	62.9
2012	62.7	62.0	62.6	62.7	63.2	63.3	63.2	62.6	62.3	63.1	66.0	66.3	63.3
2013	63.6	63.1	63.2	63.3	63.6	63.8	64.3	64.0	63.8	64.4	67.1	68.1	64.4
2014	64.4	63.9	64.2	65.2	65.4	65.6	65.6	65.2	65.0	65.7	68.1	68.7	65.6
2015	65.0	64.3	64.6	64.8	65.3	65.9	66.6	66.0	65.3	66.6	69.7	70.5	66.2
2016	66.9	66.8	67.0	67.8	67.7	67.8	68.5	67.6	67.4	69.0	70.3	70.9	68.1
2017	67.9	67.5	67.4	67.6	67.5	67.6	67.5	67.2	66.9	67.9	70.5	70.8	68.0
2018	67.4	66.7	66.6	66.6	67.1	67.1	67.0	66.7	66.2	67.2	70.0	69.8	67.4
Transportation and Utilities													
2010	61.0	60.8	60.7	61.1	61.2	61.4	61.5	62.0	61.9	62.5	62.8	63.3	61.7
2011	62.2	62.2	62.5	63.1	63.5	63.9	64.3	64.3	65.0	66.0	66.0	66.5	64.1
2012	64.7	64.4	64.5	64.3	64.6	64.7	64.7	65.3	65.9	65.8	66.6	67.6	65.3
2013	65.1	65.1	64.5	65.0	64.7	64.7	64.5	64.0	63.5	64.1	65.2	65.4	64.7
2014	63.6	63.8	64.3	64.8	64.4	64.8	64.9	65.5	65.9	67.4	68.5	68.3	65.5
2015	66.5	66.1	66.0	66.2	66.5	67.0	69.2	68.2	68.4	68.8	70.5	72.1	68.0
2016	69.5	69.0	68.9	69.4	69.7	70.8	71.0	71.0	71.0	71.7	73.6	74.0	70.8
2017	70.0	69.7	69.5	70.1	70.3	71.1	71.8	71.6	71.5	71.6	73.3	74.6	71.3
2018	71.5	71.0	71.4	71.2	71.6	72.5	72.7	72.6	73.0	73.3	76.8	76.2	72.8
Information													
2010	6.4	6.3	6.3	6.2	6.3	6.3	6.2	6.2	6.2	6.2	6.2	6.3	6.3
2011	6.2	6.1	6.1	6.1	6.2	6.1	6.1	6.1	6.0	6.0	6.0	6.0	6.1
2012	6.1	6.1	6.1	6.1	6.1	6.0	6.1	6.1	6.0	6.0	6.0	6.0	6.1
2013	5.9	5.9	5.9	5.9	6.0	6.1	6.0	6.0	6.0	6.0	6.1	6.1	6.0
2014	6.0	6.0	6.0	6.0	6.0	6.0	5.9	6.0	5.9	5.8	6.0	6.0	6.0
2015	5.8	5.8	5.8	5.9	5.9	5.9	5.8	5.8	5.7	5.7	5.8	5.9	5.8
2016	5.8	5.8	5.7	5.7	5.7	5.7	5.8	5.7	5.7	5.6	5.7	5.8	5.7
2017	5.7	5.7	5.7	5.6	5.7	5.7	5.8	5.8	5.7	5.7	5.8	5.9	5.7
2018	5.5	5.5	5.5	5.5	5.6	5.6	5.5	5.4	5.3	5.3	5.4	5.4	5.5
Financial Activities													
2010	29.7	29.6	29.5	29.2	29.1	29.0	28.9	28.8	28.5	28.2	28.0	28.1	28.9
2011	27.6	27.3	27.2	27.5	27.6	27.6	27.7	27.7	27.6	27.5	27.5	27.6	27.5
2012	27.4	27.4	27.4	27.3	27.5	27.3	27.5	27.4	27.1	27.3	27.4	27.4	27.4
2013	27.2	27.0	27.0	27.0	27.0	27.2	27.4	27.3	27.3	27.3	27.4	27.5	27.2
2014	27.1	27.1	27.1	27.4	27.6	27.6	27.6	27.6	27.4	27.5	27.5	27.5	27.4
2015	27.3	27.2	27.1	27.2	27.4	27.6	27.7	27.8	27.6	27.8	27.9	28.0	27.6
2016	27.7	27.8	27.6	27.8	27.9	28.0	28.2	28.2	28.1	28.1	28.2	28.3	28.0
2017	28.1	28.1	28.2	28.3	28.6	28.9	28.8	28.8	28.8	28.8	28.7	28.9	28.6
2018	28.8	29.1	29.2	29.2	29.4	29.5	29.5	29.5	29.6	29.7	29.9	30.0	29.5

Employment by Industry: Memphis, TN-MS-AR, 2010–2018—*Continued*

(Numbers in thousands, not seasonally adjusted)

Industry and year	January	February	March	April	May	June	July	August	September	October	November	December	Annual average
Professional and Business Services													
2010	76.5	76.0	76.6	75.8	78.6	78.3	75.6	77.2	78.2	82.2	83.2	83.5	78.5
2011	79.6	80.7	81.8	82.8	82.8	82.5	82.9	84.0	84.3	87.5	89.4	90.2	84.0
2012	82.8	84.7	84.4	84.6	85.6	86.2	84.7	86.0	87.7	90.4	94.0	94.2	87.1
2013	86.4	87.8	88.9	89.3	90.7	90.4	86.8	89.7	90.9	91.7	97.7	100.0	90.9
2014	91.4	90.1	91.1	94.9	95.7	95.1	94.0	96.2	96.6	98.7	103.0	104.9	96.0
2015	97.4	97.4	97.7	98.0	99.1	99.2	99.4	101.0	101.1	102.8	106.0	107.8	100.6
2016	99.1	98.6	98.9	99.9	99.2	98.1	97.5	99.3	100.3	100.4	103.1	103.6	99.8
2017	93.8	94.3	94.3	95.0	95.0	95.7	94.5	95.4	95.4	98.5	101.7	102.1	96.3
2018	94.2	94.9	94.8	95.8	96.6	96.7	95.2	96.6	96.5	98.3	98.9	101.5	96.7
Education and Health Services													
2010	82.4	83.1	83.8	83.5	83.3	82.8	82.6	83.0	83.0	83.6	83.9	83.8	83.2
2011	82.5	83.0	83.5	84.3	84.1	83.6	83.8	84.5	85.6	85.8	86.2	86.1	84.4
2012	85.7	86.6	87.3	86.2	86.3	85.8	85.6	87.2	88.1	88.3	88.9	89.4	87.1
2013	88.1	89.3	89.5	89.3	89.4	88.4	87.4	88.1	89.2	89.6	90.1	90.1	89.0
2014	88.8	89.4	89.4	89.6	89.0	87.8	87.6	88.9	89.5	89.6	89.6	89.6	89.1
2015	88.3	89.5	89.6	89.7	89.2	88.4	89.1	90.5	91.3	91.7	92.2	92.6	90.2
2016	91.1	91.9	92.0	92.6	92.7	91.1	91.3	92.9	93.5	93.8	93.8	93.7	92.5
2017	92.2	93.4	93.8	93.8	93.7	92.6	91.8	93.5	94.2	94.6	94.7	94.6	93.6
2018	93.0	94.3	94.6	94.8	94.7	93.5	93.1	95.0	95.7	96.9	96.3	96.0	94.8
Leisure and Hospitality													
2010	62.5	62.8	64.3	65.2	66.0	67.3	66.9	66.5	64.6	64.3	63.8	63.4	64.8
2011	62.3	62.6	63.9	65.1	65.7	66.6	65.7	64.9	63.3	61.7	61.6	61.6	63.8
2012	59.7	60.4	61.7	63.4	64.2	65.4	64.6	64.6	62.8	63.1	62.4	62.6	62.9
2013	60.8	61.1	62.1	63.7	65.0	65.8	65.2	65.0	63.5	63.5	63.6	63.3	63.6
2014	62.1	62.9	64.4	65.5	66.6	68.6	65.9	66.1	64.1	63.9	63.6	63.9	64.8
2015	62.2	62.7	62.8	65.2	66.8	67.8	67.1	66.8	64.9	65.5	65.3	66.0	65.3
2016	64.3	65.2	66.2	67.3	68.1	69.5	68.8	68.5	66.9	66.8	66.8	67.1	67.1
2017	65.7	66.7	67.8	68.9	69.8	71.0	69.7	69.7	67.9	68.2	67.9	67.9	68.4
2018	65.5	66.4	67.9	68.8	70.0	71.0	69.9	70.3	68.5	68.4	69.8	68.7	68.8
Other Services													
2010	24.4	24.4	24.6	24.8	24.7	24.7	24.4	24.1	23.7	23.9	23.6	23.4	24.2
2011	23.1	23.1	23.3	23.4	23.4	23.7	23.9	23.9	23.8	23.6	23.6	23.6	23.5
2012	23.5	23.6	23.9	24.1	24.3	24.6	24.4	24.2	24.1	24.1	24.0	24.0	24.1
2013	23.7	23.8	24.0	24.3	24.4	24.7	24.6	24.3	24.2	24.0	24.0	23.9	24.2
2014	23.7	23.9	24.0	24.0	24.1	24.5	24.3	24.1	24.1	24.0	23.8	23.9	24.0
2015	23.9	24.1	24.1	24.3	24.5	24.8	24.8	24.7	24.7	24.6	24.7	24.8	24.5
2016	24.7	24.8	25.0	25.0	25.1	25.5	25.5	25.4	25.4	25.2	25.3	25.3	25.2
2017	25.2	25.4	25.6	25.6	25.7	26.1	26.1	26.1	26.1	25.9	26.1	26.2	25.8
2018	25.9	26.4	26.6	26.7	26.8	27.3	27.3	27.2	27.1	27.2	27.7	27.6	27.0
Government													
2010	84.8	87.0	87.3	87.5	89.4	82.9	82.5	84.6	86.0	87.6	87.6	86.1	86.1
2011	85.4	86.9	86.7	86.9	85.7	79.6	79.3	83.0	84.8	85.3	85.7	84.7	84.5
2012	84.2	85.8	85.9	86.3	84.9	80.2	80.7	83.0	85.3	85.7	86.2	85.2	84.5
2013	83.9	86.2	85.9	86.8	84.5	78.8	78.1	80.9	83.1	83.5	84.1	82.5	83.2
2014	82.0	83.3	83.5	84.1	82.0	77.2	77.1	80.2	82.6	83.2	83.5	82.7	81.8
2015	81.7	84.2	84.1	83.3	80.9	76.1	76.1	79.1	82.2	83.4	83.5	82.1	81.4
2016	80.9	82.7	83.2	82.2	79.9	75.2	75.7	79.1	82.8	83.5	83.9	82.8	81.0
2017	81.9	83.8	83.7	84.0	82.0	77.5	77.8	80.8	85.0	84.7	85.3	83.9	82.5
2018	83.4	85.3	85.5	84.6	83.2	78.7	78.7	82.2	85.5	86.0	86.6	85.1	83.7

Employment by Industry: Richmond, VA, 2010–2018

(Numbers in thousands, not seasonally adjusted)

Industry and year	January	February	March	April	May	June	July	August	September	October	November	December	Annual average
Total Nonfarm													
2010	581.5	578.9	585.1	593.4	598.8	600.6	593.0	590.3	590.9	595.1	596.2	596.2	591.7
2011	586.8	589.0	593.4	600.1	600.7	602.6	601.4	598.6	601.3	607.4	610.8	609.3	600.1
2012	597.6	599.7	604.7	610.4	612.8	617.0	610.7	613.6	614.6	619.1	622.0	623.8	612.2
2013	608.6	611.3	615.7	620.9	621.1	624.2	622.0	622.9	622.9	625.1	634.1	631.9	621.7
2014	620.0	618.0	623.3	630.7	635.3	637.5	632.8	634.1	632.9	636.6	642.7	643.2	632.3
2015	632.6	632.9	635.5	644.0	649.1	652.0	651.2	652.2	655.0	662.2	668.2	666.9	650.2
2016	651.4	653.4	655.9	662.6	661.7	665.2	659.4	660.3	662.7	667.8	673.5	673.9	662.3
2017	656.4	662.1	664.9	667.5	669.7	674.9	670.3	670.4	671.3	674.3	678.3	677.8	669.8
2018	665.1	670.3	672.0	675.3	677.3	682.3	681.2	682.8	676.9	681.5	683.0	683.0	677.6
Total Private													
2010	470.2	467.1	473.0	479.9	484.6	487.3	485.5	483.5	482.2	484.3	484.4	485.0	480.6
2011	475.4	476.8	481.0	487.5	489.5	491.9	494.3	492.6	492.0	495.7	498.4	497.4	489.4
2012	486.0	486.9	491.6	498.5	502.0	506.4	505.1	507.9	506.6	509.2	510.6	512.6	502.0
2013	498.4	500.4	504.8	509.1	511.1	514.0	516.1	517.7	514.9	515.4	523.7	521.5	512.3
2014	509.9	507.7	512.5	520.0	525.3	527.5	526.3	527.2	523.6	526.1	531.5	532.0	522.5
2015	522.1	522.0	525.0	533.6	539.6	542.5	545.8	547.1	546.9	551.1	556.4	555.6	540.6
2016	541.3	541.6	543.7	550.1	551.1	554.4	552.6	554.0	552.9	556.3	561.0	561.4	551.7
2017	545.6	549.7	552.5	555.5	559.4	564.5	562.8	563.6	561.4	563.1	566.0	566.2	559.2
2018	554.4	558.1	559.6	563.3	566.5	571.5	572.3	573.3	566.1	568.8	568.3	568.8	565.9
Goods Producing													
2010	62.8	61.8	62.8	64.2	64.3	64.7	65.2	64.5	64.2	64.6	64.2	63.6	63.9
2011	61.3	61.5	62.0	62.4	62.6	62.7	63.0	62.8	62.6	63.2	63.1	63.0	62.5
2012	61.1	60.7	61.7	62.7	63.2	63.7	63.7	64.2	64.0	63.7	63.6	63.5	63.0
2013	61.9	62.5	63.3	64.0	64.3	65.1	65.2	65.2	64.8	64.2	64.1	63.6	64.0
2014	62.5	62.3	63.1	64.1	64.9	65.3	65.9	66.1	65.9	65.8	65.6	65.6	64.8
2015	64.2	64.3	65.2	66.8	67.5	67.6	68.5	68.7	68.5	68.2	67.8	67.5	67.1
2016	66.3	66.6	67.2	68.1	68.4	69.0	69.5	69.2	69.4	69.6	69.4	69.0	68.5
2017	67.2	68.0	68.8	69.5	70.0	71.1	71.5	71.6	71.5	71.1	70.6	70.5	70.1
2018	69.0	69.6	69.9	70.8	71.3	72.0	72.9	73.2	72.4	72.3	72.3	72.2	71.5
Service-Providing													
2010	518.7	517.1	522.3	529.2	534.5	535.9	527.8	525.8	526.7	530.5	532.0	532.6	527.8
2011	525.5	527.5	531.4	537.7	538.1	539.9	538.4	535.8	538.7	544.2	547.7	546.3	537.6
2012	536.5	539.0	543.0	547.7	549.6	553.3	547.0	549.4	550.6	555.4	558.4	560.3	549.2
2013	546.7	548.8	552.4	556.9	556.8	559.1	556.8	557.7	558.1	560.9	570.0	568.3	557.7
2014	557.5	555.7	560.2	566.6	570.4	572.2	566.9	568.0	567.0	570.8	577.1	577.6	567.5
2015	568.4	568.6	570.3	577.2	581.6	584.4	582.7	583.5	586.5	594.0	600.4	599.4	583.1
2016	585.1	586.8	588.7	594.5	593.3	596.2	589.9	591.1	593.3	598.2	604.1	604.9	593.8
2017	589.2	594.1	596.1	598.0	599.7	603.8	598.8	598.8	599.8	603.2	607.7	607.3	599.7
2018	596.1	600.7	602.1	604.5	606.0	610.3	608.3	609.6	604.5	609.2	610.7	610.8	606.1
Mining, Logging, and Construction													
2010	31.2	30.4	31.4	32.7	32.8	33.0	33.5	33.0	32.7	33.2	33.0	32.4	32.4
2011	30.7	30.7	31.2	31.7	31.9	31.9	32.3	32.1	31.9	32.4	32.4	32.3	31.8
2012	31.0	30.7	31.5	32.3	32.7	33.0	33.2	33.6	33.5	33.2	33.2	32.9	32.6
2013	31.6	31.9	32.7	33.3	33.4	34.0	34.1	34.2	33.9	33.3	33.2	32.7	33.2
2014	31.7	31.7	32.5	33.4	34.0	34.3	34.9	34.9	34.8	34.9	34.7	34.6	33.9
2015	33.6	33.8	34.6	36.2	36.7	36.6	37.5	37.7	37.5	37.2	36.7	36.3	36.2
2016	35.2	35.3	35.8	36.6	36.9	37.3	37.7	37.5	37.7	37.9	37.8	37.2	36.9
2017	35.7	36.2	36.9	37.3	37.8	38.7	39.0	39.1	39.1	39.0	38.6	38.5	38.0
2018	37.5	37.9	38.3	39.1	39.4	39.9	40.7	40.9	40.1	40.1	40.0	39.5	39.5
Manufacturing													
2010	31.6	31.4	31.4	31.5	31.5	31.7	31.7	31.5	31.5	31.4	31.2	31.2	31.5
2011	30.6	30.8	30.8	30.7	30.7	30.8	30.7	30.7	30.7	30.8	30.7	30.7	30.7
2012	30.1	30.0	30.2	30.4	30.5	30.7	30.5	30.6	30.5	30.5	30.4	30.6	30.4
2013	30.3	30.6	30.6	30.7	30.9	31.1	31.1	31.0	30.9	30.9	30.9	30.9	30.8
2014	30.8	30.6	30.6	30.7	30.9	31.0	31.0	31.2	31.1	30.9	30.9	31.0	30.9
2015	30.6	30.5	30.6	30.6	30.8	31.0	31.0	31.0	31.0	31.0	31.1	31.2	30.9
2016	31.1	31.3	31.4	31.5	31.5	31.7	31.8	31.7	31.7	31.7	31.6	31.8	31.6
2017	31.5	31.8	31.9	32.2	32.2	32.4	32.5	32.5	32.4	32.1	32.0	32.0	32.1
2018	31.5	31.7	31.6	31.7	31.9	32.1	32.2	32.3	32.3	32.2	32.3	32.7	32.0

Employment by Industry: Richmond, VA, 2010–2018—*Continued*

(Numbers in thousands, not seasonally adjusted)

Industry and year	January	February	March	April	May	June	July	August	September	October	November	December	Annual average
Trade, Transportation, and Utilities													
2010	105.9	104.4	105.2	106.5	107.8	108.2	107.6	107.5	106.4	107.6	109.5	111.1	107.3
2011	107.3	106.5	107.0	108.5	108.8	109.3	109.3	109.5	108.6	110.0	112.6	114.2	109.3
2012	109.7	108.6	109.4	110.0	111.1	111.1	110.2	110.6	110.9	113.8	117.1	120.7	111.9
2013	112.9	111.8	112.0	112.6	113.3	113.7	114.0	114.3	113.9	115.3	118.5	120.0	114.4
2014	115.6	114.9	115.7	116.6	117.3	118.1	117.7	118.1	117.0	117.5	119.7	121.2	117.5
2015	116.9	116.0	116.1	117.4	118.1	119.1	120.8	120.9	120.6	121.5	124.2	125.7	119.8
2016	121.1	120.2	120.4	121.2	121.5	122.2	121.1	121.4	120.7	121.3	124.6	125.3	121.8
2017	120.3	119.0	119.0	120.2	121.0	122.1	121.6	121.6	122.4	123.0	126.3	127.1	122.0
2018	122.0	121.8	121.9	122.0	122.6	123.4	123.5	123.6	122.9	123.3	125.4	127.6	123.3
Wholesale Trade													
2010	25.2	25.2	25.3	25.8	26.0	26.1	26.1	26.2	26.0	26.4	26.5	26.5	25.9
2011	26.6	26.6	26.8	26.9	26.9	27.1	27.3	27.2	27.0	26.9	27.0	27.0	26.9
2012	26.8	26.9	27.2	27.6	27.8	28.0	27.8	28.0	27.9	27.9	28.0	28.0	27.7
2013	28.0	28.1	28.2	28.2	28.2	28.3	28.4	28.3	28.2	28.2	28.1	28.1	28.2
2014	27.7	27.7	27.8	27.9	28.1	28.3	28.3	28.4	28.2	28.0	28.1	28.2	28.1
2015	28.2	28.3	28.3	28.5	28.7	28.9	28.9	28.9	28.9	28.9	29.0	29.1	28.7
2016	28.6	28.5	28.6	28.6	28.6	28.5	28.5	28.5	28.4	28.4	28.5	28.6	28.5
2017	28.3	28.4	28.6	28.6	28.7	28.9	28.7	28.8	28.8	28.6	28.7	28.6	28.6
2018	28.4	28.4	28.4	28.4	28.3	28.5	28.5	28.4	28.2	28.5	28.1	28.3	28.4
Retail Trade													
2010	63.5	62.1	62.6	63.2	64.4	64.6	64.0	63.8	62.9	63.7	65.4	66.4	63.9
2011	63.3	62.5	62.7	63.4	63.6	63.7	63.3	63.6	62.9	64.3	66.6	67.8	64.0
2012	64.4	63.3	63.6	63.7	64.5	64.2	63.6	63.8	64.1	67.1	70.1	73.0	65.5
2013	65.6	64.5	64.4	64.9	65.5	65.6	65.7	65.9	65.5	66.9	69.7	70.3	66.2
2014	66.9	66.5	67.0	67.5	67.6	67.8	67.3	67.3	66.3	66.8	68.4	69.0	67.4
2015	65.4	64.5	64.5	65.1	65.5	66.0	66.1	66.0	65.5	66.1	68.0	68.5	65.9
2016	65.7	65.4	65.5	66.2	66.5	66.9	66.7	66.8	65.9	66.6	68.7	68.9	66.7
2017	66.2	65.3	65.5	65.9	66.4	67.1	67.2	66.6	66.0	66.8	68.9	69.3	66.8
2018	66.6	66.0	66.1	66.2	66.7	67.1	66.8	66.9	66.1	65.7	67.5	68.8	66.7
Transportation and Utilities													
2010	17.2	17.1	17.3	17.5	17.4	17.5	17.5	17.5	17.5	17.5	17.6	18.2	17.5
2011	17.4	17.4	17.5	18.2	18.3	18.5	18.7	18.7	18.7	18.8	19.0	19.4	18.4
2012	18.5	18.4	18.6	18.7	18.8	18.9	18.8	18.8	18.9	18.8	19.0	19.7	18.8
2013	19.3	19.2	19.4	19.5	19.6	19.8	19.9	20.1	20.2	20.2	20.7	21.6	20.0
2014	21.0	20.7	20.9	21.2	21.6	22.0	22.1	22.4	22.5	22.7	23.2	24.0	22.0
2015	23.3	23.2	23.3	23.8	23.9	24.2	25.8	26.0	26.2	26.5	27.2	28.1	25.1
2016	26.8	26.3	26.3	26.4	26.4	26.8	25.9	26.1	26.4	26.3	27.4	27.8	26.6
2017	25.8	25.3	24.9	25.7	25.9	26.1	25.7	26.2	27.6	27.6	28.7	29.2	26.6
2018	27.0	27.4	27.4	27.4	27.6	27.8	28.2	28.3	28.6	29.1	29.8	30.5	28.3
Information													
2010	9.5	9.5	9.4	9.4	9.4	9.5	9.5	9.4	9.5	9.5	9.5	9.5	9.5
2011	9.2	9.2	9.1	8.9	8.9	8.9	9.0	7.6	8.6	9.3	9.3	9.5	9.0
2012	8.1	8.1	8.2	8.1	8.1	8.2	8.1	8.3	7.7	7.7	8.0	8.0	8.1
2013	7.8	8.0	8.1	8.5	7.9	8.1	7.9	8.0	7.8	7.8	7.9	8.0	8.0
2014	8.3	7.9	7.9	7.9	8.1	7.6	7.9	8.1	7.7	7.8	7.6	7.6	7.9
2015	7.5	7.5	7.4	7.4	7.6	7.4	7.6	7.5	7.5	7.6	7.4	7.3	7.5
2016	7.3	7.4	7.2	7.5	6.8	7.6	7.5	7.5	7.7	7.3	7.2	7.4	7.4
2017	7.1	7.4	7.5	7.3	7.5	7.5	7.4	7.5	7.7	7.6	7.9	7.7	7.5
2018	7.4	7.5	7.4	7.3	7.6	7.5	7.5	7.3	7.1	7.1	7.1	7.1	7.3
Financial Activities													
2010	41.8	41.7	41.9	42.1	42.2	42.5	42.3	42.4	42.0	42.3	42.3	42.5	42.2
2011	42.2	42.3	42.6	42.8	43.1	43.4	44.0	44.2	44.0	44.3	44.7	45.1	43.6
2012	44.4	44.7	44.9	45.4	45.6	46.1	46.2	46.4	46.2	46.2	46.4	46.5	45.8
2013	46.0	46.1	46.3	46.6	46.7	47.0	47.5	47.6	47.3	47.3	47.4	47.3	46.9
2014	47.0	47.3	47.2	47.3	47.5	47.8	47.9	48.0	47.5	47.8	48.2	48.4	47.7
2015	48.4	48.8	48.8	49.0	49.0	49.2	49.4	49.5	49.1	49.2	49.2	49.1	49.1
2016	48.0	48.0	47.9	48.5	48.7	48.8	48.8	49.1	48.8	49.0	49.4	49.6	48.7
2017	48.7	49.1	49.0	49.0	49.3	49.8	50.0	50.0	49.4	49.6	49.6	49.6	49.4
2018	49.6	50.3	50.2	50.4	50.5	50.9	51.3	51.3	50.9	51.4	51.6	51.8	50.9

Employment by Industry: Richmond, VA, 2010–2018—*Continued*

(Numbers in thousands, not seasonally adjusted)

Industry and year	January	February	March	April	May	June	July	August	September	October	November	December	Annual average
Professional and Business Services													
2010	89.9	89.9	90.6	91.9	92.1	92.4	93.4	93.5	93.7	94.4	94.5	94.7	92.6
2011	94.1	94.7	95.8	96.6	96.4	96.0	96.6	96.5	96.9	97.4	98.4	96.4	96.3
2012	95.9	96.8	96.9	98.1	98.5	99.3	99.5	100.0	100.5	101.0	100.0	99.7	98.9
2013	98.4	98.8	99.3	98.9	99.3	99.2	99.7	100.7	100.3	100.9	105.4	103.9	100.4
2014	100.7	99.1	99.6	101.2	102.7	102.6	101.6	101.5	101.8	103.6	108.3	108.1	102.6
2015	105.0	103.8	104.2	106.1	108.2	109.0	108.1	108.6	110.3	113.8	118.0	118.1	109.4
2016	111.8	111.0	110.6	111.9	112.0	111.8	110.8	111.0	112.7	114.6	116.9	119.0	112.8
2017	112.6	113.6	113.2	113.2	114.4	115.4	114.1	114.1	114.5	115.3	117.5	117.9	114.7
2018	114.7	115.2	114.6	114.9	116.0	116.7	115.9	116.6	115.4	116.3	117.7	116.7	115.9
Education and Health Services													
2010	84.4	84.3	85.0	85.0	85.7	84.9	82.4	82.1	84.2	85.5	85.7	85.3	84.5
2011	84.7	85.2	85.3	86.1	85.1	84.7	85.6	85.8	87.0	88.0	88.4	87.1	86.1
2012	87.0	87.5	87.7	88.9	87.7	87.7	87.8	88.7	90.2	90.7	90.9	90.0	88.7
2013	89.6	90.5	90.7	91.1	90.1	89.2	89.9	90.7	92.0	92.8	93.3	92.0	91.0
2014	92.0	92.4	92.8	94.1	93.0	92.5	92.4	93.0	93.6	94.7	94.8	93.6	93.2
2015	94.2	94.8	94.9	95.9	94.8	94.2	94.8	95.5	96.6	97.5	97.6	96.5	95.6
2016	96.9	97.4	97.3	97.7	96.4	95.7	95.0	96.4	97.1	98.9	99.0	97.5	97.1
2017	98.2	99.1	99.2	99.1	98.1	97.1	96.9	98.0	98.8	99.6	98.7	98.8	98.5
2018	99.1	99.7	99.8	100.0	98.3	98.2	98.6	99.3	100.1	100.6	99.5	99.4	99.4
Leisure and Hospitality													
2010	46.7	46.2	48.2	51.2	53.4	55.2	55.2	54.3	52.7	50.9	49.2	48.9	51.0
2011	47.4	48.1	49.8	52.4	54.9	56.9	56.9	56.4	54.9	54.0	52.4	52.5	53.1
2012	50.6	51.3	53.3	55.2	57.4	59.7	59.1	59.0	56.7	55.5	54.0	54.1	55.5
2013	52.3	53.0	55.1	57.1	58.9	60.8	60.8	60.1	58.0	56.3	56.4	56.1	57.1
2014	53.5	53.5	55.7	58.0	60.7	62.1	61.5	61.0	59.0	58.0	56.4	56.7	58.0
2015	55.2	56.0	57.4	60.1	63.0	64.4	64.9	64.6	62.9	61.7	60.6	60.0	60.9
2016	58.7	59.7	61.6	63.2	65.3	67.0	67.2	66.8	64.4	63.2	62.2	61.5	63.4
2017	59.6	61.5	63.5	65.3	67.1	69.2	68.8	68.5	64.9	64.6	63.3	62.7	64.9
2018	61.1	62.3	63.9	65.9	67.9	70.1	69.7	69.3	65.1	65.5	62.4	61.8	65.4
Other Services													
2010	29.2	29.3	29.9	29.6	29.7	29.9	29.9	29.8	29.5	29.5	29.5	29.4	29.6
2011	29.2	29.3	29.4	29.8	29.7	30.0	29.9	29.8	29.4	29.5	29.5	29.6	29.6
2012	29.2	29.2	29.5	30.1	30.4	30.6	30.5	30.7	30.4	30.6	30.6	30.1	30.2
2013	29.5	29.7	30.0	30.3	30.6	30.9	31.1	31.1	30.8	30.8	30.7	30.6	30.5
2014	30.3	30.3	30.5	30.8	31.1	31.5	31.4	31.4	31.1	30.9	30.9	30.8	30.9
2015	30.6	30.8	31.0	30.9	31.4	31.6	31.7	31.8	31.4	31.6	31.6	31.4	31.3
2016	31.2	31.3	31.5	32.0	32.0	32.3	32.7	32.6	32.1	32.4	32.3	32.1	32.0
2017	31.9	32.0	32.3	31.9	32.0	32.3	32.5	32.3	32.2	32.3	32.1	31.9	32.1
2018	31.5	31.7	31.9	32.0	32.3	32.7	32.9	32.7	32.2	32.3	32.3	32.2	32.2
Government													
2010	111.3	111.8	112.1	113.5	114.2	113.3	107.5	106.8	108.7	110.8	111.8	111.2	111.1
2011	111.4	112.2	112.4	112.6	111.2	110.7	107.1	106.0	109.3	111.7	112.4	111.9	110.7
2012	111.6	112.8	113.1	111.9	110.8	110.6	105.6	105.7	108.0	109.9	111.4	111.2	110.2
2013	110.2	110.9	110.9	111.8	110.0	110.2	105.9	105.2	108.0	109.7	110.4	110.4	109.5
2014	110.1	110.3	110.8	110.7	110.0	110.0	106.5	106.9	109.3	110.5	111.2	111.2	109.8
2015	110.5	110.9	110.5	110.4	109.5	109.5	105.4	105.1	108.1	111.1	111.8	111.3	109.5
2016	110.1	111.8	112.2	112.5	110.6	110.8	106.8	106.3	109.8	111.5	112.5	112.5	110.6
2017	110.8	112.4	112.4	112.0	110.3	110.4	107.5	106.8	109.9	111.2	112.3	111.6	110.6
2018	110.7	112.2	112.4	112.0	110.8	110.8	108.9	109.5	110.8	112.7	114.7	114.2	111.6

Employment by Industry: Louisville/Jefferson County, KY-IN, 2010–2018

(Numbers in thousands, not seasonally adjusted)

Industry and year	January	February	March	April	May	June	July	August	September	October	November	December	Annual average
Total Nonfarm													
2010	567.0	561.6	572.3	579.4	586.2	586.7	578.4	581.3	582.8	586.4	590.2	591.9	580.4
2011	572.0	574.3	579.2	584.9	587.4	589.7	580.4	587.2	588.8	589.9	594.8	593.1	585.1
2012	580.8	580.0	587.9	593.8	601.9	604.2	597.6	602.7	605.1	606.3	613.3	614.5	599.0
2013	598.2	599.0	603.8	610.4	614.1	615.1	607.4	617.2	617.0	618.0	623.9	624.4	612.4
2014	606.9	606.1	612.4	621.4	625.4	628.3	625.2	630.6	631.4	633.0	638.1	641.3	625.0
2015	626.5	625.9	630.1	634.0	643.7	645.8	636.4	644.5	645.0	649.2	656.2	659.2	641.4
2016	642.2	642.9	648.2	653.6	658.4	660.5	659.1	660.6	661.5	659.4	665.1	668.0	656.6
2017	651.2	651.2	655.2	660.7	665.1	668.9	665.2	667.0	669.0	669.2	675.4	675.4	664.5
2018	657.4	660.3	664.1	668.4	671.5	676.0	670.0	673.7	672.9	668.5	676.0	675.7	669.5
Total Private													
2010	489.7	484.1	493.0	499.0	504.1	506.4	502.8	504.9	505.1	508.2	512.2	514.6	502.0
2011	495.2	496.7	501.3	506.7	508.9	512.2	506.4	510.8	509.9	510.9	515.5	514.2	507.4
2012	502.5	501.4	508.8	514.7	522.7	525.9	523.4	526.2	526.4	527.2	534.3	535.7	520.8
2013	520.1	519.9	524.1	530.2	533.8	535.6	531.5	539.1	537.1	538.2	543.8	544.5	533.2
2014	528.1	527.3	533.0	541.8	546.0	549.4	549.5	552.6	551.6	553.1	558.4	561.9	546.1
2015	547.8	547.2	551.1	554.5	564.1	567.7	562.2	568.8	567.7	571.2	578.0	581.3	563.5
2016	565.0	565.8	569.9	576.1	581.1	584.2	585.3	585.6	584.8	583.6	589.1	592.3	580.2
2017	576.4	576.3	580.2	585.0	589.2	594.1	593.2	593.1	593.4	593.9	599.8	600.0	589.6
2018	583.4	585.1	588.6	593.2	596.0	600.8	598.0	599.8	597.2	593.0	600.2	600.2	594.6
Goods Producing													
2010	85.2	80.5	85.2	85.5	86.5	87.0	84.8	87.1	87.5	87.5	87.3	86.7	85.9
2011	83.2	83.4	84.1	85.6	86.0	87.4	84.6	88.0	88.3	88.1	88.7	87.9	86.3
2012	87.0	85.9	89.5	91.3	92.9	94.5	94.8	95.5	95.8	95.8	96.5	96.6	93.0
2013	94.4	94.3	94.8	95.8	96.5	97.5	95.0	98.6	98.4	98.2	98.4	98.3	96.7
2014	96.2	96.3	97.5	99.5	100.9	102.2	102.6	102.8	102.5	102.8	103.8	103.6	100.9
2015	102.1	101.9	102.3	101.0	105.3	106.6	103.8	107.4	107.3	107.3	107.5	107.7	105.0
2016	106.1	106.5	108.1	108.2	109.5	111.3	111.9	111.5	111.1	110.3	110.7	110.1	109.6
2017	107.7	107.8	108.5	109.5	110.3	111.3	112.6	112.2	112.2	111.4	112.4	111.8	110.6
2018	110.1	110.5	111.2	112.2	112.9	114.3	113.4	114.3	113.2	113.4	114.2	114.4	112.8
Service-Providing													
2010	481.8	481.1	487.1	493.9	499.7	499.7	493.6	494.2	495.3	498.9	502.9	505.2	494.5
2011	488.8	490.9	495.1	499.3	501.4	502.3	495.8	499.2	500.5	501.8	506.1	505.2	498.9
2012	493.8	494.1	498.4	502.5	509.0	509.7	502.8	507.2	509.3	510.5	516.8	517.9	506.0
2013	503.8	504.7	509.0	514.6	517.6	517.6	512.4	518.6	518.6	519.8	525.5	526.1	515.7
2014	510.7	509.8	514.9	521.9	524.5	526.1	522.6	527.8	528.9	530.2	534.3	537.7	524.1
2015	524.4	524.0	527.8	533.0	538.4	539.2	532.6	537.1	537.7	541.9	548.7	551.5	536.4
2016	536.1	536.4	540.1	545.4	548.9	549.2	547.2	549.1	550.4	549.1	554.4	557.9	547.0
2017	543.5	543.4	546.7	551.2	554.8	557.6	552.6	554.8	556.8	557.8	563.0	563.6	553.8
2018	547.3	549.8	552.9	556.2	558.6	561.7	556.6	559.4	559.7	555.1	561.8	561.3	556.7
Mining, Logging, and Construction													
2010	24.7	23.8	24.5	25.3	25.3	25.7	26.3	25.8	25.4	25.2	24.7	23.8	25.0
2011	21.9	21.9	22.9	23.9	24.2	25.1	25.5	25.4	25.2	24.8	24.7	24.2	24.1
2012	22.7	22.6	23.6	24.2	24.7	25.3	25.2	25.0	24.8	24.5	24.7	24.4	24.3
2013	22.7	22.5	23.2	24.1	24.7	25.4	26.1	26.1	26.0	25.7	25.7	25.4	24.8
2014	23.9	23.9	25.2	26.2	27.0	28.1	28.4	28.2	28.2	28.2	28.3	27.8	27.0
2015	26.3	26.4	26.6	27.7	28.7	29.4	30.4	29.6	29.3	29.2	28.9	28.7	28.4
2016	27.0	26.7	27.3	28.2	28.4	28.9	29.2	28.9	28.6	28.5	28.5	28.1	28.2
2017	26.6	26.8	27.5	28.1	28.6	29.4	30.4	29.9	29.7	29.6	29.6	29.2	28.8
2018	27.9	28.3	29.0	29.8	30.2	31.2	31.2	30.9	30.7	30.7	30.2	30.4	30.0
Manufacturing													
2010	60.5	56.7	60.7	60.2	61.2	61.3	58.5	61.3	62.1	62.3	62.6	62.9	60.9
2011	61.3	61.5	61.2	61.7	61.8	62.3	59.1	62.6	63.1	63.3	64.0	63.7	62.1
2012	64.3	63.3	65.9	67.1	68.2	69.2	69.6	70.5	71.0	71.3	71.8	72.2	68.7
2013	71.7	71.8	71.6	71.7	71.8	72.1	68.9	72.5	72.4	72.5	72.7	72.9	71.9
2014	72.3	72.4	72.3	73.3	73.9	74.1	74.2	74.6	74.3	74.6	75.5	75.8	73.9
2015	75.8	75.5	75.7	73.3	76.6	77.2	73.4	77.8	78.0	78.1	78.6	79.0	76.6
2016	79.1	79.8	80.8	80.0	81.1	82.4	82.7	82.6	82.5	81.8	82.2	82.0	81.4
2017	81.1	81.0	81.0	81.4	81.7	81.9	82.2	82.3	82.5	81.8	82.8	82.6	81.9
2018	82.2	82.2	82.2	82.4	82.7	83.1	82.2	83.4	82.5	82.7	84.0	84.0	82.8

Employment by Industry: Louisville/Jefferson County, KY-IN, 2010–2018—*Continued*

(Numbers in thousands, not seasonally adjusted)

Industry and year	January	February	March	April	May	June	July	August	September	October	November	December	Annual average
Trade, Transportation, and Utilities													
2010	124.0	122.9	123.9	125.4	126.3	127.0	127.2	127.8	127.8	129.7	132.8	136.1	127.6
2011	128.3	127.7	128.7	129.3	129.5	130.2	129.4	129.5	129.0	129.6	132.9	134.4	129.9
2012	128.3	128.0	128.5	128.8	130.0	130.8	130.4	130.5	130.7	130.6	134.2	136.4	130.6
2013	129.9	129.5	130.3	130.2	131.0	131.6	131.4	132.5	132.3	132.7	136.3	139.2	132.2
2014	132.0	131.3	131.9	132.1	133.5	134.2	134.1	135.4	135.9	137.2	140.5	144.5	135.2
2015	137.7	136.8	137.3	137.3	138.5	139.6	139.0	140.7	140.4	141.8	145.1	147.4	140.1
2016	142.9	142.0	142.3	142.8	143.7	143.9	144.8	145.1	145.1	145.3	149.0	153.4	145.0
2017	145.5	144.4	144.5	144.7	145.3	146.6	146.2	147.0	146.9	147.6	152.2	154.9	147.2
2018	149.1	147.8	148.1	147.1	147.7	149.0	148.9	148.9	148.2	147.5	151.9	154.4	149.1
Wholesale Trade													
2010	27.0	27.0	27.1	27.1	27.2	27.3	27.5	27.5	27.5	27.5	27.6	27.5	27.3
2011	27.3	27.4	27.6	27.5	27.6	27.7	27.8	27.8	27.8	27.8	27.8	28.0	27.7
2012	27.6	27.7	27.7	27.8	28.0	28.1	28.3	28.3	28.4	28.4	28.5	28.5	28.1
2013	28.5	28.7	28.7	28.6	28.6	28.7	28.7	28.9	28.9	28.8	28.9	29.0	28.8
2014	28.7	28.8	28.8	28.7	28.8	28.7	28.8	28.8	28.8	28.7	28.6	28.7	28.7
2015	28.5	28.5	28.6	28.5	28.7	28.7	28.8	29.0	29.0	29.0	29.1	29.2	28.8
2016	28.8	28.8	28.9	28.9	29.0	29.0	29.1	28.8	28.8	28.8	29.0	29.2	28.9
2017	28.6	28.6	28.5	28.9	29.0	29.2	29.1	29.1	29.0	29.1	29.1	29.4	29.0
2018	29.1	29.2	29.4	29.4	29.2	29.4	29.2	29.1	29.0	29.0	29.6	28.7	29.2
Retail Trade													
2010	58.5	57.8	58.5	58.6	59.0	59.2	59.2	59.3	58.7	59.9	61.5	62.1	59.4
2011	58.9	58.2	58.9	59.5	59.6	59.6	59.3	59.3	58.7	59.6	61.6	62.2	59.6
2012	59.6	59.1	59.6	59.8	60.5	61.0	60.8	60.7	60.3	60.9	63.2	63.3	60.7
2013	60.0	59.6	60.0	60.2	60.8	61.1	61.0	61.3	61.0	61.4	63.6	64.3	61.2
2014	60.1	59.8	60.1	60.7	61.2	61.5	61.3	61.9	61.5	62.3	64.4	65.7	61.7
2015	62.4	61.9	62.2	62.6	63.3	63.7	63.2	63.6	62.9	63.8	65.8	66.7	63.5
2016	63.6	63.6	63.8	64.4	64.8	64.8	64.7	64.6	64.3	65.1	67.4	68.3	65.0
2017	65.8	65.2	65.4	65.6	65.9	66.1	66.1	66.1	65.7	66.2	68.7	69.0	66.3
2018	65.9	65.5	65.8	65.2	65.9	65.8	65.8	65.6	64.7	64.1	66.9	68.0	65.8
Transportation and Utilities													
2010	38.5	38.1	38.3	39.7	40.1	40.5	40.5	41.0	41.6	42.3	43.7	46.5	40.9
2011	42.1	42.1	42.2	42.3	42.3	42.9	42.3	42.4	42.5	42.2	43.5	44.2	42.6
2012	41.1	41.2	41.2	41.2	41.5	41.7	41.3	41.5	42.0	41.3	42.5	44.6	41.8
2013	41.4	41.2	41.6	41.4	41.6	41.8	41.7	42.3	42.4	42.5	43.8	45.9	42.3
2014	43.2	42.7	43.0	42.7	43.5	44.0	44.0	44.7	45.6	46.2	47.5	50.1	44.8
2015	46.8	46.4	46.5	46.2	46.5	47.2	47.0	48.1	48.5	49.0	50.2	51.5	47.8
2016	50.5	49.6	49.6	49.5	49.9	50.1	51.0	51.7	52.0	51.4	52.6	55.9	51.2
2017	51.1	50.6	50.6	50.2	50.4	51.3	51.0	51.8	52.2	52.3	54.4	56.5	51.9
2018	54.1	53.1	52.9	52.5	52.6	53.8	53.9	54.2	54.5	54.4	55.4	57.7	54.1
Information													
2010	9.3	9.2	9.3	9.3	9.3	9.3	9.3	9.3	9.2	9.1	9.2	9.3	9.3
2011	9.2	9.1	9.1	9.2	9.2	9.1	9.2	9.1	9.1	9.1	9.3	9.3	9.2
2012	9.2	9.2	9.5	9.6	9.6	9.6	9.5	9.5	9.3	9.2	9.3	9.3	9.4
2013	9.4	9.4	9.4	9.4	9.5	9.5	9.5	9.6	9.4	9.3	9.3	9.3	9.4
2014	9.4	9.4	9.5	9.4	9.4	9.4	9.3	9.3	9.1	9.2	9.3	9.2	9.3
2015	9.1	9.1	9.0	8.9	9.0	8.9	9.0	9.0	8.9	9.0	9.1	9.1	9.0
2016	9.1	9.2	9.1	9.1	9.2	9.2	9.2	9.3	9.3	9.3	9.4	9.4	9.2
2017	9.3	9.3	9.4	9.4	9.4	9.4	9.3	9.3	9.3	9.4	9.2	9.1	9.3
2018	9.1	9.1	9.1	9.2	9.3	9.2	9.1	9.1	9.0	9.0	9.0	9.0	9.1
Financial Activities													
2010	41.2	41.1	40.9	40.5	40.5	40.6	40.5	40.2	39.8	40.1	40.2	40.4	40.5
2011	40.2	40.4	40.4	39.8	39.9	40.2	40.1	40.3	40.6	40.6	40.7	40.8	40.3
2012	40.5	40.4	40.6	40.3	40.7	41.2	41.5	41.6	41.7	41.8	42.0	42.4	41.2
2013	42.1	42.2	42.4	42.4	42.6	43.0	43.2	43.4	43.5	43.7	43.9	44.1	43.0
2014	43.9	43.9	44.0	44.0	44.4	44.6	44.9	45.0	45.2	45.5	45.7	46.0	44.8
2015	45.6	45.6	45.8	45.4	45.7	46.1	46.1	46.1	46.0	46.2	46.3	46.6	46.0
2016	46.3	46.4	46.3	46.4	46.6	46.9	47.2	46.8	46.8	47.0	46.9	47.2	46.7
2017	46.6	46.4	46.3	46.3	46.5	46.9	46.7	46.6	46.7	46.8	46.8	46.9	46.6
2018	45.8	45.5	45.5	45.4	45.7	46.2	46.4	46.4	46.2	46.8	46.2	46.3	46.0

Employment by Industry: Louisville/Jefferson County, KY-IN, 2010–2018—*Continued*

(Numbers in thousands, not seasonally adjusted)

Industry and year	January	February	March	April	May	June	July	August	September	October	November	December	Annual average
Professional and Business Services													
2010	68.6	68.7	69.4	71.3	71.8	72.3	71.8	71.7	72.9	72.7	73.6	74.2	71.6
2011	69.9	70.8	71.5	72.0	72.5	72.9	72.5	73.5	73.6	75.3	75.4	75.5	73.0
2012	72.1	71.4	72.1	73.5	74.7	74.6	73.9	75.4	76.3	77.5	79.0	78.9	75.0
2013	74.4	73.8	74.9	76.9	77.0	77.4	76.8	79.3	78.9	80.6	81.5	81.0	77.7
2014	77.4	76.3	77.9	80.1	80.9	81.1	81.3	82.9	82.5	83.6	84.6	85.1	81.1
2015	82.1	81.4	82.2	84.2	85.8	85.7	84.8	85.2	85.4	86.3	88.5	89.8	85.1
2016	83.9	83.2	83.1	84.8	85.7	85.7	85.2	85.8	86.3	86.8	88.5	89.0	85.7
2017	84.6	83.9	84.2	84.6	84.8	85.4	85.9	85.9	87.4	88.5	89.3	89.1	86.1
2018	84.9	85.4	85.9	87.7	86.9	87.4	86.5	87.3	87.7	87.2	88.2	87.6	86.9
Education and Health Services													
2010	81.6	81.7	82.3	82.3	82.8	82.5	82.6	82.7	83.0	83.5	83.8	83.8	82.7
2011	83.2	83.2	83.5	82.9	83.0	83.0	83.1	83.2	83.6	83.4	83.4	82.6	83.2
2012	83.3	83.5	83.6	84.0	84.2	84.4	84.0	84.3	84.6	85.1	85.5	85.7	84.4
2013	84.5	84.7	85.0	85.2	84.7	84.3	84.3	84.3	84.6	85.3	85.6	85.2	84.8
2014	84.2	84.4	84.8	85.1	84.4	84.0	84.0	84.5	85.4	85.9	85.0	85.8	84.8
2015	84.8	85.2	85.9	85.6	85.6	84.8	84.7	86.4	87.4	89.3	89.6	89.6	86.6
2016	88.3	88.8	89.2	88.7	88.7	88.2	88.8	89.3	90.2	90.6	90.8	90.9	89.4
2017	92.0	92.7	93.2	94.1	94.0	94.2	93.5	93.7	94.5	95.3	95.3	95.0	94.0
2018	94.3	95.1	95.3	96.0	95.8	95.6	94.8	95.3	96.5	96.7	98.0	97.9	95.9
Leisure and Hospitality													
2010	54.7	54.9	56.5	59.1	61.2	61.6	60.7	60.3	59.4	59.9	59.7	58.3	58.9
2011	55.8	56.5	58.2	62.1	63.0	63.3	61.3	61.3	60.0	59.3	59.6	58.0	59.9
2012	56.6	57.4	59.2	61.4	64.9	64.7	63.4	63.9	62.7	61.8	62.4	60.9	61.6
2013	59.8	60.3	61.5	64.4	66.6	66.3	65.5	65.6	64.5	63.2	63.7	62.3	63.6
2014	60.4	61.1	62.6	66.6	67.5	68.8	68.2	67.7	66.1	64.3	64.5	63.1	65.1
2015	62.0	62.6	63.8	67.5	69.3	70.6	69.5	68.6	67.2	66.0	66.3	65.6	66.6
2016	63.1	64.1	65.9	69.9	71.6	72.7	71.8	71.4	69.9	67.8	67.9	66.3	68.5
2017	65.0	65.9	67.8	69.9	72.2	73.6	72.3	71.7	70.0	68.6	68.4	67.0	69.4
2018	64.7	66.1	67.5	69.3	71.6	72.9	73.0	72.6	70.8	67.1	67.2	64.9	69.0
Other Services													
2010	25.1	25.1	25.5	25.6	25.7	26.1	25.9	25.8	25.5	25.7	25.6	25.8	25.6
2011	25.4	25.6	25.8	25.8	25.8	26.1	26.2	25.9	25.7	25.5	25.5	25.7	25.8
2012	25.5	25.6	25.8	25.8	25.7	26.1	25.9	25.5	25.3	25.4	25.4	25.5	25.6
2013	25.6	25.7	25.8	25.9	25.9	26.0	25.8	25.8	25.5	25.2	25.1	25.1	25.6
2014	24.6	24.6	24.8	25.0	25.0	25.1	25.1	25.0	24.9	24.6	25.0	24.6	24.9
2015	24.4	24.6	24.8	24.6	24.9	25.4	25.3	25.4	25.1	25.3	25.6	25.5	25.1
2016	25.3	25.6	25.9	26.2	26.1	26.3	26.4	26.4	26.1	26.5	25.9	26.0	26.1
2017	25.7	25.9	26.3	26.5	26.7	26.7	26.7	26.7	26.4	26.3	26.2	26.2	26.4
2018	25.4	25.6	26.0	26.3	26.1	26.2	25.9	25.9	25.6	25.3	25.5	25.7	25.8
Government													
2010	77.3	77.5	79.3	80.4	82.1	80.3	75.6	76.4	77.7	78.2	78.0	77.3	78.3
2011	76.8	77.6	77.9	78.2	78.5	77.5	74.0	76.4	78.9	79.0	79.3	78.9	77.8
2012	78.3	78.6	79.1	79.1	79.2	78.3	74.2	76.5	78.7	79.1	79.0	78.8	78.2
2013	78.1	79.1	79.7	80.2	80.3	79.5	75.9	78.1	79.9	79.8	80.1	79.9	79.2
2014	78.8	78.8	79.4	79.6	79.4	78.9	75.7	78.0	79.8	79.9	79.7	79.4	79.0
2015	78.7	78.7	79.0	79.5	79.6	78.1	74.2	75.7	77.3	78.0	78.2	77.9	77.9
2016	77.2	77.1	78.3	77.5	77.3	76.3	73.8	75.0	76.7	75.8	76.0	75.7	76.4
2017	74.8	74.9	75.0	75.7	75.9	74.8	72.0	73.9	75.6	75.3	75.6	75.4	74.9
2018	74.0	75.2	75.5	75.2	75.5	75.2	72.0	73.9	75.7	75.5	75.8	75.5	74.9

Employment by Industry: New Orleans-Metairie, LA, 2010–2018

(Numbers in thousands, not seasonally adjusted)

Industry and year	January	February	March	April	May	June	July	August	September	October	November	December	Annual average
Total Nonfarm													
2010	525.9	528.4	532.8	535.4	535.2	534.5	527.4	528.8	532.0	535.3	539.0	541.2	533.0
2011	533.2	536.5	539.5	541.1	541.7	536.9	533.2	536.9	538.8	542.1	546.3	548.1	539.5
2012	537.1	540.5	543.0	549.4	550.8	545.1	541.0	543.5	539.7	546.8	552.0	554.0	545.2
2013	550.2	554.2	553.3	553.1	554.1	553.0	546.3	554.7	552.3	559.6	564.7	564.0	555.0
2014	554.4	559.7	563.3	563.4	565.3	567.2	562.7	567.1	564.8	571.1	578.1	578.3	566.3
2015	569.2	572.0	573.2	579.2	580.4	577.1	573.2	574.3	572.1	580.6	581.7	583.2	576.4
2016	572.8	572.8	573.8	579.1	580.8	575.8	572.4	574.5	576.2	577.7	580.4	578.0	576.2
2017	570.3	576.8	574.2	577.5	580.8	575.7	567.5	569.9	570.4	575.3	579.4	578.7	574.7
2018	571.3	573.2	575.2	577.9	579.1	575.4	571.2	574.8	575.0	584.4	585.6	585.1	577.4
Total Private													
2010	442.0	444.0	447.7	450.5	448.7	450.0	445.5	446.1	448.9	451.8	455.2	457.9	449.0
2011	450.8	454.1	457.4	458.8	459.6	456.8	454.8	457.1	457.5	461.3	465.4	467.6	458.4
2012	458.6	461.2	464.1	469.2	470.7	466.2	464.5	465.7	461.0	467.7	472.7	474.7	466.4
2013	472.6	476.1	475.2	475.3	476.0	476.0	472.5	481.2	477.8	484.8	489.6	488.7	478.8
2014	480.8	484.8	488.1	488.8	491.0	491.1	489.8	494.2	490.5	496.3	503.1	504.1	491.9
2015	496.0	497.6	499.4	505.0	506.3	504.0	502.7	503.0	499.1	508.3	509.2	511.1	503.5
2016	501.2	500.4	501.8	506.6	506.4	503.0	502.6	504.4	505.0	505.4	508.0	505.9	504.2
2017	499.1	504.4	502.1	503.4	506.5	502.8	497.5	499.5	498.8	502.3	505.9	505.5	502.3
2018	499.3	500.2	502.5	503.4	504.4	502.2	500.9	504.3	503.3	511.9	512.7	512.8	504.8
Goods Producing													
2010	72.7	72.8	73.2	73.3	73.7	74.2	73.9	73.7	73.5	74.3	73.5	73.6	73.5
2011	72.7	72.8	73.0	73.3	73.2	72.8	73.0	72.8	72.2	72.3	72.3	72.2	72.7
2012	71.2	71.3	71.5	71.0	71.6	72.0	72.2	72.1	71.9	72.0	72.1	71.4	71.7
2013	70.0	69.8	70.2	69.7	70.3	71.0	71.1	71.1	70.9	70.5	70.0	69.4	70.3
2014	68.7	69.1	69.6	69.3	69.9	69.7	69.9	69.7	69.4	69.7	69.7	70.1	69.6
2015	70.2	69.6	68.7	69.2	69.1	69.2	69.2	68.8	68.5	68.8	67.9	67.6	68.9
2016	65.5	65.1	64.9	64.8	64.4	64.5	65.0	64.4	64.6	63.9	63.7	63.3	64.5
2017	63.7	64.2	63.9	64.0	64.4	64.5	64.3	64.2	64.2	64.6	64.5	65.0	64.3
2018	64.4	64.1	64.7	64.6	64.9	65.7	65.4	65.2	65.0	65.6	65.9	65.6	65.1
Service-Providing													
2010	453.2	455.6	459.6	462.1	461.5	460.3	453.5	455.1	458.5	461.0	465.5	467.6	459.5
2011	460.5	463.7	466.5	467.8	468.5	464.1	460.2	464.1	466.6	469.8	474.0	475.9	466.8
2012	465.9	469.2	471.5	478.4	479.2	473.1	468.8	471.4	467.8	474.8	479.9	482.6	473.6
2013	480.2	484.4	483.1	483.4	483.8	482.0	475.2	483.6	481.4	489.1	494.7	494.6	484.6
2014	485.7	490.6	493.7	494.1	495.4	497.5	492.8	497.4	495.4	501.4	508.4	508.2	496.7
2015	499.0	502.4	504.5	510.0	511.3	507.9	504.0	505.5	503.6	511.8	513.8	515.6	507.5
2016	507.3	507.7	508.9	514.3	516.4	511.3	507.4	510.1	511.6	513.8	516.7	514.7	511.7
2017	506.6	512.6	510.3	513.5	516.4	511.2	503.2	505.7	506.2	510.7	514.9	513.7	510.4
2018	506.9	509.1	510.5	513.3	514.2	509.7	505.8	509.6	510.0	518.8	519.7	519.5	512.3
Mining, Logging, and Construction													
2010	37.6	37.9	38.2	37.9	38.2	38.8	38.9	38.9	38.9	39.9	39.5	39.4	38.7
2011	38.8	38.8	39.2	40.1	39.8	39.6	39.5	39.4	39.0	39.1	39.1	39.0	39.3
2012	38.4	38.7	39.1	38.8	39.2	39.5	39.6	39.6	39.8	39.9	39.9	39.2	39.3
2013	38.1	38.2	38.6	38.2	38.4	38.8	38.9	38.9	38.9	38.5	38.1	37.7	38.4
2014	37.2	37.7	38.2	38.2	38.4	38.4	38.7	38.6	38.6	38.9	39.1	39.4	38.5
2015	39.5	39.0	38.9	38.6	38.6	38.4	38.2	37.9	37.7	38.2	37.3	36.9	38.3
2016	35.5	35.0	34.9	34.6	34.2	34.3	34.8	34.4	34.5	34.0	33.8	33.1	34.4
2017	33.2	33.5	33.4	33.7	34.0	33.9	34.0	33.9	34.1	34.5	34.3	34.6	33.9
2018	34.3	34.2	35.0	34.9	35.1	35.7	35.4	35.1	35.1	35.6	36.1	35.5	35.2
Manufacturing													
2010	35.1	34.9	35.0	35.4	35.5	35.4	35.0	34.8	34.6	34.4	34.0	34.2	34.9
2011	33.9	34.0	33.8	33.2	33.4	33.2	33.5	33.4	33.2	33.2	33.2	33.2	33.4
2012	32.8	32.6	32.4	32.2	32.4	32.5	32.6	32.5	32.1	32.1	32.2	32.2	32.4
2013	31.9	31.6	31.6	31.5	31.9	32.2	32.2	32.2	32.0	32.0	31.9	31.7	31.9
2014	31.5	31.4	31.4	31.1	31.5	31.3	31.2	31.1	30.8	30.8	30.6	30.7	31.1
2015	30.7	30.6	29.8	30.6	30.5	30.8	31.0	30.9	30.8	30.6	30.6	30.7	30.6
2016	30.0	30.1	30.0	30.2	30.2	30.2	30.2	30.0	30.1	29.9	29.9	30.2	30.1
2017	30.5	30.7	30.5	30.3	30.4	30.6	30.3	30.3	30.1	30.1	30.2	30.4	30.4
2018	30.1	29.9	29.7	29.7	29.8	30.0	30.0	30.1	29.9	30.0	29.8	30.1	29.9

Employment by Industry: New Orleans-Metairie, LA, 2010–2018—Continued

(Numbers in thousands, not seasonally adjusted)

Industry and year	January	February	March	April	May	June	July	August	September	October	November	December	Annual average
Trade, Transportation, and Utilities													
2010	103.7	103.2	104.0	104.4	104.5	104.6	104.9	104.7	104.6	106.4	108.3	109.6	105.2
2011	107.8	107.4	107.5	107.7	107.9	107.7	107.8	107.6	107.3	107.9	109.9	110.7	108.1
2012	108.0	107.4	107.8	108.1	108.3	108.2	107.8	107.8	107.3	109.3	112.3	113.2	108.8
2013	111.4	110.4	111.3	110.5	110.5	110.6	110.8	111.5	111.6	112.5	114.4	116.0	111.8
2014	112.6	112.1	112.7	112.8	113.6	114.2	114.6	115.2	114.8	115.5	118.1	120.2	114.7
2015	116.2	115.3	115.8	116.2	116.6	116.8	116.6	116.6	116.1	117.1	118.8	120.1	116.9
2016	116.4	115.5	115.8	115.9	115.8	115.6	115.5	115.7	115.0	115.6	117.4	118.7	116.1
2017	114.5	113.8	113.8	113.5	113.7	113.7	112.7	113.0	112.4	112.7	115.0	115.9	113.7
2018	113.2	112.6	112.6	112.3	112.7	112.4	112.5	113.0	112.1	112.2	113.7	114.1	112.8
Wholesale Trade													
2010	22.2	22.3	22.3	22.3	22.4	22.5	22.4	22.4	22.3	22.5	22.6	22.6	22.4
2011	23.0	23.2	23.1	22.6	22.8	22.9	22.8	22.8	22.7	22.8	22.8	22.8	22.9
2012	22.4	22.5	22.5	22.8	22.7	22.7	22.6	22.6	22.5	22.5	22.5	22.6	22.6
2013	23.1	23.2	23.3	23.1	23.1	23.2	23.2	23.3	23.3	23.4	23.4	23.5	23.3
2014	23.4	23.5	23.5	23.4	23.4	23.5	23.5	23.6	23.6	23.6	23.7	23.8	23.5
2015	23.3	23.3	23.4	23.4	23.5	23.5	23.4	23.4	23.2	23.4	23.3	23.4	23.4
2016	23.3	23.3	23.1	23.2	23.2	23.1	23.2	23.1	22.9	22.8	22.8	22.8	23.1
2017	22.3	22.3	22.4	22.5	22.6	22.6	22.5	22.5	22.4	22.4	22.4	22.4	22.4
2018	22.6	22.7	22.6	22.5	22.5	22.7	22.7	22.7	22.4	22.2	21.9	21.9	22.5
Retail Trade													
2010	57.1	56.6	57.3	57.0	56.9	56.9	56.9	56.6	56.7	57.9	59.8	60.7	57.5
2011	58.7	58.4	58.6	58.9	58.8	58.6	58.7	58.4	58.0	58.8	60.6	61.1	59.0
2012	59.2	58.4	58.5	58.5	58.7	58.6	58.6	58.3	57.9	59.5	62.1	62.6	59.2
2013	60.4	59.4	59.9	59.8	60.0	60.1	60.4	60.7	60.8	61.3	63.1	64.0	60.8
2014	61.3	60.9	61.1	61.2	61.7	62.4	62.8	62.9	62.4	63.0	65.1	66.5	62.6
2015	63.5	63.0	63.4	63.5	63.8	64.2	64.0	64.0	63.5	64.4	66.1	66.8	64.2
2016	64.1	63.6	63.9	64.1	64.1	64.3	64.1	64.1	63.6	64.4	66.1	66.8	64.4
2017	63.7	63.0	63.0	62.6	62.6	62.5	61.9	62.2	61.6	62.0	64.0	64.3	62.8
2018	62.0	61.1	61.2	60.9	61.2	60.9	60.7	60.8	60.2	60.5	61.9	62.0	61.1
Transportation and Utilities													
2010	24.4	24.3	24.4	25.1	25.2	25.2	25.6	25.7	25.6	26.0	25.9	26.3	25.3
2011	26.1	25.8	25.8	26.2	26.3	26.2	26.3	26.4	26.6	26.3	26.5	26.8	26.3
2012	26.4	26.5	26.8	26.8	26.9	26.9	26.6	26.9	26.9	27.3	27.7	28.0	27.0
2013	27.9	27.8	28.1	27.6	27.4	27.3	27.2	27.5	27.5	27.8	27.9	28.5	27.7
2014	27.9	27.7	28.1	28.2	28.5	28.3	28.3	28.7	28.8	28.9	29.3	29.9	28.6
2015	29.4	29.0	29.0	29.3	29.3	29.1	29.2	29.2	29.4	29.3	29.4	29.9	29.3
2016	29.0	28.6	28.8	28.6	28.5	28.2	28.2	28.5	28.5	28.4	28.5	29.1	28.6
2017	28.5	28.5	28.4	28.4	28.5	28.6	28.3	28.3	28.4	28.3	28.6	29.2	28.5
2018	28.6	28.8	28.8	28.9	29.0	28.8	29.1	29.5	29.5	29.5	29.9	30.2	29.2
Information													
2010	6.8	7.3	7.2	6.9	7.5	8.3	6.0	6.3	8.7	6.5	6.9	7.1	7.1
2011	6.9	6.8	8.4	7.6	8.5	8.0	6.9	6.9	7.1	7.4	7.4	8.0	7.5
2012	7.2	7.8	8.0	10.5	11.9	9.2	8.6	8.7	7.9	7.7	8.6	8.9	8.8
2013	9.1	10.1	9.2	9.6	10.2	10.5	7.6	8.3	8.0	9.6	10.6	9.1	9.3
2014	7.4	8.4	9.0	8.5	8.7	8.2	8.2	8.0	7.6	7.7	9.6	9.0	8.4
2015	6.8	8.4	8.5	9.8	10.3	9.7	9.2	8.6	8.1	9.0	9.6	9.8	9.0
2016	8.7	8.1	7.9	7.9	7.5	6.7	7.3	8.0	6.6	6.8	8.0	6.7	7.5
2017	6.5	8.3	7.6	8.2	8.7	6.7	6.4	7.2	7.0	7.1	7.2	7.0	7.3
2018	7.3	8.0	8.1	8.3	8.6	7.7	6.9	7.3	7.0	7.3	7.6	7.5	7.6
Financial Activities													
2010	26.0	26.0	26.1	26.1	26.4	26.3	26.3	26.2	26.1	26.4	26.5	26.5	26.2
2011	26.7	26.7	26.7	26.4	26.6	26.5	26.8	26.8	26.7	26.9	27.0	27.0	26.7
2012	26.7	26.8	26.8	26.8	26.9	27.0	26.9	26.9	26.8	27.0	27.1	27.1	26.9
2013	27.0	27.1	27.1	27.3	27.5	27.6	27.8	28.0	27.9	28.2	28.1	28.1	27.6
2014	28.0	28.2	28.3	28.6	28.7	28.9	29.0	29.1	28.9	29.1	29.3	29.3	28.8
2015	29.3	29.4	29.5	29.6	29.6	29.7	29.7	29.7	29.5	29.8	29.9	29.8	29.6
2016	29.6	29.6	29.6	30.0	30.2	30.1	30.3	30.3	30.5	30.5	30.3	30.2	30.1
2017	29.9	30.0	29.8	29.6	29.7	29.6	29.7	29.5	29.2	29.3	29.4	29.5	29.6
2018	29.0	29.1	29.1	29.0	29.1	29.0	29.1	29.0	28.9	29.1	28.7	28.9	29.0

Employment by Industry: New Orleans-Metairie, LA, 2010–2018—*Continued*

(Numbers in thousands, not seasonally adjusted)

Industry and year	January	February	March	April	May	June	July	August	September	October	November	December	Annual average
Professional and Business Services													
2010	66.2	67.1	67.8	69.7	69.5	69.8	69.5	69.0	68.0	68.6	68.8	68.7	68.6
2011	67.1	68.6	68.3	68.8	68.5	68.1	67.4	68.0	68.0	69.7	69.8	69.9	68.5
2012	67.8	69.0	69.5	71.4	71.0	69.4	69.8	69.1	68.1	70.5	70.4	70.0	69.7
2013	70.3	73.6	71.7	72.0	71.7	71.6	72.2	72.6	71.9	74.0	74.1	74.4	72.5
2014	73.0	74.1	74.8	75.4	74.7	75.0	74.2	74.3	73.4	75.3	75.6	75.8	74.6
2015	74.1	74.5	75.4	77.0	76.4	75.5	75.3	75.3	73.7	75.8	75.3	75.2	75.3
2016	74.0	74.6	74.7	76.9	76.7	75.4	74.6	74.8	76.3	75.9	75.3	74.3	75.3
2017	74.4	76.4	75.5	74.7	75.5	74.6	74.6	74.1	74.3	76.2	77.3	75.1	75.2
2018	74.0	74.7	75.1	75.1	74.8	74.5	74.4	74.4	74.5	77.0	75.9	76.3	75.1
Education and Health Services													
2010	77.5	77.8	78.3	79.2	76.4	75.3	75.2	76.0	77.1	78.4	78.8	78.8	77.4
2011	77.5	78.6	79.1	79.8	79.1	77.4	77.5	78.6	80.2	81.4	82.1	81.7	79.4
2012	80.0	81.0	81.8	81.7	81.7	81.0	80.4	81.9	81.9	82.7	82.9	83.0	81.7
2013	84.4	84.9	84.5	84.0	83.6	82.2	81.5	85.9	86.6	88.3	88.4	88.2	85.2
2014	87.7	88.3	88.4	88.7	88.9	88.0	88.1	91.0	91.8	92.3	92.7	92.3	89.9
2015	92.3	92.7	92.9	94.2	94.4	93.3	93.2	95.1	95.7	97.8	97.7	97.8	94.8
2016	97.1	97.4	97.7	98.8	99.1	98.2	98.3	100.0	100.8	100.5	100.9	100.8	99.1
2017	99.0	99.6	99.2	100.0	100.0	99.4	96.6	98.6	99.6	99.3	99.5	99.1	99.2
2018	98.0	98.5	98.2	99.3	99.4	97.5	98.0	100.7	101.1	103.1	103.6	102.2	100.0
Leisure and Hospitality													
2010	67.8	68.4	69.6	70.2	70.0	70.6	69.1	69.6	70.4	70.2	71.3	72.4	70.0
2011	70.9	71.9	73.0	73.6	74.2	74.5	73.6	74.6	74.3	73.8	74.9	76.1	73.8
2012	75.8	75.9	76.5	77.4	76.9	76.9	76.3	76.8	74.8	76.1	76.9	78.6	76.6
2013	77.9	77.6	78.5	79.3	79.3	79.5	78.4	80.7	78.0	78.8	81.1	80.6	79.1
2014	80.4	81.7	82.3	82.5	83.3	83.9	82.6	83.7	81.6	83.5	84.9	84.0	82.9
2015	83.8	84.3	85.2	85.3	85.9	85.8	85.3	84.8	83.6	86.1	86.1	86.9	85.3
2016	86.1	86.4	87.4	87.9	88.4	88.2	87.2	86.8	87.0	88.0	88.1	87.8	87.4
2017	86.8	87.8	88.1	89.1	90.0	89.7	88.8	88.4	87.8	88.7	88.6	89.5	88.6
2018	88.9	88.8	90.3	90.3	90.3	90.8	90.0	90.1	90.2	93.0	92.7	93.6	90.8
Other Services													
2010	21.3	21.4	21.5	20.7	20.7	20.9	20.6	20.6	20.5	21.0	21.1	21.2	21.0
2011	21.2	21.3	21.4	21.6	21.6	21.8	21.8	21.8	21.7	21.9	22.0	22.0	21.7
2012	21.9	22.0	22.2	22.3	22.4	22.5	22.5	22.4	22.3	22.4	22.4	22.5	22.3
2013	22.5	22.6	22.7	22.9	22.9	23.0	23.1	23.1	22.9	22.9	22.9	22.9	22.9
2014	23.0	22.9	23.0	23.0	23.2	23.2	23.2	23.2	23.0	23.2	23.2	23.4	23.1
2015	23.3	23.4	23.4	23.7	24.0	24.0	24.2	24.1	23.9	23.9	23.9	23.9	23.8
2016	23.8	23.7	23.8	24.4	24.3	24.3	24.4	24.4	24.2	24.2	24.3	24.1	24.2
2017	24.3	24.3	24.2	24.3	24.5	24.6	24.4	24.5	24.3	24.4	24.4	24.4	24.4
2018	24.5	24.4	24.4	24.5	24.6	24.6	24.6	24.6	24.5	24.6	24.6	24.6	24.5
Government													
2010	83.9	84.4	85.1	84.9	86.5	84.5	81.9	82.7	83.1	83.5	83.8	83.3	84.0
2011	82.4	82.4	82.1	82.3	82.1	80.1	78.4	79.8	81.3	80.8	80.9	80.5	81.1
2012	78.5	79.3	78.9	80.2	80.1	78.9	76.5	77.8	78.7	79.1	79.3	79.3	78.9
2013	77.6	78.1	78.1	77.8	78.1	77.0	73.8	73.5	74.5	74.8	75.1	75.3	76.1
2014	73.6	74.9	75.2	74.6	74.3	76.1	72.9	72.9	74.3	74.8	75.0	74.2	74.4
2015	73.2	74.4	73.8	74.2	74.1	73.1	70.5	71.3	73.0	72.3	72.5	72.1	72.9
2016	71.6	72.4	72.0	72.5	74.4	72.8	69.8	70.1	71.2	72.3	72.4	72.1	72.0
2017	71.2	72.4	72.1	74.1	74.3	72.9	70.0	70.4	71.6	73.0	73.5	73.2	72.4
2018	72.0	73.0	72.7	74.5	74.7	73.2	70.3	70.5	71.7	72.5	72.9	72.3	72.5

Employment by Industry: Salt Lake City, UT, 2010–2018

(Numbers in thousands, not seasonally adjusted)

Industry and year	January	February	March	April	May	June	July	August	September	October	November	December	Annual average
Total Nonfarm													
2010	576.8	576.4	580.6	583.9	586.8	588.3	586.3	587.6	590.4	594.4	597.1	598.4	587.3
2011	585.3	586.9	589.9	594.6	595.0	597.7	596.1	600.2	603.5	604.7	609.1	610.4	597.8
2012	600.9	603.8	607.3	617.1	621.6	624.2	616.1	620.9	624.9	629.0	635.8	635.9	619.8
2013	624.7	628.5	631.9	636.3	637.6	639.2	634.4	637.8	640.8	648.4	654.2	655.4	639.1
2014	641.3	643.8	646.3	650.3	651.7	655.1	647.1	652.4	657.6	662.8	668.5	670.7	654.0
2015	660.1	663.3	667.9	669.5	673.7	675.3	673.4	676.7	681.2	688.1	692.4	695.3	676.4
2016	682.1	687.5	690.9	694.5	696.6	698.9	698.7	701.0	706.8	709.4	712.2	712.8	699.3
2017	702.1	705.5	708.3	710.2	713.0	716.8	710.8	714.9	720.3	725.6	731.4	733.6	716.0
2018	715.8	722.3	724.1	726.9	730.2	736.0	731.4	736.0	738.8	742.1	745.5	745.5	732.9
Total Private													
2010	482.5	482.2	486.4	489.0	490.2	492.7	494.3	495.2	494.3	497.5	500.2	502.3	492.2
2011	490.1	491.6	494.5	498.3	498.6	501.2	503.4	507.0	507.1	508.6	512.4	513.5	502.2
2012	504.1	506.6	510.0	518.5	523.4	526.0	522.5	527.4	527.2	530.0	537.0	537.8	522.5
2013	527.1	530.5	534.1	536.7	537.5	538.7	538.9	542.6	540.4	545.6	551.8	553.0	539.7
2014	539.1	540.8	543.1	545.8	546.8	549.9	549.1	555.1	555.0	559.2	564.8	566.8	551.3
2015	557.0	559.4	563.3	564.2	567.9	570.5	573.3	577.8	576.7	581.6	586.3	588.9	572.2
2016	577.6	581.6	584.5	586.5	588.3	591.0	596.6	600.3	599.4	600.1	603.2	603.5	592.7
2017	594.4	596.6	599.1	600.1	602.2	607.1	608.1	612.1	611.3	614.9	620.6	622.4	607.4
2018	607.2	612.7	614.3	615.7	619.0	623.4	625.9	631.0	629.1	630.6	634.0	633.5	623.0
Goods Producing													
2010	82.4	81.7	82.2	83.6	84.7	85.4	86.0	86.7	86.8	86.9	86.1	85.2	84.8
2011	83.0	82.8	83.4	84.4	85.3	86.6	88.6	89.5	89.0	88.7	88.5	87.5	86.4
2012	85.5	86.1	86.7	88.2	90.1	90.9	90.8	91.4	91.0	90.9	90.3	89.7	89.3
2013	87.5	87.3	88.1	89.3	89.8	90.2	90.1	90.9	90.2	89.7	89.3	88.5	89.2
2014	86.6	87.0	87.7	88.7	89.5	90.3	90.5	91.3	91.2	91.7	91.2	90.5	89.7
2015	88.7	89.0	90.1	90.9	91.9	92.9	93.7	93.8	93.6	94.4	94.1	94.1	92.3
2016	92.1	92.5	93.6	94.3	95.2	95.9	96.9	97.0	97.3	97.5	97.0	96.1	95.5
2017	94.8	95.5	97.1	96.8	98.3	99.7	100.2	100.4	100.4	100.6	100.7	100.4	98.7
2018	98.7	99.5	100.3	100.8	101.9	103.5	103.7	103.8	103.3	103.2	102.4	101.4	101.9
Service-Providing													
2010	494.4	494.7	498.4	500.3	502.1	502.9	500.3	500.9	503.6	507.5	511.0	513.2	502.4
2011	502.3	504.1	506.5	510.2	509.7	511.1	507.5	510.7	514.5	516.0	520.6	522.9	511.3
2012	515.4	517.7	520.6	528.9	531.5	533.3	525.3	529.5	533.9	538.1	545.5	546.2	530.5
2013	537.2	541.2	543.8	547.0	547.8	549.0	544.3	546.9	550.6	558.7	564.9	566.9	549.9
2014	554.7	556.8	558.6	561.6	562.2	564.8	556.6	561.1	566.4	571.1	577.3	580.2	564.3
2015	571.4	574.3	577.8	578.6	581.8	582.4	579.7	582.9	587.6	593.7	598.3	601.2	584.1
2016	590.0	595.0	597.3	600.2	601.4	603.0	601.8	604.0	609.5	611.9	615.2	616.7	603.8
2017	607.3	610.0	611.2	613.4	614.7	617.1	610.6	614.5	619.9	625.0	630.7	633.2	617.3
2018	617.1	622.8	623.8	626.1	628.3	632.5	627.7	632.2	635.5	638.9	643.1	644.1	631.0
Mining, Logging, and Construction													
2010	31.1	30.6	31.1	31.9	33.1	33.5	33.8	34.3	34.6	35.0	34.2	33.3	33.0
2011	31.1	30.8	31.4	32.1	32.8	33.8	35.2	35.7	35.3	35.1	34.8	33.7	33.5
2012	32.0	32.6	32.9	34.2	35.7	36.1	35.9	36.5	36.2	35.9	35.6	34.9	34.9
2013	33.1	33.0	33.7	34.8	35.3	35.6	35.5	36.3	35.8	35.3	35.1	34.1	34.8
2014	32.5	32.8	33.5	34.5	35.3	35.9	36.4	36.9	37.1	37.4	36.9	36.0	35.4
2015	34.3	34.6	35.4	36.0	36.6	37.3	38.0	38.0	38.1	38.5	38.3	38.1	36.9
2016	36.6	36.9	38.0	38.8	39.3	39.8	40.1	40.2	40.3	40.5	40.0	38.9	39.1
2017	37.7	38.2	39.6	39.8	41.3	42.5	42.9	43.1	43.3	43.3	43.1	42.6	41.5
2018	41.4	41.8	42.6	43.0	43.9	45.0	45.1	45.4	45.0	44.7	44.0	42.9	43.7
Manufacturing													
2010	51.3	51.1	51.1	51.7	51.6	51.9	52.2	52.4	52.2	51.9	51.9	51.9	51.8
2011	51.9	52.0	52.0	52.3	52.5	52.8	53.4	53.8	53.7	53.6	53.7	53.8	53.0
2012	53.5	53.5	53.8	54.0	54.4	54.8	54.9	54.9	54.8	55.0	54.7	54.8	54.4
2013	54.4	54.3	54.4	54.5	54.5	54.6	54.6	54.6	54.4	54.4	54.2	54.4	54.4
2014	54.1	54.2	54.2	54.2	54.2	54.4	54.1	54.4	54.1	54.3	54.3	54.5	54.3
2015	54.4	54.4	54.7	54.9	55.3	55.6	55.7	55.8	55.5	55.9	55.8	56.0	55.3
2016	55.5	55.6	55.6	55.5	55.9	56.1	56.8	56.8	57.0	57.0	57.0	57.2	56.3
2017	57.1	57.3	57.5	57.0	57.0	57.2	57.3	57.3	57.1	57.3	57.6	57.8	57.3
2018	57.3	57.7	57.7	57.8	58.0	58.5	58.6	58.4	58.3	58.5	58.4	58.5	58.1

Employment by Industry: Salt Lake City, UT, 2010–2018—*Continued*

(Numbers in thousands, not seasonally adjusted)

Industry and year	January	February	March	April	May	June	July	August	September	October	November	December	Annual average
Trade, Transportation, and Utilities													
2010	117.1	116.7	116.8	116.8	117.4	117.8	117.8	118.6	118.1	118.9	121.1	122.2	118.3
2011	117.9	117.5	118.1	119.2	119.4	120.0	120.5	121.1	121.0	121.5	124.2	125.3	120.5
2012	122.2	121.8	122.8	123.9	124.7	125.5	124.8	125.5	126.0	126.7	129.8	130.1	125.3
2013	126.5	126.2	126.2	126.0	126.9	127.1	127.5	127.9	127.2	129.0	131.7	132.6	127.9
2014	127.9	127.4	127.7	128.1	128.7	129.4	128.9	129.7	130.2	131.9	134.9	136.0	130.1
2015	132.4	132.5	132.9	132.7	133.6	133.6	134.7	136.0	135.8	137.2	139.7	141.2	135.2
2016	137.2	137.5	138.1	137.7	138.4	138.3	139.2	139.9	140.1	139.9	142.7	144.4	139.5
2017	139.3	138.8	139.4	139.3	139.5	140.4	141.0	141.5	141.5	143.1	147.1	148.6	141.6
2018	142.6	142.6	143.1	143.2	144.0	145.0	146.3	147.3	148.0	148.7	150.6	151.7	146.1
Wholesale Trade													
2010	27.6	27.6	27.6	27.7	28.0	28.0	28.2	28.3	28.1	28.2	28.4	28.6	28.0
2011	28.5	28.7	29.0	29.1	29.2	29.5	29.6	29.7	29.7	29.7	29.8	29.9	29.4
2012	29.8	29.9	30.1	30.1	30.2	30.2	30.0	30.2	29.9	29.9	29.8	29.8	30.0
2013	30.1	30.1	30.0	30.0	30.2	30.1	30.1	30.2	29.9	29.9	30.0	30.0	30.1
2014	29.5	29.6	29.5	29.7	29.8	29.9	30.0	30.0	30.0	30.3	30.4	30.6	29.9
2015	30.1	30.4	30.5	30.7	31.0	31.1	31.2	31.3	31.1	31.1	31.2	31.3	30.9
2016	31.0	31.2	31.3	31.2	31.3	31.2	31.6	31.6	31.5	31.3	31.3	31.4	31.3
2017	31.0	31.1	31.2	31.3	31.5	31.6	31.7	31.7	31.6	31.8	32.0	32.1	31.6
2018	31.4	31.8	31.9	32.0	32.2	32.3	32.6	32.7	32.5	33.0	32.9	32.8	32.3
Retail Trade													
2010	62.7	62.2	62.2	62.1	62.4	62.5	62.3	62.7	62.3	62.7	64.4	64.9	62.8
2011	61.4	60.8	61.0	61.7	61.9	62.0	62.3	62.7	62.6	63.4	65.6	66.2	62.6
2012	63.5	62.9	63.5	64.1	64.7	65.3	65.6	65.8	66.3	67.0	69.9	69.9	65.7
2013	66.4	66.1	66.3	66.9	67.5	67.8	68.0	68.4	68.1	68.9	71.1	71.4	68.1
2014	67.5	67.2	67.5	67.7	68.2	68.4	68.7	69.3	69.4	70.4	72.6	73.3	69.2
2015	69.9	69.6	69.6	69.8	70.3	70.2	70.6	71.4	71.3	72.1	74.4	75.1	71.2
2016	72.0	72.2	72.6	72.4	72.8	73.0	73.2	73.7	73.7	74.0	76.1	76.7	73.5
2017	72.9	72.4	72.7	72.8	72.8	73.1	73.3	73.9	73.6	74.6	77.3	78.0	74.0
2018	74.5	73.9	74.1	74.4	74.9	75.2	76.0	76.6	76.0	76.9	78.7	79.1	75.9
Transportation and Utilities													
2010	26.8	26.9	27.0	27.0	27.0	27.3	27.3	27.6	27.7	28.0	28.3	28.7	27.5
2011	28.0	28.0	28.1	28.4	28.3	28.5	28.6	28.7	28.7	28.4	28.8	29.2	28.5
2012	28.9	29.0	29.2	29.7	29.8	30.0	29.2	29.5	29.8	29.8	30.1	30.4	29.6
2013	30.0	30.0	29.9	29.1	29.2	29.2	29.4	29.3	29.2	30.2	30.6	31.2	29.8
2014	30.9	30.6	30.7	30.7	30.7	31.1	30.2	30.4	30.8	31.2	31.9	32.1	30.9
2015	32.4	32.5	32.8	32.2	32.3	32.3	32.9	33.3	33.4	34.0	34.1	34.8	33.1
2016	34.2	34.1	34.2	34.1	34.3	34.1	34.4	34.6	34.9	34.6	35.3	36.3	34.6
2017	35.4	35.3	35.5	35.2	35.2	35.7	36.0	35.9	36.3	36.7	37.8	38.5	36.1
2018	36.7	36.9	37.1	36.8	36.9	37.5	37.7	38.0	39.5	38.8	39.0	39.8	37.9
Information													
2010	16.1	16.2	16.6	16.7	16.6	16.5	16.6	16.3	16.4	16.4	16.9	17.0	16.5
2011	16.0	16.3	16.4	16.0	16.1	16.2	16.1	16.3	16.1	16.1	16.5	16.5	16.2
2012	16.0	16.1	16.2	18.5	19.1	19.0	17.6	17.9	17.5	17.8	18.6	18.6	17.7
2013	19.3	19.4	19.4	18.0	18.1	18.1	18.0	18.2	17.8	17.8	18.5	18.6	18.4
2014	18.0	18.3	18.4	18.1	18.1	18.2	18.2	18.6	18.2	17.9	18.1	18.1	18.2
2015	17.6	17.8	17.8	17.6	17.9	17.8	18.2	18.6	18.4	18.6	19.2	19.0	18.2
2016	18.7	19.6	19.0	18.7	18.9	19.1	19.7	20.3	19.6	19.6	19.7	19.6	19.4
2017	19.8	20.5	20.0	19.9	20.0	20.5	20.9	21.4	21.2	21.7	21.5	20.9	20.7
2018	19.7	20.4	19.5	19.7	20.2	20.2	20.7	21.3	20.8	21.0	21.3	21.3	20.5
Financial Activities													
2010	45.8	45.4	45.5	45.2	45.2	45.3	45.4	45.6	45.7	46.1	46.2	46.4	45.7
2011	45.5	45.7	45.8	46.0	45.9	46.2	46.2	46.4	46.3	46.3	46.4	46.6	46.1
2012	45.9	46.0	46.1	46.4	46.5	46.8	47.0	47.6	47.4	47.5	47.9	48.4	47.0
2013	47.4	47.8	47.8	48.2	48.5	49.2	49.7	50.1	49.9	50.1	50.4	50.6	49.1
2014	49.4	49.7	49.5	49.6	49.9	50.4	50.8	51.4	51.0	51.5	51.9	52.1	50.6
2015	51.9	52.3	52.4	52.4	52.8	53.1	53.5	53.6	53.6	53.9	54.1	54.4	53.2
2016	54.2	54.7	54.7	54.8	55.3	55.7	56.3	56.7	56.2	56.6	56.9	57.0	55.8
2017	56.5	56.7	56.5	56.6	57.1	57.5	57.4	57.7	57.4	57.8	57.9	58.4	57.3
2018	57.9	58.4	58.3	58.3	58.8	59.5	59.8	60.2	59.5	59.8	60.0	60.4	59.2

Employment by Industry: Salt Lake City, UT, 2010–2018—*Continued*

(Numbers in thousands, not seasonally adjusted)

Industry and year	January	February	March	April	May	June	July	August	September	October	November	December	Annual average
Professional and Business Services													
2010	90.2	90.6	92.8	93.6	94.5	95.5	96.2	95.4	94.9	96.0	96.3	97.1	94.4
2011	94.7	95.5	96.3	97.3	97.7	98.0	98.8	99.6	100.1	101.8	102.2	102.1	98.7
2012	99.5	100.5	101.2	101.4	102.5	103.5	103.7	105.0	105.1	106.7	107.7	107.2	103.7
2013	103.0	104.8	106.0	108.6	108.0	108.4	109.0	110.1	110.1	113.1	114.2	114.0	109.1
2014	110.7	110.6	111.0	111.9	112.4	113.3	112.8	114.5	115.1	116.5	117.2	117.8	113.7
2015	114.1	114.0	115.2	116.2	117.4	118.8	119.2	120.3	120.0	121.3	121.9	122.0	118.4
2016	119.0	119.1	119.9	120.8	121.5	122.3	124.1	124.8	124.1	124.4	124.1	123.0	122.3
2017	122.0	121.1	121.2	122.1	122.8	123.8	124.8	125.6	125.7	126.2	126.6	126.2	124.0
2018	121.9	123.4	124.5	124.5	125.3	126.4	127.1	127.7	127.6	127.5	128.3	126.2	125.9
Education and Health Services													
2010	65.9	66.1	66.3	66.6	66.3	66.0	65.3	65.5	66.8	67.8	67.8	67.6	66.5
2011	67.1	67.6	67.6	68.0	67.4	66.9	65.6	66.0	67.6	68.2	68.3	68.0	67.4
2012	67.7	68.1	68.1	70.7	70.6	70.3	68.4	69.2	70.3	71.2	71.9	71.9	69.9
2013	72.3	73.0	73.3	72.7	72.7	72.0	70.5	71.3	72.2	73.3	74.0	73.7	72.6
2014	72.3	72.9	73.3	73.1	73.4	72.5	71.8	73.0	73.6	74.3	75.3	75.2	73.4
2015	75.6	76.3	76.5	76.2	76.6	76.1	74.9	75.8	76.9	78.4	79.1	78.6	76.8
2016	78.2	79.1	79.3	80.0	79.6	78.9	78.7	79.6	81.1	81.7	82.5	82.1	80.1
2017	81.5	82.5	82.6	83.0	83.0	82.1	81.1	82.4	83.0	83.8	84.6	84.2	82.8
2018	83.9	84.6	84.6	84.9	84.6	83.6	83.1	84.3	85.1	85.5	85.8	84.7	84.6
Leisure and Hospitality													
2010	47.1	47.5	47.9	48.5	47.4	48.1	48.6	48.7	47.7	47.4	47.9	49.0	48.0
2011	48.2	48.4	49.0	49.4	48.5	48.9	48.9	49.3	48.6	47.7	48.1	49.3	48.7
2012	49.2	49.7	50.4	50.9	51.1	51.2	50.9	51.4	50.9	50.2	51.8	52.8	50.9
2013	52.1	52.7	53.6	53.8	53.1	53.8	53.8	53.8	53.2	53.0	53.9	55.2	53.5
2014	54.5	54.9	55.3	55.9	54.3	55.1	54.9	55.4	55.0	54.8	55.6	56.6	55.2
2015	55.6	56.2	57.0	57.2	56.7	57.0	57.5	58.1	57.3	56.8	57.1	58.5	57.1
2016	57.4	58.1	58.7	59.1	58.2	59.2	59.8	60.0	59.4	58.9	59.0	60.0	59.0
2017	59.2	60.1	60.7	60.8	59.8	61.0	60.4	60.9	60.5	60.1	60.6	62.0	60.5
2018	61.0	62.1	62.2	62.4	62.0	62.6	62.5	63.7	62.5	62.6	63.8	66.1	62.8
Other Services													
2010	17.9	18.0	18.3	18.0	18.1	18.1	18.4	18.4	17.9	18.0	17.9	17.8	18.1
2011	17.7	17.8	17.9	18.0	18.3	18.4	18.7	18.8	18.4	18.3	18.2	18.2	18.2
2012	18.1	18.3	18.5	18.5	18.8	18.8	19.3	19.4	19.0	19.0	19.0	19.1	18.8
2013	19.0	19.3	19.7	20.1	20.4	19.9	20.3	20.3	19.8	19.6	19.8	19.8	19.8
2014	19.7	20.0	20.2	20.4	20.5	20.7	21.2	21.2	20.7	20.6	20.6	20.5	20.5
2015	21.1	21.3	21.4	21.0	21.0	21.2	21.6	21.6	21.1	21.0	21.1	21.1	21.2
2016	20.8	21.0	21.2	21.1	21.2	21.6	21.9	22.0	21.6	21.5	21.3	21.3	21.4
2017	21.3	21.4	21.6	21.6	21.7	22.1	22.3	22.2	21.6	21.6	21.6	21.7	21.7
2018	21.5	21.7	21.8	21.9	22.2	22.6	22.7	22.7	22.3	22.3	21.8	21.7	22.1
Government													
2010	94.3	94.2	94.2	94.9	96.6	95.6	92.0	92.4	96.1	96.9	96.9	96.1	95.0
2011	95.2	95.3	95.4	96.3	96.4	96.5	92.7	93.2	96.4	96.1	96.7	96.9	95.6
2012	96.8	97.2	97.3	98.6	98.2	98.2	93.6	93.5	97.7	99.0	98.8	98.1	97.3
2013	97.6	98.0	97.8	99.6	100.1	100.5	95.5	95.2	100.4	102.8	102.4	102.4	99.4
2014	102.2	103.0	103.2	104.5	104.9	105.2	98.0	97.3	102.6	103.6	103.7	103.9	102.7
2015	103.1	103.9	104.6	105.3	105.8	104.8	100.1	98.9	104.5	106.5	106.1	106.4	104.2
2016	104.5	105.9	106.4	108.0	108.3	107.9	102.1	100.7	107.4	109.3	109.0	109.3	106.6
2017	107.7	108.9	109.2	110.1	110.8	109.7	102.7	102.8	109.0	110.7	110.8	111.2	108.6
2018	108.6	109.6	109.8	111.2	111.2	112.6	105.5	105.0	109.7	111.5	111.5	112.0	109.9

Employment by Industry: Hartford-West Hartford-East Hartford, CT NECTA, 2010–2018

(Numbers in thousands, not seasonally adjusted)

Industry and year	January	February	March	April	May	June	July	August	September	October	November	December	Annual average
Total Nonfarm													
2010	535.2	540.8	543.6	551.6	552.5	549.1	542.1	539.1	553.4	560.4	562.8	563.1	549.5
2011	544.1	550.3	551.4	559.6	557.6	554.0	547.7	542.5	556.8	560.5	561.7	563.9	554.2
2012	545.6	552.9	555.5	559.6	559.4	559.0	551.6	548.2	562.3	568.7	572.4	571.6	558.9
2013	553.2	556.8	560.0	566.1	567.6	568.4	557.8	554.2	564.9	569.1	573.2	572.9	563.7
2014	557.0	559.7	562.5	571.0	573.3	572.5	562.5	559.6	571.5	577.9	580.6	581.0	569.1
2015	564.8	566.4	569.2	576.6	579.4	579.6	567.8	564.3	575.5	582.1	584.9	583.0	574.5
2016	568.0	569.7	572.6	576.5	580.0	579.0	570.9	566.5	576.7	581.4	585.1	584.2	575.9
2017	570.1	571.7	573.7	578.4	582.9	583.4	572.8	569.2	581.2	583.2	586.6	586.2	578.3
2018	572.9	574.9	576.0	579.1	585.2	586.6	576.9	574.9	584.3	588.4	591.8	591.9	581.9
Total Private													
2010	443.5	442.8	444.9	452.0	456.0	459.1	457.3	456.4	458.3	460.4	462.1	463.1	454.7
2011	452.0	452.3	453.3	460.1	463.0	465.8	464.0	461.2	462.3	461.6	462.2	464.8	460.2
2012	455.6	456.0	458.4	462.1	466.4	470.3	467.6	466.6	467.4	470.1	472.3	472.1	465.4
2013	461.3	460.4	463.1	468.3	472.8	476.7	472.3	471.5	471.9	471.8	474.9	474.8	470.0
2014	464.1	463.6	465.6	473.0	478.0	480.8	476.9	476.0	477.2	478.9	480.6	481.6	474.7
2015	470.6	469.9	472.2	478.4	484.1	488.5	482.9	481.5	481.6	484.0	485.5	485.3	480.4
2016	475.1	474.4	476.5	480.1	485.3	489.8	487.8	485.9	486.0	486.4	488.8	489.1	483.8
2017	478.9	478.0	479.5	484.0	490.1	493.6	488.4	486.9	489.4	489.9	492.5	493.0	487.0
2018	482.0	482.0	482.4	486.3	493.3	497.9	493.1	492.7	492.5	494.7	497.1	498.0	491.0
Goods Producing													
2010	71.3	70.5	70.7	72.7	73.7	74.7	74.6	74.7	75.0	75.2	75.1	74.9	73.6
2011	72.2	72.0	72.5	73.7	74.7	76.0	76.1	75.9	75.8	75.4	75.6	75.0	74.6
2012	73.1	72.7	73.0	74.1	74.7	75.7	76.1	75.9	75.3	75.5	75.4	75.1	74.7
2013	73.0	72.6	72.7	74.1	75.4	76.1	76.6	75.9	75.5	75.0	74.8	74.3	74.7
2014	71.9	71.6	71.7	73.5	74.5	75.3	75.9	75.9	75.6	75.6	75.4	75.0	74.3
2015	72.8	72.6	73.1	75.2	76.7	77.6	77.1	77.3	77.0	76.9	76.7	76.2	75.8
2016	74.2	73.5	74.2	75.8	76.8	77.8	78.3	78.2	77.5	77.5	77.3	76.9	76.5
2017	74.9	74.8	75.4	76.7	78.2	79.6	79.8	79.5	78.9	78.4	78.3	77.6	77.7
2018	75.5	75.9	76.2	77.7	79.1	80.4	80.5	80.4	79.7	79.7	79.4	78.6	78.6
Service-Providing													
2010	463.9	470.3	472.9	478.9	478.8	474.4	467.5	464.4	478.4	485.2	487.7	488.2	475.9
2011	471.9	478.3	478.9	485.9	482.9	478.0	471.6	466.6	481.0	485.1	486.1	488.9	479.6
2012	472.5	480.2	482.5	485.5	484.7	483.3	475.5	472.3	487.0	493.2	497.0	496.5	484.2
2013	480.2	484.2	487.3	492.0	492.2	492.3	481.2	478.3	489.4	494.1	498.4	498.6	489.0
2014	485.1	488.1	490.8	497.5	498.8	497.2	486.6	483.7	495.9	502.3	505.2	506.0	494.8
2015	492.0	493.8	496.1	501.4	502.7	502.0	490.7	487.0	498.5	505.2	508.2	506.8	498.7
2016	493.8	496.2	498.4	500.7	503.2	501.2	492.6	488.3	499.2	503.9	507.8	507.3	499.4
2017	495.2	496.9	498.3	501.7	504.7	503.8	493.0	489.7	502.3	504.8	508.3	508.6	500.6
2018	497.4	499.0	499.8	501.4	506.1	506.2	496.4	494.5	504.6	508.7	512.4	513.3	503.3
Mining, Logging, and Construction													
2010	15.2	14.5	14.6	16.6	17.3	17.8	18.0	18.2	18.0	18.1	17.9	17.3	17.0
2011	15.4	15.1	15.3	16.5	17.3	18.1	18.4	18.4	18.2	18.0	18.2	17.4	17.2
2012	15.8	15.3	15.7	16.8	17.2	17.7	18.2	18.3	18.1	18.2	18.1	17.6	17.3
2013	16.0	15.8	16.0	17.3	18.5	18.9	19.4	19.4	19.3	19.3	19.1	18.4	18.1
2014	16.8	16.5	16.6	18.3	19.4	19.7	20.4	20.5	20.4	20.2	20.0	19.4	19.0
2015	17.7	17.4	17.6	19.6	20.8	21.2	21.3	21.5	21.2	21.3	21.2	20.6	20.1
2016	19.0	18.3	19.0	20.4	21.3	21.7	21.9	21.9	21.4	21.2	20.9	20.0	20.6
2017	18.2	17.9	18.3	19.4	20.6	21.1	21.2	21.1	20.8	20.6	20.2	19.2	19.9
2018	17.4	17.6	17.9	19.2	20.3	20.7	20.8	20.8	20.6	20.3	20.4	19.1	19.6
Manufacturing													
2010	56.1	56.0	56.1	56.1	56.4	56.9	56.6	56.5	57.0	57.1	57.2	57.6	56.6
2011	56.8	56.9	57.2	57.2	57.4	57.9	57.7	57.5	57.6	57.4	57.4	57.6	57.4
2012	57.3	57.4	57.3	57.3	57.5	58.0	57.9	57.6	57.2	57.3	57.3	57.5	57.5
2013	57.0	56.8	56.7	56.8	56.9	57.2	57.2	56.5	56.2	55.7	55.7	55.9	56.6
2014	55.1	55.1	55.1	55.2	55.1	55.6	55.5	55.4	55.2	55.4	55.4	55.6	55.3
2015	55.1	55.2	55.5	55.6	55.9	56.4	55.8	55.8	55.8	55.6	55.5	55.6	55.7
2016	55.2	55.2	55.2	55.4	55.5	56.1	56.4	56.3	56.1	56.3	56.4	56.9	55.9
2017	56.7	56.9	57.1	57.3	57.6	58.5	58.6	58.4	58.1	57.8	58.1	58.4	57.8
2018	58.1	58.3	58.3	58.5	58.8	59.7	59.7	59.6	59.1	59.4	59.0	59.5	59.0

Employment by Industry: Hartford-West Hartford-East Hartford, CT NECTA, 2010–2018—*Continued*

(Numbers in thousands, not seasonally adjusted)

Industry and year	January	February	March	April	May	June	July	August	September	October	November	December	Annual average
Trade, Transportation, and Utilities													
2010	85.0	83.7	83.8	84.0	85.3	86.2	84.7	84.3	84.9	86.1	87.7	89.3	85.4
2011	85.8	84.9	85.0	86.2	86.4	87.1	85.3	84.9	85.7	85.9	87.7	89.4	86.2
2012	86.2	85.0	85.6	85.7	86.9	87.3	85.3	85.2	86.5	87.4	89.4	90.2	86.7
2013	87.6	86.2	86.9	87.8	88.6	89.4	87.2	87.2	88.7	89.6	91.8	92.9	88.7
2014	89.2	87.9	88.0	88.9	89.7	90.2	87.7	87.3	89.2	90.0	91.6	92.7	89.4
2015	89.4	88.1	88.1	88.6	89.7	90.4	87.7	87.5	89.5	91.0	92.8	93.9	89.7
2016	90.8	89.5	89.8	89.3	90.6	90.5	88.7	88.0	89.4	90.3	92.4	94.0	90.3
2017	90.6	88.9	88.5	88.5	90.0	90.4	88.1	88.1	91.0	92.3	94.6	95.9	90.6
2018	92.7	91.1	90.7	90.1	92.4	92.9	90.5	90.0	91.7	92.3	94.6	95.7	92.1
Wholesale Trade													
2010	18.0	17.9	17.9	18.1	18.2	18.4	18.4	18.4	18.2	18.2	18.3	18.3	18.2
2011	18.0	17.9	18.0	18.2	18.3	18.4	18.3	18.3	18.1	18.0	17.9	17.9	18.1
2012	17.7	17.7	17.7	17.8	17.9	18.0	18.1	18.0	17.9	18.1	17.9	18.0	17.9
2013	17.8	17.8	17.8	17.9	18.0	18.1	18.0	18.0	17.9	17.9	17.9	18.0	17.9
2014	17.8	17.7	17.7	17.8	17.9	17.9	17.9	17.8	17.8	17.8	17.7	17.8	17.8
2015	17.7	17.6	17.6	17.8	17.9	18.0	17.9	18.0	17.9	17.8	17.8	17.8	17.8
2016	18.0	17.9	18.0	18.1	18.1	18.2	18.1	18.0	17.9	17.8	17.8	17.9	18.0
2017	17.9	17.8	17.8	17.9	18.1	18.1	18.0	17.9	17.9	17.9	17.8	18.0	17.9
2018	17.9	17.9	17.9	17.9	18.0	18.1	18.0	17.9	17.8	17.8	17.7	17.7	17.9
Retail Trade													
2010	53.7	52.5	52.7	53.0	53.6	54.4	54.1	53.9	53.4	54.5	55.8	57.3	54.1
2011	54.6	53.7	53.6	54.5	54.5	55.0	54.3	54.3	53.9	54.3	56.1	57.5	54.7
2012	55.2	54.0	54.4	54.5	55.2	55.4	54.6	54.7	54.3	55.0	57.1	57.5	55.2
2013	55.6	54.5	54.8	55.3	55.8	56.3	55.7	56.0	55.6	56.4	58.2	58.9	56.1
2014	56.4	55.2	55.3	55.9	56.5	56.9	55.9	55.8	55.7	56.3	58.0	58.6	56.4
2015	56.2	55.1	55.2	55.3	56.0	56.5	55.5	55.5	55.2	56.1	57.6	58.5	56.1
2016	55.8	54.7	55.0	54.8	55.5	55.9	55.4	55.2	54.6	55.4	57.0	57.5	55.6
2017	56.0	54.4	54.1	54.7	55.2	55.5	55.1	55.0	54.4	55.3	57.1	57.7	55.4
2018	55.6	54.3	54.0	54.0	54.8	55.0	54.6	54.5	53.9	54.4	56.3	56.9	54.9
Transportation and Utilities													
2010	13.3	13.3	13.2	12.9	13.5	13.4	12.2	12.0	13.3	13.4	13.6	13.7	13.2
2011	13.2	13.3	13.4	13.5	13.6	13.7	12.7	12.3	13.7	13.6	13.7	14.0	13.4
2012	13.3	13.3	13.5	13.4	13.8	13.9	12.6	12.5	14.3	14.3	14.4	14.7	13.7
2013	14.2	13.9	14.3	14.6	14.8	15.0	13.5	13.2	15.2	15.3	15.7	16.0	14.6
2014	15.0	15.0	15.0	15.2	15.3	15.4	13.9	13.7	15.7	15.9	15.9	16.3	15.2
2015	15.5	15.4	15.3	15.5	15.8	15.9	14.3	14.0	16.4	17.1	17.4	17.6	15.9
2016	17.0	16.9	16.8	16.4	17.0	16.4	15.2	14.8	16.9	17.1	17.6	18.6	16.7
2017	16.7	16.7	16.6	15.9	16.7	16.8	15.0	15.2	18.7	19.1	19.7	20.2	17.3
2018	19.2	18.9	18.8	18.2	19.6	19.8	17.9	17.6	20.0	20.1	20.6	21.1	19.3
Information													
2010	11.3	11.2	11.2	11.2	11.2	11.2	11.3	11.4	11.4	11.4	11.5	11.5	11.3
2011	11.5	11.4	11.4	11.3	11.3	11.3	11.3	11.3	11.2	11.1	11.1	11.0	11.3
2012	11.0	11.1	10.9	11.1	11.2	11.2	11.2	11.3	11.3	11.3	11.6	11.3	11.2
2013	11.5	11.7	11.7	11.4	11.5	11.6	11.5	11.6	11.2	11.2	11.3	11.3	11.5
2014	11.2	11.3	11.5	11.5	11.4	11.5	11.6	11.7	11.5	11.3	11.6	11.7	11.5
2015	11.5	11.6	11.6	11.8	11.8	11.9	11.9	12.0	11.9	11.9	12.0	12.0	11.8
2016	11.7	11.6	11.6	11.5	11.6	11.6	11.6	11.6	11.4	11.2	11.1	11.1	11.5
2017	10.7	10.6	10.6	10.6	10.5	10.6	10.6	10.6	10.5	10.3	10.4	10.3	10.5
2018	10.1	10.1	9.9	10.0	9.9	10.0	10.0	9.9	9.9	9.9	10.0	10.0	10.0

Employment by Industry: Hartford-West Hartford-East Hartford, CT NECTA, 2010–2018—*Continued*

(Numbers in thousands, not seasonally adjusted)

Industry and year	January	February	March	April	May	June	July	August	September	October	November	December	Annual average
Financial Activities													
2010	61.8	61.8	62.2	61.4	61.5	62.4	62.4	62.6	62.0	62.2	62.2	62.3	62.1
2011	62.2	62.0	62.2	61.8	61.8	62.3	62.5	62.3	61.7	61.6	61.4	61.5	61.9
2012	61.1	61.1	61.3	60.7	60.7	61.6	61.6	61.1	60.5	60.3	60.1	60.1	60.9
2013	60.0	59.5	59.4	59.1	58.8	59.6	59.4	58.7	57.6	56.9	56.7	56.7	58.5
2014	57.0	56.6	56.4	56.3	56.5	57.1	57.4	57.1	56.6	56.7	56.7	56.8	56.8
2015	56.7	56.6	56.7	56.8	57.0	57.9	58.1	58.0	57.3	57.2	57.5	57.4	57.3
2016	57.2	57.0	57.2	57.3	57.3	58.2	58.1	58.0	57.3	57.1	57.1	57.0	57.4
2017	56.8	56.7	56.8	56.7	56.8	57.7	57.7	57.5	56.8	56.7	56.7	56.5	57.0
2018	56.2	56.2	56.3	56.2	56.2	57.4	57.4	57.0	56.5	57.0	57.5	57.5	56.8
Professional and Business Services													
2010	58.4	59.1	59.1	61.5	61.6	62.0	61.8	61.7	61.5	62.0	61.8	61.6	61.0
2011	60.6	60.9	60.5	62.4	62.6	63.2	63.4	63.1	63.2	63.8	63.5	64.2	62.6
2012	62.9	63.4	63.9	65.1	65.5	66.3	66.2	66.4	66.1	66.5	66.4	66.0	65.4
2013	63.7	64.5	64.5	66.0	66.6	67.6	67.5	68.1	68.5	68.5	68.9	68.9	66.9
2014	67.7	68.5	68.8	70.4	71.7	71.9	71.2	71.2	71.1	71.8	71.9	72.0	70.7
2015	70.8	71.5	72.0	72.8	73.6	74.9	73.8	73.4	72.9	73.1	73.3	72.7	72.9
2016	70.8	71.1	71.2	72.2	72.6	73.8	73.3	73.4	73.3	73.3	73.5	73.6	72.7
2017	71.8	72.0	72.3	73.8	74.3	74.9	74.7	74.4	74.2	74.0	74.5	74.3	73.8
2018	72.2	72.6	72.8	73.3	74.0	74.7	74.7	75.0	74.5	74.8	74.7	73.8	73.9
Education and Health Services													
2010	98.1	98.5	99.2	99.9	99.3	98.5	97.7	97.2	99.4	100.4	101.0	101.1	99.2
2011	100.4	101.0	101.5	102.0	101.4	100.0	99.2	98.4	100.2	100.0	99.8	100.3	100.4
2012	99.4	100.4	100.8	100.7	100.4	99.6	99.2	98.8	101.2	102.3	103.0	103.5	100.8
2013	101.5	102.1	103.0	103.1	102.5	102.0	100.6	100.8	103.2	103.5	104.3	103.9	102.5
2014	102.1	102.9	103.4	104.8	104.3	103.9	102.4	103.0	105.0	105.3	105.8	105.9	104.1
2015	103.8	104.2	104.4	105.4	105.0	104.9	103.7	103.1	104.5	105.2	105.5	105.6	104.6
2016	104.3	105.0	105.1	105.1	105.0	105.3	105.8	105.4	107.1	107.2	108.2	107.5	105.9
2017	106.9	107.7	107.8	107.9	108.4	106.9	105.2	105.4	107.5	107.8	108.2	108.8	107.4
2018	107.2	108.3	108.3	108.8	109.2	108.4	106.3	106.9	108.7	110.3	110.4	111.1	108.7
Leisure and Hospitality													
2010	37.5	38.0	38.6	41.1	43.0	43.5	44.3	44.0	43.6	42.6	42.2	41.9	41.7
2011	39.1	39.9	39.9	42.2	44.1	44.8	45.5	44.8	44.2	43.5	42.7	43.0	42.8
2012	41.4	41.8	42.6	44.2	46.2	47.4	46.8	46.6	45.3	45.2	44.6	44.8	44.7
2013	43.0	42.7	43.7	45.9	48.3	48.9	48.3	48.2	46.4	46.4	46.3	45.9	46.2
2014	44.2	44.0	44.9	46.5	48.6	49.3	49.1	48.4	46.8	46.7	46.1	46.1	46.7
2015	44.3	44.0	44.8	46.4	48.6	49.1	48.7	47.9	46.9	47.1	46.1	45.9	46.7
2016	44.5	45.1	45.7	47.2	49.5	50.4	49.8	49.2	48.2	47.9	47.4	47.1	47.7
2017	45.5	45.6	46.3	47.9	49.8	51.1	50.1	49.4	48.4	48.6	47.8	47.6	48.2
2018	45.9	45.6	45.7	47.5	49.7	50.9	50.6	50.4	48.8	48.5	47.9	49.2	48.4
Other Services													
2010	20.1	20.0	20.1	20.2	20.4	20.6	20.5	20.5	20.5	20.5	20.6	20.5	20.4
2011	20.2	20.2	20.3	20.5	20.7	21.1	20.7	20.5	20.3	20.3	20.4	20.4	20.5
2012	20.5	20.5	20.3	20.5	20.8	21.2	21.2	21.3	21.2	21.6	21.8	21.1	21.0
2013	21.0	21.1	21.2	20.9	21.1	21.5	21.2	21.0	20.8	20.7	20.8	20.9	21.0
2014	20.8	20.8	20.9	21.1	21.3	21.6	21.6	21.4	21.4	21.5	21.5	21.4	21.3
2015	21.3	21.3	21.5	21.4	21.7	21.8	21.9	22.3	21.6	21.6	21.6	21.6	21.6
2016	21.6	21.6	21.7	21.7	21.9	22.2	22.2	22.1	21.8	21.9	21.8	21.9	21.9
2017	21.7	21.7	21.8	21.9	22.1	22.4	22.2	22.0	22.1	21.8	22.0	22.0	22.0
2018	22.2	22.2	22.5	22.7	22.8	23.2	23.1	23.1	22.7	22.2	22.6	22.1	22.6
Government													
2010	91.7	98.0	98.7	99.6	96.5	90.0	84.8	82.7	95.1	100.0	100.7	100.0	94.8
2011	92.1	98.0	98.1	99.5	94.6	88.2	83.7	81.3	94.5	98.9	99.5	99.1	94.0
2012	90.0	96.9	97.1	97.5	93.0	88.7	84.0	81.6	94.9	98.6	100.1	99.5	93.5
2013	91.9	96.4	96.9	97.8	94.8	91.7	85.5	82.7	93.0	97.3	98.3	98.1	93.7
2014	92.9	96.1	96.9	98.0	95.3	91.7	85.6	83.6	94.3	99.0	100.0	99.4	94.4
2015	94.2	96.5	97.0	98.2	95.3	91.1	84.9	82.8	93.9	98.1	99.4	97.7	94.1
2016	92.9	95.3	96.1	96.4	94.7	89.2	83.1	80.6	90.7	95.0	96.3	95.1	92.1
2017	91.2	93.7	94.2	94.4	92.8	89.8	84.4	82.3	91.8	93.3	94.1	93.2	91.3
2018	90.9	92.9	93.6	92.8	91.9	88.7	83.8	82.2	91.8	93.7	94.7	93.9	90.9

Employment by Industry: Birmingham-Hoover, AL, 2010–2018

(Numbers in thousands, not seasonally adjusted)

Industry and year	January	February	March	April	May	June	July	August	September	October	November	December	Annual average
Total Nonfarm													
2010	491.9	492.8	494.1	497.1	500.4	499.8	496.3	494.7	494.1	497.8	500.2	500.3	496.6
2011	489.7	492.1	495.2	497.1	498.8	501.1	498.1	498.5	501.1	500.8	504.3	505.5	498.5
2012	498.3	500.9	505.0	508.1	508.6	510.4	504.8	505.8	507.8	508.7	512.3	511.9	506.9
2013	502.9	506.3	508.4	512.0	514.0	515.4	511.3	512.0	513.8	514.5	518.2	520.1	512.4
2014	507.8	508.8	512.8	516.1	517.2	519.0	514.9	516.8	518.2	518.6	521.3	522.9	516.2
2015	512.4	515.1	516.6	520.4	523.2	524.6	522.8	523.2	523.2	525.5	527.9	528.4	521.9
2016	518.7	521.7	522.7	526.7	527.7	528.5	527.3	527.1	528.2	528.1	530.5	531.2	526.5
2017	522.4	525.9	527.8	528.6	530.9	533.6	532.0	533.0	533.6	534.9	538.7	538.3	531.6
2018	529.9	533.0	535.0	536.6	537.6	541.1	538.2	540.0	539.4	541.9	544.1	545.5	538.5
Total Private													
2010	407.6	408.2	409.0	411.7	412.7	413.4	414.0	413.0	410.7	413.4	415.8	415.7	412.1
2011	405.6	407.8	410.8	412.7	414.2	416.8	417.0	418.0	418.3	418.3	421.7	422.8	415.3
2012	416.3	418.2	421.9	425.2	425.7	428.1	425.9	426.7	426.8	426.5	429.9	429.4	425.1
2013	421.0	424.1	426.1	429.8	432.2	433.9	432.4	433.2	433.2	433.0	436.5	438.1	431.1
2014	426.6	427.4	431.2	434.2	434.9	436.8	435.1	436.5	436.4	436.4	438.8	440.3	434.6
2015	431.0	433.3	434.6	438.2	440.8	442.2	442.4	442.2	441.3	443.1	445.2	445.4	440.0
2016	436.4	439.1	440.0	443.7	444.6	445.4	445.5	445.0	445.0	444.8	446.8	447.3	443.6
2017	439.5	442.5	444.3	445.2	447.3	449.6	449.8	450.7	450.0	451.1	454.6	453.8	448.2
2018	446.5	449.5	451.2	452.6	453.5	456.5	455.7	457.0	455.1	457.4	459.1	460.3	454.5
Goods Producing													
2010	62.2	61.8	61.6	62.1	62.0	61.9	62.3	62.3	61.7	61.3	61.5	61.4	61.8
2011	60.3	60.8	61.8	61.9	62.6	63.3	62.9	63.3	63.8	63.9	64.3	64.8	62.8
2012	63.9	63.9	64.5	64.9	65.3	65.5	65.6	65.5	65.5	65.7	65.6	65.7	65.1
2013	65.2	64.8	65.6	66.0	66.3	66.5	66.4	66.6	66.4	66.4	66.3	66.9	66.1
2014	65.3	65.2	66.2	66.1	66.3	66.6	66.4	66.5	66.6	66.5	66.7	66.7	66.3
2015	66.1	66.4	66.1	65.7	66.0	66.4	66.7	66.7	66.4	66.6	66.6	66.5	66.4
2016	65.7	65.9	66.1	66.1	66.0	66.3	66.0	65.5	65.9	65.4	65.4	65.5	65.8
2017	64.7	64.8	65.4	65.1	65.8	66.4	66.5	66.8	67.4	67.6	67.4	67.8	66.3
2018	67.2	68.0	68.6	68.7	69.0	69.7	69.8	70.5	70.6	71.5	72.1	72.6	69.9
Service-Providing													
2010	429.7	431.0	432.5	435.0	438.4	437.9	434.0	432.4	432.4	436.5	438.7	438.9	434.8
2011	429.4	431.3	433.4	435.2	436.2	437.8	435.2	435.2	437.3	436.9	440.0	440.7	435.7
2012	434.4	437.0	440.5	443.2	443.3	444.9	439.2	440.3	442.3	443.0	446.7	446.2	441.8
2013	437.7	441.5	442.8	446.0	447.7	448.9	444.9	445.4	447.4	448.1	451.9	453.2	446.3
2014	442.5	443.6	446.6	450.0	450.9	452.4	448.5	450.3	451.6	452.1	454.6	456.2	449.9
2015	446.3	448.7	450.5	454.7	457.2	458.2	456.1	456.5	456.8	458.9	461.3	461.9	455.6
2016	453.0	455.8	456.6	460.6	461.7	462.2	461.3	461.6	462.3	462.7	465.1	465.7	460.7
2017	457.7	461.1	462.4	463.5	465.1	467.2	465.5	466.2	466.2	467.3	471.3	470.5	465.3
2018	462.7	465.0	466.4	467.9	468.6	471.4	468.4	469.5	468.8	470.4	472.0	472.9	468.7
Mining, Logging, and Construction													
2010	26.9	26.7	26.8	27.1	27.2	27.4	27.6	27.8	27.2	27.0	26.8	26.8	27.1
2011	25.9	26.3	27.1	27.3	27.7	28.1	27.9	28.0	28.5	28.3	28.5	28.8	27.7
2012	27.8	27.8	28.0	28.1	28.3	28.2	28.4	28.2	28.0	28.3	28.1	28.0	28.1
2013	27.6	27.1	27.9	28.0	28.2	28.2	28.3	28.4	28.0	28.0	27.7	28.1	28.0
2014	26.9	26.7	27.4	27.3	27.5	27.6	27.7	27.8	27.8	27.9	27.8	27.8	27.5
2015	27.2	27.5	27.3	27.6	28.0	28.3	28.6	28.8	28.7	28.9	28.9	28.8	28.2
2016	28.2	28.2	28.2	28.2	28.1	28.4	28.3	27.9	28.2	28.1	28.1	28.2	28.2
2017	27.5	27.5	27.8	27.6	28.3	28.6	28.8	29.1	29.5	29.6	29.1	29.3	28.6
2018	28.9	29.4	30.0	30.0	30.3	30.7	30.8	31.3	31.3	32.0	32.0	32.5	30.8
Manufacturing													
2010	35.3	35.1	34.8	35.0	34.8	34.5	34.7	34.5	34.5	34.3	34.7	34.6	34.7
2011	34.4	34.5	34.7	34.6	34.9	35.2	35.0	35.3	35.3	35.6	35.8	36.0	35.1
2012	36.1	36.1	36.5	36.8	37.0	37.3	37.2	37.3	37.5	37.4	37.5	37.7	37.0
2013	37.6	37.7	37.7	38.0	38.1	38.3	38.1	38.2	38.4	38.4	38.6	38.8	38.2
2014	38.4	38.5	38.8	38.8	38.8	39.0	38.7	38.7	38.8	38.6	38.9	38.9	38.7
2015	38.9	38.9	38.8	38.1	38.0	38.1	38.1	37.9	37.7	37.7	37.7	37.7	38.1
2016	37.5	37.7	37.9	37.9	37.9	37.9	37.7	37.6	37.7	37.3	37.3	37.3	37.6
2017	37.2	37.3	37.6	37.5	37.5	37.8	37.7	37.7	37.9	38.0	38.3	38.5	37.8
2018	38.3	38.6	38.6	38.7	38.7	39.0	39.0	39.2	39.3	39.5	40.1	40.1	39.1

Employment by Industry: Birmingham-Hoover, AL, 2010–2018—*Continued*

(Numbers in thousands, not seasonally adjusted)

Industry and year	January	February	March	April	May	June	July	August	September	October	November	December	Annual average
Trade, Transportation, and Utilities													
2010	104.2	103.9	104.4	104.4	104.9	105.1	105.1	105.1	104.8	106.1	107.6	108.5	105.3
2011	104.7	104.6	105.0	104.7	104.9	105.1	105.2	105.6	105.5	106.1	107.9	109.0	105.7
2012	106.2	106.1	107.0	106.8	107.4	107.3	106.9	106.8	106.5	107.1	109.6	110.3	107.3
2013	106.6	106.8	107.4	107.2	107.7	108.0	108.2	108.3	108.1	108.6	111.0	112.4	108.4
2014	108.2	107.6	108.5	108.2	108.3	108.7	108.4	108.5	108.5	108.7	111.4	112.5	109.0
2015	108.2	108.1	108.8	109.5	110.1	110.4	110.3	110.2	109.7	110.4	112.5	113.3	110.1
2016	109.6	109.6	109.8	110.1	110.4	110.3	109.9	110.0	109.7	110.0	111.7	112.6	110.3
2017	109.2	109.0	109.1	108.8	109.0	109.0	108.8	108.8	108.5	109.1	111.1	111.5	109.3
2018	108.8	108.1	108.6	108.1	108.7	108.4	108.4	108.7	108.4	109.5	110.8	111.0	109.0
Wholesale Trade													
2010	28.3	28.2	28.2	28.3	28.3	28.3	28.3	28.3	28.1	28.4	28.3	28.3	28.3
2011	27.8	28.0	28.0	28.1	28.1	28.1	28.3	28.4	28.4	28.6	28.6	28.8	28.3
2012	28.5	28.8	28.9	28.8	29.1	29.0	29.0	29.0	28.9	29.0	29.1	29.2	28.9
2013	29.1	29.2	29.2	29.2	29.2	29.0	29.2	29.3	29.2	29.4	29.5	29.5	29.3
2014	28.9	29.0	29.0	28.9	29.0	29.0	29.1	29.2	29.3	29.3	29.4	29.5	29.1
2015	28.7	28.9	29.0	29.0	29.0	29.0	29.1	29.1	29.0	29.1	29.1	29.2	29.0
2016	28.8	28.9	28.9	28.9	29.0	29.0	28.9	28.9	28.7	28.9	28.8	28.9	28.9
2017	28.4	28.5	28.4	28.4	28.5	28.4	28.4	28.4	28.2	28.3	28.3	28.3	28.4
2018	28.0	28.1	28.1	27.9	28.1	28.1	28.3	28.4	28.4	28.5	28.5	28.4	28.2
Retail Trade													
2010	55.8	55.5	56.0	55.9	56.1	56.2	55.8	55.8	55.6	56.6	58.2	59.0	56.4
2011	56.0	55.5	55.8	56.0	56.1	56.3	56.1	56.4	56.2	56.6	58.4	59.1	56.5
2012	56.3	55.7	56.1	56.1	56.5	56.5	56.1	56.0	55.7	56.4	58.8	59.3	56.6
2013	55.3	55.3	55.7	55.7	56.1	56.5	56.5	56.4	56.2	56.9	59.2	60.3	56.7
2014	56.8	56.1	56.9	56.9	56.9	57.2	56.9	56.9	56.7	57.1	59.5	60.3	57.4
2015	56.9	56.8	57.3	57.9	58.5	58.7	58.3	58.2	57.9	58.4	60.4	60.9	58.4
2016	57.7	57.7	57.8	58.3	58.5	58.4	58.1	58.1	58.0	58.3	60.1	60.6	58.5
2017	57.7	57.4	57.5	57.5	57.7	57.8	57.7	57.5	57.3	57.9	59.7	59.7	58.0
2018	57.4	56.9	57.3	57.4	57.6	57.4	57.2	57.3	57.0	57.5	58.4	58.3	57.5
Transportation and Utilities													
2010	20.1	20.2	20.2	20.2	20.5	20.6	21.0	21.0	21.1	21.1	21.1	21.2	20.7
2011	20.9	21.1	21.2	20.6	20.7	20.7	20.8	20.8	20.9	20.9	20.9	21.1	20.9
2012	21.4	21.6	22.0	21.9	21.8	21.8	21.8	21.8	21.9	21.7	21.7	21.8	21.8
2013	22.2	22.3	22.5	22.3	22.4	22.5	22.5	22.6	22.7	22.3	22.3	22.6	22.4
2014	22.5	22.5	22.6	22.4	22.4	22.5	22.4	22.4	22.5	22.3	22.5	22.7	22.5
2015	22.6	22.4	22.5	22.6	22.6	22.7	22.9	22.9	22.8	22.9	23.0	23.2	22.8
2016	23.1	23.0	23.1	22.9	22.9	22.9	22.9	23.0	23.0	22.8	22.8	23.1	23.0
2017	23.1	23.1	23.2	22.9	22.8	22.8	22.7	22.9	23.0	22.9	23.1	23.5	23.0
2018	23.4	23.1	23.2	22.8	23.0	22.9	22.9	23.0	23.0	23.5	23.9	24.3	23.3
Information													
2010	9.8	9.7	9.7	9.5	9.5	9.6	9.4	9.4	9.3	9.3	9.3	9.3	9.5
2011	9.2	9.1	9.1	9.0	9.0	9.0	9.0	9.0	9.0	8.9	8.9	8.9	9.0
2012	8.9	8.9	9.0	8.8	8.8	8.9	8.9	8.9	8.9	8.8	8.8	8.9	8.9
2013	8.9	8.9	8.8	8.9	9.0	9.0	9.1	9.0	8.9	8.9	8.9	9.0	8.9
2014	8.8	8.7	8.7	8.6	8.6	8.5	8.3	8.3	8.2	8.3	8.4	8.4	8.5
2015	8.3	8.4	8.4	8.3	8.3	8.2	8.3	8.2	8.1	8.1	8.1	8.1	8.2
2016	8.0	8.0	8.0	8.0	7.9	8.0	7.9	7.9	7.8	7.9	8.0	7.9	7.9
2017	7.8	7.7	7.7	7.6	7.6	7.6	7.6	7.5	7.4	7.4	7.5	7.4	7.6
2018	7.4	7.6	7.6	8.0	7.5	7.9	7.5	7.4	7.4	7.4	7.5	7.5	7.6
Financial Activities													
2010	39.1	39.1	39.2	39.2	39.3	39.3	39.3	39.3	39.3	40.0	40.2	40.4	39.5
2011	40.0	40.1	40.0	40.2	40.1	39.7	40.1	39.9	39.8	39.8	39.9	40.0	40.0
2012	39.9	40.0	40.2	40.4	40.6	40.6	40.7	40.7	40.7	41.0	41.1	41.1	40.6
2013	40.6	40.8	40.8	41.0	41.3	41.5	41.8	42.1	42.1	42.4	42.8	42.9	41.7
2014	42.0	42.2	42.2	42.3	42.4	42.4	42.4	42.4	42.0	42.1	42.2	42.2	42.2
2015	42.1	42.1	42.2	42.2	42.3	42.3	42.4	42.4	42.2	42.3	42.3	42.3	42.3
2016	42.2	42.2	42.1	42.0	42.0	42.0	42.2	42.2	42.1	42.1	42.3	42.4	42.2
2017	42.3	42.4	42.4	42.2	42.3	42.5	42.4	42.4	42.2	42.4	42.5	42.4	42.4
2018	42.1	42.0	41.9	41.9	41.8	42.0	42.1	42.2	41.8	42.1	42.2	42.1	42.0

Employment by Industry: Birmingham-Hoover, AL, 2010–2018—*Continued*

(Numbers in thousands, not seasonally adjusted)

Industry and year	January	February	March	April	May	June	July	August	September	October	November	December	Annual average
Professional and Business Services													
2010	59.5	59.8	59.9	60.8	60.5	60.0	61.0	60.6	59.9	60.7	60.4	60.2	60.3
2011	59.3	59.9	60.2	60.9	61.0	61.8	61.8	62.0	62.6	62.2	62.3	62.8	61.4
2012	61.7	62.5	63.1	64.0	63.5	64.4	64.1	64.6	64.4	64.1	63.8	63.1	63.6
2013	61.7	63.1	63.2	63.6	63.2	63.6	63.6	63.6	63.2	63.5	63.5	63.6	63.3
2014	61.5	62.2	62.5	63.6	63.6	63.7	63.7	64.6	64.5	64.8	64.3	64.4	63.6
2015	63.1	63.8	64.5	65.0	65.3	65.4	65.8	65.8	65.6	66.2	66.2	65.9	65.2
2016	64.9	65.4	65.3	66.0	66.1	66.1	66.4	66.4	65.9	66.1	66.3	66.0	65.9
2017	65.7	66.3	66.8	67.0	67.4	68.1	68.2	68.7	68.3	68.6	68.9	68.7	67.7
2018	67.8	68.7	69.0	68.8	68.3	68.9	68.6	68.9	68.7	68.0	67.4	66.8	68.3
Education and Health Services													
2010	64.9	65.6	65.2	65.6	65.6	65.5	65.6	65.5	65.5	65.8	66.2	65.5	65.5
2011	64.5	64.8	65.4	65.3	65.4	65.1	65.3	65.5	66.1	65.9	66.6	66.0	65.5
2012	65.8	66.1	66.4	67.0	66.4	66.7	66.2	66.9	67.7	67.4	68.3	68.3	66.9
2013	67.2	68.5	67.9	68.4	68.8	68.5	67.7	68.3	68.8	68.5	69.2	69.4	68.4
2014	67.8	68.4	68.5	69.1	68.6	68.7	68.3	68.8	69.4	69.9	69.4	69.8	68.9
2015	68.7	69.5	68.9	69.9	69.9	70.1	70.1	70.4	70.8	71.2	71.0	71.3	70.2
2016	69.9	70.8	70.4	71.2	71.1	70.9	71.3	71.7	72.8	72.9	72.5	72.9	71.5
2017	71.0	72.3	72.0	72.5	72.2	72.5	72.6	72.7	73.5	73.4	74.3	74.1	72.8
2018	72.4	73.5	73.1	73.7	73.5	74.1	73.9	74.2	74.6	74.8	75.3	75.6	74.1
Leisure and Hospitality													
2010	40.7	41.0	41.6	42.7	43.3	43.8	43.0	42.8	42.7	42.5	43.0	43.0	42.5
2011	40.7	41.3	42.1	43.3	43.7	45.0	44.8	45.0	44.1	44.0	44.1	43.8	43.5
2012	42.3	42.9	43.7	45.3	45.6	46.1	44.9	45.0	45.2	44.4	44.8	44.2	44.5
2013	43.1	43.5	44.5	46.7	47.8	48.2	47.1	46.8	47.3	46.6	46.7	45.8	46.2
2014	45.0	45.1	46.3	47.9	48.5	49.5	48.8	48.8	48.7	47.7	48.0	48.0	47.7
2015	46.3	46.7	47.3	48.9	50.0	50.4	49.9	49.7	49.7	49.6	49.6	49.2	48.9
2016	47.6	48.5	49.4	51.0	51.8	52.2	52.1	51.7	51.3	50.9	50.9	50.3	50.6
2017	49.1	50.0	50.8	51.7	52.6	53.0	53.1	53.2	52.1	52.0	52.2	51.4	51.8
2018	50.5	51.2	51.8	52.8	53.9	54.4	54.4	54.1	52.7	53.4	53.0	53.9	53.0
Other Services													
2010	27.2	27.3	27.4	27.4	27.6	28.2	28.3	28.0	27.5	27.7	27.6	27.4	27.6
2011	26.9	27.2	27.2	27.4	27.5	27.8	27.9	27.7	27.4	27.5	27.7	27.5	27.5
2012	27.6	27.8	28.0	28.0	28.1	28.6	28.6	28.3	27.9	28.0	27.9	27.8	28.1
2013	27.7	27.7	27.9	28.0	28.1	28.6	28.5	28.5	28.4	28.1	28.1	28.1	28.1
2014	28.0	28.0	28.3	28.4	28.6	28.7	28.8	28.6	28.5	28.4	28.4	28.3	28.4
2015	28.2	28.3	28.4	28.7	28.9	29.0	28.9	28.8	28.8	28.7	28.9	28.8	28.7
2016	28.5	28.7	28.9	29.3	29.3	29.6	29.7	29.6	29.5	29.5	29.7	29.7	29.3
2017	29.7	30.0	30.1	30.3	30.4	30.5	30.6	30.6	30.6	30.6	30.7	30.5	30.4
2018	30.3	30.4	30.6	30.6	30.8	31.1	31.0	31.0	30.9	30.7	30.8	30.8	30.8
Government													
2010	84.3	84.6	85.1	85.4	87.7	86.4	82.3	81.7	83.4	84.4	84.4	84.6	84.5
2011	84.1	84.3	84.4	84.4	84.6	84.3	81.1	80.5	82.8	82.5	82.6	82.7	83.2
2012	82.0	82.7	83.1	82.9	82.9	82.3	78.9	79.1	81.0	82.2	82.4	82.5	81.8
2013	81.9	82.2	82.3	82.2	81.8	81.5	78.9	78.8	80.6	81.5	81.7	82.0	81.3
2014	81.2	81.4	81.6	81.9	82.3	82.2	79.8	80.3	81.8	82.2	82.5	82.6	81.7
2015	81.4	81.8	82.0	82.2	82.4	82.4	80.4	81.0	81.9	82.4	82.7	83.0	82.0
2016	82.3	82.6	82.7	83.0	83.1	83.1	81.8	82.1	83.2	83.3	83.7	83.9	82.9
2017	82.9	83.4	83.5	83.4	83.6	84.0	82.2	82.3	83.6	83.8	84.1	84.5	83.4
2018	83.4	83.5	83.8	84.0	84.1	84.6	82.5	83.0	84.3	84.5	85.0	85.2	84.0

Employment by Industry: Buffalo-Cheektowaga-Niagara Falls, NY, 2010–2018

(Numbers in thousands, not seasonally adjusted)

Industry and year	January	February	March	April	May	June	July	August	September	October	November	December	Annual average
Total Nonfarm													
2010	521.6	523.3	526.1	533.5	539.7	539.7	530.3	532.7	537.1	544.9	545.8	545.1	535.0
2011	527.2	529.4	530.2	538.2	542.6	545.4	537.2	538.5	546.4	548.4	549.2	548.8	540.1
2012	530.7	534.9	536.8	539.3	546.3	548.4	539.7	542.4	545.4	551.4	551.1	551.2	543.1
2013	532.3	535.4	537.8	541.4	548.0	550.1	543.7	545.6	550.0	556.7	556.7	555.9	546.1
2014	535.1	538.8	540.6	547.0	552.5	555.3	549.0	550.2	553.4	559.5	558.1	559.3	549.9
2015	537.8	540.9	542.8	549.1	557.4	559.9	554.7	555.4	558.0	565.6	564.8	565.4	554.3
2016	543.9	547.9	549.9	557.2	561.3	563.2	558.8	559.0	562.6	567.6	567.4	565.4	558.7
2017	548.4	552.6	554.3	556.6	563.5	566.3	560.9	562.4	565.7	570.9	572.7	571.2	562.1
2018	549.9	554.3	556.2	559.5	567.1	568.9	564.3	565.9	567.8	572.7	571.6	570.7	564.1
Total Private													
2010	427.6	427.8	430.1	437.7	442.0	444.2	443.3	445.4	446.9	450.0	450.2	449.7	441.2
2011	434.0	435.1	436.3	443.8	448.7	452.9	449.4	450.6	456.4	455.7	456.2	455.9	447.9
2012	440.3	442.3	444.3	447.4	454.1	457.6	453.7	456.8	457.6	460.4	459.8	459.8	452.8
2013	443.6	444.5	446.8	451.2	458.0	461.1	459.0	460.8	463.2	466.5	466.5	466.0	457.3
2014	448.3	449.8	451.2	457.7	463.8	467.4	465.0	466.2	467.4	470.7	469.0	470.7	462.3
2015	450.9	452.5	454.3	460.8	468.8	471.8	470.4	470.9	471.4	476.5	475.5	475.8	466.6
2016	456.4	458.8	460.5	468.0	472.0	474.4	473.5	474.0	474.5	478.0	477.6	474.8	470.2
2017	458.7	462.1	463.8	466.2	472.9	476.4	474.4	476.4	477.2	480.3	481.5	479.7	472.5
2018	460.8	463.6	465.6	469.4	476.6	478.9	477.8	479.7	479.1	481.7	480.4	479.2	474.4
Goods Producing													
2010	64.5	63.9	64.2	66.9	68.7	69.9	70.8	71.3	71.1	71.2	70.7	69.0	68.5
2011	66.7	66.4	67.0	69.4	71.2	72.9	73.4	74.1	73.5	73.1	72.4	70.5	70.9
2012	68.0	67.5	68.3	69.8	71.6	72.9	73.1	73.4	72.6	72.4	71.3	70.2	70.9
2013	67.3	66.7	67.3	68.6	71.2	72.4	72.2	73.6	73.0	73.0	72.1	70.9	70.7
2014	68.3	68.3	68.7	70.8	73.2	74.7	74.3	75.6	75.1	74.7	73.1	72.2	72.4
2015	68.6	68.2	69.0	71.1	73.8	75.0	75.6	75.5	74.9	75.4	74.7	74.1	73.0
2016	70.8	70.2	70.8	72.5	74.3	75.5	75.9	75.9	75.3	75.0	74.5	72.2	73.6
2017	70.0	69.6	69.8	71.8	73.5	74.8	74.7	75.3	74.8	74.5	73.7	72.0	72.9
2018	69.2	69.5	69.8	71.4	73.7	75.0	75.6	75.8	74.9	74.4	73.5	72.4	72.9
Service-Providing													
2010	457.1	459.4	461.9	466.6	471.0	469.8	459.5	461.4	466.0	473.7	475.1	476.1	466.5
2011	460.5	463.0	463.2	468.8	471.4	472.5	463.8	464.4	472.9	475.3	476.8	478.3	469.2
2012	462.7	467.4	468.5	469.5	474.7	475.5	466.6	469.0	472.8	479.0	479.8	481.0	472.2
2013	465.0	468.7	470.5	472.8	476.8	477.7	471.5	472.0	477.0	483.7	484.6	485.0	475.4
2014	466.8	470.5	471.9	476.2	479.3	480.6	474.7	474.6	478.3	484.8	485.0	487.1	477.5
2015	469.2	472.7	473.8	478.0	483.6	484.9	479.1	479.9	483.1	490.2	490.1	491.3	481.3
2016	473.1	477.7	479.1	484.7	487.0	487.7	482.9	483.1	487.3	492.6	492.9	493.2	485.1
2017	478.4	483.0	484.5	484.8	490.0	491.5	486.2	487.1	490.9	496.4	499.0	499.2	489.3
2018	480.7	484.8	486.4	488.1	493.4	493.9	488.7	490.1	492.9	498.3	498.1	498.3	491.1
Mining, Logging, and Construction													
2010	15.5	15.0	15.3	18.1	19.5	20.2	21.1	21.3	20.9	21.0	20.5	18.5	18.9
2011	16.5	16.1	16.7	18.6	20.3	21.4	22.2	22.5	22.2	21.8	21.0	19.1	19.9
2012	17.1	16.6	17.4	18.9	20.3	21.3	21.5	21.7	21.1	20.8	19.9	18.7	19.6
2013	16.6	16.2	16.5	17.6	20.0	20.8	21.3	21.6	21.1	21.0	20.2	18.7	19.3
2014	16.5	16.3	16.8	18.6	20.9	22.1	22.6	23.0	22.7	22.4	20.8	19.6	20.2
2015	17.2	16.6	17.1	19.1	21.6	22.3	23.1	23.2	22.9	23.1	22.4	21.5	20.8
2016	18.8	18.5	19.0	20.7	22.5	23.3	23.7	23.7	23.3	22.9	22.3	20.2	21.6
2017	18.2	17.8	18.0	20.2	21.7	22.7	23.1	23.4	23.0	22.4	21.5	19.8	21.0
2018	17.8	17.8	18.1	19.6	21.7	22.7	23.1	23.2	22.5	21.9	21.1	19.8	20.8
Manufacturing													
2010	49.0	48.9	48.9	48.8	49.2	49.7	49.7	50.0	50.2	50.2	50.2	50.5	49.6
2011	50.2	50.3	50.3	50.8	50.9	51.5	51.2	51.6	51.3	51.3	51.4	51.4	51.0
2012	50.9	50.9	50.9	50.9	51.3	51.6	51.6	51.7	51.5	51.6	51.4	51.5	51.3
2013	50.7	50.5	50.8	51.0	51.2	51.6	50.9	52.0	51.9	52.0	51.9	52.2	51.4
2014	51.8	52.0	51.9	52.2	52.3	52.6	51.7	52.6	52.4	52.3	52.3	52.6	52.2
2015	51.4	51.6	51.9	52.0	52.2	52.7	52.5	52.3	52.0	52.3	52.3	52.6	52.2
2016	52.0	51.7	51.8	51.8	51.8	52.2	52.2	52.2	52.0	52.1	52.2	52.0	52.0
2017	51.8	51.8	51.8	51.6	51.8	52.1	51.6	51.9	51.8	52.1	52.2	52.2	51.9
2018	51.4	51.7	51.7	51.8	52.0	52.3	52.5	52.6	52.4	52.5	52.4	52.6	52.2

Employment by Industry: Buffalo-Cheektowaga-Niagara Falls, NY, 2010–2018—*Continued*

(Numbers in thousands, not seasonally adjusted)

Industry and year	January	February	March	April	May	June	July	August	September	October	November	December	Annual average
Trade, Transportation, and Utilities													
2010	96.4	95.0	95.1	96.0	97.4	98.4	96.8	97.3	98.3	99.3	101.3	101.9	97.8
2011	97.3	95.8	95.9	97.0	98.2	99.6	98.2	99.1	99.9	100.7	103.1	103.9	99.1
2012	99.5	97.4	98.1	98.0	100.1	101.2	99.8	100.3	101.1	101.5	103.3	104.3	100.4
2013	99.2	97.5	97.9	98.2	99.7	101.0	99.9	99.8	100.9	101.4	104.0	105.6	100.4
2014	100.7	99.4	99.9	100.7	101.7	103.4	101.7	101.7	102.2	103.1	105.7	107.1	102.3
2015	101.9	100.8	100.8	101.5	103.1	104.2	103.0	102.8	103.3	104.3	106.2	107.5	103.3
2016	102.4	101.2	101.5	102.2	103.0	103.4	102.1	101.8	101.9	102.4	104.4	104.9	102.6
2017	100.8	98.9	99.5	98.8	100.3	101.3	99.7	99.7	100.7	101.6	103.8	104.6	100.8
2018	99.5	98.2	98.3	98.8	100.1	100.4	99.8	99.6	99.6	101.1	104.2	104.4	100.3
Wholesale Trade													
2010	20.9	20.8	20.8	20.9	21.1	21.2	21.2	21.3	21.2	21.3	21.4	21.4	21.1
2011	21.2	21.0	21.0	21.2	21.5	21.7	21.7	21.8	21.7	21.6	21.8	21.8	21.5
2012	21.6	21.5	21.6	21.5	21.7	21.9	21.8	22.0	21.8	21.9	21.8	21.9	21.8
2013	21.7	21.6	21.6	21.6	21.6	21.8	21.9	21.9	21.9	22.0	22.1	22.3	21.8
2014	22.2	22.0	22.0	22.2	22.4	22.5	22.2	22.3	22.2	22.3	22.3	22.4	22.3
2015	22.2	22.1	22.1	22.2	22.2	22.4	22.5	22.3	22.2	22.3	22.2	22.4	22.3
2016	22.0	21.9	21.8	21.9	22.0	21.9	21.9	21.7	21.3	21.5	21.6	21.6	21.8
2017	21.5	21.3	21.3	21.2	21.3	21.4	21.4	21.3	21.2	21.3	21.4	21.3	21.3
2018	20.9	20.8	20.8	21.0	21.0	21.0	21.1	21.0	20.9	20.7	20.6	20.5	20.9
Retail Trade													
2010	59.8	58.7	58.8	59.4	60.3	60.9	60.4	60.8	60.8	61.8	63.5	64.0	60.8
2011	60.4	59.3	59.5	60.3	60.8	61.7	61.4	62.3	62.0	62.9	65.0	65.5	61.8
2012	62.1	60.5	61.0	61.1	62.3	62.9	62.8	63.1	63.0	63.4	65.3	65.8	62.8
2013	61.7	60.3	60.6	60.9	61.9	62.8	62.5	62.5	62.3	62.7	65.0	66.1	62.4
2014	62.0	61.0	61.5	61.9	62.3	63.6	63.1	63.1	62.4	63.1	65.3	66.2	63.0
2015	62.5	61.7	61.7	62.3	63.2	63.8	63.6	63.8	63.3	64.0	65.9	66.6	63.5
2016	63.4	62.5	62.8	63.3	63.6	64.0	63.8	63.9	63.3	63.6	65.4	65.4	63.8
2017	62.4	60.9	61.4	61.1	61.8	62.3	61.5	61.9	61.4	62.3	64.3	64.5	62.2
2018	61.0	60.1	60.1	60.4	61.5	61.5	61.4	61.4	60.4	61.7	64.3	64.0	61.5
Transportation and Utilities													
2010	15.7	15.5	15.5	15.7	16.0	16.3	15.2	15.2	16.3	16.2	16.4	16.5	15.9
2011	15.7	15.5	15.4	15.5	15.9	16.2	15.1	15.0	16.2	16.2	16.3	16.6	15.8
2012	15.8	15.4	15.5	15.4	16.1	16.4	15.2	15.2	16.3	16.2	16.2	16.6	15.9
2013	15.8	15.6	15.7	15.7	16.2	16.4	15.5	15.4	16.7	16.7	16.9	17.2	16.2
2014	16.5	16.4	16.4	16.6	17.0	17.3	16.4	16.3	17.6	17.7	18.1	18.5	17.1
2015	17.2	17.0	17.0	17.0	17.7	18.0	16.9	16.7	17.8	18.0	18.1	18.5	17.5
2016	17.0	16.8	16.9	17.0	17.4	17.5	16.4	16.2	17.3	17.3	17.4	17.9	17.1
2017	16.9	16.7	16.8	16.5	17.2	17.6	16.8	16.5	18.1	18.0	18.1	18.8	17.3
2018	17.6	17.3	17.4	17.4	17.6	17.9	17.3	17.2	18.3	18.7	19.3	19.9	18.0
Information													
2010	7.9	7.8	7.9	7.7	7.7	7.8	7.9	7.9	7.8	7.8	7.8	7.7	7.8
2011	7.6	7.6	7.6	7.7	7.7	7.8	7.8	6.9	7.7	7.6	7.6	7.7	7.6
2012	7.6	7.6	7.6	7.6	7.7	7.8	7.7	7.6	7.6	7.5	7.6	7.6	7.6
2013	7.5	7.5	7.5	7.5	7.5	7.6	7.6	7.6	7.6	7.6	7.6	7.6	7.6
2014	7.6	7.6	7.6	7.6	7.6	7.7	7.6	7.6	7.6	7.6	7.6	7.6	7.6
2015	7.3	7.2	7.3	7.4	7.4	7.4	7.4	7.3	7.3	7.4	7.3	7.3	7.3
2016	7.1	7.1	7.0	7.1	6.5	7.2	7.1	7.1	7.1	7.0	7.0	7.1	7.0
2017	7.0	7.1	7.1	7.0	7.0	7.2	7.1	7.1	7.2	7.1	7.3	7.4	7.1
2018	7.2	7.4	7.5	7.5	7.5	7.6	7.5	7.5	7.3	7.3	7.3	7.3	7.4
Financial Activities													
2010	30.3	30.3	30.4	30.4	30.4	30.6	30.7	30.5	30.2	30.5	30.6	31.1	30.5
2011	31.1	31.1	31.2	31.5	31.1	31.4	31.4	31.7	31.5	31.4	31.5	32.2	31.4
2012	31.5	31.6	31.5	31.8	31.8	32.3	32.3	32.3	31.9	32.2	32.3	32.4	32.0
2013	31.9	31.9	32.0	31.9	31.9	32.2	32.8	32.1	31.7	32.0	32.1	32.6	32.1
2014	31.9	31.9	32.0	32.2	32.5	33.0	33.1	33.0	32.9	33.0	33.1	33.5	32.7
2015	32.9	32.9	33.0	33.3	33.7	34.0	34.3	34.4	34.1	34.2	34.4	34.6	33.8
2016	34.3	34.3	34.2	34.5	34.7	35.2	35.4	35.4	35.1	35.2	35.3	35.7	34.9
2017	36.4	36.6	36.7	36.5	36.6	37.1	37.4	37.2	36.9	36.7	36.9	37.1	36.8
2018	36.5	36.4	36.3	36.4	36.7	36.9	36.7	36.5	36.2	36.6	36.5	36.6	36.5

Employment by Industry: Buffalo-Cheektowaga-Niagara Falls, NY, 2010–2018—*Continued*

(Numbers in thousands, not seasonally adjusted)

Industry and year	January	February	March	April	May	June	July	August	September	October	November	December	Annual average
Professional and Business Services													
2010	69.2	68.9	69.4	71.6	71.7	72.6	73.5	73.5	72.8	72.6	71.5	71.5	71.6
2011	70.1	70.3	70.1	72.0	72.5	73.7	74.4	74.0	73.8	73.7	72.9	72.6	72.5
2012	71.1	71.3	71.3	72.5	72.9	74.3	74.6	74.8	73.6	74.4	73.9	73.2	73.2
2013	71.3	71.6	72.0	73.1	73.7	75.0	75.1	75.0	74.8	74.0	73.4	72.6	73.5
2014	69.9	69.8	69.2	71.0	72.0	73.4	73.8	73.4	72.8	72.9	72.2	72.4	71.9
2015	69.5	69.9	69.5	71.3	72.7	73.7	73.8	73.7	72.9	73.2	71.9	71.6	72.0
2016	69.1	69.1	69.1	70.9	71.9	72.6	73.1	72.8	72.2	72.7	71.7	71.1	71.4
2017	68.5	69.0	69.2	70.4	70.9	72.0	72.7	73.0	72.2	73.1	72.8	72.2	71.3
2018	69.5	69.9	70.4	70.9	71.8	73.6	74.2	74.1	72.9	72.2	70.8	70.1	71.7
Education and Health Services													
2010	87.8	89.7	90.2	90.5	90.0	87.8	85.8	85.7	88.9	91.0	91.5	91.3	89.2
2011	88.7	90.7	90.8	91.2	90.6	88.2	86.1	86.0	89.5	90.9	91.4	91.4	89.6
2012	89.2	91.7	91.5	91.4	91.1	88.1	86.4	86.7	90.3	92.4	92.5	92.9	90.4
2013	90.3	92.3	92.7	93.1	92.4	89.9	88.7	88.9	92.6	94.7	95.0	95.0	92.1
2014	91.9	94.5	94.7	94.4	93.5	91.4	89.8	89.6	92.5	94.9	94.8	95.1	93.1
2015	92.1	94.1	94.5	94.4	93.9	91.8	90.3	90.8	93.4	96.1	96.6	96.7	93.7
2016	93.5	96.2	96.5	96.7	95.9	93.4	92.2	91.9	95.5	98.4	98.9	98.6	95.6
2017	95.5	98.4	98.4	98.4	97.9	95.5	94.1	94.5	97.2	99.7	99.9	99.9	97.5
2018	97.4	100.1	100.1	100.5	99.8	97.0	95.0	95.5	98.7	101.0	101.5	102.0	99.1
Leisure and Hospitality													
2010	48.6	49.2	49.8	51.4	52.9	53.8	53.6	54.7	54.7	54.3	53.5	53.8	52.5
2011	49.7	50.2	50.7	51.8	54.1	55.8	54.8	55.5	57.1	55.2	54.2	54.3	53.6
2012	50.4	52.2	52.8	53.1	55.4	57.3	56.3	58.2	57.2	56.5	55.4	55.6	55.0
2013	52.5	53.4	53.7	55.1	57.6	59.0	58.7	59.6	58.6	59.3	57.8	56.9	56.9
2014	53.7	53.9	54.4	56.5	58.6	59.2	59.9	60.5	60.0	59.8	57.9	58.1	57.7
2015	54.3	55.1	55.6	57.1	59.4	60.8	61.0	61.4	60.9	60.9	59.5	58.9	58.7
2016	54.9	56.2	56.8	59.2	60.6	62.2	62.5	63.8	62.6	62.2	60.6	60.3	60.2
2017	55.8	57.7	58.2	58.3	61.7	63.3	63.3	64.3	63.2	62.3	61.9	61.4	61.0
2018	56.9	57.4	58.3	58.9	61.8	63.1	63.2	64.9	63.9	63.2	60.7	60.5	61.1
Other Services													
2010	22.9	23.0	23.1	23.2	23.2	23.3	24.2	24.5	23.1	23.3	23.3	23.4	23.4
2011	22.8	23.0	23.0	23.2	23.3	23.5	23.3	23.3	23.4	23.1	23.1	23.3	23.2
2012	23.0	23.0	23.2	23.2	23.5	23.7	23.5	23.5	23.3	23.5	23.5	23.6	23.4
2013	23.6	23.6	23.7	23.7	24.0	24.0	24.0	24.2	24.0	24.5	24.5	24.8	24.1
2014	24.3	24.4	24.7	24.5	24.7	24.6	24.8	24.8	24.3	24.7	24.6	24.7	24.6
2015	24.3	24.3	24.6	24.7	24.8	24.9	25.0	25.0	24.6	25.0	24.9	25.1	24.8
2016	24.3	24.5	24.6	24.9	25.1	24.9	25.2	25.3	24.8	25.1	25.2	24.9	24.9
2017	24.7	24.8	24.9	25.0	25.0	25.2	25.4	25.3	25.0	25.3	25.2	25.1	25.1
2018	24.6	24.7	24.9	25.0	25.2	25.3	25.8	25.8	25.6	25.9	25.9	25.9	25.4
Government													
2010	94.0	95.5	96.0	95.8	97.7	95.5	87.0	87.3	90.2	94.9	95.6	95.4	93.7
2011	93.2	94.3	93.9	94.4	93.9	92.5	87.8	87.9	90.0	92.7	93.0	92.9	92.2
2012	90.4	92.6	92.5	91.9	92.2	90.8	86.0	85.6	87.8	91.0	91.3	91.4	90.3
2013	88.7	90.9	91.0	90.2	90.0	89.0	84.7	84.8	86.8	90.2	90.2	89.9	88.9
2014	86.8	89.0	89.4	89.3	88.7	87.9	84.0	84.0	86.0	88.8	89.1	88.6	87.6
2015	86.9	88.4	88.5	88.3	88.6	88.1	84.3	84.5	86.6	89.1	89.3	89.6	87.7
2016	87.5	89.1	89.4	89.2	89.3	88.8	85.3	85.0	88.1	89.6	89.8	90.6	88.5
2017	89.7	90.5	90.5	90.4	90.6	89.9	86.5	86.0	88.5	90.6	91.2	91.5	89.7
2018	89.1	90.7	90.6	90.1	90.5	90.0	86.5	86.2	88.7	91.0	91.2	91.5	89.7

Employment by Industry: Rochester, NY, 2010–2018

(Numbers in thousands, not seasonally adjusted)

Industry and year	January	February	March	April	May	June	July	August	September	October	November	December	Annual average
Total Nonfarm													
2010	495.4	499.2	501.5	507.8	512.8	512.5	504.5	504.5	509.5	518.6	518.8	516.7	508.5
2011	499.6	504.3	506.3	515.7	518.3	519.5	511.5	512.2	519.5	525.6	525.5	525.9	515.3
2012	505.9	512.2	514.7	517.0	523.7	523.3	513.9	512.7	519.8	527.7	527.8	528.2	518.9
2013	507.8	515.1	516.5	520.8	526.1	523.9	514.4	514.7	522.2	529.3	530.6	530.4	521.0
2014	510.1	517.8	519.1	522.2	527.2	527.1	517.7	518.0	524.4	532.3	532.9	532.9	523.5
2015	513.5	519.6	520.7	526.3	532.1	532.6	524.2	524.3	529.2	539.5	539.4	538.6	528.3
2016	522.3	527.3	529.8	536.4	537.9	536.9	528.1	526.5	532.3	541.6	541.1	540.0	533.4
2017	522.1	529.3	527.8	536.4	538.6	539.0	528.6	528.7	536.0	544.8	544.7	544.2	535.0
2018	525.3	532.9	533.9	538.5	543.3	543.3	534.2	534.5	541.4	547.1	545.6	543.4	538.6
Total Private													
2010	412.9	414.6	416.9	423.0	426.5	427.4	428.5	429.6	429.5	434.3	433.8	431.4	425.7
2011	418.2	420.2	422.2	431.2	434.1	436.1	436.5	437.2	439.3	442.3	441.5	441.3	433.3
2012	425.6	428.8	431.2	434.2	440.1	440.8	439.7	439.2	440.7	445.4	445.2	444.5	438.0
2013	428.0	432.6	433.7	438.0	442.9	442.1	440.9	441.5	443.5	448.2	448.7	448.1	440.7
2014	431.6	436.7	438.0	440.9	446.1	446.6	445.2	445.5	446.3	452.0	451.4	450.7	444.3
2015	435.1	438.6	439.8	445.7	450.4	451.9	451.9	452.2	451.7	459.2	458.3	457.4	449.4
2016	443.2	446.7	448.8	455.7	456.9	456.7	452.6	454.7	455.2	461.0	460.2	458.5	454.5
2017	443.2	448.3	447.2	455.1	457.5	458.8	456.4	456.5	457.8	464.2	463.5	462.9	456.0
2018	446.5	451.9	453.0	457.6	461.9	462.5	461.2	461.2	461.9	464.7	462.3	460.1	458.7
Goods Producing													
2010	75.9	75.0	75.3	77.0	78.2	79.6	80.8	81.3	80.4	80.6	80.0	77.9	78.5
2011	76.2	75.5	75.9	77.5	79.4	81.5	82.5	82.8	81.9	81.7	80.6	79.3	79.6
2012	77.2	76.5	76.7	78.0	79.6	81.6	82.2	82.1	80.9	80.6	79.4	78.7	79.5
2013	76.3	75.3	75.4	76.8	78.6	79.8	80.5	81.0	80.0	80.0	79.2	78.0	78.4
2014	75.7	74.9	75.4	76.3	78.5	80.2	81.3	81.5	80.5	80.7	79.5	78.2	78.6
2015	76.0	75.1	75.6	77.3	79.4	80.8	81.7	81.7	80.7	81.1	80.0	78.9	79.0
2016	76.5	76.1	76.5	77.5	79.0	80.4	80.9	80.7	79.8	79.5	78.5	77.1	78.5
2017	75.1	74.9	75.1	77.0	78.2	79.4	80.1	80.4	79.6	79.6	78.1	77.1	77.9
2018	75.0	75.0	75.2	76.3	78.4	80.1	80.6	81.2	80.8	79.9	79.3	77.5	78.3
Service-Providing													
2010	419.5	424.2	426.2	430.8	434.6	432.9	423.7	423.2	429.1	438.0	438.8	438.8	430.0
2011	423.4	428.8	430.4	438.2	438.9	438.0	429.0	429.4	437.6	443.9	444.9	446.6	435.8
2012	428.7	435.7	438.0	439.0	444.1	441.7	431.7	430.6	438.9	447.1	448.4	449.5	439.5
2013	431.5	439.8	441.1	444.0	447.5	444.1	433.9	433.7	442.2	449.3	451.4	452.4	442.6
2014	434.4	442.9	443.7	445.9	448.7	446.9	436.4	436.5	443.9	451.6	453.4	454.7	444.9
2015	437.5	444.5	445.1	449.0	452.7	451.8	442.5	442.6	448.5	458.4	459.4	459.7	449.3
2016	445.8	451.2	453.3	458.9	458.9	456.5	447.2	445.8	452.5	462.1	462.6	462.9	454.8
2017	447.0	454.4	452.7	459.4	460.4	459.6	448.5	448.3	456.4	465.2	466.6	467.1	457.1
2018	450.3	457.9	458.7	462.2	464.9	463.2	453.6	453.3	460.6	467.2	466.3	465.9	460.3
Mining, Logging, and Construction													
2010	15.3	14.7	15.0	16.8	17.8	18.9	19.7	20.1	19.3	19.1	18.7	16.9	17.7
2011	15.5	15.0	15.3	16.6	18.2	19.5	20.2	20.5	20.1	19.9	19.1	18.1	18.2
2012	16.4	16.0	16.4	17.7	19.0	20.3	20.9	21.0	20.4	20.1	19.3	18.5	18.8
2013	16.9	16.5	16.6	17.6	19.6	20.5	21.1	21.2	20.6	20.6	19.8	18.8	19.2
2014	17.0	16.6	16.9	18.0	20.0	21.1	21.7	21.8	21.2	21.4	20.6	19.3	19.6
2015	17.5	16.8	17.1	18.6	20.5	21.4	21.7	21.9	21.5	21.7	20.9	19.9	20.0
2016	18.0	17.7	18.1	19.3	20.8	21.7	22.3	22.3	21.8	21.8	21.3	20.1	20.4
2017	18.6	18.2	18.5	20.5	21.7	22.4	22.9	23.3	22.7	22.5	21.4	20.5	21.1
2018	19.1	19.0	19.3	20.3	22.1	23.2	23.4	23.7	23.4	23.0	22.7	21.1	21.7
Manufacturing													
2010	60.6	60.3	60.3	60.2	60.4	60.7	61.1	61.2	61.1	61.5	61.3	61.0	60.8
2011	60.7	60.5	60.6	60.9	61.2	62.0	62.3	62.3	61.8	61.8	61.5	61.2	61.4
2012	60.8	60.5	60.3	60.3	60.6	61.3	61.3	61.1	60.5	60.5	60.1	60.2	60.6
2013	59.4	58.8	58.8	59.2	59.0	59.3	59.4	59.8	59.4	59.4	59.4	59.2	59.3
2014	58.7	58.3	58.5	58.3	58.5	59.1	59.6	59.7	59.3	59.3	58.9	58.9	58.9
2015	58.5	58.3	58.5	58.7	58.9	59.4	60.0	59.8	59.2	59.4	59.1	59.0	59.1
2016	58.5	58.4	58.4	58.2	58.2	58.7	58.6	58.4	58.0	57.7	57.2	57.0	58.1
2017	56.5	56.7	56.6	56.5	56.5	57.0	57.2	57.1	56.9	57.1	56.7	56.6	56.8
2018	55.9	56.0	55.9	56.0	56.3	56.9	57.2	57.5	57.4	56.9	56.6	56.4	56.6

Employment by Industry: Rochester, NY, 2010–2018—*Continued*

(Numbers in thousands, not seasonally adjusted)

Industry and year	January	February	March	April	May	June	July	August	September	October	November	December	Annual average
Trade, Transportation, and Utilities													
2010	80.5	79.3	79.6	80.6	81.9	83.2	82.2	82.5	81.6	83.1	83.7	84.6	81.9
2011	81.5	80.3	80.3	81.4	82.3	83.4	82.5	82.6	81.8	83.3	84.3	85.6	82.4
2012	82.2	80.3	80.7	80.8	83.1	84.3	83.4	83.2	82.6	83.9	85.0	85.7	82.9
2013	82.2	80.7	80.7	81.2	82.6	83.6	82.6	82.2	81.8	82.9	84.1	84.8	82.5
2014	81.8	80.8	80.5	81.3	82.7	83.7	82.6	82.7	82.2	83.1	84.2	85.1	82.6
2015	81.8	80.6	80.8	81.5	83.3	84.6	83.6	83.6	83.0	83.9	85.2	86.0	83.2
2016	82.9	81.9	81.9	82.9	83.6	84.5	83.9	83.8	83.7	84.5	85.7	86.0	83.8
2017	83.2	82.2	81.6	82.6	83.9	84.7	83.8	84.0	84.0	84.9	86.3	86.7	84.0
2018	83.6	82.8	82.6	83.3	84.1	84.7	84.2	83.9	83.8	84.1	85.4	85.1	84.0
Wholesale Trade													
2010	16.1	16.1	16.1	16.3	16.4	16.6	16.6	16.6	16.4	16.6	16.5	16.6	16.4
2011	16.2	16.2	16.3	16.5	16.6	16.8	16.8	16.7	16.6	17.0	16.9	16.9	16.6
2012	16.5	16.5	16.6	17.0	17.2	17.3	17.3	17.2	17.0	17.3	17.3	17.3	17.0
2013	17.2	17.1	17.1	17.2	17.3	17.4	17.4	17.3	17.3	17.2	17.1	17.2	17.2
2014	17.0	17.1	17.0	17.2	17.4	17.6	17.6	17.5	17.3	17.4	17.3	17.3	17.3
2015	17.1	17.0	17.1	17.1	17.2	17.4	17.4	17.4	17.1	17.3	17.3	17.3	17.2
2016	17.1	17.1	17.0	17.4	17.4	17.5	17.6	17.4	17.3	17.2	17.2	17.1	17.3
2017	17.1	17.1	17.1	17.2	17.3	17.4	17.2	17.4	17.4	17.4	17.4	17.3	17.3
2018	17.3	17.3	17.3	17.5	17.5	17.7	17.7	17.7	17.4	17.4	17.3	17.3	17.5
Retail Trade													
2010	54.4	53.3	53.6	54.3	55.3	56.3	56.0	56.3	55.1	56.3	57.0	57.7	55.5
2011	55.5	54.3	54.2	54.9	55.5	56.4	56.1	56.3	55.0	56.1	57.2	58.3	55.8
2012	55.8	54.0	54.3	54.1	55.8	56.7	56.5	56.4	55.4	56.4	57.6	57.9	55.9
2013	55.1	53.7	53.8	54.1	55.2	56.0	55.6	55.5	54.2	55.3	56.4	56.9	55.2
2014	54.5	53.5	53.3	53.9	54.9	55.7	55.2	55.5	54.5	55.2	56.3	57.0	55.0
2015	54.5	53.5	53.6	54.2	55.5	56.4	56.0	56.1	55.1	55.9	57.1	57.7	55.5
2016	55.5	54.5	54.5	55.0	55.6	56.3	56.1	56.2	55.4	56.3	57.3	57.5	55.9
2017	55.3	54.2	53.6	54.7	55.4	56.1	56.0	56.0	55.1	56.0	57.3	57.5	55.6
2018	55.2	54.4	54.1	54.6	55.3	55.6	55.4	55.3	54.8	54.9	56.3	56.0	55.2
Transportation and Utilities													
2010	10.0	9.9	9.9	10.0	10.2	10.3	9.6	9.6	10.1	10.2	10.2	10.3	10.0
2011	9.8	9.8	9.8	10.0	10.2	10.2	9.6	9.6	10.2	10.2	10.2	10.4	10.0
2012	9.9	9.8	9.8	9.7	10.1	10.3	9.6	9.6	10.2	10.2	10.1	10.5	10.0
2013	9.9	9.9	9.8	9.9	10.1	10.2	9.6	9.4	10.3	10.4	10.6	10.7	10.1
2014	10.3	10.2	10.2	10.2	10.4	10.4	9.8	9.7	10.4	10.5	10.6	10.8	10.3
2015	10.2	10.1	10.1	10.2	10.6	10.8	10.2	10.1	10.8	10.7	10.8	11.0	10.5
2016	10.3	10.3	10.4	10.5	10.6	10.7	10.2	10.2	11.0	11.0	11.2	11.4	10.7
2017	10.8	10.9	10.9	10.7	11.2	11.2	10.6	10.6	11.5	11.5	11.6	11.9	11.1
2018	11.1	11.1	11.2	11.2	11.3	11.4	11.1	10.9	11.6	11.8	11.8	11.8	11.4
Information													
2010	9.6	9.5	9.5	9.4	9.5	9.5	9.6	9.6	9.4	9.4	9.4	9.3	9.5
2011	9.3	9.2	9.1	9.1	9.1	9.1	9.2	9.2	9.1	9.1	9.0	9.0	9.1
2012	8.6	8.5	8.5	8.4	8.5	8.5	8.5	8.5	8.4	8.4	8.5	8.4	8.5
2013	8.3	8.2	8.2	8.3	8.3	8.3	8.4	8.4	8.1	8.1	8.2	8.2	8.3
2014	8.2	8.2	8.2	8.1	8.1	8.2	8.4	8.3	8.2	8.4	8.4	8.5	8.3
2015	8.4	8.4	8.3	8.4	8.4	8.4	8.4	8.3	8.2	8.3	8.3	8.4	8.4
2016	8.5	8.6	8.7	8.7	8.7	8.6	8.6	8.5	8.5	8.5	8.5	8.5	8.6
2017	8.2	8.1	8.1	8.1	8.1	8.1	8.1	8.1	8.0	8.0	8.0	8.1	8.1
2018	8.0	8.0	8.0	8.0	8.1	8.2	8.1	8.0	8.0	8.0	8.0	8.0	8.0
Financial Activities													
2010	20.4	20.2	20.4	20.3	20.6	21.2	21.3	21.1	20.3	20.4	20.3	20.3	20.6
2011	20.3	20.3	20.4	20.7	20.9	21.6	21.9	22.0	21.3	21.3	21.2	21.4	21.1
2012	21.3	21.3	21.2	21.3	21.5	22.2	22.3	22.4	21.6	21.6	21.5	21.7	21.7
2013	21.2	21.2	21.1	21.2	21.5	22.0	22.3	22.2	21.6	21.2	21.2	21.4	21.5
2014	21.0	20.9	21.1	21.0	21.4	22.0	22.2	22.2	21.7	21.7	21.6	21.9	21.6
2015	21.6	21.6	21.7	21.7	21.9	22.3	22.3	22.3	21.8	21.8	21.9	21.9	21.9
2016	21.8	21.9	21.9	22.1	22.3	22.7	23.1	23.1	22.4	22.4	22.2	22.4	22.4
2017	21.6	21.5	21.4	21.6	21.8	22.4	22.4	22.4	21.6	21.7	21.7	21.9	21.8
2018	21.9	21.8	21.8	21.9	22.2	22.6	22.5	22.5	21.9	21.8	21.3	21.3	22.0

Employment by Industry: Rochester, NY, 2010–2018—*Continued*

(Numbers in thousands, not seasonally adjusted)

Industry and year	January	February	March	April	May	June	July	August	September	October	November	December	Annual average
Professional and Business Services													
2010	58.9	59.3	59.5	60.3	60.3	61.8	62.6	63.1	62.1	63.3	63.2	62.4	61.4
2011	60.4	60.4	61.1	63.5	63.5	65.2	65.7	66.1	66.3	65.6	65.9	65.8	64.1
2012	64.4	64.5	64.8	66.3	66.7	67.7	67.5	67.2	66.4	67.1	67.4	66.7	66.4
2013	65.4	65.4	65.4	66.2	66.5	68.0	68.0	68.0	67.3	67.6	68.2	67.8	67.0
2014	65.6	66.2	66.5	66.4	66.8	67.6	67.5	67.3	66.7	67.1	68.0	67.8	67.0
2015	66.5	67.0	66.6	68.0	68.5	70.1	70.8	70.9	69.9	70.5	69.8	69.5	69.0
2016	68.3	68.1	68.1	69.4	69.4	69.9	69.9	69.2	68.7	69.1	69.2	68.5	69.0
2017	67.2	67.9	67.6	68.5	69.1	70.3	70.1	70.0	69.8	69.9	69.9	69.9	69.2
2018	67.7	68.0	68.2	69.2	70.1	71.0	71.9	71.6	70.5	69.6	69.1	68.8	69.6
Education and Health Services													
2010	109.6	113.6	114.1	114.6	112.3	107.2	106.1	106.0	112.9	115.7	116.3	116.4	112.1
2011	111.2	115.1	115.4	116.8	114.3	108.9	107.7	107.5	114.5	117.4	117.7	117.8	113.7
2012	111.5	117.0	117.5	117.2	114.9	108.9	107.9	108.0	115.8	119.1	119.7	120.0	114.8
2013	113.3	119.8	120.3	120.2	117.9	111.2	109.6	110.3	118.5	122.0	122.7	122.7	117.4
2014	117.4	123.1	123.5	123.5	120.5	115.6	113.7	114.4	120.5	124.4	124.5	124.4	120.5
2015	118.7	123.5	123.8	124.0	120.5	116.2	115.3	115.7	120.8	126.9	127.5	127.0	121.7
2016	122.2	127.0	127.4	128.5	124.9	120.4	119.2	119.2	124.5	130.0	130.5	130.5	125.4
2017	124.9	130.6	130.2	131.4	128.6	123.5	121.4	121.4	127.5	133.0	133.9	133.8	128.4
2018	127.6	133.1	133.3	133.8	130.9	126.0	124.4	124.0	130.0	135.4	136.1	135.4	130.8
Leisure and Hospitality													
2010	40.0	39.8	40.6	42.7	45.4	46.6	47.5	47.6	44.6	43.4	42.4	41.9	43.5
2011	40.9	41.0	41.4	43.2	45.6	47.5	48.2	48.2	45.4	44.9	43.8	43.2	44.4
2012	41.3	41.6	42.5	42.8	46.2	48.0	48.7	48.7	45.9	45.6	44.5	44.1	45.0
2013	42.3	43.0	43.5	44.9	48.1	49.9	50.2	50.0	47.1	47.2	45.8	45.7	46.5
2014	42.8	43.4	43.6	45.0	48.5	49.9	50.3	50.0	47.3	47.2	45.8	45.4	46.6
2015	43.0	43.3	43.8	45.5	49.0	50.2	50.8	50.6	48.2	47.4	46.3	46.4	47.0
2016	44.0	44.2	45.3	47.2	49.5	50.8	51.5	51.2	48.5	47.7	46.4	46.2	47.7
2017	44.0	44.1	44.2	46.5	48.4	51.0	51.3	51.3	48.2	47.9	46.4	46.2	47.5
2018	43.7	44.2	44.8	45.9	48.7	50.5	50.5	51.1	47.8	46.7	43.8	44.7	46.9
Other Services													
2010	18.0	17.9	17.9	18.1	18.3	18.3	18.4	18.4	18.2	18.4	18.5	18.6	18.3
2011	18.4	18.4	18.6	19.0	19.0	18.9	18.8	18.8	19.0	19.0	19.0	19.2	18.8
2012	19.1	19.1	19.3	19.4	19.6	19.6	19.2	19.1	19.1	19.1	19.2	19.2	19.3
2013	19.0	19.0	19.1	19.2	19.4	19.3	19.3	19.4	19.1	19.2	19.3	19.5	19.2
2014	19.1	19.2	19.2	19.3	19.6	19.4	19.2	19.1	19.2	19.4	19.4	19.4	19.3
2015	19.1	19.1	19.2	19.3	19.4	19.3	19.0	19.1	19.1	19.3	19.3	19.3	19.2
2016	19.0	18.9	19.0	19.4	19.5	19.4	19.1	19.0	19.1	19.3	19.2	19.3	19.2
2017	19.0	19.0	19.0	19.4	19.4	19.4	19.2	18.9	19.1	19.2	19.2	19.2	19.2
2018	19.0	19.0	19.1	19.2	19.4	19.4	19.0	18.9	19.1	19.2	19.3	19.3	19.2
Government													
2010	82.5	84.6	84.6	84.8	86.3	85.1	76.0	74.9	80.0	84.3	85.0	85.3	82.8
2011	81.4	84.1	84.1	84.5	84.2	83.4	75.0	75.0	80.2	83.3	84.0	84.6	82.0
2012	80.3	83.4	83.5	82.8	83.6	82.5	74.2	73.5	79.1	82.3	82.6	83.7	81.0
2013	79.8	82.5	82.8	82.8	83.2	81.8	73.5	73.2	78.7	81.1	81.9	82.3	80.3
2014	78.5	81.1	81.1	81.3	81.1	80.5	72.5	72.5	78.1	80.3	81.5	82.2	79.2
2015	78.4	81.0	80.9	80.6	81.7	80.7	72.3	72.1	77.5	80.3	81.1	81.2	79.0
2016	79.1	80.6	81.0	80.7	81.0	80.2	71.9	71.8	77.1	80.6	80.9	81.5	78.9
2017	78.9	81.0	80.6	81.3	81.1	80.2	72.2	72.2	78.2	80.6	81.2	81.3	79.1
2018	78.8	81.0	80.9	80.9	81.4	80.8	73.0	73.3	79.5	82.4	83.3	83.3	79.9

Employment by Industry: Grand Rapids-Wyoming, MI, 2010–2018

(Numbers in thousands, not seasonally adjusted)

Industry and year	January	February	March	April	May	June	July	August	September	October	November	December	Annual average
Total Nonfarm													
2010	438.2	442.5	443.8	451.1	458.1	459.0	451.7	454.4	463.2	464.6	466.1	463.9	454.7
2011	452.8	455.0	457.6	465.9	470.4	470.6	467.1	468.9	476.8	476.7	479.4	479.7	468.4
2012	471.5	473.2	477.0	483.8	488.4	488.4	482.0	484.6	492.4	494.7	496.6	495.6	485.7
2013	487.2	490.1	492.7	495.0	501.8	503.4	497.4	502.0	508.1	509.4	511.7	513.0	501.0
2014	502.6	504.7	507.1	510.5	519.5	521.0	508.2	510.9	517.4	520.7	523.0	525.0	514.2
2015	514.3	516.6	519.2	523.8	531.2	532.4	525.8	524.5	533.9	538.1	539.9	542.2	528.5
2016	532.1	534.2	536.5	539.6	544.8	547.8	539.6	540.9	546.7	549.4	551 2	552.3	542.9
2017	543.9	545.9	548.4	550.3	556.7	559.6	548.0	549.8	555.0	559.8	561.3	562.4	553.4
2018	553.1	557.3	560.9	564.2	570.2	573.6	559.0	561.3	565.4	568.0	570.0	570.7	564.5
Total Private													
2010	390.4	392.7	394.2	401.3	408.9	411.3	408.9	412.1	414.6	414.6	415.7	414.8	406.6
2011	404.7	406.1	408.2	416.2	423.1	424.1	424.6	427.1	429.4	428.3	430.4	431.6	421.2
2012	423.4	424.7	428.4	435.6	441.4	443.9	440.7	443.2	444.8	446.2	447.8	448.0	439.0
2013	440.2	442.0	444.9	447.6	455.4	458.6	457.4	461.5	461.5	461.9	464.6	466.0	455.1
2014	455.9	457.2	459.5	463.3	473.6	476.1	468.2	470.6	470.9	472.7	474.9	477.6	468.4
2015	467.5	468.9	471.6	476.2	485.2	488.0	485.0	484.2	487.4	490.2	492.1	494.5	482.6
2016	485.2	486.4	488.6	491.9	498.4	502.0	498.6	499.7	499.7	501.1	502.6	503.9	496.5
2017	496.6	497.5	500.1	502.3	509.9	513.2	506.9	508.0	507.1	510.8	512.5	513.6	506.5
2018	505.8	508.0	512.0	515.6	523.1	527.9	517.2	517.9	516.5	518.5	520.5	520.6	517.0
Goods Producing													
2010	95.3	95.3	96.3	98.5	100.8	102.5	103.1	103.9	103.5	102.1	101.9	102.0	100.4
2011	100.8	101.0	101.7	103.9	106.0	107.9	108.2	109.0	108.6	108.6	108.9	109.1	106.1
2012	107.6	107.5	108.3	110.0	111.6	113.7	114.1	114.8	114.1	113.8	113.5	113.7	111.9
2013	112.5	112.6	113.5	114.6	116.9	118.9	119.4	120.1	119.5	119.4	119.8	119.8	117.3
2014	118.4	118.9	119.6	121.0	123.4	125.7	125.9	125.8	125.3	125.1	125.3	125.5	123.3
2015	123.6	124.0	124.7	126.3	128.4	130.8	131.3	131.4	130.9	131.5	131.3	131.7	128.8
2016	130.5	130.7	131.1	132.6	133.8	135.7	136.3	136.1	135.0	135.4	135.3	135.8	134.0
2017	135.1	135.3	135.8	137.4	139.0	141.4	141.0	141.3	139.8	139.4	139.2	139.6	138.7
2018	138.6	138.8	140.0	141.4	143.0	145.6	145.4	144.8	143.6	143.8	143.9	144.4	142.8
Service-Providing													
2010	342.9	347.2	347.5	352.6	357.3	356.5	348.6	350.5	359.7	362.5	364.2	361.9	354.3
2011	352.0	354.0	355.9	362.0	364.4	362.7	358.9	359.9	368.2	368.1	370.5	370.6	362.3
2012	363.9	365.7	368.7	373.8	376.8	374.7	367.9	369.8	378.3	380.9	383.1	381.9	373.8
2013	374.7	377.5	379.2	380.4	384.9	384.5	378.0	381.9	388.6	390.0	391.9	393.2	383.7
2014	384.2	385.8	387.5	389.5	396.1	395.3	382.3	385.1	392.1	395.6	397.7	399.5	390.9
2015	390.7	392.6	394.5	397.5	402.8	401.6	394.5	393.1	403.0	406.6	408.6	410.5	399.7
2016	401.6	403.5	405.4	407.0	411.0	412.1	403.3	404.8	411.7	414.0	415.9	416.5	408.9
2017	408.8	410.6	412.6	412.9	417.7	418.2	407.0	408.5	415.2	420.4	422.1	422.8	414.7
2018	414.5	418.5	420.9	422.8	427.2	428.0	413.6	416.5	421.8	424.2	426.1	426.3	421.7
Mining, Logging, and Construction													
2010	14.8	14.6	15.0	16.1	16.9	17.5	17.8	17.8	17.4	17.0	16.5	16.0	16.5
2011	14.7	14.5	14.8	15.9	17.0	17.7	18.3	18.2	17.9	17.6	17.3	16.8	16.7
2012	15.6	15.3	15.8	16.8	17.5	18.1	18.5	18.7	18.4	18.2	17.7	17.5	17.3
2013	16.6	16.4	16.7	17.3	18.7	19.5	20.0	20.2	19.9	19.8	19.5	18.9	18.6
2014	17.9	17.9	18.2	19.0	20.3	21.2	21.4	21.5	21.3	20.8	20.5	20.0	20.0
2015	18.7	18.6	19.0	20.1	21.2	22.0	22.2	22.2	21.9	21.7	21.3	20.8	20.8
2016	19.8	19.8	20.4	21.7	22.6	23.4	23.6	23.6	23.2	23.1	22.8	22.2	22.2
2017	21.4	21.4	21.8	23.1	23.9	24.9	25.0	25.0	24.4	24.2	23.8	23.4	23.5
2018	22.5	22.6	23.3	24.4	25.3	26.3	26.3	26.2	25.8	25.8	25.4	25.2	24.9
Manufacturing													
2010	80.5	80.7	81.3	82.4	83.9	85.0	85.3	86.1	86.1	85.1	85.4	86.0	84.0
2011	86.1	86.5	86.9	88.0	89.0	90.2	89.9	90.8	90.7	91.0	91.6	92.3	89.4
2012	92.0	92.2	92.5	93.2	94.1	95.6	95.6	96.1	95.7	95.6	95.8	96.2	94.6
2013	95.9	96.2	96.8	97.3	98.2	99.4	99.4	99.9	99.6	99.6	100.3	100.9	98.6
2014	100.5	101.0	101.4	102.0	103.1	104.5	104.5	104.3	104.0	104.3	104.8	105.5	103.3
2015	104.9	105.4	105.7	106.2	107.2	108.8	109.1	109.2	109.0	109.8	110.0	110.9	108.0
2016	110.7	110.9	110.7	110.9	111.2	112.3	112.7	112.5	111.8	112.3	112.5	113.6	111.8
2017	113.7	113.9	114.0	114.3	115.1	116.5	116.0	116.3	115.4	115.2	115.4	116.2	115.2
2018	116.1	116.2	116.7	117.0	117.7	119.3	119.1	118.6	117.8	118.0	118.5	119.2	117.9

Employment by Industry: Grand Rapids-Wyoming, MI, 2010–2018—*Continued*

(Numbers in thousands, not seasonally adjusted)

Industry and year	January	February	March	April	May	June	July	August	September	October	November	December	Annual average
Trade, Transportation, and Utilities													
2010	79.9	79.2	79.3	80.2	81.1	81.6	81.2	81.2	80.4	81.6	82.7	82.8	80.9
2011	79.8	79.4	79.4	81.3	82.0	82.5	82.6	82.6	82.1	82.4	83.7	84.1	81.8
2012	81.0	80.4	81.1	82.7	83.8	84.1	83.9	84.1	83.8	84.7	86.3	86.6	83.5
2013	84.0	83.9	84.4	85.6	87.0	87.9	87.9	88.5	87.8	88.5	89.7	90.3	87.1
2014	86.5	86.3	86.7	88.0	89.5	90.4	90.4	90.5	90.1	91.1	92.8	93.6	89.7
2015	91.4	91.0	91.3	92.9	94.3	95.1	95.2	94.7	94.2	95.1	96.5	97.5	94.1
2016	94.2	93.9	93.9	95.3	96.5	96.9	96.7	96.6	95.3	96.0	97.7	97.9	95.9
2017	95.0	94.7	94.9	95.9	96.8	97.3	96.7	96.4	95.3	95.9	97.3	97.8	96.2
2018	95.5	95.1	95.4	96.4	98.3	98.8	99.0	98.8	97.5	97.4	98.4	98.3	97.4
Wholesale Trade													
2010	24.2	24.2	24.4	24.6	24.8	24.8	25.0	24.9	24.5	24.6	24.6	24.7	24.6
2011	24.3	24.3	24.3	24.9	25.1	25.4	25.5	25.6	25.3	25.3	25.4	25.4	25.1
2012	25.0	25.0	25.3	25.8	26.1	26.3	26.4	26.3	26.3	26.6	26.6	26.7	26.0
2013	26.3	26.3	26.4	26.8	27.2	27.6	27.8	28.0	27.9	28.1	28.2	28.5	27.4
2014	27.2	27.4	27.5	28.2	28.7	29.0	29.0	29.0	28.7	28.7	28.9	29.1	28.5
2015	28.9	29.0	29.1	29.6	29.9	30.2	30.4	30.4	30.2	30.4	30.7	30.9	30.0
2016	30.8	30.8	30.8	31.0	31.2	31.2	31.5	31.4	31.0	31.1	31.4	31.2	31.1
2017	30.7	30.9	31.1	31.4	31.7	31.8	31.9	31.7	31.4	31.2	31.3	31.5	31.4
2018	31.5	31.6	31.6	31.8	32.3	32.5	32.4	32.2	31.8	31.8	31.8	31.7	31.9
Retail Trade													
2010	44.1	43.5	43.4	44.0	44.6	44.9	44.4	44.6	44.0	45.0	46.0	46.1	44.6
2011	43.8	43.4	43.3	44.3	44.8	44.9	44.8	44.8	44.5	44.8	46.0	46.3	44.6
2012	44.0	43.3	43.7	44.5	45.2	45.2	45.0	45.2	44.9	45.4	46.9	46.8	45.0
2013	44.8	44.6	45.0	45.1	46.0	46.4	46.5	46.7	46.3	46.7	47.8	48.2	46.2
2014	45.8	45.5	45.7	46.2	47.1	47.5	47.5	47.6	47.3	48.3	49.6	49.8	47.3
2015	48.0	47.6	47.8	48.6	49.6	49.9	49.6	49.4	49.0	49.6	50.6	51.1	49.2
2016	48.7	48.6	48.5	49.4	50.3	50.5	50.1	50.1	49.3	49.8	51.0	51.1	49.8
2017	49.2	48.9	48.8	49.3	49.7	49.8	49.2	49.1	48.4	49.2	50.4	50.5	49.4
2018	48.6	48.2	48.4	49.1	50.3	50.5	50.6	50.5	49.6	49.4	50.4	50.3	49.7
Transportation and Utilities													
2010	11.6	11.5	11.5	11.6	11.7	11.9	11.8	11.7	11.9	12.0	12.1	12.0	11.8
2011	11.7	11.7	11.8	12.1	12.1	12.2	12.3	12.2	12.3	12.3	12.3	12.4	12.1
2012	12.0	12.1	12.1	12.4	12.5	12.6	12.5	12.6	12.6	12.7	12.8	13.1	12.5
2013	12.9	13.0	13.0	13.7	13.8	13.9	13.6	13.8	13.6	13.7	13.7	13.6	13.5
2014	13.5	13.4	13.5	13.6	13.7	13.9	13.9	13.9	14.1	14.1	14.3	14.7	13.9
2015	14.5	14.4	14.4	14.7	14.8	15.0	15.2	14.9	15.0	15.1	15.2	15.5	14.9
2016	14.7	14.5	14.6	14.9	15.0	15.2	15.1	15.1	15.0	15.1	15.3	15.6	15.0
2017	15.1	14.9	15.0	15.2	15.4	15.7	15.6	15.6	15.5	15.5	15.6	15.8	15.4
2018	15.4	15.3	15.4	15.5	15.7	15.8	16.0	16.1	16.1	16.2	16.2	16.3	15.8
Information													
2010	5.5	5.5	5.5	5.5	5.7	5.7	5.7	5.7	5.6	5.5	5.5	5.5	5.6
2011	5.4	5.4	5.4	5.3	5.4	5.4	5.4	5.5	5.3	5.4	5.4	5.5	5.4
2012	5.4	5.3	5.3	5.3	5.4	5.4	5.5	5.6	5.4	5.4	5.4	5.5	5.4
2013	5.5	5.5	5.5	5.6	5.6	5.7	5.6	5.6	5.5	5.5	5.6	5.6	5.6
2014	5.6	5.6	5.7	5.8	5.8	5.8	5.9	5.9	5.7	5.8	5.8	5.8	5.8
2015	5.5	5.5	5.6	5.5	5.6	5.6	5.6	5.5	5.4	5.5	5.5	5.6	5.5
2016	5.5	5.5	5.5	5.6	5.7	5.8	5.7	5.7	5.7	5.7	5.8	5.8	5.7
2017	6.0	6.0	6.0	6.1	6.2	6.2	6.1	6.1	6.0	6.0	6.1	6.2	6.1
2018	6.2	6.2	6.2	6.3	6.4	6.5	6.5	6.5	6.3	6.3	6.4	6.4	6.4
Financial Activities													
2010	20.7	20.8	20.6	20.7	21.1	21.1	21.4	21.4	21.6	21.8	21.9	22.2	21.3
2011	21.7	21.9	21.7	22.1	22.2	22.3	22.6	22.8	22.8	22.8	23.1	23.3	22.4
2012	22.8	22.9	23.0	23.2	23.4	23.4	23.6	23.3	23.3	23.7	23.8	23.7	23.3
2013	24.0	24.2	24.2	24.3	24.5	24.6	24.4	24.4	24.4	24.3	24.4	24.3	24.3
2014	24.6	24.3	24.3	24.5	24.7	24.8	24.9	25.1	25.0	24.7	24.8	24.9	24.7
2015	24.8	24.4	24.4	24.4	24.9	24.6	24.9	25.0	24.8	24.9	25.0	25.3	24.8
2016	25.4	25.0	25.1	25.5	25.8	25.7	25.8	25.8	25.6	25.7	25.7	25.9	25.6
2017	26.1	25.9	26.0	25.9	26.2	26.5	26.2	25.9	26.0	26.1	26.1	26.2	26.1
2018	26.1	26.1	26.3	26.3	26.7	27.1	26.5	26.5	26.4	26.4	26.6	26.6	26.5

Employment by Industry: Grand Rapids-Wyoming, MI, 2010–2018—*Continued*

(Numbers in thousands, not seasonally adjusted)

Industry and year	January	February	March	April	May	June	July	August	September	October	November	December	Annual average
Professional and Business Services													
2010	57.7	59.6	59.4	62.1	64.1	65.0	62.9	65.1	68.5	68.9	69.5	68.4	64.3
2011	65.3	66.4	67.2	69.4	71.3	70.8	70.8	71.7	73.5	72.0	72.0	72.4	70.2
2012	71.9	72.4	73.0	74.8	75.7	75.7	73.0	73.7	74.7	75.0	74.9	74.3	74.1
2013	73.4	73.9	74.0	74.6	75.9	75.5	74.3	76.0	76.8	77.3	78.0	78.7	75.7
2014	76.3	76.3	76.0	77.9	80.8	79.6	72.9	74.1	74.6	76.3	76.3	76.7	76.5
2015	74.2	74.4	74.4	75.5	77.7	76.9	74.7	74.5	76.3	78.2	78.3	78.2	76.1
2016	77.2	77.0	77.7	76.7	77.4	78.4	75.9	76.6	79.0	79.7	79.6	79.5	77.9
2017	78.0	77.9	78.5	77.0	78.8	78.2	75.1	75.4	77.5	79.3	79.7	79.4	77.9
2018	77.5	78.2	79.2	80.0	80.5	81.3	74.9	75.7	77.2	77.9	77.6	77.2	78.1
Education and Health Services													
2010	73.2	74.2	74.3	74.2	74.1	72.6	72.5	72.6	73.3	74.5	75.1	74.5	73.8
2011	73.8	74.3	74.7	75.0	74.8	73.3	73.5	73.6	75.8	77.0	77.7	77.3	75.1
2012	75.8	77.1	77.7	78.1	78.1	76.9	76.5	77.1	79.1	80.1	80.9	80.8	78.2
2013	78.6	79.9	80.7	79.9	79.6	79.0	78.8	79.6	81.2	81.5	82.7	82.5	80.3
2014	81.4	82.7	83.2	82.1	82.4	81.6	80.6	81.3	83.3	83.4	84.3	84.9	82.6
2015	83.5	84.7	85.4	85.1	85.2	84.5	82.9	83.0	86.0	86.5	87.5	87.8	85.2
2016	85.9	87.2	87.6	87.5	88.0	87.0	86.0	86.7	88.4	88.6	89.2	89.9	87.7
2017	88.4	89.4	90.0	90.3	90.8	90.1	89.1	89.9	91.4	92.9	93.5	93.9	90.8
2018	92.6	93.7	94.5	94.5	94.7	93.9	90.3	91.1	93.1	93.8	94.8	94.4	93.5
Leisure and Hospitality													
2010	36.9	37.0	37.6	38.9	40.9	41.5	41.0	41.2	41.0	39.4	38.4	38.6	39.4
2011	37.5	37.5	37.9	39.1	41.1	41.7	41.4	41.6	41.3	40.2	39.8	40.0	39.9
2012	39.6	39.7	40.4	41.5	43.2	44.1	43.6	44.1	43.9	43.0	42.4	42.6	42.3
2013	41.3	41.2	41.7	42.3	45.0	45.9	45.7	46.0	45.1	44.3	43.3	43.6	43.8
2014	41.9	41.8	42.6	42.9	45.6	46.6	46.2	46.7	45.7	45.0	44.4	44.9	44.5
2015	43.4	43.8	44.5	45.1	47.6	48.6	48.6	48.6	48.1	47.0	46.5	46.6	46.5
2016	44.8	45.4	45.9	46.6	48.9	49.8	49.6	49.8	48.6	47.7	47.2	47.0	47.6
2017	46.0	46.3	46.7	47.7	49.9	51.1	50.4	50.8	49.0	49.0	48.3	48.2	48.6
2018	47.5	48.0	48.5	48.6	51.3	52.1	52.2	52.1	50.1	50.6	50.6	51.0	50.2
Other Services													
2010	21.2	21.1	21.2	21.2	21.1	21.3	21.1	21.0	20.7	20.8	20.7	20.8	21.0
2011	20.4	20.2	20.2	20.1	20.3	20.2	20.1	20.3	20.0	19.9	19.8	19.9	20.1
2012	19.3	19.4	19.6	20.0	20.2	20.6	20.5	20.5	20.5	20.5	20.6	20.8	20.2
2013	20.9	20.8	20.9	20.7	20.9	21.1	21.3	21.3	21.2	21.1	21.1	21.2	21.0
2014	21.2	21.3	21.4	21.1	21.4	21.6	21.4	21.2	21.2	21.3	21.2	21.3	21.3
2015	21.1	21.1	21.3	21.4	21.5	21.9	21.8	21.5	21.7	21.5	21.5	21.8	21.5
2016	21.7	21.7	21.8	22.1	22.3	22.7	22.6	22.4	22.1	22.3	22.1	22.1	22.2
2017	22.0	22.0	22.2	22.0	22.2	22.4	22.3	22.2	22.1	22.2	22.3	22.3	22.2
2018	21.8	21.9	21.9	22.1	22.2	22.6	22.4	22.4	22.3	22.3	22.2	22.3	22.2
Government													
2010	47.8	49.8	49.6	49.8	49.2	47.7	42.8	42.3	48.6	50.0	50.4	49.1	48.1
2011	48.1	48.9	49.4	49.7	47.3	46.5	42.5	41.8	47.4	48.4	49.0	48.1	47.3
2012	48.1	48.5	48.6	48.2	47.0	44.5	41.3	41.4	47.6	48.5	48.8	47.6	46.7
2013	47.0	48.1	47.8	47.4	46.4	44.8	40.0	40.5	46.6	47.5	47.1	47.0	45.9
2014	46.7	47.5	47.6	47.2	45.9	44.9	40.0	40.3	46.5	48.0	48.1	47.4	45.8
2015	46.8	47.7	47.6	47.6	46.0	44.4	40.8	40.3	46.5	47.9	47.8	47.7	45.9
2016	46.9	47.8	47.9	47.7	46.4	45.8	41.0	41.2	47.0	48.3	48.6	48.4	46.4
2017	47.3	48.4	48.3	48.0	46.8	46.4	41.1	41.8	47.9	49.0	48.8	48.8	46.9
2018	47.3	49.3	48.9	48.6	47.1	45.7	41.8	43.4	48.9	49.5	49.5	50.1	47.5

Employment by Industry: Tucson, AZ, 2010–2018

(Numbers in thousands, not seasonally adjusted)

Industry and year	January	February	March	April	May	June	July	August	September	October	November	December	Annual average
Total Nonfarm													
2010	352.4	356.3	355.7	357.9	358.3	346.1	342.4	348.6	351.4	354.2	357.3	359.2	353.3
2011	350.9	354.9	355.4	356.8	356.5	342.8	338.7	350.6	355.8	359.0	362.7	362.1	353.9
2012	357.3	361.2	362.5	362.7	362.2	351.0	344.6	355.4	360.9	363.6	367.2	368.1	359.7
2013	360.4	364.4	365.8	367.3	366.4	353.0	350.4	357.9	365.1	366.2	370.1	370.6	363.1
2014	363.8	366.8	366.8	368.0	366.3	356.6	353.6	357.6	366.1	369.5	373.1	374.0	365.2
2015	367.3	370.1	370.5	370.6	367.9	355.0	352.4	360.6	368.7	371.7	375.0	376.2	367.2
2016	369.3	372.3	373.3	375.7	373.0	362.0	360.0	364.9	374.5	377.9	380.7	382.2	372.2
2017	376.6	380.0	380.4	379.3	377.8	367.2	364.3	369.3	379.0	381.6	384.4	386.0	377.2
2018	378.6	382.8	383.0	383.2	381.7	371.4	368.8	374.8	384.4	387.2	391.7	390.4	381.5
Total Private													
2010	274.3	275.6	276.3	277.1	276.0	274.5	272.1	273.2	272.1	274.7	276.4	279.0	275.1
2011	274.3	275.6	276.5	277.5	277.7	276.2	274.3	276.7	277.2	279.3	282.6	283.9	277.7
2012	279.9	281.2	282.7	282.6	282.2	281.0	277.8	280.1	280.9	283.2	286.5	287.7	282.2
2013	282.5	284.0	285.5	286.8	286.6	284.1	282.6	285.4	286.1	286.6	290.3	290.9	286.0
2014	285.4	286.9	287.3	288.5	287.9	286.0	283.6	286.4	287.7	290.2	293.3	294.9	288.2
2015	289.7	291.0	291.4	291.3	290.0	287.9	287.0	289.5	289.8	292.4	294.5	296.1	290.9
2016	291.2	292.8	293.3	296.1	295.0	292.7	291.9	294.5	295.7	298.5	300.9	302.6	295.4
2017	299.2	300.6	300.7	299.6	298.9	298.4	295.7	297.9	299.1	301.6	304.2	305.9	300.2
2018	301.1	303.1	303.6	303.5	303.1	301.9	300.3	302.8	304.1	306.9	310.7	309.6	304.2
Goods Producing													
2010	40.6	40.5	40.6	40.9	41.0	41.1	41.0	41.1	40.6	40.6	40.3	40.4	40.7
2011	39.9	39.7	39.9	39.7	39.8	40.0	39.9	39.9	39.7	39.5	39.4	39.2	39.7
2012	38.9	38.8	39.1	39.1	39.3	40.0	40.1	40.2	40.0	40.2	40.5	40.7	39.7
2013	40.0	40.1	40.4	40.7	40.8	41.3	41.5	41.4	40.9	40.4	40.2	40.0	40.6
2014	39.6	39.5	39.5	39.4	39.4	39.6	39.8	40.2	39.9	39.8	39.4	39.3	39.6
2015	38.7	38.8	38.8	39.3	39.2	39.6	39.9	39.9	39.4	39.8	39.7	39.8	39.4
2016	39.2	39.4	39.3	39.6	39.7	40.0	40.3	40.4	40.1	40.4	40.5	40.6	40.0
2017	40.5	41.2	41.1	41.2	41.5	41.9	42.2	42.4	42.1	42.3	42.4	42.7	41.8
2018	42.4	42.7	43.2	43.2	43.4	44.0	44.3	44.5	44.6	44.7	45.1	44.9	43.9
Service-Providing													
2010	311.8	315.8	315.1	317.0	317.3	305.0	301.4	307.5	310.8	313.6	317.0	318.8	312.6
2011	311.0	315.2	315.5	317.1	316.7	302.8	298.8	310.7	316.1	319.5	323.3	322.9	314.1
2012	318.4	322.4	323.4	323.6	322.9	311.0	304.5	315.2	320.9	323.4	326.7	327.4	320.0
2013	320.4	324.3	325.4	326.6	325.6	311.7	308.9	316.5	324.2	325.8	329.9	330.6	322.5
2014	324.2	327.3	327.3	328.6	326.9	317.0	313.8	317.4	326.2	329.7	333.7	334.7	325.6
2015	328.6	331.3	331.7	331.3	328.7	315.4	312.5	320.7	329.3	331.9	335.3	336.4	327.8
2016	330.1	332.9	334.0	336.1	333.3	322.0	319.7	324.5	334.4	337.5	340.2	341.6	332.2
2017	336.1	338.8	339.3	338.1	336.3	325.3	322.1	326.9	336.9	339.3	342.0	343.3	335.4
2018	336.2	340.1	339.8	340.0	338.3	327.4	324.5	330.3	339.8	342.5	346.6	345.5	337.6
Mining, Logging, and Construction													
2010	16.4	16.3	16.5	16.8	16.9	17.2	17.1	17.3	17.0	17.2	17.0	17.0	16.9
2011	16.6	16.5	16.7	16.5	16.5	16.7	16.6	16.5	16.3	16.3	16.2	16.0	16.5
2012	15.7	15.5	15.8	15.9	16.1	16.7	16.8	16.9	16.8	17.0	17.3	17.5	16.5
2013	17.1	17.1	17.5	17.7	17.8	18.2	18.2	18.1	17.8	17.5	17.4	17.4	17.7
2014	17.0	17.0	17.0	17.0	16.9	17.0	17.1	17.6	17.4	17.5	17.1	16.8	17.1
2015	16.4	16.5	16.5	16.9	16.9	17.0	17.2	17.2	16.8	17.0	16.9	16.9	16.9
2016	16.4	16.5	16.4	16.5	16.6	16.7	16.6	16.6	16.6	16.8	16.9	16.9	16.6
2017	16.8	16.9	17.1	17.2	17.4	17.6	17.7	17.8	17.7	17.9	17.9	18.0	17.5
2018	17.9	18.0	18.4	18.3	18.5	18.7	18.9	19.0	19.1	19.1	19.2	19.2	18.7
Manufacturing													
2010	24.2	24.2	24.1	24.1	24.1	23.9	23.9	23.8	23.6	23.4	23.3	23.4	23.8
2011	23.3	23.2	23.2	23.2	23.3	23.3	23.3	23.4	23.4	23.2	23.2	23.2	23.3
2012	23.2	23.3	23.3	23.2	23.2	23.3	23.3	23.3	23.2	23.2	23.2	23.2	23.2
2013	22.9	23.0	22.9	23.0	23.0	23.1	23.3	23.3	23.1	22.9	22.8	22.6	23.0
2014	22.6	22.5	22.5	22.4	22.5	22.6	22.7	22.6	22.5	22.3	22.3	22.5	22.5
2015	22.3	22.3	22.3	22.4	22.3	22.6	22.7	22.7	22.6	22.8	22.8	22.9	22.6
2016	22.8	22.9	22.9	23.1	23.1	23.3	23.7	23.8	23.5	23.6	23.6	23.7	23.3
2017	23.7	24.3	24.0	24.0	24.1	24.3	24.5	24.6	24.4	24.4	24.5	24.7	24.3
2018	24.5	24.7	24.8	24.9	24.9	25.3	25.4	25.5	25.5	25.6	25.9	25.7	25.2

Employment by Industry: Tucson, AZ, 2010–2018—*Continued*

(Numbers in thousands, not seasonally adjusted)

Industry and year	January	February	March	April	May	June	July	August	September	October	November	December	Annual average
Trade, Transportation, and Utilities													
2010	57.3	57.0	56.9	56.9	57.0	56.9	56.7	57.0	56.4	56.7	58.3	59.0	57.2
2011	57.5	57.1	57.1	57.3	57.6	57.5	57.2	58.1	57.4	58.1	60.0	60.5	58.0
2012	58.4	57.5	57.5	57.4	57.4	57.4	56.9	57.5	57.7	58.0	59.9	60.6	58.0
2013	58.5	57.9	58.1	58.2	58.6	58.4	58.5	59.5	59.5	59.6	61.5	62.6	59.2
2014	60.3	59.9	60.1	60.1	60.1	59.9	59.6	60.3	60.2	60.6	62.4	63.3	60.6
2015	60.7	59.8	59.8	59.6	59.8	59.4	59.5	60.4	60.5	60.8	62.3	62.8	60.5
2016	60.6	59.9	59.9	60.2	60.1	59.6	59.7	60.1	59.8	60.5	62.2	63.0	60.5
2017	61.4	61.1	60.7	60.9	60.8	60.6	60.4	60.9	60.8	61.4	63.0	63.6	61.3
2018	61.3	60.6	60.5	60.5	60.4	60.2	59.9	60.2	60.0	60.9	62.0	61.8	60.7
Wholesale Trade													
2010	8.3	8.3	8.2	8.3	8.3	8.2	8.2	8.1	8.0	7.9	8.0	8.0	8.2
2011	7.9	8.0	8.0	7.9	8.0	7.9	8.0	7.9	8.0	8.0	8.0	8.0	8.0
2012	7.8	7.8	7.9	7.9	8.0	8.0	8.0	8.0	8.1	8.0	8.0	8.1	8.0
2013	7.9	7.9	7.9	7.9	7.9	7.9	7.8	7.9	8.0	8.0	7.9	8.0	7.9
2014	7.8	7.8	7.9	7.9	7.9	7.9	7.9	7.8	7.9	7.8	7.8	7.8	7.9
2015	7.7	7.7	7.7	7.7	7.8	7.8	7.8	7.8	7.8	7.8	7.7	7.8	7.8
2016	7.7	7.8	7.7	7.7	7.8	7.7	7.8	7.8	7.7	7.8	7.8	7.8	7.8
2017	7.7	7.8	7.7	7.7	7.7	7.8	7.7	7.7	7.7	7.7	7.6	7.7	7.7
2018	7.5	7.5	7.5	7.5	7.5	7.6	7.4	7.4	7.3	7.4	7.4	7.4	7.5
Retail Trade													
2010	40.1	39.7	39.6	39.6	39.6	39.6	39.3	39.7	39.2	39.5	41.0	41.4	39.9
2011	39.9	39.4	39.4	39.6	39.7	39.7	39.4	40.2	39.4	40.1	41.9	42.2	40.1
2012	40.7	39.7	39.7	39.6	39.6	39.6	39.2	39.8	39.9	40.5	42.4	42.7	40.3
2013	41.2	40.6	40.9	41.1	41.3	41.2	41.2	41.9	41.8	41.9	43.8	44.5	41.8
2014	42.8	42.3	42.4	42.5	42.4	42.2	42.0	42.7	42.4	42.8	44.5	45.1	42.8
2015	42.8	41.9	41.9	41.8	41.8	41.5	41.6	42.4	42.3	42.6	43.9	44.2	42.4
2016	42.6	42.1	42.2	42.4	42.2	41.8	41.7	42.1	41.8	42.2	43.8	44.1	42.4
2017	42.9	42.3	42.2	42.3	42.1	41.8	41.7	42.1	41.8	42.2	43.7	43.9	42.4
2018	42.3	41.8	41.7	41.7	41.7	41.4	41.2	41.4	41.2	41.8	42.7	42.3	41.8
Transportation and Utilities													
2010	8.9	9.0	9.1	9.0	9.1	9.1	9.2	9.2	9.2	9.3	9.3	9.6	9.2
2011	9.7	9.7	9.7	9.8	9.9	9.9	9.8	10.0	10.0	10.0	10.1	10.3	9.9
2012	9.9	10.0	9.9	9.9	9.8	9.8	9.7	9.7	9.7	9.5	9.5	9.8	9.8
2013	9.4	9.4	9.3	9.2	9.4	9.3	9.5	9.7	9.7	9.7	9.8	10.1	9.5
2014	9.7	9.8	9.8	9.7	9.8	9.8	9.7	9.8	9.9	10.0	10.1	10.4	9.9
2015	10.2	10.2	10.2	10.1	10.2	10.1	10.1	10.2	10.4	10.4	10.7	10.8	10.3
2016	10.3	10.0	10.0	10.1	10.1	10.1	10.2	10.2	10.3	10.5	10.6	11.1	10.3
2017	10.8	11.0	10.8	10.9	11.0	11.0	11.0	11.1	11.3	11.5	11.7	12.0	11.2
2018	11.5	11.3	11.3	11.3	11.2	11.2	11.3	11.4	11.5	11.7	11.9	12.1	11.5
Information													
2010	4.7	4.7	4.7	4.6	4.6	4.5	4.5	4.4	4.4	4.4	4.4	4.4	4.5
2011	4.3	4.5	4.3	4.3	4.4	4.3	4.4	4.5	4.4	4.4	4.5	4.5	4.4
2012	4.4	4.6	4.5	4.5	4.6	4.4	4.4	4.5	4.3	4.4	4.5	4.4	4.5
2013	4.5	4.6	4.4	4.5	4.8	4.5	4.5	4.7	4.4	4.4	4.6	4.5	4.5
2014	4.5	4.6	4.4	4.4	4.5	4.4	4.4	4.4	4.3	4.4	4.5	4.5	4.4
2015	4.4	4.6	4.4	4.5	4.4	4.4	4.4	4.6	4.4	4.5	4.8	4.8	4.5
2016	4.8	5.0	5.0	5.1	5.1	5.0	5.0	5.1	5.1	5.1	5.3	5.3	5.1
2017	5.5	5.5	5.5	5.5	5.4	5.4	5.2	5.4	5.2	5.3	5.7	5.5	5.4
2018	5.6	6.1	5.6	5.7	5.6	5.6	5.5	5.5	5.4	5.5	5.7	5.7	5.6
Financial Activities													
2010	17.5	17.6	17.3	17.1	17.2	17.3	17.2	17.2	17.0	17.1	17.1	17.3	17.2
2011	17.0	17.0	17.0	16.9	16.8	16.8	16.9	16.8	16.8	16.8	16.8	17.0	16.9
2012	16.8	16.9	16.6	16.6	16.7	16.8	16.8	16.9	16.9	17.1	17.1	17.3	16.9
2013	17.0	17.1	17.2	17.0	17.1	17.3	17.2	17.2	17.2	17.5	17.5	17.7	17.3
2014	17.4	17.4	17.5	17.5	17.5	17.5	17.6	17.4	17.3	17.5	17.6	17.8	17.5
2015	17.3	17.4	17.4	17.3	17.3	17.2	17.1	17.1	17.0	17.2	17.2	17.2	17.2
2016	17.1	17.1	17.1	17.0	17.0	17.1	17.1	17.2	17.3	17.4	17.5	17.6	17.2
2017	17.4	17.4	17.5	17.4	17.4	17.7	17.6	17.6	17.6	17.9	17.9	18.0	17.6
2018	17.7	17.9	17.9	17.9	18.0	18.0	18.2	18.2	18.1	18.2	18.4	18.6	18.1

Employment by Industry: Tucson, AZ, 2010–2018—*Continued*

(Numbers in thousands, not seasonally adjusted)

Industry and year	January	February	March	April	May	June	July	August	September	October	November	December	Annual average
Professional and Business Services													
2010	46.3	46.6	46.9	46.7	45.7	45.7	45.6	45.4	45.2	46.3	46.3	47.3	46.2
2011	46.0	46.4	46.7	46.7	46.4	46.6	46.3	46.5	47.5	48.4	48.8	49.4	47.1
2012	48.2	48.7	49.3	49.1	48.7	48.7	48.4	48.4	48.6	49.4	49.8	49.8	48.9
2013	49.5	49.9	50.3	50.8	50.3	49.2	48.9	49.1	49.6	49.7	50.7	50.6	49.9
2014	49.6	49.6	49.4	49.7	49.7	49.6	48.9	49.4	50.4	50.9	51.5	51.7	50.0
2015	50.9	51.1	50.7	50.5	49.8	49.4	49.6	49.8	50.5	51.0	51.4	51.6	50.5
2016	50.1	50.5	50.3	50.8	50.4	50.1	50.2	50.8	51.7	52.1	52.1	52.7	51.0
2017	52.0	51.9	51.7	51.2	50.8	51.2	51.1	51.0	51.2	51.2	51.4	51.9	51.4
2018	51.0	51.5	51.3	51.1	51.2	50.8	51.1	51.7	52.4	53.4	54.3	53.3	51.9
Education and Health Services													
2010	58.0	58.3	58.4	58.6	58.6	58.0	57.4	58.2	58.3	58.8	58.8	59.2	58.4
2011	58.7	59.2	59.1	59.8	59.9	59.4	59.2	60.1	60.4	60.5	60.9	61.2	59.9
2012	61.1	61.2	61.5	61.3	61.2	60.7	59.7	60.4	60.8	61.2	61.4	61.7	61.0
2013	60.6	61.1	61.3	61.5	61.4	60.8	61.0	61.9	62.1	62.2	62.6	62.6	61.6
2014	60.9	61.2	61.4	61.7	61.6	61.0	60.3	61.1	61.3	62.1	62.2	62.7	61.5
2015	61.9	62.0	62.3	62.4	62.6	61.9	62.0	62.9	63.0	63.8	63.7	64.2	62.7
2016	63.9	64.3	64.5	64.8	64.8	64.3	63.8	64.8	64.8	65.3	65.5	65.8	64.7
2017	65.1	65.5	65.6	65.3	65.3	64.9	64.0	64.9	65.4	65.5	65.8	66.1	65.3
2018	65.5	65.8	66.0	66.0	66.1	65.9	65.2	66.0	66.4	66.4	67.4	67.3	66.2
Leisure and Hospitality													
2010	37.4	38.4	38.9	39.5	39.1	38.0	36.8	37.1	37.5	38.0	38.4	38.7	38.2
2011	38.4	39.0	39.7	40.1	40.1	39.0	37.8	38.4	38.7	39.1	39.6	39.6	39.1
2012	39.7	40.9	41.4	41.8	41.4	40.0	38.6	39.3	39.8	40.0	40.4	40.4	40.3
2013	39.9	40.7	41.0	41.2	40.7	39.7	38.2	38.9	39.8	40.1	40.4	40.3	40.1
2014	40.6	42.1	42.3	43.1	42.4	41.1	40.0	40.6	41.3	41.7	42.3	42.1	41.6
2015	42.6	43.9	44.3	44.3	43.5	42.6	41.4	41.9	42.3	42.5	42.7	43.1	42.9
2016	42.6	43.7	44.2	45.6	44.9	43.5	42.7	43.1	43.9	44.7	44.9	44.7	44.0
2017	44.5	45.2	45.6	45.1	44.7	43.6	42.5	43.0	44.1	44.8	44.9	44.9	44.4
2018	44.5	45.3	45.7	45.8	45.0	43.9	42.8	43.3	43.8	44.2	44.2	44.5	44.4
Other Services													
2010	12.5	12.5	12.6	12.8	12.8	13.0	12.9	12.8	12.7	12.8	12.8	12.7	12.7
2011	12.5	12.7	12.7	12.7	12.7	12.6	12.6	12.4	12.3	12.5	12.6	12.5	12.6
2012	12.4	12.6	12.8	12.8	12.9	13.0	12.9	12.9	12.8	12.9	12.9	12.8	12.8
2013	12.5	12.6	12.8	12.9	12.9	12.9	12.8	12.7	12.6	12.7	12.8	12.6	12.7
2014	12.5	12.6	12.7	12.6	12.7	12.9	13.0	13.0	13.0	13.2	13.4	13.5	12.9
2015	13.2	13.4	13.7	13.4	13.4	13.4	13.1	12.9	12.7	12.8	12.7	12.6	13.1
2016	12.9	12.9	13.0	13.0	13.0	13.1	13.1	13.0	13.0	13.0	12.9	12.9	13.0
2017	12.8	12.8	13.0	13.0	13.0	13.1	12.7	12.7	12.7	13.2	13.1	13.2	12.9
2018	13.1	13.2	13.4	13.3	13.4	13.5	13.3	13.4	13.4	13.6	13.6	13.5	13.4
Government													
2010	78.1	80.7	79.4	80.8	82.3	71.6	70.3	75.4	79.3	79.5	80.9	80.2	78.2
2011	76.6	79.3	78.9	79.3	78.8	66.6	64.4	73.9	78.6	79.7	80.1	78.2	76.2
2012	77.4	80.0	79.8	80.1	80.0	70.0	66.8	75.3	80.0	80.4	80.7	80.4	77.6
2013	77.9	80.4	80.3	80.5	79.8	68.9	67.8	72.5	79.0	79.6	79.8	79.7	77.2
2014	78.4	79.9	79.5	79.5	78.4	70.6	70.0	71.2	78.4	79.3	79.8	79.1	77.0
2015	77.6	79.1	79.1	79.3	77.9	67.1	65.4	71.1	78.9	79.3	80.5	80.1	76.3
2016	78.1	79.5	80.0	79.6	78.0	69.3	68.1	70.4	78.8	79.4	79.8	79.6	76.7
2017	77.4	79.4	79.7	79.7	78.9	68.8	68.6	71.4	79.9	80.0	80.2	80.1	77.0
2018	77.5	79.7	79.4	79.7	78.6	69.5	68.5	72.0	80.3	80.3	81.0	80.8	77.3

Employment by Industry: Fresno, CA, 2010–2018

(Numbers in thousands, not seasonally adjusted)

Industry and year	January	February	March	April	May	June	July	August	September	October	November	December	Annual average
Total Nonfarm													
2010	284.6	287.8	290.0	291.7	294.9	294.1	286.2	287.9	290.5	294.6	292.9	291.3	290.5
2011	285.4	289.7	292.1	293.8	294.7	292.7	289.5	289.4	292.6	293.3	292.4	290.4	291.3
2012	285.3	287.8	290.8	292.1	296.0	297.1	292.9	293.5	294.8	298.2	298 5	296.5	293.6
2013	292.6	297.2	300.0	300.8	303.1	303.8	299.8	302.3	305.0	307.2	307.7	307.2	302.2
2014	301.6	306.2	308.5	310.7	312.7	313.5	312.0	313.3	315.7	320.1	319.2	318.8	312.7
2015	313.7	317.2	320.1	322.3	324.1	325.7	323.2	324.4	328.0	332.3	331.7	331.3	324.5
2016	325.5	327.9	331.1	334.9	336.9	338.7	334.8	336.3	340.7	342.1	342.6	339.4	335.9
2017	333.4	337.5	340.5	343.3	345.0	345.6	340.2	342.7	346.4	346.9	348.6	347.1	343.1
2018	344.2	347.3	350.1	351.4	353.7	353.9	349.0	352.8	356.3	358.3	361.7	361.6	353.4
Total Private													
2010	218.2	218.2	219.3	221.3	224.4	225.3	224.1	226.1	226.2	227.1	226.2	225.3	223.5
2011	220.0	221.6	223.0	224.1	225.7	226.1	226.7	228.4	229.9	228.0	227.2	226.5	225.6
2012	221.8	222.5	224.6	225.7	229.6	231.4	231.3	233.9	233.2	233.4	234.1	232.9	229.5
2013	229.5	231.6	233.6	234.3	236.8	237.9	239.6	242.5	242.7	243.0	242.5	242.7	238.1
2014	237.1	239.4	240.8	242.8	244.2	245.3	248.1	251.5	251.5	253.0	251.8	251.7	246.4
2015	246.4	247.7	250.5	252.2	253.4	255.1	258.3	260.9	260.5	262.6	261.1	261.2	255.8
2016	255.4	257.0	258.9	262.1	263.7	265.5	268.7	270.6	270.4	270.0	269.7	267.4	265.0
2017	261.7	263.8	266.2	268.5	269.9	271.0	273.1	275.2	275.3	273.7	274.4	273.1	270.5
2018	269.8	271.6	272.4	274.4	276.6	277.5	280.9	284.0	283.9	284.1	285.4	285.5	278.8
Goods Producing													
2010	34.8	34.3	34.6	35.2	36.9	37.4	37.5	38.2	38.2	37.7	36.0	35.3	36.3
2011	34.0	34.0	34.1	34.4	35.5	36.3	36.9	37.5	37.8	36.5	34.9	34.6	35.5
2012	33.9	33.6	34.0	34.1	36.5	37.7	38.3	39.0	37.6	37.0	35.7	35.4	36.1
2013	34.6	34.5	34.8	34.9	36.0	36.9	38.2	39.0	38.6	37.7	36.4	36.3	36.5
2014	35.7	35.7	35.8	36.3	37.0	38.3	39.6	40.7	40.7	40.2	38.9	38.4	38.1
2015	37.9	38.1	39.0	39.3	39.7	41.1	42.9	43.4	43.3	42.6	40.6	40.2	40.7
2016	39.3	39.6	39.6	40.3	40.7	42.3	43.6	44.3	44.0	42.3	41.5	41.0	41.5
2017	40.0	40.8	41.6	42.3	43.6	43.8	44.6	45.4	45.6	44.3	43.9	43.4	43.3
2018	42.6	43.2	43.2	43.9	44.5	45.4	46.0	46.8	47.0	46.8	45.6	44.9	45.0
Service-Providing													
2010	249.8	253.5	255.4	256.5	258.0	256.7	248.7	249.7	252.3	256.9	256.9	256.0	254.2
2011	251.4	255.7	258.0	259.4	259.2	256.4	252.6	251.9	254.8	256.8	257.5	255.8	255.8
2012	251.4	254.2	256.8	258.0	259.5	259.4	254.6	254.5	257.2	261.2	262.8	261.1	257.6
2013	258.0	262.7	265.2	265.9	267.1	266.9	261.6	263.3	266.4	269.5	271.3	270.9	265.7
2014	265.9	270.5	272.7	274.4	275.7	275.2	272.4	272.6	275.0	279.9	280.3	280.4	274.6
2015	275.8	279.1	281.1	283.0	284.4	284.6	280.3	281.0	284.7	289.7	291.1	291.1	283.8
2016	286.2	288.3	291.5	294.6	296.2	296.4	291.2	292.0	296.7	299.8	301.1	298.4	294.4
2017	293.4	296.7	298.9	301.0	301.4	301.8	295.6	297.3	300.8	302.6	304.7	303.7	299.8
2018	301.6	304.1	306.9	307.5	309.2	308.5	303.0	306.0	309.3	311.5	316.1	316.7	308.4
Mining, Logging, and Construction													
2010	11.9	11.7	11.9	12.1	12.5	12.6	12.7	12.6	12.4	12.3	12.0	11.8	12.2
2011	11.2	11.3	11.6	11.6	11.7	11.9	12.3	12.3	12.2	11.8	11.4	11.5	11.7
2012	11.4	11.3	11.6	11.7	12.2	12.9	13.2	13.3	12.8	13.0	12.8	12.7	12.4
2013	12.4	12.4	12.8	13.0	13.5	13.8	14.1	14.2	14.0	13.7	13.6	13.5	13.4
2014	13.2	13.3	13.4	13.7	13.9	14.3	14.6	14.8	14.7	14.9	14.7	14.3	14.2
2015	14.0	14.1	14.6	15.0	15.2	15.7	16.1	16.0	15.7	15.9	15.8	15.8	15.3
2016	15.4	15.7	15.7	16.1	16.2	16.6	16.7	16.9	16.8	16.7	16.9	16.6	16.4
2017	15.8	16.3	16.9	17.4	17.7	18.2	18.4	18.4	18.4	18.4	18.4	18.3	17.7
2018	17.8	18.3	18.2	18.6	18.9	19.4	19.6	19.7	19.5	19.6	19.5	19.3	19.0
Manufacturing													
2010	22.9	22.6	22.7	23.1	24.4	24.8	24.8	25.6	25.8	25.4	24.0	23.5	24.1
2011	22.8	22.7	22.5	22.8	23.8	24.4	24.6	25.2	25.6	24.7	23.5	23.1	23.8
2012	22.5	22.3	22.4	22.4	24.3	24.8	25.1	25.7	24.8	24.0	22.9	22.7	23.7
2013	22.2	22.1	22.0	21.9	22.5	23.1	24.1	24.8	24.6	24.0	22.8	22.8	23.1
2014	22.5	22.4	22.4	22.6	23.1	24.0	25.0	25.9	26.0	25.3	24.2	24.1	24.0
2015	23.9	24.0	24.4	24.3	24.5	25.4	26.8	27.4	27.6	26.7	24.8	24.4	25.4
2016	23.9	23.9	23.9	24.2	24.5	25.7	26.9	27.4	27.2	25.6	24.6	24.4	25.2
2017	24.2	24.5	24.7	24.9	25.9	25.6	26.2	27.0	27.2	25.9	25.5	25.1	25.6
2018	24.8	24.9	25.0	25.3	25.6	26.0	26.4	27.1	27.5	27.2	26.1	25.6	26.0

Employment by Industry: Fresno, CA, 2010–2018—*Continued*

(Numbers in thousands, not seasonally adjusted)

Industry and year	January	February	March	April	May	June	July	August	September	October	November	December	Annual average
Trade, Transportation, and Utilities													
2010	53.6	53.3	53.3	53.8	54.1	54.8	54.7	55.6	56.1	56.7	57.8	58.0	55.2
2011	55.6	55.5	55.2	55.9	56.2	56.4	57.4	57.9	58.7	59.1	60.2	60.0	57.3
2012	56.3	55.5	55.8	56.3	57.2	57.9	58.1	58.6	59.4	59.9	61.2	61.1	58.1
2013	58.1	58.7	59.1	59.2	60.3	60.0	60.7	61.7	61.9	61.8	63.0	63.2	60.6
2014	60.2	60.3	60.6	61.0	61.1	61.4	61.7	62.2	62.6	63.2	64.1	64.6	61.9
2015	61.5	61.3	61.4	61.6	62.0	62.3	63.2	64.1	64.6	65.7	66.2	66.4	63.4
2016	63.9	63.6	63.6	64.3	65.0	65.2	65.7	66.2	66.7	67.0	68.5	67.6	65.6
2017	65.5	64.9	64.6	64.9	65.0	65.4	65.6	66.3	66.6	67.0	68.3	68.3	66.0
2018	66.0	65.6	65.2	65.8	66.3	66.3	68.7	69.4	69.5	68.9	71.6	71.5	67.9
Wholesale Trade													
2010	10.9	10.9	10.9	11.0	11.0	11.4	11.6	11.6	11.5	11.8	11.7	11.4	11.3
2011	11.9	12.0	12.0	12.0	12.1	12.2	12.6	12.6	12.7	12.7	12.7	12.4	12.3
2012	12.1	12.1	12.2	12.2	12.5	12.8	12.9	13.0	13.0	13.0	12.9	12.8	12.6
2013	12.7	12.9	13.0	13.2	13.6	13.6	13.5	13.7	13.6	13.5	13.4	13.4	13.3
2014	13.4	13.5	13.5	13.3	13.3	13.5	13.6	13.7	13.6	13.6	13.4	13.3	13.5
2015	13.1	13.1	13.0	13.0	13.1	13.4	13.7	13.8	13.8	14.2	14.0	14.0	13.5
2016	13.8	13.7	13.7	13.7	13.9	14.1	14.3	14.2	14.3	14.3	14.3	14.1	14.0
2017	14.0	13.8	13.8	13.8	13.9	14.3	14.3	14.3	14.2	14.3	14.1	14.2	14.1
2018	13.9	14.0	13.9	14.1	14.3	14.5	14.6	14.8	14.5	14.2	14.5	14.5	14.3
Retail Trade													
2010	32.5	32.2	32.2	32.4	32.5	32.6	32.3	32.8	33.3	33.6	34.6	35.2	33.0
2011	32.9	32.7	32.4	32.9	33.0	33.0	33.2	33.4	33.9	34.2	35.5	35.9	33.6
2012	33.1	32.4	32.5	32.9	33.2	33.4	33.5	33.7	34.4	35.0	36.6	36.5	33.9
2013	34.1	34.2	34.4	34.4	34.7	34.6	34.9	35.5	35.7	36.0	37.6	37.8	35.3
2014	35.4	35.2	35.6	36.1	36.1	36.1	36.0	36.2	36.6	37.3	38.6	39.2	36.5
2015	36.7	36.5	36.7	36.6	36.8	36.8	37.2	37.8	38.1	38.7	39.5	39.6	37.6
2016	37.9	37.7	37.8	38.1	38.3	38.3	38.5	38.9	39.1	39.6	41.0	40.3	38.8
2017	38.9	38.5	38.2	38.3	38.1	38.1	38.3	38.7	38.7	39.3	40.5	40.6	38.9
2018	39.0	38.5	38.2	38.6	38.8	38.6	38.9	39.1	39.2	39.2	41.2	41.1	39.2
Transportation and Utilities													
2010	10.2	10.2	10.2	10.4	10.6	10.8	10.8	11.2	11.3	11.3	11.5	11.4	10.8
2011	10.8	10.8	10.8	11.0	11.1	11.2	11.6	11.9	12.1	12.2	12.0	11.7	11.4
2012	11.1	11.0	11.1	11.2	11.5	11.7	11.7	11.9	12.0	11.9	11.7	11.8	11.6
2013	11.3	11.6	11.7	11.6	12.0	11.8	12.3	12.5	12.6	12.3	12.0	12.0	12.0
2014	11.4	11.6	11.5	11.6	11.7	11.8	12.1	12.3	12.4	12.3	12.1	12.1	11.9
2015	11.7	11.7	11.7	12.0	12.1	12.1	12.3	12.5	12.7	12.8	12.7	12.8	12.3
2016	12.2	12.2	12.1	12.5	12.8	12.8	12.9	13.1	13.3	13.1	13.2	13.2	12.8
2017	12.6	12.6	12.6	12.8	13.0	13.0	13.0	13.3	13.7	13.4	13.7	13.5	13.1
2018	13.1	13.1	13.1	13.1	13.2	13.2	15.2	15.5	15.8	15.5	15.9	15.9	14.4
Information													
2010	3.8	3.7	3.7	3.5	3.5	3.5	3.6	3.5	3.5	3.5	3.5	3.5	3.6
2011	3.4	3.4	3.4	3.4	3.5	3.5	3.5	3.5	3.6	3.6	3.7	3.6	3.5
2012	3.8	3.7	3.7	3.8	3.8	3.9	3.8	3.8	3.8	3.8	3.8	3.8	3.8
2013	3.8	3.8	3.8	3.8	3.8	3.8	3.8	3.8	3.8	3.8	3.8	3.8	3.8
2014	3.8	3.8	3.8	3.8	3.8	3.8	3.9	3.9	3.9	3.9	3.9	4.0	3.9
2015	3.9	3.9	3.9	3.9	3.9	3.9	3.9	3.9	3.8	3.8	3.9	3.9	3.9
2016	3.8	3.8	3.8	3.8	3.8	3.8	3.8	3.7	3.7	3.7	3.7	3.6	3.8
2017	3.6	3.7	3.7	3.7	3.6	3.5	3.6	3.6	3.6	3.6	3.6	3.6	3.6
2018	3.6	3.6	3.5	3.6	3.6	3.6	3.6	3.6	3.6	3.6	3.6	3.6	3.6
Financial Activities													
2010	13.5	13.4	13.3	13.4	13.4	13.4	13.4	13.4	13.3	13.4	13.3	13.3	13.4
2011	13.2	13.3	13.2	13.2	13.1	13.1	13.0	13.0	12.8	12.6	12.6	12.6	13.0
2012	12.6	12.6	12.6	12.8	13.0	12.9	13.0	13.0	13.0	12.9	12.9	13.0	12.9
2013	12.9	12.9	13.0	13.0	12.9	12.9	13.0	13.0	12.9	12.9	12.8	12.7	12.9
2014	12.7	12.7	12.7	12.7	12.8	12.8	12.8	12.7	12.7	12.9	13.0	13.0	12.8
2015	12.8	12.8	13.0	13.0	13.1	13.1	13.3	13.3	13.2	13.3	13.3	13.2	13.1
2016	13.1	13.2	13.2	13.4	13.4	13.3	13.4	13.3	13.3	13.4	13.4	13.4	13.3
2017	13.5	13.5	13.6	13.6	13.7	13.7	13.8	13.8	13.7	14.0	14.1	14.1	13.8
2018	14.0	14.0	14.0	14.2	14.2	14.2	14.2	14.2	14.1	14.3	14.2	14.2	14.2

Employment by Industry: Fresno, CA, 2010–2018—*Continued*

(Numbers in thousands, not seasonally adjusted)

Industry and year	January	February	March	April	May	June	July	August	September	October	November	December	Annual average
Professional and Business Services													
2010	26.0	26.2	26.6	27.2	27.2	27.1	26.8	26.8	26.3	26.6	26.6	26.3	26.6
2011	26.6	27.3	27.3	27.3	27.4	26.8	26.6	26.7	27.0	26.8	26.3	26.4	26.9
2012	26.4	26.7	27.1	26.7	26.2	26.1	26.1	26.4	26.6	27.3	28.4	27.1	26.8
2013	27.7	28.0	27.8	28.2	27.9	28.5	29.0	29.4	29.9	30.4	30.1	30.0	28.9
2014	29.0	30.1	30.2	29.8	30.3	30.1	31.3	32.1	32.3	32.9	31.8	31.6	31.0
2015	30.8	31.0	31.2	31.4	31.3	31.5	31.6	31.7	31.3	32.1	31.9	31.7	31.5
2016	31.1	31.1	31.4	31.8	31.9	31.8	32.6	32.3	32.6	32.8	32.2	31.4	31.9
2017	30.2	30.8	31.0	30.8	30.8	30.9	31.0	30.8	30.9	30.3	30.0	29.6	30.6
2018	30.7	31.3	31.1	31.4	31.8	31.7	31.7	32.2	32.5	32.7	33.0	33.0	31.9
Education and Health Services													
2010	51.1	51.3	51.4	52.0	51.8	51.6	51.0	51.2	51.8	52.0	52.2	52.3	51.6
2011	51.5	51.6	52.6	52.8	52.4	52.0	51.3	51.5	52.3	52.2	52.6	52.7	52.1
2012	52.2	53.2	53.6	53.6	53.5	53.2	52.5	53.1	53.6	53.7	53.7	54.0	53.3
2013	54.2	55.2	55.7	55.7	55.7	55.4	54.2	54.7	55.3	56.2	56.3	56.4	55.4
2014	55.5	55.9	56.7	57.5	56.8	56.5	56.2	56.9	57.3	58.1	58.2	58.5	57.0
2015	58.2	58.7	59.6	60.1	59.7	59.7	59.8	60.7	61.1	62.1	62.2	62.6	60.4
2016	62.0	62.9	63.9	64.4	64.1	64.1	63.8	64.5	65.0	65.4	65.6	66.0	64.3
2017	65.4	66.0	67.0	68.0	67.2	67.3	67.8	68.5	68.9	68.4	68.9	68.9	67.7
2018	68.3	68.9	69.8	69.5	69.4	69.5	69.7	70.3	70.6	71.7	71.2	72.1	70.1
Leisure and Hospitality													
2010	25.5	25.9	26.3	26.2	27.4	27.4	27.4	27.5	27.1	27.2	26.8	26.7	26.8
2011	26.0	26.6	27.3	27.1	27.6	27.9	27.9	28.0	27.3	26.8	26.5	26.3	27.1
2012	26.5	27.0	27.5	27.8	28.6	28.8	29.0	29.2	28.5	28.0	27.6	27.7	28.0
2013	27.5	27.6	28.4	28.5	29.2	29.6	30.0	29.9	29.3	29.3	29.1	29.3	29.0
2014	29.2	29.8	29.8	30.5	31.1	31.3	31.6	31.6	30.7	30.5	30.5	30.3	30.6
2015	30.1	30.5	31.0	31.3	32.1	32.1	32.2	32.2	31.5	31.3	31.3	31.5	31.4
2016	30.7	31.3	31.7	32.4	33.1	33.6	34.1	34.3	33.1	33.3	32.9	32.7	32.8
2017	32.2	32.6	33.1	33.5	34.0	34.7	35.1	34.9	34.1	34.1	33.6	33.3	33.8
2018	32.9	33.2	33.6	33.9	34.6	34.8	35.2	35.3	34.5	33.9	34.1	34.1	34.2
Other Services													
2010	9.9	10.1	10.1	10.0	10.1	10.1	9.7	9.9	9.9	10.0	10.0	9.9	10.0
2011	9.7	9.9	9.9	10.0	10.0	10.1	10.1	10.3	10.4	10.4	10.4	10.3	10.1
2012	10.1	10.2	10.3	10.6	10.8	10.9	10.5	10.8	10.7	10.8	10.8	10.8	10.6
2013	10.7	10.9	11.0	11.0	11.0	10.8	10.7	11.0	11.0	10.9	11.0	11.0	10.9
2014	11.0	11.1	11.2	11.2	11.3	11.1	11.0	11.4	11.3	11.3	11.4	11.3	11.2
2015	11.2	11.4	11.4	11.6	11.6	11.4	11.4	11.6	11.7	11.7	11.7	11.7	11.5
2016	11.5	11.5	11.7	11.7	11.7	11.4	11.7	12.0	12.0	12.1	11.9	11.7	11.7
2017	11.3	11.5	11.6	11.7	12.0	11.7	11.6	11.9	11.9	12.0	12.0	11.9	11.8
2018	11.7	11.8	12.0	12.1	12.2	12.0	11.8	12.2	12.1	12.2	12.1	12.1	12.0
Government													
2010	66.4	69.6	70.7	70.4	70.5	68.8	62.1	61.8	64.3	67.5	66.7	66.0	67.1
2011	65.4	68.1	69.1	69.7	69.0	66.6	62.8	61.0	62.7	65.3	65.2	63.9	65.7
2012	63.5	65.3	66.2	66.4	66.4	65.7	61.6	59.6	61.6	64.8	64.4	63.6	64.1
2013	63.1	65.6	66.4	66.5	66.3	65.9	60.2	59.8	62.3	64.2	65.2	64.5	64.2
2014	64.5	66.8	67.7	67.9	68.5	68.2	63.9	61.8	64.2	67.1	67.4	67.1	66.3
2015	67.3	69.5	69.6	70.1	70.7	70.6	64.9	63.5	67.5	69.7	70.6	70.1	68.7
2016	70.1	70.9	72.2	72.8	73.2	73.2	66.1	65.7	70.3	72.1	72.9	72.0	71.0
2017	71.7	73.7	74.3	74.8	75.1	74.6	67.1	67.5	71.1	73.2	74.2	74.0	72.6
2018	74.4	75.7	77.7	77.0	77.1	76.4	68.1	68.8	72.4	74.2	76.3	76.1	74.5

Employment by Industry: Tulsa, OK, 2010–2018

(Numbers in thousands, not seasonally adjusted)

Industry and year	January	February	March	April	May	June	July	August	September	October	November	December	Annual average
Total Nonfarm													
2010	406.6	408.0	411.4	415.2	417.7	416.4	410.1	409.3	412.0	417.3	418.9	419.5	413.5
2011	407.7	405.2	411.7	414.8	416.0	415.7	414.3	414.4	418.1	421.9	422.8	423.8	415.5
2012	414.3	418.0	420.6	424.6	427.1	426.8	421.8	423.0	426.0	431.4	434.7	435.0	425.3
2013	423.1	425.8	428.7	431.4	433.6	433.8	430.9	432.4	434.3	437.2	438.6	438.0	432.3
2014	431.6	434.0	436.1	438.2	440.8	440.5	437.9	438.7	441.0	446.5	448.2	449.3	440.2
2015	442.7	444.2	445.1	448.0	449.2	448.2	445.9	444.4	446.4	451.4	453.6	452.9	447.7
2016	442.9	444.6	445.6	447.0	446.8	445.2	442.5	442.3	446.0	448.0	450.5	451.0	446.0
2017	437.9	440.9	445.0	446.8	448.8	450.5	446.5	447.2	450.6	452.1	454.5	456.5	448.1
2018	447.6	449.8	454.2	452.2	454.6	456.7	453.0	454.4	455.8	457.4	461.5	460.2	454.8
Total Private													
2010	349.6	349.9	352.5	355.7	356.6	358.4	358.8	358.4	356.1	358.7	360.1	360.8	356.3
2011	351.6	348.4	354.5	357.6	359.1	360.8	362.6	362.7	363.0	364.1	364.9	365.8	359.6
2012	358.8	360.9	362.9	367.2	369.4	372.0	371.1	372.0	370.1	373.3	376.3	376.7	369.2
2013	366.9	368.0	370.6	373.3	375.6	377.8	378.0	379.6	377.7	378.2	379.1	378.6	375.3
2014	374.3	374.9	376.7	379.1	381.4	384.0	384.6	385.0	383.6	386.5	387.8	389.3	382.3
2015	385.0	384.8	385.8	388.2	389.5	391.3	392.3	390.6	388.3	390.7	392.5	392.0	389.3
2016	384.4	384.4	385.1	387.0	387.2	388.4	388.8	388.5	387.9	389.2	391.4	391.2	387.8
2017	381.1	382.3	385.7	387.7	389.5	393.2	392.2	392.8	392.2	393.1	395.2	396.9	390.2
2018	390.0	391.2	395.3	394.0	395.9	400.0	399.5	400.4	399.8	400.5	404.2	402.7	397.8
Goods Producing													
2010	74.5	74.5	75.0	75.4	75.8	76.9	77.6	77.3	77.1	78.0	78.4	78.9	76.6
2011	77.1	76.4	78.1	79.0	79.4	80.3	80.8	80.7	81.0	81.8	82.1	82.3	79.9
2012	81.2	81.6	82.2	83.1	83.8	84.3	84.4	84.7	84.5	86.6	87.0	86.6	84.2
2013	84.2	84.5	84.9	85.2	85.5	86.2	85.8	86.3	85.6	85.9	85.3	85.1	85.4
2014	84.8	85.3	85.2	85.1	85.6	86.1	86.9	87.2	87.0	87.9	87.9	88.0	86.4
2015	87.3	87.8	87.0	86.4	85.9	86.0	85.6	84.8	84.4	84.2	84.0	83.9	85.6
2016	82.4	82.3	81.7	81.2	81.0	81.3	81.0	81.0	80.8	79.9	80.0	80.1	81.1
2017	78.4	78.9	79.4	79.4	80.3	81.7	81.7	82.0	82.4	82.5	82.5	83.4	81.1
2018	83.2	84.0	84.8	84.5	85.4	86.5	86.2	86.7	86.7	86.5	88.1	88.9	86.0
Service-Providing													
2010	332.1	333.5	336.4	339.8	341.9	339.5	332.5	332.0	334.9	339.3	340.5	340.6	336.9
2011	330.6	328.8	333.6	335.8	336.6	335.4	333.5	333.7	337.1	340.1	340.7	341.5	335.6
2012	333.1	336.4	338.4	341.5	343.3	342.5	337.4	338.3	341.5	344.8	347.7	348.4	341.1
2013	338.9	341.3	343.8	346.2	348.1	347.6	345.1	346.1	348.7	351.3	353.3	352.9	346.9
2014	346.8	348.7	350.9	353.1	355.2	354.4	351.0	351.5	354.0	358.6	360.3	361.3	353.8
2015	355.4	356.4	358.1	361.6	363.3	362.2	360.3	359.6	362.0	367.2	369.6	369.0	362.1
2016	360.5	362.3	363.9	365.8	365.8	363.9	361.5	361.3	365.2	368.1	370.5	370.9	365.0
2017	359.5	362.0	365.6	367.4	368.5	368.8	364.8	365.2	368.2	369.6	372.0	373.1	367.1
2018	364.4	365.8	369.4	367.7	369.2	370.2	366.8	367.7	369.1	370.9	373.4	371.3	368.8
Mining, Logging, and Construction													
2010	25.3	25.4	25.7	25.9	26.2	26.8	27.2	27.0	27.0	27.5	27.6	27.8	26.6
2011	26.2	25.6	26.7	27.0	27.1	27.4	27.3	27.3	27.3	27.6	27.5	27.4	27.0
2012	26.4	26.4	26.7	27.1	27.5	27.6	27.9	28.1	28.1	29.7	30.3	29.7	28.0
2013	27.7	27.9	28.5	29.1	29.5	30.0	29.8	30.4	30.0	30.7	30.1	29.8	29.5
2014	29.4	29.6	29.4	28.8	29.0	29.1	29.7	30.0	29.9	30.6	30.4	30.2	29.7
2015	29.5	30.0	29.7	29.8	29.8	30.1	30.3	30.1	30.0	30.2	30.0	29.9	30.0
2016	29.1	29.0	29.0	29.1	29.3	29.6	29.5	29.6	29.6	29.0	28.7	28.8	29.2
2017	27.9	28.0	28.4	28.4	28.9	29.7	29.7	29.9	30.2	30.2	30.0	30.3	29.3
2018	29.8	30.4	30.9	30.6	31.1	31.8	31.9	32.5	32.3	32.3	32.7	33.4	31.6
Manufacturing													
2010	49.2	49.1	49.3	49.5	49.6	50.1	50.4	50.3	50.1	50.5	50.8	51.1	50.0
2011	50.9	50.8	51.4	52.0	52.3	52.9	53.5	53.4	53.7	54.2	54.6	54.9	52.9
2012	54.8	55.2	55.5	56.0	56.3	56.7	56.5	56.6	56.4	56.9	56.7	56.9	56.2
2013	56.5	56.6	56.4	56.1	56.0	56.2	56.0	55.9	55.6	55.2	55.2	55.3	55.9
2014	55.4	55.7	55.8	56.3	56.6	57.0	57.2	57.2	57.1	57.3	57.5	57.8	56.7
2015	57.8	57.8	57.3	56.6	56.1	55.9	55.3	54.7	54.4	54.0	54.0	54.0	55.7
2016	53.3	53.3	52.7	52.1	51.7	51.7	51.5	51.4	51.2	50.9	51.3	51.3	51.9
2017	50.5	50.9	51.0	51.0	51.4	52.0	52.0	52.1	52.2	52.3	52.5	53.1	51.8
2018	53.4	53.6	53.9	53.9	54.3	54.7	54.3	54.2	54.4	54.2	55.4	55.5	54.3

Employment by Industry: Tulsa, OK, 2010–2018—*Continued*

(Numbers in thousands, not seasonally adjusted)

Industry and year	January	February	March	April	May	June	July	August	September	October	November	December	Annual average
Trade, Transportation, and Utilities													
2010	74.0	73.4	73.9	74.1	74.4	74.6	74.7	74.5	73.6	74.1	75.7	76.4	74.5
2011	73.3	72.3	73.3	74.3	74.4	74.6	74.7	74.8	74.8	75.1	76.9	77.5	74.7
2012	74.9	74.5	75.0	75.4	75.9	76.5	76.1	75.9	75.6	76.6	78.8	79.3	76.2
2013	75.2	74.8	75.4	76.3	76.8	77.2	77.6	77.9	77.8	78.1	80.0	81.0	77.3
2014	78.7	78.2	78.5	78.8	79.4	80.3	80.3	80.5	80.3	81.1	82.7	83.8	80.2
2015	81.1	80.8	81.2	81.3	81.8	82.5	82.2	82.5	82.0	84.5	87.1	87.9	82.9
2016	83.4	82.5	82.8	83.3	83.3	83.2	82.8	83.2	82.8	84.7	87.7	87.2	83.9
2017	82.4	81.5	81.5	81.8	81.9	82.1	82.5	82.5	82.6	84.1	87.3	86.9	83.1
2018	83.5	82.3	82.9	82.8	83.0	83.2	83.5	84.0	84.4	86.2	88.4	86.8	84.3
Wholesale Trade													
2010	15.0	15.0	15.1	15.1	15.1	15.2	15.2	15.2	15.2	15.1	15.2	15.3	15.1
2011	14.9	14.9	15.0	15.1	15.0	15.1	15.3	15.2	15.2	15.1	15.1	15.1	15.1
2012	14.9	15.0	15.1	15.2	15.3	15.4	15.3	15.4	15.4	15.5	15.5	15.5	15.3
2013	15.2	15.2	15.2	15.4	15.4	15.4	15.5	15.6	15.6	15.5	15.5	15.5	15.4
2014	15.6	15.6	15.7	15.6	15.5	15.7	15.8	15.9	15.9	15.9	15.9	15.9	15.8
2015	15.8	15.8	15.8	15.7	15.7	15.8	15.8	15.8	15.6	15.8	15.7	15.8	15.8
2016	15.8	15.8	15.7	15.8	15.7	15.7	15.8	15.7	15.8	15.7	15.8	15.9	15.8
2017	15.8	15.9	16.0	16.2	16.2	16.3	16.2	16.3	16.2	16.3	16.3	16.4	16.2
2018	16.3	16.3	16.4	16.3	16.4	16.6	16.3	16.4	16.5	16.5	16.4	16.5	16.4
Retail Trade													
2010	44.8	44.1	44.5	44.9	45.2	45.3	45.3	45.2	44.4	45.0	46.5	46.8	45.2
2011	44.7	43.7	44.5	45.2	45.4	45.3	45.1	45.3	45.3	45.7	47.4	47.7	45.4
2012	45.5	44.8	45.3	45.5	45.8	46.2	45.9	45.6	45.4	46.3	48.4	48.7	46.1
2013	45.5	45.1	45.6	46.0	46.5	46.8	46.8	47.0	46.9	47.4	49.1	49.9	46.9
2014	47.4	47.0	47.2	47.5	48.1	48.6	48.4	48.5	48.3	48.9	50.2	51.2	48.4
2015	48.7	48.7	48.9	49.2	49.6	50.0	49.4	49.6	49.4	50.0	51.6	52.4	49.8
2016	49.8	49.6	50.1	50.3	50.4	50.4	50.0	50.0	49.3	49.9	51.7	51.7	50.3
2017	49.1	48.5	48.4	48.5	48.5	48.6	48.8	48.5	48.0	48.4	50.3	50.5	48.8
2018	48.8	48.0	48.3	48.4	48.4	48.2	48.3	48.4	48.1	49.1	50.0	49.1	48.6
Transportation and Utilities													
2010	14.2	14.3	14.3	14.1	14.1	14.1	14.2	14.1	14.0	14.0	14.0	14.3	14.1
2011	13.7	13.7	13.8	14.0	14.0	14.2	14.3	14.3	14.3	14.3	14.4	14.7	14.1
2012	14.5	14.7	14.6	14.7	14.8	14.9	14.9	14.9	14.8	14.8	14.9	15.1	14.8
2013	14.5	14.5	14.6	14.9	14.9	15.0	15.3	15.3	15.3	15.2	15.4	15.6	15.0
2014	15.7	15.6	15.6	15.7	15.8	16.0	16.1	16.1	16.1	16.3	16.6	16.7	16.0
2015	16.6	16.3	16.5	16.4	16.5	16.7	17.0	17.1	17.0	18.7	19.8	19.7	17.4
2016	17.8	17.1	17.0	17.2	17.2	17.1	17.0	17.5	17.7	19.1	20.2	19.6	17.9
2017	17.5	17.1	17.1	17.1	17.2	17.2	17.5	17.7	18.4	19.4	20.7	20.0	18.1
2018	18.4	18.0	18.2	18.1	18.2	18.4	18.9	19.2	19.8	20.6	22.0	21.2	19.3
Information													
2010	8.4	8.3	8.3	8.7	8.7	8.5	8.7	8.5	8.4	8.3	8.3	8.4	8.5
2011	8.3	8.2	8.2	8.1	8.2	8.2	8.3	8.3	8.2	8.2	8.1	8.2	8.2
2012	8.1	8.0	8.0	7.9	7.9	7.9	8.0	7.9	7.9	7.9	7.9	7.9	7.9
2013	7.8	7.8	7.8	7.9	7.9	7.9	7.9	7.8	7.7	7.7	7.6	7.6	7.8
2014	7.5	7.4	7.5	7.4	7.3	7.4	7.4	7.3	7.1	6.9	7.0	7.2	7.3
2015	7.1	7.1	7.1	7.1	7.2	7.2	7.2	7.2	7.1	7.2	7.3	7.4	7.2
2016	7.3	7.4	7.3	7.3	7.4	7.4	7.4	7.4	7.3	7.3	7.4	7.4	7.4
2017	7.4	7.4	7.4	7.4	7.4	7.3	7.3	7.1	7.0	7.0	7.0	7.2	7.2
2018	7.2	7.1	7.1	7.1	7.1	7.1	7.1	7.1	6.9	7.0	6.9	7.0	7.1
Financial Activities													
2010	23.2	23.2	23.2	23.3	23.3	23.2	23.2	23.2	23.0	23.0	22.9	23.0	23.1
2011	22.7	22.6	22.6	22.6	22.5	22.6	22.6	22.6	22.5	22.6	22.6	22.7	22.6
2012	22.4	22.5	22.4	22.2	22.3	22.4	22.5	22.5	22.4	22.6	22.6	22.7	22.5
2013	22.6	22.6	22.6	22.7	22.8	22.9	23.0	23.0	22.9	23.1	23.2	23.1	22.9
2014	22.8	22.8	22.8	22.9	22.8	22.8	22.9	22.9	22.8	22.9	23.0	23.0	22.9
2015	22.9	22.9	23.0	23.0	23.1	23.1	23.5	23.4	23.3	23.4	23.3	23.3	23.2
2016	23.2	23.2	23.1	23.1	23.2	23.2	23.3	23.2	23.1	23.2	23.1	23.3	23.2
2017	22.8	22.7	22.8	23.0	23.0	23.1	23.0	23.2	23.1	23.2	23.3	23.5	23.1
2018	23.3	23.3	23.4	23.3	23.2	23.4	23.3	23.3	23.2	23.3	23.3	23.4	23.3

Employment by Industry: Tulsa, OK, 2010–2018—*Continued*

(Numbers in thousands, not seasonally adjusted)

Industry and year	January	February	March	April	May	June	July	August	September	October	November	December	Annual average
Professional and Business Services													
2010	53.6	54.0	54.4	55.3	55.1	55.3	55.2	55.1	54.9	55.7	55.1	54.6	54.9
2011	53.0	52.8	53.7	53.7	53.8	53.9	54.6	54.8	55.4	55.6	55.1	55.1	54.3
2012	53.3	54.6	54.8	55.9	56.1	56.8	56.9	57.5	57.0	57.3	57.5	56.9	56.2
2013	55.7	56.0	56.8	57.0	57.4	57.9	58.4	58.6	58.2	58.6	58.2	57.3	57.5
2014	56.8	57.0	57.6	58.3	58.8	59.3	59.0	58.7	58.4	60.0	59.6	59.3	58.6
2015	59.5	58.6	58.9	59.9	60.2	60.0	60.5	60.0	59.0	59.6	58.9	58.5	59.5
2016	57.8	57.9	57.7	58.7	58.7	59.2	59.3	59.0	59.2	59.5	59.0	58.9	58.7
2017	57.8	58.9	60.0	60.3	60.5	61.1	60.5	60.9	60.6	60.7	60.1	60.3	60.1
2018	58.1	59.2	60.0	59.0	59.3	60.9	60.6	60.7	60.4	59.6	59.8	58.6	59.7
Education and Health Services													
2010	64.6	64.8	65.0	65.2	65.2	65.2	65.3	65.7	65.6	66.4	66.6	66.7	65.5
2011	66.0	65.4	66.1	66.3	66.7	66.6	66.8	66.8	66.7	67.0	66.6	66.6	66.5
2012	66.1	66.1	65.9	66.6	66.8	66.8	66.5	66.9	67.1	67.4	67.6	68.0	66.8
2013	67.6	68.0	68.1	67.9	67.8	67.7	67.4	67.7	68.0	68.3	68.5	68.4	68.0
2014	67.8	68.0	68.2	68.4	68.4	68.3	68.1	68.5	68.8	69.1	69.2	69.4	68.5
2015	68.8	68.7	68.9	69.1	69.0	69.1	69.9	70.1	70.5	70.3	70.5	70.0	69.6
2016	70.2	70.4	70.6	70.3	70.0	69.8	70.2	70.4	70.8	71.3	71.1	71.2	70.5
2017	70.4	70.5	70.6	70.9	71.1	71.1	70.9	71.0	71.3	71.4	71.2	71.6	71.0
2018	71.3	71.4	71.9	71.3	71.3	71.1	71.3	71.3	71.9	71.9	72.2	72.1	71.6
Leisure and Hospitality													
2010	34.4	34.8	35.7	36.8	37.2	37.4	37.1	37.3	36.8	36.5	36.4	36.2	36.4
2011	34.9	34.4	36.0	37.1	37.5	37.7	37.9	38.1	37.8	37.2	36.8	36.7	36.8
2012	36.3	37.0	37.9	38.9	39.3	39.8	39.3	39.4	38.7	38.0	38.0	38.4	38.4
2013	37.2	37.6	38.4	39.3	40.3	40.4	40.4	40.9	40.3	39.5	39.3	39.2	39.4
2014	39.0	39.2	39.9	41.0	41.7	42.0	42.1	42.2	41.6	40.9	40.7	40.8	40.9
2015	40.5	41.0	41.6	43.4	44.1	44.9	44.3	44.2	43.8	43.3	43.2	42.9	43.1
2016	42.1	42.6	43.7	44.6	45.0	45.4	45.6	45.2	44.7	44.1	43.7	43.7	44.2
2017	42.5	42.8	44.2	45.3	45.5	46.4	45.8	45.9	45.0	43.9	43.5	43.6	44.5
2018	43.1	43.4	44.5	45.3	45.8	46.5	46.2	46.4	45.4	45.1	44.6	45.0	45.1
Other Services													
2010	16.9	16.9	17.0	16.9	16.9	17.3	17.0	16.8	16.7	16.7	16.7	16.6	16.9
2011	16.3	16.3	16.5	16.5	16.6	16.9	16.9	16.6	16.6	16.6	16.7	16.7	16.6
2012	16.5	16.6	16.7	17.2	17.3	17.5	17.4	17.2	16.9	16.9	16.9	16.9	17.0
2013	16.6	16.7	16.6	17.0	17.1	17.6	17.5	17.4	17.2	17.0	17.0	16.9	17.1
2014	16.9	17.0	17.0	17.2	17.4	17.8	17.9	17.7	17.6	17.7	17.7	17.8	17.5
2015	17.8	17.9	18.1	18.0	18.2	18.5	19.1	18.4	18.2	18.2	18.2	18.1	18.2
2016	18.0	18.1	18.2	18.5	18.6	18.9	19.2	19.1	19.2	19.2	19.4	19.4	18.8
2017	19.4	19.6	19.8	19.6	19.8	20.4	20.5	20.2	20.2	20.3	20.3	20.4	20.0
2018	20.3	20.5	20.7	20.7	20.8	21.3	21.3	20.9	20.9	20.9	20.9	20.9	20.8
Government													
2010	57.0	58.1	58.9	59.5	61.1	58.0	51.3	50.9	55.9	58.6	58.8	58.7	57.2
2011	56.1	56.8	57.2	57.2	56.9	54.9	51.7	51.7	55.1	57.8	57.9	58.0	55.9
2012	55.5	57.1	57.7	57.4	57.7	54.8	50.7	51.0	55.9	58.1	58.4	58.3	56.1
2013	56.2	57.8	58.1	58.1	58.0	56.0	52.9	52.8	56.6	59.0	59.5	59.4	57.0
2014	57.3	59.1	59.4	59.1	59.4	56.5	53.3	53.7	57.4	60.0	60.4	60.0	58.0
2015	57.7	59.4	59.3	59.8	59.7	56.9	53.6	53.8	58.1	60.7	61.1	60.9	58.4
2016	58.5	60.2	60.5	60.0	59.6	56.8	53.7	53.8	58.1	58.8	59.1	59.8	58.2
2017	56.8	58.6	59.3	59.1	59.3	57.3	54.3	54.4	58.4	59.0	59.3	59.6	58.0
2018	57.6	58.6	58.9	58.2	58.7	56.7	53.5	54.0	56.0	56.9	57.3	57.5	57.0

Employment by Industry: Urban Honolulu, HI, 2010–2018

(Numbers in thousands, not seasonally adjusted)

Industry and year	January	February	March	April	May	June	July	August	September	October	November	December	Annual average
Total Nonfarm													
2010	427.9	432.8	434.8	434.0	437.0	433.1	428.9	424.9	433.3	437.9	442.9	445.4	434.4
2011	429.2	439.2	442.0	439.2	439.8	437.7	433.5	430.8	440.1	443.4	448.8	451.8	439.6
2012	430.8	444.7	446.8	447.7	450.3	448.3	441.1	446.1	449.3	453.3	461.3	461.2	448.4
2013	440.6	455.4	457.4	454.2	458.9	455.8	451.7	449.4	457.1	461.5	467.3	469.5	456.6
2014	456.2	460.6	463.3	461.4	464.0	460.4	454.1	455.4	461.8	465.0	471.4	470.0	462.0
2015	461.6	466.2	468.7	467.6	469.4	467.3	460.9	464.6	467.0	472.7	477.7	481.4	468.8
2016	465.0	472.0	473.7	471.4	474.4	471.1	466.7	468.5	474.8	475.2	481.2	479.2	472.8
2017	471.5	476.8	479.6	477.8	479.3	476.5	468.6	467.6	477.2	477.6	481.1	484.4	476.5
2018	471.5	478.0	479.9	476.9	478.9	477.8	468.8	471.0	476.1	481.2	485.0	487.8	477.7
Total Private													
2010	332.1	333.8	334.5	333.3	334.6	334.2	334.8	335.0	337.3	338.8	340.4	344.5	336.1
2011	335.2	338.7	341.0	338.5	338.4	338.7	339.9	341.3	343.8	344.2	347.9	350.4	341.5
2012	341.8	343.8	345.2	346.1	348.1	348.8	348.8	351.4	352.1	353.5	357.8	359.5	349.7
2013	351.5	354.2	355.9	355.8	356.8	357.6	359.5	359.7	360.1	361.7	366.4	368.1	358.9
2014	358.3	359.3	361.7	360.5	361.7	361.4	361.8	363.0	364.5	365.5	369.0	371.7	363.2
2015	364.1	365.5	367.6	366.7	367.7	368.4	369.3	370.1	369.7	372.7	376.9	379.6	369.9
2016	369.4	371.4	372.3	372.5	372.9	372.3	375.0	377.0	377.0	375.1	378.3	379.9	374.4
2017	374.2	375.3	378.1	376.6	377.8	378.1	377.3	378.6	379.0	377.6	379.9	382.5	377.9
2018	375.0	376.6	378.6	376.5	376.5	378.8	377.0	379.0	378.6	381.3	381.7	385.1	378.7
Goods Producing													
2010	32.0	31.8	31.8	31.7	31.7	31.5	31.8	31.7	31.9	32.4	32.4	32.6	31.9
2011	31.5	31.9	32.1	32.2	32.2	32.8	33.1	33.3	33.6	33.3	33.1	33.1	32.7
2012	32.4	32.3	32.3	32.2	32.2	32.6	32.8	33.0	33.4	33.5	33.7	33.5	32.8
2013	32.9	33.2	33.5	33.5	34.0	33.8	34.2	34.4	34.3	34.3	34.5	34.6	33.9
2014	33.7	34.0	34.2	34.0	34.4	34.9	35.4	35.7	35.7	36.0	35.9	35.8	35.0
2015	34.9	35.0	35.6	35.9	36.3	37.0	37.7	37.7	37.8	38.7	39.0	39.5	37.1
2016	38.8	39.4	39.7	39.5	39.8	39.9	40.2	40.2	39.7	39.1	39.0	38.9	39.5
2017	37.8	38.0	38.4	38.1	38.3	38.5	38.1	38.3	38.1	37.5	37.7	37.8	38.1
2018	37.2	37.3	37.6	37.4	37.5	37.8	37.9	37.7	37.6	38.5	37.4	38.3	37.7
Service-Providing													
2010	395.9	401.0	403.0	402.3	405.3	401.6	397.1	393.2	401.4	405.5	410.5	412.8	402.5
2011	397.7	407.3	409.9	407.0	407.6	404.9	400.4	397.5	406.5	410.1	415.7	418.7	406.9
2012	398.4	412.4	414.5	415.5	418.1	415.7	408.3	413.1	415.9	419.8	427.6	427.7	415.6
2013	407.7	422.2	423.9	420.7	424.9	422.0	417.5	415.0	422.8	427.2	432.8	434.9	422.6
2014	422.5	426.6	429.1	427.4	429.6	425.5	418.7	419.7	426.1	429.0	435.5	434.2	427.0
2015	426.7	431.2	433.1	431.7	433.1	430.3	423.2	426.9	429.2	434.0	438.7	441.9	431.7
2016	426.2	432.6	434.0	431.9	434.6	431.2	426.5	428.3	435.1	436.1	442.2	440.3	433.3
2017	433.7	438.8	441.2	439.7	441.0	438.0	430.5	429.3	439.1	440.1	443.4	446.6	438.5
2018	434.3	440.7	442.3	439.5	441.4	440.0	430.9	433.3	438.5	442.7	447.6	449.5	440.1
Mining, Logging, and Construction													
2010	21.4	21.3	21.3	21.3	21.3	21.2	21.5	21.3	21.4	21.9	21.8	21.9	21.5
2011	20.9	21.2	21.3	21.5	21.5	22.1	22.4	22.5	22.7	22.4	22.1	22.2	21.9
2012	21.6	21.5	21.6	21.6	21.7	22.0	22.2	22.3	22.6	22.7	22.8	22.6	22.1
2013	22.2	22.4	22.7	22.8	23.2	23.0	23.4	23.5	23.3	23.3	23.5	23.6	23.1
2014	22.9	23.2	23.3	23.2	23.6	23.9	24.2	24.4	24.6	24.7	24.7	24.5	23.9
2015	23.7	23.8	24.4	24.7	25.1	25.7	26.4	26.4	26.6	27.4	27.7	28.1	25.8
2016	27.7	28.1	28.4	28.2	28.5	28.5	28.8	28.7	28.3	27.7	27.7	27.5	28.2
2017	26.6	26.7	26.9	26.7	26.8	26.9	26.5	26.6	26.5	25.9	26.1	26.1	26.5
2018	25.6	25.8	26.1	26.0	26.2	26.6	26.7	26.6	26.5	27.3	26.4	26.9	26.4
Manufacturing													
2010	10.6	10.5	10.5	10.4	10.4	10.3	10.3	10.4	10.5	10.5	10.6	10.7	10.5
2011	10.6	10.7	10.8	10.7	10.7	10.7	10.7	10.8	10.9	10.9	11.0	10.9	10.8
2012	10.8	10.8	10.7	10.6	10.5	10.6	10.6	10.7	10.8	10.8	10.9	10.9	10.7
2013	10.7	10.8	10.8	10.7	10.8	10.8	10.8	10.9	11.0	11.0	11.0	11.0	10.9
2014	10.8	10.8	10.9	10.8	10.8	11.0	11.2	11.3	11.1	11.3	11.2	11.3	11.0
2015	11.2	11.2	11.2	11.2	11.2	11.3	11.3	11.3	11.2	11.3	11.3	11.4	11.3
2016	11.1	11.3	11.3	11.3	11.3	11.4	11.4	11.5	11.4	11.4	11.3	11.4	11.3
2017	11.2	11.3	11.5	11.4	11.5	11.6	11.6	11.7	11.6	11.6	11.6	11.7	11.5
2018	11.6	11.5	11.5	11.4	11.3	11.2	11.2	11.1	11.1	11.2	11.0	11.4	11.3

Employment by Industry: Urban Honolulu, HI, 2010–2018—*Continued*

(Numbers in thousands, not seasonally adjusted)

Industry and year	January	February	March	April	May	June	July	August	September	October	November	December	Annual average
Trade, Transportation, and Utilities													
2010	78.3	77.5	77.4	77.6	77.2	77.8	78.3	78.4	78.2	78.6	80.2	81.5	78.4
2011	79.1	78.6	78.6	78.3	78.3	78.5	78.9	79.0	79.3	80.1	81.9	82.9	79.5
2012	80.9	80.3	80.6	80.5	81.0	81.5	81.7	81.9	82.1	82.6	85.1	86.0	82.0
2013	82.7	82.5	82.8	82.5	82.6	83.1	83.2	83.4	83.2	83.5	85.5	86.7	83.5
2014	83.4	82.6	82.8	82.5	82.6	82.9	83.3	83.0	83.1	83.6	85.8	87.5	83.6
2015	84.6	84.1	84.2	83.8	83.8	84.3	84.3	84.2	83.9	84.5	86.3	87.5	84.6
2016	84.4	83.8	83.6	83.1	83.3	83.2	83.8	84.2	84.5	85.0	86.6	88.0	84.5
2017	85.4	84.4	84.4	84.1	84.3	84.8	85.1	85.5	85.6	86.1	87.7	88.6	85.5
2018	86.1	85.3	85.2	85.1	85.3	85.5	85.8	85.9	85.8	85.8	86.9	87.2	85.8
Wholesale Trade													
2010	14.1	14.0	14.1	14.1	14.1	14.1	14.3	14.2	14.2	14.2	14.2	14.3	14.2
2011	14.0	13.9	13.9	14.0	14.0	14.0	14.1	14.1	14.1	14.1	14.1	14.2	14.0
2012	14.1	14.0	14.1	14.0	14.0	14.1	14.1	14.2	14.2	14.2	14.2	14.3	14.1
2013	14.1	14.1	14.2	14.1	14.1	14.1	14.1	14.1	14.1	14.0	14.1	14.1	14.1
2014	14.0	14.0	14.0	13.9	13.9	14.0	14.0	14.0	14.0	14.1	14.2	14.4	14.0
2015	14.1	14.1	14.2	14.1	14.2	14.2	14.2	14.3	14.2	14.2	14.1	14.2	14.2
2016	14.0	13.9	13.9	14.0	14.0	14.0	14.1	14.1	14.1	14.1	14.2	14.3	14.1
2017	14.1	14.1	14.1	14.0	14.0	14.1	14.0	14.1	14.1	14.1	14.1	14.2	14.1
2018	14.0	14.0	14.0	13.9	14.0	14.0	14.0	13.9	13.9	14.2	14.4	14.2	14.0
Retail Trade													
2010	44.8	44.2	44.1	44.1	43.8	44.2	44.5	44.6	44.5	44.8	46.3	47.3	44.8
2011	45.5	45.0	45.0	44.8	44.8	44.8	45.1	45.2	45.5	46.1	47.8	48.6	45.7
2012	46.8	46.4	46.4	46.4	46.8	47.0	47.0	47.0	47.1	47.4	49.8	50.4	47.4
2013	47.8	47.4	47.5	47.2	47.2	47.4	47.5	47.6	47.4	47.6	49.5	50.4	47.9
2014	47.5	46.7	46.8	46.7	46.7	47.1	47.4	47.2	47.4	47.6	49.4	50.6	47.6
2015	48.3	47.8	47.8	47.5	47.4	47.7	47.7	47.6	47.5	48.0	49.8	50.6	48.1
2016	48.1	47.6	47.4	46.7	46.6	46.5	47.0	47.2	47.6	48.0	49.3	50.2	47.7
2017	48.2	47.2	47.2	47.1	47.2	47.4	47.7	47.8	47.7	48.0	49.8	50.4	48.0
2018	48.5	47.7	47.4	47.5	47.6	47.6	47.8	47.9	47.8	47.6	48.3	48.5	47.9
Transportation and Utilities													
2010	19.4	19.3	19.2	19.4	19.3	19.5	19.5	19.6	19.5	19.6	19.7	19.9	19.5
2011	19.6	19.7	19.7	19.5	19.5	19.7	19.7	19.7	19.7	19.9	20.0	20.1	19.7
2012	20.0	19.9	20.1	20.1	20.2	20.4	20.6	20.7	20.8	21.0	21.1	21.3	20.5
2013	20.8	21.0	21.1	21.2	21.3	21.6	21.6	21.7	21.7	21.9	21.9	22.2	21.5
2014	21.9	21.9	22.0	21.9	22.0	21.8	21.9	21.8	21.7	21.9	22.2	22.5	22.0
2015	22.2	22.2	22.2	22.2	22.2	22.4	22.4	22.3	22.2	22.3	22.4	22.7	22.3
2016	22.3	22.3	22.3	22.4	22.7	22.7	22.7	22.9	22.8	22.9	23.1	23.5	22.7
2017	23.1	23.1	23.1	23.0	23.1	23.3	23.4	23.6	23.8	24.0	23.8	24.0	23.4
2018	23.6	23.6	23.8	23.7	23.7	23.9	24.0	24.1	24.1	24.0	24.2	24.5	23.9
Information													
2010	7.3	8.1	8.3	7.7	8.9	8.3	7.0	7.5	9.4	8.3	7.9	8.8	8.1
2011	6.9	7.9	8.7	6.6	6.5	6.3	6.8	6.8	6.7	6.8	7.1	7.2	7.0
2012	6.8	7.0	7.1	7.0	7.0	6.3	6.7	6.9	6.9	7.2	7.7	7.5	7.0
2013	6.9	7.0	7.1	7.0	6.6	6.5	8.2	7.0	7.3	8.0	8.3	8.5	7.4
2014	6.9	7.0	7.1	6.9	7.4	6.7	6.8	7.3	7.3	7.1	7.3	7.4	7.1
2015	7.1	7.2	7.2	7.0	6.9	6.8	7.2	7.2	7.1	7.3	8.2	8.3	7.3
2016	6.8	7.2	7.0	7.1	7.6	7.0	7.3	8.3	7.7	7.3	8.2	7.3	7.4
2017	7.5	7.7	7.8	7.7	8.4	7.5	7.6	8.6	7.8	6.8	6.9	7.1	7.6
2018	7.0	7.5	7.6	7.5	7.5	8.0	6.8	8.4	7.9	8.0	8.3	8.4	7.7
Financial Activities													
2010	20.6	20.7	20.7	20.6	20.6	20.5	20.7	20.6	20.6	20.6	20.5	20.7	20.6
2011	20.3	20.3	20.3	20.3	20.3	20.2	20.4	20.3	20.2	20.3	20.5	20.4	20.3
2012	20.0	20.1	20.1	20.1	20.2	20.4	20.4	20.4	20.4	20.4	20.5	20.4	20.3
2013	20.1	20.2	20.4	20.4	20.5	20.6	20.6	20.5	20.6	20.5	20.5	20.7	20.5
2014	20.5	20.5	20.8	20.7	20.8	20.8	21.0	20.9	20.8	20.9	20.9	21.1	20.8
2015	20.8	20.9	21.1	21.1	21.2	21.3	21.3	21.3	21.1	21.1	21.2	21.4	21.2
2016	21.3	21.5	21.5	21.5	21.5	21.6	21.9	21.9	21.8	21.8	21.8	22.0	21.7
2017	21.8	21.8	22.0	21.9	21.9	22.0	21.9	21.8	21.9	21.9	22.0	22.2	21.9
2018	21.9	21.8	22.0	22.0	21.8	21.9	21.8	21.8	21.7	21.8	22.4	22.4	21.9

Employment by Industry: Urban Honolulu, HI, 2010–2018—*Continued*

(Numbers in thousands, not seasonally adjusted)

Industry and year	January	February	March	April	May	June	July	August	September	October	November	December	Annual average
Professional and Business Services													
2010	57.0	57.3	57.4	57.5	57.6	57.6	58.2	58.0	58.2	58.6	58.8	59.4	58.0
2011	59.1	60.0	60.6	60.5	60.1	60.3	60.1	60.9	61.1	61.0	61.5	62.6	60.7
2012	60.7	61.1	61.5	62.2	62.6	62.7	62.2	62.9	62.6	63.0	63.6	63.9	62.4
2013	63.0	63.7	64.0	63.9	63.6	63.9	64.3	64.6	64.5	65.3	66.1	66.2	64.4
2014	65.6	65.8	66.2	66.3	65.8	66.0	65.6	65.9	66.2	66.0	66.5	66.8	66.1
2015	66.0	66.2	66.5	66.2	66.0	66.2	66.2	66.0	65.6	66.0	66.2	66.1	66.1
2016	64.9	65.3	65.2	65.6	64.7	64.7	65.1	65.3	65.2	64.8	65.0	65.2	65.1
2017	64.4	64.6	64.9	64.7	64.5	65.2	65.2	65.1	64.9	64.9	65.2	65.2	64.9
2018	64.3	64.6	65.1	64.7	64.5	64.9	65.1	65.4	65.3	65.6	65.9	65.8	65.1
Education and Health Services													
2010	58.1	58.8	59.0	58.7	59.1	58.7	58.6	58.3	58.3	59.5	59.7	60.1	58.9
2011	58.1	59.5	59.6	59.5	59.8	59.1	59.2	58.9	60.0	60.1	60.8	61.0	59.6
2012	59.0	60.1	60.1	60.4	60.8	60.4	60.0	60.8	61.2	61.3	61.6	62.2	60.7
2013	60.7	61.7	62.0	62.0	62.2	62.1	61.3	61.6	62.1	61.8	62.9	62.6	61.9
2014	61.1	61.8	62.2	62.2	62.2	61.6	61.4	61.5	62.4	62.8	63.3	63.8	62.2
2015	62.9	63.9	64.4	64.4	64.5	63.9	63.5	63.8	64.6	65.0	65.3	65.8	64.3
2016	63.7	64.0	64.7	64.9	64.7	64.1	64.4	64.0	65.0	64.2	64.6	64.9	64.4
2017	64.4	64.8	65.5	65.4	65.3	64.5	63.9	63.3	64.9	64.8	65.0	65.6	64.8
2018	64.1	65.0	65.6	65.2	64.9	65.0	64.1	64.1	65.1	65.8	66.1	66.2	65.1
Leisure and Hospitality													
2010	58.9	59.4	59.6	59.5	59.5	59.9	60.2	60.4	60.7	60.7	60.9	61.4	60.1
2011	60.5	60.6	61.2	61.1	61.1	61.4	61.3	61.9	62.4	62.1	62.5	62.6	61.6
2012	62.0	62.6	63.1	63.3	63.7	64.4	64.6	64.9	64.9	64.9	65.0	65.5	64.1
2013	64.6	65.2	65.4	65.6	66.4	66.8	66.8	67.2	67.0	67.2	67.5	67.7	66.5
2014	66.4	66.8	67.4	67.2	67.7	67.7	67.6	67.8	68.0	68.1	68.2	68.1	67.6
2015	67.0	67.3	67.5	67.4	67.9	67.8	68.2	69.0	68.7	69.1	69.6	70.0	68.3
2016	68.6	69.2	69.5	69.6	70.1	70.6	71.1	71.9	71.8	71.7	71.7	72.3	70.7
2017	71.8	72.8	73.7	73.3	73.6	74.0	74.0	74.4	74.2	74.1	73.8	74.3	73.7
2018	73.2	73.7	73.9	73.2	73.7	74.2	74.0	74.3	73.7	74.4	73.1	75.2	73.9
Other Services													
2010	19.9	20.2	20.3	20.0	20.0	19.9	20.0	20.1	20.0	20.1	20.0	20.0	20.0
2011	19.7	19.9	19.9	20.0	20.1	20.1	20.1	20.2	20.5	20.5	20.5	20.6	20.2
2012	20.0	20.3	20.4	20.4	20.6	20.5	20.4	20.6	20.6	20.6	20.6	20.5	20.5
2013	20.6	20.7	20.7	20.9	20.9	20.8	20.9	21.0	21.1	21.1	21.1	21.1	20.9
2014	20.7	20.8	21.0	20.7	20.8	20.8	20.7	20.9	21.0	21.0	21.1	21.2	20.9
2015	20.8	20.9	21.1	20.9	21.1	21.1	20.9	20.9	20.9	21.0	21.1	21.0	21.0
2016	20.9	21.0	21.1	21.2	21.2	21.2	21.2	21.2	21.3	21.2	21.4	21.3	21.2
2017	21.1	21.2	21.4	21.4	21.5	21.6	21.5	21.6	21.6	21.5	21.6	21.7	21.5
2018	21.2	21.4	21.6	21.4	21.3	21.5	21.5	21.4	21.5	21.4	21.6	21.6	21.5
Government													
2010	95.8	99.0	100.3	100.7	102.4	98.9	94.1	89.9	96.0	99.1	102.5	100.9	98.3
2011	94.0	100.5	101.0	100.7	101.4	99.0	93.6	89.5	96.3	99.2	100.9	101.4	98.1
2012	89.0	100.9	101.6	101.6	102.2	99.5	92.3	94.7	97.2	99.8	103.5	101.7	98.7
2013	89.1	101.2	101.5	98.4	102.1	98.2	92.2	89.7	97.0	99.8	100.9	101.4	97.6
2014	97.9	101.3	101.6	100.9	102.3	99.0	92.3	92.4	97.3	99.5	102.4	98.3	98.8
2015	97.5	100.7	101.1	100.9	101.7	98.9	91.6	94.5	97.3	100.0	100.8	101.8	98.9
2016	95.6	100.6	101.4	98.9	101.5	98.8	91.7	91.5	97.8	100.1	102.9	99.3	98.3
2017	97.3	101.5	101.5	101.2	101.5	98.4	91.3	89.0	98.2	100.0	101.2	101.9	98.6
2018	96.5	101.4	101.3	100.4	102.4	99.0	91.8	92.0	97.5	99.9	103.3	102.7	99.0

Employment by Industry: Worcester, MA-CT, 2010–2018

(Numbers in thousands, not seasonally adjusted)

Industry and year	January	February	March	April	May	June	July	August	September	October	November	December	Annual average
Total Nonfarm													
2010	255.4	255.4	255.8	259.3	262.7	262.6	258.0	258.1	261.1	264.1	264.6	265.6	260.2
2011	259.3	260.2	261.1	263.9	265.1	264.4	262.5	261.0	265.8	268.2	269.1	269.0	264.1
2012	261.7	261.9	264.3	265.1	266.7	268.5	264.7	264.6	268.4	270.6	271.1	270.2	266.5
2013	264.6	265.1	267.1	270.6	273.1	273.5	267.1	268.4	271.3	273.6	274.5	274.7	270.3
2014	268.1	269.8	271.8	275.8	277.4	277.3	272.5	272.8	276.8	280.2	281.2	281.0	275.4
2015	272.3	273.0	275.0	278.7	282.0	281.9	276.2	276.2	279.5	283.3	284.4	284.9	279.0
2016	275.6	277.8	279.4	283.7	285.8	286.0	282.4	281.7	285.8	286.8	288.4	287.7	283.4
2017	279.7	281.7	283.4	285.7	288.3	288.9	283.8	284.1	288.3	290.3	290.9	291.5	286.4
2018	281.9	284.8	285.7	287.5	289.7	289.8	283.4	283.8	287.0	288.8	290.5	289.5	286.9
Total Private													
2010	213.9	213.6	213.9	217.2	219.7	220.6	220.0	220.3	220.1	222.4	222.5	223.3	219.0
2011	218.4	218.6	219.3	222.1	223.1	223.3	224.6	223.8	225.1	226.7	227.6	227.4	223.3
2012	221.1	220.5	222.4	223.7	225.2	227.2	226.8	226.8	227.0	228.7	228.7	227.7	225.5
2013	223.5	222.6	224.5	226.8	229.5	231.8	229.2	230.1	229.1	230.3	230.6	230.5	228.2
2014	226.1	225.9	227.8	231.1	233.1	235.1	234.0	234.2	233.8	236.2	236.3	236.3	232.5
2015	230.3	229.1	230.6	234.0	237.5	238.6	237.6	238.0	237.0	239.3	239.9	240.3	236.0
2016	233.5	233.8	234.8	239.3	241.3	243.1	243.1	242.7	242.4	242.8	243.1	243.1	240.3
2017	237.0	237.5	239.1	241.2	243.6	245.9	244.8	245.2	244.6	245.4	245.6	245.9	243.0
2018	238.6	239.8	240.8	242.4	244.6	246.0	243.9	244.3	243.1	243.8	244.8	243.9	243.0
Goods Producing													
2010	35.8	35.2	35.3	36.2	36.7	37.3	37.2	37.3	37.1	37.3	37.4	37.1	36.7
2011	35.8	35.3	35.4	36.2	37.1	37.6	38.5	38.5	38.3	38.3	38.3	38.1	37.3
2012	36.0	35.6	35.9	36.4	36.6	37.0	37.1	37.1	36.9	37.0	36.7	35.9	36.5
2013	35.0	34.8	35.0	35.6	36.3	36.9	37.1	37.3	36.9	36.7	36.4	36.2	36.2
2014	35.5	35.1	35.4	35.9	36.6	37.2	37.5	37.4	37.2	37.7	37.6	37.1	36.7
2015	36.4	35.8	36.0	37.0	37.9	38.4	38.6	38.5	38.1	38.5	38.4	38.2	37.7
2016	37.2	36.9	37.3	38.0	38.5	39.3	39.3	39.3	39.0	38.7	38.7	38.7	38.4
2017	37.2	36.7	37.0	37.8	38.5	39.2	39.3	39.5	39.1	39.3	39.1	38.8	38.5
2018	37.9	37.8	38.0	38.8	39.4	40.0	40.3	40.0	39.7	39.6	39.6	39.3	39.2
Service-Providing													
2010	219.6	220.2	220.5	223.1	226.0	225.3	220.8	220.8	224.0	226.8	227.2	228.5	223.6
2011	223.5	224.9	225.7	227.7	228.0	226.8	224.0	222.5	227.5	229.9	230.8	230.9	226.9
2012	225.7	226.3	228.4	228.7	230.1	231.5	227.6	227.5	231.5	233.6	234.4	234.3	230.0
2013	229.6	230.3	232.1	235.0	236.8	236.6	230.0	231.1	234.4	236.9	238.1	238.5	234.1
2014	232.6	234.7	236.4	239.9	240.8	240.1	235.0	235.4	239.6	242.5	243.6	243.9	238.7
2015	235.9	237.2	239.0	241.7	244.1	243.5	237.6	237.7	241.4	244.8	246.0	246.7	241.3
2016	238.4	240.9	242.1	245.7	247.3	246.7	243.1	242.4	246.8	248.1	249.7	249.0	245.0
2017	242.5	245.0	246.4	247.9	249.8	249.7	244.5	244.6	249.2	251.0	251.8	252.7	247.9
2018	244.0	247.0	247.7	248.7	250.3	249.8	243.1	243.8	247.3	249.2	250.9	250.2	247.7
Mining, Logging, and Construction													
2010	7.5	7.1	7.2	7.9	8.3	8.7	8.9	8.9	8.7	8.9	8.8	8.5	8.3
2011	7.5	7.1	7.1	8.0	8.6	9.0	9.5	9.6	9.5	9.5	9.4	9.1	8.7
2012	8.2	7.8	8.1	8.7	8.9	9.2	9.5	9.6	9.4	9.3	9.2	8.9	8.9
2013	8.2	8.0	8.1	8.7	9.3	9.8	10.0	10.1	9.8	9.6	9.4	9.0	9.2
2014	8.3	8.1	8.2	8.9	9.5	10.0	10.3	10.3	10.2	10.3	10.2	9.7	9.5
2015	8.9	8.5	8.6	9.4	10.2	10.5	10.7	10.7	10.4	10.7	10.6	10.3	10.0
2016	9.5	9.2	9.5	10.1	10.6	11.0	11.3	11.3	11.2	11.3	11.1	11.0	10.6
2017	10.0	9.5	9.7	10.5	11.1	11.5	11.8	11.9	11.7	11.8	11.6	11.2	11.0
2018	10.4	10.3	10.4	11.1	11.6	11.9	12.1	12.0	11.9	11.8	11.6	11.2	11.4
Manufacturing													
2010	28.3	28.1	28.1	28.3	28.4	28.6	28.3	28.4	28.4	28.4	28.6	28.6	28.4
2011	28.3	28.2	28.3	28.2	28.5	28.6	29.0	28.9	28.8	28.8	28.9	29.0	28.6
2012	27.8	27.8	27.8	27.7	27.7	27.8	27.6	27.5	27.5	27.7	27.5	27.0	27.6
2013	26.8	26.8	26.9	26.9	27.0	27.1	27.1	27.2	27.1	27.1	27.0	27.2	27.0
2014	27.2	27.0	27.2	27.0	27.1	27.2	27.2	27.1	27.0	27.4	27.4	27.4	27.2
2015	27.5	27.3	27.4	27.6	27.7	27.9	27.9	27.8	27.7	27.8	27.8	27.9	27.7
2016	27.7	27.7	27.8	27.9	27.9	28.3	28.0	28.0	27.8	27.4	27.6	27.7	27.8
2017	27.2	27.2	27.3	27.3	27.4	27.7	27.5	27.6	27.4	27.5	27.5	27.6	27.4
2018	27.5	27.5	27.6	27.7	27.8	28.1	28.2	28.0	27.8	27.8	28.0	28.1	27.8

Employment by Industry: Worcester, MA-CT, 2010–2018—*Continued*

(Numbers in thousands, not seasonally adjusted)

Industry and year	January	February	March	April	May	June	July	August	September	October	November	December	Annual average
Trade, Transportation, and Utilities													
2010	47.9	47.3	47.8	48.6	49.3	49.7	48.9	48.9	49.0	49.6	50.3	51.0	49.0
2011	49.2	48.7	48.8	49.0	49.3	49.3	48.8	48.8	49.4	50.5	51.2	51.9	49.6
2012	50.0	49.3	49.5	49.8	50.4	50.7	50.1	50.2	50.8	51.5	52.2	52.2	50.6
2013	50.5	49.8	50.1	50.9	51.8	52.4	51.3	51.4	51.7	52.2	53.3	53.7	51.6
2014	52.1	51.5	51.8	52.3	52.8	53.2	52.7	52.6	53.1	53.5	54.4	55.1	52.9
2015	52.2	51.3	51.6	52.1	52.7	53.1	52.4	52.6	52.6	53.2	54.1	54.7	52.7
2016	52.6	52.0	52.1	53.1	53.4	54.0	53.2	53.1	53.1	53.5	54.3	55.1	53.3
2017	53.4	52.7	52.7	53.0	53.5	54.0	53.3	53.4	53.2	53.6	54.3	54.8	53.5
2018	53.4	52.6	52.5	52.7	53.2	53.6	52.4	52.5	52.4	52.3	53.4	53.7	52.9
Wholesale Trade													
2010	10.4	10.3	10.3	10.3	10.3	10.3	10.1	10.0	9.9	10.1	10.0	9.9	10.2
2011	9.7	9.6	9.6	9.7	9.8	9.8	9.8	9.7	9.7	9.9	9.9	9.9	9.8
2012	9.9	9.8	9.9	10.0	10.1	10.2	10.2	10.2	10.2	10.5	10.5	10.3	10.2
2013	10.2	10.1	10.2	10.2	10.3	10.4	10.4	10.4	10.4	10.5	10.5	10.5	10.3
2014	10.4	10.3	10.4	10.5	10.6	10.7	10.7	10.7	10.6	10.6	10.6	10.5	10.6
2015	10.3	10.2	10.3	10.5	10.5	10.5	10.4	10.4	10.3	10.4	10.4	10.4	10.4
2016	10.2	10.2	10.2	10.4	10.4	10.5	10.5	10.5	10.4	10.5	10.4	10.4	10.4
2017	10.3	10.3	10.3	10.3	10.3	10.3	10.3	10.3	10.1	10.2	10.1	10.1	10.2
2018	10.1	10.0	10.0	10.0	10.0	10.0	9.7	9.7	9.5	9.5	9.5	9.5	9.8
Retail Trade													
2010	28.0	27.5	28.0	28.5	28.8	29.1	28.9	29.0	28.5	28.9	29.5	30.0	28.7
2011	29.0	28.5	28.5	28.8	28.9	29.0	28.9	29.0	29.1	29.8	30.4	30.9	29.2
2012	29.6	29.0	29.0	29.1	29.5	29.7	29.6	29.7	29.7	30.0	30.7	30.7	29.7
2013	29.5	28.9	29.0	29.6	30.3	30.5	30.0	30.1	29.9	30.3	31.1	31.3	30.0
2014	30.4	29.7	29.8	30.2	30.4	30.5	30.4	30.3	30.4	30.7	31.3	31.5	30.5
2015	30.2	29.4	29.5	29.8	30.3	30.6	30.3	30.5	30.0	30.5	31.1	31.3	30.3
2016	30.1	29.5	29.6	30.1	30.3	30.7	30.3	30.3	29.8	30.1	30.9	31.1	30.2
2017	30.1	29.5	29.5	29.8	30.1	30.5	30.2	30.3	29.8	30.1	30.7	30.9	30.1
2018	30.1	29.5	29.4	29.6	29.9	30.1	29.7	29.7	29.3	29.2	29.9	30.0	29.7
Transportation and Utilities													
2010	9.5	9.5	9.5	9.8	10.2	10.3	9.9	9.9	10.6	10.6	10.8	11.1	10.1
2011	10.5	10.6	10.7	10.5	10.6	10.5	10.1	10.1	10.6	10.8	10.9	11.1	10.6
2012	10.5	10.5	10.6	10.7	10.8	10.8	10.3	10.3	10.9	11.0	11.0	11.2	10.7
2013	10.8	10.8	10.9	11.1	11.2	11.5	10.9	10.9	11.4	11.4	11.7	11.9	11.2
2014	11.3	11.5	11.6	11.6	11.8	12.0	11.6	11.6	12.1	12.2	12.5	13.1	11.9
2015	11.7	11.7	11.8	11.8	11.9	12.0	11.7	11.7	12.3	12.3	12.6	13.0	12.0
2016	12.3	12.3	12.3	12.6	12.7	12.8	12.4	12.3	12.9	12.9	13.0	13.6	12.7
2017	13.0	12.9	12.9	12.9	13.1	13.2	12.8	12.8	13.3	13.3	13.5	13.8	13.1
2018	13.2	13.1	13.1	13.1	13.3	13.5	13.0	13.1	13.6	13.6	14.0	14.2	13.4
Information													
2010	3.4	3.6	3.6	3.6	3.7	3.7	3.6	3.6	3.5	3.6	3.6	3.6	3.6
2011	3.6	3.6	3.6	3.6	3.6	3.6	3.7	3.4	3.6	3.7	3.6	3.6	3.6
2012	3.6	3.6	3.6	3.6	3.7	3.7	3.7	3.8	3.7	3.6	3.7	3.7	3.7
2013	3.7	3.6	3.7	3.7	3.7	3.8	3.7	3.7	3.5	3.5	3.7	3.7	3.7
2014	3.7	3.7	3.7	3.6	3.7	3.8	3.8	3.8	3.7	3.7	3.7	3.8	3.7
2015	3.8	3.8	3.8	3.9	3.9	3.9	3.9	3.9	3.9	3.9	3.9	4.0	3.9
2016	4.0	4.0	3.9	3.9	3.7	4.0	4.0	3.9	3.8	3.8	3.7	3.7	3.9
2017	3.8	3.8	3.7	3.7	3.7	3.8	3.7	3.7	3.7	3.7	3.6	3.7	3.7
2018	3.6	3.6	3.6	3.6	3.6	3.6	3.6	3.6	3.4	3.4	3.4	3.4	3.5
Financial Activities													
2010	14.6	14.6	14.6	14.6	14.6	14.7	14.7	14.7	14.6	14.9	14.8	14.9	14.7
2011	14.7	14.7	14.7	14.7	14.7	14.7	14.9	14.9	14.9	15.0	15.0	15.0	14.8
2012	14.9	14.9	14.9	14.9	15.0	15.0	15.1	15.0	14.9	15.0	14.9	14.9	15.0
2013	14.8	14.8	14.8	14.8	14.8	15.0	14.9	14.9	14.8	14.8	14.8	14.8	14.8
2014	14.7	14.7	14.8	14.9	15.0	15.1	15.2	15.2	15.0	15.0	15.0	15.0	15.0
2015	14.8	14.8	14.8	14.9	15.0	15.0	15.2	15.2	14.9	15.0	14.9	14.9	15.0
2016	14.8	14.8	14.7	14.8	14.9	15.0	15.0	15.0	14.8	14.8	14.8	14.8	14.9
2017	14.7	14.7	14.6	14.8	14.9	15.1	14.9	14.9	14.7	14.7	14.6	14.6	14.8
2018	14.5	14.5	14.5	14.6	14.7	14.8	14.9	14.9	14.7	14.7	14.5	14.6	14.7

Employment by Industry: Worcester, MA-CT, 2010–2018—*Continued*

(Numbers in thousands, not seasonally adjusted)

Industry and year	January	February	March	April	May	June	July	August	September	October	November	December	Annual average
Professional and Business Services													
2010	25.3	24.9	25.2	25.7	26.1	26.4	26.5	26.5	26.3	26.4	26.1	26.6	26.0
2011	26.9	27.0	26.7	27.9	27.5	27.6	27.7	27.3	27.3	27.1	27.9	26.8	27.3
2012	25.8	25.4	25.8	26.1	26.0	26.5	26.4	26.5	26.0	26.3	26.2	25.9	26.1
2013	25.3	25.3	25.6	26.1	26.4	26.5	26.2	26.4	26.0	26.1	25.9	25.5	25.9
2014	25.4	25.5	25.5	26.4	26.5	26.8	26.3	26.5	26.4	26.5	26.4	26.1	26.2
2015	25.8	25.8	25.6	26.0	26.3	26.6	26.8	27.0	26.9	27.0	27.2	27.2	26.5
2016	26.1	26.4	26.4	27.5	27.8	28.1	28.4	28.4	28.3	28.4	28.4	28.2	27.7
2017	27.1	27.6	27.8	27.9	27.9	28.4	28.8	28.9	29.1	28.5	28.6	28.5	28.3
2018	27.5	27.7	28.1	27.7	28.1	28.5	28.1	28.4	28.2	28.2	28.6	28.3	28.1
Education and Health Services													
2010	57.3	58.6	58.4	58.2	57.8	56.8	56.9	57.1	58.6	59.4	59.8	59.7	58.2
2011	58.5	59.5	59.9	59.4	59.0	57.9	58.4	58.4	59.8	60.4	60.6	60.7	59.4
2012	60.0	61.0	61.6	61.4	61.1	60.6	60.7	60.6	61.9	62.7	63.0	63.0	61.5
2013	62.3	62.9	63.4	62.7	62.6	62.1	61.3	61.5	62.2	62.9	63.1	63.4	62.5
2014	61.9	62.9	63.6	64.1	63.8	63.2	62.8	62.9	63.8	64.8	65.0	65.0	63.7
2015	63.6	64.5	65.0	65.4	65.7	65.0	64.2	64.1	65.5	66.7	67.0	66.9	65.3
2016	65.0	65.9	66.2	66.7	66.6	65.3	65.3	65.2	66.8	67.6	67.7	67.6	66.3
2017	66.1	67.6	68.1	68.4	68.4	67.3	66.8	66.7	68.2	68.7	68.9	69.1	67.9
2018	66.5	68.5	68.5	68.8	68.7	67.5	67.1	67.3	68.3	68.9	69.4	68.8	68.2
Leisure and Hospitality													
2010	21.2	20.9	20.6	21.7	22.8	23.1	23.0	23.1	22.4	22.6	21.8	21.8	22.1
2011	21.2	21.2	21.4	22.4	23.0	23.5	23.4	23.4	23.0	22.9	22.2	22.4	22.5
2012	22.0	21.9	22.3	22.5	23.3	24.3	24.1	24.0	23.5	23.1	22.4	22.4	23.0
2013	22.2	21.9	22.2	23.1	23.9	24.7	24.0	24.3	23.9	24.0	23.3	23.0	23.4
2014	22.8	22.5	22.9	23.6	24.3	25.1	24.8	24.9	24.3	24.7	23.9	23.8	24.0
2015	23.4	23.0	23.5	24.3	25.4	25.7	25.3	25.5	24.6	24.4	23.8	23.8	24.4
2016	23.4	23.4	23.5	24.5	25.5	26.1	26.5	26.4	25.8	25.3	24.7	24.2	24.9
2017	24.2	23.9	24.5	24.9	25.8	26.9	26.6	26.7	25.8	26.0	25.6	25.5	25.5
2018	24.7	24.6	24.9	25.4	26.1	26.8	26.2	26.3	25.6	25.9	25.1	24.9	25.5
Other Services													
2010	8.4	8.5	8.4	8.6	8.7	8.9	9.2	9.1	8.6	8.6	8.7	8.6	8.7
2011	8.5	8.6	8.8	8.9	8.9	9.1	9.2	9.1	8.8	8.8	8.8	8.9	8.9
2012	8.8	8.8	8.8	9.0	9.1	9.4	9.6	9.6	9.3	9.5	9.6	9.7	9.3
2013	9.7	9.5	9.7	9.9	10.0	10.4	10.7	10.6	10.1	10.1	10.1	10.2	10.1
2014	10.0	10.0	10.1	10.3	10.4	10.7	10.9	10.9	10.3	10.3	10.3	10.4	10.4
2015	10.3	10.1	10.3	10.4	10.6	10.9	11.2	11.2	10.5	10.6	10.6	10.6	10.6
2016	10.4	10.4	10.7	10.8	10.9	11.3	11.4	11.4	10.8	10.7	10.8	10.8	10.9
2017	10.5	10.5	10.7	10.7	10.9	11.2	11.4	11.4	10.8	10.9	10.9	10.9	10.9
2018	10.5	10.5	10.7	10.8	10.8	11.2	11.3	11.3	10.8	10.8	10.8	10.9	10.9
Government													
2010	41.5	41.8	41.9	42.1	43.0	42.0	38.0	37.8	41.0	41.7	42.1	42.3	41.3
2011	40.9	41.6	41.8	41.8	42.0	41.1	37.9	37.2	40.7	41.5	41.5	41.6	40.8
2012	40.6	41.4	41.9	41.4	41.5	41.3	37.9	37.8	41.4	41.9	42.4	42.5	41.0
2013	41.1	42.5	42.6	43.8	43.6	41.7	37.9	38.3	42.2	43.3	43.9	44.2	42.1
2014	42.0	43.9	44.0	44.7	44.3	42.2	38.5	38.6	43.0	44.0	44.9	44.7	42.9
2015	42.0	43.9	44.4	44.7	44.5	43.3	38.6	38.2	42.5	44.0	44.5	44.6	42.9
2016	42.1	44.0	44.6	44.4	44.5	42.9	39.3	39.0	43.4	44.0	45.3	44.6	43.2
2017	42.7	44.2	44.3	44.5	44.7	43.0	39.0	38.9	43.7	44.9	45.3	45.6	43.4
2018	43.3	45.0	44.9	45.1	45.1	43.8	39.5	39.5	43.9	45.0	45.7	45.6	43.9

Employment by Industry: Bridgeport-Stamford-Norwalk, CT NECTA, 2010–2018

(Numbers in thousands, not seasonally adjusted)

Industry and year	January	February	March	April	May	June	July	August	September	October	November	December	Annual average
Total Nonfarm													
2010	377.1	377.0	379.8	385.8	392.9	395.3	395.2	391.1	391.2	393.0	394.2	396.4	389.1
2011	383.4	385.3	386.8	392.7	395.0	396.9	397.0	393.0	394.8	396.4	397.6	400.0	393.2
2012	389.1	389.5	393.0	395.7	399.0	403.3	401.8	398.2	398.9	400.1	401.9	404.7	397.9
2013	392.0	391.1	394.9	400.7	404.1	409.4	407.3	403.6	404.2	405.2	407.4	407.6	402.3
2014	395.7	394.6	397.9	403.7	407.6	410.4	409.1	406.8	406.9	409.4	412.5	413.8	405.7
2015	401.2	399.6	401.1	406.6	412.1	417.0	413.0	410.0	409.7	413.7	415.6	416.5	409.7
2016	403.6	402.5	405.7	408.7	412.6	417.7	415.5	411.3	410.8	411.8	413.0	412.5	410.5
2017	401.4	399.5	401.6	404.4	409.2	415.4	412.7	408.1	408.1	408.5	410.9	411.8	407.6
2018	400.0	400.5	401.8	404.6	410.2	416.5	412.2	407.4	408.3	408.9	413.0	413.6	408.1
Total Private													
2010	332.9	331.5	334.1	340.9	345.6	350.1	351.6	349.6	346.6	347.8	348.7	350.8	344.2
2011	339.8	340.0	341.5	346.8	349.6	353.2	355.8	353.2	350.3	350.9	352.1	354.4	349.0
2012	345.7	344.8	348.0	350.6	354.2	359.7	359.5	357.2	354.1	354.9	356.3	359.2	353.7
2013	348.1	346.1	349.6	355.5	359.2	364.6	364.4	362.2	359.5	359.8	361.5	362.0	357.7
2014	352.1	349.9	352.8	358.0	362.0	366.1	366.7	364.4	361.8	363.5	366.0	367.8	360.9
2015	357.1	354.8	356.1	361.1	366.8	371.6	370.3	368.0	364.7	368.2	369.7	371.0	365.0
2016	359.6	357.7	360.7	363.7	367.3	372.8	373.0	369.9	366.3	367.0	367.7	367.8	366.1
2017	357.7	354.9	356.8	360.1	364.4	370.9	370.7	367.0	364.1	364.0	366.3	367.7	363.7
2018	356.7	356.4	357.5	360.8	365.5	372.0	370.2	366.2	363.9	364.2	368.1	369.2	364.2
Goods Producing													
2010	42.5	42.1	42.4	43.6	44.1	44.9	45.2	45.1	44.7	44.5	44.1	43.7	43.9
2011	42.6	42.5	42.8	43.7	44.3	44.8	44.8	44.6	44.2	44.1	43.9	43.9	43.9
2012	42.6	42.5	42.4	42.6	42.9	43.7	43.6	43.4	42.9	42.8	42.8	42.8	42.9
2013	41.5	41.3	41.3	42.2	42.7	43.4	43.1	43.1	42.9	42.8	42.8	42.4	42.5
2014	41.1	40.9	41.0	41.8	42.2	42.6	42.6	42.5	42.1	42.5	42.3	41.9	42.0
2015	40.6	40.1	40.2	41.2	42.1	42.6	42.5	42.5	42.3	42.4	42.2	41.9	41.7
2016	40.7	40.5	40.8	41.5	42.0	42.5	42.6	42.5	42.0	42.0	41.8	41.4	41.7
2017	40.5	40.2	40.3	41.4	41.9	42.6	42.5	42.3	41.8	41.9	41.7	41.5	41.6
2018	39.8	39.9	39.9	40.9	41.6	42.4	42.5	42.3	41.8	41.6	41.7	41.6	41.3
Service-Providing													
2010	334.6	334.9	337.4	342.2	348.8	350.4	350.0	346.0	346.5	348.5	350.1	352.7	345.2
2011	340.8	342.8	344.0	349.0	350.7	352.1	352.2	348.4	350.6	352.3	353.7	356.1	349.4
2012	346.5	347.0	350.6	353.1	356.1	359.6	358.2	354.8	356.0	357.3	359.1	361.9	355.0
2013	350.5	349.8	353.6	358.5	361.4	366.0	364.2	360.5	361.3	362.4	364.6	365.2	359.8
2014	354.6	353.7	356.9	361.9	365.4	367.8	366.5	364.3	364.8	366.9	370.2	371.9	363.7
2015	360.6	359.5	360.9	365.4	370.0	374.4	370.5	367.5	367.4	371.3	373.4	374.6	368.0
2016	362.9	362.0	364.9	367.2	370.6	375.2	372.9	368.8	368.8	369.8	371.2	371.1	368.8
2017	360.9	359.3	361.3	363.0	367.3	372.8	370.2	365.8	366.3	366.6	369.2	370.3	366.1
2018	360.2	360.6	361.9	363.7	368.6	374.1	369.7	365.1	366.5	367.3	371.3	372.0	366.8
Mining, Logging, and Construction													
2010	9.5	9.2	9.5	10.7	11.0	11.4	11.7	11.7	11.5	11.4	11.2	10.8	10.8
2011	9.7	9.6	9.8	10.8	11.3	11.6	11.8	11.8	11.7	11.7	11.6	11.4	11.1
2012	10.4	10.3	10.5	11.2	11.5	11.9	12.1	11.9	11.7	11.6	11.6	11.5	11.4
2013	10.5	10.2	10.3	11.3	11.7	12.0	12.2	12.3	12.2	12.1	12.1	11.6	11.5
2014	10.4	10.2	10.5	11.6	12.2	12.5	12.7	12.7	12.6	12.7	12.6	12.2	11.9
2015	11.0	10.6	10.7	11.9	12.6	12.8	12.8	12.9	12.9	13.0	12.8	12.5	12.2
2016	11.4	11.1	11.5	12.3	12.7	12.9	13.0	13.0	12.9	12.9	12.7	12.2	12.4
2017	11.2	11.0	11.1	12.3	12.8	13.2	13.2	13.2	13.1	13.1	12.9	12.4	12.5
2018	11.1	11.1	11.3	12.2	12.8	13.2	13.2	13.2	13.0	12.8	12.9	12.7	12.5
Manufacturing													
2010	33.0	32.9	32.9	32.9	33.1	33.5	33.5	33.4	33.2	33.1	32.9	32.9	33.1
2011	32.9	32.9	33.0	32.9	33.0	33.2	33.0	32.8	32.5	32.4	32.3	32.5	32.8
2012	32.2	32.2	31.9	31.4	31.4	31.8	31.5	31.5	31.2	31.2	31.2	31.3	31.6
2013	31.0	31.1	31.0	30.9	31.0	31.4	30.9	30.8	30.7	30.7	30.7	30.8	30.9
2014	30.7	30.7	30.5	30.2	30.0	30.1	29.9	29.8	29.5	29.8	29.7	29.7	30.1
2015	29.6	29.5	29.5	29.3	29.5	29.8	29.7	29.6	29.4	29.4	29.4	29.4	29.5
2016	29.3	29.4	29.3	29.2	29.3	29.6	29.6	29.5	29.1	29.1	29.1	29.2	29.3
2017	29.3	29.2	29.2	29.1	29.1	29.4	29.3	29.1	28.7	28.8	28.8	29.1	29.1
2018	28.7	28.8	28.6	28.7	28.8	29.2	29.3	29.1	28.8	28.8	28.8	28.9	28.9

Employment by Industry: Bridgeport-Stamford-Norwalk, CT NECTA, 2010–2018—*Continued*

(Numbers in thousands, not seasonally adjusted)

Industry and year	January	February	March	April	May	June	July	August	September	October	November	December	Annual average
Trade, Transportation, and Utilities													
2010	67.5	66.3	66.5	66.7	68.3	69.5	68.4	68.2	68.2	69.1	70.9	72.6	68.5
2011	69.0	68.0	67.8	68.7	69.2	69.9	69.0	68.6	68.4	69.0	70.7	72.6	69.2
2012	69.8	68.2	68.7	68.5	69.4	70.3	69.0	68.8	68.8	69.5	71.4	72.7	69.6
2013	70.0	68.5	69.1	69.4	69.9	70.7	69.7	69.6	69.7	70.3	72.1	73.6	70.2
2014	70.8	69.3	69.5	69.6	70.2	71.0	69.8	69.5	69.8	70.7	72.6	74.1	70.6
2015	70.9	69.4	69.6	69.5	70.6	71.5	70.0	69.8	70.3	71.4	73.3	74.8	70.9
2016	71.0	69.7	70.1	70.2	71.1	71.5	70.3	69.7	70.4	70.7	72.5	73.8	70.9
2017	71.1	69.5	69.4	69.4	70.3	71.1	69.8	69.2	69.7	70.2	72.4	73.7	70.5
2018	70.0	68.7	68.6	68.1	69.7	70.4	68.7	68.3	69.0	69.8	72.3	73.9	69.8
Wholesale Trade													
2010	12.7	12.7	12.8	12.9	13.0	13.2	13.1	13.1	13.0	13.0	13.1	13.2	13.0
2011	13.0	13.0	13.0	13.2	13.2	13.3	13.3	13.3	13.1	13.1	13.0	13.1	13.1
2012	12.9	12.9	13.0	12.9	12.9	13.1	13.1	13.1	13.0	13.1	13.1	13.1	13.0
2013	13.0	13.0	13.1	13.1	13.1	13.2	13.3	13.2	13.1	13.2	13.2	13.3	13.2
2014	13.2	13.2	13.2	13.2	13.2	13.3	13.2	13.2	13.1	13.1	13.1	13.2	13.2
2015	13.0	13.0	13.1	13.1	13.2	13.3	13.2	13.2	13.1	13.2	13.1	13.1	13.1
2016	12.8	12.8	12.9	13.0	13.2	13.3	13.3	13.2	13.1	13.1	13.1	13.2	13.1
2017	13.0	13.0	13.0	13.0	13.0	13.4	13.4	13.5	13.4	13.4	13.4	13.6	13.3
2018	13.3	13.4	13.5	13.5	13.5	13.7	13.7	13.7	13.6	13.6	13.6	13.6	13.6
Retail Trade													
2010	45.6	44.4	44.5	44.8	45.9	46.7	46.4	46.2	45.6	46.5	48.0	49.2	46.2
2011	46.4	45.4	45.2	45.8	46.2	46.7	46.4	46.2	45.6	46.2	47.9	49.3	46.4
2012	47.1	45.5	45.9	45.8	46.5	47.2	46.7	46.6	46.1	46.6	48.4	49.3	46.8
2013	47.3	46.0	46.3	46.5	47.0	47.6	47.2	47.3	46.6	47.2	48.9	50.0	47.3
2014	47.7	46.3	46.5	46.7	47.2	47.9	47.5	47.3	46.9	47.7	49.3	50.3	47.6
2015	47.9	46.7	46.8	46.7	47.5	48.2	47.4	47.5	47.1	48.0	49.8	50.8	47.9
2016	48.2	47.0	47.2	47.2	47.7	48.1	47.7	47.4	47.0	47.4	48.9	49.7	47.8
2017	48.1	46.7	46.6	46.8	47.4	47.8	47.6	47.2	46.6	47.1	49.0	49.6	47.5
2018	47.3	46.0	45.8	46.0	46.8	47.2	46.5	46.3	46.1	46.8	49.0	50.0	47.0
Transportation and Utilities													
2010	9.2	9.2	9.2	9.0	9.4	9.6	8.9	8.9	9.6	9.6	9.8	10.2	9.4
2011	9.6	9.6	9.6	9.7	9.8	9.9	9.3	9.1	9.7	9.7	9.8	10.2	9.7
2012	9.8	9.8	9.8	9.8	10.0	10.0	9.2	9.1	9.7	9.8	9.9	10.3	9.8
2013	9.7	9.5	9.7	9.8	9.8	9.9	9.2	9.1	10.0	9.9	10.0	10.3	9.7
2014	9.9	9.8	9.8	9.7	9.8	9.8	9.1	9.0	9.8	9.9	10.2	10.6	9.8
2015	10.0	9.7	9.7	9.7	9.9	10.0	9.4	9.1	10.1	10.2	10.4	10.9	9.9
2016	10.0	9.9	10.0	10.0	10.2	10.1	9.3	9.1	10.3	10.2	10.5	10.9	10.0
2017	10.0	9.8	9.8	9.6	9.9	9.9	8.8	8.5	9.7	9.7	10.0	10.5	9.7
2018	9.4	9.3	9.3	8.6	9.4	9.5	8.5	8.3	9.3	9.4	9.7	10.3	9.3
Information													
2010	10.3	10.2	10.3	10.4	10.4	10.3	10.2	10.3	10.2	10.2	10.2	10.4	10.3
2011	10.3	10.3	10.3	10.3	10.3	10.3	10.5	10.5	10.4	10.4	10.5	10.7	10.4
2012	10.6	10.6	10.5	10.6	10.5	10.6	10.6	10.7	10.6	10.6	10.7	10.8	10.6
2013	10.9	11.2	11.2	11.1	11.3	11.5	11.7	11.5	11.5	11.4	11.5	11.5	11.4
2014	11.4	11.4	11.5	11.5	11.5	11.5	11.6	11.6	11.5	11.4	12.1	12.2	11.6
2015	12.0	12.0	12.0	12.1	12.1	12.2	12.2	12.3	12.2	12.2	12.3	12.3	12.2
2016	12.4	12.4	12.4	12.5	12.5	12.6	12.8	13.2	12.8	12.8	12.8	12.4	12.6
2017	12.1	12.3	12.3	12.3	12.0	12.3	12.3	12.3	12.2	12.3	12.5	12.5	12.3
2018	12.8	12.9	12.8	12.8	12.7	12.8	12.8	12.9	12.8	12.9	13.1	13.2	12.9
Financial Activities													
2010	42.0	42.0	42.1	42.1	42.2	42.9	43.1	43.2	42.5	42.4	42.4	42.7	42.5
2011	42.4	42.4	42.4	42.4	42.3	42.3	43.2	43.0	42.1	42.1	42.1	42.1	42.4
2012	41.7	41.6	41.6	41.5	41.6	42.2	42.3	42.0	41.4	41.5	41.4	41.5	41.7
2013	41.4	41.2	41.2	41.1	41.3	41.9	42.1	41.9	41.4	41.3	41.4	41.5	41.5
2014	40.3	40.2	40.3	40.2	40.4	41.1	41.4	41.3	40.8	40.9	41.0	41.3	40.8
2015	40.9	40.9	41.0	41.0	41.1	41.8	41.9	41.7	41.0	41.1	41.1	41.2	41.2
2016	41.0	40.8	41.0	40.8	40.8	41.2	41.4	41.1	40.5	40.6	40.7	40.6	40.9
2017	40.2	39.9	39.9	39.8	39.9	40.4	40.6	40.3	39.6	39.6	39.4	39.6	39.9
2018	39.1	38.9	38.9	38.5	38.5	39.2	39.3	39.0	38.5	39.2	39.6	39.8	39.0

Employment by Industry: Bridgeport-Stamford-Norwalk, CT NECTA, 2010–2018—*Continued*

(Numbers in thousands, not seasonally adjusted)

Industry and year	January	February	March	April	May	June	July	August	September	October	November	December	Annual average
Professional and Business Services													
2010	61.5	61.9	62.8	65.3	65.5	66.3	66.8	66.6	66.4	66.7	66.2	66.0	65.2
2011	63.9	64.6	65.1	66.6	66.9	67.4	68.0	67.6	67.3	67.5	67.4	67.2	66.6
2012	65.7	65.8	67.2	68.5	68.7	69.4	69.6	69.4	68.9	68.4	68.2	68.0	68.2
2013	65.3	65.5	66.0	68.1	68.6	69.5	69.6	69.8	69.0	68.9	68.5	67.9	68.1
2014	65.6	65.7	66.1	68.2	68.7	69.2	69.5	69.5	68.7	68.6	68.8	68.3	68.1
2015	66.2	66.2	66.1	68.1	68.8	69.3	69.5	69.6	68.6	69.9	69.9	69.4	68.5
2016	66.7	66.5	67.1	68.5	68.4	69.5	69.4	69.0	68.1	68.0	67.4	67.1	68.0
2017	64.1	63.8	64.2	65.0	65.3	66.3	66.4	66.4	65.9	65.9	66.0	65.8	65.4
2018	63.5	63.5	63.9	65.5	66.0	67.2	66.9	66.7	65.9	65.5	65.7	65.6	65.5
Education and Health Services													
2010	63.7	64.0	64.2	65.0	65.1	64.3	64.7	63.8	64.7	65.6	66.1	66.3	64.8
2011	65.2	65.7	65.9	66.2	66.1	65.6	65.6	64.9	65.9	66.3	66.9	67.1	66.0
2012	66.5	67.1	67.5	67.5	67.5	67.2	67.0	66.4	67.5	68.2	68.5	69.3	67.5
2013	67.6	67.7	68.4	69.3	69.3	69.0	68.4	67.5	68.6	69.4	69.9	69.4	68.7
2014	69.4	69.4	69.9	70.5	70.9	70.2	70.4	69.4	70.6	71.3	71.6	72.0	70.5
2015	71.3	71.3	71.5	71.7	72.2	71.9	71.1	70.3	70.9	72.2	72.5	72.4	71.6
2016	71.6	71.8	72.0	71.9	72.3	71.9	71.8	71.1	72.2	73.0	73.2	73.3	72.2
2017	72.7	72.9	73.1	73.7	74.2	73.9	73.6	72.7	74.0	73.8	74.3	74.4	73.6
2018	73.4	74.8	74.9	75.2	75.2	74.8	74.4	73.1	74.5	74.9	75.3	74.9	74.6
Leisure and Hospitality													
2010	29.9	29.6	30.2	32.1	34.0	35.5	36.5	35.7	34.0	33.4	32.8	33.1	33.1
2011	30.7	30.8	31.4	33.0	34.4	36.6	37.9	37.4	36.0	35.6	34.6	34.7	34.4
2012	32.8	32.9	34.0	35.2	37.2	39.5	40.3	39.6	37.7	37.5	36.8	37.6	36.8
2013	35.3	34.7	36.2	37.9	39.5	41.7	42.6	41.7	39.8	39.1	38.8	39.1	38.9
2014	37.1	36.7	38.0	39.6	41.2	43.4	44.0	43.3	41.5	41.2	40.6	40.8	40.6
2015	38.3	38.0	38.8	40.6	42.7	44.8	45.4	44.1	42.0	41.6	41.1	41.5	41.6
2016	39.0	38.8	40.0	40.9	42.6	45.3	46.2	45.1	42.7	42.3	41.7	41.6	42.2
2017	39.6	39.0	40.1	40.9	42.9	45.9	46.8	45.5	43.1	42.6	42.3	42.4	42.6
2018	40.7	40.4	41.1	42.1	44.0	46.8	47.1	45.7	43.8	42.9	42.8	42.9	43.4
Other Services													
2010	15.5	15.4	15.6	15.7	16.0	16.4	16.7	16.7	15.9	15.9	16.0	16.0	16.0
2011	15.7	15.7	15.8	15.9	16.1	16.3	16.8	16.6	16.0	15.9	16.0	16.1	16.1
2012	16.0	16.1	16.1	16.2	16.4	16.8	17.1	16.9	16.3	16.4	16.4	16.5	16.4
2013	16.1	16.0	16.2	16.4	16.6	16.9	17.2	17.1	16.6	16.6	16.6	16.6	16.6
2014	16.4	16.3	16.5	16.6	16.9	17.1	17.4	17.3	16.8	16.9	17.0	17.2	16.9
2015	16.9	16.9	16.9	16.9	17.2	17.5	17.7	17.7	17.4	17.4	17.3	17.5	17.3
2016	17.2	17.2	17.3	17.4	17.6	18.3	18.5	18.2	17.6	17.6	17.6	17.6	17.7
2017	17.4	17.3	17.5	17.6	17.9	18.4	18.7	18.3	17.8	17.7	17.7	17.8	17.8
2018	17.4	17.3	17.4	17.7	17.8	18.4	18.5	18.2	17.6	17.4	17.6	17.3	17.7
Government													
2010	44.2	45.5	45.7	44.9	47.3	45.2	43.6	41.5	44.6	45.2	45.5	45.6	44.9
2011	43.6	45.3	45.3	45.9	45.4	43.7	41.2	39.8	44.5	45.5	45.5	45.6	44.3
2012	43.4	44.7	45.0	45.1	44.8	43.6	42.3	41.0	44.8	45.2	45.6	45.5	44.3
2013	43.9	45.0	45.3	45.2	44.9	44.8	42.9	41.4	44.7	45.4	45.8	45.6	44.6
2014	43.6	44.7	45.1	45.7	45.6	44.3	42.4	42.4	45.1	45.9	46.5	46.0	44.8
2015	44.1	44.8	45.0	45.5	45.3	45.4	42.7	42.0	45.0	45.5	45.9	45.5	44.7
2016	44.0	44.8	45.0	45.0	44.9	44.9	42.5	41.4	44.5	44.8	45.3	44.7	44.4
2017	43.7	44.6	44.8	44.3	44.8	44.5	42.0	41.1	44.0	44.5	44.6	44.1	43.9
2018	43.3	44.1	44.3	43.8	44.7	44.5	42.0	41.2	44.4	44.7	44.9	44.4	43.9

Employment by Industry: Omaha-Council Bluffs, NE-IA, 2010–2018

(Numbers in thousands, not seasonally adjusted)

Industry and year	January	February	March	April	May	June	July	August	September	October	November	December	Annual average
Total Nonfarm													
2010	448.0	447.4	451.0	458.6	463.4	464.7	461.1	462.0	458.7	464.3	465.0	464.9	459.1
2011	453.2	453.8	455.9	463.9	467.3	467.9	464.8	465.8	464.4	467.6	469.8	469.4	463.7
2012	459.7	459.7	463.6	468.7	473.3	472.6	471.3	471.2	470.2	473.9	476.6	475.9	469.7
2013	465.7	466.2	468.4	473.9	480.3	480.6	478.6	480.4	480.0	483.4	486.1	485.5	477.4
2014	474.7	476.4	478.4	482.8	487.9	487.3	484.2	486.3	485.5	489.3	491.1	492.2	484.7
2015	480.0	481.1	484.4	490.9	495.2	496.0	493.7	495.2	493.2	498.8	499.4	500.4	492.4
2016	485.9	487.0	491.4	496.9	500.6	500.6	499.7	498.9	499.9	502.4	502.0	501.9	497.3
2017	490.5	492.9	495.6	499.7	503.0	504.0	499.0	499.0	499.1	502.9	505.0	504.3	499.6
2018	492.0	493.7	496.7	501.3	507.5	507.5	502.3	502.8	502.4	505.7	508.4	508.4	502.4
Total Private													
2010	383.5	382.6	385.2	392.1	396.1	398.2	398.5	399.0	395.0	397.9	398.6	399.2	393.8
2011	387.8	387.8	390.5	397.1	400.3	402.7	401.7	402.0	399.8	401.1	403.1	403.5	398.1
2012	393.9	393.5	397.9	402.7	406.8	409.5	408.7	408.1	405.9	408.1	410.7	410.9	404.7
2013	400.9	400.8	403.3	408.2	413.9	415.8	415.5	417.0	415.6	417.7	420.2	420.5	412.5
2014	409.4	410.4	412.9	416.7	421.1	422.9	421.2	422.5	420.1	422.5	424.3	426.2	419.2
2015	414.3	415.0	418.6	424.1	427.9	430.5	430.1	431.0	428.2	431.9	432.3	433.7	426.5
2016	419.8	420.4	424.8	429.7	432.8	434.2	436.3	436.0	433.8	435.1	434.8	435.5	431.1
2017	424.3	426.3	429.3	432.5	435.4	437.6	436.5	436.5	433.0	435.4	437.6	437.7	433.5
2018	425.2	426.5	429.7	433.9	439.6	441.1	439.6	439.4	436.0	438.3	440.4	440.9	435.9
Goods Producing													
2010	50.4	49.9	50.4	52.4	52.9	53.3	53.5	53.2	52.5	52.3	52.2	51.3	52.0
2011	49.0	49.0	49.8	51.0	51.6	52.6	52.7	52.4	51.8	52.1	52.1	52.0	51.3
2012	49.9	49.5	50.6	51.7	52.5	53.3	53.6	53.5	53.4	53.6	53.7	53.5	52.4
2013	51.6	52.0	52.4	54.0	55.4	56.0	56.9	56.9	56.7	56.5	56.3	55.0	55.0
2014	53.3	53.4	53.9	56.2	56.9	57.9	58.3	58.5	58.3	58.4	58.1	57.8	56.8
2015	55.8	56.0	56.9	58.7	59.0	59.4	59.6	59.4	59.1	59.9	59.2	58.4	58.5
2016	56.2	56.1	57.5	58.9	59.5	60.2	60.6	60.6	60.2	60.2	59.8	59.0	59.1
2017	57.5	58.3	59.3	60.1	60.6	61.4	61.7	61.5	61.2	61.7	61.8	61.5	60.6
2018	59.0	59.4	60.6	62.3	63.2	64.0	64.4	64.2	63.8	63.4	63.4	62.9	62.6
Service-Providing													
2010	397.6	397.5	400.6	406.2	410.5	411.4	407.6	408.8	406.2	412.0	412.8	413.6	407.1
2011	404.2	404.8	406.1	412.9	415.7	415.3	412.1	413.4	412.6	415.5	417.7	417.4	412.3
2012	409.8	410.2	413.0	417.0	420.8	419.3	417.7	417.7	416.8	420.3	422.9	422.4	417.3
2013	414.1	414.2	416.0	419.9	424.9	424.6	421.7	423.5	423.3	426.9	429.8	430.5	422.5
2014	421.4	423.0	424.5	426.6	431.0	429.4	425.9	427.8	427.2	430.9	433.0	434.4	427.9
2015	424.2	425.1	427.5	432.2	436.2	436.6	434.1	435.8	434.1	438.9	440.2	442.0	433.9
2016	429.7	430.9	433.9	438.0	441.1	440.4	439.1	438.3	439.7	442.2	442.2	442.9	438.2
2017	433.0	434.6	436.3	439.6	442.4	442.6	437.3	437.5	437.9	441.2	443.2	442.8	439.0
2018	433.0	434.3	436.1	439.0	444.3	443.5	437.9	438.6	438.6	442.3	445.0	445.5	439.8
Mining, Logging, and Construction													
2010	19.4	19.0	19.4	21.4	21.7	22.0	22.1	22.0	21.4	21.1	21.0	20.0	20.9
2011	18.2	18.0	18.7	19.7	20.3	21.2	21.3	21.3	21.0	21.0	20.8	20.1	20.1
2012	19.0	18.6	19.5	20.6	21.3	21.8	22.0	22.1	22.0	22.4	22.2	21.9	21.1
2013	20.3	20.4	20.8	22.2	23.2	23.6	24.3	24.3	24.1	24.0	23.6	22.4	22.8
2014	21.1	21.0	21.6	23.7	24.4	25.3	25.5	25.8	25.7	25.8	25.4	25.0	24.2
2015	23.4	23.5	24.4	26.1	26.4	26.6	26.7	26.6	26.4	27.0	26.4	25.6	25.8
2016	23.8	23.7	24.9	26.2	26.8	27.5	27.9	27.9	27.6	27.5	27.3	26.3	26.5
2017	25.0	25.5	26.5	27.1	27.5	28.1	28.1	27.9	27.7	28.1	28.1	27.5	27.3
2018	25.5	25.6	26.7	28.4	29.2	29.9	30.3	30.1	29.8	29.6	29.6	29.0	28.6
Manufacturing													
2010	31.0	30.9	31.0	31.0	31.2	31.3	31.4	31.2	31.1	31.2	31.2	31.3	31.2
2011	30.8	31.0	31.1	31.3	31.3	31.4	31.4	31.1	30.8	31.1	31.3	31.9	31.2
2012	30.9	30.9	31.1	31.1	31.2	31.5	31.6	31.4	31.4	31.2	31.5	31.6	31.3
2013	31.3	31.6	31.6	31.8	32.2	32.4	32.6	32.6	32.6	32.5	32.7	32.6	32.2
2014	32.2	32.4	32.3	32.5	32.5	32.6	32.8	32.7	32.6	32.6	32.7	32.8	32.6
2015	32.4	32.5	32.5	32.6	32.6	32.8	32.9	32.8	32.7	32.9	32.8	32.8	32.7
2016	32.4	32.4	32.6	32.7	32.7	32.7	32.7	32.7	32.6	32.7	32.5	32.7	32.6
2017	32.5	32.8	32.8	33.0	33.1	33.3	33.6	33.6	33.5	33.6	33.7	34.0	33.3
2018	33.5	33.8	33.9	33.9	34.0	34.1	34.1	34.1	34.0	33.8	33.8	33.9	33.9

Employment by Industry: Omaha-Council Bluffs, NE-IA, 2010–2018—*Continued*

(Numbers in thousands, not seasonally adjusted)

Industry and year	January	February	March	April	May	June	July	August	September	October	November	December	Annual average
Trade, Transportation, and Utilities													
2010	92.1	91.3	91.9	93.0	94.1	93.9	93.4	93.5	92.9	94.2	96.3	98.1	93.7
2011	92.6	91.9	92.4	93.1	93.6	93.3	93.0	93.5	93.5	93.9	96.6	97.5	93.7
2012	92.9	91.8	92.4	92.9	94.0	94.1	93.5	93.3	93.4	94.5	97.4	98.6	94.1
2013	93.8	92.5	92.9	93.1	94.4	94.7	94.4	95.1	95.0	95.9	99.0	100.8	95.1
2014	95.9	95.0	95.2	95.6	96.3	96.3	95.7	96.6	96.1	97.1	99.9	102.1	96.8
2015	95.8	95.1	95.6	96.6	97.4	98.0	97.3	97.9	97.2	98.3	100.8	102.4	97.7
2016	96.2	95.6	95.7	96.2	96.7	96.6	96.7	96.8	96.4	97.0	99.2	100.3	97.0
2017	95.8	95.4	95.7	96.2	97.0	96.6	96.4	96.6	96.0	96.6	99.9	100.6	96.9
2018	95.4	94.7	95.0	95.2	96.1	96.2	95.8	95.7	95.0	95.9	99.6	99.2	96.2
Wholesale Trade													
2010	17.5	17.4	17.4	17.6	17.6	17.7	17.6	17.4	17.2	17.2	17.2	17.2	17.4
2011	16.9	16.9	17.0	17.0	17.0	17.1	17.1	17.0	17.1	17.1	17.2	17.1	17.0
2012	16.7	16.7	16.8	16.8	16.9	16.9	16.9	16.8	16.7	16.7	16.8	16.8	16.8
2013	16.6	16.6	16.7	16.8	17.0	17.1	17.0	16.9	16.8	16.9	17.0	17.0	16.9
2014	16.9	16.9	17.0	17.1	17.1	17.2	17.2	17.1	17.0	16.9	17.0	17.0	17.0
2015	16.4	16.3	16.5	16.7	16.8	16.9	16.8	16.9	16.7	16.8	16.9	16.9	16.7
2016	16.7	16.6	16.7	16.7	16.7	16.8	16.9	16.9	16.6	16.6	16.7	16.6	16.7
2017	16.5	16.5	16.6	16.7	16.8	16.9	16.9	16.8	16.6	16.6	16.7	16.7	16.7
2018	16.5	16.5	16.6	16.6	16.8	17.0	16.8	16.7	16.5	16.6	16.9	16.8	16.7
Retail Trade													
2010	48.9	48.3	48.7	49.3	50.1	50.2	49.6	49.6	49.1	50.2	51.8	52.7	49.9
2011	49.3	48.7	49.0	49.6	50.1	49.9	49.7	49.9	49.6	50.3	52.7	53.4	50.2
2012	50.0	49.0	49.4	49.8	50.5	50.6	50.2	50.0	49.9	51.1	53.3	53.8	50.6
2013	50.2	49.4	49.7	50.1	50.7	50.9	51.0	51.0	51.0	52.0	54.6	55.5	51.3
2014	52.3	51.5	51.5	52.1	52.5	52.7	52.5	52.8	52.4	53.3	55.2	56.0	52.9
2015	52.7	52.3	52.5	52.9	53.3	53.8	53.3	53.4	52.9	53.8	55.7	56.4	53.6
2016	53.3	53.0	53.0	53.7	54.0	54.1	54.4	54.3	53.9	54.6	56.4	56.9	54.3
2017	53.7	53.3	53.5	54.0	54.3	54.1	54.0	54.0	53.4	54.2	56.8	57.0	54.4
2018	53.6	53.0	53.0	53.3	53.8	53.8	53.7	53.3	52.5	53.2	56.3	55.7	53.8
Transportation and Utilities													
2010	25.7	25.6	25.8	26.1	26.4	26.0	26.2	26.5	26.6	26.8	27.3	28.2	26.4
2011	26.4	26.3	26.4	26.5	26.5	26.3	26.2	26.6	26.8	26.5	26.7	27.0	26.5
2012	26.2	26.1	26.2	26.3	26.6	26.6	26.4	26.5	26.8	26.7	27.3	28.0	26.6
2013	27.0	26.5	26.5	26.2	26.7	26.7	26.4	27.2	27.2	27.0	27.4	28.3	26.9
2014	26.7	26.6	26.7	26.4	26.7	26.4	26.0	26.7	26.7	26.9	27.7	29.1	26.9
2015	26.7	26.5	26.6	27.0	27.3	27.3	27.2	27.6	27.6	27.7	28.2	29.1	27.4
2016	26.2	26.0	26.0	25.8	26.0	25.7	25.4	25.6	25.9	25.8	26.1	26.8	25.9
2017	25.6	25.6	25.6	25.5	25.9	25.6	25.5	25.8	26.0	25.8	26.4	26.9	25.9
2018	25.3	25.2	25.4	25.3	25.5	25.4	25.3	25.7	26.0	26.1	26.4	26.7	25.7
Information													
2010	11.3	11.3	11.2	11.2	11.3	11.3	11.2	11.2	11.1	11.1	11.1	11.2	11.2
2011	11.2	11.2	11.1	11.1	11.1	11.2	11.4	11.4	11.3	11.3	11.4	11.4	11.3
2012	11.3	11.4	11.4	11.4	11.3	11.3	11.3	11.2	11.2	11.1	11.1	11.1	11.3
2013	11.0	11.0	11.0	11.0	11.1	11.1	11.1	11.1	11.1	11.1	11.1	11.1	11.1
2014	11.1	11.0	11.0	11.0	11.1	11.1	11.2	11.2	11.2	11.2	11.3	11.4	11.2
2015	11.3	11.4	11.4	11.5	11.6	11.7	11.7	11.8	11.6	11.7	11.8	11.9	11.6
2016	11.8	11.8	11.8	11.8	11.8	11.8	11.8	11.8	11.8	11.8	11.8	11.9	11.8
2017	11.7	11.7	11.7	11.7	11.6	11.6	11.6	11.5	11.4	11.5	11.4	11.5	11.6
2018	11.4	11.3	11.3	11.3	11.2	11.2	11.2	11.1	11.0	11.0	11.0	11.0	11.2

Employment by Industry: Omaha-Council Bluffs, NE-IA, 2010–2018—*Continued*

(Numbers in thousands, not seasonally adjusted)

Industry and year	January	February	March	April	May	June	July	August	September	October	November	December	Annual average
Financial Activities													
2010	40.0	40.1	40.3	40.1	40.3	40.5	40.7	40.8	40.5	40.9	40.8	40.9	40.5
2011	40.9	40.9	41.0	41.2	41.4	41.4	41.4	41.3	41.3	41.3	41.5	41.7	41.3
2012	41.3	41.2	41.3	41.5	41.6	41.6	41.8	41.8	41.7	41.8	42.0	42.1	41.6
2013	41.8	41.9	41.9	42.0	42.1	42.2	42.2	42.1	42.0	42.1	42.2	42.2	42.1
2014	42.0	42.1	42.0	41.8	41.9	42.1	42.2	42.0	41.9	42.0	42.0	42.0	42.0
2015	41.5	41.6	41.5	41.7	42.0	42.3	42.4	42.4	42.3	42.6	42.7	43.1	42.2
2016	42.9	43.0	43.2	43.3	43.3	43.5	43.8	43.7	43.5	43.5	43.5	43.6	43.4
2017	43.3	43.3	43.3	43.4	43.4	43.8	43.9	43.9	43.9	44.2	44.1	44.3	43.7
2018	44.1	44.5	44.5	44.8	45.0	45.2	45.2	45.1	44.8	45.2	44.8	45.4	44.9
Professional and Business Services													
2010	61.3	60.9	61.1	62.8	63.3	63.8	64.5	64.8	64.4	65.1	65.1	65.2	63.5
2011	63.3	63.4	63.7	65.3	65.3	66.1	66.8	67.0	67.0	66.6	66.6	66.4	65.6
2012	65.6	65.8	65.8	67.1	67.4	68.6	68.6	68.2	67.8	68.6	68.9	68.7	67.6
2013	67.6	67.7	67.9	69.3	69.8	70.5	70.4	70.5	70.7	72.1	72.4	73.0	70.2
2014	70.4	71.1	71.5	71.9	72.4	72.8	72.1	72.1	71.8	72.2	72.4	72.2	71.9
2015	71.7	71.9	72.5	73.7	73.8	74.4	74.3	74.1	73.8	74.4	74.2	74.2	73.6
2016	72.4	72.6	73.2	74.6	74.5	74.8	74.9	74.6	74.1	73.8	73.5	74.2	73.9
2017	72.0	72.1	72.6	73.0	72.9	73.2	73.0	72.6	72.0	72.1	72.5	72.4	72.5
2018	70.2	70.5	70.9	71.4	72.0	72.7	72.5	72.2	72.2	73.0	73.5	73.8	72.1
Education and Health Services													
2010	70.5	71.1	71.2	71.4	71.6	71.5	71.5	71.8	71.5	72.2	72.2	72.4	71.6
2011	72.0	72.6	72.6	73.2	73.4	73.0	72.3	72.8	73.0	74.1	74.3	74.4	73.1
2012	73.4	73.9	74.6	74.5	74.7	74.3	74.1	74.8	74.9	75.4	75.7	75.5	74.7
2013	74.5	75.1	75.1	75.1	75.3	74.8	74.3	74.7	75.0	75.4	75.6	75.5	75.0
2014	74.5	75.3	75.8	75.3	75.6	74.7	74.3	75.0	75.3	76.3	76.5	76.8	75.5
2015	75.5	75.7	76.1	76.0	76.2	75.5	76.2	76.8	77.3	78.5	78.6	78.4	76.7
2016	77.0	77.6	78.5	78.2	78.7	78.1	79.2	79.5	80.2	80.9	80.7	80.7	79.1
2017	79.2	80.0	80.4	80.2	80.5	79.9	79.6	79.9	80.2	81.0	81.1	80.9	80.2
2018	80.0	80.8	81.2	80.9	81.6	80.3	79.6	80.2	80.3	80.9	80.6	81.3	80.6
Leisure and Hospitality													
2010	40.7	40.8	41.8	43.7	45.0	46.1	45.9	46.0	44.6	44.7	43.5	42.7	43.8
2011	41.5	41.6	42.6	44.8	46.5	47.5	46.6	46.3	44.7	44.6	43.5	43.0	44.4
2012	42.4	42.8	44.5	46.1	47.6	48.4	48.0	47.6	45.9	45.7	44.6	44.1	45.6
2013	43.4	43.5	44.8	46.3	48.4	49.0	48.7	49.0	47.6	47.3	46.3	45.6	46.7
2014	44.9	45.2	46.0	47.2	49.1	49.9	49.5	49.3	47.7	47.6	46.3	46.2	47.4
2015	45.1	45.6	46.9	48.1	50.0	51.2	50.5	50.6	49.2	48.6	47.2	47.4	48.4
2016	45.8	46.2	47.3	49.0	50.6	51.4	51.3	51.3	49.9	50.1	48.5	48.1	49.1
2017	47.2	47.8	48.6	50.0	51.5	53.1	52.3	52.6	50.5	50.5	48.9	48.6	50.1
2018	47.4	47.5	48.4	50.0	52.4	53.3	52.7	52.8	50.9	50.9	49.5	49.3	50.4
Other Services													
2010	17.2	17.2	17.3	17.5	17.6	17.8	17.8	17.7	17.5	17.4	17.4	17.4	17.5
2011	17.3	17.2	17.3	17.4	17.4	17.6	17.5	17.3	17.2	17.2	17.1	17.1	17.3
2012	17.1	17.1	17.3	17.5	17.7	17.9	17.8	17.7	17.6	17.4	17.3	17.3	17.5
2013	17.2	17.1	17.3	17.4	17.4	17.5	17.5	17.6	17.5	17.3	17.3	17.3	17.4
2014	17.3	17.3	17.5	17.7	17.8	18.1	17.9	17.8	17.8	17.7	17.8	17.7	17.7
2015	17.6	17.7	17.7	17.8	17.9	18.0	18.1	18.0	17.7	17.9	17.8	17.9	17.8
2016	17.5	17.5	17.6	17.7	17.7	17.8	18.0	17.7	17.7	17.8	17.8	17.7	17.7
2017	17.6	17.7	17.7	17.9	17.9	18.0	18.0	17.9	17.8	17.8	17.9	17.9	17.8
2018	17.7	17.8	17.8	18.0	18.1	18.2	18.2	18.1	18.0	18.0	18.0	18.0	18.0
Government													
2010	64.5	64.8	65.8	66.5	67.3	66.5	62.6	63.0	63.7	66.4	66.4	65.7	65.3
2011	65.4	66.0	65.4	66.8	67.0	65.2	63.1	63.8	64.6	66.5	66.7	65.9	65.5
2012	65.8	66.2	65.7	66.0	66.5	63.1	62.6	63.1	64.3	65.8	65.9	65.0	65.0
2013	64.8	65.4	65.1	65.7	66.4	64.8	63.1	63.4	64.4	65.7	65.9	65.0	65.0
2014	65.3	66.0	65.5	66.1	66.8	64.4	63.0	63.8	65.4	66.8	66.8	66.0	65.5
2015	65.7	66.1	65.8	66.8	67.3	65.5	63.6	64.2	65.0	66.9	67.1	66.7	65.9
2016	66.1	66.6	66.6	67.2	67.8	66.4	63.4	62.9	66.1	67.3	67.2	66.4	66.2
2017	66.2	66.6	66.3	67.2	67.6	66.4	62.5	62.5	66.1	67.5	67.4	66.6	66.1
2018	66.8	67.2	67.0	67.4	67.9	66.4	62.7	63.4	66.4	67.4	68.0	67.5	66.5

Employment by Industry: Albuquerque, NM, 2010–2018

(Numbers in thousands, not seasonally adjusted)

Industry and year	January	February	March	April	May	June	July	August	September	October	November	December	Annual average
Total Nonfarm													
2010	369.4	370.5	372.0	375.6	376.1	374.9	371.1	372.2	373.5	376.0	375.8	376.5	373.6
2011	367.7	371.7	372.3	375.8	375.3	373.2	370.3	370.4	373.6	373.8	372.9	371.7	372.4
2012	364.0	367.0	369.7	371.0	371.6	368.1	366.6	368.8	372.6	377.8	377.6	376.5	370.9
2013	368.9	371.9	372.6	376.3	377.2	373.7	372.4	374.2	375.1	377.8	378.8	378.8	374.8
2014	371.0	372.9	374.0	376.4	379.5	375.4	375.5	378.0	377.9	381.5	381.9	381.5	377.1
2015	373.5	376.5	377.0	380.9	381.6	379.6	378.6	380.4	381.6	385.7	388.2	386.0	380.8
2016	379.5	383.6	383.4	387.9	388.4	385.6	385.9	387.2	389.3	388.9	390.0	389.9	386.6
2017	382.9	385.9	386.8	389.8	388.6	390.0	387.2	388.4	391.0	392.3	393.6	393.8	389.2
2018	388.4	390.0	390.9	393.5	392.0	392.8	391.7	392.2	393.3	395.6	397.0	395.8	392.8
Total Private													
2010	287.8	286.7	287.6	290.4	290.6	291.8	290.9	291.4	290.4	291.4	291.2	291.7	290.2
2011	285.6	287.5	287.5	291.1	291.3	290.4	290.0	289.7	290.0	289.1	288.2	286.7	288.9
2012	282.8	283.5	285.7	287.8	288.6	289.4	288.4	289.0	289.7	293.6	293.2	291.9	288.6
2013	287.6	288.3	288.8	292.7	294.1	292.2	293.0	293.8	292.0	294.3	294.8	295.1	292.2
2014	290.1	289.9	290.4	294.2	296.6	295.2	296.3	298.0	295.9	298.9	299.0	298.5	295.3
2015	293.4	294.4	294.8	299.4	300.8	300.2	300.7	301.7	300.5	303.4	304.5	303.3	299.8
2016	298.9	300.3	299.8	304.8	305.9	304.6	306.9	307.5	306.9	306.2	306.4	306.7	304.6
2017	302.8	303.2	304.2	307.2	308.0	309.0	308.3	309.1	309.1	310.1	311.1	310.6	307.7
2018	307.6	307.7	308.3	311.1	312.1	312.1	312.7	313.0	311.6	313.0	313.9	314.1	311.4
Goods Producing													
2010	38.9	38.4	38.3	38.8	39.1	39.4	40.0	39.8	39.6	39.3	38.9	38.5	39.1
2011	37.6	37.3	38.0	38.4	38.5	38.8	39.0	38.6	37.9	37.7	37.1	36.6	38.0
2012	36.2	36.2	36.5	36.6	37.0	37.5	37.3	37.2	36.9	37.7	37.4	37.1	37.0
2013	36.3	36.4	36.7	37.2	37.6	37.9	38.0	37.8	37.4	37.8	37.2	36.8	37.3
2014	36.3	35.9	36.0	36.3	36.8	37.0	37.4	37.5	36.9	37.4	37.1	36.9	36.8
2015	36.4	36.2	36.2	36.9	37.0	37.3	37.5	37.4	37.0	37.6	37.4	37.3	37.0
2016	36.7	36.9	36.8	37.5	37.7	37.9	38.0	37.9	37.8	37.9	37.5	37.7	37.5
2017	37.3	37.2	37.6	38.1	38.3	38.9	39.2	39.4	39.4	39.6	39.6	39.7	38.7
2018	39.4	39.4	39.6	40.0	40.2	40.5	40.4	40.2	39.8	39.8	39.8	39.4	39.9
Service-Providing													
2010	330.5	332.1	333.7	336.8	337.0	335.5	331.1	332.4	333.9	336.7	336.9	338.0	334.6
2011	330.1	334.4	334.3	337.4	336.8	334.4	331.3	331.8	335.7	336.1	335.8	335.1	334.4
2012	327.8	330.8	333.2	334.4	334.6	330.6	329.3	331.6	335.7	340.1	340.2	339.4	334.0
2013	332.6	335.5	335.9	339.1	339.6	335.8	334.4	336.4	337.7	340.0	341.6	342.0	337.6
2014	334.7	337.0	338.0	340.1	342.7	338.4	338.1	340.5	341.0	344.1	344.8	344.6	340.3
2015	337.1	340.3	340.8	344.0	344.6	342.3	341.1	343.0	344.6	348.1	350.8	348.7	343.8
2016	342.8	346.7	346.6	350.4	350.7	347.7	347.9	349.3	351.5	351.0	352.5	352.2	349.1
2017	345.6	348.7	349.2	351.7	350.3	351.1	348.0	349.0	351.6	352.7	354.0	354.1	350.5
2018	349.0	350.6	351.3	353.5	351.8	352.3	351.3	352.0	353.5	355.8	357.2	356.4	352.9
Mining, Logging, and Construction													
2010	21.6	21.1	21.0	21.3	21.4	21.7	22.2	22.1	21.8	21.6	21.3	20.9	21.5
2011	20.1	19.9	20.5	20.7	20.8	21.0	21.1	20.6	20.1	19.8	19.4	18.9	20.2
2012	18.6	18.6	18.8	18.9	19.2	19.6	19.3	19.3	19.1	19.8	19.7	19.5	19.2
2013	18.8	19.0	19.4	19.8	20.2	20.4	20.5	20.3	20.1	20.5	20.2	19.8	19.9
2014	19.5	19.4	19.5	19.8	20.2	20.4	20.8	20.8	20.4	20.9	20.8	20.6	20.3
2015	20.1	19.8	19.8	20.6	20.5	20.7	20.9	20.7	20.6	20.9	20.8	20.7	20.5
2016	20.4	20.5	20.6	21.2	21.3	21.6	22.0	21.9	21.9	22.1	21.9	22.0	21.5
2017	21.7	21.7	22.1	22.6	22.8	23.3	23.5	23.7	23.7	23.8	23.8	23.8	23.0
2018	23.6	23.6	23.8	24.1	24.2	24.4	24.2	24.0	23.7	23.6	23.7	23.4	23.9
Manufacturing													
2010	17.3	17.3	17.3	17.5	17.7	17.7	17.8	17.7	17.8	17.7	17.6	17.6	17.6
2011	17.5	17.4	17.5	17.7	17.7	17.8	17.9	18.0	17.8	17.9	17.7	17.7	17.7
2012	17.6	17.6	17.7	17.7	17.8	17.9	18.0	17.9	17.8	17.9	17.7	17.6	17.8
2013	17.5	17.4	17.3	17.4	17.4	17.5	17.5	17.5	17.3	17.3	17.0	17.0	17.3
2014	16.8	16.5	16.5	16.5	16.6	16.6	16.6	16.7	16.5	16.5	16.3	16.3	16.5
2015	16.3	16.4	16.4	16.3	16.5	16.6	16.6	16.7	16.4	16.7	16.6	16.6	16.5
2016	16.3	16.4	16.2	16.3	16.4	16.3	16.0	16.0	15.9	15.8	15.6	15.7	16.1
2017	15.6	15.5	15.5	15.5	15.5	15.6	15.7	15.7	15.7	15.8	15.8	15.9	15.7
2018	15.8	15.8	15.8	15.9	16.0	16.1	16.2	16.2	16.1	16.2	16.1	16.0	16.0

Employment by Industry: Albuquerque, NM, 2010–2018—*Continued*

(Numbers in thousands, not seasonally adjusted)

Industry and year	January	February	March	April	May	June	July	August	September	October	November	December	Annual average
Trade, Transportation, and Utilities													
2010	62.3	61.6	61.7	61.6	61.9	61.9	61.9	62.4	61.9	62.5	63.6	64.3	62.3
2011	61.9	61.5	61.4	62.1	62.3	61.7	61.2	61.4	61.4	61.9	63.2	63.5	62.0
2012	61.9	61.4	61.6	61.6	61.8	61.5	61.5	61.8	61.9	62.8	64.0	64.0	62.2
2013	62.0	61.4	61.4	62.0	62.1	62.0	62.6	62.9	62.4	63.2	64.7	65.3	62.7
2014	62.7	62.3	62.4	62.8	62.9	62.6	62.9	63.1	63.1	63.8	65.1	65.5	63.3
2015	63.5	63.1	62.9	63.3	63.7	63.3	63.5	63.8	63.7	64.3	65.6	65.9	63.9
2016	63.7	63.2	63.0	63.9	63.8	63.3	63.5	63.9	63.9	64.2	65.5	65.5	64.0
2017	63.4	62.7	62.6	62.6	62.5	62.6	62.6	62.9	62.8	63.5	64.9	65.3	63.2
2018	63.6	63.2	63.0	63.2	63.7	63.2	63.4	63.8	63.3	63.7	65.0	65.0	63.7
Wholesale Trade													
2010	12.1	12.1	12.0	12.1	12.1	12.1	12.0	12.0	11.9	11.9	11.8	11.8	12.0
2011	11.7	11.7	11.7	11.8	11.8	11.7	11.7	11.7	11.6	11.6	11.6	11.6	11.7
2012	11.6	11.7	11.8	11.8	11.9	11.8	11.9	11.9	11.8	11.9	11.9	11.9	11.8
2013	11.7	11.6	11.6	11.7	11.7	11.7	11.7	11.7	11.6	11.6	11.7	11.7	11.7
2014	11.7	11.8	11.8	11.9	12.0	11.9	11.9	11.9	11.9	11.9	11.9	11.9	11.9
2015	11.8	11.8	11.8	11.9	12.0	11.9	11.9	11.9	11.9	12.0	11.9	11.9	11.9
2016	12.0	12.0	11.9	12.1	12.0	11.9	11.9	11.9	11.9	11.8	11.7	11.7	11.9
2017	11.6	11.7	11.7	11.6	11.6	11.7	11.7	11.6	11.6	11.7	11.6	11.6	11.6
2018	11.7	11.7	11.6	11.7	11.7	11.7	11.7	11.7	11.6	11.6	11.6	11.6	11.7
Retail Trade													
2010	40.7	40.0	40.3	40.1	40.4	40.5	40.6	41.0	40.5	41.0	42.1	42.6	40.8
2011	40.6	40.2	40.3	40.8	41.0	40.6	40.2	40.4	40.3	40.7	42.0	42.1	40.8
2012	40.7	40.1	40.2	40.3	40.4	40.4	40.2	40.3	40.5	41.1	42.3	42.2	40.7
2013	40.5	40.1	40.1	40.6	40.7	40.7	41.2	41.4	41.0	41.8	43.2	43.5	41.2
2014	41.3	40.8	41.0	41.3	41.2	41.1	41.3	41.4	41.3	42.0	43.2	43.4	41.6
2015	41.6	41.2	41.1	41.4	41.7	41.5	41.8	42.0	41.9	42.4	43.6	43.7	42.0
2016	41.7	41.3	41.2	41.8	41.7	41.5	41.5	41.7	41.7	42.1	43.4	43.2	41.9
2017	41.6	40.9	40.8	41.0	40.9	41.0	41.0	41.2	41.0	41.5	43.0	43.1	41.4
2018	41.6	41.2	41.2	41.1	41.6	41.3	41.5	41.7	41.2	41.6	42.7	42.6	41.6
Transportation and Utilities													
2010	9.5	9.5	9.4	9.4	9.4	9.3	9.3	9.4	9.5	9.6	9.7	9.9	9.5
2011	9.6	9.6	9.4	9.5	9.5	9.4	9.3	9.3	9.5	9.6	9.6	9.8	9.5
2012	9.6	9.6	9.6	9.5	9.5	9.3	9.4	9.6	9.6	9.8	9.8	9.9	9.6
2013	9.8	9.7	9.7	9.7	9.7	9.6	9.7	9.8	9.8	9.8	9.8	10.1	9.8
2014	9.7	9.7	9.6	9.6	9.7	9.6	9.7	9.8	9.9	9.9	10.0	10.2	9.8
2015	10.1	10.1	10.0	10.0	10.0	9.9	9.8	9.9	9.9	9.9	10.1	10.3	10.0
2016	10.0	9.9	9.9	10.0	10.1	9.9	10.1	10.3	10.3	10.3	10.4	10.6	10.2
2017	10.2	10.1	10.1	10.0	10.0	9.9	9.9	10.1	10.2	10.3	10.3	10.6	10.1
2018	10.3	10.3	10.2	10.4	10.4	10.2	10.2	10.4	10.5	10.5	10.7	10.8	10.4
Information													
2010	9.0	8.7	8.4	9.4	8.9	9.4	8.8	8.9	8.4	8.4	8.7	8.8	8.8
2011	8.6	8.6	8.6	9.2	9.5	9.2	8.7	8.1	7.8	7.9	8.0	7.8	8.5
2012	8.1	8.4	8.8	8.8	8.1	8.0	8.3	8.4	8.6	8.4	8.5	8.4	8.4
2013	8.1	8.8	8.4	8.5	8.6	8.0	7.9	7.8	7.6	7.9	8.0	7.8	8.1
2014	7.4	7.7	7.9	7.7	8.2	8.1	8.0	8.2	7.5	7.8	8.2	8.1	7.9
2015	7.4	8.0	8.2	7.9	8.3	8.0	8.1	8.7	8.3	8.1	8.4	7.7	8.1
2016	7.5	7.4	7.4	7.8	7.6	7.4	7.8	7.9	7.8	7.4	8.1	7.8	7.7
2017	7.4	7.1	7.4	7.7	7.6	7.6	7.3	7.2	7.2	7.6	7.3	7.2	7.4
2018	7.0	7.0	7.1	7.2	7.2	7.1	7.0	6.8	6.9	7.0	6.9	7.0	7.0
Financial Activities													
2010	18.3	18.1	18.3	18.0	17.9	18.0	18.0	17.9	17.7	17.8	17.7	17.7	18.0
2011	17.4	17.4	17.4	17.6	17.5	17.6	17.7	17.7	17.7	17.7	17.6	17.7	17.6
2012	17.5	17.6	17.7	17.6	17.7	17.7	17.8	17.8	17.7	17.9	17.8	17.8	17.7
2013	17.8	17.7	17.6	17.7	17.9	17.8	17.9	18.0	17.9	18.0	18.2	18.2	17.9
2014	17.7	17.8	17.8	17.7	17.8	17.7	18.0	17.9	17.8	18.0	17.9	17.9	17.8
2015	17.7	17.8	17.9	18.0	18.1	18.1	18.2	18.1	17.9	18.1	18.1	18.2	18.0
2016	18.1	18.2	18.2	18.4	18.5	18.4	18.4	18.4	18.3	18.4	18.4	18.4	18.3
2017	18.5	18.5	18.4	18.5	18.5	18.6	18.7	18.7	18.6	18.7	18.7	18.7	18.6
2018	18.6	18.7	18.6	18.7	18.6	18.7	18.9	18.8	18.7	18.6	18.5	18.9	18.7

Employment by Industry: Albuquerque, NM, 2010–2018—*Continued*

(Numbers in thousands, not seasonally adjusted)

Industry and year	January	February	March	April	May	June	July	August	September	October	November	December	Annual average
Professional and Business Services													
2010	57.8	57.8	57.5	58.1	57.6	58.4	58.2	58.5	58.6	59.0	58.6	58.6	58.2
2011	57.3	59.3	57.7	58.0	57.8	58.1	58.2	58.3	58.7	57.7	57.3	56.7	57.9
2012	55.2	55.2	55.6	55.9	56.0	56.8	56.4	56.4	56.5	57.2	57.3	56.6	56.3
2013	56.6	56.9	56.6	57.5	57.5	57.0	57.7	57.7	57.0	57.5	57.1	57.4	57.2
2014	56.7	56.8	56.3	57.7	57.7	57.1	57.8	58.0	56.8	57.5	57.2	57.3	57.2
2015	56.3	56.4	56.3	57.0	56.8	57.1	57.7	57.6	57.3	57.9	58.0	58.1	57.2
2016	57.2	57.5	57.2	58.0	58.0	58.5	59.6	59.3	59.3	59.2	58.8	59.0	58.5
2017	58.8	59.5	59.5	60.1	59.9	60.7	60.9	61.0	61.0	60.9	61.4	61.2	60.4
2018	60.4	60.4	60.3	60.9	60.6	61.2	61.5	61.8	61.6	61.8	61.1	61.3	61.1
Education and Health Services													
2010	54.3	54.5	55.0	55.1	55.2	54.3	53.8	53.7	55.0	55.4	55.6	55.8	54.8
2011	55.5	55.6	55.8	55.9	55.8	54.4	54.8	54.9	56.3	56.5	56.2	56.0	55.6
2012	56.1	56.3	56.3	56.7	56.6	55.7	55.4	55.3	56.9	57.7	57.7	57.8	56.5
2013	57.5	57.7	58.0	58.3	58.3	57.1	56.1	56.8	58.0	58.4	58.6	58.6	57.8
2014	58.7	58.8	59.0	59.5	59.7	58.8	58.2	58.8	60.2	60.8	60.8	60.5	59.5
2015	60.7	61.2	61.4	62.0	62.2	61.4	60.7	61.3	62.7	63.5	63.7	63.1	62.0
2016	63.7	64.2	64.1	64.6	64.7	63.5	63.0	63.6	64.4	64.4	64.1	64.6	64.1
2017	64.3	64.7	64.5	65.0	65.0	63.9	62.9	63.6	64.3	64.7	64.5	64.2	64.3
2018	64.5	64.6	64.6	65.1	65.1	64.4	63.6	64.2	65.0	65.6	66.8	66.8	65.0
Leisure and Hospitality													
2010	35.5	35.9	36.7	37.7	38.3	38.1	38.0	37.9	37.4	37.1	36.5	36.4	37.1
2011	35.8	36.1	36.8	38.1	38.2	38.4	38.2	38.6	38.5	38.1	37.3	36.9	37.6
2012	36.3	36.6	37.3	38.7	39.6	39.9	39.7	40.0	39.4	39.8	38.8	38.4	38.7
2013	37.8	37.8	38.5	39.8	40.5	40.6	40.9	41.0	40.2	39.9	39.4	39.4	39.7
2014	39.1	38.9	39.3	40.8	41.8	41.9	42.0	42.4	41.8	41.8	41.0	40.7	41.0
2015	40.1	40.2	40.4	42.7	43.1	43.1	43.0	42.9	42.0	42.3	41.8	41.5	41.9
2016	40.6	41.3	41.6	42.8	43.9	43.6	44.3	44.2	43.4	42.8	42.1	41.9	42.7
2017	41.6	41.8	42.5	43.3	44.2	44.3	44.3	44.2	43.9	43.3	42.9	42.5	43.2
2018	42.3	42.6	43.2	44.0	44.6	44.6	45.4	45.1	44.2	44.4	43.7	43.7	44.0
Other Services													
2010	11.7	11.7	11.7	11.7	11.7	12.3	12.2	12.3	11.8	11.9	11.6	11.6	11.9
2011	11.5	11.7	11.8	11.8	11.7	12.2	12.2	12.1	11.7	11.6	11.5	11.5	11.8
2012	11.5	11.8	11.9	11.9	11.8	12.3	12.0	12.1	11.8	12.1	11.7	11.8	11.9
2013	11.5	11.6	11.6	11.7	11.6	11.8	11.9	11.8	11.5	11.6	11.6	11.6	11.7
2014	11.5	11.7	11.7	11.7	11.7	12.0	12.0	12.1	11.8	11.8	11.7	11.6	11.8
2015	11.3	11.5	11.5	11.6	11.6	11.9	12.0	11.9	11.6	11.6	11.6	11.5	11.6
2016	11.4	11.6	11.5	11.8	11.7	12.0	12.3	12.3	12.0	11.9	11.9	11.8	11.9
2017	11.5	11.7	11.7	11.9	12.0	12.4	12.4	12.1	11.9	11.8	11.8	11.8	11.9
2018	11.8	11.8	11.9	12.0	12.1	12.4	12.5	12.3	12.1	12.1	12.1	12.0	12.1
Government													
2010	81.6	83.8	84.4	85.2	85.5	83.1	80.2	80.8	83.1	84.6	84.6	84.8	83.5
2011	82.1	84.2	84.8	84.7	84.0	82.8	80.3	80.7	83.6	84.7	84.7	85.0	83.5
2012	81.2	83.5	84.0	83.2	83.0	78.7	78.2	79.8	82.9	84.2	84.4	84.6	82.3
2013	81.3	83.6	83.8	83.6	83.1	81.5	79.4	80.4	83.1	83.5	84.0	83.7	82.6
2014	80.9	83.0	83.6	82.2	82.9	80.2	79.2	80.0	82.0	82.6	82.9	83.0	81.9
2015	80.1	82.1	82.2	81.5	80.8	79.4	77.9	78.7	81.1	82.3	83.6	82.7	81.0
2016	80.6	83.3	83.6	83.1	82.5	81.0	79.0	79.7	82.4	82.7	83.6	83.2	82.1
2017	80.1	82.7	82.6	82.6	80.6	81.0	78.9	79.3	81.9	82.2	82.5	83.2	81.5
2018	80.8	82.3	82.6	82.4	79.9	80.7	79.0	79.2	81.7	82.6	83.1	81.7	81.3

Employment by Industry: Greenville-Anderson-Mauldin, SC, 2010–2018

(Numbers in thousands, not seasonally adjusted)

Industry and year	January	February	March	April	May	June	July	August	September	October	November	December	Annual average
Total Nonfarm													
2010	345.0	347.1	350.0	353.6	357.9	355.9	353.3	354.7	356.3	358.6	360.5	361.0	354.5
2011	351.0	357.1	360.9	363.6	364.6	362.2	360.6	363.0	365.1	365.6	367.8	367.5	362.4
2012	360.8	363.6	366.8	367.5	370.8	369.8	364.9	367.5	370.3	370.6	374.8	375.1	368.5
2013	368.3	371.2	373.9	375.3	379.0	381.2	376.7	380.0	384.0	386.3	388.0	388.7	379.4
2014	378.6	380.3	385.2	386.8	389.5	389.4	384.3	387.7	390.7	393.8	397.1	398.6	388.5
2015	390.8	393.1	395.2	398.3	401.8	403.1	400.7	403.0	404.2	408.8	410.1	411.6	401.7
2016	401.3	404.3	406.4	409.4	410.4	409.3	407.3	409.4	410.7	412.7	415.1	415.5	409.3
2017	407.9	411.5	412.8	415.2	417.1	416.7	413.2	416.1	417.6	420.9	425.1	426.0	416.7
2018	419.5	422.5	424.4	424.9	427.0	427.7	420.2	422.9	422.5	426.8	429.1	431.0	424.9
Total Private													
2010	288.4	290.3	293.1	296.4	299.3	298.7	299.4	301.1	300.8	302.4	304.2	304.9	298.3
2011	295.7	301.5	305.3	307.7	308.6	307.1	307.0	309.8	309.8	309.6	311.6	311.4	307.1
2012	304.8	307.2	310.3	311.0	313.8	313.7	311.0	313.2	313.7	313.2	317.1	317.5	312.2
2013	311.0	313.7	316.0	317.2	321.1	323.6	321.7	324.6	326.5	327.9	329.7	330.3	321.9
2014	320.8	322.1	326.8	328.4	330.7	331.4	328.7	331.4	332.4	334.6	337.7	339.1	330.3
2015	332.1	333.8	335.6	338.6	341.9	343.8	343.9	345.5	344.7	348.4	349.7	350.9	342.4
2016	341.6	344.4	346.0	348.9	349.8	349.4	349.9	351.3	350.7	352.0	354.2	354.4	349.4
2017	347.8	351.1	352.0	354.1	355.8	356.1	354.8	356.8	356.4	359.0	362.9	363.7	355.9
2018	358.0	360.5	362.0	362.4	364.2	365.8	360.5	362.3	359.9	363.7	365.6	367.4	362.7
Goods Producing													
2010	62.0	61.6	61.8	62.2	62.7	62.9	63.0	63.0	62.9	62.8	63.0	63.4	62.6
2011	61.5	63.1	63.5	63.9	64.1	64.3	64.4	64.7	64.3	64.4	64.6	64.5	63.9
2012	64.0	64.3	64.8	64.9	65.4	65.3	65.1	65.6	65.6	66.0	66.3	66.4	65.3
2013	66.2	66.9	67.5	67.5	68.1	68.5	68.2	68.8	69.0	69.2	69.5	69.6	68.3
2014	68.8	69.0	69.7	69.9	70.5	70.9	70.3	70.7	70.6	70.6	70.9	71.2	70.3
2015	70.7	70.7	71.0	71.3	72.1	72.8	72.9	72.9	72.9	73.2	73.1	73.4	72.3
2016	73.3	73.5	73.9	74.5	75.0	75.3	76.0	76.0	75.6	75.6	76.1	76.4	75.1
2017	75.6	75.9	75.9	75.8	75.9	76.5	76.2	76.2	75.9	76.0	76.2	76.7	76.1
2018	76.3	76.7	76.7	76.5	76.3	77.4	77.6	77.1	77.0	76.5	76.5	77.0	76.8
Service-Providing													
2010	283.0	285.5	288.2	291.4	295.2	293.0	290.3	291.7	293.4	295.8	297.5	297.6	291.9
2011	289.5	294.0	297.4	299.7	300.5	297.9	296.2	298.3	300.8	301.2	303.2	303.0	298.5
2012	296.8	299.3	302.0	302.6	305.4	304.5	299.8	301.9	304.7	304.6	308.5	308.7	303.2
2013	302.1	304.3	306.4	307.8	310.9	312.7	308.5	311.2	315.0	317.1	318.5	319.1	311.1
2014	309.8	311.3	315.5	316.9	319.0	318.5	314.0	317.0	320.1	323.2	326.2	327.4	318.2
2015	320.1	322.4	324.2	327.0	329.7	330.3	327.8	330.1	331.3	335.6	337.0	338.2	329.5
2016	328.0	330.8	332.5	334.9	335.4	334.0	331.3	333.4	335.1	337.1	339.0	339.1	334.2
2017	332.3	335.6	336.9	339.4	341.2	340.2	337.0	339.9	341.7	344.9	348.9	349.3	340.6
2018	343.2	345.8	347.7	348.4	350.7	350.3	342.6	345.8	345.5	350.3	352.6	354.0	348.1
Mining, Logging, and Construction													
2010	14.5	14.3	14.4	14.7	14.9	15.0	15.0	14.8	14.7	14.6	14.6	14.7	14.7
2011	13.4	14.2	14.3	14.4	14.6	14.6	14.5	14.5	14.3	14.2	14.4	14.3	14.3
2012	14.1	14.3	14.6	14.4	14.7	14.7	14.6	14.7	14.6	14.8	14.9	14.9	14.6
2013	14.7	14.8	15.1	15.2	15.5	15.7	15.8	15.9	15.9	16.0	16.2	16.3	15.6
2014	15.7	15.7	16.1	16.1	16.3	16.5	16.1	16.4	16.3	16.3	16.5	16.6	16.2
2015	16.1	16.1	16.2	16.3	16.7	17.1	17.0	17.0	16.9	17.0	17.0	17.0	16.7
2016	17.0	17.2	17.5	17.8	18.2	18.4	18.7	18.6	18.3	18.2	18.3	18.3	18.0
2017	17.8	18.0	17.9	18.2	18.3	18.6	18.3	18.3	18.1	18.2	18.2	18.4	18.2
2018	18.4	18.6	18.7	18.8	19.1	19.4	19.5	19.4	19.3	19.3	19.4	19.6	19.1
Manufacturing													
2010	47.5	47.3	47.4	47.5	47.8	47.9	48.0	48.2	48.2	48.2	48.4	48.7	47.9
2011	48.1	48.9	49.2	49.5	49.5	49.7	49.9	50.2	50.0	50.2	50.2	50.2	49.6
2012	49.9	50.0	50.2	50.5	50.7	50.6	50.5	50.9	51.0	51.2	51.4	51.5	50.7
2013	51.5	52.1	52.4	52.3	52.6	52.8	52.4	52.9	53.1	53.2	53.3	53.3	52.7
2014	53.1	53.3	53.6	53.8	54.2	54.4	54.2	54.3	54.3	54.3	54.4	54.6	54.0
2015	54.6	54.6	54.8	55.0	55.4	55.7	55.9	55.9	56.0	56.2	56.1	56.4	55.6
2016	56.3	56.3	56.4	56.7	56.8	56.9	57.3	57.4	57.3	57.4	57.8	58.1	57.1
2017	57.8	57.9	58.0	57.6	57.6	57.9	57.9	57.9	57.8	57.8	58.0	58.3	57.9
2018	57.9	58.1	58.0	57.7	57.2	58.0	58.1	57.7	57.7	57.2	57.1	57.4	57.7

Employment by Industry: Greenville-Anderson-Mauldin, SC, 2010–2018—*Continued*

(Numbers in thousands, not seasonally adjusted)

Industry and year	January	February	March	April	May	June	July	August	September	October	November	December	Annual average
Trade, Transportation, and Utilities													
2010	66.2	66.2	66.6	67.4	67.9	67.9	67.8	68.0	67.7	68.7	70.0	70.4	67.9
2011	67.6	68.2	68.8	69.0	69.2	69.3	69.3	69.4	69.0	69.2	70.4	70.9	69.2
2012	68.8	68.6	69.1	69.3	69.6	69.6	69.5	69.5	69.3	69.6	71.3	71.4	69.6
2013	68.5	68.5	69.3	69.6	70.2	70.7	70.6	71.2	70.8	71.5	72.9	73.6	70.6
2014	70.2	70.1	70.5	70.8	71.3	71.9	71.5	71.9	71.7	72.8	74.3	75.3	71.9
2015	73.1	72.9	73.5	74.2	74.6	74.7	74.9	75.1	74.6	75.6	77.2	77.6	74.8
2016	74.6	74.6	74.3	74.6	75.0	74.9	75.0	75.1	75.1	75.8	77.1	78.1	75.4
2017	75.6	75.7	75.5	75.2	75.3	75.3	75.4	75.7	75.1	75.8	77.8	78.8	75.9
2018	76.4	76.3	76.4	76.5	77.5	77.1	75.9	76.2	76.2	76.5	78.2	79.1	76.9
Wholesale Trade													
2010	15.7	15.9	15.9	16.4	16.6	16.6	16.6	16.7	16.6	16.9	16.9	16.8	16.5
2011	16.8	16.9	17.1	17.0	17.0	17.1	17.2	17.2	17.2	17.2	17.2	17.3	17.1
2012	17.1	17.1	17.2	17.3	17.3	17.4	17.4	17.5	17.2	17.3	17.3	17.4	17.3
2013	17.1	17.2	17.2	17.3	17.5	17.5	17.5	17.7	17.5	17.6	17.7	17.7	17.5
2014	17.1	17.1	17.1	17.2	17.4	17.6	17.6	17.7	17.7	18.2	18.3	18.4	17.6
2015	18.7	18.7	18.9	19.0	19.1	19.1	19.1	19.1	19.1	19.3	19.3	19.4	19.1
2016	19.0	19.0	18.9	18.9	18.8	18.9	18.8	18.8	18.7	18.8	18.9	19.0	18.9
2017	18.6	18.6	18.6	18.5	18.5	18.6	18.7	18.7	18.5	18.2	18.2	18.4	18.5
2018	17.9	18.0	17.9	17.9	17.9	18.0	18.1	18.0	18.1	18.1	18.1	18.0	18.0
Retail Trade													
2010	39.7	39.5	39.9	40.1	40.4	40.4	40.3	40.4	40.2	40.8	42.0	42.5	40.5
2011	40.0	40.3	40.7	40.9	40.9	40.8	40.9	41.0	40.7	40.9	42.0	42.4	41.0
2012	40.7	40.6	40.8	40.7	41.0	40.9	40.8	40.8	40.8	40.9	42.6	42.6	41.1
2013	40.4	40.2	41.0	41.2	41.5	41.9	41.9	42.2	42.1	42.6	43.9	44.3	41.9
2014	42.0	42.0	42.3	42.2	42.4	42.8	42.5	42.7	42.5	43.1	44.5	45.1	42.8
2015	43.2	43.0	43.3	43.9	44.1	44.2	44.3	44.6	44.2	44.9	46.3	46.5	44.4
2016	44.1	44.2	43.9	44.2	44.5	44.3	44.3	44.4	44.4	44.9	46.0	46.5	44.6
2017	44.6	44.7	44.6	44.5	44.5	44.4	44.5	44.8	44.4	45.2	46.9	47.2	45.0
2018	45.6	45.5	45.6	45.6	46.5	45.9	44.5	44.9	44.9	45.1	46.6	47.4	45.7
Transportation and Utilities													
2010	10.8	10.8	10.8	10.9	10.9	10.9	10.9	10.9	10.9	11.0	11.1	11.1	10.9
2011	10.8	11.0	11.0	11.1	11.3	11.4	11.2	11.2	11.1	11.1	11.2	11.2	11.1
2012	11.0	10.9	11.1	11.3	11.3	11.3	11.3	11.2	11.3	11.4	11.4	11.4	11.2
2013	11.0	11.1	11.1	11.1	11.2	11.3	11.2	11.3	11.2	11.3	11.3	11.6	11.2
2014	11.1	11.0	11.1	11.4	11.5	11.5	11.4	11.5	11.5	11.5	11.5	11.8	11.4
2015	11.2	11.2	11.3	11.3	11.4	11.4	11.5	11.4	11.3	11.4	11.6	11.7	11.4
2016	11.5	11.4	11.5	11.5	11.7	11.7	11.9	11.9	12.0	12.1	12.2	12.6	11.8
2017	12.4	12.4	12.3	12.2	12.3	12.3	12.2	12.2	12.2	12.4	12.7	13.2	12.4
2018	12.9	12.8	12.9	13.0	13.1	13.2	13.3	13.3	13.2	13.3	13.5	13.7	13.2
Information													
2010	6.9	7.1	7.1	6.6	6.7	7.1	7.2	6.6	6.6	6.6	6.6	7.0	6.8
2011	7.1	7.0	7.3	7.1	6.9	7.0	6.8	6.8	6.7	7.5	7.5	7.5	7.1
2012	7.3	7.6	7.5	7.6	7.8	7.8	7.2	7.1	7.1	7.0	7.1	7.3	7.4
2013	7.3	7.4	7.3	7.3	7.4	7.3	7.4	7.2	7.2	7.2	7.1	7.1	7.3
2014	7.0	6.9	6.9	6.9	7.1	7.1	7.2	7.1	7.1	7.1	7.3	7.3	7.1
2015	7.4	7.4	7.4	7.3	7.4	7.5	7.4	7.4	7.4	7.4	7.4	7.5	7.4
2016	7.3	7.3	7.2	7.2	7.2	7.1	7.1	7.0	7.1	7.1	7.0	7.1	7.1
2017	7.2	7.2	7.2	7.3	7.3	7.4	7.4	7.4	7.4	7.3	7.3	7.2	7.3
2018	7.2	7.3	7.3	7.3	7.2	7.3	7.3	7.4	7.3	7.3	7.3	7.4	7.3
Financial Activities													
2010	15.1	15.2	15.2	15.2	15.3	15.2	15.1	15.1	14.9	15.2	15.3	15.2	15.2
2011	15.0	15.0	15.0	15.1	15.1	14.9	15.1	15.1	15.1	15.1	15.1	15.1	15.1
2012	14.8	14.8	15.0	14.9	15.0	15.1	15.2	15.1	15.2	15.2	15.3	15.5	15.1
2013	15.5	15.6	15.7	15.9	16.0	16.1	16.0	16.0	16.0	16.1	16.2	16.2	15.9
2014	15.7	15.7	15.9	15.9	16.0	16.2	16.3	16.4	16.3	16.3	16.4	16.6	16.1
2015	16.2	16.2	16.3	16.4	16.5	16.8	16.8	16.8	16.8	17.1	17.1	17.4	16.7
2016	17.2	17.3	17.4	17.5	17.5	17.7	17.8	18.0	18.0	18.3	18.4	18.3	17.8
2017	18.1	18.2	18.3	18.3	18.4	18.4	18.6	18.6	18.5	18.5	18.7	18.8	18.5
2018	18.6	18.7	18.7	18.5	18.7	18.9	18.9	18.7	18.5	18.5	18.7	19.0	18.7

Employment by Industry: Greenville-Anderson-Mauldin, SC, 2010–2018—*Continued*

(Numbers in thousands, not seasonally adjusted)

Industry and year	January	February	March	April	May	June	July	August	September	October	November	December	Annual average
Professional and Business Services													
2010	51.4	52.5	53.6	54.8	55.4	55.4	56.3	57.3	57.3	57.9	58.3	58.3	55.7
2011	56.4	58.2	59.3	60.4	60.5	60.4	61.0	62.6	63.1	62.4	62.5	62.4	60.8
2012	60.6	61.1	62.3	62.5	62.9	63.4	62.7	63.8	63.2	62.6	63.6	63.6	62.7
2013	62.0	62.8	63.3	62.9	64.1	65.4	64.4	65.3	66.4	66.7	66.9	66.6	64.7
2014	64.1	65.0	66.4	67.0	67.0	66.6	65.9	66.9	67.7	68.7	69.1	69.0	67.0
2015	67.0	67.6	67.4	68.6	69.7	70.0	70.5	70.9	71.2	71.8	71.5	71.6	69.8
2016	68.0	69.0	69.1	70.3	69.3	68.8	68.9	69.0	68.8	69.1	69.0	68.3	69.0
2017	67.3	68.1	68.1	69.9	70.2	70.1	69.5	70.1	71.1	72.5	73.4	73.4	70.3
2018	71.1	71.7	72.1	72.3	72.5	72.9	69.4	70.6	69.7	72.0	71.6	71.2	71.4
Education and Health Services													
2010	40.4	40.9	41.1	41.6	42.1	41.8	41.5	41.9	41.8	42.4	42.5	42.3	41.7
2011	41.5	42.3	42.5	42.0	42.1	41.9	41.5	41.6	41.6	41.4	41.6	41.6	41.8
2012	40.8	41.4	41.6	41.4	41.9	40.9	40.4	40.7	42.1	42.0	42.3	42.3	41.5
2013	41.5	42.0	42.2	42.3	42.9	42.6	42.3	42.9	43.5	43.9	44.2	44.5	42.9
2014	43.6	44.1	44.4	44.3	44.5	44.4	44.1	44.8	45.2	45.8	45.9	46.1	44.8
2015	45.1	45.8	46.1	46.3	46.4	46.6	46.0	47.1	47.1	47.6	47.9	48.0	46.7
2016	47.3	47.8	48.3	48.2	48.5	48.1	48.1	49.2	49.4	49.6	49.8	49.7	48.7
2017	48.6	49.5	49.6	49.7	50.0	49.5	49.3	50.1	50.4	50.9	50.9	50.8	49.9
2018	50.5	51.1	51.4	51.3	51.4	49.9	49.7	50.9	51.6	52.6	52.4	52.9	51.3
Leisure and Hospitality													
2010	34.5	34.8	35.6	36.4	36.9	36.2	36.6	37.3	37.3	36.6	36.3	36.1	36.2
2011	34.6	35.5	36.5	37.4	37.8	36.7	36.3	37.0	37.0	36.6	36.8	36.4	36.6
2012	35.1	35.6	36.4	36.6	37.4	37.8	37.2	37.8	37.6	37.1	37.4	37.2	36.9
2013	36.4	36.9	37.0	37.9	38.5	39.0	39.0	39.3	39.1	38.8	39.1	39.0	38.3
2014	38.0	37.9	39.3	39.9	40.5	40.5	39.8	40.1	40.3	39.8	40.2	40.1	39.7
2015	39.2	39.7	40.2	40.8	41.4	41.5	41.6	41.5	40.9	41.8	41.7	41.6	41.0
2016	40.2	41.0	41.8	42.5	43.2	43.3	42.8	42.8	42.4	42.3	42.6	42.3	42.3
2017	41.3	42.4	43.1	43.7	44.4	44.5	44.0	44.4	43.7	43.8	44.4	43.8	43.6
2018	43.6	44.3	44.9	45.5	46.0	47.7	47.2	46.9	45.1	45.9	46.5	46.4	45.8
Other Services													
2010	11.9	12.0	12.1	12.2	12.3	12.2	11.9	11.9	12.3	12.2	12.2	12.2	12.1
2011	12.0	12.2	12.4	12.8	12.9	12.6	12.6	12.6	13.0	13.0	13.1	13.0	12.7
2012	13.4	13.8	13.6	13.8	13.8	13.8	13.7	13.6	13.6	13.7	13.8	13.8	13.7
2013	13.6	13.6	13.7	13.8	13.9	14.0	13.8	13.9	14.5	14.5	13.8	13.7	13.9
2014	13.4	13.4	13.7	13.7	13.8	13.8	13.6	13.5	13.5	13.5	13.6	13.5	13.6
2015	13.4	13.5	13.7	13.7	13.8	13.9	13.8	13.8	13.8	13.9	13.8	13.8	13.7
2016	13.7	13.9	14.0	14.1	14.1	14.2	14.2	14.2	14.3	14.2	14.2	14.2	14.1
2017	14.1	14.1	14.3	14.2	14.3	14.4	14.4	14.3	14.3	14.2	14.2	14.2	14.3
2018	14.3	14.4	14.5	14.5	14.6	14.6	14.5	14.5	14.5	14.4	14.4	14.4	14.5
Government													
2010	56.6	56.8	56.9	57.2	58.6	57.2	53.9	53.6	55.5	56.2	56.3	56.1	56.2
2011	55.3	55.6	55.6	55.9	56.0	55.1	53.6	53.2	55.3	56.0	56.2	56.1	55.3
2012	56.0	56.4	56.5	56.5	57.0	56.1	53.9	54.3	56.6	57.4	57.7	57.6	56.3
2013	57.3	57.5	57.9	58.1	57.9	57.6	55.0	55.4	57.5	58.4	58.3	58.4	57.4
2014	57.8	58.2	58.4	58.4	58.8	58.0	55.6	56.3	58.3	59.2	59.4	59.5	58.2
2015	58.7	59.3	59.6	59.7	59.9	59.3	56.8	57.5	59.5	60.4	60.4	60.7	59.3
2016	59.7	59.9	60.4	60.5	60.6	59.9	57.4	58.1	60.0	60.7	60.9	61.1	59.9
2017	60.1	60.4	60.8	61.1	61.3	60.6	58.4	59.3	61.2	61.9	62.2	62.3	60.8
2018	61.5	62.0	62.4	62.5	62.8	61.9	59.7	60.6	62.6	63.1	63.5	63.6	62.2

Employment by Industry: Bakersfield, CA, 2010–2018

(Numbers in thousands, not seasonally adjusted)

Industry and year	January	February	March	April	May	June	July	August	September	October	November	December	Annual average
Total Nonfarm													
2010	226.2	226.4	229.0	233.6	233.7	233.9	224.4	227.5	230.4	232.3	233.2	234.5	230.4
2011	230.9	232.1	233.8	236.5	238.7	238.3	235.9	238.2	238.9	239.5	240.7	241.2	237.1
2012	238.8	240.7	243.7	245.6	248.2	249.0	243.6	245.3	247.4	249.8	250.8	250.5	246.1
2013	245.6	247.5	249.1	250.8	252.4	250.4	247.0	249.7	251.6	253.7	254.8	255.0	250.6
2014	250.8	252.3	254.4	256.4	258.2	255.9	252.3	256.3	258.9	259.3	261.7	261.8	256.5
2015	257.4	256.8	258.0	258.0	259.2	257.5	252.8	256.7	257.5	259.9	260.6	260.7	257.9
2016	256.1	256.0	255.6	257.2	256.5	256.1	250.1	253.0	256.1	258.7	261.0	259.9	256.4
2017	255.0	255.8	258.2	259.0	260.7	260.1	255.0	258.0	260.9	263.5	265.6	264.5	259.7
2018	262.2	263.1	264.6	265.9	267.2	268.0	261.1	266.3	268.6	270.3	272.6	273.1	266.9
Total Private													
2010	166.0	165.5	166.5	169.4	169.6	170.4	171.0	171.7	171.6	171.3	171.7	172.8	169.8
2011	170.4	171.0	172.0	174.8	176.9	176.7	179.1	180.5	180.8	179.5	180.3	180.9	176.9
2012	179.7	180.9	183.3	186.0	188.4	189.1	189.1	190.1	189.9	190.0	190.9	190.6	187.3
2013	187.1	188.2	189.3	191.1	193.1	193.0	192.6	194.4	193.8	194.1	194.8	194.8	192.2
2014	191.7	192.5	193.7	195.6	197.3	197.3	197.0	199.6	199.2	198.3	199.7	200.1	196.8
2015	196.2	195.5	195.9	195.6	196.4	196.2	196.5	197.6	196.3	196.5	197.2	197.1	196.4
2016	193.2	192.2	191.1	192.6	191.6	191.5	191.3	192.2	192.6	193.1	195.0	194.3	192.6
2017	189.8	190.2	191.8	193.0	194.8	194.2	195.0	196.0	196.5	196.6	198.1	197.5	194.5
2018	196.2	196.7	197.8	199.4	200.7	201.1	200.8	203.0	203.1	203.3	205.1	205.8	201.1
Goods Producing													
2010	34.0	33.4	33.9	34.7	35.4	35.6	36.1	36.3	36.7	36.8	36.6	37.0	35.5
2011	36.6	36.8	36.9	38.0	38.3	39.0	39.4	39.8	40.0	39.7	39.5	40.1	38.7
2012	40.5	41.0	41.7	42.5	42.8	43.5	44.0	44.4	44.5	44.0	44.0	43.3	43.0
2013	42.3	42.4	42.8	43.1	43.4	43.8	43.9	44.6	45.0	45.0	44.8	44.7	43.8
2014	44.3	44.4	44.6	45.2	45.5	45.9	46.2	46.8	46.7	46.3	46.1	45.8	45.7
2015	44.7	44.0	43.3	42.4	42.0	41.8	41.7	42.2	41.6	40.6	40.3	39.9	42.0
2016	38.8	38.0	37.0	36.6	36.3	36.3	36.7	36.9	37.5	36.9	37.0	36.8	37.1
2017	35.8	35.7	36.1	36.5	36.6	36.9	37.4	37.7	38.0	37.7	37.7	37.3	37.0
2018	37.6	37.8	37.7	37.6	38.0	38.2	38.8	39.4	39.5	39.5	39.4	39.2	38.6
Service-Providing													
2010	192.2	193.0	195.1	198.9	198.3	198.3	188.3	191.2	193.7	195.5	196.6	197.5	194.9
2011	194.3	195.3	196.9	198.5	200.4	199.3	196.5	198.4	198.9	199.8	201.2	201.1	198.4
2012	198.3	199.7	202.0	203.1	205.4	205.5	199.6	200.9	202.9	205.8	206.8	207.2	203.1
2013	203.3	205.1	206.3	207.7	209.0	206.6	203.1	205.1	206.6	208.7	210.0	210.3	206.8
2014	206.5	207.9	209.8	211.2	212.7	210.0	206.1	209.5	212.2	213.0	215.6	216.0	210.9
2015	212.7	212.8	214.7	215.6	217.2	215.7	211.1	214.5	215.9	219.3	220.3	220.8	215.9
2016	217.3	218.0	218.6	220.6	220.2	219.8	213.4	216.1	218.6	221.8	224.0	223.1	219.3
2017	219.2	220.1	222.1	222.5	224.1	223.2	217.6	220.3	222.9	225.8	227.9	227.2	222.7
2018	224.6	225.3	226.9	228.3	229.2	229.8	222.3	226.9	229.1	230.8	233.2	233.9	228.4
Mining, Logging, and Construction													
2010	21.3	20.8	21.2	21.8	22.6	22.8	23.1	23.3	23.2	23.2	23.4	23.8	22.5
2011	23.6	23.9	24.0	25.0	25.4	25.8	26.3	26.5	26.4	26.5	26.5	27.0	25.6
2012	27.7	28.1	28.7	29.4	29.7	30.0	30.3	30.5	30.2	30.1	30.2	29.6	29.5
2013	28.9	28.9	29.2	29.4	29.6	29.8	29.8	30.3	30.2	30.4	30.3	30.3	29.8
2014	30.1	30.2	30.3	30.6	31.0	31.2	31.6	31.8	31.6	31.5	31.6	31.4	31.1
2015	30.5	29.9	29.2	28.3	28.0	27.6	27.6	27.4	27.0	26.7	26.4	26.1	27.9
2016	25.4	24.6	23.6	23.3	23.0	22.9	23.1	23.1	23.2	23.2	23.5	23.4	23.5
2017	22.7	22.6	23.0	23.4	23.4	23.5	23.9	23.9	24.1	23.9	24.1	24.2	23.6
2018	24.4	24.5	24.5	24.7	25.0	25.1	25.8	26.1	26.1	26.2	26.2	26.1	25.4
Manufacturing													
2010	12.7	12.6	12.7	12.9	12.8	12.8	13.0	13.0	13.5	13.6	13.2	13.2	13.0
2011	13.0	12.9	12.9	13.0	12.9	13.2	13.1	13.3	13.6	13.2	13.0	13.1	13.1
2012	12.8	12.9	13.0	13.1	13.1	13.5	13.7	13.9	14.3	13.9	13.8	13.7	13.5
2013	13.4	13.5	13.6	13.7	13.8	14.0	14.1	14.3	14.8	14.6	14.5	14.4	14.1
2014	14.2	14.2	14.3	14.6	14.5	14.7	14.6	15.0	15.1	14.8	14.5	14.4	14.6
2015	14.2	14.1	14.1	14.1	14.0	14.2	14.1	14.8	14.6	13.9	13.9	13.8	14.2
2016	13.4	13.4	13.4	13.3	13.3	13.4	13.6	13.8	14.3	13.7	13.5	13.4	13.5
2017	13.1	13.1	13.1	13.1	13.2	13.4	13.5	13.8	13.9	13.8	13.6	13.1	13.4
2018	13.2	13.3	13.2	12.9	13.0	13.1	13.0	13.3	13.4	13.3	13.2	13.1	13.2

Employment by Industry: Bakersfield, CA, 2010–2018—*Continued*

(Numbers in thousands, not seasonally adjusted)

Industry and year	January	February	March	April	May	June	July	August	September	October	November	December	Annual average
Trade, Transportation, and Utilities													
2010	41.7	41.5	41.3	41.8	41.9	41.9	42.8	43.2	43.0	42.1	42.8	43.7	42.3
2011	42.5	42.1	42.1	43.0	44.0	43.6	44.6	44.8	44.7	44.2	44.8	45.1	43.8
2012	43.7	43.3	43.6	44.7	45.4	45.7	45.8	45.8	45.6	46.0	47.3	47.8	45.4
2013	46.0	45.9	46.1	47.0	47.4	47.5	47.7	48.1	47.8	47.9	49.1	49.7	47.5
2014	47.7	47.7	48.0	48.7	49.3	49.3	49.4	50.5	50.4	49.7	50.9	51.6	49.4
2015	49.6	49.4	49.6	50.1	50.6	50.5	51.1	51.1	50.9	51.3	52.1	52.3	50.7
2016	50.5	50.2	50.2	50.8	51.3	51.0	51.0	51.1	50.9	51.3	52.8	52.6	51.1
2017	50.6	50.1	50.2	50.6	51.3	51.2	51.7	52.2	51.9	52.4	53.7	53.7	51.6
2018	52.7	52.3	52.7	53.2	53.8	53.6	53.3	53.7	53.5	54.2	55.4	55.8	53.7
Wholesale Trade													
2010	7.0	6.9	6.6	7.1	7.1	7.5	8.4	8.6	8.6	7.3	7.2	7.2	7.5
2011	7.2	7.1	6.9	7.3	7.4	7.5	8.4	8.3	8.3	7.9	7.5	7.3	7.6
2012	7.4	7.2	7.2	7.7	7.8	8.0	7.9	7.9	7.9	8.0	8.0	8.1	7.8
2013	8.3	8.4	8.4	8.4	8.4	8.5	8.6	8.6	8.6	8.5	8.5	8.5	8.5
2014	8.5	8.6	8.6	8.8	8.7	8.8	8.6	8.8	8.7	8.6	8.7	8.7	8.7
2015	8.6	8.6	8.4	8.2	8.3	8.3	8.4	8.4	8.3	8.2	8.2	8.2	8.3
2016	8.1	8.2	8.2	8.1	8.2	8.2	8.1	8.1	8.0	8.1	8.0	8.0	8.1
2017	7.9	7.9	8.0	8.0	8.1	8.1	8.5	8.6	8.5	8.4	8.4	8.3	8.2
2018	8.3	8.2	8.3	8.3	8.4	8.4	8.4	8.4	8.3	8.3	8.4	8.4	8.3
Retail Trade													
2010	26.0	25.9	26.0	26.0	25.8	25.6	25.5	25.6	25.5	25.8	26.7	27.7	26.0
2011	26.6	26.3	26.5	26.8	27.2	27.0	27.0	27.1	26.9	27.0	28.0	28.5	27.1
2012	27.4	27.0	27.3	27.7	27.9	27.8	27.8	27.8	27.6	27.9	29.3	29.6	27.9
2013	28.1	27.9	28.0	28.7	28.9	28.8	28.9	29.1	28.8	29.1	30.3	30.7	28.9
2014	29.2	29.1	29.2	29.8	30.2	30.0	30.1	30.8	30.8	30.6	31.7	32.1	30.3
2015	30.6	30.5	30.8	31.2	31.5	31.4	31.5	31.5	31.4	31.7	32.7	32.8	31.5
2016	31.6	31.4	31.5	32.0	32.1	31.8	31.9	31.9	31.7	32.0	33.5	33.5	32.1
2017	32.1	31.6	31.5	31.6	31.8	31.7	31.7	31.8	31.5	31.9	33.1	33.2	32.0
2018	32.0	31.6	31.6	31.8	32.0	31.8	31.6	31.7	31.4	32.1	33.1	33.5	32.0
Transportation and Utilities													
2010	8.7	8.7	8.7	8.7	9.0	8.8	8.9	9.0	8.9	9.0	8.9	8.8	8.8
2011	8.7	8.7	8.7	8.9	9.4	9.1	9.2	9.4	9.5	9.3	9.3	9.3	9.1
2012	8.9	9.1	9.1	9.3	9.7	9.9	10.1	10.1	10.1	10.1	10.0	10.1	9.7
2013	9.6	9.6	9.7	9.9	10.1	10.2	10.2	10.4	10.4	10.3	10.3	10.5	10.1
2014	10.0	10.0	10.2	10.1	10.4	10.5	10.7	10.9	10.9	10.5	10.5	10.8	10.5
2015	10.4	10.3	10.4	10.7	10.8	10.8	11.2	11.2	11.2	11.4	11.2	11.3	10.9
2016	10.8	10.6	10.5	10.7	11.0	11.0	11.0	11.1	11.2	11.2	11.3	11.1	11.0
2017	10.6	10.6	10.7	11.0	11.4	11.4	11.5	11.8	11.9	12.1	12.2	12.2	11.5
2018	12.4	12.5	12.8	13.1	13.4	13.4	13.3	13.6	13.8	13.8	13.9	13.9	13.3
Information													
2010	2.7	2.6	2.6	2.6	2.6	2.6	2.9	2.8	2.7	2.7	2.7	2.8	2.7
2011	2.7	2.6	2.6	2.6	2.6	2.6	2.7	2.6	2.6	2.6	2.6	2.6	2.6
2012	2.7	2.7	2.7	2.7	2.7	2.8	2.6	2.6	2.6	2.6	2.7	2.7	2.7
2013	2.7	2.6	2.6	2.6	2.6	2.6	2.5	2.5	2.5	2.4	2.5	2.4	2.5
2014	2.4	2.4	2.4	2.4	2.4	2.4	2.3	2.4	2.3	2.4	2.4	2.4	2.4
2015	2.4	2.4	2.4	2.4	2.4	2.8	2.8	3.0	3.0	2.9	2.8	2.9	2.7
2016	2.7	2.6	2.3	2.2	2.0	2.1	2.1	2.0	2.0	2.0	2.0	2.0	2.2
2017	2.0	2.0	2.0	2.1	2.1	2.1	2.0	2.0	2.0	2.0	2.0	2.1	2.0
2018	2.0	2.0	2.0	2.1	2.1	2.1	2.1	2.0	2.0	2.0	2.0	2.0	2.0
Financial Activities													
2010	7.8	7.9	7.9	8.0	8.0	7.9	7.9	7.8	7.7	7.6	7.5	7.5	7.8
2011	7.4	7.6	7.6	7.8	7.9	7.8	8.1	8.2	8.1	8.0	8.1	8.0	7.9
2012	8.0	8.1	8.1	8.4	8.6	8.4	8.4	8.4	8.4	8.4	8.3	8.3	8.3
2013	8.4	8.3	8.3	8.4	8.5	8.5	8.4	8.4	8.3	8.4	8.4	8.3	8.4
2014	8.3	8.2	8.2	8.2	8.3	8.2	8.2	8.2	8.1	8.3	8.1	8.2	8.2
2015	8.2	8.0	8.1	8.1	8.1	8.0	8.1	8.1	8.0	8.0	7.9	7.8	8.0
2016	7.9	7.8	7.8	8.0	7.9	7.9	7.8	7.8	7.7	7.7	7.7	7.6	7.8
2017	7.8	7.7	7.8	7.7	7.7	7.7	7.7	7.6	7.6	7.7	7.6	7.6	7.7
2018	7.5	7.5	7.5	7.7	7.6	7.6	7.6	7.6	7.6	7.6	7.6	7.5	7.6

Employment by Industry: Bakersfield, CA, 2010–2018—*Continued*

(Numbers in thousands, not seasonally adjusted)

Industry and year	January	February	March	April	May	June	July	August	September	October	November	December	Annual average
Professional and Business Services													
2010	24.2	24.0	24.3	25.2	24.9	25.2	24.5	24.6	24.6	25.2	25.4	25.3	24.8
2011	25.4	25.7	26.1	26.1	26.1	25.9	26.5	26.7	27.1	26.7	26.9	26.5	26.3
2012	26.6	27.1	27.8	27.5	28.0	27.9	28.1	28.1	28.0	27.8	27.4	27.3	27.6
2013	26.9	27.6	27.6	27.4	27.8	27.8	27.5	27.7	27.4	27.3	26.9	26.7	27.4
2014	26.6	26.8	26.9	26.8	27.2	27.2	26.9	27.1	27.1	27.4	27.8	27.6	27.1
2015	27.0	26.9	27.0	26.6	26.7	26.8	26.7	26.5	26.1	26.8	27.1	27.2	26.8
2016	26.7	26.8	26.5	27.0	26.3	26.3	26.0	26.1	26.5	26.5	26.7	26.4	26.5
2017	25.9	26.1	26.4	26.1	26.4	26.2	26.2	26.2	26.4	25.9	26.0	25.9	26.1
2018	25.9	26.4	26.6	26.8	26.8	27.2	26.5	27.1	27.4	27.3	27.6	27.4	26.9
Education and Health Services													
2010	29.2	29.3	29.4	29.5	29.3	29.4	29.6	29.8	29.6	29.9	29.8	29.9	29.6
2011	29.5	29.6	29.7	29.9	30.1	29.9	30.1	30.4	30.6	30.5	30.5	30.8	30.1
2012	30.6	30.8	31.1	31.4	31.6	31.4	31.2	31.6	31.8	32.0	31.9	32.0	31.5
2013	31.6	32.0	32.1	32.4	32.6	32.1	32.1	32.4	32.3	32.5	32.6	32.5	32.3
2014	32.2	32.4	32.5	32.6	32.7	32.5	32.3	32.7	32.7	32.7	32.8	32.8	32.6
2015	32.5	32.7	32.9	33.3	33.5	33.5	33.2	33.7	33.7	34.0	34.1	34.1	33.4
2016	34.0	34.2	34.2	34.6	34.6	34.7	34.6	35.1	35.0	35.3	35.5	35.6	34.8
2017	35.3	35.9	36.1	36.5	36.7	36.1	36.2	36.5	36.6	37.0	37.2	37.1	36.4
2018	37.2	37.1	37.2	37.6	37.6	37.6	37.9	38.2	38.3	37.9	38.4	39.0	37.8
Leisure and Hospitality													
2010	19.8	20.1	20.3	20.8	20.8	21.1	20.8	20.6	20.7	20.4	20.4	20.1	20.5
2011	19.8	20.1	20.4	20.7	21.1	21.2	21.0	21.0	20.7	20.9	20.9	20.8	20.7
2012	20.6	20.8	21.2	21.6	22.0	22.2	22.0	21.9	21.7	21.8	21.9	21.9	21.6
2013	21.9	22.0	22.3	22.6	23.1	23.4	23.2	23.1	23.0	23.1	22.9	23.0	22.8
2014	22.6	22.9	23.4	23.8	24.0	24.1	24.1	24.0	24.0	23.6	23.8	24.0	23.7
2015	24.0	24.3	24.8	25.0	25.4	25.4	25.3	25.3	25.3	25.2	25.2	25.3	25.0
2016	25.2	25.2	25.5	25.8	25.7	25.8	25.6	25.3	25.2	25.4	25.4	25.4	25.5
2017	24.9	25.2	25.6	25.9	26.4	26.4	26.2	25.9	26.0	25.9	26.0	25.9	25.9
2018	25.8	26.1	26.5	26.7	27.1	27.1	26.9	26.8	26.6	26.6	26.5	26.7	26.6
Other Services													
2010	6.6	6.7	6.8	6.8	6.7	6.7	6.4	6.6	6.6	6.6	6.5	6.5	6.6
2011	6.5	6.5	6.6	6.7	6.8	6.7	6.7	7.0	7.0	6.9	7.0	7.0	6.8
2012	7.0	7.1	7.1	7.2	7.3	7.2	7.0	7.3	7.3	7.4	7.4	7.3	7.2
2013	7.3	7.4	7.5	7.6	7.7	7.3	7.3	7.6	7.5	7.5	7.6	7.5	7.5
2014	7.6	7.7	7.7	7.9	7.9	7.7	7.6	7.9	7.9	7.9	7.8	7.7	7.8
2015	7.8	7.8	7.8	7.7	7.7	7.4	7.6	7.7	7.7	7.7	7.7	7.6	7.7
2016	7.4	7.4	7.6	7.6	7.5	7.4	7.5	7.9	7.8	8.0	7.9	7.9	7.7
2017	7.5	7.5	7.6	7.6	7.6	7.6	7.6	7.9	8.0	8.0	7.9	7.9	7.7
2018	7.5	7.5	7.6	7.7	7.7	7.7	7.7	8.2	8.2	8.2	8.2	8.2	7.9
Government													
2010	60.2	60.9	62.5	64.2	64.1	63.5	53.4	55.8	58.8	61.0	61.5	61.7	60.6
2011	60.5	61.1	61.8	61.7	61.8	61.6	56.8	57.7	58.1	60.0	60.4	60.3	60.2
2012	59.1	59.8	60.4	59.6	59.8	59.9	54.5	55.2	57.5	59.8	59.9	59.9	58.8
2013	58.5	59.3	59.8	59.7	59.3	57.4	54.4	55.3	57.8	59.6	60.0	60.2	58.4
2014	59.1	59.8	60.7	60.8	60.9	58.6	55.3	56.7	59.7	61.0	62.0	61.7	59.7
2015	61.2	61.3	62.1	62.4	62.8	61.3	56.3	59.1	61.2	63.4	63.4	63.6	61.5
2016	62.9	63.8	64.5	64.6	64.9	64.6	58.8	60.8	63.5	65.6	66.0	65.6	63.8
2017	65.2	65.6	66.4	66.0	65.9	65.9	60.0	62.0	64.4	66.9	67.5	67.0	65.2
2018	66.0	66.4	66.8	66.5	66.5	66.9	60.3	63.3	65.5	67.0	67.5	67.3	65.8

Employment by Industry: Knoxville, TN, 2010–2018

(Numbers in thousands, nct seasonally adjusted)

Industry and year	January	February	March	April	May	June	July	August	September	October	November	December	Annual average
Total Nonfarm													
2010	349.6	350.3	352.6	357.8	361.1	357.8	357.9	360.5	362.2	361.7	363.6	363.1	358.2
2011	355.7	358.4	361.0	364.1	364.9	363.6	361.6	366.6	368.6	367.8	369.6	368.3	364.2
2012	361.2	362.7	365.9	367.7	368.7	366.7	364.6	368.6	369.6	370.4	372.2	372.0	367.5
2013	362.7	364.5	366.8	369.0	370.1	366.1	365.1	370.1	371.5	374.8	376.2	375.9	369.4
2014	367.9	369.2	371.9	374.8	376.7	372.2	372.5	377.7	380.8	382.6	386.3	385.1	376.5
2015	377.1	376.9	378.8	383.3	385.0	380.9	381.1	385.9	389.9	392.0	393.8	393.2	384.8
2016	383.7	386.1	389.6	393.2	393.3	390.2	388.6	392.6	397.0	397.4	399.6	397.6	392.4
2017	389.2	392.3	393.0	396.6	397.2	392.2	391.3	395.4	398.8	398.0	401.5	400.1	395.5
2018	391.7	394.3	396.2	399.9	401.9	397.2	395.8	400.4	403.7	403.4	406.4	405.1	399.7
Total Private													
2010	289.7	289.9	292.1	296.2	298.0	298.9	300.0	301.0	301.3	300.2	302.0	301.8	297.6
2011	296.5	298.9	301.5	304.3	305.1	306.6	306.5	308.0	308.8	308.0	309.2	308.3	305.1
2012	301.7	303.1	305.9	307.6	308.5	309.2	308.2	310.6	310.5	310.1	311.6	311.5	308.2
2013	303.7	305.1	307.4	308.2	309.5	309.5	309.3	312.1	312.1	312.7	315.0	314.4	309.9
2014	308.3	308.5	311.2	313.7	315.5	315.2	316.1	319.2	320.6	321.1	323.7	324.1	316.4
2015	316.9	316.7	318.8	322.7	324.8	324.5	325.0	327.5	328.7	330.2	331.1	331.8	324.9
2016	324.6	325.4	328.4	331.7	332.4	333.5	332.6	334.3	335.8	335.5	336.6	336.4	332.3
2017	330.3	331.5	332.6	335.6	336.5	335.7	335.2	337.2	338.1	336.7	339.7	339.2	335.7
2018	332.7	334.1	336.0	339.4	340.8	340.5	339.2	341.9	342.5	342.3	343.9	344.4	339.8
Goods Producing													
2010	48.1	48.3	49.0	50.0	50.3	50.9	51.4	51.3	51.5	51.5	51.5	51.4	50.4
2011	50.4	50.9	51.5	51.7	51.8	52.6	52.8	53.2	53.7	54.1	53.7	52.9	52.4
2012	51.3	51.6	51.7	51.7	52.0	52.5	52.6	52.9	53.0	52.9	52.7	52.3	52.3
2013	51.3	51.8	51.9	51.7	51.8	51.9	51.8	52.1	52.1	53.1	53.1	51.9	52.0
2014	50.8	51.2	51.6	51.7	51.6	51.7	52.1	52.6	52.9	53.3	53.8	53.4	52.2
2015	51.9	51.8	52.0	52.4	52.6	52.6	53.1	53.4	54.3	55.0	54.8	54.5	53.2
2016	54.2	54.3	55.4	55.9	55.7	56.1	56.1	56.4	56.9	57.0	56.9	56.5	56.0
2017	55.7	56.1	56.5	56.7	56.8	56.8	57.1	57.2	57.5	57.3	57.6	57.1	56.9
2018	56.6	56.7	57.3	57.8	57.9	58.3	58.8	59.0	59.4	59.9	58.8	58.8	58.3
Service-Providing													
2010	301.5	302.0	303.6	307.8	310.8	306.9	306.5	309.2	310.7	310.2	312.1	311.7	307.8
2011	305.3	307.5	309.5	312.4	313.1	311.0	308.8	313.4	314.9	313.7	315.9	315.4	311.7
2012	309.9	311.1	314.2	316.0	316.7	314.2	312.0	315.7	316.6	317.5	319.5	319.7	315.3
2013	311.4	312.7	314.9	317.3	318.3	314.2	313.3	318.0	319.4	321.7	323.1	324.0	317.4
2014	317.1	318.0	320.3	323.1	325.1	320.5	320.4	325.1	327.9	329.3	332.5	331.7	324.3
2015	325.2	325.1	326.8	330.9	332.4	328.3	328.0	332.5	335.6	337.0	339.0	338.7	331.6
2016	329.5	331.8	334.2	337.3	337.6	334.1	332.5	336.2	340.1	340.4	342.7	341.1	336.5
2017	333.5	336.2	336.5	339.9	340.4	335.4	334.2	338.2	341.3	340.7	343.9	343.0	338.6
2018	335.1	337.6	338.9	342.1	344.0	338.9	337.0	341.4	344.3	343.5	347.6	346.3	341.4
Mining, Logging, and Construction													
2010	15.6	15.7	16.3	16.9	16.9	17.2	17.7	17.7	17.8	17.8	17.7	17.6	17.1
2011	16.2	16.5	17.0	17.2	17.1	17.5	17.8	18.1	18.7	19.0	18.4	17.4	17.6
2012	15.9	16.1	16.4	16.3	16.6	17.0	17.0	17.4	17.5	17.4	17.2	16.9	16.8
2013	16.1	16.5	16.6	16.6	16.8	16.8	16.8	17.1	17.2	17.9	17.8	16.9	16.9
2014	15.9	16.2	16.5	16.7	16.7	16.7	17.0	17.3	17.6	17.9	18.2	17.8	17.0
2015	16.7	16.5	16.8	17.1	17.4	17.2	17.3	17.6	18.3	19.1	18.7	18.2	17.6
2016	16.9	16.7	17.5	17.8	17.4	17.7	17.8	17.9	18.5	18.3	18.1	17.8	17.7
2017	17.1	17.4	17.8	18.1	18.3	18.3	18.4	18.5	18.8	18.7	18.8	18.3	18.2
2018	17.7	17.7	18.2	18.4	18.6	18.8	18.6	18.6	18.9	19.2	18.2	18.4	18.4
Manufacturing													
2010	32.5	32.6	32.7	33.1	33.4	33.7	33.7	33.6	33.7	33.7	33.8	33.8	33.4
2011	34.2	34.4	34.5	34.5	34.7	35.1	35.0	35.1	35.0	35.1	35.3	35.5	34.9
2012	35.4	35.5	35.3	35.4	35.4	35.5	35.6	35.5	35.5	35.5	35.5	35.4	35.5
2013	35.2	35.3	35.3	35.1	35.0	35.1	35.0	35.0	34.9	35.2	35.3	35.0	35.1
2014	34.9	35.0	35.1	35.0	34.9	35.0	35.1	35.3	35.3	35.4	35.6	35.6	35.2
2015	35.2	35.3	35.2	35.3	35.2	35.4	35.8	35.8	36.0	35.9	36.1	36.3	35.6
2016	37.3	37.6	37.9	38.1	38.3	38.4	38.3	38.5	38.4	38.7	38.8	38.7	38.3
2017	38.6	38.7	38.7	38.6	38.5	38.5	38.7	38.7	38.7	38.6	38.8	38.8	38.7
2018	38.9	39.0	39.1	39.4	39.3	39.5	40.2	40.4	40.5	40.7	40.6	40.4	39.8

Employment by Industry: Knoxville, TN, 2010–2018—*Continued*

(Numbers in thousands, not seasonally adjusted)

Industry and year	January	February	March	April	May	June	July	August	September	October	November	December	Annual average
Trade, Transportation, and Utilities													
2010	70.9	70.3	70.5	70.8	71.0	71.0	71.6	71.8	71.6	72.0	73.4	73.7	71.6
2011	71.2	71.0	71.5	72.1	72.4	72.6	72.6	72.6	72.6	73.0	74.6	75.2	72.6
2012	72.7	72.6	73.2	73.6	73.8	73.9	74.1	74.2	74.1	74.7	76.4	76.8	74.2
2013	73.8	73.7	74.1	74.1	74.2	74.2	74.4	74.5	74.3	74.8	76.5	77.1	74.6
2014	74.3	74.1	74.7	74.8	75.0	75.4	75.9	76.2	76.1	76.6	78.1	78.9	75.8
2015	76.1	75.3	75.8	76.7	77.0	77.1	77.4	78.0	78.0	78.6	80.0	81.0	77.6
2016	78.0	77.9	78.2	78.5	78.7	78.6	78.7	78.7	78.9	79.2	80.5	81.3	78.9
2017	77.9	77.3	77.1	77.3	77.2	77.2	77.0	77.4	77.3	77.6	79.4	80.0	77.7
2018	77.1	76.7	77.3	77.9	78.2	78.2	77.9	78.3	78.3	78.6	80.6	81.0	78.3
Wholesale Trade													
2010	16.3	16.3	16.3	16.2	16.1	16.1	16.1	15.9	15.8	15.8	15.7	15.6	16.0
2011	15.6	15.6	15.7	16.0	16.1	16.2	16.2	16.2	16.2	16.2	16.3	16.4	16.1
2012	16.3	16.4	16.4	16.5	16.5	16.6	16.4	16.5	16.6	16.5	16.5	16.4	16.5
2013	16.3	16.3	16.4	16.2	16.2	16.2	16.1	16.1	16.1	16.1	16.1	16.1	16.2
2014	16.0	16.0	16.0	16.0	16.1	16.0	15.9	16.1	16.1	16.1	16.1	16.2	16.1
2015	16.1	16.1	16.1	16.2	16.2	16.2	16.3	16.3	16.4	16.5	16.5	16.6	16.3
2016	16.4	16.4	16.4	16.4	16.4	16.5	16.4	16.4	16.5	16.5	16.4	16.5	16.4
2017	16.2	16.2	16.2	16.1	16.1	16.2	16.1	16.1	16.2	16.3	16.4	16.5	16.2
2018	16.0	16.1	16.2	16.2	16.2	16.3	16.2	16.3	16.3	16.3	16.3	16.4	16.2
Retail Trade													
2010	43.9	43.4	43.5	43.7	43.9	43.9	44.0	44.3	44.1	44.5	45.8	45.9	44.2
2011	44.0	43.6	43.9	44.1	44.2	44.4	44.4	44.3	44.2	44.7	46.1	46.4	44.5
2012	44.5	44.2	44.8	45.1	45.1	45.3	45.7	45.5	45.2	45.7	47.2	47.3	45.5
2013	45.0	44.8	45.0	45.0	45.0	45.0	45.4	45.2	44.9	45.4	47.0	47.3	45.4
2014	45.1	44.8	45.1	45.2	45.2	45.7	46.2	46.0	45.8	46.1	47.5	47.9	45.9
2015	45.6	45.0	45.4	46.1	46.2	46.4	46.6	46.9	46.7	47.2	48.4	49.0	46.6
2016	47.0	46.9	47.2	47.4	47.6	47.7	47.9	47.8	47.9	48.4	49.7	50.1	48.0
2017	48.1	47.7	47.6	48.0	47.9	48.0	47.9	47.9	47.7	47.9	49.4	49.6	48.1
2018	47.6	47.4	47.8	48.3	48.4	48.5	48.2	48.0	47.9	48.2	49.9	50.0	48.4
Transportation and Utilities													
2010	10.7	10.6	10.7	10.9	11.0	11.0	11.5	11.6	11.7	11.7	11.9	12.2	11.3
2011	11.6	11.8	11.9	12.0	12.1	12.0	12.0	12.1	12.2	12.1	12.2	12.4	12.0
2012	11.9	12.0	12.0	12.0	12.2	12.0	12.0	12.2	12.3	12.5	12.7	13.1	12.2
2013	12.5	12.6	12.7	12.9	13.0	13.0	12.9	13.2	13.3	13.3	13.4	13.7	13.0
2014	13.2	13.3	13.6	13.6	13.7	13.7	13.8	14.1	14.2	14.4	14.5	14.8	13.9
2015	14.4	14.2	14.3	14.4	14.6	14.5	14.5	14.8	14.9	14.9	15.1	15.4	14.7
2016	14.6	14.6	14.6	14.7	14.7	14.4	14.4	14.5	14.5	14.3	14.4	14.7	14.5
2017	13.6	13.4	13.3	13.2	13.2	13.0	13.0	13.4	13.4	13.4	13.6	13.9	13.4
2018	13.5	13.2	13.3	13.4	13.6	13.4	13.5	14.0	14.1	14.1	14.4	14.6	13.8
Information													
2010	5.9	5.8	5.8	5.8	5.8	5.9	5.9	5.9	5.9	6.0	6.0	6.0	5.9
2011	6.1	6.1	6.0	6.0	6.0	6.0	6.1	6.0	6.0	5.9	5.9	5.8	6.0
2012	5.8	5.9	5.8	5.9	5.9	5.9	6.0	6.0	5.8	6.0	5.9	6.0	5.9
2013	6.1	6.0	6.0	6.1	6.1	6.1	6.1	6.1	5.9	6.0	6.1	6.0	6.1
2014	6.1	6.0	6.0	6.1	6.0	6.1	6.1	6.1	6.0	5.9	6.0	6.0	6.0
2015	6.1	6.0	6.0	6.0	5.9	5.9	5.9	5.9	5.9	5.8	5.9	5.9	5.9
2016	5.9	5.9	5.9	5.9	5.9	5.9	6.0	5.9	5.9	5.8	5.8	5.9	5.9
2017	5.9	5.9	6.0	5.9	6.0	6.0	6.0	6.0	6.0	5.9	5.9	5.9	6.0
2018	5.9	5.9	5.9	6.0	5.9	5.9	6.0	5.9	5.9	5.9	5.9	5.8	5.9
Financial Activities													
2010	17.8	17.8	17.8	18.0	18.0	18.0	17.9	17.8	17.7	17.6	17.7	17.7	17.8
2011	17.5	17.5	17.5	17.6	17.6	17.8	17.7	17.8	17.7	17.8	17.8	17.9	17.7
2012	17.8	17.9	18.0	18.0	18.1	18.1	18.0	18.0	17.9	17.9	17.9	18.0	18.0
2013	17.7	17.6	17.9	17.9	18.0	18.1	18.1	18.1	18.1	18.0	18.0	18.1	18.0
2014	17.9	18.0	18.0	18.1	18.1	18.2	18.3	18.3	18.3	18.4	18.5	18.6	18.2
2015	18.5	18.6	18.6	18.6	18.6	18.8	18.8	18.8	18.7	18.8	18.9	19.0	18.7
2016	18.7	18.7	18.8	18.9	19.0	19.1	19.1	19.2	19.2	19.3	19.3	19.3	19.1
2017	19.2	19.2	19.2	19.4	19.4	19.5	19.5	19.6	19.5	19.6	19.5	19.6	19.4
2018	19.5	19.6	19.7	19.7	19.8	20.0	20.0	20.0	19.9	19.5	19.5	19.7	19.7

Employment by Industry: Knoxville, TN, 2010–2018—*Continued*

(Numbers in thousands, not seasonally adjusted)

Industry and year	January	February	March	April	May	June	July	August	September	October	November	December	Annual average
Professional and Business Services													
2010	50.1	50.2	50.4	52.1	52.4	51.9	52.8	53.9	54.0	54.3	54.5	54.7	52.6
2011	54.6	55.6	56.1	56.2	56.0	55.4	55.6	56.3	56.5	56.4	56.6	56.3	56.0
2012	54.9	55.1	55.7	55.8	55.8	55.4	54.7	56.1	56.1	55.4	55.6	55.5	55.5
2013	54.5	55.0	55.3	55.4	55.7	55.5	55.4	57.0	57.2	57.2	57.6	57.8	56.1
2014	57.5	57.6	58.2	59.2	59.4	58.6	58.3	60.0	60.7	60.6	61.0	61.1	59.4
2015	60.0	59.9	60.3	61.4	62.4	61.5	61.2	62.6	63.0	63.4	62.9	63.2	61.8
2016	61.2	61.4	62.2	63.1	63.4	63.4	62.8	64.0	64.2	64.3	64.3	64.4	63.2
2017	63.5	64.1	64.6	65.5	65.6	64.8	64.2	65.0	65.5	64.6	65.2	65.1	64.8
2018	63.5	64.2	64.3	65.0	65.3	64.7	63.7	65.0	65.2	63.7	64.4	64.6	64.5
Education and Health Services													
2010	47.9	48.1	48.4	48.6	48.7	48.8	48.6	48.8	49.2	49.0	49.2	49.2	48.7
2011	48.7	49.1	49.4	50.1	50.1	50.3	50.3	50.5	50.8	50.2	50.0	49.9	50.0
2012	49.5	49.7	49.9	49.9	50.1	50.1	50.1	50.5	50.7	50.8	50.6	50.8	50.2
2013	49.6	50.0	50.2	50.2	50.2	49.6	49.5	49.8	50.1	50.1	50.4	50.6	50.0
2014	49.7	49.8	50.0	50.0	50.6	50.4	50.4	50.9	51.4	51.7	51.7	51.9	50.7
2015	51.4	51.6	52.0	51.8	52.1	52.0	51.8	52.1	52.2	52.4	52.5	52.6	52.0
2016	52.2	52.4	52.7	52.9	53.0	52.9	52.7	53.1	53.3	53.6	53.8	53.8	53.0
2017	53.8	54.1	54.1	54.1	54.2	53.8	53.8	54.1	54.1	54.3	54.5	54.4	54.1
2018	54.0	54.2	54.3	54.6	54.7	54.3	54.0	54.4	54.4	55.2	55.1	55.4	54.6
Leisure and Hospitality													
2010	34.0	34.3	35.0	36.0	37.0	37.5	37.2	37.1	37.3	35.9	35.9	35.4	36.1
2011	34.6	35.2	35.9	36.9	37.5	37.8	37.4	37.6	37.8	36.9	36.7	36.4	36.7
2012	35.8	36.4	37.6	38.4	38.5	38.8	38.3	38.6	38.6	38.3	38.5	38.2	38.0
2013	36.9	37.1	37.9	38.5	39.1	39.5	39.5	39.9	39.9	39.1	38.9	38.5	38.7
2014	37.8	37.5	38.2	39.5	40.4	40.4	40.6	40.7	40.8	40.4	40.2	39.8	39.7
2015	38.6	39.1	39.7	41.2	41.5	41.8	41.9	41.9	41.8	41.4	41.3	40.7	40.9
2016	39.7	40.0	40.4	41.5	41.9	42.6	42.3	42.2	42.6	41.5	41.2	40.4	41.4
2017	39.6	40.0	40.3	41.8	42.3	42.5	42.5	42.8	43.1	42.4	42.5	42.0	41.8
2018	41.1	41.6	41.9	43.0	43.6	43.6	43.4	43.8	43.8	43.9	44.0	43.5	43.1
Other Services													
2010	15.0	15.1	15.2	14.9	14.8	14.9	14.6	14.4	14.1	13.9	13.8	13.7	14.5
2011	13.4	13.5	13.6	13.7	13.7	14.1	14.0	14.0	13.7	13.7	13.9	13.9	13.8
2012	13.9	13.9	14.0	14.3	14.3	14.5	14.4	14.3	14.3	14.1	14.0	13.9	14.2
2013	13.8	13.9	14.1	14.3	14.4	14.6	14.5	14.6	14.5	14.4	14.4	14.4	14.3
2014	14.2	14.3	14.5	14.3	14.4	14.4	14.4	14.4	14.4	14.2	14.4	14.4	14.4
2015	14.3	14.4	14.4	14.6	14.7	14.8	14.9	14.8	14.8	14.8	14.8	14.9	14.7
2016	14.7	14.8	14.8	15.0	14.8	14.9	14.9	14.8	14.8	14.8	14.8	14.8	14.8
2017	14.7	14.8	14.8	14.9	15.0	15.1	15.1	15.1	15.1	15.0	15.1	15.1	15.0
2018	15.0	15.2	15.3	15.4	15.4	15.5	15.4	15.5	15.6	15.6	15.6	15.6	15.4
Government													
2010	59.9	60.4	60.5	61.6	63.1	58.9	57.9	59.5	60.9	61.5	61.6	61.3	60.6
2011	59.2	59.5	59.5	59.8	59.8	57.0	55.1	58.6	59.8	59.8	60.4	60.0	59.0
2012	59.5	59.6	60.0	60.1	60.2	57.5	56.4	58.0	59.1	60.3	60.6	60.5	59.3
2013	59.0	59.4	59.4	60.8	60.6	56.6	55.8	58.0	59.4	62.1	61.2	61.5	59.5
2014	59.6	60.7	60.7	61.1	61.2	57.0	56.4	58.5	60.2	61.5	62.6	61.0	60.0
2015	60.2	60.2	60.0	60.6	60.2	56.4	56.1	58.4	61.2	61.8	62.7	61.4	59.9
2016	59.1	60.7	61.2	61.5	60.9	56.7	56.0	58.3	61.2	61.9	63.0	61.2	60.1
2017	58.9	60.8	60.4	61.0	60.7	56.5	56.1	58.2	60.7	61.3	61.8	60.9	59.8
2018	59.0	60.2	60.2	60.5	61.1	56.7	56.6	58.5	61.2	61.1	62.5	60.7	59.9

Employment by Industry: Albany-Schenectady-Troy, NY, 2010–2018

(Numbers in thousands, not seasonally adjusted)

Industry and year	January	February	March	April	May	June	July	August	September	October	November	December	Annual average
Total Nonfarm													
2010	424.5	428.4	429.6	435.9	439.5	439.2	431.3	429.9	431.7	436.0	438.2	436.5	433.4
2011	421.2	427.0	427.7	435.2	436.9	437.7	433.2	432.2	435.2	440.2	442.6	440.7	434.2
2012	428.0	433.8	434.9	441.2	444.9	446.0	437.9	438.3	440.8	447.2	450.0	447.0	440.8
2013	432.8	439.6	441.0	445.9	450.1	451.4	444.2	443.2	445.6	452.2	454.6	452.2	446.1
2014	435.5	442.7	444.2	449.2	453.0	454.8	447.8	447.6	449.0	458.5	459.0	457.0	449.9
2015	445.0	449.8	450.1	455.7	460.0	461.6	455.1	454.4	455.2	464.8	464.9	463.4	456.7
2016	450.4	456.7	458.4	465.1	465.0	467.6	463.0	463.3	464.1	472.8	472.1	470.6	464.1
2017	455.7	461.9	462.9	468.8	469.8	472.7	465.8	466.7	468.2	476.7	476.8	474.8	468.4
2018	458.4	465.6	466.3	470.5	473.8	476.7	469.7	470.0	470.5	480.3	481.2	480.1	471.9
Total Private													
2010	317.3	319.5	321.1	326.8	328.6	328.8	330.0	330.7	329.5	331.8	333.4	331.9	327.5
2011	320.5	323.7	324.6	330.9	332.3	333.4	334.4	334.8	335.7	337.3	339.3	337.3	332.0
2012	327.3	330.8	332.6	338.0	341.1	343.0	341.3	342.2	341.8	345.2	347.0	344.5	339.6
2013	332.1	336.1	337.9	342.9	346.5	347.8	346.6	346.8	347.2	350.6	351.8	349.9	344.7
2014	336.3	340.4	342.0	346.8	350.5	352.4	351.2	352.0	350.6	356.7	356.9	354.7	349.2
2015	345.0	347.8	348.2	353.6	357.3	359.1	358.6	359.0	357.0	362.9	362.9	361.3	356.1
2016	350.2	354.5	356.2	362.2	362.9	365.2	365.8	366.9	364.3	370.5	369.6	367.8	363.0
2017	354.6	358.9	359.9	365.4	367.2	369.8	368.3	370.0	368.5	373.9	373.7	371.5	366.8
2018	357.2	362.9	363.5	367.9	370.5	373.5	371.8	373.5	371.2	378.1	378.5	377.2	370.5
Goods Producing													
2010	34.7	34.0	34.4	36.1	37.0	37.9	38.0	38.2	38.5	38.1	37.7	36.8	36.8
2011	35.2	34.8	35.1	37.1	38.2	39.4	40.4	40.8	40.4	40.2	39.9	38.5	38.3
2012	37.0	36.4	37.0	39.0	40.1	41.3	41.8	42.0	41.6	41.3	40.9	40.3	39.9
2013	38.7	38.5	38.9	40.2	42.0	42.8	43.4	43.5	42.9	42.8	42.4	41.3	41.5
2014	39.5	39.0	39.3	40.9	43.2	44.4	44.8	45.3	44.7	44.7	44.4	43.6	42.8
2015	42.6	42.2	42.4	43.9	45.6	46.8	47.4	47.5	46.5	46.3	45.8	44.8	45.2
2016	43.1	42.6	43.0	44.6	46.0	46.9	47.6	47.7	47.1	47.2	46.0	45.0	45.6
2017	43.5	43.2	43.9	45.6	46.7	48.0	47.7	48.0	47.7	47.6	47.1	46.0	46.3
2018	43.9	43.6	44.3	45.7	47.0	48.4	48.9	48.8	47.9	48.0	47.2	46.3	46.7
Service-Providing													
2010	389.8	394.4	395.2	399.8	402.5	401.3	393.3	391.7	393.2	397.9	400.5	399.7	396.6
2011	386.0	392.2	392.6	398.1	398.7	398.3	392.8	391.4	394.8	400.0	402.7	402.2	395.8
2012	391.0	397.4	397.9	402.2	404.8	404.7	396.1	396.3	399.2	405.9	409.1	406.7	400.9
2013	394.1	401.1	402.1	405.7	408.1	408.6	400.8	399.7	402.7	409.4	412.2	410.9	404.6
2014	396.0	403.7	404.9	408.3	409.8	410.4	403.0	402.3	404.3	413.8	414.6	413.4	407.0
2015	402.4	407.6	407.7	411.8	414.4	414.8	407.7	406.9	408.7	418.5	419.1	418.6	411.5
2016	407.3	414.1	415.4	420.5	419.0	420.7	415.4	415.6	417.0	425.6	426.1	425.6	418.5
2017	412.2	418.7	419.0	423.2	423.1	424.7	418.1	418.7	420.5	429.1	429.7	428.8	422.2
2018	414.5	422.0	422.0	424.8	426.8	428.3	420.8	421.2	422.6	432.3	434.0	433.8	425.3
Mining, Logging, and Construction													
2010	14.5	14.0	14.3	15.9	16.7	17.4	18.1	18.4	18.1	17.6	17.0	16.2	16.5
2011	14.7	14.2	14.4	15.9	16.9	17.8	18.6	19.0	18.6	18.2	17.8	16.5	16.9
2012	15.2	14.5	14.8	16.7	17.6	18.5	18.8	18.9	18.5	18.2	17.7	17.1	17.2
2013	15.2	14.9	15.2	16.4	18.0	18.4	19.2	19.4	19.0	18.9	18.4	17.4	17.5
2014	15.9	15.6	15.8	17.2	19.3	20.0	20.3	20.7	20.3	20.3	19.9	19.0	18.7
2015	18.1	17.6	17.7	19.0	20.5	21.2	21.4	21.5	20.7	20.4	19.7	18.9	19.7
2016	17.2	16.7	17.1	18.5	19.8	20.4	20.9	21.0	20.6	20.5	19.8	18.8	19.3
2017	17.6	17.2	17.3	18.9	20.1	20.9	21.2	21.1	21.0	20.7	20.2	19.1	19.6
2018	17.4	17.2	17.6	18.9	20.1	21.0	21.4	21.4	21.1	21.1	20.4	19.5	19.8
Manufacturing													
2010	20.2	20.0	20.1	20.2	20.3	20.5	19.9	19.8	20.4	20.5	20.7	20.6	20.3
2011	20.5	20.6	20.7	21.2	21.3	21.6	21.8	21.8	21.8	22.0	22.1	22.0	21.5
2012	21.8	21.9	22.2	22.3	22.5	22.8	23.0	23.1	23.1	23.1	23.2	23.2	22.7
2013	23.5	23.6	23.7	23.8	24.0	24.4	24.2	24.1	23.9	23.9	24.0	23.9	23.9
2014	23.6	23.4	23.5	23.7	23.9	24.4	24.5	24.6	24.4	24.4	24.5	24.6	24.1
2015	24.5	24.6	24.7	24.9	25.1	25.6	26.0	26.0	25.8	25.9	26.1	25.9	25.4
2016	25.9	25.9	25.9	26.1	26.2	26.5	26.7	26.7	26.5	26.7	26.2	26.2	26.3
2017	25.9	26.0	26.6	26.7	26.6	27.1	26.5	26.9	26.7	26.9	26.9	26.9	26.6
2018	26.5	26.4	26.7	26.8	26.9	27.4	27.5	27.4	26.8	26.9	26.8	26.8	26.9

Employment by Industry: Albany-Schenectady-Troy, NY, 2010–2018—*Continued*

(Numbers in thousands, not seasonally adjusted)

Industry and year	January	February	March	April	May	June	July	August	September	October	November	December	Annual average
Trade, Transportation, and Utilities													
2010	71.7	70.2	70.7	71.2	71.8	72.6	72.0	72.5	71.7	72.3	73.8	75.0	72.1
2011	71.3	70.2	70.4	71.2	71.7	72.5	72.0	72.5	72.1	72.6	74.5	75.9	72.2
2012	72.6	71.4	71.5	72.2	73.2	74.0	73.4	73.6	73.0	73.9	75.7	76.2	73.4
2013	72.3	71.4	71.6	72.2	73.2	74.4	73.9	73.9	73.7	74.8	76.4	77.1	73.7
2014	73.1	72.3	72.6	73.1	73.9	74.6	74.1	74.4	74.1	76.0	76.6	77.1	74.3
2015	73.9	72.7	72.8	73.4	74.2	75.0	74.6	74.8	74.5	76.0	77.1	77.8	74.7
2016	74.8	73.7	73.8	74.2	74.8	75.6	75.4	75.7	75.5	77.1	77.5	77.7	75.5
2017	74.4	73.1	72.9	73.5	73.9	74.5	74.4	74.6	74.4	75.7	76.6	76.8	74.6
2018	73.7	72.9	72.6	73.0	73.9	74.5	74.2	74.6	74.4	75.4	77.3	78.0	74.5
Wholesale Trade													
2010	12.7	12.7	12.7	12.8	13.0	13.0	13.0	13.1	13.0	13.1	13.2	13.2	13.0
2011	13.1	13.1	13.1	13.2	13.2	13.3	13.3	13.3	13.1	13.0	13.2	13.2	13.2
2012	13.1	13.1	13.2	13.4	13.5	13.7	13.7	13.7	13.5	13.6	13.6	13.5	13.5
2013	13.4	13.4	13.5	13.4	13.6	13.7	13.7	14.0	13.6	13.5	13.5	13.4	13.5
2014	13.4	13.4	13.4	13.7	13.8	13.9	13.9	14.0	13.8	13.9	13.8	13.8	13.7
2015	13.9	13.9	13.8	13.9	13.9	14.0	14.0	13.9	13.8	13.7	13.8	13.8	13.9
2016	13.7	13.6	13.7	13.6	13.7	13.8	13.8	13.8	13.7	13.7	13.6	13.6	13.7
2017	13.5	13.4	13.4	13.2	13.3	13.4	13.5	13.4	13.2	13.1	13.1	13.1	13.3
2018	12.9	12.9	12.9	12.8	12.9	13.0	13.2	13.2	13.1	13.1	13.1	13.0	13.0
Retail Trade													
2010	46.2	44.8	45.1	45.5	45.9	46.7	46.2	46.6	45.9	46.5	47.8	48.9	46.3
2011	46.1	45.0	45.3	45.9	46.2	46.9	46.5	46.9	46.5	47.1	48.7	49.8	46.7
2012	47.3	46.2	46.2	46.7	47.5	48.0	47.5	47.7	47.1	47.9	49.7	50.0	47.7
2013	47.0	45.9	46.1	46.6	47.2	48.1	47.8	47.8	47.5	48.5	49.8	50.3	47.7
2014	47.2	46.3	46.4	46.8	47.4	48.0	47.6	47.8	47.5	49.2	49.6	49.8	47.8
2015	47.1	46.0	46.1	46.5	47.2	47.9	47.6	47.9	47.6	48.9	49.6	50.0	47.7
2016	47.7	46.8	46.7	47.4	47.7	48.2	48.1	48.3	48.1	49.5	49.7	49.7	48.2
2017	47.3	46.2	46.0	46.7	46.9	47.4	47.4	47.5	47.3	48.7	49.3	49.2	47.5
2018	47.0	46.2	45.8	46.4	46.9	47.3	46.9	47.2	46.9	48.1	49.6	50.3	47.4
Transportation and Utilities													
2010	12.8	12.7	12.9	12.9	12.9	12.9	12.8	12.8	12.8	12.7	12.8	12.9	12.8
2011	12.1	12.1	12.0	12.1	12.3	12.3	12.2	12.3	12.5	12.5	12.6	12.9	12.3
2012	12.2	12.1	12.1	12.1	12.2	12.3	12.2	12.2	12.4	12.4	12.4	12.7	12.3
2013	11.9	12.1	12.0	12.2	12.4	12.6	12.4	12.4	12.6	12.8	13.1	13.4	12.5
2014	12.5	12.6	12.8	12.6	12.7	12.7	12.6	12.6	12.8	12.9	13.2	13.5	12.8
2015	12.9	12.8	12.9	13.0	13.1	13.1	13.0	13.0	13.1	13.4	13.7	14.0	13.2
2016	13.4	13.3	13.4	13.2	13.4	13.6	13.5	13.6	13.7	13.9	14.2	14.4	13.6
2017	13.6	13.5	13.5	13.6	13.7	13.7	13.5	13.7	13.9	13.9	14.2	14.5	13.8
2018	13.8	13.8	13.9	13.8	14.1	14.2	14.1	14.2	14.4	14.2	14.6	14.7	14.2
Information													
2010	9.0	9.0	9.0	8.8	8.9	8.9	9.0	9.0	8.8	8.8	8.8	8.8	8.9
2011	8.8	8.7	8.7	8.8	8.8	8.9	9.0	8.2	8.8	8.8	8.8	8.8	8.8
2012	8.7	8.7	8.7	8.7	8.7	8.7	8.7	8.6	8.5	8.6	8.6	8.5	8.6
2013	8.5	8.5	8.5	8.6	8.5	8.5	8.5	8.6	8.5	8.5	8.6	8.7	8.5
2014	8.6	8.7	8.7	8.7	8.7	8.8	8.5	8.5	8.4	8.4	8.4	8.4	8.6
2015	8.3	8.2	8.2	8.5	8.5	8.4	8.9	8.8	8.7	8.8	8.7	8.8	8.6
2016	8.7	8.7	8.7	8.8	8.2	8.8	8.9	8.8	8.8	8.7	8.6	8.7	8.7
2017	8.5	8.6	8.6	8.5	8.4	8.6	8.5	8.5	8.4	8.4	8.4	8.5	8.5
2018	8.6	8.7	8.7	8.6	8.7	8.8	8.6	8.7	8.5	8.5	8.6	8.5	8.6
Financial Activities													
2010	24.3	24.2	24.3	24.3	24.3	24.7	24.8	24.7	24.3	24.5	24.4	24.6	24.5
2011	24.3	24.3	24.3	24.4	24.4	24.8	25.0	25.1	24.7	24.6	24.6	24.7	24.6
2012	24.7	24.7	24.8	24.9	24.9	25.5	25.6	25.5	25.2	25.3	25.4	25.5	25.2
2013	25.0	25.0	25.1	25.2	25.3	25.7	25.7	25.6	25.2	25.3	25.2	25.3	25.3
2014	25.2	25.1	25.1	25.0	25.2	25.7	25.9	25.7	25.4	25.5	25.4	25.5	25.4
2015	25.5	25.5	25.5	25.7	25.7	26.1	26.3	26.3	25.9	25.9	25.9	26.1	25.9
2016	25.9	25.9	26.0	26.1	26.1	26.6	26.7	26.7	26.2	26.2	26.2	26.3	26.2
2017	25.9	25.8	25.8	25.9	26.2	26.7	26.6	26.6	26.3	26.3	26.3	26.4	26.2
2018	26.1	26.1	26.0	26.2	26.3	26.7	27.0	26.8	26.3	26.4	26.2	26.1	26.4

Employment by Industry: Albany-Schenectady-Troy, NY, 2010–2018—*Continued*

(Numbers in thousands, not seasonally adjusted)

Industry and year	January	February	March	April	May	June	July	August	September	October	November	December	Annual average
Professional and Business Services													
2010	49.2	49.3	49.5	50.6	50.6	51.0	52.0	51.6	50.8	51.2	51.2	51.0	50.7
2011	50.1	50.2	50.3	51.5	51.2	51.8	52.2	51.8	51.7	51.8	52.5	51.7	51.4
2012	51.4	51.5	51.8	52.7	52.8	53.4	53.2	53.2	52.4	52.7	53.2	52.0	52.5
2013	51.8	51.8	52.0	53.0	53.1	53.7	53.6	53.3	52.8	52.4	52.4	51.8	52.6
2014	51.1	51.3	51.5	52.5	53.0	53.6	53.9	53.8	53.1	53.3	53.7	53.2	52.8
2015	53.3	53.2	53.0	54.0	54.3	55.1	54.7	54.7	53.8	54.5	54.4	54.1	54.1
2016	53.8	54.2	54.6	55.8	55.6	56.7	57.5	57.6	56.5	57.0	57.1	56.6	56.1
2017	55.4	55.6	55.5	56.1	56.2	57.1	57.1	57.2	55.9	56.1	56.1	55.7	56.2
2018	54.6	55.1	55.2	55.9	56.0	57.1	57.8	58.3	56.4	57.0	57.3	57.2	56.5
Education and Health Services													
2010	80.1	83.7	83.8	84.5	83.2	80.5	79.5	79.0	82.5	84.4	85.4	84.1	82.6
2011	81.4	85.4	85.4	85.9	84.7	81.9	80.5	79.9	83.6	86.1	86.5	85.4	83.9
2012	82.9	87.0	87.3	87.5	86.6	83.8	81.9	81.2	85.5	88.3	88.8	88.2	85.8
2013	85.0	89.1	89.1	89.9	88.4	84.8	83.6	83.0	87.6	90.6	91.3	90.6	87.8
2014	86.5	91.1	91.4	91.7	89.7	87.1	85.8	85.3	88.6	92.3	92.5	91.4	89.5
2015	87.8	92.0	92.1	92.2	90.6	88.5	86.8	86.2	89.7	93.3	93.6	92.5	90.4
2016	89.1	93.9	94.3	94.7	93.0	90.0	88.5	88.3	91.1	95.0	95.2	94.8	92.3
2017	90.6	95.3	95.7	96.6	94.7	92.5	90.8	90.8	94.8	98.0	98.6	97.8	94.7
2018	92.9	98.1	98.5	98.3	96.6	95.1	91.7	92.3	96.0	99.7	100.2	99.0	96.5
Leisure and Hospitality													
2010	30.7	31.4	31.7	33.5	34.9	35.5	36.8	37.7	35.3	34.8	34.4	33.7	34.2
2011	31.8	32.4	32.7	34.1	35.3	36.4	37.3	38.5	36.4	35.5	34.8	34.5	35.0
2012	32.5	33.5	33.6	35.1	36.9	38.3	38.7	40.2	37.8	37.2	36.5	36.0	36.4
2013	33.3	34.1	34.8	36.0	38.1	39.8	39.8	40.9	38.8	38.1	37.3	36.8	37.3
2014	34.3	34.8	35.2	36.6	38.6	40.2	39.9	40.7	38.2	38.2	37.4	37.0	37.6
2015	35.3	35.6	35.8	37.4	39.8	40.6	41.2	42.2	40.0	39.6	38.8	38.5	38.7
2016	36.2	36.9	37.2	39.1	40.4	41.8	42.3	43.4	40.6	40.5	40.2	39.8	39.9
2017	37.5	38.6	38.7	40.3	42.1	43.3	44.0	45.3	42.2	42.6	41.4	41.0	41.4
2018	38.3	39.1	38.9	40.8	42.5	43.5	44.0	44.7	42.7	43.8	42.4	42.7	42.0
Other Services													
2010	17.6	17.7	17.7	17.8	17.9	17.7	17.9	18.0	17.6	17.7	17.7	17.9	17.8
2011	17.6	17.7	17.7	17.9	18.0	17.7	18.0	18.0	18.0	17.7	17.7	17.8	17.8
2012	17.5	17.6	17.9	17.9	17.9	18.0	18.0	17.9	17.8	17.9	17.9	17.8	17.8
2013	17.5	17.7	17.9	17.8	17.9	18.1	18.1	18.0	17.7	18.1	18.2	18.3	17.9
2014	18.0	18.1	18.2	18.3	18.2	18.0	18.3	18.3	18.1	18.3	18.5	18.5	18.2
2015	18.3	18.4	18.4	18.5	18.6	18.6	18.7	18.5	17.9	18.5	18.6	18.7	18.5
2016	18.6	18.6	18.6	18.9	18.8	18.8	18.9	18.7	18.5	18.8	18.8	18.9	18.7
2017	18.8	18.7	18.8	18.9	19.0	19.1	19.2	19.0	18.8	19.2	19.2	19.3	19.0
2018	19.1	19.3	19.3	19.4	19.5	19.4	19.6	19.3	19.0	19.3	19.3	19.4	19.3
Government													
2010	107.2	108.9	108.5	109.1	110.9	110.4	101.3	99.2	102.2	104.2	104.8	104.6	105.9
2011	100.7	103.3	103.1	104.3	104.6	104.3	98.8	97.4	99.5	102.9	103.3	103.4	102.1
2012	100.7	103.0	102.3	103.2	103.8	103.0	96.6	96.1	99.0	102.0	103.0	102.5	101.3
2013	100.7	103.5	103.1	103.0	103.6	103.6	97.6	96.4	98.4	101.6	102.8	102.3	101.4
2014	99.2	102.3	102.2	102.4	102.5	102.4	96.6	95.6	98.4	101.8	102.1	102.3	100.7
2015	100.0	102.0	101.9	102.1	102.7	102.5	96.5	95.4	98.2	101.9	102.0	102.1	100.6
2016	100.2	102.2	102.2	102.9	102.1	102.4	97.2	96.4	99.8	102.3	102.5	102.8	101.1
2017	101.1	103.0	103.0	103.4	102.6	102.9	97.5	96.7	99.7	102.8	103.1	103.3	101.6
2018	101.2	102.7	102.8	102.6	103.3	103.2	97.9	96.5	99.3	102.2	102.7	102.9	101.4

Employment by Industry: McAllen-Edinburg-Mission, TX, 2010–2018

(Numbers in thousands, not seasonally adjusted)

Industry and year	January	February	March	April	May	June	July	August	September	October	November	December	Annual average
Total Nonfarm													
2010	219.8	220.4	221.6	221.3	223.2	221.3	212.1	215.6	218.8	222.8	225.0	226.8	220.7
2011	224.2	225.2	226.5	227.4	228.0	226.8	220.6	224.1	225.6	226.5	229.9	231.1	226.3
2012	228.4	229.6	231.4	231.2	231.4	230.4	223.2	226.6	228.3	231.8	235.2	237.0	230.4
2013	232.3	234.6	236.2	236.5	237.2	236.7	229.5	233.8	235.1	238.1	241.8	243.7	236.3
2014	238.6	239.9	240.9	242.1	244.1	243.0	236.0	239.7	240.9	244.9	247.3	249.9	242.3
2015	245.7	247.4	248.4	248.1	250.4	249.0	242.9	245.4	246.3	248.9	251.8	253.1	248.1
2016	249.4	251.1	252.0	253.6	254.0	252.3	246.1	249.9	252.6	255.2	258.0	259.6	252.8
2017	255.9	256.2	257.7	259.0	260.3	259.0	251.1	253.7	256.7	260.1	263.6	265.6	258.2
2018	261.2	263.0	264.8	264.6	265.9	264.3	258.4	261.7	262.9	266.3	268.5	269.2	264.2
Total Private													
2010	164.1	163.9	164.8	164.4	166.1	165.0	163.5	165.1	166.0	167.4	168.9	170.9	165.8
2011	168.1	168.5	170.0	171.5	171.7	171.5	171.1	172.8	172.6	172.4	174.8	175.9	171.7
2012	173.6	174.2	175.6	176.0	176.0	175.6	174.0	175.8	175.3	176.7	179.4	181.0	176.1
2013	177.0	178.6	179.8	180.7	180.7	180.9	179.4	181.9	181.2	182.1	185.1	186.9	181.2
2014	181.9	182.8	183.5	185.4	186.1	186.0	185.0	187.1	186.6	188.2	190.0	192.2	186.2
2015	188.8	189.8	190.6	191.0	191.9	191.3	191.0	191.6	190.6	191.2	193.6	194.4	191.3
2016	191.4	192.3	193.0	194.2	194.0	193.0	192.5	194.5	194.6	195.6	198.1	199.1	194.4
2017	196.3	196.2	197.7	198.3	199.1	199.0	197.0	198.4	199.0	200.2	203.0	204.7	199.1
2018	201.8	202.3	203.6	203.5	204.2	203.6	203.5	205.2	204.2	205.4	206.9	207.2	204.3
Goods Producing													
2010	15.1	14.8	15.1	14.8	15.0	14.5	14.2	14.4	14.5	14.5	14.6	14.7	14.7
2011	14.7	14.7	14.8	14.5	14.6	14.7	14.7	15.0	15.0	15.1	15.4	15.3	14.9
2012	15.2	15.3	15.5	15.3	15.3	15.3	15.1	15.4	15.3	15.6	15.7	15.9	15.4
2013	15.6	15.8	15.9	16.0	16.0	16.1	15.9	16.2	16.0	16.2	16.3	16.4	16.0
2014	16.1	16.5	16.2	16.6	16.4	16.5	16.3	16.6	16.6	16.8	16.7	16.9	16.5
2015	16.5	16.7	16.4	16.4	16.2	16.2	15.9	15.5	15.3	15.2	15.1	15.1	15.9
2016	14.8	14.7	14.6	14.3	14.0	14.0	14.0	14.1	14.2	14.6	14.7	14.8	14.4
2017	14.9	14.9	14.9	14.8	15.1	15.3	15.2	15.4	15.2	15.2	15.6	15.7	15.2
2018	15.4	15.5	15.5	15.3	15.4	15.2	15.2	15.2	15.1	15.3	15.6	15.4	15.3
Service-Providing													
2010	204.7	205.6	206.5	206.5	208.2	206.8	197.9	201.2	204.3	208.3	210.4	212.1	206.0
2011	209.5	210.5	211.7	212.9	213.4	212.1	205.9	209.1	210.6	211.4	214.5	215.8	211.5
2012	213.2	214.3	215.9	215.9	216.1	215.1	208.1	211.2	213.0	216.2	219.5	221.1	215.0
2013	216.7	218.8	220.3	220.5	221.2	220.6	213.6	217.6	219.1	221.9	225.5	227.3	220.3
2014	222.5	223.4	224.7	225.5	227.7	226.5	219.7	223.1	224.3	228.1	230.6	233.0	225.8
2015	229.2	230.7	232.0	231.7	234.2	232.8	227.0	229.9	231.0	233.7	236.7	238.0	232.2
2016	234.6	236.4	237.4	239.3	240.0	238.3	232.1	235.8	238.4	240.6	243.3	244.8	238.4
2017	241.0	241.3	242.8	244.2	245.2	243.7	235.9	238.3	241.5	244.9	248.0	249.9	243.1
2018	245.8	247.5	249.3	249.3	250.5	249.1	243.2	246.5	247.8	251.0	252.9	253.8	248.9
Mining, Logging, and Construction													
2010	8.7	8.6	8.7	8.6	8.8	8.7	8.6	8.6	8.7	8.5	8.5	8.5	8.6
2011	8.5	8.6	8.7	8.6	8.7	8.8	8.9	9.1	9.1	9.0	9.1	9.0	8.8
2012	8.9	9.0	9.2	9.1	9.2	9.2	9.2	9.3	9.2	9.3	9.3	9.4	9.2
2013	9.0	9.1	9.3	9.5	9.6	9.8	9.7	9.9	9.8	9.8	9.8	9.9	9.6
2014	9.8	9.9	9.9	10.0	10.0	10.1	10.1	10.3	10.2	10.4	10.3	10.4	10.1
2015	10.0	9.8	9.7	9.6	9.6	9.7	9.3	9.1	9.0	8.8	8.5	8.4	9.3
2016	8.2	8.1	8.1	8.0	7.8	7.8	7.9	7.9	7.9	8.0	8.0	8.1	8.0
2017	8.1	8.1	8.2	8.2	8.4	8.6	8.6	8.7	8.5	8.5	8.5	8.5	8.4
2018	8.3	8.3	8.4	8.3	8.4	8.4	8.4	8.4	8.3	8.3	8.4	8.2	8.3
Manufacturing													
2010	6.4	6.2	6.4	6.2	6.2	5.8	5.6	5.8	5.8	6.0	6.1	6.2	6.1
2011	6.2	6.1	6.1	5.9	5.9	5.9	5.8	5.9	5.9	6.1	6.3	6.3	6.0
2012	6.3	6.3	6.3	6.2	6.1	6.1	5.9	6.1	6.1	6.3	6.4	6.5	6.2
2013	6.6	6.7	6.6	6.5	6.4	6.3	6.2	6.3	6.2	6.4	6.5	6.5	6.4
2014	6.3	6.6	6.3	6.6	6.4	6.4	6.2	6.3	6.4	6.4	6.4	6.5	6.4
2015	6.5	6.9	6.7	6.8	6.6	6.5	6.6	6.4	6.3	6.4	6.6	6.7	6.6
2016	6.6	6.6	6.5	6.3	6.2	6.2	6.1	6.2	6.3	6.6	6.7	6.7	6.4
2017	6.8	6.8	6.7	6.6	6.7	6.7	6.6	6.7	6.7	6.7	7.1	7.2	6.8
2018	7.1	7.2	7.1	7.0	7.0	6.8	6.8	6.8	6.8	7.0	7.2	7.2	7.0

Employment by Industry: McAllen-Edinburg-Mission, TX, 2010–2018—*Continued*

(Numbers in thousands, not seasonally adjusted)

Industry and year	January	February	March	April	May	June	July	August	September	October	November	December	Annual average
Trade, Transportation, and Utilities													
2010	45.2	44.7	45.1	45.5	45.9	45.8	45.4	46.0	45.8	46.5	47.6	48.7	46.0
2011	46.8	46.3	46.7	47.4	47.4	47.3	47.3	47.9	47.3	47.7	49.3	50.1	47.6
2012	48.6	48.2	48.7	48.9	49.0	49.2	49.4	50.1	49.5	49.8	52.0	52.5	49.7
2013	50.7	50.3	50.5	50.8	50.8	51.1	50.7	51.1	50.8	51.0	53.1	54.1	51.3
2014	51.4	51.0	51.2	52.1	52.1	52.5	52.7	52.8	52.4	52.9	54.9	55.8	52.7
2015	53.6	53.4	53.8	54.1	54.4	54.3	54.3	54.8	54.2	54.4	55.9	56.4	54.5
2016	54.4	54.0	54.2	54.7	54.7	54.5	54.6	55.0	54.3	54.7	56.5	56.8	54.9
2017	54.6	53.9	54.0	53.7	53.8	53.7	53.6	53.7	53.4	53.3	54.8	55.2	54.0
2018	53.6	53.1	53.2	53.3	53.4	53.2	53.0	53.2	53.0	54.0	55.4	55.6	53.7
Wholesale Trade													
2010	6.3	6.3	6.3	6.5	6.6	6.6	6.4	6.4	6.5	6.6	6.6	6.7	6.5
2011	6.6	6.6	6.8	6.9	6.8	6.7	6.7	6.7	6.7	6.7	6.7	6.8	6.7
2012	6.9	6.9	7.0	7.2	7.2	7.1	7.0	7.1	7.2	7.3	7.3	7.4	7.1
2013	7.5	7.5	7.7	7.9	7.8	7.7	7.5	7.4	7.5	7.5	7.6	7.6	7.6
2014	7.5	7.6	7.7	8.1	8.1	7.9	7.7	7.7	7.8	7.9	7.9	8.0	7.8
2015	8.0	8.1	8.2	8.4	8.4	8.3	8.2	8.2	8.2	8.2	8.2	8.3	8.2
2016	8.1	8.2	8.2	8.5	8.5	8.4	8.2	8.2	8.2	8.3	8.3	8.4	8.3
2017	8.4	8.6	8.8	8.8	8.9	8.8	8.8	8.6	8.7	8.7	8.7	8.8	8.7
2018	8.8	8.9	9.1	9.3	9.3	9.2	8.8	8.8	8.9	8.9	9.0	9.0	9.0
Retail Trade													
2010	32.0	31.5	31.9	32.0	32.1	32.0	32.0	32.5	32.2	32.8	33.9	34.7	32.5
2011	33.3	32.7	32.8	33.3	33.3	33.3	33.3	33.8	33.3	33.6	35.2	35.8	33.6
2012	34.2	33.6	33.9	34.0	34.0	34.2	34.5	35.0	34.6	34.8	36.9	37.2	34.7
2013	35.4	35.0	35.0	35.0	35.0	35.3	35.2	35.6	35.2	35.4	37.4	38.3	35.7
2014	35.8	35.4	35.5	35.9	35.9	36.5	36.8	36.9	36.4	36.7	38.6	39.2	36.6
2015	37.0	36.8	37.0	37.3	37.4	37.4	37.4	37.8	37.3	37.6	39.0	39.3	37.6
2016	37.8	37.3	37.5	37.7	37.7	37.6	37.8	38.1	37.4	37.9	39.6	39.7	38.0
2017	37.8	37.0	36.9	36.6	36.5	36.4	36.3	36.7	36.2	36.5	38.0	38.0	36.9
2018	36.6	35.9	35.8	35.7	35.7	35.6	35.7	35.9	35.6	36.6	37.8	37.8	36.2
Transportation and Utilities													
2010	6.9	6.9	6.9	7.0	7.2	7.2	7.0	7.1	7.1	7.1	7.1	7.3	7.1
2011	6.9	7.0	7.1	7.2	7.3	7.3	7.3	7.4	7.3	7.4	7.4	7.5	7.3
2012	7.5	7.7	7.8	7.7	7.8	7.9	7.9	8.0	7.7	7.7	7.8	7.9	7.8
2013	7.8	7.8	7.8	7.9	8.0	8.1	8.0	8.1	8.1	8.1	8.1	8.2	8.0
2014	8.1	8.0	8.0	8.1	8.1	8.1	8.2	8.2	8.2	8.3	8.4	8.6	8.2
2015	8.6	8.5	8.6	8.4	8.6	8.6	8.7	8.8	8.7	8.6	8.7	8.8	8.6
2016	8.5	8.5	8.5	8.5	8.5	8.5	8.6	8.7	8.7	8.5	8.6	8.7	8.6
2017	8.4	8.3	8.3	8.3	8.4	8.5	8.5	8.4	8.5	8.1	8.1	8.4	8.4
2018	8.2	8.3	8.3	8.3	8.4	8.4	8.5	8.5	8.5	8.5	8.6	8.8	8.4
Information													
2010	2.1	2.0	2.0	2.0	2.1	2.0	2.0	1.9	1.9	2.0	2.0	2.0	2.0
2011	2.1	2.1	2.1	2.1	2.1	2.1	2.1	2.1	2.0	2.0	2.1	2.1	2.1
2012	2.1	2.0	2.0	2.0	2.0	2.0	2.0	2.0	1.9	2.1	2.1	2.2	2.0
2013	2.1	2.1	2.1	2.1	2.2	2.2	2.2	2.2	2.1	2.2	2.3	2.3	2.2
2014	2.2	2.2	2.2	2.2	2.2	2.2	2.2	2.2	2.1	2.2	2.3	2.3	2.2
2015	2.3	2.2	2.2	2.2	2.3	2.3	2.4	2.4	2.3	2.2	2.3	2.3	2.3
2016	2.2	2.2	2.2	2.3	2.3	2.3	2.3	2.3	2.2	2.2	2.3	2.3	2.3
2017	2.2	2.2	2.2	2.3	2.4	2.5	2.5	2.5	2.5	2.6	2.7	2.8	2.5
2018	2.8	2.9	2.9	2.9	2.9	3.0	3.0	2.9	2.8	2.8	2.9	2.9	2.9
Financial Activities													
2010	8.0	8.0	8.0	8.1	8.1	8.1	8.1	8.1	8.2	8.3	8.4	8.5	8.2
2011	8.4	8.4	8.5	8.5	8.5	8.6	8.6	8.6	8.7	8.7	8.6	8.7	8.6
2012	8.8	8.8	8.8	8.8	8.8	8.9	8.8	8.8	8.8	8.9	8.9	9.0	8.8
2013	8.8	8.9	8.9	8.9	8.9	8.9	8.9	9.0	8.9	9.0	9.0	9.0	8.9
2014	9.0	9.0	9.0	9.0	9.1	9.1	9.0	9.0	9.0	9.1	9.1	9.2	9.1
2015	9.0	9.0	9.1	8.9	9.0	9.0	9.0	9.0	9.0	9.0	9.0	9.1	9.0
2016	8.9	8.9	8.9	8.9	8.9	8.9	8.8	8.9	8.8	8.7	8.8	8.8	8.9
2017	8.8	8.7	8.7	8.9	8.9	8.8	8.9	8.8	8.8	8.9	8.9	9.0	8.8
2018	9.0	8.9	8.9	8.9	9.0	9.0	9.2	9.1	9.0	9.0	9.0	9.1	9.0

Employment by Industry: McAllen-Edinburg-Mission, TX, 2010–2018—*Continued*

(Numbers in thousands, not seasonally adjusted)

Industry and year	January	February	March	April	May	June	July	August	September	October	November	December	Annual average
Professional and Business Services													
2010	14.0	14.2	14.0	14.0	14.0	14.1	14.0	14.1	14.1	14.3	14.4	14.7	14.2
2011	14.5	14.7	14.8	15.6	15.5	15.3	15.0	15.2	15.0	14.9	15.0	15.0	15.0
2012	15.3	15.4	15.3	15.7	15.5	15.0	15.0	15.0	15.1	15.2	14.8	14.9	15.2
2013	15.1	15.6	15.8	15.9	15.6	15.5	15.1	15.5	15.5	15.5	15.7	16.2	15.6
2014	15.5	15.7	16.0	16.1	15.9	15.7	15.3	15.8	15.6	16.1	15.5	15.8	15.8
2015	16.1	16.3	16.3	16.3	15.9	15.8	15.6	15.5	15.5	15.5	15.8	15.7	15.9
2016	15.9	16.3	16.7	16.7	16.2	16.0	16.1	16.2	16.4	16.8	16.9	16.9	16.4
2017	16.7	16.9	17.2	17.4	16.9	17.1	16.8	17.0	17.3	17.6	18.0	18.1	17.3
2018	17.9	17.9	18.1	17.9	17.6	17.4	17.1	17.2	17.2	17.4	17.2	17.6	17.5
Education and Health Services													
2010	55.7	55.9	56.1	55.8	56.4	56.1	55.8	56.3	57.2	57.4	57.6	57.9	56.5
2011	57.4	57.7	58.0	58.3	58.5	58.2	58.6	59.2	60.0	59.6	59.9	60.2	58.8
2012	59.4	59.9	60.1	59.9	60.0	59.6	58.6	59.2	59.5	59.8	60.2	60.4	59.7
2013	59.0	59.6	59.8	60.2	60.4	60.2	60.1	61.0	61.3	61.8	62.1	62.3	60.7
2014	61.2	61.6	61.6	61.9	62.5	62.0	62.0	62.8	63.1	63.4	63.9	64.2	62.5
2015	63.9	64.3	64.4	64.6	65.2	64.6	64.7	65.5	65.7	66.2	66.7	66.8	65.2
2016	66.2	66.9	66.8	67.8	68.2	67.4	67.0	68.2	69.0	69.0	69.4	70.0	68.0
2017	69.6	70.0	70.3	70.6	71.1	70.6	69.5	70.5	71.3	72.2	72.6	73.4	71.0
2018	72.9	73.4	73.6	74.3	74.7	74.5	75.1	76.3	76.2	75.9	75.9	75.4	74.9
Leisure and Hospitality													
2010	19.0	19.3	19.5	19.1	19.4	19.2	18.9	19.2	19.3	19.2	19.2	19.4	19.2
2011	19.2	19.5	20.0	20.0	19.9	20.1	19.6	19.6	19.5	19.2	19.4	19.4	19.6
2012	19.2	19.6	20.2	20.2	20.1	20.2	19.8	20.0	20.0	19.9	20.3	20.8	20.0
2013	20.5	21.0	21.5	21.4	21.3	21.3	20.9	21.3	21.2	20.9	21.1	21.2	21.1
2014	21.1	21.3	21.8	21.9	22.2	22.2	21.7	22.1	22.2	22.0	22.0	22.4	21.9
2015	21.9	22.3	22.8	22.9	23.2	23.3	23.3	23.1	23.0	23.1	23.2	23.5	23.0
2016	23.5	23.8	24.1	24.2	24.3	24.5	24.2	24.4	24.4	24.2	24.2	24.2	24.2
2017	24.2	24.3	25.0	25.2	25.5	25.5	25.1	25.1	25.1	24.9	24.9	25.0	25.0
2018	24.7	25.1	25.8	25.3	25.5	25.5	25.2	25.6	25.2	25.2	25.1	25.4	25.3
Other Services													
2010	5.0	5.0	5.0	5.1	5.2	5.2	5.1	5.1	5.0	5.2	5.1	5.0	5.1
2011	5.0	5.1	5.1	5.1	5.2	5.2	5.2	5.2	5.1	5.2	5.1	5.1	5.1
2012	5.0	5.0	5.0	5.2	5.3	5.4	5.3	5.3	5.2	5.4	5.4	5.3	5.2
2013	5.2	5.3	5.3	5.4	5.5	5.6	5.6	5.6	5.4	5.5	5.5	5.4	5.4
2014	5.4	5.5	5.5	5.6	5.7	5.8	5.8	5.8	5.6	5.7	5.6	5.6	5.6
2015	5.5	5.6	5.6	5.6	5.7	5.8	5.8	5.8	5.6	5.6	5.6	5.5	5.6
2016	5.5	5.5	5.5	5.3	5.4	5.4	5.5	5.4	5.3	5.4	5.3	5.3	5.4
2017	5.3	5.3	5.4	5.4	5.4	5.5	5.4	5.4	5.4	5.5	5.5	5.5	5.4
2018	5.5	5.5	5.6	5.6	5.7	5.8	5.7	5.7	5.7	5.8	5.8	5.8	5.7
Government													
2010	55.7	56.5	56.8	56.9	57.1	56.3	48.6	50.5	52.8	55.4	56.1	55.9	54.9
2011	56.1	56.7	56.5	55.9	56.3	55.3	49.5	51.3	53.0	54.1	55.1	55.2	54.6
2012	54.8	55.4	55.8	55.2	55.4	54.8	49.2	50.8	53.0	55.1	55.8	56.0	54.3
2013	55.3	56.0	56.4	55.8	56.5	55.8	50.1	51.9	53.9	56.0	56.7	56.8	55.1
2014	56.7	57.1	57.4	56.7	58.0	57.0	51.0	52.6	54.3	56.7	57.3	57.7	56.0
2015	56.9	57.6	57.8	57.1	58.5	57.7	51.9	53.8	55.7	57.7	58.2	58.7	56.8
2016	58.0	58.8	59.0	59.4	60.0	59.3	53.6	55.4	58.0	59.6	59.9	60.5	58.5
2017	59.6	60.0	60.0	60.7	61.2	60.0	54.1	55.3	57.7	59.9	60.6	60.9	59.2
2018	59.4	60.7	61.2	61.1	61.7	60.7	54.9	56.5	58.7	60.9	61.6	62.0	60.0

Employment by Industry: New Haven, CT NECTA, 2010–2018

(Numbers in thousands, not seasonally adjusted)

Industry and year	January	February	March	April	May	June	July	August	September	October	November	December	Annual average
Total Nonfarm													
2010	259.1	262.4	260.9	265.3	268.2	267.0	262.5	260.0	267.2	269.5	269.9	269.7	265.1
2011	262.1	264.9	263.1	269.5	270.3	269.8	263.0	261.5	269.0	270.9	272.1	272.2	267.4
2012	265.3	269.7	269.1	273.3	275.2	274.6	267.2	265.4	273.1	275.0	276.9	278.2	271.9
2013	268.2	269.5	270.8	276.6	277.1	277.5	271.9	269.9	276.6	279.1	281.3	279.9	274.9
2014	272.7	273.8	273.3	279.1	279.3	279.2	273.6	271.6	279.5	281.1	283.5	283.8	277.5
2015	275.0	276.0	275.8	280.6	282.0	281.6	274.7	272.2	280.0	283.7	286.0	286.0	279.5
2016	275.1	277.9	279.7	282.4	284.2	284.3	277.2	275.5	283.3	285.9	287.5	288.6	281.8
2017	278.9	281.2	280.7	285.7	286.6	287.7	279.2	278.3	284.2	286.9	289.9	289.8	284.1
2018	278.9	282.8	281.4	286.4	287.8	288.1	281.2	279.3	287.0	290.6	290.7	290.0	285.4
Total Private													
2010	224.1	225.9	224.9	229.0	230.8	231.2	231.3	230.0	231.7	233.6	233.5	233.6	230.0
2011	227.5	228.8	227.9	233.0	234.5	235.0	232.9	232.4	234.3	235.2	236.0	236.2	232.8
2012	231.8	233.8	233.3	237.4	240.1	240.5	237.7	237.0	239.1	240.1	241.3	242.2	237.9
2013	234.0	234.5	235.5	240.2	241.2	241.8	241.1	240.7	241.8	244.1	245.3	244.6	240.4
2014	237.9	238.0	237.5	242.6	243.5	244.0	243.1	241.8	244.0	245.7	247.2	247.9	242.8
2015	240.2	239.9	239.6	244.0	245.7	246.5	244.1	242.4	244.5	247.5	249.3	249.8	244.5
2016	240.4	241.8	243.3	245.9	247.4	248.5	246.4	245.9	248.2	250.0	251.2	252.0	246.8
2017	244.4	245.3	245.0	249.7	250.7	252.6	249.1	248.8	249.7	251.3	254.2	254.0	249.6
2018	244.8	247.3	246.0	250.9	252.4	253.4	251.3	250.3	252.4	255.4	255.2	254.4	251.2
Goods Producing													
2010	34.2	33.7	34.0	34.8	35.4	35.7	35.8	35.9	35.8	35.3	35.1	34.9	35.1
2011	33.8	33.9	34.0	34.6	35.2	35.7	35.5	35.7	35.4	35.3	35.2	35.0	34.9
2012	34.1	34.1	34.1	34.5	35.1	35.4	35.4	35.4	35.2	34.9	34.8	34.6	34.8
2013	33.6	33.3	33.6	34.1	34.6	35.0	35.6	35.5	35.2	35.3	34.8	34.6	34.6
2014	33.5	33.3	33.4	34.3	34.9	35.2	35.7	35.6	35.4	35.2	34.8	34.6	34.7
2015	33.9	33.4	33.5	34.6	35.1	35.6	35.6	35.5	35.3	35.1	34.9	34.7	34.8
2016	33.6	33.3	33.5	34.0	34.4	34.9	35.0	35.0	34.7	34.5	34.4	34.0	34.3
2017	33.3	33.1	33.1	33.5	33.9	34.5	34.6	34.6	34.2	34.2	34.1	34.0	33.9
2018	32.7	32.9	33.2	33.7	34.4	35.0	35.6	35.4	35.0	34.7	34.6	34.5	34.3
Service-Providing													
2010	224.9	228.7	226.9	230.5	232.8	231.3	226.7	224.1	231.4	234.2	234.8	234.8	230.1
2011	228.3	231.0	229.1	234.9	235.1	234.1	227.5	225.8	233.6	235.6	236.9	237.2	232.4
2012	231.2	235.6	235.0	238.8	240.1	239.2	231.8	230.0	237.9	240.1	242.1	243.6	237.1
2013	234.6	236.2	237.2	242.5	242.5	242.5	236.3	234.4	241.4	243.8	246.5	245.3	240.3
2014	239.2	240.5	239.9	244.8	244.4	244.0	237.9	236.0	244.1	245.9	248.7	249.2	242.9
2015	241.1	242.6	242.3	246.0	246.9	246.0	239.1	236.7	244.7	248.6	251.1	251.3	244.7
2016	241.5	244.6	246.2	248.4	249.8	249.4	242.2	240.5	248.6	251.4	253.1	254.6	247.5
2017	245.6	248.1	247.6	252.2	252.7	253.2	244.6	243.7	250.0	252.7	255.8	255.8	250.2
2018	246.2	249.9	248.2	252.7	253.4	253.1	245.6	243.9	252.0	255.9	256.1	255.5	251.0
Mining, Logging and Construction													
2010	7.9	7.6	7.8	8.6	9.1	9.1	9.3	9.4	9.4	9.3	9.2	8.9	8.8
2011	8.2	8.3	8.3	8.9	9.4	9.7	9.7	9.8	9.6	9.6	9.4	9.2	9.2
2012	8.5	8.5	8.5	8.9	9.3	9.5	9.7	9.8	9.7	9.5	9.5	9.2	9.2
2013	8.4	8.1	8.4	9.1	9.5	9.8	10.2	10.3	10.2	10.0	9.8	9.5	9.4
2014	8.6	8.5	8.7	9.6	10.1	10.3	10.6	10.7	10.6	10.4	10.3	10.1	9.9
2015	9.4	9.1	9.2	10.2	10.7	11.1	11.2	11.2	11.1	11.1	11.0	10.8	10.5
2016	9.9	9.7	10.0	10.6	11.0	11.3	11.4	11.4	11.3	11.1	11.0	10.5	10.8
2017	9.8	9.7	9.7	10.2	10.6	11.0	10.9	11.0	10.9	10.8	10.7	10.4	10.5
2018	9.4	9.6	9.9	10.4	10.9	11.4	11.8	11.7	11.5	11.4	11.4	11.3	10.9
Manufacturing													
2010	26.3	26.1	26.2	26.2	26.3	26.6	26.5	26.5	26.4	26.0	25.9	26.0	26.3
2011	25.6	25.6	25.7	25.7	25.8	26.0	25.8	25.9	25.8	25.7	25.8	25.8	25.8
2012	25.6	25.6	25.6	25.6	25.8	25.9	25.7	25.6	25.5	25.4	25.3	25.4	25.6
2013	25.2	25.2	25.2	25.0	25.1	25.2	25.4	25.2	25.0	25.3	25.0	25.1	25.2
2014	24.9	24.8	24.7	24.7	24.8	24.9	25.1	24.9	24.8	24.8	24.5	24.5	24.8
2015	24.5	24.3	24.3	24.4	24.4	24.5	24.4	24.3	24.2	24.0	23.9	23.9	24.3
2016	23.7	23.6	23.5	23.4	23.4	23.6	23.6	23.6	23.4	23.4	23.4	23.5	23.5
2017	23.5	23.4	23.4	23.3	23.3	23.5	23.7	23.6	23.3	23.4	23.4	23.6	23.5
2018	23.3	23.3	23.3	23.3	23.5	23.6	23.8	23.7	23.5	23.3	23.2	23.2	23.4

Employment by Industry: New Haven, CT NECTA, 2010–2018—*Continued*

(Numbers in thousands, not seasonally adjusted)

Industry and year	January	February	March	April	May	June	July	August	September	October	November	December	Annual average
Trade, Transportation, and Utilities													
2010	46.0	45.3	45.4	45.1	46.3	46.7	46.2	46.2	46.0	46.7	47.5	48.3	46.3
2011	46.1	45.4	45.5	46.4	46.8	47.1	46.3	46.4	46.6	46.9	47.8	48.5	46.7
2012	47.2	46.5	46.7	46.8	47.8	48.3	47.6	47.4	47.6	48.3	49.8	50.1	47.8
2013	48.3	47.1	47.6	48.4	49.0	49.3	48.4	48.7	48.9	49.4	50.6	51.3	48.9
2014	48.8	48.2	48.4	49.0	49.6	49.9	49.3	49.3	49.5	50.1	51.5	52.1	49.6
2015	49.7	48.6	49.1	49.2	50.3	50.6	49.6	49.3	49.7	50.9	52.8	53.2	50.3
2016	50.6	49.6	50.2	50.6	51.2	51.3	50.7	50.8	51.1	52.0	53.3	53.9	51.3
2017	52.2	50.7	50.8	51.4	52.2	52.3	51.7	51.5	51.4	52.2	54.7	54.7	52.2
2018	52.0	50.7	50.9	51.0	51.6	52.0	51.3	51.1	51.2	51.8	52.5	52.7	51.6
Wholesale Trade													
2010	11.2	11.3	11.3	11.2	11.4	11.4	11.5	11.4	11.3	11.3	11.3	11.4	11.3
2011	11.3	11.2	11.2	11.3	11.3	11.4	11.4	11.4	11.3	11.2	11.2	11.2	11.3
2012	11.1	11.1	11.1	11.2	11.3	11.3	11.3	11.1	11.1	11.1	11.2	11.2	11.2
2013	11.0	10.9	11.0	11.1	11.2	11.2	11.2	11.2	11.1	11.1	11.1	11.1	11.1
2014	10.9	10.9	10.9	11.1	11.2	11.2	11.2	11.1	11.1	11.1	11.1	11.1	11.1
2015	11.0	11.0	11.0	11.1	11.3	11.3	11.4	11.3	11.2	11.3	11.3	11.4	11.2
2016	11.3	11.3	11.5	11.5	11.6	11.6	11.7	11.6	11.6	11.6	11.6	11.7	11.6
2017	11.6	11.5	11.5	11.6	11.7	11.8	11.7	11.6	11.5	11.5	11.6	11.6	11.6
2018	11.5	11.5	11.5	11.5	11.6	11.6	11.6	11.5	11.4	11.4	11.3	11.3	11.5
Retail Trade													
2010	28.2	27.4	27.5	27.4	28.0	28.3	28.2	28.3	27.8	28.4	29.2	29.7	28.2
2011	28.2	27.6	27.6	28.2	28.5	28.6	28.3	28.5	28.3	28.6	29.5	30.1	28.5
2012	29.1	28.4	28.5	28.4	29.1	29.4	28.9	28.9	28.5	29.0	30.4	30.6	29.1
2013	29.1	28.2	28.3	28.8	29.2	29.4	29.1	29.4	29.1	29.7	30.9	31.5	29.4
2014	29.5	28.9	29.0	29.2	29.6	29.9	29.8	29.9	29.5	30.0	31.3	31.8	29.9
2015	30.0	29.0	29.3	29.2	29.8	30.1	29.6	29.6	29.5	30.5	31.7	32.0	30.0
2016	30.2	29.3	29.5	29.7	30.0	30.2	30.0	30.2	29.9	30.6	31.9	32.1	30.3
2017	31.0	29.8	29.7	30.0	30.4	30.5	30.3	30.2	29.8	30.4	31.9	31.9	30.5
2018	30.3	29.2	29.3	29.4	29.6	29.9	29.7	29.6	29.2	29.7	30.3	30.2	29.7
Transportation and Utilities													
2010	6.6	6.6	6.6	6.5	6.9	7.0	6.5	6.5	6.9	7.0	7.0	7.2	6.8
2011	6.6	6.6	6.7	6.9	7.0	7.1	6.6	6.5	7.0	7.1	7.1	7.2	6.9
2012	7.0	7.0	7.1	7.2	7.4	7.6	7.4	7.4	8.0	8.2	8.2	8.3	7.6
2013	8.2	8.0	8.3	8.5	8.6	8.7	8.1	8.1	8.7	8.6	8.6	8.7	8.4
2014	8.4	8.4	8.5	8.7	8.8	8.8	8.3	8.3	8.9	9.0	9.1	9.2	8.7
2015	8.7	8.6	8.8	8.9	9.2	9.2	8.6	8.4	9.0	9.1	9.8	9.8	9.0
2016	9.1	9.0	9.2	9.4	9.6	9.5	9.0	9.0	9.6	9.8	9.8	10.1	9.4
2017	9.6	9.4	9.6	9.8	10.1	10.0	9.7	9.7	10.1	10.3	11.2	11.2	10.1
2018	10.2	10.0	10.1	10.1	10.4	10.5	10.0	10.0	10.6	10.7	10.9	11.2	10.4
Information													
2010	5.7	5.6	5.5	5.3	5.3	5.2	5.1	5.1	5.0	4.9	4.9	4.9	5.2
2011	4.8	4.8	4.8	4.7	4.7	4.7	4.6	4.5	4.5	4.6	4.6	4.6	4.7
2012	4.5	4.5	4.4	4.3	4.3	4.3	4.3	4.3	4.3	4.3	4.3	4.3	4.3
2013	4.3	4.3	4.3	4.2	4.2	4.2	4.2	4.2	4.1	4.2	4.2	4.3	4.2
2014	4.3	4.2	4.1	4.1	4.1	4.1	4.2	4.1	4.0	3.7	3.7	3.7	4.0
2015	3.6	3.6	3.6	3.5	3.5	3.5	3.4	3.4	3.4	3.4	3.4	3.4	3.5
2016	3.4	3.3	3.3	3.4	3.4	3.4	3.4	3.5	3.4	3.4	3.5	3.5	3.4
2017	3.7	3.7	3.7	3.7	3.8	3.7	3.7	3.7	3.6	3.6	3.6	3.6	3.7
2018	3.7	3.7	3.7	3.7	3.7	3.8	3.8	3.7	3.7	3.9	3.9	3.9	3.8
Financial Activities													
2010	12.1	12.1	12.2	12.1	12.2	12.3	12.6	12.5	12.2	12.2	12.2	12.2	12.2
2011	12.3	12.3	12.3	12.2	12.2	12.3	12.3	12.3	12.0	12.0	11.8	12.0	12.2
2012	12.1	12.0	12.1	12.1	12.1	12.3	12.3	12.2	12.1	12.0	12.0	12.1	12.1
2013	12.1	12.0	12.0	12.0	12.0	12.2	12.3	12.3	12.3	12.3	12.3	12.4	12.2
2014	12.3	12.3	12.3	12.4	12.5	12.6	12.7	12.7	12.6	12.5	12.5	12.6	12.5
2015	12.5	12.4	12.4	12.5	12.6	12.7	12.7	12.7	12.6	12.6	12.5	12.5	12.6
2016	12.4	12.4	12.4	12.5	12.5	12.7	12.7	12.6	12.4	12.4	12.3	12.4	12.5
2017	12.4	12.4	12.4	12.4	12.5	12.5	12.4	12.4	12.2	12.2	12.1	12.1	12.3
2018	12.1	12.1	12.0	12.1	12.2	12.3	12.3	12.2	12.1	12.1	12.1	12.1	12.1

Employment by Industry: New Haven, CT NECTA, 2010–2018—*Continued*

(Numbers in thousands, not seasonally adjusted)

Industry and year	January	February	March	April	May	June	July	August	September	October	November	December	Annual average
Professional and Business Services													
2010	24.8	25.4	25.2	25.9	25.8	26.4	26.5	26.5	26.2	26.3	26.3	26.4	26.0
2011	25.8	26.1	25.8	26.8	26.7	27.2	27.2	27.2	27.1	27.1	27.4	27.6	26.8
2012	27.6	27.6	27.9	28.8	28.8	28.9	28.5	28.5	28.9	28.9	29.0	29.4	28.6
2013	28.8	29.0	29.0	29.2	29.4	29.8	29.9	29.8	29.3	29.6	29.9	29.9	29.5
2014	29.0	29.2	29.1	29.6	29.8	29.9	30.0	29.7	29.5	29.9	30.2	30.5	29.7
2015	29.7	30.0	29.9	30.5	30.6	30.8	30.5	30.2	30.2	30.5	30.6	30.6	30.3
2016	29.3	29.7	29.9	30.2	30.3	30.8	30.5	30.6	30.5	30.6	30.7	31.1	30.4
2017	30.2	30.2	30.6	31.4	31.0	31.7	31.6	31.4	31.1	31.1	31.4	31.4	31.1
2018	30.2	30.9	30.5	31.1	31.3	31.4	31.5	31.6	31.2	31.4	30.7	30.0	31.0
Education and Health Services													
2010	72.1	74.0	72.5	74.6	73.6	71.8	71.7	70.7	74.1	76.2	75.8	75.0	73.5
2011	74.8	75.9	74.7	76.0	75.6	73.6	72.8	72.2	75.4	76.5	76.8	75.7	75.0
2012	74.9	77.5	76.0	77.3	77.6	75.7	74.4	74.0	76.7	78.0	77.8	77.9	76.5
2013	75.4	77.7	76.7	78.5	77.2	75.4	75.1	74.8	77.6	79.3	79.7	78.6	77.2
2014	77.6	78.4	77.1	79.4	77.8	76.4	75.5	75.1	78.4	79.9	80.3	80.1	78.0
2015	78.0	79.2	77.7	79.6	78.3	76.8	76.3	75.7	78.4	80.4	80.8	80.9	78.5
2016	78.1	80.1	80.0	80.4	79.4	77.9	76.9	76.4	80.0	81.1	81.4	81.3	79.4
2017	78.0	80.4	79.4	81.2	80.1	79.2	76.8	77.0	80.2	81.2	81.5	81.8	79.7
2018	79.2	81.7	80.3	82.7	81.6	79.9	78.1	77.8	81.3	84.4	84.1	84.4	81.3
Leisure and Hospitality													
2010	19.0	19.6	19.8	20.8	21.9	22.5	22.8	22.6	21.9	21.6	21.4	21.5	21.3
2011	19.9	20.3	20.7	21.9	23.0	23.7	23.7	23.6	23.0	22.6	22.2	22.4	22.3
2012	21.0	21.2	21.7	22.9	23.8	24.9	24.5	24.5	23.8	23.1	23.0	23.2	23.1
2013	21.2	20.8	21.8	23.2	24.1	25.1	24.9	24.8	24.0	23.6	23.3	23.0	23.3
2014	22.0	22.0	22.6	23.2	24.1	25.0	24.8	24.5	24.0	23.6	23.5	23.5	23.6
2015	22.3	22.2	22.7	23.4	24.5	25.5	25.1	24.8	24.2	23.9	23.6	23.8	23.8
2016	22.4	22.8	23.2	24.0	25.3	26.4	26.2	26.1	25.2	25.1	24.8	24.8	24.7
2017	23.8	24.0	24.1	25.2	26.2	27.5	27.2	26.9	25.8	25.5	25.4	25.1	25.6
2018	23.9	24.2	24.4	25.4	26.3	27.5	27.2	27.0	26.4	25.6	25.7	25.4	25.8
Other Services													
2010	10.2	10.2	10.3	10.4	10.3	10.6	10.6	10.5	10.5	10.4	10.3	10.4	10.4
2011	10.0	10.1	10.1	10.4	10.3	10.7	10.5	10.5	10.3	10.2	10.2	10.4	10.3
2012	10.4	10.4	10.4	10.7	10.6	10.7	10.7	10.7	10.5	10.6	10.6	10.6	10.6
2013	10.3	10.3	10.5	10.6	10.7	10.8	10.7	10.6	10.4	10.4	10.5	10.5	10.5
2014	10.4	10.4	10.5	10.6	10.7	10.9	10.9	10.8	10.6	10.8	10.7	10.8	10.7
2015	10.5	10.5	10.7	10.7	10.8	11.0	10.9	10.8	10.7	10.7	10.7	10.7	10.7
2016	10.6	10.6	10.8	10.8	10.9	11.1	11.0	10.9	10.9	10.9	10.8	11.0	10.9
2017	10.8	10.8	10.9	10.9	11.0	11.2	11.1	11.3	11.2	11.3	11.4	11.3	11.1
2018	11.0	11.1	11.0	11.2	11.3	11.5	11.5	11.5	11.5	11.5	11.6	11.4	11.3
Government													
2010	35.0	36.5	36.0	36.3	37.4	35.8	31.2	30.0	35.5	35.9	36.4	36.1	35.2
2011	34.6	36.1	35.2	36.5	35.8	34.8	30.1	29.1	34.7	35.7	36.1	36.0	34.6
2012	33.5	35.9	35.8	35.9	35.1	34.1	29.5	28.4	34.0	34.9	35.6	36.0	34.1
2013	34.2	35.0	35.3	36.4	35.9	35.7	30.8	29.2	34.8	35.0	36.0	35.3	34.5
2014	34.8	35.8	35.8	36.5	35.8	35.2	30.5	29.8	35.5	35.4	36.3	35.9	34.8
2015	34.8	36.1	36.2	36.6	36.3	35.1	30.6	29.8	35.5	36.2	36.7	36.2	35.0
2016	34.7	36.1	36.4	36.5	36.8	35.8	30.8	29.6	35.1	35.9	36.3	36.6	35.1
2017	34.5	35.9	35.7	36.0	35.9	35.1	30.1	29.5	34.5	35.6	35.7	35.8	34.5
2018	34.1	35.5	35.4	35.5	35.4	34.7	29.9	29.0	34.6	35.2	35.5	35.6	34.2

Employment by Industry: Oxnard-Thousand Oaks-Ventura, CA, 2010–2018

(Numbers in thousands, not seasonally adjusted)

Industry and year	January	February	March	April	May	June	July	August	September	October	November	December	Annual average
Total Nonfarm													
2010	271.3	272.3	272.8	277.5	280.3	277.2	273.3	274.2	275.1	277.7	280.2	281.2	276.1
2011	275.2	275.9	276.1	277.9	278.3	278.4	275.0	276.0	277.6	279.9	283.3	282.7	278.0
2012	278.6	280.2	281.1	281.7	283.7	284.4	279.1	280.2	281.6	285.7	289.2	290.1	283.0
2013	285.2	287.3	287.8	287.6	289.6	288.9	285.4	287.5	288.7	292.3	296.2	297.8	289.5
2014	290.7	291.5	292.8	293.7	294.6	294.6	290.0	291.6	292.3	296.1	298.3	298.6	293.7
2015	292.2	294.3	294.6	295.4	296.0	295.7	292.4	293.6	295.7	301.0	303.0	303.7	296.5
2016	295.8	298.0	298.2	300.0	301.1	301.2	297.9	298.4	299.9	303.7	305.1	305.8	300.4
2017	298.8	300.9	302.0	304.4	306.5	307.3	302.4	303.5	305.9	309.5	311.8	311.8	305.4
2018	304.4	307.2	307.7	309.6	310.7	309.6	306.6	307.6	307.8	310.3	312.5	313.3	308.9
Total Private													
2010	228.7	229.1	229.5	231.6	232.8	232.2	232.0	231.8	231.8	232.9	234.5	235.7	231.9
2011	230.4	230.6	230.6	232.5	233.1	232.7	233.9	234.1	234.3	235.2	237.7	238.4	233.6
2012	234.7	235.6	236.5	237.2	238.8	239.7	238.6	239.3	239.2	241.9	244.7	245.9	239.3
2013	241.4	242.9	243.2	243.2	244.7	244.2	244.9	246.4	246.2	248.4	251.9	253.5	245.9
2014	247.0	247.2	248.4	249.1	250.0	250.0	249.5	249.7	249.0	251.0	252.7	253.2	249.7
2015	247.1	248.2	248.6	249.2	249.1	249.2	251.3	251.4	250.9	254.7	256.3	256.8	251.1
2016	249.4	251.0	250.8	252.9	253.3	253.2	254.3	254.4	254.4	256.7	257.6	258.1	253.8
2017	251.8	253.2	254.2	256.5	258.4	259.9	258.6	259.1	259.7	262.4	263.8	264.3	258.5
2018	257.8	259.7	260.1	261.7	262.5	262.4	262.9	263.3	261.7	263.0	264.4	265.6	262.1
Goods Producing													
2010	37.8	37.7	37.8	37.9	38.4	38.5	38.7	38.3	38.2	38.2	38.1	37.6	38.1
2011	37.3	37.2	37.2	37.3	37.3	37.3	37.5	37.5	37.4	37.3	37.4	36.8	37.3
2012	36.5	36.6	37.0	36.8	37.0	37.4	37.4	37.6	37.7	37.6	37.6	37.7	37.2
2013	37.4	37.5	37.6	37.3	37.5	37.7	38.0	38.2	38.4	38.7	39.1	38.9	38.0
2014	38.8	39.1	39.7	39.3	39.8	39.9	40.3	40.7	40.7	40.7	40.6	40.4	40.0
2015	40.6	40.5	40.6	40.7	40.6	41.0	41.5	41.7	41.3	41.4	41.4	41.3	41.1
2016	40.4	40.7	40.7	41.1	41.1	41.3	41.8	41.7	41.7	41.6	41.3	41.1	41.2
2017	40.4	40.8	41.3	41.8	42.2	42.6	42.6	42.8	42.9	43.0	43.1	43.0	42.2
2018	42.8	43.2	42.9	43.6	43.7	43.9	44.5	44.5	44.5	44.7	44.5	44.2	43.9
Service-Providing													
2010	233.5	234.6	235.0	239.6	241.9	238.7	234.6	235.9	236.9	239.5	242.1	243.6	238.0
2011	237.9	238.7	238.9	240.6	241.0	241.1	237.5	238.5	240.2	242.6	245.9	245.9	240.7
2012	242.1	243.6	244.1	244.9	246.7	247.0	241.7	242.6	243.9	248.1	251.6	252.4	245.7
2013	247.8	249.8	250.2	250.3	252.1	251.2	247.4	249.3	250.3	253.6	257.1	258.9	251.5
2014	251.9	252.4	253.1	254.4	254.8	254.7	249.7	250.9	251.6	255.4	257.7	258.2	253.7
2015	251.6	253.8	254.0	254.7	255.4	254.7	250.9	251.9	254.4	259.6	261.6	262.4	255.4
2016	255.4	257.3	257.5	258.9	260.0	259.9	256.1	256.7	258.2	262.1	263.8	264.7	259.2
2017	258.4	260.1	260.7	262.6	264.3	264.7	259.8	260.7	263.0	266.5	268.7	268.8	263.2
2018	261.6	264.0	264.8	266.0	267.0	265.7	262.1	263.1	263.3	265.6	268.0	269.1	265.0
Mining, Logging, and Construction													
2010	12.3	12.3	12.4	12.3	12.7	12.7	12.7	12.6	12.5	12.6	12.6	12.4	12.5
2011	12.4	12.3	12.3	12.5	12.5	12.5	12.7	12.8	12.6	12.8	12.8	12.6	12.6
2012	12.5	12.6	12.8	12.7	12.9	13.1	13.1	13.2	13.3	13.3	13.5	13.6	13.1
2013	13.4	13.5	13.4	13.3	13.5	13.6	13.8	13.9	14.0	14.3	14.6	14.5	13.8
2014	14.4	14.6	14.9	14.7	15.0	15.0	15.2	15.4	15.4	15.3	15.2	15.0	15.0
2015	15.0	14.8	14.9	15.0	15.0	15.3	15.6	15.6	15.2	15.2	15.3	15.2	15.2
2016	14.8	15.0	15.0	15.5	15.6	15.5	15.8	15.8	15.8	15.9	15.8	15.7	15.5
2017	15.1	15.5	15.8	16.4	16.6	16.8	17.0	17.1	17.1	17.2	17.3	17.3	16.6
2018	17.0	17.3	16.8	17.7	17.6	17.8	18.1	18.0	18.0	18.1	18.1	17.8	17.7
Manufacturing													
2010	25.5	25.4	25.4	25.6	25.7	25.8	26.0	25.7	25.7	25.6	25.5	25.2	25.6
2011	24.9	24.9	24.9	24.8	24.8	24.8	24.8	24.7	24.8	24.5	24.6	24.2	24.7
2012	24.0	24.0	24.2	24.1	24.1	24.3	24.3	24.4	24.4	24.3	24.1	24.1	24.2
2013	24.0	24.0	24.2	24.0	24.0	24.1	24.2	24.3	24.4	24.4	24.5	24.4	24.2
2014	24.4	24.5	24.8	24.6	24.8	24.9	25.1	25.3	25.3	25.4	25.4	25.4	25.0
2015	25.6	25.7	25.7	25.7	25.6	25.7	25.9	26.1	26.1	26.2	26.1	26.1	25.9
2016	25.6	25.7	25.7	25.6	25.5	25.8	26.0	25.9	25.9	25.7	25.5	25.4	25.7
2017	25.3	25.3	25.5	25.4	25.6	25.8	25.6	25.7	25.8	25.8	25.8	25.7	25.6
2018	25.8	25.9	26.1	25.9	26.1	26.1	26.4	26.5	26.5	26.6	26.4	26.4	26.2

Employment by Industry: Oxnard-Thousand Oaks-Ventura, CA, 2010–2018—*Continued*

(Numbers in thousands, not seasonally adjusted)

Industry and year	January	February	March	April	May	June	July	August	September	October	November	December	Annual average
Trade, Transportation, and Utilities													
2010	52.1	51.8	51.8	53.0	53.1	52.9	52.9	52.7	52.7	53.4	54.9	56.0	53.1
2011	53.4	52.9	52.9	53.7	53.7	53.9	54.1	54.2	53.9	54.4	56.6	57.4	54.3
2012	55.2	54.2	54.1	54.6	55.1	55.1	55.3	55.1	55.1	55.8	58.7	59.4	55.6
2013	56.6	56.4	55.9	56.0	56.5	56.6	56.7	56.9	56.5	57.1	60.0	61.0	57.2
2014	57.8	57.1	56.8	57.0	57.2	57.3	57.6	57.6	57.3	58.0	60.1	60.9	57.9
2015	58.1	57.8	57.3	57.3	57.5	57.7	58.4	58.2	57.9	59.2	60.9	61.4	58.5
2016	58.6	58.0	57.7	58.0	58.3	58.0	58.8	58.9	58.7	59.8	61.3	62.0	59.0
2017	59.3	58.4	58.2	58.8	58.9	58.9	59.1	59.2	58.8	60.0	61.7	62.1	59.5
2018	59.8	59.0	58.6	58.6	58.7	58.4	58.8	58.9	58.3	58.7	60.1	61.2	59.1
Wholesale Trade													
2010	11.7	12.0	12.1	13.0	12.9	12.7	12.5	12.2	12.0	12.1	12.3	12.2	12.3
2011	12.0	12.1	12.3	12.7	12.6	12.6	12.7	12.6	12.6	12.4	12.4	12.3	12.4
2012	12.3	12.3	12.4	12.6	12.7	12.7	12.7	12.7	12.7	12.5	12.6	12.7	12.6
2013	12.5	12.7	12.7	12.8	12.9	12.9	12.8	12.9	12.7	12.8	12.9	13.1	12.8
2014	12.8	12.8	12.8	12.8	12.8	12.8	12.7	12.7	12.5	12.6	12.6	12.7	12.7
2015	12.4	12.5	12.4	12.4	12.4	12.5	12.6	12.6	12.5	12.8	12.9	12.8	12.6
2016	12.7	12.8	12.7	12.8	12.9	12.9	13.1	13.1	13.1	13.1	13.2	13.3	13.0
2017	13.0	13.1	13.1	13.2	13.2	13.4	13.4	13.3	13.2	13.2	13.2	13.2	13.2
2018	13.1	13.2	13.1	13.1	13.2	13.2	13.2	13.2	13.1	13.1	13.2	13.2	13.2
Retail Trade													
2010	35.2	34.6	34.5	34.8	35.0	34.9	35.0	35.1	35.3	36.0	37.3	38.3	35.5
2011	36.1	35.5	35.3	35.6	35.6	35.8	35.8	36.0	35.8	36.5	38.5	39.3	36.3
2012	37.3	36.3	36.0	36.4	36.7	36.7	36.8	36.6	36.6	37.5	40.3	40.7	37.3
2013	38.4	37.9	37.5	37.4	37.8	37.9	38.0	38.1	37.9	38.4	41.1	41.7	38.5
2014	39.0	38.3	38.1	38.3	38.4	38.5	38.9	38.9	38.8	39.4	41.5	42.2	39.2
2015	39.8	39.3	39.0	38.9	39.1	39.2	39.7	39.6	39.5	40.5	42.0	42.5	39.9
2016	39.9	39.3	39.1	39.3	39.4	39.1	39.6	39.8	39.6	40.6	41.9	42.3	40.0
2017	40.2	39.3	39.1	39.5	39.6	39.4	39.6	39.8	39.5	40.6	42.2	42.4	40.1
2018	40.3	39.5	39.2	39.2	39.2	38.8	39.3	39.4	38.9	39.3	40.5	41.4	39.6
Transportation and Utilities													
2010	5.2	5.2	5.2	5.2	5.2	5.3	5.4	5.4	5.4	5.3	5.3	5.5	5.3
2011	5.3	5.3	5.3	5.4	5.5	5.5	5.6	5.6	5.5	5.5	5.7	5.8	5.5
2012	5.6	5.6	5.7	5.6	5.7	5.7	5.8	5.8	5.8	5.8	5.8	6.0	5.7
2013	5.7	5.8	5.7	5.8	5.8	5.8	5.9	5.9	5.9	5.9	6.0	6.2	5.9
2014	6.0	6.0	5.9	5.9	6.0	6.0	6.0	6.0	6.0	6.0	6.0	6.0	6.0
2015	5.9	6.0	5.9	6.0	6.0	6.0	6.1	6.0	5.9	5.9	6.0	6.1	6.0
2016	6.0	5.9	5.9	5.9	6.0	6.0	6.1	6.0	6.0	6.1	6.2	6.4	6.0
2017	6.1	6.0	6.0	6.1	6.1	6.1	6.1	6.1	6.1	6.2	6.3	6.5	6.1
2018	6.4	6.3	6.3	6.3	6.3	6.4	6.3	6.3	6.3	6.3	6.4	6.6	6.4
Information													
2010	5.2	5.2	5.2	5.2	5.2	5.2	5.2	5.2	5.1	5.0	5.0	5.0	5.1
2011	4.9	4.8	4.8	4.8	4.9	4.9	4.9	4.9	4.8	4.8	4.9	5.0	4.9
2012	5.0	5.0	5.1	5.0	5.1	5.2	5.2	5.2	5.1	5.3	5.3	5.3	5.2
2013	5.1	5.1	5.1	5.1	5.1	5.2	5.3	5.3	5.2	5.3	5.3	5.4	5.2
2014	5.4	5.4	5.4	5.4	5.4	5.5	5.4	5.3	5.2	5.2	5.2	5.3	5.3
2015	5.1	5.1	5.1	5.0	5.0	5.1	5.1	4.9	4.9	5.1	5.1	5.2	5.1
2016	4.9	4.9	4.9	4.9	5.0	5.1	5.0	5.1	5.0	4.9	5.0	5.0	5.0
2017	4.9	4.9	4.9	5.0	5.1	5.1	5.1	5.1	5.0	5.0	5.0	5.1	5.0
2018	5.0	5.0	4.9	5.0	5.1	5.1	5.1	5.0	4.9	4.9	4.9	4.9	5.0
Financial Activities													
2010	20.2	20.3	20.3	20.1	20.1	20.1	20.3	20.4	20.3	20.5	20.6	20.8	20.3
2011	20.6	20.6	20.8	20.7	20.7	20.7	20.7	20.3	20.1	20.0	19.6	19.9	20.4
2012	19.9	20.1	20.0	19.7	19.6	19.6	19.5	19.4	19.2	19.4	19.4	19.4	19.6
2013	19.1	19.1	19.2	18.8	18.8	18.7	18.8	18.9	18.9	18.9	18.9	18.9	18.9
2014	19.0	18.9	19.0	18.9	18.8	18.9	18.8	18.7	18.4	18.5	18.4	18.4	18.7
2015	18.0	17.8	17.8	17.9	17.9	17.6	17.8	17.7	17.6	17.7	17.6	17.5	17.7
2016	17.3	17.3	17.3	17.5	17.4	17.3	17.5	17.4	17.4	17.5	17.5	17.5	17.4
2017	17.1	17.1	17.0	16.9	17.0	16.9	16.9	16.8	16.8	16.9	16.9	16.7	16.9
2018	16.4	16.6	16.6	16.7	16.8	16.6	16.5	16.4	16.3	16.5	16.5	16.5	16.5

Employment by Industry: Oxnard-Thousand Oaks-Ventura, CA, 2010–2018—*Continued*

(Numbers in thousands, not seasonally adjusted)

Industry and year	January	February	March	April	May	June	July	August	September	October	November	December	Annual average
Professional and Business Services													
2010	40.2	40.1	40.4	40.1	40.1	40.3	40.3	40.4	40.2	40.2	40.1	40.4	40.2
2011	39.3	39.3	39.3	39.6	39.6	39.6	40.4	40.2	40.1	40.2	40.3	40.5	39.9
2012	40.0	40.5	40.8	40.8	40.9	41.4	41.4	41.7	41.6	42.2	42.3	42.5	41.3
2013	42.1	42.2	42.6	42.5	42.5	42.5	43.0	43.0	43.0	43.3	43.3	43.6	42.8
2014	42.2	41.5	42.0	41.9	41.6	41.6	41.7	41.4	41.2	41.3	41.1	41.0	41.5
2015	39.4	39.7	40.4	40.4	39.7	39.9	40.5	40.6	40.4	41.6	41.4	41.6	40.5
2016	40.2	40.6	40.7	41.0	40.9	41.0	41.0	40.9	40.7	41.0	41.1	41.1	40.9
2017	40.8	41.2	41.4	41.8	41.9	42.4	42.7	42.4	42.4	42.9	42.9	43.0	42.2
2018	41.4	42.0	42.4	42.9	43.3	43.0	43.1	42.9	42.8	43.5	43.7	43.2	42.9
Education and Health Services													
2010	34.6	35.3	35.1	36.0	36.0	35.6	34.8	35.0	35.3	35.9	36.1	36.2	35.5
2011	35.6	36.2	35.9	36.3	36.3	35.6	35.3	35.8	36.7	37.2	37.5	37.6	36.3
2012	37.3	38.0	38.1	38.3	38.4	38.0	37.1	37.6	38.1	39.0	38.9	39.4	38.2
2013	39.3	40.2	40.3	40.5	40.6	39.8	39.1	39.9	40.3	41.2	41.5	41.6	40.4
2014	40.6	41.6	41.4	42.1	42.1	41.4	40.4	40.8	41.4	42.5	42.6	42.6	41.6
2015	41.8	42.7	42.6	42.8	43.0	42.4	42.2	42.3	43.0	43.9	44.1	44.2	42.9
2016	43.3	44.3	44.1	44.6	44.5	44.3	43.6	43.8	44.3	45.5	45.3	45.4	44.4
2017	44.1	45.1	45.3	45.5	45.9	46.3	44.9	45.6	46.6	47.1	46.9	47.3	45.9
2018	46.4	47.3	47.7	47.4	47.1	47.5	47.2	47.9	47.8	47.7	48.0	48.7	47.6
Leisure and Hospitality													
2010	29.5	29.6	29.7	30.1	30.6	30.4	30.7	30.7	30.7	30.5	30.5	30.6	30.3
2011	30.3	30.5	30.6	31.0	31.4	31.6	31.8	32.1	32.0	31.9	31.9	31.8	31.4
2012	31.6	31.8	32.1	32.6	33.1	33.3	33.2	33.3	33.0	33.1	33.2	32.9	32.8
2013	32.4	32.9	33.0	33.4	34.1	34.1	34.2	34.4	34.1	34.1	34.0	34.3	33.8
2014	33.5	33.8	34.2	34.6	35.1	35.5	35.5	35.5	35.2	35.0	34.9	34.9	34.8
2015	34.5	35.0	35.2	35.4	35.6	35.8	36.1	36.4	36.2	36.2	36.1	36.0	35.7
2016	35.2	35.6	35.8	36.1	36.5	36.6	37.0	37.0	36.9	36.7	36.6	36.5	36.4
2017	35.8	36.1	36.5	37.1	37.6	37.9	37.6	37.6	37.6	37.8	37.7	37.6	37.2
2018	36.7	37.2	37.7	38.0	38.3	38.4	38.3	38.3	37.7	37.5	37.3	37.5	37.7
Other Services													
2010	9.1	9.1	9.2	9.2	9.3	9.2	9.1	9.1	9.3	9.2	9.2	9.1	9.2
2011	9.0	9.1	9.1	9.1	9.2	9.1	9.2	9.1	9.3	9.4	9.5	9.4	9.2
2012	9.2	9.4	9.3	9.4	9.6	9.7	9.5	9.4	9.4	9.5	9.3	9.3	9.4
2013	9.4	9.5	9.5	9.6	9.6	9.6	9.8	9.8	9.8	9.8	9.8	9.8	9.7
2014	9.7	9.8	9.9	9.9	10.0	9.9	9.8	9.7	9.6	9.8	9.8	9.7	9.8
2015	9.6	9.6	9.6	9.7	9.8	9.7	9.7	9.6	9.6	9.6	9.7	9.6	9.7
2016	9.5	9.6	9.6	9.7	9.6	9.6	9.6	9.6	9.7	9.7	9.5	9.5	9.6
2017	9.4	9.6	9.6	9.6	9.8	9.8	9.7	9.6	9.6	9.7	9.6	9.5	9.6
2018	9.3	9.4	9.3	9.5	9.5	9.5	9.4	9.4	9.4	9.5	9.4	9.4	9.4
Government													
2010	42.6	43.2	43.3	45.9	47.5	45.0	41.3	42.4	43.3	44.8	45.7	45.5	44.2
2011	44.8	45.3	45.5	45.4	45.2	45.7	41.1	41.9	43.3	44.7	45.6	44.3	44.4
2012	43.9	44.6	44.6	44.5	44.9	44.7	40.5	40.9	42.4	43.8	44.5	44.2	43.6
2013	43.8	44.4	44.6	44.4	44.9	44.7	40.5	41.1	42.5	43.9	44.3	44.3	43.6
2014	43.7	44.3	44.4	44.6	44.6	44.6	40.5	41.9	43.3	45.1	45.6	45.4	44.0
2015	45.1	46.1	46.0	46.2	46.9	46.5	41.1	42.2	44.8	46.3	46.7	46.9	45.4
2016	46.4	47.0	47.4	47.1	47.8	48.0	43.6	44.0	45.5	47.0	47.5	47.7	46.6
2017	47.0	47.7	47.8	47.9	48.1	47.4	43.8	44.4	46.2	47.1	48.0	47.5	46.9
2018	46.6	47.5	47.6	47.9	48.2	47.2	43.7	44.3	46.1	47.3	48.1	47.7	46.9

Employment by Industry: El Paso, TX, 2010–2018

(Numbers in thousands, not seasonally adjusted)

Industry and year	January	February	March	April	May	June	July	August	September	October	November	December	Annual average
Total Nonfarm													
2010	276.5	278.0	281.4	281.5	283.5	281.8	275.5	277.3	281.7	282.3	284.2	285.5	280.8
2011	281.1	281.6	283.0	284.2	284.4	282.7	280.6	281.9	285.6	283.0	285.4	286.8	283.4
2012	282.8	284.9	286.6	287.6	288.9	285.8	284.1	286.3	288.6	290.2	292.5	292.8	287.6
2013	287.0	289.3	290.4	291.1	292.3	289.1	287.5	290.5	293.3	294.6	297.5	297.6	291.7
2014	292.9	294.5	295.7	296.5	297.4	294.7	290.9	292.9	294.3	296.2	298.6	299.7	295.4
2015	296.2	297.9	298.8	300.2	302.2	300.8	298.0	300.2	302.3	305.5	307.6	307.6	301.4
2016	304.0	305.5	305.9	308.9	309.7	307.1	306.0	308.2	311.2	310.7	312.6	312.9	308.6
2017	309.6	311.8	312.0	313.4	314.4	311.3	307.3	309.2	312.9	314.6	317.5	317.9	312.7
2018	314.4	315.9	316.0	316.7	317.9	315.3	313.7	316.3	318.3	320.4	321.0	321.6	317.3
Total Private													
2010	205.9	206.6	209.7	209.8	211.1	212.6	210.5	211.9	211.2	211.4	213.0	214.2	210.7
2011	210.6	211.0	212.2	213.3	213.8	213.8	214.5	215.6	214.8	212.7	214.6	216.3	213.6
2012	212.2	214.2	215.8	217.0	218.1	218.7	218.1	220.1	219.1	219.3	221.1	221.6	217.9
2013	216.2	218.0	218.9	220.1	221.5	222.1	221.6	223.9	223.4	224.4	226.8	227.1	222.0
2014	223.5	224.6	225.8	226.1	226.9	227.1	225.4	227.0	225.3	225.9	227.8	229.0	226.2
2015	225.8	227.1	227.9	229.8	231.7	233.0	232.2	233.8	232.7	234.9	236.5	236.6	231.8
2016	233.3	234.4	234.6	237.2	237.8	238.0	239.0	240.6	239.6	238.3	240.1	240.6	237.8
2017	237.9	239.2	239.5	240.8	241.7	241.5	239.8	241.2	241.2	241.9	244.7	244.8	241.2
2018	241.9	242.8	242.9	243.5	244.7	245.0	245.5	247.6	246.2	247.1	247.6	248.1	245.2
Goods Producing													
2010	32.1	32.1	32.3	32.3	32.4	32.3	32.5	33.3	32.9	32.1	31.9	31.7	32.3
2011	31.2	31.1	31.3	31.3	31.4	31.2	31.1	31.9	31.6	30.7	30.7	30.5	31.2
2012	30.2	30.3	30.5	30.6	30.8	31.0	30.9	31.6	31.6	31.5	31.4	31.0	31.0
2013	30.4	30.9	30.8	30.9	31.0	31.0	30.9	31.6	31.5	31.3	31.1	30.9	31.0
2014	30.7	31.0	31.0	31.0	31.1	31.0	30.0	30.8	30.4	30.1	29.9	30.0	30.6
2015	29.7	30.2	30.3	30.6	31.2	31.1	31.1	31.4	31.6	31.9	31.7	31.7	31.0
2016	31.3	31.8	31.6	32.3	32.4	32.6	32.3	32.2	32.1	31.5	31.5	31.6	31.9
2017	31.6	32.1	32.5	32.6	32.8	33.0	32.2	32.1	32.1	32.1	32.1	32.0	32.3
2018	31.9	32.2	32.4	32.2	32.3	32.6	32.7	32.9	32.9	32.8	32.7	33.0	32.6
Service-Providing													
2010	244.4	245.9	249.1	249.2	251.1	249.5	243.0	244.0	248.8	250.2	252.3	253.8	248.4
2011	249.9	250.5	251.7	252.9	253.0	251.5	249.5	250.0	254.0	252.3	254.7	256.3	252.2
2012	252.6	254.6	256.1	257.0	258.1	254.8	253.2	254.7	257.0	258.7	261.1	261.8	256.6
2013	256.6	258.4	259.6	260.2	261.3	258.1	256.6	258.9	261.8	263.3	266.4	266.7	260.7
2014	262.2	263.5	264.7	265.5	266.3	263.7	260.9	262.1	263.9	266.1	268.7	269.7	264.8
2015	266.5	267.7	268.5	269.6	271.0	269.7	266.9	268.8	270.7	273.6	275.9	275.9	270.4
2016	272.7	273.7	274.3	276.6	277.3	274.5	273.7	276.0	279.1	279.2	281.1	281.3	276.6
2017	278.0	279.7	279.5	280.8	281.6	278.3	275.1	277.1	280.8	282.5	285.4	285.9	280.4
2018	282.5	283.7	283.6	284.5	285.6	282.7	281.0	283.4	285.4	287.6	288.3	288.6	284.7
Mining, Logging, and Construction													
2010	15.7	15.8	15.9	15.9	15.9	15.7	15.7	15.8	15.4	14.8	14.7	14.4	15.5
2011	14.2	14.0	14.1	14.0	14.0	13.7	13.8	14.1	13.9	13.2	13.2	13.0	13.8
2012	12.8	12.8	12.8	12.8	12.9	13.1	13.1	13.3	13.2	13.2	13.2	13.0	13.0
2013	12.5	12.8	12.7	12.7	12.9	13.0	13.1	13.4	13.4	13.5	13.4	13.3	13.1
2014	13.4	13.8	13.9	13.8	13.9	13.8	12.9	13.2	12.9	12.8	12.8	12.9	13.3
2015	12.8	13.1	13.2	13.5	14.0	14.0	14.1	14.3	14.5	14.7	14.6	14.6	14.0
2016	14.4	14.8	14.7	15.2	15.2	15.3	15.1	14.9	14.9	14.6	14.6	14.6	14.9
2017	14.7	15.0	15.4	15.5	15.8	16.0	15.5	15.5	15.5	15.4	15.4	15.5	15.4
2018	15.4	15.7	15.8	15.6	15.6	15.9	16.0	16.2	16.2	16.3	16.2	16.5	16.0
Manufacturing													
2010	16.4	16.3	16.4	16.4	16.5	16.6	16.8	17.5	17.5	17.3	17.2	17.3	16.9
2011	17.0	17.1	17.2	17.3	17.4	17.5	17.3	17.8	17.7	17.5	17.5	17.5	17.4
2012	17.4	17.5	17.7	17.8	17.9	17.9	17.8	18.3	18.4	18.3	18.2	18.0	17.9
2013	17.9	18.1	18.1	18.2	18.1	18.0	17.8	18.2	18.1	17.8	17.7	17.6	18.0
2014	17.3	17.2	17.1	17.2	17.2	17.2	17.1	17.6	17.5	17.3	17.1	17.1	17.2
2015	16.9	17.1	17.1	17.1	17.2	17.1	17.0	17.1	17.1	17.2	17.1	17.1	17.1
2016	16.9	17.0	16.9	17.1	17.2	17.3	17.2	17.3	17.2	16.9	16.9	17.0	17.1
2017	16.9	17.1	17.1	17.1	17.0	17.0	16.7	16.6	16.6	16.7	16.7	16.5	16.8
2018	16.5	16.5	16.6	16.6	16.7	16.7	16.7	16.7	16.7	16.5	16.5	16.5	16.6

Employment by Industry: El Paso, TX, 2010–2018—*Continued*

(Numbers in thousands, not seasonally adjusted)

Industry and year	January	February	March	April	May	June	July	August	September	October	November	December	Annual average
Trade, Transportation, and Utilities													
2010	55.2	55.1	55.8	56.1	56.3	56.2	56.6	56.8	56.8	57.4	58.8	59.8	56.7
2011	57.2	56.7	57.0	57.7	57.9	57.8	58.2	58.6	58.1	58.3	59.9	60.9	58.2
2012	58.6	58.3	58.5	59.4	60.0	60.2	59.7	60.2	59.6	60.0	61.9	62.4	59.9
2013	59.9	59.8	60.2	61.1	61.6	61.8	61.6	62.2	61.8	62.8	64.7	65.5	61.9
2014	63.4	62.8	63.4	63.3	63.4	63.6	63.5	63.7	63.3	63.9	65.6	66.6	63.9
2015	64.2	63.8	64.3	64.7	65.1	65.3	65.2	65.5	65.1	66.3	67.4	67.7	65.4
2016	65.9	65.5	66.0	66.6	66.7	67.0	67.3	68.3	67.9	68.4	70.2	70.3	67.5
2017	68.0	67.5	67.5	67.2	67.2	67.5	67.1	67.8	67.6	67.9	70.0	70.0	67.9
2018	67.6	67.3	67.2	67.3	67.4	67.8	68.1	68.8	68.4	69.1	70.3	70.1	68.3
Wholesale Trade													
2010	9.8	9.8	10.0	10.1	10.0	10.0	10.2	10.1	10.1	10.1	10.1	10.1	10.0
2011	9.9	10.0	10.0	10.1	10.2	10.2	10.4	10.4	10.3	10.3	10.2	10.3	10.2
2012	10.1	10.3	10.3	10.4	10.4	10.4	10.3	10.3	10.2	10.3	10.4	10.4	10.3
2013	10.3	10.3	10.3	10.4	10.5	10.6	10.6	10.7	10.7	10.7	10.8	10.8	10.6
2014	10.6	10.7	10.8	10.8	10.8	10.9	10.9	10.9	10.9	10.9	10.9	10.9	10.8
2015	10.9	10.9	11.0	11.1	11.1	11.1	11.1	11.2	11.1	11.2	11.2	11.2	11.1
2016	11.2	11.2	11.3	11.3	11.4	11.4	11.4	11.4	11.4	11.4	11.4	11.5	11.4
2017	11.3	11.4	11.5	11.4	11.5	11.6	11.5	11.6	11.7	11.8	11.8	11.9	11.6
2018	11.9	11.9	12.0	11.9	11.9	12.0	12.0	12.1	12.1	12.2	12.2	12.3	12.0
Retail Trade													
2010	33.0	32.9	33.3	33.5	33.7	33.6	33.8	34.1	34.2	34.7	36.1	37.0	34.2
2011	34.7	34.1	34.3	35.0	35.1	35.1	35.0	35.3	34.9	35.2	36.8	37.5	35.3
2012	35.7	35.1	35.2	35.9	36.3	36.4	36.0	36.4	35.9	36.2	37.9	38.4	36.3
2013	36.2	36.1	36.2	36.9	37.2	37.2	37.2	37.6	37.3	38.2	40.0	40.7	37.6
2014	38.7	38.1	38.3	38.5	38.5	38.5	38.5	38.6	38.3	38.8	40.5	41.2	38.9
2015	38.9	38.5	38.6	38.8	39.1	39.2	38.9	39.1	38.8	39.7	40.7	40.9	39.3
2016	39.0	38.5	38.7	39.2	39.2	39.4	39.6	40.6	40.1	40.7	42.4	42.3	40.0
2017	40.5	40.0	39.8	39.6	39.5	39.5	39.4	39.9	39.6	39.8	41.8	41.7	40.1
2018	39.5	39.0	38.8	39.0	39.1	39.2	39.5	40.0	39.7	40.2	41.3	40.9	39.7
Transportation and Utilities													
2010	12.4	12.4	12.5	12.5	12.6	12.6	12.6	12.6	12.5	12.6	12.6	12.7	12.6
2011	12.6	12.6	12.7	12.6	12.6	12.5	12.8	12.9	12.9	12.8	12.9	13.1	12.8
2012	12.8	12.9	13.0	13.1	13.3	13.4	13.4	13.5	13.5	13.5	13.6	13.6	13.3
2013	13.4	13.4	13.7	13.8	13.9	14.0	13.8	13.9	13.8	13.9	13.9	14.0	13.8
2014	14.1	14.0	14.3	14.0	14.1	14.2	14.1	14.2	14.1	14.2	14.2	14.5	14.2
2015	14.4	14.4	14.7	14.8	14.9	15.0	15.2	15.2	15.2	15.4	15.5	15.6	15.0
2016	15.7	15.8	16.0	16.1	16.1	16.2	16.3	16.3	16.4	16.3	16.4	16.5	16.2
2017	16.2	16.1	16.2	16.2	16.2	16.4	16.2	16.3	16.3	16.3	16.4	16.4	16.3
2018	16.2	16.4	16.4	16.4	16.4	16.6	16.6	16.7	16.6	16.7	16.8	16.9	16.6
Information													
2010	5.2	5.2	5.2	5.3	5.4	5.6	5.5	5.4	5.4	5.4	5.5	5.4	5.4
2011	5.4	5.4	5.4	5.4	5.4	5.5	5.5	5.5	5.5	5.5	5.5	5.6	5.5
2012	5.7	5.7	5.8	5.7	5.8	5.8	5.9	5.9	5.9	6.0	6.0	6.1	5.9
2013	6.1	6.0	6.1	5.9	5.9	5.9	5.8	5.8	5.8	5.8	5.9	5.8	5.9
2014	5.7	5.7	5.5	5.5	5.5	5.4	5.4	5.3	5.3	5.5	5.5	5.6	5.5
2015	5.5	5.4	5.3	5.3	5.3	5.3	5.3	5.2	5.2	5.1	5.2	5.2	5.3
2016	5.1	5.0	5.0	5.1	5.1	5.1	5.1	5.1	5.0	4.9	5.0	5.0	5.0
2017	5.0	4.9	5.0	4.9	4.9	4.9	4.9	4.9	4.8	4.8	4.8	4.8	4.9
2018	4.6	4.4	4.4	4.5	4.5	4.6	4.6	4.6	4.5	4.5	4.6	4.6	4.5
Financial Activities													
2010	11.6	11.6	11.7	11.7	11.8	11.8	11.9	11.9	11.9	12.0	12.1	12.2	11.9
2011	12.1	12.1	12.2	12.3	12.4	12.5	12.5	12.4	12.4	12.5	12.4	12.6	12.4
2012	12.4	12.6	12.6	12.6	12.6	12.7	12.7	12.7	12.6	12.6	12.5	12.5	12.6
2013	12.3	12.3	12.3	12.4	12.4	12.4	12.1	12.1	12.1	12.1	12.1	12.1	12.2
2014	11.9	12.0	12.0	12.1	12.1	12.2	11.6	11.6	11.7	11.7	11.7	11.7	11.9
2015	11.9	12.0	12.0	12.0	12.1	12.2	12.2	12.3	12.2	12.4	12.4	12.5	12.2
2016	12.4	12.6	12.5	12.5	12.5	12.4	12.5	12.5	12.7	12.6	12.6	12.6	12.5
2017	12.5	12.6	12.6	12.6	12.6	12.5	12.6	12.7	12.7	12.7	12.6	12.7	12.6
2018	12.7	12.7	12.7	12.5	12.6	12.6	12.6	12.7	12.7	12.7	12.7	12.7	12.7

Employment by Industry: El Paso, TX, 2010–2018—*Continued*

(Numbers in thousands, not seasonally adjusted)

Industry and year	January	February	March	April	May	June	July	August	September	October	November	December	Annual average
Professional and Business Services													
2010	31.4	31.4	32.3	31.5	31.3	30.9	31.0	31.1	31.0	31.5	31.5	31.5	31.4
2011	31.0	31.3	31.0	31.0	30.5	29.9	30.2	30.1	30.4	29.7	29.9	30.4	30.5
2012	29.9	30.1	30.5	30.5	30.1	29.8	30.0	30.3	30.3	30.5	30.4	30.6	30.3
2013	30.2	30.7	30.6	30.2	29.9	29.9	30.2	30.8	31.3	31.6	31.9	32.0	30.8
2014	31.4	31.5	31.5	31.6	31.4	31.1	31.3	31.5	31.1	31.7	31.7	31.5	31.4
2015	31.9	31.8	31.5	32.2	32.0	32.5	32.2	32.9	32.6	33.2	33.7	33.6	32.5
2016	33.5	33.4	32.9	33.4	33.0	32.7	33.6	33.7	33.8	33.5	33.5	33.9	33.4
2017	33.8	34.1	33.5	34.3	34.1	33.9	33.7	34.1	34.6	34.8	35.5	35.8	34.4
2018	35.5	36.0	35.4	35.2	35.1	34.9	35.1	35.3	35.6	36.0	35.2	35.7	35.4
Education and Health Services													
2010	35.2	35.2	35.7	35.9	36.1	37.7	35.8	36.0	36.2	36.3	36.4	36.7	36.1
2011	36.6	36.8	36.9	37.3	37.4	37.4	37.5	37.6	37.8	37.7	37.8	37.8	37.4
2012	37.5	38.3	38.6	38.4	38.5	38.5	38.3	38.7	38.8	39.3	39.4	39.4	38.6
2013	38.6	39.0	39.1	39.5	39.6	39.5	39.8	40.1	40.3	40.7	40.7	40.5	39.8
2014	40.3	40.9	40.9	40.9	41.1	41.0	41.0	41.2	41.1	41.5	41.8	42.0	41.1
2015	41.8	42.2	42.3	42.4	42.6	42.5	42.6	42.7	42.8	43.2	43.2	43.2	42.6
2016	43.0	43.2	43.1	43.4	43.6	43.3	43.7	44.0	44.0	44.1	44.1	44.1	43.6
2017	44.1	44.6	44.5	44.9	45.1	44.8	44.7	45.1	45.3	45.5	45.6	45.7	45.0
2018	45.6	45.8	45.7	46.1	46.4	46.2	46.1	46.7	46.6	46.9	46.9	46.9	46.3
Leisure and Hospitality													
2010	26.3	26.8	27.6	28.1	28.8	28.8	28.0	28.1	28.0	27.6	27.7	27.8	27.8
2011	28.0	28.3	29.1	29.1	29.6	29.9	29.9	29.8	29.5	28.9	29.0	29.1	29.2
2012	28.6	29.4	29.8	30.4	30.8	30.8	30.7	30.8	30.7	29.9	30.0	30.2	30.2
2013	29.5	29.9	30.5	30.9	31.7	31.8	31.4	31.5	31.0	30.8	30.9	31.0	30.9
2014	30.8	31.3	32.1	32.5	33.0	33.2	32.9	33.3	33.0	32.2	32.2	32.3	32.4
2015	31.5	32.2	32.7	33.3	34.1	34.4	33.9	34.2	33.8	33.4	33.5	33.3	33.4
2016	32.7	33.3	33.9	34.5	35.0	35.2	35.0	35.4	34.8	34.1	34.0	34.0	34.3
2017	33.8	34.3	34.7	35.3	35.9	35.7	35.4	35.4	35.1	35.0	35.0	34.8	35.0
2018	35.1	35.5	36.1	36.7	37.4	37.1	37.2	37.5	36.5	36.1	36.1	36.1	36.5
Other Services													
2010	8.9	9.2	9.1	8.9	9.0	9.3	9.2	9.3	9.0	9.1	9.1	9.1	9.1
2011	9.1	9.3	9.3	9.2	9.2	9.6	9.6	9.7	9.5	9.4	9.4	9.4	9.4
2012	9.3	9.5	9.5	9.4	9.5	9.9	9.9	9.9	9.6	9.5	9.5	9.4	9.6
2013	9.2	9.4	9.3	9.2	9.4	9.8	9.8	9.8	9.6	9.3	9.5	9.3	9.5
2014	9.3	9.4	9.4	9.2	9.3	9.6	9.7	9.6	9.4	9.3	9.4	9.3	9.4
2015	9.3	9.5	9.5	9.3	9.3	9.7	9.7	9.6	9.4	9.4	9.4	9.4	9.5
2016	9.4	9.6	9.6	9.4	9.5	9.7	9.5	9.4	9.3	9.2	9.2	9.1	9.4
2017	9.1	9.1	9.2	9.0	9.1	9.2	9.2	9.1	9.0	9.1	9.1	9.0	9.1
2018	8.9	8.9	9.0	9.0	9.0	9.2	9.1	9.1	9.0	9.0	9.1	9.0	9.0
Government													
2010	70.6	71.4	71.7	71.7	72.4	69.2	65.0	65.4	70.5	70.9	71.2	71.3	70.1
2011	70.5	70.6	70.8	70.9	70.6	68.9	66.1	66.3	70.8	70.3	70.8	70.5	69.8
2012	70.6	70.7	70.8	70.6	70.8	67.1	66.0	66.2	69.5	70.9	71.4	71.2	69.7
2013	70.8	71.3	71.5	71.0	70.8	67.0	65.9	66.6	69.9	70.2	70.7	70.5	69.7
2014	69.4	69.9	69.9	70.4	70.5	67.6	65.5	65.9	69.0	70.3	70.8	70.7	69.2
2015	70.4	70.8	70.9	70.4	70.5	67.8	65.8	66.4	69.6	70.6	71.1	71.0	69.6
2016	70.7	71.1	71.3	71.7	71.9	69.1	67.0	67.6	71.6	72.4	72.5	72.3	70.8
2017	71.7	72.6	72.5	72.6	72.7	69.8	67.5	68.0	71.7	72.7	72.8	73.1	71.5
2018	72.5	73.1	73.1	73.2	73.2	70.3	68.2	68.7	72.1	73.3	73.4	73.5	72.1

Employment by Industry: Allentown-Bethlehem-Easton, PA-NJ, 2010–2018

(Numbers in thousands, nct seasonally adjusted)

Industry and year	January	February	March	April	May	June	July	August	September	October	November	December	Annual average
Total Nonfarm													
2010	324.4	325.7	329.7	334.0	338.3	338.3	330.2	330.5	334.9	337.7	338.9	341.1	333.6
2011	328.8	330.9	334.7	339.8	343.8	344.9	337.7	337.9	342.7	344.2	345.1	346.5	339.8
2012	336.8	339.7	343.0	346.3	348.8	349.0	340.4	340.7	346.5	347.8	349.1	348.8	344.7
2013	340.2	341.3	343.8	347.6	351.1	352.3	344.8	345.6	350.4	351.5	353.8	352.7	347.9
2014	343.3	342.7	345.9	351.8	356.7	357.1	348.8	349.8	354.9	358.4	360.2	361.0	352.6
2015	348.9	348.7	351.0	355.6	360.8	360.7	355.6	356.0	360.7	365.1	367.4	367.7	358.2
2016	356.3	357.1	360.7	364.0	367.2	366.8	363.4	362.8	368.3	371.3	373.0	372.6	365.3
2017	362.7	363.3	364.9	368.2	372.2	372.2	366.5	366.0	372.3	374.2	376.8	376.4	369.6
2018	366.9	369.0	369.9	373.9	377.2	377.1	371.5	371.4	375.6	380.8	379.3	378.8	374.3
Total Private													
2010	281.7	281.7	285.4	289.3	292.5	293.4	292.1	293.1	293.2	295.3	296.0	298.4	291.0
2011	287.6	288.4	291.9	296.9	300.8	302.0	300.8	301.7	302.2	302.5	302.9	304.3	298.5
2012	295.8	297.9	301.2	304.2	306.2	307.8	305.0	305.6	306.4	306.4	307.6	307.0	304.3
2013	299.4	300.0	302.2	306.1	309.2	311.4	309.5	310.1	310.4	310.7	312.3	311.7	307.8
2014	303.0	302.0	305.0	310.7	315.3	316.4	314.0	314.6	315.2	317.8	319.2	319.9	312.8
2015	309.6	308.6	310.9	315.3	320.2	321.3	320.5	320.8	321.2	325.0	326.9	327.3	319.0
2016	317.1	317.0	320.3	323.5	326.5	327.2	327.8	327.9	328.8	331.1	332.4	331.9	326.0
2017	323.5	323.6	324.7	327.8	331.5	332.7	331.3	331.4	332.3	333.6	336.1	335.6	330.3
2018	327.5	328.5	329.4	333.2	336.3	336.9	335.8	335.7	335.5	339.8	338.0	337.7	334.5
Goods Producing													
2010	45.7	45.0	45.8	46.8	47.4	48.2	48.2	48.2	48.1	48.0	47.8	47.3	47.2
2011	45.7	45.3	46.3	47.1	48.0	48.7	48.5	48.9	48.5	47.9	47.5	47.0	47.5
2012	45.8	45.8	46.6	47.1	47.2	48.0	48.0	47.8	47.8	47.6	47.3	46.9	47.2
2013	45.8	45.5	46.0	46.8	47.5	48.0	48.1	48.2	48.1	48.3	48.1	47.6	47.3
2014	46.3	45.9	46.6	48.1	49.0	49.7	49.6	49.6	49.2	49.2	49.1	48.8	48.4
2015	47.3	46.8	47.4	48.5	49.5	49.9	50.0	50.1	49.7	50.3	50.0	49.4	49.1
2016	48.3	47.9	48.5	49.5	50.1	50.5	50.9	50.9	49.9	49.9	49.7	49.4	49.6
2017	48.2	48.4	48.9	49.8	50.7	51.4	51.4	51.6	51.2	51.3	51.4	51.2	50.5
2018	50.1	50.1	50.5	51.4	52.0	52.9	53.4	53.2	53.0	53.0	52.6	52.4	52.1
Service-Providing													
2010	278.7	280.7	283.9	287.2	290.9	290.1	282.0	282.3	286.8	289.7	291.1	293.8	286.4
2011	283.1	285.6	288.4	292.7	295.8	296.2	289.2	289.0	294.2	296.3	297.6	299.5	292.3
2012	291.0	293.9	296.4	299.2	301.6	301.0	292.4	292.9	298.7	300.2	301.8	301.9	297.6
2013	294.4	295.8	297.8	300.8	303.6	304.3	296.7	297.4	302.3	303.2	305.7	305.1	300.6
2014	297.0	296.8	299.3	303.7	307.7	307.4	299.2	300.2	305.7	309.2	311.1	312.2	304.1
2015	301.6	301.9	303.6	307.1	311.3	310.8	305.6	305.9	311.0	314.8	317.4	318.3	309.1
2016	308.0	309.2	312.2	314.5	317.1	316.3	312.5	311.9	318.4	321.4	323.3	323.2	315.7
2017	314.5	314.9	316.0	318.4	321.5	320.8	315.1	314.4	321.1	322.9	325.4	325.2	319.2
2018	316.8	318.9	319.4	322.5	325.2	324.2	318.1	318.2	322.6	327.8	326.7	326.4	322.2
Mining, Logging, and Construction													
2010	10.8	10.5	11.0	12.0	12.5	12.9	13.0	13.1	13.1	13.0	12.7	12.1	12.2
2011	10.9	10.7	11.4	12.2	12.8	13.1	13.2	13.2	13.2	13.0	12.8	12.2	12.4
2012	11.3	11.3	11.7	12.2	12.4	12.8	12.7	12.6	12.6	12.6	12.4	11.9	12.2
2013	11.1	10.9	11.4	12.1	12.7	12.9	13.0	13.1	13.3	13.4	13.1	12.5	12.5
2014	11.6	11.3	11.7	13.0	13.6	13.8	13.7	13.9	13.7	13.6	13.3	12.7	13.0
2015	11.6	11.1	11.5	12.6	13.3	13.4	13.5	13.6	13.5	14.0	13.6	13.0	12.9
2016	12.2	11.8	12.3	13.2	13.5	13.7	14.0	14.1	13.8	13.6	13.3	12.9	13.2
2017	12.0	12.1	12.5	13.1	13.7	14.0	14.0	14.2	13.9	13.9	13.8	13.3	13.4
2018	12.3	12.3	12.6	13.2	13.7	14.1	14.5	14.5	14.5	14.5	14.3	13.8	13.7
Manufacturing													
2010	34.9	34.5	34.8	34.8	34.9	35.3	35.2	35.1	35.0	35.0	35.1	35.2	35.0
2011	34.8	34.6	34.9	34.9	35.2	35.6	35.3	35.7	35.3	34.9	34.7	34.8	35.1
2012	34.5	34.5	34.9	34.9	34.8	35.2	35.3	35.2	35.2	35.0	34.9	35.0	35.0
2013	34.7	34.6	34.6	34.7	34.8	35.1	35.1	35.1	34.8	34.9	35.0	35.1	34.9
2014	34.7	34.6	34.9	35.1	35.4	35.9	35.9	35.7	35.5	35.6	35.8	36.1	35.4
2015	35.7	35.7	35.9	35.9	36.2	36.5	36.5	36.5	36.2	36.3	36.4	36.4	36.2
2016	36.1	36.1	36.2	36.3	36.6	36.8	36.9	36.8	36.1	36.3	36.4	36.5	36.4
2017	36.2	36.3	36.4	36.7	37.0	37.4	37.4	37.4	37.3	37.4	37.6	37.9	37.1
2018	37.8	37.8	37.9	38.2	38.3	38.8	38.9	38.7	38.5	38.5	38.3	38.6	38.4

Employment by Industry: Allentown-Bethlehem-Easton, PA-NJ, 2010–2018—*Continued*

(Numbers in thousands, not seasonally adjusted)

Industry and year	January	February	March	April	May	June	July	August	September	October	November	December	Annual average
Trade, Transportation, and Utilities													
2010	65.8	64.6	65.3	65.6	66.2	66.7	66.8	67.2	67.4	68.4	69.6	70.9	67.0
2011	67.8	67.0	67.5	67.9	68.8	69.6	69.5	69.8	70.2	71.3	72.8	74.1	69.7
2012	71.6	71.0	71.6	71.7	71.9	72.3	71.7	71.8	72.0	72.6	74.3	75.0	72.3
2013	72.2	71.3	71.4	71.6	72.2	72.6	71.5	72.0	72.1	72.6	74.1	75.1	72.4
2014	72.5	71.4	72.1	72.8	73.6	74.2	73.8	74.1	74.4	75.2	77.0	78.3	74.1
2015	75.4	74.3	74.9	75.0	76.3	77.1	77.1	77.4	77.2	78.1	80.0	80.9	77.0
2016	77.9	77.3	77.9	78.4	79.3	79.8	79.9	80.4	81.1	82.6	85.1	85.7	80.5
2017	82.9	81.4	81.1	81.8	82.4	83.0	82.5	82.9	83.8	84.5	87.7	88.0	83.5
2018	84.6	83.5	83.5	84.0	84.6	85.0	84.5	84.6	84.9	86.0	87.5	87.2	85.0
Wholesale Trade													
2010	12.7	12.6	12.7	13.0	13.1	13.2	13.2	13.2	13.2	13.3	13.3	13.3	13.1
2011	12.9	12.9	13.1	13.1	13.3	13.3	13.5	13.5	13.4	13.6	13.5	13.5	13.3
2012	13.4	13.4	13.5	13.6	13.5	13.6	13.5	13.4	13.4	13.3	13.2	13.2	13.4
2013	12.9	12.9	12.9	12.9	13.0	13.1	13.0	13.0	13.0	12.9	12.9	12.9	13.0
2014	12.9	12.9	13.0	13.2	13.3	13.4	13.4	13.4	13.3	13.5	13.4	13.4	13.3
2015	13.2	13.2	13.2	13.1	13.2	13.3	13.5	13.5	13.3	13.4	13.4	13.4	13.3
2016	13.1	13.2	13.3	13.4	13.5	13.6	13.6	13.6	13.5	13.8	13.8	13.9	13.5
2017	13.6	13.6	13.7	13.8	13.8	14.0	14.1	14.1	14.1	14.2	14.1	14.1	13.9
2018	13.9	14.0	14.0	14.2	14.2	14.4	14.5	14.5	14.3	14.4	14.4	14.4	14.3
Retail Trade													
2010	38.9	37.9	38.3	38.3	38.7	39.1	39.0	39.0	38.6	39.3	40.4	41.5	39.1
2011	39.3	38.5	38.7	38.9	39.3	39.7	39.4	39.6	39.0	39.5	40.8	41.9	39.6
2012	39.9	39.1	39.3	39.4	39.7	40.0	39.8	40.0	39.4	40.0	41.6	42.0	40.0
2013	40.1	39.3	39.3	39.4	39.8	40.1	39.7	39.9	39.5	40.0	41.2	42.1	40.0
2014	39.9	38.9	39.3	39.8	40.4	40.7	40.4	40.4	40.0	40.3	41.8	42.6	40.4
2015	40.4	39.3	39.5	39.7	40.5	41.0	40.8	40.9	40.3	40.8	42.3	42.5	40.7
2016	40.6	39.9	40.0	40.3	40.7	41.0	40.9	41.1	40.6	41.1	42.4	42.8	41.0
2017	41.1	40.2	40.1	40.4	40.6	40.9	40.6	40.6	40.2	40.6	42.1	42.4	40.8
2018	40.6	40.0	40.1	40.2	40.5	40.7	40.5	40.5	39.9	40.0	40.9	40.5	40.4
Transportation and Utilities													
2010	14.2	14.1	14.3	14.3	14.4	14.4	14.6	15.0	15.6	15.8	15.9	16.1	14.9
2011	15.6	15.6	15.7	15.9	16.2	16.6	16.6	16.7	17.8	18.2	18.5	18.7	16.8
2012	18.3	18.5	18.8	18.7	18.7	18.7	18.4	18.4	19.2	19.3	19.5	19.8	18.9
2013	19.2	19.1	19.2	19.3	19.4	19.4	18.8	19.1	19.6	19.7	20.0	20.1	19.4
2014	19.7	19.6	19.8	19.8	19.9	20.1	20.0	20.3	21.1	21.4	21.8	22.3	20.5
2015	21.8	21.8	22.2	22.2	22.6	22.8	22.8	23.0	23.6	23.9	24.3	25.0	23.0
2016	24.2	24.2	24.6	24.7	25.1	25.2	25.4	25.7	27.0	27.7	28.9	29.0	26.0
2017	28.2	27.6	27.3	27.6	28.0	28.1	27.8	28.2	29.5	29.7	31.5	31.5	28.8
2018	30.1	29.5	29.4	29.6	29.9	29.9	29.5	29.6	30.7	31.6	32.2	32.3	30.4
Information													
2010	5.6	5.5	5.5	5.6	5.6	5.7	5.7	5.7	5.7	5.6	5.6	5.6	5.6
2011	5.5	5.6	5.6	5.7	5.8	5.8	5.9	5.7	5.8	5.8	5.9	5.8	5.7
2012	5.7	5.8	5.9	6.0	6.0	6.1	6.0	6.1	6.1	6.0	6.1	6.1	6.0
2013	6.1	6.2	6.2	6.1	6.2	6.2	6.2	6.2	6.1	6.1	6.1	6.1	6.2
2014	6.1	6.1	6.2	6.2	6.3	6.3	6.3	6.3	6.2	6.1	6.1	6.1	6.2
2015	6.0	6.1	6.1	6.1	6.2	6.2	6.2	6.2	6.1	6.0	6.0	6.0	6.1
2016	5.9	5.9	6.0	6.1	5.9	6.1	6.1	6.1	6.0	5.8	5.7	5.6	5.9
2017	5.6	5.7	5.6	5.6	5.6	5.7	5.7	5.7	5.5	5.5	5.6	5.3	5.6
2018	5.3	5.4	5.4	5.3	5.4	5.4	5.4	5.5	5.4	5.4	5.4	5.3	5.4
Financial Activities													
2010	15.6	15.6	15.5	15.4	15.4	15.4	15.4	15.4	15.2	15.3	15.3	15.4	15.4
2011	15.2	15.2	15.2	15.2	15.2	15.3	15.1	15.0	15.0	15.0	15.0	15.1	15.1
2012	15.2	15.2	15.2	15.1	15.1	15.1	15.1	15.1	14.9	14.8	14.8	14.9	15.0
2013	14.9	15.0	15.0	15.1	15.1	15.2	15.2	15.1	14.9	14.8	14.8	14.8	15.0
2014	14.5	14.6	14.6	14.7	14.9	15.1	15.2	15.1	14.9	14.9	14.9	15.0	14.9
2015	15.0	14.9	15.0	14.9	15.0	15.1	15.1	15.1	14.9	14.8	14.8	14.7	14.9
2016	14.6	14.5	14.6	14.5	14.6	14.8	14.7	14.7	14.6	14.3	14.3	14.3	14.5
2017	14.1	14.2	14.3	14.1	14.1	14.3	14.3	14.3	14.0	13.9	13.8	13.8	14.1
2018	13.8	13.8	13.8	13.9	13.9	14.0	14.1	14.0	13.8	14.2	14.1	14.1	14.0

Employment by Industry: Allentown-Bethlehem-Easton, PA-NJ, 2010–2018—*Continued*

(Numbers in thousands, not seasonally adjusted)

Industry and year	January	February	March	April	May	June	July	August	September	October	November	December	Annual average
Professional and Business Services													
2010	41.1	41.0	41.7	42.7	42.8	43.0	42.5	42.6	42.9	44.3	45.5	47.0	43.1
2011	44.0	44.1	44.8	46.1	46.4	46.0	45.8	46.5	46.8	46.3	46.6	47.7	45.9
2012	45.3	45.2	45.5	46.2	46.2	46.5	45.8	46.0	46.5	46.8	47.2	47.5	46.2
2013	46.1	45.5	45.8	46.6	46.6	47.4	47.9	48.6	48.1	48.7	50.0	50.1	47.6
2014	48.1	47.2	47.1	48.4	48.8	49.0	48.3	48.9	49.0	49.6	51.0	51.2	48.9
2015	48.6	47.8	47.6	47.8	48.1	48.2	48.0	48.6	48.7	50.6	52.4	52.7	49.1
2016	48.9	47.9	47.8	49.2	49.2	49.6	49.8	50.0	50.6	51.7	51.9	51.8	49.9
2017	49.4	48.8	48.4	49.3	50.0	50.3	49.4	49.4	49.5	49.0	49.0	49.1	49.3
2018	48.4	48.1	47.4	48.4	48.6	48.8	48.2	47.9	48.2	48.9	48.2	47.4	48.2
Education and Health Services													
2010	65.0	67.5	68.2	67.8	67.8	65.9	65.4	66.0	67.3	68.2	68.4	68.2	67.1
2011	66.6	68.0	68.6	68.5	68.6	67.1	66.6	66.4	68.4	69.7	70.1	69.4	68.2
2012	67.9	70.2	71.1	71.1	70.6	69.1	68.2	68.0	70.7	71.5	71.6	71.0	70.1
2013	69.0	71.3	71.8	72.0	71.6	70.0	69.4	69.2	71.9	72.3	73.1	71.7	71.1
2014	69.9	71.6	72.2	72.8	72.5	70.6	69.8	69.4	72.3	73.9	74.2	73.7	71.9
2015	71.3	72.9	73.3	74.4	73.8	72.2	71.7	71.1	73.5	74.9	75.1	74.7	73.2
2016	72.6	74.4	75.3	75.5	74.8	72.5	72.3	71.6	74.3	75.3	75.6	74.8	74.1
2017	73.4	75.3	75.9	76.1	75.6	73.1	73.2	72.8	75.9	77.5	77.6	77.3	75.3
2018	75.5	77.9	78.5	78.8	78.2	75.6	75.2	75.7	78.0	79.8	79.3	79.1	77.6
Leisure and Hospitality													
2010	28.9	28.6	29.3	31.2	33.0	34.1	33.8	33.7	32.6	31.5	29.7	29.9	31.4
2011	29.0	29.4	30.0	32.3	33.8	35.0	34.9	35.1	33.5	32.5	30.9	31.0	32.3
2012	30.2	30.5	31.1	32.8	34.9	36.3	36.0	36.6	34.5	33.2	32.5	31.7	33.4
2013	31.7	31.6	32.3	34.1	36.1	37.9	37.2	36.9	35.6	34.3	32.5	32.7	34.4
2014	32.2	31.9	32.7	34.1	36.5	37.6	37.2	37.4	35.7	35.4	33.3	33.1	34.8
2015	32.5	32.4	33.0	34.8	37.3	38.6	38.4	38.4	37.4	36.5	34.8	34.9	35.8
2016	35.0	35.2	36.3	36.2	38.3	39.5	39.7	39.8	38.2	37.4	35.9	35.9	37.3
2017	35.7	35.5	36.2	36.7	38.5	40.1	40.0	40.1	38.1	37.6	36.7	36.5	37.6
2018	35.7	35.6	36.1	37.1	39.1	40.4	40.2	40.2	37.8	38.1	36.5	37.8	37.9
Other Services													
2010	14.0	13.9	14.1	14.2	14.3	14.4	14.3	14.3	14.0	14.0	14.1	14.1	14.1
2011	13.8	13.8	13.9	14.1	14.2	14.5	14.5	14.3	14.0	14.0	14.1	14.2	14.1
2012	14.1	14.2	14.2	14.2	14.3	14.4	14.2	14.2	13.9	13.9	13.8	13.9	14.1
2013	13.6	13.6	13.7	13.8	13.9	14.1	14.0	13.9	13.6	13.6	13.6	13.6	13.8
2014	13.4	13.3	13.5	13.6	13.7	13.9	13.8	13.8	13.5	13.5	13.6	13.7	13.6
2015	13.5	13.4	13.6	13.8	14.0	14.0	14.0	13.9	13.7	13.8	13.8	14.0	13.8
2016	13.9	13.9	13.9	14.1	14.3	14.4	14.4	14.4	14.1	14.1	14.2	14.4	14.2
2017	14.2	14.3	14.3	14.4	14.6	14.8	14.8	14.6	14.3	14.3	14.3	14.4	14.4
2018	14.1	14.1	14.2	14.3	14.5	14.8	14.8	14.6	14.4	14.4	14.4	14.4	14.4
Government													
2010	42.7	44.0	44.3	44.7	45.8	44.9	38.1	37.4	41.7	42.4	42.9	42.7	42.6
2011	41.2	42.5	42.8	42.9	43.0	42.9	36.9	36.2	40.5	41.7	42.2	42.2	41.3
2012	41.0	41.8	41.8	42.1	42.6	41.2	35.4	35.1	40.1	41.4	41.5	41.8	40.5
2013	40.8	41.3	41.6	41.5	41.9	40.9	35.3	35.5	40.0	40.8	41.5	41.0	40.2
2014	40.3	40.7	40.9	41.1	41.4	40.7	34.8	35.2	39.7	40.6	41.0	41.1	39.8
2015	39.3	40.1	40.1	40.3	40.6	39.4	35.1	35.2	39.5	40.1	40.5	40.4	39.2
2016	39.2	40.1	40.4	40.5	40.7	39.6	35.6	34.9	39.5	40.2	40.6	40.7	39.3
2017	39.2	39.7	40.2	40.4	40.7	39.5	35.2	34.6	40.0	40.6	40.7	40.8	39.3
2018	39.4	40.5	40.5	40.7	40.9	40.2	35.7	35.7	40.1	41.0	41.3	41.1	39.8

Employment by Industry: Columbia, SC, 2010–2018

(Numbers in thousands, not seasonally adjusted)

Industry and year	January	February	March	April	May	June	July	August	September	October	November	December	Annual average
Total Nonfarm													
2010	342.3	343.8	345.6	347.2	349.3	347.9	343.5	343.9	345.1	348.3	349.5	348.2	346.2
2011	339.8	343.8	345.8	349.1	349.6	348.3	344.5	347.4	349.1	351.3	354.8	355.4	348.2
2012	349.6	351.6	353.9	353.9	355.9	354.6	352.4	355.0	356.4	359.5	366.5	366.3	356.3
2013	355.6	358.3	359.7	362.5	364.2	362.2	360.4	361.3	365.9	368.1	375.3	376.2	364.1
2014	367.2	366.9	371.7	373.4	375.2	372.2	369.9	373.6	375.8	380.1	385.7	386.8	374.9
2015	377.1	379.7	380.7	382.7	385.0	383.7	382.3	384.6	387.7	391.8	397.6	398.9	386.0
2016	387.1	390.4	391.1	394.0	396.2	393.5	393.4	395.0	397.2	399.1	403.9	403.3	395.4
2017	393.7	395.8	397.1	398.7	399.9	399.9	397.1	393.2	393.3	397.2	402.7	402.6	397.6
2018	395.1	397.7	398.9	399.2	401.7	401.8	402.3	402.6	400.5	404.2	403.7	405.3	401.1
Total Private													
2010	260.2	261.1	262.5	263.9	264.8	265.2	264.0	264.6	264.5	266.8	267.8	266.9	264.4
2011	259.3	262.6	264.3	268.1	269.2	269.1	267.8	269.4	268.9	270.6	273.9	274.7	268.2
2012	269.4	270.2	272.4	272.5	274.3	274.0	273.7	275.7	275.7	277.6	283.9	283.8	275.3
2013	274.4	275.8	277.0	280.2	282.1	282.1	282.6	284.6	285.1	286.3	292.8	294.1	283.1
2014	285.0	283.7	288.1	289.6	291.4	290.0	289.6	292.3	292.1	295.7	301.0	302.2	291.7
2015	293.0	294.7	295.5	297.2	299.7	300.4	300.3	301.5	302.4	306.4	311.8	312.8	301.3
2016	302.5	304.9	305.1	308.1	310.2	309.2	308.9	310.6	311.2	313.0	317.5	316.5	309.8
2017	308.2	309.6	310.5	311.8	313.1	313.9	312.0	308.9	307.7	311.2	316.2	316.2	311.6
2018	309.9	311.9	312.8	313.0	315.6	316.0	317.9	318.1	314.7	318.2	317.2	318.5	315.3
Goods Producing													
2010	42.1	42.1	42.1	41.8	41.9	42.3	42.3	41.9	42.0	42.2	42.2	42.1	42.1
2011	41.1	41.6	42.0	42.2	42.4	42.6	42.6	42.8	42.5	42.4	42.5	42.6	42.3
2012	41.9	42.1	42.5	41.9	42.2	42.5	42.7	42.7	42.6	42.9	42.9	42.7	42.5
2013	41.8	42.1	42.4	42.3	42.5	42.8	43.0	43.0	43.1	43.2	43.5	43.6	42.8
2014	43.5	43.5	44.0	44.4	44.6	44.5	44.9	45.0	45.1	45.3	45.5	45.9	44.7
2015	45.7	46.0	45.9	46.2	46.3	46.6	46.5	46.5	46.8	47.4	47.4	47.3	46.6
2016	46.7	46.8	46.9	46.7	47.0	47.5	48.0	48.3	48.2	48.4	48.6	48.8	47.7
2017	49.6	49.4	49.6	49.8	50.2	50.4	50.4	47.0	46.6	46.4	46.5	46.6	48.5
2018	46.7	47.2	47.3	47.3	47.4	47.8	48.3	47.7	47.7	47.9	48.1	48.0	47.6
Service-Providing													
2010	300.2	301.7	303.5	305.4	307.4	305.6	301.2	302.0	303.1	306.1	307.3	306.1	304.1
2011	298.7	302.2	303.8	306.9	307.2	305.7	301.9	304.6	306.6	308.9	312.3	312.8	306.0
2012	307.7	309.5	311.4	312.0	313.7	312.1	309.7	312.3	313.8	316.6	323.6	323.6	313.8
2013	313.8	316.2	317.3	320.2	321.7	319.4	317.4	318.3	322.8	324.9	331.8	332.6	321.4
2014	323.7	323.4	327.7	329.0	330.6	327.7	325.0	328.6	330.7	334.8	340.2	340.9	330.2
2015	331.4	333.7	334.8	336.5	338.7	337.1	335.8	338.1	340.9	344.4	350.2	351.6	339.4
2016	340.4	343.6	344.2	347.3	349.2	346.0	345.4	346.7	349.0	350.7	355.3	354.5	347.7
2017	344.1	346.4	347.5	348.9	349.7	349.5	346.7	346.2	346.7	350.8	356.2	356.0	349.1
2018	348.4	350.5	351.6	351.9	354.3	354.0	354.0	354.9	352.8	356.3	355.6	357.3	353.5
Mining, Logging, and Construction													
2010	15.5	15.5	15.6	15.4	15.4	15.6	15.6	15.3	15.2	15.3	15.2	15.1	15.4
2011	14.4	14.7	15.0	15.1	15.2	15.2	15.3	15.4	15.3	15.4	15.5	15.5	15.2
2012	14.9	15.0	15.3	14.8	15.1	15.3	15.5	15.6	15.6	15.6	15.7	15.7	15.3
2013	15.2	15.3	15.5	15.5	15.7	15.9	16.2	16.2	16.2	16.3	16.5	16.6	15.9
2014	16.6	16.4	16.5	16.6	16.7	16.8	17.0	17.1	17.0	17.2	17.2	17.3	16.9
2015	17.0	17.0	17.0	17.2	17.4	17.5	17.4	17.4	17.6	18.0	18.1	18.4	17.5
2016	18.2	18.4	18.7	18.8	19.0	19.4	19.7	20.0	20.1	20.3	20.6	20.7	19.5
2017	21.2	21.0	21.1	21.2	21.4	21.4	21.2	17.8	17.5	17.3	17.3	17.2	19.6
2018	17.3	17.5	17.5	17.6	17.7	17.8	18.1	17.6	17.6	17.7	17.8	17.9	17.7
Manufacturing													
2010	26.6	26.6	26.5	26.4	26.5	26.7	26.7	26.6	26.8	26.9	27.0	27.0	26.7
2011	26.7	26.9	27.0	27.1	27.2	27.4	27.3	27.4	27.2	27.0	27.0	27.1	27.1
2012	27.0	27.1	27.2	27.1	27.1	27.2	27.2	27.1	27.0	27.3	27.2	27.0	27.1
2013	26.6	26.8	26.9	26.8	26.8	26.9	26.8	26.8	26.9	26.9	27.0	27.0	26.9
2014	26.9	27.1	27.5	27.8	27.9	27.7	27.9	27.9	28.1	28.1	28.3	28.6	27.8
2015	28.7	29.0	28.9	29.0	28.9	29.1	29.1	29.1	29.2	29.4	29.3	28.9	29.1
2016	28.5	28.4	28.2	27.9	28.0	28.1	28.3	28.3	28.1	28.1	28.0	28.1	28.2
2017	28.4	28.4	28.5	28.6	28.8	29.0	29.2	29.2	29.1	29.1	29.2	29.4	28.9
2018	29.4	29.7	29.8	29.7	29.7	30.0	30.2	30.1	30.1	30.2	30.3	30.1	29.9

Employment by Industry: Columbia, SC, 2010–2018—*Continued*

(Numbers in thousands, not seasonally adjusted)

Industry and year	January	February	March	April	May	June	July	August	September	October	November	December	Annual average
Trade, Transportation, and Utilities													
2010	62.5	62.0	62.3	62.3	62.4	62.4	62.2	62.4	61.8	62.3	63.2	63.9	62.5
2011	61.4	61.7	61.8	62.2	62.3	62.7	62.3	62.4	62.5	62.8	64.2	64.8	62.6
2012	63.0	62.4	62.9	62.7	63.2	63.0	63.1	63.9	63.9	64.5	66.3	66.7	63.8
2013	63.9	64.0	64.3	64.4	64.9	65.2	65.7	66.0	66.2	66.8	68.1	69.1	65.7
2014	66.9	66.7	67.4	67.1	67.6	67.7	67.7	68.3	68.1	68.8	70.2	71.4	68.2
2015	68.4	68.7	68.7	69.2	69.9	70.6	71.0	71.5	71.3	72.0	73.8	74.5	70.8
2016	72.1	72.4	72.3	73.0	73.7	73.7	74.1	74.0	73.6	74.0	75.6	75.6	73.7
2017	72.9	72.5	72.6	72.3	72.5	73.0	72.9	72.8	72.7	73.6	75.2	75.8	73.2
2018	72.7	72.7	73.1	72.7	73.8	74.2	74.7	74.6	73.7	74.4	76.9	77.2	74.2
Wholesale Trade													
2010	14.0	13.9	14.0	13.9	13.9	13.9	13.8	13.6	13.5	13.7	13.7	13.6	13.8
2011	13.5	13.6	13.6	13.6	13.6	13.6	13.6	13.5	13.6	13.4	13.5	13.5	13.6
2012	13.6	13.7	13.8	13.7	13.9	13.9	14.0	14.1	14.0	14.0	14.0	14.0	13.9
2013	13.8	13.9	14.0	14.0	14.2	14.3	14.3	14.3	14.4	14.4	14.6	14.7	14.2
2014	14.7	14.8	15.0	14.8	14.9	14.9	14.9	15.0	14.9	14.9	14.9	15.0	14.9
2015	14.8	14.8	14.8	14.9	15.0	15.1	15.0	15.1	15.1	15.2	15.3	15.4	15.0
2016	15.3	15.5	15.5	15.7	15.7	15.7	15.7	15.6	15.6	15.5	15.5	15.6	15.6
2017	15.5	15.5	15.5	15.3	15.3	15.4	15.3	15.3	15.2	15.2	15.2	15.2	15.3
2018	14.9	15.0	15.0	14.9	15.0	15.0	15.0	15.0	15.0	15.0	15.1	15.0	15.0
Retail Trade													
2010	38.0	37.6	37.8	38.2	38.3	38.2	37.9	38.3	37.9	38.1	39.0	39.7	38.3
2011	37.5	37.6	37.7	38.0	38.1	38.3	38.2	38.3	38.2	38.3	39.3	39.8	38.3
2012	38.2	37.6	38.0	37.8	38.0	37.7	37.7	38.0	37.9	38.2	39.6	39.8	38.2
2013	37.8	37.7	37.9	38.2	38.4	38.4	38.6	38.9	38.8	39.4	40.2	40.7	38.8
2014	38.9	38.5	38.8	38.7	38.9	38.9	38.9	39.2	39.0	39.5	40.6	41.2	39.3
2015	39.2	39.1	39.3	39.6	39.9	40.3	40.2	40.5	40.2	41.1	42.6	43.0	40.4
2016	41.0	41.1	41.2	41.5	41.8	41.8	41.9	42.1	41.9	42.0	43.4	43.3	41.9
2017	41.6	41.3	41.4	41.5	41.6	41.7	41.5	41.7	41.3	41.9	43.5	43.6	41.9
2018	41.6	41.5	41.8	41.5	42.3	42.3	42.7	42.5	41.4	41.9	44.0	44.2	42.3
Transportation and Utilities													
2010	10.5	10.5	10.5	10.2	10.2	10.3	10.5	10.5	10.4	10.5	10.5	10.6	10.4
2011	10.4	10.5	10.5	10.6	10.6	10.8	10.5	10.6	10.7	11.1	11.4	11.5	10.8
2012	11.2	11.1	11.1	11.2	11.3	11.4	11.4	11.8	12.0	12.3	12.7	12.9	11.7
2013	12.3	12.4	12.4	12.2	12.3	12.5	12.8	12.8	13.0	13.0	13.3	13.7	12.7
2014	13.3	13.4	13.6	13.6	13.8	13.9	13.9	14.1	14.2	14.4	14.7	15.2	14.0
2015	14.4	14.8	14.6	14.7	15.0	15.2	15.8	15.9	16.0	15.7	15.9	16.1	15.3
2016	15.8	15.8	15.6	15.8	16.2	16.2	16.5	16.3	16.1	16.5	16.7	16.7	16.2
2017	15.8	15.7	15.7	15.5	15.6	15.9	16.1	15.8	16.2	16.5	16.5	17.0	16.0
2018	16.2	16.2	16.3	16.3	16.5	16.9	17.0	17.1	17.3	17.5	17.8	18.0	16.9
Information													
2010	5.6	5.6	5.6	5.6	5.6	5.5	5.6	5.7	5.6	5.6	5.7	5.6	5.6
2011	5.4	5.4	5.4	5.3	5.4	5.4	5.4	5.4	5.3	5.3	5.4	5.4	5.4
2012	5.4	5.4	5.4	5.2	5.2	5.2	5.2	5.2	5.2	5.3	5.4	5.4	5.3
2013	5.5	5.8	5.8	5.9	5.6	5.4	5.5	5.5	5.5	5.6	5.7	5.7	5.6
2014	5.6	5.5	5.4	5.6	5.4	5.5	5.4	5.4	5.4	5.5	5.7	5.4	5.5
2015	5.5	5.5	5.4	5.5	5.6	5.4	5.4	5.4	5.4	5.4	5.5	5.6	5.5
2016	5.5	5.5	5.4	5.6	5.8	5.9	5.7	5.7	5.7	5.8	5.9	6.2	5.7
2017	5.6	5.9	5.9	5.7	5.9	5.6	5.4	5.3	5.2	5.2	5.3	5.2	5.5
2018	5.4	5.7	5.5	5.5	5.5	5.5	5.5	5.5	5.4	5.4	5.5	5.5	5.5
Financial Activities													
2010	27.7	27.7	27.6	27.3	27.3	27.3	27.0	27.0	26.8	27.0	27.0	27.0	27.2
2011	26.9	26.9	27.0	27.1	27.3	27.4	27.3	27.5	27.5	27.8	28.0	28.2	27.4
2012	28.2	28.3	28.4	28.4	28.6	28.7	28.8	28.9	29.0	29.1	29.3	29.3	28.8
2013	29.2	29.4	29.7	29.8	30.0	30.2	30.3	30.5	30.6	30.3	30.4	30.5	30.1
2014	30.1	30.1	30.1	30.1	30.2	30.2	30.1	30.2	30.2	30.1	30.1	30.2	30.1
2015	30.0	30.1	30.1	30.1	30.3	30.4	30.3	30.4	30.5	30.6	30.8	30.9	30.4
2016	30.5	30.6	30.6	30.6	30.7	30.9	30.8	31.0	31.1	31.3	31.5	31.4	30.9
2017	31.0	31.1	31.1	30.8	30.9	31.2	31.1	31.2	31.0	31.0	31.1	31.3	31.1
2018	31.2	31.2	31.2	31.0	31.0	31.1	31.3	31.3	31.8	30.7	30.9	30.5	31.1

Employment by Industry: Columbia, SC, 2010–2018—*Continued*

(Numbers in thousands, not seasonally adjusted)

Industry and year	January	February	March	April	May	June	July	August	September	October	November	December	Annual average
Professional and Business Services													
2010	38.1	38.8	39.1	39.8	40.0	40.4	40.2	40.6	40.9	41.5	41.2	40.9	40.1
2011	40.1	41.1	41.3	42.4	42.3	42.2	42.0	42.5	42.1	42.5	43.3	44.1	42.2
2012	42.8	43.0	43.3	44.0	44.5	44.5	44.4	44.4	43.9	44.4	47.8	48.3	44.6
2013	45.0	44.0	43.8	44.8	45.2	45.2	45.2	45.6	45.7	45.9	49.9	50.8	45.9
2014	46.4	44.8	46.1	45.9	46.5	45.6	45.5	46.1	46.1	47.5	51.5	51.8	47.0
2015	47.7	47.4	47.3	47.2	47.6	47.9	47.9	47.8	48.5	51.0	53.0	54.0	48.9
2016	49.3	49.7	49.3	50.1	49.9	49.2	48.3	48.9	49.7	50.0	51.5	51.4	49.8
2017	47.8	47.8	47.9	48.9	49.2	49.9	49.1	48.7	48.8	50.5	53.4	53.5	49.6
2018	50.9	51.0	51.1	51.5	52.1	52.5	52.9	53.0	51.7	53.1	52.6	53.4	52.2
Education and Health Services													
2010	42.0	42.2	42.3	42.5	42.7	42.6	42.5	42.5	42.6	43.2	43.2	43.0	42.6
2011	42.2	42.8	42.8	43.9	43.8	43.5	43.3	43.0	43.3	43.6	43.7	43.4	43.3
2012	43.0	43.3	43.4	43.3	43.3	42.6	42.5	42.7	43.3	43.6	43.7	43.5	43.2
2013	42.6	43.2	43.2	43.7	44.0	43.7	43.8	44.1	44.4	44.8	45.0	45.0	44.0
2014	44.4	44.6	45.4	45.8	46.0	45.4	45.7	45.9	46.2	46.4	46.5	46.5	45.7
2015	45.9	46.4	46.6	46.7	47.2	47.0	46.9	46.8	46.9	47.0	47.4	47.3	46.8
2016	46.7	47.3	47.5	47.7	48.2	47.8	47.9	47.9	48.4	48.6	48.8	48.8	48.0
2017	48.0	48.7	48.8	48.8	48.7	48.5	48.2	48.2	48.2	48.6	48.4	48.4	48.5
2018	47.9	48.4	48.5	48.1	48.6	48.5	49.2	49.4	48.9	49.1	47.9	47.4	48.5
Leisure and Hospitality													
2010	29.7	30.2	30.8	31.9	32.1	31.8	31.5	31.9	32.1	32.1	32.6	31.7	31.5
2011	29.8	30.7	31.5	32.3	32.8	32.2	31.7	32.6	32.5	33.1	33.6	32.8	32.1
2012	31.4	31.9	32.5	33.0	33.2	33.1	32.7	33.6	33.5	33.5	34.1	33.4	33.0
2013	31.9	32.8	33.1	34.5	35.0	34.7	34.2	34.9	34.7	34.7	35.2	34.3	34.2
2014	33.2	33.5	34.6	35.4	35.7	35.6	35.0	35.9	35.7	36.7	36.1	35.6	35.3
2015	34.4	35.1	35.8	36.7	37.0	36.7	36.5	37.2	37.2	37.2	37.9	37.1	36.6
2016	35.7	36.6	36.9	38.2	38.7	38.0	38.0	38.7	38.4	38.7	39.3	38.1	37.9
2017	37.3	38.1	38.4	39.3	39.5	39.1	38.8	39.5	39.1	39.7	40.2	39.3	39.0
2018	38.9	39.4	39.8	40.6	40.8	39.9	39.6	40.2	39.2	41.2	39.0	40.1	39.9
Other Services													
2010	12.5	12.5	12.7	12.7	12.8	12.9	12.7	12.6	12.7	12.9	12.7	12.7	12.7
2011	12.4	12.4	12.5	12.7	12.9	13.1	13.2	13.2	13.2	13.1	13.2	13.4	12.9
2012	13.7	13.8	14.0	14.0	14.1	14.4	14.3	14.3	14.3	14.3	14.4	14.5	14.2
2013	14.5	14.5	14.7	14.8	14.9	14.9	14.9	15.0	14.9	15.0	15.0	15.1	14.9
2014	14.9	15.0	15.1	15.3	15.4	15.5	15.3	15.5	15.3	15.4	15.4	15.4	15.3
2015	15.4	15.5	15.7	15.6	15.8	15.8	15.8	15.9	15.8	15.8	16.0	16.1	15.8
2016	16.0	16.0	16.2	16.2	16.2	16.2	16.1	16.1	16.1	16.2	16.3	16.2	16.2
2017	16.0	16.1	16.2	16.2	16.2	16.2	16.1	16.2	16.1	16.2	16.1	16.1	16.1
2018	16.2	16.3	16.3	16.3	16.4	16.5	16.4	16.4	16.3	16.4	16.3	16.4	16.4
Government													
2010	82.1	82.7	83.1	83.3	84.5	82.7	79.5	79.3	80.6	81.5	81.7	81.3	81.9
2011	80.5	81.2	81.5	81.0	80.4	79.2	76.7	78.0	80.2	80.7	80.9	80.7	80.1
2012	80.2	81.4	81.5	81.4	81.6	80.6	78.7	79.3	80.7	81.9	82.6	82.5	81.0
2013	81.2	82.5	82.7	82.3	82.1	80.1	77.8	76.7	80.8	81.8	82.5	82.1	81.1
2014	82.2	83.2	83.6	83.8	83.8	82.2	80.3	81.3	83.7	84.4	84.7	84.6	83.2
2015	84.1	85.0	85.2	85.5	85.3	83.3	82.0	83.1	85.3	85.4	85.8	86.1	84.7
2016	84.6	85.5	86.0	85.9	86.0	84.3	84.5	84.4	86.0	86.1	86.4	86.8	85.5
2017	85.5	86.2	86.6	86.9	86.8	86.0	85.1	84.3	85.6	86.0	86.5	86.4	86.0
2018	85.2	85.8	86.1	86.2	86.1	85.8	84.4	84.5	85.8	86.0	86.5	86.8	85.8

Employment by Industry: Baton Rouge, LA, 2010–2018

(Numbers in thousands, not seasonally adjusted)

Industry and year	January	February	March	April	May	June	July	August	September	October	November	December	Annual average
Total Nonfarm													
2010	359.9	362.0	364.9	364.9	366.1	365.6	361.4	364.1	365.4	368.3	368.9	368.5	365.0
2011	364.6	368.5	370.4	372.1	371.4	368.0	365.9	366.4	371.9	374.5	374.5	373.8	370.2
2012	369.1	373.9	376.1	376.8	376.7	374.5	368.2	374.2	377.6	380.1	382.2	380.7	375.8
2013	375.0	381.0	383.8	385.6	386.6	384.8	381.7	386.3	389.3	392.4	393.2	389.5	385.8
2014	383.7	388.6	391.7	393.2	396.5	393.9	392.4	397.1	401.2	405.7	403.9	402.3	395.9
2015	397.8	401.0	401.7	402.2	405.5	403.4	402.8	405.5	407.2	411.5	411.5	408.6	404.9
2016	400.1	403.7	406.3	407.2	407.3	404.8	402.8	399.6	404.4	408.3	407.4	404.2	404.7
2017	401.7	408.1	408.1	407.6	408.4	405.3	401.7	405.2	406.2	409.8	410.6	408.1	406.7
2018	400.9	406.6	412.6	411.0	411.8	411.5	406.2	409.4	411.5	412.6	415.1	411.4	410.1
Total Private													
2010	283.6	284.2	286.8	287.1	288.0	289.2	288.4	288.6	287.8	290.2	290.7	291.1	288.0
2011	289.7	291.5	293.7	295.1	294.6	292.9	292.9	293.9	295.1	296.9	296.7	296.6	294.1
2012	294.2	297.9	300.5	301.5	301.8	301.3	298.1	301.7	303.0	305.7	307.6	306.7	301.7
2013	303.1	307.4	310.2	312.1	313.4	313.0	313.0	315.1	315.4	318.8	319.1	316.4	313.1
2014	312.4	315.8	318.8	320.7	324.3	322.9	323.7	326.2	327.9	332.5	330.2	329.3	323.7
2015	326.6	328.2	328.8	329.5	333.1	332.2	333.8	334.2	333.6	337.5	337.0	334.6	332.4
2016	327.8	329.6	332.0	333.2	333.3	332.2	332.5	327.2	329.7	334.2	332.7	329.6	331.2
2017	328.5	333.1	332.7	332.9	333.9	332.4	331.4	332.9	331.7	335.6	335.9	333.8	332.9
2018	328.2	332.0	337.8	336.8	337.9	339.0	336.1	337.1	336.7	337.2	339.1	335.2	336.1
Goods Producing													
2010	63.5	63.4	63.5	62.8	62.6	63.8	64.5	64.7	64.6	64.8	64.0	64.0	63.9
2011	64.5	65.7	66.5	66.4	65.6	64.8	64.8	64.6	65.6	66.5	65.1	64.4	65.4
2012	65.1	67.1	67.8	67.5	67.4	67.1	66.4	67.8	68.8	70.1	70.4	69.3	67.9
2013	68.9	71.3	72.4	72.2	72.7	72.9	72.6	73.2	74.0	76.8	75.7	73.7	73.0
2014	73.7	75.9	77.0	76.3	77.6	77.2	78.8	80.2	82.2	84.1	80.2	78.5	78.5
2015	77.5	78.4	79.0	78.1	78.9	80.1	81.7	82.0	82.3	85.3	83.4	81.3	80.7
2016	79.3	80.3	80.8	79.7	79.9	81.6	82.3	79.6	81.0	84.6	81.9	79.7	80.9
2017	81.5	83.9	82.9	82.1	82.5	81.4	81.4	81.4	80.5	83.1	81.6	81.0	81.9
2018	79.1	81.5	85.1	84.2	85.7	87.5	86.2	85.8	85.6	87.1	85.6	84.5	84.8
Service-Providing													
2010	296.4	298.6	301.4	302.1	303.5	301.8	296.9	299.4	300.8	303.5	304.9	304.5	301.2
2011	300.1	302.8	303.9	305.7	305.8	303.2	301.1	301.8	306.3	308.0	309.4	309.4	304.8
2012	304.0	306.8	308.3	309.3	309.3	307.4	301.8	306.4	308.8	310.0	311.8	311.4	307.9
2013	306.1	309.7	311.4	313.4	313.9	311.9	309.1	313.1	315.3	315.6	317.5	315.8	312.7
2014	310.0	312.7	314.7	316.9	318.9	316.7	313.6	316.9	319.0	321.6	323.7	323.8	317.4
2015	320.3	322.6	322.7	324.1	326.6	323.3	321.1	323.5	324.9	326.2	328.1	327.3	324.2
2016	320.8	323.4	325.5	327.5	327.4	323.2	320.5	320.0	323.4	323.7	325.5	324.5	323.8
2017	320.2	324.2	325.2	325.5	325.9	323.9	320.3	323.8	325.7	326.7	329.0	327.1	324.8
2018	321.8	325.1	327.5	326.8	326.1	324.0	320.0	323.6	325.9	325.5	329.5	326.9	325.2
Mining, Logging, and Construction													
2010	38.9	38.7	38.8	38.2	37.8	38.9	39.6	39.8	39.7	39.7	38.9	38.8	39.0
2011	39.3	40.5	41.3	41.2	40.2	39.4	38.9	38.4	39.2	40.0	38.7	37.9	39.6
2012	38.9	40.9	41.3	41.0	40.7	40.1	39.5	40.9	41.9	43.2	43.4	42.3	41.2
2013	42.1	44.5	45.5	45.3	45.6	45.5	45.1	45.4	46.0	48.7	47.6	45.6	45.6
2014	45.2	47.5	48.6	47.8	49.0	48.4	49.9	51.3	53.0	54.8	50.9	49.2	49.6
2015	48.7	49.4	50.0	49.0	49.7	50.7	52.1	52.3	52.7	55.4	53.7	51.7	51.3
2016	50.1	51.0	51.7	50.6	50.8	52.4	53.0	50.3	51.6	55.1	52.5	50.3	51.6
2017	52.3	54.6	53.6	52.8	53.2	52.0	52.1	52.0	51.3	53.7	52.4	51.7	52.6
2018	50.1	52.4	55.9	55.1	56.4	57.8	56.5	55.9	55.8	57.2	55.8	54.7	55.3
Manufacturing													
2010	24.6	24.7	24.7	24.6	24.8	24.9	24.9	24.9	24.9	25.1	25.1	25.2	24.9
2011	25.2	25.2	25.2	25.2	25.4	25.4	25.9	26.2	26.4	26.5	26.4	26.5	25.8
2012	26.2	26.2	26.5	26.5	26.7	27.0	26.9	26.9	26.9	26.9	27.0	27.0	26.7
2013	26.8	26.8	26.9	26.9	27.1	27.4	27.5	27.8	28.0	28.1	28.1	28.1	27.5
2014	28.5	28.4	28.4	28.5	28.6	28.8	28.9	28.9	29.2	29.3	29.3	29.3	28.8
2015	28.8	29.0	29.0	29.1	29.2	29.4	29.6	29.7	29.6	29.9	29.7	29.6	29.4
2016	29.2	29.3	29.1	29.1	29.1	29.2	29.3	29.3	29.4	29.5	29.4	29.4	29.3
2017	29.2	29.3	29.3	29.3	29.3	29.4	29.3	29.4	29.2	29.4	29.2	29.3	29.3
2018	29.0	29.1	29.2	29.1	29.3	29.7	29.7	29.9	29.8	29.9	29.8	29.8	29.5

Employment by Industry: Baton Rouge, LA, 2010–2018—*Continued*

(Numbers in thousands, not seasonally adjusted)

Industry and year	January	February	March	April	May	June	July	August	September	October	November	December	Annual average
Trade, Transportation, and Utilities													
2010	64.0	63.9	64.5	64.9	65.0	64.9	64.5	64.5	64.3	65.2	66.5	67.2	65.0
2011	65.0	64.8	65.0	65.6	65.6	65.4	65.1	65.2	65.0	65.7	66.8	67.7	65.6
2012	65.9	65.8	66.4	66.5	66.7	66.4	66.0	66.3	65.8	66.8	68.7	69.1	66.7
2013	66.5	66.3	66.8	67.2	67.2	67.2	66.9	67.4	67.4	67.6	68.9	69.9	67.4
2014	67.7	67.2	67.7	67.7	67.8	67.8	67.7	67.9	67.8	68.5	70.4	71.3	68.3
2015	69.6	69.1	69.4	69.5	69.6	69.5	69.5	69.8	69.8	70.5	71.8	72.2	70.0
2016	70.3	69.8	70.4	70.2	70.2	69.5	69.8	69.5	69.5	70.4	72.0	72.6	70.4
2017	71.0	70.5	70.6	70.4	70.4	69.7	69.8	70.3	69.6	70.4	72.1	72.2	70.6
2018	70.6	70.0	70.5	70.5	70.6	69.9	69.9	70.5	70.4	69.8	71.1	71.2	70.4
Wholesale Trade													
2010	12.4	12.4	12.4	12.5	12.5	12.4	12.4	12.5	12.4	12.7	12.6	12.6	12.5
2011	12.7	12.7	12.7	12.8	12.9	12.9	12.9	12.9	12.9	13.0	13.0	13.0	12.9
2012	13.1	13.1	13.2	13.2	13.2	13.2	13.1	13.1	13.1	13.3	13.4	13.4	13.2
2013	13.6	13.6	13.8	13.9	13.8	13.7	13.6	13.6	13.5	13.6	13.5	13.5	13.6
2014	13.4	13.3	13.4	13.3	13.3	13.3	13.2	13.2	13.2	13.1	13.1	13.1	13.2
2015	13.2	13.2	13.3	13.2	13.2	13.2	13.1	13.1	13.1	13.3	13.3	13.3	13.2
2016	13.4	13.3	13.3	13.4	13.4	13.2	13.2	13.2	13.2	13.2	13.2	13.2	13.3
2017	13.0	13.1	13.1	13.1	13.1	13.1	13.1	13.3	13.2	13.3	13.3	13.3	13.2
2018	13.3	13.5	13.6	13.5	13.5	13.5	13.5	13.6	13.7	13.6	13.6	13.6	13.5
Retail Trade													
2010	40.0	39.9	40.4	40.5	40.6	40.6	40.2	40.1	40.0	40.5	41.9	42.3	40.6
2011	40.2	39.9	40.2	40.6	40.6	40.4	40.2	40.0	39.9	40.3	41.6	42.2	40.5
2012	40.5	40.5	40.9	41.0	41.0	41.0	40.9	40.8	40.5	41.3	43.0	43.2	41.2
2013	40.5	40.2	40.4	40.6	40.5	40.8	40.7	40.8	41.0	41.1	42.4	43.0	41.0
2014	40.9	40.6	40.8	40.9	40.9	41.2	41.2	41.0	41.0	41.7	43.5	44.1	41.5
2015	42.4	42.1	42.4	42.5	42.5	42.6	42.6	42.7	42.5	43.1	44.3	44.3	42.8
2016	42.8	42.7	43.1	42.9	42.8	42.9	43.0	42.5	42.5	43.5	45.0	45.7	43.3
2017	44.3	43.8	43.9	43.7	43.5	43.3	42.9	43.0	42.6	43.0	44.4	44.3	43.6
2018	42.7	41.9	42.2	42.2	42.2	42.0	41.8	41.8	41.7	41.2	42.3	42.3	42.0
Transportation and Utilities													
2010	11.6	11.6	11.7	11.9	11.9	11.9	11.9	11.9	11.9	12.0	12.0	12.3	11.9
2011	12.1	12.2	12.1	12.2	12.1	12.1	12.0	12.3	12.2	12.4	12.2	12.5	12.2
2012	12.3	12.2	12.3	12.3	12.5	12.2	12.0	12.4	12.2	12.2	12.3	12.5	12.3
2013	12.4	12.5	12.6	12.7	12.9	12.7	12.6	13.0	12.9	12.9	13.0	13.4	12.8
2014	13.4	13.3	13.5	13.5	13.6	13.3	13.3	13.7	13.6	13.7	13.8	14.1	13.6
2015	14.0	13.8	13.7	13.8	13.9	13.7	13.8	14.0	14.2	14.1	14.2	14.6	14.0
2016	14.1	13.8	14.0	13.9	14.0	13.4	13.6	13.8	13.8	13.7	13.8	13.7	13.8
2017	13.7	13.6	13.6	13.6	13.8	13.3	13.8	14.0	13.8	14.1	14.4	14.6	13.9
2018	14.6	14.6	14.7	14.8	14.9	14.4	14.6	15.1	15.0	15.0	15.2	15.3	14.9
Information													
2010	4.6	4.6	4.6	4.8	4.8	4.8	4.7	4.6	4.4	4.7	4.7	5.0	4.7
2011	4.8	4.9	4.8	4.9	4.8	4.8	4.8	4.9	4.8	5.0	4.9	5.0	4.9
2012	4.8	5.0	4.9	5.4	4.8	5.0	4.9	4.7	5.3	4.7	4.9	5.2	5.0
2013	5.5	5.9	6.3	6.7	6.7	6.7	7.2	6.4	5.8	5.9	6.1	5.6	6.2
2014	5.3	5.6	6.1	6.9	8.3	8.0	7.6	6.5	6.0	6.6	6.6	6.5	6.7
2015	7.0	7.2	6.1	6.9	8.0	7.5	7.7	6.9	6.2	5.6	5.7	5.8	6.7
2016	5.7	6.3	6.3	5.8	5.9	6.2	6.0	5.3	5.2	5.2	5.6	5.4	5.7
2017	4.9	5.4	5.6	5.9	6.0	5.9	5.5	5.0	5.0	5.0	5.1	5.1	5.4
2018	5.0	5.6	6.2	5.7	5.2	5.1	4.9	4.3	4.6	4.9	5.1	5.0	5.1
Financial Activities													
2010	17.2	17.2	17.3	17.2	17.2	17.2	16.9	16.9	16.7	16.9	16.9	17.0	17.1
2011	17.0	17.0	17.0	16.9	16.9	16.8	16.9	16.8	16.8	16.9	16.9	17.0	16.9
2012	16.9	16.9	17.0	17.0	17.0	17.0	16.9	17.1	16.9	17.1	17.3	17.3	17.0
2013	17.0	17.1	17.1	17.1	17.3	17.6	17.6	17.8	17.9	18.3	18.3	18.1	17.6
2014	17.5	17.4	17.4	17.5	17.6	17.7	18.0	18.2	18.3	18.5	18.5	18.5	17.9
2015	18.2	18.3	18.2	18.3	18.4	18.4	18.4	18.5	18.3	18.5	18.5	18.7	18.4
2016	18.5	18.5	18.5	18.5	18.8	18.7	19.0	18.9	19.0	19.0	18.9	18.8	18.8
2017	18.8	18.8	18.7	19.0	19.0	18.9	18.8	18.9	18.8	18.8	18.8	18.7	18.8
2018	18.4	18.5	18.5	18.5	18.5	18.7	18.8	18.8	18.6	18.7	18.8	18.8	18.6

Employment by Industry: Baton Rouge, LA, 2010–2018—*Continued*

(Numbers in thousands, not seasonally adjusted)

Industry and year	January	February	March	April	May	June	July	August	September	October	November	December	Annual average
Professional and Business Services													
2010	41.0	41.1	41.5	41.7	41.8	41.9	41.8	41.9	41.5	41.9	41.6	41.7	41.6
2011	41.6	41.9	42.3	42.8	42.6	42.4	42.2	42.8	43.3	43.0	42.7	42.8	42.5
2012	42.9	43.4	43.9	44.8	45.0	44.7	43.6	43.9	44.4	44.8	44.3	44.0	44.1
2013	44.0	44.8	45.0	45.3	44.9	44.5	44.7	45.3	45.3	45.5	45.3	44.8	45.0
2014	44.8	45.4	45.7	46.2	46.1	45.6	45.8	46.0	46.3	47.2	47.9	48.0	46.3
2015	48.2	48.7	49.0	49.1	49.4	48.7	49.1	49.4	49.0	49.2	48.9	48.2	48.9
2016	47.6	47.7	48.1	49.3	48.4	46.9	46.8	46.3	48.0	47.6	47.4	46.3	47.5
2017	45.7	46.3	46.4	46.5	46.3	46.1	46.4	47.0	46.8	47.4	47.4	47.0	46.6
2018	46.9	47.3	47.6	47.6	47.5	47.3	47.3	47.5	47.2	47.3	48.1	46.9	47.4
Education and Health Services													
2010	47.7	47.9	48.4	48.9	49.2	48.8	48.8	48.8	49.2	49.6	49.8	49.5	48.9
2011	49.6	49.9	50.0	49.4	49.4	49.2	49.7	49.6	50.0	50.2	50.5	50.4	49.8
2012	49.9	50.6	50.8	50.3	50.3	50.4	49.9	50.6	50.5	51.1	51.1	51.2	50.6
2013	50.9	51.3	51.3	51.5	51.7	51.3	51.3	52.3	52.3	52.5	52.8	52.5	51.8
2014	52.4	52.6	52.8	52.7	52.7	52.3	51.9	53.1	53.4	53.7	53.5	53.4	52.9
2015	53.1	53.2	53.2	53.2	53.1	52.4	52.1	52.6	52.8	53.1	53.2	53.0	52.9
2016	51.9	52.0	51.9	52.6	52.6	52.2	52.2	52.4	52.2	52.4	52.2	52.5	52.3
2017	52.4	52.8	52.9	53.0	53.1	52.9	52.2	52.6	52.9	53.3	53.7	53.7	53.0
2018	53.0	53.3	53.3	53.4	53.4	53.0	52.5	53.3	53.2	52.8	53.6	52.6	53.1
Leisure and Hospitality													
2010	31.0	31.3	32.2	32.4	32.9	33.1	32.7	32.8	32.8	32.4	32.6	32.1	32.4
2011	32.5	32.6	33.3	34.1	34.8	34.4	34.1	34.6	34.3	34.4	34.5	34.2	34.0
2012	33.7	33.9	34.5	34.7	35.3	35.2	35.2	36.1	36.0	35.8	35.6	35.5	35.1
2013	35.1	35.3	35.7	36.6	37.3	37.1	37.2	37.1	37.1	36.7	36.5	36.3	36.5
2014	35.5	36.0	36.4	37.6	38.2	38.3	37.8	38.1	37.8	37.4	36.8	36.9	37.2
2015	36.7	37.0	37.5	38.0	39.0	39.0	38.7	38.5	38.6	38.5	38.8	38.7	38.3
2016	37.9	38.4	39.1	40.3	40.6	40.2	39.8	38.8	38.4	38.7	38.3	38.0	39.0
2017	37.8	38.8	39.0	39.4	40.1	40.7	40.6	41.0	41.5	40.9	40.6	39.8	40.0
2018	38.9	39.1	40.0	40.2	40.2	40.6	39.8	40.4	40.4	39.8	40.1	39.6	39.9
Other Services													
2010	14.6	14.8	14.8	14.4	14.5	14.7	14.5	14.4	14.3	14.7	14.6	14.6	14.6
2011	14.7	14.7	14.8	15.0	14.9	15.1	15.3	15.4	15.3	15.2	15.3	15.1	15.1
2012	15.0	15.2	15.2	15.3	15.3	15.5	15.2	15.2	15.3	15.3	15.3	15.1	15.2
2013	15.2	15.4	15.6	15.5	15.6	15.7	15.5	15.6	15.6	15.5	15.5	15.5	15.5
2014	15.5	15.7	15.7	15.8	16.0	16.0	16.1	16.2	16.1	16.5	16.3	16.2	16.0
2015	16.3	16.3	16.4	16.4	16.7	16.6	16.6	16.5	16.6	16.8	16.7	16.7	16.6
2016	16.6	16.6	16.9	16.8	16.9	16.9	16.6	16.4	16.4	16.3	16.4	16.3	16.6
2017	16.4	16.6	16.6	16.6	16.5	16.8	16.7	16.7	16.6	16.7	16.6	16.3	16.6
2018	16.3	16.7	16.6	16.7	16.8	16.9	16.7	16.5	16.7	16.8	16.7	16.6	16.7
Government													
2010	76.3	77.8	78.1	77.8	78.1	76.4	73.0	75.5	77.6	78.1	78.2	77.4	77.0
2011	74.9	77.0	76.7	77.0	76.8	75.1	73.0	72.5	76.8	77.6	77.8	77.2	76.0
2012	74.9	76.0	75.6	75.3	74.9	73.2	70.1	72.5	74.6	74.4	74.6	74.0	74.2
2013	71.9	73.6	73.6	73.5	73.2	71.8	68.7	71.2	73.9	73.6	74.1	73.1	72.7
2014	71.3	72.8	72.9	72.5	72.2	71.0	68.7	70.9	73.3	73.2	73.7	73.0	72.1
2015	71.2	72.8	72.9	72.7	72.4	71.2	69.0	71.3	73.6	74.0	74.5	74.0	72.5
2016	72.3	74.1	74.3	74.0	74.0	72.6	70.3	72.4	74.7	74.1	74.7	74.6	73.5
2017	73.2	75.0	75.4	74.7	74.5	72.9	70.3	72.3	74.5	74.2	74.7	74.3	73.8
2018	72.7	74.6	74.8	74.2	73.9	72.5	70.1	72.3	74.8	75.4	76.0	76.2	74.0

Employment by Industry: North Port-Sarasota-Bradenton, FL, 2010–2018

(Numbers in thousands, not seasonally adjusted)

Industry and year	January	February	March	April	May	June	July	August	September	October	November	December	Annual average
Total Nonfarm													
2010	236.2	238.0	239.9	240.0	241.8	236.4	233.1	234.9	233.5	235.0	238.4	240.4	237.3
2011	236.4	239.6	241.2	243.2	241.0	237.0	235.1	238.4	238.2	239.6	243.9	246.1	240.0
2012	243.1	245.1	248.2	247.6	246.9	242.9	240.0	242.7	243.4	246.9	252.2	253.9	246.1
2013	250.6	254.4	256.2	256.3	256.4	252.3	251.1	253.9	254.5	258.5	265.0	267.0	256.4
2014	263.1	266.3	268.9	269.0	268.7	265.1	263.9	267.5	268.3	273.8	278.6	282.0	269.6
2015	278.7	281.4	284.3	284.4	284.3	281.1	278.1	280.9	281.2	286.4	290.1	293.2	283.7
2016	290.1	293.2	295.0	294.9	293.6	289.3	289.0	291.5	292.2	296.7	300.7	302.6	294.1
2017	299.6	301.4	304.2	302.4	301.2	297.3	295.8	299.1	292.5	302.9	306.6	308.8	301.0
2018	305.7	309.4	311.4	310.1	308.9	305.2	302.9	306.4	305.5	307.3	310.6	311.9	307.9
Total Private													
2010	208.4	210.1	211.9	212.0	212.3	210.9	207.9	208.3	206.4	207.5	210.8	212.9	210.0
2011	209.0	212.0	213.5	215.5	213.8	212.7	211.1	211.2	211.3	212.3	216.4	218.8	213.1
2012	216.0	217.7	220.7	220.3	219.7	218.7	215.9	216.7	216.6	219.6	224.9	226.6	219.5
2013	223.5	227.1	228.8	229.1	229.4	228.2	227.1	228.1	227.9	231.2	237.4	239.5	229.8
2014	236.2	239.2	241.5	241.7	241.5	241.0	239.7	241.6	241.6	246.2	250.7	254.3	242.9
2015	251.1	253.7	256.4	256.6	256.6	256.5	253.5	254.6	254.2	258.7	262.3	265.4	256.6
2016	262.4	265.4	267.0	266.9	265.6	264.2	263.9	264.6	264.7	268.7	272.8	274.8	266.8
2017	271.7	273.3	276.0	274.8	273.2	272.1	270.7	272.5	264.9	274.7	278.3	280.3	273.5
2018	277.3	280.9	282.7	281.4	280.2	279.6	277.4	279.3	277.6	279.5	282.8	284.1	280.2
Goods Producing													
2010	27.9	27.8	27.7	28.0	28.3	28.6	28.6	28.7	28.6	28.4	28.3	28.4	28.3
2011	27.5	27.7	27.9	28.4	28.6	29.1	29.1	29.2	29.4	29.3	29.5	29.6	28.8
2012	29.3	29.4	29.6	29.6	29.9	30.0	29.9	30.3	30.3	30.5	30.8	30.8	30.0
2013	30.4	30.7	30.8	30.9	31.2	31.4	31.5	31.8	31.9	32.2	32.7	32.9	31.5
2014	32.8	33.0	33.2	33.6	34.1	34.3	34.5	34.8	35.3	35.4	35.5	35.8	34.4
2015	35.3	35.6	35.7	36.0	36.3	36.6	36.5	36.9	37.1	37.3	37.3	37.6	36.5
2016	37.4	37.7	37.9	38.2	38.2	38.5	38.8	38.8	39.0	39.3	39.7	40.0	38.6
2017	39.2	39.5	39.9	39.7	39.9	40.2	40.1	40.4	38.9	40.7	41.0	41.1	40.1
2018	40.6	41.3	41.6	41.7	41.8	42.4	42.1	42.5	42.4	42.7	43.1	43.3	42.1
Service-Providing													
2010	208.3	210.2	212.2	212.0	213.5	207.8	204.5	206.2	204.9	206.6	210.1	212.0	209.0
2011	208.9	211.9	213.3	214.8	212.4	207.9	206.0	209.2	208.8	210.3	214.4	216.5	211.2
2012	213.8	215.7	218.6	218.0	217.0	212.9	210.1	212.4	213.1	216.4	221.4	223.1	216.0
2013	220.2	223.7	225.4	225.4	225.2	220.9	219.6	222.1	222.6	226.3	232.3	234.1	224.8
2014	230.3	233.3	235.7	235.4	234.6	230.8	229.4	232.7	233.0	238.4	243.1	246.2	235.2
2015	243.4	245.8	248.6	248.4	248.0	244.5	241.6	244.0	244.1	249.1	252.8	255.6	247.2
2016	252.7	255.5	257.1	256.7	255.4	250.8	250.2	252.7	253.2	257.4	261.0	262.6	255.4
2017	260.4	261.9	264.3	262.7	261.3	257.1	255.7	258.7	253.6	262.2	265.6	267.7	260.9
2018	265.1	268.1	269.8	268.4	267.1	262.8	260.8	263.9	263.1	264.6	267.5	268.6	265.8
Mining, Logging, and Construction													
2010	14.9	14.9	14.9	15.0	15.2	15.5	15.5	15.6	15.5	15.3	15.2	15.1	15.2
2011	14.5	14.6	14.8	14.9	14.9	15.1	15.1	15.1	15.4	15.3	15.4	15.4	15.0
2012	14.9	15.0	15.1	15.2	15.3	15.5	15.5	15.7	15.7	16.0	16.1	16.1	15.5
2013	15.8	16.0	16.1	16.2	16.4	16.6	16.8	17.1	17.1	17.4	17.6	17.8	16.7
2014	17.7	17.8	18.1	18.4	18.7	18.9	19.1	19.3	19.6	19.7	19.6	19.7	18.9
2015	19.5	19.6	19.7	19.9	20.1	20.2	20.2	20.5	20.7	20.9	21.0	21.2	20.3
2016	20.9	21.2	21.4	21.7	21.7	21.9	22.1	22.2	22.4	22.6	22.9	23.1	22.0
2017	22.6	22.8	23.2	23.1	23.2	23.5	23.5	23.8	22.7	24.2	24.4	24.5	23.5
2018	24.0	24.7	24.9	25.0	25.1	25.6	25.4	25.7	25.7	25.8	26.0	26.2	25.3
Manufacturing													
2010	13.0	12.9	12.8	13.0	13.1	13.1	13.1	13.1	13.1	13.1	13.1	13.3	13.1
2011	13.0	13.1	13.1	13.5	13.7	14.0	14.0	14.1	14.0	14.0	14.1	14.2	13.7
2012	14.4	14.4	14.5	14.4	14.6	14.5	14.4	14.6	14.6	14.5	14.7	14.7	14.5
2013	14.6	14.7	14.7	14.7	14.8	14.8	14.7	14.7	14.8	14.8	15.1	15.1	14.8
2014	15.1	15.2	15.1	15.2	15.4	15.4	15.4	15.5	15.7	15.7	15.9	16.1	15.5
2015	15.8	16.0	16.0	16.1	16.2	16.4	16.3	16.4	16.4	16.4	16.3	16.4	16.2
2016	16.5	16.5	16.5	16.5	16.5	16.6	16.7	16.6	16.6	16.7	16.8	16.9	16.6
2017	16.6	16.7	16.7	16.6	16.7	16.7	16.6	16.6	16.2	16.5	16.6	16.6	16.6
2018	16.6	16.6	16.7	16.7	16.7	16.8	16.7	16.8	16.7	16.9	17.1	17.1	16.8

Employment by Industry: North Port-Sarasota-Bradenton, FL, 2010–2018—*Continued*

(Numbers in thousands, not seasonally adjusted)

Industry and year	January	February	March	April	May	June	July	August	September	October	November	December	Annual average
Trade, Transportation, and Utilities													
2010	45.1	45.4	45.5	45.6	45.5	45.1	44.5	44.7	44.4	45.0	46.3	47.4	45.4
2011	46.2	46.2	46.4	46.8	46.3	46.0	45.8	45.9	46.2	46.6	48.3	49.1	46.7
2012	48.1	48.1	48.5	48.5	48.8	48.5	47.8	47.9	48.2	49.1	50.6	51.5	48.8
2013	49.8	50.2	50.1	50.4	50.4	50.3	50.2	50.3	50.3	51.2	53.2	54.0	50.9
2014	52.0	52.3	52.5	52.7	52.6	52.5	51.8	52.3	52.3	53.1	55.1	56.2	53.0
2015	54.4	54.5	54.8	54.6	54.6	54.7	54.3	54.6	54.7	55.3	57.2	58.0	55.1
2016	56.1	56.4	56.3	56.6	56.4	56.1	55.8	56.2	56.8	57.9	59.0	59.5	56.9
2017	57.5	57.2	57.3	57.0	56.4	56.2	55.9	56.6	55.5	58.1	59.7	60.0	57.3
2018	58.5	58.9	58.9	58.5	58.2	58.2	57.9	58.7	59.1	60.3	61.6	62.1	59.2
Wholesale Trade													
2010	7.0	7.1	7.1	7.1	7.2	7.1	7.1	7.1	7.0	7.1	7.1	7.2	7.1
2011	7.2	7.3	7.4	7.3	7.1	7.2	7.2	7.2	7.3	7.2	7.2	7.3	7.2
2012	7.3	7.3	7.4	7.4	7.5	7.5	7.3	7.3	7.3	7.5	7.5	7.5	7.4
2013	7.4	7.5	7.6	7.6	7.6	7.6	7.5	7.6	7.6	7.7	7.8	7.8	7.6
2014	7.6	7.7	7.7	7.8	7.9	7.9	7.9	8.0	8.0	8.1	8.2	8.3	7.9
2015	8.1	8.2	8.3	8.3	8.3	8.3	8.3	8.3	8.4	8.3	8.3	8.3	8.3
2016	8.3	8.3	8.2	8.3	8.3	8.4	8.4	8.4	8.4	8.4	8.4	8.4	8.4
2017	8.4	8.4	8.4	8.4	8.4	8.4	8.4	8.4	8.3	8.4	8.5	8.6	8.4
2018	8.4	8.6	8.6	8.6	8.6	8.7	8.7	8.8	8.8	8.8	8.8	8.9	8.7
Retail Trade													
2010	34.1	34.2	34.3	34.4	34.2	33.9	33.4	33.5	33.3	33.9	35.0	35.7	34.2
2011	34.7	34.7	34.8	35.2	35.0	34.6	34.4	34.5	34.7	35.2	36.8	37.3	35.2
2012	36.4	36.4	36.7	36.9	37.0	36.7	36.3	36.4	36.7	37.3	38.6	39.2	37.1
2013	37.9	38.1	37.9	38.2	38.2	38.2	38.1	38.1	38.1	38.8	40.5	41.2	38.6
2014	39.7	39.9	40.1	40.2	40.0	39.8	39.2	39.5	39.5	40.2	41.9	42.6	40.2
2015	41.4	41.4	41.5	41.5	41.4	41.5	41.2	41.5	41.5	42.2	43.8	44.4	41.9
2016	42.9	43.2	43.3	43.4	43.2	42.8	42.6	43.0	43.5	44.5	45.3	45.4	43.6
2017	43.9	43.7	43.7	43.4	43.0	42.6	42.4	43.0	42.2	44.6	45.7	45.5	43.6
2018	44.5	44.8	44.9	44.5	44.2	44.1	43.8	44.5	44.9	46.0	47.2	47.2	45.1
Transportation and Utilities													
2010	4.0	4.1	4.1	4.1	4.1	4.1	4.0	4.1	4.1	4.0	4.2	4.5	4.1
2011	4.3	4.2	4.2	4.3	4.2	4.2	4.2	4.2	4.2	4.2	4.3	4.5	4.3
2012	4.4	4.4	4.4	4.2	4.3	4.3	4.2	4.2	4.2	4.3	4.5	4.8	4.4
2013	4.5	4.6	4.6	4.6	4.6	4.5	4.6	4.6	4.6	4.7	4.9	5.0	4.7
2014	4.7	4.7	4.7	4.7	4.7	4.8	4.7	4.8	4.8	4.8	5.0	5.3	4.8
2015	4.9	4.9	5.0	4.8	4.9	4.9	4.8	4.8	4.8	4.8	5.1	5.3	4.9
2016	4.9	4.9	4.8	4.9	4.9	4.9	4.8	4.8	4.9	5.0	5.3	5.7	5.0
2017	5.2	5.1	5.2	5.2	5.0	5.2	5.1	5.2	5.0	5.1	5.5	5.9	5.2
2018	5.6	5.5	5.4	5.4	5.4	5.4	5.4	5.4	5.4	5.5	5.6	6.0	5.5
Information													
2010	3.4	3.4	3.3	3.3	3.4	3.4	3.4	3.4	3.4	3.4	3.5	3.5	3.4
2011	3.4	3.5	3.5	3.5	3.4	3.4	3.4	3.4	3.4	3.4	3.4	3.4	3.4
2012	3.5	3.4	3.4	3.4	3.4	3.3	3.3	3.3	3.3	3.3	3.3	3.4	3.4
2013	3.3	3.3	3.4	3.4	3.4	3.4	3.4	3.4	3.3	3.3	3.3	3.3	3.4
2014	3.3	3.3	3.3	3.4	3.4	3.4	3.4	3.4	3.4	3.4	3.4	3.5	3.4
2015	3.4	3.5	3.5	3.5	3.5	3.5	3.6	3.6	3.6	3.6	3.6	3.6	3.5
2016	3.6	3.6	3.5	3.5	3.5	3.5	3.6	3.5	3.5	3.5	3.5	3.5	3.5
2017	3.5	3.4	3.5	3.5	3.5	3.5	3.5	3.4	3.4	3.4	3.4	3.4	3.5
2018	3.5	3.5	3.5	3.5	3.5	3.6	3.5	3.5	3.4	3.5	3.5	3.5	3.5
Financial Activities													
2010	13.6	13.6	13.6	13.7	13.6	13.6	13.7	13.7	13.6	13.7	13.8	13.9	13.7
2011	13.8	13.9	14.0	13.9	14.0	14.0	14.1	14.1	14.0	14.1	14.2	14.3	14.0
2012	14.1	14.1	14.2	14.4	14.4	14.4	14.4	14.4	14.3	14.4	14.5	14.5	14.3
2013	14.3	14.3	14.3	14.5	14.4	14.4	14.5	14.5	14.5	14.5	14.6	14.7	14.5
2014	14.3	14.4	14.4	14.4	14.4	14.4	14.5	14.5	14.5	14.7	14.7	14.7	14.5
2015	14.5	14.5	14.7	14.7	14.7	14.7	14.7	14.7	14.6	14.8	14.6	14.9	14.7
2016	14.7	14.7	14.9	14.9	14.8	14.9	14.6	14.7	14.7	14.8	14.8	14.9	14.8
2017	14.9	14.9	15.0	14.8	14.8	15.0	14.9	14.8	14.7	14.9	14.9	15.1	14.9
2018	14.8	14.8	14.9	14.8	14.7	14.7	14.7	14.8	14.6	15.0	15.1	15.1	14.8

Employment by Industry: North Port-Sarasota-Bradenton, FL, 2010–2018—*Continued*

(Numbers in thousands, not seasonally adjusted)

Industry and year	January	February	March	April	May	June	July	August	September	October	November	December	Annual average
Professional and Business Services													
2010	29.0	29.2	29.6	29.6	31.1	31.1	29.9	30.1	29.2	29.0	29.8	30.1	29.8
2011	28.5	29.8	29.9	31.0	30.9	31.0	30.6	30.6	30.3	30.3	31.0	31.4	30.4
2012	30.4	30.7	31.4	31.3	31.1	31.4	31.0	31.0	31.0	32.1	33.6	33.7	31.6
2013	33.1	33.9	34.6	34.6	35.2	35.2	35.0	35.3	35.4	36.1	37.1	37.4	35.2
2014	36.2	36.7	37.1	37.2	38.0	38.2	37.9	38.4	38.5	39.7	40.2	41.0	38.3
2015	39.7	40.5	40.9	41.4	42.3	42.9	41.4	41.4	41.3	42.5	43.0	43.6	41.7
2016	43.8	44.8	45.4	45.6	45.2	45.1	45.7	45.2	45.1	45.6	46.5	46.9	45.4
2017	46.0	46.6	47.4	47.3	47.1	47.4	47.8	48.0	46.7	47.2	47.5	47.8	47.2
2018	47.5	47.7	48.0	47.7	47.8	48.4	47.2	47.7	47.1	46.4	46.5	46.2	47.4
Education and Health Services													
2010	43.3	43.7	44.0	44.1	43.8	43.5	43.3	43.5	43.5	43.8	44.0	44.2	43.7
2011	44.1	44.5	44.7	44.8	44.7	44.3	44.1	44.3	44.4	44.7	44.9	45.3	44.6
2012	44.7	45.1	45.4	45.2	45.2	44.8	44.3	44.7	45.1	45.4	45.9	45.9	45.1
2013	45.6	46.1	46.1	46.2	46.2	45.6	45.4	45.8	46.0	46.6	47.0	47.2	46.2
2014	47.1	47.7	48.0	48.0	48.1	47.8	47.4	48.0	48.0	48.7	49.0	49.5	48.1
2015	49.3	49.6	49.8	49.8	49.9	49.7	49.5	49.9	49.9	50.7	51.0	51.3	50.0
2016	50.6	51.0	51.1	50.9	51.2	50.7	50.9	51.5	51.7	52.3	52.9	53.2	51.5
2017	52.6	53.0	52.9	53.1	53.0	52.6	52.0	52.7	52.0	53.5	53.6	54.0	52.9
2018	53.5	54.2	54.4	54.5	54.3	53.9	54.0	54.6	54.7	54.7	55.3	55.9	54.5
Leisure and Hospitality													
2010	34.3	35.1	36.1	35.7	34.8	34.0	33.0	32.8	32.4	32.9	33.8	34.0	34.1
2011	34.4	35.2	35.9	35.8	34.7	33.8	33.1	32.9	32.7	33.2	34.4	35.0	34.3
2012	35.4	36.3	37.5	37.1	36.2	35.6	34.7	34.6	33.8	34.3	35.6	36.0	35.6
2013	36.3	37.8	38.6	38.1	37.6	36.9	36.3	36.1	35.5	36.1	38.0	38.5	37.2
2014	38.8	39.9	41.0	40.4	39.0	38.6	38.5	38.4	37.8	39.2	40.6	41.4	39.5
2015	42.3	43.1	44.4	44.0	42.7	41.9	41.1	41.1	40.5	41.8	42.7	43.3	42.4
2016	43.1	44.0	44.6	44.0	43.1	42.3	41.6	41.8	41.0	42.4	43.4	43.8	42.9
2017	45.1	45.7	46.9	46.2	45.3	44.0	43.3	43.2	40.6	43.3	44.4	44.9	44.4
2018	45.1	46.4	47.1	46.5	45.6	44.3	44.0	43.5	42.3	42.8	43.5	43.8	44.6
Other Services													
2010	11.8	11.9	12.1	12.0	11.8	11.6	11.5	11.4	11.3	11.3	11.3	11.4	11.6
2011	11.1	11.2	11.2	11.3	11.2	11.1	10.9	10.8	10.9	10.7	10.7	10.7	11.0
2012	10.5	10.6	10.7	10.8	10.7	10.7	10.5	10.5	10.6	10.5	10.6	10.8	10.6
2013	10.7	10.8	10.9	11.0	11.0	11.0	10.8	10.9	11.0	11.2	11.5	11.5	11.0
2014	11.7	11.9	12.0	12.0	11.9	11.8	11.7	11.8	11.8	12.0	12.2	12.2	11.9
2015	12.2	12.4	12.6	12.6	12.6	12.5	12.4	12.4	12.5	12.7	12.9	13.1	12.6
2016	13.1	13.2	13.3	13.2	13.2	13.1	12.9	12.9	12.9	12.9	13.0	13.0	13.1
2017	12.9	13.0	13.1	13.2	13.2	13.2	13.2	13.4	13.1	13.6	13.8	14.0	13.3
2018	13.8	14.1	14.3	14.2	14.3	14.1	14.0	14.0	14.0	14.1	14.2	14.2	14.1
Government													
2010	27.8	27.9	28.0	28.0	29.5	25.5	25.2	26.6	27.1	27.5	27.6	27.5	27.4
2011	27.4	27.6	27.7	27.7	27.2	24.3	24.0	27.2	26.9	27.3	27.5	27.3	26.8
2012	27.1	27.4	27.5	27.3	27.2	24.2	24.1	26.0	26.8	27.3	27.3	27.3	26.6
2013	27.1	27.3	27.4	27.2	27.0	24.1	24.0	25.8	26.6	27.3	27.6	27.5	26.6
2014	26.9	27.1	27.4	27.3	27.2	24.1	24.2	25.9	26.7	27.6	27.9	27.7	26.7
2015	27.6	27.7	27.9	27.8	27.7	24.6	24.6	26.3	27.0	27.7	27.8	27.8	27.0
2016	27.7	27.8	28.0	28.0	28.0	25.1	25.1	26.9	27.5	28.0	27.9	27.8	27.3
2017	27.9	28.1	28.2	27.6	28.0	25.2	25.1	26.6	27.6	28.2	28.3	28.5	27.4
2018	28.4	28.5	28.7	28.7	28.7	25.6	25.5	27.1	27.9	27.8	27.8	27.8	27.7

Employment by Industry: Dayton, OH, 2010–2018

(Numbers in thousands, not seasonally adjusted)

Industry and year	January	February	March	April	May	June	July	August	September	October	November	December	Annual average
Total Nonfarm													
2010	353.7	354.3	357.2	361.1	363.2	362.1	357.7	359.1	362.5	364.7	366.4	366.3	360.7
2011	358.0	359.4	362.3	366.7	367.8	366.3	362.3	363.2	368.0	369.4	371.3	370.5	365.4
2012	363.2	365.4	367.7	369.8	371.0	371.9	365.8	367.0	369.1	369.9	372.1	372.1	368.8
2013	360.9	363.7	365.2	367.9	371.2	370.4	366.0	367.8	369.1	370.4	374.1	373.1	368.3
2014	363.3	365.2	368.2	370.9	372.9	373.7	370.9	373.3	375.0	377.4	379.4	380.3	372.5
2015	370.3	371.9	373.5	378.1	380.7	380.5	380.4	381.4	380.9	384.7	387.0	388.1	379.8
2016	377.4	380.0	382.5	384.5	385.3	384.0	385.4	385.1	386.3	387.4	389.5	389.9	384.8
2017	380.5	382.5	383.9	388.3	389.3	388.6	389.0	389.6	389.3	391.4	393.9	393.0	388.3
2018	384.3	386.6	388.5	390.5	391.0	389.8	390.0	391.1	390.9	391.4	393.5	392.6	390.0
Total Private													
2010	290.2	290.0	292.4	296.0	296.4	297.0	296.7	297.7	298.8	299.6	301.4	301.4	296.5
2011	294.0	294.5	297.0	301.3	301.6	301.7	300.6	301.8	304.1	304.6	306.3	307.4	301.2
2012	300.7	301.3	303.4	305.3	306.3	308.0	305.9	306.3	305.8	306.0	308.0	308.2	305.4
2013	299.4	300.3	301.7	304.6	307.3	308.4	306.5	307.7	306.3	307.4	310.7	310.3	305.9
2014	302.5	302.4	305.1	308.7	310.7	312.6	312.3	313.7	312.2	314.1	315.8	317.0	310.6
2015	309.0	308.9	310.8	314.5	318.4	318.7	319.0	319.8	318.3	321.0	323.1	324.2	317.1
2016	316.0	316.7	319.2	320.5	322.8	321.6	323.8	323.4	322.5	323.5	325.3	325.8	321.8
2017	318.6	319.1	320.4	324.3	327.0	327.3	328.0	328.7	326.8	328.2	330.2	329.6	325.7
2018	323.0	323.7	325.5	327.5	329.4	329.1	329.9	330.6	328.5	329.0	330.9	330.2	328.1
Goods Producing													
2010	44.4	44.1	44.7	45.8	46.5	47.3	47.7	48.1	48.0	47.7	47.8	47.5	46.6
2011	46.4	46.4	47.2	47.7	48.5	49.0	49.4	49.6	49.6	49.6	49.7	49.6	48.6
2012	48.5	48.4	48.8	49.2	49.7	50.4	50.1	50.1	50.0	49.8	49.8	49.8	49.6
2013	48.4	48.5	48.9	48.9	49.8	50.3	50.0	49.9	49.6	49.7	49.9	49.7	49.5
2014	48.5	48.7	49.3	49.7	50.6	51.4	51.5	51.8	51.6	51.6	51.6	51.5	50.7
2015	50.5	50.6	50.7	51.5	52.2	52.5	52.8	53.1	52.9	53.3	53.0	53.2	52.2
2016	52.1	52.2	52.6	52.9	53.4	53.6	54.4	54.3	54.5	54.5	54.4	54.3	53.6
2017	53.3	53.2	53.4	53.9	54.5	55.3	55.4	55.5	55.2	55.3	55.2	55.2	54.6
2018	54.2	54.5	54.8	55.4	56.1	56.5	56.6	57.0	56.7	57.0	56.8	56.9	56.0
Service-Providing													
2010	309.3	310.2	312.5	315.3	316.7	314.8	310.0	311.0	314.5	317.0	318.6	318.8	314.1
2011	311.6	313.0	315.1	319.0	319.3	317.3	312.9	313.6	318.4	319.8	321.6	320.9	316.9
2012	314.7	317.0	318.9	320.6	321.3	321.5	315.7	316.9	319.1	320.1	322.3	322.3	319.2
2013	312.5	315.2	316.3	319.0	321.4	320.1	316.0	317.9	319.5	320.7	324.2	323.4	318.9
2014	314.8	316.5	318.9	321.2	322.3	322.3	319.4	321.5	323.4	325.8	327.8	328.8	321.9
2015	319.8	321.3	322.8	326.6	328.5	328.0	327.6	328.3	328.0	331.4	334.0	334.9	327.6
2016	325.3	327.8	329.9	331.6	331.9	330.4	331.0	330.8	331.8	332.9	335.1	335.6	331.2
2017	327.2	329.3	330.5	334.4	334.8	333.3	333.6	334.1	334.1	336.1	338.7	337.8	333.7
2018	330.1	332.1	333.7	335.1	334.9	333.3	333.4	334.1	334.2	334.4	336.7	335.7	334.0
Mining, Logging, and Construction													
2010	9.7	9.3	9.8	10.5	10.7	11.2	11.5	11.4	11.2	11.0	10.9	10.4	10.6
2011	9.5	9.5	9.8	10.4	11.1	11.5	11.8	11.8	11.7	11.4	11.4	11.0	10.9
2012	10.5	10.3	10.5	10.9	11.4	11.6	11.5	11.4	11.3	11.2	11.1	10.9	11.1
2013	10.1	10.2	10.6	10.8	11.5	11.8	11.7	11.7	11.6	11.6	11.6	11.2	11.2
2014	10.4	10.4	10.9	11.2	11.9	12.3	12.6	12.5	12.3	12.2	12.0	11.8	11.7
2015	11.1	11.0	11.2	12.0	12.4	12.6	12.8	12.8	12.8	12.9	12.7	12.6	12.2
2016	11.6	11.6	11.9	12.3	12.6	12.8	12.9	12.8	12.7	12.7	12.5	12.1	12.4
2017	11.5	11.6	11.8	12.3	12.7	13.1	13.2	13.3	13.1	13.0	12.9	12.7	12.6
2018	11.8	11.9	12.2	12.7	13.3	13.5	13.7	13.8	13.6	13.7	13.5	13.3	13.1
Manufacturing													
2010	34.7	34.8	34.9	35.3	35.8	36.1	36.2	36.7	36.8	36.7	36.9	37.1	36.0
2011	36.9	36.9	37.4	37.3	37.4	37.5	37.6	37.8	37.9	38.2	38.3	38.6	37.7
2012	38.0	38.1	38.3	38.3	38.3	38.8	38.6	38.7	38.7	38.6	38.7	38.9	38.5
2013	38.3	38.3	38.3	38.1	38.3	38.5	38.3	38.2	38.0	38.1	38.3	38.5	38.3
2014	38.1	38.3	38.4	38.5	38.7	39.1	38.9	39.3	39.3	39.4	39.6	39.7	38.9
2015	39.4	39.6	39.5	39.5	39.8	39.9	40.0	40.3	40.1	40.4	40.3	40.6	40.0
2016	40.5	40.6	40.7	40.6	40.8	40.8	41.5	41.5	41.8	41.8	41.9	42.2	41.2
2017	41.8	41.6	41.6	41.6	41.8	42.2	42.2	42.2	42.1	42.3	42.3	42.5	42.0
2018	42.4	42.6	42.6	42.7	42.8	43.0	42.9	43.2	43.1	43.3	43.3	43.6	43.0

Employment by Industry: Dayton, OH, 2010–2018—*Continued*

(Numbers in thousands, not seasonally adjusted)

Industry and year	January	February	March	April	May	June	July	August	September	October	November	December	Annual average
Trade, Transportation, and Utilities													
2010	59.4	58.7	59.2	59.6	59.9	60.2	59.7	59.8	59.4	60.2	61.9	62.9	60.1
2011	60.1	59.3	59.7	60.5	60.9	61.1	60.9	61.1	61.1	62.1	63.7	64.7	61.3
2012	61.9	61.3	62.0	62.2	62.7	62.6	62.3	62.5	62.4	63.1	64.8	65.3	62.8
2013	62.2	61.8	62.0	62.5	63.0	63.1	63.0	63.1	62.9	63.6	65.8	66.5	63.3
2014	63.5	62.9	63.3	63.8	64.0	64.2	64.0	64.0	63.9	64.7	66.4	67.3	64.3
2015	64.7	64.4	64.5	64.9	65.7	65.7	65.5	65.5	65.0	65.6	67.2	68.1	65.6
2016	64.9	64.4	64.7	64.7	65.1	65.0	65.1	65.2	64.6	65.3	66.7	67.5	65.3
2017	64.9	64.4	64.3	64.7	65.2	65.3	65.7	65.7	65.0	65.9	67.8	68.2	65.6
2018	65.9	65.5	65.6	65.9	66.3	66.3	66.6	66.1	65.5	66.2	67.6	68.2	66.3
Wholesale Trade													
2010	11.7	11.7	11.7	11.7	11.7	11.8	11.8	11.8	11.7	11.7	11.7	11.8	11.7
2011	12.0	11.9	12.0	12.1	12.2	12.3	12.4	12.4	12.4	12.6	12.5	12.6	12.3
2012	12.7	12.8	12.9	12.6	12.7	12.7	12.9	12.9	12.8	12.9	12.8	12.9	12.8
2013	12.7	12.6	12.6	12.6	12.6	12.7	12.6	12.5	12.5	12.5	12.6	12.6	12.6
2014	12.6	12.6	12.6	12.7	12.8	12.9	12.8	12.7	12.8	12.8	12.8	12.9	12.8
2015	13.1	13.1	13.1	13.2	13.2	13.2	13.3	13.2	13.0	13.0	13.0	13.0	13.1
2016	12.9	12.9	12.9	12.8	12.9	12.9	12.9	12.9	12.8	12.8	12.8	12.9	12.9
2017	12.8	12.9	12.9	13.2	13.3	13.4	13.5	13.5	13.4	13.6	13.7	13.8	13.3
2018	13.8	13.9	14.0	14.0	14.1	14.2	14.2	14.1	14.1	14.1	14.2	14.3	14.1
Retail Trade													
2010	37.5	36.8	37.2	37.6	37.9	37.9	37.5	37.5	37.2	37.8	39.2	39.8	37.8
2011	37.4	36.8	37.1	37.7	37.9	38.0	37.7	37.8	37.7	38.6	40.2	40.8	38.1
2012	38.3	37.6	38.2	38.5	38.8	38.6	38.2	38.3	38.2	38.7	40.3	40.5	38.7
2013	38.2	37.8	38.1	38.6	39.0	38.9	38.8	38.9	38.6	39.2	40.9	41.3	39.0
2014	38.5	38.1	38.5	38.9	38.9	39.0	38.7	38.8	38.7	39.5	41.0	41.4	39.2
2015	38.7	38.5	38.6	38.9	39.4	39.5	39.2	39.3	39.0	39.5	40.9	41.5	39.4
2016	39.2	39.0	39.2	39.5	39.8	39.6	39.6	39.7	39.2	39.8	40.9	41.4	39.7
2017	39.5	38.9	38.9	39.1	39.4	39.4	39.6	39.6	39.1	39.8	41.4	41.4	39.7
2018	39.6	39.1	39.1	39.3	39.7	39.5	39.7	39.5	38.9	39.5	40.4	40.5	39.6
Transportation and Utilities													
2010	10.2	10.2	10.3	10.3	10.3	10.5	10.4	10.5	10.5	10.7	11.0	11.3	10.5
2011	10.7	10.6	10.6	10.7	10.8	10.8	10.8	10.9	11.0	10.9	11.0	11.3	10.8
2012	10.9	10.9	10.9	11.1	11.2	11.3	11.2	11.3	11.4	11.5	11.7	11.9	11.3
2013	11.3	11.4	11.3	11.3	11.4	11.5	11.6	11.7	11.8	11.9	12.3	12.6	11.7
2014	12.4	12.2	12.2	12.2	12.3	12.3	12.5	12.5	12.4	12.4	12.6	13.0	12.4
2015	12.9	12.8	12.8	12.8	13.1	13.0	13.0	13.0	13.0	13.1	13.3	13.6	13.0
2016	12.8	12.5	12.6	12.4	12.4	12.5	12.6	12.6	12.6	12.7	13.0	13.2	12.7
2017	12.6	12.6	12.5	12.4	12.5	12.5	12.6	12.6	12.5	12.5	12.7	13.0	12.6
2018	12.5	12.5	12.5	12.6	12.5	12.6	12.7	12.5	12.5	12.6	13.0	13.4	12.7
Information													
2010	10.7	10.7	10.7	10.5	10.4	10.4	10.3	10.2	10.1	10.0	9.9	9.9	10.3
2011	9.8	9.8	9.8	9.8	9.7	9.8	9.8	9.7	9.7	9.5	9.4	9.3	9.7
2012	9.2	9.1	9.0	9.0	8.9	8.9	9.0	8.8	8.8	8.7	8.7	8.7	8.9
2013	8.7	8.7	8.7	8.7	8.7	8.8	8.8	8.7	8.6	8.5	8.5	8.5	8.7
2014	8.4	8.4	8.4	8.5	8.5	8.6	8.6	8.5	8.4	8.4	8.4	8.5	8.5
2015	8.4	8.4	8.4	8.5	8.5	8.6	8.6	8.6	8.5	8.5	8.5	8.5	8.5
2016	8.4	8.5	8.5	8.5	8.5	8.5	8.5	8.4	8.3	8.4	8.4	8.4	8.4
2017	8.4	8.3	8.3	8.4	8.4	8.4	8.5	8.4	8.3	8.3	8.3	8.3	8.4
2018	8.3	8.3	8.3	8.3	8.2	8.3	8.2	8.1	8.0	7.9	7.9	8.0	8.2
Financial Activities													
2010	16.3	16.3	16.3	16.5	16.6	16.5	16.6	16.5	16.4	16.6	16.6	16.6	16.5
2011	16.3	16.3	16.3	16.4	16.4	16.5	16.5	16.5	16.4	16.4	16.5	16.6	16.4
2012	16.4	16.4	16.5	16.7	16.7	16.8	17.0	17.0	17.0	17.0	17.1	17.1	16.8
2013	16.8	16.9	16.8	16.9	17.1	17.1	17.1	17.1	17.0	17.0	17.1	17.1	17.0
2014	16.9	17.0	17.1	17.1	17.3	17.4	17.4	17.7	17.5	17.6	17.6	17.6	17.4
2015	17.3	17.2	17.3	17.3	17.5	17.6	17.6	17.7	17.5	17.8	17.8	17.8	17.5
2016	17.5	17.6	17.6	17.7	17.7	17.8	17.9	17.8	17.8	17.9	18.0	18.2	17.8
2017	17.8	17.9	17.8	18.0	18.0	18.2	18.2	18.2	18.2	18.2	18.1	18.2	18.1
2018	18.2	18.3	18.2	18.3	18.3	18.4	18.2	18.1	17.9	17.9	17.9	18.0	18.1

Employment by Industry: Dayton, OH, 2010–2018—*Continued*

(Numbers in thousands, not seasonally adjusted)

Industry and year	January	February	March	April	May	June	July	August	September	October	November	December	Annual average
Professional and Business Services													
2010	43.6	43.9	44.1	45.4	45.4	45.9	45.8	46.5	46.1	46.2	46.3	46.1	45.4
2011	45.6	45.7	46.2	46.9	46.6	46.9	47.0	47.5	47.4	47.3	47.3	47.7	46.8
2012	46.9	47.1	47.1	47.4	47.4	47.7	47.8	47.8	47.3	47.7	47.4	47.4	47.4
2013	46.3	46.3	46.1	47.2	47.3	47.6	47.5	48.0	47.8	48.1	48.5	48.0	47.4
2014	47.2	47.0	47.4	48.5	48.6	49.2	49.6	49.8	49.2	49.9	50.0	49.9	48.9
2015	48.3	48.1	48.7	49.8	50.6	50.9	51.3	51.1	50.8	51.4	51.5	51.2	50.3
2016	50.1	50.2	51.0	50.8	51.0	50.7	51.2	50.9	50.6	50.9	51.1	50.8	50.8
2017	49.1	49.5	49.9	51.0	51.4	51.5	51.6	51.8	51.3	52.3	52.7	51.7	51.2
2018	51.1	51.2	51.8	52.6	52.5	53.0	52.9	53.0	52.7	52.6	53.5	52.3	52.4
Education and Health Services													
2010	67.9	68.5	68.7	68.2	67.0	65.5	65.3	65.4	68.3	69.4	69.6	69.6	67.8
2011	68.4	69.3	69.5	69.9	68.6	66.7	65.8	66.1	69.6	70.2	70.2	70.4	68.7
2012	69.2	70.2	70.1	69.9	68.9	68.6	67.3	67.7	69.1	69.5	69.9	69.6	69.2
2013	68.0	68.9	69.1	69.3	69.0	68.3	67.8	68.4	69.1	70.0	70.5	70.0	69.0
2014	68.6	69.2	69.6	69.9	69.6	68.7	68.4	69.1	70.3	70.9	71.1	71.5	69.7
2015	70.2	70.6	70.9	70.9	71.0	69.9	69.9	70.7	71.6	72.3	73.2	73.2	71.2
2016	71.9	72.6	73.0	72.8	73.0	71.6	72.0	72.4	73.4	73.5	73.8	73.6	72.8
2017	73.0	73.4	73.6	73.5	74.0	72.6	72.8	73.2	74.4	74.5	74.8	74.8	73.7
2018	74.1	74.4	74.5	74.1	74.1	72.3	72.8	73.5	74.3	75.1	75.6	74.9	74.1
Leisure and Hospitality													
2010	33.4	33.3	34.0	35.3	35.9	36.5	36.6	36.6	36.0	35.1	34.9	34.6	35.2
2011	33.3	33.5	34.1	35.7	36.4	37.1	36.7	36.9	36.0	35.4	35.3	35.0	35.5
2012	34.4	34.6	35.6	36.5	37.3	38.1	37.8	37.8	36.8	35.8	35.8	35.8	36.4
2013	34.7	34.7	35.5	36.3	37.5	38.3	37.7	37.9	36.9	36.2	36.2	36.3	36.5
2014	35.5	35.3	36.0	37.2	38.2	39.1	38.9	38.9	37.6	37.3	37.1	37.1	37.4
2015	36.0	36.0	36.7	37.9	38.9	39.5	39.1	39.0	38.0	38.1	38.0	38.2	38.0
2016	37.2	37.3	37.8	39.0	39.9	40.2	40.4	40.1	39.1	38.8	38.7	38.8	38.9
2017	37.9	38.2	38.8	40.4	41.1	41.5	41.4	41.5	40.3	39.7	39.4	39.3	40.0
2018	37.6	37.8	38.6	39.1	40.0	40.3	40.6	40.8	39.6	38.6	37.9	38.1	39.1
Other Services													
2010	14.5	14.5	14.7	14.7	14.7	14.7	14.7	14.6	14.5	14.4	14.4	14.2	14.6
2011	14.1	14.2	14.2	14.4	14.5	14.6	14.5	14.4	14.3	14.1	14.2	14.1	14.3
2012	14.2	14.2	14.3	14.5	14.7	14.9	14.6	14.6	14.4	14.4	14.5	14.5	14.5
2013	14.3	14.5	14.6	14.8	14.9	14.9	14.6	14.6	14.4	14.3	14.2	14.2	14.5
2014	13.9	13.9	14.0	14.0	13.9	14.0	13.9	13.9	13.7	13.7	13.6	13.6	13.8
2015	13.6	13.6	13.6	13.7	14.0	14.0	14.2	14.1	14.0	14.0	13.9	14.0	13.9
2016	13.9	13.9	14.0	14.1	14.2	14.2	14.3	14.3	14.2	14.2	14.2	14.2	14.1
2017	14.2	14.2	14.3	14.4	14.4	14.5	14.4	14.4	14.1	14.0	13.9	13.9	14.2
2018	13.6	13.7	13.7	13.8	13.9	14.0	14.0	14.0	13.8	13.7	13.7	13.8	13.8
Government													
2010	63.5	64.3	64.8	65.1	66.8	65.1	61.0	61.4	63.7	65.1	65.0	64.9	64.2
2011	64.0	64.9	65.3	65.4	66.2	64.6	61.7	61.4	63.9	64.8	65.0	63.1	64.2
2012	62.5	64.1	64.3	64.4	64.7	63.9	59.9	60.7	63.3	63.9	64.1	63.9	63.3
2013	61.5	63.4	63.5	63.3	63.9	62.0	59.5	60.1	62.8	63.0	63.4	62.8	62.4
2014	60.8	62.8	63.1	62.2	62.2	61.1	58.6	59.6	62.8	63.3	63.6	63.3	62.0
2015	61.3	63.0	62.7	63.6	62.3	61.8	61.4	61.6	62.6	63.7	63.9	63.9	62.7
2016	61.4	63.3	63.3	64.0	62.5	62.4	61.6	61.7	63.8	63.9	64.2	64.1	63.0
2017	61.9	63.4	63.5	64.0	62.3	61.3	61.0	60.9	62.5	63.2	63.7	63.4	62.6
2018	61.3	62.9	63.0	63.0	61.6	60.7	60.1	60.5	62.4	62.4	62.6	62.4	61.9

Employment by Industry: Charleston-North Charleston, SC, 2010–2018

(Numbers in thousands, not seasonally adjusted)

Industry and year	January	February	March	April	May	June	July	August	September	October	November	December	Annual average
Total Nonfarm													
2010	278.5	279.8	283.4	286.6	290.5	290.7	288.2	288.1	287.7	290.7	292.3	292.3	287.4
2011	287.9	289.5	292.2	296.5	298.7	298.5	296.7	296.3	296.9	298.0	299.3	299.5	295.8
2012	295.6	298.9	302.1	306.2	307.7	308.1	305.2	306.7	306.4	307.6	311.3	309.9	305.5
2013	303.2	305.6	308.1	311.3	313.2	314.5	313.4	314.1	314.0	315.6	317.2	317.5	312.3
2014	311.1	313.9	316.9	322.5	325.4	325.6	322.8	324.3	324.3	326.5	328.6	328.7	322.6
2015	322.9	325.9	329.3	332.5	336.2	336.0	335.8	337.1	335.5	339.7	342.5	342.0	334.6
2016	336.1	338.8	341.3	345.3	347.2	348.2	347.6	347.1	347.3	345.6	350.0	349.7	345.4
2017	345.0	348.0	350.7	353.2	356.0	356.9	356.7	355.8	353.5	357.1	359.8	359.9	354.4
2018	357.2	361.2	362.4	363.1	366.2	370.0	368.4	367.6	362.0	370.2	372.2	371.9	366.0
Total Private													
2010	218.2	219.1	222.3	225.0	227.3	229.8	228.3	228.3	226.8	229.0	230.3	230.5	226.2
2011	226.8	228.1	230.7	234.5	236.7	237.4	236.8	237.0	235.6	236.7	237.8	237.9	234.7
2012	234.5	237.3	240.1	243.8	245.3	246.2	244.4	245.4	243.5	244.5	246.0	246.4	243.1
2013	240.9	242.8	245.1	247.8	250.1	251.9	252.0	252.8	251.0	253.2	254.4	254.9	249.7
2014	249.5	251.5	254.4	259.0	261.9	263.6	262.3	262.6	261.0	262.7	264.4	264.7	259.8
2015	260.1	262.1	265.2	268.3	272.0	273.1	273.2	274.2	271.2	274.8	277.1	276.6	270.7
2016	271.3	273.8	275.8	279.7	281.7	283.3	283.2	283.8	282.1	280.8	285.1	284.5	280.4
2017	280.7	283.5	285.8	288.2	291.1	292.7	292.7	292.1	288.1	291.3	293.6	293.7	289.5
2018	291.8	295.5	296.5	296.7	300.1	304.4	303.4	302.9	295.9	303.9	305.6	305.3	300.2
Goods Producing													
2010	34.5	34.5	34.9	34.8	35.0	35.2	35.1	35.1	35.0	34.7	34.9	35.2	34.9
2011	35.0	35.1	35.4	35.7	36.2	36.6	36.6	36.6	36.6	36.5	36.7	36.7	36.1
2012	36.4	36.5	36.9	37.1	37.3	37.5	37.5	37.5	37.4	37.4	37.6	37.8	37.2
2013	37.7	38.0	38.1	38.3	38.8	39.1	39.5	39.5	39.6	39.5	39.7	40.1	39.0
2014	39.8	39.9	40.1	40.4	40.9	41.5	41.4	41.4	41.3	41.7	41.9	42.1	41.0
2015	42.1	42.7	42.5	42.4	42.9	43.5	43.7	43.7	43.7	43.9	44.2	44.1	43.3
2016	44.1	44.6	44.6	44.7	44.8	45.3	45.4	45.4	45.5	45.2	45.4	45.7	45.1
2017	45.6	46.2	46.3	46.3	46.6	46.9	47.2	47.0	46.9	47.2	47.3	47.6	46.8
2018	47.9	48.6	48.4	48.5	49.0	49.5	49.7	49.4	49.3	49.7	49.9	50.0	49.2
Service-Providing													
2010	244.0	245.3	248.5	251.8	255.5	255.5	253.1	253.0	252.7	256.0	257.4	257.1	252.5
2011	252.9	254.4	256.8	260.8	262.5	261.9	260.1	259.7	260.3	261.5	262.6	262.8	259.7
2012	259.2	262.4	265.2	269.1	270.4	270.6	267.7	269.2	269.0	270.2	273.7	272.1	268.2
2013	265.5	267.6	270.0	273.0	274.4	275.4	273.9	274.6	274.4	276.1	277.5	277.4	273.3
2014	271.3	274.0	276.8	282.1	284.5	284.1	281.4	282.9	283.0	284.8	286.7	286.6	281.5
2015	280.8	283.2	286.8	290.1	293.3	292.5	292.1	293.4	291.8	295.8	298.3	297.9	291.3
2016	292.0	294.2	296.7	300.6	302.4	302.9	302.2	301.7	301.8	300.4	304.6	304.0	300.3
2017	299.4	301.8	304.4	306.9	309.4	310.0	309.5	308.8	306.6	309.9	312.5	312.3	307.6
2018	309.3	312.6	314.0	314.6	317.2	320.5	318.7	318.2	312.7	320.5	322.3	321.9	316.9
Mining, Logging, and Construction													
2010	13.9	13.9	14.2	14.3	14.4	14.5	14.4	14.3	14.2	14.0	14.0	14.0	14.2
2011	13.8	13.8	13.9	13.9	14.2	14.3	14.1	13.9	13.8	13.6	13.6	13.4	13.9
2012	13.0	13.1	13.3	13.5	13.7	13.9	14.0	14.0	13.9	13.7	13.8	13.9	13.7
2013	14.1	14.0	14.2	14.5	14.9	15.2	15.4	15.5	15.5	15.4	15.6	15.8	15.0
2014	15.5	15.6	15.7	15.9	16.3	16.7	16.5	16.5	16.4	16.7	16.8	16.9	16.3
2015	16.7	17.0	17.2	17.2	17.5	17.9	17.9	17.9	17.8	18.1	18.4	18.4	17.7
2016	18.4	18.5	18.7	18.8	19.0	19.3	19.4	19.4	19.4	19.3	19.5	19.7	19.1
2017	19.6	19.8	20.0	20.0	20.2	20.4	20.6	20.4	20.2	20.5	20.6	20.8	20.3
2018	21.3	21.5	21.6	21.8	22.0	22.3	22.3	22.1	21.9	22.2	22.3	22.4	22.0
Manufacturing													
2010	20.6	20.6	20.7	20.5	20.6	20.7	20.7	20.8	20.8	20.7	20.9	21.2	20.7
2011	21.2	21.3	21.5	21.8	22.0	22.3	22.5	22.7	22.8	22.9	23.1	23.3	22.3
2012	23.4	23.4	23.6	23.6	23.6	23.6	23.5	23.5	23.5	23.7	23.8	23.9	23.6
2013	23.6	24.0	23.9	23.8	23.9	23.9	24.1	24.0	24.1	24.1	24.1	24.3	24.0
2014	24.3	24.3	24.4	24.5	24.6	24.8	24.9	24.9	24.9	25.0	25.1	25.2	24.7
2015	25.4	25.7	25.3	25.2	25.4	25.6	25.8	25.8	25.9	25.8	25.8	25.7	25.6
2016	25.7	26.1	25.9	25.9	25.8	26.0	26.0	26.0	26.1	25.9	25.9	26.0	25.9
2017	26.0	26.4	26.3	26.3	26.4	26.5	26.6	26.6	26.7	26.7	26.7	26.8	26.5
2018	26.6	27.1	26.8	26.7	27.0	27.2	27.4	27.3	27.4	27.5	27.6	27.6	27.2

Employment by Industry: Charleston-North Charleston, SC, 2010–2018—*Continued*

(Numbers in thousands, not seasonally adjusted)

Industry and year	January	February	March	April	May	June	July	August	September	October	November	December	Annual average
Trade, Transportation, and Utilities													
2010	51.6	51.6	52.4	52.5	53.1	53.8	53.8	53.7	53.4	54.3	55.3	55.9	53.5
2011	54.0	53.9	54.1	54.5	54.8	55.0	55.4	55.3	55.0	55.7	56.3	56.7	55.1
2012	55.3	55.5	56.0	56.5	56.9	57.1	57.1	57.1	56.7	57.4	58.9	59.3	57.0
2013	56.6	56.6	56.9	57.6	58.0	58.5	58.7	58.8	58.6	59.6	60.2	61.0	58.4
2014	58.6	58.5	58.6	59.4	59.9	60.8	60.2	60.2	59.8	60.2	61.5	61.9	60.0
2015	59.8	59.5	60.2	61.0	61.6	62.1	62.2	62.4	61.8	62.8	63.8	64.3	61.8
2016	62.0	62.2	62.4	63.3	63.7	63.9	63.8	63.8	63.6	63.4	65.2	65.8	63.6
2017	63.8	63.6	63.8	64.0	64.6	64.9	65.1	64.8	63.7	64.7	66.4	67.1	64.7
2018	65.2	65.4	65.6	65.9	67.1	68.0	67.8	67.7	66.8	68.7	70.4	70.4	67.4
Wholesale Trade													
2010	8.1	8.0	8.1	8.2	8.3	8.3	8.3	8.4	8.2	8.1	8.1	8.1	8.2
2011	8.0	8.0	8.0	8.1	8.1	8.0	8.1	8.0	7.9	7.9	7.9	7.9	8.0
2012	7.8	7.9	7.9	8.0	8.0	8.0	7.9	7.9	7.8	7.9	7.9	7.9	7.9
2013	7.7	7.7	7.8	7.9	7.9	8.0	8.0	8.0	8.0	8.0	7.9	8.0	7.9
2014	7.8	7.9	7.9	7.9	7.9	8.1	8.1	8.2	8.2	8.2	8.2	8.2	8.1
2015	8.2	8.3	8.3	8.4	8.5	8.4	8.5	8.5	8.5	8.8	8.8	8.8	8.5
2016	8.8	8.9	8.9	9.0	9.0	9.1	9.1	9.1	9.2	9.2	9.3	9.3	9.1
2017	9.3	9.4	9.4	9.4	9.5	9.6	9.6	9.6	9.5	9.5	9.6	9.6	9.5
2018	9.4	9.5	9.5	9.5	9.6	9.6	9.6	9.6	9.6	9.6	9.7	9.7	9.6
Retail Trade													
2010	33.4	33.3	33.7	33.7	34.2	34.6	34.5	34.3	33.9	34.6	35.6	35.9	34.3
2011	34.3	34.1	34.4	34.9	35.2	35.3	35.6	35.3	35.2	35.8	36.4	36.6	35.3
2012	34.9	34.9	35.3	35.5	35.8	36.0	36.1	36.1	35.8	36.2	37.6	37.7	36.0
2013	35.6	35.5	35.6	36.1	36.4	36.8	37.0	37.2	37.0	37.7	38.7	39.1	36.9
2014	37.0	36.9	37.3	37.7	38.0	38.5	38.4	38.2	37.9	38.1	39.4	39.8	38.1
2015	37.7	37.5	37.9	38.4	38.8	39.6	39.8	40.0	39.6	40.1	41.3	41.4	39.3
2016	39.5	39.6	39.7	40.3	40.7	40.7	40.7	40.6	40.3	40.0	41.5	41.8	40.5
2017	40.2	39.9	40.0	40.2	40.6	40.7	40.6	40.4	39.4	40.2	41.7	41.8	40.5
2018	40.7	40.8	40.9	41.2	42.3	43.1	42.8	42.6	41.8	43.5	45.0	44.9	42.5
Transportation and Utilities													
2010	10.1	10.3	10.6	10.6	10.6	10.9	11.0	11.0	11.3	11.6	11.6	11.9	11.0
2011	11.7	11.8	11.7	11.5	11.5	11.7	11.7	12.0	11.9	12.0	12.0	12.2	11.8
2012	12.6	12.7	12.8	13.0	13.1	13.1	13.1	13.1	13.1	13.3	13.4	13.7	13.1
2013	13.3	13.4	13.5	13.6	13.7	13.7	13.7	13.6	13.6	13.9	13.6	13.9	13.6
2014	13.8	13.7	13.4	13.8	14.0	14.2	13.7	13.8	13.7	13.9	13.9	13.9	13.8
2015	13.9	13.7	14.0	14.2	14.3	14.1	13.9	13.9	13.7	13.9	13.7	14.1	14.0
2016	13.7	13.7	13.8	14.0	14.0	14.1	14.0	14.1	14.1	14.2	14.4	14.7	14.1
2017	14.3	14.3	14.4	14.4	14.5	14.6	14.9	14.8	14.8	15.0	15.1	15.7	14.7
2018	15.1	15.1	15.2	15.2	15.2	15.3	15.4	15.5	15.4	15.6	15.7	15.8	15.4
Information													
2010	5.3	5.3	5.3	5.0	4.9	5.0	4.9	5.0	4.9	4.9	4.9	5.0	5.0
2011	5.0	4.9	4.9	5.0	5.0	5.0	5.0	5.0	4.9	4.8	4.8	4.8	4.9
2012	4.8	4.9	4.8	4.8	4.8	4.9	5.0	5.0	4.9	5.0	5.1	5.2	4.9
2013	5.0	5.0	5.0	5.1	5.0	5.1	5.1	5.0	5.0	5.0	5.0	5.1	5.0
2014	5.0	5.0	5.1	5.2	5.2	5.3	5.3	5.2	5.2	5.2	5.4	5.4	5.2
2015	5.3	5.3	5.3	5.3	5.3	5.3	5.4	5.4	5.4	5.4	6.2	5.6	5.4
2016	5.5	5.5	5.8	6.3	5.6	5.6	5.6	5.6	5.5	5.6	5.7	5.8	5.7
2017	5.7	5.7	5.8	5.8	5.9	6.3	6.0	6.0	6.2	6.1	6.1	6.5	6.0
2018	6.1	6.2	6.3	6.3	6.3	6.4	6.4	6.4	6.3	6.4	6.4	6.5	6.3
Financial Activities													
2010	11.2	11.1	11.2	11.3	11.4	11.5	11.6	11.6	11.4	11.7	11.7	11.7	11.5
2011	11.7	11.6	11.7	11.7	11.8	11.8	11.8	11.9	12.0	12.3	12.5	12.5	11.9
2012	12.4	12.6	12.5	12.4	12.4	12.6	12.4	12.6	12.5	12.6	12.7	12.9	12.6
2013	12.5	12.7	12.7	12.7	12.9	12.8	12.9	13.1	13.0	13.2	13.3	13.3	12.9
2014	12.9	13.2	13.1	13.1	13.3	13.3	13.3	13.4	13.5	13.7	13.7	13.9	13.4
2015	14.0	14.0	14.1	14.0	14.2	14.2	14.0	14.2	14.0	14.3	14.4	14.5	14.2
2016	14.3	14.4	14.1	14.4	14.5	14.5	14.5	14.6	14.5	14.7	14.8	14.7	14.5
2017	14.7	14.7	14.9	14.9	15.0	14.9	15.1	15.1	15.0	15.3	15.3	15.3	15.0
2018	15.4	15.5	15.8	15.7	15.8	16.0	16.0	16.0	15.9	16.0	16.1	16.1	15.9

Employment by Industry: Charleston-North Charleston, SC, 2010–2018—*Continued*

(Numbers in thousands, not seasonally adjusted)

Industry and year	January	February	March	April	May	June	July	August	September	October	November	December	Annual average
Professional and Business Services													
2010	39.8	40.2	40.4	41.7	41.8	42.4	41.8	42.2	41.9	42.9	43.1	42.9	41.8
2011	42.9	43.4	43.9	44.7	44.8	44.3	44.1	44.6	44.2	44.9	44.9	44.8	44.3
2012	44.6	45.6	46.1	46.9	46.9	46.6	45.3	45.9	45.9	45.9	45.8	45.9	46.0
2013	45.3	46.0	46.5	46.4	46.5	46.4	46.1	46.4	46.6	47.4	47.6	47.5	46.6
2014	46.2	47.6	48.4	48.8	49.0	48.5	48.3	48.5	48.9	49.2	49.4	49.4	48.5
2015	48.1	49.0	49.5	50.2	50.6	50.7	50.2	50.8	50.6	51.8	51.9	52.0	50.5
2016	50.8	51.6	51.9	51.9	52.2	52.2	52.7	53.2	53.0	53.0	54.2	53.3	52.5
2017	53.2	54.2	54.6	55.3	55.5	55.5	55.4	55.5	55.6	56.2	56.7	56.2	55.3
2018	56.3	57.4	57.6	57.2	57.9	58.4	58.6	58.7	57.2	58.8	58.2	57.3	57.8
Education and Health Services													
2010	33.0	33.1	33.5	33.4	33.4	33.4	33.3	33.5	33.9	34.4	34.7	34.9	33.7
2011	34.5	35.1	35.2	35.1	35.0	34.7	34.4	34.5	34.8	34.6	34.7	34.6	34.8
2012	34.1	34.6	34.7	34.6	34.7	34.3	34.2	34.4	34.7	35.2	35.3	35.2	34.7
2013	34.8	35.2	35.2	35.0	35.1	34.9	35.0	35.3	35.1	35.7	35.9	35.8	35.3
2014	35.8	36.0	36.2	36.5	36.6	36.6	36.4	36.7	36.7	37.3	37.4	37.4	36.6
2015	37.1	37.4	37.5	37.6	37.9	37.4	37.7	38.1	38.1	38.6	38.8	38.5	37.9
2016	38.0	38.4	38.3	38.4	38.6	38.4	38.4	38.8	39.2	39.2	39.3	39.4	38.7
2017	39.3	39.9	39.8	39.8	39.7	39.5	39.7	40.0	39.9	40.5	40.8	40.8	40.0
2018	40.8	41.4	41.3	41.0	41.6	42.3	41.8	42.8	42.1	42.6	42.9	42.5	41.9
Leisure and Hospitality													
2010	32.3	32.8	34.0	35.7	37.1	37.7	37.1	36.7	35.9	35.7	35.3	34.6	35.4
2011	33.4	33.7	35.1	37.2	38.3	38.9	38.2	37.9	36.8	36.6	36.4	36.2	36.6
2012	35.2	35.7	37.0	39.0	39.6	40.3	39.9	40.0	38.7	38.3	37.8	37.3	38.2
2013	36.3	36.6	37.7	39.7	40.8	41.8	41.4	41.5	40.0	39.8	39.7	39.1	39.5
2014	38.2	38.3	39.8	42.3	43.5	43.9	43.6	43.5	42.0	41.8	41.5	41.0	41.6
2015	40.2	40.7	42.5	44.1	45.6	45.9	46.0	45.7	43.9	44.3	44.0	43.7	43.9
2016	43.1	43.5	45.1	46.9	48.4	49.4	48.8	48.5	47.0	46.0	46.6	46.0	46.6
2017	44.8	45.5	46.8	48.3	49.9	50.6	50.2	49.7	46.9	47.3	47.0	46.2	47.8
2018	46.0	46.7	47.2	47.7	47.9	49.2	48.5	47.4	43.9	47.4	47.4	48.2	47.3
Other Services													
2010	10.5	10.5	10.6	10.6	10.6	10.8	10.7	10.5	10.4	10.4	10.4	10.3	10.5
2011	10.3	10.4	10.4	10.6	10.8	11.1	11.3	11.2	11.3	11.3	11.5	11.6	11.0
2012	11.7	11.9	12.1	12.5	12.7	12.9	13.0	12.9	12.7	12.7	12.8	12.8	12.6
2013	12.7	12.7	13.0	13.0	13.0	13.3	13.3	13.2	13.1	13.0	13.0	13.0	13.0
2014	13.0	13.0	13.1	13.3	13.5	13.7	13.8	13.7	13.6	13.6	13.6	13.6	13.5
2015	13.5	13.5	13.6	13.7	13.9	14.0	14.0	13.9	13.7	13.7	13.8	13.9	13.8
2016	13.5	13.6	13.6	13.8	13.9	14.0	14.0	13.9	13.8	13.7	13.9	13.8	13.8
2017	13.6	13.7	13.8	13.8	13.9	14.1	14.0	14.0	13.9	14.0	14.0	14.0	13.9
2018	14.1	14.3	14.3	14.4	14.5	14.6	14.6	14.5	14.4	14.3	14.3	14.3	14.4
Government													
2010	60.3	60.7	61.1	61.6	63.2	60.9	59.9	59.8	60.9	61.7	62.0	61.8	61.2
2011	61.1	61.4	61.5	62.0	62.0	61.1	59.9	59.3	61.3	61.3	61.5	61.6	61.2
2012	61.1	61.6	62.0	62.4	62.4	61.9	60.8	61.3	62.9	63.1	65.3	63.5	62.4
2013	62.3	62.8	63.0	63.5	63.1	62.6	61.4	61.3	63.0	62.4	62.8	62.6	62.6
2014	61.6	62.4	62.5	63.5	63.5	62.0	60.5	61.7	63.3	63.8	64.2	64.0	62.8
2015	62.8	63.8	64.1	64.2	64.2	62.9	62.6	62.9	64.3	64.9	65.4	65.4	64.0
2016	64.8	65.0	65.5	65.6	65.5	64.9	64.4	63.3	65.2	64.8	64.9	65.2	64.9
2017	64.3	64.5	64.9	65.0	64.9	64.2	64.0	63.7	65.4	65.8	66.2	66.2	64.9
2018	65.4	65.7	65.9	66.4	66.1	65.6	65.0	64.7	66.1	66.3	66.6	66.6	65.9

Employment by Industry: Greensboro-High Point, NC, 2010–2018

(Numbers in thousands, not seasonally adjusted)

Industry and year	January	February	March	April	May	June	July	August	September	October	November	December	Annual average
Total Nonfarm													
2010	331.6	331.7	334.5	336.0	337.8	337.7	333.6	337.2	337.8	341.8	340.0	340.0	336.6
2011	333.0	335.7	337.8	340.7	341.3	338.8	333.7	338.7	341.4	342.7	343.1	342.5	339.1
2012	337.2	339.6	341.1	342.6	343.9	339.3	330.7	340.7	342.6	345.7	347.5	347.9	341.6
2013	341.0	343.0	344.5	346.4	346.8	343.7	336.5	345.7	347.5	349.7	350.3	350.5	345.5
2014	342.7	342.6	345.7	349.2	350.6	346.4	339.9	347.7	350.1	353.6	354.6	354.8	348.2
2015	348.7	350.3	351.1	355.6	356.7	353.7	346.7	354.8	356.5	359.4	360.3	360.2	354.5
2016	352.7	354.7	356.4	359.0	358.8	355.5	351.0	357.1	359.1	362.3	365.4	363.9	358.0
2017	354.8	357.6	357.4	359.8	360.4	358.8	352.0	358.2	359.3	361.9	362.8	361.7	358.7
2018	356.8	358.9	360.4	361.4	362.9	360.4	353.0	359.7	360.9	363.8	363.4	360.4	360.2
Total Private													
2010	284.4	284.4	286.7	287.6	288.2	290.2	292.0	292.8	291.1	294.1	292.7	293.0	289.8
2011	286.6	289.0	290.8	293.7	294.4	295.5	295.0	296.2	295.7	296.0	296.1	295.7	293.7
2012	291.7	293.6	294.7	296.0	296.9	297.3	297.1	298.1	297.3	299.0	300.5	301.4	297.0
2013	295.0	296.7	297.7	299.9	300.2	301.0	300.9	303.1	302.3	303.8	304.0	304.4	300.8
2014	297.2	297.0	299.7	302.8	303.7	303.5	304.0	305.5	305.3	308.1	308.7	309.3	303.7
2015	303.8	305.2	306.0	310.1	311.0	311.1	311.0	313.2	312.2	314.7	315.3	315.3	310.7
2016	308.5	309.8	310.8	313.8	313.3	313.4	314.9	315.5	315.1	316.6	319.2	318.5	314.1
2017	310.2	312.5	312.2	314.4	315.0	316.8	315.7	316.3	314.8	316.9	317.8	317.0	315.0
2018	312.4	314.1	315.4	316.0	316.8	317.8	316.6	318.2	316.5	318.8	318.3	315.6	316.4
Goods Producing													
2010	62.4	62.3	62.8	63.2	63.2	63.8	64.0	64.1	63.9	63.8	63.4	63.6	63.4
2011	62.7	63.1	63.5	64.4	64.7	65.2	65.3	65.6	65.3	65.0	64.6	64.6	64.5
2012	64.6	64.9	64.9	64.5	64.8	64.9	64.9	64.8	65.1	65.1	65.2	65.7	65.0
2013	64.8	64.4	64.9	65.4	65.6	66.3	66.3	66.3	66.4	66.6	66.5	66.6	65.8
2014	65.7	65.7	66.2	66.3	66.6	67.0	66.9	66.9	67.1	67.0	67.1	67.4	66.7
2015	66.8	67.3	67.7	68.4	68.5	68.9	69.1	69.6	69.3	69.4	69.2	69.6	68.7
2016	68.9	69.1	69.5	69.5	69.7	70.1	71.0	71.0	70.9	70.8	70.9	71.2	70.2
2017	69.9	70.7	70.8	70.8	70.8	71.1	70.9	70.9	70.6	70.8	70.6	70.5	70.7
2018	70.1	70.4	70.5	70.4	70.5	71.0	70.6	70.4	70.3	70.3	70.1	70.0	70.4
Service-Providing													
2010	269.2	269.4	271.7	272.8	274.6	273.9	269.6	273.1	273.9	278.0	276.6	276.4	273.3
2011	270.3	272.6	274.3	276.3	276.6	273.6	268.4	273.1	276.1	277.7	278.5	277.9	274.6
2012	272.6	274.7	276.2	278.1	279.1	274.4	265.8	275.9	277.5	280.6	282.3	282.2	276.6
2013	276.2	278.6	279.6	281.0	281.2	277.4	270.2	279.4	281.1	283.1	283.8	283.9	279.6
2014	277.0	276.9	279.5	282.9	284.0	279.4	273.0	280.8	283.0	286.6	287.5	287.4	281.5
2015	281.9	283.0	283.4	287.2	288.2	284.8	277.6	285.2	287.2	290.0	291.1	290.6	285.9
2016	283.8	285.6	286.9	289.5	289.1	285.4	280.0	286.1	288.2	291.5	294.5	292.7	287.8
2017	284.9	286.9	286.6	289.0	289.6	287.7	281.1	287.3	288.7	291.1	292.2	291.2	288.0
2018	286.7	288.5	289.9	291.0	292.4	289.4	282.4	289.3	290.6	293.5	293.3	290.4	289.8
Mining, Logging, and Construction													
2010	12.1	12.0	12.3	12.6	12.5	12.7	12.6	12.6	12.5	12.7	12.6	12.5	12.5
2011	11.7	12.1	12.4	12.8	12.9	13.1	13.1	13.1	13.1	12.9	12.7	12.7	12.7
2012	12.5	12.4	12.5	12.2	12.2	12.3	12.4	12.4	12.3	12.3	12.2	12.2	12.3
2013	11.9	11.9	12.2	12.4	12.5	12.7	12.8	13.0	13.0	13.0	13.0	12.9	12.6
2014	12.6	12.6	12.9	12.9	13.1	13.3	13.3	13.3	13.4	13.4	13.4	13.4	13.1
2015	12.9	13.1	13.3	13.8	13.9	14.0	14.2	14.3	14.2	14.2	13.9	14.0	13.8
2016	13.8	13.8	14.0	14.3	14.3	14.4	14.9	14.9	15.0	14.9	14.8	14.8	14.5
2017	14.3	14.7	14.9	15.0	14.9	15.2	15.1	15.1	15.1	15.4	15.3	15.3	15.0
2018	15.0	15.2	15.5	15.5	15.6	15.9	15.9	15.8	15.8	15.8	15.7	15.5	15.6
Manufacturing													
2010	50.3	50.3	50.5	50.6	50.7	51.1	51.4	51.5	51.4	51.1	50.8	51.1	50.9
2011	51.0	51.0	51.1	51.6	51.8	52.1	52.2	52.5	52.2	52.1	51.9	51.9	51.8
2012	52.1	52.5	52.4	52.3	52.6	52.6	52.5	52.4	52.8	52.8	53.0	53.5	52.6
2013	52.9	52.5	52.7	53.0	53.1	53.6	53.5	53.3	53.4	53.6	53.5	53.7	53.2
2014	53.1	53.1	53.3	53.4	53.5	53.7	53.6	53.6	53.7	53.6	53.7	54.0	53.5
2015	53.9	54.2	54.4	54.6	54.6	54.9	54.9	55.3	55.1	55.2	55.3	55.6	54.8
2016	55.1	55.3	55.5	55.2	55.4	55.7	56.1	56.1	55.9	55.9	56.1	56.4	55.7
2017	55.6	56.0	55.9	55.8	55.9	55.9	55.8	55.8	55.5	55.4	55.3	55.2	55.7
2018	55.1	55.2	55.0	54.9	54.9	55.1	54.7	54.6	54.5	54.5	54.4	54.5	54.8

Employment by Industry: Greensboro-High Point, NC, 2010–2018—*Continued*

(Numbers in thousands, not seasonally adjusted)

Industry and year	January	February	March	April	May	June	July	August	September	October	November	December	Annual average
Trade, Transportation, and Utilities													
2010	67.4	67.2	67.5	67.9	68.1	68.1	68.1	68.1	68.1	68.8	69.5	70.3	68.3
2011	67.8	68.1	68.3	68.7	68.9	68.8	68.7	68.8	68.6	69.0	69.9	70.5	68.8
2012	68.9	68.9	68.9	69.7	70.2	69.9	69.8	69.8	69.8	70.3	71.7	72.2	70.0
2013	69.8	69.9	70.0	70.6	70.7	70.5	70.7	70.9	70.8	72.0	72.7	73.5	71.0
2014	70.9	70.4	71.1	72.0	72.2	72.3	71.8	72.2	71.8	72.3	73.6	74.3	72.1
2015	71.7	71.6	71.8	72.7	72.5	72.5	72.3	72.8	72.8	73.8	74.6	75.7	72.9
2016	72.5	72.1	72.3	73.0	73.0	72.9	72.8	73.0	72.6	73.3	74.4	75.3	73.1
2017	73.3	72.8	72.5	73.5	73.7	74.3	74.2	74.3	73.9	75.0	76.4	76.9	74.2
2018	74.8	74.8	74.8	74.5	74.7	74.9	74.8	75.2	75.3	75.8	77.0	76.9	75.3
Wholesale Trade													
2010	18.0	18.0	18.2	18.2	18.2	18.1	18.1	18.1	18.0	18.0	18.0	18.0	18.1
2011	17.7	18.0	18.0	18.0	18.0	17.9	17.8	17.8	17.6	17.5	17.4	17.4	17.8
2012	17.4	17.6	17.7	17.9	18.0	18.0	17.9	18.0	18.0	18.1	18.2	18.4	17.9
2013	18.1	18.3	18.4	18.5	18.5	18.5	18.5	18.6	18.6	18.6	18.6	18.6	18.5
2014	18.4	18.4	18.6	19.0	19.1	19.0	18.9	18.9	18.8	18.6	18.6	18.7	18.8
2015	18.5	18.6	18.6	18.9	18.9	18.8	18.8	18.9	18.7	18.9	18.9	19.1	18.8
2016	18.9	18.8	19.0	19.3	19.4	19.3	19.2	19.2	19.0	19.1	18.9	19.0	19.1
2017	18.8	18.9	18.9	19.0	19.0	19.2	19.2	19.3	19.1	19.3	19.3	19.5	19.1
2018	19.3	19.4	19.5	19.6	19.6	19.7	19.6	19.7	19.6	19.5	19.3	18.8	19.5
Retail Trade													
2010	34.8	34.6	34.7	34.9	35.0	34.9	34.8	34.8	34.7	35.1	35.9	36.3	35.0
2011	34.6	34.5	34.7	34.9	35.1	35.1	35.1	35.2	35.0	35.4	36.4	36.8	35.2
2012	35.6	35.4	35.2	35.7	36.1	35.9	36.0	35.8	35.8	36.0	37.4	37.5	36.0
2013	35.8	35.8	35.9	36.2	36.4	36.2	36.4	36.3	36.2	37.1	38.0	38.5	36.6
2014	36.6	36.2	36.5	36.8	36.9	37.0	36.7	37.0	36.6	37.1	38.2	38.4	37.0
2015	36.7	36.5	36.6	36.9	37.0	37.1	37.0	37.3	37.3	37.9	38.9	39.4	37.4
2016	37.4	37.3	37.3	37.7	37.7	37.7	37.7	37.8	37.7	38.3	39.4	39.7	38.0
2017	37.8	37.6	37.3	37.5	37.5	37.6	37.7	37.6	37.1	37.6	38.8	38.8	37.7
2018	37.2	37.1	37.0	37.0	37.2	37.1	37.2	37.3	37.1	37.6	38.7	38.9	37.5
Transportation and Utilities													
2010	14.6	14.6	14.6	14.8	14.9	15.1	15.2	15.2	15.4	15.7	15.6	16.0	15.1
2011	15.5	15.6	15.6	15.8	15.8	15.8	15.8	15.8	16.0	16.1	16.1	16.3	15.9
2012	15.9	15.9	16.0	16.1	16.1	16.0	15.9	16.0	16.0	16.2	16.1	16.3	16.0
2013	15.9	15.8	15.7	15.9	15.8	15.8	15.8	16.0	16.0	16.3	16.1	16.4	16.0
2014	15.9	15.8	16.0	16.2	16.2	16.3	16.2	16.3	16.4	16.6	16.8	17.2	16.3
2015	16.5	16.5	16.6	16.9	16.6	16.6	16.5	16.6	16.8	17.0	16.8	17.2	16.7
2016	16.2	16.0	16.0	16.0	15.9	15.9	15.9	16.0	15.9	15.9	16.1	16.6	16.0
2017	16.7	16.3	16.3	17.0	17.2	17.5	17.3	17.4	17.7	18.1	18.3	18.6	17.4
2018	18.3	18.3	18.3	17.9	17.9	18.1	18.0	18.2	18.6	18.7	19.0	19.2	18.4
Information													
2010	5.6	5.5	5.5	5.5	5.5	5.5	5.6	5.6	5.5	5.5	5.5	5.6	5.5
2011	5.5	5.5	5.5	5.5	5.5	5.5	5.5	5.5	5.5	5.5	5.4	5.4	5.5
2012	5.4	5.5	5.4	5.4	5.4	5.4	5.4	5.3	5.3	5.3	5.3	5.3	5.4
2013	5.2	5.2	5.1	5.0	5.0	5.0	5.0	4.9	4.9	4.9	4.9	5.0	5.0
2014	4.9	4.9	4.9	4.9	4.9	5.0	5.0	5.0	5.0	5.1	5.1	5.1	5.0
2015	5.1	5.1	5.1	5.0	5.1	5.1	5.1	5.0	4.9	4.9	4.9	4.9	5.0
2016	4.9	5.0	5.0	4.8	4.8	4.8	4.9	4.9	4.8	4.8	4.8	4.8	4.9
2017	4.7	4.8	4.8	4.6	4.6	4.6	4.7	4.7	4.7	4.7	4.8	4.8	4.7
2018	4.7	4.6	4.6	4.6	4.6	4.6	4.6	4.6	4.5	4.5	4.6	4.6	4.6
Financial Activities													
2010	20.3	20.2	20.2	20.0	19.8	19.8	19.9	19.9	19.9	19.9	19.8	19.9	20.0
2011	19.6	19.6	19.7	19.7	19.6	19.6	19.6	19.5	19.4	19.0	18.9	18.8	19.4
2012	18.3	18.4	18.4	18.4	18.3	18.4	18.4	18.5	18.5	18.7	18.7	18.8	18.5
2013	18.3	18.4	18.4	18.4	18.4	18.5	18.3	18.4	18.1	18.1	18.2	18.2	18.3
2014	18.2	18.1	18.1	17.8	17.8	17.7	17.8	17.7	17.6	17.6	17.6	17.6	17.8
2015	17.6	17.5	17.5	17.6	17.8	18.0	18.1	18.1	18.0	18.1	18.2	18.3	17.9
2016	18.2	18.2	18.2	18.1	18.0	18.0	18.2	18.1	18.0	18.0	18.2	18.2	18.1
2017	17.9	17.9	17.7	17.6	17.6	17.7	17.8	17.7	17.7	17.8	17.9	18.0	17.8
2018	18.2	18.3	18.4	18.1	18.5	18.6	18.5	18.5	18.5	18.6	18.5	18.5	18.4

Employment by Industry: Greensboro-High Point, NC, 2010–2018—*Continued*

(Numbers in thousands, not seasonally adjusted)

Industry and year	January	February	March	April	May	June	July	August	September	October	November	December	Annual average
Professional and Business Services													
2010	42.0	42.3	42.9	42.9	42.8	43.6	44.9	45.4	45.3	46.5	45.5	45.1	44.1
2011	44.2	45.1	45.7	46.1	45.9	46.1	46.4	46.7	47.3	47.6	47.6	47.1	46.3
2012	46.6	47.0	47.7	47.5	47.1	47.1	46.6	47.2	46.8	47.4	47.6	47.6	47.2
2013	46.2	47.0	46.9	47.4	47.0	47.0	47.0	48.1	48.5	49.0	48.6	48.3	47.6
2014	47.0	47.0	47.7	48.4	48.0	47.7	48.7	49.4	50.0	51.7	51.1	51.0	49.0
2015	49.5	49.7	49.4	50.4	50.1	49.8	50.0	50.9	50.5	51.7	51.6	50.5	50.3
2016	49.0	49.4	49.1	50.1	48.7	48.7	49.5	49.6	50.3	50.8	51.7	50.6	49.8
2017	48.1	48.8	48.6	49.2	49.0	49.3	49.0	49.2	49.2	49.5	49.1	48.6	49.0
2018	47.4	47.5	47.8	48.6	48.0	47.9	47.8	48.4	48.4	49.2	48.3	46.7	48.0
Education and Health Services													
2010	46.5	46.3	46.5	46.5	46.5	46.3	46.4	46.5	45.9	47.1	47.0	46.9	46.5
2011	46.1	46.4	46.3	46.7	46.6	46.4	45.9	46.3	46.7	47.4	47.5	47.3	46.6
2012	46.6	47.2	47.0	47.3	47.1	46.7	47.0	47.4	48.0	48.2	48.5	48.4	47.5
2013	47.9	48.5	48.6	48.5	48.4	47.8	47.7	48.3	48.7	48.5	48.5	48.4	48.3
2014	47.3	47.7	47.6	48.0	48.0	47.4	47.3	47.5	48.2	48.6	48.8	48.6	47.9
2015	48.9	49.4	49.3	49.7	49.7	49.3	49.1	49.4	50.1	50.2	50.5	50.4	49.7
2016	49.8	50.6	50.7	51.0	50.9	50.4	50.3	50.8	50.9	51.2	51.2	51.0	50.7
2017	50.0	50.5	50.2	50.5	50.5	50.1	49.7	50.1	50.3	51.1	51.1	50.9	50.4
2018	50.4	51.1	51.2	51.3	51.4	50.9	50.6	51.4	51.3	51.8	51.6	51.6	51.2
Leisure and Hospitality													
2010	28.1	28.4	29.1	29.5	30.2	30.9	30.9	31.1	30.6	30.5	30.1	29.8	29.9
2011	28.8	29.3	30.0	30.7	31.3	31.8	31.5	31.8	31.0	30.6	30.3	30.0	30.6
2012	29.4	29.8	30.5	31.1	31.7	32.3	32.5	32.7	31.6	31.7	31.2	31.0	31.3
2013	30.5	30.9	31.4	32.3	32.7	33.2	33.2	33.6	32.5	32.3	32.1	32.0	32.2
2014	30.9	30.9	31.7	32.8	33.5	33.5	33.6	34.0	33.1	33.2	32.9	32.8	32.7
2015	31.8	32.2	32.8	33.8	34.7	34.9	34.4	34.8	34.3	34.1	33.9	33.5	33.8
2016	33.0	33.2	33.7	34.9	35.7	35.9	35.6	35.7	35.2	35.1	35.5	35.0	34.9
2017	34.1	34.7	35.3	35.8	36.3	37.0	36.7	37.0	36.1	35.7	35.6	35.0	35.8
2018	34.6	35.1	35.8	36.2	36.7	37.2	37.2	37.2	35.9	36.2	35.9	35.0	36.1
Other Services													
2010	12.1	12.2	12.2	12.1	12.1	12.2	12.2	12.1	11.9	12.0	11.9	11.8	12.1
2011	11.9	11.9	11.8	11.9	11.9	12.1	12.1	12.0	11.9	11.9	11.9	12.0	11.9
2012	11.9	11.9	11.9	12.1	12.3	12.6	12.5	12.4	12.2	12.3	12.3	12.4	12.2
2013	12.3	12.4	12.4	12.3	12.4	12.7	12.7	12.6	12.4	12.4	12.5	12.4	12.5
2014	12.3	12.3	12.4	12.6	12.7	12.9	12.9	12.8	12.5	12.6	12.5	12.5	12.6
2015	12.4	12.4	12.4	12.5	12.6	12.6	12.9	12.6	12.3	12.5	12.4	12.4	12.5
2016	12.2	12.2	12.3	12.4	12.5	12.6	12.6	12.4	12.4	12.6	12.5	12.4	12.4
2017	12.2	12.3	12.3	12.4	12.5	12.7	12.7	12.4	12.3	12.3	12.3	12.3	12.4
2018	12.2	12.3	12.3	12.3	12.4	12.7	12.5	12.5	12.3	12.4	12.3	12.3	12.4
Government													
2010	47.2	47.3	47.8	48.4	49.6	47.5	41.6	44.4	46.7	47.7	47.3	47.0	46.9
2011	46.4	46.7	47.0	47.0	46.9	43.3	38.7	42.5	45.7	46.7	47.0	46.8	45.4
2012	45.5	46.0	46.4	46.6	47.0	42.0	33.6	42.6	45.3	46.7	47.0	46.5	44.6
2013	46.0	46.3	46.8	46.5	46.6	42.7	35.6	42.6	45.2	45.9	46.3	46.1	44.7
2014	45.5	45.6	46.0	46.4	46.9	42.9	35.9	42.2	44.8	45.5	45.9	45.5	44.4
2015	44.9	45.1	45.1	45.5	45.7	42.6	35.7	41.6	44.3	44.7	45.0	44.9	43.8
2016	44.2	44.9	45.6	45.2	45.5	42.1	36.1	41.6	44.0	45.7	46.2	45.4	43.9
2017	44.6	45.1	45.2	45.4	45.4	42.0	36.3	41.9	44.5	45.0	45.0	44.7	43.8
2018	44.4	44.8	45.0	45.4	46.1	42.6	36.4	41.5	44.4	45.0	45.1	44.8	43.8

APPENDIX

SEVENTY-FIVE LARGEST MSAs AND COMPONENTS
(as defined July 2015)

Core based statistical area	State/ County FIPS code	Title and Geographic Components	Core based statistical area	State/ County FIPS code	Title and Geographic Components
35620		**New York-Newark-Jersey City, NY-NJ-PA**		48201	Harris County
35620		Dutchess County-Putnam County, NY Div 20524		48291	Liberty County
	36027	Dutchess County		48339	Montgomery County
	36079	Putnam County		48473	Waller County
35620		Nassau County-Suffolk County, NY Div 35004	47900		**Washington-Arlington-Alexandria, DC-VA-MD-WV**
	36059	Nassau County	47900		Silver Spring-Frederick-Rockville, MD Div 43524
	36103	Suffolk County		24021	Frederick County
35620		Newark, NJ-PA Div 35084		24031	Montgomery County
	34013	Essex County			Washington-Arlington-Alexandria, DC-VA-MD-WV Div
	34019	Hunterdon County	47900		47894
	34027	Morris County		11001	District of Columbia
	34035	Somerset County		24009	Calvert County
	34037	Sussex County		24017	Charles County
	34039	Union County		24033	Prince George's County
	42103	Pike County		51013	Arlington County
35620		New York-Jersey City-White Plains, NY-NJ Div 35614		51043	Clarke County
	34003	Bergen County		51047	Culpeper County
	34017	Hudson County		51059	Fairfax County
	34023	Middlesex County		51061	Fauquier County
	34025	Monmouth County		51107	Loudoun County
	34029	Ocean County		51153	Prince William County
	34031	Passaic County		51157	Rappahannock County
	36005	Bronx County		51177	Spotsylvania County
	36047	Kings County		51179	Stafford County
	36061	New York County		51187	Warren County
	36071	Orange County		51510	Alexandria city
	36081	Queens County		51600	Fairfax city
	36085	Richmond County		51610	Falls Church city
	36087	Rockland County		51630	Fredericksburg city
	36119	Westchester County		51683	Manassas city
				51685	Manassas Park city
31080		**Los Angeles-Long Beach-Anaheim, CA**		54037	Jefferson County
31080		Anaheim-Santa Ana-Irvine, CA Div 11244			
	06059	Orange County	33100		**Miami-Fort Lauderdale-West Palm Beach, FL**
31080		Los Angeles-Long Beach-Glendale, CA Div 31084			Fort Lauderdale-Pompano Beach-Deerfield Beach, FL Div
	06037	Los Angeles County	33100		22744
				12011	Broward County
16980		**Chicago-Naperville-Elgin, IL-IN-WI**	33100		Miami-Miami Beach-Kendall, FL Div 33124
16980		Chicago-Naperville-Arlington Heights, IL Div 16974		12086	Miami-Dade County
	17031	Cook County	33100		West Palm Beach-Boca Raton-Delray Beach, FL Div 48424
	17043	DuPage County		12099	Palm Beach County
	17063	Grundy County			
	17093	Kendall County	37980		**Philadelphia-Camden-Wilmington, PA-NJ-DE-MD**
	17111	McHenry County	37980		Camden, NJ Div 15804
	17197	Will County		34005	Burlington County
16980		Elgin, IL Div 20994		34007	Camden County
	17037	DeKalb County		34015	Gloucester County
	17089	Kane County			Montgomery County-Bucks County-Chester County, PA
16980		Gary, IN Div 23844	37980		Div 33874
	18073	Jasper County		42017	Bucks County
	18089	Lake County		42029	Chester County
	18111	Newton County		42091	Montgomery County
	18127	Porter County	37980		Philadelphia, PA Div 37964
16980		Lake County-Kenosha County, IL-WI Div 29404		42045	Delaware County
	17097	Lake County		42101	Philadelphia County
	55059	Kenosha County	37980		Wilmington, DE-MD-NJ Div 48864
				10003	New Castle County
19100		**Dallas-Fort Worth-Arlington, TX**		24015	Cecil County
19100		Dallas-Plano-Irving, TX Div 19124		34033	Salem County
	48085	Collin County			
	48113	Dallas County	12060		**Atlanta-Sandy Springs-Roswell, GA**
	48121	Denton County		13013	Barrow County
	48139	Ellis County		13015	Bartow County
	48231	Hunt County		13035	Butts County
	48257	Kaufman County		13045	Carroll County
	48397	Rockwall County		13057	Cherokee County
19100		Fort Worth-Arlington, TX Div 23104		13063	Clayton County
	48221	Hood County		13067	Cobb County
	48251	Johnson County		13077	Coweta County
	48367	Parker County		13085	Dawson County
	48425	Somervell County		13089	DeKalb County
	48439	Tarrant County		13097	Douglas County
	48497	Wise County		13113	Fayette County
				13117	Forsyth County
26420		**Houston-The Woodlands-Sugar Land, TX**		13121	Fulton County
	48015	Austin County		13135	Gwinnett County
	48039	Brazoria County		13143	Haralson County
	48071	Chambers County		13149	Heard County
	48157	Fort Bend County		13151	Henry County
	48167	Galveston County			

Core based statistical area	State/County FIPS code	Title and Geographic Components
	13159	Jasper County
	13171	Lamar County
	13199	Meriwether County
	13211	Morgan County
	13217	Newton County
	13223	Paulding County
	13227	Pickens County
	13231	Pike County
	13247	Rockdale County
	13255	Spalding County
	13297	Walton County
14460		**Boston-Cambridge-Newton, MA-NH**
14460		Boston, MA Div 14454
	25021	Norfolk County
	25023	Plymouth County
	25025	Suffolk County
14460		Cambridge-Newton-Framingham, MA Div 15764
	25009	Essex County
	25017	Middlesex County
14460		Rockingham County-Strafford County, NH Div 40484
	33015	Rockingham County
	33017	Strafford County
38060		**Phoenix-Mesa-Scottsdale, AZ**
	04013	Maricopa County
	04021	Pinal County
41860		**San Francisco-Oakland-Hayward, CA**
41860		Oakland-Hayward-Berkeley, CA Div 36084
	06001	Alameda County
	06013	Contra Costa County
		San Francisco-Redwood City-South San Francisco, CA Div 41884
41860	06075	San Francisco County
	06081	San Mateo County
41860		San Rafael, CA Div 42034
	06041	Marin County
40140		**Riverside-San Bernardino-Ontario, CA**
	06065	Riverside County
	06071	San Bernardino County
19820		**Detroit-Warren-Dearborn, MI**
19820		Detroit-Dearborn-Livonia, MI Div 19804
	26163	Wayne County
19820		Warren-Troy-Farmington Hills, MI 47664
	26087	Lapeer County
	26093	Livingston County
	26099	Macomb County
	26125	Oakland County
	26147	St Clair County
42660		**Seattle-Tacoma-Bellevue, WA**
42660		Seattle-Bellevue-Everett, WA Div 42644
	53033	King County
	53061	Snohomish County
42660		Tacoma-Lakewood, WA Div 45104
	53053	Pierce County
33460		**Minneapolis-St Paul-Bloomington, MN**
	27003	Anoka County
	27019	Carver County
	27025	Chisago County
	27037	Dakota County
	27053	Hennepin County
	27059	Isanti County
	27079	Le Sueur County
	27095	Mille Lacs County
	27123	Ramsey County
	27139	Scott County
	27141	Sherburne County
	27143	Sibley County
	27163	Washington County
	27171	Wright County
	55093	Pierce County
	55109	St Croix County
41740		**San Diego-Carlsbad, CA**
	06073	San Diego County
45300		**Tampa-St Petersburg-Clearwater, FL**
	12053	Hernando County
	12057	Hillsborough County
	12101	Pasco County
	12103	Pinellas County

Core based statistical area	State/County FIPS code	Title and Geographic Components
19740		**Denver-Aurora-Lakewood, CO**
	08001	Adams County
	08005	Arapahoe County
	08014	Broomfield County
	08019	Clear Creek County
	08031	Denver County
	08035	Douglas County
	08039	Elbert County
	08047	Gilpin County
	08059	Jefferson County
	08093	Park County
41180		**St. Louis, MO-IL**
	17005	Bond County
	17013	Calhoun County
	17027	Clinton County
	17083	Jersey County
	17117	Macoupin County
	17119	Madison County
	17133	Monroe County
	17163	St Clair County
	29071	Franklin County
	29099	Jefferson County
	29113	Lincoln County
	29183	St Charles County
	29189	St Louis County
	29219	Warren County
	29510	St Louis city
12580		**Baltimore-Columbia-Towson, MD**
	24003	Anne Arundel County
	24005	Baltimore County
	24013	Carroll County
	24025	Harford County
	24027	Howard County
	24035	Queen Anne's County
	24510	Baltimore city
36740		**Orlando-Kissimmee-Sanford, FL**
	12069	Lake County
	12095	Orange County
	12097	Osceola County
	12117	Seminole County
16740		**Charlotte-Concord-Gastonia, NC-SC**
	37025	Cabarrus County
	37071	Gaston County
	37097	Iredell County
	37109	Lincoln County
	37119	Mecklenburg County
	37159	Rowan County
	37179	Union County
	45023	Chester County
	45057	Lancaster County
	45091	York County
41700		**San Antonio-New Braunfels, TX**
	48013	Atascosa County
	48019	Bandera County
	48029	Bexar County
	48091	Comal County
	48187	Guadalupe County
	48259	Kendall County
	48325	Medina County
	48493	Wilson County
38900		**Portland-Vancouver-Hillsboro, OR-WA**
	41005	Clackamas County
	41009	Columbia County
	41051	Multnomah County
	41067	Washington County
	41071	Yamhill County
	53011	Clark County
	53059	Skamania County
40900		**Sacramento--Roseville--Arden-Arcade, CA**
	06017	El Dorado County
	06061	Placer County
	06067	Sacramento County
	06113	Yolo County
38300		**Pittsburgh, PA**
	42003	Allegheny County
	42005	Armstrong County
	42007	Beaver County
	42019	Butler County
	42051	Fayette County

Core based statistical area	State/ County FIPS code	Title and Geographic Components	Core based statistical area	State/ County FIPS code	Title and Geographic Components
	42125	Washington County		47081	Hickman County
	42129	Westmoreland County		47111	Macon County
29820		**Las Vegas-Henderson-Paradise, NV**		47119	Maury County
	32003	Clark County		47147	Robertson County
17140		**Cincinnati, OH-KY-IN**		47149	Rutherford County
	18029	Dearborn County		47159	Smith County
	18115	Ohio County		47165	Sumner County
	18161	Union County		47169	Trousdale County
	21015	Boone County		47187	Williamson County
	21023	Bracken County		47189	Wilson County
	21037	Campbell County	47260		**Virginia Beach-Norfolk-Newport News, VA-NC**
	21077	Gallatin County		37053	Currituck County
	21081	Grant County		37073	Gates County
	21117	Kenton County		51073	Gloucester County
	21191	Pendleton County		51093	Isle of Wight County
	39015	Brown County		51095	James City County
	39017	Butler County		51115	Mathews County
	39025	Clermont County		51199	York County
	39061	Hamilton County		51550	Chesapeake city
	39165	Warren County		51650	Hampton city
12420		**Austin-Round Rock, TX**		51700	Newport News city
	48021	Bastrop County		51710	Norfolk city
	48055	Caldwell County		51735	Poquoson city
	48209	Hays County		51740	Portsmouth city
	48453	Travis County		51800	Suffolk city
	48491	Williamson County		51810	Virginia Beach city
28140		**Kansas City, MO-KS**		51830	Williamsburg city
	20091	Johnson County	39300		**Providence-Warwick, RI-MA**
	20103	Leavenworth County		25005	Bristol County
	20107	Linn County		44001	Bristol County
	20121	Miami County		44003	Kent County
	20209	Wyandotte County		44005	Newport County
	29013	Bates County		44007	Providence County
	29025	Caldwell County		44009	Washington County
	29037	Cass County	33340		**Milwaukee-Waukesha-West Allis, WI**
	29047	Clay County		55079	Milwaukee County
	29049	Clinton County		55089	Ozaukee County
	29095	Jackson County		55131	Washington County
	29107	Lafayette County		55133	Waukesha County
	29165	Platte County	27260		**Jacksonville, FL**
	29177	Ray County		12003	Baker County
18140		**Columbus, OH**		12019	Clay County
	39041	Delaware County		12031	Duval County
	39045	Fairfield County		12089	Nassau County
	39049	Franklin County		12109	St Johns County
	39073	Hocking County	36420		**Oklahoma City, OK**
	39089	Licking County		40017	Canadian County
	39097	Madison County		40027	Cleveland County
	39117	Morrow County		40051	Grady County
	39127	Perry County		40081	Lincoln County
	39129	Pickaway County		40083	Logan County
	39159	Union County		40087	McClain County
17460		**Cleveland-Elyria, OH**		40109	Oklahoma County
	39035	Cuyahoga County	39580		**Raleigh, NC**
	39055	Geauga County		37069	Franklin County
	39085	Lake County		37101	Johnston County
	39093	Lorain County		37183	Wake County
	39103	Medina County	32820		**Memphis, TN-MS-AR**
26900		**Indianapolis-Carmel-Anderson, IN**		05035	Crittenden County
	18011	Boone County		28009	Benton County
	18013	Brown County		28033	DeSoto County
	18057	Hamilton County		28093	Marshall County
	18059	Hancock County		28137	Tate County
	18063	Hendricks County		28143	Tunica County
	18081	Johnson County		47047	Fayette County
	18095	Madison County		47157	Shelby County
	18097	Marion County		47167	Tipton County
	18109	Morgan County	40060		**Richmond, VA**
	18133	Putnam County		51007	Amelia County
	18145	Shelby County		51033	Caroline County
41940		**San Jose-Sunnyvale-Santa Clara, CA**		51036	Charles City County
	06069	San Benito County		51041	Chesterfield County
	06085	Santa Clara County		51053	Dinwiddie County
34980		**Nashville-Davidson--Murfreesboro--Franklin, TN**		51075	Goochland County
	47015	Cannon County		51085	Hanover County
	47021	Cheatham County		51087	Henrico County
	47037	Davidson County		51101	King William County
	47043	Dickson County		51127	New Kent County
				51145	Powhatan County

Core based statistical area	State/County FIPS code	Title and Geographic Components
	51149	Prince George County
	51183	Sussex County
	51570	Colonial Heights city
	51670	Hopewell city
	51730	Petersburg city
	51760	Richmond city
31140		**Louisville/Jefferson County, KY-IN**
	18019	Clark County
	18043	Floyd County
	18061	Harrison County
	18143	Scott County
	18175	Washington County
	21029	Bullitt County
	21103	Henry County
	21111	Jefferson County
	21185	Oldham County
	21211	Shelby County
	21215	Spencer County
	21223	Trimble County
35380		**New Orleans-Metairie, LA**
	22051	Jefferson Parish
	22071	Orleans Parish
	22075	Plaquemines Parish
	22087	St Bernard Parish
	22089	St Charles Parish
	22093	St James Parish
	22095	St John the Baptist Parish
	22103	St Tammany Parish
41620		**Salt Lake City, UT**
	49035	Salt Lake County
	49045	Tooele County
25540		**Hartford-West Hartford-East Hartford, CT**
	09003	Hartford County
	09007	Middlesex County
	09013	Tolland County
13820		**Birmingham-Hoover, AL**
	01007	Bibb County
	01009	Blount County
	01021	Chilton County
	01073	Jefferson County
	01115	St Clair County
	01117	Shelby County
	01127	Walker County
15380		**Buffalo-Cheektowaga-Niagara Falls, NY**
	36029	Erie County
	36063	Niagara County
40380		**Rochester, NY**
	36051	Livingston County
	36055	Monroe County
	36069	Ontario County
	36073	Orleans County
	36117	Wayne County
	36123	Yates County
24340		**Grand Rapids-Wyoming, MI**
	26015	Barry County
	26081	Kent County
	26117	Montcalm County
	26139	Ottawa County
46060		**Tucson, AZ**
	04019	Pima County
23420		**Fresno, CA**
	06019	Fresno County
46140		**Tulsa, OK**
	40037	Creek County
	40111	Okmulgee County
	40113	Osage County
	40117	Pawnee County
	40131	Rogers County
	40143	Tulsa County
	40145	Wagoner County
46520		**Urban Honolulu, HI**
	15003	Honolulu County
49340		**Worcester, MA-CT**
	09015	Windham County
	25027	Worcester County
14860		**Bridgeport-Stamford-Norwalk, CT**
	09001	Fairfield County
36540		**Omaha-Council Bluffs, NE-IA**
	19085	Harrison County
	19129	Mills County
	19155	Pottawattamie County
	31025	Cass County
	31055	Douglas County
	31153	Sarpy County
	31155	Saunders County
	31177	Washington County
10740		**Albuquerque, NM**
	35001	Bernalillo County
	35043	Sandoval County
	35057	Torrance County
	35061	Valencia County
24780		**Greenville, NC**
	37147	Pitt County
12540		**Bakersfield, CA**
	06029	Kern County
28940		**Knoxville, TN**
	47001	Anderson County
	47009	Blount County
	47013	Campbell County
	47057	Grainger County
	47093	Knox County
	47105	Loudon County
	47129	Morgan County
	47145	Roane County
	47173	Union County
10580		**Albany-Schenectady-Troy, NY**
	36001	Albany County
	36083	Rensselaer County
	36091	Saratoga County
	36093	Schenectady County
	36095	Schoharie County
32580		**McAllen-Edinburg-Mission, TX**
	48215	Hidalgo County
35300		**New Haven-Milford, CT**
	09009	New Haven County
37100		**Oxnard-Thousand Oaks-Ventura, CA**
	06111	Ventura County
21340		**El Paso, TX**
	48141	El Paso County
	48229	Hudspeth County
10900		**Allentown-Bethlehem-Easton, PA-NJ**
	34041	Warren County
	42025	Carbon County
	42077	Lehigh County
	42095	Northampton County
17900		**Columbia, SC**
	45017	Calhoun County
	45039	Fairfield County
	45055	Kershaw County
	45063	Lexington County
	45079	Richland County
	45081	Saluda County
12940		**Baton Rouge, LA**
	22005	Ascension Parish
	22033	East Baton Rouge Parish
	22037	East Feliciana Parish
	22047	Iberville Parish
	22063	Livingston Parish
	22077	Pointe Coupee Parish
	22091	St Helena Parish
	22121	West Baton Rouge Parish
	22125	West Feliciana Parish

Core based statistical area	State/ County FIPS code	Title and Geographic Components	Core based statistical area	State/ County FIPS code	Title and Geographic Components
35840		**North Port-Sarasota-Bradenton, FL**	16700		**Charleston-North Charleston, SC**
	12081	Manatee County		45015	Berkeley County
	12115	Sarasota County		45019	Charleston County
19380		**Dayton, OH**		45035	Dorchester County
	39057	Greene County	24660		**Greensboro-High Point, NC**
	39109	Miami County		37081	Guilford County
	39113	Montgomery County		37151	Randolph County
				37157	Rockingham County